DICTIONARY OF AMERICAN HISTORY

DICTIONARY
OF
AMERICAN HISTORY

DICTIONARY OF AMERICAN HISTORY

REVISED EDITION

VOLUME VIII

INDEX

Charles Scribner's Sons · New York

1 3 5 7 9 11 13 15 17 19 V/C 20 18 16 14 12 10 8 6 4 2

Printed in the United States of America
Library of Congress Catalog Card Number 76-6735
ISBN 0-684-15078-6

EDITORIAL STAFF

LOUISE BILEBOF KETZ, *Managing Editor*

JEAN G. COOKE, *Chief Indexer*

INDEXERS

JANET BYERS

HELEN CHUMBLEY

MARGARET DONOVAN

NORMA FRANKEL

ROBERT HAYCRAFT

LELAND S. LOWTHER

DAVID WILLIAM VOORHEES

MARSHALL DE BRUHL, *Director, Reference Editorial*

INTRODUCTION

The Index to Volumes I through VII of the revised edition of the *Dictionary of American History* brings together in alphabetical order the many thousands of facts contained within the text volumes. It expands those subjects that are entries in the text by listing all references to the subject throughout the set. Thus, the reader will find a reference to the general article on a particular subject under its alphabetical heading within the appropriate volume (for instance, "Newspapers" in Volume V), plus every other reference to the subject contained in other articles. The Index can, therefore, serve both as a guide to specific information and as an outline for study of a particular subject in American history. All subjects covered in the *Dictionary* are included in the Index, whether they are article entries or not. While no biographies are included in the text volumes, every person mentioned in the set is included in the Index, along with all references to that individual.

In order to present the index material in the simplest and clearest fashion, certain devices have been incorporated. Letter-by-letter alphabetizing has been used throughout. Article headings appear in boldface capital letters; subjects that do not appear as articles are listed in lightface type. The volume, page, and column reference to an article entry always appears first, in boldface type. Column designations are "a" for the left-hand column, "b" for the right-hand column. For many of the presidents of the United States, those topics relating to their presidency have been set off by the use of an intermediate head (*—President*) from those items related to other aspects of a president's life. And, in the case of those presidents who also had outstanding military careers, such as George Washington, Andrew Jackson, and Ulysses S. Grant, an additional intermediate head (*—Military Career*) has been added.

A great deal of parenthetical information has also been included in the Index. Wherever possible, dates are provided for events, court cases, legislation, and the like. All place names are identified by territory, city, state, or country. And nearly every individual is identified by his or her main profession. A number of less familiar terms and identical entries, such as *stocks* (in finance) and *stocks* (a colonial device for punishment), are also described parenthetically. A list of abbreviations used precedes the index entries. All italicized entries have been identified with the exception of those that are titles of published books.

For further ease of use, organizations have often been listed twice—under their full title and under the key work in their name. Where information on organizations, and information in general, has not been repeated, the reader is cross-referred to the place where the page references appear. In an attempt to list all possible names and spellings for a topic, the Index is heavily cross-referenced. To enable the reader to find more easily the subject he seeks, headings for each page have been provided, identifying the first entry on the left-hand page and the last entry on the right-hand page.

While preparing the Index, certain errors in the text were discovered, and an Errata List was prepared, which immediately follows this Introduction.

L. B. K.

ERRATA LIST

VOLUMES I–VII

VOLUME I

Page 15a, line 30	*For* (June 27, 1784) *read* (June 27, 1874)
Page 97b, lines 27–28	*For* Center for Advanced Study and Behavioral Sciences *read* Center for Advanced Study in the Behavioral Sciences
Page 103a, line 9	*For* Senator John B. *read* Senator John L.
Page 117b, line 18	*For* Bonita *read* Bonito
Page 140a, line 20	*For* 1938 *read* 1937
Page 236a, line 51	*For* Lawrence *read* Lawrance
Page 249a, line 1	*For* It is official *read* It was official
Page 261b, line 1	*For* Cheeves *read* Cheves
Page 284a, line 20	*For Bookkeeping read Beekeeping*

VOLUME II

Page 7b, line 31	*For* H. W. Dow *read* H. H. Dow
Page 12a, line 49	*For* Graaf *read* Graaff
Page 62b, line 21	*For* George C. *read* George G.
Page 81a, line 50	*For Ladies' read Lady's*
Page 89b, line 46	*For* 1971 *read* 1970
Page 103b, line 36	*For* Arthur *read* John
Page 104a, line 24	*For* of Duveen *read* of Joseph Duveen
Page 123a, line 21	*For* Act of 1731 *read* Act of 1732
Page 321b, line 12	*For* at Brunswick *read* at New Brunswick
Page 359b, line 20	*For* 1916 *read* 1914
Page 385b, line 50	*For* Hardaway site, Ga. *read* Hardaway site, N.C.
Page 484b, line 40	*For* A. D. Hill's *read* A. P. Hill's

VOLUME III

Page 18b, line 19	*For* Cockrill *read* Cockrell
Page 77b, line 35	*For* Albert *read* Alexander
Page 120a, line 11	*For* (Kingston, N.Y.) *read* (Kingston, Ont.)
Page 128b, line 42	*For* Endicott *read* Endecott
Page 146a, line 11	*For* Dauphine *read* Dauphin
Page 151b, line 15	*For* parteries *read* parterres
Page 164a, line 1	*For* nautral *read* natural
Page 168a, line 29	*For* Percival *read* Perceval
Page 219b, line 44	*For* (1629–40) *read* (1625–40)
Page 232a, lines 32–33	*For* Wilmington, Del. *read* Wilmington, N.C.
Page 316a, line 35	*For* William H. Marcy *read* William L. Marcy
Page 352a, line 47	*For* 1891 *read* 1890
Page 369b, line 16	*For* Ouiatanon *read* Ouiatenon
Page 403b, line 43	*For* Médard *read* Médart
Page 408b, line 2	*For* Joseph *read* John
Page 424b, lines 32–33	*For* (*see Downes* v. *Bidwell*) *read* (*Downes* v. *Bidwell*)
Page 443a, line 52	*For* 1968 *read* 1969

ERRATA LIST

Page 454a, lines 13–14	*For* Two stations in the Arctic and twelve in the Antarctic *read* Twelve stations in the Arctic and two in the Antarctic
Page 476a, line 44	*For* Lt. Gov. Nanfan *read* Lt. Gov. John Nanfan
Page 477b, line 19	*For* Nathan G. *read* Nathan C.
Page 498b, line 1	*For* by Kirby Smith *read* by Edmund Kirby-Smith
Page 502b, line 30	*For* R. Cargill Hill *read* R. Cargill Hall

VOLUME IV

Page 8a, line 43	*For* Valverde, N.Mex. *read* Valverde, Tex.
Page 116b, line 38	*For* Kirkland *read* Kirtland
Page 126a, line 8	*For* Amendments *read* Amendment
Page 143a, lines 9–10	*For* Sons of Liberty, Revolutionary *read* Sons of Liberty (American Revolution)
Page 161a, line 35	*For Westoner read Westover*
Page 161b, lines 15–16	*For* depth, psychology *read* depth psychology
Page 165b, lines 48–49	*For* Trilling (*The Liberal Imagination read* Trilling (d. 1976) (*The Liberal Imagination*
Page 199a, line 13	*For* Jovejoy *read* Lovejoy
Page 202b, line 31	*For* 1867 *read* 1866
Page 206b, line 50	*For* 1844 *read* 1842
Page 251a, lines 49–50	*For* Lillie, then president both of MBL and of the National Academy of Sciences *read* Lillie, then president of MBL
Page 257a, line 35	*For* Gen. Kirby Smith *read* Gen. Edmund Kirby-Smith
Page 260b, lines 14–15	*For* Saint Mary's City *read* Saint Marys City
Page 260b, line 24	*For* Saint Mary's City *read* Saint Marys City
Page 261a, line 51	*For* Harry Whinnamice *read* Harry Whinna Nice
Page 276b, line 37	*For* Dauphine *read* Dauphin
Page 324a, lines 8–9	*For* Monterey *read* Monterrey
Page 353b, line 40	*For* Beacon *read* Bacon
Page 380b, lines 35–36	*For* it was located near Council Bluffs, in present-day Iowa *read* it was located in Nebraska, near Council Bluffs, Iowa
Page 410a, line 40	*For* assisted Kirby Smith's *read* assisted Edmund Kirby-Smith's
Page 431b, lines 43–44	*For Dreadnaught read Dreadnought*

VOLUME V

Page 29a, line 41	*For* 74-ton *read* 74-gun
Page 31a, line 24	*For* Stephen H. *read* Stephen A.
Page 78b, line 30	*For* 1937 *read* 1936
Page 91a, line 15	*For* Chippewa *read* Chippawa
Page 93b, line 39	*For* demolish *read* demolished
Page 135a, lines 14–16	*For* Lillie of the University of Chicago became president of the U.S. National Academy of Sciences *read* Lillie of the University of Chicago became chairman of the Committee on Oceanography at the National Academy of Sciences
Page 140a, line 49	*For* Pickawillany *read* Pickawillanee
Page 165a, line 44	*For* Spaulding *read* Spalding
Page 178b, lines 16–17	*For* The Lincoln Highway and the Union Pacific Railroad follow *read* Highways U.S. 30 and Interstate 80 now follow
Page 192b, line 16	*For* James Steuart Curry *read* John Steuart Curry
Page 236a, line 9	*For* World *read* International
Page 264b, lines 1–2	*For* Matamoras *read* Matamoros
Page 290b, line 30	*For* Clement Adler *read* Clément Ader
Page 321a, line 31	*For* 1858 *read* 1758
Page 322b, line 28	*For* Groghan *read* Croghan
Page 342b, line 42	*For* United Staes *read* United States
Page 434b, line 7	*For* 1967 *read* 1966
Page 455a, line 48	*For* (Jones Act) *read* (Jones-White Act)
Page 461a, line 21	*For* 1899 *read* 1898

VOLUME VI

Page 67b, line 8	*For* 1934 *read* 1930
Page 77b, line 8	*For* 1800 *read* 1801
Page 133a, line 19	*For* enterpreneurs *read* entrepreneurs
Page 133b, line 28	*For* 1849 *read* 1848
Page 138a, line 24	*For* Appomatox *read* Appomattox
Page 171b, lines 18–19	*For* to more productive the rural population, and others living in rural areas *read* to more productive land.
Page 187b, line 37	*For* 1821 *read* 1819

Page 193b, line 35	*For* Fort Chartres *read* Fort de Chartres
Page 193b, lines 45–46	*For* Fort Chartres *read* Fort de Chartres
Page 210b, line 29	*For* Charles *read* Carlos
Page 226a, line 37	*For* Mohican *read* Mahican
Page 260a, line 40	*For* Fowlstown *read* Fowlton
Page 320b, lines 18–19	*For* Highway U.S. 40 now follows *read* Highways U.S. 40 and Interstate 70 now follow
Page 328b, line 16	*For* Act of 1954 *read* Act of 1958
Page 341b, lines 40–41	*For Slavery and an Industrial System read Slavery as an Industrial System*
Page 346b, line 40	*For* Earl of Sterling *read* Earl of Stirling
Page 355a, lines 14–15	*For* early in 1865 (*see* Powder River Campaign). Julesburg *read* early in 1865. Julesburg
Page 432b, line 20	*For Virginia Board of Education read Virginia Board of Elections*

VOLUME VII

Page 5b, line 15	*For* 1870 *read* 1871
Page 16b, line 24	*For* Edward *read* Edwin
Page 39a, line 36	*For* Kearney *read* Kearny
Page 39b, lines 46–47	*For* Gen. Kirby Smith *read* Gen. Edmund Kirby-Smith
Page 118a, line 13	*For* (1951) *read* (1957)
Page 171a, line 6	*For* Henry J. Mayo *read* Henry T. Mayo
Page 185a, line 51	*For* December 1950 *read* December 1949
Page 188b, line 7	*For* François Margane *read* François Marie Bissot
Page 195a, line 15	*For* Appomatox *read* Appomattox
Page 226a, line 19	*For* of 1948 *read* of 1949
Page 244b, line 26	*For* betwen *read* between
Page 274a, line 31	*For* 1672 *read* 1662
Page 345a, line 44	*Delete*
Page 356b, line 35	*For* Denis Kearny *read* Denis Kearney
Page 357a, line 28	*For* N.D. *read* S.Dak.

ABBREVIATIONS USED IN THIS INDEX

act.	actor, actress
adm.	administrator
advt.	advertiser, advertising
aeron.	aeronaut, aeronautical
Afr.	Africa
agric.	agricultural, agriculturist
agron.	agronomist
Ala.	Alabama
Alg.	Algeria
Alta.	Alberta
Amer.	American
Antarc.	Antarctica
anthrop.	anthropologist
arch.	architect, architecture
archaeol.	archaeologist
archbp.	archbishop
Ariz.	Arizona
Ark.	Arkansas
art.	artist
astro.	astronaut
astron.	astronomer, astronomy
astrophys.	astrophysicist
atty. gen.	attorney general
au.	author
Aus.	Austria
av.	aviator
Az.	Azores
bact.	bacteriologist
Bah.	Bahamas
Belg.	Belgium
biblio.	bibliophile
biochem.	biochemist, biochemistry
biol.	biologist
Bor.	Borneo
bot.	botanist
bp.	bishop
Br.	British
Braz.	Brazil
Br. Hon.	British Honduras
Bur.	Burma
bus.	business, businessman
B.W.I.	British West Indies
ca.	circa
Calif.	California
Can.	Canada
capt.	captain
card.	cardinal
cartog.	cartographer, cartography
cartoon.	cartoonist
char.	character
chem.	chemist, chemistry
chor.	choreographer
cinema.	cinematographer
class.	classicist
cler.	clergyman
col.	colonial, colonist, colonizer
coll.	collector
Colo.	Colorado
Colom.	Colombia
comp.	composer, composition
Conn.	Connecticut
C.R.	Costa Rica
crim.	criminologist
crit.	critic
crystal.	crystallographer
cur.	currency
Dak.	Dakota
D.C.	District of Columbia
Del.	Delaware
Den.	Denmark
dent.	dentist, dentistry
dial.	dialect
dict.	dictator

ABBREVIATIONS USED IN THIS INDEX

dipl.	diplomacy, diplomat
dir.	director
dram.	dramatist
ecol.	ecologist
econ.	economist
ed.	editor
educ.	educator
Egy.	Egypt
elec.	electrical, electricity, electronics
emp.	emperor, empress
ency.	encyclopedia, encyclopedist
Eng.	England
eng.	engineer, engineering
engr.	engraver
entom.	entomologist
expl.	explorer
femin.	feminist
fig.	figure
fin.	finance, financier
Fla.	Florida
Fr.	France
Ga.	Georgia
geog.	geographer
geol.	geologist
Ger.	German, Germany
gov.	governor, government
Gr.	Greece
Green.	Greenland
Haw.	Hawaii
hist.	historian
Hung.	Hungary
hydrog.	hydrographer
Ice.	Iceland
ichthyol.	ichthyologist
Ill.	Illinois
illus.	illustrator
Ind.	Indiana
ind.	industrialist, industry
int.	interior
inv.	inventor
Ire.	Ireland
Is.	Island(s)
It.	Italy
Jap.	Japan
Jor.	Jordan
jour.	journal, journalist
jur.	jurist
k.	king
Kans.	Kansas
Kor.	Korea
Ky.	Kentucky
L.A.	Los Angeles
La.	Louisiana
lang.	language
law.	lawyer
Leb.	Lebanon
L.I.	Long Island
Lib.	Liberia
ling.	linguist
lit. char.	literary character
Lux.	Luxembourg
mach.	machine
mag.	magazine
Mass.	Massachusetts
math.	mathematician
Md.	Maryland
med.	medical
mer.	merchant
metal.	metallurgist
meteor.	meteorologist
Mex.	Mexico
mfg.	manufacturing
mfr.	manufacturer
mgr.	manager
Mich.	Michigan
mil.	military
min.	mineral, mineralogist
Minn.	Minnesota
Miss.	Mississippi
miss.	missionary
Mo.	Missouri
Mont.	Montana
Mor.	Morocco
mus.	music, musical, musician(s)
myth.	mythology
nat.	naturalist
navig.	navigator
nav. off.	naval officer
N.B.	New Brunswick
N.C.	North Carolina
N.Dak.	North Dakota
Nebr.	Nebraska
Neth.	Netherlands
Nev.	Nevada
Newf.	Newfoundland
news.	newspaper
N.Guin.	New Guinea
N.H.	New Hampshire
Nic.	Nicaragua
N.J.	New Jersey
N.Mex.	New Mexico
Nor.	Norway

nov.	novelist
N.S.	Nova Scotia
N.Y.	New York
N.Y.C.	New York City
off.	officer
offi.	official
Okla.	Oklahoma
Ont.	Ontario
Oreg.	Oregon
org.	organization, organizer
ornith.	ornithologist
Pa.	Pennsylvania
Pac. O.	Pacific Ocean
paint.	painter, painting
paleon.	paleontologist
Pan.	Panama
par.	parish
Para.	Paraguay
parl.	parliamentarian
path.	pathologist
period.	periodical
pharm.	pharmacologist
Phil.	Philippines
Phila.	Philadelphia
philan.	philanthropist
philol.	philologist
philos.	philosopher
phot.	photographer, photography
phys.	physicist, physics
physic.	physician
physiol.	physiologist
Pol.	Poland
pol.	political, politician, politics
pol. sci.	political science
P.R.	Puerto Rico
pres.	president
print.	printer
prod.	producer
prop.	proprietor
pseud.	pseudonym
psych.	psychiatrist, psychologist, psychology
pub.	publication, publisher
q.	queen
ref.	reformer
rel.	religion, religious
rev.	revolutionary
R.I.	Rhode Island
riv.	river
rr.	railroad
Russ.	Russia
S.	South
S.C.	South Carolina
schol.	scholar
sci.	scientist
Scot.	Scotland
sculp.	sculptor, sculpture
S.Dak.	South Dakota
sec.	secretary
sing.	singer
soc.	sociologist
sol.	soldier
Sp.	Spain, Spanish
states.	statesman
statis.	statistician
surg.	surgeon
tech.	technician, technologist
Tenn.	Tennessee
Terr.	Territory
terr.	territorial
Tex.	Texas
Thai.	Thailand
theat.	theatrical
theol.	theologian
topog.	topographer
trav.	traveler
Tun.	Tunisia
Turk.	Turkey
Univ.	University
Uru.	Uruguay
USSR	Union of Soviet Socialist Republics
Va.	Virginia
Venez.	Venezuela
vet.	veterinarian
V.I.	Virgin Islands
Viet.	Vietnam
virol.	virologist
Vt.	Vermont
W.Afr.	West Africa
Wash.	Washington
W.Ger.	West Germany
Wis.	Wisconsin
writ.	writer
W.Va.	West Virginia
Wyo.	Wyoming
zool.	zoologist

DICTIONARY
OF
AMERICAN HISTORY

INDEX ENTRIES

A

A–1 (prop craft) VI–302b
A–1E (attack plane) I–54a
A4 (attack plane) I–56b
A–6 (attack plane) I–56b–57a
A–7 (attack plane) I–57a; VI–302b
A–7D (attack plane) I–54a
A–20 (bomber) I–50a
A–26 (bomber) I–50a
A–36 (bomber) I–53b
A–37 (support plane) I–54a
AAA. *See* Agricultural Adjustment Administration; American Automobile Association
AAAS. *See* American Association for the Advancement of Science
AACHEN (Ger.) **I–1a**
World War II I–380a; III–314a; VI–285b; VII–340a
AAF. *See* Army Air Forces
Aalto, Alvar (arch.) III–136b
AAS. *See* American Anti–Slavery Society
AAUP. *See* American Association of University Professors
ABA. *See* American Bar Association
Abaco (Bah.) III–273b
Abacus II–154a
Abbe, Cleveland (meteor.) II–75b–76a; IV–317b
Abbeville (S.C.) VI–349a
Abbeville County (S.C.) III–315a
Abbey Theatre (Dublin) VII–49b
Abbot, Charles Greeley (astrophys.) VI–319a
Abbot, Downing and Company II–158a; V–178a
Abbott, Jacob (au.) I–335a
Abbott, Robert S. (pub.) V–76a
Abbott, Samuel W. (physic.) IV–149b
Abbott, W. H. (bus.) V–319a
Abbott Laboratories II–107a
Abbott Pharmaceutical Company V–274a
ABC CONFERENCE (1914) **I–1b**
Abderhalden, Emil (biochem.) I–303a
'Abdu'l-Baha (Abbas Effendi) (rel. leader) V–172a
Abel, I. W. (labor leader) IV–76a
Abel, John Jacob (pharm.) IV–3a
Abelson, Philip (phys.) I–457a
Abercrombie, Fort (N.Dak.) II–284a; III–32a
Abercrombie, James (off.) II–134a, 267a; III–116a; IV–86a; VI–162b; VII–57a
Aberdeen, Lord. *See* Gordon, George Hamilton
Aberdeen Angus cattle I–471b; VI–45a
Aberdeen Proving Ground (Md.) II–153a, 154b
Abernathy, Ralph D. (cler.) I–24a
Abigail (ship) VI–199a
ABILENE (Kans.) **I–1b**
cattle I–471b, 473a; II–31b–32a, 248b–49a, 251b; IV–26a, 280b; VI–45a
Chisholm Trail II–31b
Eisenhower Library I–167b; III–284b
ABILENE TRAIL I–2a
Abingdon (Va.) VI–202b
AB-INITIO MOVEMENT (1866–69) **I–2a**
Abiquiu (N.Mex.) III–162b
ABLEMAN* v. *BOOTH (1859) **I–2a**
ABNAKI (Indians) **I–2b**; II–31a, 321a; III–360b, 366b, 367a
Casco Treaty of 1678 I–465b
Dummer's War II–380b; V–111b
French and Indian War III–115a, 116b
Jesuit missions III–499a
Kennebec River settlements IV–37a
King Philip's War IV–47b
King William's War IV–49a; VI–201a; VII–358b
Pemaquid Point V–243b
Rogers' Saint Francis raid VI–190a
"running the gauntlet" III–154b
See also Pequawket
Abolition. *See* Antislavery
Abortion I–100b, 307a; II–263a; VI–267a; VII–314a
A.B. PLOT (1823–24) **I–3a**
ABRAHAM, PLAINS OF (Can.) **I–3b**; III–116b; VI–1b
Abraham Lincoln (sculp.) VI–243b
ABRAHAM LINCOLN, FORT (N.Dak.) **I–3b**; I–312b; II–496a; IV–168a; VI–135a,b
Abrahams, Peter V–199b
Abrams, William Penn (millwright) VII–361b
Abrams v. *United States* (1919) VI–255a
Abruzzi Mountains III–187a
Absalom, Absalom! IV–164b
Absentee ballot II–410b–11a
ABSENTEE OWNERSHIP I–3b
military tracts IV–345a
Ohio Company of Associates V–143b
"speculators' deserts" IV–99b
tenements VII–23b
Wyoming Valley VII–347a
Abstract expressionism V–192b–93a,b
Abstract of the Lawes of New England I–294a
Abstract of title. *See* Title, abstract of
"Absurdist" playwrights VII–50b–51a
AC–47 (cargo plane) I–54a
AC–119 (cargo plane) I–54a
AC–130 (cargo plane) I–49b, 54a
ACADEMIC FREEDOM I–4b; II–115b, 470b; VII–15b, 156b
Academician (jour.) II–398a
Académie des Sciences (Fr.) IV–126a
ACADEMIES I–5b; II–394b, 397a, 398b; IV–116a; VI–228b
natural history IV–348b
old field schools V–151b
scientific education VI–232a
University of Pennsylvania V–248b–49a
Academy of Natural Sciences (Phila.) I–110b; IV–348b; V–327a; VI–235b–36a, 237b
Academy of Sciences. *See* National Academy of Sciences
ACADIA I–6a; I–361a; II–92b, 126b; III–120b; IV–46b, 192a; VI–190b; VII–162b
fur trade VI–182a
Jesuit missions III–499a
maps VII–73b
Port Royal V–369b
Queen Anne's War VI–2b
Acadia (par., La.) I–6b
Acadia National Park IV–422b; V–217a, 218 (table), 220a
ACADIAN COAST I–7a; I–6b
Acadians
Evangeline II–465b
Pointe Coupee V–335a
Accardo, Tony (criminal) II–258b
Accelerators, particle II–278a; IV–119a,b; V–296a,b, 297a, 300b–01a
Accessory Transit Company III–23a–b; V–94a
ACCIDENTS I–7a; IV–151b
airplane I–69b; II–500a; III–429b
airship I–234a
automobile I–152b, 228a, 230a–b
court cases IV–19a
industrial liability laws II–440b–41b
industrial relations III–406b
insurance III–427a, 429b, 431b–32a, 435a
occupational IV–80a, 293a
railroad workers VI–20a
Safety First movement VI–185a
social legislation VI–327a
steamboat II–89a
workmen's compensation VI–328a; VII–322a
See also Disasters
Accokeek furnace (Va.) V–409b
Account of Expeditions to the Sources of the Mississippi and Through the Western Parts of Louisiana V–312a
ACE. *See* Active Corps of Executives I–59a
Acetate II–7a; V–327b; VII–44a
Acetone acid II–226b
Acetylene II–7b, 422a
Acheson, Edward G. (chem.) II–7b, 422a; III–409a
Achievement tests II–400a
"A choice, not an echo" I–430b
Achromatic lens I–241a, 349a
ACKIA, BATTLE OF (1736) **I–7b**; I–197a; II–22b; VII–70b
ACLU. *See* American Civil Liberties Union
ACOMA (N.Mex.) **I–7b**; II–461a; III–367b; V–460a; VI–162a
mesas IV–315a
San Esteven church I–159b
Acorn I–157b; III–51b, 362b
A'Court, H. Holmes (nav. off.) I–76b
Acoustical research V–289b
Acoustic mines IV–351a
Acre right. *See* Cabin rights
Acres, Birt (cinema.) IV–417a
Acrylic plastics V–328a
ACS. *See* American Colonization Society
Act Concerning Religion. *See* Act of Religious Toleration
ACT FOR THE IMPARTIAL ADMINISTRATION OF JUSTICE (1774) **I–8a**; II–93a; III–464a
"Act for the liberties of the People" (1639) III–316a–b
Act for the Punishment of Certain Crimes (1798) I–86b
Act Further to Regulate Interstate and Foreign Commerce by Prohibiting the Transportation therein for Immoral Purposes of Women and Girls, and for Other Purposes. *See* Mann Act

Acting. *See* Theater
ACTION I–8b; VI–328b
ACTION Cooperative Volunteers I–8b
***ACTIVE* CASE** (1809) **I–9a**
Active Corps of Executives I–8b, 9a
Act of Religious Toleration (1649) IV–260b
Acton (Minn.) VI–296b
Acton, Lord, John E. E. Dalberg–Acton (hist.) II–231b
Actors
moral codes IV–408a
Actor's Equity Association I–315a
Actors Studio VII–50a
Actors' Workshop (San Francisco) VII–50b
Acts of Trade and Navigation. *See* Navigation Acts
"Act to Authorize the President to Raise Mounted Volunteers for the Defense of the Frontier" (1832) I–475b
Act to Encourage Immigration (1864) II–214a
Actuarial science VII–206b–07a
Actuarial tables IV–149a
Actuaries, Institute of II–154a
Acturial Society of America III–434a
ACV. *See* ACTION Cooperative Volunteers
AD (attack plane) I–56b
ADA. *See* American Dental Association
Adaes (Robeline, La.) I–48b
Adair, John (pol.) IV–40b, 184a
Adair, William (rr. off.) I–9b
ADAIR* v. *UNITED STATES (1908) **I–9b**; II–222a; VII–354b
Adam, Robert (arch.) III–445b
Adam Forepaugh's Circus II–40b
Adam of Bremen (hist.) III–280a
Adams (corvette) III–217b, 247b
Adams, Abigail V–185a; VII–313a
Adams, Alvin (mer.) I–9b
Adams, Amos Kendall (hist.) III–282b
Adams, Charles C. (ecol.) II–391b
Adams, Charles Francis (dipl.) IV–85a
Alabama I–72b
Alabama Claims I–73a; II–65a,b
campaign of 1848 III–111b
Liberal Republican party IV–141a
Trent affair VII–116a
Adams, Charles Francis, Jr. (law., hist.) VI–157a
Adams, Edward D. (fin.) V–92a,b
ADAMS, FORT (Miss.) **I–9b**; III–108a, 232b; IV–179a
Adams, Francis W. H. VII–238a
Adams, Franklin P. (humorist) V–75a
Adams, Henry (hist.) III–260a, 282a; IV–163a
Adams, Henry Carter (econ.) IV–2b
Adams, Herbert Baxter (hist.) I–106a; III–282b
Adams, John I–120a; II–174 (table); III–260b, 262a; IV–268a; V–395 (table), 396b; VI–107a; VII–179 (table), 293b, 309a
American Academy of Arts and Sciences I–97b; IV–126a
Articles of War VI–301b; VII–143a
Boston Massacre I–346a; VII–117a–b
British debts I–366b
Continental navy VI–128a
Declaration of independence II–303b–05b, 308a; III–87b
Defence of the Constitutions V–353a
Embargo of 1807 II–437a
E pluribus unum II–455b
foreign loans II–382a–b; VI–120a
library II–107b
Loyalists VI–115b
Massachusetts Bill of Rights I–298b
Massachusetts constitution VI–390b
Molasses Act VI–321a
Peace of Paris II–318b; V–214b; VI–117a
philosophy V–287a
Plan of 1776 V–323b
prerevolutionary imperial idea III–346b
Revolution VI–114a
—*President:*
Alien and Sedition Acts I–86b
campaign of 1800 III–494b
Convention of 1800 II–215a; VI–117a; VII–348a
Cooper, Thomas, trial V–397b
court appointments IV–248b, 335b; VI–448a
educational reform II–396a
election I–417a, 475a; III–4b
Franco-American relations III–95b–96a
Fries pardon III–124a
isolationism III–480a
judicial reform IV–19b
Marine Hospital Service III–267b
Miranda's intrigues IV–361b
Napoleon IV–266b
Navy Department V–17b
newspaper attack on I–224a
political patronage VI–375a
White House VII–291b
XYZ Affair IV–347a; VII–347b
—*Vice-president:*
conservatism II–189a
elected I–416b, 417a
executive privilege II–473b
Federalist party II–325b
Gazette of the United States V–69b
presidential title V–399a
Adams, John Quincy II–175 (table); III–260b, 279b; IV–268a; V–161a, 395 (table), 396b
A.B. Plot I–3a
Adams–Onís Treaty I–10b, 126b, 154a, 174a; IV–320b; VI–359b
American system IV–193b
Amistad case I–114b
antislavery gag rule V–265b, 266b
antislavery petitions IV–267b
Arbuthnot and Ambrister case I–154a
census of 1820 I–481b
Cuba II–268a
Great Lakes disarmament III–217a
Latin-American policy IV–115a, 115b
Monroe Doctrine I–121a; III–462a–b; IV–400a; VI–364a
National Lord's Day Society IV–409a
panic of 1819 V–206b
Perry's Venezuela mission VII–170a
secessionist movement VI–250b
Smithsonian Institution VI–318b
Treaty of Ghent III–176b; VII–235b
—*President:*
astronomic observatories V–131a
campaign of 1824 I–418b; II–231a, 327a; IV–469b; V–101b; VI–421b
campaign of 1828 I–418b–19a; III–486a; V–101b
civil service II–59b
conservation policy II–187b
French spoliation claims III–121b
internal improvements III–449a,b
Monroe Doctrine V–153a
National Republican party II–327a
political patronage VI–375a
Adams, Lewis (mechanic) VII–130b
Adams, Paul D. (off.) IV–130a
Adams, Robert (pub.) II–341a–b
Adams, Samuel (states.) IV–161b; V–161a; VI–112b
Boston Committee of Correspondence I–345a
Boston Resolutions of 1767 I–347a
committees of correspondence II–140a; IV–266a
Constitution II–196a–b
Declaration of Independence II–308a
Freemasons III–109a
natural rights doctrine V–7b
Revere's ride VI–106a
Adams, Samuel Hopkins (jour.) V–466a
Adams, Sherman V–346b
Adams, Thomas S. (educ.) VII–308b
Adams, Walter Sydney (astron.) I–212a
Adams, William (dipl.) III–176b
Adams and Company I–10a
Adams County (Ohio) III–222a; IV–420b–21a
ADAMS EXPRESS COMPANY I–9b; VII–97a, 101a
Adams family III–279b; IV–256b
Adams Memorial (sculp.) VI–243b
ADAMSON ACT (1916) IV–68b; VI–21a; VII–214a
ADAMS–ONÍS TREATY (1819) **I–10b**; I–126b; III–68a; IV–115a, 197b, 198a; V–254b; VI–359b, 364a; VII–111b, 236a
Arbuthnot and Ambrister case I–154b
Arkansas River I–174a
Florida III–38b–39a, 40b, 42a; VII–277a
Greer County III–228a
Indian Country III–379a
Mexican boundary IV–320b
Nootka Sound V–109a
opposition IV–184a
Oregon II–216a
Pacific Northwest V–167b
Sabine River VI–143a
Seminole VI–259b
Texas VII–36b
Adamson v. *California* (1947) V–353b
Adams press V–411a
Adam Thoroughgood House (Princess Anne County, Va.) I–161a
Ad astra per aspera (motto) VI–393 (table)
Addams, Jane (social worker) II–18a; V–100a, 280a; VI–331b
Hull House VI–330b
slums VI–314a
Addickes, David (art.) VII–41a
Addiction, drug. *See* Drug Addiction

Adding machines I–395b, 396b
Addington, Henry (pol.) I–367
Addison, Joseph (writ., states.) III–241b
Addison, William H. (off.) VI–244b
"ADDRESS OF THE SOUTHERN DELEGATES" (1849) **I–10b**
"Address. . .to Their Constituents" (1850) IV–453b
ADDYSTON PIPE COMPANY CASE (1899) **I–11a**; VI–102a
Adelphia (Ohio) IV–250b
Aden (Yemen) III–277b
ADENA (culture) **I–11a**; I–157a; III–300a; VII–320a
Adenine II–357b, 378a; IV–389a, 390a
Ader, Clément (eng.) V–290b; VI–14b
Aderholt, O. F. III–154a
Adhesives II–239a; III–44b; IV–357b
Adirondack Mountains
conservation IV–101b
resorts VI–100b
Adirondack Park Agency Act (1971) IV–101b
Adirondack porch chair III–136a
Adjutant and Inspector General's Office IV–339b
ADKINS* v. *CHILDREN'S HOSPITAL (1923) **I–12a**; IV–70a, 80a, 353a; VII–214a, 269a,b
Adler (warship) I–144a
Adler, Stella (dir.) VII–50a
Adler and Sullivan VI–299a
Administration industrielle et générale III–406a–b
Administrative adjudication. *See* Administrative Justice
ADMINISTRATIVE DISCRETION, DELEGATION OF I–12a
ADMINISTRATIVE JUSTICE I–12b
Administrative Office Act (1939) IV–17b
Administrative Office of the U.S. Courts II–501a; IV–17b
Administrative Procedure Act (1946) I–12b, 13b; V–472a
Admiral (Md.) I–434b
ADMIRALS AND COMMODORES I–13b
chief of naval operations V–13b
Confederacy V–17a
Admiral's Cup race VII–349a
"Admiral's Map" IV–247a
Admiralty, Board of VI–128a
ADMIRALTY LAW AND COURTS I–14a
colonial smuggling VI–320b
Constitution II–202a
district courts IV–16a, 17a
Dolphin II–360a
Rule of the War of 1756 VI–169a
Springbok case VI–376b
See also Prize Cases, Civil War; Prize Courts
Admission of states. *See* State–making Process; entries under individual states
ADOBE I–15a; V–317a
forts III–78a; IV–89b, 108a, 109a
frontier army I–192b
pueblos I–166b, 377a; III–367a,b; V–460a
Spanish colonial architecture I–159b, 160a, 377b
ADOBE WALLS, BATTLE OF (1874) **I–15a**
Adopting Act (1729) I–410b
Adowa, Battle of (1896) I–21b
Adrenaline V–307a
Adrian (fashion designer) II–372b
Adriatic Sea III–106b, 235b
World War I VII–329a
"Adult book" stores II–263a
Adult education II–399b, 401b; VI–228b
See also Education
Adult Education Act (1966) II–401b
Adult Education Association of the U.S.A. II–401b
Adultery V–355b, 464b; VI–265b
divorce II–356b
Ad valorem duties. *See* Duties, Ad Valorem and Specific
Advance (brig) II–319b
Advent Christian church I–15b
ADVENTIST CHURCHES I–15a; VI–77b
Jehovah's Witnesses III–497b
New York State V–87a
physiology movement V–306a
Western Reserve VII–275a
ADVENTURE (sloop) **I–15b**
ADVENTURERS I–15b
filibustering III–22b
Adventures of Huckleberry Finn IV–163b
ADVERTISING I–16a
almanacs I–91a
blimp II–345b–46a
book matches IV–274b
brands I–359b
cereal industry I–488a
corporate II–107a
cosmetic industry II–234a
distribution of goods and services II–354b
Eastman Kodak V–292a
Federal Trade Commission II–178b, 500a; III–459a
folklore III–49a
Food and Drug Administration III–54a
fraudulent II–208b, 500a
immigration IV–94a,b
Klondike gold rush IV–52a
magazines II–354b; IV–222a,b
mail–order houses IV–225a
marketing research IV–255a
motor trucks IV–419b
newspaper II–354b; V–69a, 72a; VII–356a
pharmaceutical industry V–275a
political campaigns I–415b, 425b; V–450a
pure food and drug movement V–467a
radio I–480b; II–424a–b
Robinson–Patman Act VI–157b
self–policing II–208b
slang VI–300a
soap industry VI–323b–24a
tax III–229a
television I–480b; II–345b, 354b
vitamins V–128a
westward movement III–353b; IV–100a
yellow journalism V–71b
Advice to the People in General With Their Health III–325a
Advisory Committee on National Defense IV–69a
Advisory Council on Historic Preservation V–393a
"Advocate of Industry and Enterprise" VI–231a
Adz II–386a
AEC. *See* Atomic Energy Commission
Aedes mosquito IV–291b
A.E.F. *See* American Expeditionary Forces
AEOLUS (rr. car) **I–20b**
Aerial Experiment Association I–233a
Aerial gunship. *See* Gunships
Aerial photography I–236a, 248a, 463a–64a; II–88a; V–293a–b
"Aerodrome" I–233a
Aerodynamics IV–106a
Aeromarine Airways I–67b
Aeromedical research I–63b
Aeronautical Chart and Information Service I–464a
Aeronautical charts II–88b
Aeronautic corps I–248a
Aeronautics. *See* Aviation; Dirigibles
Aeronautics, National Advisory Committee for. *See* National Advisory Committee for Aeronautics
Aeronautics, Navy Bureau of V–18a; VII–341b
Aeronautics and Space Administration, National. *See* National Aeronautics and Space Administration
Aeronautics Board, Civil. *See* Civil Aeronautics Act
Aerosol cans V–183a; VI–213a
Aerospace Defense Command I–58a, 59a
Aerospace Industries Association IV–171a; V–400a
Aerospace industry I–237b–38a
San Diego VI–208b
Southwest VI–355b
tungsten III–15b
Aerospace Medical Association IV–289a
Aerospace Medicine, School of IV–292b
Aetatis Suiae V–186a
AFAS. *See* American and Foreign Anti-Slavery Society
AFDC. *See* Aid to families with dependent children
Affirmative action programs IV–81a; VI–8a
AFL. *See* American Federation of Labor
AFL–CIO. *See* American Federation of Labor–Congress of Industrial Organizations
Africa
astronomical observatories V–131b
coffee VI–345b
colonization movement I–101a; II–127a–b, 404b
copper deposits II–223b
Dutch trade II–383b
eclipse expedition (1889) II–88a
immigration to U.S. III–341b
labor resources II–122a
Liberia IV–141b
missions IV–409b
music IV–442b–43a
Navigation Acts V–15b
rubber trade VI–167b
slave smuggling VI–321b, 322a
slave trade IV–335a; VI–170b, 304a, 304b, 308b, 309a
U.S. civil rights movement II–59a
venereal disease VII–169a
World War II VII–338a, 340b
yellow fever VII–355a
"Africa for the Africans" I–21b; V–200a
African–American Institute I–22a
AFRICAN–AMERICAN RELATIONS I–21a; VII–87b
Liberia IV–141b
mandates IV–236b
Pan–Africanism V–199a
Point Four program V–335a
triangular trade II–119a; IV–388a; VII–86a, 119a, 277b
AFRICAN COMPANY, ROYAL I–22b; II–469b; VI–310a; VII–119b
"African iron" VII–119a,b
African Lodge (Boston) III–109a

AFRICAN METHODIST EPISCOPAL CHURCH I–23a; I–21b; IV–319a
African Methodist Episcopal Zion church I–21b; IV–319a
African Studies Association I–22a
African Union First Colored Methodist Protestant church IV–319a
Afro–American ballads. *See* Ballads; Music, Afro–American
AFRO–AMERICAN CHURCH I–23a; VI–78b
  antebellum South VI–343a
  free blacks III–102b
  Methodists IV–318b, 319a
  music IV–443a
  Reconstruction VI–59b
AFRO–AMERICAN CULTURE I–24a
  black press V–75b–76a
  folklore III–48b
  Gullah III–233b
  music IV–442b
  pottery V–379b
  slavery VI–306b–07a
Afro–American literature. *See* Literature, Afro–American
AFRO–AMERICAN MIGRATION I–25b; I–29a, 29a–b, 30a, 30a; III–438a; V–67b; VI–432b; VII–141a,b
  Chicago II–18a
  Cleveland II–75a
  Harlem III–253a,b
  New Jersey V–57b
  Reconstruction VI–59b
  segregation VI–256a–b
  slums VI–314b
  Virginia VII–196b
  World War I IV–69a
Afro–American music. *See* Music, Afro–American
AFRO–AMERICANS I–26a
  African Methodist Episcopal Church I–23a
  age composition of population V–362b–63a
  Alabama I–72a,b
  American Colonization Society I–100b
  antislavery I–136b
  army I–187a
  Association for the Study of Negro Life and History III–279b
  backlash I–239b
  Baltimore I–250b
  Baptist church I–265a
  Bedford–Stuyvesant I–282b
  birth rate V–361b
  black capitalism I–309a
  black cavalry I–309b
  Black Codes I–310b
  black infantry I–313b
  Black Laws I–314a
  Black Muslims I–315a
  black nationalism I–315b
  Black Panthers I–315b
  black power I–316a
  Blease movement I–319a
  Brooklyn I–370b
  Brownsville Affair I–371b
  Brown v. *Board of Education of Topeka* I–372b
  California I–408b
  campaign of 1876 I–423a
  campaign of 1948 I–429b
  campaign of 1968 I–431a
  carpetbaggers I–460a
  Catholics I–468a
  Charleston I–497b
  Cincinnati II–37b
  citizenship I–94b; II–370b
  civil rights movement II–55b–59a, 64b
  civil service II–61a
  Civil War prisoners II–468b
  Clinton riots II–77a
  Code Noir II–91b
  colleges II–113b–14a, 115a
  colonization movement II–127a–b; IV–141b
  Communist party members II–145b
  community action programs II–148a
  compensated emancipation II–433b–34a
  Compromise of 1890 II–151a
  Confederate army II–63b, 161a–b, 162a
  Congress of Racial Equality II–179b
  Connecticut II–181a
  consumers' cooperatives II–221a
  Creoles II–257a
  crime II–258b, 261b
  dance II–287a, 289b–90b, 290b
  Dartmouth College II–293b
  death rate V–361b
  Democratic party I–239a–b; VII–210b
  discrimination II–54a–b
  drug use II–262b
  education II–395b, 399b, 401b–02a, 403a–04b
  elected officials III–20b; VII–211a–b
  Ellenton riot II–432a
  emancipation movement II–434a
  Emancipation Proclamation II–434b, 436a
  employment II–455b–56a
  enfranchisement II–325b, 408a
  equal protection of the law II–457a
  Equal Rights Association III–91b
  eugenics movement III–158b
  Farmers' Alliance II–493b
  Fifteenth Amendment II–205a–b
  "forty acres and a mule" III–81a
  Fourteenth Amendment II–64b, 205a–b; III–86a–87a; VI–56b–57a
  free blacks III–101b
  Freedman's Savings Bank III–103a
  freedmen II–54a
  Freemasons III–109a
  gambling II–260b
  Georgia III–168b, 169a,b
  Harlem III–253a
  hat manufacture III–262a
  Houma Indians III–308a
  House Un–American Activities Committee III–308b
  Indiana III–370b
  integration III–437a
  International Exposition of 1895 III–453b
  Jim Crow laws III–502b
  jury service VI–417b
  King, Martin Luther IV–45b–46a
  labor force IV–73b, 75a, 75b
  labor movement IV–76b
  life expectancy IV–151a; V–361b
  literacy test IV–160a
  literature IV–166a
  lynching IV–208a
  Melungeons IV–301a
  Michigan IV–332a
  military service IV–339b
  minority rights IV–359a
  miscegenation IV–362b
  Moynihan Report IV–424b
  NAACP IV–460b
  National Urban League V–1a
  naturalization V–6b
  "Negro Plot" of 1741 V–32b
  Newark V–41b
  New South V–67b
  newspapers V–75b–76a
  New York City V–83b–84a
  New York Colony III–253a
  New York State V–88a
  Niagara movement V–92b
  "nigger" V–95b
  Pan–Africanism V–199a
  peonage V–260b
  Pinkster celebration V–316b
  poll tax I–451a
  poverty V–280b
  protest movement II–179b
  race relations VI–6a–b, 7a,b
  race riots I–431a; VI–8a
  radical right VI–12b
  Reconstruction III–295a–b; VI–55b
  religious education II–403a–b
  Scottsboro case VI–241b
  sectionalism VI–254a–b
  segregation I–372b–73a; II–54a–b; VI–255b
  sharecroppers IV–103a–04a
  slave insurrections VI–303a
  slavery VI–304b
  slaves to Indians II–52a
  slave trade VI–309a
  slums VI–314b–15a
  Solid South VI–337a
  South Carolina VI–348a
  Southern Christian Leadership Conference VI–351b
  Student Nonviolent Coordinating Committee VI–420b
  Thirteenth Amendment II–205a–b
  Tillmanism VII–59a
  unemployment VII–140b
  Union Army II–63b, 161a
  voter registration III–93b
  voting rights II–205b
  Washington, D.C. VII–245b–46a
  White Citizens Councils VII–291a
  woman's rights movement VII–313a, 314b
  women's clubs VII–313b
  Wyoming VII–346a
  See also African–American Relations; Fugitive Slave Acts; Integration; entries under Black, Negro, Reconstruction
Afro–American suffrage. *See* Suffrage, Afro–American
Afro–American Symphony (comp.) IV–438b
Afroyim v. *Rusk* (1967) II–475b; III–86b
AFSCME. *See* American Federation of State, County, and Municipal Employees
AFT. *See* American Federation of Teachers
Afton (Va.) I–325b
Agamemnon (steamship) I–400b
AGAMENTICUS (Maine) **I–32a**; III–200a,b
Agana (Guam) III–426a
Agassiz, Alexander (zool.) I–410b; III–27b, 29a,b; IV–119b; V–134b; VI–455a
Agassiz, Lake VI–63b
Agassiz, Louis (nat.) I–344a; II–76a, 390a; III–27a,b, 260a; IV–119b, 120a, 233a, 251a, 348b; V–134b, 196b; VI–90b
Agate Basin projectile point III–484b
Agate Fossil Beds National Monument V–217b
Agateware III–184a
Agave cactus III–398a
Agencies, federal. *See* Federal Agencies
Agencies, Indian. *See* Indian Agencies
Agency for International Development III–72a
Agency shop
  checkoff II–4a
  union agreements II–81a
Agent, colonial. *See* Colonial Agent
Agent Orange (defoliant) II–319a–b

Agents, Indian. *See* Indian Agents
Age of Enterprise VI–157a
Age of Mammals IV–232b
Age of Reason III–112a
Age of Roosevelt III–283a
"Age of the Automobile" I–231b
Agnew, Spiro T. (pol.) IV–261a; V–347a; VI–93b, 368b; VII–133a
attack on network news agencies I–480b
campaign of 1968 I–431b
campaign of 1972 I–432a
resignation V–78a, 398b
vice-presidency VII–180a
Agramonte, Aristides (physic.) VII–355b
AGRARIAN MOVEMENT I–32b; II–189a
automobiles I–226b
expansion II–474b
free silver VI–371a
Grange III–210a
Jacksonian Democracy III–486b
Jefferson, Thomas II–166a
Jeffersonian Democracy III–495b
Knights of Labor IV–64b
Nonpartisan League V–106a
North Dakota V–117b
organized labor IV–62a
Patrons of Husbandry V–228b
populism V–364b
radicals VI–13b
Republican party VI–92b
South Dakota VI–350a
taxation VII–5b–6a
third parties VII–52b
Tillmanism VII–58b
Agrarians
absentee landowners I–4a–b
banks I–130a
big business I–389a
Bourbons I–345a
calamity howlers I–404a
See also Farmers; Populists
Agreement of the People III–132b
Agricultural Act (1970) I–43a; VI–172a
Agricultural Adjustment Act (1933) I–43a; III–194a; V–44a, 47a, 402a; VI–138b, 426a; VII–7b, 13a
Bankhead Cotton Act I–254b
crop-reduction IV–103b–04a
farm relief I–391a
Hoosac Mills Case III–299a
Thomas Amendment I–302a; IV–395b; VII–54b
wheat prices VII–286b
Agricultural Adjustment Act of 1938. *See* Pope–McGill Farm Act
Agricultural Adjustment Administration IV–104a; V–44a, 48a; VII–124b
Agricultural colleges II–115a, 447b, 494a; III–151a; IV–93b, 96a, 97a,b, 103b
dairy industry II–281b
Agricultural cooperatives. *See* Cooperatives, Farmers'
Agricultural credit corporations I–44a
Agricultural Credits Act (1923) VII–231a
Agricultural Economics, Bureau of I–463b
Agricultural experiment stations I–45a, 46b–47a; II–494a, 494a; III–52b, 151a
dry farming II–376a
nutrition V–127b
Agricultural extension service II–494b
Agricultural fairs I–285a
Agricultural Land Grant College Act. *See* Morrill Act (1862)
Agricultural Library, National I–45b
AGRICULTURAL MACHINERY I–34a; I–37a–b; IV–103a
Chicago II–17b
combine II–133b
cotton picker IV–104a
Dodge City (Kans.) II–358b
flour milling III–43a–44b
Granger movement III–211a
harness III–255b
Industrial Revolution III–412a
interchangeable manufacture IV–272b
International Harvester Company III–454b
McCormick reaper IV–211a
Memphis IV–302a
mowing machine IV–424a
Oklahoma V–149b
Peoria V–260b
state fairs VI–329b
sugarcane VI–436b
thresher VII–55a
trade association VII–92b
wheat growing VII–286b
Agricultural Marketing Act (1929) I–43a
Agricultural Marketing Service V–359a
Agricultural Museum (jour.) I–45b
Agricultural Research Center (Beltsville, Md.) I–46b
Agricultural societies I–41a–42a, 45a; III–151b
education I–47a
Agricultural Society (Pa.) I–110b
Agricultural Society, United States I–41b
Agricultural Statistics, Office of IV–95a
Agricultural Trade Development and Assistance Act (1954) I–43b; III–62a
AGRICULTURE I–36a; III–52b; VI–48a
Alabama I–71a–72a
American Farm Bureau Federation I–42a
American Philosophical Society I–110b
applied genetics III–159a
Arizona I–172b
Arkansas I–173b
Bankhead-Jones Farm Tenant Act IV–104a
beet sugar VI–437a
biochemistry I–302b–03b
boll weevil I–26a; IV–103a
Brannan Plan I–360b
California I–407b, 408b; VI–365a
child labor II–23b–25a
China trade V–158a
chinch bug II–29a
Chinese labor II–29b
Civil War production II–69b
Clayton Antitrust Act II–72a
coasting trade II–90b
Colorado II–128a–b
commerce clause II–137a
commission merchant II–138a
Commodities Exchange Act II–140b
Commodity Credit Corporation I–43a, 44b
Connecticut II–180b
controlled floods III–36b
corn belt II–226b–27a
corporation farming IV–104a
cotton II–238a; IV–103a
Cotton Kingdom II–241a
county fair II–244b
credit II–255a
crop control program IV–104a
Cropland Adjustment Program I–43a
Customs Service, United States II–277a; VII–108a
Delaware II–320b
Delaware Indians II–321a
Denver II–332a
Desert Land Act II–335b
dry farming II–375b
executive agreements II–472a
exports VII–87a,b
farm banks V–455b
farmers' cooperatives II–221a
farmhand II–495a
federal nutrition programs V–129a–b
fencing III–10a,b
fertilizers III–16a
food stamp program III–56a
Four-H clubs III–84b
fruit growing III–128a
gardening III–150b
Georgia III–169a–b
government aid VII–11b
government control I–391a
government inspection III–422a
Granger movement III–210a
grasshoppers III–212b
Great Depression IV–103b
Hamilton's fiscal policies III–245b–46a,b
health hazards IV–294b
hemp III–271a
Hoosac Mills Case III–299a
horse III–303b–04a
Idaho III–328b
Illinois III–329b–30a
immigration III–336b, 491b
Indiana III–370a,b
indigo III–405b
insecticides and herbicides III–421b
insects II–391a
Intermediate Credit Banks III–447a
internal improvements III–447b
international exchange of developments V–170b
Iowa III–468b
irrigation III–477a
Italian-Americans III–483b
joint-stock land banks IV–6b
Kentucky IV–40a,b, 41b, 42a
land grant colleges II–399a; IV–300b
Land Office reports IV–95a
land systems IV–102a
livestock industry IV–169b
Long Island IV–185b
Louisiana IV–193b–94a
Maine IV–227a
manors IV–241b
McNary-Haugen bill IV–219a
Michigan IV–331b
minimum wage VII–214a
Minnesota IV–356b–57a
Mississippi IV–369a,b
Missouri IV–377a, 378a
Montana IV–403a,b
mortgage relief legislation IV–414a–b
Narragansett planters IV–451b
Natchez IV–455a
national parks V–220a
Nebraska V–31b
New Deal V–44a–b
New England V–50a; VI–170b
New Hampshire V–53b, 54a
New Haven Colony V–56a
New Jersey V–57a
New Mexico V–60a
New Plymouth Colony V–65a
New South V–67a,b
New Sweden Colony V–80b
New York State V–87a
Night Riders V–96a

AGRICULTURE (cont.)
Nonpartisan League V–106a
Norris Farm Export Act V–111b
North Carolina V–115b, 116a,b
North Dakota V–117b, 118a
oats V–129b
Ohio V–141a,b
Oklahoma V–149a
onions V–156a
open-book credit III–422b
Oregon V–165b
panic of 1857 V–207a
panic of 1893 V–207b
panic of 1929 V–209a
patents V–226a
Pennsylvania V–246b
peonage V–260b
per capita income VI–384a–b
periodicals VI–235b
Philippines V–284a
pioneers V–317a–b
plantation system V–178b, 324b; VI–341a–b
Point Four program V–335a
poor whites V–359a
Pope–McGill Farm Act V–359a
populism V–364b
potatoes V–376b
prairie V–387a
prairie dogs V–387b
prices V–405a–b, 406a
Progressive party IV–84b
public land states V–444b–45a
Puerto Rico V–461a,b
pure food movement V–465b
rainfall VI–40b
rainmaking VI–42a
ranching VI–44b, 45a
reclamation VI–53b
Reconstruction Finance Corporation VI–60a
Red River of the North VI–64b
reforestation VI–67a
relief projects VI–73b
Resettlement Administration VI–99a
revolutionary war VI–117b
Rhode Island VI–131b
ribbon farms VI–135a
rice VI–135b
Rio Grande Valley VI–143b
Rockefeller Foundation VI–158a
Rocky Mountains VI–160b
rural development VI–171b
rural life VI–174a–76a; VII–159a,b
Saint Paul VII–134a
Schenectady VI–225b
secret societies VI–253a
sectionalism VI–254a
sharecropping IV–103a–b; VI–268b
slavery VI–304b
Smith–Lever Act VI–318a
soil VI–334a
sorghum VI–340a
South Dakota VI–350a
state fairs VI–392b
state geological surveys III–165b
state universities VII–156a–b
steam engines VI–409a
subsidies II–476a; VI–426a, 471a
subsistence homesteads VI–426b
sugarcane VI–436a, 436b–37a
tariff III–20a, 113a,b; VI–465a–b, 470b
taxation VII–5b
tea VII–16a
Tennessee VII–25b, 26a
Tennessee Valley VII–28a,b
tobacco VII–66b
Trade Expansion Act VI–469b–70a
transition from frontier III–126a
Trelawney Plantation VII–114b
truck farming II–180b, 297b
unemployment VII–140b
unionization of workers IV–76b
Utah VII–162a
Vincennes VII–188b
vineyards VII–305a–b
Virginia VII–194a, 196a–b
Virgin Islands VII–204a
War Finance Corporation VII–231a
Washington State VII–247b, 248a
water law VII–256a
wild rice VII–298a
Wisconsin VII–308a
work force V–132a–b
World War I VII–327b, 328a
World War II VII–336a
See also Agrarian Movement; Agrarians; Bees; Botany; individual names of crops and products

AGRICULTURE, AMERICAN INDIAN I–47b; III–50b–51a, 318b, 356a,b, 381a
Athapascan cultures III–368b
California Indians III–362a
corn II–225b–26a
Eastern Woodlands culture III–366b
Havasupai III–262b
Hopi III–301a
irrigation III–477a
Jesuit missions III–499a
maize I–486a
Mandan, Hidatsa, and Arikara IV–235b
Mexico IV–327a
Mississippian cultures IV–370a,b
Mogollon IV–385b
Mohave IV–386a
native plants V–325b
Navaho V–8b
Pawnee V–230b
Pima–Papago V–314a,b
Plains Indians III–363b
plantation system II–52a
potato V–376b–77a
pottery III–373b
Pueblo III–367b; V–459b
religion III–392a,b
Southeast culture III–366a–b
Southwest cultures III–369a
tobacco VII–64b–65a
vegetable gardens III–150b–51a
villages III–405a
wild rice VII–298a
Woodland Tradition VII–320a
Zuni VII–372a

Agriculture, Department of I–359b, 399b; II–178b, 498a; III–52b
advertising I–19a
bacteriology I–241a–b
Bureau of Animal Industry I–45a, 241b; V–447b
Bureau of Chemistry V–447b, 465b
Bureau of Entomology III–213a
Bureau of Public Roads I–484b
cattle industry I–472a
chemistry II–10b
Civilian Conservation Corps II–51a
consumer protection II–208b
extension services I–41b, 43b
farm credit I–44b
Farm Security Administration VI–99b
farm tenancy IV–103b
Food and Drug Administration III–53b, 54a
food stamps III–56a,b
foreign agricultural service VI–389a
Four-H clubs III–84b
history I–33a, 41b, 45a–b
insecticides III–421a
Job Corps III–504a
meat inspection laws IV–279b
National Forest Service IV–95b
national parks and monuments V–217a
Office of Dry Land Agriculture II–376a
Office of Road Inquiry II–502b
ornithology and mammalogy II–390a; IV–233a
Patent Office V–226a
rainmaking VI–42a
Resettlement Administration V–46a
rural development VI–171b, 172a
scientific experiments I–46b
soil conservation VI–335b
soil surveys VI–334a
Soviet wheat deal (1972) I–43b
veterinary medicine VII–177a
Weather Bureau II–135a; VII–264a
wildlife preservation VII–297b

Agriculture, secretary of I–44b
beet sugar quotas I–285b
farm cooperative associations I–451b
livestock industry regulation VI–378b
meat inspection IV–279b
Packers and Stockyards Act V–183b
rural post roads VI–176a

"Agriculture and Commerce" (motto) VI–395 (table)
Aguayo, San Miguel de. *See* Aguayo Expedition
AGUAYO EXPEDITION (1720–22) **I–48b**; VI–210a
AGUE I–49a; II–454b; IV–229a
Aguilar, Martin d' (expl.) V–164b
Aguinaldo, Emilio (rev.) III–133a; IV–340a; V–281b, 282b; VI–361b, 362b
AH–1G (helicopter) I–49b
Ah, Wilderness! (play) VII–50b
AHA. *See* American Historical Association
Ahtena (Indians) I–80b
Aid to Families of Dependent Children V–382a; VI–74a,b
Aiken, Conrad (poet) IV–164a
Aiken, Howard (inv.) II–153b–54a, 426b
Aiken, John W. (pol.) VI–325b
Aiken County (S.C.) II–432a
Ailey, Alvin (chor.) I–25a; II–289b
AIM. *See* American Indian Movement
Aimard, Gustave (trav., writ.) III–122b
AIP. *See* American Institute of Planners
Airacobra (fighter plane) I–53a, 57b
Airacomet (jet fighter) I–53b
Air and Space Museum, National IV–469a; VI–319b
Air bases (U.S.)
Africa I–149b
Atlantic II–314b
Bermuda I–292b
Great Britain I–124a; II–314b
Iceland II–314b; III–327b
Spain VI–360b
World War II II–33a
Air brake V–247b; VI–28a
Air cargo. *See* Cargo, air

AIR CAVALRY I–49a
helicopters III–270b
Vietnam War
VII–183b–84a
Air Command and Staff School I–64b
Air Commerce Act (1926) VII–264b
Air conditioning
automobile I–299b
See also Heating and Air Conditioning
Air Corps Act (1926) I–59b
Air Corps Tactical School I–64a–b, 66b
Aircraft
accidents I–66a, 69b, 234a; II–346a–47b
aerial tankers I–52b, 61a, 62a, 237b
agriculture I–40b
aluminum I–92a
amphibian I–51b
biplanes I–50b–51b, 52b
cargo I–49b, 52b, 61b, 62b, 63a, 65a, 237b, 291a
Coast Guard II–90a
dive bombers I–55a, 56b
environmental pollution VI–213a
gunships I–49b, 62b, 63a, 65a, 291a
helicopters I–49a,b, 52a, 55b, 56b, 62a, 188a
interceptor I–53b, 54a
jet I–50b, 52a,b, 53b, 54a, 56a,b, 56b–57a, 61a,b, 62b, 63a,b, 67b, 68b, 69a, 235a, 237b, 411a; IV–363b
mine planting IV–351a
monoplanes I–50a, 51a,b, 52b, 53a, 55a
patrol I–55b
reconnaissance I–235a, 484b
rocket I–52a,b, 235a
scout bombers (VSB) I–55a
scout observation (VSO–VOS) I–55b
sea planes I–51a,b
supersonic transports I–53a, 69a
support I–54a
torpedo I–55a,b
tracker I–56b
transports I–49a,b, 51b–53a, 61a–64a, 68a–69a, 234a–35a, 236a–37a, 291a
turbojets I–52a, 68b, 237b
See also Aviation Industry
AIRCRAFT, BOMBER I–50a; II–345b; IV–364a, 431b; V–26b–27a
AD Douglas Skyraider I–56b
armament I–57b
B–9 I–236b
B–29 III–489b–90b
B–29 units I–64a
B–52 I–235a
bombing I–328a
carrier aircraft I–55a
Cuban missile crisis I–61b
development I–52a
fighter bombers I–53a–b
Korean War I–237b
Liberator V–332a
national defense II–314b
Strategic Air Command I–62a,b
Strategic Arms Limitation Talks VI–417a
torpedoes VII–76b
Vietnam War I–63a; II–316b
World War II I–60a–b, 67a,b, 207b–08a; VII–335b, 338b, 340b, 343b
XB–17 I–59b
AIRCRAFT, DEVELOPMENT OF I–50b; II–314b; IV–105b–06b, 244b, 433a–b
military helicopters III–270a
National Advisory Committee for Aeronautics IV–458a
AIRCRAFT, FIGHTER I–53a; I–55a, 57a–58a, 60a–61b, 235a, 237b; IV–431b
air battle of Germany III–174a
bomber I–50a
carrier aircraft I–57b
design I–235a
development I–55a
dirigible transport II–344b–45a
fighter interceptors I–62a
jet engines I–237b
Korean War I–61a–b
P–51 I–52a
rockets VI–159a
Soviet planes in Korea IV–56a,b
Vietnam War I–62b; VII–185b
World War I VII–326a
World War II I–60a; VII–335b, 339a, 340b, 343b
Aircraft, naval. *See* Aircraft Carriers and Naval Aircraft
AIRCRAFT ARMAMENT I–57a; V–164a
machine guns IV–215a
missile systems IV–363a
Neutrality Act (1935) IV–430a
Aircraft Board (World War I) VII–327b
AIRCRAFT CARRIERS AND NAVAL AIRCRAFT I–54a; IV–432a; V–11a–b, 25a,b, 26a, 27a; VI–279b; VII–241b
airships II–344a–45a
Battle of Midway IV–336a
Battle of the Philippine Sea V–286a
Berlin airlift I–291a
Enterprise II–350a
Five-Power Naval Treaty III–33b
Forrestal II–350a
helicopters III–270a
Lexington II–225a; IV–136b
London Naval Treaty IV–183a
national defense II–314b
naval competition V–10a,b, 11a–b
naval production V–28a
parity V–216b
prize courts V–421b
Skywarrior I–50b
Task Force 58 VII–1a
World War II I–234b; II–218b, 225a, 387b; VII–342a,b, 343a–b
Yorktown II–225a
See also Navy, United States
Aircraft hijackings. *See* Hijacking, Aerial
Aircraft Manufacturer's Association I–235b
Aircraft Production Board IV–433b
Aird, James VII–352b
AIR DEFENSE I–57b
Air National Guard I–64b
artillery I–200a,b
missile systems IV–363a
SAGE system II–156a
Air Defense Command I–58a, 62a, 64a
Airfoil IV–106a
AIR FORCE, UNITED STATES I–59a; II–315a
Aachen I–1a
aviation records I–235a
Berlin airlift I–290b
bombing I–67a–b, 328a, 411a, 431a
Bronze Star II–312a
China II–26a
Cross for Distinguished Service II–310b
disasters II–346b; IV–341b
Distinguished Service Medal II–311a
Eighth Air Force I–67a
Far East Air Forces IV–56b
Fourth Fighter–Interceptor Wing I–61a
intelligence staff III–439a
Jefferson Barracks III–494b
Korean War IV–56b–57a
Medal of Honor II–310a
medical research IV–292b–93a
Midway Islands base IV–337a
missiles IV–363b
North Dakota bases V–117b
Officers' Reserve Corps V–138b
polar exploration V–338a
recruitment VI–61a
Reserve Officers' Training Corps VI–99a
San Antonio VI–207b
slang VI–302a–b
Soldiers' and Airmens' Home VI–336b
space program IV–459a
strategic air power II–314b
strategic bomber force I–179b
XXI Bomber Command I–64a
Vietnam War VII–183b, 184b, 185a
volunteers II–451a
women VII–318b
World War I IV–83b
World War II II–237a; VII–62a
See also Aircraft; Aircraft, Bomber; Aircraft, Fighter; Aircraft Armament
AIR FORCE ACADEMY, UNITED STATES I–65a
Air Force Department II–167b, 498a
Air Force Logistics Command I–64a
Air Force Nurse Corps VII–318b
Air Force Reserve I–64b–65a
Air Force Systems Command I–64a
Air France (airline) II–347a
Airglow III–453b
Airlift, China. *See* Flying the Hump
Airlifts II–218a
Berlin I–60b, 179a, 290b
blizzards I–320a
Vietnam I–63a
Yom Kippur War (1973) II–213a
Airlines
airmail I–65b–66a
aviation industry I–236b
See also Air Transportation
AIRMAIL I–65b; III–452a; VII–102a
acts I–68a
contracts I–236a
postage stamps V–372b
private carriers I–67b, 236a
U.S. Air Corps I–59b, 68a, 233b
World War I IV–458a
Air Mail Act (1930) I–68a
Airman's Medal II–312a
Airmaster (monoplane) I–52b
Air Material Command I–64a
Air Medal II–312b
Airmobile. *See* Air Cavalry; First Cavalry Division
Air National Guard I–64b; IV–464a
Air piracy. *See* Hijacking, Aerial
Airplane disasters. *See* Aviation; Disasters
Air pollution II–224a; VI–155b
California I–408b
Clean Air Acts II–188b
electric energy II–417b
Airports IV–428b
Albany (N.Y.) I–82a
Civil Aeronautics Act II–49b
county-sponsored II–245b
federal assistance I–70a; II–499a; III–452a
federal expenditures III–450a
local government IV–172a

AIRPORTS (cont.)
Mohawk Valley IV–387a
See also Air Transportation
AIR POWER, STRATEGIC I–66a
military policy IV–344a
missile systems IV–363a
national defense II–315b
naval competition V–11b
Air raids I–66a–67b; II–50a
See also Air Force, United States; Korean War; Vietnam War; World War I; World War II
Air Reserve Forces I–64b–65a
Air rights IV–104b
Air–sea patrols II–90a
Air–search radar II–345b
Air security officers II–277b
Air Service, U.S. IV–83b
Air Service Field Officers' School I–64a–b
Air Service Tactical School I–64a–b
Airships. *See* Dirigibles
Air–Slide railroad cars III–44b
Air tankers
B–47 I–61a
KC–135 I–52b, 237b
Strategic Air Command I–62a
Air taxies I–68b
Air–to–air ordnance I–57b
AIR TRANSPORTATION I–67b; III–452a; VII–101b, 102a,b
army logistics I–190a
Chicago Air Convention VII–112b
China Clipper II–28a
Civil Aeronautics Administration II–49b
freight VII–84a,b
government inspection III–422a
hijacking III–276b
insurance III–429b
labor laws IV–467a
mail subsidies VI–425b
Midway Islands IV–337a
National Mediation Board II–157b, 500b
World War II VII–336a
Air University I–64a–b
Air War College I–64b
Airways Modernization Board II–49b
Airy, George B. (astron.) III–166b, 480b, 481a
AISNE DEFENSIVE (1918) **I–70a**; I–502a
AISNE–MARNE OPERATION (1918) **I–70a**; V–146b; VI–197a
Aitken, Robert (pub.) I–294a
Aix–la–Chapelle. *See* Aachen
Aix–la–Chapelle, Congress of (1818) I–93a
AIX–LA–CHAPELLE, TREATY OF (1748) **I–70a**; III–118a; IV–47a
Associators I–208a
cession of Louisburg IV–192b
Ajacan (Virginia) III–41a
Ajo (Ariz.) III–390b
Akagi (aircraft carrier) IV–336b, 337a
Akeley, Carl (nat.) III–19b
Akerly, Samuel (nat.) III–27a
Akron (Ohio)
cereal manufacture I–486b–87a
Ohio and Erie Canal V–145b
Pennsylvania and Ohio Canal V–249b
rubber industry V–141b; VI–167b, 168a
school system I–70b–71a
strikes V–142a
Akron (dirigible) I–51b, 234a, 236b; II–346a
Akron II (dirigible) II–345a, 346a
AKRON LAW (1847) **I–70b**
ALA. *See* Alliance for Labor Action
ALABAMA I–71a; IV–200a; VI–393 (table)
Afro–American education II–404a
Battle of Cabusto I–402a
Black Belt I–308b
black suffrage III–437b; VI–432a,b, 433a,b
boundary I–351a; III–38a, 41b
Buford expedition I–376b
campaign of 1836 I–419b
Choctaw II–33a
civil rights movement I–31a; II–58b–59a
Civil War I–71b; II–432a; III–146a; IV–382b, 405a; VI–166a
Civil War supplies II–163a
coal II–85a, 86a
constitution (1901) I–29a
cotton I–38a; II–237b–38b; VI–305b
Creek War II–256b; III–305b; IV–347b, 456a; VII–239a
Democratic party VII–210a
desegregation I–31a
double jeopardy VII–154b
fall line II–485a
Fort Charlotte I–499a
Fort Claiborne I–402a
Fort Condé I–499a
Fort Confederation II–167b
Fort Deposit II–333a
Fort Gaines III–146a
Fort Tombecbe II–167b
Fort Toulouse VII–77a
free blacks I–29a
Freedom Riders II–179b; III–107a
French settlers II–167b; III–121b
grandfather clause III–208b
Great Trading and War Path III–387b
Guntersville Dam III–323a
Hillabee Towns III–278a
horse racing III–304b
Huntsville III–318b–19a
hurricanes II–352a; III–319b
hydroelectric power II–423a
Indian slaves III–401a
Indian treaties IV–97a
Inland Waterways Corporation V–455b
iron II–163a; V–67a
Ku Klux Klan IV–58b, 59a
minimum–wage law IV–353b
Mississippi Territory IV–368a,b
Mobile IV–382a
Muscle Shoals II–423a
National Democratic party VII–53a
"New West" V–81b
New York Times libel suit III–105a–b
Old Southwest VI–356a
Peace Society VII–149a
Perdido River V–262a
poker V–336a
poll tax III–92b
port authority V–368a
prehistory II–385b
public land sales V–452b, 453a
public land states V–453a
railroad land grant IV–94a; VI–26a
railroads VI–33a, 36a,b
Reconstruction VI–57b, 59a
repudiation of state debts VI–96b
rice VI–136a
Russell Cave V–217b
Saint Stephens VI–197b
school integration II–402a
Scottsboro case VI–241b
secession II–61a; VI–250b
segregation II–179b
Seminole War VII–239a
slavery I–27b; VI–309a
Spanish exploration V–370a
Spanish settlers II–167b
statehood VII–284a
sugarcane VI–436a
taxation VII–15a
Tennessee River VII–27b
tidelands VII–57b
tobacco VII–67a
Tombigbee Valley VII–70b
tornadoes II–351a,b; VII–75b
Treaty of Fort Jackson III–383b
Tuskegee Institute VII–130b–31a
Union Rights party VII–148a
Union sentiment VII–148b
veterinary medicine VII–176b
Voting Rights of 1965 VII–211a
War of 1812 IV–383a
Wheeler Dam III–323b
Wilson Dam III–323b–24a
Yazoo fraud VII–353b
Alabama (battleship) VII–242a
Alabama (ship of the line) VI–282a
Alabama (song) VI–393 (table)
ALABAMA (warship) **I–72b**; I–438b; II–63a, 65b, 213a; IV–35a, 310b; V–17b, 20a, 23b; VI–181a, 274b; VII–147a
See also Alabama Claims
Alabama, University of I–72a
ALABAMA CLAIMS I–72a; I–121b; II–65b; III–68a–b, 456a; IV–4b; V–232b
arbitration IV–5b
neutrality doctrine V–35a
neutral rights V–39a
Treaty of Washington I–439a; VII–112b, 248b
Alabama Great Southern Railroad III–64b; VI–37a
Alabama Indians III–499b
ALABAMA PLATFORM I–73b
Alabama River I–308b; II–256b; IV–456a; VI–414b
Alabama Territory I–71a
Alabamo (Ala.) II–336b
Alachua (Indians) VI–260b
ALAMANCE, BATTLE OF (1771) **I–73b**; III–212b; VI–72a
Alamo (Tex.) VI–207b
ALAMO, SIEGE OF THE (1836) **I–74a**; VI–84a, 207a, 213a; VII–37b
Bowie, James I–355a
Alamo Canal II–130a
Alamogordo (N.Mex.)
atomic bomb test I–215b; IV–238b
Alamo Plaza (San Antonio) I–267a
Alarcón, Hernando de (expl.) II–129b, 228b
ALASKA I–74b; VI–393 (table); VII–285a
acreage purchased V–445 (table)
air defense I–58b, 62a
Alcan Highway I–439b; VI–156a
Aleut I–84a
American Indian migration III–355a
Apache V–8b
Arbor Day I–154a
Ballinger–Pinchot controversy I–274b
birch bark I–304b
boomtowns I–336b
border dispute I–122b, 439a; IV–5b
Chinook jargon II–30a–b
chromite III–13b
citizenship II–42b; V–6a
coal II–86a
coast survey II–88a
constitution VI–391b
counties II–245a
domestic shipping

IV–309a
earthquakes II–347b, 385a–b; III–164b
Eastern Orthodox church II–386b
Eskimo II–461b
exploration II–219b; V–337a,b
food III–53b
forests III–74b
fortifications III–78b
free land III–107b
gold I–302a, 439a; III–191b, 238a; IV–52a; V–405b
Haida III–238a
highways VI–156a
initiative III–418b
Kodiak Island IV–54a
land grants for education IV–93b
mackerel fisheries IV–217a–b
mineral lands I–247b–48a
national parks and monuments V–217a,b, 218 (table), 220b
Navaho V–8b
naval forces V–25a
old-age legislation VI–328a
petroleum V–122a, 271a, 272b
pipeline I–80a, 230b, 336b
placer mining V–323a
political subdivisions V–349b
prehistory III–302a
Pribilof Islands V–401a
proposed annexation II–475a
public domain V–446a
purchase I–84b, 126b; II–475a; III–68b, 347a; V–158a, 443b, 453a; VI–177b; VII–111b
railroads III–203a
recall VI–51a
referendum VI–66b
rivers VI–151a
Russia II–461b; V–164b; VI–177b, 180b–81a
salmon IV–311a; VI–201a
sealing IV–250a; VI–245b, 245b
Seattle trade VII–248a
statehood VI–400a, 401b; VII–33b
steamship lines II–91a
taxation VII–13b
territorial government VII–32a–b
territorial status III–424b
timberlands VII–61a
U.S. flag III–34b
Wells, Fargo VII–267a
wolves VII–311b
woman's suffrage III–91b; VII–315a
workmen's compensation VI–185a
World War II VII–334a, 336b
Yukon River VII–367a
Alaska (corvette) I–76b
Alaska, Gulf of IV–54a
Alaska Commercial Company VI–245b
Alaska Highway. *See* Alcan Highway
Alaska Native Claims Settlement Act (1971) V–220b
ALASKAN INDIANS **I–80b**; III–238a, 252b, 356a, 396b; V–217b
art and technology III–373a–b
Chinook V–165a
education III–380a, 390a
Eskimo III–357b–58a
Jesuit missions III–500b
Northwest Coast III–360b
subarctic culture III–358b–60b
tobacco VII–65a
See also Canadian Indians
Alaska Omnibus Act VI–401b
ALASKA-PACIFIC-YUKON EXPOSITION (1909) **I–81a**
Alaska Peninsula I–84b; IV–54a
Alaska Power Administration III–445a
Alaska Railway VII–98b
Alaska's Flag (song) VI–393 (table)
Alaska Statehood Act VI–401b
Albacore (submarine) V–286a
Albacore hull VI–423a–b
Albanel, Charles (cler.) VI–220a
Albanian Orthodox Archdiocese in America II–387a
Albany (Ga.) I–31a; V–28a
ALBANY (N.Y.) **I–81a**; II–267b
billeting VII–80a
bog iron I–327a
Burghers I–384b
capitol V–191a
charter II–383b
clay III–183a
colonial suffrage VI–434a
domestic trade VII–83b
Dudley Observatory V–131a
Dutch merchants III–475b
Erie Canal II–460a
Freemasons III–109a
freemen III–109b
French and Indian War III–115b
fur trade III–141a,b; IV–386b
Genesee Road III–157a
Great Lakes III–216a
Hudson River III–275b, 312a,b
Hudson River land patents III–313a
Hudson's exploration V–86a
Iroquois Beaver Land Deed III–476a
Iroquois trade VII–95b
Iroquois Trail III–387b
Iroquois Treaty III–476b
King William's War IV–49b
Lafayette's visit IV–84a
painters V–186a
Pinkster celebration V–316b
post roads V–374b–75a
potatoes V–376b
railroads III–450a; IV–386b; V–87a; VI–24b, 25a,b; VII–100b
revolutionary war I–384b, 436b; III–400b; V–172b; VI–217b, 385b; VII–280a
scientific research VI–238a
settlement I–492b; II–383a,b
slums VI–314a
steamboats III–131b–32a; VI–407a
train robbery VII–97b
See also Orange, Fort
Albany, Treaty of (1722) V–386a
Albany Academy V–294a
ALBANY CONGRESS (1754) **I–82a**; I–81b; II–389a; III–115b, 123a; V–85a; VI–451b
ALBANY CONVENTION (1689–90) **I–82b**
Albany County (N.Y.) III–291b
Albany Evening Journal (news.) I–132b
Albany Institute VI–236a
Albany Institute of History and Art III–137a
Albany Mall (N.Y.) V–87b
Albany Plan of Union I–82a–b; II–122a
ALBANY REGENCY (1820–48) **I–82b**; I–107b
Albany-Schenectady Railroad I–82a
Albany slip (clay) III–183a
Albatross (research ship) III–29a, 30a
ALABATROSS (trade ship) **I–83a**
Albee, Edward (dram.) IV–165b; VII–50b
ALBEMARLE (ram) **I–83a**; V–424a; VI–425a
ALBEMARLE AND CHESAPEAKE CANAL I–83a
Albemarle County (Va.) III–495b
Albemarle pippins III–128b
Albemarle Point (S.C.) VI–347a
settlement I–496a
ALBEMARLE SETTLEMENTS I–83a; I–447b; II–271a; V–115a
Albemarle Sound II–392b; V–109b, 115a
Albemarle and Chesapeake Canal I–83a
Civil War VI–156b
Lost Colony VI–42b
Raleigh's first colony VI–43b
Albers, Josef (art.) II–104b
Albert (prince consort) VII–115b
Albert, Carl (pol.) II–178 (table); VI–368b
Alberta (Can.)
Columbia River Treaty II–132a
Indians I–441b; III–363a
mustangs IV–444b
Albert of Saxony (schol.) III–481a
Albertus Magnus (philos.) III–49b
Albion (Ill.) II–450b
Albion, New. *See* Plowden's New Albion
Albright, Horace M. (offi.) V–220a
Albright, Tenley (athlete) V–154b
Albright-Knox Gallery II–106a
ALBUQUERQUE (N.Mex.) **I–83b**
Civil War VI–144a; VII–165b
Forest Service III–76b
railroads VI–27a
Whipple's expedition VII–289a
Albuquerque, Duke of I–83b
Alcalá de Henares, San Diego de. *See* San Diego
ALCALDES I–83b
Alcan Highway II–450a; VI–156a
Alcatraz Island III–397a; VI–7b, 209b
Alchemists II–278a
ALCOA. *See* Aluminum Company of America
Alcohol
corn II–226b
excise taxes VI–105a
fur trade III–140a,b
tariff VI–467a
Alcohol, Drug Abuse, and Mental Health Administration III–267b
Alcohol, industrial II–261a
Alcohol, Tobacco, and Firearms, Bureau of VII–108a
bootlegging I–339b
Alcohol Abuse and Alcoholism, National Institute of IV–159a
Alcoholic beverages
barley and rye I–486b
bootlegging I–339a
distilling II–353b
Indian III–398a–99a
Prohibition II–261a–b, 406b–07b
temperance movement VII–22a
See also Ale; Brewing; Liquor Laws
Alcoholism VI–204b
Alcott, Amos Bronson (educ.) II–158a; III–129b; VI–228b
Alcott, Louisa May (au.) I–335a; IV–223a
Alcott, William Andrus (educ., physic.) V–264b, 306a
Alden, John (col.) V–334a
ALDER GULCH (Mont.) **I–83b**; II–477b; III–270a
Alderman, Edward A. (educ.) VII–197b

Aldermanic Committee to Investigate the Relief Administration in New York City I–336b
Aldine (mag.) VII–319a
Aldine imprints II–109a
Aldrich, Larry (art coll.) II–106a
Aldrich, Nelson (pol.) III–6a; IV–468a; V–209a; VI–467b
Aldrich, Thomas Bailey (au.) I–335a–b; IV–223a
Aldrich Commission. *See* National Monetary Commission
Aldrich Report of 1911 V–209a
ALDRICH–VREELAND ACT (1908) **I–84a**; I–256b; III–6a; IV–468a; V–209a
Aldrin, Edwin E., Jr. (astronaut) I–63b, 210b; IV–406b
Aldworth, Robert (mer.) V–243b
Ale I–326a; II–353b; III–51b, 398b
Alemany, José Sadoc (cler.) II–362b
Alembert, Jean d' (math., philos.) II–444a
Alert (ship) III–224a
ALEUT (Indians) **I–84a**; I–75a; II–461b; III–358a, 396b
language I–81a
population I–79a, 85a
Aleutian archipelago I–81a, 84a; II–461b
ALEUTIAN ISLANDS I–84b
Aleut I–75a
Canton fur trade I–446a
Eskimo III–357b
exploration II–219b
migration to North America I–74b
Russian claims VI–180b
sea otter trade VI–247a,b
World War II I–439b; IV–54a, 336b; VII–336b
Alexander (Indian) IV–47a
Alexander I (czar) III–177a; IV–400a; VI–177b
Alexander VI (pope) II–323b; VII–75a
Alexander, Cosmo (paint.) V–186b, 187b
Alexander, Harold (off.) I–141a,b, 308a; IV–33a; V–113a; VI–284b
Alexander, James (col. offi.) V–56b
Alexander, John W. (paint.) V–191a
Alexander, Robert (off.) V–147a
Alexander, William, Earl of Stirling (poet) III–17b, 152a; IV–185a,b, 185b; V–369b; VI–346b; VII–359a
Alexander, William, Lord of Stirling (off.) IV–186a
Alexander Archipelago I–75a
Alexander Brown and Sons III–63b, 466a
Alexander family (Va.) I–85a; III–469b
Alexander I Island V–338a
Alexander the Great
sea power VI–247b
Alexandria (Egy.) II–334a, 479a
Alexandria (La.)
Camp Beauregard I–434b
Civil War I–279b; VI–63a
Alexandria (Minn.) IV–38b
ALEXANDRIA (Va.) **I–85a**; III–148a, 219a; IV–423a; VII–244b
ALEXANDRIA CONFERENCE (1785) **I–85a**; II–192b
Alexandrine Library and Museum IV–126a
Alfalfa II–281a; III–328b
Alfred (ship) VI–128a,b
Alfred Jenks and Son IV–433a
Alfriend, Frank H. (ed.) VI–353a
Algal studies (bot.) I–349b
Al G. Barnes Circus II–41a
Algebra
electric circuit analysis II–39a
Maya IV–327b
ALGECIRAS CONFERENCE (1906) **I–85b**; III–97a; IV–221a; V–233a, 261b; VII–113a
Alger, Andrew (col.) VI–184a
Alger, Arthur (col.) VI–184a
Alger, Horatio, Jr. (au.) I–335b, 494b
Algeria
World War II IV–32b; V–112b, 113a; VII–338a
Algerian Zouaves II–432b; VII–371b
Algernourne, Fort (Va.) IV–399b
Algiers
Barbary Wars I–266b; II–303a–b, 303a–b; V–19b; VII–111b
extraterritoriality treaty II–479a
tribute I–266a; III–168a; VII–120a,b
Algonkin (lang.) I–445b; II–17a, 497a; III–360a,b, 364a, 365a, 365a,b, 366b–67a, 476a; VII–305b, 367b
Abnaki I–2b
Algonquin I–85b
Arapaho I–151b
Bible I–294a; III–375b; V–410b
Blackfoot I–311a
Cheyenne II–16b
Chippewa II–31a
Cree II–30b
Delaware II–321a
farming I–48a
Fort William Henry massacre VII–301a
Fox III–88b
"Great Spirit" III–223a
"Happy Hunting Ground" III–251a
Mahican IV–387a
Michabous IV–330a
Mohegan IV–387a
Muskhogean languages II–51b
myth and folklore III–386b
Northeastern architecture I–166b
powwow V–386b
sachem VI–183b
Salishan tribes I–441b
wampum VII–223a
Wappinger Confederacy VII–223b
wigwam VII–294b
Algonkin Atsina (Indians) I–311a
ALGONQUIN (Indians) **I–85b**; III–365a, 475a
Champlain I–492b
Jesuit missions III–499a
Shawnee VI–270b
Vermont VII–171a
Virginia VII–192a
Algren, Nelson (au.) IV–164b
Alhambra IV–161b
Ali, Muhammad (boxer) V–154b, 423b
Ali, Noble Drew I–315b
Alianza movement VI–7b
Alibates Flint Quarries and Texas Panhandle Pueblo Culture V–217b
ALIEN AND SEDITION LAWS (1798) **I–86a**; II–53b, 326b, 332b; III–4b, 104a; V–2b; VII–117b
journalists V–69b–70a
loyalty oaths IV–202b
minority rights IV–358b
Virginia and Kentucky Resolutions VII–198a
See also Sedition Acts
Alien Contract Labor Law. *See* Contract Labor, Foreign
Alien Enemies Act (1798) I–86b; II–445a, 463a
Alien Friends Act (1798) I–86b
ALIEN LANDHOLDING I–87a
ban on IV–103b
confiscation II–168b
Japanese VI–7a
land tenants I–4a
populism V–365b
restrictions VII–356b
Alien Property Custodian, Office of II–168b, 445b; VII–327b
Alien Registration Act of 1940. *See* Smith Act
Aliens
deportation II–332b–33a
registration II–473a
restrictions I–86a–88b, 409a, 409a,b
rights I–87b–88a
Smith Act VI–317b
welfare benefits II–457b
See also Immigration; Naturalization
Aliens, enemy *See* Enemy Aliens in the World Wars
ALIENS, RIGHTS OF I–87b
citizenship VII–315b–16a
habeas corpus IV–218b
international law III–455a, 456b
Smith Act VI–255b
U.S. ships VI–165a
Aliens, undesirable III–417b
Alligator (submarine) VI–424b
Alim (Indian) V–387b
'Ali Muhammad (rel. leader) V–171b
Alinsky, Saul II–147b
Alkali II–5a, 6a–b
Al-ki (motto) VI–395 (table)
Allaire, James VI–409a
All-America Conference (football) III–57a
All-American Canal II–130a
All-American Futurity III–305a
Allan, John (bibliophile) II–108b
Allan, Maude (dancer) II–287a
ALLATOONA PASS, BATTLE AT (1864) **I–88b**
Allegany County (N.Y.) V–463b
Alleghany (merchantman) I–266b
Alleghany County (Va.) III–469b
Allegheny County (Pa.) VII–290a
Allegheny divide II–369b
Allegheny Mountains III–256b
Batts–Fallam expedition I–277b
British exploration V–32a
colonial boundary III–118a, 120a
English–French rivalry I–477a
Fort Loudoun IV–192a
land grants IV–371a
Monongahela River IV–398b
"New West" V–81b
Potomac River V–378a
settlement IV–92b
Shenandoah Valley VI–275b
stagelines VI–380a
surveys III–226a
Treaty of Long Island of Holston IV–186b
Vandalia Colony VII–166b
wagoners VII–216a
western lands IV–181b; VII–252a
Westsylvania VII–281a
ALLEGHENY MOUNTAINS, ROUTES ACROSS I–88b; III–448a; V–367a
Allegheny Portage Railroad V–247a, 247a
Boone's Gap III–223b
buffalo trace I–376a
Cumberland Gap II–477a

Wilderness Road II–477a
ALLEGHENY PORTAGE RAILWAY I–89a; I–443b; III–286a; V–247a, 250a; VI–25a
Allegheny Reservation (N.Y.) V–139b
ALLEGHENY RIVER I–89a; II–381b
canal III–448a
Céloron's voyage V–146a
Forks of the Ohio V–143a
Fort Fayette II–497b
Fort Pitt V–321a
French and Indian War IV–51a; VI–150a
Gist exploration III–182a
Holland Land Company III–291b
Indian route I–88b
Iroquois cession VI–385b
La Salle expedition V–145a
Navigator handbook V–17a
oil IV–43b, 44a; V–269b
oil pipeline V–318b
pack trains V–184a
Pittsburgh V–321b
portages V–367b
steamboats VII–271a
Treaty of Fort Stanwix III–382b
Venango VII–168b
westward movement VI–149a
Allegheny Transportation Company V–319a
Allegiance, pledge of. *See* Pledge of Allegiance
Allen, E. C. (mfr.) I–16b
Allen, Ethan (off.) III–112a; IV–86b
captured (1775) I–435b–36a
Green Mountain Boys III–226b
Montreal IV–405b
Onion River Land Company V–156a
Ticonderoga III–215b; VII–56a, 171b
Vermont III–241a
Allen, Henry T. (off.) I–192a
Allen, Henry W. (gov.) VI–274b
Allen, Ira (pol.) III–226b, 241a; V–156a
Allen, James (col.) VI–113b
Allen, James Lane (au.) IV–41a
Allen, Joel A. (zool.) IV–233a
Allen, Lewis F. (au.) II–280a
Allen, Richard (cler.) I–23a; IV–443a
Allen, Robert S. (jour.) V–75a
Allen, Samuel IV–264a
Allen, William (pol.) III–21a
Allen, Zachariah (bus.) III–430b
Allende, Salvador. *See* Gossens, Salvador Allende
Allen's Farm (Va.) V–245b
Allenstein (Pol.) VII–173a
Allentown (Pa.) III–470b; IV–142b
Allen v. *Virginia State Board of Elections* (1969) III–93b; VII–211a
Allergists, American College of IV–289a
Allergists for Mycological Investigations, Association of IV–289a
Allergy, American Academy of IV–289a
Allergy and Infectious Disease Institute IV–465a
Allergy Association, International IV–289a
Allergy Foundation of America IV–289a
Alley Dwelling Authority VII–246a
"All For Our Country" VI–394 (table)
Allgeyer v. *Louisiana* (1897) II–378a
All Hail to Massachusetts (song) VI–394 (table)
***ALLIANCE* (frigate) I–89a**; I–290b; VI–129a
Alliance for Labor Action IV–76b
ALLIANCE FOR PROGRESS I–89b; II–359b; III–62a, 70a; IV–114a; V–53a, 171a, 205b; VI–345a, 364b
Alliance Trust Company, Ltd. III–65b
Allied Chemical and Dye Company II–8b
Allied Expeditionary Forces I–108a
Allied powers
occupation of Germany (1918–23) I–191b–92a
World War I I–176b; VII–213a
World War II I–141a, 214a, 308a
See also France; Great Britain
Alligator (animal) V–62b; VI–90a
Alligator (Indian) VII–311a
Alligator (ship) V–22b
Alligator and Its Allies VI–91b
Alligewi (Indians) I–89a
Alliot, Paul (trav.) III–420b
Allis–Chalmers Company II–416a
Allison, William B. (pol.) I–90a, 318b; III–110b
ALLISON COMMISSION (1884–86) **I–90a**
"All men are created equal" II–306b, 456b
Allopathy IV–297a
Allouez, Claude Jean (miss.) III–499b; VI–192a
Great Village of the Illinois III–330b
Green Bay III–225b
Lake Superior VI–443a
Saint Joseph Mission VI–191b
Sault Sainte Marie pageant VI–219a
Wisconsin II–13b; VII–306b
Alloway (N.J.) III–182b
"ALL QUIET ALONG THE POTOMAC" I–90b
All–Star game (baseball) I–271a
Allston, Washington (paint.) V–188b
Allthorn (brush) I–494a
Allumette Island V–95a
Almanacke for New England for the Year 1639 I–90b
ALMANACS I–90b; V–69a,b
Nautical Almanac Office V–12a–b
Poor Richard's Almanac V–358b
Stamp Act VI–381b
Almanac Singers IV–441b
Almond, J. Linsey, Jr. (gov.) VII–196a
Almshouses III–306b; V–380a–b; VI–72b, 327b
Almy, John Jay (nav. off.) V–424a
Almy, William I–175a
Aloha State VI–393 (table)
Alpaca III–381a
ALPHADELPHIA ASSOCIATION I–91a
Alpha helix IV–390a
Alpine (N.Y.) II–133a
Alpine skiing VI–298a,b
Alsace–Lorraine III–86a; VII–173a, 331a
Alsatian colonists II–237a
Alsop, George (au.) IV–161a; VII–65b
Alsop, Richard (au.) III–259b
Alsop process (flour) III–45b
Alston v. *Norfolk School Board* (1940) II–401b
ALTA CALIFORNIA I–91b; IV–199b
Anza expedition I–141a
horse III–302b
Indian missions III–385b
Pious Fund controversy V–318a
San Francisco VI–209a
Spanish Inquisition III–420b
Spanish settlement I–405a
Altaic languages III–355b
Altamaha River
Fort King George IV–46b
Georgia III–168a, 171b
Indian land cession I–223b
settlement I–239a
ALTA VELA CLAIM I–91b
Alternating current II–38b–39a, 414a–15b, 416a; IV–244a
hydroelectric power III–320b
Altgeld, John P. (pol.) III–201a, 330a
Haymarket Riot III–266a; IV–65a
Altgeld, John Peter (law.) IV–67a
Altman, Benjamin (mer., philan.) II–104a
Altman and Company v. *United States* (1912) III–417b
Alto (Tex.) VI–210a
Alton (Ill.)
American Bottom I–100b
Lakes–to–Gulf waterway IV–88a
Lincoln–Douglas debate IV–156a
Lovejoy riots IV–199a; V–70b
steamboat racing VI–408a
Union prison camp V–414a,b
ALTON PETROGLYPHS I–91b; IV–7a
Alton Railroad VI–34b
Altoona (Pa.) IV–175b; VI–408a
Altorfer, A. W. (inv.) II–420b
Alum II–5a–b; V–466a
ALUMINUM I–91b; I–378b, 379a; II–7b, 422a–b; III–409b; IV–244b; V–102a, 103b–04a; VI–48b
atomic weight determination I–218b
cans VII–62a
monopoly IV–399b
New South V–67a–b
Niagara Falls power V–91b
salt VI–203a
trust–busting VII–123b
Wisconsin VII–308a
Aluminum chloride II–422b
Aluminum Company of America I–92a; II–422b; IV–399b; V–102a, 103b; VII–123b
Aluminum fluoride II–422b
Aluminum oxide II–422b; III–184b
Alvan Clark and Sons V–131b
Alvarado (Calif.)
beet sugar factory I–285a
Alvarado (Mex.) IV–252a, 322a
Alvarado, Hernañdo de (expl.) II–228b
Alvarado, Juan Bautista (col. gov.) IV–254a; VI–45b
Alvarez, Luis W. (phys.) IV–119b; V–100a, 301a,b
Alvárez de Pineda, Alonso (expl.) VII–36a
AM. *See* Amplitude modulation
AMA. *See* American Medical Association
Amadas, Philip (navig.) VI–43b
Amalfi, Tables of (maritime law) I–14b
Amalgamated Association of Iron, Steel and Tin Workers III–297a; IV–66a
Amalgamated Clothing Workers of America II–82b–83a; IV–72a, 73a, 76a, 77a

Amalgamated Copper Company III–122b
Amalgamated Iron and Steel Workers VI–410b
Amalgamated Meat Cutters v. *Jewel Tea Company* (1965) VI–103b
"Amalgamationists" II–184b
Amalgamation religions. *See* Nativistic Movements, American Indian
Amalgams
dentistry II–330a, 331a
AMANA COMMUNITY I–92b; II–147a; IV–338b–39a
Amangual, Francisco (off.) VII–36a
Amarillo (Tex.) II–251b, 382a; VII–40b
Amateur Athletic Union
basketball I–272b
Amateur Hockey Association of the United States III–287b
Amatol V–383b
Amazon River II–323b
Ambassador Hotel (Los Angeles) IV–38a
AMBASSADORS I–93a; II–201b, 202a,b, 343a, 437a–b; III–71b, 72a; VI–389a
Iroquois III–475b
Senate confirmation II–171b
U.S. Information Service V–432b
Ambergris III–413a
Ambridge (Pa.) IV–181a
Ambrister, Robert (trader) *See* Arbuthnot and Ambrister, Case of
Ambroise and Company V–5a
Ambulances
telecommunications II–425b
Amebiasis IV–291b
AMELIA ISLAND AFFAIR (1817) **I–93b**
Amelung, John Frederick (mfr.) III–182b, 184b–85a
AMEN CORNER I–94a; IV–167a
AMENDMENTS TO THE CONSTITUTION I–94a; II–203a, 204a–08a; III–2b–3a
black suffrage VI–431a,b, 432b, 433a; VII–208b
certification II–498b
child labor II–25a
Civil War II–197b
congressional power to propose II–171b, 171b
District of Columbia voting VII–132b, 208b
election of president VII–131b–32a
election of senators VII–208b
Force Acts III–59a–60a
freedom of the press V–78b–79a
human rights II–316b
inauguration of president III–350b
income taxes VII–6a,b
joint resolutions VI–100a
judicial review IV–14a,b
poll tax VII–133a, 208b
presidential disability V–397a
presidential succession VII–133a–b
presidential term VII–132b
Prohibition VII–23b
Prohibition repeal VII–132a–b
Radical Republicans VI–11a
Reconstruction VI–56b–57a,b
religious liberty VII–69a
reserved powers of states VI–97b
right of petition V–265a,b
Scopes trial VI–239b
search and seizure VI–248b
state police power V–339a
states' rights VI–404a
suffrage VI–434b–35a
third–term doctrine VII–53b–54a
vice–presidency VII–181a
voting age VII–133b, 208b
War Amendments VII–226b
Washington, D.C. VII–245b
woman's suffrage VII–208b, 315a–b
See also Bill of Rights; Constitution of the United States; entries under individual amendments
Amerada Corporation V–272a
America (blimp) II–345b
America (carrier) V–22a
America (seaplane) I–51a
America (ship–of–the–line) III–21b; VI–282a
"America" (song). *See* "My Country, 'tis of Thee"
America (towboat) VII–77b
AMERICA (yacht) **I–95b**; VII–348b
AMERICA, DISCOVERY AND EARLY EXPLORATION OF I–95b; IV–136a
artist–explorers V–184b
astronomical observations V–130b
coast mapping IV–247a
Columbus' voyages VI–216a
European land claims IV–91b
fake exploration of Pacific coast V–179b
Florida V–356a
France III–118b; V–52b
Franciscans III–94a
Grand Canyon III–208a
Great Plains III–220b
Hakluyt's *Voyages* III–240b
historical accounts III–280a
Hudson River III–312a
Hudson's voyage V–86a
Kansas IV–25a
Massachusetts IV–264b
Narragansett Bay IV–451b
Nicolet's explorations V–95a
Norsemen IV–38a–b; V–112a
Northwest Passage V–122a
Norumbega V–123a
Oklahoma V–148a
venereal disease VII–168b–69a
Vinland VII–189b
western sea VII–275a
AMERICA, NAMING OF I–97a; I–96a
America and the World War V–390b
"America fever" III–335b
AMERICA FIRST COMMITTEE I–97a; III–480a; VII–333b
American, The IV–163b
American Academy of Allergy IV–289a
American Academy of Arts and Letters IV–126b
AMERICAN ACADEMY OF ARTS AND SCIENCES I–97a; IV–126a, 267a; VI–237b
Boston culture I–344b
chemistry II–10b
Memoirs VI–235b
American Academy of General Practice IV–289a
American Academy of Medicine IV–284b
American Academy of Pediatrics IV–276a
American Agricultural Chemical Company II–8b
American Agriculturist (period.) I–45b
American Airlines
airplane crashes II–346b, 347a
flight limitation I–69a
south Pacific route I–68b
American Air Volunteers. *See* Flying Tigers
American and Foreign Anti–Slavery Society I–137b, 138a
American and Foreign Christian Union V–3a
American Annual Encyclopedia II–444b
American Anthropological Association I–129a; IV–126b
American Antiquarian Society I–477a; II–98b, 108a; III–278b, 279a, 280b, 285a; IV–126a; V–69b
American Anti–Slavery Society I–136b, 137a–b; II–434a; III–145b; IV–141a; V–145b, 266b
American Arbitration Association I–152b–54a
American Archives III–60a, 281a
American Aristotype V–291b
American Art Association–Anderson Galleries I–332b–33a
American Art Union II–101b
American Association (baseball) I–270b
American Association for Labor Legislation IV–67a, 294a; V–401a
American Association for State and Local History III–279a
AMERICAN ASSOCIATION FOR THE ADVANCEMENT OF SCIENCE I–98a; III–165b; IV–127a; VI–236a,b
forest study III–73a
Massachusetts life table IV–149a–b
scientific societies VI–237b–38a,b
American Association of Colleges of Pharmacy V–275a–b
American Association of Dental Schools II–330b
American Association of Engineers II–449a
American Association of Museums IV–436b
American Association of Planned Parenthood Physicians IV–289a
American Association of Social Workers I–495b
American Association of University Professors I–5a; IV–76a
American Association of Zoological Parks and Aquariums VII–371a
American Association to Promote the Teaching of Speech to the Deaf III–248a
American Atlantic and Pacific Ship Canal Company V–94a
AMERICAN AUTOMOBILE ASSOCIATION I–98b; I–226a, 231b
American Ballet Company II–289a
American Ballet Theatre II–289a–b
American Bankers Association V–400a; VII–92a
American Baptist Association I–265b
American Baptist Churches in the U.S.A I–265a
American Baptist Convention I–265a, 265b
AMERICAN BAR ASSOCIATION I–99a; IV–18b
Commission on Correctional Facilities and Services V–417b
legal education IV–121a–b
Morrissey nomination IV–413a
narcotics trade violations IV–451a
uniform arbitration act I–153b

uniform state laws
VI–399b
American Bar Association Journal I–99b
American Basketball Association I–273b
American Battle Monuments Commission I–478a; II–499b
American Bee Association I–284a
American Bee Journal I–284a
American Beekeeping Federation I–284a
AMERICAN BIBLE SOCIETY I–99b; I–293b; IV–366b
American Bimetallic League VI–288a
American Bimetallic Union VI–288a
American Bison Society I–375b
American Board of Commissioners for Foreign Missions III–385b; IV–364b, 366b; V–167a
AMERICAN BOTTOM I–100b; III–329a
American Boy (mag.) IV–223a
American Breeders Association III–159a
American Cargo War Risk Exchange III–428b–29a
American Carpetho–Russian Orthodox Greek Catholic Church II–387a
American Catholic Missionary Conference V–3a
American Cattle Doctor VII–176a
American Cereal Company I–487a, 488a
American Chemical Journal IV–2b
American Chemical Society II–12a, 13a; IV–126b
American Chemical Society Journal II–11b
American Christian Missionary Society II–352b
American Church History Series III–282a
AMERICAN CIVIL LIBERTIES UNION I–100b; II–50b; V–236a, 438a
American Classical League II–400b
American College Athletics (report) II–401a
American College of Allergists IV–289a
American College of Physicians IV–289a
American College of Surgeons III–307a–b; IV–289a
American Colonies in the Seventeenth Century III–282b
AMERICAN COLONIZATION SOCIETY I–100b; I–21a; II–127a, 434a
Liberia IV–141b
opposition to I–315b
Virginia III–145a
American Commonwealth V–353b
American Convention for Promoting the Abolition of Slavery and Improving the Condition of the African Race I–135b
American Convention on Human Rights (1969) III–456b
American Correctional Association V–418a
American Cotton Oil Trust VII–122a
American Council of Learned Societies II–340b; III–281b; IV–127a; VI–238b
American Cyanamid Company V–341a
American Dairyman's Association (N.Y.) II–280a
American Dental Association II–330a–b, 331b; V–468b
American Dental Convention II–330a
American dogwood VI–395 (table)
American Economic Association IV–126b; VI–468a
American Electric Heating Company II–419b
American elm VI–394 (table), 395 (table)
American Engineering Council II–449a
American Entomological Society Transactions VI–236a
American Ephemeris and Nautical Almanac V–12b
American Equal Rights Association VII–315a
American Ethnological Society I–128a
American Ethnological Society Transactions VI–236a
AMERICAN EXPEDITIONARY FORCES I–101b; IV–328a; VI–301a, 338b; VII–230a, 325b, 326b–27a
American Legion VII–175a
artillery IV–431a
D Day II–297a
landing in France IV–84a
Liberty engines IV–433b
Meuse–Argonne offensive IV–319a
military roads VI–156a
organization I–186a
psychological warfare V–440b
Saint-Mihiel VI–197a
tanks I–177a
transport VII–328b
See also World War I
AMERICAN EXPEDITIONARY FORCES IN ITALY I–102a
American Experience Table IV–149b
AMERICAN EXPRESS COMPANY I–102a; I–10a; V–255b; VII–267a
American Falls (Idaho) I–155a; III–328b
American Falls (Niagara Riv.) V–91a
American Farm Bureau Federation I–42b; V–400b
American Farmer (period.) I–45b; III–230b
American Federation of Catholic Societies I–469b
American Federation of Government Employees IV–75b
American Federation of Information Processing Societies II–156a
American Federation of Labor III–412b; IV–65a–b, 66a–b, 67a–b, 68a, 69a,b, 70a,b, 71a, 72a; VI–39a
campaign of 1924 IV–81b
campaign of 1936 IV–73a
campaign of 1944 IV–73b
immigration restriction III–342a
injunctions III–419a
labor parties IV–81b
McNamara case IV–219a
merger with CIO IV–74b
peace movements VII–236b
pressure for labor department IV–78
Progressive party IV–84b
railway shopmen's strike VI–40b
Socialist party VI–326b
social security V–46a
support of Democratic party IV–68a
unemployment insurance VI–328a
U.S. Steel VI–410b
Western Federation of Miners VII–272b
woman suffrage III–92a
AMERICAN FEDERATION OF LABOR–CONGRESS OF INDUSTRIAL ORGANIZATIONS I–102b; II–462b; IV–77a; V–400b
American Federation of Teachers IV–76a
Boston police strike I–346b
Buck Stove and Range Company case I–357a, 374b
campaign of 1924 I–428a
Communist party II–145b
contract labor II–214b
criticism IV–76b
Danbury Hatters' Case II–286b
formation II–111a; IV–74b
Knights of Labor IV–52b
lobbying IV 171a–
national health insurance IV–289b
Prohibition II–407a
American Federation of State, County, and Municipal Employees IV–75b, 76a
American Federation of Teachers IV–76a
American Female Guardian Society IV–409a
American Fish Culturists' Association III–27b
American Fisheries Society III–27b
American Football League III–57b
American forces in Germany. *See* Army of Occupation; Germany, American Occupation of
American Foreign Service Association Report (1968) III–72a
American Forestry Association II–187b; III–73a, 74a
American Foundries v. *Tri-City Council* (1921) VI–419a
American Friends Service Committee III–123b; V–280b, 470b
Nobel Peace Prize V–99b, 100a
World War I relief VII–330a
AMERICAN FUR COMPANY I–105a; III–79a, 143a, 143b, 403a; IV–415a; VII–271b
Astoria I–209a; III–226b
Chequamegon Bay post II–13b
Chicago property II–17a
Fort Assiniboine I–206a
Fort Benton I–289b; III–77b
Fort John IV–1b
Fort Kiowa IV–51a
Fort Laramie IV–108a
Fort Snelling VI–322b
Fort Union IV–403a; VII–145b
Green River rendezvous III–227a
Illinois fur brigade III–331b
Mackenzie's Treaty IV–217a
merchants VII–273b, 274a
Minnesota IV–356a
Missouri River IV–380b
North West Company V–121a
Pacific Fur Company V–180a
Pembina VI–63b
Prairie du Chien V–388a
Pratte, Chouteau and Company II–34a
Red River of the North VI–64b
rival firms II–131b
Sault Sainte Marie VI–220a
Southwest Company VI–357b
voyageurs VII–211b
American Game Conference VII–298a
American Game Protection and Propagation Association II–187b

American Gazeteer IV–413b
American Geographic Society V–337b
American Geography IV–413b
American Geological Institute IV–127a
American Girl (mag.) IV–223a
American Heritage Dictionary II–340b
American Herpetology VI–90a
AMERICAN HISTORICAL ASSOCIATION I–106a; III–279a, 282b, 284b; IV–126b
American Historical Review (jour.) I–106a
American Historical Society III–279a
American holly VI–393 (table)
American Home (mag.) II–100a
American Home Missionary Society III–331b, 469a; IV–365b
American Honey Producers Association I–284a
American Horse (Indian) VI–297a, 313a
American Hospital Association III–307b; IV–289b
American Hull Syndicate III–428b
American Humane Association I–125b
AMERICAN INDEPENDENT PARTY I–106b; VI–12b
Alabama politics I–71b–72a
backlash I–239b
campaign of 1968 I–431b; VII–52b
campaign of 1972 I–432a
AMERICAN INDIAN DEFENSE ASSOCIATION I–106b; V–49a
American Indian Mission Association III–385b
AMERICAN INDIAN MOVEMENT I–106b; V–210b; VI–164b
American Indians United V–210b
American in Paris, An (comp.) IV–438b
American Institute of Biological Sciences IV–127a
American Institute of Chemical Engineers II–448b
American Institute of Electrical Engineers II–448b, 449a
American Institute of Homeopathy III–293b
American Institute of Mining and Metallurgical Engineers II–448b
American Institute of Mining Engineers II–449a
American Institute of Physics IV–127a
American Institute of Planners II–49b
American Iron and Steel Association VI–463b
American Iron and Steel Institute VII–92a
AMERICANISM I–107a
"Americanists" IV–2a
American Jewish Committee IV–10b
American Jewish Congress IV–10b
American–Jewish Historical Society III–279b
American Joint Commission to France. *See* France, American Joint Commission to
American Journal of Archaeology IV–2b
American Journal of Conchology VI–236a
American Journal of Dental Science II–330a–b
American Journal of Education II–398b; IV–207a
American Journal of Insanity IV–305b
American Journal of Mathematics IV–2b
American Journal of Nursing V–126b
American Journal of Pharmacy V–275a
American Journal of Philology IV–2b
American Journal of Psychiatry IV–305b
American Journal of Psychology IV–2b; V–442a
American Journal of Science I–111a; II–11a; VI–235b
American Journal of Science and Arts IV–348b–49a
American Laboratory Theatre VII–50a
AMERICAN LABOR PARTY I–107a
campaign of 1936 IV–73a
F. D. Roosevelt IV–81b
American Lake I–434b
AMERICAN LAND COMPANY I–107b; IV–99b; V–452b
American Law Institute IV–18b; V–438a
American League (baseball) I–270b, 271a
AMERICAN LEGION I–108a; VII–175a
bonus movement I–331a–b
pledge of allegiance V–331b
Prohibition II–407a
veterans' benefits V–257a
American Legion Magazine I–108b; VII–175a
AMERICAN LIBERTY LEAGUE I–108b
American Library Association I–335b; II–401b; IV–145a
American Life Convention III–434a
American Light Infantry VI–415b
American literature. *See* Literature
American Locomotive Company IV–175b, 176b, 177b
American Lutheran Church IV–206b; V–123b; VI–79b
American Magazine IV–161a
American Magazine, or Monthly View IV–221b
American Mail Lines IV–312a
American Mathematical Association II–400b
AMERICAN MATHEMATICAL SOCIETY I–109a; II–154a
American Medical Association II–399b; IV–289a, 296b; V–400a
birth control I–307a
homeopathy III–293b, 294a
industrial health IV–294a
maternal and child health care IV–275a
medical education IV–284a
medical sects IV–297a
national health insurance IV–289b
pure food and drug movement V–466a, 468b
American Medical College Association IV–284b
American Mercury (mag.) I–479a
American Metals Company V–102a
AMERICAN–MEXICAN MIXED CLAIMS COMMISSION I–109b
American Mineralogical Journal IV–349a; VI–235b
American Mineralogist (jour.) IV–349a
American Miners Association II–86b
American Minerva (news.) V–69b
American Missionary Association I–114b; IV–365b
American Motors I–229a, 231a; VII–90a
American Museum, Barnum's. *See* Barnum's Museum
American Museum of Arts IV–468b
American Museum of Natural History I–128b; III–27b; IV–233a, 436b, 437a–b
American Nation: A History III–282b
American National Game of Base Ball (print) II–275a
American Naturalist (period.) VI–237a
American Nettie Mine VI–213b
American Newspaper Directory I–18a
American Newspaper Guild I–207a; V–77b
American Newspapers Publishers Association I–18a
American Nurses Association IV–289b; V–126b
American Opinion (jour.) IV–2a
American Ornithologists' Union I–305a, 306a; VII–298a
American Ornithology V–413b
American Osteopathic Association V–175a
AMERICAN PARTY I–109a; II–191a, 327b; V–3a; VI–253a; VII–149a
anti–Catholic sentiment I–283a, 467b
campaign of 1856 I–421a
campaign of 1860 I–421a
Cincinnati II–37b
homestead movement III–296b
Kansas–Nebraska Act IV–29b
Kentucky I–323a
New Orleans IV–193b
radical right VI–12b
Republican party VI–92b
Tammany Hall VI–459b
American Pathfinders V–3b
American Peace Society V–235a,b, 236a; VII–236a,b
American Pediatric Society IV–275a, 289a
American Petroleum Institute IV–170b–71a; V–400a
American Pharmaceutical Association V–468b
AMERICAN PHILOSOPHICAL SOCIETY I–110a; II–396a; IV–126a; V–277a; VI–237b
anthropology and ethnology I–128a
Bartram, John I–348b
chemistry II–10b
industrial research III–408a
museum holdings IV–435b, 436a
Transactions VI–235b
Wistar parties VII–309a
American Phrenological Journal and Miscellany V–294a
American Physical Society V–295a, 304b–05a
American Physiological Society III–325b; V–307a,b
American Political Science Association V–348a,b, 353b
American Political Science Review (jour.) V–348a,b
American Power and Light Company v. *Securities and Exchange Commission* (1946) II–137a; III–459b
American Preceptor VI–227a–b
American President Lines IV–312a
American Press Institute II–133a; V–79b
American Printing House for the Blind III–248b, 267b
American Professional Football Association III–57a
AMERICAN PROTECTIVE ASSOCIATION I–111a; V–3a
immigration restriction III–342a

little red schoolhouse IV–169a–b
radical right VI–12b
American Protestant Association I–467b
American Protestant Society V–2b
American Protestant Vindicator (news.) V–2b
American Psychiatric Association IV–305b
American Psychological Association IV–126b; V–442a,b
American Public Health Association IV–275a; V–447a
American Quarterly (jour.) I–112a
AMERICAN RAILWAY ASSOCIATION I–111b
American Railway Express Company I–10a, 102b; VII–267b
AMERICAN RAILWAY UNION I–111b; II–298b; IV–66b
Pullman strike II–17b; III–419a; V–463a
railroad brotherhoods VI–20a
Social Democracy VI–324b
strikes VI–419a
American Relief Administration V–280b; VII–329a–30b
American Renaissance (painting) V–191a–92a
AMERICAN REPUBLICAN PARTY I–111b; V–2b, 279a
American Republics, Bureau of. *See* Pan-American Union
American Republics, Consultative Meeting of Foreign Ministers of the (1939) V–200a
American Republics, International Bureau of V–205a
American Revolution. *See* Revolution, American
American River III–190b
gold I–405b; III–81b; VI–209b
American robin VI–393 (table)
Americans, The III–283a
American Samoa. *See* Samoa, American
"American Scholar" (address) IV–162a
American School of Osteopathy V–175a
American Selling Plan VI–470b, 471a
Americans for Democratic Action V–400b
American Smelting and Refining Company V–102a; VI–317a
American Social Hygiene Association V–438a
American Social Science Association I–106a
American Society for African Culture I–22a
American Society for Engineering Education II–448a
American Society for Promoting Useful Knowledge I–110b
American Society for Psychical Research V–213a,b
American Society for Testing Materials III–408b
American Society for the Judicial Settlement of International Disputes VII–236b
American Society for the Prevention of Cruelty to Animals I–125b; VI–331b
American Society for the Promotion of Temperance VII–22b
American Society of Civil Engineers II–448b
American Society of Dental Surgeons II–330a
American Society of Equity II–221b
American Society of Ichthyologists and Herpetologists III–28a; VI–91b
American Society of Limnology and Oceanography II–392a
American Society of Mammalogists IV–233a
American Society of Mechanical Engineers II–447b, 448b
American Society of Newspaper Editors V–76a, 77b
American Society of Parasitologists IV–126b
American Society of Superintendents of Training Schools for Nurses of the United States and Canada V–126b
American Speech and Hearing Association III–249a
American Spelling Book VII–266a
American Standards Association VI–185a
American States, International Conferences of V–106a
American Statesmen III–281b
American Statistical Association IV–126a; VII–206b
American Steel Foundries v. *Tri-City Trade Council* (1921) III–419a
American Student Union VII–365b
AMERICAN STUDIES I–112a; III–131a
American Sugar Refining Company VI–437b; VII–154a
American Sunday School Union I–293b, 335a; VI–442b
American Surety Building (N.Y.C.) VI–299a
American-Swedish Historical Museum III–279b
AMERICAN SYSTEM I–113b; III–113a, 449a; IV–115b; VII–268b
Louisiana IV–193b
navigation projects VI–145b
wages and prices VI–465b
"American system of manufacture" I–205b; III–442a; IV–216b, 272b
American Teacher (period.) V–96a
American Telegraph and Cable Company II–137a
American Telephone and Telegraph Company II–423b; VII–20a
institutional advertising I–19b
repeatered cable I–401a
research III–409b; V–295a
vacuum tubes VII–163a
American Temperance Union VII–22b–23a
AMERICAN TOBACCO CASE (1911) **I–114a**; I–140a; VII–155a
American Tobacco Company v. *United States* (1946) VI–103a
American Tract Society I–293b; IV–409a
American Train and Track. *See* Amtrak
American Transit Association IV–428b
American Union Against Militarism V–236a; VII–236b
American Urological Association IV–289a
American Veterans of World War II, Korea, and Vietnam VII–175a
American Veterinary Association VII–176b
American Veterinary College VII–176b
American Veterinary Journal VII–176a
American Veterinary Medical Association VII–176a,b
American Veterinary Review (period.) VII–176a,b
American Volunteer Corps. *See* Flying Tigers
American Watch, Quarter, and Station Bills VI–301b
"American way" IV–334b
American Weekly Mercury (news.) III–427a; IV–190b; V–251a
American Woman Suffrage Association VII–315a, 317a
American Woolen Company VII–321a
America's Coming of Age IV–164a
America's Cup I–95b; V–65b; VII–348b, 349a,b
America's Messenger (almanac) I–90b
Americo-Liberian elite IV–141b
Amersfoort. *See* Flatlands (N.Y.)
Ameryk, Richard I–97a
Ames, A. A. (pol.) VI–142b
Ames, Fisher (states.) II–473b; VII–309a
Ames, John C. (fed. marshal) IV–191b
Ames, Joseph (educ.) IV–3b
Ames, J. T. (mfr.) IV–433a
Ames, Mary Clemmer III–26a
Ames, Nathaniel (pub.) I–90b
Ames, Oakes (fin., pol.) II–256a; VII–147b
Ames, Oliver (mfr.) II–256a
Ames, William (cler.) V–52a
Ames Aeronautical Laboratory IV–458a
Ames Building (Boston) VI–299a
Ames Manufacturing Company III–442a
Amherst, Jeffrey (off.) II–134a; III–116a,b, 117a–b; IV–86a; V–85b
Crown Point II–267a
Fort La Galette IV–85a
Fort Ontario V–175b
Indian policy V–356b–57a
Montreal IV–405b
Rogers' Rangers VI–162b
Rogers' Saint Francis raid VI–190a,b
Ticonderoga VII–57a
Amherst, William (off.) III–117b
Amherstburg (Ont., Can.) II–338a; VI–42a; VII–45b
Amherst College I–47a; II–109b, 398a
Amiens (Fr.)
World War I I–177a; VI–338b
AMIENS, TREATY OF (1802) **I–114a**
Amino acid I–303a, 304a; II–13a, 358a; III–158a; V–127b
Amish Mennonites. *See* Mennonites
***AMISTAD* CASE** (1841) **I–114b**
Amistad Dam VI–143b
AMITE, BATTLE OF (1808) **I–114b**
Amite River III–326b, 479a
Amity and Commerce, Treaty of (1778) IV–416b; VII–109a
Amman (Jor.)
aerial hijacking III–277b
Amman, Jacob (bp.) IV–303a
Ammann, Othmar (eng.) I–364b
Ammonia II–420b; III–16b–17a,b, 409b; V–98a; VI–69b
Ammonium nitrate III–17a; V–383b
Ammonium sulfate II–5a; III–17a
Ammonium thiocyanate II–319a
Ammonoosuc River VI–190a–b
Ammunition V–163a
fur trade III–140a,b
metallic II–131a
Minié ball IV–352b
See also Munitions

AMNESTY I–114b
campaign of 1872 I–422b
Civil War II–295a; III–400a; VI–55b, 56b, 57b, 58a–b, 431b–32a
Indian hostilities VI–377b
Johnson's Proclamation of Amnesty V–425a
Mormons IV–411b
Shays's Rebellion VI–272a
Amnesty Act (1872) III–295a
Amniocentesis III–158b
"Among the Folks in History" (comic strip) V–72b
Amoskeag Company V–54a
Amoskeag Falls IV–347b
Amoskeag Falls Canal I–442b
Amos Tuck School of Business Administration II–293a
Amos Wright (ship) VI–143b
Ampère, André Marie (phys.) II–413a
Amphetamines V–468b
Amphibian planes I–51b
Amphibians and Reptiles, Society for the Study of VI–91b
Amphibians and Reptiles of Illinois VI–91b
Amphibious warfare IV–252b
Iwo Jima III–485a
World War II I–459a; VII–62a, 343a–b
Amphictyonic League IV–124a
Amphitrite (ship) IV–189a; VI–129a
Amplifier II–39a, 423b, 425b
Amplitude modulation (AM) VI–15b, 16a
Ampudia, Pedro de (off.) IV–404b
Amputation IV–284a
Amsterdam (Neth.)
colonial banking loans II–382b
dry docks II–375a
exchanges II–469b
Pilgrims V–64b, 312b
U.S. state bonds VI–96a
Amsterdam, Fort (N.Y.) II–383a
Amtrak I–391b; III–451a–b, 458b; VI–31b; VII–102b
Amundsen, Roald (expl.) *See* Amundsen Polar Expeditions
Amundsen Gulf V–122a
AMUNDSEN POLAR EXPEDITIONS I–115b; V–122a, 337a
Amur River I–75b
Amusement tax VII–7a, 11a
"A. Mutt" (comic strip) V–72a
AMVETS. *See* American Veterans of World War II, Korea, and Vietnam
***AMY WARWICK* ADMIRALTY CASE** (1863) **I–116a**
Anabaptists IV–303a; VI–80b
Anaconda (Mont.) VI–316b–17a
ANACONDA COPPER I–116a; I–116a; II–223a; III–122b; IV–90a, 466a; V–102a; VI–316b–17a
Anaconda Silver Mining Company I–116a
Anacostan (Indians) III–499a
Anacostia (Washington, D.C.) V–28a
Anacostia–Chesapeake Canal V–2a
Anacostia (D.C.) Neighborhood Museum VI–319b
Anacostia River VII–244b
Anadarkho (Indians) I–286a
An Address to the Independent Federal Electors, of the State of New York, on the Subject of the Election of Governor and Lt. Governor of the State III–276b
Anaheim Colony III–477b
ANAHUAC, ATTACK ON (1832) **I–116b**
Analog computers II–152b–53a, 156a
ANANIAS CLUB I–116b
Anarchiad III–259b
Anarchic individualism II–290b
ANARCHISTS I–116b; VI–13b
communes II–142b
excluded from immigration II–445a
freedom of speech III–104a
Haymarket Riot III–266a
labor movement IV–64a,b
Sacco–Vanzetti case VI–183a
Anarchosyndicalist movement I–104a, 117a
Anasaldo engines II–344a
ANASAZI (culture) **I–117a**; IV–385b
town construction I–157b
Utah VII–161a
Anatomy I–110b; IV–283a,b
Anchor Line VI–407a
Ancient, Fort (Ohio) IV–421a; V–140a
Ancient Arabic Order of Nobles of the Mystic Shrine III–109a–b
Ancient Monuments of the Mississippi Valley VI–320a
Ancient Order of Hibernians IV–63a
Ancient Order of United Workmen III–435a
Ancient's Lodge (N.Y.C.) III–109a
Ancient Society III–476a
Ancón, Treaty of (1833) VI–456a
Ancona (It.) III–201a; V–211b
Andalusia (Phila.) I–163a
Andalusian mule IV–426a
Andean Common Market VI–346a
Anders, William A. (astronaut) I–210b
Andersen, Hans Christian (au.) IV–223a
Anderson, Alexander (engr.) V–413b; VII–319a
Anderson, Alexander (inv.) I–488a
Anderson, Carl D. (phys.) V–100a, 295b, 299a, 302b
Anderson, Edgar (bot.) I–349a
Anderson, Jack (jour.) V–75a
Anderson, John (auctioneer) I–332b
Anderson, John (off.) I–297a
Anderson, Joseph Reid (bus.) VII–113b
Anderson, Kenneth (off.) IV–32b; V–113a
Anderson, Maxwell (playwright) VI–183a; VII–50a
Anderson, Paul (nat.) VI–91b
Anderson, Richard H. (off.) VI–186b, 216a, 376a
Anderson, Robert (off.) V–308a; VI–251a, 387a, 440b
Anderson, William (pol. sci.) V–348b
Anderson family (Va.) III–469b
Anderson Galleries I–332b
Anderson Ranch (Idaho) III–328b
ANDERSON* v. *DUNN (1821) **I–117b**
ANDERSONVILLE PRISON I–117b; I–219b, 287a; II–159b
Andover (Mass.) II–328b; IV–267a
Andover Theological Seminary III–469a; VI–81b
ANDRÉ, CAPTURE OF I–118b; I–194b
André, John (off.) IV–48a, 363a; VI–150a; VII–225a
Andrew, John Albion (gov.) IV–267b
Andrew County (Mo.) V–330a
Andrew Doria (ship) VI–128a,b
Andrew Jackson (clipper ship) I–448a; II–77b
Andrew Jackson (sculp.) VI–243a
Andrews, Charles M. (hist.) III–282b
Andrews, E. G. (eng.) II–154b
Andrews, Elisha Benjamin (educ.) I–372a
Andrews, John (physic.) IV–294a
Andrews, John (seaman) VI–186a
Andrews, Roy Chapman (nat.) IV–437b
Andrews, Samuel (ind.) VI–382b
ANDREWS'S RAID (1862) **I–118b**
Andromeda III–242a
Andros, Edmund (col. gov.) II–117b; IV–265b; V–50b, 84b, 243b; VI–140b
Connecticut charter II–182b
Dominion of New England II–121b
Duke of York's proprietary VII–359a,b
East Jersey II–388b
Ipswich protest III–469a–b
King's Province dispute IV–48b
quitrents VI–4a
Saint-Castin's trading house VI–188a
Androscoggin River V–242a, 359b; VI–149a
Andros Regime. *See* New England, Dominion of
"Andy Gump" (comic strip) V–72a
Anemia IV–229a
Anesthesia
dentistry II–331a
ANESTHESIA, DISCOVERY OF I–118b; IV–285b, 297b; V–306b
Anesthetic agents IV–284a
Anesthetizers II–374a
Anfinsen, C. B. (biochem.) I–304a; IV–391b; V–100a
Angaur Island I–459a
Angel Gabriel (ship) V–243b
Angell, C. D. V–271a
Angell, James Burrill (dipl.) II–29a
Angevin Empire IV–224a
Anghiera, Pietro Martire d' VI–167a
Anglican church
King's College II–394b
See also Church of England in the Colonies
ANGLO-AMERICAN RELATIONS I–119b; II–313b
acreage ceded to U.S. V–445 (table)
Alabama Claims I–72a; II–213a; III–68a–b; V–35a
American Samoa III–425a
Atlantic Charter I–214b
atomic bomb research IV–237b
Balfour mission I–246b
Bayard–Chamberlain Treaty I–277b
Bermuda Conference I–292b
border forts II–166b, 458b, 484b
British debts VII–230b–31a
Canada and American Revolution I–435b
Canadian–American boundary VI–189a
Canton and Enderbury islands VII–125b
Caribbean balance of power IV–188a
Chesapeake–Leopard incident II–16a, 16a, 436a

China incident II–28a–b
Clayton–Bulwer Treaty II–72b; V–200b
cod fisheries II–92b, 93b
Coercion Acts II–93a
Convention of 1818 II–92b, 215b, 215b, 284b
Creole slave case II–257b, 257b
Dallas–Clarendon Convention II–285a, 285a
Declaratory Act II–309a
defense II–314b
destroyers for bases VII–342a
Dumbarton Oaks Conference II–380b
embargo of 1807 II–436b
Essex Case II–464a
Fenian movement III–10b
fishing rights III–30b–31a
Five–Power Naval Treaty III–33b
Florida boundary VII–353b
flour trade III–43a
Great Lakes Disarmament Agreement III–217a
Halifax fisheries award III–243b
Haro Channel dispute III–256a
Hay–Pauncefote treaties III–266a; V–201a
Henry Letters III–272b–73a
Hermosa case III–273b–74a
House–Grey Memorandum III–309a
impressment of seamen III–349b
indemnities III–352a
Indian barrier state III–375a
Indian trade III–389a
international law III–455b–56a
Israel III–481b
isthmian canal IV–111a; VII–58b
Jay's Treaty II–215a, 342b; III–67b, 95b, 96b, 493a; IV–329a, 381b, 402b; VI–150b
Johnson–Clarendon Convention IV–4b
Kasson tariff treaty IV–33a
lend–lease III–60b, 69a; IV–134a; V–21b
Liberia IV–141b
Macon's Bill No. 2 IV–219b
mandates IV 236b–
Marshall Plan IV–258a
McLeod case IV–218b
Migratory Bird Treaty IV–381a
Mississippi River IV–373b; V–315b
Monroe Doctrine IV–400a–b, 401a
Monroe–Pinkney Treaty IV–402b
Mosquito question IV–416a
Napoleonic Wars III–67b
Nassau Pact IV–454a
naval parity V–216b
Netherlands award V–33a
Nicaraguan canal III–278a; V–94b; VI–378b
Nonintercourse Act V–105a
Nootka Sound affair II–342b
Nuclear Test Ban Treaty V–124b
Olney–Pauncefote Treaty V–153a
Open Door notes V–158b
Oregon II–215b–16a, 475a; III–21a, 68a, 313b; IV–6a; V–164b–65a, 167a–68a, 169b–70a; VI–151a; VII–247b
Pacific Islands III–425a
Panama Canal V–200b
Panama tolls question V–204b
panic of 1785 V–206a
panic of 1837 V–206b
panic of 1893 V–207b
Paris conferences V–215b
Parliament's peace resolutions V–237b
Patriot War V–227a
peace conferences V–232b, 233a
Perdicaris affair V–261b
Pike's upper Mississippi expedition V–312a
Potsdam Conference V–378b
Proclamation of Neutrality V–36b
radar development VI–10a–b
retaliation VI–104b
Rose intrigue VI–164b
Rouse's Point boundary controversy VI–165b
Rule of the War of 1756 VI–169a–b
Rush–Bagot Agreement III–68a
Sackville–West incident VI–183b
San Juan Island VI–214a
sealing IV–250b; V–401a; VI–282a
Sino–Japanese War VI–294b
slave trade VI–322a
Teheran Conference VII–18a
Texas VII–38b
trade I–123a; III–4b; IV–266a,b; VII–86b, 87a
treaties VII–111b, 112a,b
Treaty of Ghent III–176b
Treaty of Versailles III–285b; IV–178b
Treaty of Washington VII–248b
Trent affair II–65b, 67b; VII–115b
Tripartite Agreement VII–120b
"twisting the British lion's tail" VII–134b
U.S. aid III–61a,b
U.S. arms shipments IV–363b
U.S. bases VII–110a
U.S. boundary V–120a
U.S. Civil War II–62a, 64b–66a, 65a–b, 162a,b, 162b, 213a, 213a, 238a, 435b; III–40b; VI–274b
U.S. consul III–71a
U.S. debts II–166b, 319a
U.S. neutrality V–34b
Venezuela boundary controversy V–153a; VII–170a
Washington's Farewell Address VII–251b
Wayne's Indian campaign VII–263a
Webster–Ashburton Treaty VII–265a
western boundaries VII–269b
West Florida VII–277a
wildlife preservation VII–297b
Wisconsin VII–307a
World War I IV–319b–20a; VII–332b
World War II III–489b, 492b; V–36a, 37a, 297a; VI–199b, 284b; VII–334b–35a,b
Zimmerman telegram VII–368b
See also Revolution, American; Revolutionary War; War of 1812
Anglo–Catholics V–179b
Anglo–Catholic theology II–455a–b
Anglo–Chinese relations I–268b; II–27a, 275b
ANGLO–CHINESE WAR (1839–42) **I–125a**; V–158a
See also Opium War
Anglo–Dutch War (1664) V–82a
Anglo–French Arbitration Treaty (1904) VI–163b
Anglo–Japanese Alliance (1902–21) I–122a, 123a; III–85b
Anglo–Palladism (arch.) I–161b–62b
Anglo–Russian convention (1828) I–75a
Angmagssalik (Green.) II–461b; III–357b
Angola
slave trade I–27a; VI–309b
U.S. investments I–22a
Angostura (Venez.). *See* Ciudad Bolívar
Angostura projectile point III–484b
Anguar
World War II VII–139a
Anhalt–Zerbst (Ger.) III–172b
ANIÁN, STRAIT OF I–125a
Anik (satellite) II–143b
Aniline dyes IV–291a
Animal behavior VII–371a
parapsychology V–213b
Animal ecology II–390a, 391b
Animal feed III–54a
Animal husbandry IV–169b; V–127b
See also Livestock Industry
Animal Industry, Bureau of I–45a, 241b; V–447b; VII–177a
ANIMAL PROTECTIVE SOCIETIES I–125a
Animal psychology V–442a,b
Animals. *See* Zoological Parks
Animals, state VI–392a
Animas River. *See* Purgatoire River
Animis opibusque parati (motto) VI–395 (table)
Ankara (Turk.) I–243a
Anker Bay IV–451b
An Loc (Viet.) I–63a
Ann (ship) V–334a; VI–436a
Annaba (Alg.) IV–32b
Anna Christie (play) VII–50a
Annales de chimie (period.) VI–235a
Annalist (period.) VI–51b
Annals of Congress II–178a; III–203b, 281a; IV–8b
Anna Pavlova Company II–288b
Annapolis (Md.) IV–261b; VI–340b; VII–82b
city plan II–45a
colonial suffrage VI–434a
education II–395a
founding I–249b
libraries IV–144a
Naval Academy II–399a
newspaper V–69a
Peggy Stewart burning V–241b; VII–16b
revolutionary war IV–260b; VII–361a
stagelines VI–380a
See also Naval Academy, United States; Providence (Md.)
ANNAPOLIS CONVENTION (1786) **I–85b**, 126a; II–192b, 212a; III–459b
Annapolis Royal. *See* Port Royal
Ann Arbor (Mich.) I–211a; III–128a
Ann Arbor Railroad VI–35b
Anne (Eng. q.)
Mohegan Case IV–387a
Newark charter V–41a
Palatines V–195a
proclamation money V–424a
Queen Anne's War VI–2a
Wawayanda Patent VII–261b
Anne, Fort (N.Y.) I–385a
Annenberg School of Communications V–249b
ANNEXATION OF TERRITORY I–126a; II–313b, 474b–75b; III–68b, 347a–48a; V–445 (table)
Adams–Onís Treaty I–10b
Alaska I–75a–b
California I–405b
citizenship V–6a
Gadsden Purchase III–145a
Great Plains III–221a
Hawaii III–263a,b

ANNEXATION OF TERRITORY (cont.)
international law III–455a
jingoism III–503b
Jones v. *United States* (1890) III–417b
Louisiana IV–382b
"manifest destiny" IV–239a
Marquesas annexation IV–220b
Mexican War IV–111a
Midway Islands IV–337a
Pearl River V–240b
Philippines V–235b
Pribilof Islands V–401a
public domain V–443b
Puerto Rico III–58a; V–461a
Spanish-American War IV–111a; VI–362b
state-making process VI–400a
Texas VII–38b
treaties VII–111b
Treaty of Paris V–215a
West VII–267b–68a
Wilmot Proviso VII–303b
Annisquam (Mass.) I–447a; IV–250b, 251a
Anniston (Ala.) I–435a; III–107a
Ann McKim (schooner) I–251a; II–77a
Annotated codes. *See* Statutory Law
Annual of Scientific Discovery VI–236a
Annual Register III–280b
Ansco Company V–292a,b
Ansel, Edgar (jour.) V–74a
Anson County (N.C.) VI–71b
Anspach-Bayreuth (Ger.) III–172b
Antarctica
Amundsen expeditions I–115b
Byrd's flights I–399a
exploration I–63b; V–336b, 337a,b, 338a
International Polar Year III–454a
mapping of I–463b, 464a
naval forces V–25a
Palmer's discovery V–197b
sealing VI–245a
Wilkes expedition VII–272a, 299b
See also Polar Exploration
Antarctic Developments Projects, U.S. Navy V–338a
Antarctic Journal of the United States V–338b
Antarctic Ocean III–28b
Antarctic Service, U.S. V–337b
Antarctic Treaty (1961) V–338a
ANTELOPE (slave ship) **I–126b**; III–51a, 484a,b; VII–346a, 357b
Antelope and Deer of America IV–232b
Anthem, national. *See* "Star-Spangled Banner"
Anthony, Susan B. (ref.) III–91b; IV–439a; VII–315a, 317a
Anthony, William Arnold (phys.) II–413b
Anthony Company V–291b
Anthracite coal. *See* Coal
ANTHRACITE STRIKE (1902) **I–127a**; V–247b
ANTHRACITE-TIDEWATER CANALS I–127b
Anthropological Association, American. *See* American Anthropological Association
ANTHROPOLOGY AND ETHNOLOGY I–128a
Bureau of American Ethnology II–464b
Indian land claims III–377b
Kwakiutl studies IV–59a
National Museum II–465a; IV–468b
radiocarbon dating VI–17b
See also Indian, American, Native Cultures
Anthropology Today (jour.) I–129a
Anthropometry IV–293a
Antiaircraft
artillery I–58a
guns I–58b, 200a
missiles IV–363a, 363b
Antiballistic missiles I–58b; VI–417a
ANTIBANK MOVEMENT OF THE WEST I–129b; III–101b
Antiberiberi factor (biochem.) I–303a
Anti-Bigamy Act (1862) VII–162a
Antibiotics II–12b; III–54a, 410a, 417a; V–274a
marketing regulation V–467b
poultry preservation III–56a
Anti-Catholicism. *See* Catholicism; Nativism
Anticosti Island VI–2b
ANTIETAM, BATTLE OF (1862) **I–130a**; II–435b; III–100b; IV–262a; V–377b; VII–197b
Lee's defeat II–62b, 162b
ANTIFEDERALISTS I–130b; V–86b; VII–134b
campaign of 1792 I–417a
Constitution II–196a–97a, 326b
Genêt mission III–159b
implied powers III–348a
taxation VII–12b
Antifreeze VI–203a
Antigua (B.W.I.) V–418b
ANTI-HORSE THIEF ASSOCIATION I–131b
Anti-Imperialist League I–131b, 132a; V–235b; VII–236b
ANTI-IMPERIALISTS I–131b; V–235b–36a
dollar diplomacy II–359b
Anti-Injunction Act (1932) II–111a
Antilles II–345b
Anti-Masonic Enquirer (jour.) I–132b
ANTI-MASONIC MOVEMENTS I–132a; III–109a
Morgan trials IV–410b
New York State V–86b
radical right VI–12a,b
Vermont VII–172a
Anti-Masonic party I–132b; VII–288b
campaign of 1832 I–419a
nominating convention II–216a; V–101b
Antimissile launchers IV–364a
Antimissile missiles II–316a; IV–363b, 364a
Anti-Missourian Brotherhood V–123b
Antimonopoly movement I–87b
ANTIMONOPOLY PARTIES I–133a
campaign of 1884 I–424a
taxation VII–5b–6a
Antimony
matches IV–274a
ANTINOMIAN CONTROVERSY I–133a; II–124a; IV–447b; V–53b, 55a; VI–76a; VII–316b
fast days II–496b
Rhode Island settlers VI–131b
Antinomianism
Gortonites III–200b
Antioch College II–399a
Antiochean Orthodox Archdiocese of Toledo, Ohio, and Dependencies in North America II–387a
Antiochean Orthodox Christian Archdiocese of New York and All North America II–387a
Anti-Parliament movement IV–60b
Antiproton IV–119b
Antiquarian Society, American. *See* American Antiquarian Society
Antiques II–98b, 99a–b, 101a; III–447a
Antiques (mag.) II–100a
Antiquities Act (1906) II–187b; V–216b–17a, 392b
ANTIRENT WAR (1839–46) **I–134a**; IV–92a; V–88b
ANTI-SALOON LEAGUE I–134a; II–407a; IV–171a; V–429b; VII–23b
Anti-Semitism III–279b; IV–10a,b, 11b, 12a
National Union for Social Justice IV–472b
radical right VI–12b
Antisepsis IV–284a, 298b
ANTISLAVERY I–134b; IV–115b; VI–6a, 305a, 306a–b, 307b, 308a, 342b
"Address of the Southern Delegates" I–10b
Afro-American churches I–23b
American Colonization Society I–100b
antiwar groups VII–236a
Bible I–293b
campaign of 1856 VI–42b
Cincinnati II–37b
Clay, Henry III–329a
colonization movement II–127a
compensated emancipation II–433b
emancipation movement II–434a
Free Soil party I–420b
Frémont's emancipation orders II–434b
gag rule III–145b; IV–358b
Garrison mob III–153a
Genius of Universal Emancipation III–162b
Harpers Ferry raid III–256b
home missionary societies IV–365b
homestead movement III–296b
Hunkers III–318a
immediatism III–332b
Kansas I–341a,b, 342a; IV–25b–26a, 31a, 118b, 130b, 377b; V–51a–b; VII–72b
Kansas Free-State party IV–28a
Kansas-Nebraska Act IV–28b
Liberator IV–141a
Liberty party I–420a,b; IV–143b
Lovejoy assassination IV–199a; V–70b
Madison County war IV–220a
manumission IV–246a–b
Massachusetts IV–267b
Methodists IV–318b
Mexican War V–235a
Michigan IV–331b
Nashoba settlement IV–452b
National Liberty party I–420b
natural rights doctrine IV–140a
navy patrols V–19b
New England Antislavery Society V–50b
newspapers II–436a
New York State V–86b, 87a, 87a
North Star V–75b–76a
Oberlin movement V–130a
Oberlin-Wellington rescue case V–130b
Ohio V–141b
Ohio State Antislavery Society V–145b
pacifists V–181b
Pearl case V–239a
"peculiar institution" V–241b
Pennsylvania V–247a
petitions to Congress V–265b, 266b
Philanthropist V–279a
Phillips, Wendell II–487b
post-Revolution VI–118b

propaganda II–66b
prostitution V–437b
publications II–37b; III–105a
Quakers V–470b
Radical Republicans VI–10b
religious societies VI–77b
Ruffner pamphlet VI–168b
Saint Louis VI–194b
secessionist movement VI–250b
Shadrach fugitive slave case VI–267b
Silver Grays VI–288a
slave trade VI–310b–11b
societies IV–409a
South Carolina VI–347b
temperance movement VII–22b
Texas VII–38b
third–party support VII–52b
Uncle Tom's Cabin VII–137b
Underground Railroad VII–138a
Vermont VII–172a,b
Wakarusa War VII–218b
Whig party VII–288b
woman's rights movement VII–313a
women VII–316b
Woolly Heads VII–321b
See also Church Schisms Over Slavery Issue; Emancipation Movement
Anti–Slave Society VI–310b
Antismuggling Act (1935) II–276a
"Anti–Snappers" VI–322b
Antistrike law (1935) II–144b
Antisubmarine missile IV–363b
Antisubmarine warfare (ASW)
carrier strength I–57a
postwar fleet I–56a–b
TBF Grumman Avenger I–55b
World War I VII–328b
World War II VII–343a–b
Antisubmarine warfare carriers (CVS) I–56a–b
Antitank weapons IV–363a
Antitrust Division (Dept. of Justice) II–230a
ANTITRUST LAWS I–139b; III–458b; VII–122a,b, 123a,b, 124a, 124a
Capper–Volstead Act I–451b
fair–trade agreements II–483a
holding companies III–290b
Justice Department IV–22a
Kansas IV–26b
laissez–faire doctrine IV–85b
marine insurance III–429a
National Recovery Administration IV–469a
New Deal regulatory codes V–44b
Packers and Stockyards Act V–183a
prices V–403b
Progressive movement V–427a, 428b
regulation of corporations II–230a
restraint of trade VI–101b
strikes VI–419a
"trust–busting" VII–121b
Webb Export Act VII–264b
See also Clayton Antitrust Act; Sherman Antitrust Act
Antitrust movement
campaign of 1900 I–425b–26a
Antitrust Procedures and Penalties Act (1974) I–140b
Antivivisectionists I–125b
Antiwar groups. *See* War Opposition Organizations; Pacifism
Antiwar Moratorium (1969) V–237b
Antler Creek IV–118a
ANTWERP (Belg.) **I–140b**
World War II I–379b, 380a; IV–363a; VI–159a; VII–340a
Anuskiewicz, Richard (art.) V–193b
Anville, Jean Baptiste Bourguignon d' (geog., cartog.) VII–74a
"Anxious bench" III–25a
Anza, Juan Bautista de (expl.). *See* Anza Expedition
ANZA EXPEDITION (1775–76) **I–141a**; III–150b
Camino del Diablo route I–413a
horses III–302b
San Francisco VI–209a
Tubac VII–125b
ANZIO (1944) **I–141a**; VII–338b
Gustav Line III–235b
AP. *See* Associated Press; Great Atlantic and Pacific Tea Company
APACHE (Indians) **I–141b**; II–433b; III–220b, 365a, 367a, 368b–69a, 396b; V–8b, 314a,b
Albuquerque I–83b
Arizona I–171b, 172a
attacks on Genizaro III–162b
Black Cavalry against I–310a
Black Infantry against I–313b
Camp Grant massacre I–433a–b
Comanche II–133b
Fort Stanton VI–385a
Fort Sumner III–199b; VI–439b
Fort Union VII–145a
horse III–303a
hostilities IV–340a
Kansas IV–25a
Kiowa–Apache IV–50b–51a
language III–360a
Medicine Creek Council IV–299a
nativistic movement V–4a
New Mexico V–59b, 60a
Oklahoma V–148a,b, 149a
peace commissions III–378a
Peyote Cult V–273a
Pueblo warfare VI–224b
Santa Fe Trail VI–215a
scouts VI–242a
Spanish forts VI–168b
territory concessions III–379b
Texas VII–36b
water holes VII–256a
Apache, Fort (Ariz.) III–304a
APACHE, FORT, INCIDENT AT (1886) **I–142a**
Apache Canyon (N.Mex.) III–187b; VII–165b
APACHE PASS EXPEDITION (1861) **I–142a**; IV–236b–37a
APACHE WARS I–142a; III–127a; VI–6a; VII–239b
Fort Sill VI–287b
Mangas Coloradas Wars IV–236b
scouts VI–242a
Apalache (Ga.) III–170a
Apalachee (Indians)
Battle of Ayubale I–238b
De Soto expedition II–336a
massacre I–143a
Narváez expedition IV–452a
Apalachee Bay IV–452a; VI–196b
APALACHE MASSACRE (1704) **I–143a**; III–41a
Apalachicola River III–38b, 39a, 41b; V–254a
Florida boundary V–262a
Forbes Purchase III–59a
Fort Gadsden III–145a
Fort Saint Marks VI–196b
Apalachin (N.Y.) II–262b
Apartheid
opposition to in U.S. I–357a
Apartment hotel I–143a
APARTMENT HOUSES I–143a
slums VI–314a
See also Tenements
Apennine Mountains III–200b–01a, 235b
APIA, DISASTER OF (1889) **I–144a**
Apiculture I–283b–84a
Apis mellifera (honeybee) I–283b–84a
Apollo 8 I–210b
Apollo 11 I–210b; IV–406b
Apollo 13 I–210b
Apollo Gallery II–101b
Apollo program I–63b, 210b, 212b; II–347a; IV–460a,b; V–132a; VI–159a,b
Apollo–Soyuz Test Project (1975) I–210b
Apollo spacecraft III–15a
Apology for the True Christian Divinity Held by the Quakers III–123a
Apostle Islands II–13b
Apostle of Arizona. *See* Kino, Eusebio
Apostle of the West. *See* Allouez, Claude Jean
Apostles Scots Confession (1560) V–392a
APOSTOLIC DELEGATION I–144a
Apostolic Faith V–260a
Apostolic Lutheran Church IV–206b
Apostolic Overcoming Holy Church of God V–260a
Apothecary. *See* Pharmacy
APPALACHIA I–144a
coal III–216b
federal aid II–502b
Girl Scouts III–181a
Kentucky IV–42a
migration to Cleveland II–75a
moonshine IV–407b
poverty V–382a
unemployment VII–141a
Appalachian Coals v. *United States* (1933) VI–102b–03a; VII–123a
Appalachian Corridor VII–282a
Appalachian Highlands II–272a
Appalachian Mountain Boundary. *See* Indian Barrier State; Proclamation of 1763; Quebec Act
Appalachian Mountain Club II–187b
Appalachian Mountains II–51b; III–369b, 412a; V–271b; VII–97b
boundary III–114b
buffalo trails VI–152b
coal fields II–85a
Confederate deserters II–335b
feuds III–18a
foothills II–485a
geological survey III–163b, 165a,b
geology III–481a
gold III–191a
Great Smoky Mountains III–222a
Indian territory III–388a
Kentucky violence IV–41a
Lederer's expedition IV–131a
Mohawk Valley IV–386b
New England V–49b
Ohio River discovery V–145a,b
Ohio Valley V–146a
passes V–224a–b
Pennsylvania V–277b
Piedmont V–310a
Proclamation of 1763 V–424b
rainfall VI–41b
resorts VI–100b
westward movement

APPALACHIAN MOUNTAINS (cont.)
VII–283a
Appalachian Spring (ballet) IV–439a
***APPAM* CASE** (1917) **I–144b**; V–422a
Appeal, right of IV–16b
APPEAL OF THE INDEPENDENT DEMOCRATS (1854) **I–145a**
Appeals, courts of IV–15b, 19a,b
jurisdiction IV–16b
state IV–18a
APPEALS FROM COLONIAL COURTS I–145a; IV–15a; V–421a
"Appeal to Heaven" (motto) V–316a
Appeldore Island III–479b
Appellate courts
Privy Council IV–12b
Appendicitis IV–297b
Appert, Nicolas (chem.) I–444b–45a; III–54b–55a
Apple blossom VI–393 (table), 394 (table)
Apple Creek II–283b
Applegate, Jesse VII–217b
Applegate's Cutoff III–215a
Apple pie III–52a
Apples III–128a,b
dried II–373a
pure food laws V–466b, 467a
APPLESEED, JOHNNY (John Chapman) **I–145b**; III–128b–29a
Appleton (Wis.) III–320b
Appleton, John J. (dipl.) IV–449a
Appleton, Nathan (mfr.) VII–44b
Appleton and Company I–334a
Appleton's Annual Cyclopaedia II–444b
Appliances
sales II–332b, 354b
See also Electrification, Household
Applied Physics Laboratory (Silver Spring, Md.) IV–3b
Appointment, Council of. *See* Council of Appointment, New York
APPOINTMENTS TO GOVERNMENT OFFICE AND APPOINTING POWER I–145b
Congress and president II–472a
executive removal power VI–84b
Foreign Service III–71a–b
Garfield–Blaine–Conkling controversy III–152b
Johnson impeachment III–345b
political patronage V–227b
rotation in office VI–165a
Senate confirmation II–479a
spoils system VI–374b
Tenure of Office Act VII–31b
Appomattoc (Indians) I–277b
APPOMATTOX (Va.) **I–146b**; VI–186b; VII–195a
Army of Northern Virginia VII–197b
Civil War II–62b, 63a, 68b, 165a; VI–138a; VII–197b
Appomattox River V–145a
Civil War VI–186b, 410a–b
revolutionary war I–194a
APPORTIONMENT I–147a; II–198a, 205b, 355b, 410a; III–94a
Baker v. *Carr* I–244a
Connecticut II–180a
constitutional convention debate II–194a
Georgia III–169a
gerrymander III–175a
legal education IV–121b
slave population II–151b
state legislatures III–86b–87a
taxation III–351b; VI–377a
three–fifths compromise III–5a
Apportionment Act (1842) I–147a
APPRENTICESHIP I–148a; II–393b, 396a; IV–60b
colonial labor force IV–60a, 79a
colonial suffrage VI–434a
dentistry II–329b
farm laborers I–36b
furnituremaking III–134a
fur trade IV–237a
hatmaking III–262a; IV–242b
indentured servants II–495a
lawyers IV–120b, 121b
libraries IV–281a
medical education IV–282b–83a,b, 295a, 296a–b
minimum–wage laws IV–353b
monopolies V–225b
navy VI–301b
nonwhites IV–76b
printer's devil V–410a
silversmithing VI–289b
tramp printers V–409b
unions II–80a
Apprenticeship Act (1937). *See* National Apprenticeship Act
Apprenticeship and Training, Bureau of I–148b
APPROPRIATIONS BY CONGRESS I–148b; II–200b, 476a
Emergency Relief Administration V–44a
Food and Drug Administration III–53b; V–467b–68a
foreign policy II–171b
Indian education III–379b, 380a,b
Indian removal III–394a,b
legislative riders VI–138b
logrolling IV–181a
Manhattan Project IV–238a
Ohio and Mississippi improvements VI–145b–46a
Pacific railway surveys VI–353b
pork barrel projects V–366b–67a
Powell explorations V–384a
railroad surveys VI–39a
reclamation VI–54b
Red River raft VI–65a
rural free delivery VI–172b, 173a
rural post roads VI–176b
space activities IV–459b
subsidies VI–425a,b
telegraph VII–18b
Treasury VII–108a
Ways and Means Committee VII–263b
Wilmot Proviso VII–303b
Works Progress Administration VII–323a
World War I relief VII–329a
See also Expenditures, Federal; Government Spending
Appropriations Committee III–37b
Apricots III–128b
Aptheker, Herbert (hist.) III–436b
'Aqaba, Gulf of III–481b–82a
Aquatints V–413b
Aqueducts VII–259a
canal construction I–443a
Erie Canal II–459b
Aquia Creek V–377b
AQUIDNECK ISLAND (R.I.) **I–149a**; IV–451b; V–65b; VI–131b
Aquinas, Saint Thomas II–362b
AR–15 (rifle) VI–140a
ARAB–AMERICAN RELATIONS I–149a
Baghdad Pact I–243a
energy crisis (1973) I–231a, 391b
investment in U.S. III–67a
Israel III–481b–82b
October war settlement III–70b
oil I–124a, 231a
oil embargo III–415b; VI–472b
Palestine I–124a
Suez Canal I–124b
Suez crisis VI–429b
***ARABELLA (ship)* I–151b**
ARABIAN GOLD I–151a
***ARABIC* CASE** (1915) **I–151a**; IV–205b; VI–452b
Arab–Israeli October War (1973) III–70b, 482a
Arab–Israeli War (1948–49) III–481b
"Araby's Daughter" (poem) V–152a
Aranda, Count of (Pedro Pablo Abarca y Bolea) I–151a; II–318b–19a
ARANDA MEMORIAL I–151a
ARANJUEZ, CONVENTION OF (1779) **I–151b**; II–318b
Aranjuez, Convention of (1801) IV–196a
ARAPAHO (Indians) **I–151b**; III–220b, 365a, 396b
Atsina I–311a; IV–236a
Bent's Fort I–290a
Colorado V–437b
Fort Bascom I–269b
Fort Laramie Treaty III–383b; IV–108b
Fort Sedgwick VI–254b
Ghost Dance III–177b
Indian Country cessions III–384a
Jesuit missions III–500a,b
Kansas IV–25a
Kiowa IV–50b
language I–86a
Medicine Creek Council IV–299a
Oklahoma V–148b, 149b
peace commissions III–378a
Platte Bridge fight V–330a
Red River War VI–64a
Sioux wars VI–297a
Sun Dance VI–441b
territory concessions III–379b
warfare VI–208a; VII–239b
Wyoming VII–345b, 346a
Arapahoe County (Kans.) III–497b
Arbeiter–Zeitung (period.) III–266a
Arbeter Ring (Workmen's Circle) IV–10b
Arbitragers II–254b
Arbitrary arrest. *See* Arrest, Arbitrary, During the Civil War
ARBITRATION I–152a; II–157b
Alabama Claims I–72b, 121b, 439a
American–Mexican mixed claims I–109b
Anglo–American disputes I–120a–b, 122a
British debts I–341a, 366a, 438a
Butterfield Claims I–398b
Canadian–American I–439a
Caracas mixed commissions I–452a
collective bargaining II–110a
commercial treaties VII–112b
compulsory II–113a
fisheries I–439a
fur seals I–439a
I'm Alone Case III–332a–b
international II–471b

international law
III–456a–b
joint commissions IV–5b
Mexican oil controversy
IV–322b
miners strike (1902)
IV–67b
National Trades' and Workers' Association
IV–471b
Olney–Pauncefote Treaty
V–153a
Panama tolls question
V–204b
patents V–226a
peace conferences
V–232b–33a
Permanent Court of Arbitration V–262a
Pious Fund controversy
V–318a
railway labor disputes
IV–64b
Root Arbitration Treaties
VI–163a
sealing V–401a
Venezuela boundary controversy VI–226b
Arbitration, Permanent Court of. *See* Permanent Court of Arbitration
ARBOR DAY I–154a; II–187b; III–73a; VII–114a
Arboretum and Nature Reserve (Gray Summit, Mo.) IV–378b
Arbuthnot, Alexander (trader) *See* Arbuthnot and Ambrister, Case of (1818) I–154a
Arbuthnot, James (nav. off.) VII–253a
Arbuthnot, Marriot (nav. off.) I–496b
ARBUTHNOT AND AMBRISTER, CASE OF (1818) **I–154a**
Arcadia Conference (1941) VII–335a
Arcano Del Mare (atlas) IV–248a
Arch (arch.) I–159b, 166b
bridges I–363b, 364a,b, 377b, 378a; II–384a
ARCHAEOLOGY AND PREHISTORY, NORTH AMERICAN I–154b
Adena I–11a
alcoholic drinks III–398a
Alton petroglyphs I–91b, 91b
Anasazi I–117a
Big Bone Lick (Ky.) I–11b, 295b
Bonito in Chaco Canyon I–329b
Bureau of American Ethnology II–464b
Cahokia mounds I–402b
cave fauna II–391a
Clovis culture II–83b, 83b
copper mining II–223a
Desert culture II–334b, 334b
Eastern Archaic culture II–385b, 385b
Folsom culture III–50a
Formative culture II–386a
Great Serpent Mound III–222a
"Great Spirit" III–222b
Hohokam culture III–289a
Hopewell culture III–300a
horse III–302a
Indian land claims III–377b
Indian migration I–74b
Iroquois League III–475a
Itama culture III–484a
Kansas IV–25a
Mesa Verde ruins IV–315b
Mexican Indians IV–327a
Mississippian cultures IV–370a
Mogollon IV–385b
mounds IV–420b
Navaho V–8b
New Mexico V–59b
Norse explorations V–112a
Ohio Valley V–140a
Oklahoma V–148a
Old Copper culture II–386a
paleontology V–195a
Pima–Papago V–314a
Poverty Point V–382b
Pueblo V–459b, 460a
radiocarbon dating VI–17b
Southern Cult VI–352b
tree–ring dating VII–114a
U.S. Geological Survey III–163b
Utah VII–161a
venereal disease VII–168b–69a
Woodland Tradition VII–319b
See also Indian, American, Native Cultures; Mounds and Mound Builders
Archaic culture II–334b, 385b–86a; V–382b; VII–319b–20a
Archaic stage (prehistory) I–154b, 155b–57a
Adena culture I–11b
shell mounds IV–421b
ARCHANGEL, U.S. TROOPS AT (1918) **I–158b**; VI–284a
Archbald, Robert W. (jur.) II–134b; III–344b
Archbold, John D. (ind.) VI–383b
Arches National Park V–217a, 219 (table)
Architects Emergency Relief Committee of New York VII–17b
Architectural training I–163b–64a
ARCHITECTURE I–159a
Adam style I–497a
Chicago II–17b–18a
colonial Williamsburg VII–302a
Confederate White House VII–292a
dry docks II–375a
Faneuil Hall II–487b
Harvard University III–260b
hospitals III–307a
housing III–309b–10b
interior decoration III–445b
Jeffersonian III–495a
Johnson Hall (N.Y.) IV–4b
licensing IV–148a–b
log cabin IV–179a
Louisiana Purchase Exposition IV–198a
meetinghouse IV–300a
Monticello IV–405a
New Orleans V–62b
Niagara Falls powerhouses V–92a
Panama–Pacific Exposition V–203b
skyscrapers VI–298b
Spanish II–184b; VI–365a
tenements VII–23b
White House VII–291b
World's Columbian Exposition VII–324b
Yale University VII–351a
ARCHITECTURE, AMERICAN INDIAN I–166a; I–159a
Adena I–11b
building materials I–377a
Eskimo III–358a
Haida III–238a
Hohokam culture III–289a
Itama culture III–484b
Mesa Verde ruins IV–315b
Mexico IV–327b
Mogollon IV–385b
mounds IV–420b
Navaho V–9a
Northwest Coast culture III–361a
Pueblo III–367b; V–460a
sod house VI–332b
villages III–405a
Western cultures III–362b–63a
wigwam VII–294b
Architecture, landscape. *See* Landscape Architecture
Architecture of Country Houses III–445b
ARCHIVES I–167a; III–283b, 284a
Historical Records Survey V–46b
National Archives III–281a
Archives of American Art (N.Y.C.) VI–319b
ARCHIVE WAR (1841) **I–169b**
Archivist of the United States I–167a–68a
Arch Street Theatre (Philadelphia) VII–48b
Arc light II–413b–14a, 421b; IV–153a,b
Arctic
De Haven expedition V–23a
Eskimo II–461b
exploration II–319b; V–122a, 336b, 337a,b, 338a,b
International Polar Year III–454a
wolves VII–311b
World War II II–217b
Arctic Basin
exploration V–338b
Arctic Circle VII–367a
air defense I–58a, 62a
Amundsen expeditions I–115b
Arctic culture III–355a, 356a, 357b
Arctic: Journal of the Arctic Institute of North America V–338b
Arctic Ocean II–219b; V–367b
exploration II–353a; V–336b, 337a,b, 338a
Ringgold–Rodgers Exploring Expedition VI–142a
whaling VII–285b
Arctic Research Laboratory, U.S. Navy V–338a
Arctic Zoology IV–231b
Ardennes (Belg.)
World War II IV–230b; VI–285b; VII–340a,b
Arellano, Tristán de Luna y (expl.) V–254a
Arena Stage (Washington, D.C.) VII–50b
Arensberg, Louise II–105a
Arensberg, Walter II–105a
Arezzo (It.) III–201a
Argall, Samuel (off.) II–322a; VII–200b
Mount Desert raid IV–226a
Port Royal V–369b
Potomac River V–378a
Argand, Aimé (chem.) IV–152b
Argand lamp IV–152b–53a
Argenterie (silverware) III–140b
Argentia III–337b
Argentia Conference (1941) VII–334b–35a
Argentina IV–114a
beef II–436a
boundary dispute with Brazil IV–363a
corn production II–226b
diplomatic relations IV–115a
Drago Doctrine II–369a
education II–398a
Falkland Islands controversy II–484a–b
Hayes Award III–265b
International Exposition of 1895 III–453b
Juan Perón III–199b
Kasson tariff treaty IV–33a
meat trade IV–281a
Perry's mission VII–170a
U.S. beef quarantine IV–112a
U.S. trade VI–343b, 344a,b, 345a, 346a
World War I VI–378a
World War II IV–112a, 402a

Argersinger v. *Hamlin* (1972) III–179b
Argo (Colo.) VI–316b
Argo (ship) V–336b
Argon IV–89a
Argonaut (submarine) VI–423a
Argonne Forest (Fr.) IV–319b, 320a; VI–197a; VII–327a
Arian Christology III–497b
Arias, Arnulfo (states.) V–203a
ARID REGIONS I–170a
Agricultural Adjustment Act V–48a
climate II–76a
Department of the Interior III–445a
Desert culture II–334b
Great Basin V–194a
Great Plains III–220b
Idaho III–328b
irrigation III–477a
Jornado del Muerto IV–8a
Kansas IV–25b
mesquite IV–316a
Montana IV–403b
Nebraska IV–50a
Pueblo cultures III–367b
rainfall VI–40b
reclamation VI–53b
resorts and spas VI–101a
springs VI–377b
water holes VII–256a
water rights IV–104a–b
windmills VII–304b
Wyoming VII–345b
Arieti, Silvano (psych.) IV–306b
ARIKARA (Indians) **I–171b**; III–363b; V–230b
Leavenworth expedition IV–129b
Lewis and Clark Expedition IV–136a
Missouri River IV–380b
scouts IV–168a; VI–242a
warfare II–283a; VII–239a
Arikara and Blackfoot War (1823) VII–239a
Arikara War III–127a
Arista, Mariano (off.) V–198b; VI–97a
Aristocracy II–326a
colonial society II–125a, 325a
eliminated II–189a
Federalist V–351a
titles of nobility V–100b
Aristocratic philosophy II–189b
Aristotle (philos.) II–456b
liberty IV–142a
Social contract theory V–350b
Aristotle's Lyceum IV–126a
Aristotle's Masterpiece VI–266a
Arithmetic VI–227a
ARIZONA I–171b; VI–355a,b, 393 (table)
antiinjunction law VII–121a
Black Infantry I–313b
boundary I–352a; IV–321b
boycotts I–356b
camels in I–413a
campaign of 1964 VI–93b
Camp Grant massacre I–433a
Casa Grande Ruins National Monument V–392b
citrus industry II–43b
Civil War I–172a; IV–315b
cliff dwellings IV–315b
Colorado River Compact II–130a; III–460a
Colorado River dispute VI–398a
Colorado River Reservation III–395b
copper industry II–223a
cotton production II–238b
dairy industry II–281b
deer VII–297b
Desert culture II–334b
exploration I–24b
Fort Apache I–142a
Fort Apache Reservation IV–90a–b
Fort Yuma VII–367b
Franciscans III–94a
Gadsden Purchase II–475a; III–68a, 145b
Gila Trail III–179b
Glen Canyon Dam III–322b
gold II–477b
Grand Canyon III–208a
Havasupai III–262b
Hohokam culture III–289a
Hopi III–300b
Horsehead Crossing III–304a
Indian agriculture IV–327a
Indian missions III–385b; IV–367a,b
Indians III–367a, 369a, 396a
Japanese–Americans II–445b; III–491a
Jesuit missions III–498b, 499a
land grants for education IV–93b
lemons III–128b
manganese III–13a
martial law IV–259a
mission settlements I–159b–60a
Mogollon culture IV–385b
mustangs IV–445a
national parks and monuments V–217a,b, 218–19 (table)
Navaho V–8b, 9b; VI–439b
Oatman Indian captives V–129b
Oñate's explorations V–155a–b
outlaws VII–187a
Paiute V–194a
Pima V–314a–15a
presidios V–399b
Pueblo V–459a
Pueblo Revolt V–4a
railroad route VI–353b
ranches III–302b
recall VI–51a
reclamation VI–54a,b
Reconstruction Finance Corporation VI–60a
referendum VI–66b
resorts and spas VI–101a,b
retirement communities II–48b
River Yumans IV–386a
ruins VII–114a
sheep wars VI–273a,b
silver II–477b; VI–292b
Spanish exploration II–184b, 228b
state–making process VI–401a–b
suffrage III–92a
Tenth Cavalry I–310a
Tombstone II–477b; VII–70b
traildriving I–473b
Tubac VII–125b
U.S. flag III–34b
water holes VII–256a
woman's suffrage III–91b; VII–315a
World War I VII–325a
Zimmerman telegram VII–368b
Arizona (battleship) VII–242a
Arizona (song) VI–393 (table)
Arizonac (Ariz.) I–172a
Arizona City (Ariz.) VII–367b
Arizona Republic (news.) V–73b
Arizona–Sonora Desert Museum (Tucson) VII–371b
"Arizona strip" II–461a
Arizona v. *California* (1964) II–130b
***ARK* AND *DOVE* I–172b**; II–124b; IV–260b
ARKANSAS I–172b; III–213b; VI–393 (table); VII–253b
banks I–129b, 259a
bayous I–279a
Brooks–Baxter War I–370b
caravans I–453a
Cherokee Trail II–14b
Civil War I–174a; III–269b, 400a, 498a; IV–257a, 374b; V–222a, 238b, 316a, 389a, 402b, 403a; VI–63a, 249b
coal mines II–85a
cotton II–237b, 238b; IV–104a
Delaware Indians II–321a
Democratic party VII–210a
desegregation I–31a; II–54b; IV–341b
De Soto expedition II–184a, 336b
evolution, theory of VI–239b
exploration II–381a; III–119a
farmers' alliances V–365a
Fort Smith VI–317a
forty–niners III–82a
Hot Springs National Park V–218 (table)
Indian Country III–379a
Indian Territory III–399b
irrigation III–478b
Japanese–American relocation III–491a
land speculation IV–99b
legislators' travel allowance IV–339a
Louisiana IV–192b
military tracts IV–91a, 344b
Old Southwest VI–356a
Osage land cession V–173b
panic of 1837 III–64a
Peace and Constitutional Society VII–149a
Peace Convention I–341b
petroleum VI–356b, 357a
public land speculation I–107b
railroad survey VI–39a
rainfall VI–41b
Reconstruction III–295a; VI–56a, 58b
referendum VI–66b
repudiation of state debts VI–96b
rice I–279a, 486b; VI–136a
Santa Fe trade VI–215b
school integration II–402a
secession II–61b, 160b; VI–251b
settlement IV–457a; VII–284a
sharecroppers IV–103a
slavery VI–309a
sugarcane VI–436a
tobacco VII–66b
tornadoes II–351b, 352a
Treaty of Fort Clark III–383b
vanadium III–15b
voting VII–209a
wagon trains VII–217b
zinc VII–368b
Arkansas (Indians) I–173a, 174a; III–499b
Arkansas (ironclad) III–474b; VII–181b
Arkansas (song) VI–393 (table)
***ARKANSAS*, DESTRUCTION OF THE** (1862) **I–173b**; I–275a
Arkansas Agricultural Wheel II–493b
Arkansas Gazette (news.) V–73b
ARKANSAS POST (Ark.) **I–173b**; I–160a, 172b–73a; II–247b; III–143b; VI–215a
ARKANSAS POST, BATTLE OF (1863) **I–174a**; IV–370a, 375b
ARKANSAS RIVER I–174a; VI–147a
Adams–Onís Treaty I–10b
Arkansas Post I–173b
basin IV–25a
Becknell expedition I–282b
Bent's Fort I–290a; II–16b
Bluestem Pastures I–326a

Canadian River I–441b
Cherokee Trail II–14b
Comanche II–133b
De Soto expedition II–336b
Dodge City II–358b
exploration II–247b; III–119a,b, 329a; IV–372a; VII–271b
Fort Atkinson I–213b
Fort Gibson II–359a; III–178b
Fort Larned IV–109a
Fort Lyon IV–208b
Fort Mann IV–240a
Fort Smith VI–317a; VII–289a
Fowler expedition III–88a
fur trade IV–159b
Gran Quivira V–155a
Indian land cession IV–199a
Indians IV–108b
Jolliet and Marquette expedition IV–7a
Kansas–Oklahoma commission VI–402a–b
Kiowa IV–50b
Las Animas land grant IV–110a
Leadville IV–124a
Long's exploration IV–186b
Long's explorations IV–187a
Louisiana purchase IV–196b
Mallet brothers exploration IV–230a
Medicine Creek Council IV–299b
"Mississippi Bubble" II–237a
Nebraska V–31a
Osage II–34a; V–173b
Pike's expedition V–311b–12a
Pikes Peak gold rush V–311b
Poverty Point V–382b
Santa Fe Trail VI–215a,b; VII–256a
steamboating VI–406b, 407a
Taos Trail VI–461a
trading posts VII–96a
Treaty of Fort Clark III–383b
tributaries IV–25a
U.S. boundary II–127b; IV–320b; VI–359b
water rights III–478a; IV–27b
western routes V–224b
Wichita VII–294a
ARKANSAS RIVER, GREAT BEND OF THE I–174b; VI–215b
Arkansas River Compact (1949) IV–28a
Arkansas River Compact Administration VI–402b
ARKANSAS RIVER ROUTE I–174b
"ARKANSAS TRAVELER" (song) **I–175a**; III–19a
Arkansas Valley VII–187b
ARKS I–175a; IV–174b, 347b, 374a; VI–148a, 149b
Arkwright, Richard (inv., mfr.). *See* Awkwright Machinery
ARKWRIGHT MACHINERY I–175a; IV–157b; V–230b; VI–44b
Arlington (Va.) V–392b; VI–15a; VII–196a
Arlington House (Va.) I–175b; VII–154b
ARLINGTON NATIONAL CEMETERY I–175b; I–478a
burial of *Maine* crew IV–227b
Custis–Lee Mansion VII–154b
Unknown Soldier VII–156b
Armada (1588) II–217b
Armaments
fortifications III–78b
Fort Lafayette IV–83b
Fourteen Points III–86a
Great Lakes II–471b
ironclads IV–85a
naval V–26a–27b
See also Defense, National; Munitions
Armand, Charles, Marquis de la Rouërie (off.) III–173a; VI–129a
Armat, Thomas (inv.) IV–417a
Armed forces III–3b
command of president II–178b
desegregation II–56b; III–503a; V–1a
desertion II–334b
enlistment II–450b
expatriation II–475b
government inspection III–422a
reduced II–316b
Sedition Act II–463a–b
volunteers II–316b
women VII–318a
Armed Forces Institute of Pathology IV–292b
Armed Freedom (statue) I–451a
Armed merchantmen. *See* Merchantmen, Armed
ARMED NEUTRALITY OF 1780 I–175b; II–446b; V–324a; VI–119b, 177a
Armed robbery II–258a
Armenia
World War I relief VII–330a
Armies, disbanding of the. *See* Demobilization
Armijo, Manuel (gov.) VII–36a
"Arm-in-Arm" Convention (1866). *See* National Union ("Arm-in-Arm") Convention
ARMINIANISM I–176a; VI–81b; VII–275a
Arminian Methodists III–127b
Arminius, Jacobus (theol.) I–176b; VI–456a
Armistead, Walker K. (off.) VI–261a
ARMISTICE OF NOV. 11, 1918 I–176b; I–102a, 159a; II–438a, 468b; V–425a–b; VII–327a, 328a
American Expeditionary Forces I–101b
Fourteen Points III–86a
German reparations VII–173b
ARMORED VEHICLES I–177a
antitank weapons IV–363b; VI–140a–b
Normandy invasion V–111a
World War I VII–326a
World War II VII–334b, 338a
See also Tanks
Armories
interchangeable manufacture III–441a,b, 442a
munitions manufacture IV–432a–b
ARMOR PLATE I–179a
Civil War V–322a
Confederate rams VI–44b
floating batteries III–36a
ironclads III–474b
New Ironsides V–56a
nickel III–14a
warships VII–240b, 242a–b
Armory Show (1913) II–104b, 105b
Armour, Philip D. (ind.) III–80a; IV–280b
Armour and Company I–283b; II–17b; IV–280b; VI–414b
Armour and Swift II–282a
Arms
Civil War II–162b
Colt six-shooter II–130b
Connecticut manufacture II–181a
shipments to Cuba II–269b–70a
World War I contracts II–314a
Arms, right to bear II–204a, 313a
National Rifle Association IV–470a
United States v. *Cruikshank* VII–154a
Armsby, H. P. (biochem.) I–303a
ARMS RACE WITH THE SOVIET UNION I–179a; III–69b
Manhattan Project IV–239a
missiles I–67b; IV–363b, 364a, 432a; VI–159a–b
naval competition V–10b–11b
Rosenberg case VI–164b
SALT talks IV–364a; VI–416b
space race IV 458b–59a
Armstrong, Edwin H. (elec. eng.) II–424a, 425b; VI–15a, 16a,b
ARMSTRONG, FORT (Ill.) **I–180b**; IV–355b
Armstrong, Fort, Treaty of (1832) III–383b, 384b, 404a
Armstrong, Harry E. (med. off.) IV–292b
Armstrong, Henry (pugilist) V–423a
Armstrong, James (pol.) I–417a
Armstrong, John, Jr. (off.) V–42b
Armstrong, John (off.)
Forbes expedition III–58b
Fort Loudon IV–191b
Fort Raystown I–282b
Kittanning IV–51a; V–222a
York campaign VII–358b–59a
Armstrong, John (sec. of war) I–318a
Armstrong, Louis (mus.) IV–166b, 440a, 443b
Armstrong, Neil A. (astron.) VI–159a
moon landing I–63b, 210b; IV–406b
Armstrong, William W. (pol.) III–431a, 433b
Armstrong Commission III–433b
ARMY, CONFEDERATE I–180b; II–161a–62a; VI–373b
administration II–63a
Afro-American troops II–63b, 161a–b
Alabama I–71b
arms and ammunition II–67a
Army of Mississippi IV–369b
Army of Northern Virginia I–130a, 146b–47a, 458b; II–295a, 482b, 482b; VII–197a
Army of Tennessee VII–26b
casualties and losses II–64b
cavalry I–475b–76a
clothing II–163b
Colt six-shooter II–131a
conscientious objectors II–63b
conscription II–63a
cotton agents II–159a
desertion I–115a; II–159b, 164b, 335b; III–297b
draft II–366b
dummy battleships I–277a
Florida troops III–39b
Galvanized Yankees III–148b
Indian allies I–335b–36a
Kentucky troops IV–41a
manpower II–64a–b
marching songs IV–262a
medical service II–164b
military fines II–185a
militia II–366b
Mississippi troops IV–368b
Mosby's Rangers IV–415b
music IV–442b
North Carolina troops

ARMY, CONFEDERATE (cont.)
V–116a
ordnance II–158b, 163a
partisan bands V–222a
prisoners II–159a, 279a
railroads II–253a, 479b
rangers VI–46b
rebel yell VI–50b
recruiting II–63a
reorganization (1863) V–248a
saltpeter V–98a
slaves II–161b
soldiers' homes VI–336b
states' rights VI–405a
substitutes II–161b–62a, 185a; VI–427a
tax VII–64a
Tennessee troops VII–25b
Terry's Texas Rangers VII–34a
Texas cattle drives I–473a
"Twenty Negro Law" II–162a
uniforms I–324a
Union prisons V–414a
United Confederate Veterans VII–149b
United Daughters of the Confederacy VII–150b
Virginians VII–195a
volunteers II–366b–67a; VII–208a
war industries II–162a
West Point graduates IV–341a
See also Confederate States of America; Civil War
Army, Department of the VII–230b
Army, National. *See* National Army
Army, secretary of the
army staff organization I–189a
ARMY, UNION I–181b; IV–346a
administration II–63a
Afro-Americans I–28b; II–63b; IV–339b
arms and ammunition II–67a
Army of Potomac V–377a–b
Army of the Cumberland II–21b, 271b
Army of the James I–184b; III–488a
Army of the Mississippi IV–370a
Army of the Ohio V–142a
Army of the Potomac I–130a, 146b–47a, 184b, 249a, 382a; II–96b, 140a, 369a; IV–36a
Army of the Tennessee I–184b; VII–26b
Army of Virginia I–382a; VII–197a
artillery II–379a
balloons I–59a, 232b
border states VII–148b
bounties II–63a, 366b–67a, 451a–b
Bummers I–382b
Butler's Order No. 28 I–398a
casualties and losses II–64b
cavalry I–475b–76a
Civil War General Order No. 100 II–70a
Colt six-shooter II–131a
congressional investigation I–182b
conscientious objectors I–182b
conscription II–63a, 161a, 161a
desertions I–115a, 353b; II–164b, 335a–b
draft II–366b, 367a
draft riots II–63a, 369a, 369a
dummy battleships I–277a
"embalmed beef" II–436a
enlistment I–182a–b; II–451a–b
First New York Fire Zouaves II–433a
Florida troops III–39b
free blacks VI–308a
Galvanized Yankees III–148b
general staff II–63a
Grand Army of the Republic III–207b
Illinois troops I–433a; III–329b
Indian Brigade III–375b
Jessie Scouts III–498b
Kansas troops IV–26a
manpower II–21b, 64a–b, 451b
Massachusetts troops IV–267b
military bounties I–353a–b
Military Order of the Loyal Legion IV–343a
Minnesota troops IV–356b
music IV–442b
officers I–184b–85a
organization I–184b–85a
pensions IV–471b
prisoners II–222b, 433a, 484b; IV–139a
rangers VI–46b
recruiting II–63a, 451b
regular army II–62a
sharpshooters VI–269b
Sharps rifle VI–270a
smallpox VI–316a
southerners VI–354b
substitutes II–63a, 185a, 366b–67a; VI–426b
Swamp Angel VI–453a
Tennessee troops VII–25b
uniforms I–324a; II–371b; VII–144b
U.S. Christian Commission II–35a
volunteers II–366b–67a; VII–208a
weapons IV–430b
West Point I–184a,b; IV–341a
See also Civil War
ARMY, UNITED STATES I–182b; II–200a, 313a–14a
aeronautical division I–59a
Afro-Americans I–29b, 30a–b, 310a, 313b–14a, 371b–72a; IV–339b
Air Corps I–59b, 68a, 328a
airmail I–59b, 65b, 67b–68a, 233b; III–452a
Airmobile I–49a
Alaska I–76a,b
American Expeditionary Forces IV–84a, 319a
amnesty I–114b
Apache Wars I–142a
appropriations II–476a
armies
First I–1a, 101b–02a, 379b, 380a; III–174b, 314a–b; IV–319b; V–110b; VI–193b, 197a–b; VII–327a, 339a,b, 340a,b
Second IV–320a
Third I–191b, 273b, 380a; VII–339b, 340a,b
Fifth I–141a; III–235b; VI–199b; VII–341a
Seventh VI–284b; VII–341a
Ninth I–379b, 380a; VII–340b
Tenth V–147b
Twelfth I–379b, 380a; VII–339b
armored vehicles I–177a–79a
See also Tanks
artillery I–49a, 58a, 190b, 199b
Black Cavalry IV–339b–40a
Black Hawk War I–312a
Black Infantry IV–339b–40a
bombers I–52a
Bonus Army I–330a, 331b
Boomer movement I–336b
Bronze Star II–312a
Brownsville affair I–371b; IV–340a
cavalry, air I–49a
cavalry, horse I–475a–76a; IV–339b–40a
cavalry, mechanized I–177a–79a
chemical warfare II–9b–10a
Chief of Staff I–177b, 178a
China garrison II–25b
civil defense II–50a
Colt six-shooter II–130b–31a
commander in chief II–201b
commissioning of officers II–202a
computers II–153a
constitutional provisions IV–342b
cornets II–228a
corps
First (I) I–70b
Second (II) I–308a; IV–33a; VII–327a
Third (III) I–70b; V–147b
Fifth (V) I–379b, 380a; V–110b; VI–285b, 361b–62a
Sixth (VI) I–141b; IV–8a
Seventh (VII) I–1a; V–110b; VI–285b
Eighth (VIII) I–379b, 380a; VI–362a
Thirteenth (XIII) IV–370a
Nineteenth (XIX) I–1a; VI–285b
Courier 1B satellite II–143a
Defense Department I–60b
demobilization II–323b–24b
desertion I–114b–15b; II–334b
dirigibles II–344a
disaster aid IV–341b
Distinguished Service Medal II–310b–11a
divisions
1st Armored IV–32b, 32b
1st Cavalry I–49a,b; IV–55b; VII–183b–84a
1st Infantry I–446a; III–314b; IV–404a; V–110b; VI–197b; VII–325b, 326b, 328b
2nd Armored I–380a
2nd Infantry I–286a, 379b; IV–55b, 319b, 320a; VII–326b
3rd Infantry I–491b, 502a; VII–326b
4th Armored I–273b, 380a
4th Infantry I–379b; III–314b; V–110b, 111a; VII–327a
5th Armored III–314b
5th Infantry IV–411a, 445b
6th Infantry IV–129b–30a
7th Armored I–379b; VI–198a
7th Infantry IV–257b
8th Infantry III–314b
9th Armored I–273b, 379b; VI–84a, 198a
9th Infantry III–314b; V–184a
10th Armored I–273b, 379b
10th Infantry IV–411a
10th mountain VI–298a
11th Airborne V–213b
13th Airborne V–213b
16th Infantry IV–84a
17th Airborne V–213b
21st Infantry IV–205a
24th Infantry IV–55b, 340b
25th Infantry IV–205a, 340a
26th Infantry I–286b; VI–197b; VII–326b, 327a
27th Infantry III–180a; VI–198a,b; VII–327a, 366b
28th Infantry I–273b,

379b, 446a, 491b;
III–314b; V–147a;
VI–198a; VII–326b
29th Infantry V–110b
30th Infantry
VII–327a, 366b
32nd Infantry V–147a;
VII–327a
37th Infantry
VII–366b
42nd Infantry I–491b;
VII–326b
77th Infantry IV–189a;
V–147a; VII–327a
78th Infantry I–379b;
III–314b
81st Infantry I–459a;
V–243a
82nd Airborne I–379b;
V–110b, 213b, 214a
83rd Infantry
III–314b; V–307b
91st Infantry VII–366b
92nd Infantry IV–340b
93rd Infantry IV–340b;
VII–327a
99th Infantry I–379b
101st Airborne I–49a,
273b, 379b; V–110b,
213b, 214a
106th Infantry I–379b;
IV–257b; VI–198a
307th Infantry
IV–189b
308th Infantry
IV–189b
"doughboy" II–365b
dragoons III–80b; IV–129b,
411a
I–475b
Engineer Corps I–215b,
463b; II–449b–50a
enlistment I–181b–82b
ensign II–452a
flags III–35a
Fort Armstrong I–180b
Fort Knox IV–53b
Fort Riley VI–141b
Fort Sam Houston
VI–204b
Fort Sill VI–287a
Freedmen's Bureau
III–103a
frontier III–126b
garrisons I–371a
gas masks I–197a
general staff II–367a–b
GI II–366a
helicopters I–49a,b;
III–270b
hospitals I–102a
Indian scouts V–230b
Indian wars I–142a,b,
219a, 243a, 313a
intelligence staff III–439a
intelligence tests
V–442a–b
Jefferson Barracks
III–494b
Jet Propulsion Laboratory
III–502a–b
Kansas Border War
I–314a
Laos IV–107b
Lebanon IV–130a
liquor ration II–353b
Map Service I–464a
McCarthy hearings
IV–209b; VII–310b
Medal of Honor II–310a
medical department
IV–290a–92b
Messiah War I–243a
Mexican War
IV–323b–24a,b
military policy IV–343a,b
militia support IV–345b
missiles IV–363b
Mormon Battalion
I–172a; IV–411a
Mormon War I–363a
mutinies IV–445a–b
National Guard IV–346a,
463b
Office of Scientific Research
and Development
V–137a
Officers' Reserve Corps
V–138b
ordnance V–163a–b
Ordnance Department
I–196b
paratroops V–213b
pension plans V–256b
polar exploration
V–337a,b, 338a
posts I–190b, 192b–93a
preparedness movement
V–391a
radar II–425a
railroad strikes I–111b;
VI–38b
rangers VI–46b
recoilless rifle VI–140a
recruitment VI–60b
Regiment of Mounted Riflemen I–475b
regiments I–288b
Afro-American I–29b,
313b–14a; IV–340a
7th Cavalry IV–168a,
316a
7th Infantry
I–142a
38th Infantry
I–491b
87th mountain infantry
VI–298a
107th Infantry
IV–320a
182nd Infantry
IV–463b
332nd Infantry I–102a;
V–307b
339th Infantry
I–158b–59a
Reserve Officers' Training
Corps VI–98b
revolutionary war
VI–125a–26a
rifles VI–139b–40a
riot (1968) I–32a
rockets VI–159a
San Diego VI–208b
schools I–191a, 241b, 289a
Sea Fencibles VI–244b
Seminole Wars I–475b
sharpshooters VI–270a
Signal Corps I–59b,
90a,b; VI–285b
Signal Service II–75b
Sioux I–107a
slang VI–300b–01b
Soldiers' and Airmens'
Home VI–336b
Soldier's Medal
II–311b–12a
Spencer rifle VI–372a
supply system V–375a–b
truck-standardization-
program IV–419b
Uniform Code of Military
Justice VII–143b–44a
uniforms VII–144a
U.S. flag III–35a
volunteers II–316b, 366b;
VII–208a
War Department
VII–229b
Weather Bureau II–75b
West Point IV–340b
women VII–318a–b
Yellow Fever Commission
VII–355b
Yosemite National Park
VII–362a
See also Camps; Korean
War; Spanish–American
War; Vietnam War; War
of 1812; World War I;
World War II
Army Air Corps
Jet Propulsion Laboratory
III–502a
polar exploration V–337b
Army Air Forces I–59b–60b,
186b; VII–230b, 318b
air battle of Germany
III–174a
See also Air Force, United
States
Army Air Forces Air Trans-
port Command III–46a
Army Air Service IV–106a;
V–337a
Army and Navy Journal
VI–84b
Army and Navy Register
VI–84b
Army Appropriation Act
(1916) VII–231b
Army Appropriation Bill
(1853) I–453a
Army Aviation School
VI–287b
Army Ballistic Missile Agency
IV–459a
Army Command and General
Staff School IV–129b
Army Epidemiological Board
IV–292a
Army Ground Forces
VII–230b
Army Medical Library
IV–292a
Army Medical Museum
IV–292b
Army Medical Research Board
IV–291b
Army Medical School
IV–291b
Army Medical Specialist Corps
IV–290b
"Army mule" IV–426a
Army Nurse Corps
VII–318a,b
uniforms VII–145a
ARMY OF OCCUPATION
(1918–23) **I–191b**
debt agreement III–172a
expenses VI–87b
financing VII–213a
Army of the Ohio. *See* Ohio,
Army of the
Army of the Republic of Viet-
nam VII–183a, 184a,b
Army of the West IV–129b
ARMY ON THE FRONTIER
I–192a; I–184a, 185b;
III–126b–27a; VI–300b–01a
Fort Osage V–173b
Magee–Kearny expedition
IV–223b
military policy
IV–343a
pack trains V–184a
sutler merchant
VI–452b
See also Wars and
Campaigns, Indian
Army Ordnance Department
V–163a,b
Army Organization Act (1950)
I–189a
ARMY POSTS I–192b;
I–190b; III–126b
Fort Leavenworth
IV–129a
Fort McHenry IV–213b
Fort Ripley VI–144b
Newport Barracks V–66a
New South V–67b
Russells, Majors, and Wad-
dell VI–176b
Army Supply. *See* Army,
United States
Army surplus
ski equipment VI–298b
Army War College I–185b,
190b–91a; IV–384a
Arnhem (Neth.)
World War II III–187b;
V–213b; VII–340a
Arnim, Juergen von (off.)
I–308a; IV–32b; V–113a
Arnold, Asa (inv.) VII–43a
Arnold, Benedict (off.)
II–286a; VI–385b;
VII–171b
Battle of Freeman's Farm
I–385b; III–108b
Battle of Ridgefield
VI–139a
Battle of Valcour Island
III–234a; IV–86b;
VII–164a,b
court–martial II–246b
march to Quebec I–193b,
436a
New London burning
V–58b
Ticonderoga VII–56a
treason I–118a,b, 194a;
III–275b–76a, 313a;
VI–150a; VII–280a
Virginia raid I–194a;
VI–351b
Yorktown VII–360b
Arnold, Fort (N.Y.). *See*
Clinton, Fort
Arnold, Gottfried II–454a
Arnold, Harold DeForest
(phys.) II–423b; VII–163a
Arnold, Henry H. (off.)
III–490a
Arnold, Jacob IV–413a
Arnold, Matthew (poet, critic)
VI–342b

Arnold, Ripley A. (off.) III–80b
Arnold, Thurman (law.) VII–123b
Arnold Arboretum (Boston) IV–267b
ARNOLD'S MARCH TO QUEBEC (1775) **I–193b**; I–436a
ARNOLD'S RAID IN VIRGINIA (1781) **I–194a**; VI–351b
ARNOLD'S TREASON I–194a; III–275b–76a, 313a; VI–150a; VII–280a
  André, John I–118a–b
Arno River
  World War II VII–338b
Aronoke tobacco VII–67b
Aroostook (Maine) V–376b
Aroostook River I–194b
AROOSTOOK WAR (1838–39) **I–194b**; V–118b
ARPENT I–195a
Arrastre (tool) III–191a
ARREST I–195a
ARREST, ARBITRARY, DURING THE CIVIL WAR I–195b; II–62a, 190a
  Corning letter II–228a
  Vallandigham incident VII–164b
Arriola, Andrés de (expl.) V–254a
Arromanches (Fr.) V–111a
Arrow, Kenneth J. (econ.) V–99b
Arrow Lake II–132a
Arrowrock (Idaho) III–328b; VI–215a
Arrowsic Island VI–185b
Arrowsmith, Aaron (geog.) *See* Arrowsmith's Map
ARROWSMITH'S MAP I–196a; VII–74b
Arroyo Hondo (La.) IV–197b; V–33b; VII–36b
Arroyo Seco (Calif.) III–502a
"Arsenal of Democracy" (Detroit) II–337a
ARSENALS I–196b; V–163a–b
  Baton Rouge I–274b
  congressional control II–200a
  Fort Leavenworth IV–129b
  munitions manufacture IV–432a
  Newport Barracks V–66a
  New York City V–85b
Arsenic
  food contamination V–466b
Arsenicals III–421a,b; VI–213a
Arson
  capital punishment I–450a
Arsphenamines VII–169a
Art
  agrarianism I–32b
  black I–30a
  Cooper Union II–222a
  copyright II–224b
  See also Painting
Art, folk. *See* Folk Art
Art, Indian. *See* Indian Art and Technology
d'Artaguette, Pierre (off.) I–197a
Art dealers II–101b–02b, 105a–b
Art Deco III–446b
  furniture III–136b
Artedi, Peter (ichthyol.) III–26b
Artesian well
  irrigation III–478a–b
Art galleries II–103b–04a, 105b–06a
  Smithsonian Institution VI–319a,b
Arthritis, Metabolism, and Digestive Diseases Institute IV–465a
Arthur, Chester A. (pres.) II–176 (table); V–395 (table)
  Arrears of Pension Act V–255a
  campaign of 1880 I–423b; VI–381a
  Fort Rice VI–135b
  tariff VI–464a
  vice-presidency VII–179 (table)
Arthur, Gabriel (expl.) V–31b–32a; VII–25a
Arthur Allen House (Va.) I–161a
Arthurdale (W.Va.) VI–426b
ARTHUR D. LITTLE, INC. I–197a; III–409a, 410a; IV–268a; V–328b
Arthur Kill II–431a–b
Arthur Mervyn IV–161b
Arthurs, James (eng.) VI–409a
Artichoke III–381a
Articles for Government of the Navy. *See* Uniform Code of Military Justice
ARTICLES OF CONFEDERATION I–197b; II–4b, 165b–67b, 211b–12a; VI–117a
  Anglo-American relations I–120a
  Antifederalist support I–130b
  Committee of the States II–138b
  Constitution II–192b–93b, 194a
  courts under I–14b
  enumerated powers II–195b
  federal-state relations III–9a
  foreign relations VI–388a
  Indian affairs III–382b, 388b
  interstate boundary agreements III–459b
  judiciary IV–15b
  loyalty oaths IV–202b
  New Jersey V–57b
  patents V–225b
  postal service V–371a
  privileges and immunities of citizens V–420a–b
  ratification provision II–196a
  revision II–151b
  Rhode Island VI–132b
  state government VI–396b
  treaties under I–362b
  "United States of America" VII–153b
  war financing VI–120b
  weights and measures IV–462a
  western land claims VII–273a
Articles of War. *See* Uniform Code of Military Justice
ARTICLE X I–199a; IV–125a, 178b
Artificers
  compulsory labor IV–79b
ARTILLERY I–199b; IV–431a
  interchangeable manufacture III–440a
  machine guns IV–214b
  manufacture IV–432b
  navy V–26a–b, 27a–b
  Neutrality Act (1935) IV–430a
  recoilless rifle VI–140a
  revolutionary war IV–430a; VII–56b
  rockets VI–159a
  Swamp Angel VI–453a
  World War I VII–326a
Artillery and Guided Missile Center and School VI–287a
Art Institute of Chicago II–103a, 105a
Artisans IV–60a,b
  education IV–281a–b
  folk art III–47a,b
  Hopewell culture III–300a
Artists
  advertising I–16a–19b
  black I–25a
Artists in New York City, Society of American V–191b
Art Journal VII–319a
Art nouveau III–446b
Art of This Century Gallery II–105b
Arts and Architecture Building (Yale Univ.) I–166a
Arts and Crafts movement III–136a
Arts and Letters, American Academy of. *See* American Academy of Arts and Letters
Arts and Letters, National Institute of. *See* National Institute of Arts and Letters
Arver v. *United States* (1918) II–367b
ARVN. *See* Army of the Republic of Vietnam
Asbestos
  health hazards IV–294b
  pollution VI–213a
  sheathing I–379a
Asbury, Francis (bp.) II–39b; IV–318a,b; VI–442a
Ascension, Fort (Ill.) IV–264a
Ascorbic acid VI–244a
"AS GOES MAINE, SO GOES THE NATION" I–200b
Ashanti (people) VI–309b, 310a
Ashbery, John (poet) IV–165b
Ashburnham (Mass.) I–490b; II–79a
Ashburton, Lord. *See* Baring, Alexander, 1st Baron Ashburton
Ashburton Treaty. *See* Webster-Ashburton Treaty
Ashby (Mass.) II–79a
ASHBY'S GAP I–200b; V–224b
Ash Can school (paint.) V–192a,b
Ash Committee (1969–71) II–497b
Ashe, Arthur (athlete) VII–30b
Ashe, John (off.) I–362a
Ashe, Thomas (au.) I–295b, 367b, 368a
Asheville (N.C.) II–347a
Asheville (gunboat) III–234b
Ashford, Bailey K. (med. off.) III–298b; IV–291b
Ashfork (Ariz.) VI–273b
Ash Hollow (Nebr.) III–256a
Ash Hollow, Battle of. *See* Harney Expedition
Ashkenazim IV–9a–b; VI–79a
Ashland (Ky.) IV–41b
Ashland (Mass.) II–79b
Ashland (Va.) IV–282a
Ashland (Wis.) VI–443b
Ashley, Edward (trader)
  Castine I–466a
Ashley, James M. (pol.) VII–54a
Ashley, William Henry (fur trader) *See* Ashley Expeditions
ASHLEY EXPEDITIONS I–200b; II–477a–b; VI–318a; VII–74b
  Arikara IV–129b
  Colorado River II–129b
  Green River III–227a
  Missouri IV–377b
  Platte River Trail V–330b
  rendezvous VII–103b–04a
  Rocky Mountain Company VI–160a
  Sioux VI–296a
  Smith explorations VI–318a
  Utah VII–161a
Ashley Falls (Colorado River) II–129b
Ashley River III–16b; VI–347a
  Middleton Place I–497a, 498a
  revolutionary war I–496b
  settlement I–496a
Ashmun Institute II–404b
Ashtabula (Ohio) II–350b, 459a; III–218b
Ashwander v. *Tennessee Valley Authority* (1936) III–321b

Ash Wednesday
Mardi Gras IV–249b
Asia
Anglo-American relations I–122a
citrus trees II–43a
"color line" V–199b
immigration III–337b, 340b–41b, 342a
Indian migration I–74b; III–355a, 357b
quota system VI–4b–5a
U.S. aid III–62a
yellow peril VII–356b
Asia (warship) V–86a
ASIA, TRADE WITH I–201a; VII–86b, 87b
Kearny's mission to China IV–34b
Navigation Acts V–15b, 16a; VI–107b
Open Door policy V–157b
Perry's Japan expedition V–263a
rubber VI–167b, 168a
tea VII–16b
war with Korea (1871) IV–54b
See also China trade
Asian-Americans
civil rights II–55b–56a
Asian Development Bank VII–108a
Asiatic cholera II–33a–b, 454b
Asiatic Fleet V–24b
Asiatic influenza III–416b
Asiatic Squadron (U.S. Navy) IV–239a–b; VI–361b
ASIENTO (1713) **I–202a**; I–22b; VI–2b, 309b, 310a,b; VII–162b
Asimov, Isaac (au.) IV–165a
Askin, John (fur trader) III–403b
ASP. *See* American Selling Plan
Aspdin, Joseph I–477b
Aspen (Colo.)
silver II–128a; VI–292b
ski resort VI–101b
Asphalt IV–44a; VI–156a–b
Aspinwall, Thomas II–108b
Aspirin V–273b
Asroc (missile) IV–363b
Assam III–46a
ASSASSINATIONS, POLITICAL I–202a
Cáceres, Rámon II–361a
campaign of 1968 I–431a–b
Faisal of Saudi Arabia I–150b
Garfield, James I–146a; V–228a
Kennedy, John F. I–430b; II–58b; IV–37b–38a
Kennedy, Robert F I–431a; IV–38a
King, Martin Luther II–55b, 59a; IV–45b
Lincoln, Abraham II–64a, 349b
Long, Huey P. IV–195a
McKinley, William I–117a; V–204b–05a; VI–252a
Pottawatomie massacre V–379a
Roosevelt, Theodore I–381a
Steunenberg, Frank III–266b
Trujillo, Rafael II–361b
ASSAY OFFICES I–203b; IV–360a
Assemblies, colonial. *See* Colonial Assemblies
Assemblies of God V–260a
ASSEMBLY, FIRST AMERICAN I–204a
ASSEMBLY, RIGHT OF I–204a; I–94a, 298b, 299b; II–53b; V–265b
Civil War II–62b
Declaration of Rights II–308b
First Amendment II–171b, 204a
United States v. *Cruikshank* VII–154a
ASSEMBLY LINE I–205a; IV–272b
automobile I–227a; IV–77b
flour milling III–45b
machine tools IV–216a–b
morality of IV–408b
scientific management VI–234a–b
Assenisipia III–497a
ASSINIBOINE (Indians) **I–206a**; I–151b; II–282b, 283a, 380a; III–365a, 396b; IV–236a
Fort Union VII–145b
half-breeds III–242b
Jesuit missions III–499b, 500b
Mackenzie's Treaty IV–217a
wild rice VII–298b
ASSINIBOINE, FORT (N.Dak.) **I–206a**
Assiniboine River IV–118a
ASSISTANCE CLAUSE I–206a
ASSISTANT I–206b
general court III–155a,b
negative voice V–32a
New Plymouth Colony V–65a
Associated Aviation Underwriters III–429b
ASSOCIATED LOYALISTS OF NEW ENGLAND I–206b
ASSOCIATED PRESS I–206b; III–198b; V–74a,b, 79b; VII–152a,b
Associate Reformed Presbyterian Church IV–365b; V–392b
Associates (trading company) VII–95a
Associates of New Jersey Company V–57b
Association, freedom of IV–14b, 358b
Association football III–56b
Association for Improving the Conditions of the Poor VI–313b; VII–24a
Association for the Study of Negro Life and History III–279b
Association Island V–439a
Associationism IV–62a
Association of Allergists for Mycological Investigations IV–289a
Association of American Geologists I–98a; VI–236a
Association of American Geologists and Naturalists IV–464b; VI–237b
Association of American Law Schools II–399b; IV–121a–b
Association of American Medical Colleges II–399b; IV–284b
Association of American Railroads I–111b; III–451a; VI–28a, 29b, 30a
Association of American Universities II–400b
Association of Catholic Trade Unionists I–469a
Association of Licensed Automobile Manufacturers I–227a; VI–257a
Association of Life Insurance Presidents III–434a
Association of Medical Superintendents of American Institutions for the Insane IV–289a, 305b
Association of Pentecostal Churches in America V–29b
Association of Southern Women for the Prevention of Lynching IV–208a
Association of Westmoreland County III–250b
Association on American Indian Affairs I–106b
ASSOCIATIONS (colonial) **I–207b**; II–211a; V–440a
boycott of British goods VI–121b
tea boycott VII–15b, 17a
Associations of Adults for Mutual Education IV–207a
ASSOCIATORS (1747–48) **I–208a**
Assumption, Fort (La.) II–22a
Assumption, Fort (Tenn.) IV–301b
ASSUMPTION AND FUNDING OF REVOLUTIONARY WAR DEBTS I–208a; II–299b, 302a–b; III–245a; VII–222a
arbitration IV–5b
British debts366a
Compromise of 1790 II–149b
Continental currency II–274b
location of national capital I–448b; II–149b
national sinking fund VI–294a
Public Credit Act V–443b
public lands sales V–443b
"Assumption of risk" doctrine II–441a
Assunpink Creek V–408a
Astaire, Fred (dancer) II–290b
Astbury, W. T. (phys.) IV–389a–b
Asthma
sanitariums VI–101a
As Thousands Cheer (musical) IV–442a
Astley, Philip (showman) II–40a
Aston, F. W. (phys.) V–299b
Aston, W. (chem.) I–218b
Astor, John Jacob (fur trader, fin.) III–122b, 142b–43a, 144b, 403b; IV–377b; VII–222a
American Fur Company I–105a; II–34a, 131b; IV–217a, 217b–18a
Astoria I–209a; VI–322b; VII–95b, 247b, 271b
Fort Pierre V–310b
fortune III–79a
land speculation IV–99a, 100b, 101a
New York Public Library IV–145a
Oregon V–164b
Pacific Fur Company V–180a
Protective War Claims Association V–438b
Southwest Fur Company VI–357b
Wisconsin VII–307b
Astor, John Jacob III II–103b
Astor, John Jacob IV (bus.) VII–64a
Astor, Mary (Mrs. William Astor) III–85a
Astor Fur Company. *See* American Fur Company; Astoria; Pacific Fur Company
Astor Hotel (N.Y.C.) V–84a
Astor House (N.Y.C.) V–84a
ASTORIA (Oreg.) **I–209a**; I–83a, 296b, 477a; II–131b; III–226a; V–164b; VII–95b, 247b, 271b
Lewis and Clark Expedition IV–136b
Oregon question V–167b
Oregon Trail V–168b, 169a
Pacific Fur Company V–180a,b
Platte River Trail V–330b
Snake River VI–322b
Tonquin VII–72a
Astoria (book) III–122b
ASTOR PLACE RIOT (1849) **I–209b**
Astrogeology III–444b
Astrology
almanacs I–90b
chapbooks I–494b
ASTRONAUTICS I–209b; III–410b
information retrieval VI–232b
Jet Propulsion Laboratory III–502a

ASTRONAUTICS (cont.)
miniaturization IV–352a
moon landing IV–406b
NASA programs IV–459b–60b
National Aeronautics and Space Administration IV–458b
National Air and Space Museum VI–319b
rockets VI–159a,b
scientific education VI–232a–b
slang VI–300a
Sputnik 1 IV–363b
Astronomical Diary and Almanack I–90b
Astronomical Papers V–12b
ASTRONOMY I–211a; III–166b, 167a; V–294a
"falling of the stars" VI–387b
Hale Observatories III–241b
Naval Observatory V–12a
observatories V–130b
radio astronomy VI–16b
Yale University VII–351a
Astrophysical Observatory, Smithsonian VI–319b
Astrophysics I–211b; V–296a
Astrup, Eivind (expl.) V–240b
Asunción (Para.) V–212b
ASW. *See* Antisubmarine warfare
Aswan High Dam VI–429b
withdrawal of U.S. aid I–124b, 149b–50a
Asylum, political. *See* Political Exiles to the United States
Asylums V–380a–b; VI–256a
Atabrine IV–291b
Atanasoff, John (phys.) II–154b
A. Tappan and Company IV–307b
Atcheson, Camp (N.Dak.) II–283b–84a
Atchinson Daily Globe (news.) V–73b
ATCHISON (Kans.) **I–213a**
Atchison, Topeka and Santa Fe Railroad VI–32b
freighting V–177a
Platte River Trail V–330b
stage lines VI–379b
Atchison, David R. (pol.) IV–377b
border ruffians I–341a
Kansas–Nebraska Act IV–29a,b
sack of Lawrence IV–118b
Atchison County (Mo.) V–330a–b
Atchison Globe (news.) I–213a
Atchison, Topeka and Santa Fe Railroad VI–27a, 32b, 191b, 216a
Atchison terminal I–213a
Atlantic and Pacific I–214b; IV–94b
cattle shipments IV–280b
hide and tallow trade III–274b
Athabasca (Alta., Can.) III–209a
Athabasca, Lake II–30b; V–121a; VII–275b
Athabasca River VII–275b
Athapascan (lang.) II–30b; III–238a, 360a, 364a, 365a, 367a, 368b, 369a; V–8b; VII–367b
Alaskan Indians I–79a, 80b–81a
Apache I–141b
Arizona I–171b
Canadian Indians I–441b
Hare III–252b
Sarci I–311a
Atheism II–356a
moral standards IV–408a
Athenagoras (archbp.) II–386b, 387a
Atheneum (Phila.) I–163b
Athens (Gr.)
Olympic Games V–154a
sea power VI–247b
Athens (Ky.) I–337b
Athens (Ohio) VII–156a
Athens (Pa.) V–250b; VI–451b
"Athens of America" I–344a
"Athens of the South." *See* Nashville
Atherosclerosis V–129b
Atherton, Humphrey (speculator) I–213a
ATHERTON COMPANY I–213a
Atka (icebreaker) V–338a
Atkin, Edmund (Indian agent) III–387b
Atkins, Samuel (pub.)
America's Messenger I–90b
Atkinson, Edward (ind., econ.) I–482a; III–430b
ATKINSON, FORT (Kans.) **I–213b**; I–193a; IV–240a
Atkinson, Fort (Nebr.) IV–130a; V–30b
Atkinson, Fort, Treaty of (1853) III–404b
Atkinson, Henry (off.)
Battle of Bad Axe I–242b
Black Hawk War I–312a
Magee–Kearny expedition IV–223b
Yellowstone River expeditions VI–296a; VII–357b
Atlanta (Ga.) III–438a; V–62b, 67b; VII–211b
Afro-Americans I–29a, 32a
Camp Gordon I–434b
civil rights movement II–57b
Civil War I–88b, 213b–14a, 213b–14a; III–78b, 98a; V–56a, 238a–b; VI–26b, 278a
federal records center III–284b
Forest Service III–76b
Freedom Riders III–107a
International Exposition of 1895 III–453b
King, Martin Luther IV–46a
mayor I–32a
railroad rate wars VI–23a
railroads IV–302b, 453b; VI–33a, 34b
riot (1906) I–29b
riot (1967) I–31b; VI–9a
Southern Christian Leadership Conference VI–351b
subway III–451b
tennis VII–29a
Winecoff Hotel fire II–348b
Atlanta I (cruiser) VII–241a, 242b, 293a
Atlanta II (cruiser) VII–242b
ATLANTA CAMPAIGN (1864) **I–213b**; II–62b, 271b, 295b; III–298a; IV–314a; VI–26b, 278a; VII–26b, 27a, 34b
Army of the Ohio V–142b
Battles at New Hope Church (Ga.) V–56a
Battles on Peachtree Creek V–238a
Ezra Church II–479b
Kenesaw Mountain IV–36b
Rouseau's raid VI–166a
Atlanta Constitution (news.) V–66b, 73b, 73b, 377a
Atlanta University I–28b; II–113b; III–103b
Atlantic (mag.) IV–222a,b
Atlantic (schooner) VII–349a
ATLANTIC, BATTLE OF THE I–214a; V–21a–b; VII–342b
gunboats III–234b
torpedo warfare VII–76b
Atlantic and Gulf Railroad VI–220b
ATLANTIC AND PACIFIC RAILROAD I–214b; I–83b
land grants IV–94b, 94b
Atlantic and Pacific Tea Company II–282a; VII–123b
Atlantic and Pacific Telegraph Company VII–276b
Atlantic cable. *See* Cables, Atlantic and Pacific
ATLANTIC CHARTER I–214b; I–361b; II–471b; III–84a; VII–335a
Soviet Union VI–179a
Atlantic City (N.J.) VI–100b
Akron disaster II–346a
Jewish Chautauqua Society II–1b
Atlantic Coastal Plain II–485a
Atlantic Coast Line Railroad III–39b; VI–25a, 32a, 36b
See also Seaboard Coast Line
ATLANTIC COMMUNITY I–215a; VI–469a,b; VII–88b–89a
tariff VI–470a
Atlantic fisheries dispute. *See* Fisheries Dispute, Arbitration of
Atlantic Fleet I–14a; V–24b, 25a
Atlantic, Gulf and West Indies Steamship Company II–91a
Atlantic Intracoastal Waterway VI–148b–49a; VII–260b
Atlantic Monthly (mag.) II–298b; IV–162b
Atlantic Neptune (atlas) IV–248a
Atlantic Ocean
air bases II–314b
Florida Straits III–41b
Gulf of Mexico IV–326a
Gulf Stream III–232b
hurricanes III–319a,b
lifesaving stations IV–152a
Lindbergh's flight II–310a, 311b; IV–156b
Long Island IV–185a
mapping of coast IV–247b
Narragansett Bay IV–451b
navigational charts IV–277a
research III–29a
Atlantic–Pacific Interoceanic Canal Study V–202b
Atlantic States Marine Fisheries Commission VI–402a,b
Atlantic Telegraph Company III–215b
Atlantic Wall V–110b
Atlantis (ship) III–233b
Atlas (maps) I–462b
See also Mapping of American Coast
Atlas (missile) IV–363b, 459a; VI–159b
spaceflight I–64a
Atlas B (rocket) II–143a
Atlas Powder Company V–328a
Atlatls (throwing stick) II–83b
Atlee's Station (Va.) VII–117a
Atocha, A. J. (off.) IV–323b
Atoka (Okla.) IV–334a
Atom
splitting II–278b
structure II–12a
study II–12a
See also Physics, Nuclear
ATOMIC BOMB I–215a; III–69b, 324a, 410a; IV–363b, 432a, 433b; V–296a, 300b; VII–191a, 237a
Anglo-American relations I–123b
arms race I–179a
bombing of Japan I–67b, 328b; III–490b
cold war I–60b; II–97b
fallout IV–294b
Lawrence Radiation Laboratory IV–119a
laws of war VII–226a
Manhattan Project IV–237b
Naval Research Laboratory V–28a
Nuclear Test Ban Treaty

V–124b
Oak Ridge plant III–321b
Office of Scientific Research and Development V–137b
Rosenberg case VI–164b
Soviet Union II–315a; III–61b, 69b
U.S. Air Force I–60b
World War II VII–341a
Atomic energy IV–245a; V–295b–96a
computers II–155a
Fair Deal II–480b
federally funded research IV–471a
federal regulation II–229b–30a
information retrieval VI–232b
international control II–315a
masers and lasers IV–262a
Atomic Energy Act (1946) I–216a; III–203a
Atomic Energy Act (1954) I–216a, 217a
Atomic Energy Act (1958) I–124a
Atomic Energy Agency, International I–216b
ATOMIC ENERGY COMMISSION, UNITED STATES I–216a; II–500a; III–410b, 459a; IV–119b, 471a; V–137b; VI–230b
hydrogen bomb III–324a
judicial review IV–16b
military and strategic intelligence III–439b
particle accelerators V–297a,b
physics research V–296a
scientific education VI–232a
vanadium III–15a
Atomic energy industry
New South V–67b
Atomic energy plants
Great Britain I–124a
United States I–391b
Atomic Power Laboratories (Oak Ridge, Tenn.) VII–26a
ATOMIC POWER REACTORS I–217a; I–216b; II–416a, 417a–b
Hanford Atomic Works VII–248a
Manhattan Project IV–237b
Tennessee Valley Authority V–455b
tungsten III–15b
Atomic research VI–230b–31a
Atomic warfare
bombing I–328b
electronic weapons II–425a
military policy IV–344a
ATOMIC WEIGHT DETERMINATIONS I–218a; II–12a; V–298a
"Atoms-for-Peace" I–216b
Atom smasher. *See* Cyclotron
ATROCITIES IN WAR I–219a
Bataan–Corregidor I–274a
Battle of Waxhaw VII–262a
Civil War II–66b, 159b
Cuban war for independence II–268b
Dominican Republic II–361a–b
Fort William Henry massacre VII–301a
Goliad massacre VII–37b
Malmédy massacre IV–230b
Philippine Insurrection V–281b
scalping VI–224a
Atsina (Indians) III–229a, 365a; IV–236a
Arapaho I–151b
Attack carrier (CV) I–54b, 55b, 57a
ATTAINDER I–220a; II–53b, 200b, 274a
loyalty oaths III–153a
test laws VII–35a
Attakapas. *See* Saint Martinville
Attakullaculla (Indian) VI–455a
ATTICA (N.Y.) **I–220a**; V–417b; VII–192a
Attlee, Clement (states.)
Potsdam V–378b
Attorney General IV–21b
antitrust laws I–139b
colonial II–120b
Confederacy II–160a
Federal Bureau of Investigation II–503b
Kennedy, Robert F. I–400a
Mitchell, John I–400a
Rush, Richard I–318a
See also Justice, Department of
Attu (Alaska)
World War II I–84b–85a; IV–54a; VII–336b
Atwater, Caleb (pioneer) II–390b; III–468a
Atwater, W. O. (biochem.) I–46a, 303a; II–494a; V–127b
Atwood, William (jur.) II–121a
Atzerodt, George A. IV–154b, 155a
Aubrey, John (hist.) V–359b
Aubry, Charles Philippe (off.) IV–264a
Aubry, Francis Xavier (trader) I–221a
AUBRY'S RIDE (1848) **I–221a**
Auburn (Mass.) VI–159a
AUBURN PRISON SYSTEM I–221a; V–415a–b; VI–67b
Auchmuty, Robert (law.) I–346a
AUCTIONS I–221b
book I–332b–33a
dairy industry II–281b
decorative arts II–99a, 100a
distribution of goods and services II–354b
horse races III–304b
houses II–106b–07a, 108a
land II–70a–b, 166a; IV–90b
livestock IV–170a
Oklahoma lands V–149a,b
public lands sales V–452b
stock exchanges II–469a–70a
taxation VII–4b, 5a, 12b
tobacco II–221b; IV–41b
Audemus fura nostra defendre (motto) VI–393 (table)
Audenarde (Belg.) VII–366b
Audiffron, Marcel (inv.) II–420b
Audio-tapes II–425b
Audit
federal II–152a
governmental expenditures II–501b
Audit Bureau of Circulations I–18a
Auditorium Building (Chicago) I–164a
Audubon, John James (ornith., art.) V–190b, 413b; VII–130a
Audubon Society I–222b
Birds of America I–304b; II–477a
mammals IV–232a
Audubon, John Woodhouse (nat.) IV–232a
Audubon, Victor (nat.) IV–232a–b
AUDUBON SOCIETY, NATIONAL I–222a; II–187b
bird sanctuaries I–306a,b
Augering match VI–161b
AUGHWICK (Pa.) **I–222b**; I–358a; IV–51a, 181a
Auglaize River II–317a
Augsburg Confession IV–205b, 206a
Augusta (princess) I–223b
AUGUSTA (Ga.) **I–223a**; VI–349b
Camp Hancock I–434b
commerce VI–220b
direct-trade convention VI–352b
fall line II–485a
Machine Gun School I–289a
Masters Tournament III–198a
post road V–375a
railroads VI–33a
revolutionary war IV–44b
Augusta (It.) VI–284b
Augusta (Maine)
Fort Western VII–269b
Kennebec Trading Post IV–37b
soldiers' home VI–336b
See also Cushenoc
Augusta (schooner) II–349a
AUGUSTA (warship) **I–223a**
AUGUSTA, CONGRESS OF (1763) **I–223a**
AUGUSTA, FORT (Pa.) **I–223b**; III–115b
AUGUSTA, TREATY OF (1773) **I–223b**
Augusta Academy (Va.). *See* Washington and Lee University
AUGUSTA COUNTY (Va.) **I–223b**; III–469b; VI–275b
Auk (jour.) I–305a
Aull, James (mer.) VII–274a
Aull Company V–375b
Aulneau, Jean Pierre (miss.) III–499b
Aunuu Island III–425b
Auranches (Fr.) II–237a
AURARIA (Colo.) **I–224a**; II–477b
AURORA (news.) **I–224a**; V–70a; VII–293b
chemistry articles II–10b
Aurora (Oreg.) I–293a
Aurora Branch Railroad VI–32b
Aury, Luis (pirate) I–93b; III–149a; V–320a
Austen, Jane (au.) VI–342b
Austin (Minn.) IV–357a
Austin (Nev.) II–346b
Austin (ship) VII–41b
Austin (Tex.) VII–40a
Archive War I–169b
Johnson Library I–167b; III–284b
Austin, A. Everett II–289a
Austin, Ann (rel. leader) V–469b
Austin, Moses (col.) I–224a; IV–122a; VI–189b; VII–37a
Austin, Stephen F. (col.) VII–37a
Austin colony I–224a
Battle of Concepción II–157a
Texas IV–457a
Texas Rangers VII–39a
AUSTIN COLONY I–224a
Austin Hall (Harvard) III–260b
Austinville (Va.) IV–122a; VII–125b; 123a–
Austinville mine (Va.) IV–122a
Australia
Battle Fleet Cruise I–276b
Battle of Bismarck Sea I–307b
bauxite I–92b
Concord Coach II–158a
Dutch trade II–383b
gold II–77a, 95b
Korean War IV–55b, 56b
land titles VII–77a
lead imports IV–123b
meat trade IV–281a
Organization for Economic Cooperation and Development V–170b
Pacific cable I–401a
radio astronomy VI–17a
Rhodes scholars VI–134b
shipping IV–310b
Southeast Asia Treaty Organization VI–350b
tennis VII–30b
United Nations Declaration VII–151b
Vietnam War VII–182b

AUSTRALIA (cont.)
whaling VII–285b
World War I VI–338b
World War II II–225a; III–229a, 492b; IV–83a; VII–335a, 336b, 342a,b, 343a
Australia, National Museum of II–106b
Australian ballot I–248b–49a; IV–269a; VII–209a
Austria
Common Market VI–472a
Declaration of Paris V–214a
European Free Trade Association VI–469a; VII–89a
gold standard III–193b
Hungarian revolution (1848) IV–57b
immigration to U.S. III–337b, 339a,b
neutrality V–36a
Organization for Economic Cooperation and Development V–170b
Salzburgers VI–204b
Seven Years' War III–115b
sharpshooters VI–269b
steelmaking III–474a
trade VII–87a
Treaty of Versailles VII–173a
U.S. aid III–61b
World War I II–277a; V–308a; VII–325b, 329b, 330a, 330b
World War II V–378b; VII–334a, 341a
Austria–Hungary
Fourteen Points III–86a
immigration to U.S. III–333a, 338b, 339a, 340b
pig iron III–471 (table)
World War I VII–327a
Austrian Succession, War of the (1740–48) I–70b
Austro–Prussian War (1866) V–207a
Autecology II–392a
Automatic Electric Cooking Company II–419b
Automatic pilot I–51b
Automatic Sequence Control Calculator (Mark I) II–154a
Automatic transmission I–229a
Automatic Voting Machine Company VII–210b
AUTOMATION I–224b
auto workers IV–77b
flour milling III–43a
job security IV–75a
standards of living II–427a
technocracy movement VII–17b
textile industry VII–44b
unemployment VII–141a,b
AUTOMOBILE I–225a; III–452a; IV–244b
accidents I–152b
advertising I–17a, 19a
agrarianism I–33b
assembly line I–205a; IV–272b
automation I–224b; IV–75a
aviation industry I–235a, 237a
Bakelite V–328a
baseball I–271a
batteries V–102b
bicycles I–295a
Big Three manufacturers VII–124a
collision–avoidance devices IV–333a
copper V–103b
Detroit II–337a–b
distribution of goods and services II–354a
Du Pont family III–80a
electric battery II–421b
emission devices V–270b
excise taxes VI–105a
folklore III–49a
foreign trade VII–89b, 90a
gasoline tax III–153a
glass industry III–186a
government regulations I–449b
great fortunes III–80b
Great Lakes shipping III–218a
highways I–78a; II–302b
imports VI–471b
industrial research III–409a,b
Industrial Revolution III–410b
installment buying III–422b–23a
insurance III–426b, 431b–32a
Kentucky IV–41b
labor codes IV–71b
Lincoln Highway IV–156a
Louisiana Purchase Exposition IV–198a
machine tools IV–216a
Michigan IV–331b, 332a
monopolistic power IV–399b
no–fault insurance I–152b
panic of 1929 V–209b
passenger miles VI–155b
petroleum industry V–267a; VI–356b–57a
pollution VII–158b
prices V–402b, 406a
racing I–99a; II–244b; VI–392b
rebates VII–85a
road improvement movement VI–152a, 154b
roads III–450b–51a
rubber VI–167b, 168a
rural areas VI–175b
Saint Paul VII–134a
sales VII–84b
salt industry VI–203a
Scientific American VI–231a–b
Selden patent VI–257a
steam power VI–410a
storage battery I–276a
street paving V–230a
strikes VI–420a
taxation VII–9b, 10a, 11a
transportation VII–101b–02a, 102b
truck adaptation IV–419b
unions IV–70b, 72b
urban structure VII–159b
use taxes VI–200a
Wisconsin VII–308a
World War II industry IV–245a
See also American Automobile Association
Automobile Chamber of Commerce. *See* National Automobile Chamber of Commerce
Automobile Club, United States I–231b
Automobile Club of America I–99a
Automobile Club of Missouri I–99a
Automobile clubs
American Automobile Association I–98b–99a
good roads movement I–228b
Automobile Dealer's Day in Court Act (1956) I–230a
Automobile Manufacturers Association I–227a
Automotive Engineers, Society of II–448b
AUTOSSEE, BATTLE OF (1813) **I–232a**; II–257a
Auxiliary to the Sons of Union Veterans of the Civil War III–208a
Ava (Ohio) II–344b
Avalon, Peninsula of (Newf.) IV–260a
Avalon Bay I–466b
Avco Cup III–287b
Ave Maria (mag.) III–293a
Avenger (torpedo plane) I–55b
Avery, Clarence I–205b
Avery, Ephraim (cler.) VII–118a
Avery, John (pirate) I–151a
Avery, Milton C. (paint.) V–193a
Avery, Oswald T. (physic.) I–304a; III–157b, 158a; IV–389b, 390b
Avery, Peter I–232b
Avery, Samuel P. (art dealer) II–102b
Avery Island *See* Avery Salt Mine
AVERY SALT MINE I–232a; VI–202b
AVERYSBORO, BATTLE OF (1865) **I–232b**
AVERY'S TRACE I–232b
Avery v. *Midland County* (1968) III–87a
Avezzano (It.) III–235b
AVIATION I–232b
Advisory Committee for Aeronautics IV–458a
army I–188b
bombing I–328a–29a
Civil Aeronautics Act II–49b
Civil Aeronautics Administration II–49b
disasters II–346a–47b
Federal Aviation Agency II–498b–99a, 500a
gas turbines VII–129a,b
licensing IV–148b
Lindbergh's Atlantic flight IV–156b
Marine Corps experiments IV–252b
microwave technology IV–333a
military gliders III–187a
military slang VI–302a–b
National Advisory Committee for Aeronautics IV–106a
petroleum prospecting V–272b
polar exploration V–337a–b
radar II–425b
radio communications II–424b
research III–409b–10a
Scientific American VI–231a–b
transatlantic flight V–30a
visit and search VII–205a
weather forecasts VII–264a–b
See also entries under Air; Aircraft
Aviation Corporation I–236b
AVIATION INDUSTRY I–235b; IV–245b
broadcast regulations III–1a
California strike (1940) IV–341b
celluloid V–328a
computers II–156a
Connecticut II–181a
Fort Worth III–80b–81a
great fortunes III–80b
Long Island IV–186a
regulation II–500a
Saint Louis VI–194b
San Antonio VI–207b
Washington State VII–248a
Wichita VII–294a
World War I IV–433a; VII–328a
World War II VII–336a
See also entries under Air; Aircraft
Aviation insurance III–426b, 429b
Aviation medicine IV–292b–93a
Aviators
barnstorming I–268a
World War I IV–83b
AVIDAC (computer) II–156a
Avilés, Pedro Menéndez de. *See* Menéndez de Avilés, Pedro
"A Virtuoso's Collection" IV–436a
"A Visit From St. Nicholas" (poem) I–335b
Avitaminosis V–128b
Avocado III–129a, 381a
Avogadro, Amedeo (chem.) I–218a

Avon (brig) VII–253a
Avon Products II–234a
AWAKENING, SECOND
I–238a; VI–77a
Disciples of Christ
II–352b
Mormons IV–116b
Awful Disclosures of the Hotel Dieu Nunnery of Montreal
IV–250a
Awiehawken River VII–266b
Awl III–140a, 402b
AWSA. *See* American Woman Suffrage Association
Axel Heiberg Island V–240b, 337a
Axelrod, Julius (biochem.)
V–100a
Axel's Castle IV–165b
Axes III–402b
Archaic culture II–386a
fur trade III–140a
Axis powers I–67a, 214a, 308a
Latin America IV–112a
See also Germany; Italy; Japan
Axletree V–177a
Aycock, Charles B. (pol.)
VI–432a
Aydelotte, Frank (educ.)
III–424b
Ayer (Mass.) I–434b
Ayer, Edward Everett (ind., biblio.) II–109b; III–19a
Ayer, N. W., and Son I–18a
Ayers, Henry (bact.) I–46a
AYLLÓN, EXPEDITIONS OF DE I–238b; I–96a
Chicora II–23b
Florida III–38a
South Carolina VI–347a
Ayllón, Lucas Vásquez de (expl.). *See* Ayllón, Expeditions of de
Ayrshire cattle I–471b; II–280a, 281b
AYUBALE, BATTLE OF (1703) **I–238b**
AYUNTAMIENTO I–239a
Azikiwe, Nnamdi V–199b
AZILIA, MARGRAVATE OF I–239a
Azores II–323b, 350a
flight of NC-4 I–51a
immigrants I–447a
salt V–16a
transatlantic flight V–30a
Aztalan (Wis.) IV–370a
Aztec (Indians) III–356a, 366a, 368b; IV–327a
agriculture I–48a
alcoholic drinks III–398a
architecture I–166a
mounds IV–421a
political organization
III–391a
pulque V–314b
religion III–251a, 392a
Spanish conquest VII–36a
Aztec art III–136b
Aztec Ruins National Monument V–217b
Aztec–Tanoan (lang.)
III–301a; V–459b
Azusa Street Mission (L.A.)
V–259b

B

B–1 (bomber) I–50b
B–2 (bomber) I–50a
B–9 (bomber) I–236b
B–10 (bomber) I–50a, 57b, 236b
B–17 (bomber) I–50a, 52a, 56b, 59b, 67a, 237a
B–17F (bomber) I–50a
B–17G (bomber) I–50a
B–18 (bomber) I–50a
B–24 (bomber) I–50a, 52a, 60a
B–24H (bomber) I–50a
B–24J (bomber) I–50a
B–25 (bomber) I–50a, 57b; III–489b
B–26 (bomber) I–50a,b; II–346b
B–29 (bomber) I–50a,b, 52a, 60b, 64a, 67b; II–26a; III–485a,b, 489b–90b; V–286a; VI–198a
B–29A (bomber) I–50a
B–29B (bomber) I–50a
B–36 (bomber) I–50b, 57b, 60b, 61b
B–45 (bomber) I–50b
B–45C (bomber) I–50b
B–47 (bomber) I–50b, 61a, 237b
B–50 (bomber) I–50b
B–52 (bomber) I–50b, 57b, 61b, 62b, 63b, 67b, 235a, 237b, 411a–b; IV–431b; VII–183b, 184b, 185b
B–52G (bomber) I–50b
B–52H (bomber) I–50b
B–56G (bomber) I–50b
B–57 (bomber) I–50b
B–58 (bomber) I–50b
B–66 (bomber) I–50b
B'ab V–171b
Babbage, Charles (math.)
I–396b, 397a; II–153b; III–480b
Babbitt, Almon W. (pol.)
II–334a
Babbitt, Irving (educ.)
II–189b, 401a; IV–164a
Babbitt, Milton (comp.)
IV–439b
Babcock, Orville E. (off.)
II–362a; VII–290b
Babcock, Stephen Moulton (chem.) I–46a; II–281a–b
"Baby bonds" VI–222a
"Baby boom" V–363a
Babylon (L.I., N.Y.) II–350b
auctions I–221b
Baccalaos III–208a
Bache, Alexander Dallas (phys.) I–98a; II–447a; III–233a; V–134a,b, 294b
Bache, Benjamin Franklin (pub.) I–224a
Bache, William (art.)
VI–286b
Bachelder, John (inv.)
VI–265a
BACHELOR HOUSES
I–239a
Bachman, John (cler.)
IV–232a
Backcountry. *See* Backwoods and Backcountry
"Backfire" bomber VI–417a
Backfiring V–389a
BACKLASH I–239a
California I–408b
civil rights movement
II–59a, 59a
New South V–67b
radical right VI–12a
"Back to Africa" V–200a
"Back to Africa" movement
II–127b; IV–166b
Backus, Elijah I–319b
Backus, John II–156b
Backus Island I–319b
Backward-wave oscillator
VII–164a
BACKWOODS AND BACKCOUNTRY I–239b; V–310a
colonial land grants
IV–92a
districts II–485a
frontier merchant
III–127a
Mississippi IV–368b
North Carolina IV–48a
Regulators of North Carolina VI–71b
Regulators of South Carolina VI–72a
revivalism IV–423b
Scotch-Irish VI–240b
shooting match VI–282b
South Carolina
VI–347a–b
stump speakers VI–421b
trapping VII–104b
Whiskey Rebellion
VII–289b
Backwoodsmen
Bowie knife I–355a
bushwhackers I–388b
Bacon IV–281a
Bacon, C. E. (educ.)
III–275a
Bacon, Francis (philos.)
IV–161a; V–294a; VI–248a
Bacon, Nathaniel. *See* Bacon's Rebellion
Bacon, Robert (banker, dipl.)
VII–31a
Baconian method II–356a
Bacon's Castle (Surry County, Va.) I–161a
BACON'S REBELLION (1676) **I–240a**; II–117a, 125a; III–280b, 436b, 489a; VII–58b, 191a, 193a
BACTERIOLOGY AND VIROLOGY I–240b; III–53a
army research IV–291a
food spoilage I–445a
hygiene III–325b
medical education 284a–
pharmaceutical industry
V–273b
public health V–447a,b
tuberculosis VII–126a,b
Bacteriophages IV–389b
BAD AXE, BATTLE OF (1832) **I–242b**; VI–148a
Bad Axe River
Black Hawk War I–242b, 312a
Baden-Powell, Lord (Robert Stephenson Smyth)
I–357b
Badge of Military Merit
II–312b
Badger, Joseph (paint.)
V–186b
Badger State VI–395 (table)
Badin, Stephen T. (cler.)
V–335b
BAD LANDS (S.Dak.)
I–242b; II–284a
fossil remains V–196b
Messiah War VII–344b
Badlands National Monument (S.Dak.) I–242b; V–217b
Badoglio, Pietro (off.)
VI–199b, 284b
Bad River IV–118a; V–310b
Badwater (Calif.) II–297b
Baekeland, Leo H. (chem.)
II–7a; III–409a; V–328a
Baer, Clara I–272b
Baer, George F. (ind.)
I–127a
Baer, Max (boxer) I–488a
Báez, Buenaventura (pol.)
II–362a
Baffin, William (expl.)
III–240b; V–122a
Baffin Bay II–319b; V–122a
Baffin Island V–336b; VII–190a
Baffinland (Indians)
III–358a
Bagaduce (Maine). *See* Castine
Bagby, George William (humorist, ed.) VI–353a
BAGHDAD PACT (1955)
I–243a; I–149b
Bagley, Sarah (labor leader)
VII–316b
Bagot, Charles (dipl.)
III–217a
Bagot-Rush Agreement. *See* Great Lakes Disarmament Agreement
Bahaism (Baha'i)
V–171b–72a
Bahama Channel V–356a; VI–187b
BAHAMA ISLANDS
I–243b; II–257b
air transportation I–67b
British army VI–126b
British capture VI–130a
charter colonies I–499b
Civil War I–292a; II–213a; III–40b
Columbus' voyage I–96a
Florida Rangers III–42b
Loyalist veterans VI–131a
natural history III–26b
revolutionary war
IV–251b
shipwrecks II–443b
Watlings Island VII–261a
writs of assistance

BAHAMA ISLANDS (cont.)
VII–345a
Bahia (Braz.) III–40a; VII–212b
Bahía de la Asumpción II–131b
Bahia de San Johan Baptista IV–451b
Baikal, Lake (USSR) VI–284a
Bail and fines
Bill of Rights I–299a; II–204b
Bailer, John C. (chem.) II–12b
Bailey, Francis (jour.) II–497a; III–108b
Bailey, Gamaliel (abolitionist, ed.) V–145b, 279b
Bailey, Jacob W. (oceanog.) III–29a; V–134b
Bailey, James A. (circus owner) II–40b
Bailey, James T. (tech.) V–328b
Bailey, Liberty Hyde (bot.) II–227b
Bailey, Theodorus (nav. off.) IV–136b
Bailey v. *Alabama* (1910) V–260b
BAILEY* v. *DREXEL FURNITURE COMPANY (1922) **I–243b**; II–25a; III–247a, 459b
Baillie, Hugh (jour.) VII–152b
Baily, Francis (trav.) VI–153a
Bailyn, Bernard (hist.) VI–113a
Bainbridge (Ohio) II–329b; VII–241b
Bainbridge, Kenneth T. (phys.) I–218b; V–301a
Bainbridge, William (nav. off.) III–168a; V–19a,b
Barbary Wars I–266b
Constitution–Java engagement II–192a
Philadelphia V–278b
Baine, John (typefounder) V–411b
Baird, John L. (inv.) VII–21a,b
Baird, Spencer Fullerton (zool.) III–27b, 28b; IV–232b; V–134b; VI–90b
census of 1880 I–482a
ornithology I–304b
Smithsonian Institution IV–468b; VI–319a–b
U.S. Fish Commission III–30a; IV–251a
Baja California. *See* Lower California
Bakelite II–7a; III–409a; V–327b, 328a
Baker, Benjamin A. (act., playwright) VII–47b
Baker, Bertram (pol.) I–283a
BAKER, BOBBY, CASE I–243b; II–231b
Baker, Daniel (off.) VI–186a
Baker, E. D. (off.) I–249a
Baker, E. M. (off.) V–310a
Baker, Francis (cler.) V–229b
Baker, Fred (physic.) VI–242a
Baker, George F. (fin.) III–79b; V–462a
Baker, John (dent.) II–329b
Baker, Lafayette (detective) VI–373b
Baker, Lawrence A. VII–30b
Baker, Newton D. (states.) I–434b; VII–230a
Baker, Ray Stannard (au.) IV–424b
Baker, Richard Brown II–106a
Baker, Robert G. (Bobby) *See* Baker, Bobby, Case
Baker, Russell (humorist) V–75a
Baker, S. Josephine (physic.) IV–275b
Baker and Scribner I–334a
Baker Island VII–125b
BAKER'S CABIN MASSACRE (1774) **I–244a**
BAKER* v. *CARR (1962) **I–244a**; I–147b; II–180a, 410a, 457b; IV–133b; VI–432b, 435a
Bakeshop Case. *See Lochner* v. *New York*
Bakewell, Thomas (eng.) VI–409a
Bakewell and Brown I–164b
Bakewell cattle I–471b
Baking III–45b
apprenticeship I–148b
Baking powder V–466a
Balance Agriculture With Industry Program IV–369b
"Balance" docks II–375a
Balance of payments III–8a; VI–53a
coinage II–95a
fair trade II–484a
International Monetary Fund III–457b
Pittman Act V–321b
reciprocal trade agreements VI–53a
Balance of power
Far East II–488a
missile weapons systems IV–364a
Nixon policy II–316b
World War I I–122b
"Balance of terror" II–316a
BALANCE OF TRADE I–244b; VI–471b; VII–89b–90b, 91a, 92a
colonial trade IV–388a
South American trade VI–344b
specie payments VI–370a
Balanchine, George (chor.) II–289a, 290a–b
Balao class (submarine) VI–423a
Balboa, Vasco NÚñez de (expl.) I–96a; V–203b
Balboa Park (San Diego) VI–208b
Balch, Emily G. (econ., soc.) V–100a
BALCONES ESCARPMENT (Tex.) **I–246b**
Balconies (arch.) I–160a
Balcony House IV–315b
Bald cypress VI–394 (table)
Bald eagle II–384b–85a
Bald Eagle Creek IV–175a
Baldwin (Kans.) I–314a; V–175a
Baldwin, Abraham (pol.) II–193a, 203b
Baldwin, Frank D. (off.) VII–217a
Baldwin, F. S. (inv.) I–396a–b
Baldwin, Henry (jur.) VI–445b
Baldwin, James (au.) IV–165a, 167a
Baldwin, J. Mark (psych.) V–442a
Baldwin, Matthias (ind.) IV–175b; VI–25a, 36a
Baldwin, Samuel (col.) V–56b
Baldwin, Simeon (law.) I–99a
Baldwin, Theron (theol.) III–331b; VII–350b
Baldwin, Thomas (mfr.) I–233a
Baldwin, Thomas Scott (eng.) II–343b
Baldwin–Felts Agency II–462b
Baldwin "flexible beam" truck IV–175b
Baldwin Locomotive Works IV–175b, 176b, 177b
Baldwin–Ziegler Expedition (1901–02) V–337a
Baldwyn (Miss.) III–485a
Balén Causeway (Mex.) IV–329a
Baley, Art (mus.) IV–440b
Balfour, Arthur James (states.) I–246b
BALFOUR AND VIVIANI–JOFFRE MISSIONS (1917) **I–246b**
Balfour Declaration (1917) IV–10b
Bali
World War II IV–182a
Balikpapan (Bor.) IV–228b–29a
Baling press I–35a
BALIZE (La.) **I–246b**
Balkans
Fourteen Points III–86a
immigrants II–439b; III–338b
Ball, Joseph A. VII–238a
Ball, Mottram D. (offi.) I–76b
Ball, Thomas (sculp.) VI–243b
Ballad of Baby Doe (opera) IV–439a
BALLADS I–247a; III–49a; VI–382b
cowboy songs II–250a
"Joe Bowers" IV–1a
"Oleana" V–152b
Tin Pan Alley VII–62b
Ballet II–286b–87b, 288b–89b
music IV–438b, 439a
North Carolina V–116b
Ballet Russe II–288b–89a; VII–49b
Ballet Society II–289a
Ballets: U. S. A. II–289b
Ballet Theatre II–288b–89a
Ballet West II–289b
Ball games III–366a
Indian ceremonial II–52a
See also Baseball; Basketball; Football
Ballinger, Richard A. (law.) V–427b
Ballinger–Pinchot controversy I–247b
naval oil reserves V–13a
BALLINGER–PINCHOT-CONTROVERSY I–247b
Progressive movement V–427b
"standpatters" VI–385a
Ballistic Missile Defense System (BMDS) I–58b; II–316a
Ballistic Missile Early Warning System (BMEWS) I–58b, 62a
Ballistic Research Laboratory II–155a
Ballistics calculation II–153a, 155a
Ballistite V–383b
"Balloon" frame (arch.) I–163b, 377b; II–45b
Balloon Hoax IV–406b
BALLOONS I–248a
aerial photography V–293a
Air National Guard I–64b
flights I–232b
Signal Corps I–59a
weather observation VII–264b
World War I I–235b
BALLOT I–248b; II–408b, 410b, 457b; VII–209a
direct primary V–406b
filing fees V–341b
Massachusetts ballot IV–269a
Progressive movement V–428a
referendum III–418b
secret ballot V–347a
state laws VII–208b
Ballou, Adin (cler.) III–300a
Ballou, Hosea (cler.) II–170b
Ballroom dancing II–290b
BALL'S BLUFF, BATTLE OF (1861) **I–249a**
Ball's Ford (Va.) I–381a
Balmaceda, José Manuel (pol.) VI–3b
Balmacedistas I–250b
Balthwayt, William (offi.) IV–188b
Baltic (steamship) IV–310a
Baltic Sea II–291a–b; III–106a,b
gunboats III–235a
revolutionary war V–423b
U.S. trade IV–309b
World War II IV–313b; VII–341a

BALTIMORE (Md.)
I–249a; II–41a; IV–261a; VI–340b
Afro-Americans I–23a, 25b
Allegheny wagoners VII–216a
Bank of United States IV–211b
Barron v. *Baltimore* I–268b
canmaking VII–62a
Carrollton viaduct I–363b
Catholic church I–251a–b, 467a,b, 468b; V–3a
chamber of commerce I–491a
chemical industry II–6a
city council II–44a
city government II–44a
clothing industry II–82a
colonial labor IV–60a
Constitutional Union Party Convention II–191b
criminal gangs II–258a
Cyclops disaster II–349b
electric railway VI–40a
fall line II–485a
fertilizer III–16a–b
flag III–35a
flour III–43a, 45a
food preservation III–55b
foreign trade VII–86b
Fort McHenry IV–213b
furniture III–138a
gambling III–149b
Genius of Universal Emancipation III–162b
Hicksites III–274a
illumination II–5b; IV–153a
Johns Hopkins University IV–2a
Lafayette's visit IV–84a
Lumbee IV–203b
medical education IV–283b
Methodist church IV–318a–b
mortality statistics IV–149b
navy yard V–29a
Niles' Weekly Register V–96b
Norfolk trade V–109b
pack trains V–184a
Peale museum V–5a
pharmacy society V–275a
Pittsburgh trade V–321b–22a
port authority V–368a
pottery V–379b
presidential convention II–216a
race riots I–32a
railroad rate wars VI–23a
railroads VI–25a,b; VII–83b, 100b
railroad strike of 1877 IV–63b; VI–38b
revolutionary war III–118a
sailing packets V–183b
Scotch-Irish VI–240b
silver work VI–290a
slums VI–314a
smallpox VI–316a
social work VI–331a
Southern Commercial Convention VI–352a
stagelines VI–380a
stone fleets VI–415a
subway III–451b
sugar industry VI–437a
telegraph VII–18b
Tom Thumb VII–71a
trade unions IV–62b
War of 1812 IV–261a
water supply VII–258a,b, 259a
Weekly Museum V–71a
Young Men's Hebrew Association VII–362b
Baltimore (cruiser) IV–239b
BALTIMORE, BATTLE OF (1814) **I–250b**; I–249b; VII–234b
Baltimore, David (biochem.) IV–391a
Baltimore, Lord. *See* entries under Calvert
***BALTIMORE* AFFAIR** (1891) **I–250b**; VI–3b
Baltimore Afro-American (news.) V–76a
Baltimore Agreement (1922) VI–40b
Baltimore and Ohio Railroad I–249b; II–15b; III–332b, 449b, 450a, 451b; IV–261a; VI–24b, 25a, 32a, 33a–b; VII–83b, 100b
Aeolus I–20b
investors IV–3a
Latrobe's Folly IV–116a
locomotives IV–175a, 176a, 177a
Potomac River V–378b
rail bridges I–363b
rate wars VI–23a
strike of 1877 IV–63b; VI–38b
Tom Thumb VII–71a
Wheeling VII–287b
See also Chesapeake and Ohio Railroad
BALTIMORE BELL TEAMS I–250b
Baltimore cathedral I–163a
BALTIMORE CLIPPER I–251a; I–249b; II–77a
Baltimore College of Dental Surgery II–330a
BALTIMORE COUNCILS, PROVINCIAL AND PLENARY I–251a; I–467b; II–399b; VI–228b
Baltimore Equitable Society III–430a
Baltimore Family II–122b
Baltimore Fencibles VI–244b
BALTIMORE FIRE (1904) **I–251b**, 251b; I–250a; III–430a
***BALTIMORE* INCIDENT** (1798) **I–251b**
Baltimore Museum of Art III–137a
Baltimore oriole VI–394 (table)
BALTIMORE RIOT (1861) **I–251b**; IV–262a
Baltimore Water Company VII–258a, 259a
Balzac v. *People of Porto Rico* (1922) III–424b, 425a
Bamberger, Louis (philan.) III–423b
Ban (rel.) IV–303a
Bananas III–52b, 129a; IV–382b; VI–346a
Bancos (land tracts) IV–321b
Bancroft, George (hist.) III–281b, 282a; IV–267a; V–9b; VI–107b
Bancroft, J. S. (inv.) V–412b
Bancroft Hall (Naval Academy) V–10a
Bancroft Library (Berkeley, Calif.) III–284b, 285b
Bandelier National Monument V–217a,b
Bandits
Anti-Horse Thief Association I–131b
Bellevue War I–287a
Mexico IV–327b
Banditti II–249b
Bandy (sport) III–286b
Bangkok (Thai.)
Southeast Asia Treaty Organization VI–350b
Bangladesh
smallpox VI–316a
Bangor (Maine) III–247b
Bangor and Old Town Railroad IV–226b
Bangs, Lemuel (auctioneer) I–332b
Bangs Merwin and Company I–332b
Banister, John (bot.) I–348b; V–325b–26a
Banjo (comp.) IV–438a
Banjo clock II–79a
Bank, Federal Reserve. *See* Federal Reserve System
BANK DEPOSITS I–252a; I–255a, 256a, 257a,b, 258a; IV–392a, 395b
banking acts of 1933 and 1935 I–259b–60a
Bank of the United States VI–85b
branch and group banking I–259a
check currency II–1b, 2a–b
crash of 1929 II–470a
Federal Deposit Insurance Corporation II–500b–01a
Federal Reserve System III–5b, 8a,b
Florida III–42a
Glass-Steagall Act V–45a
gold redemption III–251b–52a
panic of 1907 V–208a–b
"pet banks" I–255b
private mint coins IV–360a–b
taxation VII–5b
See also Federal Deposit Insurance Corporation
Bankers' acceptances V–159b
Bankers Association, American VII–92a
Banker's panic of 1907. *See* Panic of 1907
Bank examining I–253b–54a
BANK FAILURES I–253a; I–257a; III–194a
banking crisis of 1933 I–260a
currency II–243b
Federal Deposit Insurance Corporation III–7a
Franklin National Bank III–66b
Great Depression III–6b
joint-stock land banks IV–6b
North Dakota V–117b
panic of 1792 V–206a
panic of 1819 V–206a
panic of 1857 V–207a
panic of 1893 V–208a
panic of 1907 V–209a
panic of 1929 VI–371a
Safety Fund System VI–185a
state banking I–259a
BANK FOR INTERNATIONAL SETTLEMENTS I–254a
German reparations VII–363b
Bank for Reconstruction and Development, International. *See* International Bank for Reconstruction and Development; World Bank
Bankhead, John H. (pol.) VI–269a
Bankhead, William Brockman (states.) II–177 (table)
BANKHEAD COTTON ACT (1934) **I–254b**
Bankhead-Jones Farm Tenant Act (1937) I–41a; IV–104a; VI–269a
Bank holding companies I–258a–59b
Bank Holding Company Act (1956) I–258b; III–290a,b
Bank Holiday Proclamation (1933) V–425b
BANKING I–245a
A.B. plot I–3a
American Express Company I–102b
American Fur Company I–105b
Anglo-American III–63b–64b
antibank movement I–129b; III–101b
auto financing III–423a
big business I–389a
bills of exchange II–467b
business forecasting I–395a
campaign of 1816 I–418a
campaign of 1832 I–419a
campaign of 1844 I–420a
charge-credit plans III–423b
China II–488b
Civil War II–63b, 69b
clearinghouses II–73a–74b, 73b–74b
colonial restrictions VI–107b
computers II–156b
credit II–254b–55a
Export-Import Bank

BANKING (cont.)
II–500b
farm credit I–44a–b
federal charter system IV–395a
Federal Deposit Insurance Company II–500b–01a
Federal Reserve System III–5b
foreign investment I–245a; III–63b, 66b–67a
free banking system III–101b
Freedman's Savings Bank III–103a
frontier III–127b
general stores VI–416a
Glass–Steagall Act III–186b; V–45a, 45a
Gold Exchange Bank III–190a
government corporations III–201b
government ownership III–202b
great fortunes III–79a,b
holding companies III–290a,b
Independent Treasury System III–354b
Industrial Revolution III–411a
interest laws III–443a
Intermediate Credit Banks III–447a
land speculation I–107b–08a
licensing IV–148b
Locofoco party IV–175a
Manhattan Company VII–258b
McFadden Banking Act IV–212b
Morris Canal and Banking Company IV–412b
National Banking Act II–2a
National Banking System II–152b
national bank notes IV–461b
National Monetary Commission IV–468a
National Union for Social Justice IV–472b
New Deal V–43b–44a
New Hampshire V–54b
New York City V–83a,b, 87b–88a
Ocala Platform V–132a
panic of 1837 V–206b
panic of 1873 V–207b
panic of 1907 V–208a–b
panic of 1929 V–209a,b, 210a
pension plans V–255b
political contributions V–448b
prices V–403b, 405a
public debt II–317a–b
Pujo Committee investigation V–462a
Reconstruction Finance Corporation V–455b; VI–59b
regulation V–347a
risks II–218b
saddlebag banks VI–184b
Safety Fund System VI–185a
San Francisco VI–209b
service corporations II–229a
specie payments VI–369b
state ownership III–204a
stock exchanges II–470a
subsidies VI–425b
Suffolk Banking System VI–430b
taxation VII–5b, 10b
Treasury Department VII–108a
trusts VII–121b
Wall Street VII–222a
Wells, Fargo VII–267a
wildcat banks II–275a, 464b
wildcat money VII–295a
World War II revenue VII–8b
See also Investment Banks

BANKING, BRANCH AND GROUP I–258a; III–7a
congressional debate III–22a
growth I–257a
McFadden Banking Act IV–212b
National Banking Act of 1863 I–256a

BANKING, STATE I–259a; I–255a; II–74a, 275a; V–455a
Arkansas I–173a
bank failures I–253a,b
banking crisis of 1933 I–260a
bank notes II–2a, 95a, 244a
Bank of Darien II–291b
Bank of the United States III–245b
branches I–258b
Civil War II–69a
Federal Reserve System III–6a
government deposits VI–85b
Green v. *Frazier* III–227a
Hunkers III–318a
Independent Treasury System III–354b
Indiana VI–390a
Kentucky IV–40b
Louisiana IV–194a
McFadden Banking Act IV–212b
Michigan IV–332a
National Banking System I–256a, 257a
North Dakota V–117b
note issues I–261a
panic of 1792 V–206a
panic of 1819 V–206a
panic of 1837 V–206b
paper–money issues IV–394a
pet banks V–264a
regulation I–255b
Safety Fund System VI–185a
South Carolina VI–349a
specie payments VI–370a,b
state debts VI–95b
Van Buren administration VII–288b
Veazie Bank v. *Fenno* VII–168a
wildcat banks II–464b

BANKING ACTS OF 1933 AND 1935 I–259b; III–7a, 186b; V–44a
bank deposits I–252b
branch and group banking I–258b
interest rates III–443a,b

BANKING CRISIS OF 1933 I–260a; III–194a; V–43b–44a; VI–51b, 371a–b
Bank Holiday Proclamation V–425b
Reconstruction Finance Corporation VI–60a

Bank moratorium (1933) I–253b, 257a, 260a
Bank Note Detectors I–255b
Bank Note Reporters I–253a, 255b; II–243b–44a
Bank notes I–252a; IV–393b
A.B. plot I–3a
as money I–258a
bank deposits I–255a,b
bank failures I–253a
Bank of the United States I–261a
Civil War II–2a
counterfeit II–243b
emergency bank note issue (1914) I–256b
Federal Reserve System III–5b
free banking system III–101b
inflation III–414b, 415a
legal tender IV–132a, 394b
National Banking System I–256a
national banks IV–395a
state taxation of federal issues IV–211b
See also Money
Bank notes, national. *See* National Bank Notes
Bank of America I–257a; VI–209b
***BANK of AUGUSTA* v. *EARLE* (1839) I–260b**
Bank of California VI–44a
Bank of China v. *Wells Fargo Bank* (1952) III–456a
Bank of Columbia v. *Okely* (1819) II–377b
***BANK OF COMMERCE* v. *NEW YORK CITY* (1863) I–260b**
Bank of Darien II–291b
Bank of England III–6b; V–113b
Bank of Kentucky I–365a
Bank of Maryland I–255a
Bank of Massachusetts I–255a
Bank of Milwaukee I–263b
Bank of New York I–255a; V–83a

BANK OF NORTH AMERICA I–260b; I–255a; II–254b; III–5b, 427b; V–277b; VI–117b

Bank of Pennsylvania III–201b
Bank of the State of South Carolina I–259b
See also South Carolina, State Bank of

BANK OF THE UNITED STATES I–260a; I–255a–b; III–5b–6a, 201b, 202b, 245b; V–277b, 455a
bank deposits I–252a
constitutionality III–348b
French spoliation claims III–122a
Independent Treasury System III–354b
interest rates III–443a
Jeffersonian Republicans VI–94a
New York Stock Exchange II–469b
paper–money issues IV–394a
prices V–405a
states' rights VI–404b
—First (1791–1811):
branches I–258a
European investments II–301a
—Second (1811–36):
Biddle's presidency IV–168b–169a
branches I–258a
British investments III–63b
campaign of 1832 I–419a
charter II–458a
charter renewal II–232a
credit expansion VI–370b
Crowbar Law of Ohio II–266b
hard money opponents III–251b
internal improvements I–330b; III–448b
Jacksonian Democracy III–486b
Jackson's opposition IV–228a; VII–288a
Jeffersonian Republicans VI–94b
McCulloch v. *Maryland* IV–211b
panic of 1819 V–206a
pet banks V–264a
removal of deposits VI–85b, 427a
specie circular VI–369b
state banking I–259b
state debts VI–96b
taxation by Ohio V–174a–b

***BANK OF THE UNITED STATES* v. *HALSTEAD* (1825) I–261b**
***BANK OF THE UNITED STATES* v. *PLANTER'S BANK OF GEORGIA* (1824) I–261b**

Bank runs I–254a, 256b
Bankruptcies
auctions I–222a
Confederation II–192b
court rules IV–17a
farms IV–415a
Mobile IV–382b

Morris Canal and Banking Company IV–412b
Penn Central VI–32a,b, 35b
railroad rate wars VI–23a
Union Pacific Railroad VII–148a
"whitewash" VII–293b
BANKRUPTCY LAWS **I–261b**; II–195b, 199b
constitutionality V–140a
contract clause II–213b
Frazier–Lemke Farm Act III–100a; V–45b
imprisonment for debt II–299a
Securities and Exchange Commission II–500b
Sturges v. *Crowninshield* VI–422a
Banks, Dennis I–107a
BANKS, EXPORT–IMPORT **I–262b**; II–500b–01a; III–201b
aid to Israel III–481b
dollar diplomacy II–359b
loans to Latin America IV–113b
Banks, foreign
investment in U.S. III–67a
Banks, investment. *See* Investment Banks
Banks, Nathaniel P. (off.) II–175 (table)
Army of Virginia VII–197a
Battle at Front Royal III–128a
Battle at Jenkins Ferry III–498a
Battle of Cedar Mountain I–476b
Battle of Pleasant Hill V–331a
Battle of Sabine Crossroads VI–182a
Battle of Winchester VII–304a
Bayou Teche expedition I–279a
Port Hudson attack IV–375a; V–369a
Red River campaign IV–457a; VI–63a
Banks, postal savings. *See* Postal Service, United States
BANKS, PRIVATE **I–263a**
Jay Cooke and Company II–218b
Banks, rural I–252a
BANKS, SAVINGS **I–263a**; II–255a; III–7a
interest laws III–443a
mutual II–220b
Banks' Ford (Va.) IV–425a
Bannack (Mont.) III–270a; IV–403a; V–333a
Bannerman's Island (N.Y.) III–275b
BANNOCK (Indians) **I–264a**; III–363a
wars VII–239b
Bannock (Idaho) III–32a
BANNOCK WAR (1878) **I–264b**; VII–239b
Bantry Bay (Ire.) VII–329a
Bao Dai (emp.) III–160b
BAPTIST CHURCHES **I–264b**; I–466a; VI–78b
Afro-American I–23a,b, 24a; VI–59b
Brown College II–394b
camp meetings I–433b
colleges II–114a
colonial society II–126a
Cotton Kingdom II–241a
Disciples of Christ II–352b
East Jersey V–57a
elementary schools II–394b
foreign missions IV–366b
Freewill Baptists V–174b
frontier preaching III–127b
Great Revival III–221b
hymns III–326a
missionary work III–385b; IV–365a,b
New Jersey IV–397b
Newport V–65b
New York State V–87a
North Carolina V–115a
publishing IV–453a
radical right VI–12a
religious liberty VI–80b; VII–69a
Rhode Island VI–132a
Rice–Campbell debates VI–135b
slavery II–36b; VI–78b
Southern Christian Leadership Conference VI–352a
sumptuary laws VI–440b
Sunday schools VI–442b
Virginia VI–75b
Western Reserve VII–275a
West Virginia VII–281a
Baptist Convention, National Primitive. *See* National Primitive Baptist Convention
Baptist Convention, U.S.A. *See* National Baptist Convention, U.S.A., Inc.
Baptist Convention of America. *See* National Baptist Convention of America
Baptist Home Mission Society IV–365b
Baptist Mahoning Valley Association VII–275a
Baptist Missionary Society IV–366a
Baraboo (Wis.) II–40b
Baraboo Range VI–218b
Baraka, Imamu Amiri (au.) I–25a, 315b; IV–166b, 167b, 443a–b
Baranov, Aleksandr (expl.) I–75a; VI–180b
Baranowski, Jan Josef (inv.) VII–210b
Bar Association, American. *See* American Bar Association
BARATARIA **I–265b**
Civil War IV–371b
pirates III–148b; V–320a
BARBADOS **I–265b**
Cromwell's western design VII–270b
demographic study II–328b
flour trade III–42b
Maryland settlers IV–260b
Quakers V–469b
settlements II–124a
slave trade I–22b
sugar IV–388a; VI–386b
tea trade VII–17a
triangular trade VII–119a
Barbados distemper. *See* Yellow Fever
Barbara Line III–235b
Barbary Coast (San Francisco) II–260a
Barbary pirates IV–299b
BARBARY WARS **I–266a**; VII–87a, 111b, 120a–b, 237a
black powder V–383a
Constitution II–190b
Decatur's cruise to Algiers II–303a
Derna expedition II–334a, 334a
gunboats III–234a
Intrepid III–464b; IV–44b
marine corps IV–251b
navy V–19a
Philadelphia capture V–278b
United States VII–153a
U.S. Navy V–19a,b, 29a
warships VII–240a
Barbastro, Luis Cancer de (miss.) III–41a
BARBECUE **I–266b**; III–53b; VI–365a
BARBED WIRE **I–267a**; II–250b–51a; III–126a; V–160b
armored vehicles I–177a
cattle rustling I–474a
Fence War III–10a,b
foreign trade VII–87b
Osage hedge V–174a
public lands fencing V–451b
BARBED WIRE PATENT CASE (1892) **I–267b**
Barbé–Marbois, François de (dipl.) IV–196b–97a
Barber, Edwin Atlee (archaeol.) II–100b
Barber County (Kans.) III–261b; VI–64a
Barbers
medicine IV–283a
Barbiturates II–373b; V–468b
Barbizon school of painting II–102a, 103b–04a
Barbour, James (states.) III–494b
Barbour, John S. (pol.) VI–49b
Barbour, Philip P. (jur.) II–174 (table); VI–445b
Barbour, Thomas (nat.) VI–91a
Barbourville (Ky.) II–273a
Barbout, James (offi.) IV–129a
Barcelona chair III–136b
Barcelona International Exhibition (1929) III–136b
Barclay, Robert (Quaker) III–123a
Barclay, Robert H. (nav. off.) II–459b; VII–266b
Bardeen, John (phys.) V–99b, 100a, 296a, 305a,b
transistor I–287b; II–425b
Bardeen–Cooper–Schrieffer theory V–305b
Bardstown (Ky.) I–467a; IV–42a, 447b
Barenblatt v. *United States* (1959) III–465b
Barents Sea IV–435a
Bargaining for a Horse (paint.) V–190b
BARGEMEN **I–267b**
Ohio River VI–147b
Barger, Harold (econ.) III–252a
Barges III–147b; IV–381b; VI–148a,b; VII–100a
coasting trade II–90b–91a
grain carriers I–40b
inland waterways VII–260b
Lakes–to–Gulf waterway IV–88a–b
milk transportation II–280a
Mississippi River IV–373a, 374a–b
See also Towboating
Baring, Alexander, 1st Baron Ashburton (dipl.) V–118b
Baring, House of III–466a
Baring Brothers and Company III–63b–64a; V–207b; VI–96a, 277b
Bark (ship) VI–280a
Barker, Bernard L. VII–255a
Barkley, Alben W. (pol.) I–429b; VII–180 (table)
Barkley, Charles (sea capt.) V–462a
Bark mills IV–127b–28a
Barley III–51b, 53a; VI–48a
bread II–219a
cereals I–486a,b
whiskey II–353b
Barlow, Joel (poet, dipl.) III–259b, 326a; VI–239a
Barlow, Samuel L. M. (law., bibliophile) II–108b
Barlowe, Arthur (navig.) VI–43b
Barmen Declaration (1934) V–392b
Barnard, Edward E. (astron.) I–211b
Barnard, Frederick A. P. (educ.) II–132b
Barnard, George (trader) VII–77a
Barnard, George G. (jur.) VII–131b
Barnard, Henry (educ.) II–397a, 398a–b, 405a–b; VI–227a
Barnard College II–132b–33a
Barnard's Trading Post (Tex.) VII–77a, 96a

BARNBURNERS I–267b; I–138b; III–111b, 318a
Barnegat (N.J.) II–346a; IV–152a
III–315b
Barnes, Albert C. (art collector) II–104b
Barnes, Al G. (circus owner) II–41a
Barnes, A. S. (pub.) I–334a
Barnes, Charles Reid (bot.) II–391b
Barnes, Joseph (jour.) V–74a
Barnett, Ross R. (pol.) IV–369b
Barney, Joshua (nav. off.) I–317b; III–234b, 320b; V–18b; VII–249b
BARN RAISING I–268a; I–284b; IV–60a, 79b
Barnstable (Mass.) I–447a; V–156a
BARNSTORMING I–268a
basketball I–273a
Barnum, Phineas T. (showman) IV–436b
advertising I–16b
American Museum VII–48a
circus II–40b
Lind's American tour IV–157a
Barnum and Bailey Circus II–40b
Barnum's Circus II–40b
BARNUM'S MUSEUM I–268b; I–435a; V–84a; VII–48a
Barnwell, John (off.) IV–46b; VII–130b
Baroque furniture III–134a–b
Baroque painting V–185a
Barr, Charlie VII–349a
Barrancas, Fort (Fla.) V–254a,b
Barrande, Joachim (paleon.) V–195b
Barras, Charles M. (playwright) V–93b
Barras, Louis de (nav. off.) VII–199a
Barrell, Joseph (geol.) III–167a, 481a
Barrett, Oliver R. I–333a
Barrett, Theodore H. (off.) V–198b
Barricourt (Fr.) IV–320a
Barriens (submarine designer) VI–422b
BARRIER FORTS, ATTACK ON (1856) **I–268b**
Barrier state, Indian. *See* Indian Barrier State
Barrin, Roland Michel. *See* La Galissonière, Marquis de la
Barrington, Fort (Ga.) III–42b
Barrios VI–7a
Barro Colorado Island (Pan.) VI–319b
Barron, James (nav. off.)
Chesapeake–Leopard incident II–16a
court-martial II–247a
duel with Decatur I–318a; II–377a
Barron, John. *See Barron* v. *Baltimore*
Barron, Samuel (nav. off.) I–266b
Barron's (mag.) V–76b
BARRON* v. *BALTIMORE (1833) **I–268b**; II–53b, 377b; III–86b; V–339b
Bill of Rights I–94a
Barrow, David I–135b
Barrow, John (off.) V–122a
Barrow, Joseph Louis. *See* Louis, Joe
Barrow, Robert (Quaker) III–41a
Barrows and Company V–318b
Barrow Strait II–319b; V–122a
Barry, John (nav. off.) I–467a; V–18b, 423b; VI–128a; VII–153a
Alliance I–89b
Lexington IV–136b
Barry, Philip (playwright) VII–50a
Barry, Thomas H. (offi.) VII–31a
Barrymore family VII–48b
BART. *See* Bay Area Rapid Transit
BARTER I–269a; IV–393b
colonial trade II–119a
flax and yarn IV–157b
frontier trade II–487a; III–127a
Barter, "Rattlesnake Dick" (outlaw) VI–379b
Barth, John (au.) IV–165a
Barth, Karl (theol.) VI–79b, 82b–83a
Barthelme, Donald (au.) IV–165a
Bartholdi, Frédéric August (sculp.) VI–405b
Bartholet, Louis (trader) IV–27a–b
Bartlesville (Okla.) VI–356b
Bartlett, E. L. (Bob) I–78a
Bartlett, Elisha (physic.) III–325a
Bartlett, Frederick Clay II–105a
Bartlett, James H. (phys.) V–302a
Bartlett, John Russell (au.) I–269a
Bartlett, Josiah (physic.) II–307b
Bartlett, Neil (chem.) II–12b
Bartlett, Robert A. (expl.) V–240b
BARTLETT'S EXPLORATIONS (1850–53) **I–269a**
Bartlett's Point (N.Y.) III–118a
Barton, Benjamin Smith (physic., nat.) I–128a, 348b–49a; II–390a; V–326a–b
Barton, Clara V–280a; VI–61b
Barton, William (off.) VI–246b
Barton, William P. C. (physic., bot.) V–326b
Bartow (Fla.) III–40a
Bartram, John (bot.) I–348b; III–29b, 151b; V–326a
American Philosophical Society I–110a
travels II–390a
Bartram, William (nat.) I–304b, 348b; II–477a; V–326a; VI–90a
Travels (1791) II–390a
Baruch, Bernard M. (fin., states.)
War Industries Board V–44a–b; VII–231b
Barus, Carl (geol.) III–167a
Bascio, Matteo da. *See* Matteo da Bascio
BASCOM, FORT (N.Mex.) **I–269b**
Bascom, George N. (off.)
Apache Pass expedition I–142a; IV–236b
BASEBALL I–269b; I–488a; II–261a, 337b
Baseball Clubs, National League of. *See* National League of Professional Baseball Clubs
Baseball Hall of Fame I–269b
Baseball Players Association. *See* National Association of Baseball Players; National Brotherhood of Baseball Players
Basement (arch.) I–160b
Bases, U.S. II–316b
Bahamas I–243b
cold war II–475b
Basil, Vasili de (ballet adm.) II–288b
Basin culture III–362a–63a, 367a, 369a
art and technology III–373b
myth and folklore III–386a–b
Basing point system V–102b; VII–123a,b
BASKETBALL I–272a; IV–220b; V–154a,b
Basketball Association, National. *See* National Basketball Association
Basketball Association in America I–273a
Basketball Committee. *See* National Basketball Committee of the United States and Canada
Basketball League, National. *See* National Basketball League
Basketball Rules Committee, Joint I–272b
Basket Maker cultures III–367a
Pueblo V–460a
Basketmaker phase (archaeol.) I–117b
Basketry III–362b, 373b, 374a, 381a–b
Archaic culture II–386a
Desert culture II–334b
Baskin, Leonard (art.) V–414a; VII–319b
Basle, Treaty of (1795) V–315b
Basov, N. G. (phys.) IV–262b
Bass (fish) III–51a, 413a
Bass, Charlotta (pub.) V–429b
Bass, Sam (outlaw) I–247a; VII–97b
Bassa (people) IV–141b
Bassett, John (metalworker) VI–290b
Bassett, John Spencer (hist.) III–486a
Bassett, Rex (inv.) II–420b
Bassett, Richard (states.) II–203b
Bassett Town (Pa.) VII–244b
BASTOGNE (Belg.) **I–273b**; I–379b, 380a; VII–340a
Bat (missile) V–164a
BATAAN–CORREGIDOR CAMPAIGN (1942) **I–273b**; V–284a; VII–336b
prisoners I–219b
Batavia (Ill.) II–388a; V–297b
Bat Cave (N.Mex.) I–48a, 157a; IV–385b
Batchelder, Samuel (mfr., inv.) IV–187b; VII–43a
BATEAU I–274a; II–265b; III–403b; IV–374a, 381b; VI–148a
revolutionary war I–193b
Bates, Ann (spy) VI–373a
Bates, David (eng.) I–442b
Bates, Elisha (abolitionist) V–279b
Bates County (Mo.) II–34a
Bateson, William (biol.) III–157a
Bates Union II–86b
Bates v. *City of Little Rock* (1960) I–204b
Bath (Maine) IV–37b
settlement VI–185b
shipbuilding IV–226b; VI–279b
Bath (N.Y.) V–463b
Bath (N.C.) V–115b
Bath County (Va.) III–469b
BATHTUBS AND BATHING I–274b
Bathurst, Henry, 3rd Earl Bathurst III–177a
Batista, Fulgencio II–269b; III–276b; IV–112b–13a
BATON ROUGE (La.) **I–274b**; III–326b; VI–359b
Afro-Americans I–25b, 29a
Civil War III–228a
Long assassination IV–184a
revolutionary war VI–365b
BATON ROUGE, BATTLE OF (1862) **I–275a**; I–173b; IV–375a; V–369a
BATON ROUGE, SEIZURE OF (1810) **VII–277a**
Battelle, Gordon I–275a
BATTELLE MEMORIAL INSTITUTE I–275a; III–410a

Batteries, floating. *See* Floating Batteries
Batterson, James G. (bus.) III–435a
BATTERY (N.Y.C.) **I–275b**; II–432b; V–368b
BATTERY, ELECTRIC I–276a; II–413a, 421b
clocks II–79b
railways VI–40a
Battery Wagner, Battle of (1863) I–497a
Battle, William C. (pol.) VII–196a
Battle Abbey (Richmond) VI–137a
Battle Creek (Mich.) I–434b; IV–471b
Battle Creek Sanitarium V–306a
Battle deaths. *See* War Losses
Battlefields, national
Antietam I–130a
Big Hole I–296a
Cowpens (S.C.) II–251b
BATTLE FLEET CRUISE AROUND THE WORLD (1907–09) **I–276b**; III–68b; IV–431b; V–20a; VII–241a
"BATTLE HYMN OF THE REPUBLIC" I–276b; II–53a
Battle Monuments Commission. *See* American Battle Monuments Commission
Battle of Bunker's Hill (paint.) V–188b
Battle of Lake Erie V–262b
"Battle of the Clouds." *See* Lookout Mountain, Battle of
"Battle of the Hedgerows" II–237a
"Battle of the Kegs" (poem) IV–35b
"Battle of the systems" II–416a
Battleships I–67a; V–25a,b; VII–241a, 241a, 241b–42a, 329a, 341b, 343b
Five-Power Naval Treaty III–33b
guns V–26b
naval competition V–10a,b
scout observation aircraft I–55b
Washington Naval Conference VII–250b
See also Warships
BATTLESHIPS, DUMMY I–277a
Battles of the American Revolution, 1775–1781 IV–180a
Batts, Nathaniel (trader) I–83a
Batts, Thomas (off.) I–277b
BATTS–FALLAM EXPEDITION (1617) **I–277a**
Batu khan (Mongol) I–180b
Baudry, Paul J. A. (paint.) V–191a
Bauer, Louis H. (med. off.) IV–292b
Bauhaus style III–136b, 446b
Baum, Frederick (off.) I–289a
Baum, L. Frank (au.) I–335b
Baum, Morton II–289a
Baumler, Joseph Michael VII–369b
Bauxite III–164a
aluminum production I–92b
Arkansas I–173a
Bavaria (Ger.)
World War II VII–341a
Bavarian Illuminati III–112a
Bawden, F. C. (plant path.) IV–389a
Baxter, Elisha (pol.) I–370b
Baxter, G. P. (chem.) I–218b
Baxter, Thomas (adventurer) VI–134a,b
Baxter Springs (Kans.) I–473a; IV–26a
Bay, Jacob (typefounder) V–411b
Bayama (Cuba) III–150b
Bayard, James A. (pol.)
Treaty of Ghent III–176b; VII–235b
Bayard, Thomas F. (states.) I–93b
campaign of 1876 I–422b
Olney Corollary V–153a
BAYARD–CHAMBERLAIN TREATY (1888) **I–277b**; II–29a
Bayard's Sugar House (N.Y.C.) VI–436b
BAYARD* v. *SINGLETON (1787) **I–277b**
Bay Area Rapid Transit III–203a, 451b; VI–209b, 429b
Bayberry candles I–444a
Bayeux (Fr.) V–110b
Bay Islands II–72b
Baylor Hospital (Dallas) III–435b
Baylor University VII–40b
Bayne, Thomas L. (off.) II–162b
Baynton, John (mer.) *See* Baynton, Wharton and Morgan
BAYNTON, WHARTON AND MORGAN I–278a; I–309a; III–141b, 403a; VI–285a
Bay of Biloxi IV–276b
Bay of Fundy IV–225b
BAY OF PIGS INVASION (1961) **I–278b**; I–454b; II–209b; III–70a, 199b, 463a,b; IV–113a; V–53a, 74a, 94b
"Bayonet bonds" VI–96b
Bayonne (N.J.) I–364b
Bayonne Bridge V–368b
Bayonne Decree (1808) III–118b, 121b; IV–449b
BAYOU I–279a
Bayou Barataria I–279a
Bayou Bend Collection (Houston) III–137a
Bayou Lafourche (La.)
Houma Indians III–308a
Isleños settlement III–479a
Last Island hurricane IV–110b
Bayou Manchac (La.) III–326b; IV–234b
Isleños settlement III–479a
Bayou Pierre I–279a
Bayou Saint John VI–191a
Bayou Teche (La.)
Acadians I–6b
BAYOU TECHE EXPEDITION (1863) **I–279a**; I–461b
BAY PATH I–279b
***BAY PSALM BOOK* I–279b**; I–294a; III–326a; V–410b
Cambridge press I–333b
Bay State VI–394 (table)
Bay van Nassau IV–451b
Baziotes, William (art.) II–105b
Bazooka IV–363a; VI–140a, 159a
Beach, Alfred Ely (inv., ed.) VI–231a; VII–128a
Beach, C. A. (inv.) II–420a
Beachey, Lincoln (av.) I–233b
Beachy Amish Mennonite Churches IV–303a
Beacon Hill (Boston) I–344a; VI–86a
Beadle, Erastus F. (pub.) II–341a–42a
Beadle, G. W. (biol.) III–157b, 158a; IV–389a; V–100a
Beadle, Irwin P. (pub.) II–341a–b
Beads
Archaic culture II–386a
Dakota II–283a
fur trade III–140b
Hohokam culture III–289b
Beal, Fred E. (labor leader) III–154a
Beal, William James (bot.) I–46a; II–226a
Beales, John Charles (col.) VI–143b
Beall, John Yates (nav. off.) *See* Beall's Raid on Lake Erie
BEALL'S RAID ON LAKE ERIE (1864) **I–280a**; I–435a; IV–5a; V–121b
Bean, Benjamin W. (inv.) VI–264b
Bean, Tarleton H. (nat.) III–28a
Bean, William (settler) VII–25a, 253a
Beans III–51a, 53b, 54b, 381a
Indian agriculture I–47b, 48a,b; IV–385b
Bear III–51a, 150a, 358b, 402b; VII–346a, 357b
Bear (whaler) III–224a
Bear, Kodiak. *See* Kodiak bear
Bear Creek VII–70b
Beard, Charles A. (hist., educ.) I–97a; II–197b; III–283a; V–348b, 353b
Beard, Charles A. (neurol.) IV–306a
Beard, Mary (hist.) III–283a
Beards III–239b
Beardslee, L. A. (nav. off.) I–76b
Beardslee telegraph machine VI–285b
BEAR FLAG REVOLT (1846) **I–280a**; I–409b; III–264b; VII–272a
BEAR HUNTERS AND BEAR STORIES I–280b; III–48b
Bear Lake (Utah) VII–104a
Bear Mountain (N.Y.) III–312b
Bear oil II–480a
BEAR PAW MOUNTAINS, BATTLE AT (1877) **I–281a**
BEAR RIVER (Calif.) **I–281a**
Bear River (Utah–Idaho)
Bonneville expedition I–330a
Oregon Trail V–168b
Sublette's Cutoff VI–422a
Walker expedition VII–220a
BEAR RIVER, BATTLE OF (1863) **I–281a**
Bear Springs, Treaty of (1846) II–363b
Beasley, Daniel (off.) IV–347b
Beat generation IV–165b
Beatles (mus.) IV–441a
Beatrice Creamery II–282a
Beattie, Edward W. (jour.) V–74a
Beaubien, Carlos IV–278a; VI–210b
Beaubien, Jean Baptiste (trader) I–281b
Beaubien, Narcisco VI–210b
BEAUBIEN LAND CLAIM I–281b
Beauchamp, John VII–219b
Beauchamp and Leverett patent I–466a
Beau Danube (ballet) II–288b
Beaufort (N.C.) V–115b
BEAUFORT (S.C.) **I–281b**; III–38a; VI–135b
Beaufort Sea V–122a, 338b
Beauharnois, Charles de (col. gov.) II–267a
BEAUHARNOIS, FORT (Minn.) **I–281b**; III–89b
Beaujeu, Daniel (off.) I–358a
Beaumarchais, Pierre Augustin Caron de (playwright) III–94b, 306a; VI–119b, 120a, 129a,b
Beaumont (Tex.) IV–334a; V–271b; VII–40b
Beaumont, Andrew (pol.) II–222a
Beaumont, William (physic.) IV–285b, 292a, 297b; V–306b; VI–196b–97a

Beaumont de La Bonninière, Gustav (au.) III–122b
Beauregard, Pierre G. T. (off.) I–181a, 468a; VI–373a
Army of Mississippi IV–370a
Drewry's Bluff II–373a, 382b
Elk River II–432a
first Battle of Bull Run I–381a
Fort Sumter VI–440b
Beautiful Nebraska (song) VI–394 (table)
Beautiful Ohio (song) VI–395 (table)
Beauty aids II–234a, 371a
Beauty parlors II–233b; III–239a
Beaux Arts I–163b–64a; VI–243b, 244a
Beaver (animal) III–133a–b, 142a, 402b; IV–422a,b; V–16a; VI–160a,b; VII–105a, 296b
Canton fur trade I–446a
Colorado II–128a
Green River III–227a
New Mexico V–59b
steel traps VI–411b
trappers' rendezvous VII–103b
Beaver (Indians) I–441b; III–360b
Beaver (Pa.) IV–216b
Beaver (ship) I–209a
Beaver, Tony (lumberman) VI–458b
Beaver Creek IV–45a; VII–252b
Beaver Dam Creek (Va.) IV–282a
Beaver Dam Creek, Battle of. *See* Mechanicsville, Battle of
BEAVER DAMS, BATTLE OF (1813) **I–281b**
Beaver Dam Station (Va.) VII–358a
BEAVER HATS I–282a; II–119a, 371b; III–133b; IV–37b, 242b
Beaver Islands VI–416b
BEAVER MONEY I–282a; II–94b, 140b, 453a; IV–392b; V–401b
Beaver State VI–395 (table)
Beaver Street (N.Y.C.) V–40a
Beaver trade. *See* Beaver; Fur Trade
Bebber, Jack van (athlete) V–154b
Bebop (mus.) IV–440b
Beccaria, Marchese di, Cesare Bonesana (econ., jur.) V–415a
Beck, Julian (dir.) VII–51a
Becker, Carl L. (hist.) IV–161b; VI–115a
Becker, George F. (geol.) III–166b–67a; V–268a
Becker, H. (phys.) V–298b
Beckett, Samuel (playwright) VII–50b–51a
Beckham, J. C. W. (pol.) III–188b
Beckley, John James (offi.) IV–146a, 148a
Beckman, James III–151a
Becknell, William (trader). *See* Becknell's Expeditions
BECKNELL'S EXPEDITIONS (1821–22) **I–282a**; I–452b; VI–215a–b; VII–217b
Santa Fe Trail II–477b
Taos VI–461a
Beckwith, E. G. (off.) VI–39a
Beckwith, George V–235b
Beckwourth's Pass (Calif.) III–215a
Becky Sharp (film) IV–418a
Becton, George Wilson III–254a
Bedacht, Max (Communist) II–144a
Bedford (N.Y.) IV–186a
Bedford (Pa.) I–358b; III–59a; VI–49a
BEDFORD, FORT (Pa.) **I–282b**; III–58b
Bedford, Gunning, Jr. (states.) II–193a, 203b
Bedford Cut Stone Company v. *Journeymen Stonecutters' Association* (1927) III–419a
BEDFORD–STUYVESANT (Brooklyn, N.Y.) **I–282b**; I–370b
Bedinger, Henry (off.) VI–170a
Bedini, Gaetano (cler.) I–283a
BEDINI RIOTS (1853, 1854) **I–283a**
Bedloe's Island. *See* Liberty Island
Bedspreads III–133b
Bedsprings III–136a
Bedsteads III–134a
Bee, G. E. (off.) I–381b
Beech (tree) III–74b; VII–59b
Beecher, Catharine Esther (femin.) II–418a
Beecher, Henry Ward (cler.) III–112a–b; V–161b; VI–243b
adultery charge VII–118b
Beecher's Bibles I–283b
phrenology V–294a
Beecher, Lyman (cler.) VI–77a; VII–22a–b
BEECHER ISLAND, BATTLE OF (1868) **I–283a**
BEECHER'S BIBLES I–283b; IV–25b; VI–270a
Beef III–52b; V–160a–b
meat-packing IV–280a,b
revolutionary war VI–120a
Beefmaster cattle I–471b
Beef steers
corn belt II–227a
"Beef Trail" I–473a
Beef trust III–443b
BEEF TRUST CASES I–283b; III–343a
Beehive State VI–395 (table)
BEEKEEPING I–283b
Beekman (N.Y.) I–284b
Beekman, Henry (landowner). *See* Beekman Patent
BEEKMAN PATENT I–284b; III–220b, 313a
Beer I–361b–62a; III–51b, 398b; V–182b
Prohibition II–407a
taxes VII–6a
Wisconsin VII–308a
World World I restrictions V–430a
Beers, Clifford W. IV–304a, 306a
Beers, Ethel Lynn (poet) I–90b
BEES (social gatherings) **I–284b**
Beeswax II–480a
Beeswax candles I–444a
Beethoven, Ludwig von (comp.) II–287b
Beetles III–421a
BEET SUGAR I–285a; VI–48a, 437a
child labor II–24b
commercial bounties I–352b
Idaho III–328b
subsidies VI–426a
Behaim, Martin (geog.) IV–247a
Behavioralism V–349a, 354a
Behavioral science
juvenile courts IV–23a
Behaviorism (psych.) V–442a
Behrman, S. N. (playwright) VII–50a
Beiderbecke, Bix (mus.) IV–166b
Beidler, John X. VII–187b
Beinecke Rare Book and Manuscript Library (Yale) III–285a; VII–351a
Beirut (Leb.) IV–130a
Beissel, Johann Conrad (cler.) II–147a, 454a
Békésy, Georg von (physiol.) V–100a
Belair Grove (Fla.) II–43a
Belasco, David (playwright, prod.) VII–48b, 49a
Belcher, Jonathan (col. gov.) VI–109b
Belcher, Supply (comp.) IV–438a
Belcourt, George A. (cler.) V–244a
Belen (N.Mex.) III–162b
Belén Gate (Mex.) I–494b
Belgian Antarctic Expedition (1897–98) I–115a
Belgian horse III–303b
BELGIAN RELIEF I–285b; VII–329a
Belgium
art nouveau III–446b
Common Market VI–469a
Confederate commission II–65b
currency upvalue III–196b
European Economic Community VII–88b
Fourteen Points III–86a
German reparations VI–87b
investments in U.S. III–63a, 66b
Korean War IV–55b
linen products IV–157b
Macedonian dispute arbitration IV–212b
mandates IV–236b
Nine-Power Pact V–96b
North Atlantic Treaty Organization V–113b
Organization for Economic Cooperation and Development V–170b
pig iron III–471 (table)
trade VII–87a
Treaty of Versailles VII–173a,b
United Nations Declaration VII–151b
Unknown Soldiers II–310a
Walloons VII–221b
Washington Naval Conference VII–251a
Western Union Defense Organization 114a–
World War I I–122b; IV–319b; VII–331a, 332a, 366b
World War II I–273b, 379a–380a; III–187a; IV–230b; VI–198a; VII–334b
Belize (Br. Hon.) IV–181b
Belknap, Cora Le Roy I–286a
BELKNAP, FORT (Tex.) **I–286a**; III–199b
Belknap, Jeremy (cler.) III–27a, 278b; IV–232a, 423b; VII–206a
Belknap, William Goldsmith (off.) I–286a
Belknap, William W. (pol.) I–286a
BELKNAP SCANDAL I–286a; V–346a
Bell, Alexander Graham (inv.) VI–14b
aviation experiments I–233a
education of the deaf III–248a
telegraph VII–19a
telephone II–413b; V–289b; VII–19b–20a
telephone patent cases VII–20b
Bell, Chichester A. (inv.) V–289b
Bell, curfew II–274b
Bell, Daniel W. (bus., off.) V–285a
Bell, Edward Price (jour.) V–74a
Bell, James Ford (ind.) I–488a
Bell, John (physic.) III–325a–b
Bell, John (states.) II–175 (table); VII–25b
campaign of 1860 I–421a; II–191b
slavery compromise II–139a

Bell, J. R. (off.) IV–187a
Bell, Peter H. (pol.) VII–35b
Bell, Robert (auctioneer)
I–332b
Bell, Tom (outlaw) VI–379b
Bella Bella (Indians)
III–362a; IV–59a
Bella Coola (Indians)
I–441b; III–362a
Bella Coola River V–164b;
VII–275b
Belladonna IV–305b
Bellah, Robert (soc.) II–52b
Bellamy, Edward (au.)
IV–163b; VI–325a, 326a
Bellamy, Francis (ed.)
V–331b
Bellamy, George A. (act.)
VI–330b
Bellanca, Giuseppe I–51b
Bell calculators II–154b
BELLEAU WOOD, BATTLE OF (1918) **I–286a**;
I–70a; IV–252b, 319b;
VII–326b
Belleek porcelain III–184a
BELLEFONTAINE (Ill.)
I–286b; I–100b
BELLEFONTAINE, FORT (Mo.) **I–286b**; V–312a
Belle Grove (Middletown, Va.)
IV–472a
Belle Isle (La.) II–350b
BELLE ISLE (Va.) **I–287a**
Belle Isle Strait VII–285a
Belles lettres. *See* Literature
Belleville (N.J.) VI–408b
Bellevue (Nebr.) I–399a,
399a; V–30b–31a
Bellevue (Ohio) VI–35a
Bellevue, Fort (Iowa)
IV–219b
Bellevue Hospital (N.Y.C.)
III–306b, 307a; V–126b
BELLEVUE WAR (1840)
I–287a
Bellicourt Canal Tunnel (Fr.)
VI–338b
Belligerents
Consolato del mare
II–190a
contraband of war
II–212b–13b
neutral ships II–446a
See also Neutrality;
Neutral Rights
Bellman, Henry (pol.)
V–149b
Bellomont, Earl of. *See*
Coote, Richard, Earl of
Bellomont
Bellot Strait V–122a
Bellow, Saul (au.) IV–165a,b
Bellow Falls Canal IV–174b
Bellows, George W. (art.)
V–414a
Bellows, Henry W. (cler.)
V–438b; VI–211a
Bellows Falls (Vt.) I–363b
Bells
fur trade III–140a
Hohokam culture
III–289b
Bell Telephone VII–20a,
276b
communication satellites
II–143a
electric circuit analysis
II–39a
microwave chains
IV–333a
BELL TELEPHONE LABORATORIES
I–287a; II–423b; V–137a
calculators II–154b
crystal diffraction V–303b
electron diffraction
V–295b
lasers IV–263a
masers IV–262b
microwave technology
IV–333a
radio astronomy
VI–16b–17a
silicon oxide masking technique IV–352b
telecommunications
II–425b
television VII–21b
transistor III–410a; V–305a;
VI–259a
vacuum tube VI–15a
Belluschi, Pietro (arch.)
I–165b
Bell v. *Maryland* (1964)
II–50b
Bell X–1 (aircraft)
VI–159a
Belmont (Colo.) VI–292a
Belmont (Mass.) IV–2a
Belmont (Miss.) IV–136b
Belmont (Mo.) I–288a
Belmont, August (banker)
II–103b; III–79b; IV–410a
BELMONT, BATTLE OF
(1861) **I–288a**
Belmont Stakes III–305a
Belote, Melissa (athlete)
V–154b
"BELOVED MAN/ BELOVED WOMAN"
I–288a
Natchez IV–455b, 456a
Belshazzar's Feast (paint.)
V–188b
Belter, John Henry III–135b
Beltrami, Giacomo III–468a;
VII–196b
Beltrán, Bernardino (sol.)
I–288b
BELTRÁN–ESPEJO EXPEDITION (1582) **I–288b**
Beltz, William (pol.) I–79a
Belvidera (ship) V–394a
Bemis Heights (N.Y.)
VI–123b
Bemis Heights, Battle of. *See*
Freeman's Farm, Battles
of
Benbow, John (nav. off.)
VI–2b
Bendix automatic washer
II–420a
Bendix G–15 (computer)
II–156a
Benedict, F. G. (biochem.)
I–303a
Benedict, Ruth (anthrop.)
I–129a
BENEFIT OF CLERGY
I–288b
Benefits, workmen's IV–70a
Benelux countries
U.S. aid III–61b
Benevolence.
See Philanthropy and
Benevolence:
Benevolent and Protective Order of Elks VI–252b
Benewah County (Idaho)
II–93b
Benezet, Anthony (educ.)
I–135a; V–279b; VI–311a
Benin, Bight of (W.Afr.)
VI–309b
Benjamin, Judah P. (pol.)
II–160a–61a; IV–326b
Bennehoff Run (Pa.) V–319a
Bennett, Edward Herbert
(landscape arch.)
IV–96b
Bennett, Floyd (av.) I–399a
Bennett, H. H. (agric. chem.)
VI–335a–b
Bennett, James Gordon (pub.)
V–73b
advertising I–17a
Associated Press I–207a
Jeannette polar expedition
V–336a
New York Morning Herald
V–71a,b
transatlantic cable I–401a;
II–137a
yellow journalism
VII–356a
Bennett, James Gordon, Jr.
(pub.) VII–349a
Bennett, John (au.) I–335b
Bennett House (N.C.)
V–116a
BENNING, FORT (Ga.)
I–289a; VI–47a, 287b
Bennington (Vt.) III–183b;
V–70a, 379b
BENNINGTON, BATTLE OF (1777) **I–289a**;
I–385a; III–226b; V–54a,
126a; VII–171b
Bennington pitcher III–184a
Benoist, Francois M. (fur trader) IV–159b
Benson, Elmer A. (gov.)
II–491b–92a
Benson, Lee (hist.) III–487a
Benson, William S. (nav. off.)
I–14a; V–13b
Bent, Charles (trader)
II–477b; III–143b;
IV–27b; VII–96a
Bent, Fort (Colo.) IV–27b
Bent, Silas (jour.) V–80a
Bent, St. Vrain and Company
IV–27b
Bent, William (trader)
II–477b; III–143b;
IV–27b; VII–96a
Bent's Fort I–289b
westward movement
I–453a
Benteen, Frederick (off.)
IV–168a, 168a,b
Bentham, Jeremy (jur., philos.)
prisons V–415a
Bentham, Samuel (inv.)
III–442a
Bentley, Arthur F. (pol. sci.)
V–348b
Bentley, Edward M. (inv.)
electric streetcars II–414b
Bentley, Elizabeth VI–428b
Bentley, William (cler.)
II–98b
Benton, Caleb (bus.) V–81b
Benton, Jessie. *See* Frémont,
Jessie Benton
Benton, Linn Boyd (inv.)
V–412b
Benton, Thomas Hart (pol.)
I–376a; III–77b;
IV–377a,b; V–161a
Bank of the United States
III–251b, 354b
duel with Lucas II–377a
Fort Benton I–289b
Fort Leavenworth
IV–129a
Graduation Act III–207a
homestead movement
III–295b
Indian factory system
I–105a; II–480a
Kansas–Nebraska Act
IV–29a,b
public land sales
VII–265b
Benton, Thomas Hart (paint.)
V–192b
Benton, William (pub.)
II–444a
Benton, Fort (Big Horn River)
VII–95b
BENTON, FORT (Mont.)
I–289b; III–32a; IV–403a,
403a
fur trade II–34a
Mullan Trail IV–426a
Piegan War V–310a
BENTONVILLE, BATTLE OF (1865) **I–289b**;
I–458b; V–116a; VII–34b
Benton v. *Maryland* (1969)
II–53b
BENT'S FORT (Colo.)
I–289b; I–174b, 293a;
II–128a; IV–208b; VII–96a
Bent's New Fort I–290a
Benz, Karl (auto. mfr.)
I–225b, 226a
Beothuk (Indians) III–355b,
360b
Berceau (corvette) I–345a;
V–15a
Berea (Ky.) IV–220a
Berea (Ohio) IV–207a
Berea College IV–220a
BEREA COLLEGE* v. *KENTUCKY (1908) **I–290a**
Berean Series VI–442b
Berg, Patty (golfer)
III–198a–b
Bergen (Nor.) V–37b
prize cases I–290b
Bergen County (N.J.)
IV–131b
BERGEN PRIZES I–290b
Berger, Raoul (hist.)
III
344a
Berger, Victor L. (ed., Socialist) II–492b; VI–324b,
326b
Bergeron, Tor (meteor.)
IV–317b
Berger v. *New York* (1967)
II–427b

Bergh, Henry (philan.) I–125b
Bergius, Petter–Jonas (physic.) VI–167a
Beriberi I–303b; IV–291b
Bering, Vitus (navig.) I–74b, 84a,b; VI–245b, 247a
Bering Sea I–439a; VII–367a
migration of Asians to America I–74b
Pribilof Islands V–401a
sealing I–84b; VI–245a, 246a
territorial waters VII–33a
See also Seal Fisheries
Bering Sea Fur Seal Arbitration (1893) III–456b
Bering Strait II–219b
Alaskan Indians I–81a
American Indian migration III–355a
Eskimo II–461b
Jeannette expedition V–336a,b
Northwest Passage V–122b
Russian claims VI–180b
whaling VII–285b
Bering Strait Indians III–358a
Berkeley (Calif.) VII–156b, 187a
Berkeley, Busby II–290b
Berkeley, George (philos.) V–186a, 287a
Yale University VII–351a
Berkeley, John, 1st Baron Berkeley of Stratton IV–398a; V–42b
Carolina proprietary I–458a
Concessions and Agreement II–157a
Long Island IV–185b
New Jersey II–124a; V–56b, 436b; VII–278a, 359b
religious liberty VII–68b
Berkeley, William (col. gov.) V–145a
Albemarle settlements I–83b
Bacon's Rebellion I–240a; III–436b
Carolina proprietary I–458a
Lederer's exploring expeditions IV–131a
Plowden's New Albion V–332b
Virginia colony II–117a
Berkeley County (Va.) VII–281a
Berkeley Hundred (Va.) VII–95a
Berkeley Warm Springs (Va.) VI–100b
Berkman, Alexander (anarchist) I–116b–117a; VI–13b
Berkner, Lloyd V. (phys.) III–454a
Berks County (Pa.) III–300b; V–251b
Berkshire Agricultural Society II–244b; VI–392b
Berkshire hog III–288b
Berkshire Mountains VI–100b
Berkshire Music Festival IV–268b
Berkshire Society II–244b
Berle, Adolph A., Jr. (dipl.) I–359b; V–43b
Berlin (Conn.) VII–62b, 63a
Berlin (Ger.) III–69b–70b; V–113b–14a
apartment houses I–143a
Communist pressure II–315b
electric railway VI–40a
Kennedy administration V–53a
Olympic Games V–154a
Open Door notes II–27a
Paris conferences V–215b–16a
partitioning III–174b, 175a
World War II I–60a; II–407b
Berlin, Irving (comp.) IV–442a
BERLIN, TREATY OF (1921) **I–290b**; III–172a; VII–174a
BERLIN AIRLIFT (1948–49) **I–290b**; I–60b–61a, 179a; II–218a; III–69b; V–114a
BERLIN BLOCKADE (1948–49) **I–291a**; III–69b; V–114a; VI–179b
campaign of 1948 V–429a
division of Europe II–98a
Paris Peace Conference V–215b
Berlin Conference on Samoa (1889) I–144a
Berlin crisis (1961–63) I–64b, 187a
Berlin Decree (1806) I–321a; II–436b–37a; III–118b, 121b; IV–449b; VI–105a
British orders in council V–162a
See also Napoleon's Decrees
Berliner, Emile (inv.) V–289b, 290a
Berlin Resolution (1962) VI–100a
BERLIN WALL I–291b; IV–384b; VI–180a, 439b
Berman v. *Parker* (1959) II–440a
Berman v. *United States* (1946) II–185b
***BERMUDA* ADMIRALTY CASE** (1865) **I–292a**; II–67b, 213a
Bermuda Company I–499b, 500a; VII–66a, 94b
BERMUDA CONFERENCE (1957) **I–292b**
Bermuda Hundred (Va.) II–373a, 382b; III–488a
BERMUDA ISLANDS I–292b
British army VI–126b
Civil War II–162b
earthquake II–385a
potatoes V–376b
privateers VI–129b
Rhodes scholars VI–134b
settlement VII–94b
Somers' voyage VI–338a
tennis VII–29a
yacht racing VII–349a
Bermuda onions V–156a
Bermuda Triangle II–346b
Bernal, J. D. (phys.) IV–389b
Bernalillo (N.Mex.) VI–162a
BERNARD, FORT (Wyo.) **I–292b**
Bernard, Francis (col. gov.) IV–266a, 422b
Bernard, John (act.) I–367b
Bernard, Mountague (law.) VII–248b
Bernhard Line III–235b
Bernhardt, Sarah (act.) IV–417b
Bernstein, Carl (jour.) V–78a; VII–255b
Bernstein, Leonard (comp., cond.) IV–438b; VII–50b
Bernstorff, Andreas Peter von (states.) I–290b
Bernstorff, Johann–Heinrich von (dipl.) VII–332b
Berrien, John M. (pol.) I–10b
Berrien County (Mich.) V–335b
Berries III–128a, 129a
Berrigan brothers VII–118a
Berry, Chuck (mus.) IV–441a
Berry, Clifford (phys.) II–154b
Berryman, John (poet) IV–165b
Berryman, O. H. (nav. off.) V–23a
Berthelot, Henri M. (off.) I–70b
Berthold, Bartholomew (fur trader) II–34a
Berthold, Fort (N.Dak.) II–284a; III–34a
Berthold, Fort, Reservation (N.Dak.) III–395b
Berthold, Saint I–455b
Bertholett, Louis. *See* Bartholet, Louis
Berthollet, C. L. (chem.) II–6a
Berthoud, James (bus.) VI–462a
Bertoia, Harry III–137a
Bertrand H. Snell Lock VI–193a
Bertrand Township (Mich.) V–335b
Bertron, S. R. VI–163b
Berwick Bay (La.) I–279b, 461b
Berwick–on–Tweed (Eng.) II–453a
Beryllium IV–294a, 294b
Berzelius, Jöns Jakob (chem.) I–218a
Bessemer, Henry (eng., inv.) III–473a
Bessemer process III–470b, 473a, 474a; IV–244a,b, 244b
Bessemer rails VI–39b
Bessemer Steel Association III–473a
Bessemer Steel Company III–473a
Bessemer steel converter II–223b
Bessey, Charles Edward (bot.) I–349a; II–391b
Beste, J. Richard I–367b, 368a
Best Friend IV–175b; VI–24b
Bestiality VI–265b
Betatron V–301a
BETHABARA (N.C.) **I–293a**; VII–350a
Bethania (N.C.) VII–350a
Bethe, Hans (phys.) V–100a, 295b, 302b, 303a
Bethel (Conn.) II–286a, 286b
Bethel African Methodist Episcopal Church I–23a
Bethel College V–259b
BETHEL COMMUNITY I–293a
Bethesda (Md.) IV–465a
BETHESDA HOUSE OF MERCY I–293a
Bethlehem (Pa.) III–124a
iron and steel industry III–470b
Moravians VII–350a
water supply VII–258a
Bethlehem Steel Company I–250a; III–14a, 79b–80a; VI–234a
creusot process I–179a
Beth Sholom Synagogue (Elkins Park, Pa.) I–165a
Betio Island III–180a; VI–462a
Betsy (merchantman) I–290b
Better Business Bureau, National V–468b
Better business bureaus II–208b
advertising I–19a
Betts v. *Brady* (1942) III–179a
Beverages, non–alcoholic. *See* Soft Drink Industry
Beveridge, Albert J. (pol., hist.) V–161a, 427b
Beverley, Robert (col. offi., hist.) III–280b; VII–206a
Beverly (W.Va.) III–332b
Beverly Ford (Va.) I–360a
Beverwyck (N.Y.) I–81b; II–383a
Bewick, Thomas (engr.) VII–319a
Bexar–Nacogdoches road II–339b
Beyond Culture IV–165b
Beyond Life IV–164b
Biacnabato, Pact of (1897) V–282b
Biard, Pierre (miss.) III–398b
Bibb (steamer) III–29a
BIBLE I–293a; VI–227a
American Bible Society I–99b
Book of Mormon IV–411a
Cherokee VI–263a
collections II–109a
colonial use II–258a
door–to–door salesmen II–444b

Eliot's Indian Bible III–375b; V–410b
Gideon Society III–179b
Higher Criticism III–275a
illustrations III–47b
missionary societies VI–77b
morals IV–408a
Moses His Judicials IV–415b
nativism V–2b
Pentecostalism V–259b
reading in schools II–398a, 400a
scientific inquiry III–112b
slavery I–23b
Society for the Propagation of the Gospel VI–332a
theocracy VII–51b
translations IV–364b, 366b
Bible, Alan (pol.) V–40a
BIBLE COMMONWEALTH I–294a; III–220a; VII–51a–b
BIBLES, PRINTING OF I–294a
Bicameral council II–44a; IV–171b
BICAMERAL LEGISLATURES I–294b; IV–133b; V–351b
American Samoa VI–205a–b
Constitutional Convention II–183a
Liberia IV–141b
Massachusetts Bay II–117a–b
North Carolina V–115b
Parliament V–220b
Plymouth colony II–117a–b
territories VI–400b
Virginia colony II–117a–b
Bickertonites IV–117a
Bickley, George (physic.) IV–52b
Bicorne VII–144a
Bicycle I–225a, 226b
interchangeable manufacture IV–272b
machine tools IV–216a
BICYCLING I–295a
road improvement movement VI–152a, 154b
rubber tires VI–167b
Biddeford (Maine) IV–227a; VI–184a
Biddeford Pool (Maine) VI–184a
Biddle, Charles A. (dipl.) I–295a
Biddle, James (nav. off.) III–302a; V–11b, 22b
Biddle, Nicholas (fin.) IV–168b
Bank of the United States I–255a, 255a, 261b
securities III–466a
Biddle, Nicholas (nav. off.) V–18b; VI–128a,b
Biddle family IV–256b
BIDDLE MISSION (1836) **I–295a**
Bidlack, Benjamin A. (dipl.) I–295b
BIDLACK TREATY (1846) **I–295b**; V–204a,b; VII–111b
Bidwell, John (pol.) II–477b; V–430b; VII–23b
Bien, Julius (map pub.) I–462b
Bien Hoa (Viet.) VII–183a, 186b
Bienville, Sieur de, Jean Baptiste Le Moyne (expl.) III–119a
Alabama settlement I–71a
Carolina settlements I–457b
Chickasaw–French War I–7b, 196b–97a; VII–70b
Côte des Allemands II–237a
Fort Assumption II–22a; IV–301b
Forte Condé II–158a
Fort Rosalie VI–164a
Fort Toulouse VII–77a
Louisiana II–22b, 91b; IV–192b
Mississippi IV–368a, 372a, 375b, 455a
Mobile IV–382a
Natchez VII–95b
New Orleans V–62a
Pensacola V–254a
Bierstadt, Albert (art.) II–102b
Bigamy V–355b; VI–399b
Big Band Era IV–440a–b
Big Bear supermarket VI–258a
Big Beaver Creek III–223b
Big Bend Dam VI–147a
Big Bend National Park V–219 (table)
Big Bethel, Battle of (1861) IV–399b
BIG BLACK RIVER, BATTLE OF (1863) **I–295b**
Big Blue River VII–280b
Big Bonanza (mine) II–157a
BIG BONE LICK (Ky.) **I–295b**; IV–39b
BIG BOTTOM MASSACRE (1791) **I–296a**
Big Brother and the Holding Company (mus.) IV–441a
BIG BROTHER MOVEMENT I–296a
Big business. *See* Business, Big
Big Dry (Mont.) V–241a
Big Elk (Indian) III–386b
Bigelow, Erastus B. (inv.) I–460b; IV–187b; VII–43b
Bigelow, Henry B. (zool.) V–135a
Bigelow, Jacob (physic., bot.) II–390b; III–408b; IV–297a; V–326b
Bigelow, John (dipl.) II–65a
Bigelow, Julian II–156a
Big Foot (Indian) IV–316a; VII–344b
Big Four of California I–406a
Big Four Railroad VI–35b
Biggs, Hermann M. (physic.) VII–126b–27a
Big Hole (Wyo.) VII–104a
BIG HOLE, BATTLE OF (1877) **I–296a**
Big Hole National Battlefield (Mont.) I–296a
Big Hole River I–296a
BIG HORN MOUNTAINS I–296a; III–119b
Bozeman Trail I–357b
Fort Phil Kearny IV–33b
Indian territory IV–108b
La Vérendrye exploration IV–118a
Bighorn River II–477a; III–32a
Fort C.F. Smith VI–317b
fur trade III–143a, 143a; VI–196a
Manuel's Fort IV–159b, 242a
Bighorn sheep VII–357b
BIG KNIVES I–296b; I–296b; III–375a
Big Lick (Va.). *See* Roanoke
Biglow, Hosea (lit. char.) I–296b
***BIGLOW PAPERS* I–296b**
BIG MOCCASIN GAP I–297a
Big Mound, Battle of (1863) II–283b
Big Mountains (Wasatch Range) IV–411b
"Big Muddy." *See* Missouri River
Bigordi, Domenico de Tommaso. *See* Ghirlandajo
"Big Pasture Lands" (Okla.) V–149a,b
Big Sandy country (Ky.) IV–39b
Big Sandy Creek VI–320a–b
Big Sandy River IV–43a
Big Sioux River II–131b, 284b; VII–106a
Big Spring River III–318b
Big Springs Convention (1855) IV–28a, 31a
"Big stick" policy I–391a; V–20a; VI–313a; VII–121b
Big Stone Lake II–380a; VII–234b
Big Three (auto ind.) IV–71b, 331b
Big Timber Creek IV–454a
Big top (circus) II–40b
Big Track (Indian) V–173b
Big Tree. *See* Sequoia VI–287b
Big Tree Reservation (N.Y.) V–139b
Bilbo, Theodore Gilmore (pol.) IV–369a
Billboards I–17b, 20a
Billerica (Mass.) II–6a
BILLETING I–297a; II–307a; VII–80a
Charter of Liberties I–500b
Mutiny Act of 1765 IV–445b
Quartering Act II–93a
Third Amendment II–204a
Bill Haley and the Comets (mus.) IV–441a
Billing, Edward (Quaker) II–388b
Billing machine I–396b
Billings (Mont.) II–419b; IV–403b
Billings, John Shaw (physic.) IV–2b, 149b, 292a–b; VII–207a
Billings, Josh (pseud.) I–91a
Billings, Warren K. (labor leader) IV–406a,b
Billings, William (comp.) III–326a; IV–438a
Bill of attainder. *See* Attainder
BILL OF RIGHTS I–297a; I–94a–b; II–204a–b; VI–391a; VII–201a
Barron v. *Baltimore* I–269b
billeting I–297a
civil rights and liberties II–53b
common law II–141b
Congress II–171b
courts IV–15b
due process II–377b, 378b
enumerated powers II–453b
Fourteenth Amendment III–86b
freedom of speech III–104a
Henry, Patrick V–161a
human rights III–316b
judicial review IV–14b
jury trial IV–21a
minority rights IV–358b
natural rights doctrine IV–140a
ratification of Constitution II–196b
right to bear arms IV–470a
Russia VI–177b
state government III–9a; VI–396b–97a
state police power V–339a,b
territorial government VII–32b
See also Constitution of the United States
Bill of Rights, English I–298b, 300b; II–191a; V–464a; VI–396a
Bill of Rights Day I–298b
BILLS OF CREDIT I–300a; III–9b
Briscoe v. *Bank of Kentucky* I–365a
Charleston (S.C.) V–404b
colonies II–94b; IV–393b; VII–3a
Continental Congress II–274b–75a, 299b
inflation III–414b
issuance by Congress IV–20a
public debt VI–94b
revolutionary war III–244b; V–123b; VI–117a–b, 120a
specie payments VI–370a
state II–200b, 253b
Bills of exchange. *See* Exchange, Bill of

BILLS OF RIGHTS, STATE **I–300b**; II–141b; VI–98a, 118b
Bill Williams River V–155b, 155b
Billy Budd IV–162a
"Billy in the Low Ground" (song) III–19a
Billy the Kid (William H. Bonney) IV–155a, 439a
Biloxi (Indians) III–367a; IV–368a
BILOXI (Miss.) **I–301a**; III–120a; IV–276b, 368a, 372a
Casket girls I–466a
Charlevoix's journey I–499a
Biloxi Bay I–301a
Biltmore (N.C.) I–164a; III–73b
Bimeler, Joseph Michael. *See* Baumler, Joseph Michael
BIMETALLISM **I–301a**; II–94a, 95a–b; III–192b, 193a; IV–392b, 395a; VI–288a–b, 289a
Bland–Allison Act I–318b
Coin's Financial School II–96a
Crime of 1873 II–264a
free silver III–110a
limping standard IV–154a
Populist party V–365b–66a
Silver League VI–288a
Silver Republicans VI–293a
specie payments VI–370b
Thomas Amendment VII–54b
Bimini (Bah.) V–356a
BINAC (computer) II–155b
Binary system II–426b
Binckes, Jacob (nav. off.) V–84a
Binder (agric. mach.) IV–211a
Binet, Alfred (physic.) III–440a
Bingham (Utah)
copper V–103b
Bingham, Caleb (educ.) VI–227a–b
Bingham, George C. (paint.) V–189b, 190b–91a
Bingham, Hiram (miss.) III–263a; IV–364b
Bingham, John A. (pol.) IV–6a
Bingham, William (fin.) I–302b; IV–89b
Bingham family V–73b
BINGHAM PURCHASE **I–302b**
Binghamton (N.Y.) I–41b
Bingo IV–191b
Binh Xuyen (gang) VII–183a
Binny, Archibald (typefounder) V–411b
Binny and Ronaldson V–411b, 413a
BIOCHEMISTRY **I–302b**; II–13a; V–307b
DNA II–357b
genetics III–157b–58a, 159a
mental health IV–287a
molecular biology IV–388b
nutrition V–127b
Rockefeller Foundation VI–158a
Biodegradable materials V–328b
Biogeography II–390a, 392a
Biography III–281a–b; IV–163a
Dictionary of American Biography II–340b
Biological research II–391a–b
Cold Spring Harbor II–97a
Marine Biological Laboratory IV–250b
Biological Sciences, Institute of. *See* American Institute of Biological Sciences
Biological Survey, Bureau of IV–233a; VII–297b
Biological warfare II–9b; VII–225b
Biology
deep-sea V–133a
electric circuit analysis II–38b–39a
fish and marine life III–26a
genetics III–157a, 158b
molecular IV–388b
physiology V–306a
plant ecology II–392a
Biomedical research I–241a; IV–465a,b
Biophysics IV–3b, 251a
Bioscope IV–417a
Biosystematic research IV–378b
Biotin V–128a
Birch (tree) III–74b; VII–59b
Birch, Francis A. (sci.) III–481a
Birch, John (miss.) IV–1b
Birch, John, Society. *See* John Birch Society
Birch, Thomas (engr.) V–413b
Birch, William (engr.) V–413b
Birch, William R. (paint.) V–188a
BIRCHARD LETTER (1863) **I–196a**, 304a
BIRCH BARK **I–304b**; III–366b
Abnaki I–2b
Algonquin I–86a
canoe I–445b; II–31a; III–381b
Chippewa II–31a
pictographs IV–335b
wigwam VII–294b
Birch Coulee, Battle of (1862) VI–296b
"Bircher." *See* John Birch Society
"Birch seal" III–226b
Bird, Henry (off.) I–306b, 367a; V–319b
Bird, Isabella I–367b–68a
Bird, William (metal.) III–300b
BIRDS **I–304b**; III–150a
Audubon, John James II–477a
Audubon Society I–222b
census II–390a
Hayden survey IV–233a
preservation V–217b; VII–296b, 297b
sanctuaries I–305b
wild turkeys VII–130a
Yellowstone Park VII–357b
Birds, state VI–392a, 393–95 (table)
Birdseye, Clarence (inv.) III–55b; VI–70a
BIRD'S INVASION OF KENTUCKY (1780) **I–306b**
Birds of America VII–130a
BIRD'S POINT (Mont.) **I–306b**
Birge, Edward A. (nat.) II–391a
Birge, Raymond T. (phys.) V–299b
Birkbeck, Morris (au.) I–367b–68a, 367b–68a; II–450b
Birkeland–Eyde process III–17a
Birkenhead (Eng.) IV–85a
Birmingham (Ala.) V–67b; VII–191a
civil rights movement I–72a; II–55a, 58b
Freedom Riders III–107a
iron and steel industry III–470b
race riots I–31a–b; VI–8b
railroads VI–34b, 36b
steel manufacture III–473b
Birmingham (cruiser) I–54a, 233b
Birmingham (Eng.) III–64b
Birmingham Cooperative Marketing Act (1922) II–221b
Birmingham Meetinghouse (Pa.) I–360a
Birney, James G. (abolitionist) I–136a, 137a
Matilda Lawrence case IV–276b
Philanthropist V–279b
presidential candidate I–138a, 420a,b; IV–143b, 143b
Birth Control League, National I–307a
BIRTH CONTROL MOVEMENT **I–307a**; IV–256b–57a; VI–266a
American Civil Liberties Union I–100b
censorship I–478b
demographic studies II–328b
Goldman, Emma I–116b
Oneida Colony V–155b
public health V–448a
venereal disease VII–169b
Birth defects III–158b
Birth of a Nation (film) IV–58b, 417b
Birthrate II–328a, 486b; V–361b–62a,b
colonial period IV–150a
Births
record-keeping VII–205b, 206b, 207a
Bisbee (Ariz.) I–172b
Bisbee copper mine II–223a
Biscay, Bay of IV–189a
Biscayne Bay III–39b; IV–302b
Biscayne National Monument V–217b
Biscuits III–52a; IV–280b
Bishop, Bridget (col.) VII–310a
Bishop, Cortland Field I–332b, 333a
Bishop, Henry (comp.) III–297a
Bishop, K. S. (sci.) V–128a
Bishop, Stephen (guide) IV–233b
BISHOP HILL COLONY **I–307b**; II–147a
Bishop's Committee for Ecumenical and Interreligious Affairs I–470a
Bismarck (N.Dak.) II–283b, 285a; V–117a, 118a
blizzard of 1888 I–320b
Fort Abraham Lincoln I–312b
railroads VI–407a
Bismarck (battleship) VII–242a
BISMARCK SEA, BATTLE OF (1943) **I–307b**
Bismuth VII–169a
Bison. *See* Buffalo
"Bisquick" III–44b
Bissell, G. A. (law.) V–269a
Bissell, Israel V–85b
Bissell, Wilson S. (law.) VI–172b
BIT (cur.) **I–308a**; II–94b
Bitter, Karl (sculp.) VI–243b
Bitterroot VI–394 (table)
Bitterroot Mountains IV–177a; V–89b, 225a; VI–413a
Bitterroot River V–178b
Bitterroot Valley III–477a; IV–403a, 403a, 403a
Bitumens IV–44a
Bituminous coal. *See* Coal
Bituminous Coal Conservation Act (1935) II–136b, 481b; III–231b
Bituminous Coal Stabilization Act (1935) V–47a–b
BIZERTE (Tun.) **I–308a**; V–113a; VII–338a
World War II IV–32b
Bjerknes, Jakob A. B. (meteor.) IV–317b
Bjerknes, Vilhelm (phys.) III–233b; IV–317b
Black (destroyer) V–22a
Black, Green Vardiman (dent.) II–331a
Black, Harold S. (phys.) I–287b; II–39a
Black, Hugo (jur.) VI–446b
Adamson v. *California* V–353b
Bill of Rights I–299b, 300a

due process of law II–378a,b
freedom of speech III–104a–b
freedom of the press III–105a
Japanese-American relocation III–491a
Black, James (pol.) V–430b
Black, Jeremiah S. (states.) I–91b; V–234b
Black, Joseph (educ.) II–10b
Black, Samuel W. (gov.) V–31b
Black, William (phot.) I–248a
"Black ball" IV–269a
BLACK BALL LINE I–308b; V–183b; VI–280b; VII–349a
Black bear I–280b
Blackbeard (Edward Teach) (pirate) I–374a
BLACK BELT I–308b; V–325a; VI–305b
Blackberries III–51a, 129a
Blackbird (Idaho) III–14a
Black Boy IV–167a
BLACK BOYS I–309a; I–278a
Fort Bedford attack I–282b
Fort Loudon IV–191b
Sideling Hill VI–285a
Blackburn, Joseph (paint.) V–186b, 187a
BLACKBURN'S FORD, BATTLE AT (1861) **I–309a**; I–381a
Black Canyon of the Colorado II–129b
Black Canyon of the Gunnison V–217b
BLACK CAPITALISM I–309a; I–316b
Black Carolina Corps VI–130a
Black Cat (patrol plane) I–55b
Black Catholics, National Office for. *See* National Office for Black Catholics
BLACK CAVALRY IN THE WEST I–309b; IV–339b–40a; VI–301a
Black cockade II–437b
BLACK CODES I–310a; IV–369a; VI–56b, 304b–05a
Kansas IV–31a
See also Code Noir
Black-Connery bill (1933) II–481b
Black Crook (play) V–93b
Blackett, P. M. S. (phys.) V–301b
Black-eyed Susan VI–394 (table)
Blackface minstrelsy IV–438a
Black Fish (Indian) I–337a
BLACKFOOT (Indians) **I–310b**; III–227a, 363b, 365a, 396b
Ashley expedition I–201a
Battle of Pierre's Hole V–310b
Fort Assiniboine I–206a
half-breeds III–242b
Henrys Fork III–273a
horse III–303a
Jesuit missions III–500a,b
language I–86a, 441a
Mackenzie's Treaty IV–217a
Manuel's Fort IV–242a
medicine III–385a
Missouri Fur Company IV–378a
Missouri River IV–380b
Montana IV–403a
Piegan War V–310a
Saint Louis Missouri Fur Company VI–196a
sign language VI–286b
warfare VII–239a
BLACK FRIDAY (1869) **I–311a**; V–346a–b; VI–413b
Black Hawk (Indian). *See* Black Hawk War
Blackhawk (Colo.) VI–292b, 316b
Black Hawk Purchase (1832) I–312a; III–383b, 384b
BLACK HAWK WAR (1832) **I–311b**; II–297a; III–88b, 127a; IV–122a; VII–239a
Fort Howard III–311b
Fort Winnebago VII–306a
Illinois III–329b
Iowa land cession III–468a
Jefferson Barracks III–494b
rangers VI–46b
Treaty of Fort Armstrong III–384b, 404a
Wisconsin VII–307b
BLACK HILLS I–312a; VI–350a
columbite mines III–14b
Custer expedition VII–272b
Dakota Indians II–283b
floods II–352a; III–37a
gold II–16b, 283b, 285a; III–191b; IV–109a; V–179a; VI–379b
Kiowa IV–50b
Sioux V–437b
Black Hills National Forest I–312b
Black Hills spruce (tree) VI–395 (table)
BLACK HILLS WAR (1876) **I–313a**; I–312b; IV–109a; VI–297a
Battle of Little Bighorn IV–167b
Battle of Slim Buttes VI–312b
BLACK HORSE CAVALRY I–313b; VI–71b
BLACK INFANTRY IN THE WEST I–313b; I–310a; IV–339b–40a
"Black is Beautiful" I–25a
Black Jack (Kans.) I–342a
BLACK JACK, BATTLE OF (1856) **I–314a**
Black Kettle (Indian) VI–208a; VII–252b
BLACK LAWS I–314a
"Black Legend" (Spain) VI–358b
BLACK LEGION I–314a
BLACKLEGS I–314b
Black liberation movement I–315b; II–56b
BLACKLISTING I–314b; II–86a; IV–61b, 471b; VII–325a
Blacklock, William I–497a
Black lung IV–293b, 294b
Blackmail
Black Horse Cavalry I–313b
Black market
inflation III–415a
World War II II–236a; V–401b
Black militancy I–136a, 138a, 315b
Black Mountain poets IV–165b
Blackmun, Harry A. (jur.) VI–447b
BLACK MUSLIMS I–315a; I–24a, 220a; V–170b–71a, 423a
BLACK NATIONALISM I–315b; III–254a; V–170b, 200a
Blackouts, power II–153a
BLACK PANTHERS I–315b
BLACK PATCH WAR (1906–08) **I–316a**; IV–41b; V–96a
Black Pioneers VI–130a, 131a
Black Point (Maine) IV–207b; VI–184a
Black powder II–7a; V–383a,b
BLACK POWER I–316a; I–25a; II–59a; V–76a; VI–315a
"Black religion" I–25a
Black River II–460a; III–199b
Black River Canal I–443b
Blackrobes. *See* Jesuit Missions; Jesuits
Black Rock (N.Y.) III–218a; V–91a; VII–220b
BLACK ROCK, BOMBARDMENT OF (1812) **I–316b**
Black Rock Desert III–215a
Blacks. *See* Afro-Americans
Blacks, Free. *See* Free Blacks
Blacksburg (Va.) II–369b
Black Sea III–106a,b
Black Sea pledges I–73b
Black-seed cotton II–237b, 240a
Black September Organization III–277b
Black's Fork (Wyo.) I–363a
BLACKSMITHING I–316a; III–77a, 413b, 472a–b; VI–291b; VII–82a
hardware III–252a
unionization IV–62a
wagon manufacture VII–216a
Blacksnake Hills VI–191b
"Black Sox" scandal (1921) I–270b
Black stem rust VII–268a
Blackstock's Hill, Battle of. *See* Enoree, Battle of
Blackstock's Plantation (S.C.) II–451b
Blackstone, Sir William (jur.) IV–120b
on jury trial IV–21a
prisons V–415a
separation of powers II–4b; V–384b–85a
Blackstone Canal IV–174b
Blackstone Rangers (gang) VI–328b
Blackstone River IV–347b; V–230b; VI–133b
Black studies II–115a, 402b
BLACK SWAMP I–317b
BLACK WARRIOR AFFAIR (1854) **I–317b**
Black Warrior River I–402a; VII–70b
Black Warrior-Tombigbee Waterway VI–147a
Black Watch III–330b
BLACKWATER, BATTLE OF (1861) **I–317b**
Blackwater Draw (N.Mex.) II–83b; III–484b
Blackwater River VII–275b
Blackwelder Manufacturing Company I–35b
Black Widow (fighter plane) I–53b
Bladensburg (Md.) I–248a
BLADENSBURG, BATTLE OF (1814) **I–317b**; IV–251b; VII–249b
rockets VI–159a
BLADENSBURG DUELING FIELD I–318a; II–376b–77a
Blaine, James G. (states.) II–175 (table); III–152b
campaign of 1876 I–422b
campaign of 1880 I–423b
campaign of 1884 I–383a, 423b, 424a; IV–425b
campaign of 1892 I–424b
Latin America policy IV–111a
Mafia incident IV–221b
Mulligan letters IV–426a
Nast cartoons IV–454b
prison reform V–415b
reciprocal trade agreements VI–343b
sealing VI–245b–46a
Blair, Chauncy II–104a
Blair, Fort (W.Va.) *See* Randolph, Fort
Blair, Francis P., Jr. (states.)
Battles on Peachtree Creek V–238b
campaign of 1868 I–422a
Blair, Francis P., Sr. (states.) IV–51a
Confederate peace negotiations II–165a; V–234b
Hampton Roads Conference III–247b
Washington Globe III–187b

Blair, James (cler., educ.) VII–300a–b
Blair, John (jur.) II–203b; VI–445a
Blair, Montgomery (law., states.) V–373a
Blair, W. Frank (nat.) VI–91b
Blair House (Washington, D.C.) I–202b
Blair's Gap I–89a
Blair v. *Williams* (1823) V–151a
Blake (steamer) III–29a, 233a
Blake, George A. H. (off.) IV–268b
Blake, Lyman R. (inv.) I–338a
Blake, Robert (nav. off.) VII–270b
Blakelock, Ralph A. (paint.) V–189b–90a
Blakely, Johnston (nav. off.) VII–253a
Blakeslee Mirror Company III–135b
Blakiston Company (pub.) I–334a
Blanca Peak (Colo.) IV–268b
Blanchard, Frank N. (nat.) VI–91a
Blanchard, Jean-Pierre (aeron.) I–248a
Blanchard, Thomas (inv.) III–441b–42a; IV–216a, 272b
Blanchet, François Norbert (cler.) V–165a
Blanc Mont (Fr.) IV–252b
Blanco Encalada (warship) VII–76a
Blanc Trust suit (1890) III–146a
Bland, Bobby (mus.) IV–440a
Bland, Humphrey (off.) VI–126a
Bland, Richard P. (pol.) III–110b; VII–300b
Bland-Allison Act I–318b
BLAND-ALLISON ACT (1878) **I–318b**; I–302a; II–96a; III–110b; IV–154a–b, 395a; VI–288b, 371a
Blankets III–402b
fur trade III–140a,b
Blashfield, Edwin Howland (paint.) V–191a
Blast furnace-converter process II–223b
Blast furnaces II–17b; III–12b
BLAST FURNACES, EARLY I–318b; III–77a, 411b, 472a–b; IV–123a
Blasting powder V–383a–b
Blatchford, Samuel (jur.) VI–446a
Blaumiler, Joseph II–147a
Blavatski, Helena Petrovna (rel. leader) V–172a; VII–51b–52a
Bleach III–408b
cotton industry II–239a
flour industry III–45b
hair styling III–239a
manufacture II–10a
Blease, Coleman L. (pol.) *See* Blease Movement
BLEASE MOVEMENT I–319a; VII–59a
Bleeding Kansas. *See* Border War; Kansas Struggle
Blennerhassett, Harman I–319b, 387b
BLENNERHASSETT ISLAND I–319b; I–388b
BLESSING OF THE BAY (bark) **I–319b**
Blickensderfer typewriter VII–136b
Blimps II–343b–45b
Blind VI–72b, 74a
education III–248a,b
library service IV–147b
social legislation VI–327b
Blind pig. *See* Speakeasy
Blind tiger. *See* Speakeasy
Bliss, Fort (Tex.) II–433a–b; VI–144a
Bliss, Tasker H. (off.) V–247b
Blister rust III–74b
Blitzstein, Marc (comp.) IV–438b
BLIZZARDS I–319b; II–351a–52a
National Weather Service VII–264a
range cattle industry V–33a
Bloch, Felix (phys.) V–100a, 295b, 304a
Bloch, Konrad (biochem.) V–100a
Block, Adriaen (expl.) II–179b; III–31a; IV–264b
Block, Herbert L. ("Herblock") (cartoon.) I–464b; V–73a
BLOCKADE I–320b; II–270b–71a, 436b, 446a–b
armed neutrality of 1780 I–175b–76a
Berlin I–60b–61a, 290b–91b; II–98a, 218b
Civil War I–73a, 116a, 121b, 245b, 292a, 321b–22a, 497a; II–61b–62a, 65a–b, 67a, 69a, 161a, 162a, 163a, 238a, 384a, 446b; III–148b, 234b; IV–20b, 371a, 383a; V–17b, 19b, 34b–35a, 116a, 421a–b, 424a; VI–220b, 405a, 425a; VII–94a, 146b, 147a
continuous voyage doctrine II–446b
Cuban missile crisis III–463b
Declaration of London V–233b
Declaration of Paris V–214a, 324a; VII–225b
enemy destination doctrine II–446a–47a
freedom of the seas III–106b
Mexican War IV–322a
Napoleonic Wars III–118b, 455b; V–162a
Napoleon's decrees IV–449b
neutral rights V–38b
Peterhoff case V–264a
retaliation in international law VI–104b
revolutionary war II–5b; VI–128b, 367b
slave trade VI–322a
Spanish-American War VI–216b, 361a–b, 363a
Texas Revolution VII–41b
Venezuela VII–169b–70a
Vietnam War V–22a
visit and search VII–204b
war contraband II–212b
War of 1812 I–325b; IV–309b; V–83a; VII–235a–b
World War I I–176b; II–12a, 446b; V–119b; VII–94a, 324b–25a
World War II I–274a, 328b
world wars III–456a
BLOCKADE RUNNERS, CONFEDERATE I–321b; II–65a, 162b–63a, 313b; V–19b; VII–146b
Albemarle I–83a
Bahamas I–243b
bayous I–279a
contraband of war II–213a
Florida III–40b
Fort Fisher III–30b
Fort Saint Marks VI–196b
Jürgen Lorentzen IV–20b
Laird rams IV–85a
Mobile IV–382b
North Carolina V–116a
prize money V–424a
stone fleets VI–415a
Block-front furniture III–134b, 138a
Block-grant program (housing) II–48a
Blockhouses
Fort King George IV–46b
Fort Kiowa IV–51a
Fort Meigs IV–300b
Fort Smith VI–317a
Fort Steuben VI–412b
Fort Union VII–145b
Fort Western VII–269b
Johnson Hall IV–4b
McIntyre Garrison IV–179a
water supply VI–377b
Wilderness Road VII–296b
Block Island V–261a; VI–134b
Block-ship III–36a
"BLOCKS OF FIVE" I–322a
Blockwood IV–181b
BLOCS I–322a
farm I–451b
Greenback party III–225a
Blodget, Samuel (mer.) III–427b
Blodgett, William T. (mfr.) II–102a
Blodgett v. *Holden* (1927) IV–12b
Bloembergen, N. (phys.) IV–262b
Blomen, Henning (pol.) VI–325b
Blommaert, Samuel (bus.) V–81a, 229a; VII–372b
"Blondie" (comic strip) V–72b
Blood
donation VI–62a
military medical care IV–291a
study of I–303a
Bloodgood, Abraham (inv.) III–36a
Blood Indians I–311a; III–365a; V–310a
"BLOOD IS THICKER THAN WATER" I–322b
Bloodletting IV–229b; VII–355b
BLOODY ANGLE (1864) **I–322b**; VI–376b; VII–197b
BLOODY ISLAND I–322b; II–377a
BLOODY MARSH, BATTLE OF (1742) **I–323a**; III–498a; VI–349a
BLOODY MONDAY (1855) **I–323a**
BLOODY POND, BATTLE OF (1755) **I–323a**; III–115b
Bloody Ridge, Battle of (1942) III–229b
BLOODY RUN, BATTLE OF (1763) **I–323b**
BLOODY SHIRT I–323b; II–64b
campaign of 1876 I–423a
Bloom, Sol (pol.) VII–151a
Bloomer, Amelia (ref.) I–323b
BLOOMER DRESS I–323b
Bloomfield Steamship Company IV–312a
Bloomingdale Asylum for the Insane II–132b
Bloomington (Ill.) V–462b
Bloor, William (mfr.) III–184b
Blount, Fort (Tenn.) II–273b
Blount, James Henderson (dipl.) II–471a
Blount, William (pol.) I–324a; II–203b
Holston Treaty III–292a
Muscle Shoals colony IV–435b
Southwest Territory II–22b; VI–358a
Blount, Winton M. (offi., pol.) V–374a,b
Blount College. *See* Tennessee, University of
BLOUNT CONSPIRACY I–324a
Blow, Henry T. (pol.) IV–6a
Blow, Susan Elizabeth (educ.) II–398b
Blowers, Sampson Salter (sol.) I–346a
Blowgun III–366b
BLS. *See* Bureau of Labor Statistics

Blubaugh, Douglas (athlete) V–154b
BLUE AND GRAY I–324a
"Blue-backed spelling book" II–394a
BLUEBACKS I–324a
Blueberries III–51a, 129a
Bluebird VI–394 (table)
Bluebonnet (flower) VI–395 (table)
"Blue Book" (mil. manual) I–183b
"Blue-collar blues" IV–77b
BLUE-COLLAR WORKERS I–324a; II–239b; IV–75a
Blue Cross III–307b, 435b, 436a
BLUE EAGLE EMBLEM I–324b; II–92a; V–44b
Blue Earth River IV–355a
Bluefish (submarine) VII–139a
Blue Grass Band IV–441b
BLUEGRASS COUNTRY I–324b; III–304b; IV–39b, 40b, 329b
Bluegrass music IV–441b
Blue Grass State VI–394 (table)
Blue hen chicken VI–393 (table)
Blue jeans II–372b
BLUE LAWS I–324b; IV–408a; VI–440a
Blue Licks (Ky.) VI–100b
BLUE LICKS, BATTLE OF (1782) **I–325b**; III–400b
  Bryan's Station I–373b
Blue Licks River VII–238b
Blue Licks Springs I–325a
"Bluelight Federalists" I–325b
BLUE LIGHTS I–325b
BLUE LODGES I–325b; VI–339b
Blue Mesa Dam II–130a
Blue Mountains V–169a
Blue Point (Maine) VI–184a
Blue Pup currency II–275a
Blue Ridge Gap V–224b
Blue Ridge Mountains III–251a, 488b; VII–201b
  agriculture VII–194a
  Ashby's Gap I–200b
  Augusta Company I–223b
  Baltimore and Ohio Railroad VI–25a
  Batts-Fallam expedition I–277b
  Chester's Gap V–224b
  Lederer's expedition IV–131a
  Shenandoah Valley VI–275b
  Spotswood's expedition IV–53a
  Treaty of Hopewell III–383a
  Tryon's Line VII–125b
  Virginia Path VII–202b
  Washington District VII–250a
  westward movement VII–283a
Blue Ridge Parkway V–220a; VII–196a
Blue Ridge Railroad I–325b
BLUE RIDGE TUNNEL I–325b
Blue River V–168b, 334b
Blues (mus.) III–48b, 49a; IV–439b–40a,b, 443a–b
Blues for Mr. Charlie (play) IV–167a
BLUE SKY LAWS I–325b; IV–26b
Blues People IV–166b
Blue spruce VI–393 (table), 395 (table)
BLUESTEM PASTURES (Kans.) **I–326a**
Bluestem wheat VII–286a
Blue Swallowtail Line V–183b
Blue whale VII–285b
BLUFFTON MOVEMENT I–326a
Blumlein, A. D. (inv.) V–290b
Blunder, Fort. *See* Rouse's Point Boundary Controversy
Blunt, James (off.) V–389a
Blyden, Edward W. (au.) I–315b
Blynman, Richard (cler.) I–446b
Blyth, Samuel (off.) II–452b
Blythe, David G. (paint.) V–189b
B'nai B'rith IV–10a,b
Board, Cornelius VI–412a
Boardly, John Beal V–187b
Board of election II–411a
Board of Engineers for Rivers and Harbors VI–146b
Board of Foreign Scholarships III–131a
Board of Governors of the Federal Reserve System I–260a
Board of Indian Commissioners III–371b, 378b; IV–387b
Board of Mediation, U.S. II–500b
Board of Mediation and Conciliation IV–68b
Board of Missions of the Presbyterian General Assembly IV–365b
Board of National Popular Education VI–299b
Board of Overseers, Harvard III–259b, 260a
Board of Tax Appeals, U.S. II–500b
Board of Trade (Washington, D.C.) VII–245a–b
BOARD OF TRADE AND PLANTATIONS I–326b; IV–188b; V–421a, 425a; VI–108b–09a,b, 363b
  agents II–116b–17a
  Alberton Company I–213a
  American defense system IV–46b
  commerce VI–110b
  councils II–119b
  Fort Stanwix Treaty VI–386a
  judiciary II–121a
  manufacturing restrictions IV–242b
  Mitchell's Map IV–381a
  naval stores V–14b
  rights of Englishmen VI–140b
  royal colonies VI–166b
Board of Trade of the City of Chicago V–320b–21a
Board of War. *See* War Department
Boards of education. *See* Education, Boards of
Boards of trade I–491a; II–141a, 281b
  See also Chambers of Commerce
Boas, Franz (anthrop.) I–128b–29a; II–465a; III–374a; IV–59a
Boates, Billy (slaver) VI–310b
"Boating acts" II–89b–90a
Boating safety II–89b–90a
Boats
  arks I–175a
  bateaux I–274a
  flatboats III–35b
  galley boats III–147b
  keelboat IV–35a
  Mackinaw boat IV–218a
  snagboats VI–322a
  See also Shipbuilding; Warships
Boatswain's Creek IV–282a
Bobby socks II–372b
Bobsledding V–154b
Bobsleds VII–168a
Bodega Bay (Calif.) VI–180b
Bodhidharma (monk) V–171b
Bodleian Library VI–18b; VII–302b
Body of Liberties. *See* Massachusetts Body of Liberties
Boehme, Jacob II–454a
Boehn, Max von (off.) I–286a, 491b
  Oise-Aisne operation V–147a
Boeing 247 (transport plane) I–51a, 236b
Boeing 307 (transport plane) I–52a
Boeing 707 (transport plane) I–52b, 68b, 237b; II–347a,b
Boeing 727 (transport plane) II–347b
Boeing 747 (transport plane) I–52b, 69a
Boeing, William E. (av.) I–51b, 235b; 236b–
Boeing Aircraft Company I–237a; III–452a; VII–248a
Boeing SST (transport plane) I–53a
Boerstler, C. G. (off.) I–281b
Boer War (1899–1902) I–122b
  neutrality III–456a
Boethuk (Indians) I–441a
Bofor (machine gun) V–27a
Bogardus, A. H. VII–298b
Bogardus, James (inv.) I–164b
Boggs, Hale (pol.) VII–238a
Boggs, Lillburn W. (gov.) II–496a; IV–377b
Boggy Creek (Okla.) IV–334a
BOG IRON MINING I–327a; III–77a; VI–218a
Bogotá (Colom.)
  Organization of American States V–171a, 205a
Bogotá Conference (1948) III–456b
Bohemia IV–409b
  immigration to U.S. III–339b, 340a
Bohemia Manor (Md.) IV–59b
Bohlen, Tommy VII–349a
Bohr, Niels (phys.) V–298a, 300a, 300a, 301b, 302a, 304a
Bohr theory of the atom IV–262a
Boies, Horace (pol.) III–468b
Boisbriant, Pierre Duque (off.) IV–32a
Bois d'arc (tree) V–174a
Bois de la Brigade Marine I–286b
Bois de Sioux VI–63b
Boise (Idaho) I–203b; III–328a,b
BOISE, FORT (Idaho) **I–327b**; V–168b; VI–185b
Boise River I–327b; V–169a
Bok, Derek Curtis (educ.) III–260b
Bok, Edward William (ed.) I–19a
Bolden, Charles ("Buddy") (mus.) IV–440a
Boleslavski, Richard (act.) VII–50a
Bolingbroke, 1st Viscount, Henry Saint John (states.) VI–2b
Bolivar (Ohio) III–223b
Bolívar, Simón (states.) IV–110b; V–203a; VII–170a
Bolivia V–233a
  Chaco War V–205a
  corn II–225a
  Dominican missions II–362b
  Franciscans III–94b
  Good Neighbor policy III–199a
  independence IV–111a
  Nitrate War III–16b
  Santiago Inter-American Congress VI–217a
  U.S. trade VI–346a
Bolling v. *Sharpe* (1954) I–372b; II–54b
Bollman, Justus Erich (adventurer) I–327b
Bollman, Wendel (arch.) I–364a
BOLLMAN CASE (1807) **I–327b**
BOLL WEEVIL I–327b; I–26a; II–238a–b; III–421a; IV–103a
Bolm, Adolph (dancer) II–288b

Bologna (It.) III–201a
School of Advanced International Studies IV–3b
Bolon, A. J. (Indian agent) VII–350a
Bolshevik Revolution (1917) III–342b; VI–178a–b, 181a, 326a,b; VII–325b, 328b
Bolsheviks VI–283b–84a
Bolshevism
Communist Party, USA II–143b
World War I peace conference VII–331a
BOLTERS I–328a
campaign of 1884 IV–425b
Silver Grays VI–288a
Silver Republicans VI–292b
Bolton, Herbert E. (hist.) V–155a
Bomarc (missile) I–58b, 62a; IV–363b
Bomb, atomic. *See* Atomic Bomb
Bombay (India) II–388a
Bombé double chests III–134b
Bombers. *See* Aircraft, Bomber; Dive Bombers; Scout Bombers
BOMBING I–328a; V–26b–27a
Cambodia I–411a
carriers VII–241a
civil rights movement II–58a–b
Germany I–67a
Haymarket Square Riot II–17b
Iwo Jima III–485b
Japan I–67b; III–489b
Laos II–316a
navy research V–28a
Normandy invasion V–111a
Ploesti oil fields V–332a
retaliation in international law VI–104b
tests I–234a
Vietnam War I–431a; II–316a; IV–107b; VII–183b, 184b
World War II III–174a–b; IV–83a; VII–335a, 337b, 339a–b, 340a, 341a, 343b
Bombs. *See* Munitions; Ordnance
Bombsight I–51a
Bonanza Creek IV–51b; V–437a
BONANZA KINGS I–329a
BONANZA WHEAT FARMING I–329a
Bonaparte, Charles Joseph (law.) II–503a
Bonaparte, Jerome III–122b
Bonaparte, Joseph III–122b; VI–218a, 359a
Bonaparte, Lucien (dipl.) VI–211a
Bonaparte, Napoleon. *See* Napoleon I
Bonapartists III–121b
Bond, Thomas (physic.) III–306b; V–251b
Bond, William C. (astron.) I–211a
Bonds
banknotes I–256a
Civil War financing II–63a, 66a, 164a, 317a
investment banking III–466a
state banking I–259a
Bonds, government I–258a
foreign investment III–65a
liberty loans IV–143a
local governments IV–172a–b
Morgan–Belmont Agreement IV–410a
national bank notes IV–461b
taxation VII–12a–b
See also Debt, Public
Bonds, municipal
taxation VII–5b, 6a,b
Bonds, state
foreign investors III–63b–64a
taxation VII–5b
Bonds, tax-exempt IV–6b
Bond transfers VII–7b
Bond v. *Floyd* (1966) III–93b
Bone (Tun.). *See* Annaba
Bone tools II–334b
Bonfils, Frederick G. (ed.) V–73b
Bonham, M. L. (off.) I–381a
Bonhomme Richard (Indiaman) VII–241b
***BONHOMME RICHARD–SERAPIS* ENCOUNTER** (1779) **I–329a**; I–89b; V–18b; VI–129a; VII–240a, 241b
Boni, Albert (pub.) I–334b
Boni, Charles (pub.) I–334b
Bonifacio, Andres (rev.) V–282b
Bonifacius VI–81a
BONITO IN CHACO CANYON I–329b; I–117b
national monument V–217b
Bonner, Robert (pub.) IV–222a
Bonnet Carre spillway V–356b
Bonnet rouge. See Liberty Cap
Bonnets II–371a–b
Bonneville, Benjamin L. E. de (off.) III–311b
See also Bonneville Expedition
Bonneville, Fort (Wyo.) I–330a; III–227a
Bonneville, Lake III–163b
Bonneville Dam I–465a; II–285b; III–322a; V–455b; VI–147a
BONNEVILLE EXPEDITION (1832–34) **I–329b**; I–453a; III–143b; VII–217a–b
Columbia River II–131b
mapping VII–74b
Oregon Trail V–168b
South Pass VI–354b–55a
Sublette's Cutoff VI–422a
Walker party VII–220a
Bonneville Power Administration III–445a
Bonneville Salt Flats (Utah) I–231b
Bonney, William H. *See* Billy the Kid
Bonney and Bush. *See* Lobdell Car Wheel Company
"BONNIE BLUE FLAG" I–330a
Bonnin, Gousse (mfr.) III–183b
Bonnin and Morris V–379b
Bonpland, Aimé (nat.) III–166a; IV–248a
BONUS ARMY I–330a; I–331b; IV–70b; V–257b, 265b; VII–246b
Bonus Bill (1924) V–257b
BONUS BILL, CALHOUN'S (1816) **I–330b**; III–448b; VI–450a
BONUSES, MILITARY I–330b
GI Bill of Rights III–178b
reenlistment II–451a
state II–303a
"Bonus Expeditionary Force" I–330b
Bonython, Richard VI–184a
BOOBY TRAPS I–332a; V–258a
BOODLE I–332a
Boogie–Woogie (mus.) IV–440a
BOOK AUCTIONS I–332b; II–108a–b, 109a–b
Book Award, National. *See* National Book Award
Book Collecting. *See* Collecting: Books and Manuscripts
Booker T. Washington National Monument V–217b
Bookkeeping machine I–396b
Bookmaking II–260a–b, 261b
Book of Common Prayer II–455a
Book of Concord IV–205b
Book of Confessions V–392a
Book of Discipline (Methodism) IV–318b
Book of Knowledge II–444b
Book of Mormon. *See* Mormon, Book of
Book of the General Lawes and Libertyes (1648) IV–265a, 271a
BOOK PUBLISHING I–333a
Bay Psalm Book I–279b
Chicago II–18b
copyright II–224b
electronic printing II–426b
Johns Hopkins University Press IV–2b
McGuffey's Readers IV–213a
Nashville IV–453a
New York City II–41b; V–83b
New York State V–87b
New York Times properties V–76b
Russell Sage Foundation VI–177a
Smithsonian Institution VI–320a
BOOKS, CHILDREN'S I–335a
early schoolbooks VI–227a
Elements of Geography IV–413b
encyclopedias II–444b
hornbook III–301b
New England Primer V–51b
Peter Parley V–264b
BOOMER MOVEMENT I–335b; I–310a; V–148b, 150a
Boompjes Hoek. *See* Gloucester (N.J.)
BOOMTOWNS I–336a
coal fields II–45b
mining IV–354a
Oklahoma V–149a
Pithole V–321a
Virginia City III–191b; VII–199b
BOONDOGGLING I–336b
New Deal V–46a
Boone, Daniel (pioneer) II–477a; III–302b; IV–185a, 303b; VI–450b; VII–239a
Big Moccasin Gap I–297a
Bluegrass Country I–324b
Boonesborough I–337a
Charleston (W.Va.) I–497b
Cumberland Gap II–272a
daughter kidnapped I–337a
Indian land titles IV–92b
Kentucky III–24b; IV–40a; VI–455a
Powell's Valley V–384b
Tennessee VII–25a
Wilderness Road VI–153a; VII–296a
Boone, Israel (pioneer) I–337b
Boone, Jemima I–337a
Boone, Nathan (off.) IV–33b
Boone, Richard II–148a
Boone and Crockett Club VII–298a
BOONE–CALLAWAY KIDNAPPING (1776) **I–336b**
Boone County (Ky.) I–295b
BOONESBOROUGH (Ky.) **I–337a**; I–324b; IV–40a; VI–356a; VII–25a, 103a, 283b, 296a
Boone–Callaway kidnapping I–336b
Cumberland Gap II–272a
Cumberland River II–273a
Indian raids III–239a
Boone's Creek (Ky.) I–337b
Boone's Gap III–223b
BOONE'S STATION I–337b

Boone's Trail III–387b
BOONTON IRON WORKS I–337b
Boonville (Calif.) II–346a
BOONVILLE, BATTLE OF (1861) **I–337b**; I–462a
Boorstin, Daniel (hist.) III–283a
BOOST, Project V–24a
Boot, Henry A. H. (phys.) VII–163b
Boot and Shoe Manufacturers Association, National I–338b
BOOT AND SHOE MANUFACTURING I–337b; VII–83a
Boston I–344b
foreign trade VII–84b, 90a
Knights of St. Crispin IV–62b
leather industry IV–128a–b
Massachusetts IV–266b, 267b
mechanization IV–62b
moccasin IV–384b
Newark V–41a–b
New Hampshire V–54b
Philadelphia Cordwainers' Case V–278b
protective organization IV–60b
rubber VI–167a,b
Salem VI–199b
trust-busting VII–124a
Boot and Shoe Workers Union, International I–338b
Booth, Catherine Mumford VI–204b
Booth, Edwin (act.) VII–49a
Booth, Evangeline Cory VI–204b
Booth, John Wilkes IV–154b, 261a; VI–285a
Booth, Sherman I–2a
Booth, Wilbur F. (jur.) I–339a
Booth, ("General") William (preacher) VI–204a–b
Boothia Peninsula V–122a
Boot Hill VII–71a
cow towns II–252a
Dodge City II–358b
Booth's Theatre (N.Y.C.) VII–49a
BOOTH* v. *UNITED STATES (1934) **I–339a**
BOOTLEGGING I–339a; VII–23b
Anti-Saloon League I–134a
Chicago II–18a
moonshine IV–407b
organized crime II–259b, 261a–62a
padlock injunction V–184b
Prohibition II–407a
Secret Service VI–252a
Boots II–370b, 371a, 372a,b
Bootstrap, Operation V–461b
Borah, William E. (pol.) III–328b, 480a; V–427b
BORAX I–340a; II–297b
Borax Company, United States. *See* United States Borax Company
Bordeaux (Fr.) II–217a
Borden, Gail (inv.) II–280a
Borden, Lizzie VII–118a
Borden Dairy Products II–282a
Bordentown (N.J.) I–443a; VI–24b–25a; VII–116a,b
BORDER FORTS, EVACUATION OF I–340b; II–484b; III–142b, 217b, 493a, 494a; V–157a; VII–270a
BORDER RUFFIANS I–341a; I–342a, 388b; II–439a; IV–25b–26a, 31a
BORDER SLAVE STATE CONVENTION (1861) **I–341b**; II–149b; VI–251a
BORDER STATES I–341b
compromise movement of 1860 II–149b
emancipation II–433b–34a, 435a,b
guerrillas III–231a
Kentucky IV–39b, 43a, 220a
manumission IV–246a,b
secession VI–251b
slavery II–434a
Union sentiment VII–148b
BORDER WAR I–342a; IV–25b–26a; V–471a
Battle of Black Jack I–314a
Battle of Osawatomie V–174a
Beecher's Bibles VI–270a
Jayhawkers III–493a
Kansas City (Mo.) IV–27b
Leavenworth IV–129a
Marais des Cygnes massacre IV–248a
National Kansas Committee IV–28a
Pottawatomie massacre V–378b–379a
sack of Lawrence IV–118b
Boré, Jean Étienne (planter) VI–436a
Borgenicht, Grace (art.) II–105b
BORGNE, BATTLE OF LAKE (1814) **I–342a**; V–63a, 224a; VII–188a
Borgne, Lake III–326b, 479a
Boric acid I–340a
Borlaug, Norman E. (agron.) I–486a–b; V–100a
Borman, Frank (astronaut) I–210b
Born, Max (phys.) V–303b
Borneo
World War II IV–138a–b; VII–139a, 337a
Borno, Louis (pres.) III–240a
Boron (Calif.) I–340b
BOROUGH I–342b; III–317b; V–349b
Boscawen, Edward (nav. off.) III–115a–b
Boskovic, R. J. (math,.astron.) III–480b
Bosnians III–339a
Bosom bottles II–233b
BOSQUE REDONDO (N.Mex.) **I–342b**; V–9a; VI–439b
BOSSES AND BOSSISM, POLITICAL I–343a; V–345a,b; VI–142a–b
caucuses I–474b
Long, Huey P. IV–184a
Mahone, William VI–49b
McManes, James V–279a
New Jersey III–237b–38a; V–58a
New York City VII–295a
nominating conventions V–102a
party machine IV–213b
Pendergast machine V–244b
public utilities IV–427b
Tweed Ring II–232a; IV–454b; VII–131a–b
BOSTON (Mass.) **I–343b**; II–41a; IV–265a, 265b, 267b; V–83a; VII–159a, 319b
Adams Express Company I–9b
aerial photographs I–248a
American Academy of Arts and Sciences II–10b
Anti-Imperialist League V–235b
apartment houses I–143a
Atlantic Intracoastal Waterway VI–146b, 148b
auction galleries II–100a
banking I–252a
bathtubs I–274b
Bible printing I–294a
billeting I–297a
Board of Customs Commissioners II–275b
book publishing I–333a–b, 334a
bossism I–343a
Boston News-Letter V–68b
Bunker Hill Centennial Exhibition II–99a
calico printing II–5a
Catholicism I–467a
chamber of commerce I–491a
Charles River Bridge I–496a
Charlestown I–498b
city directory II–343b
city hall I–166a
Civil War II–68a, 368b
clearinghouse II–73b
clipper ships II–77a–b
Cocoanut Grove fire II–348a
cod fisheries II–93a
colonial coaches VII–99b
colonial commerce II–119a; IV–265b
colonial labor IV–60a
colonial postal service V–371a
Columbian Centinel II–458a
Constitution II–190b
crime commission II–263b
crime rate II–259a
criminal gangs II–258a
distilleries II–353b
Dominion of New England VII–360a
Dorchester settlement II–364a–b
drogher trade II–373b
dry dock II–375a
earthquake II–385a
education II–397b
education of the handicapped III–248a,b
electric railway VI–40a
elevated railway II–428a; VI–429a
endowed foundations III–82a
environmental sanitation VI–211b
Faneuil Hall II–487b
ferries III–11b
fire fighting III–25a
fire of 1872 V–207a
First Church of Christ, Scientist II–35b
fish trade II–92b
food preservation III–55a
Fourth of July III–87b
freedom of the press III–104b
Freemasons III–108b, 109a
freethinking III–112a
freighting VII–100a
fugitive slaves I–138a, 387a; VI–267b
furniture III–134b, 138a
gardening III–151a,b
Garrison mob III–153a
glassmaking III–185a
Government Center II–48b
Grand Banks III–208a
graphic arts V–413b
health education III–325b
hide and tallow trade III–274b
highways VI–418a
hockey III–287b
homeopathy III–293b
Huguenots III–121a, 315a
Hutchinson letters III–320b
Intolerable Acts VI–113b
kerosine IV–44a
kindergarten II–398b
King William's War IV–49b–50a
Lafayette's visit IV–84a
Latin school IV–116a
learned societies IV–126a,b
lecture days IV–131a
Liberator IV–141a
liberty tree IV–144a
libraries IV–144a,b
Logan International Airport II–347b
mackerel fisheries IV–217a
map publication I–462b
Massachusetts General Hospital III–306b; V–126b
Massachusetts Spy V–69b

BOSTON (cont.)
meat supply IV–280a
medical inspection of schoolchildren IV–275b
microwave communications IV–333a
Middlesex Canal III–447b–48a; IV–174b, 335b
mortality statistics IV–149b
nativism V–3a
Natural History Museum I–295b
navy yard II–190b; V–27b, 28a, 29a
New England Antislavery Society V–50b
New England Hospital for Women and Children V–126b
New Hampshire trade VI–149a
newspapers V–79b
New Thought movement V–81a
nominating caucus I–474a
nonimportation agreements V–104a
Old North Church V–151b
Old South Church V–152a
paving V–230a, 230a
pharmacy V–274b, 275a
police V–339a
political bossism V–345a
population IV–268a,b
port authority V–368a
Portland disaster II–349b
Port Royal V–369b
post roads V–261a, 374b, 375a
pottery V–379b
prison ships V–418b
private schools VI–228b
Provident Institution for Savings II–255a
public health VII–157b–58a
Publick Occurrences V–68a–b
Puritans V–469a; VI–262a
Quakers V–469b
quartering acts V–471b
race riots I–31b; VI–8a
railroad rate wars VI–23a
railroads III–449b, 450a; VI–25a,b, 35b
Regicides VI–70b
Revolution VI–372b
revolutionary committees III–421b
revolutionary war I–199b, 344b–45a, 382b, 382b–83a; II–211a, 485b; IV–137a,b, 266a; V–100b, 316a; VI–106a, 123a, 125a, 128a; VII–251a,b
roads I–355a
rum VI–170b
sailing packets V–183b
scientific research VI–238a
settlement IV–265a
Shawmut VI–270a
shipbuilding III–45b, 413a; VI–279b
shipping IV–309b
silver work VI–289b, 290a
ski trains VI–298a
skyscrapers VI–299a
slums VI–313b, 314a
smallpox VI–315b
smuggled goods V–320a
soap II–15a; VI–324a
social legislation VI–327b
social work VI–331a
Sons of Liberty VI–339a
South End House VI–330b
stagelines VI–380a
steam engines VI–409b
steamship lines II–91a
stock exchange II–255b, 469b
street railways VI–418a
subtreasury III–354b; VI–427a
suburban growth VI–427b
subway IV–428a; VI–429a
Suffolk Bank VI–430b
Sugar Act VI–435b
sugar industry VI–437a
tea trade VII–15a, 17a
telephone VII–20a
temperance movement VII–22b
tenements VII–23b
textile industry VII–44b
theater VII–47a
toll bridges VII–69b
town plan II–45a
Townshend Acts VII–80b–81a
trade unions IV–61b
triangular trade VII–119a, 120a
tuberculosis VII–126b
United Colonies of New England VII–149a,b
urban renewal II–48b
veterinary medicine VII–175b, 176b
Vose Gallery II–102a
War of 1812 II–364a
Watch and Ward Society I–479a; II–263b
watchmaking II–78b
waterfront II–47b
water supply IV–428a; VI–212a; VII–259a
wheat prices V–404a,b
witchcraft VII–309b
yellow fever VII–355a
Young Men's Christian Association VII–362b
Boston (cruiser) IV–239b; V–25b; VII–241a, 242b, 293a
Boston (novel) VI–183a
Boston (privateer) I–345a; V–423b
BOSTON, SIEGE OF (1775) **I–344b**; II–485b; VI–128a; VII–56a,b
Boston and Albany Railroad VI–25a, 35b
Boston and Colorado smelter VI–316b
Boston and Lowell Railroad VI–25a, 32b
Boston and Maine Railroad III–299a; V–456a; VI–25a, 32b, 298a
Boston and Providence Railroad VI–35b; VII–101a
Boston and Sandwich Glass Company III–182b
Boston and Western Land Company IV–99b
Boston Aqueduct Corporation VII–259a
Boston Associates III–63a
Boston Athenaeum I–97b, 344b; II–101a, 109a
Boston Ballet II–289b
Boston Bay IV–152a; VI–199a
***BOSTON–BERCEAU* ACTION** (1800) **I–345a**; V–15a
Boston College IV–267b
BOSTON COMMITTEE OF CORRESPONDENCE I–345a; II–140a; IV–266a; V–244a
BOSTON COMMON I–345b; V–471b; VII–97a
Boston Gazette (news.) VII–155b
Boston Journeymen Bootmakers Society II–142a
Boston Latin School II–394a; VI–229b
Boston Lyceum Bureau IV–207b
Boston Manufacturers Mutual Fire Insurance III–430b
BOSTON MANUFACTURING COMPANY I–345b; IV–187b, 272b
BOSTON MASSACRE (1770) **I–345b**; I–297a, 345b; IV–60b, 266a; VI–112b; VII–81a, 117a–b
benefit of clergy I–289a
engraving I–464a; V–413b
Hill, Wills I–326b
Old South Church V–152a
Boston Mechanics' Lyceum IV–281b
"BOSTON MEN" I–346a
Boston Museum IV–436b
Boston Museum of Fine Arts I–344b; II–100a, 103a; IV–267b, 436b
Boston Museum of Science IV–437b
BOSTONNAIS ("Bastonais") **I–346a**
Boston Neck I–344b
***BOSTON NEWS–LETTER* I–346a**; I–344a; V–68b
advertising I–16a
Boston Opera Company VII–49b
Boston Philosophical Society VI–237b
BOSTON POLICE STRIKE (1919) **I–346b**; III–260a; IV–69b
BOSTON PORT ACT (1774) **I–346b**; I–208a; II–93a; III–464a; V–57a
Boston Post Road V–375a; VII–2b
Boston Public Library I–164b; II–108b; III–248b; IV–144b
BOSTON RESOLUTIONS OF 1767 I–347a
BOSTON RESOLUTIONS OF 1810 I–347a
Boston Society of Civil Engineers II–448b
Boston Society of Natural History IV–348b, 436a; VI–235b–36a, 237b, 238a
Boston Symphony Orchestra I–344b; IV–267b
BOSTON TEA PARTY (1773) **I–347a**; IV–266a; VI–113b, 321b; VII–3b, 16a, 81a
Coercion Acts II–93a
Freemasons III–109a
Intolerable Acts III–464a
Old South Church V–153a
Port Act I–346b
BOSTON TEN TOWNSHIPS I–347b
Boston Type Foundry V–412a
Boston University I–344b; IV–267b
Boston Veterinary Institute VII–176a
Boston Water–Works Company VII–258a
Boston Weekly News–Letter I–346a
Boston Weekly News–Letter and New England Chronicle. See Boston News–Letter
Bostwick, J. A., and Company VI–383a
Boswyck. *See* Bushwick (N.Y.)
BOTANICAL GARDENS I–347b
Missouri Botanical Garden IV–378a
Botanic Family Physician. See New Guide to Health; or, the Botanic Family Physician
Botanic Garden, U.S. VII–299b
BOTANY I–348b; I–111a; IV–250b–51a; V–249a, 325b
Boteler, Alexander Robinson (pol.) II–139b
Botetourt County (Va.) I–224a; III–469b
Bothe, Walther (phys.) V–298b
Bottle Bill
Oregon V–165b
Bottling
soft drink industry VI–333a–b
Bouchard, Hippolyte de (off.) I–350a
BOUCHARD EXPEDITION (1818) **I–350a**
Boudinot, Elias (ed.) I–99b–100a; VI–263a
Boudinot, Elias (states.) IV–329b
Boudinot, Elias Cornelius (law.)
boomer movement I–336a

BOUGAINVILLE (1943)
I–350a; II–33a, 443a; IV–253a; VII–337a
Bougainville, Louis Antoine de (off.) IV–86b
Bouguer, Pierre (hydrog.) III–166a, 480b
Boulder (Colo.) V–435a
Boulder Canyon project VI–54a
Boulder Canyon Project Act (1928) II–130a
Boulder Dam. *See* Hoover Dam
Boulevard (Nickel) Bridge VII–69b
Boundaries, range
cow custom II–251a
Boundaries, U.S.
Adams–Onís Treaty I–10b, 174a
Alaska I–75b–76a, 122b, 439a
annexation of territory I–126a
Arkansas River I–174a
Aroostook War I–194b, 194b
Canada I–73b, 121a–b, 184a, 437a–39b; II–88a; III–454b; IV–87b; V–33a; VII–265a
Canada–New York VI–165b
Canadian waterways VII–261a
Chamizal Treaty I–352a
Coast and Geodetic Survey II–88a
Convention of 1818 I–126b; II–215b; III–30b
Definitive Treaty of Peace I–126a, 340b; II–318b, 458b; III–492b
Ellicott's mission II–432a
Florida III–40b, 41b; VI–351a; VII–353b
Great Lakes III–216a
Haro Channel dispute III–256a
Indian Stream Republic III–401b
Jay's Treaty III–493a
Maine–Canada IV–226b
Mexico I–352a; II–88a; III–145a–b, 230a; IV–320b, 328a; VI–312b; VII–39a
Mississippi River IV–372b
Mitchell's Map IV–381a
Northeast V–118a
northern II–475a
Northwest II–215b–16a; V–120a–b
Nueces River V–125a
Oregon V–165a, 167b, 169b
Oregon Treaty I–126b
Pacific Northwest VII–248b
Pinckney's Treaty III–67b; V–315a
Red Line Map VI–62b
resurvey I–9b; II–167b
Rio Grande VI–143a
San Juan Island VI–214a
southern I–10b
Spanish territory II–127b
Texas VII–36b, 155a
Treaty of Guadalupe Hidalgo I–126b
Webster–Ashburton Treaty I–195a
western I–9b, 10b; II–475a; VII–269b
West Florida II–381a
See also Great Lakes Disarmament Agreement
BOUNDARY DISPUTES BETWEEN THE STATES I–350b
colonial land grants IV–92a
Georgia III–168b
Georgia–Florida III–171b
Greer County III–200a
interstate compacts VI–402a
Maryland–West Virginia III–200a
Mason–Dixon Line IV–263a
Michigan–Ohio III–128a; IV–331a
Missouri–Iowa III–297b
Mitchell's Map IV–381a
New Hampshire Grants V–88b
New York–Connecticut V–130b
New York–Massachusetts V–88b
Ohio–Michigan V–144b; VII–68b
Pennsylvania–Connecticut V–250b; VII–116b, 346b–47b
Pennsylvania–Maryland- V–251b
Pennsylvania–Virginia- V–253a
Supreme Court VI–444b
Texas VII–39a–b
Upper Peninsula of Michigan VII–157a
Boundary Waters Treaty (1909) I–440b; III–454b
Bounties
wolves VII–311b
See also Fishing Bounties; Land Bounties
BOUNTIES, COMMERCIAL I–352a
chemical industries II–5b
colonial III–204a; IV–242b, 308a; V–16a–b
Confederacy II–159b–60a
debenture plan II–477b
Hamilton's fiscal policies III–245b–46a, 246b–47a
hemp III–271a
indigo III–405b; VI–386b; VII–86a
naval stores V–14b
"normalcy" V–110a
saltpeter V–98a
sugar VI–435b, 467a
BOUNTIES, MILITARY I–352b; II–450b–51a; IV–344b–45a; VII–233a
British army VI–127a
Civil War II–63a, 302b, 335a, 366b–67a, 541a–b; VI–61a
Continental Army I–183a, 331a
Donation Lands II–363a
Georgia land III–170b
Indiana III–369b
land scrip IV–97a,b
Ohio lands III–227b
revolutionary war II–335a, 450b; VI–125b; VII–188b, 273a,b
swamplands VI–453b
Texas public lands VII–41b
Union Army I–182a
Virginia IV–92a; VII–202a
volunteers VII–208a
Washington's western lands VII–252a
western lands V–140b
Bounty brokers I–353b
BOUNTY JUMPER I–353b; II–335a
Bouquet, Henry (off.) IV–154a
Forbes expedition III–58b, 59a, 211b
Fort Bedford I–282b
See also Bouquet's Expedition
BOUQUET'S EXPEDITION (1763–65) **I–353b**; I–359a, 389a; V–90b
Fort Ligonier IV–154a
Fort Pitt V–246b, 321a
Great Trail III–223b
Raystown Path VI–49a
Bourbon (whiskey) II–354b; VII–289b
BOURBON COUNTY (Ga.) **I–354a**
Bourbon County (Kans.) I–342a; VI–241a
Bourbon County (Ky.) I–444b
Great Revival III–221b
whiskey VII–289b
Bourbon family compact II–487b
Bourbon Restoration (1815–30) III–96b
BOURBONS I–354a
Compromise of 1890 II–151a
Florida III–39b, 40a
Mississippi IV–369a
New South V–66b
Readjuster movement VI–49b
West Virginia VII–281b
Bourbon triumvirate III–169a
Bouresches (Fr.) VII–326b
World War I I–286b
BOURGEOIS I–354b
Bourgeois, Stephen II–104a
Bourgmont, Étienne Veniard de (expl.). *See* Bourgmont's Explorations
BOURGMONT'S EXPLORATIONS I–354b; III–119b
Fort Orleans III–144a; V–173a
Mississippi Valley IV–376b
Platte River V–30b
Bourlamaque, François de (off.) III–116b
Bourne, George (cler.) I–135b
Bourne, Jonathan (pol.) V–427b
Bourne, Randolph (au.) IV–164a
Boussingault, Jean Baptiste (chem.) III–16a
Bout, Jan Evertsen (col.) V–266a
Boutwell, George S. (pol.) I–131b, 311b; IV–6a
BOUWERIES I–354b
Bovard, Oliver K. (ed.) V–73b
Bow, Joseph (inv.) VI–133a
Bowditch, Henry Pickering (physiol.) IV–285b; V–307a
Bowditch, Nathaniel (astron.) I–211a, 354b–55a
BOWDITCH'S *AMERICAN PRACTICAL NAVIGATOR* I–354b
Bowdoin, James (gov.) II–101a; VI–272a
Bowdoin, James III II–101a–b
Bowdoin Bay (Green.) V–240b
Bowdoin College II–101a–b
Bowdoin family V–186b
Bowen, Daniel (art.) VII–262a
Bowen, J. S. (off.) V–369a
Bowen, Norman L. (geol.) V–268b
Bowen, William G. (educ.) V–409a
Bowers, Claude (hist.) III–486a
Bowers, Henry F. I–111a
BOWERY (N.Y.C.) **I–355a**; III–128b, 253a; IV–359b; VI–418a
Bowie, James (off.) I–74a; VII–37b
Bowie, Rezin P. I–355a
Bowie, W. F. (geol.) III–480b
BOWIE KNIFE I–355a; II–376b; III–227a
Bowlegs, Billy (Indian) I–154a; VI–261a–b
Bowler, Jack (slave) VI–304a
Bowler hat II–372a
Bowles, Samuel (ed.) III–148b; V–73b
Bowles, William Augustus (adventurer). *See* Bowles's Filibustering Expeditions
BOWLES'S FILIBUSTERING EXPEDITIONS I–355b; III–59a; VI–196b, 366b, 367a
Bowley, Arthur L. (math., econ.) VI–206b
Bowlin, James B. (dipl.) V–212b
"Bowling Alley" (Kor.) VI–301a
Bowling Green (Ky.) IV–41b, 42a; VII–34b
BOWLING GREEN (N.Y.C.) **I–356a**
Bowling Green (Ohio) III–316a

Bowls, stone II–386a
Bowman, Isaiah (educ.) IV–3b
Inquiry III–420a
Bowman, John (pioneer) IV–40a
Bowne, Borden P. (theol.) VI–82b
Bow wood V–174a
BOWYER, FORT, ATTACK ON (1814) **I–356a**
Boxelder Creek II–379b
Boxer (brig) II–452b
Boxer Indemnity Fund II–471a
Boxer Protocol (1901) II–25b, 27b, 471b
BOXER REBELLION (1900) **I–356a**; I–185b; II–27a, 29b; III–462b
guerrillas III–231a
indemnities III–352a
marines IV–252b
Peking Congress V–242a
Russia VI–178a
Boxing
Olympic Games V–154a,b
See also Prizefighting
Boxwood VII–319a
BOYCOTTING I–356b; IV–60b; V–182a; VI–419a,b
AFL I–374b; IV–65b
bus I–30b, 72a; II–55a, 56b, 57a, 58a
China I–124a; II–29b
colonies VI–112a,b; VII–313a
Cuba II–269b–70a
Danbury Hatter's Case II–286a
legal recognition IV–69a
nonimportation agreements V–104a
Norris–La Guardia Anti–Injunction Law V–112a
opposition IV–471b
prohibitions IV–69a
Pullman strike IV–66b–67a
restraint of trade VI–102b, 103b
restrictions IV–74b
revolutionary war I–208a; VI–121b; VII–316a
ruled illegal IV–67b
Taft–Hartley Act IV–467a
tea II–388a
United Farm Workers IV–76b
Boyd, James (au.) IV–164b
Boyd, John Parker (off.) II–35a
Boyd, Louise A. (expl.) V–337b
Boyd, Lynn (law.) II–175 (table)
Boyden, Seth (inv.) II–6b–7a; V–41b
Boyden, Uriah (eng.) VII–257a
Boyd's Creek, Battle of (1780) III–400b
BOYDTON PLANK ROAD, ENGAGEMENT AT (1864) **I–357a**; V–265a
Böyë, Herman (cartog.) I–462b
Boyle, Hal (jour.) V–74a
Boyle, Richard, 3rd Earl of Burlington I–161b
Boyle, Robert (phys.) VII–300b
Boyle, W. A. "Tony" (labor leader) IV–76a; VII–151a
Boylston, Zabdiel (physic.) IV–275a, 295a; VI–315b; VII–205b
BOY SCOUTS OF AMERICA I–357b; I–108b
Boys' Life (mag.) IV–223a
Boy With a Squirrel (paint.) V–187a
Bozeman (Mont.) II–432b
Bozeman, John M. (pioneer) I–357b; II–477b
Bozeman Pass V–225a
BOZEMAN TRAIL I–357b; II–477b; IV–403a
Fort C.F. Smith VI–317b
Fort Connor II–184a
Fort Phil Kearny IV–33b
Indian hostilities IV–108b
Brace, Charles Loring (social worker) V–280a
Brace, Donald (pub.) I–334b
Brachiopods III–163b
Brackenridge, Hugh Henry (law.) V–70a
Bradbury, John (nat.) VII–271b
Bradbury, Ray (au.) IV–165a
Braddock (Pa.) IV–398a
Braddock, Edward (off.) II–134a
See also Braddock's Expedition
Braddock, James J. (pugilist) V–422b
BRADDOCK'S EXPEDITION (1755) **I–358a**; I–85a; II–126b, 272a, 382a; III–58b, 115b; IV–398b; V–246b, 251b, 356b, 378b; VI–150a; VII–307a
Allegheny route I–88b
Battle of the Monongahela IV–398a
Frederick III–100b
Indian participants IV–181a
Braddock's Field (Pa.) IV–84a; VII–290a
BRADDOCK'S ROAD I–358b; I–89b; II–273a; III–219b; IV–130a; V–224b; VI–155b; VII–283a
Bradford, Andrew (pub.) IV–161a, 190b, 221b; V–251a
Bradford, John (surv.) V–70a
Bradford, William (col. gov.) IV–396a, 423b; V–65a, 312b
history of Plymouth Plantation III–280a; IV–161a
Indian trade IV–264b–65a
Kennebec Trading Post IV–37b
Mayflower Compact IV–278b
schoolteachers VI–229a
Thanksgiving Day VII–46a
Bradford, William (print.) I–294a; V–69a, 82b, 212a
Bradlee, Benjamin C. (ed.) V–78a
Bradley, Bill (athlete) V–154b
Bradley, Joseph P. (jur.) I–423a; II–378a; VI–445b
Bradley, Omar N. (off.) VI–193b; VII–339b
Battle of the Bulge I–379b
Cherbourg II–13b
Normandy invasion V–110b
Tunisian campaign I–308a
Bradley v. *Milliken* (1974) I–397b; II–54b–55a
Bradstreet, Anne (poet) IV–160b
Bradstreet, John (off.). *See* Bradstreet's Fort Frontenac Expedition; Bradstreet's Lake Erie Expedition
Bradstreet, John M. (law.) IV–307b
Bradstreet, Simon (states.) I–411b
Bradstreet Company IV–307b
BRADSTREET'S FORT FRONTENAC EXPEDITION (1758) **I–358b**; III–58b, 116a, 124b
BRADSTREET'S LAKE ERIE EXPEDITION (1764) **I–359a**; II–337b; V–90b, 357a
Sandusky VI–208b
Brady (Tex.) II–358b
Brady, Fort (Mich.) VI–197a
Brady, Mathew B. (phot.). *See* Brady Photographs
BRADY PHOTOGRAPHS I–359a; IV–147a; V–71b, 293a
Brafferton Hall (Williamsburg, Va.) I–161b; VII–300b
Bragg, Braxton (off.) I–181a
Army of Mississippi IV–370a
Army of Tennessee VII–26b
Battle of Chickamauga II–21b
Battle of Missionary Ridge IV–364b
Battle of Murfreesboro IV–434b
Battle of Ringgold Gap VI–141b
Chattanooga campaign I–502b; II–163a
Cumberland Gap II–272b
Kentucky invasion IV–42a, 426b; V–66a, 142b; VI–26b
Louisville III–485a
Perryville V–263a
Tennessee IV–54a; V–248a
Tullahoma campaign VII–127b
Bragg, Lawrence (phys.) V–303b
Bragg, William H. (phys.) IV–389a; V–303b
Bragg, W. L. (phys.) IV–389a
Brahman cattle VI–45a
Brahmanism VII–52a
Braille typewriters III–249a
Brainerd, David (miss.) III–385b
Braintree (Mass.) I–327a; III–472a
BRAIN TRUST I–359b; V–43b
Brakes
autos I–228b
power brakes IV–420a
railroads VI–28a
Bramble (ship) V–122a
Bramwell, William C. (inv.) VII–44a
Branch, John (pol.) III–39a
Branch banking. *See* Banking, Branch and Group
Branchville (S.C.) VI–349b
Brancourt–le–Grand (Fr.) VI–338b
Brand, Hennig IV–274a
Brandegee Estate (Boston) I–97b
Brandeis, Louis D. (jur.) IV–10b, 268a; V–47a, 48a; VI–446b
Bill of Rights I–299a, 300b
clear–and–present–danger rule III–105a
due process of law II–378b
minimum–wage legislation VII–269a–b
Muller v. *Oregon* IV–68b
Sedition Act VI–255a
unions II–110b
Brandenburg (Ky.) IV–410b
Brandenburg v. *Ohio* (1969) V–78b
Branding (punishment) V–464b, 465a; VI–265b
Brandon (Va.) I–194a
Brands, cattle. *See* Cattle Brands
BRANDS, PRIVATE AND NATIONAL I–359a; I–18a; II–421b, 482b; VII–93b
Brandt, Willy (states.) VI–471a
Brandy
distillation II–353b
fur trade III–140b
Indian consumption III–398a,b
Indian trade III–402b
slave trade VII–119b
BRANDY STATION, BATTLE OF (1863) **I–360a**
Brandywine (frigate) IV–84a
Brandywine Creek III–45a
BRANDYWINE CREEK, BATTLE OF (1777) **I–360a**; III–173b; VI–123b
Brandywine Mills III–45a
Brandywine River II–320b, 429b

Branford (Conn.) V–55b; VII–350b
Brangus cattle I–471b
Braniff Airways I–68b
Brannan, Charles Franklin (law.) I–360b
BRANNAN PLAN (1949) **I–360b**
Bransfield, Edward (expl.) V–198a
Branson, E. R. (inv.) VII–44a
Branson, J. L. (inv.) VII–44a
Brant, Joseph (Indian) III–400b; IV–173b, 354b; V–172b
Brantford (Ont., Can.) VI–14b
Brant Rock (Mass.) VI–15a
Branzburg, Paul (jour.) V–79a
Branzburg v. *Hayes* (1972) III–105b
Brashear City (La.) I–279b
Brasiletto wood IV–181b
Brass V–103a,b
  Connecticut II–181a
  zinc VII–369a
Brass bands IV–439b
Brass clocks II–78b–79b
Brass work VI–291b, 292a
Brattain, Walter (phys.) I–287b; II–425b; V–100a, 305a
Brattleboro (Vt.). *See* Dummer, Fort
Bratton, John (off.) VII–261b
Braun, Karl Ferdinand (phys.) II–423b; VII–21a
Braun, Wernher von (rocket expert) IV–459b
Bravay and Company IV–85a
Braxton, Carter (states.) II–308b
Bray, Thomas (cler.) IV–144a; VI–75b
Brayton, George (inv.) VI–257b
Brazil IV–114a
  ABC conference I–1b
  air disaster II–347a
  Alabama Claims VII–249a
  boundary dispute IV–363a
  corn production II–226b
  cotton production II–238b
  diplomatic recognition IV–110b
  diplomatic relations IV–115a
  Dominican Republic intervention IV–113a
  Franciscans III–94b
  Huguenots III–121a
  independence movement IV–115a
  Indians III–385b; VII–65b
  International Expostion of 1895 III–453b
  Jews IV–9a
  Mardi Gras IV–249b
  meat trade IV–281a
  orange–tree cuttings III–128b
  Panama Congress V–203b
  rubber trade VI–167b
  slave trade VI–311b
  Sugar Islands VI–437a
  Treaty of Tordesillas VII–75a
  United Nations Declaration VII–151b
  U.S. Civil War III–40a; VII–212b
  U.S. merchant marine IV–310b
  U.S. trade VI–343b, 344b, 345a,b, 346a
  World War II IV–112a
BRAZIL, CONFEDERATE EXPATRIATES TO I–360b
BRAZITO, BATTLE AT (1846) **I–361a**; II–363b
Brazos River
  Barnards' trading post VII–96a
  De Soto expedition VII–36a
  Fort Belknap I–286a
  Fort Griffin III–228a
  freight traffic VII–39a
  Texas Revolution VII–38a
Breach of peace I–205a
Bread II–219a; III–51b, 53b, 54b
  enrichment V–128b
  exports VII–86a,b
Breakers (Newport, R.I.) I–164a
Breakfast cereals. *See* Cereals, Manufacture of
"Breakfast of Champions" I–488a
Brearley, David (jur.) II–203b
Breathitt County (Ky.) III–252b
Breckinridge, John C. (off., states.) IV–40b
  Battle at Marion IV–253b
  Battle of Baton Rouge I–173b, 275a
  Battle of New Market V–59a
  campaign of 1860 VII–39b
  land speculation IV–99b
  Port Hudson siege V–369a
  vice–president I–421b, 421b; VII–179 (table)
Breckinridge, W. C. P. (jour.) IV–41a
BREDA, PEACE OF (1667) **I–361a**; I–466a; V–253b; VII–279a
Breeches II–371a–b
Breechloader III–441b
Breedlove v. *Suttles* (1937) III–93a; V–355a
Breed's Hill I–382b
Breen, Joseph I. (adm.) I–480a; IV–418b
Breen Mine IV–303b
Breese, S. (map pub.) I–462b
Bréguet, Louis Charles (eng.) III–270a
Breidenbaugh, C. F. (showman) VI–283a
Breit, Gregory (phys.) V–301b–02a
Bremen (Ger.) II–349a
Bremerton (Wash.) V–27b, 29b, 462a
Brennan, Peter J. (offi.) IV–77a
Brennan, William J. (jur.) VI–447a
  Baker v. *Carr* I–244b
  Bill of Rights I–300a
  freedom of the press III–105a–b
Brenner Pass (Aus.) VII–341a
Brent, Charles (fur trader) VI–196a
Brereton, Lewis H. (off.) V–332a
Breslin, Jimmy (au.) V–79a
Brest (Fr.) II–375a; VII–339b
Brest–Litovsk, Treaty of (1918) I–158b, 176b; VI–178b, 283b
BRETHREN I–361a; II–114a; V–181a; VI–76b
Brethren Church (Ashland, Ohio) I–361a
Brethren Churches, National Fellowship of. *See* National Fellowship of Brethren Churches
Brethren of the Coast I–373b
Brett, George E. (pub.) I–334b
BRETTON WOODS CONFERENCE (1944) **I–361b**; I–254b; III–195b, 457a; VI–468b; VII–88b, 91a
Breuckelen. *See* Brooklyn
Breuer, Marcel (arch.) III–136b
Brewer, David J. (jur.) V–354b; VI–446a
Brewer, John Hart III–184a
BREWING I–361b; III–54b
  colonial industry III–413b
  foreign investments III–63a
  Prohibition II–261a; V–429b
  refrigeration VI–70a
  Volstead Act VII–207b
  Wheeling VII–288a
  Wisconsin VII–308a
Brewster, Gilbert (inv.) VII–43a
Brewster, Jonathan (trader) V–334b
Brewster, William (col.) V–312b
Brewton, Miles, House I–162b
Breyman, Heinrich von (off.) I–289a
Brezhnev, Leonid (states.) III–70b; VI–416b
  arms race agreement I–180b
Briand, Aristide (dipl.) II–343a; IV–36a
Briand–Kellogg Pact. *See* Kellogg–Briand Pact
Briarcliff Manor (N.Y.) III–181b
BRIAR CREEK, BATTLE OF (1779) **I–362a**; III–168b
Bribery
  boodle I–332a
  impeachment II–202a
  lobbies IV–170b
  political corruption II–231a, 232b
  voters II–408b
Brice, Calvin S. (pol.) I–424b
Brices Cross Roads (Miss.) VII–128b
Brickell, John (physic.) III–26b; IV–231a
Bricker, John W. (pol.) I–429a
  See also Bricker Amendment
BRICKER AMENDMENT I–362a; VII–110a,b
Brick Market (Newport, R.I.) I–162a
Bricks. *See* Building Materials
Brickwedde, Ferdinand G. V–299b
Bridge (dent.) II–331a
Bridge of San Luis Rey IV–164b
Bridgeport (Ala.) II–253a
Bridgeport (Conn.) II–492b
Bridgeport (Nebr.) II–246b, 246b
BRIDGER, FORT (Wyo.) **I–363a**; III–215a; VI–422a; VII–96a, 161b
  California Trail I–410a
  caravan route I–453a
  Mormon expedition IV–249b, 411a
  Mormon migration IV–411b
  Oregon Trail V–168b, 169a
  Overland Trail V–178b
  pony express V–357b
Bridger, James (pioneer) III–48b, 143b; IV–422a; VI–241b; VII–103b
  Ashley expeditions I–201a
  Fort Bridger I–363a
  Great Salt Lake II–477b; III–222a
Bridger's Gap I–201a
Bridger's Pass V–178b, 225a; VI–379b
BRIDGES I–363a; I–377b–78a
  colonial construction VI–152b
  disasters II–350b–51a
  George Washington III–312b
  Golden Gate III–189a
  High Bridge VII–259a
  insurance III–429a
  Latrobe's Folly IV–116a
  Niagara suspension bridges V–93b
  Port Authority of New York and New Jersey V–368b
  railroads VI–25b–26a
  San Francisco VI–209b

BRIDGES (cont.)
tolls VII–69a
Verrazano–Narrows IV–452a
Wheeling Bridge VII–288a
Bridges, C. B. (geneticist) III–157b
Bridges, Charles (paint.) V–186a
Bridges, John VII–261b
Bridges–Reece Bill III–195a
Bridges v. *California* (1941) III–105a
Bridgewater (Can.) IV–205a
Bridgewater (Mass.) IV–47b
Bridgewater, Battle of. *See* Lundy's Lane, Battle at
Bridgman (Mich.) II–143b
Bridgman, Laura III–248b
Bridgman, Percy (phys.) V–100a
"Briefe and Plaine Scheam" for Union (1697) II–121b
Briefe and True Report of the New Found Land of Virginia (1588) III–26b
Brief Narrative of the Case and Trial of John Peter Zenger (1736) V–69a
Brief Rule to Guide the Common–People of New–England How to Order Themselves and Theirs in the Small Pocks, or Measles VI–315a
Brigadoon (musical) VII–50b
Briggs, Ansel (pol.) III–468a
Briggs, Charles A. (educ.) III–275a; V–392a; VI–78b
Briggs, Clare (cartoon.) V–72b
Briggs, Henry (cartog.) IV–248a
Briggs, Isaac (inv.) VI–408b
Briggs, L. J. (phys.) I–349b
Brigham, Amariah (physic.) IV–305b
Brigham, Clarence S. I–332b
Bright, David E. II–106b
Bright, Francis (col.) I–498b
Bright, Margaret Lucas (ref.) VII–312b
Brightman, Lehman (Indian) VII–152a
Bright tobacco VII–67a–b
Brigs (ships) VII–240a
Brill, Abraham (psych.) IV–306a
Brillat-Savarin, Anthelme (pol., writ.) III–122b
Brillouin, Léon (phys.) V–304a
Brine VI–69b
food preservation II–219a
meat–packing IV–280a
refrigeration II–421a
Brinkerhoff, Jacob (jur., pol.) VII–304a
Brinley, George (bibliophile) I–333a; II–108b
Brinton, Daniel G. (anthrop.) I–128b
Brisbane, Albert (ref.) III–85a
Brisbane, Arthur (jour.) V–72a, 75a
BRISCOE* v. *BANK OF THE COMMONWEALTH OF KENTUCKY (1837) **I–365a**
Brissot de Warville, Jean Pierre (jour.) III–122a; VI–106b
Bristlecone pine VI–18a
BRISTOE CAMPAIGN (1863) **I–365a**
Buckland Races I–374a
Bristoe Station (Va.)
Civil War I–365a, 374a, 382a
Bristol (Conn.) II–79a
Bristol (Maine) I–32a; V–243b
Bristol (R.I.) II–328b; IV–422b; VII–352a
Bristol, Mark L. (nav. off.) V–23a
BRISTOL TRADE I–365a; I–16a, 22b, 496b; IV–309b
Bristow, Benjamin H. (law.)
campaign of 1876 I–422b
Whiskey Ring VII–290b
Bristow, George F. (comp.) IV–438b
Bristow, Joseph L. (pol.)
Progressive movement V–427b
Britain, Battle of (World War II) I–58a, 66b–67a, 328a; VII–333b
radar VI–10a
Britannia metalwork VI–290b, 291a,b
British Association for the Advancement of Science I–98a
British Broadcasting Corporation II–425b
BRITISH CAMPAIGN OF 1777 I–365b; VI–123b
Albany I–81b
Battle of Oriskany V–172b
Mohawk Valley IV–386b–87a
British Columbia (Can.)
Adventure I–15b
camels in the West I–413a
dams II–132a
exploration V–164b
Haro Channel dispute III–256a
Indians III–238a, 363a, 373a–b
Jesuit missions III–500a
Northwest Coast culture III–360b
Oregon boundary V–165a
salmon VI–201a
Stikine River VI–151a
U.S. boundary VII–248b
Yukon River VII–367a
British Commonwealth of Nations
lend–lease IV–134a
BRITISH DEBTS I–366a; VI–108b; VII–86b, 270a
Canadian–U.S. relations I–438a
evacuation of border forts I–341a
Jay's Treaty III–493a, 494a
Peace of Paris VI–117a
Virginia VII–230b–31a
British East India Company. *See* East India Company, English
British Empire Before the American Revolution III–282b
British Grand Fleet VII–329a
British Guiana
Hornet–Peacock engagement III–301b
Venezuela boundary dispute I–122a; IV–401a; V–153a; VI–226b; VII–170a
British Home Guard VII–334b
British Honduras
confederate expatriates VI–274b
Dallas–Clarendon Convention II–285a
British Isles
immigrants II–75a
Norse voyages V–112a
British Labor Representation Committee IV–68a
British Legion VI–130a
British Museum IV–348a
British North America Act (1867) I–439a
British North American Provinces I–438a
British Open tournament (golf) III–198a
British Overseas Airways Corporation
hijacking III–277a
BRITISH PLAN OF CAMPAIGN IN THE WEST I–367a
British posts
Forks of the Ohio V–143a
Fort Blair VI–45b
Fort Bute III–326b
Fort Edward Augustus III–311b
Fort Halifax III–243b
Fort Hamilton III–244a
Fort Miami (Ind.) IV–329a
Fort Miami (Ohio) IV–329a–b
Fort Niagara V–90b, 91b
Fort Pitt V–321a
Fort Pownall V–386a
Fort Presque Isle V–399b
Fort Saint Marks VI–196b
Fort William Augustus V–139b
Kaskaskia IV–32a
New York V–85a,b
Ninety–Six V–97a
Number 4 V–126a
Sandusky VI–208b
See also Border Forts, Evacuation of
British spoliation claims IV–5b
BRITISH TRAVELERS IN AMERICA, EARLY I–367a; IV–436b; VI–218a
British Vickers (machine gun) I–57b
British West Indies
Civil War II–67b
colonial plans of union II–121a–b
trade II–92b, 118b–19a, 167a
U.S. balance of trade I–245a
Brittany (Fr.)
World War II VII–339a, 339b
Broad Bay (Maine) VII–219b
Broadcast Bureau III–1a
Broadcasters, National Association of I–480b–81a
Broadcasting II–424a–b
equal time laws V–448b, 450a
Federal Communications Commission III–1a
First Amendment III–106a
libel III–105a–b
New York City V–83b
public utilities 456b–
radio VI–14b
regulation III–106a
Broad construction (Constitution) II–197b, 327a
Broadened Opportunity for Officer Selection and Training. *See* Project BOOST
Broadhorn (ship) I–175a
Broadloom weaving II–239a
Broadman, Richard (cler.) IV–318a
Broad River II–382b; III–30a
BROAD SEAL WAR (1838–40) **I–368a**
BROADSIDES I–368b; IV–202a
Broad Street (N.Y.C.) III–100a; V–40a; VI–212a; VII–221b, 222b
BROADWAY (N.Y.C.) **I–368b**; III–52b; IV–237b
New Amsterdam V–40a
Niblo's Garden V–93b
subway VI–429a
theater II–290a; IV–438b, 442a; VII–50b
Tin Pan Alley VII–62b
Brock, Isaac (off.) II–338b; VI–3a
Brockenbrough, John VI–138a
Brockhaus, Friedrich (ed.) II–444a
Brockton (Mass.) IV–266b
Brockway, Zebulon R. (penologist) V–415b; VI–67b, 68a,b
Broderick, David Colbreth (pol.) I–203a; II–377a
Brodhead, Daniel (off.) IV–117b
See also Brodhead's Allegheny Campaign
BRODHEAD'S ALLEGHENY CAMPAIGN (1779) **I–369a;** VI–438a
Iroquois III–400b; VI–386a

Broglie, Louis de (phys.) V–303b
Broilers (chickens) II–320b
Broke, Philip Vere (nav. off.) II–16a; III–315b
Bromides IV–305b
Bromine II–7b; V–267a
BRONCO I–369a; VI–184b, 364b
Bronk, Detlev W. (educ.) IV–3b; VI–158b
BRONSON* v. *RODES (1868) **I–369a**; VI–95a
Brontotheriums I–242b
Bronx (N.Y.) II–428a; V–33b, 82a
Bronx River VII–258b, 293a
Bronx Zoo. *See* New York Zoological Park
Bronze
Civil War II–67b
coins II–95a–b, 95b
Indian use III–356b
Bronze Star Medal II–312a–b
Brooches II–371b, 372a
Brooke, Edward (pol.) IV–268a
Brooke, Fort (Fla.) I–451b; VII–311a
Brooke, John M. (nav. off., oceanog.) III–28b–29a; V–134b, 135a; VI–44b
Brooke, John R. (off.) II–268b
Brooke, Lord, Robert Greville II–182a
Brooke Army Medical Center VI–204b
Brooke rifles VII–26a
Brookes, Norman (athlete) VII–29b
BROOK FARM INSTITUTE OF AGRICULTURE AND EDUCATION I–369b; II–147a; III–85a; VI–325b; VII–98a
Brookfield (Mass.) IV–47b
Brookfield Zoo. *See* Chicago Zoological Park
Brookhaven National Laboratory II–133a; V–297a
Brookings, Robert S. (mer., philan.) I–370a
BROOKINGS INSTITUTION I–369b; V–400b–01a
Brookland. *See* Brooklyn
Brookline (Mass.) III–197b
BROOKLYN (N.Y.) **I–370a**; IV–185b; V–82a; VI–427b
air disaster II–347a
baseball I–270a, 271a
Bedford–Stuyvesant I–282b
colonial settlement IV–185a
directory II–343b
elevated railway II–428a
Jehovah's Witnesses III–498a
navy yard II–348b; V–27b, 28a, 29a
Perfectionist Community II–147a
revolutionary war III–498b; IV–185b, 186a; V–418b
subways VI–429a
Tammany Hall VI–460a
tenements VII–24b
Walloons VII–221b
Brooklyn (cruiser) V–261b; VI–207a, 216b, 217a
Brooklyn (sloop) II–286a; IV–371a; VI–313b
Brooklyn Americans (hockey) III–287b
Brooklyn Battery Tunnel I–275b
Brooklyn Benevolent Society III–82b
Brooklyn Botanic Garden I–348a
BROOKLYN BRIDGE I–370b; I–364b, 378a
Brooklyn Dodgers (baseball) I–271a
Brooklyn Heights (N.Y.) I–370b; IV–186a
Brooklyn Institute IV–207a
Brooklyn Museum III–137a
Brooklyn Rapid Transit Corporation VI–429a
Brooks, Alton (jur.) I–116b
Brooks, Byron A. (inv.) VII–136a
Brooks, Elisha IV–25a
Brooks, Gwendolyn (au.) I–25a
Brooks, James (jour.) II–256a
Brooks, John F. (cler.) III–331b
Brooks, Joseph (cler., pol.) I–370b
Brooks, N. C. (nav. off.) IV–337a
Brooks, Phillips (bp.) V–161b; VI–78b
Brooks, Preston Smith (pol.) I–203a, 371a; IV–31a
Brooks, Van Wyck (critic) IV–164a
Brooks, W. K. (zool.) III–29b
BROOKS–BAXTER WAR (1872–74) **I–370b**
Brooks Brothers II–81b
BROOKS–SUMNER AFFAIR (1856) **I–371a**; I–203a; IV–31a
Brooks v. *United States* (1925) II–136b
Broom (mag.) IV–190a
Broom, Jacob (pol.) II–203b
Broome County (N.Y.) I–41b, 347b
Broomfield, William S. (pol.) I–397b
Broomfield Amendment I–397b
Brotherhood of Locomotive Engineers I–386a
See also Railroad Brotherhoods
Brotherhood of Locomotive Firemen IV–66b
Brotherhood of Telegraphers of the United States and Canada VII–19b
Brotherhood of the Spirit (commune) II–142b
Brotherhoods, railroad. *See* Railroad Brotherhoods
Brotherhood War (1889–90) (baseball) I–270b
Brother Jonathan (nickname). *See* Jonathan I–334a
Brough, John (pol.) VII–146a, 164b
Brougham, John (act., playwright) VII–48a
Broughton, George (art.) II–103a
Broughton, Nicholas (nav. off.) VI–128a
Broughton, Samuel IV–169a
Broughton, William (nav. off.) V–164b
Broughton, W. R. (expl.) II–131b
Broun, Heywood (jour.) V–75a
Broward, Napoleon Bonaparte (pol.) III–40a
Browder, Earl (Communist) II–144b; V–47b
Brown, Aaron v. (states.) VI–353b
Brown, Albert G. (pol.) V–360b
Brown, Alexander, and Sons III–466a
Brown, Alice (au.) IV–163a
Brown, Arthur, Jr. (arch.) I–164b
Brown, B. Gratz (pol.) I–422b; IV–141a
Brown, Charles Brockden (au.) IV–161b
Brown, Mrs. Charles S. (golfer) III–198a
Brown, Edmund G. (pol.) I–408a, 409a
Brown, Edmund G., Jr. (pol.) I–409a
BROWN, FORT (Tex.) **I–371a**
Brown, George (dipl.) III–263a
Brown, Gordon (eng.) II–156a
Brown, Henry B. (jur.) VI–446a
Brown, Henry Kirke (sculp.) VI–243a,b
Brown, H. Rap VI–14a
Brown, Jacob (off.) I–184a; III–118a; V–91a, 139b; VII–234b
Battle of Chippewa II–31b; IV–205a
Fort Brown I–371a
Fort Erie II–458a
militia IV–345b
Sackets Harbor VI–183b
Brown, James (sing.) IV–442b
Brown, John (abolitionist) V–93a
Battle of Osawatomie V–174a
Coppoc Case II–224a
Harpers Ferry raid I–138a; III–256b, 437a, 465a; IV–252a; VI–270a, 307b, 342a, 404b
Pottawatomie massacre I–314a, 342a; II–118b; IV–26a, 31a; V–379a
trial VII–107a, 117b
Brown, John (col.) IV–37a; V–243b
Brown, John (mer.) III–153b
Brown, John (off.) I–435b; IV–86b
Ticonderoga VII–56a
Brown, John, Jr. (pol.)
Kansas prohibition IV–27a
Brown, John Carter (bus.) II–109a; IV–99b
Brown, John George (art.) II–103a
Brown, Joseph C. (surv.) VII–74b
Brown, Joseph E. (pol.) II–165a; III–169a; V–108a; VI–405a
Brown, Moses (bus.) I–175a; IV–99b; VI–133a
Brown, Nicholas (bus.) I–372a
Brown, Nicholas, family VI–132a
Brown, Noah (shipbuilder) VII–220b
Brown, Norman O. (psych.) IV–165a
Brown, Oliver. *See* *Brown* v. *Board of Education of Topeka*
Brown, Richard H. (hist.) III–487a
Brown, Samuel I–347b
Brown, Solyman (dent.) II–330a
Brown, Walter F. (offi.) I–68a; III–452a
Brown, William (trav.) V–376a
Brown, William Henry (art.) VI–286b
Brown, William Hill (au.) IV–161a
Brown, William W. I–287a
Brown Brothers III–63b
Brown Decades IV–164a
Browne, Carl (labor agitator) II–252b
Browne, Malcolm (jour.) V–74b
Browne, Ralph C. (inv.) V–119b
Browne, Robert (cler.) I–371a–b; VI–262a
Browne, Thomas (off.) III–42a
Brownell, W. C. (au.) IV–163a
Brownie Girl Scouts III–181b
Browning, John M. (inv.) IV–215a, 431b
Browning machine gun I–57b; IV–215a; V–27a
Browning rifle IV–431b; VII–326a
BROWNISTS I–371a
Brownlow, William G. (<Parson>) (jour., pol.) II–63b; V–221a; VII–148b
Brown lung IV–294b
Brown settlement (Tenn.) VII–253b
Brown's Ferry (Tenn.) I–502b

Brown Shoe Company VII–124a
Brown's Hole (Wyo.) III–291a
Brownson, Orestes A. (ed.) I–469b
Brown's Park (Wyo.) III–291a
Brownstown (Mich.) III–316a
BROWNSTOWN AND DETROIT TREATIES (1807–08) **I–371b**
Browns Valley projectile point III–484b
Brownsville (Pa.) I–364a; V–144a; VI–65b
Brownsville (Tex.)
boll weevil I–327b
Civil War V–198b, 264b; VII–39b
Mexican War IV–324b; V–198b
Rio Grande VI–143a
riots IV–340a
ship channel VII–260b
Texas Rangers VII–42a
See also Brownsville Affair
BROWNSVILLE AFFAIR (1906) **I–371b**; IV–340a
Brown Swiss cattle I–471b; II–281b
Brown thrasher (bird) VI–393 (table)
BROWN UNIVERSITY **I–372a**; II–114b, 394b; V–439b; VI–132a
Greene–Harris book collection II–108b
John Carter Brown collection II–109a
library III–285a; IV–145b
mineralogy IV–348b
BROWN* v. *BOARD OF EDUCATION OF TOPEKA (1954, 1955) **I–372b**; I–30a, 32a; II–54b–55a, 56a, 57a–b, 404a–b, 457a; III–86b, 438b, 503a; IV–359a, 461a; V–126a, 331b, 353b; VI–256b; VII–196a, 291a
Brown v. *Louisiana* (1966) II–50b
BROWN* v. *MARYLAND (1827) **I–373a**; V–172a
Brown v. *Vandergrift* (1875) V–269b
Bruce, Archibald (min.) IV–349a; VI–235b
Bruce, David, Jr. (typefounder) V–412a
Bruce, David K. (dipl.) II–28a
Bruce, James, 8th Earl of Elgin II–431a
Bruce, Louis R. (offi.) III–373a
Bruinsburg (Miss.) III–208b; V–369a
Brulé (Indians) II–283a
Brulé, Étienne (expl.) VII–73b
Lake Huron III–319a
Lake Ontario V–156b
Lake Superior VI–443a
Sault Sainte Marie IV–330b; VI–219b
Brulé–Saint Croix portage II–380a
Brulé Sioux (Indians) III–256a, 378a; VI–164b, 296b; VII–345b
Brumidi, Constantino (paint.) V–191a
Brunel, Marc Isambard (inv.) III–138b, 442a,b; VII–128a
Brunner, Emil (theol.) VI–79b, 82b–83a
Brünnow, Franz (astron.) I–211a
Brunsviga (calculating machine) I–396a
Brunswick (Ga.) II–348b; III–428b; VII–223b
Brunswick (Ger.) III–172b
Brunswick (Maine) IV–227a; V–242a
Brunswick (N.C.) I–447b; V–115b
Brush, Charles F. (inv.) I–276a; II–413b; IV–153a
Brush, George de Forest (paint.) V–192a
Brushaber v. *Union Pacific Railroad Company* (1916) VII–6b
Brush Creek (Mo.) VII–280b
"Brushpopper" (cowboy) I–494a
"Brush whiskey" IV–407b
Brush wolf II–252b
Brussels (Belg.) VI–472a
air crash II–347a
North Atlantic Treaty Organization V–113b
World War I VII–366b
Brussels Conference (1937) V–96b–97a
BRUSSELS MONETARY CONFERENCE (1892) **I–373a**
Bruton Parish Church (Williamsburg) VII–300a–b, 302a
Brutus (sloop) VII–38a, 41a–b
Bruyère, Fabry de (expl.) III–119b; IV–230a
Bryan, Charles W. (pol.) I–428a
Bryan, Thomas J. II–103a
Bryan, William Jennings (states.) IV–382a; V–31b, 161b, 343b; VI–93a; VII–236b
agrarian movement I–33a, 39a, 44a
anti-corporate policy II–327b
anti-imperialism I–131b
Bryan–Chamorro Treaty I–373a, 483b
campaign of 1896 I–425a–b; III–189a; IV–335a; V–223b, 366a; VI–293a, 371a
campaign of 1900 I–425–26a; V–235b, 281b
campaign of 1908 I–426b
campaign of 1916 III–269b
Cross of Gold speech II–266a; III–111a
dollar diplomacy II–359b
Dominican Republic relations II–361a
free silver II–96b; IV–154b
Japan V–107b
Lusitania sinking IV–205b
Manchuria IV 235a–
peace conventions VI–217a
resignation VII–324b
Root Arbitration Treaties V–232b
Scopes trial VI–239b; VII–118b
BRYAN–CHAMORRO TREATY (1914) **I–373a**; I–483b; II–359b; V–94a, 95a; VII–112b
"Bryanism" I–426a
BRYAN'S STATION (Ky.) **I–373b**; VI–377b
Bryant, Pearl I–247b
Bryant, Sturgis and Company III–274b
Bryant, William Cullen (poet, ed.) IV–160b, 223a, 267a; V–189a; VII–361b
hymns III–326b
New York Evening Post V–68a, 73a
Bryant Park (N.Y.C.) II–474b; VII–259a
Bryant's Minstrel Troupe of New York II–357a
Bryce, James, Viscount Bryce (jur., hist., dipl.) V–222a, 353b; VI–447a; VII–261a
Bryce Canyon (Utah) II–346b
Bryce Canyon National Park V–217a, 218 (table)
Buade (riv.) IV–7a
Buade, Louis de. *See* Frontenac et Palluau, Comte de, Louis de Buade
Bubonic plague V–446b
Bucareli accords (1923) I–109b
Bucareli y Ursúa, Antonio Maria I–141a
BUCCANEERS **I–373b**; III–22b
Florida Straits III–41b
logwood trade IV–181b
Providence Island Company V–439a
Treaty of London IV–182b
See also Pirates
Buchalter, Lepke (racketeer) II–258b
Buchanan (Va.) III–488a
Buchanan, Franklin (nav. off.) I–14a; IV–396b, 397a; V–9b; VII–26b
Battle of Mobile Bay IV–383a
Buchanan, James (pres.) II–175 (table); V–247b, 394b, 395 (table)
administration's finances II–66a
adventurers III–24a
campaign of 1852 I–420b
campaign of 1856 IV–31a; VI–42b
Civil War II–61b
Covode investigation II–248b
Cuban relations V–175a
Dallas–Clarendon Convention II–285a
Fort Sumter VI–440b
government printing III–202a
homestead movement III–296b
Lecompton Constitution IV–130b–131a
Mexico relations IV–323a
Mormons IV–411a,b
Morrill Act IV–412b
Santo Domingo mission VI–217a
secession of southern states VI–251a
Star of the West VI–387a
Treaty of Guadalupe Hidalgo III–230a
Trist Mission IV–324a
Buchanan County (Mo.) V–330a
Bucharest, Treaty of (1918) I–176b
Bucher, Lloyd (nav. off.) V–460b
Buchwald, Art (humorist) V–75a
Buck, Pearl (au.) V–99b
Buck, Solon J. (hist.) I–167b
Buckaroo II–250a
BUCKBOARDS **I–374a**
Buckeye (tree) VI–395 (table)
Buckeye State VI–395 (table)
Buckhannon River II–477a
Buckingham, James Silk (trav., au.) I–367b, 368a
Buck Island Reef National Monument V–217b
Buckland, Cyrus (inv.) III–442a
Buckland, William (arch.) I–162b
Buckland Mills (Va.) I–374a
BUCKLAND RACES (1863) **I–374a**
Buckley, Samuel B. (bot.) III–222b
Buckley, William F., Jr. (jour.) II–189b; V–75a
Bucklin, Joseph III–154a
Buckner, Simon B. (off., pol.) III–189a; V–147b; VII–137b
Bucks County (Pa.) III–124a; VI–267b; VII–220b
Bucks County Historical Society (Pa.) VI–411b
Buckshots. *See* Molly Maguires
BUCKSHOT WAR (1838) **I–374a**
Buckskin II–283a, 371a; III–363b, 373b–74a; IV–50b, 127b
Bucksport (Maine) IV–226b
BUCK STOVE AND RANGE CASE (1911) **I–374b**; I–356b–57a; III–419a; IV–67b

BUCKTAILS (1818–26)
I–374b
Bucyrus (Ohio) V–152b
Budapest (Hung.)
radio VI–14b
Budd, William (nav. off.)
V–424a
Buddhism V–171b; VII–52a
Budge, Don (athlete)
VII–30b
Budget, Bureau of the
II–296a, 497b; V–136b;
VII–107b
Budget, Director of the. *See*
Office of Management
and Budget
Budget, Office of Management
and. *See* Office of Man-
agement and Budget
Budget, United States III–3a
Budget and Accounting Act
(1921) I–370a; II–152a,
501a; V–136b, 398a
Budget and Accounting Proce-
dures Act (1950)
II–152a
Budget message, presidential
II–502b
Bueche, Arthur (sci.)
III–156a
Buell, Abel (engr.) V–411b,
413a; VII–74a
Buell, Don Carlos (off.)
II–271b
Army of the Ohio
V–142a,b
Battle of Perryville
V–263b
Battle of Shiloh VI–278b
Kentucky invasion
IV–42a
Louisville III–485a
Buell, George (off.) VI–64a
Buenaventura, Fort (Utah)
VII–161b
BUENAVENTURA RIVER
I–374a; III–214b
Buena Vista (Calif.) V–13a
BUENA VISTA, BATTLE
OF (1847) **I–375a**;
IV–324a; VII–39a
Buenos Aires (Arg.) II–484a
Bouchard expedition
I–350a
Inter-American conferences
V–105a, 106a, 171a,
205a
peace conference
V–232a
Buenos Aires, United Prov-
inces of V–203b
Buenos Aires Conference of
American States (1936)
III–199a, 463a
BUFFALO I–375a;
III–50a–51a, 150a;
IV–90a, 233a; V–160b;
VI–6a
Apache III–368b
Arkansas River I–174b
Clovis culture II–83b
Comanche II–133b
cow-country II–250b
cow towns II–251b
Dakota II–283a
Great Plains III–220b
hides III–274b; VI–160b
hunters II–358b
hunting I–311a, 441b;
III–318a–b
Indian religion III–392b
Indian trade III–402b
Itama culture III–484a,b
Omaha Indians V–155a
Plains hunting III–363a,b,
364a
preservation III–54b;
VII–296b–97a, 298a
robes II–128a; IV–422b
salt licks VI–202a
Staked Plain VI–380b
stampedes VI–382b
Yellowstone Park
VII–357b
Buffalo (fighter plane) I–55a
BUFFALO (N.Y.) **I–375b**;
II–41b
air crash II–346a
Amana community I–92b
basketball I–273a
Civil War I–280a
crime II–259a, 262b
domestic trade VII–83b
electric lighting II–414b
Erie Canal II–460a;
III–448a
Fenians III–11a
flour milling III–43a, 44a,
45b
Free Soil party III–111b
Great Lakes VI–146a
iron and steel industry
III–12a, 470b
Iroquois Trail III–387b
Lake Erie II–459a
National Kansas Committee
IV–28a
Niagara Falls V–92b
Pan American Exposition
V–204b
railroads III–450a; IV–386b;
V–87a; VI–25b, 34a,
35a,b; VII–100b
steamboats VII–83b, 220b
stock exchange II–469b
War of 1812 III–218a;
IV–445b; V–91a
wheat VII–134a
Young Men's Christian As-
sociation VII–363a
Buffalo Bayou, Brazos and
Colorado Railroad
VI–26a–b, 37a
"Buffalo Bill." *See* Cody,
William F.
Buffalo Bill's Wild West Show
VI–161b; VII–298b
BUFFALO CHIPS I–376a;
II–487a; III–265a
Buffalo Creek (N.Y.)
I–375b; V–139b
Buffalo Creek (W.Va.)
II–352a
Buffalo Creek, Treaty of
(1802) III–383b
Buffalo Creek Reservation
VII–293b
Buffalo Grain Pool V–358a
Buffalo grass V–33a
Buffalo Historical Society
V–205a
Buffalo Horn (Indian)
I–264b
Buffalo Hunters (Indians)
III–51a
"Buffalo Skinners" (song)
I–247a
"Buffalo soldiers" I–310a;
VI–301a
BUFFALO TRAILS I–376a;
II–272a; III–387a, 447b;
VI–152b
Great Trading and War
Path III–223a
salt licks VI–202a
Wilderness Road
VII–296a
Buffer State. *See* Indian Bar-
rier State
BUFFINGTON ISLAND
SKIRMISH (1863)
I–376a; IV–410b
Buffon, Comte Georges Louis
Leclerc de (nat.)
IV–231b
Buford, Abraham (off.)
II–14b; VII–261b–62a
Buford, Fort (N.Dak.)
IV–415a; VII–145b
Buford, Jefferson (off.). *See*
Buford Expedition
Buford, John (off.) I–360a;
II–484b
BUFORD EXPEDITION
(1856) **I–376b**; II–439a
Buggy I–461b; III–255b
Building and Construction
Trades Councils
New York IV–77a
BUILDING AND LOAN AS-
SOCIATIONS I–376b;
VI–221b
BUILDING MATERIALS
I–377a
brickmaking IV–243a
ferrous metals III–12a
logs IV–179a
retail sales II–355a
Savannah VI–220b
street paving V–230a
Vermont VII–172b
Buildings
government inspection
III–422a
public IV–96a
See also Architecture
Bukharin, Nikolai Ivanovich
(states.) II–144a
Bulfinch, Charles (arch.)
I–163a, 451a; II–487b;
III–260b
Bulganin, Nikolai Ivanovich
(states.) III–161a
Bulgaria
nationalization of U.S.
property IV–466a
Paris Peace Conference
V–215b
Treaty of Versailles
VII–173a
United States v. *Bulgaria*
III–453b
World War I VII–327a,
330b
World War II V–378b
Bulgarian Eastern Orthodox
Church II–387a
Bulgars III–339a
BULGE, BATTLE OF THE
(1944–45) **I–379a**;
III–314b; VII–340b
Antwerp I–141a
armored vehicles I–178b
Bastogne I–273b
Malmédy massacre
IV–230b
Saint-Vith VI–198a
Siegfried Line VI–285b
Bulk carriers III–218a–b;
IV–312b
Bull, Dixie (pirate) V–243b
Bull, Jonathan VI–70b
Bull, Ole (col.) V–152b
Bull, Thomas (off.) VI–70b
Bullard, Robert L. (off.)
I–446a; IV–320a; V–147b
BULLBOATS I–380a;
IV–374a; VI–148a
BULLDOZE I–380b
Bulletin of the American Den-
tal Association II–330b
Bulletin of the Atomic Scien-
tists (period.) VI–237a
Bulletin of the Johns Hopkins
Hospital IV–3a
Bullfrog Mining District (Nev.)
VI–135a
BULL GARRISON HOUSE
(South Kingstown, R.I.)
I–380b
Bullins, Ed (playwright)
IV–167b; V–96a
Bullion
bills of exchange II–468a
Confederacy II–164a
depositories IV–360a
See also Bimetallism
BULL MOOSE PARTY
I–380b; V–427a–29a
bolters I–328a
campaign of 1912 I–426b;
V–329a; VI–331a;
VII–52b, 53b
campaign of 1916 I–427a
Farmer–Labor party
II–492b–93a
"square deal" VI–378a
Taft–Roosevelt split
VI–458a
Bulloch, James D. (nav. off.)
I–72b; II–158b; IV–85a;
V–17a–b
Bullock, Leonard H. (col.)
VII–102b
Bullock, Rufus B. (pol.)
III–295a
Bullpup (missile) IV–363b
BULL RUN, FIRST BATTLE
OF (1861) **I–381a**;
I–182a; II–62b, 451a;
V–377a; VI–373a;
VII–148a
Belle Isle prisoners
I–287a
Davis–Johnston controversy
II–295a
marines IV–252a
McDowell's advance
I–309a
"On to Washington"
V–157a
railroads VI–26b
Union captives IV–139a
BULL RUN, SECOND BAT-
TLE OF (1862) **I–382a**;
II–62b; III–229a; IV–261b;
VII–197a, 197b
Battle of Cedar Mountain
I–476b
Battle of Chantilly I–493b
Porter court-martial

BULL RUN, SECOND BATTLE OF (cont.) V–368b
Bull trains V–179a
Bullwhacker IV–426a; V–177b; VII–218a
"Bully beef" II–436a
Bultmann, Rudolf (theol.) VI–79b, 83a
Bulwer, Henry (dipl.) II–72b–73a
BUMMERS I–382b
Bumstead, Dagwood (comic character) V–72b
Buna (N.Guin.) VII–336b
Bunau-Varilla, Philippe (eng.) III–265a; V–201a,b, 204a
Bunbury, M. Simmones (off.) VI–244b
Bunche, Ralph (dipl.) V–100a
Bunch of Grapes Tavern (Boston) V–143b; VII–2a
Buncombe. *See* Bunkum
Buncombe County (N.C.) I–383a
Bundles (Indian) IV–236a
BUNDLING I–382b; II–485b; VI–266a
Bundy, Omar (off.) I–286a
BUNKER HILL (1775) **I–382b**; I–344b, 498b; II–274b, 364a; IV–7b, 84a, 266a; V–161a; VI–123a; VII–115a, 251b
breastworks II–449b
Bunker Hill (Idaho) IV–122b
Bunker Hill (Va.) VII–281a
Bunker Hill Centennial Exhibition (1875) II–99a
Bunker Hill mine (Idaho) VI–292b
BUNKER HILL MONUMENT I–383a; VI–24b
Bunkers VII–115b
BUNKUM I–383a; VI–299b
Bunny hug (dance) II–290b
Bunsen, Robert W. (chem.) II–11b
Bunting v. *Oregon* (1917) IV–80a; VII–214a
Bunyan, John (au.) IV–424b
Bunyan, Paul (char.) III–49a; VI–458b
Buoys
Coast Guard II–90a
federal maintenance II–89a–90a
Burbank (Okla.) V–149a
Burch, Dean (law., offi.) I–480b
Burchard, Samuel D. (cler.). *See* Burchard Incident
BURCHARD INCIDENT (1884) **I–383a**; I–424a
Burchfield, Charles (paint.) V–192b
Burck, Jacob (cartoon.) V–73a
Burd, Fort (Pa.) VI–65b
Burd, James (off.) III–58b; IV–200a; VI–65b
Burden, Henry (inv.) III–472b
BUREAUCRACY I–383b
lobbies IV–170b
Louisiana IV–195a
Nader's Raiders IV–448b
political parties V–343b
political patronage V–227b
president V–394b
pressure groups V–400b
state government VI–398a
states' rights VI–404b
urban structure VII–159b
Bureau of Aeronautics (navy) VII–341b
Bureau of American Ethnology II–464b–65a
Bureau of Animal Industry V–447b; VII–177a
Bureau of Applied Social Research V–454a
Bureau of Biological Survey VII–297b
Bureau of Chemistry V–447b, 465b, 466a,b
Bureau of Drug Abuse Control V–468b
Bureau of Education for the Handicapped III–249a
Bureau of Engraving and Printing V–372b
Bureau of Fisheries III–29a, 30a; VII–297b
Bureau of Foreign and Domestic Commerce IV–350a
Bureau of Intelligence and Research III–439b
Bureau of International Expositions V–89a
Bureau of Labor Statistics V–406a, 425b
Bureau of Land Management III–444a; V–446a
Forest Service V–451b
grazing VI–426a
Bureau of Medicine and Surgery, Navy IV–292b
Bureau of Narcotics V–468b
Bureau of Narcotics and Dangerous Drugs IV–22a; V–468b
Bureau of Outdoor Recreation III–444b
Bureau of Public Roads VI–152a; VII–98b
Bureau of Reclamation III–445a
Bureau of Refugees, Freedmen, and Abandoned Lands III–103a
Bureau of Sports Fisheries and Wildlife III–29a
Bureau of the Budget II–296a, 497b; V–136b
Bureau of the Census. *See* Census, U.S. Bureau of the
Bureau of the Mint IV–360a
Bureau of War Risk Insurance III–428b
Burford (ship) VI–128b
Burger, Warren E. (jur.) VI–444a, 447b, 448a
Commission on Correctional Facilities and Services V–417b
exclusionary rule VI–249a
judicial review IV–14b
obscenity I–479b
pornography III–106a
Burgess, John W. (educ.) III–342b; V–347b
Burgess, W. Starling (av.) I–235b; VII–349a
Burgess Company I–51a
Burgesses, House of. *See* Colonial Assemblies
Burgesses, House of (Va.) VII–193a
Burgh, Albert Coenraets (patroon) V–229a
Burgh, Henry (humanitarian) VII–24b
BURGHERS I–384b
Burglar alarms IV–333a
Burglary II–260a
capital punishment I–450a
Burgoyne, John (off.) *See* Burgoyne's Invasion
BURGOYNE'S INVASION (1777) **I–384b**; I–365b–66a; II–340a, 406a; III–173b; IV–86b; VI–123b; VII–171b
Albany I–81b
Battle of Bennington I–289a
Battle of Oriskany V–172b
Freeman's Farm III–108a–b
Iroquois participation III–400b
Oswego (N.Y.) V–175b
Saratoga surrender II–214b–15a; III–276a; IV–211b; V–231b; VI–217a; VII–358b
Ticonderoga VII–57a
Burial, Indian. *See* Indian Burial
Burial mounds
Adena I–11a–b
American Bottom I–100b
Cahokia I–157b, 402b
See also Mounds and Mound Builders
Burials
record-keeping VII–205b
Burk, John Daly (ed.) I–86b
Burke, Edmund (states.) II–189a,b; III–280b; IV–161b; V–188a
political parties V–222b
Reflections on the Revolution in France VI–141a
representation VI–88b
representative government VI–89b
Revenue Act of 1767 VII–80b
BURKE ACT (1906) **I–385b**
Burke-Hartke Act (1971) VI–472a; VII–90b
Burks, Arthur (phys.) II–156a
Burleigh, Charles (eng.) VII–128a
Burleigh, Harry T. (comp.) III–253b
Burleigh County (N.Dak.) II–283b
Burler County (Pa.) IV–434b
Burleson, Albert Sidney (pol.) II–446a
Burlesque II–260a; VII–48a, 49a
Burley tobacco VII–67b
Burlingame, Anson (dipl.) I–386a
BURLINGAME TREATY (1868) **I–386a**; II–29a, 488a–b; V–158a; VII–356b
Burlington (Iowa) III–468a, 469a; VI–28a
Burlington (N.J.) V–56b, 57a; VII–278b
land speculation I–386a
Quaker settlers II–124a
steamboat III–32b
Burlington (Vt.) V–156a
pottery manufacture II–5a
War of 1812 IV–87a
Burlington (Wis.) VI–416b
Burlington, Lord. *See* Boyle, Richard, 3rd Earl of Burlington
BURLINGTON COMPANY I–386a; V–176a
Burlington Heights (Can.) VI–415a
Burlington Northern Railroad III–451b; IV–176b; VI–26a, 32a, 32b–33a
BURLINGTON STRIKE (1888) **I–386a**; IV–66b
Burma
independence I–124a
missionaries I–265a
Southeast Asia Treaty Organization VI–350b
World War II I–60a; II–26a, 315a; III–46b; IV–446b–47a; V–138b; VII–337b, 342b
See also Burma Road and Ledo Road
BURMA ROAD AND LEDO ROAD I–386b; II–450a; III–46b; IV–314a; VI–156a
Burnaby, Andrew (trav.) IV–79b
Burnaby, Frederick G. (trav.) V–5a
Burnap, Daniel (inv.) II–77b–78a
"Burned-over" district (N.Y.) IV–116b; VI–77b
Burnet, David G. (pol.) VII–38a
Burnet, William (col. gov.) V–85a, 157a, 175b, 195a; VI–199a
Burnett, Peter H. VII–217b
Burnham, Daniel Hudson (arch.) II–18a, 46a
Burnham, Walter Dean (au.) II–327b
Burning (punishment) V–465a
"Burning brands" I–473b
BURNING SPRING (W.Va.) **I–387a**; II–464b
Burn research IV–291a
Burns, Anthony (slave) I–387a
Burns, Arthur F. (econ.) I–391b; III–8b
Burns, James MacGregor (pol. sci.) V–222b

Burns, Lucy (ref.) VII–315a
Burns, Tommy (pugilist) V–422b
Burns, William J. (detective) V–166a
Burns Agency II–462b
BURNS FUGITIVE SLAVE CASE (1854) **I–387a**
Burnside, Ambrose E. (off.)
  Army of the Ohio V–142b
  Battle of Antietam I–130a
  Battle of Fredericksburg III–101a
  Battle of Spotsylvania Courthouse VI–376b
  First Battle of Bull Run I–381b
  General Order No. 38 III–156a–b; VII–164b
  Grand Army of the Republic III–207b
  Knoxville siege IV–54a
  "Mud March" IV–425a
  Roanoke Island VI–156b
  Second Battle of Bull Run II–62b
"Burnt cork" minstrelsy IV–438a
BURNT CORN, BATTLE OF (1813) **I–387b**; IV–347B
Burnt Corn Creek I–387b
Burr, Aaron (pol.) IV–135b; V–41b, 347a; VI–414b
  campaign of 1796 I–417a, 475a
  election of 1800 III–4b–5a; VII–131b
  election of 1800 I–94b, 388a, 417a–b; II–409a; III–494b–95a
  landholdings IV–100b
  Manhattan water supply VII–258b
  Martling Men IV–260a
  Mexican Association IV–320b
  Miranda's intrigues IV–361b
  New York City politics V–83a
  Tammany Hall VI–459a
  Texas conspiracy VII–37a
  vice-presidency VII–179 (table)
  See also Burr Conspiracy; Burr–Hamilton Duel; Burr Trial
Burr, Aaron, Sr. (cler., educ.) V–41a, 408b
Burr, George O. (biochem.) V–127b
Burr, M. M. (biochem.) V–127b
Burr, Theodore (arch.) I–363b
BURR CONSPIRACY I–387b; I–319b, 324a, 327b; II–252a; III–22b; VII–37a
  Mexican Association IV–320b
  New Orleans V–63b–64a
BURR–HAMILTON DUEL (1804) **I–388a**; II–377a; VII–266b
Burriel, Juan (off., gov.) VII–204a
Burrill, Thomas Jonathan (bot.) I–46a
Burritt, Elihu (ling., ref.) V–235b
Burroughs 220 (computer) II–156a
Burroughs, Margaret G. (au.) I–25a
Burroughs, William Seward (inv.) I–396b
Burrowes, Thomas H. (pol.) I–374a
Burrows, J. M. D. (mer.) VII–274a
Burrows, J. M. D., Company V–375b
Burrows, William (nav. off.) II–452b
BURR TRIAL (1807) **I–388b**; V–397b; VII–107a
Burschenshaften refugees V–342a
Burt, Francis (gov.) V–31a
Burt, William A. (inv.) I–395b; IV–331b; VI–441a; VII–136a
Burton, Harold H. (jur.) VI–446b
Burton, Isaac (off.) III–304a
Burton, Mike (athlete) V–154b
Burton, William H. (chem.) III–409a
Burton, William M. (chem., ind.) V–267a, 270a
Burton Act (1906) V–92a
Burundi IV–236b
Bush, Vannevar (elec. eng.) I–457a; VI–230b
  atomic bomb I–215b; IV–238a
  differential analyzer II–153a–b
  National Science Foundation IV–470b
  Office of Scientific Research and Development V–137a
Bush and Lobdell. *See* Lobdell Car Wheel Company
Bushnell, David (inv.) IV–35b; VI–422b
Bushnell, Horace (cler.) VI–78a, 82a
"Bush rangers" II–246a
Bushrod, Richard (mer.) II–364b
BUSHWHACKERS I–388b; II–165a; III–231a; IV–377b
Bushwick (N.Y.) I–370a; IV–185a
BUSHY RUN, BATTLE OF (1763) **I–389a**; I–353b
BUSINESS, BIG I–389a; IV–244b
  antitrust laws I–139b
  blacklisting I–314a
  campaign of 1888 I–424a–b
  campaign of 1904 I–426a
  canning industry I–445b
  commerce clause II–135b–37a
  conglomerates II–169a
  conservatism II–189a,b
  corporate charters II–229a–b
  crash of 1929 I–390b–91a
  Cuba II–361b
  Customs Service II–277a
  dairy industry II–282a
  distribution of goods and services II–354a–55a
  employment departments II–442b
  excess profits tax II–467a–b
  fair-trade laws II–484a
  financing II–467b–68a
  foundations III–83b
  government loans II–498b
  government regulation I–389b–91b, 449b; II–72a; III–204a–05a
  Industrial Revolution III–411a
  "interests" III–443b
  lobbies IV–170b
  monopoly IV–398b
  New Deal I–391a; V–46b
  New Freedom V–53a
  newspapers V–76a–77a
  organized crime II–258b
  panic of 1907 V–208b
  panic of 1929 V–209b
  price maintenance V–403a
  Republican party VI–93b
  robber barons VI–156b
  Sherman Antitrust Act VI–276a
  taxation VII–6b
  trade associations VII–92a
  "trust–busting" VII–121b
  trusts VII–121b
  women VII–317b
  World War I I–390b
Business, government regulation of. *See* Government Regulation of Business
BUSINESS, PUBLIC CONTROL OF I–389b
  government corporations III–201a, 202b–03a
  licensing IV–148a–b
  railroad rate wars VI–23a–b
  warehousing IV–434a–b
Business administration. *See* Industrial Management
BUSINESS CYCLES I–391b
  desertion from military II–334b–35a
  federal surplus VI–449a
  money supply IV–234a
  national income reports IV–462a
  prices V–403b
  recession of 1937 VI–51b
  standards of living VI–384a
  wool industry VII–321a
  See also entries under Panic
Business Economists Association. *See* National Association of Business Economists
Business ethics II–92a
Business exchanges II–493b
Business failures
  depression of 1920 I–334a
  panic of 1873 V–207a,b
  panic of 1893 V–208a
  panic of 1907 V–208b
BUSINESS FORECASTING I–394b
BUSINESS MACHINES I–395b
Business schools I–19a
BUSING I–397b; II–400a, 457a; III–438b, 438b; VI–8a
  Bradley v. *Milliken* II–54b–55a
  crosstown and intercounty II–402b
  legal education IV–121b
  New South V–67b–68a
  parochial schools II–400a
  See also Boycotting
Busk (rel.) III–366a
Buster Brown (comic character) V–72a
Busti, Paul (bus.) III–291b
Bustle (dress) II–372a
Bus transportation III–451b, 452a; VI–380b; VII–101b, 102a
  integration II–58a; III–107b
  municipal ownership IV–428b
  urban structure VII–159b
BUSY BEES OF DESERET I–397b
Butane V–267a–b
Butaritari Island III–180a
Bute, Earl of. *See* Stuart, John
BUTE, FORT (La.) **I–398a**; III–326b
Butler, Andrew P. (pol.) I–371a
Butler, Benjamin F. (off., pol.) I–424a; III–262a; V–347a; VII–358a
  America I–95b
  Army of the James III–488a
  campaign of 1884 III–225a
  Dutch Gap Canal II–382b
  Fort Fisher III–30b
  Gatling gun II–67a
  James River expedition VI–138a
  Johnson impeachment III–345b–46a
  land speculation I–107b
  New Orleans V–63b
  Radical Republicans VI–11b
  Sanborn contracts VI–207b
  slaves as contraband II–212a
  Soldiers and Sailors convention VI–336a
Butler, Edward (pol.) VI–142b
Butler, Elizur (miss.) VII–321b–22a
Butler, Henry (showman) VI–283a

Butler, John (off.) I–398a; V–90b; VI–130a
Battle of Oriskany V–172b
Cherry Valley Massacre II–15a
Niagara Company V–91a
rangers VI–46b
Wyoming Massacre VI–452a; VII–346b
Butler, Josephine Elizabeth (ref.) V–437b
Butler, Matthew Calbraith (off.) II–373a
Butler, Nicholas Murray (educ.) II–132b, 470b; V–100a
Butler, Pierce (jur.) II–203b; V–47a; VI–446b; VII–269b
Butler, Richard (Indian agent) V–322a
Butler, Richard (off.) III–308a
Butler, Robert (off.) IV–329a
Butler, Smedley D. (off.) II–26a
Butler, Zebulon (off.) VII–346b
Butler Act (Tenn., 1925) VI–239b, 240a
Butler bill (1927) V–10a
Butler County (Pa.) II–147a; III–255a
Butler Ring VI–142b
BUTLER'S ORDER NO. 28 (1862) **I–398a**
BUTLER'S RANGERS I–398a; VI–46b, 130a; VII–346b
Butte (Mont.) VI–101b
copper II–223a–b; V–103a
mining IV–403a
silver VI–292b
BUTTE DES MORTS COUNCIL (1827) **I–398a**
Butter II–279b, 280b–81a, 282a,b
pure food laws V–465b, 466b
Butterfat test II–281a–b
Butterfield, D. A. (bus.) I–398b
Butterfield, Daniel I–311a
Butterfield, John (fin.) III–221a; V–357b; VI–353b, 379a
BUTTERFIELD CLAIMS I–398b
BUTTERFIELD OVERLAND DISPATCH I–398b; VI–320b; VII–39a
Butterfield Overland Mail. *See* Southern Overland Mail
Butterfly violet VI–393 (table), 395 (table)
Butterick, Ebenezer (inv.) II–371b
Butterick, John (off.) IV–137a–b
Butternuts III–51a
Butternuts (Copperheads) II–222b
Butterworth v. *Dempsey* (1964) II–180a
Button, Dick (athlete) V–154b
Buying, installment. *See* Installment Buying, Selling, and Financing
Buying associations, consumer II–221a
Buzzards Bay (Mass.) I–447a; V–130a
Buzz bomb IV–363a
Byam, Ezekiel IV–274a
"By and by" (motto) VI–395 (table)
Byllynge, Edward (col.) V–56b; VII–278a–b
Byrd, Harry F. (pol.) I–343b; VII–195b, 196a
Byrd, James (off.) III–58b
Byrd, Richard E. (expl.) V–337a–b
Distinguished Flying Cross II–311b
Medal of Honor II–310a
polar expeditions I–398b
Byrd, William (planter, fur trader) I–161b, 332b; IV–161a, 231a; VI–136b; VII–201b
Dismal Swamp II–353a
library II–107b
Byrd, William II (planter, col. offi.) III–280b; VI–136b; VII–192b, 193b
Byrd family IV–256b
Virginia landholdings IV–92a
BYRD'S POLAR FLIGHTS I–398b; V–337a–b
Byrd v. *McCready* (1950) I–372b
Byrne, William M., Jr. (jur.) V–258b
Byrnes, James F. (jur.) I–429b; VI–446b
Byrns, Joseph Wellington (pol.) II–177 (table)
Byron, George Gordon, 6th Baron Byron (poet) IV–267a; V–188a
Byron, John (nav. off.) V–418b
Byssinosis IV–294b
"By the sword peace under liberty" (motto) VI–394 (table)
"By Valor and Arms" (motto) VI–394 (table)

C

CA (heavy cruiser). *See* Cruisers
C–2 (airship) II–344a; IV–312a
C–3 (freighter) IV–312a
C–5 (dirigible) II–343b
C–5A (transport plane) I–63b
C–7 (blimp) II–344b
C–46 (twin engine plane) II–346b
C–47 (transport plane) I–49b, 291a; III–46a; VI–302a–b
C–54 (transport plane) I–52a, 61a, 291a; III–46a; IV–180b
C–69 (transport plane) I–52a
C–119 (transport plane) I–49b
C–123 (transport plane) I–62a
C–124 (transport plane) I–65a; II–346b
C–130 (transport plane) I–49b, 62b, 63a, 65a
C–141 (transport plane) I–61b
CAB. *See* Civil Aeronautics Board
Cabanne, Jean Pierre (trader) I–399b; II–34a
CABANNE'S TRADING POST (Nebr.) **I–399b**
Cabarets II–260a, 261b
Cabbage III–51b, 54b
Cabell, James Branch (au.) IV–164b
Cabet, Étienne III–327a; VI–325b
Cabeza de Vaca, Álvar Núñez (expl.). *See* Cabeza de Vaca, Travels of
CABEZA DE VACA, TRAVELS OF I–399b; I–96a; II–184a; IV–452a; VII–36a–b, 372a
CABILDO (govt.) **I–399b**; I–239a
Cabildo (New Orleans) I–160a
Cabin (arch.) I–160b
Cabin Creek VII–239a
CABINET I–399b; II–498a; III–3b
appointments II–168a
attorney general IV–21b
budget V–137a
Commerce and Labor Department IV–78a
Council of National Defense II–243a
Department of Transportation VII–98a
flag III–35b
Health, Education, and Welfare Department III–267b
Housing and Urban Development II–47b; III–310b
Interior Department III–444a
Kitchen Cabinet IV–51a
Labor Department IV–78a
Lincoln's II–64a
Navy Department V–18b
New Deal V–43a–b
Nixon's proposed reorganization IV–78b–79a
post office IV–36b; V–372a, 374a
presidential disability V–397a,b
presidential succession II–207b; V–398b
revolutionary committees VI–122b
salary grab VI–198b
Senate confirmation II–171b
State Department VI–388a
Tenure of Office Act VII–31b
Treasury VII–107b
women VII–317b
See also individual cabinet departments
Cabinet, British II–191a
Cabinet, Confederate II–160a–b, 165a
Cabinet-Maker and Upholsterer's Drawing Book III–135a
Cabinetmaking I–490b; III–134a,b, 138a,b; IV–61b
CABIN RIGHTS I–400a
Cable, George Washington (au.) IV–162b
Cable Act (1922) V–7a; VII–315b
Cable cars II–414b; VI–209b, 418a
Cable communication III–1a
CABLES, ATLANTIC AND PACIFIC I–400b
American Telegraph and Cable Company II–137a
Commercial Cable Company II–137a
Great Eastern III–215b
Midway Islands IV–337a
navy assistance V–23a
telegraph VII–19a
telephone II–142b–43a, 142b–43a; VII–20b
vacuum tubes VII–163a–b
Western Union VII–276b
Yap mandate VII–353b
Cables, overland II–426a
Cable service
Interstate Commerce Commission III–458a
Cable television III–1a,b
Caborca (Mex.) V–314b
Cabot (ship) VI–128a
Cabot, John (expl.) I–6a, 96b, 401b; III–355b; IV–247a; V–122a, 246a; VII–275b
cod fisheries II–92a
Cabot, Lewis (expl.) I–401b
Cabot, Richard Clarke (physic.) VI–331a
Cabot, Sanctius (expl.) I–401b
Cabot, Sebastian (expl.) I–401b; IV–247a,b
Cabot family IV–256b
CABOT VOYAGES I–401b; IV–264b; VII–275b
American Indian III–355b
Northwest Passage V–122a
Pennsylvania V–246a
Cabral, Pedro (expl.) I–96a
Cabrillo, Juan Rodríquez (expl.). *See* Cabrillo Expedition
CABRILLO EXPEDITION (1542) **I–401b**; I–405a, 466b; IV–404b
Cabrillo National Monument V–217b

Cabrini, Saint Frances Xavier I–469b
CABUSTO, BATTLE OF (1540) **I–402a**; II–336b
Cacao II–453a; III–381a
Cácares, Rámon (pol. leader) II–361a
Cache (Okla.) IV–184b
Cache Creek VII–238b
Cache la Poudre River V–178b
Cache la Poudre Valley VII–146a
CACIQUE I–402a; III–368b; VI–348b
Cactus
 alcoholic drinks III–398a
Cactus wren (bird) VI–393 (table)
Caddo (Indians) III–367a; V–230b
 Lower Indian Reserve I–286a
 Parker's Fort attack V–216b
 Red River Post VI–64b
Caddoan (lang.) III–364a, 365a, 365b; IV–235b; V–148a
 Arikara I–171b
 Pawnee V–230b
Cadette Girl Scouts III–181b
Cadillac (auto) I–228b
Cadillac, Antoine de la Mothe (col. adm.) III–120a, 216a
 Crozat's grant VI–189b
 Detroit II–336b; IV–330b
 Fort Pontchartrain du Détroit V–356b
 Indian policy VI–219b–20a
 Louisiana II–267b
Cádiz (Sp.)
 triangular trade VII–119b
Cadman, Charles W. (comp.) IV–438b
Cadmium VI–48b; VII–369b
Cadore, Duc De. *See* Champigny, Jean Baptiste Nompère, Duc de Cadore
Cadotte, Jean Baptiste (fur trader) II–13b
Cadotte, Michel (fur trader) II–13b
Cadwalader, John (off.) II–321b
Cadwalader family IV–256b
Cadwallader, George (off.) III–31a
Caen (Fr.) V–110b; VII–339a,b
Caesar, Julius IV–163a
Cafe La Mama (N.Y.C.) VII–51a
Cage, John (comp.) IV–165a, 439b
Cahaba (Ala.) I–308b
CAHABA OLD TOWNS I–402a
Cahaba River I–402a
Cahensly, Peter Paul (rel. leader) I–469a
CAHOKIA (Ill.) **I–402a**
 architecture I–160a
 Fort Saint Joseph VI–192a
 Franciscans III–94a
 fur trade III–144a
 Holy Family Mission III–329a
 Mississippian Culture I–158a
 revolutionary war V–388a; VI–126b, 195a
 settlement I–100b
Cahokia Indians I–402a
CAHOKIA MOUNDS I–402b; IV–370a,b, 420b
CAHUENGA, TREATY OF (1847) **I–403a**; I–409b; VI–210b
Cahuenga ranch. *See* Cahuenga, Treaty of
Cahuilla (Indians) III–363a; IV–366a
Caientoton Island. *See* Manitoulin Islands
Caimanera (Cuba) III–230b
Cairo (Egy.)
 aerial hijacking III–277b
 mixed courts II–479a
 World War II VII–338a
CAIRO (Ill.) **I–403b**; II–406b
 Bird's Point I–306b
 Civil War I–288a
 floods III–37a
 Illinois Central Railroad VI–26a
 Juchereau's tannery IV–9a
 Lakes-to-Gulf waterway IV–88a
 railroad bridge I–364a
 Sultana disaster II–349a
 yellow fever II–454b
Cairo (ironclad) II–384a; VI–424b
Cairo City and Canal Company I–403b
CAIRO CONFERENCES (1943) **I–403b**; II–489a
Caisson (floating gate) II–375a
CAJON PASS I–403b; V–224b
Cajuns. *See* Acadia
Calais (Fr.) II–217a
 World War II VII–339a,b
Calais (Maine) IV–226b
CALAMITY HOWLER I–403b
Calamus IV–162b
Calash (bonnet) II–371a
Calash (coach) VII–168a–b
Calaveras grove (Calif.) VI–262b
Calcium arsenate III–421a
Calcium carbide II–7b, 422a; V–98a
Calcium chloride III–55a
Calcium cyanamide III–17a
Calcium nitrate II–43b; III–17a
Calcium oxide II–5a
Calculating machine I–395b–96a; II–153b; IV–352a
 See also Computers
Calculator, pocket VI–259a
Calcutta (India)
 trade II–388a
Caldecott, Randolph (illus.) I–335b
Calder, Alexander (sculp.) VI–244a
CALDER* v. *BULL (1798) **I–404a**
Caldwell (Kans.) I–2a, 473b; II–32a, 251b
Caldwell, Charles (physic.) V–293b
Caldwell, Earl (jour.) V–79a
Caldwell, Erskine (au.) I–479a; IV–164b
Caldwell, Frank (eng.) I–234b
Caldwell, James (theat. mgr.) I–268a
Caldwell, James H. (theat. mgr.) VII–47a
Caldwell, William (off.) I–373b
Caldwell County (Mo.) II–496a; III–262b
Caledonia (frigate) II–459a–b; III–218a
Calendrical systems III–356b, 366a; IV–327a
Calgary Stampede I–369a; VI–161b
Calhoun, John C. (states.) V–161a
 Alabama politics I–71a
 army administration I–184a
 Bluffton movement I–326a
 Bonus Bill I–330b; III–448b
 Bureau of Indian Affairs III–371a
 campaign of 1824 I–418b
 campaign of 1828 I–419a
 campaign of 1832 I–419a
 "concurrent majority" doctrine V–352b
 conservatism II–189a
 Cotton Kingdom II–241a
 Eaton affair II–389b
 Indian missions III–499b
 Indian policy III–379a,b
 Indian removal III–221a, 389a, 393b, 394a
 internal improvements VI–145b
 natural rights doctrine V–7b
 nullification III–78a; V–125b, 176b; VII–198a, 265b
 oratory IV–162b
 "peculiar institution" V–241b
 Rip Raps contract-scandal VI–145a
 slavery I–137b; II–150a, 189a; IV–377b; VI–307b
 southern rights movement VI–354a
 state sovereignty VI–403b–04a; VII–198a
 states' rights VI–347b
 Survey Act of 1824 VI–450a
 tariff III–113a; VI–465a–b, 466a
 Tarpley letter IV–453b; VII–1a
 vice-presidency VII–179 (table)
 War Department II–313b; VII–229b
 war hawks VII–231a
 Washington Republican I–3a
 Yellowstone River expeditions VII–357b
 See also Calhoun's *Disquisition on Government*; Calhoun's *Exposition*
Calhoun, Lee Q. (athlete) V–154a
CALHOUN'S *DISQUISITION ON GOVERNMENT* I–404a; V–353a; VI–403b–04a
CALHOUN'S *EXPOSITION* I–404b; V–125b; VI–347b; VII–265b
Calico Hills (Calif.) I–155a
Calico printing II–5a
CALICO RAILROAD I–404b
CALIFORNIA I–405a; VI–355a,b, 393 (table); VII–268a, 268a
 acquisition II–475a; III–263a
 aircraft industry strike IV–341b
 alcaldes I–83b
 alien landholding I–87a, 409a
 Alta California I–91b
 antimiscegenation laws IV–362b
 Anza expedition I–141a
 Bear Flag Revolt I–280a
 black officeholders VI–432b
 Border Slave State Convention I–341b
 Bouchard expedition I–350a
 boundary I–352a
 boycotts I–356b
 campaign of 1880 IV–409b
 campaign of 1948 V–429a
 cession by Mexico III–230a
 Chinese II–29b, 30a; VII–356b
 chromite III–13b
 civil service II–60a
 Civil War III–187b; V–372a
 Clayton Compromise II–73a
 Colorado River Compact II–130a–b; III–460a
 Colorado River dispute VI–398a
 Colorado River Reservation III–395b
 Compromise of 1850 II–139a, 150a–b
 conciliation process II–157b
 Concord Coach II–158a
 conquest IV–34a–b, 252a
 constitutional convention (1879) IV–33a
 courts of the Plains II–247a
 criminal procedure

CALIFORNIA (cont.)
III–320a
Death Valley II–297b
declaratory judgment laws II–309b
Democratic clubs V–345b
Desert culture II–334b
Digger Indians III–51b
discrimination in courts III–437b
divorce laws II–356b
earthquakes II–385a
emigration I–363a, 452b, 453a, 485b; II–477b; IV–25b
End Poverty in California (EPIC) II–454a
exploration I–269a, 401b, 403b, 413a, 455b–56a, 466b; II–184b, 369a; III–114b; IV–249a; VI–160a
filibustering III–23a
fish III–27a
floods V–23a
forest fires II–348b
forests III–74b
Fort Yuma VII–367a
Franciscans III–94a
freeways III–451a
Frémont expeditions III–215a; VII–271b
furniture III–139b
Garcés–Anza route III–150b
Ghost Dance III–177b
Golden Gate Bridge III–189a
Golden Gate International Exposition III–189b
grasshopper attacks III–212b
great fortunes III–79b
Great Valley III–223b
Hale Observatories III–241b
Hastings' Cutoff III–260b
Hawk's Peak episode III–264b
historic properties IV–472a
home–rule charters I–501a
horse III–302b, 303a, 304b; IV–444b
horse racing III–304b
hydroelectric power III–320b
Indians III–222b, 356a, 360b, 362a–63a, 396a,b; IV–365b; V–4a; VI–6a
In re Neagle V–30a
Italians III–338a, 483a,b
Japanese–Americans II–445b; III–491a
Jesuits III–498b, 501b
Jet Propulsion Laboratory III–502a
Jimsonweed Cult III–503a
junior colleges II–400b
juvenile courts IV–23b
Kearny–Frémont quarrel IV–34a
Kelly's Industrial Army IV–36a
Kern County Land Company II–336a
Lakewood Plan IV–172b
land management V–450a
Lassen's Post and Ranch IV–110a
law schools IV–121b
Magdalena Bay IV–223b
mail service V–177b–78a
mapping IV–247b, 248a
Mariposa land grant IV–254a
Mexican boundary IV–321b
Mexican War I–280a–b, 403a, 409b; III–34a; IV–323a, 323b–24a, 324b; V–19b; VI–184a, 210b, 214a, 414a
Midwinter International Exposition IV–337b
migration III–221a
minimum–wage law IV–352b
missions I–159b; VI–364b
Miwok IV–381b
Modoc IV–51b
Modoc War IV–51b, 384b; VII–127a
Monterey IV–404b
Monterey State Historic Park IV–472a
Morningstar commune II–142b
mountain passes V–224b
mud slides II–352a
Mussel Slough incident IV–444a
Nataqua IV–454b
national forests V–446a
national parks and monuments V–217a,b, 218–19 (table)
Native American Church V–2a
native plants V–326b, 327a
Northwestern Indian War VII–239b
Okies V–149a
overland mail V–357b
Pacific republic movement V–180b
Paiute V–194a
Panama Railroad V–203b
Panoche Grande Claim V–210b
Phoenixiana V–289a
picketing V–308b
Pious Fund controversy V–318a
poker V–336a
popular sovereignty V–155a
population growth V–88a
potash III–17a
presidios V–399b; VI–364a
private mints IV–360a–b
public ownership V–455a
Pullman strike V–463b
purchase from Mexico IV–324b
Quakers V–470a
race relations VI–7a
railroads VI–20b, 26b, 27a,b, 36b, 37a
railroad surveys VI–39a
ranches VI–45a
ranchos del rey VI–45b
recall VI–51a
Reconstruction Finance Corporation VI–60a
redwoods VI–262b
referendum VI–66b
Republican League V–345b
Republic of I–280b
resorts and spas VI–100b, 101a,b
retirement communities II–48b
rivers VI–150a
River Yumans IV–386a
roundups VI–161a
Rural Legal Assistance Program V–136a
Russian settlement VI–180b
San Diego VI–208a
San Francisco VI–209a
Santa Catalina I–466b
Santa Fe Trail VI–215b–16a
seismographic stations III–164b
settlers II–433b, 461a; VII–161b
single–tax plan VI–293b
skiing VI–298a,b
slavery II–150a,b; IV–379b
Smith explorations VI–318a
Southern Overland Mail VI–353b
southern railroad route VI–353b
Spanish and Mexican land grants IV–93a
Spanish Trail VII–256a
stage and train robberies VII–97b
state fairs VI–392b
statehood I–78b; VI–254a
telegraph V–358a
Tigre Island VII–58b
timberlands IV–97b
trails VII–100a
Trinity Dam III–323b
Union Pacific Railroad VII–147b
United Farm Workers IV–76b–77a
Vancouver's exploration VII–166a
veterinary medicine VII–176b
wagon trains VII–217b
Walker expedition VII–220a
water rights IV–104b
water supply VI–54a; VII–259a,b
westward movement V–176b, 179a; VII–284a,b
woman's suffrage III–91b; VII–315a
Workingmen's party IV–33a
Yosemite National Park VII–361b
Yurok VII–367b
—*Economic Activity:*
Adams Express Company I–10a
banking I–258b
beet sugar I–285a; VI–437a
borax I–340a–b
cattle I–472b, 473a
citrus fruit II–43a, 43b
clipper ship trade II–77a–b
contrabandistas II–212b
cotton II–238b; IV–104a
dairy industry II–281b
dried fruits II–373a
drogher trade II–373b
dry farming II–375b
fair–trade laws II–482b
farmers' cooperatives II–221b
farming VI–365a
farm labor movements I–42a
flour milling I–488a
forty–niners II–248a
fruit growing III–128b
gold I–281a, 292b, 448a, 452b, 473a; II–29b, 77a, 95b, 241b; III–81b–82a, 163a, 190b, 191a; IV–349a
Grange stores II–220b
grape boycott V–182a
hide and tallow trade III–274b
interstate trade barriers III–460b
irrigation III–477b, 478a–b
joint–stock land banks IV–6b
land speculation II–336a; IV–99b, 101a
lead–silver industry IV–122b
meat–packing IV–280b
mining IV–354a, 354a,b; VI–364b
onions V–156a
oranges II–43a
overland freighting V–177a
petroleum V–270a, 272a
placer mining V–323a
prices V–405a
rice I–486b
salmon VI–201a
seals VI–245b
sea otter trade VI–247a,b
self–service stores VI–258a
sheep VI–273a
shipping IV–310b
silver mining VI–292a
smelters VI–316b
sweet potatoes V–377a
use of camels I–412b, 413a
Wells, Fargo VII–267a
wheat I–486a; II–375b; III–44a
winemaking III–53b, 129a; VII–305a–b
wool VII–320b
California, College of II–115a
California, Gulf of I–125a; II–129a, 129a; III–362a; V–145a
exploration IV–452b; V–155b
California, University of II–115a; VII–156b
chair design III–137a
mining engineering III–166b
political science

V–348b–49a
Scripps Institution
V–135a; VI–242a
California, University of, at Berkeley
atomic bomb V–300b
Bancroft Library III–284b
free speech movement
VII–366a
Lawrence Radiation Laboratory IV–119a
particle accelerators
V–297a, 301a,b
radicals VI–14a
Survey Research Center
V–454a
California, University of, at Los Angeles
meteorological studies
IV–318a
California Academy of Sciences V–327a
CALIFORNIA ALIEN LAND LAW (1913) **I–409b**
CALIFORNIA BANK NOTES I–409b
California Basin Indians
IV–386a
CALIFORNIA BATTALION I–409b
California Big Tree
VII–220a
California Borax Company
I–340a
California College of Medicine
IV–288b
California Consolidated Mine
II–157a
California culture
III–362a–63a, 369a;
VII–367b
basketry III–373b
cremation III–376a
myth and folklore
III–386a,b
political organization
III–391b
religion III–392a
Shaker religion VI–268a
California Debris Commission
VI–146a
California Gulch (Colo.)
IV–124a
California Indians
scalping VI–224b
tobacco VII–65a
California Indian War (1851–52) VII–239a
California Institute of Technology II–448a; III–158a
Hale telescope III–242a
Jet Propulsion Laboratory
III–502a
California Lawn Tennis Club
VII–29a–b
California mine (Nev.)
I–329a
Californian (liner) VII–64a
CALIFORNIA TRAIL I–409b; V–330b; VI–154a;
VII–101a
Indian concessions
III–379b
Indian hostilities III–256a
pony express V–357b
South Pass VI–354b
wagon trains VII–217b
water approach IV–27b
water holes VII–256a
CALIFORNIA v. CENTRAL PACIFIC RAILROAD COMPANY (1888)
I–410a
Call, Richard Keith (pol.)
III–39a; VI–260b
Callahan, Edward (sheriff)
III–253a
Call-and-response, African
IV–443a
Callao (Peru) V–180a
Callaway, Elizabeth I–337a
Callaway, Flanders I–337a
Callaway, Francis I–337a
Callaway, Richard (off.)
I–337a
Callaway Gardens (Ga.)
I–348a
Callear, Moses (mfr.)
III–184b
Callender, James T. (pol. writ.)
I–86b
Caller, James (off.) I–387b
Calles, Plutarco Elías (pol.)
IV–328b
Calley, William (off.)
II–247a
Calliope (ship)
I–144a
Calliope, steam II–40b
Call money (fin.)
I–256a–b
Calls (fin.) II–470b
CALOMEL I–410a;
IV–297a; VII–355b
Calorimeter I–46a, 303a
Calorimotors I–276a
Calrod element II–420a
Calumet. *See* Pipe, Indian
Calumet, Lake IV–88a
CALUMET AND HECLA MINE I–410b; II–223a–b
Calumet–Sag route IV–88a
Calvados (Fr.) VII–339a
Calvert, Cecilius, 2nd Baron Baltimore V–332b
Battle of the Severn
VI–264b
Maryland I–172b;
II–117b, 124a, 124b;
IV–260a–b; V–436b
proprietary agents
V–435b, 436a
religious liberty
VI–80b
Saint Marys VI–197a
Calvert, Charles, 3rd Baron Baltimore
Maryland settlement
I–249b
Pennsylvania–Maryland-boundary dispute V–252a
Calvert, Charles, 4th Baron Baltimore V–252a
Calvert, George, 1st Baron Baltimore III–18a;
IV–260a; V–251b–52a,
378a
Claiborne II–70a
royal land grants IV–91b
Calvert, Leonard (col. gov.)
Claiborne II–70a
Maryland IV–260b
Calvert City (Ky.)
IV–41b
Calvert family III–501b
estate confiscation
V–436b
land speculation IV–98b
Maryland IV–263a
Calves (cattle) II–281b
Calvin, John (rel. ref.). *See* Calvinism
Calvin, Melvin (biochem.)
I–303b; IV–119b; V–100a
CALVINISM I–410b;
III–112b; V–286b, 391a,b;
VI–75b, 76b, 81a,b
Arminianism I–176a–b
Baptist churches I–264a
Bible I–293b
colonial education
II–393b
Edwardsean theology
II–406a
evangelism II–466a
frontier preaching
III–127b
Huguenots III–315a
immigration III–336b
Labadist sect IV–59b
Massachusetts Bay Colony
I–411b, 412a
Methodist theory
IV–318b
New England Primer
V–51b
Puritanism V–469a,b
Reformed churches
VI–68b
schoolbooks VI–227a
Synod of Dort VI–455b
Westminster Confession of Faith II–169b; VII–279a
Yale College II–394b
Calvo, Carlos (states.). *See* Calvo Doctrine
CALVO DOCTRINE (1885)
I–411a; II–369a;
V–105b–06a
Campbell, John (jour.)
I–346a
Cambodia
aid costs VII–229a
Geneva Accords of 1954
III–159b
Indochina War VII–182b
Mayaguez incident V–74b
Southeast Asia Treaty Organization VI–350b
surrender VII–185a,
186b–87a
Vietnam War II–316b
CAMBODIA, BOMBING OF I–411a; I–49a, 63a;
III–70b, 463a,b;
VII–184a,b, 237b, 254a,
366a
Nixon impeachment proceedings III–345a
pacifism V–181a–b, 182a
protest movement V–237b
Cambrai (Fr.)
World War I I–177a
Cambrai, Battle of (1917)
VI–338a–b
Cambria Iron Works IV–5a
Cambridge (Md.) I–31b
CAMBRIDGE (Mass.)
I–411b; IV–266b
Great Bridge I–363b
Harvard University
III–259b
Kennedy Library I–167b
migration to Connecticut
VI–151a
natural history museum
I–305a
Nautical Almanac Office
V–12b
printing and publishing
I–279b–80a, 294a, 333b;
V–410b
Regicides VI–70b
"Research Row" IV–268a
Revere's ride VI–106a
revolutionary war
II–214b; VI–125a
Smithsonian Institution
VI–319a,b
universities I–344b
Washington Elm
VII–250a
Cambridge, University of (Eng.) II–155b, 423b,
427a; V–296b, 297b;
VI–81a
CAMBRIDGE AGREEMENT (1629) **I–411b**; III–220a
Cambridge Common (Mass.)
VII–250a
Cambridge Group for the History of Population and Social Structure II–328a
CAMBRIDGE PLATFORM (1648) **I–412a**; I–410b;
II–169b; VI–75b, 223b;
VII–279a
Cambridge poets IV–162a
Camden (N.J.) III–11b;
V–57b; VI–181b
Camden (S.C.)
railroad VI–349b
revolutionary war
III–286a–b
state bank VI–349a
See also Camden, Battle of
CAMDEN, BATTLE OF (1780) **I–412a**; VI–124a–b,
129a, 351b
Camden, Lord. *See* Pratt, Charles
Camden and Amboy Railroad
II–322a; IV–175b; V–57b;
VI–24b, 36a
CAMDEN–YORKE OPINION (1769) **I–412b**
Camellia (flower) VI–393
(table)
Camels I–242b
Itama culture III–484a
Camel's hair coats II–372b
CAMELS IN THE WEST I–412b
Cameo brooches II–372a
Cameras. *See* Photographic Industry
Camera tube, electronic
II–425b
Cameron (La.) II–351b;
III–319b
Cameron, Simon (pol.)
II–63a, 68a
Cameron, William E. (gov.)
VI–49b
Cameroon, Republic of
IV–236b
CAMINO DEL DIABLO I–413a

Cammerer, Arno B. (offi.) V–220a
Cammock, Thomas (col.) VI–184a
Camouflage
Vietnam War I–63a
Campagnie de Scioto. *See* Scioto Company
Campaign for Human Development I–470a
CAMPAIGN RESOURCES I–413a; V–344a
corporations II–233a; IV–171a
corruption V–346b
corrupt practices acts II–232b
illegal contributions II–231b
"laundering" II–231b
lobbies IV–170b
misuse II–408b
national committees II–409b
"paper organizations" II–233a
political parties II–410b
publicity and corrupt-practices laws V–448a
regulation II–232b–33a
special-interest groups II–233a
third parties VII–53a
Campaigns, advertising I–18b
CAMPAIGNS, POLITICAL I–414b; II–410b; V–223b
broadcast time III–2a
congressional election of 1910 V–427b
congressional election of 1914 V–428b
corrupt practices acts II–233a; V–448a
costs I–413b–14a; II–411a
funding I–416a
Hatch Act III–261a
Michigan senate campaign of 1920 V–41b
Mississippi IV–369b
pamphleteering V–199a
party platforms V–328b
patronage V–228b
political parties V–343b–44a
pressure groups V–400b
publicity I–413b
roorback VI–163a
"Salt River" VI–203b
slogans VI–313a
Soldiers and Sailors conventions VI–336a
stump speakers VI–421b
Vare case VII–167b
whispering campaigns VII–291a
CAMPAIGNS, PRESIDENTIAL I–416a
contributions V–449a–b
costs II–411a, 411a
dark horse candidates II–292a
Idaho III–328b
issues II–410b
national committee IV–463a
Nevada V–40a
New Mexico V–60a
nominating conventions II–216a
Secret Service protection VI–252b
slogans VI–313a
third parties VII–53a
vice-presidency VII–180b–81a
voting behavior VII–210a
whispering campaigns VII–291a
1796 I–94b, 94b, 475a; III–4b, 96b
1800 I–94b, 94b, 388a, 388a; II–325b; III–4b–5a, 494b–95a; V–123a
1824 I–3a; II–231a, 231a, 327a, 458a; IV–202a, 469b; V–101b, 223a–b; VI–421b; VII–201b
1828 II–327a; V–101b; VI–459b
1832 I–255b; II–216a; VI–203b, 459b
1836 VII–288a
1840 I–138a, 200b, 432b; IV–143b, 274a; V–207a; VI–422a; VII–63b, 288b
1844 I–138a; II–292a; III–21a; IV–143b; V–170a; VI–38b, 42b, 138a, 163a; VII–288b
1846 IV–6a
1848 I–138a,b; II–184b; III–111b, 111b; IV–143b; V–152a, 329a
1856 I–110a, 138b, 139a; III–111b, 112a; V–3a; VI–42b, 92b
1860 I–432b; II–191b, 248b, 433b; III–109b, 437b; V–207a; VI–40a, 92b, 307b; VII–39b, 62b, 294b
1864 II–62b, 222b; III–81a; V–121b, 356a; VI–92b; VII–146a
1868 III–224b; IV–135a–b
1872 I–323b, 432b; III–224b; IV–63a, 63a, 141b; V–49b, 430b; VII–313b
1876 I–133a, 323b; II–38b, 231b, 231b; III–224b, 437b–38a; VI–65b, 93a; VII–344a
1880 III–152b, 225a; IV–409b
1884 I–383a–b; II–457b–58a; III–110b, 225a; IV–425b, 426b, 471b; V–430b
1888 I–322a; II–457b–58a; III–113a, 225a; V–257a; VI–183b–84a; VII–146b
1892 I–111a; III–113a; V–39b, 359a, 364b, 430b; VI–322b; VII–23b
1896 II–266a; III–111a, 189a, 201a; IV–335a; V–223b, 329a, 354b, 364b, 366a, 430b; VI–292b, 371a
1900 III–131b; V–235b, 281b; VI–287b, 293a, 324b, 325b
1904 III–197a; VI–288a
1908 IV–68a; VI–297b
1912 II–71b, 327b; III–113b; IV–68a, 331b; V–329a, 427b–28a; VI–93a, 326b, 331a, 458a; VII–122b
1916 III–269b; V–428b
1920 II–361b, 361b, 490b, 493a; V–107a, 110a; VI–15b, 326a
1924 II–492a; IV–58b, 70a, 81b, 84b
1928 III–113b; V–3b
1932 I–432b; II–327b, 407a, 492a; III–194a; IV–261a; V–43a, 106a, 430a; VI–51b–52a, 134a, 326a
1936 II–492a; IV–73a, 261a; V–47b; VI–93a, 325b
1940 II–492a; IV–73a, 134b
1944 II–480b; IV–73b
1948 I–107b; II–146b, 480b; III–9a–b; V–429a
1952 I–20a, 179b; V–429b; VI–93b, 337b; VII–57b
1956 V–124b; VI–337b
1960 I–432b; II–472b; V–3b, 124b; VI–325b, 337b
1964 I–523b–33a; III–169a, 222b; VI–13a, 93b, 337b; VII–210a
1968 II–316b; IV–77a, 261b; V–237b; VI–93b, 325b, 326a, 337b; VII–210a
1972 I–103a; V–182a; VI–71b, 327a, 337b; VII–208b–09a, 210a, 254a,b, 291a, 318a
CAMPAIGN SONGS I–432b; VI–313a
Campania (It.) VI–199b
Camp Augur (Wyo.). *See* Washakie, Fort
Camp Beauregard (La.) I–434b
Campbell, Aldrich and Nulty (arch.) I–166a
Campbell, Alexander (preacher) II–36b, 352b; VI–77b, 135b; VII–275a
Campbell, Angus (inv.) I–35b
Campbell, Bartley (playwright) VII–49a
Campbell, George A. (phys.) II–39a
Campbell, George W. (banker) VII–130b
Campbell, George Washington (dipl.) II–437a
Campbell, Hugh (off.) III–330b
Campbell, H. W. (agric.) II–376a
Campbell, James A. (spy) VI–373b
Campbell, John (col.) III–331a; V–142b
Campbell, John (off.) I–367a
Campbell, John (pub.) V–68b
Campbell, John, 4th Earl of Loudoun (off.) II–134a; III–115b, 116a; IV–86a; VI–46b
Fort Loudoun IV–192a
Fort Pitt V–321b
Campbell, John Archibald (jur.) II–160b, 161a, 165a; III–247b; VI–445b
Campbell, John B. (off.) IV–367b
Campbell, Robert (fur trader) IV–108a; VII–103b, 367a
Campbell, Thomas (cler.) II–352b
Campbell, Thomas E. VI–54a
Campbell, Walter (offi.) V–466b
Campbell, William (col. gov.) VI–347a
Campbell, William (off.) IV–48a
Campbell, William (off.) IV–329a
Campbell, W. W. (astron.) I–211b
Campbell class (gunboats) III–234b
Campbellites. *See* Disciples of Christ
Camp Bird Mine (Colo.) III–192a; VI–213b
Camp Bowie (Tex.) I–434b
Camp Brown (Wyo.). *See* Washakie, Fort
CAMP BUTLER (Ill.) **I–433a**; V–414b
Camp Charlotte, Treaty of (1774) II–381b
CAMP CHASE (Ohio) **I–433a**; I–219b; IV–5a; V–121b, 414a,b
Camp Cody (N.Mex.) I–434b
Camp Custer (Mich.) I–434b
Camp David (Md.) III–70a; VI–179b
Camp Devens (Mass.) I–434b
Camp Dix (N.J.) I–434b
Camp Dodge (Iowa) I–434b
Camp Doniphan (Okla.) I–434b
CAMP DOUGLAS (Ill.) **I–433a**; II–222b; V–121b, 414b
Camp Douglas (Utah) I–281a
Campeach wood IV–181b
Campeche (Mex.) VII–41b
Campeche Bay (Mex.) IV–181b
Camper (vehicle) I–230b; II–248a
Camp Fisk (Miss.) II–349a
Camp Fremont (Calif.) I–434b
Camp Funston (Kans.) I–434b
Camp Gordon (Ga.) I–434b
Camp Grant (Ill.) I–434b
CAMP GRANT MASSACRE (1871) **I–433a**; I–142b
Camp Green (N.C.) I–434b
Camp Hancock (Ga.) I–434b
Camp Hill (Va.) I–435a
Camphine IV–44a
Camphor II–7a; V–328a

Camp Independence. *See* Yuma, Fort
Camp Jackson (S.C.) I–434b
CAMP JACKSON AFFAIR (1861) **I–433b**; V–402b
Camp J. E. Johnston (Fla.) I–435a
Camp Kearney (Calif.) I–434b
Camp Kendrick (N.J.) II–344a
Camp Knox. *See* Knox, Fort (Ky.)
Camp Lee (Va.) I–434b
Camp Lewis (Wash.) I–434b
Camp Logan (Tex.) I–434b
Camp MacArthur (Tex.) I–434b
Camp McClellan (Ala.) I–435a
Camp Meade (Md.) I–434b
CAMP MEETINGS I–433b; I–238b; V–317b; VI–77b
  Cane Ridge revival I–444b
  Cumberland Presbyterian church III–221b–22a
  Disciples of Christ II–352b
  frontier II–487a
  Great Revival III–221b–22a
  hymns III–326a
  Leatherwood God IV–129a
  music IV–442b
  preaching III–128a
  protracted meeting V–438b
  rainmaking VI–42a
Camp Merritt (N.J.) I–435a
Camp Morton (Ind.) V–414b
Camp Moultrie, Treaty of (1823) VI–259b
CAMPOBELLO FIASCO I–434a
Camp Ordway (Washington, D.C.) I–435a
Camp Pike (Ark.) I–434b
Camp Randall (Wis.) V–414b
Camps, Indian. *See* Indian Villages
CAMPS AND CANTONMENTS OF WORLD WAR I I–434a; VII–325b
  Camp Knox IV–53b
  Plattsburg V–390b
  See also listings under Camp
Camp Sevier (S.C.) I–435a
Camp Shelby (Miss.) I–435a
Camp Sheridan (Ala.) I–435a
Camp Sherman (Ohio) I–434b
Camp Stewart (Va.) I–435a
Camp stoves II–422a
Camp Supply (Indian Terr.) I–375a
Camp Taylor (Ky.) I–434b
Camp Travis (Tex.) I–434b
Camp Union (Va.) V–335b
Camp Upton (N.Y.) I–434b
Camp Wadsworth (S.C.) I–435a
Camp Wheeler (Ga.) I–435a
CAMP WILDCAT (Ky.) **I–435a**
Canada
  Acadia I–6a
  aerial hijacking III–277b
  Alcan Highway VI–156a
  Apache V–8b
  British investment III–65b
  British law II–247b
  Carrying Place of Niagara V–90a
  cession to Britain IV–405b; V–52b, 214b
  Champlain Canal III–312b
  colonization II–149b
  Confederate expatriates VI–274b
  consumer cooperatives II–220a
  cowboys II–248b
  Declaration of Panama V–200a
  Deerfield Massacre II–312b–13a
  Dominion of I–437a, 439a
  Dummer's War II–380b
  enumerated powers II–453b
  Eskimo II–462a
  exploration I–492b–93a, 498a
  Fort George III–167b
  free blacks III–130b
  French and Indian War III–58b, 115a–17a; VI–1a–b
  French civil law II–247b
  French government II–329a
  French settlements II–246a
  fugitive slaves I–28a; VI–267b; VII–138a
  fur trade I–105a; III–139b, 141b, 142a–b, 327b, 398b; VI–411b
  Grand Banks III–208a
  Great Lakes VII–157a
  half-breeds III–242b
  hockey III–286b–87a,b
  horse breeding III–304b
  Hudson's Bay Company III–313b–14a
  Hurricane Hazel II–351b
  Hutterite communes II–142a
  immigration to U.S. III–333a,b, 337b, 338a, 339b, 341b
  independence movement III–318a
  Indian Country III–379a
  Indian Stream Republic III–401b
  International Control Commission III–452b
  International Polar Years III–454a
  iron ore III–12b; VI–281a–b
  Iroquois Beaver Land Deed III–476a
  Jesuit *Relations* III–501a
  King William's War IV–49b
  Klondike gold V–322b–23a
  Korean War IV–55b
  Kwakiutl IV–59a
  La Salle's explorations IV–109a
  Leisler Rebellion IV–134a
  Louisburg IV–192a
  Manitoulin Islands IV–239b
  Minnesota IV–355a
  missions I–451b; III–499b, 500a
  Navaho V–8b
  New France III–119b–20a
  newspapers I–18a
  Niagara Falls V–91a–92b
  nickel III–14a
  nitrogen fixation III–17a
  Norse voyages V–112b
  North Atlantic Treaty Organization II–315a; V–113b
  Northwest Coast exploration V–164b
  North West Company V–121a
  Northwest Territories II–319b
  nuclear fission V–300a
  Ohio country V–140b
  Organization for Economic Cooperation and Development V–170b
  paper exports V–212b
  Patriot War V–227a
  plank roads V–323a
  prairie dogs V–387b
  Quakers V–470b
  radar VI–10a
  radio astronomy VI–17a
  Rhodes scholars VI–134b
  Richelieu River VI–136b
  Saint Clair Tunnel VII–128a
  sales tax VI–200b
  sealing V–401a; VI–245a,b
  Sicilian campaign VI–284b
  Sioux VI–297a
  smallpox VI–316a
  Soviet espionage VI–428b
  tobacco VII–64b
  tornadoes II–352b
  trade organizations VI–471a–b
  Treaty of Utrecht VII–162b
  United Mine Workers VII–150b
  United Nations Declaration VII–151b
  Upper Louisiana IV–195b
  Vietnam III–160a
  Wells, Fargo VII–267a
  whaling VII–285a,b
  wildlife preservation VII–297a,b
  World War II III–235b; V–110b, 111a,b, 337b; VII–339a
  See also New France; Nova Scotia
CANADA, CONFEDERATE ACTIVITIES IN I–435a; II–159a
  Johnson's Island IV–5a
  Northwest Conspiracy V–121b
  Saint Albans raid VI–187a
CANADA AND THE AMERICAN REVOLUTION I–435b; III–400a–b; VI–123a,b; VII–164b
  alliance mission IV–86b
  Arnold's march to Quebec I–193b
  Battle of Bennington I–289a
  Battle of Three Rivers VII–55a
  "Bostonnais" I–346a
  British campaign of 1777 I–365b
  Burgoyne's invasion I–384b
  Fort Chambly I–491b
  Fort St. Louis I–491b; VI–195a
  land bounties IV–91a
  Loyalists VII–150b
  Montgomery's expedition IV–86b
  Montreal IV–405b
  political exiles V–342a
  Quebec Act II–247b
  Refugee Tract VI–70b
  Saint Johns siege VI–191a
CANADA AND THE WAR OF 1812 I–436b; I–120b, 436b, 438b, 438b; II–313b; V–19a–b; VII–233a,b, 234a, 235b, 249b
  Battle at Lundy's Lane IV–205a
  Battle of Chateaugay I–501b
  Battle of Lacolle Mill IV–82a
  Battle of Lake Erie II–459a
  Battle of Queenston Heights VI–3a
  Battle of the Thames VII–45b
  coast defenses II–474b
  Fort Schlosser VI–226a
  Hull's invasion II–338a–b
  Lake Champlain IV–87a, 212a
  Lake Erie II–458b
  New York invasion V–330b
  Raisin River massacre VI–42a
"Canada First" I–440a
Canadensium Plantarum V–325b
Canadian Amateur Hockey Association III–287a
CANADIAN-AMERICAN RECIPROCITY I–437a
  Elgin–Marcy Treaty II–431a, 431a
  fisheries III–31a
  Halifax fisheries award III–243b
  Migratory Bird Treaty Act II–188a
  Niagara Falls power V–91b–92b
  North American Conservation Conference II–187b
  Trade Expansion Act VI–470a

CANADIAN–AMERICAN-RELATIONS I–437a
air defense I–58a, 59a, 62a
Alabama Claims I–73a
Alaska I–75a, 76b, 122b, 439a
Bayard–Chamberlain Treaty I–277b
borders I–73b, 121a, 122b, 184a, 194b, 440a; II–313b; V–33a–b, 120a, 120a
Cahokia I–402a
Chicago Drainage Canal II–19a
Civil War II–162a; VII–115b
conscientious objectors II–185b
Definitive Treaty of Peace II–318b
DeHaven's expedition II–319b
emigration II–439b
exchange students II–471a
Fenian movement III–10b–11a
fisheries I–73b, 277b, 437a
fishing rights III–30a, 31a
flour milling III–45b
French and Indian War I–323a–b
I'm Alone Case III–332a–b
independence movement III–318a
investments in U.S. III–66b
lead imports IV–123b
Maine boundary dispute IV–226b
McLeod case IV–218a
Michigan IV–330b
Neutrality Act of 1939 V–37b
Neutrality Acts of 1935–37 V–38b
Patriot War V–227a
Prohibition II–261a
Rouse's Point boundary controversy VI–165b
salmon fishing VI–201b
San Juan Island VI–214a
sealing I–84b, 85a; VI–246a
trade I–120a–b; II–166b–67a; VI–344a; VII–87b, 91b
Treaty of Washington VII–248b
U.S. investments II–301b
Vietnam deserters II–335b
CANADIAN–AMERICAN-WATERWAYS I–440a; III–478a
Columbia River Treaty II–132a
Great Lakes pollution VII–259b
International Joint Commission III–454b
Lake Champlain IV–85b
Mississippi River IV–372a,b
New York barge system V–175b
Niagara Falls V–91a–92b
Richelieu River VI–136b
Saint Croix River VI–188b
Saint Lawrence River VI–192a
Saint Lawrence Seaway VI–193a
Sault Sainte Marie Canals VI–219a
Treaty of Washington VII–248b
Waterways Treaty VII–261a
CANADIAN ANNEXATION MOVEMENT I–441a; I–437a,b, 438b, 439a; II–474b; VI–177b–78a
Canadian Archipelago V–336b, 338a; VII–190a
Canadian Falls V–91a
CANADIAN INDIANS I–441a; III–252b, 356a, 396a
Chipewyan II–30b
Eskimo III–357a, 358a
Native American Church V–2a
snowshoes VI–323a
subarctic culture III–358b–60b
wigwam VII–295a
Canadian National Railways VI–34a,b
Canadian Pacific Railroad VI–36b
Canadian Refugee Relief Association III–318a
CANADIAN RIVER I–441b; II–359a
Battle of Adobe Walls I–15a
Camp Supply VI–443b
caravan traffic I–453a
exploration III–119b; IV–249a
Fonda's expedition III–50b
Fort Bascom I–269b
Long's explorations IV–187a; VII–271b
Mallet brothers exploration IV–230a
Oñate's explorations V–155a
sheep wars VI–273a–b
Staked Plain VI–380b
Canajoharie (N.Y.) V–323a; VI–438a
Canalboats VII–100a–b
Canal Fulton (Ohio) I–443b
CANAL RING I–442a
CANALS I–442a; III–447b–48a, 449a,b, 450b, 451b–52a; IV–174b; VI–145b, 146a,b; VII–100a, 259b, 260a,b
agriculture I–40a
Albemarle and Chesapeake I–83a
Anacostia–Chesapeake V–2a
Anthracite–Tidewater I–127b
banking II–255a
Cape Cod I–447a
Carondelet I–459b
Chesapeake and Delaware II–15b
Chesapeake and Ohio II–15b
Chicago Drainage II–19a–20b
Chicago Sanitary and Ship II–18a; IV–88a
city planning II–45b
construction II–301a, 449b; V–179a
construction materials I–477b
Delaware and Hudson I–364b; II–321b–22a
Delaware and Raritan V–57b
Ditch Gap II–382b
domestic trade IV–309a; VII–83b
Erie I–363b, 440b; II–459b
federal aid II–501b
foreign investments I–245a; II–301a, 382b; III–64a
Fox–Wisconsin Waterway III–90a, 90a
freedom of the seas III–106a
funds II–255a, 302b
Gallatin's report III–147a
geological surveys III–164b
government ownership III–202b
growth of cities II–41a
Hohokam culture III–289a
Hudson River III–312b
Hunkers III–317b
Illinois and Michigan II–17b, 20a; III–329b, 331a
Indiana III–374b
Industrial Revolution III–411b, 412a
inland lock navigation III–419b
interoceanic I–45a, 121b, 295b, 373a–b, 483b; II–72b–73a, 116a, 285a; VI–378b
See also Panama Canal
irrigation I–279a; III–477b
James River and Kanawha III–488a–b
Lake Erie–Lake Michigan V–1b–2a
Lake Erie–Ohio River V–1b
Lakes-to-Gulf deep waterway IV–87b
land grants IV–94a, 96a, 99b; V–444a
land reclamation VI–53b
land speculation IV–100a
Louisville and Portland IV–198b
Middlesex Canal IV–335b
Mohawk Valley IV–387a
Morris Canal V–41b, 57b
Morris Canal and Banking Company IV–412b
Muskingum River IV–443b
New York State V–87a
Ohio II–74b–75a; V–141b, 145b
Ohio and Erie Canal V–249b
opposition to construction I–374b
panic of 1837 V–206b
Pennsylvania I–89a, 364b; V–247a, 249b
Pennsylvania and Ohio Canal V–249b
Potomac River V–378a
public ownership V–455a
railroad competition II–75a
Richelieu River VI–136b
Saint Lawrence River VI–192b
Saint Lawrence Seaway VI–192b–93a
Santee Canal VI–216a
Sault Sainte Marie I–440b; VI–219a
showboats VI–283a
Society for Establishing Useful Manufactures VII–160b
South Carolina Canal VI–349a
state construction III–204a
state debts VI–95b
steamboat competition VI–148b
subsidies VI–425a
Survey Act of 1824 VI–450a
Tennessee River VII–27b
tunnels VII–127b
Union Canal VII–145b
Wabash and Erie VII–212a
"Washington Ditch" II–353a
waterpower IV–347b
Waterways Treaty VII–261a
Welland I–440b
westward movement VII–283b
See also Locks and Waterways
Canal towns II–45b
Canal Zone. *See* Panama Canal
Canal Zone Biological Area. *See* Smithsonian Tropical Research Institute
Canal Zone Code (1934) V–201b
Cana Movement I–469b
Canandaigua (N.Y.) III–157a
Canarsie (Indians) IV–237a
CANARY ISLANDS I–444a
Isleños III–479a
Neutrality Act of 1939 V–37b
Somers' voyage VI–338a
Texas settlement VI–207a
wine production III–129a
Canberra (cruiser) V–25b
Canby, Edward R. S. (off.) II–68b; IV–385a; VI–144a; VII–127a, 165b
Cancer I–242b; II–358a; IV–299a
deaths I–7a
occupational medicine IV–294b

Cancer Council, National Advisory IV–287b
Cancer Institute, National IV–287b
Candlenut (Kukui) VI–393 (table)
CANDLES I–444a; III–413b; IV–152b–53a; VI–323b, 372b; VII–277b, 285a
Caneadea Reservation (N.Y.) V–139b
CANE RIDGE REVIVAL (1801) **I–444b**; II–352b; III–221b; VI–77b
Cane sugar. *See* Sugarcane
Canfield, Richard (gambler) III–150a
Canister (projectile) V–26a
Cannabis IV–305b, 451a
Cannel coal IV–44a
Cannes (Fr.)
 tennis VII–30a
Canning, George (states.) I–121a; II–460b; III–349b; IV–400a, 402b
Canning, home III–55a
CANNING INDUSTRY I–444a; III–54b–55a
 aluminum V–104a
 brewing I–362a
 child labor II–24b
 chromium III–13b
 citrus industry II–43b
 food preservation II–373a–b
 fruit growing III–129a
 meat IV–280b, 281a
 pure food laws V–466a,b
 salmon VI–201a
 tin can VII–61b
 See also Packaging
Cannizzaro, Stanislao (chem.) I–218a
Cannon V–163a, 164a
 aerial I–57b
 Civil War II–67a, 163a
 navy V–26a–b
 revolutionary war IV–430a
 See also Artillery
Cannon, Clarence (parl.) VI–169b
Cannon, Howard (pol.) V–40a
Cannon, James P. (Trotskyite) II–144a
Cannon, Joseph G. (pol.) I–445b; II–176 (table); III–38a; V–427b
Cannon, Walter B. (physiol.) V–307a
Cannonball River VI–135a
Cannon House Office Building (Washington, D.C.) IV–146b
CANNONISM I–445b; VI–385a
Cannon Mountain (N.H.) VI–101a
Cannon-shot measure III–106b
CANOE I–445b; III–381a,b; V–367a; VI–148a
 birch bark I–304b; II–31a
 burial III–376a
 Eastern Woodlands III–366b
 fur trade III–403b
 Mackinaw boat IV–218a
 Mississippi River IV–372b
 Northwest Coast culture III–361a
 Ohio River VI–147b
Canonchet (Indian) IV–47b
Cañoncito (N.Mex.) III–187b
Can openers, electric II–421b
Canot, Theodore (smuggler) VI–311a
Canso (Can.) IV–46b, 192a
Canterbury (N.H.) II–147a
Canterbury, archbishop of II–455a
Canterbury, Robert (off.) IV–39a
Canterbury, See of (Eng.) IV–224a
CANTIGNY, AMERICAN ATTACK AT (1918) **I–446a**; I–102a; IV–404a; VII–326b
Cantilever truss (arch.) I–364a
Cantino, Alberto (cartog.) IV–247a
Canton (China) II–26b
 Anglo-Chinese War I–125a
 attack on Barrier Forts I–268b
 Kearny mission IV–34b; V–22b
 opium I–201b
 trade VII–86b
Canton (Ohio)
 industry V–141b
CANTON FUR TRADE I–446a; II–28b, 219b, 388a; V–158a
 Cook, James V–164b
 Pacific Fur Company V–180a
 Russia VI–180b
Canton Island III–425a; VII–125b
Cantonments
 World War I I–434a–35b
Canvas IV–157b
CANVASS I–446b; II–411a
Canyon de Chelly National Monument V–217b
Canyonlands National Park V–219 (table)
Cao Dai (rel. sect) VII–183a
CAP. *See* Community Action Program
CAPE. *See* Coalition of American Employees
CAPE ANN (Mass.) **I–446b**
 fishing II–92b
 Mariana IV–250a
 settlement II–365a; VI–199a
Cape Bon VII–338a
Cape Bonavista VII–162b
Cape Breton Island
 Acadia I–6a
 discovery I–401b
 French and Indian War III–115a–b
 French possession II–92b, 126b; VI–190b
 Treaty of Utrecht VII–162b
 See also Louisbourg
Cape Canaveral (Fla.) I–210b, 336b; III–40a, 233a; IV–406b, 460a; V–67b
 War of 1812 V–238b
Cape Catoche (Mex.) IV–181b
Cape Cinque Hommes (Mo.) V–59a
CAPE COD I–447a; II–92a; IV–449a
 exploration I–96b; IV–264b
 hurricanes III–320a
 mackerel fisheries IV–217a
 Martha's Vineyard IV–258a
 Pilgrims II–242a; IV–278b; V–64b, 313a
 Portland sinking II–349b
 ship graveyard II–89a
 Thresher sinking II–350a
Cape Cod Canal I–447a
Cape Cod National Seashore IV–268a
Cape Columbia V–241a
Cape d'Urville (Green.) V–240b
Cape Elizabeth (Maine) VI–184a
Cape Esperance, Battle of (1942) VII–68a
Cape Fear
 Yamasee War VII–352a
Cape Fear River III–30b; VI–149b
 Civil War I–277a
 exploration I–96a
 See also Fisher, Fort, Capture of
CAPE FEAR RIVER SETTLEMENTS I–447b; V–115a,b; VII–350a
Cape Finisterre (Sp.) II–453a; VI–386b
Cape Gata II–303a
CAPE GIRARDEAU I–447b; IV–195b, 376b; VI–271b
Cape Girardot. *See* Cape Girardeau
"Cape Harbor" I–447a
Capehart Company V–290b
Cape Hatteras (N.C.) VI–424b
 Gulf Stream III–232b, 233a
 mackerel fisheries IV–217a
 Monitor IV–397a
 national seashore V–220a
 settlement I–238b
Cape Henlopen V–80b, 252a; VII–359b
Cape Henry VII–199a
CAPE HORN I–448a; VII–285a,b
 clipper ships II–77a–b
 Drake's exploration I–96b
 gold rush III–81b; VI–150a
 intercoastal trade IV–309a
 Oregon voyage VI–363a
 passage II–76a, 463b
 westward movement V–176b
Cape Kennedy (Fla.). *See* Cape Canaveral
Cape May (N.J.) II–322a; III–320b; VI–100b
Cape Mendocino (Calif.) I–74b
Cape Morris K. Jesup V–240b
Cape Nome (Alaska) III–191b
Cape of Good Hope II–28b, 388a; III–190a; IV–406b; VII–285b
 ocean shipping VI–281a
 slave trade VI–311b, 322a
Cape Porpoise I–96b; III–200a
Capes (dress) II–371a,b
Cape Sabine III–224a
Cape Sable (Md.) II–5b, 6a
Cape Saint James. *See* Cape Cod
Cape San Lucas (Mex.) I–91b
Cape Sheridan V–240b, 241a
Cape Thomas Hubbard V–240b–41a
Cape Torokina (Pac. O.) I–350b
Cape Tragabigzanda. *See* Cape Ann
Cape Verde Islands II–323b; VI–363a
Cap fence VI–19a
Capistrano (Calif.) I–350a
CAPITAL, NATIONAL, LOCATION OF I–448b; I–208b–09a; VII–244b
 Federalist party III–4b
 Philadelphia V–277a
Capital crimes I–449b–450a
Capital gains tax VII–9b–10a, 12a, 12a–b
CAPITALISM I–448b
 American Indian III–361a; IV–59a
 Asian II–489b
 cold war VI–179b
 Communist party II–144b
 exchanges II–469b
 industrial II–475a
 Industrial Workers of the World III–412b
 Jacksonian Democracy III–486b
 morality of IV–408b
 New York City V–83b
 Open Door policy V–157b, 158a
 radicalism VI–13b
 syndicalism VI–455b
 woman's rights movement VII–314b
 See also Socialist Movement
CAPITAL PUNISHMENT I–449b; V–415a, 464a–b
 colonial settlements V–464b
 hanging III–249b
 narcotics violations IV–451a
 piracy V–320a–b
 sexual crimes VI–265b

CAPITAL PUNISHMENT (cont.)
slave trade VI–321b
social pacifism V–181b
Capital ships VII–242a
Five–Power Naval Treaty III–33b
London Naval Treaty (1930) IV–183a
London Naval Treaty (1936) IV–183b
Capital stock tax VII–7b, 8b, 13a,b
CAPITATION TAXES **I–451a**; II–200b; V–355a; VI–377a; VII–3a
CAPITOL AT WASHINGTON **I–451a**; V–191a; VII–244b, 246a,b, 246b, 250b
architecture I–163a
burning of I–120b
cooling III–269b
heating III–268b, 269a
inauguration of president III–350b–51a
Library of Congress IV–146a,b
sculptures VI–243a
speaker of the House VI–369b
Vietnam War protest V–266a
War of 1812 VII–249b
Capitol Reef National Park V–217a, 219 (table)
Capitol Syndicate VI–380b
Capone, Al (criminal) II–18a, 258b, 261b
Capone, Ralph (criminal) II–261b
Caporetto, Battle of (1917) VII–325b
Capote, Truman (au.) IV–165a; V–79a
Capper, Arthur (pol.) I–451b
Capper–Ketcham Act (1928) I–47a
CAPPER–VOLSTEAD ACT (1922) **I–451b**
Cap Rock escarpment VI–380b
Capron, Erastus A. (off.) I–451b
Capron, Fort (Fla.) I–451b
CAPRON TRAIL I–451b
Caps (hats) II–372a
Captain Jack. *See* Kintapuash
Captivities, Indian. *See* Indian Captivities
Captured and Abandoned Property Acts (1863, 1864) II–168a
CAPUCHINS I–451b; I–455b
Capulin Mountain National Monument V–217b
Caracas (Venez.) V–171a
CARACAS MIXED COMMISSIONS (1903) **I–452a**
CARAVANS, OUTFITTING OF I–452a
CARAVAN TRAFFIC ON THE GREAT PLAINS **I–452b**; II–158b; VI–215b
Carbine IV–430b, 433a; VI–139b
Carbohydrates I–303b; II–357b
Carbolic acid III–421b
Carbon II–84b, 422a
iron and steel manufacture III–472a,b, 473a
kerosine oil IV–44a
lamp filaments IV–88b–89a
Carbon–14 I–303b; II–12b
Carbonated drinks. *See* Soft drink industry
Carbon bisulfide III–421a
Carbon County (Pa.) VII–220b
Carbondale (Pa.) VI–33b, 416a
Carbon dioxide
anesthesia I–119a
Carbon lamp. *See* Lamp, carbon
Carbon steel III–12b
Carbon tetrachloride IV–294b
Carbon transmitter VII–20a
Carborundum (silicon carbide) II–7b, 422a; III–409a; V–91b
Cárdenas (Cuba) IV–188a
Cárdenas, García López de (expl.) II–129b, 228b
Cárdenas, Lázaro (states.) IV–322b, 328b
Carderock (Md.) V–28a
Cardiac surgery IV–297b
CARDIFF GIANT I–453b
Cardin, Louis (pol.) VI–204a
Cardinal (bird) VI–393 (table), 394 (table), 395 (table)
Cardinal, Jean Marie (trader) III–147a; V–387b
Cardiology V–307b
Cardozo, Albert (jur.) VII–131b
Cardozo, Benjamin N. (jur.) IV–10b; V–47a, 48a; VI–446b
Bill of Rights I–299b, 300a
minimum–wage legislation VII–269a–b
CARE (Cooperative for American Remittances Everywhere) V–280b
Care, Henry (pol. writ.) VI–141a
Carentan (Fr.) V–110b
Carey, Henry (comp.) IV–446a
Carey, Henry C. (econ., pub.) I–462b; VI–464a
Carey, Hugh (pol.) V–87b
Carey, James (labor leader) IV–76a
Carey, Mathew (econ., pub.) I–334a, 462b; VI–442b; VII–355b
Carey, William (miss.) IV–366a
CAREY DESERT LAND ACT (1894) **I–453b**; I–170b; III–328b, 478a; VI–53b
Carey's Atlas VII–74b
Carib (lang.) I–402a
Caribbean
buccaneers I–374a
colonization I–499b; V–439a
Cromwell's western design VII–270b
Great Migration III–219b
horse III–302a,b
hurricanes III–319b–20a
Isle of Pines III–479a
lend–lease bases V–36a
naval forces V–25a
Puerto Rico V–461a
Rhodes scholars VI–134b
slavery VI–305a, 307a
southern plantations VI–341b
U.S. fortifications III–78b
Virgin Islands VII–203b
War of Jenkins' Ear III–498a
World War II VII–342b
CARIBBEAN POLICY **I–453b**; III–68b–69a, 347a,b
Good Neighbor policy III–199a
Gulf of Mexico IV–326b
intervention II–359b; III–462a–b, 463a,b; V–105b
isolationism III–480a
Monroe Doctrine IV–399b
Mosquito question IV–416a
Neutrality Act of 1939 V–37b
Nicaragua VI–378b
Platt Amendment V–330a
Teller Amendment VII–22a
See also Latin America, U.S. Relations with
Caribou I–80b, 441b; III–358a,b, 360a
Eskimo II–462b
preservation V–217b
Caribou Indians III–358a
Caricature, cartoon IV–454b
Carillon, Fort (N.Y.) IV–86a; VII–56b
See also Ticonderoga, Fort
Carleton, Guy, 1st Baron Dorchester (off.) II–134a; III–493b; VI–123a
Battle of Valcour Island IV–86b; VII–164a
Butler's Rangers I–398a
flight from Montreal I–193b, 436a; IV–405b
New York–Quebec boundary VI–165b
Carleton, Will (au.) IV–163a
Carleton and Kissam (advt.) I–17b
Carleton Island I–340b
Carlin, William P. (off.) III–101a
CARLISLE (Pa.) **I–455a**
Civil War III–250b
Forbes Road III–59a
Fort Bedford I–282b
French and Indian War III–58b
Pontiac's War I–353b
Raystown Path VI–49a
Carlisle, Earl of. *See* Howard, Frederick I–499b
Carlisle, John Griffin (states.) II–176 (table); VI–466b
Carlisle Barracks (Pa.) I–191a
Carlisle Commission. *See* Peace Commission of 1778
CARLISLE INDIAN INDUSTRIAL SCHOOL **I–455a**; III–380a, 389b
Carlota (emp.) VI–274b
CARLOTTA, CONFEDERATE COLONY OF I–455a
Carlsbad (N.Mex.) III–17b
potash II–8a; V–376a
CARLSBAD CAVERNS **I–455b**; V–217a, 218 (table)
Carlson, Chester F. (print.) I–397a
Carlson, Evans F. (off.) IV–229a
Carlyle, Thomas (essayist, hist.) III–136a
Carmack, George Washington (prospector) IV–52a; V–437a
CARMELITES I–455b
CARMELO RIVER I–455b
Carmichael, Leonard (psych.) VI–319a
Carmichael, Stokely I–316a; II–59a; VI–14a
Carmichael v. *Southern Coal and Coke Company* (1937) IV–80b
Carmine, Al (dir.) VII–51a
Carnegie, Andrew (ind.) V–247b, 309b; VII–89b
Anti–Imperialist League I–131b
Carnegie Institution I–457a
conservatism II–189a
fortune III–79b
foundations III–83a
Hero Fund I–456b
Mesabi Iron Range IV–315b
peace movement V–236a
philanthropy V–280a
vertical combination production IV–272b
Carnegie Commission on Higher Education I–456b; II–401a
Carnegie Company
Homestead strike IV–66a
CARNEGIE CORPORATION OF NEW YORK **I–456a**; I–457b; III–83a; IV–251a
Carnegie Endowment for International Peace III–83a, 278a; V–236a,b; VII–236b
Carnegie family V–322a
CARNEGIE FOUNDATION FOR THE ADVANCEMENT OF TEACHING **I–456a**; II–401a–b; III–83a; IV–284b; V–400b–01a

CARNEGIE HERO FUND COMMISSION I–456b
Carnegie Institute of Technology IV–301a; V–307b
CARNEGIE INSTITUTION OF WASHINGTON I–457a; II–97a; III–83a
geophysical laboratory III–167a
"Jukes" Family report IV–20a
Marine Biological Laboratory IV–251a
Mount Wilson Observatory III–241b
petrographic studies V–268a,b
Saint Augustine restoration VI–188a
Carnegie–Mellon University IV–301a
Carnegie Steel Company III–297a
Carnes, Peter (aeron.) I–248a
CARNIFEX FERRY, BATTLES AT (1861) **I–457a**
Carnivals
Mardi Gras IV–249b
state fairs VI–392b
Carnivores III–150a
CAROLANA I–457b; III–268a; V–115a
Carolina (song) VI–395 (table)
CAROLINA, FUNDAMENTAL CONSTITUTIONS OF I–457b; II–117b; III–132b; VI–347a
landholding IV–242a
nobility IV–94b–95a; V–100b; VI–348b
Carolina and Northwestern Railroad VI–37a
Carolina jessamine (flower) VI–395 (table)
CAROLINA PROPRIETORS I–458a; I–83a–b, 239a, 243b, 499b; II–117b, 124a, 157a; III–212b; V–115a, 194b, 436b; VI–347a
agents V–435b
Heath Patent III–268a
manors IV–241b
proposed nobility VI–348b
quitrents VI–4a
religious liberty VI–80b; VII–68b–69a
Carolina Road. *See* Virginia Path
Carolinas
assembly II–117b
Bartram's travels II–477a
Cherokee Wars II–14b–15a
Concessions and Agreement II–117b, 157a
constitution II–157a
Creek trails II–33a
De Soto expedition II–336b
founding II–124a
freeholders II–117b
Fundamental Constitutions II–117b
Indian raids II–382a
land speculation IV–98b
mustangs IV–445a
triangular trade II–119a
CAROLINAS, SHERMAN'S MARCH THROUGH (1865) **I–458b**; I–289b, 382b; II–163b; VI–221a; VII–27a
Carolina wild rose VI–393 (table)
Carolina wren VI–395 (table)
Caroline, Fort (Fla.) III–38a; V–370a; VI–187b, 348b
***CAROLINE* AFFAIR** (1837) **I–458b**; I–438b; V–118b, 227b
McLeod case IV–218a
"Caroline gamecock." *See* Sumter, Thomas
CAROLINE ISLANDS I–459a; III–425b; VII–34a, 124b, 353b
Treaty of Paris V–215a
World War II II–387a; IV–257b; VII–337a
CARONDELET (steam gunboat) **I–459a**; II–384a; III–478b
Carondelet (Mo.) IV–376b
Carondelet, Fort (Mo.) II–34a
Carondelet, Francisco Luis Héctor de (col. gov.) I–459b; IV–213a; VI–366b
CARONDELET CANAL I–459b
CARONDELET INTRIGUE I–459b; VI–366b
Carothers, Wallace H. (chem.) II–9a; III–409b; VII–44a
Carousel (musical) IV–442a
Carousels II–244b; III–47a
Carpathia (liner) VII–64a
Carpenter, C. C. (pioneer) I–336a; V–148b, 150a
Carpenter, John A. (comp.) IV–438b
Carpenter Company II–419a
Carpenters
unionization IV–61b
CARPENTERS' HALL (Phila.) **I–459b**; III–354a; V–247a
CARPETBAGGERS I–459b; IV–58a; VI–57b
Afro-American education II–403b
churches VI–59b
corruption II–64b
restoration of home rule III–295a
scalawags VI–223b
Slaughterhouse Cases VI–303a
Wormley Conference VII–344a
Carpetho-Russian Orthodox Greek Catholic Church II–387a
CARPET MANUFACTURE I–460b; VII–43b, 44a–b
power loom IV–187b
wool VII–320b, 321b
Carr, Archie (nat.) VI–91a
Carr, Eugene A. (off.) VI–241b–42a; VII–252b
Carr, Robert (off.) V–42b–43a
Carranza, Venustiano (rev.) I–1b; IV–327b, 328b
Carrara (It.) III–201a
Carré, Ferdinand VI–69b
CARRIAGE MAKING I–460b; V–41a–b; VII–216b
Carriages VII–168a
Carriage tax VII–4b, 5a, 12b, 168a,b
CARRIAGE TAX, CONSTITUTIONALITY OF I–461a
Carrickfergus (Ire.) VI–46a
Carrier (Indians) III–360b
Carrier, air. *See* Aircraft; Aviation
Carrier, aircraft. *See* Aircraft Carriers and Naval Aircraft
Carrier, Willis H. (inv.) III–269a,b
Carrillo, José Antonio (off.) VI–210b
Carrington, Henry B. (off.) III–17b; IV–33b, 108b; VI–87a
CARRION CROW BAYOU, BATTLE OF (1863) **I–461a**
CARRIZAL, SKIRMISH OF (1916) **I–461b**; IV–327b
Carroll, Charles, of Carrollton (pol.) I–467a; VI–115b
Declaration of Independence II–305b–06a, 308a
envoy to Canada I–435b; IV–86b
Carroll, Daniel (pol.) I–467a; II–203b
Carroll, James (physic.) VII–355b
Carroll, John (cler.) I–251a, 467a; II–362b; III–334b; IV–86b
Carroll, Thomas (eng.) I–35a
Carroll, William (offi.) V–49b
Carroll County (Mo.) I–354b; III–144a
Carrollton Viaduct (Baltimore) I–363b
Carry Me Back to Old Virginia (song) VI–395 (table)
Carson, Christopher ("Kit") (trapper, scout) II–477b; III–143a; IV–422a; VI–241b
Battle of Valverde VII–165b
California conquest IV–34a
Frémont explorations III–114a
Navaho campaign V–9a; VI–439b
Taos VI–461a
Carson, John R. (phys.) IV–333a
Carson, Moses B. (fur trader) VI–196a
Carson, Pirie, Scott and Co. I–164a
Carson, Rachel (au.) III–421a
Carson City (Nev.) IV–360a; V–318a, 357b
Carson County (Utah) IV–454b
Carson Pass V–225a
Carson River II–157a; III–81b, 215a
Carson Sink VI–154a; VII–220a
Carson Valley V–39b, 317b
Carswell, George H. (jur.) VI–443b
Cartagena (Colom.) III–420b, 498a; V–269a; VII–270b
Cartagena, Republic of I–265b
CARTAGENA EXPEDITION (1741) **I–461b**; II–126b
Cartago (Costa Rica) I–438b
"Carte de La Louisiane" III–100a; VII–74a
"Carte de l'Amérique Septentrionale" III–100a
Cartels VI–102a
railroads VI–21b
Carter, Benny (mus.) IV–440b
Carter, Elliott (comp.) IV–439a–b
Carter, Harry (ed.) V–410b
Carter, James Gordon (educ.) II–397a, 398a; VI–228b
Carter, John (pioneer) I–461b–62a
Carter, Nick (lit. char.) II–341b
Carter, Robert ("King") (col. offi.) VII–192b
Carter, William, Fund III–82a
Carteret, George (col.) II–388b; IV–398a; V–42b
Carolina proprietary I–458a, 458a
Concessions and Agreement II–157a
New Jersey II–124a; V–56b, 436b; VII–278b, 359b
religious liberty VII–68b
Carteret, John, Earl Granville (states.) III–212b
Carteret, Philip (col. gov.) II–431b
Carter family (mus.) IV–441b
CARTER'S VALLEY SETTLEMENT I–461b; IV–186b
CARTER* v. *CARTER COAL COMPANY (1936) **I–462a**; II–136b, 323a, 482a; III–231b
Carthage (Afr.)
sea power VI–247b
Carthage (Ill.) IV–117a, 412a; VI–87a
CARTHAGE, BATTLE OF (1861) **I–462a**
Cartier, Jacques (expl.) I–96b, 440a; III–240b; IV–247b; V–52b; VII–275b
Lachine Rapids VI–192b–93a
Northwest passage

CARTIER, JACQUES (cont.)
III–216a; V–122a
Saint Lawrence River
VI–192a
CARTOGRAPHY I–462a; III–166b
aerial mapping V–272b
coasts IV 247a–
Franquelin's maps
III–99b
Kansas IV–25a
Mitchell's Map IV–381a
navy V–23a
polar regions V–336b, 337a, 338a,b
topographic mapping
VII–73a
U.S. Geological Survey
III–163a, 163b–64a
Cartoons V–68b
CARTOONS, POLITICAL I–464a; V–72b–73a, 431a
campaign of 1832 I–419a
"Doonesbury" V–72b
Nast, Thomas IV–454a
Pennsylvania Gazette
V–251a
Cartwright, Peter (cler.)
II–39b
Caruso, Enrico (sing.)
VI–15a
Carver, George Washington (bot.) V–217b
Carver, James (vet.)
VII–176a
Carver, John (col. gov.)
V–65a, 313a
Carver, Jonathan (trav., au.). *See* Carver's *Travels*
Carver, W. F. (showman)
VII–298b
CARVER CLAIM I–464b
CARVER'S *TRAVELS* I–464b; V–164b
Falls of Saint Anthony
VI–187a
Fox–Wisconsin Waterway
III–89b
Prairie du Chien V–388a
Sauk Prairie VI–218b
Carving
folk art III–47a,b
furniture III–138a
Cary, Thomas (col. gov.)
I–465a
Cary Arboretum I–348a
CARY'S REBELLION (1710)
I–465a
Casa Amesti (Monterey, Calif.)
IV–472a
Casablanca (Mor.)
World War II V–113a; VII–338a
CASABLANCA CONFERENCE (1943) **I–465a**; I–67a; III–174a; V–113a; VI–284b; VII–338b
Casablancas, Fernando (inv.)
VII–44a
Casa de Contratación
IV–247b; VI–363b
Casa Grande Ruins National Monument V–217b, 392b
Casa Mañana (show)
III–81a
Casas, Gonzalo de las
VI–224a
Cascade Mountains III–74b; IV–177a; V–165a; VI–412b, 413a
CASCADES OF THE COLUMBIA I–465a; V–169a
Cascade Theater (New Castle, Pa.) IV–417b
Cascade Tunnel VII–128b
Cascara sagrada III–381a
Casco Bay (Maine) II–485b; III–200a; IV–207b
Fort Loyal IV–200a
Popham Colony V–359b
settlement IV–225b
shipbuilding IV–309b; VI–279b
CASCO TREATY OF 1678 I–465b; IV–47b
CASCO TREATY OF 1703 I–465b
Case, E. C. (educ.) V–197a
Case, Jerome I. (mfr.)
VII–55b
Case, J. I., Company I–35b
Case furniture III–134b
Casein (plastic) II–7a
Case Institute II–448a
Casement, Dan (rancher)
I–326a
Case Study House (Pacific Palisades, Calif.) I–165b
Casey, Joseph J. (pub.)
III–272a
"Casey Jones" (ballad)
I–247a
Cash, Johnny (mus.)
IV–442a
Cash crop
corn II–227a
cotton II–237b
soybeans II–227a
whiskey II–353b
Cashmere shawls II–371b
Cash registers I–395b, 396a
Cash–register trusts
VII–122b
Cashtown (Pa.) III–175b
Casiguran Bay III–133a
Casilear, John W. (art.)
II–103b
Casimir, Fort. *See* New Castle
Casinos, gambling III–150a
CASKET GIRLS I–466a
Casper (Wyo.) VII–346a
Cass, George W. (eng.)
I–329a
Cass, Lewis (states.)
campaign of 1848 I–268a; III–111b
campaign of 1848 I–420b
Chicago Treaty II–21a
Compromise of 1850
II–150a
Indian affairs I–398a; III–373a
Indian factory system
I–105a
Indian removal
III–393b–94a
Michigan Territory
IV–331a
Oregon question III–21a
popular sovereignty
V–360a
Saginaw Treaty VI–186b
Treaty at Prairie du Chien
V–388b
Treaty of Chicago
III–398b
Treaty of Saint Marys
VI–197a
Winnebago War
VII–306b
Cass and Butler Almanac
I–91a
Cassard, Jacques (buccaneer)
I–374a
Cassatt, Mary (paint.)
II–103a; V–192a, 413b
Cass–Cheney farm I–329a
Cassels, Louis W. (jour.)
VII–152b–53a
Cassidy, Frederick II–340b
Cassimeres II–266a
Cassino (It.)
World War II I–141a; III–235b; IV–404a
Cass Lake (Minn.) IV–355b
Casson, François Dollier de (miss.) II–458b
Cassville (Ga.) I–213b
Castañeda, Pedro de (expl.)
III–208a
Caste system
Cotton Kingdom II–241a
Castillo de San Marcos National Monument
I–159b; V–217b; VI–188a
See also Marion, Fort
CASTINE (Maine) **I–466a**; III–120b
Fort Pentegoet V–260a
Penobscot expedition
IV–251b
revolutionary war
IV–226a; V–253b
Saint–Castin's trading house
VI–188a
War of 1812 III–247b
Castine (gunboat) III–234b
Castine, Vincent de
III–120b; V–253b
Cast–iron cookery II–219a
Cast–iron furniture III–136a
Castle, Irene (dancer)
III–239a
Castle Clinton National Monument (N.Y.) I–275b; V–217b
Castle Garden (N.Y.)
I–248a, 275b; IV–157a
Castle Island (N.Y.) II–383a
Castlereagh, Viscount. *See* Stewart, Robert
CASTLE THUNDER (Va.)
I–466a; II–159b
Castle William (Boston)
V–471b
Castle William (N.Y.C.)
III–206b; V–414a
Castner, Hamilton Y. (chem.)
II–7b, 422b
Castner Aluminum Company, Ltd. II–422b
CASTORLAND COMPANY I–466b
Castration V–465a
Castro, Cipriano (states.)
VII–169b
Castro, Fidel (dict.)
III–199b; IV–112b–13a; V–342b; VI–429a
Alliance for Progress
I–89b
Bay of Pigs invasion
I–278b, 454b
CIA plots to assassinate
II–270a
Cuban missile crisis
II–270b–71a
Guantánamo Bay
III–231a
Kennedy assassination
VII–238b
U.S. policy II–269b; VI–55a,b
Castro, José (off.) I–280b
Cataldo (Idaho) II–93b
Cataldo, Joseph (ling.)
III–500b
Catalina (patrol plane) I–55b
CATALINA, SANTA I–466b
Cataloging in Publication (Library of Congress)
IV–147b
Catalog sales. *See* Mail–Order Houses
Catalogue of Catalogues
IV–225a
Catania (It.) VI–284b
Cataract (steamboat)
VI–408a
Cataract Construction Company V–92a
Cataraqui (Ont., Can.)
I–358b; III–120a, 124b
Catawba (Indians) VI–239b, 270b
Augusta Congress I–223a
Great Warriors Path
VII–238b
Virginia trade VII–201b
Catawba grapes VII–305a
Catawba River III–31b, 322a; VI–149b; VII–261b
Catch–22 IV–164b
"Catcher's Mitt" (Viet.)
VI–301a–b
Catechism of Health
III–325a
Catechisms VI–227a,b
Caterpillar machine–gun destroyer I–177a
Caterpillar tractor I–177a
Catesby, Mark (nat.) I–304b, 348b; III–26b, 27a, 29b; IV–231a; V–326a; VI–90a
Catfish III–51a
Catfish Camp (Pa.)
VII–244b
Cathartics IV–229b
Cathay. *See* China
Cather, Willa (au.) IV–164a
Catherine I (Russ. emp.)
I–74b
Catherine II (Russ. emp.)
VI–177a
armed neutrality of 1780
I–175b
Catherine of Alexandria, Saint
I–466b
Cathode–ray oscillograph
II–423b
Cathode ray tube II–424b; VII–21a, 164a
Catholic Bishops, National Conference of. *See* National Conference of Catholic Bishops

Catholic Church Extension Society I–469a
Catholic Conference, United States. *See* United States Catholic Conference
Catholic Counter-Reformation II–393a
Catholic Education Association. *See* National Catholic Education Association
Catholic Emancipation Act (1829) V–2b
CATHOLICISM I–466b; VI–78a,b, 79b
Afro-American churches I–24a
Americanism I–107a
antebellum South VI–343a
Apostolic Delegation I–144a
Baltimore I–249b, 251a; II–124a
Bedini riots I–283a
birth control I–307a
Bloody Monday I–323a
campaign of 1928 I–428b
campaign of 1960 I–430b
Capuchins I–451b
Carmelites I–455b
censorship I–479a
Chequamegon Bay mission II–13b
Civil War II–36b
Coeur d'Alene mission II–93b
colleges II–114a–b
colonial schools II–394b
colonial suffrage VI–434a–b
Congregation de Propaganda Fide II–170b
Connecticut II–181a
divorce II–356b
Dominicans II–362b
Eastern Orthodoxy II–386b
education II–393b, 397a, 490a–b
Ephrata Community II–454a
evangelism II–466b
Fenian movement III–11a
French Canadians III–338b
frontier missions IV–366b
immigration III–334b, 337a–b, 342a
Indian education III–379b
Indian missions IV–365b
Indian nativistic movements V–4a
Indian Shaker religion VI–267b
Italian-Americans III–483b
Jesuits III–498b, 501a–b
Ku Klux Klan IV–58b
Louisiana II–91b
Maryland IV–260b
Massachusetts V–50a
Mexico II–233a
mysticism IV–448a
nativism V–2a, 279a; VII–149a, 160a–b
"Negro Plot" of 1741 V–32b
New Albion V–332b
New York State V–87a
opposition to I–110a, 111a, 139a, 283a, 323a
Oregon missions V–167a
Oxford Movement V–179b
Pacific missions IV–364b
papal states consulate V–211b
parish V–216a
parochial schools II–399b, 402b; VI–228b, 229a
Paulists V–229a
Philippines V–282a
Priests of Holy Cross III–293a
propaganda V–431b
Protestant moral standards IV–408a
Pueblo III–367b; V–459b
Puerto Rico V–462a
Puritanism V–468b
Quebec Act VI–2a
radical right VI–12a
religious liberty VI–80a; VII–68b
Saint Paul VII–134a
settlement houses VI–330b
slavery II–36b
Southwest missions IV–367a
Spanish Inquisition III–420a
suffrage VI–431a
temperance movement VII–23a
Texas II–443a
Treaty of Utrecht VII–162b
Ursulines VII–160b
Vermont VII–172b
voting behavior VII–210b
Wide-Awakes VII–294b
Wisconsin VII–307b
witchcraft VII–309b
Catholic Laity, Council of. *See* National Council of Catholic Laity
Catholic Men, Council of. *See* National Council of Catholic Men
Catholic Publication Society V–229b
Catholic Relief Services I–470a; V–280b
Catholic Rural Life Conference. *See* National Catholic Rural Life Conference
Catholic Students Mission Crusade I–469a
Catholic Summer School (Lake Champlain) II–1b
Catholic University of America (Washington, D.C.) I–169a, 468b
Catholic War Council. *See* National Catholic War Council
Catholic Welfare Conference. *See* National Catholic Welfare Conference
Catholic Women, Council of. *See* National Council of Catholic Women
Catholic World (mag.) V–229b
Catholic Youth Organization I–469b
Catlin, G. E. G. (pol. sci.) V–348b
Catlin, George (paint.) III–468a; VII–357a, 361b
See also Catlin's Indian Paintings
CATLIN'S INDIAN PAINTINGS I–470b; II–477a; IV–236a; V–189b
Cat Nation II–458b
"Cato" (pseud.). *See* Clinton, George III–241b
Caton, John Dean (nat.) IV–232b
Cat On a Hot Tin Roof (play) VII–50b
Cat-o'-nine-tails III–36b
Cato's Letters VI–113a
Cato's Revolt (1739) VI–303b
Catron, John (jur.) VI–445b
"Cats" (hay) III–265a
CATSKILL MOUNTAINS I–471a
Hudson River school of painting V–189a
Rip Van Winkle VI–145a
water supply VII–259a
Catsup
pure food and drug movement V–466a
"Cat's whisker" crystal rectifier II–423b
Catt, Carrie Chapman (ref.) III–92a; VII–315a
Cattaraugus (N.Y.) V–139b
Cattell, James McKeen (psych.) I–98b; II–470b; III–440a; V–441b, 442a
CATTLE I–471a; I–37b, 38b; III–51b; IV–169b; VI–48a
Abilene I–1b
as money II–140b
barbed wire I–267a
Bozeman Trail I–358a
Brown Swiss dairy II–281b
California I–406a
Chisholm Trail II–31b–32a, 477b
citrus industry II–43b
Colorado II–128a
cornfeed II–226a–b
cowboys II–248b
cow pony III–303a–b
cowpunchers II–251b
cow towns II–251b
disease III–53a; VII–176a, 177a
Dodge City II–358b
El Paso II–433b
feed II–43b
fencing III–10a,b
Florida III–39b
folklore III–49a
foreign investments II–301a
Fort Griffin III–228a
Fort Worth III–80b
Grand Prairie III–209b
Great Plains III–221b; VII–284b
herd law versus free grass III–273b
hide and tallow trade II–212b, 373b; III–274b
historical records III–285a
importation II–279a
Indian cultures III–368b
Jesuit missions III–499a
mavericks IV–277b
meat-packing IV–280a,b
mesquite IV–316a
Montana IV–403a
Nebraska V–31b
nesters V–33a
Nevada V–39b
New Mexico V–60a
Ohio V–141b
Oklahoma V–149b
open-range grazing V–159b
overgrazing III–75b
pesticides III–421a
prairie dogs V–387b
ranching VI–44b–45b
roundups VI–161a–b
Saint Joseph VI–191b
sales II–281b
San Antonio VI–207b
scalawag VI–224a
sheep wars VI–273a
South Dakota VI–350a
Staked Plain VI–380b
state fairs VI–392b
stockyards VI–414a
subsidies VI–426a
Tennessee VII–26a
Texas IV–30b; VI–355b, 364b; VII–40a–b
Texas longhorns IV–184b
Virginia VII–194a
wolves VII–311b
Wyoming VII–345b, 346a–b
See also Dairy Industry
Cattle and Horse Growers' Association, National I–472a
CATTLE ASSOCIATIONS I–472a; VI–161a
CATTLE BRANDS I–472b; I–473b–74a; V–160a; VI–161a
mavericks IV–277b
CATTLE DRIVES I–472b; I–1b, 471b; II–249b–50a, 251b; VI–45a
cowboys VII–96a
Goodnight-Loving Trail III–199b
Great Plains III–221b
Kansas IV–26a
long drives IV–184a
meat-packing IV–280b
mustangs IV–444b
Ogallala V–139a
Oklahoma V–148b
open-range grazing V–159b
stampedes VI–382a
Texas VII–40b
Texas longhorns IV–184b
Wichita VII–294a
Cattle eveners' pool V–358a
Cattle grub III–421a
Cattle range industry. *See* Range cattle industry

CATTLE RUSTLERS
I–473b; III–306a; VI–181a
CATTLE TICK FEVER
I–474a; I–46a, 241b; III–421a; IV–170a, 298a; VII–176a, 177a
CATV. *See* Cable television
Caucasus (Russia) I–56b
CAUCUS I–474a; III–381b
campaign of 1808 I–417b
congressional II–173a
congressional committees II–173a
floor leader selection III–37b
Jacksonian Democracy III–486b
nominations I–414b; V–101b, 406b
political parties V–343a, 344a,b
Caucus of Labor Union Women VII–314b
Caudill, Harry (au.) IV–41a
Caughnawaga Reservation (N.Y.) V–139b
Caulfield, John T. VII–254a
Caustic soda II–422b; III–421b; VI–203a
"Cavalcade of Texas" VII–41a
Cavalcade of the Golden West III–189b
Cavalla (submarine) V–286a
Cavalry, Air. *See* Air Cavalry
CAVALRY, HORSE
I–475a; I–49a, 184b; IV–303b
black cavalry I–309b
Civil War VI–377a
Continental army VI–125b
cornet rank II–228a
Horse Marines III–304a
Indian wars II–313b
Jayhawkers III–493a
Jefferson Barracks III–494b
revolutionary war II–249b
Rough Riders VI–165a
Terry's Texas Rangers VII–34a
Villa raid VII–187b
Cavalry, mechanized. *See* Armored Vehicles
"Cavalry cabinet" V–283b
CAVE-IN-ROCK (Ill.)
I–476a; IV–263a
Cavelier, Robert, Sieur de La Salle. *See* La Salle, Sieur de, Robert Cavelier
Cavendish, Fort (Ill.) I–501b
Cavendish, Lord VII–200b–01a
Cavendish, Thomas (navig.) III–240b
Cavendish Laboratory III–158a; V–297b, 301a
Cavite (Phil.) III–26a; IV–239b
Caxton, William (print.) II–107b
Cayo Hueso ("bone key") IV–44b
Cayuga (Indians) III–365b, 475a
French and Indian War III–115a
Iroquois Treaty III–476b
La Famine Treaty IV–83b
sachems VI–183a
Sullivan–Clinton campaign VI–438a
Cayuga County (N.Y.) II–460a
Cayuga Lake II–227b
Cayuse (Indians) III–363a, 500b
CAYUSE WAR (1847–50)
I–476a; VII–239a
Whitman massacre VII–221a, 294a
Cazenove, Théophile (bus. agent) III–291a,b
CBS. *See* Columbia Broadcasting System
CCC. *See* Civilian Conservation Corp; Commodity Credit Corporation
Cease-and-desist orders I–390b; IV–72a
Clayton Antitrust Act II–72a
Federal Trade Commission II–500a
Cebu (Phil.) V–282a
Cedar III–72b, 73a, 374a
Cedar Breaks National Monument V–217b
Cedar City (Utah) IV–421b
Cedar Creek (Va.) V–5a
CEDAR CREEK, BATTLE OF (1864) **I–476b**; VI–275a, 276a
Cedar Island III–479b; VII–235a
Cedar Key (Fla.) III–39b
CEDAR MOUNTAIN, BATTLE OF (1862) **I–476b**
Cedar Post (S.Dak.) IV–380b
Cedar Rapids (Iowa) I–487b
Cedar-Riverside (Minn.) II–48b
Cedar Run (Va.) I–476b
Cedar Valley II–461a
Ceilometer VII–264b
Celanese Corporation V–328a, 328b
Celebrezze, Anthony J. (offi.) III–267b
Celestial Empire. *See* China
Celestial photography V–131a,b
Celler-Kefauver Act (1950) I–140a; II–72a, 230b; III–204b; VI–103a; VII–124a
Celles (Belg.)
World War II I–380a
Cellophane III–409b
Celluloid II–7a, 8b; III–409a; V–327b, 328a
photographic film V–292a
sound recordings V–290a
Celluloid Manufacturing Company. *See* Celanese Corporation
Cellulose II–7a; V–328a
Cellulose acetate V–328b
Céloron de Blainville, Pierre Joseph de (expl.) V–367b
Falls of the Ohio V–142b
Forks of the Ohio V–143a
Logstown IV–181a
Monongahela River IV–398b
Venango VII–168b
See also Céloron's Lead Plates
CÉLORON'S LEAD PLATES I–477a; III–118a; V–146a
CEMENT I–477b
artificial I–378b
canal construction IV–174b
Erie Canal II–459b
hydraulic I–378b
iron oxides III–12a
Lincoln Highway IV–156a
natural gas V–5b
Prairie du Chien V–388a
price quotations V–402b
street paving V–230a
Cement Institute VII–123b
Cemeteries
segregation III–502b; VI–256a
CEMETERIES, NATIONAL
I–478a
Arlington I–175b, 175b
Chalmette I–490b
Confederate graves VII–150a
Custer Battlefield IV–168b
Gettysburg III–176b
Cemetery Hill (Pa.) III–175b, 176a
Cemetery Ridge (Pa.) III–175b, 176a; V–309a
CENSORSHIP I–478b
American Legion I–108a–b
book publishing I–333b
cold war V–74a
Customs Service II–277a
Federal Communications Commission III–2a
freedom of the press III–104b
motion picture industry IV–418b
Near v. *Minnesota* V–30b, 78b
Social Justice IV–472b
CENSORSHIP, MILITARY
I–481a; V–74a–b
Civil War V–71b
World War I VII–332b
World War II VII–333b, 336a
Censorship, Office of I–481a
Census
apportionment II–172a, 198a
congressional districts II–355b
demographic studies II–327b–28b
CENSUS, U.S. BUREAU OF THE I–481b; II–135a; III–284a, 444a; VI–388b; VII–206a
apportionment I–147a–b
capitation taxes I–451a
Census of Business I–489a
census of governments IV–171a
computers II–156a
department stores II–332b
farm tenancy IV–103b
farm workers II–495b
horses and mules IV–170a
import-export statistics II–277a
machine-tool industry IV–216a
mortality schedules IV–149b
school districts IV–172a
unemployment VII–140b
Census of Business
1948 I–489a
1967 I–490a
Census of Manufactures (1840) IV–127b
Census of Manufactures (1899) I–226a
Census of 1790 III–426b, 437a; V–82b–83a
Census of 1810 IV–158b, 246a
Census of 1820 V–132a
Census of 1850 IV–356a
Census of 1860 V–108a
Census of 1890 III–333b
Census of 1910 III–333b
Census of 1920 I–148a; III–333b
Census of 1930 VI–7a
Census of 1969 II–495a
CENT I–483a; II–95a–b, 341a, 384b; IV–394a, 395a
CENTENNIAL EXPOSITION (1876) **I–483a**; I–397a; V–278a
decorative arts II–98b, 99b
dynamo II–413b
furniture III–136a
industrial exhibition IV–244a
Lawrence IV–118b
National Museum IV–468b
paintings II–103a
soda fountain VI–332a
Spirit of '76 VI–374b
telephone VII–20a
Centennial State VI–393 (table)
Center Church (New Haven) VI–71a
Center for Advanced Study in the Behavioral Sciences I–97b
Center for Disease Control III–267b
Center for Metropolitan Planning IV–4a
Center for Study of Responsive Law IV–448b
Center for the Study of Man VI–319b
CENTINEL OF THE NORTH-WESTERN TERRITORY (news.)
I–483b; V–70b; VI–239a
CENTO. *See* Central Treaty Organization
Central America VI–471a–b
aerial hijacking III–277a
Afro-American colonization II–127b
colonization V–439a

diplomatic relations IV–115a
filibustering III–23a–b
Franciscans III–94b
fruit III–52b
interoceanic canal I–121b, 373a–b, 454a, 483b; II–72b–73a, 268b
intervention V–105b
meat trade IV–281a
Monroe Doctrine IV–400b
Mosquito question IV–416a
nonrecognition policy V–107b
Panama Congress V–203b
slavery VI–312a
Spanish colonies V–461a
Wells, Fargo VII–267a
See also Latin America, U.S. Relations with; Panama Canal
Central America, Federation of IV–110b
CENTRAL AMERICAN COURT OF JUSTICE I–483b; I–373b; III–456b; VII–113a
Central American Peace Conference (1907) I–483b; VII–113a
Central American Transit Company V–94a
Central Arizona Project II–130b
Central bank. *See* Federal Reserve System
Central Bank of Sweden V–99b
Central City (Colo.) IV–354a; V–311b, 437a
Central Conference of American Rabbis IV–9b
Central heating. *See* Heating and Air Conditioning
Central Highlands (Viet.) VII–183b–84a, 185a
Centralia (Ill.) VI–26a
Centralia (Wash.) IV–68a
Centralia "Massacre" (1919) VII–248a
CENTRAL INTELLIGENCE AGENCY I–484a; II–498a; III–439a–40a; V–138b; VI–374a, 389b
Bay of Pigs invasion I–278b; II–269b
Chile activities IV–113b
information retrieval VI–233a
Kennedy, John F., assassination VII–238a
National Student Association VII–365b
plots to assassinate Castro II–270a
Rockefeller investigation VII–238b
Watergate VII–255b
CENTRALIZATION I–484b; III–195a, 418b
federal–state jurisdiction VII–154b
proportional representation V–435b
Slaughterhouse Cases VI–303a
Smith–Hughes Act VI–318a
states' rights opposition III–9a,b
Centralized Traffic Control (railroads) VI–31a
Central Lyceum Bureau IV–207a
Central of Georgia Railroad VI–33a, 220b
CENTRAL OVERLAND CALIFORNIA AND PIKES PEAK EXPRESS I–485a; IV–129b; V–178a; VI–176b, 379b
Central Pacific Railroad I–406a, 485a; III–79b, 79b, 450a; V–39b; VI–37a, 37a–b
Chinese labor II–29b
land grants IV–94b; VI–425a
CENTRAL PACIFIC–UNION PACIFIC RACE I–485a; IV–94b; VI–27a, 154a–b; VII–101a, 147b
Central Park (N.Y.C.) IV–96b
Central Park Apartments (N.Y.C.) I–143b
Central Powers II–314a, 446b
Central Radio Propagation Laboratory II–88b
Central Railroad and Banking Company of Georgia VI–33a
CENTRAL ROUTE I–485b; VI–39a
overland mail V–178a
Smith explorations VI–318a
Union Pacific VII–147a
Central States Cooperative II–220b
Central trade councils. *See* Trade councils, central
Central Treaty Organization V–234a
Baghdad Pact I–243a
Central Valley (Calif.) III–223b
Central Valley Project (Calif.) I–407a; VI–54a
Central Vermont Railroad VI–34b
Centre Square (Phila.) VII–258b
Centre Square Water Works (Phila.) VII–258b
Centreville (Va.) I–365a, 381a
Century (mag.) IV–222a; VI–249a
Century Dictionary II–340a
***CENTURY OF DISHONOR* I–485b**
CENTURY OF PROGRESS INTERNATIONAL EXPOSITION (1933–34) **I–485b**; I–271a; II–18a
Ceramics. *See* Glass and Ceramics
CEREAL GRAINS I–486a
oats V–129b
prices V–404a
tariff VI–471a
wheat VII–286a
CEREALS, MANUFACTURE OF I–486b; II–226b; III–44b; V–128b; VI–191b
Cerebral palsy III–249a
Cerf, Bennett (pub.) I–334b
Cermak, Anton J. (pol.) I–202b
CERRO GORDO, BATTLE OF (1847) **I–488b**; II–324a; IV–324a
Certificates of deposit IV–393b
Certificates of indebtedness VII–8b
Certiorari, writ of VI–444b
Cervera y Topete, Pascual (nav. off.) IV–314b; VI–214a, 216b, 361a–b, 362a, 363a
Cervi's Rocky Mountain Journal (news.) V–79a
Cesare, Oscar E. (cartoon.) V–73a
Cesca chair III–136b
Cessna 310 II–347
CETA. *See* Comprehensive Employment and Training Act
Ceylon
Rhodes scholars VI–134b
Southeast Asia Treaty Organization VI–350b
Cézanne, Paul (art.) II–103b, 104b
Chaboillez, Charles (fur trader) V–244a
Chaco Canyon (N.Mex.) I–117b, 329b; III–367a; V–8b, 460a
Chaco Canyon National Monument V–217b
Chaco War (1932–35) V–205a
Chadds Ford (Pa.) I–360a; V–192b
Chadwick, James (phys.) V–298b–99a
Chafee, John H. (offi.) V–460b
Chaff VII–55a
Chaffee, Adna R. (off.) I–177b; V–281b
Chaffee, Edwin (inv.) V–327b; VI–167a
Chaffee, Roger B. (astronaut) II–347a
Chagall, Marc (art.) II–105b
Chagres River I–295a
Chaikin, Joseph (dir.) VII–51a
Chain banking. *See* Banking, Branch and Group
Chain drive IV–419b
CHAIN GANGS I–488b; II–217a
Chain reaction, nuclear V–300a–b
Chains, newspaper V–76a–b
CHAIN STORES I–489a; VII–319b
dairy industry II–282a
department stores II–332b
five–and–tens III–33a
food III–53a
livestock industry IV–170a
price–fixing V–402a, 403a
price maintenance V–403a
Robinson–Patman Act VI–157b
self–service VI–258a,b
CHAIRMAKING I–490a; III–134a,b, 135a,b, 136a,b, 137a, 138a,b
Chaise I–461a; VII–99b, 168a
Chalco, Lake II–214b
Challenge (dairy cooperative) II–282a
Challenge of Crime in a Free Society (report) II–263b; V–416b–17a
Challenger Expedition (1872–76) III–29a; V–134b
Chalmers, Lionel (au.) II–390b
Chalmette, Ignace de Lino de I–490b
Chalmette National Cemetery I–490b
CHALMETTE NATIONAL HISTORICAL PARK I–490b
Châlons (Fr.)
World War I I–491b
Chaloup Bay IV–451b
Chama River I–409b; II–461a; VI–368a
Chamberlain (S.Dak.) IV–51a
Chamberlain, C. J. (bot.) I–349a
Chamberlain, Clarence (av.) I–51b
Chamberlain, Daniel H. (gov.) III–244a; VI–348a
Chamberlain, Jacob C. I–333a
Chamberlain, John W. (inv.) II–420b
Chamberlain, Owen (phys.) IV–119b; V–100a
Chamberlin, Thomas C. (geol.) III–167a, 481a
Chamber of Commerce, U.S. I–491a; IV–461b
Chambers, Joseph (trader) VI–197b
Chambers, Thomas
settlement at Kingston (N.Y.) IV–49a
Chambers, Whittaker III–278a–b; VI–428b; VII–310b
Chambersburg (Pa.) III–59a; V–462b; VI–49a
CHAMBERSBURG, BURNING OF (1864) **I–490b**; VI–275a
CHAMBERS OF COMMERCE I–491a; II–141a; IV–70a; V–400b
Chambers Street (N.Y.C.) VII–258b
CHAMBLY, FORT (Can.) **I–491b**; I–436a; IV–86b; VI–136b, 191a
Chambly canal VI–136b
Chamizal National Memorial VI–143b
Chamizal Treaty (1967) IV–321b, 329a; VI–151a
Chamonix (Fr.) V–154a
Chamorro, Emiliano (pol.) I–373a

Chamoun, Camille IV–130a
CHAMPAGNE–MARNE OPERATION (1918) **I–491b**; IV–319b
Champagny, Jean Baptiste Nompère, Duc de Cadore (dipl.) IV–449b
CHAMPAIGN COUNTY RESCUE CASES (1857) **I–491b**
CHAMP D'ASILE I–492a
Champion, Charles IV–191b
CHAMPION'S HILL, BATTLE OF (1863) **I–492a**; I–295b
Champlain (N.Y.) IV–406a
Champlain, Lake. *See* Lake Champlain
Champlain, Samuel de (expl.) IV–82b, 330b
  Quebec III–142a
  See also Champlain's Voyages
Champlain Canal II–460a; III–312b
CHAMPLAIN'S INDIAN ALLIANCE (1608) **I–492b**
CHAMPLAIN'S VOYAGES I–492b; I–96b; III–119a; V–95a, 123a
  Cape Ann I–446b
  Cape Cod I–447a
  Crown Point II–266b
  Great Lakes III–216a; VII–157a
  Isles of Shoals III–479b
  Lake Champlain IV–85b
  Lake Huron III–319a
  Lake Ontario V–156b
  Maine IV–422b
  mapping IV–247b–48a; VII–73a–b
  Massachusetts IV–264b
  New France V–52b
  New Hampshire V–53b
  Ottawa River V–367a–b
  Richelieu River VI–136b
  Saint Croix IV–225b
  Saint Croix Island VI–189a
  Saint Lawrence River VI–192a
  Vermont VII–171a
Champlain Valley IV–86b; VII–171b
  See also Lake Champlain
CHAMPOEG CONVENTION (1843) **I–493a**; V–165b
Chamuscado, Francisco Sánchez (off.) VI–162a
CHANCELLORSVILLE, BATTLE OF (1863) **I–493a**; I–248a; II–62b; III–81a–b; V–248a; VI–430b; VII–115a, 197b
Chance music IV–439b
Chanco (Indian) III–219a
Chandler, Charles F. (chem.) IV–120a
Chandler, John (off.) VI–415a
Chandler, Thomas Bradbury (cler.) VI–112b
Chandler, William Eaton (pol.) III–224a
Chandler, Zachariah (pol.) II–140a; VI–11b
Chandler Act (1938) I–262b; III–466b
Chandler family IV–200a
Chandlers I–444a
Chandler School II–399a
"Change Alley" (London) III–62b
Channel Island National Monument V–217a
Channel Islands. *See* Santa Barbara Islands
Channing, Edward (hist.) III–260a, 282a
Channing, J. Parke (eng.) II–449a
Channing, William Ellery (cler.) II–158a, 170a; III–112a; IV–267a; VI–78a
CHANTIER I–493b
Chantier (steamship) I–398b–99a
CHANTILLY, BATTLE OF (1862) **I–493b**
Chanute, Octave (eng.) I–232b
Chapapote (asphalt) IV–44a
CHAPARRAL I–494a
CHAPBOOKS I–494a; I–335a; III–49b
Chapel Hill (N.C.) V–116b
Chapin Mine IV–303b
Chaplains VI–130b
Chaplin, Charles (act.) IV–417b
Chaplin Hills, Battle of. *See* Perryville, Battle of
Chapman I–494a
Chapman, In re (1897) III–465a
Chapman, John. *See* Appleseed, Johnny
Chapman, William (act.) VI–283a
Chapman, William S. IV–99b
Chapman's *Drawing Book* VII–319a
Chappell, P. S. (agric.) III–16b
Chappell, Thomas (agric.) III–16b
Chaps, leather II–249a
Chapultepec, Act of (1945) IV–402a; VI–142b
CHAPULTEPEC, BATTLE OF (1847) **I–494b**; IV–252a, 324a, 329a, 391b; VI–241a
Charbonneau, Tossaint IV–136a
Charcoal III–472a,b; V–97b–98a
Chargaff, Erwin (biochem.) II–357b–58a; IV–390a
Charge accounts II–74a; III–423a–b
Charge–credit plans III–423b
Chargé d'affaires I–93a
Chariot VII–99b, 168a,b
Charismatic movement I–470a
Charities, Association of Societies for Organizing. *See* National Association of Societies for Organizing Charities
Chariton (Iowa) IV–223b
Charity Hospital (New Orleans) III–306b
CHARITY ORGANIZATION MOVEMENT I–494b; V–280a, 380b
Charity Organization Society VI–327b; VII–24b
CHARITY SCHOOLS I–495b; II–395a, 396b
Charivari. *See* Shivaree
Charlemagne (emp.) I–1a
Charles I (Br. k.) II–371a; IV–265a, 269b
  Alexander grant V–369b
  Carolana grant V–115a
  Carolina patent I–458a
  colonial policy II–123a
  Great Migration III–219b
  Heath Patent III–268a
  Long Island grant VI–346b
  Maryland I–172b; IV–260a
  New Albion V–332b
  Petition of Right II–191a
  Puritans V–469a
  Regicides VI–70b
Charles II (Br. k.) V–56a
  Baron's rebellion I–240b
  Carolana III–268a
  Carolina I–458a; V–115a
  colonial policy II–123a
  Connecticut II–182a; VII–274a
  Delaware Circle II–322b
  Duke of York's proprietary V–95b, 333a; VII–347a, 359a
  Fundamental Constitutions of Carolina VI–348b
  Long Island grant IV–185b
  Lords of Trade IV–188b
  Massachusetts Bay colony IV–269a
  Massachusetts claim to Maine IV–226a
  Peace of Breda I–361a
  Penn grant III–123a–b; V–246a
  Pennsylvania–Connecticut boundary dispute V–250b
  Pennsylvania–Maryland-boundary dispute V–252a
  Regicides IV–48a
  Rhode Island II–365a; VI–132a, 134a
  Virginia V–151a
Charles III (Sp. k.) III–50b
  Aranda memorial I–151a
  colonial defense VI–168b
  New Spain VI–363b
Charles V (Sp. k.) IV–452a
  Asiento VI–309b
  Cabeza de Vaca I–399b
  Chicora grant II–23b
Charles, Fort (Maine) V–243b
Charles, Fort (Va.) IV–399b
Charles, Ray (mus.) IV–440a
Charles E. Stuart et al. v. *School District No. 1 of the Village of Kalamazoo.* *See* Kalamazoo Case
Charlesfort (S.C.) V–370a; VI–348b
Charles Mix County (S.Dak.) II–285a
Charles Pratt and Company VI–383a
Charles River I–363b, 498b; IV–269b
CHARLES RIVER BRIDGE CASE (1837) **I–496a**; II–214a; V–339b
Charles River County (Va.). *See* York County
Charless, Joseph (pub.) V–70b
Charleston (cruiser, 1889) VI–362a; VII–242b
Charleston (cruiser, 1904) VII–242b
Charleston (dance) II–290b
Charleston (Ill.) I–498b; IV–155b
Charleston (Mo.) I–306b
CHARLESTON (S.C.) **I–496a**; III–41a,b; VI–220b, 340b, 347b, 348a; VII–82b
  Afro–Americans I–25b, 29a; IV–339b
  anti–abolitionist movement I–137a
  butter II–297b
  Carolina colony I–457b
  city plan II–45a
  Civil War I–118a; II–63a, 159b; III–308a; IV–397a, 431a; V–19b, 56a; VI–221a, 387a, 415a, 422b, 424b, 453a; VII–215b
  colonial commerce II–119a
  colonial labor IV–, 60a
  directory II–343b
  direct–trade convention VI–352b
  distilleries II–353b
  earthquake II–385a
  fertilizer III–16b
  Fort Sumter II–61a–b; VI–440b
  Fourth of July III–87b
  furniture III–135b
  fur trade III–143b, 403a
  Genêt mission III–159b
  golf III–197a
  Huguenots III–121a, 315a
  indigo III–405b
  Middleton Place IV–96b
  Mississippi Valley trade IV–302b
  navy yard V–27b, 29a,b
  newspapers I–467b; V–69a
  postal service V–371a
  pottery V–379b
  prices V–404a–b
  Queen Anne's War VI–2b
  railroads IV–453b; VI–25b
  revolutionary war I–297a, 412a, 498a; II–465a; III–42b; IV–420a; VI–124a,b, 129a, 130a, 347a–b, 351b; VII–261b
  rice V–404b–05a; VI–135b
  Santee and Cooper Canal I–442a
  scientific research

VI–238a
seagoing hopper dredge VI–146a
settlement II–298a; V–370a
slave insurrections VI–303b, 304a, 307a
slave trade II–390a, 443b
South Carolina Canal and Railroad Company VI–349b
South-Carolina Gazette V–71a
South Carolina Interstate and West Indian Exposition VI–349b
South Carolina Railroad VI–24b
Southern Commercial Convention VI–352a
Spanish expeditions VI–348b, 349a
state bank VI–349a
steam power VI–409b
steamship lines II–91a
subtreasury III–354b; VI–427a
sulfuric acid works II–6b
tea party VII–16b
tea trade VII–15a
theater VII–46b, 47a
Tillmanism VII–59a
tinware VII–63a
Vesey Rebellion III–437a; VII–174a
War of 1812 VII–235a

CHARLESTON (W.Va.) **I–497b**; VII–282a, 288a
cotton market II–238a
gas springs V–5a
salt IV–25a; VI–202a,b
street paving V–230a

Charleston, Battle of (1780) I–412a, 496b
Charleston and Hamburg Railroad. *See* South Carolina Railroad
CHARLESTON GARDENS I–497b
CHARLESTON HARBOR, DEFENSE OF (1776) **I–498a**
CHARLESTON INDIAN TRADE I–498a
Charleston Library Society II–108a
Charleston Neck (S.C.) I–497a
Charleston News and Courier (news.) V–66b; VII–58b
CHARLESTOWN (Mass.) **I–498b**; IV–265a
anti-Catholic sentiment I–467b
Charles River bridge I–496a
colonial vehicles VII–168b
navy yard V–29a
Revere's ride VI–106a
revolutionary war I–382b; IV–137b
Ursuline convent burned VII–160a
Ursuline convent burning V–2b
Winthrop's settlement I–344a

Charlestown (N.H.) II–267a; V–126a; VII–171a
See also Number 4
Charles Town (S.C.) V–115a
Charles Town (Va.) III–257a
Charlestown Navy Yard (Boston) III–258b
Charlevaux Ravine (Fr.) IV–189a
Charlevoix, Pierre François Xavier de (cler.). *See* Charlevoix's Journey
CHARLEVOIX'S JOURNEY (1720–22) **I–498b**; VI–195a
Charlie Brown (comic character) V–72b
CHARLOTINA I–499a
Charlotte (N.C.)
Camp Green I–434b
Confederate government II–294b
federal mint I–204a; IV–360a
Mecklenburg Declaration of Independence IV–282a
Mecklenburg Resolves IV–282b
railroad V–117a

Charlotte, Camp (Ohio) IV–179a
CHARLOTTE, FORT (Ala.) **I–499a**; II–158b; VI–365b
CHARLOTTE, TREATY OF CAMP (1774) **I–499a**
Charlotte Amalie (St. Thomas) VII–204a
Charlotte Bay IV–302b
Charlotte Harbor V–356a
Charlottesville (Va.)
Civil War VII–117a
integration VII–196a
Monticello IV–405a
revolutionary war II–215a; IV–8b
University of Virginia VII–197b

Charlotte Temple IV–161a
Charming Polly (merchantman) I–290b
Charnel houses III–376a
Charnisay, Charles d'Aulnay III–120b
Charolais cattle I–471b; VI–45a
Charpentier, Paul (chem.) IV–306b
Charqui IV–280b
CHARTER COLONIES I–499b; VI–166a
Connecticut II–180a, 182a
Georgia III–168a
governors II–120a
Plymouth II–242a
Providence Plantations V–439a
royal disallowance VI–166b

CHARTERED COMPANIES I–500a; II–228b–29a; VII–94b, 95a
Hudson's Bay III–313a
labor recruitment IV–60a

Charter Oak. *See* Connecticut Charter of 1662
Charter of Freedoms and Exemptions (1629) V–61a
CHARTER OF LIBERTIES (1683) **I–500b**
CHARTER OF PRIVILEGES (1701) **I–500b**; IV–142b; V–246a–b
Charters
compact theory II–149a
contracts II–293b
state power over II–213b

Charters, colonial. *See* Colonial Charters
Charters, home-rule II–44b
CHARTERS, MUNICIPAL I–500b; IV–427a
home rule III–294b
Saint Louis VI–194a

CHARTRES, FORT DE (Ill.) **I–501a**; II–265b; III–120a, 329a, 330b
d'Artaguette's command I–197a
Indian trade IV–277b
Laclède's trading post VI–193b
population I–402b
settlement I–100b

CHARTRES, FORT DE, TREATY (1766) **I–501b**
Charts and Instruments, Depot of V–12a, 133a–b, 134a–b, 336b
Chase, Camp (Columbus, Ohio) V–121b
Chase, Lucia (dancer) II–288b
Chase, Martha (biol.) III–158a
Chase, Salmon P. (states.) III–417a; V–141b; VI–445b
antislavery activity IV–8a
Appeal of the Independent Democrats I–145a
banking I–256a
Bermuda admiralty case I–292a
campaign of 1860 I–421b
campaign of 1864 V–356a
Civil War financing II–66a–b
emancipation II–435a,b
fractional notes IV–394b
greenbacks III–251b
habeas corpus III–236b
Legal Tender Act IV–133a
Liberty party IV–143b
Matilda Lawrence case IV–276a
Ohio State Antislavery Society V–145b
Reconstruction Acts IV–376a
specie payments VI–370b
taxation VII–5a
test laws VII–35a
wildcat banks VII–295a

Chase, Samuel (jur.) II–305b, 308a; VI–445a
Alexandria Conference I–85b
carriage tax case I–461a
envoy to Canada I–435b; IV–86b
presidential subpoena V–397b
See also Chase Impeachment I–501b

Chase, Stuart I–20a–b
CHASE IMPEACHMENT (1804) **I–501b**; III–344a; VI–444a
Chase Manhattan Bank
art collection II–107a

Chase National Bank I–257a; III–466a
Chasseboeuf, Constantin F. de *See* Volney, Comte de La Rochefoucauld-Liancourt
Chaste, Aymar de (expl.) I–492b
Chastellux, François Jean de (off.) III–122a
Chastity IV–408a
Chateaubriand, François René de (states) III–122b
CHATEAUGAY, BATTLE OF (1813) **I–501b**; I–436b
CHÂTEAU-THIERRY-BRIDGE, AMERICANS AT (1918) **I–502a**; I–70a, 70a, 102a, 286a, 491b; IV–319b; VII–326b
Châtel, Marquis de. *See* Crozat, Antoine
Chatham (tender) VII–166a
Chatham (Can.) III–256b
Chatham (Eng.)
dry docks II–375a

Chatham Shaker Village (N.Y.) III–137a
Chatsworth (Ill.) II–350b
Chattahoochee River III–171b, 498a
Civil War I–213b; IV–37a
Creek cession III–401b
Creek War I–232a
Definitive Treaty of Peace I–351a
Florida boundary VI–351a; VII–353b
Fort Scott VI–260a
Georgia boundary III–168a,b
Mississippi IV–368a
Seminole VI–259b
Spanish mission III–170a
U.S. boundary II–381a, 432a
western boundary VII–269b

Chattanooga (Tenn.)
Civil War II–272b; III–298a; IV–36b, 42a, 314a, 435a
railroads IV–453b; VI–33a, 38a
United Confederate Veterans VII–150a
See also Chattanooga Campaign

CHATTANOOGA CAMPAIGN (1863) **I–502a**; II–21b, 62b, 163a, 271b; IV–54a; VI–26b; VII–26b, 34b, 127b
Battle of Lookout Mountain IV–187a
Battle of Missionary Ridge IV–364b
Battle of Wauhatchie

CHATTANOOGA CAMPAIGN (cont.)
VII–261b
"cracker line" II–253a
Chattanooga Creek IV–187a
Chatterton Hill (N.Y.C.) VII–293a
Chaudière River I–193b
Chaudron and Rasch VI–290a
Chauncey, Charles (cler., educ.) VI–77a
Chauncey, Isaac (nav. off.) III–218a; VI–183b
Niagara campaigns V–90b–91a
Oswego headquarters V–175b
York campaign VII–358b
Chaussegros de Léry, Gaspard–Joseph. *See* Léry, Gaspard–Joseph Chaussegros de
Chautauqua (N.Y.) II–1a; VII–312a
Chautauqua, Lake II–1a; V–367b
Chautauqua Assembly VI–442b
CHAUTAUQUA MOVEMENT II–1a; I–434a; II–399b; IV–207b
Chautauquan (mag.) II–1a
Chauvin, Louis (fur trader) VI–367a
Chavez, César E. (labor leader) I–408b; IV–76b–77a; V–182a
Cheat River III–332b; VII–283a
CHECK CURRENCY II–1a; I–252a, 255a, 256a; IV–395b
charge accounts II–74a
clearinghouses II–73b–74a
credit cards II–74a
Federal Reserve System III–6b
gold standard III–193a
hard money I–302a
inflation III–415a
service charges I–257b
state banks I–259b
See also Demand deposits
Check List of North American Amphibians and Reptiles VI–91a
CHECKOFF II–2b
Taft–Hartley Act IV–74a
Checkrow planter I–486a
CHECKS AND BALANCES II–4b; III–2a; IV–142b; V–385a
Antifederalists I–131a
bicameral legislatures I–294b
legislative power IV–12b
minority rights IV–358b
presidential veto VII–178a
state government VI–396b
Cheerios (cereal) I–488a
Cheerleaders III–56b
"Cheer'ly Men" (song) VI–301b
Cheese II–280b–81a,b; III–51b, 54b; VI–48a
colonial production II–279b
pure food laws V–465b
Cheesequake (N.J.) III–183a
Cheever, Ezekiel (educ.) II–394a; VI–227a, 229b
Chefoo (China) IV–54b
Chelsea (Mass.) IV–266b
Chelsea Hospital (pension fund) VI–127b
Chelsea (Mass.) Keramic Art Works V–379b
Cheltenham (Mo.) III–327a
Chemehuevi (Indians) III–363a
Chemical Abstracts (jour.) II–11b
Chemical Analyses of Igneous Rocks V–268b
Chemical engineers II–448b
CHEMICAL INDUSTRY II–4b; II–10a–b; IV–245a
agriculture I–46b
DuPont Company II–320b
fertilizer III–16a
foreign trade VII–87b
Kansas City (Mo.) IV–27b
Kentucky IV–41b
lead V–102b
Memphis IV–302a
New Jersey V–58a
New York State V–87b
nickel III–14a
nitrates V–98a–b
petrochemicals V–266b
Philadelphia V–278a
photography V–291a,b
plastics V–327b
Saint Louis VI–194b
Saint Paul VII–134a
salt VI–202a, 203a
South America VI–343b
synthetic rubber VI–168a
tariff VI–470b
Tennessee VII–26a
textiles VII–44a
towboating VII–77b
trade association VII–92b
Virginia VII–196a
vitamins V–128a
West Virginia VII–281b
See also Chemistry
Chemical Society, American. *See* American Chemical Society
Chemical Society of Philadelphia II–10b; IV–126b
CHEMICAL WARFARE II–9b; VI–105a; VII–225b
defoliation II–319a
Washington Naval Conference VII–251a
World War I V–258a
Chemin des Dames (Fr.) I–286a; VII–326b
Chemise II–372b
CHEMISTRY II–10a
American Chemical Journal IV–2b
atomic weight determination I–218a
biochemistry I–302a
brewing I–362a
cotton industry II–239a
detergents VI–324a
food adulteration V–465b
General Electric Research Laboratory III–156a
gold mining III–191a,b
Harvard University IV–119b
industrial research III–408a–09b
Lawrence Radiation Laboratory IV–119a
medical education IV–283b
medicine IV–287a
Mellon Institute IV–300b
mineralogy IV–349a
molecular biology IV–388b
Nobel Prizes V–99b–100a
pharmaceutical industry V–273a
quinine IV–229b
soapmaking VI–323b
soil VI–334a
U.S. Geological Survey III–163b
Chemistry, Bureau of III–53b; V–447b, 465b, 466a,b
Chemotaxonomy I–349a
Chemotherapeutic drugs V–467b
Chemung (Pa.) VI–438a
Chemung Canal IV–174b
Chenango Canal IV–174b
Chenango County (N.Y.) II–460a
Cheney, Benjamin (clockmaker) II–77b, 78b–79a
Cheney, E. P. (bus.) I–329a
Cheney, Timothy (clockmaker) II–78b
Chennault, Claire L. (off.) II–26a; III–46b
Chen Ning Yang (phys.) V–296a
CHEQUAMEGON BAY II–13b; VI–443a
CHERBOURG (Fr.) **II–13a**
Kearsarge–Alabama encounter IV–35a; VII–147a
World War II II–237a; V–110b; VII–339a
Cherokee (Indians) II–51b–52b; III–151b, 367a, 396a,b, 476a
Augusta Congress I–223a
Avery's Trace I–232b
Battle of Etchohih VI–347a
Boonesborough I–337a
British II–14b–15a
Carter's Tennessee settlement I–462a
Charleston (S.C.) I–496b
Cherokee Strip II–14a
Chickasaw Old Fields II–23a
Civil War III–400a
Creek War II–256b; III–278a
Dawes Commission II–295b
Dodge–Leavenworth expedition II–358b
Donelson's Line II–363a–b
Fort Prince George V–408a
Fort Smith Council VI–317a
French and Indian War III–117a; IV–192a
fur trade III–143b
Galphin claim III–148a
Georgia III–168b; VII–321b–22a
gold II–14a; V–178b, 311a
Great Smoky Mountains III–222a
Great Trading and War Path III–223a, 387b
Holston Treaty III–292a, 383a
Holston Valley settlements III–292b
intermarried citizen III–447a
Jesuit missions III–500a
Kentucky II–292a
Melungeons IV–301a
mounds IV–421a
Natchez relations IV–455b
New Echota Treaty V–49b
North Carolina V–115b
Oklahoma II–321a; IV–199a
Panton, Leslie and Company V–211a
political organization III–365b
removal III–389b, 393b, 394a,b, 395a; V–437b
revolutionary war II–14b–15a; III–400b
Scioto Trail VI–239b
Sequoya's syllabary VI–263a
Shawnee relations VI–270b
Tennessee V–32a; VI–357b–58a; VII–25a
Tennessee Cumberland Road II–273b
Tennessee River VII–27b
Texas VII–38b
Trail of Tears II–52b; V–148a; VII–96b
Transylvania Company VII–103a
Treaty of Hard Labor III–251a, 382b; VI–386a
Treaty of Hopewell III–300b, 383a
Treaty of Lochaber III–382b; IV–173a
Treaty of Nogales V–100b
Treaty of Sycamore Shoals III–382b; VI–455a
Treaty of Tellico III–383a
Tryon's Line VII–125b
Union Army III–375b–76a
Virginia III–380b; VII–192a, 201b, 203a
Watauga settlement VII–253a,b
western lands VI–356b
West Virginia VII–281a
See also Civilized Tribes, Five; Overhill Cherokee
Cherokee County (Tex.) II–389a
Cherokee Dam III–322a
Cherokee language III–365b

Cherokee Nation
  oil springs IV–333b
CHEROKEE NATION* v. *GEORGIA (1831) **II–14a**; V–125b
Cherokee Outlet (Okla.) V–148b
Cherokee Phoenix (news.) VI–263a
Cherokee River. *See* Tennessee River
Cherokee rose VI–393 (table)
CHEROKEE STRIP (Okla.) **II–14a**; V–148b, 149b
Cherokee Strip Livestock Association II–14b
CHEROKEE TRAIL **II–14b**; V–178b
CHEROKEE WARS (1776–81) **II–14b**; III–380b
  Battle of Long Island Flats IV–186a
  Treaty of Long Island of Holston IV–186b
Cherrington, Ernest H. (ref.) V–429b
Cherronesus III–497a
Cherry (Ill.) II–350a; III–134b
Cherry Creek (Colo.) I–224a; III–191b; IV–129b; V–311b; VI–320b
Cherry Hill Penitentiary V–252b
Cherry trees. *See* Japanese Cherry Trees
CHERRY VALLEY MASSACRE (1778) **II–15a**; III–400b; VII–293b
Cherub (sloop) II–463b
Chesapeake (frigate) V–29b, 424a
CHESAPEAKE AND DELAWARE CANAL **II–15b**; I–127b, 443b; III–449a; VI–146a, 425a
CHESAPEAKE AND OHIO CANAL **II–15b**; I–40a, 442b, 443a; III–448a–b, 449a,b; IV–61b, 261a; VI–146a, 425a
Chesapeake and Ohio Canal Company V–378a,b
Chesapeake and Ohio Canal National Monument II–15b
Chesapeake and Ohio Canal National Park II–15b
Chesapeake and Ohio Railroad III–451b; VI–32a, 33a–b
  Blue Ridge Tunnel I–325b
  James River and Kanawha Canal III–488a
Chesapeake Bay VI–340b
  Albemarle and Chesapeake Canal I–83a
  Anacostia–Chesapeake Canal V–2a
  Ayllón's settlement I–238b
  Baltimore I–249a
  canals II–15b
  Civil War V–20a
  Claiborne settlement II–70a
  Fortress Monroe IV–399b
  Gwynn's Island III–236a
  Jesuit missions III–499a
  Maryland–Virginia agreement III–459b
  navigation and commerce I–85a
  Norfolk trade V–109b
  Norse exploration I–95b
  Pennsylvania–Maryland-boundary dispute V–252a
  Plowden's New Albion V–332b
  Potomac River V–378a
  Powhatan Confederacy V–385b
  Principio Iron Works V–409a
  Raleigh's Lost Colony VI–43a
  revolutionary war III–117b; IV–136b; VI–123b, 129a; VII–198b–99a, 360b, 361a,b
  settlement IV–260b; VI–451a; VII–192b
  shipping I–251a
  showboats VI–283a
  slavery VI–305b
  Spanish exploration IV–302b
  tobacco VII–67b
  War of 1812 IV–213b; VII–234b, 235a
  War of 1812 V–393b
Chesapeake Bay Bridge and Tunnel VII–128b
Chesapeake Capes, Battle of. *See* Virginia Capes, Battle of
Chesapeake Coastal Plain III–43a
CHESAPEAKE–LEOPARD INCIDENT (1807) **II–16a**; II–247a, 436b; III–350a; VII–233b
CHESAPEAKE–SHANNON FIGHT (1813) **II–16a;** II–16a–b, 364a, 364a, 459a, 459a, 459a
Chesecocks Patent III–313a; IV–24a
Cheshire (Eng.) V–194b
Chesnutt, Charles W. (writ.) IV–166a
Chester (steamship) IV–141b
Chester (Ill.) I–100b
Chester (Pa.) III–219a
Chester, George F. VI–383a
Chester County (Pa.) I–360a; II–322b; VII–165a
Chester County Historical Society (Westchester, Pa.) III–137a
Chesterfield, Lord (Philip Dormer Stanhope) IV–241a
Chester River VI–149b
Chester's Gap V–224b
Chester White hog III–288b
Chesterwood (Stockbridge, Mass.) IV–472a
Chestnut blight III–74b
Chestnuts III–51a
Chestnut Street (Phila.) III–391b
Chests III–135a
Chests of drawers III–134a,b, 138a
Chetwynd, William V–409a
Chevalier, Michel (econ.) III–122b
"Chevaux-de-frize" III–275b
Cheves, Langdon (banker) I–261b; II–174 (table)
Chevrolet (auto) I–228b, 232a
Chew, Beverly I–333a, 333b; II–109b
Chew family III–173b
Chewing tobacco VII–67a
CHEYENNE (Indians) **II–16b**; III–220b, 365a, 396b; IV–109a, 236a
  Battle of Adobe Walls I–15a
  Battle of Beecher Island I–283a
  Bent's Fort I–290a
  Black Hills War I–313a
  Camp Supply VI–443b
  Dull Knife Campaign II–379b
  Fort Bascom I–269b
  Fort Connor II–184a
  Fort Francis E. Warren VII–237b
  Fort Laramie IV–108a
  Fort Laramie Treaty III–383b; IV–108b
  Fort Sedgwick VI–254b
  Fort Wallace VII–221a
  Germaine girl captives III–172a
  Ghost Dance III–177b
  Hancock's massacre VII–190b
  hostilities IV–340a; VII–239a,b
  Indian Country cessions III–384a
  Jesuit missions III–500a,b
  Kansas IV–25a
  Kidder massacre IV–45a
  language I–[illegible]
  Medicine Creek Council IV–299a
  migration I–151b
  Nebraska V–31a
  Oklahoma V–148b, 149b
  Pawnee Rock V–230b
  peace commissions III–378a
  Platte Bridge fight V–330a
  Red Cloud's War III–17b
  Red River War VI–64a
  removal from Colorado V–437b
  Sand Creek massacre I–219a; VI–208a
  scouts VI–242a
  Sheridan's Washita campaign VII–252b
  Sioux wars VI–297a
  South Platte route VI–355a
  Summit Springs VI–241b–42a
  Sumner's expedition VI–439b
  Sun Dance VI–441b
  territory concessions III–379b
  Wagon Train charge VII–217a
  War Bonnet Creek fight VII–227b
  war with Dakota II–283a–b
  Wyoming VII–345b
CHEYENNE (Wyo.) **II–16b**; VII–345b, 346a
  cattle I–473b, 473b; II–251b; V–139a
  Fort Francis E. Warren VII–237b
  Frontier Days VI–161b
  Goodnight–Loving Trail III–199b
  Kansas Pacific Railroad IV–30b
  Lincoln Highway IV–156a
Cheyenne Mountain I–59a
Cheyenne River III–256a; IV–415a
Chiang Kai-shek (states.) II–26a, 27b–28a, 489a; III–61b
  Cairo Conference I–403b
  Manchuria IV–235b
  World War II VII–337b
Chiapas (Mex.) III–302a
Chicaca (Ala.) II–336b
CHICAGO (Ill.) **II–17a**; I–433a; III–329b; VII–159a, 308a
  Afro-Americans I–25b; III–253b
  American Catholic Missionary Conference V–3a
  apartment houses I–143a
  architecture I–164a,b, 378a
  arc lights II–413b–14a
  Art Institute II–103a,b, 105a
  Baltimore and Ohio Railroad VI–23a
  Beaubien land claims I–281b
  black officeholders VI–432b
  blizzards I–320b
  Board of Trade II–413b–14a; V–320b
  book publishing I–334b
  bootlegging I–339b
  botanical garden I–348b
  Century of Progress Exposition I–485b
  Chicago Sanitary and Ship Canal IV–88a
  civil service reform II–60a
  Civil War V–121b
  clearinghouse II–73b
  clothing industry II–82a–b
  Columbian Museum III–19a
  Commonwealth Electric Company II–416b
  Communist party II–143b
  community action programs VI–328b
  Daley, Richard I–343b
  Democratic convention of 1968 IV–214b, 342a; VII–191b

CHICAGO (cont.)
directory II–343b
domestic trade VII–83b, 84a
education II–398b
education of handicapped III–248b
electric railway VI–40a
elevated railway II–415a, 428a; VI–429a,b
establishment I–24b
Evangelical Alliance II–465b
federal records center III–284b
Federal Reserve banks III–8a
Field Museum of Natural History III–19a
flag III–35a
foreign trade VII–89b
Fort Dearborn II–297a, 477a
furniture III–139a
fur trade VII–105a
gambling III–149b
German immigrants III–81a, 336b
grain elevators II–430a
grain storage rate-fixing IV–434a
Grant Park I–55a; II–297b; IV–96b
Great Lakes VI–146a
growth II–41b
Haymarket Riot III–266a; IV–64b–65a
hockey III–287b
hogs III–289a
Hull House V–280a
Illinois and Michigan Canal III–331a
Illinois Central Railroad VI–26a
Indian factory system II–480a
Indian population III–397b
Indian relocation VI–83b
Industrial Workers of the World IV–67b
International Electric Congress II–415b
iron and steel industry III–12a
Iroquois Theater fire II–348a; III–476b
Jolliet and Marquette expedition IV–7a
labor party movement IV–81a
labor unions II–492b
Lake Michigan IV–332b
land speculation I–107b; IV–100b, 100b
Levee II–260a
Loop II–297b
mail-order houses IV–225a
mapmaking I–462b
marine disasters II–349b, 388b
meat-packing II–37b, 436a; III–53a; IV–170a, 280a–81a; VII–84a
mechanics' institutes IV–281b
Midway Plaisance IV–337a
Minnesota rail link IV–357a
motion pictures IV–417b
music IV–440a
National Kansas Committee IV–28a
National Labor Party Convention II–492b–93a
National Trust for Historic Preservation IV–472a
natural history museum I–305a
Newberry Library II–109b; III–285a
newspapers V–79b
organized crime II–261b, 262b
parochial school fire (1958) II–348b
party machine IV–214a
paving V–230a
pharmacy society V–275a
political bossism V–345a
political cartoons V–73a
political machine VI–142b
Pullman strike IV–66b–67a; V–463b
race riots I–30a, 31b, 32a; III–436a; VI–8a, 9a
Railroad Administration VI–19b
railroad pools V–358a
railroads III–450a; IV–28b, 29a; VI–25b, 32b, 33a,b, 34a,b, 35a,b, 36a,b; VII–101b
Reconstruction Finance Corporation VI–60a
Republic Steel Company strike IV–72b
restaurants III–52b
retail trade VII–84b
riot of 1877 IV–63b
Saint Lawrence River VI–192b
skyscrapers III–269a; VI–299a
slums VI–314a,b
snowstorms II–351b
social work VI–330b, 331a
steel strikes VI–411a
stock exchange II–469b
stockyards VI–414a–b
St. Valentine's Day Massacre I–339b
subtreasury VI–427a
subway VI–429b
"swing round the circle" VI–454b
tenements VII–23b
tennis VII–29a,b
trades council IV–63b
trading house III–142b
typhoid VII–259b
urban renewal VI–86b
veterinary medicine VII–176b
wagons V–389b
Western Society of Engineers II–448b
Winnebago War VII–306b
World's Columbian Exposition I–164b; II–46a, 415a, 419a, 465b; III–11b, 19a; VII–324a
World's Parliament of Religions V–171b
Zouave Cadets II–432b
Chicago (cruiser) VII–241a, 242b, 293a–b
Chicago, University of IV–337b
atomic bomb IV–238a
atomic power reactor V–300b
atomic research VI–230b
electronic research II–423b
elementary school II–398b
law school IV–121a
meteorological studies IV–318a
political science V–348b–49a
pragmatism V–386b
radiocarbon dating VI–17b
scientific education VI–237b–38a
teachers college II–401a
Chicago Academy of Science VI–236a
Chicago Air Convention (1944) VII–112b
Chicago and Alton Railroad I–364a; V–462b; VI–34b, 36a
Chicago and North Western Railroad IV–303b; VI–25b, 33b
Chicago and Rock Island Railroad VI–25b
Chicago and Southern Air Lines I–68b
Chicago Area Projects (1930's) II–147b
Chicago Art Institute III–137a
Chicago Board of Trade II–141a, 469b
grain trade III–44a
See also "Pit"
Chicago, Burlington and Quincy Railroad III–451b; IV–403b; V–119a; VI–28a, 32a, 32b–33a; VII–308b–09a
See also Burlington Northern
Chicago Burlington Railroad v. *Chicago* (1897) II–440a
Chicago Commons VI–330b
Chicago Daily News (news.) V–73a,b
Chicago Daily Tribune (news.) V–73a,b
Chicago Defender (news.) V–76a
CHICAGO DRAINAGE CANAL II–19a; II–20a–b
Chicago–Edison Company VII–129b
Chicago Eight II–20b
CHICAGO FIRE (1871) **II–19a**; II–17b, 348a; V–230a
Mrs. O'Leary's cow IV–424b
panic of 1873 V–207a
Chicago Great Western Railroad VI–33b, 191b
Chicago Imperial Mill I–487a
Chicago, Milwaukee, Saint Paul and Pacific Railroad IV–403b; VI–33b
Chicago, Milwaukee and Saint Paul Railroad IV–303b; VI–27b, 33b
electrification VI–40a
CHICAGO, MILWAUKEE AND SAINT PAUL RAILWAY COMPANY* v. *MINNESOTA (1890) **II–19b**
Chicago Municipal Court II–157b
Chicago Opera Ballet II–288b
CHICAGO PORTAGE II–19a; III–329a, 332a; V–367b
Chicago Railway Exposition (1883) VI–40a
Chicago Resistance trial. *See* Chicago Seven
Chicago River II–17a, 18a, 19a, 297a, 349b, 388b; III–144a, 329a
Chicago Rivers and Harbors Railroad Convention (1847) VI–21a
CHICAGO ROAD II–20a; IV–331a, 332b
Chicago, Rock Island and Pacific Railroad VI–26a, 33b
Chicago Sanitary and Ship Canal II–18a; IV–88a
CHICAGO SANITARY DISTRICT CASE (1933) **II–20a**
CHICAGO SEVEN II–20b; II–18b; VII–118a
Chicago South Shore and South Bend Railroad III–461b
Chicago Sun–Times (news.) V–73a, 74b
Chicago Ten II–20a
Chicago Times (news.) II–222b
Chicago Times–Herald (news.) I–225b–26a
Chicago Transit Authority VI–429b
CHICAGO TREATIES (1821, 1833) **II–21a**; III–383b, 398b
Chicago Tribune (news.) III–19a; V–76b, 78b
Chicago Tribune Tower I–164b
Chicago Union Stock Yards IV–170a
Chicago White Sox I–270b
Chicago World's Fair (1933) VII–298b–99a
Chicago Zoological Park VII–371a
Chicanos III–338a
California I–408b
poverty V–280b
protests VI–7b
woman's rights VII–314b
See also Mexican–Americans

Chichén Itzá (Mex.)
IV–327b
Chichimec (Indians)
VI–224a
Chickadee (bird) VI–394 (table)
Chickahominy (Indians)
V–385b
Chickahominy River II–96b
Civil War III–146a–b; IV–281b; V–245a; VI–150a, 263b; VII–197b, 301b
Chickamauga (Indians)
II–15a
CHICKAMAUGA, BATTLE OF (1863) **II–21b**; I–502a; II–271b; IV–54a, 187a; VI–26b; VII–26b, 127b
Chickamauga Creek II–15a, 21b
Chickamauga Dam III–322a
Chickamauga Station (Ga.)
IV–365a
Chickasaw (Indians)
III–367a, 396b
Augusta Congress I–223a
Battle of Cabusto I–402a
Colbert's Gang II–96b
Dawes Commission
II–295b
De Soto expedition
II–336b
Fort Jefferson attack
III–494a
Jesuit missions III–499b
liquor III–398b
Memphis IV–301b
migration I–308b
Mississippi IV–368a
Natchez Trace II–33a; IV–456b
Panton, Leslie and Company V–211a
ranking I–288a
Shawnee relations
VI–270b
Spanish trade VI–366b
Tennessee VII–25a,b
treaty of 1832 IV–97a
Treaty of Hopewell
III–300b
Treaty of Natchez
IV–456a
Treaty of Nogales V–100b
Treaty of Old Town
III–383b
Treaty of Pontotoc
V–357a–b
war with French I–7b, 197a
western lands VI–356b
See also Civilized Tribes, Five
Chickasaw Bayou II–22a; III–238b
CHICKASAW BLUFFS
II–22a
Chickasaw–French War
II–22b
Fort San Fernando
VI–366b
Guion's expedition
III–232b
Hope encampment
IV–195b
Indian factory system
II–480a
Memphis IV–301b
revolutionary war II–96b
CHICKASAW BLUFFS, BATTLE OF (1862)
II–22a; VII–181b
Chickasaw–Choctaw Trail
III–387b
CHICKASAW COUNCIL HOUSE, TREATY OF (1816) **II–22a**
CHICKASAW–CREEK WAR (1793) **II–22a**
CHICKASAW–FRENCH WAR (1736–40) **II–22b**; VII–25a, 70b
Chickasaw Nation
oil springs IV–333b
CHICKASAW OLD FIELDS
II–23a
CHICKASAW TREATY (1783) **II–23a**
Chickasha (Okla.) II–32a
Chicken I–72a; III–53b; IV–280b; VI–44b
"Chicom" (slang) VI–301a
Chicopee (Mass.) III–442a; IV–347b; VII–45a
CHICORA II–23a
Chicory coffee III–53b
Chief executive. *See* Governor; President
Chief Joseph Dam III–322a
Chief Joseph's Campaign. *See* Nez Perce War
Chief justice of the Supreme Court VI–368b, 444a, 445a,b
circuits II–39b–40a
presidential impeachment
II–198b
Smithsonian Institution
VI–319a
Chief of Naval Operations
I–14a
Chihuahua (Mex.)
Apache Wars I–142b
Confederate settlement
IV–325a
Franciscans I–288b
freight traffic I–453a
Indians III–369a
Mexican boundary
IV–321a
Mexican War I–361a; II–363b; IV–323b; VI–184a
Pershing expedition
I–461b; IV–327b
Pike's expedition V–312a
Santa Fe trade VI–214b
Santa Fe Trail VI–215a
Taos trade VI–461a
CHIHUAHUA TRAIL
II–23b; I–83b
Chilcoot Pass (Alaska)
IV–52a
Child, Francis James (philol.)
I–247a
Child, Lydia Maria (ed.)
IV–223a
Child, Robert (phys.) I–412a
Child Health and Human Development Institute
IV–465a
Child health care. *See* Maternal and Child Health Care
Childhood and Society
IV–165a
CHILD LABOR II–23b; VI–331a; VII–312b
agricultural workers
II–495b
Chicago laws II–18a
commerce clause II–136b
curfew laws II–274b
dairy industry II–279b
elimination IV–71b
factories IV–61b
Fair Labor Standards Act
V–48b
interstate commerce
III–247a, 459b
legislation I–95b, 243b; IV–68b, 68b–69a, 80a,b
Massachusetts IV–293b
minimum wage IV–352b, 353a,b
National Recovery Administration IV–469b
Progressive movement
V–428b
regulation II–482a
Social Gospel VI–325a
state laws VI–328a
Supreme Court decisions
III–349a
sweatshop VI–454a
Child Labor Cases VI–98a
Child Labor Committee, National II–24b
Child Nutrition Act (1966)
I–43b
Children IV–256b–57a
citizenship V–7a
neglect IV–24a
poverty V–380b–81a
Children, Interstate Compact on the Placement of
III–460a
Children, Society for Prevention of Cruelty to. *See* Society for the Prevention of Cruelty to Children
Children of God II–142b
Children's Aid Society
III–248b; V–280a
Children's books. *See* Books, Children's
Children's Bureau III–267b; IV–78a; V–447b; VI–328a
Children's courts. *See* Juvenile Courts
Children's Cyclopaedia
II–444b
Children's Hospital (Boston)
V–340b
Children's Magazine
IV–222b
Childs, Francis (pub.) V–71a
Childs, Harwood L. (pol. sci.)
V–453a–b
Childs, Marquis W. (jour.)
V–75a
Childs, Richard IV–429b
Child welfare
American Civil Liberties Union I–100b
American Humane Association I–125b
American Legion I–108b
federal programs I–8b–9a
Russell Sage Foundation
VI–177a
See also Maternal and Child Health Care
Chile V–233a
ABC conference I–1b
Baltimore affair I–250b
borax I–340a
diplomatic recognition
IV–110b; V–107b; VI–55a
diplomatic relations
IV–115a
Dominican missions
II–362b
earthquake V–23a
horse III–302a
Inter-American Congress
VI–217a
International Exposition of 1895 III–453b
Macedonian affair
IV–212b
Marxist government
IV–113a–b
mining VI–364b
nationalization of U.S. property IV–466a
nitrates II–8a, 478a; V–97b, 98a
Nitrate War III–16b
privateering V–419b
Quinteros Bay Episode
VI–3b
saltpeter III–16b
sealing II–28b
shipping IV–310b
Tacna-Arica controversy
VI–456a
territorial waters III–107a
tobacco VII–64b
United Nations Declaration
VII–151b
U.S. operations in (1970)
II–315b
U.S. prisoners V–22b
U.S. trade VI–343b, 344b, 345a,b, 346a
World War II IV–112a
Chile nitrate. *See* Sodium Nitrate
Chiles, Joseph B. VII–217b
CHILLICOTHE (Indians)
II–25a
Chillicothe (Ohio) V–141a; VII–368a
Adena culture I–11a
Bank of the United States
II–266b; V–174b
Camp Sherman I–434b
Cumberland Road
II–273b
land office III–258a
politics II–25b, 356a
Scioto Gazette VI–239a
Chillicothe Gazette (news.)
VI–239a
CHILLICOTHE JUNTO
II–25b
Chillicothe Republicans
II–25b, 356a
Chiloe Island VII–64b
Chilton, Mary (col.) V–334a
Chimney (arch.) I–161a
Chimney Point (Vt.) II–266b
CHIMNEY ROCK II–25b; II–246b
Chimney Tops Mountain
(N.C.) IV–186b

China
Canadian trade I–439b, 440a
citrus trees II–43a
civil war (1947–49) II–26b, 315b
Communist victory (1949) II–98a; III–69b
corn production II–226b
cotton production II–238b
currency system VI–289a
Dominican missions II–362b
Geneva Accords of 1954 III–159b, 161a
gunpowder V–97b
Hawaiian labor III–263b, 264a
hydrogen bomb III–324a
Japanese II–471b; IV–106b; V–216b; VII–334a
Japanese Twenty-one Demands V–107b, 159a
Korean War II–469a
Manchuria IV–234b
Nine-Power Pact V–96b; VII–251a
Nuclear Test Ban Treaty V–125a
prostitutes II–259b
refugees V–342b
republic II–29b
revolution II–25b; V–280b
Ringgold-Rodgers Exploring Expedition VI–142a
secret protocol of 1917 VI–251b
Sino-Japanese War III–68b
Soviet Union V–114b, 124b–25a; VI–180a
tobacco VII–64b
Treaty of Versailles VII–173a
tungsten III–15b
United Nations II–28a; III–70b
United Nations Declaration VII–151b
UN Security Council V–234a
Vietnam War V–22a
Wells, Fargo VII–267a
World War I VII–331a
World War II VII–337b
China, Nationalist (Taiwan) II–27b–28a, 489a
Yalta Conference VII–351b
CHINA, U.S. ARMED FORCES IN II–25b; IV–252a,b, 253a
CHINA, U.S. RELATIONS WITH II–26b; II–488a–90a; VII–92a
Alaska-Pacific-Yukon Exposition I–81a
Anglo-Chinese War I–125a
atomic bomb I–180b, 216a
Barrier Forts attack I–268b
Battle Fleet cruise I–276b
Boxer Rebellion I–185b, 356a; III–352a, 462b
Burlingame Treaty I–386a
cold war II–97b
Communist victory (1949) I–179b
Cushing's Treaty II–275a–b
détente III–62b
dollar diplomacy II–359b–60a, 488b
Dumbarton Oaks Conference II–380b
Export-Import Bank I–263a
extraterritoriality doctrine II–275b, 479b
Flying Tigers III–46a
French Indochina revolt II–315b
grain sales to I–43b
Kearny trade mission IV–34b
Korean War I–61a–b, 124a, 219b, 332a; II–315b; IV–56a,b, 57a
Lansing-Ishii Agreement IV–106b
lend-lease IV–134a
Manchukuo V–107a
Manchuria IV–234b
most-favored-nation treaties III–68b
nationalization of U.S. property IV–466a
neutralism V–36b
Nixon policy II–316b; III–70b; IV–113a
Nixon visit II–426b; V–234b; VI–93b
nonrecognition V–108a
"no-win policy" V–124a
nuclear weapons IV–364a–b
Open Door policy I–122a; II–471b; III–68b, 347b; V–35a, 157b
Peking Congress V–242a
Peking Tariff Conference V–242b
Potsdam Declaration V–378b
Quemoy and Ma-tsu bombardment III–70a
railroad building II–359b
Reed Treaty VI–66a
Root-Takahira Agreement VI–164a
secret protocol of 1917 VI–251b
Shanghai Opium Commission II–374b
Sino-Japanese War VI–294b
Sino-Soviet dispute I–180b
subversion VI–428b
summit conferences VI–439a
Treaty of Tientsin I–386a
U.S. aid III–61b
U.S. Court for China II–479b
U.S. defenses I–56b
U.S. recognition III 456a; VI–55a
U.S. Seventh Fleet V–22b
Vietnam War I–62b; II–316b; V–258a–b
World War II I–386b–87a, 403b; III–45b–46a, 489b–90a; IV–314a, 415b, 446b–47a
yellow peril VII–356b–57a
See also China Trade
China Air Task Force III–46b
***CHINA CLIPPER* II–28a**
***CHINA* INCIDENT II–28a**
CHINA TRADE II–28b; I–201a–b; IV–309b; VII–86b, 94a
armed merchantmen IV–313a
Astor, John Jacob IV–100b
balance of trade I–245a
clipper ships II–77a
East India Company II–388a
furs I–446a–b; II–219b
ginseng III–180b–81a
Hawaii III–263a
Kearny mission I–125a
Latin-American markets IV–115b
Massachusetts IV–266a
Open Door policy IV–234b; V–157b
Philippines III–347b; V–283a
Russia VI–177b, 180b
sea otters VI–247a
trade dollar VII–92b
Chinaware II–28b; V–379b
CHINCH BUG II–29a
Chinda, Mrs. Sutemi III–491b
Chindwin River III–46a
Chinese-Americans
protest VI–8a
race riots VI–8a
"separate but equal" doctrine V–331b
"Chinese cheap labor" IV–409b
Chinese Communists
Birch, John IV–1b
Chinese elm VII–114a
CHINESE EXCLUSION ACTS II–29a; I–88a; II–29b–30a, 445a; III–342a,b, 491b, 492a; IV–64a; VII–356b
Morey letter IV–409b
United States v. *Wong Kim Ark* VII–155b
CHINESE IMMIGRATION AND LABOR II–29b; II–488b; III–333a, 335a, 340b, 341a,b, 342a
California I–405b
contract labor II–333a
Greenback party III–225a
Morey letter IV–409b
opium II–373b
opposition IV–33a, 64a
race relations VI–7a
transcontinental railroads I–406a, 406a
United States v. *Wong Kim Ark* VII–155b
Washington State VII–248a
yellow peril VII–356b
Chinese Mathematics—Acta I–109a
Chinese mulberry tree VI–286b
Chinese opium dens II–260a
Chinook (Indians) II–30a–b; III–362a
Oregon V–165a
Chinookan (lang.) II–30a
CHINOOK JARGON II–30a; I–346a; V–165a; VI–392b, 395 (table)
Chinook State VI–395 (table)
CHINOOK WINDS II–30b
CHIPEWYAN (Indians) **II–30b**; I–441b; III–360b
Chipilly Ridge (Fr.) VI–338b
Chipley, William (bus.) III–39b
Chippawa (Ont.) V–91a
Chippendale, Thomas (cabinetmaker) III–134b
Chippendale furniture III–134a–b, 138a; VI–242b
CHIPPEWA (Indians) **II–30b**; III–360b, 365a, 366b, 367a, 396a,b
Algonquin relations I–86a
Brownstown Treaty I–371b
Butte des Morts council I–398a
Cheyenne II–16b
Duluth's explorations II–380a
Fort McIntosh treaties IV–216b
Fort Ripley VI–144b
French trade III–89a
Great Indian Council at Niagara V–90b
half-breeds III–242b
Hull Treaty III–316a
land cessions IV–107b
land scrip IV–97b
language I–86a, 441a, 441a
Leech Lake uprising IV–131b; VII–239b
Midewiwin III–385a; IV–335b
Minnesota IV–355a, 356a
myth and folklore III–386b
picture writing I–304b
Pontiac's War V–357a
Red River cart traffic VI–64a
religion III–393a
removal III–394b
Saginaw Treaty III–383b; VI–186b
Sault Sainte Marie VI–219b
Sioux war VI–294b
Spring Wells Treaty VI–377b
Treaty at Prairie du Chien V–388b
Treaty of Chicago III–383b
Treaty of Fort Harmar III–255a
Treaty of Greenville III–383a
Treaty of Saint Louis III–383b

Treaty of Saint Marys VI–197a
war with Fox III–88b
war with Sioux IV–31b, 346b
wild rice VII–298a
Wisconsin VII–305b, 307b
CHIPPEWA, BATTLE OF (1814) **II–31b**; I–436b; IV–205a; VII–234b
Chippewa River II–31b
Chiricahua Apache (Indians) I–141b, 142a
Chiricahua National Monument V–217a
Chirico, Giorgio de (art.) II–104b
Chirikov, Alexei (expl.) I–84b
Chisholm, Alexander II–32a
Chisholm, Jesse (Indian) II–31b, 477b
Chisholm, Shirley (pol.) I–283a
CHISHOLM TRAIL **II–31b**; I–472b; II–249a, 251b, 477b; V–148b; VI–45a
San Antonio VI–207b
Wichita VII–294a
CHISHOLM* v. *GEORGIA (1793) **II–32a**; I–94a; II–430b; VI–403b
Chisum, John IV–155a
Chiswell, John (miner) II–32b; III–381a
CHISWELL'S MINES **II–32b**; III–251a, 381a; VII–125b
Chitose (seaplane tender) II–387b
Chittenden, Hiram M. (mil. eng., hist.) VI–53b; VII–357a
Chittenden, Russell H. (chem., educ.) V–127b
Chittenden, Thomas (pol.) III–226b, 241a; VII–171b
Chivington, J. M. (off.) VI–208a
Chivington's Massacre. *See* Sand Creek Massacre
Chloramphenicol IV–292a
Chlordane III–213a
Chlorides II–5b
Chlorine VI–203a
drinking water IV–291b
production II–7b
textile industry II–6a
Chloroform IV–284a
Chloroquine–primaquine IV–291b
Chlorpromazine IV–306b
Choate, Rufus (law.) IV–267b; V–161b
Choctaw (Indians) III–367a, 396b
Augusta Congress I–223a
Battle of Amite I–114b
boundaries I–442a; II–167b
Chickasaw–French War II–22b
Choctaw Trail II–33a
citizenship III–377a
Dancing Rabbit Creek Treaty II–291a
Dawes Commission II–295b
De Soto expedition II–336b
Fort Adams treaty I–9b
Fort Jefferson attack III–494a
Jesuit missions III–499b
land claims II–291a
land frauds II–32b
migration I–308b
Mississippi IV–368a; VII–54b
mounds IV–421a
Natchez relations IV–455b
Natchez Trace IV–456b
oil drilling rights IV–334a
Panton, Leslie and Company V–211a
political organization III–365b
ranking I–288a
religion III–393a
removal III–394a; VII–181b
Saint Stephens VI–197b
Spanish trade VI–366b
Tombigbee Valley VII–70b
treaty of 1830 IV–97a
Treaty of Doak's Stand III–383b
Treaty of Hopewell III–300b
Treaty of Natchez IV–456a
Treaty of Nogales V–100b
western lands VI–356b
See also Civilized Tribes, Five
CHOCTAW LAND FRAUDS **II–32b**
Choctaw Nation VI–379a
Choctaw Trading House, Treaty of. *See* Indian Removal
CHOCTAW TRAIL **II–33a**; VII–54b
Choir, The (songbook) IV–446a
Choiseul, Étienne François de (dipl.) III–50b
CHOISEUL RAID (1943) **II–33a**
CHOLERA **II–33a**; II–454b; III–82a; IV–295b
cities VII–158a
environmental sanitation VI–212a,b
epidemics V–447a
Fort Riley VI–141b
infant deaths IV–275a
navy research IV–292b
New Orleans V–62b
Oregon Trail V–169b
research I–241a; IV–465a
Savannah VI–220b
slums VI–313b
statistics VII–206b
Cholera, hog VII–177a
Cholesterol II–282b
Chopin, Frédéric (comp.) II–287b
Chopper–scraper culture II–334b
Choptank River VI–149b
Choreographers II–286b–90b
Choshiu clan (Jap.) VI–278b–79a
Chosin Reservoir (Kor.) IV–253a
Chou En-lai (states.) VI–439a
Chouteau, Auguste Pierre (fur trader) II–34a–b; IV–159b; VI–195b, 215a,b; VII–96a
Chouteau, Francis G. (fur trader) II–34b, 131b; IV–27b
Chouteau, Jean Pierre (fur trader) II–34a–b
Chouteau, Pierre (fur trader) II–34a; IV–159b, 380a; VI–195b; VII–271b, 280a–b
Chouteau, René Auguste (fur trader) II–34a–b; III–403b–04a; VI–193b–94a; VII–95b
CHOUTEAU AND COMPANY **II–34a**; I–105b; III–144b, 403b; IV–377b
Chouteau family II–376a
CHOUTEAU'S TRADING POSTS **II–34a**; IV–27b; VII–96a
Chowan River VI–149b
Chrisman, Jesse III–286a
Christanna, Fort (Va.) VII–201b
Christ Church (Boston). *See* Old North Church
Christ Church (Cambridge, Mass.) I–162a
Christ Church (Lancaster Co., Va.) I–161b
Christ Church (Oxford, Eng.) V–179a
Christ Church (Phila.) I–162a
Christ Church (Savannah) VI–220a
Christ Church (Washington, D.C.) I–163a
Christian, George H. (flour miller) III–43b
Christian, William (off.) IV–186b; V–335b
Christian Advocate and Journal V–166b
CHRISTIANA FUGITIVE AFFAIR (1851) **II–34b**; I–138a
Christianahamn (Del.) V–80b
Christian Alliance V–3a
CHRISTIAN AND MISSIONARY ALLIANCE **II–34b**
Christian Baptist II–352b
CHRISTIAN COMMISSION **II–35a**
Christian Cynosure (news.) I–133a
Christian Family Movement I–469b
Christianity
Bahaism teachings V–172a
freethinking III–112b
morality IV–408a–b
Christianity and Liberalism VI–82b
Christianity and the Social Crisis VI–78b, 82b
Christianizing the Social Order VI–78b
Christian Methodist Episcopal church IV–319a
Christian Nurture VI–78a, 82a
Christian Philosopher VI–81a
"Christian Quakers" IV–35b
Christian Reformed Church VI–69a, 69a
Christian Science. *See* Church of Christ, Scientist
Christian Science Association II–35b
Christian Science Monitor (news.) II–36a; V–68a, 78a
Christiansen, Parley P. (pol.) II–493a
Christiansen, William II–289b
Christian Way VI–82b
Christie's I–221b
CHRISTINA, FORT (Del.) **II–35a**; II–123b; V–42b, 80b, 246a
Christina Kill V–80a
Christmas
Puritans II–496a
Christmas Conference (1784) IV–318a–b
Christopher Columbus (whaleback) VII–285a
Christopher Wren Building (Williamsburg) VII–302a
Christy, David (au.) IV–46b
Christy Minstrels IV–359b
Chris wheat VII–286b
Chromatography II–12b
Chromite III–13b
Chromium III–12a, 13b
Chronograph I–211a
Chronological History of New England III–280b
Chrysler, Walter P. (mfr.) III–80b
Chrysler Building (N.Y.C.) I–164b
Chrysler Corporation I–229a,b, 230a; IV–72b, 331b; VII–124a
Chrysler Financial Corporation III–423a
CHRYSLER'S FIELD, BATTLE OF (1813) **II–35a**; I–436b; IV–406a
Chrysler Tower (N.Y.C.) VI–299a
Chryssa (V. Mavromichali) (sculp.) VI–244a
Chuck wagon VII–96a
Chugach (Indians) III–358a
Chukchi (Chuckchee) Sea exploration V–338b
Chu Lai (Viet.) VII–186a
Chumash (Indians) I–446a; III–363a; V–4a
Chungishnish (Indian diety) III–503a
Chungking (China) VII–337b
Church, and state, separation of
Constitution II–197a

Church, Benjamin (off.)
IV–47b; VI–2b
Church, Benjamin (physic., spy) VI–372b
Church, E. Dwight
II–109b
Church, Frederick (art.)
II–102a, 103a; V–189a
Church, John B. VII–266b
Church, William (inv.)
V–412a
Church and state, separation of
VI–80b
colonial settlements
III–334b
New England Way V–51b
Churches
archives III–284a
plantation I–23b
storefront I–24a
Churches, established. *See* Religion
Churches, National Council of
II–353a, 387a; VI–79b
Churches of Christ
II–352b
Churches of Christ, Federal Council of VI–79b
Church Hill (Richmond, Va.)
VII–292a
Churchill, Fort (Nev.)
V–357b, 358a
Churchill, John, 1st Duke of Marlborough (off.)
VI–2b
Churchill, Thomas J. (off.)
I–174a
Churchill, Winston (states.)
VII–333b
Atlantic Charter I–215a
Cairo Conference I–403b
Casablanca Conference
I–67a, 465a; VII–338b
"Iron Curtain" address
III–474b
lend–lease IV–134b
Potsdam Conference
V–378b
sea power VI–248b
Stalin VI–179a
Teheran Conference
VII–18a
United Nations Declaration
VII–151b
U.S. neutrality V–36a
World War II I–123a–b, 141a; VII–335a, 336a,b, 344a
Yalta Conference
VII–351b
"Church in Action Against the Saloon" I–134a
See also Anti–Saloon League
Churchman, John (expl.)
V–336b
Church membership
Adventists I–15b
African Methodist Episcopal church I–23a
Afro–American church
I–23b, 24a
Baptist I–265b
Brethren I–361a
Churches of the New Jerusalem V–58b
Church of the Nazarene
V–30a
Congregational churches
II–170a
Disciples of Christ
II–352b–53a
Eastern Orthodoxy
II–387a
Episcopal churches
II–455a
Jehovah's Witnesses
III–498a
Lutherans V–123b
Mennonites IV–303a
Methodists IV–319a
Moravian Brethren
IV–409b
Norwegian churches
V–123b
Oriental religions and sects
V–171b
Pentecostal churches
V–260a
Presbyterianism V–392b
Reformed churches
VI–69a
Schwenkfelders VI–230a
Shakers VI–268a
Society of Friends
III–123b
CHURCH MEMBERSHIP SUFFRAGE II–35b
Church mergers VI–79b
Church music II–352b
Church of Christ (Mormon)
IV–117a
CHURCH OF CHRIST, SCIENTIST II–35b; VI–79a
Church of England
Dissenters II–353a
divorce II–356b
Latitudinarians IV–116a
Oxford Movement
V–179a
Puritans V–468b
CHURCH OF ENGLAND IN THE COLONIES
II–36a; VI–81a, 109a, 112b
Carolina I–457b
church covenant II–248a
College of William and Mary VII–300a
colonial elementary schools
II–394b
Episcopal church II–455a
Great Migration III–220a
Huguenots III–315a
Indian education III–379b
Maryland I–466b; IV–260b
Methodism IV–318a
New England Way V–51b
New York City V–82a,b
North Carolina V–115a
Pilgrims V–64b
religious liberty VII–69a
Revolution VI–115b
Savannah VI–220a
Scotch–Irish VI–240b
Separatist VI–262a
Shenandoah Valley
VI–275b
Society for the Propagation of the Gospel VI–331b
South Carolina VI–347a
suffrage VI–434a
sumptuary laws VI–440a
Toleration Act V–470a
Virginia VI–75a,b
West Jersey V–57a
Church of God (Abrahamic Faith) I–15b
Church of God, Cleveland, Tenn. V–260a
Church of God, Original
V–260a
Church of God in Christ (Mennonite) IV–303a
Church of God in Christ (Pentecostal) V–260a
Church of God of Prophecy
V–260a
Church of Jesus Christ of Latter–Day Saints. *See* Latter–Day Saints, Church of Jesus Christ of
Church of Latter–Day Saints (Bickertonites) IV–117a
Church of the Brethren
I–361a
Church of the Higher Life
V–81a
Church of the Lutheran Brethren of America IV–206b
Church of the Lutheran Confession IV–206b
Church of the Nazarene. *See* Nazarene, Church of the
Church of the Transfiguration. *See* Little Church Around the Corner
CHURCH SCHISMS OVER SLAVERY ISSUE
II–36b; VI–78b
home missionary societies
IV–365b
Methodists IV–318b
Presbyterianism V–392a
See also Reconstruction and the Churches
Church Unity, Consultation on
VI–79b
Church World Service
V–280b
"Churka" (cotton gin)
II–240a
Churrigueresque architecture
I–159b
CHURUBUSCO, BATTLE OF (1847) **II–36b**;
I–451b; II–214b; IV–324a
Churubusco River II–37a
CIA. *See* Central Intelligence Agency
CIBOLA II–37a; II–184b, 228a; IV–367a; V–459b; VII–36a, 372a
Cicuye (N.Mex.). *See* Pecos
Cigarettes V–67a; VII–65a, 67a–b
Indians V–318a
legislation I–325a
trade association VII–92b
Cigarmakers
sweatshop VI–454a
union IV–62a, 63b
Cigars VII–64b, 67a,b
Indians V–318a
Cigar–store figures III–47a
Cilley, Jonathan II–377a
Cimarron (Kans.) II–246a; VI–215b
CIMARRON, PROPOSED TERRITORY OF II–37a
Cimarron Crossing I–174b; VI–215b
Cimarron Cutoff VI–215b
Cimarron River I–282b;
II–14b; VI–318a; VII–256a
Cinchona IV–297b
Cinchona bark IV–229b
CINCINNATI (Ohio)
II–37a; III–232b, 286b; VII–159a
barnstorming I–268b
Bedini riots I–283a
Big Brother movement
I–296a
bossism I–343a
bridges I–364a
chamber of commerce
I–491a
Civil War I–435a;
IV–410a,b; VI–378b
directory II–343b
Disabled American Veterans
VII–175a
domestic trade
VII–83b–84a
fire department III–25a
floods III–37a
Fort Greenville III–227b
Fort Washington
III–244a; VI–188b; VII–247a
fossil remains V–197a
fugitive slaves I–492a
furniture III–135b, 139a
gambling III–149b
German immigrants
III–81a, 336b; V–75b
growth II–41b
harness factory III–255b
hogs III–289a
land office III–258a
Lochry's defeat IV–173b
machine–tool industry
IV–216a
mayorship VII–53a
meat–packing IV–170a, 280a; V–141b
mechanics' institutes
IV–281b
Miami and Erie Canal
V–141b, 145b
National Association of Manufacturers IV–461b
natural history museum
I–295b
Newport Barracks V–66a
newspapers I–483b; V–70b
observatory I–211a
pewter work VI–291b
pharmacy society V–275a
Philanthropist V–279b
pottery V–379b
prices V–404b, 405a
prison reform congress
V–415b–16a
proportional representation
V–435a
publishing I–334a
race riots VI–9a
railroads VI–25a,b, 34b, 37a,b, 349b
settlement IV–329b
slavery VII–137b
soapmaking VI–323b
steamboats VI–406b
steam engines VI–409a
stockyards VI–414a

subtreasury VI–427a
sulfuric acid II–6a
town planning II–46b
trade VII–83b
Vallandigham incident VII–164b
Washington's western lands VII–252a
Western Museum IV–436b
winemaking VII–305a
See also Losantiville
Cincinnati (gunboat) II–384a
Cincinnati, New Orleans and Texas Pacific Railroad VI–37a
CINCINNATI, SOCIETY OF THE II–37b; IV–329b–30a, 343a; VII–175a
Cincinnati and Louisville Mail Line VI–407a
Cincinnati Art Museum II–103a
Cincinnati Astronomical Society V–131a
Cincinnati Commercial (news.) V–71b
Cincinnati Enquirer (news.) II–222b; V–144b
Cincinnati Gazette (news.) V–71b
Cincinnati Red Stockings I–270a
CINCINNATI RIOTS (1884) **II–38a**
Cincinnati Southern Railroad I–364a; VI–25a
Cincinnati Tennis Club VII–29a
Cincinnatti Zoo VII–370b
CINCUS. *See* Commander in chief, U.S. Navy
"Cinderella Man." *See* Braddock, James J.
CinemaScope IV–418a
Cinématographe IV–417a
Cinematography. *See* Motion Pictures
Cinerama IV–418a
CIO. *See* American Federation of Labor–Congress of Industrial Organizations; Committee for Industrial Organization; Congress of Industrial Organizations
CIPHER DISPATCHES II–38b; IV–454b
Circle in the Square (N.Y.C.) VII–51a
CIRCUIT ANALYSIS, ELECTRIC II–38b
Circuit councils IV–17b
Circuit Courts. *See* Courts, circuit; Judiciary
CIRCUIT RIDERS II–39b; II–487a; VI–77b
Methodist church IV–318b
CIRCUITS, JUDICIAL II–39b
CIRCUS II–40a; IV–220b
showboats IV–283a
See also Wild West Show
Citadel (Charleston, S.C.) I–497a
Cities
automobile I–227b–28a
bossism I–343a–b
climate II–76b
community action programs II–147b
curfew laws II–274b
CITIES, GROWTH OF II–41a
Florida III–42a
food supply III–52a
health VI–173a–b; VII–157b–58b
housing III–309b
Indian population III–397b
Jeffersonian Democracy III–495b
municipal ownership IV–427b
New York V–277b
Philadelphia V–246b
preservation movement V–393a
Saint Joseph VI–191b
Saint Louis VI–194a–b
San Diego VI–208b
San Francisco VI–209b
skyscrapers VI–298b
slums VI–313b
social settlements VI–330a
steam power VI–409b
suburban growth VI–427b
subways VI–429a
Texas VII–40b
town government VII–78b
urban renewal VI–86a
urban structure VII–159a
water supply VI–377b
water supply and conservation VII–258a–59b
Wisconsin VII–307b
Citizen and Countryman's Experienced Farrier VII–175b
Citizens, boards of IV–427a
Citizen's Alliance, National II–42a
CITIZENS' ALLIANCES II–42a
Citizens' Association (N.Y.C.) VI–313b
Citizens' committees. *See* Vigilantes
CITIZENSHIP II–42a; I–94b
Afro-Americans I–28b; IV–27b
Alien and Sedition Acts I–86a–b
American Samoa VI–205b
American seamen II–277a
Articles of Confederation I–198b
Chinese VII–356b
colonial New England V–52a
Connecticut Plan II–151b
diversity-of-citizenship cases II–460a
election to Congress II–172a
expatriation II–475b–76a
Fourteenth Amendment II–54a, 205a; III–86a–b; VI–56b, 431b
Guam III–230b
immigration laws III–334a
impressment of seamen III–349b–50a
Indians I–106b, 385b; III–377a, 390a
insular possessions III–425a, 426b
Japanese exclusion III–492a
married women VII–315b
naturalization V–6a
New Jersey Plan 151b–
Northwest Territory V–140b
Philippines IV–7b
Puerto Rico III–58a; V–461a
Seminole VI–260a
slaves II–370a–b
suffrage IV–359b
territories VII–33b, 34a
United States v. *Wong Kim Ark* VII–155b
universal military service II–313a
Virginia Plan II–151b
Virgin Islands VII–203b
voting II–410a; VII–209a
CITIZENSHIP, DUAL II–42b
married women VII–315b
Citizens' Industrial Association IV–471b
Citizens rights. *See* Civil rights and liberties
Citizens Stamp Advisory Committee V–372b
Citric acid II–43b
Citronelle (Ala.) II–68b
Citron production II–43a
CITRUS INDUSTRY II–43a; VI–48a
California I–406a
Florida III–39a, 39b–40a; VI–187b
insecticides III–421a
Rio Grande Valley VI–143b
Texas VII–40b
See also Fruit Growing
City and Suburban Homes Company VII–24a–b
City Art Museum (Saint Louis) III–137a
City Beautiful Movement II–45b–46b
City Center Joffrey Ballet II–289b
City clerk II–44b, 411a
City councilmen II–245b
CITY COUNCILS II–44a; IV–171b, 426b–27a; VI–397b
council-manager government IV–172a
municipal reform IV–429b
Washington, D.C. VII–245a,b
City Creek (Utah) III–477a
City directories II–343b
City flags III–35a
City government IV–171b–72a
merger with county government IV–172b
See also Local Government; Municipal Government
City Hall (N.Y.C.) VI–382a
"City in the sky." *See* Acoma
CITY MANAGER PLAN II–44b; IV–133b, 427a
Kansas IV–26b
municipal reform IV–429b
New England VII–78b
popularity of IV–172a
"City of sin" II–259b
CITY PLANNING II–45a
party machines IV–214b
Savannah VI–220b
skyscrapers VI–299a
suburban growth VI–428a
urban structure VII–159b
Washington, D.C. VII–244b–45a
zoning ordinances VII–370a
City Point (Va.) III–488a; V–265a
City Point Railway IV–35a
City Tavern (Phila.) III–354a, 427b
City University of New York V–83b
parapsychology V–213b
Ciudad Bolívar (Venez.) VII–170a
Ciudad Juárez (Mex.) IV–321a,b
Civic associations I–491a
Civics VI–227b
Civic understanding tests IV–160a
CIVIL AERONAUTICS ACT (1938) **II–49b**; I–68a; III–459a
Civil Aeronautics Administration II–49b, 498b; III–452a
Civil Aeronautics Authority I–68a; II–500a
See also Civil Aeronautics Board
Civil Aeronautics Board I–68a, 69b; II–49b, 167b, 498b, 500a; III–422a, 459a; V–458a
Civil and Defense Mobilization, Office of II–498a
Civil and Political Rights, International Covenant on III–457a
Civil authority
See also Military Aid to the Civil Powers
Civil contract
marriage II–486a
Civil courts. *See* Courts, civil
CIVIL DEFENSE II–49b; V–237a
CIVIL DISOBEDIENCE II–50a
civil rights movement II–57b
legal education IV–121b
martial law IV–258a
pacifists V–181b–82a
Civil Disorders, National Advisory Commission on. *See* National Advisory Commission on Civil

CIVIL DISORDERS, NATIONAL ADVISORY COMMISSION ON. (cont.)
Disorders
Civil engineering I–442a–b; II–448b
Civil Engineers, American Society of. *See* American Society of Civil Engineers
Civil government
compact theory II–149a
CIVILIAN CONSERVATION CORPS II–51a; II–188a; III–73b–74a, 76a, 503b; IV–71a; V–44a; VI–73a–b; VII–364b
national parks V–220a
Officers' Reserve Corps V–138b
reforestation VI–67a–b
soil conservation VI–335b
Civilian Public Service V–182a–b
CIVILIZED TRIBES, FIVE II–51b; III–396b
Civil War III–399b–400a
Creek nation V–254b
education III–380a
Fort Smith Council VI–317a
Indian commission III–378b
Indian Territory III–402a
intermarried citizen III–447a
land cession I–335b–36a
Oklahoma V–148a–b, 150a; VI–355a
removal I–219a
Seminole VI–259b
slaveholding III–401a
state of Sequoyah VI–262b
Treaty of Nogales V–100b
Civil marriages II–485b
Civil officers
impeachment II–202a
CIVIL RELIGION II–52b; VI–80a
Civil Rights, Commission on II–499b; VI–256b, 433a; VII–209b
Civil Rights, Committee on II–54a, 56b
Civil rights acts II–53b–55a,b, 457a,b
Civil Rights Act (1866) III–59b
Civil Rights Act (1875) III–59b, 502b; VI–58a, 255b–56a
Civil Rights Act (1886) VI–417b
Civil Rights Act (1957) I–239a; III–20a; VII–211a
Civil Rights Act (1960) III–20a
Civil Rights Act (1964) I–32a, 239b, 310b; II–50b, 137a, 402a, 455b, 456a; III–20a, 21a,b, 107b, 438a; V–339b; VI–328b, 433a; VII–209b
Community Relations Service IV–22b
employment IV–80b; VII–141a
literacy tests IV–160a
support by labor IV–76b
Civil Rights Act (1968) II–56a; III–107b; IV–208b
CIVIL RIGHTS AND LIBERTIES II–53a; I–94b
Alien and Sedition Acts V–69b–70a
arrest I–195a–b
Catholics I–467a
censorship I–478b
Civil War II–62a–b
commerce clause II–137a
Committee on Civil Rights IV–208a,b
congressional debate III–21b
Constitution II–197a, 197b, 197b
criminal suspects IV–361b
cruel and unusual punishment V–464a
electronic surveillance II–427b
equal protection of the law II–457a
executive orders II–473a
Fifteenth Amendment III–20a
Force Acts III–59b
Fourteenth Amendment II–137a; III–86a
Hague v. *Committee on Industrial Organization* III–237b
Haiti III–240a
Hatch Act III–261a–b
integration III–437b–38b
interracial marriage IV–362b
Japanese-American relocation III–490b
jury right IV–21a
Justice Department IV–22a
juvenile courts IV–23b
majority rule IV–228a
military VII–154a
minority rights IV–358a
Mormons VII–162a
Niagara movement V–92b
Penn's Holy Experiment III–293a
prisoners V–417a–b
private schools V–167a
privileges and immunities of citizens V–421a
right of revolution VI–121a
Slaughterhouse Cases VI–303a
Supreme Court IV–14a; VI–447b
United States v. *Cruikshank* VII–154a
"witch-hunt" VII–310b–11a
woman's rights movement VII–314a
Civil Rights Cases (1883) II–54a, 55a, 457a; III–60a, 438a; VI–58a
CIVIL RIGHTS MOVEMENT II–56a; I–28b–32a, 28b–32a; II–50a–b, 55a–b; III–503a; VI–256b–57a; VII–118a
AFL-CIO I–103a
Afro-American culture I–25a
Alabama I–71a, 72b
Black Power I–316a
black suffrage VI–432b, 433a
bloc I–322b
busing I–397b
campaign of 1948 I–429b
campaign of 1968 I–431a–b
Catholics I–470a
churches I–24b
constitutional amendments I–95a
education II–402b
Freedom Riders III–107a
Indians IV–464a
industrial relations III–408a
Jewish alliance IV–11b
Johnson, Lyndon, administration V–329a–b
Kennedy administration V–53a
King, Martin Luther IV–45b
Ku Klux Klan IV–59a
minority rights IV–359a
Mississippi IV–369b
mob violence IV–208a,b
NAACP IV–460b
National Guard call-up IV–341b
National Urban League V–1b
"nigger" V–95b
pacifism V–181b–82a
private property V–433b
Progressive party V–429a
race riots II–259a; VI–8b–9a
radicals VI–14a
religious debate VI–80a
Selma-Montgomery march V–265b
social legislation VI–328a,b
South Carolina VI–348a
Southern Christian Leadership Conference VI–351b
states' rights III–9b
Student Nonviolent Coordinating Committee VI–420b
student participation VII–365b
Students for a Democratic Society VI–421a
violence VII–191a,b
voting rights VII–211a
Warren Court I–408a
See also Backlash
CIVIL SERVICE II–59a; I–146a, 383b; III–3b; VI–165a, 375b
Customs Service II–277a
desegregation II–56b
establishment II–232a
fair employment II–455b–56a
Foreign Service III–72b
Hatch Act III–261a–b; V–448b
Hoover Commissions III–299b
Indian agencies III–372a–b
Indian agents III–373a
Pendleton Act V–245a
Philippines V–283a,b
political assessments V–341b
political patronage IV–214b; V–227b, 345b
reform I–422b, 423a; II–457b; IV–141a; VI–380b
ripper legislation VI–144b
rules and regulations II–473a
State Department VI–388b–89a
state government VI–398a
subversives VI–428b
Tammany Hall VI–460b
Toledo V–142a
ward leader VII–230b
women VII–317b
workmen's compensation III–431b
Civil Service Commission II–59b–60b; IV–16b; VI–375b
Civil Service League, National II–59b; V–228a
CIVIL WAR II–61a; VI–387a; VII–190b, 292b–93a
Adams Express Company I–10a
advertising I–16b
agents II–158b
agrarianism I–33a
agricultural machinery I–34a, 38a
Alabama I–71a–b, 72b
Albemarle I–83a
amnesty I–114b–15a
Amy Warwick I–116a
antisecessionist movement IV–8a
antislavery gangs IV–377b
antiwar activities I–304a; II–190a; VII–236a
arbitrary arrest II–228a
Arkansas I–173b, 275a
Army, Confederate I–180b
Army, Union I–181b, 184b–85a
Army of Potomac V–377a
Army of the James III–488a
Army of the Ohio V–142a
army slang VI–300b
artillery I–199b, 200a; IV–431a
Associated Press I–207a
Bahama Islands I–243b
balloons I–59a, 232b, 248a
Baltimore riot I–251b
bankruptcy laws I–262a
Bermuda admiralty case I–292a
Birchard Letter I–196a, 304a
Black Belt I–308b–09a
black powder V–383a
black soldiers II–468b; IV–339b
blockade I–83a, 116a, 121b, 245b, 279a, 292a, 321a; II–159a, 161a, 162a–63b,

238a, 384a, 446b
blockade runners I–73a, 321a, 497a; II–162b
Blue and Gray I–324a
bonds II–218b
bonuses I–331a
border states I–341b
bounties I–353a–b; II–302b, 335a–b, 366b–67a, 451a–b
British indemnities III–352a
British mediation V–233a
British ships I–292a
Bummers I–382b
bushwhackers I–388b
Butler's Order No. 28 I–398a
campaign of 1864 I–421b–22a
campaign of 1876 I–422b, 423a
Camp Jackson affair I–433b
Canadian relations I–435a, 438b–39a
canned meats IV–280b
capital punishment I–450a
Carondelet I–459a
cartoons I–464b
Catholics in I–468a
cavalry I–475b–76a
cemeteries I–478a
check currency II–2a
Christian Commission II–35a
churches II–36b; VI–59b
Cincinnati II–37b
civil religion II–52b–53a
clothing industry II–81b
College of William and Mary VII–300b
Colorado II–128a
Colt six-shooter II–431a
Committee on the Conduct of the War II–139b
commutation money II–185a
Compromise of 1860 II–149b
Confederacy collapse II–165a
Confederate impressment III–349a
Confederate migration to Mexico IV–325a
Confederate rams VI–44b
Confederate States of America established IV–404b–05a
Confederate tax-in-kind VII–64a
confiscation of property II–168a
confiscation of slaves II–434a–b, 435a
conscientious objectors II–185a
conscription I–181a, 182a–b, 184b, 353a–b; II–186a, 313b
constitutional amendments II–197b
II 205a–06a–
continuous voyage doctrine II–446b
contraband II–213a, 446b
contracts investigated II–140a
Copperheads II–161a, 222b
Corps of Engineers II–450a
costs II–313b, 476a; VII–228 (table), 228b
cotton II–165a, 168a, 238a, 267b; IV–157b
cotton agents II–159a
cotton as money II–267b
Cotton Kingdom II–241a
counterfeiting VI–252a
"cracker line" II–253a
Cumberland Gap II–272b
currency I–301b
death penalty II–190a
DeBow's *Review* II–298b
declaration of war VII–224b
Delaware II–320b
demobilization II–324a; IV–346a
Denver II–332a
Department of the South II–434b–35a
Department of the West II–434b
deserters II–159b, 335a–b
Dolphin Admiralty Case II–360a
draft II–314a, 366b–67a, 368b–69a, 451a–b
draft resistance III–292a
Draft Riots II–258a, 368b–69a
Dred Scott Case II–370b
dummy battleships I–277a
Eads gunboats II–384a
Ellsworth's Zouaves VII–371b
Emancipation Proclamation II–434b
"embalmed beef" II–436a
enemy trading VII–94a
enlistment II–451a–b
espionage VI–373a–b
excess profits tax II–467a
Ex parte Milligan IV–346b
federal mints IV–360a
federal surplus VI–449a–b
feuding III–18b
financing II–218b, 317a; VII–24b
Fishing Creek Confederacy III–31b
Five Civilized Tribes V–148a–b
Florida III–39b; V–254b
food supplies II–253a
foreign contract labor II–214a
foreign investments III–64b
foreign policy III–68a–b
Foreign Service III–71a
Fort Fillmore III–24a
Fort Gaines III–146a
fortifications III–78b
Fort Leavenworth IV–129a,b
Fortress Monroe IV–399b
Fort Saint John VI–191a
Fort Saint Marks VI–196b
Fort Smith VI–316a
Fourteenth Amendment III–86a, 87a
Franco–American relations III–97a
Fritchie, Barbara III–100b, 124a
Galvanized Yankees III–148b
General Order No. 38 III–156a
Georgia III–168b
Great Britain I–72b–73b, 121b; II–162a–b
See also Alabama; Alabama Claims
greenbacks III–225b; VI–94b
guerrillas III–231a
gunboats II–22a; III–234b
habeas corpus II–179a, 472b; III–237a; IV–314b
Hampton Roads Conference III–247b
Holden Peace Movement III–289b
Holmes County Rebellion III–292a
Honey Island III–297b
hospitals I–191b
Housatonic III–308a
immigration III–336a
income tax II–113b; III–351a
Indiana III–370a
Indian Brigade III–375b
Indians I–335b–36a; III–399b, 401a; VI–296b
inflation I–301b; II–2a, 235b; III–414b–15a
international law III–455b–56a
ironclad warships III–474a–b
Jayhawkers III–493a
Jefferson Barracks III–494b
Jessie Scouts III–498b
Johnson–Clarendon Convention IV–4b
Jürgen Lorentzen IV–20b
Kansas IV–26a
Kansas–Missouri relations I–342a
Kentucky IV–41a, 43a
Knights of the Golden Circle IV–52b
Know–Nothing party V–3a
Ku Klux Klan IV–57b
labor I–34a, 38a; IV–62b
Laird rams IV–85a
laws of war VII–225a,b
lead industry IV–122b
Lee's Arlington estate I–175b
Legal Tender Act IV–132b
Lexington IV–136b
logistics I–189b–90a
losses VII–232 (table), 232b
Louisiana IV–194a–b
Loyal Publication Societies IV–202a
loyalty oaths IV–202b
machine guns IV–215a
mail routes V–178a
mapmaking I–463b
marines IV–252a
maritime law III–106b
Marshall Convention IV–257a
Maryland IV–261a
McClellan's Harrison's Landing letter III–258a
medical schools IV–284a
Mexico IV–325b, 328a–b, 361a
military arrests II–222b
military censorship I–481a
military roads VI–156a
militia I–433b; II–313b, 451b
mines V–164a
minesweeping IV–351a
Minié ball IV–352b
Minnesota IV–356b
Mississippi IV–368b
Mississippi River IV–371a, 373a, 374a, 374b, 375a
Missouri IV–377b
Mobile IV–382b
mobilization IV–383b
money III–192b; IV–392b, 393a, 394b
monitors II–286a; IV–397a
Monroe Doctrine IV–400b
Morgan's raids IV–410a–b
mortars IV–413b
Mosby's Rangers IV–415b
mules IV–426a
munitions II–8a, 313b; IV–279a, 430b, 433a; V–163a, 164a
Nashville IV–453a
Nast cartoons IV–454b; V–73a
national defense II–313b
national sinking fund VI–294a
Naval Academy V–9b
naval officers I–13b–14a
Navy Department V–18a
neutral rights V–39a
New Ironsides V–56a–b
New Mexico IV–315b; V–60a
Newport Barracks V–66a
newspaper coverage V–71a–b
New York City V–83a–b, 84a
New York State V–87a
Norfolk Navy Yard V–29b
North Carolina V–116a
Northwest conspiracy V–121b
"Northwestern Confederacy" II–222b
ocean shipping III–428a; IV–310b
Ohio V–141b; VI–378b
"On to Richmond" V–157a
"On to Washington" V–157a
opium use IV–450a
Order of American Knights V–161b
Pacific republic movement V–180b
panic of 1873 V–207a
papal states V–211b

CIVIL WAR (cont.)
partisan bands V–222a
passports I–196a
peace movements II–163b, 164b–65a; V–234b, 235b; VII–149a
Pennsylvania V–247b
pensions V–257a
Peterhoff admiralty case V–264a
pharmaceutical industry V–273b
photographs I–359a; V–293a
Pittsburgh V–322a
plantation system V–325b
political prisoners IV–83b
political writings V–353a–b
Port Royal (S.C.) V–370a
postal service II–472b; V–373a–b
presidential powers II–179a, 472a–b; V–394a
price-fixing V–401b
prices V–405a–b
prisoners II–159a–b, 190a, 484b
prisons I–117b–18a, 219b, 287a, 433a, 435a, 466a–b; II–159a, 222b, 433a; V–414a
privateering IV–256a; V–214a, 419b
prize cases V–421a
prize money V–424a
profiteering V–426a
propaganda II–159a, 159b; V–221a, 432a
prostitution V–437b
protectionism II–276a
public debt II–299b
Radical Republicans VI–10b–11b
railroads I–118b, 146b; II–253a; VI–26b, 37b
rangers VI–46b
Rebellion Records III–281a
rebel yell VI–50b
recruiting II–451b
rifles VI–139b
riots I–251b, 498b
rivers VI–150a
Russia I–75b; VI–177b, 181a
Saint Augustine VI–188a
salt VI–202b
saltpeter V–98a
Sanitary Commission VI–211a
secret service I–196a
sectionalism VI–254a
sequestration of property II–168a
shipbuilding VI–279b
Singleton peace plan VI–293b
slavery I–21a, 28a–b, 34a, 38a; II–435a–b; VI–307b–08a; VII–54a
slaves as contraband II–212a
smallpox VI–316a
Sons of Liberty VI–339a
sorghum VI–340a
South Carolina VI–348a
Southern Overland Mail VI–353b
southern unionists VI–354a
specie payments suspension VI–104a
Spencer rifle VI–372a
spies I–118b; II–159b
state borrowing II–302b
state sovereignty VI–404a
states' rights VI–404b, 405a–b
steamboats II–253a; VI–407a
stone fleets VI–414b
Stonewall VI–415a
store boats VI–415b
strikes II–235b
submarines I–497a; VI–422b, 424b
substitutes II–186a, 366b, 367b
Sultana disaster II–349a–b
Supreme Court VI–447b
surrender I–146b–47a, 458b
taxation VII–5a,b, 12b
telegraph VII–18b, 19a
Tennessee VII–25b
test laws VII–34b
Texas VII–39b
tintypes VII–62b
torpedoes I–497a; II–285b–86a, 294b; VI–424b
trade I–245b
training camps I–433a
treason II–190a, 222b; VII–107a
trenches VII–115a
Trent affair III–350a; VII–115b
Union Democrats VII–146a
Union navy V–19b; VII–146b
Union party VII–148a
Union preservation II–435a, 435a,b
Union sentiment VII–148b–49a
Vallandigham incident VII–164b
venereal disease VII–169a
veterans I–331a, 424a; III–207b; IV–97b; VII–175a
Virginia VII–195a
volunteers II–186a, 302b, 313b, 366b–67a; IV–343b
Wachusett affair VII–212b
War Democrats VII–229b
warships V–25a; VII–240b
West Point graduates IV–341a
westward movement VII–284b
women VII–317a
wool industry VII–320b
zinc VII–369a
See also Confederate States of America; Indians in the Civil War; Navy, Confederate; Navy, United States; Reconstruction
—Battles and Campaigns:
Aliatoona Pass I–88b
Andrew's Raid I–118b
Antietam I–130a
Appomattox I–146b
Arkansas Post I–174a
Atlanta I–213b; IV–36b; V–56a, 238a–b; VII–26b, 27a
Averysboro I–232b
Ball's Bluff I–249a
Baton Rouge I–275a
Battery Wagner I–497a
Bayou Teche I–279a, 461b
Belmont I–288a
Bentonville I–289b, 458b; V–116a
Big Black River I–295b
Bird's Point I–306b
Blackburn's Ford I–309a, 381a
Blackwater I–317b
Bloody Angle I–322b
Boonville I–337b, 462a
Boydton Plank Road I–357a; V–265a
Brandy Station I–360a
Bristoe Station I–365a
Buckland Races I–374a
Buffington Island I–376a
Bull Run (1861) I–182a, 381a
Bull Run (1862) I–382a, 476b; VII–197a
Camp Wildcat I–435a
Carnifex Ferry I–457a
Carrion Crow Bayou I–461a
Carthage I–462a
Cedar Creek I–476b; VI–275a
Cedar Mountain I–476b
Chambersburg I–490b
Champion's Hill I–295b, 492a
Chancellorsville I–493a
Chantilly I–493b
Charleston I–497a–b; VI–453a
Chattanooga I–502a; VII–26b
Chickamauga I–502a; II–21b, 271b; VII–26b
Chickasaw Bluffs II–22a; VII–181b
Cold Harbor II–62b, 96b; VI–138a
Columbia (S.C.) II–131a
Corinth II–62b, 225b
Corrick's Ford II–231a
Crater II–253b; VI–138a
Cross Keys II–266a; III–487b
Dahlgren's and Kilpatrick's Raid II–279a
Doniphan's Expedition II–363b
Drewry's Bluff II–373a
Dug Springs II–379a
Dutch Gap Canal II–382b
Elk River II–432a
Ezra Church II–479b
Fair Oaks II–482a; V–245a
Falling Waters II–484b
Farmville I–146b
Fisher's Hill I–476b; III–31a; VI–275a
Five Forks III–33a; V–265a; VI–276a
Florida raids III–40a
Fort Brown I–371a
Fort Donelson II–363a, 363a
Fort Fisher III–30b; V–116a
Fort Henry III–272b
Fort McAllister IV–209a
Fort Pickens V–308a
Fort Pillow V–313b
Fort Pulaski V–462b
Fort Stedman V–265a; VI–410a
Fort Sumter VI–440b–41a
Fort Union VII–145a
Frayser's Farm III–100a; VII–293a
Fredericksburg III–101a
Fredericktown III–101a
Front Royal III–128a, 487b
Gaines' Mill III–146a; V–245b; VI–263b
Galveston III–148b
Gettysburg III–175b; V–309a
"Gettysburg of the Southwest" II–128a
Glasgow III–182a
Glorieta III–187b; V–60a; VI–144a
Grand Gulf III–208b
Grierson's Raid III–228a
Groveton III–229a
Haines' Bluff III–238b
Hanover cavalry engagement III–250b
Harpers Ferry III–256a
Hatteras Inlet III–262a
Helena III–269b
Holly Springs III–292a
Hood's Tennessee campaign III–98a–b, 298a; VII–26b
Huntsville III–319a
Imboden–Jones raid III–332b
Island Number Ten III–478b
Iuka III–485a
Jackson (Miss.) III–485b
Jackson's Valley campaign III–487a; V–245b
Jenkins Ferry III–498a; V–402b
Kearsarge–Alabama encounter IV–35a
Kelly's Ford IV–36a
Kenesaw Mountain IV–36b
Kentucky invasion IV–42a
Kernstown III–487b; IV–43b
Knoxville siege IV–54a
Lexington (Mo.) siege IV–137a
Lone Jack (Mo.) IV–183b
Lookout Mountain IV–187a
Malvern Hill IV–230b; V–245b
Marion IV–253b
Maryland invasion IV–261b
McDowell (Va.) IV–212b
Mechanicsville IV–281b; V–245b; VI–263b

Memphis IV–302a
Meridian IV–313b
Mill Springs IV–347a
Mine Creek IV–26a
Mine Run IV–36a, 350a
Missionary Ridge I–502b; IV–364b
Mobile Bay II–285b; IV–382b; VI–425a; VII–26b
Monitor and *Merrimack* IV–396a
Monocacy IV–398a; VI–275a
"Mud March" IV–425a
Munfordville IV–426b
Murfreesboro IV–434b
Nashville IV–453a; VII–26b
New Hope Church I–213b; V–56a
New Market V–59a
New Orleans V–63b
Norfolk V–110a
North Anna V–113b; VI–138a
Olustee V–153b
Palmito Ranch V–198b
Peachtree Creek V–238a
Pea Ridge V–238b, 402b
Peninsular campaign V–245a; VII–360a
Pennsylvania invasion V–248a
Perryville IV–41a; V–263a
Petersburg V–264b; VI–138a
Philippi V–281a
Pickett's charge III–176a; V–309a
Pilot Knob V–314a, 403a
Pine Bluff V–316a
Pleasant Hill V–331a
Port Gibson V–369a
Port Hudson V–369a
Port Republic III–487b; V–369a
Prairie Grove V–389a
Price in Missouri III–182a; V–402b
Quantrill's raid IV–26a; V–471a
Rappahannock Station VI–47a
Raymond III–485b; VI–48b
Red River IV–457a; V–331a, 402b; VI–63a
Richmond (Ky.) VI–137a
Richmond (Va.) III–21a–b; V–245a; VI–137a,b, 420b
Rich Mountain VI–138b
Ringgold Gap VI–141b
Roanoke Island VI–156b
Rousseau's Raid VI–166a
Sabine Crossroads VI–182a
Sailor's Creek I–146b; VI–186b
Saint Albans I–439a; VI–187a
Santa Rosa Island VI–216a
Savage's Station V–245b; VI–220a
Savannah VI–220b, 221a; VII–27a
Secessionville I–497a
Seven Days' Battles III–100a, 146a–b; IV–230b; V–245b; VI–137a, 263b
Shenandoah Valley VI–275a, 276a; VII–304a–b
Sherman's march through Carolinas I–458b; VII–27a
Sherman's march to the sea I–382b; VI–278a; VII–27a
Shiloh VI–278a; VII–26b
Sibley's Rio Grande operations VI–144a
Spotsylvania Courthouse VI–138a, 376a
Spring Hill VI–377a
Steele's Bayou VI–410b
Stuart's ride VI–420b
Suffolk VI–430a
Todd's Tavern VII–68a
Toms Brook VII–71a
Trevilian Station VII–117a
Tullahoma VII–127b
Tupelo VII–128b
Valverde VI–144a; VII–165b
Vicksburg I–174a, 502a–b; VII–181b
Wagner Battery VII–215b
Wauhatchie VII–261a
Westport IV–27b; V–403a; VII–280b
White Oak Swamp VII–292b
Wilderness I–322b; VI–137b–38a; VII–295b
Williamsburg V–245a; VII–301b
Wilson's Creek V–402b; VII–304a
Winchester VII–304a–b
Yazoo Pass VII–354a
Yellow Tavern VII–358a
Civil War amendments. *See* Fifteenth Amendment; Fourteenth Amendment; Thirteenth Amendment
CIVIL WAR GENERAL ORDER NO. 100 II–70a; VII–225a,b
Civil Works Administration IV–71a; V–45b, 46a; VI–73a
CL (light cruiser). *See* Cruisers
Claflin, Victoria (ref.) VI–13a–b
Clagett, William H., Jr. (pol.) VII–357b
Claiborne, F. L. (off.)
  Creek War IV–456a
Claiborne, Fort (Ala.) I–402a
Claiborne, William (col.) II–70a
Claiborne, William C. C. (pol.) V–173b
  Battle of New Orleans V–63a
  Burr conspiracy V–63b–64a
  Louisiana purchase IV–197a
  West Florida VII–277a
CLAIBORNE SETTLEMENT II–70a
CLAIM ASSOCIATIONS II–70a; V–390a, 444a, 452b
Claim clubs II–70a
CLAIM JUMPER II–70b; II–70a; V–390a
CLAIMS, FEDERAL COURT OF II–71a
Claims, land. *See* Land Claims
Claims, small I–152a
Claims commissions IV–381b, 382a
Clairvoyance V–212b, 213a
Clallam County (Wash.) V–169b
Clamorgan, Jacques (fur trader) VI–367a
Clamorgan, Loisel and Company VI–367a
Clams I–477a; III–51a,b
Clansman IV–58b
Clanton brothers VII–71a
Clapboard (arch.) I–161a, 377b
Clapp, Moses E. (pol.) IV–169a; V–427b
Clapper, Raymond (jour.) V–74a, 75a
Claremont (Calif.) I–348b
Clarendon, Earl of. *See* Hyde, Edward; Villiers, George William Frederick
Clarendon County (N.C.) I–447b; V–115a
Clari (operetta) III–297a
Clark, Abraham (law.) II–308a
Clark, Alvan (astron.) I–211a; V–13a, 131b
Clark, Alvan, and Sons V–131b
Clark, Bennett Champ (pol.) VI–24a
Clark, Billy J. (physic.) VII–22a
Clark, Charles E. (nav. off.) V–165b
Clark, Daniel (mer.) III–146a; VI–366a
Clark, Edward L. (pol.) VII–39b
Clark, E. W., and Company II–218b
Clark, Fort, Treaty of (1808) III–383b; V–173b
Clark, George Rogers (off.) I–286b, 367a; III–239a; IV–303b
  Battle of Piqua V–319b
  Detroit expedition IV–173b
  Fort Henry III–272b
  Fort Jefferson III–494a
  Fort Nelson V–32b
  galley boats III–147b
  Kentucky County IV–43a
  Loramie's store IV–188a
  "Old Chillicothe" II–25b
  Transylvania Company VII–203a
  Wisconsin VII–307a
  See also Clark's Northwest Campaign
Clark, James Beauchamp ("Champ") (pol.) I–426b; II–176 (table)
Clark, John (gov.) VII–121a
Clark, John (spy, off.) VI–373a
Clark, John B. (off.) III–182a
Clark, John Bates (econ.) VII–140a
Clark, John H. (jur.) VI–446b
Clark, Jonas (cler.) VI–106a
Clark, Joseph S., Jr. (pol.) V–278a
Clark, J. Reuben (dipl.) V–106a
Clark, Kenneth (educ.) II–148a
Clark, Mark W. (off.) I–141a,b; VI–199b
Clark, Ransome (sol.) II–278b
Clark, Thomas (off.) VI–226a
Clark, Thomas C. (jur.) VI–446b
Clark, William (fur trader) VI–195b
  American Indian museum IV–436a–b
  Fort Osage V–173b
  Fort Shelby V–388a
  Oregon missions V–166b
  Sioux VI–295b–96a
  Treaty at Prairie du Chien V–388b
  War of 1812 VII–234b
  See also Lewis and Clark Expedition
Clark, William A. (bus., pol.) III–80a; IV–403b
Clark, W. P. (off.) II–379b
Clark County (Ohio) I–492a
Clark Distilling Company v. *Western Railway Company* (1917) VII–265a
Clarke, Arthur C. (sci.) II–142b–43a
Clarke, Edward Y. IV–58b
Clarke, Elijah (sol.) IV–44b
Clarke, Gary K. VII–371a
Clarke, John (cler.) II–116b; V–65b, 185a; VI–131b, 132a, 134a
Clarke, William E. (dent.) I–119a
Clarke, William Newton (theol.) VI–78b, 82a–b
Clarke–McNary Act (1924) III–73b, 75b; VI–67a
Clark Field (Phil.) I–274a
CLARK, FORT (Ill.) **II–71a**; I–471a; V–260b
Clark, Fort (Mo.) II–34a
  See also Osage, Fort
Clark, Fort (N.C.) IV–252a
Clark Library (Los Angeles) V–191b
Clark Pass V–225a
CLARK'S NORTHWEST CAMPAIGN (1778–79) **II–71a**; I–240a, 296b; III–258b, 329a; IV–264a–b; V–140b, 142b; VI–124a, 126b, 155b, 363b
  Fort Sackville IV–53b
  Kaskaskia IV–32a

CLARK'S NORTHWEST CAMPAIGN (cont.)
Kentucky IV–40a
land bounties III–227b
Mississippi River IV–372b
Sauk Indians VI–218b
Spanish aid VI–367b
supplies V–354b
Vincennes II–338a; III–147b, 369b; IV–59b; VII–188b
Willing VII–302b
Clarkson, Thomas (abolitionist) VI–311a
Clarksville (Ind.) III–369b; VII–189b
Clark University II–470b; III–424a; IV–267b, 306a
parapsychology V–213a
psychology V–441b
scientific education VI–237b–38a
Clark v. *Tousey* I–145a
Class–action suits II–148a, 230b
Classical reform movement (Judaism) IV–9b
Classical style (landscape arch.) IV–96b, 97a
Classics (educ.) IV–2a
Classic stage (prehistory) I–117b, 156b
Classified Service. *See* Civil Service
Class structure
colonial society II–125a–b
Class warfare
Communist party II–144a,b, 145b
Clatsop, Fort (Wash.) II–131b; IV–136b
Claude, Albert (biol.) V–100a
Clawson, John L. I–333b
Clay
building I–377a
ceramics III–182b, 183a–b
glassmaking III–185a
See also Adobe
Clay, Cassius. *See* Ali, Muhammad
Clay, Cassius M. (abolitionist) IV–220a
Clay, Clement Claiborne (pol.) I–435a; V–234b
Clay, Green (off.) IV–40b
Clay, Henry (states.) II–174 (table); III–328b–29a; IV–159b; V–161a; VII–148b
Alabama support I–71a
American Colonization Society I–101a
American system I–113b; III–449a; IV–193b; VI–145b; VII–268b
Anti–Masonic party I–132b
campaign of 1824 I–418b; IV–469b; V–101b
campaign of 1832 I–419a,b; VI–203b–04a
campaign of 1844 I–420a,b; IV–143b; VI–42b
compromise doctrine IV–43a
Compromise of 1850 II–139a, 150a; IV–454a; VI–307b
conservatism II–189a
"Corrupt Bargain" II–231a
distribution bill II–333b
executive power of removal VI–84b
Force Acts III–59b
internal improvements III–449a, 450a
John Randolph duel II–377a
land distribution bill IV–91a
Latin–American independence wars IV–115a, 115b
livestock breeding I–37b, 471b
Missouri compromise VI–307b
mules IV–425b
National Republican party II–327a
oratory IV–162b
Rice–Campbell debates VI–135b
Survey Act of 1824 VI–450a
tariff VI–463b, 465b, 466a
Treaty of Ghent III–176b; VII–235b
War Hawks IV–40b, 418a; VII–231a
Whig party VII–288a,b
Clay, Lucius D. (off.) I–291a; II–449b; VI–155b
Clay County (Mo.) II–496a
Clay–eaters II–253a
Clayoquot (Can.) I–15b
Claypoole, David C. (pub.) V–71a
Claypoole, James III–111b
Clayton (N.Y.) III–118a
Clayton, Henry D. (law.) II–71b
Clayton, John (bot.) I–348b; V–326a
Clayton, John Middleton (states.) II–72b, 73a; VI–388b
CLAYTON ANTITRUST ACT (1914) **II–71b**; I–140a, 390b; II–230a; III–204b, 458b; IV–69a, 399a,b; V–112a, 462b; VI–102b, 103a, 277a; VII–122b
boycotting I–357a
Duplex Printing Press Company v. *Deering* IV–69a
flour trust III–44a
injunctions III–419a
judicial interpretation IV–69a
laissez–faire doctrine IV–85b
mergers VII–123a
strikes VI–419a
Supreme Court interpretation IV–70a
unions II–110b, 136a; III–407a; VII–124a
CLAYTON–BULWER TREATY (1850) **II–72b**; I–121b, 454a; II–285a; III–266a, 278a; V–94b, 200b; VI–378b; VII–112a
abrogation I–122a
Mosquito question IV–416a
Tigre Island VII–58b
CLAYTON COMPROMISE (1848) **II–73a**
Clean Air Act (1967) II–188b
"Clean" bomb V–124b
Cleaning and dyeing industry VII–123a
Clean Water Act (1972) VII–259b
Clear and present danger rule I–478b; III–104a, 105a; VI–225a–b
"Clear Choice" (slogan) VI–313a
Clear Creek I–317b; III–477b
Clear Fork III–228a
CLEARINGHOUSE, NEW YORK II–73a
CLEARINGHOUSES II–73b
Clear Lake I–340a
Clearwater, Alphonso T. II–100b
Clearwater River IV–108a; VI–322b
gold III–328a
CLEARWATER RIVER, BATTLE ON (1877) **II–74b**
Cleaveland, Moses (pioneer) II–74b; V–140b; VII–274b
Cleaveland, Parker (min.) IV–348b
Cleaver, Eldridge (au.) I–316a; IV–165a, 167b, 167b
Cleburne, Patrick R. (off.) IV–365a; VI–141b
Cleeton, C. E. (phys.) IV–262b
Cleeve, George (col. offi.) IV–207b, 207b; VI–184a
Clemenceau, Georges (states.) VII–331a
Clemens, Augustine (paint.) V–184b–85a
Clemens, Samuel (paint.) V–185a
Clemens, Samuel Langhorne (Mark Twain). *See* Twain, Mark
Clements, Frederic (bot.) I–350a; II–391b
Clements, William L. (ind.) II–109b
Clements Library (Ann Arbor, Mich.) III–284b
Clendenin, Charles I–497b
Clendenin, George I–497b
Cleopatra (sculp.) VI–243a
Clephane, James O. (stenographer) V–77a
Clergy
glebelands III–186b
medicine IV–283a, 295a
professional schools II–397b
Clerical workers V–132b
unionization IV–75a
Clérisseau, C. L. (arch.) I–162b
Clerke, Charles (ship capt.) II–219b
Clermont (steamboat) I–81b–82a; III–131b, 312a, 312b; IV–310a; VI–148a, 280b, 407a, 408a, 410a; VII–100b
CLEVELAND (Ohio) **II–74b**; III–218b
Afro–Americans I–32a
air transportation I–67b
bootlegging I–339b; II–262a
centennial exposition III–217b
city plan II–45b
crime II–261b
crime commission II–263b
directory II–343b
disasters II–348a,b
domestic trade VII–83b
foreign trade VII–89b
German immigrants III–336b
growth II–41b
Hiram House VI–330b
Hunters and Chasers of the Eastern Frontier III–318a
Indian relocation VI–83b
industry V–141b
La Follette party IV–84b
Lake Erie II–459a
Lewis Flight Propulsion Lab IV–458b
Loyal Leagues IV–201b
Oberlin–Wellington rescue case V–130b
ocean shipping V–142a
Ohio and Erie Canal IV–443b; V–145b
railroads VI–34a
Saint Lawrence River VI–192b
settlement V–140b
Standard Oil VI–382b–83a
typhoid VII–259b
Woman's Christian Temperance Union VII–312a
Cleveland, (Stephen) Grover (pres.) II–176 (table); V–346b, 395 (table), 396b; VII–291a
ambassadors I–93b
Anthracite Strike I–127a
campaign of 1884 I–423b–24a; IV–425b
campaign of 1888 I–322a, 424a–b; III–113a; V–184a
campaign of 1892 I–424b; III–113a; VI–322b
cattle industry V–33a
civil service reform II–59b
conservation II–187b
Democratic support II–75a
Hawaii III–263b
Idaho III–328a
Indians II–295b
In re Debs II–298b
interoceanic canal I–373b
Labor Day IV–79a
literacy test III–342b
Misiones award IV–363a
New York governorship

V–87b
North Atlantic fisheries dispute IV–385b
Olney–Pauncefote Treaty V–153b
panic of 1893 V–208a, 426a
pension bills V–257a
Porter, Fitz–John V–369a
Pullman strike I–111b; IV–67a; V–463b
Sackville–West incident VI–184a
Sherman Silver Purchase Act III–111a; VI–287b, 288b
Statue of Liberty VI–405b
tariff VI–463b, 466b–67a
third–term doctrine VII–53b
Venezuela boundary controversy I–122a; IV–401a; V–153a; VI–226b; VII–170b
vetoes VII–178a
White House I–274b
Cleveland and Mahoning Railroad V–249b
CLEVELAND DEMOCRATS II–75a
Cleveland Foundation III–83a
Cleveland Museum of Art II–104b
Cleveland Public Library IV–146a
Cleves (Ohio) VII–127b
Cliff dwellings
Anasazi I–117a
Mesa Verde IV–315b
national monuments V–217a,b
Clifford, Nathan (jur.) VI–445b
Cliff Palace (Colo.) I–117b
IV IV–315b
CLIMATE II–75b
cookery II–219a
Great Plains VII–59a–b
Gulf of Mexico IV–326a
meteorology IV–316a
National Weather Service VII–264a
plants II–391b
tea growing VII–16a
Climatic posts, U.S. Army II–75b
Climatron (Missouri Botanical Garden) IV–378b
Climax (Colo.) III–14b–15a; IV–124a, 354b
Clinch, Duncan L. (off.) VI–260b; VII–311a
Clinch, Fort (Fla.) I–451b
Clinchfield Railroad VI–36b
Clinch Mountains I–297a
Clinch River II–274a
Cumberland Gap V–224b
Great Warriors Path VII–238b
Norris Dam III–323b
settlement VII–283a
Southwest Point VI–357b
Clinch Valley College VII–197b
Clingman, Thomas L. (pol.) III–222b
Clinic Hospital (Cleveland) II–348a
Clinton (Conn.) VII–350b
Clinton (Miss.) II–77a; VI–48b
Clinton (N.Y.) IV–169a
Clinton, De Witt (states.) I–275b; VI–218a; VII–266b
Bucktails I–374b
campaign of 1812 I–418a
Erie Canal II–459b; V–86b
high–minded men III–276b
internal improvements III–450b
New York education system II–396b
opposition IV–260a
Quids VI–3b
Tammany Hall VI–459a
Clinton, Fort (N.Y.) I–275b; II–191b; III–275b; VII–279b
Clinton, George (states.) IV–49a; V–85a, 86b; VII–179 (table)
Antifederalists I–131a
campaign of 1804 I–417b
campaign of 1808 I–418b–19a
Constitution V–353a
King George's War II–267a
landholdings IV–100b
New York education system II–396b
New York judiciary II–121a
Trespass Act VII–116b
Clinton, Henry (off.) II–134a; III–108a, 276a; VI–123b, 124a,b, 373a; VII–279b, 280a
Arnold, Benedict I–194a
Battle of King's Mountain IV–48b
Battle of Monmouth IV–397b
Battle of Springfield VI–377a
Burgoyne's invasion I–385a
capture of André
Charleston (S.C.) I–496b, 498a
Fort Moultrie attack IV–420a
Highlands of the Hudson III–275b
Hudson River forts II–191a
southern campaigns VI–351a
Vermont III–241a
West Point VI–217b
Yorktown campaign VII–360b–61a
Clinton, James (off.) II–433a; IV–354b; VI–438a
CLINTON RIOT (1875) **II–77a**
CLIPPER SHIPS II–77a; I–251a; III–428a; IV–310a,b, 266b, 309a; V–183b; VI–279b; VII–87a, 348b
California goldseekers III–81b
fishing schooner IV–217a
Flying Cloud III–45b
Maine IV–226b
slave trade VI–308b–09a
Cliveden (Phila.) IV–472a
Cloche hats II–372a
CLOCK AND WATCH INDUSTRY II–77b
health hazards IV–294b
Massachusetts IV–266b
peddlers V–241b
CLOCKMAKING II–78b; III–134a, 138a; VII–352b–53a
interchangeable manufacture III–442a–b; IV–272b
Clocks, atomic V–12b
Clorox Company VII–124a
"Close" blockade I–321a
Closed–end investment companies III–467a
"Closed sea." *See Mare clausum*
CLOSED SHOP II–80a; IV–60b, 61a,b
checkoff II–3b–4a
National Labor Relations Act IV–466b
opposition IV–471b
right–to–work laws IV–74b
strikes VI–419a
Taft–Hartley Act IV–74a, 467a; VI–457b
war industries IV–73a–b
Closson, William B. (engr.) VII–319b
"Clothed with a public interest" IV–434a–b
Clothing
colonial II–370b–71a
Confederacy II–163b
Eskimo II–462a
frontier II–487a
fur trade III–140a
mass–produced II–371b
pioneers V–317b
CLOTHING INDUSTRY II–81a; IV–243b
disposables VII–44a–b
household manufacture IV–246a
linsey–woolsey IV–157b, 158a
Newark V–41a–b
New York State V–87b
ready–to–wear II–372a
sewing machine VI–265a
sheep VI–272b
sweatshop VI–454a
wool industry VII–321a
CLOTURE II–83b; III–21b–22a
Cloud seeding II–76b
Clover II–281a
Cloverdale (Calif.) III–327a
Cloverport (Ky.) IV–44a
CLOVIS CULTURE II–83b; I–155b; III–50b
Cloward, Richard (soc.) II–148a
Cloyd's Mountain VI–275a
Club House (Saratoga Springs, N.Y.) III–150a
Clurman, Harold (dir., critic, au.) VII–50a
CLUW. *See* Caucus of Labor Union Women
Clydesdale (horse) III–303b
Clymer, George (mer.) II–203b, 308b
Clymer, George E. (pressmaker) V–413a
Clytie (sculp.) VI–243b
CNO. *See* Naval Operations, Chief of
Coaches III–47a; VII–99b, 168a,b
Coahuila (Mex.) III–302b
COAHUILA AND TEXAS, STATE OF II–84a; I–48b; VI–143a, 143b–44a; VII–37a–b
Coahuiltecan (lang.) I–86a
COAL II–84a; V–267a; VI–48a,b
Alabama I–72a
Alaska I–77a
Appalachia III–216b
Arkansas I–173a
boomtowns II–45b
brown II–84b
Cincinnati II–37b
coasting trade II–90b
codes of fair competition VII–123a
Colorado II–128b
derivatives I–197a
domestic trade VII–83b, 84a,b
electric power II–416a
experiments II–10b
Fort Scott VI–241a
glassmaking III–185a–b
Great Lakes shipping III–216b, 218a,b; V–157a
Guffey Coal Acts I–462a; III–231b; V–47a–b
Industrial Revolution III–410b–11a,b, 412a
internal improvements III–447b
iron and steel manufacture III–470b, 472b, 473b
Kansas IV–25a, 26a
Kentucky IV–41b
lignate II–84b
"Little NRA" II–481b–82a
mineral rights IV–104b
mining II–350a–b; IV–350a,b, 354a
Mississippi River IV–373a, 374a
Montana IV–403b
New Jersey V–57b
New South V–67a
New York State V–87a
Norfolk V–110a
occupational medicine IV–293b, 294a
Ohio II–75a
oil distillation IV–44a
Oklahoma V–148b, 149a
paleobotany I–350a
paving V–230a
Pennsylvania II–75a; III–165a; V–247a,b
Pennsylvania canal system V–250a
petrochemical industry V–267b

COAL (cont.)
phenol derivative II–7a
pollution VII–158b
price–fixing II–481b–82a
public lands V–445b
Railroad Administration VI–19a,b
railway land grants IV–104b
Richmond VI–136b
Saint Louis VI–194b
saltmaking IV–25a
shipbuilding VI–279b
shipping IV–310b, 311a
smelting VI–316b
steam power VI–410a
synthetic gasoline II–9a
synthetic rubber II–9a
tariff VI–463a
Tennessee VII–25b
Tennessee Valley Authority VII–28b
towboating VII–77b
town sealers VI–245a
transportation II–459a; III–235a
U.S. Geological Survey III–164a
Virginia VII–196a
West Virginia II–75a; VII–281b, 282a
World War I III–129b; VII–327b
Wyoming VII–346a
zinc VII–369a
Coal Creek (Tenn.) II–350a
Coale, Edward VI–244b
Coal Flora of Pennsylvania 196b
Coal gas II–5b; III–16b; IV–153a
Coalinga (Calif.) VII–259b
Coalition of American Employees IV–76a
Coal Mine Safety Act (1960) IV–294a
Coal Mines and Safety Act (1969) VI–328a
COAL MINING AND ORGANIZED LABOR II–86a; IV–62b, 63a; VII–191b
AFL IV–66a
Anthracite Strike I–127a; IV–67a–b; V–247b
automation IV–75a
checkoff II–3a–b
communist influence IV–70b
Herrin massacre III–274a; IV–70b
Hitchman Coal Company v. *Mitchell* III–286a
Molly Maguires IV–391b
panic of 1873 V–207b
strikes II–3a–b, 86b–87a; IV–69b, 73a,b
Taft–Hartley Act VI–457a
United Mine Workers VII–150b
wage increases II–3b
"yellow–dog" contract VII–354b–55a
Coal oil. *See* Kerosine Oil
Coal tar IV–294a
health hazards IV–294b
nylon II–9a
Toluene II–8a–b
COAST AND GEODETIC SURVEY II–87a; I–211a; II–135a; V–133a, 134a,b, 294b
Alaska V–337a
cartography I–463a
congressional investigation I–90a
geophysics III–167a
Gulf Stream studies III–233a
mapping of U.S. IV–248a
marine biology III–28b, 29a
weights and measures IV–462b
Yukon River VII–367a
Coaster's Harbor Island (R.I.) V–65b
COAST GUARD, UNITED STATES II–88b; III–246a; VII–98b, 108a
Afro–Americans I–30b
Bronze Star II–312a
commissioned officers II–168a
disaster aid IV–341b
Distinguished Service Medal II–311a
ensign II–452a
flags III–35a–b
Governors Island III–206b
Great Lakes shipping III–218b
gunboats III–234b
I'm Alone Case III–332a
Key West base IV–45a
lifesaving IV–152a–b
Medal of Honor II–310a
Naval Home VI–336b
oceanography V–135a
polar exploration V–122a, 337b, 338b
revenue cutter service II–277a
San Diego VI–208b
U.S. flag III–35a
Vietnam War V–22a
women VII–318a
World War I V–20a
Coast Guard Academy, U.S. II–90a
COASTING TRADE II–90b; IV–309a,b
Constitution regulation II–200b
Embargo Act VII–233b
foreign ships III–204a; VII–72a, 83a
Navigation Acts V–15b
Panama Canal tolls V–204b; VII–69b–70a
sailing packets V–183b–84a
schooner VI–229b
ships III–413a
smuggling VI–321a–b
Coast Ranges III–223b
COASTWISE STEAMSHIP LINES II–91a
Coats II–371a; III–133b
Cobalt III–12a, 13b, 14a–b
Cobalt oxide III–14a–b, 183b
COBB, FORT (Okla.) **II–91a**; VII–252b
Cobb, Frank I. (ed.) V–73b
Cobb, Howell (law.) II–175 (table)
Cobb, Irvin S. (jour.) IV–41a; V–74a
Cobbett, William (jour.) I–367b, 368a; V–366a–b; VII–205b
Cobblers I–338a
Cobblestones V–229b, 230a
Cobb–Lippmann Memorandum II–342a
Coblenz (Ger.) I–192a
Cobra, Operation (1944) II–237a; VI–193b
Coca bush products IV–449b, 450a
Coca–Cola Company II–107a; VI–333b
Cocaine II–260a, 261a, 373b–74a; IV–449b; VII–65a–b
Coca leaf II–374a; III–385b; VII–65a–b
Cochetope Pass V–225a
Cochise (Indian) I–141b, 142a,b; III–391b; IV–236b
Cochiti (N.Mex.) I–8a; III–367b; V–460a
Cochituate Aqueduct VII–259a
Cochran, Barbara Ann (athlete) V–154b
Cochran, Thomas C. (hist.) VI–157a
Cochrane, Alexander (nav. off.) VII–249b
Cochrane, Lord Thomas IV–212b
Cockburn, George (nav. off.) VII–249b
Cockburn Island IV–239b
Cockcroft, John Douglas (phys.) II–278a; V–301a
Cocke, P. St. George (off.) I–381a
Cockrell, Jim III–253a
Cockrell, Theodore D. A. (nat.) III–28a
Cockrell, Tom (marshall) III–253a
Cockrell, Vard (off.) IV–183b
Cockspur Island V–462b
Cocoa III–53a
Cocoanut Grove fire (1942) II–348a
Coconut III–52b
Coconut oil VI–323a,b
Cocopa (Indians) III–363a; IV–386a
Cod III–52a
Coddington, William (col. gov.) V–65b; VI–131b
***CODE, UNITED STATES* II–91b**; VI–405b
espionage laws II–463b
statutory law VI–406a
Codeine IV–449b
CODE NAPOLÉON II–91b
common law II–141b
CODE NOIR II–91b
Code of Federal Regulations I–167b
"Code of Wartime Practices for the American Press" (1942) V–74a
CODES OF FAIR COMPETITION II–92a; I–324b; VII–123a
National Recovery Administration IV–469a,b
poultry industry VI–225a
COD FISHERIES II–92a; III–413a; IV–264b
Anglo–American disputes I–121b
Cape Cod I–447a
Company of One Hundred Associates II–149b
Grand Banks III–208a
Isles of Shoals III–479b
Labrador IV–82a
salt bounties III–31b
Sugar Islands trade VI–437a
Cody, William F. ("Buffalo Bill") (scout, showman) VI–241b; VII–227b, 298b
Coe Collection (Yale Univ.) III–285a
COERCION ACTS (1774) **II–93a**; I–8a, 346b–47a; II–309a; III–464a–b; VII–3b
Massachusetts Government Act IV–271a
Quartering Act V–471b
Suffolk Resolves VI–430b
COETUS–CONFERENTIE CONTROVERSY (1737–71) **II–93a**
Coeur d'Alene (Idaho)
lead–silver–zinc production IV–122b
silver mining VI–292b
strikes IV–66a; VII–272b
Coeur d'Alene (Indians) III–363a, 500a; VII–239b
COEUR D'ALENE MISSION (Idaho) **II–93b**; II–131b
Coeur d'Alene Mountains III–328a
COEUR D'ALENE RIOTS (1892) **II–93b**; IV–66a
Coffee III–53a
Brazil VI–343b
duties III–228a, 244b
East India trade II–388a
enumerated commodity II–453a
exchange II–469b
freeze drying III–55b–56a
Horizontal Tariff III–301b
imports VII–87b
makers II–417b, 419a, 421b
Puerto Rico V–461b
South America VI–345a,b
tea trade VII–17a
whiteners II–282a
Coffee, Calville and Company II–94a
Coffee, Holland (trader) II–94a; VII–238b
Coffee, John (off.) V–357a
Coffee, John F. (off.) IV–183b
Coffeehouses
advertising I–16a
clearinghouses II–73b

insurance business
III–426b, 427a
Niblo's Garden V–93b
COFFEE'S TRADING POSTS II–94a; VII–238b
Cofferdams II–375a
Coffin, Charles Albert (ind.) II–414a
Coffin, Jared (bus.) V–81b
Coffin, Levi (abolitionist) I–136a; VII–138b–39a
Coggeshall, John (legis.) VI–132a, 134a
Cohan, George M. (act., playwright, prod.) IV–442a; VII–49a
Cohasset (Mass.) IV–152a
Cohen, Wilbur J. (offi.) III–267b
COHENS* v. *VIRGINIA (1821) **II–94a**; II–195b; IV–19b
Cohn, Roy M. (law.) IV–210a–b
Coiffures II–371a–b
COINAGE II–94a; VI–94b
beaver money I–282a
bimetallism I–301a–02b
bit I–308a
Bland–Allison Act I–318b
bullion II–95a
cent I–483a
Coinage Laws Act IV–154a
colonial restrictions VI–107b
congressional powers II–199b, 208a
"Cross of Gold speech" II–266a
debased coins II–95b
dime II–341a
doubloon II–365b
eagle II–384b
E pluribus unum II–455b
federal IV–359b–60a
foreign as legal tender II–94b–95a
free silver III–110a
fugios III–129b
gold standard III–192b
hard money III–251b
In God We Trust III–417a
interstate commerce III–459a
legal tender IV–132b
liberty–cap cent IV–143a
pieces of eight V–309a–b
pistole II–365b; V–320b
private minting IV–360a
proclamation money V–424a
seigniorage VI–257a
silver dollars VI–277a
silver legislation VI–288a, 288a
specie payments VI–370a
standards II–208a
Thomas Amendment V–44a
trade dollar VII–92b
Treasury VII–108a
See also Money
Coinage acts I–301a–2b
Coinage Act (1792) II–95a
Coinage Act (1853) VI–279a
Coinage Act (1873) II–96a, 264a; IV–154a
Coinage Act (1900) IV–392b
Coinage Act (1965) VI–289a
***COIN'S FINANCIAL SCHOOL* II–96a**; III–111a; V–199a
Coit, Henry L. (physic.) II–280a; IV–275b
Coit, Stanton VI–330b
Coitus VI–266b
Coke II–84b; III–17a, 411b
coal tar II–8a
iron manufacture III–472b
Mississippi River IV–373a
nitrates V–98a
Coke, Richard (gov.) VII–40a
Coke, Thomas (cler.) IV–318b
Colbert, James (outlaw) II–96b
Colbert, Jean Baptiste (states.) IV–7a
Colbert, William (Indian) II–22a
Colbert's Ferry III–146b
COLBERT'S GANG II–96b
Colbert Shoals (Ala.) VII–27b
Colburn, Warren (educ.) II–397a
Colchester (Conn.) IV–387b
Cold, common II–373b
Colden, Cadwallader (col. adm.) I–348b; V–85b–86a; VI–211b, 382a
COLD HARBOR, BATTLE OF (1864) **II–96b**; II–62b; V–264b; VI–138a; VII–197b
COLD SPRING HARBOR BIOLOGICAL LABORATORY II–97a; II–133a; III–158a,b
COLD WAR II–97a; I–60b, 290b–92a; II–475b; III–69b–70a, 348a; VI–179b–80a
Africa I–22a
air defense I–58a
Berlin airlift I–290a
Canada I–439b
Caribbean policy I–454b
censorship V–74a
Communist party II–145b
conservatism II–189b
enemy trading VII–94a
financing II–317b
foreign aid III–61a; VII–88b
Geneva summit conference III–161a–b
Great Britain I–124a
hydrogen bomb III–324b
John Birch Society IV–1b
Korea IV–55a
lend–lease IV–134a
liberals' support IV–140b
Mexico IV–329a
missile gap IV–458b–59a
mobilization techniques IV–384a–b
neutrality V–36a
North Atlantic Treaty Organization V–114a
nuclear testing V–124b
Paris conference V–215b–16a
Point Four principle V–335a
Progressive party V–429a
Reserve Officers' Training Corps VI–99a
Rosenberg case VI–164b
scientific education VI–232a–b
Spain VI–360b
subversion VI–428b
teachers' loyalty oath VII–15b
U.S. critics V–236b–37a
U.S. Information Agency II–499a
U.S. interventions III–463a–b
U.S. missile technology IV–363a,b
Vinson Court IV–14a
See also Arms Race With the Soviet Union
Coldwater Creek I–286b
Coldwater River VII–354b
Cold wave (hair style) III–239b
Cole, Charles H. (nav. off.) IV–5a
Cole, Henry (offi.) III–136a
Cole, Nat "King" (sing.) IV–442a
Cole, Thomas (paint.) II–101b, 102b–03a; V–189a, 190b
Cole, Timothy (engr.) VII–319b
Colean, Miles L. (econ.) VI–86a
Cole Bros. Circus II–41a
Colegrove v. *Green* (1946) I–147b, 244a
Coleman (Tex.) II–358b
Coleman, McAlister (Socialist) II–492b
Coleman, Ornette (mus.) IV–440b
Coleman, Robert (metal.) III–300b
Coleman, William (pub.) V–69b
Coleman, William T. VII–238a
Coleman Vote Tally System VII–210b–11a
Coleraine (Ga.) II–480a
Coles, C. P. (inv.) IV–397a
Coles, Stephen L. II–418b
Colescott, James A. IV–58b
Coleslaw III–52a
Colfax, Schuyler (pol.) II–175 (table)
campaign of 1868 I–422a
Crédit Mobilier II–256a
vice–presidency VII–179 (table)
Colgate, William (mfr.) VI–324a
Colgate–Palmolive–Peet VI–324a
Coligny, Gaspard de (expl.) III–38a
Collagen IV–389b
Collazo, Oscar I–202a
COLLECTING II–98b
Library of Congress IV–147a
See also Museums
COLLECTIVE BARGAINING II–110a; I–152b–53a; IV–60b, 75a; VI–14a, 457a–b
AFL IV–65b
AFL–CIO I–102b, 103b
checkoff II–2b, 3b
clothing industry II–83a
colleges and universities II–115b
farmers I–42a
federal employees IV–75b
government encouragement II–230b
health insurance III–435b
industrial relations III–407a,b, 408a
IWW opposition IV–68a
judicial review IV–14a
medical care IV–294b
National Industrial Recovery Act IV–71b; V–44b
National Labor Relations Act I–314b; IV–466b–67a; V–46b–47a
National Recovery Administration IV–469a,b
pension plans V–256a
postal workers V–374b
post–World War II IV–74a
Progressive movement V–428b
railroads VI–21a
regulation II–481b
steel industry VI–411a
Taft–Hartley Act IV–467a
unions II–80a–81a
United Farm Workers IV–76b–77a
World War I VII–232b
See also Strikes
Collective living. *See* Communes
Collective naturalization II–42b
Collective security V–234a
North Atlantic Treaty Organization V–113b
pacifist opposition V–181b
Pact of Rio VI–142b
Southeast Asia Treaty Organization VI–350b
United Nations Conference VII–151a–b
Collector of customs, colonial II–275b
COLLECTOR* v. *DAY (1871) **II–113b**; VII–5b
College, Academy, and Charitable School of Philadelphia II–114b
College and Academy of Philadelphia II–10a
College Entrance Examination Board II–115a
College Entrance Requirements, Committee on II–399a
College of Apothecaries (Phila.) V–273b

College of Arms VII–300b
College of California II–115a
College of Medicine of Maryland (Baltimore) IV–283b
College of New Jersey II–108a
See also Princeton University
College of Pharmacy (Phila.) V–273b, 275a
College of Philadelphia II–114b
College of Physicians (Phila.) I–110b
College of Physicians and Surgeons (N.Y.C.) IV–283b
College of Rhode Island. *See* Brown University
College of the Province of New York II–132a
COLLEGES, AFRO-AMERICAN II–113b; I–21b, 23b; II–404a–b; III–103b
COLLEGES, DENOMINATIONAL II–114a
antebellum South VI–343a
Iowa III–468b
Log College IV–179b
COLLEGES AND UNIVERSITIES II–114b; II–393a
academic freedom I–4b, 4b
academies I–5b
advertising courses I–19a
agricultural II–447b
American studies I–112a
antiwar demonstrations V–237b
archives I–169a
astronomical observatories V–131a,b
Boston I–344b, 344b
Brown University V–439b
Clinch Valley College VII–197b
Columbia University V–79b, 347b
curriculum II–397b, 399a, 400b–01a
dance schools II–288a
deism II–320a
draft-resistance movement V–237a
Duke University V–116b
election system II–398a
faculty unionization IV–76a
farmers' institutes II–494a
football III–56b–57a
forestry schools III–73b
Gallaudet College VI–327b
George Mason College VII–197b
Harvard University III–259b; V–79b
industrial research IV–300b
Iowa III–468b
Job Corps III–504a
job placement II–442b
Johns Hopkins IV–2a; V–347b
Judaic studies IV–12a
Kent State IV–38b–39b
land grant I–33a, 47a,b, 350a; II–399a; IV–93a, 96a, 97b
learned societies IV–126b
libraries III–284b; IV–145b
lottery financing III–149b
Mary Washington College VII–197b
Massachusetts IV–267b
mechanical II–447b
medical research IV–288a
Morrill Act IV–412a–b
Nader's Raiders IV–448b
Naval Academy V–23b, 24a
Naval Reserve Officers' Training Corps V–28b
Naval War College V–24a
navy V–23b–24b
New Left II–146b
newspapers V–79a
New York City V–83b
North Carolina V–116b
nursing V–127a
oceanography V–135a
Old Dominion University VII–300b
osteopathic instruction V–175a
paleontology V–197a
parapsychology V–213a,b
particle accelerators V–297a
peace movements V–236b
Philadelphia V–278a
Presbyterianism V–391b
Princeton University V–408b
Reserve Officers' Training Corps V–139a; VI–98b
Rockefeller University VI–158b
Rutgers University VI–181b
scientific research IV–471a
secularization II–399a
sexual behavior studies VI–266b
social work VI–331a
South Carolina VI–347b; VII–59a
Students for a Democratic Society VI–421a
tax shelters III–83b
Texas VII–40b
Transylvania Medical School IV–40b
Tuskegee Institute VII–130b
University of Missouri V–79b
University of North Carolina V–115b
University of Pennsylvania V–248b
University of Virginia VII–197b
University of Wisconsin VII–308a
University Year for ACTION I–8b, 9a
veterinary medicine VII–176a,b
Virginia Commonwealth University VII–300b
war protest I–115b
Washington and Lee University VII–249a
West Virginia VII–282a
William and Mary VII–300a
woman's rights movement VII–314a
women III–91b–92a
women teachers VII–317a
Yale University VI–273b–74a; VII–350b
Yeshiva College IV–11a
See also Law Schools; Universities, State
College Settlement (N.Y.C.) VI–330b
Collegiate Athletic Association, National. *See* National Collegiate Athletic Association
Collegiate church VI–68b
Collegiate School. *See* Yale University
Collegiate School of New York VI–228b
Colles, Christopher (eng., inv.) VI–408b; VII–258a
Colleton, John I–458a
Collett Vare, Glenna (golfer) III–198a–b
Collier, John (offi.) I–106b; III–380b, 390a; V–49a
Collier, Peter F. (pub.) I–334b
Collier's (mag.) I–17b, 19a; IV–222b, 424b; V–466a
Collier Trophy IV–106b
Collin County (Tex.) VII–35b
Collins, Caspar (off.) V–330a
Collins, Edward K. (shipowner) IV–310a
Collins, J. Lawton (off.) I–1a; II–13b
Collins, Joel (outlaw) V–139a
Collins, Michael (astron.) IV–406b
Collins liquefier V–304b
Collinson, Peter (bot.) I–348b
Collision-avoidance devices IV–333a
Collodion V–291a, 327b–28a
Collot, Victor (off.) II–116a
COLLOT'S JOURNEY (1796) **II–116a**
Colman, S. (art.) II–103a
Colman's Rural World (period.) I–45b
Cologne (Ger.)
World War II VI–83b; VII–340a,b
Coloma (Calif.) III–190b, 191a
Colombaid guns I–200a
Colombia VII–243b
Cartagena I–265b
claims against IV–5b
diplomatic recognition IV–110b
diplomatic relations IV–115a
immigration to U.S. III–337b, 341b
Indians I–48a; III–356b
Korean War IV–55b
marine landings IV–252a
Panama Congress V–203b
Panama Revolution III–463a; VI–364a
United Nations Declaration VII–151b
U.S. trade VI–343b, 344a, 344b, 345a,b, 346a
War of Jenkins' Ear III–498a
COLOMBIA, CANAL CONTROVERSY WITH II–116a; IV–111a,b; V–200b–01a; VII–111b
Bidlack Treaty I–295b, 454a
Hay-Herrán Treaty III–265b
Panama Canal III–265a
Panama Revolution V–204a
Colón (Pan.) V–201b, 202a; 204a–
Colon (ship) VI–216b
Colón Cemetery (Havana) IV–227b
Colonel Carter of Cartersville IV–162b
Colonel's Dream IV–166a
COLONIAL AGENT II–116a
Mazzei, Philip IV–279b
Randolph, Edward IV–188b; VI–46a
COLONIAL ASSEMBLIES II–117a; VI–109a–10a,b, 111a
British Parliament V–220b
Duke of York's proprietary VII–359a
freemen III–109b
Indian affairs III–387b
investigatory powers III–464b
Jamestown III–489a
law enforcement IV–15a
naturalization V–6a
New Hampshire V–53b
New Jersey V–57a
New Plymouth Colony V–65a
New York Colony V–84b–85a; VII–80a
Pennsylvania V–246a
prerevolutionary imperial idea III–346b
privilege V–419b
provincial congresses V–440a
Raleigh Tavern VI–44a
Rhode Island VI–132a
royal colonies VI–166a–b
taxation VI–381a,b, 382a; VII–14b
unicameralism VII–142a
Virginia VII–193a
West Jersey VII–278b
COLONIAL CHARTERS II–118b; I–499b–500a; IV–91b; VI–390b
agents II–116b
British policy II–122a–23a, 122b
Connecticut V–56a; VII–274a
constitution III–132a
corporations II–229a
councils II–119b
Declaration of Independence II–307a

Declaration of Rights II–308b
Duke of York's proprietary VII–359a
Elizabethtown (N.J.) II–431b
Free Society of Traders III–111a
Jamestown VII–192b
land speculation IV–98b
Lords of Trade and Plantation IV–188b
loyalty oaths IV–202a–b
Massachusetts Bay III–155a; IV–265a,b, 269a, 269b–70a, 271b; V–50b
Massachusetts Government Act II–93a
mining tax III–20b
New Albion V–332b
New England Company V–51a
New Netherland V–61a
New Plymouth Colony V–313a,b
patroons V–229a
Pennsylvania V–246a
Pennsylvania–Connecticut boundary dispute V–250b
Pennsylvania–Maryland-boundary dispute V–251b
Pennsylvania–Virginia-boundary dispute V–253a
proprietary provinces V–436a
Providence Plantations V–439a
religious liberty VII–68b
Rhode Island VI–132a, 134a
rights II–308b
rights of Englishmen VI–140b
royal colonies II–229a; VI–166a
state constitutions VI–396b
trading companies VII–94b
Virginia Company of London VII–199b
western lands II–183b; VII–273a

COLONIAL COMMERCE II–118b; III–413a–b; IV–307b; VI–110b–12b, 386a–b; VII–82a–b
beaver trade II–453a
bills of credit II–94b
bills of exchange II–468a
Board of Customs Commissioners II–375b
Boston Port Act II–93a
British policy II–122a–23a
coasting trade II–90b
cod fisheries II–92a–b
Coercion Acts II–93a
coffee II–94b
commission merchants and factors II–138a, 138a
commodities as money IV–392b
copper II–223a
corporations II–229a
Council for New England II–242a
Council for Trade and Plantations II–241b
credit II–254a
Cuba II–267b
Culpeper's Rebellion II–271a
currency IV–393b
customs service II–275b
Dorchester Company II–364b
Dutch merchants at Albany II–383a
duties II–275b
East India Company II–388a
East Indies II–388a
enemy trading VII–93b
enumerated commodities II–453a
export taxes II–478a
flour III–42b, 45a
foreign trade VII–85b–86b
freedom of the seas III–106b
fur trade III–139b
government regulation III–204a
Grenville Act III–228a
hardware III–252a
hat manufacture III–262a
hemp III–271a
Hester case III–274a
household manufacturing IV–245b–46a
Indian trading posts II–480a
inland waterways VII–259b–60a
Intolerable Acts II–93a; III–464a
iron III–76b, 469b
Isles of Shoals III–479b
Jamestown III–489a
licenses to trade IV–148a
linen industry IV–157b
logwood IV–181b
maple sugar VI–436b
marine insurance III–426b, 427a–b
Massachusetts IV–265a,b
merchant marine IV–309a,b
molasses II–92b, 116b; IV–387b, 388a
Narragansett planters IV–451b
naval stores II–5a; V–14b
Navigation Acts II–5a, 120a, 122b, 241b, 271a–b, 275b; V–15b
New Haven V–55b–56a
New Jersey V–57a
Newport V–65b
New York Colony V–85a
nonimportation agreements V–104a
Norfolk V–109b
onions V–156a
Panama City V–203a
peddlers V–241b
Philadelphia V–246b
Plymouth Trading Post V–334a
potash V–375b–76a
prerevolutionary imperial idea III–346a
price–fixing V–401b
prices V–403b–04b
Providence Plantations V–439b
purchasing power IV–393a
Queen Anne's War VI–2b
Regulating Act II–388a
Restraining Acts II–93a
restrictions IV–242b
Revenue Act II–5a
Revolution VI–107b–08b
Rhode Island VI–131b, 132a
Richmond VI–136b
rivers VI–149a
Rule of War of 1756 II–464a
rum trade VI–170b–71a
Salem VI–199a
salt VI–202a
smuggling II–92b, 275b; V–320a; VI–320b
soap VI–323a–b
Stamp Act II–309a
Sugar Acts II–123a, 309a; VI–435a
Sugar Islands VI–437a
tar VI–461b
taxation VI–381b; VII–14b
tea II–5a, 388a; VII–15a–b, 16b
tidewater VII–58a
tobacco II–271a–b; VII–65b, 66a–b, 67b–68a VII 66b–
Townshend Acts II–309a, 494b; VII–80b–81a
Treaty of London IV–182b
triangular trade VII–119a, 120a, 277b–78a
War of Jenkins' Ear III–498a
West Indies II–28b, 92b, 267b
whaling VII–285a
wheat VII–286a
White Pine Acts II–123a
"whitewash" VII–293b
wool II–123a; VII–320a–b
writs of assistance VII–344b

COLONIAL COUNCILS II–119b; VII–142a
New Jersey V–57a
Pennsylvania V–246a
royal colonies VI–166a
Virginia VII–200a

Colonial Currency. *See* Money

COLONIAL DAMES OF AMERICA II–120a

Colonial general court. *See* General Court, Colonial

Colonial government II–325a
Council for Foreign Plantations II–241b
counties II–245a
freemen III–109b
fundamental constitutions III–132a
general court III–155a
Gorges' Province of Maine III–200a–b
hundred III–317b
Indian treaties III–382a
land titles IV–91b
Lords of Trade and Plantation IV–188b
Ludlow's Code IV–203b
manors IV–241b
Massachusetts Bay IV–265a, 269a, 269b–70b
Mayflower Compact IV–278b
New Amsterdam V–40a–b
New Haven Colony V–55b
New Netherland V–60b–61a, 266a
North Carolina V–115a
Penn's Holy Experiment III–293a
privilege V–419b
Privy Council V–421a
quo warranto VI–4b
rights of Englishmen VI–140b
royal disallowance VI–166b
theocracy VII–51b
tidewater VII–58a
United Colonies of New England VII–149b
Vincennes VII–188b
West Jersey Concessions VII–278b

COLONIAL GOVERNORS II–120a; III–206a; VI–109a,b, 110a, 111a, 111a, 396a; VII–142a
assemblies II–118a–b
Carolina IV–95a
councils II–119b–20a
Dominion of New England V–50b
general court III–155a
Indian III–387b
judiciary II–121a
Massachusetts IV–264b–65a
municipal government IV–426b
New Amsterdam V–40b
New England V–49b
New Hampshire V–53b
New Jersey V–57a
New Plymouth Colony V–65a
New Sweden Colony V–80b
New York V–82a,b, 84b–85a
Pennsylvania V–246a
plans of union II–121b–22a
prerevolutionary imperial idea III–346b
privilege V–419b
Revenue Act of 1767 VII–80b
Rhode Island VI–132a
royal colonies VI–166a,b

COLONIAL GOVERNORS' INSTRUCTIONS II–120b
royal disallowance VI–166b
Virginia VII–201a

Colonial industries. *See* Industries, Colonial

Colonialism III–347a
Fourteen Points III–86a
Pan-Africanism V–199a,b

COLONIAL JUDICIARY II–120b; I–145a, 326b; IV–15a–b
general court III–155b
habeas corpus III–236b
jury trial II–308b; IV–21a
justice of the peace IV–22b
libel suits IV–139b
New Amsterdam V–40b
Pembroke Resolves V–244a
Privy Council IV–188b
Revenue Act of 1767 VII–80b
royal colonies VI–166b
town gaugers III–154b
Colonial land grants. *See* Land Grants, Colonial
Colonial National Historical Park III–489a–b
Colonial Period of American History III–282b
COLONIAL PLANS OF UNION II–121a; II–311b
Association II–211a
Declaration of Rights II–308b
Dominion of New England V–50b
Galloway's plan III–148a, 346b
United Colonies of New England VII–149a
COLONIAL POLICY, BRITISH II–122a; II–5a, 388a; VI–363b, 396a
commerce VII–86a
freedom of the press III–104b
frontier defense VI–381a
Ipswich protest III–469a
land company rivalries IV–98b
letters of "Junius" IV–20b
manufacturing restrictions IV–242b
Massachusetts Bay IV–270a–b
mercantilism IV–307b
ministers' salaries V–221b
Molasses Act IV–387b
Mutiny Act of 1765 IV–445b
Nicolls' commission V–95b
Parliament V–220b
patents V–225b
prerevolutinary imperial idea III–346a
proprietary provinces V–436a
quartering acts V–471b
Quebec Act VI–2a
smuggling VI–320b
taxation VII–2b, 3b, 14a–b
tea duties VII–15a
town meetings VII–79a
Townshend Acts VII–80a
Warwick Commission VII–244a
See also Revolution, American
Colonial Policy of the United States. *See* Insular Possessions
Colonial–revival style furniture III–138b
COLONIAL SETTLEMENTS II–123a; V–316b; VI–427b
agriculture VI–174a–b
animal disease VII–175b–76a
Caribbean V–438b–39a
corporations II–229a
criminal penalties V–464b–65a
Dorchester Company II–364b–65a
Duke of York's proprietary VII–359a
education VI–227a
environmental sanitation VI–211b–12a
fencing laws III–10a
feudalism III–18a
fire fighting III–25a
fire insurance III–426b
folklore III–48a–b
folk medicine III–49b
food III–51b–52a; V–465a
Force's Tracts III–60a
freed slaves II–433b
French and Indian War III–114b
fruit growing III–128b
fugitive slaves III–130a
furniture III–133b–34b
game laws VII–296b
Georgia III–168a
Georgiana III–171a
glebes III–186b
Gorges' Province of Maine III–200a
Great Migration III–219b
headright III–267a
health VII–157b–58a
historical accounts III–280a–b
House of Hope III–309a
housing III–309b
hundred III–317b
immigration III–334a–35a
indentured servants III–352b
Indian policy III–382a–b, 387b
Indian slaves III–401a
inflation III–414b
influenza III–416a–b
inland waterways VII–259b–60a
intestate estates III–464a
Jamestown III–488b
Jesuit missions III–499a
King Philip's War III–223a
literary narratives IV–161a
local government IV–171a
Long Island IV–185a–b; VI–346b
lotteries IV–190b
Maine IV–225b–26a; VI–185b
malaria IV–229a
Maryland IV–260a–b
Massachusetts Bay Company IV–265a, 269b
militia IV–345a
missionary activity IV–365a
Nantucket IV–449a
Narragansett Bay IV–451b
New Amsterdam V–40a
Newark V–41a
New England V–49b
New England Company V–51a
Newfoundland III–180b
New Haven V–55a
New Jersey IV–397b
New Netherland V–60b
New Plymouth Colony IV–264b; V–64b, 312b–13b
New Smyrna Colony V–66a
newspapers V–68a–69b, 69a, 75a–b
New York Colony V–84b, 86a
Nicolls' commission V–95b
North Carolina V–115a
open–book credit III–422b
palatine jurisdictions V–194b
Palatines V–195a
patroons V–229a
Pejebscot Purchase V–242a
Pemaquid Point V–243b
Pennsylvania V–246a
pharmacy V–274b
Philadelphia V–277a
plantations V–324a
poor V–380a; VI–72b
Popham Colony V–359b
population growth V–361a
Port Royal (S.C.) V–370a
postal service V–370b–71a
post roads V–374b
printing V–410b
public health V–446b
public markets IV–255b
quitrents VI–4a
Raleigh's first colony VI–43b
Raleigh's Lost Colony VI–42b
redemptioners VI–62b
religion VI–75a–77a
religious liberty VI–80a–81a
Rhode Island VI–131b–32a
rivers VI–149a
river towns of Connecticut VI–151a
royal colonies VI–166a
Saco Bay VI–184a
Saint Croix VI–189a
Saint Marys VI–197a
Salem VI–199a
Salzburgers in Georgia VI–204b
Savannah VI–220a
Saybrook VI–223a
schoolteachers VI–229a
Scotch–Irish VI–240b
Shawomet VI–271b
sheep VI–272b
slave insurrections VI–303b
slavery VI–304b–05a, 310a,b
South Carolina VI–347a
Southold VI–354b
Strawberry Bank VI–417b
street paving V–229b–30a
suffrage VI–433b
Sunday schools VI–442a
surveyors VI–450b
taverns VII–2a
taxation VII–26–3b
Thanksgiving Day VII–46a
theater VII–46b
tidewater VII–58a–b
town meetings VII–78b–79a
trading companies II–231a, 288b–29a; VII–94b
transportation VII–99b
Vandalia Colony VII–166b
vehicles VII–168a
Virginia VII–199b–201a
Virginia Company of Plymouth V–333b
vital statistics VII–205a–b
voting III–91a
water supply VII–258a
western lands VII–273a
winemaking VII–305a
Zwaanendael VII–372b
See also entries under each state
COLONIAL SHIPS II–124b; VII–99b
Ark and *Dove* IV–260a
Mary and John IV–260a
Mayflower IV–278a
Somers' voyage VI–338a
Susan Constant VI–451a
Welcome VII–267a
COLONIAL SOCIETY II–125a
conservatism II–188b–89a
cost of living II–235a
crime II–257b–58a, 259b
divorce II–356b
dress II–370b–71a
dueling II–276b
entail of estate II–452a
farm families VI–174a–b
fast days II–496b
gambling II–259b; III–149a–b
Great Awakening III–214a
hair styles III–239a
heresy II–258a
indentured servants III–352b
labor force IV–60a
manners IV–240b
marriage IV–256a–b
miscegenation IV–362b
missionary activity IV–365a
mortality rate IV–149b
music IV–437b, 443a
newspapers V–68a–69a
painting V–184b
philanthropy V–279b
Pinkster celebration V–316b
primogeniture V–408a
prostitution II–259b; V–437b
race relations VI–5b–6a
sexual attitudes VI–265b–66a
smallpox VI–315a–b
Standing order VI–384b
sumptuary laws VI–440a

Swiss settlers VI–455a
temperance movement V–429b
theater VII–46b
theocracy VII–51b
tithingman VII–64b
Virginia VII–193a
witchcraft II–258a; VII–309b
See also Punishments, Colonial
COLONIAL WARS II–126a; V–52b; VII–282b
Afro-Americans IV–339b
British navy V–18b
Dummer's War V–111b
Dutch War of 1653 VI–134a
fortifications VII–115a
King George's War IV–46b, 192a
King Philip's War IV–47a
King William's War IV–49a, 200a; VI–1b–2a, 181b–82a
Maine IV–226a
militia IV–345a–b
Mohawk Valley IV–386b
nativism V–2a
New York Colony V–85a–b
partisan bands V–222a
pensions V–256b
privateering V–418b–19a
Queen Anne's War VI–2a; VII–162b
Rhode Island VI–132a
Saint Lawrence River VI–192b
Salmon Falls attack VI–201a
Society of Colonial Wars VI–332a
War of Jenkins' Ear III–498a
weapons IV–432a
Colonies
Carlotta I–455a
Carolana I–457b
Clarendon I–447b
types I–458a, 499b–500a
COLONIZATION MOVEMENT II–127a; I–101a–b, 134a, 135b–36a, 139a
manumission IV–246a–b
Nashoba settlement IV–452b
smuggled slaves VI–321b
Colony, fourteenth. *See* Fourteenth Colony
COLORADO II–127b; VI–355a,b, 393 (table)
Anasazi culture I–117a
Auraria I–224a; II–477b
beet sugar I–285a
Bent's Fort I–174b, 289b, 293a, 293a
boomtowns I–336b
borax I–340a
British mining companies III–65a
caravan traffic I–453a
cattle I–473b; II–249a; IV–184b; V–160a
Civil War VII–165b
coal mining II–86a
Cochetope Pass V–225a
Colorado River Compact II–130a
communes II–142b
desert I–141a, 340a
Dust Bowl II–382a
Fort Lancaster IV–89b
Fort Lyon IV–208b
Fort Massachusetts IV–268b
Fort Sedgwick VI–254b
Fowler expedition III–88a
Frémont explorations VII–272a
gasoline tax III–153a
geology III–163b
gold II–477b; III–191b, 221a; V–177a, 437a; VI–379a
Haywood–Moyer–Pettibone Case III–267a
hydroelectric power III–320b
Indian Country III–384a
Indian removal V–437b
Indian wars VII–239b, 252b
irrigation III–477b, 478a
James expedition III–488a
Jefferson Territory III–497a
juvenile courts IV–23b
Kansas water dispute III–478a
lead–silver industry IV–122b
Leadville mining district IV–123b
Long expedition VII–271b
Maxwell land grant IV–92b, 278a
Mesa Verde National Park IV–315b
migration VII–100b
mining I–336b, 398b; IV–354a–b
Missouri River IV–380a
Moffat Tunnel VII–128b
molybdenum III–15a
national parks and monuments V–217a,b, 218 (table)
Navaho V–8b
Nebraska panhandle V–205b
Nonpartisan League V–106b
Oklahoma panhandle V–205b
Old Spanish Trail VII–217b
Oregon Trail VI–355a
Overland Trail V–178b
Pikes Peak V–311a
Pikes Peak gold rush III–191b; V–311a
Pike's southwestern expedition V–312a
Platte Bridge fight V–330a
Populist party V–365b
private mints IV– 360b
Pueblo V–8b
racetracks II–260b
railroads VI–32b, 33b, 34a
Raton Pass VI–47a
recall VI–51a
reclamation VI–53b
Red River Indian War VI–64a
referendum VI–66b
resorts and spas VI–100b, 101a,b
Rio Grande VI–143a
roundups VI–161a
Sand Creek massacre VI–208a
Sangre de Christo grant VI–210b
San Juan Country VI–213b
scrub breeders I–267a
sheep wars VI–273b
silver III–163a; VI–292a–b
single-tax plan VI–293b
smelters VI–316b
Smoky Hill Trail VI–320b
Social Democracy VI–324b
Taos Trail VI–215b
Uncompahgre VII–137b
Union Colony VII–146a
Union Pacific Railroad VII–147b
uranium III–164a
uranium–vanadium III–15a
Ute VII–162a
vanadium III–15a
veterinary medicine VII–176b
vigilantes VII–187b
water rights IV–27b
westward movement VII–284b
woman's suffrage VII–315a
See also Denver
Colorado, University of V–307a
Colorado–Big Thompson reclamation project VI–54a
Colorado Cattle Growers' Association I–472a
Colorado City (Ariz.) VII–367b
Colorado City (Colo.) II–264b
COLORADO COAL STRIKES (1903–04, 1913–14) **II–128b**; IV–258b; VII–272b
Colorado Desert VII–217b
Colorado Fuel and Iron Company II–128b–29a
Colorado Mortgage and Investment Company III–477b
COLORADO NARROW-GAUGE RAILROADS II–129a
Colorado National Monument V–217b
Colorado potato beetle III–421a
Colorado River II–128a, 440b
California–Arizona dispute VI–398a
Fort Yuma VII–367a
freight traffic VII–39a
Gila Trail III–179b
Glen Canyon Dam III–322b
Grand Canyon III–208a
Green River III–226b
Hoover Dam III–323a
Indian missions IV–302b
Indians III–367a, 369a
Mexican boundary IV–321a,b
Mohave III–376b
River Yumans IV–386a
Spanish Trail VII–256a
U.S. boundary III–230a; VI–151a
western routes V–224b
Colorado River Aqueduct II–130a
Colorado River Basin Project Act (1968) II–130b
Colorado River Compact (1922) II–130a; III–460a, 478a
COLORADO RIVER EXPLORATIONS II–129a; I–413a; VII–275b
Coronado's expedition II–228b
Escalante–Domínquez–expedition II–461a
Oñate's explorations V–155b
Powell expeditions V–384a
Smith, Jedediah VI–318a
COLORADO RIVER PROJECTS II–130a; I–407a; III–460a; VI–54a; VII–259a
Colorado River Reservation (Ariz.–Calif.) III–395b; IV–386b
Colorado River Storage Act (1956) II–130a
Colorado River Storage project VI–54a
Colorado Springs (Colo.) I–59a; VI–100b, 101a
Colorado Territory II–128a
Colored Farmer's Alliance and Cooperative Union II–493b
"Colored Masons" III–109a
Colored Methodist Episcopal church I–23b
"Color line" V–199b
Colossus Bridge I–363b
"Colossus of the North" V–105b
Colquhoun, Patrick (land speculator) V–88b
Colquitt, Alfred Hoit (pol.) III–169a
Colson, Charles W. VII–254a
Colt, Samuel (inv.) I–205b; II–130b, 168b; IV–433a
Colter, John (trapper) II–477a; IV–242a; VI–354b
Colton, Calvin (jour.)
Clay, Henry I–113b
Coltrane, John (mus.) IV–440b
Colt revolving rifle IV–430b
COLT SIX-SHOOTER II–130b; II–168b; IV–430b; VII–42a
Columbia (blimp) II–345b
Columbia (Conn.) II–292b
Columbia (fig.)
folk art III–47b

Columbia (Md.) II–48b
Columbia (Ohio) IV–329b
Columbia (Pa.) V–249b–50a
Columbia (ship) I–446a; II–28b; III–263a; VI–244b
Columbia (S.C.) II–415b; VI–347b
 Camp Jackson I–434b
 capital I–496b
 Civil War I–458b; II–131a
 Confederate prison camp II–159b
 fall line II–485a
 railroads VI–349b
 state bank VI–349a
Columbia (spacecraft) IV–407a
Columbia (Tenn.) VI–377a
COLUMBIA, BURNING OF (1865) **II–131a**; I–458b; VI–348a
Columbia Broadcasting System VII–21b–22a
 censorship I–480b, 481a
Columbia College. *See* Columbia University
Columbia Company (Eng.) V–290b
Columbia County (N.Y.) III–313a
Columbia County (Pa.) III–31b
Columbia District (Oreg.) V–164b
Columbia District (Wash.) VII–247b
COLUMBIA FUR COMPANY II–131a
 American Fur Company I–105b
 Fort Pierre V–310b
 Missouri River IV–380b
 Red River of the North VI–64b
Columbia Institute for the Deaf and Dumb. *See* Gallaudet College
Columbia Lake II–131b
Columbian Agricultural Society II–244b
Columbian Centinel (news.) II–458a
Columbian Chemical Society of Philadelphia II–10b
Columbian engine VI–410a
Columbian Exposition *See* World's Columbian Exposition
Columbian Illuminati III–332a
Columbian Institute IV–464b
Columbian Museum of Chicago III–19a
Columbian Order VI–459a
Columbian press V–411a, 413a
Columbia Record Company V–290b
Columbia River II–30a, 219b; VI–150a; VII–248a
 atomic bomb research IV–238a
 basin improvements VI–54a, 147a
 boundary disputes VI–151a
 Dalles II–285b; III–322a–b
 dams III–322a, 323a
 Fort Okanogan V–147a
 Fort Vancouver V–170a; VII–165b
 fur trade VI–192b, 375b; VII–271b
 hydroelectric sites II–423a
 Indian nativistic movements V–4a
 Indian treaties VI–412b
 McNary Dam III–323a–b
 Oregon Trail VI–153b
 Russian expansion VI–177b
 salmon VI–201a
 Snake River VI–322b
 Yakima Wars VII–350a
COLUMBIA RIVER EXPLORATION AND SETTLEMENT II–131b; I–452b, 453a; II–477a; III–114b; V–164a–65a; VII–247a,b, 271a,b, 275b, 276a
 Astoria V–180a,b; VII–95b
 Bonneville expedition I–330a
 border dispute I–121a
 cascades I–465a
 fur trade I–83a, 83a, 209a
 Lewis and Clark Expedition IV–136b
 Navigator handbook V–17a
 Oregon Methodist Mission V–166b
 Oregon question V–167b
 Oregon Trail V–168a–b, 169a
 railroad surveys VI–39a
 Smith explorations VI–318a
 territorial claims VI–151a
 Vancouver expedition VII–166a
 wagon trains VII–217b
 Walla Walla VII–221a
COLUMBIA RIVER TREATY (1961) **II–132a**; I–440b
COLUMBIA UNIVERSITY II–132a; II–114b, 114b, 394b, 395a, 470b; V–83b
 archives I–169a
 brain trust I–359b
 Bureau of Applied Social Research V–454a
 chemistry instruction II–10a
 College of Physicians and Surgeons V–306b
 efficiency movement VI–234b
 genetic research III–157b, 158a
 law school IV–120b, 121a
 library II–108a, 108a
 library school IV–145a
 lottery financing III–149b
 Manhattan Project IV–238a
 medical school IV–283a,b
 mining engineering III–166b
 molecular generator IV–262b
 nursing V–126b
 oceanography V–135a
 oral history collection III–285a
 political science V–347b, 348b–49a
 Rockefeller Center IV–100b, 104b
 rugby III–56b
 School of Journalism V–79b
 Students for a Democratic Society VI–421b
 Teachers College II–401a
 technocracy movement VII–17b
 See also King's College
Columbia Valley III–477a; VII–286a,b
Columbine VI–393 (table)
Columbite III–14b
Columbium III–12a, 14b, 14b
Columbus (Ga.) I–289a
Columbus (Ky.) VI–34b
 Civil War I–288a; IV–374b, 375a; VI–278b
Columbus (N.Mex.) IV–327b, 328b; VII–187b
Columbus (Ohio) III–111b; V–141a
 American Federation of Labor IV–65a
 Camp Chase I–433a; IV–5a
 Civil War II–62b, 363a; V–121b; VI–26b
 Cumberland Road I–39b
 National Road IV–470b
 Ohio National Stage Company V–144b
 Ohio State Penitentiary five II–348a
 Refugee Tract VI–70b
Columbus (ship) VI–128a, 282a
Columbus, Christopher (navig.) IV–136a; V–372b; VII–75a, 275b
 citrus fruits III–128a
 food supply III–51a
 hogs III–288a
 horses III–302a
 hurricanes III–319a
 Indians I–74b
 maps IV–247a
 naming of America I–97a
 Puerto Rico V–461a
 Santa Maria VI–216a
 sugarcane VI–436a
 tobacco VII–64b
 venereal disease VII–168b–69a
 voyages to New World I–96a
 Watlings Island VII–261a
Columbus, Fort (N.Y.) III–206b; V–414a
Columbus, Knights of VI–252b
Columbus Crisis (news.) II–222b
Columnists V–75a
Colve, Anthony (nav. off.) V–82a
Colville, Fort (Wash.) II–131b; VI–375b
Colwell, N. P. (educ.) IV–284b
Colwell, Stephen (econ., law.) VI–463b–64a
COMANCHE (Indians) **II–133a**; III–119b, 220b, 228b, 363b, 396b
 Arapaho war I–151b
 attacks on Genizaro III–162b
 Battle of Adobe Walls I–15a
 Beale colony massacre VI–144a
 Camp Supply VI–443b
 Catlin's paintings I–471a
 Dodge–Leavenworth expedition II–359a
 Fort Atkinson I–213b
 Fort Bascom I–269b
 Fort Mason IV–263a
 Fort Sill VI–287b
 Fort Sumner VI–439b
 Fort Zarah VII–368a
 Ghost Dance III–177b
 Kansas IV–25a
 Kiowa alliance IV–50b
 Medicine Creek Council IV–299a
 Mexico raids II–283a
 New Mexico V–59b, 60a
 Oklahoma V–148a,b, 149a,b
 Parker's Fort attack V–216b
 peace commissions III–378a
 Pecos raids V–241a
 Peyote Cult V–273a
 Red River War VI–64a
 San Antonio VI–207b
 Sheridan's Washita campaign VII–252b
 sign language VI–286b
 Smith explorations VI–318a
 Spanish forts VI–168b
 Staked Plain VI–380b
 territory concessions III–379b
 Texas VII–36b, 38b
 trade II–34b
 wars VII–239a,b
Comanche County (Okla.) VI–287a
Combahee River I–497a
Combat Arms Regimental System I–200a
Combat Developments Command I–187b
Combat Infantry Badge II–312a
Combat Medical Badge II–312a
Combat Team, Fifth Regimental IV–55b
Combe, George (physic.) V–293b
Combers (cotton mfg.) II–239a
COMBINE II–133b; I–34b–35a, 36a; VII–55b, 286b
Combined Fleet (Japan) IV–336a

Combined Raw Materials Board VII–335a
Combined Shipping Assignment Board VII–335a
Combmaking V–327b
Comedy Overture on Negro Themes (comp.) IV–438b
Comet (brig) II–443b
Comet (plane) I–52b
Comet (steamboat) VI–408a
Comets (astron.) II–356a
Comic strips V–72a–b
  "Willie and Joe" V–68a
COMINCH. *See* Commander in chief, U.S. Navy
Cominter. *See* Communist International
Comity clause II–202b
Command and General Staff College I–190b, 191a
Commander in chief, U.S. fleet VI–302a
Commander in chief, U.S. Navy V–13b
COMMANDER IN CHIEF OF BRITISH FORCES (1754–83) **II–134a**; VI–124a
Commander in Chief's Guard. *See* Lifeguard, Washington's
Commander of Naval Forces Operating in European Waters I–14a
"Command of the Army" Act (1867) VI–57a
Commentaries on the Laws of England IV–120b
Commerce (Ill.) V–8a
  congressional authority IV–80a,b
  enemy destination II–446a
  expansion II–474b–75a
  stock exchanges II–469b
  See also Colonial Commerce; Interstate Commerce
COMMERCE, COURT OF II–134a
COMMERCE, DEPARTMENT OF II–134b; II–498a; III–1a, 35b; IV–22b; VII–108a
  Bureau of Corporations II–230a
  Bureau of Fisheries III–30a
  Bureau of Mines IV–350a
  Bureau of Public Roads II–502b
  Bureau of Standards IV–462a
  cabinet I–399b
  Census Bureau I–482b
  city planning II–47a
  Civil Aeronautics Act II–49b
  Coast and Geodetic Survey II–88a–b
  enabling legislation II–178b
  foreign commerce service VI–389a
  national income estimates IV–462a
  National Oceanic Atmospheric Administration III–29a–b
  Patent Office V–226b
  radio regulation VI–15a,b
  Shipping Board Bureau VI–281b
  transportation VII–98a–b
  Weather Bureau VII–264a
  zoning VII–370a
Commerce, interstate. *See* Interstate Commerce Commission; Interstate Commerce Laws; Trade, Domestic
Commerce and Labor, Department of I–482b; II–134b; IV–78a
Commerce and Navigation, Treaty of (1911) V–97a
COMMERCE CLAUSE II–135b; III–458b
  congressional power II–195b, 275b; III–3a
  Gibbons v. *Ogden* III–178a
  implied powers III–349a
  interpretations II–220a
  Mann Act IV–240a
  meat inspection laws IV–279b
  regulation of corporations II–229b–30a
Commerce Commission. *See* Interstate Commerce Commission
Commercial Aviation, Bureau of II–49b
Commercial banks. *See* Banking; Banks
Commercial Bureau of American Republics IV–111a
COMMERCIAL CABLE COMPANY II–137a
COMMERCIAL COMMITTEE II–137a; VI–122b; VII–302b
Commercial Convention (1815) II–215b
Commercial Credit Company III–422b
Commercial Investment Trust of New York III–422b–23a
Commercial Union of the American Republics V–233a
  See also Pan-American Union
Commission for Relief in Belgium. *See* Belgian Relief
COMMISSION GOVERNMENT II–137b; IV–172a, 427a
  cities II–44a
  North Carolina V–116a
  Washington, D.C. VII–245a,b
  Wisconsin VII–308b
COMMISSION MERCHANTS AND FACTORS II–138a; IV–243a
  fur trade III–403a,b
  hardware trade III–252a
  McCoy, Joseph G. II–248b
Commission on Civil Rights II–499b; VI–433a; VII–209b
Commission on International Labor Legislation III–454b
Commission on Life Adjustment Education for Youth II–400b
Commission on Organization of the Executive Branch of the Government (1947–49) II–497b
Commission on Political Activity of Government Personnel III–261b
Commissions, Indian. *See* Indian Commissions
Commissions of conciliation IV–381b, 382a
Commissions of inquiry IV–381b, 382a
Commission to the Five Civilized Tribes III–378b
Committee for Improving the Industrial Condition of Negroes in New York V–1a
Committee for Industrial Organization I–104b, 107a; IV–72a
  See also American Federation of Labor–Congress of Industrial Organizations
Committee for Nonviolent Action V–237a
Committee for the Reelection of the President (1972) VII–254a,b, 255a
Committee for Trade and Plantations II–242a
Committee Government in the Revolution *See* Revolutionary Committees
Committee of Commerce II–137b; VI–122b
Committee of Eleven (1787) II–194a–b
Committee of European Economic Cooperation IV–258a
Committee of Forty-eight II–492b–93a
Committee of One Hundred (N.Y.C.) V–86a
Committee of One Hundred (Phila.) V–279a
Committee of Secret Correspondence VI–122b
Committee of Seven on the Teaching of History in the Secondary Schools I–106a
Committee of Ten on Secondary School Studies II–399a
COMMITTEE OF THE STATES II–138b
COMMITTEE OF THE WHOLE II–139a; VI–65b, 369a
COMMITTEE OF THIRTEEN (1850) **II–139a**; II–150a
  Crittenden Compromise II–265a
  Omnibus Bill V–155a
COMMITTEE OF THIRTEEN (1860) **II–139a**
COMMITTEE OF THIRTY-THREE (1860) **II–139b**; II–265a
Committee of Urban Conditions Among Negroes V–1a
Committee on Civil Rights II–54a, 56b; IV–208a,b
Committee on College Entrance Requirements II–399a
Committee on Committees VI–411b
Committee on Committees for House Democrats VII–263b
Committee on Economic Development V–400b–01a
Committee on Economic Security VI–329a
Committee on Foreign Relations (Senate) IV–401b
Committee on Government Contract Compliance II–456a
Committee on Government Contracts II–456a
Committee on Government Operations IV–209b
Committee on Industrial Organization II–462b
  campaign of 1936 V–47b
  Hague v. *Committee on Industrial Organization* III–237b
Committee on Interstate Commerce II–271a
Committee on Medical Research IV–287b; V–137a
Committee on Political Education IV–77a
COMMITTEE ON PUBLIC INFORMATION II–139b; I–481a; V–74a, 440b; VII–326a, 332b–33a,b
COMMITTEE ON THE CONDUCT OF THE WAR II–139b; II–66b; VI–11a
Committee on the Conservation and Administration of the Public Domain V–451a
Committee on Western Lands III–371a
Committees, investigating. *See* Investigating Committees
Committees, party V–344b–45a
COMMITTEES OF CORRESPONDENCE II–140a; I–207b–08a; IV–266a; VI–113b, 121b
  Boston I–345a
  Hartford VII–56a
  New York City V–82b, 85b
Committees of Observation and Inspection VI–121b–22a
COMMITTEES OF SAFETY II–140a; VI–121b
  antebellum South VI–354a
  Boston IV–266a

COMMITTEES OF SAFETY (cont.)
Massachusetts VII–56a
Mecklenburg County (N.C.) IV–282a
Pittsburgh V–322b
Washington District VII–250a
"Committees of vigilance" I–405b
Committee System (Congress) II–173a
Committee to Investigate Organized Crime II–258b
Commodities, enumerated. *See* Enumerated Commodities
COMMODITIES AS MONEY II–140b; II–94b; IV–233b, 392b, 393b; V–401b, 404a
quitrents VI–4a
tobacco V–221b; VII–65b
COMMODITIES EXCHANGE ACT (1936) **II–140b**; III–207a–b
Commodity Credit Corporation I–43a, 44b; IV–2a
Commodity Distribution Program V–129a
"Commodity dollar" theory V–45a
COMMODITY EXCHANGES II–140b; II–469a–70b
Chicago Board of Trade V–320b
commission merchants II–138b
Grain Future Act III–207a
wheat VII–286b
Commodity marketing associations II–221a–b
Commodity tax VII–11b
Commodores. *See* Admirals and Commodores
Common Carrier Bureau III–1a
Common Cause IV–171a
Common defense
See also Defense, National
COMMON LANDS II–141a
COMMON LAW II–141a; VI–406a
alien landholding I–87a
arbitration I–153b
British Constitution II–191a
colonies II–257b–58a, 308b
contempt of Congress III–465b
contracts II–229a
education IV–120b
eminent domain II–440a
freedom of speech III–104a
Great Britain II–325a
habeas corpus III–236b
industrial relations III–406b–07a
industrial safety II–440b–41a
inheritance II–452a, 452a
injunctions III–419a
jury trial II–204b; IV–21a
juvenile courts IV–23a
labor organizations IV–60b
land ownership III–107b
libel IV–139b
licenses to trade IV–148a
lockout IV–174a
Magna Charta IV–224a
Massachusetts Body of Liberties IV–271a
picketing V–308b
property statutes V–434a
prostitution V–437b
restraint of trade VI–102a
rights of Englishmen VI–140b
Seventh Amendment II–204b
sexual crime VI–266a
stare decisis VI–386b
strikes VI–419a
suits II–204b
water law VII–256a
workers' rights III–431a
Zenger trial V–82b
Common-law marriages II–485b–86a
Common Man, Age of the III–486b
Common Market III–97b
currency float III–196b
Kennedy Round III–70a
reciprocal trade agreements VI–52b–53a
Common recovery doctrine II–452a
Commons, John R. (educ.) I–495a; VII–308b
Common School Almanac I–91a
***COMMON SENSE* II–141b**; IV–161b; V–198b, 353a; VI–113b, 114b; VII–61b, 82a
Commonweal of Christ II–252b
Commonwealth Edison Company of Chicago II–416a
Commonwealth Electric Company of Chicago II–416b
Commonwealth Foundation IV–286b
Commonwealth Fund VII–330b
Commonwealth of Nations
Barbados I–265b
Commonwealth status VII–13b
Puerto Rico V–461a–b
COMMONWEALTH* v. *HUNT (1842) **II–142a**; II–110b; III–407a; IV–61a; VI–103b, 419a
COMMUNES II–142a; II–486b; V–182b; VII–313b
Communicable diseases IV–287a
Communications II–424a–b
American Telegraph and Cable Company II–137a
book publishing I–334b
censorship II–277a
Commercial Cable Company II–137a
electric circuit analysis II–38b–39a
Federal Communications Commission III–1a
fire fighting III–25b
freedom of speech III–104a–b
holding companies III–290a
interstate commerce laws III–458b
microwave technology IV–333a
offtrack betting II–260a
Postal Telegraph II–137a
public utilities V–456b, 459a
radio signals II–142b
scientific information retrieval VI–232b
security exchanges II–255b
Western Union II–137a
See also Radio; Telephone; Television; Telegraph
Communications Act (1934) I–480b; III–1a; VI–15b–16a
Communications Command, U.S. Army VI–286a
Communications Commission, Federal. *See* Federal Communications Commission
Communications Satellite Corporation II–143a; IV–459b; V–456a
COMMUNICATIONS SATELLITES II–142b; II–426a–b; III–1b, 410b; IV–459b; V–293b; VI–159a,b
air force I–63b
batteries I–276b
Bell Labs I–287b
broadcasting VI–16b
congressional debate III–21b, 22a
earth resources III–444b
Jet Propulsion Laboratory III–502a–b
microwave technology IV–333a–b
Signal Corps VI–286a
Telstar VII–20b
Western Union VII–277a
Communion, Anglican V–179a
Communism
AFL-CIO I–102b
American Labor Party I–107b
anarchists I–116b
anticommunist organizations IV–1b
Arab-American relations I–149b–50a
Cambodia II–316b
capitalism I–449a
Caribbean policy I–454b
China II–26a–b, 98a
CIO IV–74b
clothing industry II–83a
coal mining unionization II–86b
cold war II–97b–98a
containment III–61a,b, 69b, 70a, 463a–b
Czechoslovakia II–98a
Eisenhower Doctrine II–407b
emblem II–437b
House Committee on Un-American Activities III–308b–09a
immigration II–445a; III–333b, 339b
Iron Curtain III–474b
Johnson Doctrine IV–4b
Ku Klux Klan enmity IV–58b
Laos II–316b; IV–107a
Latin America IV–112b–13b
loyalty testing IV–203a
McCarthy–Army hearings IV–209b
middle class IV–334b
Monroe Doctrine IV–402a
national defense II–315a; IV–343b–44a
nativism V–3b
Oneida Colony VI–325b
radical right VI–12b
radicals VI–14a
recognition policy VI–55a–b
refugees V–342b
Southeast Asia IV–107a
Southeast Asia Treaty Organization VI–350b
South Vietnam II–316b
Trade Expansion Act VI–469b–70a
Truman Doctrine II–97b; VII–121a
unions IV–70a,b, 74a, 81b
Western Hemisphere V–171a
"witch-hunt" VII–310a
Workers' Party of America II–493a
World War II VII–333a
See also Vietnam War
Communist bloc IV–56b
Communist China. *See* China, People's Republic of
"Communist conspiracy" IV–2a
"Communist-front" organizations II–499b
Communist International (Comintern) II–143b–44a
Communist International, Third (1919). *See* Third Communist International
Communist Labor party II–143b; VI–326a
Communist Manifesto VI–325b
COMMUNIST PARTY, UNITED STATES OF AMERICA II–143b; VI–326a, 327a
blacklisting I–314b
Bolshevik Revolution VI–181a
campaign of 1932 I–428b
campaign of 1936 I–429a; V–47b
campaign of 1940 IV–73a
"clear and present danger" VI–225b
Dennis v. *United States* VII–118a

Great Depression IV–70b
labor unions VI–457a,b
McCarthy investigation VI–12b
minority rights IV–359a
Progressive party V–429a
Sacco–Vanzetti case VI–183a
Scottsboro case VI–241b
Smith Act VI–317b
social security V–46a
subversion VI–428a,b
syndicalism VI–455b
Taft–Hartley Act IV–74a
"witch-hunt" VII–310b
youth movements VII–365b
Communist Party of America II–143b, 144a
Communist Party v. *Subversive Control Board* (1961) VII–310b
Communist Political Association II–145b
COMMUNITIES II–147a; IV–338b–39a; VI–13b
Amana I–92b
Bethel I–293a
Bishop Hill I–307b
Brook Farm I–369b
Ephrata II–454a
Fourierism III–85a
Fruitlands III–129b
Harmony Society III–255a
Hopedale III–300a
Icaria III–327a
Land of Shalam VI–268a
Nashoba IV–452b
New Harmony V–54b
Oneida Colony V–155b
Shakers VI–268a
Socialist movement VI–325b
Waldenses VII–219b
Zoar Society VII–369b
COMMUNITY ACTION PROGRAMS II–147b; II–502a; V–135b–36a; VI–172a, 328b
Community Chest V–280a
Community colleges II–115a, 400b
Community of True Inspiration I–92b
Community property VII–9a
Community Relations Service IV–22b
Community Renewal Program II–47b
Community Services Administration V–136a
COMMUTATION BILL (1783) **II–148b**
Commutation money II–63a, 185a, 186a
Commuter trains
disasters II–350b, 351a
Compact, state II–200b
Compact clause IV–28a
Compact for Education VI–398a
Compacts, interstate. *See* Interstate Compacts
COMPACT THEORY II–149a
Fort Hill letter III–78a
secession VI–249b, 250a
COMPAGNIE DE L'OCCIDENT II–149a; I–173b; IV–370b
Louisiana IV–193a; V–173a
Compagnie de New Yorck I–466b
Compagnie des Indes. *See* Company of the Indies
Companies, investment. *See* Investment Companies
Companies, voluntary military. *See* Military Companies, Voluntary
Company of Felt-Makers III–262a
Company of Military Adventurers III–171a
Company of New France II–149b; VI–190b
COMPANY OF ONE HUNDRED ASSOCIATES II–149a; III–142a
Company of Royal Adventurers to Africa I–22b
Company of the Indies I–466a; II–149a, 158a; IV–193a, 370b
Company of the West III–142a
Company stores II–2b–3a, 128b; IV–61a
Company towns II–2b
coal mining II–86a
planning II–45b, 46a
Pullman (Ill.) IV–66b; V–463a
"Comparative negligence" doctrine II–441a
Compass II–26b
Compendium of the Tenth Census (June 1, 1880) I–482a
Compensated emancipation II–433b–34a, 435a–b
Compensation, Workmen's. *See* Workmen's Compensation
Compleat Body of Divinity VI–81a
Complex Calculator II–154a
Compo Point (Conn.) II–286a; VI–139a
Comprehensive Drug Abuse Prevention and Control Act (1970) II–374b
Comprehensive Employment and Training Act (1972) II–442b; III–504b
Compromise Act of 1799 VI–451b, 452a
COMPROMISE MOVEMENT OF 1860 II–149b; II–139a; VII–148b
COMPROMISE OF 1790 II–149b
Compromise of 1820 VI–309a
COMPROMISE OF 1850 II–149a; I–138b, 405b; II–139a; IV–28b, 29b, 379b; V–3a; VI–250b, 307b, 355b
campaign of 1852 I–420b
Fugitive Slave Act III–130b
Georgia Platform III–171a
Higher–law doctrine III–275a
Nashville Convention IV–454a
Nevada V–39b
Omnibus Bill V–155a
Seward's opposition II–184b
states' rights VI–404b
Union Rights party VII–148a
COMPROMISE OF 1890 II–151a
COMPROMISES OF THE U.S. CONSTITUTION II–151a; II–194a
slavery VI–305a–b
Compromise Tariff of 1833 V–126a; VI–466a–b; VII–288a
Comptometer I–396b
Compton, Arthur H. (phys.) IV–238a; V–100a, 295b
Compton, Karl T. (phys.) V–137a
COMPTROLLER GENERAL OF THE UNITED STATES II–152a; II–501a–b
COMPTROLLER OF THE CURRENCY II–152b; II–74a; VII–108a
Comptroller of the treasury II–152a
Compulsory Convoy Act (1798) II–217b
Compulsory military service. *See* Draft
COMPUTERS II–152b; II–425a,b, 426b–27a; III–410a
astronomy I–212a
automation I–224b
business forecasts I–395b
communications III–1b
Customs Service II–277b
demography II–328a
dictionary compilation II–340b
digital V–304b
electric "super power systems" II–417a
mapmaking I–464a
memories V–305b
Minnesota production IV–358a
monopolistic power IV–399b
National Institutes of Health IV–465a
political campaigns I–415b
railroads IV–177b; VI–31a
scientific information retrieval VI–232b–33a
scientific management IV–273a
space exploration V–132a
stock ticker VI–413b
transistor VI–259a; VII–164a
typesetting V–413a
weather forecasts VII–264b
Western Union VII–277a
Comrie, L. J. I–397a
COMSATS (satellites) II–143a
Comstock (Mich.) I–91a
Comstock, Anthony (ref.) I–307a, 478b, 479a; VI–266b
Comstock, Billy (trapper, scout) VI–241b
Comstock, William A. (pol.) I–260a; IV–332a
Comstock Laws I–307a
COMSTOCK LODE II–156b; I–406a; II–477b; III–191b, 328a; IV–178a; VI–292a
Bonanza kings I–329a
Nevada V–39b
Ralston's ring VI–44a
Sutro tunnel VI–453a
Virginia City VII–199b
CONAD. *See* Continental Air Defense Command
Conant, James B. (educ.) I–215b; II–400b; III–175a, 260b; V–137a; VI–230b
Conant, Roger (col. gov.) II–365a; IV–265a; VI–91b
Cape Ann I–446b
Salem VI–199a
CONARC. *See* Continental Army Command
Concanen, Richard L. (cler.) II–362b
CONCEPCIÓN, BATTLE OF (1835) **II–157a**
Conception (riv.) IV–7a
Concerto in F (comp.) IV–438b
CONCESSIONS AND AGREEMENT (1664–65) **II–157a**; I–83b; II–117b, 388b; III–132b; V–56b
Concho (Ariz.) III–304a
CONCILIATION, LABOR II–157b; VII–232b
CONCILIATION COURTS, DOMESTIC II–157b
Conciliation Service, U.S. II–157b, 499a; IV–74a, 78a
Concio ad Clerum ("Advice to the Clergy") VI–81b
Concord (gunboat) IV–239b
Concord (Mass.) II–99a
Concord Group II–158a
Revere's ride VI–106a
revolutionary war IV–266a
See also Lexington and Concord
Concord (N.H.) II–158a; V–375a
Concord (N.C.) V–117a
Concord, Battle of (1775) II–211a, 468b
See also Lexington and Concord
Concord, Mass., 1840–60 (comp.) IV–439a
Concord Antiquarian Society II–99a; III–137a
Concord Bridge IV–360b; VI–283a
CONCORD COACH II–158a; I–461a; V–178a

CONCORD GROUP **II–158a**; IV–162a, 163a, 267a
Concord Hymn (poem) VI–282b
Concord River III–141a
Concrete I–364b–65a, 378a–79a, 478a
street paving V–230a
"Concurrent majority" V–352b
Concurrent Resolutions. *See* Resolutions, Legislative
CONDÉ, FORT (Ala.) **II–158a**; I–499a
Condé, Pedro García (off.) II–363b
Condensed milk II–280a, 281a
Condominiums II–49a
Condon, Edward U. (phys.) V–301a
Condon, John F. IV–156b
Condor (bomber) I–50a
Cone, James H. (theol.) VI–83a–b
Conejos River V–312a
Conemaugh Reservoir IV–5a
Conemaugh River II–351a; III–448a; VI–149a
Conemaugh Valley IV–5a
Conestoga (Indians) V–231a
Conestoga horse III–303b
Conestoga Massacre. *See* Paxton's Boys
CONESTOGA WAGON **II–158b**; II–248a; IV–89b; V–389b; VI–152b–53a; VII–100a,b, 168a, 216a
Conewago Falls Canal IV–174b
Coney Island (N.Y.C.) I–275b; VI–100b
Confederacy. *See* Confederate States of America
Confederacy, United Daughters of the. *See* United Daughters of the Confederacy
CONFEDERATE AGENTS **II–158b**
Bulloch, James D. IV–85a
Greenhow, Rose O'Neal VI–373a
Impressment Act II–163b
Indian treaties III–400a
Slidell, John IV–85a
Sons of Liberty VI–339a
Confederate Almanac and Register I–91a
Confederate Army. *See* Army, Confederate
Confederate Conscription Acts VI–427a
Confederate expatriates VI–274b
CONFEDERATE FLAG **II–159a**
Confederate Gulch (Mont.) IV–403a
Confederate Memorial Literary Society VII–292b
Confederate navy. *See* Navy, Confederate
Confederate Ordinance Bureau II–162b
CONFEDERATE PRISON CAMPS **II–159a**
Andersonville I–117b
atrocities I–219b
Belle Isle I–287a
Castle Thunder I–466a
Libby Prison IV–139a
Confederate rams. *See* Rams, Confederate
CONFEDERATE STATES OF AMERICA **II–159b**; II–61a,b, 62a,b, 313b; III–436a; VI–251a–b
Alabama I–71a–b
Alabama I–72b–73b, 121b
Albemarle I–83a
Arkansas I–173b
arrests I–196a
Avery salt mine I–232a
Bermuda admiralty case I–292a
Birchard Letter I–304a
blockade of I–83a, 116a, 121b, 245b, 279a, 292a, 321b, 497a; II–67a–b, 159a
blockade-running II–313b
cabinet II–294b
Canada I–435a, 438b–39a
church schism II–36b
commercial bounties I–352b
Confederation Act II–168a
Confiscation Acts II–168a
congress II–159a
conscientious objectors II–185a
conscription II–185a, 186a
Copperheads II–222b
cotton as money II–267b
cotton trade II–68a
counterfeiting II–244a
currency I–324a; V–405b
Davis–Johnston controversy II–295b
DeBow's *Review* II–298b
debts II–205b, 241a, 302b; VI–96b
Democratic party VII–210a
diplomacy II–64b–66a
"Dixie" anthem II–357a
Dolphin admiralty case II–360a
enemy trading VII–94a
espionage VI–373a
establishment I–71b, 115a; IV–404b–05a
excess profits tax II–467a
expatriates I–360b, 455a
Fire-eaters III–25a
Five Civilized Tribes V–148a–b
flag I–330a
Florida III–39a
Great Britain I–72b–73a, 121b, 292a; II–65a–b, 213a; VII–134b
Hampton Roads Conference III–247b
impressment III–349a
inflation II–235b; III–415a, 416a; V–405a,b
Joint Committee on Reconstruction IV–6a
Kentucky support IV–41a
"Lost Cause" IV–189b
Lower South Department II–159a
loyal governments VI–249b
Maryland support IV–261a
Mississippi River IV–374b
munitions VII–113b
newspaper support V–71b
opium use IV–450a
political prisoners II–159b
postal service V–373a–b
president II–294b–95a
price-fixing V–401b
prisons I–117b–18a, 219b, 287a, 466a–b
privateers V–419b
propaganda II–66b, 159a
Provisional Congress I–180b
railroads VI–26b, 37b–38a
Reconstruction VI–55b
seal VI–246a
slavery VII–54a
song I–330a
states' rights VI–405a
support II–434b
taxation VII–5b, 15a
tax-in-kind VII–64a
Thirteenth Amendment VII–54a–b
Trans-Mississippi Department II–159a
Trent affair VII–115b
Union sentiment VII–148b
Virginia VII–195a
war costs VII–228 (table), 228b
war losses VII–232 (table), 232b
White House VII–292a
See also Civil War
Confederate Veteran (period.) VII–150a
Confederate Veterans, United *See* United Confederate Veterans
CONFEDERATION (1781–88) **II–165b**; II–192b
Congress II–174a, 194a, 211b
debts II–302a
Dohrman's Grant II–359a
domestic trade VII–82b
Great Seal of the United States II–384b
Kentucky representation IV–42b
land grants for education IV–93a
Muscle Shoals speculation IV–435a–b
Ordinance of 1785 IV–90b
states' rights VI–404a
tariff II–276a
taxation VII–4a
western lands V–162a–b, 162a–b; VII–274a–b
Confederation, Articles of. *See* Articles of Confederation
CONFEDERATION, FORT (Ala.) **II–167b**; VI–366b; VII–270a
Confederation Générale du Travail VI–455b
Confederation of State Medical Examining and Licensing Boards IV–284b
Conference for Progressive Political Action I–428a; IV–81a, 84b
Conference of American States V–106a
Conference of Commissioners on Uniform State Laws (1922) II–309b
Conference of State and Local Historical Societies III–279a
Conferences. *See* under specific name of conference, as in Bretton Woods Conference
Confessionalism, religious
Presbyterianism VI–76b, 78a
Confession of 1967 (Presbyterianism) V–392b
Confessions, criminal IV–361b
CONFIRMATION BY THE SENATE **II–167b**
ambassadors II–437a
Federal Communications Commission III–1a
Interstate Commerce Commission III–458a
National Labor Relations Board IV–467b
presidential appointments in Philippines IV–7b
removal from office IV–446a
Supreme Court justices VI–443b–44a
Tenure of Office Act VII–31b
Confirming Act (1787) VI–451b, 452a
CONFISCATION ACTS (1861–64) **II–168a**; I–249a; II–64a, 212b, 435a; VII–54a
CONFISCATION OF PROPERTY **II–168b**
Civil War II–67b, 190a
Granville estate III–212b
Loyalists I–366a–b; III–493a; VI–117a, 118b; VII–172a
maritime warfare III–343a
Mexican War IV–325a
Radical Republicans VI–11a
revolutionary war II–481b; III–79a; IV–200b–1a; V–436b–37a
slaves II–434a–35a
Treaty of Versailles VII–173b
Van Ness Convention VII–167a
See also Nationalization of U.S. Property Abroad
Conformity Act (1872) IV–17a
Confraternity of Christian Doctrine I–468b
Confucius II–27a
Conger, Fort (Can.) III–224a; V–337a

CONGLOMERATES **II–169a**; I–391b; III–290b
antitrust legislation II–72a
broadcasting III–1b–2a
mergers VII–124a
motion picture industry IV–418b
restraint of trade VI–103a
taxation III–205a
Congo (Afr.) I–21b, 439b
Congregatio a Sancta Cruce. *See* Holy Cross, Priests of
Congregational Association of Connecticut V–324a; VII–275a
Congregational Christian Church II–170a; VI–79b
CONGREGATIONAL CHURCHES **II–169b**; VI–75b, 77a,b, 78a, 81a, 82a
American Home Missionary Society III–469a
Assemblies of God V–260a
Cambridge Platform I–412a; VII–279a
church covenant II–248a
colleges II–114a
colonial schools II–394b
colonial society II–126a
colonization of Afro-Americans I–101a
Connecticut Constitutional Convention II–183a
Dartmouth College II–394b
Disciples of Christ II–352b
East Jersey V–57a
Great Migration III–220a
hymns III–326a
Massachusetts IV–267a
meetinghouse IV–300a
missionary work III–385b; IV–365a,b, 366b
New England V–50a,b
New England Way V–52a
New Haven Colony V–55a,b
New Lights cult V–58b
New Plymouth Colony V–65a
New York State V–87a
Pilgrims V–312b
Plan of Union V–324a, 391b
religious liberty VII–69a
Salem VI–199a
Saybrook Platform VI–223b
Separatists VI–262a
sex code VI–265b
slavery II–36b
Standing order VI–384b
Sunday schools VI–442b
Synod of Dort VI–456a
Western Reserve VII–275a
Westminster Confession VII–279a
Yale Band VII–350b
Yale University VII–350b
Congregational Holiness Church V–260a
Congregational Home Missionary IV–365b
CONGREGATION DE PROPAGANDA FIDE **II–170b**; I–451b, 467a, 468a
Congregation of Holy Cross. *See* Holy Cross, Priests of
Congress (warship) IV–396b
Congress, Continental. *See* Continental Congress
CONGRESS, UNITED STATES II–171a; II–174–76 (table); III–2a, 3a,b; IV–133b
adjournment II–199a, 201b–02a
admission of states II–202b, 443a–b
Alaska representation I–76b, 77a
apportionment I–147a–b, 147a–b, 244a–b, 481b; II–194a
appropriations I–148b–49a; II–477a
Bank of the United States IV–211b
blocs I–42a, 322a–b
campaign committees V–345b
campaign contributions V–449b
carpetbaggers I–460a
caucus I–418b, 474b
Central Intelligence Agency I–484b
checks and balances II–4b
commerce clause II–135b
commerce regulation III–178a–b, 178a–b; IV–80b
commercial treaties VII–108b
Committee on Labor IV–64b
compensation II–199a
comptroller general of U.S. II–152a, 501b
comptroller of the currency II–152b
congressional districts II–355b
Congressional Record II–178a
Constitution II–198a–200b, 201a,b, 202a,b
constitutional amendments II–203a
consumer protection II–208a
contempt I–117b; II–210b
contested elections I–423a
convening II–174a, 199a, 201b, 206b
copyright law II–224b–25a
corruption II–231b
Council of National Defense II–243a
courts-martial system II–246b
declaration of war II–313a, 472a
delegated powers II–323a
delegation of administrative powers I–12a–b
election of senators VI–261b, 264a–b
elections II–199a, 408b, 410a
electoral college II–201a, 412a
enabling legislation II–178b
enumerated powers II–195b, 199b–200a, 453a
executive agreements I–363a; II–471b
executive branch reorganization II–497b
executive orders II–473a
executive power of removal IV–446a
executive privilege II–473b–74a
expenditures II–476a
extra sessions II–479a
Federal Election Commission V–449a
Federal Register III–5b
filibuster III–21b
floor leader III–37b
franked mail III–98a
freedom of speech III–104a
"full faith and credit clause" II–202b
general welfare clause III–156b
Hoover Commissions III–299b
House Committee on Un-American Activities III–308a
House Ways and Means committee VII–263b
impeachment powers III–343b
implied powers III–348a
imposts III–349a
Indian treaties III–383a
insurance regulation III–434a
interstate commerce IV–148a, 434b
interstate compacts III–459b
investigating committees III–464b
Johnson impeachment III–345b
judicial review IV–12a, 248b
labor's appeal to redress grievances IV–68a
lame-duck sessions IV–88b
land bounties IV–91a
land grants IV–96a
legal tender IV–132a,b, 133a
legislative courts IV–16b
legislative resolutions VI–100a
legislative riders VI–138b
location of I–448b
logrolling IV–181a
lotteries IV–191a
loyalty testing IV–203a
Medal of Honor II–310a
military law IV–342b
militia IV–345b
monetary powers IV–20a
monetary standard IV–392b
national defense II–313a
National Monetary Commission IV–468a
naturalization V–6a
Naval Academy appointments V–10a
New Deal legislation IV–71a
nominating system V–101b
organic law V–170a
pairing V–194a
party leadership V–344b–45a
party whip VII–288b
pocket veto V–334b
police power IV–240a
post offices V–373b
post roads V–372a
Powell Case V–383b
power of inquiry IV–45b
presidential disability II–172a
presidential election II–205a
presidential succession II–206b, 207b; V–398b
president's annual economic report II–498a
privateering IV–256a; V–423b–24a
private sector authority IV–80a
Puerto Rico V–461b
records of proceedings III–202a; IV–8b
Reed rules VI–65b
reserved powers of the states VI–97b
right to regulate labor relations IV–468a
rules of the House VI–169b
salary grab VI–198b
seceded states VI–249b
separation of powers IV–209a; V–385a
Smithsonian Institution VI–319a
speaker of the House VI–368b
State of the Union messages II–201b
state relations II–200b
Statutes at Large VI–405b
statutory law VI–406a
steering committees VI–411b
subversion VI–428a
Supreme Court packing VI–448a–49a
tariffs II–323b
taxation II–206a, 275b, 313a, 453b, 476a; IV–211a; VII–4a–b, 12a, 13b
territorial delegates VI–400b–01a
territorial governments VII–31b–32a,b
territories II–202b; III–424b
titles of nobility V–100b
travel allowances IV–339a
Treasury III–244b
treatymaking VII–109b,

CONGRESS, UNITED STATES (cont.)
110b
two–party system VII–134b
United States Code II–91b
vice–president II–205a; VII–178b
Virgin Islands representation III–425b
War Department VII–230a
war–making powers VII–223b, 226b–27b, 237a,b
war powers I–116a; IV–346b
Washington, D.C. VII–245a,b
weights and measures II–208a; IV–462a–b
White House Office II–497b
women VII–318a
See also Executive and Congress
Congresses, provincial. *See* Provincial Congresses
Congress Hall (Phila.) III–354a; V–277b
Congressional apportionment. *See* Apportionment
Congressional Budget and Impoundment Control Act (1974) II–179a
Congressional districts I–147a–48a; II–355a–b
boundaries II–172a
reapportionment II–173b
Congressional elections costs II–411a
Congressional filibuster. *See* Filibuster, Congressional
Congressional Globe II–178a; III–203b; IV–8b
Congressional Government V–353b
Congressional immunity II–172a
Congressional investigations II–171a, 210b
Attica I–220b
Ballinger–Pinchot controversy I–247b–48a
Bank of the United States V–206a
CIA activity in Chile II–113b
Civil War II–139a–40a
Committee on the Conduct of the War I–249a
committee system II–173a
Crédit Mobilier II–256a
drug industry V–468a
Elk Hills oil scandal V–13b
endowed foundations III–83b; V–281a
entertainment industry I–314b–15a
Gardiner award III–152a
House Un–American Activities Committee III–308a
interstate trade barriers III–460b–61a
Ku Klux Klan IV–58a
labor I–103a
lobbies IV–170b
Lorimer case IV–189a
McCarthy–Army hearings IV–209b
Mulligan letters IV–426a
munitions industry IV–203a, 433b; V–35b, 117b
naval oil reserves II–431b; VII–16b
organized labor IV–74b
pharmaceutical industry V–274a
Philippine Insurrection V–281b–82a
Pueblo incident V–460b
railroads II–271a
scientific agencies I–90a–b
star route frauds VI–387a
steel strikes IV–72b
Teapot Dome oil scandal V–13b
Vare case VII–167b
Washington, D.C., paving II–319b
See also Investigating Committees
***CONGRESSIONAL RECORD* II–178a**; II–172b; III–203b; IV–8b
CONGRESSIONAL REGULATORY POWERS II–178a
delegation of powers II–323a
Congressional Research Service IV–147a
Congressional rules. *See* Rules of the House
Congressional Serial Set III–203b
Congressional Union. *See* Woman's Party, National
Congressmen–at–large II–355a
Congress of Industrial Organizations III–413a; IV–72a–b, 273b; VII–191b
campaign of 1940 IV–73a
campaign of 1944 I–429b; IV–73b
merger with AFL IV–74b
See also American Federation of Labor–Congress of Industrial Organizations; Committee for Industrial Organizations
Congress of Micronesia III–426a
CONGRESS OF RACIAL EQUALITY II–179b; I–31a, 72a; VI–352a
Freedom Riders II–58a–b; III–107a
"Congress of Rough Riders of the World" VII–298b
Congress of the International Geodetic and Geophysical Union (1924) III–481a
Congress of Vienna (1815) I–93a
Congress Pottery III–184a
Congreve rockets I–318a; VI–159a
Conifers III–74b; VII–60a
Conkling, Roscoe (pol.) III–152b
campaign of 1876 I–422b
campaign of 1880 I–423b
campaign of 1884 I–424a
Joint Committee on Reconstruction IV–6a
Stalwarts VI–380b
Con men II–260a
Conn, Billy (pugilist) V–423a
Connally, John B. (pol.) IV–37b
Connally, Thomas (pol.) VII–151a
Connally Amendment (1946) III–453b, 457a
Connally "Hot Oil" Act (1935) V–270b
Conneaut (Ohio) II–459a; VII–274a
CONNECTICUT II–179b; IV–270a; V–49b; VI–393 (table)
Albany Congress I–82a
bachelor houses I–239a
bills of credit I–300a
birth and death registration IV–149a
black suffrage III–437b
blue laws VI–440a
Cambridge Platform I–412a
Cartagena expedition I–461b
chemical industry II–5a
child labor II–24b
clockmaking II–77b–79a; VII–352b–53a
colonial agents II–116b
colonial assembly II–117b, 118a
colonial council II–119b
colonial courts I–145a
colonial exiles V–342a
colonial government II–181a–83a; VI–166a,b
colonial plans of union II–121b
colonial suffrage VI–434a
committees of safety II–140b
Congregational Association of V–324a
constitution VI–390b, 396b
Convention of 1787 II–171a, 193a,b, 194a, 478a
counties V–349b
county government II–245a
currency I–483a
Declaration of Independence II–308a
Dominion of New England II–182b; V–50b
double jeopardy VII–154b
Duke of York's proprietary VII–359b
Dutch War of 1653 VI–134b
education II–396a, 398b; VI–227a
entail of estate II–452a
fast days II–497a
Federalists III–5a
"Firelands" II–183b
founding II–124a
furniture III–134b
general court III–155b
Gore III–200a
Halfway Covenant III–243a
harness and saddle hardware III–255b
Hartford Convention III–259a
historical society III–278b
House of Hope III–309a
hurricanes III–319b
incorporating act I–499b, 500a; II–229a
Indian land cession IV–387a–b
Indian villages III–405a
King Philip's War III–223a; IV–47b
King's Province claim IV–49a
King William's War IV–49b
lead industry IV–122a
leather industry IV–127b
legal tender IV–132a
Leisler Rebellion IV–134a
liquor laws IV–158b
Litchfield Law School IV–159b
Long Island IV–185b
Loyalists VII–150b
Ludlow's Code IV–203b
migration from IV–338b; V–41a
minimum–wage law IV–353a
minutemen IV–361a
Mississippi settlers III–171a
Mohegan IV–387a
Narragansett land I–213a
New England Way V–51b
New Hampshire settlers V–53b
New Haven Colony V–55a; VII–149b
New Lights cult V–58b
New Plymouth Colony V–65a
New York boundary dispute I–350b
oblong V–130b
off–track betting III–305b
Ohio lands V–140b
Pennsylvania boundary dispute V–250b; VII–116b, 347a–b, 353a–b
Pequot Indians V–261a
Pequot War V–261a
personal liberty laws V–263b
pewter work VI–291a,b
Plymouth Trading Post V–334a
price–fixing V–401b
Prohibition II–407a
property boundaries III–10a
provincial congress V–440a
public land states V–453a
Puritans V–469a
Regicides VI–70b, 71a
religion VI–81a
religious liberty VII–69a

revolutionary war V–58b, 66a; VI–125a, 139a, 186a; VII–251a–b
river towns VI–151a
Rogerenes VI–162a
rubber industry VI–167a
Saybrook VI–223a,b
Saybrook Platform VI–223b
settlement III–219b, 220a; VII–95a, 282b
silk VI–286b
slavery I–135b; VI–309a
Southampton VI–346b
Southold VI–354b
Stamp Act VI–381b
state constitutions II–182a, 183a
suffrage II–35b
Susquehanna Company VI–451a
Susquehanna settlers VI–452a
thanksgiving days II–497a
tobacco VII–66b
town surveys V–452a
Tri-State Regional Planning Commission III–460a
typefounding V–413a
United Colonies of New England IV–270a; VII–149a
U.S. Constitution II–196a, 203b
usury law III–443a
War of 1812 VI–415b
Western Reserve II–74b, 183b; III–25b; VI–204a
writs of assistance VII–345a
Wyoming Valley IV–92a, 98b; VII–346b
Yale University VII–350b
Yankee–Pennamite Wars II–183b; VII–353a
zinc VII–369a
See also New England
CONNECTICUT, FUNDAMENTAL ORDERS OF (1639) **II–181a**; II–117b; III–132b; VI–151b
CONNECTICUT, OLD PATENT OF II–182a; II–180a, 182a–b, 183b; IV–188a; VI–151b, 223a
Connecticut Academy of Arts and Sciences VI–235b
Connecticut Agricultural Experiment Station I–303a; II–226a
CONNECTICUT CHARTER OF 1662 II–182a; I–145a, 206b, 213a; II–35b, 118b, 180a, 183a; VI–166a, 390b; VII–274a, 346b–47a
assemblies II–117b
Dorr's Rebellion III–436b
Fishers Island III–31a
New Haven Colony V–56a
suffrage II–35b
Susquehanna Company VI–451b
Connecticut Code (1650) I–239a
See also Ludlow's Code
CONNECTICUT COMPROMISE (1787) **II–183a**; II–151b; VI–403b
CONNECTICUT CONSTITUTIONAL CONVENTION (1818) **II–183a**
Connecticut Hall (Yale) VII–351a
Connecticut Historical Society II–183a; III–137b
Connecticut Land Company II–74b, 183b; III–25b; V–140b; VII–273b, 274b
Connecticut Line IV–445a; VII–347b
Connecticut Path I–279b
Connecticut Rangers III–254b; VI–46b
Connecticut River II–179b, 182a; III–200a, 226b, 309a; IV–83b; VI–149a; VII–69b
Bay Path I–279b
bridge I–363b
canals IV–174b
Duke of York's Proprietary V–56a; VII–359a,b
Dutch War of 1653 VI–134b
French and Indian War VI–190a,b
fur trade III–141a; VII–104b
Indian Stream Republic III–401b
navigation VI–148a
Northeast boundary V–118a,b
patroonship V–229a
Pequot War V–261a
Plymouth Trading Post V–334a
revolutionary war II–267a
Saybrook VI–223a
settlement V–53b–54a; VI–151a
U.S. boundary VI–165b; VII–265a
Vermont VII–171a,b
Wappinger Confederacy VII–223b
waterpower IV–347b; VII–257a
westward movement VII–260a
Wethersfield V–55b
Connecticut River Valley Flood Control Commission VI–402a
Connecticut Society for Mental Hygiene IV–304a
Connecticut Society for the Reformation of Morals VII–22b
Connecticut State Library II–183a
Connecticut Valley I–279b; III–258b; VII–268a
fur trade III–140b
Number 4 V–126a
revivalism VI–76b
settlement III–309a; IV–338a; VII–282b
silk VI–287a
CONNECTICUT WESTERN LANDS II–183b; V–140b, 162b, 162b, 443b; VII–273a–b
Salt Springs Tract VI–204a
Seven Ranges survey VI–264a
Western Reserve VII–274a–75a
Wyoming Valley VII–347a–b
Connecticut Wits. *See* Hartford Wits
Connelly's Tavern (Natchez, Miss.) I–160b
Conner, David (nav. off.) IV–322a, 323b, 325a; V–19b
Conner, Patrick E. (off.) I–281a
Connestoga Creek IV–175a
Connolly, James B. (athlete) V–154a
Connolly, J. B. (au.) I–447a
Connolly, John (cler.) II–362b
Connolly, John (off.) II–183b, 381b; III–250a
Falls of the Ohio V–142b
Fort Pitt V–253a, 321b
Connolly, Richard B. ("Slippery Dick") (pol.) VI–142a; VII–131a
CONNOLLY'S PLOT (1775) **II–183b**
Connoquenessing Creek IV–434b
CONNOR, FORT (Wyo.) **II–184a**; I–357b
See also Reno, Fort (Wyo.)
Connor, James (print.) V–412a–b
Connor, Martin Sennett (pol.) IV–369a–b
Connor, Patrick E. (off.) II–184a; VII–162a
Connor, Robert D. W. I–167a
Connors, Jimmy (athlete) VII–30b, 31a
Conococheague Valley IV–191b; VI–285a
Conolly, Horace II–465b
***CONQUISTADORES* II–184a**; II–43a, 452b–53a
Afro-Americans I–24b
Penitent Brothers V–245b, 245b
Conrad, Frank (eng.) II–424a
Conrad, Joseph (au.) IV–162a; V–96a
Conrad, Timothy (paleon.) V–195b
Conscience, liberty of III–219a
CONSCIENCE WHIGS II–184b; I–138b; VII–288b, 321b
Cotton Whigs II–184b
Free Soil party III–111b
Republican party VI–92b
CONSCIENTIOUS OBJECTORS II–185a; V–181a–b, 182a–b
Civil War I–182b; II–161b; VI–426b
Jehovah's Witnesses III–497b
Osgoodites V–174b
Quakers III–123b; V–470b–71a; VII–201b
War Resisters' International VII–236b
World War I V–236a
World War II II–50b
Consciousness-raising
woman's rights movement VII–313a
CONSCRIPTION II–186a; II–366a, 450b–51a
British army VI–127a
Civil War I–180a–b, 182a–b, 184b, 353a; II–63a, 161a–62a, 185a, 313b; IV–62b; VI–354b, 405a, 426b; VII–148b
post–World War II IV–344a–b
press gangs V–399b
revolutionary war VI–118a
Vietnam War VI–61a
World War I IV–343b, 358b–59a
World War II VII–334b
Conscription, Bureau of (Confederate) II–162a
Conscription Act (1940) II–450b
Conscription Act of 1863 IV–62b, 383b; VI–426b
Consejo de Indias VI–363b
"Consent of the governed" II–304a, 306b; VII–14b
CONSERVATION II–187a
Agriculture Department I–45a–b
Alaska I–79b–80b
Civilian Conservation Corps II–51a; VI–73a–b
Coast Guard II–89b
conscientious objectors V–182b
Department of the Interior III–444a
electric power II–416b, 417b
engineering education II–448a
federal policy I–42b
fish III–28a
forests III–73a,b, 75a–b, 76a
gasoline III–153b
Girl Scouts III–181a
grazing lands IV–95b
hydroelectric power sites III–321a
interstate compacts VI–402a,b
lumber industry IV–204b
mining IV–350b
Montana IV–403b
Nader's Raiders IV–448a
national forests V–450b, 451a,b
national parks and monuments V–217a,b, 219a
natural gas V–5b
New Nationalism V–60a
New York State V–87b
Niagara Falls V–91b–92a
oil VI–357a
paper recycling V–212b
Point Four program V–335a
Progressive movement V–427b; VI–234b

CONSERVATION (cont.)
public domain V–445a–b
reforestation VI–67a
Republican party VI–93a
Resettlement Administration VI–99a
Rocky Mountains VI–160b
soil I–350a; V–44b, 47a, 48a; VI–335a–b
timberlands IV–95a–b, 96a; VII–60a, 61a–b
U.S. Geological Survey III–164a
water II–450a; VII–259a–b
wildlife preservation VII–296b
Yosemite Park VII–362a
Conservation Commission, National II–187b
Conservation Foundation II–188a
CONSERVATISM II–188b
Jacksonian Democracy III–486a–b
John Birch Society IV–1b
Louisiana IV–195a
Missouri IV–378a
National Intelligencer IV–465b
nativism V–3b
radical right VI–12b
Republican party VI–93b
South Dakota VI–350a
"standpatters" VI–384b
Virginia Democrats VII–195b
woman's suffrage VII–315a
Wyoming VII–346a
See also Radicals and Radicalism
Conservative Baptist Associations of America I–265b
Conservative Congregational Christian Conference II–170a
Conservative Jews IV–10a, 11a,b
Conservative party I–107b
Conservative United Synagogue of America IV–11a
Conservatories IV–96b
Considérant, Victor Prosper (ref.) VI–105a
"Consocial" community III–129b
***CONSOLATO DEL MARE* PRINCIPLE II–190a**; I–14b
Consolidated Aircraft Corporation I–236a, 237a
Consolidated Oatmeal Company I–487a
Consolidated Virginia Silver Mine I–329a
Consolidation (bus.) I–389a, 391b
CONSPIRACIES ACTS OF 1861 AND 1862 II–190a
Conspiracy
defined II–142a
injunctions III–419a
labor organizations IV–60b–61a
restraint of trade I–356b
riots of 1877 IV–63b
Watergate II–259a
Constable III–317b; IV–60a, 79b; V–338b; VII–79a
Constable, William (landowner) I–466b; IV–219b
Constantinople (Tur.) II–386b
Constantinople, Convention of (1888) V–201a
Constellation (aircraft carrier) II–348b
Constellation (frigate) III–21b
Anglo-Chinese War I–125a
See also
Constellation-Insurgente Encounter
Constellation-Vengeance Encounter
Constellation (transport plane) I–52a
***CONSTELLATION-INSURGENTE* ENCOUNTER** (1799) **II–190a**; IV–251b; V–15a, 19a, 423b; VII–240a
***CONSTELLATION–VENGEANCE* ENCOUNTER** (1800) **II–190b**; IV–251b; V–15a, 19a; VII–240a
CONSTITUTION (frigate) **II–190b**; II–389b; III–315b; V–19a; VII–243b
armament V–27a
Barbary Wars I–266a
figureheads III–21b
See also
Constitution–Cyane and *Levant* Engagement;
Constitution–Guerriere Engagement;
Constitution–Java Engagement
Constitution (carrier) V–22a
CONSTITUTION, BRITISH II–190b; V–352a
Constitution, Confederate IV–405a
Constitution, Fort (N.J.) IV–131b
Constitutional and Political History of the United States III–282a
Constitutional Apportionment. *See* Apportionment
Constitutionalism V–351a, 352a
Constitutionalist party III–108b
Constitutional law
See also Due Process of Law
CONSTITUTIONAL UNION PARTY II–191a
campaign of 1860 I–421a
Compromise of 1850 II–150b
See also Union Rights Party
***CONSTITUTION–CYANE* AND *LEVANT* ENGAGEMENT** (1815) **II–191b**
Constitution Day (Sept. 17, 1937) V–353b
CONSTITUTION FORT (N.Y.) **II–191b**; III–275b; VII–280a
***CONSTITUTION–GUERRIÈRE* ENGAGEMENT** (1812) **II–191b**; V–424a; VII–240a
Constitution Hall (Washington, D.C.) II–294a
Constitution Island II–191a; III–275b, 276a, 312b–13a; VII–280a
***CONSTITUTION–JAVA* ENGAGEMENT** (1812) **II–192a**
CONSTITUTION OF THE UNITED STATES II–192b; II–167a, 212a; V–351a–52b; VI–370a, 391a, 396b–97a; VII–201a
academic freedom I–5a
administrative justice I–12b
admiralty law and courts I–14b
ambassadors II–342b, 437a
American Liberty League I–108b
amnesty I–114b
annexation of territory I–126a
Antifederalists I–130b
apportionment I–147a
army I–183b
bankruptcy I–262b; VI–422a
Barron v. *Baltimore* I–269b
bill of attainder I–220a, 297b; II–53b
Bill of Rights II–53b
bills of credit I–365a
Booth v. *United States* I–339a
Bricker Amendment I–362b
British debts I–366b
capitation taxes I–451a
census I–451a, 481b
citizenship II–42a
civil disobedience II–50b
civil rights and liberties II–53b
coinage VI–94b
commerce clause I–373a; II–135b, 151b, 229b–30a, 275b; III–178a
compact clause IV–28a
compromises II–151a
concept of liberty IV–142b
Confederate Constitution II–160a
Congress II–171a–72b, 173b, 174a,b, 178a–79a, 472a
congressional elections II–408b, 410a
congressional rules and procedures II–172b
congressmen II–355b
conservatism II–189a
consumer protection II–208a
Continental Congress II–211a
contract clause II–213b, 293b
copyright II–224b
Crittenden Resolution II–149b, 265a
cruel and unusual punishment III–249b–50a
Decius Letters II–303b
declaratory judgments II–309b
defense II–313a
delegation of powers II–323a
democracy II–325b
Democratic party II–327a
direct taxes VI–377a
dispensing powers of president IV–36b
doctrine of sovereignty VI–358b
due process clause I–5a; II–377a
education II–395b
election of senators I–94b
emergency power IV–358a
enumerated powers II–453a
equal protection of the laws II–499b
Essex Junto II–464a
executive agreements I–363a; II–471b
executive power of removal IV–446b; VI–84b
export taxes II–478a
ex post facto law I–297b; II–53b
extradition II–478b
extra sessions II–478b–79a
federal agencies II–497b
federal expenditures II–476a
federal government III–2a
federal income tax III–351a–b
Federalist III–4a
Federalist party III–4a
federal-state relations III–9a
foreign trade I–120a
freedom of press II–53a
freedom of religious worship II–53a
freedom of speech II–53a; III–104a
freedom of the press III–104b
fugitive slaves II–152a; III–130a; V–263b
general welfare clause III–156b; VI–327b
Georgia ratification III–168b
government ownership V–455a
government regulation of business III–204b
habeas corpus II–53b; III–236a
Hartford Convention III–5a
Henry, Patrick V–161a
Higher-law doctrine III–275a
impeachment III–343b

implied powers II–497b; III–348a; IV–20a, 211b
import duties V–172a
imposts III–349a
inauguration of president III–350b
Independence Hall III–354a
Indian affairs III–383a, 388b
inherent powers III–417a
insular possessions III–424b–25a
international law III–455a
interstate commerce II–152a; III–458b, 460b; VI–379a; VII–82b
interstate compacts III–459b
Iroquois League III–475b
Jefferson–Burr election dispute III–494b
Jeffersonian Democracy III–496a
Jeffersonian Republicans VI–94a
judicial circuits II–39b
judicial review IV–12a, 248b
judiciary IV–15b–17b
Judiciary Act (1789) IV–9a
jury trial I–297b; II–53b; IV–21a
legal tender III–251b; IV–132a,b, 132b
Liberian constitution IV–141b
loose construction of II–327a, 453b
loyalty oaths IV–202b
majority rule IV–228a
Massachusetts ratification IV–266a
military law IV–342b
national capital VII–244b
National Guard I–64b
naturalization I–88a; V–6a
New Hampshire ratification V–54a
New Jersey Plan V–57b
New York ratification V–86b
North Carolina ratification V–116a
nullification V–125b
pamphleteering V–199a
patents V–225b
Pennsylvania ratification V–247a
Pinckney Plan V–315a
pocket veto V–334b
police power V–339a
political parties V–223a, 343a
political writings V–353a–b
postal service V–371a
presidential disability V–397a
presidential electors I–94b; II–408b–09b
presidential powers II–472a; V–394a
presidential power to use troops IV–341b
presidential succession V–398b
presidential title V–399a
presidential veto VII–177b–78a
primaries V–41b
privateering IV–256a
privileges and immunities II–53b; V–420a–b
ratification II–320a, 326b
recognition policy VI–54b
relations between states VI–401b–02a
religion I–297b
religious test for public office II–53b
reserved powers of states VI–97b
Rhode Island ratification VI–132b–33a
right of assembly I–204a; II–53a
right of revolution VI–121b
right to bear arms IV–470a
right to sue II–32a–b
rules of the House VI–169b
secession VI–249b
Senate confirmation II–167b
separation of powers I–12b; V–385a
shared powers in II–472a
slavery I–27b; II–64a, 152a; IV–8a; VI–305a–b, 312a
South Carolina I–496b
South Carolina ratification VI–347b
speaker of the House VI–368b
state election authority III–93a
state–making process VII–31b
State of the Union address V–398a
state sovereignty I–404a; VI–403a
states' rights IV–105b; VI–404a
strict construction II–327a, 327a
supremacy clause I–362b
Supreme Court I–339a; VI–444a,b, 444b, 447a
taxation II–476a; VII–4a–b
territorial governments VII–31b, 32a–b, 33b
territories VII–13b
test cases I–100b
text II–198a–208a
three–fifths clause II–151b
tidelands VII–57a
titles of nobility V–100b
treason VII–106b, 107a
treatymaking I–362b; IV–381a; VII–109b, 110a–b
treaty ratification VI–359a
"United States of America" VII–153b
vice–president II–408a; VII–178b
voter qualifications VII–208a,b
war–making powers VII–223b, 226b, 237a
Webster–Hayne debate VII–265b
weights and measures IV–462a
See also Amendments to the Constitution; Bill of Rights; and entries under individual amendments
Constitution Plaza (Hartford, Conn.) VI–86b
Constitutions, fundamental. *See* Fundamental Constitutions
Constitutions, state. *See* State Constitutions
Constitution State VI–393 (table)
Construction industry
aluminum I–92b; V–104a
copper V–103b
Federal Housing Administration II–47a
panic of 1929 V–209b
recession of 1973–75 VII–85a
Taft–Hartley Act VI–457a
unemployment VII–140b
union security provisions IV–74b–75a
work force V–132b
working conditions IV–78b
Works Progress Administration VII–323b
CONSULAR CONVENTION (1789) **II–208a**
Consular jurisdiction
Egypt II–479a–b
Consular Relations, Vienna Convention on (1962) III–457a
Consular Service. *See* Foreign Service
Consuls II–201b
Consultation on Church Unity VI–79b
Consultative Meeting of Foreign Ministers of the American Republics (1939) V–200a
Consumer
boycotts I–357a
cooperatives II–220b
corporations II–230b
dairy industry II–282a
distribution of goods and services II–354a–55a
labor grievances II–3a
research organizations I–20a
Consumer Advisory Council II–209a
Consumer Affairs, Office of II–498a
Consumer Credit Protection Act (1969) III–423b, 443b, 459a
Consumer Federation of America II–208a
Consumer Price Index (CPI) II–209b–10a, 235b–36a,b
Consumer Product Safety Commission III–54a; V–468a
CONSUMER PROTECTION II–208a; I–391b; II–355a; IV–77a
Bureau of Standards IV–462b
fair trade II–484a
Food and Drug Administration III–54a
government inspection III–422a
government regulation III–204b
interstate commerce laws III–459a
Justice Department IV–22a
Nader's Raiders IV–448b; VII–124b
pure food and drug movement V–465a
Consumer Protection and Environmental Health Service III–54a
CONSUMER PURCHASING POWER II–209a
food stamps III–56a
installment buying III–422b
National Recovery Administration IV–469b
New Deal V–45b, 46a
panic of 1837 V–206b
tariff VI–463a,b
wage and salary comparisons VII–215b
Consumer Reports II–208b
Consumer Safety Product Act (1972) I–7b
Consumers Research II–208b
Consumers Union II–208b
Consumers Unions, International Organization of II–209a
Consumption. *See* Tuberculosis
Consumption price index II–235b–36b
Contact mines (explosives) IV–351a
Container Corporation II–107a
Containerization V–183a; VI–281a
merchant marine IV–312b
Containers
tin cans VII–61b
Containment policy II–98a; III–463a–b
II 315b–
Contarini, Giovanni (cartog.) IV–247a
Contempt, criminal III–105a,b
CONTEMPT OF CONGRESS II–210b; I–117b, 117b; III–465a; IV–210b
Con–Thien (Viet.) VII–186a
CONTI, FORT (Ont., Can.) **II–210b**
Conti, Pietro (inv.) VII–136a
Continental Air Defense Command I–59a
Continental army *See* Revolutionary War, American Army in

Continental Army Command I–187b
Continental Association V–104b
CONTINENTAL CONGRESS II–211a; II–4b; V–277a; VI–113b–15a, 117a, 396a; VII–14a, 351b
Albany Congress I–82a
armed neutrality of 1780 I–176a
Articles of Confederation I–197b; II–165b–67a
"association" I–208a
Bank of North America I–260b
Bermuda delegates I–292b
bills of credit I–300a
blockades I–320b–21a
bonuses I–331a
British prison ships V–418b
Canadian alliance I–435b
capital at York VII–358b
Commercial Committee II–137a–b
committees of correspondence I–345a
committees of safety II–140a
conscientious objectors II–185a
Continental army I–183a–b, 475a; VI–125a–b
Continental navy VI–128a,b
Conway Cabal II–218a
courts-martial II–246b
currency II–274b–75a
debts II–299b, 301b–02a
Declaration of Independence II–303b
Declaration of Rights II–308b
embargoes VII–93b
Federalists III–4a
first presidential election I–416b
foreign volunteers VI–129a
French Consular Convention II–208a
Georgia III–168b
Independence Hall III–354a
independence resolution VI–161b
Indian factory system II–480a
legal tender IV–132a
location of capital I–448b
Loyalist support IV–200b
mapping I–463a
marines IV–251b
military code VII–142b–43a
national lottery IV–191a
New England militia VI–123a
New Jersey V–57a
Olive Branch Petition V–152b
Philadelphia I–459b; V–247a
president II–305b
privateering V–419a
prize money V–423a
provincial congresses V–440a
revenue VII–3b–4a
revolutionary committees VI–121b, 122a–b
Rhode Island delegations VI–132b
secret agents III–71a
secretary II–304b, 305b
Suffolk Resolves VI–431a
Thanksgiving Day VII–46a
theater ban VII–46b–47a
treaties VII–111a
"United States of America" VII–153a–b
U.S. Army I–183a
War and Ordnance Board VII–226b
war financing VI–120a,b
Washington, George I–344b
Continental divide I–201a, 209a; VI–160a; VII–345b
Continental drift III–481a
Continental Line VI–117b, 118a, 125b
Continental Marines II–450b
Continental shelf III–107a, 164b
Continental Shelf, UN Convention on the (1958) VII–33a
Continuous voyage doctrine II–213a, 446a–b, 464a
Bermuda admiralty case I–292a
Civil War I–321a; II–67b; V–35a, 39a
Dolphin case II–360a
international law III–455b–56a
London Declaration IV–182a,b
Springbok case VI–376b
See also Enemy Destination
CONTRABAND, SLAVES AS II–212a; VI–300b
***CONTRABANDISTAS* II–212b**
CONTRABAND OF WAR II–212b
armed neutrality of 1780 I–175b
Civil War II–67b
Declaration of London V–233b
Declaration of Panama V–200a
Declaration of Paris V–214a
defined II–446a–47a
freedom of the seas III–106b
free ships, free goods III–110a
international law III–455b–56a
London Declaration IV–182a
munitions definition IV–430a
Neutrality Act of 1939 V–37b
neutral rights V–38b
Peterhoff case V–264a
Plan of 1776 V–323b
Proclamation of Neutrality V–37a
Prussia treaty V–440b
retaliation in international law VI–104b
World War I VII–325a
Contraception. *See* Birth Control Movement
Contract, freedom of II–378a–b; IV–68b, 80a–b, 173b
CONTRACT CLAUSE II–213b; II–200b
mortgage moratorium acts IV–358a
property rights V–339a
Yazoo fraud IV–99a; VII–354a
Contract labor
freedmen III–103b
CONTRACT LABOR, FOREIGN II–214a; III–353a
Chinese in California IV–33a
Civil War IV–62b
deportation II–333a
Hawaii III–264a
immigration restriction III–342a
opposition IV–64a,b
Contract labor laws II–214a,b; III–353a
Contracts II–200b; III–9b
charters II–293b
Clayton Antitrust Act II–72a
corporations II–229a
Court of Claims II–71a
Fletcher v. *Peck* III–36a
Gold Clause Cases III–189a
labor-management disputes II–499a
political corruption II–232a
See also Collective Bargaining
Contracts, government II–498b
army supply V–375a–b
Civil War II–68a–b
political parties V–345b
"pork barrel" V–366b
scandals V–346b
Contrast, The (play) VII–47a,b
CONTRERAS, BATTLE OF (1847) **II–214b**; IV–324a; VI–241a
Contributions to the Natural History of the United States of America VI–90b
"Contributory negligence" doctrine II–441a
Convair Aircraft Company I–237b, 238a
"Convective" theory IV–316b
Convention (brig) I–9b
CONVENTION ARMY II–214b; VI–217b
Convention for the Pacific Settlement of International Disputes III–237a–b; V–262a
Convention for the Preservation and Protection of Fur Seals (1911) VII–33a
Convention of Law of the Sea (1958) VII–113a
CONVENTION OF 1800 II–215a; II–208a; III–67b, 96a, 96b, 118b; V–15b; VII–348a
alien landholding I–87a
arbitration IV–5b
spoliation claims III–98a, 121b
CONVENTION OF 1818 WITH ENGLAND II–215b; I–126b, 277b; II–92b, 284b; III–30b–31a, 243b; IV–6a; V–120a,b, 169b–70a; VII–111b, 270a–b
joint occupation V–164b
Louisiana purchase boundary IV–198a
mackerel fisheries IV–217a
Convention on the Continental Shelf, United Nations (1958) VII–33a
Convention on the Law of Treaties (1968) VII–113a
Convention on the Rights and Duties of States (1933) V–106a
Convention on the Territorial Sea and the Contiguous Zone, United Nations (1958) VII–33a
CONVENTIONS, PARTY NOMINATING II–216a; I–415b; II–408b, 409b; III–3b; V–101b, 102a, 223b, 344a, 344b, 406b–07a
bolters I–328a
caucus I–474b
expenditure limits V–449b
financing regulation II–232b
funding I–414b
Jacksonian Democracy III–486b
national committee IV–463a
platforms V–329a
presidential I–416a
proportional representation V–435b
Snap Convention VI–322b
two-thirds rule VII–135b
unit rule VII–155b
vice-presidency VII–180b
Conventions, provincial. *See* Provincial Congresses
Conveyor system. *See* Assembly Line
CONVICT LABOR SYSTEMS II–216b; V–415a–b, 416b
abolition movement IV–61b
Auburn Prison system I–221a
chain gangs I–488b
colonial period IV–60a, 79a
federal contracts VII–223a

Georgia III–169a
indentured servants III–353a
Louisiana IV–194a
Workingmen's Party VII–322a
Convicts
colonial importation I–451a; II–258a
immigration laws I–87b; II–445a
Convoy ONS–5 I–214b
Convoy PQ 17 IV–435a
Convoy PQ–17 I–214b
CONVOYS II–217a
Battle of the Atlantic I–214a–b
commanders I–14a
Naval War With France V–15a
submarine warfare VI–424a
warships VII–243b
World War I V–20a; VII–325b, 328b
World War II II–314b; IV–158a, 313b, 435a; VII–339a, 342a, 343a
Conway, Henry Seymour (off.) V–237b
Conway, Thomas (off.). *See* Conway Cabal
CONWAY CABAL II–218a; I–436a; VII–226b, 292b
Conyngham, Gustavus (nav. off.) VI–128b
COOCH'S BRIDGE, BATTLE OF (1777) **II–218a**
Cook, Clarence C. (art critic) II–99b; III–446b
Cook, Frederick A. (physic., expl.) V–337a
Cook, George Cram (nov., playwright) V–439b
Cook, James (expl.) II–353a; VI–247a
Alaska I–75a, 84b
Hawaii III–263a
Nootka Sound VII–247a
Northwest Passage II–219b
Oregon V–164b, 167b
Cook County (Chicago) II–17a, 18b; IV–23a, 214b; V–345a
Cooke, James W. (nav. off.) I–83a
Cooke, Jay (fin.) V–247b
COOKE, JAY, AND COMPANY II–218b; II–63b; III–466a; V–207a
Cooke, John Esten (phys.) I–410a
Cooke, J. P. (chem.) I–218b
Cooke, Morris L. IV–323a
Cooke, Philip St. George (off.) III–179b; IV–411a; VII–217b
COOKERY II–219a; II–418a, 419a,b
food preservation III–54b
Cooke's pills I–410a
Cooke's wagon road III–82a
Cookeville (Tenn.) I–232b
Cook Inlet I–81a; II–219b
COOK'S SEARCH FOR THE NORTHWEST PASSAGE (1776–80) **II–219b**; VII–247a
Coolants II–420b, 421a
Cooley, James Ewing (auctioneer) I–332b
Cooley, Thomas M. (jur.) IV–24b
Cooley and Bangs II–108a–b
COOLEY* v. *BOARD OF WARDENS OF PORT OF PHILADELPHIA (1852) **II–220a**; II–135b; IV–148a
Coolidge, Calvin II–177 (table); IV–268a; V–394b, 396 (table); VI–93a
Boston police strike I–346b
McNary–Haugen bill IV–219b
vice–presidency I–427b; VII–180 (table)
—*President:*
amnesty I–115b
Bonus Bill V–257b
Bureau of Mines IV–350a
Custer State Park I–312b
elected I–428a
Elk Hills Oil scandal II–431b
Far Eastern policy II–488b
Flag Day III–34a
Geneva Three–Power Naval Conference III–160b–61a, 162a
Havana Conference III–262b
holding companies VII–123a
immigration restriction III–333b
Latin America III–479a–b
Lindbergh's return to America IV–157a
Mexico VI–364a
military bonus I–331b
Nicaragua II–343a; III–199a; IV–401b
nonrecognition policy V–107b
radio regulation VI–15b
Soviet government VI–181a
succeeds to presidency I–427b
Tacna–Arica controversy VI–456a
third–term doctrine VII–53b
Coolidge, Susan (au.) I–335b
Coolidge, William (chem.) III–409a
Coolidge, William D. (chem.) II–417a; III–155b; IV–89a, 153b
Coolidge Auditorium (Library of Congress) IV–148a
Cooper, Anthony Ashley. *See* Shaftesbury, 1st Earl of
Cooper, D. B. (hijacker) III–277b
Cooper, James B. (nav. off.) V–11b
Cooper, James Fenimore (au.) IV–161b–62a, 387a; V–176a, 189b, 262b, 316b
Cooper, John Sherman (pol.) VII–238a
Cooper, Kent (jour.) I–207b
Cooper, Leon N. (phys.) V–100a, 305b
Cooper, Myles (cler., educ.) II–132b; V–86a
Cooper, Peter (mfr., philan.) II–222a; III–224b; IV–175a; V–438b; VI–24b; VII–71a
Cooper, Samuel (off.) I–181a
Cooper, Thomas (law., sci., educ.) I–86b; III–325a; V–7b, 397b
Cooper, William (jur.) I–386a; V–176a
Cooperative apartments I–143b
Cooperative banks. *See* Savings and Loan Associations
Cooperative Extension Service III–84b
Cooperative for American Remittances Everywhere. *See* CARE
Cooperative Forest Management Act (1950) III–76a
Cooperative Marketing Act (1922) I–43a, 451b
See also Capper–Volstead Act
COOPERATIVES, CONSUMERS' II–220a; I–389b; IV–64a; VI–358a
COOPERATIVES, FARMERS' II–221a
Capper–Volstead Act I–451b
dairy industry II–281a, 282a
electrification projects V–46a
Farmers Alliance II–493b
federal agencies I–44a,b
Granger movement III–210a, 211a
irrigation III–477b
threshing VII–55b
wheat VII–286b
Cooperatives, producers' IV–64a; VI–455b
big business I–389b
Knights of Labor support IV–52b
National Labor Union IV–63a
COOPERATIVES, TOBACCO II–221b; IV–41b; V–96a
Cooperative State Experiment Station Service I–46b
Cooperative Wholesale Society II–220b
Cooper–Hewitt Museum (N.Y.C.) III–137b; VI–319b
Cooper Institute (N.Y.C.) III–386b
Cooper–Molera Adobe (Monterey, Calif.) IV–472a
Cooper River III–315a; VI–149b
Charleston I–496a
Cypress Gardens I–498a
navy installation I–497b
Santee Canal VI–216a
South Carolina Canal VI–349a
Cooperstown (N.Y.) I–269b; V–176a
COOPER UNION FOR THE ADVANCEMENT OF SCIENCE AND ART II–222a
Coordinator of Information, Office of V–138a
Coors Brewery VI–7b–8a
Coosa River III–223a; VII–77a
Coote, Richard, Earl of Bellomont (col. gov.) III–152b; V–84b
Beekman Patent I–284b
land grants V–88a
New York oil deposits IV–43b
piracy V–320a
plan of union II–121b
Copano (Tex.) III–304a
Copano Bay VI–144a
COPE. *See* Committee on Political Education
Cope, Edward Drinker (nat.) I–110b; III–27b; IV–232b, 233a; V–196b, 197a; VI–91a
Copeau, Jacques (act., dir.) VII–49b
Copeia (jour.) III–28a; VI–91b
Copeland, E. J. (eng.) II–420b; VI–70a
Copeland, Royal S. (physic., pol.) V–467a
Copeland, Thomas (eng.) VI–409a
Copeland Report (1933) III–74a
Copenhagen (Den.) II–291a
Copland, Aaron (comp.) IV–439a
Coplay (Pa.) I–477b
Copley, John Singleton (paint.) IV–352a; V–185b, 186b, 187a,b, 188b
Copley newspaper chain V–76b
Coppage, O. B. I–9b
COPPAGE* v. *KANSAS (1915) **II–222a**; VII–354b
Copper II–422a; VI–291b–92a
Archaic culture II–386a
coinage II–95a–96a, 95b; IV–360a, 394a, 395b
colonial shops III–413b
Indian use IV–421b
silver mining VI–292a,b
silver work VI–289b
U.S. Geological Survey III–163a
Copper, Lake II–223a
Copper engraving
mapmaking I–462b
COPPERHEADS II–222a; VII–229b
antiwar activities I–195b
Charleston riot I–498b
Civil War manpower II–161a
Corning Letter II–228a
Ex parte Milligan IV–346b
Indiana IV–258b
Knights of the Golden Cir-

COPPERHEADS (cont.)
cle IV–52b
Loyal Publication Societies IV–202a
Nast cartoon IV–454b
National Union Convention IV–472b; VI–336a
newspapers III–105a; V–71b
Northwest conspiracy V–121b
Order of American Knights V–161b
Sons of Liberty VI–339a
Copper Indians III–358a
COPPER INDUSTRY II–223a; V–102a, 103a–b; VI–48b
Alaska I–77a
Anaconda Mining Company I–116a
Arizona I–172a,b
Baltimore IV–261a
Calumet and Hecla Mine I–410b
Chilean nationalization IV–466a
cobalt production III–14a
colonial trade II–119b, 453a
Confederate ordnance II–163a
domestic trade VII–84a
great fortunes III–80a
Lake Superior VI–443a–b
Michigan IV–331a
molybdenum production III–15a
Montana III–270a; IV–403a,b
Navigation Acts V–16a
Nevada V–39b
nickel production III–14a
panic of 1907 V–208a
Puerto Rico V–461b
Sault Sainte Marie Canals VI–219a
smelting VI–316b
South America VI–343b, 345b
Tennessee VII–25b
Copper Kings, War of the IV–403b
Copper Queen Mine II–223a
Copper River III–16b
Coppinger, William I–101b
Coppoc, Barclay II–224a
Coppoc, Edwin II–224a
COPPOC CASE (1859) **II–224a**
Copson, John (insurer) III–427a–b
Copyholds III–18a
COPYRIGHT II–224b; I–333b, 334a
commercial treaties VII–108b
congressional power II–195a, 200a
interstate commerce III–459a
Library of Congress IV–146b, 147a
magazines IV–222a
news VII–152a–b
Patent Office V–226b
Copyright Office II–224b
Coquina (stone) V–243a
Coracles. *See* Bullboats
Coral II–371b; III–163b
Coral Gables (Fla.) I–348b
Coral Sea
World War II IV–83a
Coral Sea (carrier) V–22a
CORAL SEA, BATTLE OF THE (1942) **II–225a**; IV–136b, 336a; V–20b, 26b; VII–337a, 342b
Corbett, Boston IV–154b
Corbett, Harrison and MacMurray VI–299a
Corbett, James J. (pugilist) V–422b
Corbin, Abel Rathbone I–311a
Corcoran, W. W. (philan.) III–152a
Corcoran Gallery II–103a
Cordage II–276a; III–271a
Cordova Valley (Mex.) I–455b; IV–325a
Corduroy roads VI–153a, 156a
Cordwainers' Case. *See* Philadelphia Cordwainers' Case
CORE. *See* Congress of Racial Equality
Corey, Giles (col.) V–400a; VII–310a
Corey, R. B. (chem.) IV–390a
Corfam IV–128b
Corfield v. Coryell (1823) V–420b
Cori, Carl (biochem.) V–100a, 127b
Cori, Gerty (biochem.) V–100a, 127b
Corinna (Maine) IV–227a
Corinne Road. *See* Virginia City–Corrine Road
Corinth (Miss.) II–62b; III–298b; VI–278b
CORINTH, BATTLE OF (1862) **II–225b**; IV–369b, 370a, 374b; V–142b, 389a
Coriolis, G. G. de (eng.) III–233b
Coriolis force (phys.) I–305b; III–233b
Corlett, Charles H. (off.) IV–257b
Corliss, George (ind.) VI–133a, 410a
CORN II–225b; III–51a, 52a, 53a, 54b, 381a; VI–48a
Agricultural Adjustment Administration V–44a
Archaic culture II–386a
bread II–219a
cereal I–486a
Florida III–39a
fodder II–279a, 281a
foreign trade VII–86b
frontier cultivation II–487a
genetic studies I–349b
hog food III–288b
Hopewell culture III–300a
Hopi III–301a
horse III–303b–04a
hybrid I–46a; II–281a
Illinois III–329b
Indiana III–370a,b
Indian cultivation I–11b, 36a, 47b–48b, 157a; III–356b, 366a,b, 367b; IV–235b, 385b, 386a; V–59b, 325b
livestock feed IV–280a
maize beer VII–65b
marketing quotas V–359a
Missouri IV–377a
molasses IV–388a
money II–140b
moonshine IV–407b
Norfolk V–109b
Ohio V–141b
penole V–254a
Peoria V–260b
prices V–404a
processing III–55a
product enrichment V–128b
production II–227a
revolutionary war VI–120a
Richmond VI–136b
soil erosion VI–335a
South I–38a
storage II–429b
Tennessee VII–25b
towboating VII–77b
whiskey II–353b; VII–289b
Woodland Tradition VII–320a
Corn and Bible Commonwealth. *See* Iowa
CORN BELT II–226b; I–486a; II–226a
draft horse III–303b
soil VI–334b
South Dakota VI–349b–50a
CORN BORER, EUROPEAN II–227a
Cornbury, Viscount. *See* Hyde, Edward
Corn clubs III–84b
Corn crib I–48b; III–366b
Corned beef III–51b; IV–280b
Cornell, Ezra (fin., philan.)
Cornell University II–227a
Western Union VII–276b
Cornell, Sarah VII–118a
CORNELL UNIVERSITY II–227a; II–447b, 470b; IV–99b
archives I–169a
Chautauqua movement II–1a
labor history collection III–285a
philosophy V–287b
political science V–349a, 349a
press I–334b
veterinary medicine VII–177a
CORNET (rank) **II–228a**
Corn flakes I–487b, 488a
Corn–hog industry II–281a
Cornhusker State VI–394 (table)
Cornhusking I–284b
peg I–36a
Corning (Iowa) III–327a
Corning, Erastus (bus.) I–107b; II–228a; III–243a
Corning Glass Works III–186a
CORNING LETTER II–228a; I–196a
Cornish, Samuel (cler.) V–75b
Corn Island V–142b
Corn Laws I–119b, 486a; III–43a; IV–310a; V–170a
Corn liquor III–52a
Cornmeal II–226b; III–45a; V–317b
Corn oil II–226b
Corn plant (arch.) I–163a
Cornplanter (Indian) III–386b
Corn pone. *See* Pot Likker and Corn Pone
Corn rights I–400a
Cornstalk (Indian) I–499a; II–381b; III–400b; V–335b; VI–45b
Cornstarch II–226b
Corn sugar and syrup II–226b
Cornut, Jacques–Philippe (physic.) V–325b
Cornwall (Pa.) III–14a
Cornwall, County of (Maine) V–50b, 243b; VII–360a
Cornwallis, Charles, 1st Marquis Cornwallis (off.) III–31b; VI–124b
Battle of Camden I–412a
Battle of Cooch's Bridge II–218a
Battle of Cowpens II–251a
Battle of Edge Hill II–393a
Battle of Eutaw Springs II–465a
Battle of Guilford Courthouse III–232a
Battle of King's Mountain IV–48a; VII–25b
Battle of Monmouth IV–397b
Battle of Princeton V–408a
Battle of Trenton II–321b
Battle of Waxhaw VII–261b
Brandywine Creek I–360a
Cherokee allies II–15a
College of William and Mary VII–300b
Fort Mercer engagement IV–308b
Fort Washington IV–131b
occupation of Philadelphia III–173b
Richmond IV–8b
1781 summer campaign I–194a
southern campaigns VI–351a
Yorktown III–117b; V–19a, 237b; VI–116b; VII–198b, 199b, 360b–61a
Cornwall Mines III–300b
Coronado (Kans.) II–245b
Coronado, Francisco Vásquez de (expl.) *See* Coronado's Expedition

Coronado, Juan Vásquez de (conquistador) V–155a
Coronado Coal Cases (1919–25) VI–103a
CORONADO'S EXPEDITION (1540–42) **II–228a**; I–96b; II–184a–b, 452b; IV–452b
Acoma I–8a
Arizona I–171b
Cibola II–37a, 336a
Colorado II–127b
Grand Canyon III–208b
Great Plains III–220b
Hopi III–301a
horses III–363a
Kansas IV–25a–b
missionaries IV–367a
Mississippi Valley IV–375b
New Mexico V–59b
Oklahoma V–148a
Pawnee V–230a–b
Pecos V–241a
Pueblo Indians III–368b
pueblos V–459b
Quivira III–211a
Rocky Mountains VI–160a
Staked Plain VI–380b
Taos Pueblo VI–461a
Texas VII–36a–b
Zuni VII–372a
Corporal (missile) III–502a
Corporal punishment II–258a, 397a
Corporate colonies II–122b, 266b
Corporation charters, colonial II–118b
Corporation farming I–39b; IV–104a
Corporation for Propagating the Gospel in New England V–410b
CORPORATIONS II–228b; IV–244b, 245a
antimonopoly parties I–133a
antitrust laws I–139b; II–72a
archives III–284a
art collections II–107a
campaign funds II–232b–33a
charters as contracts II–293b
city planning II–46b
Council for New England II–242a
credit II–255a
dairy II–281a
distilling industry II–354a
employer–worker relations IV–63a
excess profits tax II–467a
five–and–ten–cent stores III–33a
foundations III–83a–b
government II–501a; III–201a
holding company III–289b
industrial research III–409a–10b
Industrial Revolution III–411a
"interests" III–443b
interstate commerce laws III–458b
investment companies III–467a
land grants V–444a
licensing IV–148b
manufacturing IV–243a
multinational II–359b–60a; III–66a–b, 348a
newspapers V–76a
New York City V–83b
personnel departments III–407b
persons III–229a
philanthropy V–280b
political contributions V–448b
pressure groups V–400b
private police forces II–463a
prospecting V–437b
public interest V–457a
Publicity Act of 1903 V–448a
public revenue VI–105a,b
ranching VI–44b
regulation III–205a
state licenses V–420b
taxation II–300a; V–48b; VII–6a,b, 7a,b, 8a–b, 9a,b, 9a,b, 10a,b, 11b, 12a,b, 13a,b
T. Roosevelt antitrust policy IV–230a
unionization II–463a
Wealth Tax Act V–46b
Corporations, Bureau of II–135a, 230a; V–448a
Corps of Engineers. *See* Engineers, Corps of
Corpus Christi (Tex.) II–352a; IV–323b; VI–144a
Corpus Christi Bay V–125a
Corpus Christi (Tex.) *Call–Times* (news.) V–78b
Correctional Manpower and Training, Joint Commission on V–417a
Corregidor, Battle of (1942) I–219b, 273b–74a; II–26a; VII–337a
See also Bataan–Corregidor
Correo de Méjico (revenue cutter) VI–209a
CORRICK'S FORD, SKIRMISH AT (1861) **II–231a**
CORRUPT BARGAIN (1824) **II–231a**; IV–469b; VI–466a
CORRUPTION, POLITICAL II–231a; V–346a–47a; VI–142a–b
Black Horse Cavalry I–313b
California I–406a–b
campaign of 1952 I–430a
city government IV–171b
Civil War II–63a–b
colonial smuggling VI–320b
corrupt practices acts II–232b
Crédit Mobilier II–255b
election of senators VI–264a–b
elections VII–209a
Elk Hills Oil scandal II–431b
Foreign Service III–71a
Georgia III–169a
Indiana III–374b
Liberal Republican party IV–141a
local government IV–429b
Lorimer case IV–189a
Louisiana IV–195a
Manhattan Company VII–258b–59a
monopolies I–139b
narcotics trade IV–451b
Nast cartoons IV–454b
New York City V–83b, 87a–b
Nixon resignation V–98b
organized crime II–260a
party machine IV–214a–b
Pine Barren speculations V–315b
Prohibition V–430a
publicity and corrupt–practices laws V–448a
public land sales II–336a
Reconstruction VI–57b
Regulators of North Carolina VI–71b
Sanborn contracts VI–207b
San Francisco VI–209b
Tammany Hall VI–459a
Teapot Dome scandal VII–16b
Truman administration I–430a
Tweed Ring VII–131a
utilities IV–427b–28a
Vare case VII–167b
Washington Benevolent Society VII–249b
Watergate V–78a–b; VII–253b
Yazoo fraud VII–353b
CORRUPT PRACTICES ACTS II–232b; V–42a
Corsair II (attack plane) I–54a, 57a
Corsair F4U (fighter plane) I–55a
Corse, J. M. (off.) I–88b
Corsets II–371b–72a
Corsicana (Tex.) V–271b; VII–40b
Corso, Gregory (poet) IV–165b
Cort (bulk carrier) III–218b
Cort, Henry (inv.) III–472b
Cortelyou, George B. (law., pol.) V–208b
Corte–Real, Gaspar (navig.) IV–247a
Corte–Real, Miguel (expl.) II–341a
Cortes, Hernando (expl.) I–96a, 288b; III–151b, 302a; IV–247b, 326a; VII–370b
capture of Mexico II–184a
cattle II–248b
horses IV–444b
Lower California IV–199b
stock saddle VI–184b
Cortes, Hernando (offi.) III–420a
Cortina, Juan (brigand) I–371a
Cortland, Stephen (off.) III–476b
Cortland County (N.Y.) I–347b
Corvette (auto) I–232a
Corwin, Edward S. (pol. sci.) II–474a; V–348b
Corwin, Thomas (law., pol.) II–65a; V–161a
Gardiner award III–152a
Corwin amendment I–95b
CORWIN–DOBLADO TREATY (1862) **II–233a**
Corydon (Ind.) VII–189a
Coryell, John R. (au.) II–341b
Coryell's Ferry (Pa.) VII–165a
Cos, Martín Perfecto de. *See* Perfecto de Cos, Martín
Cosa, Juan de la (navig.) I–96a; IV–247a
Cosa Nostra II–262b; III–483b
Cosby, William (col. gov.) V–82b, 85a; VII–368a
Coshocton (Ohio) V–145b
COSMETICS II–233b; II–372a
advertising I–19a
government regulation III–54a
hair III–239b
pure food and drug movement V–467a, 468a
Cosmic chemistry II–12b
Cosmic rays III–453b; V–296b, 302b
Cosmographiae Introductio I–97a; IV–247a
Cosmonaut I–209b
Cosmopolitan (period.) I–17b; IV–424b
Costa Rica
Bryan–Chamarro Treaty I–373b
Central American Court of Justice I–483b
Clayton–Bulwer Treaty II–72b
Dominican Republic intervention IV–113a
interoceanic canal I–373b
Tinoco regime V–107b
United Nations Declaration VII–151b
U.S. recognition VI–55a
Costello, Frank (criminal) II–262a
Cost equalization VI–464b–65a
Costilla River VI–210b
COST OF GOVERNMENT II–234a; II–88b
COST OF LIVING II–234b
gold supply III–193a
inflation III–415a
minimum wage IV–353a
post–World War II IV–74a
taxation VII–10a–b

Cost of Living Council V–402a
Cost of Living Index II–234b–36b; V–449b
Costume. *See* Dress
CÔTE DES ALLEMANDS **II–237a**; I–173b
COTENTIN PENINSULA **II–237a**; II–14a; V–110b; VI–193b
Cottage furniture III–139a
COTTON **II–237b**; II–7a; III–126a, 381a; VI–48a
- Agricultural Adjustment Administration V–44a
- Alabama I–71a, 72a
- antebellum South VI–341b
- Arkansas I–173b; IV–104a
- Augusta (Ga.) I–223a
- Bankhead Act I–254a
- Black Belt I–308b
- black–seed II–237b, 240a
- boll weevil I–327b; IV–103a
- California IV–104a
- carpet manufacture I–460b
- Charleston (S.C.) I–497a
- checkoff II–3b
- China trade I–201a,b; V–158a
- Civil War II–65b–66a, 67b–68a, 69a–b, 162a, 165a, 168a–b; VI–405a; VII–94a
- Clayton–Bulwer Treaty II–72b
- coasting trade II–90a
- colonial trade II–119b
- contraband IV–182b
- East India trade I–201b; II–388a–b
- economic importance to South IV–46b
- El Paso II–433b
- exchange II–241a, 469b
- fabric II–266a
- factors and credit II–254b
- farmers and fertilizer II–8a
- farm tenancy I–41a
- Florida III–39a
- foreign investments III–64a
- foreign trade VII–87a,b
- free trade III–113a
- Georgia III–168b, 169a
- harvesting I–35a–b, 36a
- Hopi III–301a
- household manufacture IV–246a
- Indian cultivation I–36a, 48a; III–356b
- internal improvements III–447b
- linsey–woolsey IV–158a
- Louisiana IV–194a
- Lower South IV–200a
- Maine IV–226b–227a
- manufacturing IV–243a,b
- marketing quotas V–359a
- mechanical picker IV–104a
- Memphis IV–302a
- Mississippi IV–104a, 368b, 369b
- Mobile IV–382b
- Nashville IV–453a
- Natchez IV–455a
- New Hampshire V–54a
- New Orleans V–62b
- New Smyrna Colony V–66a
- New South V–67a
- nitrocellulose V–327b
- Norfolk V–110a
- North Carolina V–116a
- Oklahoma V–149a
- packing III–271a
- panic of 1819 V–206b
- plantation system I–38a; V–324b–25a
- Port Royal (S.C.) V–370a
- prices II–493b; V–405a
- Rhode Island textiles VI–133a,b
- sailing packets V–183b–84a
- Saint Louis VI–194b
- Santee Canal VI–216b
- Savannah VI–220b
- sharecropping VI–174b
- slavery I–27b, 34a, 38a; II–184b; VI–304b, 305a,b, 310a, 311a
- soil III–16b; VI–335a
- South American trade VI–343b
- South Carolina VI–347b
- Southwest VI–355b
- Spanish and Mexican land grants IV–93a
- steamboats VI–408b
- steam power VI–409b
- tariff VI–465a–b
- tenant farmers IV–103a
- Tennessee VII–25b, 26a
- Texas I–309b; IV–104a; VII–40a
- textiles VII–42b, 43a,b, 44a, 45a, 83a
- tidewater VII–58a
- Tombigbee Valley VII–70b
- trade I–21a, 37a, 119b, 121b, 245a, 263a
- transport III–235a
- triangular trade VII–119b
- unionization IV–73a
- Vicksburg VII–181b
- weaving IV–187b
- World's Industrial and Cotton Centennial Exposition VII–324b
- World War I VII–331b
- *See also* Cotton Gin

Cotton, John (cler.)
- Antinomian controversy I–133a,b
- Bible commonwealth I–294a
- Court of High Commission III–275a
- Massachusetts Body of Liberties IV–271a
- *Moses His Judicials* IV–415b; V–55a,b
- New England Way V–52a
- *Spiritual Milk for Boston Babes* I–335a
- theocracy VII–51b

Cotton belt II–237b, 238a,b; IV–200a; V–207a
"Cotton Belt" Railroad. *See* Saint Louis–Southwestern Railroad
Cottonclad warships VI–44b
Cotton clubs III–84b
Cotton Control Act. *See* Bankhead Cotton Act
Cotton County (Okla.) VII–238b
"Cotton–eyed Joe" (song) III–19a
Cotton Futures Act (1916) II–470a
COTTON GIN **II–240a**; II–237b; V–325a; VII–43a
- effect on slavery I–27b, 34a, 38a; VI–305b, 311a
- linen industry IV–157b
- Massachusetts IV–266b

Cotton Gin Port (Miss.) III–146b; VII–70b
COTTON KINGDOM **II–241a**; II–237b; III–64a; IV–46a–b; VI–305b
COTTON MONEY **II–241a**; II–267b
Cotton picker I–35b, 36a; II–238b; IV–104a
Cotton plant (arch.) I–163a
Cotton Pool Participation Trust Certificates V–359a
Cottonseed oil IV–457a
Cotton State VI–393 (table)
Cotton States and International Exposition. *See* International Exposition of 1895
Cotton–synthetic blends II–239b
"Cotton was King" II–162a, 237b
Cotton Whigs. *See* Conscience Whigs
Cottonwood (tree) VI–393 (table), 395 (table); VII–114a
Cottonwood Point II–131b
Cottrell, Leonard II–148a
Couch, William L. (pioneer) I–336a; V–148b, 150a
Coudray, Philippe Tronson du (off.) VI–126b, 129a
Coues, Elliot (nat.) I–304b; IV–232b
Coughlin, Charles E. (cler.) II–446a; IV–472b; V–47b; VI–12b, 269a
Coulson Packet Company II–496a
Coulter, Ernest K. I–296a
Coulter, John M. (bot.) II–391b
Council, City. *See* City Councils
COUNCIL BLUFFS (Iowa) **II–241b**; I–170a; III–468a,b
- Calico Railroad I–404b
- caravan traffic I–453a
- Fort Atkinson IV–130a
- Fort Lisa IV–380b
- James gang VII–97b
- Kelly's Industrial Army IV–36a
- Magee–Kearny expedition IV–223b
- railroads VI–37b, 407a
- steamboating VII–271a
- trading post III–353b
- westward movement IV–20b
- Yellowstone River expeditions VII–357b

Council City (Kans.) VII–187b
COUNCIL FOR FOREIGN PLANTATIONS **II–241b**; VI–363b
COUNCIL FOR NEW ENGLAND **II–242a**; I–499b, 500a; II–122b, 123b; V–436b; VII–94b
- Dorchester Company II–364b
- Duke of York's proprietary VII–359a
- Gardiner's Island III–152a
- Gorges' Province of Maine III–200a
- Laconia grant IV–82b
- Long Island IV–185a
- Lygonia grant IV–207b
- Mason title IV–263b
- Massachusetts IV–265a
- Massachusetts Bay Company IV–269b, 270a
- New England Company V–51a
- New Hampshire grant V–53b
- New Plymouth Colony III–132a,b; IV–278b; V–65a, 313b
- Pejebscot Purchase V–242a
- Pemaquid grant V–243b
- Plough Patent IV–207b
- Plymouth Company V–334a
- river towns of Connecticut VI–151b
- royal land grants IV–91b
- Saco Bay settlements VI–184a
- Waldo patent VII–219b

Council for Scientific and Industrial Research I–197a
Council for Trade and Plantations II–241b
Council for Trade of 1660 VI–363b
COUNCIL GROVE (Kans.) **II–242b**; II–248a; VI–216a
Council–manager government II–44a; IV–172a, 427a, 429b
Councilmanic office II–44b
COUNCIL OF APPOINTMENT, NEW YORK **II–243a**
COUNCIL OF CENSORS **II–243a**; VI–390b
Council of Economic Advisers II–480b, 498a; V–137a, 398a; VII–107b
Council of Europe
- human rights III–317a

Council of Federated Organizations II–58b
Council of Foreign Ministers V–215b, 378b
Council of Medical Education and Hospitals (1904) IV–284b

COUNCIL OF NATIONAL DEFENSE II–243a; II–50a; IV–69a; VII–231b, 326a, 327b, 334b
COUNCIL OF REVISION, NEW YORK II–243b; VI–391a
Council of State Governments III–459b–60a; VI–402a,b, 402b
Council of Thirteen for Virginia VII–200a
Council of Trade II–121b
Council of Trent (1545–64) II–170b
Council on African Affairs I–21b–22a
Council on Environmental Quality II–188b, 498a
Council on Foreign Relations V–400b–01a
Council on Industrial Health IV–294a
Council on International Economic Policy II–498a
Council on Policy Studies in Higher Education I–456b
Councils of safety. *See* Committees of Safety
Counsel, right to III–179a–b
 Miranda decision IV–362a
Counterculture
 drugs II–262b
 fashion II–372b
 Zen V–171b
Counterespionage
 Secret Service VI–252a
Counterfeit Detectors II–243b–44a
COUNTERFEITING II–243b
 Bank Note Detectors I–255b
 coinage II–95b
 Confederate postage stamps V–373a
 congressional power to punish II–199b
 federal–state jurisdiction VII–154b
 Secret Service VI–252a; VII–108a
Counterintelligence. *See* Intelligence, Military and Strategic
Counter–Reformation
 Capuchins I–451b
 education II–393a
Counteruniversities II–402b
Countess of Scarborough (ship) I–329b
Country and western music IV–441a,b, 453a
Country Gentlemen (period.) I–45b
Country Joe and the Fish (mus.) IV–441a
Country Life Commission VI–171a–b, 175a
Country Life in America (mag.) II–100a
"Country of the West" VI–219a
COUNTRY STORE II–244a; VI–258a; VII–84a
 Granger movement III–211a
 hardware III–252a
County agents
 agriculture I–41b–42a, 47a
County Election (paint.) V–189b
COUNTY FAIRS II–244b
COUNTY GOVERNMENT II–245a; IV–171a,b
 antebellum South VI–343a
 city government IV–172b
 elections II–411a
 home rule III–294b
 land titles IV–105b
 North Carolina V–116a
 parish V–216a
 patronage V–228a
 political subdivisions V–349b, 350a
 taxation VII–11a
 towns VII–81b
 Washington District VII–250a
 women VII–317b
 zoning VII–370b
County Poor House Act (1824) VI–327b
County school VI–227a, 227a
COUNTY-SEAT WARS II–245b
Coup, William C. (circus owner) II–40b
Coup counting III–364b; VI–224b
Couplers (railroads) VI–27b–28a
Courage To Be IV–165a
Courbet, Gustave (art.) II–103a
***COUREURS DE BOIS* II–246a**; III–119b, 142b; IV–375b
Courier and Enquirer (news.) I–207a
Courier 1B (satellite) II–143a
Cournand, André F. (physiol.) V–100a
Course of Empire (paint.) V–189a
Court, Margaret Smith (athlete) VII–30a
Court Baron of Saint Clement's Manor II–246b
COURTESY OF THE SENATE II–246a; III–152b
Court for China, U.S. II–479b
COURTHOUSE ROCK II–246b
Courthouse towns
 Virginia II–45a
COURT LEET II–246b; III–18a
Court of Appeals, U.S.
 McGuire Act II–483b
 Tax Court decisions II–500b
Court of Chancery IV–23a
Court of Claims, U.S. I–12b, 12b; IV–16b
Court of Customs and Patent Appeals IV–16b
Court of Death (paint.) V–188b
Court of General Sessions IV–22b
Court of International Justice, Permanent. *See* International Court of Justice
Court of Quarter IV–22b
Court of the Exchequer I–12b
Court painting V–186a
Courts
 Administrative Office of U.S. Courts II–501a
 admiralty I–14a
 appointing power II–201b
 arbitration I–152b, 153b
 attorneys II–168a
 civil I–13a
 collective bargaining II–110b–11a
 common law II–141b
 constitutional provisions II–195b, 200a, 202a, 453b
 contested elections II–411b
 criminal I–13a
 declaratory judgments II–309b
 diversity–of–citizenship cases II–460a–b
 divorce II–356b
 federal II–453b
 judicial review IV–12a
 See also Colonial Judiciary; Domestic Relations, Courts of; Juvenile Courts
Courts, Administrative Office of U.S. II–501a
Courts, circuit IV–15b–16a, 19a, 19b; VI–448a
Courts, constitutional IV–16b
Courts, county IV–18b
Courts, criminal
 police interrogations IV–361b
Courts, district IV–16a, 19a, 21b
 admiralty jurisdiction I–14b
Courts, legislative IV–16b
Courts, military III–103a
Courts, municipal IV–18a,b
Courts, prize. *See* Prize Courts
Courts, state IV–17b–18b, 19a
 Kansas IV–26b
Courtship II–485b–86b; IV–256b
Courtship of Miles Standish (poem) IV–162a
COURTS-MARTIAL II–246b
 Articles of War VII–143a
 conscientious objectors II–185b
 Frémont, John C. IV–34a
 Hull, William III–315b
 Mackenzie, Alexander S. VI–338a
 Milligan, Lambdin P. IV–346b
 Porter, Fitz-John V–368b–69a
 Pueblo incident V–460b
 Reno, Marcus IV–168a–b
 Uniform Code VII–144a
 Vallandigham incident VII–164b
Courts of appeals. *See* Appeals, courts of
Courts of Indian offenses. *See* Indian Tribal Courts
COURTS OF THE PLAINS II–247a; VI–161a
Coushatta Bayou VI–65a
Coushatta Massacre (1874) VII–292b
Coutances (Fr.) VII–339b
***COUTUME DE PARIS* II–247a**
Couture, Jean (trader). *See* Couture's Operations
COUTURE'S OPERATIONS II–247b; I–173b; III–143b
Couturier, Henri (paint.) V–185a–b
Couwenhoven, Jacob van. *See* Van Couwenhoven, Jacob
Couzens, James (pol.) IV–332a
COVENANT, CHURCH II–247b; V–391a
Covenanters V–3b; VII–138a
Covenant of grace doctrine I–133a
Covenant of the League of Nations. *See* League of Nations
Covent Garden Theater (London) III–297a
Coventry (Pa.) VII–165a
COVERED WAGON II–248a; IV–424a; V–177b
 Conestogas II–158b
 freighting V–177b
 Great Plains traffic I–453a
 Oregon caravans V–166a
 Oregon Trail V–168b
 westward movement VII–283b
Coverly, Nathaniel (pub.) I–494a
Covert, John (art.) II–104b
Covington (Ky.) III–88a
Covode, John (pol.) II–140a, 248b
COVODE INVESTIGATION (1860) **II–248b**
Cowan, John (prospector) III–270a
Cowans Ford Dam III–322a
COWBOYS II–248b; I–38b, 471b; V–160a; VI–364b
 broncos I–369a
 cattle drives VII–96a
 Colt six-shooter II–131a
 cow towns II–251b–52a
 Dodge City II–358b
 Fence War III–10a
 fiddle III–19a
 horses III–303a
 long drives IV–184a
 ranch VI–45a
 roundups VI–161a–b
 saddle VI–184b
 stampedes VI–382b
 Texas I–473b
 Wild West Show VII–298b
 Wyoming VII–346a

COWBOYS AND SKINNERS II–249b
COWBOY SONGS II–249b; VI–161b, 382b
"Cowboy State" VII–346a
Cow camps V–160a
Cowcatchers IV–175b
COW COUNTRY II–250b; V–160a; VI–355b
COW CUSTOM II–251a; V–160a; VI–161a
Cowell, Henry (comp.) IV–439a
Cowell, Joseph L. (act.) V–336a
Cowes (Eng.) IV–260b; VII–349a
Cowhides
  California currency I–405b, 409b
Cow horse I–369a; III–303a–b
Cowles, A. H. (eng.) II–7b, 422a,b
Cowles, E. H. (eng.) II–7b, 422a,b
Cowles, Gardner (ed.) V–73b
Cowles, Henry C. (bot.) II–391b
Cowles newspaper chain V–76b
Cowley, Malcolm (au.) IV–190a
COWPENS, BATTLE OF (1781) **II–251a**; VI–124b, 126b, 351b
Cowper, William (surg.) IV–231a
Cowperthwaite and Sons III–422b
Cowpox III–293b; IV–275a; VI–315b
COWPUNCHER II–251b; I–494a
COW TOWNS II–251b
  Abilene I–1b; II–248b
  Dodge City II–358b
  Great Plains III–221b
  Ogallala V–139a
  Wichita VII–294a
Cox, Allyn (paint.) V–191b
Cox, Archibald (law.) III–344b, 465b; V–78a; VII–255b
Cox, Edward F. (law.) V–98b
Cox, George B. (pol.) I–343a
Cox, Harvey (theol.) VI–83a
Cox, Herald R. (virol.) V–341a
COX, INSURRECTION OF (1798) **II–252a**
Cox, Jacob Dolson (off.) VI–336a
Cox, James M. (pol.) I–427b
Cox, Jesse (Socialist) VI–324b
Cox, Kenyon (paint.) V–191a
Cox, Tricia Nixon V–98b
Cox, Zachariah (land speculator) II–252a; IV–435b
Cox Committee III–83b
Coxe, Daniel (landowner, pol.) III–268a
  Carolana colony I–457b
  plan of union II–122a
  West Jersey VII–278b
Coxe, Tench (pol. econ.) I–482b; II–5b; V–199a
Coxe's Plan (1722) II–122a
Coxey, Jacob (bus., pol.). *See* Coxey's Army
COXEY'S ARMY II–252a; IV–36a, 67a; V–208a, 265b; VII–246b
Coyle Electronic voting machine VI–211a
Coyle v. *Smith* (1911) II–443b
COYOTE II–252b; III–150a, 386b; IV–233a; VII–357b
  Indian religion III–222b
  sign language VI–286b
Coyote State VI–395 (table)
Cozzens, A. M. II–103b
Cozzens, James Gould (au.) IV–164b
CPEHS. *See* Consumer Protection and Environmental Health Service
CPI. *See* Consumer Price Index
CPPA. *See* Conference for Progressive Political Action
CPUSA. *See* Communist Party, United States of America
Crabb, Henry A. (filibuster) III–23b
CRAB ORCHARD (Ky.) **II–253a**; II–272a; VII–296a
Crabs III–51a
"CRACKER LINE" II–253a
"CRACKERS" II–253a
Craddock, Charles Egbert. *See* Murfree, Mary Nouailles
Cradle (tool) I–34b
"Cradle of Liberty" II–487b
"Cradle of the Confederacy." *See* Montgomery (Ala.)
Cradle Will Rock (opera) IV–438b
Craftsman Magazine III–136a
Craftsmen
  Freemasons III–108b
  furniture III–138a
  marks I–359b, 360a
Craft unions. *See* Unions, Craft
Craig, Andrew I–386a; V–176a
Craig, Charles F. (med. off.) IV–291b
Craig, Fort (N.Mex.) VI–144a; VII–165b
Craig, Hiram II–253b
Craig, Lewis (cler.) IV–338b
Craig, Thomas E. (nav. off.) V–260b
Craig County (Va.) III–469b
Craigie, Andrew (fin.) III–291b; VI–239a
Craigie and Hulbert (pub.) II–340b
Craig's Mountain II–74b
Craig v. *Harney* (1947) V–78b
CRAIG* v. *STATE OF MISSOURI (1830) **II–253b**; I–365a
Cramer, Seed, and Hammer Company V–291b
Cramer, Zadok (pub.) V–17a
Crampton's Gap, Battle of. *See* South Mountain, Battle of
Cramp v. *Board of Public Instruction of Orange County, Florida* (1961) VII–15b
Cramton, Louis C. (hist.) VII–357a
Cranberries I–447a; III–51a, 129a
Cranch, Christopher Pearse (au.) I–335a
Cranch, Richard, and Company VI–372b
Crandall, J. B. (bus.) V–317b
Crandall, Lucien S. (inv.) VII–136a
Crane (bird) III–150a
Crane, Charles R. (ind., dipl.) IV–251a; VI–163b
Crane, Hart (poet) IV–164a, 189b
Crane, H. R. (phys.) V–300b
Crane, Ichabod (lit. char.) IV–161b; VI–312b
Crane, Stephen (au.) IV–163b; V–41b
Crane, William (nav. off.) V–19b
CRANEY ISLAND II–253b
Craps (gambling) III–149b
Crash of 1929. *See* Panic of 1929
CRATER (1864) **II–253b**; IV–339b; V–265a; VI–138a; VII–197b
Crater Lake V–165b
Crater Lake National Park V–218 (table), 445b; VI–156a
Craters of the Moon National Monument V–217b
Craven, William, Earl of Craven I–458a
Crawcour brothers (dent.) II–330a
Crawford, Cheryl (dir.) VII–50a
Crawford, Fort (Colo.) VII–137b
CRAWFORD, FORT (Wis.) **II–253b**; III–90a; IV–355b; V–388a, 388b
Crawford, John (physic.) I–240b
Crawford, Martin J. (law.) II–161a
Crawford, Thomas (sculp.) I–451a; VI–243a, 246a
Crawford, William (off.) III–272b, 400b; V–152b; VII–157b
Crawford, William H. (states.)
  A.B. plot I–3a
  campaign of 1816 I–418a
  campaign of 1824 I–418b, 475a; V–101b
Crawford County (Ohio) VII–157b
Crawford County (Pa.) V–407a
Crawford County (Wis.) V–388a
Crazy Horse (Indian) I–313a; II–283a; III–17b; VI–157b, 297a, 313a, 350a
CRAZY SNAKE REBELLION (1900–01) **II–254a**
Crazy Woman Creek VI–242a
Cream II–282b
Creameries II–280b, 281b
Cream-of-tarter V–466a
Creamware (pottery) III–183b
CREDIT II–254a
  agencies I–376b
  agricultural I–44a–45a
  Bank of the United States I–255a
  bills of exchange II–468a
  British investment in U.S. III–63a–64b
  cards I–102b, 258a; II–74a; III–423b
  colonial I–245a
  Federal Reserve System III–5b
  fiat money IV–392b
  fur trade III–403a
  gold standard III–193b
  government I–500b
  inflation II–209b
  installment I–227b; III–422b
  interest laws III–443a
  Intermediate Credit Banks III–447a
  land sales IV–90b
  mercantile agencies IV–307b
  Neutrality Acts of 1935–37 V–38a
  New Era V–52a
  open-market operations V–159b
  panic of 1785 V–206a
  panic of 1819 V–206a
  panic of 1837 V–206b, 206b
  panic of 1873 V–207a
  panic of 1907 V–208a–b
  panic of 1929 V–210a
  public lands V–444a,b, 452b; VI–75a
  Pujo Committee investigation V–462b
  sharecroppers VI–268b
Credit Control Act (1969) III–443b
CREDIT ISLAND, BATTLE OF (1814) **II–255b**
CRÉDIT MOBILIER OF AMERICA II–255b; II–231b; V–346a; VI–198b; VII–147b
CREDIT OF THE NATION II–256a; III–244b, 245a, 493b
Credit unions II–220b
Cree (Indians) II–30b; III–360b, 365a, 366b
  half-breeds III–242b
  Jesuit missions III–499b, 500a
  language I–441a

Creede (Colo.) I–336b; VI–213b
Creek (Indians) II–52a; III–366a, 367a, 396b
Apalache massacre I–143a
architecture I–166b
Augusta Congress I–223a
Battle of Burnt Corn I–387b
Bowle's expedition I–355b
Bowles's expedition VI–367a
burial III–376a
Cahaba Old Towns I–402a
Charleston (S.C.) I–496b
Cherokee Wars II–15a
Chickasaw–Creek War II–22a
Civil War III–400a
confederation III–391a
Crazy Snake Rebellion II–254a
curing III–385b
Dawes Commission II–295b
De Soto expedition II–336b
enslavement III–401a–b
Forbes Purchase III–59a
Galphin claim III–148a
Georgia III–168b
Georgia Compact VII–299b
Great Trading and War Path III–223a
Hillabee Towns III–278a
land cessions I–223a, 308b
McGillivray incident IV–213a
mounds IV–421a
Natchez relations IV–455b
Panton, Leslie and Company V–211a
Pensacola Congress V–254b
political organization III–365b
religion III–392a, 393a
removal III–393b, 394a
revolutionary war III–170a, 400b–01a
Seminole VI–259b, 260a
Seminole Wars VI–260b
Spanish trade VI–366b
state of Sequoyah VI–262b
status ranking I–288a
Tennessee VII–25a
trails II–33a
Treaties of Indian Springs III–401b
Treaty of Fort Jackson III–383b
Treaty of New York City III–383a
Treaty of Nogales V–100b
Union Army III–375b–76a
War of Jenkins' Ear III–498a
western lands VI–356b
Yamasee War VII–352a
See also Civilized Tribes, Five
Creekology–trendology V–271a
CREEK WAR (1813–14) **II–256b**; VII–236a, 239a
backwoodsmen I–240a
Battle of Autossee I–232a
Battle of Horsehoe Bend II–333a
Battle of Horseshoe Bend II–333a; III–305b
Fort Mims massacre IV–347b
Hillabee Towns III–278a
Natchez campaign IV–456a
Treaty of Fort Jackson VII–77a
Creel, George (jour.) I–407b, 481a; II–139b; V–74a; VII–332b
Creel Committee. *See* Committee on Public Information
Creeley, Robert (poet) IV–165b
Creole Jazz Band IV–440a
CREOLES II–257a
music IV–438a
New Orleans V–62a,b
***CREOLE* SLAVE CASE** (1841) **II–257b**; I–28a, 114b
Creole State VI–394 (table)
Creosote IV–378b
Cresap, Michael (off.) II–257b; IV–179a
Cresap, Thomas (trader) IV–398b; V–378b; VII–244b
CRESAP'S WAR (1774) **II–257b**
Crescent City (Calif.) II–347b
Crescit eundo (motto) VI–394 (table)
Crete
World War II III–187a
Cretinism IV–305b
Creusot (Fr.)
steel plates I–179a
CRÈVECOEUR, FORT (Ill.) **II–257b**; III–120a, 329a; IV–109b; V–260b
Crèvecoeur, M. G. J. de (writ.) III–122a; VI–114b–15a
Crèvecoueur, M. G. J. de (writ.) IV–79a,b
Cribb, Tom (boxer) V–422b
"Cribs" (prostitution) II–260a
Crick, Francis H. C. (biol.) I–304a; II–13a, 357b, 358a; III–158a; IV–390a–b, 391a
Cricket (mag.) IV–223a–b
Crim, William H. (physic.) II–100a
CRIME II–257b; VII–206a
aerial hijacking III–276b
Afro–Americans I–26a
bootlegging I–339a
bossism I–343a
Chicago II–18a
cocaine II–374a
colonial punishments V–464b
courts IV–18b
deportation of criminals II–333a
depression of 1873–78 V–207b
dime novel II–341b
education II–402a
electronic surveillance II–427b
famous trials VII–118a–b
Federal Bureau of Investigation II–503b
federal offenses III–3a
gambling III–149b
gun control IV–470a
horse stealing III–305b
hue and cry III–314a
immunity bath III–343a
Indians and liquor III–399a
"Jukes" Family IV–20a
Justice Department IV–21b
justice of the peace IV–22b
"Kallikak" Family IV–24b
kidnapping of free blacks IV–45a
Lindbergh kidnapping IV–156b
Loomis gang IV–187b
Mafia incident IV–221a
McNamara case IV–218b
Miranda decision IV–362a
narcotics trade IV–449b
New York City V–83b–84a
Night Riders V–96a
North Dakota V–118a
Northfield bank robbery V–119b
Plummer gang V–333a
prisons V–415a
Prohibition II–407a
San Francisco VI–209b
Secret Service VI–252a
sexual crimes VI–265b–66a
stagecoach robberies VI–379b
train robberies VII–97a
vigilantes VII–187a
violence VII–191b–92a
Webster–Parkman murder case VII–266a
Wickersham Commission VII–294b
CRIME, ORGANIZED II–259b
crime commissions II–263a
electronic surveillance II–427b
Italian–Americans III–483b
Prohibition V–430a
prostitution V–438a
Crime, Society for the Prevention of II–263b
Crimea V–23a
Crime against Kansas. *See* Brooks–Sumner Affair
"Crime Against Kansas" speech I–371a; IV–31a
Crime and Delinquency (jour.) II–263b
Crime and Delinquency, National Council on II–263b
Crimean War (1854–56) II–431a; III–97a; VII–225b
Declaration of Paris V–214a
ironclad warships IV–396a
photography V–293a
CRIME COMMISSIONS II–263a
Lexow Committee IV–137b
Crime Control Act (1968) IV–362a
Crime families II–262a–b
Crime in America (report) II–263b
Crime Information Center, National II–503b
CRIME OF 1873 II–264a; I–301b, 318b; III–110a–b, 188b, 192b, 251b; IV–154a, 395a; VII–92b
Criminal Justice Standards and Goals, National Advisory Commission on V–417b, 418a
Criminal law I–13a
jury trial IV–21a
juveniles IV–23a, 24a
Criminal procedure
murder accusation III–320a
Criminal trials
constitutional provisions II–204a
due process of law II–378b
Crinoline (dress) II–371b
Cripple Creek (Colo.) IV–354a
CRIPPLE CREEK MINING BOOM II–264a; I–336b; II–128b; III–191b; V–311a, 437a
CRIPPLE CREEK STRIKES (1893–94, 1903–04) **II–264b**; II–332a; VII–272b
Crippled
education III–248a
Crisis (news.) V–76a
CRISIS (pamphlet) **II–264b**; IV–161b; V–198b; VII–61b, 82a
Crisp, Charles F. (law.) II–176 (table)
Criticism and Fiction IV–163b
Crittenden, George B. (off.) IV–347a
Crittenden, John J. (law., pol.) IV–43a; VII–265b
Constitutional Union party II–191a
See also Crittenden Compromise; Crittenden Resolution VI–251a
Crittenden, T. L. (off.) IV–434b
CRITTENDEN COMPROMISE (1860–61) **II–264b**; I–341b; II–139a, 149b; VI–11a, 251a

Crittenden–Johnson resolutions (1861) VI–55b
CRITTENDEN RESOLUTION (1861) **II–265a**; II–149b; VI–55b
Croatan (Indians). *See* Lumbee
Croatians III–339a
Croatoan Island VI–43a
Crocker, Charles (fin.) I–406a; III–79b
Crocker, E. B. II–103b
Crocker, Marcellus M. (off.) VI–48b
Crocker Land Expedition (1913–17) V–337a
Crockery V–184a, 379b
Crockett, David (frontiersman) III–48b; VI–299b–300a, 458b
Alamo I–74b; VII–37b
bear hunting I–280b
cattle drive I–473a
Crockett, Fort Davy (Utah) VII–161b
Crocodilians, Lizards, and Snakes of North America VI–91a
Crofton, Walter VI–68a
Croghan, George (Indian agent) I–278a, 386a; III–403b
Forks of the Ohio V–143a
Fort Stephenson VI–412a
land speculation IV–98b
Logstown Treaty IV–181b
Otsego (N.Y.) lands V–176a
Pittsburgh Committee of Safety V–322b
"suffering traders" VI–430a
Treaty of Easton II–389a
Treaty of Fort de Chartres I–501b
See also Croghan's Expeditions to Illinois
CROGHAN'S EXPEDITIONS TO ILLINOIS (1765–66) **II–265a**; III–330b; VI–285a
Croghansville (Ohio) VI–208b
Croker, Richard (pol.) I–343a; IV–138a; V–83b; VI–460a; VII–295a
Crol, Sebastian (off.) V–60b
Croll, James (meteor.) III–166b
Cromberger, Juan (print.) V–410a, 411a
Crompton, William (inv., mfr.). *See* Crompton Loom
CROMPTON LOOM II–266a; IV–187b; VII–43a,b
Cromwell, Oliver (states.) I–361a
Colonial Board II–241b
colonial policy II–122b–23a
Massachusetts Puritans IV–265a–b
New Albion V–333a
New Netherlands V–55b
western design VII–270b
"Cronyism" IV–51a
Crook, George (off.)
Apache Wars I–142b
Sioux Council VI–295b
Sioux Wars I–313b; VI–242a, 297a, 313a
Crookes, William (chem., phys.) III–17a
Crooks, Ramsay (fur trader) I–105b; III–143a, 403b; VI–357b
Crop insurance II–501a
Crop Insurance Corporation, Federal V–359a
Cropland Adjustment program I–43a
Crop lien II–69b; IV–103a
Crop-reduction program IV–103b
Crop rotation I–37a; VI–334a
Cropsey, Jaspar F. (paint.) II–103a–b; V–190b
Crop speculation I–38b
Cros, Charles (inv.) V–289b
Crosby, Bing (sing.) IV–442a
Crosley refrigerator VI–69b
Cross and Crown (period.) II–362b
Cross-country skiing VI–298a,b
"Crossing-place on the Muskingum" III–223b
CROSS KEYS, BATTLE OF (1862) **II–266a**; III–487b; V–369a–b
"CROSS OF GOLD" SPEECH (1896) **II–266a**; I–425a; III–111a
Cross Roads Africa I–22a
"Crossroads of America" VI–393 (table)
Croswell, Edwin (pol.) I–107b
Croswell, Harry (pub.). *See* Croswell Libel Suit
CROSWELL LIBEL SUIT II–266a; IV–139b
Croton (N.Y.) VI–173b
Croton Aqueduct (N.Y.C.) V–83a; VII–128a, 259a
Croton River VII–259a
Crow (Indians) III–227a, 363b, 365a, 396b; IV–235b, 236a
fur trade IV–242a
Jesuit missions III–500a,b
relation with Blackfoot I–311a
scouts VI–242a
South Pass I–201a
war with Dakota II–283a
Wyoming VII–345b
Crow (Indian chief) II–379b; IV–403a
Crow, Hugh (slaver) VI–310b
Crow, Walter J. (settler) IV–444a
CROWBAR LAW OF OHIO (1819) **II–266b**
Crowder, Enoch H. (off.) II–269a
Crowder Commission I–454b
Crowell, Benedict (offi.) VII–230a
Crowell, Henry Parsons (bus.) I–487a, 488a
Crowell, John (Indian agent) III–394a
Crowell, Thomas Y. (pub.) I–334b
Crowell Publishing Company I–17b
"Crowing rooster" (emblem) II–437b
Crown Heights (N.Y.) I–282b
Crowninshield, Edward A. (book collector) II–108b
CROWN LANDS II–266b; IV–101b, 105a
CROWN POINT (N.Y.) **II–266b**; V–85a,b; VII–171a
Franciscans III–94b
French and Indian War I–323a; II–126b, 405b; III–115b, 116a,b; VI–162b, 190a
revolutionary war I–435b; IV–86b; VII–56b, 164a
See also Saint Frédéric, Fort
CROWN POINT TO NO. 4 (1759) **II–267a**; VII–171a
Crowns (dent.) II–331a
Crow Wing, Battle of. *See* Sioux–Chippewa Wars
Crow Wing River IV–356a; VI–144b
Croyable (schooner) V–15a–b
Crozat, Antoine (fin.). *See* Crozat Grant
CROZAT GRANT II–267b; II–91b; IV–192b, 370b; V–173a; VI–189b
Crozier, William B. (off.) V–163b
CRP. *See* Committee for the Reelection of the President
Crucible, The (play) VII–50b
Cruel and unusual punishment. *See* Punishment, Cruel and Unusual
Cruelty, physical
divorce laws II–356b
Cruisers I–54b, 55b; V–25a,b, 26a; VII–241a,b, 242a–43a,b, 341b, 343b
Confederate II–65a
London Naval Treaty II–461a
naval competition V–10a,b
Washington Naval Conference VII–250b
World World War II II–387b
See also Warships
Cruising Club of America VII–349a
Crump, Edward H. (pol.) I–343a; IV–214a
Crusader (fighter plane) I–57a
Cruse, Thomas (miner) III–270a
Cruyshautem Ridge (Belg.) VII–366b
Crystal Dam II–130a
Crystallography II–12a; IV–349a, 389a–b; V–267b–68a
DNA II–358a
See also Physics, Solid-State
Crystal Palace Exhibition, London (1851) III–412a, 442a; IV–244a, 272b
Crystal Palace Exposition (1853). *See* Exhibition of the Industry of All Nations
Crystal sets IV–271b
C.S.A. COTTON II–267b
C-T-R Company I–397a
Cub (light plane) I–52b
CUBA II–267b; III–70a; IV–111a,b, 112a, 112b–13b, 115b; VI–360a–b, 429a
aerial hijacking III–276b, 277a–b
Bay of Pigs invasion I–278b, 454b; III–463a,b
Black Warrior affair I–317b
blockade (1962) II–270b–71a
Canadian trade I–439b
cession to Spain III–38b
confiscation of U.S. property II–169a; IV–466a
dollar diplomacy II–359b
earthquake II–385a
enemy trading VII–94a
exiles III–199b; V–342b
filibustering III–352a
Florida Straits III–41b
fruit III–52b
Good Neighbor policy III–199a,b
Guantánamo Bay III–230b
guerrillas III–231a
Gulf of Mexico IV–326a,b
horse III–302a
hurricanes II–352a; III–319a
immigration to U.S. III–337b, 341b
Isle of Pines III–479a
López expeditions III–23a; IV–188a
"manifest destiny" IV–239a
marine research III–29a
Mexican relations IV–329a
Neely v. *Henkel* V–32a
piracy IV–416a; V–320b
Platt Amendment V–329b
Ponce de León expeditions V–356a
Port Royal attack VI–348b
proposed purchase by U.S. V–175a
revolution I–89b; II–359b; V–171a, 280b
revolutionary war VII–199a
silver minting by U.S. I–262b
slave trade VI–309a, 312a; VII–37a

Spanish–American War
I–185b, 454a; II–436a; III–150b, 347a,b; IV–227a, 252b, 314b; VI–165b, 213b–14a, 216b, 361a, 363a
Teller Amendment VII–22a
treaties VII–112a
Treaty of Paris (1763) V–214b
Treaty of Paris (1898) V–215a
Trent affair VII–115b
United Nations Declaration VII–151b
U.S. Caribbean policy I–453b
U.S. intervention II–315b; III–462b–63a; IV–402a; V–105b
U.S. protectorate II–475a; III–68b
U.S. recognition VI–55a,b
Virginius affair VII–204a
Watlings Island (B.W.I.) VII–261a
Wells, Fargo VII–267a
yellow fever I–241b; IV–298a; VII–355b
yellow journalism V–71b; VII–356a
Cuba (N.Y.) IV–43b, 44a
Cuba, Treaty on Relations With (1903) VII–112a
CUBAN MISSILE CRISIS (1962) **II–270a**; I–61b, 65b, 108b, 180a, 292a, 321b, 454b; II–316a; III–70a, 463a,b; IV–113a, 253a; V–11a, 53a, 74a; VI–180a, 416b, 439b; VII–205a
aerial photography V–293b
cold war II–98b
diplomacy II–343a
Nuclear Test Ban Treaty V–125a
presidential war powers VII–237a
radio communication V–22b
U.S. missile development IV–363a
Cuban refugees
drug distribution II–262b
Cub Scouts I–108b, 357b
Cuckoo Tavern IV–8b
Cucumber III–151a
Cuffe, Paul (seaman) I–101a, 315b; II–127a
Cugnot, Nicholas J. (inv.) IV–419a
Culbertson, Alexander (fur trader) III–77b; IV–403a
Culebra River VI–210b
Culiacán (Mex.) IV–452b
Cullen, Countee (au.) I–30a; IV–166b
Cullen, Michael (bus.) VI–258a
Cullom, Shelby M. (pol.). *See* Cullom Committee
CULLOM COMMITTEE **II–271a**; VI–23b
Culpeper (Va.) I–476b
Culpeper, John (surv.) II–271b
Culpeper, Thomas Lord II–481a–b
CULPEPER'S REBELLION (1677) **II–271a**
Culp's Hill (Pa.) III–175b, 176a
Cultigens II–386a
Cultivator (mach.) I–34b, 38b
Cult of the Dreamers V–4a
Cumberland (Md.) III–448a; IV–470b; V–144a
Braddock's Road I–358b
cement I–477b
Chesapeake and Ohio Canal I–40a; II–15b
Cumberland Road II–272a
Fort Cumberland II–271b
pack trains V–184a
Cumberland (warship) IV–396b
CUMBERLAND, ARMY OF THE II–271b; IV–54a, 434b; V–142b
Cumberland, Department of the V–142b
Cumberland, Duke of (William Augustus) II–272a; IV–201b
CUMBERLAND, FORT (Md.) **II–271b**; I–358a; III–58b, 115b
Cumberland and Oxford Canal I–442b
Cumberland–Appalachian plateau IV–39b
Cumberland Compact. *See* Cumberland Settlements
CUMBERLAND GAP **II–272a**; I–88b, 376a; II–253a, 477a; IV–201b; V–224b; VII–25a, 100a
Civil War II–363a; V–263b
exploration IV–39b
Great Trading and War Path III–223a–b
Great Warriors Path III–387b; VII–238b
Kentucky settlement I–324b, 337a
Powell's Valley V–384b
Scioto Trail IV–330a; VI–239b
Vandalia Colony VII–166b
Westsylvania VII–281a
Wilderness Road II–273a; VII–296a
Cumberland Head (N.Y.) IV–87a, 212a; V–331a
Cumberland Mountains II–248a; IV–43a, 201b; VII–25a, 166b
CUMBERLAND PRESBYTERIAN CHURCH **II–272b**; II–39b; III–221b; V–392b
CUMBERLAND RIVER **II–272b**; IV–201b; VI–149–50a; VII–25a
Civil War IV–410a; VI–150b, 278a
dams VII–26a
Fort Donelson II–363a
fur trade III–143b
Indian claims II–23a
long hunters IV–185a
Miami Trail IV–330a
military tract IV–344b
settlement II–274a; IV–452b
Shawnee VI–270b
steamboating VI–406b
Transylvania Company VII–103a
Treaty of Hopewell III–383a
Treaty of Sycamore Shoals III–382b; VI–455b
CUMBERLAND ROAD **II–273a**; I–39b, 358b; III–223b, 448a–b, 449a; VI–153a–b, 156a; VII–100a
Allegheny wagoners VII–216a
cattle VI–414a
construction II–449b
domestic trade VII–83a
Great Meadows III–219a
National Road IV–470a
Potomac River V–378b
Southwest Point VI–357b
Wheeling VII–287b
CUMBERLAND ROAD, TENNESSEE **II–273b**
Cumberland Road Bill. *See* Toll Gate Bill
CUMBERLAND SETTLEMENTS **II–273b**; I–232b; VI–149b; VII–103a, 253b
Carlisle I–455a
Henderson Land Company III–271b
Indian relations II–23a
Nashville VI–356a
Cumberland Synod II–272b
Cumberland Valley IV–39b
Civil War V–248a
Indian migration VI–270b
settlement VI–356a
Cumberland Valley Railroad V–462b
Cuming, Thomas B. (gov.) V–31a
Cummings, E. E. (poet) IV–164b, 189b
Cummings, Homer S. (law., pol.) V–43b
Cummings, Jonathan I–15b
Cummings, Nathan II–106b
CUMMINGS v. MISSOURI (1866) **II–274a**; IV–202b; VII–35a
Cummins, Albert B. (pol.) IV–169a; V–427b; VII–99a
Cunard, Samuel (shipowner) IV–310a
Cunard Building (N.Y.C.) V–191b
Cunard White Star Line IV–205a
Cunningham, Ann Pamela IV–423a
Cunningham, Merce (chor.) II–289b, 290a
Cunningham, Sumner A. (ed.) VII–150a
Cunningham, Winfield Scott (nav. off.) VII–218b
Cupboards III–134a
Cupeño (Indians) III–363a
Cupro–nickel coins II–95b
Curaçao
colonial trade VII–93b
Indian captives II–462b
logwood trade IV–181b
marine landing IV–251b
Naval War With France V–15a
Curare III–381a, 385b; VII–65b
CURFEW BELL **II–274b**
Curfew laws II–274b
"Curfew Must Not Ring To–Night" IV–160b
Curie, Marie (chem.) V–99b
Curing
meat–packing IV–280a
Curler, Jacob van (offi.) III–309a
Curley, James M. (pol.) I–343a; V–345a, 347a
"Curly Boss." *See* Ruef, Abraham
Currency III–204a; IV–392a, 393a–95b
Greenback movement III–224a
International Monetary Fund III–457a
under Articles of Confederation II–167a
See also Coinage; Money
Currency, Check. *See* Check Currency
Currency, Comptroller of the II–74a
CURRENCY, CONTINENTAL II–274b; V–123b–24a; VI–117b, 120a,b
bills of credit III–414b
depreciation II–212a
legal tender IV–132a
pine tree shilling V–316a
prices V–404a–b
Public Credit Act V–443b
revenue VII–3b–4a
value II–167a
CURRENCY, RED DOG AND BLUE PUP **II–275a**
Currency Act (1764) VI–110b
Current (elec.) II–39a
Curricle VII–99b
Currie, Lauchlin (offi.) VI–428b
Currie, William (physic.) II–390b; VII–205b
Currier, Edward (lithographer) II–275a
Currier, Nathaniel (lithographer) II–275a
Currier Gallery of Art (Manchester, N.H.) III–137b
CURRIER & IVES **II–275a**; I–37b; V–413b
Currituck Sound I–83a
Curry, Jabez L. M. (educ.) V–231b
Curry, John Steuart (art.) IV–26b; V–192b

Cursillo movement I–470a
Curti, Merle E. (hist.) III–283a
Curtice, Cooper VII–177a
Curtis, Benjamin R. (jur.) II–135b, 220a; V–353b; VI–445b
Curtis, Charles (pol.) IV–26b; VII–180 (table)
campaign of 1928 I–428a
campaign of 1932 I–428b
Curtis, Charles Gordon (inv.) VI–410a; VII–129b
Curtis, Cyrus H. K. (pub.) I–17b, 19a
Curtis, Edward (med. off.) IV–291a
Curtis, George W. (man of letters) V–161b
Curtis, G. G. (inv.) II–415b
Curtis, Joel (inv.) III–442b
Curtis, Samuel R. (off.) V–238b, 402b–03a; VII–280b, 368a
Curtis Act (1924) I–106b
Curtis flying boat V–30a
Curtis Publishing Company I–18a; IV–255a
Curtiss, Glenn H. (av.) I–51a, 233a–b, 235b; II–343b
Curtiss Aeroplane and Motor Company I–235b, 236a
Curtiss Aircraft Company II–344b–45a
Curtis's Botanical Magazine VI–235a
Curtiss–Wright Aircraft Company II–346a
Curtiss–Wright Corporation I–236a
Curwin, George (off.) V–185a
Curzon Line VII–351b
Cushenoc (Maine) IV–37a,b
See also Augusta
Cushing (Okla.) VI–356b
Cushing (torpedo boat) VII–76a–b, 243a
Cushing, Caleb (dipl.) I–125a; II–27a; IV–99b; V–166b
Cushing, Harvey (surg.) IV–3a; V–307a
Cushing, Thomas (pol.) VII–142b
Cushing, William (jur.) VI–445a
Cushing, William B. (nav. off.) I–83a; V–424a
CUSHING'S TREATY (1844) **II–275a**; II–27a, 479b; IV–34b; V–158a
Cushman, J. A. (paleon.) V–197a
Cushman, Robert (col.) V–313a
Custer (S.Dak.) I–312b
Custer, George Armstrong (off.) IV–45a; VI–215b, 242a
Battle at Toms Brook VII–71a
Battle at Trevilian Station VII–117a
Battle of Little Bighorn II–283b, 496a; III–127a; IV–168a; VI–297a
Black Hills War I–312b, 313a; VII–272b
Cheyenne massacre VII–190b
Cheyenne wars II–17a
Fort Abraham Lincoln I–3b
Fort Hays III–266b
Fort Sill VI–287b
Mosby's Rangers IV–415b
Soldiers and Sailors convention VI–336a
Washita Campaign VI–241b, 443b; VII–252b
Custer Battlefield National Cemetery IV–168b
Custer Battlefield National Monument V–217a,b
Custer State Park I–312b
Custis, George Washington Parke (playwright) I–175b; II–244b; VII–47b, 154b
Custis, Mary Ann I–175b
Custis–Lee Mansion (Va.) V–392b; VII–154b
Customhouses
Confederacy II–164a
weights and measures IV–462b
Customs Administration Act (1938) II–276a
Customs Agency Service II–276b
Customs Border Patrol II–276b, 277b
Customs collections, colonial VI–110b
Customs duties
Coast Guard II–88b–89b
colonial governors II–120a
Customshouse, New York V–85b
Customs Intelligence Bureau II–277a
Customs receivership
Dominican Republic II–361a
Customs revenues *See* Duties
CUSTOMS SERVICE, UNITED STATES II–275b; III–246a; VII–108a
censorship I–479b, 480a
Puerto Rico V–461b
Cutaway coats II–371b
Cutbush, James (chem.) II–10b
Cutler, Manasseh (cler.) IV–423b; V–143b; VI–238b–39a
Cutler, Timothy (cler.) VI–75b
Cutter, Charles Ammi (librarian) IV–145a
Cutter Pharmaceutical Company V–341a
Cutters, revenue II–88b–90a
Cutting, Bronson M. (pol.) I–479a
Cutting, James Ambrose (chem.) II–7a
Cutting horse III–303b
Cuyahoga (ship) II–338b
Cuyahoga Bay V–214b
Cuyahoga County (Ohio) II–74b
Cuyahoga River II–74b, 227b; III–414a
Cuyahoga Valley V–145b
Cuyler's Sugar House (N.Y.C.) VI–436b
Cuyp, Albert (art.) II–101b
Cuyuna Iron Range III–473b; IV–357a
Cuzco (Peru) IV–327b
CV. *See* Attack carriers
CVA. *See* Attack carriers
CVE. *See* Escort carriers
CVL. *See* Light carriers
CVS. *See* Antisubmarine warfare carriers
CWA. *See* Civil Works Administration
Cyanamide process III–17a; V–98a
Cyane (frigate) II–191b; V–22b
Cyanide process III–191b
Cybernation I–224b
Cyclamate sweeteners V–468a
Cycles, Business. *See* Business Cycles
Cycling
Olympic Games V–154a
Cyclones. *See* Tornadoes and Cyclones
Cyclops (collier) II–349b
CYCLOTRON II–278a; IV–119a,b; V–295b, 300b–01a
Cygnus (constellation) VI–17a
Cynthiana (Ky.) IV–410a
Cypress (tree) I–445b; IV–204a; VI–48b
Cypress Gardens (S.C.) I–497a, 498a
Cyril, Saint (Constantine) II–386b
Cystic fibrosis III–249a
Cytogenetics I–350a
Cytosine II–357b–58a; IV–389a, 390a
Czechoslovakia V–429a
Communist coup (1948) II–98a
hockey III–287b
immigration to U.S. III–337b, 338b, 339a,b, 340a
nationalization of U.S. property IV–466a
Soviet invasion V–114a,b; VI–416b
United Nations Declaration VII–151b
vacuum tubes VII–163b
World War I I–158b
World War II II–407b; VII–334a
Czechoslovak Legion VI–283b–84a
Czech settlement VI–350a
Czolgosz, Leon F. (assassin) I–117a, 202b

D

D'Abbadie, M. IV–277b
Dablon, Claude (miss.) III–501a; IV–217b; VI–190b–91a
Dabney, Virginius (ed.) V–73b
Dacres, James R. (off.) II–191b
Dadd, George H. (vet.) VII–176a
Daddi, Bernardo (art.) II–102a
Daddy Grace (cler.) I–24a
Dade, Francis L. (off.). *See* Dade Massacre
DADE MASSACRE (1835) **II–278b**; VI–260b
Daedalus (jour.) I–97b
Daggett, Ezra I–445a
Dagneaux de Quindre, Antoine (off.) I–337a
Daguerre, Louis J. M. (paint., inv.). *See* Daguerreotype
DAGUERREOTYPE II–279a; V–291a, 293a
"Dagwood" sandwich V–72b
Dagworthy, George (off.) III–58b
Dagyr, John Adam I–338a
Dahlgren, John A. (nav. off.) I–200a; V–26b
Dahlgren, Ulric (off.) II–279a
Dahlgren guns IV–431a; V–56a
DAHLGREN'S AND KILPATRICK'S RAID (1864) **II–279a**; IV–139a
Dahlonega (Ga.) IV–360a
Dahomey (people) VI–310a
Daie, Thomas (col. gov.) III–489a
Daily Mail (London news.) V–74b
Daily newspapers V–70b–71a
Daily Racing Form III–305a
Daily Worker (news.) II–144b, 146a
Daily World (news.) II–146a
Daimler, Gottlieb (eng.) I–225b
Daines Mound 2 I–11b
Daiquiri (Cuba) VI–362a
Dairen (China) IV–234b; VII–351b
DAIRY INDUSTRY II–279a; I–46a; VI–176a
cattle I–471b–72a
Connecticut II–180b
corn belt II–227a
food preservation III–54b; VI–69a
Fort Scott VI–241a
Green Bay III–226a
inspection VI–173b
Iowa III–468b
Maine IV–227a

malaria IV–229b
Minnesota IV–357a
Natchitoches IV–457a
New Hampshire V–54a
New York State V–87a
Prairie du Chien V–388a
Rhode Island IV–451b; VI–134a
tariff VI–471a
Vermont VII–172b
Virginia VII–196b
Washington State VII–248a
Wisconsin VII–308a
Dairymen's League II–282a
Daisy Bradford No. 3 (oil well) II–389a
Daito Islands III–425a
DAKOTA (Indians) **II–282b**; III–365a; IV–236a; VI–350a
Arapaho war I–151b
Black Hills War I–313a; IV–168a
Cheyenne alliance II–17a
councils III–378b
expeditions against II–283b–84a
fur trade IV–356a
Minnesota IV–355a,b
Red River cart traffic VI–64a
scalping VI–224b
Sully expedition IV–135a
Sun Dance VI–441b
Dakota Apartments (N.Y.C.) I–143b
DAKOTA EXPEDITIONS OF SIBLEY AND SULLY (1863–65) **II–283b**; III–32a; VI–296b
Battle of Killdeer Mountain IV–45b
Fort Rice VI–135a
Fort Ridgely VI–139a
Dakota Gold Rush. *See* Black Hills
DAKOTA LAND COMPANY II–284b
DAKOTA TERRITORY II–284b; II–284a; V–117a
Arikara and Blackfoot War VII–239a
Black Hills War IV–167b
black infantry I–313b, 314a, 314b
Custer expedition VII–272b
Fort Rice VI–135a
fur trade V–121a
homestead movement VII–59b
Idaho III–328a
open–range grazing V–160a
Sioux reservation VI–295b
Sioux Wars VII–239b
South Dakota VI–349b
Winnebago VII–306a
Wyoming VII–345b
Dalberg–Acton, John E. E. *See* Acton, Lord
Dale, Chester II–105a
Dale, Thomas (col. gov.) II–285a
D'Alembert, Jean *See* Alembert, Jean d'
DALE'S LAWS OF VIRGINIA II–285a
Daley, Richard J. (pol.) I–343b; II–18b; IV–214a,b; V–345a
Dali, Salvador (paint.) V–192b
Dalitz, Moe II–261b
Dall, W. H. (paleon.) V–196a
Dallas (Tex.) III–80b; VII–40b
airport I–70a
centennial exposition III–81a
flour milling III–44a
Indian relocation VI–83b
John Kennedy assassination IV–37b
railroads VI–36b
Reunion VI–105a
settlement VII–35b
Texas Centennial Exposition VII–41a
theater VII–50b
Dallas, Alexander J. (law.) II–285a; VII–5a
Dallas, George M. (states.) I–420a; II–285a; VII–179 (table)
DALLAS–CLARENDON CONVENTION (1856) **II–285a**
Dallas County (Ala.) VI–433a
Dallas Herald (news.) VII–187b
Dallas Morning News (news.) V–73b
***DALLAS REPORTS* II–285a**
Dallas Symphony Orchestra VII–40b
DALLES II–285b; II–30a; VI–379b
federal mint IV–360a
Frémont exploration VII–271b
Oregon Trail V–169a
Yakima Wars VII–350a
Dalles Dam II–285b; III–322a–b
Dall sheep V–217b
Dalmatian immigrants III–339a
Dalton (Ga.) III–298a
Civil War I–502b; IV–365a
Dalton, John (chem.) I–218a; II–11a
Dalton, John Call (physiol.) V–306b
Dalton boys (outlaws) VII–97b
Daly, Marcus (miner) I–116a; IV–403b
Daly, R. A. (geol.) III–481a
Dalyell, James (off.) VI–162b
Dalzel, James (off.) I–323b
DAME SCHOOL II–285b; II–394a; VI–229a
"DAMN THE TORPEDOES" II–285b; IV–383a; VI–425a
Dams IV–174b; VI–147a
climate II–76b
Colorado River II–130a
Columbia River II–132a
cow country II–250b
Flaming Gorge Dam II–130a
Fort Peck Dam II–449b
Hoover Dam II–76b, 130a
Illinois IV–88a
irrigation III–477b
Johnstown flood IV–5a
Libby II–132a
Mississippi Basin VI–148b
Missouri River IV–380a
Muscle Shoals VI–146b
Newlands Reclamation Act V–445a–b
Parker Dam II–130a
Quaker Bridge IV–5a
Tennessee River VII–27b
Tennessee Valley Authority VII–28a
Works Progress Administration VII–323b
See also Hydroelectric Power
Dan, Sons of II–291b
Dana, Charles A. (ed.) I–369b; V–71b, 73b, 157a
Dana, Francis (dipl.) I–176a; VI–177a
Dana, James Dwight (geol.) III–29b; IV–348b; V–195b; VI–235b; VII–299a
Dana, Richard Henry (au.) I–344a, 405b; II–373b; IV–267a
Dana, Richard Henry (law.) VI–112a; VII–224b
Dana, Samuel L. (chem.) III–408b
Da Nang (Viet.) II–450a; IV–253a; VII–185b, 186a, 186b
Danbury (Conn.) III–25b
DANBURY, BURNING OF (1777) **II–286a**; IV–361a; VI–139a, 186a
DANBURY HATTERS' CASE (1908) **II–286a**; I–356b; IV–67b; VI–103b, 419a
DANCE II–286b
African IV–442b
Afro–American I–25a
folklore III–48b
frontier II–487a
New York City V–83b
sheet music IV–438a
Dancehalls II–260a
Dance in Place Congo (comp.) IV–438b
DANCES, AMERICAN INDIAN II–290b; IV–59b; V–210b
Dance Theater of Harlem II–289b
DANCING RABBIT CREEK, TREATY OF (1830) **II–291a**; II–32b; VII–181b
Danes
Minnesota IV–356b
Danforth, Charles (inv.) VII–43a
Danforth, George (inv.) VII–43a
Danforth, Samuel (metalworker) VI–290b
Danforth, Thomas (pol.) III–200b
Danforth, William (mfr.) I–487a
Danforth family (metalworkers) VI–290b, 291a
Danger Cave (Utah) II–334b
"Danger of an Unconverted Ministry" (sermon) V–391b
Daniel, John W. (pol.) VI–49b
Daniel, Peter v. (jur.) VI–445b
Daniel Boone Escorting a Band of Pioneers (paint.) V–189b
Danielian, Leon (dancer) II–288b
Daniels, Jonathan Worth (ed.) V–73b
Daniels, Josephus (jour., states.) IV–322b; V–13a, 13b, 14a, 18a, 73b
Danish–American arbitration treaty (1888) I–398b
DANISH SPOLIATION OF AMERICAN COMMERCE II–291a
Danish West Indies
annexation proposal II–475a
See also Virgin Islands of the United States
DANITES II–291b
Dan Rice's Floating Palace VI–283a
Dan River III–232a; VI–149b; VII–202b
Dante Alighieri IV–162a
Danvers (Mass.) VI–199a; VII–309b–10a
Danville (Ky.) II–272a; IV–42b; VII–296a
Danville (Va.) VII–196a
Danzig (Pol.)
Treaty of Versailles VII–173a
DAR. *See* Daughters of the American Revolution
Darby, William O. (off.) VI–46b
Darcy v. *Allien* (1602) V–225b
Dardanelles III–86a
Dare, Ananias (col.) VI–43a
Dare, Ellinor White (col.) VI–43a
Dare, John VI–43a
Dare, Virginia (col.) VI–43a
Daredevils VI–392b
D'Arges Colony. *See* (d')Arges Colony
DARIEN, BANK OF II–291b
Darien, Isthmus of. *See* Panama, Isthmus of
DARK AND BLOODY GROUND II–291b
DARK DAY II–292a
DARK HORSE II–292a
Pierce, Franklin I–420b
Polk, James K. I–420a

Darley, F. O. C. (illus.) I–335b
Darling, Jay N. ("Ding") (cartoon.) V–73a
Darlington (Indian Terr.) II–379b
Darnall, Carl Rogers (med. off.) IV–291b
Darnall, Henry (col. offi.) V–436a
Darragh, Lydia VII–292b
Darrow, Clarence S. (law.) IV–219a; V–161b; VI–239b; VII–118b
Dart, Joseph (mer.) II–430a; III–43a
D'Artaguette, Pierre. *See* Artaguette, Pierre d'
Dartiguenave, Sudre (pres.) III–240a
DARTMOOR PRISON II–292a
Dartmouth (Eng.) IV–278b; V–313a
Dartmouth, 2nd Earl of. *See* Legge, William
DARTMOUTH COLLEGE II–292b; II–114b, 293b–94a; IV–191a; V–54a, 279b
  Chandler School II–399a
  chemistry studies II–10a
  founding II–394b
  Indian education II–293b
  lottery financing III–149b
  medical school II–293a; IV–283a
  skiing VI–298a
  technical instruction II–447a
DARTMOUTH COLLEGE CASE (1819) **II–293b**; II–114a, 213b–14a, 397b; IV–19b; V–161a, 399a–b, 457a; VII–117b, 156a
Dartmouth College v. *Woodward. See* Dartmouth College Case
Dartmouth Outing Club VI–298a
Darusmont, Frances Wright (ref.) II–297b
Darwin, Charles (nat.) II–226a, 390a; IV–163b; V–196b, 287b, 288a; VI–230a
  conservatism II–189a
  evolution theory II–391a
  influence on education II–399a
Darwin, George H. (math., astron.) III–166b
Darwinism I–349a
Darwinism, Social II–475a
"Data crunching" II–427a
Data of Geochemistry III–163b
Dates (food) III–128a, 129a
Datrua (weed) III–503b
Datsun (auto) VII–90a
Datura (weed) III–381a; VII–65a
Daubenton, Louis Jean Marie (nat.) IV–231b
Daugherty, Harry M. (law.) VI–40b
DAUGHTERS OF 1812 II–294a
DAUGHTERS OF THE AMERICAN REVOLUTION II–294a
Daughters of the Confederacy, United. *See* United Daughters of the Confederacy
Daughters of Union Veterans of the Civil War III–208a
D'Aulnay, Charles de Menou V–369b
Dauntless (bomber) I–55a
DAUPHIN ISLAND II–294a; III–146a; IV–276b
DAV. *See* Disabled American Veterans
Daveiss, Joseph Hamilton. *See* Daviess, Joseph Hamilton
Davenport (Iowa) II–255b; III–336b, 468b, 469a; VI–159b
Davenport, Charles B. (zool.) II–97a; III–159a
Davenport, George (fur trader) III–147a
Davenport, Homer (cartoonist) I–464b
Davenport, John (cler.) V–185a, 273a; VI–263b
  Court of High Commission III–275a
  New Haven Colony V–55a
  Regicides VI–70b
Davenport, Thomas (inv.) I–276a; II–413a; VI–40a
David, Henry (hist.) III–283a
David Franks and Company I–278a; III–141b
David Harum IV–163a
DAVIDS (ironclads) **II–294b**; VI–425a
Davids, James. *See* Dixwell, John
Davidson, Fort (Mo.) V–314a
Davidson, John W. (off.) VI–64a
Davidson, Mount VI–452b–53a
Davidson, Robert (inv.) VI–40a
David Taylor Model Basin (Md.) V–28a
Davie, William R. (law.) II–215a
Davies, Arthur B. (paint.) II–104a
Davies, Samuel (educ.) III–326a
Daviess, Joseph Hamilton (law.) IV–40b
Davis, John (athlete) V–154b
Davis, Alexander J. (arch.) I–163a
Davis, Benjamin (off.) II–145b
DAVIS, CAPTURE OF (1865) **II–294b**; I–324b; II–68b, 165a
Davis, Charles H. (nav. off.) III–23b, 474b; IV–302a; V–12a–b
Davis, Cummings E. (collector) II–99a
Davis, David (jur.) I–423a; III–224b; IV–63a; VI–445b
Davis, David R. (eng.) I–52a
Davis, D. Dwight (nat.) VI–91b
Davis, Dwight (offi.) I–177b
Davis, Dwight F. VII–29b
Davis, E. J. (gov.) VII–40a
DAVIS, FORT (Tex.) **II–294b**
Davis, Henry Gassaway (pol.) I–426a
Davis, Henry W. (pol.) VI–11b, 58b; VII–213a
Davis, Herbert (ed.) V–410b
DAVIS, IMPRISONMENT AND TRIAL OF II–294b; I–324b; IV–399b
Davis, Jack (outlaw) VII–97b
Davis, James S. (abolitionist) IV–220a
Davis, J. C. (off.) I–317b
Davis, Jefferson II–241a; IV–41a, 368b, 405a; V–373a; VI–246a
  amnesty I–115a
  Andersonville prison I–118a
  education I–324b
  Fort Winnebago VII–306a
  See also Davis, Capture of; Davis, Imprisonment and Trial of II–
  —*Confederate President:*
  army I–181a–b
  Army of Northern Virginia VII–197a
  Battle of Drewry's Bluff II–373a
  Bragg, Braxton II–21b
  Camp Jackson affair I–433b
  Chattanooga campaign I–502b
  Davis–Johnston controversy I–381b; II–295a
  Far West III–187b
  government organization II–160a–61b
  Hampton Roads Conference III–247b
  Hood's Tennessee campaign III–298a
  inauguration II–357a
  Lee, Robert E. II–482b
  military policy V–248a,b
  navy V–17a
  peace movement of 1864 V–234b
  Richmond evacuation VI–137b
  surrender of Confederate Army II–68b
  treason charge VII–107a
  White House VII–292a
  —*Secretary of War:*
  Army Appropriation Bill I–453a
  railroad surveys VI–39a
  —*Senator:*
  slavery in territories II–139a
  Soldiers' and Airmens' Home VI–336b
Davis, Jefferson Columbus (off.) V–32b; VII–127a
Davis, John (expl.) V–197b
Davis, John Wesley (physic., pol.) II–175 (table)
Davis, John William (law., pol.) I–427b, 428a
Davis, J. P. (engr.) VII–319b
Davis, Matthew (pol.) VI–459a
Davis, Miles (mus.) IV–440b
Davis, Ossie (act., playwright) V–96a
Davis, Ozara Stearns (comp.) III–326b
Davis, Phineas (eng.) IV–175a–b
Davis, Rennie II–20b–21a
Davis, Richard Harding (jour.) V–73b–74a
Davis, Stuart (paint.) V–192b
Davis, Sylvanus (off.) IV–200a
Davis, Varina (Mrs. Jefferson) VII–292a
Davis, William (inv.) III–55a
Davis–Bacon Act (1931) IV–78b, 353b
Davis Cup VII–29b, 30a,b
Davis Dam II–130a
DAVIS–JOHNSTON CONTROVERSY II–295a; I–324b, 381b; V–238a
Davis Lock VI–219b
Davison, Nicholas (landowner) V–243b
Davisson, Clinton J. (phys.) I–287b; V–100a, 295b, 303b
Davis Strait VII–285a
Davis v. *County School Board of Prince County* I–372b
Davy, Humphry (chem.) I–119a, 276a; II–11a, 413b; IV–128a
"Davy Crockett" (rifle) VI–140b
Davy Crockett's Almanack of Wild Sports of the West I–91a
Davys, John (navig.) III–240b; IV–37a; V–122a
Dawes, Charles G. (law., fin., pol.) V–100a
  campaign of 1924 I–427b
  vice-presidency VII–180 (table)
  See also Dawes Plan
Dawes, Henry L. (pol.) *See* Dawes Commission
Dawes, William (patriot) IV–137a; VI–106a
DAWES COMMISSION II–295b; III–378b; VI–87b–88a
DAWES GENERAL ALLOTMENT ACT OF 1887 II–295b; III–389b; IV–387b; V–148b; VI–6a
  amended I–385b
  Indian citizenship III–377a
  South Dakota VI–350a

DAWES PLAN (1924)
II–296a; I–245b; III–352b; IV–117b; V–215a; VI–87b–88a
Dawson (Alaska) VII–367a
Dawson (N.Mex.) II–350a
Dawson, Andrew (fur trader) IV–403a
Dawson, F. W. (ed.) V–66b
Dawson, Henry Barton (hist.) III–282a
Dawson City (Yukon Terr.) IV–52a
Day, Arthur L. (geol.) V–268a
Day, Benjamin H. (pub.) V–71a, 73a
Day, John (expl.) II–477a
Day, Luke VI–272a
Day, Mahlon (pub.) I–494a
Day, Matthew (print.) I–333b; V–410b
Day (Daye), Stephen (print.) I–90b, 279b, 333b, 411b; V–410b
Day, Thomas Fleming (ed.) VII–349a
Day, William Rufus (jur., states.) V–215a; VI–446a
Daybeds III–137a
Day–care centers I–9a; V–129a; VI–74a; VII–314a
DAYLIGHT SAVING TIME
II–296b; VI–139a
Day–school movement IV–11b
"Days of Real Sport" (comic strip) V–72b
Dayton (Ohio) II–44b; V–49a, 141b, 145b; VI–336b
Dayton (Tenn.) VI–239b
Dayton, Fort (N.Y.) V–172b
Dayton, Jonathan (pol.) II–174 (table), 203b; IV–329b
Dayton, William Lewis (pol., dipl.) II–65a
Dayton–Wright Company I–236a
DC–2 (transport plane) I–51b
DC–3 (transport plane) I–49b, 51b, 68a, 236b; II–346b–47a
DC–4 (transport plane) II–346b
DC–6 (transport plane) I–237b; II–346b
DC–7 (transport plane) I–237b; II–346b
DC–7C (transport plane) I–52b
DC–8 (transport plane) I–52b, 68b, 237b; II–347a
DC–9 (transport plane) II–347a,b
DC–10 (transport plane) I–52b, 69a
D DAY II–297a
See also Normandy Invasion
DDT III–421a; IV–230a; V–137b
Dead Buffalo Lake, Battle of (1863) II–283b
"Dead man's" control II–350b
Dead River I–193b
Dead Sea V–23a
Deadwood (S.Dak.) I–203b, 336b; V–179a; VI–201b
Deadwood Dick (lit. char.) II–341b
Deadwood Gulch (S.Dak.) I–312b
Deaf VI–74a
education III–248a–b
Deale County (Del.) II–322b
Dealey, George B. (ed.) V–73b
Dean, Gordon E. (law.) I–216b
Dean, John W. III (law.) VII–254b, 255a,b
Deane, Silas (dipl.)
Continental navy VI–128a
Illinois and Wabash Company III–331a
joint commission to France III–90a, 95a; VI–119b
military code VII–142b
Dean rice plantation I–498a
DEARBORN, FORT (Ill.)
II–297a; II–17a, 477a
Beaubien land claim I–281b
Indian massacre III–329b
Michigan Territorial Road IV–332b
military highway II–20a
War of 1812 VII–262a
Dearborn, Henry (off.) II–297a,b; III–108a, 315b; VII–234b
Dearborn Observatory (Ill.) V–131b
DEARBORN WAGON
II–297b
Deas, Charles (paint.) V–189b
Death duty. *See* Inheritance Tax Laws
Death of a Salesman (play) VII–50b
Death of God: The Culture of Our Post–Christian Era VI–83a
Death on the Pale Horse (paint.) V–187a, 188b
Death penalty I–449b–50b; II–190a; III–219a
See also Capital Punishment
Death Rapids II–131b
Death rates. *See* Life Expectancy
Death Route. *See* Sage Plains
Deaths
employers' liability laws II–440b–41a
epidemics II–454a
record–keeping VII–205b, 206b, 207a
trends II–328a
workmen's compensation acts II–441a–b
DEATH VALLEY II–297b; II–477b; III–215a
borax I–340a
forty–niners III–82a
national monument V–217a,b
Death Valley Scotty (mine) II–298a
DEBATABLE LAND
II–298a
Debate
cloture II–83b
Congress II–173a
literary societies IV–160b
De bello Gallico IV–163a
Debentures II–477b
Debora (ship) VI–134b
De Bow, James Dunwoody Brownson (ed.). *See* De Bow's *Review*
DE BOW'S *REVIEW* (jour.)
II–298a
Debs, Eugene v. (labor leader) IV–68a
AFL I–104a
American Railway Union I–111b; IV–66b; VI–20a
campaign of 1912 I–427a
campaign of 1920 I–427b; II–493a
imprisonment II–463b
Industrial Workers of the World III–412b; IV–67b
Pullman strike II–17b, 298b–99a; III–419a; IV–67a; V–463a; VI–419a
Socialist party II–143b, 492b; VI–324b, 326a,b
trials VII–117b
DEBS, IN RE (1895)
II–298b; III–351b; IV–67a; VI–419a
DEBT, IMPRISONMENT FOR II–299a; I–488b; VII–322a
abolishment IV–80a
abolition movement IV–61b
panic of 1819 V–206b
peonage V–260b
West Jersey VII–278b
DEBT, PUBLIC II–299b; III–8a; VII–90b–91a
Articles of Confederation VII–4a
bond issues II–63b, 300a, 317a
collection I–411a
constitutional provisions II–199b, 203a, 203a, 205b, 453b, 476a
Court of Claims II–71a
credit of the nation II–256a
federal expenditures II–476a
federal surplus VI–449a
Greenback movement III–224a
greenbacks III–225b
Hamilton's fiscal policies III–244a–45b, 246a
Hoover moratorium IV–409a
interest III–7b
internal improvements III–147b
Jeffersonian Democracy III–496a
location of national capital I–448b
monetizing II–317b
national sinking fund VI–294a
"Ohio Idea" I–422a
panic of 1929 V–209a
repudiation VI–94b
revolutionary war I–208b; II–149b, 167a
savings bonds VI–222a
Treasury VII–108a
Victory loan of 1919 VII–182b
war costs VII–228 (table)
War of 1812 VI–465a
World War I VII–326a
World War II II–301b; VII–8a
See also Foreign Investments in the United States
DEBT AND INVESTMENT, FOREIGN II–300b; VII–85a, 222a–b
Africa I–22a
Alliance for Progress IV–113a
arbitration IV–381b
China V–158a
Cuba II–268a; VI–361a
dollar diplomacy II–359b
Dominican Republic II–361a–b
Drago Doctrine II–369a, 369a
Europe II–301a
gold III–195b–96a
Haiti III–240a
Hamilton's fiscal policies III–244a–45a
International Monetary Fund III–457b
Latin American IV–111a,b
Liberia IV–141b
Mexico IV–322b, 328b
panic of 1929 V–209a
payment in silver IV–395b
petroleum V–270b
Sherman Silver Purchase Act VI–277b
South America VI–346a
Debtors
colonial labor force IV–60a
Georgia II–124b; III–168a
indenture II–299a
Debts, Civil War
Confederacy II–164a, 302b
Union II–63b, 69a
DEBTS, COLONIAL AND CONTINENTAL
II–301b; III–63a; VI–117b
British merchants II–119a, 166b, 319a
Hamilton's fiscal policies III–244b–45a
legal tender IV–132a
panic of 1785 V–206a
revenue VII–3b–4a
Shays's Rebellion VI–271b
war financing VI–120a
Debts, international
collection III–237b
DEBTS, STATE II–302a; VI–398b
Hamilton's fiscal policies III–246a
Illinois III–329b, 331a

DEBTS, STATE (cont.)
internal improvements III–449b
legal tender IV–132a
New York V–87b
panic of 1837 V–206b
Pennsylvania V–250a
Readjuster movement VI–49a
repudiation VI–95b
revolutionary war I–208a–b; VI–120b
Rhode Island VI–133a
South Carolina state bank VI–349a
Texas VII–39a
Virginia v. *West Virginia* VII–203b
Debye, Peter (phys.) V–303b
Decades of the Newe Worlde III–280a
Decalogue (Ten Commandments)
Adventists I–15b
De Casse, Henri (mfr.) III–184a
Decatur (Ala.) VI–166a
Decatur (destroyer series) VII–243a
Decatur (Ill.) III–207b
Decatur, Stephen (nav. off.) V–19a
Bank of North America I–260b
Barbary Wars I–266a; II–303a–b; IV–44b; VII–120b
Chesapeake–Leopard incident II–16a
duel with Barron I–318a; II–377a
Intrepid III–464b
nationalism V–176b
Philadelphia V–278b, 423b
President V–394a
United States VII–153a
United States–Macedonian encounter VII–240a
War of 1812 I–325b
Decatur County (Iowa) V–42a
Decatur House (Washington, D.C.) I–163a; IV–472a
DECATUR'S CRUISE TO ALGIERS (1815) **II–303a**; I–266b
Decennial Index III–203b
Deception Island V–198a
Decimal system
coinage II–95a
DECIUS LETTERS II–303b
Declaration by United Nations (1942). *See* United Nations Declaration
Declaration of Causes of Taking up Arms (1775) VI–107a
Declaration of Colonial Rights and Grievances. *See* Declaration of Rights
Declaration of Four Nations (1943) II–380a; IV–415b
Declaration of Immediate Causes (1860) VI–250b
DECLARATION OF INDEPENDENCE II–303b; II–211b, 306a, 377a; V–2a, 7b, 351a, 353a, 432a; VI–114a, 115a, 116a,b, 118b, 396a; VII–2b, 153a,b, 193b–94a, 351b
billeting I–297a
centennial I–483a
colonial courts IV–15a
common law II–141b
compact theory II–149a
conservation II–189a
contrasted with Constitution II–197a
Declaration of Rights of Man and of the Citizen I–298b
equality II–456a–b
Fourth of July III–87b
freedom II–456b
human rights III–316b
Independence Hall III–353b–54a
Jeffersonian Democracy III–495b
Mecklenburg Declaration IV–282a
Mecklenburg Resolves IV–282b
natural rights doctrine IV–358a–b
New York V–85b, 86a
Parson's Cause V–221b
reserved powers of the people VI–98b
right of petition V–265b
right of rebellion VI–50b
Rodney's ride VI–161b
slavery I–135a
writs of assistance VII–345a
Declaration of Paris (1856). *See* Paris, Declaration of
Declaration of Right (1689) V–265b
DECLARATION OF RIGHTS (1774) **II–308b**; II–211a; IV–308b; V–385a; VI–114a
Declaration of war. *See* War, Declaration of
Declaration on Taking Arms (1775) VII–153b
DECLARATORY ACT (1766) **II–309a**; III–346b; VI–112b
DECLARATORY JUDGMENT LAWS II–309b
Decoration, interior. *See* Interior Decoration
Decoration Day. *See* Memorial Day
DECORATIONS, MILITARY II–310a
Decorative arts
collecting II–98b
Indian III–373a–74b
Industrial Revolution III–136a
De Cou House (N.Y.) I–281b
Dedham (Mass.) II–328b; IV–269a; VI–430b
De Donis (1285) II–452a
Deep Space Network III–502b
Deep Throat (movie) I–480a
Deer III–51a, 150a, 361a, 362b, 364a, 368a, 402b, 484a; VII–296b, 297b, 346a
Deer Creek (Calif.) IV–110a
Deere, John (mfr.) I–34a, 37b; III–43a
Deerfield (Mass.) II–312b–13a; IV–47b, 86a; VI–2b; VII–282b
Deerfield Academy VI–228b
DEERFIELD MASSACRE (1704) **II–312b**; IV–47b
Deerfield Valley (Mass.) IV–268b
Deering, James II–103b
Deering Harvester Company III–454b
Deer Lodge (Mont.) III–32a
Deerskin I–496a; III–141b
Deerslayer IV–162a
Deer suet candles I–444a
Defence of the Constitutions of Goverment of the United States of America V–353a
Defendants, rights of IV–362a
Defender (blimp) II–345b
Defender, Cramer, and Hammer Company V–292a
Defense, Department of I–60b, 187a; II–315a, 498a; IV–344a, 471a; VII–196a, 230b
air cavalry I–49a
atomic energy I–216a
cabinet I–399b
civil defense II–50a
executive agreements II–342b
military and strategic intelligence III–439a,b
military space activities IV–459a,b
National Rifle Association IV–470a
National Security Council VI–389b
Navy Department V–18b
Pentagon Papers III–105b
police activities V–339a
pork barrel contracts V–366b
Pueblo incident V–460b
scientific education VI–232a
veterans' organizations VII–175a–b
DEFENSE, NATIONAL II–313a
atomic research VI–230b
Bureau of Mines IV–350b
chromium III–13b
Coast Guard II–90a
congressional powers II–171b, 453b
costs II–234a, 476b
dollar diplomacy II–359b
Emergency Broadcast System III–1a
Espionage Act II–463a
foreign aid III–60b
fortifications III–78a
frontier III–126b–27a
government spending III–205a
Gulf of Mexico IV–326a–b
harbors VI–147a
hydrogen bomb III–324a
Iceland III–327b
information retrieval VI–232b
inland waterways VII–260b
isolationism III–479b
Japanese–American relocation III–490b
Kennedy administration V–53a
Key West IV–45a
Manhattan Project IV–238a
military and strategic intelligence III–438b
military law IV–342b
military policy IV–343a
militia IV–345b
missiles IV–363a; VI–159b
mobilization IV–383a
National Guard IV–463b
National Science Foundation IV–470b
naval armament V–26a–27b
naval parity V–216b
navy V–18b
nickel III–14a
North Atlantic Treaty Organization V–113b
Nuclear Test Ban Treaty V–124b
Office of Scientific Research and Development V–137a
Ogdensburg Agreement V–139b
ordnance V–163a
Panama bases V–202a–b
Pearl Harbor V–239a
Pentagon Papers V–259a
Philippines V–284b, 285a
physics V–296a
preparedness movement V–390b
pressure groups V–400a
Reconstruction Finance Corporation VI–60a
recruitment VI–60b
research I–457a
river and harbor improvements VI–145b
satellites VI–159b
savings bonds VI–222a
Sea Fencibles VI–244b
Southeast Asia Treaty Organization VI–350b
space exploration IV–458b–59a
Strategic Arms Limitation Talks VI–416b
taxation VII–7a, 11b
Tennessee Valley Authority VII–28a
territorial waters VII–33a
Trade Expansion Act VI–470a
volunteers VII–207b
war costs VII–228a
War Industries Board VII–231b
war-making powers

VII–223b–25a, 226b–27b
warships VII–240a
Washington Naval Conference VII–250b
World War II expenditures VII–8a
See also entries under Army; Air Force; Coast Guard; National Guard; and Navy
Defense, secretary of IV–342b
Defense Act (1916) II–314a
Defense Calculator II–156a
Defense Condition Three III–482b
Defense contracts II–499b
Defense highways II–502b
Defense industries II–473a
Defense Intelligence Agency III–439b
Defenseless America V–390b
Defense Plant Corporation III–201b; VI–60a
Defense plants II–498b
Defense Production Act (1950) III–12a, 13a,b
Defense Reorganization Act (1958) II–316a
Deferments, military II–367a, 367b–68a
Defiance (Ohio) II–317a; V–145b
Defiance, Fort (N.Mex.) VI–439b
DEFIANCE, FORT (Ohio) **II–317a**; III–244a; VII–263a
DEFICIT, FEDERAL II–317a; III–195b–96b; VI–449a–b
taxation VII–5a
Vietnam War VII–222b
Deficit spending II–300a
Definite Synodical Program IV–206a
DEFINITIVE TREATY OF PEACE (1783) **II–318a**; II–216a; III–216a–b, 369b, 403b; V–214a–b; VI–124b
alien landholding I–87a
arbitration IV–5b
British debts I–366b
British posts I–340b–41a
British violation II–166b
confiscated property II–168b, 481b
fishing privileges II–92b; III–30b; IV–82a
Florida III–38b, 41b; IV–197b; V–254b; VII–277a
Fort Saint Marks VI–196b
Georgia boundary III–171b
Jay–Gardoqui negotiations III–493b
Jay's Treaty III–493a
Lake Erie II–458b
Lake of the Woods boundary IV–87b
Mississippi River IV–372b, 373b; V–315a; VI–365b
Mississippi Valley IV–376a
Northeast boundary V–118a
Northwest II–71b; III–24b; V–152a
Northwest boundary V–120a–b
prisoners of war II–215a
Russian relations I–176a
Saint Croix River VI–189a
state violations I–199a
Trespass Act VII–116b
U.S. boundaries I–126a, 351a; VI–165b; VII–269b
U.S. violation II–166b
Wisconsin VII–307a
See also Paris, Peace of (1783)
Deflation V–404b–05a,b
gold supply III–193a–b
Great Depression III–415a
panic of 1785 V–206a
price–fixing V–401b
DEFOLIATION II–319a; I–46b; II–9b; VII–226a
De Fonte, Bartholomew (nav. off.) V–180a
De Forest, John William (au.) IV–163b
De Forest, Lee (inv.) II–423b, 425b; VI–15a; VII–163a
DeForest, Robert W. (law.) VII–24b
De Gaulle, Charles (states.) III–97b; IV–454a; VI–470a
D'Église, Jacques (trader) IV–380b
DeGolyer, Everette L. (ind.) V–272a
DEGOLYER CASE (1874) **II–319b**
DeGolyer Company II–319b
Degoutte, Jean Marie (off.) I–70b; V–147a
DeGrey, Earl I–73b
De Haven, Edwin Jesse (nav. off.). *See* De Haven's Expedition
DE HAVEN'S EXPEDITION (1850–51) **II–319b**; V–23a, 336b
DEISM II–320a; III–112b
Deistic Ancient Order of Druids III–112a
De Jonge v. *Oregon* (1937) I–204b; III–105a; V–265b
Dekanawida (Indian) III–475a
DeKay, James E. (nat.) III–27a; IV–232a; VI–90b
De Koven, Reginald (comp.) IV–442a
De Kruif, Paul (bact.) I–242a
Delacroix, Ferdinand (paint.) V–187a, 188b
Delafield, Richard (arch.) I–364a
De Lancey, James (jur.) II–121a; V–85a–b
De Lancey, James (off.) II–249b
De Lancey, Oliver (off.) II–249b; IV–363a; VI–130a
De Lancey, Stephen III–100a; IV–354b
De Lancey family IV–200a
De Lancey's Green Jackets II–249b
De Lanoy, Peter (pol.) V–82a–b
Delany, Martin R. (jour., physic.) I–101b, 315b; II–127b
Delaplace, William (off.) III–215b; VII–56b
Delassus, Carlos Dehault (col. offi.) IV–195b, 377a
DeLaval, Carl G. *See* Laval, Carl G. de
Delavan, Edward C. (pub.) III–243a
DELAWARE II–320a; VI–393 (table)
Alexandria Conference I–85b
Annapolis Convention I–126a
archives I–168b
beet sugar I–285a
bills of credit I–300a
border state I–341b
boundary II–322b
cattle III–51b
Civil War II–61b; V–19b; VI–251b, 308a
colonial suffrage VI–434a
constitution VI–392a
Declaration of Independence II–305a, 308a
Delaware River Basin Compact III–460a
delegate convention system V–101b
Dutch settlements IV–199b
election laws I–206b
entail of estate II–452b
Federalists III–5a
feudalism III–18a
flogging III–36b
Fort Christina II–35a
holding companies III–290a
Huguenots III–315a
hundred III–317b
independence resolution VI–161b–62a
Lower Counties IV–199b
Loyalists VI–115b
Mason–Dixon Line IV–263a
New Castle V–42b
New Jersey boundary dispute I–351a,b
New Sweden Colony V–80a, 81a
political party emblems II–437b
proprietary grant V–436b
Quakers V–470a
railroads VI–36a
religious toleration II–394b
revolutionary war VI–128b
separation from Pennsylvania V–246a
settlement II–124b
slavery I–342a; VI–309a
steam navigation III–32a
Swedes III–334b
Swedish settlements IV–199b
trusts VII–122a
"turf and twig" VII–129b
unionism VI–354a
U.S. Constitution II–193a, 196a, 203b, 478a
usury law III–443a
water supply VII–259a
Zwaanendael Colony VII–372b
DELAWARE (Indians) **II–320b**; III–227b, 367a
Allegheny River I–89a
Bouquet's expedition I–353b, 389a
Bradstreet's Lake Erie expedition I–359a
Brodhead's Allegheny campaign I–369a
council III–378b–79a
Dodge–Leavenworth expedition II–358b
Firelands III–25b
Fort Laurens IV–117b
Fort McIntosh treaties III–24b; IV–216b
Fort Seybert massacre VI–267a
Fort Stanwix Treaty (1768) VI–386a
French and Indian War III–115a, 116b, 123a; IV–51a
Gnadenhutten III–187b
Jesuit missions III–500a
Logstown IV–181a
Logstown Treaty IV–181b
Maumee Convention IV–276b
migration to Ohio VI–270b–71a
Moravian missionaries II–381b
nativistic movement II–322b
Pennsylvania V–246a
Pontiac's War V–357a
removal III–393b
revolutionary war III–400b; V–152b
Schoenbrunn mission VI–226a
scouts VI–242a
Spring Wells Treaty VI–377b
Squaw Campaign VI–378a
Treaty at Pittsburgh V–322a
Treaty of Easton II–389a
Treaty of Fort Harmar III–255a
Treaty of Fort Wayne VII–262b
Treaty of Greenville III–383a
Treaty of Shackamaxon VI–267a
Treaty of 1778 III–383a
Upper Sandusky VII–157b
Vincennes cession VII–189b
Walking Purchase VII–220b
Wappinger Confederacy VII–223b

Delaware (ship) III–21b; VI–282a
Delaware, Fort (Del.) V–414b
Delaware, Lackawanna and Western Railroad I–364b; VI–34a
See also Erie Lackawanna,
Delaware, Lehigh, Schuylkill and Susquehanna Railroad VI–34b
DELAWARE, WASHINGTON CROSSING THE (1776) **II–321a**; VI–123b
DELAWARE AND HUDSON CANAL II–321b; I–443b; VI–33b
aqueduct I–364b
coal hauling I–127b
railroad IV–175b
railroads VI–24b
Stourbridge Lion locomotive VI–416a
Delaware and Hudson Canal Company I–442b; VI–33b
Delaware and Hudson Railroad VI–33b
DELAWARE AND RARITAN CANAL II–322a; I–127b, 443a; V–57b
Delaware and Raritan Canal Company I–442b
DELAWARE BAY II–322a
canal II–15b
Duke of York's proprietary VII–359a,b
New Sweden Colony V–80a–b
Pennsylvania–Maryland-boundary dispute V–252a
settlement II–147a
shipbuilding VI–148a
War of 1812 IV–135b
War of 1812 VII–235a
Zwaanendael Colony VII–372b
Delaware Canal I–443a
Delaware–Chesapeake Canal II–320b
See also Chesapeake and Delaware Canal
DELAWARE CIRCLE II–322b
Delaware Company VI–451b
Delaware Confederacy II–462b
DELAWARE COUNTIES ACT OF UNION (1682) **II–322b**
Delaware Division (Pennsylvania Canal System) I–127b; IV–174b; V–250a,b
DELAWARE PROPHET II–322b; V–4a, 356b, 357a; VI–271a
Delaware River I–443a; VII–372b
Anglo–Dutch rivalry III–258b
canals I–127b; II–322a; V–250a
Duke of York's Proprietary V–56a, 56b; VII–359a
East Jersey II–388b
exploration V–246a
ferries III–11b
Fort Mifflin IV–337b
Fort Nassau IV–454a
Hog Island Shipyard III–288a
hogs III–288b
Indians II–389a; VI–270b
Iroquois cession VI–385b
Morristown IV–413a
navigation VI–148a,b
Neshaminy Creek V–33a
New Albion V–332b
New Castle V–42b
New Haven Colony V–55b
New Jersey–Delaware boundary dispute I–351a,b
New Sweden Colony V–80a,b
patroonship V–229a
Pennsylvania–Maryland-boundary dispute V–252a
Pennsylvania Turnpike III–450b
Pennsylvania–Virginia-boundary dispute V–253a,b
Phelps–Gorham purchase V–276a
Philadelphia V–277a, 278a
Phoenix V–289a
Quakers II–124a
revolutionary war I–223a; III–36a; IV–35b, 251b; V–408a; VII–116a
Scotch-Irish VI–240b
settlement II–35a, 123b, 125b; IV–179a
Shawnee VI–270b
shipbuilding V–246b
steamboats III–32b
tide mills VII–58a
Treaty of Fort Stanwix III–382b
Walking Purchase VII–220b
War of 1812 IV–135b
water supply VII–259a
West Jersey VII–278b
Delaware River Basin Compact (1936) III–460a
Delaware River Commission VII–259a
Delaware River Valley III–214a
De La Warr, Lord (Thomas West) II–320a, 322a
De La Warre Bay II–322a
Delbrück, Max (biol.) I–304a; III–158a; IV–389b; V–100a
Delcassé, Théophile (dipl.) III–97a
DELEGATION OF POWERS II–323a
administrative discretion I–12a
Congress II–195b
executive orders II–473a
"Hot oil" Case III–307b
president V–394a
De Leon, Alonso IV–110a
De Leon, Daniel (Socialist)
Industrial Workers of the World III–412b; IV–67b
opposition to AFL I–104a
Socialist Labor Party IV–66b; VI–324b, 325a
De Leon, Edwin II–65b
De Leyba, Fernando (col. gov.) IV–376b
Delfthaven (Neth.) V–313a
Pilgrim voyage IV–278b
Delftware V–379b
Delgado, Isaac II–103b
DELIMA* v. *BIDWELL (1901) **II–323b**
Delinquents. *See* Juvenile Courts
Delisle, Guillaume (geog.) V–156b; VII–73b–74a
Delivered price system V–102b
Dellinger, David II–20b–21a; VI–14a
Dells (Wis. Riv.) III–89a
D. E. Loewe Company IV–67b
De Long, George Washington (nav. off.) V–336a,b
Delos (Gr.) II–375a
Del Rio (Tex.) I–246b; VI–143b
Delta Airlines I–68b; II–347b
Delta Dagger (airplane) I–54a
Delta Dart (airplane) I–54a
Delta Lines IV–312a
Demand-and-supply theory I–244b
Demand deposits I–252b–53a, 253b, 257a,b, 258a; II–1b–2a, 254b
DEMARCATION LINE (1494) **II–323b**; V–109a–b
Demarest Building (N.Y.C.) II–429a
Demerec, Milislav (geneticist) II–97a
Demesne land III–18a
De Mézieères y Clugny, Athanase. *See* Mézières y Clugny, Athanase de
Demilitarized Zone (Vietnam) VII–182b, 184a, 185b, 186a,b
De Mille, Agnes (chor.) II–289b, 290a,b
De Mille, Cecil B. (prod.) IV–417b
Deming (N.Mex.) VI–27a
Camp Cody I–434b
DEMOBILIZATION II–323b; IV–343a,b
Civil War I–185a; IV–346a
Korean War I–187a
revolutionary war V–42a
World War I I–186a; IV–341b
World War II I–179a, 187a
DEMOCRACY II–324b; V–351b–52a
Adams, John II–189a
Afro-Americans III–101b
campaign of 1824 I–418b
elections II–409b
equality II–456b
frontier ideal II–249b
Gettysburg Address III–202a–b
legislature IV–133b
Magna Charta IV–224b
Monroe Doctrine IV–400b
moral codes IV–408a
natural rights doctrine IV–140a
New Freedom V–53a
Plymouth colony IV–279a
public opinion V–453b; 454b–
representation VI–88a
representative government VI–89a
republic VI–92a
Republican party II–189a
town government VII–78a
U.S. Constitution II–197a
Democracy, Jacksonian. *See* Jacksonian Democracy
Democracy, Jeffersonian. *See* Jeffersonian Democracy
DEMOCRACY, WORLD SAFE FOR II–326b; IV–383b; V–124a; VII–333a
Democracy in America III–122b; V–353b
Democratic clubs V–345b
See also Jacobin Clubs
Democratic–Farmer Labor party II–492a
Democratic National Committee II–487b
DEMOCRATIC PARTY II–326b; I–415a–b; II–410b; IV–469b–70a; V–86b, 223a,b, 343b; VI–94b; VII–134b
AFL–CIO I–103a, 104b
Afro-Americans I–239a–b; III–438a
agrarianism I–33a
Alabama I–71a,b, 72a, 73b
American Labor party I–107a
American Liberty League I–108a
Antimonopolists I–133a
antislavery IV–28a
antislavery gag rule III–145b; V–266b
Appeal of the Independent Democrats I–145a
backlash I–239a
Barnburners III–111b, 318a
black suffrage III–93a; VI–431a, 431b
Bloody Monday I–323a
bloody shirt I–323b
bossism I–343a
Bourbons I–354a
Burchard incident I–383a
campaign of 1844 III–21a
campaign of 1872 IV–63a, 141a
campaign of 1876 II–38b; VII–344a
campaign of 1892 VI–322b
campaign of 1896 I–39a; II–75a, 266a; III–189a, 351b; IV–335a; V–354b, 366a
campaign of 1900 V–235b
campaign of 1904 III–197a
campaign of 1916 III–269b
campaign of 1932

V–106a, 430a
campaign of 1936 V–47b
campaign of 1944 IV–73b
campaign of 1948 III–9a–b; V–429a; VII–52b–53a
campaign of 1968 II–18b, 20b; III–70b; IV–342a; VII–191b
campaign of 1972 IV–77a
campaigns, presidential I–416a
carpetbaggers I–460a
Catholics I–467b
civil rights II–56b
Cleveland Democrats II–75a
congressional election of 1938 V–48b
congressional caucus I–474b
congressional election of 1918 IV–124b
Connecticut II–180b
Copperheads II–222a
Corning Letter II–228a
Cotton Kingdom II–241a
Daley, Richard J. II–18b; IV–214b
Delaware II–320b
direct primary V–407a
donkey symbol IV–454b; V–73a
emblems II–437b
Fair Deal II–480b
Farmer's Alliance II–493b
federal surplus VI–449a
Florida III–39b
Georgia III–168b–69a
"government by injunction" III–201a
Greenback movement III–224b
Hunkers III–317b
Idaho III–328b
Illinois III–330a; IV–156a
Independent Treasury System III–354b
Indiana III–370a
Iowa III–468a–b
Italian–Americans III–483b
Jacksonian Democracy III–486a
Kansas IV–31a; VII–345a
Kansas–Nebraska Act IV–29a,b
Kentucky factions IV–41a
labor's support IV–68a, 81b–82a
League of Nations IV–125a,b
Lecompton Constitution IV–131a
legislature IV–133b
Locofocos IV–175a
Louisiana IV–194b, 195a, 336a; VII–287a
Loyal Publication Societies IV–202a
Maine IV–226b, 227a
"manifest destiny" III–68a; IV–239a; VII–362a
Michigan IV–332a
Minnesota II–490b, 492a–b
Missouri IV–377a, 378a
Monroe–Pinkney Treaty IV–402b
Nashville Convention IV–453b
national committee IV–463a
National Union Convention VI–336a
New Departure policy V–49a
New Hampshire V–54a
New Mexico V–60a
New Orleans riots V–64a
New South V–108b
New York City V–83a,b
New York State I–267b–68a
nominating conventions II–216a; V–101b
North Carolina V–115b, 116a
Ohio V–142a
Oklahoma V–149b
one–partyism VII–135a
organization V–344b–46a
Pacific republic movement V–180b
party whip VII–289a
Pendergast machine V–244b
Pennsylvania I–374a–b; V–247b
"pop-gun" bills V–359a
populists V–365b
presidents V–395–96 (table)
Progressive movement V–427b, 428b, 429a
Progressive party IV–84b
Prohibition II–407a
proportional representation V–435b
Readjuster movement VI–49a
reciprocal trade agreements VI–51b–52a
Reconstruction III–295a–b, 437b–38a; VI–56a,b, 57a, 93a
Republican party formation VI–92b
Rhode Island VI–133b
Richmond Junto VI–138a
ripper legislation VI–144b
runoff primary V–407a
"Salt River" VI–203b
scientific information III–165a–b
Silver Democrats VI–287b
Silver party V–39b
Silver Republicans VI–293a
Sixteenth Amendment VI–297b
slavery I–110a, 138b, 139a; II–435a,b
Social Democrats VI–327a
South I–29a, 239a–b; VI–254b, 337a
South Carolina Reconstruction III–244a
South Dakota VI–350a
steering committees VI–411b
Supreme Court Packing Bills V–48a
Taft–Roosevelt split VI–458a
Tammany Hall VI–459b–60b
tariff I–326a; III–113a,b; VI–462b, 464a,b, 466b, 467a, 469b
taxation VII–6a
Tennessee VII–26a
Texas III–93a; VII–40b
third–term doctrine VII–53b
Topeka Constitution VII–72b
Treaty of Versailles IV–178b
Tweed Ring VII–131a–b
two–thirds rule VII–135a–b
Union Democrats VII–146a
Union party VII–148a
unit rule VII–155b
Vermont VII–172a,b
vice–presidents VII–179 (table), 180 (table)
Virginia VII–195b, 196a
voting behavior VII–210a–b
War Democrats VII–229b
Washington Benevolent Society VII–249b
Watergate II–259a; VII–253b
Ways and Means Committee VII–263b
Whig party VII–288a
whispering campaigns VII–291a
white primary III–20b; V–407a
Wilmington Riot VII–303a
Wilmot Proviso VII–303b–04a
Wisconsin VII–307b–08a
"witch–hunt" VII–310b
woman's suffrage VII–312b
Wyoming VII–346a
"Young America" VII–362a
Democratic republic. *See* Republic
Democratic–Republican party II–327a; IV–469b–70a
campaign of 1800 II–409a
campaign of 1832 II–216
campaigns, presidential I–417a–18a
Dartmouth College Case II–293b
election of 1800 IV–19b
Martling Men IV–260a
New York State I–374b
presidents V–395 (table)
See also Republicans, Jeffersonian
Democratic Review (period.) IV–239a; VII–362a
Democratic Societies. *See* Jacobin Clubs
Democratic Steering Committee VII–263b
Democratic Study Group I–322b
Democratic Vistas IV–162b
DEMOGRAPHY II–327b
Bureau of the Census I–482a,b
ecology II–392a
sampling methods and procedures VI–206a,b
urban structure VII–159a
westward movement VII–283b
See also Population, Growth and Movements of; Vital Statistics
DEMOLOGOS (warship) **II–329a**; III–36a, 131b; VII–240b
Demonetization
silver II–332a
See also Silver Legislation
Demonstration Cities and Metropolitan Development Act (1966) II–47b; IV–173a; V–393a; VI–328b
Demopolis (Ala.) VII–70b
Dempsey, Jack "Nonpareil" (boxer) V–423a
Dempsey, William Harrison (Jack) (boxer) I–488a; V–422b
Dempster, Arthur J. (chem.) I–218b
Demuth, Charles (paint.) V–192b
Denby, Edwin (pol.) V–13a, 346b; VII–16b
Dendrochronology. *See* Tree–Ring Dating
Dengue (virus) IV–291b
Denikin, Anton I. VI–178b
Denim work pants II–372a
Denishawn Company II–288a
Denison (Tex.) I–246b; VII–187b
Denison Dam III–322b
Denison News (news.) VII–187b
Denman, Mathias II–37b
Denmark III–106b
Bergen prizes I–290b
Butterfield claims I–398b
Common Market VI–472a
consumer cooperatives II–220a
European Free Trade Association VI–469a; VII–89a
Greenland II–46lb
immigration to U.S. III–334b, 337a
Jürgen Lorentzen prize case IV–20b
Kasson tariff treaty IV–33a
North Atlantic Treaty Organization V–113b
Organization for Economic Cooperation and Development V–170b
Pacific cable I–401a
slave trade VI–309b
Sound dues VI–340a
spoliation of American commerce II–291a–b
Stonewall VI–415a
U.S. aid III–61b
Virgin Islands III–425a;

DENMARK (cont.)
VII–112a, 203b
World War II III–327a; VI–424b; VII–334b
Dennan, Joseph (nav. off.) VI–311b
Dennis, Martin (chem.) IV–128b
Dennison, Aaron (watch mfr.) II–78b
Dennison, Howard, and Davis II–78b
Dennis v. *United States* (1951) II–146a; III–104a; IV–359a; VI–317b; VII–118a, 310b
Denny, William (col. gov.) II–389a; III–116b
DENONVILLE, FORT (N.Y.) **II–329a**
Denonville, Marquis de, Jacques René de Brisay (col. gov.)
Fort Frontenac V–156b
See also Denonville's Invasion II–329a–b
DENONVILLE'S INVASION (1687) **II–329a**; III–124b
Densmore, James (mfr.) I–396a; VII–136a
Dental Association, American. *See* American Dental Association
Dental Association, National II–330a
Dental Corps, Army IV–290b
Dental Corps, Navy IV–292b
Dental Cosmos (jour.) II–330b
Dental Educational Council II–330b
Dental engine II–331a
Dental Examiners, National Association of II–330b
Dental Faculties, National Association of II–330b
Dental Faculties Association of American Universities II–330b
Dental insurance III–436a
Dental Research Institute IV–465a
Dental School of the University of Maryland II–330a
Dental Schools, American Association of II–330b
Dental Surgeons, American Society of. *See* American Society of Dental Surgeons
DENTISTRY II–329b
army IV–290b
celluloid V–328a
education II–114b
navy IV–292b
University of Pennsylvania V–249a
women VII–317a
Works Progress Administration VII–323b
Dents, corn II–226a
Dentures, artificial II–329b, 331a
DENVER (Colo.) **II–332a**
Air Force Academy I–65a
anti-Chinese riots III–352a
Auraria I–224a
busing I–397b
Butterfield Overland Dispatch I–398b
caravan outfitting I–452a,b
cereal manufacturing I–487a
federal mint I–204a; IV–360a
federal records center III–284b
fires IV–354a
Forest Service III–76b
freighting V–177a
gold I–336b; V–311a
Goodnight-Loving Trail III–199b
Indian relocation VI–83b
Jefferson Territory III–497a
juvenile courts IV–23b
Kansas Pacific Railroad IV–30b
Leavenworth and Pikes Peak Express IV–129b; V–311b
Oregon Trail VI–355a
population II–128b
sanitariums VI–101a
smelting VI–316b
Smoky Hill Trail VI–320a,b
stage lines I–485a; VI–379b
stockyards VI–414a
Union Colony VII–146a
vigilantes VII–187b
Denver, J. W. (gov. offi.) II–332a
Denver and Rio Grande Railroad II–129a; III–64b
Denver and Rio Grande Western Railroad VI–27b, 34a
Denver and Salt Lake Railroad VI–34a; VII–128b
Denver-Auraria (Colo.) I–174b
Denver Pacific Railroad IV–30b; VI–37b
Denver Post (news.) V–73a, 73b
Deodands III–18a
Deoxyribonucleic acid. *See* DNA
Deoxyribose IV–389a
Department of Labor. *See* Labor, Department of
Department of the Lakes II–338a
Department of the West IV–129b
DEPARTMENT STORES II–332a; I–17a
foreign investment III–66b
hardware trade III–252b
mail-order sales IV–225a
self-service VI–258b
See also Chain Stores; Five-and-Ten-Cent Stores
Dependent Pension Bill (1887) V–257a
De Pere (Wis.) III–225b; IV–7a
De Peyster, Abraham (off.) IV–48b
Depletion allowance VI–12a; VII–10a
DEPORTATION II–332b; IV–209b; V–342b
DEPOSIT, FORT (Ala.) **II–333a**
DEPOSIT, RIGHT OF II–333a; VI–359a; VII–111b
Mississippi River IV–372b
New Orleans VI–150b
Pinckney's Treaty IV–196b, 373b; V–315b
DEPOSIT ACT OF 1836 II–333b; VI–449a
Deposit banking. *See* Bank Deposits
Depot of Charts and Instruments IV–276b–77a; V–12a, 133a–b, 134a–b, 336b
Depreciation allowance VII–12a
Depression (1785–88) V–206a
Depression (1837–44) I–255b; II–255a; IV–81a; V–206b
Depression (1870's) III–405b; V–207a–b
Depression (1886) II–251b
Depression (1890's) I–33a, 376b; II–252b; IV–36a; V–207b–08a
DEPRESSION OF 1920 II–333b
Nonpartisan League V–107a
reclamation VI–54a
shanty towns VI–268b
Depression (1921) II–220b
Depression (1969) III–415b
Depression, Great (1930's) I–394b; V–353b
advertising I–19a
agrarianism I–33b
agriculture I–39b, 42a, 43a, 44a
Anti-Saloon League I–134b
art collecting II–105a
auto sales I–230a
aviation industry I–236b
balance of trade I–245b
bank deposits I–252b
bank failures I–253b, 257a–b; III–6b
bankruptcy laws I–262b
bimetallism I–302a–b
blacks I–30a
book collecting II–109b
British war debts I–123a
building and loan associations I–376b
California I–407b; II–454b
campaign of 1932 I–428b
clothing industry II–83a
Connecticut II–180b
contract work V–309b
cooperative apartments I–143b
cotton industry II–238b
currency and banking IV–395b
dairy industry II–282a
dam construction III–322a
Democratic party II–327b
Detroit II–337a
education II–400a
emigration II–439b
endowed foundations III–83a
farm tenancy I–40b
federal aid II–502a
federal deficit II–317b
food supply III–53a
foreign investments II–301a
forestry programs III–73b–74a
France III–97b
government corporations III–201b
government spending III–205b
home ownership VI–222a
Home Owners' Loan Corporation III–294a
Hoover administration VI–93a
Hoover moratorium IV–409a
horse racing revenues III–305a
housing II–47a; III–310a, 310b; IV–428b
industrial research III–409b
insurance companies III–434a
interstate trade barriers III–460b
labor IV–70b–71b
land speculation IV–100b
law schools IV–121b
mapmaking I–463b
Massachusetts IV–267b
Michigan IV–332a
migrant workers II–495b
military bonuses I–331b
Minnesota mortgage moratorium IV–358a
Mississippi IV–369a–b
mortgage relief legislation IV–414b
National Employment Service Act II–442a
national sinking fund VI–294a
National Youth Administration VII–364b
nativism V–3b
New Deal V–43a
New Era V–52a
New Hampshire V–54b
Ohio V–142a
Oklahoma V–149a
Pennsylvania V–247b
petroleum industry V–270a–b
planned economy V–323b
political parties V–223a
poverty V–381b
price-fixing V–402a
prices V–406a
profit sharing V–426b

Prohibition V–430a
public control of business I–390b–91a
public debt II–300a
purchasing power of money IV–393a
Reconstruction Finance Corporation V–455b; VI–59b
relief VI–72b–73a
rubber VI–168a
Russia VI–178b
shanty towns VI–268b
share-the-wealth movements VI–269a
silver prices VI–288b
social security VI–329a
soil conservation VI–335b
South Carolina VI–348a
state borrowing II–302b
subsistence homesteads VI–426b
taxation VII–7b, 13a
technocracy movement VII–17b
tenant farmers IV–103b
tenements VII–23b
theater VII–49b–50a
unemployment VII–139b, 140a,b
union membership IV–70a
unregulated market system IV–80b
woman's rights movement VII–314a
Works Progress Administration VII–322b
See also Panic of 1929
Depressions
cost of government II–234a
desertion from army II–334b–35a
federal deficit II–317a
inflation II–236b
De Priest, Oscar (pol.) I–29b; VI–432b
Deptford (Eng.) II–375a
Depth charges V–163b
Derby, George Horatio (off., au.) V–289a
Derby, G. H. (expl.) II–129b
Derbyshire (Eng.) IV–44a
Deringer, Henry (mfr.) IV–432b
Dermatoses IV–294b
Dermer, Thomas IV–264b
Dern, George H. (pol.) V–43b
DERNA EXPEDITION (1805) **II–334a**; I–266a; IV–251b
Desalination VII–259b
De Sapio, Carmine G. (pol.) VI–460b
Des Barres, J. F. W. (off.) IV–248a
Descalona, Luis (miss.) V–241a
Desch, Joseph (eng.) II–154b
Description de la Louisiane III–272a,b
Description of New England V–53b
Description of the Province of New Albion V–332b–33a
Desegregation
armed forces II–56b
busing I–397b
campaign of 1968 I–431b
civil service II–56b
mass resistance II–54b
schools II–54b–55a
Supreme Court rulings II–54a–55b, 57a–b, 400a
See also Integration
DESERET, STATE OF **II–334a**; I–397b; IV–117a; VII–161b
Gunnison massacre III–235a
Salt Lake City VI–203b
Desert, Great American. *See* Great American Desert
DESERT CULTURE **II–334b**; I–156a, 157a; IV–385b
Anasazi I–117b
Hohokam III–289a
Pueblo V–460a
Utah VII–161a
DESERTION **II–334b**
British army VI–127b
Civil War II–63a, 67a, 159b, 164b; III–297b; IV–368b
expatriation II–475b
land bounties for enemy deserters IV–91a
revolutionary war III–173a; VI–118b, 130a
Seamen's Act of 1915 VI–246b
Valley Forge VII–165a
DESERT LAND ACT (1877) **II–335b**; I–453b; V–444b, 450b; VI–53b
Deserts
Forty-Mile III–81b
Great American Desert III–213b
Jornado I–174b
Owens Valley (Calif.) IV–104b
See also Arid Regions
Desert willow (tree) VII–114a
Deshon, George (cler.) V–229b
Design, National Academy of V–188b, 191b, 192a
Desire (slave ship) VI–308b
Desire Under the Elms (play) VII–50b
Desks III–134a,b, 135a
"Des Landes Vater" II–497a
Desmet (Idaho) II–93b
De Smet, Pierre Jean (miss.) II–477b; III–122b, 468a, 500a
Coeur d'Alene II–93b
Fort Berthold II–284a
irrigation III–477a
Montana IV–403a
Oregon missions V–167a
Sublette's Cutoff VI–422a
Des Moines (Iowa) I–434b; II–157b; III–468a,b; VI–35b
Des Moines Rapids VII–196b, 271a
Des Moines Register and Tribune (news.) V–73b
Des Moines River III–242b
floods II–351a; III–37a
Fort Kearny IV–33b
fur trade III–144b
neutral ground V–33b
De Soto, Hernando (expl.). *See* De Soto Expedition
DE SOTO EXPEDITION (1539–43) **II–336a**; I–96a–b; II–184a, 452b; III–302b
Alabama I–71a, 402a
Arkansas I–172b
Arkansas River I–174a
Battle of Mauvilla IV–277a
Five Civilized Tribes II–51b–52a
Florida III–38a
hogs III–288a–b
Louisiana V–173a
Mississippi IV–368a, 372a, 375b
Mississippi River IV–301b
Narváez patent IV–452b
Natchez Indians IV–455b
Oklahoma V–148a
Tennessee VII–24b
Texas VII–36a
vegetable gardens III–150b–51a
Des Plaines River II–19b; III–332a; IV–7a, 87b
D'Estaing, Jean Baptiste Hector (off.) VI–221a, 438a–b
D'Estaing, Valéry Giscard (states.) III–97b
Destination, Enemy. *See* Enemy Destination
Destroyer (bomber) I–50b
Destroyer escort VII–243a
Destroyers V–25a,b, 26a; VII–241a,b, 243a, 328b, 342a, 343b
aircraft launch I–55b
construction II–370a
Frank E. Evans II–350a
London Naval Treaty II–461a
naval competition V–10a,b
World War II II–225a, 387b, 443a
See also Warships
Detached house (arch.) I–164a,b, 165a
Detector, electronic II–423b
Détente III–62b, 71a; IV–113a
Detergent. *See* Soap and Detergent Industry
DETROIT (Mich.) **II–336b**; III–216a, 438a; IV–330b, 331a,b, 332a; V–123a
Afro-Americans I–25b
bootlegging I–339b
busing I–397b
Cadillac'S Indian policy VI–220a
Campus Martius II–338b
Chicago Road II–20a
city planning II–45b, 338b
civil disturbances IV–342a
colonial architecture I–160a
colonial land grants IV–93a
directory II–343b
flour milling I–488a
foreign trade VII–89b
Fort Pontchartrain III–120a; V–356b
Franciscans III–94a
French and Indian War III–117a
Grand Circus II–338b
Great Trail III–223b
hockey III–287b
Hull Treaty III–316a
Indian factory II–480a
Indian trade VII–95b
Kaskaskia trade IV–32a
Lake Erie II–459a
land tenure IV–104b
Michigan Territorial Road IV–332b
organized crime II–262b
portage V–367b
race riots I–31b, 32a; II–259a; IV–258b, 259a, 457b; VI–7a, 8a, 9a
Railroad Conspiracy VI–20b
railroads VI–34a
recall VI–51a
recording industry IV–442a–b
revolutionary war VI–130a
ribbon farms VI–135a
Saint Lawrence River VI–192b
shipbuilding III–216b
Spring Wells Treaty VI–377b
trading house III–142b
Treaty of Greenville III–227b
War of 1812 I–436b; III–217a, 217b; VII–45b
Detroit (ship) II–459b; III–218a
DETROIT, FORT (Mich.) **II–337b**; III–142b; V–356b; VII–188a
Anglo-French relations I–477a
Bourgmont, E. v. de I–354b
Bradstreet's expedition I–359a
British I–340b, 341a; VII–270a
Fort Saint Joseph VI–191b
Fox-French Wars III–89a
French II–458b; VI–162b
Hull's Trail III–316a
Indian councils II–392b
Pontiac's War I–323b; II–265b, 322b, 337a; V–90a, 357a
revolutionary war I–367a; II–71a; III–400b; IV–59b, 117b, 173b, 216b; VI–124a
Seneca attack II–339b
War of 1812 VII–234a,b
DETROIT, SURRENDER OF (1812) **II–338a**; II–458b; III–315b; VI–42a; VII–45b, 234a, 262a
Detroit, University of II–337b

DETROIT, WOODWARD PLAN OF **II–338b**; II–45b, 45b
DETROIT FIRE (1805) **II–339a**; II–338b
Detroit Free Press (news.) V–76b
Detroit Gazette (news.) V–70b
Detroit Institute of Arts II–337b; III–137b
Detroit Lions (football) II–337b
Detroit Red Wings (hockey) II–337b
Detroit River II–336b, 337b
  ferries III–11b
  Fort Pontchartrain V–356b
  Hull Treaty III–316a
  U.S. boundary VII–265a
  War of 1812 VI–42a
Detroit River Tunnel VII–128b
Detroit Tigers (baseball) II–337b
Detroit treaty (1807). *See* Brownstown and Detroit Treaties
Detroit Zoological Park VII–371a
Deuel, Wallace R. (jour.) V–74a
Deuterium II–12b; V–299b
Deuterons IV–119a
DEVALUATION **II–339a**; I–252b, 257b, 302a; II–318a; III–195b, 196a–b; VI–472b; VII–222b
  foreign investment III–66b
  gold dollar III–192a; IV–392b, 394a, 395b
  Great Depression III–7a
  New Deal V–44a, 45a
  price declines V–404a
  repudiation of public debt VI–95a,b
  Thomas Amendment VII–54b
  Tripartite Agreement VII–120b
  World Economic Conference VII–324a
Devanter, Willis Van (jur.) VI–446a
Devastator (airplane) I–55b
Deveaux, Andrew (off.) VI–130a
Development Loan Fund III–62a
Development of American Political Science: From Burgess to Behavioralism V–347b
Devereux, James P. S. (off.) VII–218b
Devereux, John H. (off.) VI–374b
Devil
  folklore III–48b
Deville, Henri Sainte-Claire. *See* Sainte-Claire Deville, Henri
Devil's Highway. *See* Camino del Diablo
DEVIL'S HOLE, AMBUSCADE OF (1763) **II–339b**
Devils Lake II–284a
Devils Postpile National Monument V–217a
Devils River VI–143b
Devil's Tower National Monument I–313a; V–217b
Devoe Manufacturing Company VI–383a
Devon cattle I–471b; II–281b
De Voto, Bernard A. (hist.) VII–268b
De Vries, David P. (navig.) II–322a; VII–372b
Dew, Thomas Roderick (econ.) VII–194b
Dewberries III–129a
Dewees, William P. (physic.) IV–275a
De Wette, Wilhelm M. L. VI–82a
Dewey, George (nav. off.) I–14a; III–25b–26a, 263b; IV–239b; V–20a, 282b; VI–361b, 362b, 363a; VII–169b
Dewey, John (philos., educ.) II–398b, 400a; V–286b, 288a–b, 386b, 387a
  Laboratory VI–228b
Dewey, Melvil (librarian) IV–145a
Dewey, Thomas E. (pol.) V–87b; VI–93b
  campaign of 1944 I–429a
  campaign of 1948 I–429b; II–480b
Dewey Decimal System IV–145a
DeWitt, Green II–339b
De Witt, Simeon (surv.) I–462a, 463a
De Witt Clinton (locomotive) IV–386b; VI–24b
DEWITT'S COLONY **II–339b**
De Young, Henry II–103b
Deystouy, Auguste (inv.) I–338a
D'Hondt quota (pol.) V–435b
DH–4B (airplane) I–233b
DIA. *See* Defense Intelligence Agency
Diacetylmorphine II–374a
Diaghilev, Sergei (ballet prod.) II–288b, 289a; VII–49b
Dial (mag.) IV–190a; VII–98a
Diamond, "Legs" (criminal) II–258b
Diamondback snake VI–47b
DIAMOND ISLAND FIGHT (1777) **II–340a**; IV–86b
Diamond Match Company IV–274b
Diamonds, synthetic III–156a
Diamond State VI–393 (table)
Diarrhea IV–150b, 151a, 275a, 299a
Diastrophism VI–237a
Diaz, Adolfo (pol.) V–94a
Diaz, Armando (off.) II–311a
Díaz, Melchior (expl.) II–129b, 228b
Díaz, Porfirio (states.) IV–328b
Dibble (tool) I–48b
Dice III–149b; VI–381b
Dichlorodifluoromethane VI–70a
Dichlorodiphenyltrichloroethane. *See* DDT
Dick Act (1903) I–185b; II–314a; IV–343b, 346a, 463b
Dickens, Charles (au.) I–367b, 368a, 403b; IV–163a; VII–245a
Dickenson, Jonathan (cler.) V–391b
Dickinson, Charles II–377a
Dickinson, J. (nav. off.) III–302a
Dickinson, John (states.) V–198b, 247a
  Annapolis convention I–126a
  antislavery I–135a
  Articles of Confederation I–197b
  Constitution II–193a, 194a, 203b
  Declaration of Independence II–304b
  Farmer's Letters II–494b; VI–111b
  "Liberty Song" VII–155b
  library II–107b
  Plan of 1776 V–323b
  "Song of Liberty" IV–142b
Dickinson, Jonathan (cler., educ.)
  Princeton University V–408b
Dickinson's Farmer's Letters VI–111b
Dickman, Joseph T. (off.) I–70b, 191b, 502a
Dickson, Robert (fur trader) III–403b
Dickson, William Kennedy Laurie (inv.) IV–417a
Dickstein, Samuel (pol.) III–308b
Dictating machine I–396a
Dictatorships II–409b
DICTIONARIES **II–340a**; VI–227a; VII–266a
DICTIONARY OF AMERICAN BIOGRAPHY **II–340b**; III–281b
Dictionary of American English II–340b
Dictionary of Americanisms II–340b
Didat Deus (motto) VI–393 (table)
Diderot, Denis (ency.) II–444a
Didrikson, Mildred ("Babe") (athlete) V–154a
Die Arbeiter Zeitung (news.) IV–64b
Diebold, John I–225a
Die-casting V–103a,b
"Died with their boots on" II–358b
Diefenbaker, John (states.) I–440a
Diegueño (Indians) III–363a; IV–366a
Diem, Ngo Dinh (pres.) III–70a, 160b; VII–182b–83a
Dien Bien Phu (Viet.) I–49a, 124b; II–489b
Dieppe school (cartog.) IV–247b
Dies, Martin, Jr. (pol.) III–308b
Diesel electric generators II–416a–b
Diesel electric locomotive II–416a–b
Diesel engine IV–420a
Dieskau, Ludwig August (off.) I–323b; III–115a–b; IV–86a, 87b
Diet. *See* Nutrition and Vitamins
Dietary allowances, recommended V–128b
Diethylene glycol V–467a
Differential analyzer II–153a
Digestion IV–292a
Digger (Indians) III–51b; V–194a
Digging stick I–36a, 48b
DIGHTON ROCK **II–341a**
Digital computers I–287b; II–152b, 154a, 426b
Digitalis IV–297b
Dikes VII–58a
Diligente (clipper) VI–308b–09a
Dill, Daniel H. (off.) VI–135a
Dillard, Harrison (athlete) V–154a
Dillard University III–103b
Dillenius, Johann (bot.) I–348b
Diller, Burgoyne (art.) II–104b
Dillion's rule I–501a
Dilworth, Richardson (pol.) V–278a
Dilworth, Thomas (educ.) VI–227a
DIME **II–341a**; II–95a
Dime Book of Practical Etiquette IV–240b
"Dime" museum VII–47b
DIME NOVELS **II–341a**; I–334a, 335b
Dimond, Anthony J. (pol.) I–78a
Dine, Jim (art.) VII–319b
Dingley, Nelson (pol.) VI–467a
Dingley Tariff (1897) II–323b; III–58a; IV–33a; VI–464a,b, 467a–b
Dinjan (India) III–46a
Dinnerware III–184b
Dinosaur National Monument V–217b, 220a
Dinosaurs III–163b
Dinsmore, Elsie (lit. char.) I–335b

Dinwiddie, Robert (col. gov.)
II–381b; III–115a, 219a; IV–130a; V–146a
Dinwiddie Courthouse (Va.)
III–33b; V–265a
See also Five Forks, Battle of
Diocese of the Armenian Church of North America
II–387a
Diomedes Islands
Eskimo I–81a
Dior, Christian (fashion designer) II–372b
Dioramas VII–47b
Diphtheria I–241b; II–280a, 454b; IV–150a,b, 275a, 295a, 299a; V–340a, 447b
Diplomacy
Articles of Confederation II–166b
Civil War II–64b–66a, 162a
cold war II–97a
commercial treaties VII–108b
Cuban relations II–269b–70a
embassies II–437a
executive agreements II–471b
indemnities III–352a
National Security Council II–498a
Pan-American Union V–205a
reprisal VI–104b
Revolution VI–116a–17a
rivers VI–150b
U.S. Information Agency II–499a
See also Dollar Diplomacy; Far Eastern Policy; Foreign Service
DIPLOMACY, SECRET II–342a
Fourteen Points VII–330b
Lansing–Ishii Agreement IV–106b
Open covenants, openly arrived at V–157b
Perdicaris affair V–261b
protocol of 1917 VI–251b
Santo Domingo mission VI–217a
Slidell mission IV–323a
Teheran protocol VII–18a
Treaty of San Ildefonso VI–210b
Trist Mission III–230a
Vietnam peace talks V–216a; VII–184b
Diplomacy, shirt-sleeve. *See* Shirt-Sleeve Diplomacy
Diplomacy for the 70's III–72a
Diplomatic corps I–93a
Diplomatic Correspondence of the American Revolution III–281a
DIPLOMATIC MISSIONS II–342b; VI–389a,b
Dana mission to Russia VI–177a
Geneva Accords of 1954 III–159b
Geneva Conferences III–160b
Great Lakes Dissarmament Agreement III–217a
international law III–455b
Jay's Treaty III–493b–94a
joint commission to France III–90a
Latin-American republics IV–115a
Monroe mission to France IV–402a
Naples claims IV–449a
papal states V–211b
peace conferences V–232b
Perry's Japan expedition V–263a
Perry's Venezuela mission VII–170a
Slidell in Mexico VI–312b
whaling VII–285a
Diplomatic Reception Room, Department of State (Washington, D.C.) III–137b
Diplomatic Relations, Vienna Convention on (1961) III–457a
Diplomatic Service. *See* Foreign Service
Diplomats. *See* Ambassadors; Ministers; Consuls; Chargé d'Affaires
Dirac, Paul (phys.) V–299a, 304a
Direct current II–414b
Direct-current distribution system IV–153b
Direct-current motors II–413a, 415b
"Direct effect" doctrine II–136b
Direct election II–194b–95a
Direction for Adventurers to New Albion V–332b
Directoire style (dress) II–371b
DIRECTORIES, CITY II–343b
Directory of Interstate Agencies VI–402a
Direct painting V–191b
Direct primary. *See* Primary, Direct
Direct tax VII–4a,b–5a,b, 6a, 12b
apportionment II–183a, 198a
Barnburners I–268a
carriage tax I–461a
Confederacy II–164a
constitutional prohibition I–451a
regulation II–200b
DIRIGIBLES II–343b; I–51b, 233a, 236b
Dirigo (motto) VI–394 (table)
Dirk, Rudolph (cartoon.) V–72a
Dirksen, Everett (states.) I–474b
"Dirty tricks" campaign (1972) VII–291a
Disability IV–294b
Disability insurance III–434b, 435b
See also Workmen's Compensation
Disabled American Veterans VII–175a
Disarmament
Geneva Conferences III–161a
Great Lakes III–217a–b
Hague peace conferences III–237a
Nuclear Test Ban Treaty V–124b
post-World War I I–290b
Students for a Democratic Society VI–421a
Treaty of Versailles VII–173a
See also Arms Race With the Soviet Union; Geneva Conferences; Strategic Arms Limitations Talks
DISASTERS II–346a
Apollo fire IV–460a
Chicago Fire IV–424b
Coast Guard rescue II–89b
conscientious objectors V–182b
Eastland II–388b
floods III–36b
forest fires III–74b
Galveston storm III–149a
Griffon IV–217b
hurricanes III–319a; IV–258b
immigration to U.S. III–339b
Iroquois Theater fire III–476b
Johnstown flood IV–5a
Last Island hurricane IV–110b
Lusitania IV–205a
martial law IV–258b
military aid IV–341b
mining town fires IV–354a
Mississippi River IV–373a, 374b
Princeton explosion V–408b
Red Cross VI–61b, 62a
relief V–280b
Sable Island VI–182a
San Francisco earthquake VI–210a
Savannah VI–220b
steamboat explosions VI–148b
Titantic VII–64a
tornadoes VII–75a
Triangle fire VII–118b
U.S. Navy V–23a
DISCIPLES OF CHRIST II–352b; VI–77b
Cane Ridge revival I–444b
frontier preaching III–127b
Rice–Campbell debates VI–135b
slavery II–36b
Western Reserve VII–275a
Disciplinary Barracks, U.S. IV–129b
"Discipline out of the Word" V–51b
Discotheques II–349a
Discount houses II–421b
Discounting II–467b
Discount stores VII–124a
Discourse of the Old Company VII–201a
Discourse on the Constitution and Government of the United States VI–403b–04a
DISCOVERY **(ship) II–353a**; II–219b, 322a; VII–166a, 192b
Discovery (colonial ship) VI–451a
"Discrete" sound system V–290b
Discretion, administrative. *See* Administrative Discretion, Delegation of
Discrimination II–55a,b
Afro-Americans I–21a, 26a, 27a–b, 31b, 101a, 357a
aliens I–88b
employment II–56b, 455b–56a; VII–141a
equal protection clause III–86b
Force Acts III–60a
gerrymandering III–175a
housing III–310b, 311a
Indians I–106b
literacy tests IV–160a
National Labor Relations Act IV–466b–67a
Niagara movement V–93a
railroads II–493a–b
segregation VI–255b
states II–54a
voting III–20a
See also Race Relations; Segregation
Disease
agriculture II–391b
Church of Christ, Scientist II–35b–36a
climate II–75b
environment II–390b
germ theory II–390b
hookworm III–298b
malaria IV–229a
military medicine IV–291a
poor whites V–358b
vital statistics VII–205b
workmen's compensation VII–322b
Disease, oral II–331b
Disease, study of. *See* Bacteriology and Virology
Disease Control, Center for III–267b
Disfranchisement of the southern black. *See* Suffrage, Afro-American
Disguised unemployment VII–139b
Dishwasher, electric II–417b, 419a
Disk plow I–34a
DISMAL SWAMP II–353a
Dismal Swamp Canal III–449a; VI–425a
Disme II–95a, 341a; IV–394a
Disney World (Fla.) III–40a

Dispensing powers IV–36b
Displaced Persons Act (1948) III–339b; V–342b
DISSENTERS II–353a
colonization I–499b
New Hampshire settlements V–53b
New York City V–82a
religious liberty VII–69a
Rogerenes VI–162a
South Carolina VI–347a
Dissenters, political
Civil War II–66b
Distant blockade I–321a
Distant Early Warning I–58a, 62a; V–338a
Distemper VII–175b–76a
Distillers and Cattle Feeders Trust VII–122a
Distillery mash II–280a
DISTILLING II–353b
colonial II–4b–5a; III–413b; IV–243a; VI–108a
moonshine IV–407b
Prohibition II–261a; V–429b
Salem II–5a
springs VI–377b
taxation VII–4b, 5a, 8b, 12b
Tennessee VII–26a
whiskey VII–289a
Whiskey Rebellion VII–290a
Whiskey Ring VII–290b
Distinguished Flying Cross II–311b
Distinguished Service Cross II–310a–11b
Distinguished Service Medal II–310b–11b
Distinguished Unit Citation IV–314a
Distribution Act. *See* Deposit Act of 1836
DISTRIBUTION OF GOODS AND SERVICES II–354a; VII–84b–85a
commerce clause II–135b
furniture III–139a–b
Hamilton's fiscal policies III–246a
hardware trade III–252a
inflation III–414a
marketing research IV–255a
monopoly IV–398b
packaging V–182b
rubber industry VI–167b
self-service stores VI–258a
Socialist movement VI–325b
work force V–132b
Distribution–Preemption Act (1841) V–444a,b
Distribution's Place in the American Economy Since 1869 III–252a
DISTRICT, CONGRESSIONAL II–355a
District attorney, U.S. II–503b
District attorneys IV–21b
District courts. *See* Courts, district
District judges II–39b–40a
District of Columbia III–438a–b
campaign of 1972 VI–93b
canal I–442b
circuit court IV–36b
compensated emancipation II–433b–34a
congressial power over II–200a
courts IV–16b
Coxey's Army II–252b
Crittenden Compromise II–265a
dueling I–318a
fair-trade law II–482b, 483b
flag III–35a
lotteries IV–191a
minimum-wage law IV–352b, 353a
osteopathy V–175a
presidental electors II–207a
presidential electors II–408b–09a
sales tax VI–200a
segregation II–54b
slavery I–137b; VI–308a
slave trade II–139a, 150a
state land cessions IV–260b
taxation VII–14a
U.S. attorney II–210b
voting rights I–95a, 431a; VII–132b, 208b
Washington public transportation IV–428b
workmen's compensation III–431b
See also Washington, D.C.
District of Columbia Redevelopment Act (1945) VII–246a
District school system II–394a, 396b, 397a
Disturnell, John (pub.) II–355b; VII–74b
DISTURNELL'S MAP II–355b; III–230a; IV–321a
Ditmars, Raymond Lee (nat.) VI–91b
Dive bombers I–55a, 56b, 328a; II–387b
Diversity–of–citizenship cases II–460a–b
Divided school VI–226b
Dividends
taxation VII–12a
DIVINE PROVIDENCES II–355b; II–496a
Divine sovereignty II–406a
Diving
Olympic Games V–154a,b
Divining rod V–271a
"Divinity School Address" IV–162a; VI–81b
Divinity schools
Yale VII–351a
DIVISION ACT OF 1800 II–356a
DIVORCE II–356b; IV–257a; V–355b
Equal Rights party II–457b
Navaho V–9a
North Dakota V–118a
rates II–486a–b
state laws VI–402a
uniform state laws VI–399a,b
woman's rights VII–313b, 314a
Dix, Dorothea Lynde (philan., ref.) IV–305b; V–280a; VI–327b; VII–206a
Dix, John A. (states.) I–107b
Dix, John D. (physic.) I–143a
Dix–Hill Cartel (1862) II–468b
DIXIE II–357a
"Dixie" (song) IV–359b, 438a
Dixiecrat party II–480b; VII–52b
Dixie Highway VII–296b
Dixie Project II–130b
Dixon, Billy (scout) VI–241b
Dixon, Jeremiah (surv.) II–322b; IV–263b; V–252b, 253a
Dixon, Jeremy VI–263b
Dixon, Joseph M. (pol.) IV–403b
Dixon, Robert VII–234b
Dixon, Thomas (au.) IV–58b
Dixon Kemp Rule VII–349b
Dixwell, John (Regicide) IV–48a; V–70b
Djesakid IV–335b
D. L. and W. Railroad. *See* Delaware, Lackawanna and Western Railroad
DMZ. *See* Demilitarized Zone
DNA II–357b; I–304a; II–13a; III–158a; IV–389a, 389b–91b
Doak's Stand, Treaty of (1820) I–441b–42a; III–383b; VII–181b
Doane, Thomas (eng.) VII–128a
Doan's Store (Tex.) II–32a, 358b
Doar, John M. (law.) III–344b
Dobbs, Arthur (col. gov.) VI–71b; VII–350a
Dobbs Ferry (N.Y.) III–117b
"Dobie" *See* Adobe
Dobie, James Frank (writ.) VII–41a
Dobrynin, Anatoly (dipl.) VI–417a
Dobson, Thomas (pub.) II–444a
Dock, Christoph (educ.) II–395a
Dock, Lavinia (educ.) V–126b
Dockery Act (1894) II–152a
Dockstader, Lew (act.) IV–359b
Dodd (pub.) I–334a
Dodds, Harold W. (pol. sci.) V–409a
Dodge, Augustus C. (pol.) III–468a–b
Dodge, David Low (mer.) V–235a
Dodge, Grenville M. (off., eng.) VI–373b; VII–147b
Dodge, Harold F. (statis.) VI–206b
Dodge, Henry (off.) II–358b–59a
Dodge, Mary Abigail (Gail Hamilton) (ed.) IV–223a
Dodge, Mary Mapes (au.) I–335a; IV–223a; V–41b
Dodge, Willam de Leftwich (paint.) V–191a
DODGE CITY (Kans.) **II–358b**; I–174b
cattle I–473b; II–32a, 251b; IV–26a, 280b; VII–294a
Dust Bowl II–382a
Fort Mann IV–240a
vigilantes VII–187b
DODGE CITY TRAIL II–358b
Dodge, Fort (Iowa) VI–374a
Dodge, Fort (Kans.) I–375a; II–358b
DODGE–LEAVENWORTH–EXPEDITION (1834) **II–358b**
Dodsley (pub.) II–466b
Doenitz, Karl (nav. off.) I–214a,b; II–217b; V–21b; VI–424b; VII–342b
Dog I–37a
coyote II–252b
Eskimos II–462a
travois VII–106b
Dog, wild III–51a
"Dogie" I–473b
"Dogie" songs II–250a
Dog races III–149b
Dogrib (Indians) III–360b
language I–441b
Dog's Head in the Porridge Pot Tavern (N.Y.) VII–2a
Dog sled III–381a
Dogtown (Mass.) I–447a
Dogwood (tree) VI–394 (table), 395 (table)
Doheny, Edward L. (oil prod.) I–407a; II–431b; VII–16b
Dohrman, Arnold Henry (dipl.) II–359a
DOHRMAN'S GRANT II–359a
Dohrn, Anton (zool.) IV–251a
Doisy, Edward (biochem.) V–100a
Dokuchaiev, v. v. (chem.) VI–334a
Dolbear, Amos E. (inv.) VII–20b
Dole, Sanford B. (pol.) III–263b
Dollar II–94b–95a
devaluation II–318a, 339a–b
dime II–341a
gold content II–339a
DOLLAR–A–YEAR MAN II–359a
DOLLAR DIPLOMACY II–359a; II–475b; VI–364a
China II–488b
Dominican Republic II–361a–b
Manchuria II–488b; IV–235a

DOLLAR SIGN II–360a
Dollier de Casson, François. *See* Casson, François Dollier de
Dolliver, Jonathan P. (pol.) V–427b
Dolly agitator II–420a
Dolores (Calif.) VI–209a
Dolores (Tex.) VI–144a
Dolores River VI–368a
Dolphin (frigate) VI–128b
Dolphin (steel ship) VII–241a, 293b
***DOLPHIN* ADMIRALTY CASE** (1863) **II–360a**
Domain, Eminent. *See* Eminent Domain
Domain, Public. *See* Public Domain
Dome (arch.) I–159b; IV–405a
Domebo (Okla.) II–83b
Domestic and Foreign Missionary Society of the Protestant Episcopal Church IV–365b
Domesticated animals I–37a, 158a
Domestic Commerce, Bureau of II–135a
Domestic Conciliation Courts II–157b
Domestic Council II–498a
Domestic insurrections. *See* Insurrections, Domestic
Domestic Medicine IV–295b
DOMESTIC RELATIONS, COURTS OF II–360a
Domestic servants II–214b, 418a–19a, 442b
Domestic Trade. *See* Trade, Domestic
Domina Scientiarum (degree) II–399a
Domínguez, Francisco Atanasio (miss.) II–461a; VII–74a, 161a
Dominic, Saint II–362b
Dominica III–117a; V–214b
DOMINICAN REPUBLIC II–360b
  Alta Vela claim I–91b
  conflict with Venezuela V–171a
  dollar diplomacy II–359b
  immigration to U.S. III–337b, 341b
  Kasson tarriff treaty IV–33a
  United Nations Declaration VII–151b
  U.S. intervention II–315b; III–199a, 348a, 463a, 463a,b; IV–4b, 111b, 113a, 252b, 253a, 385b, 401a,b, 402a; V–105b, 106a, 171a; VI–163a
  U.S. occupation I–61b, 65a, 454b; II–359b
  U.S. protectorate III–347b
  U.S. trade VI–343b
DOMINICAN REPUBLIC, PROPOSED ANNEXATION OF II–362a; II–475a; III–347a; IV–111a
DOMINICANS II–362b
Dominion of New England. *See* New England, Dominion of
Domino theory IV–107a; V–259a
Doña Ana (N.Mex.) IV–315b; VI–268a
Donaldson, Thomas (offi.) V–450b
Donation Land Law (1850) IV–218b; VII–300a
DONATION LANDS II–362b; III–296a; V–165a; VII–300a
Donck, Adriaen van der. *See* Van der Donck, Adriaen
Donck, Geerard (paint.) V–185a
Donelson, Andrew Jackson (dipl.) IV–51a
Donelson, Fort (Tenn.) I–459a
DONELSON, FORT, CAPTURE OF (1862) **II–363a**; I–433a; II–62b, 363a; III–272b; IV–374b, 375a; V–414a; VI–150b, 278a; VII–137b
Donelson, John (pioneer)
  Big Moccasin Gap I–297a
  Cumberland settlements II–273a, 274a
  Nashborough IV–452b
  See also Donelson's Line
Donelson, Rachael. *See* Jackson, Rachael Donelson
DONELSON'S LINE II–363a; III–292b; IV–173a
Don Fernando de Taos. *See* Taos
Dongan, Thomas (col. gov.) II–117b–18a
  Gardiner's Island III–152a
  Iroquois Treaty III–476b
  New York City V–82a
  Rumbout's patent VI–170a
  Tappan patent VI–461b
  See also Dongan Charters
DONGAN CHARTERS II–363b; I–81b
Doniphan (Kans.) I–354b
Doniphan, Alexander W. (off.). *See* Doniphan's Expedition
Doniphan, Camp (Okla.) VI–287b
DONIPHAN'S EXPEDITION (1846–47) **II–363b**; I–361a; VI–184a
Don Juan (film) IV–418a
Donkey, Democratic IV–454b
Donner Lake VII–217b
DONNER PARTY II–364a; VII–161b
Donner Pass V–225a
Donner Summit (Calif.) VI–101b
Donop, Carl von (off.) II–321b
Donora (Pa.) VII–158b
Donovan, William J. ("Wild Bill") (law.) V–138a
"DON'T FIRE TILL YOU SEE THE WHITE OF THEIR EYES" II–364a
"DON'T GIVE UP THE SHIP" II–364a; II–16a, 459a
"Don't Tread on Me" (motto) V–316a; VI–47b
"Don't Tread on Me" (cartoon) V–73a
Doolittle, Isaac (mfr.) V–413a
Doolittle, James H. (off.) I–60a; III–489b
Dooly, John (sol.) IV–44b
"Doonesbury" (comic strip) V–72b
Doorman, Karel (nav. off.) III–492b; IV–182a
Door-to-door salesmen II–444b, 444b
Dorade (yacht) VII–349a
Doran, George (pub.) I–334b
Dorand, René (eng.) III–270a
Dorchester (Eng.) II–364b
Dorchester (Ga.) III–169b
DORCHESTER (Mass.) **II–364a**; III–169b, 220a; IV–260a
  Dorchester Company II–364b
  migration to Connecticut VI–151a
  pewter work VI–291b
  tenements VII–23b
  voting IV–269a
Dorchester (S.C.) III–169b
Dorchester, Daniel (cler.) III–398b
Dorchester Club (Montreal) III–286b
DORCHESTER COMPANY II–364b; I–446b; V–51a; VI–199a; VII–95a
Dorchester Heights (Mass.) I–345a
Dordrecht (Neth.) VI–455b
Dorfman, Joseph (hist.) III–283a, 486b
Dorlandt, Lambert (landowner) V–286a
"Dormitory" communities II–46a
Dorr, Samuel G. (inv.) VII–43a
Dorr, Thomas Wilson (pol.). *See* Dorr's Rebellion
DORR'S REBELLION (1842) **II–365a**; III–436b; IV–206b; VI–133b; VII–107a
Dorr v. *United States* (1904) III–424b
Dorset, Marion (chem.) I–46a
Dort (Neth.) VI–455b
Dos Passos, John (au.) IV–164b, 189b, 190a
Douay Bible I–294b
Doubleday (pub.) II–340b
Doubleday, Abner (off.) I–269b
Doubleday, Frank N. (pub.) I–334b
Double eagle (coin) II–95b, 384b
Double-helix III–157a–b, 158a; IV–390a–b
Double jeopardy I–299a; II–204a; III–207a; VII–154b
Doublets II–370b–71a
DOUBLOON II–365b
DOUGHBOY II–365b; I–108a; VI–301a
DOUGHFACES II–366a; I–138b
Doughty, John (off.) III–254b
Doughty, Thomas (paint.) V–189a, 190a–b
Doughty, William (shipbuilder) VII–240a
Douglas, Camp (Chicago) II–222b; V–121b
Douglas, David (bot.) V–327a; VII–271b
Douglas, Donald W. (av.) I–51b, 236a
Douglas, Helen Gahagan (pol.) III–285a
Douglas, James (surv.) I–295b
Douglas, Lewis (pol.) V–45a
Douglas, Paul H. (pol.) II–235b
Douglas, Stephen A. (states.) III–329b; V–161a; VI–218a, 454b
  Appeal of the Independent Democrats I–145a
  campaign of 1852 I–420b
  campaign of 1860 I–421a
  Compromise of 1850 II–150a; VI–307b
  Freeport Doctrine III–109b
  internal improvements III–450b
  Kansas-Nebraska Act IV–29a
  Kansas struggle IV–31a; V–51b
  Lecompton Constitution IV–131a
  Lincoln-Douglas debates IV–155a; V–353a
  Little Giant IV–168b
  Nebraska V–31a
  Oregon question III–21a
  popular sovereignty V–351b, 360a
  Union Democrats VII–146a
  War Democrats VII–229b
Douglas, Thomas, 5th Earl of Selkirk (col.)
  Pembina IV–187a; V–244a
  Red River III–313b; V–117a, 121a; VI–64b
Douglas, William O. (jur.) VI–446b
  Bill of Rights I–299b, 300a
  First Amendment III–105a
  freedom of the press V–79a
  Securities and Exchange Commission III–466b

Douglas Aircraft Company I–236a, 237a; III–452a
Douglas Dam III–322b
Douglas fir III–74b; IV–95b, 204a; V–446a; VI–48b, 395 (table); VII–60a, 114b
Douglas Lake II–391b
Douglass, Andrew E. (astron.) VII–114a
Douglass, David (theat. mgr.) VII–46b–47a
Douglass, Frederick (lecturer, writ.) I–28a, 137a; III–256b; V–75b–76a, 93a, 280a
Douglass, William (physic.) VII–206a
Douglas World Cruisers I–51b
Douhet, Giulio (off.) I–66b, 328a
Dousman, Hercules L. (fur trader) IV–356a; V–388a
Dove (ship) II–124b
Dove, Arthur G. (paint.) II–104b
"Dove of peace" II–366a
Dover (Del.) V–43a
Dover (Eng.)
World War II VII–339a
Dover (N.H.) V–179b; VII–45a
Dover (N.Y.) I–284b
Dover (Pa.) III–250b
Dover-Foxcroft (Maine) IV–227a
Dover Point (N.H.) VI–417b–18a
DOVES II–366a
Dow, H. H. (chem.) II–7b
Dow, Neal (mer.) IV–226b; VII–23a
Dow Chemical Company II–423a; III–409b; V–237a
Dow-Corning Company IV–300b
Dowd, A. T. VI–262b
Dow Jones Company V–76b
Dowling, Dick (off.) VII–39b
Down Easter (ship) IV–226b, 310b; VI–279b
Downer, Samuel (mfr.) IV–44a
Downer Works (Boston) IV–44a
Downes v. *Bidwell* (1901) III–424b, 425a; VII–13b–14a
Downey, John G. (pol.) III–478a
Downfall of Babylon (news.) V–2b
Downie, George (nav. off.) V–330b–31a
Downing, Andrew J. (landscape arch.) I–163b; III–445b; IV–96b
Downton, R. L. (inv.) III–44a
"Down to Rowser's" (song) V–331a
Downtown Gallery II–104a, 105b
Dowse, Thomas (bibliophile) II–108b
Doyen (dipl.) I–93a
Doyle, Arthur Conan (physic., nov.) VII–49a
Doyle, Thomas (off.) IV–264a
Doyle, William M. S. (art.) VI–286b
Doylestown (Pa.) V–379b; VI–411b
DPR. *See* Korea, Democratic People's Republic of
Drabik, Alexander (sol.) VI–84a
DRAFT II–366a; IV–342b, 346b
Civil War I–182a–b, 353a; II–161b–62a, 163b, 180a, 314a, 368b–69a, 451a–b; III–31b; IV–383b; VI–426b
congressional debate III–22a
conscientious objectors II–185b; V–181b
demobilization II–323b, 324b
enlistment II–451a
Espionage Act II–463b; VI–225a
Holmes County Rebellion III–292a
National Defense Act IV–384a
naval reserve V–29a
New York draft riots IV–62b
New York State V–87a
opposition V–237a; VI–14a
peacetime I–187a
Quakers V–470b
revolutionary war II–186a, 450b
termination I–188a
Universal Military Training and Service Act IV–384b
Vietnam War I–187a–b; II–316b; VI–61a–b; VII–208a
World War I I–186a; II–186a, 314a, 451a; VII–325b
World War II I–186b; II–451a; VII–334b, 335a, 336a
See also Selective Service
Draft boards II–186b
Draft dodgers I–115b, 440a; II–335b
Draft horse III–303b
DRAFT RIOTS (1863) **II–368b**; I–468a; II–186a, 258a; IV–62b
New York City III–436a; V–83b, 87a; VI–313b; VII–191a–b
Dragging Canoe (Indian) II–15a, 292a; IV–186b
Drago, Luis M. (states.). *See* Drago Doctrine
DRAGO DOCTRINE II–369a; I–411a; V–105b–06a
Dragon (missile) IV–363b
Dragonades III–315a
Dragon boats VII–349b
Dragoons II–228a; III–494b; IV–34a, 411a
Drag racing I–231b
Drake (ship) VI–46a
Drake, Daniel (physic.) II–390b
Drake, Edwin L. (ind.) II–369b; IV–44a; V–266b, 269a, 271a; VII–295a
Drake, Francis (navig.) III–240b
Oregon V–164b, 167b
privateering V–418b
Raleigh's first colony VI–44a
Saint Augustine V–370a
slave trade VI–310a
See also Drake at California
Drake, Samuel (act.) I–268a; VII–47a
Drake, Samuel Gardner (hist.) II–108b
DRAKE AT CALIFORNIA (1579) **II–369a**; I–96a; III–190a
Drake's Bay I–401b; II–369a–b
DRAKE'S OIL WELL II–369b; II–464b; IV–44a; V–146b, 266b, 272a,b
Drama. *See* Theater
Drama Review (mag.) VII–51a
"Dram shop" acts IV–159a
Drane, Fort (Fla.) VII–311a
Draper, George (mfr.) IV–187b; VII–43b
Draper, George, and Sons VII–43b
Draper, George O. VII–43b
Draper, Ira (inv.) VII–43a
Draper, John (pub.) I–346a; II–369b
Draper, Lyman Copeland (hist.) II–108b; III–285a
Draper, Richard (pub.) I–346a
DRAPER'S MEADOWS II–369b
Draves, Victoria M. (athlete) V–154b
Drawback (rebate) VI–50a
Drawbaugh, Daniel (inv.) VII–21a
Drayton, Daniel (abolitionist) V–239a
Drayton, John Grimke (cler.) I–497a, 498a
Drayton Hall (Charleston, S.C.) I–161b
DREADNOUGHT (warship) **II–369b**; II–375b; IV–431b; VI–279b; VII–241a, 241a, 242a
Dream books II–260b
"Dream songs" IV–165b
Drebbel, Cornelis (inv.) VI–422b
Dredging, deep-sea III–29a
DRED SCOTT CASE (1857) **II–370a**; I–27b; II–54a; V–353b, 360b; VI–307b; VII–117b
campaign of 1860 I–421a
due process of law II–377b
Freeport Doctrine III–109b; IV–155b
judicial review IV–13b
Matilda Lawrence case IV–276b
states' rights VI–404b
Supreme Court VI–447b
Dred Scott v. *Sanford.* *See* Dred Scott Case
Dreer, Ferdinand J. II–108b
Dreft detergent VI–324a
Dreier, Katherine S. II–104b
Dreiser, Theodore (au.) IV–163b
Dreissiger (Grays) III–336b
Dresden Junction (Ohio) IV–444a
DRESS II–370b
army uniforms VII–144a
fur III–133b
Godey's Lady's Book III–188a
Indian III–374a, 381a
miniatures IV–352a
moccasins IV–384b
Navaho V–9a
Dresser, Horatio (mental healer) V–81a
Dresser, Julius (mental healer) V–81a
Dress patterns II–371b
Drew, Charles (physic.) IV–291a
Drew, Daniel (fin.) III–312b; VII–222a
Drew, Edward B. (dipl.) IV–55a
Drew, George F. (pol.) III–39b, 295b
Drew, John (act.) VII–48b
Drew, Louisa Lane (act., theat. mgr.) VII–48b
DREWRY'S BLUFF, BATTLE AT (1864) **II–373a**; II–382b; III–488a
Drexel, Katharine I–468a
Drexel, Morgan and Company III–79b
DRIED FRUITS AND VEGETABLES II–373a; III–413b
Dried milk II–281a
Drift fences II–251a
Driggs, Frederick E. IV–99b
Drill (mach.) I–34a–b
dentistry II–331a
gold mining III–191b
Drips, Andrew (fur trader) VI–196a
Driscoll, Joseph (jour.) V–74a
Drive-ins I–230b; V–292b
DROGHER TRADE II–373b
Dromgoole, W. A. IV–301a
Droop quota (pol.) V–435b
Drop City (Colo.) II–142b
Dropsy IV–333b
Drosophila Group (Columbia Univ.) III–157b
Drought I–38b, 170a–71a; II–76b; VI–41a–b
Civilian Conservation Corps II–51a
dry farming II–376a
Dust Bowl II–382a

fast days496b
Great Plains I–486b
migrant workers II–495b
Nebraska IV–50a
rainmaking VI–42a
Drought-resistant crops II–375b
Droulliard, George (scout) III–119b; IV–136a
Drown, Thomas M. (chem.) IV–120a
Drowne, Shem (col.) V–243b
Dr. Pepper (soft drink) VI–333b
Dr. Ralston health clubs I–487a
Drude, Oskar (bot.) II–391b
Drude, Paul (phys.) V–304a
Drug Abuse Control, Bureau of V–468b
Drug abuse education II–402b
Drug Abuse Prevention, Special Action Office for II–498a
DRUG ADDICTION II–373b; IV–450a,b
federal agencies V–468b
red light districts II–260a
slang VI–300a
Vietnam troops V–258a
See also Narcotics Trade and Legislation
Drug Enforcement Administration V–468b
Druggists, National Association of Retail V–275b
Drugs
advertising I–19a
Indian III–381a
manufacture II–10a–b
mercurials II–5b
mysticism IV–448a
opposition of osteopaths V–175a
plants I–349b
World War I scarcity II–12a
See also Narcotics Trade and Legislation; Pharmaceutical Industry
Drugstores II–355a
morphine II–260a
soda fountains VI–332a
soft drink industry VI–333a
See also Pharmacy
Drug-therapy communes II–142b
Drum
African music IV–442b–43a,b
Indian II–290b–91a
Drum, cylinder II–291a
Drum, Fort (Fla.) I–451b
Drum Lummon Mine (Mont.) III–270a
Drumm, Stella (hist.) VII–235a
Drum majorettes III–56b
Drummers (mer.) II–81a
Drummond, Gordon (off.) II–458a–b; IV–205a; V–91a
Drummond, Lake II–353a
Drummond, Roscoe (jour.) V–75a
Drummond, Thomas (bot.) V–327a
Drummond, William (col. gov.) I–83b
Drummond Island IV–239b, 240a
Drums IV–164b
Drum Taps IV–162b
Drunkenness IV–158b, 159a; V–464b; VII–22a
Drury, Newton B. (offi.) V–220a
Dry bloc I–322a
Dryden, Hugh L. (offi.) IV–458a, 459a
Dryden, John F. (bus.) III–434b
DRY DOCKS II–375a
DRY FARMING II–375b; I–170b–71a
Colorado II–128b
New Mexico V–60a
Staked Plain VI–380b
Dry goods stores II–332b
Drying
food preservation II–219a; III–54b
Dry Land Agriculture, Office of II–376a
Dry painting. *See* Sand painting
Dry states IV–159a
Dual Citizenship. *See* Citizenship, Dual
Dualism III–9a
Dual school system II–54b, 55a; IV–369b
Dual unionism II–86b
Duane, James (pol.) VII–116b, 117a
Duane, William (jour.) I–86b, 224a; V–70a I–418a
Duane, William J. (law.) VI–85b
Dubinsky, David (labor leader) IV–10a, 76a
Dublin (Ire.)
New Albion charter V–332b, 333a
Dublin, Louis I. (statis.) VII–207a
Du Bois, W. E. B. (educ.)
black nationalism I–315b
Crisis V–76a
Harlem Renaissance I–30a
NAACP IV–460b
Niagara movement V–92b
Pan-Africanism I–21b; V–199b, 200a
Dubourg, Louis (bp.) III–499b
Dubreuil, Louis (fur trader) VI–367a
Du Bridge, Lee (phys.) VI–10b
Dubuisson, Paul (off.) VI–129a
DUBUQUE (Iowa) **II–376a**; III–147a, 154b; IV–122b
Dubuque, Julien (miner) II–376a; III–147a, 467b; IV–122a
Dubuque County (Iowa) III–147a
Dubuque Mining District. *See* Galena–Dubuque Mining District
Duchamp, Marcel (art.) II–104b, 105a
Duchesne, Rose Philippine (teacher, miss.) I–469b
Duchesne River VII–137a
DUCKING STOOL II–376a; V–464b
Duck Island III–479b
Ducks III–51a, 52a, 150a
Duck stamp I–306a
Ducktown mines II–163a
Duclos, Jacques (Communist) II–145b
Duco lacquer I–228b; III–409b
Duden (Ger. immigrant) VI–194b
Dudensing, Valentine (art dealer) II–105a
Dude ranch VI–44b
Dudley, Benjamin (surg.) IV–40b
Dudley, Charles Benjamin (chem.) III–408b; IV–273a
Dudley, Joseph (col. gov.) I–465b; V–50b
Dudley, Robert (expl.) IV–248a
Dudley, Thomas (col. offi.) I–411b
Dudley, W. W. (pol.) I–322a
Dudley Observatory (N.Y.) V–131a
Dudley's Massacre. *See* Meigs, Fort
Duegueño (Indians) III–503b
DUELING II–376b
Bladensburg Field I–318a
Bloody Island I–322b
Campbell versus Gardenier II–437a
Gwinnett–McIntosh duel III–236a
Hamilton, Alexander, and Burr, Aaron VII–266b
Perry–Elliott controversy V–262b
Sandbar duel I–355a
scandals V–346b
Weehawken VII–266b
Duelling Oaks (New Orleans) II–377a
DUE PROCESS OF LAW II–377a; V–421a
Adkins v. *Children's Hospital* I–12a
American Civil Liberties Union I–100b
Bill of Rights I–299a–300a; II–53b
constitutional provision I–94a
delegated power I–12b
Dred Scott Case II–370b
eminent domain II–440a
Fifth Amendment II–204a
Fourteenth Amendment II–205b; III–86a,b
Frazier–Lemke Farm Bankruptcy Act III–100b
freedom of the press III–229a
government regulation of business III–204a,b
habeas corpus III–237a
House Committee on Un-American Activities III–308b
judicial review IV–14b; V–472b
juvenile criminals IV–23b
Legal Tender Act IV–132b
limitations on states II–54a
minimum-wage laws IV–80a–b, 353a
miscegenation IV–362b
mortgage moratorium acts IV–358a
murder accusation III–320a
natural rights doctrine IV–358b
padlock injunction V–184b
property II–214a; V–433b–34a
Railroad Pension Act VI–24a
right of assembly I–204b
right to counsel III–179a–b
Slaughterhouse Cases VI–302b
state police power V–339b, 339b
Supreme Court VI–447a
Duer, William (fin.) IV–98b; V–143b; VI–239a
Duerk, Alene B. (nav. off.) VII–318b
Duff, Mary (act.) I–268a
Dugdale, Richard L. (soc.) III–158b, 159a; IV–20a
Duggar, B. M. (bot.) IV–378b
DUGOUT (house) **II–379a**; II–487a; 160b–
Dugout canoe I–445b–46a; III–381b
DUG SPRINGS, BATTLE AT (1861) **II–379a**
Duke, Benjamin N. (ind.) III–80b
Duke, James B. (ind.) III–80a–b
Duke, Washington (ind.) III–80a
Duke Foundation IV–286b
Duke of Cumberland's Regiment VI–130a
DUKE OF YORK'S LAWS II–379a; VII–359a
Duke Power Company System III–322a
Duke University I–169a; III–285a; V–116b, 213a
DUKW (amphibious vehicle) V–137b
Dulany, Daniel (law.) VI–111b; VII–14b
Dulhut, Sieur. *See* Duluth, Sieur, Daniel Greysolon
Dulles, Allen W. (offi.) VII–238a
Dulles, John Foster (law.)
Anglo-American relations I–124b
Arab-American relations

DULLES, JOHN FOSTER (cont.)
I–124b, 149b, 150a
foreign policy II–489a
Latin American communism IV–112b
national defense II–315b
neutralism V–36a–b
Suez crisis VI–430a
Dulles Airport (Washington, D.C.) I–165b; II–347b
Dull Knife (Indian) VI–242a
DULL KNIFE CAMPAIGN (1878–79) **II–379b**; IV–109a
Duluth (Minn.) II–380a, 491a; VI–443b
architecture I–160a
Great Lakes VI–146b
railroads VI–33a
shipbuilding VII–285a
wheat VII–308a
Duluth, Sieur, Daniel Greysolon (expl.) II–246a
Denonville's invasion II–329a
rescue of Hennepin III–89b, 272a
See also Duluth's Explorations
DULUTH'S EXPLORATIONS II–379b; III–119a; IV–355a; V–52b; VI–192a, 443a; VII–73b
Dumas, J. B. (chem.) I–218b
Du Maurier, George (au.) I–334b
Dumbarton Oaks (Washington, D.C.) IV–96b
DUMBARTON OAKS CONFERENCE (1944) **II–380a**; II–380a; IV–415b; VI–179b; VII–151a
DUMMER, FORT (Vt.) **II–380b**; VII–171a
Dummer, Shubael (cler.) VII–358b
Dummer, William (col. gov.). *See* Dummer's War
Dummer Academy VI–228b
DUMMER'S WAR (1724–25) **II–380b**; III–120b; V–111a
Dummy entrymen IV–100a, 103b
Dumont Company VII–21b
DUMPLIN CREEK, TREATY OF (1785) **II–380b**
Dumplings III–52a
Dum spiro spero (motto) VI–395 (table)
Dun and Bradstreet, Inc. IV–307b
Dun and Company IV–307b
Dunant, Jean Henri (philan.) III–161b
Dunbar, David (surv.) VII–219b
Dunbar, Paul Lawrence (poet) IV–166a
Dunbar, William (off.) I–358a
Dunbar, William (sci., expl.). *See* Dunbar's Expedition
Dunbar, William (surv.). *See* Dunbar's Line
DUNBAR'S EXPEDITION (1804–05) **II–381a**
DUNBAR'S LINE II–381a; VI–351a
Duncan (Okla.) II–32a
Duncan, Alexander (pol.) VI–204a
Duncan, George B. (off.) V–147a
Duncan, Isadora (dancer) II–287a–b, 288a
Duncan, James (labor leader) VI–163b
Duncan, Joseph (pol.) VII–293b
Duncan, Matthew (pub.) V–70b
Duncan, Robert Kennedy (chem.) IV–300b
Duncan, Silas (nav. off.) II–484a
Duncan, William V–66a
Duncan Lake II–132a
Duncan v. *Kahanamoku* (1946) III–237a; IV–259a
Dundee (Scot.)
foreign investment trusts III–65a–b
Dunellon (Fla.) III–40a
Dunglison, Robley (physic.) III–325a; V–306b
Dunham, Katherine (dancer) I–25a
Dunk, George Montagu, 2nd Earl of Halifax (offi.) I–326b, 327a
Dunkards (Dunkers) V–342a
Confederate Army II–161b
conscientious objectors II–185a
Ephrata Community II–147a
immigration to U.S. III–335a
See also Brethren
Dunkirk (N.Y.) VI–34a; VII–100b
Dunlap, John (pub.) I–16b; V–71a
Dunlap, William (art., theat. mgr.) VII–47a
Dunlap's Creek VI–65b
Dunleith plantation V–325b
Dunlop, John T. (educ.) III–407b; VI–420a
Dunmore, Fort (Pa.) II–381b
Dunmore, 4th Earl of, John Murray (col. gov.) I–355b, 499a; II–184a, 381b; III–236a
Battle at Great Bridge III–215b
Battle of Point Pleasant V–335b
Falls of the Ohio V–142b
Fort Fincastle III–272b
McDonald's expedition IV–212a
Norfolk V–109b
DUNMORE'S WAR (1774) **II–381a**; II–25b; III–258a; VI–386a, 450b; VII–103a
Battle of Point Pleasant V–335b
Charleston (S.C.) I–497b
Holston Valley settlements III–292b
peace negotiations IV–179a
Treaty at Pittsburgh V–322a
Treaty of Camp Charlotte I–499a
Dunne, Edward F. (pol.) III–330a
Dunne, J. W. (eng.) I–51a
Dunning, William A. (hist.) VI–57b
Dunn v. *Blumstein* (1972) VI–71a–b, 99b, 435a
Dunstan (Maine) VI–184a
Dunster, Henry (cler., educ.) III–259b; V–410b
Dunthey Company II–421a
Duplex Printing Press Company v. *Deering* (1921) I–357a; II–72a, 110b; III–419a; IV–69a, 70a; VI–103b
Du Poisson, Paul (miss.) III–499b
Du Ponceau, Peter S. I–110b
Du Ponceau, Pierre Étienne (law., writ.) VI–129b
Du Pont, Eleuthère Irénée (ind.) III–80a
gunpowder V–383a
Du Pont, Henry Francis (ind.) II–100b; IV–437a
Du Pont, Lammot (ind.) III–408b; V–383a
Du Pont, Pierre S. (ind.) III–80b
Du Pont, Samuel F. (nav. off.) IV–397a; V–424a; VI–440b
Du Pont de Nemours, E. I., and Company II–320b; III–409a,b; V–383a,b; VII–123b
archives I–169a
atomic bomb III–410a
Celanese V–328b
Corfam IV–128b
expansion II–8b
Manhattan Project IV–238a
nylon II–9a
powder II–5b, 320b
synthetic fibers VII–44a
Du Portail (eng.) VII–165a
DuPortail, Louis Lebegue (off.) VI–129a
Du Pratz, Antoine. *See* Le Page du Pratz, Antoine
DUQUESNE, FORT (Pa.) **II–381b**; III–120a, 219b; IV–130b; V–143a, 246b, 321a,b, 399b; VI–150a, 271a, 276a
Aughwick I–222b
Braddock's defeat II–126b, 272a
Braddock's expedition I–358a; IV–398a
Braddock's Road VI–155b
Forbes expedition IV–154a
Franciscans III–94b
French and Indian War III–58b, 59a, 115b, 116a, 211b; V–144a, 146a; VII–283a
French evacuation I–359a
Duquesne de Menneville, Marquís II–381b
Durand, Asher B. (paint.) II–101b, 103a; V–189a, 190a–b
Durand, Peter (inv.) I–445a; III–55a
Durand-Ruel Gallery II–103b
Durang, John (dancer) II–286b–87a
Durango (Colo.) VI–213b, 368a
Durango (Mex.) II–23b; VI–215a
Durant, Charles Ferson (aeron.) I–248a
Durant, George II–271b
Durant, Thomas Clark (fin.) II–256a; VII–147b
Durant, Will (William James) (educ.) II–492b
Durant, William C. (ind.) I–227a; III–80b, 461a
Duranty, Walter (jour.) V–74a
Durell; E. H. (jur.) IV–336a
Durfee, Amos I–458b; IV–218a
Durfee, B. M. (eng.) II–154a
Durfee and Peck V–241a
Durgin, Samuel H. (physic.) IV–275b
Durham (Conn.)
library IV–144b
Durham (Eng.) V–194b
Durham (N.H.) II–293a; V–53b
Durham (N.C.)
Civil War II–63a, 165a; V–116a
Duke University V–116b
parapsychology V–213b
Durham, bishopric of (Scot.) IV–260a
Durham, Palatinate of V–436a
Durham cattle I–471b
Durham Station (N.C.) II–68b
Durkee, John (off.) VI–452a; VII–347a, 353a
Durocher, Laurent (fur trader) VI–367a
Duroc hog III–288b
Duryea, Charles E. (inv.) I–225b–26a
Duryea, J. Frank (inv.) I–225b–26a
Düsseldorf Academy V–188b
DUST BOWL II–382a; I–350a; V–48a, 149a
Dustin, Amos VI–296b
Dust storms VI–41b
forestry III–74a
Great Plains III–221b
Nebraska IV–50a
soil erosion VI–335b
Dutch auction I–222a
DUTCH BANKERS' LOANS (1782) **II–382a**; III–245a
Dutch East India Company II–383b; III–243a
Dutch East Indies I–201a; II–28b
Dutch elm disease III–74b

Dutchess County (N.Y.)
III–220b; IV–169a;
V–130b; VI–462a
land patents I–284b;
III–313a; VI–170a
lead industry IV–122a
revolutionary war V–86a
Dutchess Quarry Cave (N.Y.)
I–155a
Dutch Flat (Calif.) I–281a
DUTCH FORK OF SOUTH CAROLINA II–382b
DUTCH GAP CANAL II–382b
Dutch Harbor (Aleutians)
I–84b; IV–336b
Dutch Henry's Crossing
V–378b
Dutch House of Hope. *See* House of Hope
DUTCH-INDIAN WAR (1643–45) **II–382b**;
VII–223b
Dutchman IV–167b
Dutchman's Point (N.Y.)
VII–270a
DUTCH MERCHANTS AT ALBANY II–383a;
III–475b
Dutch oven III–51b
Dutch Point (Conn.)
III–309a
Dutch Reformed church
I–411b
Coetus–Conferentie Controversy II–93b
colonial education
II–393b, 394b
colonial society
II–125b–26a
home missionary societies
IV–365b
missionary work III–385b
Queens College II–395a
Rutgers University
VI–181b
Dutch settlements
Cape Horn I–448a
cattle III–51b
colonial coins II–94b
colonial dress
II–370b–71a
Connecticut II–179b
Delaware II–320a; IV–199b
Delaware Bay II–322a
effective occupation
II–406b
Esopus War II–462b
Fort Christina II–35a
Fort Nassau V–42b
fur trade III–141a,b;
IV–454a
Holland Land Company
IV–98b
House of Hope V–334b
Hudson River II–125b;
III–312a
Indians and guns
III–399a
Iowa III–468b
Iroquois alliance I–492b
Kingston (N.Y.) IV–49a
Long Island IV–185a,b
New Amsterdam V–40a
New Netherland V–60b,
86a
New York City I–275b;
II–320b; V–82a, 84a
patroons V–229a
Pennsylvania V–246a
Saybrook VI–223a
Schenectady VI–225b
sheep VI–272b; VII–320a–b
windmills VII–58a
Dutch War of 1653 VI–134a
DUTCH WEST INDIA COMPANY II–383b
Albany I–81b; II–383a
colonial settlements
II–123b
Delaware River forts
V–42b
fur trade III–141a; VI–225b
Hudson exploration
III–312a
Manhattan I–354b;
IV–237a
New Amsterdam V–40a
New Netherland V–60b,
266a
patroons V–229a
Zwaanendael Colony
VII–372b
DUTIES, AD VALOREM AND SPECIFIC
II–383b; II–478a;
VI–462b, 465a,b
collection II–88b
colonial II–5a; V–16b
constitutional provisions
II–199b, 200b, 275b
Hamilton's fiscal policies
III–244b–45a
imported fibers IV–157b
liquor IV–159a
presidential powers
II–323a
revenue II–276a–b;
VI–105a,b
tea VII–15a
Du Tisne, Claude Charles. *See* Tisne, Claude Charles du
Dutton, Clarence (geol.)
III–166b, 480b; V–384a
Dutton, E. P. (pub.) I–334a
Duval, Gabriel (jur.)
VI–445a
DuVal, William P. (pol.)
III–39a
Duveen, Joseph (art dealer)
II–105b
Duveen Brothers II–104a
Du Vigneaud, Vincent (chem.)
V–100a
Duyckinck, Evert (paint.)
V–185b
Duyckinck, Gerret (paint.)
V–185b, 186a
DUZINE II–384a
Dvina River (Russia) I–159a
Dwight, James (physic.)
VII–29a
Dwight, Jeremiah IV–99b
Dwight, John S. (mus. crit., ed.) I–369b
Dwight, Theodore W. (educ.)
IV–120b; V–415b
Dwight, Timothy (cler., educ.)
III–259b; VI–77a, 81b
Deism III–112a
hymns III–326a
Yale I–238a
Dwight D. Eisenhower Library
I–167b
Dwight D. Eisenhower Lock
VI–193a
Dyeing III–44b; IV–245a
colonies II–5a
cotton industry II–239a
fur III–133b
Germany II–7b–8a
hair coloring III–239b
textile industry II–8b
Dyer, Alexander B. (sol.)
II–67a
Dyer, E. H. (bus.) I–285a
Dyer, Eliphalet (jur.)
VI–451b
Dyer, L. C. (pol.) IV–208b
Dyer, Rolla E. (physic.)
IV–287b
Dyer, William (adventurer)
VI–134a,b
Dyes
cosmetics II–233b
indigo III–405b
research III–408b
textile industry VII–44a
World War I II–12a
Dyewoods II–119b, 453a;
V–16a; VII–119b
Dylan, Bob (mus.) IV–441a
Dylks, Joseph C. IV–129a
Dynamite III–191b; V–383b
Dynamo I–276a; II–413b,
414a; III–99b
chemical industry II–7b
electrochemical industry
II–422a
hydroelectric power
III–320b
Dysentery III–82a; IV–150b,
295b, 299a
infant deaths IV–275a
Jamestown III–488b
Jersey prison ship
III–498b
slave trade VI–310b
Dyspepsia III–52b

E

Eads, James B. (eng., inv.). *See* Eads Bridge; Eads Gunboats; Eads Jetties
EADS BRIDGE II–384a;
I–364a, 378a
EADS GUNBOATS
II–384a; I–459a
EADS JETTIES II–384b;
VI–146a
Eagan, Edward (athlete)
V–154b
Eagle (coin) II–95b, 384b
Eagle (fighter plane) I–54a
Eagle (lunar module)
IV–407a
Eagle (ship) VI–422b
EAGLE, AMERICAN
II–384b
folk art III–47b
furniture III–135a
seal of the United States
VI–246b
Eagle Ottawa Leather Company IV–128b
Eagle Pass (Tex.) VI–274b
Eagle Pull, Operation (1975)
VII–186b
Eagle Scout I–357b
Eagleton, Thomas (pol.)
I–432a
Eakins, Thomas (paint.)
II–103b; V–190a, 191a,b
Eames, Charles (arch.)
I–165b; III–136b–37a
Eames, Ray III–136b–37a
Earhart, Amelia (av.)
II–311b
Earl, Ralph (paint.) V–187b,
188a
Earle, Alice Morse II–99b
Earle, Pliny (mfr., inv.)
VII–43a
Earl of Stairs Plan (1721)
II–121b–22a
Earl Palatine of New Albion. *See* Plowden, Edmund
Early, Jubal A. (off.)
VI–373b
Bull Run I–381b
Chambersburg I–490b
Fisher's Hill III–31a
Fredericksburg I–493a
Gettysburg III–176a
Monocacy IV–398a
Shenandoah campaign
VI–275a, 276a; VII–304b
Toms Brook VII–71a
Early Bird (satellite) II–143a
Earp, Wyatt (lawman)
II–252a; VII–71a
Earth
geophysical explorations
III–166a
International Geophysical Year III–454a
isostasy III–480b
study II–88b
Earth Diver (myth.)
III–386a
Earthenware III–13a, 183a,b,
184a,b
See also Pottery
Earth history IV–348a–b
Earth lodge IV–236a
Earth-Maker III–222b
Earthquake Research, National Center for III–164b
EARTHQUAKES II–385a;
II–347b–48a
divine providences
II–356a, 496b
New Madrid V–63a
San Francisco VI–210a
U.S. Geological Survey
III–164b
U.S. Navy assistance
V–23a
Earth Technology Resource Satellite III–167b
Earthworks III–78a,b;
VII–320a
Civil War IV–426b
Fort Nonsense V–108a
Great Serpent Mound
III–222a
Hopewell culture
III–300a
Indian cultures I–11b,
157a, 166a; II–386a
Mound Builders

EARTHWORKS (cont.)
IV–421a,b
Poverty Point
V–382b
East, Edward Murray (biol.) I–46a; II–226a
Eastabrook, Arthur H. (penologist) IV–20a
East Africa I–21a, 27a
East Antarctica. *See* Wilkes Land
East Bay (San Francisco) III–11b
East Boston (Mass.) V–100b
East Canyon IV–411b
East Country Puritans III–220a
East Dubuque (Iowa) VI–26a
Easter II–496a
Eastern Airlines I–68a, 69a; II–347b
EASTERN ARCHAIC CULTURE II–385b; VII–319b–20a
Eastern bluebird VI–394 (table)
Eastern Company I–401a
Eastern Culture areas III–365a–67a
Eastern Dorsale mountains
World War II IV–32b
Eastern Europe
aerial hijacking III–276b, 277a
immigration III–338b–40b, 342a
Iron Curtain III–474b
Soviet–U.S. relations II–97b–98a
U.S. aid III–61a–b
Eastern goldfinch VI–393 (table), 394 (table)
Eastern Hemisphere
immigration quota III–334a
Eastern hemlock VI–395 (table)
Eastern Island IV–337a
Eastern Oblique Arc II–88a
EASTERN ORTHODOXY II–386a; VII–52a
EASTERN SOLOMONS, BATTLE OF THE (1942) **II–387a**; III–229b; V–21a; VII–68a
Eastern State Hospital (Williamsburg) III–306b; IV–305a
Eastern Steamship Company II–91a
Eastern Woodlands culture I–11a,b, 156b, 157a, 158a; III–300b, 360b, 365a–67a
canoe I–445b
Fox III–88b
"Great Spirit" III–223a
"Happy Hunting Ground" III–251a
scalping VI–224b
Southern Cult VI–352b
wampum VII–223a
See also Indian, American, Native Cultures
Eastern Yacht Club I–95b
Easter offensive (1972) I–63a; VII–184b, 186b
"Easter outfit" II–372b
East Florida
Bartram's travels II–477a
ceded to U.S. I–10b, 154b
donation lands II–363a
See also Florida
East Florida Rangers. *See* Florida Rangers
East Gallatin River II–432a
East Germany. *See* Germany, East
East Greenwich (R.I.) V–261a
East Hampton (N.Y.) IV–186a; VI–346b
East Hartford (Conn.) II–77b, 78b
EAST INDIA COMPANY, ENGLISH II–388a; I–201a
army VI–126b
Boston Tea Party I–347a; II–93a
monopoly II–388b
Tea Act VI–113b, 321a
tea trade I–208a; VII–15a–b, 16b
East India Marine Society IV–436a
East India Squadron IV–252a
East Indies
search for route to I–401b
World War II VII–335a
EAST INDIES TRADE II–388a; IV–266b; VII–279a
EAST JERSEY II–388b; V–56b–57a, 436b
assembly II–118a
colonial plans of union II–121b
Elizabethtown II–431b
Perth Amboy V–264a
Quakers II–124a,b
religious liberty VII–69a
Eastlake, Charles Lock (paint.) I–163b; III–136a, 446a–b
Eastlake furniture III–138b
EASTLAND **(steamer) II–388b**; II–349b
East Liverpool (Ohio) III–183b, 184b; V–379b
Eastman, Charles R. (ichthyol.) III–27b
Eastman, George (inv.) I–17b; IV–417a; V–291b–92a, 328a
Eastman, Seth (paint.) V–189b
Eastman Company V–291b
Eastman Kodak Company III–409a–b; IV–300b; V–292a,b, 293a
Eastman Kodak Research Laboratory V–292a
East New York (N.Y.) I–282b
Easton (Pa.)
canal museum I–443b
canals I–127b
Convention Army II–215a
Great Swamp VI–267b
Indian conferences III–123a
revolutionary war VI–438a
Walking Purchase VII–220b
westward movement VII–283a
Easton, David (pol. sci.) II–326b; V–347a
EASTON, TREATY OF (1758) **II–388b**; III–58b, 116b
Eastport (Maine) I–434a, 448a
East River II–346b, 349b; IV–237a
Battery I–275b
bridges I–364b, 370b
revolutionary war V–418b; VII–293a
shipbuilding VI–279b
subway VI–429a,b
tunnel VII–128b
East Saginaw (Mich.)
salt VI–202b
East Saint Louis (Ill.) III–329a
Cahokia I–402a
meat packing I–283b
Monks Mound IV–420b
race riots I–29b; VI–8a,b
railroads VI–25b
tornado II–351a
East Side House (N.Y.) VI–330b
East Tennessee. *See* Tennessee
East Tennessee, Virginia and Georgia Railroad VI–37a
EAST TEXAS MISSIONS II–389a; VII–36b
EAST TEXAS OIL FIELD II–389a
East Windsor (Conn.) II–77b
Easy Date (horse) III–305a
Easy Plan of Discipline for a Militia VI–126a
Eaton (Ohio) VI–188b
Eaton, Amos (sci.) II–447a; IV–348b
Eaton, Charles (pol.) VII–151a
Eaton, Dorman B. (law.) V–245a
Eaton, John H. (pol.) II–389b; III–39a; IV–51a; V–346b
Eaton, Margaret O'Neale. *See* Eaton Affair
Eaton, Nathaniel (educ.) III–259b
Eaton, Theophilus (mer.) V–55a,b, 273a; VI–263b
Eaton, Thomas II–395a–b
Eaton, William (off.) II–334a
EATON AFFAIR II–389b; V–346b
Eaton's Neck (N.Y.) II–349a
Eaton's Station (Tenn.) IV–186b
Ebbetts and Cutting. *See* Union Fur Company
Eben-Emael, Fort (Belg.) III–187a
Ebenezer (Ga.) III–170a; VI–204b
Ebenezer Baptist Church (Atlanta) IV–46a
Eber (ship) I–144a
E Bonds III–8b
Ebony Junior (mag.) IV–223a
ECA. *See* Economic Cooperation Administration
Eccles, Marriner (econ.) III–7b
Eccles, W. H. (eng.) II–153b
Ecclesiastical Commission of York V–312b
Ecclesiastical government II–149a
Echo (pub.) III–259b
ECHO **(slave ship) II–390a**
Echo I (balloon) II–143a
Echo Canyon IV–411b
Echternach (Lux.)
World War II I–379b
Eckert, J. Presper (math.) II–155a, 426b
Eckert, Wallace J. (astron.) I–212a
Eckert-Mauchly Corporation II–155b, 156a
Eclecticism IV–284a,b, 288a
Eclectic Readers. See McGuffey's Readers
Eclipse (steamboat) VI–407b
Eclipse expeditions II–88a
Eclipses
divine providences II–356a
Naval Observatory V–12a,b
ECO-ACTION III–181a
École des Beaux Arts (Paris) I–163b–64a; VI–243b
École Polytechnique II–447a
Ecological Monographs II–392a
Ecological Society of America II–392a
ECOLOGY II–390a
animal II–390a, 391b
Audubon Society I–222b
conservation II–187a–88b
defoliants II–319b
education II–402b
fish management III–28a
interstate compacts VI–402a,b
petroleum industry V–270b
reforestation VI–67a
soil erosion VI–335a–b
supersonic transport I–53a
timberlands VII–60a
workers' environments IV–77b
zoos VII–371a
See also Wildlife Preservation
Ecology (jour.) II–392a
Econochaca, Battle of (1813) II 257a
Economic, Social and Cultural Rights, International Covenant on III–457a
Economic Advisers, Council of. *See* Council of Economic Advisers

Economic aid. *See* Foreign aid
Economic Association, American. *See* American Economic Association
Economic Cooperation Administration IV–258a; VII–88b
Economic Cooperation and Development, Organization for. *See* Organization for Economic Cooperation and Development
Economic determinism V–353b
Economic Development Administration II–135a
Economic Geology (jour.) III–163b
Economic History of the United States III–283a
Economic internationalism V–170b
Economic Interpretation of the Constitution III–283a; V–353b
Economic Mind in American Civilization III–283a
Economic Opportunity, Office of. *See* Office of Economic Opportunity
Economic Opportunity Act (1964) I–239b; II–147b–48b; V–135b, 382a; VI–328b
  Job Corps III–503b
  rural development VI–171b–72a
Economic report, annual II–480b, 498a
Economic Research, Institute for I–370a
Economic Research, National Bureau of. *See* National Bureau of Economic Research
ECONOMIC ROYALISTS II–392a; V–47b
Economics
  laissez-faire IV–85a
  Nobel Prizes V–99b
Economic Security, Committee on VI–329a
Economy (Pa.) II–147a; III–255b
Economy, planned. *See* Planned Economy
Écores Prudhomme. *See* Prudhomme Bluffs
Ecorse (Mich.) III–316a
ECORSE RIVER COUNCIL (1763) **II–392b**; III–117b; V–357a
Ecosystem concept II–391a
Écu (coin) II–94b
Ecuador V–233a
  earthquake V–23a
  Galápagos Islands III–146b
  immigration to U.S. III–341b
  Indians III–356b
  International Exposition of 1895 III–453b
  Kasson tariff treaty IV–33a
  oil industry IV–114a–b
  territorial waters III–107a
  United Nations Declaration VII–151b
  U.S. trade VI–345b, 346a
Ecumenical Council VI–79b
Ecumenical movement II–353a
  congregational leadership II–170a
  Eastern Orthodox churches II–387a
  Methodism IV–318b
Eddis, William (col. offi.) IV–79a
Eddy, Mary Baker II–35b–36a; VI–79a
Eddystone (Pa.) IV–175b
Edelman, George W. (inv.) I–395b
Edelman, Gerald M. (biochem.) V–100a
Eden, Anthony (states.) III–161a; IV–415b; VI–430a
Eden, Charles (col. gov.) II–392b–93a
Eden, Richard (hist.) III–280a
Eden, William, 1st Baron Auckland (states.) V–232a
Eden projectile point III–484b
EDENTON (N.C.) **II–392b**; V–115b; VI–340b
Edenton Tea Party (1774) II–393a
Ederle, Gertrude (athlete) V–154b
Edes, R. (art critic) III–446b
Edgar Huntley IV–161b
Edgar S. Kaufmann House (Bear Run, Pa.) I–165a
Edgartown (Mass.) IV–258a
Edge, Walter (gov.) V–368a–b
Edgefield policy. *See* Mississippi Plan
EDGE HILL, BATTLE OF (1777) **II–393a**
Edict Concerning the Negro Slaves in Louisiana (1724) II–91b
Edict of Nantes (1598) III–315a
Edinburgh (Scot.) III–65a
  Encyclopaedia Britannica II–444a
  high school II–397b
  medical education IV–297b
Edinburgh, University of II–10b
Edison, Thomas A. (inv.) II–7b; V–227a
  battery I–276a
  Edison effect VII–163a
  electric light IV–153a–b
  electric railway VI–40a
  electrochemical industry II–422a
  incandescent light II–413b, 414a; IV–88b
  industrial research III–409a
  light filament III–186a
  mimeograph I–396a, 397a
  motion pictures I–479b; IV–417a, 418a; V–328a
  Naval Consulting Board V–14a
  phonograph V–289b, 290a
  Scientific American VI–231a
  stock ticker VI–413b
  streetcars II–414b
  telegraph II–414a; VII–19a
  telephone VII–20b
  voting machine VII–210b
Edison Company IV–153b
Edison dynamo III–320b
Edison General Electric Company II–414a–b
Edison Light Company II–414a,b
Editorial cartoons I–464b
Editorials V–68b
Editorial Writers, National Conference of V–77b
Editor & Publisher (period.) IV–272a
Edmonson County (Ky.) IV–233b
Edmunds, George F. (pol.) VI–276b
Edmunds Act (1882) VII–162a
Edmunds–Tucker Act (1887) VII–162a
Edouart, Auguste (art.) VI–286b
EDSAC (computer) II–155b, 156a
EDUCATION II–393a
  academic freedom I–4b
  academies I–5a
  adult I–47a
  advertising I–19a
  agrarianism I–33b
  agricultural I–47a
  American approach IV–2a
  antebellum South VI–343a
  apprenticeship I–148a
  automobile's effect I–227b
  Brook Farm I–369b
  Carnegie Corporation of New York I–456a
  Carnegie gifts III–79b
  Catholic I–467a,b, 468b; II–490a–b
  charity schools I–495b
  Chautauqua movement II–1a–b
  chemistry II–10a–11b
  children's magazines IV–222b
  coeducational II–114b, 399a
  colleges and universities II–114b
  costs II–234b
  crime II–258b
  dame school II–285b
  Dartmouth College Case II–293b
  democracy II–324b, 326a
  denominational colleges II–114a
  dentistry II–329b–30b
  discriminiation II–457a–b
  district school VI–226b
  encyclopedias II–444a
  engineering II–447a
  European approach IV–2a
  evolution theory VI–239b
  farmer's institutes II–494a–b
  federal aid II–501b, 502a; III–438b
  Florida III–40a
  Franciscans III–94b
  Franklin Institute III–99a
  Franklin's Academy V–248b–49a
  frontier II–487a; IV–365b
  Fulbright grants III–130b
  GI Bill of Rights III–178a; V–258a
  Girl Scouts III–181a
  government expenditures II–234b, 476a; III–205a
  Granger movement III–210a
  grants-in-aid III–211b
  Great Society III–222b
  Haiti III–240a
  handicapped III–248a
  Harvard University III–259b–60b
  Health, Education, and Welfare Department III–267b
  hornbook III–301b
  hygiene III–324b–25a,b
  Indiana III–370a,b
  Indians II–292b
  industrial management III–406a,b
  Institute for Advanced Study III–423b
  integration VI–404b–05a
  intelligence tests III–440a
  interstate compacts VI–398a, 402a,b
  Jefferson, Thomas II–325b
  Jeffersonian Democracy III–496a
  Jesuits III–501b
  Jews IV–10a–b, 11a,b, 12a
  Jim Crow practices II–56b
  Job Corps III–504a,b
  journalism V–79b
  Kalamazoo Case IV–24b
  Kentucky IV–41b
  labor movement IV–77a
  land grants IV–93a, 96a
  Latin-American students IV–114a
  Latin Schools IV–116a
  law schools IV–120b
  learned societies IV–126b
  little red schoolhouse IV–169a
  local government IV–171b, 172a
  Louisiana IV–194a,b
  lyceum movement IV–207a
  manners IV–240b–41a
  Massachusetts IV–265a, 267b
  McGuffey's Readers IV–213a
  mechanics' institutes IV–281a
  military II–293a
  mineralogy IV–348a–b, 349a
  Minnesota IV–358a
  missionary schools

EDUCATION (cont.)
IV–364b
museums IV–437a–b
National Education Association IV–463a
National Urban League V–1a
National Youth Administration VII–364b
native plants V–326a–b
Naval Academy V–9b
navy V–23b–24b
neighborhood school control IV–173a
New England V–49b–50a
New England Primer V–51b
New Haven Colony V–55b
New South V–67b
New York City V–83a, 83b–84a
New York State IV–191b; V–87a,b
New York Times properties V–76b
North Carolina V–115b, 116a,b
North Dakota V–118a
Northwest Ordinance VII–268b
Northwest Territory V–163a
Office of Economic Opportunity V–135b
old field schools V–151b
Oregon Parochial School Case V–167a
Peabody Fund V–231b
Peace Corps I–8b
Pennsylvania VI–452a
Peter Parley books V–264b
Philippines V–283a
philosophy V–287a
political science V–347b–49a
poor whites V–359a
private schools VI–228b
Progressive movement V–428b
public opinion V–454a,b
public revenue VI–105b
Puerto Rico V–461a
Quakers V–470b
reformatories VI–67b, 68a
Rhode Island VI–132a
Rhodes scholarships VI–134b
Rockefeller Foundation VI–158a
rural population VI–174b
Russell Sage Foundation VI–177a
safety movement I–7b
schoolbooks VI–227a
school lands VI–227b, 228a
science VI–231b–32b
segregation II–54b, 57a, 57a–b; III–502b; V–331b; VI–256a,b
separate–but–equal doctrine II–54a
Slade's Girls VI–299b
Smith–Hughes Act VI–318a
Smith–Lever Act VI–318a
social legislation VI–328a,b
South Carolina VI–348a
spelling bee VI–372a
state borrowing II–303a
state government VI–398b
state universities VII–156a
subsidies VI–425b
suburban areas VI–428a
taxation VII–11a,b
teachers VI–229a
teachers' loyalty oath VII–15b
teachers' loyalty oaths IV–203a
teacher unionization IV–75b–76a
tennis VII–30b
Texas VII–38b
town schools II–285b
Truman administration II–480b
universal IV–61b, 80a
Ursulines VII–160a,b
U.S. Military Academy IV–340b
Veterans Administration VII–174b
VISTA I–8b
volunteer agencies I–8b–9a
West Virginia VII–282a
wildlife management VII–297b–98a
women III–91b–92a; VII–314a, 317b–18a
Workingmen's Party VII–322a
Wyoming Valley VII–347a
Yale Band VII–350b
See also Colleges and Universities; Indian Education; Libraries; Universities, State
EDUCATION, AFRO-AMERICAN II–403a; I–28b, 32a
African students I–21b
Berea College v. *Kentucky* I–290a
Berea School IV–220a
Brown v. *Board of Education* I–372b
church support I–23b
colleges II–113b
freedmen III–103a,b
Mississippi IV–369b
race riots I–31a
radical right VI–12b
Tuskegee Institute VII–130b
White Citizens Councils VII–291a
Education, Board of National Popular VI–299b
EDUCATION, BOARDS OF II–404b; III–298b; IV–172a
Education, Bureau of II–405b; III–307a
Education, Department of II–405a
Education, Land Grants for *See* Land Grants for Education
EDUCATION, UNITED STATES OFFICE OF II–405a; II–395b, 402a; III–267b
busing I–397b
handicapped children III–248b, 249a
library reports IV–145a
National Teachers Association IV–463a
private schools VI–229a
Educational Commission of the States III–460a
Educational Orders Act (1938) V–163b
Educational Personnel, Interstate Agreement on Qualification of III–460a
Educational Testing Service I–456b
Education for Parenthood III–181b
Education of Henry Adams IV–163a
Education Professions Development Act (1967) II–401a
EDVAC (computer) II–155b
Edward (ship) IV–136b
EDWARD, FORT (N.Y.) **II–405b**; I–385a; III–115b; IV–211a; VII–301a
Edward Augustus, Fort (Wis.) III–225b–26a, 311b; VI–218b
Edwards (Okla.) V–272a
Edwards, Charles (law., au.) VI–143b
EDWARDS, FORT (Ill.) **II–406a**
Edwards, Haden (col.) III–101a; VII–37a
Edwards, Jonathan (cler.) II–406a, 466a; III–214a; VI–76b, 77a, 81a–b
mysticism IV–447b
New Lights V–58b
philosophy V–286b–87a
psychology V–441a–b
writings IV–161a
Edwards, Jonathan, Jr. (cler.) VI–81b
Edwards, Ninian (law.) I–3a
Edwards Air Force Base (Calif.) IV–458b
Edwards County (Ill.) II–450b
EDWARDSEAN THEOLOGY II–406a; VI–77a, 81a–b
Edward's Station (Miss.) I–492a
Edwards v. *California* (1941) V–420b
Edwardsville, Treaties of (1818, 1819) III–383b
Eel III–51a
Eel River Indians III–383a; VII–189b, 212b, 262b
Eel Spearing at Setauket (paint.) V–189b, 190b
EFFECTIVE OCCUPATION II–406b
Effie Afton (steamer) VI–159b
Effigy mounds IV–420b
Effigy Mounds National Monument V–217b
Effingham, Lord Howard of (col. gov.) III–476b
Egan (Indian) I–264b
Egan, Charles II–106a
Egan, Michael (bp.) III–94b
Egan, William (pol.) I–78b, 79a, 80b
Egede, Hans (miss.) II–461b
EGG HARBOR ENGAGEMENT (1778) **II–406b**
Eggleston, Edward (cler., nov.) IV–223a; VI–372a
Eggs VI–48a
freeze drying III–55b
Egmont, Earl of. *See* Perceval, Sir John
Egypt III–481b–82a,b
aerial hijacking III–277b
Baghdad Pact I–243a
Gaza Strip IV–236b
Kissinger mediations V–233a
marine landing IV–252a
relations with U.S. I–149a–150b
Suez Canal I–124a,b
Suez crisis III–352b; VI–429b
sugar beet I–285a,b
Treaty of Versailles VII–173a
United Nations Declaration VII–151b
U.S. consular jurisdiction II–479a,b
World War II V–112b; VII–338a
Yom Kippur War II–213a
"EGYPT" (Ill.) **II–406b**; IV–155b
Egyptian Secrets III–49b
E. Howard and Company II–79b
Ehrenberg, Christian G. (nat.) V–134b
Ehrenberg, Herman (prospector) II–477b
Ehrlichman, John D. VII–255b
Eielsen, Elling (rel. leader) V–123b
Eielsen Synod V–123b
Eielson, Carl Ben (expl.) V–337b
Eifel (Ger.)
World War II I–379b
Eifel Mountains
World War II VII–340a
Eiffel Tower III–11b
Eigenmann, Carl H. (educ.) II–391b
Eight, The (paints.) II–104a, 106b
EIGHTEENTH AMENDMENT II–406b; I–94b–95a; II–206a; IV–159a; V–429b–30a; VII–23b
Anti-Saloon League I–134a
bootlegging I–339a
campaign of 1928 I–428a
campaign of 1932 I–428b
Customs Service II–277a,b

federal–state enforcement VII–154b
Kansas opposition IV–27a
organized crime II–261a
repeal I–339b; II–206b, 262a, 354a; V–45a; VII–132a
Volstead Act VII–207b
Eighth Air Force I–64a
Eighth Amendment I–299a, 450b; III–250a; V–464a
Eighth (VIII) Corps. *See* entries under Army, United States
Eighth Infantry Division III–314b
Eighth International Conference of American States (1936) V–106a
Eighth Massachusetts–Marblehead Regiment IV–463b
Eight–hour–day movement II–491a; IV–62b, 63a, 64a,b, 65a, 69b; V–428b; VII–213b
Adamson Act IV–68b; VI–21a
Haymarket Riot III–266a
May Day demonstrations IV–278a
National Labor Union IV–81a
Toledo V–142a
Eighth Texas Cavalry. *See* Terry's Texas Rangers
Eight Men IV–167a; V–61b
Eights, James (geol.) V–336b
Eighty–first Infantry Divison. *See* entries under Army, United States
Eighty–second Airborne Divison. *See* entries under Army, United States
Eighty–seventh Mountain Regiment. *See* entries under Army, United States
Eighty–third Infantry Division. *See* entries under Army, United States
Eijkman, Christian (bact.) I–303a
Einem, Karl von (off.) I–491b
Einstein, Albert (phys.) III–424b; IV–237b, 262a; V–295b, 301a, 303a,b
"Eirik the Greenlanders' Bishop Went to Look for Vinland" (annal) V–112a
Eirik the Red's Saga V–112a; VII–190a
Eisenhower (carrier) I–56b
Eisenhower, Dwight D. II–177 (table); III–284b; IV–26b; V–396 (table), 396b; VII–40b
—Military Career:
Bastogne I–273b
Battle of the Bulge I–379b, 380a
European Theater command I–123a
McCarthy hearings VII–310b
Normandy invasion V–110b; VII–339a
North African campaign V–112b; VII–338a–b
occupation of Germany III–174b
psychological warfare V–441a
Sicilian campaign VI–284b
—President:
Adams, Sherman, scandal V–346b
Air Force Academy I–65a
Alaska statehood I–78a,b
arms control I–180a
atomic energy I–216b
Brazil visit II–347a
Bricker Amendment I–362b–63a
cabinet I–400a; VII–317b
campaign of 1952 I–20a, 179b, 430a,b
campaign of 1956 I–430a
China policy II–28a
civil rights movement II–56b
Committee on Government Contracts II–456a
Cuba II–269b
disability V–397a
Far Eastern policy II–489a–b
foreign aid III–62a
foreign policy III–69b–70a
Geneva summit conference III–161a
government appointments I–146a
Hawaii statehood I–78a,b
Health, Education, and Welfare Department III–267b
"Herblock" cartoons V–73a
highways VI–155b
Inland Waterways Corporation V–455b
Israel III–482a
item veto III–484b
Korean War IV–57a
Latin American policy IV–113b
Lebanon IV–130a
loyalty programs II–145b
McCarthy hearings VI–429a
Middle East II–407b
military–industrial complex IV–434a
military policy IV–344a
missile program IV–363b; VI–159b
national defense II–315b
national health insurance IV–289b
national parks V–220a
National Security Council VI–389b
"no–win policy" V–124a
nuclear weapons I–187a
Panama Canal V–202b
pocket veto V–335a
Point Four principle V–335a
Reconstruction Finance Corporation VI–60a
Reorganization Plan Number 1 III–54a
Republican party II–189b; VI–93b
Rosenberg case VI–164b
rural development VI–171b
Saint Lawrence Seaway I–440a
school integraton II–57b–58a
SCORE II–143a
Soviet relations VI–179b–80a
space program IV–459a,b
steel strikes III–419b
Suez crisis I–292b; VI–430a
summit conference VI–439a
Supreme Court appointments I–408a
Taft–Hartley Act IV–74a
taxation VII–9a
third–term doctrine VII–54a
tidelands VII–57b
Twenty–second Amendment VII–132b
U–2 incident V–216a
Unknown Soldier VII–156b
vetoes VII–178a
Vietnam VII–183a
Eisenhower, Milton S. (educ.) I–203b; IV–3b, 4a
EISENHOWER DOCTRINE (1957) **II–407b**; III–70a
Eisenhower jacket VII–145a
Eisenhower–Remón Treaty (1955) V–202b
Elaine (Ark.) I–30a
El Al Airlines III–277b, 453b
El Alamein (Egy.)
World War II IV–32b; V–113a
Elastic clause III–9a
Elazar, Daniel VI–398b
ELBE RIVER II–407b; VII–173b, 341a
Elbridge, Giles (mer.) V–243b
El Camino Real I–405a
El Caney, Battle of. *See* San Juan Hill and El Caney
El Capitan (operetta) IV–442a
El Capitan rockface VII–362a
El Chamizal (Mex.) VI–143b
Elderkin, Jedediah VI–451b
Elderly. *See* Old Age
El Diario (news.) V–75b
EL DORADO OIL FIELD II–408a
Eldridge Hotel (Lawrence, Kans.) V–471a
Election, certificates of II–411a
Electioneering II–408b
ELECTION LAWS II–408a
Force Acts III–59b
Massachusetts IV–267a
Newberry v. *United States* V–41b
residency requirements VI–99b
voter registration VI–71a
ELECTION OF THE PRESIDENT II–408b; I–94b; II–171b, 200b–01a, 411b–12b; V–343a, 394b
absentee voting II–410b
constitutional convention II–194b–95a
District of Columbia VII–132b, 208b
financing regulation II–232b
Jefferson–Burr election dispute III–494b
registered voters II–410b
residency requirements VI–99b
third–term doctrine VII–53a
Twelfth Amendment II–204b; VII–131b
two–party system VII–134b
two–thirds rule VII–135a
voter registration VI–71a–b
Election of vice–president II–409a–b
ELECTIONS II–409b; II–411a
assistance clause I–206a,b
ballots II–408b
bribery I–322a
Compromise of 1890 II–151a
contribution funds II–232b–33a
corruption V–346b
corrupt practices acts II–232b, 232b
democracy II–324b
falsification of returns II–232b
federal II–199a
judges IV–17a, 17b–18a
"law and order" issue II–259a
local government IV–171b
Louisville riot I–323a
majority rule IV–228a–b
municipal reform IV–429b
nominating system V–101b
party campaigns V–344a
party machines IV–214b
political parties V–343a
post–Civil War South IV–58a
preferential voting V–390a
proportional representation V–435b
public opinion V–454a
recall VI–50b
referendum VI–66a
repeating VI–88a
special II–172a
two–party system VII–134b
voter registration VI–71a,b
voting age II–55b, 408a–b
voting procedures VII–209a
See also Campaigns, Political; Campaigns,

ELECTIONS (cont.)
Presidential; Franchise
Elections, congressional
1800 IV–19b
1838 I–368a–b
1854 I–110a
1855 I–110a
1862 III–81a
1866 IV–472b; VI–57a
1878 III–110b, 225a
1882 III–225a
1918 IV–124b–25a
1938 V–48b
ELECTIONS, CONTESTED II–411a; II–408b
Goebel Affair III–188a
Hargis–Callahan–Cockrell feud III–252b
Hayes–Tilden VI–93a
Vare case VII–167b
See also Campaigns, Presidential: 1824, 1876; Jefferson–Burr Election Dispute
Elections, Primary. *See* Primary, Direct; Primary, Run–Off; Primary, White
Elective system (educ.) II–228a, 398a; III–260a; IV–3a
Electon beam fabrication IV–352b
ELECTORAL COLLEGE II–411b, 411b; II–201a, 201a, 204b, 408b–09b, 409a–b, 412a; V–343a
certification II–498b
constitutional convention II–194b, 194b–95a
District of Columbia VII–132b
Jefferson–Burr election dispute III–495a
third parties VII–52b
two–thirds rule VII–135a–b
Electoral Commission (1876) II–412a
Electorate. *See* Franchise
Electors, presidential I–94b; II–201a, 205b, 408b–09b
constitutional convention II–194b
District of Columbia II–409a
Electra (airliner) II–346b
Electrical and Electronic Engineers, Institute of II–449a
Electrical appliances. *See* Electrification, Household
Electrical engineering II–414a, 448b, 449a
Electrical equipment industry
checkoff II–3b
Chicago II–18b
Connecticut II–181a
copper II–223a, 224a
price–fixing II–259a
Saint Louis VI–194b
Schenectady VI–226a
Electrical Exhibition (1884) III–99a
Electrical Exposition Center (Paris) VI–14b
"Electrical jack" II–413a
Electrical workers
Communist party II–145a
unionization IV–65b, 72b
World War I II–419a
Electric arc welding I–378b
Electric Boat Company V–27b–28a
Electric cars I–276b
Electric circuitry 153a–
Electric energy II–417a,b
Electric fan III–269a
Electric flash III–136b
Electricity
aluminum I–92b
automobile I–225b
circuit analysis II–38b–39a
clocks II–79b–80a
cooperative organizations II–220b–21a
dynamo II–7b
elevated railways II–428a
price rise II–421b
Scientific American VI–231a–b
Electricity, atmospheric IV–316a–b
Electric light. *See* Electric Power and Light Industry
Electric lines, interurban. *See* Interurban Electric Lines
Electric motor
agriculture I–38b
noise pollution VI–212b–13a
ELECTRIC POWER AND LIGHT INDUSTRY II–412b; I–276a; IV–153–54a, 244a, 245b
aluminum V–104a
Bakelite V–328a
copper II–224a; V–103b
flour milling III–44a
government ownership III–203a
hydroelectric power III–320b
Industrial Revolution III–410b
Kentucky IV–41b
licensing IV–148b
locomotives IV–177a–b
municipal ownership IV–427b, 428a
Niagara Falls power V–91b
nuclear power I–217b–18a
phonograph V–290a
public ownership V–455b
public utilities V–456b
railroads VI–35b
Rural Electrification Administration V–46a
Society for Establishing Useful Manufactures VII–161a
steam power VI–410a
subsidies VI–425b
Tennessee Valley Authority VII–28a,b
tungsten III–15b
turbines VII–129a
wagons IV–419b
Electric railways. *See* Railways, Electric
Electric streetlights I–369a
Electric Theater (L.A.) IV–417b
Electric train II–413a
Electric typewriters VII–136b–37a
Electric Vehicle Company VI–257a
ELECTRIFICATION, HOUSEHOLD II–417b
Electrification Administration, Rural. *See* Rural Electrification Administration
Electrified track II–416a
Electro–Automatic Refrigerator Company II–420b
Electrochemical battery I–276a
ELECTROCHEMICAL INDUSTRY II–421b; II–7b, 415a
Niagara Falls power V–91b, 92b
Electrocution II–414b; III–249b
Electrode II–423b
Electrodynamics V–304a
Electrolysis II–7b, 421b, 422b
Electrolyte I–276a
Electrolytic process V–103a,b
Electromagnetism I–111a, 276a; II–143a, 413a–b; IV–119a; V–294b, 305b; VI–231a
Electromatic Typewriters, Inc. VII–137a
Electron I–287b; II–12a, 423a–b; V–297b, 299a
Electronic camera tube II–425b
Electronic flip–flop II–153b
Electronic music II–426b; IV–439b, 441a, 442b
Electronic Nigger (play) V–96a
Electronic Numerical Integrator and Computer. *See* ENIAC
Electronic receiver II–425b
ELECTRONICS II–423a; III–410a; IV–245a,b
astronomical observations V–132a
electric circuit analysis II–38b–39a
foreign trade VII–89b, 90a
great fortunes III–80b
imports VII–84b
Kentucky IV–41b
mapmaking I–464a
miniaturization IV–352a
Minnesota IV–357b, 358a
Naval Research Laboratory V–14b
New Hampshire V–54b
oceanographic survey V–134a
Pawtucket V–231a
radio VI–14b
research III–410a
Rhode Island VI–134a
San Diego VI–208b
semiconductors VI–259a
society of engineers II–449a
sound recording V–290b
Southwest VI–355b
tantalum III–14b
telegraphy VII–19a
telephone VII–20a–b
television VII–21a
towboating VII–77b
vacuum tubes VII–163a
Electronics Research Center (Boston) IV–460a
ELECTRONIC SURVEILLANCE II–427a
Watergate VII–254a
Electronic switching elements
computers II–153b
Electron microscope I–242a, 349b
Electrophone Company VI–14b
Electroplating II–413a, 422a, 423a; III–14a
Electroshock IV–306b
Electrostatic generator II–278a
Electrostatic tubes
computers II–155b
Elementary and Secondary Education Act (1965) II–55b; III–438b; IV–145b; VI–328b
Elementary school
colonial South II–395a–b
congressional support II–234b
curriculum II–397a–98b
growth II–399b–400a
Massachusetts Bay Colony II–393b
methodology II–398b
New Netherland II–394b
See also Education
Elementary Spelling Book VII–266a
Elementary Treatise on Mineralogy and Geology IV–348b
Elements of Geography IV–413b
Elephant I–242b; II–40a
Elephant, Republican I–464b; II–437b; IV–454b
Elephant seal VI–245a
"Elephant's Ear" (Viet.) VI–301a–b
ELEVATED RAILWAYS II–428a; III–451b; VI–429a,b
Chicago VI–40a
electrification II–415a
Elevator buildings I–378a
ELEVATORS II–428b
apartment houses I–143b
architecture I–164b
electric II–414b–15a
skyscrapers VI–298b
ELEVATORS, GRAIN II–429b
flour milling III–43a, 44a
Granger movement III 210a
Green v. *Frazier* III–227a
licensing IV–148b
Nonpartisan League V–106b
North Dakota V–117b
wheat VII–286b

Eleventh Airborne Division V–213b
ELEVENTH AMENDMENT II–430b; I–94a; II–32a–b; III–371a; VI–96b
Eleventh Naval District VI–208b
El Ferrol de Caudillo (Sp.) V–30a
Elfsborg, Fort (N.J.) IV–454a
Elgin (Ill.) II–282a
Elgin, Lord. *See* Bruce, James
Elgin Botanical Garden (N.Y.C.) I–348a
ELGIN–MARCY TREATY (1854) **II–431a**; I–437a, 438b; III–243b
El Greco. *See* Greco, El
Elijah's Manna I–487b
Eli Lilly Company V–274a
Elim Missionary Assemblies V–260a
Eliot, Charles William (educ.) II–399a,b, 470b; III–260a,b; IV–120a
Eliot, George Fielding (jour.) V–74a
Eliot, Jared (cler., physic.) VI–335a
Eliot, John (miss.) I–294a; III–375b, 385b, 416a; V–279b, 410b
Eliot, T. S. (poet) IV–164a, 165b, 190a
Eli Whitney of Whitneyville IV–433a
"Elixir Sulfanilamide" V–467b
Elizabeth (N.J.) II–321b, 431a–b; V–368b, 408b
Elizabeth (Va.) I–317a
Elizabeth I (q.) I–148a; II–406b; IV–7a; V–225b
Gilbert's patent III–180a
Kennebec settlements IV–37a
loyalty oaths IV–202a
Puritans V–468b
Raleigh's colonies V–115a; VI–43b
sea power VI–248a
slave trade VI–310a
Elizabeth II (q.) I–440a
Elizabethan Poor Law (1601) V–279b
Elizabethan style furniture III–135b, 138b
Elizabeth City (N.C.) VI–156b
Elizabeth Islands
oats V–130a
Elizabeth of York VI–205b
Elizabeth River I–83a; II–253b; III–215b
Elizabethtown (N.J.) V–56b
ELIZABETHTOWN ASSOCIATES II–431a
Elk III–51a, 364a; VI–161a; VII–297b, 346a, 357b
Elk Ferry (Md.) II–218a
Elkhart Lake (Wis.) III–461b
ELK HILLS OIL SCANDAL II–431b; V–13b; VII–16b
Elkhorn, Battle of. *See* Pea Ridge, Battle of
Elkhorn Tavern (Ark.) V–238b
ELKINS ACT (1903) **II–431b**; II–134b; III–273a, 458a; VI–22a
railroad rebates VI–50a
Standard Oil of Indiana VI–384a
Elk River I–497b
ELK RIVER, BATTLE OF (1862) **II–432a**
Elkton (Ky.) V–96a
ELLENTOWN RIOT (1876) **II–432a**
Ellery, William (law.) II–308a
Ellesmere Island II–319b; III–224a; V–240b, 337a,b, 338a
Ellet, Charles (eng.) I–364b; IV–302a
Ellicott, Andrew (surv.)
Nolan expeditions V–101a
Washington, D.C. I–162b
See also Ellicott's Mission
Ellicott, Joseph (land agent) I–375b; III–291b
ELLICOTT'S MISSION (1797–1800) **II–432a**; II–381a; III–171b; VI–351a
Ellington, Edward Kennedy ("Duke") (comp.) IV–440b
Elliot, Charles W. (educ.) IV–119b
Elliot, John L. VI–330b
Elliots, E. B. (actuary) IV–149a–b
Elliott, A. Marshall (philol.) IV–2b
Elliott, Ezekiel B. (statis.) VII–207a
Elliott, Jesse D. (nav. off.) II–459a–b; III–218a; V–262b
Elliott, R. S. (agric.) II–375b
Elliott, Stephen (off.) VI–441a
Elliott, William Yandell (pol. sci.) V–348b
Ellis (Kans.) IV–26a
Ellis, Edward S. (au.) II–341b
ELLIS, FORT (Mont.) **II–432a**
Ellis, Havelock (sci., writ.) VI–266b
Ellis, John M. (miss.) III–331b
ELLIS ISLAND II–432b; I–275b
Ellison, Ralph (au.) I–25a; IV–165a, 166b, 167a
Ellsberg, Daniel V–258b, 346a; VII–254b
Ellsworth (Kans.) II–251b
Ellsworth, Elmer E. (off.) II–432b; VII–371b
Ellsworth, Henry Leavitt (law.) I–4a, 45a
Ellsworth, Lincoln (expl.) I–116a; V–198a, 337a,b
Ellsworth, Oliver (jur., states.) II–193a, 215a; V–409a; VI–445a
ELLSWORTH'S ZOUAVES II–432b; VII–371b
Ellul, Jacques (hist.) V–454b
Elm Grove (Mo.) I–453a
Elmira (N.Y.)
reformatory V–415b; VI–67b, 68a
revolutionary war II–433a; VI–438a
Union prison V–414b
ELMIRA, BATTLE OF (1779) **II–433a**
Elmira College VI–68a,b
Elmira Female College II–399a
ELMIRA PRISON (N.Y.) **II–433a**; I–219b
El Morro. *See* Inscription Rock
El Morro National Monument V–217b
EL PASO (Tex.) **II–433a**; VII–46b
Amalgamated Clothing Worker dispute IV–77a
Chamizal IV–329a; VI–151a
Civil War VI–144a
Fort Fillmore III–24a
Gila Trail III–179b
Jornada del Muerto IV–8a
Mexican War II–363b
Oñate's explorations V–155a
Pueblo Revolt V–461a
railroads VI–37a; VII–40a
railway surveys VI–353b
Rio Grande VI–143a,b, 151a
sanitariums VI–101a
Santa Fe Trail VI–215a
Southern Overland Mail V–178a; VI–154a, 353b
stage lines VI–379a; VII–101a
U.S. boundary IV–321b
wagon trains VII–217b
El Paso County (Colo.) V–311a
El Paso County (Tex.) VI–204a
El Paso del Norte. *See* El Paso
El Reno (Okla.) II–32a; VI–87a
El Salvador
Central American Court of Justice I–483b
interoceanic canal I–373b
United Nations Declaration VII–151b
U.S. trade VI–343b
Elsenborn Ridge (Ger.) I–379b–80a
Elssler, Fanny (dancer) II–287a
El Toro Marine Base V–98b
Elvehjem, Conrad A. (biochem.) I–303b; V–128a
Elwell, Newton II–100a
Elwood (Kans.) IV–26a
Ely (Nev.) V–39b
Ely, Eugene B. (av.) I–51a, 54a, 233b
Ely, Richard T. (econ.) IV–2b; VI–82b, 325a
Emancipation I–27b, 134b–36a, 139a
Catholics I–467b
Fourteenth Amendment III–86a
New York City III–253a
EMANCIPATION, COMPENSATED II–433b
Lecompton Constitution IV–130b
EMANCIPATION MOVEMENT II–434a; VI–305a,b
Copperhead opposition II–222b
Liberator IV–141a
Radical Republicans VI–10b
EMANCIPATION ORDERS, FRÉMONT AND HUNTER II–434a; II–168a; VI–11a
EMANCIPATION PROCLAMATION (1863) **II–434b**; I–28b, 139a; II–62a, 64a, 168b, 434a; III–400a; V–248a, 425a, 432a; VI–308a–b; VII–54a, 237b
Black Codes I–310a
Civil War diplomacy II–162b
enlistment of blacks IV–339b
Reconstruction VI–55b
slavocracy VI–312a
EMANCIPATOR (news.) **II–436a**; I–137a
Emancipator and Free America (news.) II–436a
Emancipator and Free Soil Press (news.) II–436a
Emancipator and Journal of Public Morals (news.) II–436a
Emancipator and Republican (news.) II–436a
Emaniji (Dak. Terr.) II–284b
"EMBALMED BEEF" II–436a; IV–279b; V–466a
Embargo
exports to Cuba II–269b
munitions definition IV–430a
EMBARGO ACT (1807) **II–436a**; I–85a, 93b, 120b; III–67b, 118b, 455b; IV–309b; V–34b, 104b–05a; VI–104b; VII–87a, 233b
Charleston I–497a
cities II–41a
Democratic party II–327a
distillers II–353b
Essex Junto II–464a
Massachusetts IV–266b
Napoleon's decrees IV–449b
neutral rights V–38b
New England VI–397a
New York City V–83a
opposition III–5a
Rhode Island VI–133a

EMBARGO ACT (cont.)
South Carolina VI–347b
textiles III–411b
Vermont VII–172a
wool VI–272b
Embarkation camps I–435a
EMBASSIES II–437a; VI–252b
EMBLEMS, PARTY II–437b; IV–454b; V–198a
Embree, Elihu (ed.) II–436a
Embroidery II–371a
Embryology IV–250b–51a; V–307b
Embury, Philip (cler.) IV–318a
Emergency, national VII–224b
Emergency Banking Relief Act (1933). *See* Banking Acts of 1933 and 1935
Emergency Broadcast System III–1a
Emergency Farm Mortgage Act (1933) IV–6b
EMERGENCY FLEET CORPORATION II–438a; I–390b; III–201b, 288a; V–455a; VI–281b; VII–326a
Emergency Peace Federation V–236a
Emergency Planning, Office of II–498a
Emergency Preparedness, Office of II–498a
Emergency Price Control Act (1942) VII–336a
Emergency Relief Administration IV–71a; V–44a, 73a–b
Emergency Relief and Construction Act (1932) VI–60a
Emerging Rights of the Confined V–417a
Emerson, Luther Orlando (comp.) VII–264a
Emerson, Ralph Waldo (au.) I–344a; III–112a; IV–162a, 267a; V–161b, 281a, 287a–b; VII–97b–98a
agrarianism I–33a
Concord Group II–158a
Concord Hymn VI–282b
conservation II–187a
mysticism IV–448a
transcendentalism VI–78a, 81b
"Young America" VII–362a
Emerson–Thoreau Medal I–97b
Emery, Henry C. (econ.) VI–464a–b
Emetine IV–291b
EMIGRANT AID MOVEMENT II–439a
Kansas IV–28a, 31a
New England Emigrant Aid Company V–51b
Sons of thc South VI–339b
Emigrant Companies. *See* Overland Companies
Emigrant Spring (Calif.) II–297b
EMIGRATION II–439a
armed escorts III–32a
forty–niners III–81b
Independence (Mo.) III–353b
water supply VI–377b
Emigration Canyon IV–411b
EMINENT DOMAIN II–439b; III–202b; IV–105a; V–433b
contract clause II–213b
implied powers III–349a
Kohl v. *United States* (1876) III–417b
New York City V–82a
Tennessee Valley Authority V–44b
zoning VII–370a
Emissions control II–277b
Emistesigo (Indian) III–401a
Emmet, Thomas A. (law.) III–178a; VI–407b
Emmet, W. L. R. (eng.) II–416a
Emmett, Dan (act.) IV–359b
Emmett, Daniel D. (comp.) II–357a; IV–438a
Emmitsburg Road III–175b
Emmittsburg (Md.) I–467b
Emmons, Nathaniel (theol.) VI–81b
Emmons, Samuel F. (geol.) III–166b–67a
Emory, W. H. (off.) II–91a; VI–353b
See also Emory's Military Reconnaissance II–440b
EMORY'S MILITARY RECONNAISSANCE (18-46) **II–440b**; VI–90b, 353b
Emperor Jones (play) V–439b
Empire Mine (Calif.) III–191a
Empire State VI–394 (table)
Empire State Building (N.Y.C.) I–164b; II–346b; VI–16a, 299a
Empire State of the South VI–393 (table)
Empire style (dress) II–371b
Empire style furniture III–135a, 138a–b, 445b
Empire Theatre (Montgomery, Ala.) III–269b
Empire Transportation Company VI–383a
Employee loyalty investigations II–473b
Employee Retirement Income Security Act (1974) V–256b
Employees
employer's liability laws II–440b
Employees, federal
right to organize IV–75b
Employee's Compensation Act (1908) III–431b
Employer associations IV–60b, 70a
Employer–employee relations. *See* Industrial Relations
Employers
closed shop II–80a–81a
collective bargaining II–110a–13a
industrial spies II–462b–63a
"yellow–dog" contracts II–222a
Employers' Liability Act (1908) III–431a–b
EMPLOYERS' LIABILITY LAWS II–440b; IV–267b
Employment
civil rights II–55a
discrimination II–56b, 457b
elderly V–150a
federal aid II–502a
full employment II–480b–81a; IV–77a, 77b–78a
iron and steel industry III–470a, 471 (table)
minority groups II–473a–b
New York City V–83b–84a
occupation changes V–132a
party machines IV–214a–b
public sector IV–75b
race relations I–239b
space program II–426a
women II–457b, 486a–b
World War II IV–73a
See also Unemployment
Employment Act (1946) II–480b, 498a; VI–328a
Employment agencies II–441b, 442b
Employment and Manpower Act (1970) III–504b
Employment Assistance Program VI–83b
EMPLOYMENT SERVICE, UNITED STATES II–441b; IV–71a, 78b
Employment Standards Administration IV–78b
Emporia Gazette (news.) V–68a, 73b
EMPRESARIO SYSTEM II–442b; III–267a; VII–37a
EMPRESS AUGUSTA BAY, BATTLE OF (1943) **II–443a**
Empress of China (ship) I–446a; II–26b, 28b; III–180b; VII–86b
ENABLING ACTS II–443a; VI–401a
Kentucky IV–42b
Ohio VI–153a
organic law V–170a
Enamel II–419b
"Enamel Method" II–419b
Encephalitis III–416b; IV–291b
Enchiladas III–53a
ENCOMIENDA SYSTEM II–443b
ENCOMIUM (brig) **II–443b**
Encyclopaedia Britannica II–444a–b
Encyclopedia Americana II–444a–b
Encyclopedia of Religion and Ethics II–445a
Encyclopedia of Science and Technology II–445a
Encyclopedia of World Art II–445a
ENCYCLOPEDIAS II–444a; III–422b
Encyclopédie II–444a
Endangered Species Preservation Act (1966) III–76a
Endeavour (yacht) VII–348b
Endeavour II (yacht) VII–348b
Endecott, John (col. gov.) II–365a; III–128b; IV–265a, 315a; V–51a; VI–199a
Enderbury Island III–425a; VII–125b
Enders, John F. (bact.) V–100a, 340b
Endo, Ex parte (1944) III–491b
Endocrinology IV–287a; V–307b
Endogamy IV–257a
Endowed foundations. *See* Foundations, Endowed
Endowments
Johns Hopkins University IV–2a, 3a
learned societies IV–127a–b
End Poverty in California *See* EPIC
Endymion (frigate) V–394a
"Enemies" list VII–254a
ENEMY ALIENS IN THE WORLD WARS II–445a; II–463a; VII–94a
ENEMY DESTINATION II–446a; III–106b, 456a
Civil War V–35a, 39a
continuous voyage II–67b
London Declaration IV–182b
Springbok case VI–376b
Enemy property II–164a, 168b
Energy
biochemistry studies I–303a
city planning II–49a
coal II–84a, 85a–b
cost of living II–236b
Department of the Interior III–444a
"Energy certificates" VII–17b
Energy crisis (1970's) I–391b; III–415b
Alaska I–80b
appliance industry II–421b
coal II–85b
daylight saving time II–296b
Energy Reorganization Act (1974) IV–351a
Energy Research and Development Administration IV–351a
Enfield Armory (Eng.) III–442a; IV–272b
Enfield rifles II–67a; III–442a; IV–430b
Enforcement Acts. *See* Force Acts
Engagés II–246a
See also Voyageurs

Engebi Island IV–257b
Engelmann, George (bot.) I–349a; IV–378a,b
Engels, Friedrich (philos.) III–476a; VI–325b
Engineering
cyclotron II–278a
earthquake-resistant structures II–385b
Erie school I–442b
information retrieval VI–232b
Lawrence Radiation Laboratory IV–119a
Engineering Council, American. *See* American Engineering Council
ENGINEERING EDUCATION II–447a; II–114b–15a, 397b, 399a; VI–232a,b
Cooper Union II–222a
foreign students II–471a
Franklin Institute III–99b
Lawrence Scientific School IV–119a–20a
Naval Academy V–9b
navy V–24a–b
physics V–295a
Princeton University V–409a
Sheffield Scientific School VI–274a
solid-state physics V–304b
Tuskegee Institute VII–130b
U.S. Military Academy II–449b; IV–341a; VI–145b
Engineering Education, American Society for. *See* American Society for Engineering Education
ENGINEERING SOCIETIES II–448b; IV–457b
Engineers, American Association of II–449a
ENGINEERS, CORPS OF II–449b; VII–98b
atomic bomb V–137b
Cumberland River VII–26a
dam construction III–322a,b
flag III–35a
fortifications III–78a–b
Garrison Dam V–117b
inland waterways VII–77b, 261a
Lakes-to-Gulf waterway IV–88a
Manhattan Project IV–238a, 433b
military roads VI–156a
Murmansk railroad IV–435a
reclamation VI–53b
river and harbor improvements VI–145b, 146a,b, 147a
Sault Sainte Marie Canals VI–219b
U.S. Military Academy IV–340b, 341a
Engineers Club of Saint Louis II–448b
Engineers Joint Council II–449a
Engines
aircraft I–51a,b, 52a, 235a
Anasaldo II–344a
chromium III–13b
columbium III–14b
Curtiss II–343b
jet III–410a
Liberty II–344a
Maybach II–344b
Packard II–344b
Pratt and Whitney II–345a
reciprocating II–416a
Warner II–345a
England VII–66a
agricultural chemistry VI–334a
Arkwright machinery I–175a; VII–44b
art nouveau III–446b
auctions I–221b
bankruptcy laws I–261b
benefit of clergy I–288b–89a
bicycle I–295a
borax I–340b
Bourbon family compact II–487b
boxing V–422a–b
Caribbean VII–270b
Castine (Maine) I–466a
cattle II–279b; III–51b
civil war II–70a
cod fisheries II–92b
colonial administration IV–188b
colonial agents II–116a
colonial charters II–118b
colonial coinage II–94b
colonial commerce II–118b
colonial councils II–119b
colonial governors II–120a
colonial iron I–318b–19a
colonial judiciary II–120b
colonial manufactures IV–242b
colonial plans of union II–121a
colonial policy II–122a
colonial settlements II–123a
colonial trade I–245a; VII–82b, 86a,b
colonial wars I–6a; II–126a
commercial arbitration I–153a
common law II–141b
Council for New England II–242a
Court Leet II–246b, 246b
criminal code II–247b
crown lands II–266b
Crown Point II–266b
daylight saving time II–296b
Debatable Land II–298a
Declaration of Rights II–308b
Delaware Indians II–321a
Delaware settlement II–320a
Denmark relations II–291a
Dorchester Company II–364b
Drake explorations II–369a–b
dueling code II–376b
Duke of York's proprietary VII–359a
East India Company II–388a
Ecorse River Council II–392b
education II–393b
"effective occupation" II–406b
electric railways VI–40a
exploration IV–264b
export taxes II–478a
Florida IV–92b, 368a; VI–187b
Fort Charlotte II–158b
Fort Christina II–35a
free banking III–101b
free ships, free goods III–110a
French frontier posts III–119b
French rivalry in Penobscot region III–120b
French West Indies IV–135b
fur trade III–141a–b, 142a,b, 143b–44b, 398b
gasoline tax III–153a
geological surveys III–165b
Glorious Revolution II–309a; IV–134a
golf III–197b
Hakluyt's *Voyages* III–240b
high-energy physics V–296b–97a
Hudson River land patents III–313a
Hudson's Bay Company III–313b
hundred III–317b
immigration to U.S. III–334a,b, 337b; IV–60a
impeachment III–343b–44a
imprisonment for debt II–299a
indentured servitude III–353a
Indian policy II–480a; III–382a, 387b–88a
insurance III–435a
intelligence tests III–440a
Iroquois Beaver Land Deed III–476a–b
Iroquois Treaty III–476b
Isle of Orleans III–479a
King William's War VI–1b–2a
Labrador fisheries IV–82a
landscape architecture IV–96b
land systems IV–101b, 102a
land titles IV–105a,b
libel laws IV–139b
locomotives IV–175a,b
logwood trade IV–181b
Long Parliament II–122b
Louisiana IV–193a
Magna Charta II–190b; IV–224a
Maine IV–225b–26b; V–253b
marine insurance III–427a,b, 428a, 429a
maritime convoy system II–217a
mental illness IV–305a
mercantilism II–166b; IV–307b
merchant adventurers I–15b–16a
Methodist church IV–318a,b
Mexican debts IV–325b
minimum wage IV–352b
missionary societies IV–366a–b
Mississippi Valley IV–375b, 376a
Mohawk Valley IV–386b
Mormons V–8a
Natchez IV–455a
naturalization V–6a
New Amsterdam V–41a
New France V–52b
New World claims V–109a–b
New World explorations I–96b, 401b, 447b
New World mapping VII–73a,b
New York City V–82a, 84a
North Carolina I–447b
parapsychology V–213a
Peace of Breda I–361a
poor relief VI–72b
Port Royal V–370a
primogeniture V–407b
psychological warfare V–441a
Puerto Rico V–461a
Puritan Revolution II–242b
Quakers III–123a
Queen Anne's War VI–2a
radio astronomy VI–17a
railroad gauge VI–27b
rails VI–39b
Reformation VI–80a,b
refrigeration VI–69b
Regicides VI–70b, 71a
Rio Grande colonists VI–143b
royal disallowance II–121a
Russia alliance VI–177a
Salmon Falls settlement VI–201a
saltpeter V–98a
sea otter VI–247a
sea power VI–248a
sea trade III–106b
Shawnee and Delaware trade VI–271a
silversmiths VI–289b
slave trade I–22b, 202a; VI–309b–10b, 311a–b
smallpox VI–315a–b
South Carolina VI–348b
Spanish relations VI–358b–59a
steam engines VI–409a
submarines VI–422b, 423a
Sugar Island VI–437a

ENGLAND (cont.)
sweatshop VI–454a
Synod of Dort VI–455b
television VII–21a
Tennessee VII–25a
theater VII–46b, 47b
theosophical societies VII–52a
tobacco VII–64b, 66b, 67b
trading companies II–228b–29a
trading posts VII–95b
transatlantic telegraph cable VII–19a
Treaty of London IV–182b
Treaty of Paris (1763) I–351a
triangular trade VII–119b
"turf and twig" VII–129b
union with Scotland II–122a
U.S. state bonds VI–96a
U.S. tariffs VII–370a
Vermont VII–171a
Walloons VII–221b
War of Jenkins' Ear III–498a
war with France V–52b
war with Spain IV–274a, 361b
Western Hemisphere IV–115b
West India trade VII–277b
wool VII–320b
World War II II–50a; VII–334a
See also French and Indian War; Great Britain and entries under Anglo
England, John (cler.) I–467b; V–409a
English, Robert H. (off.) II–346a
English, William (labor leader) IV–61b
English, William A. (pol.) II–450a
English, William H. (pol.) IV–131a; V–334b
English-American VII–270b
English bill. *See* English Compromise of 1858
English Channel II–237a
balloon crossing I–248a
telegraphy cable I–400b
World War I IV–320a; VII–329a
World War II V–111a; VII–334a, 338a, 338b, 339a
English classical architecture I–161a,b
ENGLISH COMPROMISE OF 1858 II–450a; IV–31b, 131a
English Liberties, or the Free-born Subject's Inheritance VI–141a
English saddle VI–184b
ENGLISH SETTLEMENT (Ill.) **II–450b**
English South Sea Company I–22b
Englishtown (N.J.) IV–397b
Englund, C. R. (phys.) VI–9b
Engraving and Printing, Bureau of V–372b; VII–108a
Engravings V–413a–14a
Engrossing (bus.) IV–399a; V–225b
ENIAC (computer) II–152b
Enid (Okla.) II–32a
Eniwetok Atoll III–324a, 352a; IV–253a, 257b; VII–337a
Enlightenment II–466a; V–279b
agrarianism I–32b
American Revolution VI–118b
human rights III–316b
religious thought and writings VI–81a,b, 82a
slavery I–135a
Enlightenment philosophy
U.S. Constitution II–197a
ENLISTMENT II–450b; VII–232b
Afro-Americans IV–339b
British army VI–127a, 129b
civil rights VII–154a
land bounties IV–91a, 344b
pensions V–256b
recruitment VI–60b
revolutionary war VI–117b, 125b
short-term and demobilization II–323b–24a
Washington's eight months army VII–251a,b
ENLISTMENT IN THE UNION ARMY II–451a
Enoch Pratt Free Library (Md.) IV–261b
Enochs, Enoch (riverman) VI–147b
ENOREE, BATTLE OF (1780) **II–451b**
Enoree River II–451b
Enormous Room IV–164b
Enos, Roger (off.) I–193b
Enquiry Into the Modern Prevailing Notions of Freedom of the Will IV–161a
Enrolled shipping IV–309a, 311a
Enrollment Act (1863) I–182b, 353a; II–366b, 368a, 451b
Ensenada de Hezeta II–131b
Ense petit placidam sub libertate quietem (motto) VI–394 (table)
ENSIGN (rank) **II–452a**
Ensilage II–281a
ENTAIL OF ESTATE II–452a; III–78b, 495b; IV–102b; V–408a
ENTANGLING ALLIANCES II–452b; III–67b, 480a; IV–124b
Enteric fever II–454b
Enterprise (aircraft carrier) I–54b, 56a; II–350a, 387b; IV–336a,b, 432a; VI–280a; VII–241b
Enterprise (blimp) II–345b
Enterprise (brig) II–452b
Enterprise (schooner) V–15a
Enterprise (steamboat) VI–407b, 408a
***ENTERPRISE-BOXER* ENGAGEMENT** (1813) **II–452b**
Entertainer, The (comp.) IV–439b
Entertainment
broadcasting II–424b
literary societies IV–160a
minstrel shows IV–359b
Mischianza IV–363a
Wild West Show VII–298b
women VII–317b
Entomology II–227a, 391b
Entomology, Bureau of III–213a
***ENTRADA* II–452b**
ENUMERATED COMMODITIES II–453a; II–119a; III–346b; V–16a,b; VI–107b, 321a, 386a,b, 435b–36a; VII–81a
ENUMERATED POWERS II–453a; II–178a, 195b; III–9a, 156b; VI–391b
Enumerated rights. *See* Bill of Rights
Environment
"bill of rights" II–188b
corporations II–230b
disease II–390b
nuclear wastes II–417b
Environmental chemistry II–12b
Environmental determinism IV–408b
Environmental engineering IV–293a
Environmental Health Sciences Institute IV–465a
Environmental protection
city planning II–49a
cost of living II–236b
Customs Service II–277b
interstate compacts VI–402b
labor's support IV–77b
state government VI–398b
Tennessee Valley Authority VII–28b
Wisconsin VII–308b
Environmental Protection Agency I–391b; II–188b, 417b; VI–213a
drinking water VII–259b
pesticides III–421a,b
Environmental Quality Act (1969) III–76a
Environmental Quality Council. *See* Council on Environmental Quality
Environmental sanitation. *See* Sanitation, Environmental
Environmental Science Services Administration II–88b
Environmental studies II–402b
Envoy extraordinary I–93a
Enzymes
RNA II–358a
study of I–304a
See also Molecular Biology; Proteins
EPA. *See* Environmental Protection Agency
E. P. Charlton and Company III–32b
Épernay (Fr.)
World War I I–491b
Epervier (brig.) V–238b
Ephedrine III–381a
Ephemerides V–12b
EPHRATA (Pa.) **II–454a**; I–161a
EPIC ("End Poverty in California") **II–454a**; I–407b; VI–269a–b
EPIDEMICS II–454a; IV–295a,b
animal diseases VII–175b–76a, 177a
children IV–275a
cholera II–33a–b; V–447a
colonial hospitals III–306b
deaths IV–150a
environmental sanitation VI–212a,b
Fort Saginaw VI–186a
Indians III–357a
influenza III–416a
measles VII–294a
New Orleans V–62b
New York City V–82b, 83a
Pecos mission V–241a
pioneers V–317b
polio V–340a–b
record-keeping VII–205b, 206b
research IV–285b
Savannah VI–220b
smallpox III–34a; VI–315a,b, 316a
study of I–241a
typhoid IV–291b; VI–173b; VII–259b
urban health VII–157b
Valley Forge VII–165a–b
venereal disease VII–169b
World War I relief VII–329b, 330a
yellow fever IV–302a; V–446b; VI–362b; VII–258a, 355a–b
Epidemiology II–328a
dentistry II–331b
EPISCOPAL CHURCH II–455a; VI–78a
Afro-Americans I–23b
colleges II–114a
Cotton Kingdom II–241a
foreign missions IV–366b
glebes III–187a
home missionary societies IV–365b
hymns III–326a
Maryland IV–260b
Old North Church V–151b
Oxford Movement V–179a
parochial schools II–399b
private schools VI–228b
religious liberty VII–69a
Sunday schools VI–442b
Episcopal Corporation III–432a

E PLURIBUS UNUM
II–455b
Epoxy II–12b; V–328a
Epstein, Paul (phys.) V–295b
Equal-cost-of-production principle VI–468a
Equal Credit Opportunity Act (1974) III–423b
EQUAL EMPLOYMENT OPPORTUNITY COMMISSION II–455b; II–55b
EQUALITY, DOCTRINE OF II–456a; V–351a
Afro-Americans III–102b
democracy II–324b
frontier II–326a
moral codes IV–408a
sexes II–486a–b
"Equality Before the Law" VI–394 (table)
"Equality State" VI–395 (table); VII–346a
Equalization Fee. *See* McNary–Haugen Bill
Equalizers (elec.) II–39a
Equal opportunity
colleges and universities II–115b
employment II–55b
housing IV–429a
Equal Opportunity Act (1964) IV–76b
Equal Pay Act (1963) IV–80b
Equal pay for equal work IV–353b
"Equal population" principle I–244b
EQUAL PROTECTION OF THE LAW II–457a; II–205b; III–2b, 86a, 86b–87a, 204b; V–421a
Afro-American suffrage III–20b
American Civil Liberties Union I–100b
Brown v. *Board of Education of Topeka* VI–256b
Commission on Civil Rights II–499b
Fourteenth Amendment I–300a
judicial review IV–14b
miscegenation IV–362b
mortgage moratorium acts IV–358a
poll taxes V–434b
"separate but equal" doctrine V–331b
Slaughterhouse Cases VI–303a
United States v. *Harris* VII–154a
"Equal Rights" (motto) VI–395 (table)
Equal Rights Amendment (1972) IV–126a; VII–314a–b, 318a
Equal Rights Association III–91b
EQUAL RIGHTS PARTY II–457b
Equestrian
Olympic Games V–154b
Equine influenza VII–175b
Equipment Clause (1839) VI–311b
Equitable Building (Portland, Oreg.) I–165b
Equitable Life Assurance Society III–433a
Equitable Life Building (N.Y.C.) VI–299a
Equitable Life Insurance Company III–434b
Equity (Ohio) II–147b
Equity Cooperative Exchange V–106b
Equus caballus III–302a
ERA OF GOOD FEELING II–458a; I–418a; III–5a
Erasmus, Desiderius (scholar) III–316b
Erdman Act (1898) VI–21a, 28b; VII–354b
Ericson, Leif (expl.) I–95b–96a; VII–189b
Ericsson (speedboat) VII–243a
Ericsson, John (inv.) III–36b; IV–397a
Eric the Red II–461b
Erie (Ala.) I–402a
Erie (gunboat) III–234b
Erie (Indians) II–458b; III–399b, 475a
Ohio V–140a
Erie (Pa.) III–120a, 475a
Fort Presque Isle IV–250b; V–399b
French fort V–246b
portage V–367b
War of 1812 II–458b–59a
Erie (slave ship) VI–312a
ERIE, FORT (Can.) **II–458a**; III–11a, 167b, 218a; IV–205a; V–91a; VII–234b
Erie, Fort, Battle of (1814) I–436b
ERIE, LAKE II–458b; III–215b–16b; VII–157a
biological research station II–391b
Black Swamp I–317b
bog iron I–327a
Bradstreet's expedition I–359a
British boundary V–214b
Buffalo (N.Y.) I–375b
canals IV–443b; V–1b–2a
Carrying Place of Niagara V–90a
Civil War I–280a, 433a, 435a, 439a; V–121b
Cleveland II–74b
Delaware Prophet II–322b; V–4a
disasters II–349a
domestic trade VII–83b
Erie Canal I–40a; II–460a; III–448a; V–50a
Erie Triangle II–460b
exploration III–119a
ferries III–11b
Fort Erie II–458a
Fort Greenville III–227b
Fort Presque Isle III–115a, 118a; V–399b
Fort Saint Clair VI–188b
Four-Mile Strip III–85a
French frontier posts IV–213b
Great Lakes Exposition–Cleveland Centennial III–217b
iron ore III–473b
Iroquois Beaver Land Deed III–476a
Iroquois Trail III–387b
Johnson's Island IV–4b
Lafayette's visit IV–84a
Miami and Erie Canal V–145b
Miami–Maumee roadway IV–329b
naval disarmament III–217a
New York and Erie Railroad VI–25a
Niagara Falls V–91a
Ohio and Erie Canal V–141b, 145b
Ohio–Michigan boundary dispute V–144b
Ohio Valley II–381b
Pennsylvania and Ohio Canal V–249b, 250a
Pennsylvania panhandle V–205b–06a
port II–74b
portages V–367b
railroads VI–34a; VII–100b
revolutionary war III–400b
Toledo War VII–68b
Wabash and Erie Canal III–374b, 449a; VII–212a
Welland Canal I–440b; III–452a; V–157a; VI–193a
Western Reserve II–183b; VII–274a,b
ERIE, LAKE, BATTLE OF (1813) **II–459a**; I–436b; II–338a, 364a, 458b; III–217a; IV–118b; V–19a, 141a, 262b, 424a; VII–45b, 46a, 235a, 266b–67a, 307b
Erie, Walter (col.) II–364b
Erie Barge Canal I–443b
ERIE CANAL II–459b; II–459a; III–147b, 223b, 226a, 331a, 411b, 448a, 449b; IV–387a; V–86b, 87a, 249b, 277b; VI–145b; VII–100a, 260a
Albany I–81a
Baltimore I–249b
boomtowns I–336a
bridge I–363b
Buffalo (N.Y.) I–375b
Canadian trade I–440b, 441a
cement rock I–328b, 477b
Cleveland II–74b
cod fisheries II–93a
Detroit IV–331a
domestic trade IV–309a; VII–83b
Erie School I–442a–b
financing II–255a; VI–202a
flour shipments III–43a
foreign investments III–64a
government ownership III–202b
Great Lakes III–216b
Hudson River III–312b
iron shipments I–327a
lead marketing IV–122b
New England V–50a
New York City V–83a
Ohio V–141a
railroad rate wars VI–23a
Schenectady VI–225b
showboats VI–283a
tolls I–443a
transportation costs I–40a
westward movement VII–283b
"Erie Canal" (ballad) I–247a
Erie County (Ohio) III–25b
Erie Lackawanna Railroad V–456a; VI–34a
Erie Railroad V–87a; VI–25b, 34a; VII–83b, 100b
management IV–273a
rate wars VI–23a
ERIE RAILROAD COMPANY* v. *TOMPKINS (1938) **II–460a**; VI–454b
Erie school (eng.) I–442a–b
ERIE TRIANGLE II–460b
Erikson, Erik H. IV–165a
Erin's Hope (ship) III–10b
ERISA. *See* Employment Retirement Income Security Act
Erlanger, Joseph (physiol.) IV–3a; V–100a
Erlangers (banking house) II–164a
Ernst, Max (art.) II–105b
Eros (mag.) I–479b
Erosion II–51a; VI–334b–35b
ERP. *See* European Recovery Program
Erskine, David M. (dipl.) II–460b
Erskine, Robert (geog.) I–463a
ERSKINE'S AGREEMENT (1809) **II–460b**
Ervien v. *United States* (1919) II–443b
Ervin, Sam (pol.) VII–255a
Ervin Committee. *See* Senate Select Committee for Investigating Into Presidential Campaign Activities
Erving, Henry Wood II–99b
Escadrille Américaine. *See* Lafayette Escadrille
Escalante, Silvestra Vélez de (miss., expl.). *See* Escalante–Domínguez Expedition
Escalante Desert II–461a
ESCALANTE–DOMÍNGUEZ EXPEDITION (1776–77) **II–460b**; II–129b; VII–74a
Great Salt Lake III–222a
Paiute V–194b
Spanish Trail VI–368a
Utah VII–161a
ESCALATOR CLAUSE II–461a; II–236b; IV–183a; VI–472a
Japan V–10b
Escanaba (Mich.) IV–303b
Escape clause (tariff) III–113b–14a; VI–469a, 470a, 471a,b

Escapee Program, U.S. V–281a, 342b
Esch, John Jacob (pol.) VII–99a
Esch–Cummins Act. *See* Transportation Act of 1920
Esche, Otto (mer.) I–413a
Escheat V–433b
Escobar, Marisol. *See* Marisol Escobar
Escort carriers I–54b–55a,b, 56a
Escort fighters I–60a
Esherick, Wharton III–137a
Eskaleut (lang.) I–84a; II–462a; III–357b
Eskiminzin (Indian) I–433b
ESKIMO II–461b; III–357b–58a,b, 396b; V–217b
  Alaska I–79a, 80b–81a; II–462a
  Aleut I–84a
  architecture I–166b, 167a
  art III–374b
  burial III–376a
  Canada I–441b
  canoes I–446a
  dress III–374a, 381a
  language III–355b
  medicine III–385a
  myth and folklore III–386a,b
  Norsemen V–112b
  religion III–392b, 393a
  scalping VI–224b
  tambourine II–291a
  tobacco VII–64b
Esmeralda County (Nev.) I–340a
Esnault–Pelterie, Robert (aeron.) I–209b
Esopus (Indians). *See* Esopus Wa; Kingston (N.Y.)
Esopus River II–462b
ESOPUS WAR (1659–64) **II–462b**; IV–49a; V–61b
ESP. *See* Extrasensory perception; Parapsychology
Española I–96a
  See also Hispaniola
Espejo, Antonio de (expl.) I–8a, 172a, 288b; II–184b; III–262b; V–155a
Esperance (ship) V–423b
Espinosa, Antonio (print.) V–411a–b
Espionage VI–428a–29a
  Hiss case III–278a
  Industrial Workers of the World III–412b
  military and strategic intelligence III–438b
  Office of Strategic Services V–138a
  Watergate VII–254a,b
  World War I VII–325b
  See also Spies
ESPIONAGE, INDUSTRIAL II–462b; IV–72b
Espionage Act (1915) I–481a
ESPIONAGE ACT (1917) **II–463a**; II–445b; III–105a; VII–326a
  Customs Service II–277a
  enemy trading VII–94a
  loyalty testing IV–202b
  newspapers V–74a
  Rosenberg Case VII–107b
  Schenck v. *United States* VI–225a
  Social Justice banned IV–472b
Espionage Act (1940) II–463b
ESPIONAGE LAWS II–463a; I–450a, 478b
Espirito Santo (Braz.) I–360b
Espuela Land and Cattle Company V–160b
Espy, James Pollard (meteor.) IV–316b–17a
Esquire (mag.) I–479a
Essay on a Congress of Nations IV–82b
Essay on Calcareous Manures III–16a
"Essay on the Trade of the Northern Colonies" VI–132b
Essays (Emerson) IV–162a
Essays to Do Good VI–81a
Esse quam videri (motto) VI–395 (table)
Essex (frigate) IV–220a
***ESSEX*, ACTIONS OF THE** (1812–14) **II–463b**; IV–251b; VII–243b
***ESSEX* CASE** (1804) **II–464a**; VI–169a–b
Essex class (carrier) I–54b, 55a, 56a, 57a; VII–1b
Essex County (Mass.) II–464a; III–175a; IV–436a
Essex County (Vt.) II–464b
Essex County College (N.J.) V–41b
Essex Historical Society II–98b
Essex Institute (Salem) II–98b; III–137b; VI–205b
ESSEX JUNTO II–464a; III–259a; VI–164b, 250a
"Essex Result" II–464a
ESSEX WILDCAT BANK II–464b
Estaing, Jean Baptiste d' (nav. off.) VI–128b
Estate, entail of. *See* Entail of Estate
Estates, intestate. *See* Intestate Estates
Estate tax II–500b; III–417b–18a; VI–105b; VII–4b, 4b, 6a, 7a–b, 7a,b, 8b, 9a, 10b–11a, 13a, 14a
Esteban (expl.) II–37a, 228b; VII–372a
Estebanico (slave) I–24b; IV–452a
Estes, Richard (paint.) V–193a
Estes Park (Colo.) VI–101b
Estes v. *Texas* (1965) III–105b, 105b
Esto perpetua (motto) VI–393 (table)
Estrada, Juan de (col. gov.) IV–45a
Etchaottine (Indians) III–252b
Etchohih, Battle of (1761) VI–347a
ETERNAL CENTER (oil well) **II–464b**
Ether I–119a; IV–284a, 285b, 297b; VI–70a
Ethical Culture Society III–248b
Ethiopia II–342b; IV–252b
  Afro-American support I–21b
  Italian conquest V–35b
  Korean war IV–55b
  smallpox VI–316a
  United Nations Declaration VII–151b
  U.S. military base I–22a
  war with Italy IV–183b
Ethnic lore III–48b–49a
Ethnic studies II–402b
Ethnology I–128a–29b
  See also Anthropology
ETHNOLOGY, BUREAU OF AMERICAN II–464b
Ethyl gasoline II–7b, 9a; V–267a
Etinchem Spur (Fr.) VI–338b
Etiquette. *See* Manners
Etiquette, The Blue Book of Social Usage IV–241a
Etna, Mount (It.) VI–284b
Etowah (Ga.) IV–370a; VI–353a
Etruria IV–196a; VI–211a
Eufaula (Okla.) VI–262b
Eufaula Convention (1902–03) V–149a
Eugene (Oreg.) VII–300a
Eugenics III–158b, 159a, 342b; V–155b; VI–237a
Eugenics Record Office II–97a; III–159a
Euphrates River IV–53a
Eureka (motto) VI–393 (table)
Eureka (Nev.) VI–292b
Eurocurrency III–66b
Eurodollar III–8b, 66b
Europa (blimp) II–345b
Europe
  Africa colonies I–21a–b
  communism II–315a
  debts II–301a
  Declaration of Independence II–304a
  disarmament I–124b
  engineering education II–447a–b
  indentured servants II–495a
  Marshall Plan II–315a
  privateering IV–256a
  Prohibition II–261a
  school system II–398a
  sexual attitudes VI–265b
  technical institutions II–447b
  trade VI–193a
  U.S. Army in I–187b
  U.S. Civil War II–162b, 163a
  U.S. conscientious objectors II–185b
  World War II II–145a, 315a
European Advisory Commission (World War II) IV–415b; V–378b
European–American Bank III–66b
European Coal and Steel Community I–254b
European Economic Community I–124b; VI–469a, 470a,b, 471a,b, 472a,b; VII–88b, 89a, 91b
  tariffs VII–109a
  U.S. balance of trade I–246a
  value–added tax VI–200b
European Free Trade Association VI–469a, 472a; VII–89a
European Monetary Agreement (1958–72) I–254b
European Payments Union I–254b
European Recovery Program. *See* Marshall Plan
European Relief Council (World War I) VII–330a,b
Eustis, Henry L. (educ.) IV–120a
EUTAW SPRINGS, BATTLE OF (1781) **II–465a**; VI–351b
Eutopia (Ohio) II–147b
EVANGELICAL ALLIANCE II–465a; IV–206a
Evangelical and Reformed Church II–170a
Evangelical Calvinism I–265b
"Evangelical Catholic" II–455a
Evangelical Friends Alliance V–470b
Evangelical Lutheran Church V–123b
Evangelical Lutheran Church in America IV–206b
Evangelical Lutheran Synod IV–206b
Evangelical Mennonite Brethren IV–303a
Evangelical Methodist church IV–319a
Evangelical United Brethren IV–319a
EVANGELINE (poem) **II–465b**; I–6a; IV–162a
"Evangeline Oak" I–6b
Evangeline State Park (La.) I–6b
EVANGELISM, EVANGELICALISM, AND REVIVALISM II–465b; VI–76b–78a,b
  camp meetings I–433b
  Christian and Missionary Alliance II–34b
  Congregational church II–170a
  Edwardsean theology II–406a
  Finney revivals III–24b; V–2b
  Great Awakening III–214a
  Great Revival III–221b
  home missionary societies IV–365a

Methodists IV–318a
Mormonism IV–116b–17a
mourners' bench IV–423b
New Lights V–58b
Norwegian churches V–123b
Oberlin movement V–130a
Pentecostalism V–259b
Presbyterianism V–391b
protracted meeting V–438b
Quakers III–123b; V–470a–b
radical right VI–12a
rainmaking VI–42a
Reformed churches VI–68b
religious thought and writings VI–81a–b, 82a
Salvation Army VI–204a
Second Awakening I–238a
temperance movement VII–22b, 23b
Evans, A. W. (off.) VII–252b
Evans, George Henry (ref.) III–296a; IV–62a; VII–362a
Evans, Gil (mus.) IV–440b
Evans, Henry (inv.) VII–61b
Evans, Herbert M. (sci.) V–128a
Evans, Hiram W. IV–58b
Evans, John S. (trader) I–286a
Evans, Lewis (geog.). *See* Evans' *General Map of the Middle British Colonies in America*
Evans, Luther Harris (librarian) IV–148a
Evans, Nathan George (off.) I–381a
Evans, Oliver (inv.) III–43a, 411b
automatic flour mill IV–272b
conveyors I–205a, 224b
grain elevator II–429b–30a
milling patent V–225b
refrigeration VI–70a
steam engines VI–222b, 409a, 410a
Evans, Robley D. (nav. off.) I–276b
Evans, Samuel (nav. off.) V–424a
EVANS' *GENERAL MAP OF THE MIDDLE BRITISH COLONIES IN AMERICA* II–466b; VI–204a; VII–74a, 239a, 287b
Evans rail VI–39b
Evanston (Wyo.) VII–345b
Evansville (Ind.) III–374b; VII–212a
Evaporated milk II–281a, 282b
Evaporators, fruit II–373a
Evarts, Jeremiah (law., philan.) VII–22b
Evarts, William M. (states.) I–76b; IV–221a
Eveleth, J. G. (bus.) V–269a
Evening Graphic (news.) V–74b
Evening Star (steamer) II–349b
Everett, Edward (cler., states.) III–176b; IV–267a; V–161b
campaign of 1860 I–421a; II–191b
Harvard University III–259b–60a
land speculation IV–99b
Lawrence Scientific School IV–119b
Everett "Massacre" (1916) VII–248a
Everglades (Fla.) II–52b, 347b; III–40a, 42a, 367a
Seminole III–39a, 396b
Everglades National Park (Fla.) I–70a; V–218 (table)
Evergreens IV–97a
Evergreen State VI–395 (table)
Evermann, Barton Warren (ichthyol.) III–27b, 28a
Evers, Charles (pol.) IV–369b
Evers, Medgar W. I–203a; II–58b
Evershed, Thomas (civil eng.) V–92a
Everson Gallery of Art I–166a
Everson v. *Board of Education* (1947) I–299b
Evert, Chris (athlete) VII–31a
Evertsen, Cornelis, Jr. (nav. off.) V–84a
"Ever upward" (motto) VI–394 (table)
Everybody's Magazine IV–424b
Every Man His Own Doctor; or The Poor Planter's Physician IV–295b
Evjue, William T. (ed.) V–73b
Evolution IV–233a
botanical studies I–349a
conservatism II–189a
DNA study II–358a
freethinkers III–112a–b
genetics III–157a
paleontology V–196b–97a,b
right to teach I–100b
Evolution, theory of VI–230a–b
Scopes Trial VI–239b
Evolution of the Igneous Rocks V–268b
Ewe (people) VI–309b
Ewell, Richard S. (off.) V–248a; VI–376a
Army of Northern Virginia VII–197b
Battle of Cedar Mountain I–476b
Battle of Cross Keys II–266a
Battle of Gettysburg III–175b
Battle of Winchester VII–304a
Battles at Sailor's Creek VI–186b
Battles of the Wilderness VII–295b
First Battle of Bull Run I–381a
Ewen, H. I. (astron.) I–212a
Ewing, G. W. (fur trader) I–105b
Ewing, Thomas, Jr. (off.) V–314a; VI–336a
Ewing, W. G. (fur trader) I–105b
Ewry, Ray (athlete) V–154a
Examiner of Interferences, Office of V–226b
Exarchate of the Russian Orthodox Church in North and South America II–387a
Excelsior (motto) VI–394 (table)
Excelsior (steamer) IV–52a
Excelsior Pottery III–184a
Excelsiors (baseball team) I–270a
EXCESS PROFITS TAX II–467a; III–205a; V–46b; VII–4b, 7a,b, 8a,b, 9a, 13a,b
EXCHANGE, BILLS OF II–467b
colonial trade II–119a
express companies VII–101a
Intermediate Credit Banks III–447a
open-market operations V–159b
slave trade IV–388a
triangular trade VII–119b
EXCHANGE OF PRISONERS II–468a, 468a
Civil War II–63a–b; V–414b
Korean War IV–56b
Treaty of Versailles VII–173a
War of 1812 VII–111b
EXCHANGES II–469a
Civil War speculation II–69a
clearinghouses II–73a–74b
commodities III–207a
grain III–44a
investment banking III–465b, 465b–66a
life insurance III–434b
New Era V–52b
New York IV–237b
New York City V–83a,b, 87b–88a
Pacific Coast Stock Exchange VI–209b
panic of 1907 V–208b
panic of 1929 V–209b, 210a
regulation II–500b; V–45a
stock ticker VI–413b
Wall Street VII–221b
Exchanges, business II–493b
Exchanges, grain III–207a
EXCHANGE STUDENTS II–470b
Fulbright grants III–130b
Latin America V–232a–b; VI–365a
Excise taxes I–33a; II–353b; VI–200a; VII–3a, 4a–b, 5a–b, 6b, 7a,b, 8a, 9a,b, 10a, 11b, 12b, 13a,b
congressional powers II–199b
public revenue VI–105a
Whiskey Rebellion I–41a; II–69a
Exclusion. *See* Immigration Restriction
Exclusionary rule (law) VI–249a
Excursion boats III–218a
Execution
hanging III–249b
Rosenberg, Ethel and Julius II–463b
Executive, Chief. *See* Governor; President
EXECUTIVE AGENT II–471a; II–342b
EXECUTIVE AGREEMENTS II–471b; III–3b; VII–109b–10a,b, 111a
Bricker Amendment I–362b
commercial treaties VII–108b
foreign aid VII–112b
foreign trade VI–468a
treaties II–472a
See also Diplomacy, Secret
EXECUTIVE AND CONGRESS II–472a; II–171a; IV–133b; V–394b
executive power of removal VI–84b
item veto III–484b
League of Nations IV–125a–b
legislative resolutions VI–100a
power of removal IV–446a
presidential disability V–397a,b
presidential messages V–398a
presidential veto VII–177b
Reconstruction VI–55b, 56a–57a, 58b
separation of powers IV–209a
Tenure of Office Act VII–31b
Executive branch
authority to implement policy II–178a
checks and balances II–4b
Constitution II–200a–02a
enumerated powers II–453b
immunity II–474a
lobbies IV–170b
reorganization II–497b
Executive budget I–148b–49a
Executive Office of the President II–497b–98a
Bureau of the Budget V–136b
Indian affairs III–371b
Office of Economic Opportunity V–135b
EXECUTIVE ORDERS II–473a
Civil War II–62a
federal agencies II–497b
Federal Register III–5b
Indian reservation

EXECUTIVE ORDERS (cont.)
III–395b
Japanese–American relocation III–490b
Kennedy, John F. IV–75b
Statutes at Large VI–405b
EXECUTIVE PRIVILEGE II–473b
United States v. *Nixon* III–465b
Executive Protective Service VI–252b
Executive Reorganization Act (1949) II–497b
Exeter (cruiser) III–492b
Exeter (N.H.) V–53b, 54a
EXHIBITION OF THE INDUSTRY OF ALL NATIONS (1853) **II–474a**; II–428b; III–136a
Exiles, political. *See* Political Exiles to the United States
Existentialism V–288b; VI–79b, 83a
EXPANSION II–474b; III–68a–b, 213b–14a
agrarianism I–33a
Caribbean IV–111a
Cuba II–268a; V–174b
Florida III–38b, 40b, 42a
Great Plains III–221a
imperialism III–347a
Indian Country III–402a–b
Indian land cessions III–384a
Indian policy III–379a–b
isolationism III–479b
jingoism III–503b
Kansas–Nebraska IV–29a–b
"manifest destiny" IV–239a
Open Door policy V–35a, 157b
opposition I–131b–32a; V–49b, 235a,b
Oregon country III–21a
panic of 1857 V–207a
railroad surveys VI–39a
Spanish–American War II–314a
suburban growth VI–427b
war hawks V–34b; VII–231b
War of 1812 VII–234a
western separatism VII–276a
westward land migrations V–176b
whaling VII–285a
Whig party VII–288b
See also Explorers, Unofficial
Ex parte Garland. See Garland Case
Ex parte Merryman. See Merryman, Ex Parte
EXPATRIATION II–475b; II–439a–b
Confederate officers VI–274a–b
sculptors VI–243a
Vietnam War VI–61a
Expediting Act (1903) II–230a
EXPENDITURES, FEDERAL II–476a; III–8a, 205a–b
appropriations I–148b–49a
audit II–501b
Federal Communications Commission III–1b
federal surplus VI–449b
Food and Drug Administration III–54a
grants–in–aid III–212a
Hawaii III–264b
Health, Education, and Welfare Department III–268a
highways VI–155a
Indian land titles III–384a–b
industrial research III–410a,b
Job Corps III–504a
Kennedy administration VII–9a
Lawrence Radiation Laboratory IV–119b
Louisville and Portland Canal IV–198b
munitions IV–432b
National Science Foundation IV–471a
Naval Research Laboratory V–14a
New Deal relief VI–74a,b
panic of 1893 V–208a
pork barrel projects V–366b
pump–priming V–464a
Railroad Administration VI–19b
rapid–transit construction IV–428b
revenue VII–4a–b, 7a,b
river and harbor improvements VI–147a
roads III–451a
school integration II–402a
state agencies II–457b
taxation VII–2b, 11b
Treasury III–244b
welfare V–382a
World War II VII–8a,b
See also Appropriations by Congress; Government Spending
Experience and Nature V–288a
Experiment (schooner) V–15a
Experimental Boiling Water Reactor I–217b
Experimental Breeder Reactor No. 1 I–217b
Experimental Evolution, Stations for II–97a
Experiment clubs III–84b
Experiment Stations, Office of I–45a, 46b
Exploration Company I–116a
Exploration of the Colorado River of the West V–384b
Explorations and Surveys, Office of I–463b
Explorer I (satellite) I–72a; II–426a; III–502a; IV–458b, 459a,b
EXPLORERS, UNOFFICIAL II–477a; VII–271b
Knights of the Golden Horseshoe IV–53a
mountain men IV–422a
Pacific coast fakers V–179b
Explorer Scouts I–108b, 357b
Explosions II–348a–50b; IV–350b
Explosives II–7a, 423a; IV–350b
foreign trade VII–87b
industrial research III–409a
powder V–383a
rainmaking VI–42a
World War I II–12a
See also Munitions
EXPORT DEBENTURE PLAN II–477b
Export Embargo Act (1940) VII–334b
Export–Import Bank Act (1945) I–262b
Export–Import Banks. *See* Banks, Export–Import
Exports
nontaxable II–171b
taxing II–151b
See also Trade, Foreign
EXPORT TAXES II–478a; VII–4a–b, 10b
colonies VII–3a
Exposition International des Artes Decoratifs et Industriels (1925) III–136b
Expositions
Alaska–Pacific–Yukon I–81a
Centennial I–483a,b
Century of Progress I–485b
Chicago Railway Exposition VI–40a
Fort Worth Frontier Centennial III–81a
furniture III–139a
Golden Gate International Exposition III–189b
Great Lakes Exposition–Cleveland Centennial III–217b
International Exposition of 1895 III–453b
Jamestown Exposition III–489b
Midwinter International IV–337b
New York World's Fair V–89a
Panama–Pacific International Exposition V–203b
Pan–American Exposition V–204a
Sesquicentennial International Exposition VI–263a
South Carolina Interstate and West Indian Exposition VI–349b
Southern Exposition VI–353a
Tennessee Centennial Exposition VII–27a
Texas Centennial Central Exposition VII–41a
Trans–Mississippi Exposition VII–98a
World's Columbian Exposition VII–324a
World's Industrial and Cotton Centennial Exposition VII–324b
Ex post facto laws II–53b, 171b, 200b
Express companies
American Express I–102a
Butterfield Overland Dispatch I–398b
Central Overland California and Pikes Peak I–485a
Interstate Commerce Commission III–458a
stagecoaches VI–379b
Expression, freedom of II–446a
Expressionist dancing II–286b–87b
Express routes I–412b
Express stations VI–377b
EXPUNGING RESOLUTION II–478a
Expurgatory oath II–274a
Extension services, agricultural I–45b
EXTRADITION II–478b; II–202b
aerial hijacking III–277a
international law III–456b
relations between states VI–402a
treaties VII–112b
Webster–Ashburton Treaty VII–265a
Extrality V–159a
Extramarital affairs IV–256b
Extra–Sensory Perception V–213a, 213a
EXTRA SESSIONS II–478b
Extraterrestrial radio waves I–287b
EXTRATERRITORIALITY, RIGHT OF II–479a; VI–165a
China II–275b; V–242b
Madrid Conference IV–221a
Exxon VII–40b
Eyak (Indians) I–81a; III–362a
Eye Institute IV–465a
Eye Surgeons, Society of IV–289a
Eyles, Sir Joseph, and Company V–130b
Eyne (Belg.) VII–366b
EZRA CHURCH, BATTLE OF (1864) **II–479b**; I–213b

F

F2A (fighter plane) I–55a
F2B–1 (fighter plane) I–55a
F2F (fighter plane) I–55a
F3B–1 (fighter plane) I–55a
F3F (fighter plane) I–55a
F–4 (fighter plane) I–54a, 57a
F4F (fighter plane) I–55a
F4F–3 (fighter plane) VII–218b
F4U (fighter plane) I–55a
F5 (fighter plane) I–54a
F6F (fighter plane) I–55a; V–285b; VII–343b
F8U–1 (fighter plane) I–57a
F–9C (fighter plane) II–345a
F–14 (fighter plane) I–57b
F–15 (fighter plane) I–54a
F–80 (fighter plane) I–61a
F–84 (fighter plane) I–53b
F–84F (fighter plane) I–53b
F–86 (fighter plane) I–53b, 57b; II–347b; IV–57a
F–86A (fighter plane) I–61a
F–89 (fighter plane) I–53b, 53b, 54a
F–94 (fighter plane) I–53b
F–94C (fighter plane) I–54a
F–100 (fighter plane) I–54a
F–100C (fighter plane) I–53b
F–101A (fighter plane) I–54a
F–102 (fighter plane) I–54a
F–104 (fighter plane) I–54a
F–105 (fighter plane) I–54a; VI–302b
F–106 (fighter plane) I–54a
F–111 (fighter bomber) I–50b, 54a, 235a
FAA. *See* Federal Aviation Administration
Fabrics II–371a
  flammable III–54a
  weaving IV–187b
Fabric sizing III–44b
Fabry–Perot interferometer IV–262b–63a
Fabry–Perot resonator IV–263a
"Face on the Barroom Floor" IV–160b
Fact–finding commissions IV–5b
Factorage system II–138a
Factories
  child labor II–24b
  dairy II–280b–81a
  fire insurance III–430b
  food preparation II–219a
  government inspection III–422a
  heating III–269a
  public health V–447a
  women workers VII–313a
  work force V–132b
Factors. *See* Commission Merchants and Factors
Factory conditions legislation IV–68b
Factory dormitories IV–61a–b
Factory management. *See* Industrial Management
Factory system IV–243b
  convict labor I–221a
  opposition II–418b
  scientific management VI–233b
FACTORY SYSTEM, INDIAN II–480a; I–192b; III–389a; VII–95b
  army posts I–192b
  Fort Edward II–406a
  Fort Madison IV–219b–20a
  fur trade I–105a; III–142b
  Virginia III–380b
Factory towns II–45b
Factory workers
  wages IV–61a
Facts in Review (period.) VII–333a
Faculty tax VII–3a, 11b
Faeroe Islands V–112a
Faial (Az.) III–155a
Faïd Pass (Tun.) IV–32b
Faint the Trumpet Sounds IV–168b
Fair, James Graham (fin.) I–329a; II–157a
Fairbank, Calvin VII–265a–b
Fairbanks (Alaska) I–77b
  exploration V–338a
  gold III–191b; IV–52a
Fairbanks, Charles W. (pol.) I–426a; VII–180 (table)
Fairbanks, Richard (postmaster) V–371a
Fairburn, William A. IV–274b
Fairchild Company I–236a
Fairchild Tropical Garden (Fla.) I–348b
Fair Credit Billing Act (1974) III–423b
FAIR DEAL II–480b; III–205b; IV–140b
Fair employment practices I–391b; II–481a
Fair Employment Practices Committee II–56b, 455b–56a, 480b; IV–73b; VI–256b
Fairfax, Catherine II–481a
Fairfax, Thomas, 6th Baron Fairfax of Cameron II–481a–b
Fairfax County (Va.) V–224b; VI–275b
Fairfax Courthouse. *See* Chantilly, Battle of
Fairfax family (Va.) III–18b; IV–92a
FAIRFAX PROPRIETARY II–481a
Fairfax Resolves (1774) I–85a
Fairfield (Conn.) III–25b
Fair Housing Ordinance (Washington, D.C., 1962) VII–246a
FAIR LABOR STANDARDS ACT (1938) **II–481b**; I–95b; IV–71b, 80b, 353b; V–48a–b; VII–213b, 214a
  amended II–481a
  child labor II–23b–25a; III–247a–b
Fairmont Creamery II–282a
Fairmount Hill (Phila.) VII–258b
Fairmount Water Works (Phila.) VII–258b
FAIR OAKS, BATTLE OF (1862) **II–482a**; I–248a; II–295a; V–245a
Fairport (Ohio) II–459a
Fairs
  agricultural I–41b
  kermis IV–43b
  See also County Fairs; State Fairs
Fair Share Act (1960) V–342b
Fair Trade Enabling Act (1952) II–483a–b
FAIR TRADE LAWS II–482b; I–140a, 489b–90a; V–402a, 403a–b; VI–102b; VII–124a
Fair Trade League V–403a
Fairweather, Bill (expl.) II–477b
Fairy tales I–335a
Faisal, Ibn al Saud (k.) I–150b
Faisal II (k.) I–243a
"Faith bonds" III–39a
Faithful Narrative of the Surprising Work of God (1737) IV–161a
Faith healing III–49b; V–30a, 259b
Fajans, Kasimir (phys.) V–299b
FAJARDO CASE (1824) **II–484a**
Fake fur III–133b
Falaise (Fr.) VII–339b
Falcon (missile) I–57b; IV–363b
Falcon (ship) V–240b
FALKLAND ISLANDS II–484a; IV–252a, 400b
Fall, Albert B. (law., pol.) II–431b; V–13b, 346b, 347a; VII–16b
Fallam, Robert (au.) I–277b
FALLEN TIMBERS, BATTLE OF (1794) **II–484b**; I–183b; II–317a, 497a; III–227b, 255a, 369b; IV–53b; V–123a, 141a; VII–157b, 247a, 263a,b
Falling Creek (Va.) III–472a; VI–291b
Fallingwater (Bear Run, Pa.) I–165a
FALLING WATERS SKIRMISH (1863) **II–484b**
FALL LINE II–485a; III–43a; V–310a; VII–283a
Fallout shelters II–50a
Fall River (Mass.) IV–63b, 266b, 268a, 347b
Falls of Saint Anthony (Minn.) VII–133b
Falls of the Ohio. *See* Ohio, Falls of the
Falls View. *See* Upper Falls Bridge
Falmouth (Maine) II–485b; IV–226a
  See also Portland (Maine)
Falmouth (Mass.)
  shipbuilding I–447a
Falmouth (Va.)
  Civil War IV–425a
FALMOUTH, BURNING OF (1775) **II–485b**; IV–226a
False advertising I–19a
FAMILY II–485b
  antebellum South VI–343a
  budgets II–235b
  colonial period IV–150a
  cost of living II–234b
  courts II–360a–b
  demography II–328a
  divorce II–356b
  Eskimo II–462a
  farm II–495a
  marriage IV–256a
  rural life VI–174a–b
  westward movement VII–283b
  woman's rights movement VII–314b
FAMILY, FRONTIER II–487a; IV–424a
Family–assistance program VI–74b
FAMILY COMPACT (1761) **II–487b**; III–50b; V–109a
Family court IV–24a
Family medicine IV–285a
Family Welfare Association I–495b
Fan, electric II–417b; III–269a
Fan, folding II–371a
Faneuil, Peter (mer.) II–487b; VII–120a
FANEUIL HALL (Boston) **II–487b**; IV–191a
FANK. *See* Federal Armée National Khmer
Fannin, James W., Jr. (off.) III–198b; IV–274a; VI–213a; VII–37b
Fannin County (Tex.) III–327a; VII–238b
Fanning, Edmund (offi.) VI–72a
Farad, Wali I–315a
Faraday, Michael (chem.) I–276a; II–413a, 414b
Farah Company IV–77a
Farben–Industrie, I.G. V–292b
Far East
  markets and expansion II–475a
  music IV–439b
  U.S. merchant marine IV–310b
  U.S. territorial legitimacy V–159a
  World War I VII–329a
  World War II VII–342a

Far East Command, U.S.
IV–56b
FAR EASTERN POLICY II–488a
domino theory IV–107a
expansion III–347a,b
immigration III–342a,b; IV–209b
Lansing–Ishii Agreement IV–106b
Laos intervention IV–107a
Madrid Conference IV–221a
Magdalena Bay Resolution IV–223b
Nine–Power Pact V–96b
Open Door policy V–157b
parity V–216b
Perry's Japan expedition V–263a
Pittman Act V–321b
Point Four program V–335a
Taft–Katsura Memorandum VI–457b
See also Philippine Islands
Farewell to Arms IV–164b
Fargo (N.Dak.) V–118a
Fargo, William G. (expressman) I–102a; VI–353b; VII–267a
Faribault (Minn.) II–490a–b
Faribault, Jean Baptiste (fur trader) II–490a
FARIBAULT CLAIM II–490a
FARIBAULT PLAN II–490a
Faris, Barry (ed.) VII–153a
Farley, James A. (pol.) I–66a; V–43b
Farm and Fireside (period.) I–17b
Farm banks, federal V–455b
Farm bloc I–322a, 451b
Farm Bureau Federation I–42a; IV–171a; V–400b
Farm Credit Act (1933) IV–6b
Farm Credit Act (1953) I–44b
Farm Credit Administration I–44b; II–221a, 500b
Farm credit agencies I–44a–45a; IV–415a
Farmer, Joseph V–409a
Farmer–Labor Federation II–491b
Farmer–Labor party
campaign of 1932 I–428b
FARMER–LABOR PARTY OF 1920 II–492b; I–39a, 427b; IV–81b
Conference for Progressive Political Action IV–84b
FARMER–LABOR PARTY OF MINNESOTA II–490b; IV–70a, 81b; V–107a; VII–53a
state income tax IV–357b
Farmer organizations I–39b
Grange I–33b
Farmers
daylight saving time II–296b
government protection II–226b
Greenback movement III–224a, 225a
mortgages II–493b
sharecroppers IV–103a–b
trusts II–493b
See also Agrarians; Agrarian Movement; Agriculture; Populists
FARMERS' ALLIANCE II–493a; I–38b–39a, 41b, 42b; II–42a; V–365a–b; VI–175a
grain elevators II–430b
Kansas IV–26b
Ocala Platform V–132a
Farmer's Allminax I–91a
***FARMER'S ALMANAC* II–494a**; I–91a
Farmer's Bank of Maryland I–252a
Farmers' cooperatives. *See* Cooperatives, Farmers'
"Farmers' Declaration of Independence" (1873) III–210b
Farmers' Exchange Bank I–253a
Farmers' Fourth of July III–210b
Farmers Home Administration I–45a,b, 45b; VI–172a
FARMERS INSTITUTES II–494a; I–47a
FARMER'S LETTERS, DICKINSON'S II–494b
Farmers' Loan and Trust Company of New York III–291b
Farmers organizations
Granger movement III–210a–11a
National Farmers Organization I–42a
National Farmers Union I–41b, 42b
Farmers' State Alliance II–493b
Farmers trust VII–124b
Farmers' Union, North Dakota V–117b
Farm experiment clubs III–84b
Farm families II–495a
diet III–53b
FARMHAND II–495a; IV–61a
Farming
common lands II–141a
county fairs II–244b
dairy industry II–279b
oxen V–179a
See also Agriculture
Farming, corporation IV–104a
Farming mill I–34b
Farmington River V–334b
Farm Journal (period.) I–45b
Farm labor I–41b
employment offices II–441b
minimum–wage laws IV–353b
unionization IV–67b, 76b–77a
Farm machinery. *See* Agricultural Machinery
Farm prices I–360b; II–235a
Farm relief
mortgage legislation IV–414a–b
Farms VI–48a
Intermediate Credit Banks III–447a
land systems IV–102a
land tenure IV–102b
Farm Security Administration I–45a; III–503b; VI–99b, 269a
Farmville (Va.) I–146b
Farnsworth, Charles S. (off.) VII–366b
Farnsworth, Philo Taylor (eng.) II–425b; VII–21a–b
Farnum, Dustin (act.) IV–417b
Faro III–149b
Farr, William (jour.) V–79a
Farragut, David G. (nav. off.) I–14a; II–285b–86a; III–474b; VI–425a
Battle of Mobile Bay IV–382b, 383a; VII–26a
Hartford III–258b
New Orleans IV–374b–75a, 413b; V–63b; VII–146b, 240b
Port Hudson siege V–369a
prize money V–424a
Vicksburg VII–181b
Farrand, Beatrix (landscape arch.) IV–96b
Farrell, James T. (au.) IV–164b
Farrell Lines IV–312a
Farriers I–317a; VII–175b
Farrier's Magazine VII–176a
Farrington gang VII–97b
Farthingale (dress hoop) II–370b
Farwell, Arthur (comp.) IV–438b
Far West
Civil War III–187b
exploration III–114a–b; IV–422a; VII–74b
fish III–28a
Fort Leavenworth expeditions IV–129b
French travelers III–122b
fur trade III–143a–b
horse III–303b
Independence (Mo.) III–353b
mapping VII–74a
Mormon settlement IV–339a
overland mail V–357b–58a
per capita income VI–384a
pioneers V–316b
railroads III–450a
railroad surveys VI–39a
school lands VI–228a–b
transportation VII–101a
wagon trains VII–217a
westward movement VII–284b
FAR WEST (Mo.) II–496a
FAR WEST (stern wheeler) **II–496a**; IV–168a
Fascism
capital I–449a
House Committee on Un–American Activities III–308b
newspapers V–74a
radical right VI–12b
subversion VI–428a
World War II VII–333a
Fashion II–81a, 81a
See also Dress
Fashion designers II–372a
Fast Carrier Task Force VII–1a–2a
FAST DAYS II–496a
Fast–food chains III–53a
Fastnet race VII–349a
Father Abraham's Speech V–358b
Father Divine I–24a; III–254a–b
Fatherland (period.) VII–332b
FATHER OF HIS COUNTRY II–497a
"Father of motion pictures." *See* Edison, Thomas Alva
"Father of the Constitution" II–193a
FATHER OF WATERS (Mississippi Riv.) **II–497a**
Fats II–357b
study of I–303a
Fatti maschii, parole femine (motto) VI–394 (table)
Faucett, H. W. (prospector) IV–334a
Faulkner, C. J. (dipl.) I–196a
Faulkner, William (au.) IV–164b, 189b; V–99b
Fauna Boreali–Americana III–27a; IV–232a
Faunce, John (col.) V–334a
Faunce, Thomas (col.) V–334a
Faunce, William Herbert Perry (educ.) I–372a
Fauntleroy, Fort (Colo.) IV–208b
Fauntleroy, Thomas T. (off.) VI–141b
Faure, Edgar (states.) III–161a
Faust, Bernard (physic.) III–325a
Faustin I. *See* Soulouque, Faustin Élie
Faux, W. (trav.) I–367b, 368a
"Favored union" clause II–81a
Fay, Jones (physic., pol.) III–226b
Fayette (N.Y.) VI–87a
FAYETTE, FORT (Pa.) **II–497b**
Fayette County (Ky.) I–337b
Fayette County (Pa.) V–144a
Fayetteville (N.Y.) I–477b
Fayetteville (N.C.)
Civil War I–458b
Fayetteville, Battle of. *See* Prairie Grove, Battle at

Fayol, Henri (eng.)
III–406a–b
Fayolle, Marie Emile (off.)
IV–404a
FB–111A (fighter bomber)
I–50b
FBI. *See* Federal Bureau of Investigation
FCC. *See* Federal Communications Commission
FDA. *See* Food and Drug Administration
FDIC. *See* Federal Deposit Insurance Corporation
Fear God and Take Your Own Part V–390b
Fearon, Henry B. I–367b, 368a
Feather, Norman (phys.)
V–299b
Featherbedding
railroads VI–30b, 32a
Feather River Project
I–407b
Fechner, Robert (offi.)
II–51a
FEDERAL AGENCIES II–497b; III–3a,b
ACTION I–8b
adminstrative justice
I–12a
Alaska Power Administration III–445a
Allison Commission
I–90a,b
Atomic Energy Commission
III–439b, 459a
auditing II–501b
Bonneville Power Administration III–445a
Bureau of Indian Affairs
III–371a
Bureau of Intelligence and Research III–439b
Bureau of Outdoor Recreation III–444b
Bureau of Reclamation
III–445a
Central Intelligence Agency
I–484a,b; III–439a–40a
Civil Aeronautics Board
III–459a
class–action suits II–148b
comptroller general
II–152a
Customs Service
II–277a–b
Defense Intelligence Agency
III–439b
Department of Housing and Urban Development
III–310a
Election Commission
V–449a
Environmental Protection Agency VI–213a
Equal Employment Opportunity Commission
II–455b
executive removal power
III–317a; VI–85a
Federal Bureau of Investigation III–439b
Federal Communications Commission III–1a, 459a; VI–16a,b
Federal Home Loan Bank
VI–221b
Federal Housing Authority
III–310b–11a
Federal Power Commission
III–321a, 459a; V–5b–6a
Federal Trade Commission
III–458b–59a
Fish and Wildlife Service
III–444b
Food and Drug Administration III–53b
Forest Service III–75a
Freedmen's Bureau
III–103a
General Land Office
III–444a
government inspection
III–422a
Great Depression V–381b
Hatch Act III–261a
Health, Education, and Welfare Department
III–267b
Hoover Commissions
III–299b
Indian Office III–444a
Inland Waterways Commission III–321a
Intelligence Board
III–439a–b
Intelligence Resourses Advisory Board III–439b
Interstate Commerce Commission III–457b
Maritime Commission
III–459a; IV–254b
Mining Enforcement and Safety Administration
III–444b
National Academy of Sciences IV–457a
National Advisory Committee for Aeronautics
IV–458a
National Aeronautics and Space Administration
IV–458b
National Bituminous Coal Commission III–232a
National Bureau of Standards IV–462a
National Labor Relations Board III–459a; IV–466b
National Park Service
III–444a; V–219a
National Science Foundation IV–470b
National Security Agency
III–439b
National Security Council
III–439a,b
New Deal V–43b–47a
Office of Economic Opportunity V–135b
Office of Management and Budget V–136b
Office of Saline Water
III–445a
Office of Scientific Research and Development
V–137a
Office of Strategic Services
V–137b
Patent Office V–226a–27a
personnel offices II–60a
political corruption
II–231a
Postal Service
V–371b–74b
preservation movement
V–393a,b
Public Health Service
V–447b
quasi–judicial agencies
V–471b
Radio Commission
VI–15b
Reconstruction Finance Corporation VI–59b
scientific information retrieval VI–232b, 233a
Shipping Board III–459a
Southeastern Power Administration III–445a
Southwestern Power Administration III–445a
Tennessee Valley Authority
III–321a,b, 459a;
VII–27b
transportation VII–98a–b
Veterans Administration
VII–174b
Weather Service VII–264a
See also Government Corporations
FEDERAL AID II–501b
alcoholism IV–159a
Amtrak VI–31b
counties II–245b
desegregated schools
III–438b
farmers III–53a
federal deficit VI–449b
food programs V–129a
food stamps III–56a
Fulbright grants III–130b
GI Bill of Rights
III–178b
housing VI–314b–15a
Indians V–49a; VII–287a
internal improvements
III–448a–49b, 450a–b
irrigation III–477b–78a
land grants for education
IV–93a
learned societies
IV–127a–b
Maysville veto IV–279b
medical research
IV–285a, 285b
mental health programs
IV–307a,b
navy yard V–27b–28a
New Deal V–43a
Office of Economic Opportunity V–135b
Penn Central VI–32b
polar exploration V–337a
pork barrel projects
V–366b
public land states V–453a
Reconstruction Finance Corporation VI–59b
roads IV–156a; VI–152a, 154b–55b
scientific education
VI–232a–b
social legislation VI–327b, 327b–29a
steamship lines IV–310a,b
subsidies VI–425a
unemployment relief
V–381b
urban renewal VI–86a–b
War Finance Corporation
VII–231a
water pollution VII–259b
See also Land Grants to Railways
Federal Aid Highway Act (1916) I–78a, 99a; II–502b
Federal Aid Highway Act (1956) III–9b
FEDERAL–AID HIGHWAY PROGRAM II–502b;
VI–154b–55b
Federal Aid Road Act. *See* Rural Post Roads Act
Federal Airport Act (1946)
I–70a; III–452a
Federal Anti–Price Discrimination Act. *See* Robinson–Patman Act
Federal Armée National Khmer I–411b
Federal Arts Project
VII–323a–b
Federal Aviation Act (1958)
II–500a
Federal Aviation Administration I–69b, 69b; II–49b, 498b, 498b–99a, 500a; III–422a; VII–98b, 98b
aerial hijacking III–277a
See also Aviation
Federal Barge Line
VII–77a,b
Federal Board for Vocational Education VI–318a
Federal Bureau of Corporations III–343a
FEDERAL BUREAU OF INVESTIGATION II–503a; I–383b, 484a; IV–22a; V–259a, 339a
appointments II–168a
crime statistics II–258a
Kennedy, John F., assassination VII–238a
Ku Klux Klan IV–59a
Latin America V–138a
military and strategic intelligence III–439b
Rosenberg case VI–165a
Federal Children's Bureau
IV–275b–76a
Federal Civil Defense Agency
II–50a
Federal Commission on Industrial Relations III–83b
FEDERAL COMMUNICATIONS COMMISSION III–1a; I–13a, 480b; II–500a; III–3a, 106a, 458a, 459a; IV–271b
radio VI–15b–16a,b
television V–346b; VII–21b
Federal Corrupt Practices Act (1910) V–448b–49a
Federal Council of Churches
II–353a; IV–318b;
VII–330b
Federal Council of Churches of Christ VI–79b
Federal Council of the Churches of Christ in America
II–465b
Federal courts. *See* Courts; Judiciary
Federal Crop Insurance Corporation II–501a; V–359a
Federal Deposit Insurance Corporation I–253b–54a, 257b, 259b, 264a; II–500b–01a; III–7a, 186b,

FEDERAL DEPOSIT INSURANCE CORPORATION (cont.)
201b, 443b; V–45a, 373b
"Federal Edifice" cartoon I–464b
Federal Election Campaign Act (1971) I–414a,b; V–448b–50a
Federal Election Commission V–449a
Federal Emergency Relief Administration. *See* Emergency Relief Administration
Federal employees
political activities II–233a
Federal Employers' Liability Act (1908) II–441a
Federal Equal Pay Act (1963) IV–353b
Federal expenditures. *See* Expenditures, Federal
Federal Farm Board I–43a, 44a
Federal Farm Loan Act (1916) I–44a; IV–6b
Federal Food and Nutrition Office V–128b
FEDERAL GOVERNMENT III–2a; II–197b; IV–1b; VI–396a–b
agriculture III–52b
branches II–171a, 178a
bureaucracy I–383b
centralization I–484b
Civil Service II–59a; III–261a–b
corrupt practices acts II–232b–33a
costs II–234a
debts II–302a–b
election crimes II–408b
Employment Service II–442a–b
enumerated powers II–453a–b
essays on II–264b
franked mail III–98a
gold reserve III–190a
government contracts IV–353b
government ownership III–202b
grants-in-aid III–211a
Hoover Commissions III–299b
hospitals III–306b
housing III–310a–b
implied powers IV–211b
Indian education III–380a–b
Indian lands III–396a
Indian policy III–382b–83a, 388b
industrial relations III–407a–08a
industrial research III–409b–10a,b
inspection of industry III–422a
interstate commerce laws III–458b
interstate compacts III–459b
intrastate commerce VI–283b
judiciary IV–15a
Justice Department IV–21b
labor contracts VII–223a
labor protection IV–80a,b
land grant policy II–396a
land titles IV–105b
legislature IV–133b
library development IV–146a
licensing IV–148b
life insurance III–434a
liquor regulation IV–159a
literacy tests IV–159b
lobbies IV–170a
manpower problems II–442a–b
medical research IV–286a, 287a–88a
mortgage relief legislation IV–414b
municipal government IV–427a–b
museums IV–436b
neighborhood school control IV–173a
political party funding I–414a,b
political theories V–351a–52b
public assistance V–280b
public housing IV–428b–29a
public ownership V–454b
public revenue VI–105a
regulation of business I–389b; III–204a–05a
retirement program V–255a
separation of powers V–385a–b
spending III–205a–b
state-making process VI–399b
state sovereignty VI–403a
Supreme Court denial of power IV–43b
surplus VI–449a
taxation VII–4a–10b, 11b–14a
tidelands VII–57a
titles of nobility V–100b
treatymaking powers IV–381a
versus local government IV–13a
Virginia Plan II–193b–94a
women VII–317b
Federal Hall (N.Y.C.) III–350b; VII–221b
Federal Highway Act (1921) I–228b; II–502b
Federal Highway Administration II–502b–03a
Federal Hill (Ky.) IV–447b
Federal Home Loan Bank Board I–376b; II–501a; III–294a–b
Federal Home Loan Bank System I–376b; II–501a; VI–221b
Federal Housing Administration I–376b–77a; II–47a, 48a; III–310b–11a
mapmaking I–464a
See also Housing and Urban Development, Department of
Federal Intermediate Credit Banks. *See* Intermediate Credit Banks
Federalism I–418b; III–104a; V–351a,b
"Federalism without Washington" VI–402b
***FEDERALIST* III–4a**; I–130b; II–196b; V–199a, 350b, 351a, 352a, 353a; VII–194a, 309a
federal judiciary IV–15b
jury trial IV–21a
minority rights IV–358b
No. 84 I–297b
political corruption II–231a
representation doctrine VI–88a–b
representative government VI–89b
republic VI–92a
FEDERALIST PARTY III–4a; II–325b, 326b; V–223a, 343b; VI–94a,b; VII–117b, 134b
agrarian movement I–33a
Alien and Sedition Acts I–87a–b; IV–202b; V–2b, 69b
Anglo-French wars III–238b
backwoodsmen I–240a
Bill of Rights I–297b
black cockade II–437b
campaign of 1796 III–96b
campaign of 1800 III–494b–95a
censorship I–478b
Chase impeachment I–501b
congressional caucus I–474b
Connecticut II–180b, 183a
Constitution I–130b–31a; II–196a–97a
Dartmouth College Case II–293b
demise II–458a
embargo of 1807 VI–164b
Essex Junto II–464a
executive privilege II–473b
French Revolution II–189a
Gazette of the United States III–202a; IV–463b
government appointments I–145b
Hamilton's fiscal policies III–246a
Hartford Convention III–259a
high-minded men III–276a–b
implied powers III–348a
Jay's Treaty III–494a
Jefferson-Burr election dispute VII–131b
judiciary IV–19b, 228a, 335b; VI–448a
Louisiana Purchase VI–211a
manners IV–240b
Marbury v. *Madison* IV–248b
Marshall Court IV–13b
Massachusetts IV–266a,b
Mazzei letter IV–279b
Monroe's recall from France IV–402b
National Republican party IV–469b
New England III–273a
New Hampshire V–54a
New Jersey V–58a
New York City V–83a
New York State V–86b
North Carolina V–115b
party caucus I–474b
political patronage VI–375a
presidential campaigns I–417a–18b
presidents V–395 (table)
Quids VI–3a
secessionist movement VI–250a
Sedition Act VI–255a
successors II–327a
Tammany Hall VI–459a
taxation VII–5a, 12b
temperance movement VII–22b
titles of nobility V–100b
trade restrictions V–104b
Vermont VII–172a
vice-presidents VII–179 (table)
War of 1812 I–325b
War of 1812 V–235a
Washington Benevolent Society VII–249b
Whiskey Rebellion VII–290b
"wise, and good and rich" VII–309a
XYZ affair VII–347b
Yazoo fraud VII–354a
Federal Judicial Center IV–17b
Federal Labor Board VI–40b
Federal League (baseball) I–270b
Federal Mediation and Conciliation Service. *See* Conciliation Service, U.S.
Federal Metal and Nonmetallic Safety Act (1966) IV–350b
Federal Militia Act (1792) IV–463b
Federal Oil Conservation Board V–270b
Federal Open Market Committee V–159b
Federal Organized Reserve II–314b
Federal Power Commission II–178b, 188a, 500a; III–321a; V–458a
"Federal Procession" III–88a
Federal Property and Administrative Services Act (1949) II–498b
Federal Radio Commission III–1a; VI–15b
Federal Records Act (1950) I–168a
***FEDERAL REGISTER* III–5b**; VI–405b
Federal Register Act (1935) I–167b

Federal Regulation of Lobbying Act (1946) II–232a
Federal Reserve Act (1913) I–44a, 252b, 258b; II–73a–b, 317a; IV–395a; V–462b; VI–427a
Federal Reserve Act (1933) II–500b
Federal Reserve Bank of New York II–73b, 235a
Federal Reserve Bulletin V–159b
FEDERAL RESERVE SYSTEM III–5b; I–256b, 257a,b, 391a; II–74a, 498b; III–355a; IV–468a; VII–107b
  bank failures I–253b
  banking acts of 1933 and 1935 I–259b
  banking crisis of 1933 V–44a
  bank notes IV–395a,b
  branch and group banking I–258b–59a
  clearinghouses II–73b–74b
  credit I–258a
  demand deposits I–252a–b
  federal deficit II–317b
  food stamp program III–56a
  Glass–Steagall Act III–186b; V–45a
  gold certificates IV–394b
  gold holdings I–302b; III–190a, 192a, 194b, 196a; IV–392b–93a; V–45b; VI–371a–b
  government debts II–317b
  installment buying III–422b
  interest rates III–443a,b
  McFadden Banking Act IV–212b
  monetarist's formula IV–234b
  open–market operations V–159b
  opposition IV–2a
  panic of 1929 V–209a,b, 210a
  Pittman Act V–321b
  savings banks I–264a
  stock exchange II–470a
  subtreasuries VI–427a
  Thomas Amendment VII–54b
  Treasury deposits VII–108a
Federal Reserve–Treasury "accord" (1951) I–257b
Federal Rules of Civil Procedure II–460b
Federal Savings and Loan Insurance Corporation I–376b; II–501a; III–294b; VI–221b
Federal Securities Act (1933) V–45a, 448a
Federal Security Agency II–405b; III–54a, 267b; VII–364b
Federal sovereignty II–195a–b
Federal spending power. *See* Expenditures, Federal; Government Spending
Federal–State Cooperative Extension Service VI–175b
FEDERAL–STATE RELATIONS III–9a; III–2a,b, 3a; VI–397a–b
  agriculture education and research I–46b–47a
  Cohens v. *Virginia* II–94a
  concurrent powers VII–154b
  enumerated powers II–453a–b
  forests III–75b, 76a,b
  franchise III–93a–b
  freedom of speech III–104a
  habeas corpus III–236b–37a
  labor laws IV–467a
  McCulloch v. *Maryland* IV–211b
  narcotics laws IV–449b–50a,b
  National Governors' Conference III–206a
  National Road IV–470b
  Office of Economic Opportunity V–136a
  revenue sharing VI–10b
  rural post roads VI–176a
  Sault Sainte Marie Canals VI–219a
  Slaughterhouse Cases VI–303a
  state–making process VI–399b
  states' rights VI–404a
  subsidies VI–425b
  taxation VII–4b, 5a, 6a, 8a
  tidelands VII–57a
  Virginia and Kentucky Resolutions VII–198a
  vocational education VI–318a,b
Federal style (arch.) I–159a, 162b–63a
Federal style furniture III–138a–b
Federal Subsistence Homestead Corporation VI–426b
Federal Surplus Commodities Corporation III–53a; V–359a
Federal Surplus Relief Corporation VI–73b
Federal Theatre Project V–46a; VII–50a, 323a
Federal Trade Commission I–140a, 390b; II–71b–72a, 500a,b; III–204b, 458b–59a; VI–277a
  advertising I–19a,b, 480b; II–208b; V–467a
  codes of fair competition II–92a
  consumer protection I–391b
  enabling legislation II–178b
  executive removal power III–317a; IV–446b; VI–85a
  Federal Security Act V–45a
  judicial review IV–16b
  meat–packing I–283b
  mergers VII–124a
  Nader investigation IV–448b
  restraint of trade VI–103a
  tobacco I–20a
  Webb Export Act VII–264b
  World War I VII–94a
Federal Trade Commission Act (1914) I–139b–40a; II–230a, 483a; III–317a; VI–102b; VII–122b–23a
Federal Trade Commission v. *Brown Shoe Company* (1966) VI–103a
Federal Trade Commission v. *Cement Institute et al.* (1948) V–402b; VI–103a
Federal Trade Commission v. *Ruberoid* (1952) V–472b
Federal Triangle (Washington, D.C.) VII–246b
Federal Water Power Act (1920) II–188a
Federal Works Agency II–502b
Federal Writers' Project V–46a; VII–323a
Federated American Engineering Societies II–449a
Fédération Internationale de Basketball Amateur I–272b
Federation of American Societies for Experimental Biology IV–127a
Federation of Central America. *See* Central America, Federation of
Federation of Organized Trades and Labor Unions IV–52b, 65a
  See also American Federation of Labor–Congress of Industrial Organizations
Fee, John G. (cler.) IV–220a
Feeblemindedness III–159a, 440a
Feedback amplifier theory I–287b
Feedback circuits II–39a, 424a
Feedstuffs V–465b
Fee owner IV–104b
Fee simple III–109b, 464a; IV–101b, 102a, 105a; V–407b
Fee tail III–464a; IV–105a; V–434a
Feke, Robert (paint.) V–186a,b, 186b, 187a; VI–132a
Feld, Eliot (chor.) II–289b
Fellner, William J. (econ.) VII–141a
Fellows, John (off.) VI–217b
"Fellow–servant" doctrine II–441a
Fellowship (ship) II–364b
Fellowship of Reconciliation V–236b; VII–236b
Fels, Joseph (philan.) VI–293b
Fels Institute of State and Local Government V–249b
Felt, Dorr E. (inv.) I–396b
Felt Forum (N.Y.C.) IV–220b
Feltham, Jocelyn (off.) VII–56b
Felton, William (pol.) III–169a
Female mortality II–487a
Feminist movement II–486a–b
  birth control I–307a,b
  missionary work IV–365b
  See also Woman's Rights Movement
FENCE VIEWERS III–10a
FENCE WAR III–10a; V–451b
Fencing (sport) V–154a
FENCING AND FENCING LAWS III–10a; V–160b
  barbed wire I–267a,b
  cattle rustling I–474a
  herd law versus free grass III–273b
  mesquite IV–316a
  Osage hedge V–174a
  public lands V–451b
  rail fences VI–19a
  ranches VI–45a,b
FENIAN MOVEMENT III–10b; I–434a, 439a; VII–134b
Fenimore Cooper (ship) VI–142a
Fenner, Arthur (gov.) VI–133a
Fenner, James (gov.) VI–133a
Fenno, John (ed.) V–69b
Fenton, Christopher Webber (mfr.) III–183b
Fenton, Roger (phot.) V–293a
Fenwick, Edward Dominic (cler.) II–362b
Fenwick, George (col.) VI–223a
Fenwick, John (col.) II–388b; V–56b; VII–278a–b
FEPC. *See* Fair Employment Practice Committee
Ferber, Edna (au.) IV–442a
Ferber, Herbert (sculp.) VI–244a
Ferdinand II (k.) II–323b
Ferdinand VII (k.) I–10b
Ferdinand, Fort (Miss.) II–22a
Ferguson, Elsie (act.) III–26a
Ferguson, Harry (inv.) I–35b–36a
Ferguson, James E. (pol.) III–11a; VII–40b
Ferguson, Miriam A. (gov.) VII–40b
Ferguson, Patrick (off.) I–240a; II–15a; IV–48a; VI–351b
Ferguson, Robert (pub.) V–70b
FERGUSON IMPEACHMENT III–11a
Ferguson v. *Skrupa* (1963) II–378a

Fériana (Tun.) IV–32b
Ferlinghetti, Lawrence (poet) IV–165b
Fermentation
  food preservation III–54b
Fermi, Enrico (phys.) I–215b, 217b; IV–238a; V–295b–96a, 299a, 300a,b, 302b, 303a, 304a
Fermi National Accelerator Laboratory V–297b
Fernandina (Fla.) III–39b
Fernow, Bernhard E. (forester) III–75a
Ferral, John (labor leader) IV–61b
Ferrar, John (mer.) VII–200b
Ferrar, Nicholas (theol.) VII–200b, 201a
Ferree, Fort (Ohio) VII–157b
Ferrel, William (meteor.) III–233b; IV–317b; V–134b
Ferrelo, Bartolomé (expl.) I–401b; V–164b
FERRIES III–11a
  Great Lakes III–218a
  Harris' Ferry III–257b
  King's Ferry IV–48a
  New York City V–83a
  New York–New Jersey III–132a
  Oregon Trail V–169b
  Red River cart traffic VI–63b
Ferris, A. C. (ind.) IV–44a
Ferris, George W. G. (eng.) III–11b
FERRIS WHEEL III–11b; IV–337b; VII–324a
Ferroalloys III–12b
Ferrocolumbium III–14b
Ferromolybdenum III–15a
Ferrophosphorus III–15b
Ferrotype VII–62b
FERROUS METALS III–11b; I–378b; VI–48a,b
FERTILIZERS III–16a
  adulteration laws V–465b
  Baltimore IV–261a
  Charleston I–497b
  citrus industry II–44a
  food supply III–53a
  guano III–230b
  log ash IV–204a
  manufacture II–8a
  meat-packing industry IV–281a
  nitrates V–98a,b
  phosphorus II–6b
  potash V–376a
  Prairie du Chien V–388a
  Savannah VI–220b
  Tennessee Valley Authority V–44b–45a; VII–27b, 28a,b
Fessenden, Reginald (phys.) VI–15a
Fessenden, William P. (pol.) IV–6a
Festiniog Railway II–129a
Fête champêtre IV–363a
Fetish bundles III–366b, 367b, 368a, 392a
Fetterman, William J. (off.). *See* Fetterman Massacre
FETTERMAN MASSACRE (1866) **III–17b**; I–296b; III–378a; IV–33b; VI–297a
FEUDALISM III–17b; I–257b–58a; III–412b
  abandoned II–325a
  American colonies V–100b
  English law IV–224a
  entail of estate II–452a
  Gorges' Province of Maine III–200a
  land tenures V–433a–b
  Martha's Vineyard IV–258a
  palatine jurisdictions V–194b
  primogeniture V–407b
  property II–326a
  proprietary provinces V–436a
  quitrents VI–4a
  South Carolina VI–348b
Feuds
  Hargis–Callahan–Cockrell III–252b
  Martin–Tolliver IV–259b
FEUDS, APPALACHIAN MOUNTAIN III–18a; IV–41a
  Hatfield–McCoy III–262a
  Kentucky II–292a
Fever River V–102b
Fevers II–454b
Fever therapy IV–306b
Few, William (states.) II–203b
Feynman, Richard P. (phys.) V–100a, 296a, 297b
FF-1 (fighter plane) I–55a
FFV (First Families of Virginia) **III–18b**
FHA *See* Federal Housing Administration
Fiala–Ziegler Expedition (1903–05) V–337a
Fiat money III–111a; IV–392b, 393a, 395b
  Civil War financing IV–132b
  Coxey's Army II–252a–b
  inflation III–415a
Fiberglass IV–294b
Fibers V–267b
Fibers, synthetic III–410a
  nylon II–372b
Fichte, Johann (philos.) V–287a
Fichus II–371a
Ficklin (Tex.) III–304a
Fiction
  book publishing I–334a
  coyotes II–253a
  western II–358b
  See also Literature
"Fiddle and the Bow" (song) III–19a
FIDDLERS AND FIDDLE TUNES III–18b; I–175a; III–297b
Fidelity and Casualty Company of New York III–435a
Fiedler, Leslie (au.) IV–165b
Field, Cyrus West (mer.) I–400b; VII–19a
Field, Darby (expl.) IV–423a–b
Field, James G. (pol.) I–424b
Field, Marshall (mer.) III–19a,b, 80b; V–73b
Field, Robert (paint.) IV–352a
Field, Stanley (adm.) III–19b
Field, Stephen D. (inv.) VI–40a
Field, Stephen J. (jur.) IV–20a; V–30a; VI–445b
Field and Stream (mag.) VII–298a
Field Book of Snakes VI–91b
Field Engineering Bureau III–1b
Field Guide to Reptiles and Amphibians VI–91b
Field Guide to Western Reptiles and Amphibians VI–91b
Field hockey III–286b; V–154a
Fielding, Lewis (psych.) VII–254b
FIELD MUSEUM OF NATURAL HISTORY III–19a
Fields, Al G. (act.) IV–359b
Fields, Jeremiah (Regulator) VI–72a
Fields, William (expl.) V–337b
Field Service Regulations (U.S. Army) IV–180a
FIELD* v. *CLARK (1892) **III–20a**
Fiennes, William, 1st Viscount Saye and Sele II–182a; IV–188a
Fifteen gallon law VII–23a
Fifteen Passenger Act (1879) II–29a
Fifteenth Air Force I–64a; V–332a
FIFTEENTH AMENDMENT III–20a; I–94b; II–53b, 205b–06a, 325b, 408a, 410a; III–86a, 91b, 92a, 437b–38a; IV–359a–b; V–352b; VI–97b, 98a, 434b–35a; VII–208b, 209b, 226b, 315a
  black codes I–310b
  black suffrage VI–431a, 431b
  citizenship I–28b
  civil rights acts II–457b
  Force Acts III–59b–60a
  freedmen's rights II–151a
  Georgia ratification III–295a
  grandfather clause III–208b, 232a
  Jim Crow laws III–503a
  judicial review IV–14a
  Ku Klux Act VII–155a
  Radical Republicans VI–11b
  Reconstruction VI–58a
  residency requirements V–116a
  southern ratification VI–57b
  United States v. *Harris* VII–154b
  white primary V–407b
Fifth Air Force I–64a
Fifth Amendment I–299a
  Adair v. *United States* I–9b, 9b
  Adkins v. *Children's Hospital* I–12a
  aliens I–88a
  Barron v. *Baltimore* I–269a
  congressional investigations I–315a
  double jeopardy VII–154b
  Dred Scott Case II–370b
  due process III–86b
  eminent domain II–439b
  legal tender IV–132b
  McCarran Act VII–310b
  See also Due Process of Law
Fifth Amphibious Force III–180a
Fifth Armored Division III–314b
Fifth Army, U.S. *See* entries under Army, United States
Fifth Avenue (N.Y.C.) III–446a,b
Fifth Avenue Hotel (N.Y.C.) I–94a
Fifth (V) Corps. *See* entries under Army, United States
Fifth Fleet III–180a; V–24b, 285b; VI–198a,b; VII–1a,b, 343b
Fifth Infantry Division. *See* entries under Army, United States
Fifth Marine Regiment IV–252b
Fifth Massachusetts–Middlesex Regiment IV–463b
Fifth Regimental Combat Team IV–55b
Fifth Republic (Fr.) III–97b
FIFTHS MINING TAX III–20b
"FIFTY-FOUR FORTY OR FIGHT" III–21a; IV–6a; V–165a, 168a; VI–313a
Fifty–Niners III–477b
Fighter planes. *See* Aircraft, Fighter
"FIGHT IT OUT ON THIS LINE IF IT TAKES ALL SUMMER" III–21a
Figs III–128a
FIGUREHEADS III–21b; III–47a; VI–242b
Figure skating
  Olympic Games V–154a,b
Fiji Islands VII–299b, 342b
Filament (lamp) III–155b
Filament yarn II–239a
Filhiol, Don Juan (off.) IV–362a
FILIBUSTER, CONGRESSIONAL III–21b
  anti-poll tax law II–481a
  cloture II–83b
  fair employment practices bill II–481a

"Little group of willful men" IV–169a
FILIBUSTERING III–22b; III–352a
Bowles expeditions I–355b
Gutiérrez–Magee expedition III–235b–36a
Latin–American independence wars IV–114b
López expeditions IV–188a
Mexican support IV–320b
Mexico III–145b
Natchitoches IV–457a
Nolan expeditions V–101a
Rio Grande VI–143a
Texas VII–37a
Walker's California expedition IV–199b
Filioque clause II–386b
Filipino–American War (1899–1902). *See* Philippine Insurrection
FILLMORE, FORT (N.Mex.) **III–24a**
Fillmore, Millard (pres.) I–274b; II–175 (table); III–24a; V–263a, 395 (table); VII–106a
campaign of 1856 I–110a, 421a
Kossuth's visit IV–57b
National Intelligencer IV–465b
Silver Grays VI–288a
vice–presidency VII–179 (table)
vice–president I–420b
Film, photographic IV–417a; V–291b
Films. *See* Motion Pictures
Filson, John (hist., expl.) I–337b; II–37b
See also Filson's Map
FILSON'S MAP III–24a; VII–239a
Finance
bills of exchange II–467b
clearinghouses II–73b
holding companies III–290b
stock exchange II–470a
Finance, Superintendent of II–166a
Finance Companies, National Association of III–423a
Finance corporations I–227b
Financial ratings
Dun and Bradstreet IV–307b
Financing, installment. *See* Installment Buying, Selling, and Financing
Fincastle, Fort. *See* Henry, Fort
FINCASTLE COUNTY (Va.) **III–24b**; I–224a; II–32b; IV–43a
Finch, Robert H. (pol.) III–267b
Findlay, Fort (Ohio) III–316a
Fine, Jean G. VI–330b
Fine, Oronce (cartog.) IV–247a–b
Fine Arts, National Collection of VI–319b
Fine Arts Commission VII–246b
Fine Arts Palace (San Francisco) III–189b
Fines II–204b, 396b
Finger Lakes III–448a; IV–344b
Fingerprinting II–446a
Finisterre (yacht) VII–349a
Fink, Albert (rr. eng.) I–364a; IV–273a
Fink, Mike (folk hero) I–267b; III–48b; VI–147b, 458b
Finland
Common Market VI–472a
European Free Trade Association VI–469a; VII–89a
immigration to U.S. III–334b, 337a
Organization for Economic Cooperation and Development V–170b
Paris Peace Conference V–215b
war with Russia V–37b
World War I I–158b; IV–117b; VII–332a
World War II V–378b; VI–178b
Finlay, Carlos, J. (physic.) VII–355b
Finlay, Hugh (offi.) V–375a
Finletter Commission I–234b
Finley, James (eng.) I–364a
Finley, John (pioneer) IV–40a; VII–239a
Finley, Robert (cler.) I–101a
Finn boats VII–349b
Finnegan, Joseph (off.) V–153b
Finney, Charles G. (cler., educ.) V–2b; VI–81b; VII–275a
See also Finney Revivals
FINNEY, FORT, TREATY OF (1786) **III–24b**
Finney, John M. T. (surg.) IV–3a
FINNEY REVIVALS (1825–35) **III–24b**; II–466a; VI–77a
Finnish settlement
South Dakota VI–350a
Fir (tree) III–72b, 74b; VI–223a; VII–59b
Fire
cookery II–219a
defoliation II–319a–b
Firearms
colonial industry III–413b
Colt six–shooter II–130b–31a
fur trade III–402b
Indians III–399a
Neutrality Act (1935) IV–430a
See also Ordnance
Fire departments
broadcast regulations III–1a
FIRE–EATERS III–25a
Fire engines III–25a
Fire escapes VII–24a
Fire extinguisher III–25a
FIRE FIGHTING III–25a
conscientious objectors V–182b
forests III–74b
municipal water supply IV–428a
New York City V–82b
prairie fires V–389a
Fire insurance III–426b, 428a,b, 429b–31a
Fire insurance and underwriters map I–462b
FIRELANDS III–25b; II–183b; VII–273b, 274b
Firelands Company III–25b
Fire Next Time IV–167a
Fireplace III–268b, 269a
Fire prevention
Civilian Conservation Corps II–51a
Fire rite IV–327a
Fires II–348a–50a
Baltimore I–250a, 251b
Boston I–344a
Charleston, S.C. I–497b
Chicago II–17b, 19a–b
Iroquois Theater III–476b
Jamestown III–489a
Johnstown (Pa.) II–351a
mines II–350a–b
New York City V–83a, 86a
prairie V–388b
San Francisco VI–209b, 210a
Savannah VI–220b
Triangle fire VII–118b
Washington, D.C. VII–249b
Fires, forest III–74a–b, 75b; VII–59b, 60a, 61a
Firescreens III–134b
"Fireside chats" V–44a, 161b, 353b
Firestone Library (Princeton) V–409a
Firestone Tire and Rubber Company I–21b, 169a; IV–141b; VI–167b
"FIRE WHEN YOU ARE READY, GRIDLEY" III–25b
Fireworks III–54a, 88a; VI–159a
First African Baptist Church of Savannah I–23a
First African Meeting House in Philadelphia I–23a
First African Presbyterian Church of Philadelphia I–23a
First aid programs
Red Cross VI–61b, 62a
First Amendment I–298b–300a; III–104a, 105a,b, 106a
censorship I–478b, 479b
congressional investigations I–315a
Hatch Act III–261b
limiting federal government II–378b
picketing V–308b–09a
right of assembly I–204a,b
teachers' loyalty oath VII–16a
First American Catholic Missionary Congress I–469a
First Armored Division IV–32b
First Army, U.S. *See* entries under Army, United States
First Baptist Church of Providence, R.I. III–149b; VI–76a
First Baptist Meeting House (Providence, R.I.) I–162a
First Cavalry Division. *See* entries under Army, United States
First Church (Boston) I–133a; IV–131a
First Church of the Tae VI–268b
First Colony of Virginia. *See* Virginia Company of London
First (I) Corps I–70b
First Corps Tactical Zone (Viet.) IV–253a–b
First Day Society VI–442b
First Dragoons IV–129b
First Families of Virginia. *See* FFV
First Fleet V–25a
First Infantry Division. *See* entries under Army, United States
First International (labor org.) IV–63a,b
First International Conference of American States (1890) V–205a
First International Geological Congress (1878) V–195b
First International Polar Year (1882–83) III–454a
"FIRST IN WAR, FIRST IN PEACE, AND FIRST IN THE HEARTS OF HIS COUNTRYMEN" III–26a
FIRST LADY OF THE LAND III–26a; III–350b; VI–320a
First Lessons in Composition VI–227b
First Marine Air Wing IV–56b, 57a, 253a; VII–186a
First Marine Division IV–253a; V–242b–43a; VII–186a,b
First Marine Regiment VII–186a
First Mobile Force (Japan) IV–336b
First Mountain (Can.) IV–118a
First National Bank of New York III–79b
First National Bank of Titusville V–319a
First New York Fire Zouaves II–432b–33a; VII–371b
First Ranger Battalion V–111a
"First Report on the Public Credit" (1790) V–443a–b

First SS Panzer Division
IV–230b
First State VI–393 (table)
First Unitarian Church (Baltimore) I–250a
First U.S. Cavalry Volunteers
VI–165a
Fischer, Emil (chem.)
I–303a; II–11b
Fischer, Robert (law.)
I–220b
Fish III–53b
Department of the Interior
III–444a,b
folklore III–48b
forests III–75b
Gulf of Mexico IV–326b
preservation III–54b, 55b;
VI–69a, 70a
prices V–404a
Fish, Hamilton (states.)
Alabama Claims I–73a
Monroe Doctrine
IV–401a
Protective War Claims Association V–438b
Treaty of Washington
VII–248b
Virginius affair
VII–204a–b
Fish, Job VII–220b
Fish, state VI–392a
FISH AND MARINE LIFE
III–26a
conservation VII–296b
oceanography V–135a–b
Fish and Wildlife Service
III–444b; VII–297b
Fish and wildlife services
III–27b–28a
FISH COMMISSION, UNITED STATES III–30a;
III–27b, 28a–b; IV–251a;
V–134b
FISHDAM FORD, BATTLE OF (1780) **III–30a**
Fisher, Carl G. IV–156a
Fisher, Dorothy Canfield (au.)
IV–26b
Fisher, Fort (N.C.) II–162b
See also Fisher, Fort, Capture of
FISHER, FORT, CAPTURE OF (1864–65) **III–30b**;
IV–252a; V–56a, 116a
Fisher, H.C. ("Bud") (cartoon.) V–72a
Fisher, Irving (econ.)
IV–233b, 234a, 286a
Fisher, Mary (rel. leader)
V–469b
Fisher, Osmond (astron.)
III–166b
Fisher, Ronald (statis.)
VI–206b
Fisher, Warren, Jr. (bus.)
IV–426a–b
Fisheries
management III–27b–28b
Fisheries, Bureau of II–135a;
III–30a; VII–297b
Fisheries and Fishery Industries of the United States
III–27b
FISHERIES DISPUTE, ARBITRATION OF
III–30b; III–243b;
VII–248b
Fisheries Laboratory, Bureau of Commercial
II–391b
Fisherman's Wharf (San Francisco) VI–209b
Fishers (beaver)
III–150a
FISHER'S HILL, BATTLE OF (1864) **III–31a**;
I–476b; VI–275a;
VII–305b
FISHERS ISLAND III–31a
Fishes of Illinois III–28a
Fishes of North and Middle America III–27b
Fish Hawk (research ship)
III–29a
Fishing
Alaska I–77b
Boston I–344b
Bristol trade I–365b
Canada I–439a
cod II–92a
colonial industry III–413a
Dorchester Company
II–364b–65a
Dorchester plantation
V–51a
foreign trade VII–86a
Grand Banks III–208a
Great Lakes III–216b
Indian food supply
III–51a
interstate compacts
III–460a
Isles of Shoals III–479b
Labrador IV–82a
Lake Superior I–105b
Long Island IV–185b
mackerel IV–217a
Maine IV–227a
Maryland–Virginia agreement III–459b
Monhegan Island
IV–396a
New England IV–311a;
V–50a; VI–170b, 171a
Newfoundland I–277b
New Hampshire V–53a–b
New Plymouth Colony
V–65a
Northwest Coast culture
III–361a
Pemaquid Point V–243a,b
Pensacola V–254b
Rhode Island VI–134a
Saco Bay VI–184a
Sagadahoc VI–185b
Saint Marys River
VI–219b
Salem VI–199a
salmon VI–201a
salt duties III–31b
Savannah VI–220b
subarctic Indian culture
III–358b
Sugar Acts VI–435a
territorial waters
III–107a; VII–33a
Treaty of Ghent III–177a
Trelawney Plantation
VII–114b
triangular trade II–119a;
VII–119b, 278a
U.S. Fish Commission
III–30a
Wyoming VII–346a
FISHING BOUNTIES
III–31b; II–92b
FISHING CREEK, ACTION AT (1780) **III–31b**
FISHING CREEK CONFEDERACY III–31b
Fishing Creek Valley
III–31b
Fishing rights
Anglo–French rivalry
III–115a
boundary disputes I–351b
Canadian–American trade
I–437a
Cape Ann I–446b
Convention of 1818
II–215b
Council for New England
II–242a
Definitive Treaty of Peace
II–319a
Elgin–Marcy Treaty
II–431a
French–English conflict
II–126b
Treaty of Ghent
VII–235b
Treaty of Utrecht
VII–162b
Treaty of Washington
VII–248b
Fishing stage. *See* Stage, Fishing
Fishkill (N.Y.) VI–170a
Fishmeal VI–346a
Fisk, Clinton B. (banker)
I–424b
Fisk, James (speculator)
I–311a; VII–222a
Fisk, James Liberty (off.)
III–32a
Fiske, Harrison Grey (dram., ed.) VII–48b
Fiske, John (philos., hist.)
IV–163b; V–287b
Fiske, Minnie Maddern (act.)
VII–48b
Fiske, Thomas Scott (math.)
I–109a
FISK OVERLAND EXPEDITIONS (1862–66)
III–32a
Fisk University I–28b;
II–113b; III–103b
Fission, nuclear. *See* Nuclear fission
Fission weapons I–216a
Fitch, Henry (nat.) VI–91a
Fitch, James (cler.) II–356a
Fitch, John (inv.)
mapping VII–74b
See also Fitch's Steamboat Experiments
Fitch, Samuel S. (dent.)
II–329b
Fitch, Thomas (col. gov.)
VI–451b
Fitch, William Clyde (playwright) VII–49a
Fitchburg (Mass.) I–490a
Fitchburg Railroad III–299a
FITCH'S STEAMBOAT EXPERIMENTS III–32a;
III–131b; VI–408a, 409a;
VII–100b
Fitzgerald, Desmond
II–103b
Fitzgerald, Ella (sing.)
IV–442a
Fitzgerald, F. Scott (au.)
IV–164a, 189b
Fitzgibbon, James (off.)
I–281b
Fitzhugh, George (soc.)
VI–306b, 343a
Fitzmaurice, William Petty.
See Lansdowne, Marquis of
Fitzpatrick, Daniel R. (cartoon.) I–464b; V–73a
Fitzpatrick, Thomas (trapper)
I–201a; II–477b; III–143a;
IV–34b, 108b, 422a;
VI–354b; VII–103b
Fitzroy, Augustus Henry, Duke of Grafton (states.)
IV–20b
Fitzsimmons, Frank E. (labor leader) IV–76b
Fitzsimmons, ("Ruby") Robert (pugilist) V–422b
Fitz Simmons, Thomas (states.) I–467a; II–203b
FIVE-AND-TEN-CENT-STORES III–32b
Five Civilized Tribes. *See* Cherokee; Chickasaw; Chippewa; Chocktaw; Civilized Tribes, Five; Seminole
Five Civilized Tribes, Commission of II–295b
FIVE FORKS, BATTLE OF (1865) **III–33a**; V–265a;
VI–186b, 276a; VII–197b
Five Little Peppers I–335b
Five Lower Towns (Ind.)
II–15a
Five Nations
New York Colony V–84b
See also Civilized Tribes, Five; Iroquois
Five Points (N.Y.) IV–250a
FIVE-POWER NAVAL TREATY (1922)
III–33b; III–160b;
VII–250b–51a
5307th Provisional Unit
IV–314a
FIVE-TWENTIES III–33b;
II–218b; III–224a; V–144b
FIVE VILLAGES (N.Dak.)
III–33b; II–285a; IV–235b
Five Years Meeting *See* Orthodox Five Years Meeting
Fixed incomes
inflation II–236b
Flaco, Juan ("Lean John").
See Flaco's Ride
FLACO'S RIDE (1846)
III–34a
FLAG, PRESIDENTIAL
III–34a; III–35b
FLAG DAY (June 14)
III–34a
Flagg, Ernest (arch.)
VI–299a; VII–24a
Flagg, G. W. (art.) II–101b
Flagler, Henry M. (ind.)
III–39b; VI–34a, 382b,
383a
Flag of the Confederate States.
See Confederate Flag

"Flag of the Union" (poem) VII–155b
FLAG OF THE UNITED STATES III–34b; II–218b
pledge of allegiance V–331b
Sedition Act II–463a–b
"Star-Spangled Banner" VI–387b
FLAGS III–35a
pine tree flag V–316a
rattlesnake flag VI–47b
"Flags of convenience" IV–312a
Flagstaff (Ariz.) III–75b; V–13a; VI–101b
Flamand (ship) VI–129b
Flaming Gorge Dam II–130a
Flanagan, Hallie VII–323a
Flanders
World War I I–491b; IV–320a
Flandrau, Charles E. (jur., off.) V–81b
Flandreau (S.Dak.) II–284b
Flannagan, John B. (sculp.) VI–244a
Flapper dress II–372a
Flash floods III–37a,b
Flatbed press I–334a
FLATBOATMEN III–35b; I–476a
Mississippi River IV–372b
Ohio River VI–147b
Flatboats I–89a, 175a, 267a, 476a; IV–174b, 347b; VI–148a, 149b; VII–99b
Hit or Miss III–286a
Mississippi River IV–374a, 456b
New Orleans V–62a
Ohio River V–142b
store boats VI–415b
westward movement VII–283b
Flatbush (N.Y.) I–370a; IV–185a, 186a
Flatfoots (circus proprietors) II–40b
Flathead (Indians) III–227a, 363a, 500a,b; IV–403a; V–166b, 178b
Flathead Indian Reservation VII–297a
Flathead River III–323a; VI–375b
Flatlands (N.Y.) I–370a; IV–185a
Flat River VI–190a
Flatstoneland. *See* Helluland
Flatt, Lester (mus.) IV–441b
Flattery, Cape II–219b
Flatware V–155b
Flavin, Dan (sculp.) VI–244a
Flax III–413b; V–184a
colonial manufacture IV–157b
household manufacture IV–246a
linsey-woolsey IV–158a
tariff VI–465b
Fleeming, John (print.) I–294a
Fleet, merchant
World War I II–438a–b
Fleet, Reuben (bus.) I–236a
Fleet, United States V–24b–25a
chief of naval operations V–13b
See also Navy, United States
Fleet Marine Force IV–252b, 253b; V–20b
Fleet minelayer V–25b
Fleet submarine V–25b
Fleetwing (yacht) VII–348b–49a
Fleetwood, Battle at. *See* Brandy Station, Battle of
Fleetwood Hill (Va.) I–360a
Fleming, J. Ambrose (inv.) VII–163a
Fleming, Klas (nav. off.) V–81a
Fleming, Peggy (athlete) V–154b
Fleming, Robert (banker) III–64b, 65a
Fleming, William (off.) V–335b
Flemington (N.J.) IV–156b
Flemming, Arthur S. (offi.) III–267b
Fletcher, Benjamin (col. gov.) V–84b
Battery (N.Y.C.) I–275b
Beekman patent I–284b
Great Nine Partners' Patent III–220b
Kakiate patent IV–24a
land grants III–313a; V–88a
Philipse's patent V–286a
Fletcher, Frank J. (nav. off.) II–225a, 387b; III–229b; IV–336a,b; V–20b
Fletcher, James C. (adm.) IV–460a
Fletcher, Robert (physic.) IV–292a
Fletcher and Gardiner VI–290a
Fletcher School (Tufts) V–24b
FLETCHER v. PECK (1810) **III–36a**; II–213b, 293b; IV–19b, 99a; VII–354a
Fleur de Lys (yacht) VII–349a
Flexner, Abraham (educ.) II–401a,b; III–423b–24a; IV–284b, 298a
Flexner, Simon (path.) I–242a; IV–287a; VI–158b
Flexner Report on Medical Education (1910) III–294a; IV–284b, 298a; V–307a
Flickertail State VI–395 (table)
Flight and Pursuit (paint.) V–189b
Flint (Mich.) IV–331b; VII–76a
Flint, Austin, Jr. (physic.) V–306b
Flint, Austin, Sr. (physic.) VII–126a
Flint, Charles Louis (law, agric.) II–280a
Flint, Royal VI–239a
Flint, Timothy (miss., writ.) I–473a
Flint corn II–226a
Flint Hills (Kans.) I–326a
Flint hoe I–36a
Flint River II–23a; III–41b, 171b, 401b
Florida boundary VI–351a
Fort Scott VI–260a
western boundary VII–269b
"Flip-flops" (computers) II–153b
"Floaters" (land speculation) V–390a
FLOATING BATTERIES III–36a
FLOGGING III–36b; V–464b, 465a
British army VI–127b
Ku Klux Klan IV–58a
Pueblo V–460b
Quakers V–469b
revolutionary war IV–208a
sex crimes VI–265b
Spanish Inquisition III–420b
Flood, Curt (athlete) I–271b
Flood, James C. (fin.) I–329a; II–157a
Flood control II–450a; VI–146b, 147a,b, 148b
Bureau of Reclamation VI–54a
Canadian-American waterways I–440b
Forest Service III–76a
interstate compacts VI–402a
Tennessee River VII–27b, 28a
Tennessee Valley Authority V–44b–45a
FLOODS III–36b; II–351a–52a
Cairo (Ill.) I–403b
hurricanes III–319b
Idaho I–327b
Inland Waterways Commission III–420a
Johnstown (Pa.) IV–5a
Kaskaskia IV–32a
military aid IV–341b
Mississippi River IV–373a, 374b, 374b
Missouri River I–286b; IV–380a
National Weather Service VII–264a,b
New Orleans V–62b
Ohio Valley V–146a
rainfall VI–41b
relief V–281a
Rio Grande VI–143a,b
Vermont VII–172b
See also Disasters
FLOOR LEADER III–37b
Flora boreali-americana V–326a
Flora virginica I–348b; V–326a
Florence (Ga.) II–159b
Florence (It.)
World War II VII–338b
Florence (Wis.) IV–303b
Flores, José María (off.) VI–210b
FLORIDA III–38a; IV–115b, 200a; VI–393 (table); VII–190b
Afro-American education II–404a
Amelia Island affair I–93b
annexation I–9b, 10b, 126b, 499a; II–474b–75a; IV–110b
Apalache massacre I–143a
Arbor Day I–154a
architecture I–159b
d'Arges colony I–169b
Arthur expedition V–32a
Bartram's travels II–477a
Battle of Ayubale I–238b
black suffrage VI–433b
Blount conspiracy I–324a
Bowles's expedition VI–366b
British army VI–126b
British military grants IV–92b
campaign of 1876 II–38b
Cape Canaveral IV–406b, 407a
Capron Trail I–451b
cattle I–471a
chain gangs I–489a
Cherokee II–15a
citizenship II–42b
citrus industry II–43a–b
Civil War IV–405a; V–153b, 308a; VI–216a
coast survey II–87b
colonial land grants IV–93a
Creek Indians II–257a
Cuban refugees I–278b
dairy industry II–281b
debtor laws II–299b
Definitive Treaty of Peace IV–376a
deserters II–335b
De Soto expedition II–336a; III–288a–b
discovery V–356a
dog races III–149b
donation lands III–296a
Dunbar's Line II–381a
East Florida III–68a
English rule II–298a; III–50b; IV–368a; V–214b
exploration I–96a,b; II–184a; IV–110a
filibustering I–355b
Forbes Purchase III–59a
Fort Brooke I–451b
Fort Capron I–451b
Fort Clinch I–451b
Fort Gadsden III–145a
Fort Marion IV–253b
Fort Matanzas IV–274a
Fort Pickens II–61b
Fort Saint Marks VI–196b
Fort Tonyn III–42b
Franciscans III–94a
free land III–107b
French settlements III–240b
fruit I–40a; III–128b
fur trade III–144a

FLORIDA (cont.)
Genêt mission III–159b
Georgia boundary III–171b
Gideon Case III–179a
Gulf of Mexico IV–326a,b
Gulf Stream III–232b, 233a
horse III–302b, 304b
Huguenots III–121a, 315a; V–341b–42a
Hunter's emancipation orders II–434b
hurricanes II–351a,b, 352a; III–319b, 320a
Indian defense V–101a
Indian education III–379b
Indian missions III–385b
Jackson raid I–121a, 154a; VI–131b
Jefferson's proposed states III–496b–97a
Kemper raid IV–36b
Key West IV–44b
land speculation I–336b
Louisiana purchase IV–196b
Mississippi River V–315a
national parks and monuments V–217b, 218 (table)
natural history III–26b, 26b
naval stores V–14b
New England Emigrant Aid Company V–51b
New Smyrna Colony V–66a
newspapers V–76b
panhandle V–206a
panic of 1837 III–64a
Panton, Leslie and Company V–211a
patio gardens III–151b
Peace Society VII–149a
Pensacola V–254a
Pensacola Congress V–254b
Perdido River V–262a
phosphorus deposits II–6b
plant study V–326a
presidios V–399b
Proclamation of 1763 V–424b
Queen Anne's War II–126b
quitrents VI–4a
railroads VI–36a,b, 37a
Reconstruction III–295b; VI–58a
Republican party VI–337b
repudiation of state debts VI–96a, 96b
resorts and spas VI–101a
revolutionary war III–42b; IV–193a; VI–130a, 363b; VII–303a
rice VI–135b
right-of-reply statute V–79a
rock phosphate III–16b
Saint Augustine VI–187b
Santa Rosa complex III–300b
secession II–61a; VI–250b
Seminole II–257a; III–367a, 396b; VI–259b, 260a
Seminole Wars III–381b, 462b; V–147a–b; VI–260a; VII–239a,b, 311a
settlement IV–338a; VII–283b
shell mounds IV–421a
slavery VI–309a
Spain I–9b; II–319a, 381a; III–168a; IV–135b, 197b, 302b; VI–359a, 359b, 363b–64a, 365b, 365b, 367b; VII–270a
Spanish–American War II–436a
Spanish–English conflict II–126b
Spanish Inquisition III–420b
state bank I–259a
sugarcane I–486b; VI–436a,b, 437a
swamplands VI–453b
tafia trade VI–456b
teachers' loyalty oath VII–15b
teachers' organizations IV–76a
tidelands VII–57b–58a
tobacco VII–66b, 67a,b
Treaty of Natchez IV–456a
Treaty of Payne's Landing V–231a
tuberculosis patients VII–126a
veterinary medicine VII–176b
War of 1812 I–120b; VII–233a
War of 1812 VII–234a, 236a
War of Jenkins' Ear III–498a
whiskey manufacture II–163b
World War II VI–149a, 374a
writs of assistance VII–345a
Yamasee War VII–352a
See also East Florida; West Florida, Annexation of; West Florida Controversy
FLORIDA (warship) **III–40b**; I–72b; II–213a; V–17b; VII–212b
Florida, Gulf of III–41b
Florida, Jackson's seizure of. *See* Arbuthnot and Ambrister, Case of
FLORIDA, PURCHASE OF (1819) **III–40b**; IV–320b; V–443b; VI–400a; VII–111b
acreage V–445 (table)
land titles IV–105b
public land states V–453a
Saint Augustine VI–187b
Seminole VI–260b
FLORIDA, SPANISH MISSIONS IN III–40b; III–38a–b; IV–303a
FLORIDA, STRAITS OF III–41b; III–233a
Floridablanca, Count of, José Moxina y Redondo (dipl.) VI–365a
FLORIDA BOUNDARY III–41b, I–351a; II–319a; VI–351a, 359a–b; VII–353b
Florida City (Fla.) II–351b
Florida East Coast Railway III–39b; VI–34a
Florida Everglades. *See* Everglades
Florida Keys II–267b; III–320a; V–356a; VI–34a
Florida Land and Colonization Company II–43a
FLORIDA LAND BOOM OF THE 1920'S III–42a; III–40a
FLORIDA RANGERS III–42b; VI–130a
Florida Straits III–319a
Florida War. *See* Seminole Wars
Florissant (Mo.) III–501b
Florissant Fossil Beds National Monument V–217b
Flory, Paul J. (chem.) IV–301a; V–100a
Flotation process II–223b
FLOUR MILLING III–42b; II–219a; VII–286a,b
automatic milling IV–272b
Baltimore I–249b
colonial mills IV–243a; VI–108a
corn II–226b
exchanges II–469b
exports VII–86a, 87a, 87b
Falls of Saint Anthony VI–187a
foreign investments III–63a
grain elevators II–429b–30a
gristmills III–228b
Minnesota IV–357a; VII–134a, 308a
North Dakota V–117a,b
prices V–404b, 405b
product enrichment V–128b
public ownership V–455a
pure food laws V–465b
Richmond VII–194a
Saint Joseph VI–191b
tariff VI–463a
tax II–164b
Wisconsin VII–308a
World War I VII–329b
"Flour trust" III–44a
Flower, George (col.) II–450b
Flower Gap V–224b
Flower gardens III–151a–52a
Flower Mound (Tex.) II–48b
Flowers
landscape architecture IV–96b
Flowers, state VI–392a, 393–95 (table)
Flow graphs (elec.) II–39a
Floyd, Fort (Kans.) VI–439b
Floyd, John (off.)
Creek War I–232a; II–257a
Fort Nelson V–32b
Floyd, John (pol.) V–164b, 167b
Floyd, John B. (gov.) I–457a I–419b
Floyd, William (states.) II–308a
Floyd Bennett (airplane) I–399a
Floyd, Fort (N.Dak.) VII–145b
Flu. *See* Influenza
Fluorescent bulb manufacture IV–294a
Fluorescent lamp. *See* Lamp, fluorescent
Fluoridation II–331b
Fluorine II–9a, 12b, 423a
Fluorite II–422b
Fluorocarbons II–9a–b
Fluorosis II–331a
Flushing (N.Y.) IV–185a
Flushing Meadow (N.Y.) V–89a
Flush Times (1830–40) IV–368b
Flutes II–291a
Fluxes II–454b
Fly (ship) VI–128a
Flying boats I–237a
FLYING CLOUD (clipper ship) **III–45b**; I–448a; II–77b
Flying Dutchman (paint.) V–189b
Flying eagle (coin) II–95b
Flying Fish (ship) I–448a; II–77b
Flying Fortress I–50a, 52a, 56b, 59b, 67a
Flying shuttle II–237b
Flying Squadron VI–207a
FLYING THE HUMP III–45b; VII–337b
FLYING TIGERS III–46a; I–386b; II–26a
Flying wedge III–57b
Flynn, Ed (pol.) I–343a
Flynt, Henry II–101a
Fly shuttle IV–187b
FM. *See* Frequency modulation
FM–FM radio telemetry III–502a
F. M. Kirby and Company III–32b
Foch, Ferdinand (off.) VI–197b; VII–327a
Château-Thierry I–502a
Distinguished Service Medal II–311a
Somme offensive VI–338b
World War I armistice I–176b
Fodder II–279a, 281a
Foerderer, Robert (chem.) IV–128b
Foerster, Norman (educ.) II–401a
Fogarty International Center IV–465b
Fogarty–McGovern Act (1958) III–249a
Fogel Grip (ship) V–80a
Fokine, Michel (chor.) II–287b
Fokker, Anthony (aircraft designer) I–236a

Fokker airplane I–399a
Folger, Henry Clay (ind.) II–109b
Folger family III–233a
Folger Shakespeare Memorial Library II–109b
Folies Bergères III–189b
Folin, Otto (biochem.) I–303b
FOLK ART III–46b
painting V–187b
pottery V–379a
samplers VI–205b
Folkers, Karl A. (chem.) V–128a
FOLKLORE III–48a
childen's books I–335b
coyote II–253a
Indian III–386a
"Joe Bowers" IV–1a
Johnny Appleseed III–128b–29a
Mississippi riverboat gambler II–259b
peace pipe V–318a–b
rattlesnakes VI–47b
razorback hogs VI–49a
Rip Van Winkle VI–145a
tall stories VI–458b
FOLK MEDICINE III–49a; IV–283a
rattlesnake VI–47b
See also Indian Medicine
Folk music I–247a; IV–438b, 439a, 439b–40a, 441a–b
"My Old Kentucky Home" IV–447a
Folk rock IV–441a
Folk songs
"Joe Bowers" IV–1a
See also Ballads; Music
Follow Through (preschool project) II–402b
Folsom (Calif.) VI–26b
Folsom (N.Mex.) III–50a, 484b
Folsom, Davis E. (surv.) VII–357a
Folsom, Marion B. (offi.) III–267b
FOLSOM CULTURE COMPLEX III–50a; III–484a; V–59b
Fonck, Rene (av.) IV–156b
Fonda, John H. (expl.) III–50b
FONDA'S EXPEDITION (1823) **III–50b**
Fond du Lac (Minn.) IV–355b; VI–443a
Fong, Hiram (pol.) II–30a
Fong, March (pol.) II–30a
Fong Yue Ting v. *United States* (1893) III–417b
Fonseca, Gulf of I–373b; VII–58b
Fontaine, Pierre François Leonard (arch.) III–135a
FONTAINEBLEAU, TREATY OF (1762) **III–50b**; IV–197b, 198a, 376b; V–173a, 214b; VI–194a; VII–36b
Fontana Dam III–322b
Fontenelle, Lucien (fur trader) VI–196a
FOOD III–50b
advertising I–19a
Confederacy II–163b
fish III–26a–b
government regulation III–54a, 458b
maple sugar IV–246b
marine life III–29b
meats IV–280b–81a
mesquite IV–316a
Navigation Acts V–16a
New York State V–87b
nutrition and vitamins V–127b
penole V–254a
Philadelphia V–278a
pioneers V–317b
potatoes V–376b
pot likker and corn pone V–377a
retail stores II–354b
sales VII–84b
sanitation VI–212b
self-service stores VI–258a–b
sweet potato V–377a
turkeys VII–130a
World War I VII–327b
World War II VII–336a
See also Pure Food and Drug Movement
Food, Drug, and Cosmetic Act (1938) III–54a; V–467a
Food, Drug, and Insecticide Administration III–53b
Food Administration (World War I) I–390b; IV–135b; VII–329b
Food and Agriculture Act (1965) I–43a
Food and Drug Act (1906) I–19a
FOOD AND DRUG ADMINISTRATION III–53b; I–391b; III–267b, 422a; V–467a–68b
Nader's Raiders IV–448b
vitamin regulation V–128a
Food and Nutrition Board V–128b
Food and Nutrition Office, Federal V–128b
Food and Nutrition Service III–56b
Food–composition tables V–127b
Food Employees v. *Logan Valley Plaza* (1968) V–309a
Food for Peace III–53a
FOOD PRESERVATION III–54b; I–444b–45b; II–219a
dried fruits and vegetables II–373a
fruits III–129a
meat III–51b
nutrition V–129b
pure food and drug movement V–465b
refrigeration VI–69a
tin can VII–61b
Food processing
Chicago II–18b
Minnesota IV–357b
Food Stamp Act (1964) I–43b; III–56a
FOOD STAMP PROGRAM III–56a; I–45b; II–502b; III–53a; V–129a; VII–108a
Food stores
child labor II–23b
milk marketing II–282b
Foot and mouth disease VII–177b
FOOTBALL III–56b
betting II–261a
Detroit Lions II–337b
gambling III–149b
Green Bay Packers III–226a
New Orleans V–62b
Foote, A. E. IV–349a
Foote, Andrew H. (nav. off.)
Barrier Forts I–268b
Battle of Belmont I–403b
Fort Henry III–272b
Island Number Ten III–478b
Naval Home V–11b
slave trade VI–311b
Foote, Charles B. I–333a
Foote, Henry Stuart (pol.) II–139a, 150a
Foote, Samuel A. (pol.) VII–265b
Forage II–226b
Foraker, Joseph B. (pol.) I–372a
FORAKER ACT (1900) **III–58a**
Foraminifera III–29a
Foran Act (1885) II–214b; IV–64b
Forbes, George (eng.) V–92b
Forbes, John (off.). *See* Forbes Expedition; Forbes Road
Forbes, Stephen Alfred (nat.) II–391a; III–28a
Forbes, Thomas (bus.) V–211a
Forbes and Company V–211b
FORBES EXPEDITION (1758) **III–58a**; I–358b; II–382a; III–59a, 116a; V–143a, 246b; VI–49a
Battle of the Loyalhanna IV–200a
Fort Ligonier IV–154a
Fort Loudon IV–191b
Fort Pitt V–321a,b
Ligonier III–211b
Raystown Path VI–49a
Forbes family (silversmiths) VI–290a
FORBES PURCHASE III–59a
FORBES ROAD III–59a; I–88b, 89a, 282b; II–273a; III–58b
Hanna's Tavern III–250a
Miller's Run Gap V–224b
westward movement VII–283a
Force, Peter (pub., hist.) II–108b; III–60a, 279a, 281a; IV–146b
FORCE ACTS III–59a; V–176b
Ku Klux Act IV–57b
Reconstruction VI–58a
South Carolina nullification V–126a
Force Command I–187b
***FORCE'S TRACTS* III–60a**
Ford, Edsel (mfr.) I–205b
Ford, Gerald R. (pres.) II–178 (table); III–345a–b; V–396 (table); VI–93b, 94a; VII–118b, 133a
antitrust legislation I–140b
cabinet VII–317b
Cuba II–270a
economic policies VII–85a
fair–trade laws II–483b
floor leader III–38a
foreign policy III–70b–71a
inflation III–415b
Israel III–482b
Latin American policy IV–113b
Little League I–271b
Nixon pardon VII–255b
Nixon resignation V–98b, 99a
Office of Economic Opportunity V–136a
presidential succession V–398b
Soviet Arms agreement I–180b
Strategic Arms Limitation Talks VI–417a
veterans' benefits I–332a
vetoes VII–178a
vice–presidency VII–178b, 180a, 180a, 181a
Vietnam deserters I–115b
War Powers Act VII–225a
Warren Commission VII–238a
Ford, Henry (ind.) I–229a; III–80b, 461a; V–72b
America First Committee I–97a
assembly line II–337a; IV–272b
mass production IV–272a,b
model T I–227a
peace ship III–60a
Selden patent 257a–b–
senate campaign V–41b
subsistence homesteads VI–426b
Ford, Henry Jones (pol. sci.) V–348b
Ford, J. (archaeol.) V–382b
Ford, John S. ("Rip") VII–39a
Ford, Thomas (pol.) III–329b, 331a; IV–412a
Ford Foundation II–402b; III–83a, 503b; V–280b, 400b–01a
Ford Foundation Gray Areas Project II–148a
Fordham (N.Y.) III–313a
Fordham University V–83b
Ford Island (Haw.) V–239b
Ford Model T III–15a
Ford Motor Company I–227a,b; III–15a; IV–331b; VII–124a
aircraft I–236a; IV–433a,b

FORD MOTOR COMPANY (cont.)
archives I–169a
assembly line I–205b
automation I–224b
mass production IV–272b–73a,b
mass transit I–231b
Mustang I–229b, 232a
Thunderbird I–232a
Trimotor transport I–51b
unions I–230a
United Automobile Workers IV–72b
Ford Motor Credit Company III–423a
Fordney, Joseph W. (pol.) VI–468a
Fordney–McCumber Tariff Act (1922) VI–464b, 467b–68a
Ford of the Fathers (Colorado River) II–461a
Fordson (tractor) I–227b
FORD'S PEACE SHIP III–60a
Ford's Theatre (Washington, D.C.) IV–154b
Ford trimotor transport I–51b
Foreclosures IV–414a,b, 415a
Foreign Affairs, Department of VI–388a,b; VII–111a
Foreign affairs, secretary for II–166a, 166a
Foreign–affairs agencies III–72a
Foreign Agricultural Service I–45b
FOREIGN AID III–60b; II–301b; V–280b–81a
balance of trade I–246a
cold war II–475b
containment II–315b; III–463a
Declaration of Independence II–303b
dollar diplomacy II–359b
European Recovery Act VII–88b
federal deficit VI–449b
financing II–317b
imperialism III–348a
Israel III–481b, 482a–b
Laos IV–107a,b
Latin America IV–113b–14a
lend–lease IV–134a; VII–334b
Liberia IV–141b
Marshall Plan II–301b; IV–257b; VII–88a–b
nationalization of U.S. property IV–466b
Philippines V–284b–85a
Point Four program V–281a, 335a
post–World War II VI–179b
Russia VI–178a, 178b
South America II–359b; VI–345a
Spain VI–360b–61a
taxation VII–11b
treaties VII–112b
Truman Doctrine VII–121a–b
Vietnam III–160b
war costs VII–229a
wheat VII–286b
World War I VII–329a–30b
Foreign and Colonial Government Trust III–467a
Foreign and Domestic Commerce, Bureau of II–135a; IV–350a
Foreign Assistance Act (1961) IV–466b
Foreign Bondholders Protection Council of the United States II–361b
Foreign debt. *See* Debt and Investment, Foreign
Foreign Direct Investments, Office of II–135b
Foreign Evangelical Society V–2b–3a
Foreign exchange devaluation II–339a
Foreign Intelligence, U.S. I–484a
FOREIGN INVESTMENTS IN THE UNITED STATES III–62b; II–301a
Dutch bankers' loans II–382a
Holland Land Company III–291a
Mississippi Bubble IV–370b
panic of 1893 V–207b
ranching V–160b
Scioto Company VI–239a
specie payments VI–370b
states II–302a–b; VI–96a–b
taxation VII–9b
Foreign Investors Tax Act (1966) VII–9b
Foreign–language press V–75b
Foreign Ministers, Council of V–215b
Foreign missions. *See* Missions, Foreign
FOREIGN POLICY III–67b
aid V–280b–8la
anticommunism II–315a, 316b
campaign of 1916 I–427a
campaign of 1964 I–431a
commercial treaties VII–108b
Confederation II–192b
Congress II–178b, 195b
Cuban relations V–174b
delegated power II–323a
dollar diplomacy II–359a
Emancipation Proclamation II–435a–b
Federalist party III–4b
French in Mexico IV–361a
Good Neighbor policy III–198b
Gulf of Mexico IV–326a–b
historiography III–283a–b
Honduras III–297a–b
Honolulu Conference III–297b
Hülsemann incident III–316a
imperialism III–347a
intervention III–461b
isolationism III–479b
Jay's Treaty II–326b; IV–402b
jingoism III–503b
Kennedy administration V–53a
Latin America IV–110b–116a
League of Nations IV–125a–b
lend–lease IV–134a
liberalism IV–140b–41a
Liberia IV–141b
Magdalena Bay Resolution IV–223b
Manchuria IV–234b
Mexico IV–325b–26a, 328a–29a
military and strategic intelligence III–438b
military forces IV–343a
Monroe Doctrine IV–110b, 399b
most–favored–nation principle IV–416b
neutrality V–33b
New Deal V–48b
Nixon administration IV–113a
"normalcy" V–110a
North Atlantic Treaty Organization V–113b
nuclear testing V–124b–25a
Open Door policy V–157b
party platforms V–329a
peace conferences V–232b
peace movement opposition V–235a–37b
Philippines V–282b–85a
president II–171b, 178b; V–394b
pressure groups V–401a
Progressive party V–429a
propaganda V–431b
recognition VI–54b
Roosevelt Corollary VI–163a
Russia VI–177a–80a
Russo–Japanese War V–370b
secret diplomacy II–342a
Senate II–171b
Southeast Asia Treaty Organization VI–350b
Spain VI–358b–62b
State Department VI–388a
Strategic Arms Limitation Talks VI–416b
summit conferences VI–438b
treaties VII–110a
U.S. Navy VII–328a
Vietnam War IV–239b
Voice of America VII–207b
"watchful waiting" VII–253b
See also Foreign Aid
Foreign Relations (period.) III–281a
Foreign Scholarships, Board of III–131a
FOREIGN SERVICE III–71a; II–168a, 437a–b; III–35b; VI–388b–89a, 428b
Foreign Service Act (1946) III–71b; VI–389a
Foreign students II–402a, 470b–71a
Foreign trade. *See* Trade, Foreign
Forel, François Alphonse (nat.) II–391a
Foreman, George (pugilist) V–154b, 423a
Foreman, Richard (dir.) VII–51a
"Foreman James Monroe" (song) I–247a
Forepaugh's Circus II–40b
Forest, François de la (expl.) V–260b
Forestalling (bus.) IV–399a; V–225b
Forest and Stream (mag.) I–222b
Foresters, Society of American III–72b, 73b
Forest fires
California II–348b
Michigan II–348a
National Weather Service VII–264a
Wisconsin II–348a
Forest Hills (N.Y.) VII–29b, 30a,b
Forest Hills Village (N.Y.) II–46b
Forest Management Act (1897) IV–98a; V–450b
Forest products I–197a,b, 395a
Forest Products Laboratory III–76b
Forest Reserve Act (1891) II–187b; IV–95a
FORESTRY III–72b
conservation I–42b; II–187b; VII–266b, 297b
ecology II–392a
Interior, Department of the IV–95b
Montana IV–403b
reforestation VI–67a
timberlands VII–59b
Yale University VII–351a
See also Lumber Industry
Forestry, Division of II–187b
Forestry Association, American III–73a, 74a
Forests
Land Office reports IV–95a
sawmills VI–223a
Forests, national III–73b, 74a,b, 75a,b, 75b–76a, 164a, 444b; IV–96a; V–446a, 450b, 451a; VI–67a; VII–60a,b, 61a, 266b
Alaska I–80a
Black Hills I–312b
government inspection III–422a
grazing VI–426a
hydroelectric power sites III–321a
mining III–76a

private landholdings IV–98a
timber reserves IV–204b
wildlife sanctuaries VII–297b
Wyoming VII–346a
Forests, private III–73b, 74b–75a
Forests, state III–74a
FOREST SERVICE, UNITED STATES III–75a; I–45a,b; III–73b, 74a, 422a; IV–95b; V–451a,b
Ballinger–Pinchot controversy I–247b
harvesting VII–60a
national monuments V–217a
range lands V–446a
reforestation VI–67a
timber reserves IV–204b
Forgery
Secret Service VI–252a
FORGES, COLONIAL III–76b; IV–243a; V–108a, 230b; VI–218a–b
Principio Company V–409a
Forget–me–not VI–393 (table)
Forgings (metal) III–469b–70a
"FORGOTTEN MAN" III–77a; VI–313a
"Forks" (Red River of the North) VI–64b
Forks of the Ohio. *See* Ohio, Forks of the
Formaldehyde II–7a; V–328a
Formal style (landscape arch.) IV–96b
Forman, David (off.) III–77b
Forman, Ezekiel III–77b
Forman, Samuel S. (off.) III–77b
Forman, William (off.) III–77b
FORMAN'S COLONY (Miss.) **III–77b**; I–170a
FORMAN'S MASSACRE (1777) **III–77b**
Formative culture II–386a; VII–319b–20a
Formative stage (archaeol.) I–154b, 156b–58a
Formosa I–403b; II–27b; III–61b, 70b
Four–Power Treaty III–85b
marine landing IV–252a
summit conference VI–439a
World War II III–489b; VII–2a
See also Taiwan
Forney steam locomotive II–428a
Fornication VI–265b
Forrest, Edwin (act.) I–209b; VII–47b
Forrest, Nathan B. (off.) III–292b; IV–313b; V–313b; VII–128b
Forrestal (carrier) I–56a; II–350a; V–22a, 25b
Forrestal Campus (Princeton) V–409a
Forrester, Jay (elec. eng.) II–156a
Forsyth, Benjamin (off.) VII–358b
Forsyth, George A. (off.) I–283a
Forsyth, John (Confed. offi.) II–161a; V–118b
Forsyth, J. W. (off.) VII–344b
Forsyth's Fight. *See* Beecher Island, Battle of
Fort. *See* Under identifying name of fort, as in Recovery, Fort, except where the designation has become attached to a continuing city
Fort Ancient (Ohio) V–140a
Fort Apache Reservation (Ariz.) IV–90a–b
Fortas, Abe (jur.) I–300a; VI–447b
FORT BENTON (Mont.) **III–77b**
Fort Berthold Reservation (N.Dak.) I–171b; III–395b
Fort Collins (Colo.) III–76b
Fort Edward (N.Y.) II–406a
Forten, James (sailmaker) I–136b
Fort Frederica National Monument V–217b
Fort Gibson, Treaty of (1833) VI–259b–60a
Fort Greene (N.Y.) I–282b
Fort Hall (Idaho) I–453a
Fort Hall Reservation (Idaho) I–264b
For the Union Dead IV–165b
FORT HILL LETTER III–78a
FORTIFICATIONS III–78a
architecture I–159b, 160a
colonial wars VII–115a
Confederacy II–161a
congressional powers II–200a
earthworks IV–421a
Fort Greenville III–227b
Fort Lafayette (N.Y.) IV–83b
Fort Marion IV–253b
Fortress Monroe IV–399b
Fort Steuben VI–412a
Fort Washington (N.Y.) VII–246b
Frederica III–100b
Gothic Line III–201a
Gustav Line III–235b
Highlands of the Hudson III–275b
Indian villages III–405a
Jamestown III–489a
military policy IV–343a
national defense II–313b
Pemaquid pavements V–243a
Rip Raps Island VI–145a
Siegfried Line VI–285b
water supply VI–377b
See also Army Posts
Fort Jefferson National Monument V–217b
Fort Loudoun Dam III–322b
Fort Loyal (Maine) IV–49b
Fort Matanzas National Monument V–217b; VI–188a
Fort McHenry National Park V–217a
Fort Peck Dam II–449b; III–322b; VI–147a
Fort Pierre (Mont.) V–310b
Fort Point (Maine) III–120b
Fort Pulaski National Monument V–217b
FORTRAN (computer language) II–156b
Fort Randall Dam III–322b; VI–147a
Fort Scott (Kans.) I–131b
Fort Scott National Historic Site VI–241a
Fort Stanwix National Monument V–217b
Fort Sumter National Monument V–217a,b; VI–441a
Fort Tryon Park (N.Y.C.) IV–97a
Fortuna wheat VII–286b
Fortune (mag.) VII–333b
Fortune (ship) V–313b
FORTUNES, GREAT III–78b
Astor, John Jacob IV–100b
Rockefeller, John D., Jr. IV–100b
taxation VII–6a
Fort Union National Monument V–217b
FORT WORTH (Tex.) **III–80b**
airport I–70a
Balcones escarpment I–246b
Camp Bowie I–434b
cattle II–251b
federal records center III–284b
railroads VI–36b
settlement VII–35b
Fort Worth and Denver Railroad VI–380b
FORT WORTH FRONTIER CENTENNIAL EXPOSITION (1936) **III–81a**
"FORTY ACRES AND A MULE" III–81a
FORTY–EIGHTERS III–81a; III–336b; V–342a
"Forty–Five." *See* "Ninety–Two" and "Forty–Five"
FORTY FORT (Pa.) **III–81b**; VII–346b
Forty Mile (Yukon Terr.) IV–52a
FORTY–MILE DESERT III–81b; III–215a
FORTY–NINERS III–81b
caravans I–452b
covered wagon II–248a
food supply III–477b
"Joe Bowers" IV–1a
"Oh! Susanna" V–146b
transportation VI–379a
Forty–ninth parallel II–215b
Forty–second Infantry Division. *See* entries under Army, United States
Forty–second Street (N.Y.C.) VII–62b
Forty Thieves (N.Y.C.) VI–142a, 459b
Forum (mag.) IV–222a
"Forward" (motto) VI–395 (table)
Forward pass III–57b–58a
"Forward to Richmond." *See* "On to Richmond"
Fosdick, Harry Emerson (cler.) III–326b; V–161b, 392a
Fossil Butte National Monument V–217b
Fossil fuel II–416a, 417a
Fossils
Badlands I–242b
Big Bone Lick I–295b
fish III–27b
See also Paleontology
Foster, Charles (pol.) VI–295b
Foster, Charles H. W. I–95b
Foster, Ellis (tech.) V–328b
Foster, Emory S. (off.) IV–183b
Foster, John (print.) V–185a, 413b; VII–319a
Foster, John G. (off.) V–142b
Foster, Luther H. (educ.) VII–130b
Foster, Morrison VI–453b
Foster, Murphy J. (gov.) IV–196a
Foster, Ronald M. (math.) II–39a
Foster, Stephen C. (comp.) I–37b; IV–438a; VII–264a
"My Old Kentucky Home" IV–447a
"Oh! Susanna" V–146b
"Swanee River" VI–453b
Foster, William Z. (labor leader) II–144a,b, 145b; IV–69b, 70b
Foster Grandparent Program I–8b–9a
Foster Grant Company V–328a
Foster homes IV–23b; V–381a
Foster–Hutchinson House (Boston) I–161a
Foster v. *Neilson* (1829) VII–110b–11a
Fothergill, John (physic.) I–348b
Foulweather, Cape II–219b
Foundation Directory III–82b, 83a,b
FOUNDATIONS, ENDOWED III–82a; V–280b
Carnegie Corporation of New York I–456a,b
Carnegie Foundation for Advancement of Teaching I–456a
congressional investigations V–281a
medical research IV–286b
parapsychology V–213b
Peabody Fund V–231b
pressure groups V–400b–01a
Rockefeller Foundation VI–157b

FOUNDATIONS, ENDOWED (cont.)
Russell Sage Foundation VI–176b
Smithsonian Institution VI–319a
taxation VII–9b–10a
"Fountain of youth" II–184a; V–356a
Fountains IV–96b
Fourche Mailine (people) V–148a
Four Corners I–117a; III–15a
Fourdrinier papermaking machine I–16b
FOUR FREEDOMS III–84a
FOUR-H (4–H) CLUBS III–84b; I–43b; VI–175b
FOUR HUNDRED III–85a
Fourier, François Marie Charles (soc. sci., ref.). *See* Fourierism
FOURIERISM III–85a; I–91a,b, 369b; II–147a; IV–62a; VI–325b
Reunion VI–105a
FOUR-MILE STRIP III–85a
FOUR-MINUTE MEN III–85a; II–139b; IV–143b; VII–333a
Fourneyron, Benoît (eng.) VII–129a, 257a
"Four-piper" destroyer VII–243a
FOUR-POWER TREATY (1921) **III–85b**; III–33b; VII–250b
Four Revolutionary Plays IV–167b
Four Seas III–106b
FOURTEEN POINTS III–85b; I–215a; V–353b; VII–327a, 333a
Open covenants, openly arrived at V–157b
Russia VI–178a
Treaty of Versailles VII–174a
World War I peace conference VII–330b
FOURTEENTH AMENDMENT III–86a; I–94b, 299a–300a; II–64b, 205a–b; III–104a, 437b–38a; IV–6a; V–352b; VI–97b, 98a; VII–226b, 315a
alien landholding I–409b
aliens I–88a
amnesty I–115a,b
apportionment I–147a,b
black citizenship I–28b
black codes I–310b
black suffrage VI–431a,b
capital punishment I–450b; III–250a
centralization I–484b
citizenship II–42a, 54a
civil rights II–53b, 55a, 137a
commerce clause II–135b
Davis, Jefferson II–295a
Dred Scott Case II–370b
due process of law II–214a, 377a; IV–14b
eminent domain II–440a
equal protection II–54a, 457a–b; IV–14b
Force Acts III–59b–60a; IV–57b
freedom of press III–229a
government regulation of business III–204b
Granger Cases III–209b
habeas corpus III–237a
Hague v. *Committee on Industrial Organization* III–238a
Indian citizenship III–377a
judicial review IV–14a,b
Lochner v. *New York* IV–173b
lynching IV–208b
Maryland ratification IV–261a
minimum voting age II–55b
minimum-wage laws iv–353a
Minnesota Moratorium Case IV–358a
miscegenation IV–362b
Mississippi IV–369a
Oregon Parochial School Case V–167a
peonage V–260b
picketing V–308b–09a
poll tax I–451a; V–355a; VII–133a
price-fixing V–30b
privileges and immunities clause V–420b–21a
Radical Republicans VI–11b
Reconstruction VI–56b–57a,b, 58a,b, 59a
repudiation of state debts VI–96b
right of assembly I–204b
right of petition V–265a–b
segregation I–373a; II–57a
"separate but equal" doctrine V–331b
Slaughterhouse Cases VI–302b
Soldiers and Sailors convention VI–336a
South Carolina VI–348a
state limitation II–54a
Strauder v. *West Virginia* VI–417b
United States v. *Harris* VII–154b
United States v. *Wong Kim Ark* VII–155b
voting rights II–410a; III–20b
woman's suffrage IV–359a
"yellow-dog" contracts II–222a
"Fourteenth Amendment citizens" II–476a
FOURTEENTH COLONY III–87a
Fourteenth Illinois Infantry III–207b
Fourth Amendment I–299a
arrest I–195a
search and seizure VI–248b, 249a
Fourth Army VI–204b
Fourth Brigade (marines) IV–252b
Fourth Infantry Division. *See* entries under Army, United States
Fourth Marine Division IV–257b; VI–198a–b; VII–62a
FOURTH OF JULY III–87b; III–210b; VI–159a, 374b; VII–134b
Fourth Regular Infantry IV–224b
Fourth Republic (Fr.) III–97b
Fourth Symphony (comp.) IV–439a
Fourth term
campaign of 1944 I–429a,b
Fowle, Zechariah (print.) V–69b
Fowle and Draper (pub.) I–494a
Fowler, Harlan (eng.) I–51b
Fowler, Jacob (fur trader) III–88a, 143b; IV–25b; VI–461a
Fowler, Lorenzo N. (phrenologist) V–294a
Fowler, Melvin (archaeol.) I–402b
Fowler, Orson S. (phrenologist) V–294a
FOWLER EXPEDITION (1821) **III–88a**
Fowlers and Wells V–294a
FOWLTOWN, BATTLE OF (1817) **III–88b**; VI–260a–b
Fox I–446a; III–133a, 142a, 150a, 402b; VII–105a
Sable Island VI–182a
FOX (Indians) **III–88b**; III–366b, 396b; IV–122a
alliances I–281b
Battle of Bad Axe I–242b
Black Hawk War I–311b; III–329b
Fort Armstrong I–180b
Half-Breed Tract III–242b
Iowa III–468a
Jesuit missions III–499b
lead III–147a
neutral ground V–33b
Oklahoma lands V–148b, 149b
removal III–394b
revolutionary war VI–195a
Sioux-Chippewa War VI–294b
Sioux treaties VI–296a
Treaty at Prairie du Chien V–388b
Treaty of Fort Armstrong III–383b
Treaty of Fort de Chartres I–501b
Treaty of Prairie du Chien III–383b
Treaty of Sauk and Fox Agency III–383b
wild rice VII–298b
Fox, Dixon Ryan (hist.) III–283a
Fox, George (rel. leader) III–123a; V–469b
Fox, George W. L. (act., mgr.) III–238b; VII–48a
Fox, Gustavus v. (nav. off.) V–18a
Fox, Henry, Lord Holland (states.) III–291b
Fox, John, Jr. (au.) IV–41a
Fox, Josiah (shipbuilder) VII–240a
Fox, Justus (typefounder) V–411b
Fox, Kate VI–157b
Fox, Livingston and Company IV–415a
Fox, Margaret VI–157b
Fox, W. F. (off.) II–64a
Fox, William (prod.) IV–417b
Foxcroft, John (postmaster) V–371a
FOX-FRENCH WARS III–88b; II–337b; III–89b, 225b
Foxholes VII–115b
Fox River I–398b; III–88b, 225b
exploration III–119a, 329a
Fort Howard VI–186a
Fox-Wisconsin Waterway III–89a
fur trade III–144a
papermaking V–212a–b
Winnebago VII–305b
Fox-trot (dance) II–290b
Fox-Wisconsin Improvement Company III–90a
FOX-WISCONSIN WATERWAY III–89a; II–380b
exploration III–119a
Fort Winnebago VII–306a
Fox-French Wars III–88b–89a
Green Bay III–226a; VII–306b
Jolliet and Marquette expedition IV–7a
portage V–367b
Prairie du Chien V–387b
Sauk Prairie VI–218b
Foxy Grandpa (comic character) V–72a
Fractional currency IV–393b, 394a–b, 395b; VI–104a, 279a
Fraeb, Henry (fur trader) VII–103b
Fraktur certificates III–47a, 48a
Frame of Government (1682). *See* Penn's Frame of Government
France
Abnaki alliance I–3a
Acadia I–6a
agricultural chemistry VI–334a
aircraft I–51b
Alabama I–71a
Algeciras Conference I–85b
Algonquin alliance I–86a
Anglo-French War (1857–

58) VI–66a
apartment houses I–143a
Arab world I–149a,b, 150a
Arkansas I–172b–73a
atomic bomb I–216a
atomic power I–217b
automobile I–225b
ballet II–286b
balloon flights I–232b
Belgian relief I–285b
Berlin occupation I–291a
bicycle I–295a
bimetallism III–110a
blockades I–321a
Bourbon family compact II–487b
Boxer Rebellion I–356a
British colonial policy II–123a
Burr conspiracy I–387b
Cahokia I–402a
Canada II–246a, 247a–b
Canadian Indians I–441b
Carolina I–458a
cattle III–51b; VI–45a
Charleston Indian trade I–498a
Chequamegon Bay settlement II–13b
Chicago II–17a
Chickasaw–French War I–196b–97a; II–22b–23a
Code Napoléon II–91b
coins in colonies II–94b
colonial land grants IV–92b
colonial wars with England I–6a
Colorado claims II–127b
Common Market VI–469a, 470a–b
Compagnie de New Yorck I–466b
consumer cooperatives II–220a
Convention of Aranjuez I–151b
Creoles II–257a
Crown Point II–266b–67a
Crozat Grant II–267b
Cuba II–268a
daguerreotype II–279a
dance II–286b–87a
Dauphin Island II–294a
Declaration of Paris V–214a
Declaration of Rights of Man I–298b
Deerfield Massacre II–312b
Dominican Republic II–360b
Dummer's War II–380b
East Texas missions II–389a
École Polytechnique II–447a
education of the deaf III–248a
"effective occupation" II–406b
European Economic Community VII–88b
exploration I–24b, 96b, 447b, 492b, 498b–99a; II–17a, 247b, 458b, 497a; IV–264b; V–52b
fashions II–371b
Florida III–38a,b, 41b; IV–302b; V–254a
foreign trade VI–471a
Four–Power Treaty III–85b
freebooters II–217b
French–Chickasaw War I–7b, 197a
furniture III–135a
fur trade II–31a, 458b; III–141a–b, 142a–b, 143a, 143b–44b, 398b; IV–82b
Garde Nationale IV–463b
Geneva Accords of 1954 III–159b, 161a
Geneva disarmament conference III–161a
Geneva summit conference III–161a
Geneva Three–Power Naval Conference III–161a, 162a
geological surveys III–165b
Georgia claims II–298a
German reparations VI–87b
gold standard III–193b, 194b
Grand Banks fishing III–208a
Great Lakes III–216a; VII–157a
Gulf of Mexico IV–326a
helicopters III–270a
hydrogen bomb III–324a
Illinois II–265a; III–329a
immigration to U.S. III–333a, 337b, 341b
Indian allies II–321a, 392b; V–179b, 356b–57a
Indian captivities III–376b
Indian expeditions III–124b–25a
Indian trade II–31a, 265b
Indian wars II–329a, 380a
Indochina I–49a, 124a; III–159b; IV–107a; VII–182b
investments in U.S. III–63a, 65b, 66b
Iowa III–467b
ironclad warships IV–396a
Iroquois Beaver Land Deed III–476b
Isle of Orleans III–479a
Israeli relations III–481b, 482a
Jesuit missions III–498b–99b
King George's War II–126a–b
King William's War II–126a; VI–1b–2a, 181b–82a
Korean War IV–55b
La Salle's explorations IV–109b
letters patent I–6a
London Naval Treaty (1930) IV–183a; VI–424a
London Naval Treaty (1936) IV–183b
Louisbourg II–126b
Louisburg I–70b
Louisiana I–48b, 173b–74a, 301a, 399b; II–22b, 91b, 215b, 247a–b; IV–192b–93b, 198b, 301b, 376b; V–173a
Madrid Conference IV–221a
Maginot Line VI–285b
Maine settlements IV–225b, 226a–b
malaria research IV–229b
medical education IV–297b
medical research IV–285b
mental illness IV–305a
mercantilism II–166b
Mexico II–65a, 162a, 324a; IV–325b, 328a–b
Michigan IV–330b
Mississippi Valley I–173b; IV–375b
Missouri River IV–379b
Mobile II–33a
Mohawk Valley IV–386b
Molasses Act VI–435b
Morocco I–85b
motor truck transport IV–419a
Mount Desert claim IV–422b
Munich conference (1938) VI–285b
music IV–437b, 439a
Napoleonic Wars I–120b; V–162a; VII–233a–b
NATO withdrawal III–70a
naval competition V–10a,b
naval rivalry with England II–375a
neutral rights V–38b
Newfoundland fisheries II–92a–b
New Mexico VII–188a
New World claims V–109a–b
New World mapping VII–73a–b
New York Colony V–85a,b
Nine–Power Pact V–96b
Nootka Sound controversy V–109a
North Atlantic Treaty Organization V–113b, 114a–b
nuclear fission V–300a
nuclear physics V–298b, 302a
Nuclear Test Ban Treaty V–125a
occupation of Germany III–174b; VII–351b
Ohio claims III–118a
Oklahoma V–148a
Organization for Economic Cooperation and Development V–170b
Ostend Manifesto V–175a
Panama Canal V–201a
Peace of Paris V–214a
pharmaceutical industry V–273b
Physiocrats IV–85a
pig iron III–471 (table)
psychological warfare V–441a
Quasi War I–251b
Queen Anne's War II–126a–b; VI–2a
radar VI–l0a
radio astronomy VI–17a
refrigeration VI–69b
relations with Great Britain III–94b–95b
rivalry with Spain II–126a
Rule of the War of 1756 VI–169a
rum VI–171a, 321a
Saint Louis VI–193b–94a
Sault Sainte Marie Pageant VI–219a
Schenectady attack VI–225b
sea trade III–106b
sharpshooters VI–269b
Shawnee and Delaware trade VI–271a
sheep VI–272b
Shimonoseki expedition VI–278b
Siberian expedition VI–284a
slave trade VI–309b
Society of the Cincinnati II–38a
South Carolina I–281b, 496a; VI–348b, 349a
Southeast Asia II–315b, 489a–b
Southeast Asia Treaty Organization VI–350b, 351a
Stonewall VI–415a
submarines VI–422b
Suez Canal I–124b
Suez crisis III–352b; VI–429b
Sugar Islands VI–437a
supersonic transport I–53a, 238a
syndicalism455b
television VII–21a
Tennessee VII–25a
tennis VII–30a,b
Texas I–48b; VI–64b
Treaty of Amiens I–114a
Treaty of Breda I–361a
Treaty of Fontainebleau III–50b
Treaty of Paris V–214b
Treaty of Saint Germain–en–Laye VI–190b
Treaty of San Ildefonso VI–211a
Treaty of Tilsit II–291a
Treaty of Utrecht II–92b; VII–162b
Treaty of Versailles VII–172b
Treaty of Whitehall (1686) VII–291a
triangular trade VII–119b
United Nations Declaration VII–151b
Unknown Soldiers II–310a
UN Security Council V–234a
Ursulines VII–160b
U.S. Civil War I–468a; IV–35a, 85a
U.S. gold reserves

FRANCE (cont.)
III–195b
U.S. sedition acts VI–255a
Vermont VII–171a
vineyards III–129a
Walloons VII–221b
war contraband II–212b
war crimes trials VII–229a
warships VII–243a
wars of French Revolution I–114a
war with England V–84b
Washington Naval Conference VII–250b, 341b
Western Union Defense Organization V–114a
West Florida VII–277a
West India trade VII–278a, 278a
Wisconsin VII–306b–07a
World Economic Conference VII–324a
World War I I–70a,b, 101b–02a, 158b–59a, 246b, 286a,b, 446a, 491b, 502a; II–314a, 438a; IV–83b, 84a–b, 319b, 404a; V–20a,b, 146b–47a; VI–197a, 338a–b, 338a–b; VII–115a, 325a,b, 326a,b–27a, 328b, 329a, 330b
World War I debts VII–332a
World War II I–1a, 59b, 178a, 465a; II–315a; III–235b; V–110a–11b, 113a, 138b, 213a; VI–193b; VII–242a, 334a,b, 338a,b–40a
World War II peace settlement V–378b
Young Men's Christian Association VII–363a
See also entries under French; French and Indian War
FRANCE, AMERICAN JOINT COMMISSION TO (1777–78) **III–90a**; III–95a
France, Convention With. *See* Convention of 1800
France and England in North America IV–163a
France v. *United States* (1959) III–453a
Franchère, Gabriel (au.) III–122b
FRANCHISE III–90b; II–53a
Afro-Americans III–20a–b
Commission on Civil Rights II–499b
District of Columbia VII–132b
eighteen-year-olds VII–133b
extension IV–80a
Fifteenth Amendment II–53b; III–60a
freeholder III–107b
freemen III–109b
Jacksonian Democracy III–486b
Jeffersonian Republicans VI–94b
Jews IV–9a
literacy test IV–160a
Louisiana IV–194b
Massachusetts Bay IV–269a
Minor v. *Happersett* IV–359a
New Hampshire V–54a
New York State V–86a,b
Nineteenth Amendment V–97a
nonvoting V–108b
Philippines IV–7b; V–283a,b
political parties V–223b, 224a, 343a
Reconstruction VI–55b
Reconstruction Acts VI–58b–59a
United States v. *Reese* VII–155a
Virginia VII–195a,b, 281b
voter qualifications VII–208b–09a
Washington, D.C. VII–245a,b
women IV–26b; VII–313b–14a, 314b–15b, 317a
Wyoming VII–346a
Franchise (bus.)
quo warranto VI–4b
Franchises, utility V–458b
Francis I (Fr. k.) I–96b, 447b; IV–451b; V–52b
Francis, James B. (eng.) VII–129a, 257a
Francis, Peter (seaman) VI–186a
Francis, Philip (col. offi.) IV–20b
Francis, Sam (art.) II–107a
Francis, Thomas (sci.) V–341a
Francis, William (inv.) VII–136a
FRANCISCANS III–94a; I–96b; III–498b
Acoma I–8a
Apalache massacre I–143a
Arizona I–172a, 172a
California I–405a, 405a; IV–365b
Capuchins I–451b
Colorado River exploration II–129b
Florida I–143a; III–38b, 41a
Georgia III–170a
Hennepin, Louis III–272a; IV–109b
Hopi mission III–301a
Indian education III–379b
Indian missions III–385b
New Mexico I–288b; II–23b, 461a; V–59b
San Antonio missions VI–207b
Southwest missions IV–367a,b
Spanish Inquisition III–420b
Texas missions II–433a
Francis of Assisi, Saint III–94a
Franck, James (phys.) IV–238a; V–303a
Franco, Francisco VI–360b
FRANCO-AMERICAN ALLIANCE OF 1778 III–94b; I–194b, 194b; II–208a, 215a, 318b; III–67b, 90b, 95b, 96a, 306a, 352a, 455b, 462a; V–2a, 232a, 323b; VI–116b–17a, 119b, 124a, 368a; VII–111a, 153b, 165b, 348a
French navy V–19a
Genêt mission III–159b
most-favored-nation principle IV–416b
prize cases III–98a
Saratoga surrender VI–217b
spoliation claims III–121b
FRANCO-AMERICAN MISUNDERSTANDING (1798–1800) **III–95b**; III–96b; IV–347a
enemy trading VII–93b
naval war V–15a
spoliation claims III–121b
XYZ affair VII–347b
Franco-American Naval War (1797–1800). *See* Naval War With France
FRANCO-AMERICAN RELATIONS III–96a; VI–124b
alliance of 1778 III–94b
America VI–282a
American joint commission III–90a
American Revolution I–151a, 367a; III–306a; VI–116a–17a,b, 119a–b, 120a, 128b, 129a
atomic bomb research IV–237b
boundaries I–126a
Caribbean balance of power IV–188a
Consular Convention II–208a
Convention of 1800 II–215a
Convention of 1800 II–208a; III–67b
Convention of 1818 II–215b
Definitive Treaty of Peace II–318a
Embargo of 1807 II–436b
exchange students II–471a
extraterritoriality II–479a
Five-Power Naval Treaty III–33b
Fourteen Points III–86a
French Decrees III–118b
French in Mexico IV–361a
French refugees III–121a
Genêt mission III–159b; IV–169b
Great Britain I–120b, 120b
Indian barrier state III–375a
Indian trade III–389a
Indochina War VII–182b, 185a–b
international law III–455b, 456a
isolationism III–480a
Israel III–481b
Kasson tariff treaty IV–33a
Kellogg-Briand Pact IV–35b
Koszta case IV–57b
lend-lease ships V–21b
Liberia IV–141b
London Naval Treaty II–461a
Louisiana IV–193a,b, 196a–97b
Louisiana Purchase II–127b, 474b; VI–150b, 359a
Macon's Bill No. 2 IV–219b
mandates IV–236b
Marshall Plan IV–258a
Monroe Doctrine IV–400b
Monroe mission IV–402a
Morocco taxation III–453a–b
Naples claims IV–449a
Napoleonic Wars III–67b
Napoleon's decrees IV–449b
Nonintercourse Act V–105a
nonintervention III–462a
nuclear weapons IV–454a
Panama Canal V–201a
Panama Railroad V–204a
Paris conferences V–215b
Perdicaris affair V–261b
Proclamation of Neutrality V–36b
Quasi War I–86b, 345a; II–89a, 190a–b, 212b–13a; III–121a; V–15a
recognition VI–54b
retaliation VI–104b
revolutionary war II–5b, 449b; III–67b, 117b–18a; IV–189a; V–65b, 98a
revolutionary war debts II–301a, 302a; III–245a
revolutionary war loans III–63a
Rule of the War of 1756 VI–169a
spoliation claims III–121b
Statue of Liberty VI–405b
Texas VII–38b, 41b
trade I–245a; II–382b, 446b; VII–86b–87a, 91b
treaty negotiation VII–111a
Treaty of Amity and Commerce VII–109a
Treaty of Versailles IV–178b
Tripartite Agreement VII–120b
U.S. aid III–61b
U.S. Civil War II–64b–65b, 162a, 162a
U.S. flag III–34b
U.S. neutrality V–34b
Viviani-Joffre Mission I–246b
Washington's Farewell Address VII–251b
World War I III–309a;

IV–319b–20a
World War II V–37a
XYZ Affair II–215a; IV–347a
See also French and Indian War
FRANCO–AMERICAN WAR PRIZE CASES **III–98a**; III–121b
Franconia (N.H.) VI–298a
Franconia Aerial Tramway VI–101a
Franco-Prussian War (1870–71) I–73b; III–97a, 162a, 352b; V–207a; VII–225b, 248b
Franco-Russian Alliance of 1807 VI–177b
Franco-Spanish War (1719) IV–456b
Frank, Leo VII–118a
Frank E. Evans (destroyer) II–350a
Frankford (Pa.) I–196b, 376b
Frankfort (Ky.)
Civil War IV–42b
Goebel Affair III–188b
railroad VI–34b
railroads IV–137b
Frankfort (Maine) III–247b
Frankfort (N.Y.) I–363b
Frankfort Land Company III–173a
Frankfurter, Felix (jur.) IV–10b, 268a; VI–446b
Adamson v. *California* V–353b
apportionment I–244a
Bill of Rights I–299b
due process II–378b
freedom of speech III–104a
on power of Supreme Court IV–15a
"Frankie" (song) I–247b
FRANKING III–98a
Frank Leslie's Illustrated Newspaper IV–454a; V–73a
Franklin (Kans.) I–342a; VII–218b
Franklin (Mo.) I–282a, 282a, 453a, 453a; VI–215b
Franklin (Pa.) IV–213b; V–146b, 246b
Franklin (ship) VI–282a
Franklin (Tenn.) III–98b; VII–26b
Franklin (Va.) IV–212b
Franklin, Aretha (sing.) IV–440a
FRANKLIN, BATTLE OF (1864) **III–98a**; III–298a; VI–377a
Franklin, Benjamin I–464a; III–209a, 354a, 427a; V–186b, 247a, 277a, 372b; VI–266a, 320a; VII–153b, 155b, 205b–06a, 262a, 319a
academy V–248b–49a
advertising I–18b
Albany Plan of Union I–82a; II–122a
American Philosophical Society I–110a,b, 111a; IV–126a
apprenticeship I–148a; IV–79a
Associations I–208a
Autobiography IV–161a
Bank of North America I–260b
Bonhomme Richard I–329b
Braddock's expedition I–358a
climate II–75b–76a
code of behavior IV–240b
colonial agent II–116b
Constitution II–193a, 196a, 203b
consular convention with France II–208a
consumer cooperative II–220a
daylight saving time II–296b
Declaration of Independence II–303b, 304b, 306a, 308a
dueling II–377a
education I–5b; II–114b
electricity II–413a
endowed foundations III–82a
envoy to Canada I–435b, 438a; IV–86b
E pluribus unum II–455b
fertilizer III–16a
fire insurance II–220a
foreign loans VI–120a
Foreign Service III–71a
foreign volunteers VI–129a
Freemasons III–108b–09a
General Magazine and Historical Chronicle IV–161a, 221b
Gulf Stream study III–233a
Hutchinson letters III–320b
Indian trading posts II–480a
Kennedy-Franklin Plan of Union II–122a
land speculation IV–98b
library II–107b
life insurance III–432a
lotteries IV–190b
meteorologic experiments IV–316a
mission to France III–90a, 95a; VI–119b, 128b
Navigation Acts V–17a
New Jersey currency V–404a
ocean studies V–134a
Ohio Indians I–455a
on population V–361a
on typesetters health IV–293a
papers II–109a
Paxton Boys V–231a
Peace of Paris V–214b; VI–117a
Pennsylvania constitution VI–390b
Pennsylvania Gazette I–16b; V–68b, 72b–73a, 251a
Pennsylvania Hospital III–306b; IV–283a; V–251b
Philadelphia Academy II–395a
Philadelphia census III–427a, 430a
Philadelphische Zeitung V–75b
philanthropy V–279b
philosophy V–287a
physics V–294a–b
Plan of 1776 V–323b
Poor Richard's Almanac I–90b; V–358b
postal service V–371a,b
preliminary articles of peace II–318b
prerevolutionary imperial idea III–346b
printer's devil V–410a
printing V–411b
rattlesnakes VI–47b
Red Line Map VI–62b; VII–265a
Scotch-Irish III–335a
slavery I–135b
Stamp Act VI–381b
stove III–99b, 268b
subscription library IV–144b
Vandalia Colony VII–166b
water supply VII–258a
writings III–281a
Franklin, Fort (Pa.) VII–168b
Franklin, James, Jr. (pub.) V–65b
Franklin, John (expl.) II–319b; III–224a; IV–232a; V–23a, 122a, 336b
Franklin, John (settler) VI–451b
Franklin, Rosalind (biophys.) IV–390a
FRANKLIN, STATE OF III–98b; I–240a; II–381a; III–497b; VI–356a; VII–25b
fourteenth colony III–87a
Muscle Shoals speculation IV–435b; VI–365b
Southwest Point VI–357b
Franklin, William (col. gov.) I–368a; V–57a, 463b
Franklin, William B. (off.) I–130a; IV–425a; VI–220a; VII–293a
Franklin and Hull (pub.) II–466b
Franklin cents. *See* Fugios
Franklin College (Ga.) VII–156a
Franklin County (Ga.) V–315b
Franklin County (Kans.) V–378b
Franklin County (N.Y.) IV–219b
Franklin D. Roosevelt (carrier) V–22a
Franklin D. Roosevelt Library I–167b
Franklin Health Assurance Company of Massachusetts III–435a
Franklinia (plant) I–348b
FRANKLIN INSTITUTE III–99a; IV–281b; VI–235b–36a
Franklin Journal and American Mechanics' Magazine III–99a
Franklin Literary Society VI–168b
Franklin National Bank I–254a; III–66b, 423b
Franklin's Academy I–5b; II–395a
FRANKLIN STOVE III–99b; III–268b
Frankstown Path I–88b
Franquelin, Jean Baptiste Louis (cartog.). *See* Franquelin's Maps
FRANQUELIN'S MAPS III–99b; V–145a; VII–73b
Franz Josef Land V–337a
Frasch, Herman (chem.) II–6b; III–409a
Frasconi, Antonio (art.) V–414a
Fraser, Alexander (off.) III–330b
Fraser, Charles (paint.) IV–352a
Fraser, Simon (fur trader) VII–276a
Fraser, Simon (off.) III–311b; VII–55a
Fraser River V–121a; VI–201b; VII–247b, 275b, 276a
Fraser Valley I–441b
Fraske, Frederick (sol.) V–257b–58a
Fraternal Appeal to the American Churches IV–206a
Fraternal life insurance III–435a
Fraternities, college VI–253a
Fraud
Civil War II–63a, 68a–b
county-seat election II–245b
Desert Land Act II–336a
elections II–411a
Gardiner award III–152a
mails II–208b
marine insurance III–428b
Secret Service VI–252a
Special Agency Service II–276b
Fraud statutes I–325b
Fraudulent voting II–408b
Fraunces, Samuel III–100a
FRAUNCES TAVERN (N.Y.C.) **III–100a**; VI–339b
FRAYSER'S FARM, BATTLE OF (1862) **III–100a**; IV–230b; VII–293a
Frazer, John (fur trader) VII–168b
Frazier, E. Franklin (soc.) I–24b
Frazier, Joe (pugilist) V–154b, 423a

Frazier, Lynn J. (gov.)
V–106b, 107a
FRAZIER-LEMKE FARM BANKRUPTCY ACT (1934) **III–100a**; IV–414b; V–45b, 47a
Frazier–Lemke Farm Mortgage Moratorium Act (1935) III–100b; V–47a, 48a
Freake family V–185a
Fredendall, Lloyd R. (off.) IV–32b
FREDERICA (Ga.) **III–100b**; I–323a; IV–46b; V–217b
FREDERICK (Md.) **III–100b**
Civil War III–124a–b, 256a; IV–190a, 261b, 398a
glassmaking III–182b, 185a
pack trains V–184a
revolutionary war II–215a
Frederick VI (Den. k.) II–291b
Frederick, Christine II–418a–b
Frederick County (Md.) IV–260b
Frederick County (Va.) II–381b; VI–275b
Fredericks, Walter (phys.) V–303b
Fredericksburg (Va.) III–109a; VI–376a
Civil War I–493a; III–487b; IV–281b; VI–138a, 263b
Mary Washington College VII–197b
FREDERICKSBURG, BATTLE OF (1862) **III–100b**; I–248a; II–62b; IV–425a; VII–197b
Fredericksville (Va.) VI–376a
Fredericktown (Mo.) III–13b, 101a
FREDERICKTOWN, ACTION AT (1861) **III–101a**
Fredonia (N.Y.) II–220b; V–5a; VII–312a
Fredonia Gaslight and Waterworks Company V–5a
FREDONIAN REVOLT (1826–27) **III–101a**; IV–448b
Fred Steele, Fort (Wyo.) IV–300a
Free African Society I–23a
FREE BANKING SYSTEM **III–101b**; I–255b, 256a; VI–184b
FREE BLACKS **III–101b**; I–100b–01a; IV–246b
antebellum South VI–340b, 342a
enslavement III–130b
integration III–437b
Kansas IV–28a,b; VII–73a
Louisiana II–91b
military service IV–339b
New Amsterdam III–253a
personal liberty laws V–263b
revolutionary war VI–118a, 125b
slave insurrections VI–304a
suffrage III–91b; VI–431a,b
Underground Railroad VII–138b
Union army VI–308a
Washington, D.C. VII–246a
See also Kidnapping of Free Blacks
Freeboldsen, Freebold VI–458b
Freebooters I–373b–74a; II–217b
Freebooting. *See* Filibustering
Free Democratic party I–138b, 139a
Free disposition, doctrine of II–452a
Freedman's Bank Act (1865) III–103a
FREEDMAN'S SAVINGS BANK III–103a
Freedmen
civil rights III–59b
elections II–151a
farm tenancy IV–103a
"forty acres and a mule" III–81a
Fourteenth Amendment III–87a
Ku Klux Klan IV–57b, 58a
Liberian colonization IV–141b
FREEDMEN'S BUREAU **III–103a**; I–460a; V–280a; VI–56b, 71b
education II–399b, 403b
ministers VI–59b
Radical Republicans VI–11b
"Freedom and Unity" (motto) VI–395 (table)
Freedom from arrest V–419b
Freedom from fear I–215a; III–84a
Freedom from molestation V–419b
Freedom from want I–215a; III–84a
Freedom of assembly. *See* Assembly, Right of
Freedom of conscience. *See* Religious Liberty II–157a
Freedom of contract II–378a
Freedom of expression I–100b, 116b
motion pictures IV–418b
Smith Act (1940) II–446a
Freedom of Information Center V–79b
Freedom of Information Act (1966) V–472a
Freedom of Information Act (1975) V–79a
Freedom of petition. *See* Petition, Right of
Freedom of religion. *See* Religious Liberty
FREEDOM OF SPEECH **III–104a**; I–94a, 204b, 298b, 299a; II–53b, 171b, 324b; III–84a; IV–358b; V–78b
Alien and Sedition Laws I–86a
censorship I–478b
Civil War II–62a
colonial governments V–419b
First Amendment II–204a
Fourteenth Amendment III–86b
Jeffersonian Democracy III–496a
judicial review IV–14b
New Harmony settlement V–55a
newspapers V–77b
picketing V–309a
Schenck v. *United States* VI–225a
sedition acts VI–255b
Smith Act VI–317b
Supreme Court VI–447b
FREEDOM OF THE PRESS **III–104b**; I–94a, 204b, 297b, 298b, 299a; II–53b, 171b; IV–358b; V–77b–78a, 78b–79a
Alien and Sedition Laws I–86a, 87a; V–69b–70a
censorship I–478b
Civil War II–62a–b
Croswell libel suit II–266a, 266a
democracy II–324b
First Amendment II–204a
"Forty–Five" V–97b
Grosjean v. *American Press Company* III–229a
Jeffersonian Democracy III–496a
judicial review IV–14b
libel IV–139b
Lovejoy assassination V–70b
mass media IV–272a
Near v. *Minnesota* V–30b
Pentagon Papers V–258b
sedition acts VI–255b
Zenger trial V–69a, 82b, 85a; VII–117a, 368a
FREEDOM OF THE SEAS **III–106a**; III–69a, 428a
armed merchantmen IV–313a,b
Atlantic Charter I–215a
Civil War II–67b
Fourteen Points III–86a
free ships, free goods III–110a
Geneva Three–Power Naval Conference III–162a
immunity of private property III–343a
mare clausum IV–249b
Plan of 1776 V–323b
territorial waters VII–32b
Trent affair VII–115b
World War I IV–205b; VII–324b–25a
World War I armistice I–176b; III–86a
World War I peace conference VII–330b
Freedom of the Will VI–81b
Freedom of worship. *See* Religious Liberty
FREEDOM RIDERS **III–107a**; I–31a; II–55a, 58a, 179b
Freedoms, Four. *See* Four Freedoms
Freedoms and Exemptions, Charter of (1629) V–61a
Freedom's Journal (news.) V–75b
Free–electron theory V–304a
Free enterprise I–390a; II–214a
Free French Forces I–465a
Freehold (N.J.) IV–397b
FREEHOLDER **III–107b**; I–3b, 4a
Carolina II–117b
Jeffersonian Democracy III–495b–96a,b
manors IV–241b–42a
Massachusetts IV–265b
quitrents VI–4a
suffrage VI–433b–34a,b
See also Freemen
Free–in–county mailing III–98a
FREE LAND **III–107b**; IV–94b, 96a, 100a, 103b; VII–267b
Homestead Act IV–95a
homestead movement III–295b; IV–91a
Jeffersonian Democracy III–495b
panic of 1857 V–207a
Taylor Grazing Act IV–96a
Texas VII–35b, 37a, 39a, 41b
West VII–268a
Free list IV–182b
Free love VI–13a
Freeman, Douglas Southall (ed., hist.) V–73b
Freeman, Edward A. (hist.) V–347b
Freeman, Mary Eleanor Wilkins (au.) IV–163a
Freeman, Rowland G. (physic.) IV–275b
Freeman, Samuel T. (auctioneer) I–332b
Freeman, Thomas (eng.) I–9b; VI–351a
Freeman, W. (psych.) IV–306b
FREEMAN'S EXPEDITION (1805–06) **III–108a**; II–381a
FREEMAN'S FARM, FIRST BATTLE OF (1777) **III–108a**; I–385a–b
FREEMAN'S FARM, SECOND BATTLE OF (1777) **III–108a**; VI–217a
FREEMAN'S JOURNAL **III–108b**; I–483b; VI–239a
Free market system I–449b
FREEMASONS **III–108b**; II–454a; VI–246b, 252b, 253a
anti–Masonic movements I–132a
Deism III–112a
Illuminati of New England III–332a
Morgan trials IV–410b
opposition to I–132a–33a
radical right VI–12a
Vermont VII–172a

FREEMEN III–109b; I–342a; VII–95a–b
colonial governors II–120a
general court III–155a,b
Maryland II–117b
Massachusetts Bay II–35b, 117a–b; IV–269a
New Plymouth Colony II–117a–b; V–65a
proprietary provinces V–436a
town meetings VII–79a
Free Methodist church of North American IV–319a
"Free Micronesia" movement III–426a
Free Museum of Science and Arts V–249a–b
Freeport (Ill.). *See* Freeport Doctrine
Freeport (Tex.) VII–259b
FREEPORT DOCTRINE III–109b; IV–155b; V–360b
Freer, Charles Lang (ind.) II–103b; VI–319b
Free range. *See* Open Range Cattle Period
Freer Gallery of Art VI–319b
Free School Society. *See* Public School Society
Free School Society of New York City II–396b
FREE SHIPS, FREE GOODS III–110a; I–175b; II–213a, 190a; III–455b
armed neutrality of 1780 I–175b
Declaration of Paris V–324a
Franco–American misunderstanding III–95b
Plan of 1776 V–323b
FREE SILVER III–110a; I–44a, 302a; III–113a; VI–371a, 466b
Bland–Allison Act I–318b
Bryan, William Jennings II–96b
campaign of 1896 II–266a; III–189a; V–3a
Cleveland Democrats II–75a
Crime of 1873 IV–154a–b
debtor relief IV–414a
Gold Bugs III–188b
Greenback movement III–225a
Greenback party III–224b; VI–333b
Nevada V–39b
Ocala Platform V–132a
Populist party V–365b–66a
radicals VI–13b
seigniorage VI–257a
Sherman Silver Purchase Act VI–277a
Silver Democrats VI–287b
Silver League VI–288a
FREE SOCIETY OF TRADERS III–111a; VI–267b
Free soil
Mason–Dixon Line IV–263a
"Free soil, free speech, free labor and free men" III–111b
"FREE SOIL, FREE SPEECH, FREE MEN AND FRÉMONT" III–111b
FREE SOIL PARTY III–111b
antislavery VII–52b
Appeal of the Independent Democrats I–145a
Barnburners I–268a
Black Laws I–314a
campaign of 1848 I–420b; V–329a
campaign of 1852 I–420b
Compromise of 1850 II–150a
Conscience Whigs II–184b
homestead movement III–296a–b
Liberty party I–138a; IV–143b
New York State V–86b
Ohio State Antislavery Society V–145b
Radical Republicans VI–10b
Republican party VI–92b
Topeka Constitution VII–73a
Vermont VII–172a
Free Speech movement (1964) I–408b; VII–366a
Free State (news.) IV–118b
Free–State Hotel(Lawrence, Kans.) IV–118b
Free–state movement I–342a; IV–30a–b, 31a
Free State of Van Zandt. *See* Van Zandt, Free State of
Free–State party. *See* Kansas Free–State Party
FREETHINKING III–112a
FREE TRADE III–112b; III–460b; VI–462b, 471a, 472b; VII–88b, 90b
Open Door policy V–157b
versus protection II–276b
"Free–trade party" VI–462b
Free universities II–402b
Freewill Baptists V–174b
Free–willers III–353a
Freeze drying III–55b–56a
Freezers III–55b
Freezing
food preservation III–54b, 55b–56a
Freighters
Lake Erie II–459a
See also Merchant Marine
Freighting
canals II–460a
cow towns II–251b
truck IV–420a
Freighting, overland. *See* Overland Freighting
Frelinghuysen, Frederick Theodore (states.) I–420a; V–41b
Frelinghuysen, Theodore J. (cler.) III–214a; V–391b; VI–76b
Fremont (Nebr.) IV–338b
Fremont (Ohio) III–223b; VI–208b, 412a
Frémont, Jessie Benton (Mrs. John C.) III–498b
Frémont, John C. (off., pol.) II–449b
Army of Virginia VII–197a
Battle of Port Republic V–369a
campaign of 1856 I–139a, 420b–21a; III–111b; IV–254b; VI–42b, 92b
Civil War I–288a; II–266a
Colt's revolvers II–68a
conquest of California IV–34a
emancipation orders II–168a, 434a, 435a; VI–11a
Fort Uintah VII–137a
Hawk's Peak episode III–264b
Jessie Scouts III–498b
Kansas exploration IV–25b
Kansas Pacific Railroad IV–30b
Lassen's Post and Ranch IV–110b
Mariposa land grant IV–254a
Mexican War I–280a, 403a, 409b; IV–323b–24a, 325a; VI–210b
quarrel with Kearny IV–34a
Stockton–Kearny quarrel VI–414a
western routes V–224b, 225a
See also Frémont's Explorations
Frémont–Kearny quarrel. *See* Kearny–Frémont Quarrel
Frémont Pass V–225a
FRÉMONT'S EXPLORATIONS (1842–54) **III–114a**; II–477b; V–227a; VII–271b–72a
Buenaventura River I–374b
Colorado II–128a
Great Basin III–214b
Great Salt Lake III–222a
mapping VII–74b
Nebraska V–31a
Smoky Hill Trail VI–320a
South Pass VI–354b
South Platte IV–89a
Utah VII–161a
Frémont's Peak III–114a
French
Kaskaskia IV–31b
Mohawk River V–224a
Northwest Territory V–122b–23a
Pass Christian V–224a
Saint Paul VII–134a
South Dakota VI–350a
French, A. B. (showman) VI–283a
French, Daniel (inv.) VI–408a.b
French, Daniel Chester (sculp.) VI–243b, 283a
French, S. G. (off.) I–88b
French Academy of Sciences V–289b
French alliance. *See* Franco–American Alliance of 1778
FRENCH AND INDIAN WAR (1754–63) **III–114b**; II–126a, 458b; III–120a; IV–265b; VI–110a–b, 381a; VII–267b
Albany Congress I–82a
Augusta Congress I–223a
Battle of Bloody Pond I–323a,b
Battle of Bushy Run I–389a
Battle of Grant's Hill III–211b
Battle of Great Meadows III–219a
Battle of La Belle Famille IV–60a
Battle of Lake George IV–87b
Battle of the Loyalhanna IV–200a
Battle of the Monongahela IV–398a
billeting I–297a
border forts I–340b
Braddock's expedition I–358a
Bradstreet's Fort Frontenac expedition I–358b
British rangers VI–46b
Canada I–438a
Charleston (W.Va.) I–497b
Cherokee II–14b
Colorado II–127b
Delaware Indians VII–220b
Detroit II–336b, 337b
enemy trading VII–93b
financing II–302a
Forbes expedition I–282b; III–58a
Fort Duquesne II–381b–82a
Fort Edward II–405b
Fort La Galette IV–85a
Fort Ligonier IV–154a
Fort Loudoun IV–192a
Fort Niagara V–90b
Fort Pentegoet V–260a
Fort Pitt V–321a
Fort Pownall V–386b
Fort Saint Frederic II–267a
Fort Seybert massacre VI–267a
forts Ontario and Oswego V–175b
Fort William Henry massacre VII–301a
French defeat VI–119a
Georgia II–298a; III–168a
German Flats III–172b
Indian support III–387b
Kittanning campaign IV–51a
Lake Champlain

FRENCH AND INDIAN WAR (cont.)
IV–86a–86b
Logstown Indians IV–181a
Louisiana IV–193a
Loyal Land Company IV–201b
Maine IV–226a
militia I–183a
Mississippi IV–368a
Mississippi River IV–373a
Mobile I–499a; IV–382a
Montreal IV–405b
New York V–86a
New York Colony V–85a–b
Northwest Territory IV–355b
Ohio V–140b
Ohio Company of Virginia V–144a
Ohio Valley I–477a
Oklahoma V–148a
partisan bands V–222a
Pennsylvania V–246b; VI–271a
Pennsylvania Hospital V–251b
prices V–404a
privateering V–419a
Proclamation of 1763 V–424b
Quakers I–135a; III–122b–23a; V–470a
Quebec VI–1a–b
rattlesnake flag VI–47b
Raystown Path VI–49a
recruitment IV–345b
Redstone Old Fort VI–65b
Richelieu River VI–136b
rivers VI–150a
Rogers' Rangers VI–162b
Saint Francis raid VI–190a
smuggling VI–321a
Tennessee Valley VII–27b
Ticonderoga I–358b; VII–57a
Treaty of Aix-la-Chapelle I–70b
Treaty of Easton II–389a
Treaty of Paris V–214b
westward movement VII–283a
Wyoming Valley VII–347a
French Antique style furniture III–135b
FRENCH ARMY, MARCH OF ROCHAMBEAU'S (1781) **III–117b**; V–66a
French Broad River II–380b–81a; III–292a,b
Douglas Dam III–322b
Great Warriors Path VII–238b
settlement VII–283a
Tennessee River VII–27a–b
French-Canadians I–437b, 438a, 440a
coureurs de bois II–246a
explorers II–285b
immigration to U.S. III–338a–b
New Hampshire V–54b
Prairie du Chien V–388a
Quebec Act VI–2a
revolutionary war I–435b
Saint Paul VII–134a
Vermont VII–172b
Walla Walla VII–221a
Willamette Valley VII–300a
FRENCH CLAIMS IN OHIO III–118a; I–477a; II–381b–82a; III–58a–b, 59a, 120a, 141b, 375a; V–140a–b, 146a
French colonial architecture I–160a,b
French Creek (Pa.) VII–168b
FRENCH CREEK, ACTION AT (1813) **III–118a**
FRENCH DECREES III–118b; I–497a; II–436b; III–95b; IV–449b
French-Eversole Feud (1885–94) III–18b
French Expeditionary Corps III–235b
FRENCH EXPLORATION IN THE WEST III–118b; I–441b; II–379b–80a; III–313a
Arkansas River I–174a
Fox-Wisconsin Waterway III–89b
Franciscans III–94a–b
Great Lakes III–216a
Great Plains III–220b
Green Bay III–225b
Illinois III–329a, 331b
Indiana III–369b
Indians III–399a–b
Jolliet and Marquette expedition IV–6b
Kansas IV–25b
Lake Michigan IV–332a–b
La Vérendrye expedition IV–117b–18a
lead industry IV–122a
mapping III–99b
Michigan IV–330b
Minnesota IV–355a–b
Mississippi River IV–372a
Mississippi Valley IV–368a, 375b
Missouri IV–376b
Missouri River I–354b; IV–379b
Natchitoches IV–456b–57a
Ohio River V–142b, 145a,b
Platte River V–30b
Prairie du Chien V–387b
Red River of the North VI–64a–b
Rocky Mountains VI–160a
Saint Lawrence River VI–192a
Texas IV–197b; VII–36b
French Five Hundred III–148a
"French flats" I–143b
FRENCH FRONTIER POSTS III–119b; III–118a, 142a–b; IV–109b; VII–171a
Albany III–312a
Arkansas Post I–173b
Balize I–246b
Baton Rouge I–274b
boundary conflicts with English IV–46b
Carillon VII–56b
Fort Beauharnois I–281b, 281b; III–89b
Fort Carillon IV–86a
Fort Caroline V–370a
Fort Chambly IV–86b
Fort Condé I–499a; II–158a
Fort Crévecoeur II–257b
Fort de Chartres I–501a,b
Fort Detroit II–336b–37a, 337b
Fort Duquesne V–143a
Fort Frontenac III–124b
Fort La Baye III–311b
Fort La Galette IV–85a
Fort LeBoeuf IV–130a
Fort Machault IV–213b
Fort Massac IV–264a
Fort Maurepas IV–276b
Fort Miami IV–329a
Fort Niagara V–90a, 91b
Fort Orleans V–173a
Fort Ouiatenon V–176a
Fort Pentegoet V–260a
Fort Pimitoui V–315a
Fort Pontchartrain de Détroit V–356b
Fort Presque Isle V–399b
Fort Rosalie IV–455a; V–210b; VI–164a
Fort Saint Antoine VI–187a
Fort Saint Charles VI–188a
Fort Saint Frédéric II–267a; IV–86a, 87b
Fort Saint John IV–86b
Fort Saint Joseph VI–191b
Fort Saint Louis (Ill.) VI–195a
Fort Saint Louis (Tex.) VI–195a
Fort Saint Pierre VII–181a
Fort Tombecbee II–167b; VII–70b
Fort Toulouse VII–77a
Fort Wayne VII–262a
Franciscans III–94a–b
French and Indian War III–114b
Great Lakes III–216a; V–175b
Green Bay III–225b
Illinois Country III–330a–b
Indiana III–369b
Indian trade VII–95b
Isle aux Noix IV–86b
King William's War IV–49b–50a
Lake Nipigon IV–117b
Louisburg IV–192a
Mackinac IV–217b
Magazin Royal V–90a
Marin expedition IV–250b
Minnesota IV–355a–b
Mississippi Valley IV–193a
Natchitoches IV–456b; VI–189b
New York V–85a,b
Ohio Valley V–146a
Pennsylvania V–246b
Pointe Coupee V–335a
Port Royal V–369b, 370a
Prairie du Chien V–387b
Prudhomme Bluffs V–440b
Red River of the North VI–64b
Richelieu River IV–86a
Sandusky VI–208b
Sault Sainte Marie VI–219b
Susquehanna River I–223b
Venango VII–168b
Vincennes VII–188a
FRENCH GRANTS III–120a; III–148a
French Indochina II–315b
FRENCH IN THE PENOBSCOT REGION III–120b; I–466a; V–214b, 243b, 253b; VI–188a
French-language press V–75b
French Lick (N.C.) II–274a; III–271b; IV–452b
French Marine Ordinance (1681) I–14b
FRENCH MILLS (N.Y.) **III–120b**; IV–406a
French Morocco
World War II II–345a
French New Panama Canal Company V–201a
French North Africa
World War II IV–32b
French Northwest Africa I–308a
French Panama Canal Company V–201a, 204a
French Prairie VII–300a
FRENCH PRIVATEERS III–121a; IV–192a
FRENCH REFUGEES III–121a; III–315a
Champ d'Asile I–492a
South Carolina settlement II–124a
Tombigbee Valley VII–70b
French Revolution (1789) III–96a, 238b
British retaliation VI–104b
exiles V–342a
Federalist party VI–94a
Jacobin Clubs III–487b
liberty cap IV–143a
political refugees III–121a–b
Rights of Man VI–141a
Rule of the War of 1756 VI–169a
Spain VI–359a
U.S. neutrality V–34a, 36b
U.S. recognition III–456a
French Revolution (1830) III–96b, 122a
French Revolution, wars of the (1793–1802) I–114a, 126a

campaign of 1796 I–417a
Charleston trade I–496b–97a
Code Napoléon II–91b
Convention of 1800 II–215a
Federalists II–189a
Polly Admiralty Case V–355a
U.S. policy IV–402a–b
French's New Sensation (showboat) VI–283a
FRENCH SPOLIATION CLAIMS III–121b; II–215a; III–95b, 352a; V–15b
arbitration IV–5b
Naples claims IV–449a
prize cases III–98a
Frenchtown (Mich.) III–316a; VI–42a
See also Monroe
French Town (Wash.) VII–221a
FRENCH TRAVELERS IN AMERICA, EARLY III–122a
French West Indies
colonial trade II–92b, 118b–19a, 446b
Treaty of Paris II–126b
Freneau, Philip (ed.) III–108b; IV–161b, 463b; V–69b
Frenkel, Yakov (phys.) V–304a
FRENZIED FINANCE III–122b; III–433b; IV–424b
Freon II–9a, 421a; VI–213a
Freon 12 VI–70a
Frequency modulation (FM) II–424a, 425b; VI–16a–b
Frequent Wind, Operation (1975) VII–187a
Freud, Sigmund (psych.) IV–164a, 306a
Freudianism IV–408b
Frick, Henry Clay (ind.) III–80a; VI–455a; VII–89b
art collection II–104a
attempted assassination I–117a
Homestead Strike III–297a; IV–66a
Frick family V–322a
Fried, Rose II–105b
Friedan, Betty (ref.) VII–317b
Friedman, Milton (econ.) III–8b; IV–234a
Friedrichshafen (Ger.) II–344b
FRIENDLY ASSOCIATION III–122a
Friendly Botanic Societies IV–288a
FRIENDS, SOCIETY OF III–123a; VI–76a
Hicksites III–274a
Keith controversy IV–35b
pacifism VII–236a
slavery I–135a
Friends General Conference III–274b
Friendship (Maine). *See* Medumcook VI–395 (table)
FRIENDS OF DOMESTIC INDUSTRY III–124a
Friends of the New Germany III–172a
Friends' Public School of Philadelphia II–395a
Friends Service Council V–470b
Friends Society. *See* Sons of the South
Friends United Meeting V–470b
Friends World Committee for Consultation V–471a
Friends Yearly Meeting III–123b
Fries, John. *See* Frie's Rebellion
Friesenhahn Cave (Tex.) I–155a
FRIES'S REBELLION (1799) **III–124a**; I–41a; III–436b; VII–107a
Frigates II–313b; III–474b; V–25a,b, 26a; VII–240a,b, 241b, 242a, 242a, 243a–b
Alliance I–89a,b, 290b
Constellation II–190a–b
Constitution II–190b
President V–393b
Quasi War II–217b
War of 1812 II–217b
See also Warships
Frigidaire Company II–420b, 421b
Frigidaire refrigerator II–418a
FRINK AND WALKER STAGE LINES III–124a
Frio County (Tex.) V–139a
Frisch, Otto R. (phys.) V–300a
"Frisco." *See* Saint Louis–San Francisco Railroad
Frist Special Service Force VI–46b–47a
FRITCHIE, BARBARA, AND THE FLAG III–124a; III–100b
Frobisher, Benjamin (mer.) III–403b
Frobisher, Joseph (mer.) III–403b
Frobisher, Martin (expl.) III–240b; V–122a
Frock coat II–371b
Froebel, Friedrich (educ.) II–398b
Froehlke, Robert F. I–372a
"Frogmen" VII–139a
Frog Pond (Boston) I–345b
Frohman, Charles (theat. mgr.) VII–48b
Froines, John II–20b
Frolic (warship) V–424a; VII–252b
Fromme, Lynette ("Squeaky") VII–118b
Fromm–Reichman, Frieda (psych.) IV–306b
Frontenac, Comte de Palluau et de, Louis de Buade (col. gov.) III–124b–25a; IV–7a
Duluth explorations II–379b
Fort Frontenac V–156b
King William's War II–126a; IV–49b–50a, 200a; VI–2a
New France IV–109a–b
Salmon Falls attack VI–201a
Schenectady VI–225b
FRONTENAC, FORT (Ont., Can.) **III–124b**; I–358b–59a; III–58b, 116a; IV–109b; V–157a, 139b, 156b
Frontenac, Lake V–156b
FRONTENAC DESTROYS ONONDAGA (1696) **III–124b**
Frontera (Mex.) IV–252a, 322a, 325a
FRONTIER III–125a; VII–282b
animal husbandry IV–169b
cowboys II–249b
democracy II–326a
equality II–326a
expansionist movement I–33a
family II–485b–86a, 487a–b
fencing laws III–10a
folklore III–48b
food supply III–52a
free land III–107b
Great Plains III–220b
Great Revival III–221b
Harrison Land Act III–257b
homestead movement III–295b
Honkey–donk girls III–297b
housing III–309b
Indians and liquor III–398b
inland waterways VII–260a
Jeffersonian Democracy III–495b
land policy I–4a,b
land speculation IV–435a
log buildings IV–179b
logrolling IV–181a
long hunters IV–185a
lynching IV–208a
maple sugar IV–246b
McGuffey's Readers VI–227b
missionary activity IV–365a,b
Mississippi Valley IV–376a
newspaper V–70b
"New West" V–81b
pioneers V–316b
population growth II–326a
preemption V–389b
society II–259b
stagelines VI–379a, 380a
stump speakers VI–421b
surveyors VI–450a
tomahawk claims VII–70a
Turner theory III–282b
West VII–267b
westward movement II–326a
whiskey II–353b
wolves VII–311b
women VII–313a
FRONTIER, TRANSITION FROM III–126a
Minnesota IV–357a
Frontier days celebrations I–369a; VII–346b
FRONTIER DEFENSE III–126b; II–313b
Afro–American troops IV–339b
Cahaba Old Towns I–402a
Camp Supply VI–443b
Civil War III–400a
colonial plans of union II–121a–22a
fall line II–485a
Fort C.F. Smith VI–317b
Fort Francis E. Warren VII–237b
Fort Franklin VII–168b
Fort Hays III–266b
Fort Howard III–311b
fortifications III–78a
Fort Jesup III–501b
Fort King George IV–46b
Fort Leavenworth IV–129a
Fort Mason IV–263a
Fort Massachusetts IV–268b
Fort Owen V–178b
Fort Prince George V–408a
Fort Recovery VI–60a
Fort Riley VI–141b
Fort Scott VI–241a
Fort Sedgwick VI–254b
Fort Smith VI–317a
Fort Snelling VI–322b
Fort Stanton VI–385a
Fort Stanwix VI–385a
Fort Steuben VI–412a
Fort Washington (Ohio) VII–247a
Fort Wayne VII–262a
Fort Winnebago VII–306a
Fort Yuma VII–367a
Fort Zarah VII–368a
Galvanized Yankees III–148b
Indians and guns III–399a
Kansas IV–25b
Kentucky IV–42b
Middle Plantation VII–301a
militia IV–345b
Minnesota IV–355b
Nacogdoches IV–448b
Paxton Boys V–231a
presidios V–399b
Redstone Old Fort VI–65b
San Antonio VI–207b
Sandusky VI–208b
Southwest Point VI–357b
Stamp Act financing VI–381a
Texas VII–36b, 38a,b
Texas Rangers VII–42a
Washington District VII–250a
Watauga Association VII–253b
Frontier in American History III–203a

FRONTIER MERCHANT
III–127a; VII–273b–74a
general stores VI–416a
store boats VI–415b
sutlers VI–452b
Tarascon, Berthoud and Company VI–462a
See also Peddlers
Frontier missions. *See* Missions, Frontier
FRONTIER PREACHING
III–127b; IV–367a; V–77b
Frontiersmen I–278a, 309a; V–211a
See also Pioneers
Frontier trading posts. See Trading Posts, Frontier
"Front porch" campaign (1896) I–416b, 425b
Front Royal (Va.) VII–304a
FRONT ROYAL, BATTLE AT (1862) **III–128a**; III–487b
Frosch, Carl (elec. eng.) IV–352b
Frost, D. M. (off.) I–433b
Frost, Robert (poet) IV–164a
FROST-BITTEN CONVENTION (1836) **III–128a**
Frost v. *Leighton* (1739) I–145a
Froth flotation process V–103a
Frothingham, A. L., Jr. (archaeol.) IV–2b
Frothingham, Octavius Brooks (cler.) V–287a
Frothingham v. *Mellon* (1923) III–211b
Frozen foods II–43b; III–55b; VI–70a
FRUIT GROWING
III–128a
alcoholic beverages II–353b
Delaware II–320b
Idaho III–328b
imports VII–90a
refrigeration VII–84a
South America VI–343b
Southwest VI–355b
storm warnings VII–264a
Virginia VII–194a
Washington State VII–248a
See also Citrus Industry
FRUITLANDS III–129b; VII–98a
Fruits II–373a–b; III–52b, 53b, 54b
Fry, D. W. (phys.) V–301a–b
Fry, Edmund V–412a
Fry, John (monk) I–452a
Fry, Joseph (sea capt.) VII–204a
Fry, Joshua (surv.) III–219a,b; VII–74a
Fry, Thornton (math.) II–154b
Fry, William Henry (comp.) IV–438b
Fryeburg (Maine) IV–199a
Frying pan, electric II–419a
FTC. *See* Federal Trade Commission
Fuca, Juan de (Apostolos Valerianos) (expl.) V–180a
Fuchs, Klaus I–123b; VI–428b
Fuel
buffalo chips II–487a
coal II–86a
daylight saving time II–296b
Geological Survey III–163a
jet engine IV–44b
liquid IV–350b
Osage hedge V–174a
resources VI–48a–b
tariff VI–471a
FUEL ADMINISTRATION
III–129b; I–390b; IV–135b
Fuel cells I–276b
Fuel shortage (1973–74) I–69b, 230b–31a
Fugill, Thomas VI–263b
FUGIOS III–129b; I–483a
Fugitives (org.) I–33b
Fugitives from justice
constitutional provision II–202b
extradition II–478b
FUGITIVE SLAVE ACTS
III–130a; I–138a; VI–307b
colonization movement II–127a
Compromise of 1850 II–150a
constitutionality I–2a,b
federal–state enforcement VII–154b
Hamlet case III–247a
Higher–law doctrine III–275a
kidnapping of free blacks IV–45a
nullification V–125b; VI–397a
Oberlin–Wellington rescue case V–130b
opposition to I–135b
personal liberty laws V–263b
Prigg v. *Pennsylvania* V–406b
Shadrach case VI–267b
slaves as contraband II–212b
Supreme Court ruling IV–43b
trials VII–117b
Uncle Tom's Cabin VII–137b
upheld by Supreme Court IV–8a
Fugitive slaves VI–307a
Burns case I–387a,b
Champaign County I–491b
Christiana Affair II–34b
Civil War II–67a
constitutional provision II–202b
contraband II–212a
Pearl case V–239a
recovery II–152a
return of I–10b
Seminole VI–259b, 260a
Underground Railroad VII–138a
Webster–Fairbank trials VII–265a
Fulbright, J. William (states.) II–362a; III–130b–31a
FULBRIGHT ACT AND GRANTS III–130b; II–401a, 470b–71a
Fulbright-Hays Act (1961) II–401a; III–130b
Fuld, Mrs. Felix (philan.) III–423b
FULL DINNER PAIL
III–131b; I–426a; VI–313a, 463b
Full employment II–480b–81a
Full Employment Act (1946) III–8a; IV–78a; V–398a; VII–140a–b
Fuller, Buckminster (builder) I–165b
Fuller, Horace S. II–99b
Fuller, Loie (dancer) II–287a,b, 288a
Fuller, Margaret (critic, soc. ref.) VII–98a
Fuller, Melville W. (jur.) II–136a; III–351b; IV–14a; VI–446a
Fuller, Sidney IV–120a
Fuller and Lord I–337b
Full faith and credit II–202b; III–9b
Fullinwider, S. P. (off.) V–119b
Fulminate of mercury II–163a
Fulton (Mo.) III–474b
FULTON (steamship)
III–131b; V–212b; VII–240b
Fulton, Robert (eng.) III–312a
Clermont I–81b; III–131b, 312b; IV–310a; VI–280b; VII–100b
Demologos II–329a; III–36a; VII–240b
Hudson steamboat monopoly III–131b–32a
Nautilus V–8a; VI–422b
steamboat monopoly III–178a, 178a; V–289a; VI–407a
steamboat patents V–63a
steamboats IV–374a; VI–148a–b, 408a, 409a, 410a; VII–260a
Fulton focus (culture) V–148a
FULTON'S FOLLY
III–131b; VI–407a; VII–100b
Fulton the First (steam warship). *See Demologos*
Functionalism (psych.) V–442a
FUNDAMENTAL CONSTITUTIONS III–132a; II–117b; IV–94b
Fundamental Constitutions of Carolina. *See* Carolina, Fundamental Constitutions of
Fundamentalism II–466a; V–78a, 392a; VI–79a, 82a
Christian and Missionary Alliance II–34b
theory of evolution VI–230a–b, 239b
Fundamentalist–modernist controversy V–470b
Fundamental Methodist church IV–319b
Fundamental Orders of Connecticut. *See* Connecticut, Fundamental Orders of
Fundamentals (tracts) VI–79a
Fund for Adult Education II–401b
Funding Act (1790) II–274b; IV–393b; VI–294a
Funding of revolutionary debt. *See* Assumption and Funding of Revolutionary War Debts
Fundy, Bay of V–214b
Fungi I–241a
Funk, Casimir (biochem.) I–303a
Funk, I. K. (pub.) I–334b
Funk and Wagnall II–340a
Funny papers V–72a–b
Funston, Frederick S. (off.) III–133a; V–281b
FUNSTON'S CAPTURE OF AGUINALDO (1901)
III–133a
Fu–ping prefecture (Kor.) II–54b
FUR AND FUR-BEARING ANIMALS III–133a; III–150a
frontier merchants III–127a
Great Lakes III–142a
Indian trade III–402b
Northwest Coast culture III–361a
Fur-Bearing Animals: A Monograph of North American Mustelidae IV–232b
Fur cloth II–334b
Fur farming III–133b
Furman v. *Georgia* (1972) I–450b; III–250a; V–464b
Furnace, electric II–7b, 422a–b
Furnace, resistance II–422a
Furnaces III–269a
"Furnishing merchant" II–238a
Furnishings, home. *See* Interior Decoration
FURNITURE III–133b; I–163b; VI–242b
collecting II–98b
folk art III–47a
fur III–133b
interior decoration III–445a
retail stores II–354b
sales II–332b
Shakers VI–268a
White House VII–292a
FURNITURE INDUSTRY
III–138a; III–413b; VII–82b
chairmaking I–490a

Grand Rapids IV–331b
Massachusetts IV–266b
New South V–67a
North Carolina V–116b
Tennessee VII–26a
Virginia VII–196a
Furniture workers
union IV–63b
Furor (destroyer) VI–216b
Furriers unions IV–70b
FUR TRADE III–139b;
II–477a; III–133a–b, 150a, 413b; VII–82b
Albany I–81b; II–383a; III–312a
Allegheny Mountains I–88b
American Fur Company I–105a,b, 289b, 399a; III–226b
Anglo–French rivalry II–458b; III–114b–15a
Arizona I–172a
Astoria I–83a, 209a
Bad Lands I–242b
Battle of Pierre's Hole V–310b
beaver I–282a; VII–296b
Bent's Fort I–174b, 290a
Big Horn Mountains I–296b
Bonneville expedition I–329b–30a
bourgeois I–354b
British posts III–375a; VII–270a
California I–280a
chantier I–493b
Chequamegon Bay II–13b
Cherokee III–380b
Chicago II–17a
China I–446a,b; II–28b, 219b; III–181a
Chippewa II–30b–3la
Chouteau family II–34a–b, 376a
colonial II–119b, 453a; VI–108a
Colorado II–128a
Colorado River II–129b, 131b
Columbia River II–l3lb
Connecticut Valley III–309a
coureurs de bois II–246a
Courthouse Rock II–246b
Dalles II–285b
Detroit II–71a, 336b–37a
Dutch West India Company V–61a
East Indies II–388a
exports VII–86a
Forks of the Ohio V–143a
Fort Benton III–77b–78a
Fort Boise I–327b
Fort Bridger I–363a
Fort Crawford II–254a
Fort Hall III–243b
Fort John IV–1b
Fort Kiowa IV–51a
Fort Laramie IV–108a
Fort Mortimer IV–415a
Fort Nassau IV–454a
Fort Niagara V–90a–b
Fort Okanogan V–147a
Fort Ouiatenon V–176a
Fort Pierre V–310a
Fort Snelling VI–322b
Fort Uintah VII–137a
Fort Union VII–145b
Fort Vancouver VII–165b
Fort William Augustus V–139b
Fox Indians III–88b
French exploration III–118a
frontier III–126b
Gila Trail III–179b
Grand Portage III–209a
great fortunes III–78b, 79a
Great Valley III–223b
Green Bay III–226a
Green River III–227a
Griffon III–228b
Gros Ventre III–229a
Henrys Fork III–273a
holes of the mountains III–291a
Hudson's Bay Company III–313a
hunting grounds III–318a–b
Idaho III–327b
Illinois fur brigade III–331b
Indiana III–369b
Indian factory system II–480a
Indians III–398b, 402b–04a
Iroquois Beaver Land Deed III–476b
Iroquois raids III–399b
irrigation III–477a
Kansas IV–25b
Kennebec Trading Post IV–37b
Laconia grant IV–82b
Lake Ontario V–156b
Lake Superior VI–443a
La Vérendrye, Sieur de IV–117b
Lisa and Company IV–159b
Mackinac IV–218a, 332b
mangeurs de lard IV–237a
Manuel's Fort IV–242a
Michigan IV–330b
Minnesota IV–355b–56a
Missouri IV–27b, 377b
Missouri River IV–379b, 380b
Mohawk Valley IV–386b
Montana IV–403a
mountain men IV–422a
mountain passes V–224a,b
Navigation Acts V–16a
Nebraska V–30b
Nevada V–39b
New France IV–109b
New Hampshire V–53b
New Netherland V–62a
New Orleans V–62a
New Plymouth Colony V–65a
New Sweden Colony V–80b
New York V–86a
North West Company V–121a
Northwest Territory IV–355b
Ogden's Hole V–140a
Ohio V–140a–b
Ohio River V–145a–b
Ohio Valley VI–271a
Oregon V–164b, 165a, 167a, 167b
Oregon Trail V–168a–b; VI–153b
Pacific Fur Company V–180a
Pacific Northwest III–263a
pack trains V–184a
Pembina V–244a
Pemmican War V–244b
Pennsylvania V–246b
Pensacola Congress V–254b
Pikes Peak V–311a
pioneers V–316b
Platte River Trail V–330b
Prairie du Chien V–387b–88a
Proclamation of 1763 VI–110b, 112a–b
Radisson's *Voyages* VI–18b
Red River cart traffic VI–63b
Red River of the North VI–64b
Rocky Mountain Fur Company VI–160a
Rocky Mountains VI–160a–b
routes I–340b–41a
Russia I–74b; VI–180b
Sagadahoc VI–185b
Saint Lawrence River VI–192b
Saint Louis IV–376b; VI–194a
Saint Louis Missouri Fur Company VI–195b
Saint Paul VII–134a
Santa Fe IV–377a; VI–215a
Sault Sainte Marie VI–220a
Savannah VI–220a
Schenectady VI–225b
Scioto Trail VI–239b
sealing VI–245a
sea otter VI–247a
Smith explorations VI–318a
Snake River VI–322b
snowshoes VI–323a
South Carolina VII–352a
Southwest Fur Company VI–357b
Spanish–Missouri Fur Company VI–367a
Spokane House VI–375b
steel trap VI–411b
Sublette's Cutoff VI–422a, 422a
Taos VI–461a
Taos Trail VI–461a
Tennessee VII–25a
Tonquin VII–72a
trading posts VII–95b
transportation I–380a–b, 445b
trappers' rendezvous VII–103b
trapping VII–104b
Utah VII–161a,b
Venango VII–168b
Vermont VII–171a
Vincennes VII–188b
Virginia VII–201b
voyageurs VII–211b
wagon trains VII–217a–b
Walker expedition VII–220a
Washington State VII–247a,b
western merchants VII–273b
Wisconsin VII–306b–07a,b, 307b
wolves VII–312a
Yellowstone River VII–357b–58a
Fur Traders Descending the Missouri (paint.) V–191a
Furuseth, Andrew (labor leader) VI–246b
Furuseth Seamen's Act. *See* Seamen's Act of 1915
Fur workers' union II–145a
Futa Pass (It.) III–201a
Futures market II–430a, 470b
F. W. Woolworth and Company III–32b, 33a
Fyrd IV–345a, 346b

G

Gabarus Bay IV–192a
Gable, Dan (athlete) V–154b
Gabrielino (Indians) I–446a; III–363a, 503a; IV–366a
GABRIEL'S INSURRECTION (1800) **III–145a**; III–437a; VI–303b, 304a, 307a
Gadsden, Christopher (off., pol.) VI–47b, 128a, 347a
GADSDEN, FORT (Fla.) **III–145a**
Gadsden, James (dipl.) III–145b; IV–199b; V–231a
GADSDEN PURCHASE (1853) **III–145a**; I–126b, 352a; II–475a; III–68a, 230a; IV–328a; V–443b; VI–355a–b; VII–111b
acreage V–445 (table)
Arizona territory I–172a
exploration II–477b
Lower California IV–199b
Mesilla IV–315b
Mexican boundary IV–321b
southern railroad route VI–353b
GAF. *See* General Aniline and Fil; German Air Force
Gafsa (Tun.) IV–32b
Gagarin, Yuri (cosmonaut) I–209b; VI–159b
Gage, Thomas (off.) II–134a; IV–266a; VI–199a, 372b
Connolly's plot II–184a
Fort William and Mary VII–300b

GAGE, THOMAS (cont.)
Indian trade I–278a
Lexington and Concord VI–123a
Pontiac's War II–337b
Quartering Act V–471b
reserve troops VII–80a
Stamp Act VI–111a–b
Gage, Thomas (trav.) VII–270b
GAG RULE, ANTISLAVERY III–145b; I–137b, 138b; IV–358b; V–265b, 266b
Gail Hamilton. *See* Dodge, Mary Abigail
Gaine, Hugh (print.) I–335a
Gaines, Edmund P. (off.) III–88b; VI–260a; VII–311a
GAINES, FORT (Ala.) **III–146a**
Gaines, Fort (Minn.). *See* Ripley, Fort
Gaines, George S. (mer.) III–146b; VI–197b
GAINES CASE (1834–90) **III–146a**
GAINES' MILL, BATTLE OF (1862) **III–146a**; I–248a; V–245b; VI–263b
GAINES' TRACE III–146b
Gaines v. *Canada* (1938) I–372b; II–401b, 457a; VI–256b
Gainesville (Va.) I–374a
Gaines wheat VII–286b
Gaithersburg (Md.) IV–462b
GALAHAD. *See* Merrill's Marauders
GALÁPAGOS ISLANDS III–146b; II–463b
Galaus, Jean François de, Comte de La Pérouse (expl.) III–238a
Galbraith, John Kenneth (econ.) VII–139b
GALCIT Rocket Research Project III–502a
Gale, Leonard D. (chem.) I–276a; VII–18b
Gale, William A. (fur trader) III–274b
Galena (Ill.) III–147a, 450a; IV–122a; VII–307b
Galena (min.) IV–122b
Galena and Chicago Union Railroad VI–25b, 33b
GALENA-DUBUQUE MINING DISTRICT III–147a; IV–122a,b; VII–307b
Galena River III–147a
Galenson, Walter (econ.) VII–141a
Galerie (arch.) I–160b
Gales, Joseph, Jr. (pub.) I–3a; IV–465b
Galesburg (Ill.) III–493a; IV–155b, 338b
Galey, John H. V–271b–72a
Galinée, René de Bréhant (expl.) II–458b
Gall (Indian) I–313a; VI–295b
Gall, Franz J. (physic.) V–293b
Galland, Pierre Victor (paint.) V–191a
Gallatin, Albert (fin., states.) VI–455a
bank deposits I–252a
canal construction IV–87b
Coast and Geodetic Survey II–87a–b
constitutional system II–326b
Convention of 1818 II–215b
embargo of 1807 II–437a
federal surplus VI–449a
internal improvements III–147a, 448b; VI–145b, 450a
national sinking fund VI–294a
report on manufactures III–147a
Treaty of Ghent III–176b; VII–235b
Gallatin, Albert (ling. schol.) I–128a
Gallatin, Albert E. (paint.) II–105a
Gallatin River IV–378a, 379b; V–225a
GALLATIN'S REPORT ON MANUFACTURES (1820) **III–147a**
GALLATIN'S REPORT ON ROADS, CANALS, HARBORS, AND RIVERS (1808) **III–147a**; III–448b; VI–145b, 450a
Gallatin Valley IV–403a
Gallaudet, Edward M. (educ.) III–248a
Gallaudet, Thomas H. (educ.) III–248a
Gallaudet College III–248a, 267b; VI–327b
Gallaudet Company I–236a
Gallego mills VII–194a
Galleons II–217b
Gallery of the Pennsylvania Academy of the Fine Arts II–101a
GALLEY BOATS III–147b; IV–374a
GALLIPOLIS (Ohio) **III–148a**; III–120b; VI–239a
Galloway, G. N. (hist.) IV–8a
Galloway, Joseph (law.) VII–165a
See also Galloway's Plan of Union
GALLOWAY'S PLAN OF UNION (1774) **III–148a**; III–346b; VI–114a
Gallup (N.Mex.) I–106b, 329b; VII–372a
Gallup, George H. (pollster) V–453b
Gallup Poll V–453b
Gallwitz Army Group VI–197b
GALPHIN CLAIM III–148a
Galt family IV–305a
Galt Hotel (Louisville) V–32b
Galtier, Lucian (cler.) VII–134a
Galton, Francis (psych.) III–440a
Galvanic deflagrators I–276a
Galvanization
zinc V–103a
GALVANIZED YANKEES III–148b; VI–300b
Galveston (Tex.)
commission government II–137b
Mina expedition IV–348a
Texas Revolution VII–38a
Galveston, Harrisburg and San Antonio Railroad VI–37a
GALVESTON, LOSS AND RECAPTURE OF (1862, 1863) **III–148b**; II–63a; VII–39b
Galveston Bay IV–452a
Galveston Island (Tex.)
French refugees I–492a
GALVESTON PIRATES III–148b; I–93b; V–320a
GALVESTON STORM (1900) **III–149a**; II–351a; III–37a, 319b
Gálvez, Bernardo de (col. adm.) III–38b; IV–193a; VI–363b, 365b, 367b
capture of Fort Bute I–398a
capture of Manchac IV–234b
Fort Panmure V–210b
New Orleans I–367a
Pensacola V–254b
seizure of Mobile IV–382a
Willing expedition VII–303a
Gálvez, José de (states.) I–405a
Galveztown (La.) III–479a
Gambier, James (nav. off.) III–176b
Gamblers IV–52b, 64a
GAMBLING III–149a; VI–301a; VII–312b
cow towns II–252a
crime II–258a
electronic surveillance II–427b
horse racing III–304b–05a
houses II–261b
laws II–260b
moral codes IV–408a
Nevada V–40a
Ohio River VI–147b
organized crime II–259b–63a
padlock injunction V–184a
poker V–336a
Revenue Act of 1951 V–339b
saloons VI–201b
state-run II–263a
steamboat racing VI–407b
stock exchange II–470a–b
syndicates II–258b
temperance movement VII–22b
GAME, EARLY ABUNDANCE OF III–150a; VII–296b–97a
wolves VII–311a
Game laws VII–296b–98a
Game preserves VII–297b
Games theory IV–121b
Game Warden, Operation (1966) V–22a
Gamma globulin IV–292a
polio V–340b
Gamma rays V–298a,b, 299a, 305b
Gamow, George (phys.) V–300b, 301a, 303a
Gandhi, Mohandas II–50b
Gangs, criminal II–258b
Chicago II–18a
Gangsters. *See* Crime, Organized
Gannett newspaper chain V–76b
Gans, David (phys.) V–299b, 301b
Gans, Joe (pugilist) V–423a
Gansevoort, Peter (off.) V–172b
Gant, Captain (trapper) VII–104b–05a
Gant and Blackwell expedition (1831) VII–104b–05a
"Gantlope" III–154b
Gantt, Henry L. VI–234b
Gaps, mountain. *See* Passes, Mountain
GAR. *See* Grand Army of the Republic
Garand rifle. *See* M-1 Rifle
Garay grant III–145b
Garbage collectors
Memphis strike (1968) IV–75b
unionization IV–75b
Garbage removal. *See* Sanitation, Environmental
Garber Field (Okla.) IV–334a
Garcés, Francisco (miss.) I–172a, 403b; III–150b; IV–367b; VI–368a
GARCÉS-ANZA ROUTE III–150b
Garcia, Calixto (rev.) VI–362a
GARCÍA, MESSAGE TO (1898) **III–150b**; VI–373b
García Íñiguez, Calixto (rev.). *See* García, Message to
Garcitas Creek VI–195a–b
Gardeau Reservation (N.Y.) V–139b
Garden, Alexander (nat.) I–497a; III–26b, 29b; V–326a
Gárdenas, García López de (expl.) III–208a
Garde Nationale IV–463b
Garden cities II–46b
Garden clubs III–151b
Gardenier, Barent (pol.) II–437a
GARDENING III–150b
ornaments III–47a
vegetable IV–96b
windmills VII–305a
Garden of the Gods V–311a

Garden State VI–394 (table)
Gardiner, David III–152a
Gardiner, George A. (landowner) III–152a
Gardiner, John III–152a
Gardiner, Lion (off.) III–152a; VI–223a
GARDINER AWARD III–152a
Gardiner's Bay III–152a; IV–185b
GARDINER'S ISLAND III–152a
Gardner (Mass.) I–490b; IV–266b
Gardner, Frank (off.) V–369a
Gardner, John W. (offi.) III–267b
Gardner, Rowland (settler) VI–374a
Gardner's Hole (Wyo.) III–291a
Gardoqui, Diego de (dipl.) I–169b; III–77b, 492b; V–59a; VI–359a, 365b
Garfield (Utah) III–14a
Garfield, James A. II–176 (table); V–142a, 394b, 395 (table), 398b; VI–93a, 243b; VII–178a
—*Congressman:*
census of 1880 I–482a
Crédit Mobilier II–256a
Degolyer Case II–319b
—*President:*
assassination I–146a, 202b; III–152b; V–228a; VI–375b
campaign of 1880 I–423b; III–152b; IV–409b
disability V–397a
Garfield, James Rudolph (law., offi.) VII–31a
GARFIELD–BLAINE–CONKLING CONTROVERSY III–152b
Garibaldi, Giuseppe III–338a
Garigliano River III–235b
Garland, Alexander H. (pol.) IV–376a
Garland, Augustus Hill (law.) III–152b–53a
Garland, Fort (Colo.) IV–268b
Garland, Hamlin (au.) IV–163b
GARLAND CASE (1867) **III–152b**; IV–202b; V–99a; VII–35a
Garman, Samuel (zool.) VI–90b–91a
Garment cutters IV–64a
Garment industry
Chicanos IV–77a
Jewish influence IV–10a
support of F. D. Roosevelt IV–81b
unemployment VII–140b
union security provisions IV–74b–75a
Garner, John Nance (pol.) II–177 (table); VII–40b
campaign of 1932 I–428b
campaign of 1936 I–429a; V–47b
Committee on Un–American Activities VI–428a
vice–presidency VII–180 (table)
Garner v. *Louisiana* (1961) II–50b
Garnet, Henry Highland (cler.) I–138a
Garnett, Deborah VII–316a
Garnett, Robert S. (off.) VI–138a
Garrad, T. T. (off.) I–435a
Garraty, John A. (hist.) II–341a
Garret, Thomas (mer.) VII–138b
Garrett, Mary E. (philan.) IV–3a
Garrett, Richard H. (farmer) IV–154b, 155a
Garrison, Lindley M. (law., offi.) VII–325a
Garrison, William Lloyd (abolitionist) I–28a, 136a, 137a; III–153a; IV–267b; V–235b, 280a; VI–13b
Genius of Universal Emancipation III–162b
Liberator II–436a; IV–141a
opponents IV–143b
"peculiar institution" V–241b
Garrison Dam III–322b; V–117b, 455b; VI–147a
GARRISON MOB III–153a
Garrison's *Liberator. See Liberator*
Garry, Fort (Can.) V–244a; VI–63b
Garter snakes VI–91a
Garvan, Francis P. (law.) II–100b
Garvey, Marcus (black nationalist) I–21b; II–127b; III–254a; IV–166b; V–200a
Gary (Ind.) III–438a, 473b
Gary, Elbert H. (law., bus.) IV–69b; VI–157a
Gas III–249b
chemical warfare II–9a, 12a
coal II–84b
cooking II–418a
fires and explosions II–348a–49a
heating II–418a
municipal ownership IV–427b, 428a
U.S. Geological Survey III–164a
See also Gasoline; Natural Gas Industry
Gas acetylene II–422a
Gas Belt VII–369a
Gas coolant II–418a
Gascoyne–Cecil, Robert, 3rd Marquis of Salisbury (states.) V–153a; VII–170b
Gas discharge tubes III–156a
Gas gangrene IV–291a, 298a
"Gasless Sundays" III–129b
Gaslight II–412b, 413b–14a; IV–153a,b
Gas mask I–197a
Gasoline III–409a,b; V–267a–b, 270a; VI–203a, 356b–57a
advertising I–19a
ethyl I–228b
lead additives V–102b
price quotations V–402b
rationing I–230a
shortage (1973–74) I–230a–31a; VI–472b
synthetic II–9a
World War II III–174a; VII–336a
Gasoline engine I–35b, 228b; IV–420a
agriculture I–38a
automobile I–225b, 226a,b, 227a
trucks IV–419b
Gasoline service stations II–354b; VII–85a
GASOLINE TAXES III–153a; III–450b; VII–7b, 10b, 11a
Oregon V–165b
road construction VI–152a, 155b
sales taxes VI–200b
Gaspar River I–434a
***GASPÉE*, BURNING OF THE** (1772) **III–153b**; II–93a; VI–112b, 132b; VII–81a
Gaspée Point (R.I.) III–153b
Gaspé Peninsula I–492b
Gasser, Herbert S. (physiol.) V–100a; VI–158b
Gaston County v. *United States* (1969) III–93b
Gastonia (N.C.) III–154a; IV–70b
GASTONIA RIOTS (1929) **III–154a**
Gastrointestinal disorders II–373b; IV–150a
Gasworks II–5b
Gat (Libya) I–266b
Gatch, T. L. (aeronaut) I–248b
Gates, Horatio (off.) III–276a; IV–211b; V–42b; VI–170a
Battle of Camden I–412a,b; VI–124b, 351b
battles of Freeman's Farm III–108a–b
Bemis Heights VI–123b
Burgoyne's invasion I–385a,b
Conway Cabal II–218a
invasion of Canada I–436a,b
Saratoga VI–217b
Sullivan–Clinton campaign VI–438a
War and Ordnance Board VII–226b
Gates, John W. (speculator) I–267a; III–79b
Gates, Thomas (col. adm.) VI–338a; VII–199b
Gates, William, Jr. (inv.) IV–274a–b
Gates Commission VII–208a
Gates County (N.Y.) II–147a
Gateway Arch VI–194b
"Gateway to the West." *See* Pittsburgh
Gatlin (Ariz.) III–289b
Gatling, Richard J. (inv.). *See* Gatling Gun
GATLING GUN III–154a; I–49b; II–67a; IV–215a, 431a
Gato class (submarine) VI–423a
GATT. *See* General Agreement on Tariffs and Trade
Gauge, railroad VI–27b
GAUGERS, TOWN III–154b
Gauley River I–457a
Gault, In re (1967) IV–23b
"GAUNTLET, RUNNING THE" III–154b; III–376b
Gauss, Carl Friedrich (math., astron.) III–454a; VI–206b
Gautier, Théophile (au.) II–287a
Gavelkind III–464a
Gavilan Peak. *See* Hawk's Peak Episode
Gavins Point Dam VI–147a
Gayoso de Lemos, Manuel (col. gov.) II–22a; IV–456a; V–100b
Gaza Strip III–481b; IV–236b; VI–430a
Gazette of the United States (news.) III–202a; V–69b, 181a
Gazette Times. See Pittsburgh Gazette
G. C. Murphy and Company III–33a
G. D. Searle Company V–274a
Gear drive IV–419b
Geary, John W. (pol.) I–342a; IV–31a; VII–261b
Geary Act (1892) II–29a
Geary County (Kans.) VI–141b
Gebhart v. *Bolton* I–372b
Geddes, Henry (nav. off.) V–15a
Geddes, James (eng.) I–442b
Geddes, Patrick (biol.) II–46b
Gedrioz, K. K. (chem.) VI–334a
Gee, Joshua V–409a
Geechee (dial.). *See* Gullah
Geese III–51a, 150a
Geiger, Hans (phys.) V–298a
Gela (It.) VI–284b
Gelelemend (Indian). *See* Killbuck
Gellatly, Arthur (bus.) II–103b
Gell–Mann, Murray (phys.) V–100a, 296a, 297b
GELPCKE* v. *DUBUQUE (1864) **III–154b**
Gemini Project I–63b, 64a, 210a–b; IV–459b–60a; VI–159a
Gem lamp IV–89a
"Gems" (photog.) VII–62b
Gems, state VI–392a
Gem State VI–393 (table)
Genealogical libraries II–294a

Genealogy
census records I–482b
demography II–327b
General (locomotive) I–118b
General Accounting Office II–152a, 501a–b
General Agreement on Tariffs and Trade III–113b–14a, 161a; VI–52b, 468b–69a, 469b, 470a–b, 471a; VII–88b, 89a, 109a, 112b
General Aniline and Film V–292b
GENERAL ARMSTRONG (privateer) **III–155a**
General Assembly of the Presbyterian Church III–385b
General Association of Regular Baptist Churches I–265b
General Chemical Company II–8b
General Church of the New Jerusalem V–58b
General Conference (Quakers) V–470b
General Conference of Mennonite Brethren Churches IV–303a
General Conference of the Mennonite Church IV–303a
General Convention (Swedenborgian Church) V–58b
General Conventions (Episcopal church) V–179b
GENERAL COURT, COLONIAL III–155a; VII–94b, 95a–b
Connecticut VI–151b
Gorges' Province of Maine III–200a
land grants IV–91b
lecture days IV–131a
Massachusetts II–35b; III–259b; IV–60b, 269a, 269b–70a,b, 271a, 271a; VI–358b
negative voice V–32a
New Plymouth Colony V–65a
plantations V–324a
training day VII–97a
General Dynamics I–238a
General Education Board III–83a; IV–286b
General Electric Company II–412b, 414a–16a, 419b–20b, 421b, 423b–24a; IV–268a; VI–226a; VII–124a
fair-trade prices II–483a
lamp manufacture IV–153b
laser development IV–263a
locomotives IV–177b
Niagara Falls power V–92b
radio VI–15a, 16b
silicone II–12b
television VII–21a
vacuum tubes VII–163a,b
GENERAL ELECTRIC RESEARCH LABORATORY III–155b; II–417a; III–409a; IV–153b, 154a, 300b; V–295a
incandescent lamp IV–88b
vacuum tube VI–15a
General Exchange Act (1922) III–75b
General Federation of Women's Clubs V–466a
General Fireproofing III–137a
General Foods Corporation I–487b
General Forfeiture Act (1890) IV–94b
General History of Virginia, New England, and Summer Isles III–280a
General Jessup (steamer) II–129b
General Land Office. *See* Land Office, U.S. General
General Magazine and Historical Chronicle IV–161a, 221b
General Managers' Association V–463a
General Medical Sciences Institute IV–465a
General Mills I–488a; III–44b, 45b
General Missionary Convention of the Baptist Denomination III–385b
General Monk (brig) III–320b
General Motors Acceptance Corporation I–227b; III–423a
General Motors Corporation I–227a, 229a; II–420b; III–80a; IV–273a, 331b; VII–123b, 124a
aircraft IV–433a
Freon II–9a
industrial research III–409b
locomotives IV–177b
mass-transit I–231b
refrigeration VI–70a
research I–197b
strike IV–74a
United Auto Workers I–230a; IV–72b
General Mound Area IV–420b
General Munitions Board VII–231b
General Neighborhood Renewal Plan II–47b
GENERAL ORDER NO. 38 (1863) **III–156a**; VII–164b
See Civil War General Order No. 100
General Revision Act (1891) V–445a
General Seafoods Corporation III–29a
General Services Administration I–168a; II–135a, 498b
General Services Agency III–299b
General Sherman (schooner) IV–54b
General Sherman tree VI–262b
General Slocum (steamer) II–349b
General Staff, Army I–188b–89a
General Staff, College I–191a
General Staff Corps I–188b
General stores. *See* Stores, General
General Synod (Lutheran church) IV–206a
General Taylor's Rough and Ready Almanac I–91a
General Theological Seminary (N.Y.) II–455a; V–179b; VI–78a
General Theory of Employment, Interest and Money III–195a
General Time Convention I–111b; VI–28a
General Tire and Rubber Corporation VI–168a
General Tom Thumb (Charles Stratton) I–268b
General Treaty of Inter-American Arbitration (1929) VII–112b
GENERAL WELFARE CLAUSE III–156b; II–197a, 199b; VII–4a–b
congressional powers II–171b, 195b, 453b
congressional spending II–178b, 476a
education II–395b
police power II–440a
General William T. Sherman (sculp.) VI–243b
"General Winter" I–438b
Genera of North American Plants, and a Catalogue of the Species, to the Year 1817 V–326b
Genera of North American Reptiles and a Synopsis of the Species VI–90a
Generating plants, electric II–415a–16b
Generators
electrostatic II–278a
hydroelectric power III–320b
self-excited II–413b
Genesee Castle (N.Y.) VI–438a
Genesee County (N.Y.) V–91a, 463b
Genesee River IV–99a; VII–293b
aqueduct II–459b
Iroquois III–475a
Phelps-Gorham purchase I–375b
waterpower IV–347b
GENESEE ROAD III–157a
Genesee Valley II–460a; III–43a, 45a, 291a–b
Genêt, Edmond Charles (dipl.) III–487b; V–422a
See also Genêt Mission
Genêt, Jean (playwright) VII–50b
Gene theory III–157a
Genetic code III–157b
GENETICS III–157a; I–304a; II–13a
botanical experiments I–349b–50a
Carnegie Institution I–457a
defoliants II–319b
DNA II–357b
Eskimo II–461b–62a
"Jukes" Family IV–20a
"Kallikak" Family IV–24b
molecular biology IV–388b
Rockefeller Foundation VI–158a
GENETICS, APPLIED III–158b
Genetics Department of the Carnegie Institute II–97a
GENÊT MISSION (1793) **III–159b**; III–96a–b, 455b; IV–196a, 402b
campaign of 1796 I–417a
Little Sarah IV–169b
Louisiana IV–193b
Geneva (N.Y.) III–157a
Geneva (Switz.)
International Labor Office III–455a
penal congresses V–416a
Young Women's Christian Association VII–364a
Geneva, University of II–396a
GENEVA ACCORDS OF 1954 III–159b; I–124b; II–489b; III–161a; VII–182b, 183a
Geneva Agreement (1930). *See* General Agreement on Tariffs and Trade
Geneva Arbitration (1871) I–121b; III–352a
Geneva award (1872) IV–4b, 5b
Geneva College (Pa.) I–272a
GENEVA CONFERENCES III–160b; V–233b
Alabama Claims VII–248b, 249a
disarmament V–35b
General Agreement on Tariffs and Trade VI–469b; VII–89a
Indochina War III–159b–60a
Kennedy Round VI–470a–b
Laos cease-fire III–452b
law of the sea III–457a
laws of war VII–225b, 226a
naval parity IV–183a
partition of Indochina IV–107a
Three-Power Naval Conference III–162a
GENEVA CONVENTIONS III–161b; II–213a; V–233a; VI–61b
Geneva Conventions on the Law of the Sea (1958) III–457a

Genevan Bible I–293b
Geneva Protocol (1925) II–9b; VII–225b
GENEVA THREE-POWER NAVAL CONFERENCE (1927) **III–162a**; III–160b–61a; V–10a; VI–424a
Geneva Tribunal (1872) II–213a
Genie (missile) IV–363b
GENIUS OF UNIVERSAL EMANCIPATION (period.) **III–162b**; II–436a
GENIZARO (Indians) **III–162b**
Genoa (It.) III–106b
bills of exchange II–467b
sea power VI–247b
Genoa (Nev.) VI–298a
Genoa Conference (1922) III–193b
Genocide VII–226a
Genocide Convention (1949) VII–113a, 226a
Genre painting V–185b, 188a, 189a–b, 190b–91a
Gentleman and Wife (paint.) V–188a
"Gentleman highwayman" VI–379b
Gentleman's Magazine II–455b
Gentlemen Prefer Blondes (musical) VII–50b
Gentlemen's Agreement (1907) II–471b, 488b; III–68b, 492a; VII–357a
Gentlemen's agreements (bus.) I–390a,b
Geochemistry II–12b; IV–349a
Geodesy III–166a,b, 480b; V–294b
Geodetical Association, International II–88a
Geodetic and Geophysical Union, Congress of the International (1924) III–481a
Geodetic survey. *See* Coast and Geodetic Survey
Geodetic surveys
Air Force I–63b
Geodynamics Project (1974–79) III–167b
GEOGRAPHER'S LINE **III–163a**; VI–264a
Geographical, Historical, Political, Philosophical and Mechanical Essays II–466b
Geographical and Geological Survey of the Rocky Mountain Region II–464b
Geography (atlas) IV–247a
Geography Made Easy. *See* Morse Geographies
Geological Congress, First International (1878) V–195b
Geological Exploration of the Fortieth Parallel V–268a
Geological Institute, American. *See* American Geological Institute
GEOLOGICAL SURVEY, UNITED STATES **III–163a**; III–165b–66a, 444a–b; IV–349a; V–195b–96a,b, 384b; VII–75a, 272b
Alaska exploration V–337a
Bureau of Mines IV–350a
chemical laboratory III–167a
Colorado River mapping II–129b
congressional investigation I–90a
petrography V–268a,b
topographic mapping I–463b
GEOLOGICAL SURVEYS, STATE III–164b
Massachusetts IV–348b
paleontology V–195a–b
reports VI–236a
Geologists, Association of American VI–236a
Geologists and Naturalists, Association of American IV–464b
Geology IV–348a–b
American Philosophical Society I–110b
Association of American Geologists I–98a
fossil studies V–195a
isostasy III–480b
National Museum IV–468b
Geology of the Eastern Portion of the Uinta Mountains V–384b
Geomagnetism III–453b, 454a
GEOPHYSICAL EXPLORATIONS III–166a
International Geophysical Year III–453b
oceanography V–135a
petrography V–268a
Powell expeditions V–384a
Geophysical Laboratory (Carnegie Institution) I–457a
Geophysical Research Corporation V–272a
Geophysical Year, International. *See* International Geophysical Year
Geophysics V–294b
George II (Br. k.) II–405b–06a
colonial judiciary II–121a
death II–121a
Elizabethtown II–431b
George III (Br. k.) I–223b, 356a; II–4b; V–5a; VII–299b
colonial judiciary II–121a
Declaration of Independence II–304a–b, 305a, 306b, 307a–b; VI–115a
German mercenaries III–172b
Grand Ohio Company III–209a
Holland Patent III–291b
Massachusetts petition IV–271a
New Albion V–333a
N.Y. Chamber of Commerce I–491a
Olive Branch Petition V–152b
revolutionary war VI–127a
Russia alliance VI–177a
Ticonderoga VII–57a
GEORGE, FORT (Can.) **III–167b**; II–458a; III–218a; V–91a
George, Fort (Fla.) VI–365b
George, Fort (Maine) V–242a
George, Fort (N.Y.) I–281b; VI–382a; VII–56b
George, Fort (N. Dak.) IV–415a
George, Fort (Va.) IV–399b
George, Fort (Wash.) I–209b; VII–165b
George, Henry (econ.) III–202b; IV–81a, 101a,b, 163b; V–426b–27a; VI–13b, 293a–b
George, Lake. *See* Lake George
George, Milton (ed.) II–493a
George, Walter (pol.) V–48b
George C. Marshall Space Flight Center (Ala.) I–72a
George Dewey (frigate) V–26a
George Mason College VII–197b
George Peabody and Company III–79b
George Peabody College for Teachers II–401b
Georges Island (Maine) I–96b
Georgetown (Colo.) VI–292a
Georgetown (Ky.) IV–410a
Georgetown (Maine) IV–225b
Georgetown (Md.) I–318a; II–15b
Georgetown (S.C.) VI–135b, 347b
Georgetown (Washington, D.C.) II–380a; VI–86a; VII–244b
Georgetown Academy I–467a
Georgetown Island IV–37b; VI–185b
Georgetown University I–169a; III–501b
George Washington (sculp.) VI–242b
GEORGE WASHINGTON (ship) **III–168a**; I–266a
George Washington (submarine) I–180a; VI–423b
George Washington Birthplace National Monument V–217b; VII–219b
George Washington Bridge I–364b; III–312b; V–368b
George Washington Bridge Bus Terminal V–368b
George Washington Carver National Monument V–217b
George Washington University V–24b
GEORGIA III–168a; IV–200a; VI–393 (table)
Archaic culture II–385b–86a
auctions I–168b
Augusta Congress I–223a
Augusta Treaty I–223b
Bank of Augusta I–260b
Bartram's travels II–477a
bills of credit I–300a
black suffrage VI–432a, 433a,b
blue laws I–325a
boll weevil II–238b
boundary disputes I–350b, 351a, 351a, 352a
Bourbon County I–354a
Buford expedition I–376b
candlemaking I–444b
chain gangs I–489a; II–217a
Cherokee II–14a–15a; V–437b; VII–96b, 321b–22a
Chisholm v. *Georgia* (1793) II–32a–b
Civil War I–118b, 213b–14a, 502b; II–62b, 163b, 271b, 479b; III–298a; IV–209a, 405a; V–56a, 238a–b; VI–26b, 138a, 141b, 278a; VII–26b
colleges and universities II–114b
colonial government VI–166b
colonial suffrage VI–434a,b
colonial trade II–119a
Compromise of 1850 II–150b; III–171a
congressmen II–198b
constitution VI–391a
Continental Congress II–211a, 308b
cotton I–38a; II–237b, 238b; V–325a
"crackers" II–253a
Creek Indians I–223b
Creek War I–232a; II–256b; VII–239a
debatable land II–298a
Declaration of Independence II–305a, 308a
Democratic party VII–210a
De Soto expediton II–336b
employer liability laws II–441a
excess profits tax II–467a
exploration I–96a
fall line II–485a
Florida attack VI–349a
foreign study II–470b
Fort Barrington III–42b
Fort Benning I–289a
Fort King George IV–46b
Fort Pulaski V–462b
Fort Wilkinson VII–299b
Franciscan missions III–38b
Frederica III–100b
fruit growing III–128b
fur trade III–141a,b, 143b, 144a

GEORGIA (cont.)
gold III–191a; V–437a
grandfather clause III–208b
Great Trading and War Path III–387b
Gullah III–233b
historical society III–278b
horse racing III–304b
Hunter's emancipation orders II–434b
hurricanes III–319b
Indian attacks V–101a
Indian removal III–394a,b, 401b
International Exposition of 1895 III–453b
iron industry III–472a
item veto III–484b
Jesuit missions III–499a
Ku Klux Klan IV–58b, 59a
landholding I–4a
land speculation I–354a
legislature IV–133b; VII–142a
Loyalists IV–200a; VI–115b
lynching legislation IV–208b
martial law IV–259a
minimum-wage law IV–353b
Moravian settlement IV–409b
national monuments V–217b
naval stores V–14b
North American Land Company V–113a
nullification V–125b
Old Southwest VI–356a
paper industry V–212b
Peace Society VII–149a
Pine Barren speculations V–315b
pioneers V–316b
plantation system V–325a
plant study V–326a
port authority V–368a
presidios V–399b
primogeniture V–408a
private mints IV–360a
railroads VI–25a, 33a, 36b, 37b
Reconstruction III–171b, 295a; VI–57b
referendum VI–66b
Regulators VI–71b
religious liberty VI–80b; VII–68b, 69a
repudiation of state debts VI–96b
revolutionary war II–15a, 251a; III–42b, 170a, 401a; IV–44b; VI–118a, 124a, 130a, 351a; VII–71b, 360b
rice I–486b; VI–135b, 136a, 386b
Salzburgers IV–206a; V–342a; VI–204b
Savannah VI–220a
school segregation II–402a
secession II–61a; VI–251a
Seminole VI–259b
Seminole War VII–239a
Seminole Wars III–88b; VI–260a
settlement II–124b
sharecroppers IV–103a
silk VI–286b
slavery II–151b, 305a; VI–309a; VII–223b
Spanish missions IV–303a
Spanish posts III–38a; IV–302b
stagelines VI–380a
state university II–395b; VII–156a
suffrage III–92a,b
sugarcane VI–436a
taxation VII–15a
test garden III–151b
tobacco VII–66b, 67a,b
tornadoes VII–75b
Treaties of Indian Springs III–401b
Treaty of Fort Jackson III–383b
Treaty of New York City III–383a
Troup and Clark parties VII–121a
Union Rights party VII–148a
Union sentiment VII–148b
U.S. Constitution II–193a,b, 196a, 203b, 478a
veterinary medicine VII–176b
Voting Rights Act of 1965 VII–211a
War of 1812 VII–235a
War of Jenkins' Ear I–323a; III–498a
western boundary VII–269b–70a
western lands II–166a; III–170b, 389a, 393b; V–443b; VI–356a–b, 358a; VII–273a,b, 353b–54a
westward movement VII–283a
whiskey II–163b
Yamasee War VII–352a
Yazoo fraud II–166a; III–36a; IV–99a; VI–356b; VII–353b
GEORGIA (cruiser) **III–169b**
Georgia (song) VI–393 (table)
GEORGIA, PURITAN MIGRATION TO III–169b
Georgia, Southern and Florida Railroad VI–37a
GEORGIA, SPANISH MISSIONS IN III–170a; III–41a
GEORGIA, WAYNE'S OPERATIONS IN (1782) **III–170a**
GEORGIA COMPACT (1802) **III–170b**; III–168b; VII–299b
Georgia Institute of Technology II–448a
GEORGIA LAND LOTTERY SYSTEM III–170b
GEORGIA–MISSISSIPPI COMPANY III–170b
GEORGIANA III–171a; IV–92b
Georgiana Land Company IV–98b
Georgian architecture III–495a
Georgian Bay III–216a, 319a; V–95a; VII–157a, 307a
GEORGIA PLATFORM III–171a
Georgia Railroad. *See* Western and Atlantic Railroad
GEORGIA'S SOUTHERN BOUNDARY III–171b
Georgia v. *South Carolina* (1922) I–351a
GEORGIA* v. *STANTON (1867) **III–171b**; IV–209a; VI–58a
Gérard, Conrad (dipl.) III–331a
Gerard, John (bot.) I–348b
Gerhard, William W. (physic.) IV–297b, 285b, 298a
Géricault, Jean (paint.) V–187a, 188b
Germain, Lord George. *See* Sackville Germain, George
Germaine, Adelaide VII–217a
Germaine, Julia VII–217a
GERMAINE GIRL CAPTIVES III–172a; VII–217a
GERMAN–AMERICAN BUND III–172a; IV–58b
GERMAN–AMERICAN DEBT AGREEMENT (1930) **III–172a**; III–172a; V–215a
German–Americans
isolationism III–480a
Minnesota politics II–491a
World War I II–445b
World War II III–491a
German Catholic Central Verein I–469b
German Coast. *See* Côte des Allemands
German Customs Union VII–173a
GERMAN FLATS (N.Y.) **III–172b**; III–291b; V–195a; VII–282b
German immigrants
labor unions IV–63b
slums VI–314a
Germanium V–304b, 305a; VI–259a
German-language press V–75b
German measles II–445b; IV–292a
GERMAN MERCENARIES III–172b; I–360a, 365b; VI–126b; VII–116a
German Mills American Oatmeal Company I–486b
German Missouri Synod V–123b
GERMANNA (Va.) **III–173a**; VI–376a
Germanopolis (Pa.) III–173b
German Protestantism V–194b–95a, 310b
German Reformed church I–410b; III–335a
German settlements IV–338a
Cincinnati II–37b
Cleveland II–75a
Côte des Allemands II–237a
Frederick III–100b
Germantown III–173b
Iowa III–468b
Minnesota IV–356b
New Ulm V–81a
North Carolina V–115b
North Dakota V–117b
Pennsylvania IV–89b
pottery V–379a–b
Saint Louis VI–194b
Saint Paul VII–134a
Shenandoah Valley V–378a; VI–275b
South Carolina II–382b
South Dakota VI–350a
Virginia III–173a
West Virginia VII–281a
westward movement I–38b; VII–282b, 283a
Wisconsin VII–307b
Yadkin River VII–350a
Zoar VII–369b
GERMANTOWN (Pa.) **III–173a**
charity organization I–494b
German Bible I–294a
Mennonite Community II–147a
newspaper V–75b
paper mill V–212a
revolutionary war III–173b
typefounding V–411b, 413a
GERMANTOWN, BATTLE OF (1777) **III–173b**; VI–123b
German university system IV–2a, 126b
Germany
agricultural chemistry VI–334a
Algeciras Conference I–85b
American Samoa III–425a
Apia disaster I–144a
Appam case I–144b
art nouveau III–446b
astronomy I–211a
automobile I–225b
aviation I–60b, 234b
Berlin I–290b–92a
Berlin Treaty (1921) I–290b
Boer War I–122b
Boxer Rebellion I–356a
calculating machine industry I–396b
Caroline Islands V–215a
chemical industry II–7b–9a
chemical training II–11a–b
clocks II–77b

coal industry V–267b
cold war II–98a
commerce II–359b
conquest of Western Europe II–314b
consumer cooperatives II–220a
currency upvalue III–196a,b
detergents II–9a; VI–324a
education II–470b
employers' liability insurance III–431b
exchange students II–470b, 471a
extraterritoriality II–479a
Franco-Prussian War III–352b
free ships, free goods III–110a
Geneva disarmament conference III–161a
glassmaking III–185b–86a
gold standard I–301b; III–193b
immigration to U.S. II–125b; III–81a–b, 333a, 334b, 335a, 336a–37a, 339a,b, 341b, 370a; IV–60a, 206a, 209b, 310a; V–3a, 99b
indentured servants III–353a
industrial research III–408b; IV–300b
inflation III–415b
intelligence tests III–440a
investments in U.S. III–63a, 64b, 65a,b
iron and steel manufacture III–471 (tables), 474a
Joachimsthal (coin) II–94b
Liberia IV–141b
log construction IV–179b
Louisiana Purchase Exposition IV–198a
Luftwaffe I–328a
Madrid Conference IV–221a
medical education IV–284a, 297b, 298a
medical research IV–285b–86a
Micronesia VII–125a
missile development IV–363a,b
multinational corporations III–66b
music IV–437b, 438b, 439a
nitrates V–98a,b
nitrocellulose V–327b
nitrogen fixation III–17a
nuclear fission I–215b; IV–237b
nuclear physics V–298b, 302a,b
Nuremberg trials I–219b
Open Door notes V–158b
Pacific Islands III–425b–26a
petrography V–268a
pharmaceutical industry V–273b–74a
philosophy V–287a
photographic industry V–292b
pietism V–310b
political exiles V–342a
political science V–347b
potash II–8a; V–376a
potassium III–17a
psychology V–441b
radar VI–l0a
revolutionary war I–289a,b, 385a
Rhodes scholars VI–134b
rockets VI–159a
Russian relations I–158b
Samoa Islands VI–205a
scientific periodicals VI–235a
Siberia VI–283b
Synod of Dort VI–455b
trade II–213a; VII–87a
universities II–397b, 399a
U.S. balance of trade I–246a
U.S. loans I–245b
U.S. national defense II–314b
U.S. naval competition V–10a
U.S. shipping IV–311a
vacuum tubes VII–163b
Venezuela II–369a; IV–401a; VII–169b
Walloons VII–221b
Washington Naval Conference VII–250b
Wheaton's Zollverein Treaty VII–370a
workmen's compensation VII–322a
Zeppelin I–232b, 236b; II–344b
See also entries under Berlin
—*World War I:*
air combat IV–83b
Aisne–Marne operation I–70a,b
Allied propaganda V–441a
American Expeditionary Forces I–101b–02a
armistice I–176b–77a; III–86a
Army of Occupation VII–213a
Belgium I–122b
Belleau Wood I–286a,b
blockade II–12a
bombing I–66b
Cantigny attack I–446a
Champagne–Marne operation I–491b
Château-Thierry I–502a
contraband II–447a; IV–182b
history VII–324b–27a
Lusitania sinking IV–205a
mandated colonies IV–236a
Meuse–Argonne offensive IV–189a–b, 319a
mixed claims commission IV–381b
Montdidier–Noyon operation IV–404a
navy V–20a
North Sea mine barrage V–119b
Oise–Aisne operation V–146a
propaganda VII–332b
relief VII–330a
reparations II–296a–b; III–97b, 352b; IV–117b; V–215a; VI–87b; VII–363b
Russia I–158b
Saint-Mihiel VI–197a
ships seized II–277a
Somme offensive VI–338b
submarine blockade I–321b
submarine warfare I–122b, 151a; II–213a, 217b, 314a–b; IV–311b, 313b; VI–280b, 423a, 423a, 424a; VII–328a–b
Sussex Case VI–452b
torpedo warfare VII–76b
Treaty of Versailles IV–125a; VII–172b, 330b–31a
U.S. neutrality V–35b
U.S. relief VII–329b
warships VII–329a
Zimmerman telegram VII–368b
—*World War II:*
Aachen I–1a
air combat I–60a
American occupation III–174b
Antwerp siege I–140b–41a
Anzio I–141a
Appam Case V–422a
Argentina IV–112b
Battle of the Atlantic I–214a,b
Battle of the Bulge I–273b, 379a–80a
Bizerte I–308a
bombing of I–60b, 67a, 328b
booby traps I–332a
Casablanca Conference I–465a
Cherbourg II–13b–14a
commerce raiding II–217b
declares war on U.S. II–315a
Elbe River II–407b
enemy aliens II–446a
exchange of prisoners II–469a
gliders III–187a
Gothic Line III–200b
Gustav Line III–235a
history VII–334a,b, 335b, 336a–b, 338a–41a
Huertgen Forest III–314a
Luftwaffe II–217b
Malmédy massacre IV–230b
Monte Cassino IV–404a
naval supremacy II–314b
navy V–20b
Normandy V–110a; VI–193b
North African campaign V–112b
Office of Strategic Services VI–374a
panzer invasions I–177b
paratroops V–213b
Paris peace conferences V–215b
Ploesti air raids V–332a
Potsdam Conference V–378b
propaganda VII–333a
property confiscated II–169a
raids on England I–67a; II–50a
recoilless rifle VI–140b
Remagen VI–83b
reparations III–352b
Salerno VI–199b
Siegfried Line VI–285b
Soviet Union II–145a, 315a; VI–178b–79a,b
submarine warfare I–214a; II–213a, 314b, 345a; IV–313b; VI–424b; VII–342b
Teheran Conference VII–18a
torpedo warfare VII–76b
Tunisia campaign IV–32b
underwater defenses VII–139a
U.S. aid to Allies IV–134b, 135a
U.S. Navy V–21a–b
U.S. neutrality V–36a, 37a,b, 39a
war crimes trials VII–229a,b
warships VII–242a
wolf packs II–217b
Yalta Conference VII–351b
GERMANY, AIR BATTLE OF III–174a
GERMANY, AMERICAN OCCUPATION OF (1944–55) **III–174b**; I–102a, 188a, 191b–92a; V–432b; VII–351b
women VII–318b
Germany, West III–69b, 175a
aerial hijacking III–277b
Common Market VI–469a
currency VII–91a
European Economic Community VII–88b
gunboats III–235a
International Court of Justice III–453a
investments in U.S. III–66b
North Atlantic Treaty Organization V–113b
Organization for Economic Cooperation and Development V–170b
Organization of European Economic Cooperation IV–258a
Paris Peace Conference V–215b
U.S. aid III–61b
U.S. military pact III–70a
Volkswagon VII–90a
Germer, Lester (phys.) V–303b
Germ scalpers III–43b–44a
Germ theory of disease I–240b; II–390b
Geronimo (Indian) I–141b, 142a, 310a; III–391b; VI–242a, 287b; VII–239b
See also Apache Wars

Gerrard, Thomas II–246b
Gerry, Elbridge (states.) III–175a; V–199a
Bill of Rights I–297b
campaign of 1812 I–418a
constitutional convention II–193a, 194b
Declaration of Independence II–305b–06a, 308a
vice-presidency VII–179 (table)
XYZ Affair III–96a; IV–347a; VII–347b
GERRYMANDER II–175a; I–147b; II–355b, 355b; VI–432a,b
Gershwin, George (comp.) IV–438b, 442a
Gesner, Abraham (surg.) V–269b
Gessner, Abram (ind.) IV–44a
Gestring, Marjorie (athlete) V–154a
Getty, George W. (off.) I–269b
Getty, J. Paul (ind.) III–80b
Gettysburg (Pa.) II–484b; III–176b; IV–156a, 206a
GETTYSBURG, BATTLE OF (1863) **III–175b**; I–200b; II–62b, 162b, 164a–b; III–100b; IV–85a; V–247b, 248b; VII–127b, 197b
Army of Northern Virginia VII–197a
Hanover cavalry engagement III–250b
Mosby's Rangers IV–415b
Pickett's charge V–309a
GETTYSBURG ADDRESS (1863) **III–176b**; III–202a–b; IV–162b; V–353b
"Gettysburg of the Southwest" II–128a
"Gettysburg of the West." *See* Westport, Battle of
Gettysburg Theological Seminary II–465a
Geysers VII–357b
Yellowstone National Park VI–160b
G. Fox digg'd out of his Burrowes (tract) VII–82a
GG-1 (locomotive) IV–177a
Ghana
Afro-Americans I–22a
black power I–316b
mandate IV 236b–
missions II–362b
music IV–443a
Pan-Africanism V–199b
Rhodes scholars VI–134b
Ghandi, Mahatma (states.) V–181b
GHENT, TREATY OF (1814) **III–176b**; I–120b, 209b, 438b; II–92b, 216a, 292b, 338a, 458b–59a, 464b; III–68a, 216b; IV–87a; V–232b; VI–377b; VII–111b, 235b
arbitration IV–5b
Canadian–U.S. boundary V–33a; VI–165b
Fort Niagara V–90b
Great Lakes V–331a
Indian Barrier State III–375b; V–120b
Norfolk trade V–109b
Northeast boundary V–118a
Northwest boundary VII–270a
Ohio country V–141a
slave trade VI–322a
Wisconsin VII–307b
Ghettos I–26a, 29b; VI–7a, 314b
Bedford–Stuyvesant I–282b, 370b
black power I–316b
community action program II–148a
crime II–261b, 262b
Harlem I–30a
Los Angeles I–408b
religious life I–24a
Ghirardelli Square (San Francisco) VI–209b
Ghirlandajo (Domenico de Tommaso Bigordi) (paint.) II–102a
GHOST DANCE III–177a; II–283b; III–251a, 391b; V–4a, 194b, 272b, 434b–35a; VI–242a
Battle of Wounded Knee VII–344a
Messiah War IV–316a; VI–297a
Ghosts
folklore III–48b
"Ghost shirts" III–177b
Ghost towns IV–101b
mining towns IV–354b
Oklahoma V–149a
Rhyolite VI–135a
Virginia City VII–199b
GI II–366a; VI–301a
Giaever, Ivar (phys.) V–100a
Giannini, Amadeo P. (banker) III–483b
Giant ground sloth V–195a
Giant sequoia VII–114b
Giard, Basil (trader). *See* Giard Tract
GIARD TRACT III–177b; III–467b
Giauque, William (chem.) VII–99b–100a
Gibbon, John (off.) I–296a; II–432b
Gibbon Pass V–225a
Gibbons, Ambrose (col. agent) IV–250a
Gibbons, Floyd (jour.) V–74a
Gibbons, James (cardinal) I–469a
Gibbons, James Sloan (abolitionist) VII–263b
Gibbons, Thomas (law., pol.) III–178a, 178a
GIBBONS* v. *OGDEN (1824) **III–178a**; I–373a; II–135b, 197b, 220a; III–132a, 458b; IV–19b, 148a; V–353b; VI–145b, 407b; VII–83b
Gibbs, David (off.) VI–286a
Gibbs, James (arch.) I–162a
Gibbs, Josiah Willard (chem.) II–11a,b; V–295a
Gibbs, Oliver Wolcott (chem.) II–10b, 11a
Gibbstown (N.J.) III–409a
GI BILL OF RIGHTS III–178b; I–108b, 331b; II–115a, 401a; V–258a
Gibraltar I–151b; II–318b–19a; VI–116b, 359a; VII–119b
Gibraltar, Strait of II–345a
Gibraltar of the West. *See* Louisburg
Gibson, Alexander (off.) VI–60b
Gibson, Charles Dana (art.) IV–241a
GIBSON, FORT (Okla.) **III–178b**; II–14b, 359a; VI–241a
Gibson, George (off.) III–179a
Gibson, Henry C. II–103b
Gibson, John (off.) IV–179a
Gibson, Kenneth A. (pol.) V–41b
Gibson focus (culture) V–148a
Gibson girl II–372a
"Gibson Girl" (radio) VI–302b
GIBSON–LINN EPISODE (1776–77) **III–178b**; III–38b
Gibson v. *Florida Legislature Investigation Committee* (1963) I–204b
Giddings, Joshua R. (pol.) V–145b, 239a
Gideon, Clarence Earl III–179a
GIDEON CASE (1963) **III–179a**
GIDEON SOCIETY III–179b
Gideon v. *Wainwright*. *See* Gideon Case
Giessen (Ger.) VII–341a
Gifford, Sanford R. (paint.) V–189a
Gift of God (ship) V–333b, 359b
Gift tax III–418a; VI–105b; VII–4b, 6a, 7a–b, 8b, 9a, 13a
GI Joe V–74a
Gila Bend (Ariz.) III–289b
Gila Cliff Dwellings National Monument V–217b
Gila Range I–413a
Gila River II–129b, 440b; III–179b; IV–34b
California Trail I–410a
Camino del Diablo I–413a
Fort Yuma VII–367a
Hohokam culture III–289a–b
Mexican boundary IV–321a,b
Mormon Battalion IV–411a
Pima V–314a
southern railroad route VI–353b
U.S. boundary III–230a
wagon trail VII–217b
Gila River County (Ariz.) III–491a
GILA TRAIL III–179b; I–170b; V–224b
stagelines VI–379a
wagon trains VII–217b
Gila Valley II–130a; III–367a
Gila Wilderness (N.Mex.) III–73b, 75b
Gilbert, Adrian (navig.) III–240b; IV–37a
Gilbert, Cass (arch.) I–164b; VI–299a
Gilbert, Charles Henry (ichthyol.) III–27b
Gilbert, Grove Karl (geol.) III–163b, 166b, 222a; V–384a
Gilbert, Henry F. B. (comp.) IV–438b
Gilbert, Humphrey (navig.) I–16a; II–122b, 123b, 124b; III–180a; V–324a; VI–43b
Gilbert, John V–360a
Gilbert, Joseph H. (agric., chem.) III–16a
Gilbert, Mathew VI–263b
Gilbert, Raleigh (nav. off.) V–359b
GILBERT ISLANDS III–180a
World War II IV–229a, 257b; VII–1b–2a, 337a, 343a
GILBERT'S PATENT III–180a
Gilbreth, Frank B. VI–234b
Gilbreth, Lillian E. VI–234b
GILDED AGE III–180b; IV–162b
Four Hundred III–85a
manners IV–241a
philanthropy V–280a
robber barons VI–156b
scientific publication VI–236a,b
Gilded Age III–180b; IV–162b, 162b
Gilder, Richard Watson (poet, ed.) VII–24a
Gildersleeve, Basil L. (philol.) IV–2a,b
Gilding
furniture III–138a
Giles Resolutions (1793) III–245a
Gill, Irving (arch.) I–165a
Gill, Theodore N. (zool.) III–27b
Gillem, Alvan C. (off.) VII–127a–b
Gillespie, Archibald H. (off.) III–34a; VI–214b
Gillespie, John Birks ("Dizzy") (mus.) IV–440b
Gillett, Frederick H. (law.) II–176 (table)
Gillette, William (playwright, act.) VII–49a
Gillian, C. C. v. (off.) II–311a
Gilliland, Will (sol.) VII–56a
Gillis, James M. (nav. off.) V–12a,b

Gillmore, Quincy A. (off.) V–462b; VII–215b
Gilman, Arthur D. (arch.) I–143a
Gilman, Daniel Coit (educ.) I–457a; II–470b; III–423b–24a; IV–2a, 3b, 4a, 145b
Gilman, Kendall, and Post VI–299a
Gilman, Nicholas (pol.) II–203b, 203b
Gilman Country Day School VI–228b
Gilmer, Thomas W. (pol.) V–408b
Gilmor, Harry (off.) III–498b
Gilmore, James R. (mer.) V–234b
Gilmore, Robert II–101b
Gilmore's Garden IV–220b
Gilpin, Thomas (mfr.) V–212a
Gilpin, William (off., law.) IV–240a; VI–210b, 215b–16a
Gimbel Brothers VI–258b
Gimcrack (sloop) VII–348b
Gimpel, René II–104a
Gimpel and Company II–104a
Ginger II–119b, 453a; V–16a
Ginsberg, Allen (poet) IV–165b
GINSENG, AMERICAN III–180b; II–28b, 388a; III–127a; V–184a
Ginzburg, Ralph (pub.) I–479b
Giogo Pass (It.) III–201a
Giovanni, Nikki Di (au.) I–25a
Giovanni's Room IV–167a
Gipson, Lawrence Henry (hist.) III–282b
Girard, Charles Frederic (ichthyol.) III–27b; VI–90b
Girard, Stephen (bus., philan.) I–255a, 263b, 274b; III–79a; V–279b
Girard College (Phila.) I–163a
Girard College Trust III–82b
Girard Life Insurance, Annuity and Trust Company III–432b
Girl Guides of England III–181a
Girl in Doorway (sculp.) VI–244a
GIRL SCOUTS OF THE UNITED STATES OF AMERICA III–181a
Girls' rite III–360a, 363a, 368b
Girty, George H. (paleon.) V–196a
Girty, Simon (frontiersman) I–373b; VI–60b
Giselle (ballet) II–287a, 289b
Gist, Christopher (expl., off.) I–358b
  See also Gist, Travels and Journals of
Gist, George. *See* Sequoya
GIST, TRAVELS AND JOURNALS OF (1750–53) **III–182a**; VI–450b
  Allegheny Mountains I–88b
  Big Bone Lick I–295b
  Forks of the Ohio V–143a
  Kentucky IV–39b
  LeBeouf mission IV–130a
  Logstown IV–181a–b
  Monongahela River IV–398b
  Murdering Town IV–434b
  Ohio Company of Virginia V–144a
  Pickawillanee V–308a
Gist, William H. (gov.) VI–250b
Gitlow, Benjamin II–144a
Gitlow v. *New York* (1925) I–299a; II–53b, 378b; III–104a; V–78b; VI–255a–b
Gitskan (Indians) III–362a
Gitt, Josiah W. (pub.) V–74b
"GIVE ME LIBERTY OR GIVE ME DEATH!" III–182a; III–281a; V–161a; VI–137a
Gjoa (sloop) I–116a
Glacier Bay National Monument V–217a
Glacier National Park V–218 (table), 445b; VI–160b
Glaciology II–76a,b; III–453b
Glackens, William (art.) II–104b
Gladden, Washington (cler.) VI–78b, 82b, 325a
Gladwin, Henry (off.) II–337b; V–357a
Glaize River VII–263a
Glance at New York in 1848 (play) VII–47b
Glanton, John VII–367a
Glarner, Fritz (art.) II–104b
Glaser, Donald A. (phys.) IV–119b; V–100a
Glasgow (Mo.) I–364a
GLASGOW, ACTION AT (1864) **III–182a**
Glasgow, Ellen (au.) IV–162b, 164a
Glasgow Mechanics' Institute IV–281a
Glaspell, Susan (writ.) V–439b
Glass
  duties II–276a; VI–110b
  furniture III–136b
  Revenue Act of 1767 VII–80b
  use in buildings I–161a, 165b, 379a
Glass, Carter (pol.) III–6a; VI–432a; VII–195b
Glass, Hugh (trapper) I–201a, 280b
Glass, safety plate I–228b
GLASS AND CERAMICS III–182a
  cobalt oxide III–14a–b
  collecting II–99a–b, 100b
  tariff VI–465b
Glassboro (N.J.) III–70b
Glasses, drinking III–185b–86a
Glassford, William A. II (nav. off.) IV–228b
GLASSMAKING III–184b; II–4b–5a, 10a; III–182b–83a
  bottles V–328b; VI–333a–b
  child labor II–24b
  colonial III–413b; IV–243a; VI–108a
  health hazards IV–294b
  Kentucky IV–41b
  log ash IV–204a
  monopolistic power IV–399b
  Ohio V–141b
  Oklahoma V–149b
  Pittsburgh V–322a
  potash V–375b
  Sandwich (Mass.) I–447a
  soda II–6b
  trade association VII–92b
  Wheeling VII–288a
Glass Menagerie (play) VII–50b
GLASS–STEAGALL ACT (1933) **III–186b**; II–2a, 470a; V–45a
Glavis, L. R. (offi.) I–247b
Glazes, ceramic I–340b
Glazing
  cotton industry II–239a
Gleanings in Bee Culture I–284a
Gleason, Roswell (metalworker) VI–291b
Gleaves, Albert (nav. off.) VII–329a
GLEBES III–186b
Glen, James (col. gov.) V–408a
Glen Canyon Dam II–130a; III–322b
Glendale (Va.) III–100a
Glendale, Battle of (1862). *See* Frayser's Farm, Battle of
Glenn (Okla.) VI–356b
Glenn, Hugh (mer.) III–88a; VI–215a–b
Glenn, John H., Jr. (astronaut, pol.) I–210a; V–142a
Glennan, T. Keith (educ.) IV–459a
Glenn Fowler expedition (1821). *See* Fowler Expedition
Glennon, James H. (nav. off.) VI–163b
Glidden, Carlos (inv.) I–396a
Glidden, Joseph F. (inv.) I–267a
Glidden Tours I–226a
Gliddon, George (anthrop.) I–128b
Glider flights I–232b
GLIDERS, MILITARY III–187a
  Normandy invasion V–110b; VII–339a
  Sicilian campaign VI–284b
Glinka, K. D. (chem.) VI–334a
GLOBE, WASHINGTON (news.) **III–187b**; I–419b; VI–85b
Globemaster (transport plane) II–346b
Globe Tavern (Va.) V–265a
Glocester (R.I.) I–253a
Glooscap (myth.) III–386b
GLORIETA, BATTLE OF (1862) **III–187b**; II–128a; V–60a; VI–144a; VII–165b
Glorious Revolution (1688) I–466b; II–36a, 125a, 309a, 325a; III–316b; IV–134a; V–52b; VI–75b, 396a; VII–291b
Gloskap. *See* Michabous, God of Michilimackinac
Gloucester (Mass.)
  cod fisheries II–93a
  colonial trade IV–265a
  deep-sea fishing I–446b
  fishing fleet IV–311a
  mackerel fisheries IV–217a
  schooners VI–229b
  Universalist church II–170b
  whaling I–447a
Gloucester (N.J.)
  Walloons VII–221b
Gloucester (ship) VI–216b
Gloucester, Duke of II–108a
Gloucester County (N.J.) IV–454a; V–42b
Gloucester (Eng.) *Journal* VI–442a
Glover, Goody (col.) VII–309b
Glover, James W. (prof.) IV–149b
Glover, Josse (cler.) I–333b; V–410b
Glucose VI–340a
Glue
  matches IV–274a
  meat-packing industry IV–281a
GNADENHUTTEN (Ohio) **III–187b**; III–25b; IV–351b; VI–226a
Gnaeus Pompeius Magnus (off., states.) VI–247b
GNP. *See* Gross national product
Go, Mississippi (song) VI–394 (table)
Goat IV–169b
Goat Island V–91a
God
  folklore III–48b
God and Christ VI–82a
Goddard, George W. (off.) V–293b
Goddard, Henry Herbert (psych.)
  "Kallikak" Family IV–24b
Goddard, Luther (watchmaker) II–78a
Goddard, Robert H. (phys.) I–210a; VI–159a
Goddard, William (print.) V–413a, 439b
Goddard family III–134b, 138a

Goddard Space Flight Center
IV–459b
Godefroy, Maximilien (arch.)
I–250a
"God enriches" (motto)
VI–393 (table)
Godey, Louis (pub.). *See* Godey's Lady's Book
GODEY'S LADY'S BOOK (mag.) **III–188a**; II–81a, 371b; IV–222a
Godfrey, Edward (col. gov.)
III–200b
Godin, Antoine (trapper)
V–310b
Godkin, Edwin L. (ed.)
V–71b, 73b; VI–157a
Godman, John D. (physic.)
IV–232a
Godman Army Air Field (Ky.)
IV–53b
Godoy, Manuel de (states.)
VI–211a
"God Save the King" (song)
IV–446a
Godspeed (ship) VI–451a; VII–192b
Godthaab (Green.) V–112b
Godwin, Mills E. (pol.)
VII–196a
Godyn, Samuel (patroon)
V–229a; VII–372b
Godyn's Bay II–322a
Goebbels, Joseph (pol.)
VII–333a
Goebel, William (pol.). *See* Goebel Affair
GOEBEL AFFAIR
III–188a; I–203a; IV–41a–b
Goeppert-Mayer, Maria (phys.) V–100a
Goethals, George W. (eng.)
I–190a; II–450a; VII–230a
Panama Canal V–201b
Goethals Bridge V–368b
Goethe, Johann von (poet)
III–259b; IV–267a
Goff, John W. (pol.)
IV–138a
Goffe, William (off.) IV–48a; VI–70b
Goforth, William (physic.)
I–295b
Gogebic Iron Range
III–473b
Goheen, Robert F. (educ.)
V–409a
Gokstad ship V–112a
Gold
assaying I–203b–04a
atomic weight I–218b
banking crisis of 1933
V–44a
beaver money I–282a
bills of exchange II–468a
Black Friday I–311a,b
Chicago Board of Trade
V–320b
Civil War price II–63b
coinage I–301a–02b; II–95a–96a, 95b, 365b, 384b; IV–359b–60a
dentistry II–331a
devaluation II–339a–b
Federal Reserve III–7a, 8a–b
New Deal V–45a–b
open-market operations
V–159b
panic of 1920 II–333b
panic of 1893
V–207b–08a
panic of 1907 V–208b
price-fixing V–401b, 402a
Resumption Act VI–104a
speculation III–188b
ten-forties VII–24b
U.S. dollar II–339a
GOLD ACT (1864)
III–188b
"Gold and silver" (motto)
VI–394 (table)
Gold and Stock Telegraph Company VI–413b
Gold Beach (Fr.) V–110b, 111a
Goldberg, Arthur J. (jur.)
I–300a; VI–447a
Goldberger, Joseph (physic.)
I–303b; IV–305b; V–128a
GOLD BUGS III–188b
Gold certificates III–188b, 190a, 192a, 194a, 196a; IV–394b
Gold clause VI–95a, 371b
Gold Clause Act (1935)
V–45b
GOLD CLAUSE CASES (1935) **III–188b**; III–194a–b; VI–95a–b
Gold Coast (Africa) V–199b; VII–119a
Gold cyanide III–191b
GOLD DEMOCRATS
III–189a; II–75a
Gold Dust Corporation
III–45b
Gold eagle (coin) I–301a,b; IV–394a
"Golden age of conservatism"
II–188a
Golden Bowl IV–163b
GOLDEN GATE BRIDGE
III–189a; I–364b; VI–60a, 209b
Golden Gate Bridge and Highway District III–189a
GOLDEN GATE INTERNATIONAL EXPOSITION (1939) **III–189b**
Golden Gate Park (San Francisco) IV–337b; VI–210a
Golden Gate Park Bridge
I–364b
Golden Gate renewal project
VI–86b
"Golden Gospels" II–109a
Golden Hill (N.Y.C.)
III–189b
GOLDEN HILL, BATTLE OF (1770) **III–189b**; V–85b; VI–112b
GOLDEN HIND (ship)
III–189b; II–369a
Golden poppy VI–393 (table)
Goldenrod VI–394 (table), 394 (table)
Golden Rod (showboat)
VI–283a
Golden State VI–393 (table)
Golden Triangle (Pittsburgh)
V–322a
Goldenweiser, E. A. (econ.)
III–195b
GOLD EXCHANGE
III–190a; VI–472b
International Monetary Fund III–457b
Gold Exchange Bank
III–190a
Gold exchange standard
III–193b
Goldfield (Nev.) III–191b; V–39b; VI–135a
Gold Hill (Colo.) IV–354b
GOLD HOARDS, FEDERAL
III–190a; VI–371b
GOLD IN CALIFORNIA
III–190b; I–405b; III–191a, 213b, 221a; IV–349a; V–437a; VI–160b, 355b; VII–100b
Bear River I–281a
Cape Horn travel I–448a
caravan traffic I–452b
clipper ships III–428a
effect on cattle industry
I–473a
Forty-Mile Desert
III–81b
forty-niners III–81b
labor activity IV–62a
Lassen's Post and Ranch
IV–110b
Mariposa area IV–254a
mining camp law
IV–354a
outlaws VII–187a
overland freighting
V–177a
Panama Railroad V–200b
panic of 1857 V–207a
placer mining V–322b
prairie schooner V–389b
San Francisco VI–209b
Santa Fe Trail V–59b
skiing VI–298a
stagecoach robberies
VI–379b
Sutter's Fort VI–453a
trails I–410a
transportation VI–150a, 244b, 379a
U.S. shipping IV–310a
westward movement
V–176b; VII–284a
Goldman, Emma (anarchist)
I–116b, 117a, 202b; VI–13b
Goldman, Eric (hist.)
III–283a
Goldman-Sachs II–254b
Goldmark, Peter Carl (eng.)
VII–21b
GOLD MINES AND MINING III–191a; IV–177b
Alaska I–77a, 79b–80a, 302a, 439a; VII–248a
Alder Gulch (Mont.)
I–83b–84a
Appalachians I–301b
Arizona I–142b, 172a; II–477b
Australia II–77a
Black Hills I–312b–313a; II–283b, 285a
bonanza kings I–329a
boomtowns I–336a,b
California I–405b–06a; II–29b, 77a, 241b; III–190b
Cherokee land II–14a
Chinese labor II–29b
Colorado I–174b, 224a, 398b, 452b; II–128a, 477b
Comstock Lode II–156b, 477b
copper II–224a
Cripple Creek II–264a
Custer expedition
VII–272b
Denver II–332a
express companies
VII–101a
Fisk expeditions III–32a
great fortunes III–80a
Helena mining camp
III–269b
Idaho II–284a; III–328a
Klondike I–77a; IV–51b–52a
Leadville IV–123b
Mariposa IV–254a–b
mining camp law
IV–354a
Montana I–289b, 357b; II–284a, 477b; III–77b–78a
Nevada V–39b
Nez Perce War V–89b
Oregon V–165b
Pikes Peak V–311a–b
placer mining V–322b
prices V–405a,b
private mints IV–360a
prospectors V–437a
Rocky Mountains
III–221a; VI–160b
San Juan Country
VI–213b
silver VI–292a
smelters VI–316b
South Africa I–302a
South Dakota VI–350a
Southwest VI–355b
Tombstone VII–70b
U.S. Geological Survey
III–163a
westward movement
VII–284b
Wyoming II–16b
GOLD PURCHASE PLAN (1933–34) **III–192a**; III–194b
Gold repositories
Fort Knox IV–53b
GOLD RESERVE ACT (1934) **III–192a**; I–302a; III–190a, 194b; IV–234a, 394b; VI–371b
Gold reserves III–195b–96a, 196a,b; VII–90b–91a
Legal Tender Act
IV–132b
Morgan-Belmont Agreement IV–410a
Gold rush (1849). *See* Gold in California
Goldsboro (N.C.) II–68b
Civil War I–458b
railroad V–117a
Goldsborough, Louis M. (nav. off.) V–12a
Goldsborough, T. Alan (jur., pol.) II–86b; IV–234a
Gold Settlement Fund
II–74a

Goldsmiths VI–289b
GOLD STANDARD
III–192b; I–301b–02a; II–75a, 264a; III–6b, 193b, 193b–94a, 251b–52a; IV–392b, 394a,b; VI–95a–b, 289a, 370a, 371a–b; VII–91a
abandonment IV–234a
campaign of 1892 I–424b
campaign of 1896 I–425a; V–366a
campaign of 1904 I–426a; III–197a
"Cross of Gold" Speech II–266a
elimination VII–222b
free silver movement III–110a
Gold Bugs III–188b
limping standard IV–154a
panic of 1893 V–207b–08a
post–World War I III–457b
Silver Republicans VI–292b
Tripartite Agreement VII–120b
World Economic Conference VII–324a
Gold Standard Act (1900) III–111a, 193a; IV–395a; VI–371a
Goldstine, Herman (off.) II–155a, 156a
GOLD TELEGRAM OF PARKER (1904) **III–197a**
Goldwater, Barry (pol.) VI–13a, 93b
campaign of 1964 I–430b–31a; V–343b
conservatism II–189b
Louisiana IV–195a
Nixon resignation V–99a
Goldwyn, Samuel (prod.) IV–417b
GOLF III–197a
segregation VI–256a
Works Progress Administration VII–323b
Goliad (Tex.). *See* Goliad, Massacre at
GOLIAD, MASSACRE AT (1836) **III–198b**; VI–84a; VII–37b
Gomberg, Moses (chem.) II–12b
Gómez, Esteban (expl.) I–447a; III–312a
Gomez, Vicente P. (gov.) V–211a
Gomillion v. *Lightfoot* (1960) VI–432b
Gompers, Samuel (labor leader) IV–10a, 65a,b, 66a–b, 68a, 70a–b
American Federation of Labor I–104a
Buck Stove and Range Case I–374b; IV–67b
campaign of 1920 II–493a
Clayton Act II–72a, 110b
International Labor Organization III–454b
McNamara case IV–219a
Populist movement IV–81b
War Industries Board VII–231b
woman suffrage III–92a
World War I government boards IV–69a
Gondra Convention (1923) VI–217a
Gone With the Wind (film) IV–418a
Gong v. *Rice* (1927) V–331b
Gonorrhea V–438a; VII–169a
Gonzales (Tex.) VI–213a
GONZALES, BATTLE OF (1835) **III–198b**; II–339b; VII–37b
Gonzales, Richard ("Pancho") (athlete) VII–30b
Gooch, Daniel W. (pol.) II–140a
Goodbye, Columbus IV–165a
Goode, George Brown (adm.) III–27b, 28a; IV–437a, 468b
Good Hope, Fort. *See* House of Hope
Good Housekeeping (mag.) I–17b
Goodman, Benny (mus.) IV–440b
Goodman, Paul (au.) II–326b
"Good Message" III–249b
GOOD NEIGHBOR POLICY III–198b; I–454b; III–69a, 347b, 463a; IV–114a; VI–364b
F. D. Roosevelt administration IV–112a
Mexico IV–328b
reciprocal trade agreements V–45b
Good News for Modern Man (Bible) I–100a
Goodnight, Charles (cattleman) III–199b; VI–273a–b
GOODNIGHT–LOVING TRAIL III–199b; I–473b; III–304a
Goodnow, Frank J. (educ.) IV–3b; V–347b
Goodrich, B. F., Company VI–167b
Goodrich, Charles A. (cler., au.) VI–227b
Goodrich, Samuel Goodrich (au.)
See also Peter Parley
Goodrich, Samuel Griswold (au.) I–335a; II–397a; VI–227b
Good Roads movement. *See* Road Improvement Movement
Goods, distribution of. *See* Distribution of Goods and Services
Goodsonn, William (nav. off.) VII–270b
Goodwin, Hannibal W. (cler., inv.) IV–417a; V–41b
Goodwin, John (mfr.) III–184b
Goodwin, Martha (col.) VII–309b
Goodwin, Philip L. (arch.) I–165a
Goodwin, William A. R. (cler.) VII–302a
Goodyear, Anson Conger I–333a
Goodyear, Charles (inv.) II–7a, 331a
vulcanization VI–167a
Goodyear, Charles, Jr. (inv.) I–338a
Goodyear, Moses (mer.) VI–184a; VII–114b
Goodyear Tire and Rubber Company II–345b–46a; VI–167b
Goodyear Zeppelin Corporation I–234a, 236b; II–344a–b
Gookin, Daniel (off.) VI–70b
"Gooney Bird" (C–47) VI–302a–b
"Goophered Grapevine" (short story) IV–166a
Gooseberries III–129a
Goose Creek I–497a; III–215a
Goosefoot (plant) I–157a
Goose Lake III–215a
Gopher State VI–394 (table)
Gordillo, Francisco (expl.) I–96a
Gordon, George A. (cler., theol.) VI–82a
Gordon, George Hamilton, 4th Earl of Aberdeen (states.) V–170a
Gordon, John B. (off.) I–146b; III–169a; VI–186b; VII–150a
Fort Stedman assault VI–410a
Gordon, J. P. (phys.) IV–262b
Gordon, Lincoln (educ.) IV–4a
Gordon, Nathaniel (sea capt.) VI–311b
Gordon, Thomas (pol. writ.) VI–113a
Gordon Creek (Colo.) III–484b
GORE III–199b; III–227b
Gorgas, Josiah (ed.) II–163a
Gorgas, William C. (surg., off.) IV–229b, 291b
Panama Canal V–201b
yellow fever VII–355b
Gorgeana (Maine) I–32a; III–200b
Gorges, Ferdinando (col. prop.)
Bristol trade I–365b
Council for New England II–242a, 364b; IV–265a, 270a
Virginia Company of Plymouth V–333b–34a
See also Gorges' Province of Maine
Gorges, Robert (gov.-gen.) II–242a
Gorges, Thomas (col. gov.) III–200a,b
GORGES' PROVINCE OF MAINE III–200a; III–17b–18a, 18a; IV–207b, 225b–26a, 263b; V–436b
Agamenticus I–32b
Duke of York's proprietary VII–359a
Isles of Shoals III–479b
Laconia grant IV–82b
New Hampshire V–53b
Randolph's Commission VI–46a
Trelawney Plantation VII–114b
Gorham, Nathaniel (states.) II–203b; IV–98b; V–88b, 276a
Gorham silver VI–290a
Göring, Hermann VII–229b
Gorky, Arshile (paint.) V–192b
Gorman, Arthur P. (pol.) VI–467a
Gorman–Wilson tariff (1894) V–354b
Gorrell, James (off.) III–225b
Gorrie, John (physic.) III–269b; VI–69b
Gorsuch, Edward (farmer) II–34b
Gorton, Samuel (rel. leader) III–200b; VI–271b
Warwick VI–131b
GORTONITES III–200b
Gosiute (Indians) VII–161a
Gosnold, Bartholomew (navig.) V–130a, 359b
Cape Cod I–96b, 447a; II–92a; IV–264b
Jamestown III–488b
Maine coast IV–37a
Martha's Vineyard IV–258a
Nantucket IV–449a
"Gospel of Wealth" (essay) III–83a
Gospel songs III–326a; IV–440a, 442a–b
Gosport (Va.) II–253b
Gosport Navy Yard V–17a, 29a
Goss, A. H. (inv.) II–420b
Gossens, Salvador Allende (states.) IV–113a; VI–344b
Gossip column IV–241b
Go Tell It on the Mountain IV–167a
Gotham Court (N.Y.C.) VII–24b
Gotha raids I–66b
Gothic cottage (arch.) I–163b
GOTHIC LINE III–200b
Gothic revival architecture I–163a
Gothic style furniture III–135b
Goths
exploration of America IV–38a
Gottschalk, Louis Moreau (comp.) IV–438a
Gott strafe England VI–302a
Goudsmit, Samuel (phys.) V–295b
Gough, John B. (lecturer) VII–23a
Goulburn, Henry (dipl.) II–215b; III–176b

Gould, A. A. (zool.) III–29b
Gould, Benjamin Apthorp (educ.) I–211a
Gould, Charles N. (geol.) V–272a
Gould, James (educ.) IV–159b
Gould, Jay (fin.) III–466a; VII–222a
  Black Friday I–311a,b; VI–413b
  fortune III–79a
  Kansas Pacific Railroad IV–30b
  railroad strikes IV–64a–b; VI–38b
  telegraph companies VII–276b
Gould, R. T. (hist.) V–198a
Goulding, John (inv.) VII–43a
Goupil and Company II–102a
Gouraud, Henri J. E. (off.) I–491b
Gourd I–157a
Gourd seed corn II–226a
Gourgues, Dominique de (off.) III–38a
Gouzenko, Igor VI–428a–b
Government, cost of. *See* Cost of Government
Government, federal. *See* Federal Government
Governmental Research, Institute for I–370a
"GOVERNMENT BY INJUNCTION" III–201a
Government Contract Compliance, Committee on II–456a, 456a
Government contracts IV–71b
  employment II–455b–56a
  munitions IV–432b–34a
  patronage V–227b, 228b
  protective regulations IV–80a
Government Contracts, Committee on II–456a, 456a
Government Corporation Act (1945) II–152a; III–201b
GOVERNMENT CORPORATIONS III–201a; III–203a
  Amtrak III–458b
  Home Owners' Loan Corporation III–294a
  Virgin Islands Corporation VII–204a
  War Finance Corporation VII–231a
Government employees
  political assessments V–341a
  protective regulations IV–80b
Government expenditures. *See* Expenditures, Federal
Government issue (GI) III–178b
GOVERNMENT NEWSPAPERS III–202a
"GOVERNMENT OF THE PEOPLE, BY THE PEOPLE, FOR THE PEOPLE" III–202a
GOVERNMENT OWNERSHIP III–202b; III–204a; V–454b–56a
  corporations III–201a
  municipalities IV–427b
  munitions manufacture IV–432a,b
  North Carolina railroads V–117a; VI–25a
  populism V–365b
  salt works VI–202a–b
  scandals V–346a
  Tennessee Valley Authority III–321b
Government Printing Office II–501a; III–202a, 203b; IV–8b
GOVERNMENT PUBLICATIONS III–203a; III–281a
  Federal Register III–5b
  Journal of Congress IV–8b
  survey reports VI–236a
GOVERNMENT REGULATION OF BUSINESS III–203b; V–456a
  air transportation III–452a
  capitalism I–449a
  commodity exchanges III–207a–b
  exchanges II–470a
  Food and Drug Administration III–53b
  grain elevators II–430b
  Granger Cases III–209b
  Greenback party III–225a
  Guffey Coal Acts III–231b
  Hepburn Act III–273a
  holding companies III–290a–b
  inspection III–422a
  installment credit III–423b
  insurance industry III–434a–b
  Interstate Commerce Commission III–457b
  interstate commerce laws III–458b
  investment banking III–466a–b
  McFadden Banking Act IV–212b
  natural gas industry V–5b–6a
  New Deal V–43b–48b
  New Nationalism V–60a
  planned economy V–323b
  private property V–433b
  public utilities V–456a
  Railroad Administration VI–19a, 29a
  railroads III–451a–b; VI–23b, 30a,b, 32a–b
  southwestern oil fields VI–357a
  World War I VII–327b–28b
GOVERNMENT SPENDING III–205a
  Office of Management and Budget V–136b
  panic of 1929 V–210a
  pump-priming V–463b
  veterans' benefits V–257b, 258a–b
  wheat prices VII–286b
  See also Appropriations by Congress; Expenditures, Federal
GOVERNOR III–206a; V–344a; VI–118b, 396b, 397b
  colonial II–120a–b
  extradition II–478b; VI–402a
  item veto III–484b
  martial law IV–258b
  National Guard IV–341b, 464a
  New Jersey V–58a
  nominating system V–101b
  political parties V–345b
  proclamations V–425a
  Raleigh Conference of Southern Governors VI–42b
  removal power VI–85a–b
  Senate vacancies II–172a
  state constitutions VI–390b, 391a
  state party committee V–344b
  taxation VI–398b
  territories VI–400b
Governor and Company of Adventurers of England Trading Into Hudson's Bay. *See* Hudson's Bay Company
GOVERNORS, CONFERENCES OF III–206a
Governors, territorial
  Indian affairs III–372b
GOVERNORS ISLAND III–206b; V–40a, 60b
Gowen, Franklin B. (law., bus.) IV–392a
Gower, Anne VI–205b
"GO WEST, YOUNG MAN, GO WEST" III–206b
Grace, Robert (inv.) III–99b
Grace Line IV–312a
GRADUATION ACT (1854) **III–207a**; IV–100a; V–444a
Grady, Henry W. (ed.) V–66b, 161b
Graff, Frederick (eng.) VII–258b
Graffenried, Christopher de VI–455a
Graff House (Phila.) III–354a
Graft
  boodle I–332a,b
  New York City IV–137b
Grafton (W.Va) VI–138b
GRAFTON* v. *UNITED STATES (1907) **III–207a**
Graham, Albert B. (educ.) III–84b
Graham, Billy (cler.) II–466a
Graham, Isaac (fur trader) I–280a
Graham, John D. (art.) II–104b
Graham, Katharine (pub.) VII–317b
Graham, Martha (dancer) II–288a, 289b
Graham, Sylvester (ref.) V–306a; VI–266a,b
Graham Cave (Mo.) II–385b
Graham Land (Antarc.) V–198a
Graham's Crossing VI–63b
Graham–Tewksbury feud VI–273b
Graham v. *Richardson* (1971) I–88a
Grahn, Lucile (dancer) II–287a
Graig, James H. (states.) III–273a
Grain III–53b
  alcoholic beverages II–353b
  bonanza farms I–38a
  Chicago Board of Trade V–320b
  China trade V–158a
  colonial trade VII–82b
  cultivation I–34a,b
  Delaware II–320b
  exchanges II–469b
  exports II–430b
  farm tenancy I–41a
  foreign trade VII–86a, 87a
  Georgia III–169a
  gristmills III–228b; VII–257a
  harvesting I–34b
  Kansas City (Mo.) IV–27b
  Kaskaskia IV–32a
  Lake Erie transportation II–459a
  Lake Ontario shipping V–157a
  liquor laws V–430a
  Ogdensburg V–139b
  prices V–404a
  Saint Joseph VI–191b
  shipping IV–310b
  transport I–40a
  See also Cereal Grains
Grain Corporation (World War I) IV–135b
Grain elevators. *See* Elevators, Grain
Grain exchanges III–207a
GRAIN FUTURES ACT (1922) **III–207a**
Grains Futures Administration III–207a
Grain Standards Act (1916) II–470a
Grain terminals I–376a; II–491a
Gramercy Apartments (N.Y.C.) I–143b
Grammar VI–227a,b
Grammar of the English Language VI–227b
Grammar school II–393a,b, 397a
  colonial New York II–394b
  Massachusetts IV–116a
  technical II–448a
Grammatical Institute of the English Language VI–227a; VII–266a

Gramme, Zénobe T. (eng.) II–413b
Grampus (whaler) VII–285b
Granada (Calif.) III–491a
Granada (Mass.) II–22a
Granada (N.Y.) II–48b
Granada (Nic.) III–23a
Gran Chaco VI–224a
Grand Alliance (World War II) II–97b
GRAND ARMY OF THE REPUBLIC III–207b; IV–301a; VII–150a, 175a
GRAND BANKS III–208a; II–93a; III–115a, 232b; IV–311a; VII–278a
See also Newfoundland fisheries
GRAND CANYON III–208a; I–171b; II–346b; VII–357b
discovery II–129b, 228b
Indians III–362a, 369a
Grand Canyon National Park III–208b; V–217a, 218 (table), 445b
Grand Canyon State VI–393 (table)
Grand Central Station (N.Y.C.) IV–177a
Grand Coulee Dam III–203a, 323a; V–455b; VII–248a
Grand Cyclops (Ku Klux Klan) IV–58a
Grand Dragon (Ku Klux Klan) IV–58a
Grand Ecore (La.) IV–457a; VI–63a, 182a
Grande Ronde Valley V–169a
GRANDFATHER CLAUSE III–208b; I–29a; III–20a, 92b, 93a, 232a; IV–461a; VI–432a,b
Grand Forks (N.Dak.) V–117b; VI–64b
Grandfort, Marie (trav.) III–122b
Grand Gulf (Miss.) III–208b; V–369a
GRAND GULF, BATTLE AT (1863) **III–208b**
Grand Island (Nebr.) I–285a; IV–33b; V–330b
Grand jury II–204a
Grand Logistics IV–180b
Grand Manitoulin Island IV–239b
Grand Marias River I–323b
Grand Medicine Lodge. *See* Midewiwin
GRAND OHIO COMPANY III–208b; I–278b; III–370b; VII–166b
Grand Old Party. *See* Republican Party
"Grand Ole Opry" (radio show) IV–441b
Grand period (Pueblo III) I–329b
GRAND PORTAGE III–209a; IV–355a,b; VI–443a
fur trade V–121a; VI–192b
Hudson's Bay Company III–313b
national monument V–217b
GRAND PRAIRIE III–209a
Grand Rapids (Mich.) III–139a; IV–331b
Grand Rapids Public Museum III–137b
Grand Review (1865) VII–27a
Grand River (Can.) II–458b
Grand River (Colo.) VI–368a
Grand River (Mich.) II–21a
Grand River (Mo.) IV–376b, 380a; V–173a
Grand River (Okla.) II–34a; IV–333b
Grand River (S.Dak.) IV–130a, 316a; VI–313a
Grand River Massacre. *See* Messiah War
Grand River valley V–145a
Grand Teton National Park V–217a, 218 (table), 220a; VI–161a; VII–346a
Grand Titan (Ku Klux Klan) IV–58a
Grand Trunk Western Railroad VI–23a, 34a–b; VII–128a
Grand Union Hotel (Saratoga Springs) VI–218a
Grand Wash Cliffs (Ariz.) III–208a,b
Grand Wizard (Ku Klux Klan) IV–58a
Grangeno (shrub) I–494a
Granger (Wyo.) V–168a
Granger, Francis (law.) I–419b; II–184b; VI–288a
Granger, Gordon (off.) II–21b; VI–336a
GRANGER CASES (1877) **III–209b**; III–211a; IV–434a
Granger laws III–209b, 211a
GRANGER MOVEMENT III–210a; I–33b, 41b, 42b; II–220b–21b; VI–175a
Antimonopoly parties I–133a
Department of Agriculture I–45a
food laws V–465b
free delivery VI–172b
grain elevator monopoly II–430b
Greenback movement III–224b
Kansas IV–26b
Patrons of Husbandry V–228b
prices V–402a
railroad rate laws V–457b; VI–21b, 23b, 28b
See also Patrons of Husbandry
Grangula. *See* Otreouati
Granite
Minnesota IV–357a
New Hampshire VI–149a
shipping IV–311a
Vermont VII–172b
Granite Railway VI–24b
Granite State VI–394 (table)
Granite State (ship) VI–282a
Granola I–487b, 488b
GRAN QUIVIRA III–211a; I–125a; II–228b
national monument V–217b
Oñate's explorations V–155a
Spanish missions IV–367a
Gran Sasso (It.) III–187a
Grant, Charles (off.) IV–191b
Grant, George (eng.) I–397a
Grant, James (off.) III–117a, 211b; VI–347a
Grant, Madison (law.) III–342b
Grant, Ulysses S. III–345b; IV–444b; V–141b, 142a, 377b, 394b, 395 (table); VI–93a; VII–137b
Personal Memoirs IV–163a
secretary of war VI–57a
—*Military Career:*
armies IV–370a
Army of the James III–488a
Army of the Potomac II–140a
Army of the Tennessee VII–26b
Battle at Grand Gulf III–208b
Battle at Trevilian Station VII–117a
Battle of Iuka III–485a
Battle of Jackson III–485b
Battle of North Anna V–113b
Battle of Raymond VI–48b
Battle of Ringgold Gap VI–141b
Battle of Shiloh IV–136b; VI–278a
Battle of Spotsylvania Courthouse VI–376a
Battle on Lookout Mountain IV–187a
Battles of the Wilderness VII–68a, 295b
Belmont (Mo.) I–288a
Big Black River I–295b
Bird's Point (Mo.) I–306b
Cairo (Ill.) I–403b
Chattanooga campaign I–502a; II–21b; IV–364b; VI–150b; VII–261a
Chickasaw Bluffs II–22a
Cold Harbor II–96b
commission I–185a
Confederate surrender I–146b–47a; II–63a, 68b; IV–257a; VII–195a
Crater II–253b
Drewry's Bluff II–373a
espionage VI–373b
Fort Donelson II–363a
Fort Henry III–272b
Galvanized Yankees III–148b
Georgia Reconstruction III–171b
Holly Springs III–292a
Meridian campaign IV–313b
North Carolina I–289b
Petersburg siege V–264b
Port Gibson V–369a
Richmond I–213b; III–21a–b; VI–137a, 137b
Shenandoah campaign VI–275a; VII–304b
Sherman's march to the sea VI–278a
Spotsylvania VII–358a
Steele's Bayou expedition VI–410b
succeeds Rosecrans II–21b
Union cotton trade II–68a
Vicksburg I–279b, 492a; III–228a, 238b; IV–375a, 375b; V–248a, 369a; VII–127b, 181b–82a
Virginia I–458b; II–62b
Wilderness campaign I–322b
Yazoo Pass expedition VII–354b
—*President:*
administration scandals I–286a, 422b–23a; II–231b
Alabama Claims I–73b
anti-imperialist I–131b
Belknap scandal V–346a
Black Friday I–311a,b; V–346a–b
Brooks–Baxter War I–370b–71a
campaign of 1864 I–421b
campaign of 1868 I–422a; IV–135a–b
campaign of 1872 I–422b; IV–141a
campaign of 1880 I–423b; VI–380b–81a
Civil Service Commission II–59b
Clinton riot II–77a
Crédit Mobilier VII–147b
Cuba II–268a; VI–360a
Dominican Republic II–360b–61a, 362a
habeas corpus IV–57b
Indian policy I–142b, 433b
item veto III–484b
Liberal Republican party IV–141a
military bonuses I–331a
Monroe Doctrine IV–401a
New Orleans riots V–64a
panic of 1873 V–207a
Penal Congress V–416a
Radical Republicans VI–11b
Reconstruction III–295a; VI–57a–b
Sanborn contracts VI–207b
Supreme Court packing IV–20a, 133a; VI–448b
tax–evasion scandal V–346a
Tenure of Office Act VII–31b
term of office II–175 (table)
test oath VII–35b
third–term doctrine VII–53b
Vicksburg riots VII–182a

GRANT, ULYSSES S. (cont.)
Whiskey Ring V–346a; VII–290b
Yellowstone Park VII–357a
Grant, W. T., and Company III–33a
Grant County (Ind.) IV–367b
Grant Park (Chicago) II–18a, 297b; III–19b; IV–96b
GRANT'S HILL, BATTLE OF (1758) **III–211b**; III–58b, 116a; IV–154a
GRANTS-IN-AID III–211b; VI–425b; VII–10b
American Printing House for the Blind III–248b
centralization I–484b
civil service II–60b
cost of government II–234a–b
federal expenditures II–476b
forests VII–266b
government inspection III–422b
historic preservation V–392a
housing III–310b
Israel III–481b
law enforcement V–417a
local government IV–172b
localities II–476b
medical research IV–286b, 287b
Micronesia III–426a
poor relief VI–73a–b
recreation areas III–444b
roads III–450b
social security V–381b; VI–328a
states II–476b, 502a; III–9b; VI–105b
tax revenue III–156b
vocational education VI–318a,b
See also Land Grants for Education; Land Grants for Railways
Grantsville (Md.) I–358a
Granville, Lord. *See* Leveson-Gower, Granville George, 2nd Earl Granville
Granville County (N.C.) VI–71b, 72a
GRANVILLE GRANT III–212b; I–458a; V–436b, 437a; VII–103a
Grape boycott (1965–70) V–182a
Grapefruit II–43b
Grape-nuts I–487b
Grape phylloxera III–421a
Grapes II–353b, 407a; III–51a,b, 128a, 129a, 151b; VII–305a–b
Grapeshot V–26a
Grapes of Wrath IV–164b
Graphite, artificial II–422a
Graphophones V–290a
Graselli Company II–6b
Grass II–227a, 279a–b; III–51b
Grass, John (Indian) VI–295b
Grasse, François Joseph de (nav. off.) III–117b; VI–124b; VII–198b, 361a
Grasshopper (locomotive) IV–175b
GRASSHOPPERS III–212b; I–46a; III–51b
Grasslands, national III–76a,b
Grasso, Ella (pol.) II–180b
GRASS ROOTS CONFERENCE (1935) **III–213a**
Grass Valley (Calif.) III–191a
Grateful Dead (mus.) IV–441a
Gratiot Road IV–331a
Gratiot Street Prison (Saint Louis) V–414a
Grattan, John L. (off.) III–213a–b; VI–296b
Grattan family (Va.) III–469b
GRATTAN INCIDENT (1854) **III–213a**; IV–108a
GRATTAN MASSACRE (1854) VI–296b
Gratz, Bernard (mer.) III–331a
Grätzel, Richard (chem.) II–422b
Grave Creek VII–252a
Grave Creek Mound (W.Va.) I–11b; IV–420b
Gravel
towboating VII–77b
Graver (tool) III–50a, 484b
Graves, Thomas (nav. off.) I–498b; VII–199a
Graves, William II–377a
Graves, William S. (off.) VI–284a
Gravesend (N.Y.) I–370a; IV–185a
Gravesend Bay (N.Y.) IV–186a
Gravestones III–47b; VI–242b
Graves v. *O'Keefe* (1939) VII–8a
Graveyards, ship II–89a
Gravier, Jacques (cler.) VI–189b
Graving docks II–375a
Gravitational equilibrium. *See* Isostasy
Gravity III–453b
Gray, Asa (bot.) I–15b, 349a; II–390a; IV–163b; V–326b, 327a; VII–299a
Gray, C. E. (bact.) I–46a
Gray, Elisha (inv.) V–374b
Gray, Horace (jur.) VI–446a
Gray, L. Patrick (offi.) II–503b
Gray, Robert (expl.) I–84b; III–263a; V–462a; VII–86b
China trade II–28b
Columbia River II–131b, 477a; V–164b, 167b; VII–166a, 247a
Gray County (Kans.) II–246a
Gray Herbarium V–327b
Gray's Bay II–131b
Grayson, William (off., pol.) IV–99b
Grayson v. *Virginia* (1789) III–371a
Gray Summit (Mo.) IV–378b
Gray wolf VII–311b
Grazing II–250b
forests III–75b
government lands III–444a
public domain VI–426a
public lands V–450b, 451a
regulation IV–95b
Grazing, Division of V–446a
Great Abaco Island I–292a
GREAT AMERICAN DESERT III–213b; I–170a; III–220b–21a; VI–160b; VII–268a
Nebraska V–31a
transcontinental railroad IV–28b
westward movement VII–284b
Great American Water Circus VI–283a
Great Atlantic and Pacific Tea Company I–489b; VI–258b
GREAT AWAKENING III–214a; II–466a; VI–76b–77a
Baptist churches I–264b
Brethren I–361a
Congregational churches II–169b
Dartmouth College II–292b
education II–395a
Edwards, Jonathan II–406a
New Lights V–58b
Presbyterianism V–391b
Princeton University V–408b
Quakers I–135a
Reformed churches VI–68b
religious writings VI–81a,b
West Virginia VII–281a
Great Bahama Banks III–41b
Great Barrington (Mass.) II–414b
GREAT BASIN III–214b; II–334b
Bonneville expedition I–330a
caravan trade I–452b
exploration VII–271b, 272a
grasshopper attacks III–212b
Idaho III–328a
Indians II–291a; III–301a; IV–327a
Native American Church V–2a
Paiute V–194a
tobacco VII–64b, 65a
Ute VII–162a
western route V–224b
See also Basin culture
Great Basin Indians I–264a
Great Bear Lake III–252b
Great Bend (Kans.) VII–368a
"Great Books" discussion programs II–401b
Great Bridge (Cambridge, Mass.) I–363b
GREAT BRIDGE, BATTLE AT (1775) **III–215b**
Great Britain
abolition I–136a
Active case I–9a
admiralty law I–14a
aircraft I–50a, 52b, 238a
air defense I–62a
air force I–66b
Alabama I–71a
Algeciras Conference I–85b
ambassador to I–93b
Amiens Treaty I–114a
antibiotics V–274a
Appam case I–144b
apprenticeship I–148a
Arab relations I–149b–50a
Arbuthnot and Ambrister case I–154a
Arctic exploration V–122a
Atlantic Charter I–215a
atomic bomb I–215b
Baghdad Pact I–243a
Bahama Islands I–243b
Barbados I–265b–66a
Baton Rouge I–274b
beaver hats I–282a
Belgian relief I–285b
Bergen prizes I–290b
Berlin airlift I–291a
Bermuda admiralty case I–292a
Bills of Exchange Act II–467b
blockades I–122b, 321a,b
Bloodless Revolution II–325a
Blount conspiracy I–324a
Board of Trade I–213a, 326b
Boer War I–122b
border forts I–340b–41a, 340b–41a
Boston Massacre I–345b–46a
Boston Tea Party I–347a,b
Boxer Rebellion I–356a
British Constitution II–190b
Brussels Monetary Conference I–373a
Burr conspiracy I–387b
California I–141a
Campobello fiasco I–434a
Canadian-American relations I–437b–40a
Carnegie Corporation of New York I–456a
Caroline affair I–458b
Cartagena expedition I–461b
Cary's Rebellion I–465a
Castine (Maine) I–466a
Challenger Expedition III–29a
charity organization move-

ment I–494b
charter colonies I–499b–500a
chemical industry II–6a, 7a–8a
Chile saltpeter III–16b
Coercion Acts I–8a, 346b–47a
cold war II–97b–98a
colonial courts I–145a
colonial currency I–145a, 300a
colonial debts I–366a–67a
colonial office I–325b–27a
colonial trials I–8a
commercial bounties I–352a
common law II–191a, 325a
Common Market III–97b; VI–470a–b, 472a
Communist China I–124a
Confederate navy V–17a
consumer cooperatives II–220a
continuous voyage doctrine II–446b
convoys II–217b
corporations II–228b–29a
cotton II–162a, 237a, 238a
Council for Foreign Plantations II–241b–42a
Court of High Commission III–274b
coutumes II–247b
Cuba II–268a
Declaration of Paris V–214a
democratic institutions II–325a
Detroit II–336b–38a
devaluation VII–91b
Dominican Republic II–360b
Dreadnought II–370a
due process of law II–377a
Dunmore's War I–499a
education of the deaf III–248a
Egyptian campaigns IV–278a
enemy destination II–446b
European Free Trade Association VI–469a; VII–89a
exchange students II–470b
extraterritoriality II–479a
Falkland Islands II–484a–b
Far Eastern policy II–488a
Fenian movement III–10b
fishery disputes III–106b
Florida III–38b, 41b, 50b; V–254a
Fort Charlotte I–499a
Fort de Chartres I–501b
Four-Power Treaty III–85b
France III–94b–95b
freedom of the seas II–67b
French claims in Ohio III–118a
French Decrees III–95b, 118b
French Revolution VI–104b
fur trade III–403a,b; VI–411b
Geneva Accords of 1954 III–159b, 161a
Geneva summit conference III–161a
Geneva Three-Power Naval Conference III–160b–61a, 162a
German mercenaries III–172b
German reparations VI–88a
Glorious Revolution II–125a, 191a, 325a
gold standard I–301b; III–110a, 193b–94a
Grand Banks fishing III–208a
Great Lakes III–216a–17a; IV–332b
Green Bay III–225b
Gulf of Mexico IV–326a,b
habeas corpus III–236b, 237a
Honduras proposed loan treaty III–297a
hydrogen bomb III–324a
hymns III–326a
Iberville River III–326b
Idaho III–327b
Illinois Country I–240a, 402b, 501b; II–265a; III–329a, 330a–b; VI–285a
immigration to U.S. III–333a, 337b, 339b
Indiana III–369b
Indian allies II–52a
Indian captivities III–376b
Indian wars IV–367b
Industrial Revolution III–411a–12a
International Monetary Fund III–457b
interoceanic canal I–454a; II–72b–73a
investment companies III–467a
investments in U.S. III–62b–66b
Irish immigration III–335b–36a
iron imports III–469b
Japan II–479b
Japanese Alliance I–122a
Jay's Treaty I–126a, 245a; VII–347b
jet engine I–234b
King William's War VI–181b–82a
Korean War IV–55b
Lake Erie II–458b
land charters I–3b
Latin-America IV–115a,b; VI–360a
lend-lease II–314b
loans to II–301b
London Naval Treaty (1930) II–461a; IV–183a
London Naval Treaty (1936) IV–183b
Louisiana IV–376b
machine tools IV–215b
Mackinac Island IV–217b
Madrid Conference IV–221a
marine science V–134b
mechanics' institutes IV–281a
Mexican oil controversy IV–322b
Michigan IV–330b
military justice VII–142b
multinational corporations III–66b
Munich conference (1938) VI–285b
music IV–437b
Napoleon's decrees IV–449b
naval competition V–10a,b
naval stores V–14b
Navigation Acts V–15b
neutral rights V–38b
Nicaragua relations VI–378b
Nine-Power Pact V–96b
nonintervention policy III–463b
Nootka Sound controversy V–109a
Northeast boundary V–118a
Northwest Territory IV–355b
nuclear fission V–300a
occupation of Germany III–174b; VII–351b
Ohio Valley I–477a; V–140a–41a, 146a
Opium War II–27a, 28b
orders in council V–162a
Oregon I–126b, 493a; IV–239a
Ostend Manifesto V–174b
Palestine III–481b
Pan-Africanism V–199a–b
Parliament I–294b; II–191a; V–220b
Patriot War V–227a
Peace of Paris V–214a
Peking Tariff Conference V–242b
Pensacola I–498b
Philippines V–282a
polio V–340a
political parties V–222b
Pontiac's War II–392b; V–356b
potash V–375b–76a
Prairie du Chien V–387b–88a
prerevolutionary imperial idea III–346a
press gangs V–399b
Privy Council II–118a, 120b, 121a, 123a, 241b
prize cases V–422a
prize courts II–464a
Proclamation of 1763 V–424b
Quasi War I–251b
radar II–425a; VI–9b–10a
Red River of the North VI–64b
representative government II–325a
revolutionary war treaties II–318a–b
royal disallowance I–145a
Royal Navy II–343b, 452a
Rule of the War of 1756 II–446b; VI–169a
Russia I–158b–59a; VI–180b–81a, 181a
Samoa I–144a; VI–205a
sealing I–84b; VI–246a
sea otter hunting VI–247b
sea power II–313b
Seminole VI–259b
Shimonoseki expedition VI–279a
shipbuilding VI–279a–b
Siberian expedition VI–283b
South Carolina I–281b, 496a,b
Southeast Asia rubber VI–168a
Southeast Asia Treaty Organization VI–350b
Suez Canal I–124a
Suez crisis III–352b; VI–429b
supersonic transport I–53a
Sussex Case VI–452b
tariff VI–465a,b
television II–425b
tennis VII–29a,b, 30b
Texas I–121b, 121b, 126b
textile industry II–6a, 237b; VII–42b–43a,b
Townshend Acts I–347a
trading companies I–500a
transatlantic cables I–400b–01a
Treaty of Madrid IV–220b
Treaty of Paris II–126b; IV–197b; V–214b
Treaty of Tientsin VI–66a
Treaty of Utrecht VII–162b
Treaty of Versailles VII–172b
Treaty of Westminster VII–279a
Treaty of Whitehall VII–291a
trial by jury II–191a
trusts VII–124b
United Nations Declaration I–215a
Unknown Soldiers II–310a
UN Security Council V–234a
U.S. boundaries I–126a,b
U.S. Civil War I–72b–73a, 72b–73b, 73a, 121b; IV–85a
U.S. ranching V–160b
U.S. shipping IV–311a
Vancouver Island VII–166a
Venezuela II–369a
Venezuela blockade VII–169b
Venezuela boundary controversy VII–170a
wages and unemployment VII–141a
war contraband II–212b–13a
war crimes trials

GREAT BRITAIN (cont.)
VII–229a
War of 1812 I–317b–18a, 375b, 451a
warships VII–242a, 243a
war with Spain III–117a; IV–372b
Washington Naval Conference VII–250b, 341b
western posts I–340b–41a
West Florida I–398a; VII–277a
wool industry VI–272b
workmen's compensation VII–322a
World War I I–158b–59a, 246b, 491b; II–213a, 343b; IV–182b, 351a–b; V–20a, 119b, 432a; VI–338b, 424a–b; VII–324b–25a,b, 327a, 328b, 329a, 330b, 332a, 332b, 366b
World War II I–140b–41a, 141a,b, 308a, 328a,b, 379b, 380a, 386b, 403b; II–13b–14a, 213a, 315a; III–174a–b, 187a, 201a, 235b, 327a–b; IV–32b, 182a; V–20b, 21a,b, 110b, 111a,b, 112b, 147b, 332a; VI–424b; VII–333b, 334a,b, 335b, 337b, 338a, 338a,b–39a,b, 340a–41a, 342a,b
Yalta Conference VII–351b
Young Women's Christian Association VII–363b
Yucatán VII–366b
See also entries under Anglo, British, Canada, Colonial, and England; French and Indian War; Revolution, American; Revolutionary War; War of 1812
Great Carrying Place II–405b
Great Christian Doctrine of Original Sin Defended VI–81b
Greatcoats II–371a
Great Compromise (1787) II–171a, 194a–b
Great Corn Island I–373b
Great Council of the Iroquois III–475b
Great Depression. *See* Depression, Great
GREAT EASTERN (ship) **III–215b**; I–401a
Greater American Exposition. *See* Trans–Mississippi Exposition
Greater Miami (Fla.) II–263b
Greater New York IV–237b; V–83b
Great Falls (Md.) I–442a
Great Falls (Mont.) I–201a; IV–403b; V–367b
Great Fire of London (1666) III–430a
Great Freeze (1895) III–39b
Great Gatsby IV–164a
Greathead, James H. (eng.) VII–128a
Greathouse, Daniel (Indian) II–257b
"GREAT JEHOVAH" III–215b
Great Kanawha River I–88b; II–381b; III–148a
Jefferson's proposed states III–497a
Scioto Trail VI–239b
Great Kanawha Valley VII–252a
GREAT LAKES III–215b; II–318b, 380a, 471b; V–224a, 367a
Battle of Lake Erie II–459a
beet sugar VI–437a
boundary I–121a, 126a
British control II–458b
British forts IV–40a
Buffalo (N.Y.) I–375b
canal subsidies VI–425a
Carrying Place of Niagara V–90a
Charlotina I–499a
Chicago Drainage Canal II–20b
Chippewa VI–294b
Detroit II–337a–b
domestic shipping IV–309b
domestic trade VII–83b, 84a
Erie Canal I–82a; II–459b; III–312b
exploration I–464b, 498b; III–119a; IV–109b
fish III–27a,b
forest resources IV–96a
Fort Saint Joseph VI–191b
Fox–Wisconsin Waterway III–89a
French and Indian War III–116a,b
French posts III–115a, 118a, 120a
French settlement III–88b, 114b
fur trade III–140a, 141a, 141b–43a, 144a, 403b; VI–357b
Gallatin's report III–147b; VI–145b
grain warehouses II–430a
Griffon III–228b
Illinois Waterway VI–148b
improvements VI–146a,b
Indian agriculture III–366b
Indian Barrier State III–375a,b; V–120b
Indian removal VI–6a
Indians I–304b; II–31a; III–51a, 360b, 365a, 376a; VII–65a
Industrial Revolution III–412a
iron and steel industry III–12a
iron ore II–75a; IV–303b
Jesuit *Relations* III–501a
Jesuits III–499a,b, 501b
Lake Huron III–319a
Lake Michigan IV–332a
Lake Ontario V–156b
Lakes–to–Gulf waterway IV–87b
Lake Superior VI–443a
lifesaving stations IV–152b
Long's explorations IV–187a
Manitoulin Islands IV–239b
mapping VII–73b
Michigan III–475a
Minnesota IV–355a
Mississippi River II–20a
Mohawk Valley IV–387a
Mound Builders IV–421b
National Waterways Commission report V–1b
New France V–52b
Niagara Falls V–91b, 92a
Norsemen VII–190a
Ohio Valley V–146a
Old Northwest V–152a, 180b
Oswego (N.Y.) V–175b
pollution I–440b
Pontiac's War V–356b
railroads VI–25b, 33a,b
rumrunners II–277b
Saint Lawrence River VI–192a,b
Saint Lawrence Seaway I–440a
sawmills VI–223a
Shawnee Prophet VI–271a
shipping IV–312b; VI–193a, 279b
Straits of Mackinac IV–217b
timberlands VII–59b, 60a
transportation VII–102a
Treaty of Ghent III–176a, 177a
Upper and Lower Lakes VII–157a
Walk-in-the-Water IV–331a
War of 1812 V–331a; VI–183b, 248a; VII–45b
water supply VII–259b
western posts I–120a
western sea VII–275b
Wisconsin VII–306b, 308a
Woodland Tradition VII–320a
GREAT LAKES, NAVAL POWER ON THE III–216b
GREAT LAKES DISARMAMENT AGREEMENT (1817) **III–217a**; I–121a, 438b, 438b; II–458b–59a, 471b; III–216b; VII–111b, 157a
GREAT LAKES EXPOSITION–CLEVELAND CENTENNIAL (1936–37) **III–217b**
Great Lakes Indians III–222b; VI–224b
GREAT LAKES NAVAL CAMPAIGN OF 1812 III–217b; II–459a; VI–183b
Great Lakes Pilotage Administration VII–98b
Great Lakes–Saint Lawrence Seaway system. *See* Saint Lawrence Seaway
Great Lakes Shipping Association III–218b
GREAT LAKES STEAMSHIPS III–218a; VII–220b
Great Lakes Water Quality Agreement (1972) VII–259b
GREAT LAW OF PENNSYLVANIA (1682) **III–219a**; V–415a
Great League of the Iroquois III–365b
Great Manitoulin Island IV–240a
GREAT MASSACRE (1622) **III–219a**; IV–116a
GREAT MEADOWS (Pa.) **III–219a**; II–382a; III–115a, 219a,b
Great Miami River I–477a; II–25b; III–24b
GREAT MIGRATION (1630–40) **III–219b**; I–344a, 498b; II–124a; IV–260a, 269b
Cambridge Agreement I–412a
Dorchester Company II–364b
Salem settlement VI–199a
"Great Migration" of 1843 V–176b
GREAT NINE PARTNERS' PATENT III–220b; III–313a
Great Northern Railroad III–79b, 451b; IV–403b; V–119a; VI–27b, 32a, 32b, 33a, 37b; VII–101a, 128b
Fisk trails III–32a
foreign investments III–65a
locomotives IV–177a
Marias Pass VI–413a
strike against IV–66b
See also Burlington Northern Railroad
Great Osage *See* Osage
"Great Path" III–223a–b
Great Pineries IV–204a
GREAT PLAINS III–220b; IV–29a; VII–268b
agriculture I–38a
alien landholding I–87b
buffalo I–375a,b, 376a; VII–297a
caravans I–452b–53a
cattle V–33a, 160a,b; VI–161a
Courts of the Plains II–247a
cow country II–250b
Dakota Indians II–282b
Desert culture II–334b
drought I–486b; VI–40b
dry farming II–375b
Dust Bowl II–382a
exploration III–119a,b; IV–230a
farm mortgage relief IV–414a–b
forests III–74b
forty–niners III–82a
freighting IV–426a

grasshopper attacks
III–213a
hay burning III–265a
hide and tallow trade
III–274b
horse III–303a
hunting grounds
III–318a,b
Indian Country III–384a
Indian hostilities I–184b, 192a, 193a
Indian removal VII–190b
Indian reservations
III–396a
Indians III–51a, 357b
Indian treaties III–378a
irrigation III–478b
James expedition III–488a
livestock I–38b, 170b
Mandan, Hidatsa, and Arikara IV–235b
Pawnee V–230a
plagues I–486b
Pony Express VII–101a
populism V–365a
prairie V–387a
prairie dogs V–387b
prairie schooner V–389b
public lands V–444b
rainfall VI–40b, 41b
rainmaking VI–42a
range cattle industry
V–451b
resorts and spas VI–101a
Santa Fe Trail VI–215a
Scandinavians V–75b
scouts VI–241b
Sioux wars VI–297a
sod houses VI–332b
Texan–Santa Fe expeditions
VII–36a
Timber Culture Act
VII–59a
timberlands VII–59b, 60a
tobacco VII–64b
transition from frontier
III–126a–b
tree planting III–76a; VII–113b
Union Pacific Railroad
VII–147b
voting behavior VII–210a
westward movement
VII–284b
wheat VII–286a,b
windmills VII–257a
wolves VII–311b
See also Plains Indian culture
Great Plains Conservation program I–43b
Great Republic (ship)
I–448a
GREAT REVIVAL (1801)
III–221b; II–272b; III–112a; VII–275a
Great Revolt (1909) II–82b
Great Salt Desert III–214a, 260b; VI–318a
GREAT SALT LAKE
III–222a; I–201a; II–241b, 364a; III–214b, 215a; VII–161a
Central Route I–485b
discovery II–477b
exploration III–114b; VI–318a, 385a; VII–271b
fur trade VI–160a; VII–103b
Mormon Battalion
IV–411a
Mormons I–453a; IV–117a, 412a
Ogden's Hole V–140a
pony express V–357b
Salt Lake City VI–203b
transcontinental railroad
VI–27a
Walker expedition
VII–220a
Great Salt Lake Valley
II–461a
Great Sand Dunes National Monument V–217b
Great Seal of the United States. *See* Seal of the United States
Great Separation (Quakers)
III–123b; V–470a
GREAT SERPENT MOUND (Ohio) **III–222a**; III–300a; V–140a
Great Sioux Reservation (S.Dak.) I–312b, 313a; VI–295a–b, 350a
Great Slave Lake II–30b
GREAT SMOKY MOUNTAINS III–222a; III–396b
Great Smoky Mountains National Park V–218 (table), 220a
GREAT SOCIETY
III–222b; II–472b; IV–140b
AFL–CIO I–103a
campaign of 1964 I–431a
municipal housing
IV–428b, 429a
support by labor IV–76b
Great South Bay IV–185b
"GREAT SPIRIT"
III–222b; II–31a; III–251a, 366b; IV–90a; V–3b
Great Sun (Indian rank)
IV–455b, 456a
Great Swamp (Pa.) VI–267b
GREAT SWAMP FIGHT (1675) **III–223a**; IV–47b; VI–132a
GREAT TRADING AND WAR PATH III–223a; II–33a; III–387b
GREAT TRAIL III–223b
Great Treaty. *See* Shackamaxon, Treaty of
GREAT VALLEY III–223b; II–163a
Great Village of the Illinois. *See* Illinois, Great Village of the
Great War for Empire (1689–1763) I–438a
Great Warrior Path
III–387b
Great Western (steamship)
IV–310a
Great Western Railroad
III–450a
Great Western Railway Company IV–175b
Great Western Trail V–148b
Great White Fleet. *See* Battle Fleet Cruise Around the World
"Great White hope." *See* "White hope"
Great White Way I–369a
Greb, Harry (pugilist)
V–423a
Greco, El (paint.) II–103a
Greece
democracy I–456b
dry docks II–375a
extradition II–478b
Great Britain II–98a
immigration to U.S.
III–333a, 337b, 340a, 341b
Korean War IV–55b, 56b
North Atlantic Treaty Organization V–113b
Organization for Economic Cooperation and Development V–170b
revolution V–280b
Truman Doctrine
VII–121a
United NatiOns Declaration
VII–151b
U.S. aid I–124a, 179a; II–98a, 315b; III–61a,b; VI–179b
U.S. intervention
III–463a,b
U.S. Sixth Fleet V–22b
Greece, Ancient
Amphictyonic League
IV–124a
Greek (lang.) II–394a
Greek New Testament
I–294b
Greek Orthodox Archdiocese of North and South America II–387a
Greek revival architecture
I–163a
Greek Slave (sculp.)
VI–243a
Greeley (Colo.) II–251b; III–477b; V–178b; VII–146a
Greeley, Horace (jour., pol.)
II–220b; III–206b–07a; V–410a; VII–101a, 146a, 361b
Associated Press I–207a
campaign of 1872 I–422b; IV–141a
Civil War peace movement
II–63b; V–234b
Crystal Palace Exhibition
II–474a–b
emigrant aid II–439a
federal aid to education
IV–93b
free land IV–96a
homestead movement
III–296a
Kansas politics IV–28b
Nast cartoons IV–454b
New Departure policy
V–49a–b
New York Tribune
V–71a, 73b, 75a
phrenology V–294a
Prayer of Twenty Millions
II–435b
Republican party V–86b
"Greeley is the Real True Blue" I–432b
Greely, Adolphus W. (off., expl.). *See* Greely Arctic Expedition
GREELY ARCTIC EXPEDITION (1881–84)
III–223b; III–454a; V–337a
Green, Bartholomew (print.)
I–346a; V–68b, 68b
Green, Duff (jour., pol.)
III–187b
Green, Edward Lee (bot.)
V–327a
Green, Hetty IV–101a
Green, H. L. III–33a
Green, Samuel (physic.)
IV–58b
Green, Samuel (print.)
I–333b; V–410b
Green, William (labor leader)
I–104a; IV–70a–b, 71a, 74b
Green Act (1943) VI–289a
Green amendment (1967)
V–136a
Greenback clubs III–224b
Greenback Labor party
III–224b, 468b; IV–63b, 81a–b, 81b; VI–13b
GREENBACK MOVEMENT
III–224a
Bland–Allison Act I–318b
Farmers' Alliance
II–493b
labor's support IV–63b
National Labor Union
IV–81a
radicalism VI–13b
taxation VII–5b–6a
Union Labor party
VII–146b
Greenback party
III–224b–25a, 251b
free silver III–110b
platforms V–329a
soft money VI–333b
Greenback Party, National
I–44a
GREENBACKS III–225b; III–110a,b, 190a, 192b, 251b; IV–394b; VI–94b, 277b, 370b–71a
agrarian movement
VII–52b
Civil War II–63b, 66a–b, 317a
depreciation III–188b
Five–Twenties III–33b
inflation III–414b–15a
legal tender IV–132a,b
Legal Tender Act
IV–132b
Ohio Idea I–422a; V–144b
Resumption Act VI–104a
Green Bank (W.Va.) I–212b
GREEN BAY (Wis.)
III–225b; III–228b, 399a; VII–307a
boundary disputes I–351b
exploration III–119a, 329a; IV–109b; VII–73b, 306b
Fort Howard III–311b; 355b–
Fox–French Wars III–89a
Fox–Wisconsin Waterway
III–89a–90a
fur trade VII–104b
Indian Country III–379a
Indian factory II–480a

GREEN BAY (cont.)
Jolliet and Marquette expedition IV–7a
Lake Superior VI–443a
Nicolet's explorations V–95a
paper industry V–212b
Sauk VI–218b
trading house III–142b
Winnebago VII–305b
Green Bay Packers (football) III–226a
Greenbelt (Md.) II–46b; IV–459b
"Greenbelt" towns II–46b; V–46a
GREENBRIER COMPANY III–226a
Greenbrier River III–488a; V–335b
Greenbrier Valley III–226a; VII–281a
Green County (Wis.) III–337a; VI–455a
Greendale (Wis.) II–46b
Greene, Albert G. (poet, jur.) II–108b
Greene, Catherine II–240b
Greene, Charles III–136a
Greene, Christopher (off.) IV–308b
Greene, Francis v. (eng.) VI–156a–b
Greene, Henry III–136a
Greene, Nathanael (off.) II–240b; VI–124b, 132b; VII–360b
Battle of Camden I–412b
Battle of Cowpens II–251a
Battle of Eutaw Springs II–465a
Battle of Germantown III–173b
Battle of Guilford Courthouse III–232a
Battle of Hobkirk's Hill III–286a–b
Battle of Springfield VI–377a
capture of André I–118b
Charleston VI–347a–b
Ninety-Six V–97a
southern campaigns VI–351b
Sullivan in Rhode Island VI–438a
trenches VII–115a
Washington's eight months army VII–251b
Wayne's operations in Georgia III–170a
Greene, Theodore Francis (gov.) VI–133b
Greene and Greene (arch.) I–165a
Greene County (N.Y.) II–462b
Greenglass, David VI–164b
Green Grow the Lilacs (play) VII–50b
"Green Grow the Rushes O" (song) III–228b
Greenhills (Ohio) II–46b
Greenhouses III–151a, 269a
Greenhow, Rose O'Neal (spy) VI–373a
Green Islands VII–337a
Greenland
air defense I–58b, 62a
Danish settlement II–461b
Eskimo I–441b; II–461b, 462a; III–357b, 358a
exploration V–336b, 337a,b
fisheries III–106b
missions IV–409b
navy base V–338a
Norsemen I–95b; II–461b; V–112a,b
Northwest Passage V–122b
Peary's exploration V–240b
sealing VI–245a
whaling VII–285a
Greenlanders' Saga V–112a; VII–190a
Greenland Sea V–338b
Greenleaf, James (fin.) V–113a
GREEN MOUNTAIN BOYS III–226b; IV–86b; V–222a; VII–171b
Crown Point II–267a
Onion River Land Company V–156a
Ticonderoga VII–56a
Green Mountains III–226b, 299a; IV–102a
Green Mountain State VI–395 (table)
Greenough, Horatio (sculp.) VI–243a
Greenough, John J. (inv.) VI–264b
Greenpoint (N.Y.) V–379b
GREEN RIVER III–226b; II–129b, 477a; III–208b; VII–345b
Bonneville expedition VII–217b
exploration I–201a, 330a; V–384a
fur trade VI–160a
Miami Trail IV–330a
Mormon expedition IV–411a
Oregon Trail VI–153b
Spanish Trail VI–368a; VII–256a
Transylvania Company VII–103b
trappers' rendezvous IV–422a; VII–103b, 104a
Walker expedition VII–220a
Green River (Ky.) IV–426b
GREEN RIVER KNIFE III–227a
Greens. *See* Forty-Eighters
Greensboro (N.C.) I–31a; II–58a; V–117a; VI–173b
Greensburg (Pa.) III–250b
Green-seed cotton II–237b, 240a
Green Spring, Battle of. *See* Hot Water, Battle of
Green Spring Plantation III–308a
Greenstein, Jesse (astron.) VI–17a
Green Tree. *See* Mutual Assurance Company
GREEN* v. *FRAZIER (1920) **III–227a**
Greenville (Del.) IV–437a
Greenville (Ga.) VII–211b
Greenville (Ohio) III–227b
Fort Jefferson III–494a
Wayne campaign VII–262b–63a
Greenville (S.C.) I–435a
GREENVILLE, FORT (Ohio) **III–227b**; II–484b
GREENVILLE, TREATY OF (1795) **III–227b**; I–371b; II–17a, 297a; III–24b, 255a, 383a, 384b, 404a, 414a; IV–216b, 330a, 330b; V–123a; VI–60b, 208b, 270b; VII–17b–18a, 263a
Greenville, Treaty of (1814) IV–188a; VI–377b
Greenway, Robert (shipmaster) VII–267a
Greenway Court (Va.) II–481b
Greenwich (Conn.) III–25b, 258b
Greenwich House (N.Y.C.) VI–330b
Greenwich Village (N.Y.C.) III–253a; IV–100b; V–439b; VI–460b; VII–51a
Greenwood (Pa.) III–175b
Greenwood, Caleb VII–217b
Greenwood, John (paint.) V–186b, 187a
Greenwood's Cutoff. *See* Sublette's Cutoff
Greer (destroyer) I–214a
Greer County (Okla.). *See* Greer County Dispute
GREER COUNTY DISPUTE III–228a; III–200a; V–148b, 150a
Gregg, David (off.) VII–358a
Gregg, John (off.) VI–48b
Gregg, Josiah (trader, au.) VI–215b
Gregg County (Tex.) II–389a
Gregory XVI (pope) I–467b
Gregory, John H. (miner) V–311b
Gregory, McLeod and Company V–121a
Grenada (B.W.I.)
Proclamation of 1763 V–424b
Grenade I–178b
Grenade launcher I–49b
Grenville, George (states.) III–228a; V–221a; VI–110b
Florida grant V–66a
Stamp Act VI–381b
Sugar Act VI–435b
Grenville, Richard (nav. off.) VI–43a,b, 44a
Grenville, William Wyndham (states.) III–493b
GRENVILLE ACT (1764) **III–228a**; VI–111a
Gresham, Newt (labor leader) I–41b
Gresham, Walter Q. (states.) I–424a; VI–282a
Gresham's Law (econ.) I–301a
Gressaire Wood (Fr.) VI–338b
Greville, Robert, Baron Brooke IV–188a
Grey, Charles (off.) V–211b
Grey, Edward (dipl.) III–309a
Grey Beard (Indian) VII–217a
Greysolon, Daniel. *See* Duluth, Sieur, Daniel Greysolon
Greytown (Nic.) III–23b
Gribeauval, Jean B. v. de (off.) III–441a
Grider, Henry (pol.) IV–6a
Gridley, Charles v. (nav. off.) III–25b
Grier, Robert C. (jur.) IV–133a; VI–445b
Grierson, Benjamin H. (off.) III–228a; VII–129a
GRIERSON'S RAID (1863) **III–228a**
Grievance strike VI–418b
GRIFFIN, FORT (Tex.) **III–228a**; I–452b; II–358b; VII–187b
Griffin, Roger B. (chem.) I–197a
Griffin v. *County School Board of Prince Edward County* (1964) II–54b
Griffith (steamer) II–349a
Griffith, D. W. (dir.) IV–58b, 417b
Griffith, F. (physic.) IV–389b
Griffiths, In re (1973) I–88a
GRIFFON (ship) **III–228b**; II–458b; IV–109b, 217b
Griggs County (N.Dak.) II–283b
Grimes, James W. (pol.) III–346a, 468b; IV–6a
Grimké, Angelina Emily (ref.) I–137a; VII–316b
Grimké, Sarah Moore (ref.) V–294a; VII–316b
Grimké Sisters I–136a
Grimley, In re (1890) VII–154a
"Grin and Bear It" (comic strip) V–72b
Grinding stones III–484b
Grindstone Ford (Miss.) I–279a
GRINGO III–228b
Grinnell (Iowa) III–469a
Grinnell, George Bird (nat.) I–222b; VII–298a
Grinnell, Henry (mer., philan.) II–319b; V–336b
Grinnell Land II–319b; III–224a, 454a; V–240b
Gris, Juan (art.) II–104b
Griscom, John H. (physic.) III–325a; VI–313b; VII–24a
Griscom, John H., Jr. V–415b

Grissom, Virgil I. (astronaut) I–63b; II–347a
GRISTMILLS III–228b; III–320b; VII–82a
Providence Plantations V–439a
Tennessee VII–26a
waterpower VII–256b, 257a
Griswald v. *Connecticut* (1965) I–299b
Griswold, Fort (Conn.) V–58b
Grito de Dolores IV–322b
Grits II–226b
Grizzly bear I–280b; II–290b; V–217b
Grizzly Giant (sequoia) VII–362a
Grocery stores I–490a; II–282a; IV–170a; VI–258a
Grog
U.S. Navy V–11b
Groggeries II–259b
Grolier Club II–109a
Gronna, Asle J. (pol.) IV–169a
Gronovius, Johann Friedrich (bot.) I–348b; III–26b; V–326a
Gropper, William (paint.) V–192b
Groseilliers, Sieur de, Médart Chouart (expl.) II–13b, 246a; III–313a, 403b; VI–18a–b; VII–307a
bush ranger II–246a
Chequamegon Bay II–13b
Lake Superior VI–443a
Minnesota IV–355a
Mississippi Valley IV–375b
Grosh, Allen (prospector) II–477b
Grosh, Hosea (prospector) II–477b
GROSJEAN* v. *AMERICAN PRESS COMPANY (1936) **III–229a**; V–78b
Gross, Courtlandt (fin.) I–236b
Gross, Robert (fin.) I–236b
Grosscup, Peter S. (jur.) V–463b
Gross National Product I–393 (table); II–300a–b
government spending III–205b
Great Depression I–394b
personal saving II–300b
tax revenue VII–11b
Grosvenor, Mason (cler.) III–331b
Grosvenor House (N.Y.C.) I–143b
GROS VENTRE (Indians) **III–229a**; IV–236a
Battle of Pierre's Hole V–310b
Jesuit missions III–500b
Montana IV–403a
Grosz, George (paint.) V–192b
Grotius, Hugo (jur., states.) III–106b, 316b; VII–225a
Groton (Conn.) III–25b; V–27b–28a
Grouchy, Emmanuel de (off.) III–122b
Ground Control Approach I–234b
Groundhog thresher I–34b
Ground Observer Corps I–58a
Ground rent IV–104b
Group banking. *See* Banking, Branch and Group
Group health plans II–220b
Group insurance III–434b, 435b; V–255b, 426b
Group of Ten I–254b
Group Theatre VII–50a
Group theory of politics V–354a
Grouse III–51a
Grove focus (culture) V–148a
Grover, Sharp (scout) VI–241b
Grover, Wayne C. I–167b
Grover and Baker Sewing Machine Company VI–265a
Groves, Leslie R. (off.) I–123b, 215b; II–449b; IV–238a,b
GROVETON, BATTLE OF (1862) **III–229a**; I–382a
Grovey v. *Townsend* (1935) V–407b; VI–432b
Grow, Galusha Aaron (pol.) II–175 (table); III–296b
Growth of American Thought III–283a
Grubb, Peter (miner) III–300b
Grubs III–51b
Grueby Faience Company V–379b
Gruening, Ernest (ed., offi.) I–78b; V–73b
Grundy, Felix (pol.) VII–231a
GUADALCANAL (1942–43) **III–229a**; II–387a; IV–229a, 253a; V–20b; VII–68a, 336b, 343a
Guadalcanal (carrier) I–54b–55a
GUADALUPE HIDALGO, TREATY OF (1848) **III–230a**; I–109b, 126b; II–342b, 355b, 468b, 475a; III–68a, 145a–b, 152a; IV–322a, 324b, 328a; VI–151a, 355a–b, 364a; VII–39a, 111b
acreage ceded V–445 (table)
Arizona I–172a
California I–405b
Colorado II–128a
Lower California IV–199b
Nevada V–39b
Rio Grande I–351a, 352a; VI–143a
Texas V–125a; VII–57b
Trist mission VII–121a
U.S. boundary IV–321a
Guadalupe massacre (1847) I–219b
Guadalupe Mountains National Park V–219 (table)
Guadalupe Pass III–179b; VII–217b
Guadalupe River II–339b
Guadeloupe V–214b–15a
British capture II–116a
naval war with France I–345a; II–190b
Queen Anne's War VI–2b
Guaiacum VII–169a
Gualé (Ga.) III–41a; IV–302b
GUAM III–230b; III–425a–b; VII–32b, 34a, 334a
acquisition III–68b; VI–360b
annexation II–475b; III–347a
cession I–126b; VII–112a
citizenship V–6a
National Governors' Conference III–206b
Pacific cable I–401a
Spanish–American War IV–252b; VI–362a,b
Treaty of Paris V–215a
World War II III–490a; IV–253a; V–285b; VII–139a, 336b, 337a
Yap mandate VII–353b
Guanahani (is.). *See* Watlings Island
Guanine II–357b–58a; IV–389a, 390a
GUANO III–230b; III–16b; VI–343b
Guano Island I–91b
Guano Islands Act (1856) III–16b; VII–125a–b
Guano War III–16b
GUANTÁNAMO BAY III–230b; III–479a; IV–252b
naval base II–269b; VII–112a
Spanish–American War VI–361b, 362a
Guaranteed annual income VI–74b
Guarantee Securities Company III–422b
Guaranty Securities Company I–227b
Guardians of Liberty V–3b
Guard of Honor IV–164b
Guatemala IV–112b; V–94b
Bay of Pigs invasion I–278b
Central American Court of Justice I–483b
corn I–47b–48a
Guzmán regime I 454b–
Indians III–355b, 386a
interoceanic canal I–295a
revolution III–70a
United Nations Declaration VII–151b
U.S. intervention II–315b; III–348a, 463a,b; IV–402a
U.S. trade VI–343b
Guaycurú (Indians) VI–224b
Guernsey cattle I–471b; II–281b
Guernsey County (Ohio) IV–129a
Guerrière (warship) II–190b, 303a; V–424a
GUERRILLAS III–231a
Civil War I–388b; II–63a; IV–41a, 377b
Haiti III–240a
Jayhawkers III–493a
Jessie Scouts III–498b
Laos IV–107b
Loyalists IV–200b
military policy IV–344a
partisans V–222a
Philippine Insurrection V–281b, 282b
Popular Front for the Liberation of Palestine III–277b
Quantrill's raid V–471a
Red Legs VI–62b
revolutionary war II–249b; VI–351b
Seminole Wars VI–260b
Vietnam War IV–363b
war atrocities I–219a
Guffey, James M. V–271b
GUFFEY COAL ACTS (1935, 1937) **III–231b**; I–462a; II–86b; V–47a–b
Guffey–Snyder Act (1935). *See* Guffey Coal Acts
Guggenheim, Benjamin (bus.) VII–64a
Guggenheim, Meyer (bus.) III–80a; VI–316b, 317a
Guggenheim, Peggy II–105b
Guggenheim Aeronautical Laboratory, California Institute of Technology III–502a
Guggenheim Exploration Company IV–52a
Guggenheim Museum (N.Y.C.) I–165a
Guidance systems, missile II–316a
Guide in the Wilderness V–176a
Guide to Archives and Manuscripts in the United States III–285b
Guignas, Ignace (miss.) III–499b
Guildhall (Vt.) II–464b
Guilds
closed shop II–80a
colonial period IV–79a
medieval IV–85b
Guilford (Conn.) V–55b
Guilford, Earl of II–108a
Guilford, J. P. (psych.) III–440b
GUILFORD COURTHOUSE, BATTLE OF (1781) **III–232a**; III–286a; V–115b; VI–124b, 126b, 351b
Guilt by association III–105a
Guinea
bauxite I–92b
Guinea pig III–381a
"Guinea pig" books II–208b
GUINN AND BEAL* v. *UNITED STATES (1915) **III–232a**; VI–432a–b
Guion, Isaac (off.) III–232b

GUION'S EXPEDITION (1797) **III–232a**
Guiteau, Charles J. (assassin) I–202a–b; III–152b
Gulf, Mobile and Northern Railroad VI–34b
Gulf, Mobile and Ohio Railroad III–451b; VI–34b
See also Illinois Central Gulf
Gulf and South American Line IV–312a
Gulf Intra–Coastal Canals VII–77b
Gulf Intracoastal Waterway VI–148b; VII–260b
Gulf Oil Company IV–300b; V–272a; VII–40b
Gulfport (Miss.) V–11b
Gulf Squadron IV–252a
GULF STREAM III–232b; II–76a
Florida Straits III–41b
Franklin's observations IV–316b
Grand Banks III–208a
marine research III–29a
Gulf Stream (paint.) V–190a
Gullagher, Christian (paint.) V–188a
GULLAH (dial.) **III–233b**
Gum tree VI–48b
Gunboat diplomacy II–6b; III–234b; IV–466a
GUNBOATS III–234a; V–25a; VI–148a; VII–241a
Civil War II–22a, 363a; IV–374a, 374b, 375a, 375a
Eads gunboats II–384a
galley boats III–147b
gundelow III–235a
national defense II–313a
technological advances VII–147a
Union navy VII–146b
War of 1812 IV–212a
Gun control IV–470a
Guncotton II–7a; V–327b
GUNDELOW III–235a
Gunn, John B. (phys.) IV–333b
Gunn, John C. (physic.) IV–295b
Gunnies II–388b
Gunnison, John W. (off.) III–235a; VI–39a
GUNNISON MASSACRE (1853) **III–235a**
Gunn oscillator IV–333b
Gunpowder II–5a,b, 8a, 8a, 26b
bounties IV–308b
Civil War II–163a
colonial mills IV–243a
manufacture II–10a–b
nitrates V–97b–98a
Gunpowder Plot (1605) IV–202a
Gunpowder Trade Association V–383b
Gunrunning VI–209a
Guns V–163a–64a
antiaircraft I–200a
Eskimos II–462a
gatling gun III–154a
Indians III–399a
Maxim gun IV–277b
naval mortars IV–413b
Parrott gun V–26b
Sharps rifle I–283b
smoothbore II–313b
turret I–57b
See also Artillery; Machine gun; Munitions; Rifle; Warships
Gunships I–49b
Vietnam War I–63a
Gunsmiths I–317a; VI–291b
Gunston Hall (Fairfax Co., Va.) I–162b
Guntersville Dam III–323a
Gunther, John (jour.) IV–164b
Gun tubes V–163a
Gun turret IV–397a
Gurley, Royal (auctioneer) I–332b
Gurney, R. W. (phys.) V–301a
GUSTAV LINE III–235a; I–141a; IV–404a
Gutch, Robert (col.) IV–37b
Gutenberg Bible II–109a; IV–147a
Guthrie (Okla.) I–336b
Guthrie, Tyrone (dir.) VII–50b
Guthrie, Woody (mus.) IV–441a
Gutiérrez de Lara, Bernardo (adventurer) III–235b–36a; IV–457a
GUTIÉRREZ–MAGEE EXPEDITION (1812–13) **III–235b**
Gutta–percha I–400b; V–327b
Guy, Francis (paint.) V–188a
Guyana
bauxite I–92b
See also British Guiana
Guyasuta. *See* Kiasutha
Guyot, Arnold Henry (geog.) III–222b
Guys and Dolls (musical) IV–442a
Guzik, Jake (criminal) II–258b
Guzmán, Jacobo Arbenz (pol.) I–454b
Guzzoni, Alfredo (off.) VI–284b
Gwin, William M. (pol.) V–180b, 357b
Gwinnett, Button (legis.) II–308a; III–236a
GWINNETT–MCINTOSH DUEL (1777) **III–236a**
GWYNN'S ISLAND III–236a
Gymnastics
Olympic Games V–154a
Gypsum III–16a; VI–220b
Gypsy moth III–421a

H

Haarlem (Holland) III–253a
Haas, Gregory (friar) I–452a
Haaskouan. *See* Otreouati
HABEAS CORPUS, WRIT OF III–236a; I–297b
accused aliens IV–218b
arbitrary arrest I–195b
civil rights II–53b
Civil War II–62a, 161a, 165a, 179a, 472b; VI–405a
Constitution II–200a
Ex parte Merryman IV–314b
Japanese–American relocation III–491b
Ku Klux Act IV–57b, 58a
Supreme Court VI–444a
Habeas Corpus Act (1679) III–236b
Habeas Corpus Act (1867) VII–35a
Haber, Al VI–421a
Haber, Fritz (chem.) V–98b; VI–334b
Haberdashery stores II–81b
Haber process III–17a; V–98b
Habersham, Joseph (postmaster) V–372a
Hachett, Charles (chem.) III–14b
Hackensack (N.J.) II–321b; V–229a
Hacker, Hoystead (nav. off.) VI–128a
Hacker, Louis M. (hist.) VI–157a
Hackett, David II–148a
Hackyackawck patent. *See* Kakiate patent
Haddock III–52a
Hadfield, George (arch.) I–162b
Hadley (Mass.) VI–70b, 71a
Hadnott v. *Amos* (1969) III–93b
Haematoxylen campechianum (tree) IV–181b
Haenke, Thaddaeus (expl.) V–326b
Hagen, Walter (golfer) III–197b
Hagen, Winston I–333a
Hagenbeck, Karl VII–371a
Hagenbeck–Wallace Circus II–40b
Hagerstown (Md.) II–184a; III–256a; IV–261b; V–184a, 248b
Haggenmacher, Carl (inv.) III–44a
Haggin, James B. (law.) I–116a
Haggin and Carr II–336a
Hagley Museum (Greenville, Del.) IV–437a
Hague (Neth.) I–277b; II–382a; V–262b
Hague, Frank (pol.) I–343a; III–237b; V–58a
Hague, James D. IV–120a
Hague Agreement (1930) I–254a
Hague Convention Concerning the Rights and Duties of Neutral Powers in Naval War (1907) V–422a
Hague Court. *See* International Court of Justice
Hague Court of Arbitration. *See* Permanent Court of Arbitration
Hague Opium Convention (1912) II–374b; IV–450a
HAGUE PEACE CONFERENCES (1899, 1907) **III–237a**; II–70a; III–452b, 456a; IV–82b; V–231a–b, 422a; VII–112b, 113a
chemical weapons II–9b
Drago doctrine I–411a; II–369a
Geneva Conventions III–162a
immunity of private property III–343a
international prize court IV–182a
laws of war VII–225b
neutrality laws V–35a
neutral rights V–38b–39a
partisan bands V–222a
Permanent Court of Arbitration V–262a
submarine warfare VI–423b
Hague Tribunal of Arbitration (1910) II–92b
HAGUE* v. *COMMITTEE ON INDUSTRIAL ORGANIZATION (1939) **III–237b**
Hahn, Otto (phys.) V–300a
Hahn, William C. (phys.) VII–163b
Hahnemann, Samuel (physic.) III–293b; IV–288b
HAIDA (Indians) **III–238a**; I–79a, 441b; III–361a–b, 362a; IV–59a, 228b
Haig, Alexander M., Jr. (off.) V–99a
Haig, Douglas (off.) II–311a; IV–320a
Haight House (N.Y.C.) I–143b
Hail, South Dakota (song) VI–395 (table)
Hail, Vermont (song) VI–395 (table)
"HAIL COLUMBIA" (song) **III–238b**
Hail! Minnesota (song) VI–394 (table)
Haines (Alaska) I–80a
HAINES' BLUFF (1863) **III–238b**
Haiphong (Viet.) I–57a, 62b; V–21b, 22a; VII–184b
mines IV–351b; V–27b

Hair brooches II–371b
"HAIR BUYER" III–238b
Hair oil II–233b
Hair powder II–233b
Hair seal VI–245a
HAIR STYLES III–239a; II–372b
Hairy Ape (play) VII–50a
Haish, Jacob (inv.) I–267b
Haiti III–437a
- Bretton Woods Conference I–361b
- Dominican Republic II–360b, 361a
- Hurricane Hazel II–351b
- refugees V–342a
- Santo Domingo VI–217a
- slave revolt VI–303b, 304a
- slave trade VI–309a
- United Nations Declaration VII–151b

HAITI, INTERVENTION IN (1915–34) **III–239b**; I–454b; II–359b, 360b; III–463a; IV–111b, 112a; V–105b, 106a; VI–163a
- marine landings IV–252b
- Monroe Doctrine IV–401b
- U.S. protectorate III–347b

Hake (fish) III–413a
Hakluyt, Richard (geog.) I–365b; VI–43b
- *See also* Hakluyt's *Voyages*

HAKLUYT'S *VOYAGES* III–240b; III–280a; IV–161a; V–274b
Hakluytus Posthumus. See Purchas, His Pilgrims
Halberstam, David (jour.) V–74b
Halchidhoma (Indians) III–363a; IV–386a
Haldeman, H. R. VII–254b, 255b
Haldimand, Fort (Can.) I–340b
Haldimand, Frederick (off.) I–341a
- Fort Ontario V–157a
- Saint Louis attack VI–195a
- *See also* Haldimand Negotiations

HALDIMAND NEGOTIATIONS (1780) **III–240b**; IV–86b; VII–172a
Hale, Edward Everett (au.) II–439a
Hale, Enoch (physic.) I–363b
HALE, EXECUTION OF (1776) **III–241a**; VI–373a; VII–225a
Hale, George Ellery (astron.) I–211b; III–241b–42a; VI–230b
Hale, Horatio Emmons (ethnol.) VII–299a
Hale, John P. (states.) I–138b, 420b
- campaign of 1848 IV–143b
- campaign of 1852 III–112a

Hale, Lucretia P. (au.) I–335b; IV–223a
Hale, Matthew (fin.) VII–309b
Hale, Nathan. *See* Hale, Execution of
Hale, Sarah Josepha (writ., ed.) I–335b; III–188a; IV–223a
Haleakala National Park V–219 (table), 220a
Haleiwa (Haw.) V–239b
HALE OBSERVATORIES III–241b; V–131b
Hale reflector I–212a
Hale rockets VI–159a
Hales Bar Dam III–323b
Hale telescope III–242a–b
HALF-BREEDS III–242b; III–399b, 403b; IV–97a,b
"Halfbreeds" (pol. term.) VI–380b
HALF-BREED TRACT III–242b
Half disme IV–394a
Half–dollar II–264a, 384b
Half–eagle (coin) II–95a, 384b; IV–394a
***HALF MOON* (ship) III–243a**; I–81a, 471a; III–312a; V–86a, 246a
Halford, William (seaman) VI–186a
HALFWAY COVENANT III–243a; II–169b
Halfway houses V–416b
Haliaeetus leucocephalus (bald eagle) II–384b
Haliburton, Thomas Chandler (jur., humorist) VI–207a
Halibut III–52a, 413a; VII–33a
Halifax (N.C.) V–115b
Halifax (N.S.) III–315b; VI–182a
- British prison ships V–418b
- fisheries commission VII–248b
- French and Indian War III–116a
- hockey III–286b
- Loyalist veterans VI–131a
- privateers VI–129b
- transatlantic flight V–30a
- War of 1812 III–247b; VII–352a

Halifax (ship) II–16a
Halifax, Earl of. *See* Dunk, George Montagu, 2nd Earl of Halifax
HALIFAX, FORT (Maine) **III–243b**; I–345a; V–370a
HALIFAX FISHERIES AWARD III–243b
Hall, A. Oakey ("O.K.") (pol.) VI–142a; VII–131a
Hall, Asaph (astron.) V–13a
Hall, Basil (nav. off.) I–367b, 368a
Hall, Charles Francis (expl.) IV–457a; V–336b
Hall, Charles Martin (chem.) I–92a; II–7b, 422b; V–103b
Hall, Cherokee (lit. char.) V–336a

Hall, David (print.) V–68b, 251a
Hall, Donald (eng.) I–51b
HALL, FORT (Idaho) **III–243b**; III–215a, 260b
- Oregon Trail V–168b, 169a; VI–154a
- Snake River VI–322b
- South Pass V–225a
- stagelines VI–379b
- wagon trains VII–217b

Hall, George I–453b
Hall, G. Stanley (psych., educ.) II–470b; III–424a; IV–2b; V–441b, 442a
Hall, Henry (fin.) III–243b
Hall, James (geol., paleon.) III–480b; V–195b, 196a, 197a
Hall, John H. (inv.) III–441b; IV–272a
Hall, Joseph (print.) V–70a, 322b
Hall, Lyman (physic.) II–308a
Hall, Prince (cler.) III–109a
Hall, Samuel Read (educ.) II–398a; VI–228b
Hall, William (print.) V–251a
Hall, William, Jr. (print.) V–251a
Hallam, Lewis (theat. mgr.) VII–46b
Halle, University of V–310b–11a
Halleck, Henry W. (off.) II–63a; III–21a; IV–370a; V–245b, 377b
- Battle of Shiloh VI–278b
- Red River campaign VI–63a

Haller, Granville O. (off.) VII–350a
Hallet, Stephen (arch.) I–451a
Hallett, Samuel IV–30b
Halliday, Simeon (lit. char.) VII–138b
Hallidie, A. S. (eng., inv.) III–191b
Hallinan, Vincent W. (law.) V–429b
Hallmark Cards II–107a
Hallock, William (nav. off.) VI–128a
Hall of Fame, Baseball I–269b
Hall rifle IV–430b
Halls Stream III–200a; V–118b
Hallucinogens VII–65b
Halogens (chem.) II–12b
Halogen salts V–291a,b
Halpert, Edith Gregor II–105b
Halprin , Ann (chor.) II–290a
Hals, Frans (paint.) V–185a
Halsey, Frederick R. H. II–109b
Halsey, R. T. Haines II–100b
Halsey, William F. (nav. off.) I–14a, 459a; VII–337a–b, 343b
- Battle of Leyte Gulf IV–138a
- psychological warfare V–441a
- Third Fleet V–24b

Halske, Johann (eng.) VI–40a
Halsted, William S. (surg.) IV–3a, 298a
Ham III–52a, 53b; IV–280b, 281a
Hambleton, T. Edward (theat. mgr.) VII–51a
Hamburg (Ger.) II–407b
- World War II I–66b; VII–341a

Hamburg (S.C.) VI–24b, 349b
Hamburger III–53a
HAMBURG RIOT (1876) **III–244a**; VI–65b
Hamel (Fr.) VI–338b
Hamer, Philip M. (lib.) III–285b
Hamersly, L. R. VI–301b
Hamet (of Tripoli) II–334a
Hamill, Pete (writ.) V–79a
Hamilton (Can.) VII–45b
Hamilton (Ohio) III–244a
Hamilton, A. J. (pol.) I–2a
Hamilton, Alexander (states.) VII–15b, 291a
- Annapolis Convention I–126a
- Antifederalists II–326b
- Bank Message II–197b
- Bank of North America I–260b
- Bank of the United States I–255a, 261a
- Bill of Rights I–297b
- bimetallism I–301a; VI–370a
- British trade III–493b
- Burr duel I–387b, 388a; II–377a; VII–266b
- campaign of 1792 I–417a
- campaign of 1800 III–5a
- Coast Guard II–88b–89a
- coinage II–95a
- Constitution II–192b–93a, 196a–b, 197b, 203b
- criticism IV–463b
- Croswell libel suit II–266a; IV–139b
- Essex Junto II–464a; VI–250a
- European capital II–301a
- *Federalist* I–130b; II–196b, 325b; III–4a; IV–15b, 21a; V–353a; VII–309a
- Federalist party I–33a; III–4b; V–83a, 86b; VI–94a
- federal mint IV–394a
- federal surplus VI–449a
- financial reports to Congress V–353a
- fiscal policies III–244a
- Franco–American relations II–215a
- *Gazette of the United States* III–202a
- general welfare clause III–156b
- Genêt mission III–159b
- implied powers III–348a–b
- Jefferson–Burr election dis-

HAMILTON, ALEXANDER (cont.)
pute III–495a
Jeffersonian Democracy III–495b
Loyalists VII–116b–17a
Miranda's intrigues IV–361b
monarchy II–189a
national capital I–448b
national sinking fund VI–294a
natural rights doctrine V–7b
Neutrality Proclamation V–181a
newspapers V–69b
People v. *Croswell* VII–117b
political theories V–350b, 352a
public credit V–443a–b
public lands V–443b–44a
report on manufactures III–246b; IV–432b; VI–465a
report on military IV–432a–b
representation doctrine VI–88a
representative government VI–89b
revolutionary war debts I–208a,b; II–88b, 149b, 299b–300a, 302a; VI–120a,b
Reynolds, Maria V–346b
slavery I–135b
Society for Establishing Useful Manufactures V–57b; VII–160b
state sovereignty VI–403b
tariff II–88b; VI–463a–b
taxation VII–4b, 12b
Treasury VII–107b
Whiskey Rebellion VII–82b, 290b
Yorktown campaign VII–361a
Hamilton, Alice (physic.) IV–294a
Hamilton, Andrew (col. gov.) V–371a
Hamilton, Andrew (law.) III–354a; V–69a; VII–117a
Zenger trial IV–139b; VII–368b
Hamilton, Andrew J. (gov.) VII–39b
Hamilton, Charles A. (pioneer) IV–248a–b
Hamilton, Charles S. (off.) III–485a
Hamilton, F. E. (eng.) II–154a
HAMILTON, FORT (Ohio) **III–244a**; IV–330a
Hamilton, George E. (comp.) III–469a
Hamilton, H. C. (inv.) II–420a
Hamilton, Henry (col. adm.) II–71a–b; III–238b–39a; VI–124a
Hamilton, James (pol.) III–78a
Hamilton, John Randolph (off.) III–36b
Hamilton, Morgan (pol.) I–2a
Hamilton, Philip VII–266b
Hamilton County (Northwest Terr.) V–123a
HAMILTON'S FISCAL POLICIES III–244a; III–4b; VII–289b
bimetallism VI–288a
import duties III–493b
national bank III–101b
opposition II–326b
trade with Great Britain III–63a
Hamilton's Plan (1699) II–121b
HAMILTON'S REPORT ON MANUFACTURES (1791) **III–246b**; IV–246a, 432b; VI–465a
Hamilton Standard Propeller Company I–234b
Hamlet, James III–247a
HAMLET CASE (1850) **III–247a**
Hamlin, Hannibal (pol.) I–421b; VII–179 (table)
Hamline, Leonidas L. (cler.) IV–83a
Hamline University I–272a
Hammer and sickle II–437b
Hammerstein, Oscar II (playwright, librettist) IV–442a; VII–50b
Hammerstones III–484b
HAMMER* v. *DAGENHART (1918) **III–247a**; II–25a, 136b; III–459b; VII–117b
Hammock III–381a
Hammond, Bray (hist.) III–486b
Hammond, George (dipl.) III–375a–b, 493b
Hammond, George Henry (meat packer) I–366b
Hammond, James H. (pol.) I–137b; IV–46b; VI–349a
Hammond, John (hist.) IV–79a
Hammond, W. A. (physic.) I–410a
Hammond–Harwood House (Md.) I–162b
Hammond typewriter VII–136b
HAMPDEN EXPEDITION (1814) **III–247b**
Hampshire hog III–288b
Hampton (N.H.) V–53b
Hampton (Towson, Md.) IV–96b
Hampton (Va.) IV–106a, 458a; VI–336b
Hampton (Robb), Isabelle A. (nurse) IV–3a; V–126b
Hampton, Wade (off.) I–281a; VI–348a
Battle at Trevilian Station VII–117a
Battle of Chateaugay I–501b
Buckland Races I–374a
burning of Columbia II–131a
Canadian defeat IV–87a
First Battle of Bull Run I–381b
Red Shirts VI–65b
Tillmanism VII–59a
Hampton Institute II–113b; III–103b
Hampton Roads (Va.) III–40b, 236a; VI–145a
Battle Fleet cruise I–276b
Chesapeake–Leopard incident II–16a
Civil War IV–396b, 397a, 397a; VII–147a, 212b
coal IV–311a; VII–196a
ferries III–11b
Jamestown Exposition III–489b
railroad VI–33a
revolutionary war I–194a
Wilkes Exploring Expedition VII–299a–b
HAMPTON ROADS CONFERENCE (1865) **III–247b**; II–63b; V–234b–35a
Ham's Fork (Wyo.) III–227a; VII–104a
Hamtramck, John F. (off.) IV–53b; VI–412b; VII–262a
Han (Indians) I–80b; III–252b, 360b
Hanaman, Franz (chem.) IV–89a
Hancock (carrier) V–22a
Hancock, John (states.) V–152a; VI–113b; VII–17a, 358b
campaign of 1788 I–417a
Constitution II–196b
Continental Congress II–305b
Declaration of Independence II–305b–06a, 307b
Essex Junto II–464a
Liberty seizure VI–436a
Revere's ride VI–106a
Hancock, Ralph (hort.) III–152a
Hancock, Thomas (inv.) VI–167a
Hancock, Thomas (mer.) III–127b
Hancock, Winfield Scott (off.) V–247b
Battle of Spotsylvania Courthouse VI–376b
Boydton Plank Road engagement I–357a
campaign of 1876 I–422b
campaign of 1880 I–423b
Cheyenne expedition IV–109a; VII–190b
railroad strike of 1877 VI–38b
Hancock County (Ill.) IV–412a; V–8a
Hancock County (Tenn.) IV–301a
Hancock Script V–412a
Hand, Edward (off.) V–321b; VI–378a, 438a
Hand, Learned (jur.) V–103b; VII–123b
Handball
Olympic Games V–154a
Handbills I–16b
Handbook of Lizards VI–91a
Handbook of Snakes of the United States and Canada VI–91a
Handbook of Turtles VI–91a
Handcarts IV–411b
Hand crank I–228b
Handel and Haydn Society of Boston IV–267a, 437b
Hanford (Calif.) IV–444a
Hanford (Wash.) II–423a
Handicapped
social security VI–329a–b
HANDICAPPED, EDUCATION OF THE III–248a; II–405b; V–280a, 380b; VI–327b
Pratt-Smoot Act IV–147b
typewriter VII–136a
Handicapped Children's Educational Assistance Act (1968) III–249a
Handly's Lessee v. *Anthony* (1820) I–351b
Hand's Cove (N.Y.) VII–56a
HANDSOME LAKE CULT III–249b; III–476a; V–4a
Handy, W. C. (comp.) IV–302a, 440a, 443b
"Handy Man's Workshop" (mag. column) VI–231b
Hanford Atomic Works (Wash.) IV–238a; VII–248a
HANGING III–249b; V–464b, 465a, 469b; VI–311b
HANGING ROCK, ACTION AT (1780) **III–250a**; VII–261b
Hangman's knot III–250a
Hangtown (Calif.) VI–154a
Hanham, Thomas VII–199b
Hanks, John (pol.) VI–40a
Hanley, T. Edward II–106b
Hanna, Clinton R. (eng.) V–290a
Hanna, Gordie C. (sci.) I–35b
Hanna, Louis B. (gov.) V–106b
Hanna, Marcus A. (pol.) I–380b, 425b, 426a
Hanna, Robert III–250a
Hannah (ship) III–153b; VI–128a
HANNASTOWN (Pa.) **III–250a**
HANNASTOWN RESOLUTION (1775) **III–250b**
Hanna v. *Plumer* (1965) II–460b
Hannibal (slave ship) VI–308b
HANNIBAL AND SAINT JOSEPH RAILROAD III–250b; IV–380a; VI–26a, 191b
Hano (Indians) III–301b
Hano (N.Mex.) V–459b
Hanoi (Viet.) I–57a, 62b, 63a
Hanover (N.H.) II–292b; VI–298a
Hanover (Pa.) III–250b

HANOVER CAVALRY ENGAGEMENT (1863) **III–250b**
Hanover County (Va.) V–221b; VI–442a
Hanover Courthouse (Va.) I–161b; V–113b; VI–376b
Hanover Junction (Va.) V–113b
Hanovertown (Va.) V–113b
Han River (Kor.) IV–55a
Hans and Fritz (comic character) V–72a
Hansa towns VII–370a
Hansberry, Lorraine (au.) IV–167a
Hans Brinker, or the Silver Skates I–335a; V–41b
Hansell, Haywood S. (off.) III–490a
Hansen, Morris H. (statis.) VI–206b
Hansen, W. W. (phys.) V–301a–b
Hanson, John (legis.) III–100b
Hanson, John G. (abolitionist) IV–220a
Hapgood, Andrew S. (bus.) VI–201a
"Happiness is. . . ." V–72b
"Happy Days Are Here Again" (song) I–432b; VI–313a
Happy Hooligan (comic character) V–72a
"HAPPY HUNTING GROUND" III–250b; II–31a; III–223a, 366b, 392a
"Happy Valley" (Ger.) VI–302b
Hapsburg Empire III–338b
Harbison (S.C.) II–48b
Harbord, James (off.) I–286b
Harbor facilities
municipal ownership IV–427b
Harbor fortifications II–313a
Harbor improvements. *See* River and Harbor Improvements
Harcourt, Alfred (pub.) I–334b
Harcourt, Brace (pub.) I–334b
Hardaway site (N.C.) I–156a; II–385b
"Hard Cider and Log Cabin" campaign (1840) I–420a
Hardee, William J. (off.) I–232b; IV–365a
Army of Tennessee VII–26b
Battle of Missionary Ridge IV–365a
Battles on Peachtree Creek V–238a
Savannah siege VI–221a
Harden, Arthur (biochem.) V–127b
Hardenbergh, Henry Janeway (arch.) I–143b
Hardenbergh patent IV–354b
Harder, D. S. (bus.) I–224b
Hardin County (Ill.) I–476a; IV–263a
Harding, Chester, Jr. (off.) III–182a
Harding, Chester A. V–190a
Harding, Warren G. (pres.) II–177 (table); V–142a, 346b, 394b, 396 (table), 398b; VI–93a; VII–291a
campaign of 1920 I–427b; VII–134b
coal strike II–3b
death I–427b
Debs pardon II–463b
Far Eastern policy II–488b
Foreign Service III–72a
military bonus I–331b
naval oil reserves V–13a; VII–16b
nonrecognition policy V–107b
"normalcy" V–110a
Philippines V–283b
radio broadcasts II–424b
railway shopmen's strike VI–40b
Soviet government VI–181a
Tomb of the Unknown Soldier VII–156b
HARD LABOR, TREATY OF (1768) **III–251a**; III–382b; IV–173a; V–425a; VI–386a
HARD MONEY III–251b
antibank movement I–129b
Independent Treasury System III–354b
prices V–404a,b
See also Bimetallism; Soft Money
"Hards" (Hunkers) III–318a
HARDWARE TRADE III–252a; II–355a; III–402b; IV–448b
Hardwoods III–74b; IV–204b; VII–59b, 60b
Hardy, Harriet (physic.) IV–294a
Hardy, R. W. H. (expl.) II–129b
Hardy, Thomas (nav. off.) VI 415a–b–
Hardy, William (col. gov.) II–121a
HARE (Indians) **III–252b**; III–360b
Hare, Robert (chem.) I–276a; II–10b; III–408a–b
Hare quota (pol.) V–390b, 435b
Hargis, James (jur.). *See* Hargis–Callahan–Cockrell Feud
HARGIS–CALLAHAN–COCKRELL FEUD (1899–1903) **III–252b**; III–18b
Hargous, P. A. III–145b
Hargreaves, James (inv.) II–237b
Harkaway, Jack (lit. char.) II–341b
Harkins, William D. (chem.) V–298b, 299b, 301b
Harkness, Edward S. (philan.) II–104a; III–260b; VII–351a
Harkness, Rebekah II–289b
Harkness, Stephen v. (ind.) VI–382b, 383a
Harkness Ballet II–289b
Harlan, John Marshall (b. 1833, jur.) VI–445b
Bill of Rights I–299a, 300a
United States v. *Texas* VII–155a
Harlan, John Marshall (b. 1899, jur.) VI–447a
Bill of Rights I–299b
due process II–378a
freedom of speech III–104a
Harlan, Richard (nat.) IV–232a; VI–90a
Harland, Thomas (clockmaker) II–77b–78a
HARLEM (N.Y.C.) **III–253a**; II–261b; V–82b
Black Muslims V–171a
literature IV–166a
race riots VI–7a, 8a
HARLEM, BATTLE OF (1776) **III–254b**; III–253b; VI–373a; VII–293a
Harlem Globetrotters (basketball) I–273a
Harlem Renaissance I–30a; III–254a; IV–166a–b, 167a, 443b
Harlem River I–368b; III–117b, 254b; IV–237a; VII–258b, 259a
Harleston's Green (Charleston, S.C.) III–197a
Harley, Henry (bus.) V–319a
Harley, Robert, 1st Earl of Oxford (states.) VI–2b
"Harlot, Slavery" I–371a
Harman, Ephraim (law.) VII–130a
HARMAR, FORT (Ohio) **III–254b**; VII–247a
Harmar, Josiah (off.) II–484b; III–127a, 254b
See also Harmar's Expedition
HARMAR FORT, TREATIES OF (1789) **III–255a**
HARMAR'S EXPEDITION (1790) **III–255a**; VI–188b; VII–212b, 262b
Fort Washington VII–247a
Harmonic analyzer II–153a, 155a
Harmonic synthesizer II–153a
Harmony Mission VII–274a
HARMONY SOCIETY III–255a; II–147a; IV–338b; V–55a
Harmsworth, Alfred Charles, Lord Northcliffe (pub.) V–74b, 240b
HARNESS III–255b; III–413b
Harness racing III–305a–b
Harney, William S. (off.) VI–261a
See also Harney Expedition
HARNEY EXPEDITION (1855) **III–256a**; III–213b; IV–108a; VI–296b
Harney Peak I–312b
HARO CHANNEL DISPUTE III–256a
Haro Strait III–256a; VI–214a
Harpe, Bernard de la (expl.) IV–456b
Harpe Brothers I–476a
Harper (pub.) I–334a
Harper, Fletcher (pub.) III–257a
Harper, John L. V–174b
Harper, Robert Goodloe (pol.) III–4b; IV–347a
Harper, William R. (educ.) III–275a
Harper and Brothers III–257a
Harper and Gillespie I–274b
Harper's (mag.) II–298b
Harper's Bazar (mag.) I–17b; II–371b
Harper's *Bible* VII–319a
Harpers Ferry (W.Va.)
arms manufacturing III–441b, 442a
arsenal I–196b; IV–432b; V–163a; VI–139b
bridge I–442b
Niagara movement V–93a
Potomac River V–378a
Shenandoah Valley VI–275b
HARPERS FERRY, CAPTURE OF (1862) **III–256a**; I–130a; IV–190a, 261b
HARPERS FERRY RAID (1859) **III–256b**; I–138a; II–224a; III–437a, 465a; IV–252a; VI–270a, 302b, 342a, 404b; VII–107a
Harper's New Monthly Magazine VII–319a
***HARPER'S WEEKLY* III–257a**; IV–222a,b
cartoons I–464b; IV–454a,b; V–73a
engravings V–414a
Tammany Hall VI–459b
Harper's Young People (mag.) IV–223a
Harper v. *Virginia Board of Elections* (1966) III–93b; IV–371b; V–355a, 434b; VI–432b, 435a; VII–133a
Harpoons II–376b, 462a
Harp seal VI–245a
Harpur, Robert (prof.) VI–165b
Harrigan, Edward (playwright) VII–49a
Harriman (Tenn.) I–232b
Harriman, Edward H. (ind.) I–116b; III–79b; V–119a; VI–37b; VII–148a
Harriman, Mrs. Edward Henry II–97a
Harriman, W. Averell (pol.) II–134b; V–87b
Harriman Alaska Expedition (1899) V–337a
Harrington, Henry B. (hist.) IV–180a
Harriot, Thomas (math.) I–348b; III–26b

Harris, Albert W. III–19b
Harris, Benjamin (pub.) I–335a; V–68a
Harris, B. G. (pol.) II–222b
Harris, Caleb Fiske (biblio.) II–108b
Harris, Chapin Aaron (dent.) II–329b, 330a
Harris, Fred (skier) VI–298a
Harris, Ira (pol.) IV–6a
Harris, Joel Chandler (au.) I–335b; IV–162b, 223a
Harris, John (settler) III–257b
Harris, John (dent.) II–329b
Harris, John, Jr. III–257b
Harris, R. D. (biol.) II–97a
Harris, Roy (comp.) IV–439a
Harris, Stephen R. (nav. off.) V–460b
Harris, Townsend (dipl.) II–488b
Harris, William Torrey (educ.) II–398b
Harrisburg (Pa.) III–257a, 257b; V–247a
  Pullman service V–462b
  railroad IV–177a; VI–36a
Harrisburg (Tex.) VII–38a
HARRISBURG CONVENTION (1827) **III–257a**; VI–465b
HARRIS' FERRY (Pa.) **III–257b**
Harrison (Ohio) IV–410b
Harrison (Pa.) VI–49a
Harrison, Benjamin (pres.) II–176 (table), 294a; V–142a, 395 (table); VI–93a; VII–300b
  conservation II–187b
  election of 1888 I–322a, 424a,b; II–409b; VI–184a
  free silver VI–277a
  In re Neagle V–30a
  Latin American relations IV–111a
  Mafia incident IV–221b
  Oklahoma settlement V–149b; VI–340a
  pledge of allegiance V–331a
  pocket veto V–334b
  Rustler War VI–181b
  Sherman Silver Purchase Act VI–288b
  tariff VI–467a
Harrison, Benjamin (rev. leader) II–306a, 308b; IV–8b
Harrison, Caroline Scott II–294a
Harrison, Carter H. (pol.) III–266a
Harrison, Elizabeth (nun) VII–160b
HARRISON, FORT (Ind.) **III–257b**; VII–63a,b
Harrison, Fort (Va.) V–265a
Harrison, Francis Burton (law., pol.) V–283b
Harrison, H. C. (eng.) V–290a
Harrison, James (clockmaker) II–79a
Harrison, John (chem.) II–5b; III–408b
Harrison, Joseph, Jr. I–471a
Harrison, Peter (arch.) I–162a
Harrison, Robert (pol.) I–416b
Harrison, Robert H. (jur.) VI–445a
Harrison, Wallace K. (arch.) I–165b
Harrison, William Henry II–175 (table); III–257b; V–395 (table), 398b
  Division Act of 1800 II–356a
  Harrison Land Act III–257b
  Indian treaties III–372b–73a, 384b, 404a; VI–377b, 378a; VII–189a, 262a,b
  territorial governor III–369b; VII–189a
  War of 1812 II–338a, 458b, 459b
  —Military Career:
  Battle of Lake Erie VII–267a
  Battle of Mississinewa IV–367b
  Battle of the Thames VII–45b, 234b
  Battle of Tippecanoe V–435a; VI–271b; VII–18a, 63a, 234a
  Detroit III–217a
  Fort Ferree VII–157b
  Fort Meigs IV–300b; VI–412a
  —President:
  Baltimore affair I–250b
  campaign of 1836 I–419b
  campaign of 1840 I–420a; VI–422a; VII–63b–64a, 288b
  inauguration III–351a
  Independent Treasury System III–354b
Harrison Acts (1914) IV–450a,b
Harrison Almanacs I–91a
Harrisonburg (Va.) II–266a; III–332b; VI–275b
  Civil War V–359a–b
HARRISON LAND ACT (1800) **III–257b**; II–356a; IV–90b; VI–75a
Harrison Narcotics Act (1914) II–261a, 374b; V–276a
Harrison's Landing (Va.) III–258a; IV–230b; V–245b; VI–263b
HARRISON'S LANDING LETTER, MCCLELLAN'S (1862) **III–258a**
Harris Poll V–453b
Harrisse, Henry (hist.) IV–163a
Harris Votomatic voting machine VII–211a
Harrod, James (pioneer) III–258a; IV–40a; VI–450b
HARRODSBURG (Ky.) **III–258a**; I–324b; III–239a; IV–40a, 43a
Harrow I–34a
Harry Briggs, Jr. v. *R. W. Elliot* I–372b
Harry S. Truman Library I–167b
Hart, Albert Bushnell (hist.) III–282b; IV–8a
Hart, Charlie. *See* Quantrill, William Clarke
Hart, David (col.) VII–102b
Hart, John (farmer) II–308a
Hart, Lorenz (lyricist) IV–442a
Hart, Nathaniel (col.) VII–102b, 103a
Hart, Shaffner and Marx II–82b
Hart, Thomas (col.) VII–102b
Hart, William A. (gunsmith) V–5a
Harte, Bret (au.) I–405b; IV–163a, 223a; V–336a
Hartford (Conn.) I–274b; II–99a, 181a, 182a, 182b, 348a; VI–151a–b; VII–282b
  ballet II–289a
  city planning II–46a
  Colt six-shooter II–130b
  constitutional convention II–183a
  Constitution Plaza II–48b
  directory II–343b
  harness factory III–255b
  House of Hope III–309a,b; V–334b
  Huguenots III–315a
  munitions manufacture IV–433a
  Pequot War V–261a,b
  pewter work VI–290b
  publishing I–334a
  Regicides VI–70b
  school for the deaf III–248a
  settlement II–179b
  Sharps rifle VI–270a
  urban renewal VI–86b
  Wide-Awakes VII–294b
HARTFORD (sloop-of-war) **III–258b**; II–286a; IV–383a; VI–313b; VII–240b
HARTFORD, TREATY OF (1650) **III–258b**; IV–185b; V–62a
Hartford and New Haven Railroad VI–35b
HARTFORD CONVENTION (1814–15) **III–259a**; III–5a; V–2b, 235a; VI–250a, 404b; VII–235b
  campaign of 1816 I–418a
  Essex Junto II–464b
  New Hampshire V–54a
  nullification V–125b
Hartford Retreat IV–305b
Hartford, Treaty of (1786) I–347b; V–276b
HARTFORD WITS III–259a
Harth, Mingo VI–304a
Hartley, David (dipl.) V–214b
Hartley, Fred (pol.) VI–456b
Hartley, Robert M. (ref.) II–280a; V–280a
Hartline, Haldan K. (physiol.) V–100a
Hart Mountain (Wyo.) III–491a
Hart-Parr Company I–35b
Hartsuff, George L. (off.) VI–261a
Hartsville (Tenn.) IV–410a, 410a
Hartt, Edmund (shipbuilder) II–190b
Hartt, Mills D. (settler) IV–444a
Hartzog, George B., Jr. (offi.) V–220b
Harvard (Mass.) III–129b
Harvard (trawler) III–29a
Harvard, John (cler.) III–259b; V–279b
Harvard Business Review VII–317b
Harvard College. *See* Harvard University
Harvard Computation Laboratory II–154a
HARVARD UNIVERSITY III–259b; I–344b, 411b; II–394b; IV–191a, 265a; V–49b–50a; VI–440b
  archives I–169a
  bacteriology studies I–241a
  chemistry II–11a
  computers II–154a, 426b
  curriculum II–397b
  Divinity School VI–81b
  education report II–401a
  elective system II–115a, 398a, 399b
  endowment V–279b
  football III–56b
  founding II–114a–b
  Gray Herbarium V–327b
  Houghton Library III–285a
  industrial medicine IV–294a
  Lawrence Scientific School II–399a; IV–119b
  law school IV–120b
  library II–107b; IV–144a, 145a,b
  lottery financing III–149b
  medical school IV–283a, 284b, 298a, 348b; V–306b, 307a
  Museum of Comparative Zoology IV–233a
  Nader's Raiders IV–448b
  navy personnel V–23b
  Nieman Foundation V–79b
  observatory I–211b; V–131a
  parapsychology V–213a
  Peabody Museum III–19a
  political science V–348b–49a
  pragmatism V–386b
  psychology V–441b
  public health V–447b
  radio astronomy VI–17a
  radio Research Laboratory VI–10b
  rugby III–56b
  scientific education VI–232a, 237b
  social work VI–331a
  Students for a Democratic Society VI–421b

technical instruction II–447a
tennis VII–29b
theater VII–46b
Webster–Parkman murder case VII–266a
Harvard Yard III–260b
Harvest
thanksgiving II–497a
Harvesters I–35a; II–133b
Harvesting
hay IV–424a
Harvey, John (baker) II–339a
Harvey, John (col. gov.) II–117a
Harvey, William Hope "Coin" (econ.) II–96a–b; III–111a
Harvey process (steel mfg.) I–179a
Harwood, H. J. (inv.) IV–274b
Harwood Foundation VI–461a
Hasbrouck House (N.Y.) V–392b
Hascall, J. (inv.) I–34b–35a
Hasidim IV–11a
Haskin, De Witt C. VII–128a
Haskins, Caryl P. (adm., sci.) I–457a
Haslam, John (vet.) VII–176a
Hass, Eric (pol.) VI–325b
Hassam, Childe (paint.) V–192a
Hassler (steamer) III–29a; V–134b
Hassler, Ferdinand R. (eng.) I–211a; II–87b; V–131a
Hastings, Francis Rawdon–, 1st Marquis of Hastings (Lord Rawdon) I–412a; III–286a–b; V–97a
Hastings, Lansford W. III–260b
HASTINGS' CUTOFF III–260b; III–215a; VII–161a–b
Haswell, Anthony (ed.) V–70a
Hat Act (1732) II–123a; IV–242b
Hatch, Carl III–261a
Hatch Act (1887) I–45a, 46a; II–227b
HATCH ACT (1939) **III–261a**; II–233a; IV–203a; V–341b, 448b
Hatcher's Run (Va.) I–357a; V–265a
Hatcher's Run, Battle of. *See* Boydton Plank Road, Engagements at
HATCHET, CARRIE NATION'S III–261b; IV–27a
Hatch Experiment Station Act (1887) VII–156b
Hat Creek (Nebr.) VII–227b
Hatfield, Anderson (Anse) III–262a
Hatfield, Ellison III–262a
HATFIELD MCCOY FEUD (1880–90) **III–262a**; III–18b
Hat manufacture I–282a
mercury poisoning IV–293b
unionization IV–61b, 62a
HAT MANUFACTURE, COLONIAL RESTRICTIONS ON III–262a; III–346b; V–16b; VI–107b, 108a
Hats
army uniforms VII–144a,b
beaver III–133b
silk I–282a
three–cornered II–371a
Hatteras (Indians) IV–203b
HATTERAS INLET, CAPTURE OF (1861) **III–262a**; IV–252a; VII–146b
Hattiesburg (Miss.) I–435a
Hauge, Hans Nielsen (rel. leader) V–123b
Haugen, Gilbert N. (pol.) IV–219a
Hauge's Synod V–123b
HAUN'S MILL MASSACRE (1838) **III–262b**
Haupt, Paul (Semitic schol.) IV–2b
Hauptmann, Bruno II–258b; IV–156b; VII–118a
Haüy, R. J. (crystal.) IV–348b
Havana (Cuba) I–67b; II–336a, 349b; III–230b
British seizure III–117a; IV–326a
gambling II–262a
Inter–American Conference V–205a
Johnson–Willard fight V–422b
logwood trade IV–181b
Maine VI–84b
malaria IV–229b
native American plants V–327a
Sixth International Conference of American States V–106a
Spanish–American War IV–227a; VI–363a
Spanish settlement IV–326a
steamship lines II–91a
Havana (Ill.) II–391a
HAVANA CONFERENCE (1928) **III–262b**; III–456b; IV–112a
Havasu, Lake II–130a
HAVASUPAI (Indians) **III–262b**; III–369a
Havemeyer, Henry O. (ind.) II–103a; III–80a
Haven, Samuel F. (librarian) II–98b–99a
Havens Relief Fund Society III–82b
Haverhill (Mass.) VI–2b, 324b
Haverly's Minstrel Show IV–359b
Haverstraw (N.Y.) I–118a
Haviland, William (off.) III–117a; IV–86b, 405b
Havoc (bomber) I–50a
HAWAII III–262b; II–30a; III–347a, 425a; VI–393 (table)
acreage annexed V–445 (table)
air defense I–58a
Alaska–Pacific–Yukon Exposition I–81a
annexation I–126b; II–475a,b; III–68b; V–158a, 443b; VII–111b
archives I–168b
army deployment I–187b
Battle Fleet cruise I–276b
China trade V–156b
Chinese population II–30a
citizenship V–6a
constitution VI–391b
Cook expediton II–219b
domestic shipping IV–309a
fortifications III–78b
fruit growing III–129a
habeas corpus III–237a
horse III–302b
legislators' travel allowance IV–339a
"manifest destiny" IV–239a
marine landings IV–252a
martial law IV–259a
missionary activity IV–364b
national parks V–218–19 (table)
naturalization of citizens II–42b
naval forces V–25a
Pacific cable I–401a
Palmyra VII–125b
Panama–Pacific Exposition V–203b
Pearl Harbor I–59b; V–239a
Ringgold–Rodgers Exploring Expedition VI–142a
Saginaw rescue VI–186a
salmon trade VI–201a
sandalwood II–28b
statehood I–78a; VI–400a, 401b; VII–33b
sugarcane I–486b; VI–436b, 437a
taxation VII–13b
territorial government VII–32a–b
territorial status III–424b
U.S. flag III–34b
Wells, Fargo VII–267a
whaling VII–285a
workmen's compensation VI–185a
World War II VII–334a, 343a
Hawaiian goose (nene) VI–393 (table)
Hawaiian Organic (Territorial) Act (1900) IV–259a
Hawaii Ponoi (song) VI–393 (table)
Hawaii v. *Mankichi* (1903) III–424b, 425a
Hawaii Volcanoes National Park V–218 (table)
Hawdon, Michael IV–24a
Hawes–Cutting Act. *See* Tydings–McDuffie Act
Hawikuh (pueblo) II–228b; III–208a
Hawkes, John (au.) IV–165a
Hawkeye State VI–393 (table)
Hawkeye State (steamboat) VI–408a
Hawkins, Benjamin (Indian agent) II–256b
Hawkins, Coleman (mus.) IV–440b
Hawkins, Erick (chor.) II–290a
Hawkins, James (expl.) I–96b
Hawkins, John (nav. off.) I–96b; V–418b; VI–309b–10a
Hawkins, William (expl.) I–96b
HAWKS (pol.) **III–264b**; II–366a; V–124a
Hawks, John (arch.) I–162a
HAWK'S PEAK EPISODE (1846) **III–264b**; I–280a
Hawk (bird) IV–233a
Hawk (fighter plane) I–53a
Hawk 75 (fighter plane) I–53a
Hawk (missile) IV–363b
Hawley, Gideon (law.) II–396b
Hawley, Thomas V–130b
Hawley Lake IV–90a
Hawley–Smoot Tariff Act (1930) III–113b
HAW RIVER, BATTLE OF (1781) **III–265a**
Hawthorn (flower) VI–394 (table)
Hawthorne, Nathaniel (au.) I–335a, 344a; IV–162a, 267a, 436a; V–281a; VI–199b
Brook Farm I–369b
Concord Group II–158a
diplomatic service III–71a
Evangeline II–465b
Peter Parley books V–264b
Hawthorne Experiment VI–234a–b
Haxel, O. (phys.) V–302b
Hay I–35a; VII–248a
exchanges II–469b
foreign trade VII–86b
harvesting IV–424a
imports II–279b
town sealers VI–245a
Hay, James, 1st Earl of Carlisle VI–151b
Hay, John (states.) IV–163a
arbitration treaties VI–163b
Boxer Rebellion I–356a
Chinese relations II–27a–b
Florida Reconstruction VI–58b
Hay–Bunau–Varilla Treaty III–265a
Hay–Herrán Treaty III–265b
Hay–Pauncefote treaties III–266a

HAY, JOHN (cont.)
 Hay–Pauncefote Treaty I–122a
 Olney–Pauncefote Treaty V–153b
 Open Door policy II–488b; III–68b; IV–34b, 234b; V–157b, 242a; VI–294b
 Panama Revolution V–204a,b
 peace movement of 1864 V–234b
 Perdicaris affair V–261b
 Venezuela blockade VII–169b
HAY–BUNAU–VARILLA TREATY (1903) **III–265a**; II–116a; V–201a–b, 202a,b, 204a; VII–34a
Hayburn, William III–265b
HAY BURNING III–265a
HAYBURN'S CASE (1792) **III–265a**; I–12b
Hay–Calvo protocol (1900) V–94b
Hay–Corea protocol (1900) V–94b
Hayden, Ferdinand v. (geol.) I–110b; VII–74b, 272b, 357b
Hayden, Horace H. (dent.) II–330a
Hayden, Lewis (slave) VII–265a
Hayden, Tom II–20b, 21a; VI–421a
Hayden Survey IV–233a
Hayes, Anna Mae (off.) VII–318b
Hayes, H. K. (bot.) II–226a
Hayes, Isaac I. (physic., expl.) V–336b
Hayes, John L. (bus.) VI–464a
Hayes, Lucy Webb (Mrs. Rutherford B.) III–26a
Hayes, Max S. (pol.) II–493a
Hayes, Rutherford B. (pres.) II–176 (table); III–26a, 260b; V–142a, 395 (table)
 administration opposition VI–380b
 Bland–Allison Act I–318b; VI–288b
 campaign of 1876 I–28b, 422b; II–409b; III–437b–38a; VI–93a; VII–344a
 Chinese exclusion acts II–29a
 Conkling, Roscoe III–152b
 free silver III–110b
 Hayes Award III–265b
 Mussel Slough incident
 Panama Canal V–200b
 political corruption II–231b
 prison reform V–415b
 railroad strike of 1877 IV–63b; VI–38b
 Reconstruction III–295b; VI–58a
 resumption of specie payments VI–104a
Hayes, Vertis (art.) I–25a
HAYES AWARD (1878) **III–265b**
Hayes–Tilden controversy. *See* Campaigns, Presidential: 1876
Hay fever II–374a
Hayford, J. F. (geol.) III–167a, 480b–81a
Hayford spheroid III–481a
HAY–HERRÁN TREATY (1903) **III–265b**; II–116a; III–265a; V–201a, 204a; VII–112a
Haymarket (Va.) I–374a
HAYMARKET RIOT (1886) **III–266a**; II–17b; IV–64b–65a; VII–117b
Hayne, Robert Y. (pol.) VII–265b
Haynsworth, Clement F., Jr. (jur.) VI–443b
Hay–o–wei (Indian). *See* Yellow Hand
HAY–PAUNCEFOTE TREATIES (1900, 1901) **III–266a**; I–122a, 454a; II–73a; IV–401a; V–94b, 201a, 204b; VII–69b–70a, 112a
Hay–Quesada Treaty (1925) III–479a
Hays (Kans.) II–251b
Hays, Anna Mae Violet McCabe (off.) IV–290b
Hays, Arthur Garfield II–492b
HAYS, FORT (Kans.) **III–266b**; IV–25b
Hays, John Coffee VII–39a, 42a
Hays, Samuel S. (offi.) VI–463b–64a
Hays, Seth II–242b
Hays, Upton (off.) IV–183b
Hays, Will H. (law., pol.) I–480a
Hays City (Kans.) III–266b
Hays Office I–480a
Haywood, Spencer (athlete) V–154b
Haywood, William D. (labor leader) III–266b–67a; VII–117b
 Industrial Workers of the World III–412b; IV–67b
 Socialist party VI–326b
 Western Federation of Miners II–93b–94a
HAYWOOD–MOYER–PETTIBONE CASE III–266b
Hazard, Ebenezer (bus.) III–427b
Hazard, Erskine (eng.) I–364b
Hazard, John (nav. off.) VI–128a
Hazard, Paul II–287a
Hazard of New Fortunes IV–163b
Hazardous–duty pay IV–107b
Hazard Powder Company V–383b
Hazel Patch (Ky.) VII–296a
Hazelwood, John (nav. off.) I–223a
Hazelwood Mission III–267a
HAZELWOOD REPUBLIC III–267a
Hazen, Harold (eng.) II–153b
Hazen, William B. (off.) II–91a; IV–209a
Hazen Land V–240b
Hazlett, R. H. (rancher) I–326a
Hazzan (cantor) IV–9a
H bonds III–8b
Head, Howard (mfr.) VI–298b
Heade, Martin J. (paint.) V–189a
Head of Elk VII–361a
Head of the Passes III–474a; IV–371a
"HEADQUARTERS IN THE SADDLE" III–267a
HEADRIGHT III–267a; I–4a; III–170b; IV–92a
Head Start II–148b, 402b; V–135b, 136a; VI–328b
Head tax. *See* Capitation Taxes; Poll Tax
Heald, Henry (au.) II–297b
Heald, Nathan (off.) II–297a
Healers
 folk medicine III–49b–50a
Health I–8b–9a
 Customs Service II–277a
 federal aid II–502a
 industrial workers IV–80a
 physiology V–306a
Health, boards of III–325a; V–446b, 447a; VI–212a,b
HEALTH, EDUCATION, AND WELFARE, DEPARTMENT OF III–267b; I–391b, 399b, 495b; II–405a–b, 498a; III–3b, 54a, 299b, 422a, 503b; VII–317b
 Children's Bureau VI–328a
 civil service II–60b
 desegregation III–438b, 438b
 Girl Scouts III–181b
 Indian Health Service III–371a–b
 Interstate Compact on Placement of Children III–460a
 National Institutes of Health IV–465a
 National Library of Medicine IV–292a
 National Nutrition Center V–128b
 Office of Economic Opportunity V–135b, 136a
 research funds IV–287b
 Social and Rehabilitation Service VI–330a
 Social Security VI–328a, 330a
 welfare assistance qualifications II–178b
Health, National Board of IV–285b; V–447a–b
Health, public. *See* Public Health
Health care
 coal mining IV–350b
 medical sects IV–288a
 mental illness IV–304a–07b
 military medicine IV–290a
 occupational medicine IV–293a
Health insurance II–220b, 408b; III–426b, 427a, 434b, 435a–36a; V–448a
 Medicare IV–289b
Health Insurance Institute III–435b
Health resorts. *See* Resorts and Spas
Health Resources Administration III–267b
Health sciences IV–279a
Health services IV–3b
Hearing aids IV–352a; VI–259a
Hearst, George (mining magnate) I–116a; III–80a
Hearst, Patricia II–258b
Hearst, William Randolph (pub.) I–17b; II–258b; III–80a; V–71b, 72a, 73b, 74b, 75a, 76b
 campaign of 1936 V–47b
 International News Service VII–152a
 New York Journal II–268b
 yellow journalism VI–360a; VII–356a
Hearst publications V–79b
Hearst's Comic Weekly: Puck V–72a
Heart and Lung Institute IV–465a
Heartbreak Hotel (song) IV–441a
Heart disease I–7a; IV–287a, 299a; V–129b
Heart failure II–356a
Heart of Atlanta Motel v. *United States* (1964) II–55b, 137a; V–339b
Heart of Dixie VI–393 (table)
Heart of the Andes (paint.) II–102a
Heart River I–3b; III–33b; IV–45b
Heath, Perry S. (pol.) VI–173a
Heath, Robert (col. prop.) I–457b, 458a; III–18a, 268a; V–115a
Heath, William (off.) VII–361a
Heath hen VII–296b
HEATH PATENT (1629) **III–268a**
HEATING AND AIR CONDITIONING III–268a
 appliances II–419b
 electricity II–413a, 417b–18a, 419a
 Franklin stove III–99b
 gas II–418a, 422a
 kerosine IV–44b
 natural gas V–5b
 railroad cars VI–29b
Heat shields III–184b
Heat studies I–97b
Heavy hydrogen I–303b

Hebrew Culture IV–11a
Hebrew Scriptures I–298b
Hebrew Union College IV–9b
Hebrides Islands IV–263b
Hebron (Conn.) IV–387b
Heceta, Bruno (expl.) VII–247a
Hecker, Isaac Thomas (cler.) V–229b
Heckewelder, John (miss.) III–398a; IV–90a; VI–226a
Hedge, Frederic Henry (cler.) V–287a
Hedge fences III–10b
Hedgerows, Battle of the (1944) VI–193b
Hedges, Cornelius (jur.) VII–357b
Hedges, Isaac (off.) VI–340a
Hedging (bus.) V–320b
Hedspeth's Cutoff. *See* Sublette's Cutoff
Heemstede. *See* Hempstead (N.Y.)
Heerewegh (Heere Straat) (N.Y.C.) I–368b
Hegel, Georg (philos.) V–287a,b, 288a
Heijo (Kor.) IV–54b
Heil, A. (phys.) VII–163b
Heil, O. (phys.) VII–163b
Heilbroner, Robert L. (econ.) VII–141b
Heinlein, Robert A. (au.) IV–165a
Heinrich, John (arch.) I–165b
Heintzelman, Samuel P. (off.) VII–367a
Heinze, F. Augustus (bus.) V–208b
Heinze, Frederick A. (miner) IV–403b
Heinze–Morse banks V–208b
Heirs of Livingston and Fulton v. *Reuben Nichols and Steamboat Constitution* VI–407b
Heisenberg, Werner (phys.) V–299a, 304a, 304a
Heiskanen, W. (sci.) III–481a
Heiskell, John N. (ed.) V–73b
Heister, Leopold Philip von (off.) III–173a
"HE KEPT US OUT OF WAR" III–269b; VI–313a
Hektoen, Ludvig (bact.) I–242a
Helderberg War. *See* Anti-rent War
Heldman, Gladys VII–31a
Helena (Ark.) III–269b; VII–354b
Helena (Mont.) I–203b, 336b; III–32a
HELENA, BATTLE OF (1863) **III–269b**
HELENA MINING CAMP (Mont.) **III–269b**; IV–403a
Helena Rubenstein II–234a
Helen Birch Bartlett Memorial Collection II–105a
Helicopters
  cattle tending II–249b
HELICOPTERS, MILITARY III–270a; I–237b; V–25b; VI–301a
  Air Cavalry I–49a
  antihelicopter missiles IV–363b
  Coast Guard II–90a
  disaster aid IV–341b
  evacuation of wounded IV–290b
  Korean War IV–431b
  marine use IV–253a
  minesweeping IV–351b
  polar exploration V–338a
  rocket–firing I–178b
  Sikorsky I–52a, 234b
  slang VI–302b
  Soviet Union V–11b
  Vietnam War I–62a, 188b; VII–183a, 184a, 185b, 186a, 186b
  World War II I–52a
Heliograph VI–286a
Helium I–51b, 234a; II–344b; IV–350b; V–13a; VI–48b
"Hell Among the Yearlings" (song) III–19a
Hellcat (fighter plane) I–55a; V–285b
Helldiver (bomber) I–55a
Heller, Ben II–106b
Heller, Joseph (au.) IV–164b
Hell Gap (Wyo.) III–484b
Hell Gap projectile point III–484b
Hell Gate Bridge I–364b
Hellman, Lillian (playwright) VII–50a
"Hello Lyndon" (song) I–433a
"HELL ON WHEELS" III–270b; II–16b
Helluland. *See* Baffin Island
Helm, Leonard (off.) VII–188b
Helmholtz, Hermann von (phys.) IV–2a
Helovët Sluys (Holland) IV–196a–b
Helper, Hinton Rowan (au.) III–270b–71a
"Helperites" III–271a
Helper's Impending Crisis Dissected III–271a
HELPER'S *IMPENDING CRISIS OF THE SOUTH* III–270b
Helsinki (Finn.) VI–417a
Helvering v. *Davis* (1937) III–157a
"Helvidius." *See* "Pacificus" and "Helvidius"
Helwys, Thomas (cler.) I–264b
Hematinics V–128a
Hematite ore I–327a; IV–315a,b
Hemel Hempstead (Eng.) III–271b
Hemingway, Ernest (au.) IV–164b, 189b, 190a; V–99b
Hemlock IV–128a; VI–48b
Hemoglobin IV–391b
HEMP III–271a
  colonial trade II–453a
  duties II–276a
  linsey–woolsey IV–158a
  Missouri IV–377a
  Navigation Acts V–16a,b
  Saint Louis VI–194b
  smoking VII–64b
  tariff VI–465b
HEMPSTEAD (N.Y.) **III–271b**; II–350b, 379a; III–198a; IV–185a
Hempstead, Thomas (fur trader) VI–196a
Hemshall, James A. (nat.) III–28a
Hench, Philip S. (physic.) V–100a
Hencock (Indian) VII–130b
Henderson (N.Y.) I–248a
Henderson, Alexander (cler., dipl.) I–85b
Henderson, David (mfr.) III–183b
Henderson, David B. (pol.) II–176 (table)
Henderson, Fletcher (mus.) IV–440b
Henderson, J. (mfr.) III–183b
Henderson, John Brooks (pol.)
  Thirteenth Amendment VII–54a
Henderson, Lawrence J. (biochem.) I–303b
Henderson, Richard (col.) III–24b, 271b; IV–92b; VI–72a
  Boonesborough II–272a; IV–40a
  Transylvania Company II–274a; IV–98b; VI–356a; VII–25a, 102b, 103a, 203a
  Treaty of Sycamore Shoals VI–455a
Henderson, Robert (miner) IV–52a
Henderson, Samuel (pioneer) I–337a
Henderson County (Tex.) VII–167a
Henderson Field (Guadalcanal) III–229b; VII–68a
HENDERSON LAND COMPANY III–271b
Hendricks, Thomas A. (pol.) I–422b, 424a; VII–179 (table)
Hendrik (Indian) IV–87b
Heney, Francis J. (law.) V–166a
Hening, William Waller (ed.) III–271b
***HENING'S STATUTES* III–271b**
Henkels, Stan v. (auctioneer) I–332b
Hennepin (Ill.) III–162b
Hennepin, Louis (miss., expl.) III–89b, 119a, 228b, 272a; V–52b; VII–73b
  Falls of Saint Anthony VI–187a
  Great Lakes III–216a
  Mississippi exploration IV–109b
  Niagara Falls V–91b
  Twin Cities VII–133b
HENNEPIN NARRATIVES III–272a; VII–73b
Hennessey, David C. IV–221a
Hennessey Field (Okla.) IV–334a
Henning, Anne (athlete) V–154b
Henri, Robert (paint.) II–104a; V–192a
Henrico (Va.) VII–300a
Henrico County (Va.) III–437a; VI–307a
Henrietta (q.)
  Maria IV–260b
Henrietta (Tex.) I–2a
Henrietta (yacht) VII–348b–49a
Henrietta Island V–439a
Henry IV (Fr. k.) I–492b; III–315a
Henry VII (Eng. k.) I–96b, 401b; II–375a
Henry VIII (Eng. k.) IV–202a
Henry, Alexander (fur trader) II–13b; III–403b; V–244a; VI–63b; VII–275b
Henry, Andrew (fur trader) I–201a; II–477b; III–273a; VI–195b; VII–74b, 103b
  Utah VII–161a
Henry, Fort (Tenn.) IV–136b
HENRY, FORT (W.Va.) **III–272b**; I–277a, 459a; III–77b; IV–399b; V–31b–32a, 145a; VII–287b
HENRY, FORT, CAPTURE OF (1862) **III–272b**; II–62b, 363a; IV–374b, 375a; VI–150b, 278a
Henry, James D. (off.) I–312a
Henry, John (offi.) III–272b–73a
Henry, Joseph (phys.) I–98a, 111a, 276a; V–294a, 409a; VI–232a; VII–18b
  circuit analysis II–39a
  climate II–75b
  electromagnetism experiments II–413a
  Lighthouse Board IV–152b
  Smithsonian Institution IV–468b; VI–319a,b
  weather reports IV–317a–b
Henry, Louis (hist.) II–328a
Henry, Patrick (states.) III–182a, 272b, 302b; V–161a, 354b; VI–137b; VII–287b
  Antifederalists I–131a
  Camden–Yorke opinion I–412b
  Constitution II–196a–b, 303b
  Decius Letters II–303b
  flees Charlottesville (1781) IV–8b
  Parson's Cause V–221b, 221b
  Virginia constitution VI–390b
  Virginia Resolves VII–203a
  Wirt's biography III–281a

Henry, William (paint.) V–187a
Henry Clay Almanac I–91a
Henry County (Ill.) I–307b
Henry Draper Catalogue I–211b
Henry E. Huntington Library (San Marino, Calif.) II–109a–b; IV–145b
Henry Ford Museum (Dearborn, Mich.) II–101a; III–137b
Henry Frank (steamboat) VI–408b; VII–77b
Henry Harly and Company V–319a
HENRY LETTERS (1809) **III–272b**
Henry Phipps Psychiatric Clinic IV–3b
Henry rifle IV–430b; VI–139b
Henry's Bend V–318b
HENRYS FORK (Mont.) **III–273a**; III–227a; VII–104a
Henry Street Settlement (N.Y.C.) V–280a; VI–330b, 331a
Henry the Navigator VI–309b
Henry v. *City of Rock Hill* (1964) I–204b–05a
Henry Ward Beecher (sculp.) VI–243b
Henson, Josiah VII–138b
Henson, Matthew (expl.) V–240b, 241a
Hepatitis IV–292a
HEPBURN ACT OF 1906 III–273a; I–390a; III–458a; V–208b; VI–22a; VII–101b
railroad rebates VI–50b
Hepburn v. *Griswold* (1870) III–251b; IV–20a, 133a; VI–94b
Hepplewhite, George (cabinetmaker) III–134b
Herald Island VI–142a
Herald of Freedom (news.) IV–118b
Herbalists III–49b
Herbaria V–327a–b
Herbarium, U.S. VII–299b
Herbart, Johann Friedrich (educ.) II–398b
Herbert, Hilary A. (pol.) I–90a
Herbert, Victor (comp.) I–466a; IV–442a
Herbert Hoover Library I–167b
Herbicides. *See* Insecticides and Herbicides
"Herblock." *See* Block, Herbert L.
Herbs IV–288a
Hercules Plastics Corporation V–328a
HERD LAW VERSUS FREE GRASS III–273a
Heredia, José A. (off.) VI–184a
Heredia, José de (dipl.) VII–167a
Heredity
DNA II–357b
racial theories III–342b
See also Genetics; Genetics, Applied
Hereford cattle I–471b; VI–45a
Heresy II–258a; III–274b, 420b
Here We Have Idaho (song) VI–393 (table)
Hergesheimer, Joseph (au.) IV–164b
Hering, Constantine (physic.) III–293b
Heritage Foundation (Old Deerfield, Mass.) III–137b
Herjolfsson, Bjarni (mariner) VII–189b
Herkimer (N.Y.) III–172b; VII–282b
Herkimer, Nicholas (off.) I–385a; V–172b
Herkimer County (N.Y.) V–195a
Herman Baker and Company IV–433a
Herman Miller, Inc. III–136b, 137a
Hermann-Paasche formula II–236a
Hermanos Penitentes. See Penitent Brothers
HERMITAGE (Tenn.) **III–273b**
Hermit thrush VI–395 (table)
***HERMOSA* CASE III–273b**
Herne, James A. (act., playwright) VII–48b
Hero (sloop) V–197b
Herodotus (hist.) I–221b
Heroes of America II–164b; VII–149a
Hero Fund Commission. *See* Carnegie Hero Fund Commission
Heroin II–262a,b, 373b–74b; IV–449b, 450b, 451a
Heroism
decorations II–310a–12b
Herold, David E. IV–154b, 155a
Héroult, Paul (metal.) I–92a; II–422b; V–103b
Herpetologica (period.) VI–91b
Herpetologists' League VI–91b
Herpetology. *See* Reptiles
Herrán, Tomás (dipl.) III–265b
Herrera, Antonio de (cartog.) IV–248a
Herrera, José Joaquín IV–323a
Herrera, Simon de (off.) V–33b
Herreshoff, Nathanael G. VII–349b
Herrick, Myron T. (dipl.) IV–157a; VII–30a
Herring III–413a
HERRIN MASSACRE (1922) **III–274a**; IV–70b
Herrman, Augustin (cartog.) VII–73b
Herrman, Augustine (rel. leader) IV–59b
Herrnhut IV–409b
Herron, Francis (off.) V–389a
Hersch, Seymour (jour.) V–74b
Herschel, John (astron.) III–480b; IV–406b
Herschel Island VII–285b
Hersey, John (au.) IV–165a
Hershberger, W. D. (eng.) VI–10a
Hershey, Alfred D. (biol.) I–304a; III–158a; V–100a
Herskovits, Melville J. (anthrop.) I–24b, 129a,b
Hertel, François VI–201a
Herter, Christian A. (states.) IV–268a; VI–470a
Herter Brothers (cabinetmakers) III–445b–46a,b
Herter Report (1962) III–72a
Hertz, Heinrich (phys.) VI–14b
Herzegovinians III–339a
Hesse, Don (cartoon.) V–73a
Hesse, Emmanuel (off.) VI–195a
Hesse-Cassel (Ger.) III–172b
Hesse-Hanau (Ger.) III–172b
Hesselius, Gustavus (paint.) V–186a
Hesselius, John (paint.) V–186b, 187a,b
Hessians. *See* German mercenaries
***HESTER* CASE III–274b**; V–264a
Hetch Hetchy Valley I–407a; VII–220a, 362a
Heth, Henry (off.) II–484b; III–176a; V–309a
Heurne (Belg.) VII–366b
HEW. *See* Health, Education, and Welfare, Department of
Hewes, Joseph (legis.) II–308a, 393a; VI–128a
military code VII–142b
"He who transplanted still sustains" (motto) VI–393 (table)
Hewit, Augustine (cler.) V–229b
Hewitt, Abram S. (philan.) II–222a; IV–244b
Hexachlorophene V–468a
Hey, J.S. (astron.) VI–17a
Heyes, Pieter (shipmaster) VII–372b
Heyward, Thomas, Jr. (jur.) II–308b
Heywood, DuBose (au.) IV–438b
Heywood, Joseph (bank teller) V–119b
Hezeta, Bruno (expl.) II–131b
H Hour II–297a
Hiawatha (Indian) III–366b, 386b, 475a
Hiawatha (train) III–452a
Hiawatha, Song of (poem) II–31b
Hibben, John G. (educ.) V–409a
Hibbins, Ann (col.) VII–309b
Hibernians *See* Ancient Order of Hibernians
Hibiscus (Pua Aloha) VI–393 (table)
Hickel, Walter (pol.) I–79a, 80b
Hickel, Walter J. (pol.) VII–152a
Hickenlooper Amendment IV–466b
Hickman, Henry Hill I–119a
Hickok, James Butler ("Wild Bill") II–252a
Hays City III–266b
Hickok, Laurens P. (philos., cler.) V–441b
Hickok, "Wild Bill." *See* Hickok, James Butler
Hickory III–74b; VII–59b
Hickory Ground (Ind. Terr.) II–254a
Hickory nuts III–51a
Hickory Point (Kans.) I–342a
Hickory wood IV–280b
Hicks, Elias (Quaker). *See* Hicksites
HICKSITES III–274a; III–123b; V–470a–b
Hidalgo y Costilla, Miguel (cler., rev.) VII–37a
Hidatsa (Indians) III–229a
See also Mandan, Hidatsa, and Arikara
HIDE AND TALLOW TRADE III–274b; II–119b, 453a, 469b; III–402b; VI–161a
East Indies trade II–388b
Fort Griffin III–228b
Pembina V–244a
Santa Catalina I–466b
soap VI–323a
South America VI–343b
Hides
See also Leather Industry
Higbee (destroyer) V–22a
Higgins, Patillo (prospector) V–271b; VI–356b
Higgins family IV–200a
Higginson, Francis (cler.) VI–199a
High Backbone (Indian) III–17b
Highboys III–134a, 135b
High Bridge (N.Y.C.) VII–259a
HIGH COMMISSION, COURT OF III–274b
High crimes and misdemeanors II–202a
High energy physics. *See* Physics, High Energy
HIGHER CRITICISM III–275a
Higher Education. *See* Colleges and Universities; Graduate Schools
Higher Education Act (1965) II–401a; IV–147b

Higher Education Act (1972) I–397b
HIGHER-LAW DOCTRINE III–275a
High-fidelity broadcasting VI–16b
Highjump, Operation. *See* Antarctic Developments Projects, U.S. Navy
Highland County (Va.) III–469b
Highland Park (Mich.) I–227a
Highland patent. *See* Philipse's Patent
Highland Regiment III–58b
Highland Scots VI–115b
HIGHLANDS OF THE HUDSON III–275b
revolutionary war I–385b
Wawayanda Patent VII–261b
West Point VII–279b, 280a
HIGH LICENSE III–276a
HIGH-MINDED MEN III–276a
High Plains III–484a
High Point (N.C.) III–139a
High Rock Springs VI–217b
High schools II–397a–b, 398b–99a, 398b–99a
Afro-American II–404a
football III–56b
See also Education
High Street (Philadelphia) VI–263a
Highway Act (1962) II–503a
Highway Beautification Act (1965) I–20a
Highway Beautification Program II–503a
Highwaymen I–476a; IV–263a
Highway Revenue Act (1956) III–450b; VI–155b
Highways
Alaska I–77b, 78a
American Automobile Association I–99a
automobile I–228b
bicycles I–225a
Chicago II–18b
Chicago Road II–20a
construction I–39b–40a
county programs II–245b
Cumberland Gap II–272b
farms I–39b
federal aid II–502b–03a
federal-state relations III–9b
financing II–234b, 302b–03a
gasoline taxes III–153a
government construction III–204b
grants-in-aid III–211b
Interstate Highway Act I–99a, 230a
Kentucky IV–41b
Mexico II–23b
Mohawk Valley IV–387a
Norfolk V–110a
North Carolina V–116b
state construction VI–398b
toll-free I–230a
War of 1812 II–20a
See also Roads; Turnpikes
Highway Safety Act (1966) I–7b; VII–98b
Highway Trust Fund I–230a, 231a; III–153b; VI–155b
Higinbotham, Harlow (philan.) III–19a
Hijacking. *See* Crime, organized
HIJACKING, AERIAL III–276b; I–203b, 203b; II–277b
air security officers II–277b
Cuban agreement II–270a; IV–113a
Hildebrand, Joel (chem.) II–12b
Hildreth, Richard (hist.) III–282a
Hilgard, E. W. (geol.) VI–334a
Hill 609 (Tun.) I–308a
Hill, A. P. (off.) VI–376b
Army of Northern Virginia VII–197a,b
Battle of Antietam I–130a
Battle of Frayser's Farm III–100a
Battle of Gettysburg III–175b
Battle of Mechanicsville IV–282a
Battles of the Wilderness VII–295b
Bristoe campaign I–365a
Falling Waters skirmish II–484b
Harpers Ferry IV–261b–62a
Pennsylvania invasion V–248a,b
Hill, Carla (offi.) VII–317b
Hill, David B. (pol.) I–424b; II–75a; VI–322b
Hill, David H. (off.) IV–190a
Hill, George W. (astron.) I–211b
Hill, Isaac (pol.) V–54a
Hill, James J. (fin.) II–103b; III–79b; V–119a; VI–33a
Hill, Nathaniel P. (chem.) VI–292b, 316b
Hill, Samuel Eugene III–179b
Hill, Wills, 1st Earl of Hillsborough (states.) I–326b; III–209a; V–424b
HILLABEE TOWNS III–278a
Hill and M'Gunnegle V–375b
Hillbilly music IV–441b
Hill-Burton Act (1946) VI–402b
Hilliard, Henry W. (law., off.) I–71b
Hillman, Sidney (labor leader) I–429b; II–82b; IV–10a, 73a, 73a,b; V–47b
Hillquit, Morris (law., Socialist) VI–326b
Hillsboro (N.C.)
Regulators of North Carolina VI–72a
revolutionary war I–412a,b
Hillsboro (Ohio)
Woman's Temperance Crusade VII–312a
Hillsborough, Earl of. *See* Hill, Wills, 1st Earl of Hillsborough
Hillyar, James (off.) II–463b
Hilton, Edward (col.) V–53b; VI–418a
Hilton, William (col.) I–447b
Hilton Head (S.C.) III–197a
Himalayas I–386b; III–46a, 480b
Hindenburg (dirigible) I–51b, 234a; II–344b, 346a
Hindenburg, Paul von (off.) IV–320a
Hindenburg Line I–177a; VI–338b
Hindman, Fort (Ark.). *See* Arkansas Post
Hindman, Thomas C. (off.) V–389a; VI–274b
Hinds, Asher C. (parl.) VI–169b
Hinduism V–171b
Hindus
immigration to U.S. III–341a
Hines, Thomas H. (off.) V–121b
Hines, Walker D. (law.) VI–19b
Hinged arch I–364a
Hinges
"Holy Lord" III–293a
Hingham (Mass.) II–328b; IV–149b–50a, 150a, 265a
Hingston, Edward P. (trav.) IV–436b
Hints on Household Taste III–136a, 446a–b
Hippodamus (arch.) II–45a
Hirabayashi v. *United States* (1943) III–491a
Hiram House (Cleveland) VI–330b
Hired hand II–495a
Hires Company VI–333b
Hiring halls II–3b–4a, 80b, 80b
Hirohito (emp.) V–239b
Hiroshima (Jap.)
atomic bomb I–215b; III–490b; IV–238b; V–21a; VII–191a, 341a
Hiroshima (report) IV–165a
Hirshhorn, Joseph H. II–106a
Hirshhorn, Joseph H., Museum and Sculpture Garden VI–319b
Hiryu (aircraft carrier) IV–336b, 337a
Hise, Elijah (dipl.). *See* Hise Treaty
HISE TREATY (1849) **III–278a**; VI–378b
Hispanic-Americans
New York City V–83b–84a
New York State V–88a
Hispaniola
citrus fruits III–128a
Columbus VII–64b
hogs III–288a
horse III–302a
logwood trade IV–181b
Santa Maria VI–216a
See also Española
Hiss, Alger (offi.) *See* Hiss Case
HISS CASE III–278a; III–308b; V–346a, 347a; VI–428b; VII–118a, 310b
Histoire des arbres forestiers de l'Amérique septentrionale V–326b
Histoire des chênes de l'Amérique V–326a
Histoire naturelle (Buffon) IV–231b
Historical areas, national. *See* Parks, National, and National Monuments
Historical determinism V–353b
Historical Magazine III–282a
Historical Manuscripts Commission I–106a
Historical Records Survey III–281a; V–46a
HISTORICAL SOCIETIES III–278b; III–280b–81a, 285a
Buffalo II–205a
furniture collections III–137a–b
museums IV–435b
National Trust for Historic Preservation IV–471b
preservation V–393b
United Daughters of the Confederacy VII–150b
See also Learned Societies
Historical Society of Pennsylvania I–110b; II–108a,b; III–285a
Historic Deerfield II–101a
Historic Preservation (mag.) IV–472a
Historic preservation movement *See* Preservation Movement
Historic Sites Act (1935) V–220a, 392b–93a
HISTORIOGRAPHY, AMERICAN III–280a; IV–163a; VII–206a
frontier theory III–125a–26a
Historical Records Survey V–46b
historical societies III–278b
Jacksonian Democracy III–486a
Johns Hopkins IV–2b
Library of Congress IV–146b
moral values IV–408b
National Museum IV–468b
political science V–347a,b
Reconstruction VI–57b
Revolution VI–106b
robber barons VI–157a
Turner's frontier theory V–81b
HISTORY, AMERICAN, SOURCES OF III–283b
conquistadores II–184b
Force's Tracts III–60a
fur trade III–403b

HISTORY, AMERICAN, SOURCES OF (cont.)
government publications III–203a
Hakluyt's *Voyages* III–240b
Hennepin *Narratives* III–272b
Jesuit *Relations* III–501a
Niles' Weekly Register V–96b
Phoenixiana V–289a
Radisson's *Voyages* VI–18a
scientific periodicals VI–236b–37a
westward movement VII–283b
History and Digest of the International Arbitrations to Which the United States Has Been a Party IV–5b
History and Present State of Virginia III–280b
History and Technology, National Museum of VI–319b
History of American Life series III–283a
History of Little Goody Two Shoes I–335a
History of New England VII–355a
History of Newfoundland VI–379a
History of New Hampshire III–27a; IV–232a, 423b
History of New York by Diedrich Knickerbocker IV–161b
History of the American Revolution III–280b
History of the Conquest of Mexico IV–163a
History of the Dividing Line Betwixt Virginia and North Carolina III–280b; IV–161a
History of the Navy of the United States of America V–262b
History of the People of the United States From the Revolution to the Civil War III–282a
History of the Province of New York III–280b
History of the Revolution in South Carolina III–280b
History of the Rise, Progress, and Termination of the American Revolution III–280b
"History of the Standard Oil Company" (article) IV–424b
History of the United States (Channing) III–282a, 282a
History of the United States During the Administrations of Jefferson and Madison III–282a; IV–163a
History of the United States From the Compromise of 1850 III–282a
History of the United States from the Discovery of the American Continent III–281b
History of the United States Under the Constitution III–282a
History of the U.S. (Goodrich) VI–227b
History of the Warfare of Science With Theology in Christendom IV–163b
History painting V–187a,b, 188a,b, 189b
Hitchcock, Edward (geol.) I–98a; III–165a; VI–230a
Hitchcock, Ethan Allen (off., au.) VI–53b–54a
Hitchcock, Gilbert M. (pol.) III–285b; IV–178b
Hitchcock, Henry–Russell (arch.) I–165a
Hitchcock, Lambert (cabinetmaker) III–134b
Hitchcock, Mary II–293a
Hitchcock, Phineas W. (pol.) VII–114a
Hitchcock chairs III–134b
Hitchcock Museum (Riverton, Conn.) III–137b
HITCHCOCK RESERVATIONS III–285a
Hitchiti (Indians) II–51b, 52b
Hitchiti (lang.) VI–259b
HITCHMAN COAL COMPANY* v. *MITCHELL (1917) **III–286a**; VII–355a
Hite, Jost (col.) VI–275b
Hitler, Adolf V–124a, 342a–b; VII–174a, 334a, 341b
American Jewish communities IV–10b, 11a
Battle of Cherbourg II–14a
Battle of the Bulge I–379a,b, 380a
Fortress Europe I–328b
German Air Force III–174b
German–American Bund III–172a
Gothic Line III–200b
Gustav Line III–235b
Normandy invasion V–111a
Poland II–145a
propaganda VII–333a
Sicilian campaign VI–284b
Siegfried Line VI–285b
U.S. neutrality V–36a
V–2 rockets I–179b
"Hitlerism" VII–151b
HIT OR MISS (flatboat) **III–286a**
H. L. Green III–33a
Hoadley, Silas (clockmaker) II–79a
Hoa Hao (rel. sect) VII–183a
Hoar, Ebenezer Rockwood (jur.) VII–248b
Hoar, George Frisbie (law., states.) I–131b; VI–276b
Hoard, William D. (ed.) II–280b
Hoarders
Civil War II–163b, 165a
Hoaxes
moon hoax IV–406b
Hoban, James (arch.) I–162b, 451a; VII–291b
Hobart, Garret A. (pol.) I–425a; VII–179 (table)
Hobart, John H. (bp.) II–455a; V–179a; VI–78a
Hobbes, Thomas (philos.) II–356a, 456a; V–350b, 354a; VI–396a
liberty IV–142a
representation VI–88b
Hobble skirts II–372a
Hobbs, William H. (geol.) V–337b
Hobby, Charles (off.) VI–2b
Hobby, Oveta Culp (offi.) III–267b; VII–317b
HOBKIRK'S HILL, BATTLE OF (1781) **III–286a**; VI–351b
Hoboken (N.J.) II–348a; III–60a; V–57b, 289a; VII–266b
Hudson and Manhattan Tubes VI–429b
railroad VI–34a
Hobson, James (eng.) VII–128a
Hobson, Richmond Pearson (nav. off.) IV–314b
HOBSON'S CHOICE III–286b
Hoch, Edward W. (pol.) IV–27a
Hoch Deutsch Americanische (almanac) I–91a
Ho Chi Minh (states.) III–159b; VII–183a, 184b
Ho Chi Minh Trail IV–107b; VII–183b, 184a,b
Hockaday and Liggett Stage VI–176b
HOCKEY III–286b
Detroit Red Wings II–337b
Madison Square Garden IV–220b
Hocking River VI–239b; VII–368a
Hodge, Charles (theol.) VI–78a, 82a
Hodge, F. W. (ethnol.) II–465a
Hodges, Courtney H. (off.) III–174b; VI–84a
Hodgkin, Dorothy Crowfoot (phys.) IV–389b
Hodgson, Richard (psych.) V–213a
Hoe I–34b; III–140a
Hoe, R., and Company V–77a
Hoe, Richard M. (inv.) V–77a
Hoe, Robert (ind.) I–333a; II–103b, 109a; V–77a
Hoe and Company V–413a
Hoecake III–52a
Hoefly, E. Ann (off.) VII–318b
Hoen, August (print.) I–462b
Hoen Company I–462b
Hoff, Max ("Boo Boo") II–261b
Hoffa, James R. (labor leader) IV–76b
Hoffman, Abbie II–20b, 21a
Hoffman, Frederick L. (statis.) VII–207a
Hoffman, John T. (gov.) VI–459b; VII–131a
Hoffman, Julius J. (jur.) II–20b–21a
Hoffman, Major (off.) I–213b
Hoffman, Malvina (sculp.) III–19b
Hoffman, Nicholas von (writ.) V–79a
Hoffman, Ogden (jur.) IV–254a
Hoffman, Paul G. (adm.) VII–88b
Hoffman, Paul J. IV–258a
Hoffman, William (off.) V–414a–b
Hofmann, August (chem.) II–11b
Hofmann, Hans (paint.) V–192b
Hofstadter, Richard (hist.) III–486b
Hofstadter, Robert (phys.) V–100a
Hogan (dwelling) V–9a
Hogan, Ben (golfer) III–198a
Hogan, Frank J. I–333a
Hogarth, William (paint.) III–134a; V–186a, 187b
Hog cholera I–46a
Hogee. *See* Hockey
Hoge family (Pa.) VII–244b
"Hog Eye" (song) III–19a
Hogg, James (col.) VII–102b–03a
Hogg, James S. (gov.) VII–40b
Hog Island IV–311b
HOG ISLAND SHIPYARD III–288a; II–438a
HOG REEVE III–288a
HOGS III–288a; III–51b; VI–48a
Agricultural Adjustment Administration V–44a
cholera VII–177a
diet II–226a–b, 280b
hog reeve III–288a
Illinois III–329b
Indiana III–370a,b
meat–packing IV–280a,b
Ohio V–141b
razorbacks VI–49a
triangular trade VII–277b
See also Swine
Hogshead staves V–319a
Hoh (Indians) III–395b
Hohman, John George III–49b
HOHOKAM (culture) **III–289a**; I–157b; III–367a, 369a; IV–385b; V–217b, 314a,b
Hohokam–Pima National Monument V–217b

Hoisington, Elizabeth P. (off.) VII–318b
Hoists II–428b
Hokan (lang.) III–262b; VII–367b
Hokan–Coahuiltecan (lang.) III–369a
Hokan–Siouan (lang.) II–282b; III–364a, 369a, 476a; V–230b
Holabird and Roche VI–299a
Holand, Hjalmar R. (hist.) IV–38a–b
Holbrook, John Edwards (nat.) III–27a; VI–90b
Holbrook, Josiah (educ.) II–399b; IV–207a
HOLC. *See* Home Owners' Loan Corporation
Holcombe, James P. (law.) I–435a; V–234b
Holden, Oliver (comp.) III–326a; IV–438a
Holden, William W. (jour., pol.) II–165a; III–289b, 295a; VII–148b
HOLDEN PEACE MOVEMENT (1863–64) **III–289b**
Holden v. *Hardy* (1898) IV–173b
Holder, Charles F. (nat.) III–28a
Holder, John (pioneer) I–337a
HOLDING COMPANY III–289b; I–390a; II–229b–30a; VII–123a
American Cereal Company I–487a
banking I–258b–59a
electric utilities II–416b
New Deal V–46a,b
Northern Securities Company V–119a
panic of 1929 V–209b
public utilities V–459a
Public Utility Holding Company Act V–46b
taxation VII–7b
"Hold the Fort" (song) I–88b
HOLES OF THE MOUNTAINS III–291a
Holford, James (fin.) VI–96b
Holiday, Billie (sing.) IV–442a
Holidays
Flag Day III–34a
Fourth of July III–87b
Labor Day IV–79a
May Day IV–278a
Memorial Day IV–301a
Muster Day IV–445a
Peggy Stewart Day V–242a
Pinkster V–316b
proclamations V–425b
Thanksgiving Day VII–46a
Holiness Church of Christ V–29b–30a
Holiness Movement IV–318b
Holladay, Ben (bus.) I–398b, 485a; VI–176b, 379a
See also Holladay Overland Stage Company
HOLLADAY OVERLAND STAGE COMPANY III–291a
mail service V–178a
Overland Trail V–178b
Holladay's Overland Mail VI–320b
Holland
land systems IV–101b
Peace of Breda I–361a
religious liberty VI–80a
revolutionary war debts III–245a
World War II VII–334b
See also Netherlands
Holland, George (act.) IV–168b
Holland, John P. (inv.) III–291b–92a; VI–422b
Holland, Lord. *See* Fox, Henry
Holland, Samuel (off.) IV–248a
Holland, T. E. (jur.) VI–50b, 358a
Hollandaer, Peter (col. gov.) V–80b
HOLLAND LAND COMPANY III–291a; I–4a; V–88b
Phelps–Gorham purchase I–375b
speculation IV–98b
Treaty of Buffalo Creek III–383b
HOLLAND PATENT III–291b
Holland Purchase IV–127b
Holland Reserve (N.Y.) IV–98b
Hollandsche Land Compagnie. *See* Holland Land Company
HOLLAND SUBMARINE TORPEDO BOAT III–291b; VI–423a
Holland Tunnel III–312b; V–368b; VII–128b
Hollerith, Herman (inv.) I–397a, 482a; IV–292a–b
Hollerith tabulating machine VII–207a
Holley, Alexander L. (metal.) III–473a
Holley, Myron (pol.) I–138a; IV–143b
Holley, Robert W. (biochem.) I–304a; V–100a
Hollidaysburg (Pa.) I–89a, 443b; III–286a; V–250a
Hollings, Ernest F. (gov.) VI–348a
Hollins, George N. (nav. off.) V–22b
Hollis Hall (Harvard Univ.) I–161b
Holly, James T. (cler.) I–315b
HOLLY SPRINGS (Miss.) **III–292a**; II–22a, 225b; VII–181b
Hollywood (Calif.) I–407a
crime II–262a
fashion II–372b
motion pictures IV–417b, 418b
Hollywood Ten I–314b, 315a
Holm, Jeanne M. (off.) VII–318b
Holmden, Thomas V–321a
Holme, Thomas (surv.) V–277a
Holmes, Hogden (inv.) II–240b
Holmes, John Haynes (cler.) II–492b; III–326b
Holmes, Oliver Wendell (jur.) I–269b, 344a
Adkins v. *Children's Hospital* I–12a
Bill of Rights I–300a
Bricker Amendment I–362b
commerce clause II–136a
judicial review IV–12b
Schenck v. *United States* V–353b; VI–225a–b
Sedition Act VI–255a
taxes VII–2b
unions II–110b
Holmes, Oliver Wendell, Jr. (jur.) VI–446a
clear–and–present–danger rule III–104a, 105a
press censorship I–478b
Holmes, Oliver Wendell (man of letters) IV–162a, 267a
hymns III–326b
medical research IV–285b
"Old Ironsides" II–190b
on anesthesia IV–297b
physiology V–306b
Holmes, Theophilus H. (off.) I–381b; III–100a, 269b; V–389a
Holmes, William (off.) III–309b; V–334b
Holmes, William H. (archaeol.) V–384a
HOLMES COUNTY REBELLION (1863) **III–292a**
HOLMES* v. *WALTON (1780) **III–292a**
Holst, Hermann Eduard von (hist.) III–282a
Holstein–Friesian cattle I–471b; II–281b
Holston, Stephen (expl.) III–292b
Holston River II–274a; III–223a, 292a, 292b; VI–149b
Cherokee Dam III–322a
Cumberland Gap V–224b
Donelson's Line II–363a
Great Warriors Path VII–238b
Indian hostilities II–15a
settlement I–461b–62a; VII–253a,b
Southwest Point VI–357b
Tennessee River VII–27a–b
HOLSTON TREATY (1791) **III–292a**; II–14a, 273b; III–383a
HOLSTON VALLEY SETTLEMENTS III–292b; IV–452b; VII–253b, 283a
Holt, Henry (pub.) I–334b
Holt, John (pr., jour.) III–292b
Holt County (Mo.) V–330a
Holton, A. Linwood, Jr. (pol.) VII–196a
HOLT'S *JOURNAL* III–292b
Holum, Dianne (athlete) V–154b
Holy Alliance IV–115b
Holy Cross, College of the IV–267b
HOLY CROSS, PRIESTS OF III–293a
HOLY EXPERIMENT III–293a; II–124b; III–123b; V–246a–b, 470a
pacifism V–181a
religious liberty VII–68b
Holy Family Church (Cahokia, Ill.) I–160a
Holy Family Mission (Ill.) III–329a
Holy Ground (Ala.) IV–456a
"HOLY LORD" HINGES III–293a
Holy Name Society II–362b
Holyoake, George (soc. ref.) II–220b
Holy Office. *See* Inquisition, Spanish
Holyoke (Mass.) IV–347b; VII–45a
Holy Scriptures. *See* Bible
Holy See I–468a; II–490a–b
Homans, Sheppard (statis.) III–433a; VII–207a
Home IV–167b
Home Building and Loan Association v. *Blaisdell* (1934). *See* Minnesota Moratorium Case
Home Buildings (N.Y.C.) VII–24b
Home Department III–371a, 389b
Home Economics, College of II–227b
Home–financing institutions II–501a
Home furnishings
cotton industry II–239b
sale II–332b
Home Life Insurance Building (Chicago) I–378a; VI–299a
Home Loan Bank Board. *See* Federal Home Loan Bank Board
Home Loan Bank System III–201b; VI–221b
Home loans II–501a
Home lot IV–102a
Home Market Club V–110a
Home Means Nevada (song) VI–394 (table)
Home on the Range (song) II–250b; VI–393 (table)
HOMEOPATHY III–293b; IV–284a,b, 288a,b, 295b, 297a
Home ownership. *See* Housing
Home Owners Loan Act (1933) I–376b; V–44a; VI–221b
HOME OWNERS' LOAN CORPORATION III–294a; V–44a

Homer, Winslow (paint.)
II–103b, 105a; V–190a, 191a, 192a, 414a
HOME RULE III–294b
charters I–500b–01a; II–44b, 44b, 245b; IV–427a,b
prerevolutionary agitation IV–60b
Washington, D.C. VII–245a,b
HOME RULE IN THE SOUTH, RESTORATION OF III–295a; III–437b–38a; VI–56a–b, 57b, 58b; VII–39b–40a, 344a
Homespun II–371a, 487a; IV–157b, 158a
Homespun society II–485a
Home Squadron IV–322a
Homestake Mine (S.Dak.) I–312b; III–80a, 192a; VI–350a
Homestake Mining Company IV–293b
Homestead (Fla.) III–320a
Homestead (Pa.) I–424b; III–297a; IV–66a
Homestead Act (1862) I–38b, 42b; II–336a; III–107b, 295b, 296b–97a; IV–95a, 96a, 100a; V–380b, 444a,b, 450b; VI–273a; VII–139b, 268b–69a
agrarian movement I–33a
caravan traffic I–452b
food exports I–245b
immigration III–336b
land speculation IV–99b
Mesabi Iron Range IV–315a
military bounties I–353a
Oregon land frauds V–166a
reclamation VI–53b
Homestead allowance IV–184a
Homestead associations. *See* Savings and Loan Associations
Homesteading IV–28b
Homestead laws I–421b; II–63b
HOMESTEAD MOVEMENT III–295b; I–38b
Beaubien land claim I–281b
Boomers I–336a
campaign of 1848 III–111b
cattle I–471b; V–33a
cattle trails IV–184a
Civil War veterans IV–97b
Desert Land Act II–335b–36a
hay burning III–265a
Homestead Act IV–99b
Kinkaid Act IV–50a
legislation IV–100a
Mesabi Iron Range IV–315a
Montana IV–403a
Nebraska IV–33b
North Dakota V–117b
Oklahoma V–148b–49a,b
open–range V–160a,b
public domain IV–91a, 104b
railroad land IV–94b
ranching VI–45a
Republican party VI–92b
Texan Emigration and Land Company VII–35b
Texas VII–38b
Timber Culture Act VII–59b
timberlands VII–60a
Homestead National Monument V–217b
Homesteads, subsistence. *See* Subsistence Homesteads
HOMESTEAD STRIKE OF 1892 III–297a; IV–66a; V–247b; VI–410b; VII–107a
"HOME SWEET HOME" (song) **III–297a**
Homewood Corporation IV–3b, 4a
Hominy III–51a, 366a, 413b; V–317b
Homma, Masaharu (off.) I–274a; IV–158a
Homogenization I–471b
Homophile communes II–142b
Homosexuality VI–266b
Honan, Daniel IV–24a
Honduras V–22b
British claims II–72b; III–219b
Bryan–Chamorro Treaty I–373b
canal negotiation VII–58b
Central American Court of Justice I–483b
Dallas–Clarendon Convention II–285a
Dominican Republic intervention IV–113a
International Exposition of 1895 III–453b
interoceanic canal I–454a
logwood trade IV–181b
Louisiana lottery IV–196a
United Nations Declaration VII–151b
U.S. intervention IV–252b; VI–163a
U.S. trade VI–343b
HONDURAS PROPOSED LOAN TREATY (1911) **III–297a**
Honesdale (Pa.) II–322a; VI–416a
Honest John (missile) IV–363b
Honey I–283–84b
Honeybee I–283b–84b
Honey Hill (Ga.) VI–221a
HONEY ISLAND III–297b
Honey Lake Valley (Calif.) IV–454b
Honey locust VII–114a
Honey Springs, Battle of (1863) VI–260a
HONEY WAR (1839) **III–297b**
Hong Kong
air service II–28a
Chinese immigration II–30a
Chinese refugees V–342b
clipper ships III–45b
exchange students II–471a
immigration to U.S. III–337b, 341a,b
Southeast Asia Treaty Organization VI–350b
tariff VI–470b
wool VII–321b
Hönigschmidt, Otto (chem.) I–218b
HONKEY–DONK GIRLS III–297b
Honolulu (Haw.) III–263a
HONOLULU CONFERENCE (1966) **III–297b**
Honolulu race VII–349a
Honorable Company of Edinburgh Golfers III 197b–
"Honored Men." *See* "Beloved Man" and "Beloved Woman"
Honor system
West Point IV–340b
Honshu (Jap.) III–490a
Hood, Godley and Fouilhoux VI–299a
Hood, John B. (off.) II–62b; VI–278a
Atlanta campaign I–213b–14a
Battle at Allatoona Pass I–88b
Battle of Ezra Church II–479b
Davis–Johnston controversy V–238a
See also Hood's Tennessee Campaign
Hood, John B. (pub.) V–70b
Hood, Mount V–165b; VI–101b
Hood, Raymond (arch.) I–164b
Hood, Samuel (nav. off.) VII–198b–99a
Hooded seal VI–245a
HOOD'S TENNESSEE CAMPAIGN (1864) **III–298a**; II–295b
Army of Tennessee VII–26b
Army of the Ohio V–142b
Battle of Franklin III–98a
Nashville IV–453a
Spring Hill engagement VI–377a
Hoof–and–mouth–disease IV–112a
Hooker, Joseph (off.) II–62b; VI–300b
Army of Potomac command III–101a
Ashby's Gap I–200b
Battle of Antietam I–130a
Battle of Brandy Station I–360a
Battle of Chancellorsville I–493a,b
Battle of Missionary Ridge IV–365a
Battle of Ringgold Gap VI–141b
Battle of Wauhatchie VII–261b
Battle on Lookout Mountain IV–187a, 364b
Chattanooga campaign I–502b; VI–26b
"Mud March" IV–425a
Pennsylvania invasion V–248a
Hooker, Thomas (cler.) I–279b, 411b; II–149a; III–275a; V–273a
Hooker, Worthington (physic.) IV–296b
Hooker telescope III–242a
HOOKWORM III–298b; I–241b
medical research IV–291b
poor whites V–358b, 359a
Rockefeller Foundation VI–157b–58a, 173b
Rockefeller Sanitary Commission V–447b
Hooper, William (law.) II–308a
Hoops (dress) II–371a
Hoopskirt I–323b
HOOSAC MILLS CASE (1936) **III–299a**; III–156b–57a; VII–7b
Hoosac Mountains III–299a; VII–128a
HOOSAC TUNNEL III–299a
HOOSIER III–299a; V–72b
Hoosier Schoolmaster VI–372a
Hoosier State VI–393 (table)
Hoover, Ethel D. II–235a
Hoover, Herbert (pres.) II–134b, 177 (table); V–396 (table); VI–93a
American Relief Administration V–280b
Belgian relief I–286a
civil service reform II–59b
defeated for reelection II–189b
elected president I–428b
employment service act II–442a
engineering II–449a
Great Depression I–407b; IV–70b
Haiti intervention III–240b
Hoover Commissions III–299b
Latin American policy IV–112a
London Naval Treaty IV–183a
military bonuses I–330a,b, 331b
mortgage relief legislation VI–221b
National Commission on Law Observance and Enforcement V–416a–b
National Park Service V–220a
nonrecognition policy V–107b
Parker appointment VI–443b
Philippines VII–135b
presidential library III–284b
public lands V–451a
public works employment

V–44b
pump–priming V–464a
radio regulation VI–15b
Reconstruction Finance Corporation VI–59b
relief VI–73a; VII–323a
Roosevelt Corollary I–454b
scientific research VI–230b
Soviet government VI–181a
Tacna–Arica controversy VI–456a–b
tariff VI–468a
taxation VII–7b
veterans' benefits V–257b
warships V–10a
Wickersham Commission VII–294b
World Economic Conference VII–324a
World War I VII–326a
World War I relief VII–329b
See also Moratorium, Hoover
Hoover, J. Edgar (law., crim.) II–503a–b; VII–254a
Hoover, W. H. (ind.) II–421a
Hoover Commission on the Reorganization of the Executive Branch I–168a; II–497b
HOOVER COMMISSIONS III–299b
postal service V–374a
transportation VII–98a
Hoover Dam I–407a; II–76b, 130a; III–323a; V–40a; VI–54a
Hoover Gap (Tenn.) VII–127b
Hoover Library I–167b
Hoover mission to Russia VI–178b
Hoover–Stimson Doctrine. *See* Stimson Doctrine
Hoover–Taylor annual price index V–404b
"Hope" (motto) VI–395 (table)
Hope and Company VI–96a
Hopedale (Mass.) VII–43b
HOPEDALE COMMUNITY (Mass.) **III–300a**; II–147a
Hope Diamond VI–320a
Hope Encampment (La.) IV–195b
HOPEWELL (culture) **III–300a**; I–11b, 157a; IV–421a; V–140a; VII–320a
mounds I–11b
Hopewell (N.J.) IV–156b
Hopewell (S.C.) III–300b
Hopewell (Va.) I–336b; VII–196a
HOPEWELL, TREATY OF (1785) **III–300b**; III–292b, 383a, 393b
HOPEWELL IRON WORKS III–300b; III–300b
HOPI (Indians) **III–300b**; II–228b; III–208a, 367a,b, 368a,b, 396b; V–459b–60a; VII–372a
Acoma I–7b
missions I–172a; IV–367b
Navaho V–8b, 9a
Hopkins (Ohio) VII–265a
Hopkins, Asa (inv.) III–442b
Hopkins, C. G. (chem.) VI–334a
Hopkins, Esek (nav. off.) VI–47b, 128a, 132b
Hopkins, Frederick Gowland (biochem.) I–303a
Hopkins, Harry L. (adm., pol.) II–134b; V–43b
diplomatic missions II–343a
Emergency Relief Administration V–44a; VI–73a
National Youth Administration VII–364b
New Deal agencies IV–71a
Office of Scientific Research and Development V–137a
social work VI–331b
Works Progress Administration V–46a; VII–323a
Hopkins, J. A. H. (pol.) II–492b
Hopkins, John B. (nav. off.) VI–128a,b
Hopkins, Johns (mer., philan.) I–250a; IV–2a
Hopkins, Lemuel (physic., writ.) III–259b
Hopkins, Mark (bus.) I–406a
fortune III–79b
Hopkins, Samuel (theol.) VI–81b
Hopkins, Stephen (mer., legis.) II–306a, 308a; V–198b; VI–128a, 132b
Hopkins Grammar School (New Haven) VI–228b
Hopkinson, Francis (states.) II–308a; IV–35b, 161b, 438a
Hopkinson, Joseph (jur.) III–238b
Hopkinsville (Ky.) V–96a–b
Hopper, Edward (paint.) V–192b, 414a
Hopper, Henry (metalworker) VI–291b
Hopperdozer III–213a
Hoppe–Seyler, Ernst Felix (chem.) I–302b, 303a
Hops (plant) II–407a
Horizontal integration (bus.) I–389a
HORIZONTAL TARIFF BILL (1872) **III–301b**
Hormones II–12b, 319a, 358a; IV–281a; V–274a
Hornaday, William T. (zool.) I–375b
Hornblower, Joseph (mfr.) VI–408b
HORNBOOK III–301b; II–285b; VI–227a
Hornby, John (land speculator) V–88b
Horner, Henry (pol.) III–330a
Hornet (carrier) I–54b, 60a; III–489b; IV–336a,b, 407a
Hornet (sloop) VI–128a
***HORNET–PEACOCK* ENGAGEMENT** (1813) **III–301b**
***HORNET–PENGUIN* ENGAGEMENT** (1815) **III–302a**
HORSE III–302a; III–51a,b; IV–169b
agriculture I–37a, 39a,b
branding I–472b
bronco I–369a
canal boats I–443b
cattle drives VII–96a
circus II–40a–b
Clovis culture II–83b
colonial trade II–119b
colonial vehicles VII–168a
Comanche II–133a
conquistadores II 184b–
environmental sanitation VI–212b
feed V–130a
foreign trade VII–86b
fossil I–242b
harness III–255b
ice industry VI–69a
Indian paths VI–152b
Indians I–151b, 206a, 264a
mesquite IV–316a
mustangs IV–444b
Narragansett pacer IV–451b
Ohio V–141b
Oregon caravans V–166a
Oregon Trail V–169a,b
pack trains V–184a
Paiute V–194b
Plains Indians II–283a; III–363a–b
railways VI–24b
ranching VI–44b, 45b
range I–369a
Red River cart traffic VI–63b, 64a
replacement by tractor IV–170a
roundups VI–161a
Sable Island VI–182a
saddles VI–184b
Santa Fe Trail VI–215b, 216a
Spain VI–364b
stagecoach service V–178a
stampedes VI–382b
streetcars II–414b
street paving V–230a
street railways VI–418a
threshing VII–55a,b
transportation VII–99a
travois VII–106b
triangular trade VII–277b
Ute VII–162b
versus oxen V–179a
veterinary medicine VII–175b, 176b
wagon trains VII–281a
westward movement VII–283b
Horse Creek (Wyo.) I–292b, 330a; III–227a; VII–104a
HORSEHEAD CROSSING III–304a; III–199b
Horse hoe I–34b
Horseless Age (jour.) I–225b
HORSE MARINES III–304a
HORSE RACING III–304a; III–303b
county fairs II–244b
crime II–260a,b
frontier 11–487a
gambling III–149b
harnessmaking III–255b
pari–mutuel betting II–261b
rodeos VI–161b
Saratoga Springs VI–218a
state fairs VI–392b
state laws IV–191b
HORSESHOE BEND, BATTLE OF (1814) **III–305b**; II–333a
Horseshoe Falls V–91a
Horseshoes III–472a
HORSE STEALING III–305b; I–131b; II–70b, 259a
Indians III–303a
Loomis gang IV–187b
mustangs IV–444b
Regulators of South Carolina VI–72a
vigilantes VII–187b
Horse trading IV–1a
Horse tramways VI–24a
Horsford, Eben N. (chem.) II–11a; IV–119b
Horta (Port.) V–30a
HORTALEZ AND COMPANY III–306a; III–95a
Horticulture III–151b
Horton, Alonzo E.(mer.) VI–208b
Horton, James Edwin (jur.) VI–241b
Horton, Lester (dancer) II–288a
Hortus Cliffortianus V–326a
Hosack, David (physic.) III–325a
Hosiery II–3b; VII–44a
Hosmer, Frederick Lucian (comp.) III–326b
Hosmer, Walter II–99b
Hosmer, Zelotes II–108b
Hosogaya, Moshiro (nav. off.) IV–54a, 336b
Hospital Association, American IV–289b
Hospital Cove (S. Shetland Is.) V–198a
Hospital for the Ruptured and Crippled III–248b
Hospital insurance. *See* Health insurance
HOSPITALS III–306a; IV–298b
air conditioning III–269a,b
army I–191a,b
Catholic I–467a,b
children IV–275a
government inspection III–422a
Johns Hopkins IV–2a,b
medical education IV–285a, 286a

HOSPITALS (cont.)
Medicare IV–289b
mentally ill IV–304b–05b, 306a, 307a
Naval Home V–11b
nursing V–126b
Pennsylvania Hospital IV–283a; V–251b
public health V–447a
segregation III–502b; VI–256a
Shriners III–109b
social work VI–331a
state construction II–303a
unionization IV–75b, 76b
Hostelries. *See* Taverns
"Hot boxes" (railroads) VI–31a
"Hot cargo" contracts IV–467a
Hotchkiss (machine gun) V–27a
Hotchkiss, Hazel (athlete) VII–29b, 30a
Hot dogs I–271a
Hotel, Business, and Public Administration, School of II–227b–28a
Hotel Dieu convent (Montreal) IV–250a
Hotel Pelham (Boston) I–143a
Hotels
discrimination II–457b
fires II–348b
Florida III–42a
Natural Bridge of Virginia V–5a
Saratoga Springs VI–218a
segregation III–502b; VI–256a
See also Taverns
"Hot lines" IV–364b; VII–19b
"HOT OIL" CASE (1935) **III–307b**; II–473a
Hotpoint Division of General Electric II–419b
Hot rod I–230b
Hot Springs (Ark.) VI–100b; VII–357b
Hot Springs (Ark.) II–381a
Hot Springs National Park V–218 (table), 445b
HOT WATER, BATTLE OF (1781) **III–308a**
"Hot Water Rebellion" (1799) III–124a
Hotze, Henry II–65b, 159a
Houdon, Jean Antoine (sculp.) III–122b; VI–137a, 242b
Houdry, Eugene J. (eng.) V–270a
Houffalize (Belg.) I–380a
Hough, Franklin B. (forester) III–75a
Houghton, Douglass (geol.) IV–331a
Houghton, Norris (theat. mgr.) VII–51a
Houghton Library (Harvard Univ.) III–285a
Houghton Mifflin (pub.) I–334a
HOUMA (Indians) **III–308a**
Hound Dog (missile) IV–363b
Hours of labor IV–61a,b; VII–213b–14a,b
colonial period IV–79b
twelve-hour day IV–69b
See also Wages and Hours of Labor, Regulation of
HOUSATONIC (sloop of war) **III–308a**; VI–422b, 424b
Housatonic River II–180a; IV–387a
House, Edward M. (dipl.) I–246b; II–343a; III–86a; VII–326a
House–Grey Memorandum III–309a
Inquiry III–420a
House, Royal Earl (inv.) VII–276b
House Appropriations Committee I–149a
House Behind the Cedars IV–166a
House Committee on Banking and Currency I–258b
HOUSE COMMITTEE ON UN-AMERICAN ACTIVITIES III–308a; I–315a; II–145b; III–465b; VI–428a,b
Almanac Singers IV–441b
Hiss case III–278a
"HOUSE DIVIDED" III–309a; III–477a; IV–155a; VI–313a
HOUSE–GREY MEMORANDUM (1916) **III–309a**
Household economy II–494b
Household electrification. *See* Electrification, Household
"Household engineer" II–418a
Household industry. *See* Manufacturing, Household
Households II–328b
House Judiciary Committee III–344b–45a
Houseman, John (prod.) VII–50a
House of Commons II–191a, 309a; V–419b–420a
House of Heat III–366a
HOUSE OF HOPE (Conn.) **III–309a**; II–179b; III–141a; V–334b; VI–134b
House of Lords II–191a, 309a; IV–15a
House of Mirth IV–164a
House of Night IV–161b
House of Representatives
apportionment II–151b
assassination attempts in I–203a
campaign contributions V–449b
candidates II–232b
checks and balances II–4b
Committee of the Whole II–139a
committee on budget II–179a
Committee on Un-American Activities II–145b
Constitution II–194b–95a, 198a,b, 199a, 201a, 205a,b
contempt I–117b; II–210b
copyright committee II–225a
election II–410a
election districts II–355a–b
election of president II–409a, 412a
election of 1824 I–418b
farm bloc I–322a
Jefferson–Burr election dispute I–418a; III–494b
Labor and Education Committee II–442b
Powell Case V–383b
rules VI–169b
Statuary Hall I–163a
See also Congress, United States; Speaker of the House of Representatives
House of the Seven Gables IV–162a; VI–199b
HOUSING III–309b; VII–11b
apartment houses I–143a
associations II–220b
Baltimore I–250b
blacks I–26a, 29b, 31b, 32a, 239b; IV–461a
congressional debate III–22a
discrimination II–55a,b, 56a–b, 457b
dugout II–379a, 487a
electrification II–419a
farmers I–45a
farm tenancy I–40b
federal aid II–502a
Great Depression II–47a
heating and air conditioning III–268b
Home Owners' Loan Corporation III–294a–b
igloo II–462a
Indian III–397a
integration III–438b; VI–404b–05a
low income IV–77a
mortgage insurance agency II–47a
municipal owned and constructed IV–428b–29a
National Housing Act V–48b
National Urban League V–1a
New Amsterdam V–40b
New Deal V–46a
New York City V–83a–84b
Norfolk V–110a
public ownership V–455a
relief VI–73b
savings and loan associations VI–221b
segregation III–502b; VI–256a,b
settlement houses VI–330b–31a
slums VI–313b
social legislation VI–327b, 328a
sod house II–379a, 487a; VI–332b
subsidies VI–426a
tenements VII–23b
Truman administration II–480b–81a
urban renewal VI–86a–b
urban structure VII–160a
Veterans Administration VII–174b
VISTA I–8b–9a
Housing, Department of VII–317b
Housing Act of 1949 II–481a; VI–86a–b
Housing Act of 1975 VI–86b
Housing Administration. *See* Federal Housing Administration
Housing and Community Development Act (1974) II–48a; III–311b
HOUSING AND URBAN DEVELOPMENT, DEPARTMENT OF III–310a; I–399b, 495b; II–47b, 498a; III–3b; VI–328b
Housing and Urban Development Act (1968) III–311a
Housing and Urban Development Act (1965) VI–172a
Housing and Urban Development Act (1968) II–47b; III–310b
Housing Authority, U.S. II–47a
Houston (Tex.) V–62b, 67b; VII–40b, 370a
Archive War I–169b
Camp Logan I–434b
Civil War III–148b
Fourierism VI–105a
moon landing IV–407a
race riots IV–340a; VI–7a
railroads VI–26a–b, 35a
spacecraft center IV–460a
Houston (cruiser) III–492b
Houston, Captain I–9b
Houston, E. and W. T. R. Company v. *United States* (1914). *See* Shreveport Rate Case
Houston, Edward James (eng.) II–413b
Houston, Sam (off., pol.)
Alamo I–74a,b; VI–84a
Archive War I–169b
Battle of San Jacinto VI–213a
expedition into Mexico IV–337b
secession VI–251a
slavery VII–39b
Texas navy VII–41b
Texas presidency VII–38a–b
Texas Revolution III–304a; VII–37b–38a
Torreys' trading post VII–77a
Houston and Texas Central Railroad VII–40a
Houston family (Va.) III–469b
HOUSTON SHIP CHANNEL III–311b; VII–40b
Houston Symphony Orchestra VII–40b
Hovenweep National Monument V–217b

Hovercraft III–11b
Howard, A. W. III–44b
Howard, Bronson (playwright) VII–49a
Howard, Charles H. (pol.) VI–204a
Howard, E., and Company II–79b
Howard, Ebenezer (ref.) II–46b
Howard, Edward (mfr.) II–78b
HOWARD, FORT (Wis.) **III–311b**; III–89b–90a, 226a; IV–355b; VI–186a
Howard, Frederick, 5th Earl of Carlisle (states.) V–232a
Howard, Henry Frederick, Lord Maltravers III–268a
Howard, Jacob M. (pol.) IV–6a
Howard, John (ref.) V–415a
Howard, Martin VII–189b
Howard, Oliver O. (off.) I–264b, 493b; II–74b
Army of the Tennessee VII–27a
Battle of Wauhatchie VII–261b
Freedmen's Bureau III–103a
Nez Perce War V–89b
Sherman's march to the sea VI–278a
Howard, R. J. (chem.) V–466b
Howard, Roy W. (pub.) V–76a–b
Howard, Sidney (playwright) VII–50a
Howard University I–316b; II–113b; III–103b, 267b; VII–246a
Howe, Edgar Watson (jour.) I–213a; V–73b
Howe, Elias (inv.) II–81b, 371b; VII–43b
sewing machine VI–264b
Howe, George Augustus (off.) VII–57a
Howe, John J. (inv.) VI–167a
Howe, Julia Ward (poet, ref.) I–276b–77a; VII–315a
Howe, Richard (nav. off.) V–247a; VI–124a, 123a
Howe, Robert (off.) III–42b; V–253a
mutinies IV–445a–b
Howe, Samuel Gridley (humanitarian) III–248a,b; V–280a, 294a
Howe, William (off.) II–134a; VI–123a,b, 124a,b, 373a
Battle of Brandywine Creek I–360a
Battle of Cooch's Bridge II–218a
Battle of Edge Hill II–393a
Battle of Germantown III–173b
Battle of Long Island IV–185b, 186a
Battle of Oriskany V–172b
Battle of Trenton VII–116a
Battle of White Plains V–33b; VII–293a
Bunker Hill I–382b–83a
Burgoyne's invasion I–384b, 385a
Fort Mercer engagement IV–308b
Philadelphia IV–363a; V–211b; VII–358a–b
Howell, Clark (ed.) V–73b
Howell, David (jur.) VII–117a
Howell, Edward (col.) VI–346b
Howell, William Henry (physiol., educ.) I–303b; V–306b–07a
Howells, John Mead (arch.) I–164b
Howells, William Dean (au.) IV–163b
Howe milling machine III–442a
Hower, Ralph (educ.) I–20b
Howes, Seth B. (circus owner) II–40b
Howitzer IV–431a
Howland, Andrew M. (philan.) VI–268a
Howland Island VII–125b
How the Other Half Lives VII–24a
Hoyt, Charles H. (playwright) VII–49a
Hoyt, George W. VI–62b
Hoyt, Palmer (ed.) V–73b
Hoyt, Sherman VII–348b
HSS–1 Seabat (helicopter) I–56b
HSS–2 Sea King (helicopter) I–56b
HUAC. *See* House Committee on Un-American Activities
Huachuca, Fort (Ariz.) VII–70b
Hub (Boston) I–344a
Hubard, Master (art.) VI–286b
Hubbard, Elbert (au.) III–136a, 150b
Hubbard, Frank McKinney ("Kin") (cartoon.) V–72b
Hubbard, Gordon (expl.) II–477a
Hubbard, Gurdon S. (fur trader) III–332a
Hubbard, Kin (humorist) V–75a
Hubbardton (Vt.) IV–86b
See also Hubbardton, Battle of
HUBBARDTON, BATTLE OF (1777) **III–311b**; I–385a; III–226b; VII–171b
Hubbell, Gaylord (ref.) VI–67b
Hubble, Edwin P. (astron.) I–211b
Hube, Hans-Valentine (off.) VI–284b
Hubert, Pirsson and Company I–143b
HUD. *See* Housing and Urban Development, Department of
Hudson (N.Y.) I–444b
Hudson, Henry (navig.) III–240b, 312a; VII–275b
Albany I–81a
Cape Cod I–447a
Delaware Bay II–322a
Delaware River V–246a
Half Moon III–243a
Hudson River III–312a
liquor for Indians III–398a
Manhattan IV–237a
New York Harbor V–86a
Northwest Passage V–122a
Hudson and Manhattan Railroad VII–128a
Hudson and Manhattan Tubes VI–429a–b
Hudson Bay III–313a–14a; IV–355a
ceded to England II–126b
Chipewyan II–30b
Eskimo II–461b, 462a
exploration I–96b; V–336b
fur trade II–380b; V–121a
Indians I–441b
King William's War VI–182a
Mitchell's Map V–120a
Norsemen VII–190a
Radisson's *Voyages* VI–18b
Treaty of Utrecht VII–162b
whaling III–358a
Hudson Company (auto mfg.) I–229a
Hudson County (N.J.) III–237b
HUDSON-FULTON CELEBRATION (1909) **III–312a**; II–100b
Hudson Guild (N.Y.C.) VI–330b
HUDSON RIVER III–312a; III–243a; V–367a
Acadia I–6a
Albany I–81b
Battery I–275b
canal II–322a, 460a
coal shipments VI–33b
discovery II–383a
Duke of York's Proprietary V–56b; VII–359b
Dutch settlements I–492b; II–125b; III–18a
English fortifications V–175b
Erie Canal I–40a; III–448a
estates IV–96b
exploration V–86a
ferries III–11a–b
Fort Edward II–405b
Fort Washington VII–246b, 247a
French and Indian War III–115b
fruit growing III–128b
fur trade III–141a, 142a; VII–104b
Highlands III–275b–76a
icehouses VI–69a
Indians II–462b
inland lock navigation III–419b
Iroquois III–475a
Kayoderosseras Patent IV–33a
King's Ferry IV–48a
Lake Champlain link IV–85b
Manhattan IV–237a
Morristown IV–413a
navigation VI–148a,b
New York City V–83a
New York–New Jersey boundary V–368b
packets VI–148a
patroonship V–229a
Pequot War V–261b
railroads VI–25b, 34a
revolutionary war I–384b, 385a,b; II–191a; III–117b, 275b–76a; IV–131b; V–229b; VI–123a,b, 150a, 415b; VII–293a
Richelieu River VI–136b
Rip Van Winkle VI–145a
Saratoga Springs VI–217b
settlement V–60b; VII–282b
steamboat monopoly III–131b–32a, 178a, 178a; VI–407a
steamboats IV–310a; VI–280b
subway VI–429b
Tappan patent VI–461a
tunnels VII–128a,b
Vermont VII–171b
Wappinger Confederacy VII–223b
Weehawken VII–266b
West Point VII–279b
westward movement VII–260a
HUDSON RIVER CHAIN III–312b; III–275b, 276a; VII–280a
HUDSON RIVER LAND PATENTS III–313a; I–4a
Hudson River Museum (Yonkers, N.Y.) III–137b
Hudson River Railroad III–312b; VI–35b
Hudson River School (paint.) II–101b, 106a; V–189a
Hudson's Bay (Can.) IV–118a; V–367b
HUDSON'S BAY COMPANY III–313a; I–200b; II–30b, 228b; III–140a, 143b, 144b; VII–94b, 104b, 271b, 307a
Alaska I–75a
Arrowsmith's map I–196b; VII–74b
British colonial policy II–122a
Columbia River VI–151a
Five Villages III–33b
Fort Boise I–327b
Fort Hall III–243b
Fort Okanogan V–147a
Fort Vancouver VII–165b
Great Valley III–223b
Idaho III–327b
Indian relations I–206a

HUDSON'S BAY COMPANY (cont.)
irrigation III–477a
Jesuit missions III–499b
La Vérendrye explorations IV–380a
Northwest Coast III–238a
North West Company V–121a
Ogden's Hole V–140a
Oregon V–164b, 165a, 165a, 167a, 170a
Pembina V–244a
Pemmican War V–244b
Proclamation of 1763 V–424b
Radisson's *Voyages* VI–18b
Red River of the North VI–64b
salmon VI–201a
San Francisco VI–209a
San Juan Island VI–214a
Sault Sainte Marie VI–219b
Snake River VI–322b
Spokane House VI–375b
steel trap VI–411b
trading posts VII–95b
transportation I–380a
trappers' rendezvous VII–104a
Treaty of Utrecht VII–162b
Utah VII–161a
voyageurs VII–211b
Washington State VII–247b
Whitman massacre VII–294a
Willamette Valley settlements VII–300a
Hudson Valley V–186a
dairy industry II–279b
Dutch manors IV–102b
ginseng III–180b
Mahican IV–387a
settlement V–195a
Hudson Wasp (news.) IV–139b
Hudspeth's Cutoff III–215a
Hue (Viet.) VII–184a, 186a
HUE AND CRY III–314a
Huebner, Clarence Ralph (off.) I–1a; III–175a
Huebsch, Ben W. (pub.) I–334b
Hueco (Tex.) VII–256a
Huerfano River IV–110a; VI–215b, 461a
Huerta, Victoriano (rev.) I–1b; IV–157a, 328b; V–107b
Veracruz incident VII–171a
HUERTGEN FOREST (Ger.) **III–314a**
Huet, Charles (cler.) II–93b
Huey (helicopter gunship) I–49b
Huggins, Charles (surg.) V–100a
Huggins, Nathan I. (hist.) IV–166b
Hughes, Charles Evans (jur.) V–47a, 48a; VI–446a, 446b
Bill of Rights I–300a
campaign of 1916 I–381a, 427a; V–428b
Chile recognition VI–55a
commerce clause II–136a
Dominican Republic II–361b
freedom of the press III–105a
German reparations VI–87b
Income Tax Cases III–351b
Japan V–107b
Latin America policy III–479a–b
minimum-wage legislation VII–269a–b
Monroe Doctrine IV–401b
New York governorship V–87b
New York insurance investigation III–433b; V–208a
right of assembly I–204b
Sixth International Conference of American States V–106a
Supreme Court packing bill VI–448b
Washington Naval Conference VII–250b
Hughes, George (inv.) II–419b
Hughes, Henry (soc.) VI–343a
Hughes, Howard R. (ind.) III–80b
Hughes, John (archbp.) I–468a
Hughes, Langston (au.) I–25a, 30a; IV–166b
Hughes, Robert Ball (art.) VII–262a
Hughes Electric Heating Company II–419b
Hughes Research Laboratories IV–263a
Hugoton (Kans.) II–245b–46a
Huguenin, Thomas A. (off.) VI–441a
HUGUENOTS III–314b; III–121a, 334b; V–341b–42a
Florida III–38a, 41a
New Paltz II–384a
Port Royal V–370a
South Carolina VI–347a
Walloons VII–221b
Huichol (Indians) V–273a
Huidekoper, F. L. (au.) V–390b
Huisache (plant) I–494a
Huizar, Pedro (sculp.) I–159b
Hukawng Valley (Burma) IV–314a
Hukbalahap movement V–284b–85a
Hukwang Valley (China) I–386b
Hulbert, Edwin J. (surv.) I–410b
Hull (Eng.) II–344a
Hull, Albert W. (phys.) VII–163b
Hull, Cordell (states.) V–100a
Buenos Aires Peace Conference V–232a
Convention on the Rights and Duties of States V–106a
Good Neighbor policy III–199a
Japanese ambitions in Asia V–159a
Manchuria IV–235a
Mexican oil controversy IV–322b
Moscow Conference of Foreign Ministers IV–415b
munitions industry investigation IV–433b–34a
New Deal V–43b
non-intervention policy IV–112a
Panay incident V–205b
Reciprocal Trade Agreement Act V–45b
reciprocity treaties VII–88a
tariff III–113b; VI–468a
Trade Agreements Act VI–52a
United Nations V–234a
World Economic Conference VII–324a
HULL, COURT-MARTIAL OF (1814) **III–315b**; II–338b
Hull, Edward (adventurer) VI–134a
Hull, Isaac (nav. off.) V–17b, 19a; VII–240a
Constitution II–191b
Constitution–Guerriere encounter V–423b–24a
escape from Broke's squadron III–315b
Hull, John (silversmith) VI–289b
Hull, William (off.) II–338a–b; VII–46a
court-martial III–315b
Detroit surrender VI–42a; VII–234a
Detroit Treaty I–371b
Fort Dearborn II–297a
Hull's Trail III–316a
Michigan Territory IV–331a
Hull House (Chicago) II–18a; V–280a; VI–330b, 331a
HULL'S ESCAPE FROM BROKE'S SQUADRON (1812) **III–315b**
HULL'S TRAIL III–316a
HULL TREATY (1807) **III–316a**; I–371b
Hülsemann, Chevalier J. G. (dipl.) III–316a
HÜLSEMANN INCIDENT (1849–50) **III–316a**
Humane Slaughter Act (1958) I–43b
Humane societies I–125a,b
See also Animal Protective Societies
Humanism, intellectual II–170b
Humanitarianism IV–365a; V–279b
Humanities II–471a
Human Physiology V–306b
Human resources management. *See* Industrial Relations
HUMAN RIGHTS III–316a
American Convention on Human Rights III–456b
Declaration of Independence VI–115a
international convention VII–113a
Magna Charta IV–224a
religious liberty VI–80a
treaties I–362b
United Nations III–457a
Human Rights party I–138a
Humble Attempt at Scurrility (tract) VII–82a
Humble Oil Company VII–40b
Humboldt, Alexander von (nat., states.) II–390a–b; III–166a–b, 167b; IV–248a
Humboldt River III–215a
Bonneville expedition I–330a
California Trail VII–256a
Central Route I–485b
Forty-Mile Desert III–81b
forty-niners III–82a
Walker expedition VII–220a
Humboldt Sink III–215a
Humboldt Trail III–215a
Hume, David (philos.) V–286b
Hume, George (bus.) VI–201a
Hume, John (bus.) VI–201a
Hume, William (bus.) VI–201a
Humiliation, days of II–496a–b
Hummel, Jacob F. (inv.) VI–167a
Humors of the body IV–297a
Hump, flying the. *See* Flying the Hump
Humphrey, Andrew A. (off.) VI–186b
Humphrey, Doris (dancer) II–288a
Humphrey, H. L. (eng.) III–308a
Humphrey, Hubert H. (pol.)
campaign of 1964 I–430b
campaign of 1968 I–431a,b; VI–93b
campaign of 1972 I–432a; VII–254b
presidential disability V–397a
vice-presidency VII–180a
Humphrey, J. O. (jur.) III–343a
Humphrey, William E. (offi.) III–317a; IV–446b; VI–85a
Humphreys, David (off., dipl.) III–259b

Humphreys, Joshua (shipbuilder) II–190b; VI–128a; VII–153a, 240a
Humphreys–Abbot Mississippi study VI–146a
HUMPHREY'S EXECUTOR* v. *UNITED STATES (1935) **III–317a**; IV–446b; VI–85a
Humphry, John (col.) V–439a
Humpty Dumpty (pantomime) VII–48a
HUNDRED (terr. unit) **III–317b**
Hundred Years' War V–52b
Hungarian Revolt (1956) II–146a–b; V–342b
Hungarian Revolution (1848) III–316a; IV–57b; V–42a; VI–177b
Hungarians
  Indiana III–370a
Hungary
  corn production II–226b
  immigration to U.S. III–338b, 339a,b, 340b
  nationalization of U.S. property IV–466a
  Paris Peace Conference V–215b
  political exiles V–342a,b
  revolt III–69b
  World War I VII–330b
  World War II peace settlement V–378b
Hunger V–128b–29b
Hungnam (Kor.) IV–56a, 253a
Hungry Horse Dam III–323a; V–455b
HUNKERS III–317b
Hunkpapa (Indians) II–283a
Hunley (submarine) VI–422b, 424b
Hunley, Horace L. VI–422b
Hunnewell (Mo.) II–251b
Hunt, E. Howard, Jr. VII–254b–55a,b
Hunt, Frazier (jour.) V–74a
Hunt, Haroldson L. (ind.) III–80b
Hunt, Isaac (cler., au.) VII–82a
Hunt, John (pioneer) III–318b
Hunt, Lamar (bus.) VII–30b
Hunt, Richard Morris (arch.) I–143a, 163b; III–446b; VI–299a; VII–324b
Hunt, Theodore (fur trader) VI–196a
Hunt, Ward (jur.) VI–445b
Hunt, William E. (nav. off.) VI–217a
Hunt, William Morris (paint.) II–102a; V–191a
Hunt, Wilson Price (fur trader) II–477a; III–226b; V–180a
  Astoria post I–83a, 209a, 296b
Hunter (gunboat) IV–322a
Hunter, C. G. (nav. off.) IV–322a
Hunter, David (off.) I–490b; VII–117a
  emancipation order II–168a, 434b–35a
  Shenandoah campaign VI–275a
Hunter, George (chem.) II–381a
Hunter, Robert (col. gov.) V–85a
Hunter, Robert (writ.) V–381a
Hunter, Robert M. T. (pol.) II–139a, 165a, 175 (table); III–247b
Hunter, William (physic.) II–331a–b
Hunter, William (postmaster) V–371a
Hunter family (Pa.) VII–244b
HUNTERS AND CHASERS OF THE EASTERN FRONTIER III–318a; I–438b
  Patriot War V–227a
Hunter's Point (Calif.) V–29b
Hunting
  Eskimo II–461b, 462a
  frontier II–487a
  Indian III–51a
  national parks V–220a
  Plains Indians II–283a
  wildlife preservation VII–297a
  Wyoming VII–346a
HUNTING GROUNDS III–318a; III–24b
  Blackfoot V–310a
  long hunters IV–185a
  Sioux–Chippewa War VI–294b
  Tecumseh's crusade VII–18a
Huntington (N.Y.) IV–185b
Huntington (Oreg.) V–168a
Huntington, Collis P. (rr. magnate) I–406a; II–104a; III–79b
Huntington, Henry E. (bus.) II–109a
Huntington, Samuel (jur.) I–417a; II–308a
Huntington Library (San Marino, Calif.) III–285a
Huntress (slave ship) VI–309a
HUNTSVILLE (Ala.) **III–318b**; I–72a; IV–459b
Huntsville (W.Va.) II–347b
Hupa (Indians) III–362a, 363a; VII–367b
HUP–1 (helicopter) I–56b
Hurd, Henry Mills (psych.) IV–3a
Hurd, Jacob (silversmith) VI–290a
Hurd v. *Railroad Bridge Company. See* Rock Island Bridge Case
Hurdy–Gurdies. *See* Honkey–Donk Girls
Hurlbut, Stephen A. (pol.) III–207b
Hurley, Edward Nash (ind.) II–438a
Hurley, Patrick J. (law.) III–285a
Hurling (sport) III–286b
Huron (Indians) III–319a, 367a, 475a
  Battle of Bushy Run I–389a
  Champlain I–492b; V–156b
  Great Indian Council at Niagara V–90b
  half–breeds III–242b
  Iroquois raids III–399b
  Jesuit missions III–499a
  Mackinac IV–217b
  Nicolet's explorations V–95a
  Radisson's voyages VI–18a
  Saint Ignace Mission VI–190b
  Wisconsin VII–307a
Huron (Ohio) II–459a
Huron (S.Dak.) I–320b
HURON, LAKE III–319a; III–215b–16b; V–367b; VI–219b, 443a; VII–307a
  domestic trade VII–83b
  exploration III–119a; VI–192a; VII–73b, 157a
  France VI–219a
  fur trade III–331b; V–121a
  Hull Treaty III–316a
  Mackinac IV–217b, 330a
  Manitoulin Islands IV–239b
  Radisson's voyages VI–18b
  Sault Sainte Marie Canals VI–219a
Huron County (Ohio) III–25b
Huronia III–216a; IV–239b
Huron River III–316a
Hurricane Agnes (1972) II–352a; III–37a, 319b; IV–258b
Hurricane Audrey (1957) II–351b; III–319b
Hurricane Betsy (1965) III–320a
Hurricane Camille (1969) II–352a; III–319b
Hurricane Carol (1954) II–351b; III–320a
Hurricane Celia (1970) II–352a
Hurricane Diane (1955) II–351b; III–319b
Hurricane Donna (1960) II–351b
Hurricane Edna (1954) III–320a
Hurricane Hazel (1954) II–351b
HURRICANES III–319a; II–351a–52a
  Galveston II–137b
  Last Island (La.) IV–110b
  National Weather Service VII–264a
  New England III–76a
  New Orleans V–62b
  protection against II–76b
  rainfall VI–41b
  research IV–316b, 318a
  Savannah VI–220b
  Wilkes–Barre IV–258b
Hurston, Zora Neale (au.) IV–166b
HURTADO* v. *CALIFORNIA (1884) **III–320a**
Husayn 'Ali (Bahaullah) (rel. leader) V–172a
Husband–man's Guide VII–175b
Huse, Caleb (off.) II–158b
Hush puppies (food) III–52a
Hussakoff, Louis (nat.) III–27b
Hussey, Obed (inv.) IV–211a, 424a
Hussite movement IV–409b
Hustler (bomber) I–50b
Huston, Tom Charles VII–254a
Hutchins, Robert Maynard (educ.) II–401a
Hutchins, Thomas (geog.) I–462a, 463a; III–163a; VI–264a, 451a; VII–25a, 74a, 188b, 239a
Hutchin's Almanac I–91a
Hutchinson (Kans.) VI–202b
Hutchinson, Anne I–133a; II–124a; IV–270a, 447b; VI–76a; VII–316b
Hutchinson, J. W. I–432b
Hutchinson, Thomas (col. gov.) I–347b; II–140a; III–320a–b; V–242a
Hutchinson, William (col. offi.) III–280b
Hutchinsonian Controversy. *See* Antinomian Controversy
HUTCHINSON LETTERS III–320a
Hutchinson's Republican Songster for the Campaign of 1860 I–432b
Hutspot (hodgepodge) III–51b
Hutterian Brethren II–142a, 147a; IV–303a
Hutton, William R. (eng.) I–364a
Huxley, T. H. (biol.) III–112a; IV–2a
Hwachon Reservoir Dam I–57a
Hwai–Hai, Battle of (1949) II–26b
Hyakutaku, Haruyoshi (off.) III–229b
Hyatt, Alpheus (zool.) IV–119b, 251a
Hyatt, John W. (inv.) II–7a; III–409a; V–328a, 328b
Hyatt, Thaddeus (inv.) IV–274a
Hybrid corn II–281a
Hyde, Edward, 1st Earl of Clarendon (states.) I–73a–b, 458a
Hyde, Edward, 3rd Earl of Clarendon (Viscount Cornbury) (col. gov.) V–84b–85a
  assemblies II–118a
  Beekman patent I–284b
  Cary's rebellion I–465a
  land grants V–88a
  Minisink patent IV–354b
  royal land grants IV–91b
  Wawayanda Patent

HYDE, EDWARD, 3RD EARL OF CLARENDON (cont.)
VII–261b
Hyde, Henry, 2nd Earl of Clarendon IV–92a
Hyde, Henry B. (bus.) III–433a,b
Hyde, Udney (farmer) I–491b–92a
Hyde Expedition (1896–99) I–329b
Hyde Park (N.Y.) I–167b; III–284b
HYDER ALI (merchantman) **III–320b**
Hydesville (N.Y.) VI–157b
Hydrant systems III–25a
Hydraulic turbines II–422a
Hydrochloric acid II–6a
Hydrocyanic acid gas III–421a
HYDROELECTRIC POWER III–320b; II–415a; VI–147a,b; VII–257b
Bureau of Reclamation VI–54a
Canadian–American waterways I–440b
chemical industry II–7b
Colorado River II–130a–b
Columbia River II–132a, 423a; VII–248a
Department of the Interior III–445a
generating stations II–416b
government control II–188a
Hanford (Wash.) II–423a
Kentucky IV–41b
Missouri River IV–380a; VI–350a
Muscle Shoals II–423a; V–98a–b
Nashville IV–453a
Niagara Falls I–376a; II–422b, 423a; V–91b–92b
Oswego (N.Y.) V–176a
public lands V–446a
public ownership V–455b
regulation II–500a
resources II–416b
Snake River VI–322b
Spray (N.C.) II–422a
subsidies VI–425b
Tennessee VII–26a
Tennessee River VII–27b, 28a,b
Tennessee Valley Authority II–423a; V–44b–45a
Tuolumne River dam VII–362a
turbines VII–129a
Yukon River VII–367a
Hydrofoil III–11b; VII–243a
Hydrogen II–344a–b; III–17a, 17b; V–98b
HYDROGEN BOMB III–324a; I–123b–24a, 179b, 180a, 216a; III–69b; V–300b
Hydrographic Bureau, International V–133b
Hydrographic Office I–463b, 464a; II–76a; IV–317a; V–28a, 133a,b, 134a
HYDROGRAPHIC SURVEYS III–324b; II–87b; V–12a, 338b
See also Oceanographic Survey
Hydrological Decade, International (1965–75) III–454a–b
Hydrometallurgy II–223b
Hydropathy IV–284a, 288a,b; V–294a
Hydrophobia. *See* Rabies
Hydrophone IV–351a
Hydroplane II–28a
Hydroponics III–151a
Hydrostatics I–36a; V–294a
HYGIENE III–324b
Civil War IV–284a
colonial life expectancy IV–149b
dentistry II–331b
frontier II–487a
hospitals V–126b
hydropathy IV–288b
lead industry IV–122b
National Institutes of Health IV–465a
physiology V–306a, 307b
public health V–447a
pure food and drug movement V–466a
slums VI–313b
urban health VII–158a
Hygienic Laboratory I–242a; IV–286a, 287a, 465a
Hylton v. *United States* (1796) I–461a; III–351b; VII–6a
Hymnals I–279b–80a, 294a
HYMNS III–326a; IV–437b–38a
Afro–American music IV–442b, 443a
"Battle Hymn of the Republic" I–276b
civil religion II–52b–53a
"Hail Columbia" III–238b
"My Country, 'Tis of Thee" IV–446a
Hymn Society of America III–326b
Hypnosis, Society for Clinical and Experimental IV–306b
Hypnotherapy IV–306b
Hypodermic syringe II–374a
Hyslop, John Hervey (psych.) V–213a

I

Ia Drang Valley (Viet.) I–49a; VII–183b–84a
Iakovos (archbp.) II–387a
I Am Curious (Yellow) (movie) I–480a
I Am movement V–172a
Iberian immigration III–334b, 338b
Iberville, Sieur d', Pierre Lemoyne (expl.) II–294a; III–120a, 326b; VI–189b
Biloxi I–301a
Fort Maurepas IV–276b
Lake Pontchartrain V–356a–b
Louisiana IV–192b
Mississippi IV–368a, 372a, 375b
Natchez Indians IV–455b
IBERVILLE RIVER III–326b
Florida boundary III–41b
Fort Bute I–398a
Isleños settlement III–479a
Isle of Orleans III–479a
Manchac post IV–234b
Ibiza (Sp.) VI–472a; VII–90b
IBM. *See* International Business Machines.
IBM 650 (computer) II–156a
IBM 701 (calculator) II–156a
IBM 7010 (computer) VI–233a
Ibn–Muhammed Raisuli, Ahmed (bandit) V–261b
Ibo (people) VI–309b
IBRD. *See* International Bank for Reconstruction and Development
Ibsen, Henrik (poet, dram.) VII–49b
ICARIA III–327a; II–147a
Icaria–Speranza Community III–327a
ICBM. *See* Intercontinental ballistic missiles
ICC. *See* Interstate Commerce Commission
Ice
coasting trade II–90b
cod fisheries II–93a
shipping IV–311a
storage II–219a
Ice Age (New World) I–155a
Icebergia I–75b
Icebox II–420b–21a; III–55a,b
Icebreakers II–90a; III–218b; V–338a
Ice cream II–282b
Ice cream soda VI–333a
Ice Harbor Dam III–323a
Ice Hockey. *See* Hockey
Iceland
Common Market VI–472a
fisheries III–106b
Norse voyages V–112a
North Atlantic Treaty Organization V–113b
Organization for Economic Cooperation and Development V–170b
United Nations Declaration VII–151b
World War II V–337b
ICELAND, U.S. FORCES IN III–327a; II–314b; IV–252b–53a; VII–110a
Ice lodge II–462a
ICEM. *See* Intergovernmental Committee for European Migration
Ice milk II–282b
Ice Patrol, International II–90a; V–134b, 135a
Ice sheet II–76b
Ichthyologia III–26b
Ichthyologists and Herpetologists, American Society of III–28a; VI–91b
Ichthyology. *See* Fish and Marine Life
Ickes, Harold L. (law., pol.) I–80a; IV–71a, 95b; V–43b, 44b; VII–323a
Iconoscope VII–21b
"Icyball" refrigerator VI–69b
IDAHO III–327b; V–180b; VI–393 (table)
Bannock Indians I–264a
boomtowns I–336b
boundary I–351a
buffalo VII–297a
cobalt III–14a
Coeur d'Alene riots II–93b; IV–66a
Columbia River II–132a; VI–150a
forest fires III–74b
Fort Boise I–327b
Fort Hall III–243b–44a
gold II–284a; III–32a, 191b; VII–221b
Haywood–Moyer–Pettibone Case III–267a
Indians III–363a
Indian wars VII–239b
initiative III–418b
Japanese–American relocation III–491a
Jesuit missions III–500a
lead–silver industry II–93b; IV–122b
lead–silver–zinc production IV–122b
martial law IV–258b
national parks and monuments V–217b, 218 (table)
Nez Perce War I–281a; V–89b
Nonpartisan League V–106b
Oregon boundary V–165a
Palisades Dam III–323b
panhandle V–205b
Pierre's Hole V–310b
public land states V–453a
recall VI–51a
reclamation VI–53b
referendum VI–66b
Sage Plains VI–185b
settlement IV 108a–; VII–161b
sheep wars VI–273b
silver mining VI–292b
Snake River VI–322b
suffrage III–92a
Sun Valley VI–101b
westward movement VII–284b
woman's suffrage VII–315a
Wyoming VII–345b
Yakima Wars VII–350a
Yellowstone National Park VII–357a
Idaho Springs (Colo.) V–437a

Idaho Territory III–328a; IV–403a; VII–247b
Ide, William B. I–280b
Identification cards
enemy aliens II–446a
"I Didn't Raise My Boy to Be a Soldier" (song) VI–313a
Idiots
immigration II–445a
"I direct" (motto) VI–394 (table)
Idlewild Airport II–347a
Ieper (Belg.). *See* Ypres
Ieper–Lys operation. *See* Ypres–Lys Operation
Ie Shima V–147b
"If you seek a pleasant peninsula, look about you" (motto) VI–394 (table)
IGC. *See* International Geophysical Cooperation
I. G. Farben–Industrie V–292b
Igloo I–166b; II–462a
Iglulik (Indians) III–358a
Iguaçu River IV–363a
IGY. *See* International Geophysical Year
"I HAD RATHER BE RIGHT THAN BE PRESIDENT" III–328b
"I Have a Dream" (speech) V–161b
"I have found it" (motto) VI–393 (table)
"I have not yet begun to fight" I–329b; V–18b; VI–129a
Il, Nam (off.) IV–57a
Île Dernier (La.) II–351a
Île d'Orléans VI–1a
Île d'Ouessant III–169b
Ilford Company V–292a
ILGWU *See* International Ladies' Garment Workers' Union
"Iliad of the Nineteenth Century." *See* Exhibition of the Industry of All Nations
Ilion (N.Y.) V–195a
ILLIAC (computer) II–156a
Illinoia III–497a
ILLINOIS III–329a; VI–393 (table)
administrative reorganization III–206a
alien landholding I–87b
apples III–129a
Archaic culture II–385b
archives I–168b
Augusta County I–223b
banks I–129b, 259a
Bishop Hill Colony II–147a
Black Hawk War I–311b; VII–239a, 307b
black officeholders VI–432b
boundary dispute I–351a,b
butter production II–279b–80b
Cahokia settlement I–402a,b
Camp Butler I–433a
Camp Douglas I–433a
canal construction IV–87b–88a
Charleston riot I–498b
Cheyenne II–16b
Chicago Board of Trade V–320b
Chickasaw–French War II–22b
circuit riders II–39b
Civil War I–433a; II–61b, 271b; V–121b
coal mines II–85a, 86a
Copperheads II–222b
corn II–226b, 227a
crime study commission V–416a
Cumberland Road II–273b; III–448b
discrimination in courts III–437b
distilling VII–289b
domestic trade VII–83b
"Egypt" II–406b
English settlement II–450b
farm experiment clubs III–84b
farm tenancy IV–103b
federal–state jurisdiction VII–154b
fencing laws III–10b
fish III–28a
Fort Clark II–71a
Fort de Chartres I–501a
Fort Edwards II–406a
Fort Jefferson III–494a
Fort Johnson II–406a
Fort Massac IV–264a
Fort Saint Louis VI–195a
fossil plants V–196b
Fox–French Wars III–89a
French I–498b; II–126b; III–120a, 228b; IV–376b
Frink and Walker Stage Lines III–124a
frontier merchants III–127b
fur trade III–144a
grain monopoly II–430b
Granger Cases IV–434a
Granger laws III–209b, 210b–11a
Greenback party III–224b
Herrin massacre III–274a
homeopathy III–293b
Hopewell culture III–300a
Illinois and Michigan Canal III–331a, 449a,b; VI–425a
Indian land grants IV–4a
Indian removal III–394b
Indian trade I–278a
Indian treaties II–21a–b
interurban electric lines III–461b
iron and steel industry III–12a
Italian population III–338a
Jesuit missions III–499b
joint-stock land banks IV–6b
Juvenile court IV–23a
Kansas settlers V–360b
Kickapoo III–393b
Lake Michigan IV–332b
land speculation I–107b; IV–99b, 101a
La Salle exploration III–272a; IV–109b, 110a
lead III–147a; IV–122a,b, 123a; V–102b
legislators' travel allowance IV–339a
limnology II–391a
Lorimer case IV–189a
medical societies IV–289a
military tract IV–91a, 344b, 345a
minimum-wage law IV–353a
missionaries III–331b
Mormons II–496a; IV–339a; V–8a; VII–107a
Mormon War IV–412a
mounds III–365a; IV–420b
National Road IV–470b
New England settlers V–50a
"New West" V–81b
oats V–130a
Peoria V–260b
Peoria War VII–239a
petroleum V–272a
plank roads V–323a
Polish exiles V–342a
Populist party V–365b
Potawatomi II–21a
prairie V–387a
public land sales V–452b
public land states V–453a
Quakers V–470a
railroad land grants IV–94a; VI–26a
railroads III–450a; VI–25a, 32b, 33b, 34a,b, 35a; VII–83b
reptile survey VI–91b
retail sales VII–84b
revolutionary war I–296b; II–71b; IV–59b
Sauk VI–218b
Scotch-Irish VI–240b
seismic activity II–385a
senatorial campaign of 1858 IV–155a
settlement IV–338b
snowstorms II–351b
Starved Rock VI–388a
state fairs VI–392b
statehood VII–284a
stay and valuation acts VI–406a
stockyards VI–414a
swamplands VI–453b
tariff VI–465b
Tecumseh's crusade VII–233b
toll roads III–450b
tornadoes II–351a, 352a; VII–75b
Trail of Tears VII–96b
train robberies VII–97b
Treaties of Edwardsville III–383b
Treaty of Saint Louis III–383b
Treaty of Vincennes III–383b
veterinary medicine VII–176b
voting behavior VII–210b
westward movement VII–100a, 283b
wheat VII–286a
Winnebago War VII–306b
woman's suffrage VII–315a
Yale Band VII–350b
zinc VII–368b–69a
See also Chicago
Illinois (Indians) II–265b; III–88b, 331b, 399b; VII–305b
Jesuit missions III–499b
La Famine treaty IV–83b
land grants IV–4a
Starved Rock VI–388a
trade IV–277b
Illinois (song) VI–393 (table)
ILLINOIS, BRITISH ATTEMPTS TO REACH III–330a
ILLINOIS, GREAT VILLAGE OF THE III–330b; III–329a; VI–388a
Kaskaskia tribe IV–31b
Illinois, University of I–241a; II–227b, 391a; IV–412b; V–348b–49a
ILLINOIS AND MICHIGAN CANAL III–331a; II–17b, 20a; III–329b, 449a,b; IV–87b; VI–425a
ILLINOIS AND WABASH COMPANY III–331a
ILLINOIS BAND III–331b
Illinois Central Gulf Railroad VI–34b
Illinois Central Railroad I–403b; II–351a; III–64b, 451b; IV–94a, 101a; VI–26a, 34b
Illinois College III–331b; VII–350b
ILLINOIS COUNTRY III–331b; II–329a; III–329a–b
British I–501b; III–330a
Croghan's expedition II–265a; VI–285a
Fort de Chartres I–501a
Fort Jefferson III–494a
Fort Pimitoui V–315a
Franciscans III–94a
French occupation II–458b
Indians II–265b
Kaskaskia IV–31b
land company claims III–331a
legal system II–247b
Loftus expedition IV–178b
Mississippi River IV–372b
revolutionary war I–367a; V–354b; VI–124a
Treaty of Paris (1763) III–330a
ILLINOIS COUNTY III–331b; V–260b
Illinois Creek, Battle of *See* Prairie Grove, Battle at
ILLINOIS FUR BRIGADE III–331b
Illinois Herald (news.) V–70b
Illinois Industrial University *See* Illinois, University of

Illinois Institute of Technology I–165a
Illinois Land Company III–331a
Illinois Natural History Survey III–28a
Illinois Regiment VI–126b
Illinois River II–19a, 20a; III–119a, 329a, 330b, 331b; VI–192a
exploration III–329a; IV–372a
Fort Crèvecoeur II–257b
Fort Pimitoui V–315a
fur trade III–144a,b, 332a
Gulf Intracoastal Waterway VI–148b
Illinois and Michigan Canal III–331a
Jolliet and Marquette expedition IV–7a
Lakes-to-Gulf waterway IV–87b
La Salle's explorations IV–109b
military reserve IV–345a
Peoria V–260b
portage V–367b
research station II–391a
Starved Rock VI–388a
steamboating VI–406b
Treaty of Saint Louis III–383b
Illinois State Laboratory of Natural History II–391a
Illinois State Medical Society IV–289a
Illinois Territory I–286b; IV–32a; VII–307a
Illinois Waterway IV–88a; VI–148b
Illiteracy II–333a; III–438a
Illuminati VI–12a
ILLUMINATI OF NEW ENGLAND III–332a
Illumination. *See* Lighting
I Love You, California (song) VI–393 (table)
Ima Hogg's Bayou Bend II–101a
***I'M ALONE* CASE** (1929) **III–332a**; I–439b
Imboden, John D. (off.) I–381b; III–332b; V–59a
IMBODEN–JONES RAID (1863) **III–332b**
IMF. *See* International Monetary Fund
Immaculate Conception Mission (Ill.) III–329a
IMMEDIATISM III–332b; V–50b
Immigrant labor
agriculture II–495a
coal mining II–86a
distribution II–442a
Industrial Workers of the World IV–67b
IMMIGRATION III–332b; II–439a
agriculture I–36b, 39b
Americanization programs II–401b
balance of trade I–245a
big business I–389a
black enterprise I–309b
bossism I–343a
Boston IV–267b
campaign of 1880 IV–409b
Canadians I–440a
canal construction I–443b
Catholic church I–468b–69a
Chicago II–17a, 18a
Chinese I–386a; IV–64a
city planning II–46a
Civil War II–63b
Cleveland II–75a
clothing industry II–82a
Coast Guard II–89b
colonial labor force IV–60a
colonial society II–125a–b
Connecticut II–181a
contract labor II–214a
Customs Service II–277a
deportation II–332b–33a
elderly V–150a
Ellis Island II–432b
ethnic newspapers V–75a–b
eugenics movement III–159a
folklore III–48b–49a
French refugees III–121a
frontier II–326a
Gentlemen's Agreement III–68b
German III–81a–b; IV–310a; VI–194b
government inspection III–422a
Great Migration III–220a
growth of cities II–41b
Hamilton's fiscal policies III–245b
Harlem III–253b
Hawaii III–264a
homestead movement III–296b
housing I–143a; III–310a
Illinois II–450b
indentured servants III–353a
Indiana III–370b
inspection center II–432b
Irish IV–267a, 310a
Italian III–483a
Japanese II–471b; III–68b; VI–164a
Jeffersonian Democracy III–495b
Jews IV–9b, 10a, 11a–b
job competition IV–61b
land policy I–4a
literacy tests IV–159b
Lutheran churches IV–206a–b
McCarran–Walter Act IV–209b
medical inspection IV–287a
Minnesota IV–356b
Missouri IV–378a
Mohawk Valley IV–387a
morals IV–408b
nativism V–2a
Nazi Germany V–99b
Newark V–41b
New England V–49b, 50a
New Jersey V–57b
New Orleans V–62b
New York City I–275b; V–83a
New York State V–88a, 88a
North Dakota V–117a,b
Ohio V–141a
opposition to I–110a, 111a, 111b
organized crime II–258a
Palatines V–195a
Pennsylvania III–293a
per capita funds III–63a
political exiles V–342a–b
population changes V–361a–b
prizefighters V–422b
quotas II–333a, 432b; VI–4b
race relations VI–7a
radical right VI–12a, 12b
redemptioners VI–62b
religion VI–78a–b
Rhode Island VI–133b
sailing packets V–183b
Scotch-Irish VI–240b
Scottish and Irish II–369b
segregation VI–255b
slums VI–314a,b
social settlements VI–330a,b
Spain VI–365a
sweatshop VI–454a
Swiss VI–454b
Tammany Hall VI–459b, 460b
taxes I–451a
Texas VII–37a
Union Pacific Railroad VII–147b
urban structure VII–159a–b
Utah settlement VII–161b
Vermont VII–172b
Walloons VII–221b
western lands IV–100a
West Virginia VII–282a
westward movement I–38b
Wisconsin VII–307b
work force V–132b
World War I I–25b, 29b; II–418b–19a
Wyoming VII–346a
Young Men's Hebrew Associations VII–362b
Immigration Act (1891) II–333a
Immigration Act (1917) II–445a
Immigration Act (1921) III–333b, 342b
German quota III–337a
Immigration Act (1924) II–488b; III–333b, 337a, 340a, 492a; IV–209b; VI–4b
Immigration Act (1965) III–333b–34a, 341b, 342b
Immigration and Nationality Act (1952). *See* McCarran–Walter Act
Immigration and Naturalization, Bureau of II–442a; IV–78a
Immigration and Naturalization Service II–277a; IV–22a; V–6b–7a
employment office II–442a
IMMIGRATION RESTRICTION III–341b; II–30a, 445a; III–333a–34a
AFL support IV–65b
Chinese II–29a, 488b
Italians III–483b
Japanese II–488b; III–491b
Jews IV–10a
legislation I–87b–88a, 117a
McCarran–Walter Act IV–209b
quotas I–88a; VI–4b
retaliation VI–104b
yellow peril VII–356a
Immorality. *See* Morals
Immunity, federal VII–154b–55a
IMMUNITY BATH III–343a
IMMUNITY OF PRIVATE PROPERTY III–343a
IMPATT diode IV–333b
IMPEACHMENT III–343b; II–198b
Chase, Samuel I–501b
executive immunity II–473b–74a
Ferguson, James E. III–11a
judges V–346b
Nixon, Richard M. V–99a; VII–254a
Ohio judiciary VI–454b
Oklahoma governors V–149a
pardoning II–201b
power of Congress II–172a
president II–202a
Reconstruction governors III–295a
state judges IV–18a
Supreme Court VI–444a
trial II–198b
Tweed Ring judges VII–131b
See also Presidential Exemption From Subpoena
IMPEACHMENT TRIAL OF ANDREW JOHNSON (1868) **III–345b**; III–344a–b; VI–11b, 57a, 84b; VII–31b
Impending Crisis. See Helper's *Impending Crisis of the South*
Imperial Beach (Calif.) V–28a
Imperial-Coachella Valley II–130a
Imperial Dam II–130a
Imperial Hotel (Tokyo) I–165a
IMPERIAL IDEA, PREREVOLUTIONARY III–346a
IMPERIALISM III–347a
campaign of 1900 I–425b–26a
opposition V–235a,b
Philippines V–281b
Treaty of Paris V–215a
Imperial Maritime Customs Service V–158b
Imperial school of historians III–282b
Imperial Valley (Calif.) IV–104b

IMPLIED POWERS **III–348a**; III–3a, 9a, 157a; VI–97b
bank chartering IV–211b
federal agencies II–497b
federal education II–395b
Juilliard v. *Greenman* IV–20a
Marshall Court IV–13b
Implosion
atomic bomb IV–238b
Imports
federal financing II–500b
taxation VII–7a
See also Duties; Tariff; Trade, Foreign
IMPOSTS **III–349a**; II–199b, 200b; VII–4a–b, 10b
Impressionist painting V–190a, 192a
Impressionist printmaking V–413b
Impressionists (art) II–103a–b, 104b
Impressment IV–60a, 79a
IMPRESSMENT, CONFEDERATE **III–349a**; II–163b, 165a; VII–148b
Impressment Act (1863) II–163b
IMPRESSMENT OF SEAMEN **III–349b**; II–436b; III–106b, 455b; V–320a; VII–87a, 233b, 235b, 236a
Monroe–Pinkney Treaty IV–402b
Napoleon's decrees IV–449b
press gangs V–399b
Treaty of Ghent III–176b, 177a
War of 1812 I–438b
Imprisonment
Civil War II–190a
debt II–299a–b
Improved Dwellings Association VII–24a
Improvements, internal. *See* Internal Improvements
Inalienable rights II–325a
INAUGURATION OF THE PRESIDENT **III–350b**; IV–88b
Inca (Indians) I–48a, 166a; II–336a; IV–421a
Incandescent lamp. *See* Lamp, Incandescent
Incendiaries II–9b; V–26a
Inchon (Kor.) I–61a; IV–57a, 253a; V–21b; VII–139a
Income, minimum IV–184a
Income, national IV–462a
Income, real II–235a, 236a
Income redistribution II–502a
Income splitting VI–12a
Income tax VI–14a, 200b, 397a; VII–3a, 4b, 5a,b, 6a,b, 7a, 8a–10b, 10a,b, 11a, 11b–13b, 14a
campaign of 1892 V–365b
campaign of 1896 I–425a
Civil War II–69a, 113b, 164b
Florida III–42a
Greenback party III–225a
inherited property III–417b–18a
"normalcy" V–110a
Ocala Platform V–132a
political contributions V–341b
Progressive movement V–427b, 428b
public debt II–300a
public revenue VI–105a–b
rebates V–464a
regulations II–178b
Sixteenth Amendment I–94b; II–206a; VI–297b
Supreme Court rulings V–354b
Tax Court II–500b
Wealth Tax Act V–46b
Wisconsin VII–308b
See also Taxation
Income tax, graduated IV–64a
INCOME TAX CASES (1895) **III–351a**
Incorporated territories III–424b
Incorporating statutes II–229a
Incubation tests I–445a
In Darkest England and the Way Out VI–204a
INDEMNITIES **III–352a**
Boxer Rebellion V–242a–b
I'm Alone Case III–332b
Jay's Treaty III–493b–94a
Monroe–Pinkney Treaty IV–402b
Panama Revolution V–204b
Panay incident V–205b
Russo-Japanese War V–370b
Shimonoseki expedition VI–279a
Virginius affair VII–204b
See also Indian Claims Commission
INDENTURED SERVANTS **III–352a**; II–125a–b, 258a, 495a; IV–60a, 79a, 102b
agriculture I–36b
antebellum South VI–341b
blacks I–26b, 27a
debtors II–299a
immigration III–334b
interracial marriage IV–362b
New Amsterdam III–253a
New Netherland V–60b
New Smyrna Colony V–66a
poor relief VI–72b
poor whites V–358b–59a
redemptioners VI–62b
runaways III–130a
schoolteachers VI–229b
slavery VI–304b, 310a
Virginia I–21a, 26b; VII–193a–b
wages VII–215a
women VII–313a
Indentures
apprenticeship I–148a
Independence (Kans.) III–354b
INDEPENDENCE (Mo.) **III–353b**; II–25b
Civil War V–403a; VII–280b
mail service V–177b
merchants VII–273b
Mormons IV–339a; VI–87a
Oregon Trail V–168b, 169a
Santa Fe Trail IV–27b; VI–215b
stagelines VI–379a
trading VII–280b
Truman Library I–167b; III–284b
wagon trains II–248a
westward movement I–174b, 453a, 485b; IV–20b
Independence (ship of the line) V–19b; VI–282a
Independence (sloop) VII–38a, 41a–b
Independence (steamboat) IV–380a
Independence, Fort (N.Y.) VII–171b
Independence Bay (Green.) V–240b
INDEPENDENCE HALL (Phila.) **III–353b**; I–161b; III–268b; V–247a, 277a
Independence Mine (Colo.) II–264a; III–191b
Independence National Historic Park III–354a; IV–143a
INDEPENDENCE ROCK (Wyo.) **III–354a**; V–168b
Independence Square (Phila.) III–354a
Independent (mag.) III–257a
Independent Chronicle (news.) II–30b
Independent Journal (news.) III–4a
Independent Labor party II–492b
Independent National party III–224b
Independent Order of Oddfellows VI–252b
Independents. *See* Separatists
Independent theater movement VII–49b
INDEPENDENT TREASURY SYSTEM **III–354b**; I–255b, 256b; II–73a; III–6a, 251b; V–206b–07a
Independent Whig VI–113a
Index-Medicus IV–292a
Index of the Cost of Living. *See* Consumer Price Index
India
atomic bomb I–216a
British power II–488a
cotton II–162a, 238b, 240a
Everest survey III–480b
exchange students II–471a
gunpowder V–97b
ice production VI–69a
immigration to U.S. III–340b, 341a,b
independence I–124a
International Control Commission III–452b
missions IV–366a
Nuclear Test Ban Treaty V–125a
Pittman Act V–321b
Rhodes scholars VI–134b
shipping IV–310b
smallpox VI–316a
Southeast Asia Treaty Organization VI–350b
theosophical societies VII–52a
trade I–201a,b, 301b, 345b, 466a; II–388b; IV–309b
United Nations Declaration VII–151b
Vietnam III–160a
World War II I–386b–87a; II–26a; III–489b, 490a; VII–337b
Indian, American
Alaska I–76a–b
antebellum South VI–340b
Big Knives I–296b
birch bark I–304b
body paints II–233b
British allies VII–270a
buffalo I–375a
buffalo trails I–376a
bullboats I–380a
Catlin paintings I–470b; II–477a
census I–481b, 482a
Century of Dishonor I–485b
Champlain's alliance I–492b
Chicago II–17a, 21a–b, 297a
Civilian Conservation Corps II–51a
civil rights movement II–55b–56a
congressional apportionment II–198a, 205b
Connecticut II–179b
coureurs de bois II–246a
Dawes Commission II–295b
Dawes General Allotment Act II–295b–96a
enfranchisement I–385b
eugenics movement III–158b
federal expenditure II–476a
flower gardening III–151a–b
folk motif III–47b
food preservation III–54b
Georgia I–223a
half-breeds III–242b
horse I–369a; III–302b–03a; IV–444b
hunting grounds III–318a
Illinois Country II–265a–b
Indian New Deal V–48b–49a
Indian Reorganization Act II–296a
Kentucky II–291b–92a
Lake Erie II–458b
land frauds II–231b
land titles I–412b

INDIAN, AMERICAN (cont.)
New Plymouth Colony V–64b
Northwest Territory V–122b
Ohio Valley I–477a
paintings of V–184b, 189b
portrayal in dramas VII–47b
poverty V–280b
powwow V–386b
Quakers III–123a; V–470b
race relations VI–5b–6a, 7b
Raleigh's colonies VI–43a,b
Rhode Island VI–131b–32a
river navigation VI–148a
scouts VI–241b
segregation VI–255b
slave insurrections VI–303b
smallpox II–52a; VI–315a
Spanish relations VI–366a
subject in music IV–438b
Treaty of Ghent III–176b
War of 1812 VII–234b–35a, 262a
water rights VII–256a
White Woman of the Genesee VII–293b
wild turkey VII–130a
See also American Indian Defense Association; American Indian Movement; Agriculture, American Indian; Archaeology and Prehistory, North American; Canadian Indians; Dance, American Indian; Factory System, Indian; Nativistic Movements, American Indian; Spanish–Indian Relations; Wars and Campaigns, Indian
INDIAN, AMERICAN, NATIVE CULTURES III–355a; I–128–29b
Abnaki I–2b, 2b
Acoma I–7b
Adena I–11a, 157a
Alaska I–79a
Algonkin VII–70a
Algonquin I–85a
Anasazi I–117a,b, 157b
animal care VII–175b
Apache I–141b
Archaic stage I–11b, 154b, 155b–57b
Arizona I–171b–72a
art and technology III–373a
Assiniboine I–206a
ball games II–52a
Bannock I–264a,b
Basin Indians
Commanche IV–50b
Modoc IV–51b
Bella Bella IV–59a
Blackfoot I–310b
burial III–376a
California I–405a
California mission Indians IV–365b
Cheyenne II–16b
Chipewyan II–30b
chopper–scraper culture II–334b
Clovis II–83b
consumer cooperatives II–221a
councils III–378b
Dakota II–282b
Eskimo I–79a, 80b–81a, 84a, 166b, 167a, 441b, 446a; V–217b
Eyak I–81a
Five Civilized Tribes I–335b; II–51b
Folsom complex III–50a
food III–50b–51b
Fox I–242b; III–88b
Genizaro III–162b
"Great Spirit" III–222b
Haida III–238a; IV–59a
Hare III–252b
Havasupai III–262b
Hohokam III–289a
Hopewell III–300a
Hopi III–300b
Houma III–308a
Indians of the 1970's III–396b
interracial marriage IV–362b
inventions and discoveries III–381a
Iroquois III–475a
Iroquois–speaking VII–70a
Itama III–484a
Kiowa IV–50b
Klamath IV–51b
Kwakiutl IV–59a
liquor III–398a
Llano II–83b–84a
Lumbee IV–203b
Mahican IV–387a
Makah IV–228b
Mandan, Hidatsa, and Arikara IV–235b
medicine III–384b
Mexico IV–327a
Mississippian cultures IV–370a
Miwok IV–381b
Mogollon IV–385b
Mohave IV–386a
Mohegan IV–387a
Mound Builders IV–420b
myth and folklore III–386a
Natchez IV–455a
Navaho V–8a
New Mexico V–59b
Nootka IV–59a
Northwest Coast I–81a
Ohio V–140a
Oklahoma V–148a
Omaha V–154b
Oregon V–165a, 165b
Paiute V–194a
Pan–Indianism V–210a
Pawnee V–230a
Pennsylvania V–246a
petroglyphs II–341a
Peyote Cult V–272b
philanthropy V–279b
Pima V–314a
pipe V–318a
political organization III–390b
Pueblo V–459a
Pueblo culture III–300b
religion III–391b
Sauk I–242b
scalping VI–224a
Shawnee VI–270b
slaveholding III–401a
study of II–464b–65a
Tlingit I–81a; IV–59a
tobacco and narcotics VII–64b
Tsimshian IV–59a
Utah VII–161a
Ute VII–162a
Virginia VII–192a
wampum VII–223a
Winnebago VII–305b
Woodland Tradition VII–319b
Yurok VII–367b
Zuni VII–372a
Indian, wooden. *See* Wooden Indian
INDIANA III–369b; VI–393 (table); VII–253b
Adena I–11a
apples III–129a
Augusta County I–223b
banking I–253a, 255b, 259a
Battle of Tippecanoe VI–271b
birth and death registration IV–149a
black officeholders VI–432b
bond issue IV–412b
bossism I–343b
boundary dispute I–351a,b
campaign of 1888 I–322a
canal construction I–442b
checkoff II–4a
circuit riders II–39b
civil disturbances IV–341b
Civil War II–61b, 271b; IV–410b, 435a; V–121b
coal mines II–85a, 86a
conciliation process II–157b
Copperheads II–222b
corn II–226b, 227a
Cumberland Road II–273b; III–448b
Delaware Indians II–321a; III–393b
disasters II–348b, 351a,b, 352a
discrimination in courts III–437b
domestic trade VII–83b
Ex parte Milligan IV–346b
farm tenancy IV–103b
Fort Harrison III–257b
Fort Knox IV–53b
Fort Miami IV–329a
Fort Ouiatenon V–176a
Fort Wayne VII–262a
gores III–200a
Greenback party III–224b
Harmony Society II–147a; IV–338b
Harrison Indian treaties III–384b
historical society III–278b
homeopathy III–293b
Hoosiers III–299a
Indian campaigns VII–212b
Indian lands IV–4a, 181b
Indian removal III–394b
interurban electric lines III–461b
Iowa jurisdiction III–467b
iron and steel industry III–12a
Iroquois cession VI–385b
Italian population III–338a
Jesuit missions III–499b
Kansas settlers V–360b
Ku Klux Klan IV–58b
La Balme's expedition IV–59b
Lake Michigan IV–332b
land speculation IV–99b
La Salle's explorations IV–109b
libraries IV–144b
limnology II–391a
lynching legislation IV–208b
martial law IV–258b
National Road IV–470b
natural gas V–5a
New Harmony V–54b–55a
"New West" V–81b
Northwestern Indian War VII–239a
oil boomtowns I–336b
personal liberty laws V–263b
petroleum V–270a
"Pocket" V–334b
political organizations IV–52b
Populist party V–365b
prairie V–387a
public land states V–453a
Quakers V–470a
railroads VI–25a, 33b, 34a; VII–83b
retail sales VII–84b
school lands VI–228a
Scotch–Irish VI–240b
settlement III–227b; IV–338b
Shawnee VI–270b
social legislation VI–327b
state fairs VI–392b
statehood VII–284a
tariff VI–465b
taxation VII–11a
Tecumseh's crusade VII–233b
territorial government VII–32a
tobacco VII–66b
toll roads III–450b
tornadoes VII–75b
train robberies VII–97a–b
Treaty of Chicago III–383b
Treaty of Greenville III–383a
Underground Railroad VII–138b, 139a
Vincennes IV–59b; VII–188a, 189a
voting behavior VII–210b
Wabash Canal III–449b
Western Reserve III–414a
West Virginia migration VII–282a
westward movement

VII–100a, 283b
Indiana (battleship)
VI–216b; VII–242a
Indiana, University of
II–391b; IV–93b; V–349a;
VI–266b
INDIANA COMPANY
III–370b; I–278a; IV–98b,
371a; VI–430a
INDIAN AFFAIRS, BUREAU OF III–371a;
III–390a,b, 444a,b;
IV–95a; V–210b; VI–6a
agencies III–372a
Alaska I–79b
Black Hills War IV–167b
education III–379b–80a,b
fencing of reservations
V–160b
Indian agents III–373a
Indian occupation (1972)
III–397a; VI–7b
Indian personnel V–49a
Indian protest I–106b
Indian removal III–389a
Indians and liquor
III–399a
Indian wars I–192b
opposition IV–463a, 464a
reclamation VI–54a–b
reservations III–395b,
396a
tribal courts III–404b
Wheeler–Howard Act
VII–287a
Indiana Gazette (news.)
V–70b
INDIAN AGENCIES
III–372a; III–371b
agents III–372b
Fort Peck V–241a
Fort Snelling
VI–294b–95a, 322b
Mission Agency at Riverside IV–366a
Red Cloud VI–157a
reservations III–395b–96a
Sioux uprising VI–296b
Standing Rock VII–344b
Uncompahgre VII–137b
Washita River II–91a
INDIAN AGENTS
III–372b; II–116b
Butler, Richard V–322a
Croghan, George
IV–181b
Crowell, John III–394a
Fitzpatrick, Thomas
IV–108b
Great Plains III–221a
Lovely, W. L. IV–199a
Meeker, N.S. IV–300a
Morgan, George III–400b
Royer, R. F. IV–316a
Weiser, Conrad IV–89b
western merchants
VII–274a
Indiana party column (ballot)
I–249a
Indianapolis 500 (auto race)
I–231b; III–224b
Indianapolis (Ind.)
American Legion VII–175a
Central Canal III–374b
Civil War VI–26b
government IV–172b
Grand Army of the Republic III–207b
National Democratic party
III–189a
railroad III–374b
State Bank of Indiana
VI–390a
wagons V–389b
Indianapolis Journal (news.)
III–299a
Indian Appropriation Act
(1889) V–148b
Indian architecture. *See* Architecture, American Indian
INDIAN ART AND TECHNOLOGY III–373a;
III–381b
bow making V–174a
copper II–223a; V–103a
Eskimo III–358a
furniture design III–136b
iron oxides III–12a
Jesuit missions III–499a
lead mining VI–189b
leather production
IV–127b
Makah IV–228b
Mexico IV–327b
Mississippian cultures
IV–370a,b
moccasin IV–384b
Mogollon IV–385b
Mohave IV–386a
mounds IV–420b
natural gas IV–333b
Navaho III–369a;
V–8b–9a,b
Northwest Coast culture
III–361b
Pan–Indianism V–210b
Pueblo III–367b
salt VI–202a
travois VII–106b
Western cultures
III–362b–63a
INDIANA STATE CANALS
III–374b; VII–212a
Indiana Territory II–356a;
V–123a, 141a;
VII–188b–89a
Indian affairs
III–372b–73a
Michigan IV–331a
Wisconsin VII–307a
Indiana v. *Kentucky* (1890)
I–351b
INDIAN BARRIER STATE
III–375a; III–403b;
V–120b; VII–235b
Jay's Treaty III–493b
Treaty of Ghent III–176b
INDIAN BIBLE, ELIOT'S
III–375b; V–410b
INDIAN BRIGADE
III–375b; III–400a
INDIAN BURIAL
III–376a; I–11a,b
Hopewell culture
III–300a
Itama culture III–484b
mounds IV–420b, 421a,b
INDIAN CAPTIVITIES
III–376a; II–94a
Boone–Callaway I–336b
Genizaro Indians
III–162b
Germaine girls III–172a
Hennepin, Louis III–272a
Jemison, Mary VII–293b
Jogues, Isaac III–499a
Kentucky IV–40a
McCrea, Jane IV–211a
Oatman girls V–129b
Parker, Cynthia V–216b
revolutionary war
IV–216b
"running the gauntlet"
III–154b
Spirit Lake massacre
VI–374a
Whitman massacre
VII–294a
York attack VII–358b
INDIAN CITIZENSHIP
III–377a; I–106b;
II–42a–b; V–6a
Burke Act I–385b
intermarried citizen
III–447a
Indian Civil Rights Act (1968)
II–56a
Indian Claims Act (1946)
III–390a
INDIAN CLAIMS COMMISSION III–377a; III–390a,
397a
Seminole VI–260a
Sioux VI–295a
Indian Commissioners, Board
of III–371b, 378b
INDIAN COMMISSIONS
III–377b; VI–295b
Indian corn. *See* Maize
INDIAN COUNCIL
III–378b
Duluth's mission IV–355a
Ecorse River Council
II–392b
Fort Laramie Treaty
IV–108b
Fort Leavenworth
IV–129b
Fort Smith VI–317a
Great Council at Niagara
V–90b
hunting grounds III–318b
Iroquois III–475b
League of the Iroquois
III–365b
leasing of land and mineral
rights IV–90a
Leech Lake IV–131b
Logstown IV–181a
Medicine Creek IV–299a
Navaho V–9a
Sioux–Chippewa War
VI–295a
Sioux Council of 1889
VI–295a
Torreys' trading post
VII–77a
Washington Territory
VI–412b
Wheeler–Howard Act
V–49a
INDIAN COUNTRY
III–379a; II–284a–b;
III–221a, 402a
Fort Laramie treaties
IV–108b–09a
gold prospectors III–32a
Great Plains III–221a
land cessions III–384a,b
preemption rights V–389b
trade III–387b
Virginia factory III–380b
Indian dances. *See* Dance,
American Indian
Indian Department. *See* Indian Affairs, Bureau of
INDIAN EDUCATION
III–379b; II–394b, 395b;
III–377b, 389b, 390a–b,
397a
Carlisle School I–455a
College of William and
Mary VII–300b
colleges II–115a
Dartmouth College
II–292b
Jesuit missions III–499a
Wheeler–Howard Act
V–49a; VII–287a
INDIAN FACTORY OF VIRGINIA III–380b
Indian Factory System. *See*
Factory System, Indian
Indian Head (Md.) V–28a
Indian Health Service
III–371a
Indian Historical Press
V–76a
INDIAN INVENTIONS AND
DISCOVERIES
III–381a
snowshoes VI–297b, 323a
subarctic culture III–360a
tobacco smoking
V–318a–b
"Indianist" movement (mus.)
IV–438b
INDIAN KEY MASSACRE
(1840) **III–381b**
INDIAN LAND CESSIONS
III–381b; IV–90a;
VI–296a–b
Carver claim I–464b,
464b
Cherokee II–14a, 14b–15a;
III–400b; V–49b
Chicago II–17a, 21a–b,
297a
Chickasaw lands II–23a
Choctaw land frauds
II–32b
colonial policy III–388a–b
Connecticut IV–387a
Creek lands II–256b–57a
Cumberland settlements
II–273b
Florida III–59a; V–231b
Fort Niagara treaties
V–90b
Fort Stanwix treaties
VI–385b–86a
Four-Mile Strip III–85a
frontier III–126b
Georgia I–223a; III–88b
Great Plains III–221a
Illinois III–329b
Indian Country III–379a,
379b
Indian Territory III–402a
Iowa III–468a; V–33b;
VII–106a
Kayoderosseras Patent
IV–33a
Lovely's purchase
IV–199a
Michigan I–371b; III–316a;
IV–107b, 331a; VI–186b,
197a
Mille Lac IV–97b
Minnesota IV–355b, 356a;

INDIAN LAND CESSIONS (cont.)
VII–106a
Mississippi II–291a; IV–368b; V–357a–b; VII–54b
Nebraska V–31a
New Haven Colony V–55b
New York Colony V–84b
New York State V–88b
Ohio III–227b; IV–216a; VII–263a
Old Northwest III–24b; VII–17b–18a
Osage lands V–173b
Pennsylvania IV–216b
Phelps–Gorham purchase V–276b
removal III–393b–94b
Sauk and Fox I–311b–12a
Sioux claims commission VI–295a
Sioux Council VI–295a
State of Franklin II–381a
Tennessee IV–186b; VI–357b–58a
Tennessee River II–22a
Texas Panhandle IV–299b
Treaty of Fort Harmar III–255a
Treaty of Fort Stanwix III–208b–09a
Treaty of Indian Springs III–401b
Upper Sandusky VII–157b
Vincennes VII–189a
Virginia III–251a; IV–173a
Wabash River VII–262b
Western Reserve III–414a
westward expansion IV–99b
Wisconsin IV–107b; VII–307b
Indian Land Cessions in the United States III–384a
Indian land grants. *See* Land grants, Indian
Indian land titles IV–91b, 92b
Indian languages I–110b; III–355b, 396b
Algonkin III–360a, 365a,b, 366b–67a; IV–330a, 387a; V–410b; VII–367b
Athapascan III–360a, 367a, 368b, 369a; IV–50b; V–8b; VII–367b
Aztec–Tanoan III–301a, 301a; V–459b
Caddoan III–365b; IV–235b; V–148a, 230b
Cherokee III–365b
Chinook jargon I–346a; V–165a
Eskaleut I–84a; III–357b
Hitchiti VI–259b
Hokan VII–367b
Hokan–Coahuiltecan III–369a
Hokan–Siouan III–369a, 476a; V–230b
Hopi III–301a
Iroquoian III–365b, 367a, 475a, 476a
Keresan III–367b; V–460a
Klamath–Modoc IV–51b
Muskhogean III–308a
Muskogean III–365b; VI–259b
Na–Déné III–360a
Nahuatl V–410a
Nootka V–165a
Penutian phylum IV–51b, 381b
Plains Indians III–364a, 365a
Salishan III–362b
Sequoya's syllabary VI–263a
Shoshonean III–301a, 367a; IV–50b; V–194a, 459b; VII–162b
sign language VI–286a
Siouan III–365a,b, 367a, 476a; IV–235b; V–155a, 173b; VII–305b
Siouan–Yuchi III–365b
Tanoan III–301a, 367b; IV–50b; V–459b
Tewa III–301b, 367b; V–459b–60a
Tiwa III–367b; V–460a
Towa III–367b; V–460a
Ute VII–162b
Uto–Aztecan III–301a, 362b, 367a,b, 369a; IV–50b, 327a; V–314a, 459b; VII–162b
Wakashan IV–59a, 228b
Yuman III–262b; IV–386a
Zunian III–367b
INDIAN MEDICINE III–384b; III–49b, 393a; IV–283a
Eskimo III–358a
fossil remains V–195a
Iroquois III–476a
medicine show IV–299b
Midewiwin IV–335b
Navaho III–369a; V–9a
petroleum IV–43b; V–269a
Saratoga Springs VI–217b
INDIAN MISSIONS III–385b; II–389a; III–389b, 391b; IV–367a; V–279b; VI–364b
California IV–365b
Coeur d'Alene II–93b
Dartmouth College II–292b
education III–379b, 390a–b
Florida III–41a
Georgia III–170a
Guardian Angel II–17a
Hazelwood Republic III–267a
Hopi III–301a
Hudson's Bay Company III–313b
Immaculate Conception III–329a
Jesuits III–498b–500b
La Présentation V–139b
Lapwai IV–108a
Oregon II–285b; V–165a, 166b–67a
Pecos V–241a
Penobscot region III–120b
Pima V–314a,b
Pokagon village V–335b
Pueblo V–459b
Red River Post VI–64b
Rodríguez–Chamuscado expedition VI–162a
Saint Francis VI–190a
Saint Ignace VI–191a
San Francisco de los Tejas VI–210a
Sault Sainte Marie VI–219b
Schoenbrunn VI–226a
Southwest IV–367a–b
Spanish Inquisition III–420b
Texas IV–302b
INDIAN MYTH AND FOLKLORE III–386a; III–392a
coyote II–253a
Eastern Woodlands culture III–366b
Fox–Wisconsin Waterway III–89b
Iroquois League III–475a
Maiden's Rock IV–224b
Michabous IV–330a
Midewiwin IV–335b
Starved Rock VI–388a
wolf VII–312a
Indian New Deal V–48b–49a
Indian Ocean
navigational charts IV–277a
Neutrality Act of 1939 V–37b
World War II VII–342a
Indian oil lands V–173b
Indianola (ironclad) I–277a
INDIAN ORATORY III–386b; III–355b, 391b; V–161a
folklore III–386a
Logan's speech IV–179a
Otreouati IV–83b
Indian paintbrush (flower) VI–395 (table)
INDIAN PATHS III–387a; VI–152b
Chicago Road II–20a
Cumberland Gap II–272a
Great Warriors Path VII–238b
Scioto Trail VI–239b
Three Notch Road VII–54b
Virginia Path VII–202b
INDIAN POLICY, COLONIAL III–387b; III–382a–b, 388b, 404a; VI–5b–6a
Albany Congress I–82a
Augusta Congress I–223a
Bacon's Rebellion I–240a
barrier state III–375a
colonial plans of union II–121a–22a
courts I–145a
Detroit VI–219b–20a
Dutch–Indian War II–382b
Florida V–254b
Great Indian Council at Niagara V–90b
Iroquois allies IV–386b
Iroquois Treaty III–476b
King Philip's War IV–47a
New Amsterdam V–40b
New Netherland V–61a–b
New York Colony V–84b, 85a
Ohio V–140b
Powhatan Confederacy V–385b
Proclamation of 1763 V–424b
segregation VI–255b
suffrage VI–434b
INDIAN POLICY, NATIONAL III–388b; III–213b, 221a, 444b; VI–6a, 7b, 327b
Bureau of Indian Affairs III–371b, 372a,b
Camp Grant massacre I–433b
education III–379b–80a
Indian commissions III–377b, 377b
Indian Country III–379a
Indian New Deal V–48b
Indian removal III–393a
Jesuit missions III–499b–500a
Lake Mohonk Conference IV–387b
land cessions III–382b–84b
National Congress of American Indians IV–463a
National Indian Youth Council IV–464a
Northwest Territory V–163a
segregation VI–255b
termination of reservation system VI–97a
treaties III–404a
voluntary relocation program VI–83b
Wheeler–Howard Act VII–287a
INDIAN POLITICAL ORGANIZATION III–390b
council III–378b
Hopi III–301a
Iroquois League III–475a–b
Klamath–Modoc IV–51b
Kwakiutl IV–59a
Mahican IV–387a
Mexico IV–327a
Mississippian cultures IV–370a,b
Miwok IV–381b
Mogollon IV–385b
Mohave IV–386a
Mohegan IV–387a
Natchez IV–455b–56a
Navaho V–9a
Northwest Coast culture III–361b
Pima–Papago V–314b
Plains Indians III–365a
Powhatan Confederacy V–385b
Pueblo V–459b
reservations III–395b
sachem VI–183a
Southeast culture III–365b
subarctic culture III–360a
wampum VII–223a
Wheeler–Howard Act V–49a

INDIAN QUEEN (hostelry) (Phila.) **III–391b**; VII–2b
INDIAN RELIGION III–391b
Apache III–368b
dance II–291a
Delaware Prophet II–322b
effigy mounds IV–420b–21a
Eskimo III–358a
Five Civilized Tribes II–52a
Ghost Dance III–177a
Great Serpent Mound III–222a
"Great Spirit" III–222b
Handsome Lake Cult III–249b
"Happy Hunting Ground" III–250b
Hopi III–301a
Iroquois III–476a
Jimsonweed Cult III–503a
Kwakiutl IV–59b
land ownership concept IV–90a
medicine III–385a–b
Mexico IV–327a–b
Michabous IV–330a
missions III–385b
Mohave IV–386a
Natchez IV–455b
Native American Church V–2a
nativistic movements V–3b
Navaho V–9a
Northwest Coast culture III–361b
Pawnee V–230b
Peyote Cult V–272b
Pima–Papago V–314b
Plains Indians III–364b
prehistoric IV–370a,b
Prophet Dance V–434b
Pueblo III–367b, 368a, 386b; V–459b
scalping VI–224b
Southeast culture III–366a
Southern Cult VI–352b
subarctic culture III–360a
Sun Dance VI–441b
symbolic art III–374a,b
tobacco VII–65a
water holes VII–256a
western cultures III–363a
Winnebago VII–306a
INDIAN REMOVAL III–393a; II–52a–b; III–213b, 221a, 384a,b, 389a–b; VI–6a; VII–190b, 274a
Cherokee V–49b; VII–96b
Five Civilized Tribes V–148a–b
fur trade III–144a
Georgia III–168b, 170b
gold discoveries V–437a–b
Indiana III–370a
Indian Country III–379a
Indian Territory III–402a
Indian Trade and Intercourse Act III–402a
Jesuit missions III–499b–500a
Kansas II–241b; IV–25b
Medicine Creek Council IV–299b
Mississippi V–357a; VII–181b
Modoc IV–384b
Ogden purchase V–139b
Oklahoma V–148a–b
Removal Act of 1830 VI–85b
Seminole V–231b; VI–259b–60a, 260b, 261a–b
treaties III–404a–b
Treaty of Indian Springs III–401b
Utah VII–161b
Winnebago VII–305b, 306b
Indian Removal Act (1830) III–384b, 389a, 394a, 399b, 404a
Indian Reorganization Act (1934). *See* Wheeler–Howard Act
INDIAN RESERVATIONS III–395a; II–133b, 379b; III–384a; VI–6a, 7b, 255b; VII–268b
Apache I–172a
Arapaho I–151b
Arizona I–142a,b, 172a
army defense I–192a
Bannock I–264b
Bosque Redondo I–342b–43a
Bureau of Indian Affairs III–371b–72b
California IV–366a
Colorado River Reservation IV–386b
Dakota Indians II–283b
Dakotas II–283b
Dawes General Allotment Act II–295b, 295b; III–389b
Department of the Interior III–444b
Flathead (Montana) VII–297a
Fort Apache IV–90a–b
Fort Berthold I–171b
Fox Indians III–88b
Girl Scouts III–181a
Great Sioux I–312b, 313a; VI–295a–b
Indian Reorganization Act III–390a
Indians of the 1970's III–396a,b
Jesuits III–501b
Kansas IV–25b
Klamath IV–51b
Klamath–Modoc IV–385a
land leasing IV–90a
Lincoln County (N.Mex.) VI–385a
liquor III–399a
Lower Indian Reserve I–286a
Michigan VI–186b
migration to cities III–397b
Minnesota River VI–139a
Navaho V–9b
Nez Perce V–89b
Ogden purchase V–139b
Oklahoma V–148b
open–range cattle period V–160a,b
Oregon V–165b
Osage County (Okla.) V–173b
preemption rights V–390a
Proclamation of 1763 V–424b–25a
Qualla III–395a
Red River War VI–64a
Rosebud Reservation VI–164b
Santee Sioux VI–296a–b
self–government VII–287a
Seminole VI–260a
Sioux VI–296a; VII–106a
South Dakota IV–108b–09a; VI–350a
Stevens' treaties VI–412b
Tama III–468a
termination of reservation system VI–97a
tribal courts III–404b
unemployment III–397a
Upper Sandusky VII–157b
U.S. Army posts I–192a
voluntary relocation program VI–83b
Wild River VII–244a
Wind River VII–346a
Winnebago Long Prairie VI–144b
Yuma VII–367b
INDIANS, AMERICAN, OF THE 1970'S III–396a; III–390b; VI–7b
American Indian Movement VI–164b
minority rights IV–359a
National Congress of American Indians IV–463a
National Indian Youth Council IV–464a
newspapers V–76a
Pan–Indianism V–210a
United Native Americans VII–152a
INDIANS, URBAN AMERICAN III–397b; III–396a
liquor III–399a
religion III–393a
voluntary relocation program VI–83b
INDIANS AND LIQUOR III–398a; I–289b; III–395b; IV–158b; VII–65a,b
Fort Benton III–77b
fur trade III–140b, 143b, 402b
Leech Lake uprising IV–131b
Pima V–314b
rum trade VII–278a
Shawnee Prophet VI–271a
tafia VI–456b
Vermont VII–171a
INDIANS AND THE GUN III–399a
Colt six–shooter II–131a
Fox–French Wars III–89a
fur trade III–140a
Iroquois III–475b
Merry Mount trading post IV–315a
Indian Service. *See* Indian Affairs, Bureau of
INDIANS IN THE CIVIL WAR III–399b
disruption of mail services V–178a
Fort Smith Council VI–317a
Pike's partisan band V–222a
Seminole VI–260a
slaveholders III–401a
INDIANS IN THE REVOLUTION III–400a; III–187b–88a, 239a; VI–124a
Battle of Bennington I–289a
Battle of Olentangy V–152b
Battle of Oriskany V–172b
Battle of Piqua V–319b
British campaign in the West I–306b, 367a
British campaign of 1777 I–365b
Burgoyne's invasion I–385a, 385a
Butler's Rangers I–398a
Cherokee V–115b
Clark's Northwest campaign II–71a
Connolly's Plot II–184a
Fort Henry VII–287b
Georgia III–170a
Iroquois III–249b; VI–130a
Jay's Treaty III–493a–b
Kentucky VI–239b
Miami Indians IV–59b
Minisink raid IV–354b
Mohawk I–398a
murder of Jane McCrea IV–211a
Ohio V–140b
Saint Louis VI–195a
Sandusky VI–208b
Sauk VI–218b
Seminole VI–259b
Squaw Campaign VI–378a
Sullivan–Clinton campaign VI–437b
Tennessee VII–25b
Treaty at Pittsburgh V–322a
Washington District VII–250a
Wisconsin VII–307a
Wyandot VII–157b
Wyoming massacre VII–346b
Indians in the War of 1812
Fort Stephenson VI–412a
Raisin River massacre VI–42a
Sackets Harbor VI–183b
INDIAN SLAVEHOLDERS III–401a; II–52a; III–376a, 399b
Five Civilized Tribes V–148a,b
Shawnee V–322a,b
INDIAN SLAVERY AMONG WHITES III–401a; II–495a; VI–309a, 341b
New Netherland V–61b
Tuscarora War VII–130b

INDIAN SPRINGS, TREATIES OF (1821, 1825) **III–401b**
INDIAN STREAM REPUBLIC III–401b; III–200a
Indian Suite (comp.) IV–438b
INDIAN TERRITORY III–402a; I–336b; III–379b, 384a, 394a,b, 395a, 399b; V–149b–150a; VI–355a
- Abilene Trail I–2a
- Black Cavalry I–310a
- Black Infantry I–313b
- Boomer movement I–310a, 335b
- cattle drives V–160a
- Civil War III–376a
- Crazy Snake Rebellion II–254a
- Dull Knife campaign II–397b
- Five Civilized Tribes II–51b, 52b
- Fort Cobb II–91a
- Fort Gibson III–178b
- Fort Reno VI–87a
- Fort Smith Council VI–317a
- homesteading I–336a
- Jesuit missions III–500b
- Kansas Indians IV–26a
- Mississippi River III–171a
- oil IV–334a
- Oklahoma V–148b–49a
- partisan bands V–222a
- railroad I–214b
- Red River War VI–64a, 242a
- Sheridan's Washita campaign VII–252b
- Sooners VI–339b–340a
- state of Sequoyah VI–262b
- Wagon Train charge VII–217a
- wagon trains VII–217b
- wars VII–239b
- whiskey towns VII–290b

Indian Trade, Office of the Superintendent of II–480a; III–371a
INDIAN TRADE AND INTERCOURSE ACT (1834) **III–402a**; IV–90a
INDIAN TRADE AND TRADERS III–402b; VII–82b
- annuities III–384b
- barrier state III–375a
- Baynton, Wharton and Morgan I–278a, 309a
- Bent's Fort I–174b, 290a
- bootlegging I–339a
- British posts I–120a
- bullboats I–380a
- Bureau of Indian Affairs III–371a
- Charleston (S.C.) I–496a–b, 496a,b, 497a–b, 498a–b, 498a–b, 498a,b
- Coffee's Trading Post II–94a
- colonial regulation III–387b–88a
- Colorado II–128a
- congressional regulation II–199b
- Couture, Jean II–247b
- Croghan's Illinois expedition VI–285a
- Delaware River V–42b
- federal trading houses III–389a
- Fort Assiniboine I–206a
- Fort Hall III–243b
- Fort Laramie IV–108a
- Fort Lisa IV–159b
- Fort Madison IV–219b
- Fort Osage V–173b
- Fort Peck V–241a
- Fort Prince George V–408a
- Fort Saint Marks VI–196b
- Fort Stanwix VI–385a
- Fort Wayne VII–262a
- Fort Western VII–269b
- Fox–French Wars III–88b
- fur trade II–30b–31a, 34a–b, 285b; III–139b, 140a–b, 141a, 142a, 143b, 144a,b; VII–103b, 104b
- Galphin claim III–148a
- Giard, Basil III–177b
- government trading houses III–372a,b
- Great Trading and War Path III–223a
- Great Trail III–223b
- guns III–399b
- hunting grounds III–318a
- Independence (Mo.) III–353b
- Indiana Company III–370b
- Kennebec Post IV–37b
- Laclède's trading post VI–193b
- liquor III–398b
- Logstown IV–181a
- Loramie's store IV–188a
- Manuel's Fort IV–242a
- Maxent, Laclede and Company IV–277b, 376b
- Merry Mount IV–314b
- Minnesota IV–356a
- mountain men IV–422b
- Natchitoches IV–456b
- New France IV–109a–b
- New Netherlands V–62a
- North Carolina I–83a
- Ohio Company of Virginia V–144a
- Ohio Valley V–146a
- Oswego V–175b
- Panton, Leslie and Company V–211a
- paths III–387b
- Pickawillanee V–308a
- Popham Colony V–359b
- Proclamation of 1763 V–424b
- Radisson's voyages VI–18a–b
- rum VII–119b
- Saint Castin's trading house VI–188a
- Saint Stephens VI–197b
- Sandusky VI–208b
- Santa Fe VI–215a
- Sault Sainte Marie VI–219b
- Shawnee and Delaware VI–271a
- Sioux treaties VI–296a
- snowshoes VI–323a
- South Carolina VI–348b
- Spain VI–366a–b
- steel trap VI–411b
- Stites, Benjamin IV–329b
- "suffering traders" VI–430a
- tafia VI–456b
- Tennessee VII–25a
- tomahawk VII–70a
- trading posts VII–95b
- Treaty of Ghent I–438b
- Trelawney Plantation VII–114b
- Vermont VII–171a
- Virginia VI–341a
- Virginia factory III–380b
- Virginia Indian Company VII–201b
- Walla Walla settlements VII–221a
- Washington State VII–247a
- Wayne campaign VII–263a
- western merchants VII–273b
- Westport VII–280b
- Wisconsin VII–307a
- Wyoming Valley VII–347a

Indian trails I–39b; III–381b, 447b
- Allegheny Mountains I–88b
- Gaines' Trace III–146b
- Miami Trail IV–330a

INDIAN TREATIES III–404a; I–192b, 455a; II–295b–96a
- Albany V–386a
- Brownstown I–371b
- Butte des Morts I–398a,b, 398b
- Camp Charlotte I–499a, 499a–b
- Camp Moultrie VI–259b
- Carlisle (Pa.) I–455a
- Casco I–465b; IV–47b
- Cherokee II–15a
- Chicago II–21a–b
- Chickasaw II–23a
- Chickasaw Council House II–22a
- Choctaw I–9b
- claims commission III–377b
- colonial policy III–388a
- Council of Fort Smith VI–317a,b
- Dancing Rabbit Creek VII–181b
- Dawes General Allotment Act II–295b
- Detroit I–371b, 371b
- Doak's Stand VII–181b
- Dumplin Creek II–380b
- Easton II–388b
- education provisions III–379b
- Firelands III–25b
- Fort Crawford II–254a
- Fort de Chartres I–501b, 501b
- Fort Finney III–24b
- Fort Gibson VI–259b–60a
- Fort Harmar III–255a
- Fort Jackson III–88b
- Fort Laramie IV–108b; VI–295b
- Fort McIntosh IV–216b
- Fort Niagara V–90b
- Fort Stanwix VI–385a,b–86a
- Fort Wayne VII–262a,b, 262b
- gifts of liquor III–398b
- grants of citizenship III–377a
- Greenville II–297a; III–227b; IV–330a; VI–208b; VII–263a
- Half-Breed Tract III–242b
- Hard Labor III–251a; VI–386a
- Holston II–14a; III–292a
- Hopewell III–300b
- Hull III–316a
- Indian Country boundary III–379a
- Indian representative III–390b–91a
- Indian Springs III–401b
- Iroquois Beaver Land Deed IV–386b
- Iroquois Treaty III–476b
- Kansas Territory IV–26a
- La Famine IV–83b
- Lake Erie I–359a
- Lancaster IV–89b
- land allotments scrip IV–97a–b
- land cessions III–382a–84b, 389a
- La Pointe IV–107b
- Laramie (1851) I–358a
- Lochaber IV–173a
- Logstown IV–181b; V–144a
- Long Island of Holston IV–186b
- Mackenzie's Treaty IV–217a
- McGillivray incident IV–213a
- Medicine Lodge VI–64a
- Mendota Treaty VII–106a
- Minnesota Chippewa IV–356a
- Natchez IV–456a
- Natchez Trace right-of-way IV–456b
- national policy VI–6a
- Navaho V–9a,b
- New Echota Treaty V–49b
- New York I–355b
- Nez Perce V–89b
- Nogales V–100b
- Payne's Landing III–39a; V–231a; VI–259b–60a
- Peace of Massasoit IV–264b
- Pensacola IV–213a; VI–366b
- Pensacola Congress V–254b
- Pittsburgh V–322a
- Pontotoc V–357a
- Prairie du Chien V–388b
- removal III–393b–94b, 395a
- reservations III–395b

revolutionary war III–400b
Saginaw VI–186b
Saint Marys VI–197a
Sauk and Fox I–311b–12a
Seminole Treaty of 1866 VI–260a
Shawnee I–369a
Sioux I–313a–b; VI–295a–96a
slaveholding III–401a
Spring Wells Treaty VI–377b
Stevens' treaties V–89b; VI–412b
Sycamore Shoals VI–455a
Tellico VI–357b–58a
Traverse des Sioux VI–139a; VII–106a
Ute VII–162b
Vicennes VII–189a
Western Reserve III–414a
Wyandot I–369a; VII–157b
See also Sioux Treaties
INDIAN TRIBAL COURTS III–404b
INDIAN VILLAGES III–404b
Aughwick I–222b
Council Bluffs II–241b
Eastern cultures III–365b
Five Villages III–33b
Gnadenhutten III–187b
Gran Quivira III–211a
Great Village of the Illinois III–330b
hunting grounds III–318b
Iroquois III–476a
Kaskaskia IV–31b
Logstown IV–181a
Mesa Verde IV–315b
Mogollon IV–385b
New Mexico I–329b
Northwest Coast culture III–360b–61a
Pickawillanee V–308a
Pima–Papago V–314b
Pokagon V–335b
Powhatan Confederacy V–385b
Pueblo III–367a–68a; V–459b–60a
Venango VII–168b
Vincennes VII–188a–b
Western cultures III–362a,b
Zuni VII–372a
Indian wars and campaigns. *See* Wars and Campaigns, Indian
Indies, Company of the V–173a, 173a; VII–160b
See also Mississippi Bubble
Indigent persons
immigration II–445a
INDIGO CULTURE III–405b; VI–386b, 436a
bounties I–352a; IV–308a
Charleston (S.C.) I–496a
colonial trade II–5a, 119b, 453a; VI–108a; VII–82b
East India trade II–388b
foreign trade VII–86a
Indians I–36b
Natchez IV–455a
Navigation Acts V–16a,b
New Smyrna Colony V–66a
research III–408a
Savannah VI–220a
slavery VI–305a
South I–37a; VI–341a–b
South Carolina VI–347a
tidewater II–485a; VII–58a
Indios mansos I–369a
Individualism
laissez-faire IV–85b
moral values IV–408a–09a
Republican party II–189a
"Individualists" I–116b
Individual liberty
Constitution II–197b
Indochina
bombing of (1965–72) I–328b
France III–97a
French I–124a
partition IV–107a
U.S. aid to French III–61b
See also Laos; Southeast Asia; Vietnam War
Indochina War (1946–54) III–159b, 161a; VII–182b
Indonesia
immigration to U.S. III–341a
Philippines V–285a
Southeast Asia Treaty Organization VI–350b
U.S. operations in II–315b
World War II VII–342b
In Dubious Battle IV–164b
Industrial accidents II–440b, 441a–b
Industrial and Labor Relations, School of (Cornell Univ.) II–227b–28a
Industrial Areas Foundation II–147b
Industrial armies
Coxey's II–252b
Kelly's IV–36a
Industrial banks II–255a
INDUSTRIAL BROTHERHOOD III–405b
Industrial capitalism II–475a
Industrial codes II–481b
Industrial College of the Armed Forces I–64b, 191a
Industrial Congress (1874) III–405b
Industrial corporations
assets II–230b
concentration of control II–230b
employees II–230b
farmers cooperatives II–221b
sales II–230b
Industrial Democracy, League for VI–421a,b
Industrial Diseases, U.S. Conference on IV–294a
Industrial espionage. *See* Espionage, Industrial
Industrial fairs III–99a
Industrial Health and Safety Act (1970) IV–294b
Industrial Hygiene, Journal of IV–294a
Industrial insurance II–255a; III–434b–35a
Industrialization
cost of living II–235a
Delaware II–320b
effect on morality IV–408b
effect on unionization IV–62a
immigrant labor IV–65b
machine tools IV–215b
occupations V–132b
INDUSTRIAL MANAGEMENT III–405b
personnel III–407b, 408a
Industrial medicine. *See* Medicine, Occupational
Industrial Medicine, Journal of IV–294a
Industrial parks
Norfolk V–110a
Industrial pollutants II–502a
INDUSTRIAL RELATIONS III–406b
Industrial Relations, Federal Commission on III–83b
INDUSTRIAL RESEARCH III–408a; IV–244b–45a; V–295a,b
Arthur D. Little, Inc. I–197a
Bureau of Mines IV–350b
Franklin Institute III–99b
General Electric III–155b
incandescent lamp IV–89a
machine tools IV–215b
Massachusetts IV–267b, 268a
Mellon Institute IV–300b
National Bureau of Economic Research IV–462a
physics V–296a
power and light II–417a
Progressive movement V–428b
Research Triangle Park V–116b
INDUSTRIAL REVOLUTION III–410b
agriculture I–34a
apprenticeship I–148a
capital I–449a
cotton VI–341b
factory towns II–45b
interchangeable manufacture III–442b
Jefferson, Thomas I–32b
Jeffersonian Democracy III–495b
labor I–37a
machine tools IV–215b
Massachusetts IV–266b
middle class IV–334b
morality IV–408b
New South V–66b
slave trade VI–312a
wool industry VII–320b
Industrial Safety Council. *See* National Industrial Safety Council
Industrial slums II–45b–46a
"Industrial state" II–230b
INDUSTRIAL WORKERS OF THE WORLD III–412b; I–104a, 117a; IV–67b–68a; VI–13b, 326b
Lawrence strike IV–120a
pressure groups V–401a
sabotage VI–182b
syndicalism VI–455b
Washington State VII–248a
Western Federation of Miners VII–272b
World War I opposition V–236a
INDUSTRIES, COLONIAL III–413a; IV–243a; VII–82a–b
blacksmithing I–316b–17a
blast furnaces I–318b–19a
boot and shoe manufacture I–337b–38a
brewing I–361b
candlemaking I–444a; VI–372b
carpets I–460a
carriagemaking I–460b–61a
chairmaking I–490a–b
distilling II–353b
flour milling III–42b–43a, 45a
furniture III–138a
glassmaking III–182b, 184b
government regulation III–204a
hardware III–252a
hat manufacture III–262a
household manufacturing IV–245b–46a
indigo II–5a
iron I–327a; II–32b; III–12a, 77a, 469b, 472a–b; VI–376a
lead V–102b
leather industry IV–127b
linsey-woolsey IV–158a
manufacturing I–245a, 352a
maple sugar IV–246b
Massachusetts IV–265a
meat-packing IV–280a
monopolies V–225b
munitions IV–432a
North Carolina V–115b
paper and pulp V–212a
Pawtucket V–230b
pottery III–183a; V–379a–b
printing I–333a–b
publishing I–90a, 333a–b
research III–408a
restrictions on manufacture IV–242b
Revenue Act of 1767 VII–80b
rum manufacture II–92b
Saugus furnace VI–218a
sawmills VI–222b
textiles II–5a
trade retrictions III–346b
Industry
British colonial policy II–122a–23a
demobilization II–323b
employers liability laws II–440b
excess profits tax II–467a–b
fair-trade laws II–482b
Gilded Age III–180b
growth of cities II–41b

INDUSTRY (cont.)
National Recovery Administration II–481b
World War I mobilization II–243a
"Industry" (motto) VI–395 (table)
INDUSTRY, FORT (Ohio) **III–414a**
Industry, Fort, Treaty of (1805) III–25b
Industry, Friends of Domestic. *See* Friends of Domestic Industry
Infanta Maria Teresa (ship) VI–216b, 217a
Infantile paralysis. *See* Poliomyelitis
Infant mortality II–487a; III–52b; IV–149a–50a, 151a,b
Infantry School I–289a
Infant schools II–397a, 402b
Infant-school societies I–495b
Infirmaries. *See* Hospitals
INFLATION III–414a; III–7a,b, 8b; VI–94b; VII–222b
Articles of Confederation II–167a
automobile industry I–231a
balance of trade VII–90b
bank deposits I–252b
business cycles I–394a
check currency II–2a
Civil War II–2a, 69a, 164a; IV–62b
cost of living II–234b
currency II–2a
depression II–236b
devaluation V–45a
election of 1878 III–110b
fair-trade laws II–484a
federal deficit II–317a
food costs V–129a–b
Gilded Age III–180b
gold standard II–195a,b; III–193a–b
government regulation of business I–449b
government spending III–205b
Greenback party VI–333b
International Monetary Fund III–457b
Jeffersonian Democracy III–496a
Kentucky IV–40b
Korean War II–236b
Massachusetts IV–266a
New Deal V–44a
Nixon administration VI–471b, 472a,b
Ohio Idea V–144b
panic of 1873 V–207a
paper money standard III–251b
post–World War I II–2a, 317a–b
post–World War II II–236a, 317b; IV–74a
price-fixing I–391a; V–401b, 402a
prices V–404a,b, 405a,b, 406a
purchasing power II–209b
railroad rates VI–22a
railroads VI–31a
recession of 1973–75 VII–85a–b, 91b
relief costs VI–74b
Revolution II–2a; VI–117b, 120b
II 235a–
taxation VII–10a,b, 11a–b
Thomas Amendment VII–54b
unemployment II–236b; VII–141a,b
Vietnam War II–236b
wage controls VII–214b
wage-fixing I–391a
World War I IV–69b
INFLATION IN THE CONFEDERACY III–416a; III–415a
Influence mines IV–351b
Influence of Sea Power Upon History VI–362b
"Influence peddling" II–231b
INFLUENZA III–416a; I–242a; II–454b–55a; IV–298b–99a
army research IV–292a
pandemic of 1918–19 V–447b
Informal style (landscape arch.) IV–96b
Information Agency, U.S. II–499a; V–432b
Voice of America VII–207a
Information and Education Act (1948). *See* Smith–Mundt Act
Information Center Service V–432b
Information retrieval, scientific. *See* Scientific Information Retrieval
Information Service, U.S. V–432b
Information theory I–287a
Ingalik (Indians) I–80b
Ingalls (Kans.) II–246a
Ingalls, Jeremiah (comp.) IV–438a
Ingersoll, E. P. (ed.) I–225b
Ingersoll, Jared (jur.) II–203b
campaign of 1812 I–418a
Philadelphia Cordwainers' Case V–278b
Stamp Act VI–381b
Ingersoll, Robert G. (law.) III–112a; V–161b
campaign of 1876 I–422b
Ingles, Mary I–387a; II–369b
Ingles, Thomas II–369b
IN GOD WE TRUST III–417a; VI–393 (table)
Ingot steel III–471 (table)
Ingraham, Duncan (nav. off.) V–22b
Ingraham, Prentiss (au.) II–341b
Ingram, David (expl.) IV–37a, 396a
Ingstad, Helge (archaeol.) V–112a–b; VII–190a
INHERENT POWERS III–417a; II–304a
INHERITANCE TAX LAWS III–417b; II–452a; VII–4b, 5a, 6a,b, 7b, 10b, 12b
Florida III–42a
"normalcy" V–110a
Progressive movement V–428b
Wealth Tax Act V–46b
INITIATIVE III–418a; II–408b; III–91a; VI–51a, 66b
Oregon System V–165b, 168a
Progressive movement V–428a
reserved power of the people VI–98a
state constitutions VI–392a
Washington State VII–248a
INJUNCTIONS III–419a; IV–67a, 69a,b
Buck Stove and Range Case I–357a, 374b
campaign of 1896 I–425a
Clayton Antitrust Act II–72a
coal strikes II–86b
Coeur d'Alene riots II–93b
Hitchman Coal Company v. *Mitchell* III–286a
industrial relations III–407a
In re Debs II–298b
Norris–La Guardia Act IV–71a; V–112a
padlock injunction V–184a
Pullman Strike I–111b; V–463b
pure food and drug enforcement V–467a
strikes VI–103b, 419a,b
Truax v. *Corrigan* VII–121a
unions II–110b–11a
"yellow-dog" contract VII–355a
Inkpaduta (Indian) VI–374a
Inland Empire IV–204a
INLAND LOCK NAVIGATION III–419b
James River III–488b
Inland marine insurance III–426b, 429a–b
Inland Sea VII–343a
Inland Steel IV–72b
Inland Steel Case (1949) V–256a
Inland waterways. *See* Waterways, Inland
INLAND WATERWAYS COMMISSION III–419b; II–187b; III–321a,b; V–1b; VII–260b
Inland Waterways Corporation V–455a–b; VII–77a, 260b
Inman, Henry (art.) II–102b
Inmost Leaf IV–165b
In Nature's Wonderland (paint.) V–189a
Inner Light IV–447b
Innes, Harry (law.) VI–366a
Inness, George (paint.) V–190b, 192a
Innocent VII (pope) VII–309b
"Innocents." *See* Plummer Gang
Innocents Abroad IV–163b
Inns. *See* Taverns
Inns of Court (London) IV–120b
Inoculation
smallpox IV–275a; VI–315a–b
Inönü, Ismet (states.) I–403b
Inoue, T. (phys.) V–302b
INQUIRY (org.) **III–420a**
Inquiry, congressional power of IV–45b
Inquiry Into the Effects of Spirituous Liquors on the Human Mind and Body VII–22a,b
INQUISITION, SPANISH III–420a
Insane, treatment of the. *See* Mental Hygiene Movement; Mental Illness
Insanity, American Journal of IV–305b
INSCRIPTION ROCK III–420b
Insect disease vectors IV–170a
Insecticide Act (1910) III–53b
INSECTICIDES AND HERBICIDES III–420b; I–46b; VI–203a
forest protection III–74b
grasshopper control III–213a
kerosine IV–44b
pollution VI–213a
pure food and drug movement V–467a,b
Insects III–163b
forests III–74b, 75b, 76a
plagues I–486b
Inside Passage IV–52a
Inside shops II–81b
Insignia of rank
army I–189a,b
Signal Corps VI–286a
Insolvency II–213b, 213b, 299a
INSPECTION, COMMITTEES OF III–421b
INSPECTION, GOVERNMENTAL III–422a; III–460b
Inspirationists I–92b–93a
INSTALLMENT BUYING, SELLING, AND FINANCING III–422b
automobile I–227b
land sales IV–90b
mutual funds III–467b
panic of 1929 V–209b
sewing machine VI–265a
Instamatic camera V–293a
INSTITUTE FOR ADVANCED STUDY III–423b; II–156a
Institute for Economic Research I–370a

Institute for Government Research I–370a; III–380a, 390a
Institute of Actuaries II–154a
Institute of Electrical and Electronic Engineers II–449a
Institute of Living IV–305b
Institute of Medicine IV–457b
Institute of Northern Forestry III–76b
Institute of Pacific Islands Forestry III–76b
Institute of Radio Engineers II–449a
Institute of Social and Religious Research IV–365b
Institute of the History of Medicine (Johns Hopkins Univ.) IV–3b
Institute of Tropical Forestry III–76b
Institut National d'Études Démographiques II–328a
Instructions for the Government of Armies in the Field. *See* Civil War General Order No. 100
Instrumentalism V–288a–b, 387a
Instrument Landing Systems I–68a, 234b
INSULAR CASES (1901–22) **III–424b**; II–323b; III–426a–b; VII–13b, 32a–b, 33b
INSULAR POSSESSIONS III–425a; VII–33b–34a
  taxation VII–13b
  Virgin Islands VII–203b
  See also Anti–imperialists
Insulating materials III–156a; IV–204b
Insulin III–54a; V–274a, 467b
Insulin shock IV–306b
Insull, Samuel (bus.) II–18a, 416b–17a, 478b; V–209b
INSURANCE III–426b
  accident IV–68b
  actuarial tables VII–206b–07a
  banking I–257b, 259b–60a, 263b
  city planning II–46b
  corporations II–229a
  credit II–254b
  Customs Service II–277a
  Dallas VII–40b
  employee IV–70a, 74a
  enemy aliens VII–94a
  foreign investment III–63a, 66b
  government trust funds II–234a
  hail V–106b
  Industrial Revolution III–411a
  inflation III–414b
  life tables IV–149b
  marine II–277a
  Massachusetts IV–268a
  medical IV–293b–94a
  Medicare IV–289b
  mortgages III–310b–11a
  nationalization of U.S. property IV–466b
  Newark V–41b
  New Hampshire V–54b
  New Jersey V–58a
  New York City V–83a
  no–fault I–152b; IV–19a
  ocean shipping IV–255a
  old–age IV–71b; V–150b
  panic of 1907 V–208a,b
  pension plans V–255b
  Progressive movement V–428b
  public health V–447b
  railroad brotherhoods VI–20a
  Reconstruction Finance Corporation VI–59b–60a
  social security VI–329a
  survivors' IV–71b
  taxation VII–5b, 10b
  tontine plan VII–72a–b
  unemployment IV–80b; V–46a; VII–13a, 140a
  Veterans Administration V–258a; VII–174b
  Wall Street VII–222a
  war–risk IV–310b
  workmen's compensation VII–322b
  See also Unemployment insurance
Insurance, national health IV–77a
Insurance Company of North America III–427b, 429a, 430a
Insurgente (frigate) II–190a; V–15a, 19a, 423b
Insurgents V–427b; VI–458a; VII–306b
INSURRECTIONS, DOMESTIC III–436a; I–23a,b; II–307b; VII–191a
  Alien and Sedition Acts I–86b
  Antirent War I–134a
  Bacon's Rebellion I–240a
  Civil War II–62a
  constitutional provisions II–200a; IV–342b
  Culpeper's Rebellion II–271a, 271a–b
  Declaration of Independence II–307b
  Espionage Act II–463a
  federal troops IV–341b
  Fries's Rebellion I–41a; III–124a
  Harlem V–82b
  Leisler Rebellion IV–134a
  Nat Turner's Rebellion I–23b, 28a; II–403b
  president's power to suppress II–313a
  Shays's Rebellion I–41a; II–167a; VI–271b
  slave insurrections VI–303a
  Vesey's Rebellion I–23a, 28a
  Whiskey Rebellion I–41a; VII–290a
"Insurrection" statutes IV–341b
Integrated circuits II–156b, 426b
INTEGRATION III–437a; V–331b
  Alabama I–72a
  American Independent party I–106b
  armed forces I–187a; IV–340b
  Baltimore I–250b
  baseball I–271a
  Brown v. *Board of Education* I–372b
  busing I–397b
  bus terminals II–58a
  Catholic churches I–468a
  Catholic schools I–468b
  civil rights movement II–56a–59a
  Congress of Racial Equality II–179b
  higher education II–401b–02a
  housing III–311a
  Kentucky I–290a,b
  Ku Klux Klan IV–59a
  Little Rock (Ark.) I–207b
  Louisiana IV–195a
  Mississippi IV–369b
  NAACP IV–460b
  National Urban League V–1a
  North Carolina V–116b
  public schools II–404a
  Southern Christian Leadership Conference VI–352a
  states' rights VI–404b–05a
  Virginia VII–195b–96a
  See also Segregation
Integrators, ball and disc II–153a
INTELLIGENCE, MILITARY AND STRATEGIC III–438b
  army organization I–189a
  Central Intelligence Agency I–484a; II–498a
  Normandy invasion V–111a
  Office of Strategic Services V–137b
  photography V–293a
  Pueblo incident V–460a
  spies VI–372b
Intelligence Board, U.S. III–439a–b
  CIA I–484a
Intelligence quotient III–440b
Intelligence Resources Advisory Board III–439b
INTELLIGENCE TESTS III–440a; II–400a; V–442a–b
Intellofax system VI–233a
Intelsat. *See* International Telecommunications Satellite Consortium.
Intelsat 1 (satellite) II–143a
Intelsat 4 (satellite) II–143a
Inter–American Conferences IV–111a–b, 112a–b; V–171a, 205a,b, 232a
  See also Havana Conference (1928)
Inter–American Conferences on Problems of War and Peace IV–402a
Inter–American Congress, Santiago. *See* Santiago de Chile Inter–American Congress
Inter–American Development Bank IV–113b–14a; VII–108a
Inter–American Foundation II–501a
Inter–American Treaty of Reciprocal Assistance (1947) IV–112b, 402a; VI–142b
Interborough Rapid Transit Company (N.Y.C.) VI–429a
Interceptor planes I–53b, 54a
INTERCHANGEABLE MANUFACTURE III–441a; IV–243b, 272a
  firearms IV–432b; V–163a
  machine tools IV–216a–b
  wagons VII–216b
Intercoastal Shipping Act (1933) IV–254b
Intercollegiate Athletics Association. *See* National Association for Intercollegiate Athletics
Intercollegiate Football Association III–56b
Intercollegiate Socialist Society VII–365a
Intercolonial Congress (1689–91) II–121b
Intercontinental ballistic missiles I–62a, 210a; IV–363a,b; VI–159a,b
  arms race IV–432a, 458b–59a
  nuclear deterrent I–56b
  Soviet Union I–179b; II–316a
  Strategic Air Command I–67b, 328b
  warning systems I–58b
Interdisciplinary Research Relevant to the Problems of Our Society IV–471a
Inter–District Settlement Fund II–74a
Interest arbitration I–152a
INTEREST LAWS III–443a; VII–12a
Interest payments I–252a, 257b, 449a
Interest rates III–7b
  credit II–254a
  investment II–210a–b
  loansharking II–262a
  open–market operations V–159b
  public debt II–300b
"INTERESTS" III–443b
  public opinion V–453b
Intergovernmental Committee for European Migration V–342b
Intergovernmental Relations, Commission on VI–397a
Intergovernmental Relations, Office of II–498a
Intergovernment Personnel Act (1970) II–60b

INTERIOR, DEPARTMENT OF THE III–444a; I–399b; II–187b, 498a; VI–388b; VII–108a
Alaska I–79b
Alaska Indians I–79b
American Samoa III–425b; VI–205a; VII–34a
Bureau of Indian Affairs III–371a,b
Bureau of Labor IV–78a
Bureau of Mines II–135a; IV–350a,b
Bureau of Outdoor Recreation II–188b
census reports I–482b
Civilian Conservation Corps II–51a
forest reserves III–75a
forestry development IV–95b
Fort Yuma VII–367b
General Land Office IV–95a
Geological Survey III–163a
Grazing Division V–446a
Guam administration III–230b
Indian affairs III–378b, 389b
Job Corps III–504a
national cemeteries I–478a
national parks and monuments V–217a
National Park Service V–219a
naval oil reserves II–431b; V–13a–b; VII–16b
Office of Education II–405b
Patent Office V–226b
Pension Bureau VI–336b
railroad surveys VII–74b
reclamation I–453b; VI–53b
surveys VII–272b
territorial governments VII–32b
Trust Territory of the Pacific III–426a; VII–34a, 125a
veterans' pensions VII–174b
Virgin Islands III–425b; VII–204a
wildlife refuge I–306a
INTERIOR DECORATION III–445a
Interior Decorator (mag.) III–446b
Interlocking directorates I–140a; II–72a, 230a
INTERMARRIED CITIZEN III–447a
INTERMEDIATE CREDIT BANKS III–447a; VII–231a
Intermediate-range ballistic missile IV–363b
Internal combustion engine I–225b; V–267a; VI–257a; VII–101b
Internal Improvement Act (1855) III–39a
INTERNAL IMPROVEMENTS III–447b; IV–29a
American system I–113b
campaign of 1816 I–418a
canals VII–260a,b
Confederacy II–160a
Corps of Engineers II–449b
Democratic party II–327a
Democratic-Republicans II–327a
foreign investments I–245a; II–302b; III–63b–64a
funds I–330b
Gallatin's report III–147b
geological surveys III–164b
government spending III–205a
Hamilton's fiscal policies III–246a
Hunkers III–317b–18a
Illinois III–329b
Indiana State Canals III–374b
Jeffersonian-Republicans VI–94b
Louisiana IV–194a,b
mapmaking I–463a
Maysville veto IV–279a
National Road IV–470b
Ohio state canals V–145b
Old South II–298a
panic of 1792 V–206a
panic of 1837 V–206b
panic of 1873 V–207a–b
Pennsylvania canal system V–249b
pork barrel projects V–366b
Potomac Canals V–378a
prices V–403b
public land sales revenues V–455a
Red River raft VI–65a
repudiation of state debts VI–95b
rivers and harbors VI–145b
roads VI–152b
Sault Sainte Marie Canals VI–219a
sectionalism VI–253b–54a
societies favoring I–110b
state debts II–302b
states' rights VI–404b
subsidies VI–425a
Survey Act of 1824 VI–450a
tax revenue III–156b
urban renewal VI–86a
Internal Revenue Act (1865) VI–463b–64a
Internal Revenue Code VII–14a
Internal Revenue Service I–383b; VII–4b, 5a,b, 12b–13b
illegal gambling II–263a
income tax regulations II–178b
Tax Court I–13a
Whiskey Ring VII–290b
Internal Security Act (1950). *See* McCarran Act
Internal Security Committee II–146a; III–308b
International Academic Union IV–127a
International Air Transport Association III–277a
International Allergy Association IV–289a
International Alliance of Theatrical State Employees II–262a
International and Great Northern Railway VII–40a
International arbitration. *See* Treaties With Foreign Nations
International Association of Fire Fighters IV–76a
International Association of Machinists II–51a
International Atomic Energy Agency I–216b
International Bank for Reconstruction and Development I–361b; II–301b; III–60b–61a, 457a; VII–88b, 108a, 222b
International Bible Students. *See* Jehovah's Witnesses
International Boot and Shoe Workers Union I–338b
International Boundary Commission (U.S.–Mex.) VI–143b
International boundary disputes. *See* Alaska; Mexican Boundary; Northeast Boundary; Northwest Boundary Controversy
International Brotherhood of Teamsters I–103a
International Bureau of the American Republics V–205a
International Business Machines Corporation (IBM) I–397a; III–504a; IV–292b
art collection II–107a
calculators II–154a, 156a
computers II–426b
electric typewriter VII–137a
laser development IV–263a
International Church of the Foursquare Gospel V–260a
International Civil Aviation Association III–277a
International Claims Settlement Act (1949) II–169a
International Commerce, Bureau of II–135b
International Commission of Jurists V–202b
International Conference of American States (1889) IV–111a
International Conference on Naval Limitation. *See* Washington Naval Conference
International Congress on Mental Hygiene (1930) IV–304a
INTERNATIONAL CONTROL COMMISSION (Viet.) **III–452b**; III–160a
International Council for Philosophy and Humanistic Studies IV–127a
International Council for the Exploration of the Sea V–134b
International Council of Scientific Unions III–454a; IV–127a
INTERNATIONAL COURT OF JUSTICE III–452b; III–22a, 237b, 457a; IV–5b, 82b, 125a; V–234a, 262a; VII–110b, 113a
International Covenant on Civil and Political Rights III–457a
International Covenant on Economic, Social and Cultural Rights III–457a
International Decade of Ocean Exploration (1970–80) III–454b
International Economic Policy, Council on II–498a
International Electrical Congress (1893) II–39a, 415b
International Encyclopedia of the Social Sciences II–445a
International Exchange Service (Smithsonian) VI–319b
International Exposition in Vienna (1883) II–419a
INTERNATIONAL EXPOSITION OF 1895 III–453b
International Expositions, Bureau of V–89a
International Falls (Minn.) IV–357a–b
International Federation of Air Line Pilots Association III–277a
International Geodetical Association II–88a
International Geophysical Cooperation (1959) III–453b
INTERNATIONAL GEOPHYSICAL YEAR (1957–58) **III–453b**; III–167b; VI–159b
Explorer I III–502a
polar exploration V–338a
U.S. satellite IV–458b
INTERNATIONAL HARVESTER COMPANY III–454b; I–34b, 35b; V–428a
International Hydrographic Bureau V–133b
International Hydrological Decade (1965–75) III–454a–b
International Ice Hockey Federation III–287b
International Ice Patrol II–90a; V–134b, 135a
International Industrial Assembly of North America IV–62b

International Information Administration V–432b
INTERNATIONAL JOINT COMMISSION III–454b
International Kindergarten Union V–72a
International Labor Defense VI–241b
International Labor Office III–455a; VII–173b
INTERNATIONAL LABOR ORGANIZATION III–454b; I–290b; IV–69b; VII–113a
International Labor Union IV–63b
International Ladies' Garment Workers' Union II–82b–83a; IV–67b, 72a
INTERNATIONAL LAW III–455a
armed neutrality of 1780 I–175b
contraband of war II–212b–13b; IV–182b; V–37a
conventions VII–113a
effective occupation II–406b
enemy destination II–446a
executive agreements II–471b
freedom of the seas III–106a
Geneva Accords of 1954 III–159b
Hague peace conferences III–237a
immunity of private property III–343a–b
impressment of seamen III–349b
indemnities III–352a
International Court of Justice III–452b
intervention III–461b
Ladd's peace plan IV–82b
League of Nations IV–124a
military law IV–342b
mixed commissions IV–381b
nationalization of property IV–466a
neutrality V–33b–34a
neutral rights V–38b
prize courts V–421b
Proclamation of Neutrality V–36b
retaliation VI–104a
submarine warfare VI–423b
territorial waters VII–32b
trade with the enemy acts VII–93b
Treaty of Washington VII–249a
visit and search VII–204b
war VII–225a
International Law Commission, United Nations III–457a
International Lawn Tennis Federation VII–30a,b
International League (baseball) I–271a
International Longshoremen's Association II–74b
International Meditation Society V–171b
International Monetary and Economic Conference (1933) V–45a
INTERNATIONAL MONETARY FUND III–457a; I–254b, 361b; II–301b; III–60b–61a, 195a–96a, 196a, 453a; VI–468b, 470a–b, 471a, 472b; VII–88b, 91a, 108a, 222b
International News Service I–207a; V–79b; VII–152a
International News Service v. *Associated Press* (1918) VII–152a
International New Thought Alliance V–81a
International Niagara Commission V–92a
International Nickel Company of Canada, Ltd. V–102a
International Offshore Rule (yacht racing) VII–349a, 349b
International Olympic Committee V–153b
International Opium Conference (1911–12) II–374b
International Opium Convention (1912) IV–450a
International Organization of Consumers Unions II–209a
International Pacific Salmon Fisheries Commission VI–201b
International Penal and Penitentiary Congress (1872) V–416a
International Pentecostal Assemblies V–260a
International Petroleum Company IV–466a
International Polar Years (1882–83, 1932–33) III–454a; V–337a
International Prison Commission V–416a
International Prison Congress (1872) VI–68a
International Rapids VI–193a
International Refugee Organization V–342b
International Research Council IV–127a
International Settlements, Bank for. *See* Bank for International Settlements
International Socialist Congress (1889) IV–278a
International Social Science Council IV–127a
International Society of Weekly Newspaper Editors V–77b
International style (arch.) I–165a,b
International Telecommunications Satellite Consortium (Intelsat) II–143a
International Telecommunications Union II–143a
International Telephone and Telegraph Company III–504a; V–374b
International trade. *See* Trade, Foreign
International Trade Organization VI–468b–69a
International Union of Electrical, Radio, and Machine Workers VI–471b
International Union of Electrical Workers IV–76a
International Union of Mine, Mill, and Smelter Workers. *See* Western Federation of Miners
International Upper Mantle Project (1968–72) III–167b
International Whaling Convention VII–285b–86a
International Workers of the World II–445b
International Year of the Quiet Sun (1964–65) III–454a
International Zoo Yearbook VII–371b
Internship (med.) IV–285a
Interoceanic canal
Bryan–Chamorro Treaty I–373a,b, 483b
Clayton–Bulwer Treaty I–454a, 454a
projected I–454a
See also Panama Canal
Interoceanic routes
Gulf of Mexico IV–326b
Interposition, doctrine of II–57b
Interracial marriage. *See* Miscegenation
Interrogation, custodial IV–362a
Interrogation, relay (law) IV–362a
Interstate Agreement on Qualification of Educational Personnel III–460a
Interstate commerce
airline regulation II–500a
Annapolis Convention II–192b
Congress II–171b, 178b, 195b, 199b, 220a
Cullom Committee II–271a
Federal Power Commission II–500a
illegal conspiracies I–11a
licensing regulations IV–148a
livestock industry VI–379a
Northern Securities Company V–119a–b
organized crime II–262b
original package doctrine V–172a
presidential power to protect IV–341b
Pullman strike II–298b–99a
railroad hour regulation I–10a
steamboat monopolies III–178a, 178a
sugar trust VI–437b
See also Commerce Clause; Trade Domestic
Interstate Commerce, Committee on II–271a
Interstate Commerce Act (1887) I–389b, 390a; II–134b, 135b, 271a, 432a; III–458a, 458b; VI–21b, 23b
railroad rebates VI–50a
railroads VII–124b
World War I VI–29a
INTERSTATE COMMERCE COMMISSION III–457b; I–12a, 390a; II–500a; III–1a, 3a, 422a, 458b; V–458a, 471b
airmail I–68a
aviation II–49b
Court of Commerce II–134b
delegated power II–323a
desegregation II–58a; III–107a–b
Hepburn Act III–273a
judicial function IV–16b
Nader's Raiders IV–448b
Pope–McGill Farm Act V–359a
Progressive movement V–427b
Railroad Administration VI–19b
railroad pools V–358a
railroad rates V–208b; VI–21b–22a, 23b; VII–309a
railroad rebates VI–49b
railroads III–451b; VI–28a–b, 29a,b
segregation VI–256a
Shreveport Rate Case VI–283b
transportation rates IV–312b
water carriers V–2a
INTERSTATE COMMERCE LAWS III–458b; II–134b
Commodities Exchange Act II–140b
Connally "Hot Oil" Act V–270b
desegregation III–107b
Elkins Act II–431b
Employer's Liability Act II–441a; III–431a–b
equal protection of the law II–457b
Fair Labor Standards Act II–481b; IV–353b
fair-trade agreements II–483a–b
government inspection III–422a
grain storage IV–434b
Hepburn Act III–273a
"Hot oil" Case III–307b
Keating–Owen Act III–247a
Lacey Act VII–297a
Mann Act IV–240a
Miller–Tydings Act VII–123b
narcotics trade IV–450b
National Industrial Recov-

INTERSTATE COMMERCE LAWS (cont.)
ery Act VI–225a
National Labor Relations Act IV–467a–b, 467b–68a
Natural Gas Act V–5b
panic of 1785 V–206a
prices V–402a, 403a
Progressive movement V–428b
railroad pools V–358a
Railroad Retirement Board v. *Alton Railroad Company* VI–24a
Rap Brown law II–20b–21a
Webb–Kenyon Act VII–265a
Interstate Compact for the Supervision of Probationers and Parolees III–460a–b
Interstate Compact on the Placement of Children III–460a
INTERSTATE COMPACTS III–459b; III–9b; VI–398a, 402a–03a
Arkansas River Compact IV–28a
conservation VII–266b
Interstate Oil Compact VI–357b
Kansas–Missouri IV–28a
Kansas–Nebraska IV–28a
Kansas–Oklahoma IV–28a
Port Authority of New York and New Jersey III–201b; V–368b
water rights III–478a
Interstate Compact to Conserve Oil and Gas III–460a; VI–402b
Interstate Highway Act (1956) I–99a, 230a; VI–152a
Interstate Highway System II–502b; VI–152a, 156a
Kansas IV–26b
Interstate Oil Compact (1935) V–270b; VI–357b
Interstate Oil Compact Commission IV–334b; VI–357b
INTERSTATE TRADE BARRIERS III–460b; VII–82b
Interstate transportation IV–80b
Inter-Tribal Indian Ceremonial I–106b
INTERURBAN ELECTRIC LINES III–461a; VII–101b
Interurban transportation II–416a, 503a
INTERVENTION III–461b
Caribbean II–359b
Cuba III–231a; V–330a; VII–22a
Dominican Republic II–360b–62a
F. D. Roosevelt administration IV–112a
Good Neighbor policy III–199a
Haiti III–239b
Laos III–70a
Latin America III–69a; IV–111b–12a; V–45b
Lebanon III–70a; IV–130a
Mexican Revolution III–69a
Monroe Doctrine III–456b; IV–401a,b
Nicaragua V–94a
Roosevelt Corollary III–68b
Santo Domingo III–70a
World War I IV–134b
See also Nonintervention Policy
INTESTATE ESTATES III–464a
In the Tennessee Mountains IV–163a
INTOLERABLE ACTS (1774) **III–464a**; II–93a; VI–2a, 113b
Intoxicating liquors
Eighteenth Amendment II–206a, 406b–07b
Intoxication
crime II–258a, 259a
Intracoastal Waterway VI–146b
Intrastate commerce
original package doctrine V–172a
INTREPID (ketch) **III–464b**; I–266a; IV–44b; V–278b, 423b
Intruder (attack plane) I–56b–57a
Intruders. *See* Oklahoma Squatters; Sooners
Inuit. *See* Eskimo
Invader (bomber) I–50a
Inventions
patents V–225b
Scientific American VI–231a,b
Inventions and discoveries, Indian. *See* Indian Inventions and Discoveries
Inverness (Scot.)
World War I V–119b
Invertebrata of Massachusetts III–29b
INVESTIGATING COMMITTEES III–464b; II–173a
communism VI–14a
Haitian revolt III–240a
House Committee on Un-American Activities III–308a
New York insurance investigations III–430b–31a, 433b
Permanent Investigations Subcommittee IV–209b
Pujo Committee V–462a
Rip Raps contract–scandal VI–145a
Senate Munitions Committee III–480a
subversion VI–428b–29a
trusts VII–123b
Watergate VII–255a,b
See also Congressional investigations
Investigation, Bureau of II–503a
Investment Bankers Association III–466b
INVESTMENT BANKS III–465b; IV–244b; VII–222a–b
banking act of 1933 I–259b
Glass–Steagall Act II–470a; V–45a
Jay Cooke and Company II–218b
stock market speculation I–257a
INVESTMENT COMPANIES III–467a; II–218b, 500b
V–209b
Investment Company Act (1940) III–466b, 467a
Investment Company Institute III–467b
Investment Guarantee Program IV–466b
Investments
consumer purchasing power II–210a–b
exchanges II–469a–70b
inflation III–414b
land speculation IV–98a
New South V–66b–67a
railroads IV–94b
Wall Street VII–222a
See also Debt and Investment, Foreign
Investments, foreign *See* Foreign Investments in the United States
Invincible (sloop) VII–38a, 41a–b
Invisible Empire of the South. *See* Ku Klux Klan
Invisible Man IV–165a, 167a
Involuntary servitude II–205a; IV–60a, 79a
See also Peonage
Ionesco, Eugene (playwright) VII–50b–51a
IOWA III–467b; VI–393 (table)
Amana Community I–93a; II–147a; IV–338b–39a
banking I–129b, 259b
Black Hawk War I–311b
bond issue III–154b–55a
boundary disputes I–351b
butter production II–280b
Citizens' Alliances II–42a
claim associations II–70b
coal mines II–85a
corn II–226b, 227a
dairy cooperatives II–281a
discrimination in courts III–437b
Effigy Mounds National Monument V–217b
entail of estate II–452a–b
fencing laws III–10b
Fort Lisa IV–380b
Fort Madison IV–219b
forty-niners III–82a
Four-H clubs III–84b
Fox Indians III–88b, 396b
frontier merchants III–127b
Giard Tract III–177b
Granger laws III–209b
Half-Breed Tract III–242b
homeopathy III–293b
Honey War III–297b
horse III–303b
Icaria III–327a
Indian Country III–379a,b
Indian relocation III–394b
Jesuit missions III–499b, 500a
joint-stock land banks IV–6b
landholding I–4a
land speculation IV–101a
lead III–147a; IV–122a,b
liquor laws IV–425b
minimum-wage law IV–353b
Missouri River IV–380a
Mormons IV–411a, 411b
mounds IV–420b
neutral ground V–33b
New Buda V–42a
Nonpartisan League V–106b
oats V–130a
original package doctrine V–172a
prostitution V–438a
Quakers V–470a
railroads I–404b
Reformed churches VI–69a
Sioux land cession VII–106a
Sioux Wars VII–239b
Spirit Lake massacre VI–374a
state fairs VI–392b
statehood I–78b; III–39a
swamplands VI–453b
tornadoes II–352a; VII–75b
trading posts III–353b
transcontinental railroad VI–39a
Treaty of Fort Armstrong III–383b
Treaty of Prairie du Chien III–383b
Treaty of Sauk and Fox Agency III–383b
Treaty of Traverse des Sioux III–383b
Union Pacific Railroad VII–147a
westward movement IV–29a; VII–284a
Winnebago VII–305b, 306a
See also Council Bluffs; Dubuque
Iowa (battleship) VI–216b; VII–242a
Iowa (Indians) III–363b, 365a, 468a; VII–305b, 306a
Oklahoma lands V–148b, 149b
Treaty at Prairie du Chien V–388b
Iowa, University of I–272a; II–399a; V–349a
television VII–21a
IOWA BAND III–469a

Iowa Banking System
I–255b
Iowa City (Iowa) I–404b; III–468b; IV–411b
Iowa College II–154b; III–469a
IOWA CORN SONG III–469a
Iowa Injunction and Abatement Law (1909)
V–438a
Iowa River III–468a
Iowa State University
VII–176b
Iowa Territory II–284b
Iowa v. *Illinois* (1893)
I–351b
Ipatiev, Vladimir N. (chem.)
V–267a
Ipecac III–381a, 385b
I. P. Morris Company
V–92a
Ipswich (Mass.) II–328b, 464a; III–469a
IPSWICH PROTEST III–469a
IQ. *See* Intelligence quotient
IQ test III–159a
Iran
Anglo-American relations
I–124b
Baghdad Pact I–243a
citrus fruits III–128b
immigration to U.S.
III–341a
investment in U.S.
III–67a
military aid II–315b
Soviet Union II–97b, 315b
United Nations Declaration
VII–151b
U.S. relations I–149b; II–315b
World War II VII–18a, 338a
Iraq
Baghdad Pact I–243a
mandate IV–236b
revolution (1958) I–124b
United Nations Declaration
VII–151b
U.S. relations I–150a
IRBM. *See* Intermediate-range ballistic missile
Iredell, James (jur.) I–461a; II–40a, 393a; V–199a; VI–390b, 445a
Ireland
Campobello Fiasco
I–434a
colonial trade II–453a
Common Market
VI–472a
exchange students
II–470b
exploration of America
I–96b
Fenian movement III–10b
immigration II–125b, 258a; III–333a; IV–60a, 209b; V–3a
Navigation Acts
V–16a
OECD V–170b
Palatines V–195a
potatoes V–376b
Rio Grande colonists
VI–143b
Scotch-Irish VI–240a
universal education
II–393b
U.S. aid III–61b, 61b
World War I VII–329a
Ireland, John (archbp.)
I–468b; II–490a
Ireson, Floyd VI–462a
Ireton, Henry (off.) III–132b
Iris VI–395 (table)
Irish
campaign of 1884 I–383b
Chesapeake and Ohio Canal strike IV–61b
clothing industry II–82a
Know-Nothing party
II–37b
laborers and Erie Canal
II–460a
Minnesota IV–356b
Molly Maguires IV–392a
New York draft riots
IV–62b
organized crime II–260b
Saint Paul VII–134a
South Dakota VI–350a
Vermont VII–172b
Irish, Ned I–272b–73a
Irish hospital sweepstakes
IV–191b
Irish immigration III–334b, 335b–36a, 337b, 339b–40a
Indiana III–370a
slums VI–314a
Irish potatoes III–381a
Irish potato famine IV–310a; V–280b
Irish prison system VI–68a
Irish Republican Brotherhood
III–10b
IRISH TRACT III–469b
Iron
Alaska I–80a
bridges I–363b–64a
buildings I–378a,b
cobalt production III–14a
colonial exports II–119b, 453a
East India trade II–388a
flour III–44b
mineral rights IV–104b
mines II–32b, 75a, 491a
pack trains V–184a
Puerto Rico V–461b
railway land grants
IV–104b
U.S. Geological Survey
III–163a
See also Ferrous Metals
Iron, wrought
blacksmithing I–317a
bridges I–363b
building I–378a
IRON ACT OF 1750 III–469b; II–123a; III–77a; IV–242b
Iron and Steel Engineers' Association VI–185a
IRON AND STEEL INDUSTRY III–469b; III–11b–13a; VI–48a,b; VII–89b–90a
Alabama I–72a
automation IV–75a
Baltimore IV–261a
bridges II–384a
Buffalo (N.Y.) I–376a
Chicago II–18b
child labor II–23b
city planning
II–46a
Cleveland II–74b–75a
coal mining II–86a
coasting trade II–90b, 90b
colonial I–318b–19a; III–346b; IV–242b
construction I–164b, 363b–65a, 378a–b
domestic trade VII–84a,b
dry docks II–375a
foreign investment
III–66b
foreign trade VII–86a
government regulation
I–449b
great fortunes
III–79b–80a
Great Lakes exposition
III–217b
Great Lakes shipping
III–216b, 218a,b
Homestead Strike
III–297a
Indiana III–370b
Industrial Revolution
III–410b–11a,b, 412a
internal improvements
III–447b
Korean War II–473a
Liberia IV–141b
machine tools IV–215b
manganese III–13a
Menominee Iron Range
IV–303b
Mesabi Iron Range
IV–315a
Michigan IV–331b
Minnesota IV–357a
Mississippi River
IV–373a, 374b
molybdenum III–15a
monopolies IV–399a
New Jersey V–57b
New South V–67a
Ohio V–141b
panic of 1873 V–207b
Pawtucket V–230b
Pennsylvania V–246b, 247a,b
pension plans V–256a
Philadelphia V–277b
Pittsburgh II–18b, 18b; V–322a
price quotations V–402b
rails VI–39b
Safety First movement
VI–185a
Saint Louis VI–194b
Savannah VI–220b
shipbuilding IV–310b; VI–279b
South American trade
VI–345b
steam engines
VI–409b–10a
steel strikes VI–410b
Stove plates III–268b
tariff VI–465b, 471a,b
Tennessee VII–25b
trade association VII–92a
Tredegar Iron Works
VII–113b
tungsten III–15b
unionization IV–66a, 72b
U.S. Steel Corporation
strike IV–69b
vanadium III–15a–b
vertical combination production IV–272b
West Virginia VII–282a
World War I VII–327b
Iron and Steel Institute, American VII–92a
IRON AND STEEL MANUFACTURE III–472a; II–10a, 423a; IV–243a,b, 244a,b
Alabama I–72a
Baltimore I–250a
Bessemer process
III–180b
colonial III–76b, 408a, 413b; VI–107b, 108a
Confederate ordnance
II–67b, 163a
duties II–276a
Hudson River chain
III–313a
Iron Act of 1750
III–469b
Navigation Acts V–16a,b
Principio Company
V–409a
Saugus furnace VI–218a
Sault Sainte Marie Canals
VI–219a
scientific management
VI–234a
Spotswood's furnaces
VI–376a
Sterling Iron Works
VI–412a
Ironclad documents. *See* "Yellow-Dog" Contract
IRONCLAD OATH III–474a; VI–55b, 59a; VII–34b
IRONCLADS, CONFEDERATE, ON INLAND WATERS III–474a; II–384a–b; V–17b
IRONCLAD WARSHIPS III–474b; III–36a; IV–375a,b, 431b; VII–147a
Battle at Grand Gulf
III–208b
Cairo VI–424b
Civil War III–478b; V–17a,b, 25a
Confederate rams
VI–44b
gunboats III–234b
inland waters
III–474a–b
Laird rams IV–85a
Merrimack IV–396a
Monitor and *Merrimack*
VII–240b
monitors IV–397a
Stonewall VI–415a
Tennessee IV–383a
IRON CURTAIN III–474b; VI–179b
Irondequoit Bay
II–329a–b
Iron-manganese alloys
III–13a
Iron molders
unionization IV–62a,b,
Iron Mountain (Mich.)
IV–303b

Iron Mountain railroad
III–101a
Iron Mountains III–222a
Iron oxides III–12a
Iron River (Mich.) IV–303b
Irons, electric II–417a–b
Irons, Martin (labor leader)
IV–64b; VI–38b
IRON SHIP III–475a;
VI–148a
Ironside, William E. (off.)
I–159a
"Iron Triangle" (Kor.)
VI–301a
Iron work VI–291b, 292a
blacksmithing I–316b
Boonton (N.J.) I–337b
Iron Works Pike (Ky.)
III–206b
Iroquoian (lang.) II–51b;
III–365b, 367a, 475a, 476a
IROQUOIS (Indians)
III–475a; III–365a,b,
366a,b, 367a; VII–307a
agriculture I–2b
Albany Congress I–82a
art III–374b
British alliance IV–386b
British land claims
III–118a
captivities III–376b
Champlain's alliance
I–492b
Champlain's attack
V–156b
Cherokee II–51b
confederation I–288a
Delaware Indians II–321a
Denonville's invasion
II–329a
food III–51a
Fort Crèvecoeur II–257b
Fort Plain V–323a
Fort Stanwix treaties
III–24b, 382b, 383a;
IV–216b; VI–385b–86a;
VII–203a
French and Indian War
III–115a,b, 116b; V–175b
French expeditions against
III–124b–25a
French settlements V–52b
fur trade III–141a, 142a
gardening III–151b
Great Indian Council at
Niagara V–90b
Great Lakes III–216a
Great Trading and War
Path III–223b
Great Village of the Illinois
III–330b
guns III–399b
Handsome Lake Cult
III–249b; V–4a
Hiawatha II–31b
housing I–166b
Jemison, Mary VII–293b
Jesuit missions
III–499a,b, 500a
King William's War
IV–49b, 50a; VI–181b–82a
Lake Erie II–458b
Lake Ontario V–367a
Logstown IV–181a
Logstown Treaty IV–181b
Mahican and Mohegan relations IV–387a
migration VI–271a
Minisink raid IV–354b
Mohawk River V–224a
myth and folklore
III–386b
New France IV–109a
New York I–81b; V–84b,
85a; VII–282b
New York and Genesee
Company V–81b
Ogden purchase V–139b
Ohio V–140a
Ohio River V–145a
Ohio Valley V–146a
"Onontio" V–156b
Radisson's *Voyages*
VI–18a,b
religion III–366a
revolutionary war
II–433a; III–400a,b;
VI–130a
Richelieu River VI–136b
"running the gauntlet"
III–154b
sachem VI–183a
Seneca VII–130b
study of I–128b
"suffering traders"
VI–430a
Sullivan–Clinton campaign
VI–438a
tomahawk VII–70a
trading posts VII–95b
Treaty of Albany V–386a
Treaty of Easton II–389a
Treaty of Lancaster
III–382b
Treaty of Utrecht
II–267a; VII–162b
Tuscarora VII–130b
Vermont VII–171a
Virginia VII–192a
Walking Purchase
VII–220b
wampum VII–223a
West Virginia VII–281a
wigwam VII–294b
Woodland Tradition
VII–320a
Wyoming massacre
VII–346b
Iroquois, League of the
III–365b, 391a, 405a,
475a–b, 476a; VI–183a–b
French and Indian War
III–115a
IROQUOIS BEAVER LAND DEED (1701) **III–476a**;
IV–386b; V–84b
IROQUOIS THEATER FIRE (1903) **III–476b**; II–348a
Iroquois Trail III–387b
IROQUOIS TREATY (1684)
III–476b
Irradiation process I–303b
Irrawaddy River III–46a;
IV–314a, 446b–47a
"IRREPRESSIBLE CONFLICT" III–477a
IRRIGATION III–477a;
VI–334a, 335a
agriculture I–48b
arid regions I–170b–71a
Arizona I–172b
Bureau of Reclamation
III–445a
California I–407a
canals I–279a
citrus industry II–44a
Colorado II–128b; IV–27b
Colorado River II–130a
desert lands I–453b, 453b
government projects
IV–104a
Indian cultures III–289a,
369a
interstate compacts
III–460a
Kansas IV–26b, 27b
land speculation II–336a
Missouri River IV–380a
national parks V–220a
Nebraska V–31b
Newlands Reclamation Act
V–445b
New Mexico V–60a
reclamation VI–53b
Rio Grande VI–143b
Rocky Mountains
VI–160b
Snake River VI–322b
subsidies VI–425b
U.S. Geological Survey
III–164a
Washington State
VII–248a
water law VII–256a
water rights IV–104a–b
Waterways Treaty
VII–261a
windmills VII–305a
Irvine (Calif.) II–48b
Irvine, William (off.) V–321b
Irving, Washington (au.)
III–122b, 215b, 281b;
IV–161b; V–189b;
VI–312b
Adventures of Captain Bonneville I–330a
children's books I–335a
Rip Van Winkle I–471a;
VI–145a
Irwin, Theodore II–109a
Irwin, William H. ("Will")
(jour.) V–74a, 80a
Irwinville (Irvinville) (Ga.)
II–68b, 165a, 294b
Isaac, Harold R. (au.)
II–27a
Isabella (Sp. q.) II–323b
Iselin, C. O'D. (oceanog.)
III–233b
Ishii, Kikujiro (dipl.)
IV–106b; VI–251b
Isis Unveiled V–172a
Islam I–315a; V–171b, 172a
Islamic law II–479a
ISLAND NUMBER TEN, OPERATIONS AT (1862)
III–478b; I–459a;
IV–370a, 374b, 375a
Island of Palmas Case (1928)
III–456b
Isle aux Noix III–116b;
IV–86b
Isle La Motte VII–171a
ISLEÑOS III–479a
ISLE OF ORLEANS
III–479a; III–50b, 326b;
IV–193a, 196a,b
ISLE OF PINES III–479a;
V–329b
Isle of Portland I–477b
Isle of Wight I–172b
Isle Percé I–492b
Isle Royal II–223a
Isle Royale National Park
V–218 (table)
ISLES OF SHOALS
III–479b; IV–82b, 264a;
V–53a–b
Isleta (N.Mex.) II–461a;
III–367b; V–460a, 460a
Islip (N.Y.) VI–134b
ISOLATIONISM III–479b;
IV–343a,b; V–233a
America First Committee
I–97a
American Legion I–108b
Civil War III–68a
Convention of 1800
II–215b
entangling alliances
II–452b
League of Nations
IV–124b
lend-lease IV–134b
liberalism IV–140b
neutrality policy V–35a,b
neutral rights V–39a
propaganda VII–333a–b
Republican party VI–93b
World War II
VII–333b–34a
Isoniazid VII–127a
ISOSTASY III–480b;
III–166b
Isotopes II–12a; V–298b,
299b
Isotopic tracers I–303b
Israel
attack by New Left
IV–12a
Baghdad Pact I–243a
community centers
VII–362b
immigration to U.S.
III–341a
industrial relations
III–408a
October war (1973)
III–70b
Palestine IV–236b
Suez Canal I–124a,b
Suez crisis VI–430a
support of U.S. Jews
IV–11a,b, 12a
U.S.–Arab relations
I–149b–50b
Israel, lost tribes of IV–116b
Israel–Arab conflict
aerial hijacking III–277b
ISRAELI-AMERICAN RELATIONS III–481b;
V–233a
British in Palestine
I–124a
military aid II–315b
Yom Kippur War
II–213a
See also Arab-American
Relations
Israeli War (1967) IV–11b
Isthmian Canal Commission
V–94b, 201a,b
Italia (ship) I–116a
ITALIAN-AMERICANS-
III–482b
clothing industry II–82a
Indiana III–370a
Mafia incident IV–221b
organized crime
II–261b–63a

race riots VI–8a
slums VI–314a
World War II III–491a
Italianate *putti* I–161a
Italian Counter-Reformation architecture I–160a
Italian Renaissance architecture I–161a, 164b
Italo-Ethiopian War (1935–36) V–38a–b
Italy
airships II–344a
Alabama Claims VII–249a
borax I–340a
citrus fruits III–128b
Common Market VI–469a; VII–88b
corn II–226b
criminal behavior patterns II–258b
enemy aliens II–446a
Ethiopia V–35b
Ethopia I–21b
exchange students II–470b
Five-Power Naval Treaty III–33b
Fourteen Points III–86a
Geneva Three-Power Naval Treaty III–161a, 162a
immigration to U.S. III–333a, 336a–b, 337b–38a, 341b, 342a 339a,b
investments in U.S. III–66b
London Naval Treaty (1930) II–461a; IV–183a; VI–424a
London Naval Treaty (1936) IV–183b
Mafia incident IV–221b
mental illness IV–305a
music IV–437b
Napoleonic Wars V–162a
naval competition II–314b; V–10a
Nine-Power Pact V–96b
North Atlantic Treaty Organization V–113b
Organization for Economic Cooperation and Development V–170b
Paris Peace Conference V–215b
pistole V–320b
radar VI–l0a
tennis VII–30a
Treaty of San Ildefonso VI–211a
Treaty of Versailles VII–172b
Unknown Soldiers II–310a
U.S. aid III–61b
U.S. national defense II–314b
Venezuela II–369a; IV–401a; VII–169b
Washington Naval Conference VII–250b, 341b
World War I I–120a; V–307b–08a; VII–325b, 331a, 332a
World War II I–60a, 141a,b, 178b, 214a, 308a, 308a, 465a; II–315a; III–200b–01a, 235a–b; IV–32b, 382a; V–20b, 112b, 113a, 332a, 378b; VI–199b, 284b, 298a; VII–242a, 334b, 335a, 338a–b, 340b, 341a
ITAMA III–484a
Itasca, Lake IV–355a, 372a
ITEM VETO III–484b; VI–138b
"It grows as it goes" (motto) VI–394 (table)
Ithaca (N.Y.) II–227b
Ithaca (N.Y.) *Chronicle* (news.) VI–163a
Iturbide, Agustín de (off., emp.) I–350a
IUKA, BATTLE OF (1862) **III–485a**; IV–370a
Ives, Brayton I–333a
Ives, Charles (comp.) IV–439a
Ives, Chauncey (lithographer) II–275a
Ives, Herbert Eugene (phys.) VII–21b
Ives, James M. (lithographer) II–275a
Ives, Joseph (clockmaker) II–78a
Ives, Joseph C. (expl.) II–129b; III–208a
Ives, Levi S. (bp.) V–179b
Ives-Quinn Act V–87b
Ivory
dentistry II–329b, 331a
portrait painting IV–351b
Ivory soap I–17b; VI–323b
Ivy League
tennis VII–29a,b
IWO JIMA III–485a; I–85a, 207b; III–490a; IV–253a; V–21a; VII–2a, 139a, 337a, 343a
I Wonder As I Wander IV–166b
IWW. *See* Industrial Workers of the World
Izaak Walton League I–80a; II–188a
Izard, Mark W. (gov.) V–31b
Izmir (Turk.) V–22b, 23a

J

J. A. Bostwick and Company VI–383a
Jack, Captain. *See* Kintapuash
"Jack Armstrong, The All-American Boy" I–488a
Jackets (dress) II–372a,b
Jackling, Daniel C. (eng., metal.) V–103b
Jackman, S. D. (off.) III–182a
Jackson (Ky.) III–253a
Jackson (Mich.) IV–331b; VI–92b
Jackson (Miss.) III–485b
Bayou Pierre I–279a
civil rights movement II–58a
Civil War I–492a; VI–48b; VII–182a
southern rights convention IV–453b
Jackson, Andrew II–175 (table); III–21b, 47b; IV–453a; V–151b, 190a, 280a, 395 (table), 396a; VI–243a; VII–25b, 261b, 291a
campaign of 1824 I–418b; IV–469b; V–101b; VI–421b; VII–201b
congressional caucus I–475a
Hermitage III–273b
Memphis settlement IV–302a
Robards, Rachel V–346b
—Military Career:
Arbuthnot and Ambrister case I–10b, 121a, 154a
Battle at Villere's Plantation VII–188a
Battle of Horseshoe Bend III–305b
Battle of New Orleans II–464b; IV–193b, 339b; V–63a; VII–234b
censorship I–481a
Creek War II–256b–57a; III–404a; VII–77a, 236a
Dickinson duel II–377a
Florida III–39a, 42a, 145a; VI–359b; VII–277b
Fort Deposit II–333a
Fort Saint Marks VI–196b
Iberville River III–327a
Indian campaign III–384b
militia IV–345b
New Echota Treaty V–49b
Pensacola V–254b
Rhea Letter VI–131b
riflemen VI–269b
Seminole War III–462b; VI–259b, 260b
Treaty of Chickasaw Council House II–22a
troop mutiny IV–445b
War of 1812 I–184a, 342b, 490b
—President:
Alabama politics I–71a
amnesty I–114b
antislavery mail I–137a, 478b
attempted assassination I–202a
backwoodsmen I–240a
Bank of the United States I–255b, 259b, 261b; III–251b, 354b; IV–228a; VI–85b
banks II–464b
Buckshot War I–374b
cabinet I–107b; II–389b
campaign of 1828 V–54a, 101b; VI–94b
campaign of 1832 I–132b, 419a–b; VI–203b
campaign of 1836 I–419b
Cherokee VII–322a
civil service II–59b
democracy II–189a
Democratic party II–327a
Denmark claims II–291b
Deposit Act II–333b
Douglas's support IV–168b
Eaton affair II–389b; V–346b
election of judges IV–17b
Falkland Islands II–484a
Faneuil Hall reception II–487b
Force Acts III–59b
French spoliation claims III–96b, 121b–22a; VI–104b
gold devaluation IV–392b
government appointments I–146a
homestead movement III–295b
inauguration (1829) I–240a; III–351a
Indian policy III–379b
Indian removal II–52a; III–221a, 365b, 389a, 393b, 394a; VI–85b
individualism II–189a
internal improvements III–449a–b
Jacksonian Democracy III–486a
Kendall v. *United States* IV–36b
Kitchen Cabinet IV–51a
labor's support IV–61b
martial law in New Orleans IV–258b
Missouri support IV–377a
National Intelligencer IV–465b
Northeast boundary V–118b
nullification V–125b–26a, 176b
Panama Canal I–295a
pet banks V–264a
portrait II–101b
postal service V–372a–b
removal of deposits VI–427a
removal power VI–84b
roads VI–153b
rotation in office VI–165a
Seminole War VI–260b
Specie Circular V–206b; VI–369b, 370b
spoils system I–384a; III–71a; V–227b; VI–375a–b
Tammany Hall VI–459b
tariff VI–466a
Texas independence IV–410a
third-term doctrine VII–53b
veto VII–178a
Washington Globe III–187b
Whig party V–86b; VII–288a
Wilkes Exploring Expedition VII–299a

JACKSON, BATTLE OF (1863) **III–485b**
Jackson, Charles T. (chem.) I–119a
Jackson, Claiborne Fox (gov.) I–433b, 462a; V–402b
Jackson, David E. (fur trader) I–452b; III–143a–b, 486a; VI–160a; VII–103b
Jackson, Fort (Ala.). *See* Toulouse, Fort
Jackson, Fort (La.) I–247a; III–78b, 258b; IV–374b–75a, 413b; V–63b
Jackson, Fort, Treaty of (1814) II–257a; III–88b, 383b, 384b, 404a
Jackson, Francis James (dipl.) I–347a
Jackson, Fred S. (law.) IV–27a
Jackson, George (prospector) V–437a
Jackson, Helen Marie Hunt (au.) I–485b
Jackson, Henry M. (pol.) I–80b
Jackson, Howell E. (jur.) III–351b; V–354b; VI–446a
Jackson, James (pol.) VII–354a
Jackson, Jesse L. (cler.) I–24a
Jackson, Mahalia (sing.) IV–442a
Jackson, Martha II–105b
Jackson, Mount VII–71a
Jackson, Rachel Donelson II–274a, 274a; V–346b
Jackson, Richard (law.) II–116b
Jackson, Robert (jur.) III–104a, 105a
Jackson, Robert H. (jur.) III–491a; V–472b; VI–446b
Jackson, Thomas J. ("Stonewall") (off.) V–377b
Army of Northern Virginia VII–197a,b
Battle at Front Royal III–128a
Battle at Kernstown IV–43b
Battle at McDowell IV–212b
Battle at Savage's Station VI–220a
Battle at White Oak Swamp VII–293a
Battle of Antietam I–130a
Battle of Cedar Mountain I–476b
Battle of Chancellorsville I–493a; VII–295b
Battle of Chantilly I–493b
Battle of Frayser's Farm III–100a
Battle of Gaines' Mill III–146b
Battle of Groveton III–229a
Battle of Mechanicsville IV–282a
Battle of Port Republic V–369a
Battle of Winchester VII–304a
First Battle of Bull Run I–381b, 382a
Fritchie, Barbara III–100b, 124b
Harpers Ferry III–256a; IV–261b
Lee's lost order IV–190a
Seven Days' Battles VI–263b
Shenandoah campaign II–266a, 482a–b; III–487a–b; V–245a
Jackson, W. H. (phot.) VII–357b
Jackson County (Iowa) I–287a
Jackson County (Mo.)
Civil War IV–183b
Mormons IV–377b
Jackson County (Ohio) VI–202a
JACKSON HOLE (Wyo.) **III–486a**; III–143a, 291a
JACKSONIAN DEMOCRACY III–486a; IV–162a; V–223b, 247a, 343b, 344a; VII–288a
agrarianism I–33a
banking I–129b; III–101b
campaign of 1828 I–419a
labor IV–61a
Locofoco party IV–175a
Mississippi IV–368b
Missouri IV–377a
municipal government IV–426b–27a
natural rights IV–140a
New Jersey V–58a
New York City V–83a
opposition II–189a
pharmacists' licensing V–276a
state geological surveys III–165a–b
Union sentiment VII–148b
Jacksonian Democrats II–216a, 231a; IV–61b
Jackson Lake II–477a
Jackson Park (Chicago) II–18a; III–19b
Jackson Purchase IV–39b
Jackson State College VII–191b
JACKSON'S VALLEY CAMPAIGN (1862) **III–487a**; III–128a; V–245a
Jacksonville (Fla.) VI–187b
Afro-Americans I–25b, 29a
Camp J. E. Johnston I–435a
government IV–172b
hurricanes III–319b
railroad III–39a,b; VI–34a
Jacksonville (Ill.) III–331b; IV–168b; VII–350b
Jacob, F. (geneticist) III–158a
Jacob, Henry (cler.) I–264b; V–52a
Jacobean baroque architecture I–161a
Jacob Ford Mansion (N.J.) IV–413b
Jacobi, Abraham (physic.) I–307a; III–81a; IV–275a
JACOBIN CLUBS III–487b; IV–143a; VI–94a
Jacob's Creek (Pa.) II–350a
Jacquard loom I–397a, 460a; II–153b; VII–43b
Jacques Seligmann and Company II–104a
Jacquet-Droz, Pierre (inv.) VII–136a
Jadwin Plan (1928) VI–147a
Jaeger rifle VI–139b
Jaffee, Irving (athlete) V–154b
Jail Rock II–246b
Jaime I (battleship) V–26b
Jalap VII–355b
Jalapa (Mex.) I–488b; IV–324a; VI–312b
Jalisco (Mex.) IV–325a
Jam III–54b, 129a
Jamaica (N.Y.) II–431a
colonial settlement IV–185a
revolutionary war IV–186a
Jamaica (W.I.)
American Revolution VI–126b, 130a; VII–198b
bauxite I–92b
Cartagena expedition I–461b
Cromwell's western design VII–270b–71a
flour trade III–42b
horse III–302a
immigration to U.S. III–341b
logwood trade IV–181b
Loyalist veterans VI–131a
Rhodes scholars VI–134b
slave poll taxes I–22b
theater VII–46b
Jamaica Bay (N.Y.) II–347a
Jamaica wood IV–181b
James I (k.) II–370b
Cape Ann I–446b
charter colonies I–499b
Indian education III–379b
Jamestown III–488b; VII–192b
loyalty oaths IV–202a
Pilgrims V–65a
Scotch-Irish VI–240a
Virginia grant IV–185a, 190b; VII–274a
Waldo patent VII–219b
James II (k.) IV–134a, 226a
abdication V–50b
colonial charters II–182b
Fairfax patent II–481a
New York colonial assemblies II–118a
See also York, Duke of
James, Absolom I–23a
JAMES, ARMY OF THE III–488a
James, Edward T. (ed.) II–341a
James, Edwin (bot.) I–349a; III–488a; IV–186b; V–311a
James, Fort (N.Y.) IV–134a; V–84a
James, Frank (outlaw) V–119b; VII–97b
James, Henry (au.) IV–163b, 164a
James, Jesse (outlaw) I–247a; V–119b; VII–97b
James, Sidney II–105b, 106b
James, Thomas (trader) VI–215a–b
James, William (psych., philos.) III–260a; IV–163b, 164a; V–286a, 287b–88a, 386b, 387a, 441b, 442a
parapsychology V–213a
religion IV–448a
James Baines (ship) I–448a
James Bay I–441a
"James Bird" (ballad) I–247a
JAMES EXPEDITION (1820) **III–488a**
James Forrestal Campus (Princeton) V–409a
James gang III–231a; VII–97b
James H. Lucas (steamboat) VI–408a
James Island (S.C.) I–496a, 497a
James Madison Memorial Building (Washington, D.C.) IV–146b
Jameson, J. Franklin (hist.) I–106a
James Peak (Colo.) VII–128b
James River I–88b; III–258a, 488a–b; IV–396b; VI–149b
Belle Isle I–287a
Boulevard Bridge VII–69b
canal IV–174b
Civil War II–96b; III–100a, 488a; IV–397a; V–245a,b, 264b, 265a, 377b; VI–138a, 150a, 263b, 420b
collector of customs II–275b
Dutch Gap Canal II–382b
Hurricane Camille III–319b
Jamestown III–488b
Powhatan Confederacy V–385b
railroads VI–35a
revolutionary war I–194a; VII–360b
Richmond VI–136b
settlement II–123b; VII–192b
Shenandoah Valley VI–275b
ships graveyard II–438b
Spanish exploration I–96a, 238b
tobacco VII–67b
waterpower IV–347b
westward movement VII–260a
Williamsburg VII–301a
James River (Dakotas) II–284b; V–388b
James River and Kanawha Canal III–448a; VI–137a

JAMES RIVER AND KANAWHA COMPANY
III–488a; III–448a, 488b; VII–249a
JAMES RIVER COMPANY
III–488a
JAMESTOWN (Va.)
III–488b; III–219a; VI–340b, 341a; VII–94b, 192a–b, 193a–b
agriculture VI–335a
architecture I–161a
arrival of blacks I–26b, 27a, 36b
Bacon's Rebellion I–240b; III–436b
blacksmithing I–316b–17a
Church of England II–36a
colonial dress II–370b
colonial government I–204a
corn II–226a
cotton II–237b
criminal code II–285a
food preservation III–54b
fruit growing III–128b
glass II–4b
glassmaking III–182b, 184b
hogs III–288b
naval stores II–4b
oats V–130a
pottery V–379a
public market IV–255b
Raleigh's Lost Colony VI–43a
revolutionary war VII–360b
salt VI–202a
saltpeter II–4b; V–98a
salt works II–4b
slavery VI–310a
slave trade VI–304b
Society of Colonial Wars VI–332a
Somers' voyage VI–338a
starving time VI–388a
Susan Constant VI–451a
tobacco warehouses VII–67b
Jamestown (S.C.) III–315a
Jamestown (ship) I–76b
Jamestown, Battle of. *See* Hot Water, Battle of
JAMESTOWN EXPOSITION (1907) **III–489b**; II–100a
Jamestown Island (Va.) III–489a,b
Jamestown Ter-Centennial Exhibition (1907). *See* Jamestown Exposition
Jamieson, T. F. (sci.) III–481a
Janitors
unionization IV–75b
Janney, Eli H. (inv.) VI–28a
Jansky, Karl G. (astron.) I–212a, 287b; VI–16b–17a
Janson, Charles William I–367b, 368a
Jansson, Erik (col.) I–307b
Japan
Alaska–Pacific–Yukon Exposition I–81a
Anglo–Japanese Alliance I–122a
auctions I–222a
automobile I–229b; VII–90a
baseball I–271b
Battle Fleet cruise I–276b
Boxer Rebellion I–356a; III–352a
cherry trees gift III–491b
Chiang Kai-shek II–27b
China interests II–471b; IV–106b
cold war II–97b
consular jurisdiction II–479b
consumer cooperatives II–220a
currency III–196b; VII–91a
electronics VII–84b
extraterritoriality II–479b
Five–Power Naval Treaty III–33b
foreign trade I–201b; VI–471b; VII–90a, 91b
Four–Power Treaty III–85b
Franciscans III–94b
Geneva Three–Power Naval Treaty III–160b–61a, 162a
Gentlemen's Agreement III–68b
Hawaii III–263b
Hawaiian labor III–263b, 264a
immigration II–471b, 488b; III–335a, 340b, 341a,b; VI–7a
industrial development II–489b
investments in U.S. III–66b
iron and steel manufacture III–470a, 474a
Korea III–68b
linen products IV–157b
London Naval Treaty II–461a; IV–183a, 183b; VI–424a
Louisiana Purchase Exposition IV–198a
mackerel fisheries IV–217b
Magdalena Bay IV–199b, 223b
Manchukuo V–107a
Manchuria II–488b–89a; III–69a; IV–234b; V–35b; VII–251a, 341b
mandates III–85b
marine landing IV–252a
Micronesia VII–125a
minesweeping IV–351b
multinational corporations III–66b
naval competition V–10a,b, 11a, 216b
Nine–Power Pact V–96b
nuclear fission V–300a
nuclear physics V–302b
occupation I–188a
Open Door policy V–158b–59a
Organization for Economic Cooperation and Development V–170b
Pacific Islands III–425a, 426a
Panay incident V–205b
Peabody Museum collections IV–436a
Peking Tariff Conference V–242b
per capita income VI–384a
Perry's expedition II–488b; III–68b; IV–252a; V–22b, 263a; VII–285a
photographic industry V–292b–93a
radar VI–10a
Ringgold–Rodgers Exploring Expedition VI–142a
Root–Takahira Agreement VI–164a
rubber VI–168a
Russian trade VI–180b
Russo–Japanese Neutrality Pact VI–178b–79a
Russo–Japanese War IV–234b–35a
salmon fishing VI–201b
sealing I–85a; V–401a; VI–245b, 246a
sea otter hunting VI–247b
secret protocol of 1917 VI–251b
Shimonoseki expedition III–352a; VI–278b
Siberia V–107b; VI–283b–84a
silk VI–287a
Sino–Japanese War III–68b, 352b; VI–294b
South American trade VI–344a,b, 346a
steel III–471 (table); VII–89b
Stonewall VI–415a
Taft–Katsura Memorandum VI–457b
textiles VII–90a
tobacco VII–64b
Treaty of Portsmouth V–370b
Treaty of Versailles VII–172b
Twenty–one Demands V–107b
U.S. balance of trade I–246a
U.S. foreign policy II–488a–90a
U.S. national defense II–314b
U.S. naval forces V–25a
U.S. occupation V–432b
vacuum tubes VII–163b
war with China III–46a–b
Washington Naval Conference II–314b; VII–250b, 341b
Wells, Fargo VII–267a
wool VII–321a,b
Yap mandate IV–236b; VII–353b
yellow peril VII–356b–57a
—*World War I:*
peace conference VII–331a
Zimmerman telegram VII–325a, 368b
—*World War II:*
air war III–489b–90b
Aleutian Islands I–84b–85a, 439b
atomic bomb attacks I–215b, 216a, 328b
balloon warfare I–248a
Bataan–Corregidor I–274a
Bismarck Sea I–307b–08a
bombing of I–50a, 60b, 67b
booby traps I–332a
Bougainville I–350b
Burma Road I–386b
Caroline Islands I–459a
China III–45b–46a
Choiseul II–33a
Coral Sea I–55b; II–225a; IV–136b
disarming and demobilization II–26b, 324a
Eastern Solomons II–387a–b
Empress Augusta Bay II–443a
enemy aliens II–446a
Gilbert Islands III–180a
Guadalcanal III–229a
Guam III–230b
Hiroshima IV–238b
history VII–333b–34a, 335a,b–38a, 341a,b, 342a,b–43a, 342a,b–43a
Iwo Jima III–485a
Java Sea III–492b
Lae and Salamaua IV–83a
Leyte Gulf IV–138a
Lingayen Gulf IV–157b
Lombok Strait IV–182a
Makassar Strait IV–228b
Makin raid IV–229a
Marshall Islands IV–257a
Midway I–55b–56a; IV–336a, 337a
Myitkyina IV–446b
Nagasaki IV–238b
navy V–20b–21a
Okinawa I–55b; V–147b
Pearl Harbor I–58a, 59b, 66b–67a, 274a, 328a, 484a; II–247a, 315a, 425a; III–69a, 480a; V–239b–40a; VII–333b
Peleliu V–242b
Philippines II–315a; V–284a
Philippine Sea I–56a; V–285b
Potsdam Conference V–378b
prisons I–219b
property confiscated II–169a
Rabaul VI–5a
sinking of *Langley* I–54b
Solomon Islands II–387a–b
Southeast Asia II–315a
surrender II–324a
Tarawa VI–462a
Teheran Conference VII–18a
Tinian VII–62a
Tokyo Express VII–68a
torpedo warfare VII–76b
underwater defenses VII–139a
Wake VII–218b
war crimes trials I–219b; VII–229b
warships VII–242a

JAPAN (cont.)
Yalta Conference VII–352a
Japan (merchant ship) III–169b
JAPAN, AIR WAR AGAINST (1942–45) **III–489b**; II–26a; IV–253a
Japan, Sea of VII–343a
Japanese–American Agreement. *See* Lansing–Ishii Agreement
JAPANESE-AMERICAN-RELOCATION III–490b; I–408a,b; II–445b–46a; IV–359a; VI–7b; VII–118a, 227b, 357a
Japanese–Americans
Buddhism V–171b
California Alien Land Law I–409a
Wyoming VII–346a
JAPANESE CHERRY TREES III–491b
JAPANESE EXCLUSION ACTS III–491b; III–342a,b; VI–164a
Japanese–language press V–75b
Japanese "Monroe Doctrine" V–96b
Japanese warlords V–124a
Japanning III–134a, 138a
Jaquess, James F. (cler.) V–234b
Jardin des Plantes (Paris) IV–231b
Jarrell, Randall (poet) IV–165b
Jarves, Deming (mfr.) III–182b
Jarves, James Jackson II–102a
Jarvis, Edward (physic., statis.) VII–206a
Jarvis Island VII–125b
Jasper, William (off.) VI–221a
Java II–488a
World War II III–492b; VII–336b
Java (frigate) II–192a
JAVA SEA, BATTLE OF (1942) **III–492b**
Jaworski, Leon (law.) VII–255b
Jay (Fla.) II–348b
Jay, Fort (N.Y.C.) III–206b
Jay, James (phys.) VI–373a
Jay, John (jur., states.) III–180b; V–199a; VI–445a
American Minerva V–69b
Bank of North America I–260b
British posts IV–329a
campaign of 1788 I–416b
campaign of 1800 III–494b
Constitution II–196a–b
Federalist I–130b; II–196b; III–4a; V–353a
Federalist party III–4a; V–86b
free navigation of Mississippi IV–373b
French Consular Convention II–208a
Jay–Gardoqui negotiations III–492b; VI–359a; VII–276a
Jay's Treaty I–120b, 366b; II–215a, 342b; III–493b–94a; IV–402b
Loyalists VII–117a
New York constitution VI–390b
Peace of Paris V–214b; VI–117a
preliminary articles of peace II–318b
representative government VI–89b
slavery I–135b
Spanish negotiations VII–111a
Jaybird Association III–93a
Jay Cooke and Company. *See* Cooke, Jay, and Company
JAY-GARDOQUI NEGOTIATIONS (1785–86) **III–492b**; V–315b; VI–359a; VII–111a, 260a, 276a
free navigation of Mississippi IV–373b
JAYHAWKERS III–493a; VI–71b
Jayhawker State VI–393 (table)
JAY'S TREATY (1794) **III–493a**; I–126a; II–342b; III–67b, 375b, 455b, 456a; IV–373b; V–232b; VI–359a; VII–111b, 270a, 276b
alien landholding I–87a
Antifederalist opposition II–326b
arbitration IV–5b
British debts I–366b–67a
British posts IV–330b
campaign of 1796 I–417a
Carrying Place of Niagara V–90a
Convention of 1800 II–215a
Detroit II–337a, 338a
expiration IV–402b
extradition VII–112b
Fort Miami IV–329a
Fort Niagara V–90b
Fort Oswegatchie V–139b
Franco–American misunderstanding III–95b, 121a; IV–402b; VII–347b, 348a
Mississippi River VI–150b
negotiation IV–381b
Northwest boundary V–120b
Ohio V–141a
Saint Croix River V–118a; VI–189a
U.S. balance of trade I–245a
western posts I–120b, 341a, 438b; II–458b
Jazz IV–166b, 439a, 440a–b, 443b
Afro–Americans II–261b
Chicago II–18a
dance II–290b
New Orleans V–62b
slang VI–300a
Jazz Messengers IV–440b
Jazz Singer (movie) II–290a
Jeanes, Anna T. II–401b
Jeannette (steamer) V–336a,b
Jebb, Joshua VI–68a
Jedburgh Operation (World War II) V–138b
Jeffers, W. N. (nav. off.) V–212b
Jefferson (Mo.) III–448b
Jefferson (Pa.) III–250b
Jefferson (Tex.) I–473a
JEFFERSON, FORT (Ill.) **III–494a**
Jefferson, Fort (Fla.) IV–155a; V–217b
JEFFERSON, FORT (Ohio) **III–494a**; VI–188b
Jefferson, Peter (cartog.) VII–74a
Jefferson, Thomas II–174 (table), 215a, 320a; III–47b; IV–103b, 161b; V–187b, 306b, 383a, 395 (table); VI–44a, 92b, 451a; VII–193b, 194a, 206a, 267b, 300b
agrarianism I–32b
agriculture I–37a, 46a
American Philosophical Society I–110b, 128a
anarchism I–116b
anniversary dinner (1830) V–176b
Antifederalists II–326b
antislavery VI–305a
architecture III–495a
Articles of War VII–143a
Aurora V–70a
Bank of North America I–260b
Bank of the United States III–245b
Bill of Rights I–297b, 298b
British debts I–366b; VI–108b
British posts IV–329a
British trade III–493b
campaign of 1796 I–417a
chemistry library II–10a
climatology IV–316b
code of manners IV–240b
coinage II–95a
College of William and Mary II–395b–96a
colonization of Afro–Americans II–127a
compact theory II–149a
Compromise of 1790 II–149b
congressional caucus I–475a
Declaration of Independence II–303b–04a, 305a–b, 308b, 377a; III–354a; VI–114a, 118b; VII–2b
Democratic–Republican party IV–465b
district schools VI–227a
dueling II–377a
education II–114b, 325b, 396a, 470b
E pluribus unum II–455b
Federalists III–4b
federal mint IV–394a
flees Charlottesville IV–8b
fossils V–195a
French Revolution III–456a
Garden Book II–390b
Genêt mission III–159b; IV–169b
implied powers III–348a–49a
interchangeable manufacture III–441a
Jeffersonian Democracy III–495b
Jeffersonian Republicans VI–94a
Kentucky Resolutions V–353a; VII–198a
Lafayette's visit IV–84a
law education IV–120b
library I–333a; II–107b, 108b
lotteries IV–190b
mammal studies IV–231b
Mazzei letter IV–279b
Mecklenburg Declaration of Independence IV–282a
Mediterranean Fund IV–299b
Missouri Compromise IV–379a
moldboard plow I–34a
Monticello IV–405a–b
national capital location I–448b
National Gazette IV–463b; V–69b
Natural Bridge of Virginia V–5a
natural rights doctrine V–7b
Notes on the State of Virginia III–26b–27a; IV–179a
Ordinance of 1784 III–98b; V–162b
painting collection II–101a
patents V–225b–26a
philosophy V–287a
plow VI–335a
political parties V–223a
potatoes V–376b
prerevolutionary imperial idea III–346b
Proclamation of Neutrality V–36b
proposed western states III–496b; VII–74a–b
public lands V–443b–44a
public school system II–396a
recognition policy VI–54b–55a
religious liberty VI–80b
Revolution VI–107a
revolutionary war debts I–208b; II–149b, 302a
right of revolution VI–121b
slavery I–135a
State Department VI–388b
University of Geneva II–396a
University of Virginia II–396a, 398a; VII–156a, 197b
vice–presidency VII–179 (table)

Virginia and Kentucky Resolutions I–87a, 417a; VI–397a
Virginia capitol VI–137a
Virginia Company of London records VII–201a
Virginia Resolves VII–203a
western land policy II–166a
XYZ affair VII–347b
Yazoo land fraud IV–99a
See also Republicans, Jeffersonian
—*President:*
Adams' judicial appointments IV–335b
Algiers tribute III–168a
amnesty I–114b
architecture of capital I–162b–63a
army and navy cutback II–313a
Barbary Wars VII–111b
bimetallism I–301a
Bollman case I–327b
broad construction of Constitution II–327a
Burr conspiracy I–387b–88a
Burr trial V–397b
campaign of 1800 I–33a, 94b, 388a, 417a–b; II–189a, 325b, 409a; III–4b–5a, 494b–95a; VI–250a; VII–131b
campaign of 1804 I–417b
Chesapeake–Leopard incident II–16a
climate study II–75b
Coast and Geodetic Survey II–87a–b; V–134a
Corps of Engineers II–449b
Croswell libel suit II–266a–b; IV–139b
Dunbar's expedition II–381a
embargo I–120b; II–41a, 436a–37a; III–5a, 67b, 411b, 455b; IV–266b, 449b; V–34b, 38b, 83a, 105a; VI–104b, 133a, 164b, 347b; VII–87a, 233b
entangling alliances II–452b
Essex Junto II–464a
Florida VI–359b
foreign policy IV–399b
Freeman's expedition III–108a
government appointments I–145b
gunboat construction V–19a
impressment of seamen III–350a
inaugural address II–452b
Indian factory system I–192b
Indian territory III–389a, 393b
internal improvements III–147b
isolationism III–480a
judiciary IV–228a
Latin-American independence wars IV–115b
Lewis and Clark Expedition I–170a; IV–136a; V–164b; VII–271a
Library of Congress IV–146a
Louisiana government V–173b
Louisiana Purchase I–126a; II–313a, 327a; IV–196b, 198a; VI–150b, 211a; VII–36b, 83a
Marbury v. *Madison* IV–248b
Miranda's intrigues IV–361b
Monroe–Pinkney Treaty IV–402b
Napoleonic Wars III–234a
national defense II–313a
National Intelligencer III–202a
Nonimportation Act V–104b
Ohio statehood V–123a
political patronage VI–375a,b
Quids VI–3b
revenue VII–5a
river and harbor improvements VI–145b
Sedition Act VI–255a
Shahaka visit VI–195b
silver dollars IV–394a
states' rights II–325b
Supreme Court VI–447b
third-term doctrine VII–53b
warships VII–240a
West Florida IV–382b
West Point II–313a; IV–340b
White House VII–291b
Woodward plan of Detroit II–338b
Jefferson Airplane (mus.) IV–441a
JEFFERSON BARRACKS (Mo.) **III–494a**; I–287a
supply V–375b
JEFFERSON-BURR ELECTION DISPUTE (1801) **III–494b**; I–94b, 388a, 417a–b; III–4b–5a; VII–131b
Jefferson City (Mo.) II–273b; V–403a
Jefferson County (Ky.) VI–173b
Jefferson County (N.Y.) IV–219b
Jefferson Fork (Missouri Riv.) IV–136b
JEFFERSONIAN ARCHITECTURE III–495a
JEFFERSONIAN DEMOCRACY III–495b; II–144b, 325b
agrarian movement I–32b
antibank movement III–101b
Hartford Wits III–259b
Kentucky IV–40b
natural rights doctrine IV–140a
Pennsylvania V–247a
primogeniture V–408a
Virginia VII–194b
Jeffersonian Republicans. *See* Democratic-Republicans; Republicans, Jeffersonian
Jefferson Memorial VII–246b
Jefferson National Expansion Memorial VI–194b
Jefferson River IV–378a, 379b
JEFFERSON'S PROPOSED STATES III–496b; VII–74a–b
JEFFERSON TERRITORY III–497a; II–128a
Jeffersonton (Va.) I–382a
Jeffrey, Edward Charles (bot.) I–349a
Jeffries, David (landowner) V–242a
Jeffries, G. (au.) VII–175b
Jeffries, James J. (pugilist) V–422b
Jeffries, John (physic.) I–248a
Jeffrie's Ford (Pa.) I–360a
JEHOVAH'S WITNESSES III–497b; IV–358b
Jello I–487b
Jelly industry II–43b
Jemez (N.Mex.) III–367b; V–460a
Jemez River I–8a
Pueblo V–460a
Jemison, Mary. *See* White Woman of the Genesee
Jenckes, Joseph V–230b
Jenifer, Daniel of St. Thomas (pol.) I–85b; II–203b
Jenkins, Charles Francis (inv.) IV–417a; VII–21a
Jenkins, Charles J. (pol.) III–171a, 171b
Jenkins, Robert (seaman) III–498a
JENKINS' EAR, WAR OF (1739–43) **III–498a**; II–126b, 298a; III–168a
Battle of Bloody Marsh I–323a
debatable land II–298a
JENKINS FERRY, BATTLE AT (1864) **III–498a**; V–402b; VI–63a
Jenkins Laboratories (Washington, D.C.) VII–21a
Jenkins Television Corporation VII–21a
Jenkins v. *Georgia* (1974) III–106a
Jenks, Joseph (mfr.) III–472a
Jenner, Albert E. VII–238a
Jenner, Alfred (law.) III–344b
Jenner, Edward (physic.) V–273b; VI–315b
Jenness, J. C. (off.) VII–215b
Jennewein, Paul (sculp.) VI–244a
Jenney, Elisha (cler.) III–331b
Jenney, William Le Baron (arch.) II–17b; VI–299a
Jennings, Abraham (mer.) IV–396a
Jennings, O. B. (ind.) VI–382b
Jennings, Paul (labor leader) IV–76a
Jennings, Robert (vet.) VII–176b
Jennison, Charles R. (off.) III–493a
Jennison, Doc IV–377b
Jensen, J. H. D. (phys.) V–302b
Jerkins, leather II–370b
Jerky III–51a; IV–280b
Jerome (Ariz.) I–172b
Jerome (Ark.) III–491a
Jerome, Chauncey (inv.) II–78a, 79b
Jerome, William Travers (law.) III–150a
Jersey (fabric) II–371b
Jersey (Channel Is.) V–42b
Jersey cattle I–471b, 472a; II–281a–b
Jersey Central Lines VI–36a
Jersey Central Railroad II–350b; V–456a
Jersey City (N.J.) I–343a; V–57b; VI–429b
Lincoln Highway IV–156a
porcelain III–183b
pottery III–184a; V–379b
Jersey Homesteads (N.J.) VI–426b
Jersey Porcelain and Earthenware Company III–183b
JERSEY PRISON SHIP III–498b; V–418b
Jerusalem III–482a; V 4b–
Jerusalem Community II–147a
Jervis, John (eng.) I–442b
JESSIE SCOUTS III–498b
Jessup, Philip C. (dipl.) VII–310b
Jessup family IV–200a
JESUIT MISSIONS III–498b; III–385b
Arizona I–172a, 172a; VII–125b
Arkansas I–174a
Chicago II–17a
Council Bluffs II–241b
coureurs de bois II–246a
Florida III–41a; IV–302b
Fort Beauharnois I–281b, 381b
Georgia III–170a
Green Bay III–225b
Huronia IV–239b
Kaskaskia IV–31b
Mackinac Island IV–330a
Montana IV–403a
Mount Desert IV–226a, 422b
Pacific IV–364b
Penobscot region III–120b
Pima V–314a,b
Pious Fund controversy V–318a
Saint Ignace VI–190b
Saint Mary's V–178b
Sault Sainte Marie VI–219b
Southwest IV–367a,b

JESUIT *RELATIONS*
III–501a; II–458b; III–154b; IV–330a
maps VII–73b
JESUITS III–501a
Acadia I–6a
colonial Catholics I–467a
Great Lakes III–216a
Indian education III–379b
Indian religion III–223a, 251a
Maryland III–94b
Mississippi Valley I–452a
New England I–465b
JESUP, FORT (La.)
III–501b
Jesup, Thomas S. (off.)
IV–205a; VI–260b–61a
Jesup North Pacific Expedition (1897–1902) V–337a
Jesus, Society of. *See* Jesuits
Jesus People II–142b
Jet (dress) II–372a
Jetersville (Va.) I–146b; VI–186b
Jet propulsion I–52a
JET PROPULSION LABORATORY
III–502a; I–212b; IV–459a
Jet Star (transport plane) I–52b
Jewel Cave (S.Dak.) I–313a
Jewel Cave National Monument V–217b
Jewelry II–422b; V–9b; VI–133a
Jewett, Frank B. (elec. eng.) V–137a
Jewett, Sarah Orne (au.) IV–163a
Jewish Chautauqua Society II–1b
Jewish Joint Distribution Committee VII–330a
Jewish novel IV–165a
Jewish Theological Seminary Association IV–11a
Jewish Welfare Board VII–362b
Jewry, European
World War II III–481b
Jews
House Un-American Activities Committee III–308b
immigration III–334b, 339a, 340b, 342a
Ku Klux Klan enmity IV–58b
Morocco IV–221a
Nazi persecution III–158b
slums VI–314a
See also Judaism, American
Jews, Russian V–342a
Jew's harp III–140b
Jewtraw, Charles (athlete) V–154a
JHU Studies in Historical and Political Science IV–2b
Jicarilla Apache (Indians) I–141b; II–133b
Jig (dance) II–287a
"Jiggs and Maggie" (comic strip) V–72a
Jigs (tools) IV–272a
"Jim Crow" (char.) IV–359b
JIM CROW LAWS
III–502b; I–21a; II–54a, 56b; III–437b, 438a; IV–208a
Black Codes I–310b
court tests I–29a
Louisville housing IV–461a
Niagara movement V–93a
slave insurrections VI–303a
Jiménez, Fortún (navig.) IV–199b
Jimi Hendrix Experience (mus.) IV–441a
Jimsonweed VII–65a,b
JIMSONWEED CULT
III–503a
JINGOISM III–503b
Jivaro (Indians) VI–224b
J. J. Newberry and Company III–33a
J Jour II–297a
J. M. White (steamboat) VI–408b
Joachimsthal (coin) II–94b
JOB CORPS III–503b; III–76a; V–135b; VI–172a, 328b
Jocelyn, Henry (col. gov.) III–200a
JOCKEY HOLLOW (N.J.)
IV–1a; IV–413b
Jodo-Shinshu sect V–171b
"JOE BOWERS" (song)
IV–1a; I–247a
Joffre, Joseph (off.) I–246b; II–311a
Joffrey, Robert (dancer) II–289b
Jogues, Isaac (miss.) III–216a, 499a; VI–219b, 443a
Johannsen, Wilhelm (geneticist) III–157b
John (Eng. k.) III–18a; IV–224a
John (ship) I–333a
John XXIII (Pope) VI–79b
JOHN, FORT (Wyo.)
IV–1b; II–34a; IV–108a
John Ames Office Building (Boston) I–164a
JOHN BIRCH SOCIETY
IV–1b
"John Brown's Body" (song) I–277a
John Bull (locomotive) VI–25a
John Carter Brown Library (Brown Univ.) III–285a; IV–145b
John Day Fossil Beds National Monument V–217b
John E. Fogarty International Center IV–465b
John F. Kennedy Center for the Performing Arts VI–319b
John F. Kennedy Library I–167b–68a
John Forbes and Company III–59a
John F. Slater Fund III–82b; V–231b
John Gilpin (ship) I–448a
John Hancock (ship) VI–142a
"John Henry" (song) I–247b
John Laird and Sons IV–85a
John Martin Reservoir IV–28a
JOHNNIAC (computer) II–156a
Johnnycake II–226a
John of the Cross, Saint I–455b
John P. Kennedy (ship) VI–142a
John Robinson's Circus II–41a
Johns, Jasper (paint.) II–107a; V–193a, 414a
Johns Hopkins Hospital III–307a; IV–284b, 292a
nursing school V–126b
Johns Hopkins Studies in Historical and Political Science (jour.) V–347b
JOHNS HOPKINS UNIVERSITY IV–2a; I–250a; II–115a, 399b, 470b; III–423b; IV–261b
bacteriology I–241a
biochemistry I–303b
chemistry II–11b
hockey III–287b
library IV–145b
medical school IV–284b, 286a, 298a; V–306b–07a
oceanography V–135a
Phipps Psychiatric Clinic IV–306a
polio research V–340b
political science V–347b, 349a
psychology V–441b
public health V–447b
School of Hygiene and Public Health III–325b
scientific education VI–232a, 237b–38a
Johns Hopkins University Press IV–2b
Johnson, Fort (S.C.) I–497a
Johnson, Allen (hist.) II–340b; III–281b
Johnson, Andrew II–175 (table); IV–453a; V–108a, 395 (table); VII–25b
apprenticeship I–148a
Committee on the Conduct of the War II–140a
Crittenden resolution II–265a
Fishing Creek Confederacy III–32a
homestead movement III–296a
Senate seat VI–249b
vice-presidency VII–179 (table)
War Democrats VII–229b
—*President:*
amnesty I–115a
campaign of 1864 I–421b–22a; VI–92b; VII–146a
Confederate lands III–103b
Davis, Jefferson II–294b–95a
Dominican Republic II–360b, 362a
Garland pardon III–153a
impeachment I–91b, 115b; III–344a–b, 345b; VI–57a
Indian peace commissions III–378a
Johnson-Clarendon Convention I–73a
Lincoln assassination IV–155a
Maysville veto IV–279b
Nast cartoons IV–454b
National Union Convention IV–472b
Proclamation of Amnesty V–425a
Radical Republicans VI–11a–b
Reconstruction I–71b; II–179a; IV–6a, 369a, 376a; VI–56a–57a,b, 59a; VII–54a, 213a
removal power VI–84b
Republican party VI–93a
Soldiers and Sailors convention VI–336a
Supreme Court VI–448b
"swing round the circle" VI–454b
Tenure of Office Act VII–31b
test laws VII–34b, 35a
Johnson, Charles S. (au.) I–30a
Johnson, C. L. (av. eng.) I–52b
Johnson, Edward (col.) III–280a; IV–161a
Johnson, Edward (off.) IV–212b
Johnson, Edward Austin (pol.) I–29b
Johnson, Eldridge R. (mfr.) V–290a
Johnson, Evan M. (off.) V–147a
Johnson, Fort (Ill.) II–406a
Johnson, Fort (S.C.) I–496a
Johnson, Frank L. (nav. off.) V–460b
Johnson, Frank W. (off.) IV–274a
Johnson, George A. (expl.) II–129b
Johnson, Guy (Indian agent) III–387b, 388a, 400a; V–90b
Johnson, Henrietta (art.) V–185b
Johnson, Henry (nav. off.) IV–136b; VI–128b
Johnson, Herschel v. (jur.) I–421a
Johnson, Hiram W. (pol.) I–406b, 408a, 427b; III–480a; V–428b
Johnson, Horace III–291b
Johnson, Hugh S. (law., off.) I–324b; IV–469a; V–44b
Johnson, James (fur trapper) IV–236b
Johnson, James Weldon (au.) I–30a; IV–166b, 166b, 461a

Johnson, J. B. (civ. eng.) I–287b
Johnson, J. B. (off.) II–379b
Johnson, J. J. (bus.) V–241b
Johnson, John (off.) I–398a; IV–86b; V–172b; VI–441a
Johnson, John A. (Jack) (pugilist) V–422b, 423a
Johnson, John G. (law.) II–103a–b
Johnson, Jonathan Eastman (art.) II–103b
Johnson, Lady Bird (Claudia Alta) II–188b; VII–292a
Johnson, Lyndon Baines I–474b; II–177 (table); V–380a, 396 (table), 397a; VII–40b
floor leader III–38a
presidential library III–284b
succeeds to presidency I–430b
vice-presidency I–430b; VII–180a
—President:
Advisory Commission on Civil Disorders I–31b
AFL–CIO I–103a
Alliance for Progress IV–114a
antiwar demonstrations VII–254a
Arab–American relations I–150a
backlash I–239a
Baker, Bobby I–244a
cabinet I–400a
campaign of 1964 I–431a, 432b–33a; VI–93b; VII–134b, 210a
China policy II–28a
civil disorders IV–457b
civil rights legislation II–55a–b, 58b–59a; V–329b
conservation policy II–188b
consumer protection II–209a
Detroit riots IV–258b
Dominican Republic II–361b–62a
expenditures III–8b, 205b
foreign aid III–62a
foreign policy III–70a–b
Great Society II–472b; III–222b; IV–76b, 428b
Honolulu Conference III–297b
Indian education III–380a
Indian reservations VI–97a,b
Job Corps III–503b
Johnson Doctrine IV–4b
King, Martin Luther, assassination IV–46a
Labor and Commerce departments IV–78b
labor's support IV–77a
Manila Conference IV–239b
Medicare IV–289b
military draft II–368a
military policy IV–344a
Morrissey nomination IV–413a
National Advisory Commission on Civil Disorders VI–9a
National Park Service V–220b
National Security Council VI–389b
New York World's Fair V–89a
"no-win policy" V–124a
Pentagon Papers V–258b
postal service V–374a
Rio Grande VI–143b
Strategic Arms Limitation Talks VI–416b
tariffs VI–53a
taxation VII–9a,b
Tonkin Gulf Resolution VII–72a
Transportation Department VII–98b
vetoes VII–178a
Vietnam War I–63a; II–316a–b, 489a–b; III–264b; V–216a, 237a–b; VII–183a–b, 184a,b, 185b, 224b, 237b
doves II–366a
violence study I–203b; VII–192a
wage and price controls V–401b–02a
War on Poverty II–147b; V–135b, 382a; VI–328b
Warren Commission VII–238a
Johnson, Magnus (pol.) II–491a–b
Johnson, Marmaduke (print.) III–375b; V–410b
Johnson, Nathaniel (off.) I–496a
Johnson, Philip (arch.) I–165b; VI–299a
Johnson, Philip C. II–106a
Johnson, Reverdy (pol.) IV–6a
Johnson, Richard M. (pol.) I–419b; IV–40b, 40b; VII–46a, 179 (table), 231a
Johnson, Robert (col. gov.) VI–347a
Johnson, Samuel (au.) II–340a
Johnson, Samuel (cler.) II–132a–b, 394b
Johnson, Samuel (cler., educ.) V–287a
Johnson, Samuel (lexicog.) VII–14a,b
Johnson, Samuel William (chem.) II–494a
Johnson, Seth III–291b
Johnson, Thomas (jur.) III–100b; VI–445a
Johnson, Virginia E. (psych.) VI–266b
Johnson, William (col. offi.) III–115a,b, 116b, 117a, 387b; IV–4b, 43b; V–100b, 425a; VI–217b
Battle of Bloody Pond I–323a
Bouquet's expedition I–353b
Croghan's Indian expedition II–265b
Crown Point II–267a, 405b
Fort Niagara attack V–90b
Fort Stanwix Treaty VI–385a,b
Four-Mile Strip III–85a
French and Indian War IV–86a, 87b
Great Indian Council at Niagara V–90b
Indiana Company I–278a
Indian affairs I–82a
Iroquois IV–386b; V–85a
Kayoderosseras Patent IV–33a
landholdings IV–98b
peace treaty with Pontiac V–175b
Wyoming Valley VII–347a
Johnson, William (jur.) II–377b; III–178b; VI–445a
Johnson, William Samuel (jur., educ.) II–203b; VI–403b, 404a
Johnson Act (1924) III–333b, 492a
JOHNSON AND GRAHAM'S LESSEE* v. *MCINTOSH (1823) **IV–4a**
Johnson Building (Racine, Wis.) I–165a
JOHNSON–CLARENDON CONVENTION (1869) **IV–4b**; I–73a
Johnson County (Wyo.) VI–181a
Johnson County War. *See* Rustler War
Johnson C. Smith University (Charlotte, N.C.) I–28b; II–113b
Johnson Debt Default Act (1934) IV–134b; VII–332a
JOHNSON DOCTRINE (1965) **IV–4b**
JOHNSON HALL (Johnstown, N.Y.) **IV–4b**
Johnson Library I–167b
Johnson–O'Malley Act (1934) III–380a, 390a
Johnson–Reed Act (1924) III–342b
JOHNSON'S ISLAND **IV–4b**; V–121b, 414a,b
Civil War I–280a, 433a, 439a
Johnston, Albert (pol.) III–342b
Johnston, Albert Sidney (off.) I–181a
Army of Kentucky IV–369b
Battle of Shiloh VI–278b
Mormon expedition IV–249b, 411a; V–177a; VII–162a
Terry's Texas Rangers VII–34b
Johnston, Alexander (hist.) I–196a
Johnston, Anna Fellows (au.) IV–41a
Johnston, George (dipl.) V–232a
Johnston, Joseph E. (off.) I–181a; II–62b; V–116a; VII–182a, 197a
Army of Tennessee IV–365a; VII–26b
Atlanta campaign I–213b
Battle of Averysboro I–232b
Battle of Bentonville I–289b
Battle of Fair Oaks II–482b
Battle of Jackson III–485b
Battle of Kenesaw Mountain IV–36b
Battle of Raymond VI–48b
Battle of Williamsburg VII–301b
Battles at New Hope Church V–56a
feud with Davis II–295a
First Battle of Bull Run I–381a,b
North Carolina I–146b
Peninsular campaign V–245a
replacement by Hood V–238a
surrender I–458b; II–63a, 68b, 165a; VII–27a
Johnston, Samuel (pol.) II–393a
Johnston, William (col.) VII–103a
Johnston, William H. (off.) VII–366b
Johnstown (N.Y.) IV–4b
Johnstown (Pa.) III–286a; V–250a
portage railway I–89a, 443b
See also Johnstown Flood
JOHNSTOWN FLOOD (1889) **IV–5a**; II–351a; III–37a
Johnstown Historical Society IV–4b
John Street Theatre (N.Y.C.) VII–46b
Joiner, C. M. ("Dad") II–389a
"Join or Die" (cartoon) I–464a; V–72b–73a
Joint Allied Finance (World War I) VII–329b
Joint Anti-Fascist Refugee Committee v. *McGrath* (1951) II–378b
Joint Basketball Rules Committee I–272b
Joint Chiefs of Staff V–138a; VI–389b
Joint Chiefs of Staff Intelligence Committee III–439a
Joint Commission on Correctional Manpower and Training V–417a
Joint Commission on Mental Health and Illness V–416b
JOINT COMMISSIONS **IV–5b**
Bayard–Chamberlain Treaty

JOINT COMMISSIONS (cont.)
I–277b
International Joint Commission III–454b
Jürgen Lorentzen prize case IV–20b
revolutionary war III–90a–b
Joint Committee on Interpretation and Complaint III–429a
JOINT COMMITTEE ON RECONSTRUCTION IV–6a; II–179a; VI–56b
Joint Congressional Committee on Atomic Energy III–324a
Joint Distribution Committee, Jewish V–280b
Joint International Boundary Commission IV–240a
JOINT OCCUPATION IV–6a; III–21a, 313b; V–164b–65a, 167b–68a; VII–247b
Oregon Memorial of 1838 V–166b
Oregon Treaty of 1846 V–169b
San Juan Island VI–214a
Joint Oceanographic Institutes Deep Earth Sampling Program III–167b
Joint resolutions. *See* Resolutions, Legislative
Joint-stock companies
Amana Community I–93a
colonization I–16a, 500a
Dorchester Company II–364b
Hopedale Community III–300a
New England Company II–365a
securities marketing II–469b
See also Trading Companies
Joint Stock Companies Acts (1862, 1867) III–467a
JOINT-STOCK LAND BANKS IV–6b
Joliet (Ill.) II–400b
Joliot-Curie, Frédéric (phys.) V–298b, 299a,b
Joliot-Curie, Irène (phys.) V–298b, 299a,b
Jolliet, Louis (expl.) III–99b
Lake Erie II–458b
Lakes-to-Gulf waterway IV–87b
See also Jolliet and Marquette Discovery
JOLLIET AND MARQUETTE DISCOVERY (1673) **IV–6b**; III–89b, 119a, 216a, 272a, 329a; IV–217b; VI–192a; VII–306b
Alton petroglyphs I–91b
Arkansas I–172b
Arkansas River I–174a
Chicago II–17a, 20a
Great Village of the Illinois III–330b
Iowa III–467b
Lake Michigan IV–332b
mapping VII–73b
Memphis IV–301b
Mississippi River IV–372a
Mississippi Valley IV–376b
Missouri River IV–379b
Ohio River V–145a
Prairie du Chien V–387b
Starved Rock VI–388a
Tennessee VII–25a
"Jolly Green Giant" (helicopter) VI–302b
Jolson, Al (act.) IV–418a
Jomini, Baron Henri IV–180a
JONATHAN (nickname) **IV–7b**; VII–47b
Jonathan (Minn.) II–48b
Joncaire, Chabert (off.) IV–213b
Joncaire, Daniel de (col. offi.) V–90a
Joncaire, Louis Thomas de (col. offi.) V–90a
Jones, Anson (pol.) VII–38b
Jones, Catesby ap Roger (nav. off.) IV–396b
Jones, Christopher (seaman) IV–278a
Jones, Donald F. (biol.) I–486a; II–226a
Jones, D. R. (off.) I–381a
Jones, Eliot (econ.) VII–121b
Jones, Gabriel (law.) VII–203a
Jones, George W. (pol.) I–196a; III–468b
Jones, Herman (oil driller) V–318b
Jones, Herschel (jour.) I–333a
Jones, Inigo (arch.) I–161a
Jones, Jacob (nav. off.) V–424a; VII–252b
Jones, Jesse (offi.) III–466b
Jones, John Coffin (offi.) III–263a
Jones, John Gabriel (pioneer) IV–43a
Jones, John Paul (nav. off.) III–21b; V–18b; VI–128b, 129a
Bank of North America I–260b
Bergen prizes I–290b
Bonhomme Richard–Serapis fight I–329b; VII–240a
Ranger–Drake engagement VI–46a
U.S. flag III–34b
Jones, John S. (bus.) IV–129b; VI–176b
Jones, John W. (law.) II–175 (table)
Jones, Joseph W. (inv.) V–290a
Jones, LeRoi. *See* Baraka, Imamu Amiri
Jones, Margaret (col.) VII–309b
Jones, Margo (dir., prod.) VII–50b
Jones, Marvin (pol.) VI–269a
Jones, Owen (antiquary) III–136a
Jones, Robert (fur trader) VI–196a
Jones, Robert Edmond (theat. designer) VII–49b
Jones, Robert T. ("Bobby"), Jr. (golfer) III–197b, 198a
Jones, Sam (Indian) VI–261a
Jones, Samuel M. ("Golden Rule") (pol.) V–142a
Jones, S. J. (sheriff) IV–118b
Jones, Thomas A. (farmer) IV–154b, 155a
Jones, Thomas ap Catesby (nav. off.) I–342b; IV–404b; VII–299a
Jones, Thomas Hudson (arch.) VII–157a
Jones, William (col.) V–250b; VI–70b
Jones, William (mer.) I–261a
Jones, William Carey (law.) IV–254a
Jones, William E. III–332b
JONES ACT (1916) **IV–7b**; II–441a; V–283b
Jones Act (1929) I–339b
Jones and Laughlin Steel Corporation IV–467b
Jonesboro (Ill.) IV–155b
Jonesboro (Tenn.) II–436a; III–98b, 162b; VII–25a
JONES COUNTY, SECESSION OF IV–8a
Jones–Ketcham bill II–477b
Jones v. *United States* (1890) III–417b
JONES* v. *VAN ZANDT (1846) **IV–8a**
Jones–White Act (1929) II–438b; IV–311b
Joplin (Mo.) IV–123a; V–103a
Joplin, Scott (comp.) VI–439b
Joques, Isaac (miss.) V–41a; VII–157a
Jordan I–124b; III–481b, 482a
aerial hijacking III–277b
immigration to U.S. III–341a, 341b
Palestine IV–236b
Jordan, David Starr (zool.) I–131b; III–27b, 28a
Jordan, F. W. (eng.) II–153b
Jordan, Robert (cler.) VII–114b
Jordan, Thomas (off.) VI–373a
Jordan River V–23a; VI–203b
***JORNADA DEL MUERTO* IV–8a**; I–174b
Joseph (Indian) I–281a, 296a; II–74b; III–386b; V–89b
Joseph E. Seagram and Sons II–107a
Joseph H. Hirshhorn Museum and Sculpture Garden II–106a; VI–319b
Josephine Ford (airplane) I–399a
Josephites I–468a
Josephson, Brian (phys.) V–305b
Josephson, Matthew (hist.) VI–157a
Josephson effect V–305b
Joshua Tree National Monument V–217b
Josiah Macy, Jr., Foundation IV–286b
Josselyn, John (trav., writ.) III–26b, 128b; IV–231a, 348a, 423b; VI–244b
Jouett, John, Jr. (off.) IV–8b
JOUETT'S RIDE (1781) **IV–8b**
Journal and Guide (news.) V–76a
Journal der Physik (period.) VI–235a
Journal des sçavans (period.) VI–235a
Journalism
apprenticeship I–148a
Chicago II–18a
Fulbright grants III–131a
women VII–317b
See also Newspapers
Journalists, Society of Professional: Sigma Delta Chi V–77b
Journal of Biological Chemistry II–11b
***JOURNAL OF CONGRESS* IV–8b**; II–199a
Journal of Dental Research II–330b
Journal of Experimental Medicine IV–3a
Journal of Experimental Psychology V–442b
Journal of Geology VI–237a
Journal of Herpetology VI–91b
Journal of Industrial and Engineering Chemistry II–11b
Journal of Industrial Hygiene IV–294a
Journal of Industrial Medicine IV–294a
Journal of Parapsychology V–213a
Journal of Pharmacology and Experimental Therapeutics IV–3a
Journal of Physical Chemistry II–11b
Journal of Speculative Philosophy V–287b
Journal of the American Chemical Society II–11b
Journal of the American Dental Association II–330b
Journal of the American Veterinary Medical Association (period.) VII–176a
Journal of the Franklin Institute III–99a
Journal of the Times VII–81a
Journals, scientific. *See* Scientific Periodicals
Journals of the Continental Congress IV–8b; VII–153a–b
Journal Square Transportation Center V–368b

Journeymen
closed shop II–80a
Joutel, Henri (off.) III–119a
Joyce, James (au.) I–479a; IV–164b, 190a
Joy loading machines II–85b
J. P. Morgan and Company III–64b, 79b
Juan de Fuca Strait I–121b; II–219b; V–180a; VI–214a
Indians IV–228b
Oregon Treaty of 1846 V–169b
Puget Sound (Wash.) V–462a
Vancouver's exploration VII–166a
Juan José (Indian) IV–236b
Juáres, Juan (miss.) III–94a
Juarez (Mex.) II–433a
Juárez, Benito (states.) II–65b; IV–325b, 361a; VI–274b
Juba (dancer) II–287a
JUCHEREAU'S TANNERY IV–9a
Judah (schooner) VI–216a
Judah, Theodore (eng.) I–406a
Judaic studies IV–12a
Judaism
Bahaism teachings V–172a
JUDAISM, AMERICAN IV–9a; VI–79a
Afro-Americans I–24a
American-Jewish Historical Society III–279b
antebellum South VI–343a
colonial society II–125b
colonial suffrage VI–434a
Connecticut II–181a
Louisiana II–91b
Newport V–65b
newspapers V–75b
organized crime II–261b, 263a
Protestant moral standards IV–408a
religious liberty VII–68b
Rhode Island VI–132a
schools II–394b, 397a, 399b; VI–228b
settlement houses VI–330b
suffrage VI–431a
voting behavior VII–210b
World War I relief VII–330a
Young Men's and Young Women's Hebrew Associations VII–362b
See also Israeli-American Relations
Juday, Chancey (sci.) II–391a
Judge, William Q. (theosophist) VII–52a
Judge Advocate General, Office of the V–18a
Judges
circuit court II–39b–40a
compensation I–339a; II–202a
district court II–39b–40a
journalistic critics III–105a
Supreme Court II–39b–40a
term II–202a
"Judges' Cave" VI–70b
Judicial Conference IV–17b
Judicial Procedure Reform Act (1937) V–48a,b
JUDICIAL REVIEW IV–12a; III–3a–b; IV–15b; V–352a
administrative agencies I–12b
agency adjudication I–13b
colonies I–145a
commerce clause II–135b–37a
Ex parte McCardle IV–209a
Habeas Corpus Act VII–35a
Holmes v. *Walton* III–292a
Judiciary Act (1801) IV–19b
Legal Tender Acts IV–20a
Marbury v. *Madison* IV–248b
martial law IV–258b
National Labor Relations Board IV–467b
quasi-judicial agencies V–471b
rule of reason VI–168b
state constitutions VI–392a
state legislation IV–19a–b
statutory law VI–406a
Supreme Court VI–447a
Trevett v. *Weeden* VI–132b; VII–117a
unions III–407a
See also Bill of Rights
JUDICIARY IV–15a; II–178a
American Bar Association I–99b
American Samoa VI–205a
Arizona recall clause VI–401b
checks and balances II–4b
circuit courts II–39b–40a
civil rights II–56b–58a
colonial II–120b–21a
common-law powers IV–36b
Confederacy II–160a
Constitution II–178a, 195a, 202a–b, 204b, 453b
Declaration of Independence II–307a
district attorneys IV–21b
divorce II–356b
domestic relations courts II–360a
Federalists III–5a
federal laws VII–198b
guarantee of fair procedures II–377b
impeachment III–344a–b
judicial review IV–12a
Judiciary Act (1789) IV–19a
Judiciary Act (1801) IV–19b
jury trial IV–21a
justice of the peace IV–22b
juvenile courts IV–23a
Kentucky old court–new court struggle V–150b
Marbury v. *Madison* IV–248b
midnight judges IV–335b
military law IV–342b
Morrissey nomination IV–413a
naturalization V–6b, 7a
Ohio Sweeping Resolution VI–454b
packing bills VI–448a–49a
patents V–226a,b
patronage V–227b
Philippines V–283a
poor relief VI–74b
prison reform V–417a–b
prize courts V–422a
Progressive movement V–428b
public utility regulation V–457a
Puerto Rico V–461b
punishment for contempt I–117b
Roosevelt reorganization V–47b–48a
scandals V–346b
separation of powers IV–209a; V–385b
state constitutions VI–391a
state government VI–396b
statutes of limitations VI–405b
Supreme Court VI–443b
surrogate's court VI–450a
territorial governments VII–32a
Virginia Plan II–194a
Virgin Islands VII–204a
JUDICIARY ACT OF 1789 IV–19a; II–195b, 460a; IV–15b; VI–443b
habeas corpus III–236b
office of attorney general IV–21b
Supreme Court size VI–448a
writ of mandamus IV–249a
JUDICIARY ACT OF 1801 IV–19b; IV–228a; VI–448a
Judiciary Act of 1925 VI–444b
Judiciary Committee of the House of Representatives III–344b–45a
Judo
Olympic Games V–154a
Judson, Adoniram (miss.) I–265a
Judson, Edward Z. C. ("Ned Buntline") (au.) II–341b
Judson Memorial Church (N.Y.C.) VII–51a
Judson Poets' Theater (N.Y.C.) VII–51a
Jueces del Campos II–247a
Juengling, Frederick (engr.) VII–319b
JUILLIARD* v. *GREENMAN (1884) **IV–20a**; IV–133a; VI–94b–95a
Juin, Alphonse (off.) III–235b
Jukeboxes V–290b
"JUKES" FAMILY IV–20a; III–158b
Julesburg (Colo.) I–357b; VI–355a
Julian, George W. (pol.) II–140a; VI–11b
Julius Caesar (play) VII–50a
Jumano (Indians) IV–302b, 367b
"Jumbo Dynamo" II–414a
Jumbo Mill I–487a
Jumel, Eliza Bowen VI–218a
Jumel Mansion (N.Y.C.) I–161b; III–253b
Jumper (Indian) VI–259b
Jumping Frog of Calaveras County V–336a
JUMPING-OFF PLACES IV–20b; III–353b
Junandot, Fort (Ohio) VI–208b
Junction City (Kans.) VI–35a
Juneau (cruiser) VII–242b
Juneau (Alaska) II–347b; III–76b
Jungle, The III–53a; IV–281a, 424b; V–466a; VI–414b
Juniata River I–88b, 222b; III–448a; V–250a
Juniata Valley V–184a
Junior colleges II–115a, 400b
See also Education
Junior Davis Cup VII–29b
Junior high school II–400a–b
Junior Red Cross VI–62a
Junior Reserve Officers' Training Corps VI–98b
Junior Wightman Cup VII–29b
Juniper VII–59b
JUNIUS, LETTERS OF (1769–72) **IV–20b**
"Junk sculpture" VI–244a
Juno Beach (Fr.) V–110b, 111a
Junto (social club) IV–144b
Jupiter (locomotive) V–430b
Jupiter (planet)
radio noise I–212b
space probes I–210b
Jupiter missile I–62a; IV–363b
***JÜRGEN LORENTZEN* PRIZE CASE** (1861) **IV–20b**
Jurimetrics IV–121b
Jury service
Afro-Americans III–59b
JURY TRIAL IV–21a
Bill of Rights I–94a, 299a
civil rights II–53b
colonies I–145a
common-law suits II–204b
constitutional guarantee II–202a
contempt cases IV–69a
Declaration of Independence II–307a
due process clause IV–14b

JURY TRIAL (cont.)
fugitive slaves V–263b, 263b
Great Britain II–191a
Holmes v. *Walton* III–292a
juvenile courts IV–23b
sedition VI–255a,b
state constitutions I–278a
territorial government VII–32b
Texas VII–37b
West Jersey VII–278b
Jus sanguinis II–42b, 476a
Jussieu, Bernard de (bot.) I–349a
Jus soli II–42a
Just, Alexander (chem.) IV–89a
JUSTICE, DEPARTMENT OF IV–21b; I–399b; II–498a; IV–17b
antitrust I–140a; II–230a; III–290b
desegregation of airports III–107b
Federal Bureau of Investigation II–503a–b
Law Enforcement Assistance Administration V–417a
loyalty testing IV–202b
naturalization V–6b
Pentagon Papers V–258b
police activities V–339a
southern elections VII–209b
tidelands ruling VII–58a
Watergate VII–254b, 255b
Justice, International Court of. *See* International Court of Justice
JUSTICE OF THE PEACE IV–22b; II–247a; IV–18a
colonial judiciary IV–15a
hundred III–317b
territorial courts VII–32a
"Justices of the quorum" IV–22b
Justin Morgan (horse) III–303b
Jute IV–310b
Jutland, Battle of (1916) V–20a
Jupiter (collier) I–54b
JUVENILE COURTS IV–23a; II–360a; VI–331a
Chicago II–18a, 18a
domestic relations courts II–360a
Juvenile delinquency II–402a; VII–294b, 312b
Juvenile Miscellany (mag.) IV–223a
Juvigny (Fr.) V–147a
J. W. Hampton, Jr., and Company v. *United States* (1928) VI–464b

K

K-74 (blimp) II–345a
Kachina III–392a
Kadiak Island. *See* Kodiak Island
Kaesong (Kor.) IV–56a
Kaga (aircraft carrier) IV–336b, 337a
Kagoshima (Jap.) VI–279a
Kahanamoku, Duke P. (athlete) V–154b
Kahn, Louis (arch.) I–165b
Kahn, Otto H. (banker) III–79b
Kaibab Plateau VII–297b
Kaiser, Henry J. (ind.) III–80b
Kaiser Aluminum and Chemical Company V–103b
Kajioka, Sadamichi (nav. off.) II–225a; VII–219a
KAKIATE PATENT IV–24a; III–313a
Kalakaua (k.) III–263b
KALAMAZOO CASE (1874) **IV–24b**; II–398b
Kalanianaole, Jonah Kuhio (pr.) III–264b
Kalb, Johann (off.) I–412a; VI–126b, 129a, 351b
Kales Plan. *See* Missouri Plan
Kalinin, Michael I. VI–179b
Kalispel (Indians) III–500a
Kallet, Arthur V–466b
"KALLIKAK" FAMILY IV–24b
Kallman, McKinnell and Knowles I–166a
Kall River III–314a–b
Kalm, Pehr (bot.) I–348b; III–29b; IV–79b, 231a–b; V–326a, 376b
Kalmar Nyckel (ship) V–80a
Kalmbach, Herbert W. (law.) VII–254a
Kalmus, Herbert T. (inv.) IV–418a
Kamaiakan (Indian) VII–350a
Kamaing–Mogaung corridor (Bur.) IV–447a
Kamchatka (Russ.)
sea otters VI–247b
World War II IV–54a–b
Kamehameha I (k.) III–263a
Kamehameha III (k.) III–263b
Kamiah (Idaho) II–74b
Kamikaze V–27a, 147b; VII–2a
Kamin, Reuben (biochem.) I–303b
Kaministikwia, Fort (Minn.) VI–443a
Kaministikwia portage II–380a
Kaministikwia River VI–443a
Kanagawa, Treaty of (1854) V–263a
Kanakuk (Indian prophet). *See* Shawnee Prophet
Kanauga (Ohio) II–350b
Kanawha, Battle of the. *See* Point Pleasant, Battle of
Kanawha River I–497b; II–363a
Cherokee claims III–251a
Dunmore's War V–335b
Fincastle County III–24b
Fort Randolph VI–45b
Indian lands IV–173a
Iroquois cession VI–385b
James River and Kanawha Canal III–488a
oil deposits IV–44a
petroleum V–266b
KANAWHA SALT WORKS (W.Va.) **IV–25a**; II–5b; VI–202b
Burning Spring I–387a
petroleum V–266b
Kanawha Valley VII–281a,b
Kandinsky, Vasili (art.) II–104b, 105a
Kane, Elisha Kent (nav. off.) V–336b
Kanesville (Iowa) II–241b
Kankakee River IV–109b
Kansa (Indians) I–354b; III–363b, 365a, 383b, 500a; IV–25a; V–155a
KANSAS IV–25a; III–353b; VI–355a, 393 (table)
alien landholding I–87a,b
antislavery activity III–256b; IV–28a
army peacekeeping I–184b, 309b, 310a
blizzards I–320b
Blue Lodges I–325b
Blue Sky laws I–325b–26a
Bluestem Pastures I–326a
Border War IV–248a–b
buffalo VII–297a
Buford expedition I–376b
cattle I–1b, 38b; II–249a; IV–184b, 280b; VII–40b
Chisholm Trail II–477b
Citizens' Alliances II–42a
Civil War III–376a; V–222a, 471a
claim associations II–70b
coal mines II–85a
Colorado water dispute III–478a
Comanche II–133b
Coronado expedition III–211a
Council Grove II–242b
county-seat wars II–245b
cowtowns II–251b
Creek Indians III–400a
declaratory judgment laws II–309b
Delaware Indians II–321a
Dodge City II–358b
Dodge City Trail II–358b
Dust Bowl II–382a
emigrants I–283b; V–51a
entail of estate II–452b
exploration I–96b; II–184b, 228b; III–119a
Farmers' Alliance II–493a
farmers' debts V–365a
fire insurance rates III–430b
floods II–351b
Fort Atkinson I–193a, 213b
Fort Hays III–266b
Fort Larned IV–109a
Fort Mann IV–240a
Fort Riley VI–141b
Fort Scott VI–241a
Fort Wallace VII–221a
Fort Zarah VII–368a
Fowler expedition III–88a
Fox Indians III–88b
Free-State party IV–28a
Frémont explorations VII–272a
Grange stores II–220b
Gran Quivira V–155a
homestead movement VII–59b
Indian Country III–379b, 384a
Indian raids VII–252b
Indian relocation III–394b
Indian wars I–283a; VII–239b
industrial court VII–311a–b
interstate river compacts IV–28a
irrigation III–478b
Jayhawkers III–493a
Jefferson Territory III–497a
Jesuit missions III–500a
Kansas–Nebraska Act IV–28b
Kansas Pacific Railroad IV–30b
land speculation IV–101a
Leavenworth IV–129a–b
liquor laws IV–425a
livestock industry I–326a
midcontinent oil region IV–334a
minimum-wage IV–353a
Missouri River IV–380a
natural gas IV–123a
Nonpartisan League V–106b
oil II–408a; IV–333b; V–270a; VI–356b
Oklahoma panhandle V–205b
open-range cattle period V–159b–60a
Oregon Trail V–168b
Osage V–173b
Pawnee Rock V–230b
Pikes Peak gold rush V–311b
Pike's southwestern expedition V–312a
pioneers V–317a
Populist party V–365b
Pottawatomie massacre V–378b
prairie dogs V–387b
Quakers V–470a,b
railroads VI–35a
recall VI–51a
Red Legs VI–62b
Red River Indian War VI–64a

Roosevelt (Theodore) tour VI–378a
salt VI–202a,b
settlement IV–338b; VII–113b, 284a,b
ship parts II–438a
slavery I–283b, 376b; IV–377b; V–360a–b
Smith explorations VI–318a
Sons of the South VI–339b
Squatters' Claim Association VII–187b
stage lines I–485a
statehood I–78b
state line IV–27b
Sumner's Cheyenne expedition VI–439b
tornadoes VII–76a
Treaties of Saint Louis III–383b
tree planting VII–114a
veterinary medicine VII–176b
voting behavior VII–210a
water rights IV–27b
westward movement I–453a
wheat III–44a, 45b; VII–286a
Wichita VII–294a
woman's suffrage III–91b; VII–315a
Wyandotte Constitution VII–345a
See also Border War
Kansas, City of. *See* Kansas City
"Kansas, Crime Against" *See* Brooks–Sumner Affair
KANSAS, PROHIBITION IN IV–26b; V–429b
Kansas, Town of (Mo.) IV–27a,b
Kansas, University of IV–300b
Kansas Agricultural Experiment Station VII–286b
Kansas City (Kans.) III–119b; IV–27b; VII–345a
cattle I–1b
Fort Osage V–173b
Kansas Pacific Railroad IV–30b
KANSAS CITY (Mo.) **IV–27a**; III–353b; IV–378a
Civil War VII–280b
crime commission II–263b
electric railway VI–40a
federal records center III–284b
flour milling III–44a, 45b
freighting V–177b
meat-packing I–283b; IV–280b
music IV–440a
organized crime II–262b
Pendergast machine I–343a; IV–214a; V–244b
race riots I–32a
railroad rate wars VI–23a
railroads VI–34b, 35a,b, 36a, 37b
Santa Fe Trail VI–215b
skyscrapers VI–299a
Smoky Hill Trail VI–320b
stockyards VI–414a
Veterans of Foreign Wars VII–175a
veterinary medicine VII–176b
Westport II–242b; VII–280a
Kansas City Evening Star (news.) V–73b
KANSAS–COLORADO WATER RIGHTS IV–27b
KANSAS COMMITTEE, NATIONAL IV–28a
KANSAS FREE–STATE PARTY IV–28a; IV–25b, 30a, 31a
Battle of Osawatomie V–174a
Beecher's Bibles VI–270a
Jayhawkers III–493a
Marais des Cygnes massacre IV–248a
National Kansas Committee IV–28a
New England Emigrant Aid Company V–51b
Topeka Constitution VII–72b
Warkarusa War VII–218b
Kansas Historical Society III–278b; IV–25b
KANSAS–NEBRASKA ACT (1854) **IV–28b**; I–145a; III–353b; V–3a, 31a; VI–92b, 307b, 355b; VII–39b
Indian Country III–379b, 384a
Kansas struggle IV–31a
Kansas Territory IV–25b
opposition to I–325b
party disruption I–110a, 139a
popular sovereignty V–360a
states' rights VI–404b
Whig party V–86b
Kansas–Oklahoma Arkansas River Commission VI–402a
KANSAS PACIFIC RAILROAD IV–30b; VI–37b
Abilene I–1b
cattle shipments IV–280b
dry farming II–375b–76a
effect on buffalo I–375a
foreign investments III–65a
Fort Hays III–266b
hide and tallow trade III–274b
Smoky Hill Trail VI–320b
Kansas River II–34b; IV–25a
floods II–351a; III–37a
Fort Riley VI–141b
French exploration IV–379b
French frontier posts V–173a
Indians III–394b
Kansas City (Mo.) IV–27a,b
Nebraska V–31a
Pawnee V–230b
Santa Fe Trail VI–215b
Smoky Hill Trail VI–320a
Sumner's expedition VI–439b
trading post IV–27b
KANSAS STRUGGLE IV–31a; VI–307b, 309a; VII–284a
Battle of Osawatomie V–174a
English Compromise II–450a
Fort Riley VI–141b
Lecompton Constitution IV–130b
New England Emigrant Aid Company V–51a
Quantrill's raid IV–377b
Red Legs VI–62b
states' rights VI–404b
Topeka Constitution VII–72b
Wakarusa War VII–218b
Kansas Territory
emigrant aid movement II–439a
slavery issue I–139a, 341a, 342a
Kansas Valley
free–state migrants IV–31a
freighting route V–177a
Kansas v. *Colorado* (1907) III–417b, 478a
Kant, Immanuel (philos.) V–287a, 441b; VII–97b
Kaplan, Mordecai (prof.) IV–11a
KAPOSIA, BATTLE OF (1842) **IV–31b**; VI–295a
Kappel, Frederick R. (bus.) V–374a
Karankawa (Indians) III–367a; VII–36b
Karcher, J. C. (phys.) V–272a
Karlskrona (Swed.) II–375a
Karlsruhe (Ger.) II–45a
Kármán, Theodore von (phys.) I–52a; III–502a; V–303b
Karnes Well (oil) II–464b
Karok (Indians) III–362a, 363a; VII–367b
Karolik, Maxim II–100b
Kaska (Indians) I–441b; III–360b
KASKASKIA (Ill.) **IV–31b**; III–119a, 329a,b
architecture I–160a
Fort de Chartres I–501a
French exploration I–498b–99a
fur trade III–144a; V–176a
Illinois Herald V–70b
Indian trade I–278a
lead trade VI–189b
revolutionary war I–240a; II–71b; VI–126b; VII–302b
settlement I–100b, 402b
Kaskaskia Indians I–501b; III–329a, 330b, 379b; IV–31b
removal III–394b
Treaty of Greenville III–383a
Treaty of Vincennes III–383b; VII–189b
Kaskaskia River III–329a; IV–31b, 376b
KASSERINE PASS, BATTLE OF (1943) **IV–32a**; V–113a; VII–338a
Kasson, John Adam (dipl.) IV–33a
KASSON TREATIES IV–33a
Kataka (Indians) VI–64a
Kathio, Battle of. *See* Mille Lacs, Battle of
Katlean (Indian) I–76b
Katmai National Monument V–217a
Katsura, Taro (states.) VI–164a, 457b
Katyusha (missile) IV–363a
Katzenbach, Nicholas (law.) VII–224b
Katzenbach v. *McClung* (1964) II–55b, 137b
Katzenbach v. *Morgan* (1966) III–93b
Katzenjammer Kids (comic strip) V–72a
Katz v. *United States* (1967) II–427b
Katz v. *Walkinshaw* (1902) III–478b
Kaufmann (Desert) House (Palm Springs, Calif.) I–165b
Kaukakee River
portage V–367b
Kawana, Koichi (landscape arch.) IV–378b
Kaw River. *See* Kansas River
Kay, John (inv.) II–237b; IV–187b
Kayak I–446a; III–358a, 381a
Kayak Island I–74b
KAYODEROSSERAS PATENT (N.Y.) **IV–33a**
Kazan, Elia (act., dir.) VII–50a
Kazin, Alfred (critic) I–113a; IV–165b
KC–135 (tanker transport plane) I–52b, 237b
K. C. Ranch (Wyo.) VI–181a
KDKA (Pittsburgh) II–424a; VI–15b, 16b
Kean, Edmund (act.) VII–47b
Keaney, Frank (coach) I–273a
Kearney, Denis (labor leader)
Chinese II–29a; III–342a; VII–356b
Workingmen's Party I–406a; IV–33a, 64a
KEARNEYITES IV–33a
Kearny (destroyer) I–214a
KEARNY, FORT (Nebr.) **IV–33b**; III–256a
pony express V–357b, 358a
Sumner's expedition VI–440a
wagon trains VII–218a
KEARNY, FORT PHIL (Wyo.) **IV–33b**; VI–317b
Bozeman Trail I–358a
Fetterman Massacre III–378a

KEARNY, FORT PHIL (cont.)
Red Cloud's War III–17b
Wagon Box fight VII–215b
Kearny, Lawrence (nav. off.) I–125a
China trade mission IV–34b
Chinese trading rights II–29a
Kearny, Philip (off.) I–494a
Kearny, Stephen W. (off.) I–172a; III–468a; IV–323b, 325a; VII–39a
Battle of San Gabriel VI–210b
Battle of San Pasqual VI–214a
Fort Kearny IV–33b
Magee–Kearny expedition IV–223b
Mexican War II–363b, 440b
Santa Fe VI–214b
Stockton quarrel VI–414a
Yellowstone River expedition VII–358a
See also Kearny–Frémont Quarrel; Kearny's March to California III–179b
KEARNY–FRÉMONT QUARREL (1847) **IV–34a**; I–409b, 409b
KEARNY'S MARCH TO CALIFORNIA (1846) **IV–34a**; III–179b; IV–323b–24a; VI–353b
KEARNY'S MISSION TO CHINA (1842) **IV–34b**; II–29a; V–22b
***KEARSARGE* AND *ALABAMA* ENCOUNTER** (1864) **IV–35a**; I–72b; II–63a; VII–147a
Keating, William H. (chem.) III–99a; IV–224b
Keating–Owen Act (1916) III–247a; IV–68b
Keats, John (poet) IV–166b
Keayne, Mr. (shopkeeper) VI–358b
Keayne, Robert (ship capt.) IV–144a
Kedrov, Mikhail S. (off.) I–159a
KEELBOAT IV–35a; I–274b; III–35b; IV–374a; V–184a; VI–148a; VII–100a
Allegheny River I–89a
Arkansas River I–174b
folklore III–48b
Mississippi River IV–372b
Missouri River IV–380a, 381a
New Orleans V–62a
Ohio River VI–147b
Keelboatmen I–267b, 280b
Keelers I–267b
Keep–America–out–of–the–war movement IV–203a
"Keeper of the Wampum" III–475b
Kefauver, Estes (pol.) I–430a; II–262b, 263b; V–468a
Keflavik (Ice.) III–327b
KEGS, BATTLE OF THE (1778) **IV–35b**
Keifer, Joseph W. (law.) II–176 (table)
Keil, William (ref.) I–293a
Keim, Nicholas (mer.) III–252a
Keimer, Samuel (print.) V–68b, 251a
Keith, B. F. (theat. mgr.) VII–167b
Keith, George (Quaker) IV–35b
Keith, Myron R. VI–383a
KEITH CONTROVERSY (1691–99) **IV–35b**
Keller, Helen III–248b
Keller Mansion (Saint Charles Parish, La.) I–160b
Kelley, B. F. (off.) V–281a
Kelley, Clarence M. II–503b
Kelley, Edward J. (pol.) II–18b
Kelley, Oliver Hudson (agric. org.) I–41b; III–210a; V–175a
Kelley, Truman L. (statis.) III–440b
Kellicot, David S. (sci.) II–391b
Kellogg (Idaho) II–350b
Kellogg, Albert (physic., bot.) I–349a
Kellogg, Frank B. (states.) II–491a; V–100a; VI–456a
See also Kellogg–Briand Pact VI–163b
Kellogg, John Harvey (surg.) I–487a–b; V–306a
Kellogg, William K. (cereal mfr.) I–487a–88a
Kellogg, William P. (pol.) IV–336a; V–64a; VII–287a
KELLOGG–BRIAND PACT (1928) **IV–35b**; II–343a, 488b–89a; III–69a, 457a; IV–235a, 401b; V–107a, 159a, 233b–34a; VI–163b; VII–113a
Kellogg's Sanitas Food Company I–487b
Kellogg Toasted Corn Flake Company I–487b–88a
Kelly, Charles T. (labor leader) IV–36a
Kelly, Eleanor Mercein (au.) IV–41a
Kelly, Ellsworth (paint.) V–193b
Kelly, Howard A. (physic.) IV–3a
Kelly, James K. (off.) VII–350b
Kelly, John (nav. off.) V–22b
Kelly, John (pol.) I–424a; V–83b; VI–460a; VII–295a
Kelly, John B., Sr. (athlete) V–154b
Kelly, Walt (cartoon.) V–72b
Kelly, William (ironmaster) III–473a; IV–244a; V–247b
Kelly Air Force Base (Tex.) VI–207b
Kelly Air Mail Act (1925) I–68a, 234a, 236a
KELLY'S FORD (Va.) **IV–36a**
KELLY'S INDUSTRIAL ARMY IV–36a
Kelso (horse) III–305a
Kelvin, Lord (William Thomson) (math., phys.) II–153a; V–92a
Kelvinator Company II–420b, 421a
Kemble, Charles (act.) VII–47b
Kemble, Fanny (Frances Anne) (act.) VII–47b
Kemble, Gouverneur (mfr.) IV–432b
Kemeny, John G. (educ.) II–293a
Kemper, Nathan (adventurer) IV–36b
Kemper, Reuben (adventurer) IV–36b
Kemper, Samuel (adventurer) III–236a; IV–36b
KEMPER RAID (1804) **IV–36b**
Kenai Peninsula I–79b–80a
Kendall, Amos (jour.) I–107b; IV–36b, 51a; VI–85b
Kendall, Edward C. (biochem.) V–100a
Kendall, George (col. offi.) III–488b
KENDALL v. UNITED STATES (1838) **IV–36b**
Kendrew, John C. (molecular biol.) IV–389b, 391b
Kendrick, Douglas B. (physic.) IV–291a
Kendrick, John (navig.) I–15b, 84b; II–28b
Kendrick, John W. (econ.) V–425b
Kenel (S.Dak.) VI–196a
KENESAW MOUNTAIN, BATTLE OF (1864) **IV–36b**; I–213b
Kenly, John R. (off.) VII–304a
Kennan, George (hist.) III–424b
Kennebec County (Maine) IV–48a
Kennebec River
colonial land grants IV–263b
Fort Western VII–269b
Lygonia IV–207b
Norridgewock fight V–111a
Pemaquid Point V–243a
revolutionary war I–193b, 436a
KENNEBEC RIVER SETTLEMENTS IV–37a; II–123b; IV–225b
Fort Halifax III–243b
Gorges' province III–200a
Pejebscot Purchase claims V–242a
Plymouth Company V–333b
Popham Colony I–319b; V–359b
Sagadahoc VI–185b
KENNEBEC TRADING POST (Maine) **IV–37b**; VII–269b
Kennecott, Robert (expl.) VII–367a
Kennecott Copper Corporation IV–466a
Kennedy, Archibald (offi.) II–122a
Kennedy, Edward (pol.) IV–268a, 413a
Kennedy, Jacqueline (Mrs. John F.). *See* Onassis, Jacqueline Kennedy
Kennedy, John F. II–177 (table), 312a; III–260b; IV–268a; V–3b, 396 (table), 396a, 398b
gravesite I–175b
—President:
AFL–CIO I–103a
Alliance for Progress I–89b; IV–114a; VI–345a
ambassadors' authority II–437b
and Congress II–472b
antidelinquency programs II–148a
Arab–American relations I–150a
atomic energy I–217a
backlash I–239a
Bay of Pigs invasion I–278b; II–269b
Berlin Wall I–291b
cabinet I–400a
campaign of 1960 I–430b, 432b; VI–93b
Catholicism I–470a
China policy II–28a
civil defense V–237a
civil rights movement II–55a, 58b, 473a
civil service II–60a
Committee on Equal Employment Opportunity II–456a
conservation policy II–188a
Consumer Advisory Council II–209a
Cuban missile crisis I–180a; II–270a–71a, 343a; IV–113a; V–22b; VII–237a
defense reorganizations I–188a; V–163b
disability V–397a
executive orders II–473a
Far Eastern policy II–489a–b
federal employees IV–75b
foreign aid III–62a
foreign policy III–70a
Foreign Service VI–389a–b
gold III–196a
Halberstam, David V–74b
housing acts VI–328a–b
Indian reservation system VI–97a
Khrushchev summit conference VI–439a,b
Laos III–161b; IV–107a–b
library III–284b
military policy IV–344a
Nassau Pact IV–454a
national defense II–315b–16a

national health insurance IV–289b
National Security Council VI–389b
New Frontier V–53a
"no-win policy" V–124a
reciprocal trade agreements VI–52b–53a
Seattle World's Fair VI–249a
space program I–210a; II–426a; IV–406b–407b; VI–159b
tariff II–276a; VI–469b, 470a
taxation VII–9a
Trade Expansion Act VII–89a, 109a
vetoes VII–178a
Vienna Summit Conference VI–180a
Vietnam War V–259a; VII–183a, 185b
KENNEDY, JOHN F., ASSASSINATION (1963) **IV–37b**; I–95a, 202b, 203a, 430b; II–58b; VII–118b, 192a
Soviet Union VI–180a
Warren Commission VII–238a
Kennedy, John Pendleton (au.) IV–162b
Kennedy, Joseph P. (bus., dipl.)
Maritime Commission II–438b
Morrissey nomination IV–413a
Kennedy, Robert F. (pol.) II–148a; IV–268a
attorney general I–400a
campaign of 1964 I–430b
campaign of 1968 I–431a
KENNEDY, ROBERT F., ASSASSINATION (1968) **IV–38a**; I–202b, 203a–b; VII–192a
Kennedy Center for the Performing Arts VII–246b
Kennedy farm (Md.) III–256a
Kennedy–Franklin Plan (1751) II–122a
Kennedy International Airport II–347a,b
Kennedy Library I–167b–68a
Kennedy Round (1964–67) III–114a; VI–53a, 470a–b; VII–89a, 109a
Kennelly, Arthur E. (eng.) II–39a
Kenner, Duncan Farrar (legis.) II–164b
Kennett Square (Pa.) I–348a
Kenney, David D. (inv.) II–421a
Kenosha (Wis.) IV–332b; V–389b; VII–307b
Kensett, John Frederick (paint.) II–102b, 103a,b; V–189a
Kensett, Thomas, Sr. (bus.) I–445a
Kensington (Pa.) VI–267a
KENSINGTON STONE IV–38a; I–96b
Kent (Ohio) IV–38b
Kent, Henry Watson II–100b
Kent, Jacob F. (off.) VI–362a
Kent, James (jur.) VI–407b
Kent, Rockwell (art.) I–19b; VII–319b
Kent County (Del.) II–320b, 322b; IV–199b
Kent Island Colony II–70a
Kenton, Simon (pioneer) I–324b; II–477a; IV–40a
KENT STATE PROTEST (1970) **IV–38b**; IV–342a; VII–191b, 366a
Kent State University (Ohio). *See* Kent State Protest
Kentucke Gazette (news.) V–70a
KENTUCKY IV–39b; VI–394 (table); VII–253b, 268a
American Colonization Society I–101a
Archaic culture II–385b
d'Arges Colony I–169b–70a
Arthur expedition V–32a
Augusta County I–223b
banking I–365a
Battle of Fallen Timbers II–484b
Big Bone Lick I–295b
black officeholders VI–432b
Black Patch War I–316a
Bluegrass region I–37b, 324b
boundary dispute I–351a,b
Bryan's Station I–373b
bushwhackers I–388b
Cane Ridge revival I–444b
Carondelet intrigue I–459a
cattle I–37b
Chickasaw Treaty II–23a
circuit riders II–39b
Civil War I–435a; II–61b, 271b, 363a; III–298a; IV–43a, 347a, 374b; V–66a, 222a, 263a; VI–251b, 308a
coal mines II–85a, 86a
Constitution Union party II–191b
Crab Orchard II–253a
Cumberland Gap I–89a; II–272a
Cumberland Presbyterian Church II–272b
"Dark and Bloody Ground" II–291b
debtor laws II–299a
Deism III–112a
desegregation I–31a
distilleries VI–377b
Dominicans II–362b
exploration III–182a; IV–201a
Falls of the Ohio V–142b
feuds II–292a; III–18a; IV–259b
Filson's Map III–24a
Fincastle County III–24b
Fort Knox III–190a–b; IV–53b
Fort Nelson V–32b
fugitive slaves I–491b–92a; IV–43b
Goebel Affair III–188a–b
Great Revival III–221b
Great Warriors Path VII–238b
Harrodsburg III–258a
Hatfield–McCoy feud III–262a
hemp III–271a
horse breeding III–304b
Indiana settlers III–369b
Indian captivities III–376b
Indian lands II–291b–92a; IV–92b
Indian raids II–71a; VII–212b
Jesuits III–501b
Kentucky County IV–43a
Kentucky Dam III–323a
land surveys V–452a
legislators' travel allowance IV–339a
Lexington and Ohio Railroad IV–137b
libraries IV–144b
liquor laws VII–132a
Logan's Fort IV–179a
lyceum movement IV–207a
Madison County Antislavery War IV–220a
Mammoth Cave IV–233b; V–218 (table)
mapping of state III–164a
Maysville Turnpike Road Company IV–279b
"men of western waters" IV–303b
Miami Trail IV–330a
military tract IV–344b
Mississippi River V–59a
Missouri settlers IV–377a; VI–194a
motto VII–155b
mountain passes V–224a–b
mules IV–425b
"My Old Kentucky Home" IV–447b
Newport Barracks V–66a
"New West" V–81b
Night Riders V–96a
Nolan expeditions V–101a
North American Land Company V–113a
nullification V–125b
old court–new court struggle V–150b
Old Southwest VI–356a
petroleum V–269a
plantation system V–325a
Powell's Valley V–384b
racetracks II–260b
railroads VI–25a, 34b
referendum VI–66b
revivalism II–466a
revolutionary war I–306b, 325a, 367a; III–400b; IV–48a; V–140b; VI–124a, 239b
riflemen VI–269b
saltpeter II–5b; V–98a
school for the deaf III–248a
Scioto Trail VI–239b
Scotch-Irish VI–240b
secessionist movement VI–250a
segregation I–290a
seismic activity II–385a
settlement II–273a; IV–338b, 376a; VII–283b
slavery I–342a; VI–309a
Spanish Conspiracy V–101a; VI–365b–66a
statehood I–78b; VI–400a
stay and valuation acts VI–406a,b
steam engines VI–409a
suffrage III–91a, 92a
tariff VI–465b
theater VII–47a
tobacco VII–66b, 67b
tornadoes II–351a, 351b; VII–75b
Trail of Tears VII–96b
trails VI–153a
train robberies VII–97b
Trans-Appalachia VII–97b
Transylvania Company III–271b; VII–103a,b
trapping VII–104b
Treaty of Hopewell III–383a
Treaty of Old Town III–383b
Treaty of Sycamore Shoals VI–455a
ungranted land V–443b
unionism VI–354a
Union sentiment VII–148b
U.S. flag III–34b
Virginia and Kentucky Resolutions VII–198a
voting procedure VII–209a
western lands VII–273a,b
western separatism VII–276a
westward movement V–179a; VII–284a
whiskey VII–289b
whiskey tax II–353b
Wilderness Road VII–296a
See also Kentucky, Invasion of (1862)
Kentucky, Army of IV–369b–70a
KENTUCKY, INVASION OF (1862) **IV–42a**; IV–370a; VI–26b
Army of the Ohio V–142b
Battle of Richmond VI–137a
Morgan's raid IV–410a–b
Munfordville IV–426b
Kentucky, Synod of II–272b
Kentucky and Virginia Resolutions. *See* Virginia and Kentucky Resolutions.
Kentucky boats I–175a; VI–148a
KENTUCKY CONVENTIONS (1784–92) **IV–42b**; IV–40b

KENTUCKY COUNTY (Va.) **IV–43a**; I–240a; VII–203a
Kentucky Dam III–323a; IV–41b
Kentucky Derby III–305a
Kentucky rifle IV–430a; VI–139b
Kentucky River II–273a; III–227b; IV–40a; VII–296a
  Boonesborough I–336b, 337a
  bridge I–364a
  Cumberland Gap V–224b
  Great Warriors Path VII–238b
  Indiana Territory V–123a
  Long hunters IV–185a
  Miami Trail IV–330a
  Northwest Territory II–356a
  settlement II–363a
  trail II–272a
  Transylvania Company VII–103a
  Treaty of Sycamore Shoals III–382b; VI–455b
KENTUCKY'S NEUTRALITY DOCTRINE (1861) **IV–43a**; I–341b, 341b–42a
KENTUCKY* v. *DENNISON (1861) **IV–43b**
Kentucky whiskey II–354a
Kenya
  Dominican missions II–362b
  Pan-Africanism V–199b
Kenyatta, Jomo V–199b
Kenyon, Cox and Company V–207a
Keokuk (Indian) I–311b–12a
Keowee (S.C.) V–408a
Keowee River V–408a
Keratin IV–389b; V–327b
Kerenski, Aleksandr F. VI–164a, 178a, 181a
Keresan (lang.) I–7b–8a, 402a; III–367b, 368a; V–460a
KERMIS (fair) **IV–43b**
Kern, Edward (expl.) III–215a
Kern, Jerome D. (comp.) I–333a; IV–442a
Kern, O. J. (educ.) III–84b
Kern, R. H. (art.) III–420b
Kern County Land Company II–336a
Kerner, Otto (gov.) III–330a; IV–457b; VI–9a
KERNSTOWN, BATTLE AT (1862) **IV–43b**; III–487b
KEROSINE OIL IV–43b; V–266b, 267a, 269b, 270a; VI–356b
  insecticides III–421a,b
  lighting IV–153a
Kerr, Michael C. (pol.) II–176 (table)
Kerr, Philip Henry, 11th Marquis of Lothian (dipl.) I–333a
Kerr, Robert S. (pol.) I–244a
Kershaw, Joseph (off.) VI–376a
Kerst, Donald W. (phys.) V–301a
Kesselring, Albert (off.) I–141a; III–235b; VI–199b
KETCH IV–44b
Ketchell, Stanley (pugilist) V–423a
Ketchikan (Alaska) I–80a
Ketchum (Idaho) VI–101b
Ketchup III–55a
Ketochten Association I–265a
Kettering, Charles F. (elec. eng.) III–409b
Kettle (Indians) III–500a,b
KETTLE CREEK, BATTLE OF (1779) **IV–44b**; III–168b
Kettle Falls II–131b
Kettle Hill, Battle of (1898) VI–362a
Kettles III–140a,b, 402b
Keuka, Lake I–223a
Keweenaw Peninsula I–410b
Key, Francis Scott (law., comp.) I–249b; III–100b; IV–213b, 261a; VI–387b
Key, Philip Barton (nav. off.) VI–130b
Key, V. O., Jr (pol. sci.) V–354a, 454a,b
Keya Paha River V–31a
Keyes, W. S. (metal.) VI–292b
"Keyhole" (Viet.) VI–301a–b
Keyishian v. *Board of Regents of University of State of New York* (1967) I–5a
Keynes, John M. (econ.) II–378a; III–193b–94a, 195a; V–210a; VI–449b
Keynesian unemployment VII–139b–40a
Keystone (S.Dak.) I–312b
Keystone Aircraft Corporation I–50a
Keystone biplane I–50a
Keystone State VI–395 (table)
Key to Theosophy V–172a
KEY WEST (Fla.) **IV–44b**; III–381b
  air transportation I–67b; II–345a–b
  Atlantic Intracoastal Waterway VI–148b–49a
  hurricanes II–351b; III–319b
  marine research III–29a
  navy V–25a
  navy yard V–28a
  railroad III–39b; VI–34a
  riots III–352a
  Spanish-American War V–165b; VI–361a, 363a
Khe Sanh (Viet.) I–63a; VII–184a, 186a
Khmer Issarak III–160a
Khorana, H. G. (chem.) I–304a; IV–391a; V–100a
Khrushchev, Nikita (states.) III–69b, 70a; VI–179b–80a
  arms control I–180a
  Berlin Wall I–291b
  Communist party II–146a
  Cuban missile crisis II–271a; V–11a
  Laos III–161b
  summit conference III–161a; VI–439a
  U-2 incident V–216a
Kiallmark, George (comp.) V–152a
Kiasutha (Indian) III–250a–b
Kichisaburo, Nomura (dipl.) IV–235a
Kickapoo (Indians) I–501b; II–265b; III–24b, 88b, 366b
  Jesuit missions III–500a
  Oklahoma lands V–148b, 149b
  Pontiac's War V–357a
  removal III–393b, 394b
  Shawnee Prophet V–4a
  Treaty of Fort Wayne VII–262b
  Treaty of Greenville III–383a
  Vincennes cession VII–189b
  Wabash Towns VII–212b
  wars VII–239a,b
Kickapoo Treaty of 1862 III–377a
Kidd, Meredith H. II–295b
Kidd, William (pirate) III–152a–b
Kidder, L. S. (off.) IV–45a
Kidder Counts (N.Dak.) II–283b
KIDDER MASSACRE (1867) **IV–45a**
Kidnapping I–203b; II–258b
  Boone-Callaway I–336b–37a
  capital punishment I–450a
  indentured servants III–353a
  See also Indian Captivities
KIDNAPPING OF FREE BLACKS IV–45a; III–130b, 247a
Kids (mag.) IV–223a
Kieft, William (col. gov.) II–383a; III–271b; V–40b, 61a–b, 266a
Kiel Canal (Ger.) VII–173b
Kier, Samuel M. (ind.) IV–44a
Kier's Petroleum or Rock Oil IV–44a
Kikuchi, Chihiro (phys.) IV–262b
Kilauea (steamer) VI–186a
Kilborne, E. L. (bact.) I–241b
Kilbourn, Hallett IV–45b
Kilbourne, Fred L. VII–177a
KILBOURN* v. *THOMPSON (1880) **IV–45b**; III–465a
Kilburn, Lorenz (paint.) V–186b
Kilgore, Harley M. (pol.) V–470b
Kilingworth (Conn.) VII–350b
Killbuck (Indian chief) VI–267a
KILLDEER MOUNTAIN, BATTLE OF (1864) **IV–45b**; II–284a
Killens, John O. (au.) I–25a
Kilns IV–243a
Kilpatrick, Hugh Judson (off.) III–250b
  Battle of Averysboro I–232b
  Buckland Races I–374a
  Falling Waters skirmish II–484b
  Richmond raid II–279a
  Sherman's march to the sea VI–278a
Kilpatrick, James J. (jour.) V–75a
Kilpatrick, William H. (educ.) II–400a
Kimball, James P. IV–120a
Kimball, J. Horace (au.) I–137a
Kimball, Moses (showman) IV–436b
Kimball, Nathan (off.) IV–43b
Kimball, Sumner I. IV–152a
Kimmel, H. E. (nav. off.) V–240a
Kindergarten II–398b, 400a; VI–228b
Kindred Spirits (paint.) V–189a, 190b
Kinetograph camera IV–417a
Kinetoscope I–479b; IV–417a
King, A. F. A. (physic.) IV–229b
King, Albert (sing.) IV–442b
King, B. B. (mus.) IV–440a
King, Billie Jean (athlete) VII–30a
King, Charles (mer., educ.) II–132b
King, Clarence (geol.) I–482a; III–166b–67a; V–268a; VII–74b, 272b
King, Coretta V–161b
King, Ernest J. (nav. off.) I–14a; V–13b, 20b, 24a; VII–336b, 344a
King, F. H. (agric.) VI–334a
King, Fort (Fla.) II–278b; VI–260b
King, James (ed.) V–73b, 73b
King, Leicester (abolitionist) V–145b
KING, MARTIN LUTHER, ASSASSINATION (1968) **IV–45b**; I–31b, 202a, 203a; II–55b, 59a; IV–76b, 259b; VII–192a
  riots IV–458a; VI–8b
King, Martin Luther, Jr. (cler.) I–24a; V–100a, 161b
  Birmingham bus boycott I–72a
  civil disobedience II–50b
  civil rights movement II–55a, 57a–58b
  "Letter From Birmingham Jail" VII–118a
  nonviolence V–182a
  non-violent philosophy IV–167b
  radicalism VI–14a
  Selma-Montgomery march V–265b
  Southern Christian Leader-

ship Conference VI–351b
King, Rufus (law., states.)
American Minerva V–69b
British debts I–367a
Burr–Hamilton duel I–388a
campaign of 1808 I–417b
campaign of 1816 I–418a
Constitution II–193a, 196a, 203b
Miranda's intrigues IV–361b
Northwest boundary V–120b
papal states minister V–211b
King, Rufus (off.)
Second Battle of Bull Run I–382a
King, Samuel Ward (physic.)
Dorr's Rebellion II–365b
King, William (gov.) IV–226b
King, William Lyon Mackenzie (states.) I–439b
Ogdensburg Agreement V–139b
King, William R. (pol.) I–420b; VII–179 (table)
Kingbury furnace (Md.) V–409b
"King Caucus" I–418b
"KING COTTON" IV–46a
Civil War II–162a
diplomacy II–165a
King crab IV–54a
King Cullen market VI–258a
Kingdom of God in America VI–83a
"Kingfish." *See* Long, Huey
Kingfisher (scout plane) I–55b
KING GEORGE, FORT (Ga.) **IV–46b**
KING GEORGE'S WAR (1744–48) **IV–46b**; II–126a; III–498a; IV–265b
Crown Point II–267a
Louisburg expedition IV–192a
Louisiana IV–193a
Maine IV–226a
peace treaty I–70b
Port Royal V–369b
privateering V–419a
recruitment IV–345b
Six Nations alliance IV–89b
See also War of Austrian Succession
King Island I–81a
King James Bible I–293b, 294a
King John (play) IV–224a
King Philip (Indian). *See* King Philip's War
KING PHILIP'S WAR (1675–76) **IV–47a**; I–380b, 465b; V–253b; VII–96b–97a, 282b
atrocities I–219a
captives III–376b, 401a
days of humiliation II–496b
Great Swamp Fight III–223a
New Hampshire V–53b
Pequot IV–387a
Providence Plantations V–439a
Regicides VI–70b
Rhode Island VI–132a
Saco Bay VI–184a
King Ranch (Tex.) VI–44b
King's Arms Tavern (N.Y.) VII–2a
Kingsbury, Jacob (off.) I–286b
Kings Canyon National Park V–219 (table)
King's Carolina Rangers VI–130a
King's Chapel (Boston) I–162a
King's College (N.Y.C.). *See* Columbia University
King's College (Wilkes–Barre, Pa.) III–293a
Kings County (N.Y.) I–370a; IV–185b, 186a; V–82a
See also Brooklyn
King's County (R.I.) IV–49a
KING'S FERRY (N.Y.) **IV–48a**; VI–415b
King's Highway I–85a
KING'S MESSENGER IV–48a
"King's Mill" (Mex.) IV–391b
KING'S MOUNTAIN, BATTLE OF (1780) **IV–48a**; I–240a; VI–124b, 126a,b, 195a, 351b; VII–25a
Kingsport (Tenn.) III–381a; IV–186b
KING'S PROVINCE (R.I.) **IV–48b**; V–50b
KINGSTON (N.Y.) **IV–49a**
Delaware and Hudson Canal II–322a
Esopus War II–462b
Fort Cataraqui III–120a
Holt's *Journal* III–292b
Huguenots III–315a
Indian wars V–61b
revolutionary war VII–279b
settlement III–312a
Kingston (Ont., Can.) I–358b; III–124b; V–156b
Fort Frontenac IV–109b
hockey III–286b
War of 1812 III–218a; IV–406a; VII–358b
Kingston (R.I.) II–99a
Kingston (Tenn.) VI–357b
Kingswood (N.H.) IV–49a
KING'S WOODS IV–49a
Kingville (S.C.) VI–349b
King William Parish (Va.) III–315a
King William's Secondary School II–395a
KING WILLIAM'S WAR (1689–97) **IV–49a**; II–121b, 126a; IV–265b; VII–291b
financing II–302a
Fort Loyal IV–200a
Louisiana IV–192b
Peace of Ryswick VI–181b
Phips's Quebec attack VI–1b
privateering V–418b
recruitment IV–345b
Saint-Castin's trading VI–188a
Salmon Falls VI–201a
York attack VII–358b
Kinkaid, Thomas C. (nav. off.) IV–138a–39a
Kinkaid Act (1904) IV–50a
KINKAIDERS IV–50a
Kinley, David (educ.) I–252a
Kinney, Henry L. (filibuster) III–23b
Kinney, N. C. (off.) VI–317b
Kinney Shoe Company III–33a; VII–124a
Kinnikinnick (tobacco) III–140b
Kino, Eusebio Francisco (miss.) II–248b; III–302b, 499a; IV–367b
Arizona I–172a
California I–91b
Camino del Diablo I–413a
Pima–Papago V–314a–b
Kinsey, Alfred C. (sci.) IV–50a–b; VI–266b
KINSEY REPORT IV–50a
Kinsley, Appolos (inv.) VI–408b
Kinsman, Delos O. (econ.) VII–308b
Kintpuash (Captain Jack) (Indian) IV–51b, 385a; VII–127a
Kinyoun, J. J. (bact.) I–242a
Kinzie, John H. (Indian agent) VII–306a
KIOWA (Indians) **IV–50b**; II–359a; III–228b, 363b, 365a
Battle of Adobe Walls I–15a
Camp Supply VI–443b
Chouteau's posts II–34b
Fort Atkinson I–213b
Fort Bascom I–269b
Fort Mason IV–263a
Fort Sill VI–287b
Fort Zarah VII–368a
horse III–303a
hostilities IV–340a; VII–239b
Kansas IV–25a
Medicine Creek Council IV–299a
Oklahoma V–148a,b, 149a,b
peace commissions III–378a
Peyote Cult V–273a
Red River War VI–64a
relations with Cheyenne II–17a
reservations II–133b
Sheridan's Washita campaign VII–252b
Sun Dance VI–441b
territory concessions III–379b
Texan–Santa Fe expeditions VII–36a
KIOWA, FORT (S.Dak.) **IV–51a**
Kiowa–Apache (Indians) IV–50b–51a
Kipling, Rudyard (au.) I–334b, 447a; IV–223a
Kipp, Jacobus VI–170a
Kirby, James B. (inv.) II–420b
Kirby, Rollin (cartoon.) V–73a
Kirby, Thomas E. (art dealer) I–332b
Kirby, William (cler.) III–331b
Kirby, William F. (pol.) IV–169a
Kirby–Smith, Edmund (off.) I–181a; II–68b, 272b; VI–274b
Battle at Jenkins Ferry III–498b
Battle at Pine Bluff V–316a
Battle of Perryville V–263b
Battle of Richmond VI–137a
Kentucky invasion IV–42b
Marshall Convention IV–257a
Morgan's raids IV–410a
Red River campaign VI–63a,b
surrender II–165a
Kircher, Athanasius (schol.) I–240b
Kirchhoff, Gustav (phys.) II–38b
Kirk, Russell (au.) II–189b
Kirk, Samuel (silversmith) VI–290a
Kirkland, Caroline M. (au.) VI–372a
Kirkland, John T. (cler., educ.) III–259b
Kirksville (Mo.) V–175a
Kirstein, Lincoln II–289a
Kirtland (Ohio) IV–116b, 339a; VII–275a, 275a
Kiska Island I–84b, 85a; VII–336b
Kissimmee, Fort (Fla.) I–451b
Kissinger, Henry (states.) II–343a; III–70b; V–100a, 233a; VI–94a, 388b
Arab–American relations I–150b
Cuba II–270a
Latin American policy IV–113b
Nixon resignation III–345a; V–98b, 99a
Strategic Arms Limitation Talks VI–417a
Vietnam peace talks V–216a; VII–184b
War Powers Act VII–225a
Watergate VII–254a
Kiss of peace I–361a
Kit Carson Pass III–114b
KITCHEN CABINET IV–51a
Kittanning (Pa.) VII–281a
KITTANNING CAMPAIGN (1756) **IV–51a**; V–222a
Kittanning Path V–184a

Kittery (Maine) III–200a; IV–225b, 226a
Kittinger Company III–137a
Kitt Peak National Observatory I–212b
Kittredge, George Lyman (educ.) I–247a
Kittredge Family I–497a
Kittson, Norman W. (fur trader) VI–63b
"Kitty Fisher" (song) VII–352b
Kitty Hawk (aircraft carrier) V–22a
Kittyhawk (fighter plane) III–46b
Kitty Hawk (N.C.) I–233a
"Kitty O'Neal" (song) III–19a
Kiva I–117b, 166b; III–367b, 368a, 392b; V–459b
Kix (cereal) I–488a
KKK. *See* Ku Klux Klan
Klamath Lake III–114b
KLAMATH-MODOC (Indians) **IV–51b**; III–363a
  Modoc War IV–384b
  reservation system VI–97a
  Rogue River War VII–239b
Klassen, E. T. (offi.) V–374b
Klauber, Laurence M. (elec. eng., nat.) VI–91b
Klee, Paul (art.) II–105a
Klikitat (Indians) VII–239b, 350a–b
"Kling Chautsh" I–346a
KLONDIKE RUSH
  IV–51b; I–77a, 439a; V–322b–23a, 437a; VII–367a
Klopfer, Donald (pub.) I–334b
Klors v. *Broadway Hale Stores* (1959) VI–102b
Kloss, George II–108a
Klystron IV–333a; VII–163b–64a
Knauss, Friedrich von (inv.) VII–136a
Kneeland, Abner (cler.) III–112a
"Kneel-ins" I–31a
Knickerbocker Apartments (N.Y.C.) I–143b
Knickerbocker Baseball Club I–269b
Knickerbockers (pants) II–372a
Knickerbocker snowstorm (1922) I–320b
Knickerbocker Trust Company V–208b
Knickerbocker Village (N.Y.C.) VII–24b
Knife River IV–45b
Knight, John S. (ed.) V–73b
Knight, Peter (av.) I–52b
Knight, Sarah (trav.) VII–69b
Knight and Ridder Newspapers V–76b
Knights, Will J. III–179b
Knights of Columbus VI–252b; VII–330b
KNIGHTS OF LABOR
  IV–52a; IV–64a–b, 65a, 66a,b; VI–13b, 325a
  blacklisting I–314b
  Burlington strike I–386a
  Catholic church I–469a
  child labor laws II–24b
  coal miners II–86b
  Greenback Labor party IV–81a–b
  immigration restriction III–342a
  Industrial Brotherhood III–405b
  labor department IV–78a
  lobbying activities IV–64b
  railroad strikes of 1886 VI–38b, 39a
  taxation VII–5b–6a
Knights of Luther V–3b
Knights of Pythias VI–252b
KNIGHTS OF THE GOLDEN CIRCLE IV–52b; III–31b; V–161b; VI–253a
  Civil War propaganda II–63b, 66b
  Copperheads II–222b
  Pacific republic movement V–180b
KNIGHTS OF THE GOLDEN HORSESHOE
  IV–53a; V–145a; VI–275b
KNIGHTS OF THE WHITE CAMELIA IV–53a; III–295a
Knight v. *Board of Regents of University of State of New York* (1967) VII–16a
Knipping, Paul (phys.) V–303b
Knitting II–239a
Knitting machine VII–44a,b
Knives III–402b
  Archaic culture II–386a
  Folsom culture III–50a
  fur trade III–140a
  Itama culture III–484b
Knives, electric II–421b
Knobs (Ky.) I–324b
Knoedler, Michael (art dealer) II–102a
Knoll International III–136b, 137a
Knopf, Alfred A. (pub.) I–334b
Knorr, Nathan Homer (cler.) III–497b
Knowland, William F. (pol.) I–408a
Knowles, Lucius J. (inv.) VII–43b
Knowlton, Charles (physic.) I–307a
Knowlton, Frank (paleon.) V–196b
Knowlton, Thomas (off.)
  rangers VI–46b
Knowlton v. *Moore* (1900) VII–6b
"KNOW YE" PARTY
  IV–53b
KNOX, FORT (Ind.)
  IV–53b
KNOX, FORT (Ky.)
  IV–53b; IV–360a
  gold hoards III–190a–b
Knox, Frank (pub., pol.) I–428b–29a; V–47b; VII–334b
Knox, Henry (off.) I–302b; IV–53b
  McGillivray treaties IV–213a
  Miranda's intrigues IV–361b
  Society of the Cincinnati II–38a; VII–175a
  state sovereignty VI–403a
  Ticonderoga ordnance VII–56b
  Waldo patent VII–220a
  War and Ordnance Board VII–226b
Knox, John Jay (fin.) I–253a
Knox, Philander C. (states.) II–361a, 488b; IV–235a
Knox, Seymour H. II–106a
Knox College IV–338b
Knox County (Ind.) VII–188b
Knox County (Northwest Terr.) V–123a
Knoxville (Tenn.) II–272a; III–292a; IV–452b; VI–357b
  Civil War IV–410a; V–263b
  race riot I–30a
  Southern Commercial Convention VI–352a
  Tennessee River VII–27a
KNOXVILLE, SIEGE OF (1863) **IV–54a**; I–502b; VII–34b
  Army of the Ohio V–142b
  Battle of Missionary Ridge IV–364b
Knoxville Gazette (news.) V–70b
Knox v. *Lee* (1871) III–417b; IV–133a; VI–94b
  See also Legal Tender Cases
Knutson-Vandenberg Act (1930) III–75b–76a; VI–67b
Knyphausen, Wilhelm von (off.) I–360a; II–218a; III–173a
Koan V–171b
Kobe (Jap.) III–490a, b
Koblenz (Ger.)
  World War II VII–340a,b
Koch, Kenneth (poet) IV–165b
Koch, Robert (physic., bact.) I–241a; III–53a; V–273b; VII–126a–b
Kodak camera I–17b; V–291b–92a
Kodiak bear IV–54a
KODIAK ISLAND IV–54a; VI–247a,b
Kodish, Battle of (1918) I–159a
Kofoid, Charles Atwood (zool.) V–135a
Kohl v. *United States* (1876) III–417b
Kokomo (Colo.) IV–354b
Kolchak, Aleksandr v. (nav. off.) VI–178b, 284a
Kölreuter, Josef (bot.) III–157a
KOMANDORSKIYE ISLANDS, BATTLE OF (1943) **IV–54a**; I–84b
Kompfner, Rudolf (phys.) VII–164a
Kona Packet (schooner) VI–186b
Kondo, Nobutake (nav. off.) IV–336b
Kono, Tommy (athlete) V–154b
Konoye, Fumiamaro (dipl.) V–239a
Konversations Lexikon II–444a
Kooning, Willem de (paint.) II–107a; V–192b
Kootenay River II–132a; VI–375b; VII–276a
Kootz, Sam II–105b, 106a
Koprowski, Hilary (virol.) V–341a
Korafuto III–85b
Korea
  Cairo Conference I–403b
  division II–489a
  exchange students II–471a
  ginseng III–180b
  immigration to U.S. III–341a,b
  Japanese hegemony III–68b
  marine landings IV–252a
  Sino-Japanese War VI–294b
  Taft-Katsura Memorandum VI–457b
  Treaty of Portsmouth V–370b
  treaty with U.S. V–22b
  U.S. naval forces V–25a
  World War II II–26a
Korea, North
  embargo VII–94a
  Geneva Accords of 1954 III–161a
  Pueblo incident V–460a
  See also Korean War
Korea, South II–348b; VII–243b
  aid costs VII–229a
  Geneva Accords of 1954 III–161a
  steel VII–89b
  tariff VI–470b
  Vietnam War VII–182b
  wool VII–321b
  See also Korean War
KOREA, WAR WITH (1871) **IV–54b**
KOREAN WAR (1950–53)
  IV–55a; II–179a, 315b, 489a–b; III–69b, 348a, 463a,b; VII–190b–91a, 227a, 237a
  Afro-American troops IV–340b
  Air Force reservists I–65a
  Air National Guard I–64b
  air transport logistics IV–180b
  Air University I–64b
  aluminum I–92a
  amnesty I–115b
  Anglo-American relations I–124a

army reserves II–316b, 324b
army slang VI–301a
aviation industry I–237b
backyard gardening III–151a
bombing I–328b
booby traps I–332a
business cycles I–392 (table)
campaign of 1952 I–430a
censorship V–74a
Chinese Communists II–27b–28a
cold war II–98a
collective security V–36a, 39a
conscientious objectors II–185b
Corps of Engineers II–450a
costs VII–228 (table), 229a
defoliation II–319a
desertion I–115b; II–335b
draft II–367b
enemy trading VII–94a
evacuation of wounded IV–290b
excess profits tax II–467a; III–205a
exchange of prisoners II–469a
Fair Deal II–481a
federal deficit VI–449b
financing II–317b
foreign aid III–61b
foxholes VII–115b
guerrillas III–231b
helicopters I–188b; III–270b
Hoover Commissions III–299b
hospitals I–191b
inflation II–236b
Latin America V–171a
logistics I–49a
losses VII–232 (table)
machine guns IV–215a
Marine Corps IV–253a
mine planting IV–351b
missilery IV–363a–b
munitions IV–430b, 431b
North Atlantic Treaty Organization V–114b
"no-win policy" V–124a
opposition V–237a
paratroops V–213b
press censorship I–481b
price-fixing V–401b
prison camps I–219b
Progressive party V–429a
propaganda V–432b
public debt VI–294a
ranger companies VI–47a
reserve forces IV–384b
Reserve Officers' Training Corps VI–99a
Small Defense Plants Administration II–498b
snipers VI–270a
Soviet Union I–179b; VI–179b
Spain VI–360b
state debts II–303a
steel mills seizure I–473a; II–179a
tank battalions I–178b
Task Force 77 VII–2a
taxation VII–9a, 12a, 13b
underwater demolition teams VII–139a
Unknown Soldier II–310a; VII–156b
U.S. Army strength I–187a,b
U.S. balance of trade I–246a
U.S. Navy I–14a, 56b–57a; V–21b
veterans I–108a
veterans' benefits I–331b–32a; V–257b, 258a
veterans' organizations VII–175a
warships VII–242a
women VII–319a
KOREAN WAR, AIR COMBAT IN IV–56b; I–56b–57a, 61a–b
bombers I–50b
fighter aircraft I–53b
missilery IV–363b
Korematsu v. *United States* (1944) III–491a; VII–118a, 227b
Kornberg, Arthur (biochem.) V–100a
Kosciusko, Thaddeus (off.) III–276a; VI–126b, 129a; VII–279b
Kosloski's ranch III–187b
Kossuth, Lajos (rev.) V–342a; VI–177b
See also Kossuth's Visit
KOSSUTH'S VISIT (1851) **IV–57a**; III–316a
Koster and Bial's Music Hall (N.Y.C.) IV–417a
Kosygin, Aleksei (states.) III–70a
Koszta, Martin (rev.) IV–57b
KOSZTA CASE IV–57b
See also New Buda
Kotzebue, Albert L. (off.) II–407b
Koyukon (Indians) I–80b; III–360b
Kpelle (people) IV–141b
Kraenzlein, Alvin (athlete) V–154a
Kraft Cheese Company II–282a
Krag–Jörgensen rifle IV–430b; VI–140a
Kramer, Jack (athlete) VI–30b
Krapp, George P. (educ.) III–234a
Krause, Allison (student) IV–39a
Krauth, Charles Philip (theol.) IV–206a
Krazy Kat (ballet) IV–438b
Kresge, S. S., Company III–32b, 33a; VI–258b
Kress, Samuel H. (mer.) II–104a, 105a
Krock, Arthur (jour.) IV–41a; V–75a
Kroeber, A. L. (anthrop.) I–129a; II–465a
Kropotkin, Peter (rev.) I–116b
Kru (people) IV–141b
Kruell, Gustav (engr.) VII–319b
Krulak, Victor H. ("Brute") (off.) II–33a
Krumen (people) VI–310a
Krupp process (steel mfr.) I–179a
Krutch, Joseph Wood (au.) IV–164a
Ksaira hill (Tun.) IV–32b
Kubitschek, Juscelino (states.) IV–113b
Kuhn, Fritz III–172a
Kühn, Justus Englehardt (paint.) V–186a
Kuhn, Loeb, and Company III–79b
Kühne, Wilhelm (physiol.) I–302b, 303a
Kuklick, Bruce (hist.) I–113a
KU KLUX ACT (1870–71) **IV–57b**; III–59b, 60a; IV–58a, 259a; VII–154a,b, 155a
SA Force Acts
KU KLUX KLAN IV–57b; IV–53a, 371b; VI–71b, 253a
black suffrage VI–431b
bulldozing I–380b
campaign of 1924 I–428a
Civil War amnesty I–115b
Force Acts III–59b; IV–57b
immigration restriction III–342a
Lumbee (Indians) IV–203b
lynching I–30a
membership I–204b
nativism I–467b; V–3b
New South V–67b
Oklahoma V–149a
radical right VI–12b
Reconstruction III–295a; VI–58a
revival II–57b
Secret Service VI–252a
Texas VII–40a
Union League of America IV–202a
whispering campaigns VII–291a
Kumon Range (Bur.) III–46a; IV–314a, 447a
K'un-ming (China) I–386b; III–46a, 46b; VII–337b
Kunstler, William M. (law.) II–20b–21a
Kuomintang (pol. faction) II–26a; IV–235b
Kuribayashi, Tadamichi (off.) III–485a,b
Kurile Islands V–239b; VI–180b; VII–351b
Kurita, Takeo (nav. off.) IV–138a–39a
Kurland, Bob (athlete) V–154b
Kusaie Island V–215a
Kusch, Polycarp (phys.) V–100a
Kuskokwim River I–80b
Kutchin (Indians) I–80b; III–253a, 360b
Kutenai (Indians) I–441b; III–363a, 500a,b
Kuznets, Simon (econ.) V–99b; VI–384a
Kuznets cycles VI–384a
Kvale, Ole J. (pol.) II–491a
Kwajalein VII–219a, 337a
World War II IV–253a, 257b; VII–139a
KWAKIUTL (Indians) **IV–59a**; I–441b; III–361b, 362a
Kwakiutl–Nootka (Indians) IV–228b
Kwantung Province (China) II–29b
Ky, Nguyen Cao (states.) III–297b
Kyoto (Jap.)
penal congress V–416a
Kyushu (Jap.) III–489b; V–21a

L

L-1011 TriStar (transport plane) I–52b; II–347b
Labadie, Jean de (rel. ref.) IV–59b
Labadie, Sylvester (fur trader) VI–195b
Labadist Community of Protestant Mystics II–147a
LABADISTS IV–59b
La Bahia (Tex.) IV–184a; VI–144a
La Balme, Augustin Mottin de (off.) IV–59b
LA BALME'S EXPEDITION (1780) **IV–59b**
La Bamboula (comp.) IV–438a
La Barre, Antoine Le Febvre de (col. gov.) III–124a; IV–83b; VI–187b
La Bayadère (ballet) II–289b
La Baye (Wis.) I–498b; III–89b, 142b, 225b, 311b
trade III–144b
See also Green Bay
La Baye des Puans III–225b
Labeling II–500a; III–54a
copyright II–224b
regulation V–466a,b, 467a
LA BELLE FAMILLE, BATTLE OF (1759) **IV–60a**
La Belle Rivière V–145a
Labe River II–407b
Labiche, Emmeline I–6b
LABOR IV–60a
Adair v. *United States* I–9b
AFL–CIO I–102b
Afro-Americans I–25b, 29a,b; V–1a

LABOR (cont.)
agency shop II–81a
agriculture I–36b, 37a,b, 39a; II–495b
antiinjunction law VII–121a
apprenticeship I–148a
arbitration I–152a
blacklisting I–314b
bloc I–322b
Boston Journeymen Bootmakers Society II–142a
boycott I–357a
California I–408a
campaign of 1892 I–424b
campaign of 1936 V–47b
campaign of 1948 I–429b
Catholics I–469a
checkoff II–2b
Chinese II–29b
civil service II–59a
Civil War I–34a; II–63b, 69a, 69a
Clayton Act II–110b
closed shop II–80a, 80b–81a
clothing industry II–81a, 82a–b
coal mining II–85a–87a
coastwise steamship lines II–91a
codes IV–71b
collective bargaining II–80a–81a, 110a, 110b
commerce clause II–136a, 137a
Commonwealth v. *Hunt* II–142a, 142a
Communist party II–144b–45b
Conference for Progressive Political Action IV–84b
Confiscation Acts II–168a
contract labor II–214a, 214a; III–103b
convicts II–216b–17a
Coxey's Army II–252b
Danbury Hatters' Case II–286a–b
Democratic party II–327b
employment offices II–441b–42b
Employment Service II–441b
Erie Canal II–460a
"escalator clause" II–236b
exchanges II–220a
Greenback movement III–224b–25a
Hamilton's policies III–246b
Haymarket Riot II–17b; III–266a
Haywood–Moyer–Pettibone Case III–266b
Herrin massacre III–274a
history sources III–285a
Hitchman Coal Company v. *Mitchell* III–286a
homestead movement III–296a
Homestead Strike III–297a
immigration I–25b, 29b; II–418b–19a; III–342a, 491b–02a
indentured servants I–27a; III–352b
Indian I–48b
industrial armies IV–36a–b
Industrial Brotherhood III–404b
industrial espionage II–462b
industrial life insurance III–434b–35a
industrial management III–405b–06b
industrial relations III–406b
Industrial Revolution I–37a; III–411a, 412a
Industrial Workers of the World III–412b
injunctions II–110b–11a; III–419a
integration III–438b
International Labor Organization III–454b
Irish III–335b
journals IV–93b
judicial review IV–14a
Kansas industrial court VII–311a–b
Kearneyites IV–33a
Knights of Labor IV–52a
laissez-faire doctrine IV–85b
Lawrence strike IV–120a
legal protection of IV–80a
lockout IV–174a
Los Angeles IV–218b
mass labor IV–272a
mass–production IV–273b
May Day IV–278a
McNamara case IV–218b
merchant marine VI–281a
migrant workers VI–365a
minimum–wage legislation IV–352a
Molly Maguires IV–391b
Mooney case IV–406a
National Farmers Union I–41b
National Mediation Board II–500b
National Nonpartisan League V–106b
National Trades' and Workers' Association IV–471b
New Deal V–44b, 46a,b–47a
New Jersey V–57b
New Nationalism V–60a
newspapers V–77b
New York State V–87b
"normalcy" V–110a
occupational medicine IV–293a
occupation changes V–132b
Ohio V–142a
Pennsylvania V–247b
pension plans V–256a
peonage V–260b
Philadelphia cordwainers V–278b
Philippines V–284a
picketing V–308b
piecework V–309b
plantation system V–178b, 324b
political contributions II–232b; V–448b
political parties IV–81a–82a
prisons V–415a–b
productivity V–425b
profit sharing V–426b
Progressive movement V–427a
Progressive party IV–84b
Pullman strike V–463a
radicalism VI–13b
railroad brotherhoods VI–19b, 28b
railroads VI–28b, 30a,b, 32a
railroad strikes VI–38b, 40b
relief projects VI–73a–74a
restraint of trade VI–103b
road working days VI–156b
rural life VI–174a
sabotage VI–182b
Sacco–Vanzetti case VI–183a
Safety First movement VI–185a
Sherman Antitrust Act VI–276b–77a
shop committees VI–282b
silk industry VI–287a
Single Tax movement V–427a
Social Democratic party VI–324b
Social Gospel VI–325a
Socialist Labor party VI–325a
Socialist party of America VI–326b
Sovereigns of Industry VI–358a
steel strikes VI–410b
sweatshop VI–453b
syndicalism VI–455b
taxation VII–5b–6a
teachers IV–463b
textile industry VII–44b, 45b
unemployment VII–139b
unemployment insurance VI–328a
union activists II–462b
unionization restrictions IV–358b
union monopoly VII–124a
United Mine Workers VII–150b
Universal Peace Union V–235b
urban structure VII–159a,b
voting behavior VII–210b
wages and hours regulation VII–213a
wages and salaries VII–214b
walking delegate VII–220b
War Industries Board VII–231b
War Labor Board VII–232a
Washington State VII–248a
Western Federation of Miners VII–272b
woman's rights movement VII–313a,b, 314b
women VII–316b, 317a–b
Workingmen's Party VII–322a
workmen's compensation III–431a–b; VII–322b
World War I I–25b, 26a, 29a; VII–326a
World War II VII–334b, 336a
"yellow–dog" contract II–222a; VII–354b
See also Slavery; Strikes
Labor, Bureau of IV–64b, 78a; V–425b
Labor, Committee on (House of Rep.) IV–64b
LABOR, DEPARTMENT OF IV–78a; I–399b; II–135a, 498a; IV–22a, 69a; V–428b; VII–108a, 317b
antisubversive programs II–143b
apprenticeship training I–148b
black migration survey I–26a
Bureau of Labor Statistics II–209b
child labor laws II–24a–b
Civilian Conservation Corps II–51a
Coast and Geodetic Survey II–88a
Conciliation Service II–157b, 499a; IV–74a
employers' liability insurance III–431b
Employment Service II–442a
immigration III–334a
industrial espionage II–463a
Job Corps III–504b
Moynihan Report IV–424b
Occupational Safety and Health Act IV–77b
Office of Economic Opportunity V–135b
unemployment insurance VI–330a
Wage and Hour Division II–482a
Labor and Education Committee II–442b
Laboratory of Hygiene IV–465a
Labor conciliation. *See* Conciliation, Labor
"Labor conquers all things" (motto) VI–395 (table)
Labor contracts, foreign. *See* Contract Labor, Foreign
LABOR DAY IV–79a; IV–278a
LABOR IN THE COLONIES IV–79a; II–122a, 125b; IV–60a–b
Afro–Americans I–24b
apprenticeship I–148a
LABOR LEGISLATION AND ADMINISTRATION IV–79b; III–407a
AFL support IV–65b
Clayton Act II–71b; III–459a
Fair Labor Standards Act

II–481b–82a
laissez-faire doctrine IV–85b
Landrum–Griffin Act IV–467a
minimum wages IV–352b
National Industrial Recovery Act V–44b
National Labor Relations Act; IV–466b, 467b–68a
National Recovery Administration IV–469a
Norris–La Guardia Anti-Injunction Law V–112a
Railroad Mediation Acts VI–21a
Taft–Hartley Act IV–467a; VI–456b
wages and hours II–481b–82a
Walsh–Healy Act VII–223a
See also Medicine, Occupational
Labor–Management Relations Act (1947). *See* Taft–Hartley Act
Labor–Management Reporting and Disclosure Act (1959) *See* Landrum–Griffin Act
Labor–Management Services Administration IV–78b
Labor omnia vincit (motto) VI–395 (table)
LABOR PARTIES IV–81a
Farmer–Labor party of 1920 II–492b
Farmer–Labor party of Minnesota II–490b
free silver III–110b
Union Labor party VII–146b
Workingmen's party IV–33a
Labor racketeering II–261b, 262a
Labor schools I–469b
"Labor's Fourteen Points" II–492b
Labor's Nonpartisan League. *See* Nonpartisan League, Labor's
Labor Statistics, Bureau of II–209b, 495b; IV–78a,b
cost of living II–235b–36a
productivity studies V–425b
wholesale price index V–406a
Labrador II–461b; III–218b
eclipse expedition II–88a
Eskimo culture I–441b
exploration V–336b
Norsemen I–95b; V–112a; VII–190a
sealing VI–245a
Labrador (icebreaker) V–122a
Labrador (Indians) III–358a
LABRADOR FISHERIES IV–82a; II–92a–93a, 215b; III–30b
La Butte, Fort (N.Dak.) IV–118a
La Casa Pacifica V–98b
Laccolith III–163b
Lacey, John F. (pol.) VII–298a
Lacey Act (1900) VII–297a,b
Lachine Rapids I–96b; VI–192b–93a
Lackawanna Valley VI–34a
Lackawaxen (Pa.) I–443a
Lackawaxen ford (N.Y.) IV–354b
Laclede Ligueste, Pierre (fur trader) III–144a–b, 404a; IV–277b, 376b
Saint Louis VI–193b–94a; VII–95b
LACOLLE MILL, BATTLE OF (1814) **IV–82a**; IV–87a
See also Montreal, Wilkinson's Expedition Against
Lacolle River IV–82a
La Condamine, Charles Marie de (geog.) III–166a, 167b
Laconia Company IV–82b; V–53b
LACONIA GRANT IV–82b; IV–264a
Isles of Shoals III–479b
Strawberry Bank VI–417b
Lacquer
automobile I–228b
La Croix, Edmund (inv.) III–43b
Lacrosse (sport) III–287a, 366a
La Crosse (Wis.) I–242b
Lacrosse Playing Among the Sioux (paint.) V–189b
"Lac St Louis" V–156b
"La Danse de Feu" (dance) II–287b
Ladd, George Trumbull (psych., philos.) V–441b
Ladd, William (sea capt., farmer) IV–82b; V–235a; VII–236a
LADD'S PEACE PLAN IV–82b
Ladies Home Journal (mag.) I–17b, 19a
Ladies Magazine III–188a
Ladies of the Grand Army of the Republic III–207b–08a
LADIES' REPOSITORY (period.) **IV–82b**
Ladies' Tea Party (1774) VII–16b
Ladinos III–242b
Ladue, Joseph IV–52a
Lady Elgin (steamer) II–349a
Lady Franklin Bay III–224a; V–337a
Lady's Book (period.) III–188a
Lady's slipper (flower) VI–394 (table)
Lady Washington (merchant ship) II–28b
LAE AND SALAMAUA (1942–43) **IV–83a**; I–307b–08a
Laemmle, Carl (prod.) IV–417b
LA FAMINE, TREATY OF (1684) **IV–83b**
La Farge, John (paint.) V–191a
Lafayette (Ind.) II–265b; III–369b
Fort Ouiatenon V–176a
railroad III–374b
saloons VI–201b
Wabash and Erie Canal VII–212a,b
LAFAYETTE, FORT (N.Y.) **IV–83b**; V–414a
Lafayette, Marquis de, Marie Joseph du Motier (off.) I–89b, 275b; II–487b; III–122b; IV–57b, 84a–b, 425b; VI–126a–b, 129a; VII–245a
American troops VI–118a
Arnold's raid in Virginia I–194a
Bunker Hill monument I–383a
Garde Nationale IV–463b
invasion of Canada I–436a,b
Sullivan in Rhode Island VI–438a
Yorktown VII–199a, 360b–61a
"LAFAYETTE, WE ARE HERE" IV–84a; VII–325b
Lafayette class (submarines) VI–423b
LAFAYETTE ESCADRILLE IV–83b
Lafayette Flying Corps. *See* Lafayette Escadrille
Lafayette National Park IV–422b
LAFAYETTE'S VISIT TO AMERICA (1824–25) **IV–83b**; III–96b
Laffite, Jean (pirate) I–265b, 279a, 492a; III–149a; IV–184a, 193b; V–320a
Laffite, Pierre (pirate) I–265b
Laffite brothers VII–37a
Laflin and Rand V–383b
La Follette, Philip Fox (pol.) VII–308a
La Follette, Robert M. (pol.) V–161a; VII–308a
arming of merchant ships IV–169a
campaign of 1912 I–426b; V–427b–28a
campaign of 1924 I–428a; II–492a; IV–70a, 81b, 84b
direct primary V–407a
Progressives II–492b–93a; IV–84b; V–427b
Seamen's Act of 1915 VI–246b
Taft–Roosevelt split VI–458a
Wisconsin Idea VII–308a,b
La Follette, Robert M., Jr. (pol.) IV–72b; VII–308a
LA FOLLETTE PROGRESSIVE PARTY IV–84b; IV–70a; VII–52b
Wisconsin VII–53a, 308b
woman's suffrage III–91b–92a
La Follette Seaman's Act. *See* Seamen's Act of 1915
La Forest, François Dauphin de (expl.) V–315a
Lafourche, Bayou (La.) I–6b
LaFramboise, Joseph (trader) V–310a–b
LA GALETTE, FORT (N.Y.) **IV–85a**
La Galissonière, Marquis de, Roland Michel Barrin (col. gov.) III–115a
La Grand, Pierre (buccaneer) I–374a
La Grande Jatte (paint.) II–105a
La Grange (Ill.) IV–88a
La Grange (N.Y.) I–284b
La Grange (Tenn.) III–228a
La Guardia, Fiorello (pol.) I–107b; II–50a; V–83b; VI–459b, 460b
La Guardia Airport (N.Y.) II–346b, 347a; V–368b
Laguna (N.Mex.) I–8a; II–461a; III–367b; V–460a
Laguna Beach man I–155b
Laguna Indians IV–90a
Laguna Madre IV–452a
Lahaina (Haw.) III–263a
La Harpe, Benard de (off.) I–174a
Lahontan, Baron de, Louis Armand de Lom d'Arce (cartog.) III–222a; VII–73b
Lailson's Circus II–40a
Laird, John, and Sons I–73a
Laird, Melvin (pol.) V–460b; VII–227b
LAIRD RAMS IV–85a
La Isla Española. *See* Hispaniola
LAISSEZ-FAIRE IV–85a; III–202b; IV–140a; VII–117b
capitalism I–449b
conservatism II–189a
Dartmouth College Case II–293b
Fifth Amendment II–378a
Fourteenth Amendment II–378a
free banking III–101b
Hamilton's fiscal policies III–246a,b
Jacksonian Democracy III–486b
National Association of Manufacturers IV–461b
Progressive movement V–427a
Social Gospel VI–82b
Supreme Court IV–14a
La Jemerais, Christophe Du-Frost de (expl.) VI–188a
La Jolla (Calif.) VI–242a
La Jonquière, Marquis de, Pierre-Jacques de Taffanel V–308a
La Junta (Colo.) I–174b, 290a
La Junta (Tex.) IV–367b
Lake, C. D. (eng.) II–154a
Lake, Simon (inv.) VI–422b, 423a

"Lake as a Microcosm" (essay) II–391a
Lake Bonneville (monograph) III–222a
Lake Carriers Association III–218a
LAKE CHAMPLAIN IV–85b; III–119a; V–367a
canal II–460a
Catholic Summer School II–1b
Crown Point II–266b
Erie Canal III–448a
exploration I–492b; VI–192a
Fort Ticonderoga VII–56b
French and Indian War III–115b, 116b, 117a; IV–405b; VI–190a
French settlement III–114b
Indian trails II–405b
inland lock navigation III–419b
King William's War IV–49b
Laconia IV–82b
Mahican IV–387a
naval disarmament III–217a
Onion River Land Company V–156a
revolutionary war I–81b, 193b, 385a; III–234a, 235a; VI–123a,b; VII–56a,b, 57a, 164a
Richelieu River VI–136b
U.S. boundary VII–265a
Vermont VII–171b
War of 1812 IV–212a, 406a; V–19a–b, 330b, 424a; VII–234b, 235a
Lake City (Fla.) III–39a
Lake County (Calif.) I–340a
Lake County (Ill.) II–263b
Lake Erie and Western Railroad VI–35a
Lake Erie–Lake Michigan Canal V–1b–2a
Lake Erie–Ohio River Canal V–1b
Lake George II–340a; IV–85b
Fort Ticonderoga VII–56b
Fort William Henry VII–301a
French and Indian War III–116a; IV–86a; VI–162b
inland lock navigation III–419b
revolutionary war I–193b, 385a
Vermont VII–171a
LAKE GEORGE, BATTLE OF (1755) **IV–87b**; I–323a; II–405b; III–115b; IV–86a
Lakehurst (N.J.) II–344a; V–28a
Lakehurst Naval Air Station II–344a–b
Hindenburg explosion II–346a
Lake limnology II–391a
Lake Meadows (Chicago) VI–86b
Lake of the Woods IV–118a; VI–443a; VII–275b
Fort Saint Charles IV–355a; VI–188a
fur trade V–121a
LAKE OF THE WOODS BOUNDARY PROBLEM IV–87b; I–121a; II–215b, 319a; IV–198a; V–120a–b; VII–269b, 270a–b
Lake Placid (N.Y.) VI–101a, 298a
Lake Point Tower (Chicago) I–165b
Laker (ship) III–218a–b
Lakes, Department of the II–338a
Lakes, Great. *See* Erie, Lake; Great Lakes; Huron, Lake; Michigan, Lake; Ontario, Lake; Superior, Lake
Lake Shore and Michigan Southern Railroad VI–35b
LAKES–TO–GULF DEEP WATERWAY IV–87b
Lake Superior III–27a
Lake Tahoe Regional Planning Commission III–460a
Lakewood Plan IV–172b
Lakota (Indians) II–283a
LaLande, Jean Baptiste (trader) VI–215a,b, 461a
Lallemand, Frédéric (off.) I–492a
La Mama Experimental Theatre Club (N.Y.C.) VII–51a
Lamar (Colo.) IV–28a
Lamar, Charles A. I. VII–223b
Lamar, Joseph R. (jur.) VI–446a
Lamar, Lucius Q. C. (jur.) VI–446a
Lamar, Mirabeau B. (states.) VII–36a, 38a,b, 41b
Lamas, Carlos Saavedra (dipl.) V–232a
Lamb VI–273a
Lamb, Joseph (comp.) IV–439b
Lamb, Thomas (arch.) IV–220b
Lamb, Willis, Jr. (phys.) V–100a
Lambert, Henry (off.) II–192b
LAME-DUCK AMENDMENT IV–88b; I–95a
La Mesa, Battle of (1847) VI–210b
L'Amistad slave case. *See Amistad* Case
Lamont–Doherty Geological Laboratory II–133a
Lamp II–414a, 417a
See also Lighting
Lamp, carbon II–414a, 417a; IV–88b, 153b
Lamp, fluorescent IV–89a, 154a
LAMP, INCANDESCENT IV–88b; II–413b, 414a–b, 415a, 417b; III–155b, 156a; IV–153a–b, 154a, 244a; V–289b
Lamp, kerosine IV–44b
Lamp, mercury vapor IV–154a
Lamp, tungsten IV–153b
Lampasas County (Tex.) II–493b
La Navidad VI–216a
Lancashire (Eng.) V–194b
Lancashire furnace (Md.) V–409b
Lancaster (Conn.) IV–47b
Lancaster (Ohio) II–273b; VII–368a
Lancaster (Pa.) III–32b, 99b; VII–350a
canals IV–174b–75a
Conestoga Massacre V–231a
Ephrata Community II–454a
Forbes Road III–59a
fur trade III–141b
Indian trade I–278a
national capital V–247a
turnpike IV–89b
LANCASTER, FORT (Colo.) **IV–89a**
LANCASTER, TREATY OF (1744) **IV–89b**; III–382b
Lancaster County (Pa.) III–13b, 300b; V–251b
Lancaster Gap (Pa.) III–13b
LANCASTER PIKE IV–89b; VI–153a
Lancaster Sound V–122a
Lancaster Turnpike. *See* Lancaster Pike
Lancastrian schools II–397a
Lance (missile) IV–363b
Lance points III–50a
Lances
dueling II–376b
Land
absentee ownership I–3b–4b
gore III–199b
great fortunes III–78b–79a
single tax VI–293a–b
taxation III–351b
See also Agriculture; Soil
Land, Edwin H. (inv., ind.) V–268a, 293a
Land, free. *See* Free Land
Land, Indian
Dawes Commission II–295b
Dawes General Allotment Act II–295b
Indian Reorganization Act II–296a
See also Indian Land Cessions
LAND, INDIAN CONCEPT OF OWNERSHIP OF IV–90a; I–48b; III–382a
hunting grounds III–318a
Tecumseh's crusade V–141a; VII–18a
LAND, LEASING OF AMERICAN INDIAN IV–90a; V–81b
LAND ACT OF 1796 IV–90b; III–257b; IV–99a–b; VII–189a
Land Act of 1800. *See* Harrison Land Act
LAND ACT OF 1820 IV–90b; VI–75a
Landais, Pierre (nav. off.) I–89b, 290b
Land allotment, Indian III–389b, 390a; V–49a
Land and Water Conservation Fund III–444b
Land and Water Fund Conservation Act (1965) III–76a
Landau, Lev (phys.) V–304a
Land bank associations I–44b
Land Bank Commission IV–6b
Land banks; I–44a, 44a,b, 255a, 256a, 259a; IV–6b, 393b; V–456a
LAND BOUNTIES IV–91a; IV–97a
Dohrman's grant II–359a
Loyalist veterans VI–131a
military bonuses I–353a
military tracts IV–344b
Ohio III–227b
Patriot War V–227a
revolutionary war II–450b; VI–117b; VII–273a,b
Virginia military reserve VII–202a
Washington's western lands VII–252a
western lands V–140b
See also Bounties, Military
Land cessions, Indian. *See* Indian Land Cessions
Land claims IV–97a,b
arbitration IV–95a
Spanish and Mexican land grants IV–93a
Land classification board III–164a
Land companies
American Land Company I–107b–08a
Greenbrier Company III–226a
Henderson Land Company III–271b
Holland Land company I–4a; III–291a
Illinois and Wabash Company III–331a
Indiana Company III–370b
New York Land Company III–243a
Northwest Territory V–140b
Ohio Company of Associates V–143b
Onion River Land Company V–156a
Transylvania Company VII–102b
LAND DISTRIBUTION BILL, CLAY'S IV–91a
See also Surplus Revenue, Distribution of

Lander (Wyo.) VII–244a
Land Forfeiture Act (1890) IV–100a
Land Grant College Act (1862). *See* Morrill Act
Land grant colleges I–33a
  Alaska I–77b
  botanical studies I–350a
  experiment stations I–46a
  industrial research IV–300b
  West Virginia University VII–282a
  wildlife management VII–297b–98a
Land grants IV–105a
  French settlers III–120a
  Illinois and Michigan Canal IV–87b
  issuance IV–95a
  Lecompton Constitution IV–131a
  Macomb purchase IV–219b
  Otsego (N.Y.) lands V–176a
  title IV–105a
LAND GRANTS, COLONIAL IV–91b; III–107b; IV–102b, 105a; VI–166b
  Carolina I–83a,b
  Council for New England II–242a
  Duke of York's proprietary VII–359b
  Fairfax proprietary II–481a–b
  Falls of the Ohio V–142b
  Gardiner's Island III–152a
  Georgia III–169b
  Georgiana III–171a
  glebes III–186b
  Gorges' Province of Maine III–200a
  Granville grant III–212b
  Great Nine Partners' Patent III–220b
  Greenbrier Company III–226a
  headright III–267a
  Heath Patent III–268a
  Hudson River III–313a
  Indiana Company III–370b
  Indian territory III–388a
  Laconia grant IV–82b
  Mason title IV–263b
  Minisink patent IV–354b
  Mississippi Company of Virginia IV–371a
  New Albion V–332b
  New Hampshire V–53b, 54b
  New Smyrna V–66a
  New York V–84b, 88a
  patroons V–61a, 229a
  Pemaquid Point V–243b
  Proclamation of 1763 V–424b; VI–356a
  proprietary provinces V–436a
  royal charters II–118b
  Saco Bay VI–184a
  Schenectady VI–225b
  speculators IV–98b
  Spotwood's Virginia grant VI–376a
  Trelawney Plantation VII–114b
  Vandalia VII–166b
  Vermont III–226b
  Wawayanda Patent VII–261b
  western lands VII–273a
LAND GRANTS, SPANISH AND MEXICAN IV–93a; VI–365a
  Austin colony I–224a
  Beale's colony VI–143b–44a
  Dubuque III–147a
  Garay grant III–145b
  Giard Tract III–177b
  Iowa III–467b
  land titles IV–105b
  Las Animas grant IV–110a
  Louisiana IV–377a
  Mariposa IV–254a
  Maxwell grant IV–278a
  New Madrid V–59a
  Panoche Grande Claim V–210b
  Sangre de Christo grant VI–210b
LAND GRANTS FOR EDUCATION IV–93a; II–227a,b; III–52b, 211b; VI–227b–28b
  Miami purchase IV–329b
  military training VI–98b
  Morrill Act IV–97b, 412b
  Ordinance of 1785 II–396a
  Oregon land frauds V–166a
  public schools IV–96a
  Rutgers University VI–181b
  scientific education VI–232a
  Sheffield Scientific School VI–274a
  speculation IV–99b
  state universities VII–156a,b
  Texas public lands VII–41b
LAND GRANTS FOR RAILWAYS IV–94a; I–4a,b; III–450a; V–444a,b; VI–26a, 425a
  Atlantic and Pacific Railroad I–214b
  Central Pacific–Union Pacific VII–101a
  forfeiture IV–103b
  Illinois Central VI–34b
  Iowa III–468b
  land scrip IV–97b
  land titles IV–105a
  mineral rights IV–104b
  Mussel Slough incident IV–444a
  opposition IV–100a
  Oregon and California Railroad IV–95b
  speculation IV–99b
  Texas VII–39a
  transcontinental routes VI–27a
  Union Pacific VII–147a,b
LANDGRAVE IV–94b; VI–348b
Landholding, alien. *See* Alien Landholding
Landing craft II–375b; V–25a; VII–343b
Landing craft carriers II–375b
Landing gear (aircraft) IV–106a
Landing ship docks II–375b
Landing ship tank. *See* LST
Landis, James M. (law., educ.) II–50a
Landis, Kenesaw Mountain (jur.) I–270b; VI–384a
  Standard Oil fine V–208b
Land League movement III–11a
Landlordism I–4a
Landlords
  farm tenancy IV–102b, 103a,b, 104a
Land lottery system III–170b
Land Management, Bureau of IV–95b; V–446a, 451b
Landmark preservation II–47b, 49a
Land of Enchantment VI–394 (table)
LAND OFFICE, U.S. GENERAL IV–95a; I–463a; III–444a
  Ballinger–Pinchot controversy I–247b
  Division of Grazing V–446a
  Florida lands III–39a
  forest reserves III–75a
  land scrip IV–97a
  mapping I–463a
  public land commissions V–450a,b
  public lands fencing V–451b
Land of Opportunity VI–393 (table)
Land of the Midnight Sun VI–393 (table)
Land O' Lakes Cooperative II–282a
Landon, Alfred M. (pol.)
  campaign of 1936 I–428b–29a; IV–26b; V–47b; VI–93a
Land ordinances. *See* Ordinances of 1784, 1785, and 1787
LAND POLICY IV–95b; I–42a–b
  Clay's land distribution bill IV–91a
  Donation Lands II–362b
  eminent domain II–439b
  farm tenancy IV–103a
  free land III–295b
  mineral patent law IV–349b
  national land system IV–102b
  Ohio V–140b
  preemption rights V–389b
  public domain V–443b
  public land commissions V–450a
  public lands revenue IV–91a
  public sales IV–90b
  reclamation VI–53b
  Relief Act of 1821 VI–75a
  reservation of land V–143b
  Resettlement Administration VI–99a
  school lands VI–227b
  states' rights VI–404b
  Timber Culture Act VII–59b
Landrace hog III–288b
Land reclamation. *See* Reclamation
Land reform movement III–111b; IV–100a, 101a
Landrum–Griffin Act (1959) I–103a; II–80b, 111a; III–407a; IV–74b, 78b, 467a; VI–457b
  See also National Labor Relations Act
Land runs II–14b
Lands, Public. *See* Public Domain; Public Land Commissions; Public Land Sales; Public Land States
Lands, western. *See* Western Lands
LANDSCAPE ARCHITECTURE IV–96b; III–151b
  Panama–Pacific Exposition V–203b
  skyscrapers VI–299a
Landscape painting V–185b, 187a,b, 188a, 189a,b, 190a,b, 192a
LAND SCRIP IV–97a; IV–93b, 315a
LAND SPECULATION IV–98a
  absentee ownership I–3b–4a
  bank loans I–255b
  bankruptcy laws I–262a
  boomtowns II–45b
  Burlington Company I–386a
  Carey Desert Land Act I–453b
  Carver claim I–464b
  Choctaw land frauds II–32b
  claims associations II–70a
  Dakota Territory V–117a
  Desert Land Act II–336a
  East Florida III–38b
  farm tenancy IV–103a
  Florida I–336b; III–42a–b; V–254b
  Fort Stanwix Treaty VI–385b
  Georgia I–354a
  Grand Ohio Company III–208b
  Great Nine Partners' Patent III–220b
  Greenbrier Company III–226a
  Half-Breed Tract III–242b–43a
  Holland Land Company III–291a
  Illinois and Wabash Company III–331a
  Indian land I–213a; II–32b; IV–97a–b
  Indian removal III–393a

LAND SPECULATION (cont.)
Kansas IV–30a
Land Act of 1796 III–257b
land bounties IV–91a
land scrip IV–98a
Loyal Land Company IV–201a
military tracts IV–345a
Muscle Shoals IV–435a
New England IV–102b
New South V–66b
New York I–375b; V–88a
North American Land Company V–113a
North Carolina western lands III–98b
Ohio Company of Associates V–143b
Ohio Company of Virginia V–144a
Onion River Land Company V–156a
panic of 1837 V–206b; VI–370b
Panic of 1857 V–207a
Phelps–Gorham purchase V–276a
Pine Barren speculations V–315b
preemption rights V–389b
public lands I–107b–08a; IV–96a; V–444a–b, 452b
school lands VI–228a
Scioto Company III–120b; VI–238b
surveyors VI–450b
Tennessee VII–25a
Texas II–443a
Vandalia Colony VII–166b
Vermont VII–171b
Virginia VII–195a
Virginia military reserve VII–202a
Washington, D.C. VII–245a
Washington's western lands VII–252a
West VII–268b
western lands II–166a; V–206a
Western Reserve VII–274b
western separatism VII–276a
Yazoo fraud III–36a; VII–273b, 353b
See also Land companies
Landsteiner, Karl (path.) V–100a
Land Surveying. *See* Public Lands, Surveying of
Landsverk, O. G. (au.) IV–38b
LAND SYSTEM, NATIONAL IV–101b
tomahawk claims VII–70b
township system VII–81a
See also Land Titles
LAND TENURE IV–102b; I–40b–41a, 42a–b; V–433a–b
absenteeism I–3b–4b
alien landholding I–87a
freeholder III–107b
Indians I–48b
leasehold IV–127b
LAND TITLES IV–105a; IV–101b–02a, 102b; V–433b, 434a
cabin rights I–400a
colonial land grants IV–91b
Half-Breed Tract III–242b
Indian Country III–379a
Indian treaties III–404a,b
leasehold IV–127b
McLoughlin land claim IV–218b
metes and bounds IV–318a
New Jersey V–56b–57a
North Carolina V–115a
Oregon V–166b
quitrents VI–4a
Texas VII–35b
tomahawk claims VII–70a
Torrens systems VII–76b
Land–use planning I–222b; VI–398b
Land warrants I–331a; IV–97a
Lane (Oreg.) VII–300a
Lane, Fitz Hugh (paint.) V–189a
Lane, Franklin K. (pol.) V–219b–20a
Lane, Harry (pol.) IV–169a
Lane, James H. (pol.) IV–377b; V–471b
Kansas IV–25b, 28a,b, 31a
Topeka Constitution VII–72b
Wakarusa War VII–218b
Lane, Joseph (pol.) I–421a; V–97b, 165b, 180b
Lane, Ralph (col. gov.) V–115a; VI–42b–43a, 43b–44a
Lane, William Henry (Juba) (dancer) II–287a
Lane Seminary debates (1834) I–136a
Lane Theological Seminary V–130a
LANE* v. *OREGON (1869) **IV–105b**
Langdell, Christopher Columbus (educ.) III–260a; IV–120b, 121a
Langdon, John (mer., pol.) I–418a; II–203b; V–54a; VI–128a
Fort William and Mary VII–300b
Lange Eylandt. *See* Long Island
Langer, William (gov.) V–117b
Langford, Nathaniel (offi.) VII–357b
Langlade, Charles de (off.) I–367a; V–308a; VI–218b; VII–307a
Langley (carrier) I–54b, 56b
Langley (Va.) VII–196a
Langley, Samuel P. (av.) I–59a, 232b–33a; VI–319a,b
LANGLEY AERONAUTICAL LABORATORY IV–105b; IV–458a
Langley Field (Va.) I–64a; II–154b, 344a
Langmuir, Irving (chem.) II–12b, 76b, 417a, 423b; III–155b, 409a; IV–89a, 153b; V–99b; VII–163a
Langrage V–26a
Langstroth, Lorenzo L. (cler.) I–284a
Language
computer II–156b
dictionaries II–340a–b
See also Slang, American; Slang, Military
Lanier, Sidney (poet) IV–2b
Lankenau Hospital (Phila.) III–307a
Lankhof Farm (Belg.) VII–366b
Lannuier, Charles–Honoré (cabinetmaker) III–135a
La Noue, Zacharie Robutel de (expl.) VI–443a
Lansdowne, Marquis of, Sir William Petty, 2nd Earl of Shelburne (states.)
Proclamation of 1763 V–424b
L'Anse aux Meadows (Newf.) V–112a–b; VII–190a
Lansing, John (jur.) II–193a
Lansing, Robert (states.) IV–182b; V–157b
LANSING–ISHII AGREEMENT (1917) **IV–106b**; II–471b; IV–235a; V–96b, 159a; VI–251b
Lansky, Meyer II–261b, 262a
Lanston, Tolbert (inv.) V–412b
Laos
communist control VII–185a
Geneva Accords of 1954 III–159b
Geneva conference (1961) III–161b
Indochina War VII–182b
International Control Commission III–452b
Southeast Asia Treaty Organization VI–350b
LAOS, INTERVENTION IN (1954–74) **IV–107a**; II–316a–b, 489a; III–70a, 463a,b; V–53a; VII–183b, 184a, 186b, 227a
air operations I–61b, 62b, 63a, 328b
costs VII–229a
prisoners of war II–469a
La Pérouse, Comte de. *See* Galaus, Jean François de
La Plata, United Provinces of IV–110b
La Pointe (Madeline Is.) II–13b
LA POINTE, TREATY OF (1842) **IV–107b**
La Pointe à la Chevelure (N.Y.) II–266b
La Porte (Calif.) VI–298a
La Présentation (N.Y.) V–139b
La Présentation Mission IV–85a
Lapsley v. *Brashears* (1823) V–151a
Lapwai Creek (Idaho) IV–108a
Lapwai Indian Council. *See* Nez Perce War
LAPWAI MISSION (Idaho) **IV–108a**
Lapwai Reservation (Idaho) V–89b
La Radiere, Louis de (eng.) VII–279a
Laramie (Wyo.) III–44a; VII–345b, 346a
LARAMIE, FORT (Wyo.) **IV–108a**; III–256a; IV–1b; VII–96a
Black Hills gold discovery I–312b
Bozeman Trail I–357b; II–477b
Fort Bernard I–292b
Grattan incident III–213b
Indian treaties IV–108b–09a
Mormon migration IV–411b
Oregon Trail V–168b, 169a; VI–355a
Platte Bridge fight V–330a
pony express V–357b
Red Cloud's War III–378a
Sioux treaties VI–295b
Sioux Wars IV–33b; VI–296b
LARAMIE, FORT, TREATY OF (1851) **IV–108b**; I–358a; III–383b
LARAMIE, FORT, TREATY OF (1868) **IV–108b**; I–312b, 313a; III–378a; VI–296a, 297a, 350a
Black Hills War IV–167b
Fort Phil Kearny IV–34a
Sioux Council VI–295b
Laramie, Jacques (expl.) II–477a
Laramie Plains V–178b
Laramie River
Fort John IV–1b
Fort Laramie IV–108a
fur trade VII–104b–05a
Larch III–74b
L'Archevêque, Juan de VII–188a
Larch sawfly III–74b
Larcom, Lucy (ed.) IV–223a
Lard III–288b
Lardner, Ring (au.) IV–223a
Laredo (Tex.) VI–35a
La Reine, Fort (Can.) IV–118a
Large, Daniel (eng.) VI–409a
Lariat II–249a; VI–184b
Lark bunting (bird) VI–393 (table)
Larkin, Thomas O. (dipl.) IV–323a
Larkin Building (Buffalo, N.Y.) I–165a
Larned, B. F. (off.) IV–109a
LARNED, FORT (Kans.) **IV–109a**; IV–25b

La Roche Wood (Fr.) I–286b
Larsen, Henry A. (off., expl.) V–122a
La Saline (Okla.) II–34b
La Salle (Ill.) II–20a; III–329a, 330b, 331a; VI–33b, 408a
LA SALLE, EXPLORATIONS OF IV–109a; III–119a, 272a, 329a; V–52b; VI–192a, 192a, 195b
  Arkansas I–172b, 173b
  Chicago II–17a
  Chicago Road II–20a
  Falls of the Ohio V–142b
  Fort Conti II–211a
  Fort Crèvecoeur II–257b; V–260b
  Fort Frontenac III–124b
  Fort Prudhomme II–22a
  Great Lakes II–458b; III–216a; IV–332b
  Griffon III–228b
  Illinois II–16b
  Indiana III–369b
  Lake Ontario V–157a
  mapping III–99b
  Michigan VI–191b
  Mississippi IV–368a, 372a, 375b, 376b
  Mississippi River II–247b
  Mississippi Valley IV–7b
  Natchez Indians IV–455b
  Ohio V–140a
  Ohio River V–145a
  Ohio Valley V–146a
  Oklahoma V–148a
  Texas VII–36b
La Salle, Sieur de, Robert Cavelier (expl.) III–118a, 120a
  Fort Saint Louis VI–388a
  Franciscans III–94a
  Griffon IV–217b
  Louisiana V–173a
  Prudhomme Bluffs V–440b
  Texas IV–302b
LA SALLE, SPANISH SEARCHES FOR IV–110a; VI–195b
LAS ANIMAS LAND GRANT IV–110a
La Savane (comp.) IV–438a
"Lasca" (ballad) VI–382b
Las Casas, Bartolomé de (miss.) VI–309a–b
Lascaux Cave (Fr.) VI–18a
Lasers. *See* Masers and Lasers
Las Guásimas (Cuba) VI–165b, 213b
Lashio (Burma) I–386b; VII–337b
LASH (lighter-aboard-ship) system VI–281a
Laski, Harold (pol. sci.) III–260a
Lasky, Jesse L. (prod.) IV–417b
Las Moras Creek VI–144a
Lassallean socialism IV–63b
Lassen, Peter (pioneer) IV–110b
Lassen's Meadow (Nev.) III–215a
Lassen's Road III–215a
LASSEN'S TRADING POST AND RANCH (Calif.) **IV–110a**
Lassen Volcanic National Park V–217a, 218 (table)
Lassiter, William (off.) VI–456a
Last Chance Gulch (Mont.) III–269b–70a
Last Frontier VI–393 (table)
LAST ISLAND CATASTROPHE IV–110b
Last Judgment I–15b
Last of the Mohicans IV–161b, 387a
Las Vegas (Nev.) II–346a; V–40a; VI–135a
  gambling II–262a; III–150a
  land scrip IV–98a
  organized crime II–262b
  Santa Fe Trail I–174b
  water supply II–130b
Las Vegas (N.Mex.) II–251b
Las Vegas Hot Springs (N. Mex.) VI–100b
Laswell, Harold D. VII–333a
La Sylphide (ballet) II–289b
Late Lithic culture II–83b
Late Wisconsin period III–50a–b
Latex III–137a
Latham (Colo.) V–178b
Latham, Grey (inv.) IV–417a
Latham, Otway (inv.) IV–417a
Latham, Woodville (inv.) IV–417a
Lathan, Multon S. (pol.) V–180b
Lathe III–441b
Lathrop, Julia C. (social worker) IV–275b
Latin (lang.) II–394a; IV–283b
Latin Accidence, A Short Introduction to the Latin Tongue VI–227a, 229b
Latin America
  Anglo-American rivalry I–121b
  Indians and liquor III–398a
  slavery VI–307a
  territorial waters VII–33a
LATIN AMERICA, U.S. RELATIONS WITH IV–110b; II–475b; III–456b; V–171a; VI–364a–b
  aerial goodwill tour (1926–27) I–51b
  Alliance for Progress I–89b; III–62a
  Argentina-Brazil boundary dispute IV–363a
  Buenos Aires Peace Conference V–232a
  Cuban missile crisis II–270b
  Declaration of Panama V–200a
  diplomatic missions II–343a
  dollar diplomacy II–359b
  Drago Doctrine II–369a
  expansion III–347a
  Federal Bureau of Investigation V–138a
  filibustering III–22b
  Good Neighbor policy III–69a, 198b
  Havana Conference III–262b
  interoceanic canal I–295b
  intervention III–462b–63a
  Isle of Pines III–479a
  Johnson Doctrine IV–4b
  loans I–245b
  Macedonian affair IV–212b
  mediation of conflicts V–233a
  Monroe Doctrine I–121a,b; III–68b, 462a–b; IV–399b
  nationalization of U.S. property IV–466a
  New Deal V–45b
  nonintervention policy V–105a
  nonrecognition policy V–107b
  Panama Canal V–200b
  Panama Congress V–203b
  Panama Revolution V–204b
  Pan-American conferences VII–113a
  Pan-American Union V–205a
  Paraguay Expedition V–212b
  Perry's Venezuela mission VII–170a
  piracy V–320a–b
  Plan of 1776 V–323b–24a
  Point Four program V–335a
  Polk Doctrine V–354a
  proposed purchase of Cuba V–174b–75a
  Quinteros Bay Episode VI–3b
  Rio de Janeiro Conference VI–142b
  Roosevelt Corollary VI–163a
  Santiago Inter-American Congress V–217a
  Santo Domingo VI–217a
  Tacna-Arica controversy VI–456a
  trade VII–87b
  Venezuela blockade VII–169b
  Venezuela boundary controversy V–153a; VI–226b; VII–170a
  Wachusett affair VII–212b
  whaling VII–285a
  See also Cuba; Dominican Republic; South America, Commerce With
Latin American Free Trade Association VI–346a
LATIN-AMERICAN REPUBLICS, RECOGNITION OF IV–114b; III–96b, 456a, 462a–b; VI–55a,b, 360a
  trade VI–343b
LATIN-AMERICAN WARS OF INDEPENDENCE (1808–25) **IV–115a**; IV–110b
  privateers V–419b
  U.S. recognition IV–114b
Latin grammar school I–5b; II–394a–b
LATIN SCHOOLS IV–116a; VI–229a
LATITUDINARIANS IV–116a
La Tour, Charles (col. gov.) V–369b
La Tour, Claude de (col.) V–369b
La Tourette, Sieur de, Claude Greysolon (expl.) II–380a; VI–443a
Latreille, Pierre André (entom.) VI–90a
Latrobe (Pa.) VI–49a
Latrobe, Benjamin H., Jr. (eng.)
  Thomas Viaduct IV–116a
Latrobe, Benjamin Henry (arch., eng.)
  Baltimore architecture I–250a
  Capitol building I–162b–63a, 451a; III–268b
  Philadelphia waterworks VII–258a
  steam engines VI–409a
  White House VII–291b
Latrobe, J. H. B. (law., inv.) I–101b
LATROBE'S FOLLY IV–116a
LATTER-DAY SAINTS, CHURCH OF JESUS CHRIST OF IV–116b; VI–77b
  Book of Mormon IV–410b
  Haun's Mill massacre III–262b
  Missouri IV–377b
  Mormon Tabernacle VI–456a
  New York State V–87a
  polygamy V–355b; VI–266b, 401a
  Reorganized Church VI–87a
  Salt Lake City VI–203b
  Strangite Kingdom VI–416b
  theater VII–48a
  treason trials VII–107a
  Utah VII–161b–62a
  wagon trains VII–218a
  See also entries under Mormon
Laud, William (archbp.) III–220a, 274b; IV–270a
Laudanum II–373b
Laud Commission II–123a
Laudonnière, René Goulaine de (expl.) I–348b; III–38a
Laue, Max von (phys.) V–303b
Laufer, Berthold (nat.) III–19b; V–376b

"Laundering" of campaign funds II–231b
Laundry, home II–420b
Laun-Dry-Ette II–420b
Laura Spelman Rockefeller Memorial VII–330b
Laurel, José P. V–284a
Laurel County (Ky.) I–435a; VII–296a
Laurel Mountain VI–138b
LAURENS, FORT (Ohio) **IV–117a**; III–400b
Laurens, Henry (states.) II–318b; VI–347a, 436a; VII–153b, 358b
Laurent, Robert (sculp.) VI–244a
Laurentian ice mass I–155b
Laurents, Arthur (dram.) VII–50b
Laurier, Wilfred (states.) I–437a
Lauritsen, Charles C. (phys.) V–300b
LAUSANNE AGREEMENT (1932) **IV–117b**; IV–236a; VI–88a
Lauson, Jean de (col. gov.) VI–18a
Laussat, Pierre-Clément (col. offi.) IV–197a
Lauzun, Duc de, Armand Louis de Gontaut (off.) III–117b
Lava Beds National Monument V–217b
La Vaca River II–339b; VI–195a
Laval, Carl G. P. de (eng.) II–280b; VII–129b
Laver, Rod (athlete) VII–31a
Laveran, Alphonse (physic.) IV–229b
La Vérendrye, Sieur de, Pierre Gaultier de Varennes (expl.). *See* La Vérendrye Explorations
LA VÉRENDRYE EXPLORATIONS **IV–117b**; III–119b; VI–192a–b
Big Horn Mountains I–296b
Fort Saint Charles VI–188a
Indians IV–236a
Lake Superior VI–443a
Minnesota IV–355a–b
Missouri River IV–380a, 380b
Red River of the North VI–64a–b
Rocky Mountains VI–160a
LA VÉRENDRYE PLATE **IV–118a**; V–310b
La Veta Pass VI–461a
Lavoisier, Antoine (chem.) II–5b, 10a; III–16a; IV–152b; V–273b
Law, Andrew (comp.) IV–438a
Law, Harvey (inv.) IV–274a
Law, international. *See* International law
Law, James (vet.) VII–177a
Law, John (fin.)
Arkansas River I–173b
Crozat's grant VI–189b
Louisiana II–91b
Louisiana government V–173a
Mississippi Bubble II–149a, 237a; IV–370b
Western Company IV–192b–93a
Law and order
American Legion I–108a
Coolidge, Calvin I–346b
political issue II–259a
Law Enforcement and Administration of Justice, Commission on II–263b
Law Enforcement Assistance Administration IV–22b; V–417a,b
Lawes, John B. (agric.) III–16a
Law Library (Library of Congress) IV–146b
Lawns
landscape architecture IV–96b
Lawn tennis. *See* Tennis
Law Observance and Enforcement, National Commission on. *See* Wickersham Commission
"Law of storms" IV–316b
Lawrance, Charles L. (av. eng.) I–236a
LAWRENCE (brig) **IV–118b**; II–459a–b; V–262b
Lawrence (Kans.)
Civil War V–471a
Quantrill's raid IV–377b
Wakarusa War VI–270a; VII–218b
See also Lawrence, Sack of
Lawrence (Mass.) IV–67b, 120a; VII–45a
Lawrence, Abbott (ind.) IV–119b
Lawrence, Amos (mer.) II–439a; IV–99b
Lawrence, Cornelius V. R. (pol.) V–83a
Lawrence, D. H. (au.) I–479a
Lawrence, Ernest O. (phys.) II–12a, 278a; IV–119a,b; V–100a, 295b, 297a, 300b–01a, 303a
Lawrence, Fort (Ohio) III–223b, 227b
Lawrence, James (nav. off.) II–16a, 364a, 459a; III–301b
Lawrence, John (biol.) IV–119a
Lawrence, Matilda (slave) IV–276a
Lawrence, Richard I–202a
LAWRENCE, SACK OF (1856) **IV–118b**; I–342a; IV–25b, 28a, 30a, 31a
See also Border War
Lawrence, Thomas (paint.) V–188b
Lawrence, William (off.) I–356a
Lawrence Berkeley Laboratory. *See* Lawrence Radiation Laboratory
Lawrence Hall (Harvard Univ.) IV–119b
Lawrence Livermore Laboratory IV–119a
Lawrence-Mead, Andrea (athlete) V–154b
LAWRENCE RADIATION LABORATORY **IV–119a**
Lawrence raid (1863). *See* Quantrill's Raid
LAWRENCE SCIENTIFIC SCHOOL **IV–119b**; II–11a, 399a
LAWRENCE STRIKE (1912) **IV–120a**
"Laws, Concessions, And Agreements." *See* West Jersey Concessions
Laws Agreed Upon in England (1682) III–219a; V–246a
LAW SCHOOLS **IV–120b**; II–397b
Center for Study of Responsive Law IV–448b
Harvard University III–259b, 260a,b
Litchfield IV–159b
University of Pennsylvania V–249a
William and Mary VII–300b
Yale University VII–351a
Lawson, Alexander (engr.) V–413b
Lawson, Ernest (art.) II–104a
Lawson, John (trav.) III–26b; IV–231a
Lawson, Thomas W. (fin.) III–122b, 433b; IV–424b
Lawson, Victor F. (ed.) V–73b
Lawton, Henry W. (off.) VI–213b, 362a
Lawyers
American Bar Association I–99a
exclusion from Knights of Labor IV–52b, 64a
women VII–317a
Lawyer's Dream (paint.) V–189b
Lay, Benjamin (Quaker ref.) I–135a
Lazarus, Emma (poet) I–275b
Lazear, Jesse W. (physic.) IV–3a, 298a; VII–355b
Lazzaroni I–98a
Lea, Albert M. III–468a
Lea, Homer (sol.) II–367a
Lea, Isaac (pub.) I–110b
Lea, L. (cartog.) I–462b
Lea, Tom (art.) VII–41a
LEAA. *See* Law Enforcement Assistance Administration
Lea and Febiger (pub.) I–334a
Leaching
copper industry II–223b
Lead
colonial duties VI–110b
earthenware glazing III–183a
food contamination V–466b
silver mining VI–292a,b
U.S. Geological Survey III–163a
Lead (S.Dak.) I–312b; III–192a; VI–350a
Lead arsenate III–421a
Lead carbonate IV–122b
Lead colic IV–122b, 293b
Leaded gasoline V–267a
Leader, James VI–218a
Leader, Richard (mfr.) III–472a
LEAD INDUSTRY **IV–122a**; II–224a; V–102a,b; VI–48b
Coeur d'Alene riots II–93b–94a; IV–66a
domestic trade VII–84a
Dubuque (Iowa) II–376a
Fort Crawford (Wis.) II–254a
fuel IV–334a
Galena III–147a; VII–307b
health hazards IV–294b
Helena mining camp III–270a
Idaho III–328a
Kansas IV–25a, 26a
lead colic IV–293b
Leadville district IV–123b
Louisiana II–267b
Oklahoma V–149a
pack trains V–184a
pollution VI–213a
Sainte Genevieve district VI–189b
Saint Louis VI–194b
tariff VI–465b
Wisconsin III–90a
Wytheville (Va.) II–163a
"Lead" pencils II–422a
Lead poisoning IV–294a
Lead sulfide IV–122b
Leadville (Colo.) II–128a; IV–124a; VI–292a,b
LEADVILLE MINING DISTRICT **IV–123b**; I–336b; II–128a; IV–122b, 354b
smelters VI–316b
strikes VII–272b
Leaflets
psychological warfare V–441a
League for Industrial Democracy VI–421a,b; VII–365a,b, 366a
League Island V–56b
League Island Park (Philadelphia) VI–263a
League of Armed Neutrality. *See* Armed Neutrality of 1780
LEAGUE OF NATIONS **IV–124a**; III–69a, 237b, 457a; IV–82b; V–233b; VII–151a, 331a
campaign of 1920 I–427a,b
campaign of 1924 I–428a
Covenant IV–36a
domestic opposition to IV–401b

Franco–American relations III–97a–b
Geneva disarmament conference III–161a
Hitchcock Reservations III–285b
International Labor Organization IV–69b
Japanese mandates III–426a
Liberia IV–141b
Lodge Reservations IV–178a
Manchukuo V–107a
Manchuria IV–235a
mandates IV–236a, 236b
open diplomacy V–157b
Permanent Court of International Justice V–234a
Senate defeat VII–110b
Treaty of Versailles VII–173a,b
U.S.–Canadian relations I–439b
U.S. isolationism III–480a
U.S. rejection I–122b, 123a, 290b; II–472b; VII–113a
Western Samoa VI–205a
Yap mandate VII–353b
League of Nations, Pan–Am Indians V–210b
League of Nations Covenant Article X I–199a
League of Neutrals I–176a
League of New York Theatres I–315a
League of Red Cross Societies VI–62a
League of the Ho–Dé–no–sau–nee, or Iroquois III–476a
League of the Iroquois III–391a, 405a, 475a–b, 476a
LEAGUE OF UNITED SOUTHERNERS IV–125b; VI–354a
League of Universal Brotherhood V–235b
LEAGUE OF WOMEN VOTERS OF THE UNITED STATES IV–126a; V–400b
League to Enforce Peace IV–124a,b; V–390b; VII–236b
Leahy, Patrick J. (pol.) VII–172a
Leahy, William D. (nav. off.) I–14a
Lea–McCarren Civil Aeronautics Act (1938) II–49b
"Lean John." *See* Flaco, Juan
Lear, William P. I–52b
Learjet I–52b
LEARNED SOCIETIES IV–126a
American Philosophical Society I–110a
museums IV–435b
Learner, Max (jour.) V–75a
Learning theory V–442a,b, 443a
Leasburg (Mo.) V–314a
Lease, Mary E. (pol.) I–39a
LEASEHOLD IV–127b; I–134a; V–81b
Leasing
Indian reservations IV–90a
"Leather Breeches" (song) III–19a
LEATHER INDUSTRY IV–127b
colonial III–413b
dress II–372b
furniture III–136b–37a
meat–packing by–products IV–281a
Newark V–41a,b
Pennsylvania V–247b
preparation II–5a
Salem VI–199b
tariff VI–463a
Leatherstocking series IV–161b–62a
LEATHERWOOD GOD IV–129a
Leatherwood Valley (Ohio) IV–129a
LEAVENWORTH (Kans.) **IV–129a**
freighting V–177a
Mexican War VI–353b
Smoky Hill Trail VI–320b
Squatters' Claim Association VII–187b
trade IV–27b
LEAVENWORTH, FORT (Kans.) **IV–129a**; I–190b; III–172a; IV–25b, 129a; V–174a
Army War College I–191a
Fort Mann IV–240a
Fort Scott VI–240b
Fort Towson VII–81b
Harney expedition III–256a
Kearny expedition IV–323b
military reconnaissance II–440b
Mormons IV–411a, 411a
Platte River Trail V–330b
Sumner's Cheyenne expedition VI–439b
supplies V–375b; VI–176b
Leavenworth, Henry (off.) II–490a
Fort Leavenworth IV–129a
Fort Snelling VI–322b
Magee–Kearny expedition IV–223b
Yellowstone River expedition VII–358a
Leavenworth, Pawnee and Western Railroad. *See* Kansas Pacific Railroad
LEAVENWORTH AND PIKES PEAK EXPRESS IV–129b; V–311b; VI–176b, 379a,b
LEAVENWORTH EXPEDITION (1823) **IV–129b**
Leaverett, Thomas VII–219b
Leaves of Grass IV–162b
Leavitt, George A. (auctioneer) I–332b
Leavitt, Humphrey H. (jur.) I–492a
Le Bananier (comp.) IV–438a
Lebanon
immigration to U.S. III–341a
Lebanon (Conn.) II–292b
library IV–144b
Lebanon (Pa.) VII–127b
LEBANON, U.S. LANDING IN (1958) **IV–130a**; I–124b; II–315b; III–70a, 348a, 463a,b; IV–253a
Lebanon County (Pa.) III–300b; V–251b
Le Blanc, Honoré (off.) III–441a,b
Leblanc, Nicholas (chem.) II–6a, 7a
LeBoeuf, Fort (Pa.) II–381b; III–118a, 120a; IV–250b; V–399b
LEBOEUF, FORT, WASHINGTON'S MISSION TO (1753–54) **IV–130a**; III–115a, 182a, 219a; IV–181a, 434b; V–143a, 146a; VI–150a
Le Bourget airfield (Paris) IV–157a
L. E. Cann (bark) III–428b
Le Cap aux Isles I–446b
Le Caron, Joseph (miss.) III–319a
Lecherous Father (myth.) III–386a
Lecompton (Kans.) IV–130b
LECOMPTON CONSTITUTION IV–130b; II–450a–b; IV–28b, 31a–b; V–360b
LeConte, John Eaton (entom.) VI–90a
Le Conte, Joseph (geol.) IV–119b
LECTURE DAYS IV–131a
Lectures
copyright II–224b
Lectures on Revivals of Religion VI–81b
Lectures on Systematic Theology VI–81b
Lederberg, Joshua (genet.) V–100a
Lederer, John (trav.) IV–131a
LEDERER'S EXPLORING EXPEDITIONS IV–131a
Lederle Division V–341a
Ledo (India)
World War II I–386b
See also Burma Road and Ledo Road
Le Duc Tho. *See* Tho, Le Duc
Ledyard, Isaac VII–117a
Ledyard, John (expl.) III–263a
Lee (ship) VI–128a
Lee, Ann (rel. mystic) II–147a
Lee, Arthur (dipl.) III–90a, 94b, 95a; IV–371a; VI–119b
Lee, Charles (off.) III–179a; IV–397b; VII–251b
Lee, Custis VII–154b
Lee, Fitzhugh (off.) I–374a; VII–117a
LEE, FORT (N.J.) **IV–131b**; V–41a; VII–247a
Lee, Fort (W.Va.) I–497b
Lee, Francis Lightfoot (states.) II–308b
Lee, George Washington Custis (off.) I–175b; VII–154b
Lee, Henry ("Light Horse Harry") (off., states.) III–26a, 265a; IV–48b; V–229b
Lee, H. J. (expl.) V–240b
Lee, Jason (miss.) II–477b; III–243b; V–165a, 166b, 166b–67a; VII–300a
Lee, John D. (farmer) IV–421b, 422a
Lee, Mary Ann (dancer) II–286b, 287a
Lee, Mary Custis VII–154b
Lee, Peggy (sing.) IV–442a
Lee, Richard Henry (states.) I–197b; IV–8b; V–199a; VII–192b, 252a
Articles of Confederation II–165b
Continental navy VI–128a
Declaration of Independence II–303b, 305b, 308b
independence VI–115a, 161b
land speculation IV–98b
"Letters of a Federal Farmer" V–353a
ratification of Constitution II–196a
Virginia Resolves VII–203a
Lee, Robert E. (off.) I–175b, 181a; II–62b, 64a, 161a, 450a, 482b; VII–195a
Antietam II–162b
Army Corps of Engineers I–323a
Army of Northern Virginia VII–197a
Ashby's Gap I–200b
Battle of Antietam I–130a
Battle of Brandy Station I–360a
Battle of Cedar Mountain I–477a
Battle of Chancellorsville I–493a
Battle of Frayser's Farm III–100a; VII–293a
Battle of Fredericksburg III–101a
Battle of Gaines' Mill III–146b
Battle of Gettysburg III–175b; V–309a
Battle of Malvern Hill IV–230b
Battle of Mechanicsville IV–281b
Battle of North Anna V–113b; VI–376b
Battle of Winchester VII–304b
Battles at Sailors's Creek VI–186b
Battles of the Wilderness

LEE, ROBERT E. (cont.)
IV–54a; VII–295b
Bloody Angle I–322b
Bristoe campaign I–365a
Buckland Races I–374a
Cold Harbor II–96b
Dahlgren's and Kilpatrick's raid II–279a
Davis–Johnston controversy II–295a
Falling Waters II–484b
Fort Fisher III–30b
Hanover cavalry engagement III–250b
Harpers Ferry III–256a–b, 257a
Jackson's Valley campaign III–487b
lost order IV–190a
Maryland invasion IV–261b
Mexican War I–488b
Mine Run campaign IV–350a
Peninsular campaign V–245a
Pennsylvania invasion V–248a
Petersburg V–265a
resignation from U.S. Army I–182a
Richmond campaign V–59a; VI–137b–38a; VII–115a
right of secession VI–121b
Second Battle of Bull Run I–382a; III–229a
Seven Days' Battles VI–137a, 263b, 263b; VII–197a
Shenandoah campaign VI–275a
Sherman's march through Georgia VI–278a
Stuart's ride VI–420b
Suffolk operations VI–430b
surrender I–146b, 458b; II–63a, 68b, 165a; IV–257a
Virginia campaign IV–42a
Washington and Lee University VII–249a
Lee, Robert E., Foundation VI–417b
Lee, Sammy (athlete) V–154b
Lee, Samuel P. (nav. off.)
prize money V–424a
Lee, S. D. (off.) II–479b
Lee, Stephen Louis VI–210b
Lee, Thomas IV–371a
Lee, Thomas, of Stratford VI–417b
Leech Lake IV–355b; V–312a
LEECH LAKE, INDIAN COUNCIL AT (1806) **IV–131b**
LEECH LAKE UPRISING (1898) **IV–131b**; VII–239b
Lee-Enfield rifle VII–326a
Lee family IV–256b
Lee House (Richmond) VI–137a
Lee Mansion (Westmoreland Co., Va.) I–161b
Lee newspaper chain V–76b
Leesburg (Va.) IV–472a
Leeser, Isaac (cantor) IV–9b
Lee's Ferry II–461a
Leete, William (col. gov.) V–56a; VI–70b
Leeuwenhoek, Anthony van (nat.) I–240b
Leeward Islands III–42b
Leflore, Greenwood (Indian) II–291a
Lefoulon, Michel (mfr.) III–184a
Left (pol.) III–412b; IV–81b
Legal aid V–136a; VI–74b
Legal education. *See* Law Schools
LEGAL TENDER IV–132a; II–200b; VI–94b–95a
Coinage Act of 1873 II–264a
colonies II–94a–b; VII–3a
commodities II–140b
foreign coins II–95a; IV–394b
gold III–192b
greenbacks III–224a, 225b, 251b; VI–371a
implied powers III–349a
Legal Tender Act IV–132b
Legal Tender Cases IV–133a
notes I–255a
private mints IV–360a–b
Resumption Act VI–104a
silver coins VII–92b
silver dollar IV–154b
soft money VI–333b
specie payments VI–369b
trade dollar VII–92b
Treasury notes III–111a
LEGAL TENDER ACT (1862) **IV–132b**; II–66a–b; IV–105b; VI–94b
constitutionality IV–132b, 133a
Supreme Court rulings IV–20a
LEGAL TENDER CASES (1870–71) **IV–133a**; IV–132b; VI–94b–95a
Juilliard v. *Greenman* IV–20a
Knox v. *Lee* (1871) III–417b
Supreme Court packing VI–448b
Legal tender notes. *See* Greenbacks
Legazpe, Miguel López V–282a
"Legend of Sleepy Hollow" VI–312b
Legends
children's books I–335b
cowboys II–248b
message to García III–150b
Léger, Fernand (paint.) II–105b
Legge, William, 2nd Earl of Dartmouth (states.) II–292b; III–400a
Leggett, William (labor leader) IV–61b
Legion of Decency I–480a
Legion of Merit II–311a–b, 312b
Legislation
judicial review IV–12a
Legislation Reference Bureau (Wis.) VII–308b
Legislative branch. *See* Congress, United States
Legislative Budget Office II–179a
Legislative courts. *See* Courts, legislative
Legislative Reference Service II–501a
Legislative Reorganization Acts (1946, 1970) II–152a; IV–170b
Legislators
travel allowances IV–339a
LEGISLATURE IV–133b; V–351b
bicameral I–294b–95a
blocs I–322a
colonial II–306b–07a
divorce by II–356b
expunging resolutions II–478a–b
investigatory power III–464b
lobbies IV–170b
pairing V–194a
political parties V–344a
referendum VI–66b
separation of powers IV–209a
state constitutions VI–390b, 391a
state emblems, nicknames, mottos, and songs VI–392a
state government VI–396b, 397b
statutory law VI–406a
steering committees VI–411b
taxation VI–398b
territorial governments VII–32a
territories VI–400b
unicameralism VII–142a
Le Havre (Fr.)
sailing packets V–183b
shipping IV–310a
Lehi (Utah) I–285a
Lehigh Canal I–127b, 442b, 443a,b; V–250a
Lehigh Coal and Navigation Company I–442b; V–250b
Lehigh County (Pa.) V–251b
Lehigh River
canal I–127b; IV–412b; V–250a
Walking Purchase VII–220b
Lehigh Valley I–477b
Lehigh Valley Railroad IV–176a, 412b–13a; V–250b, 456a; VI–34b
Lehleitner, George (bus.) I–78b
Lehman, Herbert H. (pol.) I–107b; V–87b; VI–460a–b
Lehman, Philip II–104a
Lehman, Robert II–104b
Lehman Caves National Monument V–217b
Leibniz, G. W. (philos., math.) I–395b
Leibowitz, Samuel (law.) VI–241b
Leicester sheep VI–273a
Leiden (Neth.)
medical education IV–297b
Pilgrims IV–278b; V–64b, 312b
Leidy, Joseph (nat.) I–110b, 241a; III–29b; IV–232b; V–196b
Leighton, Clare (art.) VII–319b
Leinster House (Dublin) VII–291b
Leipzig (Ger.)
World War II VII–341a
Leisler, Jacob (off.) IV–49b
See also Leisler Rebellion
LEISLER REBELLION (1689) **IV–134a**; I–82b; II–125a; IV–49b; V–82a–b, 84b
Leisure Village II–48b
Leisure World II–48b
Leisy v. *Hardin* (1890) IV–158b–159a
See also Original Package Doctrine
Leland, Waldo Gifford (hist.) I–106a
Le Madrillon (Bastogne, Belg.) I–273b
Le Maire, Jakob (navig.) I–448a
Le Mans (Fr.) III–293a
LeMay, Curtis E. (off.)
air war against Japan III–490a,b
campaign of 1968 I–106b, 431b
Strategic Air Command I–61a, 67b
Lemhi Pass V–225a
Lemke, William F. (pol.) V–47b; VI–269a
Lemon, George E. (pub.) IV–471b
Lemons II–43b; III–128a,b
Lemont (Ill.) I–217b
Lemos, Manuel Gayoso de (off.) VI–366b
Le Moyne, Charles, Baron de Longueuil (col. gov.) I–295b; V–308a
Lemoyne, Jacques (art.) III–38a
Lemoyne, Pierre. *See* Iberville, Sieur d', Pierre Lemoyne
Le Moyne, Simon (miss.) VI–192a
Lena River V–336a,b
LEND-LEASE IV–134a; II–301b; III–60b, 69a; V–36a; VII–88a, 237b, 332a, 334b
balance of trade I–245b, 246a
China I–387a; III–46a
costs VII–228b
Great Britain I–123a
Soviet Union IV–435a;

VI–179a
warships V–21b; VII–243a,b
Lend–Lease Act (1941)
II–314b; III–60b;
IV–134a–b
L'Enfant, Pierre Charles (eng., off.) II–449b; V–187b;
VI–129a
Washington, D.C. I–162b;
II–45b, 46a, 338b;
VII–244b
White House VII–291b
Lenglen, Suzanne (athlete)
VII–30a
Lenin, Nikolai II–144a;
VI–164a, 325a
Leningrad (USSR)
World War II V–11a
Leninism VI–327a
Le nouveau voyage III–272a
Lenox, James (philan.)
II–102b, 109a; IV–145a
Lenox Library II–109a
Lent
Mardi Gras IV–249b
Lent, Lewis B. (circus owner)
II–40b
Leo XIII (pope) I–107a,
144a; II–156a
Leominster (Mass.) V–327b
León, Alonso de (expl.)
II–184b, 184b; VI–195b;
VII–36b
Leon, Edwin de VII–362a
Leonard, Benny (pugilist)
V–423a
Leonard, John W. (off.)
VI–84a
Leonard, Joseph (auctioneer)
I–332b
Leonard, William B. (inv.)
VII–43a
Leonard, Zenas VII–104b
Leonardo da Vinci. *See* Vinci, Leonardo da
Leonora (opera) IV–438b
Leontief, Wassily (econ.)
V–99b
Leopard. See Chesapeake–Leopard Incident (1807)
Leopold (Afr. k.) I–21b
Leopold I (emp.) VI–2a
Leopold, Aldo (forester)
VII–297b
Leopoldine Foundation
I–467a
Leopold–Loeb case VII–118a
Leoti (Kans.) II–245b
Le Page du Pratz, Antoine (hist.) IV–455a
Le Petit (hist.) IV–455a
Le Prince, Ringuet (cabinet-maker) III–445b
Lerner, Alan Jay (lyricist)
IV–442a; VII–50b
Lernoult, Fort (Mich.)
II–338a
See also Pontchartrain du Détroit, Fort
Léry Gaspard–Joseph Chaussegros de V–157a
Lesbians
woman's rights movement
VII–314b
Lescarbot, Marc (cartog.)
VII–73b
Lesley J. McNair, Fort (Washington, D.C.) I–191a
Leslie, Charles Robert (paint.)
II–102b
Leslie, John (math., phys.)
VI–69b
Lesovsky, Stepan S. (nav. off.)
VI–181a
Lesquereux, Leo (paleobot.)
I–110b; V–196b
Lessay–Périers–Saint–Lô road VI–193b
Lesseps, Ferdinand de (eng.)
V–201a
Lesser Antilles VI–126b
Lessouda hill (Tun.) IV–32b
Lesueur, Charles A. (art., nat.)
III–27a; VI–90a
Le Sueur, Pierre (expl.)
II–13b; IV–355a; VI–189b
Letcher, John (pol.) V–108a;
VI–168b
Letchworth (Eng.) II–46b
L'Etoile du Nord (motto)
VI–394 (table)
Letter cutting V–411a–b
"Letter From Birmingham Jail" VII–118a
Letter From Jamaica
V–203b
Letterman, Jonathan (off., physic.) I–191b; IV–290b
Letterpress V–411a
Letters
censorship II–277a
Letters From a Farmer in Pennsylvania to the Inhabitants of the British Colonies. See Farmer's Letters, Dickinson's
Letters From America
IV–79a
Letters From an American Farmer III–122a; IV–79a;
VI–114b–15a
"Letters of a Federal Farmer"
V–353a
Letters of marque and reprisal. *See* Marque and Reprisal, Letters of
Letters patent. *See* Patents and U.S. Patent Office
"Let the welfare of the people be the supreme law" (motto) VI–394 (table)
Lettuce III–151a
"LET US HAVE PEACE" IV–135a
Leutze, Emanuel (paint.)
II–103a, 321b; V–188b
Levant (sloop of war)
II–191b
Levassor, Émile Constant (inv.) I–225b
Levee (Chicago) II–260a
Levelers III–123a
Level walkers I–443b
Levene, P. A. T. (chem.)
II–357b
Levene, Phoebus (chem.)
I–304a
Lever, A. F. (pol.) IV–135b
LEVER ACT (1917)
IV–135b; III–129b
Lever Brothers II–234a;
VI–324a
Lever House (N.Y.C.)
I–165b; VI–299a
Leveson–Gower, George Granville, 2nd Earl Granville (states.) I–73b; VII–248b
Leviathan (ship) VII–329a
Levine, Charles (av.) I–51b
Levis (dress) II–372a
Lévis, François Gaston de (off.) III–117a; IV–405b;
VI–136b
Levi–Strauss, Claude (anthrop.) I–129b
LEVY IV–135b
Levy, Julian (art dealer)
II–105a
Levy, Uriah (nav. off.)
IV–405a
Lewes (Del.) II–322a;
IV–135b; VII–372b
LEWES, BOMBARDMENT OF (1813) **IV–135b**
Lewes Creek VII–372b
Lewin, John (col. offi.)
V–436a
Lewis, Alma I–25a
Lewis, Andrew (off.)
III–226a, 236a
Battle of Point Pleasant
V–335b
Burning Spring I–387a
Dunmore's War I–497b,
499a; II–381b
Lewis, Anthony (jour.)
V–75a
Lewis, Charles (off.) V–335b
Lewis, Clarence (philos.)
V–386b, 387a
Lewis, Fort (Mont.) I–289b;
III–77b
Lewis, Francis (mer.)
II–308a
Lewis, George W. (offi.)
IV–458a
Lewis, Gilbert N. (chem.)
II–12a; V–295a
Lewis, J. O. (art.) V–388b
Lewis, John (col.) IV–201a;
VI–275b
Lewis, John (mus.) IV–440b
Lewis, John L. (labor leader)
I–104b; IV–69b, 70b, 72a,
73b
campaign of 1936 IV–73a;
V–47b
Congress of Industrial Organizations II–462b
steel industry
VI–410b–11a
United Mine Workers
II–86b, 87a; VII–151a
Lewis, Meriwether (expl.)
See also Lewis and Clark Expedition
Lewis, Morgan (gov.) VI–3b
Lewis, Reuben (fur trader)
VI–195b
Lewis, Sinclair (writ.)
I–242a; IV–164a; V–99b
Lewis, Thomas (col.)
VI–184a
Lewis, William Berkeley (pol.)
IV–51a
Lewis, William H. (off.)
II–379b
Lewis Alfred Henry (au.)
V–336a
LEWIS AND CLARK CENTENNIAL EXPOSITION (1905) **IV–136a**
LEWIS AND CLARK EXPEDITION (1804–06)
IV–136a; I–209a; II–477a;
III–119b; VI–411b;
VII–74b, 104b, 247b,
271a, 275b
American Philosophical Society I–110b, 128a
Arikara I–171b
birds and mammals
IV–232a
botany I–349a
Columbia River II–131b;
V–164b, 167b
Dakota Territory II–285a
fish species III–27a
Fort Mandan IV–235b
fur trade III–143a, 144b
Great Plains III–220b
grizzly bear I–280b
horse III–303a
Idaho III–327b
Iowa III–468a
Kansas IV–25b
mammoth bones
IV–231b, 231b
Mandan, Hidatsa, and Arikara IV–236a
Missouri River IV–378a,
380a
Montana IV–403a
Nebraska V–30b
Oregon Trail V–168b
plant study V–326b
portages V–367b
Rocky Mountains
V–225a; VI–160b
Sacagawea III–33b
Snake River VI–322b
weather data II–75b
Lewisburg (Pa.) V–250a
Lewisburg (W.Va.) I–497b
Lewis County (N.Y.)
I–466b; IV–219b
Lewis family (Va.) III–469b
Lewis Flight Propulsion Laboratory IV–458b
Lewis' Ford (Va.) I–381a
Lewis machine gun I–57b;
IV–431b
Lewis River. *See* Snake River
Lewiston (Idaho) IV–108a
Lewiston (Maine) IV–227a;
VII–45a
Lewiston (N.Y.) II–339b;
V–90a, 91a, 91b
Lewiston suspension bridge
V–93b
Lewisville site (Tex.) I–155a
Lexicography II–340a–b
LEXINGTON (ship name)
IV–136b
carrier I–54b, 55b; II–225a;
V–20b
Continental brig VI–128b
steamboat II–349a
store ship II–484a–b
Lexington (Ky.) III–206b
Bluegrass country I–324b
Bryan's Station I–373b
Civil War IV–410a;
VI–137b
fugitive slaves VII–265a
hemp III–271a
industry IV–41b

LEXINGTON (cont.)
Kentucke Gazette V–70a
natural history museum I–295b
railroad IV–137b; VI–34b
Rice–Campbell debates VI–135b
steamboating VII–280b
Lexington (Mass.)
public library IV–144b
Revere's ride V–151b; VI–106a
Lexington (Mo.) I–453a
Civil War IV–137a; V–402b
merchants VII–273b
Lexington (Okla.) VII–290b
Lexington (Va.) VI–275b; VII–249a
LEXINGTON, SIEGE OF (1861) **IV–137a**; IV–377b
"Lexington alarm lists" IV–360b
LEXINGTON AND CONCORD (1775) **IV–137a**; I–344b, 383a; II–211a, 468b; IV–266a; V–69b, 85b; VI–107a, 123a, 125a, 282b–83a, 372b; VII–3b
minutemen IV–360b, 361a
Pittsburgh Resolutions V–322b
Revere's ride VI–106a
Society of Colonial Wars VI–332a
"Lexington and Concord" of the South IV–407b
LEXINGTON AND OHIO RAILROAD IV–137b
Lexow, Clarence (pol.) IV–138a
LEXOW COMMITTEE IV–137b; VI–460a
Leyba, Fernando de (off.) VI–363b
LEYTE GULF, BATTLE OF (1944) **IV–138a**; I–60a; V–21a; VI–1b–2a; VII–139a, 337a, 343a
LGP–30 (computer) II–156a
L'Huillier, Fort (Minn.) IV–355a
Liability insurance. *See* Insurance
Liability laws, employers. *See* Employer's Liability Laws
Liaotung Peninsula V–370b
Liautard, Alexandre (vet.) VII–176a,b
Libbie, C. F., and Company I–332b
Libby, Edward Drummond II–105a
Libby, McNeill and Libby IV–280b
Libby, Willard F. (chem.) II–12b; V–100a; VI–17b
Libby and Son IV–139a
Libby Dam II–132a
LIBBY PRISON (Va.) **IV–139a**
LIBEL IV–139b; II–266a; III–105b
Congress II–172a
Croswell suit II–266a–b
freedom of the press III–104b
New York Times Company v. *Sullivan* V–78b
sedition acts I–86b, 87a; VI–255a
Zenger trial V–69a, 82b; VII–368b
Liberal arts II–401a; IV–2a
Liberal bloc I–322b
Liberal Catholic Church V–172a
Liberal Imagination IV–165b
LIBERALISM IV–140a
break with labor IV–77a
campaign of 1924 IV–70a
Minnesota IV–357b
Vietnam War V–237a
World War I V–236a
Liberalism and Social Action V–387a
Liberal party. *See* American Labor Party
LIBERAL REPUBLICAN PARTY IV–141a; I–422a; V–49a; VI–57b
Liberator (bomber) I–50a, 52a, 55b, 60a; V–332a
LIBERATOR (news.) **IV–141a**; I–137a; III–153a
LIBERIA IV–141b; V–22b
Bretton Woods Conference I–361b
colonization I–101a; II–127a; VI–321b
Echo case II–390a
founding I–21a
France III–97a
freed slaves II–434a
iron ore III–12b
merchant marine VI–281a,b
ship registry IV–312a
sorghum VI–340a
Treaty of Versailles VII–173a
United Nations Declaration VII–151b
Libertarians
New Left II–189b
Nixon, Richard M. II–189b
Libertion Red Cross VII–94a
Liberty (fig.) III–47b
Liberty (mag.) IV–222b
Liberty (sloop) VI–436a; VII–38a, 41a–b, 81a
LIBERTY, CONCEPT OF IV–142a; V–351a
Constitution II–197a
democracy II–324b
due process II–377a–78b
Magna Charta IV–224a
Northwest Territory V–163a
Liberty, religious. *See* Religious Liberty
"LIBERTY, SONG OF" IV–142b
"Liberty and Independence" (motto) VI–393 (table)
"Liberty and Prosperity" (motto) VI–394 (table)
"Liberty and Union, Now and Forever, One and Inseparable" (motto) VI–395 (table)
LIBERTY BELL IV–142b; III–354a
Liberty–Bell Mine (Colo.) III–192a; VI–213b
Liberty bonds I–257a; II–300a; III–6b, 188b; VI–95a
Liberty Boys. *See* Sons of Liberty (American Revolution)
"Liberty cabbage" II–445b
LIBERTY CAP IV–143a
LIBERTY–CAP CENT IV–143a
Liberty engine I–51a, 233b; II–344a; IV–433a–b
Liberty Enlightening the World. *See* Statue of Liberty
Liberty Gap (Tenn.) VII–127b
"Liberty gardens" II–50a
Liberty Hall Academy (Va.). *See* Washington and Lee University
Liberty Island (N.Y.C.) I–275b; VI–405b
Liberty League V–47b
"Liberty Line." *See* Underground Railroad
LIBERTY LOANS IV–143a; II–317a; III–85a; VI–222a; VII–7a, 331b
Liberty Lobby V–400b
"Liberty measles" II–445b
Liberty of conscience III–219a
LIBERTY PARTY IV–143b
abolitionists I–138a
antislavery VII–52b
campaign of 1840 I–420a
campaign of 1844 I–420a
campaign of 1848 I–420b
campaign of 1932 I–428b
Free Soil party III–111b
LIBERTY POLES IV–143b; III–189b; VI–112b, 339a
"Liberty pups" II–445b
Liberty ships IV–312a; VI–279b, 280b; VII–344a
"Liberty Song" (poem) VII–155b
Liberty trees. *See* Liberty Poles
Liberty Warehouse Co. v. *Burley Tobacco Growers Co-operative Marketing Association* (1928) II–221b
Librarians VII–317a
LIBRARIES IV–144a; II–401a
banking IV–468a
book collecting II–107b–10a
book publishing I–334b
Carnegie gifts III–79b
county–sponsored II–245b
Enoch Pratt Free Library IV–261b
facilities for the blind III–248b
government publications III–203b
historical libraries III–279b
information retrieval VI–232b
Johns Hopkins Medical School IV–3b
Library of Congress II–501a; IV–146a
mechanics' institutes IV–281b
National Library of Medicine IV–292a
New York City V–83b
presidential III–284a,b
private I–333a
public I–456a
Truman library III–353b
universities III–284b–85a
Works Progress Administration VII–323b
Yale University VII–351a
See also American Library Association
Library Company of Philadelphia II–108a; IV–144b, 145b
Library Journal (period.) IV–145a
Library of American Biography III–281b
LIBRARY OF CONGRESS IV–146a; II–395b, 501a; III–284b; IV–145a–b; VII–246b
copyrights II–224b; V–226b
facilities for the blind III–248b
Force's historical collection II–108b
Franklin's papers II–108b–09a
Jefferson's library II–108b
murals V–191a
National Union Catalog of Manuscript Collections III–285b
Virginia Company of London records VII–201a
Librascope II–156a
Libre (commune) II–142b
Libya
U.S. air bases I–149b
World War II IV–32b; V–112b, 113a, 332a
Lice III–421a
LICENSE CASES (1847) **IV–148a**
License fees II–396b; III–153b
LICENSES TO TRADE IV–148a; III–204a
communications III–1a
liquor traffic III–276a
medical profession IV–284a,b
National Recovery Administration IV–469a
ocean shipping IV–254b
out–of–state practitioners V–420b
pharmacists V–275b–76a
revenue VII–11a
taxation VII–5a,b
traveling salesmen VII–105b
License taxes II–164b
Lichtenau (Ohio) VI–226a
Lichtenstein, Roy (art.) II–107a; V–193a

Lick, James (fin., philan.) V–131a–b
Licking County (Ohio) V–145b
Licking River I–325a; II–37b; IV–329b, 330a; V–66a; VII–238b
Lick Observatory (Calif.) I–211b; V–131b
Liddy, G. Gordon VII–254b–55a
Lieb, Michael (pol.) VI–460b
Lieber, Francis (educ.) II–70a, 444a; III–81a, 456a; V–347b; VII–225a,b
Loyal Publication Societies IV–202a
Liebig, Justus von (chem.) I–46a, 302b, 303a; II–11a; III–16a, 17a; IV–2a, 119b; VI–334a
Liebling, A. J. (jour.) V–80a
Liechtenstein III–453a
Liège (Belg.)
World War II I–380a; VII–340a
Lieu scrip IV–98a
Life (mag.) IV–222b; VI–300a; VII–333b
"Life, Liberty and the Pursuit of Happiness" V–351a
Life and Demography of the Side–blotched Lizard VI–91b
Life and Times of Benjamin Franklin IV–163a
Lifeboats II–89b
LIFE EXPECTANCY IV–148b; IV–299a; V–362a–b
acturarial tables VII–207a
elderly population V–150a
Indian III–397a
infants and children IV–274b
insurance III–433a
rural population VI–174a
urban health VII–158a,b
1750 IV–295a
LIFEGUARD, WASHINGTON'S IV–152a
Life insurance III–426b, 432a–35a
business forecasts I–395a
pension plans V–255b
secret societies VI–253a
See also Insurance
Life insurance companies II–220b, 255a
"Life of the land is perpetuated in righteousness" (motto) VI–393 (table)
Life of Washington III–215b
Lifesaving II–310a
Life Saving Benevolent Society of New York IV–152a
LIFESAVING SERVICE IV–152a; II–89b
Life Studies IV–165b
Life zones (ecol.) II–390b
Liggett, Hunter (off.) I–70b; IV–320a
Liggitt's Gap Railroad VI–34a
Light, Edwin B. (pol.) VI–288a
Light, speed of V–294b
Light, study of I–97b
Light amplification by stimulated emission of radiation. *See* Masers and Lasers
Light Antitank Weapon VI–140a
Light carriers (CVL) I–54b, 55b, 56a
Lighter aboard ship. *See* LASH system
Lighter–than–air craft. *See* Dirigibles
LIGHTHOUSE BOARD IV–152b
"Lighthouse clock" II–79a
Lighthouses III–246a; VI–146a,b
arc lights II–413b
Argand lamp IV–153a
Coast Guard II–89b–90a
construction II–449b
Lighthouses, Bureau of II–135a; IV–152b
Lighthouse Service II–89a
Light in August IV–164b
LIGHTING IV–152b
candles I–444a
coal gas II–5b
electrical energy II–413a
Eskimo stone lamp II–462a
fluorescent III–156a, 409b
gas I–444a; V–5a
glass industry III–186a
hydroelectric power III–320b
incandescent lamp IV–88b
kerosine oil I–444a; IV–44a–b; V–269b
New York City V–82b, 83a
Pintsch gaslight V–463a
Savannah VI–220b
whale oil VII–285a
Lightning I–53a, 57b, 60a
Franklin's experiments IV–316a–b
insurance III–430b
Lightning arrester II–413b
"Light sculptures" VI–244a
Lights of New York (film) IV–418a
Ligneris, François Marchand de (off.) III–58b
Ligonier (Pa.) III–58b
Forbes Road III–59a
French and Indian War IV–200a
Miller's Run Gap V–224b
Raystown Path VI–49a
LIGONIER, FORT (Pa.) **IV–154a**; III–211b
Ligueste, Pierre Laclede. *See* Laclede Ligueste, Pierre
Ligurian Sea III–106b
Like–a–fish–hook (Indian village) III–34a
Lilienthal, David E. (adm., law.) I–216a,b; VII–28a,b
Tennessee Valley Authority V–45a
Liliuokalani (q.) III–263b
Lillie, Frank R. (zool.) IV–251a; V–135a
Lillie, Gordon W. ("Pawnee Bill") VII–298b
Lillooet (Indians) I–441b; III–363a
Lilly, Eli, Company V–274a
Lily (jour.) I–323b
"Lily white" primaries I–29a
Lima (Peru)
printing V–410b
Lima, Declaration of (1938) III–69a, 456b
Lima Inter–American Conference (1938) V–205a, 232a
Lima Locomotive Works IV–176b, 177a
Lime II–5a, 43b; III–16b; IV–174b, 311a
Limes (fruit) III–128a,b
Limestone (Ky.). *See* Maysville I–477a–78a; II–75a; III–17a
Fort Scott VI–241a
Great Lakes shipping III–218a
iron industry III–472a
New South V–67a
Limestone Bridge (Ala.) II–432a
Limestone County (Tex.) V–216b
Limestone springs VI–377b
Lime–sulfur III–421a
Limitations, statutes of. *See* Statutes of Limitation
"Limited" mail coaches VI–380a
Limners V–185a, 186a
Limnology II–390a–91b
Limnology and Oceanography (jour.) II–392a
Limnology and Oceanography, American Society of. *See* American Society of Limnology and Oceanography
LIMPING STANDARD IV–154a; IV–392b
Lincecum, Gideon (physic.) IV–299b
Lincoln (Mass.) VI–106a
Lincoln (Nebr.) V–31b
Lincoln (N.Mex.) IV–155a
Lincoln, Abraham I–324b, 333a; II–144b, 175 (table); III–47b, 329b; IV–41a; V–161a, 351b, 385b, 395 (table), 396a, 398b; VI–243b, 336b, 404a, 451a; VII–155b, 291a, 311a
civil religion II–53a
Declaration of Independence VI–115a
doctrine of sovereignty VI–358a
Farmer's Almanac I–91a
"House Divided" III–309a, 477a
Lincoln–Douglas debates IV–155a; V–353a
popular sovereignty V–360b
Rock Island Bridge Case VI–160a
—President:
agrarian movement I–33a
amnesty I–115a
arbitrary arrest II–62a
Atlanta campaign I–213b–14a
balloon reconnaissance I–248a
Battle of Ball's Bluff I–249a
Birchard Letter I–304a
blockade I–321a; II–161a
border states II–434a, 435a–b
campaign of 1860 I–139a, 421a–b; II–17b, 61a, 149b; VI–40a, 92b
campaign of 1864 I–422a; VI–92b
Charleston (Ill.) riot I–498b
Civil War I–173a; II–61b, 165b; VII–148b, 224b, 264a
colonization of Afro–Americans II–127b
Committee on the Conduct of the War II–140a
compensated emancipation II–433b–34a
Confiscation Act II–434a–35a
conscientious objectors II–185b
Copperhead opposition II–222b
Corning Letter II–228a
Crittenden Compromise II–265a
Dahlgren's and Kilpatrick's Raid II–279a
Dakota Land Company II–284b
Department of Agriculture I–45a; II–10b
Emancipation Proclamation II–62a, 64a, 162b, 434a; IV–339b; V–425a, 432a; VI–308a
equality doctrine II–456b
First Battle of Bull Run I–381a
Fishing Creek Confederacy III–32a
foreign policy III–68a
Fort Rice VI–135a
Fort Sumter II–161a; VI–440b
Frémont and Hunter's emancipation orders II–168a
Gettysburg Address III–176b, 202a–b; IV–162b; V–353b
habeas corpus I–195b–96a; II–179a; III–237a; IV–314b
Hampton Roads Conference III–247b
Homestead Law III–296b
inaugural addresses V–353b
Jackson's Valley campaign III–487b
Loyal League support IV–201b
McClellan's Harrison's Landing letter III–258a
Mississippi River IV–375a
mobilization IV–383b
Morrill Act IV–412b

LINCOLN, ABRAHAM (cont.)
Nast cartoons V–73a
Nevada V–39b
newspaper opposition V–71b
peace movement of 1864 V–234b
peace negotiations II–165a
Pomeroy Circular V–356a
Powhatan incident V–386a
privateers V–419b
Proclamation of 1861 V–425a
Radical Republicans VI–11a
railroads VI–38a
raising of army II–161a
Reconstruction II–68b; IV–194a–b, 202b; VI–55b–56a, 58a–b
Savannah occupation VI–278a
seceded states VI–249b
secession II–160b; VI–251a–b
Sherman's march through Carolinas VI–221a–b
Singleton peace plan VI–293b, 294a
slavery I–28a; VI–307b–08a, 311b
spies VI–373b
spoils system VI–375b
test laws VII–34b
Texas opposition VII–39b
Thanksgiving Day VII–46a
Thirteenth Amendment II–435b
transcontinental railroad II–241b; VI–27a; VII–101a
Trent affair I–121b; VII–115b–16a
troop call IV–346a
Union Army I–182a
Union navy VII–147a
Vallandigham incident III–156b; VII–164b
Vicksburg VII–146b
Virgin Islands VII–203b
Wade–Davis Bill VII–213a
War Democrats VII–229b
war policy opposition IV–52b
war powers II–472a–b; V–394a, 421a; VII–237a,b
West Virginia statehood VII–281b
Wilmot Proviso VII–303b
Yosemite Valley VII–361b
LINCOLN, ASSASSINATION OF (1865) **IV–154b**; I–115a, 202a; II–294b–95a, 349b; IV–261a; V–211b–12a; VI–285a
Lincoln, Benjamin (off.) III–117b
Battle of Camden I–412a
campaign of 1788 I–417a
Charleston VI–124a, 351b
Savannah siege VI–221a
Shays's Rebellion III–436b; VI–272a
War Department VII–226b
Lincoln, Mary Todd I–324b
Lincoln Center (N.Y.C.) II–289a; IV–237b; VI–86b
Lincoln County (Ky.) II–253a
Lincoln County (Maine) V–243a
Lincoln County (Miss.) VII–291a
Lincoln County (N.Mex.) VI–385a
LINCOLN COUNTY WAR (1876–78) **IV–155a**
LINCOLN–DOUGLAS DEBATES (1858) **IV–155a**; III–109b, 329b; V–161a, 353a, 360b
LINCOLN HIGHWAY IV–156a; V–178b; VI–49a, 154b
Lincoln Highway Association I–228b; IV–156a
Lincoln Laboratory (Mass.) I–212b; IV–263a
Lincoln Memorial V–353b; VI–243b; VII–246b, 250b
Lincoln Park (Chicago) II–18b; VII–370b
Lincoln Portrait (comp.) IV–439a
Lincoln–Roosevelt Republican League I–406b
Lincoln Tunnel V–368b
Lincoln University II–113b, 404b
Lind, Jenny (singer) I–275b; IV–157a
Lind, John (pol.) II–471a–b; IV–157a
Linda Vista (Calif.) I–434b
Lindbergh, Anne Morrow II–258b
Lindbergh, Charles A. (av.) II–310a, 311b, 346b; VII–118a
Greenland survey flight V–337b
isolationism III–480a
Spirit of St. Louis I–51b
See also Lindbergh Kidnapping Case; Lindbergh's Atlantic Flight
Lindbergh, Charles A., Sr. (pol.) II–490b, 491a; V–106b
LINDBERGH KIDNAPPING CASE (1932–36) **IV–156b**; II–258b; VII–118a
LINDBERGH'S ATLANTIC FLIGHT (1927) **IV–156b**; I–68a, 234a, 236b; II–344b; VI–320a
Lindenmeier (Colo.) II–83b; III–484b
Lindens (Danvers, Mass.) I–161b
Lindenthal, Gustav (civ. eng.) I–364b
Lindgren, Waldemar (geol.) III–163a–b
Lindo, Moses (agric.) III–405b
LIND'S AMERICAN TOUR (1850–51) **IV–157a**; I–275b
Lindsay, Vachel (poet) IV–164a
Lindsey, Ben (jur.) IV–23b
LIND'S MISSION TO MEXICO (1913–14) **IV–157a**; II–471a–b
Lindy (dance) II–290b
Linear accelerators II–278a
Linear mounds IV–420b
Line boats I–443b
LINEN INDUSTRY IV–157b
bounties IV–308a; V–16a–b
tariff VI–465b
Linens II–371a
Line-of-battle ships. *See* Ships of the Line
Line of Demarcation II–323b
Ling, James J. (ind.) II–169b; III–80b
Ling, Matthew IV–354b
LINGAYEN GULF IV–157b; V–284a; VII–139a
Ling–Temco–Vought II–169b
Linguistics I–128b–29a
Linguistics, Indian II–464b–65a
Link, Arthur (biog.) III–283a
Linn, Lewis F. (pol.) V–166b, 167b
Linn, William (off.) III–178a
Linnaeus, Carl (bot.) I–348b; II–390b; III–26b, 29b; V–326a; VI–90a
Linn County (Kans.) I–342a; VII–187b
Linotype V–77a–b, 412b
LINSEY-WOOLSEY IV–158a; II–81a; III–413b; IV–157b; V–317b
Linton, Ralph (anthrop.) I–129a
Linton, William J. (engr.) VII–319b
Linus (comic character) V–72b
Linz (Aus.) VII–341a
Lipan Apache (Indians) I–141b; II–133b
wars VII–239a,b
Lipids (chem.) II–13a
Lipmann, Fritz A. (biochem.) V–100a
Lippincott, J. B., Company I–334a
Lippmann, Walter (jour.) IV–164a; V–75a
Lippstadt (Ger.) VII–341a
"Lips That Touch Liquor Can Never Touch Mine" IV–160b
Lipton, Seymour (sculp.) VI–244a
Lipton, Thomas VII–348b
Liquor III–52b
Eighteenth Amendment II–406b
fur trade III–140a–b, 143b
government distribution III–203a
moonshine IV–407b
retail stores II–355a
smuggling II–277b
taverns VII–2a
taxation II–164b; VII–4a,b, 5a,b, 7a, 8b, 10b, 11b, 12b, 13a
temperance movement VII–22a
woman's rights movement VII–313b
Liquor and Indians. *See* Indians and Liquor
LIQUOR LAWS IV–158b; VII–132a–b
high license III–276a
Indian III–395b
Kansas IV–26b, 26b–27a, 425a
Maine IV–226b
McConnelsville Ordinance IV–210b
mulct law IV–425b
price maintenance V–403b
Prohibition V–429b
Raines Law VI–40b
sales tax VI–200b
South Carolina VII–59a
Twenty-first Amendment V–45a
Vermont VII–172a
Virginia VII–195b
Volstead Act VII–207b
Webb–Kenyon Act VII–265a
whiskey towns VII–290b
Liquor stores, government-owned II–234a
Liquor witnesses IV–131b–32a
Liri Valley (It.) III–235b; IV–404a
LISA, FORT (Nebr.) **IV–159a**; IV–380b; V–30b; VI–196a; VII–95b
Lisa, Manuel (fur trader) II–477a; III–143a, 144b, 468a; IV–159b; VII–271b
Fort Lisa IV–159a; V–30b
Manuel's Fort IV–242a
Missouri Fur Company VI–196a
Missouri River IV–380a
Saint Louis Missouri Fur Company VI–195b
War of 1812 VII–234b
Yellowstone River IV–403a
LISA AND COMPANY IV–159b; III–143a
Lisbon (Port.)
commercial agent II–359a
transatlantic flight V–30a
triangular trade VII–119b
Lister (plow) I–34a
Lister, Joseph (surg.) I–241a; IV–284a, 298b; V–273b
Liston, Robert (dipl.) I–324a
Liston, Sonny (pugilist) V–423a
Litchfield (Conn.) IV–159b; VI–229b; VII–22b
Litchfield, Edward Hubert I–333a
Litchfield County (Pa.) VII–347b

LITCHFIELD LAW SCHOOL IV–159b; IV–120b
Literacy
book publishing I–333b
Louisiana IV–195a
LITERACY TEST IV–159b; III–20a, 92b, 93a,b; VI–435a; VII–208b, 209b, 209b, 211a
Alabama I–29a
black suffrage VI–432b, 433a
immigration restriction III–342b
Mississippi Plan IV–371b
Solid South VI–337a
Virginia VII–195b
Williams v. *Mississippi* VII–302b
Literary and Scientific Circle II–1a
Literary Digest (mag.) IV–222a
LITERARY SOCIETIES IV–160a
libraries IV–145a
LITERATURE IV–160b
antislavery I–137a
book publishing I–333a
chapbooks I–494a
children's books I–335a
Hartford Wits III–259a
historiography III–281b
Lost Generation IV–189b
magazines IV–221b
Massachusetts IV–267a
McGuffey's Readers IV–213a
muckrakers IV–424b
Nobel Prizes V–99a,b
Sam Slick VI–207a
slang VI–299b–300a
Southern Literary Messenger VI–353a
Uncle Tom's Cabin VII–137b
LITERATURE, AFRO-AMERICAN IV–166a; I–25a, 30a; V–95b–96a
Literature, National Organization for Decent. *See* National Organization for Decent Literature
Lithic culture I–154b–56b; II–385b
Lithium I–218b
Lithography I–462b; II–275a; III–48a; V–412b, 413b–14a
Lithuania
immigration to U.S. III–340a
Littell, Isaac W. (off.) I–434b
Littell's Living Age (mag.) IV–222a
Little, Arthur D. (chem., eng.) III–409a
Little, Brown Publishers I–334a
Little, George (nav. off.) I–345a; V–423b
Little, Henry (off.) III–485a
Little, Malcolm. *See* Malcolm X
Little America (Antarc.) I–399a; V–337b
Little Bahama Banks III–41b
Little Bay De Noc IV–303b
Little Belt (sloop) V–393b
LITTLE BIGHORN, BATTLE OF (1876) **IV–167b**; I–296a,b, 312b, 313a; II–283b, 432b, 496a; III–127a; V–217a,b; VI–297a, 312b
"Little Brass Wagon" (song) V–331a
Little Butte des Morts I–398a
LITTLE CHURCH AROUND THE CORNER (N.Y.C.) **IV–168b**
Little Colorado River III–304a
Little Corn Island I–373b
Little Corporal (mag.) IV–223a
Little Cottonwood Canyon (Utah) IV–122b
Little Crow (Indian) IV–31b, 356b; VI–296b, 297a; VII–319b
Little Democrat (ship) IV–169b
Little Dog (Indian) III–500a
Little Egg Harbor (N.J.) II–388b; IV–152a; VII–278b
"Little Egypt" (dancer) IV–337b; VII–324a
Little Falls (Minn.) V–312a
Little Falls (N.Y.) I–442a
Littlefield, Catherine II–288b
Littlefield, Ephraim VII–266a
Littlefield Ballet II–288b
LITTLE GIANT (nickname) **IV–168b**
"LITTLE GROUP OF WILLFUL MEN" IV–169a
Little Hatch Acts III–261b
Little Horse (Indian) III–17b
Little Italies III–483a, 484a
Little Jimmy (comic character) V–72a
Little Kanawha River I–319b; III–182a, 370b; VII–252a
Little League baseball I–271b
Little Manitoulin Island IV–239b
Little Meadows (Md.) I–358a
Little Miami River II–25b
Indian trail IV–330a
Military Reserve VII–273a
revolutionary war V–319b
settlement IV–329b
Virginia military reserve VII–202a
Washington's western lands VII–252a
Little Miami Valley VII–247a
Little Missouri River III–33b
Little Mountains (Wasatch Range) IV–411b
Little Niagara. *See* Niagara, Carrying Place of
Little Niagara, Fort (N.Y.) V–90a
LITTLE NINE PARTNERS' PATENT IV–169a
"Little NRA" II–481b–82a
Little Osage (Indians). *See* Osage
Little Pittsburg Mine IV–124a
LITTLE RED SCHOOLHOUSE IV–169a
Little Review (mag.) IV–190a
Little Rhody VI–395 (table)
Little River II–381a; III–292b, 309a; V–224b; VI–134b
Little Rock (Ark.)
Camp Pike I–434b
capital I–173a
Civil War I–174a; III–498b; VI–63a
desegregation IV–341b
martial law IV–259a
school integration I–207b; II–57b–58a
Southern Overland Mail VI–154a
westward movement I–452a
Little Rock and Fort Smith Railroad IV–426a
Little Sandy Creek III–120a
LITTLE SARAH (privateer) **IV–169b**; III–159b
Little Steel IV–72b, 73b
"Little Steel" strike (1937) V–142a; VI–410b, 411a
Little Stone Fort (N.Y.) II–267a
"Little Sure Shot." *See* Oakley, Annie
Little Tennessee River II–381a; III–117a, 292b
Fontana Dam III–322b
Fort Loudoun IV–192a; VII–25a
Great Trading and War Path III–387b
Needham–Arthur expedition V–32a
Little theater V–439b; VII–49b
Little Thunder (Indian) III–256a
Little Truckee River III–215b
Little Turtle (Indian) II–484b; III–398b–99a; IV–59b
Little v. *Barreme* (1804) VII–224a
Little Wolf (Indian) II–379b
Little Women I–335a
Litton Industries III–504a
Liturgy V–179b
Litvinov, Maksim (dipl.) V–45b
Litvinov Assignment (1933) III–352b
Liuzzo, Viola IV–59a
"Live Free or Die" (motto) VI–394 (table)
Live oak (tree) VI–393 (table)
Livermore, T. L. II–64a
Liverpool (Eng.) III–64b
Black Ball Line VI–280b
customshouse I–496b
merchants I–22b
sailing packets V–183b
shipping IV–310a
slave trade VI–310b
LIVESTOCK INDUSTRY IV–169b; I–170b; IV–103a
Agricultural Adjustment Administration V–44a
Alabama I–72a
Arizona I–172a
Bluestem pastures I–326a
Chicago II–17b
Civil War II–69a
colonial I–37a; IV–451b
Connecticut II–180b
corn belt II–227a
corn feed II–226b
Dodge City II–358b
fencing III–10b
Georgia III–169a
herd law versus free grass III–273b
hogs III–288a
Illinois III–329b
internal improvements III–447b
Iowa III–468b
Kansas IV–26a
Kansas City (Mo.) IV–27b
Kentucky IV–40a
meat-packing IV–280a
Middle West I–38b
Minnesota IV–357a
Montana IV–403b
national parks V–220a
Navaho V–8b
oats V–130a
Oregon V–165b
Packers and Stockyards Act VI–378b
public lands V–446a, 450b
railroad pools V–358a
Saint Joseph VI–191b
Saint Paul VII–134a
sheep VI–272b; VII–320a–21a
state fairs VI–392b
stockyards VI–414a
tenancy I–41a
town sealers VI–245a
transportation VII–101b
veterinary medicine VII–177a
War Finance Corporation VII–231a
Wisconsin VII–308a
wolves VII–311b
See also Cattle; Hogs; Horse
Liv Glacier Pass I–399a
Living Newspaper VII–323a
"Living Newspapers" VII–50a
Livingston, Fargo and Company I–102a
Livingston, Henry B. (jur.) VI–445a
Livingston, John (bus.) V–81b

Livingston, John Henry (cler.) II–93b
Livingston, Philip (legis.) II–308a
Livingston, Robert (landowner) III–313a
  Albany charter II–363b
  plan of union II–121b
Livingston, Robert R., Jr. (law., dipl.) II–303b
  Articles of War VII–143a
  Louisiana purchase IV–196b–97a; VI–150b
  Loyalists VII–117a
  Phelps–Gorham purchase V–276b
  steamboats III–131b–32a, 178a; V–63a, 289a; VI–408a, 409a
Livingston, William (law.) II–203b
Livingston County (N.Y.) V–463b
Livingston family (N.Y.) I–4a; IV–92a; V–86b
Livingston's Sugar House (N.Y.C.) VI–436b
Living Theatre (N.Y.C.) VII–51a
Lizard peninsula (Eng.) VII–349a
Lizards VI–91a,b
Llama III–381a
Llano culture II–83b–84a
Llano Estacado. *See* Staked Plain
Llano River IV–263a
Llewellyn, Karl N. VI–386b
Llewellyn Iron Works IV–219a
Lloyd, Edward III–427b
Lloyd, Henry Demarest (writ.) VI–157a
Lloyd, Thomas (pol.) IV–35b
Lloyd, William Alvin (spy) VI–373b
Lloyd George, David (states.) VII–328b
Lloyd's of London III–427a, 429a,b
Loan associations. *See* Savings and Loan Associations
Loans
  balance of trade I–245b
  banking I–255a, 256b, 257a, 258a, 259a, 261a
  farmers I–41a, 44a,b
  federal aid II–502a
  Home Owners' Loan Corporation III–294a
  installment buying III–422b
  interest laws III–443a
  Intermediate Credit Banks III–447a–b
  Nicaragua V–94a
  Provident Loan Society I–495a
  revolutionary war VI–120a,b
  savings banks I–263b
  small business II–498b
  tenant farmers IV–104a
LOBBIES IV–170a
  Alaska government I–77a
  American Civil Liberties Union I–100b
  American Legion I–108b
  American Medical Association IV–289b
  business I–389b
  Charity Organization Society VI–327b
  Civil War II–63b
  consumer protection II–209a
  controls II–232a
  dairy industry II–281a
  equal rights amendment VII–318a
  farm I–33b
  free silver III–110b
  labor I–103a, 104a, 322a
  National Association of Manufacturers IV–461b
  National Congress of American Indians IV–463a; V–210b
  National Education Association IV–463a
  National Rifle Association IV–470a
  New England Mississippi Land Company VII–354a
  Office Of Economic Opportunity V–136a
  pressure groups V–400a
  pure food and drug movement V–467a
  tariff VI–467b
  veterans' organizations VII–174b
  wildlife preservation VII–298a
  Workers' Alliance VII–323b
Lobdell Car Wheel Company VII–105b
Lobotomy IV–306b
Lobsters III–51a
LOCAL GOVERNMENT IV–171a
  balance of power VI–397b
  civil service reform II–60a–b
  consumer protection II–208b–09a
  corruption II–232a
  costs II–234a
  expenditures III–205a–b
  federal subsidies VI–425b
  food stamps III–56b
  government corporations III–201b
  grants–in–aid III–211b
  home rule III–294b
  initiative III–418b
  internal improvements III–448a
  justice of the peace IV–22b
  legislature IV–133b
  Mecklenburg Resolves IV–282b
  municipal government IV–426b
  municipal ownership IV–427b
  municipal reform IV–429b
  New England towns VII–78a–79b
  Panic of 1929 V–209a,b
  parish V–216a
  pension plans V–255a
  political assessments V–341b
  political patronage V–227b, 228a.b
  political scandals V–346b
  political subdivisions V–349a
  poor relief V–380b
  port authorities V–368a
  public revenue VI–105b
  referendum VI–66a,b
  relief VI–74a,b
  residency requirements for voting VI–99b
  ripper legislation VI–144b
  selectmen VI–257b
  social legislation VI–327b
  statistics VII–206a
  taxation VII–10b, 11a,b
  third parties VII–53a
  toll bridges VII–69b
  township system VII–81a
  versus federal government IV–13a
  zoning VII–370b
Local option IV–158b, 159a; V–429b; VII–23b
Locarno treaties (1925) IV–36a, 382a
LOCHABER, TREATY OF (1770) **IV–173a**; II–363a–b; III–251b, 292b, 382b; IV–201b; V–425a
  Big Moccasin Gap I–297a
LOCHNER* v. *NEW YORK (1905) **IV–173b**; II–378a; IV–68b; V–339b; VII–117b
Lochry, Archibald (off.) IV–173b
LOCHRY'S DEFEAT (1781) **IV–173b**
Lockard, Ray W. (comp.) III–469a
Locke, Alain (educ.) I–30a; IV–166b
Locke, John (philos.) II–325a, 377b; V–441b
  Fundamental Constitutions I–457b, 458a; VI–347a
  liberalism IV–140a
  liberty IV–142a
  religion VI–80b, 81a
  Second Treatise of Government II–456b
  See also Locke's Political Philosophy
Locke, Richard A. (jour.)
  moon hoax IV–406b
LOCKE'S POLITICAL PHILOSOPHY IV–173b; II–191a; VI–391a, 396a
  Bill of Rights I–298b
  compact theory II–149a; VI–113a
  equal rights of man II–456a–b
  extraconstitutional powers V–394a
  human rights III–316b
  Loyalists VI–116a
  natural rights V–7b
  right of rebellion VI–50b
  right of revolution VI–121a
  titles of nobility V–100b
Lockheed Aircraft Corporation I–51b, 52a,b, 53a,b, 54a, 57b, 60a, 61b, 69a, 235a, 236b, 237a,b, 484b; II–346b; III–452a
LOCKOUT IV–174a
  coal mining II–86b
  opposition IV–471b
  Universal Peace Union V–235b
  World War I VII–232b
Lockport (Ill.) II–19a; IV–88a
Lockport (N.Y.) IV–218a; VII–210b
Lockport flight I–443b
LOCKS AND WATERWAYS IV–174b
  Illinois IV–88a
  Monongahela River V–250a
  Saint Lawrence Seaway VI–192b
  Sault Sainte Marie Canals VI–219a
  Soo locks VI–146b
  waterpower IV–347b
Lock tenders I–443b
Lockwood, Belva A. (law.) II–458a
Lockwood, Charles A. (nav. off.) VII–343b
Lockwood, Luke Vincent II–100a
Lockyer, Captain (nav. off.) I–342b
Locofoco matches IV–175a, 274a
LOCOFOCO PARTY IV–175a; IV–61b
Locomotive Engineers, Brotherhood of IV–62b; VI–19b, 20a, 28b
Locomotive Firemen and Engineers, Brotherhood of VI–20a, 28b
LOCOMOTIVES IV–175a; II–413a, 416a, 416a; V–25b; VI–24b–25a, 29b, 30b
  De Witt Clinton IV–386b
  diesel traction III–409b
  electric VI–40a
  elevated railways II–428a, 428a
  Industrial Revolution III–411b
  interchangeable manufacture IV–272b
  Latrobe's Folly IV–116b
  Philadelphia V–277b
  Schenectady VI–226a
  standardization VI–19b
  steam engines VI–409b, 410a
  Stourbridge Lion VI–416a
  Tom Thumb VII–71a
Locusts III–212b
LODE MINING IV–177b; V–322b
  claim size IV–354a
  gold III–191a,b
  regulation IV–349b
  silver VI–292a
Lodge, Henry Cabot (states.) III–37b, 286a; IV–268a
  immigration restriction III–342b

League of Nations IV–124b, 125a
Magdalena Bay Resolution IV–223b
See also Lodge Reservations
Lodge, Henry Cabot II (pol., dipl.)
campaign of 1960 I–430b
Lodge Pole Creek VI–254b
Lodgepole pine III–74b
LODGE RESERVATIONS IV–178a; III–286a; IV–125a–b
Lodge Resolution (1912). *See* Magdalena Bay Resolution
Lodges (Indian) IV–51a
Lodge Trail Ridge III–17b
Loening, Grover (eng.) I–51b
Loesch, Claude (inv.) I–34b
Loesch, Leo (inv.) I–34b
Loesser, Frank (comp.) IV–442a
Loew, Marcus (theat. mgr.) VII–167b
Loewe, Dietrich (bus.) II–286a
Loewe, Frederick (comp.) IV–442a; VII–50b
Loewe Company. *See* D. E. Loewe Company
Loewe v. *Lawler* (1908). *See* Danbury Hatters' Case
Loew Pictures V–292b
Loftus, Arthur (off.) III–330b; IV–178b
LOFTUS HEIGHTS IV–178b; I–9b
Logan (Indian) I–244a; II–257b; III–386b
Logan, Benjamin (pioneer) IV–40a, 179a; V–319b
Logan, Daniel II–275a
Logan, Daniel Boone IV–259b
Logan, James (states.) II–107b; V–277a, 436a
Logan, John (Tahgah–jute) (Indian) IV–179a
Logan, John A. (off., pol.) III–207b; IV–301a; VI–11b, 48b
Logan Act (1799) II–343a
Logan County (Ky.) I–434a; III–221b
Logan family (Ky.) IV–259b
Logan International Airport II–347b
LOGAN'S FORT (Ky.) **IV–179a**; III–239a
Logansport (Ind.) VII–212a, 212b
LOGAN'S SPEECH (1774) **IV–179a**
LOG CABIN IV–179a; V–317a
Texas settlement VII–35b
Log Cabin and Hard Cider Campaign. *See* Campaigns, Presidential: 1840
Log Cabin Song Book I–432b
LOG COLLEGE IV–179b; V–33a, 391b; VI–76b
Log furnace IV–122a–b
Logging III–73a
oxen V–179a
timberlands VII–60b, 61b
See also Lumber Industry
LOGISTICS IV–180a
army I–189b–90a,b
Naval War College V–24a
polar bases V–337b
LOGROLLING IV–181a; I–284b; V–317b
LOGSTOWN (Pa.) **IV–181a**; IV–130b
Indian trade V–146a
Indian treaty IV–181b
Raystown Path VI–49a
LOGSTOWN, TREATY OF (1752) **IV–181b**; V–144a, 308a
LOGWOOD TRADE IV–181b
Loisel, Regis (trader) IV–380b
Lok, Michael (mer.) V–179b–80a
Loki (rocket) III–502a
Lolita IV–165a
Lo Lo Pass V–225a
Lolo Trail II–74b
Lomax, Lunsford L. (off.) VII–71a, 358a
Lombard, Carole (act.) II–346a
Lombard Street (London) VII–222a
LOMBOK STRAIT, BATTLE OF (1942) **IV–182a**
Lôme, Enrique Dupuy de (dipl.) VI–360a; VII–356a
L'Onanisme VI–266a
London (Eng.) III–64b; V–231b
clearinghouse II–73b
colonial trade VII–86a
department stores II–332b
Evangelical Alliance II–465a
exchanges II–469b
Freemasons III–108b
fur market III–142b
gambling II–262a
Kinetoscopes IV–417a
merchant adventurers I–16a
penal congress V–416a
radio VI–14b
sailing packets V–183b
Salvation Army VI–204a
shipping IV–309b, 310a
trade II–388b
U.S. envoy II–342b
World Economic Conference VII–324a
World War I I–66a
World War II I–66b–67a; IV–363a; VI–159a
Wren's plan II–45a
LONDON, DECLARATION OF (1909) **IV–182a**; V–35a, 38b–39a, 233b; VII–113a
London, Port of V–368a
London, Protocol. *See* London Naval Treaty of 1936
LONDON, TREATY OF (1604) **IV–182b**
London Agreement of 1945 VII–226a
London and Bristol Company VII–94b
London Associates V–88b
London Cabinet–Makers Book of Prices III–135a
London Charity Organization Society I–494b
London Chronicle (news.) IV–5a
London Coffee House of Philadelphia III–427b
London Company of Virginia. *See* Virginia Company of London
London Daily Mail (news.) V–74b
Londonderry (N.H.) III–52a
London Illustrated News V–62b
London Mathematical Society I–109a
London Metropolitan Police V–339a
London Missionary Society IV–364b
London Monetary Conference (1933) I–123a
London Naval Conference (1909) II–446b; III–237b; IV–182a
London Naval Conference of 1935 V–10b
LONDON NAVAL TREATY OF 1930 IV–183a; III–33b; V–10a,b, 216b; VII–341b
escalator clause II–461a
submarines VI–424a
LONDON NAVAL TREATY OF 1936 IV–183b; II–461a; VII–225b
submarines VI–424a,b
London Public Advertiser (news.) IV–20b
London Public Record Office V–68b
London purple III–421a
London Yearly Meeting (Quaker) IV–35b
London Zoological Society VII–371b
LONE JACK, ACTION AT (1862) **IV–183b**
Lonely Crowd IV–165a
Lonergan, Philip J. (cattleman) V–139a
Lonergan, Thomas (cattleman) V–139a
Lone Star State VI–395 (table)
Long, Alexander (pol.) II–222b
Long, Crawford W. (surg.) I–119a
LONG, HUEY, ASSASSINATION (1935) **IV–183b**; I–203a
Long, Huey P. (pol.) I–343b; III–229a; IV–194b, 194b–95a; V–347a, 377a
newspaper gag act V–78b
Share–the–Wealth movement V–46b, 47b, 401a; VI–269a; VII–79b
Long, James (adventurer) VII–37a
See also Long Expedition
Long, John (fur trader) III–403b
Long, Pierse VII–300b
Long, Stephen H. (off., expl.)
bridge patents I–363b
Fort Smith VI–317a
See also Long's Explorations
Long Beach (Calif.) IV–104b; V–28a, 29b
Long Beach (cruiser) VII–241b, 242b
Long Branch (N.J.) VI–100b
Long Day's Journey Into Night (play) VII–50b
LONG DRIVE IV–184a; I–471b
Longevity II–328b
LONG EXPEDITION (1819) **IV–184a**; IV–320b, 457a
Longfellow, Henry Wadsworth (poet) I–344a; IV–162a, 223a, 267a,b
Evangeline I–6a; II–465b
Harvard University III–259b
"My Lost Youth" II–452b
Paul Revere's Ride VI–106a
"Song of Hiawatha" II–31b
"The Slave in the Dismal Swamp" II–353a
"Wreck of the Hesperus" I–447a
LONGHORNS, TEXAS IV–184b; I–471b; VI–45a
Fence War III–10a
stampedes VI–382b
Longhouse of the Iroquois I–166b; III–249b, 476a
LONG HUNTERS IV–185a; II–272a, 273a; IV–40a, 303b
LONG ISLAND (N.Y.) **IV–185a**; III–152a
Brooklyn I–370a
colonial laws II–379a
Delaware Indians II–320b
Duke of York's proprietary VII–359a
Dutch–Indian War II–383a
Dutch War of 1653 VI–134b
ferries III–11a
Fishers Island III–31a
Hempstead III–271b
horse racing III–304b
hurricanes II–351b; III–320a
Indian wars V–61b
lifesaving stations IV–152a
manors IV–241b
New England settlers V–50a
oil refining VI–383a
Pinkster celebration V–316b
rainstorms II–349b
revolutionary war III–241b; IV–186a; VI–373a

LONG ISLAND (cont.)
Sag Harbor VI–185b
shipping IV–310a
Southampton VI–346b
Southold VI–354b
tide mills VII–58a
Treaty of Hartford III–258b
War of 1812 VII–235a
whaling III–413a; VII–285a
World War II VI–374a
LONG ISLAND, BATTLE OF (1776) **IV–186a**; III–254b; IV–185b; V–82b; VI–123a
Long Island Biological Laboratory II–133a
LONG ISLAND FLATS, BATTLE OF (1776) **IV–186a**
Long Island of Holston (Tenn.) III–381a, 387b; IV–173a, 186b
LONG ISLAND OF HOLSTON, TREATY OF (1777) **IV–186b**; III–400b
Long Island Oil Company VI–383a
Long Island Railroad II–350b; III–451a
Long Island Sound IV–185a
Connecticut II–179b; V–130b
Dutch War of 1653 VI–134b
revolutionary war VI–128b, 186a
Saybrook VI–223a
settlement V–55a,b
shipping IV–310a
steamship lines II–91a
Long Island University V–83b
Long Knives. *See* Big Knives
Longleaf pine V–14b
Long Lost Friend III–49b
Long Parliament II–122b
Long-playing record II–424b, 425b; V–290b
Long rifles VI–139b
Longrope's Last Guard VI–382b
Long Sault Rapids IV–406a
LONG'S EXPLORATIONS (1819–20, 1823) **IV–186b**; I–349a; II–128a; VI–90a; VII–271a,b
Great American Desert I–170a, 170a; III–213b; V–31a
Great Plains III–220b
James expedition III–488a
Kansas IV–25b
narrative IV–224b
Pembina V–244a
Pikes Peak V–311a
Platte River Trail V–330b
Rocky Mountains VI–160b
Yellowstone River VII–358a
Longshoremen
Communist party II–145a
unionization IV–72b
Longshoremen's and Harbor Workers' Act (1948) III–431b
Long's Peak (Colo.) IV–186b
Longstreet, James (off.) V–248a
Army of Northern Virginia VII–197a,b
Battle of Antietam I–130a
Battle of Blackburn's Ford I–309a
Battle of Chancellorsville I–493a
Battle of Chickamauga II–21b; VI–26b
Battle of Frayser's Farm III–100a
Battle of Gettysburg III–175b
Battle of Mechanicsville IV–282a
Battle on Lookout Mountain IV–187a
Battles of the Wilderness VII–295b
Chattanooga campaign I–502b
First Battle of Bull Run I–381a,b
Second Battle of Bull Run I–382a
siege of Knoxville IV–54a, 364b
Suffolk operations VI–430a
Longstreet, William (inv.) VI–408b
Long Strike (1870's) II–86b
Long Trail I–473b
Longueuil, Baron de. *See* Le Moyne, Charles
Longview (Tex.) I–30a
Long Wharf (Newport) V–65b
Longwood Cricket Club (Brookline, Mass.) VII–29b
Longwood Gardens (Del.) III–151b
Longwood Gardens (Pa.) I–348a
Longworth, Nicholas (hortic.) VII–305a
Longworth, Nicholas (law., pol.) II–177 (table); III–38a
Lon Nol (pres.) VII–186b
Look (mag.) IV–222b; VI–300a
Look Homeward, Angel IV–164a
Looking Backward IV–163b
Lookout, Fort (S.Dak.) IV–51a
Lookout, Fort, Treaty of (1825) VI–296a
Lookout Mountain VII–261a
LOOKOUT MOUNTAIN, BATTLE OF (1863) **IV–187a**; I–502b; II–271b; IV–364b–65a
Lookout Point Dam III–323a
LOOM IV–187b; VII–42b, 43a,b–44a
colonial textiles III–413b
cotton industry II–239a
Crompton II–266a
Navaho V–9a
silk industry VI–287a
slave trade VI–311a
wool manufacture VII–320b
Loomis, Elias (math., astron.) II–75b; IV–316b, 317a
LOOMIS GANG IV–187b
Loon VI–394 (table)
Loop (Chicago) II–18a; VI–429b
Loose construction. *See* Constitution of the United States
López, Francisco (miss.) I–288b; IV–367b; VI–162a
López, Narciso. *See* López Filibustering Expeditions
López, Nicholás (cler.) IV–302b
LÓPEZ FILIBUSTERING EXPEDITIONS (1850–51) **IV–188a**; II–268a; III–23a
Lorain (Ohio) II–459a
Lorain, John II–226a; VI–335a
Loramie, Peter. *See* Lorimier, Pierre Louis
Loramie Creek III–227b
LORAMIE'S STORE (Ohio) **IV–188a**
Lord, Nathan (educ.) II–293a
Lord and Taylor I–17a
Lord Nelson (schooner) III–217b
LORDS AND GENTLEMEN IV–188a
Lord's Day Alliance I–325a
LORDS OF TRADE AND PLANTATION IV–188b; I–326b; II–123a, 242a; IV–270b; VI–108b
Lords of Trade Plan of Union (1721) II–122a
Lords proprietors. *See* Proprietary Provinces
Lordstown (Ohio) IV–77b
Lorenson, Coby, Jr. (sci.) I–35b
Lorentz, Hendrick (phys.) V–304a
Lorenz, Konrad VII–371a
Lorettsville (Va.) II–346a
Lorien (commune) II–142b
L'ORIENT (Fr.) **IV–189a**
Lorimer, William (pol.) IV–189a
LORIMER CASE IV–189a
Lorimier, Pierre Louis (trader) I–448a; IV–122b, 188a
Loring, Edward G. (offi.) I–387a
Lorrain, Claude (paint.) V–187b
Lorraine (Fr.) IV–319b; VII–326b, 327a
Lorraine Motel (Memphis) IV–45b
LOS ADAES (La.) **IV–189a**
Los Alamos (N.Mex.)
hydrogen bomb III–324a
Manhattan Project IV–238b; V–296a, 297a
nuclear research center V–60a
nuclear weapon testing I–215b
Los Angeles (Calif.) I–280a; III–438a, 477b; VI–427b
ayuntamiento I–239a
Azusa Street Mission V–259b
black mayor I–32a
black population I–25b
bootlegging I–339b
California capital IV–404b
campaign of 1948 V–429a
Clark Library V–191b
colonial land grants IV–93a
earthquakes II–347b–48a, 385b
federal records center III–284b
gold III–190b, 191a
"good government" movement I–406b
Indian population III–397b
Indian relocation VI–83b
"industrial army" II–252b
McNamara case IV–218b
Mexican-Americans VI–7b
Mexican War I–409b; III–34a; IV–34b, 323b; VI–210b
motion pictures IV–417b
Mount Wilson Observatory III–242b
port authority V–368a
race riots I–31b; II–259a; IV–457b; VI–8b–9a
railroad VI–37b
railroad survey VI–39a
recall VI–51a
retail trade VII–84b
Robert Kennedy assassination IV–38a
sanitariums VI–101a
Spanish Trail VI–368a; VII–256a
stock exchange II–469b
subway VI–429b
unionization IV–218b
urban development II–49a
wagon trains VII–217b
water rights IV–104b
western routes V–224b
Whipple's expedition VII–289a
Los Angeles (submarine) V–25b
Los Angeles (zeppelin) II–344b
Los Angeles class (submarine) VI–423b
Los Angeles County (Calif.) II–348b; III–503a; IV–366a
Los Angeles man I–155b
Los Angeles Museum II–100b
Los Angeles River VI–210b
Los Angeles Star (news.) V–180b
Los Angeles State and County Arboretum I–348b
Los Angeles Times (news.) IV–218b; V–73b, 76b, 79a
Watergate V–78a
Losantiville (Ohio) II–37b; IV–329b; V–140b
Los Pinos (Colo.) VII–137b
Lossberg, Friedrich Wilhelm von (off.) III–173a

LOST BATTALION
IV–189a; IV–320a
"LOST CAUSE" IV–189b
Lost Cause IV–189b
Lost Colony. *See* Raleigh's Lost Colony
LOST GENERATION
IV–189b; IV–408b
Lost Lady IV–164a
LOST ORDER, LEE'S
IV–190a; III–256a
Lost River IV–385a
Lotbinière, Marquis de VII–56b
Lothian, Marquis of. *See* Kerr, Philip Henry
LOTTERIES IV–190a; II–260b; III–149a–b
American Art Union II–101b
canal financing I–442b
Civil War draft II–368b–69a
colonies II–302a
commerce clause II–136a
conscription II–186b
education funds II–396b
Genesee Road III–157a
Georgia land lottery III–170b
Louisiana IV–195b
Philadelphia and Lancaster Turnpike Company IV–89b
revolutionary war financing VI–120a
South Carolina Canal VI–349a
state–established II–263a
tontine plan VII–72a
World War I draft II–367b
LOUDON, FORT (Pa.) **IV–191b**; VI–49a, 285a
Loudon County (Va.) VII–202b
Loudoun, Earl of. *See* Campbell, John
LOUDOUN, FORT (Tenn.) **IV–192a**; III–117a; VII–25a
Loudspeaker III–156a
Loughead Company I–236a
Loughhead, Allan (aircraft designer) I–51b, 235b
Louis XIV (k.) II–458b; III–239b, 272a, 335a
colonial wars II–126a
coutume de Paris II–247a
Edict of Nantes III–315a
La Salle's exploration IV–109b
Louisiana IV–192b
Minnesota claim IV–355a
New France III–120a; V–52b
Sault Sainte Marie Pageant VI–219a
Louis XV (k.) I–354b; III–50b; IV–301b; VI–194a
Code Noir II–91b
Crown Point II–267a
Louis XVI (k.) III–306a
Louis, Joe (pugilist) V–422b–23a
Louis, Morris (paint.) V–193a–b
Louis, Pierre (statis.) VII–206b
Louisa County (Va.) V–221b
Louisa Land Company. *See* Transylvania Company
Louisa Railroad VI–33a
Louisburg (Pa.). *See* Harrisburg I–70b, 359a; II–126b; III–115a–b, 116a,b; IV–46b, 47a; V–369b; VI–1a
LOUISBURG EXPEDITION (1745) **IV–192a**; IV–226a; VI–199a; VII–115a
Louis de la Mobile, Fort (Ala.) II–158a
Louis d'or (coin) V–320b
LOUISIANA IV–192b; III–213b; IV–200a; VI–394 (table); VII–277b, 287a
Acadians I–6a,b, 7a
Adams–Onís Treaty VI–364a
antibank movement I–129b
Archaic culture II–386a
d'Arges Colony I–169b
Arkansas Post I–173b
Balize I–246b
Barataria I–265b
Baton Rouge I–274b
bayous I–279a
black suffrage I–29a; III–92b; VI–11a, 432a, 433a,b
Blount conspiracy I–324a
bossism I–343b
boundary disputes I–351b
campaign of 1876 II–38b
Capuchins I–455b
Carmelites I–455b
Carondelet intrigue I–459b
Casket Girls I–466b
Catholicism I–468a; II–91b
cession to France VI–150b, 211a, 359a
cession to Spain III–50b; IV–376b; VI–194a
Chickasaw–Creek War II–22b
citizenship II–42b
citrus industry II–43b
Civil War I–275a, 279b, 461b; II–432a; III–498a–b; IV–257a, 374b, 405a; V–63b, 369a; VI–63a, 182a, 249b
Code Napoléon II–91b, 141b
Code Noir II–91b
colonial history V–173a–b
colonial land grants IV–93a
colonial wars II–126b
Compagnie des Indes II–149a
constitution VI–391a,b
Convention of 1800 II–215b
cotton II–237b; VI–305b
county government II–245a
coutume de Paris II–247a–b
Creoles II–257a
Crozat Grant II–267b
Democratic party VII–210a
Emancipation Proclamation II–434b
exploration I–498b–99a; III–108a
filibusters III–235b–36a
Florida boundary III–41b
food III–53b
Fort Jesup III–501b
Fort Miro IV–362a
Fort Saint John VI–191a
Franciscans III–94a
free blacks II–91b
Freemasons III–109a
French claims IV–372a
French exiles I–492a
French forts IV–276b; V–173a
French rule II–247b; III–168a
fur trade III–143b–44a; IV–159b
Genêt mission III–159b
grandfather clause III–208b
Grosjean v. *American Press Company* (1936) III–229a
gubernatorial election of 1872 IV–336a
Hennepin narrative III–272a
historical society III–278b
historic properties IV–472a
horse III–302b
hospitals III–306b
Houma Indians III–308a
hurricanes II–351a,b, 352a; III–319b, 320a
Indian defense V–100b–01a
Indian trade VI–366b
Iowa jurisdiction III–467b
irrigation III–478b
Isleños III–479a
Jesuits III–499b, 501b
Jews II–91b
Ku Klux Klan IV–58b
Lake Pontchartrain V–356a
land measurement I–195a
La Salle's claim for France IV–109b, 110a
Last Island hurricane IV–110b
lead mining II–267b
Long assassination IV–184a
Los Adaes IV–189a
lotteries IV–191a
Memorial of the Planters and Merchants IV–301b
Mississippi Bubble II–149a; IV–370b
Mississippi River V–315a
Missouri IV–376b–77a
Mobile IV–382a
Natchitoches IV–456b
New Madrid V–59a
New Orleans V–62a, 64a
newspaper V–75b
"New West" V–81b
Nolan expeditions V–101a
oil IV–334a; V–272a; VI–356b, 357a; VII–57b
Old Southwest VI–356a
onions V–156a
parish V–216a, 349b
Perdido River V–262a
pharmacists V–275b
Pike expedition VII–74b
piracy V–320a
Pointe Coupee V–335a
poker V–336a
Poverty Point V–382b
privateers V–419b
public health V–447a; VI–212b
racetracks II–260b
railroad convention VI–20b
railroads VI–33b, 36b–37a
recall VI–51a
Reconstruction III–295b; VI–56a, 58a,b
Red River Post VI–64b–65a
Red River raft VI–65a
Regulators VI–71b
repudiation of state debts VI–96b
revolutionary war VI–365b, 367b
rice I–486b; VI–136a
Sabine War VII–239a
savings and loan associations VI–221b
school integration II–402a
secession II–61a; VI–251a
segregation II–54a; V–331b
Shreveport Rate Case VI–283b
Slaughterhouse Cases II–377b–78a; VI–303a
slavery II–91b; VI–309a, 335b–36a
Spain I–399b; II–389a; III–38b; VI–168b, 363b, 365b–66a
Spanish Inquisition III–420b
Spanish missions II–389a
Spanish trade VI–189b
steamboats III–132b; VI–407b
steam engines VI–409a
sugarcane I–486b; VI–341a, 436a,b, 437a
sulfur deposits II–6b
swamplands VI–453b
tafia VI–456b
tariff VI–466b
tidelands VII–57b
tobacco VII–66b
tornadoes II–352a
Treaty of Fontainebleau VII–36b
tuberculosis patients VII–126a
uniform state laws VI–399b
veterinary medicine VII–176b
Voting Rights Act of 1965 VII–211a
wagon trains VII–217b
War of 1812 I–492a; V–63a
West Florida IV–368a,b; V–240b

LOUISIANA (cont.)
White League VII–292b
See also Orleans, Territory of
Louisiana, District of IV–31b
LOUISIANA, UPPER IV–195b
Louisiana Conservative party VII–287a
Louisiana Farmer's Union II–493b
LOUISIANA LOTTERY IV–195b
LOUISIANA PURCHASE (1803) **IV–196a**; I–114a, 126a; II–216a, 474b–75a; III–68a, 96b; IV–193b, 377a; V–173b, 443b; VI–150b, 363b, 400a; VII–83a, 111b, 260a, 267b, 268b, 271a
acreage V–445 (table)
agrarian expansion I–33a
arbitration IV–5b
bond issue III–63b
Colorado section II–127b
Dakota Territory II–284b
exploration II–381a
Federalist opposition III–5a
Florida III–41b
fur trade III–143a, 144a
Great Plains III–220b
Gulf of Mexico IV–326a
Iberville River III–327a
indemnities III–352a
Indian removal III–389a, 393b
Iowa III–467b
Isle of Orleans III–479a
Kentucky support IV–40b
land titles IV–105b
Lewis and Clark Expedition IV–136a
Mississippi River IV–372b, 373b
Mississippi Valley IV–376a
Montana IV–403a
New Orleans V–62a
Oklahoma V–148a
Pike's southwestern expedition V–311b–12a
right of deposit II–333b
secessionist movement VI–250a
slavery IV–379a
Treaty of San Ildefonso VI–211a
Upper Louisiana IV–195b
weather data II–75b
West Florida III–38b; IV–36b; VII–277a
LOUISIANA PURCHASE, BOUNDARIES OF IV–197a; V–120b; VI–359a–b
American Bottom I–100b
joint occupation of Oregon Country IV–6a
Mexico IV–320b
Missouri Territory IV–378b–79a
Mobile Act IV–382b
Rio Grande VI–143a
Rocky Mountains VI–160b
Texas VI–355b; VII–36b
LOUISIANA PURCHASE EXPOSITION (1904) **IV–198a**; IV–136a, 349a; VI–194b
Louisiana Purchase Treaty (1803)
spoliation claims III–121b
LOUISIANA REVOLUTION OF 1768 IV–198a
LOUISIANA SPECIE RESERVE BANKING SYSTEM IV–198b; I–253a, 255b, 259a,b; II–255a; III–101b
Louisiana Territory I–301a
Louisiana v. *Mississippi* (1906) I–351b
Louisiana v. *United States* (1965) VI–435a
Louis Philippe (k.) III–96b, 122a
Louisville (gunboat) II–384a
Louisville (Ga.) VI–278a
Louisville (Ky.) III–182a, 227b, 369b; VII–159a
American Printing House for the Blind III–248b
bargemen I–267b
black population I–29a
campaign of 1832 VI–203b
Camp Taylor I–434b
canal IV–198b
cement rock I–477b
Civil War III–485a; IV–42a–b; V–263b; VI–26b
dairy industry II–279b
Falls of the Ohio V–142b
floods III–37a
Fort Nelson V–32b
harness factory III–255b
industry IV–41b
labor conference (1865) IV–78a
Lafayette's visit IV–84a
La Salle expedition V–145a
lifesaving station IV–152b
meat-packing IV–280a
mechanics' institutes IV–281b
Nelson–Davis quarrel V–32b
Ohio River bridge I–364a
oil refining VI–383a
public health VI–173b
railroads IV–137b; VI–33a, 34b, 37b
Southern Exposition VI–353a
steamboats VI–406b, 407b, 408a,b; VII–357a
steam engines VI–409a
Tarascon, Berthoud and Company VI–462a
trade VII–83b
unionization IV–62b
Wilderness Road VII–296a
Louisville and Nashville Railroad I–9b; II–272b; IV–273a, 426b; VI–25a, 33a, 34b–35a, 36b
LOUISVILLE AND PORTLAND CANAL IV–198b; III–449a; VI–146a
subsidy VI–425a
Louisville, Cincinnati and Charleston Railroad Company VI–349b
Louisville Courier–Journal (news.) V–73b, 79a
Louisville Medical Institute I–410a
Loundes County (Ala.) VI–433a
Lousberg Park (Aachen, Ger.) I–1a
Louther, Fort (Pa.) I–455a
Louvigny, Sieur de, Louis de la Porte (off.) III–89a
Love, Alfred (mer.) V–235b; VII–236a
Love, P. R. (off.) II–346b
Love County (Okla.) II–94a; VII–238b
Lovejoy, Arthur O. (educ.) II–470b
Lovejoy, Elijah P. *See* Lovejoy Riots
LOVEJOY RIOTS (1837) **IV–199a**; V–68a, 70b
Lovelace, Francis (col. gov.) V–84a
Lovelace, John (col. gov.) V–88a
Lovell, James A., Jr. (astronaut) I–210b
Lovell, Mansfield (off.) V–63b; VII–181b
Lovell, Solomon (off.) V–254a
Lovell House (Los Angeles) I–165a
Lovell's Island (Mass.) IV–152a
Lovelock (Nev.) III–215a, 215a
Lovely, W. L. (Indian agent) IV–199a
LOVELY'S PURCHASE IV–199a
Lovestone, Jay II–144a
Lovewell, John (off.) IV–199a
LOVEWELL'S FIGHT (1725) **IV–199a**
Loving, Oliver (cattleman) III–199b
Loving v. *Virginia* (1967) IV–362b
Low, Frederick F. (dipl.) IV–54b
Low, Juliette Gordon III–181a
Low, Seth (pol., educ.) II–132b; VI–459b
Lowantica Valley. *See* Spring Valley (N.J.)
Lowboys III–134a
Low Countries
divorce II–356b
kermis IV–43b
Lowden, Frank O. (law., pol.) I–427b; III–206a
Lowe, Ralph P. (pol.) III–468b
Lowe, Thaddeus S. C. (aeron.) I–232b, 248a
Lowell (Mass.) II–6a
labor unions VII–316b
Middlesex Canal IV–174b, 335b
mills I–345b
railroads III–449b; VI–25a
textiles II–266a; IV–266b; VII–44b–45a
trade with India II–388b
waterpower IV–347b; VII–257a
water supply VII–259b
Lowell, A. Lawrence (educ.) III–260a–b; V–222a, 347b
Lowell, Francis Cabot (mfr.) I–345b; III–63a; IV–61a; VII–44b–45a
Lowell, James Russell (poet, dipl.) I–344a; IV–162a, 267a,b
Biglow Papers I–296b
Harvard University III–259b
hymns III–326b
Peter Parley books V–264b
Lowell, Robert (poet) IV–165b
Lowell family IV–256b
Lowell Institute IV–207a
Lowenstein, Frederick (inv.) VII–163a
Lower Bonnington II–132a
LOWER CALIFORNIA IV–199b; I–405a
exploration I–91b
filibustering III–23a
horse III–302b
Indians III–362a, 363a
Jesuit missions III–499a
Magdalena Bay Resolution IV–223b
sea otter trade VI–247a
winemaking VII–305b
Lower Canada
loyalism I–438a
LOWER COUNTIES–ON–DELAWARE IV–199b
New Castle V–43a
Pennsylvania–Maryland-boundary dispute V–252a
Lower Creek (Indians) II–256b; VII–352a
Lower East Side (N.Y.C.) VII–23b
Lower Indian Reserve (Tex.) I–286a
Lower Lakes. *See* Upper and Lower Lakes
Lower Palatinate V–195a
Lower Sandusky. *See* Fremont (Ohio)
Lower Sioux Agency (Minn.) IV–356b
LOWER SOUTH IV–200a; II–61a
Low Hampton (N.Y.) I–15a
Lowie, Robert (ethnol.) I–129a
Lowndes County (Ala.) IV–456a
Lowndes County (Miss.) VI–7b
Lowry, Robert (off.) III–297b
LOYAL, FORT, CAPTURE OF (1690) **IV–200a**
Loyal American Rangers VI–130a

Loyal Americans (Royal Refugee Corps) II–249b
Loyal Associated Refugees I–206b
LOYALHANNA, BATTLE OF THE (1758) **IV–200a**; III–58b, 116a–b
LOYALISTS IV–200a; VI–106a, 115a–16a, 124b
Afro-Americans IV–339b
American historiography III–280b
associations I–208a
Augusta (Ga.) I–223b
Battle of Bennington I–289a, 289a
Battle of Elmira II–433a
Battle of King's Mountain IV–48b
British army and navy VI–129b
British campaign of 1777 I–365b
Burgoyne's invasion I–385a
burning of Danbury II–286a
Butler's Rangers I–398a
Cherokee Wars II–14b–15a
colonial debts I–366a,b
committees of safety II–140b
conscientious objectors II–185a
"Cowboys" II–249b
East Florida III–38b
emigration II–439b
flight to Canada I–438a
Fort Augusta I–223b
Georgia IV–44b
German mercenaries III–173a
Hutchinson letters III–320a
Jay's Treaty III–493a
Natchez IV–455a
New Hampshire V–54a
New Jersey V–57a–b
Newport V–65b
New York City V–86a
New York State V–86b, 88a
nonimportation agreements V–104a
Norfolk V–109b
North Carolina IV–407b; V–115b
pamphleteering V–198b
Panton, Leslie and Company V–211a
Piedmont area II–485a
postwar treatment I–341a
property confiscated II–168b, 481b; III–79a; VI–118b
Quakers VII–201b
Rivington's Gazette VI–152a
South Carolina IV–44b
Sullivan-Clinton campaign VI–437b
tar and feathers VI–462a
Trespass Act VII–116b
United Empire Loyalists VII–150b
Vermont III–241a; VII–172a
Virginia II–32b
Virginia–North Carolina frontier III–400b
Wyoming massacre VI–452a; VII–346b, 347b
See also Revolutionary War, Loyalist Troops in
LOYAL LAND COMPANY IV–201a; II–272a, 273a; IV–98b
LOYAL LEAGUES IV–201b
Loyal Legion, Military Order of the. *See* Military Order of the Loyal Legion of the U.S.A.
Loyal Legion Historical Journal IV–343a
Loyal Order of Moose VI–252b
LOYAL PUBLICATION SOCIETIES IV–202a; II–63b
Loyal Refugees VI–130a
LOYALTY OATHS IV–202a
Ex parte Garland III–152b
ironclad oaths III–474a
Reconstruction VI–55b, 58a–b
teachers VII–15b
test laws VII–34b
union leaders IV–74a
Wade-Davis Bill VII–213a
See also Test Laws
Loyalty programs VII–310b
Communist party II–145b
Loyola, Saint Ignatius III–501a,b
LSD (drug) II–262b; V–468b
LSD (landing ship dock) II–375b
LST (landing ship tank) VII–343b
Lubbock (Tex.) VII–40b, 76a
Lubbock, John W. (astron., math.) III–454a
Lubbock, Thomas S. (off.) VII–34b
Lucas, Anthony F. (prospector) IV–334a; V–271b; VI–356b
Lucas, Charles II–377a
Lucas, Eliza. *See* Pinckney, Eliza Lucas
Lucas, John (off.) I–141b
Lucas, Robert (off.) II–496a
Lucas, Robert (pol.) III–468a
Lucban, Vicente (rev.) V–281b
Luce, Stephen B. (nav. off.) V–23b, 24a
Luciano, Charles ("Lucky") II–258b, 261b, 262a
"Lucifer." *See* Matches
Luck of Roaring Camp IV–163a
Lucy (comic character) V–72b
"Lucy Locket" (song) VII–352b
Ludecke v. *Watkins* (1948) II–445a
Ludendorff, Erich F. W. (off.) IV–320a; VI–84a
Ludington, Wright II–106b
Ludlow (Colo.) II–86b; VII–191b
Ludlow, Israel (pioneer) II–37b; IV–329b
Ludlow, Louis (pol.) IV–203a
Ludlow, Noah Miller (act., theat. mgr.) I–268a; VII–47a
Ludlow, Roger (col. offi.) II–181b; IV–203b, 338a; VI–151b; VII–282b
Ludlow Commission V–94b
Ludlow massacre (1914) II–129a
LUDLOW RESOLUTION IV–203a; VII–227a–b
LUDLOW'S CODE IV–203b; I–239a; II–181b
Ludlow Street jail (N.Y.C.) VII–131b
Ludwig, Carl (physiol.) IV–285b
Ludwig, Daniel K. (shipping magnate) III–80b
Ludwig-Missionsverein (Munich) I–467a
Lufthansa
aerial hijackings III–277b, 278a
Luftwaffe I–60a, 67a, 328a; III–187a
Luge
Olympic Games V–154a
Luiseño (Indians) III–363a; IV–366a
Luks, George (paint.) II–104a
LUMBEE (Indians) **IV–203b**; IV–301a
Lumber
as money II–140b
LUMBER INDUSTRY IV–203b; VI–48b
Arkansas I–173a
bounties IV–308a
Cape Fear I–447b
Charleston (S.C.) I–496b
Chicago II–17b
coasting trade II–90b
codes of fair competition VII–123a
colonial trade II–453a; III–413a; IV–243a; VII–82b
company landholdings IV–100a
domestic trade VII–83b
Dubuque II–376a
Falls of Saint Anthony VI–187a
Florida III–39a
folklore III–49a
foreign investments III–63a
foreign trade VII–86a,b, 87a,b
furniture III–138b
Georgia III–169a
great fortunes III–80a
Great Lakes III–216b
Green Bay III–226a
Idaho III–328b
Indiana III–370a,b
Jamestown III–489a
Lake Ontario shipping V–157a
Maine IV–227a; VI–149a
Memphis IV–302a
Michigan IV–331b
Minneapolis VII–134a
Minnesota IV–357a
Mobile IV–382b
Natchitoches IV–457a
national parks V–220a
Navigation Acts V–16a,b
New England VI–170b
New Hampshire V–53b, 54a–b; VI–149a
Ogdensburg V–139b
Oregon V–165b, 166a
Pennsylvania V–247b
pine IV–331b
public lands V–450b
reforestation VI–67b
retail sales II–355a
roads III–447b
Rocky Mountains VI–160b
Saco Bay VI–184a
sales VII–84b
Savannah VI–220a,b
sawmills VI–222b
sequoia VI–262b
shipbuilding VI–279a
shipping IV–311a
tariff VI–463a
Texas VII–40b
timberlands VII–60a
triangular trade VII–119b, 277b, 278a
Vermont VII–172b
Washington State VII–247b
West Virginia VII–281b
Wisconsin VII–308a
Lumber State VI–394 (table)
Lumber workers
unionization IV–67b
Lumière, Auguste (inv.) IV–417a
Lumière, Louis (inv.) IV–417a
Luminism (paint.) V–189a
Luna, Tristán de (col.) III–41a
Lunar landing *See* Moon Landing
"LUNATIC FRINGE" IV–204b
Lunatics
excluded from immigration II–445a
Lundeen, Ernest (pol.) II–346a, 492a
Lundin, Thomas, Lord Drummond VI–114b
Lundy, Benjamin (abolitionist) I–28a, 135b; III–162b; V–279b
LUNDY'S LANE, BATTLE AT (1814) **IV–204b**; I–436b; II–458a; V–91a; VII–234b
Lunéville (Fr.) IV–319b
Lunging Island III–479b
Lupton, Fort (Colo.) II–128a
See also Lancaster, Fort
Luray (Va.) VI–275b
Luray Valley III–128a
Luria, S. E. (biol.) I–304a; III–158a; IV–389b; V–100a

Lurton, Horace H. (jur.) VI–446a
***LUSITANIA*, SINKING OF THE** (1915) **IV–205a**; IV–319a; VII–72b, 324b
Lusk, Clayton R. (pol.) IV–205b
LUSK COMMITTEE IV–205b
Lusterware III–184a
Luther, Martin (rel. ref.) I–294a; II–465b
Lutheran Brethren V–123b
LUTHERAN CHURCHES IV–205b; II–465b; VI–76b, 78b, 79b
colonial society II–125b
foreign missions IV–366b
German immigrants III–336b
hymns III–326a
immigration III–335a, 336b
Norwegian churches V–123a
pietism V–310b
private schools VI–228b
Salzburgers in Georgia VI–204b
schoolbooks VI–227a
schools II–394b, 399b
Separatists III–255a–b
Shenandoah Valley VI–275b
universal education II–393b
Wisconsin VII–307b
Lutheran Church in America IV–206b
Lutheran Church–Missouri Synod IV–206b
See also Missouri Synod
Lutheran Council in the United States IV–206b
Lutheran Free Church V–123b, 123b
LUTHER* v. *BORDEN (1848) **IV–206b**; VI–133b
Luttig, John (fur trader) VII–235a
Luttrell, John (col.) VII–102b
Lutuamian. *See* Klamath–Modoc
Luxán, Diego Perez de (sol.) I–288b
Luxburg, Count (dipl.) VI–378a
Luxembourg
Battle of the Bulge I–379a,b
Common Market VI–469a
European Economic Community VII–88b
investments in U.S. III–66b
Korean War IV–55b
North Atlantic Treaty Organization V–113b
Organization for Economic Cooperation and Development V–170b
Treaty of Versailles VII–173a
United Nations Declaration VII–151b
Western Union Defense Organization V–114a
World War II VII–334b
Luxury tax II–276a; VII–7a,b
Luzerne County (Pa.) II–222a
Luzon (Phil.) III–133a; IV–157b, 158a; V–282a
Hukbalahap movement V–285a
Philippine Insurrection V–281b
Spanish–American War V–282b
World War II I–59b, 274a; VII–139a
Lvov, Prince Georgi Evgenievich VI–164a
LYCEUM MOVEMENT IV–207a; II–399b; IV–281a,b; VII–206a
Franklin Institute III–99a
natural history IV–348b
science VI–232a
Lyceum of Natural History (N.Y.) IV–348b; VI–235b–36a, 237b
Lyceum Village (Ohio) IV–207a
Lydius, John VI–451b
Lye III–413b; VI–323a,b
Lyell, Charles (geol.) I–367b, 368a
Lyford, John (cler.) II–365a
LYGONIA IV–207b; III–200a; IV–37b; VII–114b
Lykes Brothers IV–312a
Lyman, Fort (N.Y.) II–405b
Lyman, Phineas (off., law.) II–405b; III–171a; VI–451b
Lyman's Colony. *See* Georgiana
Lynch, Charles (off.) II–32b; IV–208a
Lynch, Thomas, Jr. (legis.) II–308b
Lynch, William (nav. off.) V–23a
Lynchburg (Va.) III–488a; VI–137a, 275a
LYNCHING IV–207b; I–30a; II–32b, 247a, 258a; III–438a; VI–8a; VII–191a,b
Ku Klux Klan IV–58a
legislation V–48b
Mafia incident IV–221b
Mississippi I–31a
NAACP IV–461a
Lynch's "slave pen" (Saint Louis) V–414a
Lynde, Isaac (off.) III–24a
Lyndhurst (Tarrytown, N.Y.) I–163a; IV–472a
Lyndon Baines Johnson Library I–167b
Lynn (Mass.)
blacksmithing I–317a
bog iron I–327a
ironworks III–472a; VI–291b
Long Island settlement IV–185a–b
Saugus furnace VI–218a
shoe manufacturing I–338a
Southampton settlers VI–346b
Lynn, James T. (offi.) III–311b
Lynn Canal (Alaska) IV–52a
Lynne (Conn.) IV–387b
Lynnhaven Bay VII–199a
Lynx III–133a, 150a; VII–105a
LYON, FORT (Colo.) **IV–208b**; I–290a; VI–208a
Lyon, Irving II–99b
Lyon, Matthew (off.) I–86b
Lyon, Nathaniel (off.) I–290a
Battle at Dug Springs II–379a
Battle of Boonville I–337b
Battle of Carthage I–462a
Battle of Wilson's Creek VII–304a
Camp Jackson I–433b; V–402b
Lyons (Fr.) II–371a
Lyons, Iowa, Central Railroad I–404b
See also Calico Railroad
Lysander (N.Y.) II–48b
Lyttelton (Pa.) VI–49a
LZ-126 (zeppelin) II–344b

M

M–1 (rifle) IV–39a, 430b; VI–140a
M–4 (cannon) I–57b
M–14 (rifle) IV–431a; VI–140a
M–16 (rifle) IV–430b–31a
M16 A1 (rifle) VI–140a
M18 (rifle) VI–140b
M20 (rifle) VI–140b
M28 (rifle) VI–140b
M29 (rifle) VI–140b
M 31 (galaxy) III–242a
M40 A1 (rifle) VI–140b
M–60 (machine gun) I–49b; IV–215a
M67 (rifle) VI–140b
M72 (rocket launcher) VI–140a
M–79 (tear-gas launcher) IV–39a
Mabie brothers (circus owners) II–40b
Mabila (Ala.) I–71a
Macabebes (people) III–133a
Macadamizing V–230a
MacArthur, Arthur (off.) V–281b
MacArthur, Douglas (off.) II–450a; V–21a
army mechanization policy I–177b
conservatism II–189b
Korean War I–124a; IV–55b, 56a
Lae and Salamaua IV–83a
Lingayen Gulf IV–157b
Office of Strategic Services V–138a
Philippines V–284a
removal from command I–179b; V–124a
Seventh Fleet V–24b
World War II I–60a, 274a, 459a; VII–336b–37b
Macbeth. William II–104a
Macbride, David (physic.) IV–128a
MacCollum, William George IV–229b
Macdermott, Gilbert Hastings (mus.) III–503b
MacDonald, Dwight (anarchist) I–117a
MacDonald, Flora I–447b
MacDonald, John A. (states.) I–439a; VII–248b
MacDonald, Ramsay (states.) IV–183a
Macdonald–Wright, Stanton (paint.) V–192a–b
Macdonough, Thomas (nav. off.)
prize money V–424a
See also Macdonough's Lake Champlain Fleet
MACDONOUGH'S LAKE CHAMPLAIN FLEET IV–212a; III–177a; IV–87a; V–19a–b, 330b
MacDougal, D. T. (bot.) I–349b
MacDowell, Edward (comp.) IV–438b
MacDowell, Joseph (off.) IV–48a
MACEDONIAN (merchant ship) **IV–212b**
Macedonian (frigate) III–21b; VII–153a, 240a
Macfadden, Bernarr (pub.) V–74b
Macgowan, Kenneth (writ., theat. prod.) VII–49b
Machado y Morales, Gerardo (pol. leader) II–269a–b
MACHAULT, FORT (Pa.) **IV–213b**; III–115a, 120a; V–399b; VII–168b
Machen, August W. (pol.) VI–173a
Machen, J. Gresham (theol.) VI–82b
Machias River IV–226a
Machiavelli, Niccolò (philos.) V–354a; VI–396a
Machicoulis redoubt II–267a
Machin, Thomas (off.) III–313a
MACHINE, PARTY IV–213b; I–363a; V–343b, 345a; VI–142b
Albany Regency I–82b
Chicago II–18b
Indiana III–370a
municipal reform IV–429b
New Hampshire V–54a
New York City V–83a,b
patronage V–228a.b
Pendergast machine V–244b
political campaigns I–417a
public utilities IV–427b
Readjuster movement

VI–49b
spoils system VI–375a
Tammany Hall I–417a; VI–459b–60b
Virginia VII–195b
MACHINE GUNS **IV–214b**; III–154a; IV–431a–b; V–27a, 164a
British Vickers I–57b
Browning I–57b
Gatling gun I–49b
helicopters III–270b
Lewis gun I–57b
M–60 I–49b
Neutrality Act (1935) IV–430a
Oerlikon I–57b
World War I I–177a; VII–326a
Machine Gun School (Augusta, Ga.) I–289a
Machine politics *See* Machine, Party
Machine-Readable Cataloging Distribution Service IV–147b
Machinery
alternating current II–415a–b
coal mining II–85b
food processing III–55a
manufacture I–344b; II–244b; IV–245b
New York State V–87b
Ohio V–141b
MACHINE TOOLS **IV–215a**; III–442a
Industrial Revolution III–412a
interchangeable manufacture III–441a,b
iron industry VI–409b–10a
manufacture II–181a
motors II–415b
rubber VI–167b
Wisconsin VII–308a
Machinists, International Association of II–51a
Machinists Union IV–62a; V–400a
Mach number I–235a
MacIntosh, Douglas Clyde (theol.) VI–83a
Mack, Alexander (rel. leader) I–361a; VI–76a
Mackay, Alexander (fur trader) V–180a
Mackay, Alexander (trav.) I–367b, 368a
Mackay, James (fur trader) VI–367a
Mackay, John W. (fin.) III–80a
cables I–401a; II–137a
Comstock Lode II–157a
Postal Telegraph Company V–374b
wheat farming I–329a
MacKaye, Steele (act., theat. mgr.) VII–49a
Mackenzie, Alexander (expl.) I–84b; III–252b; V–164b; VII–247b, 275b
Mackenzie, Alexander S. (nav. off.) VI–338a
MacKenzie, Donald (fur trader) V–180a; VII–221a
Mackenzie, Fort (N.Dak.) II–34a
Mackenzie, Kenneth (fur trader) IV–217a
Fort Union IV–403a
Mackenzie, R. S. (off.) VI–64a, 242a
Mackenzie, William (mer.) II–107b
Mackenzie, William Lyon I–458b; V–227a
Mackenzie River I–441b; II–461b; V–121a
MACKENZIE'S TREATY (1831) **IV–217a**
Mackerel III–52a, 413a
MACKEREL FISHERIES **IV–217a**
MACKINAC, STRAITS OF, AND MACKINAC ISLAND **IV–217b**; I–498b; III–225b, 226a; V–367b; VI–191b, 196b
American Fur Company III–331b
British II–338b; VII–270a
ferries III–11b
fur trade III–143a; IV–332b; VI–192b, 357b
Indian factory II–480a
Indian religion IV–330a
Nicolet's explorations V–95a
railroads VI–33a, 35b
Saint Ignace Mission IV–7a, 330b; VI–190b
trading house III–142b
Treaty of Greenville III–383a
War of 1812 III–89b
Mackinac Bridge IV–218a
MACKINAW BOAT **IV–218a**; I–274a; IV–381a
Mackinaw City (Mich.) IV–217b, 218a
Mackinaw Company. *See* Michilimackinac Company
Maclay, William (law.) II–473b
MacLeish, Archibald (librarian) IV–148a
MacLeod, C. M. (biochem.) III–157b; IV–389b
Maclura (tree) V–174a
MacMillan, Donald B. (expl.) V–337a
Macmillan, Harold (states.) I–292b; IV–454a
Macmillan Company I–334b; II–340b
MacMonnies, Frederick W. (sculp.) VI–243b
MacNeil, Hermon A. (sculp.) VI–243b
Macomb, Alexander (landowner). *See* Macomb Purchase
Macomb, Alexander (off.) IV–87a; V–330b
MACOMB PURCHASE **IV–219b**; I–466b
Macon (dirigible) I–51b, 234a, 236b; II–345a
Macon (Ga.)
Camp Wheeler I–435a
railroads VI–33a, 220b
Union prisoners I–118a; II–159b; IV–139a–b
Macon, Nathaniel (law.) II–174 (table)
Macon, Uncle Dave (mus.) IV–441b
Macon County (Ala.) VII–130b
Maconochie, Alexander (off.) VI–68a
MACON'S BILL NO. 2 (1810) **IV–219b**; III–118b; V–105a; VII–233b
Macpherson's Directory for the City and Suburbs of Philadelphia (1785) II–343b
Macready, John (av.) I–51a
Macready, William Charles (act.) I–209b; VII–47b
Macune, Charles William (farm leader) II–493b
Macy, Jesse (pol. sci.) V–348b
Macy, John (au.) IV–164a
Macy, R. H., and Company I–17a; VI–258b
Madagascar
France III–97a
pirates I–151a
rice I–486b
slave trade I–27a
Maddox (destroyer) VII–71b
Madeira Islands II–191b; VI–274b
Navigation Acts V–16a
Sugar Acts VI–435b
War of 1812 VII–253a
wine production III–129a
Madelia (Minn.) V–119b
Madeline Island II–13b
Madero, Francisco (rev.) IV–157a
Madison (Ind.) III–374b
Madison (Maine) V–111b
Madison (Wis.) IV–420b; VII–308a
Madison, Dolley Payne (hostess) III–26a
MADISON, FORT (Iowa) **IV–219b**; III–468a
Madison, James II–10a, 174 (table); IV–220a; V–395 (table), 409a; VII–193b–94a,b, 198a
Annapolis Convention I–126a
armed neutrality of 1780 I–176a
Bank of the United States III–245b
Bill of Rights I–297b, 298a,b
British trade III–493b
code of manners IV–240b
colonization of Afro-Americans II–127a
compact theory VI–250a
Compromise of 1790 II–149b
Constitution II–192b, 193a, 194a, 196a, 196b, 203b
constitutional amendments I–94a
educational reform II–396a
election of president II–409a
executive power of removal VI–84b
Federalist I–130b; II–196b, 231a; III–4a; V–353a
Federalist party I–131a; III–5a
general welfare clause III–156b–57a
Marbury v. *Madison* IV–248b
minority rights IV–358b
Miranda's intrigues IV–361b
national museum IV–468b
Patent Office V–226a
political corruption II–231a–b
political parties V–223a
religious liberty VI–80b
representative government VI–89b
separation of powers V–385a
state sovereignty VI–403b
tariff of 1789 VI–465a
taxation VII–4b
Twelfth Amendment VII–132a
Virginia and Kentucky Resolutions I–87a, 417a; V–353a; VI–397a; VII–198a
Virginia constitution VI–390b
—President:
amnesty I–114b
Anglo-American relations I–347a
blockades I–321a
Bonus Bill I–330b; VI–450a
campaign of 1808 I–417b–18a; VI–94a
campaign of 1812 I–418a
conscription II–186a
Florida I–275a; IV–368a–b; VI–359b, 363b–64a; VII–277a
foreign policy III–67b–68a
French spoliation claims III–121b
Henry Letters III–273a
Hull pardon II–338b; III–315b
inauguration III–351a
Indian removal III–393b
internal improvements III–448b
Latin-American policy IV–114b
Mobile IV–383a
National Intelligencer III–202a
neutrality proclamation IV–110b; V–181a
Non-Intercourse Act II–437a
Pike expedition VII–271b
pocket veto V–334b
taxation VII–5a
Thankgiving Day VII–46a
third-term doctrine VII–53b
War of 1812 I–318a; VI–404b; VII–233b, 234a

MADISON, JAMES (cont.)
Washington Benevolent Society VII–249b
Madison, James (cler., educ.) IV–316b
Madison (Wis.) *Capital Times* (news.) V–73b
Madison County (Ala.) II–23a; III–318b
Madison County (Ky.) I–337a; IV–40a; VI–137b
Madison County (N.Y.) IV–187b
MADISON COUNTY ANTISLAVERY WAR (1859) **IV–220a**
Madison River IV–378a, 379b
MADISON'S ISLAND IV–220a
Madison Square (N.Y.) IV–220b
MADISON SQUARE GARDEN (N.Y.C.) **IV–220b**
basketball I–273a
Louis–Schmeling fight V–423a
tennis VII–30b
Madison Square Theatre (N.Y.C.) VII–49a
MADM (computer) II–156a
Madokawando (Indian) VII–358b
Madras (India) II–388a; IV–47a
Madrid (Sp.)
Morocco agreement I–85b
U.S. minister at I–154a
Van Ness Convention VII–167a
Madrid, Pact of (1953) VI–360b, 361a
MADRID, TREATY OF (1670) **IV–220b**; II–406b; III–41b; V–109b
Madrid, Treaty of (1795) V–62a
MADRID CONFERENCE (1880) **IV–221a**
Madriz, José (pol.) V–94a
"Mae West" (lifepreserver) VI–302b
Maffitt, John N. (nav. off.) III–40b
Maffitt's Channel VI–415a
Mafia II–262b; III–483b
MAFIA INCIDENT (1890) **IV–221a**; III–352a
Magaguadavic River VI–189a
Magallanes, Nicholas (dancer) II–288b
Magaung (Bur.) IV–447a
Magazine of American History IV–8a
MAGAZINES IV–221b; I–90b; IV–271b; V–69b
advertising II–354b
architecture I–163b
Catholic I–469b, 470b
Catholic World V–229b
Dow Jones Company V–76b
Drama Review VII–51a
Godey's Lady's Book III–188a
Harper's Weekly III–257a; V–73a
historical societies III–279b
Historic Preservation IV–472a
illustrators V–192a
Interior Decorator III–446b
literary IV–161a, 162b
muckrakers IV–424b
New York Times properties V–76b
Scientific American VI–231a
scientific articles IV–286a
slang VI–300a
Smithsonian Institution VI–320a
Social Justice IV–472b
Southern Literary Messenger VI–353a–b
Sunday School Magazine VI–442b
Survey VI–331b
United Press VII–152b
veterans' organizations VII–175a
veterinary medicine VII–176a
wood engravings VII–319a
World War II propaganda VII–333b
See also Scientific Periodicals
MAGAZINES, CHILDREN'S IV–222b
Magazin Royal. *See* Niagara, Carrying Place of
Magdalena Bay I–276b
MAGDALENA BAY RESOLUTION (1912) **IV–223b**; IV–199b
Magdalen Islands II–215b; III–30b
Magdeburg (Ger.) II–407b
Magee, Augustus (adventurer) III–235b–36a; IV–457a; VII–37a
Magee, Matthew J. (off.) IV–223b
Magee–Gutiérrez Expedition. *See* Gutiérrez–Magee Expedition
MAGEE-KEARNY EXPEDITION (1820) **IV–223b**
Magellan, Ferdinand (navig.) IV–247b; VII–275b
Guam III–230b
Philippines V–282a
Magellan, Straits of I–276b, 448a; II–388a; III–190a
Maginot Line VI–285b, 338b
MAGNA CHARTA (1215) **IV–224a**; I–298b, 300b; II–190b
due process of law II–377a–b
habeas corpus III–236b
right of petition V–265b
Magnalia Christi Americana III–280b; IV–161a; VI–81a
Magnesium II–423a; V–103b; VI–48b
Magnesium salts II–423a
Magnesium trip flares II–348b
Magnetic bubbles II–156b
Magnetic–core memory II–156a
Magnetic drums II–155b
Magnetic field II–88b
Magnetic hysteresis, law of II–415b
Magnetic Ink Character Recognition II–156b
Magnetic mines IV–351a
Magnetic resonance accelerator II–278a
Magnetic tape II–424b
Magnetic telegraph II–75b
Magnetic Telegraph Company VII–19a
Magnetism V–294b
Magnetogenerators II–413a–b
Magnetron IV–333a; VI–10a; VII–163b
Magnetron oscillator IV–262b
Magnets II–278a–b, 413a; III–14a, 156a, 184b
Magnin, Antoine (bact.) I–241b
Magnolia (flower) VI–394 (table)
Magnolia Gardens (Charleston, S.C.) I–497a, 498a
Magnolia State VI–394 (table)
Magoffin, Beriah (law.) IV–43a
Magoon, Charles (law.) II–269a
Magoun v. *Illinois Trust and Savings Bank* (1898) VII–6b
Magruder, Jeb Stuart VII–254b
Magruder, John B. (off.) III–148b; IV–396b; VI–220a, 274b
Magruder, Patrick (librarian) IV–148a
Magsaysay, Ramon V–285a
MAGUAGA, BATTLE AT (1812) **IV–224b**
Maguire, Molly IV–391b
Maguire–Keogh Act (1952) VI–102b
Mahalanobis, P. C. (statis.) VI–206b
Mahan, Alfred Thayer (nav. off., hist.) II–314a; III–176b; IV–343b; V–20a, 24a, 262b, 394a; VI–248a, 360a, 362b
Maharishi Mahesh Yogi V–171b
Mahican (Indians). *See* Mohegan and Mahican
Mahogany
furniture III–134b, 135a
Mahone, William (off., pol.) VI–49a,b; VII–195b
Mahoney, William (pol.) II–491a
Mahonic Baptist Association II–352b
Mahoning River VI–204a
MAIDEN'S ROCK IV–224b
Maid of Cashmere (dance) II–287a
Maidu (Indians) III–363a; IV–381b
Maier, Frank I–333a
Mail *See* Air Mail; Postal Service, United States; Post Roads; Overland Mail and Stagecoaches
Mail coaches II–433b; VI–380a
Mailer, Norman (au.) IV–164b, 165a; V–79a
Mail–order catalog I–16b, 17b
MAIL-ORDER HOUSES IV–225a; II–332b; VII–84a
hardware trade III–252b
price maintenance V–403b
rural free delivery VI–173a
Sears, Roebuck and Company I–489b
Mail routes
army posts I–193a
Central Route I–485b
Cumberland Gap II–272a
Cumberland Road II–273a
New York–Boston I–355a
Tennessee Cumberland Road II–273b
Mails
advertising I–17a, 19b
antislavery publications I–137a
aviation II–49b
censorship I–481a, 481b
fraud II–208b
Pullman strike I–111b; II–298b–99a
subsidies IV–310b
World War II II–446a
Maiman, T. H. (phys.) IV–263a
Maimonides Hospital (N.Y.C.) V–213b
Main Currents in American Thought III–283a
MAINE IV–225a; V–49b; VI–394 (table)
Abnaki I–2b–3a
Acadians I–6a
Agamenticus I–32a
Aroostook War I–194b–95a
birth and death registration IV–149a
black suffrage VI–431b
boundary disputes I–194b–95a, 438b; VII–134b
clockmaking II–78b
colonial land grants IV–263b
colonial land speculation IV–98b
Dominion of New England V–50b
dried fruit II–373a
Duke of York's proprietary VII–359a
Dummer's War II–380b; V–111b
election of 1936 V–47b
election prediction I–200b
exploration I–96b
feudalism III–18a

fishing colonies II–92b
Fort Halifax III–243b
Fort Pentegoet V–260a
Fort Pownall V–386a
Fort Western VII–269b
founding II–124a
French settlements III–120b
fur trade III–141a
gores III–199b
grasshopper attacks III–212b
historical society III–278b
Indian hostilities V–179b
Indian population III–396b
Indian trade IV–315a
Isles of Shoals III–479b
Kennebec settlements II–123b; IV–37a
King Philip's War IV–47b
king's woods IV–49a
King William's War IV–49b
Laconia grant IV–82b
license fees III–153b
liquor laws IV–158b; V–429b
Lovewell's fight IV–199a
lumber industry IV–204a; VI–149a
lyceum movement IV–207a
Lygonia IV–207b
Massachusetts Province Charter IV–265b
meat-canning IV–280b
migration from IV–338b
missionaries I–451b
missions III–498b, 499a
Monhegan Island IV–395b
Mount Desert IV–422b
national parks and monuments V–217b, 218 (table)
Northeast boundary V–118b
patent IV–270a
Pejepscot Purchase V–242a
Pemaquid Point V–243a
Pemaquid proprietors V–243b
Penobscot V–253b
Plymouth Company I–16a; V–333b
Popham Colony V–359b
port authority V–368a
potatoes V–376b
proprietary grant I–499b; V–436b
Queen Anne's War VI–2b
railroads VI–32b
referendum VI–66b
revolutionary war V–253b–54a; VI–130a
Saco Bay VI–184a
Sagadahoc VI–185b
Saint-Castin's trading house VI–188a
Saint Croix Island VI–189a
Saint Croix River VI–188b
Saint John River VI–151a
shipbuilding VI–279b
statehood I–194b; IV–379a; VI–400a
suffrage III–91b
sugar beets I–285a
temperance movement VII–23a
toll roads III–450b
town government VII–78a
trade with Massachusetts Bay IV–37b
Trelawney Plantation VII–114b
trusts VII–122a
"turf and twig" VII–129b
ungranted land V–443b
United Colonies of New England VII–149a
voting behavior VII–210a
Waldo patent VII–219b
War of 1812 III–247b
Webster–Ashburton Treaty VII–265a
See also Gorges' Province of Maine; New England
***MAINE*, DESTRUCTION OF THE** (1898) **IV–227a**; I–438b; II–268b; VI–61a, 84a, 360b, 361a; VII–356a
Afro-American sailors IV–340a
yellow journalism V–71b
Maine, Gulf of V–135a
Maine Baptist Missionary Association IV–365a
Maine Boundary Dispute. *See* Aroostook War; Northeast Boundary; Webster–Ashburton Treaty
Maine Prohibitory Law (1846) IV–26b
Maine Times (news.) V–79a
Main Street IV–164a
Maison Carrée III–495a
Maize II–225b–26b; III–51a
cereal I–486a,b
colonial cultivation I–37a
distilling II–353b
Indian cultivation I–36a; II–321a; III–476a; IV–235b, 327a
See also Corn
Maize beer III–398a; VII–65b
Majorbagwaduce Peninsula I–466a
Majoribanks, John (off.) II–465a
Majority leader (Congress) VII–288b
MAJORITY RULE IV–228a; V–351b
elections II–409b
minority rights IV–358b
nominating conventions VII–135b
public opinion V–453b
republic VI–92a
Major medical insurance III–435b
Majors, Alexander (bus.) V–178a; VI–176b
Majuro Island IV–257b
MAKAH (Indians) **IV–228b**; III–362a
MAKASSAR STRAIT, BATTLE OF (1942) **IV–228b**
Makin
World War II III–180a; VII–337a
Making of Index Numbers IV–233b
MAKIN RAID (1942) **IV–229a**; IV–253a, 257b
Malacca, Strait of II–217b
Malacology I–110b
Malaeska II–341a
Malamud, Bernard (au.) IV–165a
MALARIA IV–229a; II–454b; IV–295a,b
air cooling VI–69b
army research IV–291b
deaths IV–150a,b
Fort Leavenworth IV–129a–b
Jamestown III–488b; VII–192b
Louisiana IV–194b
Panama Canal V–201b
poor whites V–358b, 359a
research I–46a, 241a
Rockefeller Foundation VI–158a
Malay (people) V–282a
Malaya
independence I–124a
World War II VII–76b, 342a,b
Malay Archipelago III–230b
Malaysia
gutta-percha V–327b
Philippines V–285a
Rhodes scholars VI–134b
World War II V–239b
Malbone, Edward Greene (paint.) IV–352a
Malcolm, Daniel (mer., sea capt.) VI–435b
Malcolm X (Malcolm Little) (rel. leader) I–315a; II–59a; V–170b–71a; VII–192a
Malden (Can.) II–338b, 459a
Malden (Mass.) II–6a
Malden (Mich.) VI–377b
Malden (W.Va.) I–387a
Maldonado, Lorenzo Ferrer (expl.) V–179b
Malecite (Indians) I–2b; III–367a
"MALEFACTORS OF GREAT WEALTH" IV–230a
Malevich, K. S. (paint.) II–104b
Malheureux Island I–342b
Malheur River VI–185b
Malina, Judith (dir.) VII–51a
Malinowski, Bronislaw (anthrop.) I–129a
Malinta Tunnel (Phil.) I–274a
Mall (Washington, D.C.) VII–244b, 250b
Mallet, John W. (chem.) I–218b
Mallet, Paul (expl.). *See* Mallet Brothers Explorations
Mallet, Pierre (expl.). *See* Mallet Brothers Explorations
MALLET BROTHERS EXPLORATIONS (1739–42) **IV–230a**; III–119b; VI–215a,b
Mallet locomotive IV–176a,b
Malleus Maleficarum VII–309b
Mallory, Stephen R. (pol.) II–160a; IV–396b; V–17a, 19b
MALMÉDY MASSACRE (1944) **IV–230b**
Malnutrition IV–150a, 295a, 299a; V–128b–29b, 358b
Malolos (Phil.) V–282b
Malone (N.Y.) III–11a
Malone, Dumas (hist.) II–340b; III–281b
Maloney, Joseph H. (pol.) VI–325b
Maloney Act (1938) III–466b
Malpractice IV–284a
Malt
whiskey VII–289b
Malta
Rhodes scholars VI–134b
Maltese mule IV–425b
Maltravers, Lord. *See* Howard, Henry Frederick
Malvar, Miguel (rev.) V–281b
Malvern Hill (Va.) VII–358a
MALVERN HILL, BATTLE OF (1862) **IV–230b**; III–100a, 234b; V–245b; VII–293a
Mammalogists, American Society of IV–233a
MAMMALS IV–230b
fossils V–196b
Mammals of the Adirondacks IV–233a
Mammoth (fossil) I–242b; II–83b
MAMMOTH CAVE (Ky.) **IV–233b**; V–98a
Mammoth Cave National Park V–218 (table)
Mammoth Elephant Menagerie and Circus II–40b
Mammoth Oil Company VII–16b
Man, Center for the Study of VI–319b
Manabozhu. *See* Michabous, God of the Michilimackinac
Manadas IV–444b
MANAGED MONEY IV–233b; IV–395b; V–45b; VII–120b
Management, industrial. *See* Industrial Management
Management and Budget, Office of. *See* Office of Management and Budget
Manager government. *See* City Manager Plan
Managers, professional courts IV–18b, 19a
Managua (Nic.) V–94a
Manakintowne (Va.) III–315a
Man and Nature III–73a
Manassas (ironclad) III–474a; IV–371b

Manassas, Battle of. *See* Bull Run, First Battle of; Bull Run, Second Battle of
Manassas Junction (Va.) I–309a, 382a; III–229a; VI–26b
Manayunk (Pa.) I–363b, 364a
MANCHAC (La.) **IV–234b**; I–398a; III–144a, 326b; VI–365b
Manche, Department of (Fr.) VI–193b
Manchester (Eng.) II–388b; III–64b
Manchester (N.H.) IV–347b; V–54a; VI–144b; VII–45a
Manchester (N.Y.) V–91a
Manchester (Ohio) VII–202a
Manchester (Va.) I–194a
Manchester, University of (Eng.) V–296b
Manchester Pan-African Conference (1945) I–22a
Manchu dynasty II–25b; IV–234b
Manchukuo. *See* Manchuria and Manchukuo
MANCHURIA AND MANCHUKUO IV–234b; II–26a–b; III–69a, 457a; IV–55a, 183a; VII–251a
  Cairo Conference I–403b
  dollar diplomacy II–488b
  Japan II–488b–89a; IV–106b; V–35b, 96b; VII–334a, 341b
  nonrecognition V–107a
  Open Door policy V–158b–59a
  Russia I–75b; VI–178a
  Treaty of Portsmouth V–370b
  U.S. opposition V–239a–b
  World War II III–489b
  Yalta Conference VII–351b
Mancusi, Vincent R. (prison offi.) I–220a
Mandamus, writ of
  Hayburn's Case III–265b
  Marbury v. *Madison* IV–248b–49a
  Supreme Court VI–444a
MANDAN, FORT (N.Dak.) **IV–235b**
MANDAN, HIDATSA, AND ARIKARA (Indians) **IV–235b**; I–171b, 171b; II–282b–83a; III–119b, 363b, 365a
  agriculture V–230b
  bullboats I–380a
  Catlin's paintings I–471a
  Five Villages III–33b
  Fort Mandan IV–235b
  La Vérendrye explorations IV–118a, 380a
  Lewis and Clark Expedition IV–136a; VII–271a
  steel trap VI–411b
  War of 1812 VII–234b–35a
MANDATES IV–236a
  Japan III–85b, 426a
  Marshall Islands IV–257b
  Micronesia VII–125a
  Treaty of Versailles VII–173a
  Western Samoa VI–205a
  World War I peace conference VII–331a
  Yap VII–353b
Mandeville, Lambert (off.) IV–9a
Mandingo (people) VI–309b
Manebush (myth.) III–366b, 386b
Manganese III–12a, 13a–b; VI–48b
  Brazil VI–346a
Mangas Coloradas (Indian). *See* Mangas Coloradas Wars
MANGAS COLORADAS WARS IV–236b; I–142a, 310a
MANGEURS DE LARD **IV–237a**; VII–212a
Mangin, Charles M. E. (off.) I–70a; IV–404a; V–147a
Mango (fruit) III–129a
Mangum, W. P. (pol.) I–419b
Manhattan (Indian) IV–237a
MANHATTAN (N.Y.C.) **IV–237a**; V–82a,b
  Battery I–275b
  bouweries I–354b
  Bowery I–355a
  Broadway I–368b–69a
  charter of 1665 II–363b
  colonial dress II–370b–71a
  commerce V–87a
  Delaware Indians II–320b
  Dutch-Indian War II–383a
  elevated railways II–428a
  ferries III–11a–b
  Fort Washington VII–246b
  Governors Island III–206b
  Harlem III–253a
  Holland Tunnel III–312b
  Huguenots III–315a
  immigrants II–432b
  land speculation IV–100b
  Leisler Rebellion IV–134a
  "Negro Plot" of 1741 V–32b
  New Amsterdam V–40a, 60b
  Port Authority V–368b
  purchase II–320b
  revolutionary war III–254b; IV–186a; V–86a, 229b; VI–123b, 128b, 373a; VII–279b
  settlement II–383b
  springs VI–377b
  subway VI–429a–b
  tunnels VII–128b
  Walloons VII–221b
  Wall Street VII–221b
  Wappinger Confederacy VII–223b
  water supply VII–258b
Manhattan (tanker) I–80a; V–122b
Manhattan Bridge I–370b
Manhattan College V–83b
Manhattan Company I–263b; VII–258a,b
MANHATTAN PROJECT IV–237b; II–9a–b, 449b; III–410a; IV–433b; V–28a, 137b, 296a, 297a; VI–230b
Manheim (Pa.) III–182b
MANIAC (computer) II–156a
"MANIFEST DESTINY" IV–239a; II–474b–75a; III–68a; IV–324b; VII–268a, 362a
  agrarianism I–33a
  Canada I–437b
  Cuba II–268a; VI–360a
  filibustering III–22b–23a
  folklore III–48b
Manigault, Gabriel (mer.) III–79a
Manila (Phil.) III–133a; VII–334a
  air service II–28a
  federal mint IV–360a
  Lingayen Gulf IV–157b
  Philippine Insurrection V–281a
  Spanish-American War V–282b
  World War II I–274a; IV–158a; V–284a–b; VII–336b, 337a
Manila, Treaty of (1954) VI–350b, 351a
Manila Bay
  World War II I–276b
MANILA BAY, BATTLE OF (1898) **IV–239a**; III–25b–26a, 263b; V–20a, 282b; VI–361b, 362b–63a; VII–328a
MANILA CONFERENCE (1966) **IV–239b**
"Man in Quaker Garb" I–487a
Manioc I–48a; III–381a
Manitoba (Can.) III–119b
  exploration VI–192a
  Indians I–206a, 441a
  Red River of the North VI–64a
Manitou. *See* Michabous, God of the Michilimackinac
Manitou Hot Springs V–311a
MANITOULIN ISLANDS IV–239b; VI–219a
Mankato (Minn.) I–477b; IV–355a; VI–296b
Manley, John (nav. off.) VI–128a
Manlius (N.Y.) IV–445b
Manly, Charles (eng.) I–233a
Manly, William L. (expl.) II–477b
"Manly deeds, womanly words" (motto) VI–394 (table)
Manly-Hunt emigrants II–297b
Mann, A. Dudley (dipl.) II–65b, 162a; III–316a
MANN, FORT (Kans.) **IV–240a**; I–221a
Mann, Horace (educ.) II–396b, 398a–b, 404b; IV–267b
  district school VI–227a
  education of the deaf III–248a
  phrenology V–294a
MANN ACT (1910) **IV–240a**; V–438a
Manned Orbital Laboratory I–63b
Manned Spacecraft Center (Houston) IV–460a
Mann-Elkins Act (1910) I–390a; III–458a; VI–22a
Männerchor III–337a
MANNERS IV–240b
  antebellum South VI–342b
  Gilded Age III–180b
  McGuffey's Readers IV–213a
Manners, William (nav. off.) VII–253a
Manning, James (educ.) I–372a
Manning, John (off.) V–84a
Mannington (W.Va.) II–350b
MANORS IV–241b; III–18a, 313a; IV–102b; V–407b–08a; VI–348b
Manos (tool) II–386a; III–484b
Manpower Administration III–504b; IV–78b
Manpower Development and Training Act (1962) IV–78b, 80b
Manpower Report of the President (1974) II–442b
Mansard roof I–143a
Mansfield (La.) VI–63a
Mansfield, Battle of. *See* Sabine Crossroads, Battle of
Mansfield, Joseph (off.) I–130a
Mansfield, Mike (pol.) III–37b; IV–403b
Manship, Paul (sculp.) VI–244a
Manslaughter II–258a
Manson, Charles VII–118b
Manson, Mahlon D. (off.) VI–137b
Manteo (Indian) VI–43a
Mantle clocks II–79b
Manua Islands III–425b; VI–205a
Manual of the Botany of the Northern United States V–327a
Manuel, Fort (S.Dak.) VI–196a
Manuel Lisa and Company. *See* Lisa and Company
MANUEL'S FORT (Mont.) **IV–242a**; IV–159a–b, 159b
Manufacturers, National Association of. *See* National Association of Manufacturers
Manufacturer's Mutual Fire Insurance Company III–430b
Manufactures, colonial. *See* Industries, Colonial
MANUFACTURES, RESTRICTION OF COLONIAL IV–242b; III–204a; VI–107b–08a,b

See also Hat Manufacture, Colonial Restrictions on
MANUFACTURING **IV–243a**; VII–83a,b
aircraft I–235a–38a
Albany I–82a
antebellum South VI–352a
assembly line I–205a
automobile I–226b–27b
census I–481b
chemical industry II–4b
Chinese labor II–29b
Cincinnati II–37b
Civil War II–63b, 69a–b, 163b
coasting trade II–90b
Colorado II–128b
commercial bounties I–352a
commission merchant II–138a–b
Connecticut II–180b, 180b
corporate charters II–229a–b
corporate form II–230a
cotton II–238b–40a
credit II–255a, 255b
dairy industry II–279b
Detroit II–337a–b
distilling II–353b
distribution of goods and services II–354a–b
drogher trade II–373b
electrical power II–412b, 413a, 415b, 416b
El Paso II–433b
Florida III–40a
Food and Drug Administration III–54a
foreign investment III–66b, 67a
free trade III–112b
frontier merchant III–127b
furniture III–135b, 138a
Gallatin's report III–147a
Georgia III–169b
glassmaking III–182b, 184b
government regulation III–204b
Great Lakes III–216b
Hamilton's policies III–244b, 245b, 246b–47a
harness III–255b
hat I–282a
holding companies III–290b
Idaho III–328b
Illinois III–330a
immigration III–337a
Indiana III–370a,b
industrial management III–405b
industrial research III–408a
Industrial Revolution III–410b, 412a
interchangeable manufacture III–441a
interstate commerce III–459b
iron and steel III–469b–74a
Jeffersonian Democracy III–495b
Kansas IV–26a–b
Kansas City (Mo.) IV–27b
Kentucky IV–41b–42a
leather industry IV–127b
machine tools IV–215a
Massachusetts IV–267b–68a
mass production IV–272a
Michigan IV–331b
Minnesota IV–357b
Mississippi IV–369a,b
munitions IV–432a–34a
Nashville IV–452b, 453a
National Association of Manufacturers IV–461b
Newark V–41a–b
New England V–50a
New Hampshire V–54a–b
New Jersey V–57b
New South V–67a
New York City V–83a
New York State V–87a
North Carolina V–115b
Ohio V–141b
Oklahoma V–149b
Oneida Colony V–155b
panic of 1857 V–207a
paper and pulp V–212a
Pawtucket V–230b–31a
Philadelphia V–277b, 278a
photographic industry V–291a
Pittsburgh V–322a
pottery III–183a–84b
Prairie du Chien V–388a–b
prices V–406a
printing press V–413a
prison labor II–216b
Republican party VI–92b
Rhode Island VI–133a,b
Richmond VI–137a
rubber VI–167a–68a
rural life VI–175a
safety and health legislation IV–80a
Saint Louis IV–378a
Saint Paul VII–134a
Salem VI–199b
sales taxes VI–200a,b
Savannah VI–220b
scientific management VI–233b
sewing machine VI–265a–b
shipbuilding VI–279a
silk VI–286b
Society for Establishing Useful Manufactures VII–160b
South American trade VI–343b, 345a, 346a
steam engines VI–409b
tariff VI–462b, 463a,b, 465a,b, 466a,b, 470b
taxation VII–5b, 7b, 8b, 11a
textiles II–81a, 266a; VII–42b
trade associations VII–92a
Trade Expansion Act VI–471b
trademarks VII–93a
traveling salesmen VII–105b
trusts VII–122b
Vermont VII–172b
vitamins V–128a
wagons VII–216b
waterpower VII–257a,b
Wheeling VII–288a
Wisconsin VII–308a
wool II–266a; VI–272b–73a; VII–320a
World War II IV–332a; VII–88a
Wyoming VII–346a
See also Industries, Colonial
MANUFACTURING, HOUSEHOLD **IV–245b**; II–418b; III–413b
brewing I–361b
hemp III–271a
New York State V–87a
soap VI–323a
textiles VII–42b
triangular trade VII–277b
women VII–316b
wool VII–320b
MANUMISSION **IV–246a**; I–135b, 136a; VI–309a
Manumission Society of Tennessee II–436a
Manure, animal III–16a
Manuscripts III–283b, 284b
Manzanita oak I–494a
Manzunao (Calif.) III–491a
Mao Tse-tung I–124a; II–27b–28a, 489a–b; IV–235b
"Ma Perkins" (soap opera) VI–323b
Maple III–74b, 134a,b; VI–48b
Maple Leaf Rag (comp.) IV–439b
MAPLE SUGAR **IV–246b**; I–36b; III–51a, 140b, 413b; VI–436b
Map of the British and French Dominions in North America With Roads, Distances, Limits, and Extent of the Settlement IV–381a
Mapping
army engineers I–184b
Coast and Geodetic Survey II–88b
Far West I–329b–30a
See also Cartography
MAPPING OF AMERICAN COASTS **IV–247a**; I–463b
Mapp v. *Ohio* (1961) VI–249a
Maps
Arrowsmith's I–196a,b
copyright II–224b
Evans' II–466b
Filson's III–24a
Red Line VI–62b
MARAIS DES CYGNES MASSACRE (1858) **IV–248a**; I–342a
Marauder (bomber) I–50a
Marble
furniture III–135a
Vermont VII–172b
Marble Canyon III–208a
Marble Faun IV–162a
Marblehead (Mass.) II–93b; IV–360b; VI–374b, 462a
Marble Hill (N.Y.C.) IV–237a
"Marble Palace" (N.Y.C.) I–17a
Marburg (Ger.) VII–341a
Marbury, William. *See Marbury* v. *Madison*
MARBURY* v. *MADISON (1803) **IV–248b**; II–232a, 370b; IV–12a–b, 13b, 19b, 336a; V–352a, 353b; VII–117a
Marbut, Curtis F. (geol.) I–46a; VI–334a
Marcellus of Bordeaux III–49b
March, John (off.) VI–2b
March, Peyton C. (off.) I–189a; V–247b; VII–230a
March, R. B. (off.) IV–249a
Marchegiano, Rocco. *See* Marciano, Rocky
Marches (mus.) IV–438a
March of Dimes V–340a
March on Washington (1963) V–1b
March on Washington Movement (1941) II–56b
March to the Sea, Sherman's. *See* Sherman's March to the Sea
Marconi, Guglielmo (elec. eng., inv.) II–423b; VII–19a
radio VI–14b
Marconi Wireless Telegraph Company of America II–424a; VI–15a
Marco Polo. *See* Polo, Marco
Marcos, Ferdinand V–285a
Marcotte, Leon (cabinetmaker) III–445b
Marcuse, Herbert (philos.) V–288b
Marcy, Randolph B. (off.) I–453a; IV–240a, 411a; VI–90b
Marcy, William L. (states.) VI–374b
China relations I–268b
Cuban relations V–175a
Declaration of Paris V–214a
Elgin–Marcy Treaty II–431a
Hülsemann incident III–316a
Koszta case IV–57b
Sound dues VI–340a
Spanish relations I–317b
spoils system V–227b
MARCY'S EXPLORING EXPEDITION (1852) **IV–249a**; VI–90b
MARCY'S MARCH (1857) **IV–249b**
Mardi IV–162a
MARDI GRAS **IV–249b**; V–62b
MARE CLAUSUM **IV–249b**; III–106b
Bering Sea VI–246a
Gulf of Mexico IV–326b

Mare Island (Calif.) II–375a; V–27b, 29b
Mare liberum III–106b; IV–249b
Marengo (It.) III–96a
Mares, José (off.) VII–36a
Marest, Gabriel (miss.) IV–31b
Mareth (Tun.) IV–32b; V–113a
Margaret Fleming (play) VII–49a
Margaretta (ship) IV–226a
Marggraf, Andreas (chem.) I–285a
Margil de Jesús, Antonio (miss.) IV–367b; VI–207b
Margin (credit) transactions II–470a
Marguerite Bay V–198a
MARIA MONK CONTROVERSY IV–250a
MARIANA (Mass.) **IV–250a**; IV–263b, 264a
Mariana Islands III–230b, 425a,b, 426a; VII–34a, 124b, 125a
  mandate VII–353b
  World War II I–60b; III–485a, 490a; IV–257b; V–285b–86a; VI–198a; VII–1b–2a, 62a, 337a, 343a
  See also Philippine Sea, Battle of the
Marianas Political Status Commission III–426a
"Marianas Turkey Shoot" (1944) V–285b
Marianna (Fla.) III–39b
Marias Pass VI–413a
Marias River V–310a
Maricopa (Indians) IV–386a
Mariculture III–29b
Marie Antoinette (q.) IV–250b
Marie Byrd Land V–337b
Marienwerder (Pol.) VII–173a
MARIETTA (Ohio) **IV–250b**; II–348b; III–147b, 148a; IV–99a, 338b; V–123a
  canals IV–444a
  Céloron's lead plates I–477a
  Fort Harmar III–255a
  Fourth of July III–88a
  land office III–258a
  settlement V–140b, 143b–44a
  shipbuilding VI–148a
Marijuana II–259a, 262b, 263a, 373b; IV–450b
MARIN, EXPEDITION OF (1753) **IV–250b**; V–399b
Marin, John C. (paint.) V–192b, 414a
Marín, Luis Muñoz (gov.) V–461a–b
Marin, Paul (off.). *See* Marin, Expedition of
Marin County (Calif.) VI–180b
Marine Biological Association of San Diego VI–242a
MARINE BIOLOGICAL LABORATORY, WOODS HOLE IV–250b; II–133a, 391b; V–135a
  Albatross IV III–29a
  Fish Commission III–28a–b, 30a
Marine communications
  radar II–425b
  radio II–424b
MARINE CORPS, UNITED STATES IV–251b
  amphibious warfare II–314b
  blacks I–29b, 30b
  Bronze Star II–312a
  China II–25b–26b
  disasters V–23a
  Distinguished Service Medal II–311a
  Dominican Republic I–454b; II–361b–62a; IV–4b
  draft II–367b
  enlistment II–451a
  established II–313a
  First Amphibious Corps I–350a
  flags III–35a
  Guadalcanal III–229b; V–20b
  Guantánamo Bay III–231a
  Haiti III–240a
  Harpers Ferry raid III–257a
  helicopters III–270b
  Horse Marines III–304a
  Iwo Jima III–485a
  Korean War IV–55b, 56a
  Lebanon IV–130a
  mechanized warfare II–314b
  Medal of Honor II–310a
  military slang VI–302a
  Naval Home VI–336a–b
  Navy and Marine Corps Medal II–312a
  Nicaragua II–343a; V–94a–b
  Okinawa V–147b
  Peleliu V–242b
  Reserve Officers' Training Corps VI–99a
  Saipan V–285b; VI–198a
  Tarawa VI–462a
  transports I–61a
  Veracruz incident VI–104b; VII–171a
  Vietnam War VII–185b
  Wake VII–218b
  women VII–318a,b
  World War I I–286b; IV–319a; V–20b
  World War II II–33a, 387b; IV–229a; 459a–
  See also Vietnam War, Marines in
Marine disasters II–349a–50a, 388b
Marine Hospital (N.Y.C.) IV–465a
Marine Hospital Service I–242a; II–277a; III–267b, 306b; IV–287a, 292a, 293a–b; V–447b
Marine Inspection and Navigation, Bureau of II–89a
Marine insurance III–426b, 427a–29b
Marine life. *See* Fish and Marine Life
Marine mammal protection II–277b
Marine Mammals of the North-western Coast of North America IV–232b
Marine Office of America III–429a
Marine painting V–188a
Mariner (patrol plane) I–55b
Marine research stations II–391b
Mariner spacecraft I–212b; III–502b
Marine safety II–88b–90b
Marinettes II–372a; VII–318a
Marion (Ala.) I–402a
Marion (N.C.) IV–70b
Marion (Va.) IV–253b
MARION, BATTLE AT (1864) **IV–253b**
MARION, FORT (Fla.) **IV–253b**; I–142a; VI–187b, 188a
  See also Castillo de San Marcos National Monument
Marion, Francis (off.) II–451b; III–31b, 231a; IV–253b; V–222a; VI–347a–b, 351b
Marion County (Kans.) I–326a
Mariposa County (Calif.) IV–254a
Mariposa Grove (Calif.) VII–361b
MARIPOSA LAND GRANT IV–254a
Marisol Escobar (sculp.) VI–244a
Maritain, Jacques (philos.) V–288b
Maritime Act (1970) III–218b
Maritime Administration II–135a; IV–311b
Maritime Canal Company of Nicaragua V–94a, 94b
MARITIME COMMISSION, FEDERAL IV–254b; II–438b; III–459a; IV–311b; VI–281b
  freighter designations IV–312a
  shipbuilding VI–279b
  war risk insurance III–428b
Maritime law
  admiralty courts I–14a
  Alabama Claims I–73a
  Coast Guard II–88b–90a
  consolato del mare II–190a
  Declaration of Paris V–214a
  freedom of the seas III–106a
  free ships, free goods III–110a
  impressment of seamen III–349b–50b
  jurisdiction II–202a
  mare clausum IV–249b
Maritime Provinces
  Loyalist veterans VI–131a
Maritime workers
  Seamen's Act (1915) IV–68b
  unionization IV–72b
Mark I (calculator) II–154a–55a
Mark II (computer) II–154a
Mark III (computer) II–154a
Mark IV (computer) II–154a
Mark, E. L. (zool.) III–29b
Market-Garden, Operation (1944) III–187a–b
Marketing II–355a
  agents II–244b
  cooperatives II–221a, 282a
  dairy products II–281b–82b
  grain elevators II–430a
  tobacco II–221b
MARKETING RESEARCH IV–255a
  distribution of goods and services II–354b
  public opinion V–454a
MARKETS, PUBLIC IV–255b; IV–427b
Market-sharing agreements IV–399a
Market Time, Operation (1965–73) V–22a
Markham, J. (au.) VII–175b
Markham's Maister-peece VII–175b
Markland. *See* Labrador
Markoe, Frances (offi.) IV–464b
Marksmen. *See* Sharpshooters
Marksville complex III–300b
"MARK TWAIN" IV–256a
Marl (lime) III–16b
Marland, Sidney P., Jr. (educ.) III–249a
Marlatt, Earl (comp.) III–326b
Marlette Lake II–157a
Marlow (Okla.) II–32a
Marmaduke, John S. (off.) I–337b; V–389a; VII–280b
Marmalade III–54b
Marmaton River VI–241a
Marne River
  World War I I–70a, 102a, 286a, 491b, 502a; IV–404a; V–146b; VII–115a, 326b
  See also Aisne-Marne Operation
Maroon societies VI–307a
MARQUE AND REPRISAL, LETTERS OF IV–256a; I–265b; V–419a–b
  congressional power II–200a,b
  Laffites I–265b
  revolutionary war V–18b
Marquesas Islands II–463b; IV–220a
Marquette (Wis.) VI–443b
Marquette, Jacques (miss., expl.) III–499b
  Chequamegon Bay II–13b

Indiana III–369b
Saint Ignace Mission VI–190b
Sault Sainte Marie VI–219b
See also Jolliet and Marquette Discovery
Marquette Iron Range III–473b; IV–303b
Marquis, Don (humorist) V–75a
Marquis wheat VII–286a
MARRIAGE IV–256a; I–478b; II–356b, 485b–86b
age II–328b
civil II–485b
common law II–485b–86a
communes VII–313b
divorce II–356b–57a
Indian V–210b
interracial II–457b; IV–362b
Kinsey Report IV–50b
Oneida Colony V–155b
polygamy II–443b; V–355b
record-keeping VII–205b, 207a
shivaree VI–282b
trends II–328a
uniform legislation II–457b; VI–399b
woman's rights VII–314a
women's citizenship VII–315b
women workers IV–61a
See also Miscegenation
Marriner, Peter V–332b
Marrow of Tradition IV–166a
Marryat, Frank (trav.) VI–154a
Marryat, Frederick (nav. off.) I–367b, 368a; III–52b, 468a
Mars (planet) I–210b, 212b; III–502b; V–13a
Marsden, Ernest (phys.) V–298a
"Marseillaise" (song) III–238b
Marseilles (Fr.)
heroin II–262a
Marsh, A. L. (inv.) II–419b
Marsh, C. Dwight (educ.) II–391a
Marsh, Edward (watchmaker) II–78b
Marsh, George Perkins (law.) I–350a; II–187a, 390b–91a; III–73a
Marsh, Grant Prince (capt.) II–496a
Marsh, Henry (engr.) VII–319b
Marsh, O. C. (paleon.) I–453b; IV–232b; V–196b, 197a
Marsh, Reginald (paint.) V–414a
Marshak, Robert E. (phys.) V–302b
Marshall (Tex.) IV–257a; V–373a; VI–37a, 38b
Marshall, Charles H. (ship capt.) I–308b
Marshall, George C. (off.) III–61a; V–100a, 247b
armored forces I–178a
army general staff I–189a
China II–26b, 27b
Marshall Plan IV–257b; VII–88a–b
McCarthy hearings VII–310b
Pearl Harbor investigation V–240a
War Department VII–230a
World War II VII–334b, 336b
Marshall, Humphrey (pol.) IV–40b
Marshall, James W. (pioneer) III–81b, 190b, 191a
Marshall, John (jur.) II–5b, 395b; IV–142b, 347a; V–385b; VI–375a, 445a, 447b; VII–117b, 198b, 300b
Bank of the United States v. *Planter's Bank of Georgia* I–261b
bankruptcy laws V–140a
Barron v. *Baltimore* I–269a
Bill of Rights I–299a; II–53b
bills of credit II–253b
Bollman case I–327b
broad construction of Constitution II–197b
Brown v. *Maryland* I–373a
Burr trial I–388b; V–397b; VII–107a
Charles River Bridge case I–496a
Cherokee VII–321b–22a
Cohens v. *Virginia* II–94a
colonization of Afro-Americans II–127a
commerce clause II–135b, 220a; III–178a
conservatism II–189a
contract clause II–213b
Dartmouth College Case II–293b
Fairfax proprietary II–481b
Federalist party III–4b
Fletcher v. *Peck* III–36a
Gibbons v. *Ogden* V–353b; VII–83b
implied powers III–348b; IV–13b
interstate commerce III–458b
judicial review IV–13b
Marbury v. *Madison* II–232a; IV–12a–b, 248b–49a; V–353b; VII–117a
Martin v. *Hunter's Lessee* IV–259b
McCulloch v. *Maryland* IV–211b; V–353b
steamboat monopolies III–132a; VI–407b
taxation of Bank of the United States V–174b
Virginia constitution VII–194b
Washington's death III–26a
XYZ affair III–96a; VII–347b
Yazoo fraud IV–99a; VII–354a
Marshall, R. C., Jr. (off.) I–434b
Marshall, Robert C. I–336b
Marshall, Thomas R. (pol.) I–426b–27a; VII–180 (table)
Marshall, Thurgood (jur.) VI–447b
Bill of Rights I–300a
desegregation II–55a
NAACP IV–461a
MARSHALL CONVENTION (1865) **IV–257a**
Marshall County (W.Va.) IV–420b
Marshall Field (Chicago) I–164a
Marshall Field and Company III–80b
MARSHALL ISLANDS IV–257a; III–425b; VII–34a, 124b, 125a
mandate VII–353b
World War II III–180a; V–21a; VII–1b–2a, 337a, 343a
MARSHALL PLAN IV–257b; II–301b, 315a; III–61a–b, 69b; V–113b–14a, 280b; VI–468a–b; VII–88a, 332a
administration V–170a
Brookings Institution I–370a
cold war II–98a
England I–124a
France III–97b
Spain VI–360b
West Germany I–291b
Marshall Space Flight Center III–319a; IV–459b, 460a
Marshall University II–347b
Marshals (lawmen) I–482b; II–252a; III–3a; IV–21b
Marsh hay II–279a
Marston v. *Lewis* (1973) III–94a
Marteau (Martiau), Nicholas III–315a; VII–360a
Martelaer's Rock (N.Y.) II–191a; III–275b
Marten III–150a
Marten, Benjamin (bact.) I–240b
MARTHA'S VINEYARD (Mass.) **IV–258a**; III–375b; VII–359a
Martí, José (law.) II–268b
MARTIAL LAW IV–258a; IV–342b
Civil War VII–164b
Coeur d'Alene riots IV–66a
county-seat wars II–245b
Luther v. *Borden* IV–206b
New Orleans V–63b
New York City V–86a
Philippines V–285a
proclamations V–425a
San Francisco earthquake VI–210a
Veracruz incident VII–171a
Martiau, Nicholas. *See* Marteau, Nicholas
Martin 440 (plane) II–347b
Martin, Abe (comic character) V–72b
Martin, Abraham (ship pilot) I–3b
Martín, Esteban (print.) V–410a
Martin, Glenn L. (av., mfr.) I–233b, 235b
sea planes I–51b
Martin, Glenn L., Company I–236a
Martin, Henry Newell (physiol.) IV–2a; V–306b–07a
Martin, Jacob L. (dipl.) V–211b
Martin, John IV–259b
Martin, Joseph (pioneer) V–384b
Martin, Joseph W. (pol.) V–124a
Martin, Joseph W., Jr. (pol.) II–177 (table)
Martin, Luther (law.) V–199a
Martin, Thomas Commerford (ed.) II–418b
Martin, Thomas S. (pol.) VII–195b
Martin, William McChesney (econ.) III–7b, 8b
Martin Aircraft Company I–237b, 238a
Martin clippers I–237a
Martineau, Harriet (au.) I–367b, 368a
Martínez, Pedro (miss.) III–41a
Martinique III–117a; V–214b–15a
logwood trade IV–181b
Mount Pelée eruption V–23a
yellow fever VII–355a
Martinsburg (W.Va.) IV–63b; VI–38b; VII–108a
Martin's Station (Ky.) I–306b
MARTIN-TOLLIVER FEUD (1884–87) **IV–259b**; III–18b
MARTIN* v. *HUNTER'S LESSEE (1816) **IV–259b**; II–195b, 481b; IV–19b
MARTIN* v. *MOTT (1827) **IV–259b**
Martiny, Philip (sculp.) VI–243b
MARTLING MEN IV–260a
Martling's Tavern (N.Y.C.) IV–260a; VI–459a
Martyrs. *See* Florida Keys
Martyr's Rock II–191a
Marvin, C. F. (off.) VII–264b
Marvin, William (jur.) II–360a
Marvin Miller v. *California* (1973) III–106a
Marx, Karl (philos.) III–476a; VI–325b
Marx, Leo (schol.) I–113a

Marxian socialism IV–63b, 64a, 67a, 68a
Marxism V–352b; VI–325b–26a
Asia II–489b
black nationalism V–170b
Black Panthers I–315b
Iroquois III–476a
labor I–102b, 103b, 104a
moral values IV–408b
Old Left I–117a
Socialist Labor party VI–325a
Mary I (q.) I–293b
Mary II (q.) I–82b; IV–134a, 226a; V–84b; VII–300a
MARY AND JOHN (ship) **IV–260a**; II–364b; V–333b, 359b
Mary Ann (merchantman) I–266b
Mary D. Hume (whaler) VII–285b
Marye's Heights (Md.) III–101a
Mary Hitchcock Medical Center II–293a
Maryknoll (N.Y.) I–469a
Maryknoll Fathers I–469a
MARYLAND IV–260a; VI–394 (table)
Acadians I–6a
Albany Congress I–82a
Alexandria Conference I–85a,b; II–192b
American Colonization Society I–101a
Anglicanism VI–75b, 81a
archives I–168b, 168b
Ark and *Dove* I–172b; II–124b
Articles of Confederation I–198a; II–211b
Baltimore I–249a
Baltimore and Ohio Railroad VI–24b
Bank of the United States III–348b
Battle of the Severn VI–264b
bill of rights I–300b
bills of credit I–300a
blacks IV–246b
black suffrage VI–431a,b
boundary disputes I–351b; III–200a, 459b; IV–263a–b; V–251b
British debts I–366a,b
canal society I–444a
Cartagena expedition I–461b
Catholics I–466b; II–36a; III–334b
Chesapeake and Ohio Canal II–15b; III–448a
chromite III–13b
Church of England II–36b
Civil War I–130a, 341b–42a; II–61b, 484b; III–100b–01a, 256a, 332b; IV–43a, 190a, 261b–62a; V–248b; VI–251b, 275a, 308a; VII–304b
Claiborne settlement II–70a
collector of customs II–275b
colonial assembly II–117b
colonial charter V–436a
colonial exiles V–342a
colonial government VI–166a
colonial land grants IV–91b–92a
colonial land speculation IV–98b
colonial punishments V–464b, 465a
colonial suffrage VI–434a
colonial vehicles VII–168a
colonization I–172b
Committee of Safety II–184a
commodities as money II–140b
conscientious objectors II–185a
constitution VI–390b, 391a
Court Leet II–246b
Crittenden Compromise II–265a
cruel and unusual punishment V–464a
Cumberland Road II–273a–b; IV–470b
Declaration of Independence II–308a
District of Columbia VII–132b
dueling I–318a
education II–395a
Federalists III–5a
fencing laws III–10a
feudalism III–18a
flour trade III–42b
foreign trade VII–86a
founding II–124a
Franciscans III–94b
Frederick III–100b
freemen II–117b
fugitive slaves III–130a; V–406b
geological survey III–165a
Glorious Revolution II–125a
Great Trading and War Path III–223b
Harpers Ferry raid III–257a
historical society III–278b
horse breeding III–304b
Huguenots III–315a
human rights III–316b
hundred III–317b
hurricanes III–319b
indentured servants III–353a
Indiana settlers III–369b–70a
Indian treaties IV–89b
internal improvements III–447b
iron manufacture V–409b
Jefferson–Burr election dispute III–495a
Jesuits III–94b, 501b
justice of the peace IV–22b
King William's Secondary School II–395a
Labadist colony II–147a; IV–59b
lead industry IV–122a
Loyalists VI–115b
manors IV–241b–42a
marble I–451a
Mason–Dixon Line IV–263a
McCulloch v. *Maryland* IV–211b
minutemen IV–361a
miscegenation IV–362b
Monongahela River IV–398b
national parks and monuments V–217a,b
navy facilities V–28a
original package doctrine V–172a
pack trains V–184a
patents V–225b
"Peggy Stewart Day" V–242a
Pinkster celebration V–316b
plantation system V–325a
poll tax V–355a
Potomac River V–378a,b; VII–82b
presidential electors I–416b
Principio Iron Works V–409a
privateers V–419a
proprietary agents V–435b, 436a
proprietary grant I–499b, 500a; II–118b, 122b; V–194b, 436b
Quakers V–469b, 470a
quitrents VI–4a,b
racetracks II–260b
referendum VI–66b
religious liberty II–394b; V–332b; VII–68b, 69a
revolutionary war II–251a; VI–125a, 130a
roads VII–99b
Saint John's College II–395a
Saint Marys VI–197a
Scotch–Irish VI–240b
sectionalism VI–253b
slavery I–341b; VI–309a
slave trade VI–305b
state flag III–35a
state song IV–262a
suffrage III–91a
taxation VII–3a, 4a
tobacco VI–341a, 386a; VII–66b, 67a, 67b
tobacco as money VII–65b, 66a
Union sentiment VI–354a; VII–148b
U.S. Constitution II–193a, 196a, 198b, 203b, 478a
usury law III–443a
Vandalia Colony VII–166b
War of 1812 I–318a
Washington, D.C. IV–428b; VII–244b, 245b
western lands I–198a; II–166a; VII–273a, 274a
westward movement VII–260a, 283a
wheat VII–286a
whiskey VII–289b
Wilderness Road VII–296a
workmen's compensation II–441a; IV–68b; VII–322a
writs of assistance VII–345a
MARYLAND, INVASION OF (1862) **IV–261b**; I–130a
Maryland, University of II–329b
Maryland Charter (1632) IV–263a
Maryland Historical Society III–285a
Maryland Institute IV–281a
Maryland Magazine of History III–279b
Maryland Mission III–501b
"MARYLAND! MY MARYLAND!" (song) **IV–262a**; IV–261a; VI–394 (table)
Marysville (Calif.) VI–379b
Marysville Buttes (Calif.) I–280a
"Mary Washington" (rose) III–151b
Mary Washington College VII–197b
Mascouten (Indians) II–265b; III–89b, 467b; IV–7a, 9a
MASERS AND LASERS IV–262a; IV–363b
Mashuda (frigate) I–266b; II–303a
Masillon (Ohio) IV–72b
Masked dancing II–291a
Mason (Tex.) II–358b
Mason, A. T. (pol.) I–318a
Mason, Charles (surv.) II–322b; IV–263b; V–252b, 253a
Mason, Daniel G. (comp.) IV–438b
Mason, Fort (Mo.) IV–263a
MASON, FORT (Tex.) **IV–263a**
Mason, George (states.) I–162b; V–199a; VI–285a; VII–193b
Alexandria Conference I–85b
Antifederalists I–131a
Bill of Rights I–297a–b, 298a
ratification of Constitution II–196a
Virginia bill of rights I–300b
Virginia constitution VI–390b
Virginia Declaration of Rights VII–201a
Virginia Resolves VII–203a
Mason, Haven IV–429b
Mason, James Murray (law.) II–65b, 162a; VII–115b
Mason, John (col.) II–124a; IV–263b–64a; V–261a
cattle I–471a
Isles of Shoals III–479b
Maine grant IV–82b, 225b
Mariana territory IV–250a

New Hampshire grant V–53b
Norwich tract IV–387b
Strawberry Bank VI–417b
Mason, John Tufton IV–264a
Mason, John Y. (dipl) V–175a
Mason, Lowell (mus., educ.) II–397a; IV–446a
Mason, Robert (col.) VI–46a
Mason, Samuel (pirate) I–476a; IV–263a
Mason, S. J. (sci.) II–39a
Mason, William (inv.) IV–187b
Mason and Slidell Incident. *See* Trent Affair
MASON BAND IV–263a
Mason County (Tex.) IV–263a
MASON–DIXON LINE IV–263a; II–357a; VI–253b
Pennsylvania–Maryland-boundary dispute V–246b, 252b
Pennsylvania–Virginia-boundary dispute V–253a,b
sectionalism VI–342a–b
slavery III–437b; VI–310a
survey VI–450b
Masonia (Maine) IV–264a
Masonic College (Lexington, Mo.) IV–137a
Masonry I–363b, 377b; II–375a
Masons. *See* Freemasons
Mason's Fort (Pa.) IV–263a
MASON TITLE IV–263b; VI–46a
MASSAC, FORT (Ill.) **IV–264a**
Massachuset (Indians) V–410b
MASSACHUSETTS IV–264b; III–263a; IV–158b; V–49b; VI–394 (table)
agriculture VI–170b
Albany Congress I–82a
American Academy of Arts and Sciences I–97b
Antinomian controversy VI–131b
apprenticeship I–148a
Aroostook War I–194b
Articles of War VII–142b
Bay Path I–279b
Bible commonwealth I–294a
bills of credit I–300a
Bingham Purchase I–302b
birth and death registration IV–149a
black suffrage VI–431a
blast furnace I–319a
Body of Liberties (1641) IV–265a
Boston I–343b
Boston Resolutions I–347a
Boston Ten Townships I–347b
boundary disputes I–350b, 351a; V–88b
Brook Farm Association II–147a
Brotherhood of the Spirit commune II–142b
bureau of labor IV–78a
Cambridge I–411b
Cambridge Platform I–412a
campaign of 1836 I–419b
campaign of 1972 VI–93b
Canada I–435b
canal society I–444a
Cape Ann I–446b–47a
Cape Cod I–447a
Cartagena expedition I–461b
cattle disease VII–177a
chairmaking I–490a
charities board VI–327b
Charlestown I–498b
child labor laws II–24b
church organization VI–223b
Circular Letter I–326b
city planning II–46a
civil service act II–60a
clockmaking II–77b, 79a–b; VII–352b–53a
cod fishing I–447a
Coercion Acts I–8a; II–93a; IV–271b
coinage I–483a; II–384b; V–316a
colonial education IV–116a
colonial post office V–371a
colonial punishments V–464b
colonial suffrage VI–434a
colonial wage controls IV–60a–b, 79b
committee of correspondence I–345b
constitution I–204b; VI–390b, 391a,b
Convention Army II–214b
Conway Cabal II–218a
cranberries I–447a
cruel and unusual punishment V–464a
curfew laws II–274b
dairy industry II–279b, 280a
Declaration of Independence II–308a
Declaration of Rights II–308b
Declaration of Rights of the Commonwealth I–300b
Dighton Rock II–341a
earthquake effects II–385a
education II–396a,b, 397b, 398a, 404b
embargo of 1807 II–437a
Erie Triangle II–460b
Essex Junto II–464a–b
Federalists III–5a
fish III–26b, 28a
Fort Massachusetts IV–268b
franchise IV–269b
freedom of the press III–104b
Freemasons III–108b, 109a
freemen III–109b
geological survey III–165a,b; IV–348b
gerrymandering III–175a
gores III–199b
Granite Railway VI–24b
Great Awakening III–214a
great fortunes III–79a
Halfway Covenant III–243a–b
Hartford Convention III–259a
Harvard University III–259b; IOI–394b
hat manufacture III–262a
historic properties IV–472a
Hoosac Tunnel III–299a
Hopedale Community II–147a
horse breeding III–303b
Hutchinson letters III–320a
Indian factory system II–480a
Intolerable Acts II–211a; III–464a–b; VI–113b
iron industry III–472a
ironmaking III–12a
Jim Crow laws III–502b
judicial review I 145a–
justice of the peace IV–22b
juvenile criminals IV–23a
King George's War IV–192a,b
King Philip's War IV–47a
King's Province claim IV–49a
King William's War IV–49b; VI–1b
labor legislation IV–293b
lead industry IV–122a
leather industry IV–127b
Leisler Rebellion IV–134a; V–84b
life expectancy IV–150b
life insurance III–432a,b
lifesaving service IV–152a
life tables IV–149a,b
Lords and Gentlemen IV–188a
lotteries IV–191a
Loyalists VII–150b
loyalty oaths IV–203a
lyceum movement IV–207a
mackerel fisheries IV–217a
Mahican IV–387a
Maine IV–225b–26b; V–436b; VI–400a
managed money IV–233b
marble I–451a
Mariana IV–250a, 263b
Marine Biological Laboratory IV–250b
Martha's Vineyard IV–258a
May Day IV–278a
meat-canning IV–280b
merchant adventurers I–16a
Merry Mount IV–314b
Middlesex Canal IV–174b, 335b
military service II–366a–b
militia IV–346a
minimum-wage IV–68b, 352b
Minots Ledge Lighthouse VI–146a
minutemen II–366b; IV–360b
miscegenation IV–362b
mission societies IV–364b
Mississippi settlers III–171a
molasses VI–171a
Molasses Act VI–435a
Nantucket IV–449a
naval militia V–28b
New Hampshire V–53b
New Plymouth Colony V–64b, 65a
New York and Genesee Company V–81b
Nicolls' commission V–95b
Northeast boundary V–118b
Number 4 V–126a
oceanographic survey V–133b
Ohio lands V–140b
paper-money issue IV–393b
Pemaquid Point V–243b, 244a
Pembroke Resolves V–244a
pewter work VI–290b, 291a,b
Phelps–Gorham purchase V–276a
pine tree flag V–316a
piracy V–320a
plans of union II–121b–22a
population enumerations VII–205b
pottery V–379a
powwow V–386b
presidential electors I–416b
price-fixing V–401b
primogeniture V–408a
privateers V–419a
private schools VI–228b
property qualifications for voting V–434b
provincial congress V–439b, 440a
public health V–447a
public ownership V–455a
Puritans III–169b; V–342a, 469a
Queen Anne's War VI–2b
railroads III–449b–50a; VI–25a, 32b
referendum VI–66b
Regicides VI–70b, 71a
religion VI–81a
religious liberty VII–69a
reptile survey VI–90b
revivals VI–76b
revolutionary war I–344b; II–211a, 468b; III–400a; IV–137a; V–85b, 253b, 419a; VI–123a, 125a; VII–251a
rubber industry VI–167a
Sacco–Vanzetti case VI–182b

MASSACHUSETTS (cont.)
Safety First movement VI–185a
safety laws IV–80a
Salem VI–199a
salt I–447a
Saugus furnace VI–218a
school for the deaf III–248a
schools VI–226b, 227a
seafood industry I–447a
Seneca Lake cession V–86b
separation of powers V–385a
settlement IV–269b–70b; VI–427b; VII–95a
sexual attitudes VI–265b
Shamut VI–270a
Shays's Rebellion II–167a, 192b, 196b; III–436b; VI–271b
sheep III–51b; VI–272b
shipbuilding I–447a; IV–309b
shoe manufacturing I–338a
slavery I–135b; VI–309a
slave trade VI–304b
Social Democratic party VI–324b
soda fountains VI–332a
Sow Case VI–358b
spring fast II–497a
Stamp Act Congress VI–382a
state fairs VI–392b
state flag III–35a
statistics VII–206b, 207a
steam engines VI–409a
Strawberry Bank VI–418a
strikes VI–419a
Suffolk Banking System VI–430b
Suffolk Resolves VI–430b
suffrage III–91b; IV–269a
sumptuary laws VI–440a,b
tariff VI–465a
temperance movement VII–22b, 23a
textile industry VII–44b–45a,b
Thanksgiving day II–497a
tide mills VII–58a
tobacco VII–66b
town surveys V–452a
triangular trade VII–119b
unions II–142a
United Colonies of New England VII–149a
U.S. Constitution II–193a,b, 196b, 198a, 203b, 478a
usury law III–443a
voter registration VI–71a
voting IV–269a
Warwick Commission VII–244a
waterpower IV–347b
water supply IV–428a
western lands V–443b; VII–273a
West Rexburg Community II–147a
whaling I–447a; VII–285a,b
witchcraft VII–309b–10a
wolf bounties VII–311b
World War II VI–149a
writs of assistance VII–344b
yellow fever VII–355a
See also New England
Massachusetts (battleship) VI–216b; VII–242a
MASSACHUSETTS, FORT (Colo.) **IV–268b**; II–128a; IV–249b
MASSACHUSETTS, FORT (Mass.) **IV–268b**
Massachusetts, Fort (N.Mex.)
Mormon expedition IV–411a
Massachusetts Antislavery Society V–50b
MASSACHUSETTS BALLOT IV–269a; I–248b, 249a; VII–209a
MASSACHUSETTS BAY, FRANCHISE IN IV–269a; IV–270a,b
Massachusetts Bay Colony I–151b–52a; II–122b, 124a; III–219b, 220a, 220a; IV–260a, 265a–b; V–51a, 55a,b, 316b
Antinomian controversy IV–447b; VI–76a
assembly II–117a, 118a
Assistants I–206b
Bay Psalm Book I–279b
Brownists I–371b
Cambridge Platform II–169b
Casco treaties I–465b
charter II–118b; VI–4b
church membership suffrage II–35b
cod fishing II–92b
coinage II–94b
commerce II–119a
Connecticut II–182b; III–309b; VI–151a
conscientious objectors II–185a
council II–119b
Court of Assistants II–117a
Dissenters II–353a
Dominion of New England V–50b
dress II–371a
Dummer's War II–380b
education II–393b–94a
eminent domain II–440a
freemen II–35b, 117a
fur trade III–140b–41a
general court III–155a
Gorges' Province of Maine III–200b
Gortonites III–200b
government IV–415b
hard money V–404a
hogs III–288b
Hutchinson, Anne VII–316b
Iroquois Treaty III–476b
King George's War II–267a
King Philip's War III–223a
land title VI–4a
laws II–379a–b
loyalty oaths IV–202b
Lygonia grant IV–207b
Mariana IV–250a
Merry Mount trading post IV–315a
migrations from IV–338a
monopolies V–225b
negative voice V–32a
New England Way V–51b
New Plymouth Colony V–313a–b
paper currency II–302a
patent and charter II–242a
Pequot War V–261a
Plymouth Trading Post V–334b
Puritans VI–262a
Quakers V–469b
Randolph's Commission VI–46a
roads VI–152b
Shawomet VI–271b
shipbuilding II–124b
society II–125b
theocracy II–35b; VII–51a
trade IV–37b
westward movement VII–282b
Winthrop's journal III–280a
MASSACHUSETTS BAY COMPANY IV–269b; II–228b; III–62b; IV–265a–b; V–51a; VII–94b, 95a
Body of Liberties III–132b
charter I–152a, 411b–12a, 499b, 500a
Connecticut II–179b, 181b
Dorchester Company II–364b
Mariana IV–250a
New Haven Colony V–55a
plantations V–324a
Puritans V–469a
Randolph's Commission VI–46a
Salem VI–199a
shipbuilding I–319b
MASSACHUSETTS BODY OF LIBERTIES IV–271a; III–132b; IV–415b
Massachusetts Centinel (news.) I–464b
MASSACHUSETTS "CIRCULAR LETTER" IV–271a; IV–143b; V–97b
Massachusetts Codes I–239a
Massachusetts Committee of Safety I–344b
Massachusetts Emigrant Aid Company. *See* New England Emigrant Aid Company
Massachusetts General Hospital I–344b; III–306b; IV–267a, 297b; V–126b
MASSACHUSETTS GOVERNMENT ACT (1774) **IV–271a**; II–93a; III–464a; VII–79a
Massachusetts Health Insurance Company of Boston III–435a
Massachusetts Historical Society II–98b, 108a,b; III–278b, 279b, 280b, 285a; IV–126b, 267a, 435b–36a
Massachusetts Institute of Technology I–344b, 411b; II–399b, 447b, 448a; IV–120a, 267b, 268a
Arthur D. Little, Inc. I–197b
bacteriology instruction I–241a
computers II–156a, 426b
DNA research II–358a
industrial management III–406a
laser development IV–263a
meteorological studies IV–318a
political science V–349a
public health V–447b
radar research VI–10b
Radiation Laboratories IV–333a
school of architecture I–164a
School of Public Health III–325b
solid-state physics V–304b
Massachusetts Medical Society IV–267a
Massachusetts Missionary Society IV–365a
Massachusetts Province Charter IV–265b
Massachusetts Provincial Congress I–344b
Massachusetts Spy (news.) V–69a–b, 70a
Massachusetts State Board of Health I–241a
Massachusetts State House (Boston) I–163a
Massachusetts Sunday School Union VI–442b
Massachusetts v. *Laird* (1970) VII–227b
Massachusetts v. *Mellon* (1923) III–211b
Massacre, Conestoga. *See* Paxton's Boys
Massacre Island II–294a
Massacres VII–190b
Apalache I–143a
Baker's Cabin I–244a
Beale colony VI–144a
Big Bottom I–296a
Boston I–326b, 345b
Camp Grant I–142b, 433a
Cherry Valley II–15a
Chinese workers II–29b
Conestoga Indians V–231a
Dade II–278b
Deerfield II–312b–13a
Fetterman III–17b, 378a
Forman's III–77b
Fort Dearborn II–17a
Fort Loudon III–117a
Fort Mims IV–347b
Fort Pillow V–313b
Fort Seybert VI–267a
Fort William Henry VII–301b
Gnadenhutten III–188a;

IV–351b
Goliad III–198b; VII–37b
Great Massacre III–219a
Gunnison massacre III–235a
Haun's Mill III–262b
Herrin III–274a
Indian Key III–381b
Ludlow II–129a
Marais des Cygnes I–342a
Mountains Meadows IV–421b
My Lai II–247a
Occaneechee Indians I–240b
Oyster River V–179b
Piegan War V–310a
Pottawatomie I–314a, 342a; V–379a
Quantrill's raid V–471a
Raisin River VI–42b
Sand Creek VI–208a
Smith explorations VI–318a
Spirit Lake III–468a; VI–374a
St. Valentine's Day I–339b
Tuscarora War VII–130b
Whitman mission V–167a; VII–293b
Wounded Knee III–177b; VII–344a
Wyoming massacre VII–346b
Yellow Creek II–257b
Zwaanendael VII–372b
Massapeague (Indians) III–271b
Massaponax (Va.) VI–376a
Massasoit (Indian) IV–47a
Massasoit, Peace of (1621) IV–264b
Mass consumption I–227b
Massena (N.Y.) I–378b; VI–193a
Massey, John E. (cler.) VI–49a,b
Massey–Harris Company I–35a
Massiac, Fort (Ill.). *See* Massac, Fort
Massiac, Marquis de IV–264a
Massie, Nathaniel (pol.) II–25b; VII–202a
Massie's Station (Ohio). *See* Manchester
Massillon (Ohio) II–252a–b; V–145b; VI–411a
Massine, Léonide (dancer) II–288b
MASS MEDIA IV–271b
advertising III–49a
campaign funds II–411a
freedom of the press III–104b
magazines IV–221b
newspapers V–68a
propaganda V–431a
public opinion V–454a,b
slang VI–300a
United Press VII–152a
Vietnam War I–115b
violence VII–192a
woman's rights movement VII–314b
women VII–317b
World War II propaganda VII–333b
MASS PRODUCTION IV–272a; II–502a
automobile I–227a,b
clothing II–371b
furniture III–139a
glass III–186a
Industrial Workers of the World III–413a
installment selling III–423a
interchangeable manufacture IV–216b
Liberty engine IV–433b
muskets IV–432b
pottery V–379b
See also Assembly Line
Mass transit II–46a; III–153b; IV–428a–b; VI–155b
Master Car Builders' Association VI–28a
Masterman, Charles VII–332b
Master of philosophy II–403a
Masters, Edgar Lee (poet) IV–26b, 164a
Masters, Inc. II–483b
Masters, William H. (physic.) VI–266b
Master Skylark I–335b
Masters Tournament (golf) III–198a
Mastico (ship) *See Intrepid*
Mastodon I–295b, 376a
Masts II–453a; III–413a; IV–308a
Masturbation VI–266a,b
Matador Company V–160b
Matagorda (Tex.) VII–39b
Matagorda Bay III–119a; VI–195a; VII–36b
Matamoros (Mex.) II–67b; IV–274a; VI–144a
Confederate exports from II–162b
Mexican War IV–324a
Peterhoff case V–264b
Rio Grande VI–143a
MATAMOROS EXPEDITION (1835) **IV–274a**
MATANZAS, FORT (Fla.) **IV–274a**; V–217b; VI–188a
See also Fort Matanzas National Monument
Matanzas River IV–274a
MATCHES IV–274a; VII–288a
Matchless Mine IV–124a
MATERNAL AND CHILD HEALTH CARE IV–274b; IV–299a; VI–328a; VII–314a
cities VII–158b
grants–in–aid III–211b
social security VI–329b
Maternal mortality IV–150a, 151a
Maternity and Infancy Act (1921) IV–276a; VI–328a
Mathematical Association of America I–109a
Mathematics
American Journal of Mathematics IV–2b
Indians III–356b
Maya IV–327b
Mather (Pa.) II–350b
Mather, Cotton (cler.) II–101a, 107b, 356a, 496b; IV–150a; VI–81a; VII–126a
bacteriology I–240b
charity V–279b
code of behavior IV–240b
genetics I–349b
Magnalia Christi Americana III–280a–b; IV–161a
smallpox IV–295a; VI–315b; VII–205b
venereal disease VI–266b
witchcraft VII–309b
Mather, Increase (cler.) II–107b, 356a
Boston Philosophical Society VI–237b
Harvard College III–259b
Regicides VI–71a
Saybrook Platform VI–223b
Mather, Richard (cler.) I–412a; V–185a, 413b; VII–319a
Mather, Stephen T. (offi.) V–219b–20a
borax I–340b
Mathew, Theobald (cler.) VII–23a
Mathews, John (mfr.) VI–332a
Mathews, Lucia Elizabeth (Mme. Vestris) (act.) VII–47b
Mathews, M. M. (pub.) II–340b
Mathews, Shailer (theol.) VI–82b, 325a
Mathias, Robert (athlete) V–154a
Mathieson Alkali Company II–7b
Matianuck (Conn.) V–334b
MATILDA LAWRENCE CASE IV–276a
Matisse, Henri (paint.) II–104b, 105a
Matisse, Pierre (art dealer) II–105a
Matrix, scattering (elec.) II–39a
"Matrix" sound system V–290b
Ma–tsu (China) II–489a; III–70a
Matta (art.) II–104b
Mattaponi River V–385b
Matteo da Bascio (monk) I–451b
Matthaei, J. H. (biochem.) IV–391a
Matthaei Botanical Garden I–348a,b
Matthew, Stanley (jur.) VI–446a
Matthews, Herbert L. (jour.) V–74a
Matthews, James Brander (educ.) IV–163a
Mattresses III–136a
Mauch Chunk (Pa.) V–250a; VI–34b
Mauchly, John W. (math.) II–155a, 426b
Maud (ship) I–116a
Maudslay, Henry (eng.) I–205a; III–442a
Mauldin, William Henry ("Bill") (cartoon.) V–68a, 73a
Maumee (Ohio) IV–300b
Maumee Bay V–144b; VII–157a
MAUMEE INDIAN CONVENTION (1793) **IV–276b**
Maumee Rapids I–371b; II–484b; VI–42a
Maumee River III–128a
Black Swamp I–317b
British boundary V–214b
Fort Defiance II–317a
Fort Industry III–414a
Fort Jefferson III–494a
Fort Meigs IV–300b
Fort Miami (Ind.) IV–329a
Fort Miami (Ohio) IV–329a
Fort Recovery VI–60b
Fort Washington VII–247a
Fort Wayne VII–262a
French settlement V–146a
fur trade III–141b
Hull's Trail III–316a
Miami and Erie Canal V–145b
Miami purchase IV–329b
Ohio–Michigan boundary dispute VII–157a
Pontiac's War V–357a
portages V–367b
proposed settlement I–499a
Toledo War VII–68b
Wabash and Erie Canal VII–212a
War of 1812 II–338a; VI–412a
Wayne's Indian campaign VII–263a
Maumee Valley III–227b, 244a
Maumelle (Ark.) II–48b
MAUREPAS, FORT (Miss.) **IV–276b**; I–301a
Maurepas, Lake III–326b, 479a
Mauritius II–388a; III–243a
Maury, James (cler.) V–221b
Maury, Matthew F. (nav. off., oceanog.) I–455a; III–28b, 169b; V–23a, 28a, 133b, 134a–b
Gulf Stream III–233a
meteorology II–75b, 76a
Naval Observatory V–12a
polar expeditions V–336b
See also Maury's Charts
MAURY'S CHARTS IV–276b; IV–317a; V–12a, 133b
Mauvilla (Ala.) II–336b; IV–277a

MAUVILLA, BATTLE OF (1540) **IV–277a**
MAVERICK (horse) **IV–277a**; V–160a
cow custom II–251a
Maverick (missile) IV–363b
Maverick, Samuel A. (law.) IV–277a–b
Mavromichali, Chryssa v. *See* Chryssa (V. Mavromichali)
Mawhood, Charles (off.) V–408b
Maxent, Antoine IV–277b
Maxent, Gilbert Antoine de Saint. *See* Saint Maxent, Gilbert Antoine de
MAXENT, LACLEDE AND COMPANY IV–277b; III–144a–b
Maxfield, Joseph P. (eng.) V–290a
Maxim, Hiram S. (inv.) IV–215a, 277b–78a, 431a–b
Maxim, Hudson (au.) V–390b
MAXIM GUN IV–277b; IV–215a, 431a–b
Maximilian, Ferdinand (emp.) I–455a; III–97a; IV–325b–26a, 328a, 400b
Confederate expatriates IV–325b; VI–274b
Convention of Miramar IV–361a
Maxwell, George H. VI–53b
Maxwell, Lucien IV–278a
Maxwell, William (jour.) I–483b; V–70b
Maxwell, William (off.) II–218a; VI–438a
Maxwell, William Henry (educ.) II–398b
Maxwell Field (Ala.) I–64b, 66b
MAXWELL LAND GRANT IV–278a; IV–92b
Maxwell Ranch (N.Mex.) I–174b
May, Cornelius Jacobsen (mer.) IV–454a
May, Henry (pol.) I–196a
May, Hugh (arch.) I–161a
Maya (Indians) III–356a, 368b; IV–327a–b; VII–366b
agriculture I–48a
architecture I–166a,b
art III–373a
mounds IV–421a
writing III–355b, 386a
Mayaguez incident (1975) V–74b
Maybach, William (inv.) I–225b
Maybach engine II–344b
Maybeck, Bernard Ralph (arch.) I–165a
MAY DAY IV–278a; IV–314b
Mayer, Maria Goeppert (phys.) V–302b
Mayer, Robert II–106b
Mayes County (Okla.) IV–333b
Mayflower (blimp) II–345b
Mayflower (flower) VI–394 (table)
Mayflower (galley boat) III–147b
MAYFLOWER **(ship) IV–278a**; II–124b; IV–264b, 278b; V–64b, 312b, 313a,b; VI–280a
MAYFLOWER COMPACT (1620) **IV–278b**; II–149a; III–132b; IV–264b, 265a; V–65a, 313b, 353a
Mayhew, Thomas (mer.) IV–258a
Maynard, Edward (inv.) IV–279a
MAYNARD TAPE PRIMER IV–279a
Mayo (Indians) III–369a; IV–367a
Mayo, Charles H. (physic.) IV–279a
Mayo, George Elton (educ.) III–406a; VI–234a
Mayo, Henry T. (nav. off.) I–14a; VII–171a
Mayo, William J. (physic.) IV–279a
Mayo Clinic IV–279a
MAYO FOUNDATION IV–279a
Mayo Graduate School of Medicine IV–279a
Mayor–council government II–44a
Mayors II–44b; IV–171b, 426b–27a; VII–211b
Maypole IV–278a, 314b
"May she endure forever" (motto) VI–393 (table)
Maysville (Ky.) VII–368a
Maysville, Washington, Paris and Lexington Turnpike Road Company IV–279a–b
MAYSVILLE VETO (1830) **IV–279a**; III–449a
Maytag Company II–420a–b
Maywood, Augusta (dancer) II–286b, 287a
Mazda lamps II–417a
Mazinghien (Fr.) VI–338b
Mazzei, Philip (physic., mer.) IV–279b
MAZZEI LETTER IV–279b
MB–1 (bomber) I–50a, 53a
MB–1 Genie (missile) I–57b
McAdams, Clark (ed.) V–73b
McAdoo, William G. (law.)
campaign of 1920 I–427b
campaign of 1924 I–428a
Railroad Administration VI–19a–b
McAfee brothers (frontiersmen) IV 40a
McAlester, C. C. (miner) V–148b
MCALLISTER, FORT, CAPTURE OF (1864) **IV–209a**; VI–221a
McAllister, Ward (law.) III–85a
McArthur, Duncan (land speculator) IV–345a
McArthur, Fort (Ohio) III–316a
McAuliffe, Anthony C. (off.) I–273b
McCabe, Thomas (econ.) III–7b
McCain, John S. (nav. off.) VII–1b
McCall, Edward (off.) II–452b
McCall, George A. (off.) IV–282a
McCallum, Daniel C. IV–273a
McCalmont Brothers III–65a
McCardell, Claire II–372a
MCCARDLE, EX PARTE (1869) **IV–209a**; VII–35a
McCarran, Patrick A. (pol.) V–40a; VI–289a
McCarran Act (1950) VII–310b
McCarran–Ferguson Act (1945) III–429a, 434a
MCCARRAN-WALTER ACT (1952) **IV–209b**; II–445a; III–333b, 342b, 492a
Asians VII–357a
German quota III–337a
national origins system VI–5a
naturalization V–6b
McCarroll v. *Dixie Greyhound Lines* (1940) II–137a
McCarthy, Charles VII–308b
McCarthy, Eugene (pol.) I–431a; V–237b
McCarthy, Harry I–330a
McCarthy, J. M. I–318b
McCarthy, Joseph R. (pol.) III–308b–09a; V–72b; VI–12b, 14a, 416b; VII–308b, 310b
radical right II–189b
subversion hearings VI–428b–29a
See also McCarthy Army Hearings
MCCARTHY-ARMY HEARINGS (1954) **IV–209b**; VII–310b
McCarthy Committee. *See* Committee on Government Operations
McCarthyism I–314b; IV–209b; VI–13b; VII–118a
McCarthy patent II–421a
McCarty, M. (biochem.) III–158a; IV–389b
McCauley, Mary ("Molly Pitcher") VII–316a, 318a
McCausland, John (off.) I–490b–91a
McClary, John (off.) VI–197b; VII–54b
McClary's Path VII–54b
McClellan, George B. (off.) II–62b, 63a; V–247b
"All Quiet Along the Potomac" I–90b
Army of Potomac V–377a
Battle at Kernstown IV–43b
Battle at Savage's Station VI–220a
Battle at White Oak Swamp VII–292b
Battle of Antietam I–130a; III–101a
Battle of Ball's Bluff I–249a
Battle of Fair Oaks II–482a
Battle of Frayser's Farm III–100a
Battle of Gaines' Mill III–146a
Battle of Malvern Hill II–230b
Battle of Mechanicsville IV–281b
Battle of Richmond VI–420b; VII–264a
Battle of Rich Mountain VI–138b
Battle of Williamsburg VII–301b
Bull Run VII–197a
campaign of 1864 I–422a
Corps of Engineers II–449b
Harpers Ferry III–256a
Harrison's Landing letter III–258a
Lee's lost order IV–190a
Maryland defense IV–261b
Peninsular campaign III–487a,b; IV–230b, 397a, 399b; V–245a
Porter court–martial V–368b–69a
Radical Republicans VI–11a
recruiting II–451b
Seven Days' Battle VI–150a
Seven Days' Battles VI–263b
Stevens' railroad survey VI–412b–13a
McClellan, John L. (pol.) I–103a; IV–74b
McClellan committee (1963) II–262b
McClellan saddle VI–184b
McClellan's Creek VII–217a
McClellan Stores Company III–33a
McClernand, John A. (off.) I–174a; IV–370a; V–369a; VI–278b, 336a
McClintock, James (eng.) VI–422b
McCloskey, John (card.) I–468a
McCloy, John J. (off.) III–175a; VII–238a
McClure, David (miss.) IV–90a
McClure, George (off.) V–91a
McClure, R. J. L. M. (nav. off., expl.) V–122a
McClure, S. S. (pub.) I–334b
McClure's Magazine IV–424b
McCollum, Elmer v. (chem.) I–303a; IV–3b; V–128a

McComb (Miss.) III–107a
McCone, John A. (ind.) I–216b–17a
McConnell, Felix G. (pol.) III–296a
MCCONNELSVILLE ORDINANCE (1869) **IV–210b**
McCook, Alexander McDowell (off.) IV–434b
McCook Field I–234b
McCord, James W., Jr. VII–255a
McCormack, John W. (pol.) II–177 (table)
McCormick, Cyrus H. (inv.) I–34b; III–19a, 80a
reaper IV–211a, 424a
McCormick, Cyrus H., Jr. (bus.) III–454b; VI–163b
McCormick, Patricia Keller (athlete) V–154b
McCormick, Robert (inv.) IV–211a
McCormick, Vance C. (pub.) VII–244a
McCormick Bay (Green.) V–240b
McCormick family (Chicago) III–279b; V–73b
McCormick family (Va.) III–469b
McCormick Harvesting Machine Company III–454b
McCormick Institute for Infectious Diseases I–242a; IV–298b
MCCORMICK REAPER **IV–211a**; III–43a; IV–424a
McCosh, James (philos., educ.) V–409a
McCoul's House (Va.) VI–376b
McCoy, Isaac (miss.) III–398b; VII–280a–b
McCoy, John C. (trader) IV–27b; VII–280a–b
McCoy, Joseph G. (cattleman) I–1b, 471b, 473a; II–248b
McCoy, Kid (pugilist) V–423a
McCoy, Randolph III–262a
McCoy, Tim (showman) VII–299a
MCCRAY* v. *UNITED STATES (1904) **IV–211a**
MCCREA, JANE, MURDER OF (1777) **IV–211a**
McCready, Benjamin W. (physic.) IV–293b
McCrory, J. J. (mer.) III–32b
McCrory Corporation III–33a
McCue family (Va.) III–469b
McCullagh, Joseph B. (jour.) V–71b
McCullagh, William B. (ed.) V–73b
McCullers, Carson (au.) IV–165a
McCulloch, Ben (off.) V–238b; VII–304a
McCulloch, Hugh (law., banker) VI–371a
McCulloch, James W. (banker). *See McCulloch* v. *Maryland*
MCCULLOCH* v. *MARYLAND (1819) **IV–211b**; II–197b; III–348b; IV–19b; V–174b, 353b
McCulloh, Henry VII–350a
McCullough, Hugh (law., banker) II–218b
McCully, J. (mfr.) III–184a
McCully Pottery III–184a
McCumber, Porter James (pol.) IV–178a–b; VI–468a
McCune, Joseph (inv.) I–35b
McCunn, John H. (jur.) VII–131b
McCurdy, James (av. eng.) I–51a
McCutcheon, George Barr (au.) I–333a
McCutcheon, John T. (cartoon.) V–73a
McDonald, Angus (off.) II–381b; IV–212a
McDonald, David (labor leader) IV–76a
McDonald, Finan (expl.) II–131b
McDonald, William (hist.) III–486a
McDonald oil field (Pa.) V–271b
MCDONALD'S EXPEDITION (1774) **IV–212a**
McDonnell, Miles (gov.) V–244b
McDonnell Douglas I–52b, 54a, 56b, 57a, 69a
McDougal, Duncan (fur trader) I–209a; V–180a
McDougall, Alexander (shipbuilder) VII–285a
McDougall, Alexander (off.)
Battle of White Plains VII–293a
McDougall, Walt (pol. cartoonist) I–464b; V–73a
MCDOWELL, BATTLE AT (1862) **IV–212b**
McDowell, Ephraim (surg.) IV–40b
McDowell, Irvin (off.) V–377b
Army of Virginia VII–197a
Battle of Bull Run I–309a, 381a; VI–373a
Battle of Mechanicsville IV–281b
Jackson's Shenandoah campaign V–245a
Jackson's Valley campaign III–487b
Richmond campaign VI–137b
Seven Days' Battles VI–263b
McDowell, Mary VI–330b
McDowell family (Va.) III–469b
McDowell's Medical College (Saint Louis) V–414a
McEnery, John (pol.) V–64a
MCFADDEN BANKING ACT (1927) **IV–212b**; I–258b
McFadden–Pepper Act (1927). *See* McFadden Banking Act
McFarlane Strait (S. Shetland Is.) V–198a
McGarrahan, William V–210b–11a
McGee, William John (geol.) II–416b
McGill, James (mer.) III–403b
McGill, Ralph (ed.) V–73b
McGillivray, Alexander (Indian). *See* McGillivray Incident
MCGILLIVRAY INCIDENT **IV–213a**; I–355b; VI–366b
McGill University (Can.)
hockey III–287a
skiing VI–298a
McGlachlin, Edward F. (off.) I–191b–92a
McGloin, Patrick (col.) VII–37a
McGovern, George S. (pol.) I–432a; II–270b; V–182a, 343b; VI–93b, 327a
campaign of 1972 IV–77a; VII–254b, 255a
McGrain v. *Daugherty* (1927) II–210b; III–465a
McGraw, John IV–99b
McGraw–Hill Building (N.Y.C.) I–164b
McGready, James (cler.) I–238a; III–221b
McGregor (Iowa) III–177b
McGregor, Gregor (adventurer) I–93b
McGrory, Mary (jour.) VII–317b
McGuffey, William Holmes (educ.). *See* McGuffey's Readers
MCGUFFEY'S READERS **IV–213a**; II–398b; V–152a; VI–227b
McGuire, J. C. II–103a
McGuire, Peter J. (labor leader) IV–79a, 79a
McGuire–Keogh Act (1952) I–140a; II–483a–b; VII–124a
MCHENRY, FORT (Md.) **IV–213b**; IV–314b
national monument V–217a
Sea Fencibles VI–244b
"Star-Spangled Banner" VI–387b
Union prisons V–414a
War of 1812 I–249b
War of 1812 IV–261a; VI–159a
McHenry, Fort (Miss.) VII–181a
McHenry, James (legis.) II–203b; IV–213b
McIntire, Rufus (land agent) I–194b
McIntire, Samuel (carver) III–138a; VI–242b
MCINTOSH, FORT (Pa.) **IV–216b**
MCINTOSH, FORT, TREATIES OF (1785) **IV–216b**; III–24b, 255a
McIntosh, James M. (off.) II–379a; V–238b
McIntosh, Lachlan (off.) III–236a; IV–117b, 216b
McIntosh, William (Indian) III–394a; IV–4a
McIntyre, O. O. (humorist) V–75a
McIntyre, Peter (sales.) VII–105b
McIntyre, Thomas A. (bus.) III–44a
McIntyre Garrison (Maine) IV–179a
McKay, Claude (poet) I–30a; IV–166b
McKay, David (pub.) I–334b
McKay, Fort (Wis.) V–388a
See also Shelby, Fort
McKay, Frederick S. (dent.) II–331a
McKay, George L. I–332b
McKay, Gordon (ind.) I–338a; IV–120a
McKay, Robert B. (educ.) I–220b
McKean, Fort (N.Dak.) I–3b
McKean, Thomas (states.) II–305b, 308a; VI–3b, 161b
McKee, Alexander (Indian agent) IV–173b, 276b
McKee, Alexander (pioneer) V–143a
McKeesport (Pa.) II–116a; VII–49a
McKees Rocks (Pa.) V–143a
McKendree, William (bp.) I–238a
McKenna, Joseph (jur.) VI–446a
McKenna, Richard (au.) III–234b
McKenney, Thomas L. (bus., au.) I–398a
McKenzie (Indians) III–358a
McKenzie, Alexander (pol.) V–117b
McKenzie, Kenneth (fur trader) VII–145b
McKim, Charles F. (arch.) I–164a,b; VII–246b, 324b
McKim, Mead and White I–164b; III–260b, 446b; VI–299a
McKinley, John (jur.) VI–445b
McKinley, William (pres.) II–176 (table); V–142a, 396 (table), 398b; VI–93a
assassination I–117a, 202b, 426a; V–204b–05a; VI–252a
campaign of 1896 I–111a, 425b; III–189a; V–366a
campaign of 1900 I–132a, 426a; III–131b; V–281b
Cuba III–462b–63a
expansion V–158a
message to García

MCKINLEY, WILLIAM (cont.)
III–150b
Olney–Pauncefote Treaty V–153b
Philippines V–235a, 282b
Spanish–American War II–472b; VI–360b, 361a
McKinley–Adkins bill II–477b
McKinley Tariff (1890) I–424b; II–151a; III–20a, 263b; VI–343b, 464a,b, 467a
"pop–gun" bills V–359b
Sherman Silver Purchase Act VI–277a
McKinney, Fort (Wyo.) VI–181b
McKinnon, Archibald S. II–295b
McKonkey's Ferry (N.J.) VII–116a
McLain, William I–101a
McLane, Louis (bus.) V–317b–18a
MCLANE–OCAMPO TREATY (1859) **IV–218a**
McLaughlin, James (Indian agent) VI–295b
McLaughlin, Patrick (prospector) VI–292a
McLaughlin v. *Florida* (1964) IV–362b
McLaurin v. *Oklahoma State Regents* (1950) I–372b; II–56b, 401b
McLean, John (jur.) I–419b; V–375a; VI–445a
McLean, Wilmer (off.) I–146b
McLean's Ford (Va.) I–381a
McLeod, Alexander (sheriff). *See* McLeod Case
McLeod, Hugh (off.) VII–36a
MCLEOD CASE IV–218a; I–458b; V–227b; VII–265a
McLoughlin, John (fur trader) III–313b; IV–218b; VII–166a, 247b
McLoughlin, Maurice E. (athlete) VII–29b
MCLOUGHLIN LAND CLAIM IV–218b
McMahon, William (off.) VI–60b
McMahon Act (1946) I–123b
McManes, James (pol.) I–343a; V–279a
McManigal, Ortie IV–219a
McMaster, James (jour., law.) I–469b
McMaster, John Bach (hist.) III–282a; IV–163a
McMechen Narrows (W.Va.) III–77b
McMillan, Edwin M. (phys.) IV–119b, 119b; V–100a, 300b, 301b
McMillan, James (pol.) VII–246b
McMillan, William (athlete) V–154b
McMillan Commission VII–246b
McMorris, Charles H. (nav. off.) IV–54a
McMurray's map VII–74a
McMurtrie, Douglas C. (hist.) V–70a
McNair, Lesley J. (off.) I–178a,b
McNair, Robert E. (gov.) VI–348a
McNamara, James B. IV–219a
McNamara, John J. IV–219a
McNamara, Robert S. (offi.) I–400a
Ford Motor Company IV–273a
National Guard IV–464a
nuclear–powered carriers I–56b
Pentagon Papers V–258b
MCNAMARA CASE IV–218b
McNamee's Creek IV–186b
McNary, Charles L. (pol.) I–429a; III–37b; IV–219a
McNary Act (1921). *See* Norris Farm Export Act
McNary Dam III–323a–b; V–455b
MCNARY–HAUGEN BILL IV–219a; I–42a, 43a; II–477b; VII–286b
McNaughton, John T. II–347a
McParlan, Jâmes (detective) IV–63a, 392a
McPhedris–Warner House (Portsmouth, N.H.) I–161b
McPherson, Aimee Semple (evangelist) V–260a
McPherson, James B. (off.) V–238a, 369a; VI–48b, 278b; VII–27a
McQueen, Robert VI–409a
McRae, Alexander (off.) VII–165b
McRae, C. J. II–158b
McRae, Milton A. (pub.) V–76a
McReynolds, James C. (jur.) I–299a; V–47a; VI–446a; VII–269b
McSween, Alexander A. IV–155a
McSweeney–McNary Act (1928) III–75b
McTavish, Simon (mer.) III–403b
M–derived filters (elec.) II–39a
Mdewankanton (Indians) II–283a
Me 163 (fighter plane) VI–159a
Mead (pub.) I–334a
Mead, Elwood (eng.) III–478a; VI–54a
Mead, George Herbert (philos.) V–386b
Mead, Henry (mfr.) III–183b
Mead, James R. (trader) VII–294a
Mead, Lake II–76b, 130a; III–323a; VI–54a
Mead, Margaret (anthrop.) I–129a,b
Meade, Fort (Fla.) I–451b
Meade, George G. (off.) I–365a; II–62b; V–247b, 377b
Battle of Gettysburg III–175b
Jetersville VI–186b
Kelly's Ford attack IV–36a
Mine Run campaign IV–350a
Pennsylvania invasion V–248b
Meade, Richard (nav. off.) V–22b
Meadowbrook Golf Club III–198a
Meaning of Revelation VI–83a
Means, Russell (Indian activist) I–107a
Meany, George (labor leader) I–103a, 104a; IV–74b, 77a
Meares, John (sea capt.) V–462a
Mears, John O. III–152a
Measles II–454b; IV–288a; VII–294a
colonial period IV–295a
deaths IV–150b
Indians I–476b
Measurement
standards IV–462a,b
town gaugers III–154b
Meat VI–48a
"embalmed beef" II–436a
foreign trade VII–86a, 87a
frontier merchant III–127a
government inspection III–422a
markets IV–255b
preservation II–373b; III–54b, 55b, 56a; VI–69a, 70a
prices V–404a
pure food laws V–465b, 468b
refrigeration VI–70a
South American trade VI–344a, 346a
tariff VI–471a
See also Food
Meat industry VI–176a
Meat Inspection Act (1906) III–459a; IV–279b, 281a
MEAT INSPECTION LAWS IV–279b; III–53a; V–466a
MEAT–PACKING IV–280a; IV–170a
automation IV–75a
Beef Trust cases I–283b
Chicago II–17b, 18b, 37b
Cincinnati II–37b
colonial period VI–108a
conveyors IV–272b
foreign investments III–63a
Fort Worth III–80b
great fortunes III–80a
hogs III–288b–89a
inspection III–53a
leather industry IV–128a–b
Minnesota IV–357a
muckraking IV–424b
Ohio V–141b
Packers' Agreement V–183a
Packers and Stockyards Act V–183a
pure food and drug movement V–466a
refrigeration VII–84a
Saint Joseph VI–191b
Saint Louis II–37b
salt VI–203a
stockyards VI–414a,b
Mechanical arts colleges IV–93b, 97b
Mechanical energy II–412b, 417b
Mechanical engineering II–448a,b
Mechanical Engineers, American Society of. *See* American Society of Mechanical Engineers
Mechanick Exercises on the Whole Art of Printing V–410b–11a
Mechanics IV–60a, 79a,b; V–294a
Mechanicsburg (Ohio) I–491b–92a
MECHANICS' INSTITUTES IV–281a; III–99a; VI–232a
Mechanics Union of Trade Associations IV–61b
MECHANICSVILLE, BATTLE OF (1862) **IV–281b**; III–146a; V–245b; VI–263b
Mechanism of Mendelian Heredity III–157b
Mechanization
agriculture II–495a–b
butter production II–280b
cotton production II–238b
woodworking III–138b–39a
Mechem, Edwin L. (pol.) V–60a
MECKLENBURG DECLARATION OF INDEPENDENCE IV–282a
MECKLENBURG RESOLVES (1775) **IV–282a**
Mecury arc IV–177a
Medal of Honor II–310a–11b
Afro–Americans IV–340a
Baldwin, Frank D. VII–217a
Black Cavalry I–310a
Black Infantry I–313b–14a
York, Alvin C. VII–26a
See also Decorations, Military
Medary (Dak. Terr.) II–284b
Medford (Mass.) I–319b; IV–265a; VI–106a
Mediation
See also Arbitration; Labor

Mediation and Conciliation, Board of. *See* Board of Mediation and Conciliation
Mediation and Conciliation Service, Federal II–157b, 499a; IV–74a
See also Conciliation Service
Mediation Board, National II–500b, 500b; VI–21a
Mediation Commission IV–69a
Medicaid VI–328b–29a
Medical almanacs I–91a
Medical and Chirurgical Faculty of Maryland IV–283b
Medical and Surgical History of the War of the Rebellion IV–292b
Medical care
industry IV–293b
New York State V–87b
Medical College Association, American IV–284b
Medical Colleges, Association of American IV–284b
MEDICAL EDUCATION IV–282b; II–401b, 470b; IV–295b, 296a–b, 297b–98a
air force IV–292b
clinical lectures V–251b
dentistry II–329b
Harvard University III–259b, 260a
homeopathy III–294a
hospitals III–306b
hygiene III–325b–26a
Johns Hopkins University IV–2b–3b, 4a
Mayo Foundation IV–279a
National Institutes of Health IV–465a
navy IV–292b
New York City V–83b
nursing V–126b, 127a
pharmaceutical schools V–273b, 275a–b
physiology V–306b–07b
public health V–447b
Rockefeller Foundation VI–158a
Rockefeller University VI–158b
study abroad II–471a
Transylvania Medical School IV–40b
University of Pennsylvania V–249a,b
vital statistics VII–206b
William and Mary VII–300b
Yale University VII–351a
Medical Education and Hospitals, Council of (1904) IV–284b
Medical Examining and Licensing Boards, Confederation of State IV–284b
Medical insurance
Medicare IV–289b; V–150b
public assistance VI–74a
social security VI–329b–30a
See also Health insurance
Medical Repository (period.) VI–235b
MEDICAL RESEARCH IV–285a
conscientious objectors V–182b
funding IV–285a, 471a
Houston VII–40b
Jet Propulsion Laboratory III–502b
malaria IV–229b–30a
marijuana IV–451a
Mayo Foundation IV–279a
mental illness IV–305b
National Institutes of Health IV–465a
New York City V–83b
Office of Scientific Research and Development V–137a
pharmacy V–273b, 274a
physiology V–306b–07a
public health V–447a–b
Rockefeller Foundation VI–157b
Rockefeller University VI–158b
Saint Martin's stomach VI–196b
sampling methods and procedures VI–206a
smallpox VI–315–16a
tuberculosis VII–126a
vital statistics VII–206b–07a
See also Military Medicine
Medical residency system IV–3a
MEDICAL SECTS IV–288a; III–293b; IV–297a,b
Medical Service Corps IV–290b
MEDICAL SOCIETIES IV–288b; IV–457b
Medical Society of the City and County of New York IV–283b
Medical Society of the State of New York IV–293b
MEDICARE IV–289b; III–3a, 436a; V–150b; VI–74a, 328b–29a; VII–263b
Medicine, American Academy of IV–284b
Medicine, folk. *See* Folk Medicine
Medicine, Indian. *See* Indian Medicine
Medicine, Institute of IV–457b
MEDICINE, MILITARY IV–290a
Civil War IV–284a
hospitals III–306b
malaria IV–229b–30a
navy research V–28a
navy women V–23b–24a
opium IV–450a
public health V–447a
Repose V–28a
shell shock IV–306b
soldiers' homes VI–336a
women VII–318b
MEDICINE, OCCUPATIONAL IV–293a
Medicine, veterinary. *See* Veterinary medicine
MEDICINE AND SURGERY IV–295a
amphitheater V–251b
atomic energy I–217a
chemistry II–10a
drugs II–373b–74b
environmental sanitation VI–211b
homeopathy III–293b
hookworm III–298b
hospitals III–306a
hygiene III–324b
Jesuit missions III–499a
Journal of Experimental Medicine IV–3a
licensing IV–148a–b
malaria IV–229a
maternal and child health care IV–274b
Mayo Clinic IV–279a
mental illness IV–304a–07b
narcotics IV–450a,b
National Institutes of Health IV–465a
Nobel Prizes V–99a,b, 100a
nursing V–126a
osteopathy V–175a
periodicals VI–235a, 235b
petroleum IV–333a; V–269a
pharmacy V–273a, 274b
phrenology II–390b
physiology V–306b
smallpox VI–315a
tuberculosis VII–126a
urban health VII–157b
venereal disease VII–168b
women VII–317a, 318b
World War I relief VII–329b–30a
yellow fever VII–355a
Medicine Bow Peak (Wyo.) II–346b
Medicine bundles II–283b; III–384b–85a
Medicine Creek (S.Dak.) IV–299a–b
MEDICINE CREEK COUNCIL (1867) **IV–299a**; III–378a
Medicine Creek Treaty (1854) VI–412b
"Medicine Garden" I–293a
Medicine Lodge, Treaty of (1867) VI–64a
Medicine man. *See* Indian Medicine; Shamanism
Medicines, proprietary V–466a,b, 467a
MEDICINE SHOW IV–299b; VII–48a
"Medicine wolf" II–253a
Medieval Academy of America IV–126b–27a
Medill, Joseph (ed.) V–73b
Medina, Harold R. (jur.) III–466b
Meditation V–171b
MEDITERRANEAN FUND IV–299b
Mediterranean Sea
NATO fleet II–315b
shipping VI–280b
Sixth Fleet V–25a
telegraphy cable I–400b
tribute VII–120a,b
U.S. Air Force I–60a
U.S. trade IV–309b
World War I VII–329a
World War II I–308a; II–217b, 315a; IV–313b; VII–338b
Mediterranean wheat VII–286a
Medium of exchange. *See* Money
Mediums, psychic V–213a
Medora (N.Dak.) II–251b
Medumcook (Maine) VII–219b
Meech, Levi W. (actuary) IV–149b
Meehan, John Sylva (librarian) IV–148a
Meek, F. B. (paleon.) V–196a
Meeker, Ezra (pioneer) II–248a
Meeker, Leonard C. (pol. sci.) VII–223b, 227a
Meeker, Nathan C. (jour.) III–477b; VII–146a
Meeker, N. S. (Indian agent) IV–300a
MEEKER MASSACRE (1879) **IV–300a**
Meek's Cutoff *See* Sublette's Cutoff
Meeropol, Michael VI–165a
Meeropol, Robert VI–165a
Mees, C. E. K. (chem.) III–409b; V–292a
MEETINGHOUSE IV–300a
Megalonyx (sloth) IV–231b
Megalopolis VII–160a
MEIGS, FORT (Ohio) **IV–300b**
War of 1812 V–141a; VI–412a; VII–45b
Meigs, Montgomery C. (off.) II–450a; V–308b
Meigs, Return Jonathan (off.) VI–186a
Meigs County (Ohio) I–376a
Meiji Restoration (Jap.) I–201b
Meikle, Andrew (inv.) VII–55a
Meitner, Lise (phys.) V–300a
Mekamie, Francis V–391a
Mekong Delta (Viet.) VI–301a; VII–185b
Mekong River I–386b; III–46a; V–22a
Melainotype VII–62b
Melamine V–328a
Melampus (ship) II–16a
Melanchthon (ref.) IV–205b
Melbourne (carrier) II–350a
Melcher, Frederic G. (ed.) I–335b
Melges, H. ("Buddy") VII–349b

Melish, John (trav., geog.)
I–367b, 368a, 462b;
IV–320b; VII–74b
Mellon, Andrew W. (fin.)
II–104a, 105a; VI–449b
fortune III–79b
Mellon Institute IV–300b
war debts VII–331b
Mellon, James R. (fin.)
III–79b
Mellon, Paul (fin.)
II–106b
Mellon, Richard B. (fin.)
III–79b; IV–300b
Mellon, Thomas (banker)
III–79b
Mellon family V–322a
MELLON INSTITUTE OF INDUSTRIAL RESEARCH IV–300b; I–275a; III–410a
Mellon Institute of Science
IV–301a
Mellorine, nondairy
II–282b
Melon III–51a
MELUNGEONS IV–301a
Melville, Herman (au.)
IV–162a, 267a; VI–301b
Membré, Zénobe (miss., expl.)
III–272a
Memel (USSR) VII–173a
Memminger, Christopher G.
(fin.) II–160a, 164a;
V–108a; VI–349a; VII–5b
Memoirs of Hecate County
IV–165b
"Memorandum of Understanding" (Cuba–U.S.,1973)
III–276a–b
MEMORIAL DAY IV–301a; II–53a
Memorial Day Massacre
(1937) VII–191b
Memorial movement (Episcopal church) II–455a
MEMORIAL OF THE PLANTERS AND MERCHANTS OF LOUISIANA IV–301b
Memory unit (computer)
II–153b, 155b, 156a
MEMPHIS (Tenn.)
IV–301b; II–22a,b, 349a;
IV–453a
assassination of King
I–31b; IV–45b, 76b
bossism I–343a
bridge I–364a
Civil War II–22a, 62b;
III–485a; IV–313b;
VI–38a; VII–26b,
128b–29a, 181b, 182a
cotton trade II–68a
Crump machine IV–214a
gambling III–149b
Mississippi River IV–372a
music IV–440a
Nashoba IV–452b
Piggly Wiggly Stores
VI–258a
railroad conventions
VI–20b
railroads IV–28b, 302b;
VI–25b, 33b, 34b, 35a, 36b
Reconstruction VI–57a
riots III–103b
Southern Commercial Convention VI–352a
Southern Overland Mail
VI–353b
Southwestern Convention
(1845) VI–352b
Spanish post VII–270a
stagelines VI–379a
Memphis (steamer) IV–157a;
V–424a
MEMPHIS, NAVAL BATTLE AT (1862)
IV–302a; IV–374b, 375a
MEMPHIS AND CHARLESTON RAILROAD IV–302a
Memphis, El Paso and Pacific
Railroad VI–37a
Memphremagog, Lake
VI–190a
Menace (news.) V–3b
Menagerie II–40a–b
Menard, Pierre (fur trader)
IV–159b, 380b; VI–195b,
196a
Ménard, René (miss.)
II–13b; VI–443a
Menasha (Wis.) V–212b
Mencken, H. L. (ed.)
I–250a; II–189b; IV–408b
American Mercury
I–479a
Prejudices IV–164a
Mendel, Gregor (bot.)
II–226a; III–157a,b
Mendel, Lafayette B. (chem.)
I–303a; V–127b, 128a
Mendelian laws I–46a;
III–157a,b, 159a
Mendon (Mass.) IV–47b
Mendota (Minn.) VI–63b,
322b
Mendota, Treaty of (1851)
VI–296a; VII–106a
Mendoza, Antonio de (col.
gov.) I–96b; IV–452b
Mendoza, Juan Dominguez
(miss.) IV–302b
MENDOZA EXPEDITION (1683–84) **IV–302b**
Menéndez de Avilés, Pedro
(nav. off.) II–298a;
III–38a, 41a, 302b;
IV–302b; VI–187b
MENÉNDEZ IN FLORIDA AND GEORGIA IV–302b; VI–187b
Meningitis IV–292a
Menke brothers VI–283a
Menlo Park (Calif.) III–164b
Menlo Park (N.J.) II–413b,
414a; IV–88b, 153b
MENNONITES IV–303a;
V–342a
communities II–147a
Confederate Army
II–161b
conscientious objectors
II–185a
Germantown III–173a
immigration to U.S.
III–335a
migrations IV–338b
pacifism V–181a
Pennsylvania VI–76a–b;
VII–283a
wheat growing VII–286a
Menno Simons (rel. ref.)
IV–303a
"MEN OF THE WESTERN WATERS" IV–303a
MENOMINEE IRON RANGE IV–303b;
III–473b
Menominee River IV–303b
Menomini (Indians) I–398a;
III–366b
Great Indian Council at
Niagara V–90b
reservation system VI–97a
revolutionary war
VI–195a
wild rice VII–298b
Wisconsin VII–307b
Menou d'Aulnay, Charles de
V–253b
Mental defectives II–333a
Mental Health, National Institute of V–442b
Mental Health and Illness,
Joint Commission on
V–416b
Mental health programs
Kansas IV–26b
MENTAL HYGIENE MOVEMENT IV–304a;
III–325b; V–442b
social pacifism V–181b
state government VI–398b
MENTAL ILLNESS, TREATMENT OF IV–304b; I–100b; V–280a,
416b; VI–72b, 327b;
VII–206a
conscientious objectors
V–182b
health insurance III–435b
hospitals III–306b
phrenology V–294a
Quakers V–470b
segregation III–502b
social security VI–330a
Mental testing. *See* Intelligence Tests
"Mentor." *See* Ledyard,
Isaac
Menzel, Donald H. (phys.)
I–212a; V–299b
Menzies, Archibald (bot.)
V–327a
Menzies, William II–108b
Meo tribesmen (Laos)
IV–107b
MERCANTILE AGENCIES IV–307b
MERCANTILISM IV–307b; IV–243a
balance of trade I–244b
bills of exchange II–468a
British colonial policy
II–122a–23a
colonial governors
II–120a
colonial period
VI–107b–08b
European IV–85b
exchanges II–469b
middle class IV–334b
monopolies I–390a
prerevolutionary imperial
idea III–346a–b
Mercator, Gerhardus (geog.)
I–97a; IV–247b
Mercedita (warship) I–292a
Mercenaries
German III–172b
MERCER, FORT, ENGAGEMENTS AT (1777)
IV–308b; I–223a
Mercer, Hugh (off.) III–58b,
58b; V–408b
Mercersberg theologians
VI–78a, 82a
Merchant, frontier. *See* Frontier Merchant
Merchant adventurers. *See*
Adventurers
Merchant Fleet Corporation
II–438a; V–455a
See also Emergency Fleet
Corporation
MERCHANT MARINE IV–309a; I–245a; II–135a;
III–428a,b; VII–87b
Civil War II–64b, 66a;
IOI–217b; V–23b, 424a
Coast Guard II–89b
enemy destination
II–446b
enlargement II–436b
federal aid V–20a;
VI–327b
figureheads III–21b
flag III–35a
French spoliation claims
III–352a
Great Lakes III–218a–b
impressment of seamen
III–349b
Lighthouse Board
IV–152b
mail subsidies VI–425b
naval reserve V–28b
Naval War With France
V–15a
shipbuilding VI–279b,
280a,b
Shipping Board V–455a;
VI–281b
submarine warfare
VI–424a–b
Tonnage Act VII–72a
World War I II–217b,
314a–b, 438a–b
World War II II–213a,
218b; VII–343b–44a
Merchant Marine Act (1920)
IV–254b; V–455a;
VII–123a
Merchant Marine Act (1936)
IV–254b, 311b; VII–341b
Merchant Marine Act (1970)
IV–312b; VI–280a
MERCHANTMEN, ARMED IV–313a; III–456a; V–19a,
25a; VII–240a, 241b–42a
British II–217b
Hyder Ali III–320b
Naval War with France
V–419a, 423b
Neutrality Act of 1939
V–37b
submarine warfare
VI–424a
World War I VII–325a
World War II IV–435a
Merchants Exchange (N.Y.C.)
V–83a
Merchants Exchange of Saint
Louis II–141a

"Merchants of death"
IV–433b
Mercure (ship) VI–129a
Mercurials II–5b
Mercury VII–169a
fish contamination
V–468a
New Idria Mine V–211a
pollution VI–213a
Mercury (planet) I–212b;
III–502b
Mercury cadmium IV–294b
Mercury–gold amalgamation
III–191a
Mercury ore VI–48b
Mercury poisoning IV–293b
Mercury Project I–63b, 64a,
209b–10a; IV–459b, 460a;
VI–159a
Mercury–Redstone flight
(1961) I–210a
Mercury Theatre VII–50a
Mer Douce. *See* Huron, Lake
Meredith, Hugh (pub.)
V–68b, 251a
Meredith, James I–316a;
II–58b; IV–369b
Merengue (dance) II–290b
Mergenthaler, Ottmar (inv.)
V–77a, 412b
Mergers
antitrust laws II–72a
banks II–501a
big business I–390b, 391b
Burlington Northern
VI–32b
corporations II–230a–b
cotton industry II–240a
football leagues III–57b
monopoly power IV–399b
motion picture industry
IV–418b
New Jersey II–229b
power companies
III–321b
railroads VI–32a
regulation II–230a–b
restraint of trade VI–103a
trusts VII–123a, 124a
Meriam Report (1928)
III–380a, 390a
Meriam's Corner (Mass.)
IV–137b
Merici, Angela VII–160b
Meridan Britannia Company
VI–291b
Merideth, Robert (educ.)
I–112b
MERIDIAN CAMPAIGN
(1864) **IV–313b**
Merino sheep II–244b;
VI–272b; VII–320b
Meritorious Service Citation
Certificates II–312b
Merit system I–146a, 384a;
II–59b–60a
civil service V–228a
Foreign Service III–71b;
VI–389a
Hatch Act III–261a
Kansas IV–26b
Merkur, Operation (1941)
III–187a
Merlin engine I–52a
Merman, Ethel (act.)
IV–442a
Merriam, Charles (pub.)
II–340a–b
Merriam, Charles E. (pol. sci.)
V–348b
Merriam, C. L. (pol.)
IV–233a
Merriam, Clinton Hart (nat.)
II–390a–b; IV–233a
Merriam, Frank F. (pol.)
I–407b
Merriam, George (pub.)
II–340a–b
Merriam, John C. (educ.)
I–457a
Merrick (Indians)
III–271b
Merrick, Samuel (bus.)
III–99a
Merrill, A. S. (off.) II–443a
Merrill, Frank D. (off.)
IV–314a, 447a; VI–46b
Merrill, Joshua (chem.)
IV–44a
MERRILL'S MARAUDERS
IV–314a; VI–46b
***MERRIMAC*, SINKING OF**
(1898) **IV–314b**
Merrimack (ironclad)
III–474b; IV–396b–97a,
397a; V–17a, 29b, 245a;
VI–44b; VII–240b,
243b
See also *Monitor* and
Merrimack, Battle of
Merrimack Manufacturing
Company III–408b
Merrimack River VI–149a
bridge I–363b
canals IV–174b
colonial land grants
IV–263b–64a
fur trade III–141a
Gorges grant IV–225b
lead mines VI–189b
Mariana IV–250a
Middlesex Canal I–442a;
III–447b; IV–335b
settlement IV–269b;
V–53b–54a
waterpower IV–347b;
VII–257a
Merrimack Valley Textile Museum (North Andover,
Mass.) IV–437a
Merritt, Edwin A., Jr. (pol.)
III–430b–31a
Merritt, Ezekial I–280b
Merritt, Leonidas (prospector)
IV–315a
Merritt, Wesley (off.)
IV–300a; V–281a–b;
VI–362a; VII–71a, 227b,
358a
Merritt, William Hamilton
(eng.) VI–193a
Merritt Committee III–430b
Merriwell, Frank (lit. char.)
II–341b
MERRYMAN, EX PARTE
(1861) **IV–314b**; I–196a;
II–62a
Merryman, John. *See Merryman, Ex Parte*
Merrymeeting Bay V–359b;
VI–185b
MERRY MOUNT (Mass.)
IV–314b; IV–278a
Merry's Museum for Boys and Girls (mag.)
IV–222b–23a
Merton, Robert K. IV–214a
Merton, Thomas (cler.)
IV–448a
Merwin Dam III–323b
MESA IV–315a
MESABI IRON RANGE
IV–315a; III–12a, 218b,
473b; IV–357a; VI–443b
Mesa Central (Mex.)
IV–444b
Mesaiger, Charles (miss.)
III–499b
MESA VERDE, PREHISTORIC RUINS OF
IV–315b; I–117b; II–461a;
III–367a; V–8b, 217a,
460a
Mesa Verde National Park
IV–315b; V–218 (table);
VI–213b
Mescalero Apache (Indians)
I–141b, 342b; V–273a;
VI–385a, 439b
Mescalero Ridge VI–380b
Meserve projectile point
III–484b
MESILLA (N.Mex.)
IV–315b
Mesilla Valley IV–328a
Mesons II–278b; IV–119b;
V–302b
MESQUITE IV–316a;
I–494a; VII–305a
Mesquite beans IV–386a
Messerschmitt 262 (fighter
plane) III–174b
MESSIAH WAR (1890–91)
IV–316a; I–243a; VI–297a;
VII–344a
Messianic cults. *See* Nativistic Movements, American Indian
Messina (It.) VI–284b, 285a
Messina, Strait of VI–199b;
VII–338b
Messner v. *Journeymen Barbers* (1960) V–308b
Mesteños. *See* Mustangs
Mestizo (people) III–242b;
VI–6b–7a
Metabolic studies I–303b;
V–127b
Metacom (Indian). *See* Philip
Metallic magnesium II–423a
Metallurgical engineers
II–448b
Metallurgical Laboratory, University of Chicago
VI–230b
Metallurgy I–275a
coal II–84b
electrical manufacture
II–423a
General Electric Research
Laboratory III–156a
research IV–244b
sulfur production II–6b
Metalworking
apprenticeship I–148b
machine tools IV–215a
Rhode Island VI–133a
Metamora, or the Last of the Wampanoags (play)
VII–47b
Metates II–386a
Metcalf, George Forrest
(phys.) VII–163b
METEOROLOGY IV–316a;
II–75b–76b; III–167a;
V–294b
Air Force I–63b
Coast Guard II–89b
International Geophysical
Year III–453b
military medicine
IV–291a
polar stations V–337b
rainmaking VI–42a
scientific periodicals
VI–235b
tornadoes VII–75a
Weather Service VII–264a
METES AND BOUNDS
IV–318a; V–452a
Methadone II–374b
Methodist Book Concern
IV–82b
Methodist Episcopal church
II–39b; IV–318b, 319a
missions III–385b; IV–365b,
366b
Sunday schools VI–442b
Methodist Episcopal church,
South I–23b; IV–318b
Methodist Protestant church,
South IV–319a
Methodist Publishing House
IV–453a
METHODISTS IV–318a;
VI–77b, 78b
African Methodist Episcopal church I–23a
Afro–American I–24a;
IV–443a; VI–59b
camp meetings I–434a
Chautauqua movement
II–1a
Church of the Nazarene
V–30a
circuit riders II–39b
colleges II–114a
Cotton Kingdom II–241a
Dissenters II–353a
Evangelicals II–465b–66a
foreign missions IV–366b
frontier preaching
III–127b
Great Revival III–221b
home missionary societies
IV–365b
hymns III–326a
New York State V–87a
Oregon missions II–285b;
V–166b
Pentecostalism V–259b
publishing IV–453a
radical right VI–12a
revival III–214a
schism II–36b
slavery II–36b
slavery issue VI–78b
Sunday schools VI–442a
Underground Railroad
VII–138a
Western Reserve
VII–275a
West Virginia VII–281a
Willamette Valley
VII–300a
Methodist Social Creed
IV–318b

Methodius, Saint II–386b
Methods of Religious Living VI–83a
Métis (people) I–441b; III–242b
Metrazol IV–306b
Metric system IV–462b
interchangeable manufacture III–442b
Metroliner railroad service VI–31b
Metropolis (Ill.) I–364b
Metropolitan Life Insurance Company III–416b, 435b
Metropolitan Museum of Art (N.Y.C.) II–100b, 102b, 103a; III–137b; IV–237b, 352a, 436b, 437a; VI–243a,b
Metropolitan Opera (N.Y.C.) II–289a; IV–237b; VI–15a
Metropolitan Statistical Areas. *See* Standard Metropolitan Statistical Areas
Metropotamia III 497b
Metsu, Gabriel (paint.) II–103b
Metz (Fr.)
World War I V–213b
Metz, Christian I–92b
MEUSE–ARGONNE OFFENSIVE (1918) **IV–319a**; I–59b, 102a, 177a; VII–327a
Lost Battalion IV–189a
marines IV–252b
Meuse River
World War II I–273b, 380a; VII–340a
Mexia, Captain I–143a
Mexicali Valley II–130a
Mexican–Americans VI–6b–7a,b
California I–408b
civil rights II–55b
eugenics movement III–158b
labor unions IV–76b–77a
segregation VI–255b
Mexican Army
U.S. deserters II–335a
MEXICAN ASSOCIATION IV–320a
MEXICAN BOUNDARY IV–320b; I–269a, 352a; IV–328a; VI–364a; VII–39a, 111b, 272a
Nueces River V–125a
Rio Grande VI–143a–b, 150b–51a
Slidell's mission VI–312b
Treat Mission VII–108b
Mexican cession. *See* Guadalupe Hidalgo, Treaty of
MEXICAN DECREE (1830) **IV–322a**
MEXICAN GULF PORTS, BLOCKADE OF (1846–48) **IV–322a**; IV–323b, 325a
Mexican laborers
deportation II–333a
importation II–495b
MEXICAN OIL CONTROVERSY IV–322b; I–109b; III–199a, 352b; IV–328b
Mexican Revolution (1914–17) III–69a
Mexican–United States General Claims Commission I–109b
MEXICAN WAR (1846–48) **IV–323a**; I–111b, 184a–b; II–313b; III–68a, 228b; IV–110b; VI–143a, 150b–51a, 312b, 355b; VII–190b
Anglo–American rivalry I–121b
Arizona I–172a
artillery I–199b
Battle of Molino Del Rey IV–391b
Battle of Palo Alto V–198b
Battle of Resaca de la Palma VI–97a
Battle of Sacramento VI–184a
Battle of San Gabriel VI–210a
Battle of San Pasqual VI–214a
Battles of Monterrey IV–404b
Bent's Fort I–290a
Biglow Papers I–296b
bounties I–353a
Brazito I–361a
British mediation V–233a
Buena Vista I–375a
burial of U.S. dead I–478a
California I–409b
California Battalion I–409b
Cerro Gordo I–488b
Chapultepec I–494b
Churubusco I–451b; II–36b
claims commission I–109b
Colorado II–128a
Contreras II–214b
costs VII–228 (table)
Cotton Kingdom II–241a
daguerrotypes V–293a
declaration of war VII–224b, 237a
demobilization II–323b–24a
desertions II–335a
Doniphan's expedition II–363b
Emory's reconnaissance II–440b
enemy trading VII–93b–94a
exchange of prisoners II–468b
financing II–317a
Fort Brown attack I–371a
guerrillas III–231a
Hawk's Peak episode III–264b
horse cavalry I–475b
hospitals I–191a
Jefferson Barracks III–494b
Kearny's march to California IV–34b
land acquisitions I–412b; II–334a, 475a
land bounties IV–91a
laws of war VII–225a
losses VII–232 (table)
"manifest destiny" IV–239a
marines IV–252a
massacres I–219b
Mexico City IV–329a
mobilization IV–383b
Monterey (Calif.) IV–404b
Mormon Battalion IV–411a
Natchitoches IV–457a
newspaper coverage V–71a–b
opposition V–235a
pensions V–257a
privateers V–419b
prize money V–424a
profiteering V–426a
propaganda I–296b
rangers Vi–60b; VI–46b
recruitment VI–60b
San Francisco VI–209b
Santa Fe VI–214b
Santa Fe Trail VI–215b
Scott–Pillow quarrel VI–241a
sectionalism VI–254a, 342a
slavery I–138b
Stockton–Kearny quarrel VI–414a
Tennessee VII–25b
territories ceded IV–111a
Texas VII–39a
Texas Rangers VII–42a
Treaty of Cahuenga I–403a
Treaty of Guadalupe Hidalgo II–342b; III–230a; VII–111b
trenches VII–115a
Trist mission VII–121a
U.S. boundary IV–321a
veterans I–331a; IV–97a
volunteers II–367a; IV–343b; VII–208a
war loan III–64a
weapons IV–430b
West Point graduates IV–341a
Whig party VII–288b
MEXICAN WAR, NAVY IN IV–324b; V–19b
Gulf ports blockade IV–322a
Lexington IV–136b
MEXICAN WAR CLAIMS IV–325a
arbitration IV–5b
Gardiner award III–152a
mixed commission IV–381b
Mexican Water Treaty (1944) II–130a
Mexico IV–53a, 114a; VI–471a–b
Adena I–11b
agriculture I–47b–48a
architecture I–160a
Arizona I–172a
Austin Colony I–224a
Bear Flag Revolt I–280a
boll weevil I–327b
California I–405a–b
cattle IV–184b
Central American Peace Conference I–483b
Champlain's voyages I–492b
Chihuahua Trail II–23b
Coahuila and Texas II–84a
colonial land grants IV–93a
Colorado II–128a
Concord coach II–158a
corn II–225a, 226b
Coronado's expedition II–228b
courts of the plains II–247a
cowboys II–248b
Cuba IV–113a
currency system VI–289a
Desert culture II–334b
deserters II–335b
De Soto expedition II–336a
Encomienda System II–443b
fifths mining tax III–20b
filibustering III–23a
Fredonian Revolt III–101a
Galveston pirates III–149a
gold rush route III–81b, 82a
Hague peace conference III–237a
horse III–302b
hurricanes III–319a
immigration to U.S. III–333a,b, 337b, 338a, 339b–40a, 341b
independence I–282b; II–23b; IV–115a, 448b; VII–37a
Indian land tenure I–48b
La Salle's exploration IV–109b, 110a
Las Animas land grant IV–110a, 110a
Latin American Free Trade Association VI–346a
Lower California IV–199b
Mina expedition IV–348a
Montezuma's zoo VII–370b
Morelos Dam II–130a
Nevada V–39b
Oñate's explorations V–155a
Panama Congress V–203b
petroleum IV–114b; V–272a
peyote V–272b
presidios V–399b
printing V–410a–b, 411a–b
ranching I–472b–73a; VI–45a
"Remember the Alamo" VI–84a
revolution (1821) I–160a
revolution (1910) I–109b
Rockefeller Foundation VI–158a
Rocky Mountains VI–160a
Santa Fe Trail VI–215a
Santiago Inter–American Congress VI–217a
seals VI–245b
sea otter trade VI–247a
sheep VI–272b

slavery VI–312a
Spanish conquest I–24b, 96a; II–184a, 248b
Spanish exploration IV–452b
Spanish role V–461a
Spanish rule IV–135b, 320b
steel VII–89b
Texas colonization II–339b, 442b–43a
Texas Revolution I–74a, 116b, 121b; II–157a; III–22b, 198b; VII–41a–b
town mayors I–83b
United Nations Declaration VII–151b
Wells, Fargo VII–267a,b
wolves VII–311b
World War I VII–325a
World War II IV–112a
Zimmerman telegram VII–368b
See also Mexican War

MEXICO, CONFEDERATE MIGRATION TO IV–325a; I–455a, 455a–b

MEXICO, FRENCH IN IV–325b; I–492a; II–65a–b, 162a, 324a; III–68b, 97a; IV–326a, 328a, 361a–b
filibustering III–23a–b
Monroe Doctrine IV–400b–01a

MEXICO, GULF OF IV–326a; II–294a, 336b, 350a, 384b
antebellum South VI–341b
boundaries III–38a
Civil War IV–371a, 375a; VI–38a, 216a
cotton VI–305b
exploration III–326b; IV–109b–10a, 110a, 452a
Florida Straits III–41b
French colonies V–437b
French posts III–120a
Galveston storm III–149a
Gulf Stream III–232b
Houma Indians III–308a
Houston Ship Canal III–311b; VII–40b
hurricanes III–319a,b, 320a; IV–110b; VI–41b
Indian agriculture IV–327a
Indians III–365a, 392a
Isle of Orleans III–479a
Isle of Pines III–479a
lifesaving stations IV–152a
Louisiana IV–192b
Mexican War IV–322a; V–19b
Mississippi River IV–372a; VI–148b
Mobile IV–382a
mounds IV–420b
Natchez Indians IV–455b
New Orleans V–62a
oil IV–311a; V–62b, 270a, 271b; VI–356b, 357a; VII–57b
Pass Christian V–224a
Pensacola V–254a
Perdido River V–262a
piracy III–148b–49a; V–319b, 320a
railroad rate wars VI–23a
railroads III–450a; IV–94a; VI–32b, 35a, 38a
revolutionary war VI–365a
Rio Grande VI–143a
Rio Grande colony VI–143b–44a
Spanish territory IV–382b
steamship lines II–91a
Tennessee River VII–27b
Texas VII–36a, 39b
Texas Revolution VII–38a, 41a–b
tornadoes VII–75b
U.S. boundary I–10b; III–230a; IV–320b, 321a,b
War of 1812 V–63a
World War II VII–336b, 342b

MEXICO, INDIANS OF IV–327a; III–301a, 356a–b, 357a,b, 367a, 368b, 369a; V–314a,b; VII–366b
alcoholic drinks III–398a
Apache I–141b
art III–373a
conquest by Cortes III–302a–b
flower gardening III–151b
Folsom culture III–50a
Hohokam culture III–289b
horse III–303a
metallurgy III–381b
missions IV–367a
Mound Builders IV–421a
peyote V–272b
political organization III–391a
religion III–251a, 392a
rubber VI–167a
scalping VI–224a
smoking V–318a
Southeast culture III–365a
tobacco VII–65a

MEXICO, PUNITIVE EXPEDITION INTO (1916–17) **IV–327b**; I–59a, 185b, 461b, 461b, 476a; III–463a; VI–156a; VII–188a, 237a

MEXICO, RELATIONS WITH IV–328a; VI–364a
ABC Conference I–1b
Archive War I–169b
boundary IV–320b
cession of California III–190b
Chamizal Treaty VI–151a
confederate expatriates VI–274a
conservation II–187b
Corwin–Doblado Treaty II–233a
diplomatic recognition IV–110b
diplomatic relations IV–115a
El Paso II–433b
exchange students II–471a
expropriation of U.S. property IV–466a
French in Mexico IV–361a
Gadsden Purchase III–145a; V–443b
Good Neighbor policy III–199a
guerrillas III–231b
lead imports IV–123b
Lind mission II–471a–b; IV–157a
Long's Texas expedition IV–184a
McLane–Ocampo Treaty IV–218a
meat trade IV–281a
Mesilla IV–315b
Mexican Revolution III–69a
Mexican War claims IV–325a
munitions embargo IV–430a
Neutrality Acts of 1935–37 V–38b
nonrecognition policy V–107b
oil controversy IV–322b
overland freighting III–353b
Pious Fund controversy V–318a
Rio Grande VI–143a,b
Salt War VI–204a
San Antonio VI–207a,b
San Diego VI–208a
San Felipe–Correo affair VI–209a
San Francisco VI–209a–b
Santa Fe VI–214b
Slidell's mission VI–312b
Southwest VI–355a–b
support against France IV–325b
territory acquired III–111b
Texan–Santa Fe expeditions VII–36a
Texas IV–322a, 337b; VII–37a–38a,b, 39a,b
Texas Revolution III–304a; IV–274a; VI–213a
trade IV–111a
treaties VII–111b
Treat Mission VII–108b
Treaty of Guadalupe Hidalgo III–230a
Trist mission II–471a
U.S. Civil War II–65a–b, 67b, 158b–59a, 163a
Veracruz incident VI–104b; VII–171a
Villa raid VII–187b
"watchful waiting" VII–253b
water rights III–478a
Wilmot Proviso VII–303a
Wilson administration II–343a
Yucatán VII–366b
See also California; Mexican War

Mexico, Valley of IV–327a
Mexico City (Mex.)
confederate expatriates VI–274b
Inter-American Conference V–205a
Long expedition IV–184b
Mexican War II–37a, 214b; IV–324a,b, 329a, 391b
printing V–410a
Spanish Inquisition III–420a,b

MEXICO CITY, CAPTURE OF (1847) **IV–329a**; IV–252a, 324a; V–19b; VII–39a

Mey, Cornelis Jacobsen (navig.) II–322a
Meyer, Adolf (psych.) IV–3b, 306a
Meyer, Balthasar H. (educ.) VII–308b
Meyer, Deborah (athlete) V–154b
Meyer, George von Lengerke (pol., dipl.) V–18a
Meyers, Jacob (inv.) VII–210b
Meyers, Marvin (hist.) III–487a
Meyer v. *Nebraska* (1923) I–299a; II–378b
Mezes, Sidney E. (educ.) III–420a
Mézières y Clugny, Athanase de (expl.) IV–457a
Mezzotint prints V–413b
Miami (Fla.)
railroads III–39b; VI–34a
Villa Viscaya IV–96b
Miami (Fla.) III–42a, 381b
airport I–70a
air service I–67b
crime II–262a,b
hurricanes III–319b, 320a
Miami (galley boat) III–147b
Miami (warship) I–83a

MIAMI, FORT (Ind.) **IV–329a**, 329a; III–369b; IV–109b; V–176a

Miami, Fort (Mich.) III–120a

MIAMI, FORT (Ohio) **IV–329a**
Wayne's Indian campaign VII–263a

Miami, University of V–135a
Miami and Erie Canal V–141b, 145b
See also Ohio State Canals
Miami Beach (Fla.) VI–101a
Miami Canal III–449a
Miami–Dade County (Fla.) IV–172b
Miami Herald (news.) V–73b
Miami Herald Publishing Company v. *Tornillo* (1974) V–79a
Miami Indians I–501b; III–24b, 227b, 366b, 383a
Battle of Mississinewa IV–367b
Fort Washington expeditions VII–247a
Iowa III–467b
Jesuit missions III–500a
Logstown Treaty IV–181b
Maumee Convention IV–276b
Ohio V–140a
Pickawillanee V–308a
Pontiac's War V–357a
removal III–394b

MIAMI INDIANS (cont.)
revolutionary war III–400b; IV–59b
Saint Clair's expedition VI–188b
Spring Wells Treaty VI–377b
Treaty of Fort Wayne VII–262b
Vincennes cession VII–189b
Miami–Maumee portage IV–188a
MIAMI PURCHASE (1788) **IV–329b**; II–37a; VII–247a
Miami River IV–39b
Céloron's voyage V–146a
exploration III–182a
Fort Hamilton III–244a
Indian trail IV–330a
Northwest Territory V–123a
Pickawillanee V–140a
portage V–367b
settlement IV–329b
Shawnee VI–270b
Miamisburg Mound (Ohio) IV–420b
MIAMI TRAIL IV–330a
Miami University (Ohio) VII–156a
Miami Valley V–140a; VII–247a
Miangas Case (1928) III–456b
Miantonomo (Indian) V–261b
Miantonomoh (ship) V–26b
Mica Creek II–132a
Micanopy (Indian) VI–259b
Mice III–51b
MICHABOUS, GOD OF MICHILIMACKINAC IV–330a
Michael (archbp.) II–387a
Michaelius, Jonas (cler.) V–40b
Michaux, André (bot.) I–497a, 498a; III–122b; V–326a
garden I–348a
Michaux, François André (bot.) V–326b; VII–16a
Michelangelo (art.) I–451a
Michelson, Albert A. (phys.) II–153a; V–100a, 294b
MICHIGAN IV–330b; VI–394 (table)
annexation to Indiana V–123a
banking I–255b, 259b, 260a
birth and death registration IV–149a
Black Legion I–314a
blizzards I–320a
bond issue IV–412b
bootlegging I–339b
business receipts tax VI–200b
canals I–442b; III–449a
capital punishment I–450a
cereal industry I–487a
Chicago Treaty II–21a
Chippewa land cession VI–197a
Civil War II–271b, 294b
coal mines II–85a, 86b
colonial land grants IV–93a
conciliation process II–157b
copper I–410b; II–223a–b; V–103a
Detroit II–336b–38b
education II–398b
ferries III–11b
forest fires II–348a; VI–61b
Fort Saginaw VI–186a
Fort Saint Joseph VI–191b
French posts III–120a
furniture III–139b
homeopathy III–293b
Indian factory system II–480a
Indian land cessions I–371b; IV–107b; VI–186b
Indian wars III–399b
interurban electric lines III–461b
Iowa jurisdiction III–467b
iron II–75a; III–12a, 216b, 473b
Isle Royale National Park V–218 (table)
Jefferson's proposed states III–497a
Jesuit missions III–499b
Kalamazoo Case II–398b
Lake Huron III–319a
Lake Michigan IV–332b
land speculation IV–99b
limnology study II–391a
lumber industry IV–204a
Mackinac Bridge IV–218a
Menominee Iron Range IV–303b
military tracts IV–344b
Mormons VI–87a
New England settlers V–50a
Nicolet's explorations V–95a
Northwest Territory III–329b
Ohio boundary dispute I–351a; III–128a; V–144b
plank roads V–323a
Pokagon village V–335b
Polish exiles V–342a
Populist party V–365b
Potawatomi II–21a
public employee labor relations acts IV–75b
public land sales V–452b
public land speculation I–107b
public land states V–453a
public schools IV–24b
Railroad Conspiracy VI–20a
railroads III–449b; VI–25a, 34a; VII–83b
recall VI–51a
referendum VI–66b
Reformed churches VI–69a
repudiation of state debts VI–96a
retail sales VII–84b
Saginaw Treaty III–383b
salt VI–202b
Sault Sainte Marie VI–219a,b
senate campaign of 1920 V–41b
settlement IV–332b, 338b; VII–284a
snowstorms II–351b
Socialist party VI–327a
Stannard Rock Lighthouse VI–146b
state fairs VI–392b
statehood I–78b, 351a
swamplands VI–453b
Tecumseh's crusade VII–233b
timberlands IV–99b; VII–60a
Toledo War V–141b; VII–68b
tornadoes II–351b; VII–75b, 76a
Treaty of Chicago III–383b
Treaty of Greenville III–383a
United States v. *Clark* VII–154a
Upper Peninsula VII–157a
veterinary medicine VII–176b, 177a
War of 1812 III–217a; IV–224b; VI–42a; VII–45b
western lands VII–273a
Western Reserve III–414a
West Virginia migration VII–282a
westward movement VII–283b
wool VII–320b
Michigan (battleship) II–370a; VII–241a, 242a
Michigan (gunboat) I–280a; III–475a; IV–5a
MICHIGAN, LAKE IV–332a; II–297a; III–215b–16b, 225b
boundary disputes I–351a; V–144b
British occupation I–341a
Chicago I–24b; II–17a
Chicago drainage canal II–19a
Chicago portage II–20a
Chicago treaties II–21a
disasters II–346b, 349a, 388b
domestic trade VII–83b
exploration III–119a, 329a; IV–7a, 109b; V–95a; VII–157a
ferries III–11b
Fox Indians III–88b
Fox-Wisconsin Waterway III–90a
fur trade III–144b, 331b–32a
Illinois III–329b
Illinois and Michigan Canal III–331a
iron III–470b, 473b; IV–303b
Lake Erie–Lake Michigan Canal V–1b–2a
Lake Huron link IV–217b
Lakes-to-Gulf waterway IV–88a
Mackinac Island IV–330a
plant ecology II–391b
portages V–367b
Radisson's voyages VI–18b
railroads VI–33a, 35b
revolutionary war VI–363b
settlements VII–307b
Strangite Kingdom VI–416b
Upper Peninsula VII–157a
Waterways Treaty VII–261a
Michigan, My Michigan (song) VI–394 (table)
Michigan, University of I–241a; IV–93b
biological research station II–391a–b
Clements' Library II–109b; III–284b
Greenland expeditions V–337b
herbarium V–327a
library IV–145b
medical school IV–298a
pharmacy V–275a
polio vaccine V–341a
political science V–348b–49a
Survey Research Center V–454a
technical instruction II–447a
Michigan Central Railroad III–449b; VI–20a, 25b, 35b; VII–128b
Michigan City (Ind.) IV–332b; VI–192a
Michigan Fish Commission II–391a
Michigan Historical Collections III–284b
Michigania III–497a
Michigan Southern Railroad III–449b; VI–25b
Michigan State University II–227b; VII–156b, 177a
MICHIGAN TERRITORIAL ROAD IV–332b
Michigan Territory II–284b; IV–331a
Butte des Morts Council I–398a
Indian affairs III–373a
Indian land cession III–316a
Toledo War V–141b
Wisconsin VII–307a
Michigan v. *Wisconsin* (1926) I–351b
Michilimackinac
border forts I–340b, 341a
revolutionary war I–367a
See also Mackinac, Straits of, and Mackinac Island
Michilimackinac, Fort (Mich.) III–89b, 120a, 142b
Michilimackinac Company I–105a; VI–357b
Micmac (Indians) I–2b; II–31a; III–366b, 367a, 398a
See also Abnaki
Microbiology I–242a; IV–286a, 287a

Microelectronic technology. *See* Miniaturization
Microfilm I–168b, 482b
Microfossils V–197a–b
Micronesia IV–364b; V–242b; VII–125a
See also Trust Territory of the Pacific
Micronesia, Congress of III–426a; VII–34a, 125a
Microscope IV–298a
achromatic I–241a
bacteriology I–240b, 241a,b
botany I–349a
electron I–242a
petrography V–267b–68a
Microscopical Petrography V–268a
Microscopy IV–291a
Microwave amplification by stimulated emission of radiation. *See* Masers and Lasers
Microwave oven IV–333a
MICROWAVE TECHNOLOGY IV–332b; II–143a; IV–262b; V–304b; VII–20b, 163b
MIDCONTINENT OIL REGION IV–333b; VI–355b, 356b
Middle America IV–327a–b, 370b, 385b
Middle Cimarron Spring II–14b
MIDDLE CLASS IV–334b
colonial society II–125a
democracy II–326a
folk art III–47a–b
protest movement IV–75a
share-the-wealth movements VI–269a
suburban growth VI–428a
woman's rights movement VII–314a
Middle East
aerial hijacking III–276b, 277a
cold war III–69b
Eisenhower Doctrine II–407b
Soviet aid III–69b
Strategic Arms Limitation Talks VI–417a
U.S. aid III–62a
U.S. naval forces V–25a
See also Arab–American Relations; Israeli–American Relations
Middle East War (1973) II–213a
MIDDLE-OF-THE-ROAD POPULISTS IV–335a
MIDDLE PASSAGE IV–335a; VI–310b; VII–119b
Middle Plantation (Va.) VII–301a
Middle school II–400b, 402b
MIDDLESEX CANAL IV–335b; I–442a; III–447b–48a; IV–174b; V–179a
Middlesex County (N.J.) III–183a
Middle Temple (London) II–494b
Middle Tennessee. *See* Tennessee
Middleton, Arthur (rev. leader) II–308b
Middleton, "Doc" (outlaw) V–139a
Middleton, Drew (jour.) V–74a
Middleton, Henry (legis.) I–497a, 498a
Middleton Barony (S.C.) VII–16a
Middleton Place (Charleston, S.C.) I–497a, 498a; IV–96b
Middletown (Conn.) III–441a
Middletown (N.J.) IV–397b
Middletown (Pa.) VII–146a
Middletown (Va.) IV–472a
Middle West Utilities Company II–416b
Middlings purifier III–43b, 45a
Mide. *See* Midewiwin
MIDEWIWIN IV–335b; II–31b; III–366b, 385a, 393a
Midgley, Thomas, Jr. (chem.) II–9a, 421a; VI–70a
MIDNIGHT JUDGES IV–335b; VI–375a
MIDNIGHT ORDER (1872) **IV–336a**
Midshipman (rank) II–452a
Midvale Steel Company VI–234a
Midway
county fairs II–244b
Midway (carrier) I–56a, 57a
MIDWAY, BATTLE OF (1942) **IV–336a**; I–55b–56a, 84b; II–225a; IV–337a; V–20b, 26b; VI–10a; VII–337a, 343a
Midway District (Ga.) III–169b
Midway Gardens (Chicago) I–165a
MIDWAY ISLANDS IV–337a; III–425a
World War II IV–253a, 336a; VII–342a
MIDWAY PLAISANCE (Chicago) **IV–337a**; VII–324a
Midwifery IV–283a; VII–316a
MIDWINTER INTERNATIONAL EXPOSITION (1894) **IV–337b**
Midwout. *See* Flatbush (N.Y.)
Mier (Mex.) IV–337b
Miera y Pacheco, Don Bernardo (expl.) II–461a; VII–161a
MIER EXPEDITION (1842) **IV–337b**
Miescher, Johann Friedrich (Fritz) (physiol.) II–357b
Mies Van Der Rohe, Ludwig (arch.) I–165a–b; II–18a; III–136b; VI–299a
MIFFLIN, FORT (Pa.) **IV–337b**
Mifflin, Thomas (mer., pol.) II–203b; IV–338a; V–187a; VI–373a
MIG–15 (fighter plane) I–61a; IV–57a
MIG–17 (fighter plane) I–62b
Mighty Mouse (rocket) I–57b
Migis IV–335b
Mignano (It.) III–235b
Migrant population
Cleveland II–75a
crime II–258b
Migrant workers II–495b; VI–365a, 454a
child labor II–25a
government inspection III–422a
Mexico IV–328b–29a
Okies V–149a
Migration
Cherokee II–52b
Cheyenne II–16b
city to suburb II–41a–b
coureurs de bois II–246a
rural to urban II–41a–b
See also Westward Movement
Migration, Afro-American. *See* Afro-American Migration
Migration, Great. *See* Great Migration
MIGRATION, GROUP IV–338a
Great Migration III–219b
Great Path III–223b
New England V–50a
river towns of Connecticut VI–151a–b
Union Colony VII–146a
Migratory Bird Treaty (1916) IV–381a
Migratory Bird Treaty Act (1918) II–188a
Mikasuki (Indians) VI–260a,b
Miko (chief) I–288a
Mikuma (cruiser) IV–337a
Milam, Ben (col.) VII–37a
Milam Building (San Antonio) III–269b
Milan (It.) II–287a
Milan (N.Y.) IV–169a
Milan Decree (1807) I–321a; II–436b; III–118b, 121b; IV–449b; VI–105a
See also Napoleon's Decrees
Milbank Foundation IV–286b
Milbank Memorial Fund III–83a
Milbourne, Jacob (off.) V–84b
MILEAGE IV–339a
Miles, Nelson A. (off.)
Apache Wars VII–256a
Battle of Little Bighorn IV–168b
Germaine girl captives III–172a
Indian scouts VI–242a, 242a
Indian Territory expedition VII–217a
Messiah War IV–316a
Nez Perce War I–281a; V–89b
Red River Indian War VI–64a
Sioux wars VI–297a
Spanish–American War VI–361b, 362a
Miles, Samuel (off.) IV–186a
Miles City (Mont.) II–251b
cattle IV–280b
Milford (Conn.) III–315a; V–55b; VI–70b, 134b
Milford (Mass.) III–300a
Milieu therapy IV–307a
Militant (news.) II–446a
MILITARY, AFRO-AMERICANS IN THE IV–339b; I–29b
"buffalo soldiers" VI–301a
Civil War IV–383b–84a; VI–308a
Confederate army II–63b, 161a–b, 162a
desegregation VI–256b
revolutionary war VI–118a, 125b, 130a, 131a
Spanish–American War VI–362a
Union Army II–63b, 161a
MILITARY ACADEMY, UNITED STATES IV–340b; I–184a, 190b, 191a; II–313a, 313a,b, 395b–96a, 399a; III–267a; VI–145b; VII–280a
Civil War I–184b–85a
engineering II–447a, 449b; VI–232a
frontier officers I–193a
Mexican War I–184b
Thayer, Sylvanus I–184a
World War I I–186a
Military aid
cold war II–475b
containment policy II–315b
dollar diplomacy II–359b–60a
Marshall Plan II–301b
South America II–359b
U.S. Navy assistance V–23a
See also Foreign Aid
MILITARY AID TO THE CIVIL POWERS IV–341b
Hawaii III–264a
Lighthouse Board IV–152b
martial law IV–258a
Military Airlift Command I–65a
Military Air Transport Service I–61b
Military Assistance Advisory Group, Vietnam VII–182b–83a
Military Assistance Command, Vietnam VII–183a,b
Military bonuses. *See* Bonuses, Military
Military cemeteries II–499b
MILITARY COMPANIES, VOLUNTARY IV–342a; II–432b;

MILITARY COMPANIES, VOLUNTARY (cont.) IV–346a
Military Company of Adventurers. *See* Georgiana
Military courts II–246b
Military decorations. *See* Decorations, Military
Military District, U.S. (Ohio) I–331a
Military districts. *See* Military Tracts
Military fines
Civil War II–185a
Military flags III–35a
Military highways. *See* Roads, Military
Military–industrial complex IV–434a
atomic research VI–230b
lobbying IV–171a
space program IV–460a
Military intelligence. *See* Intelligence, Military and Strategic
Military justice IV–342b
Military Justice, Uniform Code of. *See* Uniform Code of Military Justice
MILITARY LAW IV–342b
civilians under IV–259a
civil rights VII–154a
General Order No. 100 II–70a
habeas corpus III–237a
mutiny IV–445a
Uniform Code of Military Justice VII–142b
Military Lodge (Boston) III–109a
Military medicine. *See* Medicine, Military
Military Merit, Badge of II–312b
MILITARY ORDER OF THE LOYAL LEGION OF THE U.S.A. IV–343a
Military ordnance. *See* Ordnance
Military pensions. *See* Pensions, Military and Naval
MILITARY POLICY IV–343a
indemnities III–352a
Vietnam War V–259a–b
Military prisons
Elmira (N.Y.) II–433b
Point Lookout (Md.) II–433b
Military rank
ensign II–452a
lieutenant II–452a
Military schools I–5b
scientific education VI–232a
Military service
desertion II–334b
draft II–366a
universal II–313a; V–390b
U.S. concept II–185b
volunteers II–366b–67a
Military slang. *See* Slang, Military
Military substitutes II–366b, 367a
Military Telegraph, U.S. VI–286a
Military Tract, U.S. VI–70b
MILITARY TRACTS IV–344b
Illinois IV–99b
land warrants IV–97a
New York VI–450b
Ohio IV–91a; VII–273a
War of 1812 land bounties IV–91a
Military Unification Act (1949) III–299b
Military Unpreparedness of the United States V–390b
Military warrants. *See* Bounties, Military; Land Bounties
MILITIA IV–345a; II–186a, 313a–b, 366b, 450b–51a
army organization I–183a
bounties I–352b–53a
British army VI–126b
Civil War I–433b; II–61b–62a
Coeur d'Alene riots IV–66a
colonial munitions IV–430a
Confederate army I–181a
congressional regulation II–200a
conscientious objectors II–185a
conscription II–186a
constitutional provisions IV–342b
demobilization II–323b
Homestead strike IV–66a
military policy IV–343a–b
minutemen IV–360b
mobilization IV–383b
Mormon War IV–412a
Muster Day IV–445a
National Guard I–185a; IV–463b
naval militia V–28b
New England VII–96b–97a
Osgoodites V–174b
presidential call IV–259b–60a
railroad strike of 1877 IV–63b; VI–38b
Regulators of North Carolina VI–72a
revolutionary war VI–117b–18a, 125b, 126a, 126b; VII–251a–b
slave insurrections VI–303b
"Squirrel Hunters" VI–378b
Union army I–182a
volunteers VII–208a
War of 1812 I–184a
Whiskey Rebellion VII–290a
Militia Act (1792) I–475b; II–313a, 314a, 366b; IV–345b, 346a
Militia Draft Act (1862) I–353a
Milk II–280a, 281a–b, 282a,b; III–52b, 53b
Delaware II–320b
enrichment V–128a–b
freeze drying III–55b
price–fixing V–402a
public health IV–275b
school programs V–129a
Milk River IV–300a
Milky Way I–211b; III–242a; VI–17a
Mill, Henry (eng.) I–395b; VII–135b
Mill, John Stuart (philos., econ.) V–441b; 89a,b–
Millbury (Mass.) IV–207a
Mill cities II–45b
Mill Creek III–320b; IV–347b
Milledgeville (Ga.) III–171a; VI–278a; VII–55a, 299b
Mille Lacs (Minn.) II–380a; IV–97b, 355a
exploration VII–73b
MILLE LACS, BATTLE OF (ca. 1745) **IV–346b**; VI–294b
Millen (Ga.) II–159b; VI–278b
Millenarianism V–279b
Millenarian sects III–112b
Millennial Dawnists. *See* Jehovah's Witnesses
Millennialism
Shakers VI–268a
Miller, Adam (col.) VI–275b
Miller, Alfred Jacob (paint.) V–189b
Miller, Arnold R. (labor leader) IV–76a; VII–151a
Miller, Arthur (playwright, au.) IV–165b; VII–50b
Miller, Bonnamy and Company I–355b; VI–196b
Miller, Douglas (hist.) III–487a
Miller, Elizabeth Smith I–323b
Miller, Emily C. H. (ed.) IV–223a
Miller, George M. (art.) VII–262a
Miller, James (off.) IV–205a
Miller, Jeff (student) IV–39a
Miller, Joaquin (au.) IV–163a
Miller, Lewis (inv.) II–1a
Miller, Perry (hist.) III–283a
Miller, Phineas (mfr.) II–240b
Miller, Samuel (pub.) V–70b
Miller, Samuel F. (jur.) VI–303a, 445b
Miller, Thomas (col. prop.) II–271b
Miller, Webb (jour.) V–74a
Miller, William (hist.) VI–157a
Miller, William (rel. leader) I–15a; VI–77b
Miller, William E. (pol.) I–431a
Miller, Willoughby Dayton (dent.) II–331b
Miller, Zach T. (showman) VII–298b
"Miller Boy" (song) V–331a
Miller Brothers (showmen) VII–298b
Miller Company II–107a
Miller farm (Pa.) V–318b–19a
Millerites I–15b
Millers of Oklahoma VI–161b
Miller's Run Gap V–224b
Miller–Tydings Act (1937) I–140a, 489b; II–483a,b; V–403b; VI–102b; VII–123b
Millet, Francis D. (art.) V–191a
Millet, Frédéric (art.) II–102a
MILLIGAN, EX PARTE (1866) **IV–346b**; I–196a; II–62a; IV–209a, 258b; VII–35a
Milligan, L. P. II–222b
Millikan, Robert A. (phys.) II–12a, 423b; V–100a, 295a,b; VI–230b
Milliken's Bend (La.) IV–339b
Milling, flour. *See* Flour Milling
Milling machine III–441a,b, 442a; IV–272a
Milling stones III–484b
Millinocket (Maine) IV–227a
Millionaires III–79a–80b
"MILLIONS FOR DEFENSE, BUT NOT ONE CENT FOR TRIBUTE" IV–347a
Mill River IV–347b
Mills III–413b; IV–243a
cotton II–238a
elevators II–428b
steam engines VI–409a
waterpower VII–256b–57a
Mills, Clark (sculp.) VI–243a
Mills, Robert (arch., eng.) I–163a; VII–250b, 292a
Mills, Roger Q. (pol.) VI–467a
Mills, Wilbur D. (pol.) VI–472b
MILL SPRINGS, ENCOUNTER AT (1862) **IV–347a**; II–271b, 363a
MILL STREAMS IV–347b; VII–256b
Millwood (Ohio) VII–252a
Millwrighting III–43a
Milroy, Robert H. (off.) III–487b
Milton (Fla.) III–39b
Milton (Mass.) VI–430b
Milton, John (poet) I–298b; III–316b; IV–161a
Milton, John (pol.) I–417a
Milwaukee (Wis.) I–381a; IV–332b; VII–307b, 308a
brewing industry I–362a
cement rocks I–477b
chamber of commerce I–491a
city planning II–46b
flour III–45a
Forest Service III–76b
fugitive slaves I–2a
German immigrants III–81a, 336b; V–75b
grain elevators II–430a
Grand Trunk Railroad VI–23a
mayorship VII–53a
National Safety Congress

I–7a
railroads V–388a; VI–34a
soldiers' home VI–336b
Milwaukee Harvester Company III–454b
Milwaukee Journal (news.) V–73b
Milwaukee Leader (news.) V–74a
Milwaukee Railroad IV–177a
Mimbreño Apache (Indians) I–142a; IV–236b
Mimbres River IV–321a
Mimeograph I–396a, 397a
MIMS, FORT, MASSACRE AT (1813) **IV–347b**; II–256b; IV–456a
Mims, Samuel IV–347b
Mina, Francisco Xavier (adventurer). *See* Mina Expedition
Minabozho IV–335b
MINA EXPEDITION (1816–17) **IV–348a**; IV–320b
Mindanao (Phil.) V–281b, 282a, 285a
World War II VII–337a
Mind and the World-Order V–387a
Mind-healing movement V–81a
Mind That Found Itself IV–304a, 306a
Mine and Mine Laborers, National Federation of II–86b–87a
Mine Laboratory. *See* Naval Ordnance Laboratory
Mine La Motte (Mo.) IV–122a
Mineral Deposits III–163a
Mineral Facts and Problems IV–350b
Mineral leases V–102b
Mineral Leasing Act (1920) II–188a; III–164a; IV–349b; V–445b
Mineral Location Law (1872) IV–349b
Mineralogical Society of America IV–349a, 349a
MINERALOGY IV–348a
American Mineralogical Journal VI–235b
salt IV–25a
MINERAL PATENT LAW IV–349a; III–21a; IV–354a
Mineral rights IV–90a, 95b, 104b; V–451a
Minerals
Department of the Interior III–444a,b
forests III–75b
Land Office reports IV–95a
state geological surveys III–164b
U.S. Geological Survey III–163a
U.S. resources VI–48a–b
MINERAL SPRINGS IV–349b; VI–333a, 377b
resorts and spas VI–100a
Saratoga Springs VI–217b
Minerals Yearbook IV–350b
Miners' and Laborers' Benevolent Association II–86b
"Miner's anemia." *See* Hookworm
MINE RUN CAMPAIGN (1863) **IV–350a**; IV–36a
Minerva (period.) IV–279b
Mines (explosives) V–27b, 28a, 163b, 164a; VII–241a
Civil War VI–424b–25a
Neutrality Act (1935) IV–430a
retaliation in international law VI–104b
revolutionary war IV–35b
World War I V–119b
World War II VII–343a
MINES, U.S. BUREAU OF IV–350a; II–135a; III–444b
foreign service VI–389a
petroleum industry V–270b
MINESWEEPING IV–351a; V–25b
underwater demolition teams VII–139a
Vietnam War V–22a
World War II VII–338b
Mine warfare ship V–25b
Mingo (Indians) III–400b; IV–351b; VII–239a
Baker's Cabin massacre I–244a
Battle of Bushy Run I–389a
French and Indian War III–115a
Treaty at Pittsburgh V–322a
MINGO BOTTOM (Ohio) **IV–351b**
Mingus, Charles (mus.) IV–440b
Minh, Duong van (off.) VII–185a
MINIATURES IV–351b; II–101a; VII–262a
MINIATURIZATION IV–352a; II–156b
Miniconjou (Indians) II–283a; III–17b
Minidoka (Idaho) III–328b, 491a
Minidress II–372b
Minié, Claude Étienne (off.) IV–352b
MINIÉ BALL IV–352b; VI–139b
Minigun I–49b
MINIMUM-WAGE LEGISLATION IV–352b; II–481a; III–3a; IV–80a–b; VII–213b, 214a, 214a
Fair Labor Standards Act V–48a–b
farm workers I–43b
judicial review IV–14a
laissez-faire doctrine IV–85b
National Industrial Recovery Act V–44b
National Recovery Administration IV–469a,b
New York State V–47b
party machines IV–214b
Progressive party V–428b
Supreme Court ruling IV–70a
Truman administration II–481a
Washington State V–48a
West Coast Hotel Company v. Parrish VII–269a
Mining
Alaska I–77a, 79b–80a
Bullfrog Mining District VI–135a
chemistry II–11b
child labor II–23b, 24b
Chinese labor II–29b
chromium III–13b
cobalt III–14a
Colorado II–128b, 264a–b, 332a
columbium III–14b
contract labor II–214b
convict labor II–217a
copper II–223a
crown lands II–266b
Death Valley II–297b–98a
disasters II–350a–b
Dubuque (Iowa) II–376a
El Paso II–433b
federal government IV–73b
federal lands II–188a
folklore III–49a
foreign investments II–301a; III–63a, 65a
forests III–75b, 76a
government inspection III–422a
great fortunes III–80a
holding companies III–290b
iron III–12a–13a, 473b
Louisiana II–267b
manganese III–13a–b
Michigan IV–332a
molybdenum III–14b–15a
Montana IV–403a,b
national parks V–220a
New Mexico V–60a
New York State V–87b
nickel III–13b–14a
nonferrous metals V–102a
panic of 1907 V–208a
prospectors V–437a
steam engine VI–408b
subsidies VI–426a
tantalum III–14b
taxation III–20b
tungsten III–15b
tunnels VII–127b
Utah VII–162a
vanadium III–15a–b
Washington State VII–247b
Western Federation of Miners VII–272b
work force V–132b
work hazards IV–293b, 294b
See also Ferrous Metals; Nonferrous Metals; and separate articles on individual metals
Mining Act of 1872 V–451b
MINING CAMP, LAW OF THE IV–354a; III–497b
Mining Enforcement and Safety Administration III–444b; IV–350b
Mining engineers II–448b–49a; III–166b
Mining Law (1866) IV–349b
Mining Magazine VI–236a
Mining schools IV–93b
MINING TOWNS IV–354a; II–259b, 259b; IV–52a
MININSINK INDIAN RAID (1779) **IV–354b**
MINISINK PATENT IV–354b
Ministers, colonial salaries V–221b
Ministers plenipotentiary I–93a
Ministers resident I–93a
Ministries Act of 1693 VI–75b
Ministry
education II–394b–95b
Mink III–133a, 142a, 150a, 402b; VI–44b
Minneapolis (Minn.) III–272a; IV–356a; VII–133b–34a
Ames Ring VI–142b
bootlegging I–339b
cereal industry I–488a
chamber of commerce I–491a
conciliation II–157b
Falls of Saint Anthony VI–187a
flour III–43b, 45a; V–117a
labor strike IV–71b
labor vote II–491a
teachers strike IV–75b
truckers' strike II–491b
waterpower IV–347b
wheat VII–308a
See also Twin Cities
Minneapolis Chamber of Commerce V–106b
Minneapolis Flour Manufacturing Company III–44a
Minneapolis-Saint Louis Railroad III–44a
Minneapolis, Saint Paul and Sault Sainte Marie Railroad. *See* Soo Line Railroad
MINNESOTA IV–355a; VI–394 (table)
blizzards I–320a,b
Border Slave State Convention I–341b
censorship V–78b
cereal grains I–486b
Chippewa II–31a; III–360b, 394b
Civil War regiments II–271b
"cooperative commonwealth" II–491b
dairy cooperatives II–281a
Dakota Indians II–282b–83b
Democratic party II–490b, 492a–b
exploration II–380a; III–313a
Falls of Saint Anthony VI–187a
Farmer-Labor party II–490b; V–107a; VII–53a
Farmers' Alliance II–493a
farmers' cooperatives

MINNESOTA (cont.)
II–221b
farm mortgage moratorium II–491b
flour milling III–44a
forest fires III–74b
Fort Beauharnois I–281b
Fort Ridgely VI–139a
Fort Ripley VI–144b
Fort Saint Charles VI–188a
Fort Snelling II–490a; VI–322b
fur trade V–121a
Grand Portage III–209a
Granger movement III–209b, 210a
grasshopper attacks III–212b
Hazelwood Republic III–267a
historical society III–278b
Hudson's Bay Company III–313b
Hutterite communes II–142a
income tax II–491b
Indian land cessions III–379b; IV–107b, 107b
Indian population III–396a,b
Indian wars II–283b, 284b
Iowa Territory III–468a
iron ore II–75a; III–216b, 473b; IV–303b
Jesuit missions III–499b
joint-stock land banks IV–6b
Lake of the Woods IV 87b; VII 269b
Lake Superior VI–443a
land grants for education IV–94a
Leech Lake uprising IV–131b
legislature IV–133b
lumber industry IV–204a
Mesabi Iron Range IV–315a
Mille Lac Indian lands IV–97b
minimum-wage law IV–353a
Missouri River IV–380a
mounds IV–420b
national parks and monuments V–217b, 219 (table)
Near v. *Minnesota* V–30b
New Deal II–491b
New Ulm V–81a
nickel III–14a
Nonpartisan League II–490b, 491a; V–106b
Northwest boundary V–120a–b
Northwest Territory III–329b
oats V–130a
old-age pensions II–491b
Populists II–492a; V–365b
prairie V–387a
public employees IV–75b
railroads II–19b
Red River cart traffic VI–63b
Red River of the North VI–64a
Republican party II–490b–92b
Rice, Henry M. VI–135a
school lands VI–228a–b
Sioux–Chippewa War IV–346b; VI–294b
Sioux land cession VII–106a
Sioux treaties VI–295a–b, 296a
Sioux uprising VI–295a, 296a; VII–319b
Sioux Wars VII–239b
statehood I–78b
steamboating VII–196b
Stillwater Convention VI–413a
swamplands VI–453b
territorial government VII–32a
three-party system VII–135a
timberlands IV–97b; VII–60a
tobacco VII–67a
Treaty of Prairie du Chien III–383b
Treaty of Traverse des Sioux III–383b
Twin Cities VII–133b
unemployment relief II–491b
union recognition II–491b
U.S. boundary II–319a
veterinary medicine VII–176b
wheat III–43b, 45a; VII–286a
wild rice VII–298a
Winnebago III–377a; VII–305b
Minnesota (warship) IV–396b, 397a
Minnesota, University of I–112a; IV–121a, 279a; V–127a, 349a
Minnesota Historical Society III–285b
Minnesota Moratorium Act (1933) IV–414b
MINNESOTA MORATORIUM CASE (1934) **IV–358b**; II–214a; IV–414b
Minnesota Railroad and Warehouse Commission II–19b
Minnesota Rate Cases (1913) II–136a
Minnesota River II–16b, 31a
exploration IV–355a,b
Fort Snelling IV–355b–56a; VI–295b, 322b; VII–133b
Indian trade IV–277b
New Ulm V–81a–b
Red River cart traffic VI–63b
Santee Sioux VI–295a, 296b
Sioux land cession IV–355b
Sioux reservations VI–139a
Sioux uprising VI–150b, 297a
Traverse des Sioux Treaty VII–106a
Minnesota State Federation of Labor II–491a
Minnesota State School of Agriculture I–272a
Minnesota Territory II–284b
Minnesota Theatre Company VII–50b
Minor, Benjamin Blake (ed.) VI–353a
Minor, Robert (cartoon.) V–73a
Minor, Stephen VI–351a
Minor, Virginia L. IV–359a
Minorities
affirmative action programs IV–81a
aid to business of I–8b
education I–456a
employment II–473a–b
labor legislation IV–80b
Minority Business Enterprise, Office of II–135b
Minority leaders II–172b
"Minority presidents" II–412a
MINORITY RIGHTS IV–358a; IV–228a
MINOR* v. *HAPPERSETT (1875) **IV–359a**
Minot (N.Dak.) IV–118a; V–117b
Minot, George R. (physic.) V–100a
Minot, Stephen (landowner) V–242a
Minots Ledge Lighthouse VI–146a
Minquez, Juan (cler.) VII–188a
Minshall, Robert (av.) I–51b
MINSTREL SHOWS IV–359b; II–290a, 357a; IV–438a; VII–48a
MINT, FEDERAL IV–359b; III–245b; IV–394a; VII–108a
assaying I–203b–04a
cents I–483a
Coinage Act of 1873 II–264a
Confederacy II–164a
free silver III–110a
Hamilton's fiscal policies III–244b
monetary standard IV–392b
Philadelphia II–95a
privately minted coins IV–360b
Mint Act (1792) IV–394a
Minton, Sherman (jur.) VI–446b
Mints
Boston I–344a
MINTS, PRIVATE IV–360a
Minturno (It.) III–235b
Minuet, Peter (col. off.) III–315a
Minuit, Peter (col. offi.) V–60b, 61a
Fort Christina II–35a
Manhattan purchase IV–237a
New Sweden Company V–81a
Minuteman (missile) I–62a, 67b; IV–364a; VI–159b
Minute Man of Concord (sculp.) VI–243b, 283a
MINUTEMEN IV–360b; II–366b; V–69b; VI–124b–25a
Indians III–400a
Lexington and Concord IV–137a
Massachusetts IV–266a
Miquelon Island II–92b; V–214b
Miracle (film) I–479b
Miracle healing III–49b
MIRAMAR, CONVENTION OF (1864) **IV–361a**; IV–325b
Miranda, Francisco (rev.) II–470b; IV–135b, 361b
Miranda, Guadalupe IV–278a
MIRANDA'S INTRIGUES IV–361b
MIRANDA* v. *ARIZONA (1966) **IV–361b**; V–339b
Miró, Esteban (col. gov.) I–6b, 169b–70a; IV–362a; V–59a; VI–366b
MIRO, FORT (La.) **IV–362a**; II–381a
Miró, Joan (art.) II–104b, 105a; V–193a
Mirrors III–135b, 138a
fur trade III–140a
glass III–186a
Hohokam culture III–289b
MIRV. *See* Multiple, independently targeted reentry vehicle
MISCEGENATION IV–362b; III–437b, 503a; V–116a; VI–256a, 265b, 304b–05a
MISHIANZA (1778) **IV–363a**
Mishongoi (Ariz.) III–300b
MISIONES AWARD (1895) **IV–363a**
See also Tordesillas, Treaty of
Misiones Territory (S.Amer.) IV–363a
Missile Defense Center (Colo.) I–59a
MISSILES, MILITARY IV–363a; I–67b; III–69b, 78b; IV–432a, 458b–59a,b; V–11a,b, 27a, 163b, 164a; VI–159a–b
air defense I–58b, 62a
air-to-air I–57b
antiballistic I–58b
antitank I–178b
aviation industry I–237b
ballistic I–237b
Corps of Engineers II–450a
Cuban missile crisis II–270a–71a, 316a
Great Britain I–124b, 292b
guided I–235a
gunboats III–235a
helicopters III–270b
hydrogen bomb III–324b
intercontinental ballistic

I–56b, 62a, 63b, 67b, 179b, 328b; II–316a
intermediate range ballistic I–124b
Jet Propulsion Laboratory III–502a–b
letter designations V–25b
long-range II–316a
miniaturization IV–352a
Naval Research Laboratory V–14b
sites II–316a
slang VI–302b
space launch systems I–63b–64a
Strategic Arms Limitation Talks VI–417a
submarines II–316a; VI–423a–b
transistors VI–259a
Vietnam War I–62b
warships VII–241b, 243b
See also Rockets
Missile tracking stations
Bahama Islands I–243b
Mission 66 (1956–1966) II–188a; V–220a
Mission Agency at Riverside IV–366a
Missionaries
China II–488a
Franciscans III–94a
Mormon IV–117a
Oregon IV–108a
training II–292b
MISSIONARY ACTIVITY IN THE PACIFIC IV–364b
Hawaii III–263a
Missionary and Bible Society of the Methodist Episcopal Church IV–365b
MISSIONARY RIDGE, BATTLE OF (1863) **IV–364b**; I–502b; II–271b; IV–187a; VI–141b
Missionary Sisters of the Sacred Heart I–469b
MISSIONARY SOCIETIES, HOME IV–365a; IV–366b; VII–206a, 365a
archives I–169b
Slade's Girls VI–299b
Missionary Society of Connecticut IV–365a
Mission churches
architecture I–159b–60a
Mission Concepción II–157a
Mission furniture III–136a
MISSION INDIANS OF CALIFORNIA IV–365b; III–385b, 503a
Mission of the Guardian Angel II–17a
Mission of the Holy Family I–402a
Mission of the Immaculate Conception IV–31b
"Mission pods" (bombs) I–50b
Mission River IV–367b
Missions II–170b
Capuchins I–451b
Franciscan II–23b, 433a, 461a
French II–13b
Georgia III–170a
Jesuit II–17a, 93b
La Présentation IV–85a
Moravian Brethern IV–409b
Paulists V–229b
Saint Ignace IV–7a
Spanish II–389a
Spanish Florida III–40b
Sulpician II–458b
See also Dominicans; Franciscans; Indian Missions; Jesuit Missions
Missions, diplomatic. *See* Diplomatic Missions
MISSIONS, FOREIGN IV–366a; I–469a; III–347a; V–280b; VI–77b
Arab nations I–149b
Baptist I–265a
Catholic I–469a
China VI–66a
Jesuits II–501b
Liberia IV–141b
Pacific IV–364b
Priests of Holy Cross III–293a
Society for the Propagation of the Gospel VI–331b
MISSIONS, FRONTIER IV–366b; IV–365a,b
Arkansas Post I–173b
Franciscans III–94a–b
Hudson's Bay Company III–313b
Illinois III–329a
Illinois Band III–331b
Iowa Band III–469a
Jesuits III–498b–500b
Oregon V–166b–67a; VII–247b
Whitman mission VII–221a
Willamette Valley VII–300a
See also Indian Missions
Missions, Spanish
Georgia III–170a
hide and tallow trade III–274b
MISSIONS OF THE SOUTHWEST IV–367a; VI–364b
Acoma I–8a
California I–141a
Franciscans III–94a
Gran Quivira III–211a
New Mexico V–59b
Pecos V–241a
presidios V–399b
Pueblo Revolt V–459b, 460b
Rodríguez–Chamuscado expedition VI–162a
San Antonio VI–207a,b
San Francisco VI–209a
San Francisco de los Tejas VI–210a
Texas I–48b; VII–36b
Tubac VII–125b
Missisquoi Bay VI–190a
MISSISSINEWA, BATTLE OF (1812) **IV–367b**
MISSISSIPPI IV–368a; IV–200a; VI–394 (table)
Afro-American education II–404a
Afro-American suffrage III–92b
Anglo–Spanish rivalry III–38b
banks I–259a
bayous I–279a
Biloxi I–301a
Black Belt I–308b
Black Codes I–310b
black suffrage IV–371b; VI–432a, 433a,b
black voter registration III–93b
boundary disputes I–351b
Chickasaw I–197a; II–22b–23a; V–357a–b
Choctaw II–33a, 291a; III–396b
civil rights movement I–24b, 31a, 316a; II–58b
Civil War I–295b, 492a, 502b; II–22a, 225b; III–208b, 228a, 238b, 292a, 485a, 485b; IV–8a, 42a, 136b, 257a, 313b, 405a; V–142b, 369a; VI–48b; VII–26b, 128b–29a, 181b–82a
Clinton riot II–77a
colonial land grants IV–93a
Compromise of 1850 II–150b
constitution I–27b
cotton II–237b, 238b; IV–104a; VI–305b
cotton money II–241a
Creek Indians III–401b
Creek War II–256b–57a; IV–456a; VII–239a
Democratic party VII–210a
entail of estate II–452b
evolution theory VI–239b
Forman's Colony III–77b
Fort Maurepas IV–276b
Fort Panmure V–210b
Fort Rosalie VI–164a
freedom riders II–179b; III–107a
Honey Island III–297b
horse racing III–304b
Houma Indians III–308a
hurricanes II–352a; III–319b
Indian treaties IV–97a
land speculation IV–99b
literacy test VII–209b, 302b
Louisiana IV–192b
lynching I–31a
minimum-wage law IV–353b
Natchez IV–455a
Natchez Indians IV–455b
Natchez Trace IV–456a
"New West" V–81b
Old Southwest VI–356a
panic of 1837 III–64a
Pass Christian V–224a
Peace Society VII–149a
Pearl River V–240b
poor whites V–358b
public land sales V–452b, 453a
public land speculation I–107b
public land states V–453a
race relations VI–7b
railroad land grants IV–94a; VI–26a
Reconstruction II–77a; IV–209a; VI–56b, 57b
repudiation of state debts VI–96a,b
rice VI–136a
secession II–61a; VI–250b; VII–1a
segregation II–179b, 402a
sharecroppers IV–103a
slavery I–27b; VI–309a; VII–223b
slaying of Medgar Evers II–58b
southern rights convention IV–453b
Spanish occupation VI–356b
statehood VII–284a
sugarcane VI–436a
territorial government VII–32a
Three Notch Road VII–54b
tidelands VII–57b
Tombigbee Valley VII–70b
tornadoes II–351b, 352a; VII–75b
Treaty of Doak's Stand III–383b
Treaty of Natchez IV–456a
Union Rights party VII–148a
Vick estate VII–181a
Vicksburg VII–181a
Voting Rights Act of 1965 VII–211a
West Florida III–41b; VII–277b
White Caps VII–291a
White Citizens Councils VII–291a
workmen's compensation laws II–441b
Yazoo fraud VII–353b
Mississippi (ship) IV–322a
MISSISSIPPI, CONFEDERATE ARMY OF IV–369b; VII–26b
MISSISSIPPI, UNION ARMY OF THE IV–370a
Mississippi, University of I–207b; II–58b; IV–369b
MISSISSIPPIAN CULTURES IV–370a; I–158a; VI–352b; VII–320a
Mississippi Barge Lines V–455a–b
MISSISSIPPI BUBBLE IV–370b; II–149a, 237a, 267b
Mississippi Colony IV–92b
Mississippi Company. *See* Compagnie de l'Occident
MISSISSIPPI COMPANY OF VIRGINIA IV–371a; III–171a; IV–98b
Mississippi Delta II–352a
MISSISSIPPI DELTAS, BLOCKADE OFF THE (1861–62) **IV–371a**
Mississippi Gazette (news.) V–70b

Mississippi Passes IV–413b
MISSISSIPPI PLAN
IV–371b; III–295a
"Mississippi question"
IV–372b
MISSISSIPPI RIVER
IV–372a; II–96b;
III–369b; IV–368a;
VI–149a–b; VII–267b
Acadian migration I–6b
agrarianism I–33a
Arkansas River I–173a
Barataria I–265b
barge line VII–260b
Bird's Point I–306b
Bloody Island I–322b
Bonnet Carre spillway
V–356b
boundary IV–87b
bridges I–364a; II–384a
British expedition to Illinois
III–330b
Burr conspiracy I–387b;
V–63b
Cahokia I–402a
Cahokia Mounds I–402b
Cairo (Ill.) I–403b
canals III–449a; VI–425a
Chalmette National Historical Park I–490b
Cherokee land cession
V–49b
Chicago II–17b, 297a
Chickasaw II–22a–b, 23a
Chippewa II–31a
Choctaw II–32b, 33a
Civil War I–275a; II–63a,
163a; III–474a,b,
478b–79a; IV–302a, 371a,
374b–75b; V–19b, 238b,
313b, 369a; VI–38a, 48b,
63a, 150a–b, 410b;
VII–146b, 181b
Côte des Allemands
II–237a
cotton I–38a
Cumberland Road
VI–153b
dams and locks IV–175a
Davenport bridge
III–468b
Definitive Treaty of Peace
II–318b
delta I–279a
De Soto expedition
III–288b
discovery I–96b; II–184a,
336b; IV–6b–7b
domestic trade IV–309a,
310a; VII–83b, 84b
Dunbar's Line II–381a
Eads jetties II–384b
exploration I–24b, 354a,
354b, 464b; II–17a, 247b;
III–119a,b, 216a, 329a;
IV–276b; V–148a
Falls of Saint Anthony
IV–347b; VI–187a
Father of Waters II–497a
ferries III–11b
flatboats III–35b
flood control VI–146b,
147a
floods I–100b; III–36b, 37a
Florida III–41b; VI–351a;
VII–277a
folklore III–48b
Forks of the Ohio V–143a
Fort Adams I–9b
Fort Armstrong I–180b
Fort Assumption II–22a
Fort Bellefontaine I–286b
Fort Bute I–398a
Fort Crawford II–254a
Fort de Chartres I–501a;
II–265b
Fort Ferdinand II–22a
Fort Jefferson III–494a
Fort Kearny IV–33b
Fort Madison IV–219b
Fort Pickering II–22a
Fort Prudhomme II–22a
Fort Ripley VI–144b
Fort Saint Antoine
VI–187a
Fort Snelling
IV–355b–56a; VI–322b
Fox–Wisconsin Waterway
III–89a
French claims III–118a;
VI–160b
French exploration
IV–109b–10a
French posts III–115a,
120a
French settlements
III–114b; IV–376b
French–Spanish rivalry
I–70b
fur trade I–105b; III–140a,
141a,b, 142a, 143b–44b;
IV–380b; V–388a;
VI–357b; VII–307a
galley boats III–147b
gambling III–149b
Georgia boundary
III–168b
Giard Tract III–177b
Great American Desert
III–213b
Gulf of Mexico
IV–326a,b
Half-Breed Tract
III–242b
Hennepin exploration
III–272a
Holston exploration
III–292b
Hope Encampment
IV–195b
Iberville River III–326b
Illinois and Michigan Canal
III–331a
Illinois Country III–331b
Illinois military reserve
IV–345a
improvements VII–77b
Indiana III–370a
Indian agriculture I–48a
Indian attacks V–101a
Indian Barrier State
III–375a; V–120b
Indian Country III–379a
Indian cultures
III–356a–b
Indian removal
III–393a,b, 395a, 401b;
V–357a; VI–85b
Indians III–365a
Indian territory III–388a
Indian trade IV–277b
Industrial Revolution
III–412a
Isle of Orleans III–479a
Jefferson Barracks
III–494a
Jefferson's proposed states
III–497a
Jesuit missions III–499a,b
Kaskaskia IV–31b
Kentucky IV–39b
Lake Huron III–319a
Lakes-to-Gulf waterway
IV–87b, 88a
land grants III–170a;
IV–371a
La Salle expeditions
VI–195b
lead III–147a; IV–122a;
VI–189b
Loftus Heights IV–178b
Louisiana IV–192b,
196a,b, 197b
lumber industry II–376a
Magee–Kearny expedition
IV–223b
malaria IV–229a
Mallet Brothers expedition
IV–230a
Manchac post IV–234b
mapping VII–73b, 74a
Memphis IV–301b
"men of western waters"
IV–303b
midcontinent oil region
IV–333b
Minnesota IV–355a
missions I–452a
Missouri–Kentucky boundary dispute I–351a
Missouri River IV–379b,
380a
Mormon settlement
IV–339a
mounds IV–420b
mustangs IV–444b
Natchez IV–455a, 456a
Natchez Indians IV–455b
Natchez Trace IV–456a
Natchitoches IV–456b
neutral ground V–33b
New Orleans V–62a;
VII–187a
Northwest Territory
V–123a
Ohio River V–145a
Old Northwest V–152a
Orleans Territory V–173a
Pike's expedition
III–468a; V–312a;
VII–271a
Pinckney's Treaty I–459b
piracy I–355a; IV–263a
Plains Indians III–363b
Pointe Coupee V–335a
Pontiac's War V–357a
portages V–367b
Prairie du Chien V–387b
Prudhomme Bluffs
V–440b
Quebec Act VI–2a
railroad rate wars VI–23a
railroads II–218b; VI–25b,
33b, 37b, 153b
railroad surveys VI–39a
rainfall VI–41b
Red River cart traffic
VI–63b
revolutionary war
III–179a; VI–130a, 195a,
365a, 367b; VII–303a
Saint Lawrence River
II–20a
Saint Louis VI–193b
Santa Fe trade VI–215b
seismic activity II–385a
settlements I–246b–47a,
447b, 499a; III–38b, 171a;
IV–92b, 338a
showboats VI–283a
Sioux–Chippewa War
IV–31b; VI–295a
Sioux land cession
IV–355b
Sioux treaties VI–295b
source II–380a
Spanish claims IV–382b
Spanish posts I–367a;
III–232b; V–100b
stagelines VI–380a
steamboating III–35b,
132b; V–62a, 336a;
VI–406b, 407a, 407b,
408a; VII–100b, 196b,
271a
Sultana disaster
II–349a–b
tobacco VII–68a
towboating VII–77b
trading posts II–34a
transportation
VII–100a–b
Treaty of Fort Armstrong
III–383b
Treaty of Old Town
III–383b
Treaty of Paris V–214b
Treaty of Saint Louis
III–383b
Twin Cities VII–133b
U.S. boundary I–126a;
II–319a; III–40b;
V–120a–b
Vicksburg VII–181a
Villere's plantation
VII–188a
War of 1812 II–255b
War of 1812 V–63a;
VII–235a
western boundary
VII–269b, 270a
western lands VII–273a
West Florida V–240b
westward movement
V–176b; VII–283b, 283b,
284a
Willing VII–302b
Willing expedition
III–147b
Wisconsin River
VII–306b
MISSISSIPPI RIVER, FREE NAVIGATION OF
IV–373a; II–166b, 333a–b;
IV–372b, 372b; V–59a,
120b; VI–150b, 359a,
359a, 365b; VII–260a,
290a, 307a
Jay–Gardoqui negotiations
III–492b; VII–111a
Kentucky enabling act
IV–42b
Pinckney's Treaty
IV–193b; V–315a
road construction
VI–153a
Spanish conspiracy
VI–365b
Treaty of Ghent
VII–235b
Treaty of Paris V–214b
western separatism

VII–276a
MISSISSIPPI RIVER, NAVIGATION ON IV–374a; IV–372b; VI–148a,b
bargemen I–267b
bateaux I–274a,b
improvements VI–145b–46a,b
"mark twain" IV–256a
Navigator handbook V–17a
snags VI–322a
steamboating I–459a; VI–407a
Virginia IV–356a
MISSISSIPPI RIVER, OPENING OF THE IV–374b
Mississippi riverboats gambling II–259b
Mississippi River Commission IV–373a, 374b; VI–146a
Mississippi Shipping Company (Delta Lines) IV–312a
MISSISSIPPI SQUADRON IV–375a; II–384a
Mississippi Summer Project (1964) VI–7b; VII–365b
Mississippi Territory III–318b; VI–358a
Alabama I–71a
Battle of Amite I–114b
Battle of Autossee I–232a
boundary VII–353b
Creek War IV–456a
homestead movement III–295b
MISSISSIPPI VALLEY IV–375b; IV–368a; V–224a
Anglo–French rivalry III–143b–44a
buffalo trails VI–152b
Carolina claim I–457b
Civil War V–63b; VI–278b
colonial land speculation IV–98b
Cumberland Road II–273a
export trade IV–302b
farm tenancy IV–103a,b
floods III–37a
foreign trade VII–260a
free navigation IV–373a
French exploration IV–6b–7b, 376b
French posts III–120a
German immigrants III–336b
Granger movement III–210a
Great Serpent Mound III–222a
Indian agriculture IV–327a
Indian barrier state III–375a
Indian mounds I–128a
Indian trade VII–95b
Jesuits III–501a–b
Jolliet and Marquette exploration VII–25a
La Salle's claim for France IV–109b
lead IV–122a; VI–189b
Louisiana IV–192b, 196a, 197a, 198a
Marksville complex III–300b
Memphis IV–301b
Minnesota IV–355a
mounds IV–420b, 421b
New France V–52b
New Orleans V–62b
Ohio Valley V–146a
Pennsylvania canal system V–250a
Pike's exploration IV–355b
pioneers V–316b
Pittsburgh V–321b
"prairie triangle" II–226b
prehistory I– 370a
rafting VI–18b
railroads IV–94a–b; VI–25a, 37b
resorts and spas VI–100b
Sauk VI–218b
Scandinavians V–75b
sorghum VI–340a
steamboats VI–408a
sugarcane VI–436b
tafia trade VI–456b
theater VII–47a
timberlands VII–59b
trade IV–372b; VII–95b
Ursulines VII–160b
westward movement VII–284a–b
wild game III–150a
Mississippi Valley Historical Association III–279a
MISSISSIPPI v. *JOHNSON* (1867) IV–209a, 376a; VI–58a; VII–35a
Missoula (Mont.) III–76b
MISSOURI IV–376b; VI–394 (table); VII–253b
alien landholding I–87b
Archaic culture II–385b
banking I–129b, 259a,b
Becknell's expeditions I–282a
Bird's Point I–306b
Blue Lodges I–325b
border ruffians I–341a
border state I–341b
boundary disputes I–351a, 352a
boycotts I–356b
bushwhackers I–388b
campaign of 1864 I–421b
Cape Girardeau I–447b
caravans I–453a
cattle drives I–1b, 473a
Civil War I–288a, 307a, 317b, 337b, 341b–42a, 433b, 462a; II–61b, 379a; III–81a, 101a, 182a, 400a; IV–137a, 183b; V–121b, 222a, 238b, 314a, 402b–03a, 471a; VI–251b, 308a; VII–280b, 304a
coal mines II–85a, 86a
colonial land grants IV–93a
constitution II–274a
corn II–226b, 227a
Craig v. *State of Missouri* II–253b
crime commission II–263b; V–416a
Delaware Indians II–321a
Democratic party IV–29a
De Soto expedition III–288b
Dred Scott Case II–370a–b
emigration to Kansas IV–31a
fair–trade laws II–482b
Far West II–496a
floods II–351b
forests III–74b
Fort Osage I–330a; V–173b
forty–niners III–82a
Fowler expedition III–88a
Frémont's emancipation orders II–434b–35a; VI–11a
frontier merchants III–127b
fur trade I–290a; II–34a; IV–422a–b
George Washington Carver National Monument V–217b
grasshopper attacks III–212b
Hannibal and Saint Joseph Railroad III–250b
Haun's Mill massacre III–262b
hemp III–271a
homeopathy III–293b
home–rule charters I–500b
Honey War III–297b
horse racing III–304b
Icaria III–327a
Independence III–353b
Indian Country III–379a
Indian relocation III–394b
Indian trade I–290a
Iowa jurisdiction III–467b
ironclad oath VII–35a
Jesuits III–501b
joint–stock land banks IV–6b
Kansas Border War III–493a; V–51b, 174a
Kansas City IV–27a
Kickapoo III–393b
lead IV–122a,b, 123a,b; V–102b
Leavenworth IV–129a
military tract IV–91a, 344b
Mormons II–496a; IV–116b; V–8a; VI–87a; VII–107a
New Madrid V–58b
"New West" V–81b
nickel III–13b
Oregon caravans V–166a
Osage land cession V–173b
panhandle V–205b
Pendergast machine V–244b
Pikes Peak gold rush V–311b
Platte purchase V–330a
prairie V–387a
proslavery activity IV–30a
referendum VI–66b
reptile survey VI–91b
Saint Genevieve Lead District VI–189b
Saint Joseph VI–191b
Saint Louis VI–193b
Santa Fe Trail VI–215a,b
Scotch–Irish VI–240b
seismic activity II–385a
Shaw's expedition VI–271b
single–tax plan VI–293b
slave raids III–257a
slavery I–341a, 342a; II–366a; VI–309a, 458b
soldiers' homes VI–337a
Sons of the South VI–339b
State Guard II–379a
statehood I–173a; VII–284a
stay and valuation acts VI–406a,b
tariff VI–465b
tobacco VII–66b
tornadoes II–351a, 351b; VII–76a
Trail of Tears VII–96b
Treaties of Saint Louis III–383b
Treaty of Fort Clark III–383b
Treaty of Prairie du Chien III–383b
Union sentiment VI–354a; VII–148b
veterinary medicine VII–176b
wagon trains VII–217b
Westport VII–280a
westward movement IV–29a; VII–100a
wild turkey VII–130a
zinc V–103a; VII–368b
Missouri (battleship) VII–242a, 341a
Missouri (ironclad) III–474b
Missouri, Kansas and Texas (Katy) Railroad VI–35a; VII–40a
MISSOURI, THREE FORKS OF THE IV–378a; VI–196a
Missouri, University of III–285a; IV–461a; V–79b, 327a
Missouri Basin Interagency Committee IV–380a
Missouri bateau I–274a
MISSOURI BOTANICAL GARDEN IV–378a; I–348a, 349a; V–327a–b; VI–194b
MISSOURI COMPROMISE (1820) **IV–378b**; II–265a, 370b; V–360a; VI–92b, 307b, 347b, 458b
Kansas struggle IV–31a
Nashville Convention IV–453b
Nebraska V–31a
repeal IV–28b
secessionist movement VI–250a
Wilmot Proviso VII–303b
Missouri ex rel. Gaines v. *Canada* (1938) II–54b
Missouri Fur Company III–143a; VI–195b, 196a
Leavenworth expedition IV–130a
Missouri River IV–378a, 380b

MISSOURI FUR COMPANY (cont.)
Yellowstone River IV–403a
See also Saint Louis Missouri Fur Company
Missouri Gazette (news.) V–70b
Missouri Indians I–354b; III–363b, 365a; V–31a
Missouri Mounted Volunteers II–363b; VI–184b
Missouri Pacific Railroad VI–25b, 35a
Missouri Plan IV–18a
Missouri Republican (news.) VII–103b
MISSOURI RIVER IV–379b; VII–268a
Arikara IV–129b
Arikara and Blackfoot War VII–239a
bargemen I–267b
basin development VI–147a
boundary disputes I–351b
bridges I–213a, 364a; III–468b
buffalo I–375a
bullboats I–380a,b
Butterfield Overland Dispatch I–398b
cattle freighting I–473a
Cheyenne II–16b
Civil War I–337b; IV–137a; V–471a
Council Bluffs II–241b
dams III–322b
domestic trade VII–83b
exploration I–170a, 354b, 499a; III–119b; IV–242a; VI–192a; VII–275b
Five Villages III–33b
flooding II–351a; III–37a
Fort Abraham Lincoln I–3b
Fort Assiniboine I–206a
Fort Bellefontaine I–286b
Fort Buford VII–145b
Fort Kiowa IV–51a
Fort Lisa IV–159b
Fort Orleans V–173a
Fort Osage V–173b
Fort Peck V–241a
Fort Pierre III–256a; V–310a
Fort Rice III–32a; VI–135a
Fort Union II–285a; VII–145b
freighting III–353b; V–179a
Great American Desert III–213b
Great Sioux Reservation VI–295b
Gulf Intracoastal Waterway VI–148b
Indian agriculture I–48a
Indian Country III–379a
Indians I–171b, 311a; IV–403a; V–31a
Indian trade IV–277b
Indian warfare II–283b, 284a; VI–150a
Kansas City (Mo.) IV–27a,b
Kiowa IV–50b
Lakes-to-Gulf waterway IV–88a
La Vérendrye exploration IV–118a, 118a
Leavenworth IV–129a
Lewis and Clark Expedition III–468a; IV–136a,b; VII–271a
Magee–Kearny expedition IV–223b
Mallet brothers expedition IV–230a
Mandan, Hidatsa, and Arikara IV–235b, 235b
Mississippi River IV–372a
Missouri boundary V–330a
Mormon migration IV–411b
Mullan Trail IV–426a
Navigator handbook V–17a
Nebraska V–31a
Omaha Indians V–154b
Oregon Trail V–168a,b
overland freighting V–177a
overland mail V–178a
Piegan War V–310a
Platte River Trail V–330b
proslavery settlements IV–31a
railroads II–218b; VI–26a, 33b, 34b, 37a
Rocky Mountains V–225a
Saint Joseph VI–191b
Saint Louis VI–193b
Santa Fe Trail VI–215a,b
settlements IV–376b
Sioux reservation IV–108b–09a
Smith explorations VI–318a
South Dakota VI–350a
steamboating I–206a; IV–403a; VI–406b, 407a, 408a; VII–260b, 271a, 357a
telegraph V–358a
territorial boundary II–284b
Three Forks IV–378a
trading posts I–289b, 399a
Treaty of Fort Clark III–383b
Treaty of Fort Laramie VI–296a
tributaries IV–25a
War of 1812 VII–234b–35a
Westport VII–280a
westward movement I–485b; VII–283b
Yellowstone River VII–357b, 357b
Missouri River Commission VI–146a
MISSOURI RIVER FUR TRADE IV–380b; II–34a; III–140a, 141b, 142b, 143a–b; VI–160a–b, 296a; VII–103b, 104b, 271b, 307a
American Fur Company I–105a
Ashley expedition I–201a
Fort Benton III–77b
Fort Lisa IV–159b
Laclède's post VI–193b
Lisa and Company IV–159b
Mackenzie's Treaty IV–217a
Missouri Fur Company VI–196a
Rocky Mountain Fur Company VI–160a
Saint Louis Missouri Fur Company VI–195b
Spanish–Missouri Fur Company VI–367a
trading posts VII–95b
Missouri State Guard III–101a; IV–137a; VII–304a
Missouri Synod III–336b; IV–206b
Missouri Territory I–173a; II–284b
Missouri Valley VI–320a
MISSOURI* v. *HOLLAND (1920) **IV–381a**; I–362b; VII–110b
Missouri v. *Kentucky* (1871) I–351a
Missouri v. *Nebraska* (1904, 1905) I–351b
Missouri Waltz (song) VI–394 (table)
Missouri Wildcats IV–421b
Mistick (Mass.) I–319b
Mistletoe VI–395 (table)
Mistress IV–256a–b
M.I.T. *See* Massachusetts Institute of Technology
Mitchel, Colin III–59a
Mitchel, Ormsby (off.) II–432a
Mitchel et al. v. *United States* (1835) III–59a
Mitchell, Arthur (dancer) II–289b
Mitchell, Charles (fin.) III–466a
Mitchell, Elisha (cler., geol.) III–165a
Mitchell, John (atty. gen.) I–400a; II–474a; VII–254b, 255b
Mitchell, John (labor leader) I–127a, 374b; II–87a; IV–67b; V–247b; VII–150b
Mitchell, John (physic., cartog.) I–410a; III–29b
See also Mitchell's Map
Mitchell, John C. (off.) VI–441a
Mitchell, John Purroy (pol.) VI–459b
Mitchell, Samuel Augustus (pub.) VII–74b
Mitchell, Sidney Z. (bus.) V–209b
Mitchell, Silas Weir (physic., au.) IV–306a; V–306b
Mitchell, Wesley C. (econ.) I–391b; V–209a
Mitchell, William (astron.) V–131a, 213b
bombing tests V–26b
court-martial I–234a, 328a; II–247a
strategic bombing I–50a, 66b
World War I I–59b
Mitchell bomber I–50a, 57b
Mitchell's Ford (Va.) I–381b
MITCHELL'S MAP IV–381a; V–120a; VI–62b, 189a; VII–74a
Mitchel v. *Reynolds* (1711) VI–102a
Mitchill, Samuel Latham (physic., pol.) III–27a
Mitla (Mex.) IV–327b
Mitrailleuse (gun) IV–214b
Mitscher (frigate) VII–243b
Mitscher, Marc A. (nav. off.) I–459a; V–285b–86a; VII–1b, 337b
Mitterofer, Peter (inv.) VII–136a
MIWOK (Indians) **IV–381b**; III–362b, 363a
Mix, Elijah VI–145a
MIXED COMMISSIONS IV–381b
Canadian–U.S. boundary V–33a–b
Halifax fisheries award III–243b
International Control Commission III–452b
Jay's Treaty III–493b–94a
Northeast boundary V–118a
Mixers, electric II–421b
Mixtec (Indians) IV–327a
MOBILE (Ala.) **IV–382a**; III–38b, 146b, 330a,b; V–240b
Black Belt products I–308b
Chickasaw–French War II–22b
Civil War II–63a; III–40b; IV–313b, 382b; VI–26b
coal I–72a
commerce IV–435a
cotton I–72a; II–238a
Creek War IV–456a
Fort Adams I–9b
Fort Condé I–499a
Fort Stoddert VI–414b
French II–33a; III–119a, 120a; IV–326a
fur trade III–144a
hospitals III–306b
Indian trade VI–366b
Indian trail II–33a
integration I–72a
Loftus expedition IV–178b
oil IV–347b
port authority V–368a
railroads III–450a; V–62a; VI–34b, 37a
revolutionary war II–96b; VI–365b
settlement IV–368a
Three Notch Road VII–55a
trading post VII–95b
Yamasee War VII–352a
MOBILE ACT (1804) **IV–382b**; VI–359b; VII–277a
Mobile and Ohio Railroad VI–26a, 34b; VII–129a
Mobile Bay II–294a
Fort Gaines III–146a
French settlement

IV–372a
Mobile IV–382a
War of 1812 I–356a
MOBILE BAY, BATTLE OF (1864) **IV–382b**; II–285b–86a; III–258b; IV–382b; VI–425a; VII–26b
Mobile Centinel (news.) V–70b
Mobile homes I–377a; II–48b; III–422b
Mobile River II–167b; IV–382a
forts II–158a
Mobiles (sculp.) VI–244a
MOBILE SEIZED (1813) **IV–383a**; I–71a; IV–382b; VI–359b
Mobile telephones IV–333a
MOBILIZATION IV–383a; II–323b–24a
logistics IV–180b
preparedness movement V–390b
World War I II–243a
World War II VII–334a–36b
Mobilization for Youth Project II–148a
Moby Dick IV–162a
Moccasin Gap V–224b
MOCCASINS IV–384b; III–363b, 368a, 381a
Mocha (Yemen) II–388a
Mocino, Mariano (bot.) V–326b–27a
Mock blockade I–321a
Mockingbird VI–393 (table), 394 (table), 395 (table)
Model 1842 U.S. Rifle IV–352b
Model cities III–311a; IV–173a; VI–315a, 328b
federal aid II–47b
Model farms III–151a
Model N Ford I–227a
Model T Ford I–205b, 227a,b; II–337a; IV–272a
Modern architecture I–163b–64a
Modern art V–192a–93a
Modern dance. *See* Dance
Modern Horse Doctor VII–176a
Modern Instance IV–163b
Modernism (rel.) V–392a; VI–79a,b
Modernistic landscapes IV–97a
Modern Jazz Quartet IV–440b
Modern Language Association II–400b; IV–2b
Modern Language Notes (jour.) IV–2b
Modern Rules of Criminal and/or Civil Procedure IV–18b
Modern Temper IV–164a
Modern Times (N.Y.) II–147b
Modified Mercalli Scale II–385a
Modoc (Indians). *See* Klamath–Modoc
MODOC WAR (1872–73) **IV–384b**; III–127a; IV–51b; VII–127a–b, 239b
Modular transportation systems I–231b
***MODUS VIVENDI* IV–385a**
Moeller, Philip (theat. dir.) VII–49b
Moffat Tunnel VI–34a; VII–128b
Moffett, William A. (nav. off.) I–236a; VII–341b
Moffett Field (Calif.) IV–458a
Mogaung Valley (Burma) IV–314a
MOGOLLON (culture) **IV–385b**; I–117b, 157b
Mohammed V–172a
Mohammed Mossadegh I–124b
MOHAVE (Indians) **IV–386a**; III–362a, 363a, 369a
captivities III–376b; V–129b
scouts VI–242a
Smith massacre VI–318a
territory III–395b
Mohave, Lake II–130a
Mohave County (Ariz.) III–208a
Mohawk (Indians) II–462b; III–255a, 365b, 475a
French and Indian War III–115a; IV–87b
guns III–399b
hockey III–286b
Iroquois Treaty III–476b
Jesuit missions III–499a
Kayoderosseras Patent IV–33a
King Philip's War IV–47b
Lancaster Treaty IV–89b
La Présentation mission V–139b
Minisink raid IV–354b
Pequot War V–261b
Rogers' Rangers VI–190a
sachems VI–183a
Saratoga Springs VI–217b
Schenectady VI–225b
trade with French III–312a
MOHAWK AND HUDSON RAILROAD IV–386b; V–87a; VI–24b, 35b, 225b
Mohawk Gateway II–459b
Mohawk River I–385a; III–291b, 312a; V–224a
Erie Canal III–448a
Fort Plain V–323a
Fort Stanwix VI–385a
fur trade III–141a, 142a
German Flats III–172b
inland lock navigation III–419b
Iroquois III–387b
Kayoderosseras Patent IV–33a
navigation IV–174b
revolutionary war IV–387a; V–172b; VI–150a, 438a
Schenectady VI–225b
settlements V–195a; VII–282b, 283a
waterpower IV–347b
MOHAWK VALLEY IV–386b
Alleghenies I–88b
French and Indian War I–358b
Iroquois III–475a
Johnson Hall IV–4b
migration from IV–338b
New England settlers V–50a
Palatines V–85a
revolutionary war I–81b, 384b; IV–86b; V–175b
Schenectady VI–225b
westward movement VII–260a
MOHEGAN AND MAHICAN (Indians) **IV–387a**; III–367a
Pequot War V–261a,b
Schoenbrunn missions VI–226a
Wappinger Confederacy VII–223b
MOHEGAN CASE IV–387a
Mohole Project III–167b
Moholy–Nagy, László (paint.) II–104b
MOHONK, LAKE, CONFERENCE IV–387b
Mohr, Charles (jour.) V–74b
Mohs, Friedrich (min.) IV–348b
Mohurs (coins) I–151a
Mojave (Calif.) I–340a
Mojave Desert I–340b, 403b
potash V–376a
Spanish Trail V–224b
Mojave River VI–368a; VII–256a
Mokcsa, Agoston Haraszthy de VII–305b
MOLASSES ACT (1733) **IV–387b**; II–92b, 116b; III–346b; IV–308a, 388a–b; V–221a; VI–107b, 171a, 435a–b; VII–93b, 119b
opposition IV–265b–66a
smuggling VI–321a
West India trade VII–278a
MOLASSES TRADE IV–388a; II–92b, 453a; IV–309b; VI–386b; VII–86a
duties III–228a; VI–110b
Molasses Act IV–387b
Navigation Acts V–16a
Norfolk V–109b
rum II–353b; VI–170b
South America VI–343b
Sugar Acts VI–435a
Sugar Islands VI–437b
towboating VII–77b
triangular trade II–119a, 119b; VI–310b; VII–119b, 277b
Moldboard plow I–34a
MOLECULAR BIOLOGY IV–388b; I–304a, 349b
genetics III–159a
Rockefeller Foundation VI–158a
Moley, Raymond (jour., prof.) I–359b; V–43b
Molineaux, Tom (slave) V–422b
Molineaux, William (mfr.) II–5a
Moline Plow Company V–44b
MOLINO DEL REY, BATTLE OF (1847) **IV–391b**; IV–324a
Moll, Herman (cartog.) VII–74a
Moll, John (law.) VII–130a
Mollet, Guy (states.) VI–430a
Mollusks III–163b
MOLLY MAGUIRES IV–391b; II–86b; IV–63a; VI–253a; VII–117b
"Molly Pitcher." *See* McCauley, Mary
Molniya 1 (satellite) II–143b
Molotov, V. M. (states.) IV–415b
Molton, Robert (shipwright) I–319b
Molucca Islands II–369a
Moluntha (Indian) I–337a
Molybdenite III–15a
Molybdenum II–224a; III–12a, 14b–15a; VI–48b
Colorado II–128b; IV–124a, 354b
tungsten production III–15b
Molybdenum sulfide III–15a
Monaco V–133b; VI–96b
Monarch Mine (Mont.) III–270a
Monarchy II–189a, 325a, 326a, 473b
opposition IV–140a
third–term doctrine VII–53b
Monash, John (off.) VI–338b
Moncada, José María (pol., off.) V–94b
Monck, George, First Duke of Albemarle I–458a
Monclova (Mex.) I–48b
Mondrian, Piet (paint.) II–104b; V–192b
Monet, Claude (paint.) II–103a
Monetarist economists III–8b; IV–234a–b
Monetary Association, National IV–234a
MONEY IV–392a; III–8a–b
balance of trade I–244b
bank deposits I–252a, 257a, 258a
bank notes II–1b–2a, 254b, 339a
Bank of the United States III–245b
barter I–269a
beaver I–282a
beaver skins II–94b
bills of credit I–300a
bills of exchange II–467b, 468a
bit I–308a
blue pup currency II–275a
check currency II–1b
Civil War II–63b

MONEY (cont.)
coin scarcity IV–360a–b
colonial coinage II–94b
colonial paper currency III–346b
colonial restrictions VI–107b, 108a, 110b
commodities as II–140b
congressional powers I–198a–99a
Continental Congress VI–120a
cotton money II–241a
counterfeiting II–243b; VI–252a
devaluation VII–91b
dime II–341a
doubloon II–365b
foreign policy II–171b
foreign trade VII–90b, 91a
free silver III–110a
Gilded Age III–180b
gold clause III–189a
gold exchange III–190a
gold standard III–192b
Greenback movement III–224a
Hamilton's fiscal policies III–244a–b
hard money III–251b
Independent Treasury System III–354b
inflation III–414a
International Monetary Fund III–457a
land scrip IV–97a
legal tender IV–132a
Legal Tender Act IV–132b
Legal Tender Cases IV–20a, 133a
limping standard IV–154a
managed money IV–233b
national bank notes IV–461b
National Monetary Commission IV–468a
Nixon administration VI–472b
North Carolina V–115b
old and new tenor VII–31a
open–market operations V–159b
panic of 1893 V–208a
panic of 1907 V–208b–09a
panic of 1929 V–209a,b
paper money IV–53b
pistole II–365b
Pittman Act V–321b
populism V–365b
prices V–403b
proclamation money V–424a
profiteering V–426a
purchasing power II–209a–b, 236b
red dog currency II–275a
repudiation of public debt VI–94b
Rhode Island VI–132a,b
Sherman Silver Purchase Act VI–277a
shinplasters VI–279a
soft money VI–333b
Spanish dollar VI–366a
specie circulars VI–369b
specie payments VI–369b
Thomas Amendment V–44a; VII–54b
tobacco VII–65b
trade dollar VII–92b
treasury notes II–63b, 317a
Tripartite Agreement VII–120b
U.S. Constitution II–171a, 199b, 208a
wildcat money VII–295a
World Economic Conference VII–324a
See also Coinage; Currency; Greenbacks
Money–back guarantee I–17a
Money bills II–172b
Money brokers II–243b
Money Diggers (paint.) V–189b
Money orders I–102b
Money Trust III–443b; V–462a
Monge, A. (au.) IV–38b
Mongolia
horse III–302a
Mongoloid race I–155b
Mongols I–180b
Monguagon (Mich.) III–316a
MONHEGAN ISLAND IV–395b; I–96b; II–92b, 452b; IV–37a–b, 225b; V–243a
Moniteur (period.) IV–279b
Monitor (ironclad) III–36b; V–19b
guns V–26b
See also Monitor and *Merrimack*, Battle of III–474b
***MONITOR* AND *MERRIMACK*, BATTLE OF** (1862) **IV–396a**; III–474b; IV–399b; VI–44b; VII–147a, 240b
Monitorial schools II–397a
MONITORS IV–397a; II–286a; III–234b; IV–375b, 382b, 396b; VI–422b; VII–241a
Monk, Maria IV–250a
"Monkey meat" II–436a
Monkey trial. *See* Scopes Trial
Monks Mound (Ill.) I–402b–03a; IV–420b
MONMOUTH, BATTLE OF (1778) **IV–397b**; V–57b; VI–124a; VII–165b
Monmouth, Fort (N.J.) IV–209b
Monmouth Courthouse (N.J.) IV–397b; VI–124a
MONMOUTH PURCHASE IV–397b
Mono (Indians) III–363a
Monocacy (ship) IV–54b
MONOCACY, BATTLE OF THE (1864) **IV–398a**; III–100b; VI–275a
Monocacy Creek I–443a
Monocacy River IV–398a; VII–202b
Monod, J. (biochem.) III–158a
Monogamy IV–256a
Monongah (W.Va.) II–350a
MONONGAHELA, BATTLE OF THE (1755) **IV–398a**
MONONGAHELA RIVER IV–398b
Allegheny River I–89a
Braddock's Road I–358b
canals IV–174b
coal II–85a
exploration III–182a
Forks of the Ohio V–143a
Fort Pitt V–321a
French and Indian War III–115b
locks and dams V–250a
Navigator handbook V–17a
Ohio Company fort IV–181b
Pittsburgh V–321b
Redstone Old Fort V–144a; VI–65b
Scotch–Irish VI–240b
settlement V–378b
westward movement VI–149a
Monongahela Valley V–253b; VII–281a, 290a
Monongalia County (Va.) I–223b
Mono–Paviotso (Indians) V–194a
Monoplane I–50a, 51b, 52b, 53a
MONOPOLY IV–398b; IV–61b
Aluminum Company of America V–103b
antitrust laws I–139b; III–458b
Associated Press I–207a
automobile patent I–227a
baseball I–270b, 271a
California I–406a
campaign of 1900 I–425b–26a
capitalism I–449b
Clayton Antitrust Act II–71b–72a
codes of fair competition IV–469a
commerce clause II–135b
commodity marketing associations II–221b
flour milling III–44a, 45a
free trade III–113a–b
fur trade I–105a; III–403a
grain elevators III–210a–b
grain industry II–430a–b
investment banking III–466b
Jackson, Andrew I–496a
labor opposition IV–64a
land I–107b–08a
meat–packing I–283b; V–183a–b
mercantilism I–390a
National Football League III–57b
Navigation Acts V–16a
New Deal V–45b
New Jersey V–58a
Ohio National Stage Company V–144b
patents V–225b, 226b
petroleum industry VI–354b
postal service V–371a,b, 372b, 373b, 375a
"public interest" V–30b, 457a
public utilities IV–427b; V–459a
railroad rebates VI–50a
railroads I–406a
restraint of trade VI–103a
robber barons VI–156b–57a
Sherman Antitrust Act VI–276a
Single Tax movement V–427a
Slaughterhouse Cases VI–303a
slave trade I–22b
state banking I–259b
steamboating VI–407a
steamship I–406a
sugar refining I–390b; VI–437b
Supreme Court I–11a; VI–447b
tariff VI–463b
tea trade VII–15a–b
telegraph VII–18b, 19a
telephone VII–20a
tobacco I–114a
trading companies II–229a
trusts VII–121b
unions II–80b, 110b–11a
wheat trade V–106a
Monorail II–428b
Monotype V–412b
Monroe (Ala.) I–402a
Monroe (La.) IV–362a
Monroe (Mich.) III–316a
Monroe, Bill (mus.) IV–441b
MONROE, FORTRESS (Va.) **IV–399b**; I–190b; III–78b
Civil War IV–397a
Davis, Jefferson II–68b, 294b
fugitive slaves II–212b
Peninsular campaign V–245a
Monroe, James I–260b; II–174 (table), 395b; III–5a; V–395 (table); VII–194a,b, 198a, 300b
campaign of 1808 I–417b; VI–3b
code of manners IV–240b
colonization of Afro–Americans II–127a
foreign policy III–68a
Franco–American misunderstanding III–95b, 118b
Gabriel's Insurrection VI–304a
Louisiana purchase IV–196b–97a; VI–211a
mission to France IV–402b
mission to Spain VI–359b
Monroe–Pinkney Treaty IV–402b
Northwest boundary V–120b
See also Monroe Doctrine
—*President:*
Cumberland Road

II–273b
election I–418a–b
Era of Good Feeling II–458a
executive agents II–471a
Florida III–39a
French spoliation claims III–121b
Indian missions III–499b
Indian policy III–379a,b
Indian removal III–221a, 393b–94a
internal improvements III–448b–49a
Lafayette's visit IV–83b
Latin-American policy IV–115a, 115b
National Intelligencer III–202a
National Road IV–470b
Perry–Elliott controversy V–262b
post roads V–372a
Rhea letter VI–131b
Rush–Bagot Agreement III–217a
Seminole wars VI–260b
Survey Act of 1824 VI–450a
third-term doctrine VII–53b
U.S. flag III–34b
War of 1812 I–318a
White House VII–292a
Monroe, Jay R. (bus.) I–396b
Monroe Calculating Machine Company I–396b
Monroe County (N.Y.) V–463b
Monroe County (Pa.) VII–220b
MONROE DOCTRINE IV–399b; I–121a, 454a; II–360b; III–68a,b, 456b, 462b; IV–110b, 124b; VI–360a, 364a,b, 378b
anti-imperialists I–132a
Clayton–Bulwer Treaty II–73a; VII–112a
Cuban missile crisis VI–180a
Falkland Islands II–484a
France II–65b; III–96b
French in Mexico IV–326a, 328a–b, 361a–b
Iceland III–327b
isolationism III–480a
jingoism III–503b
Johnson Doctrine IV–4b
League of Nations Covenant I–199a
Lodge Corollary IV–199b, 223b
Lodge Reservations IV–178a
Mosquito question IV–416a
national defense II–313b
Olney Corollary V–153a
Panama Canal V–200b
Polk Doctrine V–354a
Roosevelt Corollary II–361a, 475b; V–105b, 106a; VI–163a
Russia VI–177b
Treaty of Versailles III–285b
U.S. interventions III–463a
U.S. neutrality V–35a
Venezuela blockade VII–169b
Venezuela boundary controversy VII–170b
Yucatán VII–366b
See also Polk Doctrine
MONROE MISSION TO FRANCE (1794–96) **IV–402a**
MONROE–PINKNEY TREATY (1806) **IV–402b**
Monrovia (Lib.) IV–141b
Mons (Belg.) VII–339b
Monsanto Chemical Company II–8b
Monschau (W.Ger.) I–379b
Montagnais (Indians) III–366b
Montagnais–Naskapi (Indians) I–441a; III–360b
Montagu, George (off.) VI–130a
Montague, Andrew J. (gov.) VII–195b
Montalvo, García Ordóñez de (au.) I–405a
MONTANA IV–403a; III–328a; VI–394 (table)
Alder Gulch II–477b
army posts IV–339b
Assiniboine I–206a
Big Horn Mountains I–296a,b
Blackfoot I–311a
Black Hills War I–313a
Black Infantry I–314a
boomtowns I–336b
boycotts I–356b
Bozeman Trail IV–108b
cattle I–38b, 358a; II–249a
cereal grains I–486b
Cheyenne II–16b, 379b
chromite III–13b
Columbia River II–132a
Comanche II–133a
copper I–116a; II–223a; III–80a
Custer Battlefield National Cemetery IV–168b
Dakota Indians II–282b
Dakota Territory II–284b
elk VII–297b
Farmer–Labor party of 1920 II–493a
forest fires III–74b
Fort Benton I–289b; III–77b
Fort C.F. Smith VI–317b
Fort Ellis II–432b
Fort Owen V–178b
Fort Peck V–241a
Fort Peck Dam III–322b
fur trade III–143a
gold I–83b–84a, 289b, 357b; II–284a, 477b; III–32a, 191b
Helena mining camp III–269b
Henrys Fork III–273a
Hungry Horse Dam III–323a
Hutterite communes II–142a
Idaho panhandle V–205b
Indians III–363a, 396a,b
Indian wars VII–239b
Jesuit missions III–499a, 500a,b
lead industry IV–123a
lead–silver industry IV–122b
manganese III–13a
Manuel's Fort IV–242a
Marias Pass VI–413a
Missouri River IV–379b, 380a
mountain passes V–225a
Mullan Trail IV–426a
National Bison Range VII–297a
national parks and monuments V–217a,b, 218 (table)
Nez Perce War I–281a, 296a; II–74b
Nonpartisan League V–106b
open-range grazing V–160a
Oregon boundary V–165a
Oregon Territory III–328a
paleontology V–196b
Piegan War V–310a
Plummer gang V–333a
public lands I–247b
railroads VI–32b
ranches VI–45a
reclamation VI–54b
referendum VI–66b
seismic activity II–385a
sheep wars VI–273b
silver mining I–116a; II–223a; VI–292b
stagecoach service V–178a
statehood VII–248a
Three Forks of the Missouri IV–378a
Treaty of Fort Laramie III–383b
vigilantes VII–187b
westward movement VII–284b
wheat VII–286a
woman's suffrage VII–315a
workmen's compensation IV–68b
Yellowstone National Park VII–357a
Montana (song) VI–394 (table)
Montana Stock Grower's Association I–472a
Montani semper liberi (motto) VI–395 (table)
Montauk (N.Y.) II–343b; IV–186a
Montauk Point (N.Y.) IV–185a; VI–362b
Mont Blanc (Fr.) IV–320a
Montcalm, Louis Joseph de (off.) III–115b, 116a–17a; IV–86b; V–175b; VI–136b
death I–3b
Fort Oswego V–157a
Fort William Henry IV–86a; VII–301a
Quebec VI–1a–b
Ticonderoga VII–57a
MONTDIDIER-NOYON OPERATION (1918) **IV–404a**
Monte Albán (Mex.) IV–327b
MONTE CASSINO (It.) **IV–404a**; III–235b; VII–338b
Montecristi VII–93b
Montegny, Jolliet de (expl.) III–329a
Montenegrins III–339a
MONTEREY (Calif.) **IV–404b**; I–350a; II–461a; III–264b; VI–364b
architecture I–163a
Bear Flag Revolt I–280a
Carmelo River I–455b
exploration I–330a
historic properties IV–472a
Mexican War IV–324a, 324b
navy postgraduate school V–24b
ranchos del rey VI–45b
salmon fisheries VI–201a
Walker expedition VII–220a
Monterey (Tenn.) I–232b
Monterey, Bay of I–405a
Monterey State Historic Park IV–472a
Monterrey (Mex.) I–375a; VI–274b
MONTERREY, BATTLES OF (1846) **IV–404b**; IV–324a
Montesquieu, Baron de, Charles de Secondat (law., philos.) II–4b; VI–391a, 396a,b
liberty IV–142a,b
prisons V–415a
separation of powers V–384b–85a
Montevideo (Uru.) V–106a, 107b, 205a
Montevideo, Treaty of (1960) VI–346a
Montevideo Conference (1933) III–456b, 463a
Montevideo Convention on Extradition (1933) VII–112b
Montezuma VII–370b
Montezuma Castle National Monument V–217b
Montfaucon (Fr.) IV–319b
Montgolfier brothers I–248a
Montgomerie, John (gov.) I–332b; II–107b
Montgomery (Ala.) II–348b; VI–137a, 433a
Afro-Americans I–25b, 29a
Battle of Mauvilla IV–277a
bus boycott I–30b; VI–433a
Camp Sheridan I–435a
civil rights movement II–55a, 56b–58b; V–182a, 265b
Civil War VII–113b
Confederacy I–71b; IV–404b–05a
constitutional convention

MONTGOMERY (cont.)
(1861) II–159b–60a
Freedom Riders III–107a
railroads VI–36b
Southern Commercial Convention VI–352a
state capital I–308b
Montgomery, Archibald (off.) III–117a
Montgomery, Bernard L. (off.) I–380a; VII–340a
Battle of Kasserine Pass IV–32b
Normandy invasion V–110b; VII–339a,b
North African campaign V–113a
Salerno VI–199b
Sicilian campaign VI–284b
Montgomery, Fort (N.Y.) II–191b; III–275b; VI–166a
Montgomery, James (off., pol.) II–303b; VI–270a
Montgomery, J. E. (nav. off.) IV–302a
Montgomery, J. J. (av.) I–232b
Montgomery, John B. (off.) VI–209b
Montgomery, Richard (off.) VI–136b
death I–193b, 436a
Fort Chambly VI–191a
invasion of Canada I–346a, 435b; IV–86b
Montreal IV–405b
Montgomery, Robert (col.) I–239a
MONTGOMERY CONVENTION (1861–62) **IV–404b**; VI–251a
Montgomery County (Ga.) V–315b
Montgomery County (Ohio) IV–420b
Montgomery County (Va.) III–469b
Montgomery Improvement Association II–57a; VI–351b
Montgomery Ward II–371b; IV–225a
Monthly American Journal of Geology and Natural Science VI–237a
Monthly Catalog of United States Government Publications III–203b
Monthly Miscellany, or Memoirs for the Curious V–180a
MONTICELLO (Va.) **IV–405a**; I–163a; III–495a; IV–84a, 316b
Mont Kemmel (Belg.) VII–366b
Montmagny, Charles Huault de (col. gov.) V–156b
Montmorency River VI–1a; VII–115a
Montojo y Pasarón, Patricio (nav. off.) IV–239b
Montojoy Pasarón Patricio (nav. off.) VI–361b
Montour (mestiza). *See* Queen Ester
Montreal (Can.) III–209a
American evacuation I–436a
citrus industry II–43b
exploration I–440a
Fort La Galette IV–85a
Fox Indians III–89a
French and Indian War II–267a, 382a; III–116b, 117a; VI–1b
French–Indian relations IV–83b
fur trade I–341a; III–141b–42a,b, 142a, 403a; VI–192b; VII–306b–07a
Great Lakes shipping III–218b
hockey III–286b, 287b
Jolliet at IV–7a
King George's War IV–46b
King William's War IV–49b
La Salle's seigniory IV–109a
Leisler Rebellion V–84b
New York Colony V–85a,b
railroads VI–33b, 35b; VII–172b
revolutionary war IV–86b; VI–191a
Richelieu River VI–136b
Saint Lawrence River VI–192a,b
Saint Lawrence Seaway VI–192b
skiing VI–298a
U.S. trade VI–149a
War of 1812 I–502a
War of 1812 III–118a; IV–406a
MONTREAL, CAPTURE OF (1760) **IV–405b**; III–89b
MONTREAL, CAPTURE OF (1775) **IV–405b**; I–193b, 435b–36a
MONTREAL, WILKINSON'S EXPEDITION AGAINST (1813–14) **IV–406a**; II–35a; III–167b; VII–234b
Montreal Royals (baseball) I–271a
Montresor, John (off.) II–458a
Montrose (Colo.) VII–137b
Montrose (Nebr.) VII–227b
Montross, N. E. II–104a
Monts, Sieur de, Pierre du Guast (expl.) I–6a, 492b; IV–225b; V–369b; VI–189a
Mont-Saint-Michel and Chartres IV–163a
Monuments, national. *See* Parks, National, and National Monuments
Moody, Dwight Lyman (evangelist) II–466a
Moody, Paul (inv.) VII–43a
Moody, William H. (jur.) III–343a; VI–446a
Moon
communication satellites II–143a
Depot of Charts and Instruments V–12a
exploration III–502b
mapping III–164b
space missions I–210a,b
studies I–212b; IV–460a–b
Mooney, Thomas J. (labor leader). *See* Mooney Case
Mooney, William (pol.) VI–459a
MOONEY CASE IV–406a; VII–117b
MOON HOAX (1835) **IV–406b**
MOON LANDING (1969) **IV–406b**; I–63b; III–410b; IV–460a; V–268b–69a
Moons, artificial II–143a
MOONSHINE IV–407b; I–339a
Moore, Addison W. (philos.) V–386b
Moore, Alfred (jur.) VI–445a
Moore, Archie (pugilist) V–423a
Moore, Clement C. (au.) I–335b
Moore, Douglas (comp.) IV–439a
Moore, Edwin W. (nav. off.) VII–41b
Moore, Ely (labor leader) IV–62a
Moore, H. (inv.) I–34b–35a
Moore, Henry (col. gov.) IV–33a; VI–165b
Moore, H. T. (nav. off.) IV–20b
Moore, James (col. gov.) III–170a; VI–348b–49a; VII–130b
Apalache massacre I–143a
Battle of Ayubale I–238b
Fort Marion IV–253b
Moore, J. H. I–355a
Moore, John Bassett (au.) IV–5b
Moore, Marianne (poet) IV–164a
Moore, Stanford (chem.) I–304a; V–100a
Moore, Thomas (farmer) III–55a
Moore, Thomas (poet) II–353a; V–152a
Moore and Schley V–208b
Moorefield (W.Va.) III–332b
Moore-McCormack Lines IV–312a
Moore School of Electrical Engineering II–153a, 155a; V–249b
MOORE'S CREEK BRIDGE, BATTLE AT (1776) **IV–407b**; V–115b
Mooresville (Ala.) II–432a
Moors II–443b
Moor's Indian Charity School II–292b
Moos, Malcolm (pres. aide) VII–132b
Moose I–80a; III–51a, 358b; IV–231b; VII–346a, 357b
Moose, Loyal Order of VI–252b
Mooseburgers III–53b
Moose Lodge #107 v. *Irvis* (1972) III–86b
Moqui (Indians) IV–367b
Mora County (N.Mex.) VII–145a
Moraga, José Joaquin (off.) I–141a
Morales, Juan Ventura (col. offi.) IV–196b
Moral Man and Immoral Society VI–83a
MORALS IV–408a; VII–312a
censorship I–478b
crime II–261a
education II–397a
family system II–485b–87a
Gilded Age III–180b
Ku Klux Klan IV–58b
liquor laws IV–158b
Mann Act IV–240a
manners IV–240b
McGuffey's Readers IV–213a
miscegenation IV–362b
Prohibition V–429b
prostitution V–437b
sumptuary laws VI–440a
temperance movement VII–22a
tithingmen VII–64b
venereal disease VII–169a
MORAL SOCIETIES IV–409a
Moral treatment (med.) IV–305a–b
Moran, Thomas (paint.) V–192a
MORATORIUM, HOOVER (1931) **IV–409a**; I–245b; IV–117b; VI–88a; VII–332a
Moravia III–339b, 340a; IV–409b
MORAVIAN BRETHREN IV–409b
Bethlehem VII–258a
Delaware Indians II–321a
foreign mission IV–366a
Gnadenhutten III–187b
immigration to U.S. III–335a
Indian missions III–385b
North Carolina I–293a
Pennsylvania I–293a; VI–76b
pietism V–311a
pottery V–379a,b
Schoenbrunn mission VI–226a
Yadkin River VII–350a
Moravian Church in America (Northern Province) IV–409b, 409b
Moravian Indians VII–46a
Moravian Massacre (1782). *See* Gnadenhutten
Moravian Pottery V–379b
Moravian Town, Battle at (1813). *See* Thames, Battle of

Mordkin, Mikhail (dancer) II–288b
More, Nicholas III–111b
More, Paul Elmer (philos.) II–189b; IV–164a
More, Thomas (states.) VI–80b
Moreau, Basil Anthony (cler.) III–293a
Morehead (Ky.) IV–259b
Morehead, Charles S. (pol.) I–196a; VI–274b
Morehead City (N.C.) V–116b
Morehead v. *Tipaldo* (1936) IV–353a
Morehouse College I–28b; IV–46a
Morelos Dam II–130a
Moretum II–455b
Morey, Samuel (inv.) VI–408b
MOREY LETTER IV–409b
Morfit, Henry M. IV–410a
MORFIT'S REPORT (1836) **IV–410a**
Morfontaine, Treaty of. *See* Convention of 1800
Morgan, Arthur E. (eng., educ.) V–45a; VII–28a
Morgan, Charles (ind.) II–91a
Morgan, Daniel (off.) I–385a; II–251a; III–108a
  Battle of Guilford Courthouse VI–351b
  rangers VI–46b
  sharpshooters VI–269b
Morgan, Edmund (hist.) III–283a
Morgan, Edwin D. (pol.) V–87a
Morgan, Fort (Ala.) III–78b; IV–382b
Morgan, Fort, seizure of. *See* Mobile Bay, Battle of
Morgan, George (Indian agent) I–278b; III–147b, 400b; V–322a
  New Madrid V–58b
Morgan, George Washington (off.) II–272b
Morgan, Harcourt A. (entom., educ.) VII–28a
Morgan, Helen M. (hist.) III–283a
Morgan, Henry (buccaneer) I–374a; V–203a
Morgan, James (mfr.) III–183a
Morgan, John (physic.) II–10a; IV–283a; V–251b
Morgan, John Hunt (off.). *See* Morgan's Raids
Morgan, Jonathan (inv.) IV–274a
Morgan, J. P. (fin.) III–466a
  art collection II–104b
  bank failures I–256b
  book collection II–109a
  Edison Light Company II–414a
  fortune III–79b
  Niagara Falls power V–92a
  Northern Securities Company V–119a
  panic of 1893 V–426a
  panic of 1907 III–6a; V–208b
  private banks I–263b
  Pujo Committee V–462a
  U.S. gold supply IV–410a
  U.S. Steel IV–399a; V–428a
Morgan, J. P., and Company III–64b, 79b; VII–222b
Morgan, Julia (landscape arch.) IV–96b
Morgan, Junius S. (banker) III–79b, 466a
Morgan, Kemp VI–458b
Morgan, Lewis H. (law., ethnol.) I–128b; III–476a
Morgan, Morgan ap VII–281a
Morgan, T. H. (zool.) III–157b, 158a; V–100a
Morgan, William (Freemason) III–109a; IV–410b
  See also Morgan Trials
Morgan, Willoughby (off.) IV–223b
MORGAN–BELMONT AGREEMENT (1895) **IV–410a**
Morgan Library II–109b
MORGAN'S RAIDS (1862–64) **IV–410a**; I–376a; II–37b, 222b
Morganton (N.C.) VII–219b
MORGAN TRIALS (1827–31) **IV–410b**; I–132a
Morgan v. *Tennessee Valley Authority* (1940) VI–85a
Morgan v. *United States* (1885) VII–42b
Morgenthau, Henry, Jr. (law., dipl.) VI–371b
  gold standard IV–234a
  lend–lease IV–134b
  New Deal V–43b
  savings bonds VI–222b
  World War I relief VII–330a
Morin, Relman (jour.) I–207b
Morison, Robert (bot.) I–348b
Morison, Samuel Eliot (hist.) V–21b
Morley, E. W. (chem.) I–218b
MORMON, BOOK OF IV–410b; I–397b; II–334a; IV–116b
MORMON BATTALION IV–411a; III–179b; VII–217b
Mormon Community II–147a
MORMON EXPEDITION (1857–58) **IV–411a**; I–363a; IV–249b; V–177a; VII–107a, 161b
MORMON HANDCART COMPANIES IV–411b
Mormon Road VII–289a
Mormons
  campaign of 1856 I–421a
  Council Bluffs II–241b
  Danites II–291b
  Fort Bridger I–363a
  Gunnison massacre III–235a
  Idaho III–328b
  Illinois II–496a
  Indian raids I–281a
  irrigation III–477a
  Missouri II–496a
  Mountain Meadows massacre IV–421b
  Nauvoo settlement V–8a
  prairie schooner V–389b
  Salt Lake City II–45b
  settlements IV–339a
  Stansbury exploration VI–385a
  Utah III–213b, 221a; VII–100b, 284a
  Western Reserve VII–275a
  See also Latter–Day Saints, Church of Jesus Christ of
Mormon schools II–114a
Mormon Tabernacle. *See* Tabernacle, Mormon
MORMON TRAIL IV–411b; I–453a; V–330b; VI–154a, 160b; VII–161b
MORMON WAR (1844–46) **IV–412a**; V–8a
Morning Light (warship) IV–20b
Morningside Heights (N.Y.C.) III–254b
Morningstar (commune) II–142b
Morning star ceremony V–230b
Morningstar East (commune) II–142b
Morocco II–345b; III–97a
  Algeciras Conference I–85b
  extraterritoriality II–479a
  France v. *United States* (1959) III–453a
  Madrid Conference IV–221a
  Perdicaris affair V–261b
  Treaty of Peace and Friendship VII–111a
  Treaty of Versailles VII–173a
  tribute I–266a; VII–120a
  U.S. air bases I–149b
  World War II V–21b, 112b
Moros (people) V–282a
Morotai VII–337a
Morphine II–260a, 373b–74a; IV–449b
Morrill, Justin S. (pol.). *See* Morrill Act (1862)
Morrill, Lot M. (pol.) IV–6a
MORRILL ACT (1862) **IV–412a**; I–33a, 47a; II–115a, 399a, 447b; III–52b, 211b; IV–93b; VII–177a
  Cornell University II–227a
  land grants for education IV–97b
  military training VI–98b
  scientific education VI–232a
  state universities VII–156a–b
Morrill Act (1890) II–115a, 227b, 399a
Morrill County (Neb.) II–25b
Morrill Tariffs VI–466b–67a
Morris, Charles (nav. off.) III–247b
Morris, Charles D. (class.) IV–2a
Morris, George Anthony (mfr.) III–183b
Morris, George Pope (au.) VII–155b
Morris, George S. (philos.) IV–2b
Morris, Gouverneur (states.) I–366b; III–159b
  Constitution II–193a, 194a, 203b
  executive agent to London II–471a
  landholdings IV–98b
  ministry to France IV–402a–b
  New York constitution VI–390b
  Nootka Sound affair II–342b
Morris, I. P., Company V–92a
Morris, John A. (fin.) IV–195b
Morris, Lewis (states.) II–308a; VII–368a
Morris, Nelson (mer.) VI–414b
Morris, Richard (jur.) VII–116b
Morris, Robert (fin., states.) III–180b
  Bank of North America I–255a, 260b; III–427b; V–277b
  bimetallism I–301a
  coinage II–95a
  Commercial Committee II–137b
  Declaration of Independence II–305b
  Dutch loans II–382b
  Federalist party III–4a
  federal mint IV–359b, 394a
  Illinois and Wabash Company III–331a
  landholdings IV–98b, 99a
  land speculation V–88b
  North American Land Company V–113a
  Pine Barren speculations V–315b
  Plan of 1776 V–323b
  profiteering VI–121a
  Pulteney purchase V–276b, 463b
  revolutionary war financing II–167a; VI–117b, 120b
Morris, William (poet, art.) I–163b; III–136a, 446a
Morris, Wright (au.) IV–165a
Morris and Company I–283b
Morrisania (N.Y.) II–249b; III–313a
Morris Canal I–127b, 442b; V–57b
  Boonton Iron Works I–337b
  locks I–443b
  Newark V–41b

MORRIS CANAL AND BANKING COMPANY **IV–412b**; II–255a
Morris County (Kans.) II–243a
Morris County (N.J.) I–337b
Morris Island VI–387a; VII–215b
Morrison, Frank (labor leader) I–374b
Morrison, William (fur trader) IV–159b; VI–195b, 196a
Morrison, William R. (pol.) VI–466b
Morrissey, Francis J. X. (jur.) IV–413a
Morrissey, John (boxer) III–150a
MORRISSEY NOMINATION (1965) **IV–413a**
Morristown (N.J.) *See* Morristown, Encampment at
MORRISTOWN, ENCAMPMENT AT IV–413a; II–321b; IV–1a; V–408b; VI–377a
  Fort Nonsense V–108a
  marines IV–251b
  Pennsylvania troop IV–445a
  Pennsylvania troop mutiny V–252b
Morris Turnpike V–57b
Morro Castle (Havana) I–355b
Morro Castle (steamer) II–349b–50a
Morrow, Dwight W. (dipl.) IV–328b; V–416a
Morrow, Jeremiah (pol.) III–295b
Morrow, Prince A. (physic.) V–438a
Morrow Board I–234a, 236a
Morrow Point Dam II–130a
Morse, Charles (bus.) V–208b
Morse, David A. (offi.) III–455a
Morse, Frances Clary II–100a
Morse, Jedidiah (cler., geog.) II–397a, 444a; VI–227a; VII–206a
  geography IV–413b
  Illuminati of New England III–332a
  temperance movement VII–22b
Morse, John T., Jr. (hist.) III–281b
Morse, O. M. (inv.) III–44a
Morse, Samuel F. B. (inv.) I–276a; V–188b, 190a
  daguerreotype II–279a
  telegraph I–119a; VII–18b
Morse, Sidney E. (inv.) I–462b
Morse Code VI–14b; VII–18b
MORSE GEOGRAPHIES **IV–413b**; II–444a; VI–227a
Mortality rate III–433a; IV–298b–99a
  frontier II–487a
  infants and children IV–274b, 276a
  maternal IV–275a, 276a
  See also Life Expectancy
Mortar (tool) II–386a
MORTARS, CIVIL WAR NAVAL IV–413b; III–478b
Môrtefontaine, Château (Fr.) II–215a
Mortgage Association, National V–456a
MORTGAGE RELIEF LEGISLATION IV–414a
  Frazier–Lemke Farm Bankruptcy Act III–100a
  Home Owners' Loan Act V–44a
  Minnesota Moratorium Case IV–358a
  savings and loan associations VI–221b
Mortgages
  building and loan association I–376b
  federal insurance III–310b–11a
  foreign investments III–63a, 65a,b
  Home Owners' Loan Corporation III–294a
  panic of 1929 V–209a,b
  taxation VII–11a
MORTIMER, FORT (N. Dak) **IV–415a**
Mortise–and–tenon joints I–377b
Morton, George (col.) IV–423b
Morton, John (surv.) II–308a
Morton, J. Sterling (agric.) I–154a; II–187b; VII–114a
Morton, Levi P. (pol.) I–424a; VII–179 (table)
Morton, Oliver P. (pol.) I–422b; V–32b
Morton, Rogers (sec. of int.) I–80b
Morton, Rose and Company III–64b
Morton, Samuel G. (physic.) I–128a,b
Morton, Thomas (adventurer) III–26b; IV–161a, 314b
Morton, William T. G. (dent.) I–119b; IV–285b; V–306b
Mosaics III–289b
Mosby, John S. (off.). *See* Mosby's Rangers
MOSBY'S RANGERS **IV–415b**; V–222a; VI–46b
Mosca Pass V–224b
Moscow (USSR)
  Orthodox church II–386b
  Seventh World Congress II–144b
  Sixth World Congress II–144b
  World War II V–11a
Moscow Art Theatre VII–50a
MOSCOW CONFERENCE OF FOREIGN MINISTERS (1943) **IV–415b**; I–361b; II–471b; V–378b
Moseley, Henry G. J. (phys.) V–298a
Moseley, William (pol.) III–39a
Moselle River (Fr.) VI–197a–b
Moses, Robert (offi.) V–89a
MOSES HIS JUDICIALS **IV–415b**; V–55a,b
Mose the Bowery Bhoy (char.) VII–47b
Mosher, Hugh (sol.) VI–374b
Moskogee Indians
  food III–51a
Mosley, Charles (watchmaker) II–78b
Mosquito IV–172a, 229b, 291a,b; VII–355b
Mosquito aircraft I–61b
Mosquito Coast (Nic.) IV–181b, 416a–b
MOSQUITO FLEET **IV–416a**
Mosquito Indians VI–378b
Mosquito Inlet (Fla.) V–66a
MOSQUITO QUESTION **IV–416a**; II–72b
Mössbauer, Rudolf (phys.) V–305b
MOST–FAVORED–NATION PRINCIPLE **IV–416b**; I–386a; III–113b; VI–468a; VII–88a, 109a, 112a
  China III–68b; IV–34b; V–22b
  Cushing's Treaty II–275a–b
  Jay's Treaty IV–402b
  reciprocal trade agreements VI–52a
  Sino–American Treaty II–27a
  Trade Expansion Act VI–469b–70a
Motard, Joseph (fur trader) VI–367a
"Moth" (dance) II–287b
Mother Bethel African Methodist Episcopal Church IV–443a
Mother Earth (jour.) I–116b
Mother Goose's Melodies I–335a
Mother Lode (Calif.) IV–178a
Mother of Us All (opera) IV–439a
Mothers' pension laws V–381a
Motherwell, Robert (paint.) II–105b
Motion
  electrical energy II–413a
Motion–and–time study III–408a
Motion Picture and Television Service V–432b
Motion Picture Patents Company IV–417b; V–292a
Motion Picture Producers and Distributors of America I–480a
MOTION PICTURES **IV–416b**; V–292a–b; VI–355b
  California I–407a
  celluloid IV–244b; V–328a
  censorship I–479b–80a; II–277a
  copyright II–224b
  cowboy songs II–250b
  crime II–262b
  dance II–290a
  development II–424b
  folklore III–49a
  Fort Lee IV–131b
  industry investigation I–314b
  Jewish participation IV–10b
  military photography V–293b
  rural areas VI–175b
  slang VI–300a
  theaters VII–49a
  trade association VII–92b
  U.S. Information Agency II–499a
  vaudeville VII–167b–68a
  World War II propaganda VII–333b
Motion Pictures, Catholic Office for. *See* National Catholic Office for Motion Pictures
Motley, John L. (hist., dipl.) III–281b; IV–163a
Moton, Robert Russa (educ.) VII–130b
Motor, battery–powered II–413a
Motor, domestic service II–417b
Motor, electric II–413a–15b, 418a, 419a–20a, 429b
Motor Carrier Act (1935) III–458a
Motorcycle racing II 245a
Motorcycles I–295a
Motor–generator sets II–224a
MOTOR TRUCK TRANSPORTATION **IV–419a**; VII–84a,b, 101b, 102a–b
  agriculture I–40a,b
  brewing I–362a
  freight mileage on VI–155b
  gasoline shortage VII–85a
  government regulation III–458b; V–459a
  Interstate Commerce Commission III–458a
  long–distance I–227b, 228b
  meat–packing IV–280b
  North Carolina V–116b
  public utilities V–456b
  railroad competition VI–22a
  refrigeration III–55b
  urban structure VII–159b
Motor Vehicle Air Pollution Act (1965) I–230a
Motor Vehicle Manufacturers Association I–227a
Motown Records IV–442b
Mott, John R. V–100a; VI–163b
Mott, Lucretia (ref.) VI–261b; VII–313b, 317a
Mott, S. G. (nat.) III–27a
Motto, U.S. II–455b; III–417a

Mottos, state VI–392a, 393–95 (table)
Mott Street (N.Y.C.) VII–23b
Moulthorpe, Reuben (art.) VII–262a
Moulton, F. R. (astron.) III–167a
Moulton, James T. II–99a
Moulton, Jeremiah (off.) V–111b
Moultrie, Fort (S.C.) VI–387a, 440b
MOULTRIE, FORT, BATTLE OF (1776) **IV–420a**
Moultrie, William (off.) I–496b, 498a; IV–420a
Mound-and-plaza complex I–157b; IV–370a,b
Mound City (gunboat) II–384a
Mound City (Ohio) III–300a; IV–421a
Mound City Group National Monument V–217b
MOUNDS AND MOUND BUILDERS IV–420b; I–128a; III–365a
Adena culture I–157a
American Bottom I–100b
Archaic culture II–386a
Cahokia I–402b
Great Serpent Mound III–222a
Hopewell culture I–157a; III–300a
Mississippi Valley I–166a; IV–370a,b
national monuments V–217b
Ohio Valley V–140a
paths III–387a
Poverty Point V–382b
Redstone Old Fort VI–65b
Southern Cult VI–353a
trails I–376a
Woodland Tradition VII–320a
Moundsville (W.Va.) III–77b
Moundville (Ala.) IV–370a; VI–352a
Mount, William Sidney (paint.) II–101b; V–189b, 190b, 191a
Mount Agamenticus I–32a
Mountain bluebird VI–393 (table), 394 (table)
Mountain dew I–339a
"Mountaineers are always free men" (motto) VI–395 (table)
Mountain goats V–217b
Mountain laurel VI–393 (table), 395 (table)
Mountain lion III–150a; VII–357b
MOUNTAIN MEADOWS MASSACRE (1857) **IV–421b**; VI–368a
MOUNTAIN MEN IV–422a; II–477a–b
Bowie knife I–355a
Colorado II–128a
coyote II–253a
explorations VII–271b
Fort Bonneville I–330a
fur trade III–143a–b; VII–103b, 104b
Green River III–227a
Green River knife III–227a
horses IV–444b
Idaho III–327b
New Mexico V–59b
revolutionary war IV–48a,b
Rocky Mountains VI–160b
Utah VII–161a,b
Willamette Valley VII–300a
Wyoming VII–345b
Mountain passes. *See* Passes, Mountain
Mountain sheep III–361a
Mountain State VI–395 (table)
Mount Airy (Richmond County, Va.) I–162a
Mount Alexander (Va.) IV–53a
Mount Cadillac IV–422b
Mount Calvary (Wis.) I–452a
Mount Defiance (N.Y.) VII–57a
MOUNT DESERT (Maine) **IV–422b**; IV–226a; V–446b
Mounted Volunteer Ranger companies I–475b
Mount George (Va.) IV–53a
Mount Gulian (N.Y.) II–38a
Mount Hope (Mass.) IV–47a
Mount Hope (N.Y.) III–197b
MOUNT HOPE (R.I.) **IV–422b**
Mount Independence (N.Y.) I–385a; VII–57a
Mount Lebanon (N.Y.) II–147a
Mount McKinley I–76a
Mount McKinley National Park V–217b, 218 (table)
Mount Olympus National Monument V–217a
Mount Pleasant (Ohio) III–162b; V–279a–b
Mount Pleasant, Fort (Md.) II–272a
Mount Rainier Act (1899) IV–98a
Mount Rainier National Park IV–98a; V–218 (table), 445b
Mount Rushmore National Memorial I–312b–13a
Mount Savage Rolling Mill VI–39b
Mount Union College (Ohio) I–272a
Mount Vernon (Ohio) III–156b; VII–164b
MOUNT VERNON (Va.) **IV–423a**; III–137b; IV–96b, 472a
Alexandria Conference I–85b
gardening III–151a,b
oats V–130a
preservation II–99a; V–392b
Mount Vernon Ladies' Association IV–423a; V–392b
MOUNT WASHINGTON, EARLY EXPLORATION OF IV–423a
Mount Wilson Observatory I–211b, 457a; V–131b
See also Hale Observatories
Mount Wollaston IV–314b
Moureau (N.Y.) VII–22a
MOURNERS' BENCH IV–423b; V–438b
Mourning pictures III–47a,b
Mourt, G. *See* Morton, George
***MOURT'S RELATION* IV–423b**
Mouse River II–284a
Mousteroid culture I–155b; II–84a
MOVERS IV–423b
Movies. *See* Motion Pictures
Movie star system IV–417b
Movie theaters II–262a; IV–417b, 418b
Movietone films IV–418a
Moving school II–394a; VI–226b
Mowat, Henry (off.) II–485b
Mower I–35a, 38a
MOWING MACHINE IV–424a
Mowrer, Paul Scott (jour.) V–74a
Moxon, Joseph (print.) V–410b–11a
Moyer, Charles H. (labor leader) II–94a; III–266b–67a
Moyer v. *Peabody* (1909) IV–258b
Moylan, Mary Ellen (dancer) II–288b
Moylan, Stephen (off.) I–467a
Moynihan, Daniel Patrick (pol.). *See* Moynihan Report
MOYNIHAN REPORT (1965) **IV–424b**; III–203b
Mozambique I–22a
"Mr. Madison's War." *See* War of 1812
MRS. O'LEARY'S COW IV–424b
MUCKRAKERS IV–424b; V–75a
New York City V–83b
pure food and drug movement V–466a, 467a
robber barons VI–157a
trust-busting III–443b–44a
Mudd, Samuel Arnold (physic.) IV–154b, 155a
Muddy Brook (Mass.) IV–47b
Muddy Pass V–225a
Mud-floods III–37b
Mud Fort IV–337b
Mud Island (Pa.) IV–337b
"MUD MARCH" (1863) **IV–425a**
Mudra, Bruno von (off.) I–491b
Muffs III–133b
MUGLER* v. *KANSAS (1887) **IV–425a**
MUGWUMPS IV–425b; I–424a; III–81a–b; IV–454b
Muhammad, Elijah (rel. leader) V–171a
Muhammad Speaks (news.) V–76a
Muhlenberg, Frederick A. C. (cler., pol.) II–174 (table); VI–368b
Mühlenberg, Henry Melchior (cler.) IV–206a; V–311a; VI–76b
Muhlenberg, William Augustus (cler.) II–455a
Muir, Charles H. (off.) V–147a
Muir, James (seaman) VI–186a
Muir, John (nat.) I–407a; IV–96a; VII–361b, 362a
Muir Woods National Monument V–217b
Mulberries III–151b
Mulberry Grove Plantation (Ga.) II–240a
Mulberry operation (1944) V–111a–b
MULCT LAW IV–425b
Mulde River II–407b
MULE IV–425b; III–303a, 304a; IV–103a, 169b
agriculture I–39b
Arkansas I–173b
army supplies I–192a
canals I–443b
caravans I–452a
cultivation III–255b
freighting IV–426a
Kearny's march to California IV–34a
Oregon caravans V–166a
overland freighting V–177b
prairie schooner V–389b
replacement by tractor IV–170a
Russell, Majors, and Waddell VI–176b
Santa Fe trade IV–377a
Santa Fe Trail VI–215a,b, 216a
stagecoach service V–178a
versus oxen V–179a
wagon trains VII–218a
Mule driver. *See* Mule Skinner
MULE SKINNER IV–426a
Muley saws VI–222b
Mulford, John (pol.) V–7b
Mullan, John (off.) IV–426a
MULLAN TRAIL IV–426a; IV–403a
Muller, H. J. (geneticist) III–157b, 159a; V–100a
Muller, Steven (educ.) IV–4a
Muller v. *Oregon* (1908) IV–68b; VII–213b
Mulligan, Gerry (mus.) IV–440b
Mulligan, J. A. (off.) IV–137a
Mulligan, James IV–426b
MULLIGAN LETTERS IV–426a
Mulliken, Robert S. (chem.) V–100a

Multinational corporations II–230b; III–66a,b; IV–75a, 75a; VII–85a
Multiple, independently targeted reentry vehicle (MIRV) IV–364a
Multiple–line insurance III–426b
Multiple–Use Mining Law (1955) III–76a
Multiple Use–Sustained Yield Act (1960) II–74a; III–76a
Multiplying machine I–396a
Mu meson V–302b
Mumford, Lewis (writ.) IV–164a; VI–86a
Mumford, L. Quincy (librarian) IV–148a
Mundt, Karl E. (pol.) VI–428b
Munfordville (Ky.) IV–42a, 426b
MUNFORDVILLE, CAPTURE OF (1862) **IV–426b**
Munger, Theodore T. (cler., theol.) VI–82a
Munich Conference (1938) V–48b, 259a; VI–285b
Municipal bonds II–213b, 457b
Municipal colleges II–114b
MUNICIPAL GOVERNMENT IV–426b; IV–171a,b, 172b
  balance of power VI–397b
  city councils II–44a
  city manager plan II–44b
  commission government II–137b
  food laws V–465b
  home rule II–294b
  housing III–309b–10b
  Iowa liquor law IV–425b
  licenses to trade IV–148a,b
  loyalty oaths IV–203a
  New York City V–82a,b
  political subdivisions V–349a
  public health VI–173b
  public schools II–396b
  public utilities IV–427b; V–458b
  recall VI–51a
  reform IV–429b
  ripper legislation VI–144b
  state relations VI–398a
  taxation VII–10b–11a, 10b–11b
  Washington, D.C. VII–245a–b
  woman's suffrage VII–315a
  women VII–317b
  zoning ordinances VII–370a
Municipalities
  daylight saving time option II–296b
  employment offices II–441b
MUNICIPAL OWNERSHIP IV–427b; III–203a
MUNICIPAL REFORM IV–429b; IV–427a–b, 427b–28a
Municipal warrants V–159b
MUNITIONS IV–429b
  Civil War II–65a, 67a–b, 69a, 313b
  congressional investigation V–35b
  industrial research III–408b
  industry investigation V–117b
  Latin–American wars IV–115b
  Lusitania sinking IV–205a
  Neutrality Act of 1939 V–38a
  Neutrality Acts of 1935–37 V–38a
  neutral rights V–38b
  profiteering V–426a
  prohibition of sales III–417a–b
  Sterling Iron Works VI–412a
  taxation VII–7a
  Tredegar Iron Works VII–113b
  War Industries Board VII–232a
  World War I II–314a; VII–326a, 327b, 331b
  zinc V–103a
Munitions Assignment Board VII–335a
Munitions Industry, Senate Special Committee Investigating the III–480a; IV–433b
Munn, Orson D. (pub.) VI–231a
Munn and Company VI–231a,b
Munn and Scott IV–434a
MUNN* v. *ILLINOIS (1877) **IV–434a**; II–430b; III–209b, 211a; V–456a, 457b; VI–21b, 22a
Munro, George P. (pub.) II–341b, 342a
Munro, William B. (pol. sci.) V–348b
Munsee (Indians) II–462b
Munsey, Frank A. (pub.) V–428a
Munsey's (period.) I–17b
Munson–Williams–Proctor Institute (Utica, N.Y.) III–137b
Münsterberg, Hugo (psych.) III–260a
Muon. *See* Mu meson
Mural painting V–191a–b
Murat, Joachim (k.) IV–449a
Murchison, Charles F. *See* Osgoodby, George
Murchison Letter. *See* Sackville–West Incident
Murder II–258a; VII–191b–92a
  capital punishment I–450a
  organized crime II–261a
"Murder Act" (1774) I–8a
MURDERING TOWN (Pa.) **IV–434b**
Murdock, George (anthrop.) I–129a
Murfree, Mary Nouailles (au.) IV–163a
MURFREESBORO, BATTLE OF (1862–63) **IV–434b**; II–271b; VII–34b, 127b
MURMANSK (USSR) **IV–435a**
  World War I I–158b
  World War II IV–313b
Muroc Dry Lake (Calif.) I–234b
Murphy, Charles Francis (pol.) I–343a; V–83b; VI–460a; VII–295a
Murphy, Frank (pol., jur.) I–300a; III–105a; IV–332a; V–284a; VI–446b
  commerce clause II–137a
  Japanese–American relocation III–491a
Murphy, G. C., and Company III–33a
Murphy, George (pol.) V–136a
Murphy, George M. (phys.) V–299b
Murphy, Henry C. I–333a; II–108b
Murphy, L. G. (off.) IV–155a
Murphy, Robert C. (zool.) V–337a
Murphy, William P. (physic.) V–100a
Murphy wagons V–389b
Murrah, Pendleton (gov.) VI–274b
Murray, G. R. (physic.) IV–305b
Murray, James (off.) III–117a; IV–405b
Murray, John (cler.) II–170b
Murray, John (col. gov.) *See* Dunmore, Lord
Murray, John (off.) IV–87a
Murray, Lindley (grammarian) VI–227b
Murray, Philip (labor leader) I–104b; IV–72b, 73a, 74b
Murray, William (land agent) III–331a
Murray, William Vans (dipl.) II–215a
Murray Hill (N.J.) I–287b; III–409b
Murray v. *Hoboken Land and Improvement Company* (1855) II–377a
Murthering Town. *See* Murdering Town
Musashi (battleship) IV–138b
Muscat II–479b
"Muscle cars" I–229b
Muscle Shoals (Ala.) III–146b; VI–146b
  hydroelectric power II–423a; V–98a–b
  nitrogen plant V–383b
  river navigation I–442b
  settlement VII–70b
  Tennessee River VII–27b
  Tennessee Valley Authority VII–27b–28a
MUSCLE SHOALS SPECULATION IV–435a; III–98b; VI–365b
Musconetcong Lake I–443b
Muscongus Bay VII–219b
Muscongus Patent III–120b
Muscular dystrophy III–249a
Muse: Susan Walker Morse (paint.) V–188b
Museum for the Arts of Decoration (N.Y.C.) II–222a
Museum of Comparative Zoology (Harvard) III–27b; IV–233a
  reptile study VI–90b
Museum of Early Southern Decorative Arts (Winston–Salem, N.C.) III–137b
Museum of Fine Arts (Boston) III–137b
Museum of History and Technology (Washington, D.C.) III–137b; IV–469a; VI–319b
Museum of Modern Art (N.Y.C.) I–165a; II–105a; III–136b, 137b; IV–237b
  Aldrich purchase fund II–106a
  Janis collection II–106b
  sculpture VI–244a
Museum of Natural History (Washington, D.C.) IV–469a
Museum of Science (Boston) VI–236a
Museum of the City of New York III–137b
Museum of the Confederacy (Richmond) VI–246a; VII–292b
MUSEUMS IV–435b; II–103a, 104a–b, 106b
  Boston II–100a–b
  corporation gifts II–107a
  Field Museum of Natural History III–19a
  Fort Snelling VI–323a
  Fraunces Tavern III–100a
  furniture collections III–137a–b
  Johnson Hall IV–4b
  mammals IV–232b–33a
  Manhattan IV–237b
  Museum of the Confederacy VII–292b
  National Museum IV–468b
  National Trust properties IV–472a
  natural history IV–232b–33a
  New York City II–100b; V–83b
  North Carolina V–116b
  Philadelphia II–101a; V–278a
  sculpture VI–243a,b, 244a
  Smithsonian Institution VI–319a–20a
  Texas VII–40b–41a
Mushashi (battleship) V–10b
MUSIC IV–437b
  "blues" IV–302a
  Chicago II–18a
  copyright II–224b–25a
  cowboy songs II–249b–50b
  electronic II–426b
  fiddle tunes III–18b

folklore III–49a
hymns III–326a
Nashville IV–453a
Newport Jazz Festival V–65b
printed II–454a
singing schools VI–293a
slang VI–300a
Tin Pan Alley VII–62b
vaudeville VII–167b
MUSIC, AFRO-AMERICAN IV–442b; I–25a; III–48b; IV–438a,b, 439b–40b; VI–307a
Gullah songs III–234a
Musical comedy VII–50b
Musical Fund Society of Philadelphia IV–437b
Musical plays II–290a
Music for the Theater (comp.) IV–439a
Musicians
unionization IV–65b
Musick, Edwin C. (av.) II–28a
Music Pass V–224b
Music schools I–250a
Musket II–130b; IV–430a,b, 432b, 433a; VI–125b, 127b
interchangeable manufacture III–441a,b
mass IV–272a
Muskhogean (lang.) II–51b–52b; III–308a; VI–259b
Muskhogee (Indians) II–52a
Muskie, Edmund S. (pol.) I–431b, 432a; IV–227a; VII–254b
Muskingum River IV–39b
canals IV–175a
Fort Harmar III–254b
Indian hostilities I–296a, 353b; II–381b
Marietta settlement IV–250b
public land sales III–257b–58a
Shawnee villages IV–212a
tomahawk claims VII–70a
Zane's grants VII–368a
MUSKINGUM RIVER CANAL ROUTE IV–443b
Muskingum Valley V–140a
Muskogean (lang.) I–86a; III–365b; IV–455a; VI–259b
Muskogee (Okla.) VI–262b–63a
Muskogee Convention (1905) V–149a
Muskogee Creek II–52b
Muskogee Indians I–288a
Musk-oxen III–358b
Muskrat III–133a, 142a, 150a, 402b; VII–105a
Muslims V–282a
Muslin II–371b
Mussels III–51b
MUSSEL SLOUGH INCIDENT (1880) **IV–444a**
Mussolini, Benito III–187a; V–124a; VI–284b
Mustang (auto) I–232a
Mustang (fighter plane) I–52a, 53b, 60a, 61b
Mustang (yacht) VII–349a
Mustang Creek III–50b
Mustang Desert IV–444b
MUSTANGS (horse) **IV–444b**; I–369a; III–302b, 303a; VI–364b
Muste, A. J. (pacifist) VI–14a
MUSTER DAY IV–445a; IV–345b
Mutations. *See* Genetics
Mutilation (col. punishment) V–465a
MUTINY IV–445a
Frémont, John C. IV–34a
La Salle's crew IV–110a
revolutionary war IV–1a; V–252b; VI–118a, 377a
slave I–28a, 114b
Somers VI–338a
MUTINY ACT OF 1765 IV–445b; I–297a
"Mutt and Jeff" (comic strip) V–72a
Mutton III–52a; IV–280a; VI–45a
Mutton sheep VI–273a
Mutual aid societies
free blacks III–102b
strikes VI–418b
Mutual Assurance Company III–430a
Mutual Assurance Society of Virginia III–430a,b
Mutual Benefit Insurance Company V–41b
Mutual benefit societies IV–293a, 294a
Mutual Defense Assistance Act (1949) VII–182b, 185a–b
Mutual Defense Treaty (Phil.) (1951) V–285a
Mutual Education and Culture Exchange Act (1961) III–130b
Mutual funds III–467a–b
check currency II–2b
investments II–2b
regulation III–466b
See also Investment Companies
Mutual insurance cooperatives II–220b
Mutual Life Insurance Company of New York III–426b, 432b, 433a
Mutual savings and loan associations II–220b
Mutual savings banks I–263b–64a; II–220b
Mutual telephone societies II–220b
"MY COUNTRY, 'TIS OF THEE" IV–446a; III–238b
Myer, Albert James (army surg.) VI–285b
Myer, Fort (Va.) II–343b, 346a
Myers, Abraham Charles (off.) II–163b
Myers, Fort (Fla.) VI–261a
Myers, Frank S. (offi.) IV–446b; VI–85a
Myers, Gustavus (au.) VI–157a
Myers, Myer (silversmith) VI–290a
MYERS* v. *UNITED STATES (1926) **IV–446a**; III–317a; V–472b; VI–85a
My Fair Lady (musical) IV–442a; VII–50b
MYITKYINA, BATTLE OF (1944) **IV–446b**; I–386b; IV–314a
My Lai massacre (1968) I–219b; V–74b; VII–184a, 191a
My Life on the Plains VI–215b
"My Lord Delaware's Bay" II–322a
Myoglobin IV–391b
"MY OLD KENTUCKY HOME" (song) **IV–447a**; VI–394 (table)
Myra (whaler) VI–186a
Myrdal, Gunnar (pol. sci.) II–56b
Myrtle Street Prison (Saint Louis) V–414a
Mysterious Stranger IV–163b
Mystic (Conn.) II–77b; IV–437a; V–261b
MYSTICISM IV–447b
Eastern Orthodoxy II–386b
Gortonites III–200b
Quakers III–123b
Western Reserve VII–275a
Mystic River I–382b
Myths
Chicora II–23a–b

N

NAACP. *See* National Association for the Advancement of Colored People
Nabesna (Indians) I–80b
Nabokov, Vladimir (au.) IV–165a
NACA. *See* National Advisory Committee for Aeronautics
Naches Pass VI–413a
Nacionalista party V–283b
Naco (Ariz.) II–83b
NACOGDOCHES (Tex.) **IV–448b**; IV–197b; VII–36b
Long expedition IV–184a
missions II–389a
neutral ground V–33b
Nolan expeditions V–101a
Na-Déné (lang.). *See* Athapascan
Nader, Ralph (consumer advocate) II–355a; IV–448b; V–468a
NADER'S RAIDERS IV–448b; VII–124b
Nadzab (N. Guin.) IV–83a
Nagasaki (Jap.)
atomic bomb I–215b; III–490b; IV–238b; V–21a; VII–191a, 341a
Nagoya (Jap.) III–490b; IV–351b
Nagumo, Chuichi (nav. off.) IV–336b
Nahant (Mass.) VII–29a
Nahuatl (lang.) V–410a
Nahum Keike (Salem, Mass.) II–365a
"Nail City." *See* Wheeling
Nails I–377b; III–252a, 413a,b, 470b, 472a
NAILS, TAX ON IV–448b; II–276a
Naismuth, James (educ.) I–272a,b
Naive art III–47a
Nakagawa, Kunio (off.) V–242b, 243a
Nakaidoklini (Indian) V–4a
Nakashima, George III–137a
Naked and the Dead IV–164b
Nakota (Indians) II–283a
NAM. *See* National Association of Manufacturers
Nambe (N.Mex.) III–367b; V–459b
Namquit Point (R.I.) III–153b
Namur Island IV–257b
Nancarrow, John (eng.) VI–409a
Nancy (brig) VI–128a
"Nancy Dawson" (song) VII–352a–b
Nanfan, John (col. offi.) III–476a
Nankeens II–28b
Nanking (China) V–205b
Nanking, Treaty of (1842) II–28b
Nansemond Point (Va.) II–253b
Nansemond Stream II–353a
Nantasket Beach (Mass.) IV–315a
Nanticoke (Indians) VII–223b
Nanticoke River VI–149b
NANTUCKET (Mass.) **IV–449a**
candlemaking VI–372b
colonists I–446b
Duke of York's proprietary VII–359a
exploration I–96b
whaling III–413a; VII–285a,b
Napalm I–219b; V–237a; VII–191a
Napa Valley (Calif.)
spa VI–100b
Naphthalene III–421a
Naples (It.)
World War II I–141a; III–235b; IV–404a; VII–338b
NAPLES, AMERICAN CLAIMS ON IV–449a

Napoleon I (emp.) III–135a, 462a
British Levy IV–135b
Code Napoléon II–91b
Convention of 1800 II–215a; III–96a
economic decrees IV–449b
exile I–492a
Franco–American relations III–96b
Louisiana I–114a; III–467b; IV–193b, 196a–97a; V–62a
Naples claims IV–449a
Nonintercourse Act V–105a
Peninsular War III–231a
prize cases III–98a
Spanish–American relations VI–359b
submarines V–8a
sugar beet industry I–285a
Treaty of San Ildefonso VI–211a, 363b
Napoleon III (emp.) I–92a; III–97a
field artillery IV–431a
Mexico IV–325b, 326a, 328a–b, 361a
monitors IV–397a
Monroe Doctrine II–65b
Nicaraguan canal project V–94b
U.S. Civil War II–62a, 162a; IV–35a
"Napoleon" gun IV–431a
Napoleonic exiles I–492a
Napoleonic Wars (1803–15) II–388b; III–67b–68a, 234a; VI–294a; VII–233a,b
blockades I–321a; II–446b
British orders in council V–162a
economic warfare VI–104b–05a
foreign trade VII–87a
French Decrees III–118b
habeas corpus III–237a
Loyalist veterans VI–130b–31a
neutrality III–455b; V–34a,b
neutral rights V–39a
Rule of the War of 1756 VI–169a
Russia VI–177b
spoliation claims III–121b
textile industry VI–133a
U.S. trade I–245a, 496b–97a; II–436a
NAPOLEON'S DECREES **IV–449b**; II–436b, 437a; III–118b, 121b; V–162a; VI–104b–05a; VII–233a,b
Narcissistic dance II–290b
Narcotics, Bureau of V–468b; VII–108a
Narcotics and Dangerous Drugs, Bureau of V–468b
NARCOTICS TRADE AND LEGISLATION **IV–449b**; II–258b, 262b; V–276a; VII–312b
Bureau of Narcotics and Dangerous Drugs IV–22a
Customs Service II–277b
deportation of violators II–333a
East India trade II–388b
foreign intelligence III–439b
ghetto distribution II–262b
investigative methods II–427b
Office for Drug Abuse Law Enforcement IV–22a
Office of National Narcotics Intelligence IV–22a
opium I–201b; IV–34b
organized crime II–259b–60a, 261a, 262a–63a
political corruption II–232a
See also Drug Addiction; Tobacco and Narcotics, American Indian
Narraganset (Indians) I–380b; III–223a, 367a; IV–451b; VI–271b
Aquidneck Island I–149a
King Philip's War IV–47a,b; VI–132a
land sales I–213a
Pequot War V–261b
Narragansett (ship) V–22b
NARRAGANSETT BAY **IV–451b**; VI–131b; VII–347a
Aquidneck Island I–149a
exploration I–96b
King's Province IV–48b
revolutionary war III–117b
Shawomet VI–271b
smuggling III–153b
Narragansett colony
dairy industry II–279b
Narragansett Country. *See* King's Province
Narragansett pacer III–303b; IV–451b
NARRAGANSETT PLANTERS IV–451b
Narrative and Critical History of the Americas III–282b
Narrative painting V–188a,b
Narrow construction (Constitution) II–327a
NARROWS (N.Y.) **IV–452a**; IV–83b
Narváez, Pánfilo de (expl.). *See* Narváez Expedition I–71a
NARVÁEZ EXPEDITION (1528–36) **IV–452a**; II–43a, 184a
Alabama I–71a
Florida I–96a, 399b; III–38a
Franciscans III–94a
NASA. *See* National Aeronautics and Space Administration
Nash, Thomas (clockmaker) II–77b
Nashborough (Tenn.) *See also* Nashville
Nashborough, Fort (Tenn.) IV–452b
Nash–Kelvinator I–229a
NASHOBA (Tenn.) **IV–452b**
Nash Rambler (auto) I–229b
NASHVILLE (Tenn.) **IV–452b**; VI–149b, 340b, 356a
barnstorming I–268b
Chickasaw Treaty II–23a
Civil War IV–375a, 434b–35a; VI–26b, 278b, 377a; VII–261b
Confederate Veteran VII–150a
Cox Insurrection II–252a
government IV–172b
Henderson Land Company III–271b
Hermitage III–273b
Ku Klux Klan IV–58a
music IV–441b
Natchez Trace III–387b; IV–455a, 456a
race riot I–31b
railroads I–9b; VI–34b
settlement II–274a
southern rights convention IV–453b
Southwest Point VI–357b
state centennial VII–27a
steamboats VI–150a
Tennessee Cumberland Road II–273b
United Daughters of the Confederacy VII–150b
Nashville (warship) V–204a; VII–26a
NASHVILLE, BATTLE OF (1864) **IV–453a**; II–62b; III–98b, 298a; VII–26b
Nashville, Chattanooga and Saint Louis Railroad IV–453b
NASHVILLE AND CHATTANOOGA RAILROAD **IV–453b**
NASHVILLE CONVENTION (1850) **IV–453b**; II–150a; IV–453a; VI–250b
Tarpley Letter VII–1a
Union Rights party VII–148a
Naskapi (Indians) III–366b
Nason, A. W. (metal.) VI–292b
Nason, Thomas (art.) VII–319b
Nassau (Bah.)
adventurers I–93b
Civil War I–292a; II–162b; VI–376b
Creole slave case II–257b
Encomium slave case II–443b
Hermosa case III–273b–74a
slave mutiny I–28a
NASSAU, FORT (N.J.) **IV–454a**; V–42b
Nassau, Fort (N.Y.) II–383a
Nassau County (N.Y.) III–271b; IV–185b, 186a
Nassau Hall (Princeton Univ.) V–408b
NASSAU PACT (1962) **IV–454a**
Nasser, Gamal Abdel (states.) I–149b–50a; III–482a
Nast, Thomas (cartoonist). *See* Nast Cartoons
NAST CARTOONS **IV–454a**; I–464b; III–257a; V–73a; VI–459b–60a
NATAQUA, PROPOSED TERRITORY OF **IV–454b**
NATCHEZ (Indians) **IV–455a**; III–367a
architecture I–166b
burial III–376a
enslavement III–401a
Fort Rosalie IV–455a; VI–164a
fur trade III–143b
Jesuit missions III–499b
Louisiana warfare IV–193a
Mississippi IV–368a
mounds IV–421a
Natchitoches attack IV–456b
status ranking I–288a
NATCHEZ (Miss.) **IV–455a**; VI–340b; VII–181b
bargemen I–267b
boundaries IV–456a
Bourbon County I–354a
colonial land grants IV–93a
Cox Insurrection II–252a
De Soto expedition II–336b
Dunbar's expedition II–381a
Forman's Colony III–77b
Fort Adams I–9b
Fort Panmure V–210b
Fort Rosalie VI–164a
gambling I–314b; III–149b
Guion's expedition III–232b
Holston exploration III–292b
Long's Texas expedition IV–184a
mineral springs IV–350a
Mississippi Gazette V–70b
Natchez Trace III–387b; IV–456a
Nolan expeditions V–101a
revolutionary war VI–130a, 365b; VII–303a
Saint Stephens VI–197b
settlement I–462a; III–171a; IV–368a
Spain II–432a; VI–356b; VII–270a
steamboats IV–374a; V–63a; VI–148b
Three Notch Road VII–54b
trading post VII–95b
Natchez (steamboat) VI–407a,b
NATCHEZ, TREATY OF (1790) **IV–456a**
NATCHEZ CAMPAIGN OF 1813 IV–456a
Natchez country II–33a

Natchez District (Miss. Terr.) IV–456a
NATCHEZ TRACE **IV–456a**; III–146b, 387b; IV–455a
Bayou Pierre I–279a
flatboatmen III–35b
Fort Adams I–9b
piracy IV–263a
Natchez Trace National Parkway IV–456b
"Natchez Under the Hill" (song) III–19a
Natchitoch (Indians) IV–456b
NATCHITOCHES (La.) **IV–456b**; III–108a, 119a, 235b; IV–197b
Civil War VI–63a, 182a
Fort Jesup III–501b
Fort Towson VII–81b
French in I–48b
Indian factory II–480a
Los Adaes garrison IV–189a
neutral ground V–33b
Neutral Ground Agreement VII–36b
Pike's expedition V–312a
Saint-Denis' expedition VI–189b
steamboats VI–65a
trading post VII–95b
Nation (news.) VI–157a
Nation, Carrie (ref.) III–261b; IV–27a
Nation, credit of the II–256a–b
National Academy of Design V–188b, 191b, 192a
National Academy of Engineering II–449a; IV–457b
NATIONAL ACADEMY OF SCIENCES **IV–457a**; I–98a; II–11a, 449a; VI–238a,b
aeronautics research IV–458a
conservation II–188a
National Advisory Cancer Council IV–287b
NATIONAL ADVISORY COMMISSION ON CIVIL DISORDERS **IV–457b**; I–31b; VI–9a
National Advisory Commission on Criminal Justice Standards and Goals V–417b, 418a
National Advisory Commission on Intergovernmental Relations III–212a
NATIONAL ADVISORY COMMITTEE FOR AERONAUTICS **IV–458a**; I–233b; IV–106a, 459a; VII–327b
aircraft development I–51a, 52a
"area rule" I–235a
jet propulsion I–234b
National Aeronautics and Space Act (1958) IV–459a
NATIONAL AERONAUTICS AND SPACE ADMINISTRATION **IV–458b**; I–235a; II–498b; III–410b; IV–471a; VI–159b; VII–196a
Air Force I–63b
astronaut training I–209b
Cape Canaveral III–40a
information retrieval VI–233a
Jet Propulsion Laboratory III–502a,b
Langley Aeronautical Laboratory IV–106b
lunar landing I–210a
medical research IV–292b–93a
National Advisory Committee for Aeronautics IV–458b
satellites I–212b; II–143a
scientific education VI–232a–b
weather forecasting VII–264b
National Aeronautics and Space Council II–498a
National Agricultural Library IV–145b
National Air and Space Museum VI–319b
National American Woman Suffrage Association III–91b, 92a; VII–312b
National anthem. *See* "Star-Spangled Banner"
National Anti-Tuberculosis Association IV–304a
National Apprenticeship Act (1937) I–148b
National Archives Act (1934) III–281a
National Archives and Records Service I–106a, 168a; II–498b; III–284a
National Army II–367a
camps and cantonments I–434a
NATIONAL ASSOCIATION FOR THE ADVANCEMENT OF COLORED PEOPLE **IV–460b**; I–30b; II–55a, 56b, 57b, 58a–b; III–438a, 503a; V–93a,b; VI–352a
black intelligentsia IV–166b
Crisis V–76a
lobbying IV–171a
mob violence IV–208a,b
records III–284b
right of assembly I–204b
National Association of Baseball Players I–270a
National Association of Business Economists I–394b
National Association of Dental Examiners II–330b
National Association of Dental Faculties II–330b
National Association of Finance Companies III–423a
National Association of Home Builders V–400b
National Association of Intercollegiate Athletics I–273a
National Association of Life Underwriters III–434a
NATIONAL ASSOCIATION OF MANUFACTURERS **IV–461b**; IV–67b; V–400b, 401a
lobbying IV–170b, 171a
social security V–46a
National Association of Milk Producers V–400b
National Association of Security Dealers III–467a
National Association of Social Workers VI–331a
National Association of Societies for Organizing Charities I–495a
National Association of State Highway Officials VI–402b
National Association of Wool Manufacturers VII–321b
National Audubon Society. *See* Audubon Society, National
National Automobile Chamber of Commerce I–227a
National Bakers Association V–128a
National Bank. *See* Bank of the United States
National Banking Act (1863) I–256a, 258b, 259b, 263b; II–2a, 73a, 74a, 464b; III–443a; IV–395a; VI–430b
National Banking System I–252a, 253a, 256a–57a, 259b; II–63b, 69a; III–6a, 101b; IV–395a; VI–370a, 427a
bank notes IV–461b
comptroller of the currency II–152b
Greenback movement III–224a
Ocala Platform V–132a
See also Banking
NATIONAL BANK NOTES **IV–461b**; I–252a; II–2a; III–6a, 192b, 194b, 245b, 251b; IV–395a,b
Greenback party VI–333b
National banks I–256a–57a
branch banking I–258b
charters II–229b
check currency II–2a
failures I–253a–b
note issues I–84a
political campaigns II–232b
reserve requirements I–252b
National Baptist Convention, U.S.A., Inc. I–265a
National Baptist Convention of America I–265a,b
National Baptist Publishing Board IV–453a
National Baptist Sunday School Publishing Board IV–453a
"National Barn Dance" (radio show) IV–441b
National Basketball Association I–273a
National Basketball Committee of the United States and Canada I–272b
National Basketball League I–273a
National battlefields. *See* Battlefields, National
National Better Business Bureau V–468b
National Bimetallic Union VI–288a
National Biscuit Company I–18a, 487a
National Bison Range VII–297a
National Bituminous Coal Commission III–232a
National Board of Fire Underwriters III–430b
National Board of Health IV–285b; V–447a–b
National Board of Review I–480a
National Bond and Investment Company of Chicago III–422b–23a
National Book Award I–335b
National Broadcasting Company VII–21b
National Brotherhood of Baseball Players I–270b
NATIONAL BUREAU OF ECONOMIC RESEARCH **IV–462a**; I–394a; V–425b
NATIONAL BUREAU OF STANDARDS **IV–462a**; II–87b, 135a; III–408b; V–295a
Central Radio Propagation Laboratory II–88b
computer development II–156a
dentistry II–331b
National Business League I–309b
National Cancer Institute IV–287b, 465a
National Capital Park and Planning Commission VII–246b
National Capital Planning Association VII–246a
National Cash Register Company I–396a, 397a; II–154b
National Catholic Education Association I–468b
National Catholic Office for Motion Pictures I–480a
National Catholic Rural Life Conference I–469a
National Catholic War Council I–469b
National Catholic Welfare Conference I–469b
National Catholic Welfare Council VII–330b
National cemeteries. *See* Cemeteries, National
National Center for Earthquake Research III–164b
National Child Labor Committee II–24b; IV–67a
National Christian Association I–132b–33a
National Citizens' Alliance II–42a

National City Bank of New York I–257a; III–79b, 240a, 466a
National Civic Federation IV–67a; V–401a
National Civil Service League II–59b; V–228a
National Collection of Fine Arts VI–319b
National Collegiate Athletic Association I–272b, 273a
National Commission on Accreditation for Corrections V–417b–18a
National Commission on Law Observance and Enforcement. *See* Wickersham Commission
National Commission on the Causes and Prevention of Violence VII–192a
NATIONAL COMMITTEE IV–462b; II–409b; V–223b
National Committee for a Sane Nuclear Policy V–237a; VII–236b
National Committee for Mental Hygiene III–325b; IV–304a, 304a, 306a,b
National Conference of Catholic Bishops I–469b
National Conference of Commissioners on Uniform State Laws I–153b; III–423b; VI–399a–b, 402b
National Conference of Editorial Writers V–77b
NATIONAL CONGRESS OF AMERICAN INDIANS IV–463a; IV–464a; V–210b
National Congress on Penitentiary and Reformatory Discipline (1870) VI–68a
National Conservation Commission II–187b
National Consumers' League IV–67a
National Convention of Insurance Commissioners VI–402b
National conventions. *See* Conventions, Party Nominating
National Cordage Company V–208a
National Council for the Prevention of War VII–236b
National Council of Catholic Laity I–469b
National Council of Catholic Men I–469b
National Council of Catholic Women I–469b
National Council of Churches II–353a, 387a; IV–206a; VI–79b
National Council of Negro Women III–504a
National Council on Crime and Delinquency II–263b
National Council on Public Polls V–454a
National Crime Information Center II–503b
National Currency Act (1863). *See* National Bank Act
National Dairy Products II–282a
National Deaf-Mute College III–248a
National debt. *See* Debt, Public
National defense. *See* Defense, National
National Defense Act (1916) V–138b
National Defense Act (1916) I–186a, 188b; IV–343b, 384a, 463b; V–391a; VI–60b, 98b; VII–230a, 325a, 326a
National Defense Act (1920) I–177a, 186a, 189a; IV–343b, 463b; VII–208a
National Defense Committee
Manhattan Project IV–238a
National Defense Education Act (1958) II–115a, 401a, 448a; IV–145b; VI–328b
National Defense Mediation Board IV–73a
National Defense Research Committee V–137a; VII–334a
National Democratic party I–425a; II–75a; III–189a; VII–53a
National Dental Association II–330a
NATIONAL EDUCATION ASSOCIATION IV–463a; II–389b–400b; IV–76a
National Electric Light Association II–419b
National Emblem Act (1940) II–385a
National Emigration Convention of Colored People (1854) II–127b
National Employment Service Act (1933) IV–71a
National Environmental Policy Act (1969) II–188b; V–393a, 472a
National Farmers' Alliance. *See* Farmers' Alliance
National Farmers' Alliance and Industrial Union II–493b; V–365a–b; VI–175a
National Farmers Organization I–42a
National Farmers Union I–41b, 42b
National Federation of Miners and Mine Laborers II–86b–87a
National Federation of Priests' Councils I–470b
National Federation of State High School Athletic Associations I–272b
National Fellowship of Brethren Churches I–361a
National Firearms Act (1934) IV–450b
National Flag Conference of the American Legion (1923–24) V–331b
National Flag Day Bill (1949) III–34b
National Football League III–57a–b
National forests. *See* Forests, national
National Formulary V–466a
National Foundation for Infantile Paralysis V–340a,b
National Foundation on the Arts and the Humanities Act (1965) V–393a
National Four-H Club Foundation III–84b
National Four-H Service Committee III–84b
National Fraternal Congress III–435a
National Front for the Liberation of South Vietnam III–162a; VII–94a, 183a
National Gallery of Art (Washington, D.C.) I–166a; II–105a; VI–319b; VII–246b
NATIONAL GAZETTE (news.) **IV–463b**; I–224a; V–69b
National Geographic Society I–329b; V–337a,b
National government. *See* Federal Government
National Governors' Conference III–206a
National Grange of the Patrons of Husbandry. *See* Granger Movement; Patrons of Husbandry
National Greenback Party. *See* Greenback Party, National
NATIONAL GUARD IV–463b; I–183a, 434a,b; II–314a,b, 367a, 368a; III–3a; IV–343b, 346a; V–28b; VI–98b
aviation unit I–64b
blacks in I–29b, 30a
broadcast regulations III–1a
camps I–434b–35a
civil disturbances IV–341b
dual oaths VII–208a
expansion I–186a
federalization IV–259a
Kent State protest IV–38b–39b; VII–191b
Ludlow strike VII–191b
Mexican border strife IV–328a
National Defense Act VII–325a
National Rifle Association IV–470a
riots I–31a, 32a; VI–8b–9a; VII–191a
Somme offensive VI–338b
southwestern oil fields VI–357a
Spanish-American War II–314a; VI–361b
state militias I–185a
strike breakers II–314a
World War I II–314a; IV–319a
World War II VII–334b, 335a
See also Military Aid to the Civil Powers
National Heart Institute IV–465a
National Highway Traffic Safety Administration II–502b
National Historical Publications and Records Commission III–285a
National Historic Landmarks
Faneuil Hall II–487b
National Historic Preservation Act (1966) II–47b, 188a; V–393a
National Historic Preservation Fund IV–472a
National Hockey Association III–287b
National Hockey League III–287b, 288a
National Home for Disabled Volunteer Soldiers VI–336b
National Housing Act (1934) I–376b; II–47a; III–310b
National Housing Act (1937) II–47a; V–48b
National Housing Act (1949) II–47a
National Housing Act (1954) II–47a
NATIONAL INDIAN YOUTH COUNCIL IV–464a; V–210b
National Industrial Recovery Act (1933) I–152b, 391a; II–86b, 92b, 111a, 136b, 144b, 481b; IV–71a,b, 72a, 469a; V–44b, 46b–47a; VI–419b, 457a; VII–123a, 213b
coal industry III–231b
constitutionality VI–225a
"Hot oil" Case III–307b
naval construction VII–341b
oil industry regulation VI–402b
restraint of trade VI–102b
rural development VI–171b
subsistence homesteads VI–426b
wage- and price-fixing V–402a
See also National Recovery Administration
National Industrial Safety Council I–7a
National Institute. *See* National Institute for the Promotion of Science
National Institute for Mental Health IV–307a
NATIONAL INSTITUTE FOR THE PROMOTION OF SCIENCE IV–464a; IV–468b
National Institute of Alcohol Abuse and Alcoholism IV–159a
National Institute of Arts and Letters IV–126b

National Institute of Dental Health II–331b
National Institute of Education II–405b
National Institute of Mental Health II–148a; V–442b
National Institute of Occupational Safety and Health IV–294a
NATIONAL INSTITUTES OF HEALTH IV–465a; I–242a, 304a; III–54a, 267b; IV–471a; V–137b
dental research II–331b
genetic research III–158a,b
German measles vaccine IV–292a
Marine Biological Laboratory IV–251a
medical education IV–285a
medical research IV–287a,b
physiology research V–307b
scientific education VI–232a
NATIONAL INTELLIGENCER (news.) **IV–465b:** III–202a; VII–249b–50a
Pomeroy Circular V–356a
National Intelligencer and Washington Advertiser (news.) IV–465b
National Invitational Tournament (basketball) I–273a
National Irrigation Association VI–53b
Nationalism VI–325a, 326a
Era of Good Feeling II–458a
Federalists I–130b
tariff VI–468a,b
Webster–Hayne debate VII–265b
Nationalist bloc
constitutional convention II–193a–95b
Nationalist China. *See* China, Nationalist (Taiwan)
Nationality
McCarran–Walter Act IV–209b
Nationalization of industries II–492b; VII–124b
NATIONALIZATION OF U.S. PROPERTY ABROAD IV–465b
indemnities III–352b
Mexican oil deposits IV–322b, 328b
National Kansas Committee IV–118b
National Labor Board IV–71b; VI–457a
National Labor party II–492b–93a; IV–81b
National Labor Reform party III–224b; IV–63a
NATIONAL LABOR RELATIONS ACT (1935) **IV–466b**; II–144b; III–407a; IV–72a, 72a; V–46b–47a, 47a, 48a; VI–410b, 419b, 456b, 457a
amendment IV–76b
blacklisting I–314b
checkoff II–4a
closed shop II–80a,b
collective bargaining I–153a; II–111a
lockouts IV–174a–b
picketing V–308b
unionization I–230a
validity upheld IV–467b
"yellow–dog" contract VII–355a
National Labor Relations Board I–13a; II–500a–b; III–3a, 459a; IV–72a,b, 74a, 74b, 75b, 466b, 467a,b; V–47a; VI–457a
checkoff II–4a
closed shop II–80a–b
collective bargaining II–112a
extension of jurisdiction IV–76b
judicial review IV–16b–17a
secondary boycotts VI–103b
strikes VI–419b
"yellow–dog" contracts VII–355a
National Labor Relations Board v. *Fan Steel Corporation* (1939) VI–419b
National Labor Relations Board v. *General Motors* (1963) II–4a
NATIONAL LABOR RELATIONS BOARD* v. *JONES AND LAUGHLIN STEEL CORPORATION (1937) **IV–467b**; II–136b, 378a
National Labor Union IV–62b–63a, 78a, 81a
National League for the Protection of Colored Women V–1a
National League of Nursing Education V–126b, 127a
National League of Professional Baseball Clubs I–270a, 271a
National Liberty party. *See* Liberty Party
National Library of Medicine IV–145b, 292a, 465a
National Linseed Oil Trust VII–122a
National Lord's Day Society IV–409a
National Marine Fisheries Service III–29a
National Mediation Board II–157b, 500b; VI–21a
Railway Labor Act VII–202a
National Mental Health Act VI–331b
National Monetary Association IV–234a
NATIONAL MONETARY COMMISSION IV–468a; I–84a, 252a; III–6a; V–209a
National monuments. *See* Parks, National, and National Monuments
National Mortgage Association V–456a
NATIONAL MUSEUM IV–468b; II–465a; IV–436b, 437a; VI–319b
reptiles VI–90b, 91a
Wilkes expedition collection VII–299b
National Museum Act (1966) V–393a
National Museum of Australia II–106b
National Museum of Natural History VI–319b
National Naval Volunteers Act (1916) V–28b
National Negro Committee IV–460b
National Negro Conventions I–137a
National News Council V–77b–78a
National Nonpartisan League. *See* Nonpartisan League
National Nursing Accrediting Service V–127a
National Nutrition Center V–128b
National Nutrition Conference for Defense (1941) V–128b
National Nutrition Plan V–128b
National Nutrition Policy Study V–128b
National Observer (mag.) V–76b
National Oceanic and Atmospheric Administration II–88b, 135a; III–29a–b; V–134a; VII–264a
National Oceanographic Data Center V–133b–34a
National Oceanographic Instrumentation Center V–134a
National Ocean Survey V–133a
National Office for Black Catholics I–468a
National Opinion Research Center V–453b
National Organization for Decent Literature I–479a
National Organization for Public Health Nursing V–127a
National Organization for Women VII–314a,b, 317b
National Origins Quota Act (1924) I–88a
National origins quotas. *See* Quota System
National origins system IV–160a, 209b; VI–4b–5a
National Packing Company I–283b
National parks and monuments. *See* Parks, National, and National Monuments; Park Service, National, and National Park System
National Park Service Act (1916) II–188a
National party III–224b
National Peace Action Committee
lobbying IV–171a
National Peace Conference VII–236b
National Personnel Records Center I–168a
National Portrait Gallery VI–319b
National Primitive Baptist Convention I–265b
National Probation and Parole Association II–263b
National Program for Acquisitions and Cataloging IV–147b
National Progressive party II–492b; VII–52b
National Progressive Republican League V–427b, 428a
National Prohibition Act (1919). *See* Volstead Act
National Quadraphonic Radio Committee VI–16b
National Railroad Adjustment Board VI–21a
National Railroad Passenger Corporation. *See* Amtrak
NATIONAL RECOVERY ADMINISTRATION IV–469a; I–324b; II–481b; IV–71b; V–44b, 46a,b, 47a
clothing industry II–83a
forestry III–74a
petroleum industry V–270b
trade associations VII–92b
National Reform Association III–296a
National Register for Historic Places V–393a
National Repository (period.) IV–83a
NATIONAL REPUBLICAN PARTY IV–469b; II–327a
business interests I–33a
campaigns of 1828 and 1832 I–418b–19a
campaign of 1836 I–419b
convention of 1831 II–216a
nominating convention V–101b
"Salt River" VI–203b
Whig party VII–288b
National Research Council IV–127a, 457a–b; VI–238b
flour enrichment III–44b
Food and Nutrition Board V–128b
genetic research III–158b
penicillin IV–306b
physics fellowships V–295b
sedimentation V–268b
National Research Project V–425b
National Reserve Association III–6a; IV–468a
National Resources Committee and Planning Board I–171a, 464a
NATIONAL RIFLE ASSOCIATION IV–470a
NATIONAL ROAD IV–470a; VI–153a,b, 156a; VII–100a
agriculture transport I–39b

NATIONAL ROAD (cont.)
Braddock's Road I–358b
construction II–273a–b
growth of cities II–45b
Ohio V–141a–b
Ohio National Stage Company V–144b
Zane's Trace VII–368a
National Road (Fr.) V–147a
National Safety Congress I–7a
National Safety Council I–7a,b; IV–294a; VI–185a
National School Celebration (1892) V–331b
National School Lunch Act (1946) I–43b; II–400a; V–129a
National Science Board IV–471a
NATIONAL SCIENCE FOUNDATION IV–470b; II–448a, 498b; V–137b; VI–230b
genetic research III–158b
Marine Biological Laboratory IV–251a
Office of Polar Programs V–338b
particle accelerators V–297a
physics research V–296a
scientific education VI–232a
National Sculpture Society VI–243b
National seashore. *See* Seashores, national
National security
electronic surveillance II–427b
executive privilege II–473b
military and strategic intelligence III–438b
National Security Act (1947) I–60b, 328b, 484a; II–498a; III–439a–b; V–18b; VII–230b
National Security Agency III–439b
National Security Council I–484a; II–498a; III–439a,b; VI–389b
National Security League V–390b
National Security Resources Board II–50a
National Service Life Insurance III–434a
National Silver party I–425a
National Socialists (Ger.) VII–334a
National Society of Professional Engineers II–449a
National Stereophonic Radio Committee VI–16b
National Student Association VII–365b
National Student Federation of America VII–365a
National Student Forum VII–365a
National Student League VII–365b
National supremacy doctrine II–194a–95b; III–348b
National Survey of Secondary Education II–400b
National Survey System IV–318a
National Teachers Association IV–463a
National Technical Information Service II–135b
National Television Systems Committee VII–21b
National Temperance League I–134b
National Textile Workers Union III–154a
NATIONAL TRADES' AND WORKERS' ASSOCIATION IV–471b
National Trades Union IV–62a
National Trades Union Convention III–296a
National Traffic and Motor Vehicle Safety Act (1966) I–230a; VII–98b
NATIONAL TRIBUNE (news.) **IV–471b**; V–255a
NATIONAL TRUST FOR HISTORIC PRESERVATION IV–471b; V–393a,b
National Turnpike II–273a
National Typographical Union IV–62a
National Unification Plan (Lib.) IV–142a
National Union Catalog, Pre-1956 Imprints IV–147b
National Union Catalog of Manuscript Collections III–285b
National Union Convention (1864) I–421b
NATIONAL UNION ("ARM-IN-ARM") CONVENTION (1866) **IV–472b**; VI–336a
NATIONAL UNION FOR SOCIAL JUSTICE IV–472b; VI–269a
National Union party III–81a; VII–148a, 179 (table)
National university II–15b, 395b–96a
NATIONAL URBAN LEAGUE V–1a; I–30b; II–58a; III–284b; VI–352a
National War College I–64b, 191a
National War Labor Board IV–73a,b; VII–326a, 328a, 336a
NATIONAL WATERWAYS COMMISSION V–1b; III–420a; VI–146b
National Weather Service. *See* Weather Service, National
National Wilderness Preservation System II–188b
National Wildlife Refuge System I–306a
National Woman's Loyal League VII–317a
National Woman's Party. *See* Woman's Party, National
National Woman Suffrage Association VII–315a, 317a
National Woolgrowers' Association VII–321b
National Youth Administration. *See* Youth Administration, National
National Zoological Park VI–319b
"Nation buster" (nuclear weapon) IV–363a
NATIVE AMERICAN CHURCH V–2a; V–273a; VII–65b
Native American Party I–111b
Native Americans (org.) VI–12b
Native Claims Settlement (Alaska) I–80b
Native Son IV–167a
NATIVISM V–2a; I–467b; III–342a–b
eugenics movement III–159a
Italians III–483b–84a
Kansas–Nebraska Act IV–29b
Maria Monk controversy IV–250a
Order of United Americans VII–149a
party alignments I–139a
Philadelphia riots V–279a
radical right VI–12a–b
Tammany Hall VI–459b
Ursuline convent burned VII–160a
voting tests VII–209b
Wide-Awakes VII–294b
NATIVISTIC MOVEMENTS, AMERICAN INDIAN V–3b; III–391b
Delaware Prophet II–322b
Ghost Dance III–177a
Handsome Lake Cult III–249b
Peyote Cult VII–65b
Prophet Dance V–434b
Shaker religion VI–267b
Shawnee Prophet VI–271a
Smohalla V–89b
NATO. *See* North Atlantic Treaty Organization
Nattleton, Asahel (cler.) VI–77a
NAT TURNER'S REBELLION (1831) **V–4b**; I–23b, 28a; III–437a; VI–303b, 304a, 307a, 342a; VII–191a, 194b
Natural areas, national. *See* Parks, National, and National Monuments
NATURAL BRIDGE OF VIRGINIA V–5a
Natural Bridges National Monument V–217b
"Natural" foods III–151a
Natural Gas Act (1938) II–500a; V–5b
NATURAL GAS INDUSTRY V–5a; VI–48b
ammonia III–17b; VI–334b
depletion allowance VII–10a, 12a
distribution II–414b
Fort Scott VI–241a
government leases III–444a
Gulf of Mexico IV–326b
interstate compacts VI–402b
Joplin (Mo.) IV–123a
Kansas IV–25a, 26a,b, 123a
Louisiana IV–194b
midcontinent oil region IV–333b
mineral patent law IV–349b
Montana IV–403b
New Mexico V–60a
New South V–67b
Oklahoma IV–123a; V–149a
petrochemicals V–267b
shipping IV–313a
Southwest VI–355b, 356b, 357a
Staked Plain VI–380b
tideland deposits VII–57b
urban drilling IV–104b
West Virginia VII–281b
zinc smelters VII–369a
Natural history
ecology II–392a
fish and marine life III–26a
mammals IV–230b
mineralogy IV–348b
museums IV–437a, 468b
Natural History, Field Museum of. *See* Field Museum of Natural History
Natural History, National Museum of VI–319b
Natural History of Carolina, Florida and the Bahama Islands III–26b, 27a; V–326a; VI–90a
Natural History of North American Amphibians and Reptiles VI–91b
Natural History of North Carolina III–26b; IV–231a
Naturalism (paint.) V–190a–91a, 191b
NATURALIZATION V–6a
American Republican Party I–111b
American Samoa VI–205b
citizenship II–42a–b
congressional powers II–195b, 199b
Constitution I–88a
Declaration of Independence II–307a
dual citizenship II–43a
expatriation II–475b
Indians III–377a
Japanese exclusion III–492a
Know-Nothing party I–110a
literacy tests IV–159b
married women's citizenship VII–315b
McCarran–Walter Act IV–209b
residency requirements I–86a–b
United States v. *Wong Kim Ark* VII–155b
yellow peril VII–356b

Naturalization Act (1798)
I–86a
Natural law V–286b
Bill of Rights I–298b
compact theory II–149a
human rights III–316b
Locke, John II–191a
Natural philosophy
chemistry II–10a
electricity II–413a
Natural resources
conservation II–187a
democracy II–326a
Department of the Interior
III–444a
interstate compacts
VI–402a,b
Natural Right and History
V–354a
NATURAL RIGHTS V–7b;
II–325a; V–350b–51a
British Constitution
II–191a
concept of liberty
IV–142a
Declaration of Independence II–304a, 306a–b
domestic insurrections
III–436b
equality II–456a–b
liberalism IV–140a
Locke's philosophy
IV–174a
manumission IV–246a–b
minorities IV–358a
revolutionary war IV–12b
right of revolution
VI–121a
state constitutions
VI–391b
Nature IV–162a
Nature and Destiny of Man
VI–83a
Nature and Elements of Poetry
IV–163a
Nature and the Supernatural
VI–82a
Nature of True Virtue
VI–81b
Naugatuck River II–181a
Naughty Marietta (operetta)
I–466a; IV–442a
Naumkeag (Mass.) V–51a
"Naumkeck" River IV–250a
Nautical Almanac Office. *See* Naval Observatory and Nautical Almanac Office
Nautilus (atomic submarine)
I–179b; V–11a; VI–280a, 423a; VII–241b
NAUTILUS (diving boat)
V–8a; VI–422b
Nautilus (submarine)
IV–336b; V–337b
Nauvoo (Ill.) III–327a
NAUVOO, MORMONS AT
V–8a; IV–116b, 339a, 411b, 412a; VII–161b, 284a
Nauvoo House (Ill.) V–8a
NAVAHO (Indians) **V–8a**;
III–367a, 368b–69a, 396a,b; V–314a
Bosque Redondo reservation
I–342b–43a
buckskin III–374a
education III–380a
Fort Sumner III–199b; VI–439b
horse III–303a
language III–360a
medicine III–385b
Native American Church
V–2a
New Mexico V–59b
population II–31a
potato cultivation V–376b
Pueblo warfare VI–224b
religion III–393a
treaties II–363b
wars VII–239a,b
war with Hopi III–301a
Navajo Dam II–130a
Navajo National Monument
V–217b
Navajoo River II–461a
NAVAL ACADEMY, UNITED STATES V–9b;
II–313b, 396a, 399a, 459a; III–21b; IV–261b; V–23b, 24a
America I–95b
Saginaw's gig VI–186b
slang VI–302a
Naval Aircraft Factory (Phila.)
I–236b
Naval Asylum. *See* Naval Home
Naval Aviation Cadet program
V–29a
Naval bases
Bermuda I–292b
Charleston (S.C) I–497b
Dominican Republic
I–454a; II–360b, 362a
Far Eastern III–33b
Ford Island V–239a
Guantánamo Bay
II–269b; III–230b; VII–112a
Isle of Pines III–479a
Newport V–65b
Norfolk VII–196a
parity V–216b
Pearl Harbor III–264a; V–239a
Pensacola V–254b
polar regions V–338a,b
San Diego VI–208b
Spain VI–360b
NAVAL COMPETITION
V–10a; II–370a; VII–341b
Geneva Three-Power Naval Conference III–162a
Great Lakes III–217a
parity V–216b
Washington Naval Conference VII–250b
Naval Consulting Board
V–14a
Naval Encyclopaedia
VI–301b
Naval Engineering Experiment Station VI–363a
Naval Gun Factory V–27b, 29b
NAVAL HOME V–11b;
VI–336a
Naval Intelligence, Office of
VI–373b
Naval limitation conferences. *See* Fourteen Points; Geneva Three-Power Naval Conference; Great Lakes Disarmament Agreement; Hague Peace Conferences; London Naval Treaty of 1930; London Naval Treaty of 1936; Washington, Naval Treaty of; Washington Naval Conference
Naval Medical School
IV–292b
Naval Militia IV–346a
NAVAL OBSERVATORY AND NAUTICAL ALMANAC OFFICE
V–12a; I–211a, 211a; V–28a, 131a,b, 133a–b; VII–299b
Naval Oceanographic Office
III–324b; V–133a, 134a
NAVAL OIL RESERVES
V–13a; II–431b; VII–16b
NAVAL OPERATIONS, CHIEF OF V–13b;
V–18a,b
Naval Ordnance Laboratory (Md.) V–28a
Naval Proving Ground (Md.)
V–28a
Naval Research, Office of
IV–471a; V–28a, 137b, 296a
NAVAL RESEARCH LABORATORY V–14a;
I–212b; V–28a
radar VI–10a
Vanguard project
IV–459a
Naval reserve V–28b–29a
Naval Reserve Officers' Training Corps V–24a, 28b
Naval School. *See* Naval Academy, United States
NAVAL STORES V–14b;
II–4b
bounties I–352a; III–204a
Cape Fear region I–447b
colonial manufacture
IV–242b, 308a
colonial trade II–5a, 119b, 453a, 453a; III–413a; VI–108a
Confederacy II–164b
enumerated commodities
II–453a
exchanges II–469b
foreign trade VII–86a, 87a
king's woods IV–49a
lumber industry IV–204a
Mobile IV–382b
Navigation Acts V–16a,b
Norfolk V–109b
Savannah VI–220b
tar VI–461b
taxation VII–5b
Naval Support Force, U.S.
V–338b
Naval Torpedo Station (Newport) V–28a
Naval Transport Force (World War I) VII–329a
Naval Treaty of Washington (1922). *See* Five-Power Naval Treaty
Naval Volunteers Act, National (1916) V–28b
Naval War College V–24a, 65b
NAVAL WAR WITH FRANCE (1798–1800)
V–15a; I–83b, 120b, 345a; II–89a; III–67b, 96a, 96b, 428a, 462a; IV–347a; V–320a; VII–87a, 237a
Anglo-American relations
I–120b
armament V–27a
armed merchantmen
V–423b
Baltimore incident I–251b
Boston–Berceau action
I–345a
Constellation–Insurgente encounter II–190a, 190a
Constellation–Vengeance encounter II–190b,
contraband II–212b–13a, 212b–13a
Convention of 1800
II–215a, 215a
convoys II–217b
Federalists III–4b
Loyalist veterans VI–130b
Navy Department V–17b
neutral rights V–38b
privateering III–121a; V–419a
prize cases III–98a
revenue cutters II–89a
United States VII–153a
U.S. Navy II–313a; V–19a, 29a
warships VII–240a
Navarro, José de (arch.)
I–143b
Navasota River V–216b
Navidad (Mex.) I–401b
Navigable waterways
commerce clause II–137a
federal safety rules
II–230b
Navigation V–294a
Bowditch's *Practical Navigator* I–355a
Canadian-American waterways VII–261a
Coast Guard II–89a–b, 90a
commercial treaties
VII–108b
Depot of Charts and Instruments V–133a–b
government control
III–422a; IV–152b
hydrographic surveys
III–324b
Inland Waterways Commission III–419b
interstate compacts
III–460a
Maryland-Virginia agreement III–459b
Maury's charts IV–276b, 317a
Mississippi River
II–333a–b
Naval Observatory V–12a
oceanography V–135a
Navigation, Bureau of
II–135a; V–18a
NAVIGATION ACT OF 1817
V–15b; II–90b
NAVIGATION ACTS
V–15b; I–119b; II–117a, 119a, 122b; III–204a;

NAVIGATION ACTS (cont.)
IV–308a; VI–110a;
VII–2b, 3b, 81a
Barbados IV–388a
Board of Trade I–326b
Canary Islands I–444a
chemical industry II–5a
coasting trade II–90b
Culpeper's Rebellion
II–271b
customs II–275b
Dominion of New England
V–50b
enforcement II–120a,
241b
logwood trade IV–182a
Massachusetts IV–265b;
VI–46a
molasses trade IV–388b
prerevolutionary imperial
idea III–346b
prices V–403b
Revolution
VI–107b–08a,b
shipbuilding IV–309b;
VI–279a,b
shipping IV–310a
smuggling V–320a;
VI–320b
NAVIGATOR **(handbook)**
V–17a
NAVY, CONFEDERATE
V–17a; VII–147a
America I–95b
Arkansas I–173b
Battle of Mobile Bay
II–285b–86a; IV–382b
Battle of *Monitor* and *Merrimack* IV–396a
Beall's raid on Lake Erie
I–280a
British indemnities
III–352a
Davids II–294b
flag II–159a
flag officers I–14a
floating batteries III–36b
Florida III–40b
foundry II–163a
Georgia III–169b
ironclads III–474a–b;
IV–396b
Kearsarge–Alabama encounter IV–35a
Laird rams IV–85a
Mississippi River
IV–371a, 374b–75a
raiders IV–310b
rams I–83a; VI–44b
Shenandoah VI–274b
ships II–158b; V–25a
Stonewall VI–415a
submarines VI–422b,
424b
Tennessee VII–26a
torpedoes VI–424b
Union commerce II–63a
United Daughters of the
Confederacy VII–150b
NAVY, DEPARTMENT OF
THE V–17b; II–498a;
V–19a; VI–122b
aircraft contracts VI–425b
Coast and Geodetic Survey
II–87b
Constitution II–190b
Depot of Charts and Instruments IV–276b–77a
Kearny–Frémont quarrel
IV–34a
military reserve II–367a
Mississippi Squadron
IV–375b
navy yards V–29b
oil reserves II–431b;
V–13a; VII–16b
Trust Territory of the Pacific VII–125a
Virgin Islands VII–204a
Navy, secretary of the
chief of naval operations
V–13b
Committee on Public Information II–139b
Navy and Marine Corps
Medal II–312a
Navy, Union. *See* Union
Navy
NAVY, UNITED STATES
V–18b; II–89a, 313a,b,
314a, 368a
admirals and commodores
I–13b
Afro–Americans I–29b,
30b; IV–339b, 340a
aircraft I–54a, 233b;
IV–106a
aircraft carriers I–54a,
179b, 214b; II–225a
aircraft simulator II–156a
airships II–344a–45b
Algerian War II–303a
American Samoa
III–425b; VI–205a;
VII–34a
Articles for the Government
of the Navy VII–143a–b
Asiatic Squadron
IV–239a–b
atomic power reactors
I–217b
aviation industry I–236a
balloons I–248b
band II–347a
Battle Fleet cruise I–276b
battleships II–314a
bombing I–328b
Bronze Star II–312a
chief of naval operations
V–13b
China II–26b
Chinese Revolution of 1911
II–25b
Coast Guard II–88b–89a
Confederate officers
V–17b
constitutional provisions
II–200a, 201b, 313a;
IV–342b
Continental navy VI–128a
Cuban missile crisis
II–270b
Defense Department
I–60b
dirigibles I–51b
disasters II–346a, 347a,
349b, 350a; IV–341b
Distinguished Service Medal
II–311a
Dominican Republic
II–361b
draft II–367b
Dreadnoughts II–370a
dry docks II–375a–b
enlistment II–451a
ensign II–452a
Fajardo case II–484a
Fast Carrier Task Force
VII–1a–2a
federal surplus VI–449b
Fifth Amphibious Force
III–180a
Fifth Fleet III–180a;
V–285b
figureheads III–21b
First Marine Air Wing
IV–56b
flags III–35a
flying boat I–233b–34a
Great Lakes III–217a–b
Guadalcanal III–229b
Guam III–230b, 425b
Gulf Stream study
III–233a
gunboats III–234a
helicopters III–270a–b
intelligence staff III–439a
Key West IV–45a
Kodiak Island IV–54a
Korean War IV–55b, 57a
Liberia IV–141b
London Naval Treaty
II–461a
Lower California IV–199b
Maine inquiry VI–361a
marine biology III–28b
Medal of Honor II–310a
medical research IV–292b
Mexican War IV–322a,
324b–25a
Michigan III–475a
midshipman II–452a
Midway Islands IV–337a
military policy IV–343a,b
militia IV–346a
Mosquito Fleet IV–416a
mutiny IV–445b
Nautical Almanac Office
V–12a
Naval Academy V–9b
naval competition V–10a
Naval Home V–11b;
VI–336a–b
Naval Observatory V–12a
oceanographic survey
V–133a, 134a–b
Office of Scientific Research
and Development
V–137a
ordnance V–163b–64a
Pacific Fleet III–180a
Paraguay expedition
V–212b
Pearl Harbor V–239a
pension plans V–256b
Perry–Elliott controversy
V–262b
Perry's Japan expedition
V–263a
Perry's Venezuela mission
VII–170a
piracy V–320a, 419b
polar exploration V–336b,
337a,b, 337a,b
preparedness movement
V–391a
privateers V–419a
prize money V–423a
Pueblo incident V–460a
Quasi War II–190a–b,
212b, 313a; V–15a
Quinteros Bay Episode
VI–3b
radar I–58a; II–425a
radio communications
II–424a
recruitment VI–61a
Reserve Officers' Training
Corps VI–98b–99a
Saipan and Tinian
III–426a
sea power VI–248a–b
Seventh Fleet II–26b, 90a;
IV–56b, 138a
sharpshooters VI–270a
ships of the line VI–282a
shipyards V–29a
slang VI–301b–02a
sloops VI–313b
Spanish–American War
VI–362b
stone fleets VI–414b
submarines VI–423a–b
Texas navy VII–38a, 41b
Third Fleet IV–138a
Tonkin Gulf episode
VII–71b
torpedo boats I–307b–08a
Torpedo Squadron 8
I–55b
torpedo warfare VII–76a
transatlantic flight V–30a
Tripolitan War II–313a
twenty–one gun salute
VII–132a
underwater demolition
teams VII–139a
Uniform Code of Military
Justice VII–143b–44a
United States VII–153a
U.S. flag III–35a
Veracruz incident
VI–104b
Vietnam War
VII–184a,b
Virgin Islands
III–425b
War of 1812 II–292a,
313b, 338a; III–217b–18a;
V–423b–24a; VII–235a
Battle of Lake Erie
II–459a–b
Demologos II–329a
Enterprise–Boxer
engagement II–452b
warships IV–431b;
VII–240a
war with Korea (1871)
IV–54b
Washington Naval Conference II–314b
whiskey II–353b
"White Squadron"
VII–293a
Wilkes Exploring Expedition VII–299a–b
women VII–318a
See also Revolutionary
War, Continental Navy in;
Union Navy; World War
I, Navy in; World War II,
Navy in
Navy and Marine Corps Medal
II–312a
Navy Battalion of Mounted
Riflemen I–409b
Navy Bureau of Aeronautics
I–236a
Navy Commissioners, Board of
V–17b

Navy Cross II–310b
Navy Depot of Charts and Instruments I–463b
Navy Hydrographic Office I–90a
Navy Island I–458b; III–216b
Navy Medal of Honor II–310a
Navy Nurse Corps VII–318a,b
Navy Ordnance Department V–163a
Navy Tactical Data System I–56a
Navy Training Corps, Student V–28b
NAVY YARDS V–29a; V–27b–28a
Civil War V–17a
munitions manufacture IV–432a,b–33a
Norfolk V–110a
Pensacola V–254b
Puget Sound V–462a
ships of the line VI–282a
work hours VII–214a
Navy Yards and Docks, Bureau of V–17b
NAWSA. *See* National American Woman Suffrage Association
Naylor and Company IV–433a
NAZARENE, CHURCH OF THE V–29b
Nazareth (Pa.) IV–409b
Nazi party II–144b
Nazism IV–11b
National Union for Social Justice IV–472b
newspapers V–74a
opposition III–172a
propaganda VII–333a
subversion VI–428a
U.S. neutrality policy V–35b
Nazi–Soviet Pact (1939) II–145a, 146b
NBA. *See* National Basketball Association; National Broadcasting Company
NBS–1 (bomber) I–50a
NC–1 (flying boat) V–30a
NC–3 (flying boat) V–30a
NC–4 (flying boat) I–51a, 233b
NC–4, FLIGHT OF (1919) **V–30a**
NCIC. *See* National Crime Information Center
NDRC. *See* National Defense Research Committee
NEA. *See* National Educational Association
Neagle, David (marshal) V–30a
NEAGLE, IN RE (1890) **V–30a**
NEA Journal IV–463b
Neale, Thomas (postmaster) V–371a
Neale, Walter (col.) VI–417b
Neamathla (Indian) VI–260a
Near East Foundation V–280b
NEA Research Bulletin IV–463b
"Near money" IV–392a
NEAR* v. *MINNESOTA (1931) **V–30b**; III–105a; V–78b
NEBBIA* v. *NEW YORK (1934) **V–30b**; V–458b
NEBRASKA V–30b; VI–394 (table)
alien landholding I–87b
Arbor Day I–154a; VII–114a
archives I–168b
Arikara I–171b
black cavalry I–310a
boundary disputes I–351b
caravans I–453a
cattle II–249a; IV–280b
Chimney Rock II–25b
citizens' alliances II–42a
claim associations II–70b
corn II–226b, 227a
corn belt I–486a
county-seat wars II–245b
Dakota Territory II–284b
education II–400a
exploration III–220b
Farmers' Alliance II–493a
Fort Robinson II–379b; VI–157a
Great Sioux Reservation VI–295a–b
high license III–276a
homesteaders IV–50a; VII–59b
Idaho Territory III–328a
Indian Country III–384a
Indians III–396b; VII–306a
irrigation III–478b
Kansas–Nebraska Act IV–28b
Kansas struggle IV–31a
legislature I–294b; IV–133b; V–344a; VII–142b
midcontinent oil region IV–333b, 334a
minimum-wage law IV–352b, 353b
Missouri River IV–380a
national monuments V–217b
Nonpartisan League V–106b
Ogallala V–139a
Omaha Indians V–154b
open–range cattle period V–159b–60a
panhandle V–205b
Pawnee V–230b
phytogeographical survey II–391b
pioneers V–317a
Platte River Trail V–330b
Populist party V–365b
Prohibition II–407a
prohibition laws V–429b
public ownership V–455a
Quakers V–470a
ranches VI–45a
referendum VI–66b
school lands VI–228a
settlement IV–338b; VII–113b, 284b
Sumner's Cheyenne expedition VI–439b
trading posts III–353b
Trans–Mississippi Exposition VII–98a
Union Pacific Railroad VII–147b
Villasur expedition VII–188a
Nebraska City (Nebr.) IV–33b; V–177a,b
Nebraska Territory IV–411b
Nebraska v. *Iowa* (1892) I–351b
Necator americanus. *See* Hookworm
Necessary and proper clause II–195b, 200a, 453b; III–348a–b
Necessity, Fort (Pa.) III–219b; IV–181a; VII–252a
Neches River II–389a; VI–210a
"Neck Battery." *See* Wagner Battery, Siege of
Neckties II–372a
"Ned Buntline" (pseud.) II–341b
Neddermeyer, Seth H. (phys.) V–302b
Needham, James (expl.). *See* Needham–Arthur Expeditions
NEEDHAM–ARTHUR EXPEDITIONS (1673–74) **V–31b**; VII–201b
Tennessee VII–25a
Needles III–140a, 402b
Needle trades II–82a,b; IV–70b
Neef, Joseph (educ.) II–398a
NEELY* v. *HENKEL (1901) **V–32a**
Neenah (Wis.) V–212a–b
NEGATIVE VOICE V–32a
Negotiable Instruments Act VI–399b
Negro *See* index listings under Afro–American; Black
Negro Ensemble Company I–25a
Negroes and Allied Veterans I–30b
Negro Family: A Case for National Action. *See* Moynihan Report
Negro Life and History, Association for the Study of III–279b
"NEGRO PLOT" OF 1741 V–32b; V–465a
Negro Spirituals (dance) II–288a
Negro Women, National Council of III–504a
Negro World (news.) I–21b
Neighborhood government IV–173a
Neighborhood Guild VI–330b
Neighborhood Legal Service VI–74b
Neighborhood Playhouse (N.Y.C.) VII–49b
Neighborhood school. *See* School, District
Neighborhood Youth Corps V–135b
Neill (Primary) Act (1917) III–169a
Neilson, James (inv.) III–472b
Neilson, Sandra (athlete) V–154b
Neisner Brothers III–33a
Nelson, Battling (pugilist) V–423a
Nelson, Byron (golfer) III–198a
NELSON, FORT (Ky.) **V–32b**
Nelson, George (furniture designer) III–137a
Nelson, John (dipl.) IV–449a
Nelson, Samuel (jur.) VI–445b; VII–248b
Nelson, Thomas (mer., gov.) II–308b; III–226a; IV–8b; V–32b
Nelson, William (off.) V–32b; VI–137b
Nelson, William Rockhill (ed.) V–73b
NELSON–DAVIS QUARREL (1862) **V–32b**
Nemacolin (Indian) IV–398b
Nemacolin's Trail VII–244b
Nematology I–349b
Nemo (comic character) V–72a
Neoclassical style furniture III–134b–35a, 138a–b
Neoclassic architecture I–162b–63a
Neoclassic dancing II–289a
Neoclassic gowns II–371b
Neoclassicism (painting) V–185b, 187a,b, 188a,b
Neoclassic style furniture III–445b
Neodesha (Kans.) V–271b
Neo–Lamarckism VI–237a
Neolin (Indian) II–322b
Neolithic culture I–377a
Neosho River II–242b; III–178b
Nepera Chemical Company V–291b
Neptunium II–12b; IV–119a; V–300b
Nernst, W. H. (phys.) II–423b
NESHAMINY (creek) **V–33a**; IV–179b
Nesmith, J. W. (off.) VII–350b
Nespelem (Indians) III–363a
Nessler, Charles III–239a
NESTERS AND THE CATTLE INDUSTRY V–33a; I–473b
Net Assessment Group III–439b
Netherlands II–318a–b
Albany II–383a–b
American Revolution VI–119b
cattle II–279b
clockmaking II–77b
colonial settlements II–123b
colonial trade II–382b
commercial treaty VII–111a

NETHERLANDS (cont.)
Common Market VI–469a
currency upvalue III–196a
Dutch Reformed churches II–93b
Dutch West India Company II–123b, 383a
education II–393b
European Economic Community VII–88b
exchange students II–470b
fishery disputes III–106b
Hague peace conferences III–237a–b
Hudson River land patents III–313a
immigration to U.S. III–335a
investments in U.S. II–382b; III–62b, 63a, 65a,b, 66b
Korean War IV–55b
loans to U.S. II–302a
Maine–New Brunswick boundary I–194b
Napoleonic Wars V–162a
naval rivalry II–375a
Navigation Acts V–15b
Nine–Power Pact V–96b
North Atlantic Treaty Organization V–113b
Organization for Economic Cooperation and Development V–170b
patroons V–229a
Peace of Paris V–214a
Pilgrims V–64b, 312b
Puerto Rico V–461a
Queen Anne's War VI–2a
radar VI–10a
radio astronomy VI–17a
Reformed churches VI–68b
revolutionary war loans II–301a; VI–117b, 120a
Rule of the War of 1756 VI–169a
rum VI–170b–71a, 321a
Shimonoseki expedition VI–278b
Siegfried Line VI–285b
slave trade VI–309b
Southeast Asia possessions II–489a
States General II–383b
Sugar Islands VI–437a
Synod of Dort VI–455b
trade VII–87a
Treaty of Westminster VII–279a
United Nations Declaration VII–151b
Walloons VII–221b
Washington Naval Conference VII–251a
Western Union Defense Organization V–114a
West India trade VII–278a
World War II II–315a; III–492b; IV–182a; V–213b; VI–285b
NETHERLANDS AWARD **V–33a**; V–118a–b; VI–165b–66a
Netherlands East Indies
World War II IV–182a, 228b
Netsilik (Indians) III–358a
Nettleton, Asahel (cler.) III–326a
Nettuno (It.) I–141b
Neuberger, Roy R. II–106a
Neumann, Blessed John Nepomucene (bp.) I–469b
Neumann, J. B. (art dealer) II–105a
Neumann, John von (math.) II–155b, 156a, 426b
Neurasthenia IV–306a
Neurobiology IV–251a
Neurological Diseases and Stroke Institute IV–465a
Neurology IV–305b–06a
Neuroses IV–306a
Neutra, Richard J. (arch.) I–165a
Neutral (Indians) III–499b
Neutral Conference for Continuous Mediation III–60a–b
NEUTRAL GROUND **V–33b**; II–249b; IV–197b, 456b
Neutral Ground Agreement (1806) IV–197b, 456b; VII–36b
NEUTRALITY **V–33b**; III–456a,b, 462a; V–233a
American Revolution VI–119b
Anglo–French wars III–96a–b, 238b; VI–66a
armed neutrality of 1780 I–175b–76a
British orders in council V–162a
China in Korean War IV–56a
Civil War II–66a; IV–43a
consolato del mare II–190a
contraband II–212b–13b, 446a
Customs Service II–277a
Declaration of Panama V–200a
Declaration of Paris V–214a
Espionage Act II–463a
Federalists III–4b
freedom of the seas III–106b
French privateers III–121a
Genêt mission III–159b
Hague peace conference III–237b
Indians in the Revolution III–400b
international law III–455b, 456a
Kellogg–Briand Pact IV–36a
Laos IV–107a–b
Latin America independence wars IV–110b
munitions definition IV–430a
Napoleonic Wars II–436b; III–493b
Napoleon's decrees IV–449b
New York Colony V–85a
Panama Canal V–201a
Patriot War V–227b
Perry's Venezuela mission VII–170a
prize cases V–422a
Proclamation of Neutrality V–36b
Progressive movement V–428b
Quinteros Bay Episode VI–3b
Rule of War of 1756 II–464a; VI–169a
Spanish civil war VI–360b
territorial waters VII–33a
Treaty of Washington VII–249a
Trent affair VII–115b
U.S. shipping IV–309b
visit and search VII–204b
World War I II–446b; III–69a; VII–325a, 327b, 332b
World War II II–213a
NEUTRALITY, PROCLAMATION OF (1793) **V–36b**; III–159b, 455b, 462a
Neutrality Act of 1794 III–455b; V–37b
NEUTRALITY ACT OF 1939 **V–37a**; II–213a; III–428b; IV–313b; V–35b–36a, 38b
NEUTRALITY ACTS OF 1935, 1936, AND 1937 **V–38a**; III–69a, 480a; IV–203a, 433b; V–35b–36a, 37a,b, 38a, 117b, 236b
philanthropy control V–280b
prohibited munitions IV–430b
Spain VI–360b
NEUTRAL RIGHTS **V–38b**; V–33b–35b, 34a
Anglo–American relations I–120b
China incident II–28a
enemy destination II–446b
freedom of the seas III–106b
free ships, free goods III–110a
French Decrees III–118b
impressment of seamen III–349b
Jay's Treaty III–493a–94a
Jürgen Lorentzen prize case IV–20b
laws of war VII–225a,b
Napoleonic Wars III–67b, 455b
Napoleon's Decrees VII–233a–b
Plan of 1776 V–323b
Proclamation of Neutrality V–36b
Quasi War II–313a
Spain VI–359a,b
Treaty of Ghent VII–235b, 236a
War of 1812 II–313a
War of 1812 I–438b
Western Hemisphere IV–115b
World War I II–314a; III–69a
Neutrino V–296b, 299a
Neutron IV–119a; V–298b–99a, 299b, 300a, 302a,b, 304b
Neuve–Chapelle (Fr.) V–293a
NEVADA **V–39b**; VI–394 (table)
Agate Fossil Beds V–217b
bill of rights I–300b
borax I–340a
British mining companies III–65a
California Trail VII–256a
camels in I–413a
Colorado River Compact II–130a–b
Comstock Lode II–477b; III–191b, 328a; VI–44a
Death Valley II–298a
exploration III–114b
Forty–Mile Desert III–81b
Frémont exploration III–214b–15a; VII–271b
gambling III–149b
geology III–163b
gold II–477b; III–192a
Great Basin III–214b
horse III–303a
Indians III–51b, 373b
Indian wars VII–239b
inheritance tax III–418a
Lake Tahoe VI–101b
land speculation IV–99b
lead industry IV–123a
lead–silver industry IV–122b
migration VII–100b
outlaws VII–187a
Paiute III–177a; V–194a
Powell explorations V–384a
prostitution V–438a
public ownership V–455a
racetracks II–260b
railroad surveys VI–39a
recall VI–51a
reclamation VI–54a,b
referendum VI–66b
Rhyolite VI–135a
seismic activity II–385a
settlement VII–161b
sheep wars VI–273b
silver mining I–301b, 329a; II–477b; III–80a, 163a; VI–292a
train robberies VII–97b
Union Pacific Railroad VII–147b
Virginia City VII–199b
wagon trains VII–217b
Walker expedition VII–220a
western routes V–224b, 224b
westward movement VII–284b
woman's suffrage VII–315a
Nevada City (Calif.) IV–354b

Nevadaville (Colo.) IV–354b
Nevelson, Louise (sculp.) VI–244a
Neville, John (off.) V–321b; VII–290a
Nevin, John W. (theol.) VI–78a, 82a
Nevins, Allan (hist.) VI–157a
Nevis Island II–190a
New Albion. *See* Plowden's New Albion
New American Cyclopaedia II–444b
New American Museum (N.Y.C.) I–268b
New Amstel (Del.). *See* New Castle
NEW AMSTERDAM **V–40a**; V–60b, 61b, 332b; VII–94b
- Bowery I–355a
- Broadway I–368b
- Brooklyn I–370a
- cattle I–471a
- coastwise trade I–319b
- distilleries II–4b–5a, 353b
- Dutch investment III–63a
- environmental sanitation VI–211b
- food III–51b
- founding II–123b
- Harlem III–253a,b
- Huguenots III–315a
- Jewish community IV–9a
- kermis IV–43b
- New Sweden Colony V–80b
- painting V–185a–b
- patroons V–229a
- paving V–229b
- petition and remonstrance V–266a
- public market IV–255b
- rivalry with Swedish V–42b
- shipbuilding VI–148a
- slave trade VI–308b
- surrender to British V–82a
- tariffs V–62a
- *See also* New York City

New Archangel (Alaska) I–75a
NEWARK (N.J.) **V–41a**; III–438a; V–56b, 57b
- citrus industry II–43b
- College of New Jersey V–408b
- harness factory III–255b
- Hudson and Manhattan Tubes VI–429b
- Port Authority of New York and New Jersey V–368b
- race riots I–31b, 32a; II–259a; IV–457b; VI–9a
- Rutgers University VI–181b
- water supply VII–259b

Newark (Ohio) IV–421a; V–145b
Newark Bay II–350b, 431b
Newark International Airport V–41b, 368b
Newark Museum (N.J.) III–137b
Newark Village (Can.) V–91a
Newark Works (Ohio) IV–421a
New Avesnes. *See* Manhattan
New Bahama Channel III–41b
New Bedford (Mass.)
- population IV–268b
- stone fleets VI–415a
- textiles IV–266b
- whaling I–447a; VII–285b

New Bern (N.C.) I–162a; V–115b, 116a; VI–340b, 455a
Newbern (Tenn.) VII–63a
Newberry, J. J., and Company III–33a
Newberry, J. S. (geol.) III–208a; V–196a–b
Newberry, Truman H. (pol.) V–41b–42a
Newberry, Walter L. (mer., philan.) IV–100b
Newberry Library (Chicago) II–109b; III–285a; IV–145b
Newberry medal I–335b
NEWBERRY* v. *UNITED STATES (1921) **V–41b**
Newbery, John (pub.) I–335a
New Birth II–466a
New Bordeaux (S.C.) III–315a
New Bremen Glass Manufactory III–182b
New Bridge (N.J.) V–229b
- *See also* Hackensack

New Britain Island
- World War II I–350a; IV–253a; VI–5a

Newbrough, John B. (rel. leader) VI–268a
New Brunswick (Can.)
- boundary I–194b–95a
- Fenian movement III–10b
- Loyalists I–438a; VII–150b
- lumber industry IV–204a
- Saint Croix River VI–188b
- Saint John River VI–151a
- tobacco VII–64b
- Webster–Ashburton Treaty VII–265a

New Brunswick (N.J.) V–289a
- race riot VI–9a
- revolutionary war II–321b; V–408b
- Rutgers University VI–181b

New brutalism (arch.) I–166a
NEW BUDA V–42a
New Buffalo (commune) II–142b
Newburgh (N.Y.) II–331b; V–42a
- Deism III–112a
- Hasbrouck House V–392b

NEWBURGH ADDRESSES (1783) **V–42a**
Newburyport (Mass.) I–193b, 363b; III–235a; IV–268a
NEW CAESAREA V–42b
New Caledonia
- World War II VII–342b

New Caledonia (Can.) V–165a
New Castel (Pa.) VII–267a
NEW CASTLE (Del.) **V–42b**; II–322b; IV–454a; V–80b; VII–129b–30a, 359b
Newcastle (Maine) V–243b
New Castle (Pa.) IV–417b
Newcastle, Duke of, Thomas Pelham–Holles (states.) I–326b; III–115a–b
New Castle County (Del.) II–320b, 322b; IV–199b; V–43a
New Castle Island VII–300b–01a
Newcomb, Simon (astron.) I–211a; IV–2b, 120a, 233b
Newcomb College I–272b
Newcombe, John (athlete) VII–31a
Newcomen, Thomas (inv.) VI–408b, 410a
New Communities Act (1968) II–48b
NEW DEAL V–43a; II–472b; IV–228a; VI–14a, 93a–b, 313a
- Afro-Americans I–30a; III–438a,b
- Agricultural Adjustment Administration IV–104a
- agriculture I–30a
- American Labor party I–107a
- American Liberty League I–108b
- antitrust laws I–391a
- boondoggling I–336b
- brain trust I–359b
- bureaucracy I–384a
- Civilian Conservation Corps II–51a
- civil service I–146a
- collective bargaining III–111a
- commerce clause II–136b
- Communist party II–144b–45a
- Congress I–322a
- conservatism II–189b
- currency legislation IV–395b
- due process of law II–378a
- economic planning II–189b
- Farmer–Labor party I–39a
- farmers cooperatives II–221a
- government spending III–205b
- grants–in–aid III–211b
- historiography III–283a
- housing programs II–47a
- Indians I–106b
- Jim Crow laws II–56b
- labor I–104b; IV–71a–72a
- malaria programs IV–229b
- Minnesota II–491b
- National Recovery Administration IV–469a
- National Youth Administration VII–364a
- New York City V–83b
- opposition IV–472b
- planned economy V–323b
- presidential campaigns I–416b, 428b–29a
- pressure groups V–401a
- progressivism IV–140b
- pump–priming V–464a
- Reconstruction Finance Corporation VI–60a
- regulation of business I–389b, 391a, 391a; V–458b
- relief VI–73a–74a
- Resettlement Administration VI–99a
- scientific research IV–470b
- share–the–wealth movements VI–269b
- Socialist movement VI–326a
- Socialist party platforms V–329a–b
- social planning II–189b
- Social Security Act VI–328a
- South Carolina VI–348a
- statutes held unconstitutional IV–14a
- Supreme Court II–378a; VI–447b
- taxation VII–7b, 13a
- third–party influence VII–53a
- unemployment VII–140a
- unionization II–111a
- Works Progress Administration VII–322b

NEW DEAL INDIAN ADMINISTRATION V–48b
NEW DEPARTURE POLICY V–49a
New Dictionary of Medical Science and Literature V–306b
New Dime Novels II–341b
New Discovery of a Very Large Country Situated in America III–272a,b
NEW ECHOTA, TREATY OF (1835) **V–49b**; III–394b; VII–96b
"New Economic Era." *See* "New Era"
Newell, Frederick H. (eng.) II–449a; VI–54a
Newell, William A. (pol.) IV–152a
NEW ENGLAND V–49b; III–279a, 334a
- Afro-American music IV–442b, 443a
- antislavery VII–137b
- architecture I–161a
- beaver hats IV–242b
- blizzards I–320b
- Boston Resolutions I–347a
- bundling II–485b; VI–266a
- canals IV–174b
- candlemaking VI–372b
- cattle II–279b; III–51b
- China trade V–157b
- church covenant II–247b

NEW ENGLAND (cont.)
Church of England II–455a
civil marriages II–485b
Civil War VI–274b
cod fisheries II–92b
Coercion Acts II–93a; IV–271a–b
colonial commerce VI–107b–08a,b
colonial government II–325a
colonial land grants IV–91b
colonial land system IV–101b, 102a
colonial painting V–184b–85a,b
colonial paper money IV–393b
colonial punishments V–464b
colonial society II–125a
colonial suffrage VI–434a
colonial wars IV–86a
Colorado settlers VII–146a
columbium III–14b
commerce II–118b, 436b
commodities as money II–140b
common lands II–141a
communes VII–313b
Concord Group II–158a
Conway Cabal II–218a
country schools IV–169a
county fairs II–244b
county government II–245a
dairy produce II–279b
dame schools II–285b
"Dark Day" II–292a
demographic study II–328b
distilling II–353b
divine providences II–355b–56a
divorce II–356b
earthquakes II–385a
education II–285b, 393b, 394a–b, 394a,b, 396a
embargo of 1807 II–436b; VI–164b
exploration I–446b–47a, 492b; IV–263b
factory fire insurance III–430a
family system II–485b
farm IV–102b
Farmer's Almanac II–494a
fast days II–496a–97a
Federalist party V–2a; VI–94a
fence viewers III–10a
fish III–26b
fishing III–413a; IV–82a, 217a; VI–201a, 379a
floods III–37a
folk art III–47a,b
food III–51b, 52a, 53b
foreign trade VII–86a
forests III–74b
Fort Pentegoet V–260a
Freemasons III–108b
freemen III–109b
free trade III–113a
French and Indian War IV–86a; VI–190a
French Canadians III–338a–b
French raiding parties II–267a
Friends of Domestic Industry III–124a
fruit growing III–128b
fundamental constitutions III–132b
furniture III–135b, 139a
fur trade III–140a, 140b–41a
gardens III–151b
general court III–155a
glassmaking III–185a
glebes III–186b
grasshopper attacks III–212b
gravestones VI–242b
great fortunes III–78b
Great Migration III–219b
Green Mountain Boys III–226b
group migration IV–338a
gundelow III–235a
Hartford Convention III–259a; VI–404b
hat manufacture III–262a
Hawaii trade III–263a
historical accounts III–280a,b
hog reeve III–288a
hogs III–288b
home missionary societies IV–365a–b, 366b
horse breeding III–303b
hurricanes II–351b; III–76a, 319b, 320a
hymns III–326a
Iberian immigration III–338b
Illuminati III–332a
immigration restriction III–342a
Indian agriculture III–366b
Indiana settlers III–370a
Indian missions III–385b
Indians I–465b; III–360b; VI–183b
Indian slaves III–401a
industrial research III–408a,b
Industrial Workers of the World IV–120a
intestate estates III–464a
Ipswich protest III–469a
ironworks III–77b
Italian population III–338a
King George's War IV–46b
King Philip's War IV–47a
king's woods IV–49a
King William's War IV–49a; VI–1b–2a, 188a
labor impressment IV–79a–b
Lafayette's visit IV–84a
landholding policy I–3b
land speculation V–88b
land system IV–93a
land title VI–4a
Latin schools IV–116a
lecture days IV–131a
libraries IV–144a,b
literature IV–161a, 162a
local government IV–171a,b; VII–78b–79a
log cabin construction IV–179a–b
Long Island settlements IV–185a–b
Louisburg II–126b; IV–192a
Loyalists I–206b; IV–200a; VI–129b
lumber industry IV–204a
lyceum movement IV–207a
malaria IV–229a
mammals IV–231a
manufacturing IV–243a; VII–83a
mapping VII–73b
mapping of coast IV–247b
marine life III–29b
Massachusetts Bay Company IV–269b
meat-packing IV–280a
medical education IV–283a
meetinghouse IV–300a
merchant marine IV–309a,b
militia I–385a,b; IV–345b
mill towns II–45b
mineralogy IV–348a,b
Mohegan IV–387a
Molasses Act II–116b; IV–388a
monetary standard IV–392b
Monhegan Island IV–396a
mounds IV–420b
music IV–437b–38a, 439a
Narragansett Bay IV–451b
National Trust for Historic Preservation IV–472a
natural rights doctrine V–7b
naval stores V–14b
Navigation Acts V–16b–17a
New Hampshire V–53a
New Haven Colony V–55a
New Lights cult V–58b
New Netherland V–61b–62a
New Plymouth Colony V–64b
New York, New Haven and Hartford Railroad VI–35b
New York Colony V–85a
New York settlers V–87a
nickname Jonathan IV–7b
Nicolls' commission V–95b
nonimportation agreements I–347a
Non-Separating Puritans II–169b
Norsemen VII–190a
ocean currents IV–316b
panic of 1873 V–207b
Patrons of Husbandry V–229a
Pembroke Resolves V–244a
philosophy V–286b, 287a
Pilgrims V–312b
Pine tree emblem V–316a
piracy V–320a
plans of union II–121a
plantation V–324a
political subdivisions V–349b
Popham Colony V–359b
Port Royal V–369b
postal service V–370b–71a
potash V–376a
pottery III–183b
Presbyterianism V–391b
price-fixing V–401b
prices V–404a,b
primogeniture V–408a
Puritans II–35b; V–469a–b; VI–262b
Quakers V–469b, 470b
Queen Anne's War VI–2b, 2b
rainstorms II–349b
Regicides VI–70b, 71a, 71a
religion VI–75a–76a,b, 82a; VII–275a
revolutionary war VI–123a, 125a; VII–251a,b
Richelieu River VI–136b
rights of Englishmen VI–140b
roads VI–152b; VII–168a
rubber industry VI–167b
rum III–413b; VI–170a, 170b; VII–289b
sabbath-day houses VI–182a
Sable Island VI–182a
samplers VI–205b
Sam Slick VI–207a
savings and loan associations VI–221b
schools VI–226b
schoolteachers VI–229a,b
sealing V–336b
secession movement III–272b–73a; VI–250a, 397a
sectionalism VI–253b
selectmen VI–257b
separatism I–347a
settlement II–242a, 364b–65a; IV–278b; V–51a; VI–185b
sexual attitudes VI–265b
Shays's Rebellion VI–271b
sheep VI–272b
shipbuilding II–119a, 124b; VI–148a, 279a
shipping IV–310a
shivaree VI–282b
silk VI–286b
skiing VI–101a, 298a,b
Slade's Girls VI–299b
slavery VI–304b, 305a
slave trade VI–310a,b
smallpox VI–315a
snowshoes VI–323a
snowstorms II–352a
Standing order VI–384b
Suffolk Banking System VI–430b
Sugar Acts VI–435a
Sugar Islands trade VI–437a
sumptuary laws VI–440a,b

Sunday schools VI–442a
surveyors VI–450b
tariff VI–465b, 466a
taverns VII–2a
taxation VII–3a,b, 4a, 11b
temperance movement VII–22b
tennis VII–29a
textile industry II–237b, 239b, 255a; III–413b; IV–61a; V–67a; VII–42b, 44b–45a
Thanksgiving Day VII–46a
theocracy VII–51a
theology VI–81b
tidewater VII–58a
timberlands VII–60a
tithingmen VII–64b
tobacco VII–67a
town gaugers III–154b
town government II–245a; VII–81b
town meeting II–44a
town plans II–45a
town sealers VI–245a
training day VII–96b
transcendentalism V–58b; VII–97b
triangular trade VII–86a, 119b–20a, 277b–78a
United Colonies of New England IV–270a
Vermont VII–171a
voter registration VI–71a
voting IV–269a; VII–210a
War of 1812 II–192a
War of 1812 V–235a; VII–235a,b
Washington Benevolent Society VII–249b
watermills VII–257a
westward movement VII–260a, 282b
whaling V–336b; VI–209a
wild turkey VII–130a
witchcraft V–464b; VII–309b
wool VII–320b, 320b, 321a
World War I VII–231b
Yamasee War VII–352a
Yankee notions VII–352b
Yazoo fraud VII–354a

NEW ENGLAND, DOMINION OF V–50b; I–499b, 499b; II–121b; VII–359a–60a
colonial assembly II–118a
Connecticut II–182b
franchise IV–269a
King William's War IV–49b
Lords of Trade and Plantation IV–188b
Maine III–200b
Massachusetts IV–265b, 270b
New York Colony V–84b

NEW ENGLAND ANTI-SLAVERY SOCIETY V–50b; I–136b; IV–141a

NEW ENGLAND COMPANY V–51a; II–365a; III–220a

New England Confederation. *See* United Colonies of New England

New England Council. *See* Council for New England

New England Courant (news.) V–68b

NEW ENGLAND EMIGRANT AID COMPANY V–51a; IV–25b, 30a, 118b
Kansas Free-State party IV–28b
National Kansas Committee IV–28a
Sharps rifles VI–270a

New England Farmer (period.) I–45b

New England Hospital for Women and Children (Boston) V–126b

New England Interstate Water Pollution Control Commission III–460a

New England Labor Reform League VII–316b

New England Library II–107b

New England Life Insurance Company IV–149b

New England Loyal Publication Society IV–202a

New England Magazine IV–8a

New England Mind III–283a

New England Mississippi Land Company III–170a–b; VII–354a

***NEW ENGLAND PRIMER* V–51b**; I–335a; II–394a; V–68a; VI–227a

New England Rarities III–26b, 128b; IV–231a, 423b

New Englands Prospect IV–231a

New England Watch and Ward Society I–478b; II–263b

"NEW ENGLAND WAY" V–51b

New English Canaan III–26b; IV–315a

"NEW ERA" V–52a

New Era (gunboat) V–313b

New Era (steamship) II–349a

Newfield, Jack (writ.) V–79a

Newfoundland (Can.)
awarded to England II–92b, 126b
Beothuk Indians III–355b, 360b
Calvert grant IV–260a
exploration I–96b
fisheries I–121b, 365b; II–92a–93a, 119b, 215b, 364b; III–177a; IV–82a; VI–379a
fishing rights III–30b
French and Indian War III–117b
Gilbert's colony III–180b, 240b
Grand Banks III–208a
immigration to U.S. III–338a
Indians I–441a
Norsemen V–112b; VII–190a
North American Conservation Conference II–187b
oats V–130a
Peace of Paris VI–117a
revolutionary war VI–130a
sealing VI–245a
settlement I–16a; II–123b; VII–94b
tea trade VII–17a
Treaty of Fontainebleau V–214b
Treaty of Utrecht VII–162b
triangular trade II–119a
waters I–277b
whaling VII–285a

Newfoundland Company I–500a

NEW FRANCE V–52b; II–126b; VI–199a
British conquest II–337b
Carrying Place of Niagara V–90a
colonization II–149a
coureurs de bois II–246a
Crown Point II–266b
exploration I–477a, 493a, 499a
Franquelin maps VII–73b
frontier posts III–119b
fur trade III–142a
governors V–156b
Indians I–492b; IV–83b
Indian warfare III–399b
Jolliet and Marquette expedition IV–6b–7b
King William's War IV–200a
La Salle's explorations IV–109a–10a
New England trade III–140b
Raddison's trade expedition VI–18a
Richelieu River VI–136b
Saint Croix Island VI–189a
Salmon Falls attack VI–201a
Treaty of Saint Germain–en–Laye VI–190b, 190b
See also Canada

NEW FREEDOM V–53a; II–71b, 472b; IV–140b; VII–122b–23a

NEW FRONTIER V–53a; I–103a; IV–140b; VI–313a

New Georgia
World War II IV–253a

New Glarus (Wis.) III–337a; VI–455a

New Granada (Colom.) V–200b
I 295b–

New Granada Treaty. *See* Bidlack Treaty

New Guide to Health; or, the Botanic Family Physician IV–288a

New Guide to the English Tongue VI–227a

New Guinea I–55b
World War II II–225a; IV–83a; V–20b, 213b; VI–5a; VII–1b–2a, 336b–37a, 342b, 343a

NEW HAMPSHIRE V–53a; IV–232a; V–49b; VI–394 (table)
Albany Congress I–82a
bills of credit I–300a
birth and death registration IV–149a
black suffrage VI–431a–b
boundary disputes I–351a; IV–92a
cattle I–471a
colonial exiles V–342a
colonial land grant IV–263b–64a
colonial suffrage VI–434a
committees of safety II–140b
commutation bill II–148b
Connecticut River VI–149a
constitution VI–391a,b
dairy industry II–279b
Dartmouth College II–292b
Dartmouth College Case II–293a
Declaration of Independence II–307b
diphtheria epidemic IV–275a
Dominion of New England V–50b
double jeopardy VII–154b
enfranchisement of Jews IV–9a
fish III–27a
Freemasons III–109a
Hartford Convention III–259a
Indian Stream Republic III–401b
Isles of Shoals III–479b
King Philip's War IV–47b
king's woods IV–49a
legislature VII–142a
life table IV–149a
lottery III–149b
Merrimack River VI–149a
Middlesex Canal IV–335b
militia I–385a
minimum-wage law IV–353a
minutemen IV–361a
mortality statistics VII–207a
Number 4 V–126a
Osgoodites V–174b
plans of union II–121b–22a
port authority V–368a
presidential electors I–416b
provincial congress V–439b, 440a
religion VI–81a
revolutionary war VII–251a
ripper legislation VI–144b
settlement II–124a
silver mining VI–292a
skiing VI–101a, 298a
suffrage III–91b
town government VII–78a
Twelfth Amendment VII–132a
U.S. Constitution

NEW HAMPSHIRE (cont.)
II–167a, 193a, 196b, 198a, 203b, 478a
usury law III–443a
Vermont III–87a–b, 226b; VII–172a
Vermont Gore III–200a
voting behavior VII–210a
White Mountains IV–423a
writs of assistance VII–345a
New Hampshire (ship) VI–282a
New Hampshire Gazette (news.) V–54a
NEW HAMPSHIRE GRANTS V–54b; II–267a; V–53b, 88b, 156a; VII–171b
New Hampshire Historical Society III–137b, 278b
New Harbor (Maine) V–243b
New Harlem II–363b; III–253a,b
NEW HARMONY SETTLEMENT (Ind.) **V–54b**; II–147a, 220a
New Haven (Conn.) II–181a; III–25b
city plan II–45a
clockmaking II–77a
colonial relics exhibition II–99a
early schoolteachers VI–229b
gun manufacture II–130b
infant death rate IV–151a
low-cost housing IV–429a
munitions manufacture IV–432b
observatory I–211a
railroad VI–35b
Regicides VI–71a
shipbuilding III–413a
Yale University VII–351a
New Haven (steamboat) IV–415a
NEW HAVEN COLONY V–55a; I–239a; II–124a, 180a; III–258b
absorbed by Connecticut VII–149b
Bible Commonwealth I–294a
blue laws I–325a; VI–440a
church membership suffrage II–35b
fundamental orders III–132b
general court III–155b
laws II–379b
Long Island settlement IV–185a
Moses His Judicials IV–415b
New Sweden Colony V–80b
"phantom ship" V–273a
plans of union II–121b–22a
political organization VII–51a
Regicides VI–70b
"seven pillars" VI–263b
Southold settlement VI–354b
United Colonies of New England IV–270a; VII–149a
New Haven Colony Historical Society III–137b
New Haven Hospital V–126b
New Haven Railroad I–10a; V–261a
New History III–283a
New Holland Company I–35a
NEW HOPE CHURCH, BATTLES AT (1864) **V–56a**; I–213b
Newhouse newspaper chain V–76b
Newhouse trap VI–411b
New Humanists II–189b
New Iberia (La.) I–232a, 461b; IV–472a
New Icarian Community III–327a
Newichawannock River III–200a
New Idria Quicksilver Mine V–211a
NEW IRONSIDES (ironclad) **V–56a**; II–294b; III–474b; VI–425a
NEW JERSEY V–56b; II–37b; VI–309a, 394 (table)
Annapolis Convention I–126a
Articles of Confederation I–198b
Bill of Rights I–298b
bills of credit I–300a
birth and death registration IV–149a
black officeholders VI–432b
black suffrage III–437b
boundary dispute I–351a,b
Broad Seal War I–368a
canals IV–412b
Cartagena expedition I–461b
civil service II–60a
clay III–183b
coinage II–455b
colonial assembly II–118a, 431b
colonial land speculation IV–98b
colonial suffrage VI–434a
colonial trade II–119a
commutation bill II–148b
Concessions and Agreement II–157a
Continental Congress II–148b
crime families II–262a–b
Declaration of Independence II–308a
Delaware Indians II–320b
Delaware River Basin Compact III–460a
delftware V–379b
Dominion of New England V–50b; VII–360a
Duke of York's proprietary VII–359b
East Jersey II–388b
Elizabethtown Associates II–431a
exploration II–322a
Federalists III–5a
fencing laws III–10a
ferries III–11a–b, 132a
feudalism III–18a
foreign trade VII–86a
Fort Lee IV–131b
Fort Nassau IV–454a
Fort Nonsense V–108a
Fourierist communities II–147a
glassmaking III–184b
Hester case III–274a
hogs III–288b
holding companies III–290a
Holland Tunnel III–312b
Holmes v. *Walton* III–292a
incorporating acts II–229a–b, 230a
Indiana Company III–371a
iron works I–337b
Italian population III–338a
lifesaving stations IV–152a
lotteries IV–191b
medical societies IV–289a
militia IV–345b
minimum-wage law IV–353a
Monmouth Purchase IV–397b
Morris Canal I–337b
Newark V–41a
New Caesarea V–42b
New England settlers V–50a
New Sweden Colony V–80a
Palatines V–195a
Perth Amboy V–264a
Plowden's New Albion V–332b
Port Authority III–201b; V–368a; VI–402a
pottery III–183a,b, 184a
prison system V–417a
privateers V–419a
prohibition II–407a
proprietary grant V–436b
proprietors I–499b; II–431b
public ownership V–455a
Puritans II–431b
Quakers V–470a
Queen's College II–395a
Quintipartite Deed II–388b
railroads III–312b; VI–24b, 36a
referendum VI–66b
Reformed churches VI–69a
religious liberty II–394b; VII–68b–69a
resorts and spas VI–100b
retail sales VII–84b
revivalism VI–76b
revolutionary war II–249b, 321a–b; IV–397b; V–41a, 229b, 252b, 408a–b; VI–128b, 373a, 377a; VII–116a–b
ripper legislation VI–144b
rubber industry VI–167a
rumrunners VI–170a
Rutgers University VI–181b
schools II–393b
settlement II–124a–b, 431a–b
settlement in Ohio IV–330a
sheep VI–272b
ship channel VII–260b
silk VI–287a
slavery I–135b
snowstorms II–352a
Society for Establishing Useful Manufactures VII–160b
state banking I–259a
Statue of Liberty V–217b
steamboating VI–409a
steamboat monopoly III–178a, 178a; VI–407b
steam navigation III–32a
Stevens Institute of Technology II–448a
sugar trust VI–437b
sweet potatoes V–377a
Tappan patent VI–461b
taxation VII–4a
toll roads III–450b
town meetings VII–79b
Tri-State Regional Planning Commission III–460a
trusts VII–122a
U.S. Constitution II–151b, 193a, 194a, 195a, 196a, 198b, 203b, 478a
water supply VII–259a
Weehawken VII–266b
West Jersey VII–278a
windmills VII–304b
wiretap legislation II–427b
woman's suffrage VII–315a
writs of assistance VII–345a
zinc VII–368b
See also East Jersey; West Jersey
New Jersey (battleship) V–26b; VII–242a
New Jersey, College of. *See* Princeton University
New Jersey College of Medicine and Dentistry of Newark V–41b
New Jersey Company, Associates of V–57b
New Jersey Institute of Technology V–41b
New Jersey Iron Company I–337b
New Jersey Plan V–57b
New Jersey Railroad V–41b
New Jersey State Museum III–184a
New Jersey Turnpike V–455a
New Jersey v. *Delaware* (1934) I–351a
New Jersey Volunteers VI–130a
NEW JERUSALEM, CHURCHES OF THE V–58a
New journalism IV–165a; V–79a

Newlands, Francis G. (pol.)
V–445a; VI–53b
Newlands Act. *See* Reclamation Act of 1902
IV–68b; VI–21a, 28b
"New lead belt" IV–123a
New Left I–117a; II–146b, 189b; III–283a; IV–12a; VI–421a; VII–366a
NEW LIGHTS V–58b; V–391b, 408b
New Line (packet) V–183b
New London (Conn.)
III–25b; IV–387b
Coast Guard Academy II–90a
Pequot Trail V–261a
Pequot War V–261b
post road V–375a
prison ships V–418b
revolutionary war V–58b; VI–128b
Rogerenes VI–162a
stone fleets VI–415a
War of 1812 VI–415b; VII–153a
New London (Tex.) II–348a
NEW LONDON, BURNING OF (1781) **V–58b**
New Look (fashion) II–372b
NEW MADRID (Mo.)
V–58b; II–385a; IV–195b; V–63a
Newman, Albert H. II–106b
Newman, Robert VI–263b
Newman, W. P. (showman) VI–283a
Newman's Ridge (Tenn.) IV–301a
New Market (Va.) V–59a; VI–275a
NEW MARKET, BATTLE OF (1864) **V–59a**
NEW MEXICO V–59b; VI–355a,b, 394 (table)
Anasazi culture I–117a,b
Apache I–141b, 142a, 342b
Basin Indians III–362a
bill of rights I–300b
Black Cavalry I–310a
Black Infantry I–313b
Bonito pueblo I–329b
Bosque Redondo I–342b
boundary I–351a, 352a
caravans I–453a
Carlsbad Caverns I–455b
cattle drives II–249a; V–160a
cession by Mexico III–230a
Chicano protests VI–7b
Chihuahua Trail II–23b
Cibola II–37a
Civil War III–187b; IV–315b; VI–144a–b; VII–39b, 165b
Clayton Compromise II–73a
cliff dwellings IV–315b
colonial land grants IV–93a
Colorado River Compact II–130a–b
Compromise of 1850 II–139a, 150a; IV–28b
Compromise of 1850 V–39b
constitution VI–391b
cotton II–238b
donation lands II–363a
Dust Bowl II–382a
exploration I–24b, 269a, 269a, 288b; II–184b, 228b, 452b–53a, 460b–61a; III–220b
Folsom culture III–50a
Fort Bascom I–269b
Fort Fillmore III–24a
Fort Leavenworth IV–129a
Fort Stanton VI–385a
Fort Sumner VI–439b
Fort Union VII–145a
Franciscans III–94a
fur trade III–144a
Gadsden Purchase III–145b
gasoline tax III–153a
Genizaro Indians III–162b
Gila Wilderness III–73b, 75b
Gran Quivira III–211a
Hohokam culture III–289a
Indian agriculture IV–327a
Indian missions III–385b
Indians III–367a,b, 396a
Indian wars VII–239a,b
Inscription Rock III–420a
irrigation III–478b
Laguna Indians IV–90a
land grants for education IV–93b
Land of Shalam VI–268a
Lincoln County War IV–155a
Louisiana boundary IV–197b
manganese III–13a
Manhattan Project IV–238b
Maxwell land grant IV–92b, 278a
Mesilla IV–315b
Mexican boundary IV–321a,b
Mexican War I–361a; IV–323a,b
Mogollon culture IV–385b
molybdenum III–15a
mountain passes V–224b
national parks and monuments V–217a,b, 218 (table)
Navaho I–342b; V–8b, 9a
Old Spanish Trail VII–217b
Oñate's explorations V–155a–b
Pecos V–241a
Penitent Brothers V–245b
petroleum IV–334a; VI–356b, 357a
Pike's expedition V–312a
political party emblems II–437b
popular sovereignty V–155a
potash III–17b
presidios V–399b; VI–364a
Pueblo V–8b, 459a
Pueblo Revolt V–4a, 460b
purchase from Mexico IV–324b
railroads VI–33b
ranches III–302b
Red River Indian War VI–64a
referendum VI–66b
resorts and spas VI–100b, 101a
Rio Grande VI–143a,b
ruins VII–114a
Sangre de Christo grant VI–210b
Santa Fe VI–214b
Santa Fe Trail VI–215a,b
settlement II–127b, 184b; VII–284a
Shaw's expedition VI–271b
sheep wars VI–273a
silver mining I–354b; VI–292a
slavery II–150a–b; V–360a
southern railroad route VI–353b
Spanish Inquisition III–420b
Spanish missions IV–367a,b; VI–162a
Staked Plain VI–380b
state-making process VI–401a–b
Taos VI–460b
Texan–Santa Fe expedition VII–38b
Texan–Santa Fe trade VII–36a
Texas cession II–150b
trail driving I–473b
trails VII–100a
Vial's Road VII–178b
vigilantes VII–187b
Villa raid VII–187b
wilderness area III–73b
World War I VII–325a
Zimmerman telegram VII–368b
Zuni III–301a, 395b; V–460a; VII–372a
New Mexico Territory
acquisition II–475a
Arizona I–172a
Newmire (Colo.) III–15a
NEW NATIONALISM V–60a; IV–140b; V–427b–28a; VI–458a
New Negro IV–166b
NEW NETHERLAND V–60b; II–124a; III–334a; V–86a; VII–94b
blacksmiths I–317a
Catskill Mountains I–471a
Connecticut settlement III–309a–b
Duke of York's proprietary VII–359a,b
Dutch–Indian War II–382b
Dutch West India Company II–383b
England I–361a; V–41a; VII–279a
feudalism III–18a
Fort Christina II–35a
fur trade III–141a; VII–104b
Harlem III–253a–b
kermis IV–43b
Long Island settlements IV–185a,b
Lutheran churches IV–206a
New England trade III–140b
New Haven Colony V–55b
oats V–130a
patroonships IV–241b
petition and remonstrance V–266a
schools II–393b, 394b
sheep III–51b
Walloons III–121a; VII–221b
New Netherland (ship) V–60b
New Netherland Company III–141a
"New Norway" (Pa.) V–152b
New Orange V–41a
NEW ORLEANS (La.)
V–62a; II–252a, 347a; III–330a–b; IV–194a, 368a, 372a, 455a; V–67b, 173a; VI–340b; VII–159a
Acadians I–6b
agrarianism I–33a
American party IV–193b
architecture I–160a, 160a,b
Balize I–246b
Barataria I–265b
bargemen I–267b
barnstorming I–268b
candlemaking I–444b
capital I–301a
Carondelet Canal I–459b
Casket Girls I–466a
cattle I–473a
cession to Spain VI–194a
cholera II–33b
Civil War I–398a; II–68b, 164a; IV–371a,b; V–63b; VII–181b
coasting trade II–90b
Côte des Allemands I–173b
cotton II–68a, 238a
Creole slave case I–28a
crime commission II–263b
DeBow's *Review* II–298a
directory II–343b
dueling II–376b
Duelling Oaks II–377a
Eads jetties II–384b
exploration I–354b, 499a; III–119a
federal mint I–204a; IV–360a
filibuster III–352a
flatboat commerce III–35b
Forest Service III–76b
Fort Saint John VI–191a
French II–126b; III–114b, 115a, 120a; IV–326a
furniture III–135b
fur trade III–140a, 144a
Gaines Case III–146a
gambling III–149b
growth II–41a
hospitals III–306b
Houma Indians III–308a
Indian factory system

NEW ORLEANS (cont.)
II–480a
jazz IV–440a
Kaskaskia trade IV–32a
Knights of the White Camelia IV–53a
Kossuth's visit IV–57b
Lafayette's visit IV–84a
Lake Pontchartrain V–356a
lead III–147a; IV–122b
lotteries IV–196a
Louisiana purchase IV–196b
Mafia incident III–352a; IV–221a
Mardi Gras Iv–249b
martial law V–63b
Mexican commerce IV–320b
Mexican War II–324a
Mina expedition IV–348a
Mississippi trade IV–302b; VI–149a–b
organized crime II–262b
panic of 1857 IV–198b
Pass Christian V–224a
Pittsburgh trade V–321b
prices V–404b
race riots III–103b, 154a; VI–8a
railroads VI–25a, 27a, 34b, 35a, 36b, 37a
Reconstruction riots V–64a; VI–57a
red light district II–261a
retrocession to France VI–150b
revolutionary war I–367a; III–38b, 179a; IV–193a; VI–363a, 367b; VII–303a
right of deposit II–333a–b; IV–373b; V–315b; VII–111b
sailing packets V–183b
shipping IV–374a,b
Slaughterhouse Cases VI–303a
slums VI–314a
Southern Commercial Convention VI–352a
Southwestern Railroad Convention VI–20b
Spanish–Indian relations V–101a
Spanish rule I–399b; III–326b–27a; VII–276a,b
steamboating V–63a; VI–148b, 406b, 407b, 408a
steamship lines II–91a
Storyville II–260a
street paving V–230a
street railways VI–418b
subtreasury VI–427a
sugar industry VI–437a
Sullivan–Corbett fight V–422b
Sultana disaster II–349a
tennis VII–29a
trade VII–83a,b
trade unions IV–61b
trading post VII–95b
transcontinental railroad IV–28b
Treaty of Paris IV–197b
United Confederate Veterans VII–149b
Ursulines I–467a; VII–160b
U.S. acquisition II–333b
Vieux Carré VII–187a
War of 1812 III–36a; IV–258b; V–63a; VI–191a
White League VII–292b
World's Industrial and Cotton Centennial Exposition VII–324b
yellow fever II–454b; VII–355b
New Orleans (ship of the line) VI–282a
NEW ORLEANS (steamboat) **V–63a**; III–132a; IV–372b, 374a; VI–148b, 406b, 408a,b
NEW ORLEANS, BATTLE OF (1815) **V–63a**; I–342a,b, 490b; VII–188a, 234b
Afro-American soldiers IV–339b
backwoodsmen I–240a
marines IV–251b–52a
navy V–19b
NEW ORLEANS, CAPTURE OF (1862) **V–63b**; II–63a; IV–371b, 375a, 413b; V–19b; VII–146b, 240b
NEW ORLEANS, MARTIAL LAW IN (1806–07) **V–63b**
New Orleans, Opelousas and Great Western Railroad VI–36b
New Orleans and Northeastern Railroad VI–37a
New Orleans Delta (news.) VI–241a
New Orleans Public Belt Highway Bridge I–364b
NEW ORLEANS RIOTS (1873–74) **V–64a**
New Paltz (N.Y.) II–384a; III–315a
New Panama Canal Company III–265b
New Path I–279b
New Philadelphia (Ohio) VI–226a
NEW PLYMOUTH COLONY V–64b; II–364b–65a; IV–264b–65a,b, 423b; V–324a; VI–427b; VII–95a
adventurers I–16a
agriculture I–36b
apples III–128b
assembly II–117a
blacksmithing I–317a
Boston I–344a
Cape Ann settlers I–446b
Castine (Maine) I–466a
Connecticut trading post V–334a–b
conservation II–187a
corn II–226a
demographic study II–328b
Dominion of New England V–50b
dress II–370b–71a
dueling II–376b
fishing rights I–446b
food preservation III–54b
Fort Pentegoet V–253b, 260a
founding II–123b
freemen II–117a
fur trade III–140b
general court III–155b
glassworks II–4b
historical account III–280a
Indian trade IV–314b–15a
King Philip's War III–223a
lack of capital I–449a
land title VI–4a
Massachusetts Bay II–124a
Mayflower IV–278b
Mount Hope IV–422b
Pilgrims V–312b
plans of union II–121b–22a
Puritans V–469a
religion VI–75b
Rhode Island claims I–350b
salt II–4b; VI–202a
schoolteachers VI–229a
Separatists I–371b; VI–199a, 262a
starving time VI–388a
suffrage II–35b
Sunday schools VI–442a
supplies from Maine IV–37a
Thanksgiving Day VII–46a
trade IV–37b
United Colonies of New England IV–270a; VII–149a
Weston's settlement VII–279a
NEWPORT (R.I.) **V–65b**; I–149a; III–326a; IV–452a; V–186a; VI–100b, 131b, 132a; VII–82b
candlemaking VI–372b
colonial assembly II–117b
colonial commerce II–119a
conservation II–187a
furniture III–134b
game laws VII–296b
Naval Academy V–9b
Naval Torpedo Station V–28a
Naval War College V–24a
navy yard V–28a
newspaper V–69a
nonimportation agreements V–104b
Officer Candidate School V–29a
Providence Plantations V–439a
Quakers V–469b
Redwood Library IV–144b
revolutionary war V–65b; VI–438a–b
settlement II–124a
smuggled goods V–320a
tennis VII–29a,b
triangular trade VII–119a,b, 120a
Newport (Va.)
revolutionary war VI–124b
Newport, Christopher (mariner) II–124b; III–488b
Richmond VI–136b
Somers' voyage VI–338a
Susan Constant VI–451a
NEWPORT, FRENCH ARMY AT (1780–81) **V–65b**; III–117b
NEWPORT BARRACKS (Ky.) **V–66a**
Newport Casino VII–29a
Newport Folk Festival V–65b
Newport Jazz Festival V–65b
Newport Mercury (news.) V–65b
Newport News (Va.) VII–196a
Appam Case V–422a
Camp Hill I–435a
Camp Stewart I–435a
Civil War IV–396b
revolutionary war VII–199a
Newport-style furniture II–99a
New Regulation of Presidios (1772) VI–168b
New Richmond (Ohio) V–279b
New River I–88b, 277b; II–369b; III–223a, 251a, 292b, 488a; V–145a; VII–125b
New Rochelle (N.Y.) III–315a; VII–293a
Newsboy V–71a
New School Presbyterians II–36b; III–469a
News commentators II–424b
New Siberian Islands I–116a; V–336a
New Side, Presbyterianism. *See* New Lights
New Smyrna (Fla.) III–38b
NEW SMYRNA COLONY V–66a
Newson, Henry W. (phys.) V–299b
NEW SOUTH V–66b
Afro-Americans I–28b–32a
Afro-American suffrage III–20a–b, 92b–94a
American Independent party I–106b
backlash I–239a
Black Codes I–310a
black power I–316a
campaign of 1868 I–422a
campaign of 1876 I–422b–23b
campaign of 1948 I–429b
carpetbaggers I–459b–60a
chain gangs I–489a
child labor II–24b
civil rights I–316a,b; II–56a
convict labor II–217a
Democratic party II–327a–b; VII–134b
desegregation II–57b–58b
farm tenancy I–40b–41a
freedmen III–103a–b
free trade III–113b
hookworm III–298b
industrialization I–33b
Mason-Dixon Line IV–263a
missionaries I–460a

New Deal V–48b
Peabody Education Fund III–82b
poor whites V–359a
populism V–365a
radical right VI–12b
Reconstruction I–354a, 380b; III–295a–b
runoff primary V–407a
sectionalism VI–254a–b
"separate but equal" doctrine II–54a–b
Student Nonviolent Coordinating Committee VI–420b
textile industry VII–45a
Tredegar Iron Works VII–113b
voting behavior VII–210a
White Citizens Councils VII–291a
white primary V–407a
white supremacy II–57b
wool industry VII–321a
See also Alabama; Black Codes
New Spain
California I–405a
exploration I–96b, 141a, 399b
Mississippi River I–459b
Newspaper Editors, American Society of V–76a, 77b
Newspaper Editors, International Society of Weekly V–77b
Newspaper Guild V–77b; VI–420a–b
NEWSPAPERS V–68a; III–283b; IV–271b–72a
abolitionists I–137a
advertising II–354b; VI–323b
American Antiquarian Society III–285a
American Weekly Mercury V–251a
Associated Press I–206b
Atlanta Constitution V–66b
Aurora VII–293b
bills of mortality VII–205b
Boston Gazette VII–155b
campaign of 1896 I–425b
Catholic I–467b, 469b, 470b
censorship I–481a, 481a
Charleston News and Courier V–66b; VII–58b
Cherokee Phoenix VI–263a
Chicago Tribune III–19a
Constitution I–131a
constitutional debate V–353a
copyright II–224b
Cuban revolution II–268b
Dallas Herald VII–187b
Denison News VII–187b
Dubuque (Iowa) II–376a
Emancipator II–436a
freedom of the press III–104b
Freeman's Journal III–108b
Genius of Universal Emancipation II–436a
government newspapers III–202a
Grosjean v. *American Press Company* III–229a
Independent Journal III–4a
Ithaca (N.Y.) *Chronicle* VI–163a
Jeffersonian Republicans VI–94a
Liberator II–436a; IV–141a
Los Angeles Star V–180b
mailing privileges III–98a
Militant II–446a
Missouri Republican VII–103b
muckrakers IV–424b
Nation VI–157a
National Gazette IV–463b
National Intelligencer IV–465b; V–356a; VII–249b–50a
National Tribune IV–471b
New Hampshire Gazette V–54a
New Orleans Delta VI–241a
Newport Mercury V–65b
New York City V–82b
New York Evening Post VII–264a
New York Herald V–336a; VII–23a
New York Journal VI–84b
New York Morning Herald VII–356a
New York State V–87a
New York Sun II–256a; IV–406b
New York Times V–258b, 443a; VI–459b
New York Tribune II–222b; III–296a; V–157a
New York Truth IV–410a
New–York Weekly Journal VII–368a–b
New York World II–268b; VII–356a
Niles' Weekly Register V–96b
North Carolina V–115b
North Carolina Standard II–165a; III–289b
Observer IV–199a
organized crime II–262b
Pennsylvania Gazette V–251a
Pennsylvania Journal II–264b
People VI–325a
Philadelphia Daily American Advertiser VII–251a
Philanthropist II–37b; V–279a
Pittsburgh Gazette V–322b
political advertising V–450a
political campaigns I–415b
Porcupine's Gazette V–366a
Portland Standard V–180b
postal service V–371a
Preservation News IV–472a
presidential messages V–398b
Providence Gazette V–439b
Republic IV–465b
Rescuer V–130b
Richmond Enquirer VI–138a
Richmond Whig VI–49a
Rivington's Gazette VI–151b
Roosevelt, Theodore I–116b
rural free delivery VI–172b, 173a
San Francisco Chronicle V–180b
San Francisco Examiner VII–356a
Saturday Press V–30b
science VI–230b, 235a
Scientific American VI–231a
Scioto Gazette VI–239a
Sheppard trial VII–118a–b
slang VI–300a
Social Justice II–446a
society columns IV–241a,b
Sonora Democrat V–180b
Spanish–American War IV–227b
Springfield (Mass.) *Republican* III–148b
Stamp Act VI–381b
Stars and Stripes IV–471b
subsidies VI–425b
Topeka Commonwealth VII–187b
United Press VII–152a
Washington Globe III–187b; VI–85b
Washington National Era VII–137b
Washington Post VII–255b
Watergate VII–254a–b, 255b
Western World VI–366a
women journalists VII–317b
World War I II–445b; VII–332b–33a
World War II VII–333b, 336a
yellow journalism VII–356a
Newsprint V–77a, 212b
Newsprint magazines II–341b
New Student (news.) VII–365a
NEW SWEDEN COLONY V–80a; V–80b, 246a
Fort Christina II–35a; V–42b
leather industry IV–127b
Lutheran churches IV–205b–06a
New Haven Colony V–55b
NEW SWEDEN COMPANY V–80b; II–123b
Newsweek (mag.) IV–222b
News wire services V–79b
NEW THOUGHT MOVEMENT V–81a
Newt Kash Shelter (Ky.) I–11b
Newton (Kans.) I–2a; II–251b; IV–26a; VII–294a
Newton, A. Edward I–333a
Newton, Battle of. *See* Elmira, Battle of
Newton, Huey P. I–315b, 316a
Newton, Isaac (philos., math.) I–45a; III–166a, 480b
Newton, John (slaver) VI–310b
Newtown (Mass.) VI–151a
Newtown (N.Y.) VI–438a
colonial settlement IV–185a
revolutionary war II–433a
New Towne (Mass.) I–411b
New Ulm (Minn.)
Farmer–Labor party II–491a
NEW ULM, DEFENSE OF (1862) **V–81a**; II–283b; VI–296b
New unionism IV–65a
New Utrecht (N.Y.) I–370a; IV–185a
New Village (N.Y.) II–462b
New Voyage to Carolina III–26b; IV–231a
"NEW WEST" V–81b; V–70b
New World
English colonizing projects IV–182b
Norumbega V–123a
New World (news.) I–334a
New York (cruiser) VI–206b, 216b, 217a, 282a
New York, City University of V–213b
New York, Port of II–432b; V–87b
New York, Treaty of (1790) I–355b; III–383a; V–101a; VI–366b
See also McGillivray Incident
New York, University of the State of II–396b, 404b; VI–158b; VII–156b
New York Academy of Sciences VI–235b–36a, 237b
New York American (news.) III–276b
New York Amsterdam News (news.) V–76a
New York and Boston Illinois Land Company IV–99b, 345a
New York and Erie Railroad VI–25a, 34a

NEW YORK AND GENESEE COMPANY V–81b
New York and Harlem Railroad VII–127b
New York and Mississippi Valley Printing Telegraph Company VII–276b
New York Aquarium I–275b
New York Association for Improving the Condition of the Poor I–495a; V–280a; VI–327b
New York Audubon Society VII–298a
New York Bank for Savings II–255a
New York Bay IV–237a, 452a
New York Botanical Garden I–348a
New York Call (news.) V–74a
New York Central Railroad III–79a, 312b; IV–386b; V–87a; VI–25b, 32a, 35a, 35b; VII–83b, 100b
Mohawk and Hudson VI–24b
"public be damned" V–443a
rate wars VI–22b, 23a
strike of 1877 IV–63b
New York Chamber of Commerce I–153b
New York, Chicago and Saint Louis Railroad VI–35a
New York Cigarmakers Union IV–65a
NEW YORK CITY V–82a; II–41a,b; V–277b; VII–266b
Adams Express Company I–10a
Afro-Americans I–23a, 25b, 30a; IV–339b
air service I–67b
American Federation of Teachers IV–76a
American Telephone and Telegraph III–409b
antiwar demonstrators IV–77a
apartment houses I–143a,b
archives I–169a
art galleries II–104a–06b
assay office I–203b; IV–360a
Astor investments III–79a
Atlantic Intracoastal Waterway VI–148b–49a
avant-garde art V–192a–93a
ballet II–288b–89a
banking II–73a–b; III–79b
Barnum's Museum VII–48a
baseball I–269b
Battery I–275b; II–432b
Battery Park City II–49a
Bellevue Hospital III–306b; V–126b
Black Ball Line VI–280b
blizzards II–351a
Board of Education II–396b
Board of Health II–33b
book publishing I–333b, 334a; II–18b, 41b
boondoggling I–336b
bootlegging I–339b; II–262a
boroughs IV–185b
bossism I–343a,b
Boston post road V–261a
boweries I–354b
Bowery I–355a
Bowling Green I–356a
bridges I–364a,b
Broadway I–368b
Brooklyn I–370a
Brooklyn Navy Yard II–348b; V–28a, 29a
Bryant Park II–474b
burghers I–384b
business district fire (1835) III–430b
campaign of 1948 V–429a
campaign of 1952 V–429b
canals II–322a,b
capital market III–64b, 67a
Catholic diocese I–467a
cattle I–473a
Central Park II–46a; IV–96b
chamber of commerce I–491a
chemical education II–10b
child health care IV–275b
cholera II–33b
Christian and Missionary Alliance II–34b
citrus industry II–43b
city council II–145b
Civil War I–435a; VI–181a
clipper ships III–45b
clothing industry II–81b–82b
coast-to-coast mail service V–178a
colonial commerce II–119a; V–57a
colonial labor IV–60a
colonial suffrage VI–434a,b
Columbia University II–132a
conciliation process II–157b
Cooper Union II–222a
crime II–258a; IV–23a, 137b–38a
Crystal Palace Exhibition II–474a; III–136a
Customs Intelligence Bureau II–277a
death records IV–149a
Deism III–112a
Democratic clubs V–345b
Democratic-Republican party IV–260a
diphtheria IV–150b
directory II–343b
disasters II–346b, 346b, 347a,b, 349a,b, 350b
domestic trade VII–83b
draft riots I–468a; II–186a, 258a, 368b; III–436a; IV–62b; VII–191a–b
earthquake II–385a
education of handicapped III–248b
electric railway VI–40a
electric station II–414a
elevated railway II–428a; VI–429a,b
elevator buildings I–378a
Elgin Botanical Garden I–348a
environmental sanitation VI–211b, 212a,b
Erie Canal II–460a; III–448a; V–50a
Evangelical Alliance II–465b
exhibitions II–99a
Farmer–Labor party II–492b
Father Knickerbocker IV–161b
federal capital I–208b
federal records center III–284b
Federal Reserve banks III–6b, 7b, 8a
Fenian movement III–10b
Fifth Avenue Hotel I–383a
firemen II–432b–33a
First International (labor org.) IV–63b
fiscal crisis V–87b; VI–398b
flag III–35a
foreign trade VII–86b
Forest Hills II–46b
Fort Amsterdam II–383a
Fort Clinton I–275b
Fort Lafayette IV–83b
Fort Nassau II–383a
Fort Tryon Park IV–97a
Fort Washington VII–246b
Four Hundred III–85a
Fraunces Tavern III–100a
Freemasons III–109a
freemen III–109b
Free School Society II–396b
freighting VII–100a
French and Indian War III–116a, 117a
fruit growing III–128b
Fulton III–131b
furniture III–135b, 138a, 139a
fur trade III–403a; VII–105a
gambling III–149b, 150a
General Seminary II–455a
Girl Scouts III–181b
gold exchange III–190a
Governors Island III–206b
Grolier Club II–109a
Harlem II–261b; III–253a
health department I–241a; IV–286a
Henry Street Settlement V–280a
Hicksites III–274a
hockey III–287b
Holt's *Journal* III–292b
homeopathy III–293b
hospitals IV–275a
Hudson–Fulton celebration III–312a
Hudson River III–312a
Huguenots III–121a
ice industry VI–69a
industry VI–225a
infant death rate IV–151a
intercoastal trade IV–311b
Italian immigrants III–337b
Kinetoscopes IV–417a
Kossuth's visit IV–57a–b
Labor Day IV–79a
labor party movement IV–81a
Lafayette's visit IV–84a
land speculation IV–100b
Leisler Rebellion V–84b
letter carriers strike V–374a
liberty pole IV–144a
libraries IV–145a
Lincoln Center II–48b, 289a
Lindbergh's Atlantic flight IV–156b
Lind's tour IV–157a
Little Church Around the Corner IV–168b
Longacre Square I–368b–69a
lotteries IV–191a
Loyalist troops VI–129b
Lyceum of Natural History IV–348b
Madison Square Garden IV–220b
Manhattan IV–237a–b
manners IV–241a
manufacturing exposition IV–244a
mapmaking I–462b
meat supply IV–280b
mechanics' institutes IV–281a–b
medical education IV–283a,b
Metroliner railroad VI–31b
Metropolitan Museum of Art II–100b, 102b, 103a
microwave communications system IV–333a
milk trade II–280a
minstrel shows IV–359b
Mississippi Valley trade IV–302b
Morgan Library II–109a–b
motion pictures IV–417a,b, 418a
movie censorship I–480a
museums I–305a; IV–436b
Narrows IV–452a
National Association of Manufacturers IV–461b
"Negro Plot" of 1741 V–32b
neighborhood school control IV–173a
New South V–66b
newspapers V–69a,b, 71a,b 72a, 73a,b, 74b, 75a,b, 76a,b, 77a, 78a,b, 79a,b
New-York Historical Society III–278b
Niblo's Garden V–93b
nonimportation agreements V–104a,b

Norfolk trade V–109b
Oxford Movement VI–78a
painters V–186a
Panama-Pacific Exposition V–203b
Panama Railroad V–203b
panic of 1837 V–206b
panic of 1857 VI–370b
Paulists V–229b
paving V–229b–30a
Pennsylvania Railroad IV–177a
pewter work VI–290b, 291b
pharmacy society V–275a
police V–339a
population II–41b
porcelain III–183b
port I–40a
postal service V–371a,b, 372a,b
post roads V–374b–75a
pottery V–379b
Presbyterianism V–391b, 392a
price-fixing V–401b
prices V–404a,b, 405a,b
price war II–483a
prison ships VI–118a
private schools VI–228b
proportional representation V–435a
Protective War Claims Association V–438b
public health V–447a; VI–173b; VII–158a
Quakers V–470b
race riots I–31b, 32a; IV–457b; VI–7a, 8a,b
radio broadcasting VI–15a, 16a
railroad pool V–358a
railroad rate wars VI–23a
railroads III–450a; V–62a; VI–33b, 34a,b, 35b, 36a; VII–100b, 102b
Raines Law VI–40b
rapid transit system I–370b; IV–428b; V–41b
recording industry IV–442b
Reservoir Square II–474b
restaurants III–52b
retail trade VII–84b
Revolution III–189b; VI–112b
revolutionary committees III–421b
revolutionary war III–117b, 498b; IV–49a, 185b, 186a; VI–123a,b, 124a, 126b, 372b–73a, 422b; VII–199a,b, 246b–47a, 293a, 303a, 360b–61a,b
Richelieu River VI–136b
Rivington's Gazette VI–151b
Rockefeller University VI–158b
Russell Sage Foundation VI–177a
sailing packets I–308b; V–183b
Sailor's Snug Harbor VI–186b
security exchanges II–255b
shipbuilding VI–279b
silk VI–286b–87a, 287a
silversmithing VI–289b
silver work VI–290a
ski trains VI–298a
skyscrapers VI–299a
slave insurrections III–437a; VI–303b
slavery VI–311b
slave smuggling VI–322a
slave trade VI–309a
Sloan mansion III–446a
slums I–355a; VI–313b, 314a,b
Smithsonian Institution VI–319a,b
smuggled goods V–320a
social work VI–330b
Society of the Sons of the Revolution VI–339b
soda fountains VI–332a
Sons of Liberty VI–339a
Sons of the American Revolution VI–339a
southern V–325a
southern trade VI–340b
stagelines VI–380a; VII–99b
Stamp Act Congress VI–382a
Stamp Act riot VI–382a
Statue of Liberty VI–405b
steamboats III–131b; IV–310a; V–57b; VI–407a
steam engines VI–409a
steamship lines II–91a; IV–310a
stone fleets VI–415a
street lighting IV–153b
street railways VI–418a,b
subtreasury III–354b; VI–427a
suburban growth VI–427b
subway II–428a; IV–428a; VI–429a–b; VII–128a
sugar house prisons VI–436b
sugar industry VI–437a
sulfuric acid manufacture II–6a
Sunday schools VI–442b
sweatshop VI–454a
Tammany Hall I–417a; IV–214a; V–345a, 459a; VI–460b; VII–295a
tea party VII–16a
tea trade VII–15a, 17a
telephone VII–20a
television VII–21b
temperance movement III–261b
"Tenderloin" II–260a
tenements VII–23b, 24a–b
theater VII–46b, 47a, 49a,b, 50a,b, 50b–51a
Theosophical Society VII–52a
Times Square I–368b–69a
Tin Pan Alley VII–62b
toll bridges VII–69b
trade unions IV–61b
Trespass Act VII–116b
Triangle fire II–82a; IV–68b; VII–118b
triangular trade VII–119b, 120a
tuberculosis VII–126b–27a
tunnels VII–127b, 128a
Tweed Ring II–232a; IV–454b; VI–142a; VII–131a
typhoid IV–150b
Vanderbilt mansion III–446b
veterinary medicine VII–175b–76a,b
Vietnam demonstration V–237a
volunteer firemen III–25a
voting behavior VII–210b
Wall Street VII–221b, 222b
War of 1812 II–329a; V–394a; VII–235a,b, 240b
Washington's inauguration III–350b–51a
water supply I–263b; VII–258a,b–59a
waterworks VI–408b
Wells, Fargo VII–267a
Workingmen's Party VII–322a
world's fair V–89a
World Trade Center II–49a
Young Women's Christian Association VII–364a
Young Women's Hebrew Association VII–362b
Zenger trial V–69a
zoning II–46b–47a; VII–370a
See also Manhattan; New Amsterdam; Staten Island
NEW YORK CITY, CAPTURE OF (1673) **V–84a**; V–82a
NEW YORK CITY, PLOT TO BURN V–84a
New York City Ballet II–289a–b; IV–237b
New York City Center II–289a
New York City Central Labor Union IV–79a
New York City Opera IV–237b
New York City Passenger Ship Terminal V–368b
New York Clearinghouse. *See* Clearinghouse, New York
New York Coffee Exchange II–141a
New York College of Veterinary Surgeons VII–176b
NEW YORK COLONY V–84b; II–124a; V–86a; VI–346b
Afro-Americans III–253a
Anglicanism VI–75b
Arabian gold I–151a
assembly II–117b–18a, 309b
beaver hats I–282a; IV–242b
billeting I–297a; VII–80a
bills of credit I–300a
Cartagena expedition I–461b
charter II–383b
Charter of Liberties I–500b
Church of England II–36a
commodities as money II–140b
Connecticut II–182b
Dominion of New England V–50b; VII–360a
Duke of York's laws II–379a
education II–394b–95a
entertainment IV–43b
Esopus War II–462b
fire fighting III–25a
flour milling III–42b
Fort Amsterdam II–383a
Fort Edward II–405b–06a
Fort La Galette IV–85a
Fort Nassau II–383a
Fort Orange II–383a
French raiding parties II–267a
Great Nine Partners' Patent III–220b
hat manfacture III–262a
Hester case III–274a
historical account III–280b
horse racing III–304b
Indian relations IV–33a
intestate estates III–464a
judiciary II–121a
justice of the peace IV–22b
King George's War IV–46b
King William's War IV–49b; VI–1b–2a
leasehold IV–127b
Leisler Rebellion II–125a; IV–134a
liquor laws IV–158b
Long Island IV–185b
manors IV–241b
militia IV–345b
Monhegan Island IV–396a
Mutiny Act of 1765 IV–445b
natural rights doctrine V–7b
naval stores V–14b
New England trade III–140b
New Jersey settlers V–57a
oil deposits IV–43b
painting V–185a–b
Pemaquid Point V–243b
Pinkster celebration V–316b
plans of union II–121b–22a
primogeniture V–408a
proprietary agents V–435b–36a
proprietary grant I–499b; V–436b
provincial congress V–439b
punishments V–464b
Quakers V–470a
Quartering Act VI–112a
Queen Anne's War VI–2b
religious toleration II–394b
settlement II–123b
sheep VI–272b
suffrage III–91a; VI–434a
sugar refining II–5a
taxation VI–111b
wars IV–226a

NEW YORK COLONY (cont.)
woman's suffrage VII–314b
writs of assistance VII–345a
Zenger trial III–104b
See also New Amsterdam; New Netherland
New York cordwainers' case (1809–10) IV–61a
New York Cotton Exchange II–141a, 469b
New York County (N.Y.) V–82a
New York Crystal Palace Exhibition (1853). *See* Exhibition of the Industry of All Nations
New York Daily Advertiser (news.) V–71a
New York Daily Graphic (news.) V–74b, 77a
New York Daily Mirror (news.) V–74b
New York Daily News (news.) V–72a, 75a, 76b
New York Daily Times (news.) V–73b
New Yorker (mag.) IV–222b
New York Evening Journal (news.) V–73b
New York Evening Post (news.) IV–161b; V–68a, 69b, 71b, 73a, 73a,b, 73b; VII–264a
New York ex rel. Bryant v. *Zimmerman* (1928) I–204b
New York Eye Infirmary III–306b
New York Foundation III–83a
New York Gazette (news.) V–69a, 82b
New York General Trades Union IV–61b–62a
"NEW YORK GETS THE NEWS" V–85b
New York Giants (baseball) I–271a
New York Harbor III–51a, 312a; IV–83b; V–82a, 83a; VI–146a
New York Herald (news.) I–17a, 401a; III–81b; V–336a; VII–23a
New York Herald Building I–164b
New York Historical Society II–101b, 103a, 108a; III–137b, 278b, 285a
New York Hospital III–306b
New York Illustrated Daily News (news.) V–74b
New York Insurance Office (Phila.) III–427b
New York Journal (news.) I–464b; II–268b; IV–227b; V–76b
comic strips V–72a
Maine VI–84b
New York Journall (news.) V–82b, 85a
New York Journal of Commerce I–207a
New York Land Company III–243a
New York Ledger (mag.) IV–222a
New York Life Insurance Building (Kansas City) VI–299a
New York Mathematical Society I–109a
New York Missionary Society III–385b
New York Moral Reform Society IV–409a
New York Morning Herald (news.) V–71a,b, 73b; VII–356a
New York Naval Militia VI–282a
New York, New Haven and Hartford Railroad VI–25a, 32a, 35b
robbery VII–97a
See also Penn Central
New York Philharmonic Society IV–437b
New York Produce Exchange II–141a, 469b
New York Protestant Association V–2b
New York Public Library II–102b, 109a; IV–145a, 292b
New York Renaissance (basketball) I–273a
New York School (poets) IV–165b
New York School of Philanthropy I–495a
New York Scientific and Mechanic Institution IV–281a
New York Society for the Prevention of Cruelty to Children VI–331b
New York Society for the Suppression of Vice I–478b
New York Society Library II–108a
New York Staats-Zeitung (news.) V–75b
NEW YORK STATE V–86a; VI–394 (table)
Adirondack Park Agency Act IV–101b
Albany I–81a
Albany Congress I–82a
Amana Community II–147a
American Fur Company I–105a
American party I–109b
Annapolis Convention I–126a
Antirent War I–134a; IV–92a
Articles of Confederation I–199a
banking I–107b–08a, 253a, 259b; IV–198b; VI–185a
bankruptcy laws V–140a; VI–422a
Barnburners I–267b; III–111b, 318a
black officeholders VI–432b
black suffrage III–437b; VI–431a
blizzards I–320b
bossism I–343a,b
Boston Ten Townships I–347b
boundary disputes I–350b–51a; IV–92a
boycotts I–356b
Bucktails I–374b
buffalo (animal) I–375a, 375b
building and loan associations I–376b
campaign of 1828 I–418b
campaign of 1848 III–111b
campaign of 1948 V–429a
Canal Ring I–442a
canals I–374b, 375b, 443b; IV–174b, 412b
canal society I–444a
canal system V–250b
Catskill Mountains I–471a
cattle disease VII–177a
cement rock I–378b; IV–174b
Chinese population II–30a
city planning II–46a
Civil Service Act II–60a
coinage II–384b
colonial land grants IV–92a
colonial land speculation IV–98b, 98b
colonial wars IV–85b–86b
Colorado settlers VII–146a
conciliation process II–157b
constitution I–134a; II–243a, 243a–b; VI–390b, 391a
Cornell University II–227a
corrupt practices act II–232b
Council of Appointment II–243
Council of Revision II–243b
county agent I–42a
County Poor House Act VI–327b
court of appeals II–377b
crime II–262a–b
crime commission II–263b; V–416a
Croswell libel suit II–266a–b
Crown Point II–267a
dairy industry II–279b, 280a,b
death penalty I–450b
debtor laws II–299a
Declaration of Independence II–305a, 308a
Delaware River Basin Compact III–460a
Democratic party I–267b–68a
divorce II–356b
Dominicans II–362b
double jeopardy VII–154b
Dutch manors IV–102b
education II–396b, 403a
education of handicapped III–248a,b
Elmira Female College II–399a
Elmira Prison II–433a
enfranchisement of Jews IV–9a
Erie Canal I–40a, 442a,b, 443a; II–459b; III–64a, 202b, 448a
Erie Triangle II–460b
factory laws II–82a; IV–68b
fair-trade laws II–483a
Federalists III–4b
Federal Reserve Bank II–235a
Finney revivals III–24b
fish III–27a, 28a
Fishers Island III–31a
flour trade III–43a, 44a
folk art III–47a
foreign trade VII–86a
Fort Anne I–385a
Fort Clinton I–275b
Fort Plain V–323a
Fort Stanwix VI–385a
Franciscans III–94b
free banking system III–101b
Freemasons III–109a
French and Indian War IV–86a, 87b, 405b; VI–136b, 162b, 190a; VII–301a
French posts III–120a
furniture III–139b
fur trade III–141a,b, 142a,b
gambling III–150a
Genesee Road III–157a
geological survey III–165a,b; V–195b
German Flats III–172b
glassmaking III–185a
Gore III–200a
government at Kingston IV–49a
Hawaiian constitution III–263a
Hempstead III–271b
historic preservation V–392b
historic properties IV–472a
Holland Land Company III–291a–b
home missionary societies IV–365a–b, 366b
horse racing III–304b
hours of labor regulation IV–173b
Hudson River III–312a
Huguenots III–315a; V–342a
Hunkers III–317b
hurricanes II–351b, 352a; III–319b
immigrants II–432b
incorporating statute II–229a
incorporation laws III–204a
Indiana settlers III–370a
Indian missions III–385b
Indian removal III–394b
Indians I–398a,b; III–396b
inheritance tax III–418
inland lock navigation III–419b
insurance investigations III–430b–31a, 433b–34a; V–208a,b
internal improvements

III–447b
interurban electric lines III–461b
Iroquois III–475a; VI–386a
Italian population III–338a
Jacksonian Democracy III–487a
Jesuits III–498b, 499a, 501b
juvenile courts IV–23b
Kakiate patent IV–24a
Ku Klux Klan IV–58b
Labadist colony IV–59b
Lake Champlain IV–85b
Lake Mohonk Conference IV–387b
landholding I–4a, 284b
land reform IV–101a
leasehold IV–127b
libel laws II–266a–b; IV–139b
life insurance cooperative II–220b
Little Nine Partners' Patent IV–169a
Locofoco party IV–175a
Long Island IV–185a
lotteries IV–191a,b
lottery III–149b
Loyalists VI–115b, 116a; VII–150b
Lusk Committee IV–205b
lyceum movement IV–207a
Macomb purchase IV–219b
Mahican IV–387a
mammals IV–231b
maple sugar IV–246b–47a
Masons I–132b
McLeod case IV–218a
meat-packing IV–280b
military tracts IV–344b
minimum-wage law IV–353a; V–48a
Minisink patent IV–354b
Mohawk and Hudson Railroad IV–386b
Mohawk Valley IV–386b
movie censorship I–479b
narcotics violations IV–451a
National Guard IV–463b
national monuments V–217b
natural gas V–5a
navy yard II–375a
Nebbia v. *New York* (1934) V–30b
New Hampshire Grants V–53b, 54b
New York and Genesee Company V–81b
New York City fiscal crisis VI–398b
Niagara Company V–91a
Niagara Falls V–91a–92b
oats V–130a
oblong V–130b
offtrack betting II–263a; III–305b
Ogden purchase V–139b
Ogdensburg V–139b
Ohio lands V–140b
oil V–269a; VI–356b
Oneida Colony V–155b; VI–325b
Order of United Americans VII–149a
Oswego V–175b
Otsego lands V–176a
Palatines V–195a
Panama Railroad V–200b
Pan-American Exposition V–204b
parole system V–221b
Phelps-Gorham purchase V–276a
Philipse's patent V–286a
political corruption I–313b
political parties I–107b
population VII–205b
Port Authority III–201b; V–368a; VI–402a
potash V–376a
pottery III–183b
presidential elections I–416b
Prohibition party V–430b
public employees IV–75b
public ownership V–455a
Pulteneny Purchase V–463b
Quakers V–470a
Quebec boundary VI–165b
Quids VI–3a,b
railroads VI–25a,b, 32b, 33b, 34a, 35b, 36a; VII–83b
Raines Law VI–40b
Reformed churches VI–69a
reptile survey VI–90b
resorts and spas VI–100b, 101a, 101a
retail sales VII–84b
revivalism VI–77b
revolutionary war I–384b, 398a; II–335a; III–108a–b; IV–86b, 354b; V–33b, 172b; VI–117b, 123b, 124a, 130a, 217a–b, 377a, 437b–38a; VII–164a
revolutionary war debts I–208b
Rip Van Winkle VI–145a
rivers VI–149a
roads III–450b; V–323a; VI–152b
rubber industry VI–167a
rum VI–170a; VII–278a
Rumbout's patent VI–170a
salt VI–202a,b
Saratoga Springs VI–217b
Schenectady VI–225b
schools VI–226b, 227a
secessionist movement VI–250a
Second Awakening IV–116b
settlement IV–338a; VII–282b, 283a,b
shoe manufacturing I–338b
single-tax plan VI–293b
slavery I–135b; VI–305a, 309a
Sleepy Hollow VI–312b
Snap Convention VI–322b
snowstorms II–352a
Southold VI–354b
steamboat monopoly III–131b–32a, 178a–b; V–289a; VI–407b
steam navigation III–32a
strikes VI–419a
suffrage III–91b
sugar trust VI–437b
Sulzer impeachment III–344b
Tammany Society I–374b
Tappan patent VI–461b
tariff VI–466a
taverns VII–2a
taxation VII–4a, 6b
teachers' loyalty oaths VII–16a
teachers' organizations IV–76a
teacher training II–396b
temperance movement VII–22b
Thanksgiving Day VII–46a
timberlands VII–60a
tobacco VII–66b
town meetings VII–79b
Treaty of Buffalo Creek III–383b
Treaty of Fort Stanwix III–383a
Trespass Act VII–116b
Tri-State Regional Planning Commission III–460a
Tuscarora War VII–130b
Urban Development Corporation II–48a
U.S. Constitution II–193a, 193b, 196b, 198b, 203b; III–4a; VII–53b
usury law III–443a
Vassar College II–399a
Vermont III–226b, 240b; VII–171b, 172a
Vermont Claims V–156a
War of 1812 III–118a, 120b; IV–406a; V–330b; VI–3a, 183b, 209a, 226a
Washington Benevolent Society VII–249a
water supply VII–259a
Wawayanda Patent VII–261b
western lands II–166a, 183b; V–162a, 162a, 443b; VII–273a
West Point VII–279b
westward movement VII–260a
wheat I–486a
Whig party VI–288a
White Woman of the Genesee VII–293b
windmills VII–304b
winemaking III–129a; VII–305b
wiretap legislation II–427b
woman's suffage VII–315a
workmen's compensation IV–68b, 294a
Zouaves VII–371b
See also Albany; Long Island

NEW YORK STATE, LAND SPECULATION IN V–88a; I–107b–08a; V–86a
New York State Antislavery Society V–145b
New York State Barge Canal II–460a; III–216b, 452a; VI–225b
New York State Correctional Facility at Attica. *See* Attica
New York State Education Department III–248b
New York State Kansas Committee IV–28a
New York State Temporary Relief Administration V–43b
New York State Thruway V–87b
New York State University Regents VI–235b
New York Stock Exchange II–255b, 469b; III–269b, 466a; VII–221b
panic of 1873 V–207a
panic of 1893 V–207b
stock ticker VI–413b
New York Sun (news.) I–207a; II–256a; IV–406b; V–71a,b, 73a, 73b
New York Sunday World (news.) V–71b
New York Times (news.) V–68a, 73a,b, 74b, 75a, 76b, 78a; VI–459b
Alabama libel suit III–105a–b
on manners IV–241b
Pentagon Papers III–105b; V–78b–79a, 258b; VII–254b
"public be damned" V–443a
Watergate V–78a–b
New York Times Company v. *Sullivan* (1964) III–104a,b; V–78b; VI–255a
New York Times v. *United States* (1971) V–258b
New York Tribune (news.) III–206b, 353b; IV–93b, 96a; V–73b, 75a, 77a
Copperheads II–222b
homestead movement III–296a
"On to Richmond" V–157a
New York Truth (news.) IV–410a
New York Typographical Union No. 6 VI–420a
New York University II–105a, 401b; V–83b, 135a
New York v. *New York Central Railroad Company* VII–309a
New York Wanderers (basketball) I–273a
New York Warehouse and Securities Company V–207a
New York Weekly Journal (news.) I–478b; V–69a; VII–368a–b
New York Weekly Tribune (news.) V–71a
New York Working Man's Advocate (jour.) IV–62a

New York World (news.)
I–464b; V–71b, 73a,b, 75a; VII–356a
comic strip V–72a
Spanish–American War II–268b
NEW YORK WORLD'S FAIRS (1939–40, 1964–65) **V–89a**; VII–21b
New York Yacht Club VII–348b
New York Zoological Park VII–371b
New York Zoological Society VII–371a
New Zealand
Battle Fleet cruise I–276b
International Monetary Fund I–361b
Korean War IV–55b
minimum wage IV–352b
Organization for Economic Cooperation and Development V–170b
Pacific Island claims III–425a
Rhodes scholars VI–134b
Southeast Asia Treaty Organization VI–350b
transpacific cable I–401a
United Nations Declaration VII–151b
Vietnam War VII–182b
Western Samoa VI–205a
World War II III–235b; VII–336b
Nez Perce (Indians) III–227a, 363a, 500a,b; VII–237b
Nez Perce, Fort (Wash.) VII–221a
Nez Perce Pass V–225a
NEZ PERCE WAR (1877) **V–89b**; I–76a; VII–239b
Battle at Bear Paw Mountain I–281a
Battle of Big Hole I–296a
Battle on Clearwater River II–74b
NFO. *See* National Farmers Organization
Ngo Dinh Diem. *See* Diem, Ngo Dinh
Nguyen Van Thieu. *See* Thieu, Nguyen Van
NHL. *See* National Hockey League
Niacin III–44b; V–128a
Niagara (Can.) V–91a
Niagara (N.Y.) III–228b
Lafayette's visit IV–84a
War of 1812 I–281b; IV–406a
Niagara (frigate) II–459a–b; V–262b; VI–313b
Niagara (steamship) I–400b
NIAGARA, CARRYING PLACE OF V–90a; V–91b
Fort Niagara V–90a
NIAGARA, FORT (N.Y.) **V–90a**; III–120a, 142b; V–85a,b, 139b, 175b
British post VII–270a
evacuation by British I–340b, 341a; V–157a
Four–Mile Strip III–85a
Franciscans III–94b
French and Indian War I–359a; II–126b, 339b; III–116a,b; IV–60a, 213b; V–90a
French possession II–458b
Indian council V–90b
Niagara Falls V–91b
Pontiac's War V–357a
revolutionary war I–398a; VI–124a
War of 1812 V–90b, 91a
NIAGARA, GREAT INDIAN COUNCIL AT (1764) **V–90b**
NIAGARA CAMPAIGNS (1812–14) **V–90b**; VII–234a
Stoney Creek VI–415a
NIAGARA COMPANY V–91a
Niagara Diversion Treaty (1950) V–91b, 92b
NIAGARA FALLS V–91a; III–272b
ABC Conference I–1b
bridges I–364b
Buffalo (N.Y.) I–375b
Carrying Place of Niagara V–90a
La Salle's expeditions III–228b
Long's explorations IV–187a
shipbuilding III–216b
War of 1812 IV–205a
Waterways Treaty VII–261a
Niagara Falls, Peace Conference at. *See* Peace Movement in 1864
NIAGARA FALLS POWER V–91b; I–376a; II–415a; III–320b, 321a
chemical industry II–7b
electrochemistry II–423a, 442b
Niagara Falls Power Company V–91a–b
Niagara Genesee Company V–276b
Niagara Gorge V–93b
NIAGARA MOVEMENT V–92b; IV–460b
Niagara River
Caroline affair I–458b; V–118b
Carrying Place of Niagara V–90a
Devil's Hole ambuscade II–339b
Fort Conti II–210b
Fort Denonville II–329a
Fort Erie II–458a
Fort George III–167b
Fort Niagara V–90a
Four–Mile Strip III–85a
hydroelectric power VII–257b
La Salle's trading post V–157a
locks VI–193a
Niagara Falls V–91a
Phelps–Gorham purchase V–276b
Seneca cession V–90b
War of 1812 I–436b; III–218a; V–90b; VI–3a, 226a
NIAGARA SUSPENSION BRIDGES V–93b; I–364b
Niantic (Indians) V–261b
Niantic River V–261a
NIBLO'S GARDEN (N.Y.C.) **V–93b**
Nicaragua
Dominican Republic intervention IV–113a
filibuster expeditions III–23a–b
gold rush route III–81b
United Nations Declaration VII–151b
Nicaragua, Lake V–94b
NICARAGUA, RELATIONS WITH V–93b
Bryan–Chamorro Treaty II–359b
canal route IV–324b
Clayton–Bulwer Treaty II–72b
Dallas–Clarendon Convention II–285a
dollar diplomacy II–359b
earthquake refugees V–281a
Kasson tariff treaty IV–33a
Mosquito question IV–416a
Panama Canal negotiations I–295a, 483b
revolution II–343a, 471b
Squier Treaty VI–378b
trade VI–343b
U.S. intervention III–199a, 463a; IV–111b, 112a, 252a,b, 401b; V–105b, 106a; VI–163a
U.S. protectorate III–347b
Nicaraguan Canal Association V–94b
NICARAGUAN CANAL PROJECT V–94b; I–373a, 454a; III–266b, 278a; V–94a, 200b, 201a; VI–378b
Nicene Creed II–386b
Nicholas I (Saint) II–386b
Nicholas II (czar) III–237a; V–233b
Nicholas, George (pol.) IV–40b
Nicholas, John (law.) II–303b
Nicholas, Samuel (nav. off.) VI–128a
Nicholls, Francis T. (pol.) III–295b; IV–195b
Nichols, Edward L. (phys.) V–295a
Nichols, John T. (ichthyol.) III–28a
Nicholson, A. O. P. (law., jur.) V–360a
Nicholson, Francis (col. gov.) IV–86a; V–84b, 369b; VI–2b; VII–201b
Nicholson, John (fin.) V–113a
Nicholson, John H. III–179b
Nicholson, Samuel (nav. off.) VI–128b
Nichrome wire resistor II–419b
Nickajack Dam III–323b
Nickel III–12a, 13b–14a; VI–48b
cobalt production III–14a
coinage II–95b–96a
Lake Superior VI–443b
ocean deposits III–13b
Puerto Rico V–461a
Nickel alloys II–415b, 419b
Nickel Bridge. *See* Boulevard Bridge
Nickel industry V–102a
foreign investment III–67a
health hazards IV–294b
Nickelodeons IV–417b
Nickel Plate Railroad VI–32a, 35a
Nicklaus, Jack (golfer) III–198a
Nicknames
Jonathan IV–7b
states VI–392a, 393–95 (table)
Nicol, William (phys.) V–267b
NICOLET, EXPLORATIONS OF V–95a; III–119a, 399a
Green Bay III–225b
Lake Michigan III–216a; IV–332a
mapping VII–73b
Mississippi Valley IV–375b
Sault Sainte Marie VI–219b
Upper Lakes VII–157a
Wisconsin VII–306b
Nicolet, Jean (expl.). *See* Nicolet, Explorations of
Nicoline (whaler) VII–285b
Nicolis, Richard (col. gov.) V–82a
Nicollet, Joseph Nicholas (math., expl.) III–468a
Nicollet County (Minn.) VI–139a
Nicolls, Matthias (col. gov.) II–379a
Nicolls, Richard (col. gov.) II–363b, 431a; III–304b; IV–398a; V–95b
NICOLLS' COMMISSIONS V–95b
Nicotinic acid. *See* Niacin
Niebor, H. J. VI–341b
Niebuhr, H. Richard (theol.) VI–79b, 83a
Niebuhr, Reinhold (theol.) VI–79b, 83a
Nielson, A.C., survey tennis VII–31a
Nieman, Lucius W. (ed.) V–73b
Nieman Foundation V–79b
Niemotko v. *Maryland* (1951) I–205a
Niepce, Joseph Nicéphore (phys.) II–279a
Nier, Alfred O. (chem.) I–218b
Nieuwe River IV–451b
Nieuw Haarlem III–253a,b

Nigeria I–21a
Dominican missions II–362b
mandate IV–236b
Pan–Africanism V–199b
Rhodes scholars VI–134b
Nigerian–Biafran Civil War (1967–70) I–22a
Niger River
slave trade VI–309b
"NIGGER" V–95b
Nigger (play) V–96a
Nigger Heaven V–96a
Nigger of the Narcissus V–96a
Night blindness VI–244b
Nightclubs
fires II–348a, 349a
Prohibition V–430a
Night Hawks (Ku Klux Klan) IV–58a
Night herder V–177b
Night horse III–303b
Nightingale (clipper) VI–309a
Nightingale School (Eng.) III–307a
NIGHT RIDERS V–96a; II–221b; VII–291a
Night watch V–338b
New York City V–82b
"Nigra" V–96a
NIH. *See* National Institutes of Health
Niishiwa, Jo (student) II–470b
Nijinsky, Waslaw (dancer) II–288b
Nike (missile) I–58b, 62a
Nike–Hercules (missile) IV–363b
Nikolais, Alwin (chor.) II–290a
Nile River VI–429b
flooding III–36b
Niles (Mich.) VI–191b
Niles (Ohio) VI–204a
Niles, Hezekiah (pub.) V–96b, 206b
NILES' WEEKLY REGISTER (news.) **V–96b**
on group migration IV–338b
Nil sine numine (motto) VI–393 (table)
Nimitz (aircraft carrier) I–56b; V–11a–b
Nimitz, Chester W. (nav. off.) I–14a; III–234b, 485a; VII–337b
Battle of Midway IV–336a
Gilbert Islands III–180a
Marshall Islands IV–257b
Pacific Fleet (World War II) I–459a
Saipan VI–198a
Nimmo Report (1885) I–87a
Niña (yacht) VII–349a
Nine Men V–61b, 266a
Nine Mile Point Nuclear Station (N.Y.) V–176a
NINE–POWER PACT (1922) **V–96b**; III–33b; IV–235a; V–159a, 216b; VII–251a
NINETEENTH AMENDMENT V–97a; I–95a, 297a, 415a; II–206a, 325b, 408a, 410a; III–92a; VI–97b, 435a; VII–208b, 314a, 315a–b, 317a
Alaska I–77b
campaign of 1920 I–427b
National Woman's Party VII–312b
Nineteenth (XIX) Corps. *See* entries under Army, United States
"Ninety–day wonder" course V–29a
Ninety–first Infantry Division VII–366b
Ninety–ninth Infantry Division I–379b
Ninety–second Infantry Division IV–340b
NINETY–SIX (S.C.) **V–97a**; II–251a; VI–351b
Ninety–third Infantry Division IV–340b; VII–327a
"NINETY–TWO" AND "FORTY–FIVE" V–97b; IV–143b
Ninth Air Force V–332a
Ninth Amendment I–299a; II–204b, 453b; III–316b
Ninth Armored Division. *See* entries under Army, United States
Ninth Army, U.S. *See* entries under Army, United States
Ninth Bridgewater Treatise III–480b
Ninth Cavalry IV–340a; VI–301a, 362a
Ninth Infantry Division III–314b
Ninth International Conference of American States (1948) V–171a
Ninth Marine Amphibious Brigade VII–186b, 187a
Ninth Marine Expeditionary Brigade IV–253a; VII–185b–86a
Niobrara River V–31a
Nipigon, Lake II–380a; IV–117b
Nipissing (Indians) III–499b; V–95a
Nipissing, Lake III–319a; VII–157a, 307a
Nipkow, Paul G. (inv.) VII–21a
Nipmuck (Indians) IV–47b
Nipsic (warship) I–144a; VII–213a
NIRA. *See* National Industrial Recovery Act
Nirdlinger, Charles Frederic (playwright) III–26a
Nirenberg, Marshall W. (biochem.) I–304a; III–158a; IV–391a; V–100a
Nisei III–490b
Nishimura, Shoji (nav. off.) IV–138b
Nisi prius II–40a
NISQUALLY, FORT, ATTACK ON (1849) **V–97b**
Niter II–163a
Nitrated toluene (TNT) II–8a–b
NITRATES V–97b; II–8a; VI–334b
Chile II–478a
Muscle Shoals VII–27b
powder V–383a,b
public lands V–445b
shipping IV–310b
Nitrate War (1879–83) III–16b
Nitre and Mining Bureau, Confederate II–163b
Nitric acid II–7a; III–17a
Nitric oxide III–17a
Nitrocellulose V–327b–28a
Nitrocellulose plastics II–7a, 8a
Nitrogen II–423a; VI–48b
fertilizer III–16a,b
incandescent lamp IV–89a
nitrates V–97b
Nitrogen–15 I–303b
Nitrogen fixation II–8b; III–17a; V–98a,b
Nitrogen oxide gases II–10b
Nitroglycerine III–191b
Nitrous oxide I–119a
Nitti, Frank (criminal) II–258b
Nixon, Patricia (Mrs. Richard M.) V–98b; VII–292a
NIXON, RESIGNATION OF (1974) **V–98b**; II–474a; III–3b, 345a; V–398b; VI–93b, 368b; VII–133a, 254a
Nixon, Richard M. I–409a; II–178 (table); V–385b, 396 (table); VI–93b
campaign of 1960 I–430b
Eisenhower disability V–397a
Hiss Case III–308b; VI–428b
presidential library III–284b
vice–presidency I–430a; VII–180a
—President:
AFL–CIO I–103a
Agnew resignation VII–133a
Alliance for Progress IV–114a
ambassadors II–437b
antiwar demonstrations V–237b
Arab–American relations I–150a
armed forces reduction II–316b
atomic energy I–217a
busing I–397b
campaign of 1968 I–431b
campaign of 1972 I–431b; VI–337b; VII–134b, 291a
China policy II–28a, 316b; VI–55a
China trade VII–94a
China visit II–426b; V–234b
civil service II–60b
Clean Water Act VII–259b
community–action programs II–148b
congressional appropriations II–477a
conservatism II–189b
criminal justice commission V–417b
Cuba II–270a
devaluation II–339a–b
dollar diplomacy II–359b–60a
"Doonesbury" comic strip V–72b
draft II–186b, 368a
economic policies VI–471b–72a; VII–91a–b
Executive Protective Service VI–252b
Far Eastern policy II–489b
foreign aid III–62b
foreign policy III–70b–71a; IV–113a–b
Foreign Service VI–389b
foreign trade VII–91b
gold policy III–8a–b, 196a; VI–95b, 371b
government spending III–205b
grants–in–aid III–212a
guaranteed income VI–328b
"Herblock" cartoons V–73a
housing II–47b; III–311b
impeachment proceedings I–103a; III–344b–45b
Indian reservation system VI–97a–b
inflation II–236b
injunctions III–419b
Israel III–482b
Job Corps III–504b
Kent State protest IV–38b
Kissinger, Henry II–343a
Labor Department IV–78b–79a
labor movement IV–77a
Latin America VI–345a
Louisiana support IV–195a
military policy IV–344a–b
Mitchell, John I–400a
model cities program II–47b
moon landing IV–407a
national defense policy II–316b
National Park Service V–220b
National Security Council VI–389b
North Atlantic Treaty Organization V–114b
Office of Economic Opportunity V–136a
Office of Management and Budget V–136b
oil embargo VII–85a
Pentagon Papers V–78b–79a, 258b
Philadelphia Plan II–473a–b
postal service V–374a
price controls III–415b
radio and television control I–480b
reelected I–430a, 432a,b
relief VI–74b

NIXON, RICHARD M. (cont.)
rural development VI–172a
scientific research IV–471a
shipbuilding IV–312b–13a
Soviet Union II–316b, 426b; VI–180a
Strategic Arms Limitation Talks VI–416b–17a
subpoena of tapes V–397b–98a
Subversive Activities Control Board II–499b
summit conferences VI–439a
Supreme Court appointments IV–14b; VI–443b, 448a
tariffs VI–53a
taxation VII–9b–10b
vetoes VII–178a
Vietnam War I–411a; II–316b; V–182a; VII–184b, 185b, 237b
wage and price controls V–402a
War Powers Act VII–224b
Watergate I–409a; II–231b, 474a; III–465b; V–78a–b, 347a; VII–118b, 253b
welfare programs II–472b, 502b; V–382a–b
White House Conference on Food, Nutrition and Health V–128b
wool imports VII–321b
Nixon and Kemp Circus II–40b
Nixon Doctrine (1969) II–316b
Nixon Nitration Company V–328a
"Nixon Shock" VI–472a
Nixon v. *Condon* (1932) VI–432b
Nixon v. *Herndon* (1927) III–93a; V–407b; VI–432b
Niza, Marcos de (miss., expl.) I–96b, 171b; II–228a; IV–367a; V–459b
Cibola II–37a
Zuni VII–372a
Nketia, J. H. Kwabena (au.) IV–443a
Nkrumah, Kwame (states.) I–22a; V–199b–200a
NLRA. *See* National Labor Relations Act
NLRB. *See* National Labor Relations Board
Nobel, Alfred B. (mfr., inv.) V–383b
NOBEL PRIZES V–99a; II–11b, 13a
American Friends Service Committee V–470b
Bardeen, John II–425b
Bell Laboratories I–287b
Borlaug, Norman I–486a
Brattain, W. H. II–425b
Compton, Arthur H. V–295b
Davisson, Clinton J. V–295b
DNA research II–358a
high–energy physics V–297b
International Labor Organization III–455a
Langmuir, Irving II–76b, 423b; III–155b
Lawrence Radiation Laboratory IV–119b
Libby, Willard F. VI–17b
medicine IV–298b
Michelson, Albert V–294b
Millikan, R. A. II–423b
Millikan, Robert V–295b
National Institutes of Health IV–465b
physics V–296a
Richards, Theodore W. II–11b–12a
Roosevelt, Theodore V–370b
Shockley, W. B. II–425b
Nob Hill (San Francisco) VI–209b
Nobile, Umberto (off.) I–116a
NOBILITY, TITLES OF V–100b; I–95b; II–171b, 200b; V–351a
landgrave IV–94b
president V–399a
South Carolina VI–348b
Nobleborough (Maine) V–243b
"Noble experiment" II–354a
Noble Order of the Knights of Labor. *See* Knights of Labor
Noble's Road III–215a
Nock, Albert Jay (educ.) II–189b, 401a
Nocone, Peta (Indian) V–216b
Nodaway County (Mo.) V–330a–b
No–fault insurance I–152b; III–432a; IV–19a
Nogales (Ariz.) I–172a
Nogales, Fort (Miss.) II–22b; V–100b; VI–366b; VII–181a
See also McHenry, Fort
NOGALES, TREATY OF (1793) **V–100b**; II–167b; VI–366b
Nohoroco, Fort (N.C.) VII–130b
Noise–level tolerance IV–293a
Noise pollution VI–212b–13a
NOLAN, EXPEDITIONS OF (1792–98) **V–101a**; IV–457a; VII–37a
Nolan, Philip (horse trader) III–302b
See also Nolan, Expeditions of
Nolichuckey River IV–186b; VII–238b, 250a, 253b
Nolichuckey Valley III–400b
No Man's Land (Okla.) V–148b
See also Cimarron, Proposed Territory of
Nome (Alaska) IV–52a, 354a; V–337a
NOMINATING SYSTEM V–101b; II–409b–10a
caucus I–474a
direct primary V–406b
political parties V–343a,b
runoff primary V–407a
state chairman VI–390b
two–thirds rule VII–135a–b
unit rule VII–155b
Nominations. *See* Campaigns, Political
Noncombatants
conscientious objectors II–185a
Geneva Conventions III–161b
Noncomformists. *See* Dissenters
Nondegradable electrical resistance II–419a
Nonfat dry milk solids II–282b
NONFERROUS METALS V–102a; VI–48b
aluminum I–91b
Lake Superior VI–443b
South American trade VI–345b–46a
zinc VII–368b
NONIMPORTATION AGREEMENTS V–104a; I–207b, 208a, 347a; II–211a; IV–266a; VII–3b, 80b
committees of inspection III–421b
Napoleon's decrees IV–449b
New York City V–82b, 85b
North Carolina V–115b
tea VII–15a, 17a
NONINTERCOURSE ACT (1809) **V–104b**; II–437a; III–67b, 118b, 455b; IV–219b, 309b; VI–104b; VII–233b
NONINTERVENTION POLICY V–105a
Good Neighbor policy III–199a
Havana Conference III–262b
isolationism III–479b
North Dakota V–117b
See also Intervention
Nonpartisan League, Labor's V–47b
NONPARTISAN LEAGUE, NATIONAL V–106a; I–42b, 107a; II–490b–91a, 493a
campaign of 1936 IV–73a
Conference for Progressive Political Action IV–84b
grain elevators II–430b
North Dakota V–117b; VII–53a
Nonproliferation Treaty (1967) III–70a
NONRECOGNITION POLICY V–107a; III–456a
Manchuria III–69a; V–96b
Nonrigid airship. *See* Dirigibles
NONSENSE, FORT (N.J.) **V–108a**; I–330a
Non–Separating Congregationalists I–264b
Non–Separating Puritans II–169b
Nonsigners clause II–483a,b
NONSLAVEHOLDERS IN THE SOUTH V–108a
NONVOTING V–108b
NOODLES ISLAND SKIRMISH (1775) **V–100b**
Nooten Island III–206b
Nootka (Indians) I–441b; II–30a; III–362a; IV–59a, 228b
Nootka Convention (1790) V–167b
Nootkan (lang.) II–30a; V–165a
Nootka Sound I–15b; V–164b
Cook's expedition VII–247a
Indian hostilities I–209a
sea otters VI–247b
NOOTKA SOUND CONTROVERSY V–109a; II–342b; III–479a; IV–193b
"NO PEACE BEYOND THE LINE" V–109a; IV–182b
NORAD. *See* North American Air Defense Command
Nord Americanische Kalender II–497a
Nordenskjöld, Otto (expl.) V–198a
Nordheim, Lothar (phys.) V–304a
Nordyke and Marman IV–433a
NORFOLK (Va.) **V–109b**; III–258b; V–176b; VII–193b
Civil War IV–396b, 397a; V–17a; VII–153a
direct–trade convention VI–352b
dry docks II–375b
Freemasons III–109a
integration VII–196a
Jamestown Exposition III–489b
navy yard V–27b, 29a,b; VI–282a
Old Dominion University VII–300b
port authority V–368a
railroads VI–36a,b
revolutionary war III–215b, 236a
Ringgold–Rodgers Exploring Expeditiion VI–142a
Spanish–American War VI–363a
steamboats VI–137a
War of 1812 II–253b
Norfolk and Western Railroad I–10a; VI–32a, 35a–b; VII–195b
Adams Express Company I–10a
locomotives IV–176b, 177a
Norfolk County III–268a
"Norfolk Discipline" VI–126a

Norfolk jacket II–372a
Norfolk *Journal and Guide* (news.) V–76a
Norfolk Naval Base VII–196a
Norfolk Navy Yard VI–44b
Norfolk Prison Colony VI–68a
Norge (airship) I–116a
Noria VII–256b
"NORMALCY" V–110a
Normal schools I–5b; II–115a, 399b, 401a; IV–93b; VI–228b, 229b
Norman, Montagu (econ.) III–6b
Normandie (ship) VI–9b
NORMANDY INVASION (1944) **V–110a**; I–123a–b, 141a; II–13b, 237a, 297a; III–174a–b; VI–193b; VII–338b
Army Air Force I–60b
gliders III–187a
paratroops V–213b
tank warfare I–178b
underwater demolition teams VII–139a
U.S. Navy V–21b
Norman's Woe (reef) I–447a
NORRIDGEWOCK FIGHT (1724) **V–111b**; I–3a; II–380b
Norris, Frank (Benjamin Franklin Norris) (au.) I–406a; IV–163b
Norris, Frank (pol.) IV–169a
Norris, George W. (pol.) V–31b
Farm Export Act V–111b
Progressive movement V–427b
Tennessee Valley Authority II–472b; VII–28a
Twentieth Amendment IV–88b
Norris, Isaac, Jr. (mer.) II–107b
Norris, William (eng.) IV–175b
Norris Dam III–323b; VI–147a
NORRIS FARM EXPORT ACT (1921) **V–111b**
NORRIS–LA GUARDIA ANTI-INJUNCTION LAW (1932) **V–111b**; II–86b, 111a; III–407a, 419b; IV–71a; V–463b; VI–103b, 419b; VII–124a
"yellow-dog" contract VII–355a
Norris v. *Alabama* (1935) VI–241b
NORSEMEN IN AMERICA V–112a; I–95b–96a; II–461b, 461b; III–280a; VII–189b–91a
Cape Cod I–447a
Dighton Rock II–341a
Indian contact III–356b
Kensington Stone IV–38a
Massachusetts IV–264b
North, Charles (physic.) IV–275b
North, Frank (off.) VI–241b; VII–298b
North, Frank Mason (comp.) III–326b
North, Frederick (Lord North) (states.) V–221a; VI–127a
Coercion Acts I–347a
Intolerable Acts III–464b
Massachusetts Government Act IV–271b
peace commission III–95a
Regulating Act II–388a
North, John W. (col.) III–477b
North, Luther H. (off.) VI–241b
North, Simeon (mfr.) III–441a,b; IV–272a, 432b
North Africa
Neutrality Act of 1939 V–37b
petroleum V–272b
NORTH AFRICAN CAMPAIGN (1942–43) **V–112b**; I–465a; VII–338a–b
carrier air strikes I–55b
paratroops V–213b
Spain VI–360b
tank warfare I–178b
U.S. Air Force I–60a
North American Air Defense Command I–59a, 62a, 439b
North American Airlines I–237a
North American Aviation, Inc. I–50a,b, 52a,b, 53b, 54a, 57b, 60a, 61b, 236b
North American Conservation Conference (1909) II–187b
North American Herpetology VI–90b
North American Kerosine Gas Light Company of New York IV–44a
NORTH AMERICAN LAND COMPANY V–113a
North American Phalanx (1843–56) II–147a
North American Regiment III–58b
North American Reptilia, Part I, Ophidia VI–91a
North American Review (jour.) II–341b; III–281a; IV–233b
North American Rockwell I–238a
North American Wildlife Conference VII–298a
Northampton (Mass.) III–214a; VI–76b, 272a
Northampton County (Pa.) III–124a; V–251b; VII–220b
North Andover (Mass.) IV–437a
NORTH ANNA, BATTLE OF (1864) **V–113b**; VI–138a, 376b
North Anna River II–96b; V–113b; VI–150a, 376b
North Atlantic Coast Fisheries Arbitration (1910) III–456b
North Atlantic fisheries dispute IV–385b
North Atlantic Pact (1949) III–69b
North Atlantic Squadron VI–361a
NORTH ATLANTIC TREATY ORGANIZATION V–113b; I–124a, 439b; II–98a, 315a–b; III–69b; V–234a; VI–179b, 471a; VII–113a
arms race I–179b
Atlantic Community I–215a
collective security policy V–36a
France III–70a, 97b
Iceland III–327b
missile development IV–363a,b
Nassau Pact IV–454a
Portuguese colonies I–22a
rifle standards VI–140a
sea power VI–248b
Spain VI–360b
standardized cartridge IV–431a
Strategic Arms Limitation Talks VI–417a
U.S. forces in Germany III–175a
U.S. military assistance III–61b
U.S. naval forces V–25a
North Bend (Ohio) IV–330a
North Bergen (N.J.) I–339b
North Bridge (Concord, Mass.) IV–137a
North Briton (news.) V–97b
NORTH CAROLINA V–115a; VI–395 (table)
Albemarle I–83a, 447b
Anglicanism VI–75b
antimiscegenation laws IV–362b
archives I–168b
Augusta Congress I–223a
Avery's Trace I–232b
Bayard v. *Singleton* I–277b
black suffrage VI–431a, 432a, 433b
boundary disputes I–350b, 352a; II–274a
bounties I–352a
British debts I–366b
buffalo I–375a
Cape Fear settlements I–447b
Cartagena expedition I–461b
Cary's rebellion I–465a
cattle I–37a
chain gangs I–489a
Cherokee II–15a, 51b, 52b; III–395a; IV–186b
Chickasaw Treaty II–23a
chinch bug II–29a
Church of England II–36a
Civil War I–232b, 289b, 458b; II–62b, 162b, 163b, 165a; III–30b; IV–252a; VI–138a, 156b, 249b
Civil War peace movement III–289b
colleges and universities II–114b, 395b
colonial exiles V–342a
colonial suffrage VI–434a,b
colonial trade II–119a
commodities as money II–140b
constitution VI–390b
convict labor system V–416b
cotton I–38a; II–238b
Cowans Ford Dam III–322a
"crackers" II–253a
cruel and unusual punishment V–464a
Culpeper's Rebellion II–271a
Cumberland settlements II–274a
debtor laws II–299a
Declaration of Independence II–308a
Edenton II–392a
education II–393b, 404a
fall line II–485a
fencing laws III–10a
feudalism III–18a
feuds III–18a
fish III–26b, 28a
Fontana Dam III–322b
foreign trade VII–86a
French refugees III–121a
fugitive slave acts III–130a
Fundamental Constitution I–457b
Fundamental Constitutions I–457b
furniture III–139a,b
fur trade III–141a,b, 143b, 144a
Gastonia riots III–154a
geological survey III–165a
gold III–191a
grandfather clause III–208b
Granville grant III–212b
Great Smoky Mountains III–222a; V–218 (table)
Great Warriors Path VII–238b
Heath Patent III–268a
Henderson Land Company III–271b
Heroes of America VII–149a
Holston Treaty III–383a
Holston Valley settlements III–292b
horse drives I–473a
horse racing III–304b
hurricanes II–351b; III–319b
incorporation laws VII–222a
Indiana settlers III–369b–70a
Indian languages II–282b
Indian Path VII–202b
Indian population III–396a,b
Indian slaves III–401a
indigo I–352a
justice of the peace IV–22b
lead industry IV–122a
literacy test III–92b
lottery I–232b

NORTH CAROLINA (cont.)
Loyalists VI–115b
Lumbee IV–203b
lynching legislation IV–208b
mammals IV–231a
Mecklenburg Declaration of Independence IV–282a
Mecklenburg Resolves IV–282a
military tract IV–344b
Missouri settlers IV–377a; VI–194a
Moravians I–293a; IV–409b
mounds IV–420b
mountain passes V–224a–b
Nashville settlement IV–452b
naval stores I–352a; V–14b
newspapers V–76b
Norfolk trade V–109b
North American Land Company V–113a
Occaneechi Trail III–387b
Old Southwest VI–356a
Outer Banks II–89a
Palatines V–195a
pine barrens IV–204a
pioneers V–316b
plantation system V–325a
plant study V–326a
poor whites V–358b
port authority V–368a
pottery V–379b–80a
presidios V–399b
prices V–404b
primogeniture V–408a
privateers V–419a, 419b
private mints IV–360a
proprietors I–458a, 465a
provincial congress V–439b
Quakers I–465a; V–469b
Queen Anne's War VI–2b
railroads VI–25a, 36b, 37b
Raleigh Conference of Southern Governors VI–42b
Raleigh's first colony VI–43b
Raleigh's Lost Colony VI–42b
Reconstruction III–295a
record-keeping VII–205b
referendum VI–66b
Regulators I–73b–74a; III–436b; VI–71b
religious liberty VII–69a
revolutionary war II–15a, 465a; III–232a, 265a, 400b; IV–48a, 407b; VI–117b, 124b, 130a, 130a, 351a–b, 351b; VII–261b, 360b
rice I–352a
royal colony I–458a
Scotch-Irish VI–240b
secession II–61b, 160b; VI–251b
settlement II–124a
ships graveyard II–89a
showboats VI–283a
slavery II–443b; VI–309a
smuggled goods V–320a
Southwest Point VI–357b
Southwest Territory VI–358a
Spanish exploration V–370a
stagelines VI–380a
state debts VI–96b
State of Franklin III–87a, 98b
state university VII–156a
Swiss settlers VI–455a
tar VI–461b
taxation VII–3a, 15a
Tennessee VI–400a; VII–25a,b, 276a
tobacco VI–386a; VII–66b, 67a
tobacco as money VII–65b, 66a
tornadoes VII–75b
Transylvania Company II–274a; VII–103a,b
Treaty of Hopewell III–383a
Treaty of Sycamore Shoals VI–455a
Tryon's Line VII–125b
Tuscarora III–475a
Tuscarora War VII–130b
Union sentiment VII–148b
U.S. Constitution II–193b, 196a–97a, 198b, 203b, 478a; VII–111a
usury law III–443a
Voting Rights Act of 1965 VII–211a
Waldenses VII–219b
Washington District VII–250a
Watauga settlement VII–253a
Waxhaw VII–261b
western lands V–443b; VI–356a; VII–273a,b
westward movement VII–283b
Wilderness Road VII–296a
Wilmington Riot VII–303a
witchcraft VII–310a
writs of assistance VII–345a
Yadkin River settlements VII–350a
Yamasee War VII–352a
See also entries under Carolina
North Carolina (battleship) VI–282a; VII–242a
North Carolina, University of III–284b–85a; V–115b, 116b; VII–156a
political science V–349a
North Carolina Agricultural and Technical University I–31a; II–58a
NORTH CAROLINA RAILROAD V–117a
North Carolina Standard (news.) II–165a; III–289b
North Cascades National Park V–219 (table)
North Church (Boston). *See* Old North Church
Northcliffe, Viscount. *See* Harmsworth, Alfred Charles
North Conway (N.H.) VI–101a
Northcote, Stafford Henry, 1st Earl of Iddesleigh (states.) VII–248b
NORTH DAKOTA V–117a; VI–395 (table); VII–284b
Arikara I–171b
army posts IV–339b–40a
badlands I–243a
blizzards I–320a
cereal grains I–486b
Chippewa II–31a
Conciliation Act II–158a
county-seat wars II–245b
Dakota Indians II–282b, 283b
Dakota Territory II–284b–85a
double jeopardy VII–154b
exploration III–119a
Farmers' Alliance II–493a
Fisk expedition III–32a
Five Villages III–33b–34a
Fort Abraham Lincoln I–3b; II–496a
Fort Berthold Reservation III–395b
Fort Mandan IV–235b
Fort Mortimer IV–415a
Fort Union IV–380b; VII–145b
fur trade V–244a
Garrison Dam III–322b
grain elevators II–430b
Green v. *Frazier* III–227a
Hudson's Bay Company III–313b
hunting VII–297a
Indian population III–396a,b
Indian wars II–283b–84a
Iowa Territory III–468a
Lewis and Clark Expedition IV–136a; VII–271a
Mandan, Hidatsa, and Arikara IV–235b
Missouri River IV–380a
Nonpartisan League II–490b, 492b; V–106b–07a; VII–53a
Pembina V–244a
Populist party V–365b
prairie fires V–388b–89a
prohibition laws V–429b
railroads VI–36b
ranches VI–45a
recall VI–51a
Red River cart traffic VI–63b
Red River of the North VI–64a
referendum VI–66b
Safeguard missile site I–58b
school lands VI–228a–b
Standing Rock Agency VII–344b
statehood VII–248a
Sully's Indian expedition IV–45b
three-party system VII–135a
Treaty of Fort Laramie III–383b
voting behavior VII–210a
War of 1812 VII–234b
wheat I–486a; III–43b, 45a; VII–286a
North Dakota Farmers' Union V–117b
North Dakota Hymn (song) VI–395 (table)
North Dennis (Mass.) I–447a
North East (N.Y.) IV–169a
NORTHEAST BOUNDARY V–118a; VII–111b, 134b
Jay's Treaty III–494a
Red Line Map VI–62b
Webster–Ashburton Treaty VII–265a
Northeast culture area. *See* Eastern Woodlands culture
Northeastern University I–344b; IV–267b
North East forge (Md.) V–409b
North Easton (Mass.) III–293a
Northeast Passage I–116a
Northerly Lands III–280a
Northern Area Force (Japan) IV–336a–b
Northern Baptist Convention I–265a
Northern Cheyenne (Indians) I–313a
Northern Cross Railroad VI–35a–b
Northern Farmers Alliance II–493a
Northern Forestry, Institute of III–76b
Northern Inland Lock Navigation Company III–419b
Northern Ireland
linen IV–157b
Northern Line VI–407a
Northern Missionary Society III–385b
Northern Neck Proprietary II–481a–b
"Northern Pacific panic" (1901) V–119a
Northern Pacific Railroad I–329a; II–218b; III–79b, 451b; IV–403b; V–119a; VI–27a, 32a, 32b, 33a; VII–101a, 248a
foreign investments III–65a
land grants IV–94b
Minnesota IV–357a
See also Burlington Northern
Northern Pacific Railway Company VI–135b
Northern Securities Company II–230a; III–290b, 466a
NORTHERN SECURITIES COMPANY* v. *UNITED STATES (1904) **V–119a**; VII–122b
Northern Virginia, Army of VII–150a
Northfield (Mass.) IV–47b; VII–282b
NORTHFIELD BANK ROBBERY (1876) **V–119b**

North Fork of the Platte V–168b
North Frederick (Lord North) (states.)
colonial taxation VI–114a–b
North Kingstown (R.I.) VI–132a
North Korea. *See* Korea, Democratic People's Republic of
North Landing River I–83a
North magnetic pole I–116a
North Main Street (Providence, R.I.) V–439a
North Pacific Exploring and Surveying Expedition. *See* Ringgold–Rodgers Exploring Expedition
North Pacific Fisheries Convention (1952) VI–201b; VII–33a
North Pacific Sealing Convention (1911) V–401a
North Platte (Nebr.) III–378a; VII–188a
North Platte River
Fort Laramie IV–108a
Indian territory IV–108b
La Vérendrye exploration IV–118a
Platte Bridge fight V–330a
stage route V–178b
Villasur expedition VII–188a
North Point (Md.) IV–261a
North Pole V–122b
Byrd's explorations I–398b–99a; II–310a, 311b
exploration V–336b, 337a,b, 338a
Jeannette expedition V–336a
Peary expeditions V–240b–41a
North River I–83a; V–418b
North Rock Springs (Wyo.) VI–273b
Northrop, James H. (inv.) IV–187b; VII–43b
Northrop, John (av. designer) I–51b
Northrop, John H. (chem.) I–304a; IV–389a; V–99b
Northrop, Lucius (off.) II–163b
Northrop Aircraft, Inc. I–53b, 54a, 237a; II–155b
North Saskatchewan River I–311a
North Sea
petroleum V–272b
revolutionary war VI–128b
World War II II–217b
NORTH SEA MINE BARRAGE V–119b; IV–351a–b; V–20a, 27b; VII–329a
"North Star" (motto) VI–394 (table)
North Star (news.) V–75b–76a
Northstar–at–Tahoe VI–101b
North Star Mine (Calif.) III–191a
North Star Mine (Mont.) III–270a
North Star State VI–394 (table)
"North to the Future" (motto) VI–393 (table)
Northumberland (Pa.) V–250a
Northumberland County (Pa.) VI–452a; VII–353a
Northwest, Old VI–356a; VII–284a
Northwest Airlines II–346b; III–277b
NORTHWEST ANGLE V–120a; IV–87b; V–33a–b; VI–188a
Northwest Atlantic Fisheries Convention (1949) VII–33a
NORTHWEST BOUNDARY CONTROVERSY V–120a; VII–134b, 269b–70b
Northwest Coast culture I–81a; III–238a–b, 358b, 360b–62a; VII–367b–68a
art and technology III–373a, 374a,b
burial III–376a
"Great Spirit" III–222b
Makah IV–228b
myth and folklore III–386a,b
political organization III–391a–b
religion III–392b, 393a
scalping VI–224b
Shaker religion VI–268a
NORTH WEST COMPANY V–121a; I–105a, 209a,b; II–131b; III–142b, 144b, 209a, 403a; V–180a,b; VII–104b, 247a,b
Fort Okanogan V–147a
Fort Walla Walla VII–221a
Hudson's Bay rivalry III–313b
Lake Superior VI–443a
Leech Lake Indian council IV–131b
Long's explorations IV–187a
Minnesota IV–355b
Oregon V–164b
Pembina V–244a
Pemmican War V–244b
Red River IV–187a; VI–64b
Saint Lawrence River VI–192b
Sault Sainte Marie VI–220a
Sault Sainte Marle VI–219a
Southwest Fur Company VI–357b
Spokane House VI–375b
voyageurs VII–211b
NORTHWEST CONSPIRACY (1864) **V–121b**; I–435a; IV–53a; VI–339a
Northwestern Alliance V–365a–b
Northwestern Confederacy II–222b; VI–339a
Northwestern Consolidated Milling III–44a, 45a
Northwestern Farmers Alliance II–493a–b
Northwestern Indian Confederacy I–341a
See also Wayne Campaign
Northwestern Pike I–88b
Northwestern University V–131b, 349a
Northwestern University Dental School II–330b
Northwestern University Settlement VI–330b
"Northwest gun" III–140a
Northwest Ordinance. *See* Northwest Territory; Ordinances of 1784, 1785, and 1787
Northwest Orient Airlines I–68b
NORTHWEST PASSAGE V–122a; III–216a; VI–367a; VII–275b
Amundsen expedition I–115b–16a
Carver's travels III–89b
Hudson Bay III–313a
mapping VII–73a
Radisson's *Voyages* VI–18b
search for I–75a, 238b, 465a, 498b; II–219b
NORTHWEST TERRITORY V–122b; II–484b; IV–355b; V–140b–41a; VI–358a; VII–188b–89a
abolition III–437b
campaign of 1840 VI–422a
canals I–40a
Cincinnati II–37b
Connecticut "Firelands" II–183b
coutume de Paris II–247b
Division Act of 1800 II–356a
Fort Knox (Ind.) IV–53b
Fourth of July III–88a
Illinois III–329b
Illinois County III–331b
Indian captivities III–376b
Indians III–369b
Marietta IV–250b
Maumee Indian Convention IV–276b
Michigan IV–330b
migration III–227b
newspapers I–483b
Old Northwest V–152a
Ordinances of 1784, 1785, and 1787 V–162a–63a
public schools II–396a
Quaker settlers V–470a
religious liberty VII–69a
Saint Clair's defeat VI–188b
state universities VII–156a
suffrage III–91b
surveys VI–451a
Tecumseh's crusade VII–63a
trails VI–153a
Trumbull County II–183b
Upper Peninsula of Michigan VII–157a
U.S. Army I–192a
Vincennes defection VII–189a
War of 1812 VII–45b
Wisconsin VII–307a
Norton, Benjamin Pitkin (chem.) II–11a
Norton, Charles Eliot (au., educ.) III–260a; IV–163a
Norton, E. L. (phys.) II–39a
Norton, John (mfr.) III–183b
Norton, John Pitkin (agric. chem.) VI–273b
Norton, Julius (mfr.) III–183b
Norton and Fenton III–183b
Norton Sound III–357b
NORUMBEGA V–123a; IV–37a
Norwalk (Conn.) III–25b
Norway
Common Market VI–472a–b
European Free Trade Association VI–469a; VII–89a
exploration IV–38a
immigration to U.S. III–333a, 337a, 340a
mackerel fisheries IV–217b
meteorological studies IV–318a
nitrogen fixation III–17a
North Atlantic Treaty Organization V–113b
Olympic Games V–154a
Organization for Economic Cooperation and Development V–170b
sealing VI–245a
United Nations Declaration VII–151b
U.S. aid III–61b
World War I V–119b; VII–329a
World War II III–327a; VI–424b; VII–334b
Norway (Mich.) IV–303b
Norway pine IV–204a; VI–394 (table)
Norwegian–American Historical Association III–279b
Norwegian Augustana Synod V–123b
NORWEGIAN CHURCHES V–123a
Norwegian–Danish Conference V–123b
Norwegian Lutheran Church of America V–123b
Norwegian School of Hydrodynamic Meteorology and Oceanography IV–317b
Norwegian Sea V–338b
Norwegian settlement
Minnesota IV–356b
Oleana V–152b
South Dakota VI–350a
Norwegian Synod of the American Lutheran Church V–123b
Norwich (Conn.) II–77b, 78a; IV–387b

No–strike pledge IV–73a; VI–411a, 420a
Nostrums, proprietary IV–450a
"No substitute for victory" V–124a
"No taxation without representation." *See* Taxation Without Representation
Notebook (Lowell) IV–165b
Notes of a Native Son IV–167a
Notes on Novelists IV–163b
Notes on the State of Virginia III–26b–27a; IV–179a, 231b
"Nothing without Providence" (motto) VI–393 (table)
Notman, John (arch.) I–163b
Notre Dame, University of III–293a
Nott, J. C. (anthrop.) I–128b
Nottingham sermon (1741) V–391b
"NOT WORTH A CONTINENTAL" V–123b; II–167a, 274b; IV–394a; VI–117b, 120a
Nouveau Voyage dans les États-Unis de l'Amérique Septentrionale, fait en 1788 III–122a
Nouvelle découverte d'un très grand pays situé dans l'Amérique III–272a
Nova Belgica. *See* New Netherland
Nova Caesarea. *See* New Caesarea
Novarkhangelsk (Aleutians) I–446b
Nova Scotia (Can.) VI–182a
  awarded to Great Britain II–92b, 126b
  British army VI–126b
  British claims I–6a; V–214b
  discovery I–401b
  exploration I–492b
  fishing VI–379a
  French and Indian War III–117b
  Indians and liquor III–398a–b
  Louisburg IV–192a
  Loyalists III–173a; VII–150b
  Port Royal V–369b
  quitrents VI–4a
  revolutionary war I–438a
  tea trade VII–17a
  writs of assistance VII–345a
Novels, dime. *See* Dime Novels
Novocaine III–381a
NOW. *See* National Organization for Women
"Now I lay me down to sleep" (prayer) V–51b
"NO-WIN POLICY" V–124a
Noyes, John Humphrey (ref.) V–155b; VI–13b, 325b
Noyes, Oliver (landowner) V–242a
Noyon (Fr.)
  World War I IV–404a
NRA. *See* National Recovery Administration
NRL. *See* Naval Research Laboratory
NROTC. *See* Naval Reserve Officers' Training Corps
NSA. *See* National Security Agency; National Student Association
NSC. *See* National Security Council
NSF. *See* National Science Foundation
NTA. *See* National Teachers Association
Nuclear chemistry II–12a
"Nuclear club" V–124b
Nuclear fission II–12b; V–300a–b, 302a
Nuclear fusion III–324a; V–300b
Nuclear Nonproliferation Treaty (1968) III–161b
Nuclear physics. *See* Physics, Nuclear
Nuclear power I–222b
  aircraft carriers IV–432a
  submarines IV–432a; VI–423a
Nuclear power plants I–216b, 217b–18a; V–176a
Nuclear reactors. *See* Atomic Power Reactors
NUCLEAR TEST BAN TREATY (1963) **V–124b**; I–484b; III–70a, 161b; V–53a, 237a; VI–180a
Nuclear testing I–292b
  indemnities III–352a
  opposition V–237a
  Pacific III–426a
  Pacific Northwest I–440a
  student movements VII–366a
Nuclear warfare I–328b; II–316a
Nuclear warheads V–27a
Nuclear warships VII–241b
Nuclear weapons IV–363b, 364a–b, 432a
  air power I–67b
  army strength I–187a
  atomic bomb I–215a
  convoys II–218a
  Geneva conferences III–161b
  military policy IV–344a
  Nassau Pact IV–454a
  national defense II–313a, 315b
  underground tests II–316a
  withheld in Korea IV–56a
  See also Arms Race With the Soviet Union
Nucleic acid II–358a
Nucleons V–302a–b
Nucleotides II–357b; III–158a; IV–389a, 390b
NUECES RIVER V–125a; IV–323a, 444b; VII–39a
Nuku Hiva. *See* Madison's Island
NULLIFICATION V–125b; II–241a; VI–397a; VII–288a
  centralization III–9a
  Charleston (S.C.) I–497a
  Essex Junto II–464a
  Fort Hill letter III–78a
  Jackson, Andrew V–176b
  Jefferson's proposed states III–496b
  loyalty oaths IV–202b
  palmetto cockades V–198a
  personal liberty laws V–264a
  sectionalism VI–342a
  slavery issue I–10b
  South Carolina III–59b; VI–250b, 254a, 347b
  states' rights I–404a
  tariff VI–466a
  Virginia and Kentucky Resolutions I–87a; VI–250a; VII–198a
  Webster–Hayne debate VII–265b
NUMBER FOUR (N.H.) **V–126a**; VI–190b; VII–171a
Numbers game II–261b, 262b; III–149b
Numerology IV–143b
Numismatics II–96a
Nunivak Island I–81a
Nuremberg Charter VII–226a
Nuremberg trials I–219b; III–317a; VII–229a
Nurse Corps, Army IV–290b
Nurse Corps, Navy IV–292b
Nursery schools II–220b, 400a
Nurses Associated Alumnae of the United States and Canada V–126b
Nurses Association, American IV–289b; V–126b
NURSING V–126a; III–307a; VII–316b, 318b
  army IV–290b; VII–145a
  Johns Hopkins IV–3a
  navy IV–292b
  public health V–447b
  public school IV–275b
  Red Cross VI–61b, 62a
  Tuskegee Institute VII–131a
  University of Pennsylvania V–249b
  Works Progress Administration VII–323b
  Yale University VII–351a
Nursing Education, National League of V–126b
Nursing homes
  Medicare IV–289b
Nurturant socialization II–485b
Nut Island. *See* Governors Island
Nutmeg State VI–393 (table)
Nutria III–133a; VII–105a
Nutrition, School of (Cornell Univ.) II–227b
Nutrition and Human Needs, Select Committee on V–128b, 129b
NUTRITION AND VITAMINS V–127b; I–303a,b; III–52a–b; V–274a
  biochemistry II–13a
  flour III–44b
  physiology V–306a, 307b
  Red Cross VI–62a
  research II–12a; IV–286a, 288a
  scurvy VI–244a
  urban health VII–158b
Nutrition Center, National V–128b
Nutrition Plan, National V–128b
Nutrition Policy Study, National V–128b
Nuts III–51a
Nuttall, Thomas (bot., ornith.) I–349a; V–326b; VII–271b
Nutten Island III–206b
Nutting, Mary Adelaide (prof.) V–126b
NWLB. *See* National War Labor Board
NWSA. *See* National Woman Suffrage Association
NYA. *See* Youth Administration, National
Nydia, The Blind Girl of Pompeii (sculp.) VI–243b
Nye, Gerald P. (pol.) III–480a; IV–433b; V–117b
Nye County (Nev.) VI–135a
Nyerere, Julius (Afr. leader) I–22a
Nylon II–9a, 12b, 372b; III–409b; V–328a; VII–44a
Nylon stockings II–372b
Nyquist, H. (sci.) I–287b

O

O2U–1 (bomber) I–55a
Oacpicagigua, Luis (Indian) V–314b
Oahe Dam VI–147a
Oahspe: A New Bible VI–268a
Oahu (Haw.) III–264a; V–239a
Oak III–72b, 73a, 74b; IV–204a; VI–48b, 393 (table); VII–59b
  furniture III–134a, 136a
  tanning IV–128a
Oak Creek (N.Y.) V–176a
Oak Grove, Battle of (1862) III–146a
Oakhurst, John (lit. char.) V–336a
Oakland (auto) I–228b, 315b; IV–67a; V–463b; VI–37b, 83b
Oakland–Bay Bridge III–11b
Oakland Mole (Calif.) III–11b

Oakley, Annie (Phoebe Anne Oakley Mozee) VII–298b
Oakley, Thomas J. (law.) III–178a; VI–407b
Oak Ridge (Tenn.) I–215b; III–321b; IV–238a; V–67b, 455b; VII–26a, 28a
OAS. *See* Organization of American States
OASDHI. *See* Old–Age, Survivors, Disability, and Health Insurance
"Oath of a Free–man" V–410b
Oath of office
president II–201b
Oatlands (Leesburg, Va.) IV–472a
Oatman, Lorenzo V–129b
Oatman, Mary Ann V–129b
Oatman, Olive V–129b
OATMAN GIRLS V–129b; III–376b
Oatmeal I–486b–87a
Oatmeal Millers Association I–487a
OATS V–129b; I–486a,b; VI–48a
bread II–219a
corn belt II–227a
Ohio V–141b
OAU. *See* Organization of African Unity
Oaxaca (Mex.) III–302a
Oberlin (Ohio) I–134a; IV–338b; V–130b
Oberlin Association VII–275a
Oberlin College IV–338b; V–130a,b
Oberlin Collegiate Institute II–399a
OBERLIN MOVEMENT V–130a
OBERLIN–WELLINGTON RESCUE CASE V–130b
Oberth, Hermann (astron.) I–210a
OBLONG (N.Y.) **V–130b**
Obookiah IV–364b
Obregón, Álvaro (pol.) IV–328b; V–107b
O'Brien, Lawrence F. (offi.) V–374a; VII–254b
O'Brien, William S. (capitalist) I–329a; II–157a
Obscenity
censorship I–478b–79a
electronic media I–480b
motion pictures IV–419a
Supreme Court rulings III–105b–06a
OBSERVATORIES, ASTRONOMICAL V–130b; I–211b–12b; V–12a; VI–319b
Observer (news.) IV–199a; V–68a, 71a
Obstetrics V–175a
Ocala (Fla.) II–42a; III–40a; V–132a
Ocala Demands III–40a
OCALA PLATFORM (1890) **V–132a**
Ocampo, Francisco Xavier de (engr.) V–411b
Occaneechi (Indians) I–240b; IV–131a
Occaneechi Trail III–387b
Occanneechees Islands VII–202b
Occhialini, G. P. S. (phys.) V–302b
Occult V–213b
Occupational and Safety Administration IV–78b
Occupational medicine. *See* Medicine, Occupational
Occupational Safety and Health Act (1970) I–7b; IV–77b, 78b; VI–328a
Occupational therapy
mental illness IV–305a
OCCUPATIONS, CHANGES IN V–132a
Occupation tax II–164b; VII–6a
Ocean Exploration, International Decade of (1970–80) III–454b
Ocean Grove (N.J.) I–434a
Oceania I–81a; III–333b; VII–87b
Oceanic and Atmospheric Administration. *See* National Oceanic and Atmospheric Administration
Oceanic Steamship Company IV–312a
Ocean Island VI–186a
Ocean mining III–13b
Oceanographic Data Center, National V–133b–34a
Oceanographic Instrumentation Center, National V–134a
OCEANOGRAPHIC SURVEY V–133a
OCEANOGRAPHY V–134a; II–76a, 390a
Coast and Geodetic Survey II–88a–b
Coast Guard II–89b, 90a
Franklin's experiments IV–316a,b
Gulf Stream III–232b
hydrographic surveys III–324b
International Geophysical Year III–453b
marine life III–28b–29a
Maury's observations IV–317a
Naval Research Laboratory V–14b
polar exploration V–338b
Scripps Institution VI–242a
Ocean shipping. *See* Shipping, Ocean
Ocean Springs (Miss.) I–301a; IV–276b
Ocharte, Pedro (print.) V–410b
Ochoa, Severo (biochem.) IV–391a; V–100a
Ochs, Adolph S. (pub.) V–73b
Ochsner, Albert (surg.) VI–455a
Ocmulgee National Monument V–217b
Oconee River VII–299b
O'Connor, Basil (law.) V–340a
O'Connor, Flannery (au.) IV–165a
O'Connor, John (pol.) V–48b
Ocracoke Inlet (N.C.) VI–415a
October Revolution (1917) I–122b
Oddfellows, Independent Order of VI–252b
Odell, Moses F. (pol.) II–140a
Odell, William (off.) VI–130a
Odell typewriter VII–136b
Oder River VII–173b
Odessa (USSR)
World War II V–11a
Odets, Clifford (playwright) VII–50a
Odhner, Willgodt (inv.) I–396a
Odiorne's Point (N.H.) V–53b
O'Donnell, James (pol.) VI–172b
OECD. *See* Organization for Economic Cooperation and Development
OEEC. *See* Organization for European Economic Cooperation
OEO. *See* Office of Economic Opportunity
Oerlikon (machine gun) I–57b; V–27a
Oersted, Hans Christian (phys.) I–92a; II–413a; VII–18b
Oerter, Al (athlete) V–154a
O Fair New Mexico (song) VI–394 (table)
O'Fallon, Benjamin (Indian agent) VII–358a
Off–Broadway VII–50b–51a
Office for Drug Abuse Law Enforcement IV–22a
Office furniture III–136a, 139b
Office holding
Afro–Americans III–59b
Confederacy II–205b
freehold III–107b
limitations II–200b
right to IIO–324b
Office of Censorship (World War II) V–74a
Office of Civil and Defense Mobilization II–50a, 498a
Office of Civil Defense II–50a
Office of Construction of Weights and Measures IV–462b
Office of Consumer Affairs II–498a
Office of Criminal Justice IV–22a
Office of Dry Land Agriculture II–376a
OFFICE OF ECONOMIC OPPORTUNITY V–135b; II–148b, 498a, 502a
Job Corps III–504a
neighborhood government IV–173a
Office of Economic Stabilization VII–336a
Office of Education, U.S. *See* Education, United States Office of
Office of Emergency Planning II–498a
Office of Emergency Preparedness II–498a
Office of Examiner of Interferences V–226b
Office of Indian Affairs. *See* Indian Affairs, Bureau of
Office of Intergovernmental Relations II–498a
Office of Law Enforcement Assistance IV–22b
OFFICE OF MANAGEMENT AND BUDGET V–136b; II–498a; VII–107b
Office of National Narcotics Intelligence IV–22a
Office of Naval Research IV–471a; V–28a, 137b
Office of Preservation Services IV–472a
Office of Price Administration V–401b; VII–123b, 336a
Office of Price Stabilization V–401b
Office of Production Management IV–73a
Office of Records Management I–168a
Office of Road Inquiry II–502b
Office of Saline Water III–445a
Office of Science and Technology II–498a
OFFICE OF SCIENTIFIC RESEARCH AND DEVELOPMENT V–137a; IV–287b, 470b; V–296a
Manhattan Project IV–238a
World War II VII–334a–b
Office of Special Commissioner of the Revenue VI–464a
OFFICE OF STRATEGIC SERVICES V–137b; I–484a; III–439a; VI–373b–74a; VII–338a
partisans III–231b
psychological warfare V–441a
Office of Telecommunications Policy II–498a
Office of Territories VII–32b
Office of the Alien Property Custodian II–168b, 445b
Office of the Comptroller of the Currency Act (1863) II–152b
Office of the Coordinator of Information III–439a; V–138a

Office of the Special Representative for Trade Negotiations II–498a
Office of the Superintendent of Indian Trade III–371a, 389a
Office of Vocational Rehabilitation III–267b
Office of War Information V–138a, 432b; VII–333b, 336a
  propaganda V–441a
Office of Water Research and Technology III–445a
Officer Candidate School (Newport) V–24a, 29a
OFFICERS' RESERVE CORPS V–138b; VI–98b
Official Museum Directory IV–436b
Off-off-Broadway VII–51a
Offset printing V–77b, 412b
Offshore oil drilling V–272b; VII–57b
Off-track betting III–149b, 305b
  New York II–263a
Off-track bookmaking syndicates II–260a
Ofo (Indians) III–367a
OGALLALA (Nebr.) **V–139a**; II–251b; IV–280b
Ogallala (Wyo.) I–473b
Ogden (Utah) III–76b, 291a; IV–94b; V–140a; VII–104a
Ogden, Aaron (law.) III–178a, 178a
Ogden, Amos (off.) VI–190a,b
Ogden, David Bayard V–140a
Ogden, Edmund A. (off.) VI–141b
Ogden, Peter Skene (trapper) V–140a
Ogden, Samuel (off.) V–139b
Ogden, William B. (pol.) II–17a
Ogden Company V–139b
OGDEN PURCHASE V–139b
OGDENSBURG (N.Y.) **V–139b**; III–55a
  Fort La Galette IV–85a
  War of 1812 III–217b
Ogdensburg Declaration (1940) I–439b; V–139b
OGDEN'S HOLE (Utah) **V–140a**; III–291a
OGDEN* v. *SAUNDERS (1827) **V–140a**; II–213b
Ogeechee River I–223b; IV–209a
Ogeechee Road (Ga.) III–170a–b
Oglala Sioux (Indians) II–283a; III–17b, 378a; VI–297a
  Battle of Slim Buttes VI–313a
  Black Hills War I–313a
  Wyoming VII–345b
Oglesby, Richard J. (pol.) VI–40a
Oglethorpe, James Edward (philan.) IV–46b, 274a; V–274b
  Augusta I–223a
  Florida attack VI–349a
  Fort Marion IV–253b
  Frederica III–100b
  Georgia III–168a
  royal land grants IV–91b
  Salzburgers VI–204b
  Savannah VI–220a
  Savannah plan II–45b
  War of Jenkins' Ear I–323a; III–498a
O'Gorman, James A. (pol.) IV–169a
Ogunquit (Maine) III–200b
Oh, Wisconsin! (song) VI–395 (table)
O'Hara, Frank (poet) IV–165b
O'Hara, James (trader) V–184a
OHIO V–140a; VI–395 (table)
  Adena I–11a
  Akron Law I–70b
  Antioch College II–399a
  apples III–129a
  army campaigns III–127a
  Augusta County I–223b
  banking I–259b
  Bank of the United States II–266b; V–174a–b
  Black Laws I–314a
  black officeholders VI–432b
  Black Swamp I–317b
  bog iron I–327a
  campaign of 1836 I–419b
  Camp Chase I–433a
  Camp Perry I–289a
  Canadian refugees V–342a
  canals I–442b; II–459a; III–202b, 449b; IV–175a
  canal society I–444a
  Case Institute II–448a
  cattle industry I–37b
  checkoff II–3a
  cheese industry II–280b
  Chillicothe II–25a
  Chillicothe Junto II–25b
  Cincinnati II–37a
  circuit riders II–39b
  civil service II–60a
  Civil War I–376a; II–61b, 271b; IV–410a,b; V–121b
  Civil War militia VI–378b
  Cleveland II–74b
  coal mining II–75a, 85a, 86a
  Colorado settlers VII–146a
  conciliation process II–157b
  constitution II–302b; VII–345a–b
  Copperheads II–222b
  corn II–226b, 227a
  corn belt I–486a
  courts II–38a
  Coxey's Army IV–36a
  criminal syndicalism law V–78b
  Crowbar Law II–266b
  Cumberland Road II–273a–b; III–448b
  dairy industry II–279b
  Delaware Indians II–321a
  discrimination in courts III–437b
  distilling VII–289b
  Dohrman's grant II–359a
  domestic trade VII–83b
  Dominicans II–362b
  Dunmore's War II–381a
  exploration V–145a
  farm experiment clubs III–84b
  federal–state jurisdiction VII–154b
  Firelands III–25b
  floods and tornadoes II–351b
  football III–57a
  Fort Hamilton III–244a
  Fort Harmar III–254b
  Fort Jefferson III–494a
  Fort Laurens IV–117a
  Fort Miami IV–329a
  Fort Recovery VI–60a
  Fort Saint Clair VI–188a
  Fort Washington VII–247a
  Franciscans III–94b
  French grants III–120a
  French refugees III–121b
  Friends of Domestic Industry III–124a
  fugitive slaves IV–43b
  furniture III–135b
  Gallipolis III–148a
  Gnadenhutten III–187b
  Grange stores II–220b
  Great Serpent Mound III–222a
  Great Warriors Path VII–238b
  historical society III–278b
  Holmes County Rebellion III–292a
  homeopathy III–293b
  Hopewell culture III–300a
  horse III–303b
  impeachment III–344b
  Indiana settlers III–370a
  Indiana State Canals III–374b
  Indian land cessions III–227b; IV–216b; VII–17b–18a
  Indian lands I–371b; IV–181b
  Indian raids III–239a
  Indian removal III–394b
  Indian wars VI–188b
  interurban electric lines III–461a,b
  iron and steel industry III–12a
  Italian population III–338a
  Kansas settlers V–360b
  Kent State protest IV–38b
  Ku Klux Klan IV–58b
  Lake Michigan IV–332b
  lake ports II–459a
  land offices III–258a
  land speculation IV–99a; V–143b
  libraries IV–144b
  limnology II–391a
  liquor laws IV–210b
  Loramie's store IV–188a
  lynching legislation IV–208b
  maple sugar IV–246b
  Marietta IV–250b
  meat-packing IV–280a
  Miami Trail IV–330a
  Michigan boundary dispute III–128a; V–144b
  migration to Missouri I–293a
  Military District I–331a; VII–273a
  military tracts IV–91a, 344b; VII–202a
  miminum-wage law IV–353a
  Mingo Bottom IV–351b
  Mississippi River V–59a
  mounds IV–420b, 421a; V–217b
  National Road II–273a; IV–470a
  natural gas V–5a
  New England settlers V–50a
  "New West" V–81b
  Northwestern Indian War VII–239a
  Northwest Territory V–123a
  Oberlin Collegiate Institute II–399a
  Oberlin movement V–130a
  Oberlin-Wellington rescue case V–130b
  oil V–270a; VI–356b
  oil boomtowns I–336b
  Pennsylvania Turnpike III–450b
  Pickawillanee V–308a
  plank roads V–323a
  potash V–376a
  Prohibition party V–430b
  property qualifications for voting V–434b
  public lands I–331a; V–453a
  Quakers V–470a,b
  railroads VI–25a; VII–83b
  rainfall VI–41b
  referendum VI–66b
  retail sales VII–84b
  revolutionary war V–152b, 319b; VI–378a
  sales tax VI–200b
  Sandusky VI–208b
  Schoenbrunn mission VI–226a
  school for the deaf III–248a
  school lands VI–228a
  Scotch-Irish VI–240b
  settlement III–227b; IV–329b, 338b
  Seven Ranges Survey VI–451a
  Shawnee VI–270b
  snowstorms II–351b
  social legislation VI–327b
  stagecoach lines V–144b
  Standard Oil Company VI–382b
  state fairs VI–392b
  State Fish Hatchery II–391b
  statehood VI–401a
  Sweeping Resolution VI–454b
  Tammany society VI–460b
  tariff VI–465b, 466b

Tecumseh's crusade VII–233b
tobacco VII–66b, 67a
Toledo War VII–68b
toll roads III–450b
tornadoes VII–75b
townships VII–81b
Treaty of Greenville III–383a; VII–263a
Underground Railroad VII–138a,b, 139a
Upper Sandusky VII–157b
Vallandigham incident VII–164b
veterinary medicine VII–176b, 177a
Visable Admixture Law VII–204b
voting behavior VII–210b
War of 1812 VI–412a
Western Reserve III–414a; VI–264a; VII–273a–b, 274a
West Virginia V–205b; VII–282a
westward movement V–179a; VII–283b, 284a
wheat VII–286a
Wilberforce University II–113b
winemaking III–129a; VII–305a
wool VII–320b
Zane's Trace VII–368a
Zoar Society II–147a; IV–338b; VII–369b
Ohio (ship) VI–282a; VII–240b
OHIO, ARMY OF THE V–142a; II–271b; VI–278b; VII–26b
OHIO, FALLS OF THE V–142b
Cumberland Gap V–224b
exploration V–145a
Fort Nelson V–32b
Jefferson's proposed states III–497a
lifesaving station IV–152b
Louisville and Portland Canal IV–198b
New Orleans V–63a
revolutionary war IV–40a
Wilderness Road VII–296a
OHIO, FORKS OF THE V–143a; V–146a
Allegheny River I–89a
Fort Prince George V–144a
French and Indian War III–219a,b; VI–150a
French occupation VI–271a
Great Trail III–223b
land grants IV–92a
Logstown IV–181a
Pittsburgh V–321b
Virginia claims V–253a
western passage V–224a–b
westward movement VII–283a
Ohio Agricultural and Mechanical College. *See* Ohio State University
Ohio and Erie Canal V–141b, 145b, 249b
See also Ohio State Canals
Ohio Banking System I–255b
Ohio City (Ohio) II–74b
Ohio College of Dental Surgery II–330a
OHIO COMPANY OF ASSOCIATES V–143b; I–296a, 358b; IV–329b; V–140b, 162b–63a; VI–239a
Gallipolis III–120b
land speculation IV–99a
Marietta IV–250b, 338b
surveys VI–451a
OHIO COMPANY OF VIRGINIA V–144a; II–271b–72a, 382a; III–118a, 219a, 226a; IV–371a; V–140a
backwoods land grants IV–92a
expeditions of IV–398b
Forks of the Ohio V–143a, 253a
Gist explorations III–182a
Kentucky exploration IV–39b
land speculation IV–98b
Logstown Treaty IV–181b
Potomac River V–378b
trails VI–153a
Ohio County (Va.) I–223b
Ohio Enabling Act (1802) V–144b
OHIO IDEA V–144b; I–422a; III–224a
Ohio Indians II–265b, 484b, 497b; III–58b
Loramie's store IV–188a
Ohio Land Company. *See* Ohio Company of Virginia
Ohio Life Insurance and Trust Company VI–370b
Ohio Life Insurance Company of Cincinnati V–207a
OHIO–MICHIGAN BOUNDARY DISPUTE V–144b; I–351a, 352a; IV–331a; V–141b; VII–157a
OHIO NATIONAL STAGE COMPANY V–144b
"Ohio Plan" I–134a
Ohio River III–286b; IV–130a,b; V–224a,b; VI–203b, 253b; VII–293b
Acadians I–6a
Allegheny wagoners VII–216a
army posts III–126b
Arthur expedition V–32a
Baker's Cabin massacre I–244a
bargemen I–267b
Big Bone Lick I–295b
Blennerhassett Island I–319b, 387b
Bluegrass country I–324b
boats I–274a
boundary disputes I–351b
bridges I–364a,b
buffalo trails I–376a
Cairo (Ill.) I–403b
canals I–40a; II–15b; III–449a; IV–443b–44a; V–141b; VII–260b
canal subsidies VI–425a
Cave-in-Rock I–476a
Céloron's voyage V–146a
Central Canal III–374b
channel improvement VII–77a–b
Cherokee claims III–251a
Cincinnati II–37b
Civil War I–288a; II–363a; IV–42a, 374b, 410b; VI–38a
Clark's Detroit expedition IV–173b
Cleveland II–74b
Cresap's War II–257b
Croghan's expedition II–265b
Cumberland Road III–448b
dams and locks IV–175a
disasters II–350b
Dunmore's War V–335b
exploration III–118a, 182a
Falls of the Ohio V–142b
Fincastle County III–24b
fish III–27a
floods III–37a
Forks of the Ohio V–143a
Fort Duquesne II–382a
Fort Harmar III–254b
fortifications I–306b
Fort Jefferson III–494a
Fort McIntosh IV–216b
Fort Randolph VI–45b
Fort Steuben VI–412b
Fort Washington VII–247a
French and Indian War III–116a
French posts III–115a; IV–213b
French settlement III–120a
fur trade III–141b, 143b, 144a
galley boats III–147b
Gallipolis III–148a
gambling III–149b
Geographer's Line III–163a
Great Trail III–223b
Great Warriors Path VII–239a
Harmony Society III–255b
Illinois Country III–330b
Indiana III–370a
Indian Barrier State III–375b, 493b; V–120b
Indian land cessions III–227b, 382b
Indian removal III–394a
Indians I–499b
Indian trade I–278a
Indian Treaty at Pittsburgh V–322a
Indian villages I–337a
Indian wars VI–150a; VII–212b, 253b
industrialization IV–41b
Iroquois cession VI–385b, 386a
James River and Kanawha Canal III–488a
Jesuit missions III–499b
Kentucky IV–39b
Lafayette's visit IV–84a
Lake Erie–Ohio River Canal V–2a
land grants IV–371a
land speculation IV–99a
Logstown (Pa.) IV–181a
maize complex I–48a
Massie's Station VII–202a
"men of western waters" IV–303b
Miami and Erie Canal V–145b
Miami purchase IV–329b
Miami Trail IV–330a
Mississippi River IV–372a
Monongahela River IV–398b
mounds III–365a
navigation VI–145b–46a,b, 147a, 148a,b
Navigator handbook V–17a
Northwest Territory II–356a; V–123a
Ohio and Erie Canal V–145b
Ohio Company of Associates V–143b
Old Northwest III–369b; V–152a, 180b
pack trains V–184a
Pennsylvania and Ohio Canal V–249b
piracy IV–263a
"Pocket" V–334b
portages V–367b
Potomac River canals V–378a
pottery III–184b
proposed colony I–499a
Prudhomme Bluffs V–440b
Quebec Act V–425a; VI–2a
railroad rate wars VI–23a
railroads IV–137b; VI–25b, 33a–b, 37b; VII–100b
revolutionary war II–71a; III–147b; V–140b, 354b; VI–124a
rivermen VI–147b
Scioto Trail VI–239b
settlements III–171a, 209a; IV–92b, 181b; V–144a
Seven Ranges survey VI–264a
Shawnee VI–270b
showboats VI–283a
snags VI–322a
Southwest Territory VI–358a
steamboating IV–372b, 470b; VI–406b, 407a, 408a; VII–100b
store boats VI–415b
Tarascon, Berthoud and Company VI–462a
Tennessee River VII–27b
tomahawk claims VI–70a
trade VII–83a,b
Trans–Appalachia VII–97b
transportation VII–100a–b

OHIO RIVER (cont.)
urban communities IV–42a
Vandalia Colony VII–166b
Wabash and Erie Canal III–374b; VII–212a
Wayne's Indian campaign VII–262b
western lands VII–273a,b
Westsylvania VII–281a
westward movement VII–283b
Wheeling VII–287b
Wheeling Bridge VII–288a
Wilderness Road VII–296a
Zane's Trace VII–368a
OHIO RIVER, EARLY DISCOVERY OF V–144b; III–292b
OHIO STATE ANTISLAVERY SOCIETY V–145b
OHIO STATE CANALS V–145b; II–74b–75a; V–141b; VII–100a
Muskingum River Canal IV–443b
Pennsylvania and Ohio Canal V–249b
Wabash and Erie VII–212a
Ohio State Penitentiary II–348a
Ohio State University II–391b; VII–156a
land grants VII–202a
Ohio Turnpike II–302b
OHIO VALLEY V–146a; I–324b; VII–268a
Adena culture I–11a
Anglo–French rivalry III–115a
Carrying Place of Niagara V–90a
Cumberland Road II–273a
dairy industry II–279b
English in II–458b; IV–375b
exploration III–182a; V–144b
Forbes Road III–59a
French and Indian War II–126b; III–58b
French claims III–118a, 120a; V–246b
French control II–381b–82a
French–English rivalry I–477a; IV–46b
fur trade III–140a, 141a,b, 403b
homestead movement III–295b
Indian agriculture III–366b
Indian barrier state III–375a
Indian land cession III–24b
Indian migration VI–270b
Indian trade VII–95b
Indian wars II–389a; VII–262b–63a
land speculation VI–238b–39a
Mississippi River IV–372b
Mound Builders IV–421a,b
mules IV–426a
Ohio Company of Virginia V–144a
panic of 1857 V–207a
Pennsylvania canal system V–250a
Potomac River V–378b
prehistory V–140a
railroads VI–37b
rivermen VI–147b
settlement III–227b; V–123a; VI–149a
Shawnee VI–270b
sheep VI–272b
stagelines VI–380a
timberlands VII–59b
Venango VII–168b
Washington's western lands VII–252a
West Virginia VII–281a,b
Ohio Yearly Meeting of Friends III–123b
Ohlin, Lloyd II–148a
Ohm, Georg S. (phys.) II–38b
Ohman, Olof IV–38a
"OH! SUSANNA" (song) **V–146b**; IV–438a
Oil
Middle East I–124b, 149b–50b, 231a
See also Petroleum Industry; Petroleum Prospecting and Technology
Oil, fish VI–379a
Oil and Gas, Interstate Compact to Conserve III–460a; VI–402b
Oil City (Pa.) I–336b; V–146b, 318b
petroleum V–321a
Oil Conservation Board, Federal V–270b
Oil Creek (Pa.) V–266b, 271a, 318b, 321a; VII–295a
Oil Creek Railroad V–318b, 319a
Oil Dealers' Exchange V–146b
Oil embargo (1973–74) VI–472b; VII–91b
OIL EXCHANGES, EARLY V–146b
Oil reserves, naval. *See* Naval Oil Reserves
Oil Scandals. *See* Elk Hills Oil Scandal; Naval Oil Reserves; Teapot Dome Oil Scandal
Oil slick
midcontinent oil region IV–333b
Oil spills VI–281b
Audubon Society I–222b
Coast Guard II–90a
regulation IV–255a
Oil trust III–443b; VI–383b
Oil wells
boundary disputes I–351b
Drake's II–369b
East Texas II–389a–b
El Dorado II–408a
OISE–AISNE OPERATION (1918) **V–146b**
Ojeda, Alonso de (expl.) I–96a; IV–247a
Ojibwa. *See* Chippewa
Okalona (Miss.) IV–313b
Okanogan (Indians) III–500a,b
OKANOGAN, FORT (Ore.) **V–147a**
Okanogan River I–209a; V–147a
O. K. Corral VII–71a
OKEECHOBEE, BATTLE OF (1837) **V–147a**; VI–261a
Okeechobee, Lake II–351b; III–320a
Seminole Wars V–147a
sugarcane VI–436b
O'Keeffe, Georgia (paint.) V–192b
Okies V–149a
OKINAWA V–147b; I–55b; IV–253a; V–21a, 27a; VII–2a, 139a, 337a, 343a
OKLAHOMA V–148a; VI–355a,b, 395 (table)
black suffrage VI–432a,b
blizzards I–320b
Bluestem Pastures I–326a
boundary disputes I–351a,b
boycotts I–356b
Camp Supply VI–443b
Cherokee II–321; VII–96b
Cherokee strip II–14a
Cherokee Trail II–14b
Cheyenne II–379b
Chippewa II–31a
Chisholm Trail II–31b–32a
Cimarron II–37a
coal mines II–85a
Comanche II–133a–b
constitution VI–391b
Delaware Indians II–320b–21a
Denison Dam III–322b
De Soto expedition II–184a
Dodge City Trail II–358b
Dust Bowl II–382a
exploration III–119b; IV–230a
flour milling I–488a
Fonda's expedition III–50b
forests III–74b
Fort Gibson III–178b
Fort Reno VI–87a
Fort Sill I–289a; VI–287a
Fort Smith VI–317a
Fort Towson VII–81b
fur trade II–34a–b
grandfather clause III–208b, 232a
Greer County dispute III–200a, 228a
horse racing III–304b
impeachment III–344b
Indian Country III–379b
Indian land cession IV–199a
Indian population III–396a,b
Indian reservations II–133b; VI–64a
Indians III–365b, 401a
Indian Territory II–51b, 52b; III–402a, 402b
Jesuit missions III–500b
Kansas–Oklahoma Arkansas River Commission VI–402a
Kiowa raids IV–50b
land grants for education IV–93b
martial law IV–259a
Natchez Indians IV–455b
Native American Church V–2a, 273a
natural gas IV–123a
No Man's Land II–37a
Nonpartisan League V–106b
oil boomtowns I–336b
Osage V–173b
Osage pastures I–326a
panhandle V–205b
party emblems II–437b
petroleum IV–333b, 334a; V–270a; VI–356b, 357a
Platt National Park V–218 (table)
prairie V–387a
prairie dogs V–387b
Public Land Strip II–37a
railroads VI–36a
rainfall VI–41b
referendum VI–66b
Santa Fe trade VI–215b
Seminole VI–259b, 260a
settlement VII–284b
Shawnee VI–270b
Socialist party VI–326a,b
soldiers' homes VI–337a
Sooners VI–339b
statehood II–52b, 443b
state of Sequoyah VI–262b
teachers' loyalty oath VII–15b
train robberies VII–97b
Treaties of Saint Louis III–383b
unassigned lands I–335b–36a
veterinary medicine VII–176b
Warren's trading posts VII–238b
wheat III–44a; VII–286a
Whipple's expedition VII–289a
Wichita Mountains Wildlife Refuge IV–184b
Oklahoma (battleship) VII–242a
Oklahoma! (musical) II–290a; IV–442a; VII–50b
Oklahoma! (song) VI–395 (table)
Oklahoma, University of III–285a; IV–461a; V–272a
Oklahoma City (Okla.) I–336b; IV–104b; VI–83b, 357a
Oklahoma colony I–336a
Oklahoma Geological Survey V–272a

OKLAHOMA OPENINGS **V–149b**; V–148b–49a
OKLAHOMA SQUATTERS **V–149b**; V–149a
Oklahoma v. *Texas* (1926) I–351b
Oklawaha River V–231a
Okoboji Lakes VI–374a
O'Laughlin, Michael IV–155a
Olcott, Henry Steel (theosophist) VII–52a
Old Abraham (Indian) IV–186b
OLD AGE **V–150a**
family structure IV–256b
insurance I–428b
life expectancy IV–151b
Medicaid and Medicare IV–289b; VI–328b–29a
minority rights IV–359a
Nader's Raiders IV–448b
New Deal V–46a
nutrition programs V–129a
pensions I–77b; II–236b
population V–363a
Progressive movement V–428b
Sailor's Snug Harbor VI–186b
share–the–wealth movements VI–269a
social legislation VI–327a, 328a
social security VI–329a–b
tontine plan VII–72a
Townsend Plan VII–79b
Old–Age Revolving Pension. *See* Townsend Plan
Old–Age, Survivors, Disability, and Health Insurance V–255a–b
Old Age, Survivors Insurance VI–329b
Old Bay State VI–394 (table)
Old Black Joe (song) IV–438a
"Old Cap Collier" (dime novel) II–341b
Old Capitol prison I–466a
Old Chariton (Mo.) IV–380a
Old Chillicothe (Ohio) II–25b; V–319b
Old City Hall (Phila.) III–354a
Old Colony State VI–394 (table)
Old copper culture II–386a
OLD COURT–NEW COURT STRUGGLE **V–150b**; VI–406b
Old Crossing IV–118a
Old Crow Flats (Can.) I–155a
Old Dearborn Distributing Company v. *Seagram Distillers Corporation* (1936) II–483a
Old Deluder Satan Act (1647) II–393b–94a
"Old Ditch." *See* Chesapeake and Ohio Canal
OLD DOMINION **V–151a**; VI–395 (table)
Old Dominion University VII–300b
Oldenburg, Henry (nat., philos.) VI–235a
Old Faithful (geyser) VII–357b
OLD FIELD SCHOOLS **V–151b**; II–395a
Old Folks at Home (song) IV–438a; VI–393 (table) *See also* "Swanee River"
Old Fort Vancouver. *See* Vancouver, Fort
Old Franklin (Mo.) IV–380a
"OLD FUSS AND FEATHERS" **V–151b**
Old German Baptist Brethren I–361a
Old Guard I–426b, 429a
Oldham, John (col.) V–261a; VI–184a
Old Head of Kinsale (Ire.) IV–205a
"OLD HICKORY" **V–151b**; VI–313a
Old House of Representatives (paint.) V–190a
Old Insurance Office (Phila.) III–427b
Old Ironsides (locomotive) VI–25a, 36a
"Old Ironsides" (warship). *See Constitution*
"Old lead belt" IV–123a
Old Left II–146b; VI–14a
Old Line State VI–394 (table)
Old Line Whigs II–184b
Old Louisiana Code II–91b
"Old Lutherans" III–336b
Old Manse II–158a
Oldmixon, John VII–66a
Old New Hampshire (song) VI–394 (table)
"Old No. 1" (tractor) I–35b
OLD NORTH CHURCH (Boston) **V–151b**; VI–106a
Old North State (song) VI–395 (table), 395 (table)
OLD NORTHWEST **V–152a**; I–340b–41a; III–279a, 369b; V–140b, 180b; VII–100a, 273b
Centinel of the North-Western Territory VI–239a
emigration to Kansas IV–31a
Erie Canal III–448a
exploration II–353a, 381a, 477a, 477a–b
Fort Saint Joseph VI–191b
free blacks III–102a
French missions II–13b
Indian land cession III–24b
Lake Michigan IV–332b
Miami purchase IV–329b
Northwest Territory V–122b
Quakers VI–347b
Quebec Act I–340b
railroads VII–100b
revolutionary war III–400b
settlement I–100b, 286b
supply routes VI–155b
Tecumseh's crusade V–141a
Trans–Appalachia VII–97b
transcontinental railroad VII–147a
Wayne Campaign III–404a
"OLD OAKEN BUCKET" (poem) **V–152a**
Old Oklahoma I–336a
Old Order Amish Church IV–303a
Old Order (Wisler) Mennonite Church IV–303a
Old Patent Office Building (Washington, D.C.) VI–319b
Old Path I–279b
Old Point Comfort (Va.) III–489b; VI–145a; VII–361a
Old Post Road V–375a
Old Providence (R.I.) VII–94b
Old Providence Colony (Honduras) III–219b
"OLD ROUGH AND READY" **V–152a**
Olds, Ransom E. (auto mfr.) I–227a; II–337a
Old Saratoga (N.Y.) VI–217b
Old Saybrook. *See* Saybrook
Old School Presbyterians II–36b
Old Side, Presbyterianism V–391b
"Old Sleuth" II–341b
Oldsmobile (auto) I–229b
Olds Motor Company IV–433a
Old South. *See* South, Antebellum
OLD SOUTH CHURCH (Boston) **V–152a**
"Old sow" (cannon) VII–56b
Old Spanish Trail *See* Spanish Trail
Old Square (New Orleans). *See Vieux Carré*
Old Sturbridge Village (Mass.) III–137b
Old Taos Trail. *See* Taos Trail
Old Town (Calif.) VI–208a,b
Oldtown (Md.) V–378b
Oldtown (N.C.) I–293a
Old Town, Treaty of (1818) III–383b
OLEANA (Pa.) **V–152b**
O'Leary, Catherine II–19a–b; IV–424b
Ole Creole Days IV–162b
OLENTANGY, BATTLE OF (1782) **V–152b**
Oleomargarine II–281a, 282a; IV–211a; V–465b
Oleomargarine Act (1902) II–281a
Oleopolis (Pa.) V–319a
Oleron (maritime law) I–14b
Olga (warship) I–144a
Oliekoeken III–52a
Oligarchy V–351b
Oliphant, Patrick B. (cartoon.) V–73a
Olitski, Jules (paint.) V–193a
OLIVE BRANCH PETITION (1775) **V–152b**; VI–114b
Oliver, James A. (zool.) VI–91b
Oliver, Joseph ("King") (mus.) IV–440a
Olives III–128a
Olmec (Indians) IV–327a
Olmstead, Gideon I–9a
Olmstead et al. v. *Rittenhouse's Executives* (1809) I–9a
Olmsted, Denison (sci.) III–165a
Olmsted, Frederick Law (landscape arch.) II–46a; IV–96b; VII–246b
Olmsted, Frederick Law, Jr. (landscape arch.) V–219a
Olmsted Brothers (landscape arch.) IV–96b–97a
Olney, Joseph (nav. off.) VI–128b–29a
Olney, Richard (states.)
Income Tax Cases III–351b
In re Debs II–298b
Pullman strike IV–67a
Venezuela boundary controversy I–122a; VII–170b
OLNEY COROLLARY **V–153a**; I–122a
OLNEY–PAUNCEFOTE TREATY (1896) **V–153a**
Olonnais, François l' I–374a
Olson, Charles (poet) IV–165b
Olson, Culbert L. (pol.) I–407b; IV–406b
Olson, Floyd B. (pol.) II–491b, 492b; IV–357b
Olson, Harry (elec. eng.) VI–16b
OLUSTEE, BATTLE OF (1864) **V–153b**; III–39b; IV–339b
Olympia (cruiser) I–158b; III–25b; IV–239b
Olympic Club (Seattle) VII–29a
Olympic Committee, International V–153b
Olympic Committee, U.S. V–153b
OLYMPIC GAMES **V–153b**; II–426a–b
basketball I–272b
hockey III–286b, 387b–88a
Lake Placid (1932) VI–101a
prizefighters V–423a
skiing VI–298a,b
yacht racing VII–349b
Olympic National Park V–217a, 217a, 219 (table), 220a
Olympic Peninsula (Wash.)
Makah IV–228b
Olyphant, R. M. II–102b–03a
OMAHA (Indians) **V–154b**; II–131b; III–363b, 364a, 365a, 396b

OMAHA (cont.)
farming IV–235b
land allotment treaty III–389b
Mormon migration IV–411b
Nebraska V–31a
trade IV–159b
Winnebago VII–306a
Omaha (Nebr.) V–30b–31a, 31a
Cabanne's trading post I–399a
fur trade VI–196a
Lincoln Highway IV–156a
meat-packing I–283b; IV–170a, 280b, 281a
People's party V–365b
railroad pool V–358a
railroad rate wars VI–23a
railroads VI–33b, 35a,b, 37b; VII–101a
steamboating VII–357a
stockyards VI–414a,b
Trans-Mississippi Exposition VII–98a
Union Pacific IV–94a
westward movement VII–284b
wild west shows VII–298b
Omaha Beach (Fr.) V–110b, 111a,b; VII–339a
O'Mahoney, Joseph C. (pol.) VII–123b
O'Mahony, John (pol. leader) I–434a; III–10b–11a
OMB. *See* Office of Management and Budget
Ombudsman III–422a; V–472b
OMNIBUS BILL (1850) **V–155a**; II–150a
Omori, S. (off.) II–443a
Onandaga (Indians)
Fort Plain V–323a
Onassis, Jacqueline Kennedy II–372b; IV–37b; VII–292a
Oñate, Juan de (expl.). *See* Oñate's Explorations
OÑATE'S EXPLORATIONS (1598–1608) **V–155a**; II–452b–53a; III–420b
Acoma I–8a
Colorado River I–172a
El Paso II–433a
Mohave IV–386a–b
New Mexico II–184b; III–302b; V–59b; VI–162a
Taos Pueblo VI–461a
Ondine (yacht) VII–349a
O'Neale, Margaret (Peggy) II–389b
One-horse shay I–461a
101st Airborne Division. *See* entries under Army, United States
101st Engineer Battalion IV–463b
103rd Pursuit Squadron
World War I IV–83b
106th Infantry Division. *See* entries under Army, United States
107th Infantry Regiment. *See* entries under Army, United States
182nd Infantry Regiment. *See* entries under Army, United States
Oneida (Indians) III–365b, 400b, 475a
education III–379b
French and Indian War III–115a, 117a
Frontenac expedition III–125a
Iroquois Treaty III–476b
La Famine treaty IV–83b
sachems VI–183a
Oneida (N.Y.) VI–385a
Oneida (ship) III–217b
ONEIDA COLONY V–155b; I–307a; II–147a, 486a; V–87a, 355b; VI–13b, 266b, 325b, 411b
Oneida Company V–155b
Oneida Lake V–172b
O'Neill, Eugene (playwright) IV–165b; V–99b; VII–49b, 50a–b
Provincetown Players V–439b
O'Neill, James (act.) VII–48b
One man, one vote II–172a, 180a, 410a, 457b; III–87a; IV–133b; VII–132b
100,000,000 Guinea Pigs V–466b
One old cat (game) I–269b
119 (locomotive) V–430b
Oneonta (N.Y.) III–461b
101 Ranch VI–161b
"101 Ranch Real Wild West Show" VII–298b–99a
One Third of the Nation's Land (report) V–451a
Onion, Stephen V–409a
Onion River III–226b; V–156a
ONION RIVER LAND COMPANY V–156a
ONIONS V–156a; III–51a
Onís, Luis de (dipl.) I–10b; VI–359b
On-line data processing II–427a
On Native Grounds IV–165b
Onondaga (Indians) III–365b, 475a,b; V–139b
French and Indian War III–115a
Frontenac expedition III–124b–25a
Iroquois Treaty III–476b
La Famine treaty IV–83b
sachems VI–183a
Saint Lawrence River VI–192a
Sullivan-Clinton campaign VI–438a
Onondaga (N.Y.) II–5b, 7b; III–475b; VI–202a,b
"ONONTIO" V–156b
ONS-5 (convoy) I–214b
Onsager, Lars (chem.) V–100a
Ontario (Can.) V–156b
Chippewa III–360b
French and Indian War III–117a
Hurricane Diane III–319b
Indians I–86a, 441a; II–31a
Lake Huron III–319a
Loyalists VI–131a; VII–150b
Niagara movement V–93a
power blackout II–417a
Quakers V–470a
Sudbury mining district VI–443b
War of 1812 VI–42a
Ontario (ship) V–22b
Ontario, Fort (N.Y.) I–340b; V–157a
French and Indian War V–175b
See also Oswego
ONTARIO, LAKE V–156b; III–215b–16b; V–367a; VII–157a
Carrying Place of Niagara V–90a
Erie Canal III–448a
exploration III–119a; VI–192a
ferries III–11b
Fort Conti II–210b
Fort Denonville II–329a
Fort George III–167b
Four-Mile Strip III–85a
French and Indian War I–358b; III–115b, 116a; IV–405b
Frontenac expedition III–125a
inland lock navigation III–419b
Iroquois Beaver Land Deed III–476a
Laconia IV–82b
La Salle expedition V–145a
naval disarmament III–217a
Niagara Falls V–91a
Oswego (N.Y.) V–175b
plants II–390a; V–326a
railroads VI–34a
revolutionary war I–384b
shipbuilding VI–282a
War of 1812 III–217a, 217b–18a; VI–183b, 209a, 415a; VII–45b
Welland Canal I–440b; III–452a; VI–193a
Ontario County (N.Y.) V–463b
On the Banks of the Wabash Far Away (song) VI–393 (table)
On the Extinct Mammalia of Dakota and Nebraska IV–232b
Ontological-Hysteric Theater VII–51a
"ON TO RICHMOND" V–157a
"ON TO WASHINGTON" V–157a
On Your Toes (musical play) II–290a
Oohenonpa (Two Kettle) (Indian) II–283a
Op art V–193b
OPEC. *See* Organization of Petroleum Exporting Countries
Opechancanough (Indian) III–219a; V–385b, 386a
Opelika (Ala.) VI–166a
Opelousas (La.) I–6b, 279b, 461b; VII–292b
Open-admissions II–115b
Open Bible Standard Churches V–260a
Open-book accounts IV–393b
OPEN COVENANTS, OPENLY ARRIVED AT V–157b; II–342a; III–85b–86a; VI–438b; VII–331a
OPEN DOOR POLICY V–157b; II–27a–b, 471b, 488a–89a; III–68b; IV–34b; V–35a, 242a; VI–294b; VII–110a
Anglo-American relations I–122a
Lansing-Ishii Agreement IV–106b
Manchuria and Manchukuo IV–234b
Morocco I–85b
Nine-Power Pact V–96b; VII–251a
Root-Takahira Agreement VI–164a
Russo-Japanese War VI–178a
Open-end investment companies. *See* Mutual funds
Open field farming II–141a
Open-hearth process II–223b; III–470b, 473a, 474a
Open Housing Act (1968) I–239b
OPEN-MARKET OPERATIONS V–159a; III–6b–7a, 7a,b; VI–469b
Open-pit mining
copper II–223b
Open-Price movement VII–92a
OPEN RANGE CATTLE PERIOD V–159b; I–471b; II–251a, 358b; III–273a–b; VI–45a
barbed wire I–267a
Chisholm Trail II–477b
closing I–38b
Colorado II–128a
cowboys II–248b
cow country II–250b
cow customs II–251a
cow towns II–251b
Fence War III–10a,b
fencing II–249a
Great Plains III–221b
mesquite IV–316a
nesters V–33a
public lands V–451b
roundups VI–161a
sheep wars VI–273a
Texas VII–40a
Wyoming VII–345b
Open shop IV–67b, 68a, 70a, 71b; VI–410b
"Open skies" inspection plan III–161a
Open society II–197a
Open Theater VII–51a

Open tournaments (golf) III–197b, 198a,b
Open university II–402b
Opequon (Va.) VI–275a
Opequon Creek VII–304b
Opera IV–437b, 438b–49a, 439a; V–83b, 116b
Operant conditioning IV–307a
Operation Big Switch (1952) II–469a
Operation Bootstrap V–461b
Operation Cobra (1944) VI–193b
Operation Eagle Pull (1975) VII–186b
Operation Frequent Wind (1975) VII–187a
Operation Highjump. *See* Antarctic Developments Projects, U.S. Navy
Operation Killer (Kor. War) IV–56a
Operation Little Switch (1952) II–469a
Operation Market–Garden (1944) III–187a–b
Operation Merkur (1941) III–187a
Operation Navigation Extension Winter Season III–218b
Operation NEWS III–218b
Operation Overlord. *See* Normandy Invasion
Operation Starlight (1965) VII–186a
Operation Varsity (1945) III–187b
Operation Windmill
  Antarctic Developments Projects, U.S. Navy
Operon model III–158a
Ophir lode. *See* Comstock Lode
Ophthalmoscope IV–298a
Opinion polls. *See* Public Opinion
Opinion Research Corporation V–453b
Opium I–201b; II–373b–74b; IV–297b, 305b, 449b–50b
  ban on trade IV–34b
  crime II–260a, 261a
  pure drug laws V–465b
Opium Conference (1911–12) II–374b
Opium War (1840–42) II–27a, 28b, 275b; IV–34b
  Kearny mission V–22b
Opossum III–133a; IV–231a; VII–105a
Oppenheimer, J. Robert (phys.) I–215b; III–424b; V–303a
  hydrogen bomb III–324a
  Lawrence Radiation Laboratory IV–119a
  Manhattan Project IV–238b; V–296a, 300b
Opper, Frederick (cartoonist) I–464b
Opportunity theory II–148a
Opryland, U.S.A. (Nashville) IV–453a
Optical art. *See* Op art
Optical master I–287b
Optics II–153a; V–294a
Optlandt, Fort (Del.) VII–372b
Oquendo (ship) VI–216b
Oraibi (Ariz.) II–461a; III–300b
Oral defamation. *See* Libel
Oral hygiene II–331b
Oran (Alg.)
  World War II V–113a; VII–338a
Orange, Fort (N.Y.) I–81b; II–123b; V–40a, 60b
  Dutch–Indian War II–383a
  Huguenots III–315a
  Indian wars V–61a,b
  Rensselaerswyck V–229a
  Walloons VII–221b
  See also Albany
Orange and Alexandria Railroad I–381a; IV–36a
Orange blossom VI–393 (table)
Orangeburg (S.C.) III–405b; VII–191b
Orange County (N.Y.) III–313a, 313a; IV–354b; VI–412a; VII–261b
Orange County (N.C.) VI–71b, 72a
Orange County (Va.) I–223b; III–173a; VI–137b
Orange industry II–43b; III–478b; VI–187b
Orange juice III–55b, 128b
"Orange Quarter" (S.C.) III–315a
Oranges III–52b, 128a,b
ORATORY V–161a; IV–162b
  Fourth of July III–88a
  Indian III–386b
  stump speakers VI–421b
  "twisting the British lion's tail" VII–134b
  "United We Stand, Divided We Fall" VII–155b
  Webster–Hayne debate VII–265b
Orbital weapons platforms II–316a
Orbiter spacecraft I–212b
Orchard, Harry (assassin) II–93b–94a; III–266b
Orchards
  See also Fruit Growing
Orchestras IV–439b
  New York City V–83b
  New York Philharmonic IV–437b
  North Carolina V–116b
  Philadelphia Symphony V–278a–b
  Saint Louis Symphony Orchestra VI–194b
Orchids IV–378b
Ord, E. O. C. (off.) III–485a, 488a; IV–209a
Ord, George (nat.) IV–232a
Ord, Pacificus V–211a
Ordaz, Gustavo Díaz (pol.) VI–143b
ORDER OF AMERICAN KNIGHTS V–161b; II–222b; IV–52b–53a; VI–339a
Order of Carmelite Sisters I–455b
Order of Friars Minor. *See* Franciscans
Order of Preachers II–362b
Order of the Knights of St. Crispin IV–62b
Order of the Star-Spangled Banner. *See* American Party
Orders and Wills of York County (Va.), *1709–16* VI–411a–b
ORDERS IN COUNCIL V–162a
Orderville (Utah) II–147a
Ordinance and Hydrography, Bureau of V–12a
ORDINANCES OF 1784, 1785, AND 1787 V–162a; II–166a–b; IV–90b, 93a–b, 95b, 99a; V–143b; VII–268b, 273b
  fugitive slaves III–130a
  Geographer's Line III–163a
  Indiana III–369b
  Jefferson's proposed states III–496b
  Jones v. *Van Zandt* IV–8a
  Lake Michigan IV–332b
  land survey VI–441a
  Marietta settlement IV–250b
  Miami purchase IV–329b
  Michigan III–128a; IV–330b; VII–68b
  Mississippi Territory IV–368a
  Northwest Territory V–122b
  Ohio V–140b, 144b
  religious liberty VII–69a
  school lands II–396a; VI–228a
  Seven Ranges survey VI–264a
  slavery I–135b; VI–305b, 309a; VII–54a, 189a
  state-making process VI–400b–01a
  state universities VII–156a
  territorial governments VII–31b, 33b
  township system V–452a; VII–81a,b
  Upper Peninsula of Michigan VII–157a
  Wisconsin VII–307a
Ordinaries. *See* Taverns
ORDNANCE V–163a
  arsenals I–196b
  artillery I–199b
  bombing I–328a
  Civil War IV–215a
  Confederate Army II–163a
  Jet Propulsion Laboratory III–502a
  Korean War IV–57a
  merchantmen IV–313a
  See also Cannons; Guns; Machine Guns; Miniguns; Missiles, Military; Munitions; Rockets
Ordnance and Hydrography, Bureau of V–17b
Ordnance Department, Army I–196b
ORDVAC (computer) II–156a
Oreana (Nev.) VI–292b
OREGON V–164a; III–213b; V–180b, 443b; VI–395 (table); VII–247b, 268a
  acquisition II–475a; III–263a
  Adams–Onís Treaty II–216a; IV–320b
  Alaska laws I–76b–77a
  arid regions I–170a,b
  Border Slave State Convention I–341b
  boundary disputes I–351b
  campaign of 1844 I–420a
  cattle I–473a
  Champoeg Convention I–493a
  chromite III–13b
  Clayton Compromise II–73a
  Columbia River II–132a
  constitution VI–391b
  Convention of 1818 II–215b
  Dalles II–285b
  donation lands II–363a; III–296a
  Douglas fir III–74b; IV–95b
  emigrants IV–25b
  exploration III–114b; VII–271b, 272a
  forest fires III–74b
  free land III–107b
  fur trade I–209a; III–143b; V–121a, 180a; VI–160a
  gasoline VI–200b
  gasoline tax III–153a
  gold VII–221b
  horse III–303a
  Hudson's Bay Company III–313b
  hydroelectric power III–320b
  immigrants I–363a
  Indian Country III–379a,b
  Indian reservation system VI–97a
  Indians III–362a, 363a
  Indian wars VII–239a,b
  initiative III–418b
  Japanese-Americans II–445b
  joint occupation II–215b–16a, 475a; III–21a; IV–6a
  Klamath IV–51b
  Labor Day IV–79a
  labor laws IV–68b
  Lewis and Clark Expedition IV–136b
  Lookout Point Dam III–323a
  Louisiana purchase IV–198a
  McLoughlin land claim IV–218b
  McNary Dam III–323a–b
  Modoc War IV–384b; VII–127a

OREGON (cont.)
mountain passes V–225a
national forests V–446a
national parks and monuments V–217b, 218 (table)
New England settlers V–50a, 51b
Nez Perce War V–89b
nickel III–13b–14a
Nonpartisan League V–106b
Pacific republic movement V–180b
Paiute V–194a
private mints IV– 360b
public land states V–453a
Quakers V–470a
railroads VI–20b
recall VI–51a
redwoods VI–262b
referendum VI–66b
single–tax plan VI–293b
slavery IV–379b
Smith explorations VI–318a
South Pass VI–160b
Spanish cession VI–364a; VII–111b
stagecoach service V–178a
statehood I–78b
steamship lines II–91a
suffrage III–92a
Tillamook Lighthouse VI–146b
Treaty of Table Rock III–384a
Vancouver's exploration VII–166a
westward movement V–176b, 179a; VII–284a,b
Willamette Valley VII–300a
woman's suffrage III–91b; VII–315a
work–hours laws VII–213b, 214a
Yakima Wars VII–350a
Yurok VII–367b
OREGON (battleship) **V–165b**; VI–216b, 361a, 363a; V201a–
Oregon, My Oregon (song) VI–395 (table)
Oregon, Territory of V–275b
Oregon, University of V–349a
Oregon and California Railroad IV–95b
OREGON CARAVANS **V–166a**; I–452b; V–169a–b; VII–217b
Great Plains III–221a
"Oh! Susanna" V–146b
prairie schooner V–389b
Oregon Caves National Monument V–217b
Oregon City (Oreg.) IV–218b
"Oregon for America" II–248a
Oregon grape VI–395 (table)
OREGON LAND FRAUDS **V–166a**
OREGON MEMORIAL OF 1838 **V–166b**
Oregon Methodist Mission V–165a, 166b
OREGON MISSIONS **V–166b**; II–285b; V–165a, 167b
OREGON PAROCHIAL SCHOOL CASE (1925) **V–167a**
OREGON QUESTION **V–167a**; III–68a, 313b–14a; V–120b–21a, 164b–65a; VI–151a; VII–303b
"Fifty–Four Forty or Fight" III–21a
Fort Okanogan V–147a
"manifest destiny" IV–239a
Monroe Doctrine IV–400b
Nootka Sound controversy V–109a
Oregon Treaty of 1846 V–169b
Oregon Railroad and Navigation Company V–168a; VI–27a
Oregon Railway and Transportation Company III–65a
OREGON SHORT LINE RAILWAY **V–168a**; VI–27a, 37b
Oregon State College I–303b
Oregon State University V–135a
OREGON SYSTEM **V–168a**; V–165b, 167a
Oregon Territory I–121a; III–328a; V–97b
OREGON TRAIL **V–168a**; II–246b, 477a–b; III–215a; V–165a,b, 166a, 176b; VI–153b–54a; VII–84a, 101a, 256a
alternate route V–178b
Bozeman Trail I–357b
caravans I–452b, 453a
exploration III–114a
Fort Bernard I–292b
Fort Boise I–327b
Fort Bridger I–363a
Fort Hall III–243b
Fort Kearny IV–33b
Fort Laramie IV–108a
Frémont exploration VII–271b
fur trade I–201a
Independence (Mo.) III–353b
Independence Rock III–354a
Indian concessions III–379b
Mormon migration IV–411b
Platte River Trail V–330b
pony express V–357b
Snake River VI–322b
South Pass VI–354b
South Platte route VI–355a
Sublette's Cutoff VI–422a
wagon trains VII–217a
Westport VII–280b
westward movement VII–284a
OREGON TREATY OF 1846 **V–169b**; I–121a, 126b; II–475a; III–21a; IV–6a; V–121a, 165a, 168a; VI–151a; VII–111b, 247b
acreage ceded V–445 (table)
Fort Hall III–244a
Haro Channel III–256a
Idaho III–327b
public land states V–453a
Oregon v. *Mitchell* (1970) III–92a; VI–99b
Oregon–Washington Railway and Navigation Company VI–37b
Oregon Yearly Meeting III–123b
O'Reilly, Alexander (off.) I–399b; II–247b; IV–193a, 301b
O'Reilly, John Boyle (poet, ed.) I–495a
Ores, refractory II–332a
Oreto (ship) III–40b
Organic Act of the Philippine Islands. *See* Jones Act (1916)
Organic chemistry II–7b, 12b
Organic gardening III–151a
ORGANIC LAW **V–170a**
Alaska I–76b, 77a, 79a
Guam III–230b, 425b
Hawaii III–264a
Jones Act IV–7b
Kansas VII–73a
Oregon V–165b
Puerto Rico III–424b
Virgin Islands III–425b; VII–204a
Wisconsin VII–307b
ORGANIZATION FOR ECONOMIC COOPERATION AND DEVELOPMENT **V–170a**
Organization for European Economic Cooperation III–61b; IV–258a; V–170a–b; VII–88b
Organization of African Unity V–200a
ORGANIZATION OF AFRO–AMERICAN UNITY **V–170b**
Organization of American Historians III–279a
ORGANIZATION OF AMERICAN STATES **V–171a**; II–270a; IV–112b; V–234a; VII–113a
Alliance for Progress IV–114a
collective security policy V–36a
Cuba I–454b; II–269b
Cuban missile crisis IV–113a
Dominican Republic II–362a; IV–113a
Monroe Doctrine IV–402a
Panama V–202b
Pan–American Union V–205a
Organization of Petroleum Exporting Countries IV–114a–b; V–270b; VI–345b
Organize, right to IV–71b
Organized crime. *See* Crime, Organized
Organized Reserve (U.S. Army) I–183a, 186a; V–138b
Organized Reserve (Marine Corps) IV–253b
Organ Pipe Cactus National Monument V–217a
ORIENTAL RELIGIONS AND SECTS **V–171b**; IV–448a
Orientals
naturalization V–6b
prejudice II–445b
Orient Point (N.Y.) IV–185a
Original Celtics (basketball) I–273a
Original Dixieland Jazz Band IV–440a, 443b
ORIGINAL PACKAGE DOCTRINE **V–172a**
"Origin of a New Species" (comic strip) V–72a
Origin of Species V–287b
O'Riley, Peter (prospector) VI–292a
Orinoco Steamship Company Case (1910) III–456b
Oriskany (carrier) V–22a
ORISKANY, BATTLE OF (1777) **V–172b**; I–385a; IV–387a
Orizaba (Mex.) IV–325b
Orkney Islands
World War I V–119b; VII–329a
Orlando (Fla.) III–40a
Orleans (steamboat) IV–374a
ORLEANS, FORT (Mo.) **V–173a**; I–354b; III–119b, 144a; IV–376b
ORLEANS, TERRITORY OF **V–173a**; II–91b; IV–195b
Orleans boats I–175a
Orly Airport (Paris) II–347a
Ormsbee, Elijah (inv.) VI–408b
Orne River V–110b; VII–339a
Ornithology I–304b–05b
Ornithology and Mammalogy, Division of II–390a
Oro City (Colo.) VI–292a
Orogeny III–167a
Oronoco tobacco VII–67a
O'Rourke, Matthew J. (jour.) VII–131a
Oroville (Calif.) IV–354b
Oro y plata (motto) VI–394 (table)
Orphanages I–293a, 467b; V–381a
Orphan Annie (comic character) V–72b
Orphans VI–327b
immigration to U.S. III–339b
World War I VII–330b
Orr, Carey (cartoon.) V–73a
Orr, James Lawrence (law.) II–175 (table)
Orteig, Raymond IV–156b
Orth, Franklin L. (adm.) IV–470a
Orthodox churches. *See* Eastern Orthodoxy

Orthodox Church in America II–387a
Orthodox Five Years Meeting V–470b
Orthodox Jews IV–10a, 10b–11a,b
Orthodox Presbyterian Church V–392b
Orthodox Quakers V–470a–b
Orton, William A. (bot.) I–46a
O'Ryan, John F. (off.) VII–366b
OS2U (scout plane) I–55b
OSAGE (Indians) **V–173b**; II–358b; III–119b, 363b, 365a, 396b; VII–306a
farming IV–235b
fur trade III–144a; IV–159b
Jesuit missions III–500a,b
Kansas IV–25a
oil IV–334a
Oklahoma IV–199a; V–148a,b, 149b
Omaha relations V–155a
Osage hedge V–174a
removal III–393b
Santa Fe Trail II–242b
scouts VI–241b
trade II–34a; IV–376b; V–173b
Treaties of Saint Louis III–383b
Treaty of Fort Clark III–383b
OSAGE, FORT (Mo.) **V–173b**; I–330a; VI–196a
See also Clark, Fort (Mo.)
Osage County (Okla.) I–326a; V–173b
OSAGE HEDGE V–174a; II–487a
Osage orange. *See* Osage Hedge
Osage River IV–159b; V–173b
Osage Trail VI–215b
Osaka (Jap.) III–490b
OSAWATOMIE, BATTLE OF (1856) **V–174a**; I–342a
Osborn, Charles (abolitionist) V–279a
Osborn, Henry Fairfield (paleon.) IV–232b, 437b
Osborn, Ralph V–174b
Osborne, Richard (eng.) I–363b
Osborne, Thomas B. (biochem.) I–303a; V–127b, 128a
Osborne, Thomas Mott (penologist) V–416a
OSBORN v. BANK OF THE UNITED STATES (1824) **V–174a**; II–266b
Oscar II (ship) III–60a
Osceola (Indian) III–39a; VI–260a, 260b; VII–311a
Osceola (Mo.) V–471b
Oscillograph, cathode-ray II–423b
Osgood, Herbert Levi (hist.) III–282b
Osgood, Jacob (rel. leader) V–174b
Osgood, Samuel (off., pol.) V–371b
Osgoodby, George VI–183b–84a
OSGOODITES V–174b
Osler, William (physic.) I–119a; IV–3a, 292a, 298a
Osmeña, Sergio V–283b, 284a,b
Osprey (warship) I–76b
OSRD. *See* Office of Scientific Research and Development
OSS. *See* Office of Strategic Services
Ossabaw Sound IV–209a
Ossuaries III–376a
Ostend (Belg.) II–436b
OSTEND MANIFESTO (1854) **V–174b**; I–317b; II–268a; VI–360a
Osteology of the Reptiles VI–91a
OSTEOPATHY V–175a; IV–288a,b; VII–282a
Ostfriedsland (ship) V–26b
Ostrogorski, Moisei Yakovlevich (pol. sci.) V–222a
Ostwald, Wilhelm (chem.) II–11b
O'Sullivan, John L. (ed.) IV–239a
Oswald, Lee Harvey I–202b; IV–37b; VII–118b, 238a
Oswald, Richard (dipl.) II–318a
Oswald, Russell G. (offi.) I–220a
Oswegatchie (Indians) IV–85a
Oswegatchie (N.Y.) VII–270a
Oswegatchie, Fort (N.Y.) V–139b
Oswegatchie River IV–85a
OSWEGO (N.Y.) **V–175b**; III–400a; V–157a, 157a
British evacuation I–340b, 341a; II–126b
British fort V–85a, 90a; VII–270a
Erie Canal II–460a
French and Indian War I–358b; III–115b–16a
fur trade III–141b
Iroquois trade VII–95b
revolutionary war V–172b, 173a
War of 1812 VI–209a
Oswego County (N.Y.) IV–219b
Oswego River III–124b; V–172b, 175b
"O Tannenbaum" (song) IV–262a
OTB. *See* Offtrack betting
Otis, Arthur S. (psych.) III–440b
Otis, Elisha (inv.) II–428b–29a
Otis, Elwell S. (off.) V–281b, 282b
Otis, Harrison Gray (states.) III–259a; V–73b
Otis, James (states.) V–161a; VI–396a
antislavery I–135a
Boston Committee of Correspondence I–345a
Rights of the British Colonies Asserted and Proved VI–141a
taxation VII–14a–b
Vindication of the British Colonies VII–189b
writs of assistance VII–117a, 344b, 345a
Otis Company II–429b
Otis intelligence test III–440b
Oto (Indians) III–363b, 365a
farming IV–236a
Nebraska V–31a
trade IV–159b
Oto (lang.) VII–305b
Otranto (S.C.) I–497a
Otreouati (Indian) IV–83b
Otsego Hall (N.Y.) V–176a
Otsego Lake V–176a
OTSEGO LANDS (N.Y.) **V–176a**; I–386a
Ottawa (Indians) III–117a, 365a, 367a; V–308a
Fort McIntosh treaties IV–216b
Fort Pitt attack V–321b
Great Indian Council at Niagara V–90b
Hull Treaty III–316a
Jesuit missions III–499b
lands I–371b; III–394b
Ohio V–140a
Pontiac's War V–357a
Radisson's voyages VI–18a
revolutionary war III–400b
Saint Ignace Mission VI–191a
Spring Wells Treaty VI–377b
Treaty at Pittsburgh V–322a
Treaty of Chicago III–383b
Treaty of Fort Harmar III–255a
Treaty of Greenville III–383a
Treaty of Saint Louis III–383b
Wisconsin VII–307a, 307b
See also Algonquin
Ottawa (Ill.) III–330b; IV–155b
Ottawa River I–85b; III–119a, 216a, 319a; V–367a–b; VI–192a; VII–307a
fur trade V–121a
Great Lakes VII–157a
Nicolet's explorations V–95a
Otter I–446a; III–142a, 402b
Otter Creek I–337a; III–226b; IV–87a, 212a; VII–296a
Otter Valley VII–172a
Otto, Nicholas (inv.) I–225b
Otto engine VI–257b
Ottoman Empire I–149b; III–86a, 168a
Ottoman Turks VII–64b
Ottway newspapers V–76b
Ouachita Mountains V–268a
Ouachita Post (La.) IV–362a
Ouachita River II–381a; IV–362a; VI–407a; VII–271b
Ouachitite (rack) V–268a
Ouiatenon (Indians) III–24b
OUIATENON, FORT (Ind.) **V–176a**; II–265b; III–330b, 369b
Ouimet, Francis D. (golfer) III–197b
Oumessourit. *See* Missouri River
"Our American Cousin" (play) IV–154b
Ouray (Colo.) VI–213b
Ouray (Indians) IV–300a
"OUR COUNTRY, RIGHT OR WRONG" V–176b
Ourcq River I–70b
Our Delaware (song) VI–393 (table)
"OUR FEDERAL UNION! IT MUST BE PRESERVED!" V–176b
Our Lady of the Angels (school) II–348b
"Our Liberties We Prize and Our Rights We Will Maintain" (motto) VI–393 (table)
Our Young Folks (mag.) IV–223a
Ouspenskaya, Maria (act.) VII–50a
Outagamie County (Wis.) IV–338b
Outboard motors II–462a
"Outcasts of Poker Flat" V–336a
Outcault, Richard F. (cartoon.) V–72a
"Yellow Kid" comic strip V–71b
Outdoor Recreation, Bureau of III–444b
Outdoor Recreation Resources Review Commission II–188a
Outdoor relief V–380b; VI–72b
Outerbridge, A. Emelius VII–29a
Outerbridge, Mary Ewing VII–29a
Outerbridge Crossing V–368b
Outer Continental Shelf Lands Act (1953) VII–57b
Outer Mongolia VII–351b
Outfitting towns V–177a
Outlaws
bandits I–131b
Bellevue War I–287a
Plummer gang V–333a
U.S. Army I–192b
western II–258a
Outline of Christian Theology VI–82b
Outreach services II–147b
Outsider IV–167a
Outside shops II–81b–82a
Ovens II–219a
Overdraft II–2a–b

Overhill Cherokee (Indians) II–15a, 381a; III–223a; VI–455a; VII–103a
Cherokee Wars IV–186a
Great Warriors Path VII–238b
revolutionary war VII–250a
Overland California Mail Bill (1857) VI–154a
OVERLAND COMPANIES V–176b
forty-niners III–82a
Oregon Trail V–169a–b
Texan Emigration and Land Company VII–35b
Overland express. *See* Pony Express
OVERLAND FREIGHTING V–177a; I–452b–53a; IV–426a; VII–83a, 100a
Allegheny wagoners VII–216a
colonial vehicles VII–168a
Cumberland Road III–448b
Great Plains III–221a
Independence (Mo.) III–353b
Leavenworth IV–129a
oxen V–179a
pack trains V–184a
prairie schooner V–389b
roads VI–152b–53a,b, 154a
Russell, Majors, and Waddell VI–176b
wagon trains VII–217a
OVERLAND MAIL AND STAGECOACHES V–177b; VII–101a
Central Overland California and Pikes Peak Express I–485a
Fort Riley VI–141b
Great Plains III–221a
Holladay Company III–291a
Indian hostilities I–281a
Leavenworth and Pikes Peak Express IV–129b
Perth Amboy V–264a
Pioneer Stage Line V–317b
pony express V–357b
roads VI–152b–53a,b
Santa Fe Trail VI–215b, 216a
skiing VI–297b–98a
Smoky Hill Trail VI–320b
Southern Overland Mail VI–154a, 353b
South Platte route VI–355a
Wells, Fargo VII–267a
Overland Mail Company V–357b
Overland Route. *See* Overland Trail
OVERLAND TRAIL V–178b; II–294b; V–31a, 177a, 330b
Overlord, Operation. *See* Normandy Invasion
Overman Act (1918) VII–326a
Overseas Private Investment Corporation II–501a; IV–466b
OVERSEER V–178b; VI–306b
Over-the-counter markets III–466b
Overtime IV–80b, 353b
Overton, John (jur.) II–22a
Overy, O. T. (biochem.) II–357b
Oviedo y Valdéz, Gonzalo Fernández (col. gov.) IV–451b; V–269a
Ovington, Mary White (social worker) IV–460b
OWEN, FORT (Mont.) **V–178b**
Owen, John (off.) V–178b
Owen, Robert (ind., ref.) III–407b; VI–325b
Owen, Robert Dale (social ref.) I–307a; II–147a, 220a; V–54b, 334b; VII–322a
Owen-Glass Act (1913) I–256b; III–5b
Owenites. *See* New Harmony Settlement
Owens, Jesse (athlete) V–154a
Owens, Michael (inv.) III–185b
Owensboro (Ky.) IV–41b
Owens bottle machine III–185b
Owen's Lake VII–217b
Owens River VII–259a
Owens Valley (Calif.) I–407a; IV–104b
Owl IV–233a
Owl Woman (Indian) I–290a
"Oxbow" route VI–379a
OXEN V–179a; III–255b, 303a–b
agriculture I–37b, 39b
caravans I–452a; V–166a
cattle freighting I–473a
food source IV–280b
freighting IV–426a; V–177a,b
Indian paths VI–152b
"Joe Bowers" IV–1a
Oregon Trail V–169a,b
prairie schooner V–389b
Red River cart traffic VI–63b, 64a
Russell, Majors, and Waddell VI–176b
Santa Fe Trail VI–216a
stampedes VI–382b
wagon trains VII–218a
westward movement VII–283b
Oxenstierna, Axel (states.) V–81a
Oxford (Eng.) I–294a
Oxford (Miss.) IV–259a, 342a
Oxford (Ohio) VII–156a
Oxford, University of VI–18b, 134b
Oxford English Dictionary II–340a–b
OXFORD MOVEMENT V–179a; II–455a; VI–78a
Oxford Pledge VII–365b
Oxford Provident Building Association VI–221b
Oxide ores II–224a
Oxydol soap VI–323b
Oxygen-hydrogen torch II–10b
Oxygen masks I–234b
Oxygen process (steelmaking) III–474a
Oxyhydrogen blowpipe III–408b
Oyster Bay (N.Y.) III–258b; IV–185b
Oyster fishing I–351b, 447a; IV–185b
Oyster mines (explosive) IV–351a
OYSTER RIVER RAID (1694) **V–179b**
Oysters III–51a, 52a; VII–247b
Oyster shells I–477a
Ozark River I–174b
Ozawa, Jisaburo (nav. off.) IV–138a–39b; V–285b
Oz books I–335b
Ozone layer VI–213a

P

P-26 (fighter plane) I–53a
P-35 (fighter plane) I–53a
P-36 (fighter plane) I–53a
P-38 (fighter plane) I–53a,b, 57b, 60a
P-39 (fighter plane) I–53a, 57b
P-40 (fighter plane) I–53a; III–46b
P-47 (fighter plane) I–53a,b, 60a; VI–302a
P-51 (fighter plane) I–52a, 53b, 60a, 61b
P-61 (fighter plane) I–53b
P-80 (fighter plane) I–53b
P-82 (fighter plane) I–53b
Pablos, Juan (print.) V–410a–b, 411a,b
Paca, William (jur.) II–308a
Pace, Richard (col.) III–219a
Pacer, Narragansett III–303b
Pachácamac (Peru) IV–327b
Pacific, War of the V–233a
Pacific Antisubmarine Force V–25a
Pacific blockade I–321b
Pacific cable. *See* Cables, Atlantic and Pacific
Pacific Charter VI–350b
Pacific coast
lifesaving stations IV–152b
Midwinter International Exposition IV–337b
timberlands VII–59b, 60a,b, 61a
transcontinental railroad IV–94a–b
PACIFIC COAST, FAKE EXPLORATION OF V–179b
Pacific Coast Cooperative Union II–220b
Pacific Coast Hockey Association III–287a
Pacific Coast Stock Exchange VI–209b
Pacific Cooperative League II–220b
Pacific Fleet V–24b, 25a
Battle of Midway IV–336a
Fast Carrier Task Force VII–1a–2a
Pearl Harbor V–239a
PACIFIC FUR COMPANY V–180a; III–403a
Astoria I–209a; VII–247b
Fort Okanogan V–147a
Oregon V–164b, 165a, 167b
Platte River Trail V–330b
War of 1812 I–83a
Pacific Islands III–263b; IV–436a
Pacific Islands Forestry, Institute of III–76b
Pacific mackerel IV–217a
Pacific Mail Steamship Company II–91a
PACIFIC NORTHWEST V–180b; VII–268a
Chinook winds II–30b
dry farming II–375b
exploration I–15b; VII–299b
fur trade II–285b; III–263a; VI–411b
Idaho III–328a
Indian reservations III–395b, 396a
Indians I–441a–b
Indian slaveholding III–401a
Jesuits III–499b, 501b
Lapwai Mission IV–108a
Mullan Trail IV–426a
Oregon V–164a
Oregon missions V–167a
Oregon Question V–167a
Oregon Short Line Railway V–168a
paleontology V–195b
Patrons of Husbandry V–229a
railroads VI–27a–b
Russia VI–177b, 180b
sawmills VI–223a
settlement VII–284a
Stevens' railroad survey VI–412b
timberlands VII–59b
trading posts VII–95b
trails VII–100a
Washington State VII–247a
Wilkes expedition VII–272a
Yakima Wars VII–350a–b
Pacific Ocean
Adams-Onís Treaty I–10b
Apollo 11 splashdown IV–407a

buccaneers I–374a
discovery I–96a
exploration III–28b
Lewis and Clark Expedition IV–136b
mapping I–463b
NATO fleet II–315b
navigational charts IV–277a
Neutrality Act of 1939 V–37b
nuclear weapons tests III–324a,b
Panama–Pacific Exposition V–203b
polar exploration V–336b
Puget Sound V–462a
territorial waters VII–33a
U.S. boundary IV–320b, 321a,b
whaling VII–285a,b
Wilkes expedition VII–299b
Pacific Power and Light Company III–323b
Pacific Railroad Bill (1862) VI–39a
Pacific Railroad Conventions VI–20b–21a
Pacific Railroad of Missouri VI–25b, 35a
Pacific Railroad Reports (1855–60) VII–272a
Pacific Railroad surveys IV–232b
Pacific Railway acts I–485a; IV–30b
PACIFIC REPUBLIC MOVEMENT V–180b
Pacific Squadron IV–252a, 324b–25a
Pacific Telegraph V–372a
Pacific Trust Territory. *See* Trust Territory of the Pacific
Pacific tuna III–28b
"PACIFICUS" AND "HELVIDIUS" V–181a
Pacific Yearly Meeting III–123b
PACIFISM V–181a
anarchists I–117a
antiwar groups VII–236a
conscientious objectors II–185a
isolationism III–479b
"lunatic fringe" IV–204b
Mennonites IV–303a
peace movements V–235a
Quakers III–123a,b; V–470a,b; VII–201b
revolutionary war V–247a
Schoenbrunn mission VI–226a
youth movements VII–365b
Pacing White Mustang IV–444b
PACKAGING V–182b
aluminum V–104a
government regulation V–467b
self-service stores VI–258a
Packard, Alpheus Spring (entom.) II–391a
Packard, S. B. (pol.) III–295b
Packard Company IV–433a,b
Packard engine II–344b
Packenham, Edward (off.) V–63a,b
Packer, Philip S. (law.) III–315b
PACKERS' AGREEMENT (1920) **V–183a**
PACKERS AND STOCKYARDS ACT (1921) **V–183a**; VI–378b
Packets, canal I–443b
PACKETS, SAILING V–183b; IV–309a, 310a,b, 313a; VI–148a, 279b; VII–348b, 349a
Gulf Stream III–233a
transatlantic I–308b
Packhorse. *See* Horse
Packing houses
dairy industry II–282a
Kansas City (Mo.) IV–27b
Kentucky IV–41b
public ownership II–491a
See also Meat–Packing
Packsaddle VI–185a
PACK TRAINS V–184a
Pact of Paris (1928). *See* Kellogg–Briand Pact
Pact of Rio (1947). *See* Inter–American Treaty of Reciprocal Assistance
Paddlewheels VII–240b, 256b
Paderborn (Ger.) VII–341a
Padilla, Juan de (miss.) IV–367a
PADLOCK INJUNCTION V–184a; VII–207b
Padlock Law (1901) IV–27a
Padouca (Indians) I–354b
Padron Real (atlas) IV–247b
Paducah (Ky.) IV–41b; V–67b, 455b; VII–27b
Paff, Michael (art dealer) II–101b
Page, Charles G. (phys.) I–276a; II–413a
Page, R. M. (eng.) VI–10a
Page, Ruth (dancer) II–288b
Page, Thomas J. (nav. off.) V–23a; VI–415a
Page, Thomas Nelson (au.) IV–162b
Page County (Va.) VI–275b
Page–Stone Company II–288b
Pagoda (coin) I–151a
Pago Pago (Amer. Samoa) VI–205a
Paine, Robert Treat (jur.) II–308a
Paine, Sidney B. II–415b
Paine, Thomas (philos., au.) II–320a; IV–161b; VI–106b, 118a; VII–61b, 82a
Alliance I–89b
antislavery I–135a
Bill of Rights I–298b
Common Sense II–141b; V–353a; VI–113b, 114b
Crisis II–264b
Deism III–112a
Loyalists IV–200b
natural rights doctrine V–7b
pamphleteering V–198b
Rights of Man V–353a; VI–141a
Paine, Thomas O. (adm.) IV–460a
Paint III–44b, 156a; V–267b
colonial duties VI–110b
iron oxides III–12a
lead V–102b
Revenue Act of 1767 VII–80b
Painted Desert (Ariz.) III–300b
Painter, Theophilus (zool.) III–158a
Paint industry II–8b, 10a; VI–220b
PAINTING V–184b
collecting II–101a–07a
folk art III–46b
furniture III–134a, 138a
miniature IV–351b
national art galleries VI–319b
Spirit of '76 VI–374b
White House VII–292a
See also Indian Art and Technology
PAIRING V–194a
Pai River I–322b
PAIUTE (Indians) **V–194a**; I–264a; II–297b; III–363a
Bannock War VII–239b
Ghost Dance III–177b; V–4a–b
Nevada V–39b
Utah VII–161a
Pakenham, Edward (off.) VII–234b
Pakistan
Baghdad Pact I–243a
independence I–124a
military aid II–315b
missionary work II–362b
Rhodes scholars VI–134b
Southeast Asia Treaty Organization VI–350b, 351a
Palace of Fine Arts (Chicago) III–19b
Palache, Charles (crystal.) IV–349a
Palade, George E. (biol.) V–100a
Palanan (Phil.) III–133a
Palast–Hotel Quellenhof (Aachen) I–1a
Palatinate
World War II VII–340a,b
PALATINE JURISDICTIONS V–194b
PALATINES V–194b; III–335a; V–342a; VII–282b
German Flats III–172b
Hudson Valley III–312a
naval stores V–14b
New York Colony V–85a
Pennsylvania V–246b, 251b
Palau Islands I–459a; V–242b; VII–1b–2a, 125a, 337a
Paleobotany I–350a
Paleoecology V–197b
Paleo–Indian culture I–48a; III–50a–b
Paleolithic period I–155a,b
PALEONTOLOGY V–195a; I–110b; III–163b; IV–232b–33a
Paleozoic era III–163b
Palermo (It.) VI–284b
Palestine III–481b
Anglo–American relations I–124a
Arab–American relations I–150a,b
citrus fruits III–128b
mandate IV–236b
U.S. Jews IV–11a
World War I relief VII–330a
Palestine, Popular Front for the Liberation of III–277b
Palestinian guerrilla movements III–277a,b
Palfrey, John Gorham (cler., hist.) IV–267a
Palisades (Idaho) III–328b
Palisades Dam III–323b
Pal Joey (musical) IV–442a
Palko v. *Connecticut* (1937) I–299b; III–86b
Palladia III–366a, 392b
Palladian architecture I–160a, 162a
Palladino, Lawrence B. (hist.) III–500b
Palladio, Andrea (arch.) I–161b; III–134a–b, 495a; IV–405a
Palladium II–224a
Pallas (merchant ship) VII–86b
Palma, Tomás Estrada (pol.) II–269a
Palm Beach (Fla.) VI–249a
Palmer, A. Mitchell (law., pol.) I–427b; VI–255a
coal strike of 1919 IV–69b
Palmer, Arnold (golfer) III–198a
Palmer, Edward (bot.) V–327a
Palmer, Elihu (deist) III–112a
Palmer, Erastus Dow (sculp.) VI–243a
Palmer, George S. II–99b
Palmer, J. M. (pol.) III–189a
Palmer, Joel (offi.) VI–412b
Palmer, John M. (law., pol.) I–425a
Palmer, Joseph III–239b
Palmer, Nathaniel Brown (expl.) V–197b
Palmer, Potter (mer.) IV–100b
Palmer, Timothy (eng.) I–363b
Palmer, William A. (gov.) VII–172a
Palmer, William Jackson (off.) II–129a
Palmer–Pendleton Expedition (1829–31) V–336b

Palmer Peninsula (Antarc.) V–198a
PALMER'S DISCOVERY OF ANTARCTICA V–197b
Palmerston, 3rd Viscount, Henry John Temple (states.) II–162b; VII–116a
Palmetto VI–395 (table)
PALMETTO COCKADES V–198a
Palmetto State VI–395 (table)
PALMITO RANCH, BATTLE OF (1865) **V–198b**; VII–39b
Palm oil VI–323a,b
Palms, Francis IV–99b
Palm Sunday tornadoes (1965) VII–75b
Palmyra Island VII–125b
Palo Alto (Calif.) I–434b
PALO ALTO, BATTLE OF (1846) **V–198b**; VI–97a
Palo Duro Canyon VI–273b
Palomar, Mount I–212a; III–241b–42b
Palomar Observatory (Calif.) V–131b
  See also Hale Observatories
Paloo (Indians) VII–239b
Palos (ship) IV–54b
Palos (Sp.) I–96a
Palouse River VII–248a
Paloverde VI–393 (table)
Palynology V–197b
Pamlico River VI–149b
Pamlico Sound III–262a; V–109b
PAMPHLETEERING V–198b
  Constitution V–353a
  Loyal Publication Societies IV–202a
  newspaper editorials V–69b
  Paxton Boys V–231a
  Revolution V–432a
  Ruffner Pamphlet VI–168b
  Stamp Act VI–381b
  tea trade VII–15b
  western settlement IV–100a
Pamphlets
  chapbooks I–494a,b
  religious IV–409a
Pamunkey (Indians) I–240b
Pamunkey River
  Civil War V–113b; VI–220a, 263b; VII–117a
  Powhatan Confederacy V–385b
Pan-African Congresses V–199a–b
PAN-AFRICANISM V–199a; I–21b, 22a
Panagra (airline) I–68b
Panama
  air defense I–58a
  botanical research IV–378b
  gold rush route III–81b
  Hay–Bunau–Varilla Treaty III–265a
  independence V–204a
  isthmian canal route IV–324b
  marine landing IV–252a,b
  merchant marine VI–281a
  settlement I–405a
  ship registry IV–312a
  United Nations Declaration VII–151b
  U.S. protectorate III–347b; IV–112a
  U.S. recognition VII–112a
  World War II VII–334a
  See also Panama Canal
PANAMA, DECLARATION OF (1939) **V–200a**; V–36a
Panama, Isthmus of I–96a; V–200b; VII–111b–12a
  exploration V–23a, 203b
  Panama City V–203a
  Panama Congress V–203b
  steamship lines II–91a; IV–310a
  War of Jenkins' Ear III–498a
  westward movement V–176b
  whaling VII–285b
PANAMA CANAL V–200b; III–68b–69a, 428a; IV–111a,b, 113b; V–165b; VI–364a; VII–111b–12a
  Cape Horn decline I–448a
  construction I–185b, 188a; II–449b
  federal surplus VI–449b
  fortifications III–78b
  France III–97a
  government-owned railroad III–203a
  Hay–Bunau–Varilla Treaty III–265a
  Hay–Herrán Treaty III–265b
  Hay–Pauncefote treaties III–266a–b
  intercoastal trade IV–309a, 311b
  intervention policy V–105b
  Magdalena Bay IV–223b
  mail service V–178a
  malaria IV–229b
  military medical research IV–291b
  Monroe Doctrine IV–401a
  negotiations I–122a, 295a, 454a; II–116a, 474b, 475b
  Panama City V–203a
  Panama–Pacific Exposition V–203b
  Panama Revolution III–463a; V–204a
  revenue VII–4b
  South American trade VI–344a
  steamships IV–309a
  Tigre Island VII–58b
  tolls V–204b; VII–69b
  U.S. imperialism III–347b
  U.S. rights VII–34a
  World War II IV–322b
  yellow fever VII–355b
  See also Nicaraguan Canal Project
Panama Canal Act (1912) V–201b
Panama Canal Company II–501a; III–201b; V–201b–02a, 204a, 455a
PANAMA CITY (Pan.) **V–203a**; V–201b, 202a
PANAMA CONGRESS (1826) **V–203a**; IV–400a
PANAMA–PACIFIC INTERNATIONAL EXPOSITION (1915) **V–203b**; II–423b
PANAMA RAILROAD V–203b; V–200b, 201b–02a, 455a
  Panama City V–203a
Panama Refining Company v. *Ryan* (1935) II–323a, 473a
  See also "Hot oil" Case
PANAMA REVOLUTION (1903) **V–204a**; I–295b; II–116a; III–146b; V–201a–b; VI–364a; VII–112a
PANAMA TOLLS QUESTION V–204b
Pan-American Conferences IV–401b
  international law III–456b
PAN-AMERICAN EXPOSITION (1901) **V–204b**; I–202b
Pan-Americanism
  International Exposition of 1895 III–453b
  Panama Congress V–203a
  Rio de Janeiro Conference VI–142b
  See also Latin America, U.S. Relations With
Pan-American Petroleum Company II–431b
PAN-AMERICAN UNION V–205a; IV–111a,b, 112b; V–171a
  Buenos Aires Peace Conference V–232a
  Havana Conference III–262b
  Santiago Inter-American Congress VI–217a
Pan American World Airways I–68a,b, 69a; III–277b, 278a
Pananapapi (Indian) III–500a
Panax quinquefolium. *See* Ginseng, American
***PANAY* INCIDENT** (1937) **V–205b**; II–26a; III–234b
  Panay sunk II–26a
Pangenesis III–157b
PANHANDLE V–205b
  Oklahoma V–148a
  Texas IV–299b
  Whipple's expedition VII–289a
PANIC OF 1785 V–206a
PANIC OF 1792 V–206a; VI–239a, 294a
PANIC OF 1819 V–206a; VI–370b
  Bank of the United States I–255a,b
  Era of Good Feeling II–458a
  Kentucky IV–40b; V–150b
  state banking I–259b
  stay and valuation acts VI–406a
PANIC OF 1837 V–206b; VI–370b
  Adams, Alvin I–9b
  American Fur Company IV–356a
  American Land Company I–107b
  antibank movement I–129b
  antislavery movement I–137b
  bank failures I–173a, 255b
  Bank of the United States I–259b
  bankruptcy laws I–262a
  campaign of 1840 I–420a
  credit II–255a
  Democratic party VII–288b
  European investments I–245a
  factory workers IV–61b
  federal surplus VI–449a
  Florida III–39a
  foreign investments III–64a
  Illinois and Michigan Canal III–331a
  Indiana VII–212a
  Indians III–374b
  internal improvements III–449b
  land speculation IV–100a
  Louisiana IV–194a, 198b
  mercantile agencies IV–307b
  Mississippi IV–368b
  Mormons IV–116b
  New Jersey canal IV–412b
  rubber industry VI–167a
  Specie Circular VI–369b
  State Bank of Indiana VI–390a
  state banks I–259a
  state debts II–302b; VI–96a
  state ownership III–202b
  trade unions IV–62a
  Treasury surplus II–333b
PANIC OF 1857 V–207a; VI–370b
  federal deficit VII–5a
  land speculation IV–100a
  Louisiana banking IV–198b
  merchant marine IV–310b
  New York Clearinghouse II–73a
  Pikes Peak gold rush V–311b
  public debt VI–294a
  State Bank of Indiana VI–390a
  state banks I–259a–b
  tariff VI–466b
  unionization IV–62b
PANIC OF 1873 V–207a; III–6a, 110b; VI–288b
  Atlantic and Pacific Railroad I–214b
  Chicago II–17b
  depression I–245b, 318b
  foreign investments

III–65a–b
Granger movement III–224b
land speculation IV–100a
National Banking System I–256b
Radical Republicans VI–11b
railroad rate wars VI–23a
Ralston's ring VI–44a
Reconstruction VI–57b
Republican party VI–104a
repudiation of state debts VI–96b
trade unions IV–63a
Panic of 1884 III–6a
National Banking System I–256b
PANIC OF 1893 V–207b, 207b; III–6a, 111a, 113a; VI–467a
bank failures I–253b
bankruptcy laws I–262b
Colorado II–128a–b, 332a
Kelly's Industrial Army IV–36a
National Banking System I–256b
nativism I–111a
populism I–39a; V–364b
Populist party V–365b
profiteering V–426a
Pullman strike V–463a
railroad brotherhoods IV–66b
Sherman Silver Purchase Act VI–277b
Union Pacific Railroad VII–148a
Panic of 1903 VII–122b
PANIC OF 1907 V–208a, 208a; III–6a, 113a; VI–371a
Aldrich–Vreeland Act I–84a
"malefactors of great wealth" IV–230a
National Banking System I–256b
postal savings banks V–373b
Panic of 1914 I–256b
Panic of 1920. *See* Depression of 1920
PANIC OF 1929 V–209a; II–255b, 470a; III–6b; VI–157a, 371a; VII–222b
foreign trade VII–87b–88a
gold standard III–194a
investment advisers I–257a
investment banks III–466a
investment companies III–467a
labor movement IV–70b
New Era V–52a
Reconstruction Finance Corporation VI–59b
securities V–405b
Townsend Plan VII–79b
See also Depression, Great
PAN-INDIANISM V–210a; III–222b, 396b, 397b; VII–152a
Panmunjom (Kor.)
peace negotiations at IV–56a,b
PANMURE, FORT (Miss.) **V–210b**; VI–164b
PANOCHE GRANDE CLAIM V–210b
Panoche Grande Quicksilver Company V–211a
Panoche Grande Rancho V–211a
Panofsky, Erwin (hist.) III–424b
Panoramas VII–47b
Panpipes II–291a
Pantages, Alexander (theat. mgr.) VII–167b
Pantasote Leather Company III–434b
Pantheon III–495a
Pantograph V–289b
Panton (N.Y.) VII–171b
Panton, Forbes and Company V–211a
PANTON, LESLIE AND COMPANY V–211a; I–355b; V–254a–b; VI–196b, 366b
Panton, William (bus.). *See* Panton, Leslie and Company
Pantothenic acid V–128a
Pants II–372b
Pánuco River II–336b
Panzer divisions IV–230b
Paola (Kans.) IV–333b
Paola (Okla.) IV–334a
PAOLI, BATTLE OF (1777) **V–211b**
Paolo, Giovanni di (art.) II–103b
Papago (Indians) I–413a; III–369a, 396b; V–314a–b
Arizona I–171b
Camp Grant massacre I–433b
Jesuit missions III–500b
scalping VI–224b
scouts VI–242a
wine VII–65b
Papal bull of 1493 V–122a
PAPAL STATES, DIPLOMATIC SERVICE TO V–211b
Papaya III–129a
Papen, Franz von (off.) VII–332b
PAPER AND PULP INDUSTRY V–212a; I–16b; II–5a, 10a; IV–204b
colonial duties VI–110b; VII–80b
colonial mills IV–243a
Green Bay III–226a
imports VII–87b
Kentucky IV–41b
Maine IV–227a
Minnesota IV–357a–b
New Hampshire V–54a–b
New South V–67a
newspapers V–77a
research I–197a,b
Savannah VI–220b
timberlands VII–61b
Vermont VII–172b
Wisconsin VII–308a
Paperback books I–334a; IV–271b
Paper ballot I–248b
Paper birch I–304b
Paper commodities II–469a–b
Paper containers II–282b
Paper money III–251b–52a
bills of credit I–300a
Black Friday I–311a
British debts I–366b
Confederate I–324a
Locofoco party IV–175a
See also Money
Paper Money party. *See* "Know Ye" Party
"Paper organizations" II–233a
Papers of the American Historical Association I–106a
Pappas, Paul (jour.) V–79a
Pará (Braz.) I–360b
Paracelsus (physic.) III–49b
Paradise of the Pacific VI–393 (table)
Paraffin IV–44b
Paraguay I–399b
Chaco War V–205a
Hayes Award III–265b
Jesuit missions III–500a
United Nations Declaration VII–151b
PARAGUAY EXPEDITION (1858) **V–212b**; III–131b; V–22b
Paramedics IV–304a
Paramilitary operations V–138a
Paramount Pictures V–292b
Paraná (Braz.) I–360b
Paraná River V–22b, 212b
PARAPSYCHOLOGY V–212b
Para rubber VI–167b
Parasitologists, Society of. *See* American Society of Parasitologists
Parasitology IV–291b
Parasols II–371b, 372a
PARATROOPS V–213b; IV–83a
Choiseul raid II–33a
gliders III–187a
Normandy invasion V–110b; VII–339a
Sicilian campaign VI–284b
Sicily invasion VII–338b
Parcel post I–17a; IV–225a; VI–173a, 175a
Pardons
Mooney, Thomas J. IV–406b
Nixon, Richard M. V–99a
presidential powers II–201b
See also Amnesty
Paregoric II–373b
Parenthood II–485b–86b
Parenthood, Education for III–181b
Parent's Creek I–323b
Parent–teacher association II–400a
Parent–to–parent relations II–360a–b
Paresis IV–306b
Parham, Charles F. (cler.) V–259b
Parian ware V–379b
Pari–mutuel racing II–261b; III–304b, 305a
Paris (Fr.)
American Expeditionary Forces IV–84a
apartment houses I–143a
art nouveau III–446b
city plan II–45a
dance II–286b–87b
Definitive Treaty of Peace II–318a–19a
department stores II–332b
Hay Memorandum II–27a
Kinetoscopes IV–417a
Lindbergh's Atlantic flight IV–156b, 157a
Lost Generation IV–189b
Mardi Gras IV–249b
medical education IV–297b
medical research IV–285b
Organization for Economic Cooperation and Development V–170a
prostitutes II–259b
radio VI–14b
U.S. embassy II–437a
World War I I–70a, 102a; VII–326b
World War II VII–339b
XYZ affair VII–347b–48a
Paris (Ky.)
Cane Ridge Revival II–352b
PARIS, DECLARATION OF (1856) **V–214a**; I–321a; III–455b; V–324a
blockades II–67b, 446a–b
immunity of private property III–343a
laws of war VII–225b
neutrality laws V–34b
neutral rights V–38b
privateering IV–256a, 313a; V–419b
Paris, F. J. (col. offi.) V–436a
Paris, Pact of. *See* Kellogg–Briand Pact
PARIS, PEACE OF (1783) **V–214a**; VI–117a; VII–111a,b
British posts I–120a
Canadian relations I–438a–b
Florida VI–363b
Mackinac IV–217b
Old Northwest V–140b
Red Line Map VI–62b
U.S. boundaries IV–381a–b
See also Definitive Treaty of Peace
PARIS, TREATY OF (1763) **V–214b**; I–438a; II–92b, 126b; III–94b, 117b, 120b; VI–359a
Baton Rouge I–274b
British posts I–501b
Colorado II–127b
Florida III–38b
Fort Saint Marks

PARIS, TREATY OF (cont.)
VI–196b
France VI–119a–b
Illinois III–329a
Illinois country II–265a; III–330a; IV–178b
Isle of Orleans III–479a
Louisiana purchase boundaries IV–197b
Maine–Canadian boundary dispute IV–226b
Mississippi River boundary I–351a
New Orleans V–62a
Proclamation of 1763 V–424b
South Carolina VI–347a
PARIS, TREATY OF (1898) **V–215a;** III–58a; VI–360b, 362b; VII–112a
arbitration IV–4b
Guam III–230b
Philippines V–281a, 282b
Platt Amendment V–329b
Puerto Rico V–461a
territories VII–33b
Paris Academy of Sciences VI–237b
PARIS AGREEMENT (1925) **V–215a**
Paris Agreement (1973) II–469a
Paris–Bordeaux–Paris Race (1895) I–225b
PARIS CONFERENCES V–215b
Vietnam War III–70b; VII–184b, 186b
World War I VII–330b
Paris Exposition (1867) II–102b; IV–244a
Paris Exposition (1889) III–11b
Paris green III–421a
PARISH V–216a; V–349b
Parish (rel.) VI–75a,b
Parish Prison (New Orleans) IV–221a
Paris Opera School II–287a
Paris Peace Conference of 1946 V–215b
Paris Salon V–188b
PARITY V–216b
Parity–price program V–402a
Park, Edwards Amasa (cler.) VI–81b
Park, Mungo (slaver) VI–310a
Parka III–381a
Parke, Davis and Company V–274a
Parke, John G. (off.) VI–39a, 353b
Parke–Bernet Galleries I–333a; II–106b
Parker, Alton B. (jur., pol.) I–426a; VI–288a
campaign of 1904 III–197a
Parker, Charlie ("Bird") (mus.) IV–440b
Parker, Cynthia Ann V–216b
Parker, Francis Wayland (educ.) II–398b
Parker, Gilbert (nov.) VII–332b
Parker, John (col.) IV–37b
Parker, Peter (nav. off.) I–496b, 498a; IV–420a
Parker, Quanah (Indian) V–216b
Parker, Theodore (cler.) III–112a; IV–131a; V–287a; VI–78a, 81b–82a
Parker, William II–34b
Parker County (Tex.) II–493b
Parker Dam II–130a
Parkersburg (W.Va.) I–319b; VI–138b
PARKER'S FORT (Tex.) **V–216b**
Parker v. *Davis* (1871) IV–133a; VI–94b
Parkes, Alexander (chem.) II–7a
Park Forest South (Ill.) II–48b
Parkinson, John (bot.) I–348b
Parkinson's Ferry (Pa.) VII–290b
Parkland Hospital (Dallas) IV–37b
Parkman, Francis (hist.) I–344a; III–281b, 499a; IV–163a
Parkman, George (physic.) VII–266a
Park River III–309a
Park Row (N.Y.C.) V–40a
Parks
landscaping IV–96b
local government IV–172a
segregation VI–256a
PARKS, NATIONAL, AND NATIONAL MONUMENTS V–216b; III–73b; IV–96a; V–445b
Acadia National Park IV–422b
Alaska I–80b
Badlands I–242b
Carlsbad Caverns I–455b
Castle Clinton I–275b
Chaco Canyon I–329b
Chalmette I–490b
Colonial National Historical Park III–489a–b
Death Valley II–298a
Devils Tower I–313a
Fort Laramie IV–108a–b
Fort Pulaski V–462b
Fort Sumter VI–441a
Fort Union Post VII–145b
George Washington Birthplace VII–219a
government inspection III–422a
Grand Canyon III–208b
Gran Quivira III–211a
Great Smoky Mountains National Park III–222b
Independence National Historical Park III–354a
Inscription Rock III–420b
Mammoth Cave IV–233b
Mesa Verde VI–213b
Mesa Verde National Park IV–315b
National Park Service V–219a
Pecos National Monument V–241a
preservation movement V–392b
public lands V–446b
Rocky Mountains VI–160b
Saint Augustine VI–188a
San José Mission VI–207b
San Juan Island National Park VI–214a
Sequoia National Park VI–262b
Wind Cave I–312b
Wyoming VII–346a
Yellowstone II–188a; VII–357a
Yosemite II–187b; VII–361b
Parks, Rosa II–57a
Parks, state
Blue Licks Battlefield I–325a
Custer I–312b
Fort Bridger I–363a
Mackinac Island IV–218a
Monterey State Historic Park IV–472a
North Carolina V–116b
Parksene (plastic) II–7a
PARK SERVICE, NATIONAL, AND NATIONAL PARK SYSTEM V–219a; I–340b; III–203a, 444a,b; V–217a,b, 445b
Mission 66 II–188a
Naval Home V–11b
preservation movement V–393a
wildlife preservation VII–297b
Park Street Church (Boston) IV–446a
Park Theater (N.Y.C.) II–101a; III–297a
Parkway, national V–220a
Parkways
landscaping IV–96b
Parlange (Pointe Coupee Parish, La.) I–160b
Parley, Peter. *See* Peter Parley
Parley's Magazine IV–222b
PARLIAMENT, BRITISH V–220b; II–325a
colonial laws IV–15a
colonial policy II–122a–23a
colonial taxation VI–141a–b
Declaration of Independence II–304a–b, 305a
Declaration of Rights II–308b
Declaratory Act II–309a
investigatory powers III–464b
peace resolutions of 1782 V–237b
prerevolutionary imperial idea III–346b
right of petition V–265b
taxation without representation VII–14b
Parlin, Charles Coolidge IV–255a
Parlor caucus I–474a–b
Parlor houses II–260a
Parochial schools I–468b; II–397a, 399b, 400a
Middle Colonies II–395a
Oregon Parochial School Case V–167a
public funds II–490a
PAROLE SYSTEM V–221a; V–418a; VI–68a
Parral (Mex.) IV–327b
Parran, Thomas (physic.) IV–287b
Parrant, Pierre (trader) VII–133b–34a
Parrington, Vernon Lewis (hist.) III–283a, 486a
Parris, Samuel (cler.) VII–309b–10a
Parrish, Maxfield (paint.) V–192a,b
Parris Island V–370a; VI–348b
Parrot Mine II–223a
Parrott, Robert P. (off., inv.) I–200a; IV–431a, 433a
Parrott gun III–258b; IV–431a; V–26b, 56a; VI–453a
Parry Island IV–257b
PARSON BROWNLOW'S BOOK (1862) **V–221a**
Parson Capen House (Topsfield, Mass.) I–161a
Parsons, Betty (art.) II–105b
Parsons, Charles A. (eng.) II–415b; VII–129b
Parsons, Mary (col.) VII–309b
Parsons, Samuel H. (off.) V–143b; VI–204a, VII–279b
Parsons, Talcott (anthrop.) I–129a
PARSON'S CAUSE V–221b; V–161a; VII–135a
Parthenon (Nashville) VII–27a
Particles, elementary. *See* Physics, High-Energy; Physics, Nuclear
Particle theory V–296a
Particular Baptists I–264b
Parties, political. *See* Political Parties
PARTISAN BANDS V–221b
Parton, James (hist.) III–486a; IV–163a
Partridge III–51a, 150a
Partridge, Alden (off.) IV–340b
Party ballot I–248b–49a
Party chairman, national I–416b
Party Emblems. *See* Emblems, Party
PARTY GOVERNMENT V–222a
Party lines VII–19b
Partymiller, Walt (cartoon.) V–73a
Party platform. *See* Platform, Party
Party strip ballots I–248b
Pasadena (Calif.) III–242a, 502a; VI–51a, 101a

Pasarell, Charles (athlete) VII–30b
Pascagoula (Indians) IV–368a
Pascal, Blaise (philos., math.) I–395b
Pascal House (New Orleans) I–160b
Pas de Calais (Fr.) V–110b, 111a
Paso. *See* Ciudad Juárez
Paso de Bartolo (Calif.) VI–210b
Pasqueflower VI–395 (table)
Pass, John IV–142b
Passaconaway (Indian) III–48b
Passaic River II–431b; IV–347b; V–41a; VII–161a
Pass à L'Outre IV–371a
Passamaquoddy (Indians) I–2b; III–367a, 396b
Passchendaele, Battle of (1917) VII–325b
PASS CHRISTIAN (Miss.) **V–224a**
Passenger Act (1819) VI–327b
Passenger pigeon III–51a, 150a; VII–296b
PASSES, MOUNTAIN V–224a; I–403b; VI–354b, 413a
Passing of the Great Race III–342b
PASSPORTS V–225a
Civil War I–196a
Espionage Act II–463a
Pasteur, Louis (chem.) III–53a, 55a, 325b; V–273b
bacteriology I–241a
canning I–444b, 445a
Pasteur Institute (Paris) III–158a
Pasteurization I–362a; II–280a–b; IV–275b
Pastore, John (gov.) VI–133b–34a
Pastorius, Francis Daniel (law., au.) III–173a
Pasture grasses II–279b
Patapsco (ship) V–15a
Patapsco River I–249a; IV–116b
Patch, Alexander (off.) III–229b
Pate, Captain I–314a
Patent Fire Arms Company IV–433a
Patent Interferences, Board of V–226b
Patent leather II–6b–7a
Patent medicines I–19a; II–208b; IV–299b; V–466a
PATENTS AND U.S. PATENT OFFICE V–225b; II–135a; III–444a; IV–95a; VI–319b, 388b
aeronautics IV–458a
agriculture I–45a
American Museum of Arts IV–468b
atomic energy I–216a
automobile I–225b, 227a
aviation industry I–235b
barbed wire I–267b
Bessemer process III–473a
congressional powers II–195b, 200a
dentistry II–331a
Ellsworth, Henry L. I–4a, 45a
enemy–alien applications VII–94a
farm machinery I–37b
federally funded research IV–470b
interstate commerce III–459a
matches IV–274a,b
monopolistic power IV–399b
Motion Pictures Patent Company IV–417b
papermaking V–212a
phonograph V–289b
photographic film IV–417a
records V–290a
rubber VI–167a
Scientific American VI–231a,b
Selden patent VI–257a
sewing machine VI–264b–65a
stock ticker VI–413b
telephone VII–20b–21a
television VII–21b
vacuum–cleaner II–421a
Patent system, English IV–399a
Paternity IV–24a
Paterson (N.J.) II–130b; IV–67b–68a; VII–161a
silk industry VI–287a
Society for Establishing Useful Manufactures V–57b
trade unions IV–61b, 63b
waterpower IV–347b
Paterson, William (jur.) I–461a; II–203b; V–409a; VI–445a; VII–161a, 167a
Convention of 1787 II–151b, 193a
New Jersey Plan V–57b
war-making powers VII–224a
Path Deed VI–455b
Patheske (Indian) V–4a
Pathetic Song (paint.) V–190a
Pathet Lao III–160a, 161b; IV–107a–b
Pathfinder IV–162a
"PATHFINDER" (John C. Frémont) **V–227a**; VII–271b
Pathfinder of the Seas. *See* Maury, Matthew F.
Pathogens IV–407a
Paths, Indian. *See* Indian Paths
PATH System. *See* Port Authority Trans–Hudson System
Patios (arch.) I–160a
Patkai Range III–46a
Patman, Wright (pol.) III–83b; IV–234a; VI–157b
Patoka (tanker) II–344b
Patowmack Company Canal I–442a
Patrick, Frank III–287a
Patrick, Lester III–287a
Patrick Henry (submarine) V–25b
Patrick Henry, Fort (Ind.) IV–53b
"Patrimonial zone" III–107a
PATRIOT WAR (1837–38) **V–227a**
Patrol frigate VII–243b
Patrol gunboat III–234b, 235a
Patrol plane I–55b
Patrol ship V–25b, 26a
PATRONAGE, POLITICAL V–227b; II–472b; V–345b
bossism I–343a
boycotting I–356b
civil service II–59b, 59b–60a
corruption II–231a
corrupt–practices laws V–448b
government appointments I–145b–46a
government newspapers III–202a
Hunkers III–318a
party machines IV–214b
party organization V–344b
Pendergast machine V–244b
postal service V–374a
post office V–372a
readjuster movement VI–49b
rotation in office VI–165a
senatorial courtesy II–246a
Speaker of the House VI–369a,b
spoils system VI–374b
Tammany Hall VI–459b
ward leader VII–230b
PATRONS OF HUSBANDRY V–228b; I–38b, 38b, 41b; II–220b; III–210a, 211a; VI–358a
Industrial Congress III–405b
See also Granger Movement
Patroon painters V–186a
PATROONS V–229a; V–61a
colonial estates IV–92a
Rensselaerswyck II–383a; IV–241b
Patten, William Gilbert (au.) II–341b
Patterns, dress II–371b
Patterson, Daniel Todd (nav. off.) V–19b
Patterson, Floyd (pugilist) V–154b, 423a
Patterson, Frederick D. (educ.) VII–130b
Patterson, James Willis (pol.)
Crédit Mobilier II–256a
Patterson, John (chem.) III–158a
Patterson, John Henry (mfr.) I–396a, 397a
Patterson, Joseph M. (pub.) V–74b
Patterson, Robert (off.) I–381a,b
Patterson, Robert (proprietor) II–37b; IV–329b
Pattie, James O. (fur trader) I–280a; III–143b; VI–461a
Pattie, Sylvester (fur trader) III–143b; IV–25b
Pattison, Edward (tinsmith) VII–62b
Pattison, William (tinsmith) VII–62b
Patton, George S. (off.) I–177a; IV–420a; V–113a; VI–284b
IV–32b
Patton, James (expl.) III–292b
Patton family (Va.) III–469b
Patuxent (ocean tug) III–29a
Patuxent Indians III–499a
Patuxent River I–317b; VI–149b
Paul I (czar) VI–180b
Paul IV (pope) II–386b
Paul VI (pope) I–470b; V–89b
Paul, Alice (ref.) VII–312b, 315a
Paul, Robert W. (inv.) IV–417a
Paul Bunyan (folk hero) V–72b
Paulding, Hiram (nav. off.) III–23b
Paulding, John (sol.) I–118b
Paul Drey Gallery II–104a
Pauli, Wolfgang (phys.) V–299a, 304a
Pauling, Linus Carl (chem.) II–12b; IV–390a; V–99b, 100a
Paulino, Don (dipl.) VI–311b
Paulist Press V–229b
PAULISTS V–229a
Paulli, Ensign VI–208b
Paul Revere's Ride (poem) VI–106a
Paulus Hook (N.J.) V–57b, 229b
PAULUS HOOK, SURPRISE OF (1779) **V–229b**
Paul v. *Virginia* (1868) III–432b
Pauncefote, Julian (dipl.) I–93b; III–266a; V–153a–b
Pauperism. *See* Poverty and Pauperism
Pauper–labor doctrine VI–466a
Pauw, Michiel (patroon) V–229a
PAVING V–229b
asphalt VI–156b
environmental sanitation VI–212b
New York City V–83a
panic of 1929 V–209b
Pemaquid pavements V–243a
Savannah VI–220b
Washington, D.C. VII–246b

Paviotso (Indians) V–194a
Pavlov, Ivan P. (physiol.) VII–371a
Pavlova, Anna (dancer) II–288b
Pavonia (N.Y.) II–383a; V–229a
Pavy, B. H. (jur.) IV–184a
Pawcatuck River IV–48b; V–261a
Pawling (N.Y.) I–284b
PAWNEE (Indians) **V–230a**; I–171b; II–359a; III–220b, 363b, 396b
Arikara IV–235b
horse III–303a
Kansas IV–25a
medicine III–385a
Oklahoma V–148b, 149b
Pike's southwestern expedition V–312a
Quivira III–211a
scouts VI–241b
sign language VI–286b
trade IV–159b
Villasur expedition VII–188a
"Pawnee Bill." *See* Lillie, Gordon W.
Pawnee Fork I–221a
Pawnee Indian Village Museum (Kans.) IV–25a
Pawnee Pict (Indian Terr.) II–359a
Pawnee River IV–109a
PAWNEE ROCK (Kans.) **V–230b**; I–174b
Pawnee wheat VII–286b
Paw Paw Tunnel I–443a
PAWTUCKET (R.I.) **V–230b**; VI–133b
Arkwright machinery I–175a,b
Sunday schools VI–442b
textile strike IV–61b; VII–316b
waterpower IV–347b
Pawtucket Falls (R.I.) V–230b; VI–133a; VII–257a
Pax Britannica II–217b
Paxton (Pa.) V–231a
PAXTON BOYS V–231a; VI–452a; VII–58b, 353a
Pay Board V–402a
Payne, Cecilia H. (astron.) I–212a
Payne, David L. (pioneer) I–336a; V–148b, 150a
Payne, John Howard (act., dram.) III–297a; VII–47a
Payne, Lewis IV–154b, 155a
Payne, Sereno E. (pol.) VI–467b
Payne–Aldrich Tariff Act (1909) V–427b; VI–385a, 458a, 464a,b, 467a–b; VII–306b, 321b
PAYNE'S LANDING, TREATY OF (1832) **V–231a**; III–39a; VI–259b–60a
Payroll savings plan VI–222b
Payroll tax VI–105b; VII–7b, 10b, 11a,b
Payson, Mrs. Charles S. II–106b
Pay–TV III–1b
PB4–Y Consolidated Privateer (patrol plane) I–55b
PBM Martin Mariner (patrol plane) I–55b
PBY Consolidated Catalina (patrol plane) I–55b
Peabody, Elizabeth Palmer (educ.) II–398b
Peabody, George (philan.) I–250a; II–401b; III–82b, 466a
Peabody Fund V–231b
Peabody College V–231b
PEABODY FUND V–231b; III–82b
Peabody Institute of Music I–250a; IV–261b
Peabody Museum (Salem, Mass.) IV–436a; VI–199b
Peabody Museum of American Archaeology and Ethnology (Harvard) I–128b; III–19a
Peace and Constitutional Society VII–149a
Peace and Friendship, Treaty of (1786) VII–111a
Peace Bridge I–376a
Peace churches II–185a
PEACE COMMISSION OF 1778 V–231b; III–95a
PEACE CONFERENCE AT BUENOS AIRES (1936) **V–232a**; IV–401b
PEACE CONFERENCES V–232b
Civil War III–247b
Paris Peace Conference of 1946 V–215b
Vietnam War VII–184a–b, 186b
World War I IV–124a; VII–330b
Peace Convention (1861). *See* Border Slave State Convention
Peace Corps I–8b; III–62a, 70a; V–53a, 281a
Africa I–22a
Appalachia I–144b
Peace Democrats. *See* Copperheads
Peace Kingdoms III–254a
"Peacemaker" (gun) V–408b
PEACE MOVEMENT OF 1864 V–234b
PEACE MOVEMENTS V–235a
antiwar groups VII–236a
Bible I–293b
Civil War II–63b, 66b–67a, 163b, 164b; V–234b; VII–149a
Communist party II–145a
Copperheads II–222b
Ford's peace ship III–60a
Holden Peace Movement III–289b
Nobel Prizes V–99a,b, 100a
pacifism V–181a
Quakers III–123b
radicals VI–13b
Vietnam War VII–254a
Washington, D.C. VII–246b
See also Youth Movements
Peace of Aix-la-Chapelle. *See* Aix-la-Chapelle, Treaty of
Peace officers II–247a, 252a, 258a
Peace pipe. *See* Pipe, Indian
PEACE RESOLUTIONS OF BRITISH PARLIAMENT V–237b
Peace River III–40a; V–121a; VII–275b
Peace Society VII–149a
"PEACE WITHOUT VICTORY" V–238a; V–353b
Peach blossom VI–393 (table)
Peaches III–128a,b
Peach Orchard (Pa.) III–176a
Peach State VI–393 (table)
PEACHTREE CREEK, BATTLES ON (1864) **V–238a**; I–213b
Peacock (brig) III–263a, 301b
***PEACOCK–EPERVIER* ENGAGEMENT** (1814) **V–238b**
Peake, William (nav. off.) III–301b
Peale, Charles Willson (paint.) III–268b, 354a; IV–231b, 232a, 352a, 436a; V–186b, 187b, 188a, 190a
Peale, James (paint.) IV–352a; V–190a
Peale, Raphael (paint.) III–268b
Peale, Rembrandt (paint.) II–101b; V–5a, 188b
Peale family II–102b
Peale Museum (Washington, D.C.) IV–232b
Peanuts I–36a; III–381a; VII–196b
"Peanuts" (comic strip) V–72b
Pearce, Richard (metal.) VI–316b
Pearce, Roy Harvey (hist.) I–112b–13a
PEA RIDGE, BATTLE OF (1862) **V–238b**; III–400a; V–402b
Pearl ash III–413a; VII–82b
***PEARL* CASE V–239a**
PEARL HARBOR V–239a; III–264a
dry docks II–375b
Enterprise explosion II–350a
Japanese attack I–58a, 66b–67a, 328a, 484a; II–247a, 315a, 425a; III–69a, 439a, 480a; IV–253a, 336a, 384a; V–10b; VII–76b, 242a, 333b, 335a, 342a
navy yard V–29b
oil storage V–13b
radar VI–10a
Second Fleet V–25a
PEARL RIVER V–240b; III–41b
boundary dispute I–351b
Honey Island III–297b
West Florida VII–277a
Pearlstein, Philip (paint.) V–193a
Pearl Street (N.Y.C.) III–100a; IV–153b; V–40a, 229b
Pears III–128b
Pearson, Drew (jour.) V–75a
Pearson, Egon (statis.) VI–206b
Pearson, Karl (sci.) VI–206b
Pearson, Lester B. (states.) I–440a
Pearson, Richard M. (jur.) II–160b
Peary, Robert E. (expl.). *See* Peary's Polar Expeditions
Peary Arctic Club V–240b
PEARY'S POLAR EXPEDITIONS (1891–1909) **V–240b**; V–337a
Peas III–51a, 55a
Peasant art III–46b
Pease, Durrell O. (inv.) VII–44a
Pease, Seth II–45b
Pease Creek VI–261a
Peat II–84b
Pecan VI–395 (table)
PECK, FORT (Mont.) **V–241a**
Peck, John M. VI–387a
Peckham, Rufus W. (jur.) I–11a; VI–446a
Peconic Bay IV–185b
PECOS (N.Mex.) **V–241a**; V–460a
Pecos (pueblo) II–228b; VI–162a
Pecos Bill (folk hero) III–49a; VI–458b
Pecos National Monument V–217b, 241a
Pecos River I–342b; III–199b, 304a
Fort Sumner VI–439b
Navaho V–9a
Pecos Trail. *See* Goodnight–Loving Trail
Pecos Valley III–478b
PECULIAR INSTITUTION V–241b
Pedagogy II–398a
PEDDLERS V–241b; III–127a; VI–416a
tinware VII–62b
wagons II–297b
Yankee notions VII–352b
Pediatrics IV–275a–b; V–127b
Pediatric Society, American IV–289a
Peebles Farm (Va.) V–265a
Pee Dee River VI–149b, 303b, 453b
Peek, Frank William (elec. eng.) II–416b
Peek, George N. (ind.) V–44a–b, 45b
Peep–show Kinetoscopes IV–417a
***PEGGY STEWART*, BURNING OF** (1774) **V–241b**; IV–260b; VII–16b
Pegler, Westbrook (jour.) V–74a

Pegram, John (off.) VI–138b
Pegram, W. J. (off.)
VII–197a
Pei, I. M. (arch.) I–166a
Peierls, Rudolf (phys.)
V–304a
Peiper, Joachim (off.)
IV–230b
Peirce, Charles S. (math., phys.) III–260a; IV–2b; V–287b, 288a, 386b–87a
Peirce, John (col.) V–313a
Peirce's Metaphysical Club
IV–2b
Pejepscot Falls IV–37a
PEJEPSCOT PURCHASE V–242a
Pejepscot River V–359b
Pekin (Ill.) IV–201b
Peking (China)
Boxer Rebellion I–356a; IV–252b
Legation Quarter II–25b
Nixon trip II–28a
Peking commission (1926)
II–479b
PEKING CONGRESS (1900–01) **V–242a**; I–356a
PEKING TARIFF CONFERENCE (1925) **V–242b**
Peki–tan–oui. *See* Missouri River
Pelagic sealing. *See* Sealing
Pélagie (Indian) II–490a
Pelée, Mount V–23a
PELELIU V–242b
World War II I–459a; IV–253a; V–21a; VII–139a
Pelham (N.Y.) III–313a
Pelham, Henry (paint.)
IV–352a; V–413b
Pelham, John (off.)
Army of Northern Virginia
VII–197a
Pelham, Peter (paint.)
V–186a, 187a, 413b
Pelican (ship) I–170a; III–189b
Pelican (bird) VI–394 (table)
Pelican Island VII–297b, 298a
Pelican State VI–394 (table)
Pelisipia III–497a
Pellagra I–303b; IV–288a, 305b; V–128a, 358b, 359a; VI–173b
Pellam–Holles, Thomas. *See* Newcastle, 1st Duke of
Pell family (N.Y.) VII–56b
Pelton, Lester A. (eng.)
VII–129a, 257b
Pemaquid (Maine)
King William's War
IV–49b, 50a
settlement IV–225b
PEMAQUID PAVEMENTS V–243a
PEMAQUID POINT V–243a; IV–37a,b
fishing II–92b
Popham Colony V–359b
PEMAQUID PROPRIETORS V–243b; IV–396a; VII–360a
Pemaquid River VII–359a
Pemberton, Ebenezer (cler.)
I–332b
Pemberton, Fort (Miss.)
VII–354b
Pemberton, John C. (off.)
III–485b; VI–48b
Battle at Big Black River
I–295b
Battle at Prairie Grove
V–389a
Battle of Champion's Hill
I–492a
Chickasaw Bluffs II–22a
Vicksburg II–295a; VII–181b–82a
Pemberton family IV–200a
PEMBINA (N.Dak.) **V–244a**; IV–187a; VI–63b, 64b
War V–244b
Pembina River V–244a
Pembroke (Mass.) V–244a
Pembroke College I–372a
PEMBROKE RESOLVES V–244a
Pemell, Richard B., 1st Earl Lyons (states.) VII–115b
Pemetic. *See* Mount Desert
Pemmican III–140b, 360a, 361a; IV–280b; V–244a,b; VI–63b
PEMMICAN WAR V–244b
Penal and Penitentiary Commission, International
V–416a
Penal and Penitentiary Congress, International (1872)
V–416a
Penal colonies I–489a; V–465a
Pence (coin) II–94b
Pend d'Oreille (Indians)
III–500a
Pender, William D. (off.)
III–176a; V–309a
Pendergast, James (pol.)
V–244b
Pendergast, Thomas (pol.). *See* Pendergast Machine
PENDERGAST MACHINE V–244b; I–343a; IV–214a
Pendleton, Charles L.
II–100a
Pendleton, George H. (pol.)
I–422a; V–245a
PENDLETON ACT (1883) **V–245a**; I–146a, 384a; II–59b, 61a, 232a–b; III–261a; V–288a; VI–375b
Pendleton County (W.Va.)
VI–267a
Pendleton District (Va.)
III–292b
Pendleton Roundup VI–161b
Penguin (brig) III–302a
Penicillin III–410a, 417a; V–137b, 274a
venereal disease IV–306b; VII–169a
Penikese Island (Mass.)
IV–251a
PENINSULAR CAMPAIGN (1862) **V–245a**; II–482b; III–487a; IV–397a; V–377b
Battle of Frayser's Farm
III–100a
Fortress Monroe IV–399b
Malvern Hill IV–230b
Peninsula State VI–393 (table)
PENITENT BROTHERS V–245b
Penitentiaries. *See* Prisons and Prison Reform
Penn, Hannah V–246b
Penn, John (col. offi.)
II–118a; V–231a, 246b
Penn, John, Jr. II–308a; V–246b
Penn, Richard (col. offi.)
V–152b, 246b
Penn, Thomas (col. offi.)
II–35a; V–246b; VII–220b
Penn, William II–120a; III–123a–b; V–195a; VI–76a
brewery I–361b
charity V–279b
charter IV–263a–b
Charter of Privileges
I–500b
conscientious objectors
II–185a
conservation II–187a
Delaware II–320a; V–436b
Delaware Indians II–321a
East Jersey II–388b
fifths mining tax III–20b
frame of government
V–246a
Free Society of Traders
III–111a
German immigration
IV–206a
Germantown III–173a
Great Law III–219a; V–415a
Holy Experiment
III–293a; V–470a
Indian treaties III–382b
land grants IV–91b; VII–347a, 359b
Lower Counties–on–Delaware IV–199b
manors IV–242a
New Castle V–43a; VII–129b–30a
New Jersey VII–278a–b
pacifism V–181a
Pennsylvania II–124b; V–246a, 277a, 436b; VII–267a
Pennsylvania–Connecticut boundary dispute
V–250b
Pennsylvania–Maryland-boundary dispute V–251b
Pennsylvania–Virginia-boundary dispute V–253a
Philadelphia plan II–45a
plan of union II–121b
proprietary agents
V–435b, 436a
religious liberty VI–80b; VII–68b
Treaty of Shackamaxon
VI–267a
tree–cutting ordinance
III–73a
Union Canal VII–146a
Walking Purchase
VII–220b
West Jersey V–56b
West Jersey Concessions
II–157b; VII–278b
witchcraft VII–309b
Penn, William (nav. off.)
V–246a; VII–359b
Cromwell's western design
VII–270b
land grant VII–274a
Pennacook (Indians) I–2b, 465b
Pennamite and Yankee Wars. *See* Yankee–Pennamite Wars
Pennamites VII–346b–47b, 353a–b
Pennant, Thomas (nat.)
IV–231b
Penn Center (Philadelphia)
VI–86b
Penn Central Railroad
III–451a,b; V–278a; VI–32a,b, 35b
Penn family IV–98b; V–436b
Pennington, William (pol.)
II–175 (table); V–41b
Pennsburg (Pa.) VI–230a
Pennsbury (Pa.) I–361b
Penn's Delaware Territories. *See* Delaware Counties Act of Union; Lower Counties–on–Delaware
PENN'S FRAME OF GOVERNMENT V–246a; III–132b
Penn's Holy Experiment. *See* Holy Experiment
Penn's Treaty With the Indians (paint.) VI–267b
PENNSYLVANIA V–246a; VI–395 (table)
Acadians I–6a
Adena culture I–11a
Albany Congress I–82a
Alexandria Conference
I–85b
American army VI–125a
Annapolis Convention
I–126a
Anthracite Strike I–127a
antimiscegenation laws
IV–362b
auctioneers I–332b
bills of credit I–300a
Black Boys I–309a
black officeholders
VI–432b
blacksmiths I–317a
black suffrage III–437b; VI–431a,b
bossism I–343b
boundary disputes
I–223b–24a; III–250a; IV–263a–b
Bouquet's expedition
I–353b
Buckshot War I–374a,b
buffalo I–375a
building and loan associations I–376b
campaign of 1828 I–418b
campaign of 1836 I–419b
canals IV–174b–75a
canal society I–444a
capital punishment
I–450a
Carlisle borough I–455a
Carlisle Indian School
I–455a
Cartagena expedition
I–461b
Catholics I–466b

PENNSYLVANIA (cont.)
cereal grain V–404a
charter II–118b
Charter of Privileges I–500b
child labor laws II–24b; IV–80a
chromite III–13b
Civil War I–490b–91a; II–484b; III–31b, 175b–76a, 250b; IV–190a; V–248a–b
coal II–75a, 84b–85a, 86a, 321b; V–157a
cobalt production III–14a
colonial agent II–116b
colonial assembly II–118a
colonial charter V–436a
colonial council II–119b
colonial government VI–166a
colonial judiciary II–121a
colonial land grants IV–92a
colonial land speculation IV–98b
colonial punishments V–464b
colonial suffrage VI–434a,b
colonial trade II–119a–b
Colorado settlers VII–146a
commodities as money II–140b
Conestoga wagon II–248a; VII–168a
Connecticut western lands II–183b
conscientious objectors II–185a
constitution II–157b, 243a; VI–390b
Council of Censors II–243a
Cumberland Road II–273a–b
Cumberland Valley V–462b
dairy industry II–279b, 280b
Declaration of Independence II–305a, 308a
Delaware Bay grant VII–359b
Delaware counties II–320a
Delaware Counties Act of Union II–322b
Delaware River Basin Compact III–460a
Dickinson's Letters II–494b
distilleries VI–377b
domestic trade VII–83a,b, 84a
donation-lands II–363a
Drake oil well II–464b
education II–395a
election laws I–206b
Ephrata II–454a
Erie Triangle II–460b
feudalism III–18a
fish III–28a
floods II–351b; III–37a
folk art III–47a
football III–57a
Forbes Road III–59a
foreign trade VII–86a
forestry III–72b
Forks of the Ohio V–143a
Fort Augusta I–223b
Fort Bedford I–282b
Fort Ligonier IV–154a
Fort Loudon IV–191b
Fort McIntosh IV–216b
Fort Mifflin IV–337b
Fort Presque Isle V–399b
Forty Fort III–81b
fossil plants V–196b
Franciscans III–94b
Freemasons III–109a
freemen III–109b
Free Society of Traders III–111a
French and Indian War I–358a–b; III–58b, 219a–b; IV–51a, 154a, 398b; VI–271a
French forts III–120a; IV–130a, 213b, 250b
French refugees III–121a,b
Friendly Association III–122b–23a
Fries's Rebellion III–124a, 436b
fugitive slaves V–406b
furniture III–135b
fur trade III–141a,b, 142b
Geographer's Line III–163a
geological survey III–165a
German settlement IV–206a; V–251a
Germantown III–173a
glassmaking III–184b, 185a
Great Law of Pennsylvania III–219a
Great Trading and War Path III–223b
Hannastown III–250a
Harmony Society III–255b; IV–338b
Harris' Ferry III–257b
Hayburn's Case III–265b
historical society III–278b
historic properties IV–472a
hogs III–288b
Holland Land Company III–291a
Holy Experiment III–293a
Hopewell Iron Works III–300b
Huguenots III–315a
hurricanes III–319b; IV–258b
Hyder Ali III–320b
immigrants III–334b, 335a
impeachment III–343b, 344b
Independence Hall III–354a
Indiana Company III–370b
Indiana settlers III–370a
Indian lands IV–181b, 216b–17a; VI–386a
Indian raids II–382a
Indian trade II–480a
Indian treaties III–382b
internal improvements III–447b
interurban electric lines III–461b
intestate estates III–464a
iron and steel III–12a, 472a, 473b
Italian population III–338a
Jefferson's proposed states III–497a
Johnstown flood IV–5a
Ku Klux Klan IV–58b
Lancaster Pike IV–89b
landholding I–4a
lead industry IV–122a
legislature IV–133b; VII–142a
lime kiln II–5a
Lincoln University II–113b
lotteries IV–191a
Lower Counties-on-Delaware IV–199b
lumber industry IV–204a
mammals IV–231b
manors IV–242a
map I–462b
Mason–Dixon Line IV–263a
Masons I–132b
Mennonites IV–303a
military service II–366a
militia I–251b
Minisink patent IV–354b
Molly Maguires IV–63a, 391b
Monongahela River IV–398b
Moravian missionaries III–187b
Moravians I–293a; IV–409b
Mormons VI–87a
mountain passes V–224a,b
Murdering Town IV–434b
navy V–18b
New England settlers V–50a
New Sweden Colony V–80a
New York barge system V–175b–76a
nickel III–13b
North American Land Company V–113a
oats V–130a
Ohio Company of Virginia V–144a
Ohio Valley traders V–146a
Oleana V–152b
pack trains V–184a
panhandle V–205b
panic of 1873 V–207b
paper and pulp industry V–212a
paper mill II–5a
paper money II–118a
Paxton Boys V–231a
Penn settlement VII–267a
Penn's frame of government V–246a
petroleum IV–43b, 44a, 153a; V–269a,b, 271a,b, 272a; VI–354b, 356b
Philadelphia V–277a
Pinkster celebration V–316b
pioneers V–316b
Pittsburgh V–321b
plans of union II–121b–22a
political exiles V–342a
politics I–374a
pottery III–183b
presidential electors I–416b
primogeniture V–408a
proprietary agent V–435b, 436a
proprietary colony I–499b, 500a
proprietary grant V–436b
public ownership V–455a
Quakers III–123a–b; IV–35b, 447b; V–181a, 470a; VII–201b
Quids VI–3a–b
quitrents VI–4a
railroads VI–25a, 34a, 36a
Raystown Path VI–49a
record-keeping VII–205b
redemptioners VI–62b
Redstone Old Fort VI–65b
religious liberty VII–68b
religious toleration II–394b
retail sales VII–84b
revolutionary war I–398a; II–321a; III–173b–74a, 250b; IV–1a; V–211b; VI–117b, 130a, 130b, 437b–38a; VII–164b–65a
ripper legislation VI–144b
roads VI–152b
rubber industry VI–167a
rum trade VII–278a
school for the deaf III–248a
Scotch-Irish V–115b; VI–240b
settlement II–124b; IV–89b, 338a; VI–76a–b
Seven Ranges survey VI–264a
shipyards II–438a
Sideling Hill VI–285a
silk VI–287a
single-tax plan VI–293b
slavery I–135a,b; VI–309a
snowstorms II–352a
stagecoach lines V–144b
Stamp Act VI–381b
state courts I–9b
state fairs VI–392b
state navy VI–128b
state ownership III–204a
state university VII–156a
steam engines VI–409a
steam navigation III–32a
Susquehanna Company VI–451b
Susquehanna settlers VI–452a
Swiss settlers VI–455a
tanning II–5a
tariff VI–465a, 465b, 466a
taverns VII–2a
taxation II–118a; VII–3a, 4a, 6b
timberlands VII–60a
tobacco VII–66b, 67a
trading posts IV–181b

Treaty of Easton II–388b
Treaty of Fort Stanwix III–383a
Treaty of Shackamaxon VI–267b
"turf and twig" VII–129b
Underground Railroad VII–138b
U.S. Constitution II–193a,b, 196a–b, 198b, 203b, 478a
Vanhorne's Lessee v. *Dorrance* VII–167a
Vare case VII–167b
Venango VII–168b
Virginia rivalry II–381a–b
Walking Purchase VI–270b–71a
War of 1812 I–250b
Washington (city) VII–244b
Washington's western lands VII–252a
water supply VII–259a
Western Reserve VII–275a
West Virginia panhandle V–205b
westward movement VII–260a, 282b–83a
wheat I–486a
whiskey VII–289b
Whiskey Rebellion III–436b; VII–82b, 289b
Wilderness Road VII–296a
wild turkey VII–130a
Women in the Wilderness commune II–147a
writs of assistance VII–345a
Wyoming massacre VII–346b
Wyoming Valley IV–92a, 98b; VII–347b
Yankee–Pennamite Wars II–183b; VII–353a
York VII–358a
zinc VII–368b–69a
Zouaves VII–371b
Pennsylvania (cruiser) I–54a, 233b; VI–282a
Pennsylvania, Bank of III–201b
Pennsylvania, Historical Society of I–110b, 110b; II–108a, 108a,b
PENNSYLVANIA, INVASION OF (1863) **V–248a**
PENNSYLVANIA, UNIVERSITY OF V–248b; II–114b, 395a
archives I–169a
bacteriology I–241a
chemistry II–10a
computer program II–426b
medical school IV–283a,b, 284b; V–306b
psychology V–441b
technical instruction II–447a
veterinary medicine VII–176a,b
Pennsylvania Academy of Art V–192a
Pennsylvania Academy of Fine Arts V–278a; VI–267b
PENNSYLVANIA AND OHIO CANAL V–249b; V–250a
Pennsylvania Avenue (Washington, D.C.) III–350b; VII–244b, 291b
Pennsylvania Ballet II–289b
Pennsylvania Canal Company V–250a–b
PENNSYLVANIA CANAL SYSTEM V–249b; I–127b; III–202b, 286a, 448a, 449b; IV–174b; V–277b; VI–36a
Allegheny Portage Railway I–89a
bridge I–364b
Conemaugh Reservoir IV–5a
Main Line I–442b
showboats VI–283a
Union Canal VII–145b
Pennsylvania Central Airlines II–346a
Pennsylvania Company for Insurance on Lives and Granting Annuities III–432b
PENNSYLVANIA–CONNECTICUT BOUNDARY DISPUTE V–250b; V–246b; VI–451b
Trenton decree VII–116b
Wyoming Valley VII–346b–47b
Yankee–Pennamite Wars VII–353a
Pennsylvania Continentals VII–360b
Pennsylvania Dutch. *See* Pennsylvania Germans
Pennsylvania Evening Post and Daily Advertiser (news.) V–71a
"Pennsylvania Fireplace." *See* Franklin Stove
Pennsylvania Fiscal Agency II–256a
Pennsylvania Friends V–470a
Pennsylvania Friends' Meetings IV–35b
PENNSYLVANIA GAZETTE (news.) **V–251a**; I–16b, 464a; IV–190b; V–68b, 72b
PENNSYLVANIA GERMANS V–251a; III–334b, 335a; V–115b, 246b, 316b; VI–76a–b; VII–283a
almanacs I–91a
Conestoga horse III–303b
folk art III–47a,b
furniture III–138b
Germantown III–173a
Lancaster settlement IV–89b
Palatines V–195a
pottery V–379a–b
redemptioners VI–62b
revolutionary war VII–165a
rifles VI–139b
Schwenkfelders VI–230a
Virginia VII–192b–93a
PENNSYLVANIA HOSPITAL V–251b; III–269a, 306b; IV–283a,b, 295b, 304b–05a; V–187a
Pennsylvania Journal (news.) II–264b
Pennsylvania Line III–308a; IV–445a
Pennsylvania Main Line Canal I–442b, 443b
PENNSYLVANIA–MARYLAND BOUNDARY DISPUTE V–251b; IV–263a–b; V–246b
Pennsylvania New York Central Transportation Company VI–35b
Pennsylvania Packet and Daily Advertiser (news.) V–71a
Pennsylvania Packet and General Advertiser (news.) I–16b
PENNSYLVANIA PRISON SYSTEM V–252b; V–415a; VI–67b
Pennsylvania Property Company V–113b
Pennsylvania Railroad II–350b; III–312b; IV–89b; V–250a, 277b; VI–32a, 35b, 36a, 383a; VII–83a, 83b, 100b
Adams Express Company I–10a
Allegheny Portage Railway I–89a
Camden and Amboy VI–24b
Delaware and Raritan Canal II–322a
electrification II–416a
express service V–443a
foreign investments III–64b
industrial research III–408b
Johnstown flood IV–5a
locomotives IV–175b, 176b, 177a
New Jersey politics V–58a
quality control IV–273b
rate wars VI–22b, 23a
strike of 1877 IV–63b
tunnel VII–128a–b
See also Penn Central
Pennsylvania rifle IV–430a; VI–139b
Pennsylvania Road I–88b; VII–216a
Pennsylvania Rock Oil Company II–369b; V–269a
Pennsylvania Society of Journeymen Cabinetmakers IV–293b
Pennsylvania State Building VI–263a
Pennsylvania Station (N.Y.C.) IV–177a, 220b
Pennsylvania Study (1926–38) I–456b
PENNSYLVANIA TROOPS, MUTINIES OF V–252b; IV–445a,b; VI–118a
Pennsylvania Tubing and Transportation Company V–319a
Pennsylvania Turnpike II–302b; III–450b
PENNSYLVANIA–VIRGINIA BOUNDARY DISPUTE V–253a; I–223b–24a; II–381a–b; III–250a; IV–263b; V–246b; VII–281b
Pennsylvania v. *Nelson* (1956) V–339b
Penny Capitalists II–220a
"Penny dreadfuls" II–249a
Penny press V–71a
Penny Provident Fund I–495a
PENOBSCOT V–253b; I–2b; II–31a; III–360b, 367a, 396b
Castine (Maine) I–466a
revolutionary war III–400a
Penobscot Bay I–466a
Monhegan Island IV–395b
Pemaquid Point V–243a
revolutionary war V–254a
Saint-Castin's trading house VI–188a
PENOBSCOT EXPEDITION (1779) **V–253b**; IV–251b
Penobscot River V–214b
exploration IV–37a
Fort Pownall V–386a
French settlement III–120b
logging VI–149a
Norumbega V–123a
Waldo patent VII–219b
War of 1812 III–247b
PENOLE V–254a
Penrose, Boies (pol.) I–343b; V–347a
Penrose, Charles B. (law., pol.) I–374a
PENSACOLA (Fla.) **V–254a**; III–38b, 39b; VI–187b
British acquisition I–498b
Civil War III–131b; V–17a, 308a; VI–216a
dry dock II–375a
fur trade III–144a
hurricanes III–319b
navy yard V–27b, 29a
port authority V–368a
revolutionary war I–367a; II–96b; VI–130a, 365b
Spanish settlement IV–326a
trading post VII–95b
PENSACOLA, CONGRESS OF (1765) **V–254b**
Pensacola, Treaty of (1784) IV–213a; VI–366b
Pensacola Bay V–254a, 308a, 356a
PENSION ACT, ARREARS OF (1879) **V–255a**
federal surplus VI–449b
Pension Bureau IV–95a; VI–336b; VII–174b
Pensioners II–4a, 236b
Pension Office, U.S. III–444a

PENSION PLANS V–255a; II–255a; IV–70a
Carnegie Foundation I–456b
disclosure act (1958) IV–78b
federal old-age II–236b
Hayburn's Case III–265a
post–World War II IV–74a
profit sharing V–426b
Railroad Pension Act VI–24a
railroad retirement acts VI–23b
Townsend Plan VII–79b
PENSIONS, MILITARY AND NAVAL V–256b; I–330b
Arrears of Pension Act V–255a
Civil War II–64b
Customs Service II–277a
federal expenditures II–476a
Grand Army of the Republic III–207b
Medal of Honor winners II–310a
National Tribune IV–471b
Naval Home V–11b
prize money V–423b
Veterans Administration VII–174b
War Department powers I–12a
Pensions, old age. *See* Old Age; Pensions Plans; Social Security;Townsend Plan
PENTAGON PAPERS V–258b; III–105b; V–78b–79a, 346a; VII–254b
Pentecostal Assemblies of the World V–260a
PENTECOSTAL CHURCHES V–259b; IV–318b; V–29b
Pentecostal Church of America V–260a
Pentecostal Holiness Church V–260a
Pentecostal movement I–470a
PENTEGOET, FORT (Maine) **V–260a**; V–253b
Saint-Castin's trading house VI–188a
Pentegoet Peninsula I–466a
Penutian phylum (Indian lang.) IV–381b
PEONAGE V–260b; IV–103a
Peony VI–393 (table)
People (news.) VI–325a
"People of the Sea" V–95a
People of the State of New York v. *North River Sugar Refining Company* (1887) VI–437b
"People rule" VI–393 (table)
"People's choice" II–409a
People's Convention (1841) VI–133b
People's Council of America for Democracy and Terms of Peace V–236a
"Peoples democracies" II–325a
People's Liberation Army IV–235b
Peoples Party I–39a, 42b; II–42a, 493b; III–468b; V–365b
See also Populist Party
People's Republic of China. *See* China
People's war II–145a
People v. *Croswell* (1804) VII–117b
PEORIA (Ill.) **V–260b**; III–329a
Fort Clark II–71a
Fort Crèvecoeur II–257b
Fort Pimitoui V–315a
Fort Saint Joseph raid VI–192a
Lakes-to-Gulf waterway IV–88a
railroads VI–35a
Peoria (Indians) III–366b, 394b, 467b; IV–277b
Peoria, Lake III–329a; IV–109b; V–260b, 315a
Peoria County (Ill.) V–260b
Peoria War (1813) VII–239a
Pepin, Lake I–281b; IV–224b, 355a; VI–187a–b
Pepin County (Wis.) IV–224b
Pepper II–388a
Pepper, George Wharton (pol.) VII–167b
Pepperell, William (off.) I–359a; IV–192a, 226a; V–100b
Peppers II–227a; III–51a
Pepsi-Cola Company VI–333b
Peptide bonds IV–388b
Pepys, Samuel (diarist) I–221b; VI–18b
Pequawket (Indians) IV–199a
Pequot (Indians) III–367a; IV–387a; V–261a
PEQUOT TRAIL V–261a
PEQUOT WAR (1636–37) **V–261a**; I–219a; II–181b; IV–47a; VII–149b
Indian captives III–401a
New Haven Colony V–55a
Saybrook VI–223a
Peralta, Pedro de VI–214b
Peratrovich, Frank (pol.) I–79a
Percé Rock I–492b
Perceval, John, 1st Earl of Egmont (pol.) III–17b, 168a
Perch III–51a
Percheron (horse) III–303b
Percier, Charles (arch.) III–135a
Percy, Henry (off.) I–356a
Percy, Hugh (off.) IV–137b
Perdicaris, Ion V–261b
PERDICARIS AFFAIR (1904) **V–261b**
PERDIDO (riv.) **V–262a**; III–327a; IV–382b
Baton Rouge I–275a
boundary III–41b; VI–359a–b
French claims IV–197b
Gulf of Mexico IV–326a
West Florida VII–277a
Père Marquette Railroad VI–33a
Pérez, Juan (expl.) V–164b; VII–247a
Perez v. *Brownell* (1958) II–54a
Perfectionism I–307b; II–34b, 147a; V–155b; VI–81b
Perfecto de Cos, Martín (off.) VI–213b
Perfect Tribute (period.) III–176b
Performance Group (theater) VII–51a
Perfume II–233b
Peril point judgment (tariff) III–113b–14a; VI–469a
Periodicals
copyright II–224b–25a
education II–399b
Farmer's Almanac II–494a
See also Advertising
Periodicals, scientific. *See* Scientific Periodicals
Periodic table V–298a,b, 299b, 300a
Peripheral rights I–299b–300a; III–317a
Perjury I–450a
Perkin, William Henry (chem.) III–408b
Perkins, Frances (offi.) III–455a; V–43b; VII–317b
Perkins, George W. (fin.) V–428a,b
Perkins, Jacob (inv.) VI–70a
Perkins, Joseph (fur trader) VI–196a
Perkins, Thomas Handasyd (mer.) V–188b–89a
Perky, Henry (mfr.) I–487a
Permanent Bridge I–363b
PERMANENT COURT OF ARBITRATION V–262a; III–237b, 452b, 456b; VII–112b, 113a
Pious Fund controversy V–318a
Root Arbitration Treaties VI–163b
U.S. fishing rights III–31a
Venezuela debts VII–169b
Permanent Court of International Justice. *See* International Court of Justice
Permanent Investigations Subcommittee
McCarthy-Army hearings IV–209b
Permanent Joint Board on Defense I–439b
Permanent press II–239b
Permanent wave III–239a–b
Permian Basin (Tex.) IV–334a
Perón, Juan (pol.) III–199b
Péronne (Fr.) VI–338b
Perpetua, Cape II–219b
Perrine, Henry III–381b
Perrot, Nicolas (expl.) II–246a; III–89b, 147a
Fort Saint Antoine VI–187a
Fort Saint Nicolas V–387b
Green Bay III–225b
Minnesota IV–355a
Wisconsin VII–307a
Perry, Camp (Ohio) I–289a
Perry, Captain (adventurer) III–149a, 236a
Perry, John D. IV–30b
Perry, Matthew C. (nav. off.)
Mexican War IV–322a, 325a; V–19b
See also Perry's Expedition to Japan
Perry, Oliver Hazard (nav. off.) IV–331a; V–262b; VII–266b
Battle of Lake Erie I–436b; II–338a, 364a, 458b, 459a; V–19a; VII–45b, 266b–67a, 307b
Battle of the Thames III–217a
Lawrence IV–118b
prize money V–424a
Venezuela mission VII–170a
Perry, William E. (expl.) V–122a
Perry County (Ohio) IV–44a
PERRY-ELLIOTT CONTROVERSY V–262b
PERRY'S EXPEDITION TO JAPAN (1852–54) **V–263a**; I–201b; II–488b; V–22b, 22b; VII–285a
marines IV–252a
oceanographic survey V–133b
PERRYVILLE, BATTLE OF (1862) **V–263a**; II–271b, 272b; IV–41a, 42b, 434b
Perry v. *United States* (1935) VI–95a–b
Pershing, John J. (off.) II–310b
American Expeditionary Forces I–101b, 186a; IV–84a–b, 319b–20a; VI–301a, 338b; VII–325b, 326a–27a
army general staff VII–230a
army organization I–189a
Mexican expedition I–476a; IV–327b; VII–188a
Saint-Mihiel VI–197b
Tacna-Arica controversy VI–456a
World War I armistice I–176b
Pershing Division I–434b
Persia
citrus fruits III–128b
consular jurisdiction II–479b
Persian Gulf
oil tankers VI–281a
petroleum V–272b

World War II VII–338a
Persimmons III–366a–b
Personality, presidential V–394b, 396a,b
Personality theory V–442b
Personal liberty. *See* Liberty, Concept of
PERSONAL LIBERTY LAWS V–263; V–125b, 406b
Great Britain II–325a
Personnel for the New Diplomacy (report) III–72a
Personnel management. *See* Industrial Relations
Personnel Records Center. *See* National Personnel Records Center
Perth (cruiser) III–492b
PERTH AMBOY (N.J.) **V–264a**; II–388b; V–56b, 57a
Hester case III–274a
pottery III–183a
Peru V–233a
aerial hijacking III–276b
cinchona bark IV–229b
claims against IV–5b
colonial commerce V–203a
corn I–48a; II–225a
diplomatic recognition IV–110b
Dominican missions II–362b
earthquake V–23a
explorations I–24b
Franciscans III–94b
geophysical exploration III–166a
guano III–16b, 230b
Inca II–336a
independence war IV–115a
Indian land tenure I–48b
Indians III–356a–b, 381b, 385b
International Exposition of 1895 III–453b
lead IV–123b
Macedonian affair IV–212b
nationalization of U.S. property IV–466a
Nitrate War III–16b
ouster of Spain III–68b
Panama Congress V–203b
relations with Cuba IV–113a
Santiago Inter-American Congress VI–217a
Spanish intervention VI–360a
Tacna-Arica controversy VI–456a
territorial waters III–107a
United Nations Declaration VII–151b
U.S. trade VI–343b, 344b, 345a,b, 346a
Perutz, Max F. (molecular biol.) IV–389b, 391b
Pesaro (It.) III–201a
Pescadores Islands I–403b; III–85b
Peshtigo (Wis.) II–348a
Peso (coin) II–94b–95a, 360a
Pessen, Edward (hist.) III–487a
Pestalozzi, Johann Heinrich (educ.) II–397a, 398b; VI–227b
Pest Control Act (1947) III–76a
Pesthouses III–306b; V–446b
Pesticide control II–277b
Pesticides. *See* Insecticides and Herbicides
Pestle (tool) II–386a
Pétain, Henri (off.) II–311a; IV–320a; V–147a
PET BANKS V–264a; III–354b; VI–427a
American Land Company I–108a
government deposits I–255b
specie circular VI–369b
Peter the Great (Peter I) I–74b
Peter, Hugh (cler.) VI–199a
Peterborough (N.H.) IV–144b
***PETERHOFF* ADMIRALTY CASE** (1863) **V–264a**; II–67b, 446b
Peterkin Papers I–335b
PETER PARLEY (Samuel G. Goodrich) **V–264b**; I–335a; II–397a; IV–222b; VI–227b
"Peter Porcupine" (pseud.) V–366a
Peters, Andrew J. (pol.) I–346b
Peters, Richard (jur.) VII–226b
Peters, Samuel A. (cler.) I–324b–25a; VI–440a
Peters, W. S. VII–35b
Petersburg (Va.) V–145a
Camp Lee I–434b
Civil War II–96b, 373a; VI–430a
Fort Henry I–277a–b; V–31b–32a
Occaneechi Trail III–387b
railroads VI–35a
revolutionary war I–194a; VII–360b
PETERSBURG, SIEGE OF (1864–65) **V–264b**; I–146b, 357a; II–62b; VI–137b, 138a, 410a–b; VII–115a, 195a, 197b
Civil War III–30b; VI–186b
Petersburg Railroad VI–25a
Peters Colony Company. *See* Texan Emigration and Land Company
Petersen, Hjalmar (gov.) II–491b
Peter Sergeant House (Boston) I–161a
Petersham (Mass.) VI–272a
Peterson, Martha E. (educ.) II–133a
Petit, F. (astron.) III–480b
PETITION, RIGHT OF V–265a; I–94a, 204b, 298b, 298b; II–171b, 204a, 308b
antislavery gag rule III–146a
antislavery petitions V–266b
West Jersey VII–278b
PETITION AND REMONSTRANCE OF NEW NETHERLAND (1649) **V–266a**; V–61b
Petition of Right (1628) I–298b, 300b; II–191a
Petitions
referenda VI–66b
PETITIONS, ANTISLAVERY V–266b; I–137b
Petiver, James (au.) V–180a
Petrel (gunboat) IV–239b
Petrified Forest National Park V–217a, 219 (table)
PETROCHEMICAL INDUSTRY V–266b; III–409b
New Orleans V–62b
New South V–67b
pollution VI–213a
profiteering V–426a
Puerto Rico V–461b
Petrodollars III–67a
Petroglyphs II–341a
Petrograd (Russ.) IV–435a; VI–164a, 178a
PETROGRAPHY V–267b
Petroleum Centre (Pa.) V–146b
PETROLEUM INDUSTRY V–269a; I–149b–50b; II–6b, 354b; IV–244a; VI–48a,b
Alaska II–462a; V–122a–b
ammonia III–17b
army logistics I–190a
automobile I–228a
Baton Rouge I–274b
California I–407a
Charleston (S.C.) I–497b
checkoff II–3b
Civil War II–69a
coasting trade II–90b
codes of fair competition VII–123a
Colorado II–128b
depletion allowance VII–10a, 12a
embargo III–415b; VII–85a
energy crisis (1973) I–391b
ferrous metals III–12a
foreign investment III–66b
foreign trade VII–87b
Fort Scott VI–241a
Fort Worth III–80b
gasoline taxes III–153a
government oil leases III–444a
government regulation I–449b
great fortunes III–80a,b
Gulf of Mexico IV–326b
historical records III–285a
"Hot oil" Case 307b–
Industrial Revolution III–410b
interstate compacts VI–402b
Interstate Compact to Conserve Oil and Gas III–460a
Kansas IV–25a, 26a,b
kerosine oil IV–43b
Louisiana IV–194b; V–62b
Mexican oil controversy I–109b; IV–322b
midcontinent oil region IV–333b
Mississippi River IV–373a, 374a
molybdenum III–15a
Montana IV–403b
Natchez IV–455a
natural gas V–5a
naval oil reserves V–13a; VII–16b
New Mexico V–60a
New South V–67b
nickel III–14a
North Dakota V–117b
oceanography V–135a
oil exchanges V–146b
Oklahoma V–149a
paving V–230a
Pennsylvania V–247a,b
Perth Amboy V–264a
Peruvian nationalization IV–466a
petrochemicals V–266b
Philadelphia V–278a
pipelines V–318b–19a
Pithole V–321a
profiteering V–426a
Rockefeller's monopoly IV–399a
Saint Paul VII–134a
Salt Lake City VI–203b
Seminole lands VI–260a
shipping III–429a; IV–311a, 313a; VI–280b–81a
shortages I–230b–31a
South America VI–345a–b
South Improvement Company VI–354b
Southwest VI–355b
southwestern oil fields VI–356b, 356b
Staked Plain VI–380b
Standard Oil Company VI–382b
Standard Oil Trust VI–383b; VII–122a
subsidies VI–426a
tariffs VI–53a–b
Texas VII–40b
towboating VII–77b
Trade Expansion Act VI–470a
transportation VII–84b
Venezuela VI–344b
West Virginia VII–281b
Wichita VII–294a–b
wildcat drilling VII–295a
World War I III–129b
World War II VII–336b
Wyoming VII–346a
Petroleum Institute, American V–400a
PETROLEUM PROSPECTING AND TECHNOLOGY V–271a; V–269b, 270a, 437b
Alaska I–79b, 80a
ammonia VI–334b
boomtowns I–336b
colonial discoveries

PETROLEUM PROSPECTING AND TECHNOLOGY (cont.)
IV–43b–44a
folklore III–49a
kerosine lamp IV–153a
kerosine oil IV–43b
mineral patent law IV–349b
mining towns IV–354a
Pennsylvania IV–44a
public lands V–445b
research III–408b, 409a
tidelands VII–57b
urban areas IV–104b
U.S. Geological Survey III–164a
West Virginia II–464b
Petrology III–163b; V–267b
Pettaquamscutt (R.I.) III–223a
Pettenkofer, Max Josef von (biochem.) I–302b, 303a
Petterssen, Sverre (meteor.) IV–317b
Pettibone, Daniel III–269a
Pettibone, George A. (labor leader) II–94a; III–267a
Petticoats II–371a–b
Pettigrew, James J. (off.) II–484b; III–175b; V–309a
Petty, Sir William. *See* Shelburne, 2nd Earl of.
Petty, William (pol. econ., statis.) VII–206a
Peubla (Mex.) IV–324a
Pewter VI–289b, 290a–91b
Peyote VII–65b
PEYOTE CULT V–272b; III–391b; V–2a; VII–65b
Peyton family III–18b
PFLP. *See* Popular Front for the Liberation of Palestine
PG. *See* Patrol gunboat
PGH 2 (gunboat) III–235a
PG School (navy) V–24a–b
Phage group II–97a
Phantom II (fighter plane) I–54a, 57a
"PHANTOM SHIP" V–273a
Pharmaceutical Association, American V–275b, 468b
PHARMACEUTICAL INDUSTRY V–273a; V–275a
foreign investment III–67a
Germany II–7b–8a; III–408b
governmental regulation III–54a
meat-packing by-products IV–281a
Memphis IV–302a
morphine II–374a
pure food and drug movement V–465b, 466b
vitamins V–128a
Pharmacopoeia
Indian medicine IV–335b
Pharmacopoeia, United States V–466a
PHARMACY V–274b; II–12a; III–381a
Journal of Pharmacology and Experimental Therapeutics IV–3a
mental illness IV–306b–07a
Phegan, Mary VII–118a
Phelps, Anson G. (mer., philan.) III–24b
Phelps, Oliver (land speculator) IV–98b; V–88b, 276a
Phelps Dodge Corporation II–223b; V–102a
Phelps–Gorham Company V–91a
PHELPS–GORHAM PURCHASE (1788) **V–276a**; I–347b, 375b; V–88b, 91a, 463b
Phelps–Stokes fund II–401b
Phenix Cheese Company II–282a
Phenol II–7a; V–328a
Phenology II–390b
Phenylalanine IV–391a
PHI BETA KAPPA SOCIETY V–276b; VI–44a; VII–300b
PHILADELPHIA (Pa.) **V–277a**; II–41a, 350b; V–83a, 246b, 247a,b; VII–82b, 159a
Academy of Natural Sciences IV–348b
Adams Express Company I–10a
African Methodist Episcopal Church I–23a
agricultural societies III–151b
Allegheny wagoners VII–216a
Arabian gold I–151a
archives I–169a
Argo polar expediton V–336b
Associators I–208a
auction galleries II–100a
balloon ascent I–248a
Bartram's Garden I–348a; V–326a
bathtubs I–274b
Bible I–294b
billeting I–297a
book publishing I–333b, 334a
bootlegging I–339b
bossism I–343a
bridges I–363b
canals II–322a
candlemaking VI–372b
capital market II–255b
Carpenters' Hall I–459b
carpet manufacture I–460a
Catholic diocese I–467a
Centennial Exposition I–483a; IV–468b
central trade council IV–61b
chair manufacture I–490a,b
charitable organizations III–82a,b
chemical industry II–5b, 10a–b
circus II–40a
citrus industry II–43b
city council II–44a
city government II–44a
city planning II–45a,b
Civil War V–56b
clearinghouse II–73b
Cliveden IV–472a
colonial commerce II–119a; V–57a
colonial labor IV–60a
colonial vehicles VII–99b
Constitutional Convention I–126a
Continental Congress II–305b, 308b; VI–113b
Continental navy VI–128a
Convention of 1787 II–167a, 192b
crime commission II–263b
criminal gangs II–258a
dairy industry II–279b
Deism III–112a
directory II–343b
domestic trade VII–83a
education of handicapped III–248b
elevated railway II–428a
epidemics II–33b, 454b
Episcopal Church II–455a
Fairmont Park I–483a
fall line II–485a
Father Divine III–254a–b
federal capital I–208b
federal records center III–284b
ferries III–11b
flour III–42b, 45a
Forbes Road V–224b
Fort Mifflin IV–337b
Fourth of July III–87b, 88a
Franklin Institute III–99a
Franklin's Academy I–5b
Friends' Public School II–395a
furniture III–134b, 135b, 138a
fur trade III–141b, 403a
Genêt mission III–159b
Genius of Universal Emancipation III–162b
graphic arts V–413b
graving dock II–375a–b
Hicksites III–274a
homeopathy III–293b
hospitals I–467b; III–306b; IV–275a; V–251b
immigrants III–334b
Independence Hall III–353b
Indian factory system II–480a
Indian Queen III–391b; VII–2b
industrial research III–408a–b
inflation VI–117b
insurance business III–426b, 427a–b, 430a
Jacobin Clubs III–487b
Jay Cooke and Company II–218b
Knights of Labor IV–52a
Lafayette's visit IV–84a
Lancaster Pike IV–89b
land speculation IV–100b
learned societies IV–126a,b
Liberty Bell IV–142b
Library Company II–108a
Lincoln Highway IV–156a
locomotive building IV–175b
lotteries IV–190b–91a
Main Line canal V–249b
mapmaking I–462b
meat-packing IV–170a
mechanics' institutes IV–281b
medical education IV–283a
Military Order of the Loyal Legion IV–343a
minstrel organization IV–359b
mint II–95a; IV–143a, 359b, 360a
mortality IV–149b, 150a
motion pictures IV–417b
museums II–101a
National Gazette IV–463b; V–69b
National Union Convention IV–472b
natural history museum I–295b, 305a; IV–232a
Naval Home V–11b; VI–336a–b
navy yard IV–62a; V–27b, 29a,b
Neshaminy Creek V–33a
newspapers I–224a; V–69a, 79b
nonimporation agreements V–104a,b
oil refining VI–383a
organized crime II–261b
orphanage I–467b
Pacific Railroad Conventions VI–20b
panic of 1837 V–206b
paving V–230a
Paxton Boys V–231a
Pennsylvania Evening Post and Daily Advertiser V–70b
Pennsylvania Gazette V–68b, 251a
Pennsylvania–Maryland-boundary dispute V–252a
Pennsylvania Railroad IV–177a; V–250a
pewter work VI–290b
pharmaceutical industry V–273b
Phoenix V–289a
Pine Barren speculations V–315b
Pittsburgh trade V–321b–22a
plantation trade V–325a
Poor Richard's Almanac V–358b
porcelain III–183b
Porcupine's Gazette V–366a
postal service V–371a, 372a
post roads V–375a
pottery V–379b
Presbyterianism V–391a–b
prices V–404a,b, 405a,b
printing presses V–413a
private schools VI–228b
Protective War Claims Association V–438b
Quakers V–470a,b;

VII–201b
race riots I–31b, 32a; VI–8a
railroad rate wars VI–23a
railroads VI–25a,b, 33b, 36a; VII–101b
red light district II–261a
revolutionary war I–360a, 385a; II–321a, 393a; III–36a, 117b, 179a; IV–35b, 251b, 363a, 397b; V–211b, 253a, 354b; VI–123b, 124a, 128b, 129a, 373a; VII–116a, 165a, 292b, 358b, 361a
ripper legislation VI–144b
Rumseian Society VI–170b
sailing packets V–183b
savings and loan cooperative II–220b
Scotch–Irish VI–240b
Sesquicentennial International Exposition VI–263a
shipbuilding III–413a
shipping IV–309b
ships graveyard II–438b
silk VI–286b
silver work VI–290a
slums VI–313b, 314a
smallpox VI–315b
smuggled goods V–320a
soapmaking VI–324a
Society for the Promotion of Public Schools II–396b
Society Hill II–47b
soda fountains VI–332a
Soldiers and Sailors convention VI–336a
stagecoach lines V–82b; VI–380a
steamboating V–57b; VI–409a
steam engines VI–408b, 409a,b
stock exchange II–469b
street lighting II–413b
street railways VI–418a
subtreasury VI–427a
subway II–428a; VI–429b
sugar industry VI–437a
Sunday schools VI–442b
Tammany society VI–460b
tea party VII–16a–b
tea trade VII–15a, 17a
theater VII–46b, 47a
triangular trade VII–119b, 120a
typefounding V–411b
Underground Railroad VII–138b
United States VII–153a
University of Pennsylvania V–248b
urban renewal VI–86b
veterinary medicines VII–175b–76a,b
Walnut Street jail V–415a
War of 1812 VII–235b
Washington's inaugural III–351a
water supply VI–212a; VII–258a–b, 259a
Whiskey Rebellion VII–290a
William Penn Charter School II–395a
Wistar parties VII–309a
workingmen's parties IV–61b; VII–322a
yellow fever I–410a; VII–158a, 355b
Philadelphia (gunboat) III–234a
***PHILADELPHIA*, CAPTURE OF THE** (1803) **V–278b**; I–266a; III–464b; V–423b
Philadelphia, College, Academy, and Charitable School of II–114b
Philadelphia, College and Academy of II–10a
Philadelphia, College of II–395a; IV–283a
Philadelphia, Germantown and Norristown Railroad VI–25a, 36a
Philadelphia, Synod of (1729) VII–279a
Philadelphia Academy of Natural Sciences III–29b
Peary's explorations V–240b
Philadelphia and Lancaster Turnpike IV–89b; V–247a; VI–153a; VII–165a
Philadelphia and Reading Railroad IV–63a, 392a; V–208a; VI–36a
Philadelphia *Aurora*. *See Aurora*
Philadelphia Ballet II–288b
Philadelphia Baptist Association I–264b
Philadelphia Centennial Exposition (1876). *See* Centennial Exposition
Philadelphia Coal and Iron Company IV–392a
Philadelphia College of Pharmacy. *See* College of Pharmacy
Philadelphia Contributorship for the Insurance of Houses from Loss by Fire II–220a; III–430a
PHILADELPHIA CORDWAINERS' CASE (1806) **V–278b**; IV–61a; VI–103b, 223b, 418a–19a
Philadelphia County (Pa.) V–277b
Philadelphia Daily American Advertiser (news.) VII–251b
Philadelphia Exposition (1876). *See* Centennial Exposition
PHILADELPHIA GAS RING V–279a; VI–142a
Philadelphia General Hospital III–306b
Philadelphia Inquirer (news.) V–76b
Philadelphia Mars Iron Works VI–409a
Philadelphia Museum of Art II–102b, 103b, 105a; III–137b; IV–220b; V–278a; VI–242b
PHILADELPHIA RIOTS (1844) **V–279a**; I–467b; V–2b
Philadelphia Savings Fund Society I–263b
Philadelphia smelter (Colo.) VI–316b
Philadelphia Society for Promoting Agriculture I–41a
Philadelphia State House IV–142b; V–277a
Philadelphia Stock Exchange III–466a
Philadelphia Symphony Orchestra V–278a–b
Philadelphia Tribune (news.) V–76a
Philadelphia Yearly Meeting of New Jersey and Pennsylvania Friends I–135a
Philadelphia Zoological Garden VII–370b
Philadelphische Zeitung (news.) V–75b
PHILANTHROPIST (news.) **V–279a**; II–37b
PHILANTHROPY AND BENEVOLENCE V–279b
Baltimore I–250a
Carnegie gifts III–79b
charity organization movement I–494b
endowed foundations III–82a
hookworm research III–298b
hospitals III–306b
learned societies IV–127a–b
Mayo Foundation IV–279a
medical research IV–286a–b
medical schools IV–296a
Mellon Institute IV–300b
New York City V–83a
Peabody Fund V–231b
physiology research V–307b
poor relief VI–72b
Rockefeller gifts III–80a
Russell Sage Foundation VI–176b
Sailor's Snug Harbor VI–186b
Salvation Army VI–204a
Sanitary Commission VI–211a
Sheffield Scientific School VI–273b
Shriners III–109b
Smithsonian IV–464b; VI–318b
social welfare VI–327a–b
taxation VII–9b–10a
Philco Corporation II–421b; III–504a
Philip (Indian). *See* King Philip's War
Philip V (k.) I–83b
Philip, Fort (La.) V–63b
PHILIPPI, SKIRMISH AT (1861) **V–281a**
Philippine–American War. *See* Philippine Insurrection
Philippine Commission, second. *See* Taft Commission
Philippine Constabulary V–281b
Philippine Economic Adjustment Act (1939) VII–135b
Philippine Government Act (1902) V–283a
PHILIPPINE INSURRECTION (1899–1902) **V–281a**; II–314a, 324a; III–347b; V–282b; VI–362b; VII–190b
Afro–American troops IV–340a
anti–imperialists I–132a
army strength I–185b
atrocities I–219a–b
capture of Aguinaldo III–133a
desertions II–335b
guerrillas III–231a–b
marines IV–252b
military roads VI–156a
opposition in U.S. V–235a,b
U.S. Navy V–20a
volunteers VII–208a
PHILIPPINE ISLANDS V–282a; III–425a
acquisition I–126b; II–475a–b; III–68b; VI–360b
Alaska–Pacific–Yukon Exposition I–81a
annexation III–347a,b; V–158a
anti–imperialists I–132a
army occupation I–188a
Battle Fleet cruise I–276b
Chinese laborers II–29b
Dominican missions II–362b
federal mint IV–360a
fortifications III–78b
Franciscans III–94b
Hawaiian labor force III–263a
immigration to U.S. III–337b, 341a,b
Korean War IV–55b
Louisiana Purchase Exposition IV–198a
Manila Conference IV–239b
migration to Hawaii III–264b
military medical research IV–291b
missionary activity IV–364b
opium control II–374b
Organic Act IV–7a
Panama–Pacific Exposition V–203b
Southeast Asia Treaty Organization VI–350b
Spanish–American War I–185b; IV–239a–b; VI–361b, 362a–b
Spanish cession VII–112a
steel VII–89b
Taft Commission VI–456b
Taft–Katsura Memorandum VI–457b
taxation VII–13b
territorial status III–424b
transpacific cable I–401a

PHILIPPINE ISLANDS (cont.)
Treaty of Paris V–215a
Tydings–McDuffie Act VII–135b
United Nations Declaration VII–151b
Vietnam War VII–182b
World War II I–59b, 60a, 459a; II–26a, 315a, 425a; IV–138a, 157b, 253a; V–21a, 213b, 239b, 242b, 285; VII–1b–2a, 335a, 336b, 337a, 342a, 343a
Yap mandate VII–353b
Philippine Rehabilitation Act (1946) V–284b
Philippine Revolution (1896–97) V–282b
PHILIPPINE SEA, BATTLE OF THE (1944) **V–285b**; I–55b, 56a; V–21a; VI–198b; VII–343a
Task Force 58 VII–1b–2a
Philippine Trade Act (1946) V–284b
Philips, A. W. (econ.) VII–141a
Philips, John F. (jur.) VI–87a
Philips, William (off.)
Yorktown VII–360b
Philipsborough (N.Y.) III–313a; V–286a
Philipse, Adolphe (landowner) V–286a
Philipse, Frederick (mer.). *See* Philipse's Patent
Philipse family IV–92a, 200a
PHILIPSE'S PATENT V–286a; III–313a
Philips Viaduct I–363b
Philistine (mag.) III–150b
Phil Kearny, Fort (Wyo.). *See* Kearny, Fort Phil
Phillips, Alonzo D. IV–274a
Phillips, David Graham (au.) IV–424b
Phillips, E. W. (eng.) II–154b
Phillips, Gifford II–106b
Phillips, Isaac (nav. off.) I–251b
Phillips, Major I–465b
Phillips, Portugee (frontiersman) IV–33b
Phillips, Wendell (ref.) II–487b; IV–267b; V–161a
Phillips, William (off.) I–194a
Phillips Andover Academy II–397a–b; IV–267a; VI–228b
Phillips Exeter Academy II–397a–b; VI–228b
Phillips Petroleum Company v. *Wisconsin* (1954) V–5b–6a
Phillips v. *Savage* (1737) I–145a; III–464a
Philology IV–2b, 2b
Philo Parsons (steamer) I–280a
Philosophical Hall (Philadelphia) VII–309b
Philosophical toy II–413a, 419a
Philosophical Transactions of the Royal Society of London VI–235a
PHILOSOPHY V–286a
Eastern V–171b–72a
Harvard University III–260a
laissez–faire IV–85b
Locke, John IV–173b
physics V–294a
political theories V–350a
pragmatism V–386b
psychology V–441a–b, 442a
theosophy VII–51b
transcendentalism VII–97b
Philosophy and Humanistic Studies Council. *See* International Council for Philosophy and Humanistic Studies
Philosphical Enquiry Into the Origin of Our Ideas of the Sublime and the Beautiful V–188a
Phipps Psychiatric Clinic IV–306a
Phips, William (col. gov.) I–346a; IV–265b; V–100b, 369b
Fort William Henry V–243b
King William's War IV–49b
Quebec attack VI–1b
Phnom Penh (Cambodia) VII–186b
"Phocion" (pseud.) VII–116b
Phoebe (frigate) II–463b
Phoenicia
citrus trade II–43a
exploration in America II–341a
exploration of America I–96b
maritime law I–14b
Phoenix (Ariz.) I–172b; II–130b; VI–101a
Phoenix (missile) I–57b
PHOENIX **(steamship) V–289a**
Phoenix, John. *See* Derby, George Horatio
PHOENIXIANA **V–289a**
Phoenix Theatre (N.Y.C.) VII–51a
Phonautograph V–289a
Phong Saly (Laos) III–160a
PHONOGRAPH V–289a; I–396a; II–424b
imports VII–90a
records V–327b
Phosphate III–16a–b, 164a; VI–48b
Florida III–40a
ores III–15b
public lands V–445b
rock III–17b
Phosphorus II–6b, 357b, 423a; III–15b, 16a
matches IV–274a, 294a
Phossy jaw IV–274b, 294a
Photius (patriarch) II–386b
Photochemistry II–12a
Photoelectricity I–212a
Photoelectric tubes II–424b
Photoengraving IV–222a; V–77a
Photogrammetry V–133b
PHOTOGRAPHIC INDUSTRY V–291a; III–48a
collodion V–327b–28a
Eastman Kodak III–409a–b
film II–7a; V–328b
Fort Lee IV–131b
magazines IV–222a
motion pictures IV–416b
newspapers V–77a
tintype VII–62b
Photographic typesetting V–412b
Photographs
censorship II–277a
copyright II–224b
daguerreotype II–279a
Photography
aerial I–236a, 248a, 463b, 464a; V–133b
agriculture I–46b
celestial I–211b
telegraphy VII–19a
television VII–21a
Photography, aerial. *See* Aerial photography
Photography, celestial. *See* Celestial photography
PHOTOGRAPHY, MILITARY V–293a; VI–286a
Photometry V–131b
Photon V–302b, 303b
Photorealism V–193a
Photostat machine I–397a
Photosynthesis I–303b
Phototubes VII–21a
Phouma, Souvanna IV–107a,b
PHRENOLOGY V–293b; V–441b; VI–237a
Phthisis. *See* Tuberculosis
Phuoc Long province (Viet.) VII–185a
Phyfe, Duncan (cabinetmaker) III–135b, 138a
Phylloxera III–129a; VII–305b
Phylogeny I–349a
Physical Geography of the Sea III–28b, 233a; IV–317a; V–133b
Physical Review (jour.) V–295a, 303a
Physicians
Knights of Labor IV–52b, 64a
Physick, Philip Syng (physic.) V–251b
PHYSICS V–294a
Applied Physics Laboratory IV–3b
Bell Labs I–287b
electric circuit analysis II–38b
electronics II–423a
International Geophysical Year III–453b
microwave technology IV–333a
Nobel Prizes V–99a,b, 100a
vacuum tubes VII–163a
Yale University VII–351a
Physics, American Institute of. *See* American Institute of Physics
PHYSICS, HIGH ENERGY V–296b
vacuum tubes VII–164a
PHYSICS, NUCLEAR V–297b; III–156a; V–295b–96a, 296b–97a
cyclotron II–278a
hydrogen bomb III–324a
Lawrence Radiation Laboratory IV–119a
Los Alamos research center V–60a
Manhattan Project IV–237b
masers and lasers IV–262a
PHYSICS, SOLID–STATE V–303a; II–39a, 425b, 425b
masers IV–262b
microwave technology IV–333a
semiconductors VI–259a
telephone VII–20b
Physiocrats IV–85a
PHYSIOLOGY V–306a; I–303a
American Indian III–355a–b
autecology II–392a
Marine Biological Laboratory IV–250b–51a
Nobel Prizes V–100a
Noble Prizes V–99a
parapsychology V–213b
psychology V–441b
research IV–285b
Rockefeller Foundation VI–158a
Physiomedical practitioners IV–288a
Phytogeographical surveys II–391b
Piankashaw (Indians) I–501b; III–24b
land grants IV–4a
Treaty of Greenville III–383a
Vincennes cession VII–189b
Piano. *See* Music
Piano Quartet (comp.) IV–439a
Piano Sonata no. 2 (comp.) IV–439a
Piano Variations (comp.) IV–439a
Piasa I–91b
PIAVE RIVER, OPERATIONS ON (1918) **V–307b**; I–102a
Picabia, Francis (paint.) II–104b
Picasso, Pablo (paint.) II–104b, 105a; V–193a
Picatinny (N.J.) I–196b
Piccard, Paul (eng.) V–92a
Pick, Lewis A. (off.) I–387a
Pickaway County (Ohio) II–25b; IV–179a
Pickaway Plains I–499a; II–381a

PICKAWILLANEE (Ohio) **V–308a**; V–140a
Pickens, Andrew (off.) II–251a; IV–44b; V–222a; VI–347a–b, 351b
PICKENS, FORT (Fla.) **V–308a**; II–61b, 161a
Civil War V–254b; VI–216a
Powhatan incident V–386a
Pickerel III–51a
Pickering, Charles (nat.) VI–90b; VII–299a
Pickering, Edward C. (astron.) I–211b
Pickering, Fort (Tenn.) II–22a
Pickering, Timothy (states.) VI–126a
Alien and Sedition Acts I–86b
embargo of 1807 II–437a
French privateers III–121a
Rose intrigue VI–164b
secession VI–250a
War and Ordnance Board VII–226b
PICKETING V–308b
AFL IV–65b
antiinjunction law VII–121a
boycotting I–356b
federal regulations IV–74b
injunctions III–419a
legal recognition IV–69a
National Labor Relations Act IV–467a
Norris–La Guardia Anti-Injunction Law V–112a
woman's rights movements VII–312b
Pickett, George E. (off.) III–33b; V–309a; VII–197b
Battle of Five Forks V–265a
Battle of Gettysburg III–176a
Pickett, John T. (dipl.) II–65b
Pickett–Pettigrew charge. *See* Pickett's Charge
PICKETT'S CHARGE (1863) **V–309a**; III–176a; VII–197b
Pickford, Mary (act.) IV–417b
Pickles III–55a
Pickling II–219a; III–54b
Pickman, Benjamin (off.) VI–199a
Pickpockets II–260a
Pick–Sloan Plan VI–147a
"Pick's Pike" I–387a
Pickwick Landing Dam III–323b
Pic–Nic (paint.) V–189a
Pico, Andrés (off.) I–403a, 409b; VI–210b, 214a
Pico della Mirandola, Giovanni (philos.) III–316b
Picolata, Fort (Fla.) III–42b
Pico Peak (Vt.) VI–101a
Picpus Cemetery (Fr.) IV–84a
Picquet, François (miss.) IV–85a; V–139b
Pictorial Elementary Spelling Book VII–266a
Picturesque style (landscape arch.) IV–96b, 97a
Picuris (N.Mex.) III–367b; V–460a
Pidgin's ranch III–187b
PIECES OF EIGHT V–309a; II–94b; V–424a; VI–366a
PIECEWORK V–309b
clothing industry II–81b–82a, 83a
women VII–313a
Piedmont (Va.) VI–275a
Piedmont Airlines II–347a
PIEDMONT REGION V–310a; II–485a; VII–268a
climate observations IV–316b
De Soto expedition II–336b
reports V–117a
settlement V–115b; VII–193a, 283a
tidewater VII–58b
timberlands VII–59b
tobacco VII–66b
wheat III–43a
Piedras Negras (Mex.) VI–274b
Piegan (Indians) III–365a
Jesuit missions III–500a,b
massacre of I–219a
military federation I–311a
trade I–206a
See also Blackfoot
PIEGAN WAR (1869–70) **V–310a**
Piel, Gerard (ed.) VI–231b
Pierce, Franklin (pres.) II–175 (table); V–394b, 395 (table)
campaign of 1852 V–54a
Compromise of 1850 II–150a
Cuba II–268a; V–174b
elected I–420b
Free-State party IV–28b
Gadsden Purchase III–145b, 230a
Galápagos Islands III–146b
Kansas–Nebraska Act IV–29a–b, 30a–b
Kansas struggle V–51b
land grants for railways III–450a
social legislation VI–327b
Pierce, George (hort.) III–151b
Pierce, Henry A. (dipl.) VI–186b
Pierce, John D. (educ.) II–397a
Pierce, John R. (phys.) VII–164a
Pierce, Richard (print.) V–68a
Pierce, Sarah (educ.) VI–229b
Pierce v. *Society of the Sisters of the Holy Names of Jesus and Mary* (1925). *See* Oregon Parochial School Case
Pierie, George W. (print.) V–251a
Piermont (N.Y.) VI–34a
Piernas, Pedro (col. offi.) IV–195b; VI–194a
Pierpont, Francis H. (law., gov.) VII–281b
Pierpont limner V–186a
Pierre IV–162a
Pierre (S.Dak.) IV–380b; VI–438b
PIERRE, FORT (S.Dak.) **V–310a**; II–34a, 284a; III–256a
La Vérendrye plate IV–118a
Pierre Chouteau, Fort. *See* Pierre, Fort
Pierre's Hole (Idaho) III–143a, 291a; VII–104a
PIERRE'S HOLE, BATTLE OF (1832) **V–310b**
Pierson, Abraham (cler.) V–41a; VII–351a
Pierson, Thomas (surv.) II–322b
Pieta (sculpture) V–89b
PIETISM V–310b; I–361a
colonial society II–125b
Lutheran churches IV–206b
Moravian Brethern IV–409b
Pennsylvania V–470a
Piety, societies of V–310b
Pig clubs III–84b
Pigeon III–150a
Pigeon Cove (Mass.) I–447a
Pigeon River III–209a
Pigeon service, army VI–286a
Piggly Wiggly Stores VI–258a
Piggybacking (transport) IV–420a; VI–30b, 31a–b
Pig iron I–319a; III–77a, 469b, 470b, 471 (table), 472a, 473a
Pigments II–233b; III–13b
lead V–102b
Pigs. *See* Hogs
Pigtails III–239b
Pigwacket (Maine) IV–199a
"Pig War." *See* San Juan, Seizure of
Pike (fish) III–51a
Pike, Albert (law., off.) II–357a; III–400a; V–222a
Pike, Nicholaus (educ.) VI–227a
Pike, Zebulon M. (off., expl.) I–170a; II–127b; III–213b, 488a; VI–47b; VII–74b
Fort Snelling VI–322b
Leech Lake Indian council IV–131b
Natchitoches IV–457a
Twin Cities VII–133b
York campaign VII–358b
See also Pike's Peak; Pike's Southwestern Expedition; Pike's Upper Mississippi Expedition
Pike County (Mo.) IV–1a
Pike County (Pa.) VII–220b
"Piker" IV–1a
Pike's Island II–490a; IV–355b; VI–295b
PIKES PEAK V–311a; II–264a; IV–186b; VII–268a, 271b
Arkansas River route I–174b
botanized I–349a
James expedition III–488a
Jefferson Territory III–497a
Leavenworth and Pikes Peak Express IV–129b
PIKES PEAK GOLD RUSH V–311a; II–128a; III–191b; IV–129b; V–437a; VI–160b
Arkansas River route I–174b
Auraria I–224a
Hannibal and Saint Joseph Railroad III–250b
overland freighting V–177a
placer mining V–322b–23a
Smoky Hill Trail VI–320a,b
"Pikes Peak Humbug" V–311b
"Pikes Peak or Bust" V–311a
PIKE'S SOUTHWESTERN EXPEDITION (1806–07) **V–311b**; III–88a; VII–74b, 271a–b
Great American Desert III–213b
Great Plains III–220b
Kansas IV–25b
Oklahoma V–148a
Rocky Mountains VI–160b
Santa Fe VI–215a
PIKE'S UPPER MISSISSIPPI EXPEDITION (1805–06) **V–312a**; III–468a; V–388a; VII–74b, 271a
Falls of Saint Anthony VI–187a
Minnesota IV–355b
Sioux land purchase VI–295b
Pilcher, Joshua (fur trader) IV–130a; VI–196a
Pilcomayo River III–265b
Pilgrim (blimp) II–345b
Pilgrim Hall (Mass.) I–447a; VI–205b
PILGRIMS V–312b
Brownists I–371b
Cape Cod settlement I–447a
cattle I–471a
colonization II–123b
Council for New England II–242a
dress II–370b–71a
food III–51a,b
lack of capital I–449a
land grants VII–95a
Mayflower IV–278b
Mayflower Compact III–132b; IV–278b
Mourt's Relation IV–423b

PILGRIMS (cont.)
New Plymouth Colony I–16a; IV–264b–65a; V–64b, 324a
Plymouth Rock V–334a
trade IV–37a,b
trapping VII–104b
Weston's settlement VII–279a
Pilgrim Society II–98b
Pilgrim's Progress IV–424b–25a
Pillager band IV–131b
Pillar-and-scroll style furniture III–138b
Pillbox hat II–372b
PILLORY V–313b; V–465a
Pillow, Fort (Tenn.)
Civil War IV–374b, 375a
PILLOW, FORT, "MASSACRE" (1864) **V–313b**; IV–339b
Pillow, Gideon J. (off.) I–288a, 494b; IV–391b; VI–241a
Pillsbury, Charles A. (flour miller) III–43b
Pillsbury, John E. (nav. off.) III–233a; V–134b
Pillsbury Company III–44a, 45a
Pillsbury Flour Mills III–45b
Pillsbury–Washburn Flour Mills Company III–45a
Pilmoor, Joseph (cler.) IV–318a
Pilot Ace (computer) II–156a
PILOT KNOB, BATTLE OF (1864) **V–314a**; V–403a
Pilots
World War I IV–83b
PIMA (Indians) **V–314a**; I–171b, 172a; III–179b, 369a, 396b
Jesuit missions III–499a, 500b
national monument V–217b
Oatman captives V–129b
scalping VI–224b
wine VII–65b
PIMA REVOLT (1751) **V–314b**; VII–125b
Pimento II–453a
Pimeria Alto V–314b
Pi meson V–302b
PIMITOUI, FORT (Ill.) **V–315a**; II–257b; VI–195a
See also Saint Louis, Fort
Pinchebeck, Alys VI–205b
Pinchot, Gifford (pol.) I–247b–48a; II–187b, 416b; III–73b, 75a; V–427b, 450b
conservation IV–95b, 96a
public lands V–446a
"Tennis Cabinet" VII–31a
Vare case VII–167b
wildlife preservation VII–298a
Pinckney, Charles (law., dipl.) VI–359b
executive privilege III–465b
free blacks VI–347b
Pinckney Plan V–315a
sectionalism VI–253b
Pinckney, Charles Cotesworth (states.) VI–342a
campaign of 1800 I–417b; III–494b
Constitution I–261b–62a; II–193a, 196a, 203b, 478a
Franco-American misunderstanding III–95b, 96b
XYZ Affair IV–347a; VII–347b
Pinckney, Eliza Lucas (Mrs. Charles) III–405b; VI–347a
Pinckney, Thomas (dipl., pol.)
campaign of 1796 I–417a, 475a
See also Pinckney's Treaty II–342b
PINCKNEY PLAN V–315a
PINCKNEY'S TREATY (1795) **V–315a**; I–126a; II–167b, 342b, 432a; III–67b, 232b; V–101a; VI–150b, 359a, 366b; VII–111b, 260a, 270a, 276b
Adams–Onís Treaty I–10b
Carondelet intrigue I–459b
Dunbar's Line II–381a
Florida boundary IV–368a; VII–353b
Fort Panmure V–210b
Georgia boundary III–171b
Louisiana IV–193b
Mississippi River IV–372b, 373b
Natchez IV–455a
right of deposit II–333a; IV–196b
U.S. boundaries III–41b, 42a
Pindray, Marquis de (filibuster) III–23a
Pine II–5a; III–72b, 74b; VI–395 (table)
furniture III–134a
Michigan IV–331b
naval stores V–14b
sawmills VI–223a
timberlands VII–59a, 60a
Pine, Robert Edge (paint.) V–188a
Pineapple III–52b, 129a, 381a; V–461b
Hawaii III–264a
Pinebark beetle III–74b
PINE BARREN SPECULATIONS V–315b
PINE BLUFF, BATTLES AT (1863, 1865) **V–316a**
Pine cone and tassel VI–394 (table)
Pine Coulie, Battle of. *See* Kaposia, Battle of
Piñeda, Alonzo Alvares de (expl.) I–71a
Pine Mountain (Ga.) I–348a
Pine Plains (N.Y.) IV–169a
Pine Point (Maine) VI–184a
Pine Ridge (S.Dak.)
Messiah War IV–316a
Pine Ridge Agency (S.Dak.) IV–316a
Pine Ridge campaign (1890–91) I–310a, 314a
Pine Ridge Indian War. *See* Messiah War
Pine Ridge Reservation (S.Dak.) III–397a
Pinet, François (miss.) II–17a
PINE TREE FLAG V–316a; III–35a
PINE TREE SHILLING V–316a; II–94b; IV–393b
Pine Tree State VI–394 (table)
Pine weevil III–74b
Pinewood torches IV–152b
Piney Fork (Wyo.) IV–33b
Piney woods people II–253a
Pingree, Hazen (ref.) IV–427b
Ping-yang (Kor.). *See* Pyongyang
Pink bollworm I–328a
Pinkerton, Allan (detective) I–10a; VI–373b
Pinkerton Detective Agency IV–63a
Homestead strike IV–66a
industrial espionage II–462b
Molly Maguires IV–392a
Reno gang VII–97b
star route frauds VI–387a
Pinkney, William (law., pol.) IV–402b, 449a; V–120b, 161b
PINKSTER V–316b
Pinnacles National Monument V–217b
Pinon (nut pine) VI–394 (table)
Piomingo (Indian) II–22a, 23a
Pion. *See* Pi meson
"Pioneer" (railroad car) V–463a
Pioneer (submarine) VI–422b
Pioneer 3 (satellite) IV–333a
Pioneer Hi-Bred Corn Company II–226a
Pioneer International Hotel II–348b
PIONEERS V–316b
buffalo trails III–387a
farming IV–103a
frontier III–126a
frontier family II–487b
Independence Rock III–354a
jumping-off places IV–20b
Kentucky settlements IV–40a
log cabins IV–179b
McGuffey's Readers IV–213a
mountain men IV–422a
movers IV–423b
Oregon Trail V–168a
Pawnee Rock V–230b
prairie V–387a
prairie schooner V–389b
sectionalism VI–253b
slang VI–299b–300a
sod house VI–332b
timberlands VII–59b
West VII–267b
Wilderness Road VII–296b
women VII–313a, 316a
Pioneers, The IV–161b
Pioneer's Home (Alaska) I–77b
PIONEER STAGE LINE V–317b
Pioneer Village (Mass.) VI–199b
PIOUS FUND CONTROVERSY V–318a; III–456b; V–262a
PIPE, INDIAN V–318a; III–365b, 381a; VII–65a, 70a, 223b
Abnaki I–2b
council III–378b
Pipelines VII–84a,b
Interstate Commerce Commission III–458a
Kansas IV–26b
natural gas V–5a–b
PIPELINES, EARLY V–318b; V–269b; VI–383a,b
Pipe Line Under the Ocean. *See* Pluto
Piper, Leonora E. (medium) V–213a
Piper aircraft I–52b, 188b
Piper Cherokee (plane) II–347a
Pipe smoking VII–67a
Pipe Spring National Monument V–217b
PIPE STAVES V–319a
Pipestone National Monument V–217b
Piqua (Ohio) V–308a, 319b
PIQUA, BATTLE OF (1780) **V–319b**; II–25b
PIRACY V–319b; II–258a; V–419b
admiralty courts I–14b
aerial hijacking III–276b
Algiers IV–251b
Arabian gold I–151a
armed merchantmen IV–313a
Bahama Islands I–243b
Barbary pirates IV–299b
Barbary Wars I–266a
Bowie knife I–355a
buccaneers I–374a
Cave-in-Rock I–476a
colonies II–275b
congressional powers II–200a
Fajardo case II–484a
freedom of the seas III–106a–b
Galveston Island III–148b
gunboats III–234b
Laffite, Jean I–279a, 492a
Louisburg IV–192a
Louisiana I–265b
marine operations IV–252a
Mason band IV–263a
Napoleonic Wars III–118b
North Carolina I–447b, 458a; V–115a

slave trade II–390a; VI–311a–b, 321b
Spanish Inquisition III–420a
U.S. Navy V–19b, 29a
visit and search VII–205a
West Indies IV–416a
Pirie, N. W. (biochem.) IV–389a
Piro (Indians) III–211a
Pirogue I–445b; IV–372b, 381b; VI–148a
Piroplasmosis. *See* Cattle Tick Fever
Pisa (It.) III–201a
Piscataqua River I–32a; III–200a; V–53b
Gorges grant IV–225b
Laconia grant IV–82b
logging VI–149a
New Hampshire boundary IV–264a
revolutionary war V–54a
sawmills VI–222b
settlement VI–417b
Piscataway (Indians) III–499a
PISTOLE (coin) **V–320b**; II–365b
Pistols IV–432b
Civil War manufacture II–67b
Colt revolver IV–430b
dueling II–376b
interchangeable manufacture III–441a
Piston, Walter (comp.) IV–439a
"PIT" (Chicago Board of Trade) **V–320b**
Pitcairn, John (off.) I–383a; IV–137a
Pitch II–140b; V–14b
See also Naval Stores
Pitchers (pottery) III–183b
PITHOLE (Pa.) **V–321a**; V–269b, 318b, 319a
Pithouses I–117b
Pitkin, Henry (watchmaker) II–78b
Pitkin, James (watchmaker) II–78b
Pitney, Mahlon (jur.) VI–446a
PITT, FORT (Pa.) **V–321a**; III–188a, 330a,b; V–143a, 146a, 246b
coal mine II–85a
Continental army I–183b
Croghan's expedition VI–285a
Dunmore's War II–381b
Fort Bedford I–282b
Fort Fayette II–497b
French and Indian War I–389a; IV–154a
Pontiac's War I–353b–54a; II–265b, 337b; V–357a
revolutionary war I–369a; II–183b–84a; III–179a, 400b; VI–124a, 438a; VII–303a
Virginia's capture V–253a
Wayne's expedition I–190b
Pitt, William, the Elder (states.) IV–161b; V–187b, 321a,b; VI–111a; VII–14b
Declaratory Act II–309b
French and Indian War II–126b; III–116a,b
Revenue Act of 1767 VII–80b
sea power VI–248a
Pitt, William, the Younger (states.) III–493b; VI–114a
Pittman, Key (pol.) V–40a; VII–324a
Pittman, Phillip (cartog.) VII–74a
PITTMAN ACT (1918) **V–321b**; I–302a
Pitt River VI–185b
Pitts, Hiram (mfr.) III–43a; VII–55b
Pitts, John (mfr.) III–43a; VII–55b
Pittsburg (N.H.) III–401b–02a
PITTSBURGH (Pa.) **V–321b**; III–255b; V–143a; VII–159a
air pollution VII–158b
Allegheny wagoners VII–216a
arsenal IV–432b–33a
baseball I–271a
Bethel Community I–293a
bridges I–364b–65a, 378b
broadcasting II–424a
Civil War naval mortars IV–413b
directory II–343b
domestic trade VII–83a, 84a
Federation of Organized Trades and Labor Unions IV–65a
floods III–37a
Forbes Road III–59a
Fort Fayette II–497b
Fort Pitt V–321a
French and Indian War III–115a, 211b
frontier posts V–246b
galley boats III–147b
Gist exploration III–182a
glassmaking III–185a
Hannastown III–250a
Indian trade I–278a
iron and steel II–18b; III–12a, 470b, 473b; V–247b
Lincoln Highway IV–156a
Main Line canal V–249b–50a
medicinal petroleum IV–44a
mountain passes V–224a–b
New Orleans V–63a
oil refining VI–383a
pack trains V–184a
Pennsylvania and Ohio Canal V–249b, 250a
Pennsylvania Railroad V–250a, 277b
Pennsylvania–Virginia boundary dispute II–381b; V–253a
Pontiac's War I–389a
post road V–375a
radio VI–15b
railroads VI–25a,b, 36a; VII–100b, 101b
railroad strike of 1877 IV–63b; VI–38b
Raystown Path VI–49a
revolutionary war I–369a; V–322b
riots I–32a
shipbuilding VI–148a
Soldiers and Sailors convention VI–336a
stagelines VI–380a
steamboats VI–406b, 408b
steam engines VI–409a,b
Sunday schools VI–442b
textiles III–412a
Wheeling Bridge Case VII–288a
Whiskey Rebellion VII–290a
See also Fort Duquesne
Pittsburgh (gunboat) II–384a; III–478b
PITTSBURGH, INDIAN TREATY AT (1775) **V–322a**
Pittsburgh, University of IV–300b, 301a
Pittsburgh and Lake Erie Railroad VI–35b
Pittsburgh and Steubenville Railroad I–364a
Pittsburgh Chemical and Physiological Society II–10b
Pittsburgh Couriers (news.) V–76a
PITTSBURGH GAZETTE (news.) **V–322b**; V–70a
"Pittsburgh plus" pricing system III–470b
Pittsburgh Reduction Company I–92a; V–103b
PITTSBURGH RESOLUTIONS (1775) **V–322b**
Pittsburg Landing. *See* Shiloh, Battle of
Pittsfield (Mass.) II–244b
Pittsylvania III–209a
Pitzer, Kenneth (chem.) II–12b
Pizarro, Francisco (expl.) II–336a
PLACER MINING V–322b; III–191a–b; IV–178a; V–437a; VI–364b
Idaho III–328a
Leadville district IV–124a
Montana IV–403a
Pikes Peak V–311b
regulation IV–349b
Placerville (Calif.) V–317b, 318a, 357b; VI–297b–98a
Plagues II–496b; IV–292a
insect I–46a, 486b
Plaidsilks II–371b
PLAIN, FORT (N.Y.) **V–323a**
Plainfield (N.J.) VI–9a
riots I–31b
Plains, Great. *See* Great Plains
Plains Indians II–359a; III–358b, 362b, 363a–65a; VI–6a; VII–147b, 306a
Arapaho I–151b
architecture I–166a
Arikara I–171b
Assiniboine I–206a
Bannock I–264a–b
Blackfoot I–310b, 441a
buckskin III–374a
burial III–376a
camps III–405a
Cheyenne II–16b
Comanche II–133a
Cree II–30b
Dakota II–282b
drums II–291a
Fort Hays III–266b
Fox III–88b
Ghost Dance III–177b; V–4b
"Great Spirit" III–223a
half-breeds III–242b
horse VI–364b
horses II–184b
horse stealing III–305b–06a
medicine III–384b–85a
Oklahoma V–148b
Omaha V–154b
Pan-Indianism V–210b
Pawnee V–230a
Peyote Cult V–272b
pipe V–318a,b
political organization III–391a
pottery III–373b
religion III–392a–b, 393a
reservation population III–396b
scalping VI–224b
sign language VI–286a
Sioux VI–295a
sod house VI–332b
Sun Dance I–167a; II–291a
travois VII–106b
Ute VII–161a, 162b
wars I–190b
Plains of Abraham. *See* Abraham, Plains of
Plainview projectile point III–484b
Planetesimal hypothesis III–167a
Planets, motion of I–211b
Plank canals I–446a
Plankhouses I–166b
PLANK ROADS V–323a; VI–153a
North Carolina V–116a
Right of Way Law VI–140b
PLANNED ECONOMY V–323b
Planned Parenthood Federation of America I–307a,b
Planned Parenthood Physicians, American Association of IV–289a
Planning, city. *See* City Planning
"Planning, Programming, Budgeting" V–136b–37a
Plano culture III–484a,b
PLAN OF 1776 V–323b; III–90a–b; V–440b
Plan of 1784 V–440b
Plan of 1916 V–10a

PLAN OF UNION (1801) **V–324a**; II–170a; V–391b; VII–275a
Plano Manufacturing Company III–454b
Plansifter III–44a
Plans of union, colonial. *See* Colonial Plans of Union
Plant, Henry B. (ind.) III–39b
Plantagenet, Beauchamp V–332b
Plantation government IV–396a
PLANTATIONS V–324a; III–103a–b; IV–102b, 103a
colonial trade IV–242b
Florida III–39a
food III–52a
Indian II–52a
iron III–413b, 472b
Manors IV–241b–42a
millionaire families III–79a
Mount Vernon IV–423a
New Haven Colony V–55b
penal I–489a
rivers VI–149b
tanneries IV–127b
Trelawney VII–114b
Weston's settlement VII–279a
PLANTATION SYSTEM OF THE SOUTH V–324b; I–4a, 36b–37a, 40b; III–126a; IV–102a; VI–174b, 340b, 341a–43a
agricultural workers II–495a
Black Belt I–308b
Civil War II–69b
colonial trade VII–82b
cotton I–38a; VII–45a
Cotton Kingdom II–241a
foreign trade VII–86a
Maryland IV–260b
mules IV–425b–26a
North Carolina V–116a
overseer V–178b
rice VI–136a
Savannah VI–220b
slave churches I–23b
slavery V–422b; VI–304b, 305a,b–06a, 310a
"sold down the river" VI–335b
steam engines VI–409b
sugarcane VI–436a
tidewater region II–485a
Virginia VII–192b
Plant ecology II–390a, 391b, 392a
Planters' Bank (Miss.) VI–96a
Plant integration (ind.) IV–272b–73a
Plants, domesticated II–386a
PLANTS, NATIVE, STUDY OF V–325b; I–348a–50a; III–16a, 28b
Plasmodium (protozoa) IV–229a,b
Plaster industry IV–243a
PLASTICS V–327b; II–6b–7a, 12b; III–410a; IV–244b–45a; V–212a; VI–168a
Bakelite III–409a
building construction I–379a
celluloid III–409a; V–292a
containers II–282b
fashion II–372b
fibers II–9a
furniture III–136b
motion pictures IV–417a
petroleum products V–267b
salt VI–203a
transportation VII–84b
Vinylite V–290b
Plat, Richard VI–239a
Plateau Indians III–362a–63a
art and technology III–373b
"Great Spirit" III–222b
myth and folklore III–386a–b
political organization III–391b
Prophet Dance V–434b
religion III–392b–93a
scalping VI–224b
Plate tectonics III–481a
PLATFORM, PARTY V–328b; I–416a; V–343b
Jacksonian Democracy III–486b
presidential campaigns I–419a–432a
Platform shoes II–372b
Platinum II–224a, 419a–b
Platner, Warren III–137a
Plato's Academy IV–126a
Platt, C. F. (off.) II–484a
Platt, Orville H. (pol.) V–329b
Platt, Thomas Collier (pol.) I–94a, 343b
PLATT AMENDMENT V–329b; I–454a,b; II–269a–b; III–68b, 69a, 231a, 479a; VII–112a
PLATTE BRIDGE FIGHT (1865) **V–330a**
Platte County (Mo.) V–330a
PLATTE PURCHASE (1836) **V–330a**
Platte River III–119b; V–30b
Black Hills War I–313a
bullboats I–380b
Cheyenne Indians II–16b
exploration I–354b
Fort Kearny IV–33b
forty-niners III–82a
French exploration IV–379b–80a
fur trade III–144a; VI–160a; VII–104b–05a
Indians IV–108b
Long's explorations IV–186b
Mallet brothers exploration IV–230a
Mormon migration IV–411b
Oregon Trail V–168b; VI–153b
Overland Trail V–178b
Pawnee V–230b
wagon trains VII–218a
See also North Platte River; South Platte River
PLATTE RIVER TRAIL V–330b; V–225a; VI–215b
Bonneville expedition I–330a
caravans I–452b
gold seekers I–410a
immigrants I–485b
Leavenworth and Pikes Peak Express IV–129b
Muddy Pass V–225a
Pikes Peak gold rush V–311b
Platte Valley V–31a, 177a
Platt National Park V–218 (table)
Plattsburgh (N.Y.) V–390b
War of 1812 III–121a; IV–82a, 87a, 406a
PLATTSBURGH, BATTLE OF (1814) **V–330b**; IV–87a, 212a–b; VII–234b
Plattsburgh Bay (N.Y.) V–331a
Playboy (mag.) IV–222b
Player, Gary (golfer) III–198a
Playfair, William VI–239a
PLAY PARTY V–331a; III–19a
Playwrights' Company VII–50a
Playwrights' Theater (N.Y.C.) V–439b
Playwriting VII–47a
Pleasant, Richard (dancer) II–288b
PLEASANT HILL, BATTLE OF (1864) **V–331a**; III–498a; VI–63a
Pleasanton, Stephen (auditor) IV–152b
Pleasants, John H. (jour.) II–377a
Pleasonton, Alfred (off.) I–130a, 360a; V–403a; VII–280b
Pleated sheets (chem.) IV–390a
PLEDGE OF ALLEGIANCE V–331a; III–35a, 497b–98a; IV–202a
Pleiku (Viet.) VII–183b
Plei Me (Viet.) I–49a
Pleistocene epoch I–154b, 155b, 156a; III–163b
PLESSY* v. *FERGUSON (1896) **V–331b**; I–29a; II–399b, 404a, 457a; III–86b, 438a, 503a; VI–256a
Berea College v. *Kentucky* I–290b
Brown v. *Board of Education* I–372b, 373a; II–54a, 57a
Pleuropneumonia I–474a; VII–177a
Pliny (scholar) III–49b
Pliny, Jenson (au.) II–107b
Plockhoy, Peter II–147a
PLOESTI OIL FIELDS, AIR RAIDS ON (1941–44) **V–332a**; I–60a; VII–340b
Plough patent III–200a; IV–37b
See also Lygonia
Plow I–34a, 34a,b, 36b, 37b–38a, 48b; II–238b; III–43a
Plow and Harrow Tavern (N.Y.) VII–2a
Plowden, Edmund (col.) V–332b
Plowden, Francis (writ.) V–333a
Plowden, Mabel Marriner V–332b
PLOWDEN'S NEW ALBION V–332b
Pluck and Luck (mag. series) II–341b
Plukenet, Leonard (bot.) I–348b
Plumb, Glenn E. (law.) V–333a
Plumbe, John (railroadman) VI–39a
"Plumbers" unit VII–254b–55a,b
PLUMB PLAN V–333a
"Plumed Knight" I–422b
Plumer, William (pol.) I–418b
Plumes II–371a–b, 372a
Plummer, Henry (outlaw). *See* Plummer Gang
Plummer, J. B. (off.) III–101a
PLUMMER GANG V–333a; VII–187b
Plummet II–386a
Plum pudding III–52a
Plums III–151b
Plunger (submarine) VI–422b
Plunkitt, George Washington VI–460a
Pluralism I–316b; II–325b; IV–358b
Plurality. *See* Majority Rule
PLUTO (Pipe Line Under the Ocean) V–111a
Pluton (destroyer) VI–216b
Plutonium I–215b–16a, 217b; II–12b; IV–119a, 238a,b; V–300b
Plymouth (Conn.) clockmaking II–78a, 79a
Plymouth (Eng.) I–51a; III–220a; V–313a
Pilgrims IV–278b; V–64b
Raleigh's Lost Colony VI–42b
Somers' voyage VI–338a
transatlantic flight V–30a
Plymouth (Mass.) IV–264b
Pilgrim Society II–98b
settlement IV–264b; V–64b–65a
whaling III–413a
See also New Plymouth Colony
Plymouth (N.C.) I–83a; V–116a
Plymouth (ship) V–22b
Plymouth (Wis.) II–282a
PLYMOUTH, VIRGINIA COMPANY OF V–333b; I–16a; II–228b; VII–95a, 199b–200a
Council for New England II–242a
Kennebec River settlement II–123b

Long Island IV–185a
patent II–122b
Popham Colony V–359b
royal land grants IV–91b
Plymouth Church (Brooklyn, N.Y.) I–283b
Plymouth Colony. *See* New Plymouth Colony
PLYMOUTH ROCK V–334a
PLYMOUTH TRADING POST V–334a; VI–151b
Plywood III–136b; IV–204b; V–320b; VI–220b
Pneumatics V–294a
Pneumatic tire IV–419b; VI–167b
Pneumococci I–241b; IV–389b
Pneumonia IV–151a
deaths IV–150b
influenza III–416b, 417a
Pneu-Vac Company II–421a
Poaching VII–297a
Pocahontas (Indian) III–280a; V–385b; VII–319b
Pocantico River VI–312b
Pocasset (Mass.) IV–47a
"POCKET" (Ind.) **V–334b**
POCKET VETO V–334b; II–199b; VII–177b
Pocono Mountains VII–220b
Poe, Edgar Allan (poet, writ.) IV–162b, 406b; VI–353a; VII–198a
Poe Lock VI–219b
Poetical Works IV–161a
Poetry IV–160b, 162a,b, 163a, 164a, 165b
Afro-American IV–166a
Biglow Papers I–296b
children's I–335b
"Old Oaken Bucket" V–152a
Poe v. *Ullman* (1961) II–378a
"Pogo" (comic strip) V–72b
Pogroms IV–10a
Poictiers (ship of the line) VII–253a
Poincaré, Raymond (states.) IV–84a
Poinsett, Joel R. (dipl.) I–110b; III–59b; IV–114b, 464b; VII–299a
Point (Tex.) I–41b
Point, Fort (Maine) V–386b
Point, Nicholas (miss.) II–93b; III–500a
Point Barrow (Alaska) III–454a; V–122b, 337a,b, 338a
Point Christian (Maine) III–200b
Point Comfort (Va.) IV–399b
Point Delgada II–385a
Point du Sable, Jean Baptiste (expl.) I–24b
Pointe au fer (N.Y.) VII–270a
POINTE COUPEE (La.) **V–335a**; I–6b
Pointe du Hoe (Fr.) V–111a
POINT FOUR V–335a; III–61b, 62a, 481b; V–281a; VI–468a–b
Point Lookout (Md.) II–433a; V–414b
Point Moss V–240b
Point of Rocks (Kans.) IV–240a
Point Pleasant (W.Va.) II–350b
Céloron's lead plates I–477a
Fort Randolph VI–45b
POINT PLEASANT, BATTLE OF (1774) **V–335b**; I–497b, 499a; II–381b; VII–103a, 253b
Point Riche VII–162b
Poirier, Richard (au.) IV–165b
Poison gas IV–430a, 431b
Poisonous Snakes of North America VI–91a
Pojoaque (N.Mex.) V–459b
POKAGON VILLAGE (Mich.) **V–335b**
Pokegama, Lake VI–295a
POKER V–335b; III–149b; VI–161b
Poland
Corfam IV–128b
Fourteen Points III–86a
immigration to U.S. III–333a, 337b, 338b, 339a,b, 340a, 341b
International Control Commission III–452b
Liberia IV–141b
most-favored-nation status VI–470a
nationalization of U.S. property IV–466a
revolt III–69b
Treaty of Versailles VII–173a
United Nations Declaration VII–151b
Vietnam III–160a
World War I VII–330a
World War II I–178a, 328a; II–145a; III–235b; VII–18a, 334a
Yalta Conference VII–351b
Poland Act (1874) VII–162a
Poland China hog III–288b
Polar (Indians) III–358a
Polar bear V–217b
POLAR EXPEDITION OF THE *JEANNETTE* (1879–81) **V–336a**
POLAR EXPLORATION V–336a
Byrd, Richard E. I–398b–99a
Greely Arctic expedition III–224a
International Polar Years III–454a
Northwest Passage V–122a
Palmer's Antarctica expedition V–197b
Peary's expeditions V–240b
Polaris expedition IV–457a
submarines VI–423a
Wilkes Exploring Expedition VII–299b
Polaria (Alaska) I–75b
Polaris (ship) IV–457a; V–336b
Polaris missile I–56b; IV–363b–64a; V–11a, 164a; VI–159b, 423b
Polaris submarine I–124b; V–11a,b, 23b, 25b, 26a, 27a
Polaroid Corporation IV–268a; V–293a
Polar Programs, Office of V–338b
Polar Record (jour.) V–338b
Polar Sea V–337a
Polar Years, International (1882–83, 1932–33) III–454a
"Po' Laz'us" (ballad) I–247b
Polhem, Christopher (eng.) I–205a
POLICE V–338b
broadcast regulations III–1a
colonial courts II–246b
interrogation of suspects IV–361b–62a
New York City IV–137b–38a
organized crime II–260b
race riots I–31b; VI–8b–9a
radio communications II–424b
right of assembly I–205a
scandals V–346b
wiretapping II–427a–b
Police action
Korea IV–56b
POLICE POWER V–339a; III–238a
commerce clause II–136a
general welfare II–440a
government inspection III–422a
government regulation of business III–204b
hours of labor regulation IV–173b
interstate commerce V–172a–b
land use II–46b
lotteries IV–191b
Mann Act IV–240a
military aid to civil powers IV–342a
property V–433b
states II–293b–94a
zoning ordinances VII–370a
Police strike, Boston. *See* Boston Police Strike
Policy gambling II–260b, 261b; III–149b
New York City IV–138a
POLIOMYELITIS V–340a; I–242a; III–249a; IV–288a
Polish National Catholic Church I–469a
Polish rebellion (1830) VI–177b
Political Action Committee IV–73b
Political assassinations. *See* Assassinations, Political
POLITICAL ASSESSMENTS V–341a; VI–374b–75a
Political asylum
aerial hijackers III–277b
Political bosses. *See* Bosses and Bossism, Political
Political campaigns. *See* Campaigns, Political; Campaigns, Presidential
Political contributions. *See* Campaign Resources
Political conventions. *See* Conventions, Party Nominating
Political corruption. *See* Corruption, Political
POLITICAL EXILES TO THE UNITED STATES V–341b
French refugees III–121a
Hungarian Revolution V–42a
Italy III–338a
Regicides VI–70b
Political Greenhouse for the Year 1798 III–259b
Political machine. *See* Bosses and Bossism, Political; Machine, Party
Political organization, Indian. *See* Indian Political Organization
POLITICAL PARTIES V–343a; II–324b, 325b; III–3b
academic freedom I–5a
American Independent party I–106b
American Labor party I–107a,b
American Republican party I–111b
antislavery movement I–138b–39a
Arizona I–172b
Arkansas I–173a
assessments V–341a–b
ballots I–248b; VII–209a
bolters I–328a
Bull Moose party I–380b
campaign resources I–413a
campaigns I–414b–32a
caucus I–474a
Connecticut II–180b
corrupt practices acts II–232b–33a
Cotton Kingdom II–241a
dark horse candidates II–292a
direct primary V–406b
elections II–410b
electoral college II–412a
emblems II–437b
Equal Rights party II–457b
federal funding I–414b
Federalist party III–4a
Free Soil party III–111b
gerrymander II–355b
Greenback movement III–224b–25b
Jeffersonian Republicans VI 94a–
Liberal Republican IV–141a
Liberty IV–143b
Locofoco IV–175a
Mugwumps IV–425b
National Democratic party

POLITICAL PARTIES (cont.)
III–189a
National Republican party IV–469b
New York I–107a–b
New York City V–82a
nominating conventions II–216a
party government V–222a
party machine IV–213b
patronage V–227b
platforms V–328b
presidential elections II–409b
pressure groups V–400b
primaries II–216a
Progressive party I–380b–81a; VI–378a
propaganda V–433a
Quids VI–3a
radical right VI–12a
Readjuster party VI–49a–b
Republican party VI–92b
runoff primary V–407a
Silver party V–39b
Social Democratic party VI–324b
Socialist Labor party VI–325a
spoils system I–146a; VI–374b
Stalwarts VI–380b
state legislatures IV–133b
third parties IV–70a; VII–52a
two–party system VII–134b
Union Labor party VII–146a
Union party VII–146a, 148a
Union Rights party VII–148a
voting behavior VII–209b–10a
Whig party VII–288a
Workingmen's Party VII–322a

POLITICAL PARTIES, ORGANIZATION OF V–344b; V–343a–b
floor leader III–37b
national committee IV–462b
party government V–223a,b
party whip VII–288b
speaker of the House VI–369a
state chairman VI–390a
third parties VII–52b
ward leader VII–230b

Political Parties in the American System IV–214a
Political patronage. *See* Patronage, Political
Political prisoners
Civil War II–159b; IV–83b
Political rights. *See* Civil Rights and Liberties
Political rings. *See* Rings, Political

POLITICAL SCANDALS V–346a
Baker, Bobby I–243b–44a
Belknap scandal I–386a
campaign of 1876 I–422b
Crédit Mobilier VII–147b
Elk Hills oil reserves V–13b; VII–16b
Nast cartoons IV–454a
Pentagon Papers V–258b
Philadelphia Gas Ring V–279a
Rip Raps contracts VI–145a
Sanborn contracts VI–207b
Teapot Dome V–13b; VII–16b
Watergate V–99a; VII–253b
Whiskey Ring VII–290b
Yazoo fraud VII–353b

POLITICAL SCIENCE V–347a; II–222a; IV–2b
party government V–222a
Political Science Association, American V–348a,b, 353b
Political Science Quarterly (jour.) V–347b

POLITICAL SUBDIVISIONS V–349a
parish V–216a

POLITICAL THEORIES V–350a; V–287a
anarchism I–116b
Calhoun, John C. II–189a
church covenant II–248a
consent of the governed VII–14b
feudalism III–18a
Jacksonian Democracy III–486a
Jeffersonian Democracy III–495b
judicial review IV–12a
Locke, John II–191a; IV–173b
natural rights doctrine V–7b
nullification V–125b
pacifism V–181a
public opinion V–454b
Puritans V–286b
representation VI–88a
representative government VI–89a
right of rebellion VI–50b
right of secession VI–249b
rights of Englishmen VI–140b
separation of powers V–384b
sovereignty VI–358a
state sovereignty VI–403b
theocracy VII–51a
third–term doctrine VII–53b

POLITICAL WRITINGS V–352b
Calhoun's *Exposition* V–125b
Federalist III–4a
Magna Charta IV–224a
New Freedom V–53a
"Pacificus" and "Helvidius" V–181a
pamphleteering V–198b
Rights of Man VI–141a
Rights of the British Colonies Asserted and Proved VI–141a
Taxation No Tyranny VII–14a,b
tracts VII–82a

Politics
AFL–CIO I–102b–04b
Alaska I–78a–79a
almanacs I–91a
American Legion I–108a
antislavery movement I–137b–39a
barbecue I–267a
blocs I–322a
bossism I–343a
Broad Seal War I–368a
Brooks–Baxter War I–370b
Buckshot War I–374a
Bucktails I–374b
bunkum I–383a
Burchard incident I–383a
bureaucracy I–384a
calamity howler I–403b
California I–406a–b, 407b, 408a
Canal Ring I–442a
canvassing I–446b
carpetbaggers I–459b
cartoons I–464a
Catholics I–470a
caucus I–474a
censorship I–478b
government appointments I–145b–46a
Italian–Americans III–483b
Jewish participation IV–10b
Kentucky I–323a
New South I–354a
newspaper editors V–69b
New York I–82b, 107a–b, 442a
Pennsylvania I–374a–b
Reconstruction I–354a
South Carolina I–319a–b
spoils system I–384a

Politics, Parties and Pressure Groups V–354a
Polizzi, Alfred II–261b
Polk, James K. (pres.) II–175 (table); III–318a; IV–453a; V–395 (table); VI–369b; VII–25b
antislavery I–138b
campaign of 1844 I–420a–b; II–292a; IV–143b; VI–163a; VII–288b
foreign policy III–68a
Frémont pardon IV–34a
Hise Treaty III–278a
Independent Treasury System III–251b, 354b
Mexican War I–109b, 403a; IV–323a,b, 324a,b; V–125a; VII–94a
Missouri Compromise IV–379b
Monroe Doctrine IV–400b, 401a; V–354a
Oregon question III–21a; IV–6a
Oregon Treaty of 1846 V–165a, 168a, 170a
Scott–Pillow quarrel VI–241a
Slidell's mission to Mexico VI–312b
Texas annexation VII–38b
Treaty of Guadalupe Hidalgo II–342b; III–230a
Wilmot Proviso VII–303a
Yucatán VII–366b

Polk, Leonidas (off.) I–288a; III–297b; IV–313b

POLK DOCTRINE V–354a; IV–400b; VII–366b
Pollard, Edward Alfred (journ.) IV–189b
Pollard limner V–186a
Pollock, Jackson (art.) II–105b, 106b; V–192b
Pollock, Oliver (trader, fin.) III–179a; VII–303a
See also Pollock's Aid to the Revolution
Pollock, Thomas (trader) VII–303a

POLLOCK'S AID TO THE REVOLUTION V–354a; VI–363b, 367b

POLLOCK* v. *FARMERS LOAN AND TRUST COMPANY (1895) **V–354b**; I–94b; III–351a,b; VI–297b; VII–5b, 6a,b

POLL TAX V–355a; I–451a; III–20a, 92b–93a,b, 351b; VII–4a,b, 6a, 208b, 209a–b
Alabama I–29a
black suffrage VI–432a,b, 433a
colonies VII–3a
legislation II–481a
Massachusetts III–91b
Mississippi Plan IV–371b
outlawed I–95a, 451a; II–207b, 408a, 410a
road construction VI–152a
slaves I–22b
Solid South VI–337a
Twenty–fourth Amendment V–434b; VI–435a; VII–133a
Virginia VII–195b

Pollution
agriculture I–39b
Audubon Society I–222b
automobile I–230a; III–451a; VII–102b
California I–408b
Canadian–American waterways I–440b
chemical fertilizers III–17b
Clean Air Acts II–188b
copper industry II–224a
Environmental Protection Agency I–391b
environmental sanitation VI–211b
federal aid II–502b
forests III–75b
Great Lakes III–216b
Gulf of Mexico IV–326b
high seas III–107a
interstate compacts III–460a
Justice Department IV–22a
Lake Michigan IV–332b
National Weather Service VII–264b

Ohio Valley V–146a
Pittsburgh V–322a
plastics V–328b
public utilities V–459a
Saint Louis IV–378b
territorial waters VII–33a
urban health VII–158b
water VII–259b
West Virginia VII–282a
***POLLY* ADMIRALTY CASE** (1802) **V–355a**; II–464a; VI–169a
Polo, Marco (expl.) II–26b; V–95a
Polo Grounds (N.Y.C.) III–252a
Polopel's Island (N.Y.) III–275b
Polybius VI–391a
Polycarbonate V–328a
Polyethylene V–327b, 328a
POLYGAMY V–355b
Mormons IV–117a; VI–87a, 266b; VII–162a
Utah II–443b; VI–401a
Polygyny III–377b
Polymers I–287b; II–12a,b; III–409b; V–328b; VII–44a
Polypotamia III–497a
Polypropylene V–328a
Polysulfone V–328a
Polytechnic institutes II–11a, 447a
Polyuridylic acid IV–391a
Polyvinyls IV–128b, 294b
Pomeroy, Samuel C. (pol.) I–213a; V–356a
POMEROY CIRCULAR (1864) **V–366a**
Pomery, Lemuel (mfr.) IV–432b
Pomo (Indians) III–363a; IV–381b
Pomone (frigate) V–394a
Pompey. *See* Gnaeus Pompeius Magnus II–357a
Pompidou, Georges (states.) III–97b; VII–91b
Pomutz, George V–42a
Ponape VII–125a
Ponca (Indians) III–363b, 365a, 396b
fur trade VI–367a
Jesuit missions III–500a
Nebraska V–31a
Omaha relations V–155a
Ponce de León, Juan (expl.) II–184a; III–233a; VI–187b
citrus fruits II–43a
Puerto Rico V–461a
Ponce de León, Juan (off.)
Mexican War I–361a
PONCE DE LEÓN'S DISCOVERY (1513) **V–356a**; I–96a; III–38a; VII–36a
Poncho III–381a
Pond, James B. IV–207b
Pond, Peter (fur trader) III–403b; VII–275b
Pond Creek VII–221a
Ponderosa pine III–74b; V–446a; VI–394 (table); VII–60a
Ponderson, John VI–263b
Ponies III–303a–b
Ponta Delgada (Port.) V–30a
Pontchartrain, Comte de, Louis de Phélypeaux (states.) V–356a–b
PONTCHARTRAIN, LAKE V–356a; III–36a, 326b
Carondelet Canal I–459b
Civil War IV–371b
Fort Saint John VI–191a
Isle of Orleans III–479a
New Orleans V–62a
Orleans Territory V–173a
railroad VI–25a
PONTCHARTRAIN DU DÉTROIT, FORT (Mich.) **V–356b**; II–337b; III–120a
Pontiac (Indian). *See* Pontiac's War
PONTIAC'S WAR (1763–64) **V–356b**; II–265b, 337b–38a, 392b; III–117a,b, 330a–b; IV–92b, 330b; V–4a; VI–381a,b, 450b; VII–80a
Battle of Bloody Run I–323b
Bouquet's expedition I–353b
Bradstreet's Lake Erie expedition I–359a
British navy III–217a
Delaware Prophet II–322b
Detroit V–90a
Fort Bedford I–282b
Fort Ligonier IV–154a
Fort Miami IV–329a
Fort Pitt V–321b
Fort Presque Isle V–399b
Fort Saint Joseph VI–191b
Green Bay III–225b
Indiana Company III–370b
Paxton Boys V–231a
peace treaty V–175b
Pennsylvania V–246b
Proclamation of 1763 V–424b–25a
Sandusky VI–208b
"suffering traders" VI–430a
Treaty of Fort Stanwix VII–166b
PONTOTOC, TREATY OF (1832) **V–357a**
Pontotoc County (Miss.) V–357a
PONY EXPRESS V–357b; I–485a; V–178a, 372a; VI–176b, 380a; VII–101a
Bridger's Pass V–225a
Great Plains III–221a
Saint Joseph VI–191b
Wells, Fargo VII–267a
Pool, Lake II–223a–b
Poole, A. W. (marshal) IV–444a
Poole, Charles A. I–314a
Poole, Frederick C. (off.) I–158b, 159a
Poolrooms IV–138a
POOLS, RAILROAD V–358a; IV–177b; V–458a; VI–21b
Pooploop's Kill III–275b
Poor. *See* Poverty and Pauperism; Relief
Poor, Charles Henry (nav. off.) IV–371a
Poor, Enoch (off.) VI–438a
Poor, Henry Varnum III (art.) IV–26b
Poore, Ben Perley II–99a
Poor farms VI–72b
Poorhouses V–380b–81a
Poor Law (1601) I–148a; III–335a–b; VI–327b
Poor laws I–494b; II–299a; V–380a–b
Poor People's Campaign (1968) V–1b, 265b–66a; VII–246b
Poor Potter of Yorktown V–379b
***POOR RICHARD'S ALMANAC* V–358b**; I–90b
POOR WHITES V–358b
antebellum South VI–340b
Blease movement I–319a
crackers II–253a
nonslaveholders V–108a
slavery I–28a
Pop art II–106b; V–193a
Popcorn II–226a
Popé (Indian) V–4a, 460b; VI–461a
Pope, Albert A. (mfr.) I–295a
Pope, Camp (Minn.) II–283b
Pope, Clifford H. (herpetol.) VI–91a
Pope, Jacob (mfr.) VII–55b
Pope, John (off.) II–62b, 283b; III–267a; V–377b; VI–353b
Army of the Mississippi IV–370a
Army of Virginia VII–197a
Battle of Blackwater I–317b
Battle of Cedar Mountain I–476b
Battle of Chantilly I–493b–94a
Battle of Groveton III–229a
Boomer movement I–336a
Fort Hays III–266b
Georgia Reconstruction III–171b
Island Number Ten operations III–478b
Porter court-martial V–368b
railroad surveys VI–39a
Second Battle of Bull Run I–382a; IV–261b
Pope–Leighey House (Mount Vernon, Va.) IV–472a
Pope Manufacturing Company I–226a
POPE–MCGILL FARM ACT (1938) **V–359a**; I–43a; V–47a, 48a
Pope's Well (N.Mex.) III–199b
Popeye (comic character) V–72b
"POP–GUN" BILLS V–359a
Popham, George (col.) V–334a
See also Popham Colony
Popham, John (col.) IV–225b; V–333b
POPHAM COLONY V–359b; I–319b; II–123b; IV–37a, 225b; V–243b; VI–185b
Popish Plot (1678) IV–188b
Poplar III–72b
Poplar Forest (Va.) III–495a
"Pop" music IV–441a
Popo Agie (Wyo.) VII–104a
Popolopen Creek III–275b
Popov, Andrei A. (nav. off.) VI–181a
Popple, Henry (cartog.) VII–74a
Popple's map V–156b
Popular Front (Communist party) II–144b–45a
Popular Front for the Liberation of Palestine III–277b
Popular Science Monthly VI–236a–b
POPULAR SOVEREIGNTY V–360a; V–7b, 286b, 351b; VI–121a
Compromise of 1850 IV–379b
Dred Scott Case III–109b
fundamental constitutions III–132b
Kansas IV–31a; VII–73a
Kansas Free-State party IV–28b
Omnibus Bill V–155a
reserved powers of the people VI–98a
state constitutions VI–391b
Utah Territory II–150b
Popular vote
presidential elections II–409a–b, 412a
POPULATION, GROWTH AND MOVEMENTS OF V–361a; II–41a–b
Afro-American I–29b; III–253b, 437a,b
antebellum South VI–341a
apportionment I–147b
Arkansas I–173b
Baltimore I–249b, 250a
Baton Rouge I–275a
Boston I–344a,b
Brooklyn I–370a,b
California I–408b; VI–154a
census of 1790 III–426b, 437a
Charleston (S.C.) I–497b
Cincinnati II–37b
Cleveland II–75a
Colorado II–128a–b
Connecticut II–181a
cost of government II–234a
demography II–327b
Denver II–332a
Detroit II–337a,b

POPULATION, GROWTH AND MOVEMENTS OF (cont.)
elderly V–150a
El Paso II–433b
Eskimo II–461b
Florida III–40a, 42a
food supply III–53a; V–129a–b
free blacks III–101b–02a
frontier II–326a
Great Plains III–221b
Hawaii III–263b, 264b
Huntsville III–319a
Illinois III–329b
Indian III–356b–57a, 396a, 397b; VI–83b
Indiana III–369b–70a
Iowa III–468b–69a
Italian–Americans III–482b–83a
local government IV–172b
Long Island IV–186a
Maine IV–226b
Massachusetts IV–268b
Minnesota IV–356a,b, 357b
Mississippi IV–369b
Missouri IV–377a
Montana IV–403b
Nashville IV–453a
Natchez IV–455a
Navaho V–8b
Nevada V–40a
New Hampshire V–53b–54a, 54b
New Jersey V–57a
New Orleans V–62b
New South V–67b
New York City V–82b–83a,b
North Carolina V–116b
North Dakota V–117b, 118a
Ohio V–141b
Pennsylvania V–246b–47a
Pensacola V–254b
Peoria V–261a
Philadelphia V–277a,b
Puerto Rico V–462a
Rhode Island VI–132a, 133b
Richmond VI–137a
Roman Catholic I–467b, 470b
rural VI–171b, 174a, 175a, 175b
Saint Joseph VI–191b
Saint Louis VI–194b
San Francisco VI–209b
Savannah VI–220b
Schenectady VI–226a
Scotch–Irish VI–240b
sharecroppers VI–269a
slaves VI–6b, 305a, 306a
state government VI–398b
state–making process VII–32a
suburban growth VI–427b
Tennessee VII–25b, 26a
Texas VII–37a, 38b
Twin Cities VII–134a
urban structure VII–159a
Utah VII–162a
Vicksburg VII–181b
Virginia VII–193b, 196b
Washington, D.C. VII–245b
Washington State VII–248a
West Virginia VII–282a
westward movement VII–100a, 283b, 284a
Willamette Valley VII–300a
Williamsburg VII–301b
Wisconsin VII–307b
World War II VII–88a
Wyoming VII–345b
zero growth II–486b
See also Immigration; Life Expectancy; Vital Statistics
POPULISM V–364b; I–39a; III–225b
Afro–Americans III–438a
agrarian movement I–32b; VII–52b
antibank movement I–130a
Bourbons I–354a
government ownership III–202b–03a
Grange I–41b
Idaho III–328b
Kansas IV–26b
liberalism IV–140b
Nebraska V–31b
North Dakota V–117b
orators V–161b
pamphleteering V–199a
radicals VI–13b
Republican party VI–93a
Sherman Antitrust Act I–139b
Socialist movement VI–326a,b
South Dakota VI–350a
taxation VII–5b–6a, 6a
Wyoming VII–346a
Populist party IV–81b
agrarian movement VII–52b
bank deposits I–252a
calamity howler I–403b
California I–406b
campaign of 1888 III–225a
campaign of 1892 I–424b; VII–52b
campaign of 1896 I–425a
campaign of 1904 I–426a
coinage II–96a
Coxey's Army II–252b
currency II–2a
decline IV–67a
demand deposits II–2a
Farmer–Labor party II–492a,b
Farmers' Alliance II–493b
Florida III–40a
Georgia III–169a
grain elevator monopoly II–430b
Louisiana IV–194b
Middle–of–the–Road Populists IV–335a
Nevada V–39b
platforms V–329a
Silver Republicans VI–293a
soft money VI–333b
Solid South VI–337a
southern states I–29a
Poque (game) V–335b
Porcelain II–331a; III–182b, 183a, 183b, 184a,b; V–379b
Porches (arch.) I–160b
Porcupine III–48b
Porcupine River VI–151a
PORCUPINE'S GAZETTE (news.) **V–366a**
Porgy and Bess (opera) IV–438b
Po River III–201a
Pork III–51b
meat–packing IV–280a,b
revolutionary war VI–120a
See also Hogs
"PORK BARREL" V–366b; VI–146b
Pork Chop Hill (Kor.) VI–301a
"Pork eaters." *See Mangeurs de Lard*
"Porkopolis." *See* Cincinnati
Pornography I–478b–80b; II–259a, 260a, 263a
motion pictures IV–419a
Supreme Court rulings III–106a
Porphyry deposits II–224a
Porpoise (ship) III–28b; VI–142a, 217a
Porsche (auto) I–232a
Portage (Ohio) III–316a
Portage (Wis.) V–367b
Portage, Fort (Wis.) II–297a
Portage des Sioux (Mo.) VI–295b
Portage la Prairie (Can.) IV–118a
PORTAGES AND WATER ROUTES V–367a; V–224a–25a
Carrying Place of Niagara V–90a
Fox–Wisconsin Waterway III–89a
fur trade III–403a–b
Grand Portage III–209a
Great Lakes II–380a
Indian paths III–387a
Lake Huron III–319a
Maumee–Wabash VII–262a
Miami–Maumee IV–188a
North West Company V–121a
Saint Joseph–Kankakee VI–191b
Portal (N.Dak.) VI–36b
Portal–to–Portal Act (1947) IV–353b
Port Arthur (China) IV–234b; VI–178a; VII–351b
Port Arthur (Tex.) II–350a
Port–au–Prince (Haiti) III–240a
PORT AUTHORITIES V–368a; VI–428a
Port Authority Bus Terminal (N.Y.C.) V–368b
PORT AUTHORITY OF NEW YORK AND NEW JERSEY V–368a; III–201b, 460a; IV–428b; VI–398a, 402a
Port Authority Trans–Hudson System V–368b
Port Chester (N.Y.) I–378b; II–349a
Port Clinton (Ohio) VII–274a
Porte, J. C. (nav. off.) I–51a
Porter, Augustus V–91a
Porter, Cole (comp.) IV–442a
Porter, David D. (nav. off.) I–14a; V–247b; VII–285a
Battle at Grand Gulf III–208b
Battle of Arkansas Post I–174a
Board of Navy Commissioners V–17b
Essex II–463b
Fajardo Case II–484a
Fort Fisher III–30b
Fort Pickens V–308b
Madison Island IV–220a
Mississippi River blockade IV–371a
Mosquito Fleet IV–416a
Naval Academy V–9b
naval mortars IV–413b
Powhatan incident V–386a
prize money V–424a
Quasi War II–190a
Santo Domingo mission VI–217a
Steele's Bayou expedition VI–410b
Vicksburg VII–182a
Yazoo Pass expedition VII–354b
Porter, Fitz–John (off.)
Battle of Antietam I–130a
Battle of Gaines' Mill III–146a
Battle of Mechanicsville IV–281b
Chickasaw Bluffs II–22a
court–martial V–368b–69a
Second Battle of Bull Run I–382a
Seven Days' Battles VI–263b
Porter, Horace (off.) I–311a
Porter, John Addison (chem.) VI–273b
Porter, John L. (nav. constructor) VI–44b
Porter, Peter B. (off., pol.) II–458b; IV–87b, 205a; V–91a, 91a; VII–231a
Porter, Rufus (pub.) VI–231a
Porter, Sylvia (econ.) V–75a
Porter, William (metalworker) VI–291a
Porter brothers (mfrs.) II–78a
PORTER CASE V–368b
Porterfield, G. A. (off.) V–281a
Porterfield scrip IV–97b, 98a
Porter Heroin Act (1924) IV–450a,b
Port Foster (S. Shetland Is.) V–198a
PORT GIBSON, BATTLE AT (1863) **V–369a**; VI–48b

PORT HUDSON, SIEGE OF (1863) **V–369a**; II–63a; III–258b; IV–375a, 375b; VII–182a
Port Huron (Mich.) IV–331a; VI–34a; VII–128a
"Port Huron Statement" (1962) VI–421a
Portico (arch.) IV–405a
Portillo (Cuba) III–150b
Port Jefferson (N.Y.) IV–185b
Portland (Maine) II–485b; IV–225b
cod fisheries II–93a
Eastern Cemetery II–452b
railroads VI–34b
See also Fort Loyal
Portland (Oreg.) II–285b; III–293a
Forest Service III–76b
Lewis and Clark Exposition IV–136a
railroads V–168a; VI–33a, 37b
Southern Overland Mail VI–154a
stage lines VII–101a
Portland (steamer) II–349b; IV–52a
Portland, Isle of I–477b
Portland, University of III–293a
Portland cement I–477b
Portland (Maine) *Evening News* (news.) V–73b
Portland Mine (Colo.) III–191b
Portland Oregonian (news.) V–73b
Portland Standard (news.) V–180b
Port Lyautey (Mor.) II–345a
Port Moresby (N.Guin.) I–55b; II–225a; VII–336b
Portneuf River III–243b
Port Newark (N.J.) V–41b
Port of New York Authority. *See* Port Authority of New York and New Jersey
Portolá, Gaspar de (off., gov.) I–405a; III–302b
Monterey IV–404b
San Diego VI–208a
San Francisco VI–209a
Port Orford cedar IV–204a
Porto Rico v. *Tapia* (1918) III–424b
Portrait Gallery, National VI–319b
Portrait Gallery of Distinguished American Citizens VI–286b
Portrait miniatures II–279a; IV–351b
Portrait of a Lady IV–163b
Portrait painting II–101a; III–47a,b; V–184b–86b, 187a,b, 188b, 190a
Portrait silhouettes VI–286b
PORT REPUBLIC, BATTLE OF (1862) **V–369a**; III–487b
PORT ROYAL (N.S.) **V–369b**; VI–189a
capture by British II–126b
Capuchins I–451b
King William's War IV–49b; VI–1b
Queen Anne's War VI–2b
return to France VI–190b
See also Annapolis Royal
PORT ROYAL (S.C.) **V–370a**
Beaufort I–281b
Civil War V–19b; VII–146b
Ribault expedition VI–347a, 348b
War of 1812 VII–235a
Yamasee War VII–352a
Port Royal (Va.) IV–154b
Ports
Coast Guard II–90a
growth of cities II–41a–b
Portsmouth (N.H.) V–54a; VI–201a
Civil War draft riot II–368b
dry dock II–375a
Freemasons III–109a
Isles of Shoals III–479b
Laconia IV–82b
navy yard V–27b, 29a,b
post road V–375a
revolutionary war IV–189a; VII–300b–01a
settlement V–53b
shipbuilding VI–282a
Strawberry Bank VI–418a
tea party VII–16a–b
Portsmouth (Ohio) IV–443b; V–145b
Portsmouth (R.I.) I–149a; II–124a; III–235a; V–65b
colonial assembly II–117b; VI–134a
Moses His Judicial IV–416a
Providence Plantations V–439a
settlement VI–131b
shipbuilding III–413a
Portsmouth (sloop) I–268b
Portsmouth (Va.) II–253b
Constitution II–190b
navy yard V–29a
revolutionary war I–194a; VI–129a; VII–361a
shipbuilding VII–196a
PORTSMOUTH, TREATY OF (1905) **V–370b**; IV–235a; VI–178a, 179a, 457b
Portsmouth and Roanoke Railroad VI–36b
Port Tobacco (Md.) I–455b
Portugal
Angola I–22a
British colonies IV–221a
colonial coins II–94b
Common Market VI–472a
European Free Trade Association VI–469a; VII–89a
explorations II–341a
expulsion of Jews IV–9a
Grand Banks fishing III–208a
Hawaiian labor III–263b
immigration to U.S. I–447a; III–334b, 337b, 338b, 341b
Line of Demarcation II–323b
Maine exploration IV–225b
New World claims V–109a; VII–75a
Nine–Power Pact V–96b
North Atlantic Treaty Organization V–113b
Organization for Economic Cooperation and Development V–170b
Salem trade VI–199a
sea trade III–106b
slave trade VI–309b
Sugar Islands VI–437a
tobacco VII–64b
triangular trade II–119a
U.S. aid III–61b
War of 1812 III–155a
Washington Naval Conference VII–251a
Portuguese Guinea I–22a
Port Williams (S. Shetland Is.). *See* Port Foster
Pory, John (geog.) I–204a
Poseidon (missile) IV–364a; V–164a; VI–159b, 423b
Posey County (Ind.) III–255b; V–54b
Positivism V–354a
Positron V–299a
Posses I–474a
Possessions, insular. *See* Insular Possessions
Post, Charles W. (bus.) I–487b, 488a; IV–471b
Post, Christian Frederick (miss.) II–389a; III–58b
Post, Emily IV–241a
Post, George B. (arch.) VI–299a
Post, Wiley (av.) I–51a
Postage currency IV–394b; VI–279a
Postage stamps IV–394b; V–372b, 373a; VII–108a
Postal Act (1967) I–479b
Postal Affairs, Committee on V–373b
Postal Rate Commission V–374b
Postal Reorganization Act (1970) V–374a–b
Postal savings banks III–204b; V–365b, 373b
Postal Savings System I–264a; V–209a
POSTAL SERVICE, UNITED STATES V–370b; II–498a–b; III–1a, 201b, 203a; VII–108a
abolitionist publications I–137a
airmail I–65a, 67b–68a, 223b; VII–102a
aviation II–49b
censorship I–478b, 479a,b, 481a
Civil War II–472b
congressional powers II–195b, 199b
executive removal power VI–85a
franking III–98a
fraudulent advertising I–19b
general stores VI–416a
government inspection III–422a
government ownership V–456a
Kendall v. *United States* IV–36b
lotteries IV–191a, 196a
mail–order houses IV–225a
overland mail V–178a
periodicals IV–222a
Postal Savings System I–264a
post roads V–374b
Pullman strike V–463b
revenue VII–4b, 5a
rural free delivery VI–172b
rural post roads VI–176a
Southern Overland Mail VI–154a, 353b
stagelines VI–380a
star route frauds VI–387a
strike IV–75b
subsidies VI–425b
unionization IV–75b
war savings certificates VII–56a
World War II II–446a
Postal Service Act (1969) V–374a
Postal Telegraph, Inc. VII–277a
Postal Telegraph Cable Company. *See* Postal Telegraph Company
POSTAL TELEGRAPH COMPANY V–374b; II–137a
Post exchange VI–452b
Post–impressionist painting II–105a
Postmaster general
Confederacy II–160a
discretionary powers I–12a
Postmasters' provisionals V–372b
Post No. 4 (Vt.) II–267a
Post Office Act (1792) V–371b–72a
Post offices
Boston I–344a
Poston (Ariz.) III–491a
Poston, Charles Debrill (expl.) II–477b
Post painterly abstractionists V–193a–b
POST ROADS V–374b; V–371a, 372a
congressional powers II–199b
mapping VII–74a
Pequot Trail V–261a
rural areas VI–176a
star route frauds VI–387a
Tennessee Cumberland Road II–273b
Wheeling Bridge VII–288a
Posts, Army. *See* Army Posts
POSTS, ARMY SUPPLY V–375a; III–126b; VI–87a
Post Toasties I–487b
Postum I–487b

POTASH V–375b; II–5a, 6a–b; III–16a, 17a–b; V–184a; VI–48b
colonial production III–413a; IV–243a
colonial trade II–119b, 453a; VII–82b
imports II–8a
Jamestown II–4b
New Mexico V–60a
public lands V–445b
Savannah VI–220a
U.S. Geological Survey III–164a
Potassium II–5a, 10b, 421b; III–16a, 17a; IV–274a
Potassium carbonate. *See* Potash
Potassium cyanide III–191b
Potassium iodide V–128a
Potassium nitrate V–97b, 98a
See also Saltpeter
Potassium salts II–8a
POTATOES V–376b; III–52a, 381a; VI–48a
freeze drying III–55b
harvesting I–35b
Idaho III–328b
Indian cultivation I–36a; III–356b
Maine IV–227a
South America I–48a
whiskey VII–289b
Potato famines III–336a
Potawatomi (Indians) I–371b; III–24b, 366b–67a
citizenship treaty III–377a
Council Bluffs II–241b
Fort Dearborn II 17a
Hull Treaty III–316a
Iowa III–468a
Jesuit missions III–499b, 500a
Michigan cession II–21a
nativistic movement V–4a
Oklahoma lands V–148b, 149b
Pokagon village V–335b
Pontiac's War V–357a
removal III–394b
Spring Wells Treaty VI–377b
Treaty at Prairie du Chien V–388b
Treaty of Chicago III–383b
Treaty of Fort Harmar III–255a
Treaty of Fort Wayne VII–262b
Treaty of Greenville III–383a
Treaty of Saint Louis III–383b
Vincennes cession VII–189b
wild rice VII–298b
Wisconsin VII–307b
Woodland Tradition VII–320a
Poteau River VI–317a
Poteaux-en-terre (arch.) I–160a
Potier and Stymus (cabinetmakers) III–445b
Potlatch I–441b; III–361a,b
Haida III–238a
Kwakiutl IV–59a,b
Makah IV–228b
POT LIKKER AND CORN PONE V–377a
Potofsky, Jacob (labor leader) IV–76a
Potomac (Md.) III–181b
POTOMAC, ARMY OF V–377a; I–184b; II–96b; III–101a
Army of the James III–488a
Bull Run VII–197a
Hanover cavalry engagement III–250b
hospitals I–191b
Kelly's Ford attack IV–36a
medical care IV–290b
Mine Run campaign IV–350a
Peninsular campaign V–245a
POTOMAC COMPANY V–378a; II–15b, 395b; III–201b; V–378b
Potomac Park (Washington, D.C.) III–491b; VII–246b
POTOMAC RIVER V–378a; VI–149b
Alexandria I–85a
Alexandria Conference I–85a
Arlington National Cemetery I–175b
Braddock's Road I–88b, 358b
bridges I–442b
canals I–40a; IV–174b
Chesapeake and Ohio Canal II–15b
Civil War II–484b; III–176a; IV–262a, 397a, 415b; V–248a,b, 377a; VI–150a, 275a; VII–304b
Cumberland Road III–448b
exploration I–172b, 238b
Fairfax Proprietary II–481a
floods III–37a
Fort Cumberland II–271b
French and Indian War VI–267a
fugitive slaves V–239a
fur trade VII–104b
Jesuit missions III–499a
Maryland–Virginia dispute III–459b; VII–82b
Monongahela River IV–398b
Mount Vernon IV–423a
national capital I–448b; II–149b
Naval Observatory V–12a
Naval Research Laboratory V–14a
navigation VI–148a
Ohio Company of Virginia V–144a
Princeton explosion V–408b
Saint Marys VI–197a
Scotch-Irish VI–240b
Shenandoah Valley VI–275b
Stratford Hall VI–417b
tobacco VII–67b
Virginia Path VII–202b
Wakefield VII–219a
War of 1812 III–234b
Washington, D.C. VII–244b
Washington's Le Boeuf expedition VI–150a
waterpower IV–347b
westward movement VI–149a; VII–260a
POTSDAM CONFERENCE (1945) **V–378b**; II–97b, 169a, 471b, 489a; VI–179a; VII–110a
Pottawatomie County (Kans.) I–326a
Pottawatomie Creek I–314a; V–378b
POTTAWATOMIE MASSACRE (1856) **V–378b**; I–342a; IV–26a, 118b
Potter, David I–20b
Potter, John Fox (pol.) VII–34b
Potter, Orlando B. (law) VI–265a
Potter, Thomas M. II–99a
Potter County (Pa.) I–89a; V–152b
POTTERY V–379a; II–5a; III–182b, 183a–84b
Archaic culture II–386a
colonial production IV–243a
Indian I–48b, 157a; III–373b, 374a, 381a
Mississippian cultures IV–370a,b
Mogollon culture IV–385b
Mound Builders IV–421b
Pueblo Indians III–367b
Woodland Tradition VII–320a
See also Glass and Ceramics
Pottsville (Pa.) VII–127b
Poughkeepsie (N.Y.) I–364a; III–292b, 312b; VII–223b
Poughkeepsie Convention (1788) V–86b
Poulsen, Valdemar (inv.) V–290a
Poultry III–53b; VI–176a
codes of fair competition VI–225a
feed II–226a–b
Georgia III–169a
Maine IV–227a
Natchitoches IV–457a
preservation III–56a
Rhode Island VI–134a
Poultry Case. *See Schechter Poultry Corporation* v. *United States*
Pound, Ezra (poet) IV–164a, 165b
Pound, Roscoe (bot.) II–391b
Pourtalès, Louis François de (nat.) V–134b
Poussin, Nicolas (paint.) II–101b
Po Valley
World War II VII–338b
POVERTY AND PAUPERISM V–380a; VII–206a
Appalachian Kentucky IV–42a
charity organization movement I–494b
community action programs II–147b
Connecticut II–180a
depression of 1873–78 V–207b
elderly V–150b
Great Society III–222b
indentured servants III–353a
minority rights IV–359a
mortality rates IV–150b
New Deal V–46a
Office of Economic Opportunity V–135b
pauper schools II–395a, 396b
political machines IV–214a–b
poor whites V–358b
public health V–447a
Puerto Rico V–461b–62a
record-keeping VII–206b
relief VI–72b
rural population VI–176a
shanty towns VI–268b
share-the-wealth movements VI–269a
Single Tax movement V–427a
slums VI–313b
social legislation VI–327a
social settlements VI–330a
taxation VII–10a,b
tenements VII–23b
tuberculosis VII–127a
Washington, D.C. VII–246a
See also Foundations, Endowed; Philanthropy and Benevolence
POVERTY POINT (La.) **V–382b**; I–156a, 157a; II–386a
POWDER V–383a; V–163a
Du Pont mills II–320b
manufacture IV–432a, 433a
potash V–375b
revolutionary war V–354a–b; VI–116b
rockets VI–159a
Powder, hair II–371a
Powderly, Terence v. (labor leader) IV–64a,b, 81b, 81b; V–247b
Powder River I–357b; IV–109a; VI–87a
Powder River campaign (1865) I–358a; II–184a
See also Sioux Wars
Powell, Adam Clayton, Jr. (pol., cler.) I–24a, 316b; III–254a; V–383b–84a
Powell, Adam Clayton, Sr. (cler.) III–253a
Powell, Ambrose (expl.) V–384b
Powell, Cecil F. (phys.) V–302b

Powell, George (expl.)
V–198a
Powell, James (off.)
VII–215b
Powell, John (comp.)
IV–438b
Powell, John Wesley (geol.)
V–196b, 384a–b; VII–74b
American ethnology
II–464b
arid regions survey
I–170b; II–76a, 391a
Bureau of American Ethnology I–128b
census of 1880 I–482a
Colorado River II–129b
government survey
VII–272b
Grand Canyon
III–208a–b
public land commission
V–450a
Powell, Lake II–130a
Powell, Lazarus Whitehead (law.) II–139a
Powell, Lewis F., Jr. (jur.)
II–378b, 427b; VI–447b
POWELL CASE (1967–69)
V–383b
Powell River II–274a
POWELL'S EXPLORATIONS (1869, 1871–72)
V–384a; III–208b
POWELL'S VALLEY
V–384b; VII–103b, 238b, 283a
Powell v. *Alabama* (1932)
III–179a; VI–241b
Powell v. *McCormack* (1969)
V–384a
Power, electric. *See* Electric Power and Light Industry
Power blackout (1965)
II–417a
Power brakes I–229b
Power Commission, Federal
I–391b; II–500a; III–459a; V–5b–6a
Power of Music (paint.)
V–190b
Power of Sympathy IV–161a
Power pools III–321a–b
Powers (Mich.) IV–303b
Powers, Bertram A. (labor leader) VI–420a
Powers, Hiram (sculp.)
VI–243a
Powers, James (inv.) I–397a
Powers, John E. (advt.)
I–18b
POWERS, SEPARATION OF V–384b; II–4b; III–2a,b; V–351b
administrative adjudication
I–12b–13a
Antifederalists I–131a
congressional investigations
III–465b
Ex parte McCardle
IV–209a
judicial review IV–12b, 13a
judiciary IV–15b, 18b
legislature IV–133b
Mississippi v. *Johnson*
IV–376a
Montesquieu on IV–142b
party government V–222b
state government VI–396b
Power steering I–229b
Power weaving I–460b
Powhatan (Indian) III–219a, 367a; V–385b–86a; VI–43a
Powhatan (warship)
IV–371a; V–386a
POWHATAN CONFEDERACY V–385b; VII–192a
***POWHATAN* INCIDENT**
(1861) **V–386a**
Powhatan River VI–451a
See also James River
POWNALL, FORT (Maine)
V–386a
Pownall, John (offi.) I–327a
Pownall, Thomas (col. gov.)
III–120b; V–386a
POWWOW V–386b;
III–381b; V–210b
Poyas, Peter VI–304a
Poznán (Pol.)
Treaty of Versailles
VII–173a
PQ–17 (convoy) I–214b
PRAGMATISM V–386b;
III–112b; V–287b, 288a
Pragmatism, political
VII–52b
PRAIRIE V–387a; II–390b;
III–118b
ecology II–392a
forage crops IV–424a
Grand Prairie III–209b
Osage hedge V–174a
pioneers V–316b, 317a,b
Red River cart traffic
VI–64a
Sauk Prairie VI–218b
settlement III–10b
soil III–16a; IV–103a
sorghum VI–340a
wheat IV–211a
windmills VII–257a
wolf II–252b
Prairie, The IV–161b
PRAIRIE DOGS V–387b;
VI–458b
PRAIRIE DU CHIEN (Wis.)
V–387b; III–89b;
VII–306b
Fort Crawford II–253b;
IV–355b
fur trade II–34a
Giard Tract III–177b
Indian factory II–480a
Indian hostilities I–242b;
II–297a
Sioux treaties VI–296a
trading house III–142b
War of 1812 VII–307b
PRAIRIE DU CHIEN, INDIAN TREATY AT (1825)
V–388b; III–383b;
VI–296a
Prairie du Rocher (Ill.)
I–100b
Prairie Farmer (period.)
I–45b
PRAIRIE FIRES V–388b;
II–251a
PRAIRIE GROVE, BATTLE AT (1862) **V–389a**
Prairie hen III–150a
Prairie Island (Minn.)
IV–355a
Prairie Kings I–4a
Prairie Land and Cattle Company V–160b
Prairie rose VI–395 (table)
"Prairies" (poem) IV–161b
PRAIRIE SCHOONERS
V–389b; II–158b, 248a;
III–82a; VII–100b, 217a, 218a
Prairie State VI–393 (table)
Prairie States Forestry Project
III–74a
Prairie style (arch.) I–165a
Prairie Traveler IV–240a
"Prairie triangle" II–226b
Prat, Don Pedro (physic.)
VI–244b
Pratt, Caleb (eng.) I–363b
Pratt, Charles, and Company
VI–383a
Pratt, Charles, 1st Earl Camden (jur., pol.) I–412b;
VII–14b
Pratt, Enoch (philan.)
I–250a
Pratt, John H. (astron.)
III–166b, 480b, 481a
Pratt, Orson (Mormon)
III–477a
Pratt, R. H. (off.) I–455a
Pratt, Roger (arch.) I–161a
Pratt, Thomas (eng.) I–363b, 364a
Pratt and Whitney I–236a
Pratt and Whitney and Wright
I–51a
Pratt and Whitney engine
II–345a
Pratte, Bernard (fur trader)
II–34a
Pratte, Chouteau and Company I–105b; II–34a
Pratt-Smoot Act (1931)
IV–147b
Prayer healing III–49b
Prayer meetings III–326a
"Prayer of Twenty Millions"
II–435b
Prayers
banned in schools II–400a
Preaching
frontier III–127b; IV–365b
Preakness III–305a
Preble, Edward (nav. off.)
I–266a,b; II–190b; V–19a
Precedents of the House of Representatives VI–169b
Precinct, political V–345a
Precisionism (paint.) V–192b
Precognition V–212b, 213a
PREEMPTION V–389b;
I–400b; V–444a, 453a
Clay's land distribution bill
IV–91a
Hungarian exiles V–42a
New York and Genesee Company V–81b
Texas VII–35b
Preemption Act (1841)
II–70b, 336a; IV–100a, 315a; VII–268b
Preetorius, Emil (pub.)
V–75b
Prefabricated building
I–379a
Preface to a Twenty-Volume Suicide Note IV–167b
Preface to Morals IV–164a
PREFERENTIAL VOTING
V–390a
Prehistoric cultures. *See* Archaeology and Prehistory, North American
Premedical program IV–3a
Premont (Fr.) VI–338b
Prendergast, Maurice B. (paint.) II–104a; V–192a
Prentice, David (eng.)
VI–409a
Prentiss, B. M. (off.)
III–269b
Prentiss, Seargent Smith (law., legis.) V–161a; VII–181a
"Prepared in mind and resources" (motto) VI–395 (table)
PREPAREDNESS V–390b;
II–314a; IV–457a
Preparedness Day (1916)
IV–406a
Pre-Raphaelite style
III–445a, 446a
Presbytere (New Orleans)
I–160a
Presbyterian and Reformed Review (period.) VI–82b
Presbyterian Church in the United States II–272b
Presbyterian Church in the United States, Southern
V–392a,b
Presbyterian Church in the United States of America
V–392a
PRESBYTERIANISM
V–391a; VI–76b, 77b, 78a, 78a,b, 82a
Afro-American churches
I–23a–24a
American Home Missionary Society III–469a
Assemblies of God
V–260a
Calvinism I–410b
camp meetings I–434a
church-covenant II–248a
circuit riders II–39b
College of New Jersey
II–395a
colleges II–114a
colonial missions
IV–365a,b
colonial schools II–394b
colonial society II–125b
colonization of blacks
I–101a
Cotton Kingdom II–241a
Cumberland Presbyterian Church II–272b
Dissenters II–353a
East Jersey V–57a
foreign missions IV–366b
frontier preaching
III–127b
Great Revival III–221b
Huguenots III–315a
hymns III–326a
Indian Shaker religion
VI–267b
Lapwai Mission IV–108a
Log College IV–179b
Massachusetts Bay colony
I–412a
missionaries I–476a;
III–385b

PRESBYTERIANISM (cont.)
New England I–412a
New England Way V–52a
New Lights V–408b
New York State V–87a
parochial schools VI–228b
Plan of Union II–170a; V–324a
religious education II–399b
Rice–Campbell debates VI–135b
Saint Louis Observer V–70b
Saybrook Platform VI–223b
Second Awakening I–238b
Separatists VI–262a,b
Shenandoah Valley VI–275b
slavery schism II–36b
Soctch–Irish VI–240a
Synod of Dort VI–456a
Virginia VI–75b
Western Reserve VII–275a
Westminster Confession VII–279a
Yale Band VII–350b
Presbyterian Ministers' Fund III–426b, 432a
Presbyterian Synod IV–179b
Preschool education II–400a, 402b
Prescott (Ariz.) I–142b; II–251b
Prescott (Can.) III–318a
Prescott, Samuel (patriot) VI–106a
Prescott, Samuel Cate (sci.) I–444b, 445a
Prescott, William (off.) I–382b; II–364a
Prescott, William H. (hist.) III–281b; IV–163a, 267a
Preservation, food. *See* Food Preservation
PRESERVATION MOVEMENT V–392b; I–165b
collecting II–98b–99a, 101a
colonial Williamsburg VII–301b
federal legislation II–47b
Independence National Historical Park III–354a
Mount Vernon IV–423a
national parks and monuments V–216b, 219a
National Trust for Historic Preservation IV–471b
Saint Augustine VI–188a
Society of the Sons of the Revolution VI–339b
Stratford Hall VI–417b
See also Museums
Preservation News (news.) IV–472a
Preservation Services, Office of IV–472a
Preservatives
pure food and drug movement V–466a
Preserves III–129a
PRESIDENT V–394a; II–453b; III–2a, 3a,b
alien and sedition laws I–86b
ambassadors I–93a; II–202a, 437a
amnesty I–114b
appointments II–167b–68a, 201b, 479a
blockade powers I–116a
bureaucracy I–384a–b
cabinet I–400a; II–201b, 498a
census reports I–482b
Central Intelligence Agency III–439b
checks and balances II–4b
Civil Aeronautics Administration II–49b
civil service II–59b–60b
Coast Guard II–89a
commander in chief I–183a; II–313a
commercial treaties VII–108b–09a
Commodity Credit Corporation I–44b
compensation II–201b
comptroller general II–152a, 501b
comptroller of the currency II–153b
Congress II–171a, 174–78 (table), 201b–02a, 472a–73a
congressional appropriations I–148b–49a
courts–martial procedures VII–143b
Customs Service II–276b
democratization V–223b
diplomatic missions II–342a–43a
disability V–397a
discretionary powers I–12a,b
dispensing powers IV–36b
enemy trading VII–93b
executive agents II–471a
executive agreements II–471b
executive branch reorganization II–497b
executive orders II–473a
executive privilege II–473b
exemption from subpoena V–397b
extension of powers IV–57b
extra sessions II–172b, 478b
federal agencies II–497b–501b
Federal Election Commission V–449a
Federal Register III–5b
federal troops IV–341b
First Lady III–26a
flag III–34a, 35b
foreign policy II–171b, 178b, 323a
habeas corpus III–237a
impeachment II–198b, 202a; III–343b
inauguration III–350b
inherent powers III–417a
Interstate Commerce Commission III–458a
item veto III–484b
legal counsel IV–21b
legislation II–199b
loyalty oath IV–202b
martial law IV–258b
Medal of Honor II–310a
messages to Congress V–398a
military law IV–342b
militia IV–259b–60a
National Guard IV–463b, 464a
National Labor Relations Board IV–467a,b
national party committee V–344b
National Security Council III–439a
Neutrality Acts of 1935–37 V–38a–b
Nixon resignation V–98b
nominating system II–216a; V–101b
oath of office II–201b
Office of Management and Budget V–136b
officers commissions II–202a
Philippines IV–7b
pocket veto V–334b
political party leadership V–344a,b
proclamations V–425a
qualifications II–201a
radio broadcasts II–424b
reciprocal trade agreements VI–52a,b, 53a
recognition power VI–54b
removal power III–317a; IV–446a; VI–84b
salary grab VI–198b
Secret Service VI–252a; VII–108a
senatorial courtesy II–246a
separation of powers V–385b
speaker of the House VI–369a
succession to office V–398b
Supreme Court VI–443b–44a, 448a
tariff II–323a; III–20a; VI–464b–65a, 469a,b–70a; VII–89a
term of office I–95a; II–200b, 206b, 207a; VII–132b
territorial governments VII–31b
third–term doctrine VII–53a
title V–399a
treatymaking II–201b, 471b; IV–385a; VII–109b–10a,b
veto II–199b; VII–177b
vice–president II–172a, 207b; VII–178b
Virginia Dynasty VII–201b
war–making powers VII–223b–25a, 226a–27b
Washington, D.C., government VII–245a,b
White House II–497b; VII–291b
See also Election of the President
PRESIDENT (frigate) **V–393b**
"President" (railroad car) V–463a
President Adams (galley) III–147b
Presidential candidates. *See* Campaigns, Presidential; Election of the President
PRESIDENTIAL DISABILITY V–397a; II–172a, 479b
Presidential Elections. *See* Campaigns, Presidential; Election of the President; Electoral College
PRESIDENTIAL EXEMPTION FROM SUBPOENA V–397b; I–388b
Burr trial I–388b
Presidential libraries I–167b; III–284a,b
PRESIDENTIAL MESSAGES V–398a; II–201b, 481a
PRESIDENTIAL SUCCESSION V–398b; II–201a–b
Nixon resignation V–98b
secretary of state VI–388b
speaker of the House VI–368b
Twelfth Amendment VII–131b–32a
Twentieth Amendment II–206b
Twenty–fifth Amendment I–95a; II–207b; VII–133a
vice–presidency VII–178b
PRESIDENTIAL TITLE V–399a
President James A. Garfield (sculp.) VI–243b
President pro tempore (Senate) II–207b; V–398b, 449a
President's Advisory Council on Executive Organization II–497b
"President's Birthday Balls" V–340a
President's Commission on Higher Education II–401a
President's Commission on Law Enforcement and Administration of Justice II–263b, 374b; V–416b–17a
President's Committee on Administrative Management II–497b
President's Committee on Consumer Interests II–209a
President's Committee on Education Beyond High School II–401a
President's Committee on Juvenile Delinquency II–148a
President's Committee on Rural Poverty (1966) I–43b
President's Emergency Employment Committee VI–73a
President's Emergency Relief Organization VI–73a
"President's March" (song) III–238b

Prince, Thomas (cler., hist.) II–107b; III–280b
Prince, Walter Franklin V–213a; VI–440a
Prince Edward County (Va.) VII–196a
Prince Edward Island (Can.) VI–130a; VII–150b
Prince George, Fort (Pa.) V–144a
PRINCE GEORGE, FORT (S.C.) **V–408a**
Prince Hall Grand Lodge (Boston) III–109a
Prince of Wales (battleship) I–67a; VII–76b
Prince of Wales American Volunteers 130a VI–130a
Prince of Wales Island III–238a
Prince of Wales Strait V–122a
Princeton (N.J.) IV–251b; V–96a–b
Princeton (N.J.) III–423b; V–253a
Princeton (warship) V–408b; VII–240b
PRINCETON, BATTLE OF (1777) **V–408a**; II–321b; IV–413a; VI–123b; VII–116b
***PRINCETON*, EXPLOSION ON THE** (1844) **V–408b**; III–99b
Princeton conservatism (rel.) VI–82a,b
Princeton Seminary. *See* Princeton University
PRINCETON UNIVERSITY V–408b; II–114b; IV–179b; V–41a
  archives I–169a
  chemistry II–10a
  football III–56b
  Institute for Advanced Study III–424a
  library II–108a
  political science V–348b–49a
  rugby III–56b
  Washington and Lee University VII–249a
Prince William Sound II–385b
Principall Navigations, Voiages, and Discoveries of the English Nation. *See* Hakluyt's *Voyages*
PRINCIPIO COMPANY V–409a
Principles and Practice of Medicine VII–126a
Principles of Psychology IV–163b; V–288a
Principles of Scientific Management III–406a
Pring, Martin (expl.) IV–37a, 264b; V–53b, 359b
Pringle, John (expl.) II–477a
Pringle, Samuel (expl.) II–477a
Printers, public I–3a
PRINTERS, TRAMP V–409b; V–77b
PRINTER'S DEVIL V–410a
"Printer's grammars" V–410b
Printer's Ink (jour.) I–18b, 19a
PRINTING V–410a; V–69b
  apprenticeship I–148b
  Bay Psalm Book I–279b
  book publishing I–333b–34a
  colonial III–413b
  cotton industry II–239a
  magazines IV–222a
  Minnesota IV–358a
  music II–454a
  newspapers V–77a–b
  New York State V–87b
  printer's devil V–410a
  tramp printers V–409b
  type manufacture III–441b
  See also Newspapers
Printing, government. *See* Government Publications
PRINTING PRESS, EARLY AMERICAN V–413a; II–454a; III–173b; IV–108a; V–77a, 410a–11a
Printing press, electric II–413a
"Printing-press money" II–256a
PRINTMAKING V–413a
Prints
  copyright II–224b
Printz, Johan Björnsson (col. gov.) V–80b, 332b
Prior discovery, right of II–406b
Priorities Board (World War I) VII–328a
Prison Association of New York IV–20a; V–415b
Prison camps, confederate. *See* Andersonville; Castle Thunder; Confederate Prisons
PRISON CAMPS, UNION V–414a
  atrocities I–219b
  Camp Butler I–433a
  Camp Chase I–433a
  Camp Douglas I–433a; II–222b
  Canadian plots against I–435a
  Castle Thunder I–466b
  Elmira II–433a
  Fort Lafayette IV–83b
  Governors Island III–206b
  Johnson's Island I–433a; IV–4b
  Northwest conspiracy V–121b
  Point Lookout II–433a
Prison Commission, International V–416a
Prisoners, exchange of. *See* Exchange of Prisoners
Prisoners of war
  atrocities I–219b
  exchange II–468a
  Galvanized Yankees III–148b
  Geneva Conventions III–161b
  Korea IV–56b
  Red Cross VI–62a
  Treaty of Versailles VII–173a
  Vietnam War VII–184b, 186b, 226a
  War of 1812 II–292a–b
  Young Men's Christian Association VII–363a
Prison labor. *See* Convict Labor Systems
Prisons, Bureau of VI–68b
PRISONS AND PRISON REFORM V–415a; VII–312a
  American Civil Liberties Union I–100b
  Attica I–220a
  Auburn system I–221a
  Charity Organization Society VI–327b
  colonial punishment V–464b
  federal system IV–22a; VI–327b–28a
  flogging III–36b
  Fort Leavenworth IV–129b
  "Jukes" Family IV–20a
  juvenile criminals IV–23a,b
  minority rights IV–359a
  parole V–221a
  Pennsylvania prison system V–252b
  phrenologists V–294a
  Quakers V–470b
  reformatories VI–67b
  riots VII–192a
  segregation VI–256a
  separate system I–221a
  silent system I–221a
  Social Gospel VI–325a
  social pacifism V–181b
  social work VI–331a
  solitary system I–221a
  state government VI–398b
  Virginia VII–195b
PRISON SHIPS V–418b; I–219b; III–498b; VI–118a
Pritchard, Benjamin D. (off.) II–294b
Privacy, right of I–100b; II–378b
Private enterprise
  capitalism I–448b
  Fifth Amendment II–378a
  Fourteenth Amendment II–378a
Privateer (patrol plane) I–55b
PRIVATEERS AND PRIVATEERING V–418b; V–25a; VII–348b
  armed merchantmen IV–313a
  artillery V–26a
  Baltimore clipper I–251a
  Civil War II–63a; V–17b
  Declaration of Paris I–321a; V–34b, 214a; VII–225b
  Dutch War of 1653 VI–134a
  France III–121a
  freedom of the seas III–106a–b
  Galveston pirates III–148b
  Genêt mission III–159b
  immunity of private property III–343a
  Laffites I–265b
  Latin-American independence wars IV–114b, 115b
  letters of marque and reprisal IV–256a
  Little Sarah affair IV–169b
  Louisburg IV–192a
  Loyalists VI–129b
  merchantmen VII–241b–42a
  Naval War With France V–15a
  piracy V–320a
  prize money V–423a
  Queen Anne's War VI–2b
  revolutionary war I–438a; II–258a; IV–432a; V–18b, 54a; VI–199b, 365a
  Rhode Island VI–132a
  War of 1812 V–19a
  Yankee VII–352a
Private property
  Civil War confiscation II–168a
  contract clause II–213b
  See also Search and Seizure, Unreasonable
Private property, immunity of. *See* Immunity of Private Property
Private schools. *See* Schools, Private
PRIVILEGE IN COLONIAL GOVERNMENTS V–419b
Privileges and Elections Committee IV–210b
PRIVILEGES AND IMMUNITIES OF CITIZENS V–420a; VI–402a
  Fourteenth Amendment II–205a; III–86a,b
  Slaughterhouse Cases VI–303a
  voting II–410a
PRIVY COUNCIL V–421a; VI–363b
  colonial administration IV–188b; VI–109a
  colonial agents II–116b
  colonial assemblies II–118a
  colonial commerce IV–242b
  colonial governors II–120b
  colonial judiciary II–121a
  colonial policy II–123a
  colonial rule V–220b
  colonial statutes IV–12b
  Council for Foreign Plantations II–241b
  Council for New England II–242a
  Court of High Commission III–274b
  Heath Patent III–268a
  Hutchinson letters III–320b
  orders in council V–162a
  Parson's Cause V–221b

right of appeal IV–15a
royal disallowance VI–166b
Prize Act (1941) V–421b
PRIZE CASES, CIVIL WAR V–421a; VII–224b
Amy Warwick I–116a
Bermuda I–292a
Dolphin II–360a
Jürgen Lorentzen IV–20b
Springbok VI–376b
PRIZE COURTS V–421b; II–447a; III–237b; IV–182a, 256a
Articles of Confederation I–14b
prize money V–423a
Rule of the War of 1756 VI–169a
visit and search VII–205a
world wars III–106b
PRIZEFIGHTING V–422a
PRIZE MONEY V–423a; VII–242a
Franco-American prize cases III–98a
revolutionary war financing VI–120
Shenandoah VI–274b
Probate court. *See* Surrogate's Court
Probation IV–23a,b; V–418a
Probation and Parole Association, National II–263b
Probationers and Parolees, Interstate Compact for the Supervision of III–460a–b
Proceedings of the American Electro-chemical Society II–11b
Prochett, Matteo VII–219b
PROCLAMATION MONEY V–424a
PROCLAMATION OF 1763 V–424b; I–340b; IV–92b, 330b, 371a; V–144a; VI–110b, 112a–b, 165b, 385b
Florida government III–38b
Indian territory III–388a
Loyal Land Company IV–201b
Old Southwest VI–356a
Tryon's Line VII–125b
western lands VII–273a
westward movement VII–283a
Proclamation of Amnesty (1865) V–425a, 425a
PROCLAMATIONS V–425a; VI–246b
Procter and Gamble I–17b; VI–323b, 324a; VII–124a
Proctor, F. F. (theat. mgr.) VII–167b
Proctor, Henry A. (off.) IV–300b, 329b; VI–42a, 412a; VII–45b
Produce Exchange (N.Y.C.) I–378b
Produce exchanges II–281b, 469b
Produce Loan Act (1862) II–164a
Producers' cooperatives. *See* Cooperatives, producers'
Production Code (motion pictures) IV–418b
Production Code Administration I–480a
Production credit associations I–44b; III–447a
PRODUCTIVITY, CONCEPT OF V–425b
Industrial Revolution III–411a
inflation III–414a
labor VI–469b
scientific management VI–233b
wages VII–213b
Productivity Trends in the United States V–426a
PROFITEERING V–426a
Civil War II–63a, 68a–b
munitions IV–433b
revolutionary war III–79a; VI–120b
PROFIT SHARING V–426b; IV–70a; V–255a,b
***PROGRESS AND POVERTY* V–426b**; IV–163b; VI–293a–b
Progressive Education Association II–400b
Progressive Labor party VI–421b
Progressive Mine Workers of America II–4a
PROGRESSIVE MOVEMENT V–427a; VII–135a, 135a
antitrust legislation II–71b
automobile patent-sharing I–227a
California I–406b
campaign of 1912 I–426b–27a
campaign of 1916 I–427a
campaign of 1924 I–428a
Chicago Area Projects II–147b
child labor III–247a–b
commerce clause II–136a–b
direct primary V–407a
efficiency movement VI–234b
Farmer-Labor party of Minnesota II–490b
Farmer-Labor party of 1920 II–492b
historiography III–282b–83a
initiative III–418b
Kansas IV–26b
La Follette party IV–84b
liberalism IV–140b
Louisiana IV–194b
mental health IV–304a
Michigan IV–331b
Mississippi IV–369a
muckraking IV–425a
New Nationalism V–60a
New York City V–83b
New York State V–87b
Niagara movement V–93a
Nonpartisan League V–106b
Philadelphia V–278a
philanthropy V–280a
pressure groups V–400b, 401a
public utilities IV–427b–28a
railroad rates VI–22a
recall VI–51a
referendum VI–66b
regulation of business I–389b
Republican party VI–93a
robber barons VI–157a
South Dakota VI–350a
"standpatters" VI–385a
taxation VII–6b
unicameralism VII–142b
Washington State VII–248a
Wyoming VII–346a
PROGRESSIVE PARTY (1947–52) **V–429a**; II–480b
American Labor party I–107b
campaign of 1948 I–429b
Communist party II–146b
Progressive party, La Follete (1924). *See* La Follette Progressive Party
Progressive party of 1912–16. *See* Bull Moose Party
PROHIBITION (1919–33) **V–429b**; II–263b; IV–159a; V–73a; VII–23b, 289b, 294b
Anti-Saloon League I–134a
blue laws I–325a
bootlegging I–339a
brewing industry I–362a
campaign of 1928 I–428b
campaign of 1932 I–428b
Canadian relations I–439b
Chicago II–18a
congressional debate III–22a
crime II–258b
Customs Service II–277a–b
distilling II–354a
federal-state enforcement VII–154b
I'm Alone Case III–332a
Iowa IV–425b
Kansas opposition IV–26b
Maine IV–226b
moonshine IV–407b
padlock injunction V–184b
Progressive movement V–427a
repeal II–262a, 277b, 354a; VII–132a–b
smuggling I–292b; II–277b; VI–170a
speakeasies VI–368a
taxation VII–13a
Tennessee VII–26a
territorial waters VII–33a
Volstead Act VII–207b
winemaking VII–305b
Woman's Christian Temperance Union VII–312a
See also Eighteenth Amendment
PROHIBITION PARTY V–430b; V–400b, 429b; VII–23a–b
campaign of 1884 I–424a
campaign of 1888 I–424b
campaign of 1904 I–426a
campaign of 1932 I–428b
campaign of 1936 I–429a
platforms V–329a
Progressive movement V–428b
Project Apollo IV–460a,b
Project BOOST V–24a
Project Gemini IV–459b–60a
Project Headstart II–148b
Projectile points II–334b, 386a; III–484a,b
Projectiles, unmanned II–426a
Project Mercury I–209b–10a; IV–459b, 460a
Project Mohole III–167b
Projector, motion picture IV–417a
Project Skylab IV–460b
Prokhorov, A. M. (phys.) IV–262b
Proletarian party VI–326a
Promissory note II–1b–2a
PROMONTORY POINT (Utah) **V–430b**; I–485b; VI–27a; VII–101a, 147b, 161b
PROPAGANDA V–431a
agencies II–499a
book publishing I–334b
campaign slogans VI–313a
Civil War II–63b, 65b, 66b–67a, 159a–b
cold war II–97b
committees of correspondence VI–121b
Council of National Defense II–243b
fast days II–497a
folksongs IV–441a
House Committee on Un-American Activities III–308a
Illuminati of New England III–332a
intervention III–461b
Jeffersonian Republicans VI–94a
military photography V–293b
nativism V–2b–3b, 279a
Office of Strategic Services V–138a
Order of United Americans VII–149a
pamphleteering V–199a
Parson Brownlow's Book V–221a
peace movements V–235a–b
pressure groups V–400a
psychological warfare V–440b
public opinion V–453b, 454a,b
revolutionary war I–345a; II–140a; IV–142b; VII–61a
Sons of Liberty VI–339a
summit conferences VI–439a
tracts VII–82a

PROPAGANDA (cont.)
treason VII–106b
Uncle Tom's Cabin VII–137b
World War I II–139b; V–74a
yellow journalism VII–356a
See also World Wars, Propaganda in the
Propane V–267a–b
PROPERTY V–433a
boundary laws III–10a
community property VI–364b
contract clause II–213b
corporation holdings II–229a
democracy II–326a
due process II–377a–78b; III–204b
eminent domain II–439b
flood damage III–37b
income taxes V–354b
inheritance tax laws III–417b
insurance III–426b
intestate estates III–464a
Jeffersonian Democracy III–496a
mortgage relief legislation IV–414a
political theories V–352b
protection of I–299a
"public interest" V–456a
quitrents VI–4a
radicalism VI–13b
right to do business III–419a
slaves II–370b, 377b
state police power V–339a–b
statutes of limitations VI–405b
stay and valuation acts VI–406a
strikes VII–121a
taxation II–164b, 245b, 502a; III–153b, 351b; VI–105b, 152a; VII–3a–b, 5a–6a, 9a–11b, 12b
title II–309b
"turf and twig" VII–129b
uniform legislation II–457b
See also Confiscation of Property; entries under Land
Property, immunity of private. *See* Immunity of Private Property
PROPERTY QUALIFICATIONS V–434b; III–91a,b; V–108b; VI–431a, 432a, 434b; VII–208b
colonial settlements VI–433b–34a
New York III–437b
North Carolina V–115b
office-holding II–325b
Solid South VI–337a
South Carolina III–92b
state constitutions VI–390b
Supreme Court rulings III–94a
Virginia VII–193a, 194a–b
voting II–325b
PROPHET DANCE V–434b
PROPHET'S TOWN (Ind.) **V–435a**; VII–63a,b
PROPORTIONAL REPRESENTATION V–435a; II–410a; V–390b
Proposal for Reducing Delinquency and Expanding Opportunities II–148a
PROPRIETARY AGENT V–435b
PROPRIETARY PROVINCES V–436a; III–18a, 78b; VI–396a
agents V–435b
British colonial policy II–122b
Carolina I–457b–58a; II–124a; III–212b; V–115a
charters I–499b, 500a; II–118b
colonial courts I–145a
councils II–119a
crown lands II–266b
Delaware II–124a
Duke of York's proprietary VII–359a
fundamental constitutions III–132a,b
Gorges' Province of Maine III–200a–b
governors II–120a
Laconia IV–82b
Manors IV–241b
Martha's Vineyard IV–258a
Maryland I–172b; IV–260a
New Hampshire II–124a
New Jersey II–124a; V–56b
New York II–124a
palatine jurisdictions V–194b
Pejebscot Purchase V–242a
Pennsylvania II–124a–b; V–246a–b
quitrents VI–4a; VII–3a
religious liberty VI–80b
royal colonies VI–166a
Saco Bay VI–184a
South Carolina VI–347a
Virginia VII–200a–b
West Jersey VII–278a–b
Proprietors
colonial economy II–229a
colonial governors II–120a
colonial land speculation IV–98b
common lands II–141a
local land titles IV–91b
Maryland II–36a, 117b
New Jersey II–431b
New York II–117b
Pennsylvania II–157a
South Carolina I–496a,b, 498a
Virginia II–481a–b
Proprietors, Carolina. *See* Carolina Proprietors
Propulsion IV–106a
Prosopography III–281b
PROSPECTORS V–437a; II–477b; III–32a
Prosser, Gabriel. *See* Gabriel's Insurrection
PROSTITUTION V–437b; II–258a–b, 259b; V–355b; VII–206a, 312b
army slang VI–300b
cow towns II–252a
deportation II–333a
depression of 1873–78 V–207b
immigration laws I–87b; II–445a
Mann Act IV–240b
New York City IV–138a
organized crime II–259b–60a, 261a
padlock injunction V–184a
political corruption II–232a
punishment II–376b
"Raines Law" hotels VI–40b
saloons VI–201b
venereal disease VI–267a
woman's rights movement VII–313b
Protection. *See* Tariff
PROTECTIVE WAR CLAIMS ASSOCIATION V–438b
Proteins I–303a–04a, 303b; II–12b, 357b, 358a; III–158a
See also Molecular Biology
Protein synthesis III–157b
Pro temporibus et causis II–496b
Protestant (period.) V–2b
Protestant Conference IV–206b
Protestant Episcopal Church II–36b, 455a–b
Protestant ethic IV–334b
Protestantism II–465b–66b
antebellum South VI–343a
Connecticut II–181a
Episcopal church V–179b
Evangelical Alliance II–465a
foreign missions IV–366a–b
frontier missions IV–366b–67a
Georgia III–168a
missions II–13b
moral code IV–408a
mysticism IV–448a
nativism V–2a
New York State V–87a
Puritanism V–469a
schools II–397a
Protestant Reformation II–393a; III–316b
Protestant Reformation Society V–2b
Protestant Reformed Church in America VI–69a
Protestant Revolution (1689) IV–260b
Protestants, French. *See* Huguenots
Protest songs IV–441a–b
Protoceras I–242b
"Protocol of Peace" II–82b
Protons II–278a,b; IV–119a; V–298b–99a,b, 302a
Protozoology IV–251a
PROTRACTED MEETING V–438b
Proud, Robert (hist.) III–280b
Prout's Neck (Maine) VI–184a
Providence (Md.) VI–264b
Providence (R.I.) V–230b; VI–132a, 133a,b; VII–82b
Arkwright machinery I–175a
Baptist church I–264b
bathtubs I–274b
Brown University I–372a
College Hill II–47b
colonial assembly II–117b
electric railway VI–40a
Gaspée burning III–153b
health department I–241a
King Philip's War IV–47b
limestone I–477a
organized crime II–262b
Pequot Trail V–261a
pewter work VI–291b
post road V–375a
public health V–447a
railroads VI–25a, 35b
religion VI–76a
revolutionary war V–66a
scarlet fever IV–150b
settlement II–124a
silver work VI–290a
stagecoach lines VI–380a
statistics VII–206b
Vose Gallery II–102a
Providence (ship) VI–128a, 129a
Providence, divine. *See* Divine Providences
Providence Agreements III–132b
Providence College (R.I.) II–362b
Providence Gazette (news.) V–439b
Providence Island I–499b; V–439a
PROVIDENCE ISLAND COMPANY V–438b; I–500a
PROVIDENCE PLANTATIONS V–439a; V–65b; VI–131b–32a
Providence Public Library (R.I.) IV–146a
Providences, doctrine of II–356a
Provident Institution for Savings I–263b; II–255a
Provident Loan Society I–495a
Province Forts IV–268b
Provincetown (Mass.) I–447a; IV–264b
Pilgrims IV–278b; V–313b
PROVINCETOWN PLAYERS V–439b; VII–49b
Provincial art III–47a
PROVINCIAL CONGRESSES V–439b; VI–121b, 122a
Massachusetts IV–360b

New Jersey V–57a
New York V–85b, 86a
South Carolina VI–347a
state constitutions VI–390b
Washington District VII–250a
Provincial Councils of Baltimore. *See* Baltimore Councils, Provincial and Plenary
Provoost, Samuel (cler.) II–455a
Provost, Étienne (guide) I–201a; II–477b; VII–103b
Prowse, D. W. (au.) VI–379a
Proximity fuse I–200a; II–425a; IV–3b, 352a; V–27a, 137b, 164a, 296a; VII–335b, 343b
Prudential Insurance Company I–18a; III–434b; V–41b
Prudential Steamship Company IV–312a
Prudhoe Bay I–80a
Prudhomme, Fort (Miss.) II–22a
PRUDHOMME BLUFFS V–440b
Prussia
Declaration of Paris V–214a
French and Indian War III–115b
slave trade VI–309b
PRUSSIA, TREATIES WITH V–440b; I–245a; VII–86b, 111a, 370a
Przhevalski's horse III–302a
Psalmody III–326a
Psalm-singing IV–443a
Psalter VI–227a
Psychedelic drugs II–262b; IV–451a
Psychiatric Association, American IV–305b
Psychiatry IV–304a, 306a,b, 307a
Henry Phipps Clinic IV–3b
mental hygiene movement IV–304a
parapsychology V–213b
Psychiatry, American Journal of IV–305b
Psychical Research, American Society for V–213a,b
Psychical Research, Society for V–213a
Psychic powers
theosophy VII–52a
See also Parapsychology
Psychoanalysis IV–306a, 307a; V–442b
Psychohistory III–281b
Psychokinesis V–212b, 213a
Psychological Association, American V–442a,b
Psychological Review (jour.) V–442a
PSYCHOLOGICAL WARFARE V–440b; V–432a
World War II VII–333b, 335b
PSYCHOLOGY V–441a; IV–307a
advertising I–18b–19a
American Journal of Psychology IV–2b
drug abuse IV–451a
industrial relations III–408a
intelligence tests III–440a
mental hygiene movement IV–304a
mysticism IV–448a
occupational medicine IV–293a
parapsychology V–213a
phrenology V–293b
pragmatism III–112b
public opinion V–454a
slavery I–28a
Psychology, American Journal of V–442a
Psychology, Journal of Experimental V–442b
Psychopharmacology IV–306b
Psychosurgery IV–306b, 307a
Psychotherapy IV–307a
Psychotics. *See* Mental Illness, Treatment of
Psywar. *See* Psychological Warfare
PT 109 II–312a
Ptolemy (astron., geog.) IV–247a
Puaráy (N.Mex.) I–288b; IV–367b
Public Archives Commission I–106a
Publications, government. *See* Government Publications
"PUBLIC BE DAMNED" V–443a
Public Contracts Act (1936) II–24a; IV–78b
Public corporations. *See* Government Corporations
PUBLIC CREDIT ACT (1790) **V–443a**
Public debt. *See* Debt, Public
Public defender systems III–179b
PUBLIC DOMAIN V–443b; IV–61b
Alaska I–80b
arid regions I–170b–71a
Ballinger–Pinchot controversy I–247b
cabin rights I–400a
cattle I–471a; II–251a; V–33a
claim associations II–70a–b, 70a–b
conservation II–188a
Cornell University II–227a
Department of the Interior III–444a
Desert Land Act II–335b
distribution of land and revenue IV–91a
donation–lands II–363a
enabling acts II–443b
Erie Triangle II–460b
fencing V–451b
forests III–73a,b, 74a,b, 75a–76b
free land III–107b
frontier defense III–126b
government policy IV–95b–96a
grants–in–aid III–211b
grazing III–273b; V–159b
Greenback party III–225a
Harrison Land Act III–257b
Homestead Act VII–268b–69a
homestead movement III–295b; IV–103b
Indian reservations III–395b
Indian Territory I–336a
Jefferson, Thomas II–166a
Justice Department IV–22a
land grants for education IV–93a
land grants for railways IV–94a; VI–26a
land policy IV–102b
land sales V–452b
land scrip IV–97a
land titles IV–105a
military bonuses I–330b–31a
minerals III–164a; IV–104b, 349a–b
naval oil reserves V–13a
New South V–66b
Northwest Territory V–152a
Oregon land frauds V–166a
preemption rights V–389b
public land commissions V–450a
reclamation VI–53b
Refugee Tract VI–70b
regulation IV–95a–b
Right of Way Law VI–140b
school lands VI–227b
sectionalism VI–253b
speculation IV–98b, 103a
timberlands VII–61b
Twelve–and–a–Quarter Million Acres Bill VI–327b
water resources III–321a
Webster–Hayne debate VII–265b
western land cessions VII–273b
Public funds. *See* Revenue, Public
PUBLIC HEALTH V–446b; I–495b; II–328a; IV–150b
army statistics IV–291a
automobile I–228a
Boston IV–67b
Charity Organization Society VI–327b
dentistry II–331b
environmental sanitation VI–211b
government inspection III–422a,b
grants–in–aid III–211b
Health, Education, and Welfare Department III–267b
Hill–Burton Act VI–402b
hookworm III–298b
hospitals III–306a
housing III–310a
hygiene III–324b–26a
Indians V–49a
Institute of Medicine IV–457b
laboratories I–241a,b
local government IV–171b
maternal and child health care IV–274b
meat inspection laws IV–279b
mining III–444b
National Board of Health IV–285b
National Institutes of Health IV–465a
National Science Foundation IV–470b
National Urban League V–1a
nursing V–127a
nutrition V–128a–29b
occupational medicine IV–293a
Philippine Islands V–281b
police power II–440a
product quality control II–230b
prostitution V–437b
Puerto Rico V–461a
Red Cross VI–61b
Rockefeller Foundation VI–157b
rural population VI–173a
slums VI–313b
smallpox VI–315a
statistics VII–206a–b
tuberculosis VII–126b–27a
venereal disease V–437b
veterinary medicine VII–177b
water supply VII–258a
See also Medical Research; Urban Health
Public Health Association, American V–447a
Public Health Service II–277a; III–35b, 267b; IV–229b–30a, 286a, 287a,b, 292a; V–447b
dairy industry II–280b
Division of Industrial Hygiene and Sanitation IV–294a
employee benefits I–478b
rural health VI–173b
vaccines V–467b
vitamin research I–303b
Public Information, Committee on. *See* Committee on Public Information
"Public interest" V–433b, 456b
PUBLICITY ACTS (1903, 1909) **V–448a**; III–459a
PUBLICITY AND CORRUPT–PRACTICES LAWS V–448a; I–415b; II–232b; V–228b, 341b, 347a
Publick Occurrences Both Foreign and Domestick (news.) V–68a–b
Public land. *See* Public Domain
PUBLIC LAND COMMISSIONS V–450a

Public Land Law Review Commission V–451a
PUBLIC LANDS, FENCING OF V–451b; III–10b
PUBLIC LANDS, SURVEY OF V–452a; I–463a; IV–95a
corruption V–450a
Land Act of 1796 IV–90b
Northwest Territory V–122b
Refugee Tract VI–70b
Seven Ranges survey VI–264a
townships V–350a
Public lands, Texas. *See* Texas Public Lands
PUBLIC LAND SALES V–452b; V–443b–44a
Ballinger–Pinchot controversy I–247b
Clay's land distribution bill IV–91a
compensated emancipation II–433b
corruption II–336a
cow custom II–251a
Deposit Act of 1836 II–333b
Desert Land Act II–335b
education funds II–396b
Graduation Act III–207a
Harrison Land Act III–257b
Land Act of 1796 IV–90b
Land Act of 1820 IV–90b
Macomb purchase IV–219b
national sinking fund VI–294a
Nebraska IV–33b
Oklahoma V–149a
preemption rights V–389b
reclamation VI–53b
Refugee Tract VI–70b
Relief Act of 1821 VI–75a
revenue I–113b, 453b; III–448b; VI–105a; VII–4b, 5a; 455a–
specie circular VI–369b
speculation II–45b, 336a
U.S. Treasury surplus II–333a
PUBLIC LAND STATES V–453a; IV–94a; V–444b–45a; VI–400b
Ordinance of 1785 IV–93b
railway land grants IV–94a
Right of Way Law VI–140b
swamplands VI–453a
Public Land Strip II–37a
Public Libraries in the United States of America (report) IV–145a
Public markets. *See* Markets, Public
PUBLIC OPINION V–453a
antebellum South II–298a
civil religion II–53a
committees of correspondence II–140a
Constitution II–190b
Davis, Jefferson II–295a
democracy II–324b
dueling II–377a
elections II–409b
League of Nations IV–124b
minority rights IV–358b
political polls I–416b
presidential messages V–398b
Prohibition II–407a
ratification of Constitution II–196b
Vietnam War VII–184a,b
World War I II–139b, 445b; VII–326a
PUBLIC OWNERSHIP V–454b
Cincinnati Southern Railroad VI–25a
Farmer–Labor party II–491a,b, 493a
Ohio utilities V–142a
Plumb Plan V–333a
postal service V–374a–b
Progressive movement V–428b
utilities V–456b
Public protest, right of I–100b
Public records. *See* Archives
Public relations
political campaigns I–416b; II–409b, 410b
Public Revenue. *See* Revenue, Public
Public Roads, Bureau of I–484b; II–135a, 502b, 502b; VI–152a; VII–98b
Public Salary Act (1939) VII–8a
Public schools. *See* Schools, public
Public School Society of New York City II–396b; VI–228b
PUBLIC UTILITIES V–456a; V–433b
business forecasts I–395a
electric power and light II–412b, 416b, 418a, 418a–b
federal regulation III–459a
gas II–418a
government inspection III–422a
government ownership II–234a; V–456a,b
holding companies III–290a,b
municipal ownership III–203a; IV–427b
nationalization II–492b
National Union for Social Justice IV–472b
New Deal V–46a,b
New York State V–87b
panic of 1929 V–209b
Philippines V–284b
prices V–402a, 403b
"public interest" V–30b
regulation I–390a; II–500b; III–458b; V–347a
securities II–255b
taxation VII–11a
trusts VII–121b, 123a
Public Utility Holding Company Act (1935) II–500a; III–290a,b; V–46b
Public works
labor's support IV–71a
state corporations II–302b
state financing II–303a
Public Works Administration IV–71a; V–44b; VI–74a–b, 425b; VII–323a
Pennsylvania Turnpike III–450b
pump-priming V–464a
Publishing. *See* Book Publishing; Magazines; Newspapers
Publius (pseud.) III–4a; V–353a
Puebla (Mex.) I–47b–48a; IV–252a
PUEBLO (Indians) **V–459a**; III–356a, 367a–68b, 396b; IV–315b; V–314a
Acoma I–7b
Apache I–141b, 142a
buckskin III–374a
cacique I–402a
Cibola II–37a
dance II–291a
drums II–291a
habitat I–288b
Hopi III–300b
irrigation VI–143b
Kansas IV–25a
liquor III–399a
medicine III–385a–b
missions IV–367a,b
myth and folklore III–386b
national monument V–217b
Navaho relations V–8b, 9a
New Mexico V–59b
Pecos V–241a
political organization III–391b
religion III–251a, 392a,b, 393a; V–459b
Rodríguez–Chamuscado expedition VI–162a
scalping VI–224b
smoking V–318a
Taos VI–461a
tobacco VII–65a
Zuni VII–372a
Pueblo (Colo.) II–382a; III–88a
railroad VI–35a
smelting VI–316b
western route V–224b
***PUEBLO* INCIDENT** (1968) **V–460a**; I–64b
Pueblo prehistoric culture phases I–117b, 157b, 329b
PUEBLO REVOLT (1680–96) **V–460b**; I–8a, 142a; III–368b; IV–367b; V–4a, 59b, 459b
Hopi III–301b
Santa Fe VI–214b
Taos VI–461a
Pueblos (arch.) I–159b, 166b; II–228b; III–405a
Bonito I–329b
building materials I–377a
Puerco River III–304a
Puerperal fever IV–275a, 285b
Puerto Bello (Pan.) III–498a
Puerto Plata (Santo Domingo) IV–251b
Puerto Ricans
civil rights II–55b–56a
drug distribution II–262b
El Diario V–75b
New York State V–88a
slums VI–314b
PUERTO RICO V–461a; II–346b; III–425a; VII–32b, 33b
annexation III–347a,b; IV–111a
army occupation I–188a
cession to U.S. I–126b, 454a; II–474b–75b; III–68b; VI–360b; VII–112a
citizenship V–6a
Delima v. *Bidwell* II–323b
domestic shipping IV–309a
encomiendas II–443b
gambling III–150a
government III–58a
hookworm III–298b; IV–291b
industry I–197b
minimum-wage law IV–352b, 353a
National Governors' Conference III–206b
nationalists I–202b, 203a
naturalization II–42b
piracy V–320b
Plymouth Company expedition V–333b
Ponce de León expedition V–356a
port authority V–368a
Spanish-American War III–150b; IV–252b; VI–362a,b, 363a
sugarcane VI–436b, 437a
tariff VII–13b–14a
territorial status III–424b
Treaty of Paris V–215a
workmen's compensation VI–185a
Puerto Soledad (Falkland Is.) II–484a
Pufendorf, Samuel von (jur.) II–149a; III–316b
Puffed rice I–488a
Puffed wheat I–488a
"Puff the Magic Dragon" (gunship) I–49b
Puget, Peter (nav. off.) V–462a
PUGET SOUND V–462a; I–441b; V–165a; VII–247b
dry docks II–375b
ferries III–11b
Fort Nisqually V–97b
Indian agency III–371b
Indian nativistic movement V–4a
Indians III–356a, 360b, 361b; IV–228b
Medicine Creek Treaty VI–412b
salmon VI–201a
Stevens' railroad survey VI–413a
Vancouver's exploration VII–166a

Yakima Wars VII–350a
Puget Sound Navy Yard V–29b
Pugin, Augustus W. N. (arch.) I–163b
Pujo, Arsène (pol.). *See* Pujo Committee
PUJO COMMITTEE V–462a; III–6a, 466a
Pulaski (Tenn.) IV–57b
Pulaski, Casimir (off.) II–406b; V–462b; VI–126b, 129a, 221a
PULASKI, FORT (Ga.) **V–462b**; III–78b; V–217b; VI–220b
Pulaski County (Ky.)
Civil War IV–347a
Pulitzer, Joseph (jour.) V–75a,b, 79b
New York World II–268b; V–71b, 73b
yellow journalism VI–360a; VII–356a
Pulitzer Prize I–207b; V–72b, 79b
Pulkova (Russ.) I–211a
Pulkovo Observatory (Leningrad) V–131b
Pulliam, Eugene C. (ed.) V–73b
Pullman (Ill.) II–46a; IV–66b; V–463a
Pullman, George M. (inv.) III–80a; IV–100b; VI–36a; VII–101a
Field Museum III–19a
sleeping cars V–462b
subsistence homesteads VI–426b
Pullman Company IV–66b; VI–36a; VII–123b
Pullman Palace Car Company V–463a
PULLMANS V–462b; VI–36a; VII–101a
PULLMAN STRIKE (1894) **V–463a**; II–17b, 298b–99a; III–201a; IV–66b–67a; VI–419a
American Railway Union I–111b
Debs trial VII–117b
injunction III–419a
railroad brotherhoods VI–20a
U.S. Army II–252b
Pulp. *See* Paper and Pulp Industry
Pulp paper magazines II–341b
Pulque III–398a
Pulsars VI–17a
Pulteney, William. *See* Pulteney Purchase
Pulteney Associates IV–135b; V–463b
PULTENEY PURCHASE V–463b; V–88b
Pummelo (fruit) II–43a
Pumpelly, Raphael (geol.) I–482a
Pumpkin I–36a, 47b, 157a; III–51a, 381a
"Pumpkin papers" VII–310b
PUMP-PRIMING V–463b
New Deal V–45b, 48a,b; VI–425b
Pumps (shoes) II–372b
Puncher (cowboy) II–251b
Punished Women's Fork II–379b
PUNISHMENT, CRUEL AND UNUSUAL V–464a; II–204b
Bill of Rights I–299a; II–204b
hanging III–249b
"running the gauntlet" III–154b
PUNISHMENTS, COLONIAL V–464b; IV–240b
ducking stool II–376a–b
flogging III–36b
hanging III–249b
hue and cry III–314a
pillory V–313b
piracy V–320a
pressing to death V–400a
Rogerenes VI–162b
sex crimes VI–265b
stocks VI–413b
sumptuary laws VI–440b
tar and feathers VI–462a
Punta del Este (Uru.) V–171a
Punta del Este Charter (1961) V–205b
Purcell (Okla.) II–34b; VII–96a
Purcell, Edward M. (phys.) I–212a; V–100a
Purcell, James VI–215a,b
Purcell, Joseph (cartog.) VII–74a
Purchas, His Pilgrimes III–240b, 280a
Purchas, Samuel (compiler) III–240b, 280a
Purchase, Thomas (col.) IV–37a; V–242a
Purchasing power IV–393a
gold supply III–193a
inflation III–414b, 415a,b
See also Consumer Purchasing Power; Money
Purchasing Power of Money IV–233b
Purdue University IV–412b; VII–176b
Pure Food and Drug Act (1906) II–208b, 374a–b; III–2b, 53a,b; V–208b, 276a, 466a,b
PURE FOOD AND DRUG MOVEMENT V–465a
Food and Drug Administration III–53b
interstate commerce laws III–459a
meat inspection laws IV–279b
muckrakers IV–424b
urban health VII–158a,b
Virginia VII–195b
Pure Milk Association II–282a
Purgatoire River IV–110a, 208b; VI–215b
Purina whole wheat cereal I–487a
Purine base II–357b
Purísima Concepción Mission VI–207b
Puritan Revolution II–242b; IV–270a; V–469b; VI–396a
PURITANS AND PURITANISM V–486b; II–466a; VI–75a–76a,b
authoritarian government II–325a
Baptist movement I–264b
Bible Commonwealth I–294a
biography IV–163a
Body of Liberties III–132b
Cambridge Agreement I–411b
charity V–279b
Christmas II–496a
church membership suffrage II–35b
civil religion II–52b
colonial punishments V–464b
Court of High Commission III–274b–75a
divine providences II–496a
Dominion of New England V–50b
Dorchester Company II–364b
dress II–371a
Easter II–496a
East Jersey II–388b
education II–393b
Fort Pentegoet V–253b
Genevan Bible I–293b
Georgia III–169b
Great Migration III–220a
historiography III–280a–b
"holy society" II–125b
human rights III–316b
Illinois Band III–331b
Long Island settlements IV–185a
Magna Charta IV–224a–b
marriage IV–256a
Maryland I–466b; IV–260b; VI–264b
Massachusetts I–294a, 499b; II–125b, 242b; IV–269a,b
meetinghouse IV–300a
Merry Mount trading post IV–315a
moral code IV–408a,b
mysticism IV–447b
Newark V–41a
New England V–49b
New England Company V–51a
New England Way V–51b
New Haven II–180a; V–55a
New Jersey II–431b
philosophy V–286b
Pilgrims V–312b
Plymouth colony IV–264b
Providence Island Company V–439a
psalm-singing IV–437b
Quakers V–469b
religious liberty VII–69a
Revolution VI–113a
saints' days II–496a
Salem VI–199a
Separatists VI–262a
settlement II–124a; V–342a
sexual attitudes VI–265b
social welfare VI–327b
Westminster Confession of Faith V–391a
Purple finch VI–394 (table)
Purple Heart, Order of the II–311b, 312b
Purple lilac VI–394 (table)
Purple violet VI–394 (table)
Pursell, Henry D. (eng.) III–24a
Purses II–371b
Pursh, Frederick (bot.) I–349a
Purvis, Robert VII–138b
Purysburg (S.C.) III–315a
Pusan (Kor.) II–450a; IV–55b, 57a, 253a
Pusey, Edward B. (cler.) V–179a
Pusey, Nathan M. (educ.) III–260b
Pussey, Joshua IV–274b
Put-in-Bay II–458b, 459a
Put-In Bay Naval Battle. *See* Erie, Lake, Battle of
Putnam (pub.) I–334a
Putnam, Fort (N.Y.) VII–279b, 280a
Putnam, Frederick W. (anthrop.) I–128b; III–19a; IV–119b
Putnam, Gideon VI–218a
Putnam, Herbert (librarian) IV–145a, 147a, 148a
Putnam, Israel (off.) I–382b; VI–162b
Battle of Long Island IV–186a
Bunker Hill II–364a; VII–115a
Hudson River III–275b
Washington's eight months army VII–251b
Putnam, Paul A. (off.) VII–219a
Putnam, Rufus (off.) IV–250b; V–143b; VI–451a
Putnam County (N.Y.) III–313a; V–130b, 286a
Puts (fin.) II–470b
PWA. *See* Public Works Administration
Pygmalion (play) IV–442a
Pyle, Ernest T. ("Ernie") (jour.) V–74a, 147b
Pyle, Howard (illus.) I–335b; V–192a
Pynchon, John IV–280a
Pynchon, Thomas (au.) IV–165a
Pynchon, William (fur trader) III–140b–41a
Pyongyang (Kor.) IV–55b, 56a
See also Heijo
Pyramiding (bus.) III–290b; V–46b, 209b
Pyramids I–157b; III–289b
Pyrethrum III–421a
Pythias, Knights of VI–252b

Q

Quaboag River IV–47b
Quackenbos, G. P. (educ.) VI–227b
Quacks
dentistry II–329b–30a
Quadraphonic Radio Committee, National VI–16b
Quadraphonic sound V–290b–91a
Quahogs III–51a
Quail (bird) III–150a
Quail missile IV–363b
Quaker Bridge dam IV–5a
Quaker Hill, Battle at. *See* Rhode Island, Sullivan in
Quaker Oats I–486b–87a
Quaker Oats Company I–488a
QUAKERS V–469b; III–123a–b; V–342a
Afro-Americans II–403a
American Friends Service Committee V–280b
antislavery I–134b, 135a; V–247a; VI–305a, 347b
asylums III–306b
capital punishment V–415a
Civil War II–63b, 161b
colonial punishments V–464b
colonial schools II–394b
colonial society II–126a
conscientious objectors II–185a
Delaware II–124a–b
demographic study II–328b
Dissenters II–353a
East Jersey II–124b, 388b
flogging III–36b
Fort Christina II–35a
Friendly Association III–122b
fugitive slaves VII–138a,b
Germantown III–173a
Handsome Lake Cult III–249b
Hicksites III–274a–b
Holy Experiment III–293a
Keith controversy IV–35b
London Yearly Meeting IV–35b
Loyalists VI–115b
Massachusetts VI–440b
mysticism IV–447b
New Hampshire V–53b
New Jersey IV–397b; V–57a
Newport V–65b
North Carolina I–83b, 465a; V–115a
pacifism V–181a; VII–236a,b
Pennsylvania II–118a; V–246b
persecution IV–265a
philanthropy and benevolence V–279b
prison reform V–415a
private schools VI–228b
religious liberty VI–80b; VII–69a
revolutionary war V–247a; VII–201b
Rhode Island II–124a; VI–132a
River Rouge settlement IV–338b
Shaker beliefs VI–268a
slavery II–36b
suffrage VI–431a
tontine III–432b
West Jersey V–56b, 436b; VII–278a–b
World War I relief VII–330a
See also Friends, Society of
"Quality stabilization" bill (1964) II–483b
Qualla Reservation (N.C.) III–395a
Quang Nam province (Viet.) VII–186b
Quang Tri province (Viet.) VII–186a
Quantico (Va.) IV–252b, 253a; VII–196a
Quantitative Classification of Igneous Rocks V–268b
Quantrill, William Clarke (off.). *See* Quantrill's Raid
QUANTRILL'S RAID (1863) **V–471a**; IV–26a, 377b
Quantum electrodynamics V–296a
Quantum mechanics V–295b, 299a, 301a, 303a–b, 304a,b, 305a
Quantum statistics V–303b, 304a
Quantum theory IV–262a; V–295a, 303b, 304b, 305a; VI–259a
Quapaw (Indians) I–173b
Quarantine IV–285b, 287a; VII–157b–58a
astronauts IV–407a
public health V–446b, 447b
smallpox VI–315a
yellow fever VII–355a
Quarantine of Cuba (1962) I–321b; II–270b–71a
Quarter (coin) II–94b, 384b
Quarter-eagle (coin) II–95a, 384b
Quartering (punishment) V–465a
QUARTERING ACT (1765, 1766, 1774) **V–471b**; I–297a; II–93a; III–464a; VI–110b, 112a
Boston VII–81a
New York VII–80a
Quartering of troops. *See* Billeting
Quartermaster Corps III–35a
"Quarter sales" I–134a
"Quarter twain" IV–256a
Quartz III–270a, 328a; IV–403a
Quasars VI–17a
QUASI-JUDICIAL AGENCIES V–471b; II–499b–500a; IV–16b–17a
executive power of removal III–317a
National Labor Relations Board IV–467b
National Railroad Adjustment Board VI–21a
Quasi-public agencies II–457a
Quasi-War (1798–1800). *See* Naval War With France
Quay, Matthew Stanley (pol.) I–343b, 424a
Quebec (Can.) III–119a
Abnaki I–3a
Algonquin I–85b
British army VI–126b
cholera II–33b
colonial wars IV–226a
earthquakes II–385a
founding I–492b–93a
French and Indian War I–3b; III–115b–17a
Frontenac expedition III–125a
fur trade III–142a
Illinois III–329a
Indians III–358b, 360b
Jesuit missions III–499a
King George's War IV–46b
King William's War IV–49b; VI–1b–2a
Loyalists VI–131a; VII–150b
Michigan IV–330b
Montagnais-Naskapi I–441a
privateers VI–129b
Proclamation of 1763 V–424b
Radisson's voyages VI–18a
return to France VI–190b
revolutionary war I–193b–94a, 435b, 436a; IV–86b, 405b; VI–123a, 130a, 191a
Richelieu River VI–136b
Saint Francis mission VI–190a
Saint Lawrence River VI–192a
settlement V–52b
U.S. boundary VI–165b
U.S. trade VI–149a
War of 1812 III–247b
writs of assistance VII–345a
QUEBEC, CAPTURE OF (1759) **VI–1a**; II–126a–b; III–116b; IV–405b; VII–115a
QUEBEC, PHIPS'S ATTACK ON (1690) **VI–1b**
Quebec, Seminary of I–402a
QUEBEC ACT (1774) **VI–2a**; I–340b; II–247b, 309a; III–464a; V–425a
Illinois III–329a
Michigan IV–330b
Ohio country V–140b
western lands VII–273a
Quebec Conference (1943) I–123b
Queen Anne architecture I–164a
Queen Anne furniture III–134a–b, 136a, 138a
Queen Anne's Creek II–392b
QUEEN ANNE'S WAR (1702–13) **VI–2a**; II–126a; IV–265b
Apalache massacre I–143a
Indian allies I–465b
Louisiana IV–192b
New York Colony V–85a
privateering V–418b
recruitment IV–345b
Treaty of Utrecht VII–162b
Queen Charlotte (frigate) II–459b
Queen Charlotte Island III–238a
Queen City of the South. *See* New Orleans
"Queen City of the West" II–37b
Queen Elizabeth (film) IV–417b
Queen Ester (mestiza) VII–346b
Queen Maude Mountains I–399a
Queen of France (ship) VI–128b–29a
Queens (N.Y.) V–82a; VI–460a
Queen's American Rangers VI–46b, 130a, 131a
Queensborough Patent. *See* Kayoderosseras Patent
Queens College (N.J.). *See* Rutgers University
Queen's College (N.Y.) II–114b, 395a
Queens County (N.Y.) III–271b; IV–185b, 186a; V–86a
Queenston (Ont., Can.) V–91b
V–90b–91a
QUEENSTON HEIGHTS, BATTLE OF (1812) **VI–3a**; I–281b, 316b, 436b
Queenstown (Ire.) VII–328b
Queensware V–379b
Queet (Indians) III–395b
Quemoy (China) II–489a; III–70a
Quero (ship) VI–199b
Questa (N.Mex.) III–15a
Questioner and the Sphinx (paint.) V–190a
Queue (hair style) III–239b
Quezon, Manuel V–283b, 284a
Quicklime II–5a
Quidor, John (paint.) V–189b
QUIDS VI–3a
campaign of 1808 I–417b
Quiet Sun, International Year of the (1964–65) III–454a

Quigley, Martin (pub.) IV–418b
Quileute (Indians) III–395b
Quilting parties V–317b
Quilts III–48a
Quimby, Phineas P. (mental healer) V–81a
Quinault (Indians) III–362a, 395b
Quinault Reservation (Wash.) III–395b
Quinby, Moses (beekeeper) I–284a
Quincy (Ill.) IV–155b
Quincy (Mass.) II–398b; III–279b; IV–278a, 314b; VI–24b
Quincy, Josiah (law., pol.) IV–267a; VI–250a; VII–117a–b
Quincy, Josiah, Jr. (law.) I–346a; II–437a
Qui Nhon (Viet.) VII–183b
Quinine III–381a, 385b; IV–229b, 230a; VII–65b
Quinn, John I–333a
Quinnipiac (Conn.) V–55a–b
Quinnipiac River II–179b
Quinn v. *United States* (1915) III–93a
Quintero, John (Juan) II–65b, 158b
Quintero, José (dir.) VII–51a
QUINTEROS BAY EPISODE (1891) **VI–3b**
Quintipartite Deed (1676) II–388b; V–56b; VII–278b
Quitman, John A. (off.) I–494b; IV–329a
Qui transtulit sustinet (motto) VI–393 (table)
QUITRENTS VI–4a; III–18a; IV–101b, 102b; V–437a; VII–3a
crown lands II–266b
New Jersey V–56b
North Carolina V–115a
Transylvania Company VII–103a
West Jersey VII–278b
Quivira. *See* Gran Quivira
Quonset Point (R.I.) V–28a
Quorum
Congress II–199a
QUOTA SYSTEM VI–4b; II–432b; III–333b–34b III 342b–
Chinese II–30a
German refugees V–342a–b
Germany III–337a
McCarran–Walter Act IV–209b
National Origins Quota Act I–88a
Yugoslavia III–340a
QUO WARRANTO VI–4b

R

R–5D (cargo plane) I–291a
R–38 (airship) II–344a
RABAUL, AIR CAMPAIGN AGAINST (1943–44) **VI–5a**; I–307b, 350a; II–33a; III–229a; V–21a
Rabbeth, Francis J. (inv.) VII–43b
Rabbi IV–9a, 11a
Rabbinical Assembly of America IV–11a
Rabbinical Council of America IV–11a
Rabbit III–133a, 358b, 362b, 368a; IV–280b
Rabbit Redux IV–165b
Rabi, I. I. (phys.) V–100a, 302a
Rabies I–241a; IV–291b; VII–176a
Rabinowitch, Eugene (biophys.) VI–230b
Raccoon III–133a, 142a, 150a, 402b; VII–105a
Racehorses II–260b
RACE RELATIONS VI–5b
Afro–Americans in the Military IV–339b
antebellum South VI–341a, 342a
backlash I–239a
Baptist church I–265a
California I–405b, 408b
Chicago II–18b
city planning II–47b, 49a
civil disobedience II–50b
civil rights movement II–56a
Community Action Program II–148a
Congress of Racial Equality II–179b
equal protection of the law II–457a
miscegenation IV–362b
Mississippi IV–369a,b
National Advisory Commission on Civil Disorders IV–457b
New South V–67b
Niagara movement V–93a
Pan–Africanism V–199a
Radical Republicans VI–11b
referendum VI–67a
religious debate VI–80a
riots VI–8a
slavery VI–304b–05a, 306a,b
slums VI–314b–15a
states' rights III–349a
urban structure VII–159b
Washington, D.C. VII–246a
White Caps VII–291a
White League VII–292b
yellow peril VII–356a
RACE RIOTS VI–8a; I–29b, 30a, 31b–32a; II–59a, 259a; VI–7a,b; VII–191a
Chicago III–436a
Detroit II–337b; IV–258b, 258b
Houston IV–340a
King, Martin Luther, assassination IV–46a
Memphis III–103b
National Advisory Commission on Civil Disorders IV–457b
Newark V–41b
New Orleans III–103b
New York City III–253a
slums VI–314b, 315a
Springfield (Ill.) IV–460b
Washington, D.C. VII–246a
Watts II–259a
Wilmington VII–303a
"Race to the Sea" (1914) VII–115a
Racetracks
crime II–260a,b
Racial Equality, Congress of. *See* Congress of Racial Equality
Racial integration. *See* Integration
Racial segregation. *See* Segregation
Racine (Wis.) VII–307b
Racing. *See* Automobile;Horse Racing; Yacht Racing
Racism I–25b–26a, 29a
black nationalism I–315b
German–American Bund III–172a
Indians I–106b
Knights of the White Camelia IV–53a
Racketeering
bossism I–343b
unions I–103a
RADAR VI–9a; II–425a,b–26a; III–410a; IV–333a; V–14a, 164a, 296a, 304b; VI–259a
air defense I–58a, 62a
air search II–345b
aviation I–69b, 234b
calculators II–153b
cannon I–57b
guided missiles IV–363b
hurricanes II–76b
Naval Research Laboratory V–28a
Office of Scientific Research and Development V–137b
sets II–423b
Signal Corps VI–286a
submarines VI–423a
systems I–287b; II–38b
telescopes I–212b
towboating VII–77a,b–78a
U–boats I–214b; II–218a
vacuum tubes VII–163b, 164a
Vietnam War V–22a
weather forecasts VII–264a,b
World War II VII–335b, 342b, 343b
Radburn (N.J.) II–46b
Radcliffe–Brown, A. R. (anthrop.) I–129a
Radcliffe College IV–267b
Radial engines I–236a
Radiation
control I–391b; V–467b
Food and Drug Administration III–54a
Van Allen belts II–426a
Radiation Biology Laboratory (Rockville, Md.) VI–319b
Radiation Laboratories (M.I.T.) IV–333a
Radical Monotheism in Western Culture VI–83a
Radical Reconstruction. *See* Reconstruction
RADICAL REPUBLICANS VI–10b; II–64a; VI–13b, 57b, 58b, 92b–93a
abolition VI–308a
Afro–American suffrage III–20a, 92a–b
Alabama I–71b
American Colonization Society I–101a
amnesty I–115a
bloody shirt issue I–323b
Committee on the Conduct of the War II–140a
election of 1866 IV–228a
emancipation II–435a
Ex parte McCardle IV–209a
Freedmen's Bureau III–103b
Hamburg riot III–244a
ironclad oath III–474a
Johnson impeachment III–345b
Joint Committee on Reconstruction IV–6a
loyalty oaths VII–35a
Mississippi IV–369a
New Departure policy V–49a
opposition IV–472b
Pomeroy Circular V–356a
Porter court-martial V–369a
Reconstruction Acts IV–376a; VI–59a
Red Shirts VI–65a
restoration of home rule III–295a
scalawags VI–223b
Slaughterhouse Cases VI–303a
Soldiers and Sailors conventions VI–336a
Supreme Court packing VI–448b
Tenure of Office Act VII–31b
Union League of America IV–201b
Wade–Davis Bill VII–213a
War Amendments VII–226b
woman's rights movement III–91b
RADICAL RIGHT VI–12a
Radicals (chem.) II–12b

RADICALS AND RADICALISM VI–13a
Democratic party I–267b–68a
depression of 1873–78 V–207b
Haymarket Riot III–266a
Industrial Workers of the World III–412b
Jews IV–10a
labor strikes IV–63b
loyalty oaths IV–203a
Lusk Committee IV–205b
philanthropy V–281a
Puritans V–469a
Radical Republicans VI–10b
radical right VI–12a
railroad strike of 1877 VI–38b
Socialist labor movement IV–68a
Socialist party VI–326b–27a
Sons of Liberty (Revolution) VI–338b
Students for a Democratic Society VI–421a
U.S. Steel strike IV–69b
Western Federation of Miners VII–272b
World War I newspapers V–74a
youth movements VII–365a–66a
RADIO VI–14b; I–39b; III–409b; IV–222b, 271b
automobiles I–229b
censorship I–480a–b, 481a–b
cereal advertising I–488a
communications II–423b–24a
cowboy songs II–250b
electronic amplifier circuits II–39a
Federal Communications Commission I–13a, 480b
folklore III–49a
guidance systems III–502a
imports VII–90a
libel IV–139b
microwaves IV–333a
miniaturization IV–352a
minstrel shows IV–359b
networks I–19b
news V–79b; VII–152b
New York Times properties V–76b
political campaigns I–415b, 416b
prices V–406a
psychological warfare V–441a
public utilities V–456b
regulation II–229b–30a; III–1a–b; IV–272a
rural areas VI–175b
sales II–332b
science VI–230b
Signal Corps VI–286a
slang VI–300a, 302b
soap advertising VI–323b
stereophonic broadcasts V–290b
storage battery I–276a
taxation VII–7b
transatlantic communication II–142b
transistors VI–259a
treaties VII–113a
two-way I–51a
U.S. Information Agency II–499a
vacuum tubes VII–163a
Voice of America VII–207a
weather forecasts VII–264a,b
See also Advertising; Radar
Radioactivity II–278a; IV–294b; V–298a–b, 299b–300a
Radio Act (1912) VI–15a,b
Radio Act (1927) VI–15b
RADIO ASTRONOMY VI–16b; I–212a–b, 287b; IV–262b; V–132a
Radio Astronomy Observatory, National I–212b
RADIOCARBON DATING VI–17b; II–12b; IV–421b; VII–114b
Radiochemistry II–12a
Radio Commission, Federal I–480b; III–459a; VI–15b
Radio Corporation of America I–242a; II–424a; VI–15a, 16a,b
television VII–21b, 22a
transistors VI–259a
Radio detecting and ranging. *See* Radar
Radioelements II–278a; V–299b
Radio Engineers, Institute of II–449a
Radioisotopes I–303b; II–278b
Radiological weapons II–9b
Radiometric dating VII–114b
Radio–phonographs V–290b
Radiosonde VII–264b
Radiotelegraphy II–423a–b
Radiotelephony VI–15a
Radio telescopes I–212a–b
Radio time signal V–133b
Radio tube III–156a
Radischev, Aleksandr N. VI–177b
Radisson, Pierre Esprit (expl.) II–246a; III–403b
See also Radisson's *Voyages*
RADISSON'S *VOYAGES* VI–18a; III–313a; VI–192a; VII–307a
Lake Superior VI–443a
Minnesota IV–355a
Mississippi Valley IV–375b
Wisconsin II–13b; VII–307a
Radium IV–350b
RAF. *See* Royal Air Force
Rafinesque, Constantine S. (nat.) III–27a; VI–90a, 237a
RAFTING, EARLY VI–18b; IV–347b; VII–99b
Raft River III–215a
RAGC. *See* Royal and Ancient Golf Club
Ragtime II–290b; IV–439b
Ragtown (Nev.) III–215a
Raguet, Condy (econ.) I–252a
Raikes, Robert (ed.) VI–442a
Railcar ferries III–11b
RAIL FENCES VI–19a; III–10b
Rail Passenger Act (1970) III–458b
Rail Passenger Service Act (1971) III–451a
RAILROAD ADMINISTRATION, U.S. VI–19a; VI–29a; VII–99a
Plumb Plan V–333a
rates VI–22a
RAILROAD BROTHERHOODS VI–19b; IV–62b, 66a,b; VI–28b
American Railway Union I–111b
campaign of 1924 IV–70a
Conference for Progressive Political Action IV–84b
strike of 1946 IV–74a
Railroad compensation tax VII–4b
RAILROAD CONSPIRACY (1849–50) **VI–20a**
RAILROAD CONVENTIONS VI–20b
Railroad Labor Board VI–21a, 29b; VII–99a
Railroad land grants. *See* Land Grants for Railways
RAILROAD MEDIATION ACTS VI–21a; II–157b, 500b; VI–29b–30a, 419b, 419b
Adamson Act I–10a
Railway Labor Act III–407a; IV–467a; VII–202a
railway shopmen's strike VI–40b
Railroad Pension Act (1934) VI–24a
Railroad pools. *See* Pools, Railroad
RAILROAD RATE LAW VI–21b; II–323a; III–458a; V–358a, 458a
Elkins Act II–431b
Hepburn Act III–273a; V–208b
Transportation Act of 1958 VI–30b
Wisconsin VII–308b–09a
RAILROAD RATE WARS VI–22b; VI–49b–50a
Railroad rebates. *See* Rebates, Railroad
RAILROAD RETIREMENT ACTS VI–23b; V–45b, 45b, 47a; VI–29b, 30b; VII–13a
RAILROAD RETIREMENT BOARD* v. *ALTON RAILROAD COMPANY (1935) **VI–24a**; VI–23b–24a
Railroad retirement system V–255a
RAILROADS VI–24a; III–223b, 449b–50a,b, 451a–b, 452a; IV–244a; VII–100b, 101a–b, 102a,b, 272a
Aeolus I–20b
agriculture I–38b, 40a, 42b
airmail I–65b
air rights IV–104b
Alaska I–77b, 78a
Albany I–82a
Albuquerque I–83b
Allegheny Portage I–89a, 443b; V–247a
American Railway Association I–111b
Amtrak I–391b; III–451a–b, 458b; VII–102b
antebellum South VI–352a
Anthracite Strike I–127a
antimonopoly parties I–133a
arbitration of labor disputes IV–64b
Arkansas I–173a
army defense I–192a,b, 193a
Atchison (Kans.) I–213a
Atchison, Topeka and Santa Fe I–213a, 214b; VI–191b, 216a
Atlantic and Gulf VI–220b
Atlantic and Pacific I–214b
Baltimore and Ohio III–449b, 450a, 451b; VI–23a, 38b; VII–71a, 83b, 100b
Baltimore riot I–251b
bankruptcy laws I–262b
big business I–389a
Blue Ridge I–325b
Board of Mediation and Conciliation IV–68b
boomtowns II–45b
Boston and Maine V–456a; VI–298a
Boston and Providence VII–101a
brewing industry I–362a
bridges I–363b, 363b–64a
buffalo trails I–376a
Burlington I–386a–b
Burlington Northern III–451b
Burlington strike I–386a
Camden and Amboy II–322a; V–57b
car ferries III–11b
cattle I–473b; II–248b–49a, 358b
cement rock I–477b
Central of Georgia VI–220a
Central Pacific I–485a–b; III–450a; V–430b; VI–425a; VII–147b
Charleston and Hamburg III–450a
Chesapeake and Ohio I–325b; III–451b, 488a
Chicago II–17b, 20a
Chicago and Alton V–462b
Chicago, Burlington and

Quincy III–451b; V–119a; VII–308b–09a
Chicago Great Western VI–191b
Chihuahua Trail II–23b
Chinese labor II–29b
Chisholm Trail II–32a
circus II–40b–41a
cities II–41b
city planning II–45b–46a
Cleveland II–75a
Cleveland and Mahoning V–249b
coasting trade II–90b
Colorado II–128a
Colorado Narrow-Gauge II–129a
Columbia River Valley II–131b
commerce cause II–135b–36b
congressional investigation II–271a
construction gangs II–251b
contract labor II–214b
convict labor II–216b
Council Bluffs II–241b
Court of Commerce II–134a–b
cow country II–250b
cow towns II–251b
Coxey's Army II–252b
dairy industry II–280b
Denver II–332a
Denver and Salt Lake VII–128b
desegregation III–107b
disasters II–350b–51a, 350b–51a, 351b
discrimination II–493a–b
domestic trade VII–83b, 84a,b, 87a–b
dry farming II–375b–76a
Elkins Act II–431b–32a
Erie V–87a; VI–23a; VII–83b, 100b
Erie Canal II–460a
Erie Lackawanna V–456a
European investments I–245a
export of equipment I–263a
express companies I–102b
federal aid II–501b
federal takeover (1943) IV–73b
financing II–218b
Florida III–39a,b, 42a; V–254b
flour trade III–44b
folklore III–49a
food shipment III–52b
foreign investments III–63b–65b
foreign loans II–301a
Fort Worth and Denver VI–380b
Gadsden Purchase III–145a
government ownership II–491a; III–202b, 203a
government regulation I–389b, 390a; III–204a,b; V–457b–58a, 459a
government survey VI–39a
grain elevators II–430a
Grand Trunk VI–23a
Grand Trunk Western VII–128a
Granger laws III–209b
Granger movement III–210a
great fortunes III–79a–b
Great Northern III–451b; V–119a; VI–413a; VII–101a, 128b
Great Western III–450a
Gulf, Mobile and Ohio III–451b
Hannibal and Saint Joseph III–250b; IV–380a; VI–191b
Hepburn Act III–273a
hide and tallow trade III–274b
holding companies III–290a,b
Hoosac Tunnel III–299a
Houston and Texas Central VII–40a
Hudson and Manhattan VII–128a
Hudson River III–312b
Idaho III–328a,b
Illinois Central I–403b; III–451b
Indiana III–370b
Indian opposition IV–109a
Industrial Revolution III–411b, 412a
International and Great Northern VII–40a
Interstate Commerce Act II–135b, 432a; VII–124b
Interstate Commerce Commission III–458a
investment VI–370b
Iowa III–468b
Isthmus of Panama I–295a
Jersey Central V–456a
Kansas IV–26a,b
Kansas City (Mo.) IV–27b
Kansas-Nebraska Act IV–28b
Kansas Pacific IV–30b; VI–320b
land grant mineral rights IV– 104b
land grants IV–94a, 96a, 101a; V–444a,b
landholdings IV–100a
land scrip IV–97b, 98a
land speculation IV–99b, 100a
Lehigh Valley V–250b, 456a
Lexington and Kentucky IV–137b
livestock VI–414a
locomotives IV–175a
Long Island III–451a
Louisville, Cincinnati and Charleston VI–349b
machine tools IV–216a
Maine IV–226b
management techniques IV–273a
meat-packing IV–170a
Memphis and Charleston IV–302a
Menominee Iron Range IV–303b
Michigan Central III–449b; VI–20a–b; VII–128b
Michigan Southern III–449b
Minnesota IV–357a
Mississippi IV–369a
Missouri IV–378a
Missouri, Kansas and Texas VII–40a, 187b
Mobile and Ohio VII–129a
Mohawk and Hudson IV–386b; V–87a; VI–225b–26a
Mohawk Valley IV–387a
monopoly powers I–225a
Montana IV–403a
Mussel Slough incident IV–444a
Nashville and Chattanooga IV–453b
National Mediation Board II–157b, 500b
Naval Observatory time V–12b
Nebraska V–31a
New England V–50a
New Hampshire V–54a
New Haven Railroad V–261a
New Jersey V–41b
New Mexico V–60a
New Orleans V–62a
New South V–66b–67a
New York, New Haven and Hartford VII–97a
New York and Harlem VII–127b
New York Central III–312b; V–87a, 443a; VI–22b, 23a; VII–83b, 100b
New York City V–83a
Norfolk V–109b–10a
Norfolk and Western VII–195b
North Carolina V–116a,b, 117a
North Dakota V–117a
Northern Pacific I–329a; III–451b; V–119a; VII–101a, 248a
Northern Securities Company v. *United States* V–119a
Ogdensburg V–139b
Ohio V–141b
Oil Creek V–318b, 319a
oil transport V–269b
Oklahoma V–148b
Orange and Alexandria I–381a
Oregon Short Line V–168a
ore transportation IV–123a
overland freighting V–177b
Panama V–200b, 203b
panic of 1837 V–206b
panic of 1857 V–207a
panic of 1873 V–207a–b
panic of 1907 V–208a
panic of 1929 V–209b
Penn Central III–451a,b; V–278a
Pennsylvania III–312b; V–247a,b, 277b, 443a; VI–22b, 23a, 383a; VII–83a, 83b, 100b, 128a–b
Pennsylvania canal system V–250a
Pennsylvania Railroad III–408b; IV–89b; V–250a
Philadelphia and Reading V–208a
"piggybacking" (transport) IV–420a
Plumb Plan V–333a
pools V–358a
populism V–364b–65a, 365b
postal service V–372a
Prairie du Chien V–388a
price-fixing IV–399a; V–402a
private banks I–263b
Progressive movement V–427b
"public be damned" V–443a
public utilities V–456b
Pullman (Ill.) II–46a
Pullmans V–462b
Pullman strike II–17b, 298b–99a; V–463a
Railroad Retirement Board II–499a, 499b
rails VI–39b
rainmaking VI–42a
ranching VI–45a
Reading II–86b; V–278a
rebates VI–49b
Reconstruction Finance Corporation VI–59b–60a
reforestation VI–67a
refrigerator cars III–55a; IV–281a
Republican party VI–92b
resorts and spas VI–101a
retirement plans V–255b
Richmond (Va.) VI–137a
Right of Way Law VI–140b
road construction VI–153b
robberies VII–97a
Rock Island III–449b
Rock Island Bridge Case VI–159b
Rocky Mountains VI–160b
Saint Louis VI–194b
Saint Louis and San Francisco I–214b
Santa Fe VI–208b; VII–289a
Sante Fe VII–294a
Sante Fe-Southern Pacific VII–101a
"sea train" VI–281a
securities I–16b
segregation I–372b; III–502b; VI–255b–56a
shipping III–218a–b
sleeping cars II–17b
soap advertising VI–323b
South Carolina VI–349b
Southern Pacific VII–40a, 40a, 367b
southern route VI–353b
Spokane, Portland and Seattle III–451b

RAILROADS (cont.)
stagelines VI–380a–b
state debts VI–95b
state fairs VI–392b
state geological surveys III–164b
state regulation III–209b–10a
station architecture I–164a
steamboat competition VI–148b
steam engines VI–409b
steamship lines II–91a
strikes III–407a; IV–63b, 64a, 66b–67a, 69b, 74a
subsidies VI–425a,b
Sunbury and Erie V–250b
surveys III–221a
telecommunications II–425b
telegraph VII–18b
Tennessee VII–26a
Texas VII–39a, 40a, 41b–42a
Texas and Pacific VI–38b; VII–40a
transcontinental I–172a–b, 453a; II–29b, 229b, 230a, 433b; IV–94a, 101a
Transportation Act of 1920 VII–99a
trust VII–155a
tunnels VII–127b–28a
Union Pacific I–485a–b; III–450a; V–119a, 139a, 168a, 430b; VI–191b, 425a; VII–147a, 345b, 346a
Utah VII–161b
Utah Central VI–203b
Vermont VII–172b
versus airlines I–69a,b
versus canals I–127b
versus stage lines V–178a
Virginia VII–195a–b
Virginia Central I–325b
wartime controls I–390b
Washington VII–221b
West Virginia VII–282a
whaling VII–285b
Wichita VII–294a
work force V–132b
World War I III–129b; IV–69a–b, 419b; VI–19a–b; VII–326a
"yellow-dog" contract VII–354b
See also Interurban Electric Lines
Railroads, Association of American III–451a; VI–28a, 29b, 30a
Railroad Safety Appliance Act (1893) III–458a
RAILROADS IN THE CIVIL WAR VI–37b; II–69a,b, 163b, 165a, 253a; VI–26b
Andrews' raid I–118b
Appomattox I–146b
Baltimore and Ohio III–332b
Battle at Tupelo VII–129a
Battle of Ezra Church II–497b
Battle of Raymond VI–48b
Iron Mountain railroad III–101a
Louisville and Nashville IV–426b
Nashville and Chattanooga IV–453b
Petersburg siege V–265a
Union army logistics I–190a
West Point and Montgomery Railroad VI–166a
"Railroads on Trial" (article) IV–424b
RAILROAD STRIKE OF 1877 VI–38b; IV–63b, 258b; V–207b; VI–419a
RAILROAD STRIKES OF 1886 VI–38b
RAILROAD SURVEYS, GOVERNMENT VI–39a; I–453a; VII–74b, 272a–b
arid regions I–170b
fish collections III–27b
southern railroad route VI–353b
Stevens, Isaac I. VI–412b
survey VI–90b
transcontinental I–188a, 463b
Whipple's expedition VII–289a
Railroads' War Board VI–19a, 29a
Railroad Trainmen, Brotherhood of VI–20a, 28b
Railroad Wage Commission IV–69a
RAILS VI–39b; III–471 (table), 472b; VI–30b, 36a
Rails–end towns III–270b
"RAIL SPLITTER" VI–40a
Railway Administration. *See* Railroad Administration, United States
Railway and Locomotive Historical Society III–279a
Railway Commission of Louisiana VI–283b
Railway Conductors, Order of VI–19b–20a, 28b
Railway Express Agency I–102b
Railway Labor Acts. *See* Railroad Mediation Acts
Railway Labor Executives Association VI–29b
Railway Passengers Assurance Company III–435a
RAILWAYS, ELECTRIC VI–40a; II–415a; VI–418a–b
elevated II–428a
signaling apparatus II–414b
Railways, street. *See* Street Railways
Railway Service, United States V–456a
RAILWAY SHOPMEN'S STRIKE (1922) **VI–40b**; VI–21a, 29b
Railway viaducts I–378a
Rainbow (blimp) II–345b
Rainbow (yacht) VII–348b
Rainbow Bridge V–93b
Rainbow Bridge National Monument V–217b
Rain dance II–291a
Raines, John (pol.) VI–40b
RAINES LAW VI–40b
Rainey, Gertrude ("Ma") (sing.) IV–440a, 443b
Rainey, Henry Thomas (law.) II–177 (table)
RAINFALL VI–40b; VII–264b
disasters II–349b
hurricanes III–319b–20a
Johnstown flood IV–5a
man-made II–76b
tree planting VII–114a
RAINMAKING ON THE GREAT PLAINS VI–42a
Rains, Gabriel J. (off.) VII–350a–b
Rains, George Washington (inv.) II–163a
Rains, James S. (off.) II–379a
Rainy Lake VI–443a
Rainy Season in the Tropics (paint.) V–189a
Raisin in the Sun IV–167a
Raisin River III–316a
RAISIN RIVER MASSACRE (1813) **VI–42a**
Rajchmann, Jan (phys.) II–156a
Rakes, horse-drawn IV–424a
Raleigh (N.C.) V–116b; VII–211b
civil rights movement II–58a
Civil War I–458b; II–68b
fall line II–485a
North Carolina Standard II–165a
Raleigh (cruiser) IV–239b
Raleigh, Fort (N.C.) VI–43a,b
Raleigh, Sir Walter (navig., hist.) III–240b; IV–37a; V–324a; VII–64b
See also Raleigh's Lost Colony; Raleigh's Patent and First Colony
RALEIGH CONFERENCE OF SOUTHERN GOVERNORS (1856) **VI–42b**
RALEIGH LETTER (1844) **VI–42b**
Raleigh News and Observer (news.) V–73b
Raleigh Register (news.) IV–282a
RALEIGH'S LOST COLONY VI–42b; IV–203b; V–115a; VI–44a; VII–192b
RALEIGH'S PATENT AND FIRST COLONY VI–43b; I–16a; II–122b; III–180b; V–115a
RALEIGH TAVERN (Va.) **VI–44a**; VII–302a
Rall, Johann (off.) II–321a–b; VII–116a,b
Ralston, William C. (fin.) II–157a; VI–44a–b
Ralston Creek (Colo.) gold V–311a
Ralston-Purina Company I–487a
RALSTON'S RING VI–44a
Ram (ship) IV–85a
Ramage, Adam (mfr.) V–413a
Ramage, John (paint.) IV–352a
Ramapo Mountains VI–412a
Rambault, Charles (miss.) VI–443a
Rambouillet Decree (1810) III–121b; IV–449b
RAMS, CONFEDERATE VI–44b; VII–181b
Ramsay, David (hist.) III–280b; V–199a
Ramsey, Alexander (gov.) IV–356a,b
Ramusio, Giambattista (cartog.) IV–452a
RANCH VI–44b; III–126a, 302b
alien landholding I–87b
cattle industry I–471b
foreign investments III–63a, 65a,b
Fort Lancaster IV–89b
hide and tallow trade III–274b
Montana IV–403a
mustangs IV–444b–45a
prairie dogs V–387b
roundup VI–161a
South Dakota VI–350a
Trinchera Ranch VI–210b
Wyoming VII–346a
XIT Ranch VI–380b
Rancheros II–247a
Rancho Cahuenga. *See* Cahuenga, Treaty of
Rancho Santa Ana Botanic Garden I–348b
RANCHOS DEL REY (royal ranches) **VI–45b**
Ranchos de Taos (N.Mex.) VI–461a
Randall, Fort (S.Dak.) I–314a; II–284a; III–256a
Randall, James Ryder (educ.) IV–262a
Randall, John Ryder (educ.) IV–261a
Randall, John T. (phys.) VII–163b
Randall, Robert R. (mer.) VI–186b–87a
Randall, Samuel J. (pol.) II–176 (table); VI–466b, 467a
Randall's Island IV–237a
Rand Corporation V–258b
Randin, Hughes (expl.) II–380a; V–156b
Rand McNally Building (Chicago) I–378a
Randolph (frigate) V–18b
Randolph, A. Philip (labor leader) II–56b
Randolph, Benjamin (craftsman) III–138a
Randolph, Edmund (states.) III–493b; V–346a, 347a; VII–300b
attorney general IV–21b
Bank of the United States

III–245b
Convention of 1787
II–193a,b, 194a
flees Charlottesville (1781)
IV–8b
Proclamation of Neutrality
V–36b
Virginia Plan II–151b
Randolph, Edward (col. offi.)
IV–188b, 265b, 270b;
VI–46a
RANDOLPH, FORT (W.Va.)
VI–45b
Randolph, John (of Roanoke)
(states.) V–161a
American Colonization Society I–101a
Doughfaces II–366a
duel with Clay II–377a
embargo of 1807 II–437a
Federalist party III–5a
Quids I–417b; VI–3b
tariff VI–466a
Virginia constitution
VII–194b
Yazoo land fraud IV–99a
Randolph, Peyton (law.)
VII–300b
Randolph, Thomas Jefferson
(fin.) VII–194b
Randolph, William (planter, adm.) VII–192b
Randolph Bluffs (Mo.)
IV–27b
Randolph County (Ill.)
I–501a; IV–277b
Randolph family IV–92a,
256b
RANDOLPH'S COMMISSION (1676) **V–46a**
Random House I–334b;
II–340b
Range, electric II–417b
Range cattle industry. *See* Open Range Cattle Period
Ranger (blimp) II–345b
Ranger (carrier) I–54b
Ranger (warship) III–34b;
IV–313a; VI–46a, 129a
Ranger (yacht) VII–348b
***RANGER-DRAKE* ENGAGEMENT** (1778)
VI–46a
Ranger project III–502b
RANGERS VI–46b; V–222a
Mexican War VI–60b
Paxton Boys V–231a
Rogers' Rangers VI–162b
Terry's Texas Rangers
VII–34a
Texas Rangers VII–42a
Rangoon (Burma)
World War II I–386b;
III–46b
Rank, army insignia of. *See* Insignia of rank
Rankin, John (abolitionist)
I–135b
Ranklin, Lee J. (law.)
VII–238a
Ranney, Austin (pol. sci.)
V–222b
Ransdell Act (1930)
IV–465a
Ransom II–468a
Ransome, Ernest (eng.)
I–364b, 378b
Ranters III–123a
Raousset-Boulbon, Count Gaston Raoul de (filibuster)
III–23a
Rap Brown law II–20b–21a
Rape
colonial punishment
V–465a
Rapidan River I–365a
Civil War IV–350a;
V–248b; VI–137b, 150a;
VII–295b
revolutionary war
VII–360b
Rapid City (S.Dak.) II–352a
Rapido River (It.)
World War II III–235b;
IV–404a
Rapid transit I–143a;
III–451b; IV–428b
Chicago II–18a
elevated railways II–428a
Newark V–41b
New York City I–370b
Rapp, George (rel. leader)
II–147a; III–255a;
IV–338b
Rappahannock River
VI–149b, 376a
Civil War I–360a, 365a,
374a, 382a, 493a,b;
III–101a; IV–36a, 350a,
425a; V–248a; VI–150a
Fairfax proprietary
II–481a
settlements VII–192b
Spotswood's expedition
IV–53a
RAPPAHANNOCK STATION, BATTLE AT
(1863) **VI–47a**
Raritan Bay III–183a
Raritan River II–322a, 431b;
IV–397b
Rasles, Sebastian (miss.)
I–3a; II–380b; V–111b
Rasmussen v. *United States*
(1905) III–424b
Raspberries III–51a, 129a
Rateau, C. E. A. (eng.)
VII–129b
Rathbun, John P. (nav. off.)
VI–129a
Rathbun (Humphrey's Executor) v. *United States*
(1935) II–499b–500a;
V–472b
Rationing
petroleum V–270b
World War II V–406a;
VII–336a
RATON PASS I–174b;
VI–215b; VII–256a
Rattlesnake (privateer)
V–423b
Rattlesnake district (Mont.)
III–270a
RATTLESNAKE FLAG
VI–47b
RATTLESNAKES VI–47b;
V–387b; VI–91b
Rattletrap (galley) III–147b;
VII–303a
Raulston, John T. (jur.)
VI–239b
Rauschenberg, Robert (paint.)
V–193a
Rauschenbusch, Walter (cler.)
VI–78b, 82b, 82b, 325a
Rauschner, Johan Christian
(art.) VII–262a
Ravalli, Anthony (arch.)
III–500b
Ravalli, Anthony (miss.)
IV–403a
Ravazza, Guiseppe (inv.)
VII–136a
Raven III–222b, 386b
Ravenel, St. Julien (agric.)
III–16b
Ravenna (Ohio) I–487a
Ravenswood (Ohio)
VII–252a
Rawdon, Lord. *See* Hastings, Francis Rawdon
Rawinsonde VII–264a
Rawle, Francis (econ.)
III–427a–b
Rawlins (Wyo.) VII–345b
Rawlinson, Henry (off.)
VI–338b
Rawls, Betsy (golfer)
III–198b
RAW MATERIALS, RESOURCES OF VI–48a;
IV–244a
commodity exchanges
II–469b
imports VII–87b
Industrial Revolution
III–410b
tariffs II–276a
Ray, James Earl IV–46a
Ray, John (nat.) I–348b
Ray, Man (phot., paint.)
II–104b
Ray, P. Henry (off.) V–337a
Ray, Robert (trader) VI–49a
Ray, Ted (golfer) III–197b
Rayburn, Sam (pol.) I–474b;
II–177 (table); VI–368b;
VII–40b
Rayburn, W. F. V–11a
RAYDAC (computer)
II–156a
Raymbault, Charles (expl.)
III–216a; VI–219b;
VII–157a
Raymond, Anna Louise (philan.) III–19b
RAYMOND, BATTLE OF
(1863) **VI–48b**; III–485b
Raymond, Fort (Mont.)
IV–159b
Raymond, Henry J. (jour., pol.) I–297a; V–73b
Raymond, Rossiter Worthington (eng.) II–448b
Rayon II–3b; VI–203a;
VII–44a
Raystown (Pa.) VI–49a
See also Bedford (Pa.)
Raystown, Fort (Pa.)
I–282b, 358b
RAYSTOWN PATH
VI–49a; V–184a
Raytheon Corporation
II–156a
RAZORBACK HOGS
VI–49a; IV–184b
RCA. *See* Radio Corporation of America
REA. *See* Rural Electrification Administration
Reactance theorem (elec.)
II–39a
Reactors. *See* Atomic Power Reactors
Read, Albert C. (nav. off.)
V–30a
Read, Daniel (comp.)
III–326a; IV–438a
Read, George (states.)
II–203b, 305b, 308a;
VI–161b
Read, George W. (off.)
VI–338b
Read, Nathan (inv.)
VI–408b
Read, Thomas Buchanan
(poet) VI–276a
Reade, Benjamin VII–360a
Reade, Frank (lit. char.)
II–341b
Reader's Digest (mag.)
IV–222a; VII–333b
Reader's Digest Foundation
III–181b
Read Family II–364a
Reading (Mass.) VI–2b
Reading (Pa.) III–252a;
VII–146a
Reading, James (dent.)
II–329b
Reading Company VI–36a
Reading Railroad II–86b;
V–278a; VI–25a, 36a
READJUSTER MOVEMENT
VI–49a; VII–195b
Readjustment Benefits Act
(1966) III–178b
Ready-to-wear clothing
II–81b, 371b, 372a
Reagan, John H. (law., jur.)
II–160a; V–373a–b
Reagan, Ronald (pol.)
I–408b–09a, 431b; V–136a;
VI–94a
Real (coin) I–308a; II–94b;
IV–393b
Real estate
Bank of the United States
I–261a
barter I–269a
Florida III–42a
foreign investment
III–67a
great fortunes III–79a
land title IV–105a
loans I–255b, 256a, 257b,
263b
panic of 1929 V–209b
speculation IV–100b
taxes VI–377a; VII–11a
Realist painting
V–190a–91a,b, 192a
Real Property Inventory
VII–23b
Reaper I–34b, 35a, 38a
See also Agricultural Machinery; McCormick Reaper
Reapportionment
Baker v. *Carr* I–244b;
II–410a
congressional seats
II–355b
See also Apportionment

Reason the Only Oracle of Man III–112a
Reaugh, Frank (art.) VI–382b
REBATES, RAILROAD VI–49b; II–432a; VI–22b, 354b
Rebellion. *See* Insurrections, Domestic
REBELLION, RIGHT OF VI–50b
Rebellion Records III–281a
REBEL YELL VI–50b
Reber, Grote (radio eng.) VI–17a
RECALL VI–50b; II–408b, 409b–10a; III–91a; VI–66b
Arizona VI–401b
Kansas IV–26b
Oregon system V–168a
Progressive movement V–428a
Washington State VII–248a
Receiver, electronic II–425b
Receiver, radio II–424b
Recession I–392–93 (tables)
business cycles I–394b
California I–408a
cost of living index II–236b
energy crisis III–415b
Federal Reserve System III–8a
foreign investment II–301b
public debt II–300a
pump-priming V–463b
1974–75 IV–75a
Recession of 1880's II–214b
RECESSION OF 1937 VI–51b; III–7a; V–48a
pump-priming V–464a
Recession of 1966 III–8b
Recession of 1971 VII–10a
RECIPROCAL TRADE AGREEMENTS VI–51b; II–276a; III–113b–14a; VII–86b, 88a, 109a, 112a, 263b
Canada I–437a
Elgin–Marcy Treaty I–437a
executive agreements II–471b
Hawaii III–263b
Kasson Treaties IV–33a
Kennedy administration V–53a
McLane–Ocampo Treaty IV–218a
most-favored-nation principle IV–416b
New Deal V–45b
Roosevelt (F. D.) administration II–359b
South America VI–343b
tariff I–246a; VI–464a, 467a, 468a–72b
Wheaton's Zollverein Treaty VII–370a
Reciprocal Trade Agreements Act (1934) III–69a; V–45b; VI–52a,b, 468a, 469a,b; VII–88a, 109a
Reciprocating engine II–416a; VI–410a
Reciprocity. *See* Canadian–American Reciprocity; Reciprocal Trade Agreements; Tariff
Reciprocity Treaty of 1854. *See* Elgin–Marcy Treaty
RECLAMATION VI–53b
Bureau of Reclamation III–445a
Civilian Conservation Corps II–51a; V–44a
desert land I–453b
Idaho III–328b
Inland Waterways Commission III–420a
Mineral Leasing Act V–445b
Rocky Mountains VI–160b
subsidies VI–425b
Reclamation, Bureau of I–407a; VI–54a
dam construction III–322b, 323a,b
Pick–Sloan Plan VI–147a
Reclamation Act (1902) I–407a, 453b; II–187b; III–478a; V–445a; VI–53b, 425b
Reclamation Extension Act (1914) VI–54a
Reclamation Service, U.S. III–328b; VI–54a
RECOGNITION, POLICY OF VI–54b; III–456a
Israel III–481b
Latin America IV–110b, 114b
Liberia IV–141b
Panama V–201a, 204a,b
Santo Domingo VI–217a
Venezuela VII–170a
See also Nonrecognition Policy
Recojedas II–247a
Recollects. *See* Franciscans
Recommended dietary allowances V–128b
Reconnaissance I–235a, 484b
Cuba II–271a
missile II–316a
RECONSTRUCTION VI–55b; III–437b–38a
Ab-Initio movement I–2a
Afro-American gains I–28b–29a
Afro-American suffrage III–92b
Arkansas I–173a
Black Codes I–310b, 310b
black suffrage VI–431b–32a
Bourbons I–354a
bulldoze I–380b
campaign of 1868 I–422a
campaign of 1876 I–422b
carpetbaggers I–459b
Charleston (S.C.) I–497b
churches VI–59b
Clinton riot II–77a
colonization movement II–127b
Confederate migration to Mexico IV–325a
Confiscation Acts II–168b
congressional committee II–179a
constitutional amendments I–94b
Ellenton riot II–432a
Ex parte McCardle IV–209a
Ex parte Milligan IV–346b
Florida III–39b
freedmen IV–103a
Freedmen's Bureau III–103a
Georgia III–168b
ironclad oath III–474a
Jim Crow laws III–502b
Johnson's plan I–71b
Joint Committee on Reconstruction IV–6a
Ku Klux Klan IV–57b
Liberal Republican party IV–141a
Lincoln's assassination IV–155a
Louisiana IV–194b
Loyal Leagues IV–201b
lynching IV–208a
Mississippi II–77a; IV–369a
National Union Convention IV–472b; VI–336a
New Orleans riots V–64a
New South V–66b
North Carolina V–115b, 116a
occupation troops II–324a
opposition IV–53a
Peabody Fund V–231b
plantation system V–325b
Radical Republicans IV–228a; VI–11a–b
Red Shirts VI–65a
Regulators VI–71b
Republican party VI–93a, 337a
repudiation of state debts VI–96b
restoration of home rule III–295a–b
scalawags VI–223b
sectionalism VI–254a
segregation I–25b; VI–255b
sharecropping VI–268b
Slaughterhouse Cases VI–303a
South Carolina III–244a; VI–348a
specie payments VI–104a
Supreme Court IV–13b–14a; VI–447b
Supreme Court packing VI–448b
"swing round the circle" VI–454b
test laws VII–34b
Texas I–2a; VII–39b–40a, 42a–b
Thirteenth Amendment VII–54a
Tillmanism VII–59a
Vicksburg riots VII–182a
Virginia VII–195a
Wade–Davis Bill VII–213a
women VII–317a
RECONSTRUCTION, LINCOLN'S PLAN OF VI–58a; III–345b; VI–55b–56a
loyalty oaths IV–202b
Radical Republicans VI–11a
RECONSTRUCTION ACTS (1867–68) **VI–58b**; I–460a; IV–6a; VI–57a,b
Georgia opposition III–171b
judicial review IV–209a
Mississippi v. *Johnson* IV–376a
Thirteenth Amendment VII–54b
Virginia VII–195a
RECONSTRUCTION AND THE CHURCHES VI–59b; I–23b
RECONSTRUCTION FINANCE CORPORATION VI–59b; I–391a; III–201b, 466b; V–455b; VI–73a, 425b; VII–231a
banking crisis of 1933 I–260a
brain trust I–359b
building and loan associations I–376b
Export–Import Banks I–262b
farm credit I–44a–b
Gold Purchase Plan III–192a
pump-priming V–464a
Reconstructionist movement (Judaism) IV–11a
Reconversion Tax Act (1945) VII–8b
Recording, sound. *See* Phonograph
Recording industry II–424b; III–49a
Records, long playing II–424b, 425b
RECOVERY, FORT (Ohio) **VI–60a**; II–356a; III–227b
Indian attack II–484b
Saint Clair's defeat VI–188b; VII–247a
Wayne campaign VII–262b–63a
Recovery Administration, National. *See* National Recovery Administration
Recreation
automoblie I–228a
forests III–73b, 75b, 76a,b
public lands IV–95b
Red Cross VI–62a
social welfare I–495b
timberlands VII–60a, 61b
Recreation, Bureau of Outdoor II–188b; III–444b
Recreational areas. *See* Parks, National, and National Monuments; Park Service, National, and National Park System
Recreational vehicles I–230b
RECRUITMENT VI–60b
Afro-Americans IV–339b
bounties I–352b
Civil War labor shortages IV–62b
colonial wars IV–345b
Espionage Act VI–225a
navy V–23b
Navy Department V–18a
Newport Barracks V–66a
opposition V–237a

revolutionary war
VI–117b–18a, 125b
Union Army II–451b
See also Draft; Enlistment
Rectangular system (surv.)
IV–90b
Recycling
iron products III–474a
paper V–212b
Red, Booger (cowboy)
VI–161b
Red Army I–158b–59a;
IV–235b
Red ash VII–114a
Red Badge of Courage
V–41b
Red Bank (N.J.) IV–308b
Red Bird (Indian) VII–306b
Red Bird Uprising (1827)
III–311b
Redbud VI–395 (table)
Red China. *See* China, People's Republic of
Red Cloud (Indian) II–283a;
III–378a, 386b, 391b;
IV–109a; VI–350a
Red Cloud Agency (Nebr.)
VI–157a; VII–227b
Red Cloud's War (1866–67)
I–358a; II–184a; III–17b;
VII–215b
See also Sioux Wars
Red clover VI–395 (table)
RED CROSS, AMERICAN
VI–61b; V–280a
San Francisco earthquake
VI–210a
World War I II–372a;
VII–330a,b
Red Cross, International
III–161b, 162a
Vietnam War VII–226a
Red Cross Convention (1854)
VII–112b–13a
Red Cross Youth Service Programs VI–62a
Red Danish Cattle II–281b
Red Dog (Calif.) I–281a
Red dog currency II–275a
Red Eagle (Indian) II–257a;
III–305b
Redeemers. *See* Bourbons
REDEMPTIONERS
VI–62b
agriculture I–36b
colonial labor force
IV–60a
immigration III–334b
indentured servants
III–352b–53a
Redeye (missile) IV–363b
Redfield, Robert (anthrop.)
I–129a
Redfield, William C. (meteor.)
II–75b; IV–316b
Red Fife wheat VII–286a
Red Horn (Indian) V–310a
"Red Iron Ore" (ballad)
I–247a
Red Jacket (clipper ship)
IV–226b
Red Jacket (Indian)
III–386b; V–161a
Red Lake IV–355b; VI–64b
RED LEGS VI–62b
Redlich, Fritz (psych.)
IV–306b
Redlich, Norman VII–238a
Red–light districts II–260a,
261a–b; V–437b
RED LINE MAP VI–62b;
VII–265a
Red Lion Broadcasting Company v. *Federal Communications Commission* (1969)
III–106a
Red maple VI–395 (table)
Red Mill (operetta) IV–442a
Red Mountain (Mont.)
III–270a
"Rednecks" IV–369a,b
Red oak VI–394 (table)
Redon, Odilon (art.) II–103b
Red oxide II–5b
Redpath, James (educ.)
IV–207b; V–379a
Red pine VI–394 (table)
Red Poll cattle II–281b
Red River III–50b
Abilene Trail I–2a
Acadians I–7a
Balcones escarpment
I–246b
cattle II–358b
Chisholm Trail II–32a
Civil War I–279b;
III–474b; V–331a, 369a;
VI–63a
cotton IV–194a
Denison Dam III–322b
exploration II–381a;
III–108a, 119a; IV–249a;
VII–271b
Fort Jesup III–501b
Fort Kearny IV–33b
Fort Towson VII–81b
Gore III–200a
Grand Prairie III–209a
Great Warriors Path
VII–238b
Greer County dispute
III–228a; V–150a
Long's explorations
IV–186b, 187a
Natchitoches IV–189a,
456b, 457a
navigation improvement
VI–146a
north fork II–359a
Oklahoma–Texas boundary
I–351b
Pembina V–244a
Pike's expedition
V–311b–12a
plantations I–38a
Pointe Coupee V–335a
railroad VII–187b
Spanish settlements
VII–36b
steamboating VII–260b
sugar IV–193b–94a
trading posts II–94a
U.S. boundary I–10b;
IV–320b; VI–359b
Warren's trading posts
VII–238b
RED RIVER CAMPAIGN
(1864) **VI–63a**; IV–375b;
V–402b; VI–150b
Battle of Pleasant Hill
V–331a
Battle of Sabine Crossroads
VI–182a
Natchitoches IV–457a
RED RIVER CART TRAFFIC VI–63b; III–313b
Pembina V–244a
RED RIVER INDIAN WAR
(1874–75) **VI–64a**;
VI–443b
RED RIVER OF THE NORTH VI–64a
cart traffic VI–63b
Civil War IV–136b
exploration I–96b
fur trade VI–411b
Minnesota IV–355a
Selkirk Colony III–313b;
V–117a, 121a
settlements VII–134a
Sioux land cession
VII–106a
steamboatiog VI–407a
wheat farming I–329a
RED RIVER POST
VI–64b; IV–118a
RED RIVER RAFT
VI–65a; IV–374a
Red River Rebellion (1869)
III–242b
Red River Valley
Civil War IV–375a
Indian inhabitants I–151b
politics II–491b
wheat IV–357a
Red Rock IV–162b
"Red scare" (1919–20)
I–108b; VI–255a
RED SHIRTS VI–65a;
III–295a
Red Sleeves. *See* Mangas Coloradas
Red Star Line V–183b
Red Sticks (Indians)
II–256b–57a
REDSTONE OLD FORT
(Pa.) **VI–65b**; IV–181b;
V–144a
Redware III–183a,b, 184a
Redwood (Minn.) VI–296b
Redwood and Sons I–340b
Redwood Ferry (Minn.)
VI–296b
Redwood highway
III–189a–b
Redwood Library (Newport)
I–162a; IV–144b; VI–132a
Redwood National Park
V–219 (table)
Redwood tree III–74b;
IV–204a; VI–48b, 223a,
262b, 393 (table)
Reece Committee III–83b
Reed, Ebenezer (pub.)
V–70b
Reed, Joseph (states.)
V–252b–53a
Reed, Lowell (educ.) IV–3b
Reed, Luman II–101b
Reed, Rebecca Theresa
VII–160a
Reed, Stanley (jur.)
III–105a; VI–446b
Reed, Thomas B. (pol.)
II–176 (table); III–38a;
VI–65b, 467a
Reed, Walter (physic.)
IV–3a, 291a–b, 298a;
VII–198a
yellow fever I–188a, 241b;
VII–355b
Reed, William B. (dipl.)
treaty VI–66a
Reeder, Andrew H. (pol.)
I–341a; IV–28a, 30a, 31a
REED RULES VI–65b
REED TREATY (1858)
VI–66a
Reedy River VII–125b
Reef Points (Naval Academy handbook) VI–302a
Reel, Estelle (educ.)
VII–346a
Reel folk dances II–287a
Rees, Albert (econ.) II–235b
Reese, Albert M. (zool.)
VI–91b
Reese, John (trader) V–39b
Reeve, Tapping (educ.)
IV–159b
Reeves, Joseph M. (nav. off.)
VII–341b
Reference books
dictionaries II–340a
Dictionary of American Biography II–340b
encyclopedias II–444a
REFERENDUM VI–66a;
II–408b, 409b; III–91a,
418b; VI–51a
declaration of war
VII–227b
Kansas IV–26b
Oregon System V–165b,
168a
Progressive movement
V–428a
public opinion V–453b
reserved power of the people VI–98a–b
state constitutions
VI–392a
Washington State
VII–248a
Refineries, oil II–354b;
IV–44b
Reflation III–415a; V–402a,
406a
Reflections on the Revolution in France VI–141a
REFORESTATION
VI–67a; VII–59b, 61a–b
Civilian Conservation Corps
II–51a; III–74a
Girl Scouts III–181a
Tennessee Valley Authority
V–44b; VII–28a
Reform, municipal. *See* Municipal Reform
Reformation, Protestant
VI–83a
Lutheran churches
IV–205b
religious liberty VI–80a–b
REFORMATORIES
VI–67b; V–416a
Elmira V–415b
juvenile courts IV–23a
REFORMED CHURCHES
VI–68b; VI–75b, 79b
Coetus–Conferentie controversy II–93a
Episcopal II–455b
foreign missions IV–366b
home missionary societies
IV–365b
Lutheranism IV–206a
New Netherland V–61a
Prebyterianism V–391a

REFORMED CHURCHES (cont.)
Puritanism V–469a
Reformed Church in America II–93b; VI–69a
Reformed Church in the United States VI–69a
Reformed Mennonite Church IV–303a
Reformed Methodist Union Episcopal church IV–319a
Reformed Presbyterian Church of North America V–392b
Reformed Zion Union Apostolic church IV–319a
Reform Judaism IV–11a
Reform movements
civil service V–228a
eugenics III–158b, 159a
Fourierism III–85a
Jacksonian Democracy III–486b
liberalism IV–140a
"lunatic fringe" IV–204b
muckrakers IV–424b
Nader's Raiders IV–448a
Progressive movement V–427a
pure food and drug movement V–465a
Socialist party VI–327a
temperance VII–22b, 312a–b
third parties VII–53a
Reform schools IV–93b
REFRIGERATION VI–69a; II–417a, 420b–21a; III–269b
agriculture I–40a
butter production II–280b
copper V–103b
food preservation II–373a–b; III–55a–b
Frigidaire II–418a
fruit growing III–129a
industrial research III–409b
meat-packing IV–170a, 280b, 280b
natural gas V–5b
petroleum products V–267b
public utilities V–456b
railroad cars VII–84a
Refugee Relief Act (1953) III–339b; V–342b
Refugees
immigration to U.S. III–339b
World War I VII–330a,b
See also Political Exiles to the United States
Refugees, Freedmen, and Abandoned Lands, Bureau of III–103a
REFUGEE TRACT VI–70b
Refuges, wildlife. *See* Wildlife refuges
Refugio, Gulf del IV–451b
Refugio Mission IV–367b
Regensburg (Ger.) I–60a
Regents' Inquiry into the Character and Cost of Public Education in New York State II–400b
Regents of the University of the State of New York II–132b
REGICIDES VI–70b; IV–48a
Regina Company II–421a
Register of Dams in the United States III–322a
Register of Debates II–178a; III–203b; IV–8b
REGISTRATION OF VOTERS VI–71a; II–408a, 408a–b, 408b, 410a–b; VII–208b
Afro-Americans III–20b; VI–431a, 433a–b
civil rights movement II–58b
corrupt practices acts II–232b, 232b
Force Acts III–59b
Freedmen's Bureau III–103b
Jim Crow laws III–503a
Mississippi III–92b; IV–369b
nonvoting V–109a
party machine IV–214b
poll tax V–355a
qualifications II–410a–b
repeating VI–88a
Student Nonviolent Coordinating Committee VI–420b
Voting Rights Act III–93a–b
Regnat populus (motto) VI–393 (table)
Regrating (bus.) IV–399a; V–225b
Regulating Act. *See* Massachusetts Government Act
Regulations for the Order and Discipline of the Troops of the United States VI–126a
REGULATORS VI–71b; III–18b
REGULATORS OF NORTH CAROLINA VI–71b; III–436b; VII–58b, 253a, 283a
REGULATORS OF SOUTH CAROLINA VI–72a; III–436b
Rehn, Frank K. M. II–104a
Rehnquist, William H. (jur.) II–427b, 474a; VI–447b
Rehoboth (seaplane tender) V–133b
Reich, Steve (comp.) IV–442b
Reichelderfer, F. W. (offi.) VII–264b
Reichert, Frederick III–255a
Reid, Henry J. E. (adm.) IV–106a
Reid, Robert (bot.) II–226a
Reid, Robert R. (offi.) III–39a
Reid, Thomas Mayne (au.) II–341b
Reid's yellow dent II–226a
Reid v. *Covert* (1957) I–362b; VII–110b
Reighard, Jacob E. (ecol.) II–391a
Reihle, Antoine (fur trader) VI–367a
Reims (Fr.) I–70a, 491b
Reindeer (brig) VII–253a
Reinhard and Hofmeister VI–299a
Reinhardt, Max (theat. dir.) VII–49b
Reisenweber's Restaurant IV–440a
Reis Hammida II–303a
Reisman, Michael W. (law.) VI–403a
Rejet-de-Beaulieu (Fr.) VI–338b
Relations, Jesuit. *See* Jesuit *Relations*
Relations of 1673 by Claude Dablon III–501a
Relativity, theory of V–295a, 301a
Relay (Md.) I–363b; IV–116b
Released time education II–400a
Reliance (blimp) II–345b
Reliant (monoplane) I–52b
RELIEF VI–72b; V–380a–82b
American Friends Service Committee III–123b
Bureau of Indian Affairs III–390b
charity organization movement I–494b
Civilian Conservation Corps II–51a–b
colonial education II–394b
Community Action Program II–147b
education II–395b, 396b
elderly V–150b
endowed foundations III–82a
farmers I–44b–45a
farm surpluses I–43b
federal expenditures II–302b
Federal Theatre Project VII–50a
Freedmen's Bureau III–103a
grants-in-aid VI–105b
mortgage legislation IV–414a
National Urban League V–1a
National Youth Administration VII–364a
New Deal IV–71a–b; V–43a
Office of Economic Opportunity V–135b
panic of 1819 V–206b
Pennsylvania V–247b
Progressive party V–429a
rural development VI–171b–72a
slums VI–314b
social legislation VI–327a
social settlements VI–330a
state borrowing II–302b
stay and valutation acts VI–406a
subsistence homesteads VI–426b
taxation VII–7b
technocracy movement VII–17b
unemployment VII–140a
vocational training II–393b
waiting periods V–420b
Works Progress Administration VII–322b
World War I VII–329a
RELIEF ACT OF 1821 VI–75a
RELIGION VI–75a
Adventist churches I–15a
African Methodist Episcopal Church I–23a
Afro-American church I–23a
Amana Community I–92b
Americanism I–107a
antebellum South VI–343a
Antinomian controversy I–133a
Arminianism I–176a
Baptist churches I–264b
Bishop Hill Colony I–307b
Black Muslims V–170b–71a
Book of Mormon IV–410b
Brethren I–361a
Brownists I–371a
Calvinism I–176a–b, 410b
Cambridge Agreement I–411b
Cambridge Platform I–412a
Cane Ridge Revival I–444b
Capuchins I–451b
Carmelites I–455b
Catholicism I–466b
children's magazines IV–222b
church covenant II–247b, 497a
Churches of the New Jerusalem V–58a
Church of England II–36a
Church of Jesus Christ of Latter-Day Saints IV–116b
Church of the Nazarene V–29b
circuit riders II–39b
civil II–52b
Civil War II–36b, 63b
colleges II–113b, 114a–b
colonial education II–394a–95a
colonial settlements III–334b
colonial society II–125b–26a
compact theory II–149a
Congregational churches II–169b
Congregation de Propaganda Fide II–170b
Connecticut II–181a
conscientious objectors II–63b, 185a
Cotton Kingdom II–241a
Cumberland Presbyterian Church II–272b

deism II–320a
democracy II–325b, 326a
Disciples of Christ I–444b; II–352b
Dissenters II–353a
divine providences II–355b–56a
Dominicans II–362b
Dorchester Company II–364b–65a
Dunkers II–147a
early schoolbooks VI–227a
Eastern Orthodoxy II–386a
education I–5a; II–397b, 398a, 399b, 399b, 403a–b
Edwardsean theology II–406a
Episcopal church II–455a
fast days II–496a
Finney revivals III–24b
foreign–language press V–75b
foreign missions IV–364b, 366a
Franciscans III–94a
Freemasons I–132a–b
freethinking III–112a
frontier II–487a; III–127b; IV–366b
Gortonites II–200b
Great Awakening III–214a
Great Revival III–221b–22a
Halfway Covenant III–243a–b
Higher Criticism III–275a
home missionary societies IV–365a
Hopedale Community III–300a
Huguenots III–315a
hymns III–326a
Illuminati of New England III–332a
Indian III–391b; IV–108a
Indian education III–379b, 380a
instruction II–400a
Jehovah's Witnesses III–497b
Jesuits III–501a
Judaism, American IV–9a
Keith controversy IV–35b
Labadists IV–59b
Latitudinarians IV–116a
lecture days IV–131a
Lutheranism IV–205b; V–123b
manumission IV–246a–b
Maria Monk controversy IV–250a
marriage IV–256a
McGuffey's Readers IV–213a
medicine III–324b
meetinghouse IV–300a
Mennonites II–147a; IV–303a
Methodists IV–318a
morals IV–408a–b
moral societies IV–409a
Moravian Brethren IV–409b
Mormons I–397b
mourners' bench IV–423b
mysticism IV–447b
New England Way V–51b
New Jersey V–57a
New Lights V–58b
New Thought movement V–81a
New York State V–87a
Norwegian churches V–123a
officeholding I–297b
Oneida Colony V–155b
Oriental religions and sects V–171b
Osgoodites V–174b
Oxford Movement V–179a
pacifism V–181a,b
Palatines V–195a
Paulists V–229a
peace movement V–236a
Pentecostal churches V–259b
Perfectionists II–147a
pietism V–310b
Pilgrims V–312b
Plan of Union V–324a
pragmatism V–386b
Presbyterianism V–391a
Priests of Holy Cross III–293a
private schools VI–228b
protracted meeting V–438b
Puritanism V–468b
Quakers V–469b
radical right VI–12a–b
Reconstruction and the churches VI–59b
Reformed churches VI–68b
Reorganized Church of Jesus Christ of Latter-Day Saints VI–87a
revivals I–238a; II–406a
Rice–Campbell debates VI–135b
Rogerenes VI–162a
sabbath–day houses VI–182a
Salem VI–199a–b
Salvation Army VI–204a
Saybrook Platform VI–223b
Schwenkfelders VI–230a
Scopes trial VI–239b
Separatists II–147a; VI–262a
"seven pillars" VI–263b
Shakers II–147a; VI–268a
Social Gospel VI–324b
Society for the Propagation of the Gospel VI–331b
Society of Friends III–123a
Southwest missions IV–367a
Strangite Kingdom VI–416b
sumptuary laws VI–440a,b
Sunday schools VI–442a
Synod of Dort VI–455b
theocracy VII–51a
theosophy VII–51b
voting behavior VII–210b
Waldenses VII–219b
Western Reserve VII–275a
Westminster Confession VII–279a
woman's rights movement VII–313a,b
women VII–316b
See also Church membership; Indian Religion
Religious Education Association VI–442b
Religious Experience and Scientific Method VI–83a
RELIGIOUS LIBERTY VI–80a; II–53b; III–104a, 316b
Baptists I–265b
Bill of Rights I–94a, 299b, 498b
Charter of Privileges I–500b
colonies II–123b–24b
Columbia University II–132a
Connecticut VI–162b
democracy II–325b
First Amendment II–204a
Gorges' Province of Maine III–200b
Indians V–49a
Jeffersonian Democracy III–496a
judicial review IV–14b
Maryland IV–260b
minority rights IV–358b
New Albion V–332b
New England V–50a, 53b
New Jersey V–57a
New Madrid V–59a
New Netherland V–61a
Newport V–65b
Northwest Territory V–163a
Penn's Holy Experiment III–293a
Pennsylvania V–246a
Pilgrims V–64b
post–Revolution VI–118b
Providence Plantations V–439a; VI–131b
Rhode Island VI–132a
Supreme Court VI–447b
toleration acts VII–68b
United Colonies of New England VII–149b
Vermont VII–171b
West Jersey VII–278b
Religious painting V–188a
Religious qualifications III–91a
Religious schools
constitutionality II–400a
public funds II–399b
Religious Societies. *See* Moral Societies
Religious Society of Friends (General Conference) III–123b, 123b
Religious Society of Friends, Kansas Yearly Meeting III–123b
Religious tests II–203a
RELIGIOUS THOUGHT AND WRITINGS VI–81a; V–288b
Christian Nurture VI–78a
freethinking III–112a
Ladies' Repository IV–82b
Lutheranism IV–206a
morals IV–408a–b
mysticism IV–447b
philosophy V–286b–87a
publishing IV–453a
Rauschenbusch, Walter VI–78b
tracts VII–82a
Religious toleration
Carolinas I–457b
Charter of Liberties I–500b
colonies II–126a, 394b
Relocation, Japanese–American. *See* Japanese–American Relocation
RELOCATION PROGRAM, VOLUNTARY VI–83b; III–396a, 397b
REMAGEN (Ger.) **VI–83b**; VII–340b
Rembrandt House (N.Y.C.) I–143b
Rembrandt van Rijn (paint.) V–185a
"REMEMBER THE ALAMO" VI–84a; I–74b; VII–38a
"REMEMBER THE *MAINE*" VI–84a; IV–227b
"Remember the River Raisin" VI–42b
Remington, Frederic (paint.) I–281a; V–73b–74a, 192a; VI–382b
Remington and Sons I–396a; IV–433a; VII–136a
Remington Rand Company I–397a
Remington rifle IV–430b
Remington typewriter VII–136b
Removal. *See* Recall
REMOVAL, EXECUTIVE POWER OF VI–84b; V–472b
independent agencies III–317a
Myers v. *United States* IV–446a
Tenure of Office Act III–345b; VI–57a; VII–31b
REMOVAL ACT OF 1830 VI–85b; VI–260b
REMOVAL OF DEPOSITS VI–85b; VI–427a
Remsen, Ira (chem.) II–11b; IV–2a,b, 3b
Renaissance, American IV–96b, 96b; V–191a–92a
Renaissance architecture I–160b–61a
Renaissance classism (arch.) I–161a, 164b
Renaissance fortification architecture I–159b
Renaissance revival architecture I–163b
Renaissance Society of America IV–126b–27a
Renaissance style furniture III–135b, 138b
Renault, Philip VI–189b
Rendezvous. *See* Trappers' Rendezvous

Rendezvous With Destiny III–283a
Renegotiation Board II–499b
RENEWAL, URBAN **VI–86a**; VI–328a–b; VII–160a
federal–state relations III–9b
Housing and Urban Development III–311a
Job Corps III–504b
low–rent housing IV–429a
Rhode Island VI–134a
tenements VII–24a
Washington, D.C. VII–246a
Reno (Nev.) V–40a
Reno, Charles IV–168b
RENO, FORT (Okla.) **VI–87a**
Brownsville affair I–371b
RENO, FORT (Wyo.) **VI–87a**; I–358a; II–184a
See also Connor, Fort
Reno, Jesse L. (off.) VI–87a
Reno, Marcus (off.) II–496a; IV–168a, 168a–b
Reno brothers (outlaws) VII–97a–b
Renoir, Pierre Auguste (paint.) II–103b, 104b
Renshaw (Dak. Terr.) II–284b
Rensselaer family (N.Y.) I–4a
Rensselaer Polytechnic Institute I–47a; II–399a, 447a; VI–232a
Rensselaerswyck (N.Y.) II–383a; III–313a; IV–102b, 241b; V–61a,b, 229a
Rent control VII–336a
Rents IV–105a
land grants IV–101b–02a
taxation VII–6a, 12a
Renville, Joseph (fur trader) II–131a
Renwick, James (arch.) I–163a,b
Renwick, James (phys.)
canal construction IV–412b
Renwick Gallery VI–319b
Reorganization Plans, presidential II–499a, 500a, 501a; III–54a, 267b
Customs Service II–276b
Maritime Commission IV–254b
Office of Management and Budget V–136b
REORGANIZED CHURCH OF JESUS CHRIST OF LATTER-DAY SAINTS **VI–87a**; IV–117a
REPARATION COMMISSION (1920–30) **VI–87b**; VII–173b
Young Plan VII–363b
Reparations
Dawes Plan II–296a–b
Germany I–122b, 123a, 176b, 245b, 254a, 290b; II–296a–b
Hoover moratorium IV–409a
indemnities III–352a
International Court of Justice III–453a
Lausanne Agreement IV–117b
Paris Agreement V–215a
World War I III–86a; VII–213a, 331a
World War II V–378b
Young Plan II–296b
Repatriation II–439b
Korean War II–469a; IV–56b
World War II IV–56b
Repeatered cables I–401a
REPEATING (pol.) **VI–88a**; VI–71a
Repeating rifle II–67a; IV–430b
"Reply to Sen. Robert Y. Hayne of South Carolina" V–161a
Report of the Committee of Fifteen on Elementary Education II–398b
Report of the Joint Congressional Committee on Forestry (1941) III–74a
Report on National Vitality, Its Wastes and Conservation IV–286a
Report on the Laws of the Arid Region V–450a
Report on the Zoophytes III–29b
Repose (hospital ship) V–28a
REPRESENTATION **VI–88a**; II–485a; V–351b
British constitution II–191a
colonies II–117a–18b
Declaration of Independence II–306b
Great Britain II–325a
legislature IV–133b
proportional V–435a
republic VI–92a
unicameral legislatures VII–142a
REPRESENTATIVE GOVERNMENT **VI–89a**; V–351b
Massachusetts IV–270a
nominating system V–101b
public opinion V–453b
republic VI–92a
taxation without representation VII–14a
third parties VII–52b
See also Representation
Representatives, House of *See* Congress, United States
Reprieves II–201b
Reprint magazines IV–222a
Reprisal (internat. law) VI–104b
Reprisal (ship) VI–128b
Reprisal, letters of. *See* Marque and Reprisal, Letters of
Reproducing machines I–396a, 397a
Reproductive biology I–307b
Reptile Book VI–91b
REPTILES **VI–90a**
Reptiles of Missouri VI–91b
Reptiles of Western North America VI–91a
REPUBLIC **VI–92a**; V–350b, 351a–b
representation VI–88a–b
titles of nobility V–100b
Republic (news.) IV–465b
Republican Fork (Kansas Riv.) V–230b
Republicanism V–351a,b, 352b
Republican League V–345b
REPUBLICAN PARTY **VI–92b**; I–415a; V–108b, 223a,b, 343b; VII–134b
Afro–Americans I–28b; III–254a, 437b
antislavery I–138b, 139a
Appeal of the Independent Democrats I–145a
Barnburners I–268a
black suffrage VI–431b
bribery I–322a
Bricker Amendment VII–110a
California I–406b
campaign of 1856 III–111b
campaign of 1876 II–38b; VII–344a
campaign of 1888 VI–184a
campaign of 1896 III–189a; V–329a, 366a
campaign of 1900 III–131b
campaign of 1912 V–428a,b
campaign of 1916 V–428a,b
campaign of 1936 V–47b
carpetbaggers I–459b
caucus I–474b
Civil War II–64a
Civil War financing II–66b
compensated emancipation II–433b
Compromise of 1890 II–151a
congressional election of 1938 V–48b
Connecticut II–180b
conservatism II–189a,b
Crittenden Compromise II–265a; VI–251a
Cuban missile crisis II–270b
Delaware II–320b
direct primary V–407a
election of 1862 II–62b
election of 1864 II–62b
elections of 1918 IV–124b
elephant symbol I–464b; IV–454b; V–73a
emblems II–437b
emigrant aid movement V–51a–b
Force Acts III–59b
freedmen IV–58a
Free Soil party III–112a
Georgia III–169a
gold standard III–195a
Grass Roots Conference III–213a
Helper's *Impending Crisis* III–271a
Homestead Law III–296b
Idaho III–328b
Illinois IV–156a
Indiana III–370a
Iowa III–468b
Kansas IV–26b, 28b; VII–345a
Kansas Border War IV–118b
Kansas–Nebraska Act IV–29b
Ku Klux Act IV–57b
labor's grievance appeal IV–68a
League of Nations IV–125b
Lecompton Constitution IV–131a
legislature IV–133b
lend–lease IV–135a
Lincoln–Douglas campaign IV–155b
Louisiana IV–194b, 195a, 336a; VII–287a
Maine IV–227a
"manifest destiny" IV–239a
McCarthy–Army hearings IV–210b
McCLellan's Harrison's Landing letter III–258a
Michigan IV–331b
Minnesota II–490b–92b; IV–357b
Missouri IV–378a
Mugwumps IV–425b
national committee IV–463a
national conventions II–216a
National Union Convention VI–336a
Nebraska V–31b
New Hampshire V–54a
New Mexico V–60a
New Orleans riots V–64a
New South V–67b
New York State V–86b
Nonpartisan League V–106b
North Carolina V–115b
North Dakota V–117b–18a
Ohio V–142a
organization V–344b–46a
Panama Canal tolls VII–70a
panic of 1857 V–207a
party whip VII–289a
Pennsylvania V–247b
Philadelphia Gas Ring V–279a
Philippines V–283a
"pop–gun" bills V–359b
popular sovereignty V–360b
presidential campaigns I–420b–32b
presidents V–395–96 (table)
Progressive movement V–427a
Progressive party I–328a, 380b–81a
Prohibition II–407a
Radical Republicans VI–10b, 13b
Readjuster movement VI–49a

Reconstruction
III–295a–b; VI–56a,b, 57b, 58a, 59a
reform element IV–141a
Resumption Act VI–104a
ripper legislation VI–144b
Scioto Gazette VI–239a
Silver Republicans VI–292b
Sixteenth Amendment VI–297b
slavery I–110a; II–327a
social reform II–189a
Solid South VI–254b, 337a
South Dakota VI–350a
Stalwarts VI–380b
"standpatters" VI–384b
states' rights VI–404b
steering committees VI–411b
Supreme Court packing VI–448b
Taft–Hartley Act VI–456b
Taft–Roosevelt split I–248a; VI–458a
tariff III–113a,b; VI–464a,b, 467a,b; VII–306b
taxation VII–6b
Tennessee VII–26a
Texas VII–40a
third–term doctrine VII–53b
Topeka Constitution VII–73a
Treaty of Versailles IV–178a
Tweed Ring VII–131a
Union Democrats VII–146a
Union party VII–148a
unit rule VII–156a
Vare case VII–167b
Vermont VII–172a
vice–presidents VII–179 (table), 180 (table)
Virginia VII–195b, 196a
voting behavior VII–210a–b
Washington State VII–248a
West Virginia VII–281b
Whiskey Ring VII–290b
White League VII–292b
Wide–Awakes VII–294b
Wilmot Proviso VII–303b
Wisconsin VII–307b–08a
Wisconsin Progressives VII–53a
"witch–hunt" VII–310b
World War II isolationism III–480a
Wyoming VII–346a
Republican–Progressive League VI–458a
Republican River IV–45a, 129b; VI–141b
REPUBLICANS, JEFFERSONIAN VI–94a; III–4b–5a; V–86b, 223a, 343b; VI–92b; VII–22b
agrarianism I–33a
Alien and Sedition Acts I–86a–87a; V–69b–70a; VI–255a; VII–117b
Anglo–French wars III–238b
Antifederalists I–131a,b
Aurora I–224a
Bank of the United States I–255a; III–354b
campaign of 1800 V–123a
campaign of 1824 IV–469b; V–101b
caucus I–474b, 475a
censorship I–478b
Chase impeachment I–501b
Chillicothe Junto II–25b
Connecticut II–180b, 183a
election of 1800 III–494b–95a
government appointments I–145b
Hamilton's fiscal policies III–246a
Indiana III–370a
Jay's Treaty III–493b, 494a
liberty cap IV–143a
Louisiana IV–193b
Marbury v. *Madison* IV–248b
Massachusetts III–175a
National Intelligencer IV–465b
National Road IV–470b
New Hampshire V–54a
New Jersey V–58a
New York City V–83a
Nonimportation Act V–104b
opposition III–259a
political patronage VI–375a
Quids VI–3a
Richmond Junto VI–138a
Scioto Gazette VI–239a
secessionist movement VI–250a
Supreme Court packing VI–448a
Tammany Hall VI–459a
Vermont VII–172a
vice–presidents VII–179 (table)
"wise, and good and rich" VII–309a
XYZ affair VII–347b
Yazoo fraud VII–354a
See also Democratic Republicans
Republicans, Radical. *See* Radical Republicans
Republic Aviation Corporation I–53a,b, 54a, 60a
Republic Steel Company IV–72b; VI–411a
REPUDIATION OF PUBLIC DEBT VI–94b
REPUDIATION OF STATE DEBTS VI–95b
Mississippi IV–368b
panic of 1837 III–64a; V–206b
Repulse (cruiser) I–67a; VII–76b
Resaca de Guerrero (Mex.) VI–97a
RESACA DE LA PALMA, BATTLE OF (1846) **VI–97a**; V–198b
Resale price maintenance II–482b–84a
Resa til Norra America IV–231b; V–326a
Rescue (brig) II–319b
Rescuer (news.) V–130b
Research, industrial. *See* Industrial Research
Research, military
Lawrence Livermore Laboratory IV–119a
Research, scientific VI–205b
aeronautics IV–458a–b
Arthur D. Little, Inc. I–197a
astronautics IV–459a
Battelle Memorial I–275a
Bureau of Standards IV–462b
Carnegie Institution I–457a
Cold Spring Harbor II–97a
education VI–232a–b
engineering II–448a
Food and Drug Administration III–53b–54a
Franklin Institute III–99a–b
General Electric Laboratory III–155b
genetics III–157a, 158b
Greely Arctic expedition III–223b
information retrieval VI–232b
International Geophysical Year III–453b
Jet Propulsion Laboratory III–502a
National Research Council IV–457a
National Science Foundation IV–470b
National Weather Service VII–264b
native plants V–325b
Naval Observatory V–12a
Naval Research Laboratory V–14a
navy V–28a
New Jersey V–58a
nutrition and vitamins V–127b
oceanographic survey V–133a
oceanography V–134a
Office of Scientific Research and Development V–137a
paleontology V–195a
patents V–227a
pesticides III–421b
petrography V–267b
phonograph V–289a
physics V–294a
polio V–340b–41a
popularization of science VI–230a
radar VI–9b–10a
radio VI–14b–15a
refrigeration VI–69b–70a
Research Triangle Park V–116b
Rockefeller Foundation VI–157b
scientific societies VI–238a
Scripps Institution of Oceanography VI–242a
Smithsonian Institution VI–318b
state geological surveys III–164b
state universities VII–156b
telephone VII–19b
textiles VII–44a
U.S. Geological Survey III–163a
vacuum tubes VII–163a
Vancouver's exploration VII–166a
Wilkes Exploring Expedition VII–299a
Research and Development, Office of Scientific V–137a
Research and Development Board, U.S. III–410a
Research Applications Directorate IV–471a
Research Grants Office IV–287b
"Research Row" (Cambridge, Mass.) IV–268a
Research Triangle Park (N.C.) V–116b
Reservations, Indian. *See* Indian Reservations
RESERVATION SYSTEM, TERMINATION OF VI–97a; III–390b, 397a; IV–51b
Reserve, naval. *See* Naval reserve
Reserve Corps, Army I–186a
Reserve Corps, Officers'. *See* Officers' Reserve Corps
RESERVED POWERS OF STATES VI–97b; II–204b, 453b; III–9a
interstate commerce III–458b
public ownership V–455a
RESERVED POWERS OF THE PEOPLE VI–98a; II–204b, 453b; III–9a
RESERVED POWERS OF THE STATES V–352b
implied powers III–348b–49a
Jeffersonian Democracy III–496a
police power V–339a
Reserve Forces Act (1955) IV–464a
Reserve Officer Candidate program V–28b–29a
RESERVE OFFICERS' TRAINING CORPS VI–98b; I–186a; II–367a; IV–38b, 341a; V–139a
Reservoirs VI–147a,b
Colorado II–128b
Colorado River II–130a
irrigation III–477b
land reclamation VI–53b
Reservoir Square (N.Y.C.) II–474b
RESETTLEMENT ADMINISTRATION VI–99a; I–44b–45a; II–46b, 188a; V–46a

Residency program (med.) IV–285a, 298a
RESIDENCY REQUIREMENTS FOR VOTING VI–99b; II–410a; VI–71a–b, 435a; VII–208b, 209b
colonial settlements VI–434b
Mississippi III–92b
North Carolina V–116a
presidential elections III–93b
Resolute (blimp) II–345b
Resolution (warship) II–219b, 353a
RESOLUTIONS, LEGISLATIVE VI–100a; IV–115a; VII–177b–78a
RESORTS AND SPAS VI–100a
Cape Cod I–447b
Catskills I–471a
Isles of Shoals III–479b
Key West IV–45a
Lake Champlain IV–85b
Lake Michigan IV–332b
Last Island (La.) IV–110b
Long Island IV–186a
Mackinac IV–217b, 218a
Manitoulin Islands IV–240a
Martha's Vineyard IV–258a
mineral springs IV–350a; VI–377b
Monterey (Calif.) IV–404b
Mount Desert IV–422b
Nantucket IV–449a
New Hampshire V–54b
New Jersey V–58a
Newport V–65b
North Carolina V–116b–17a
Perth Amboy V–264a
Port Royal (S.C.) V–370a
Sag Harbor VI–186a
Saint Augustine VI–187b
Santa Catalina I–466b
Saratoga Springs VI–218a
skiing VI–298a,b
Southampton VI–346b
Sun Valley III–328b
tuberculosis VII–126b
Vermont VII–172b
Virginia Beach VII–196a
Yellow Springs (Pa.) VII–165a
Resources for the Future (org.) II–188a
Restaurants III–52b; VII–84b, 85a
discrimination I–457b
government inspection III–422a
segregation VI–256a
Reston (Va.) II–48b
Reston, James (jour.) V–75a
"Restook War." *See* Aroostook War
Restoration, historic
Johnson Hall IV–4b
Kansas forts IV–25b
"Restorationist" teachings II–352b
Restoration-style furniture III–134a
Restored Government (W.Va.) VII–281b, 288a
Restraining acts. *See* Coercion Acts
RESTRAINT OF TRADE VI–101b; I–390b; V–402a
American Tobacco Case I–114a
Clayton Antitrust Act II–72a
collective bargaining III–407a
corporations II–229b
injunctions III–419a–b
International Harvester Company III–454b
labor organizations IV–69a
railroads VII–155a
rule of reason VI–168b
Sherman Antitrust Act VI–276b
Standard Oil of New Jersey VI–383b
strikes VI–419a
sugar trust VI–437b; VII–154a
trusts VII–121b
RESUMPTION ACT (1875) **VI–104a**; I–301b, 422b; III–192b, 224b, 225b; VI–333b, 371a
Resurrection City (1968) IV–259b; VII–246b
Retail trade II–332a–b, 354b; IV–225a
Retaliation (schooner) V–15a–b
RETALIATION IN INTERNATIONAL LAW VI–104a
Retired Senior Volunteer Program I–8b, 9a
Retirement
judges IV–17a, 18a
Retirement income VII–215a
See also Pension Plans
Retortion (internat. law) VI–104b
Reuben James (destroyer) I–214a
REUNION (Tex.) **VI–105a**
Reuther, Walter (labor leader) I–104b; IV–74a, 74b, 76b
Revaluation (currency) II–339a
Revelle, Roger (oceanog.) VI–242b
Revenue, customs. *See* Duties
REVENUE, PUBLIC VI–105a
British colonial policy II–123a
comptroller general II–152a
Confederation II–167a
cost of government II–234a–b
duties II–276a
education funds II–396b
export taxes II–478a
Federal Communications Commission III–1b
federal expenditures II–476a
Federalists III–4b
federal–state relations III–9b
federal surplus VI–449a
gambling II–263a
gasoline taxes III–153a
government ownership V–455b
Hamilton's fiscal policies III–244b–45a
highways VI–155b
hunting licenses VII–297a
income taxes III–351a–b; VI–297b
land policies III–295b; IV–91a
land sales II–166a; IV–95a, 95b; V–389b, 445a, 452b, 455a
license fees IV–148b
liquor taxes V–45a
lotteries III–149a–b; IV–190b–91b
Minnesota IV–358a
national sinking fund VI–294a, 294a
Nevada V–40a
panic of 1837 V–206b
panic of 1893 V–208a
pari–mutuel tax III–305a
public schools IV–24b
school lands VI–228a
tariff VI–462b–63a
taxation III–156b–57a; VII–2b
ten–forties VII–24b
Tennessee Valley Authority VII–28b
thrift stamps VII–55b
tidelands VII–57b
Treasury VII–107b, 108a
Ways and Means Committee VII–263b
Revenue Act (1764). *See* Sugar Acts
Revenue Act (1767) II–5a; VII–15a, 80b–81a, 344b–45a
Revenue Act (1789) II–88b
Revenue Act (1924) II–500b
Revenue Act (1942) II–500b
Revenue Act (1950) III–83b
Revenue Act (1951) V–339b
Revenue Act (1962) VII–9a
Revenue Act (1964) VII–12a, 13b
Revenue Act (1971) I–414a–b; VII–10a
Revenue and Expenditure Control Act (1968) VII–9b
Revenue commissions VI–463b–64a
Revenue Cutter Service II–88b–90b, 277a; IV–152a
Revenue Marine, U.S. II–88b–89a
Revenue Marine Service IV–152a
Revenue sharing II–245b; III–212a,b; VII–10b, 11a–b, 263b
See also Grants–in–aid
Revenue–sharing act (1972) II–234b
Revere, Paul (engr., patriot) V–254a; VI–106a
engravings V–413b
espionage VI–372b
Fort William and Mary VII–300b
political cartoons I–464a
silver work VI–290a
Suffolk Resolves VI–431a
REVERE'S RIDE (1775) **VI–106a**; IV–137a, 266a; V–69b, 151b, 371b
Reversion religions. *See* Nativistic Movements, American Indian
Revised General Act for the Pacific Settlement of International Disputes IV–382a
Revitalization movements. *See* Nativistic Movements, American Indian
Revivals
Cane Ridge I–444b
Great Awakening III–214a–b
Second Awakening I–238a
See also Evangelism, Evangelicalism, and Revivalism
Revival style furniture III–136a
REVOLUTION, AMERICAN VI–106a; II–325a; VII–93b
André affair I–118a
Bahamas' support I–243b
Bermuda's support I–292b
Boston Massacre I–345b
Boston Tea Party I–347a
British debts I–366a,b
Canada IV–86b
Church of England II–36a
civil religion II–52b
Coercion Acts II–93a
colonial society II–125b
Columbia University II–132b
committees of correspondence I–345a
committees of inspection III–421b
Common Sense II–141b
Congregational churches II–170a
conservatism II–189a
Continental Congress II–165b
Conway Cabal I–436a; II–218a
Crisis II–264b
East India Company II–388a
Faneuil Hall II–487b
Floridas IV–326a
Georgia III–168b
Hannastown Resolution III–250b
Henry, Patrick III–182a
historical accounts III–280b, 281a
Holt's *Journal* III–292b
inflation II–2a, 235a
Intolerable Acts III–464a
Lafayette, Marquis de IV–84a
land bounties IV–91a
letters of "Junius" IV–20b
Locke's philosophy

IV–174a
Loyalists IV–200a; VII–150b
loyalty oaths IV–202b
Maryland IV–260b
Massachusetts IV–266a
Massachusetts Government Act IV–271b
Michigan cession IV–330b
Natchez IV–455a
natural rights doctrine IV–140a
New England V–49b
New Hampshire V–54a
New Jersey V–57a
New York V–86a
New York City V–82b, 85b
nickname Jonathan IV–7b
"Ninety-Two" and "Forty-Five" V–97b
nonimportation agreements V–104a
North Carolina V–115b
Northwest Territory IV–355b
Olive Branch Petition V–152b
oratory V–161a
pamphleteering V–198b
panic of 1785 V–206a
paper shortage I–16b
Peggy Stewart burning V–241b
Pennsylvania V–247a
pine tree flag V–316a
postal service V–371b
press gangs V–400a
propaganda V–432a; VII–61a
provincial congresses V–439b
purchasing power of money IV–393a
Quakers V–470a; VII–201b
quartering of troops IV–445b
Quebec Act VI–2a
religion VI–77a
religious liberty VI–81a
Restraining Acts II–93a
Rhode Island VI–132a–b
right of rebellion VI–50b
Rivington's Gazette VI–152a
Rodney's ride VI–161b
Russia VI–177a
Schenectady VI–225b
slavery I–135a
"Song of Liberty" IV–142b
Sons of Liberty IV–143b–44a; VI–338b
South Carolina VI–347a
Suffolk Resolves VI–430b
sugar house prisons VI–436b
tar and feathers VI–462a
taxation without representation VII–14a
tea duties VII–15a
tea parties VII–16a
tea tax II–388a
Tondee Tavern VII–71b
town meetings VII–79a
treason VII–107a
Trespass Act VII–116b
veterans IV–97a
woman's rights VII–313a
REVOLUTION, DIPLOMACY OF THE VI–119a
French alliance I–151a–b; III–94b
Hortalez and Company III–306a
joint commission to France III–90a
Olive Branch Petition V–152b
Parliament's peace resolutions V–237b
peace commission of 1778 V–231b
Spain VI–359a, 363b, 365a
Spanish alliance I–151a–b
REVOLUTION, FINANCING OF THE VI–120a; II–274b–75a, 317a; IV–393b; VI–117a–b
Bank of North America I–255a, 260b
bills of credit V–123b–24a
debts II–301a, 302a–b
Dutch loans II–382a–b
foreign loans III–63a
French loans III–95a,b
Pittsburgh Resolutions V–322b
Pollock, Oliver V–354b
Spain VI–359a, 363b
taxation VII–3b
REVOLUTION, PROFITEERING IN THE VI–120b; III–79a; V–426a
REVOLUTION, RIGHT OF VI–121a; II–149a; VI–98b
Declaration of Independence II–304a, 306b
Locke's philosophy IV–174a
REVOLUTIONARY COMMITTEES VI–121b; VI–113b
Associations I–207b
Commercial Committee II–137a
committees of correspondence II–140a
committees of inspection III–421b
committees of safety II–140a
New York V–85b
provincial congresses V–440a
Revolutionary Cult of Reason III–112a
REVOLUTIONARY WAR VI–122b; VI–107a, 114a; VII–190b
Afro-Americans IV–339b
assumption of state debts I–208a
Augusta (Ga.) I–223a
Baltimore I–249b
Battle at Great Bridge III–215b
Battle at Moore's Creek Bridge IV–407b
Battle of Bennington I–289a; V–54a, 126a
Battle of Brandywine Creek I–360a
Battle of Breed's Hill I–382b
Battle of Briar Creek I–362a
Battle of Bunker Hill I–344b, 345b, 498b
Battle of Camden I–412a,b
Battle of Charleston I–412a
Battle of Cooch's Bridge II–218a
Battle of Cowpens II–251a
Battle of Edge Hill II–393a
Battle of Elmira II–433a
Battle of Enoree II–451b
Battle of Eutaw Springs II–465a
Battle of Fishdam Ford III–30a
Battle of Fort Moultrie IV–420a
Battle of Freeman's Farm I–385b
Battle of Germantown III–173b
Battle of Golden Hill III–189b
Battle of Guilford Courthouse III–232a
Battle of Harlem III–254b, 254b
Battle of Haw River III–265a
Battle of Hobkirk's Hill III–286a
Battle of Hot Water III–308a
Battle of Hubbardton I–385a; III–311b
Battle of Kettle Creek (Ga.) IV–44b
Battle of Lexington I–344b, 383a
Battle of Long Island IV–185b, 186a
Battle of Monmouth IV–397b
Battle of Olentangy V–152b
Battle of Oriskany I–385a
Battle of Paoli V–211b
Battle of Piqua V–319b
Battle of Princeton V–408a
Battle of Ridgefield VI–139a
Battle of Springfield VI–377a
Battle of the Kegs IV–35b
Battle of Trenton VII–116a
Battle of Valcour Island III–234a; IV–86b; VII–164a
Battle of Virginia Capes VII–198b
Battle of Waxhaw VII–261b
Battle of White Plains VII–293a
Battle of Wyoming III–81b
Battles of Freeman's Farm III–108a–b
Bemis Heights (N.Y.) I–385a
Bird's invasion of Kentucky I–306b
Bonhomme Richard-Serapis encounter I–329a
Boonesborough I–337a,b
Boston I–344a, 344b–45a
bounties II–450b
British campaign in the West I–367a
British campaign of 1777 I–365b; V–172b
British navy III–217a
Bunker Hill I–382b
Burgoyne's defeat IV–211b
Burgoyne's invasion of New York I–384b; IV–86b
Butler's Rangers I–398a
Canada I–435b
Canadian refugees V–342a
Catholics I–467a
Chad's Ford I–360a
Charleston (S.C.) I–496b, 498a
Cherokee II–14b–15a
Cherry Valley massacre II–15a
Clark's Northwest Campaign II–71a; IV–31b, 59b
Connecticut III–25b
Connolly's plot II–184a
conscientious objectors II–185a
Continental Congress II–211a–b; VII–358a–b
costs VII–228 (table), 228b
cowboys and skinners II–249b
Creek Indians II–52a
Crown Point I–435b; II–267a; IV–86b
Danbury II–286a
Delaware V–43a
Detroit II–338a
draft II–366a
Edenton Tea Party II–393a
Egg Harbor engagement II–406b
enlistment II–450b
espionage VI–372b
exchange of prisoners II–468a–b
Falmouth II–485b
fast days II–497a
Fishing Creek III–31b
Florida III–38b
Fort Anne engagement I–385a
Fort Blair VI–45b
Fort Chambly (Can.) I–491b
Fort Henry III–272b; VII–287b
Fort Lee IV–131b
Fort McIntosh IV–216b
Fort Mercer engagements IV–308b
Fort Mifflin IV–337b–38a
Fort Niagara V–90b
Fort Pitt V–321b
Fort Plain V–323a
Fort Sackville IV–53b
Fort Saint Joseph VI–191b–92a
Fort Stanwix (N.Y.) I–385a

REVOLUTIONARY WAR (cont.)
Fort Washington (N.Y.) VII–246b–47a
Fort William and Mary VII–300b–01a
French munitions III–94b–95a
French supplies IV–189a
galley boats III–147b
Georgia III–168b
German Flats III–172b
Green Mountain Boys IV–86b
guerrillas III–231a
gunpowder V–383a
Gwynn's Island III–236a
Hale, Nathan III–241a–b
Hanging Rock (S.C.) III–250a
Highlands of the Hudson III–275b
Holston Valley settlements III–292b
hospitals I–191a
Hudson River II–191a
Hudson River chain III–312b
Hyder Ali III–320b
Illinois III–329a
Indian allies of British III–388a
inflation V–404b
Jersey prison ship III–498b
Jockey Hollow encampment IV–1a
Jouett's ride IV–8b
Kaskaskia I–240a
King's Ferry (N.Y.) IV–48a
King's Mountain IV–48b
Kingston (N.Y.) IV–49a
La Balme's expedition IV–59b
Lake Champlain region IV–86b
land bounties IV–344b
laws of war VII–225a
Lochry's defeat IV–173b
long rifles VI–139b
losses VII–232 (table)
Louisiana IV–193a
Maine IV–226a
maps VII–74a
marines IV–251b
Maryland troops IV–260b
military justice VII–142b
military medicine IV–290a–b
military roads VI–155b
militia laws II–366b
minutemen IV–360b
Mississippi River IV–372b
Mobile IV–382a
Mohawk Valley IV–386b–87a
Montreal I–436a; IV–405b
Morristown encampment IV–413a
munitions IV–122a
Neshaminy Creek V–33a
neutral ground V–33b
Newark V–41a
New Hampshire V–54a
New Jersey V–57a–b
New London burning V–58b
Newport V–65b
New York City V–82b, 85b, 86a
Ninety-Six V–97a
Noodles Island skirmish V–100b
Norfolk V–109b
Norfolk Navy Yard V–29b
North Carolina V–115b
Ohio V–140b
Ohio Valley V–146a
Oswego (N.Y.) V–175b
pacifism V–181a
Parliament's peace resolutions V–237b
partisan bands V–222a
Paulus Hook attack V–229b
peace commission of 1778 V–231b
Peace of Paris V–214a
Pennsylvania Hospital V–251b
Penobscot expedition V–253b
Pensacola V–254b
Perth Amboy V–264a
Philadelphia IV–363a
Piedmont region II–485a
Pollack's aid V–354a
Prairie du Chien V–388a
prices V–404b
prison ships V–418b
privateering II–258a; IV–256a; V–419a, 423b
Property confiscation II–168b
Ranger–Drake engagement VI–46a
rangers VI–46b
Revere's ride V–151b; VI–106a
Richelieu River VI–136b
Richmond VI–137a
rivers VI–150a
Sag Harbor VI–185b–86a
Saint Johns siege VI–191a
Saint Lawrence River VI–192b
Saint Louis VI–195a
Salem VI–199a–b
saltpeter V–98a
Saratoga I–385a–b, 436a; III–276a; IV–86b; VI–217a
Savannah VI–220a–b, 221a
Scioto Trail VI–239b
sea power VI–248a
sharpshooters VI–269b
Skenesboro engagement I–385a
Society of the Sons of the Revolution VI–339b
Sons of the American Revolution VI–339a
South Carolina VI–347a–b
southern campaigns VI–351a
Spanish capture of British posts VI–365a
Spanish supplies III–179a; VI–367b
Stony Point VI–415b
Sullivan–Clinton campaign VI–437b
Sullivan in Rhode Island VI–438a
Susquehanna settlements VI–452a
Tennessee VII–25a–b
Three Rivers VII–55a
Ticonderoga I–345a, 385a, 435b; II–267a; III–215b; IV–86b; VII–56a, 57a
tidewater II–485a
trenches VII–115a
Valley Forge VII–164b
Vermont VII–171b
Vincennes I–240a; III–369b; VII–188b
Virginia VII–193b
volunteers VII–207b–08a
voyageurs VII–212a
War and Ordnance Board VII–226b
Washington crossing the Delaware II–321a
Washington District VII–250a
Watauga settlement VII–253b
weapons IV–432a
West Point VII–279b–80a
whaling VII–285a–b
Whitemarsh VII–292b
Williamsburg VII–301b
Willing expedition III–147b; VII–302b
women VII–316a, 318a
Wyoming massacre VII–346b
Wyoming Valley invasion I–398a
Yorktown VII–198b, 360a
See also Indians in the Revolution

REVOLUTIONARY WAR, AMERICAN ARMY IN VI–124b; I–183a–b; VI–117b–18a, 123a
artillery I–199b
bounties I–352b; II–335a
cavalry I–475a–b
conscription II–186a
cornets II–228a
Corps of Engineers II–449b
demobilization II–323b
desertion II–335a
draft II–450b
enlistment II–450b; V–256b
ensign II–452a
insignia of rank I–189a
logistics I–189b
militia I–475b; IV–345b
munitions IV–430a
mutinies IV–445a–b; V–252b
Newburgh Addresses V–42a
pensions V–256b–57a
smallpox VI–315b
substitutes II–366a
supplies VI–120b–21a
uniforms VII–144a
Valley Forge VI–124a; VII–165a
Washington's eight months army VII–251a
Washington's Lifeguard IV–152a

REVOLUTIONARY WAR, BRITISH ARMY IN VI–126b; VI–123a
Afro-Americans IV–339b
deserters IV–91a
German mercenaries III–172b
Loyalist troops VI–129b
Philadelphia IV–363a
quartering V–471b

REVOLUTIONARY WAR, CONTINENTAL NAVY IN VI–128a; II–359a; V–18b–19a, 423b; VII–251b
Alliance I–89a
armament V–27a
Augusta I–223a
Bergen Prizes I–290b
floating batteries III–36a
gunboats III–234a, 235a
Lake Champlain fleet VI–123a
Lexington IV–136b
New Hampshire V–54a
Ranger–Drake engagement VI–46a
Turtle VI–422b
warships VII–240a

REVOLUTIONARY WAR, FOREIGN VOLUNTEERS IN VI–129a; VI–126a–b, 124a,b
French navy VI–128b; VII–198b
Galvez, Bernardo de IV–193a
German dragoons I–289a–b
Hessians I–360a, 385a
La Balme, A. M. de IV–59b
Pulaski, Casimir II–406b
Rochambeau's army III–117b; V–65b
Sullivan in Rhode Island VI–438a
Yorktown VI–117b; VII–360b–61a

REVOLUTIONARY WAR, LOYALIST TROOPS IN VI–129b; II–249b; IV–200b; VI–124a
Associated Loyalists of New England I–206b
Battle at Great Bridge III–215b
Battle at Moore's Creek Bridge V–115b
Battle of Haw River III–265a
Butler's Rangers I–398a
Florida Rangers III–42b
New Jersey V–57a–b
rangers VI–46b
Virginia revolt II–32b
Revolution of 1768 IV–193a
Revolution of 1848 (Ger.) III–81a
Revolver II–130b–31a; IV–430b, 433a
Reynard the Fox II–253a
Reynolds, Barrington (nav. off.) VI–311b
Reynolds, Charlie (trapper, scout) VI–241b

Reynolds, Jeremiah N.
VII–299a
Reynolds, John F. (off.)
III–175b
Reynolds, Joshua (paint.)
V–187a,b
Reynolds, Maria V–346b
Reynolds, Quentin (jour.)
V–74a
Reynolds Metals Company
V–103b
Reynolds v. *Sims* (1964)
I–147b–48a, 244b;
II–457b; III–86b–87a;
IV–133b; VII–142b
Rezanov, Count Nikolai Petrovich VI–180b
RFD. *See* Rural Free Delivery
R. G. Dun and Company
IV–307b
Rhapsody in Blue (comp.)
IV–438b
Rhea, John (pol.) VI–131b
RHEA LETTER VI–131b
Rhee, Syngman IV–55a
Rheims (Fr.) VII–341a
Rhenish Palatinate V–195a
Rhenium II–224a
Rhett, Alfred (off.) VI–440b
Rhett, Robert Barnwell
(states.) I–326a; III–25a
Rheumatism IV–333b
Rhine, Joseph Banks (pysch.)
V–213a
Rhineland VII–173a,b, 334a
Rhinelander's Sugar House
(N.Y.C.) VI–436b
Rhineland High Commission
I–192a
Rhine River
Treaty of Versailles
VII–173a,b
World War II II–450a;
III–187b; VI–83b–84a;
VII–340a,b
R. H. Macy and Company
II–483a
Rhode and Lusk's express
VI–379b
RHODE ISLAND VI–131b;
IV–270a; V–49b; VI–395
(table)
agriculture VI–170b
Albany Congress
I–82a
Antinomian controversy
I–133a
Arabian gold I–151a
Articles of Confederation
I–199a
bills of credit I–300a
birth and death registration
IV–149a
boundary disputes
I–350b, 351a
Brown University
I–372a
candlemaking VI–372b
Cartagena expedition
I–461b
coal II–84b
colonial agents II–116b
colonial assembly
II–117b, 118b
colonial council II–119b
colonial courts I–145a
colonial exiles V–342a
colonial government
III–132b; VI–166a,b
colonial suffrage VI–434a
constitution VI–390b,
396b
corporate colony
I–499b–500a; II–118a
counties V–349b
county fairs II–244b
Declaration of Independence II–308a
district schools VI–227a
Dominion of New England
V–50b
Dorr's Rebellion II–365a;
III–436b; IV–206b
education II–394a, 398b
Gaspée burning III–153b
general court III–155b
Gortonites III–200b
Great Swamp Fight
III–223a
Hartford Convention
III–259a
historical society III–278b
horse breeding III–303b
Huguenots III–315a
Iberian immigration
III–334b
inflation II–167a
intestate estates III–464a
King Philip's War
IV–47b–48a
King's Province IV–48b
Landholder's Constitution
II–365a–b
legislators' travel allowance
IV–339a
Loyalists I–206b
Luther v. *Borden* (1848)
IV–206b
martial law IV–259a
Massachusetts claims
I–350b
minimum-wage law
IV–353a
Molasses Act VI–435a
Mount Hope IV–422b
Narragansett I–213a;
IV–451b, 451b
New England Way V–51b
Newport V–65b
Pawtucket V–230b
People's Constitution
II–365a–b
Pequot Indians V–261a
piracy V–320a
plans of union II–121b,
122a
population enumerations
VII–205b
primogeniture V–408a
Prohibition II–407a
Providence Plantations
V–439a
provincial congress
V–440a
purchase from Indians
I–149a
Quakers II–124a; V–469b
religion VI–76a
religious liberty II–394b;
VI–80b; VII–68b
revolutionary war
III–117b; V–66a, 419a;
VI–124b, 125b, 438a–b;
VII–251a–b
revolutionary war debts
IV–53b
rubber industry VI–167a
settlement II–124a;
III–219b; VII–95a
Shawomet VI–271b
slavery I–22b, 135b;
VI–305a, 309a
slave trade VI–304b
squatter colony I–499b;
II–118b
suffrage III–91a
Tammany society
VI–460b
taxation VII–4a
textile mills IV–272b
triangular trade II–119a
United Colonies of New
England VII–149a
U.S. Constitution
II–192b, 196a–97a, 198a
usury law III–443a
witchcraft VII–310a
writs of assistance
VII–345a
Yale University VII–351a
See also New England
Rhode Island, Battle of. *See*
Quaker Hill, Battle of
Rhode Island, College of
II–114b
RHODE ISLAND, COLONIAL CHARTERS OF
VI–134a; I–145a, 350b;
II–116b, 117b, 118b, 365a;
VI–132a, 166a; VII–244a
Rhode Island, University of
V–135a
Rhode Island College. *See*
Brown University
I–372a
Rhode Island Historical Society III–137b
RHODE ISLAND IN THE DUTCH WAR OF 1653
VI–134a
Rhode Island red VI–395
(table)
Rhode Island School of Design
II–100a
Rhode Island School of Design
Museum of Art (Providence) III–137b
Rhode Island State College
I–273a
Rhode Island v. *Massachusetts*
(1846) I–350b, 351a
Rhodes, Cecil J. (states., fin.)
VI–134b
Rhodes, James Ford (hist.)
II–64a; III–282a; IV–163a
Rhodesia
Rhodes scholars VI–134b
RHODES SCHOLARSHIPS
VI–134b; II–470b
Rhododendron VI–395
(table)
Rhone Valley
World War II VII–339b
Rhumba (dance) II–290b
"Rhumbatron" VII–163b
RHYOLITE (Nev.)
VI–135a; IV–354b
Rhythm and blues
IV–440b–41a
Riall, Phineas (off.) II–31b;
IV–205a
Ribault, Jean (nav. off.)
III–38a; V–370a, 370a;
VI–347a, 348b
Ribbentrop, Joachim von
VII–229b
RIBBON FARMS VI–135a
Ribbons II–310a–12b,
371a–b
Ribeauville (Fr.) VI–338b
Ribicoff, Abraham A. (pol.)
III–267b
Riboflavin III–44b
Ribonuclease I–304a
Ribonucleic acid II–358a;
III–158a; IV–389a,
390b–91b
Ribose IV–389a
Ricardian unemployment
VII–139b
Ricardo, Antonio (print.)
V–410b
Rice, cooked III–52a, 53b
Rice, C. W. (phys.) VI–9b
Rice, Dan (circus owner)
II–40b; VI–283a
Rice, David (abolitionist)
I–135b
Rice, Elmer (playwright)
VII–50a
RICE, FORT (Dak. Terr.)
VI–135a; II–284a; III–32a
Rice, Henry M. (pol.)
VI–135a
Rice, Nathan Lewis (cler.)
VI–135b
Rice, Thomas D. (act.)
IV–359b
Rice, wild III–51a
RICE–CAMPBELL DEBATES (1845) **VI–135b**
Rice cereal I–487b
RICE CULTURE AND TRADE VI–135b;
I–486a,b; VI–386a
Agricultural Adjustment
Administration V–44a
Charleston (S.C.)
I–496a,b
colonial trade II–119b,
453a; VI–108a; VII–82b
commodity money
II–140b
exports VII–86a, 87a
Florida III–39a
irrigation III–478b
marketing quotas V–359a
Navigation Acts V–16a,b
New Smyrna Colony
V–66a
North Carolina I–447b
plantation system
V–324b–25a
prices V–404b
product enrichment
V–128b
Savannah VI–220a,b
slavery IV–79a; VI–304b,
305a, 310a
South I–37a, 38a;
VI–341a–b
South Carolina III–405b;
VI–347a,b
steam power VI–409b
taxation II–164b
Texas I–279a
tidewater II–485a; VII–58a
triangular trade II–119a;
VII–119b

RICE CULTURE AND TRADE (cont.)
wild rice VII–298b
Rice Krispies I–487b
Rice's Station (Va.) VI–186b
Rice University VII–40b
"Rich, and good and wise." *See* "Wise, and Good and Rich"
Rich, Lorimer (arch.) VII–157a
Rich, Nathaniel VII–66a–b
Rich, Obadiah (silversmith) VI–290a
Rich, Robert, 2nd Earl of Warwick (col. adm.) II–122b; III–220a
Connecticut patent II–182a; VI–151b
Rhode Island charter VI–134a
Shawomet VI–271b
Richard II (k.) I–14b
Richards, A. Newton (chem.) V–137a
Richards, Dickinson W. (physic.) V–100a
Richards, Theodore W. (chem.) I–218b; II–11b–12a; V–99b
Richards, Vincent (athlete) VII–30a
Richards, William Trost (paint.) V–192a
Richards Medical Research Building (Phila.) I–165b
Richardson, A. D. (jour.) VII–187b
Richardson, Elliott (law.) III–267b; IV–268a; V–78a
Richardson, George (metalworker) VI 291b
Richardson, Henry Hobson (arch.) I–164a; III–136a, 260b; VI–299a
Richardson, John (nat.) III–27a; IV–232a; V–122a
Richardson, Joseph, Sr. (silversmith) VI–290a
Richardson, Lewis F. (meteor.) IV–317b
Richardson, Robert E. (nat.) III–28a
Richardson, W. A. (jur.) VI–207b
Richardson, William A. (gov.) V–31b
Richardson Highway (Alaska) I–78a
Richardson Romanesque architecture I–164a
Richberg, Donald R. (adm.) IV–469a
Richelieu, Cardinal (Armand Jean du Plessis) II–149a
RICHELIEU RIVER VI–136b; V–367a; VI–149a
Champlain's voyage VI–192a
exploration I–492b
Fort Chambly I–491b
French and Indian War III–116b, 117a
French fortifications IV–86a, 86b
revolutionary war I–193b, 436a; VI–191a
"Rich man's panic." *See* Panic of 1907
Richman Stores III–33a
Richmond (Ind.) II–348b
Richmond (Ky.) VI–137a
Richmond (N.Y.) VI–460a
Richmond (Tex.) VI–26a–b
RICHMOND (Va.) **VI–136b**; VII–193b, 301b
Afro-American churches I–23a
air crash II–347a
Boulevard Bridge VII–69b
busing I–397b
canals III–488a–b; IV–174b
capitol III–495a
chemical industry VII–196a
Civil War I–249a, 381a, 493a; II–272b, 279a, 482a; III–21b, 101a, 487a, 488a; IV–261b, 281b, 397a; V–113b, 248b, 373a, 377b; VI–186b, 263b, 275b; VII–113b, 195a, 197a, 293a
Civil War prisons I–287a, 466a–b; II–159b
Confederate capital II–160b
Confederate White House VII–292a
directory II–343b
direct-trade convention VI–352b
electric railway VI–40a
fall line II–485a
flour milling III–45a; VII–194a
Gabriel's Insurrection III–145a, 437a; VI–304a
Independent Chronicle II–303b
iron and steel industry VII–113b
Lederer's expeditions IV–131a
Libby Prison IV–139a
locomotive building IV–175b
Montgomery Convention IV–405a
prices V–405b
railroads VI–36b, 37b, 38a
revolutionary war I–194a; IV–8b; VII–360b
Southern Commercial Convention VI–352a
Southern Literary Messenger VI–353a–b
state capitol I–162b; VI–242b
steam power VI–409b
streeetcars II–415a
tinware VII–63a
Tredegar Iron Works II–163a
Union administration VII–148b
Virginia Commonwealth University VII–300b
waterpower IV–347b
RICHMOND, BATTLE OF (1862) **VI–137a**; III–100a; V–245a; VI–420b
RICHMOND, BURNING AND EVACUATION OF (1865) **VI–137b**; I–146b; III–33a–b
Confederate seal VI–246a
RICHMOND, CAMPAIGN AGAINST (1864–65) **VI–137b**; I–213b, 476b; II–62b; V–59a; VII–115a
Cold Harbor II–96b
Drewry's Bluff II–373a
Dutch Gap Canal II–382b
espionage VI–373b
Petersburg siege V–264b
Richmond, Mary Ellen (soc. worker) VI–331b
Richmond and Danville Company V–117a
Richmond and Danville Railroad I–146b; VI–37a
Richmond and Petersburg Railroad VI–36b
Richmond County (N.Y.) V–82a
See also Staten Island
Richmond Enquirer (news.) VI–138a
Richmond, Fredericksburg and Potomac Railroad VI–25a
RICHMOND JUNTO VI–138a
Richmond Locomotive Works IV–175b
Richmond News Leader (news.) V–73b
Richmond's Island (Maine) IV–207b; VI–184a; VII–114b
Richmond Stage Road I–146b
Richmond Times-Dispatch (news.) V–73b
Richmond Whig (news.) VI–49a
RICH MOUNTAIN, BATTLE OF (1861) **VI–138a**; II–231a
Rickard, George Lewis ("Tex") (bus.) IV–220b; V–422b
RICKERT RICE MILLS, INC. v. FONTENOT (1936) **VI–138b**
Rickets I–303b
Ricketts, John William (circus owner) II–40a
Rickover, Hyman G. (nav. off.) I–179b, 217b; V–11a
Ricks, Willie I–316a
Rico (Colo.) VI–213b
Riddell, John L. (physic., bot.) I–241a
Riddle (Oreg.) III–13b–14a
Riddle, Eliza (barnstormer) I–268a,b
Riddleberger, H. H. (pol.) VI–49b
Riddleberger Bill (1882) VI–49b
RIDERS, LEGISLATIVE VI–138b
Ridge, John (Indian) V–49b
Ridgefield (Conn.) II–106a, 286a; III–25b
RIDGEFIELD, BATTLE OF (1777) **VI–139a**
RIDGELY, FORT (Minn.) **VI–139a**; II–283b; VI–296b, 374a
Ridgeway, James F. (writ.) V–79a
Ridgway, Matthew B. (off.) IV–56a, 300b–01a
Riel, Louis III–242b
Riesman, David (soc. sci.) IV–165a
Rietveld, Gerrit III–136a
"Riffing" VI–144b
RIFLE VI–139a; II–130b; IV–430a–31a, 431b, 433a
breech-loader V–26b
Civil War II–67a
dueling II–376b
interchangeable manufacture III–441b–42a; IV–272b
Maynard tape primer IV–279a
Minié ball IV–352b
mounted III–78b
Parrott V–56a
revolutionary war VI–125b
sharpshooters VI–269b
Sharps rifle VI–270a
Spencer rifle VI–372a
World War I VII–326a
World War II VII–335b
RIFLE, RECOILLESS VI–140a
Rifle Association, National. *See* National Rifle Association
Riflemen I–385a; VI–269b
Rifle-musket VI–139b
Rigaud, Pierre François de, Marquis de Vaudreuil-Cavagnal. *See* Vaudreuil-Cavagnal, Marquis de
Rigby, Alexander IV–207b
Rigby, Edward IV–207b
Rigdon, Sidney (Mormon) VI–87a
Riggs, Lynn (playwright) VII–50b
Riggs, Robert L. ("Bobby") (athlete) VII–30b
Riggs, Romulus (land speculator) IV–345a
Riggs, Stephen R. (cler.) III–267a
Righeimer's Saloon (Chicago) VI–201b
Right of rebellion. *See* Rebellion, Right of
RIGHT OF WAY LAW OF 1852 VI–140b
Rights, civil. *See* Civil Rights and Liberties
Rights, human. *See* Human Rights
Rights, natural. *See* Natural Rights
Rights, peripheral I–299b–300a
RIGHTS OF ENGLISHMEN VI–140b; II–191a, 308b; V–220b; VI–111b–12a; VII–189b
colonial charters II–118b
colonial judiciary II–121a
committees of correspondence II–140a

Declaration of Independence II–304a
Stamp Act VI–381b, 382a
RIGHTS OF MAN **VI–141a**; V–353a
RIGHTS OF THE BRITISH COLONIES ASSERTED AND PROVED **VI–141a**
Right to bear arms I–300b; III–317a
Right to counsel (law) IV–14b
Right to privacy III–316b–17a
Right to Read Program II–402b
Right–to–work laws IV–74b
Riis, Jacob A. (jour., writ.) VI–314a; VII–24a
Riley, Bennett C. (off.) VI–141b; VII–358a
Riley, C. v. (entom.) I–46a
Riley, Edward (comp.) III–469a
RILEY, FORT (Kans.) **VI–141b**; I–190b, 434b; IV–25b
Riley, James Whitcomb (au.) IV–163a
Riley, Terry (mus.) IV–442b
Rillieux, Norbert (inv.) VI–436b
Rimini (It.) III–201a
Rimmer, William (paint.) V–189b
Rinderpest vaccine IV–291b
Rinehart, William (sculp.) VI–243b
Ringgold (Tex.) II–32a
Ringgold, Cadwalader (nav. off.) V–336b; VI–142a
RINGGOLD GAP, BATTLE OF (1863) **VI–141b**; I–502b; IV–365a
RINGGOLD–RODGERS EXPLORING EXPEDITION (1853–59) **VI–141b**; V–23a, 336b
Ringling Brothers, Barnum and Bailey Circus II–348a
Ringling Brothers and Barnum & Bailey Combined Shows II–40b
Ringmann, Mathias (schol.) I–97a
Ring–necked pheasant VI–395 (table)
RINGS, POLITICAL **VI–142a**
Philadelphia Gas Ring V–279a
Tweed Ring VII–131a
Ringwood (N.J.) IV–445b
"Rin–Tin–Tin" (radio show) I–488a
Rio Abajo I–83b
Rio Arriba County (N.Mex.) VI–7b
Río Bravo del Norte. *See* Rio Grande
Rio Chama VI–214b
Rio Colorado I–441b
Rio de Janeiro (Braz.)
Battle Fleet cruise I–276b
Confederate expatriates I–360b
disasters II–346b–47a, 349b
inter–American conferences V–171a, 205a
slave trade VI–311b
RIO DE JANEIRO CONFERENCE (1947) **VI–142b**; IV–402a
Rio de la Plata V–212b; VI–344a; VII–162b
Rio del Norte IV–34a
Rio de Sonoita I–413a
RIO GRANDE **VI–143a**; VII–46b
Apache Wars I–142b
Arkansas River route I–174b
boundary VII–108b
boundary disputes I–352a
California Trail I–410a
Civil War III–187b; V–198b, 264b; VI–144a–b; VII–165b
confederate expatriates VI–274b
El Paso II–433a
exploration III–119a
Fort Massachusetts IV–268b
Fowler expedition III–88a
fruit growing VI–355b
fruits and vegetables I–40a
Gila Trail III–179b
Gulf of Mexico IV–326a,b
Intracoastal Waterway VI–146b
longhorn cattle IV–184b
Louisiana purchase boundary IV–197b
Mesilla IV–315b
Mexican War IV–323a,b; VI–97a
Mier expedition IV–337b
mustangs IV–444b
Navaho campaigns VI–439b
Nolan expeditions V–101a
Oñate's explorations V–155a
Pike expedition V–312a; VII–271b
presidios VI–364a
Pueblo I–8a, 402a; III–301a, 367b; V–459b, 460a, 461a
railroads I–83b
Salt War VI–204a
Sangre de Christo grant VI–210b
Santa Fe trade VI–215a
Spanish exploration IV–452a
Spanish settlement V–59b
Spanish Trail VII–256a
survey II–440b
Taos VI–460b
Texas VII–36b
Texas boundary V–125a; VII–38a,b
Texas Rangers VII–42a
U.S. boundary III–230a; IV–321a,b; VI–150b–51a, 359a; VII–39a–b
wagon trains VII–217b
RIO GRANDE, ENGLISH COLONY ON **VI–143b**
RIO GRANDE, SIBLEY'S OPERATIONS ON (1861–62) **VI–144a**; V–60a
Rio Grande Pueblo II–228b; III–396b
Rio Grande Valley VII–40b
Rio Napestle (Napeste) I–174a,b
Rio Pact (1947). *See* Inter–American Treaty of Reciprocal Assistance
Rio Panuco IV–452a
Rio Piedras (P.R.) III–76b
Riot Act of 1792 IV–259b
Riots I–26a
anti–Catholic I–283a
Attica V–417b
campaign of 1968 I–431a; II–18b, 20b
Charleston (Ill.) I–498b
Cincinnati II–38a
Clinton (Miss.) II–77a
Coeur d'Alene (Idaho) II–93b
county–seat wars II–245b
Ellenton (S.C.) II–432a
Haymarket Square II–17b
indemnities III–352a
Johnson–Jeffries bout V–422b
King, Martin Luther, assassination IV–46a
Little Rock (Ark.) I–207b
Louisville (Ky.) I–323a
military aid IV–341b
National Guard II–314a
prisons I–220b–21a; V–416a, 417b
railroad strike of 1877 VI–38b
right of assembly I–204a
See also Insurrections, Domestic
Riots, race. *See* Race Riots
Rio Verde III–226b
Riparian rights III–478a,b
Ripley (Ohio) VII–138a
Ripley, Eleazar (off.) IV–205a
RIPLEY, FORT (Minn.) **VI–144b**
Ripley, George (cler., ref.) I–369b; II–444b
Ripley, S. Dillon (zool.) VI–319a
Ripon (Wis.) VI–92b; VII–307b
RIPPER LEGISLATION **VI–144b**
RIP RAPS CONTRACT–SCANDAL **VI–145a**
Rip Raps Island VI–145a
RIP VAN WINKLE (lit. char.) **VI–145a**; I–471a; IV–161b
Rip Van Winkle (opera) IV–438b
Rise of American Civilization III–283a
Rise of Silas Lapham IV–163b
Rise of the New West V–81b
Rising, Johan (col. gov.) V–42b, 80b
Rising Sun Chair III–354a
Ritchie, Albert C. (gov.) IV–261a
Ritchie, Thomas (jour., pol.) II–377a; VI–138a
Ritner, Joseph (gov.) I–374a–b
Rittenberg, David (biochem.) I–303b
Rittenhouse, David (astron.) I–211a; V–130b
Rittenhouse, William (cler., mfr.) V–212a
Rittenhouse stove III–268b
Ritter, William E. (zool.) V–135a; VI–242a
Ritty, James (bus.) I–396a
RIVER AND HARBOR IMPROVEMENTS **VI–145b**; VI–148b–49a; VII–77a–b
army engineers I–188a
Corps of Engineers II–450a
federal surplus VI–449b
fortifications III–78a
Gallatin's report III–147a
inland waterways VII–260b–61a
Mississippi IV–373a, 374a,b, 374b
National Waterways Commission V–1b
pork barrel projects V–366b
Saint Lawrence River VI–192b
Saint Lawrence Seaway VI–192b
snagboats VI–322a
Society for Establishing Useful Manufactures VII–160b
Tennessee River VII–27b
Tennessee Valley Authority VII–27b
Vicksburg VII–181b
West Virginia VII–282a
See also Internal Improvements
River boats I–267b; IV–35a
Riverdale (N.Y.) IV–237a
River Des Peres IV–376b
Riverine Assault Force V–22a
River "Long" III–222a
RIVERMEN OF THE OHIO **VI–147b**
RIVER NAVIGATION **VI–148a**
Mississippi IV–372b, 373a, 374a
Red River raft VI–65a
Rock Island Bridge Case VI–159b
Savannah River VI–220b
snagboats VI–322a
steamboats VI–149b
Tennessee River VII–26a, 27b
Tombigbee River VII–70b
towboating VII–77b–78a
Wheeling Bridge VII–288a
"River of the West." *See* Columbia River
River pirates II–258a

River Queen (ship) II–165a; III–247b
River Rouge (Mich.) IV–338b
RIVERS VI–149a; VII–259b–61a
 agriculture I–39b, 40a
 boundary disputes I–351a,b
 fall line II–485a
 Falls of the Ohio V–142b
 floods III–36b
 Forks of the Ohio V–143a
 Green River III–226b
 Horsehead Crossing III–304a
 Hudson III–312a
 hydroelectric power III–320b
 Iberville III–326b
 Inland Waterways Commission III–419b
 interstate compacts III–459b, 460a; VI–402a
 limnology II–391a
 locks and waterways IV–174b
 Mississippi IV–372a
 Missouri IV–379b
 Nueces V–125a
 Ohio River V–144b–45b
 Pearl River V–240b
 Perdido V–262a
 portages and water routes V–367a
 Potomac V–378a
 prizes V–421b
 rainfall VI–41b
 Red River of the North VI–64a
 Richelieu VI–136b
 Rio Grande VI–143a
 Saint Croix VI–188b
 Saint Lawrence VI–192a
 Snake River VI–322b
 steamboat monopolies VI–407a
 steamboats VII–100b
 Tennessee River VII–27a
 transportation I–39b; VII–99b
 urban structure VII–159a
 waterpower VII–257a
 western sea VII–275b
 Yukon VII–367a
Rivers, Ralph J. (legis.) I–78b
Riverside (Calif.) IV–366a
Riverside Buildings (N.Y.C.) VII–24b
Riverside Colony III–477b
Riverside Magazine IV–223a
RIVERS IN AMERICAN DIPLOMACY VI–150b; IV–373a
Riverton (N.Y.) II–48b
RIVER TOWNS OF CONNECTICUT VI–151a; II–179b, 181a, 182a; VII–282b
 Pequot War V–261a
 Saybrook agreement VI–223a
River Yumans. *See* Mohave
Rives, William C. (dipl.) III–122a
Riviera, French
 World War II VII–339b
Rivière aux Chevaux I–375b
Rivière des Ark I–174a
Rivière des Iroquois. *See* Richelieu River
Rivière d'Ozark I–174a
Rivington, James (jour.) VI–152a
RIVINGTON'S GAZETTE (news.) **VI–151b**
Rizal, José (rev.) V–282b
RKO (Radio–Keith–Orpheum) V–292b
RNA (ribonucleic acid) II–358a
Road gangs I–489a
Road houses II–261a
ROAD IMPROVEMENT MOVEMENT VI–152a; IV–420a; VI–154b; VII–101b
 road working days VI–156b
 Vermont VII–172b
Road Inquiry, Office of II–502b
"Road ranches" II–45b
Roadrunner (bird) VI–47b, 394 (table)
ROADS VI–152b; III–448a–49a, 450a–51a; VII–99b, 100a, 102a,b
 agriculture I–39b–40a, 41a
 army construction I–192a
 bicycles I–295a
 Blue Ridge Parkway V–220a
 city growth II–41a
 colonial I–460b
 colonial vehicles VII–168a
 convict labor II–217a
 Corps of Engineers II–449b
 Crown Point to No. 4 II–267a
 Cumberland Road II–273a
 domestic trade VII–83a
 eminent domain II–440a
 fall line II–485a
 Federal–Aid Highway Program II–502b
 Forbes Road III–58b, 59a
 Gaines' Trace III–146b
 Gallatin's report III–147a
 gasoline taxes III–153a–b
 Genesee Road III–157a
 government inspection III–422a
 grants–in–aid VI–105b
 Indians paths III–387a
 Kansas IV–26b
 Kentucky IV–41b
 land grants IV–96a
 land speculation IV–100a
 licensing IV–148b
 Lincoln Highway IV–156a
 local government IV–171b
 log ash surfacing IV–204a
 Louisiana IV–194b
 Maysville veto IV–279b
 Michigan IV–331a,b
 Michigan Territorial Road IV–332b
 Mohawk Valley IV–387a
 Morris Turnpike V–57b
 Natchez Trace IV–456a
 National Road IV–470a
 New Jersey V–57b
 New South V–67b
 New York State V–86b–87a
 New York Thruway V–87b
 North Carolina V–116b
 Ohio V–141a,b
 Oregon Trail V–168a
 paving V–230a
 Pennsylvania IV–89b
 Pequot Trail V–261a
 Philadelphia–Lancaster Turnpike V–247a
 plank roads V–323a
 post roads V–374b
 public ownership V–455a
 Raystown Path VI–49a
 Right of Way Law VI–140b
 Rocky Mountains VI–160b
 salting VI–203a
 Santa Fe Trail VI–215a
 star routes VI–387a
 state geological surveys III–164b
 state thruway authorities III–201b
 Survey Act of 1824 VI–450a
 taverns VII–2a
 taxation VII–9a
 Tennessee Cumberland Road II–273b
 Three Notch Road VII–55a
 tolls VII–69a
 truck transportation IV–419a
 urban structure VII–159a
 Vial's Road VII–178b
 water supply VI–377b
 West Virginia VII–282a
 Wilderness Road VII–296a
 Zane's Trace VII–368a
 See also Highways; Turnpikes
Roads, Bureau of Public II–135a, 502b, 502b
ROADS, MILITARY VI–155b
 Burma and Ledo I–386b
 Chicago Road II–20a
 Fort Kearny IV–33b
 Fort Scott VI–241a
 Michigan IV–331a
Road Survey Bill. *See* Survey Act of 1824
ROAD WORKING DAYS VI–156b
Roane, Spencer VI–138a
Roanoke (Va.) II–437a; VII–195a–b, 196a
Roanoke County (Va.) III–469b
Roanoke Island
 distilling II–353b
 Raleigh's colonies I–16a; II–123b; VI–42b, 43b
 settlement V–115a
 wildlife III–26b
ROANOKE ISLAND, CAPTURE OF (1862) **VI–156b**
Roanoke River I–83a, 88b; VI–149b; VII–202b
Roanoke Settlement. *See* Raleigh's Patent and First Colony; Raleigh's Lost Colony
Roaring Camp (Calif.) V–336a
Robards, Rachel. *See* Jackson, Rachel Robards
ROBBER BARONS VI–156b
Robbins, Frederick (physic.) V–100a, 340b
Robbins, Jerome (chor.) II–289a,b, 290b
Robbins, Kendall and Lawrence Company III–442a; VI–270a
Robbins and Lawrence rifle IV–272b
Robbins Mound (Ky.) I–11b
Robbins v. *Taxing District* (1887) VII–105b
Robe, The (film) IV–418a
Robeline (La.) I–48b
Robert E. Lee (steamboat) VI–407a,b
Robert E. Lee Foundation VI–417b
Robert E. Lee Mine IV–124a
Robert Joffrey Ballet II–289b
Robert Moses Power Plant V–91b
Roberts, Bartholomew (buccaneer) I–374a
Roberts, Elizabeth Madox (au.) IV–41a
Roberts, Gideon (mfr.) II–79a; III–442a
Roberts, Nathan (eng.) I–442b
Roberts, O. E. S. (nav. off.) V–424a
Roberts, Owen J. (jur.) V–47a, 48a; VI–446b
 Agricultural Adjustment Act VI–138b
 general welfare clause III–156b–57a
 Japanese–American relocation III–491a–b
 minimum–wage legislation VII–269a–b
 Pearl Harbor investigation V–240a
 Supreme Court packing bill VI–448b
Roberts, Samuel (jour.) IV–41a
Robertson, James (pioneer) IV–92b; VII–253a,b
 Cumberland settlements II–273a
 Nashborough IV–452b
 Watauga settlements II–274a, 477a
Robertson, O. C. S. (nav. off.) V–122a
Robertson, Oscar (athlete) V–154b

Robertson, William D. (off.) II–407b
Robertson, William Henry (law.) III–152b
Roberts Tunnel II–332a
Robeson, Paul (act., sing.) I–21b
Robeson Channel V–240b
Robeson County (N.C.) IV–203b
Robidou, Antoine (fur trader) II–477b; VII–137a
Robidou, Fort (Utah) II–477b
Robidou, Joseph (fur trader) VI–191b, 367a
Robie House (Chicago) I–165a
Robin VI–394 (table), 395 (table)
Robinhood (Indian) IV–37b
Robin Hood (operetta) IV–442a
Robin Moor (merchantman) II–213a
Robinson, Charles (gov.) IV–28b, 31a; VII–73a, 218b
Robinson, Edwin Arlington (poet) IV–164a, 166b
ROBINSON, FORT (Nebr.) **VI–157a**; II–379b; VII–227b
Robinson, Frederick (dipl.) II–215b
Robinson, George Frederick Samuel (Viscount Goderich) 1st Marquis of Ripon (states.) VII–248b
Robinson, Jackie (John R.) (athlete) I–271a
Robinson, John (col.) V–312b
Robinson, James Harvey (hist.) III–283a
Robinson, John ("Yankee") (circus owner) II–40b, 41a; VI–283a
Robinson, John (col.) III–488b
Robinson, John (col. legis.) III–79a, 226a
Robinson, Joseph T. (pol.) I–428b; III–37b; VI–157b
Robinson, Samuel M. (nav. off.) VII–342a
Robinson Commission Company I–487a
ROBINSON–PATMAN ACT (1936) **VI–157b**; I–140a; II–72a; V–403a; VI–102b; VII–123b
Rochambeau, Comte de, Jean Baptiste Donatien de Vimeur (off.) III–117b; V–65b, 65b; VI–124b; VII–198b–99a
Rochdale Associationism IV–62a
Rochdale Society of Equitable Pioneers II–220a; VI–358a
Roche à Davion IV–178b
Rochembeau, Comte de, Jean Baptiste Donatien de Vimeur (off.) VII–361a
Rochester (cruiser) VII–242b
Rochester (Minn.) IV–279a
Rochester (N.Y.) I–336a; III–387b, 477a; VI–157b
  directory II–343b
  Eastman Kodak Company III–409b
  Erie Canal II–460a
  flour milling III–45a
  migration from IV–338b
  race riots I–31b; IV–457b
  railroad III–450a
  waterpower IV–347b
Rochester, University of V–349a
Rochester Anti–Masonic Enquirer (news.) I–132b
ROCHESTER RAPPINGS (1848–49) **VI–157b**
Rock and roll II–290b; IV–440b–41a
Rock Around the Clock (song) IV–441a
Rockaway (N.Y.) V–30a
Rockaway Indians III–271b
Rockaway River I–337b
Rockbridge County (Va.) III–469b; V–5a
Rockcastle Hills (Ky.) I–435a
Rock Cave, Fort (Oreg.) I–155a; II–334b
Rock Creek Park (Washington, D.C.) VII–246b
Rockefeller, Andrews and Flagler VI–382b
Rockefeller, David (banker) II–106b
Rockefeller, John D. (ind., philan.) II–189a; V–141b; VII–124b
  Afro–American education II–401b
  art collection II–104a
  fortune III–80a
  hookworm research III–298b
  medical research IV–286b
  Mesabi Iron Range IV–315b
  petroleum industry VI–354b
  petroleum monopoly IV–399a
  Rockefeller Foundation VI–157b
  Rockefeller University VI–158b
  Standard Oil II–75a; V–269b; VI–382b, 383a,b
Rockefeller, John D., III (bus., philan.) III–80a
Rockefeller, John D., Jr. (ind., philan.) III–80a
  colonial Williamsburg VII–300b, 302a
  landholdings IV–100b
  national parks V–220a
  Rockefeller Center IV–104b
Rockefeller, Laurance S.
  national parks V–220a
Rockefeller, Nelson A. (pol.)
  art collection II–106b
  Attica Prison riot I–220a,b
  campaign of 1964 I–430b
  campaign of 1968 I–431b
  CIA investigation VII–238b
  New York governorship V–87b
  vice–presidency V–398b; VI–94a; VII–180 (table), 181a
  vice–president VII–133a
Rockefeller, William (ind.) V–269b; VI–382b, 383a
Rockefeller Center (N.Y.C.) I–164b; IV–104b; VI–86a, 299a
Rockefeller Commission's Report (1975) VII–238b
ROCKEFELLER FOUNDATION VI–157b; III–82b, 83a; IV–286b, 298b; V–280b, 400b–01a, 447b
  corn experiments II–226b
  genetic research III–158b
  Hale telescope III–242a
  hookworm IV–291b; VI–173b
  malaria research IV–229b
  Marine Biological Laboratory IV–251a
  physics fellowships V–295b, 303a
  Woods Hole Oceanographic Institution V–135a
  World War I relief VII–330b
Rockefeller Institute for Medical Research I–242a, 303b; III–157b; IV–286b; VI–158b
Rockefeller Sanitary Commission III–298b; V–447b
ROCKEFELLER UNIVERSITY VI–158b; I–303b; V–307b
Rocket (train) III–452a
Rocket Launcher (bazooka) VI–140a
Rocket–powered planes I–52a–b
Rocket–propelled engines I–235a
ROCKETS VI–159a; II–9b; IV–245a; V–163b, 164a, 296a
  aircraft armament I–49b, 57b, 67b
  army research IV–459b
  astronautics I–210a
  astronomical observations I–212b; V–132a
  German development V–26b
  gunboats III–234b–35a
  helicopters III–270b
  International Geophysical Year III–454a
  Jet Propulsion Laboratory III–502a–b
  research station IV–458b
  Russian development I–179a; II–426a
  U.S. development I–179b–80a
  V–2 I–179b
  warships VII–242a
  World War II VII–340b
  See also Missiles, Military
Rockfish Gap (Va.) I–325b
Rockford (Ill.) I–434b
Rock gardening III–151b–52a
Rock Hill (S.C.) VI–348a
Rockhill, William W. (dipl.) V–242a
Rocking chair I–490a
Rockingham, Charles (states.) II–318a
Rockingham County (N.H.) V–376b
Rockingham County (Va.) III–469b
Rockingham ware III–184a; V–379b
Rock Island (Ill.) VI–33b, 159b
  arsenal I–196b
  Black Hawk War I–311b–12a
  Confederate prison I–219b
  Fort Armstrong I–180b; IV–355b
  Union prison V–414b
ROCK ISLAND BRIDGE CASE (1857) **VI–159b**
Rock Island Railroad III–449b; VI–25b–26a
Rockland (Maine) IV–226b
Rockland County (N.Y.) IV–24a, 48a
"Rock of Gibraltar" I–18a
"Rock of the Marne" I–491b
Rock phosphate III–16b
Rock River I–180b, 312a; II–21a; VI–218b
Rocks. *See* Petrography
"Rocks and Shoals." *See* Articles for the Government of the Navy
Rock Springs (Wyo.) II–29b; III–352a; VII–345b, 346a
Rockville (Md.) VI–319b
Rockville Center (N.Y.) II–350b
Rockwell, George Lincoln (Amer. Nazi Party leader) I–203a
Rockwell International I–238a
ROCKY MOUNTAIN FUR COMPANY VI–160a; I–200b; III–143a–b, 227a; VII–103b, 104a
  Leavenworth expedition IV–129b
  Missouri River IV–380b
  Platte River Trail V–330b
  Smith explorations VI–318a
  Snake River VI–322b
  wagon trains VII–217a
Rocky Mountain Quakers V–470b
Rocky Mountain Region, Geographical and Geological Survey of the II–464b
ROCKY MOUNTAINS VI–160a; II–272a; III–209a; VII–357b
  Basin Indians III–362a
  Big Horn Mountains I–296a
  Bonneville expedition I–330a
  buffalo I–375a
  buffalo trails VI–152b
  cattle drives IV–184a

ROCKY MOUNTAINS (cont.)
Chinook winds II–30b
coal III–218b
Denver II–332a
Deseret II–334a
Desert culture II–334b
domestic trade VII–84a
exploration I–200b–01a; III–114b, 119a,b; V–31a
fish III–28a
folklore III–48b
forty-niners III–82a
fur trade III–140a, 143a–b, 398b; VII–103b, 104b
gold III–221a
Great American Desert III–213b
Great Plains III–220b
horse III–303a
irrigation III–478a
Lewis and Clark Expedition IV–136b; VII–271a
locomotives IV–177a
longhorn cattle IV–184b
Long's exploration VII–358a
Long's explorations IV–186b
Louisiana IV–196a
Louisiana Purchase boundary IV–6a, 198a
Mallet brothers exploration IV–230a
midcontinent oil region IV–333b
mining III–65a; IV–122b
Mormon settlement IV–339a
mountain men IV–422a
mustangs IV–444b
national forests V–446a
Ogden's Hole V–140a
Oregon Trail V–169a
Oregon Treaty of 1846 V–165a, 168a, 169b
overland freighting V–177a
Pacific Northwest V–167b
passes V–224a, 224b–25a
Pikes Peak V–311a
Plains Indians III–363b
plateau I–15a
prairie dogs V–387b
railroads VI–33b, 34a
resorts and spas VI–101a,b
routes II–14b
settlements VII–146a
sheep VI–273a
South Pass V–330b; VI–354b
stagelines VI–379b
Stevens' railroad survey VI–413a
Taos Trail VI–461a
timberlands VII–60a,b
tree planting VII–114a
Upper Louisiana IV–195b
U.S. boundary V–120b
vigilantes VII–187a–b
Wells, Fargo VII–267a
Western Federation of Miners VII–272b
zinc VII–369a
Rocky Mountains National Park V–218 (table); VI–160b–61a
Rocky Mountains Region, Survey of the V–384b
Rococo furniture III–134a–b, 135b, 138b, 445b
Rodents II–253a
Rodeo (ballet) IV–439a
RODEOS VI–161a; I–285b, 369a; VI–364b
Courts of the Plains II–247a
state fairs VI–392b
Wyoming VII–346b
See also Wild West Show
Roderick Random VI–301b
Rodgers, Jimmie (sing.) IV–441b
Rodgers, John (nav. off.) I–266b; II–190a; V–17b, 336b; VI–142a
President V–393b
war with Korea (1871) IV–54b
Rodgers, Lincoln P. (av.) I–233b
Rodgers, Richard (comp.) IV–442a; VII–50b
Rodgers and Hart II–290a
Rodin, François (sculp.) III–19b
Rodino, Peter W. (pol.) III–344b
Rodman, Thomas J. (off.) I–200a; IV–431a
Rodney, Caesar (jur.) II–308a; V–278b
RODNEY'S RIDE (1776) **VI–161b**
Rodríguez, Augustin (miss.) I–288b; IV–367b; VI–162a
RODRÍGUEZ–CHAMUSCADO EXPEDITION (1581) **VI–162a**; I–288b
Rodrique Hortalez and Company. *See* Hortalez and Company
Roebling, John A. (eng.) I–364b; V–247b
Brooklyn Bridge I–164b, 370b, 378a
Niagara railroad bridge V–93b
Roebling, Washington (eng.) I–370b
Roebling cable aqueduct I–443a
Roebuck, John A. (pol.) II–162b
Roer River (Ger.) III–314a,b
Roetgen Forest (Ger.) III–314a
Roethke, Theodore (poet) IV–165b
Roe v. *Wade* (1973) II–378b
ROGERENES VI–162a
Rogers, Andrew J. (pol.) IV–6a
Rogers, Henry Darwin (geol.) III–165b
Rogers, Henry H. (bus.) V–208b
Rogers, John (Rogerene) VI–162a
Rogers, John (sculp.) VI–243a
Rogers, John, II (nav. off.) IV–375a
Rogers, L. A. (bact.) I–46a
Rogers, Mahlon (eng.) VI–409a
Rogers, Randolph (sculp.) VI–243b
Rogers, Robert (off.) I–465a; IV–86a,b; VI–46b, 162b, 190a
Rogers, Samuel Lyle (offi.) IV–149b
Rogers, Will (humorist) V–75a
Rogers, William (states.) VII–224a
Rogers, William Barton (geol.) I–98a; II–447b; III–165b
Rogers, William P. (states.) VI–472a
Rogers Act (1924) III–71b; VI–389a
Rogers Brothers Silverware Company VII–105b
ROGERS' RANGERS VI–162b; III–116b; IV–86a,b, 329a; VI–46b, 190a
Rogers' Rock (N.Y.) VI–162b
Rogers v. *Bellei* (1971) II–475b–76a; III–86b
Rogersville (Ky.) VI–137b
Roget's *International Thesaurus* V–96a
Rogue River I–401b
Rogue River Indians III–384a
Rogue River War (1851–56) V–165b; VII–239b
Rogue's Island IV–53b
Rohmer (Ark.) III–491a
Roi Island IV–257b
ROK. *See* Korea, Republic of
Rolette, Joseph (fur trader) V–388a
Rolfe, John (col.) III–489a; V–385b; VII–66b
Rolla (Mo.) VII–304a
Rollergin II–240a–b
Rolles, Dennis (col.) III–38b
Rollestown (Fla.) III–38b
Rolling mill products III–469b–70a,b, 471 (table), 472b
Rollins, Sonny (mus.) IV–440b
Rollo books I–335a
Roma (dirigible) II–344a
Roman, André Bienvenu (pol.) II–161a
Roman architecture III–495a
Roman Catholic Church. *See* Catholicism
Roman Curia I–468a
Roman empire
circus II–40a
dry docks II–375a
elevators II–428b
Romanesque architecture I–163b, 164a; VI–299a
Romania
corn production II–226b
immigration to U.S. III–339a
nationalization of U.S. property IV–466a
Paris Peace Conference V–215b
Unknown Soldiers II–310a
World War I I–176b
World War II V–332a
World War II peace settlement V–378b
Romanian Orthodox Episcopate of America II–387a
Roman law II–141a
Roman Maison Carrée (Nîmes, Fr.) I–162b
Roman Nose (Indian) I–283a; IV–45a
Romans, Bernard (off.) VII–70b, 74a
Romanticism
antebellum South VI–342b
Romantic painting V–185b, 187a, 188a–90a
Rome (It.)
aerial hijacking III–278a
maritime law I–14b
papal states consulate V–211b
World War II I–141a; III–200b, 201a, 235b; IV–404a; VI–284b; VII–338b
Rome (N.Y.) VI–385b
Romer, Alfred S. (zool.) VI–91a
Romer, John Irving (ed.) I–18b
Romig, Harry (statis.) VI–206b
Romilly, Samuel (law., ref.) V–415a
Rommel, Erwin (off.) IV–32b; V–113a
Romney, George (pol.) IV–258b
Ronaldson, James (typefounder) V–411b–12a
Ronde, Louis Denis de la (fur trader) II–13b
Rondout (N.Y.) VI–33b
Ronne, Finn (expl.) V–338a
Ronne Antarctic Expedition (1947–48) V–338a
Ronnel III–421a
Rook, T. (print.) III–24a
Rookwood Pottery V–379b
ROORBACK VI–163a
Roorback, Baron von (trav.) VI–163a
Roosevelt (ship) V–240b, 241a
Roosevelt, Anna Eleanor (writ.) I–30a
Roosevelt, Eleanor III–457a; V–46a; VII–364b
Roosevelt, Franklin Delano II–177 (table), 480b; III–260b; V–161b, 385b, 396 (table), 396a, 398b; VI–93a; VII–291a
campaign song I–432b
"Forgotten Man" address III–77b
poliomyelitis V–340a
presidential library III–284b
Progressive Party V–429a
progressivism V–87b
Tammany Hall

VI–460a–b
vice–presidential nomination I–427a
—*President:*
air war against Japan III–489b
American Labor party I–107a
American Liberty League I–108b
Anglo–American relations I–123a,b
Atlantic Charter I–214b; VII–334b–35a
atomic bomb IV–237b; VII–341a
attempted assassination I–202b
bank crisis of 1933 I–260a
Bank Holiday Proclamation V–425b
Bataan campaign I–274a
Battle of the Atlantic I–214a
brain trust I–359b
Buenos Aires Peace Conference V–232a
bureaucracy I–384a
Bureau of Mines IV–350b
cabinet I–400a; VII–317b
Cairo Conference I–403b
campaign of 1932 IV–261a; V–223b; VI–134a, 313a
campaign of 1936 IV–73a; VII–134b
campaign of 1940 IV–73a
campaign of 1944 IV–73b
Casablanca Conference I–67a, 465a; VII–338b
Civilian Conservation Corps II–51a
civil service reform II–60a
coal industry III–231b
Coast Guard II–89b
commerce clause II–136b
Committee on Un–American Activities VI–428a
Communist party II–144b
Congress II–472b
conservation II–188a
conservatism II–189b
Cuba II–269a–b
declaration of war VII–224b
deflation III–415a
dollar diplomacy II–359b
economic policies III–195a
economic royalists II–392a
elected I–428b; II–327b
equal employment opportunity II–56b, 455b–56a
executive orders II–473a
Farmer–Labor party II–491b, 492a
farm tenancy I–40b–41a
Federal Communications Commission VI–15b–16a
federal deficit VI–449b
Fireside Chats V–353b
Flying Tigers III–46b
foreign policy III–69a
Four Freedoms III–84a; V–353b
gold I–302a; III–190a, 192a, 194a–b; IV–234a, 395b; VI–95a, 371a–b
Good Neighbor Policy I–454b; III–199a, 463a; IV–112a
Great Depression I–391a
Hatch Act III–261a
hemispheric solidarity II–314b
Indian affairs III–371b
International Labor Organization III–455a
interstate trade barriers III–460b
Japanese–American relocation II–445b–46a; III–490b
Japanese negotiations V–239a
Jewish support IV–10b
labor legislation II–481b–82a; IV–80b
labor policies IV–73b
labor's support IV–81b
Latin–American policy IV–401b
lend–lease IV–134b; VII–237b
Ludlow resolution IV–203a
Manchuria IV–235a–b
Mexican oil controversy IV–328b
military bonuses I–331b
National Industrial Recovery Act VII–123a
National Nutrition Conference for Defense V–128b
National Park Service V–220a
National Recovery Administration IV–469a
National Youth Administration VII–364b
navy VII–341b–42a
neutrality V–39a
Neutrality Acts IV–430a; V–35b–36a, 37a–b, 38a–b
New Deal IV–71a–72a, 228a, 472b; V–43a, 83b, 329a–b, 381b; VII–53a, 140a
New York World's Fair V–89a
nonintervention policy V–106a
Office of Civil Defense II–50a
Office of Scientific Research and Development V–137a
Office of Strategic Services V–137b; VI–373b
Ogdensburg Agreement I–439b; V–139b
Pearl Harbor attack V–240a
pump–priming V–464a
pure food and drug movement V–467a
racial discrimination II–473a
railroad retirement acts VI–23b
reciprocal trade agreements III–113b
reelections I–429a–b
relief programs VI–73a–b
removal power III–317a; VI–85a
Reorganization Plan Number 4 III–54a
savings bonds VI–222a–b
Science Advisory Board IV–287a
social security IV–276a; VI–328a, 329a
Soviet government VI–181a
state of emergency (1939) II–311b
Supreme Court III–105a; IV–17a; VI–443b, 448a,b
taxation VII–7b
Teheran Conference VII–18a
Tennessee Valley Authority VII–28a
terms of office I–95a; VII–53b, 132b
territories VII–32b
Thanksgiving Day VII–46a
United Nations V–234a; VII–151a,b
veterans' benefits V–257b
vetoes VII–178a
war powers II–179a; VII–227a
Works Progress Administration VII–322b
World Economic Conference VII–324a
World War II IV–383b; VI–179a; VII–334b–35a, 336b, 344a
Yalta Conference II–97b; VII–351b
Roosevelt, Nicholas J. (inv.) IV–374a; V–63a; VI–409a
Roosevelt, Theodore II–176 (table); III–260b; V–161b, 385b, 396 (table), 396a
attempted assassination I–202b, 381a
Battle of San Juan Hill VI–213b–14a
Bull Moose party I–380b
campaign of 1912 I–328a, 380b, 426b–27a; II–327b; IV–331b; V–427b–28b; VI–331a; VII–52b, 53b
campaign of 1916 V–428b
conservationist activities IV–96a
"lunatic fringe" IV–204b
New York governorship V–87b
N.Y.C. mayoral election (1886) IV–101a
N.Y.C. police commissioner IV–138a
preparedness movement V–390b
Rough Riders VI–61a, 165b, 362a
Spanish–American War IV–239a–b; VI–361b
Taft split VI–458a
Tenement House Commission VII–24b
vice–presidency I–425b–26a; VII–180 (table)
—*President:*
Alaska boundary I–122b, 439a
Algeciras Conference V–233a
Anthracite Strike I–127a; IV–67a–b
antitrust policy I–140a; IV–230a
Battle Fleet cruise I–276b; VII–241a
big business I–391a
Brownsville affair I–371b; IV–340a
campaign of 1904 VI–313a
campaign of 1908 I–426a–b
Caribbean policy III–463a
civil service reform II–59b
conservation II–187b–88a; III–73b, 75a, 321a
Country Life Commission VI–171a–b, 175a
Cuba II–269a
dollar diplomacy II–359b
Dominican Republic II–361a; IV–385a
elected I–426a
Far Eastern policy II–488b
foreign policy III–68b–69a
Foreign Service III–71b; VI–389a
Inland Waterways Commission III–419b
Isthmus of Panama I–295b
Japan V–158b
Japanese Exclusion Acts III–492a
Manchuria IV–234b–35a
mineral lands V–445b
Monroe Doctrine IV–401a–b
Morocco I–85b
muckraking IV–424b–25a
National Governors' Conference III–206a
Newlands Act VI–53b
New Nationalism V–60a
Nobel Peace Prize V–99b, 100a
Oregon land frauds V–166a
Panama Canal V–201b
Panama Revolution V–204b
panic of 1907 V–208b
Perdicaris affair V–261b–62a
Philippine Insurrection V–282b–83a
press I–116b
Progressive movement V–427a
public lands I–247b–48a; IV–104b; V–446a, 450b
pure food and drug movement V–466a–b
Republican party VI–93a
Roosevelt Corollary V–105b; VI–163a
Root Arbitration Treaties VI–163b
Russo–Japanese war V–233a

ROOSEVELT, THEODORE (cont.)
Sampson–Schley controversy VI–207a
Secret Service VI–252a
Sherman Antitrust Act VI–277a
Smith, Jacob I–219a
"square deal" VI–378a
Taft–Katsura Memorandum VI–457b
tariff VI–467a–b
"Tennis Cabinet" VII–31a
timberlands V–445a
Treaty of Portsmouth V–370b; VI–178a
"trust-busting" III–466a; VII–121b, 122b
Venezuela blockade VII–169b
warships VII–328a
White House VII–292a
White House Conference on Children IV–275b
wildlife I–306a; VII–298a
Roosevelt, Theodore, Jr. (off., pol.) I–108a
ROOSEVELT COROLLARY VI–163a; I–454a–b; II–361a; III–68b–69a; IV–401a–b; V–105b; 475b–
intervention in Latin America IV–111b
Johnson Doctrine IV–4b
Kellogg–Briand Pact IV–402a
Monroe Doctrine V–106a
Roosevelt family IV–256b
Roosevelt Field (N.Y.) IV–156b, 157a
Roosevelt Island (N.Y.) II–48b; IV–237a
Roosevelt's Sugar House (N.Y.C.) VI–436b
Roosevelt University (Chicago) I–164a
Root, Elibu (states.) V–100a
Root, Elihu (states.)
army reforms I–185b, 190b; II–314a
Army War College I–191a
Cuba II–269a
international court III–456b–57a
Panama Canal tolls VII–70a
Philippines V–283a
Platt Amendment V–329b
Russia mission VI–163b
War Department VII–230a
Waterways Treaty VII–261a
See also Root Arbitration Treaties; Root Takahira Agreement V–232b
Root, Erastus (pol.)
Workingmen's Party VII–322a
"ROOT, HOG OR DIE" VI–163b
ROOT ARBITRATION TREATIES (1908–09) **VI–163a**; V–232b; VII–112b
Root lice III–421a
ROOT MISSION TO RUSSIA (1917) **VI–163b**
ROOT–TAKAHIRA AGREEMENT (1908) **VI–164a**; II–488b; V–158b
Rope III–413a
Roper, Charles F. (inv.) VII–43b
Roper, Daniel C. (law.) V–43b
ROSALIE, FORT (Miss.) **VI–164a**; IV–455a; V–210b
Rosario Strait III–256a
Rosa setigera III–151b
Rose VI–394 (table)
Rose, Billy (showman) III–81a, 217b
Rose, George (states.) VI–164b
Rose, John (states.) I–73b; VII–248b
Rose, Wickliffe (educ.) V–231b
Rosebay rhododendron VI–395 (table)
Rosebud Creek I–313a; IV–168a
ROSEBUD INDIAN RESERVATION (S.Dak.) **VI–164b**
Rosecrans, William S. (off.) I–468a
Army of the Cumberland II–271b; V–142b
Army of the Mississippi IV–370a
Battle at Corinth II–225b
Battle of Chickamauga II–21b
Battle of Iuka III–485a
Battle of Murfreesboro IV–434b
Battle of Rich Mountain VI–138b
Battles at Carnifex Ferry I–457a
Chattanooga campaign I–502b
Tullahoma campaign VII–127b
Rose gardening III–151b
ROSE INTRIGUE (1808) **VI–164b**
Rosenau, Milton (surg.) I–242a
Rosenbach, A. S. W. (book dealer) II–109b
Rosenberg, Ethel II–463b; VI–164b, 428b; VII–107b, 118a, 310b
Rosenberg, Julius II–463b; VI–164b, 428b; VII–107b, 118a, 310b
ROSENBERG CASE (1951) **VI–164b**; VII–107b, 118a, 310b
Rosendale (N.Y.) I–477b
Rosenquist, James (art.) V–193a
Rosenthal, Joe (phot.) I–207b
Rosenwald, Julius (mer., philan.) II–401b
Rosicrucianism II–454a; V–172a
Rosier, James V–243b
Rosin II–5a, 453a
Ross, Alexander (fur trader) VII–221a
Ross, David (trader) III–381a
Ross, Edward A. (educ.) II–470b
Ross, Fort (Calif.) VI–180b, 453a
Ross, George (jur.) II–308a; III–331a
ROSS, IN RE (1891) **VI–165a**
Ross, John (expl.) V–122a
Ross, John (Indian) III–400a; VI–317a
Ross, John (off.) III–330b
Ross, Lewis (Indian) IV–333b
Ross, Lillian (au.) V–79a
Ross, Nellie Tayloe (pol.) VII–346a
Ross, Robert (off.) I–250b, 317b–18a; VII–249b
Ross, Ronald (physic.) IV–229b
Rossby, Carl-Gustav A. (meteor.) III–233b; IV–317b
Ross County (Ohio) II–25b; IV–421a
Rosser, Thomas (off.) VII–71a
Ross Ice Shelf V–337b
Rossiter, Clinton (hist.) II–188b; III–283a
Ross Sea V–338a
Rost, Pierre A. (dipl.) II–65b, 162a
Roszak, Theodore J. (sculp.) VI–244a
Rotary engine I–229b; VI–410a
ROTATION IN OFFICE VI–165a; I–146a
bureaucracy I–384a
spoils system VI–374b, 375a
Rotation of crops I–37a
ROTC. *See* Reserve Officers Training Corps
Roth, Henry (au.) IV–165a
Roth, Philip (au.) IV–165a
Roth, Philip (mus.) III–238b
Rothko, Mark (art.) II–106b; V–192b
Rothschild and Sons (London) III–63b
Rothschild family IV–410a
Rothstein, Arnold (racketeer) II–258b
Roth v. *United States* (1957) III–104b
Rotogravure V–77b
Rotors II–415b
"Rotten boroughs" VII–14b
Rotterdam (Neth.)
World War II I–328a
Roubideau Pass V–224b
Rouen (Fr.) V–8a
Rouërie, Marquis de la. *See* Armand, Charles, Marquis de la Rouërie
Rouge II–233b
Rough Creek (Ky.) VII–252a
Roughing It IV–162b
ROUGH RIDERS VI–165a; VI–61a, 213b–14a, 362a; VII–40b
Roulette III–149b, 150a
Roulstone, George (pub.) V–70b
Roundabout trade. *See* Triangular Trade
Round Bottom (Ohio) VII–252a
Round dance II–291a
Round Hill School VI–228b
Round houses I–11b
Round-log houses I–160b
Round Tower (Fort Snelling) VI–323a
Roundup I–285a, 471a; V–160a
cow custom II–251a
longhorn cattle IV–184b
stampedes VI–382a
supervision I–472a
See also Rodeos
Rous, Francis Peyton (path.) V–100a
ROUSE'S POINT BOUNDARY CONTROVERSY VI–165b
Rousseau, Jean Jacques (philos., au.) VI–89b
Rousseau, L. H. (off.) VI–166a
ROUSSEAU'S RAID (1864) **VI–166a**
Route and Distances to Oregon and California (guidebook) V–168b
Rouville, Hertel de (off.) II–312b
Rowan, Andrew Summers (off.) III–150b; VI–373b
Rowan, Carl T. (jour.) V–75a
Rowan, John (jur.) IV–447b
Rowan County (Ky.) IV–259b
Rowell, Chester (jour.) I–406b
Rowell, George P. (advt.) I–17b–18a
Rowing
Olympic Games V–154a,b
Rowland, David III–137a
Rowland, Henry A. (phys.) IV–2a; V–294b–95a
Rowlandson, Mary III–376b; IV–47b, 161a
Rowson, Susanna Haswell (au.) IV–161a
Roxas, Manuel (states.) V–284b
Roxbury (Mass.) I–344b; II–79b; VI–106a, 167a
Roxbury Latin School (Mass.) VI–228b
Roxbury Rubber Company VI–167a
Royal Academy of Art V–187a, 188a
Royal Adventure Trading Company VI–310a
Royal African Company. *See* African Company, Royal

Royal Air Force III–174a–b
bomber aircraft I–50b
World War II I–60a, 67a, 67a, 328b
Royal Air Force Coastal Command VII–342b
Royal Americans III–58b
Royal and Ancient Golf Club III–197b
Royal Baking Powder Company I–17b
Royal Canadian Mounted Police II–503b
Royal charters. *See* Colonial Charters
Royal College of Surgeons I–295b
ROYAL COLONIES VI–166a; I–499b–500a; V–436b; VI–396a
British colonial policy II–122b
Carolina III–212b
Connecticut II–180a, 182a
councils II–119b–20a
courts I–145a; II–120b–21a
governors II–120a–b
Jamestown VII–192b
Massachusetts Bay II–242b
New France IV–109a–10a
New Hampshire V–53b
New York VII–360a
North Carolina V–115a
quitrents VI–4a–b
South Carolina I–458a; VI–347a
Virginia VII–201a
ROYAL DISALLOWANCE VI–166b; I–145a; II–121a
judicial review IV–12b
New York currency bill V–85b
Parson's Cause V–221b
Privy Council V–421a
Two Penny Act VII–135a
Royal George (ship) III–218a
Royal governors. *See* Colonial Governors
Royal Horticultural Society V–327a
Royall, Isaac V–186b
Royall House (Medford, Mass.) I–161b
"Royal Mineral Succedaneum" II–330a
Royal Navy
convoys II–217b
impressment of seamen III–349b
Laird rams IV–85a
U.S. national defense II–313a
Royal New Yorkers VI–130a
Royal Ocean Racing Club VII–349a
Royal Refugee Corps II–249b
Royal Small-Arms Commission III–442a
Royal Society I–240b; IV–126a, 231a; VI–235a, 237b
Philosophical Transactions I–110b
weather records II–75b
Winthrop mineral collection IV–348a
Royal Yacht Squadron I–95b
Royce, Charles C. (hist.) III–384a
Royce, Josiah (philos.) III–260a; IV–163b; V–287b, 386b
Royer, R. F. (Indian agent) IV–316a
Royko, Mike (jour.) V–75a
Rozhdestvenski, Z. P. (nav. off.) V–11a
RS–1 (airship) II–344a
Ruanda-Urundi IV–236b
RUBBER INDUSTRY VI–166b
Baton Rouge I–275a
Brazil VI–343b
Communist party II–145a
Connecticut II–181a
exchanges II–469b
imports VII–87b
Indian III–381a
iron oxides III–12a
Liberia I–21b; IV–141b
Ohio V–141b
paving V–230a
petrochemical V–267b
plastics V–327b
refrigeration VI–70a
synthetics II–9a, 12b; III–409b; VII–336a
transportation VII–84b
unionization IV–72b
vulcanization II–7a
Rubí, Marqués de VI–168a
Rubin, Jerry II–20b, 21a
RUBÍ'S TOUR VI–168b
Ruby, Jack IV–38a; VII–118b, 238a
Ruck, John (landowner) V–242a
Ruckelshaus, William D. (offi.) II–503b
Rucker, Fort (Ala.) VI–287b
Rudder (mag.) VII–349a
Ruddle's Station (Ky.) I–306b
Rudolph, Paul (arch.) I–166a
Rudolph, Wilma (athlete) V–154a
Ruef, Abraham (pol.) I–343a, 406b; IV–214a; VI–142b
Ruffed grouse VI–395 (table)
Ruffin, Edmund (agric.) III–16a, 25a; IV–125b; VI–335a; VII–194a
Ruffin, Frank G. (off.) VI–49a,b
Ruffner, David (bus.) VI–202b
Ruffner, Henry (cler., educ.) VI–168b
Ruffner, Joseph (bus.) IV–25a; VI–202b
RUFFNER PAMPHLET VI–168b
Ruffs II–370b
Rugby III–56b, 287a
Rugelys Mill (S.C.) I–412a
Ruggles, John (pol.) V–226a
Ruhr River
World War II VII–340a,b–41a
Ruhr Valley (Ger.) VI–302b
"Rule of capture" V–269b, 271a
RULE OF REASON V–168b; I–140a; II–71b–72a; VI–102a–b; VII–122b
RULE OF THE WAR OF 1756 VI–169a; I–175b; II–446b, 464a; III–455b; V–323b
enemy trading VII–93b
Polly Admiralty Case V–355a
Rules for a Printed Dictionary Catalogue IV–145a
Rules for the Regulation of the Navy of the United Colonies VII–143a
Rules of Land Warfare VII–225b
RULES OF THE HOUSE VI–169b; VII–263b
Rules of War. *See* War, Laws of
"Rum, Romanism and Rebellion" I–383b, 424a
Rumania. *See* Romania
Rumbout, Francis. *See* Rumbout's Patent
RUMBOUT'S PATENT VI–170a; III–220b
Rumford (Maine) IV–227a
Rumford, Count. *See* Thompson, Benjamin
Rumford Premium I–97b
Rumford stove III–268b
Rum River (Minn.) IV–346b
Rum River, Battle of (1839) VI–295a
RUM ROW VI–170a
Rum-running I–292b; II–277b; III–332a; V–430a; VI–170a
Rumseian Society VI–170b
Rumsey, James (inv.). *See also* Rumsey's Steamboat
RUMSEY'S STEAMBOAT VI–170a; V–225b; VI–408a,b; VII–100b
RUM TRADE VI–170b; IV–309b; VI–386b; VII–86a, 289b
colonies II–92b
duties VI–111a
embargo of 1807 II–353b
enemy trading VII–93b
excise tax II–353b
Georgia III–168a
Indians III–140b, 402b
Jamaica VII–271a
molasses IV–388a
Norfolk V–109b
Prohibition VI–170a
smuggling VI–320b, 321a
Sugar Acts VI–435a–b
sugarcane VI–436a
Sugar Islands VI–437b
tafia VI–456b
triangular trade II–119a; VI–310b; VII–119a, 277b–78a
Virgin Islands VII–204a
War of 1812 II–353b
West and East Africa I–21a
Rundstedt, Gerd von (off.) I–379b; V–111a
Rune Stone Museum (Alexandria, Minn.) IV–38b
Runic inscriptions. *See* Kensington Stone; Norsemen in America
Runkle, John D. (math.) IV–120a
Runnels, Hardin (pol.) VII–39b
"Running the gauntlet." *See* "Gauntlet, Running the"
Runnymede (Eng.) IV–224a
"Run on the bank" I–254a, 256b
Runyon, Damon (au.) IV–26b
Rupertus, William H. (off.) V–242b–43a
RURAL DEVELOPMENT VI–171a; IV–225a
Rural Development Act (1972) VI–172a
Rural electric associations II–220b
Rural electrification I–39b; VI–175b
Rural Electrification Administration I–44b–45a,b; II–221a, 417a; V–46a
Rural Environmental Assistance Program VI–335b
RURAL FREE DELIVERY VI–172b; I–17a; IV–225a; VI–175a–b
RURAL HEALTH VI–173a; VI–171b, 176a
Rural Legal Assistance Program, California V–136a
RURAL LIFE, CHANGES IN V–174a
antebellum period I–37b
automobile I–227b
farm technology IV–104a
health VI–173a
rural free delivery VI–173a
urbanization II–41b
See also Urban Structure
Rural migration II–46a; V–363b–64a
Rural New Yorker (period.) I–45b
RURAL POST ROADS ACT (1916) **VI–176a**; I–228b; VI–152a, 154b
Rural Rehabilitation Division VI–73b
Rush, Benjamin (physic.) I–410a; III–325a; IV–297a; V–279b–80a, 409a; VII–22a,b
chemistry II–10b
Declaration of Independence II–306a, 308a
educational reform II–396a
malaria IV–229b
mental illness IV–305a
national museum IV–468b
Pennsylvania Hospital V–251b
Porcupine's Gazette V–366b

RUSH, BENJAMIN (cont.)
sexual attitudes VI–266a
slavery I–135b
Sunday schools VI–442b
veterinary medicine VII–176a
yellow fever VII–205b, 355b
Rush, Otis (sing.) IV–442b
Rush, Richard (dipl.) I–318a
Convention of 1818 II–215b
Great Lakes Disarmament Agreement III–217a
Miranda's intrigues IV–361b
Spanish-American republics IV–400a
Rush, William (sculp.) III–21b; VI–242b
Rush-Bagot Agreement (1817). *See* Great Lakes Disarmament Agreement
Rusk, Dean (states.)
Cuba IV–113a
Rusk, Jerrold (pol. sci.) III–92b
Rusk County (Tex.) II–389a
Ruskin, John (arch.) I–163b; III–136a
Russel, Samuel (cler.) VII–350b
Russell, Benjamin (jour.) I–464b
Russell, Bertrand, 3rd Earl Russell (math., philos.)
Cuban missile crisis II–271a
Russell, Bill (athlete) V–154b
Russell, Charles Edward (jour.) VI–163b
Russell, Charles M. (art., au.) I–281a; VI–382b
Russell, Charles Taze (cler.) III–497b
Russell, David A. (off.) VII–238a
Russell, Donald S. (gov.) VI–348a
Russell, Frederick F. (med. off.) IV–291b
Russell, Gilbert (off.) I–402a
Russell, Green (prospector) II–477a; VI–320b
Russell, H. H. (law., cler.) I–134a
Russell, H. N. (astron.) I–212a
Russell, John (cler.) VI–70b
Russell, John, 1st Earl of Russell of Kingston Russell (states.) I–72b–73a; II–65b, 162b; IV–85a; VII–115b
Russell, John H. (off.) III–240a
Russell, Jonathan (dipl.) III–176b; VII–235b
Russell, Morgan (paint.) V–192a–b
Russell, Nathaniel (mer.) I–497a
Russell, Osborne (trapper) VII–105a
Russell, Richard B. (pol.) VII–238a
Russell, Ross IV–440b
Russell, William (educ.) II–398a
Russell, William (mer.) V–409a
Russell, William E. (pol.) II–75a
Russell, William G. (miner) V–311b, 437a
Russell, William H. (bus.) VI–176b
Leavenworth and Pikes Peak Express IV–129b
Pony Express I–485a; V–178a, 357b
Russell Amendment (1943) II–456a
Russell Cave National Monument V–217b
Russell Gulch (Colo.) V–437a
Russellites. *See* Jehovah's Witnesses
RUSSELL, MAJORS AND WADDELL VI–176b; I–473a; IV–426a; V–177a,b; VI–379a
Holladay Overland Stage Company III–291a
Leavenworth IV–129a
oxen V–179a
pony express V–357b
stagecoach mail V–178a
RUSSELL SAGE FOUNDATION VI–176b; II–46b; III–83a
Russellville (Ky.) V–96a
Russia I–444b
Alaska V–164b
Arctic exploitation II–461b
armed neutrality of 1780 I–175b
ballet II–287b, 288b
Black Sea pledges I–73b
Boxer Rebellion I–356a
California I–141a
coinage I–301b
colonization III–68a
consumer cooperatives II–220a
Declaration of Paris V–214a
Eastern Orthodox church II–386b
French and Indian War III–115b
Hague peace conference III–237a
immigration to U.S. III–333a, 340b
Jewish refugees V–342a
Manchuria IV–234b
Murmansk IV–435a
nuclear physics V–310b
pogroms IV–10a
Polish uprising V–342a
potash V–375b–76a
railroads IV–175b
revolution I–158a
sealing VI–245b
sea otter trade VI–247a,b
Siberia expansion II–461b
Sputnik I–235a
submarines VI–422b, 423a, 423b
tobacco VII–64b
Treaty of Tilsit II–291a
warships VII–242a, 243a
World War I I–158b–59a; VII–325b, 328b, 329a, 329b, 330a
World War I armistice I–176b
World War I debts VII–331b
World War II I–67a, 214a–b, 403b; VII–334a, 338a, 341a, 342b
RUSSIA, U.S. RELATIONS WITH VI–177a; III–69b–70b; V–234a–b
Alaska I–74b–75b, 84b, 126b; III–68b; VII–111b
Aleutian Islands I–84a–b
American Revolution I–176a; III–172b
Apollo-Soyuz Project I–210b; IV–460b
arms race I–179a
Berlin airlift I–291a
Berlin Resolution VI–100a
Berlin Wall I–291b
boundary disputes II–313b
Canton I–446a
cold war I–22a; V–236b–37a; VII–88b
containment policy III–463a–b
Cuban missile crisis I–180a, 321b
debts II–301a
Dumbarton Oaks Conference II–380a
expropriation of U.S. property IV–465b–66a
foreign aid III–61a–62b
Fourteen Points III–85b
Geneva summit conference III–161a–b
indemnities III–352b
Israel III–481b–82b
Kennedy administration V–53a
Korean War IV–56a
lend-lease II–314b; IV–134a; V–21b; VII–243b
Manchuria IV–234b
Marshall Plan IV–258a
military policy IV–343b–44a
missile rivalry IV–363b, 364a
Monroe Doctrine IV–400a
Moscow Conference of Foreign Ministers IV–415b
naval competition V–10b–11b
neutralism V–36b
Nixon administration II–316b, 426b; VI–93b
North Pacific Sealing Convention V–401a
"no-win policy" V–124a
Nuclear Test Ban Treaty V–124b, 237a
Olympic basketball I–272b
Open Door policy V–158b, 159a
Oregon boundary II–216a
Pacific Northwest claims V–165a, 167b
Paris conferences V–215b
Potsdam Conference V–378b
Pribilof Islands V–401a
Progressive party V–429a
rapprochement I–22b
recognition of Soviet Union V–45b; VI–181a
Root mission VI–163b
Russian claims VI–180b
sealing I–85a; IV–250a; VI–246a
Siberian expedition VI–283b
space race IV–458b–59a, 459b, 460a
Strategic Arms Limitation Treaty I–63b; VI–416b
summit conferences VI–439a
Teheran Conference VII–18a
trade I–262b–63a; VII–87a, 92a
Treaty of Ghent VII–235b
Treaty of Portsmouth V–370b
Truman Doctrine VII–121a
United Nations Conference VII–151a–b
U.S. Civil War II–162b, 162b; VI–181a
U.S. intervention (1918) I–122b, 158a
U.S. recognition III–456a; VI–55a
Vietnam War V–258a–b
War of 1812 III–176b; V–233a
war with Finland V–37b
wheat sales I–43b; VII–286b
World War I III–463a
World War II IV–313b, 435a
See also Arms Race With the Soviet Union; entries under Soviet Union
Russian-American Company I–74a–75b, 84b; VI–180b, 245b
RUSSIAN CLAIMS VI–180b; II–461b; VI–177b
RUSSIAN FLEETS, VISIT OF (1863–64) **VI–181a**; VI–177b
Russian mulberry VII–114a
Russian olive VII–114a
Russian Orthodox church II–386b–87a
Russian Orthodox Church Outside Russia II–387a
RUSSIAN RECOGNITION VI–181a; VI–178a–b
Russian settlements VII–286a
Kodiak Island IV–54a
South Dakota VI–350a
Russo, Anthony J. V–258b
Russo-Japanese Neutrality Pact (1941) VI–178b–79a
Russo-Japanese War (1904–05) III–68b; V–158b; VI–178a; VII–351b
Manchuria IV–234b–35a

neutrality III–456a
radiocommunications II–424b
Roosevelt mediation V–233a
Taft–Katsura Memorandum VI–457b
Treaty of Portsmouth V–370b
Russwurm, John B. (pub.) V–75b
Rust (disease) V–130a
Rust, John (inv.) I–35b
Rust, Mack (inv.) I–35b
Rust, Mrs. H. L. VII–219a
Rust, Samuel (pressmaker) V–413a
Rustlers. *See* Cattle Rustlers
RUSTLER WAR (1892) **VI–181a**
Ruston, John V–409a
Rusty Lizard VI–91b
Rutgers, Henry (off.) VI–181b
RUTGERS UNIVERSITY VI–181b; II–114b; V–41b
football III–56b
Rutgers v. *Waddington*. *See* Trespass Act
Ruth, George Herman ("Babe") (athlete) I–270b, 488a
Ruthenians III–339a, 340a
Rutherford, Ernest (phys.) II–278a; V–296b, 297b–98b, 300b, 301a,b
Rutherford, ("Judge") Joseph Franklin (cler.) III–497b
Rutherfurd, Lewis M. (astron.) V–131a
Ruthven, Alexander G. (educ.) VI–91a
Ruth v. *United States* (1957) I–479a
Rutland (Mass.) II–215a
Rutland (Vt.) II–368b; VI–101a
Rutledge, Edward (law.) II–308b
Rutledge, John (states.) VI–347a, 445a, 445a
Articles of War VII–143a
campaign of 1788 I–417a
Constitution II–193a, 196a, 203b
South Carolina Canal VI–349a
South Carolina constitution VI–390b
Rutledge, Wiley B. (jur.) I–300a; VI–446b
Ruysch, Johann (cartog.) IV–247a
Rwanda IV–236b
Ryan, Harris J. (eng.) II–416b
Ryan, John A. (cler.) I–469a
Ryan monoplane IV–156b
Ryder, Albert P. (art.) II–105a; V–189b, 192a,b
Rye I–37a, 486a,b; II–219a
whiskey VII–289b
Rye Patch (Nev.) III–215a
Ryerson, Martin A. (philan.) II–103b
Rye whiskey II–353b
RYSWICK, PEACE OF (1697) **VI–181b**; I–374a; II–92b; III–118a; IV–50a; V–85a, 369b; VI–2a
Ryujo (carrier) II–387b
Ryukyu Islands III–425a; V–147b

S

S–2D (airplane) I–56b
S–2E (airplane) I–56b
S2F (airplane) I–56b
S2F–3 (airplane) I–56b
S2F–3s (airplane) I–56b
Saab (auto) I–229b
Saar (Ger.) VI–285b; VII–173a
Saarinen, Eero (arch.) I–165b; III–136b, 137a; VI–194b
Saarinen, Eliel (arch.) I–165b
Sabacola (Ga.) III–170a
Sabal palm VI–393 (table)
Sabbath I–324b–25a; IV–408a
SABBATH-DAY HOUSES VI–182a
Sabbathday Lake (Maine) II–147a
Sabena Airlines II–347a
Sabin, Albert (virol.) V–341a
Sabin, Florence R. (anat.) IV–3a
Sabin, L. S. (nav. off.) V–21b
SABINE CROSSROADS, BATTLE AT (1864) **VI–182a**; V–331a
Sabine Pass, Battle of (1863) VII–39b
Sabine River I–10b
Fort Jesup III–501b
Gulf of Mexico IV–326b
Los Adaes IV–189a
neutral ground IV–197b; V–33b
Texas VII–36b
U.S. boundary IV–320b; VI–359b
Sabine War (1836–37) VII–239a
Sabin's Tavern (Providence, R.I.) III–153b
Sable III–402b
Sable, Jean Baptiste Point du (expl.) I–24b; II–17a
SABLE ISLAND VI–182a
SABOTAGE VI–182a; VI–374a
Civil War II–67a, 165a; VII–149a
Federal Bureau of Investigation II–503b
guerrilla warfare III–231a
navy ships II–368a
Office of Strategic Services V–138a
syndicalism VI–455b
Watergate VII–254a,b
Sabre (fighter plane) I–53b, 57b; IV–57a
Sabrejet (fighter plane) II–347b
Sac (Indians)
Half-Breed Tract III–242b
Treaty of Fort Harmar III–255a
See also Sauk
Sacagawea (Indian) III–33b; IV–136b
Sacasa, Juan Bautista (pol., off.) V–94b
Saccharin V–466a
Sacco, Nicola. *See* Sacco–Vanzetti Case
SACCO-VANZETTI CASE VI–182b; I–100b; V–75a; VII–117b–18a
Sacerdotal system IV–117a
SACHEM VI–183a; III–365b
Connecticut villages III–405a
Iroquois III–391a, 475b
Philip IV–47a
See also Tammany Hall
Sackets Harbor VI–282a
SACKETS HARBOR, OPERATIONS AT (1812–14) **VI–183b**; III–121a, 217b–18a; VI–209a
IV–406a
Sackville, Fort (Ind.) IV–53b
Sackville–Germain, George, 1st Viscount Sackville (off.) VI–123b, 127a
Vermont III–240b–41a
Sackville–West, Lord Lionel (dipl.). *See* Sackville–West Incident
SACKVILLE-WEST INCIDENT (1888) **VI–183b**; I–424b
SACLANT. *See* Supreme Allied Command Atlantic
Saco (Maine) IV–207b; VI–2b, 184a; VII–45a
SACO BAY, SETTLEMENT OF VI–184a
Saco River VI–149a
Sacramento (Calif.) II–347b; III–81b, 190b
Bear Flag Revolt I–280a
Central Pacific Railroad IV–94b
Lincoln Highway IV–156a
mail service V–177b
overland express I–398b
Pacific Railroad conventions VI–20b
Pioneer Stage Line V–317b
Pony Express V–357b; VII–101a
railroads VI–26b, 27a; VII–101a
Sage Plains VI–185b
Sutter's Fort VI–453a
SACRAMENTO, BATTLE OF (1847) **VI–184a**; II–363b
Sacramento Northern Railroad VI–37b
Sacramento River III–223b; VI–150a
improvements VI–146b
Indians III–357a, 362a
Mexican War VI–184a
salmon VI–201a
Sacramento Valley I–280a
borax I–340a
Lassen's Post and Ranch IV–110b
railroads VI–26b
Sacramento Valley Railroad VI–37a
Sacred College I–468a
Sacred Congregation de Propaganda Fide. *See* Congregation de Propaganda Fide
Sadat, Anwar (states.) I–150a
SADDLEBAG BANKS VI–184b
"Saddle Old Spike" (song) III–19a
Saddler (missile) IV–432a
SADDLES VI–184b; III–255b, 363a
Saddle shoes II–372b
Safe Drinking Water Act (1974) VII–259b
Safeguard (missile) I–58b; IV–363b
Safes II–79b
Safety I–7a–b
aviation II–498b–99a
Civil Aeronautics Board II–49b
Interstate Commerce Commission III–458a
Iriquois Theater fire III–476b
Nader's Raiders IV–448a
navigable waterways II–230b
occupational medicine IV–293a
police power II–440a
Red Cross VI–61b
Seamen's Act of 1915 VI–246b
state laws IV–80a
steamboat engines II–230b
working conditions IV–78b
Safety and Special Radio Services Bureau III–1a
Safety Congress. *See* National Safety Congress
Safety Council, National. *See* National Safety Council
SAFETY FIRST MOVEMENT VI–185a; VI–33b
Safety Fund Act (1829) VI–185a–b
SAFETY FUND SYSTEM VI–185a; I–255b
Safeway Stores II–282a
Safire, William (jour.) V–75a
SAGADAHOC (Maine) **VI–185b**; III–120b; VII–94b, 358b
Plymouth Company V–333b
Popham Colony V–359b
Sagamores IV–37a
See also Sachem

Sage, Henry W. (mer.) II–227b; IV–99b
Sage, Margaret Olivia (Mrs. Russell) VI–176b
Sage, Russell (fin.) III–79b
SAGE Air Defense system II–156a
Sagebrush VI–394 (table); VII–345b
Sagebrush State VI–394 (table)
SAGE PLAINS VI–185b
Sage School (Cornell) V–287b
SAG HARBOR (N.Y.) **VI–185b**; IV–185b
Saginaw (Mich.) IV–331a; VI–186a
Saginaw (ship) VI–186a
SAGINAW, FORT (Mich.) **VI–186a**
Saginaw Bay III–383b
Saginaw River VI–186a
Saginaw Road IV–331a
***SAGINAW'S* GIG, CRUISE OF THE** (1870) **VI–186a**
SAGINAW TREATY (1819) **VI–186b**; III–383b
Sagoyewatha. *See* Red Jacket
Saguaro cactus VI–393 (table); VII–65b
Saguaro National Monument V–217a
Saguenay River I–492b
Saigon (Viet.) I–62b; II–316b; VI–301a,b; VII–183a, 184a, 185a
Sailcloth IV–157b, 308b; VI–107b
Sailing Directions IV–277a
Sailing packets. *See* Packets, Sailing
Sailing ships II–90b–91a, 313b; VII–240a–b, 243a–b
Sailor hat II–372a
SAILOR'S CREEK, BATTLES AT (1865) **VI–186b**
SAILOR'S SNUG HARBOR VI–186b
Sails III–413a
Saint Albans (Vt.) III–11a
Saint Alban's Naval Hospital (N.Y.) V–28a
SAINT ALBANS RAID (1864) **VI–187a**; I–435a, 439a; V–84a, 121b
Saint Andrews Golf Club III–197b
Saint Andrew's Lodge (Boston) III–109a
Saint Ange, Louis (off.) I–501a
Saint Anthony (Minn.) IV–356a; VI–187a; VII–134a
  See also Minneapolis; Twin Cities
SAINT ANTHONY, FALLS OF VI–187a; III–272a
  waterpower III–45a; IV–347b
Saint Anthony, Fort (Minn.) III–313b; IV–355a,b
  See also Snelling, Fort
SAINT ANTOINE, FORT (Wis.) **VI–187a**
Saint Asaph Station (Ky.) IV–179a
Saint Augustin, Marie Tranchepain de VII–160b
SAINT AUGUSTINE (Fla.) **VI–187b**; I–24b, 96a, 496a; III–128b, 302b; V–66a, 243a, 254b, 370a; VI–348b, 349a
  architecture I–159a
  ayuntamiento I–239a
  Florida Rangers III–42b
  Fort Marion IV–253b
  Fort Matanzas IV–274a
  Key West settlers IV–45a
  logwood trade IV–181b
  missions III–41a
  patio gardens III–151b
  Ponce de León expedition V–356a
  privateers VI–129b
  Queen Anne's War I–143a, 238b; VI–2b
  railroad VI–34a
  revolutionary war VI–130a
  settlement III–38a,b
  Spanish colonization IV–302b
  War of Jenkins' Ear III–498a
  Yamasee War VII–352a
Saint Augustine's College II–113b
Saint Boniface College VI–188a
Saint-Castin, Jean-Vincent d'Abbadie de I–466a; VI–188a
SAINT-CASTIN'S TRADING HOUSE (Maine) **VI–188a**; IV–49b
Saint Catherine River III–77b
Saint Catherine's Creek IV–455b
Saint Charles (Md.) II–48b
Saint Charles (Mo.) IV–195b, 376b
SAINT CHARLES, FORT (Minn.) **VI–188a**; IV–355a
Saint Charles River VI–1b
Saint Christopher. *See* Saint Kitts
Saint Christopher Island I–361a; VII–162b
Saint Clair, Arthur (off.) I–385a; III–127a; VII–274b
  Battle of Hubbardton III–312a
  Battle of Princeton V–408a
  Cincinnati II–37b; IV–329b
  Division Act II–356a
  Fort Harmar treaties III–255a
  Fort Jefferson III–494a
  Marietta IV–250b
  Northwest Territory V–123a
  Ticonderoga IV–86b; VII–57a
  See also Saint Clair's Defeat
SAINT CLAIR, FORT (Ohio) **VI–188a**
Saint Clair, Lake II–391a; V–90b; VII–45b
Saint Clair County (Ill.) I–402b; III–21a; V–123a
Saint Clair River VI–34a–b
SAINT CLAIR'S DEFEAT (1791) **VI–188b**; II–484b; III–244a, 375a, 464b; VI–60b; VII–212b, 247a, 262b
Saint Clair Tunnel VII–128a
Saint Clement Danes (London) V–333a
Saint Clement's Island IV–260b
Saint Clement's Manor (Md.) II–246b
Saint Cloud (Minn.) IV–357a
Saint Cosmé, Jean François Buisson de (cler.) III–329a; VI–195a
SAINT CROIX (riv.) **VI–188b**; I–6a
  Duke of York's proprietary VII–359a
  Indian land cessions IV–355b, 356a
  logging VI–149a
  Northeast boundary V–118a
  portage II–380a
  Sioux–Chippewa War VI–295a
  U.S. boundary III–494a; V–33a
Saint Croix (V.I.) III–425b
  See also Virgin Islands of the United States
Saint Croix, Lake IV–31b
Saint Croix Falls VI–294b
Saint Croix Island National Monument V–217b
SAINT CROIX SETTLEMENT VI–189a; IV–225b
Saint Cyr, Hyacinthe (fur trader) VI–367a
Saint-Denis, Louis Juchereau de (expl.) *See* Juchereau's Tannery; Saint-Denis' Expedition
SAINT-DENIS' EXPEDITION (1714) **VI–189b**; III–119a; IV–456b; VII–95b
St. Denis, Ruth (dancer) II–287a,b
Sainte-Clair Deville, Henri (chem.) I–92a; II–422a–b
Sainte Foy (Can.) IV–405b
Sainte Genevieve (Mo.) I–447b; IV–195b, 376b; VI–189b–90a, 193b, 195a
SAINTE GENEVIEVE LEAD MINING DISTRICT VI–189b
Sainte-Laguë quota (pol.) V–435b
Saint Elizabeth's Church (Aachen, Ger.) I–1a
Saint Eustatius VII–93b
Saint Francis (Indians) III–400a
  See also Saint Francis, Rogers' Expedition Against
SAINT FRANCIS, ROGERS' EXPEDITION AGAINST (1759) **VI–190a**; III–116b; IV–86b; VI–162b
Saint Francis River I–3a; V–59a, 118a,b
Saint François County (Mo.) VI–190a
Saint François Xavier, Fort. *See* Green Bay
Saint Frédéric, Fort (N.Y.) II–267a
  Fort Ticonderoga VII–56b
  Franciscans III–94b
  French and Indian War IV–86a, 87b
  See also Crown Point
Saint-Gaudens, Augustus (sculp.) I–345b; IV–220b; VI–243b; VII–246b
Saint George, Fort (Maine) V–333b, 359b
Saint George Island VI–245a
Saint Georges (Maine) VII–219b
Saint George's Methodist Episcopal Church (Phila.) I–23a
SAINT GERMAIN-EN-LAYE, TREATY OF (1632) **VI–190b**; I–466a; II–92b
Saint Helena (is.) I–492a
Saint Ignace (Mich.) IV–217b, 218a
SAINT IGNACE MISSION VI–190b; IV–7a, 330b
Saint Ignatius (Mont.) III–500a
Saint James (La.) I–6b
Saint James (Mich.) VI–416b
Saint James Church (Goose Creek, S.C.) I–161b
Saint Jean, Fort. *See* Saint John, Fort
Saint John (N.B.) V–37b, 369b
  See also Virgin Islands of the United States
Saint John (V.I.) III–425b
Saint John, Bayou (La.) I–459b
SAINT JOHN, FORT (La.) **VI–191a**
Saint John, Henry. *See* Bolingbroke, 1st Viscount
Saint John, Issac (eng.) II–163b
Saint John, John P. (pol.) I–424a
Saint John, Vincent (labor leader) III–412b; IV–67b
Saint John River III–38a, 41a; VI–34a, 149b, 151a
  Northeast boundary V–118a,b
  War of Jenkins' Ear III–498a
  Webster–Ashburton Treaty VII–265a
Saint John's (Newf.) I–51a; II–344b; IV–405b
  French and Indian War III–117b

Saint Johns (Que.) IV–86b
See also Saint Johns, Siege of
SAINT JOHNS, SIEGE OF (1775) **VI–191a**; I–436a; IV–86b; VI–136b
Saint John's Berkeley (S.C.) III–315a
Saint John's Church (Richmond) VI–137b
Saint John's College II–395a
Saint John's University V–83b
Saint Jones County (Del.) II–322b
SAINT JOSEPH (Mo.) **VI–191b**; III–353b
freighting V–177a
gold in California III–81b
Oregon Trail VI–153b
Platte River Trail V–330b
Pony Express III–250b; V–357b; VII–101a
railroads VI–37b, 407a
stage lines I–485a; VI–176b
steamboat racing VI–408a
westward movement IV–20b
SAINT JOSEPH, FORT (Mich.) **VI–191b**; III–120a, 142b, 144b; IV–332b; VI–363b
Saint Joseph–Kankakee route I–498b
Saint Joseph Mission (Mich.) V–335b; VI–191b
Saint Joseph River IV–109b, 329a, 332b; V–335b; VII–262a
Saint Joseph's Hospital (Memphis) IV–46a
Saint Joseph's Island VI–144a
Saint Josephs River portage V–367b
Saint Kitts (B.W.I.) II–190a; VII–270b
Saint Lawrence, Gulf of IV–217a; V–214b; VII–285a
Saint Lawrence County (N.Y.) IV–219b
Saint Lawrence Island I–81a
SAINT LAWRENCE RIVER VI–192a; V–367a; VI–149a,b, 151a, 219b
Anglo–French rivalry I–70b
British claims V–214b
colonial wars IV–86a
earthquake II–385a
exploration I–96b, 492b; III–119a
French and Indian War III–115b, 116a, 117a; IV–405b; VI–1a–b
French posts III–120a
French settlements III–114b, 216a
fur trade III–140a, 141b, 403b; VII–104b
Gallatin's report III–147b
Great Lakes VII–157a
Indian agriculture III–366b
Indians I–48a, 492b
Jesuit missions III–499b
Laconia IV–82b
Lake Champlain link IV–85b
La Salle expedition V–145a
mapping VII–73a–b
Minnesota IV–355a
Mississippi River system II–20a
Neutrality Act of 1939 V–37b
New France V–52b
Northeast boundary V–118a,b
Ogdensburg V–139b
Queen Anne's War VI–2b
Radisson's *Voyages* VI–18b
revolutionary war I–193b, 384b; III–400b; VII–55a
Richelieu River VI–136b
transportation I–440a–b
Treaty of Utrecht VII–162b
U.S. boundary VI–165b
Vermont VII–171a,b
voyageurs VII–211b
War of 1812 I–502a; II–35a; III–118a, 120b, 217b; IV–406a; VI–248a
western sea VII–275b
Wisconsin VII–306b
SAINT LAWRENCE SEAWAY VI–192b; I–440b; VI–147a; VII–102a, 260b
Buffalo (N.Y.) I–375b
foreign trade VII–89b
Great Lakes III–216b
Great Lakes steamships III–218b
Illinois Waterway VI–148b
Lake Erie II–459a
Lake Huron III–319a
Lake Michigan IV–332b
Lake Ontario V–157a
Ohio V–142a
Oswego (N.Y.) V–176a
Sault Sainte Marie Canals VI–219b
shipping IV–312b
Saint Lawrence Seaway Authority VI–193a
Saint Lawrence Seaway Development Corporation II–501a; III–201b; VI–193a; VII–98b
Saint Lawrence Valley III–303a
Saint Leger, Barry (off.)
Battle of Oriskany V–172b
Burgoyne's invasion I–384b; V–175b
Burgoyne's surrender I–81b
Fort Stanwix VI–385b
Mohawk Valley IV–386b–87a
SAINT-LÔ (Fr.) **VI–193b**; I–178b; VII–339a–b
SAINT LOUIS (Mo.) **VI–193b**; III–50b, 120a, 220b; IV–436a; V–62b; VII–159a
American Fur Company III–143a
architecture I–160a, 379a
balloon launch I–248a
bargemen I–267b
barnstorming I–268b
Bloody Island I–322b; II–377a
bootlegging I–339b
bridges I–364a, 378a
Butler Ring VI–142b
candlemaking I–444b
capital market II–255b
caravans I–452a,b
cattle drives I–473a
chamber of commerce I–491a
chemical industry II–8b
Civil War I–433b; III–101a; V–314a, 402b; VI–38a
crime commission II–263b
Cumberland Road VI–153b
directory II–343b
Eads Bridge II–384a
Engineers Club II–448b
express service I–10a
Farmer–Labor party II–492b
Farmers' alliances convention V–365b
flour III–45a
Fort Saint Joseph VI–192a
French settlement III–114b
fur trade I–105b; III–144b, 403a,b; IV–380b, 422a; VI–367a; VII–103b, 104b, 273b
gambling III–149b
German immigrants III–81a, 336b; V–75b
Illinois County I–402a
Indian factory II–480a
Jefferson Barracks III–494a
Jesuit missions III–499b, 500a
kindergarten II–398b
Kossuth's visit IV–57b
Lakes-to-Gulf waterway IV–88a
lead industry VI–189b–90a
Lewis and Clark Expedition IV–136a,b; VII–271a
Long's explorations IV–186b
Louisiana Purchase Exposition IV–198a
Magee–Kearny expedition IV–224a
manufacturing IV–378a
Maxent, Laclede and Company IV–277b
meat–packing II–37b; IV–280a
Merchants Exchange II–141a
Mission of the Immaculate Conception IV–31b
Mississippi River IV–374b, 379b; VI–149a–b
Missouri Botanical Garden I–348a; IV–378a
Missouri constitutional convention IV–379a
Missouri Gazette V–70b
municipal housing IV–429a
Murphy wagons V–389b
National Electric Light Association II–419b
Observer IV–199a
overland freighting III–353b
Pacific Railroad Conventions VI–20b
pharmacy society V–275a
philosophy V–287b
Pike's upper Mississippi expedition V–312a,b
Platte River Trail V–330b
prostitution V–437b
railroad rate wars VI–23a
railroads IV–28b; VI–25b, 32b, 33b, 34b, 35a,b, 36a,b, 37a; VII–100b
revolutionary war I–367a; V–388a; VI–363b
riot of 1877 IV–63b
riots I–32a
river port VI–146a
Santa Fe trade VI–215a,b
settlement IV–376b
Sioux treaties VI–295b–96a
skyscrapers VI–299a
Smith explorations VI–318a
Southern Overland Mail VI–154a, 353b
stagelines VI–379a; VII–101a
steamboating IV–380a; VI–406b, 407a; VII–196b
steamboat racing VI–407b, 408a
stockyards VI–414a
subtreasury III–354b; VI–427a
subway VI–429b
tornadoes II–351a,b; VII–76a
trade VII–83b
trading post VII–95b
Upper Louisiana IV–195b
Vial's Road VII–178b
wagon trains VII–217a
War of 1812 II–255b; VII–307b
yellow fever II–454b
Saint Louis (gunboat) II–384a
SAINT LOUIS, BRITISH ATTACK ON (1780) **VI–195a**; I–367a
SAINT LOUIS, FORT (Ill.) **VI–195a**; III–120a, 329a; V–260b, 315a; VI–388a
SAINT LOUIS, FORT (Tex.) **VI–195a**; I–48b; III–119a; VII–36b
Saint Louis, Treaties of (1823) III–383b
Saint Louis, Treaty of (1816) III–383b
Saint Louis Academy of Science VI–236a
Saint Louis and San Francisco Railroad I–214b

Saint Louis Art Museum III–137b
St. Louis Blues (comp.) IV–440a
Saint Louis County (Mo.) III–494b; VI–194a,b
Saint Louis Globe–Democrat (news.) V–73a,b, 77b, 78b
Saint Louis Medical Journal IV–293b
SAINT LOUIS MISSOURI FUR COMPANY **VI–195b**; II–34a; III–143a, 144b, 403a; VII–103b
  Henrys Fork III–273a
  Missouri River fur trade IV–380b
  Oregon Trail V–168b
Saint Louis Municipal Theater VI–194b
Saint Louis Observer (news.) V–70b
Saint Louis Post–Dispatch (news.) I–464b; V–73a,b
Saint Louis River VI–443a
Saint Louis–San Francisco Railroad VI–36a
Saint Louis–Southwestern Railroad VI–36b
Saint Louis University III–501b
Saint Louis World's Fair. *See* Louisiana Purchase Exposition
Saint Louis Zoological Park VII–371a
Saint Lucia V–214b–15a
Saint Lucie County (Fla.) I–451b
Saint Lucie Inlet IV–302b
Saint Luke's Church (Isle of Wight County, Va.) I–161a
Saint Lusson, Sieur de, Simon François Daumont (expl.) IV–239b–40a; V–52b; VI–219a
Saint–Malo (Fr.) VI–128b
Saint Marks (Fla.) III–39a, 59a; VII–260b
SAINT MARKS, FORT (Fla.) **VI–196b**; I–154a, 335b; IV–253b
Saint Mark's Church–in–the–Bowery (N.Y.C.) VII–51a
St. Martin, Alexis (voyageur). *See* St. Martins Stomach
ST. MARTIN'S STOMACH **VI–196b**; IV–292a, 297b
Saint Martinville (La.) I–6b
SAINT MARYS (Md.) **VI–197a**; VI–340b
  settlement I–159a, 172b, 249b; IV–260b
SAINT MARYS, TREATY OF (1820) **VI–197a**
Saint Marys Falls Ship Canal III–473b; VI–425a
Saint Mary's Jesuit Mission V–178b
Saint Marys River III–170a, 319a; V–367b
  Florida boundary III–41b; VI–351a
  Fort Miami IV–329a
  Fort Tonyn III–42b
  Fort Wayne VII–262a
  Georgia boundary III–168a, 171b
  Lake Superior VI–443a
  Mackinac Island IV–217b
  Sault Sainte Marie VI–219b
  Sault Sainte Marie Canals VI–219a
  U.S. boundary III–41b
  western boundary VII–269b
Saint Mary's Seminary (Baltimore) I–467a
Saint Maxent, Gilbert Antoine de (col. adm.) VI–366a–b
Saint–Mémin, Charles Fevret de (paint.) V–187b–88a
Saint Mère Église (Fr.) II–237a
Saint Michael (Alaska) IV–52a
Saint Michael's Church (Charleston, S.C.) I–162a
SAINT–MIHIEL, OPERATIONS AT (1918) **VI–197a**; I–102a, 177a; IV–252b, 319b; VII–327a
Saint Nazaire (Fr.) VII–328b
St. Nicholas, An Illustrated Magazine for Young Folks IV–223a
"St. Nicholas League" IV–223a
Saint–Nicolas, Fort (Wis.) V–387b
Saint–Ours (Can.) VI–136b
Saint Patrick's Cathedral (N.Y.C.) I–163a
Saint Paul (Minn.) IV–356a; VII–133b–34a, 212a
  bootlegging I–339b
  Farmer–Labor party II–491a
  Forest Service III–76b
  fur trade VII–105a
  German immigration III–336b
  meat–packing IV–280b
  railroad surveys VI–39a
  Red River cart traffic VI–63b
  steamboat racing VI–408a
  stockyards VI–414a
  westward movement III–32a
  See also Twin Cities
Saint Paul and Pacific Railroad III–65a; IV–357a; VI–33a
Saint Paul Island VI–245a
Saint Paul's Chapel (N.Y.C.) I–162a
Saint Peters (Iowa) IV–223b
Saint Petersburg (Fla.) I–67b; III–42a
Saint Petersburg (Russ.) II–27a
Saint Peters River IV–187a, 223b, 224b, 277b
Saint Philip. *See* Missouri River
Saint Philip, Fort (La.) I–247a; III–258b; IV–374b–75a, 413b
Saint Philip, Fort, Surrender of. *See* Mississippi River, Opening of the
Saint Pierre, Fort (Miss.) VII–187a
Saint Pierre Island II–92b; V–214b
Saint–Quentin (Fr.) IV–320a
Saint Raphael Societies I–469a
Saint Roch (schooner) V–122a
Saints' days II–496a
Saint Simon Island III–100b, 498a; IV–274a; VI–204b
SAINT STEPHENS (Ala.) **VI–197b**; III–318b
  Gaines' Trace III–146b
  Spanish post VII–270a
  Three Notch Road VII–54b
Saint Thomas (V.I.) I–398b; II–484a; III–425b; V–264b
  See also Virgin Islands of the United States
Saint Valentine's Day massacre (1929) I–339b; II–258b
Saint Vincent Island (B.W.I.) V–214b
Saint Vincent's Hospital (N.Y.C.) III–307a
SAINT–VITH (Belg.) **VI–198a**; I–379b
Saint Vrain, Ceran (trader) II–477b; III–143b; VII–96a
  Bent's Fort I–289b
  Las Animas land grant IV–110a
  Missouri IV–27b
SAIPAN **VI–198a**; III–426a, 490a; IV–253a; V–21a, 285b; VII–62a, 125a, 139a, 337a
SAIS *See* School of Advanced International Studies
Sakata, S. (phys.) V–302b
Sakhalin Island III–85b; V–370b; VII–351b
Sakonnet River IV–451b
Salamander Works III–184a
Salamaua (N.Guin.) IV–83a
Salaries. *See* Wages and Salaries
SALARY GRAB **VI–198b**
Salas, Juan Pablo IV–45a
Salée River (Kor.). *See* Han River
SALEM (Mass.) **VI–199a**; II–99a; IV–265a; VII–94b, 95a
  demographic study II–328b
  distillery II–5a
  East Indies trade II–388a
  Essex Institute II–98b
  foreign trade IV–309b
  furniture III–135b
  Mariana IV–250a
  Peabody Museum IV–436a
  pewter work VI–291a
  pottery V–379a
  Puritans VI–262a
  settlement II–365a; V–51a
  shipbuilding III–413a
  slave trade VI–308b, 309a
  voting IV–269a
  whaling III–413a
  witchcraft III–280b; IV–265b; V–400a; VII–309b
Salem (N.J.) V–56b; VII–278b
Salem (N.C.) III–183b; IV–409b; VII–350a
Salem (Oreg.) VII–300a
Salem County (N.J.) VII–58a
Salem East India Marine Society VI–199b
Salem Maritime Historical Site VI–199b
"Salem sarcoid" IV–294a
SALERNO (It.) **VI–199b**; VII–338b
Salesman, traveling. *See* Traveling Salesmen
Salesmen, door–to–door II–444b
SALES TAXES **V–200a**; II–502a; VII–7b, 10b–11a,b
  Confederacy II–164b
  state revenue VI–105b
  Townsend Plan VII–80a
Salina (N.Y.) VI–202a
Salina (Okla.) II–34b
Saline River III–498b; VI–63a
Salineville (Ohio) I–376a; IV–410b
Salinger, J. D. (au.) IV–165a
Salisbury (Conn.) IV–144b
Salisbury (Mass.) I–89a
Salisbury (N.C.) II–159b; V–117a; VII–350a
Salisbury, J. H. (sci.) VII–169a
Salisbury, Lord, Robert Gascoyne–Cecil. *See* Gascoyne–Cecil, Robert
Salishan (lang.) I–441b; III–361b, 362b
Salk, Jonas (physic.) V–340b–41a
Salk vaccine I–242a
  See also Poliomyelitis
"Sally Good'–in" (song) III–19a
Salmon III–55a, 356a, 360b, 361a,b, 362b; IV–59a, 228b
Salmon, Daniel E. (vet.) I–241b; VII–177a
Salmon, Norvell (nav. off.) III–23b
Salmon, Thomas W. (psych.) IV–304a, 306b
Salmon Falls (N.H.) III–200a; IV–49b; V–53b; VI–201a
SALMON FALLS, ATTACK ON (1690) **VI–201a**
Salmon Falls Creek V–168b
SALMON FISHERIES **VI–201a**
  Alaska I–77a,b, 79a,b, 80a; IV–311a
  Columbia River VII–247b
  Indians I–81a, 441b; III–51b
  Lake Michigan IV–332b
  territorial waters VII–33a
  Yukon River VII–367a

Salmon Fisheries Commission, International Pacific VI–201b
Salmon River I–330a; III–328a; IV–83b
  Rogue River War VII–239b
  War of 1812 IV–406a
SALOONS VI–201b; VI–301a
  crime II–260a
  Honkey–donk girls III–297b
  Kansas IV–27a
  Nation, Carrie III–261b
  New York City IV–138a
  Prohibition V–429b
  speakeasies VI–368a
  whiskey towns VII–290b
  Woman's Christian Temperance Union VII–312a
Salsbury, Nate (showman) VII–298b
SALT VI–201b; II–4b, 5a,b, 6a,b; VI–48b
  Avery Island I–232a
  Big Bone Lick I–295b
  brine II–7b
  Burning Spring I–387a
  Cape Cod I–447a
  Civil War VI–196b
  colonial industry II–119b
  domestic trade VII–83b
  fishing bounties III–31b
  food preservation I–444b; II–219a, 373a; III–54b
  Great Salt Lake III–222a
  herbicides III–421a–b
  Kanawha Salt Works IV–25a
  Kansas IV–25a, 26b
  Louisiana IV–194b
  meat preservation III–51b, 52a; IV–280a
  Navigation Acts V–16a
  New England III–408a
  pack trains V–184a
  petroleum IV–333b; V–269a, 271a
  potash III–17a,b
  potassium iodide V–128a
  potassium salts V–376a
  price–fixing V–402a
  profiteering V–426a
  rainmaking VI–42a
  river deposits IV–44a
  roads III–447b
  Salt Springs Tract VI–204a
  stoneware glazing III–183a
  tariff VI–463a
  taxation VII–5a
  triangular trade VII–119b
Salter, William (cler.) III–469a
Salt Fork I–286a
Saltillo (Mex.) I–375a; II–363b
SALT I treaty (1972). *See* Strategic Arms Limitation Talks
SALT LAKE CITY (Utah) **V–203b**; II–45b; III–328b; V–177a,b
  assay office I–203b
  Ballet West II–289b
  Camp Douglas I–281a
  caravans I–452a,b; II–297b
  Deseret II–334a
  forty–niners III–82a
  irrigation III–477a
  Lincoln Highway IV–156a
  mail service V–177b, 178a
  Mormons IV–411b; V–39b; VI–456a
  Mountain Meadows massacre IV–421b
  pony express V–357b
  railroads VI–27b, 34a, 37b
  smelting VI–316b
  stage lines I–485a; VI–176b, 379a,b
  theater VII–48a
  wagon trains VII–217b
Salt Lake Desert I–330a; VII–161b
Salt Lake–Los Angeles road III–215a
Salt Lake Valley I–410a; IV–411b; VII–161b
Saltonstall, Dudley (nav. off.) V–253b; VI–128a
Saltonstall, Leverett (pol.) IV–268a
Saltonstall, Richard (col.) V–184b
Saltpeter II–4b, 5a,b; III–16b; V–97b–98a
  Confederacy II–67b
  East India trade II–388b
  gunpowder V–383a
  Mammoth Cave IV–233b
  See also Potassium Nitrate
Salt River I–410a; III–289a; IV–40a
  Pima V–314a
"SALT RIVER" (pol. term) **V–203b**
Salt River Reclamation Project VI–54a
Salts Cave (Ky.) I–157a
SALT SPRINGS TRACT V–204a
Salt Trust IV–25a
Salt Valley III–367a
Saltville (Va.) II–7b; IV–253b; VI–202a
SALT WAR (1877) **VI–204a**
Saltza, Chris von (athlete) V–154b
Saluda River II–382b
Salvage IV–45a; VII–113a
SALVATION ARMY VI–204a
Salvatorberg (Aachen, Ger.) I–1a
Salween River I–386b; III–46a
Salyer Land Company v. *Tulare Lake Basin Water Storage District* (1973) III–94a
Salzburg (Aus.)
  Lutherans IV–206a
SALZBURGERS IN GEORGIA VI–204b; V–342a
SAM (missile) IV–363b
Sam, Vilbrun Guillaume (off.) III–240a
Samaná Bay II–360b, 360b, 362a
Samar (Phil.) V–281b
Samba (dance) II–290b
Sambre River VI–338b
SAM HOUSTON, FORT (Tex.) **VI–204b**; VI–207b
Sam Neua (Laos) III–160a
SAMOA, AMERICAN V–205a; III–347a, 425a,b; V–22b; VII–32b, 34a
  annexation II–475b
  marine landings IV–252a,b
  migration to Hawaii III–264b
  missionary activity IV–364b
  National Governors' Conference III–206b
  tripartite government I–144a
Samoset (Indian) IV–396a; V–243b
SAMPLERS VI–205b
SAMPLING METHODS AND PROCEDURES VI–205b
Sampson, William T. (nav. off.) VI–206b–07a, 361a–b, 362a, 363a
  Merrimac sinking IV–314b
  Santiago V–20a, 165b; VI–214a, 216b–17a
SAMPSON–SCHLEY CONTROVERSY VI–206b; VI–217a
SAM SLICK (lit. char.) **VI–207a**
Samuels, Samuel ("Bully") VII–349a
Samuelson, Paul A. (econ.) V–99b
Sananandа (N.Guin.) VII–336b
San Andreas fault II–385a
SAN ANTONIO (Tex.) **VI–207a**; VI–144a; VII–36b
  Alamo VI–84a
  architecture I–160a
  Camp Travis I–434b
  capture by Mexico IV–337b
  caravans I–452a, 453a
  Chisholm Trail II–31a
  Civil War VI–144a
  Fort Sam Houston VI–204b
  French claims I–48b
  Gutiérrez–Magee expedition III–236a
  Long expedition IV–184a
  Los Adaes garrison IV–189a
  Mexican raid (1862) I–169b
  newspapers V–79b
  Nolan expeditions V–101a
  railroads VI–35a
  Rough Riders VI–165b; VII–40b
  sanitariums VI–101a
  Santa Fe expeditions VII–36a
  Spanish government I–239a
  Spanish mission II–389a
  stagelines VI–379a
  Texas Rangers VII–42a
  Texas Revolution I–74a; II–157a; III–198b; IV–274a; VII–37b
San Antonio de Valero Mission VI–204b, 207b
SAN ANTONIO MISSIONS VI–207b; I–159b; VI–207a, 210a
San Antonio Ranch (Tex.) II–48b
Sanatoriums
  tuberculosis VII–126b, 127a
San Augustine (Fla.) IV–253b
San Benito County (Calif.) II–385a; V–211a
San Bernardino Mountains I–403b
San Bernardino Strait IV–138b
San Blas (Mex.) IV–136b
Sanborn, Franklin Benjamin (jour., ref.) V–415b; VI–67b
Sanborn, John B. (off.) III–378a
Sanborn, John D. VI–207b
SANBORN CONTRACTS VI–207b
Sanborn Map Company I–463a
San Carlos Apache (Indians) I–141b
San Carlos de Austria, Fort (Fla.) V–254a
San Carlos Reservation (Ariz.) I–142a,b
San Cayetán del Tumacácori (Ariz.) IV–367b; VII–125b
Sánchez, José (miss.) III–94a
Sanchez–Merry protocol (1901) V–94b
San Clemente (Calif.) V–98b
San Cosmé (Mex.) I–494b
San Cosmé Gate (Mex. City) IV–252a, 329a
Sand
  glass II–5a; III–182b
  towboating VII–77b
Sandals II–334b
Sandalwood I–201b; II–28b; III–263a; V–158a
Sandbar Duel (1827) I–355a
Sandburg, Carl (poet) II–18a; IV–164a
SAND CREEK MASSACRE (1864) **VI–208a**; I–219a
Sanders, Fort (Tenn.) IV–54a
Sanders, George Nicholas (fin., rev.) VII–362a
Sanders, Wilbur Fisk (pol.) V–333a
Sanderson (brigantine) VII–119a–b
Sanderson, Deacon Elijah III–135b
Sanderson, Robert (silversmith) VI–289b
Sandersville (Ga.) VI–278a
Sand hillers II–253a
Sandia (N.Mex.) IV–367b; V–460a
Sandia culture III–50b; V–59b

SAN DIEGO (Calif.)
VI–208a; I–405a; VII–367a
Kearny expedition IV–323b
Mexican boundary IV–321a
Mexican War IV–34b, 324b; VI–214b, 353b, 414a
Mormon Battalion IV–411a
Mount Palomar Observatory III–242b
naval training V–24a
ranchos del rey VI–45b
resorts and spas VI–101a,b
Scripps Institution of Oceanography VI–242a
stagelines VI–379a
U.S. boundary III–230a
wagon trains VII–217b
western routes V–224b
winemaking VII–305b
San Diego (cruiser) VII–242b
San Diego Bay I–401b
San Diego County (Calif.) II–348b; III–503b
San Diego Marine Biological Institution. *See* Scripps Institution of Oceanography
San Diego Zoo VI–208b
Sandiford, Ralph (abolitionist) I–135a
Sandino, Augusto César (pol., off.) V–94b
Sand Island IV–337a
San Domingo. *See* Santo Domingo
Sandoski, Fort. *See* Sandusky
Sand painting III–369a, 374a; V–9a
Sand Pebbles III–234b
Sands, James (nav. off.) III–29a
Sandstone I–377a,b
SANDUSKY (Ohio)
VI–208b; II–459a; III–115a
Civil War I–433a
Moravian Indians III–188a
revolutionary war VI–378a
Scioto Trail VI–239b
trading house III–142b
Upper Sandusky VII–157b
Sandusky Bay I–280a; IV–4b
"Sandusky Plains" VII–157b
Sandusky River I–359a; VI–208b, 412a; VII–157b
Sandwich (Mass.) I–447a; III–182b, 185a
Sandwich Islands. *See* Hawaii
SANDY CREEK, BATTLE OF (1814) **VI–209a**
Sandy Hill Pass V–224b
Sandy Hook (N.J.) I–194a; IV–152a, 397b; V–84a; VII–349a
Sandy Lake (Minn.) IV–355b; VI–294b
Sandys, Edwin (col. adm.) III–472a; VII–66a, 200b, 201a
Sandys–Southhampton group II–117a
Sandzen, Sven Berger (art.) IV–26b
SANE. *See* National Committee for a Sane Nuclear Policy
San Elizario (Tex.) VI–204a
San Felipe (N.Mex.) I–8a; III–367b; V–460a
San Felipe (ship) VI–209a
San Felipe, Fort (S.C.) V–370a
***SAN FELIPE–CORREO* AFFAIR** (1835) **VI–209a**
San Felipe de Albuquerque (N.Mex.) I–83b
San Fernando, Fort (Tenn.) IV–302a; VI–366b
San Fernando Valley (Calif.) II–385b
San Fernando Veteran's Administration Hospital II–347b–48a
Sanford, Edward T. (jur.) I–12a; VI–446b
Sanford, Henry S. (dipl.) II–43a
SAN FRANCISCO (Calif.)
VI–209a; III–190a; IV–404b; VI–427b; VII–159a
air service II–28a
anti–Chinese riot II–29a; VI–8a
architecture I–164b
assay office I–204a
Barbary Coast II–260a
Battle Fleet cruise I–276b
Bay Area Rapid Transit III–203a
bridges I–364b
Buddhism V–171b
cable cars VI–418a,b
Chinese labor II–29b
Chinese population II–30a
Civil War VI–181a
clipper ships III–45b
Comstock Lode II–157a
crime II–259b
directory II–343b
dry docks II–375b
Embarcadero II–48b–49a
federal mint IV–360a, 360b
federal records center III–284b
ferries III–11b
fires IV–354a
Flaco's Ride III–34a
flour milling III–44a
Forest Service III–76b
gold I–336a; VI–150a
Golden Gate Bridge III–189a
Indian Historical Press V–76a
Indian population III–397b
industrial army II–252b
intercoastal trade IV–311b
Japanese Trade and Cultural Center II–49a
Jeannette polar expedition V–336a
King, James, murder V–73b
Klondike gold shipment IV–52a
labor strike (1934) IV–71b
Lincoln Highway IV–156a
mail service V–178a
marine insurance III–428a
mechanics' institutes IV–281b
Mexican War IV–324b
Midwinter International Exposition IV–337b
Mooney case VII–117b
music IV–441a
National Trust for Historic Preservation IV–472a
navy yard V–28a, 29b
New Thought movement V–81a
Oregon voyage VI–363a
Pacific cable I–401a
Panama–Pacific Exposition V–203b
political corruption I–343a, 406b
port authority V–368a
Preparedness Day parade IV–406a
prices V–404b, 405b
railroads VI–37b; VII–40a, 147b
Ralston's ring VI–44a
ranchos del rey VI–45b
rapid transit III–451b; IV–428b
Ruef Ring IV–214a; VI–142b
settlement I–141a
smelting VI–292b
Sons of Revolutionary Sires VI–339a
Southern Overland Mail VI–154a, 353b
stagelines VI–379a; VII–101a
steamship lines II–91a; IV–310a
stock exchange II–469b
street lighting II–413b
subtreasury VI–427a
subway VI–429b
sugar industry VI–437a
tennis VII–29a
theater VII–50b
trolleys IV–428a
Union Labor party IV–81a
United Nations VII–151a, 351b
United Native Americans VII–152a
urban renewal VI–86b
Vietnam War demonstration V–237a
vigilantes VII–187a
Wells, Fargo VII–267a
whaling VII–285b
Workingmen's Party of California IV–64a
yellow peril VII–356b
San Francisco Ballet II–289b
San Francisco Bay II–369a; III–189b; VI–209a,b
Anza expedition VII–125b
exploration VII–299b
Mexican War IV–324a
Miwok IV–381b
salt VI–202b–03a
San Francisco Bay Area Rapid Transit System (BART) II–428b
San Francisco Bay Guardian (news.) V–79a
San Francisco Bulletin (news.) V–73b
San Francisco Californian (news.) III–81b
San Francisco Chronicle (news.) V–72a, 180b
San Francisco de Asís Mission I–141a; VI–209a
San Francisco de la Espada VI–210a
San Francisco de los Neches. *See* San Francisco de los Tejas
SAN FRANCISCO DE LOS TEJAS VI–210a
SAN FRANCISCO EARTHQUAKE (1906)
VI–210a; I–226a; II–347a, 385a; V–23a, 280b
San Francisco Examiner (news.) V–71b, 72a, 76b; VII–356a
San Francisco group (poets) IV–165b
San Francisco–Oakland Bay Bridge VI–209b
San Francisco Vigilance Committee V–73b; VII–187a
San Gabriel (Calif.) I–141a
SAN GABRIEL, BATTLE OF (1847) **VI–210a**
San Gabriel de Guevavi (Ariz.) IV–367b
San Gabriel Mission (Calif.) II–43a; III–94a
San Gabriel Mountains I–403b
San Gabriel River VI–210b
Sangamon County (Ill.) II–363a
Sanger, Margaret Higgins (ref.) I–307a
Sanger, W. W. (physic.) V–437b
San Geronimo de Taos (N.Mex.) I–159b
SANGRE DE CHRISTO GRANT VI–210b
Sangre de Cristo Mountains IV–110a, 278a; V–312a; VI–210b, 461a
Sangre de Cristo Pass III–88a; V–224b
Sangro River III–235b
Sanguinet, Charles (fur trader) IV–159b; VI–367a
San Ildefonso (N.Mex.) III–367b; V–459b
SAN ILDEFONSO, TREATY OF (1800) **VI–210b**; IV–193b, 196a; V–173a; VI–150b, 359a, 363b
Mississippi River IV–372b
New Orleans V–62a
Oklahoma V–148a
SANITARY COMMISSION, UNITED STATES
VI–211a; V–280a, 447a
Civil War I–277a; II–63b,

66b
Protective War Claims Association V–438b
Sanitary Corps, Army IV–290b
Sanitary ware III–183b, 184b
SANITATION, ENVIRONMENTAL VI–211b; III–325b; V–446b–47a,b
auto emissions V–270b
Canal Zone V–201b, 202a
cholera II–33b
consumer protection II–208b
Girl Scouts III–181a,b
public utilities V–456b
research IV–285b
Savannah VI–220b
state regulation III–458b
territorial waters VII–33a
urban health VII–157b
water supply VII–258a
Waterways Treaty VII–261a
Sanitation Worker's Union IV–45b
San Jacinto (sloop) VI–313b; VII–115b
SAN JACINTO, BATTLE OF (1836) **VI–213a**; I–74b; VI–84a, 207a; VII–38a, 41b
Horse Marines III–304a
San Jacinto River VI–213b
San Joaquin River III–223b, 357a, 362a; VI–150a
San Joaquin Valley I–407a; II–336a; III–114b; IV–104b
Tehachapi Pass V–225a
Walker expedition VII–220a
San Jose (Calif.) I–280b; V–131b; VI–83b
San José (C.R.) V–171a
San José del Tumacácori I–172a
San Jose Indiano (ship) VII–352a
San José Mission National Historical Site VI–207b
San Jose scale III–421a
San José y San Miguel de Aquayo I–159b
San Juan (Colo.) III–191b–92a
San Juan (N.Mex.) V–459b, 460b
San Juan (Nic.) III–278a
San Juan (P.R.) II–503b
fortifications I–159b
Spanish–American War VI–362a, 363a
San Juan (Tex.) III–119a; V–155a
San Juan, Fort. *See* Saint John, Fort
San Juan Archipelago III–256a
San Juan Bautista (Mex.) II–385a; IV–252a
SAN JUAN COUNTRY VI–213b
San Juan de Pinos (Fla.) IV–253b
SAN JUAN HILL AND EL CANEY, BATTLES OF (1898) **VI–213b**; VI–362a
Rough Riders VI–165b
San Juan Island I–439a; VII–248b
SAN JUAN ISLAND, SEIZURE OF (1859) **VI–214a**
San Juan Island National Park VI–214a
San Juan Mountains V–225a; VI–143a, 213b; VII–272a
San Juan Province (Arg.) II–133a
San Juan River I–373b; II–72b, 461a; III–367b
Anasazi culture VII–161a
Navaho V–8b
Spanish Trail VII–256a
San Juan River (Nic.) V–94b
Sankikan. *See* Trenton (N.J.)
San Lorenzo, Treaty of. *See* Pinckney's Treaty
San Luis (Colo.) VI–210b
San Luis Potosí (Mex.) III–152a; IV–325a; V–155a
San Luis Valley IV–268b; VI–210b
gold V–437a
San Marco, Fort. *See* Marion, Fort
San Marcos, Fort (S.C.) V–370a
San Marino III–453a
San Marino (Calif.) II–109a–b; III–285a
San Mateo (Fla.) III–38a
San Miguel (N.Mex.) III–50b
San Miguel de Gualdape (S.C.) I–238b; VI–347a
San Miguel Island I–155a
San Pablo (seaplane tender) V–133b
SAN PASQUAL, BATTLE OF (1846) **VI–214a**; IV–34b
San Patricio Artillery Battalion II–335a
San Patricio Trail VI–144a
San Pedro (Calif.) VI–242a
San Pedro, Los Angeles and Salt Lake Railroad VI–27b, 37b
San Pedro River VII–70b
Sanpoil (Indians) III–363a
San Saba River V–263a
San Salvador Island I–96a
See also Watlings Island
Sans Arcs (Indians) II–283a
San Simeon (Calif.) IV–96b
Sanson, Nicolas (expl.) V–156b; VII–73b
Santa Ana (N.Mex.) I–8a; III–367b
Santa Ana River III–477b
Santa Anna, Antonio López de (off.) IV–323b; VI–144a; VII–37b–38a, 41a–b
Alamo I–74a; VI–207a
Battle of Buena Vista I–375a; IV–324a
Battle of Cerro Gordo I–488b
Battle of Churubusco II–36b
Battle of Contreras II–214b
Battle of San Jacinto VI–213a
Gadsden Purchase III–145b
Mexico City IV–329a
Santa Barbara (Calif.) I–288b, 350a; IV–34b; VI–101a
Santa Bárbara (Mex.) VI–162a
Santa Barbara Hot Springs (Calif.) VI–100b
Santa Barbara Islands I–401b, 446a
Santa Catalina, *See* Catalina, Santa (Calif.)
Santa Clara (N.Mex.) III–367b; V–459b
Santa Clara River VI–368a
Santa Cruz, Alonso de (cartog.) IV–247b
Santa Cruz Islands, Battle of (1942) VII–68a
Santa Cruz River VII–125b
Santa Elena. *See* Port Royal (S.C.)
SANTA FE (N.Mex.) **VI–214b**; I–170a; II–461a; III–213b, 221a; V–59b, 241a; VI–460b; VII–367a
architecture I–159b, 160a
Arkansas River I–174a,b
Cajon Pass I–403b
Canadian River I–442a
Civil War III–187b; V–144a; VII–165b
exploration III–119b; IV–249a
Fonda's expedition III–50b
Fort Mann IV–240a
Fowler expedition III–88a
Genizaro Indians III–162b
Gila Trail III–179b
horse III–303a
Indian Country III–379a
Indian villages I–329b
Kearny expedition IV–323b
Kearny's march to California IV–34a
Louisiana purchase boundary IV–197b
mail service V–177b
Mallet brothers exploration IV–230a
Mexican War II–363b, 440b; VI–214b; VII–39a
Missouri trade IV–377a
Oñate's explorations V–155a
Pike's expedition V–311b–12a
prairie schooner V–389b
Shaw's expedition VI–271b
Smith explorations VI–318a
Spanish settlements IV–25b
Spanish Trail I–409b; VI–368a; VII–256a
stagelines VI–379a
Texas cession II–150b
Texas expedition VII–38b
Texas trade VII–36a
trade I–282a,b, 293a; V–173a
Utah VII–161a
Vargas expedition V–461a
Villasur expedition VII–188a
wagon trains VII–217b
western routes V–224b
Santa Fe Railroad I–83b; II–358b; VI–27a, 208b
Kansas IV–26a
See also Atchison, Topeka and Santa Fe Railroad
Santa Fe–Southern Pacific Railroad VII–101a
Santa Fe–Texan Expeditions. *See* Texan–Santa Fe Expeditions
SANTA FE TRAIL VI–215a; II–477b; IV–25b; V–59b; VI–154a, 214b; VII–84a
Arkansas River I–174b
Bent's Fort I–290a
caravan traffic I–452b, 453a
Cherokee Trail II–14b
Chihuahua Trail II–23b
Civil War III–187b
Council Grove II–242b
Dodge City II–358b
Fort Atkinson I–213b
Fort Leavenworth IV–129a
Fort Smith VI–316a
Independence (Mo.) III–353b
Kansas City (Mo.) IV–27b
Kearny expedition IV–323b
mapping VII–74b
Oregon Trail V–169a
pack trains V–184a
Pawnee Rock V–230b
Raton Pass VI–47b
Taos Trail VI–461a
trade I–282a,b
water holes VII–256a
Westport VII–280b
Santa Gertrudis cattle I–471b; VI–45a
Santa Helena (Ga.) III–170a
SANTA MARIA (ship) **VI–216a**
Santa Maria, Juan de (miss.) VI–162a
Santa Marta (Colom.) VII–270b
Sant' Ambrogio (It.) III–235b
Santa Mesa (Phil.) V–282b
Sant'Ana (N.Mex.) V–460a
Santana, Pedro (states.) II–360b
Santander (Sp.) VII–349a
Santa Rosa (ship) I–350a
Santa Rosa complex III–300b
Santa Rosa Island I–155a; V–308a
SANTA ROSA ISLAND, BATTLE ON (1861) **VI–216a**; V–254b

Santa Rosa Peninsula (Fla.) II–187b
Santayana, George (poet, philos.) III–260a; IV–164a; V–288b
SANTEE CANAL VI–216a; I–442a
Santee Dakota (Indians) II–283a
Santee River III–315a; VI–149b, 349a
canal VI–216a
Santee Sioux (Indians) IV–356b; VI–295a, 296a
Sante Fe Railroad VII–289a, 294a
Santiago (Chile)
inter–American conference V–171a, 205a
SANTIAGO, BLOCKADE AND BATTLE OF (1898) **VI–216b**; II–450a; III–154a; IV–252b; V–20a; VI–213b, 361b–62a, 363a; VII–328a
Merrimac sinking IV–314b
Oregon V–165b
Sampson–Schley controversy VI–206b
SANTIAGO DE CHILE INTER–AMERICAN CONGRESS (1923) **VI–217a**
Santo Cleaner Company II–421a
Santo Domingo I–73b; III–121b; IV–196b; V–174b
Cromwell's western design VII–270b
Indian slaves III–401a
pirates IV–416a
refugees I–497a
Spanish intervention IV–400b; VI–360a
sugarcane I–486b
U.S. intervention III–70a
U.S. relief V–280b
See also Dominican Republic; Hispaniola
Santo Domingo (N.Mex.) III–367b; V–460a
SANTO DOMINGO, SECRET MISSION TO (1844) **VI–217a**
Santos (religious effigies) III–47a
Santos–Dumont, Alberto (aeron.) I–232b
San Xavier del Bac (Ariz.) I–160a, 172a; III–500b; IV–367b; VII–125b
Sao Paulo (Braz.) I–360b
Sapir, Edward (anthrop.) I–129a
Sapiro, Aaron (law.) II–221b
Sapolio (cleaner) I–17b
Sappa Creek (Kans.) II–379b
Sarajevo (Yug.) VII–324b
Saranac Lake (N.Y.) VII–126b
Saranac River IV–87a; V–330b, 331a
Saratoga (carrier) I–54b; II–387b; V–22a
Saratoga (Jefferson's proposed state) III–497a
Saratoga (ship) V–331a
SARATOGA, SURRENDER AT (1777) **VI–217a**; I–81b, 194b, 385a–b, 436a; III–95a, 276a; IV–86b; VI–123b; VII–358b, 361a,b
Convention of Saratoga II–214b
French alliance VI–116b, 119b
peace proposal V–231b
Saratoga Association for the Improvement of the Breed of Horses VI–218a
Saratoga County (N.Y.) VII–22a
SARATOGA SPRINGS (N.Y.) **VI–217b**; III–150a; IV–350a; VI–100b
Sarazen, Gene (golfer) III–198a
Sardinia
Declaration of Paris V–214a
Sargasso Sea III–233b
Sargent, John Singer (paint.) II–103b; V–191b
Sargent, Winthrop (gov.) II–252a; VII–189a
Northwest Territory V–123a
Sargo (submarine) VI–423a
Saric (Mex.) V–314b
Sarnia (Ont.) VII–128a
Sarnoff, David (exec.) VII–21b
Sarpy, Fort (Mont.) II–34a
Sarpy, Gregoire (fur trader) IV–159b, 380a
Sarpy, John B. (fur trader) IV–1b
Sarpy, Peter A. (fur trader) I–399a
Saskatchewan (Can.) I–206a, 441a; III–50a
Saskatchewan River I–441a; V–121a; VI–192b; VII–275b
Saskatchewan Valley IV–355b
Sasqua Swamp (Conn.) V–261a
Sassacus (Indian) V–261b
Sassamon, John IV–47a
Satank (Indian) VI–287b
Satanstoe V–316b
Satanta (Indian) III–386b; VI–287b
Satellite communications. *See* Communications Satellites
Satellites IV–458b
agriculture I–39b, 46b
air defense I–58b
astronomical observations I–212a
Earth Technology Resource Satellite III–167b
Explorer 1 I–72a
Explorer I II–426a
International Geophysical Year III–454a
mapmaking I–464a
oceanographic survey V–134a
photography I–463a
Project Mercury I–209b
reconnaissance I–180a; V–125a
Sputnik I–179b; II–426a; IV–363b
traveling–wave tube VII–164a
U.S. military IV–364b
weather forecasts VII–264a,b
Satellites, spy VI–416b, 417a
Satolli, Francesco (archbp.) I–144a
Satori V–171b
Satsung Range III–46a
Saturday Evening Post (mag.) IV–222b
Saturday Press (news.) V–30b
Saturn launch vehicles I–210b; IV–406b, 459b
Saucier, Jean Baptiste (eng.) I–501a
Saudi Arabia I–149b, 149b–50b; VII–151b
Sauerkraut II–445b; III–54b
Saugerties (N.Y.) VII–282b
Saugus (Mass.) IV–265a
Saugus Creek VI–218a
SAUGUS FURNACE VI–218a
Saugus River III–472a; VI–291b
Sauk (Indians) III–88b, 366b
Black Hawk War I–242b, 311b; III–329b
Fort Armstrong I–180b
Fort de Chartres Treaty I–501b
Iowa III–468a
Jesuit missions III–499b
neutral ground V–33b
Oklahoma lands V–148b, 149b
removal III–394b
revolutionary war VI–195a
Sauk Prairie VI–218b
Sioux treaties VI–296a
Treaty at Prairie du Chien V–388b
Treaty of Fort Armstrong III–383b
Treaty of Prairie du Chien III–383b
Treaty of Sauk and Fox Agency III–383b
wild rice VII–298b
See also Fox
Sauk and Fox Agency, Treaty of (1842) III–383b
Sauk County (Wis.) VI–218b
SAUK PRAIRIE VI–218b
Sauk Rapids VI–63b
Saul and the Witch of Endor (paint.) V–188b
Saulteaux (Indians) II–31a; III–367a
Saulters VI–219b
Sault Sainte Marie (Mich.) II–31a, 380a; III–216a, 452a; VI–443b
exploration VII–73b
Indian land cession VI–197a
railroad VI–36b
SAULT SAINTE MARIE, GREAT PAGEANT AT (1671) **VI–219a**
SAULT SAINTE MARIE CANALS VI–219a; I–440b; III–452a; VI–146b, 192b, 193a
iron ore III–473b
Lake Superior VI–443b
SAULT SAINTE MARIE MISSION AND TRADING POST VI–219b; III–142b, 209a; IV–6b, 330b; VI–443a
Saunders, Alvin (gov.) V–31b
Saunders, Clarence (bus.) VI–258a
Saunders, Fort (Kans.) I–342a
Saur, Christopher (print.) III–173b
Sausage III–51b; IV–281a
Saussure, Nicholas–Théodore de (chem.) III–16a
Savage, Edward (paint.) V–188a
Savage, James D. (off.) VII–361b
Savage, Thomas (off.) V–185a
Savage Mine (Nev.) VI–453a
SAVAGE'S STATION, BATTLE AT (1862) **VI–220a**; III–100a; V–245b
SAVANNAH (Ga.) **VI–220a**; I–498a–b
Afro–Americans I–23a, 25b, 29a; IV–339b
city plan II 45a
Civil War I–458b; IV–209a; V–19b; VI–221a, 278a
cotton market II–238a
Freemasons III–109a
furniture III–135b
Girl Scouts III–181b
golf III–197b
Gwinnett–McIntosh III–236a
orphanage I–293a
porcelain V–379b
port authority V–368a
Pulaski, Fort V–462b
railroads VI–25b, 33a
revolutionary war III–42b, 168b, 170a,b, 401a; IV–44b; VI–124b, 221a, 351a
rice VI–135b
roads VII–99b
settlement III–168a
Southern Commercial Convention VI–352a
sugar industry VI–437a
tinware VII–63a
Tondee Tavern VII–71b
War of 1812 V–238b; VII–235a, 253a
SAVANNAH (steamship) **VI–221a**; IV–310a; VI–280a
SAVANNAH, SIEGE OF (1779) **VI–221a**; VI–220b
SAVANNAH, SIEGE OF (1864) **VI–221a**; VI–220b, 278a; VII–27a

Savannah River III–315a; VI–220a,b
Atlantic Intracoastal Waterway VI–148b
Augusta I–223a
Civil War VI–278a
exploration I–96b
Georgia III–168a
Hamburg VI–349b
Port Royal V–370a
Pulaski, Fort V–462b
revolutionary war III–170a
Salzburgers VI–204b
settlement I–238b, 239a
Shawnee VI–270b
Savanna portage II–380a
Save-the-Redwoods League II–188a
Savings I–252a,b, 264a
commercial banks I–258a
consumer purchasing power II–210a
inflation III–414b
insurance I–253b
panic of 1929 V–209a,b
thrift stamps VII–55b
SAVINGS AND LOAN ASSOCIATIONS VI–221b; I–257b, 258a, 264a, 376b–77a
cooperative II–220b
deposits III–8b
mutual II–220b
Savings and Loan Insurance Corporation. *See* Federal Savings and Loan Insurance Corporation
Savings banks. *See* Banks, Savings
SAVINGS BONDS VI–222a; VII–8b, 108a
inflation II–236b
World War II V–406a
Savings stamps VI–222b
Savo Island, Battle of (1942) III–229b; V–25b
Saw gin II–240b
Sawmill Brook (Mass.) IV–47b
SAWMILLS VI–222b; IV–204a–b; VII–60a
convict labor II–217a
Piscataqua River VI–149a
Washington State VII–247b
waterpower VII–256b, 257a
Saxony
Hussites IV–409b
Saxton, Joseph (inv.) II–413a
Say, Jean Baptiste (econ.) VII–139b–40a
Say, Thomas (entom.) II–29a; IV–187a; VI–90a
SAYBROOK (Conn.) **VI–223a**; III–152a; VI–151b; VII–359b
Lords and Gentlemen IV–188a
New Haven Colony V–55b
Pequot War V–261a,b
settlement II–179b–80a
Yale College VII–351a
Saybrook Fort (Conn.) V–261a
SAYBROOK PLATFORM (1708) **VI–223b**; I–412a
Saye and Sele, Lord. *See* Fiennes, William
Sayler's Creek (Va.) I–146b
Saylor, David O. (mfr.) I–477b
Sayres, Edward (abolitionist) V–239a
Sazerzc Saloon (New Orleans) VI–201b
SB2C Curtiss Helldiver (scout bomber) I–55a
SB2U Vought Vindicator (scout bomber) I–55a
SBC (scout bomber) I–55a
SBD (scout bomber) VII–343b
SBD Douglas Dauntless (scout bomber) I–55a
Sbeïtla (Tun.) IV–32b
Sbiba (Tun.) IV–32b
SBU (scout bomber) I–55a
SC–1 (dirigible) II–343b
SCAB VI–223b
coal mining II–86a
Scajaquada Creek VII–220b
SCALAWAG VI–223b; II–64b, 403b; IV–58a; VI–57b
Scali, John (dipl.) II–343a
SCALPING VI–224a; III–363b; IV–199a
Scammon, Charles M. (nat.) IV–232b
Scandals. *See* Corruption, Political; Political Scandals
Scandinavia
explorations II–461b
Ford's peace mission III–60a–b
geophysical exploration III–166a
gold standard I–301b
log construction IV–179b
marine science V–134b
Reformation VI–80a
Scandinavians I–38b; II–75a; III–337a
Iowa III–468b
Minneapolis VII–134a
Minnesota IV–356b, 357b
newspapers V–75b
North Dakota V–117b
skiing VI–297b
Wisconsin VII–307b
Scarboro (Maine) VI–184a
Scarff ring I–57b
Scarlet carnation VI–395 (table)
Scarlet fever II–280a, 454b; IV–150b, 275a; V–447b
Scarlet Letter IV–162a
Scarlet Ribbon Club (Chicago) VII–29a
Scarp (missile) IV–432a
Scarsdale (N.Y.) III–313a
Scaticook (N.Y.) IV–47b
Schaefer, W. A., Pen Company V–403b
Schaff, Philip (hist.) II–465a; III–282a; VI–78a, 82a, 455a
Schattschneider, Elmer E. (pol. sci.) V–222a
Schaudinn, Fritz R. (zool.) VII–169a
Schawlow, Arthur (phys.) IV–262b
Schechner, Richard (dir.) VII–51a
Schechter, Solomon (Hebraist) IV–11a
Schechter Poultry Corporation V–47a
SCHECHTER POULTRY CORPORATION* v. *UNITED STATES (1935) **VI–225a**; II–136b, 323a, 481b; IV–72a, 469b; VII–123b
Schéhérazade (ballet) II–288b
Scheiber, Peter (inv.) V–290b
Schelde estuary I–140b
Scheldt River VII–366b
Schenck, Charles T. (Socialist) VI–225a
Schenck, Robert C. (law., pol.) I–381b; VII–248b
SCHENCK* v. *UNITED STATES (1919) **VI–225a**; I–478b; III–104a; V–353b
SCHENECTADY (N.Y.) **VI–225b**; II–383b
French expedition against IV–86a
General Electric Research Laboratory III–155b, 409a; IV–89a
King William's War IV–49b; VI–323a
Leisler Rebellion V–84b
locomotive building IV–175b
railroads IV–386b; V–87a; VI–24b
See also Albany
Schereschewsky, J. W. (physic.) IV–294a
Schermerhorn, John F. (offi.) V–49b
Schermerhorn family IV–101a
Schetterly, H. R. I–91a–b
Scheuer, Sandra (student) IV–39a
Schieffelen, Ed (prospector) II–477b; VII–70b
Schiff, Jacob H. (banker) III–79b
Schildkraut, Rudolph (theat. mgr.) VII–49b
Schiller, Karl (econ., offi.) VI–472b
Schimmel, Wilhelm (art.) III–47a
Schimmelpenninck (banking house) III–291a
Schimper, A. F. W. (bot.) II–391b
Schine, G. David (sol.) IV–210a,b
Schipporeit, George (arch.) I–165b
Schizophrenia IV–306b
Schlesinger, Arthur, Jr. (hist.) III–283a, 486b
Schlesinger, Arthur, Sr. (hist.) III–486b
Schlesinger, Arthur M. (hist.) III–283a
Schlesinger, Frank (astron.) I–211b
Schlesinger, James R. (offi.)
Atomic Energy Commission I–217a
Schlesinger and Meyer I–164a
Schleswig (Ger.) VII–173a
Schley, John Thomas (col.) III–100b
Schley, Winfield Scott (nav. off.) III–224a; VI–206b–07a, 216b–17a, 361b, 363a
Schlink, F(rederick) J(ohn) V–466b
SCHLOSSER, FORT, ATTACK ON (1813) **VI–226a**
Schmeling, Max (pugilist) V–422b–23a
Schmidt (Ger.) III–314b
Schmidt, Harry (off.) III–485a; IV–257b
Schmidt, Karl P. (nat.) VI–91b
Schmidt camera III–242b
Schmidt telescope I–212a
Schmitz, John G. (pol.) I–432a
Schmucker, Samuel S. (theol.) II–465a; IV–206a
Schnee Eifel Ridge (Belg.) VI–198a
Schneider's Hollow (N.Y.) I–471a
Schoenberg, Arnold (comp.) IV–439b
SCHOENBRUNN VI–226a
Schoenbrunn Village State Memorial VI–226a
Schoenheimer, Rudolf (biochem.) I–303b
Schoepf, Johann David (nat.) III–27a; VI–90a
Schofield, Arthur III–63a
Schofield, John M. (off.) II–68b; III–264a
Army of the Ohio V–142b
Battle of Franklin III–98a
Hood's Tennessee campaign III–298a; VI–377a
Schofield Barracks (Haw.) III–264a
Schoharie (N.Y.) V–195a
Schoharie Creek aqueduct I–443b
Schoharie River VII–282b
Schoharie Valley V–323a
Scholarships
football III–57a
higher education II–115b
Rhodes scholarships VI–134b
United Daughters of the Confederacy VII–150b
Scholastic (mag.) IV–223a
Scholey v. *Rew* (1874) VII–6b
Schomburgk, Robert Hermann (geog.). *See* Schomburgk Line

SCHOMBURGK LINE
VI–226b; VII–170a,b
Schönbein, C. F. (chem.) II–7a
Schoodiac River VI–189a
School, country IV–169a
SCHOOL, DISTRICT VI–226b
School and Society V–387a
School boards II–394a
SCHOOLBOOKS, EARLY VI–227a; VI–229b
hornbook III–301b
magazines IV–222b
McGuffey's Readers IV–213a
New England Primer V–51b
Peter Parley V–264b
Webster's speller IV–213a; VII–266a
Worcester's Readers IV–213a
Schoolcraft, Henry Rowe (anthrop.) I–128a; II–31b; III–468a
School districts II–405a; IV–171a, 172a; V–350a
elections II–411a
financing II–402b
political patronage V–228a
School enrollment II–402a
School food programs I–43b; II–501b, 502b; III–53a; V–129a
School for Artillerists and Engineers IV–340b
School for Flight Surgeons IV–292b
Schoolhouse, little red IV–169a
SCHOOL LANDS VI–227b
School Lunch Act, National (1946) V–129a
School of Advanced International Studies (Washington, D.C.) IV–3b
School of Aerospace Medicine IV–292b
School of Application for Infantry and Cavalry I–190b
School of the Arts (N.C.) V–116b
Schools
Bible II–398a
Catholic I–468a–b; II–362b
child labor laws II–24b, 25a
Dame School II–285b
dental programs II–331b
desegregation I–408a; II–54b–55b, 57a–58a, 400a
disasters II–348a,b
encyclopedias II–444b, 445a
government inspection III–422a
Indian I–455a
prayer and chapel attendance IV–408a
public health V–447a
religion II–398a
safety regulations II–348b
secondary I–5b, 47a
segregation II–457a
town schools II–285b
Works Progress Administration VII–323b
Schools, military VI–343a
Schools, old field. *See* Old Field Schools
Schools, parochial IV–194a; VI–228b, 229a
SCHOOLS, PRIVATE VI–228b; II–397a, 400a; VI–226b
colonial South II–395a
education of women VI–229b
Oregon Parochial School Case V–167a
Virginia VII–196a
Schools, public I–5b; II–393b, 396a–97a, 398a; V–380b
academic high school II–398b–99a
book publishing I–334b
Catholics I–111a
education of handicapped III–248a,b, 249a
health IV–275b
Indian education III–380a
integration I–72a, 250b; II–401b–02a, 404a
Kalamazoo Case IV–24b
land grants IV–93a–b, 96a
local government IV–171b, 172a
lottery financing III–149b
lyceum movement IV–207a
Minnesota IV–358a
neighborhood control IV–173a
parochial schools I–468b
rural areas I–39b
South I–28b
Supreme Court decisions II–400a
teachers' unions IV–76a
Virginia VII–195a,b, 196a
See also Education
School System, Army I–190b–91a
SCHOOLTEACHERS, EARLY VI–229a
SCHOONER VI–229b; VI–280b; VII–99b
Baltimore clipper I–251a; II–77a
clipper fishing schooner IV–217a
coasting trade II–90b
Great Lakes III–218a
racing VII–348b
shipping IV–311a
slave ships VI–308b
War of 1812 III–217b
warships VII–240a
Schottische (dance) II–290b
Schouler, James (hist.) III–282a; IV–163a
Schouten, William (navig.) I–448a
Schrank, John N. I–202b
Schrieffer, J. Robert (phys.) V–100a, 305b
Schrödinger, Erwin (phys.) V–304a
Schroeder (comic character) V–72b
Schroeder, Ted (athlete) VII–30b
Schroeder, Theodore (au.) I–479a
Schroeder, William (student) IV–39a
Schuchert, C. (prof.) V–197a
Schultz, George P. (offi.) VI–472b
Schultz, Jackson (chem.) IV–128b
Schultz, Sigrid (jour.) V–74a
Schulz, Charles (cartoon.) V–72b
Schumacher, Ferdinand (mfr.) I–486b–87a, 488a
Schurman, Jacob Gould (educ.) II–227b
Schurz, Carl (pol.) I–131b; II–187b; III–81a–b
forestry III–73a
Liberal Republican party IV–141a
Nast cartoons IV–454b
robber barons VI–157a
Westliche Post V–75b
Schurz, Margarethe (Mrs. Carl) II–398b
Schuster, M. Lincoln (pub.) I–334b
Schuykill River III–173b
Schuyler, Fort (N.Y.) III–157a
Schuyler, Peter (col. offi.) II–383b; V–84b; VI–2b
Schuyler, Philip (off., states.) V–86b
Burgoyne's invasion of New York I–81b, 385a
invasion of Canada I–435b
military code VII–142b
Saint Johns attack VI–191a
trenches VII–115a
Washington's eight months army VII–251b
Schuyler, Philip J. (off., states.) VI–385b
Loyalists VII–117a
Schuyler, Robert L. (ed.) II–341a
Schuyler family I–4a; IV–256b
Schuylerville (N.Y.) VI–217b
Schuylkill Canal I–127b, 443a; VII–127b
Schuylkill River
bridges I–363b, 378a
canals I–127b; VII–145b
Fort Christina V–246a
Fort Mifflin IV–337b
New Sweden Colony V–80b
revolutionary war VII–164b, 165a
toll bridge VII–69b
waterpower IV–347b
water supply VII–258b
Schuylkill Water Works I–274b
Schwab, Charles M. (ind.) III–79b–80a
Schwammenauel Dam III–314a
Schwartz, Maurice (theat. mgr.) VII–49b
Schwarzschild, Martin (astron.) I–212a
Schwegmann Brothers v. *Calvert Distillers Corporation* (1951) II–483a
Schweinfurt (Ger.) I–60a
Schwenkfeld, Kasper (rel. ref.) VI–230a
SCHWENKFELDERS VI–230a; V–342a
Schwimmer, Rosika (femin.) III–60a
Schwinger, Julian S. (phys.) V–100a, 296a
Science (period.) I–98b; VI–236b, 238a
applied genetics III–158b
astronomical observatories V–130b
Constitution II–200a, 224b
genetics III–157a
high–energy physics V–296b
industrial research III–408a
nuclear physics V–297b
nutrition and vitamins V–127b
oceanography V–134a
paleontology V–195a
parapsychology V–212b
petrography V–267b
phrenology V–293b
physics V–294a
physiology V–306a
psychology V–441a
solid–state physics V–303a
theosophy VII–51b
women VII–317b
Science, history of I–14a
SCIENCE, POPULARIZATION OF VI–230a; I–97a–98a; VI–238a
Science and Health With a Key to the Scriptures VI–79a
Science and Technology, Office of II–498a
Science fiction I–209b; IV–165a
Science Information Exchange, Inc. VI–319b
Science Museum (London) I–233a
Sciences. *See* individual entries, e.g., Biochemistry; Medicine and Surgery; Physics
Science Service VI–230b
Science—The Endless Frontier (report) IV–470b
SCIENTIFIC AMERICAN (mag.) **VI–231a**; V–289b; VI–236a–b
Scientific American Publishing Company VI–231b
Scientific American Supplement VI–231b
SCIENTIFIC EDUCATION VI–231b; II–399a
Cooper Union II–222a
exchange students II–471a
Field Museum of Natural History III–19b
Franklin Institute III–99a

Franklin's Academy V–249a
Fulbright grants III–131a
Johns Hopkins University IV–2a
Lawrence Radiation Laboratory IV–119a
Lawrence Scientific School IV–119b
Marine Biological Laboratory IV–250b
mechanics' institutes IV–281a
mining engineering III–166b
National Science Foundation IV–470b, 471a
nuclear physics V–303a
physics V–294b, 295a, 295b
Princeton University V–409a
psychology V–441b–42a,b
Scheffield Scientific School VI–273b
scientific societies VI–237b–38a
Scripps Institution of Oceanography VI–242b
solid–state physics V–304a–b
state universities VII–156a,b
veterinary medicine VII–176a–77a
See also Engineering Education; Medical Education
SCIENTIFIC INFORMATION RETRIEVAL VI–232b; VI–236b, 319a,b
SCIENTIFIC MANAGEMENT VI–233b; I–205b; IV–255a, 273a
forestry III–72b
Scientific Monthly (mag.) I–98b
SCIENTIFIC PERIODICALS VI–235a
American Journal of Nursing V–126b
American Journal of Pharmacy V–275a
American Journal of Psychology V–442a
American Journal of Science and Arts IV–348b–49a
American Mineralogical Journal IV–349a
American Mineralogist IV–349a
American Phrenological Journal V–294a
Antarctic Journal of the United States V–338b
Arctic V–338b
Copeia VI–91b
Economic Geology III–163b
Herpetologica VI–91b
information retrieval VI–232b
Johns Hopkins University Press IV–2b, 3a
Journal of Experimental Psychology V–442b
Journal of Herpetology VI–91b
Journal of Parapsychology V–213a
Journal of the Franklin Institute III–99a
marine life III–29b
Minerals Yearbook IV–350b
Physical Review V–295a, 303a
Polar Record V–338b
Psychological Review V–442a
Science VI–238a
Science Service VI–230b
Scientific American V–289b; VI–231a
veterinary medicine VII–176a
Scientific research. *See* Research, scientific
Scientific Research and Development, Office of V–137a
SCIENTIFIC SOCIETIES VI–237a
Academy of Arts and Sciences I–97a
American Association for the Advancement of Science I–98a
American Philosophical Society I–110a
American Physical Society V–295a
American Physiological Society V–307a,b
American Psychological Associaton V–442a
American Society for Psychical Research V–213a,b
American Society of Ichthyologists VI–91b
collections IV–436a
Herpetologists' League VI–91b
mechanics' institutes IV–281a
medicine IV–288b
mineralogy IV–348b, 349a
National Academy of Sciences IV–457a
National Institute for the Promotion of Science IV–464b
periodicals VI–235a
pharmacy V–275a,b
Society for Psychical Research V–213a
Society for the Study of Amphibians and Reptiles VI–91b
veterinary medicine VII–176a,b
zoological societies VII–371b
See also Learned Societies
Scientific Unions, International Council of III–454a
SCIOTO COMPANY VI–238b; VII–273b
French grants III–120b
Gallipolis III–148a
land scpeculation IV–99a
Ohio Company of Associates V–143b
Scioto County (Ohio) III–120a, 148a
SCIOTO GAZETTE (news.) **VI–239a**
Scioto River I–359a; II–356a
exploration III–182a
Great Warriors Path III–387b; VII–238b
land speculation VI–239a
Military Reserve VII–273a
Northwest Territory V–123a
Refugee Tract VI–70b
salt VI–202a
Scioto Trail VI–239b
Shawnee VI–270b
Vandalia Colony VII–166b
Virginia military reserve VII–202a
Westsylvania VII–281a
Zane's grants VII–368a
SCIOTO TRAIL VI–239b
Miami Trail IV–330a
Scioto Valley II–25b; V–140a, 145b; VI–239b
Sciotoville (Ohio) I–364b
Scissor–tailed flycatcher VI–395 (table)
SCLC. *See* Southern Christian Leadership Conference
Scofield (Utah) II–350a
Scofield, Cyrus I. (theol.) VI–79a, 82b
Scofield Reference Bible VI–79a, 82b
Sconchin (Indian) IV–385a
Scopes, John Thomas (educ.). *See* Scopes Trial
SCOPES TRIAL (1925) **VI–239b**; III–112b; VI–230b; VII–118b
SCORE (satellite) II–143a
Scorpion (fighter plane) I–53b, 54a
Scorpion (submarine) II–350a
Scotch Convenanters V–370a
SCOTCH–IRISH VI–240a
antebellum South VI–341a
East Jersey V–57a
immigration to U.S. II–125b; III–334b–35a
Irish Tract III–469b
Maine VII–219b
New Hampshire V–53b
North Carolina V–115b
Pennsylvania I–455a; IV–89b, 338a; V–246b, 251b
pioneers V–316b
potatoes V–376b
Presbyterianism V–391a,b
redemptioners VI–62b
religion VI–76b
Shenandoah Valley V–378a; VI–275b
South Carolina VI–347a–b
Virginia VII–192b
West Virginia VII–281a
westward movement VII–283a
Yadkin River VII–350a
Scotch Presbyterians II–388b, 393b
Scotland
colonial trade II–453b
consumer cooperatives II–220a
education II–393b
education of the deaf III–248a
electric railways VI–40a
golf III–197a,b
immigration to America IV–60a
indentured servants III–353a
investments in U.S. III–65a–b
medical education IV–297b
Navigation Acts V–16a
Reformation VI–80a
union with England II–122a
U.S. ranching V–160b
World War I V–119b
Scotland, Church of V–391a; VII–279a
Scotland Yard IV–188b
Scots
antebellum South VI–341a
fur trade III–141b, 142b
immigrants II–125b
Minnesota IV–356b
South Carolina I–281b
Scott, Charles (eng.) II–416b
Scott, Charles (off.) II–317a; VII–212b
Scott, Fort (Ga.) III–88b; VI–260a
SCOTT, FORT (Kans.) **VI–241a**; IV–25b
Scott, Howard (eng.) VI–269a; VII–17b
Scott, Hugh L. (off.) VI–163b
Scott, Léon (inv.) V–289a–b
Scott, Riley (inv.) I–51a
Scott, Robert F. (expl.) I–116a
Scott, Thomas A. (bus.) V–247b
Scott, Walter IV–267a
Scott, Winfield (off.) V–151b; VI–241a
Aroostook War I–195a
Battle at Lundy's Lane IV–205a
Battle of Queenston Heights VI–3a
campaign of 1852 I–420b
Cherokee removal III–394b; VII–96b
"King's Mill" IV–391b
Mexican War I–375a, 488b, 494b; II–36b, 214b, 323b–24a; IV–252a, 322a, 324a, 325a
Mexico City IV–329a; V–19b
military commissions VII–225a
Niagara campaigns V–90b–91a
Pillow quarrel VI–241a
Protective War Claims Association V–438b
recapture of York

SCOTT, WINFIELD (cont.) VII–359a
Seminole War VI–260b
Treaty of Guadalupe Hidalgo III–230a
War of 1812 I–184a
Battle of Chippewa II–31b
Fort Erie II–458a
War of 1812 VII–234b
Scott Act (1888) II–29a
Scott Field (Ill.) II–344a
Scottish Highlanders V–115b
Scottish Rite Freemasons III–109a
SCOTT-PILLOW QUARREL VI–241a
Scott Polar Research Institute V–338b
Scottsbluff (Nebr.) V–357b
Scotts Bluff National Monument V–217b
Scottsbluff projectile point III–484b
SCOTTSBORO CASE VI–241b; VII–118a
Scottsdale (Pa.) III–32b
Scourge (ship) IV–322a
Scout aircraft I–55a–b
SCOUTING ON THE PLAINS VI–241b; IV–422b; V–230b
Scout wheat VII–286b
Scovill Manufacturing Company V–291a–b; VII–105b
Scranton (Pa.) IV–81b
Scrap drives II–50a
Scraper (tool) II–334b; III–50a, 140a, 484b
Scrap metal II–438b
Screen projection (phot.) IV–417a, 418a
Screw making III–441a,b
Screw threads III–99a
Scribner's (mag.) IV–222a
Scribner's Monthly (mag.) VII–319a
Scrip. *See* Land Scrip
Scripps, Edward W. (pub.) V–76a; VI–230b, 242a; VII–152a
Scripps, Ellen VI–242a
Scripps, George H. (pub.) V–76a
Scripps, James E. (pub.) V–76a
Scripps–Howard Publications V–76a
SCRIPPS INSTITUTION OF OCEANOGRAPHY VI–242a; V–135a
Scripps–McRae League of Newspapers V–76a
Scrooby (Eng.) V–312b; VI–262a
Scrub breeders I–267a
Scrub cattle II–280a
Scruggs, Earl (mus.) IV–441b
Scudder, Horace E. (ed.) IV–223a
Scudder, Vida Dutton (educ.) VI–330b
Scudder's American Museum (N.Y.C.) I–268b
Scull, John (pub.) V–70a, 322b
Scull, Robert C. (art collector) II–106a
Scully, William I–4a, 87b
SCULPTURE VI–242b
architecture I–165b–66a
copyright II–224b
folk art III–47b
Hoffman's races of man III–19b
landscape architecture IV–96b
Statue of Liberty VI–405b
Sculpture Society, National VI–243b
SCURVY VI–244a; I–303b, 405a; II–124b; III–81b; IV–150a, 295b
Scythe I–34b
SDC Curtiss Seagull (scout aircraft) I–55b
SDS. *See* Students for a Democratic Society
Sea Adventure (ship) VI–338a
Sea–Air–Land approaches VII–139a–b
Seabat (helicopter) I–56b
Seaboard Air Line Railroad VI–32a, 36b
Seaboard Coast Line Railroad VI–32a, 36b
Seaborg, Glenn (chem.) V–100a
Seaborg, Glenn T. (chem.) I–217a; II–12b; IV–119b; V–300b
Seabury, Samuel (bp.) II–455a; VI–112b
Seabury investigations V–83b; VI–460a
SEAC (computer) II–156a
SEA FENCIBLES VI–244b
Seafood I–301a; III–53b, 55a
Seagram Building (N.Y.C.) I–165b; VI–299a
Sea grant program V–135a
Sea gull (bird) VI–395 (table)
Seagull (scout aircraft) I–55b
Sea Gull (steamer) VII–240b
Sea Island cotton II–240a
Sea King (helicopter) I–56b
Sea King (ship) VI–274b
Seal (animal) IV–233a
Seale, Bobby G. I–315b, 316a; II–20b–21a
SEALERS, TOWN VI–245a; II–208b
Sea Level (N.C.) VI–187a
SEALING VI–245a; I–201b
Alaska I–76a, 77a, 81a
Aleutian Islands I–84a,b, 85a
arctic waters V–336b
Canada I–439a
China trade I–201b, 446a,b; II–28b
Coast Guard II–89b
Eskimo III–358a
Eskimos II–462a
Fajardo Case II–484a
Great Britain VI–282a
Indians I–441b; III–392b
mare clausum IV–249b–50a
Northwest Coast culture III–361a
Pribilof Islands V–401a
Sable Island VI–182a
Santa Catalina I–466b
territorial waters VII–33a
treaty (1892) VII–112b
See also Fur seal
SEAL OF THE CONFEDERATE STATES OF AMERICA VI–246a
SEAL OF THE UNITED STATES VI–246a; II–455b, 463a
eagle II–384b
presidential flag III–34a
SEALs. *See* Sea–Air–Land approaches
Seamen, impressment of. *See* Impressment of Seamen
SEAMEN'S ACT OF 1915 VI–246b; IV–68b
Sea of Tranquility (moon) IV–407a
SEA OTTER TRADE VI–247a; I–201b
Aleutian Islands I–84a,b
China I–446b; II–28b
Santa Catalina I–466b
Washington State VII–247a
Sea Pines Plantation (S.C.) III–197a
Seaplanes I–51a, 233a, 234a
SEA POWER VI–247b
British II–313b
Mahan doctrine II–314a
military policy IV–343b
Union navy VII–146b
See also Navy, United States
Search, right of. *See* Search and Seizure, naval; Search and Seizure, Unreasonable; Visit and Search
Search and seizure, naval I–121b, 127a
Civil War II–65b
I'm Alone Case III–332a
SEARCH AND SEIZURE, UNREASONABLE VI–248b
constitutional prohibition I–94a, 299a
due process clause IV–14b
Fourth Amendment II–204a, 204a
U.S. vessels IV–219b
writs of assistance VII–344b
See also Arrest
Search warrants. *See* Writs of Assistance
Searle, G. D., Company V–274a
Searles Lake I–340b
potash III–17a; V–376a
Sears, Barnas (educ.) V–231b
Sears, F. R., Jr. VII–29a
Sears, Isaac III–189b
Sears, Mrs. J. Montgomery II–103a
Sears, Paul B. (ecol.) I–350a
Sears, Richard D. (athlete) VII–29a
Sears, Roebuck and Company I–17b, 489b; II–444a; III–136b; IV–225a; V–403a
Searsport (Maine) IV–225b, 226b
Sears Tower (Chicago) VI–299a
Seas, freedom of the. *See* Freedom of the Seas
Seashores, national V–220a
Cape Cod I–447b
Seasonal employment
clothing industry II–83a
coal mining II–86a
Sea Sparrow (missile) IV–363b
SEATO. *See* Southeast Asia Treaty Organization
Seaton, William W. (pub.) I–3a; IV–465b
"Sea train" VI–281a
Seattle (Wash.) VII–248a
assay office I–203b
federal records center III–284b
flour milling III–44a
Indian relocation VI–83b
railroads VI–33a, 37b
recall VI–51a
tennis VII–29a
trolleys IV–428a
Seattle General Strike (1919) IV–69b; VII–248a
SEATTLE WORLD'S FAIR (1962) **VI–249a**
Seaver, James E. (au) VII–293b
Seaver Hall (Harvard) III–260b
Seawater II–423a
Sea wave, seismic II–385b
Seaweed III–16a
Sea Witch (ship) I–448a
Sebastian, Benjamin (law.) VI–366a
Sebasticook River III–243b
SEC. *See* Securities and Exchange Commission
SECEDED STATES, CONGRESSIONAL REPRESENTATION OF VI–249b; VI–56b
SECESSION, ORDINANCE OF (1860–61) **VI–249b**; VI–250b–51a, 440b
nullification VI–56b
South Carolina VI–347b–48a
Texas VII–42a
SECESSION, RIGHT OF VI–249b; VI–121b
Jefferson's proposed states III–496b
New England V–49b
Pacific republic movement V–180b
Virginia and Kentucky Resolutions VII–198a
SECESSION OF SOUTHERN STATES VI–250b; II–61a–b, 64b; III–9a; VI–249b, 307b, 397a
Ab-Initio movement I–2a
Alabama I–71b
Bluffton movement I–326a
border states I–341b
Charleston (S.C.) I–497a
compromise movement of

1860 II–149b
Compromise of 1850 II–150a,b
Constitutional Union party II–191b
cotton II–241a
Cotton Kingdom II–241a
DeBow's *Review* II–298b
federal deficit VII–5a
Fire-eaters III–25a
Georgia III–168b
Homestead Law III–296b
Kentucky neutrality IV–43a
League of United Southerners IV–125b
Louisiana IV–194a
Mississippi IV–368b
Nashville Convention IV–453a, 454a
North Carolina V–116a
Radical Republicans VI–11a
Republican party VI–92b
right of rebellion VI–50b
South Carolina VI–341b
southern rights movement VI–354a
Tarpley Letter VII–1a
Tennessee VII–25b
Texas VII–39b
Union Rights party VII–148a
Union sentiment VII–148b
Virginia VII–281b
West Virginia VII–287b–88a
Whig party VII–288b
Secessionville, Battle at (1862) I–497a
Second Army IV–320a
Secondary enrichment (geol.) III–163a
Secondat, Charles de. *See* Montesquieu, Baron de La Brède et de
Second Awakening *See* Awakening, Second
Second Bank of the United States. *See* Bank of the United States
Second Bull Run Campaign. *See* Bull Run, Second Battle of
Second Central American Conference (1922–23) V–107b, 107b
Second Colony of Virginia. *See* Plymouth, Virginia Company of
Second Coming of Christ I–15a–b
Second (II) Corps *See* entries under Army, United States
Second Cumberland Presbyterian Church V–392b
Second Fleet V–25a
"Second Industrial Revolution" II–425a–b
Second Infantry Division. *See* entries under Army, United States
Second International Polar Year (1932–33) III–454a
Second Marine Division IV–252b; VI–198a–b; VII–62a
Second Republic (Fr.) III–96b–97a
Second Town-House (Boston) I–161b
Sécretan, M. (fin.) II–223b
Secretariat (horse) III–305a
Secret ballot I–249a; II–410a; IV–269a
"Secret Committee." *See* Commercial Committee
Secret Doctrine V–172a
SECRET PROTOCOL OF 1917 VI–251b
Secret Service (play) VII–49a
SECRET SERVICE, UNITED STATES VI–252a; I–196a; VII–108a, 238a
SECRET SOCIETIES VI–252b
Afro-American suffrage VI–431b
American party I–109b
American Protective Association I–111a
antirent I–134a
Black Legion I–314a
Blue Lodges I–325b
Civil War IV–5a
Confederacy II–164b
Freemasons III–108b
Granger movement III–210a
Hunters and Chasers of the Eastern Frontier III–318a
John Birch IV–2a
Knights of Labor I–314b; IV–52a, 64a
Knights of the Golden Circle IV–52b; V–180b
Knights of the White Camelia IV–53a
Ku Klux Klan IV–57b
labor movement IV–64a
Mafia IV–221a
Masons I–132a–b
Midewiwin IV–335b
Molly Maguires IV–391b
National Farmers' Alliance and Industrial Union II–493b
North Carolina V–116a
Order of American Knights V–161b
Patrons of Husbandry V–228b
Phi Beta Kappa V–276b
Red Legs VI–62b
Sons of Liberty (Civil War) VI–339a
Sons of the South VI–339b
southern Unionists VII–149a
SECTIONALISM VI–253a
antebellum South VI–342a–b
Brooks-Sumner affair I–371a
campaign of 1824 I–418a–b
Compromise of 1850 II–149b
Constitutional Union party II–191b
Democratic party II–327a
Dred Scott case II–370b
Era of Good Feeling II–458a
fall line II–485a
free trade III–113a
Georgia III–168b
Hartford Convention III–259a
historiography III–282b
homestead movement III–296b
Jay-Gardoqui negotiations IV–373b
Mississippi Valley IV–376a
New England V–49b
Piedmont and Tidewater V–310a
Republican party VI–92b
slavery I–10b; IV–453b; VI–307b, 458b
Southern Commercial Conventions VI–352b
tariff VI–466a
transcontinental railroad VI–39a
Virginia VII–194b–95a
Webster-Hayne debate VII–265b
West VII–268a
Whig party VII–288b
Secular City VI–83a
Securities
blue sky laws IV–26b
Civil War II–66a
employee purchases V–426b
exchanges II–255b
Federal Securities Act V–45a
holding companies III–289b
investment banks III–465b
investment companies III–467a
New Era speculation V–52b
open-market operations V–159a–b
panic of 1929 V–405b
Progressive movement V–428b
Publicity Acts V–448a
regulation II–500b
revenue VII–4b
taxation VII–5b, 11a
Securities Act (1933) I–326a; II–470a, 500b; III–7a, 466a, 467a
Securities and Exchange Commission II–500b; III–467a; V–45a; VII–222b
bankruptcies I–262b
investment banking III–466b
Securities Exchange Act (1934) I–326a; II–470a; III–7a, 459a, 466a, 467a; V–448a
Security, national. *See* National security
Security Council (UN) VII–151b
Security Dealers, National Association of III–467a
Sedalia (Mo.) I–473a
Sedan (Fr.) IV–319b; VII–327a
SEDGWICK, FORT (Colo.) **VI–254b**; I–357b; IV–45a
Sedgwick, John (off.) I–493a,b; IV–350a; VI–376a
Sedgwick, Robert (off.) V–369b
Sedgwick, Theodore (jur.) II–174 (table)
Sedgwick, William T. (bact.) I–242a
Sedgwick County Zoo (Wichita) VII–371b
SEDITION ACTS (1798, 1918) **VI–254b**; I–478b; II–463a–b; III–104b
libel suits IV–139b
Smith Act II–446a
World War I V–74a; VII–326a
See also Alien and Sedition Acts
Seditious libel I–478b
Seeburg Company V–290b
Seed-gathering cultures II–334b; IV–51b
Seeding, cloud II–76b
Seedtime of the Republic III–283a
Seeger, Pete (mus.) IV–441a,b
Seersucker (cloth) II–239b
Segal, George (sculp.) VI–244a
Sego lily VI–395 (table)
Segrè, Emilio (phys.) IV–119b; V–100a, 295b–96a, 303a
SEGREGATION VI–255b; I–27a, 32a; III–437b–38b; VI–6a–b, 7a,b
Alaska I–79a
black nationalism V–200a
Brown v. *Board of Education of Topeka* III–86b; IV–359a; V–126a
busing I–397b
California I–408b
Catholic churches I–468a
civil rights movement II–54a–55b, 57a–58a
de facto II–457a
education I–372b–73a; II–399b, 401b, 403b–04a
equal protection clause II–457a
Fourteenth Amendment IV–14b
Freedom Riders III–107a
Jim Crow laws III–502b
legislation I–29a
military IV–340a–b
Mississippi IV–369b
NAACP IV–461a
New South V–67b
North Carolina V–116a
Plessy v. *Ferguson* V–331b
race riots I–31a,b
railroads I–372b
Reconstruction I–25b
South Carolina VI–348a
Southern Regional Education Board VI–402a
Student Nonviolent Coor-

SEGREGATION (cont.)
dinating Committee VI–420b
Virginia VII–195b–96a
Washington, D.C. VII–246a
White Citizens Councils VII–291a
yellow peril VII–356b
See also Integration
"Segregation academies" V–67b
Seguin Island V–359b
Seicheprey (Fr.) IV–319b
SEIGNIORAGE VI–257a; VII–4b
Seine River II–436b; VII–339a
Seip Mounds (Ohio) IV–421a
Seiscor Voting Machine VII–210b
Seismic activity. *See* Earthquakes
Seismographic prospecting V–272a,b
Seismology III–453b
Seitz, Frederick (phys.) V–304a; VI–158b
Seizure. *See* Arrest; Search and Seizure, naval; Search and Seizure, Unreasonable
Selby, Thomas H. (metal.) VI–292b
Selden, George B. (law., inv.) I–227a; VI–257a
Selden, John (jur., states.) III–106b
SELDEN PATENT VI–257a
Seldes, George (jour.) V–80a
Seldon, Samuel L. (bus.) VII–276b
Select Committee on Improper Activities in the Labor of Management Field I–103a
Selective Service Act (1917) II–185b, 186a, 367a; VII–208a, 325b
Selective Service Act (1917) bounties I–353a
Selective Service and Training Act (1940) I–30a; II–186b, 367b; V–181b; VII–334b, 335a
Selective Service System II–314b, 315a, 367b–68a; IV–384b; V–139a
conscientious objectors V–182b
desertion II–335b
terminated II–316b
World War I I–186a
See also Draft
SELECTMEN VI–257b; VII–78a–b, 79a
Connecticut III–9a
Massachusetts IV–265a
Selectron tube II–156a
Selenium VII–21a
Sele River VI–199b
Self-employment V–133a; VI–329a
Self-excited generator II–413b
Self-government II–166a; V–360a
See also Home Rule
Self-improvement clubs VII–313a
Self-incrimination (law) III–320a; IV–14b, 23b
Self-preservation, right of II–456a; IV–142a
Self-raker IV–211a
Self-Realization Fellowship V–171b
Selfridge, Thomas E. (av.) II–346a
SELF-SERVICE STORES VI–257b
supermarkets II–282b, 421b
variety stores III–33a
Self-starter I–228b
Seligman (Ariz.) VI–273b
Seligman, Jesse (banker) III–79b
Seligman, Joseph (banker) III–79b
Selkirk, Earl of. *See* Douglas, Thomas
Selkirk, Fort (Can.) VII–367a
Selle River (Fr.) VI–338b
Sellers, Coleman (eng.) II–447b
Sellers, Isaiah (river pilot) IV–256a
Sellers, William (print.) V–251a
Selling, installment. *See* Installment Buying, Selling, and Financing
Sellow and Company VI–291b
Sells-Floto Circus II–40b; VII–298b
Selma (Ala.)
civil rights movement I–31a; II–55b, 58b; V–182a, 265b; VI–433a
Civil War IV–313b
Civil War foundry II–163a
martial law IV–259a
Selwyn, John VII–350a
Semi-Automatic Ground Environment I–58b
SEMICONDUCTORS VI–259a; III–156a; IV–333b; V–303a, 304a,b, 305a; VII–20b
Seminaries I–5b
Seminary Ridge (Pa.) III–175b, 176a; V–309a
SEMINOLE (Indians) **VI–259b**; III–39a, 367a, 396b
Creek War II–257a
Dawes Commission II–295b
Forbes Purchase III–59a
Jackson's campaign I–154a
pacification I–219a
removal III–394b
scouts VI–242a
Treaty of Payne's Landing V–231a
Union Army III–375b–76a
See also Civilized Tribes, Five
Seminole County (Okla.) VI–260a
Seminole Treaty of 1866 VI–260a
SEMINOLE WARS VI–260a; II–52b; III–39a, 127a, 462b; VI–259b–60a; VII–239a,b
army I–184a
Battle of Fowltown III–88b
Battle of Okeechobee V–147a
Battles at Withlacoochee River VII–311a
campaign of 1840 I–420a
Colt six-shooter II–130b
Dade massacre II–278b
gunboats III–234b
horse cavalry I–475b
Indian Key Massacre III–381b
marines IV–252a
militia IV–383b
Pensacola V–254b
Saint Augustine VI–187b
Treaty of Payne's Landing V–231a
Semirigid airship II–344a
Semisubmarine II–294b
Semitrailer IV–419b, 420a
Semmes, Raphael (nav. off.) I–14a, 72b
Alabama IV–35a; VII–147a
Confederate navy V–17a
Mexican War IV–322a
Sumter escape IV–371a
Semper Fidelis (comp.) IV–441b
"Semper Paratus" VII–318a
Senat, Antoine (miss.) III–499b
Senate, United States II–171b, 172a,b, 173a,b, 194b–95a, 198b, 199a–b, 201a,b, 206a,b
Bill of Rights I–298a–b
Bobby Baker case I–243b–44a
budget committee II–179a
cabinet I–400a
campaign contributions V–449b
campaign costs II–411a
checks and balances II–4b
cloture II–83b
confirmation by II–167b
Connecticut Plan II–151b
contempt of II–210b
courtesy II–168a, 246a
election of president II–205a
extra sessions II–479a
farm bloc I–322a
impeachment I–501b
"influence peddling" II–231b
journal II–178a
McCarthy, Joseph R. IV–210b
treaty power II–471b
vice-presidency VII–178b
vice-president II–204b–05a, 412a
See also Congress, United States
Senate Appropriations Committee I–149a
Senate Committee of Thirteen. *See* Committee of Thirteen
Senate Foreign Relations Committee VII–224b
Senate Internal Security Subcommittee VI–428b, 429a
Senate Permanent Committee on Investigations III–465a–b
Senate Select Committee for Investigating Into Presidential Campaign Activities III–465b
Senatorial courtesy. *See* Courtesy of the Senate
Senatorial patronage II–168a
Senator Ross (galley) III–147b
SENATORS, ELECTION OF VI–261b; I–94b; II–173b, 194a, 199a
corruption II–231b
Ocala Platform V–132a
Progressive movement V–428a
Seventeenth Amendment II–206a; VI–264a
Seneca (Indians) I–369a; III–365b, 475a,b; VI–377b
Denonville's invasion II–329b
Devil's Hole Ambush II–339b
Dodge-Leavenworth expedition II–358b
Fort Niagara V–90a
French IV 83b
French and Indian War III–115a
Handsome Lake Cult III–249b, 476a; V–4a
Iroquois Treaty III–477a
Jemison, Mary VII–293b
Jesuit missions III–500a
Magazin Royal V–90a
Niagara cession III–85a; V–90b
Ogden purchase V–139b
Oklahoma V–148b
Pontiac's War V–357a
sachems VI–183a
Sullivan-Clinton campaign VI–438a
Treaty at Pittsburgh V–322a
Treaty of Buffalo Creek III–383b
Tuscarora War VII–130b
See also Iroquois
Seneca (Ohio) VII–267a
Seneca County (N.Y.) II–460a
Seneca Falls (N.Y.) I–323b; VI–261b
SENECA FALLS CONVENTION (1848) **VI–261b**; III–91b; V–87a, 97a; VII–313b, 315a, 316b–17a
Seneca Falls Declaration of Rights and Sentiments VII–317a
Seneca Lake III–419b; IV–174b; V–86b, 276b; VI–438a

"Seneca Oil" IV–44a
Senegal
  slave trade I–27a
Senegal River VI–309b
Sengstacke, John H. (jour.) V–76a
Senior Companion Program I–8b–9a
Seniority system
  Congress II–173a
Sense of the Past IV–163b
Seoul (Kor.) I–61a; IV–55b, 56a, 57a, 253a
Seoul River (Kor.). *See* Han River
"Separate but equal" doctrine I–290b, 372b–73a; II–54a–b, 399b, 404a, 457a; III–86b; V–331b; VI–256a,b
Separate Puritan Congregation I–264b
"Separate state action" I–326a
Separation of powers. *See* Powers, Separation of
Separatism
  black nationalism I–315b
  black power I–316b
SEPARATISTS VI–262a; V–469a
  Brownists I–371b
  communities II–147a
  Dissenters II–353a
  Harmony Society III–255a
  New England Way V–52a
  Pilgrims V–64b, 312b
  Plymouth colony II–364b–65a; IV–264b
Separatists Society of Zoar VII–369b
Separators, hand II–280b
Sephardic Jews VI–79a
Sephardim IV–9a
Sequestration of property
  Civil War II–168a
Sequin, Armand (chem.) IV–128a
SEQUOIA VI–262b; VII–220a
  Yosemite VII–361b, 362a
Sequoia National Park V–218 (table), 445b; VI–262b
Sequoya (Indian) VI–263a
SEQUOYAH, PROPOSED STATE OF VI–262b; V–149a
SEQUOYA'S SYLLABARY VI–263a; II–52a
Serapis (warship) I–89b, 329a–b; V–18b; VI–129a
Serbia
  World War I relief VII–330a
Serbian Eastern Orthodox Diocese II–387a
Serbs III–339a
Serfdom
  Carolinas I–457b
Sergeant (missile) III–502a; IV–363b
"Sergeant Preston of the Yukon" I–488a
Seri (Indians) III–363a
Sericulture. *See* Silk Culture and Manufacture
Serpent Mound (Ohio) IV–420b–21a
Serra, Junípero (miss.) I–405a; IV–365b–66a
Serrano (Indians) III–363a
Servants II–418a–19a; IV–79a,b
Servants, indentured. *See* Indentured Servants
Service areas (gov.) IV–172a–b
Service Center for Teachers of History I–106a
Service Corps of Retired Executives I–8b–9a
Service excise tax VII–11b
Servicemen's Readjustment Act (1944) I–331b; II–115a; III–178b
Service occupations IV–75a
Services, distribution of. *See* Distribution of Goods and Services
Service stations (auto) I–228a; II–354b
Service to Military Families VI–61b
Servomechanism Laboratory II–156a
Servomechanisms II–153b, 425a
"Sesame Street" (television show) II–402b; V–72b
SESQUICENTENNIAL INTERNATIONAL EXPOSITION (1926) **VI–263a**
Sessé, Martín (bot.) V–326b–27a
Sessions, Roger (comp.) IV–439a
Setauket (N.Y.) IV–185b
Seton, Saint Elizabeth Bayley I–467a
Settlement work. *See* Social Settlements
Seurat, Georges (art.) II–105a
Seven Cardinal Principles of Secondary Education (1918) II–400b
Seven Cities of Cibola. *See* Cibola
SEVEN DAYS' BATTLES (1862) **VI–263b**; III–258a; V–245b, 377b; VI–150a
  Army of Northern Virginia VII–197b
  Frayser's Farm III–100a
  Gaines' Mill III–146a
  Malvern Hill IV–230b
  Richmond VI–137a
"SEVEN PILLARS" VI–263b
Seven Pines. *See* Fair Oaks, Battle of
SEVEN RANGES SURVEY VI–264a; III–163a; VI–451a
  Fort Harmar III–255a
  Fort Steuben VI–412b
  Ohio Company of Associates V–143b
  townships VII–81b
"Seven Sisters" V–58a
Seven Songs for the Harpsichord IV–438a
Seventeenth Airborne Division V–213b
SEVENTEENTH AMENDMENT VI–264a; I–94b; II–173b, 206a; VI–261b; VII–208b
Seventh Air Force I–64a
Seventh Amendment I–299a
Seventh Armored Division. *See* entries under Army, United States
Seventh Army, U.S. *See* entries under Army, United States
Seventh Cavalry IV–168a, 316a
Seventh (VII) Corps *See* entries under Army, United States
Seventh Day Adventists I–15b, 487a
  See also Adventist Churches
Seventh Day Baptists I–15b
Seventh Fleet V–22a,b, 24b, 25a; VII–2a
  Korean War IV–56b
  World War II IV–138a
Seventh Infantry Division IV–257b
Seventh Infantry Regiment I–142a
Seventh International Conference of American States (1933) V–106a, 107b
Seventh Kansas Cavalry III–493a
Seventh Marine Regiment VII–186a
"Seventy" agents I–136b, 137b
Seventy–eighth Infantry Division. *See* entries under Army, United States
Seventy–seventh Infantry Division. *See* entries under Army, United States
Seven Years War (1756–63) III–114b
  British Sea power VI–248a
  Rule of the War of 1756 VI–169a
  See also French and Indian War
Severance, John L. II–104b
Severance pay VII–215a
SEVERN, BATTLE OF THE (1655) **VI–264b**
Severn, Fort (Md.) V–9b
Severn County (Ga.) I–362b
Sevier, John (off., pol.) II–15a
  Battle of King's Mountain IV–48a; VII–25b
  Muscle Shoals colony IV–435b
  State of Franklin II–381a; III–98b
  Watauga settlement II–477a
Sevier River VI–368a; VII–256a
Seville (Sp.) II–217b
Sewall, Henry (physiol.) V–306b–07a
Sewall, Samuel (jur.) VII–310a
Seward (Alaska) I–77b
Seward, George F. (dipl.) IV–54b
Seward, William Henry (states.) II–475a; V–158a
  Alabama Claims I–72b
  Alaska I–75a–b
  Alta Vela claim I–91b
  Antirent War I–134a
  antislavery IV–8a; VI–288a
  Burlingame Treaty I–386a
  campaign of 1860 I–421b
  Civil War II–64b–65a, 161a, 165a, 435a, 451b
  Committee of Thirteen II–139a
  Compromise of 1850 II–184b
  Dominican Republic II–360b, 362a
  foreign policy III–68a–b
  Fort Pickens V–308b
  French in Mexico III–97a; IV–361a, 400b
  Hampton Roads Conference III–247b
  Higher–law doctrine III–275a
  "irrepressible conflict" III–477a
  "manifest destiny" IV–239a
  Mexican relations IV–325b–26a
  Nast cartoons IV–454b
  Powhatan incident V–386a
  Republican party V–86b
  Shimonoseki expedition VI–279a
  Trent affair VII–116a
Seward's Folly I–75b
Seward's Polar Bear Garden I–75b
Sewell, Samuel (Puritan) I–135a
Sewell's Point (Va.) IV–396b
Sewers IV–172a; VI–211b–12a,b
  government inspection III–422a
  New York City VI–377b
  public health V–447a
SEWING MACHINE VI–264b; VII–43b
  Civil War uniforms II–417b
  clothing industry II–81b
  Elias Howe II–371b
  harnessmaking III–255b
  interchangeable manufacture IV–272b
  machine tools IV–216a
  silk VI–287a
Sex discrimination
  Nineteenth Amendment V–97a
Sex education II–402b; V–294a
Sexes, equality of II–486a–b

SEXUAL ATTITUDES VI–265b
colonial crime II–258a
interracial marriage IV–362b
Kinsey Report IV–50a
moral codes IV–408a
motion pictures IV–418b–19a
obscenity rulings III–105b–06a
prostitution V–437b
Shakers VI–268a
sumptuary laws VI–440b
Sexual Behavior in the Human Female IV–50a
Sexual Behavior in the Human Male IV–50a
Seybert, Adam (physic., pol.) I–481b; II–5b; IV–348a
SEYBERT, FORT, MASSACRE AT (1758) **VI–267a**
Seymour, Horatio (pol.) I–422a; II–368b; III–243a, 318a; V–87a
Seymour, Richard (cler.) V–359b
Seymour, Truman (off.) V–153b
Seymour, W. J. (cler.) V–259b
Seyss–Inquart, Artur von VII–229b
Shackamaxon (Pa.) VI–267a
SHACKAMAXON, TREATY OF (1683) **VI–267a**; III–382b
Shackelford County (Tex.) III–228a
Shad III–51a
SHADES OF DEATH VI–267b
Shadow (cargo plane) I–54a
Shadows–on–the–Teche (New Iberia, La.) IV–472a
SHADRACH FUGITIVE SLAVE CASE VI–267b
SHAEF. *See* Supreme Headquarters, Allied Expeditionary Force
Shaffer farm (Pa.) V–319a
Shafter, William R. (off.) VI–213b, 217a, 361b–62a
Shaftesbury, Anthony Ashley Cooper, 1st Baron Ashley and 1st Earl of Shaftesbury (states.) I–457b, 458a; II–271b; VI–347a
Shaft mining III–473b
Shahaka (Indian) VI–195b
Shahn, Ben (paint.) V–192b, 414a; VI–183a
SHAKER RELIGION, INDIAN VI–267b; V–4a
SHAKERS VI–268a; II–30b
communities II–142a, 147a
furniture III–135b, 138b
Western Reserve VII–275a
Shakopee (Minn.) VI–295a
SHALAM, LAND OF (N.Mex.) **VI–268a**
Shale IV–44a
Shaler, Nathaniel S. (geol.) IV–120a
Shamanism III–358a, 360a, 363a, 366a, 368a, 376b, 385a, 391b, 392b, 393a, 503b; V–4a
"Shame of the Cities" (article) IV–424b
Shamrock (yacht) VII–348b
Shanewis (opera) IV–438b
Shanghai (China) II–26a, 479b; V–22b; VII–334a
Shanghai Opium Commission II–374b
"Shangri La" raid (1942) I–55b
Shankara order V–171b
Shanker, Albert (labor leader) IV–76a
Shannon (frigate) II–16a–b, 364a, 459a; III–315b
Shannon, Claude E. (math.) I–287b; II–154b, 155a
Shannon, William (pol.) IV–31a
Shannon, William V. (jour.) V–75a
Shannon, Wilson (pol.) IV–118b; VII–218b
Shannopin's Town (Pa.) VI–49a
Shantung province (China) VII–331a
SHANTY TOWNS VI–268b
Shantz, H. L. (plant ecol.) I–349b
Shapiro v. *Thompson* (1969) V–420b
Shapley, Harlow (astron.) I–211b
SHARECROPPER VI–268b; II–69b, 495a; III–103b; IV–103a–04a; V–325b; VI–174b–75a
Afro–American migration I–26a, 41a
Arkansas I–173b
cotton production II–238a,b
government subsidies VI–426a
Great Depression I–30a, 40b
poor whites V–359a
Reconstruction I–29a
Shared revenues II–234b, 502a
Shared taxes II–234a–b, 245b
Share–Our–Wealth Clubs VI–269a
SHARE–THE–WEALTH MOVEMENTS VI–269a; V–46b, 47b; VII–79b
Long, Huey P. IV–184a
pressure groups V–401a
Sharkey, William L. (pol.) IV–376a
Sharon, William (bus.) II–157a
Sharpe, George Henry (off.) VI–373b
Sharpe, Horatio (col. gov.) I–161b; II–134a
Sharpe's Rifle Manufacturing Company IV–433a
Sharps, Christian (inv.) VI–270a
Sharpsburg (Md.) I–130a; III–256b
Civil War III–101a; IV–261b–62a
See also Antietam, Battle of
SHARPSHOOTER VI–269b
SHARPS RIFLE VI–270a; I–283b; IV–430b
emigrant aid movement V–51b
sharpshooters VI–269b
Sharps Rifle Company VI–270a
Shasta (Indians) III–363a
Shasta Dam V–455b; VI–147a
Shattuck, Lemuel (mer., statis.) VII–206b
Shaumberg, Bartholomew (off.) VI–414b
Shaw, Anna Howard (ref.) VII–315a
Shaw, George Bernard (playwright, au.) IV–442a; VII–49b
Shaw, Henry (mer.) I–349a; IV–378a
Shaw, H. W. (humorist) I–91a
Shaw, John (off.) VI–271b
Shaw, John (paint.) V–188a
Shaw, Lemuel (jur.) III–407a; IV–61a
Shaw, Leslie M. (law., banker) VI–427a
Shaw, Robert Gould (off.) I–345b
Shaw, Samuel (jur.) VII–266a
Shawanese Oldtown (Md.) V–378b
SHAWMUT (Mass.) **VI–270a**; I–344a
Shawn, Edwin Meyers (Ted) (dancer) II–287b
SHAWNEE (Indians) **V–270b**; II–321a; III–24b, 227b, 366b
Allegheny River I–89a
Big Bottom massacre I–296a
Boone–Callaway kidnapping I–337a
Cherokee Wars II–14b
Chickasaw territory II–23a
Draper's Meadows attack II–369b
Dunmore's War I–499a; II–381b; V–335b; VI–386a
Fort Randolph VI–45b
Fort Stanwix Treaty VI–386a
French and Indian War III–115a, 116b, 117a
Great Trading and War Path III–223b
Great Warriors Path VII–238b
Jesuit missions III–500a
Kentucky II–292a
Logstown IV–181a
Logstown Treaty IV–181b
Maumee Convention IV–276b
McDonald's Expedition IV–212a
mounds IV–421a
Ohio V–140a
Oklahoma V–148b, 149b
Pennsylvania V–246a
Pontiac's War I–353b–54a, 359a, 389a; V–357a
removal III–393b, 394b
revolutionary war III–400b; V–152b, 319b
Spring Wells Treaty VI–377b
Tecumseh IV–90a
treaties I–369a
Treaty at Pittsburgh V–322a
Treaty of Greenville III–383a
Vincennes cession VII–189b
SHAWNEE AND DELAWARE MIGRATION VI–270b
SHAWNEE PROPHET VI–271a; III–257b; V–4a, 141a; VI–270b; VII–262b
Battle of Tippecanoe VII–63b
Prophet's Town V–435a
Tecumseh's crusade VII–18a
Shawneetown (Ill.) I–267b; VI–202a
Shawnee Trail V–148b
SHAWOMET (R.I.) **VI–271b**
SHAW'S EXPEDITION (1809) **VI–271b**
Shaw University I–28b
Shay, one–horse I–461a
Shays, Daniel (off.). *See* Shays's Rebellion
SHAYS'S REBELLION (1786–87) **VI–271b**; I–41a; II–167a, 192b, 196b; III–436b; IV–266a, 345b; VII–191a
Shea, John Gilmary (hist.) III–282a
Sheaffe, Roger H. (off.) VI–3a; VII–358b
Sheboygen (Wis.) III–461b
Sheean, Vincent (jour.) IV–164b
Sheehan, Neil (jour.) V–74b
SHEEP VI–272b; I–37b, 38b; III–51b; IV–169b
county fairs II–244b
coyote II–253a
Indian cultures III–368b
Montana IV–403a
Navaho V–8b
Nevada V–39b
New Hampshire V–54a
Ohio V–141b
overgrazing III–75b
ranching VI–44b, 45a–b
ranchos del rey VI–45b
state fairs VI–392b
subsidies VI–426a
triangular trade VII–277b
Vermont VII–172a
wolves VII–311b
wool VII–320a–21b
Wyoming VII–346a

Sheepeater (Indians) I–264b; VII–239b
Sheepscot Bay (Maine) IV–37b
SHEEP WARS VI–273a; I–38b; IV–50a; VI–45a–b
Sheet music IV–438a
Sheffield, Joseph E. (ind., philan.) VI–273b
SHEFFIELD SCIENTIFIC SCHOOL VI–273b; II–11a, 399a; IV–120a; VII–351a
Shehab, Fuad IV–130a
Shelburne, Lord. *See* Lansdowne, Marquis of
Shelburne, 2nd Earl of, William Petty (states.) II–318a; III–251a, 388a
Shelburne Museum, Inc. (Shelburne, Vt.) III–137b
Shelby, Fort (Detroit). *See* Pontchartrain du Détroit, Fort
Shelby, Fort (Wis.) V–388a
Shelby, Isaac (off.) IV–40b, 48a; VI–450b
Shelby, Joseph O. (off.) III–182a; VI–274a; VII–280b
Shelby County (Mo.) I–293a
SHELBY'S MEXICAN EXPEDITION (1865) **VI–274a**
Shelbyville (Ind.) II–347a
Sheldon, Charles Monroe (cler., au.) VI–325a
Sheldon, Edward (playwright) V–96a
Sheldon, Edward A. (educ.) II–398b
Sheldon, John P. (pub.) V–70b
Shelford, Victor E. (physiol.) II–391b
Shelikof (Shelekhov), Grigori (mer.) IV–54a
Shellac V–327b
Sheller, Charles (paint.) V–192b
Shelley, Percy Bysshe (poet) IV–161b
Shell mounds IV–420b, 421a,b
Shells III–289b, 362a
Shell shock IV–304a, 306a–b
Sheltered Life IV–164a
Shelton, Robert M., Jr. IV–58b–59a
Shelton v. *Tucker* (1960) I–204b
SHENANDOAH (cruiser) **VI–274b**; I–73a; II–213a; IV–54b; V–17b
Shenandoah (dirigible) I–51b, 234a, 236b; II–344b
SHENANDOAH CAMPAIGN (1864) **VI–275a**; VI–187a, 276a; VII–304b
Shenandoah Hunting Path. *See* Virginia Path
Shenandoah Mountains VII–71a
Shenandoah National Park V–218 (table)
Shenandoah River IV–53a; V–145a, 369b
SHENANDOAH VALLEY VI–275b; II–481b
agriculture VII–194a
Ashby's Gap I–200b
Civil War I–381a, 476b; II–266a, 482a–b; III–487a–b; IV–43b, 261b, 282a; V–59a, 245a, 248a; VI–26b, 263b, 275a; VII–304a–b
Great Trading and War Path III–223a
James River navigation III–488b
land speculation VII–195a
mountain passes V–224b
Scotch-Irish VI–240b
settlement V–378a; VII–193a, 283a
westward movement VII–100a
Sheninjee (Indian) VII–293b
Shepard, Alan B., Jr. (astronaut) I–210a
Shepard, Charles Upham (min.) IV–348b
Shepard, Charles Upham, Jr. (chem.) VII–16a
Shepard, Thomas (cler.) I–411b
Shepard, William (off.) VI–272a
Shepheard and Pratt Mental Hospital (Md.) IV–261b
Shepherd, Alexander R. (pol.) II–319b; VII–246a
Shepherd, Samuel (pub.) III–272a
Shepherdstown (W.Va.) VI–170a, 275b
Shepley, Rutan, and Coolidge VI–299a
Sheppard, Morris (pol.) V–430a
Sheppard, Samuel (physic.) VII–118a–b
Sheppard–Towner Act (1921) IV–276a
Sheppard v. *Maxwell* (1966) III–105b
Sheraton, Thomas III–135a
Sherbet II–282b
Sheridan (Wyo.) VII–346a
Sheridan, Fort (Colo.) III–266b
Sheridan, Philip H. (off.) II–62b
Battle at Toms Brook VII–71a
Battle at Yellow Tavern VII–358a
Battle of Cedar Creek I–476b
Battle of Five Forks III–33b; V–265a
Battle of Little Bighorn IV–167b–68a, 168a
Battle of Murfreesboro IV–434b
Battle of Trevilian Station VII–117a
Battle of Winchester III–31a; VI–373b; VII–304b
Battles at Sailor's Creek VI–186b
buffalo population I–375a
Fort Bascom I–269b
Fort Hays III–266b
Fort Sill VI–287a
Mosby's Rangers IV–415b
Red River Indian War VI–64a
Shenandoah campaign VI–187a, 275a, 276a
Todd's Tavern action VII–68a
Warren controversy VI–276a
Washita operations VII–252b
SHERIDAN'S RIDE (1864) **VI–276a**; I–476b
Sheridan's Scouts VI–373b
SHERIDAN-WARREN CONTROVERSY VI–276a
Sheriffs V–338b, 339a
Sherley Amendment (1912) V–466b
Sherlock Holmes VII–49a
Sherman, Frederick C. (nav. off.) VII–1b
Sherman, George H. (off.) IV–364b–65a
Sherman, James S. (pol.) I–426b; VII–180 (table)
Sherman, John (states.) III–271a; VI–276b
Reconstruction Acts VI–59a
specie payments I–318b; VI–104a
See also Sherman Silver Purchase Act
Sherman, John B. (mer.) VI–414a
Sherman, Mrs. VI–358b
Sherman, Roger (states.)
Declaration of Independence II–303b, 308a
U.S. Constitution II–183a, 193a, 203b
Sherman, Sidney (off.) VI–84a
Sherman, Stuart P. (critic) IV–164a
Sherman, William Tecumseh (off.) II–62b; III–81a; V–116a, 141b; VI–138a, 243b
Andersonville Prison I–118a
Army of the Tennessee VII–26b–27a
Atlanta campaign I–213a–14b; II–271b; IV–36b–37a; V–56a, 238a; VI–26b, 166a
Battle at Allatoona Pass I–88b
Battle at Tupelo VII–128b–29a
Battle of Arkansas Post I–174a
Battle of Averysboro I–232b
Battle of Bentonville I–289b
Battle of Chickasaw Bluffs II–22a
Battle of Ezra Church II–479b
Battle of Jackson III–485b
Battle of Kenesaw Mountain IV–36b
Battle of Shiloh VI–278b
Bummers I–382b
burning of Columbia II–131a
Confederate surrender IV–257a
First Battle of Bull Run I–381b
Fort Sill VI–287b
Fort Sumter VI–441a
Haines' Bluff III–238b
Hood's Tennessee campaign III–298a
logistics IV–180b
march through Georgia III–168b; VI–278a
march to the sea IV–209a
Meridian campaign IV–313b
post–Civil War army I–185a
Savannah seige VI–220b
Steele's Bayou expedition VI–410b
surrender of Johnston II–63a, 68b
Vicksburg VII–181b
Yazoo Pass expedition VII–354b
See also Carolinas, Sherman's March Through
SHERMAN ANTITRUST ACT (1890) **VI–276a**; I–139b–40a, 389b, 390b; II–229b, 230a; III–113a, 204b, 458b, 459b; IV–399a,b; VI–405b; VII–122a,b
Addyston Pipe Company Case I–11a
Associated Press I–207a
Beef Trust Cases III–343a
boycotts I–356b–57a; IV–67b
commerce clause II–135b–36a
Danbury Hatters' Case II–286a
Du Pont Company V–383b
electrical manufacturers case II–259a
fair–trade agreements II–483a
flour trust III–44a
In re Debs II–298b
International Harvester Company III–454b
labor union exemptions VI–138b
laissez–faire doctrine IV–85b
Miller–Tydings Amendment I–489b
Northern Securities Company V–119a
open–shop campaign IV–67b
organized labor IV–69a
price maintenance V–403a,b
prices V–402a
Pullman Strike I–111b

SHERMAN ANTITRUST ACT (cont.)
railroad rate agreements V–358a
railroads VI–22a
railroad trust VII–155a
restraint of trade VI–102a,b, 103a,b
rule of reason VI–102b, 168b
Standard Oil V–270a; VI–383b
strikes VI–419a
sugar trust VI–437b; VII–154a
tobacco industry I–114a
"trust-busting" VII–121b
unions II–110b; III–407a
See also Clayton Antitrust Act
SHERMAN SILVER PURCHASE ACT (1890) **VI–277a**; I–302a; II–96a; III–110b–11a; IV–154a–b, 395a; VI–95a, 288b, 371a, 467a
Brussels Monetary Conference I–373a
campaign of 1890 I–424b
Compromise of 1890 II–151a
panic of 1893 V–208a
repeal II–75a; VI–292b
Silver Democrats VI–287b
SHERMAN'S MARCH TO THE SEA (1864) **VI–278a**; I–214a, 214a, 382b, 382b; II–131a, 163b; III–103a, 298a; VII–26b
Army of the Tennessee VII–27a
Fort McAllister IV–209a
Georgia III–168b
Savannah VI–221a
Sherry III–52a
Sherwood, Justus (off.) III–241a
Sherwood, Robert E. (playwright) VII–50a
Shewhart, Walter A. (statis.) VI–206b
Shibasaki, Keiji (nav. off.) VI–462a
Shields, James (off.) I–488b; IV–43b
Shi'ite sect V–171b
SHILOH, BATTLE OF (1862) **V–278a**; II–62b, 225b, 271b; III–234b; IV–42a; VII–26b, 34b
Army of the Ohio V–142a
Lexington IV–136b
newspaper coverage V–71b
Shima, Kiyohide (nav. off.) IV–138a,b
Shimkin, Leon (pub.) I–334b
SHIMONOSEKI EXPEDITION (1864) **VI–278b**; III–352a
Shimonoseki Strait III–490b; VI–278b–79a
Shinano (battleship) V–10b
Shingles (build.) I–161a, 164a, 377b
Shinn, Everett (art.) II–104a
Shinny (ball game) III–366a
SHINPLASTERS VI–279a; II–95b–96a; IV–394a; VI–104a
Shinty (sport) III–286b
SHIPBUILDING VI–279a; III–428a,b, 429a; IV–310b, 311b, 312a,b; VI–148a, 148a, 280b–81b; VII–86b
Baltimore I–249b–50a
Cape Horn passage I–448a
colonial II–119a,b, 124b–25a; III–413a; VI–108a
Continental navy VI–128a
dry docks II–375a
England II–375a
Falmouth (Mass.) I–447a
great fortunes III–80b
Great Lakes III–216b, 218b
Hog Island Shipyard III–288a
ironclads III–474b
Long Island IV–185b
lumber IV–204a
Maine IV–226b
Massachusetts IV–265b
Mobile IV–382b
naval competition V–10a
navy V–27b–28a; VII–147a, 341b–42a
navy yards V–29a
New England III–220a; IV–309b
New Hampshire V–53b
Newport V–65b
Pennsylvania V–246b, 247a
Perth Amboy V–264a
public-lands timber III–73a
Sackets Harbor VI–183b
San Diego VI–208b
schooners VI–229b
Shipping Act of 1916 VI–281b
steamboats VI–406b
tar VI–461b
triangular trade VII–278a
Virginia VII–196a
warships VII–240a
Washington Naval Conference VII–250b
Washington State VII–248a
whalers IV–449a
Wheeling VII–288a
World War I II–438a–b; VII–326a, 327b, 328a,b, 329a
World War II VII–344a
Ship Carpenters and Caulkers International IV–62b
Ship disasters II–349a–50a
Ship graveyards II–89a
Shipp, Jerry (athlete) V–154b
Shippen, William (physic.) IV–283a; V–251b
Shippensburg (Pa.) VI–49a
SHIPPING, OCEAN VI–280a; VII–86a, 87a,b
armed merchantmen IV–313a
army logistics I–190a
Civil War VII–147a
coasting trade II–90b
colonial II–122a–23a
Confederacy II–163b
convoys II–217a
drogher trade II–373b
Embargo Act II–436a
Espionage Act II–463a
Great Lakes VI–193a
hijacking II–270a
insurance III–427a–29a
merchant marine IV–309a
Naples claims IV–449a
Napoleon's decrees IV–449b
navigational charts IV–277a
New Orleans V–62a
Newport V–65b
New York City V–83a–b
Ohio V–142a
Panama tolls question V–204b
Plan of 1776 V–323b
privateering IV–256a
regulation IV–254b
Rule of the War of 1756 VI–169a
sailing packets V–183b
Saint Lawrence River VI–192b
Saint Lawrence Seaway VI–192b
Salem VI–199b
shipbuilding VI–279a
steamboats VI–408a
tariff VI–465a,b
territorial waters VII–32b
Tonnage Act VII–72a
visit and search VII–204b
War of 1812 VII–235a–b
World War I VII–325b, 328b
World War II VII–336a–b, 342b, 343a
SHIPPING ACT OF 1916 VI–281b; I–390a; III–459a; IV–254b; V–455a
Shipping Act of 1920 III–429a
SHIPPING BOARD, UNITED STATES VI–281b; II–438a; III–459a; IV–311b; V–455a; VII–326a, 327b
Shipping Board Bureau, United States VI–281b
Shippingport (Pa.) II–417a
Ships
Baltimore Clipper I–251a
blacksmiths I–317a
Coast Guard II–89b–90b
figureheads III–21b
Lakers III–218a–b
slave ships VI–308b
sloop VI–313b
See also Clipper Ships; Warships
Ship Sales Act (1946) III–429a
SHIPS OF THE LINE VI–281b; V–25a; VII–240a–b, 241b, 242a, 243a
Shipstead, Henrik (pol.) II–491a,b, 492a
Ship-timber II–119b
Shipwrecks
Cape Cod I–447a
lifesaving service IV–152a
Shipyards, naval. *See* Navy Yards
Shiras, George, Jr. (jur.) VI–446a
Shire (horse) III–303b
Shirley, Fort (Pa.) I–222b; IV–51a
Shirley, William (off.) II–134a, 267a; III–116a; IV–192a; V–90b, 175b
SHIRT-SLEEVE DIPLOMACY VI–282a
Shirtwaists II–372a
SHIVAREE VI–282b
Shively, J. M. V–168b
S. H. Knox and Company III–32b
S. H. Kress and Company III–32b–33a
Sho ("Victory") IV–138a
Shockley, William (phys.) I–287b; II–425b; V–100a, 296a, 305a; VI–259a
Shockoe Hill (Va.) VII–292a
Shock therapy IV–306b
Shock troops V–213b
Shoddy (cloth) II–68a
Shoemaker, Vaughan (cartoon.) V–73a
Shoe manufacturing. *See* Boot and Shoe Manufacturing
Shoho (carrier) I–55b; II–225a
Shokaku (carrier) II–225a, 387b
Sholes, Christopher L. (inv.) I–395b–96a; VII–136a
Shonkinite V–268a
Shonkin Sag (Mont.) V–268a
Shooting
Olympic Games V–154a,b
SHOOTING MATCH VI–282b; II–487a
Shooting Star (fighter plane) I–53b
SHOP COMMITTEE VI–282b
Shopping centers II–354a; III–33a
Shore Line Railroad VI–35b
Short, Eugene (dipl.) III–245a
Short, Luke (outlaw) V–139a
Short, Walter C. (off.) V–240a
Shorter, Eli IV–99b
Shorthorn cattle I–471b, 472a; II–280a, 281b; VI–45a, 45a
Short-leaf pine VI–393 (table)
Shortridge, Eli C. D. (gov.) V–117b
Short selling II–470a
Short Symphony (comp.) IV–439a
Shoshone (Indians) I–264b; III–363a
Bannock War VII–239b
Fort Laramie Treaty IV–108b
Fort Washakie VII–244a

Jesuit missions III–500a
Nevada V–39b
scouts VI–242a
Wyoming VII–345b, 346a
Shoshonean (lang.) II–133a; III–367a; V–459b; VII–162b
Hopi III–301a
Paiute V–194a
Shoshone Lake (Wyo.) VI–322b
Shotguns II–376b
"SHOT HEARD ROUND THE WORLD" VI–282b
Shotwell, James T. (hist.) II–343a
Shoup Voting Machine Company VII–210b
"Shout" music IV–442b
Show Boat (musical) IV–442a
SHOWBOATS VI–283a; VII–47a
Show business
blacklisting I–315a
Show Me State VI–394 (table)
Shredded Wheat Company I–487a
Shreve, Henry M. (steamboat capt.) III–147a; IV–35a–b, 374a; VI–322a
Red River raft VI–65a
steamboats VI–408a
Washington VI–148b
Shreve, Lamb and Harmon I–164b; VI–299a
Shreveport (La.) VI–65a, 283b
Afro-Americans I–25b
cattle market I–473a
Civil War III–498a; IV–457a; V–331a; VI–63a, 182a
SHREVEPORT RATE CASE (1914) **VI–283b**; II–136a; VI–22a
Shrewsbury (Mass.) II–78a
Shrewsbury (N.J.) IV–397b
Shrine (Freemasonry) III–109a–b
Shriners. *See* Freemasons
Shrink packaging V–183a
Shriver, Sargent (pol.) I–432a; III–504a
Shropshire sheep VI–273a
Shrove Tuesday IV–249b
Shrubbery
landscape architecture IV–96b
Shubert, Jacob J. (theat. mgr.) VII–48b
Shubert, Lee (theat. mgr.) VII–48b
Shubert, Sam S. (theat. mgr.) VII–48b
Shubrick, William B. (nav. off.) V–22b, 212b
Shufeldt, Robert W. (nav. off.) V–22b
Shu-fly (helicopter unit) VII–185b
Shull, George Harrison (bot.) I–46a; II–226a
Shumagin Islands I–84a
Shuri (Okinawa) V–147b
Shurlock, Geoffrey (adm.) IV–418b
Shurt, Abraham (col.) IV–37a, 396a; V–243b
Shuswap (Indians) I–441b; III–363a
Siam
consular jurisdiction II–479b
See also Thailand
Siberia I–56b
birch bark I–304b
Japan V–107b
Jeannette expedition V–336a,b
Russian expansion II–461b
tobacco VII–64b
Western Union VII–367a
World War I relief VII–330a
SIBERIAN EXPEDITION (1918–20) **VI–283b**; III–463a
marines IV–252b
Siberian Indians III–358a, 386a
Sibirtsev, N. M. (chem.) VI–334a
Sibley, George (expl.) V–148a
Sibley, Henry H. (fur trader) II–283b–84a; IV–356a; VI–139a
Battle of Valverde VII–165b
Battle of Wood Lake VII–319b
Rio Grande operations V–60a; VI–144a
Sioux Minnesota uprising VI–296b
Stillwater Convention VI–413a
Sibley, Hiram (bus.) VII–276b
Sibley, John (off.) VII–39b
Sibley, Solomon II–21a
Sibuyan Sea IV–138b
Sicard, Montgomery (nav. off.) VI–186a
SICILIAN CAMPAIGN (1943) **VI–284b**; I–60a, 308a, 465a; V–110b; VII–338b
gliders III–187a
paratroops V–213b
Sicily (It.)
crime II–258b
earthquake V–23a
sulfur mines II–6b
"Sick Chicken Case." *See Schechter Poultry Corporation* v. *United States*
Sickle I–34b
Sickle-cell anemia IV–391a
Sickles, Daniel E. (off., dipl.) VII–204b
***SIC SEMPER TYRANNIS* VI–285a**; VI–395 (table)
Sideboards III–135a
SIDELING HILL (Pa.) **VI–285a**
Sidesaddle VI–184b–85a
Sidewalks V–230a
"Sidewalks of New York" (song) VI–313a
Side-wheelers VI–408a
Sidewinder (missile) I–57b; IV–363b
Sidi bou Zid (Tun.) IV–32b
Sidney, Margaret (au.) I–335b
Siebert, Wilbur H. (hist.) VII–138a
Siecheprey (Fr.) VII–326b
Siegel, Ben ("Bugsy") II–261b
SIEGFRIED LINE VI–285b; I–1a; III–314b; VI–193b
Siegfried's Bridge (Coplay, Pa.) I–477b
Siemens, William (eng.) II–422a; VI–40a
Siemens-Martin process. *See* Open-hearth process
Sierra Blanca (Tex.) VI–27a, 37a
Sierra Club I–80b, 407a; II–187b; VII–298a
Sierra Leone I–21a
black Loyalists VI–131a
colonization II–127a; VI–321b
smuggling of slaves VI–322a
Sierra Madre I–142b; IV–367a, 452b; VII–289a
Sierra Nevada II–477b; III–214b; VII–289a
Basin Indians III–362a
California Trail VI–154a
Central Route I–485b
Deseret II–334a
exploration I–330a; VII–271b
gold III–190b
Great Valley III–223b
Hastings' Cutoff III–260b
Indian nativistic movement V–4a
Paiute V–194a
passes V–224b–25a
Pioneer Stage Line V–317b
railroads VI–37a
Sequoia VI–262b
skiing VI–101b, 297b–98a
Smith explorations VI–318a
wagon trains VII–217b
Walker expedition VII–220a
water supply II–157a, 297b; VII–259a
Sigel, Franz (off.) I–462a; III–81a
Battle at Wilson's Creek VII–304a
Battle of New Market V–59a
Shenandoah campaign VI–275a
Sigerist, H. E. IV–285b
Sigma Delta Chi. *See* Society of Professional Journalists: Sigma Delta Chi
SIGNAL CORPS, U.S. ARMY VI–285b
flag III–35a
polar stations V–337a
radar VI–10a
Weather Service VII–264a
Signal Office I–463b
Signal Service, U.S. Army. *See* Signal Corps, U.S. Army
Signal stations
Galápagos Islands III–146b
Significance of Sections in American History VI–342a
"Significance of the Frontier in American History" III–125b, 282b, 486a; VII–269a
SIGN LANGUAGE VI–286a; II–30a; III–364a
Sign method of communication III–248a
Sigsbee, Charles D. (nav. off.) IV–227a
Sihanoukville (Cambodia) VII–184a
Sihasapa (Indians) II–283a
Sikorsky, Igor Ivan (aeron. eng.) I–51b, 52a, 234b, 236a; III–270a
Sikorsky clippers I–237a
Siksika (Indians) I–310b–11a
Silage II–226b, 281a; IV–170a
Silent Brigade. *See* Night Riders
Silent films IV–417b
"Silent gerrymander" III–175a
Silent panic. *See* Panic of 1907
Silent Spring III–421a
Silesia, Upper VII–173a
SILHOUETTES VI–286b
Silicon V–304b, 305a; VI–259a
Silicon carbide III–184b, 409a
Silicon dioxide III–182b
Silicone II–9a, 12b; III–156a; V–328a
Silicon oxide masking technique IV–352a–b
Silicosis IV–294b
Silk brocades II–371a
SILK CULTURE AND MANUFACTURE VI–286b; VII–44a, 87a,b
bounties IV–308a,b
China trade II–28b; III–181a
colonial bounties V–16b
colonial trade II–119b, 453a, 453a
commodity exchange II–469b
Georgia III–168a
tariff VI–465b
Silk stockings II–372a
SILL, FORT (Okla.) **VI–287a**; I–190b; II–91a; V–149a; VII–252b
Belknap scandal I–286a
Camp Doniphan I–434b
Infantry School I–289a
Sill, Joshua W. (off.) VI–287a
Sillery (Can.) V–156b
SILLIAC (computer) II–156a
Silliman, Benjamin, Jr. (chem.) I–283b; II–11a; III–408b; V–269a, 272a; VI–235b

SILLIMAN, BENJAMIN, JR. (cont.)
273b
Silliman, Benjamin, Sr. (chem.) I–98a; II–11a; III–408b; IV–44a, 348b; VI–232a
Silliman, Gold S. (off.) II–286a; VI–139a
Silo II–281a, 430b
Silo missile site IV–364a
Silver
banking crisis of 1933 V–44a
bills of exchange II–468a
Chicago Board of Trade V–320b
coinage I–301b–02b, 373a; II–94b, 95a, 95a–96a, 151a, 264a; IV–359b–60a
Crime of 1873 III–188b
demonetization II–264a
price–fixing V–401b
prices V–404a
Silver, free. *See* Free Silver
SILVER, PEWTER, AND OTHER METALWORK VI–289a; VII–82b
collecting II–98b–100b, 98b–99a
Oneida Colony V–155b
Rhode Island VI–133a
sculpture VI–244a
tinware VII–62b–63a
traveling salesmen VII–105b
Silver as money. *See* Bimetallism; Bland–Allison Act; Free Silver; Money; Pittman Act; Sherman Silver Purchase Act; Silver Legislation; Trade Dollar
Silver Bridge II–350b–51a
Silver certificates III–110b; IV–395a,b
Silver Cliff (Colo.) VI–292b
Silver Creek (Mont.) III–270a
SILVER DEMOCRATS VI–287b
campaign of 1896 I–425a
Nevada V–39b
Silver dollar I–301a,b; II–28b, 95a, 96a, 264a, 384b; III–110a,b, 192b; IV–392b–93a, 394a, 395a,b; VI–288b, 366a
SILVER GRAYS VI–288a; II–184b
Silver iodide II–76b; VI–42a
Silver Lake Mine VI–213b
SILVER LEAGUE VI–288a
SILVER LEGISLATION VI–288a; II–96a; III–110b–11a, 193a, 251b
Bland–Allison Act I–318b; IV–154a–b
Cleveland Democrats II–75a
Compromise of 1890 II–151a
Crime of 1873 VII–92b
Sherman Purchase Act VI–277a
Sherman Silver Purchase Act IV–154a–b
Thomas Amendment VII–54b
Silver party V–39b
Silver Plume (Colo.) II–347b
SILVER PROSPECTING AND MINING VI–292a; II–223a; IV–177b
Arizona I–172a
assaying I–203b–04a
Bonanza Kings I–329a, 329a
boomtowns I–336a,b
California I–405b–06a
Coeur d'Alene II–93b; IV–66a
Colorado II–128a
Comstock Lode I–406a; II–156b, 477b; III–191b
copper mining II–224a
disasters II–350b
Emigrant Spring (Calif.) II–297b
free silver III–110a
great fortunes III–80a
Helena mining camp III–270a
Idaho III–328a
Leadville district IV–123b
legislation VI–288a,b
Montana I–116a; IV–403a
Nevada I–301b; V–39b
Rocky Mountains IV–122b
San Juan Country VI–213b
Santa Fe IV–377a; VI–215a,b
smelters VI–316b
Sutro tunnel VI–453a
Tombstone II–477b; VII–70b
U.S. Geological Survey III–163a
westward movement VII–284b
Silver Purchase Act (1934) II–96a; VI–288b–89a
Silver Reef (Utah) VI–292b
SILVER REPUBLICAN PARTY VI–292b; I–425a
Silver Spring (Md.) IV–3b
Silver standard III–193b
Silver Star II–311a
Silver State VI–394 (table)
Silverton (Colo.) VI–213b
Simcoe (schooner) III–218a
Simcoe, John Graves (off.) I–194a; III–308a; IV–329a; VI–130a
Simcoe, Lake V–156b
Simitère, Pierre Eugène du II–101a, 107b
Simkhovitch, Mary Kingsbury VI–330b
Simmons, Edward Emerson (paint.) V–191a
Simmons, ("Col.") William J. IV–58a
Simmons College IV–267b; VI–331a
Simms, William Gilmore (au.) IV–162b
Simon, Leslie (off.) II–155a
Simon, Neil (playwright) VII–50b
Simon, Norton II–106b
Simon, Trent, Levy and Franks I–278a
Simon and Schuster I–334b
Simonds, Frank H. (jour.) V–74a
Simone, Nina (sing.) IV–442b
Simonetti, Anthony G. (law.) I–220b
Simons, Menno. *See* Menno Simons
Simonson, Lee (theat. designer) VII–49b
Simonton, John W. IV–45a
Simplex Electric Heating Company II–419b
Simpson, A. B. (cler.) II–34b
Simpson, George (fur trader) VII–165b
Simpson, George B. (inv.) II–417b
Simpson, Jeremiah (pol.) I–404a
Simpson, J. H. (off.) III–420b
Simpson, Kirke L. (jour.) I–207b
Simpson, "Sockless Jerry" (pol.) I–39a
Simpson, Thomas (nav. off.) VI–129a
Sims, J. Marion (physic.) IV–285b, 297b
Sims, William S. (nav. off.) I–14a; V–247b; VI–363a; VII–325b, 328b
Sims Bill. *See* Plumb Plan
Simsbury (Conn.) II–223a
Simson, Gary J. (law.) VI–403a
Sinai Peninsula III–481b; VI–430a
Sinaloa (Mex.) IV–452b
Sinatra, Frank (sing.) IV–442a
Sinclair, Harold (au.) V–62b
Sinclair, Harry F. (bus.) VII–16b
Sinclair, Upton (au., pol.) I–407b; II–454a; III–53a; IV–281a, 424b; V–466a; VI–183a, 269a, 414b
Sinclair Oil Corporation IV–322b
Siney, John (labor leader) II–86b; IV–62b
Singapore
World War II VII–336b
Singer, I. M., and Company VI–265a
Singer, Isaac M. (inv.) II–81b; VI–265a
Singer Sewing Machine Company III–422b
Singer Tower (N.Y.C.) VI–299a
SINGING SCHOOLS VI–293a; IV–437b
Single–leaf pinon VI–394 (table)
Single–member district. *See* Congressional District
SINGLE TAX VI–293a; II–492b; IV–101a
Populist party V–365b
Progress and Poverty V–427a
radicals VI–13b
Single Tax League IV–84b
Singleton, Esther (ed., music crit.) II–100a
Singleton, James Washington (pol.) VI–293b
SINGLETON PEACE PLAN VI–293b
Sing Sing Prison (N.Y.) VI–164b
SINKING FUND, NATIONAL VI–294a; III–245a, 246a
SINO–JAPANESE WAR (1894–95) **VI–294b**; II–26a; III–68b, 352b
Sino–Japanese War, Second (1937–45)
U.S. recognition V–38b
Sinoloa (Mex.) II–184a
Sino–Soviet dispute I–180b; II–489b
Sinusitis II–374a
Siouan (lang.) II–282b; III–364a, 365a,b, 367a, 476a; IV–235b; VII–305b
Assiniboine I–206a
Indian population III–396b
Mandan and Hidatsa I–171b
Omaha V–155a
Osage V–173b
Siouan–Yuchi (lang.) II–282b; III–364a, 365b
Sioux (Indians) II–131b, 184a, 336b, 432a–b; III–220b, 396a,b; IV–131b; V–437b
Battle of Little Bighorn IV–167b
Battle of Wounded Knee VII–344a
capture of Hennepin III–272a,b
Carver claim I–464b
Catlin's paintings I–471a
Chippewa IV–31b, 346b
claims commission VI–295a
Dakota II–282b
Dull Knife campaign II–379b
Duluth's explorations II–380a
Faribault claim II–490a
Fisk expedition III–32a
Five Villages III–34a
Fort Francis E. Warren VII–237b
Fort Laramie IV–108a
Fort Laramie treaties III–383b; IV–108b–09a
Fort Sedgwick VI–254b
French posts I–281b, 498b, 499a
French territory VI–187b
French trade III–89a
Ghost Dance III–177b; IV–316a
Grattan incident III–213b
Harney expedition III–256a
Hazelwood Republic III–267a
Iowa III–468a
Jesuit missions III–499b
land cessions III–379b
land scrip IV–97b

Leavenworth expedition IV–130a
Maiden's Rock legend IV–224b
Messiah War I–243a
Minnesota lands VI–139a
Minnesota uprising V–81a
Montana IV–403a
Mound Builders IV–421a
Nebraska V–31a
neutral ground V–33b
peace commissions III–378a
Platte Bridge fight V–330a
Red Cloud agency VI–157b
revolutionary war VI–195a
Rosebud Reservation VI–164b
scouts VI–242a
South Dakota VI–350a
Spirit Lake massacre VI–374a
Sully's expedition IV–45b
trading posts IV–380b
Treaty of Prairie du Chien III–383b; V–388b
Treaty of Traverse des Sioux III–383b
War of 1812 VII–234b–35a
wild rice VII–298b
Wisconsin VII–307b
Wyoming VII–345b
See also Dakota
SIOUX-CHIPPEWA WAR VI–294b; IV–31b, 355a
Sioux City (Iowa) II–284a; IV–280b; V–179a; VI–147a
SIOUX CLAIMS COMMISSION VI–295a
SIOUX COUNCIL (1889) **VI–295a**; VI–296a
Sioux Falls (S.Dak.) II–284a,b; V–117a
Sioux Half-Breed scrip IV–98a
Sioux State VI–395 (table)
SIOUX TREATIES VI–295b; IV–355b, 356a
Fort Laramie IV–108b–09a
Mendota Treaty VII–106a
Traverse des Sioux Treaty VII–106a
SIOUX UPRISING IN MINNESOTA (1862) **VI–296a**; III–127a; IV–356b; VI–150b, 297a; VII–106a, 305b–06a
Battle of Wood Lake VII–319b
claims commission VI–295a
Fort Ridgely VI–139a
New Ulm V–81a
SIOUX WARS VI–296b; VI–208a; VII–239b
Beecher Island I–283b
Black Hills War I–313a; IV–167b
Bozeman Trail I–358a; IV–108b
Fetterman massacre III–17b
Fort C.F. Smith VI–317b
Fort Phil Kearny IV–33b–34a
Fort Sully VI–438b
peace commissions III–378a
Scouts VI–242a
Wagon Box fight VII–215b
Wounded Knee I–107a, 219a
Sipuel v. *University of Oklahoma* (1948) I–372b; II–56b, 401b
Si quaeris peninsulam amoenam circumspice (motto) VI–394 (table)
Sir Adam Beck Generating Stations V–91b
Sir Christopher Wren Building (Williamsburg) VII–300b
Sirhan, Sirhan (assassin) I–202b; IV–38a
Sirica, John (jur.) II–474a; III–345a; VII–118b, 255a
Sirius (steamship) IV–310a
Sir William Johnson Papers VI–411b
Siskiyou Pass V–225a
Sisseton (Indians) II–283a; III–365a, 383b
Sister Carrie IV–163b
Sisters of Charity of Saint Joseph I–467a
Sisters of the Blessed Sacrament I–468a
Sit-down strike VI–418b, 419b
Sitgreaves, Lorenzo (off.) VI–90b
Sit-ins I–31a; II–50b, 55a, 58a, 179b; V–181b–82a
Sitka (Alaska) I–75a, 76a, 80a; IV–54a
Sitka Sound VI–247b
Sitka spruce V–446a; VI–393 (table)
Sitting Bull (Indian) II–283a; III–386b, 391b; VI–242a, 350a; VII–227b, 344a
Black Hills War I–313a
Black Infantry I–314a
Messiah War IV–316a
Sioux Council VI–295b
Sioux wars VI–297a
wild west show VII–298b
"Siwash Illahie" V–165a
Six-Day War (1967) III–482a; V–22b; VI–281a
Six-mile limit III–107a
Six Nations III–378b
Albany Congress I–82a
Easton council III–58b
Fort Harmar Treaty III–255a
French and Indian War III–115a
Handsome Lake Cult III–249b
Indiana Company I–278a; III–370b
Lancaster Treaty IV–89b
Susquehanna Company VI–451b
Treaty of Fort Stanwix III–208b–09a
Tuscarora VII–130b
Wyoming Valley VII–347a
See also Iroquois
Sixpence (coin) II–94b
Six-shooter. *See* Colt Six-Shooter
SIXTEENTH AMENDMENT VI–297b; I–94b; II–206a; III–351a; V–354b; VII–6a,b, 12a,b
Sixteenth Infantry Division IV–84a
Sixteen-to-one *See* Bimetallism
Sixth Amendment I–299a,b; III–344a; IV–21a
Sixth Brigade (marines) IV–252b
Sixth (VI) Corps *See* entries under Army, United States
Sixth Fleet V–22b, 25a
Sixth Infantry Division. *See* entries under Army, United States
Sixth International Conference of American States (1928) V–106a
Sixth Marine Regiment IV–252b
Six Tribes III–475a
Sixty-ninth Infantry Division II–407b
Skagit (Indians) III–362a
Skagway (Alaska) IV–52a
Skate (submarine) VI–423a
Skating
Olympic Games V–154a,b
Skelton, Samuel (cler.) VI–199a
Skenesboro engagement (1777) I–385a; IV–86b
Sketch Book of Geoffrey Crayon, Gent. IV–161b; VI–145a, 312b
Sketches and Burlesques. See Phoenixiana
Sketches of the Rise, Progress, and Decline of Secession. See Parson Brownlow's Book
Skidi (Indians) I–171b; IV–235b; V–230b
Skidmore, Owings and Merrill I–165b; VI–299a
Skidmore, Thomas (labor leader) IV–61b
Skiff IV–374a
Skiff, Frederick J. v. (geol.) III–19b
SKIING VI–297b
Olympic Games V–154a,b
resorts VI–101a–b
Sun Valley III–328b
Vermont VII–172b
Skillins family VI–242b
"Skim" cheese II–281a
Skim milk II–280b
Skin dressing III–373b
Skinner, B. F. (psych.) II–142b; IV–307a
Skinner, Cortland (off.) II–249b
Skinner, Halcyon (inv.) I–460b
Skinner, John S. (agric., ed.) III–230b
Skinner, R. C. (dent.) II–329b
Skinner and Chapman II–421a
Skinners. *See* Cowboys and Skinners
Skin printing II–283a
Skins
clothing II–487a
Indian trade II–480a
Skipjack class (submarine) VI–423b
"Skippy" (radio program) I–488a
Skowhegan (Maine) IV–227a
"Skraelings" II–461b
Skunk III–133a–b, 150a
Skybolt (delivery system) I–124b
Sky bus II–428b
Skyhawk (attack plane) I–56b
Skyjacking. *See* Hijacking, Aerial
Skykomish (Wash.) IV–177a
Skylab I–63b, 210b; IV–460b; V–132a
Sky marshals II–277b; III–277a
Skymaster (transport plane) I–52a
Skyraider (fighter plane) I–54a, 56b
SKYSCRAPERS VI–298b; I–164b, 165b
Chicago II–17b–18a
construction I–378b
elevators II–414b
heating III–269a
Skyscrapers (ballet) IV–438b
Sky warrior (attack plane) I–50b
Slacks II–372b
Slade, Joseph A. (outlaw) V–333a
Slade, William (pol.) VI–299b
SLADE'S GIRLS VI–299b
Slag III–472a,b
Slalom VI–298a
Slander V–465a
See also Libel
SLANG, AMERICAN VI–299b; II–340b
SLANG, MILITARY VI–300b
GI III–178b
Slate (min.) I–377b; VII–172b
Slate projectile points II–386a
Slater, John (phys.) V–304a
Slater, John F. (philan.) II–401b
Slater, John F., Fund III–82b; V–231b
Slater, Samuel (ind.) I–175a; III–63a; IV–272b; V–230b; VI–133a; VII–44b
Slater Museum (Pawtucket, R.I.) I–175b
Slaughter, Alanson (dairyman) II–280b
SLAUGHTERHOUSE CASES (1873) **VI–302b**; II–377b–78a; III–86b; V–420b, 421a; VI–58a

Slaughterhouses IV–170a, 280a,b
"Slaughter on Tenth Avenue" (dance) II–290a
Slave (Indians) I–441a; III–252b, 360b
Slave clocks II–79b
Slave Coast VI–309b
Slave codes. *See* Black Codes
SLAVE INSURRECTIONS VI–303a; I–28a; III–436b–37a; VI–307a, 347b; VII–191a
Amistad Case I–114b
Gabriel's Insurrection III–145a
Nat Turner's rebellion V–4b
slave codes VI–305a
Vesey Rebellion VII–174a
Slave representation. *See* Compromises of the U.S. Constitution
SLAVERY VI–304b; I–26b–28b; VI–174b
abolishment I–94b; V–260b; VII–54a
Afro-American music IV–442b–43a
agrarianism I–33a
agriculture I–36b
Alabama I–71a
Alabama Platform I–73b
antebellum South VI–340b, 341b, 342a,b, 352a
d'Arges Colony I–169b
Arkansas I–173a
assassination attempts I–203a
Baptist church split I 265a
Barbados I–266a
Barnburners I–268a
benefit of clergy I–289a
Bible I–23b
Black Belt I–308b
Border Slave State Convention I–341b
border states IV–220a
Brooks–Sumner affair I–371a
Calhoun, John C. I–404a–b
California I–405b; II–150b
campaign of 1840 I–420a
campaign of 1844 I–420a–b
campaign of 1848 I–420b; V–329a
campaign of 1852 I–420b
campaign of 1856 I–421a; VI–42b
campaign of 1860 I–421a–b
Carolinas I–457b
Catholics I–467b
Charleston (S.C.) I–496b, 497a
Civil War I–34a; II–64a, 64a, 66b, 69a,b, 159b, 161b, 162b, 165a; III–349b
Clayton Compromise II–73a
Code Noir II–91b
colonial labor force IV–60a, 79a
colonial punishments V–465a
colonial staples VI–386b
colonies II–125a, 188b
colonization I–100b–01b; II–127a; IV–141b
compensated emancipation II–433b
compromise movement of 1860 II–149b
Compromise of 1850 II–139a, 149b
Confiscation Acts II–168a
Congregational Churches II–170a
Connecticut II–180a
Connecticut Compromise II–151b, 183a
Conscience Whigs II–184b
contraband II–212a
Corwin amendment I–95b
cotton I–34a, 38a; II–184b, 238a
Cotton Kingdom II–241a
Creole Case II–257b
Crittenden Compromise II–264b
Crittenden Resolution II–265a
Cuba II–268a; V–174b
curfew II–274b
DeBow's *Review* II–298b
Declaration of Independence II–304b–05a
Delaware II–320b
doughfaces II–366a
Douglas, Stephen A. I–145a
Dred Scott case II–370a, 377b
emancipation I–23b; II–434a
Emancipation Proclamation II–168b, 434b
Fire-eaters III–25a
Florida III–39a
folklore III–48b
free blacks III–101b
Freedmen's Bureau III–103a
Freeport Doctrine III–109b
Free Soil party III–111b
fugitive slave laws III–130a; IV–8a
Gadsden Purchase III–145b
gag rule III–145b; V–265b
Georgia III–168a, 169b
Helper's *Impending Crisis* III–271a
Hermosa case III–273b–74a
home missionary societies IV–365b
"house divided" III–309a
Illinois III–329b
indentured servants III–353a
Indians III–401a; IV–47b
Indian slaveholders III–401a
indigo culture III–405b; VII–86a
insurrections VI–303a
integration III–437a
irrepressible conflict III–477a
Jacksonian Democracy III–487a
Jamestown III–489a
Jefferson's proposed states III–496b
Kansas I–213a, 283b, 341a, 342a, 376b; II–439a, 450a–b; IV–25b–26a, 28a, 31a; V–51a–b; VII–72b–73a, 187b, 345b
Kansas Free-State party IV–28a
Kansas–Nebraska Act IV–28b
Kentucky IV–40b–41a
kidnapping of free blacks IV–45a
Know-Nothing party I–110a
labor force I–24b, 40b; II–495a
land grant policy I–42b
Lecompton Constitution IV–130b
Lincoln–Douglas debates IV–155b
Lovejoy riots IV–199a; V–70b
manumission IV–246a
Maryland IV–260b, 261a
Mason–Dixon Line IV–263a
Matilda Lawrence case IV–276a
Methodist church IV–318b
miscegenation IV–362b
Mississippi IV–368a,b
Missouri IV–377a,b; VI–194a,b
Missouri Compromise IV–379a
morality of IV–408b
narratives IV–166a
Nashoba settlement IV–452b
Nashville Convention IV–453b
natural rights doctrine V–7b
Nebraska V–31a,b
New Orleans V–62b
New York Colony III–253a
North America I–22b
North Carolina V–116a
Northwest Territory V–163a; VII–189a
Ohio Valley V–146a
Old Northwest V–122b
Omnibus Bill V–155a
overseer V–178b
"peculiar institution" V–241b
personal liberty laws V–263b
plantation system IV–102b; V–324b
political parties V–223b
political theories V–351b, 352b
political writings V–353a–b
poll tax VII–3a
polygamy V–355b
popular sovereignty V–360a
Presbyterianism V–392a
prizefighting V–422b
Quakers III–123b
race relations VI–6a,b
Radical Republicans VI–10b
Reconstruction VI–55b, 56a,b
religious education II–403a–b
Republican party II–327a; VI–92b
revolutionary war troops I–366b; VI–118a
rice growing VI–136a
runaways I–28a
rural life VI–174b
Savannah VI–220b
secessionist movement VI–250b
secret societies I–325b
sectionalism VI–254a
segregation VI–255b
Shenandoah Valley VI–275b
slave states VI–309a
slave trade VI–309a
slavocracy VI–312a
"sold down the river" VI–335b
Sons of the South VI–339b
South Carolina VI–347a,b
southern congressmen I–10b–11a
Southern Literary Messenger VI–353a
southern nonslaveholders V–108a
southern rights movement VI–354a
Southwest VI–355b
state bills of rights I–300b
state-making process VI–401a
states' rights VI–404b
statistics VII–206a
Tallmadge Amendment VI–458b
taxation II–164b; VII–4b–5a, 12b
territories I–10b–11a
Texas VII–37a–b, 39a, 39b
textile industry VII–45b
Thirteenth Amendment II–53b, 205a
tidewater region II–485a
tobacco farming I–36b–37a
Uncle Tom's Cabin VII–137b
Underground Railroad VII–138a
Union Army I–184b
Union Democrats VII–146a
Vermont VII–171b
Virginia II–495a; VII–192b, 193a–b, 194a,b
Virginia Resolutions VII–202b
Wakarusa War VII–218b
Washington, D.C. VII–246a
Webster–Hayne debate VII–265b
West Indies I–22b
Whig party II–327a;

V–86b; VII–288b
Wilmot Proviso
VII–303b, 303b
women VII–313a
See also Afro-American Culture; Antislavery
Slavery, church schisms over. *See* Church Schisms Over Slavery
Slavery, Indian. *See* Indians as Slaveholders
Slavery and an Industrial System VI–341b
Slaves, fugitive
Ableman v. *Booth* I–2a
Burns case I–387a
Champaign County cases I–491b
Christian Affair II–34b
Slave Ship IV–167b
SLAVE SHIPS VI–308b; VI–310b, 311a
Baltimore clipper I–251a
Creole II–257b
Echo II–390a, 390a
Encomium II–443b
middle passage IV–335a
Wanderer VII–223b
SLAVE STATES VI–309a; IV–29b; VI–308a
border states I–341b
Crittenden Compromise II–265a
Cuba II–268a
Florida III–39a
free blacks III–102a
freedmen II–370b
Kansas IV–25b–26a
Louisiana IV–194a
Nashville Convention IV–453b
slavocracy VI–312a
Sons of the South VI–339b
three-fifths compromise III–5a
Union sentiment VI–354a
SLAVE TRADE VI–309a; I–21a, 135a; II–151b–52a; VI–304b, 305a,b; VII–86a
abolished I–93b
Amistad case I–114b
antebellum South VI–352b
Antelope Case I–126b
auctions I–16b, 221b
Catholics I–467b
Civil War I–121b
Confederate Constitution II–159b
Declaration of Independence II–305a
District of Columbia II–139a, 150a
Encomium case II–443b
England I–26b–27a, 202a, 365b
Galveston pirates III–149a
great fortunes III–78b–79a
middle passage IV–335a
Narragansett planters IV–451b
opposition I–101a, 135a
Perth Amboy V–264a
revolution II–215b
Rhode Island VI–132a
Royal African Company I–22b
rum VI–170b
ships VI–308b
slavocracy VI–312a
smuggling VI–321b
sorghum I–486b
South Carolina VI–347b
Southern Literary Messenger VI–353a
Sugar Islands VI–437b
taxes I–451a; II–200a
Texas VII–37a
treaties VII–113a
Treaty of Ghent III–177a
Treaty of Utrecht VII–162b
triangular trade II–119a; IV–388a; VII–119a–b, 277b–78a
visit and search VII–205a
Webster-Ashburton Treaty VII–265a
yellow fever VII–355b
SLAVOCRACY VI–312a; III–102b
campaign of 1824 I–418b
Slavs III–342a, 370a
Sledges VII–168a
Sleds II–462a
Sleepers IV–391b
Sleeping Beauty (ballet) II–288b, 289b
Sleeping cars. *See* Pullmans
Sleep-ins II–58a
SLEEPY HOLLOW (N.Y.) **VI–312b**
Sleepy Hollow Restorations, Inc. (Tarrytown, N.Y.) III–137b
Sleighs VII–168a
Slemmer, Adam J. (off.) V–308a; VI–216a
Slepian, Joseph (eng.) V–290a
Slidell, John (dipl.) II–65b, 162a
Laird rams IV–85a
land speculation IV–99b
Trent affair VII–115b
See also Slidell's Mission to Mexico VI–312b
SLIDELL'S MISSION TO MEXICO (1845–46) **VI–312b**; IV–323a; VII–39a
SLIM BUTTES, BATTLE OF (1876) **VI–312b**; VI–297a
Slippers II–371b
Sloan, Alfred P. (ind.) I–229a; IV–273a
Sloan, John (paint.) II–104a; V–192a, 414a
Sloan-Kettering Institute IV–298b
Sloan mansion III–446a
Sloat, John D. (nav. off.) I–280b; IV–324a, 404b; V–19b; VI–414a
Slocum, Henry W. (off.) I–232b; VI–278a
Slocum, John (Indian) V–4a; VI–267b
Sloep Bay IV–451b
SLOGANS, CAMPAIGN VI–313a; I–416b
"Back to normal" V–110a
"Free soil, free speech, free man and Frémont" III–111b
Full Dinner Pail III–131b
"He kept us out of war" III–269b
"Rail Splitter" VI–40a
"Tippecanoe and Tyler Too" VII–63b
Sloo, A. G. III–145b
SLOOP VI–313b; VI–280b; VII–99b
navy II–313b
New Ironsides V–56a
racing VII–348b
warships VII–240a,b
Wasp VII–252b
Slop-milk systems II–280a
Slop shops II–81b
Slosson, Edwin E. (chem.) VI–230b
Sloth IV–231b; V–195a
Slot machines II–261b
Slough, John P. (off.) VI–144a
Slough Creek I–342a
Sloughter, Henry (col. gov.) IV–134a; V–84b
Sloup Bay IV–451b
Slovakia
immigration to U.S. III–339a,b, 340a
Slovenians III–339a
SLUMS VI–313b; III–310a; VII–50a
Baltimore I–250a–b
clearance II–47a, 49a, 481a, 502a; IV–429a
effect on morality IV–408b
federal aid VI–328b
industrial II–46a
Jewish communities IV–10a
New York City I–355a; V–83a
public health V–447a; VII–158a
Puerto Rico V–461b
social settlements VI–330a
tenements VII–23b
urban renewal VI–86a
Washington, D.C. VII–246a
Sly and the Family Stone (mus.) IV–441a
Small Arms Firing School I–289a
Small business
fair-trade laws II–484a
Small Business Administration I–9a; II–498b; VI–60a
Small claims I–152a
Small Defense Plants Administration II–498b
Smaller War Plants Corporation II–498b
Smallman, James (eng.) VI–409a
SMALLPOX VI–315a; II–454b; III–293b, 306b; IV–275a, 299a; VII–355b
Blackfoot V–310a
cities VII–158a
colonial period IV–295a; V–446b
Continental navy VI–128a
deaths IV–150a,b
Indians I–264b; II–52a; III–34a; IV–236a; V–173b
Jersey prison ship III–498b
record-keeping VII–205b
revolutionary war IV–413a
Rock Island prison camp V–414b
slave trade VI–310b
vaccine V–273b
Valley Forge VII–165a–b
Welcome VII–267a
Smallwood, William (off.) V–211b
Smart bomb IV–363b; V–26b
SMAS. *See* Standard Metropolitan Statistical Areas
Smeaton, John (civ. eng.) I–477a
SMELTERS VI–316b; II–128a, 332a; V–102b–04a
air pollution II–224a
colonial III–413b
iron III–12a
phosphate ore III–15b
Saugus furnace VI–218a
silver VI–292b
Spotswood's furnaces VI–376a
Tennessee VII–25b, 26a
Western Federation of Miners VII–272b
zinc VII–368b–69a
See also Iron and Steel Industry; Lead Industry
Smibert, John (art.) II–101a, 105a, 487b; V–185b, 186a–b; VI–132a
Smiles, Samuel (au.) I–494b
Smiley, Albert K. (educ.) IV–387b
Smiley, Jim (lit. char.) V–336a
Smith, George (cabinetmaker) III–135a
Smith, Adam (econ.) II–378a; III–246b; IV–85a, 140a, 308b; V–406a, 457b; VI–468b
Smith, Alfred E. (pol.) I–470a; VII–291a
campaign of 1920 I–427b
campaign of 1928 I–428a–b; V–3b; VI–313a
campaign of 1936 V–47b
New York governorship V–87b
Port Authority of New York and New Jersey V–368a
Tammany Hall VI–460a
Smith, Andrew Jackson (off.) VI–63a; VII–128b
Smith, Bessie (sing.) IV–440a, 443b
Smith, Charles F. (off.) VI–278b, 317b
Smith, Charles Shaler (eng.) I–364a
Smith, David (sculp.) VI–244a

Smith, Edwin Burritt I–131b
Smith, Ellison DuRant ("Cotton Ed") (pol.) V–48b
Smith, Erwin F. (bact.) I–46a, 241b
Smith, F. Hopkinson (au.) IV–162b
SMITH, FORT (Ark.) **VI–317a**; I–453a; VII–289a
exploration IV–249a
Indian council VI–317a
railroad survey VI–39a
Southern Overland Mail VI–353b
stagelines VI–379a
western caravans I–452a
westward movement IV–20b
SMITH, FORT, COUNCIL OF (1865) **VI–317a**
SMITH, FORT C. F. (Mont.) **VI–317b**; I–358a
Smith, Francis M. ("Borax") (fin.) I–340b
Smith, Frederick (comp.) V–152a
Smith, George (banker) I–263b
Smith, George T. (inv.) III–43b
Smith, George Washington (dancer) II–287a
Smith, Gerald L. K. (cler.) V–47b; VI–269a
Smith, Gerrit (philan.) IV–99a
antislavery I–136a, 138a
campaign of 1848 I–420b
Emigrant Aid II–439a
Liberty party IV–143b
Smith, Gilbert (bot.) I–349b
Smith, G. W. (off.) II–482b
Smith, Hamilton L. VII–62b
Smith, Henry (gov.) IV–274a
Smith, Henry Nash (hist.) I–112a,b
Smith, Hobart M. (herpetol.) VI–91a
Smith, Holland M. (off.) III–180a, 485a; VI–198a
Smith, Hugh M. (nat.) III–28a
Smith, Hyrum (Mormon) IV–412a; VI–87a
Smith, Jacob H. (off.) I–219a; V–281b
Smith, James (frontiersman) I–282b, 309a
Smith, James (jur.) VI–462a
Smith, James (law.) II–308a
Smith, James (physic.) VI–316a
Smith, James (physic.) II–10a
Smith, Jedediah S. (fur trader) II–477b; III–143a; IV–25b; VI–318a; VII–74b, 103b, 271b
Ashley expeditions I–201a
Cajon Pass I–403b
California I–280a
caravan west I–452b
Great Valley III–223b
Paiute V–194b
Rocky Mountain Fur Company VI–160a
Santa Fe Trail VII–256a
Spanish Trail VI–368a
Smith, Jerome v. C. (nat.) III–27a
Smith, John (col.) III–26b, 128b, 488b–89a; VII–65b, 70a
Boston I–343b
Cape Ann I–446b
Cape Cod I–447a
History of Virginia III–280a
Isles of Shoals III–479b
literary narratives IV–161a
mapping IV–247b; VII–73b
Massachusetts exploration IV–264b
New England fisheries II–92b; IV–396a
New Hampshire V–53b
Pemaquid Point V–243b
Potomac River V–378a
Separate Puritan Congregation I–264b
Virginia colony I–449a
Smith, James (frontiersman) VI–285a
Smith, John Broadfoot III–135b
Smith, John Stafford (comp.) VI–387b
Smith, Joseph (Mormon) II–496a; IV–116b–17a, 377b; VI–77b, 87a, 416b
Book of Mormon IV–410b
Mormon War IV–412a
Smith, Joseph III (Mormon) VI–87a
Smith, Joshua Hett I–118a
Smith, Josiah (mer.) I–497a
Smith, Julian C. (off.) VI–462a
Smith, Landgrave Thomas I–447b
Smith, Lillian (au.) I–479a; IV–164b
Smith, Margaret Chase (pol.) VII–318a
Smith, Maria Catherine V–185a
Smith, Melancton (law., mer.) I–83a; V–199a
Smith, Nathan (physic.) II–293a
Smith, Peter (landowner) IV–99a; V–413a
Smith, Philip W. (zool.) VI–91b
Smith, Ralph C. (off.) VI–198b
Smith, Robert (states.) II–460b
Smith, Robert Pearsall (mapmaker) I–462b
Smith, Samuel F. (au.) IV–446a
Smith, Samuel Harrison (pub.) IV–465b
Smith, Samuel Stanhope (cler.) I–128a
Smith, Solomon (comedian) I–268a; VI–283a; VII–47a
Smith, Sooy (off.) IV–313b
Smith, Theobald (path.) I–46a, 241b; IV–298a; VII–177a
Smith, Thomas (col. adm.) VII–200a
Smith, Thomas (paint.) V–185a
Smith, Thomas A. (off.) II–253b; VI–317a
Smith, "Uncle Billy" V–269a
Smith, William (cler.) II–10a
Smith, William (inv.) III–442a
Smith, William (jur., hist.) III–280b
Smith, William Farrar (off., eng.) II–373a
Smith, William S. (off., dipl.) IV–361b
Smith, Willoughby (eng.) VII–21a
Smith, Winthrop B. (pub.) IV–213a
SMITH ACT (1940) **VI–317b**; II–146a, 445a, 446a; VI–255b; VII–310b
Smith College I–272a; IV–267b
Smith–Connally War Labor Disputes Act (1943) IV–73b
Smith County (Tex.) II–389a
SMITH EXPLORATIONS VI–318a
Smithfield County (Va.) III–53b
Smithfield ham III–53b; VII–196b
SMITH–HUGHES ACT (1917) **V–318a**; I–47a; II–400b
Smith Island I–447b
Smithland (Ky.) II–252a
SMITH–LEVER ACT (1914) **VI–318a**; I–42a, 47a; II–494b; III–84b
Smith–Mundt Act (1948) II–401a; V–432b
Smith–Premier typewriter VII–136b
Smith's Garrison House (R.I.) III–223a
Smithson, James (chem., min.) III–82b; IV–464b, 468b; V–280b; VI–318b
Smithsonian (mag.) VI–320a
Smithsonian Accord (1971) II–339b; VII–91b
Smithsonian Associates VI–320a
Smithsonian Astrophysical Observatory I–411b; VI–319b
SMITHSONIAN INSTITUTION VI–318b; I–111a; II–498b; III–27a–b, 82b; IV–436b, 464b, 465a; V–196a; VI–243a; VII–246b
American Association for the Advancement of Science I–98b
architecture I–163b
Catlin's paintings I–471a
ethnology II–464b
geophysics III–167a
library IV–146b
mammalogy IV–232b
meteorology II–75b; IV–317a–b
National Museum IV–468b
Philadelphia III–234a
publishing VI–236a
research V–294b
"Star-Spangled Banner" VI–388a
Walcott, Charles D. IV–106a
Wright Brothers plane I–233a
Smithsonian Press VI–320a
Smithsonian Tropical Research Institute VI–319b
Smith Sound III–358a; V–336b
Smith v. *Allwright* (1944) II–56b; III–20b, 93a; V–407b; VI–432b, 435a
Smith v. *Maryland* (1855) I–351b
Smog I–408a–b; VII–158b
Smohalla (Indian) V–4a, 89b
Smoked food I–444b; II–219a; III–54b,55a; IV–280b–81a
Smokehouses IV–280b
Smoking (tobacco) I–20a
See also Pipe, Indian
Smoky Hill River IV–25a; V–311b; VI–320a; VII–221a
SMOKY HILL TRAIL VI–320a; I–398b
Smoky Hill Valley III–119b
Smollett, Tobias (au.) VI–301b
Smoot–Hawley Tariff (1930) I–479a; VI–464b, 467b–68a, 472a; VII–88a, 109a
Smooth–bore guns II–313b
"Smothers Brothers" (television show) I–481a
Smuggler–Union Mine (Colo.) III–192a; VI–213b
Smuggling
alcoholic beverages I–339a
Amelia Island I–93b
Avalon Bay I–466b
Customs Service II–276a,b
I'm Alone Case III–332a
Louisiana I–265b
narcotics II–374b; IV–450b
Prohibition II–277b; VI–170a
territorial waters VII–33a
SMUGGLING, COLONIAL VI–320b; II–92b, 275b; V–320a; VI–108b; VII–348b
molasses IV–388a; VI–171a, 435b
Narragansett Bay III–153b
tea VI–113b; VII–17a
SMUGGLING OF SLAVES VI–321b
Smut (disease) V–130a
Smuttynose Island III–479b
Smyrna (Turk.) V–22b
Smyth, Alexander (off.) VII–234a
Smyth, Newman (cler., theol.) VI–82a,b
Smyth, William Henry (inv., soc. ref.) VII–17b

Smyth v. *Ames* (1898)
V–458a
SNAGBOATS VI–322a
Snake Dance III–301a
Snake fence VI–19a
Snake Indians III–227a
horse III–303a
Jesuit missions III–500a
SNAKE RIVER VI–322b
Bannock I–264a
caravans I–453a
exploration III–114b
Fort Hall III–243b
fur trade I–209a, 327b; VI–160a; VII–103b
Henrys Fork III–273a
Ice Harbor Dam III–323a
Lewis and Clark Expedition IV–136b
Oregon Trail V–168b, 169a; VI–153b
Palisades Dam III–323b
Smith explorations VI–318a
Yakima Wars VII–350b
Snakes VI–47b
folklore III–48b
Snaketown (Ariz.) III–289a
SNAP CONVENTION (1892) **VI–322b**
Snark intercontinental cruise missiles I–62a
SNCC. *See* Student Nonviolent Coordinating Committee
Snead, Sam (golfer) III–198a
SNELLING, FORT (Minn.) **VI–322b**; I–193a; II–284a, 490a; III–313b, 468a; IV–355b–56a; VII–133b
Leech Lake uprising IV–132a
Long's explorations IV–187a; V–244a
Red River cart traffic VI–63b
Sioux–Chippewa War VI–294b–95a
Sioux treaties VI–295b
Sioux uprisng VI–296b
steamboats VII–196b
supply V–375b
Snelling, Josiah (off.) VI–322b
Snipers VI–270a
Snoopy (comic character) V–72b
"Snoopy's Nose" (Viet.) VI–301a
Snoqualmie Pass VI–413a
Snoquamish (Indians) V–97b
Snorkel VI–423a
Snorkel truck III–25b
Snow, Edgar (jour.) IV–164b
Snow, Elisha (shipmaster) VII–352a
Snow–Bound (poem) IV–162a
Snow class (slave ship) VI–308b
Snowden, Thomas (off.) II–361b
Snow Hill (N.C.) VII–130b
Snow house I–441b
Snowmobile II–462a
SNOWSHOES VI–323a; III–381a; VI–297b
Snowshoes, Battle of (1758) VI–162b
Snowstorms. *See* Blizzards
Snow Telescope III–242a
Snuff VII–4b, 12b, 67a,b
Snug Harbor. *See* Sailors' Snug Harbor
Snyder, Gary (poet) IV–165b
Snyder, John (nat.) III–28a
SOAP AND DETERGENT INDUSTRY VI–323a; II–6b, 9a; III–410a
colonial II–5a; III–413b
hexachlorophene V–468a
log ash IV–204a
petroleum products V–267b
potash V–375b
salt VI–203a
Soap operas VI–323b
Soapstone carving III–374b
"Soapsuds Row" VI–300b
Soapweed IV–8a
Sobel, Morton VI–164b
Sob–sister stories V–71b–72a
Socage III–107b; V–433b
Soccer III–56b, 286b, 288a; V–154a
Social and Economic Statistics Administration II–135a
Social and Rehabilitation Service III–267b; VI–330a
Social Bands. *See* Sons of the South
Social Christianity III–112b
Social compact VI–391b
See also Compact Theory
Social contract theory IV–174a; V–350b, 351a
Social dancing II–290b
Social Darwinists III–68b
Social Democracy of America IV–66b; VI–324b, 326a
Social Democratic Federation VI–327a
SOCIAL DEMOCRATIC PARTY VI–324b; VI–326a,b
Social Democratic Workingmen's party of North America VI–325a
Social Democrats USA VI–327a
Social fascists II–144b
SOCIAL GOSPEL VI–324b; II–170a, 455b; V–280a; VI–78b, 82b, 83a
Methodism IV–318b
morality IV–408b
Socialism
morality IV–408b
New Harmony settlement V–55a
versus capitalism I–449a
Socialist First International (1864) VI–325a
SOCIALIST LABOR PARTY VI–325a; IV–81b; VI–324b, 326a,b; VII–52b
campaign of 1904 I–426a
campaign of 1912 IV–68a
campaign of 1932 I–428b
campaign of 1936 I–429a
labor unions I–104a
opposition to AFL IV–66a–b
radicals VI–13b
taxation VII–6a
trade unions IV–63b–64a
SOCIALIST MOVEMENT VI–325b; VI–324b, 325a–b, 326–27a
black power I–316b
class–consciousness IV–68a
Fourierism III–85a
government ownership III–203a
Industrial Workers of the World IV–67b
labor unions I–104a
May Day IV–278a
New York State I–107a–b
Oneida Colony V–155b
pamphleteering V–199a
political exiles V–342a
political parties VII–52b
radicals VI–13b
Socialist Labor party IV–81b
South Dakota VI–350a
students VII–365a
syndicalism VI–455b
theater VII–50a
woman's rights movement VII–313b
World War I V–74a
SOCIALIST PARTY OF AMERICA VI–326b; IV–66b, 81b; VI–324b, 325b, 326a; VII–52b, 365a
campaign of 1904 I–426a
campaign of 1912 I–427a
campaign of 1920 I–427b
campaign of 1924 I–428a
campaign of 1932 I–428b
campaign of 1936 I–429a; V–47b
Communist party II–143b, 144b
emblem II–437b
Farmer–Labor party II–492b
labor unions I–104a
mayorships VII–53a
Nonpartisan League V–106b
platforms V–329a–b
Populist party V–365b
pressure groups V–401a
Progressive party IV–84b
radicals VI–13b, 14a
records III–285a
Schenck v. *United States* VI–225a
taxation VII–6a
World War I II–445b; V–236a–b
Socialist Second International (1917) VI–326b
Socialist Trade and Labor Alliance IV–66b, 67b
Socialist Workers party VI–326a; VII–52b
"Socialized medicine" IV–289b
Social Justice (mag.) II–446a; IV–472b
Social Justice, National Union for. *See* National Union for Social Justice
Social Justice movement V–47b
SOCIAL LEGISLATION VI–327a; II–472b
Greenback party III–225a
laissez–faire doctrine IV–85b
organized labor IV–62a
Progressive movement V–427a, 428b
Tammany Hall VI–460a,b
workmen's compensation VII–322a
Social reform
big business II–189a
city planning II–46b
pacifism V–181b
Republican party II–189a
Social Science Council. *See* International Social Science Council
Social Science Prize (American Academy of Arts and Sciences) I–97b
Social Science Research Council IV–127a; V–348b; VI–238b
Social sciences II–222a, 471a; IV–408b, 462a; VI–177a
SOCIAL SECURITY VI–329a; I–391a, 495b; II–481a; III–3a; V–45b, 46a, 255b, 280b, 329b; VI–14a, 73b, 328a,b; VII–140a, 323a
adoption IV–80b
civil service II–60b
employment taxes VII–108a
farm operations I–43b
federal expenditures II–476a
Florida III–40a
judicial review IV–14a
laissez–faire doctrine IV–85b
Medicare IV–289b
occupational medicine IV–294a–b
old–age benefits V–150b
party machines IV–214b
pensioners abroad II–439b
railroad retirement acts VI–29b
revenue VI–105a
Social Security Act (1935) IV–71b
taxes VII–4b, 7b, 9a,b, 9b, 10a–b, 11a, 13a
Ways and Means Committee VII–263b
Social Security Act (1935) II–442a; III–9b; IV–71b, 80b, 276a; V–46a, 47a, 48a, 381a,b; VI–328a, 329a, 331a–b; VII–7b, 140a
industrial hygiene units IV–294a
medical research IV–287b
old–age benefits V–150b
public health VI–173b–74a
Social Security Act (1950) II–481a
Social Security Administration III–267b; VI–330a
Social Security Board VI–328a, 330a

SOCIAL SETTLEMENTS VI–330a; VI–314a, 331a; VII–365a
Chicago II–18a
Hull House V–280a
Social Gospel VI–325a
Social Sources of Denominationalism VI–83a
Social welfare
federal aid II–502a–b
financing II–317b
state government VI–398b
Truman's proposals II–481a
SOCIAL WORK VI–331a; I–9a, 495a–b; VI–327b
industrial relations III–406b–07a
juvenile courts IV–23a, 24a
mental hospitals IV–306a
missionary activity IV–365b
National Urban League V–1a
Russell Sage Foundation VI–177a
See also Philanthropy and Benevolence
Social Workers, National Association of VI–331a
Societé Anonyme: Museum of Modern Art II–104b
Societies, historical. *See* Historical Societies
Societies, literary. *See* Literary Societies
Societies, secret. *See* Secret Societies
Societies for Ethical Culture IV–409a
Society
colonial II–125a
Cotton Kingdom II–241a
family II–485b–87a
Four Hundred III–85a
middle class IV–334b
Society column IV–241a,b
Society for Clinical and Experimental Hypnosis IV–306b
Society for Propagating the Gospel Among the Indian and Others in North America III–385b
Society for Psychical Research V–213a
Society for the Preservation of New England Antiquities, Inc. (Boston) III–137b; IV–472a
Society for the Prevention of Crime II–263b
SOCIETY FOR THE PREVENTION OF CRUELTY TO ANIMALS VI–331b
Society for the Promotion of Christian Knowledge VI–75b
Society for the Promotion of Collegiate and Theological Education at the West (1843) II–114a
Society for the Promotion of Public Schools of Philadelphia II–396b
Society for the Propagation of the Faith I–467a, 469a
Society for the Propagation of the Gospel VI–75b
SOCIETY FOR THE PROPAGATION OF THE GOSPEL IN FOREIGN PARTS VI–331b; II–36a, 394b
Society for the Reformation of Morals IV–409a
Society for the Study of Amphibians and Reptiles VI–91b
Society for the Supression of Vice II–263b
Society Hill (Phila.) V–278a
Society Islands VI–142a
Society of Adventurers. *See* Virginia Company of London; Plymouth, Virginia Company of
Society of American Archivists I–169a–b
Society of American Artists in New York City V–191b
Society of American Foresters III–72b, 73b
Society of Arts of London V–376a
Society of Automotive Engineers II–448b
Society of Cincinnati. *See* Cincinnati, Society of
SOCIETY OF COLONIAL WARS VI–332a
Society of Constitutional Republicans VI–3b
Society of Eye Surgeons IV–289a
Society of Fellows (Harvard) III–260a–b
Society of Free-Enquirers III–112a
Society of Friends. *See* Friends, Society of; Quakers
Society of Jesus. *See* Jesuits
Society of Missionary Priests of Saint Paul the Apostle. *See* Paulists
Society of Professional Journalists: Sigma Delta Chi V–77b
Society of Saint Tammany VI–459a
Society of St. Andrews Golfers III–197b
Society of Surgeon Dentists of the City and State of New York II–329b, 330a
Society of the Sons of the Revolution. *See* Sons of the Revolution, Society of the
Socinians VII–68b
Socony Vacuum Oil Company v. *United States* (1940) VI–102b–03a
Socorro (N.Mex.) IV–34a
Sod I–160b, 213b
Sod, Fort (Kans.) I–213b
Soda II–5a, 6a–b, 7a–b; V–375b
SODA FOUNTAINS VI–332a; VI–333a
Soda Springs (Idaho) III–215a; VII–256a
Oregon Trail V–168b
Soda water VI–333a
Soddy, Frederick (chem.) II–278a; V–299b
Soderholtz, E. E. (au.) II–100a
SOD HOUSE VI–332b; I–166b, 192b; II–379a, 487a
Sodium II–7b, 421b, 422a
Sodium carbonate I–340a; VI–203a
Sodium chloride. *See* Salt
Sodium hydroxide II–422b; VI–203a
Sodium nitrate III–16b; V–97b, 98a
Sodium tetraborate I–340a
Sodium vapor lamp III–156a
Sodom, Fort (Kans.) I–213b
Sofas III–134b, 135a,b, 138a
SOFT DRINK INDUSTRY VI–333a; VI–332a
Soft goods II–332b
SOFT MONEY VI–333b; III–252a; V–404b
"Softs" (Barnburners) III–318a
Softwood VII–60b, 61a
Soho works (N.J.) VI–409a
SOIL VI–334a
conservation I–39b, 45a, 350a
exhaustion V–115b
fertilizers III–16a
geological surveys III–165a,b
improvement programs II–188a
Nebraska homestead movement IV–50a
New England V–50a
prairie V–387a
sharecropping IV–103a
southern plantation system V–325a,b
Soil Bank program I–43a
Soil Conservation and Domestic Allotment Act (1936) V–47a, 359a; VI–67b, 335b
Soil Conservation Service I–45b; II–188a; III–74a; VI–335b
Soil Erosion a National Menace VI–335b
Soil Erosion Service II–188a; VI–335b
Soissons (Fr.)
World War I I–70a; IV–252b, 404a; V–147a; VII–326b
Sokolsky, George E. (jour.) V–75a
Solar batteries I–287b
Solar cells I–276b
Solar compass. *Scc* Sun Compass
Solar eclipse expedition (1870) II–88a
Solar heat IV–317b
Solar observatories V–132a
Solar spectrum I–212b
"SOLD DOWN THE RIVER" VI–335b
Soldering I–340a
"Soldier president" IV–471b
Soldiers' and Airmens' Home (Washington, D.C.) VI–336b
Soldiers' and Sailors' Additional Homestead Act (1872) IV–97b, 98a
SOLDIERS AND SAILORS CONVENTIONS (1866) **VI–336a**
SOLDIERS' HOMES VI–336a; VII–174b
Soldier's Medal II–311b–12a
Soldier Spring VII–252b
Solicitor general IV–21b
SOLID SOUTH VI–337a; II–64b; V–67b; VI–93a
campaign of 1904 I–426a
campaign of 1956 I–430a
sectionalism VI–254a–b
voting behavior VII–210a
Solid-state amplifiers II–39a
Solid-state battery I–276b
Solid-state electronics I–287b
See also Physics, Solid-State
Soling boats VII–349b
Solitary confinement V–252b
Solomon, Isaac (chem.) III–55a
Solomon Fork VI–439b
Solomon Islands I–350a; II–33a, 387a–b, 443a; III–229b; VI–5a; VII–336b–37a
Solomon's Lodge (S.C.) III–109a
Solow, Robert M. (educ., econ.) VII–141b
Solus populi suprema lex esto (motto) VI–394 (table)
Solvay, Ernest (chem.) II–7a–b
Sombrero II–249a
Somers (brig) IV–322a
Somers (N.Y.) II–40b
Somers, George (navig.) VI–338a; VII–199b
Somers, Richard (nav. off.) III–464b
Somerset (Ohio) II–362b
Somerset Courthouse (N.J.) II–321b
Somerset House (London) I–162a
Somerset Island V–122a
Somers Island VII–201a
Somers Isles. *See* Bermuda Islands
***SOMERS* MUTINY** (1842) **VI–338a**; IV–445b
SOMERS' VOYAGE TO VIRGINIA (1609–10) **VI–338a**; I–292b
Somersworth (N.H.) VII–45a
Somervell, Brehon B. (off.) I–190a; II–450a
Somerville (Mass.) I–344b
Somerville, Alexander (off.) IV–337b

Some Thoughts Concerning the Present Revival IV–447b
Somit, Albert (pol. sci.) V–347b, 348a
SOMME OFFENSIVE (1918) **V–338a**
Sommerfeld, Arnold (phys.) V–304a
Somme River (Fr.) I–70a; VI–338b
Somoza family V–94b
Somoza Garcia, Anastasio (pol.) V–94b
Sonar III–270b; V–14a
Songbooks IV–437b–38a
Song of Hiawatha (poem) IV–162a
Song of Iowa VI–393 (table)
Song of Louisiana VI–394 (table)
Songs
  African IV–442b
  "Battle Hymn of the Republic" I–276b
  "Bonnie Blue Flag" I–330a
  fiddle tunes III–19a
  "Home Sweet Home" III–297a
  Iowa Corn Song III–469a
  "Jim Crow" IV–359b
  "Joe Bowers" IV–1a
  "My Country, 'Tis of Thee" IV–446a
  "My Old Kentucky Home" IV–447a
  "Oh! Susanna" V–146b
  "Old Oaken Bucket" V–152a
  "Swanee River" VI–453b
  Tin Pan Alley VII–62b
  "We Are Coming, Father Abraham" VII–263b
  "Yankee Doodle" VII–352a
  See also Ballads; Hymns; Music
Songs, state VI–392a, 393–95 (table)
Sonic boom I–69a
Sonic depthfinder V–133b, 135a
Sonoita (Mex.) I–413a; V–314b
Sonoma (Calif.) I–280b, 405a; IV–323b; VII–305b
Sonora (Mex.) II–228b; III–150b; IV–34b; VI–209a; VII–367a
  Apache Wars I–142b
  California Trail I–409b
  Camino del Diablo I–413a
  Civil War III–187b
  confederate expatriates VI–274b
  Confederate settlement IV–325a
  exploration I–141a; IV–452b
  filibuster expeditions III–23a,b
  Indian missions IV–367a
  Indians III–369a
  Pima Revolt V–314b
  presidios VI–364a
Sonora Democrat (news.) V–180b
Sonora Desert VII–371b
Sonora Pass V–225a
Sons of Dan II–291b
SONS OF LIBERTY (American Revolution) **VI–338b**; I–207b–08a; IV–143b–44a; VI–113b, 116a, 122a, 253a
  Boston Tea Party I–347b
  New York City III–189b, 206b; IV–60b; V–82b, 85b, 86a
  nonimportation agreements IV–266a; V–104b
  "Song of Liberty" IV–142b
  Stamp Act riot VI–382a
SONS OF LIBERTY (Civil War) **VI–339a**; II–63b; IV–52b–53a; V–161b
  Copperheads II–222b
  Northwest conspiracy V–121b
Sons of Revolutionary Sires VI–339a
Sons of Saint Tammany VI–459a
SONS OF THE AMERICAN REVOLUTION, NATIONAL SOCIETY OF THE VI–339a
SONS OF THE REVOLUTION, SOCIETY OF THE VI–339b; III–100a
SONS OF THE SOUTH VI–339b; I–325b
Sons of Union Veterans of the Civil War III–208a
Sontag and Evans gang VII–97b
Soo Canal III–218b, 452a
  See also Sault Sainte Marie Canals
Soo Line Railroad VI–36b
SOONERS VI–339b; V–149a, 150a
Sooner State VI–395 (table)
Sopwith, Thomas O. M. VII–348b
Sorauf, Frank J. (pol. sci.) IV–214a
Sorby, Henry C. (geol.) V–268a
Sorel (Can.) IV–405b
SORGHUM VI–340a; I–486a,b; II–358b
Sorin, Edward (cler.) III–293a
Soryu (aircraft carrier) IV–336b, 337a
Sotheby of London I–221b, 333a
Sotheby Parke Bernet, Inc. I–333a
Soto la Marina (Mex.) IV–348a, 452a
Soucek, Apollo (av. designer) I–51a
Soucek, Zeus (av. designer) I–51a
Souel, Jean (miss.) III–499b
Soul City (N.C.) II–48b
Soule, John Babsone Lane (jour.) III–206b
Soulé, Pierre (dipl.) I–317b; II–268a; V–174b
Soulé, Samuel (inv.) I–396a
Soul music IV–440a
Soul on Ice IV–167b
Soulouque, Faustin Élie (Faustin I) II–360b, 360b
Sound
  motion pictures IV–418a
Sound, speed of I–235a
Sound and Belts III–106b
Sound and the Fury IV–164b
Sound barrier I–235a
SOUND DUES VI–340a
Sound money II–96a
Sound navigation ranging. *See* Sonar
Sound recording. *See* Phonograph
Soup III–52a, 56a; IV–280b, 281a
Source of Human Good VI–83a
Souris River II–284a
Sour mash (whiskey) VII–289b
Sousa, John Philip (comp.) IV–441b–42a
SOUTH, ANTEBELLUM VI–340b; V–66b, 67b
  Afro-Americans I–26a–28b
  agriculture I–36b–37b, 38a
  antislavery I–135b
  backwoods VI–282b
  benefit of clergy I–289a
  Calhoun's *Disquisition on Government* I–404a
  Church of England II–455a
  colonial land policy I–4a
  colonial punishments V–465a
  colonial settlements III–334a,b
  colonial trade I–245a
  commission merchants II–138a
  cotton industry IV–46a–b
  Cotton Kingdom II–237b, 241a
  cotton money II–241a
  credit II–254b
  Cuba I–453b–54a
  curfew law II–274b
  "Dixie" II–357a–b
  dueling II–376b
  embargo of 1807 II–436b
  entail of estates II–452a
  family system II–485b
  fertilizers III–16a
  filibustering III–22b
  Fire-eaters III–25a
  food III–52a
  free trade III–113a
  fugitive slaves VII–138a
  Helper's *Impending Crisis* III–270b
  homestead movement III–296b
  horse stealing III–306a
  inns VII–2a
  intestate estates III–464a
  land speculation V–88b
  land tenancy IV–102b
  literature IV–162b
  livestock industry I–37a
  Lower South IV–200a
  Mason-Dixon Line IV–263a
  Methodist Church II–466a
  missionary societies IV–365b
  Mississippi IV–368b
  "My Old Kentucky Home" IV–447a
  Nashville IV–453a
  Nashville Convention IV–453b
  New Orleans IV–194a
  newspaper coverage V–71a
  nonslaveholders V–108a
  old field schools V–151b
  panic of 1837 V–206b
  panic of 1857 V–207a
  plantation system I–38a, 40b; V–178b, 324b
  poker V–336a
  poor whites V–108a, 358b
  postal service V–371a–b
  public education II–403b–04a
  railroads IV–453b
  Raleigh Conference of Southern Governors VI–42b
  revivalism II–466a
  Ruffner pamphlet VI–168b
  scalawags VI–224a
  schools VI–226b
  sectionalism VI–253b, 254a
  slave polygamy V–355b
  slavery I–10b–11a; VI–305b–07b, 309a; VII–202b
  slavocracy VI–312a
  South Carolina VI–347a–348a
  Southern Commercial Conventions VI–352a
  southern rights movement VI–354a
  states' rights VI–404b, 405a–b
  steam power VI–409b
  sweet potato V–377a
  tariff II–276a; VI–465b–66a
  taxation VII–4a
  tea growing VII–16a
  Thanksgiving Day VII–46a
  tobacco IV–179b
  transcontinental railroad VII–147a
  Whig party VII–288a
  See also Civil War; Confederate States of America; New South; Slavery
South, Department of the II–434b–35a
South, New. *See* New South
Southack, Cyprian (cartog.) I–447a
South Africa
  African nationalism I–21b
  Concord Coach II–158a
  gold I–302a; V–405b
  Korean War IV–55b, 56b
  moon hoax IV–406b

SOUTH AFRICA (cont.)
Pan-Africanism V-199b
Rhodes scholars VI-134b
United Nations Declaration VII-151b
U.S. investments I-22a
South Alex Field (Okla.) IV-334a
South Amboy (N.J.) III-183a,b, 184a
South America VI-471a-b
aerial hijacking III-277a
airship bases II-345a
astronomical observatories V-131b
British investment III-65b
Concord Coach II-158a
copper II-223b
cowboys II-248b
Creoles II-257a
dollar diplomacy II-359b
Indian cultures III-355b, 356a,b
Indians III-357a; VII-65a-b
Line of Demarcation II-323b
Monroe Doctrine IV-399b
navy exploration V-23a
prehistory I-47b-48a
revolutions I-126b
Spanish colonies V-461a
Spanish possessions IV-135b
World War II II-314b
See also entries under Latin America
SOUTH AMERICA, COMMERCE WITH **VI-343a**; II-365b; IV-111a; VII-87a, 87b
armed merchantmen IV-313a
Export-Import Bank I-263a
flour III-43a
furniture III-135b
ice VI-69a
Kasson Treaties IV-33a
salmon VI-201a
SOUTHAMPTON (N.Y.) **VI-346b**; IV-185b, 186a, 415b
Pilgrim voyage IV-278b
Southampton, 3rd Earl of, Henry Wriothesley VII-200b
Southampton County (Va.) II-403b; V-4b; VI-304a, 307a; VII-194b
Southampton Indians III-358a
South Bay II-322a
South Bend (Ind.) III-293a; IV-109b; V-367b
South Boston (Mass.) IV-44a
South Braintree (Mass.) VI-182b
SOUTH CAROLINA **VI-347a**; IV-200a; VI-395 (table)
Afro-American education II-403b, 404a
agricultural societies III-151b
Anglicanism VI-75b
archives I-168b
Arthur expedition V-32a
Augusta Congress I-223a
banking I-259a,b
bills of credit I-300a
black III-92b
Black Codes I-310b
black suffrage VI-432a, 433b
Blease movement I-319a
Bluffton movement I-326a
boll weevil II-238b
boundary disputes I-350b, 351a
buffalo I-375a
campaign of 1828 I-418b
campaign of 1832 I-419a-b
campaign of 1836 I-419b
campaign of 1876 II-38b
candlemaking I-444a,b
cattle I-37a
chain gangs I-489a
Charleston I-496a
Civil War I-458b, 458b, 497a; II-62b, 131a, 163b; III-103a; IV-397a, 405a; V-19b; VI-138a, 278a
colonial government I-238b, 496a, 496b
colonial land grants IV-92a
colonial land tenure IV-102b
colonial suffrage VI-434a,b
colonial trade II-119a
commercial bounties I-352a
commodities as money II-140b
Compromise of 1850 II-150b
Confederate flag I-330a
confiscation of property II-168b
constitution VI-390b
Continental Congress II-478a
cotton I-38a; II-237b, 238b; V-376a; VI-341b
debtor laws II-299a
Declaration of Independence II-305a, 308b
Democratic party VII-210a
divorce II-356b
dueling II-376b
Dutch Fork II-382b
election of electors II-195a
Ellenton riot II-432a
emancipation orders II-434b
Emancipation Proclamation II-434b
fall line II-485a
feudalism III-18a
Florida settlers IV-45a
Force Acts III-59b
foreign trade VII-86a
Fort Prince George V-408a
Fort Sumter V-217a,b; VI-440b
founding II-124a
Freemasons III-109a
French and Indian War IV-192a
Fundamental Constitutions I-457b
fur trade III-141a,b, 143b, 144a
geological survey III-165a
German settlements II-382b
golf III-197a-b
grandfather clause III-208b
Gullah III-233b
habeas corpus IV-57b
Haitian refugees V-342a
Hamburg riot III-244a
Heath Patent III-268a
historical account III-280b
horse racing III-304b
Huguenots III-121a, 315a; V-342a
hurricanes III-319b
Indiana settlers III-369b-70a
Indian missions III-170a
Indian slaves III-401a
indigo I-352a; II-5a; III-405b; VI-341a, 386b
justice of the peace IV-22b
Kansas Border War I-376b
landholdings I-4a
Lederer's exploring expeditions IV-131a-b
legislature VII-142a
Loyalists IV-200a; VI-115b
lynching legislation IV-208b
malaria IV-229a
mammals IV-231a
martial law IV-259a
migration to Alabama I-71a
minimum-wage law IV-353b
mounds IV-420b
naval stores I-352a
New England settlers V-50a
Ninety-Six V-97a
North American Land Company V-113a
North Carolina commerce V-115b-16a
nullification I-404a-b; III-9a, 59b; IV-202b; V-125b-26a; VI-254a, 397a, 466a
Occaneechi Trail III-387b
Ohio Valley traders V-146a
Old Southwest VI-356a
personal liberty laws V-264a
phosphate III-16b
phosphorus II-6b
pine barrens IV-204a
pioneers V-316b
plank roads V-323a
plantation system V-325a
plant study V-326a
poll taxes I-22b
poor whites V-358b
port authority V-368a
Port Royal V-370a
presidios V-399b
prices V-404a-b
privateers V-419b
proprietors I-496a
provincial congress V-440a
Puritans III-169b
Queen Anne's War II-126b; VI-2b
quitrents VI-4a
railroads III-450a; VI-36b, 37b
Raleigh Conference of Southern Governors VI-42b
Reconstruction III-244a, 295a-b; VI-57b, 58a
record-keeping VII-205b
Red Shirts VI-65a
Regulators III-436b; VI-72a
religious liberty VII-69a
repudiation of state debts VI-96b
revolutionary movement (1719) I-458a
revolutionary war II-451b, 465a, 465a; III-30a-b, 31b, 170a, 250a, 286a-b; IV-48a, 420a; V-97a; VI-118a, 124a,b, 130a, 351a; VII-360b
rice I-352a, 486b; VI-135b, 341a, 386b
roads VII-99b
royal colony I-458a
Santee Canal VI-216a
school segregation II-402a
Scotch-Irish VI-240b
secession II-61a; VI-250b, 251a
settlement I-281b
Shawnee VI-270b
slave insurrections III-437a; VI-303b
slavery VI-305a, 309a
slave trade II-151b
smuggled goods V-320a
Southwest Territory VI-358a
Spanish-English conflict II-126b
Spanish missions IV-303a
stagelines VI-380a
States' Rights party V-198a
sugarcane VI-436a
Swiss settlers VI-455a
tariff I-326a
tea growing VII-16a
tea party VII-16b
Tennessee settlement VII-25a
Tillmanism VII-58b
tobacco VII-66b, 67a,b
tornadoes VII-75b
town surveys V-452a
Tryon's Line VII-125b
Tuscarora War VII-130b
U.S. Constitution II-193a, 193b, 196b, 198b, 203b

usury law III–443a
Vesey Rebellion III–437a; VII–174a
Voting Rights Act of 1965 VII–211a
Waxhaw VII–261b
western lands V–443b; VI–356a; VII–273a,b
Whig party VII–288a
whiskey II–163b
Wilkes Fund dispute VI–112b; VII–299b
winemaking VII–305a
writs of assistance VII–345a
Yamasee War VII–352a
See also entries under Carolina
South Carolina (battleship) VII–241a, 242a
South Carolina (frigate) V–26a
South Carolina (warship) II–370a
SOUTH CAROLINA, PROPOSED NOBILITY IN VI–348b
SOUTH CAROLINA, SPANISH EXPEDITIONS AGAINST VI–348b
SOUTH CAROLINA, STATE BANK OF VI–349a
South Carolina, University of VII–156a
South Carolina and Georgia Railroad Company VI–349b
SOUTH CAROLINA CANAL VI–349a
South Carolina Canal and Railroad Company IV–175b; VI–24b, 349b
South Carolina College V–347b; VI–347b
See also South Carolina, University of
South Carolina Exposition and Protest. See Calhoun's *Exposition*
South-Carolina Gazette (news.) V–71a
South Carolina Golf Club III–197a–b
SOUTH CAROLINA INTERSTATE AND WEST INDIAN EXPOSITION (1901–02) **VI–349b**
SOUTH CAROLINA RAILROAD VI–349b; IV–175b; VI–24b, 37a
South Carolina Railway Company VI–349b
South Carolina Royalists VI–130a
South Carolina Society for Promoting and Improving Agriculture I–41a
South Carolina v. *Katzenbach* (1966) III–93b; VII–211a
South Charleston (Ohio) I–492a
SOUTH DAKOTA VI–349b; VI–395 (table); VII–284b
badlands I–242b
Battle of Wounded Knee V–4b
birth and death registration IV–149a
Black Hills I–312a
Cheyenne II–16b
Chippewa II–31a
columbium III–14b
county-seat wars II–245b
Dakota Indians II–282b, 283b
Dakota Territory II–284b–85a
dams VI–147a
Farmer–Labor party of 1920 II–493a
Farmers' Alliance II–493a
floods III–37a
Fort Kiowa IV–51a
Fort Randall Dam III–322b
Fort Sully VI–438b
fur trade II–131b
gold III–80a, 191b, 192a
Hutterite communes II–142a
Indian population III–396a,b
initiative II–418b
Iowa Territory III–468a
legislators' travel allowance IV–339a
Messiah War IV–316a
Missouri River IV–380a
national parks and monuments V–217b, 218 (table)
Nonpartisan League V–106b
Populist party V–365b
prairie dogs V–387b
prairie fire V–388b
railroads VI–36b
ranches VI–45a
referendum VI–66b
Rosebud Indian Reservation VI–164b
sheep VII–321a
Sioux IV–108b–09a; V–437b; VI–296a, 297a
Sioux Wars IV–109a; VII–239b
statehood VII–248a
voting behavior VII–210a
wheat III–43b, 45a
South Dakota (battleship) VII–242a
South Dakota Historical Society II–115b
Southeast Asia
communism II–316a
Japan II–489a
rubber VI–167b, 168a
Seventh Fleet V–25a
tobacco VII–64b
World War II III–489b–90a; VII–335a
See also Cambodia, Bombing of; Laos, Intervention in; Vietnam War
SOUTHEAST ASIA TREATY ORGANIZATION VI–350b; II–315b, 489b; V–234a; VII–113a
Philippines V–285a
South Vietnam VII–182b
Southeast cultures III–365a–67a, 374b, 376b, 391a
Southeastern ceremonial complex. *See* Southern Cult
Southeastern Power Administration III–445a
Southeby and Company II–106b
South End House (Boston) VI–330b
Southern, Eileen (au.) IV–442b–43a
Southern Agrarians II–189b
Southern Air Lines I–68b
Southern Alliance II–42a; V–132a
See also National Farmers' Alliance and Industrial Union
Southern and Western Literary Messenger and Review (mag.) VI–353a
Southern Association of Colleges and Schools VII–131a
Southern Baptist Convention I–265a,b; III–385b
SOUTHERN BOUNDARY, SURVEY OF THE VI–351a
Southern California Colony Association III–477b
Southern California Tennis Association VII–29b
SOUTHERN CAMPAIGNS (1780–81) **VI–351a**
SOUTHERN CHRISTIAN LEADERSHIP CONFERENCE VI–351b; I–30b–31a; II–57b, 58a
SOUTHERN COMMERCIAL CONVENTIONS VI–352a; VI–354a
SOUTHERN CULT VI–352b; IV–370a–b
Southern Cultivation (period.) I–45b
Southern Department (col. adm.) VI–109b
SOUTHERN EXPOSITION (1883–87) **VI–353a**
Southern Express Company I–10a
Southern Farmers' Alliance II–493b–94a
Southern Growth Policies Agreement (1971) III–460a
Southern Growth Policies Board VI–398a
Southern Historical Association III–279a
Southern Historical Collection III–285a,b
Southern History Association III–279a
SOUTHERN LITERARY MESSENGER (mag.) **VI–353a**
Southern Methodist church IV–319a
Southern Methodist University VII–40b
Southern Nevada Water Project II–130b
SOUTHERN OVERLAND MAIL VI–353b; III–221a; V–178a; VI–154a, 379a
Southern Pacific Company IV–444a
Southern Pacific Railroad I–214b, 406a,b; II–91a; III–79b; VI–26b, 27a, 36b–37a; VII–40a, 40a
Fort Yuma III–179b; VII–367b
land grants IV–94b
medical care IV–293b
Southern Pacific v. *Arizona* (1945) V–339b
Southern pine IV–204a; VI–48b, 393 (table)
Southern Plantation (N.C.) I–83a,b
Southern Power Company III–321a
Southern Presbyterian Church II–272b
Southern Quarterly Review (jour.) II–298a
SOUTHERN RAILROAD ROUTE VI–353b
Southern Railway II–272b; III–39b; V–117a; VI–24b, 25a, 37a, 349b; VII–202b
Southern Regional Education Board VI–398a, 402a,b
Southern Regional Education Program II–401a
SOUTHERN RIGHTS MOVEMENT VI–354a; II–150b; IV–453b
Southern Tenant Farmers Union I–40b; IV–104a
Southern Transcontinental Railroad VI–37a
SOUTHERN UNIONISTS VI–354a; VII–148b
Southey, Robert (poet) IV–267a
Southfield (gunboat) I–83a
South Fork (Pa.) II–351a
South Georgia Island V–337a
SOUTH IMPROVEMENT COMPANY VI–354b; VI–382b
South Kingstown (R.I.) I–380b; III–223a
South Korea. *See* Korea, Republic of
South Manchuria Railway V–370b
South Meadow (Conn.) III–309a
South Mountain III–256a; IV–261b
South Mountain, Battle of (1862) III–100b
SOUTHOLD (N.Y.) **VI–354b**; IV–185a; V–55b; VI–134b, 346b
South Orkney Islands V–198a
South Pacific
whaling II–463b
Wilkes expedition VII–272a
World War II II–33a
South Pacific (musical) IV–442a
SOUTH PASS VI–354b; I–201a, 209a; III–215a; V–225a; VI–160b; VII–345b

SOUTH PASS (cont.)
Bonneville expedition VII–217b
Central Route I–485b
exploration VII–271b
forty-niners III–82a
Oregon Trail V–168b, 169a; VI–153b
Platte River Trail V–330b
pony express V–357b
Smith explorations VI–318a
Sublette's Cutoff VI–422a
wagon trains I–453a
South Platte River II–379b; VI–355a
Fort Lancaster IV–89a
Fort Sedgwick VI–254b
gold V–311b
Ogallala V–139a
Oregon Trail V–168b
Overland Trail V–178b
SOUTH PLATTE ROUTE VI–355a; I–224a, 357b
South Pole I–116a, 399a; V–336b, 337b
Southport (Conn.) V–261b
South River. *See* Delaware River
South Saint Paul (Minn.) IV–31b, 357a
South Sea I–277b; V–145a
South Sea Company I–202a; II–122a; VI–2b; VII–162b
South Sea Expedition. *See* Wilkes Exploring Expedition
South Sea Islands II–28b
South Seas IV–364b
South Shetland Islands V–198a
South Side Elevated Railway II–415a
Southside Railroad I–146b; V–265a; VI–35a
South Vietnam. *See* Vietnam
Southview Cemetery (Atlanta) IV–46a
Southwark Theatre (Philadelphia) VII–46b
Southwell, Robert (offi.) IV–188b
SOUTHWEST VI–355a; VII–268a
acquisition III–68a
adobe V–317a
archaeological dating VII–114b
architecture I–159a
cattle III–10b
exploration I–399a, 441b; III–114a–b
floods and tornadoes II–351b
Fort Worth III–80b
fur trade III–143a
gambling III–149b
Great Trading and War Path III–223b
Havasupai III–262b
horse III–302b, 303a
Horsehead Crossing III–304a
horse stealing III–305b
Indian agriculture IV–327a
Indian art III–374a
Indian cultures III–356a–b, 367a–69a
Indian drugs VII–65b
Indian reservations III–396a
Indians II–358b–59a; III–360a, 396a–b
Indian treaties III–378a
irrigation III–477a
Jesuit missions III–499a
livestock industry I–38b
mesas IV–314a
mesquite IV–316a
migrant workers VI–365a
Mogollon culture IV–385b
Mohave IV–386a
mule-breeding IV–426a
mustangs IV–444b
natural gas V–5b
Navaho V–8a
patio gardens III–151b
petroleum VI–356b–57a
Pike's expedition V–311b, 312a
Pima V–314a
Pueblo Revolt V–4a
railroad conventions VI–20b–21a
rainfall VI–41b
ranching IV–45a,b
Rio Grande VI–143b
Santa Fe VI–214b
sectionalism VI–254a
ship channels VII–260b
slavery VI–312a
Spain II–184b; VII–270a
Spanish Trail VI–368a
stagelines VI–379a
timberlands VII–59b
Tombstone VII–70b
trading posts VII–95b, 96a
transcontinental railroad IV–28b
tuberculosis patients VII–126a
wheat III–45b
SOUTHWEST, OLD VI–356a
literature VI–300a
missions IV–367a
Natchez Trace IV–456a–b
penole V–254a
presidios V–399b
settlement VII–284a
Tennessee Valley VII–27b
Tombigbee Valley VII–70b
Watauga settlement VII–253b
Southwest Boundary. *See* Adams–Onís Treaty; Louisiana Purchase, Boundaries of; Mexican Boundary
Southwest cultures III–367a–69a, 390a, 396b
Southwestern Cattle Growers' Association of Kansas I–472a
Southwestern Convention (1845) VI–352b
SOUTHWESTERN OIL FIELDS VI–356b; VI–355b
Southwestern Power Administration III–445a
Southwestern Railroad conventions VI–20b–21a
Southwestern Virginia, Department of IV–410b
Southwestern War (1936–37). *See* Sabine War
SOUTHWEST FUR COMPANY VI–357b; I–105a
South West Pass IV–371a
SOUTHWEST POINT VI–357b
SOUTHWEST TERRITORY VI–358a; VI–356b; VII–32a, 277a
Holston Treaty III–292a
suffrage III–91b
territorial government VI–401b
South Weymouth (Mass.) II–345a–b
Southworth, George C. (phys.) I–212a, 287b; IV–333a,b
Soutine, Haim (art.) II–104b
Sovereign, James R. (labor leader) IV–64b
"Sovereign of the individual" I–116b
SOVEREIGNS OF INDUSTRY VI–358a; II–220b; III–405b
SOVEREIGNTY, DOCTRINE OF VI–358a
Canal Zone V–202a,b
League of Nations IV–124a
majority rule IV–228a
Nine-Power Pact V–96b
Soviet Jews IV–12a
Soviet Mathematics–Doklady I–109a
Soviet Union
aircraft I–61a, 62b
air defense I–58b
Arab relations I–149b–50a, 243a; II–315b; III–69b
atomic bomb I–61a, 179b, 216b; II–315a; III–69b, 324a
atomic power reactors I–217a,b
ballistic missiles II–316a
Berlin blockade II–98a; V–114a
Bretton Woods Conference I–361b
cold war II–97a
communism II–315a
Communist Party, United States of America II–143b–46b
corn II–226b
cotton II–238b
Cuban missile crisis IV–113a
Cuban relations II–296b
Cuba relations I–278b
Czechoslovakia invasion VI–416b
espionage VI–428a–b
Far Eastern policy II–489a
Geneva Accords of 1954 III–159b, 161a
Geneva disarmament conference III–161a
Geneva summit conference III–161a–b
gunboats III–235a
hockey III–286b, 287b–88a
Hungarian Revolution II–146a
hydrogen bomb III–69b, 324a
immigration to U.S. III–333a, 339b, 340b
industrial relations III–407b
iron and steel manufacture III–470a, 471 (tables)
Iron Curtain III–474b
Korean War II–315b, 489a; IV–56a, b, 57a
Laos relations IV–107a
Manchuria II–26b
Middle East III–481b–82b
missilery IV–363b, 432a
Molniya satellites II–143b
naval competition V–10b–11b
naval power II–316a
North Atlantic Treaty Organization V–113b–14a,b, 115a
nuclear fission V–300a
Nuclear Test Ban Treaty III–70a
nuclear tests I–53b
nuclear weapons II–316a
occupation of Germany III–174b; VII–351b
Olympic Games V–154a
polio vaccine V–341a
radar VI–10a
radio astronomy VI–17a
rocketry II–426a; VI–159a–b
space flights I–209b–10a; II–426a
Sputnik II–143a, 426a; III–69b
submarines I–56a,b
Suez Canal I–124b
Suez Crisis III–481b; VI–429b
supersonic transport I–53a, 238a
totalitarianism I–179a
United Nations II–380b
United Nations Declaration VII–151b
UN Security Council V–234a
U.S. "witch-hunt" VII–310b
vacuum tubes VII–163b
Vietnam War I–62b; II–316b; V–22a; VII–182b
war crimes trials VII–229a
Washington Naval Conference VII–250b
World War II II–145a, 315a, 324a, 407b; V–332a
Yalta Conference VII–351b
Yom Kippur War II–213a
See also Russia, U.S. Relations with
SOW CASE (1643–44) **VI–358b**
Sower, Christopher, Jr. (pub.) V–413a

Sower, Christopher, Sr. (pub.) I–293b, 294a; V–75b, 413a
Soybeans II–134a, 227a, 430b; VI–48a
Illinois III–329b
towboating VII–77b
Soyuz (spacecraft) IV–460b
Spaatz, Carl (off.) I–60b
Space (arch.) I–165b
Spacecraft I–209b–10a, 276b; II–426a; III–15a, 184b
Space Detection and Tracking System I–58b
Space exploration I–235a; III–410b
astronomical observations V–132a
aviation industry I–238a
Cape Canaveral I–336b
engineering II–448a
expenditures II–317b, 476a
financing I–391a
food I–349b
helium production IV–350b
International Geophysical Year III–454a
Langley Aeronautical Laboratory IV–106a
manned flights I–209b–10a; II–426a
medical studies IV–292b
moon landing IV–406b
National Aeronautics and Space Administration IV–458b
New Frontier V–53a
rockets VI–159a,b
Soviet Union IV–406b
Space for Peace IV–459a
Space glider I–63b
Space launch systems I–63b–64a
Space Treaty (1968) IV–364a
Spaight, Richard Dobbs (legis.) II–203b
Spain
Vial's Road VII–178b
Alabama I–71a, 499a; II–167b
Albuquerque I–83b
Arizona I–171b–72a
Arkansas I–172b–73a
Arkansas River I–174a–b
Bahama Islands VI–130a
Bourbon family compact II–487b
buccaneers I–373b
Burr conspiracy I–387b
California I–91b, 141a, 141a, 350a, 401b, 405a, 466b; II–212b; III–190b; VI–45b
Canary Islands I–444a
Caribbean colonies V–439a
Carolina I–458a
cattle I–471a, 472b–73a
citrus fruits II–43a; III–128b
civil war V–280b
claims against IV–5b
coins II–94b, 365b
colonial land grants IV–92b, 93a
colonial trade II–446b
Columbus' voyages VI–216a
conquistadores I–24b; II–184a
convoys II–217a–b
Creoles II–257a
Cromwell's western design VII–270b
Cuba II–268a–b; IV–188a; V–174b–75a
Dominican Republic II–360b
Drake expedition II–369a
effective occupation II–406b
encomienda system II–443b
exploration I–96a–b; III–118b; IV–264b, 452a
California II–373b
Cibola II–37a
Colorado II–127–28a
Columbia River II–131b
conquistadores II–184a
Coronado's expedition II–228a
Delaware Bay II–322a
Great Plains III–220b
Green River III–226b
Mississippi IV–368a, 372a
Potomac River V–378a
Rocky Mountains V–224b; VI–160a
Southwest II–461a
expulsion of Jews IV–9a
fifths mining tax III–20b
Florida I–9b, 10b, 126b, 143a, 238b, 274b, 275a, 324a, 398a; II–22b, 23a, 319a; III–38a–b, 40b–41a, 41b–42a, 145a; IV–302b, 368a, 452a; V–254a,b, 356a; VI–351a; VII–234a
Fort Miro IV–362a
Fort Nogales VII–181a
Fort Panmure V–210b
Fort Saint Marks VI–196b
Fort Sam Houston VI–204b
French and Indian War II–126b
fur trade III–141b, 142a, 143a; VI–367a
Genêt mission III–159b
Georgia I–354a; II–298a; III–168a, 170a, 171b; IV–46b
Grand Banks fishing III–208a
guerrillas III–231a
Gulf of Mexico IV–326a,b
Iberville River III–326b
immigration to U.S. III–334b, 338b, 341b
indemnities III–352a
Iowa III–467b
Isle of Orleans III–479a
King George's War I–461b
La Salle IV–110a
Latin–American independence wars IV–114b
Lewis and Clark Expedition VII–271a
Line of Demarcation II–323b
logwood trade IV–181b
Los Adaes garrison IV–189a
Louisiana I–9b, 247a, 274b, 324a, 399b, 448a, 459b; II–22a–b, 215a, 215b, 247b, 333b, 389a; III–108a; IV–192b–93b, 376b, 376b–77a, 456b; V–100b–01a, 173a, 335a
Louisiana Revolution IV–198a, 301b
Madrid Conference IV–221a
Mexican debts IV–325b
Mexico IV–320b
Micronesia VII–125a
military posts VI–168b
missions IV–365b, 367a
Mississippi River III–232b; VI–148a
Mississippi Valley IV–375b, 376a
Missouri I–354b
Missouri River IV–379b
Natchez IV–455a; VI–356b
Newfoundland fisheries II–92a
New France V–52b
New Madrid V–59a
New Mexico I–8a; II–460b–61a; V–59b
New Orleans VII–276a–b
New World claims V–109a–b; VII–75a
Nolan expeditions V–101a
Nootka Sound controversy V–109b
North Carolina I–447b
Northwest Territory IV–355b
Oklahoma V–148a
Oñate's explorations V–155a
Oregon V–164b, 167b
Organization for Economic Cooperation and Development V–170b
Panama Canal V–200b
Peace of Paris V–214a
Pemaquid Point V–243a
Peru III–68b; IV–111a
Philippines I–126b; V–281a, 282a–b
pieces of eight V–309a
Pike's southwestern expedition VII–271b
pistole V–320b
Plymouth Company expedition V–333b
Prairie du Chien V–388a
presidios V–399b
privateering V–419a,b
Providence Island I–499b
Prudhomme Bluffs V–440b
Puerto Rico V–461a
Queen Anne's War II–126b; VI–2a
Raleigh's Lost Colony VI–43a
Red River Post VI–64b
revolutionary war treaties II–318a
rum trade VI–170b–71a
Saint Augustine VI–187b
Saint Louis VI–194a
Saint Stephens VI–197b
Salem trade VI–199a
San Antonio VI–207a,b
San Francisco VI–209a
Santa Fe VI–214b
sea otter trade VI–247a
sea trade III–106b
Seminole Wars VI–260b
silver mining VI–292a
slave trade I–202a; VI–309a–b
smelters VI–316b
solar eclipse expedition II–88a
South America colonies I–265b
South Carolina I–281b, 496a, 498a; V–370a; VI–348b
Southwest VI–355a
Staked Plain VI–380b
State of Franklin IV–435b
steel VII–89b
submarines VI–422b
Taos VI–461a
Texan–Santa Fe expeditions VII–36a
Texas I–48b, 48b, 224, 492a; III–235b–36a; IV–302b, 456b; VI–189b; VII–36a–37a
tobacco VII–64b
trading posts VII–95b
Treaty of Fontainebleau III–50b
Treaty of London IV–182b
Treaty of Madrid II–406b; IV–220b
Treaty of Paris (1763) V–214b
Treaty of Paris (1898) V–215a
Treaty of San Ildefonso VI–211a
Treaty of Utrecht VII–162b
triangular trade VII–119b
Tubac settlement VII–125b
Utah VII–161a
Vancouver Island VII–166a
War of Jenkins' Ear I–323a; II–126b; III–498a
war with Britain III–117a; IV–274a, 372b; VI–124b
Washington State VII–247a
Yucatán VII–366b
Spalding, Gilbert (circus owner) II–40b
Spalding, Henry H. (miss.) IV–108a; V–165a, 167a
Spalding and Rogers VI–283a
Spander, Murray (inv.) II–421a
Spanish America. *See* entries under Latin America, South America
Spanish–American independence wars (1810–24) II–268a
SPANISH–AMERICAN RELATIONS VI–358b; II–342b

SPANISH–AMERICAN RELATIONS (cont.)
Adams–Onís Treaty I–10b, 351a; III–68a
Alta Vela claim I–91b
Amelia Island affair I–93b
American Revolution I–151a–b, 306b, 367a; III–306a; VI–116b–17a,b, 119b, 120a
Aranda Memorial I–151a
Aranjuez Convention I–151b; II–318b
Arbuthnot and Ambrister case I–154a
d'Arges colony I–169b
Black Warrior affair I–317b
Caribbean policy I–453b–54a
commerce II–166b
Cuban trade II–268b
Definitive Treaty of Peace VII–270a
Fajardo case II–484a
filibustering I–355b
Florida III–462b; VII–353b
Indian barrier state III–375a
international law III–455b
Jay–Gardoqui negotiations III–492b; VII–111a
Kemper raid IV–36b
Latin American mediation V–233a
loans to U.S. II–302a
Louisiana II–216a; IV–193a–b, 196a,b, 197a,b
McGillivray incident IV–213a
Mexican boundary IV–320b
Mississippi River II–166b; IV–372b, 373a; VI–150b
Monroe Doctrine IV–400a,b
Morocco I–85b
Neutrality Act of 1939 V–37b
Nootka Sound affair II–342b
Pike's southwestern expedition V–311b–12a
Pinckney's Treaty I–126a; II–167b, 333a–b, 342b; III–67b, 232b; V–315a
piracy V–320b
revolutionary war II–96b; III–63a, 90b, 95a, 179a, 245a; IV–367b; VI–365a–b
Rio Grande VI–143a
Spanish–American War VI–361a
Spanish conspiracy VI–365b
Teller Amendment VII–22a
Texas boundary VII–36b
treaty negotiation VII–111b
Treaty of Nogales V–100b
triangular trade II–119a
U.S. boundaries I–351a; II–127b, 313b, 432a
U.S. Civil War II–65b
Van Ness Convention VII–167a
Virginius affair VII–204a
visit and search VII–205a
War of 1812 IV–383a
western separatism VII–276a
West Florida III–68a; IV–382b; V–240b; VII–277a–b
Spanish–American revolution VII–170a
Spanish–Americans
Connecticut II–181a
Wyoming VII–346a
SPANISH–AMERICAN WAR (1898) **VI–361a**; II–268b, 314a, 472b; III–68b, 347a; IV–111a; VI–360a–b; VII–26a, 190b, 328a
Afro-American troops IV–340a
Anglo–American relations I–122a
anti-imperialists I–131b
antiwar movement VII–236b
army organization I–185a–b
army uniforms VII–144b
artillery I–200a
brown powder V–383a
burial procedures I–478a
cavalry I–476a
censorship I–481a
costs VII–228 (table)
counterespionage VI–252a
Cuba III–230b–31a; V–32a
declaration of war VII–237a
demobilization II–324a
desertions II–335b
destruction of the *Maine* IV–227a
"embalmed beef" II–436a
espionage VI–373b
exchange of prisoners II–468b
federal deficit VI–449b
financing II–317a
France III–97a
Geneva Conventions III–162a
Guam III–230b
guerrillas III–231a
gunboats II–25b
gunpowder II–8a
Hawaii III–263b
hospitals I–191b
I$Merrimac sinking IV–314b
Jefferson Barracks III–494b
losses VII–232 (table)
Maine VI–84a
"manifest destiny" IV–239a
marines IV–252a–b
message to García III–150b
mobilization IV–384a
neutrality III–456a
opposition V–235a,b
Oregon V–165b
pensions V–257a,b
Philippines V–281a, 282b; VII–208a
photography V–293a
Puerto Rico III–58a; V–461a
recruitment VI–61a
Red Cross VI–61b
rifle IV–430b
Rough Riders VI–165b; VII–40b
Sampson–Schley controversy VI–206b
San Juan Hill and El Caney VI–213b
Santiago II–450a; VI–216b
Silver Star II–311a
taxation VII–6a, 12b
Teller Amendment VII–22a
territories II–474b–75a
territories acquired I–126b, 454a; III–425a
Treaty of Paris V–215a; VII–112a
veterans I–331
veterans' organizations VII–175a
volunteers II–314a, 367a; IV–343b, 346a
War Department VII–230a
warships VII–241a
yellow journalism V–71b, 73b–74a; VII–356a
SPANISH–AMERICAN WAR, NAVY IN VI–362b; V–20a; VI–361a–62a
Afro-American troops IV–340a
Asiatic Squadron VI–361b
Battle of Manila Bay III–25b–26a; IV–239a
destruction of the *Maine* IV–227a
Navy Department V–18a
North Atlantic Squadron VI–361a–b
prize money V–424a
sinking of the *Merrimac* (1898) IV–314b
SPANISH AND SPANISH–AMERICAN INFLUENCE VI–363b
food III–51b
fruit growing III–128a–b
gardens III–151b
hogs III–288a
horse III–302a–b, 363a; IV–444b
irrigation III–477a
mule IV–425b
Penitent Brothers V–245b
penole V–254a
saddles VI–184b
sheep V–8b; VI–272b, 273a; VII–320b
Southwest culture II–184b
Taos VI–461a
water rights VII–256a
Spanish architecture I–159a–60a
SPANISH CAPTURE OF BRITISH POSTS (1779–81) **VI–365a**; VI–363b
Fort Saint Joseph VI–192a
Manchac IV–234b
Mobile IV–382a
Natchez IV–455a
Spanish Civil War (1936–39)
battleships V–26b
Spanish Commercial Company. *See* Spanish–Missouri Fur Company
SPANISH CONSPIRACY VI–365b; IV–373b; V–101a; VII–276b
defeated IV–42b–43a
SPANISH DOLLAR VI–366a; I–483a; IV–393b, 394a; VI–364b
Spanish fever I–474a; II–249a
"Spanish flats" I–143b
Spanish Fort. *See* Saint John, Fort
SPANISH–INDIAN RELATIONS VI–366a; III–385b; VI–359a
Acoma I–8a
Apache I–142a–b
Battle of Cabusto I–402a
Chickasaw–Creek War II–22b
Delaware Indians II–321a
De Soto's expedition II–336a–b
Georgia III–170a
Gran Quivira III–211a
Havasupai III–262b
horses IV–444b
Indian slavery III–401a
Jay–Gardoqui negotiations III–492b
liquor III–398a
Louisiana IV–193a
McGillivray incident IV–213a
missions III–385b, 498b–99b; IV–366a, 367a
Navaho V–9a
New Mexico V–59b
Panton, Leslie and Company V–211a
Pima Revolt V–314b
presidios VI–168b
Pueblo III–368b; V–459b
Pueblo Revolt V–460b
Red River Post VI–64b
San Francisco de los Tejas VI–210a, 210a
Sauk Prairie VI–218b
Seminole VI–259b
Texas VII–36b
Texas missions II–389a; VI–207a,b
trade II–34a, 480a
Treaty of Nogales V–100b
Yamasee War VI–349a; VII–352a
Zuni VII–372a
Spanish Indies IV–361b
Spanish Inquisition. *See* Inquisition, Spanish
Spanish Longhorn. *See* Longhorns, Texas
Spanish Main VI–130a
SPANISH–MISSOURI FUR COMPANY VI–367a; III–144b
Missouri River IV–380b
Spanish posts on the Mississippi, surrender of. *See* Guion's Expedition;

Southern Boundary, Survey of the
Spanish Succession, War of the. *See* Queen Anne's War
SPANISH SUPPLIES FROM NEW ORLEANS VI–367b; III–38b, 179a; IV–193a; V–353b
SPANISH TRAIL VI–368a; I–409b; III–114b, 215a; V–224b; VII–217b
forty-niners III–82a
Frémont explorations VII–272a
water holes VII–256a
Spann, Otis (sing.) IV–442b
Spar (ship) V–122a
Sparkman, John J. (pol.) I–430a
Sparkman and Stevens VII–349a
Sparks (Nev.) III–215a
Sparks, Jared (hist.) III–281a,b; IV–267a
Sparks, Richard (expl.) V–148a
Sparks, William A. J. (offi.) IV–95a
Sparks Circus II–41a
Sparrow (missile) I–57b
Sparrow-Hawk (ship) I–447a
Sparrows Point (Md.) III–470b
SPARs VII–318a
Spartanburg (S.C.) I–435a
Spas. *See* Resorts and Spas
Spaulding, A. G. (athlete) I–269b
Spaulding, Elbridge G. (fin.) II–66a
SPEAKEASY VI–368a; I–339a; II–261a, 407a; V–430a
SPEAKER OF THE HOUSE OF REPRESENTATIVES VI–368b; II–172b, 174–78 (table), 198b; VI–65b, 169b; VII–288b
Blaine, James G. IV–426a
Cannonism I–445b
Democrats VI–466b
Federal Election Commission V–449a
floor leader III–37b
presidential succession II–207b; V–398b; VI–388b
War Powers Act VII–224b
"Speaking in tongues" V–259b
Special Action Office for Drug Abuse Prevention II–498a
Special Agency Service II–276b
Special Commission on Revolutionary Claims (Mexican) I–109b
Special districts (gov.) IV–171a, 172a–b; V–349b, 350a
Special Drawing Rights VII–91a, 222b
Special Forces, U.S. Army VI–47a
Special Inter-American Conference for the Maintenance of Peace (1936) V–105a
Special Land Stations VI–15a
Special Operations Executive, British V–138a
Special sessions (Congress) II–172b, 478b
Specie. *See* Bimetallism; Hard Money; Money
SPECIE CIRCULAR (1834–36) **VI–369b**; I–107b; V–206b; VI–370b
SPECIE PAYMENTS, SUSPENSION AND RESUMPTION OF VI–369b; III–190a, 192b, 194a
Bland-Allison Act I–318b
campaign of 1872 I–422b
Civil War II–63b; IV–392b, 394b
Greenback movement III–224a, 225a
Independent Treasury System III–354b
inflation III–415a
panic of 1819 V–206a
panic of 1837 V–206b
Resumption Act (1875) VI–104a
resumption of Jan. 1, 1879 IV–63b
soft money VI–333b
Specie Circular VI–369b
War of 1812 I–255a; VII–235b
Specific Duties. *See* Duties, Ad Valorem and Specific
Specimen Days and Collect IV–162b
Speckle wood II–453a
Spectroscopy II–12a–b; IV–2a, 262a–b; V–131a,b
Speculation
art collecting II–107a
banking I–256a–b, 257a
blockade runners I–322a
Commodities Exchange Act II–140b
Confederacy II–164b
Constitution II–197b
gold III–188b, 190a, 193a
Kansas Territory I–342a
Mississippi Bubble IV–370b
national debt I–208a
private banks I–263b
railroad rate wars VI–23a
stock market II–63b, 69a, 470a–b
See also entries under Panic
Speculation, land. *See* Land Speculation
"Speculator deserts" I–4b; IV–91a, 99b
Speech, freedom of. *See* Freedom of Speech
Speech defectives
education III–248a, 249a
Speech therapy III–249a
Speedboat V–27b
Speed frames II–239a
Speed limit III–415b
Speed skating
Olympic Games V–154a,b
"Speed-up" (labor) IV–273b
Speedwell (ship) IV–278b; V–313a
Speeler, Henry (mfr.) III–184b
Speiss, Mathias (hist.) III–405a
SPELLING BEE VI–372a; I–285a
Spelling schools II–487a
Spelman College IV–46a
Spencer, Ambrose (offi.) IV–445b
Spencer, Christopher M. (inv.) VI–372a
Spencer, Herbert (philos.) II–189a, 378a; V–287b, 441b
Spencer, Joseph (off.) VII–251b
Spencer, Phillip (nav. off.) IV–445b; VI–338a
Spencer Arms Company IV–433a
SPENCER RIFLE VI–372a; IV–430b; VI–139b
Spener, Philip Jacob (cler.) V–310b–11a
Spermaceti I–444a; III–413a; VII–285a
SPERMACETI TRUST VI–372b
Sperm candles I–444a
Sperm oil III–413a
Sperry, Charles S. (nav. off.) I–276b
Sperry, Elmer A. (eng.) II–413b
Sperry, Lawrence (instrument maker) I–51b
Sperry, Richard (farmer) VI–70b
Sperry Electric Light, Motor and Car Brake Company II–413b
Sperry Gyroscope Company I–51b
Sperry Messenger (airplane) II–344a
Sperry-Rand II–426b
Speyer, James (banker) III–79b
Spices II–388b; III–54b; VI–343b
Spiegler, Caesar (av.) II–343b
Spier, Leslie (anthrop.) I–129a
SPIES VI–372b
Civil War I–118b, 280a; II–159b
Hale, Nathan III–241a–b
Hiss case III–278a
House Committee on Un-American Activities III–308b
industrial II–462b, 463a
labor IV–70a
McCarthy-Army hearings IV–209b
revolutionary war I–118a–b; VI–118a
Rosenberg case VI–164b; VII–107b
Spies, August (ed.) III–266a
Spikes III–413a; IV–448b
Spindletop (Tex.) IV–334a; V–271b–72a; VI–356b; VII–40b
Spingarn, Arthur B. (law.) IV–461a
Spingarn, Joel (au.) IV–164a
Spinning (av.) IV–106a
Spinning (cloth mfg.) I–175a; II–81a, 237b, 239a
Spinning jenny II–237b
Spinning mills
child labor II–23b
Spinning wheel VII–42b, 320b
Spinoza, Baruch (philos.) III–316b
Spiring, Peter (dipl.) V–81a
SPIRIT LAKE MASSACRE (1857) **VI–374a**; III–468a
SPIRIT OF '76 (paint.) **VI–374b**
Spirit of Laws V–384b
Spirit of St. Louis (airplane) I–51a; IV–156b
Spiritualism V–87a, 213a,b
Rochester rappings VI–157b
theosophy VII–52a
Western Reserve VII–275a
Spiritual Milk for Boston Babes I–335a
Spirituals (mus.) III–48b; IV–442b, 443a
Spiro (Okla.) IV–370a; VI–353a
Spiro Mound V–148a
Spitaals-Bosschen (Belg.) VII–366b
Spitalfields (Eng.) II–371a
Spithead (Eng.) V–394a
Spitsbergen (Nor.) I–398b–99a; V–337a,b
Spitz, Mark (athlete) V–154b
Spock, Benjamin (physic.) VII–118a
Spofford, Ainsworth Rand (librarian) IV–148a
SPOILS SYSTEM VI–374b; III–486a,b; V–227b, 228a
Albany Regency I–82b
bureaucracy I–384a
civil service II–59b
corruption II–231b
Foreign Service III–71a
party machine IV–214a–b
Union Army I–182b
Spokane (Wash.) III–328b; VI–375b
lumber industry IV–204a
railroads VI–37b
Yakima Wars VII–350b
Spokane, Portland and Seattle Railway III–451b
SPOKANE HOUSE (Wash.) **VI–375b**
Spokane Indians III–363a, 500a,b; VII–239b
Spokane River I–209a; VII–247b
Spoliation claims, French. *See* French Spoliation Claims
Spoliation claims, Spanish V–315b

Sponge fishing II–89b
Spooky (gunship) I–54a; VI–302b
Spooner, Ephraim (col.) V–334a
Spooner Act (1902) V–201a,b
Spoor, John I–333a
Sporting goods
taxation VII–7b
Sports
baseball I–269b
basketball I–272a
fishing III–26a, 28a
football III–56b
golf III–197a
hockey III–286b
horse racing III–304a
integration III–438b
Madison Square Garden IV–220b
Olympic Games V–153b
prizefighting V–422a
segregation VI–256a
skiing VI–297b
tennis VI–28b
yacht racing VII–348b
Sports, Fisheries, and Wildlife, Bureau of I–306b; III–29a
Sports Car Club of America I–232a
Sports cars I–232a
Sportswear II–372b
Spotswood, Alexander (col. gov.) V–145a; VI–275b
exploring expedition IV–53a
Germanna III–173a
iron works VI–376a
postal service V–371a
Virginia Indian Company VII–201b
Spotswood family (Va.) IV–92a
SPOTSWOOD'S IRON FURNACES VI–376a
SPOTSYLVANIA COURTHOUSE, BATTLE OF (1864) **VI–376a**; II–62b; III–21a; V–113b; VI–137b; VII–197b, 296a
Bloody Angle I–322b
Civil War VII–68a, 358a
Spotted hog III–288b
Spotted Tail (Indian) VI–296b, 350a
Sprague, Frank J. (eng.) II–414b–15a; VI–40a
Sprague, Ralph I–498b
Sprague, Richard I–498b
Sprague, William I–498b
Sprague, William P. (mfr.) I–460a
Sprague Electric Railway and Motor Company II–414b–15a
Spray (N.C.) II–422a
Spreckels, Claus (mfr.) III–80a
Sprengel, Christian (chem.) III–16a
***SPRINGBOK* ADMIRALTY CASE** (1862) **VI–376b**; II–67b, 213a;
Springdale, Cedar County (Iowa) II–224a
Springer (N.Mex.) IV–278a
Springer Amendment V–148b
SPRINGER* v. *UNITED STATES (1881) **VI–377a**; III–351a–b
Springfield (Conn.) II–181b
Springfield (Ill.) III–309a
Camp Butler I–433a
Grand Army of the Republic III–207b
Grass Roots Conference III–213a
race riot I–29b; IV–460b
railroad VI–36a
Springfield (Ky.) II–362b
Springfield (Mass.) VI–151a; VII–282b
armory I–196b; IV–432b, 433a; V–163a
fur trade III–141a
population IV–268b
railroad III–449b; VI–35b
Shays's Rebellion VI–272a
witchcraft VII–309b
Springfield (Minn.) VI–374a
Springfield (Mo.)
cattle drives I–473a
Civil War I–462a; V–402b; VII–304a
railroads I–214b
Springfield (N.J.) II–321b; VI–377a
Springfield (Ohio)
race riot I–29b
revolutionary war V–319b
SPRINGFIELD, BATTLE OF (1780) **VI–377a**; V–57b
Springfield Armory (Mass.) III–441b, 442a; IV–430b
Springfield (Mass.) *Republican* (news.) III–148b; V–73b
Springfield rifle II–67a; IV–430b, 433a; VII–326a
Springfield Township (Ohio) III–84b
Springfield v. United States VII–6a
SPRING HILL, ENGAGEMENT AT (1864) **VI–377a**; III–98a, 298a
SPRINGS VI–377a
mineral springs IV–249a
salt VI–202a
Spring Valley (N.J.) IV–413a
Springwells (Mich.) III–316a
SPRING WELLS, TREATY OF (1815) **VI–377b**
Spring wheat I–329a; VII–286a
Spruance, Raymond A. (nav. off.) III–180a; IV–336a,b; VII–343b
Battle of the Philippine Sea V–285b
Fifth Fleet V–24b
Saipan VI–198a
Spruce III–72b, 74b; VI–48b; VII–59b
Spruce budworm III–74b
Spruce Tree House IV–315b
Spuds, copper II–386a
Spunky, Fort (Tex.) VII–77a
***"SPURLOS VERSENKT"* VI–378a**
Spurs II–249a
Spurwink (Maine) IV–207b; VI–184a
Spurzheim, Johann K. (physic.) V–293b
Sputnik (satellite) I–179b, 235a; II–143a, 426a, 448a; III–69b; IV–363b, 406b; VI–159b
Spuyten Duyvil Creek IV–237a
Squadron Office School I–64b
Squanto (Indian) IV–264b, 265a
"SQUARE DEAL" VI–378a
Square Deal (period.) IV–471b
Squared–log houses I–160b
Square–riggers I–448a; IV–310b, 311a; VI–279b, 280a–b
Squash I–36a, 47b, 48a, 157a; II–386a; III–51a, 366b, 367b, 381a; IV–385b; V–383a
Squatters I–499b; II–118b; VI–151b
Cimarron II–37a
claim associations II–70a–b
claim jumper II–70b
free land III–107b
Half–Breed Tract III–243a
Kansas Territory I–342a
land surveys VI–450b
military tracts IV–345a
Oregon IV–218b; V–165a–b
preemption II–70b; V–389b
public lands I–400b; V–444a
See also Oklahoma Squatters
Squatters' Claim Association VII–187b
Squatter sovereignty I–73b; V–360a
See also Popular Sovereignty
SQUAW CAMPAIGN (1778) **VI–378a**
Squawkie Hill Reservation (N.Y.) V–139b
Squaw Man (film) IV–417b
Squaw Valley VI–101b, 298b
Squibb, Edward R. (mfr.) IV–292b
Squier, Ephraim G. (dipl., archaeol.) I–128a; V–93b–94a; VI–378b
SQUIER TREATY (1849) **VI–378b**; V–93b–94a
Squirrel III–150a
"SQUIRREL HUNTERS" VI–378b
SR–71 (reconnaissance plane) I–52b, 235a
SS–7 (missile) IV–432a
SS–9 (missile) IV–432a
SS–11B1 (missile) IV–363b
S. S. Kresge stores III–32b, 33a
SST. *See* Supersonic transport
S. S. White Dental Manufacturing Company II–330b
Stabiles (sculp.) VI–244a
Stabilization Fund. *See* Gold Standard
Stabilizing the Dollar IV–233b
Stable Money Association IV–234a
Stable Money League IV–234a
Stack, John (av. designer) I–52a
Stackhouse, Mark (eng.) VI–409a
Stadnitski and Son (banking house) III–291a
Stadt Huis (New Amsterdam) V–40b
Staël, Madame de (writ.) III–259b
Stafford, T. F. (bus.) VI–378b
Stafford Springs (Conn.) VI–100b
STAFFORD* v. *WALLACE (1922) **VI–378b**; II–136b
STAGE, FISHING VI–379a
Stagecoaches I–461a
Stagecoaches, overland. *See* Overland Mail and Stagecoaches
STAGECOACH LINES OF THE SOUTHWEST VI–379a
Central Overland California and Pikes Peak Express I–485a
Fort Yuma VII–367b
Great Plains III–221a
Hockaday and Liggett VI–176b
STAGECOACH ROBBERIES VI–379b; VII–97b
STAGECOACH TRAVEL VI–379b; VII–99b–100a, 101a, 168a, 218a
Apache territory I–142a
Concord Coach II–158a
Frink and Walker III–124a
harness III–255b
horses III–303a
Lancaster Pike IV–89b
Michigan Territorial Road IV–332b
New York City V–82b
Ohio National Stage Company V–144b
Richmond VI–137a
routes VI–379a–b
taverns VII–2a
Texas VII–39a
water supply VI–377b
Stag–Hound (clipper ship) II–77a
Stainless steel III–12a, 12b–13a, 13b, 14a, 15a
Stair, Earl of (John Dalrymple) (dipl.) II–121b
Stake, burning at the I–197a
STAKED PLAIN VI–380b; II–228b
exploration II–184b
mustangs IV–444b
Red River Indian War VI–64a

sheep wars VI–273b
Texas Rangers VII–42a
Wagon Train charge VII–217a
Stakman, E. C. (bot.) I–46a
Stalin, Joseph I–179b, 403b; II–28a; III–61b, 69b; VI–179a,b, 416b
Communist party II–144a–b
Manchuria IV–235b
Potsdam Conference V–378b
Soviet missile development IV–363b
Soviet navy V–10b
Teheran Conference VII–18a
U.S.–Soviet arms race I–179a–b
Yalta Conference VII–351b
Stallings Island (Ga.) I–157a; II–386a
STALWARTS VI–380b
Stam, Mark (arch.) III–136b
Stamford (Conn.) III–271b; V–55b; VI–134b
STAMP ACT (1765) **VI–381a**; I–110b, 145a; II–123a, 309a; III–346b; V–161a, 221a; VI–110b, 111a, 112a; VII–3b
cartoon I–464a
letters of "Junius" IV–20b
Maine IV–226a
Maryland IV–260b
Mutiny Act of 1765 IV–445b
New Jersey V–57a
New York City V–85b
nonimportation agreements V–104a
North Carolina V–115b
opposition I–207b; IV–265b–66a
repeal II–309a
Sons of Liberty VI–113b, 338b
STAMP ACT CONGRESS (1765) **VI–382a**; I–82b; V–82b, 85b
Stamp Act Crisis III–283a
STAMP ACT RIOT (1765) **VI–382a**
Stamp Advisory Committee, Citizens V–372b
Stamp duties VII–4b
STAMPEDES VI–382a; II–250a; IV–184b; VI–364b; VII–96a
Stamping Act (1906) VI–290a
Stamps, postage. *See* Postage stamps
Stamp tax VII–5a,b, 6a
Stanbery, Henry (law.) IV–376a; VI–59a
Standard and Poor index V 210a–
Standard City Planning Enabling Act (1924) II–47a
Standard Metropolitan Statistical Areas V–364a–b
Standard of value. *See* Money
STANDARD OIL COMPANY VI–382b; III–80a, 113a–b, 122b; V–141b, 269b–70a; VI–383b; VII–122a
Baton Rouge refinery I–274b
Cleveland II–75a
dissolved II–230a
kerosine stove IV–44b
muckrakers VI–157a
New Jersey politics V–58a
Panay incident V–205b
panic of 1907 V–208b
railroad rebates VI–50a
research III–409a,b
Standard Oil Company of Indiana V–267a, 270a; VI–384a
STANDARD OIL COMPANY OF NEW JERSEY* v. *UNITED STATES (1911) **VI–383b**; I–114a, 140a; II–71b; VI–102a–b, 169a; VII–117b, 122b, 124b, 155a
Standard Oil Trust Agreement VI–383b
Standards, National Bureau of. *See* National Bureau of Standards
Standards Association, American VI–185a
STANDARDS OF LIVING VI–384a; II–235b
automation II–427a
capitalism I–449a
consumer purchasing power II–209b
food III–53b
health VI–212b
Indian III–396b–97a
inflation II–209b
Norway VI–472a–b
public health VI–173b
rural health VI–174a
rural population VI–175b
sectionalism VI–254b
social legislation VI–327a
social settlements VI–330a–b
technological development II–427a
Standards of Weights and Measures, Office of Superintendent of II–87b
Standard time V–131a; VI–28a
Standerin, Ann Lee (rel. leader) VI–268a
Standing armies IV–345b, 383b
billeting I–297a
colonies II–308b–09a
Declaration of Independence II–307a
Standing Committee on Antiquities I–128a
Standing committees VI–122b, 411b
STANDING ORDER VI–384b; VII–22b
Standing Rock Agency (N.Dak.) VII–344b
Standing Rock Sioux VI–295b
"Stand–ins" I–31a
Standish, Burt L. (William Gilbert Patten) (au.) II–341b
Standish, Laura VI–205b
Standish, Myles (col.) IV–264b–65a, 315a
Cape Ann I–446b
Fort Pentegoet V–253b
Weston's settlement VII–279a
"STANDPATTERS" VI–384b; VII–306b
Stand Watie (Indian) VI–317a
Stanfield–Worley Bluff Shelter (Ala.) I–156a; II–385b
Stanford (Ky.) IV–179a
Stanford (N.Y.) IV–169a
Stanford, Leland (ind., pol.) I–406a; III–79b; V–430b; VII–101a
Stanford–Binet intelligence test III–440a–b
Stanford University
genetic research III–157b
Klystron VII–163b
microwave technology IV–333a
parapsychology V–213a
political science V–349a
Stanhope press V–411a
Stanislavski, Konstantin (act., prod.) VII–50a
Stankiewicz, Richard (sculp.) VI–244a
Stanley, Ann Lee. *See* Standerin, Ann Lee
Stanley, Frederick Arthur (states.) III–287a
Stanley, Robert (prospector) III–270a
Stanley, Wendell M. (biochem.) I–349b; IV–389a; V–99b
Stanley Company V–291b
Stanley Cup III–287a
Stanley Steamer (auto) I–226a
Stannard Rock Lighthouse VI–146b
Stansbury, Howard (off.). *See* Stansbury Exploration
STANSBURY EXPLORATION (1849–50) **VI–385a**; III–222a; VI–90b
Stanton (N.Dak.) IV–235b
Stanton, Charles E. (off.) IV–84b; VII–325b
Stanton, Edwin M. (law.) V–141b, 377b
Confederate surrender II–68b
General Order No. 100 II–70a
Georgia Reconstruction III–171b
Johnson impeachment III–345b
military censorship I–481a
peace movement of 1864 V–234b
recruitment II–451b
removal by Johnson VI–57a, 84b; VII–31b
Soldiers and Sailors convention VI–336a
War Department II–63a
Stanton, Elizabeth Cady (ref.) III–91b; V–87a
Senaca Falls convention VI–261b
Seneca Falls Convention V–97a; VII–313b, 315a, 317a
STANTON, FORT (N.Mex.) **VI–385a**
Stanton, Henry B. (law., ref.) I–137b
Stanton, T. W. (paleon.) V–196a
STANWIX, FORT (N.Y.) **VI–385a**
Indian land cession III–382b
national monument V–217b
revolutionary war I–81b, 385a; IV–387a; V–172b
STANWIX, FORT, TREATY OF (1768) **VI–385b**; I–278a; III–24b, 209a, 382b; IV–201b; V–425a; VI–385a, 386a
Holston Valley settlements III–292b
Indiana Company III–370b
"Indiana" grant VII–166b
"suffering traders" VI–430a
Virginia cession VII–203a
Watauga settlement VII–253a
western settlement IV–371a
STANWIX, FORT, TREATY OF (1784) **VI–386a**; III–255a, 383a; IV–201b, 216b; VI–385b
Stanwix, John (off.) III–116b; V–321a; VI–385a
STAPLES, COLONIAL VI–386a
tafia VI–456b
tobacco VII–66b
Staple Singers IV–442b
Stapleton Airport (Denver) II–332a
Stapp, John Paul (med. off.) IV–293a
Star (emblem) II–437b
Star boats VII–349b
Starch III–44b, 408a; V–376b
Star Chamber III–274b
Star–delta transformation II–39a
***STARE DECISIS* VI–386b**; IV–14b
Starfighter (plane) I–54a
Starfire (plane) I–54a
Star Island III–479b
Stark, Harold R. (nav. off.) V–240a; VII–334b
Stark, John (off.) V–126a; VI–162b
Battle of Bennington I–289a; V–54a
Bunker Hill I–382b
Burgoyne's invasion of New York I–385a

Starlight, Operation (1965) VII–186a
Star Mound (Can.) IV–118a
"Star of the North." *See* Minnesota
STAR OF THE WEST (merchantman) **VI–387a**; VI–251a
Starr, Ellen Gates (soc. worker) II–18a; VI–330b
Starr, Harris E. (ed.) II–340b
Starr, James H. (postmaster) V–373a
Starr, Jehosaphat (inv.) VI–408b
Starr, Nathan (mfr.) IV–432b
Starr Arms Company IV–433a
STAR ROUTE FRAUDS VI–387a
Star route mail service V–372a
STARS, FALLING OF THE (1833) **VI–387b**
Stars and Stripes (news.) IV–471b; V–68a, 73a
Stars and Stripes Forever (comp.) IV–441b
"STAR-SPANGLED BANNER" VI–387b; I–249b; II–357b; III–34b; IV–213b, 261a, 446a; VI–320a
"Starvation Trail." *See* Smoky Hill Trail
STARVED ROCK (Ill.) **VI–388a**; II–257b; III–119a, 329a; VI–195a
Starved Rock State Park VI–388a
STARVING TIME VI–388a; IV–295a
  Jamestown III–489a; VII–192b
  New Plymouth Colony V–64b
  Virginia V–385b
Stas, J. S. (chem.) I–218b
Stassen, Harold E. (pol.) II–492a
Stassfurt (Ger.) III–17a
STATE, DEPARTMENT OF VI–388a; I–359b, 383b, 399a; II–498a,b; VI–122b
  arbitrary arrest I–196b
  armed merchantmen IV–313b
  Bureau of Intelligence and Research III–439b
  census reports I–482a,b
  embassies II–437a,b
  Export–Import Banks I–263a
  foreign contract labor II–214a
  Foreign Relations III–281a
  Foreign Service III–72a,b
  Hiss Case III–278a–b
  International Information Administration V–432b
  McCarthy hearings VII–310b
  Mint III–245b
  most-favored-nation principle IV–416b
  Office of Strategic Services V–138b
  Office of War Information II–499a
  party platforms V–329a
  passports V–225a
  patents V–225b–26a
  reciprocal trade agreements VI–52a,b
  Statutes at Large I–167b
  tariff VI–468b
  Tariff Board VI–464b
  territorial governments VII–32b
  U.S. shipping protection IV–255a
  War Trade Board VII–244a
State, secretary of VII–201b
  ambassadors I–93a
  Committee on Public Information II–139b
  Pan-American Union IV–111b
  presidential success V–398b
  seal of the United States VI–246b
State and Local Assistance Act (1972) VI–10b
State banking. *See* Banking, State
STATE BANK OF INDIANA VI–390a
State boundary disputes. *See* Boundary Disputes Between the States
STATE CHAIRMAN VI–390a
STATE CONSTITUTIONS VI–390b; VI–396b, 397b, 398a,b, 401a
  bills of rights VI–118b
  black suffrage VI–431a, 432a
  California VI–364b
  cruel and unusual punishment V–464a
  debt limits II–302b
  Florida III–39a,b
  free-press provisions V–78b
  grandfather clause III–208b
  habeas corpus III–236b
  Illinois III–330a
  impeachment III–343b
  initiative III–418a
  Iowa III–468a,b
  judicial review IV–13a
  jury trial IV–21a
  Kansas IV–26a, 28a–b; V–429b; VII–73a, 345a–b
  Kentucky IV–42b, 43a
  Lecompton Constitution IV–130b
  legislative riders VI–138b
  literacy test VII–209b
  Louisiana IV–195a
  Maryland IV–260b
  Michigan IV–331a
  Mississippi IV–368b, 369a, 371b
  Missouri VII–35a
  natural rights V–7b
  Nebraska V–31b
  New Jersey V–57a, 58a
  New York V–86a,b
  North Carolina V–115b, 116a
  Ohio VII–204b
  organic law V–170a
  Pennsylvania V–247a
  police power V–339b
  Reconstruction VI–57a,b
  referenda VI–66b
  reserved powers of the people VI–98a–b
  Rhode Island VI–133b
  right of petition V–265a
  Separation of powers IV–133b; V–385a
  South Carolina VI–347b, 348a
  Texas VII–39a
  treason VII–106b
  Vanhorne's Lessee v. *Dorrance* VII–167a
  Vermont VII–171b
  Virginia VII–194a–b, 195a,b, 281b
  Virginia Declaration of Rights VII–201a
State corporations II–302b
State debts. *See* Debts, State
State Department Task Forces Report (1970) III–72a
State Dispensary (S.C.) VII–59a
STATE EMBLEMS, NICKNAMES, MOTTOS, AND SONGS VI–392a
  Kentucky VII–155b
  Maryland IV–262a
  Minnesota IV–355a
  Sic semper tyrannis VI–285a
  Wyoming VII–346a
State Fair Park (Dallas) VII–41a
STATE FAIRS VI–392b
  Iowa III–468b
State flags III–35a
STATE GOVERNMENT VI–396a
  administrative agencies I–13b
  admiralty courts I–14b
  antebellum South VI–343a
  apportionment I–147a–48a; III–86b–87a
  Articles of Confederation I–197b; II–165b–67a, 211b–12a, 275b
  bicameral legislatures I–294b
  Bill of Rights I–269a, 299a,b
  bills of credit I–365a; II–253b
  bills of rights I–297b
  birth and death registration IV–149a
  boards of education II–404b–05a
  boards of nurse examiners V–127a
  business regulation I–391b
  canal financing I–442b
  capital punishment V–464b
  centralization I–484b
  child labor I–243b; II–24b
  circuit courts II–40a
  citizenship II–42a
  civil service II–60a–b
  commerce clause II–135b–37a, 220a
  commercial bounties I–352b
  common law II–141b
  congressional districts II–172a, 355b
  constitutional amendments I–94a–95b
  consumer protection II–208b
  contract clause II–213b
  convict labor II–217a
  corporation charters II–229a, 293b; V–457a
  corporation regulation I–133a
  corruption I–343a–b; II–231b, 232a
  corrupt practices acts II–232b–33a; V–450a
  county government in II–245a
  debts II–302a–03a
  discrimination II–457a; III–60a
  due process of law II–378b
  eminent domain II–440a
  employment service II–441b–42a
  equal protection of the law II–457a,b
  executive removal power VI–85a–b
  expenditures II–234a; III–205a–b
  extradition II–478b
  fair-trade laws II–483b
  federal aid II–476b, 501b, 502b
  federal revenue distribution IV–91a–b
  federal-state relations III–9a
  fish and wildlife services III–27b–28a
  food laws V–465a
  food stamps III–56a
  Fourteenth Amendment III–86a
  freedom of speech III–104a
  geological surveys III–164b
  governors III–206a
  Granger laws III–209b, 211a
  grants-in-aid III–211b
  habeas corpus III–236b–37a
  highway construction VI–155a
  holding companies III–290a
  home rule III–294b
  housing III–310b
  impeachment III–344b
  implied powers III–348b–49a
  industry inspection III–422a
  industry regulation III–204a–b
  inheritance tax laws

III–418a
initiative III–418b
insurance III–432a,b
internal improvements
III–63b–64a, 448a, 449b, 450a,b, 451a,b
interstate commerce
III–458b
interstate compacts
III–459b
judicial review III–36a, 292a
labor conciliation II–157b
labor protection IV–80a,b
legislature IV–133b
licenses to trade
IV–148a–b
liquor laws I–95a; IV–158b; V–45a
literacy tests IV–159b–60a
local governments
IV–172a–b
lotteries IV–191b
loyalty oaths IV–203a
martial law IV–258b
maternal and child health care IV–275b–76a
medical profession
IV–284a,b
mortgage relief legislation
IV–414a
municipal charters
I–500b; IV–427a
national defense II–313a
National Guard IV–346a
New Jersey V–58a
Ohio Sweeping Resolution
VI–454b
patronage V–228a,b
pension plans V–255a
police V–339a, 339a
political assessments
V–341b
political contributions
I–414a,b
political patronage
I–145b–46a; V–227b
political subdivisions
V–349a
poll tax V–355a
poor relief VI–72b, 73a,b, 74a,b
privileges and immunities of citizens V–420b
property laws
V–433b–34a
provincial congresses
V–440a
public business enterprises
III–201b, 202b
public ownership V–455a
public revenue VI–105b
public schools IV–24b
public utilities V–458b
railroad rate laws VI–21b
referendum VI–66a,b
reserved powers of the people VI–98a–b
reserved powers of the states VI–97b
residual power III–417b
Rhode Island VI–133b
ripper legislation VI–144b
separation of powers
V–385a
social legislation VI–327b
state consitutions
VI–390b
state fairs VI–392b
state-making process
VI–399b
statistics VII–206b
statutes of limitations
VI–405b
suffrage III–91a–93b
Supreme Court VI–447a
surrogate's court VI–450a
taxation II–266b; VII–4a,b, 6b, 7b, 10b–11b
teachers' loyalty oath
VII–15b
third parties VII–53a
tidelands VII–57a
tolls VII–69a,b
town government VII–78a
travel allowances IV–339a
treaties I–362b–63a
unemployment relief
V–381b
uniform state laws
VI–399a,b
universities VII–156a
voter qualifications
V–434b; VI–99b; VII–208a–09a
voter registration VI–71a
woman's suffrage II–325b
women VII–317b
workmen's compensation
III–431a,b
State Governments, Council of
III–459b–60a; VI–402a,b
State Highway Officials, National Association of
VI–402b
State House of Pennsylvania (Phila.) I–161b
State laws
civil rights and liberties
II–53b
debtors II–299a
declaratory judgment
II–309b
elections II–216a, 408b–09a, 410a–11a, 412a, 480a–b
employers' liability
II–441a
gambling II–263a
labor II–482a
military service II–186a, 366b–67a
Prohibition II–407a
wiretapping
II–427b
workmen's compensation
II–441b
STATE LAWS, UNIFORM
VI–399a; II–309b; VI–402b, 403a
consumer credit III–423b
horse racing IV–191b
Swift v. *Tyson* VI–454b
See also National Conference of the Commissioners on Uniform State Laws
STATE-MAKING PROCESS
VI–399b; II–202b, 443a, 443a–b, 453b; VII–31b–32a
Staten Island (N.Y.)
II–347a, 349a; V–82a, 368b
Delaware Indians II–320b
ferries III–11a–b
revolutionary war
IV–186a; VI–377a
Sailor's Snug Harbor
VI–186b
ship graveyard II–438b
tide mills VII–58a
Walloons VII–221b
Staten Island Cricket and Baseball Club VII–29a
State of Maine Song VI–394 (table)
State of Prisons and of Child-Saving Institutions in the Civilized World V–415b
State of the Prisons in England and Wales V–415a
State of the Union message
II–201b; III–3a; V–398a
State parks. *See* Parks, state
STATES, RELATIONS BETWEEN THE VI–401b; VI–398a
boundary disputes I–350a
Hartford Convention
III–259a
inheritance taxes III–418a
interstate commerce
III–178a–b
interstate compacts
III–459b
interstate trade barriers
III–460b
legal controversies
II–202a
privileges and immunities of citizens V–420a
Supreme Court jurisdiction
VI–444b
uniform state laws
VI–399a
water rights III–478a
State songs. *See* State Emblems, Nicknames, Mottos, and Songs
STATE SOVEREIGNTY
VI–403a; I–404a; VI–397a
New York V–86b
right of secession VI–250a
state laws VI–399a
states' rights VI–404a
Virginia and Kentucky Resolutions VII–198a
"State Sovereignty, National Union" VI–393 (table)
State-space concept II–39a
STATES' RIGHTS
VI–404a; II–325b; III–9a–b; VI–397a, 403b–04a
agrarianism I–33a
Alabama I–71a,b
Antifederalists I–130b
Bank of the United States
V–174a–b
Bourbons I–354a
Calhoun's *Disquisition on Government* I–404a
campaign of 1856 I–421a
Chisholm v. *Georgia*
II–32a
Civil War II–160b, 165a
Convention of 1787
II–193 –95b
Eleventh Amendment
II–431a
fair-trade laws II–484a
federal surplus VI–449a
Georgia III–168b; VII–121a
Hartford Convention
III–259a
implied powers III–349a
interstate trade barriers
III–461a
Jackson, Andrew V–176b
judicial review of state legislation IV–19b
Nashville Convention
IV–453b
New Jersey Plan II–151b
nullification I–87a; V–125b
pamphlets II–264b
public land states V–453a
Pullman strike IV–67a
Richmond Junto VI–138a
secession VI–250b
slavery VI–307b
Sons of Liberty VI–339a
South Carolina VI–347b
taxation IV–105b
U.S. Constitution II–202b
Virginia and Kentucky Resolutions VII–198a
Webster-Hayne debate
VII–265b
States' Rights Democratic Party I–71b, 429b
STATES' RIGHTS IN THE CONFEDERACY
VI–405a; VI–404a
States' Rights party II–480b; III–9b; V–198a
State Street (Boston) V–230a
State Street (Chicago)
IV–100b
State Theater (N.Y.C.)
II–289a
Statistical Association, American VII–206b
Statistical Atlas I–482a
Statistics
Census Bureau
I–481b–82b
parapsychology V–213a
sampling VI–205b
See also Vital Statistics
Statuary Hall I–163a
STATUE OF LIBERTY
VI–405b; I–275b; II–432b; III–97a; V–217a,b
Statute of Artificers (1563)
I–148a
Statute of Monopolies (1623)
IV–399a; V–225b
Statute of Virginia for Religious Freedom
VII–193b–94a
Statute of Westminister II (1285) II–452a
STATUTES AT LARGE, UNITED STATES
VI–405b; I–167b; II–91b–92a; III–203b; IV–209b; VII–113b
STATUTES OF LIMITATIONS VI–405b
STATUTORY LAW
VI–406a
cow custom II–251a
judicial review IV–12a
Justice Department
IV–22a
state debt limitations
VI–398b
Staunton (Va.) II–44b; IV–172a, 201a; VII–194a

Staunton River VII–202b
Staves V–319a–b
STAY AND VALUATION ACTS VI–406a; II–213b
Stayner, Richard (nav. off.) VII–270b
Stazione Zoologica (Naples) IV–251a
Steak III–52b
STEAMBOATING ON WESTERN WATERS VI–406b; IV–310a; VI–148b, 408a, 409a; VII–260a,b
domestic trade IV–309a
Falls of the Ohio V–142b
Iowa III–468a
Mississippi River III–35b; IV–372b, 373a, 374a; VI–407b
Missouri River IV–380a, 381a, 403a
Nashville IV–452b
Natchez IV–455a
New Orleans V–63a
Ohio River IV–470b
Prairie du Chien V–388a
railroad rate wars VI–23a
Red River IV–457a
Red River of the North V–117a
Red River raft VI–65a
Western Engineer VII–271a
Yellowstone VII–357a
Yellowstone River expeditions VII–357b
Steamboat Inspection Service II–89a, 135a; III–422a
STEAMBOAT MONOPOLIES VI–407a; III–131b 32a, 178a; V–289a
STEAMBOAT RACING VI–407b; VII–100b
STEAMBOATS VI–408a; III–428a; IV–35b, 266b; VI–148a–b; VII–100b
Atlantic cable I–400b
canal locks IV–175a
Carondelet I–459a
Civil War II–253a
clipper ships II–77a
coasting trade II–90b–91a
Columbia River settlement II–131b
Demologos II–329a
disasters II–89a, 349a–b
domestic trade VII–83a–b
engine VI–408b–10a
explosion research III–99a
federal safety rules II–230b
Fitch experiments III–32a
Fulton III–131b
Fulton's Folly III–131b
gambling III–149b
great fortunes III–79a
Great Lakes III–218a–b
growth of cities II–41a
Hudson–Fulton celebration III–312a
Hudson River I–81b–82a; III–131b–32a, 312b
Industrial Revolution III–411b, 412a
inland waterways VII–260a,b
James River II–382b
Lake Erie II–459a
"mark twain" IV–256a
Mississippi River V–62a
Missouri River I–206a; III–143b
New Jersey V–57b
New Orleans IV–194a; V–63a
New York City V–83a
New York State V–86b–87a
Panama Canal IV–309a
patent V–225b
Phoenix V–289a
Pittsburgh V–321b–22a
poker V–336a
postal service V–372a, 375a
river navigation VI–149b–50a
Rumsey's steamboats VI–170b
Saint Paul VII–134a
shipping IV–310a,b, 311a
snagboats VI–322a
Tombigbee River VII–70b
Vicksburg VII–181b
Virginia VI–137a
Virginia III–468a; VII–196b
Walk-in-the-Water IV–331a; VII–83b, 220b
West, Edward VII–280b
Western Engineer III–468a; VII–271a
westward movement VII–283b
whalebacks VII–285a
Wheeling VII–287b
Wheeling Bridge VII–288a
Yellowstone VII–357a
Steamboat Springs (Colo.) VI–101b
Steam Engineering, Navy Bureau of V–18a
Steamers, ironclad IV–85a
STEAM POWER AND ENGINES VI–408b; I–276a; II–412b–13a, 415b; VII–257b
agriculture I–35b, 38a
automobile I–225b
elevators II–428b, 429a
fire engines III–25a
flour milling III–44a
furniture industry III–138b–39a
gold mining III–191a
grain elevators II–430a; III–43a
heating III–269a
Industrial Revolution III–410b–11a,b
leather industry IV–128a
locomotives II–416a, 428a; IV–175a–77a
Massachusetts industry IV–266b–67a
naval vessels IV–431b
Niagara Falls power V–92b
ocean shipping VI–280b
printing press V–77a
railroads VI–24b
refrigeration VI–69b
rice production VI–136a
Savannah VI–221a
sawmills VI–222b–23a
shipping IV–309b–10a,b
steamboats VI–408a
street railways VI–418a
sugarcane VI–436a
textile industry II–237b; VI–133a
towboats VII–77b
transportation VII–100b
turbines VII–129a–b
wagons IV–419b
warships III–36a
water supply VII–258a,b
whalers VII–285b
wheat growing VII–286b
wool industry VII–320b
See also Steamboats
Steamship Historical Society of America III–279a
Steamship lines II–91a; V–183b
Steam wagon V–177b
Steam warships VII–240b–41b, 243b
Stearine IV–153a
Stebbins, James H. (art collector) II–103b
Stebbins, Robert C. (herpetol.) VI–91b
Stebbins house (Mass.) II–312b
Stedman, Edmund Clarence (au.) IV–163a
STEDMAN, FORT, ASSAULT ON (1865) **VI–410a**; V–265a
Stedman, John II–339b
Steedman, J. B. (off.) VI–336a
Steel
armor plate I–179a
automobile I–228a
bridges I–364a,b
building construction I–378a–b, 379a
furniture III–137a
ships II–438a–b
See also Iron and Steel Industry; Iron and Steel Manufacture
Steel alloys III–14b, 15a
Steele, A. T. (jour.) V–74a
Steele, Frederick (off.) III–498a; VI–63a
Steele, Matthew Forney (off.) II–367b
STEELE'S BAYOU EXPEDITION (1863) **VI–410b**
Steel Institute VI–218b
STEEL STRIKES VI–410b; IV–72b
Homestead strike IV–66a
U.S. Steel IV–69b
STEEL TRAP VI–411a
Steel trust III–443b; V–208b
Steel Workers' Organizing Committee IV–72b; VI–410b–11a
Steelworkers Union VI–411a
Steenbock, Harry (biochem.) I–303a–b
STEERING COMMITTEES VI–411b
Steers, George VII–348b
Steffe, William (comp.) I–277a
Steffens, Lincoln (au.) IV–424b, 427b; V–278a
Stegg, Thomas (trader) VI–136b
Steiglitz, Alfred (art dealer) II–104a
Stein, Clarence (arch.) II–46b
Stein, Gertrude (writ.) IV–3a, 164a
Lost Generation IV–189b, 190a
music IV–439a
Stein, William H. (biochem.) I–304a; V–100a
Steinbeck, John (au.) IV–164b; V–99b
Steinem, Gloria (writ.) V–79a
Steinkraus, William (athlete) V–154b
Steinman, David B. (eng.) II–449a
Steinmetz, Charles P. (eng.) II–39a, 415b; III–409a
Stejneger, Leonhard Hess (nat.) VI–91a
Stella, Frank (paint.) V–193b
Stella, Joseph (paint.) V–192b
Stellar astronomy I–211b
Steller, Georg Wilhelm (nat.) I–74b; VI–245b
Stellingen (Ger.) VII–371a
Stencil paintings III–47a
Stengrum, Henry (inv.) II–420b
Stephen, Adam (off.) III–173b
Stephens, Alexander H. (states.) II–160a, 165a; III–247b; IV–405a; VI–56b, 405a
Stephens, Ann S. (au.) II–341a
Stephens, Captain (trapper) VII–105a
Stephens, Samuel (off.) I–83a; VI–190b
Stephens, Uriah S. (labor leader) IV–52a, 64a
Stephens, William (pol.) IV–406a
Stephenson, Benjamin F. (physic.) III–207b
STEPHENSON, FORT, DEFENSE OF (1813) **VI–412a**; VI–208b
Stephenson, George (inv.) VI–27b
Stephenson, John G. (librarian) IV–148a
Steptoe, Edward J. (off.) VII–350b
Stereochemistry II–12a
Stereophonic Radio Committee, National VI–16b
Stereophonic sound II–424b–25b; III–410a; V–290b; VI–14b, 16b
Stereotype (print.) V–77a
Sterilization I–445a; III–159a
Sterling (Mass.) II–494a
Sterling Iron and Railway Company VI–412a

STERLING IRON WORKS VI–412a; III–313a
Sterlington (N.Y.) VI–412a
Sterling v. *Constantin* (1932) IV–258b
Stern, Louis William (psych.) III–440b
Stern, Otto (phys.) V–100a
Sternberg, George M. (physic.) I–241b; IV–291a,b
Sternwheeler II–496a; VI–408a
Sterols IV–281a
Stethoscope IV–298a
Steuart, Andrew (pub.) I–494a
STEUBEN, FORT (Ohio) **VI–412a**
Steuben, Friedrich Wilhelm von (off.) I–183b; II–38a, 218a; VI–124a, 126a, 129b, 351b; VII–226b, 358b
  Valley Forge VII–165b
  Washington's Lifeguard IV–152a
  West Point VII–279b–80a
  Yorktown VII–360b
Steuben County (N.Y.) V–463b
Steuben Glass Company III–186a
Steubenville (Ohio) I–244a, 364a; III–258a; IV–351b
  See also Steuben, Fort
Steunenberg, Frank (pol.) II–93b; III–266b
Stevens, Edwin A. (eng.) I–179a; III–36a–b
Stevens, Henry N. (bookman) II–109a, 466b
Stevens, Isaac I. (off.) I–494a; IV–403a
  Piegan War V–310a
  railroad survey VI–412b
  See also Steven's Indian Treaties; Stevens' Railroad Survey
Stevens, John (inv.) I–179a; III–36a
  locomotives IV–175a
  Phoenix V–289a
  railroads V–57b; VI–24b
  steamboat VI–408b
Stevens, John C. (nav. off.) VII–348b
Stevens, John F. (eng.) V–201b; VI–163b
Stevens, John H. (pioneer) VII–134a
Stevens, John L. (dipl.) III–263b
Stevens, Robert L. (eng., inv.) I–179a; III–36a–b
  "T" rail VI–36a, 39b
Stevens, Robert T. (offi.) IV–210a
Stevens, Thaddeus (law., pol.)
  Anti–masonic movements I–132b
  Buckshot War I–374a
  Civil war finances II–66a
  Radical Republicans VI–11b, 12a, 13b
  Reconstruction Acts VI–59a
  Reconstruction policy IV–6a
Stevens, Wallace (poet) IV–164a, 165b
Stevens, W. H. (min.) IV–124a
Stevens Battery (ironclad) III–474b
Stevens County (Kans.) II–245b
Steven's House (N.Y.C.) I–143b
STEVENS' INDIAN TREATIES (1854–55) **VI–412b**
  Nez Perce V–89b
Stevens Institute of Technology II–448a
Stevens–Murphy–Townsend wagon train VII–217b
Stevenson, Adlai E. (states.) III–330a
  campaign of 1892 I–424b
  campaign of 1952 I–430a
  vice–presidency VII–179 (table)
Stevenson, Andrew (dipl.) II–175 (table), 444a
Stevenson, Robert Louis (au.) IV–223a
STEVENS' RAILROAD SURVEY VI–412b; IV–403a; VI–39a
Steward, Ira (labor leader) IV–62b
Steward, Julian H. (ethnol.) I–129b; II–465a
Stewart, Alexander (off.) II–465a
Stewart, Alexander Turney (mer.) I–17a; II–103b
Stewart, Alvan (law.) I–137b–38a
Stewart, Anthony (mer.) IV–260b; V–241b–42a
Stewart, Charles (nav. off.) II–191b
Stewart, Ellen (dir.) VII–51a
Stewart, George E. (off.) I–158b
Stewart, Lazarus (ranger) V–231a; VII–353a
Stewart, Potter (jur.) II–378b; VI–447a
Stewart, Robert, Viscount Castlereagh (states.) I–126b; III–176b, 217a
Stewart, William Drummond (trav.) VII–104a
Stewartsville (Tex.) VII–35b
Stibitz, George (eng.) II–153b, 154a
Stickley, Gustav III–136a
Stickney, Josiah H. (vet.) VII–176b
Sticks and Stones IV–164a
Stick style architecture I–164a
Stiegel, Henry William (mfr.) III–182b, 184b
Stikine River VI–151a
Stiles, Charles Wardell (zool.) I–241b; III–298b
Stiles, Ezra (cler.) VI–451b; VII–205b
Still, Andrew T. (physic.) IV–288b; V–175a
Still, Clyfford (art.) II–105b
Still, William (ref.) VII–138b
Still, William Grant (comp.) IV–438b
Stillingfleet, Benjamin (nat.) II–390b
Still life painting V–185b, 190a
Stillman, James (banker) II–103a; III–79b
Stills (liquor) I–339a,b; IV–407b
Stillwater (Minn.) II–490a–b; IV–356a; VI–295a, 413a
Stillwater, Battles of. *See* Freeman's Farm, Battles of
STILLWATER CONVENTION (1848) **VI–413a**
Stilwell, Joseph W. (off.) I–386b, 387a; II–26a; IV–314a, 447a; VII–337b
Stilwell, Silas M. (law., au.) VI–143b
Stilwell Road I–386b
Stimson, Henry L. (states.) VII–334b, 336a
  Chile V–107b
  Manchukuo III–457a; V–107a
  Manhattan Project IV–433b
  Nicaragua II–343a, 471b; V–94a
  nonrecognition doctrine V–96b, 159a
  Philippines V–283b
  War Department VII–230a
Stimson Doctrine II–489a; III–69a; V–107a,b
Stinkards IV–456a
Stinson Aircraft Division of Voltec Aircraft, Inc. I–52b
Stinson Reliant (monoplane) I–52b
Stirling, Earl of. *See* Alexander, William
Stirling, Thomas (off.) III–330b
Stirling Iron Works. *See* Sterling Iron Works
Stites, Benjamin (trader) IV–329b
Stitt, Edward R. (med. off.) IV–292b
Stobnicza, Johannes de (cartog.) IV–247b
Stockbridge (Mass.) IV–387a, 472a
Stockbridge Indians III–379b, 400a
  Rogers' Rangers VI–190a
Stock exchanges. *See* Exchanges
Stock farming I–267b; III–10b
Stock feed II–227a
Stockholm (Swed.) V–416a
Stockings, nylon II–372b
Stockings, silk II–371a, 372a
Stock market
  crash of 1929 I–390b
  See also Exchanges
Stock market crash (1929) II–416b, 417a, 500b
  See also Panic of 1929
Stockpiling II–498a
Stock roundups II–247a
Stocks (fin.)
  absentee ownership I–3b
  banking I–256b, 257a
  Blue Sky laws I–325b
  employee ownership IV–70a
Stocks (fin.)
  depression of 1920 II–333b
STOCKS (punishment) **VI–413b**; V–313b, 464b, 465a
Stock saddle VI–184b
Stock savings banks I–264a
STOCK TICKER VI–413b; I–396a
Stockton (Calif.) V–30a
Stockton, Frank (au.) I–335b
Stockton, Richard (law.) II–308a; V–409a
Stockton, Robert F. (nav. off.) IV–324a; V–19b, 408b; VI–214b
  Battle of San Gabriel VI–210b
  Bear Flag Revolt I–409b
  California conquest IV–34a
  Kearny quarrel VI–414a
  Liberia V–22b
  surrender of Los Angeles III–34a
STOCKTON–KEARNY QUARREL VI–414a
Stockton's Dental Intelligencer (jour.) II–330b
STOCKYARDS VI–414a
  Chicago IV–170a, 280b
  federal regulation VI–379a
  Packers' Agreement V–183a
  Packers and Stockyards Act V–183a
  public utilities V–456b
  Saint Joseph VI–191b
  Saint Paul VII–134a
Stoddard, Amos (off.) IV–377a
Stoddard, Solomon (cler.) III–214a; VI–76b
Stoddert, Benjamin (bus., pol.) V–17b, 19a, 29a; VI–414b
STODDERT, FORT (Ala.) **VI–414b**; IV–456a
Stoeckl, Eduard (dipl.) I–75b
"Stogies" V–389b
Stokes, Anthony (jur.) II–253a
Stokes, Benjamin M. (pub.) V–70b
Stokes, I. N. Phelps (arch.) VII–24b
Stokes, Richard L. (jour.) V–74a
Stokes, Thomas L. (jour.) V–75a
Stokowski, Leopold (cond.) V–278b
Stommel, Henry (oceanog.) III–233b
Stone, Barton W. (evangelist) I–238a; II–352b; VI–77b
Stone, C. P. (off.) I–249a

Stone, Edward Durell (arch.) I–165a
Stone, Harlan F. (jur.) I–300a; V–47a, 48a; VI–446b, 446b
civil liberties IV–14a
Federal Bureau of Investigation II–503a
First Amendment III–105a
Gold Clause Cases III–189a
Japanese–American relocation III–491a
minimum–wage legislation VII–269a–b
Stone, John (trader) V–261a
Stone, Lucy (ref.) VII–315a
Stone, Melville E. (jour.) I–207a
Stone, Thomas (law.) I–85b; II–308a
Stone, William (col. gov.) VI–264b
Stone, William (nav. off.) VI–128a
Stone, William J. (pol.) IV–169a
Stone Age IV–421b
Stone and Webster IV–238a
Stone Bridge (Va.) I–381a,b
STONE FLEETS VI–414b
Stonehill College (North Easton, Mass.) III–293a
"Stone" line I–477a
Stoneman, George (off.) IV–253b
Stone Mountain IV–58b
Stone River VII–26b
Stone River, Battle of *See* Murfreesboro, Battle of
STONEWALL (ironclad) **VI–415a**
Stoneware III–183a–b, 184a; V–379b; VI–108a
STONEY CREEK, BATTLE OF (1813) **VI–415a**; I–436b
STONINGTON, BOMBARDMENT OF VI–415a
Stonington Island V–337b
Stono (S.C.) III–437a; VI–303b
Stony Lake, Battle of (1863) II–283b
STONY POINT, CAPTURE OF (1779) **VI–415b**; III–276a; IV–48a; V–229a; VI–126a; VII–280a
Stop–and–frisk cases (1968) I–195b; VI–249a
STORE BOATS VI–415b
Storefront churches I–24a
Store of value. *See* Money
Storer, David Humphreys (physic., nat.) III–28a; VI–90b
STORES, GENERAL VI–416a; II–244a, 332b; V–274b; VI–452b
frontier III–127a,b
hardware III–252a
Storis (ship) V–122a
Storke, Thomas M. (ed.) V–73b
Stormer, F. Carl M. (math.) III–454a
Storm King Mountain (N.Y.) III–275b
Storms
disasters II–351a–52b
divine providences II–356a
See also Hurricanes; Meteorology
Storm troopers III–172a
Stormy Weather (yacht) VII–349a
Storrow, James J. (law.) I–346b
Story, Joseph (jur.) IV–120b; VI–445a
Dartmouth College case II–214a
Fugitive Slave Acts V–406b
presidential call of militia IV–260a
Supreme Court's jurisdiction IV–259b
Story, William Wetmore (sculp.) VI–243a
Story Parade (mag.) IV–223a
Storyville (New Orleans) II–260a
Stouder, Sharon (athlete) V–154b
Stoudinger, Charles (eng.) VI–409a
Stoughton, Israel (off.) V–261b
STOURBRIDGE LION (locomotive) **VI–416a**; VI–24b
Stout, Elihu (pub.) V–70b
Stout, William B. (eng.) I–51b, 236a
Stoveplates III–47a
Stover, Charles B. VI–330b
Stoves II–219a, 417a, 422a; III–51b, 99b, 268b–69a; IV–44b
Stow, Charles IV–142b
Stowe, Harriet Beecher (au.) I–137a; II–127a, 418a; IV–162b; VI–307b; VII–48a
Uncle Tom's Cabin VII–137a, 138b
Stowe–Day Foundation (Hartford, Conn.) III–137b
Strachey, William (col.) VII–70a
Straddles (fin.) II–470b
Strafford (Vt.) II–5b
Strafford, 1st Earl of, Thomas Wentworth (states.) V–332b
Strahan, Edward (au.) II–103b
Straight College III–103b
Straight ticket (pol.) II–437b
Strang, James J. (Mormon) VI–87a, 416b
STRANGITE KINGDOM VI–416b
Strasberg, Lee (dir.) VII–50a
Strasburg (Va.) III–31a, 128a, 487b; VI–275b
Civil War VI–276a; VII–71a, 304a
Strasser, Adolph (labor leader) IV–65a
Strassmann, Fritz (phys.) V–300a
Strategic Air Command I–61a, 64a, 67b, 328b
bomber aircraft I–50b, 63b
fighter aircraft I–53b
retaliatory capabilities I–61b–62a
Strategic air power. *See* Air Power, Strategic
Strategic and Critical Materials Stock Piling Act (1946) III–13a
STRATEGIC ARMS LIMITATION TALKS VI–416b; III–70b, 161b; IV–364a; VI–439a
Polaris submarines V–11b
SALT I treaty I–58b, 63b, 180b, 484b
Strategic Bombing Survey Board I–67a
Strategic Communications Command, U.S. Army VI–286a
Strategic intelligence. *See* Intelligence, Military and Strategic
Strategic Services, Office of. *See* Office of Strategic Services
Strategy, military IV–180a–b
Stratford. *See* Lee Mansion
STRATFORD HALL (Va.) **VI–417b**
Stratofortress I–50b
See also B–52
Stratojet *See* B–47
Strato Lab V I–248b
Stratton, Charles ("Gen. Tom Thumb") I–268b
Stratton, Samuel Wesley (phys.) II–153a
Stratton, W. S. (miner) II–264a
STRAUDER* v. *WEST VIRGINIA (1880) **VI–417b**
Straus, Leo (pol. philos.) V–354a
Straus, Nathan (philan.) II–280b; IV–275b
Strauss, Joseph B. (eng.) I–364b
Strauss, Levi (mfr.) II–372a
Strauss, Lewis L. (banker) I–216b
Straw II–279a
Strawberries III–129a
STRAWBERRY BANK (N.H.) **VI–417b**; V–53b
Strawbridge, Robert (cler.) II–39b; IV–318a
Straw hats II–372a
Strawn, Silas Hardy (dipl.) V–242b
Street, Fort (Mich.) II–338a
Streetcar Named Desire (play) VII–50b
Street cleaning. *See* Sanitation, Environmental
Streeter, Alson J. (pol.) I–424b; III–225a; VII–146b
Streeter, Thomas Winthrop I–333a
Streeter Collection (Yale Univ.) III–285a
Street lighting II–413b; IV–153a, 154a
STREET RAILWAYS VI–418a; III–461a
advertising I–17b; VI–323b
electrified II–414b–15a
great fortunes III–80a
New York City V–83a; VI–429a
segregation III–502b
Streisand, Barbra (sing.) IV–442a
Streptomycin VII–127a
"Stretch–out" (labor) IV–273b
Strickland, William (nav. off.) III–233a
Strict construction II–433b
Lane v. *Oregon* IV–105b
See also Constitution of the United States
Strikebreakers Act (1936) VI–419b
STRIKES VI–418b; IV–60b, 61a, 71b
AFL IV–65b
AFL–CIO I–102b, 103b, 104a
Anthracite Strike I–127a
antiinjunction law VII–121a
arbitration I–152a,b
Boston police I–346b
Buck Stove and Range Company I–374b
Burlington I–386a
California aircraft industry IV–341b
checkoff II–3a–b
Chicago II–17b
cigarmakers IV–65a
Civil War II–235b
clothing industry II–82b
coal miners IV–70b
coal (1897) II–3a
coal (1902) II–87a
coal (1919) II–86b
Coeur d'Alene II–93b
collective bargaining II–112b
Colorado coal strikes II–128b
Communist party II–145a
contract labor II–214b
cost of living II–236a
Cripple Creek II–264b, 264b
federal troops used against I–185a; IV–61b, 63b
first by women IV–61b
Gastonia riots III–154a
Great Revolt II–82b
Herrin massacre III–274a
Homestead Strike III–297a
injunctions III–419a; VI–103b
Knights of Labor IV–64a,b
Lawrence textile workers IV–120a
lead miners II–93b
legal recognition IV–69a
letter carriers V–374a
lockout IV–174a

National Labor Relations Act IV–466b
National Labor Relations Board II–80a
newspapers V–77b
Norris–La Guardia Anti–Injunction Law V–112a
no–strike pledge I–153a
Ohio V–142a
opposition IV–471b
panic of 1873 V–207b
panic of 1893 V–208a
Pawtucket mills VII–316b
Pennsylvania V–247b
Philadelphia cordwainers V–278b
Philadelphia craftsmen II–235a
postal workers V–374b
post–World War I IV–69b
post–World War II IV–74a
presidential proclamations V–425a
price–fixing V–401b
public employee IV–75b
Pullman I–111b; II–298b; V–463a
Railroad Mediation Acts VI–21a
railroads VI–29b, 30a
railroad strike of 1877 IV–63b; VI–38b
railroad strikes of 1886 VI–38b
railway shopmen's strike VI–40b
revolutionary war VI–117b
scabs VI–223b
Seattle General Strike VII–248a
silver miners II–93b
sit–down IV–72b
Socialist Labor party VI–325a
steel industry VI–410b
strikebreaking II–86b, 462b
syndicalism VI–455b
Taft–Hartley Act IV–74a, 467a; VI–457a
teachers IV–76a
Telegraphers' strike VII–19b
textile workers IV–67b–68a, 70b
United Mine Workers VII–151a
Universal Peace Union V–235b
violence VII–191b
Western Federation of Miners VII–272b
wildcat IV–77b
World War I VII–232b
World War II IV–73b
Strike Up the Band (musical) IV–442a
String beans II–227a
Stringfellow, B. F. (off.) I–341a
Stringham, S. H. (nav. off.) III–262a
Strip farming VI–335b
Strip mining I–222b; II–85b; III–473b; VII–28b
Appalachia I–144b
farmland IV–104b
Kentucky IV–41b
Montana IV–403b
Stripper, cotton I–35a
Stroke (med.) I–7a; IV–299a
Strong, Benjamin (banker) III–6b
Strong, George T. (law.) IV–297a
Strong, James G. (pol.) IV–234a
Strong, William (jur.) VI–445b
Strong, William L. (pol.) VI–459b
Stroud (cloth) III–140b, 402b
Strutt, Jedediah (inv.) VII–44b
Struve, Otto (astron.) I–212a
Stuart, Charles E. IV–24b
Stuart, David (fur trader) V–180a
Stuart, Gilbert (paint.) II–101b; V–187b, 190a; VI–132a
Stuart, J. E. B. (off.) VI–420b
Army of Northern Virginia VII–197a
Ashby's Gap I–200b
Battle at Yellow Tavern VII–358a
Battle of Brandy Station I–360a
Battle of Gettysburg III–176a
Buckland Races I–374a
Hanover engagement III–250b
Harpers Ferry raid III–257a
Mosby's Rangers IV–415b
Peninsular campaign V–245a
Pennsylvania invasion V–248a–b
Todd's Tavern action VII–68a
Stuart, Jesse (au.) IV–41a
Stuart, John (Indian agent) I–223a; II–363a; III–251a, 388a; V–254b; VI–130a, 385b, 386a; VII–74a
Stuart, John, 3rd Earl of Bute I–398a
Stuart, John Robert (mfr.) I–487a, 488a
Stuart, Robert (fur trader) I–105b, 209a; V–168b, 330b; VI–354b
Stuart family (Va.) III–469b
Stuart plasterwork I–161a
STUART'S RIDE (1862) **VI–420b**
Stuart's Town (S.C.) VI–348b
Stucker, John (pol. sci.) III–92b
Student activism VII–156b, 365a–66a
Kent State University IV–38b–39b
Student League for Industrial Democracy VI–421a
Student Navy Training Corps V–28b
STUDENT NONVIOLENT COORDINATING COMMITTEE VI–420b; I–31a, 316a; II–58a–b; IV–461a; VI–352a; VII–365b
Student Peace Union V–237a; VII–366a
Students, exchange. *See* Exchange Students
STUDENTS FOR A DEMOCRATIC SOCIETY VI–421a; VI–14a; VII–366a
Kent State University IV–38b
Vietnam War opposition V–237a
Student Volunteer Movement VII–365a
Studs Lonigan IV–164b
STUMP SPEAKERS VI–421b
Stunt pilots I–268b
Sturbridge (Mass.) IV–268a, 437a
Sturgeon III–413a
Sturgeon, William (phys.) II–417a
Sturgeon class (submarine) VI–423b
Sturges, Mary D. III–19a
STURGES* v. *CROWNINSHIELD (1819) **VI–422a**; II–213b
Sturgis, Jonathan II–103b
Sturgis, Samuel D. (off.) VII–128b
Sturtevant, A. H. (zool.) III–157b, 158a
Sturtevant, Julian M. (theol.) III–331b; VII–350b
Stuyvesant, Peter (col. gov.) I–355a; V–40b, 61b–62a, 185a,b
Esopus War II–462b
Fort Casimir IV–454a; V–42b, 80b
fruit growing III–128b
New Netherland V–266a
Schenectady VI–225b
surrender to British V–82a
Treaty of Hartford III–258b
Stuyvesant, Rutherford I–143a
Stuyvesant Apartments (N.Y.C.) I–143a
Styrene V–328a
Suarez, Diego (landscape arch.) IV–96b
Subarctic culture III–355a, 356a, 358b, 362a
Sublette, Milton G. (fur trader) I–201a; III–143b
Sublette, William L. (fur trader) II–477b; III–143b; IV–27b; V–310b; VI–160a, 422a; VII–217a
caravan traffic I–452b
Fort Laramie IV–108a
Sublette and Campbell Fort William IV–415a
Sublette brothers (fur traders) VII–103b
SUBLETTE'S CUTOFF VI–422a; II–477b; III–215a
Submarine cables I–400b–01a
SUBMARINES VI–422b; IV–431b–32a; V–25a,b, 26a; VII–241a,b
Arabic case I–151a
atomic I–179b
Battle of the Philippine Sea V–285b
compression still I–197b
disasters II–350a
George Washington V–11a
helicopters III–270b
Holland submarine torpedo boat III–291b
London Naval Treaty II–461a; IV–183a
mine planting IV–351a
missiles I–67b; IV–363b, 364a; V–164a; VI–159b
Nautilus V–8a, 11a
naval competition V–10a,b, 11a
navy medical research IV–292b
neutral rights V–39a
North Sea mine barrage V–119b
Northwest Passage V–122b
nuclear II–316a, 345b; VI–280a
oceanographic studies V–135a
polar exploration V–337b, 338b
Polaris I–124b, 180a
"S4" disaster I–447a
Strategic Arms Limitation Talks VI–417a
torpedoes V–27b; VII–76b
Trident IV–364a; V–11b
U-boats II–217b
World War I I–122b, 321b; II–217b, 314a–b; V–20a; VI–378a; VII–324b–25b, 328a–b, 329a, 368b
World War II I–54b–55a, 56a,b, 214a; II–213a, 217b, 314b; V–21a; VII–334b, 336a–b, 337a, 337b, 338b, 342b, 343a
SUBMARINES AND INTERNATIONAL LAW VI–423b; III–456a; VII–113a, 225b
retaliation VI–104b
Sussex Case VI–452b
Washington Naval Conference VII–251a
SUBMARINES AND TORPEDOES, CIVIL WAR VI–424b; I–497a; III–308a; V–164a; VI–422b
Battle of Mobile Bay II–285b
Charleston harbor I–497a
Confederate navy V–17b

SUBMARINES AND TORPEDOES, CIVIL WAR (cont.)
Davids II–294b
Submerged Lands Act (1953) VII–57b, 58a
Subroc (missile) IV–363b
SUBSIDIES VI–425a
Agricultural Adjustment Administration V–44a
Amtrak III–451b
canals VI–146a
exports VI–471a
federal II–501b
Florida land III–39a,b
Great Lakes shipping III–218b
housing III–311a; IV–429a
interstate commerce III–459a
New England fisheries III–204a
"normalcy" V–110a
Post Office V–374b; VI–380a
public transportation IV–428b
sectarian schools III–380a, 390b
shipping IV–311b–12a,b
soldiers' homes VI–336b–37a
tax revenue III–156b
Union Pacific Railroad VII–147b
SUBSISTENCE HOMESTEADS VI–426a
SUBSTITUTES, CIVIL WAR VI–426b; II–161b, 186a, 366b–67a; VII–233a
conscientious objectors II–185a
recruitment VI–61a
Subsurface rights IV–104b
SUBTREASURIES VI–427a; III–354b; V–132a
SUBURBAN GROWTH VI–427b; II–46a, 354a
apartment houses I–143a
automobile I–227b
Connecticut II–180a
housing III–310b
New Jersey V–57b
population II–41b
Suburban house (arch.) I–164a
SUBVERSION VI–428a
deportation II–333a
Federal Bureau of Investigation II–503b
guerrilla warfare III–231a
House Committee on Un-American Activities III–308a
immigration IV–209b
McCarthy–Army hearings IV–209b
Schenck v. *United States* VI–225b
Sedition Act VI–255a
Smith Act VI–317b
Southeast Asia Treaty Organization VI–350b
teachers' loyalty oath VII–15b
World War I V–35b
Subversive Activities Control Act (1950) II–499b
Subversive Activities Control Board II–499b
SUBWAYS VI–429a; III–451b
Chicago II–18b
elevated II–428a
municipal ownership IV–428a–b
New York City I–368b; VII–128a
Succotash III–366a
Sudbury (Mass.) VI–2b
Sudbury mining district (Ont.) VI–443b
Suess, Edward (geol., paleon.) III–481a
Suess, H. E. (phys.) V–302b
Suez Canal I–124b, 276b; III–481b
minesweeping IV–351b
nationalization III–352b
panic of 1873 V–207b
steamships IV–310b
tankers VI–281a
World War II IV–313b
SUEZ CRISIS (1956) **VI–429b**; I–124b, 292b; III–69b, 481b; V–202b
campaign of 1956 I–430a
Canada I–439b
France III–97b
indemnities III–352b
U.S. Sixth Fleet V–22b
"Suffering towns" III–25b
"SUFFERING TRADERS" VI–430a; I–278a
Suffolk (Va.) VI–430b; VII–196b
SUFFOLK, OPERATIONS AT (1863) **VI–430a**
Suffolk Assizes (1664) VII–309b
SUFFOLK BANKING SYSTEM VI–430b; I–255b
Suffolk County (Mass.) IV–430b
Suffolk County (N.Y.) IV–185b, 186a
SUFFOLK RESOLVES (1774) **VI–430b**
Suffrage II–325b
church membership II–35b
Commission on Civil Rights II–499b
Connecticut II–180a
poll tax I–451a
universal III–91a–92a
See also Franchise; Voting; Woman's Suffrage
SUFFRAGE, AFRO-AMERICAN VI–431a; III–92a–93a; VI–6b, 256b, 435a; VII–208b, 209b, 315a
colonial settlements VI–434b
Compromise of 1890 II–151a
disfranchisement III–437b, 438a
Fifteenth Amendment II–205b; III–20a
Force Acts III–59b
free blacks III–91b, 102a
freedmen IV–58a
Freedmen's Bureau III–103b
Georgia III–169a
grandfather clause III–208b
Jim Crow laws III–503a
literacy test IV–160a; VII–209b, 302b
Mississippi IV–369a,b
Mississippi Plan IV–371b
NAACP IV–461a
National Urban League V–1b
Niagara movement V–93a
nonvoting V–108b
poll tax V–355a
Radical Republicans VI–11a–b
Readjuster movement VI–49b
Reconstruction VI–56a,b, 57a,b, 58a, 59a
Selma–Montgomery march V–265b
Solid South VI–337a–b
South Carolina VI–348a; VII–59a
United States v. *Reese* VII–155a
Virginia VII–195b
Visible Admixture Law VII–204b
Voting Rights Act of 1965 III–438a; VII–211a
white primary V–407a
SUFFRAGE, COLONIAL VI–433b
Massachusetts IV–265b, 269a
Pennsylvania III–219a
property qualifications VII–58b
Rhode Island VI–134a
women VII–314b
SUFFRAGE, EXCLUSION FROM THE VI–434b; VI–89a
Chinese VI–7a
colonial settlements VI–434a–b
Confederates VI–58b
educational tests VII–209b
Virginia VII–194a–b
Washington, D.C. VII–245a
women IV–359a–b; VII–314b–15a
See also Suffrage, Afro-American
Suffrage, Woman's. *See* Woman's Suffrage
Suffragettes VII–312b, 317a
Sugar, maple. *See* Maple Sugar
Sugar Act (1937) II–24a–b
SUGAR ACTS (1733, 1764) **VI–435a**; II–309a; VI–107b, 381b; VII–3b, 80b, 81a, 119b–20a
colonial smuggling VI–321a
Grenville Act III–228a
Maine opposition IV–226a
molasses trade IV–388a, 388b
Rhode Island VI–132b
rum trade VI–171a
See also Molasses Act (1733)
Sugar beets. *See* Beet Sugar
Sugar Bowl V–62b
Sugar-camp rights I–400a
SUGARCANE VI–436a; III–51b, 52a
cereal grains I–486a,b
Florida III–39a
Hawaii III–263b, 264a
Louisiana IV–193b
maple sugar IV–246b
Navigation Acts V–16a
New Smyrna Colony V–66a
Norfolk V–109b
plantation system V–324b, 325a
Puerto Rico V–461a,b
rum distillers II–353b
Spanish and Mexican land grants IV–93a
tuberculosis patients VII–126a
Virgin Islands VII–204b
West India trade III–42b; IV–309b; VII–277b, 278a
Sugar Creek (Ark.) V–238b
Sugar Hill (N.Y.) VII–57a
SUGAR HOUSE PRISONS VI–436b
SUGAR INDUSTRY VI–436b; II–13a, 164b; III–53a, 53b; VI–386b
antebellum South VI–341a–b
Barbados I–266a
bounties VI–467a
colonial trade II–92b, 119b, 453a
commerce clause II–136a
commercial bounties I–352b
commodity exchange II–469b
Cuba II–269b, 359b; VI–361a
Dominican Republic II–361a
duties III–228a
East India trade II–388b
food preservation II–373a; III–54b
great fortunes III–80a
imports VII–87b
Jamaica VII–271a
Molasses Act IV–388a
New Orleans V–62b
New York II–5a
pack trains V–184a
profiteering V–426a
Puerto Rico V–461b
refining monopoly I–390b
rum trade VI–171a
Saint Louis VI–194b
Savannah VI–220b
shipping IV–310b
slavery VI–310a
sorghum VI–340a
South I–37a, 38a
South America VI–343b, 346a
steam engines VI–409b
subsidies VI–426a
tariff VI–463a,b, 466b
tariffs I–285b; IV–308a,b
taxation VII–4b, 5a, 12b

trade association VII–92a
triangular trade VII–119b
United States v. *E. C. Knight Company* VII–154a
See also Beet Sugar
SUGAR ISLANDS VI–437a; IV–309b; VII–119b, 277b
Sugar maple VI–394 (table), 395 (table), 395 (table); VII–59b
Sugar pine V–446a
SUGAR TRUST VI–437b; III–443b; VI–276b; VII–122a, 154a
Sugerman v. *Dougall* (1973) I–88a
Suggs, Louise (golfer) III–198b
Suicide VII–192a
Suisun Bay III–11b
Suitland (Md.) III–284b
Suits (dress) II–371a, 372a
Suits, C. G. (phys.) III–156a
Sulfa drugs V–274a
Sulfamylon IV–291a
Sulfanilamide V–467a
Sulfonamides III–417a
Sulfur II–6b, 7b, 8a, 67b; VI–48b
Gulf of Mexico IV–326b
gunpowder V–97b
Louisiana IV–194b; V–62b
New South V–67b
Sulfur–dioxide II–420b–21a
Sulfuric acid II–5a, 6a–b, 8a, 10a, 224a; III–16a–b, 408a; V–267a; VII–369a
Sulfuric ether I–119a
Sulfurous products II–224a
Sulkies I–461a
Sulky plow I–34a
Sullivan, Fort (Pa.) VI–438a
Sullivan, Harry Stack (psych.) IV–306b
Sullivan, James (law.) II–437a
Sullivan, John (off.) II–433a; VI–386a
Battle of Brandywine Creek I–360a
Battle of Germantown III–173b
Battle of Trenton VII–116a
Fort William and Mary VII–300b–01a
Indian campaign VI–438a
Indian expedition VII–293b, 346b
invasion of Canada I–436a
Iroquois expedition IV–354b
Rhode Island campaign VI–438a–b
Sullivan, John L. (pugilist) V–422b
Sullivan, Leon (cler.) I–24a
Sullivan, Louis H. (arch.) I–164a; II–18a
World's Columbian Exposition VII–324b
Sullivan, T. V. VII–363a
Sullivan and Considine and Orpheum VII–167b
SULLIVAN–CLINTON CAMPAIGN (1779) **VI–437b**; IV–354b
Iroquois III–400b
Sullivan County (N.Y.) IV–354b
SULLIVAN IN RHODE ISLAND (1778) **VI–438a**
Sullivan mines (Idaho) VI–292b
Sullivan's Island I–496b, 498a; IV–420a; VI–440b
Sully, Alfred (off.) II–283b–84a; III–32a
Camp Supply VI–443b; VII–252b
Dakota expeditions IV–45b; VI–296b
Fetterman massacre III–378a
Fort Rice VI–135a
Fort Sully VI–438b
SULLY, FORT (S.Dak.) **VI–438b**
Sully, Thomas (paint.) II–101b; IV–436b; V–188b–89a, 190a
Sulpicians I–467a; II–458b
Sultana (steamer) II–349a–b
Sulu Archipelago (Phil.) V–22b, 282a, 285b
Sulu Sea IV–138b
Sulzberger, C. L. (jour.) V–74a, 75a
Sulzer, William (pol.) III–344b
Sumac IV–128a
Sumatra II–388a; IV–252a
Summer resorts. *See* Resorts and Spas
Summers, Carol (art.) V–414a
"Summer soldier and sunshine patriot" VII–61b
Summer stock companies VII–50b
Summerville (S.C.) I–498a; VII–16a
SUMMIT CONFERENCES VI–438b
Big Four V–215b–16a
Eisenhower–Khrushchev III–69b, 70a; VI–179b
Ford–Brezhnev (1974) VI–417a
Geneva (1955) III–161a–b
Kennedy–Khrushchev III–161b; VI–180a
Nixon–Brezhnev III–70b
Strategic Arms Limitation Talks VI–417a
Summit Spring massacre (1868) I–219a
Summit Springs (Colo.) VI–242a; VII–252b
Sumner, Charles (states.) IV–267b; V–161a
Alabama Claims I–73a
Alaska I–75b
attack by Brooks I–203a, 371a
Civil Rights Act III–59a
"Crime Against Kansas" speech IV–31a
Dominican Republic II–362a
Liberal Republican party IV–141a
Radical Republicans VI–11b, 13b
Thirteenth Amendment VII–54a
Sumner, Edwin v. (off.) I–130a, 314a; VI–220a, 439b; VII–145a
SUMNER, FORT (N.Mex.) **VI–439b**; I–342b
Goodnight–Loving Trail III–199b
Navaho V–9b
Sumner, James B. (biochem.) I–304a; IV–389a; V–99b
Sumner, John S. (ref.) I–479a
Sumner, William Graham (educ.) II–189a; III–77a, 486a
SUMNER'S EXPEDITION (1857) **VI–439b**
SUMPTUARY LAWS AND TAXES, COLONIAL VI–440a
Sumpweed I–157a; II–386a
Sumter (S.C.) IV–429b
Sumter (warship) IV–371a; VI–181a
SUMTER, FORT (S.C.) **VI–440b**; I–497a; II–61a, 65a, 161a; III–78b
Civil War I–173a; III–36b; V–308a; VI–251a, 307b, 348a, 387a
national monument V–217a,b
Powhatan incident V–386a
Radical Republicans VI–11a
Wagner Battery VII–215b
Sumter, Thomas (off.) I–412a; II–451b; III–30a; V–222a; VI–347a–b, 351b
Fishing Creek action III–31b
Hanging Rock action III–250b
Sumurun (play) VII–49b
Sun Also Rises IV–164b, 189b
Sun Anti-Masonic Almanac I–91a
Sunbeam Corporation II–483a
Sunbury (Ga.) III–169b
Sunbury (Pa.) I–223b
Sunbury and Erie Railroad V–250b
Sun City II–48b
SUN COMPASS VI–441a; VI–450b
SUN DANCE VI–441b; II–283a, 291a; III–364b, 392b
lodge I–166b–67a
Mandan, Hidatsa, and Arikara IV–236a
Ute VII–162b
Sunday, Billy (William Ashley) (evangelist) II–466a; VI–79a
Sunday newspapers I–16b
Sunday School Magazine VI–442b
SUNDAY SCHOOLS VI–442a
Chautauqua movement II–1a
children's magazines IV–222b
evangelism II–466a–b
hymns III–326a
societies I–495b
Sunday School Society. *See* First Day Society
Sunflower I–157a; II–386a; III–151b; VI–393 (table)
Sunflower River VI–410b
"Sunflower State." *See* Kansas
Sunglasses II–372b
Sunkist Growers Inc. II–221a
Sunnyside Gardens (N.Y.) II–46b
Sunset Crater National Monument V–217a
Sunshine Silver Mine II–350b
Sunshine State VI–393 (table), 394 (table), 395 (table)
Sun studies I–211b, 212a
Sun Temple IV–315b
Sun Valley (Idaho) III–328b; VI–101b
skiing VI–298a
Sun Yat-sen (states.) II–27b
Super Bowl III–57b
Super Chief (train) III–452a
Superconductivity V–303a, 305a–b
Super Constellation (transport plane) I–52b; II–346b, 347a
Superfluidity V–305b
Superfortress (bomber plane) I–50a
See also B–29
Superheterodyne II–424a; VI–15a,b
Superior (Wis.) VI–443b
SUPERIOR, LAKE VI–443a; III–215b–16b; VI–219b
British occupation I–341a
Chequamegon Bay II–13b
copper I–410b; II–223a; V–103a
domestic trade VII–84a
exploration I–498b; II–380a; III–119a; VII–73b, 157a, 275b, 307a
fish III–27a
fisheries I–105b
France VI–219a
French posts I–281b; IV–117b–18a
fur trade III–142b, 313a; V–121a
Grand Portage III–209a
Indian land cession IV–107b
Indian missions VI–190b
iron II–459a; III–12a, 163a, 473b; IV–303b; VII–102a
Jolliet and Marquette expedition IV–6b
Lake Huron link IV–217b
Long's explorations IV–187a
Mackinac Island IV–330a

SUPERIOR, LAKE (cont.)
mining IV–244a
Minnesota IV–355a
Northwest boundary V–120a
portages V–367b
Radisson's *Voyages* VI–18b
railroads II–218b; VI–33a
Saint Lawrence Seaway VI–192b
Sault Sainte Marie Canals I–440b; VI–219a
shipping III–218b
Treaty of Saint Marys VI–197a
U.S. boundary VII–265a
Supermarkets III–53a; VI–258a–b
foreign investment III–66b
See also Self-Service Stores
Superphosphate II–6b, 8a
Superphosphate fertilizer III–16a–b
Super pumper III–25b
Superrealist school (art) II–106a
Super Sabre (fighter plane) I–54a
Supersonic flight I–52a
Supersonic transport I–53a, 235a, 238a
flight ban I–69a
Super Spooky (gunship) I–54a
Suppawn III–51b, 52a
SUPPLY, CAMP (Okla.) **VI–443b**; VII–252b
Supremacy clause I–362b; V–339b
Supreme Allied Command Atlantic V–114b
SUPREME COURT **VI–443b**; II–195b, 201b, 202a, 453b; III–2a; VII–154b
abortion II–263a
academic freedom I–5a
acquisition of territory III–417b
Afro-American suffrage VI–432a–b
Agricultural Adjustment Act I–43a, 254b; VI–138b
agriculture regulation III–299a
Alaska I–78a
alien landholding I–87a
aliens I–88a; III–417b
American Tobacco Company II–230a
"Andy Gump" dispute V–72a
antiinjunction law VII–121a
appointees II–167b–68a
apportionment I–147a–48a, 244a–b; II–172a, 180a, 355b, 410a, 457b; III–86b–87a, 94a; IV–133b
arbitrary arrest II–62a
arrest and seizure I–195a
Associated Press I–207a
attorney's oath152b
Bank of Kentucky I–365a
Bank of the United States IV–211b; V–174a–b
bankruptcy laws V–140a; VI–422a
barbed wire patents I–267b
baseball I–271b
Bill of Rights I–269a, 299a–300a; II–53b
bills of attainder II–274a
bills of credit II–253b; VI–370a
Bituminous Coal Conservation Act II–481a; III–231b
black jury service VI–417b
boycotts I–356b–57a; IV–67b
broad construction of Constitution II–197b
Bureau of Indian Affairs III–390b
busing I–397b; II–54b–55a
capital punishment I–450b; III–250a; V–464b
carriage tax I–461a
Catholic schools I–468b
censorship I–479b–80a
checkoff II–4a
Cherokee II–14a; V–125b; VII–321b–22a
Chicago drainage canal II–20a–b
child labor I–243b; II–24b–25a, 136b; III–247a–b, 349a; IV–68b–69a
citizenship II–42a–b, 54a, 370b; III–86b; IV–359a–b; VII–155b
citizen's right to sue a state II–32a, 430a
civil disobedience II–50b
civil liberties IV–362a
civil rights I–32a; II–54a, 55a–b; IV–208b
Civil War blockade V–421b
Clayton Antitrust Act II–72a; IV–69a, 70a, 70a
Clayton Compromise II–73a
closed shop II–80b
codes of fair competition IV–469b; VI–225a
collective bargaining II–110b–11a
Colorado River II–130b
commerce clause I–373a, 410a; II–135b–37a, 220a, 230a, 299a; III–178a–b
commerce interpretation IV–80a
Communist party II–146a
Communists VII–310b
Confederate Texas government VII–40a
congressional investigations II–210b; III–465a–b; IV–45b
conscientious objectors II–185b; V–181b
constitutionality of legislation IV–248b–49a
constitutional provisions IV–15b, 16a
constitutional rights VII–154a
constitutional system II–195b
contempt of Congress II–210b; III–465a
continuous voyage I–292a; II–67b
contract clause II–213b–14a, 293b; IV–99a
contracts I–496a; III–36a, 154b–55a
copyrighting of news VII–152a
corporations II–230a–b; V–457a
Crowbar Law of Ohio II–266b
Cuba status V–32a
Custis-Lee estate I–175b; VII–154b–55a
Dallas Reports II–285a
declaratory judgment laws II–309b
delegation of powers II–323a, 323a, 473a
desegregation II–54b–55b, 58a, 400a, 402a, 457a; III–438b; VII–291a
direct primary III–93a
dispensing powers of president IV–36b
diversity-of-citizenship cases II–460a–b
double jeopardy III–207a; VII–154b
draft II–367b
drug addiction II–374b
Dubuque settlers claims II–376a
due process clause II–19b, 53b, 370b, 377a–79a; III–86b
due process for juveniles IV–23b
eighteen-year-olds suffrage III–92a
election laws II–408a
electronic surveillance II–427b
eminent domain II–439b–40b; III–417b
enabling acts II–443b
enemy aliens II–445a
equal protection of the law II–457a; III–86b; VII–154a–b
executive orders II–473a
executive power of removal III–317a–b; IV–446a; V–472b; VI–85a
executive privilege II–474a; III–465b
expatriation II–475b–76a
ex post facto law I–404a
expurgatory oaths II–274a
extradition II–478b
extraterritoriality VI–165a
Fair Labor Standards Act II–482a; III–247a–b
fair-trade laws II–483a
Federal Court of Claims II–71a
federal courts I–261b
federal land cessions VI–401b
federal law over state law V–30a
Federal Register III–5b
federal sovereignty II–20a–b; VII–230b–31a
Fifth Amendment I–12a
Forbes Purchase III–59a
Force Acts III–59b–60a
foreign corporations I–260b
Fourteenth Amendment II–53b–55b, 57a; III–86b–87a; VI–302b
Frazier-Lemke Farm Bankruptcy Act III–100b; V–47a
Frazier-Lemke Farm Mortgage Act V–48a
freedom of speech III–104a; V–78b–79a; VI–225a
freedom of the press III–104b–06a, 229a, 229a; V–30b
fugitive slave laws I–2a–b; IV–8a; V–263b, 406b
fugitive slaves IV–43b, 276b
Fulton steamboat monopoly VI–407b
general welfare clause III–156b–57a
gerrymandering III–175a
gold clause III–189a
government control of industries V–458b
grandfather clause III–20b, 93a, 208b, 232a; IV–461a
grants-in-aid III–211b
Granville grant III–212b
Greer County (Okla.) V–148b
Guffey Coal Act I–462a
habeas corpus III–236b, 237a
Hatch Act III–261a–b
Hayburn's Case III–265a
hours of labor IV–80a, 173b
human rights III–315b–17a
immigration restriction III–342a
implied powers III–348b
income tax III–351a–b; V–354b; VI–297b, 377a
Independence Hall III–354a
independent regulatory commissions II–499b
Indian land grants IV–4a
Indian reservations III–395b
Indian rights III–371b–72a
inherent powers III–417a
injunctions III–419a; IV–67a
insular possessions III–424b, 426a–b
insurance regulation III–432b, 434a
integration I–30b, 271a, 290a–b, 372b–73a; II–401b, 401b; III–438a,b; IV–461a
internal affairs of nation III–417b
International Harvester Company III–454b

interstate commerce
I–11a, 462a; III–458a, 458b, 459a–b; IV–148a, 158b–159a; V–119a–b; VI–283b
interstate trade barriers
III–460b
interstate transportation
I–410a
interstate travel V–420b
Iowa–Missouri boundary
III–297b
Japanese–American relocation III–491a–b; VII–227b
Jefferson Davis trial
II–295a
Jim Crow laws IV–461a
judicial circuits II–39b
judicial review III–3a–b; IV–12a, 19a, 209a; V–352a
Judiciary Act of 1789
II–460a–b; IV–19a
jurisdiction I–9a–b; VI–454b
Kansas–Colorado water rights IV–28a
Kansas industrial court
VII–311a–b
Ku Klux Act IV–57b; VII–155a
labor legislation IV–68b
labor organizations
III–407a
labor unions II–110b, 286a–b
legal tender III–417b; IV–20a; VI–94b–95a
Legal Tender Act
IV–105b, 132b, 133a, 133a
licenses to trade IV–148b
literacy test III–93a; IV–160a; VII–302b
livestock industry regulation
VI–378b
lotteries IV–191b
loyalty oaths IV–202b, 203a; VII–35a
Mann Act IV–240a
Mariposa land grant
IV–254a
martial law IV–206b
McConnelsville ordinance
IV–211a
McKinley Tariff Act
III–20a
military trial of civilians
IV–258b, 259a, 346b–47a
militia call-up
IV–259b–60a
minimum-wage legislation
I–12a; IV–70a, 80a–b, 353a; VII–214a, 269a
minority rights IV–358b, 359a
miscegenation IV–362b
Missouri Compromise
II–370b, 377b
Monaco versus Mississippi
VI–96b
monopolistic practices
I–283b, 496a
Mormons VII–162a
mortgage moratorium acts
IV–358a
mortgage relief legislation
IV–414b
motion picture censorship
IV–418b
murder indictments
III–320a
narcotics trade IV–450a,b
National Industrial Recovery Act III–307b; IV–72a; V–47a; VI–225a
National Labor Relations Act IV–467b; V–48a
National Recovery Administration II–481b
natural gas industry
V–5b–6a
naval oil reserves VII–16b
navigation monopolies
VII–83b
New Deal V–47a
Nixon tapes V–99a
nominees IV–413a
Norris–La Guardia Anti-Injunction Law V–111b
number of justices
IV–16a, 17a, 19b
obscenity I–479b; III–105b–06a
opinions V–353b
original package doctrine
V–172a
padlock injunction
V–184b
paper money III–251b
pardons V–99a
pension plans V–256a
Pentagon Papers
III–105b; V–78b–79a, 258b
peonage V–260b
Peterhoff admiralty case
V–264a
picketing V–308b–09a
Pledge of Allegiance
III–35a
police power
III–237b–38a
poll tax I–95a, 451a; II–408a; III–93a; IV–371b; V–355a, 434b; VI–432b; VII–133a
popular sovereignty
V–360b
pornography II–263a
Powell Case V–384a
presidential subpoena
V–397b–98a
presidential war powers
II–62a; III–417a–b; IV–314b
price-fixing V–402a,b
price maintenance V–403a
primaries V–42a
private schools V–167a; VI–228b
privileges and immunities clause III–86b; V–420b, 421a
prize cases V–422a
prohibitory taxes IV–211a
property qualifications
III–94a
property rights V–339a–b
"public interest" V–30b, 456b
public protection IV–425a
public protest I–100b
Puerto Rico II–323b
Pullman Strike II–299a
racial discrimination
III–86b
railroad rates II–19b; V–458a; VI–21b, 22a, 28b; VII–308b–09a
railroad retirement acts
V–47a; VI–23b–24a
railroad trust VII–155a
Railway Labor Act
VII–202a
recognition of governments
III–456a
Reconstruction
VI–57b–58a
Reconstruction Acts
III–171b; IV–376a–b
relief waiting periods
V–420b
reserved powers of states
VI–97b, 98a
residency requirements for voting VI–99b
restraint of trade
VI–102a–03b
retired judges pay I–339a
Revenue Act of 1951
V–339b
right of assembly
I–204b–05a
right of petition
V–265a–b, 266a
right to bear arms
IV–470a
right to counsel
III–179a–b
Roosevelt reorganization
V–47b–48a
rule of reason I–140a; II–71b; VI–168b
rules of practice
IV–17a–b
salary grab VI–198b
Scottsboro case VI–241b
sedition acts VI–255a–b
segregation I–372b–73a; II–54a–55b, 56b–58a, 404a,b; III–438a, 502b–03a; V–126a; VI–256a,b
selection of cases
IV–16a–b
"separate but equal" doctrine II–54a–b, 457a; V–331b
Sheppard case
VII–118a–b
Sherman Antitrust Act
II–230a; VI–276b–77a
slave mutiny I–114b
slavery II–370b
slave trade I–127a
Smith Act VI–317b
Social Security Act V–48a
soldiers' rights VII–154a
Standard Oil Company
V–270a; VI–383b–84a
state boundary disputes
I–350b–51b
state corporations I–261b
state court rulings II–94a; IV–259b
state police power
V–339b
state rate-fixing IV–434b
state regulation of business
III–209b–10a, 211a
state regulation of commerce V–457b
state sovereignty VI–403b
state taxation of federal agencies II–266b; IV–211b
state taxing power
III–227a
steamboat monopolies
III–132a
steel mills seizure
VI–411a
strikes VI–419a
suffrage VI–435a
sugar trust VI–437b
suits between states
II–431a
Taft–Hartley Act
VI–457a
taxation II–113b; III–229a; VII–4b, 5b, 6a,b, 7b, 8a, 12a, 168a
teachers' loyalty oath
VII–15b
telephone patents VII–21a
Tennessee Bond Cases
VII–27a
Tennessee Valley Authority
III–321b
territorial governments
VII–33b
territories VII–13b–14a, 32a–b
Texas boundary VII–155a
Texas Confederate government VII–42a–b
tidelands VII–57b
tobacco cooperatives
II–221b
traveling salesmen
VII–105b
treason VII–106b
treaties I–362b; VII–110b–11a
treaty-making power
III–417b; IV–381a
trial by military commission
I–196a
trusts VII–122a,b, 123a,b, 124a,b, 154a
unionization of coal miners
III–286a
unions IV–61a
Vallandigham incident
VII–164b
Vick estate VII–181a
voter registration
VI–71a–b
Voting Rights Acts
III–93b–94a; VII–133b, 211a
voting rights of Confederates I–115a
war-making powers
VII–224a,b, 227b
Warren court I–408a
Washington State Minimum Wage Act V–48a
Watergate VII–255b
water rights III–478a
Webb–Kenyon Act
VII–265a
white primary III–20b; V–407b
women's labor law
VII–213b
work-hours laws
VII–214a
workmen's compensation
VI–328a; VII–322a,b
Yazoo fraud III–36a; VII–354a
"yellow-dog" contracts
II–222a; VII–354b–55a

SUPREME COURT (cont.)
zoning II–47a; VII–370a
See also Judiciary
Supreme Court decisions
Ableman v. *Booth* (1859) I–2a
Abrams v. *United States* (1919) VI–255a
Adair v. *United States* (1908) I–9b; II–222a; VII–354b
Addyston Pipe Company Case (1899) I–11a; VI–102a
Adkins v. *Children's Hospital* (1923) I–12a; IV–70a, 80a, 353a; VII–214a, 269a,b
Afroyim v. *Rusk* (1967) II–475b; III–86b
Allen v. *Virginia State Board of Elections* (1969) III–93b; VII–211a
Allgeyer v. *Louisiana* (1897) II–378a
Altman and Company v. *United States* (1912) III–417b
Amalgamated Meat Cutters v. *Jewel Tea Company* (1965) VI–103b
American Foundries v. *Tri-City Council* (1921) VI–419a
American Power and Light Company v. *Securities and Exchange Commission* (1946) II–137a; III–459b
American Steel Foundries v. *Tri-City Trade Council* (1921) III–419a
American Tobacco Company Case (1911) I–114a, 140a; VII–155a
American Tobacco Company v. *United States* (1946) VI–103a
Amy Warwick Admiralty Case (1863) I–116a
Anderson v. *Dunn* (1821) I–117b
Appalachian Coals v. *United States* (1933) VI–103a; VII–123a
Appam Case (1917) I–144b
Argersinger v. *Hamlin* (1972) III–179b
Arizona v. *California* (1964) II–130b
Arver v. *United States* (1918) II–367b
Ashwander v. *Tennessee Valley Authority* (1936) III–321b
Avery v. *Midland County* (1968) III–87a
Bailey v. *Alabama* (1910) V–260b
Bailey v. *Drexel Furniture Company* (1922) I–243b; II–25a; III–247a, 247a
Baker v. *Carr* (1962) I–147b, 244a; II–180a, 410a, 457b; IV–133b; VI–432b, 435a
Balzac v. *People of Porto Rico* (1922) III–424b, 425a
Bank of Augusta v. *Earle* (1839) I–260b
Bank of China v. *Wells Fargo Bank* (1952) III–456a
Bank of Columbia v. *Okely* (1819) II–377b
Bank of Commerce v. *New York City* (1863) I–260b
Bank of the United States v. *Halstead* (1825) I–261b
Bank of the United States v. *Planter's Bank of Georgia* (1824) I–261b
Barbed Wire Patent Case (1892) I–267b
Barenblatt v. *United States* (1959) III–465b
Barron v. *Baltimore* (1833) I–94a, 268b; II–53b, 377b; III–86b; V–339b
Bates v. *City of Little Rock* (1960) I–204b
Bedford Cut Stone Company v. *Journeymen Stonecutters' Association* (1927) III–419a
Beef Trust Cases I–283b; III–343a
Bell v. *Maryland* (1964) II–50b
Benton v. *Maryland* (1969) II–53b
Berea College v. *Kentucky* (1908) I–290a
Berger v. *New York* (1967) II–427b
Berman v. *Parker* (1954) II–440a
Berman v. *United States* (1946) II–185b
Bermuda Admiralty Case (1865) I–292a; II–67b, 213a
Betts v. *Brady* (1942) III–179a
Blodgett v. *Holden* (1927) IV–12b
Bolling v. *Sharpe* (1954) I–372b; II–54b
Bollman Case (1807) I–327b
Bond v. *Floyd* (1966) III–93b
Booth v. *United States* (1934) I–339a
Bradley v. *Milliken* (1974) I–397b; II–54b–55a
Brandenburg v. *Ohio* (1969) V–78b
Branzburg v. *Hayes* (1972) III–105b
Breedlove v. *Suttles* (1937) III–93a; V–355a
Bridges v. *California* (1941) III–105a
Briscoe v. *Bank of the Commonwealth of Kentucky* (1837) I–365a
Bronson v. *Rodes* (1868) I–369a; VI–95a
Brooks v. *United States* (1925) II–136b
Brown v. *Board of Education of Topeka* (1954, 1955) I–30b, 32a, 372b; II–54b–55a, 56a, 57a–b, 404a,b, 457a; III–86b, 438b, 503a; IV–359a, 461a; V–126a, 331b, 353b; VI–256b; VII–291a
Brown v. *Louisiana* (1966) II–50b
Brown v. *Maryland* (1827) I–373a; V–172a
Brushaber v. *Union Pacific Railroad Company* (1916) VII–6b
Buchanan v. *Warley* (1917) IV–461a
Buck Stove and Range Case (1911) I–356b–57a, 374b; III–419a; IV–67b
Bunting v. *Oregon* (1917) IV–80a; VII–214a
Butterworth v. *Dempsey* (1964) II–180a
Byrd v. *McCready* (1950) I–372b
Calder v. *Bull* (1798) I–404a
California v. *Central Pacific Railroad Company* (1888) I–410a
Carmichael v. *Southern Coal and Coke Company* (1937) IV–80b
Carter v. *Carter Coal Company* (1936) I–462a; II–136b, 323a, 482a; III–231b
Champion v. *Ames* (1903) IV–191b
Chapman, in re (1897) III–465a
Charles River Bridge Case (1837) I–496a; II–214a; V–339b
Cherokee Nation v. *Georgia* (1831) II–14a; V–125b
Chicago, Burlington Railroad v. *Chicago* (1897) II–440a
Chicago, Milwaukee and Saint Paul Railway Company v. *Minnesota* (1890) II–19b
Chisholm v. *Georgia* (1793) I–94a; II–32a, 430b; VI–403b
Civil Rights Cases (1883)55a; II–54a, 55a, 457a; III–60a, 438a; VI–58a
Clark Distilling Company v. *Western Railway Company* (1917) VII–265a
Cohens v. *Virginia* (1821) II–94a, 195b; IV–19b
Colegrove v. *Green* (1946) I–147b, 244a,b
Collector v. *Day* (1871) II–113b; VII–5b
Colorado v. *Kansas* (1907) IV–28a
Commonwealth v. *Hunt* (1842) II–110b; III–407a; IV–61a; VI–103b
Communist Party v. *Subversive Control Board* (1961) VII–310b
Cooley v. *Board of Wardens of Port of Philadelphia* (1852) II–135b, 220a; IV–148a
Coppage v. *Kansas* (1915) II–222a; VII–354b
Coronado Coal Case (1919–25) VI–103b
Coyle v. *Smith* (1911) II–443b
Craig v. *Harney* (1947) V–78b
Craig v. *State of Missouri* (1830) II–253b
Cramp v. *Board of Public Instruction of Orange County, Florida* (1961) VII–15b
Cummings v. *Missouri* (1866) II–274a; IV–202b; VII–35a
Danbury Hatters' Case (1908) I–356b; II–136a, 286a; IV–67b; VI–103b, 419a
Dartmouth College Case (1819) II–114a, 213b–14a, 293b, 397b; IV–19b; V–161a, 339b, 457a; VII–117b, 156a
Debs, in re (1895) II–298b; III–351b; IV–67a; VI–419a
De Jonge v. *Oregon* (1937) I–204b; III–105a; V–265b
Delima v. *Bidwell* (1901) II–323b
Dennis v. *United States* (1951) II–146a; III–104a; IV–359a; VI–317b; VII–118a, 310b
Dorr v. *United States* (1904) III–424b
Downes v. *Bidwell* (1901) III–424b, 425a; VII–13b–14a
Dred Scott Case (1857) I–27b, 421a; II–54a, 370a, 377b; III–109b; IV–13b, 155b, 276b; V–353b, 360b; VI–307b, 404b, 447b; VII–117b
Duncan v. *Kahanamoku* (1946) III–237a; IV–259a
Dunn v. *Blumstein* (1972) VI–71a–b, 99b, 435a
Duplex Printing Press Company v. *Deering* (1921) I–357a; II–72a, 110b; III–419a; IV–69a, 70a; VI–103b
Edwards v. *California* (1941) V–420b
Endo, ex parte (1944) III–491b
Erie Railroad Company v. *Tompkins* (1938) II–460a; VI–454b
Ervien v. *United States* (1919) II–443b
Estes v. *Texas* (1965) III–105b
Everson v. *Board of Education* I–299b
Federal Trade Commission v. *Brown Shoe Company* (1966) VI–103a
Federal Trade Commission v. *Cement Institute et al.* (1948) V–402b; VI–103a
Federal Trade Commission

v. *Ruberoid* (1952) V–472b, 472b
Ferguson v. *Skrupa* (1963) II–378a
Field v. *Clark* (1892) III–20a
Fletcher v. *Peck* (1810) II–213b, 293b; III–36a; IV–19b, 99a; VII–354a
Fong Yue Ting v. *United States* (1893) III–417b
Food Employees v. *Logan Valley Plaza* (1968) V–309a
Foster v. *Neilsen* (1829) VII–110b–11a
Frothingham v. *Mellon* III–211b
Furman v. *Georgia* (1972) I–450b; III–250a; V–464b
Gaines v. *Canada* (1938) I–372b; II–54b, 401b, 457a; IV–461a; VI–256b
Garland Case (1867) III–152b; IV–202b; V–99a; VII–35a
Garner v. *Louisiana* (1961) II–50b
Gaston County v. *United States* (1969) III–93b
Gault, in re (1967) IV–23b
Gelpcke v. *Dubuque* (1864) III–154b
Georgia v. *South Carolina* (1922) I–351a
Georgia v. *Stanton* (1867) III–171b; IV–209a; VI–58a
Gibbons v. *Ogden* (1824) I–373a; II–135b, 197b, 220a; III–132a, 178a, 458b; IV–19b, 148a; V–353b; VI–145b, 407b; VII–83b
Gibson v. *Florida Legislative Investigation Committee* (1963) I–204b
Gideon Case (1963) III–179a
Gitlow v. *New York* (1925) I–299a; II–53b, 378b; III–104a; V–78b; VI–255a–b
Gold Clause Cases (1935) III–189a; VI–95a–b
Gomillion v. *Lightfoot* (1960) VI–432b
Gong v. *Rice* (1927) V–331b
Grafton v. *United States* (1907) III–207a
Graham v. *Richardson* (1971) I–88a
Granger Cases (1877) III–209b; IV–434a
Graves v. *O'Keefe* (1939) VII–8a
Green v. *Frazier* (1920) III–227a
Griffin v. *County School Board of Prince Edward County* (1964) II–54b
Griffith, in re (1973) I–88a
Grimley, in re (1890) VII–154a
Griswald v. *Connecticut* (1965) I–299b
Grosjean v. *American Press Company* (1936) III–229a; V–78b
Grovey v. *Townsend* (1935) V–407b; VI–432b
Guinn and Beal v. *United States* (1915) III–232a; IV–461a; VI–432a–b
Hadnott v. *Amos* (1969) III–93b
Hague v. *Committee on Industrial Organization* (1939) III–237b
Hammer v. *Dagenhart* (1918) II–25a, 136b; III–247a, 459b; VII–117b
Handly's Lessee v. *Anthony* (1820) I–351b
Hanna v. *Plumer* (1965) II–460b
Harper v. *Virginia Board of Elections* (1966) III–93b; IV–371b; V–355a, 434b; VI–432b, 435a; VII–133a
Hawaii v. *Mankichi* (1903) III–424b, 425a
Hayburn's Case (1792) I–12b
Heart of Atlanta Motel v. *United States* (1964) II–55b, 137a; V–339b
Helvering v. *Davis* (1937) III–157a
Henry v. *City of Rock Hill* (1964) I–204b–05a
Hepburn v. *Griswold* (1870) III–251b; IV–133a; VI–94b, 94b
Hirabayashi v. *United States* (1943) III–491a
Hitchman Coal Company v. *Mitchell* (1917) III–286a; VII–355a
Holden v. *Hardy* (1898) IV–173b
Home Building and Loan Association v. *Blaisdell* (1934) II–214a; IV–358a
Hoosac Mills Case III–299a
Humphrey's Executor v. *United States* (1935) II–499b–500a; III–317a; IV–446b; V–472b; VI–85a
Hurtado v. *California* (1884) III–320a
Hylton v. *United States* (1796) I–461a; III–351b; VII–6a
Indiana v. *Kentucky* (1890) I–351b
Inland Steel Case (1949) V–256a
Insular Cases (1901) III–424b; VII–13b, 32a–b, 33b
International News Service v. *Associated Press* (1918) VII–152a
Iowa v. *Illinois* I–351b
Jenkins v. *Georgia* (1974) III–106a
Johnson and Graham's Lessee v. *McIntosh* (1823) IV–4a
Joint Anti-Fascist Refugee Committee v. *McGrath* (1951) II–378b
Jones v. *United States* (1890) III–417b
Jones v. *Van Zandt* (1842) IV–8a
Juilliard v. *Greenman* (1884) IV–20a; VI–94b–95a
J. W. Hampton, Jr., and Company v. *United States* (1928) VI–464b
Kansas v. *Colorado* (1907) III–417b
Katzenbach v. *McClung* (1964) II–55b, 137a
Katzenbach v. *Morgan* (1966) III–93b
Katz v. *United States* (1967) II–427b
Kendall v. United States (1838) IV–36b
Kentucky v. *Dennison* (1861) IV–43b
Keyishian v. *Board of Regents of University of State of New York* (1967) I–5a
Kilbourn v. *Thompson* (1880) III–465a; IV–45b
Klors v. *Broadway Hale Stores* (1959) VI–102b
Knight v. *Board of Regents of University of State of New York* (1967) VII–16a
Knowlton v. *Moore* (1900) VII–6b
Knox v. *Lee* (1871) III–417b; VI–94b
Kohl v. *United States* (1876) III–417b
Korematsu v. *United States* (1944) III–491a; VII–118a, 227b
Lane v. *Oregon* (1869) IV–105b
Legal Tender Cases (1871) IV–132b, 133a
Leisy v. *Hardin* (1890) IV–158b–59a; V–172a
Liberty Warehouse Co. v. *Burley Tobacco Growers Co-operative Marketing Association* (1928) II–221b
Little v. *Barreme* (1804) VII–224a
Lochner v. *New York* (1905) II–378a; IV–68b, 173b; V–339b; VII–117b
Louisiana v. *Mississippi* (1906) I–351b
Louisiana v. *United States* (1965) VI–435a
Loving v. *Virginia* (1967) IV–362b
Ludecke v. *Watkins* (1948) II–445a
Luther v. *Borden* (1848) IV–206b; VI–133b
Magoun v. *Illinois Trust and Sarvings Bank* (1898) VII–6b
Marbury v. *Madison* (1803) II–232a, 370b; IV–12a–b, 13b, 19b, 248b, 336a; V–352a, 353b; VII–117a
Martin v. *Hunter's Lessee* (1816) II–195b; IV–19b, 259b
Martin v. *Mott* (1827) IV–259b
Marvin Miller v. *California* (1973) III–106a
Massachusetts v. *Laird* (1970) VII–227b
Massachusetts v. *Mellon* (1923) III–211b
Mayer v. *Peabody* (1909) IV–258b
McCardle, ex parte (1869) IV–209a; VII–35a
McCarroll v. *Dixie Greyhound Lines* (1940) II–137a
McCray v. *United States* (1904) IV–211a
McCulloch v. *Maryland* (1819) II–197b; III–348b; IV–19b, 211b; V–174b
McGrain v. *Daugherty* (1927) II–210b; III–465a
McLaughlin v. *Florida* (1964) IV–362b
McLaurin v. *Oklahoma State Regents* (1950) I–372b; II–56b, 401b
Merryman, ex parte (1861) II–62a; IV–314b
Meyers v. *United States* (1926) V–472b
Meyer v. *Nebraska* (1923) I–299a; II–378b
Miami Herald Publishing Company v. *Tornillo* (1974) V–79a
Michigan v. *Wisconsin* (1926) I–351b
Milligan, ex parte (1866) I–196a; II–62a; IV–209a, 258b, 346b; VII–35a
Milligan Case (1864) II–62a
Minnesota Moratorium Case (1934) II–214a; IV–414b
Minnesota Rate Cases (1913) II–136a
Minor v. *Happersett* (1875) IV–359a
Miranda v. *Arizona* (1966) IV–361b; V–339b
Mississippi v. *Johnson* (1867) IV–209a, 376a; VI–58a; VII–35a
Missouri v. *Holland* (1920) I–362b; IV–381a; VII–110b
Missouri v. *Kentucky* (1871) I–351a
Missouri v. *Nebraska* (1904, 1905) I–351b
Mitchel et al. v. *United States* (1835) III–59a
Moose Lodge #107 v. *Irvis* (1972) III–86b
Morehead v. *Tipaldo* (1936) IV–353a
Morgan v. *Tennessee Valley Authority* (1940) VI–85a
Morgan v. *White* (1885) VII–42b

SUPREME COURT DECISIONS (cont.)
Mugler v. *Kansas* (1887) IV–425a
Muller v. *Oregon* (1908) IV–68b; VII–213b
Munn v. *Illinois* (1877) III–209b, 211a; IV–434a; V–456b, 457b; VI–21b, 22a
Murray v. *Hoboken Land and Improvement Company* (1855) II–377a
Myers v. *United States* (1926) III–317a; IV–446a; VI–85a
National Labor Relations Board v. *Fan Steel Corporation* (1939) VI–419b
National Labor Relations Board v. *General Motors* (1963) II–4a
National Labor Relations Board v. *Jones and Laughlin Steel Corporation* (1937) II–136b, 378a; IV–467b
Neagle, in re (1890) V–30a
Near v. *Minnesota* (1931) III–105a–b; V–30b, 78b
Nebbia v. *New York* (1934) V–30b, 458b
Nebraska v. *Iowa* (1892) I–351b
Neely v. *Henkel* (1901) V–32a
Newberry v. *United States* (1921) V–41b
New Jersey v. *Delaware* (1934) I–351a
New York ex rel. Bryant v. *Zimmerman* (1928) I–240b
New York Times Company v. *Sullivan* (1964) III–104a,b; V–78b; VI–255a
New York Times v. *United States* (1971) V–258b
New York v. *New York Central Railroad Company* VII–309a
Niemotko v. *Maryland* (1951) I–205a
Nixon v. *Condon* (1932) VI–432b
Nixon v. *Herndon* (1927) III–93a; V–407b; VI–432b
Norris v. *Alabama* (1935) VI–241b
Northern Securities Company v. *United States* (1904) II–230a; V–119a; VII–122b
Ogden v. *Saunders* (1827) II–213b; V–140a
Oklahoma v. *Texas* (1926) I–351b
Old Dearborn Distributing Company v. *Seagram Distillers Corporation* (1936) II–483a
Olmstead et al. v. *Rittenhouse's Executives* (1809) I–9a,b
Oregon Parochial School Case (1925) V–167a; VI–228b; VII–15b
Oregon v. *Mitchell* (1970) III–92a; VI–99b
Osborn v. *Bank of the United States* (1824) II–266b
Palko v. *Connecticut* (1937) I–299b; III–86b
Panama Refining Company v. *Ryan* (1935) II–323a, 473a; III–307b
Parker v. *Davis* (1871) VI–94b
Paul v. *Virginia* (1868) III–432b
Pennsylvania v. *Nelson* (1956) V–339b
Perez v. *Brownell* (1958) II–54a
Philadelphia Cordwainers' Case (1806) VI–103b
Phillips Petroleum Company v. *Wisconsin* (1954) V–5b
Plessy v. *Ferguson* (1896) I–29a, 290b, 372b, 373a; II–54a,b, 57a, 399b, 404a, 457a; III–86b, 438a, 503a; V–331b; VI–256a
Poe v. *Ullman* (1961) II–378a
Pollock v. *Farmers Loan and Trust Company* (1895) I–94b; III–351a,b; V–354b; VI–297b; VII–5b, 6a,b
Porto Rico v. *Tapia* (1918) III–424b
Powell v. *Alabama* (1932) III–179a; VI–241b
Powell v. *McCormack* (1969) V–384a
Prigg v. *Pennsylvania* (1842) V–263b, 406b
Prize Cases (1863) VII–224b
Quinn v. *United States* (1915) III–93a
Railroad Retirement Board v. *Alton Railroad Company* (1935) VI–23b–24a
Rasmussen v. *United States* (1905) III–424b
Red Lion Broadcasting Company v. *Federal Communications Commission* (1969) III–106a
Reed v. *Covert* (1957) I–362b; VII–110b
Reynolds v. *Sims* (1964) I–147b–48a, 244b; II–457b; III–86b–87a; IV–133b; VII–142b
Rhode Island v. *Massachusetts* (1846) I–351a
Rickert Rice Mills, Inc. v. *Fontenot* (1936) VI–138b
Robbins v. *Taxing District* (1887) VII–105b
Roe v. *Wade* (1973) II–378b
Rogers v. *Bellei* (1971) II–475b–76a; III–86b
Ross, in re (1891) VI–165a
Roth v. *United States* (1957) I–479a; III–104b
Salyer Land Company v. *Tulare Lake Basin Water Storage District* (1973) III–94a
Schechter Poultry Corporation v. *United States* (1935) II–136b, 323a, 481b; IV–469b; V–47a; VI–225a; VII–123b
Schenck v. *United States* (1919) I–478b; III–104a; VI–225a
Scholey v. *Rew* (1874) VII–6b
Schwegmann Brothers v. *Calvert Distillers Corporation* (1951) II–483a
Shapiro v. *Thompson* (1969) V–420b
Shelley v. *Kraemer* (1948) IV–461a
Shelton v. *Tucker* (1960) I–204b
Sheppard v. *Maxwell* (1966) III–105b
Shreveport Rate Case (1914) II–136a; VI–22a, 283b
Sipuel v. *University of Oklahoma* (1948) I–372b; II–56b, 401b; IV–461a
Slaughterhouse Cases (1873) II–377b–78a; III–86b; V–420b, 420b; VI–58a, 302b
Smith v. *Allwright* (1944) II–56b; III–20b, 93a; IV–461a; V–407b; VI–432b, 435a
Smith v. *Maryland* (1855) I–351b
Smyth v. *Ames* (1898) V–458a
Socony Vacuum Oil Company v. *United States* (1940) VI–103a
South Carolina v. *Katzenbach* (1966) III–93b; VII–211a
Southern Pacific v. *Arizona* (1945) V–339b
Springbok Admiralty Case II–213a
Springer v. *United States* (1881) III–351a–b; VI–377a; VII–6a
Stafford v. *Wallace* (1922) II–136b; VI–378b
Standard Oil Company of New Jersey v. *United States* (1911) I–114a, 140a; II–71b; VI–102a–b, 169a, 383b; VII–117b, 122b, 124b, 155a
Sterling v. *Constantin* (1932) IV–258b
stop-and-frisk cases (1968) VI–249a
Strauder v. *West Virginia* (1880) VI–417b
Sturges v. *Crowninshield* (1819) II–213b; VI–422a
Sugerman v. *Dougall* (1973) I–88a
Swann v. *Charlotte-Mecklenburg Board of Education* (1971) I–397b; II–54b–55a
Sweatt v. *Painter* (1950) I–372b; II–56b, 401b; IV–461a
Sweezy v. *New Hampshire* (1957) I–5a
Swift and Company v. *United States* (1905) I–283b; II–136a
Swift v. *Tyson* (1842) II–460a; VI–454b
Talbot v. *Seeman* (1801) VII–224a
Teamsters v. *Vogt* (1957) V–309a
Tennessee Bond Cases (1885) VII–27a
Terminal Railroad Association Case (1912) VII–122b
Terry v. *Adams* (1953) III–93a
Texas v. *White* (1869) VII–35b, 40a, 42a
Thornhill v. *Alabama* (1940) V–308b
Times-Mirror Company v. *Superior Court* (1941) V–78b
Trop v. *Dulles* (1958) IV–15a
Truax v. *Corrigan* (1921) VII–121a
Union Pacific Railroad Company v. *Botsford* (1891) II–378b
United Mine Workers v. *Pennington* (1965) VI–103b
United States of America v. *Richard M. Nixon* (1974) II–474a
United States Steel Case (1920) II–230a–b
United States v. *American Tobacco Company* (1911) VI–169a, 277a; VII–122b
United States v. *Arnold Schwinn and Company* (1967) VI–102b
United States v. *Belmont* (1937) VII–111a
United States v. *Brown Shoe Company* (1962) VI–103a
United States v. *Burr* (1807) V–398a
United States v. *Butler* (1936) III–156b–57a; VII–7b
United States v. *California* VII–57b
United States v. *Columbia Steel Company* (1948) VI–103a
United States v. *Cruikshank* (1876) III–60a; V–266a; VI–58a; VII–154a
United States v. *Curtiss-Wright Export Corporation* (1936) III–417b
United States v. *Darby Lumber Company* (1941) II–136b, 482a; III–247b; IV–80b; VII–214a
United States v. *Debs* (1894) VI–276b–77a

United States v. *E. C. Knight Company* (1895) I–11a; II–136a,b, 230a; III–351b; VI–437b; VII–122a, 154a
United States v. *General Electric et al.* (1961) V–402a
United States v. *Guy W. Capps, Inc.* VII–111a
United States v. *Harris* (1883) III–60a; IV–57b; VII–154a
United States v. *Hutcheson* (1941) VI–103b
United States v. *International Harvester Company* (1914) III–454b
United States v. *Kahriger* (1953) V–339b
United States v. *Kauten* (1943) II–185b
United States v. *Lanza* (1922) VII–154b
United States v. *Lee* (1882) VII–154b
United States v. *McGowan* (1938) III–395b
United States v. *National Lead* (1947) VI–102b
United States v. *Nixon* (1974) III–465b; V–99a, 397b–98a
United States v. *Perkins* (1896) VII–6b
United States v. *Philadelphia National Bank* (1963) VI–103a
United States v. *Pink* (1937) VII–111a
United States v. *Reese* (1876) III–60a, 438a; VI–58a; VII–155a
United States v. *Saint Louis Terminal Railway Association* (1912) VI–169a
United States v. *Smith* (1806) VII–224a
United States v. *South-eastern Underwriters Association et al.* (1944) III–434a
United States v. *States of Louisiana, Texas, Mississippi, Alabama, and Florida* (1960) VII–57b
United States v. *Texas* (1892) VII–155a
United States v. *Trans-Missouri Freight Association* (1897) VII–155a
United States v. *Trenton Potteries Company* (1927) V–402a; VI–102b
United States v. *United States District Court for the Eastern District of Michigan* (1972) II–427b
United States v. *Wong Kim Ark* (1898) II–42a; VII–155b
Vallandigham Case (1864) II–62a
Veazie Bank v. *Fenno* (1869) VII–168a
Vermont v. *New Hampshire* (1933) I–351a
Village of Euclid v. *Ambler Realty Company* (1926) II–47a; VII–370b
Virginian Railway Company v. *System Federation No. 40* (1937) VII–202a
Virginia v. *West Virginia* (1915) VII–203a
Wabash, Saint Louis and Pacific Railroad Company v. *Illinois* (1886) II–135b; III–210a, 458a; V–457b; VI–21b, 28b
Ware v. *Hylton* (1797) VII–230b
Washington v. *Oregon* (1908) I–351b
Watkins v. *United States* (1957) II–210b; III–465b
Wesberry v. *Sanders* (1964) I–147b; II–172a, 355b
West Coast Hotel Company v. *Parrish* (1937) I–12a; IV–80b, 353a; VII–214a, 269a
West Virginia State Board of Education v. *Barnette* (1943) III–35a; IV–358b
Wheeling Bridge Case (1849) VII–288a
White Motors Company v. *United States* (1963) VI–102b
Wieman v. *Updegraff* (1952) VII–15b
Wiener v. *United States* (1958) IV–446b; VI–85a
Williams v. *Mississippi* (1898) IV–371b; VII–302b
Wilson v. *New* (1917) I–10a
Wisconsin Railroad Commission v. *Chicago, Burlington and Quincy* (1922) II–136b; VII–308b
Wisconsin v. *Chicago* (1933) II–20a–b
Wisconsin v. *Michigan* (1936) I–351b
Wolff Packing Company v. *Court of Industrial Relations* (1923) VII–311a
Wolf v. *Colorado* (1949) VI–249a
Wood v. *Brown* (1932) I–147b
Worcester v. *Georgia* (1832) VII–321b
Wynhamer v. *People* (1856) V–339b
Yates v. *United States* (1957) VI–317b; VII–118a
Yerger, ex parte (1868) III–236b
SUPREME COURT PACKING BILLS VI–448a; IV–14a; V–47b–48a; VI–443b
Supreme Economic Council (World War I) VII–329b
Supreme Headquarters, Allied Expeditionary Force VI–301a
Suretyship insurance III–426b
Surgeon Dentists of the City and State of New York, Society of II–329b–30a
Surgery. *See* Medicine and Surgery
Suribachi, Mount III–485a,b
Surigao Strait IV–138b
Surinam
bauxite I–92b
SURPLUS, FEDERAL VI–449a
land sales income IV–91a
tariff VI–464a, 466a,b, 467a
Surplus Property Act (1944) III–131a; V–393a
Surprise (ship) VI–128b
Surratt, John H. IV–155a; V–211b–12a
Surratt, Mary E. IV–154b–55a
Surrealists II–105a
SURROGATE'S COURT VI–450a
Surtax VII–7b, 9a,b, 12a, 13b
Survey (mag.) VI–331b
Survey, oceanographic. *See* Oceanographic Survey
Survey Act of 1807 II–87b
SURVEY ACT OF 1824 VI–450a; II–20a; VI–145b
Survey Act of 1832 II–87b
Surveying
army I–184b, 188a
canals I–442a
Corps of Engineers II–449b
Land Act of 1796 IV–90b
public domain I–463a
railroads I–83b
Southwest II–440b
western lands II–166a
See also Public Lands, Surveying of
Survey of the Coast II–87b
Surveyor General, Office of IV–90b
Surveyor project I–212b; III–502b
SURVEYORS, EARLY VI–450a; VII–272a–b
Dunbar, William II–381a
Ellicott, Andrew II–381a
Geographer's Line III–163a
king's woods IV–49a
metes and bounds IV–318a
Vancouver's exploration VII–166a
See also Topographic Mapping
Surveys, consumer I–19b–20a
Survival in the Air Age I–234b
Survivors benefits V–256a
Susa, Treaty of (1629) VI–190b
SUSAN CONSTANT (ship) **VI–451a**; VII–192b
Suspending Act (1767) VII–80a
Suspension bridges I–364a–b
Brooklyn Bridge I–164b
building materials I–378a
Verrazano-Narrows IV–452a
See also Bridges
Susquehanna (Indians) III–399b; V–246a
Susquehanna and Tidewater Canal I–127b
SUSQUEHANNA COMPANY VI–451a; II–183b; III–81b; V–231a; VI–452a; VII–347a,b
Pennsylvania-Connecticut boundary dispute V–250b
Wyoming Valley (Pa.) IV–98b
Yankee-Pennamite Wars VII–353a
Susquehanna Division canal V–250b
Susquehanna River VII–358b
Boston Ten Townships I–347b
canals III–448a; IV–174a–75b
Chemung Canal IV–174b
coal transport I–127b
Conewago Falls Canal IV–174b
forks I–223b
Fort Augusta III–115b
Harris' Ferry III–257b
Hurricane Agnes IV–258b
Indian migration VI–270b
Otsego lands V–176a
Pennsylvania canal system V–249b–50a
revolutionary war VI–438a, 438a
Scotch-Irish VI–240b
settlements VI–451b, 452a
Shawnee VI–270b
Treaty of Easton II–389a
Union Canal VII–145b
West Branch I–88b
westward movement VI–149a; VII–260a
Wyoming Valley VII–347a
Susquehanna River Basin Company (1969) III–460a
SUSQUEHANNA SETTLERS VI–452a
Susquehanna Valley VI–49a
Sussex, Duke of II–108a
***SUSSEX* CASE** (1916) **VI–452b**; VII–325a
Sussex County (Del.) II–320b, 322b; IV–199b
Sussman, Barry (ed.) V–78a
Sutherland, Earl W., Jr. (physiol.) V–100a
Sutherland, George (jur.) V–47a; VI–446b; VII–269b
SUTLER MERCHANT VI–452b
Sutro, Adolph (eng.) II–157a; VI–44a, 452b–53a
SUTRO TUNNEL VI–452b
Ralston's ring VI–44a
Sutter, John A. (pioneer) I–281a, 405b; III–81b, 191a; VI–453a
SUTTER'S FORT (Calif.) **VI–453a**; I–280b, 448a; III–114b, 190b; VII–95b–96a

Sutton, May (athlete) VII–29b
Sutton, Walter (biol.) III–157b
Suwannee River I–154a; III–39a; VI–260b, 453b
Svedberg, T. (chem.) IV–388b–89a
Sverdlovsk (Russ.) VI–179b
Sverdrup, Harald U. (oceanog.) VI–242b
SWAC (computer) II–156a
Swains Island III–425b; VI–205a
SWAMP ANGEL VI–453a; IV–431a
Swamp Fight. *See* Great Swamp Fight
"Swamp Fox." *See* Marion, Francis
Swamp Land Act (1850) VI–453b
SWAMPLANDS VI–453a
Swan, Timothy (comp.) III–326a
"SWANEE RIVER" (song) **VI–453b**
Swan Hill Pottery III–184a
Swan Lake (ballet) II–288b, 289b
Swann v. *Charlotte–Mecklenburg Board of Education* (1971) I–397b; II–54b–55a
Swans III–150a
Swansea (Mass.) IV–47a
Swanson, Claude A. (pol.) V–43b; VII–195b
Swanton (Vt.) IV–87a
Swarthmore College III–274a
Swartwout, Samuel (mer., pol.) I–327b; VI–143b; VII–293b
Swatara (ship) V–22b
Swayne, Noah H. (jur.) II–378a; VI–445b
Sweat bathing III–385b
Sweaters II–372b
SWEATSHOP VI–453b; IV–10a
  clothing industry II–82a, 372a
  morality of IV–408b
  Triangle fire VII–118b
Sweatt v. *Painter* (1950) I–372b; II–56b, 401b
Sweden
  commercial treaty VII–111a
  Common Market VI–472a
  European Free Trade Association VI–469a; VII–89a
  exchange students II–470b
  Fort Elfsborg IV–454a
  fur trade III–141b
  hockey III–287b
  immigration to U.S. III–333a, 337a, 339b–40a
  investments in U.S. III–66b
  iron III–469b
  meteorological studies IV–318a
  naval stores V–14b; VI–461b
  Organization for Economic Cooperation and Development V–170b
  polio V–340a
  reciprocity treaties VII–86b
  slave trade VI–309b
  Sound dues VI–340a
  submarines VI–422b
  trade treaties I–245a
  U.S. aid III–61b
  Vietnam deserters II–335b
  World War I VI–378a
Sweden, New. *See* New Sweden Colony
Swedenborg, Emanuel (sci., philos.) V–58a
Swedenborgianism. *See* New Jerusalem, Churches of the
Swedish Nightingale. *See* Lind, Jenny
Swedish Royal Academy of Science V–326a
Swedish settlements II–35a, 123b, 125b, 320a; III–334b
  cattle III–51b
  Delaware IV–199b
  Duke of York's proprietary VII–359b
  log cabins IV–179a
  Minnesota IV–356b
  New Sweden Colony V–80a
  New Sweden Company V–80b
  Philadelphia V–277a
  sheep VI–272b; VII–320b
Sweeny, Peter B. ("Brains") (pol.) VI–142a; VII–131a
SWEEPING RESOLUTION (1810) **VI–454b**
Sweet corn II–226a
Sweet mash (whiskey) VII–289b
Sweet potato I–48a; III–51a, 52a, 381a; V–376b–77a
  See also Potato
Sweetwater V–168b
Sweetwater River III–354a; VII–103b
Sweezy v. *New Hampshire* (1957) I–5a
Swift, Gustavus F. (meat-packer) III–80a
Swift, Joseph G. (off.) IV–340b
Swift and Company I–283b; II–17b; IV–280b; VI–414b
Swift and Company v. *United States* (1905) I–283b; II–136a
"Swift" boats V–22a
Swift Run Gap (Va.) IV–43b
SWIFT* v. *TYSON (1842) **VI–454b**; II–460a
Swimming
  Olympic Games V–154a,b
Swine I–37b; IV–169b
  corn belt II–227a
  See also Hogs
Swine cholera I–241a
Swing, Raymond Gram (jour.) V–74a
Swing Era IV–440a,b
"SWING ROUND THE CIRCLE" (1866) **VI–454b**; VI–57a
Swinnerton, James (art.) V–72a
Swissair III–277b
Swiss–American Historical Society III–279b
SWISS SETTLERS VI–454b; II–125b; V–379a
Switchboards VII–20a
Switchmen's Union of North America VI–20a, 28b
Switzerland
  Alabama Claims arbitration VII–249a
  alienage of Swiss citizens I–87a
  Bank for International Settlements I–254a
  Common Market VI–472a
  currency upvalue III–196b
  European Free Trade Association VI–469a; VII–89a
  immigration to U.S. III–337a
  International Court of Justice III–453a
  investments in U.S. III–63a, 65b, 66b
  neutrality V–36a
  Organization for Economic Cooperation and Development V–170b
  pharmaceutical industry V–273b, 274a
  Siegfried Line VI–285b
  Synod of Dort VI–455b
  U.S. aid III–61b
Switzerland County (Ind.) III–337a; VI–455a
Sword Beach (Fr.) V–110b
Swords II–376b; IV–432b
Sybil (ship) I–89b
Sybrant, Jan (landowner) V–286a
SYCAMORE SHOALS, TREATY OF (1775) **VI–455a**; II–273b–74a, 292a; III–382b
Sydenham, Thomas (physic.) II–390b
Sydney–Hobart race VII–349a
Syllabub III–52a
Sylvania III–497a
Sylvester, J. J. (math.) IV–2a,b
Sylvester–William, Henry (law.) V–199a
Sylvis, William (labor leader) IV–62a, 62b, 63a
Symbionese Liberation Army II–258b
Symington, Stuart (pol.) I–60b
Symmes, John Cleves (off.) IV–99a, 329b, 330a; VII–299a
Symmes, Thomas (cler.) IV–199a
Symmes purchase. *See* Miami Purchase
Syms, Benjamin (educ.) II–395a–b
Syms–Eaton School II–395a–b
Synagogues IV–9a, 10a, 11a,b; V–65b
Synchrocyclotron II–278b
Synchromists (paint.) V–192a–b
Synchrotron II–278b; V–301b
Syncom 2 (satellite) II–143a
SYNDICALISM VI–455b; I–117a; VI–13b
  Brandenburg v. *Ohio* V–78b
  Industrial Workers of the World III–412b
  sabotage VI–182b
  Socialist party VI–326b
Syndicated newspapers V–76b–77a
Synecology II–392a
Syng, Philip (silversmith) III–430a
Syngman Rhee II–489a
SYNOD OF DORT VI–455b
Synod of Evangelical Lutheran Churches IV–206b
Synod of Kentucky II–272b
Synod of Philadelphia VII–279a
Synods, Presbyterian IV–365a
Synopsis of the Fishes of North America III–27b
Synthetic building materials I–379a
Synthetic fibers I–460b; II–372b; VII–44a, 67b
Synthetic leather I–338b
Synthetic rubber VI–168a
Syphilis IV–306b; V–438a; VI–266b
  See also Venereal Disease
Syracuse (It.) VI–284b
Syracuse (N.Y.)
  canal museum I–443b
  fugitive slaves I–138a
  Oneida Colony V–155b
  railroad III–450a
  salt II–5b
  state fair VI–392b
Syracuse Action for Youth II–148b
Syracuse Convention (1850) II–184b
Syria I–150a; III–481b, 482a
  marine landings IV–252b
  U.S. landing in Lebanon IV–130a
  World War I relief VII–330a
  Yom Kippur War II–213a
Syrian Orthodox Church of Antioch II–387a
Syringa VI–393 (table)
Systema naturae III–26b, 29b; VI–90a
Systematic Theology VI–82a
System of Dante's Hell IV–167b
System of Mineralogy IV–348b

Systems analysis III–406b, 407b
Szilard, Leo (phys.) IV–237b, 238b; V–303a; VI–230b

T

T4M-1 (torpedo plane) I–55a
T-34 (dirigible) II–344a
T-171 Vulcan (cannon) I–57b
Tabasco (Mex.) IV–322a, 325a; VII–41b
Tabasco River IV–252a, 322a
Taber (Alta., Can.) I–155a
TABERNACLE, MORMON VI–456a
Table Rock, Treaty of (1853) III–384a
Tables III–135a,b
Tableware VII–288a
Tabloids IV–271b; V–68a, 74b–75a
Tabor, Horace A. W. (miner) IV–124a, 439a
Tacloban (Phil.) I–60a
TACNA-ARICA CONTROVERSY VI–456a; VI–217a
Tacoma (Wash.) VI–33a; VII–248a
Tacoma Building (Chicago) VI–299a
Taconite III–12a–b, 218b; IV–315b, 357b–58a
Tacos III–53a
Tactical Air Command I–53b, 54a, 61b, 64a
Tactical Air Navigational System I–56a
Tactics, military IV–180a–b
Tae, First Church of the VI–268b
TAFIA VI–456b
Taft, Helen Herron (Mrs. William Howard) III–491b
Taft, Robert A. (pol.) II–189b
  campaign of 1940 I–429a
  campaign of 1952 I–430a
  Taft-Hartley Act IV–74a; VI–456b
Taft, Robert A., Jr. (pol.) V–142a
Taft, William Howard II–176 (table); V–142a, 394b, 396 (table); VI–446b
  Cuba Intervention II–269a
  double jeopardy VII–154b
  Fifth Amendment I–12a
  interstate commerce VI–379a
  League to Enforce Peace IV–124a
  restraint of trade VI–102a
  right to strike VI–419a
  Taft-Katsura Memorandum VI–457b
  War Department VII–230a
  See also Taft Commission VI–456b
  —President:
  antitrust laws I–140a
  Ballinger-Pinchot controversy I–247b
  campaign of 1908 I–426b
  campaign of 1912 I–426b–27a; II–327b
  Canadian-American relations I–437a, 439a
  China policy III–347b
  Department of Labor IV–78a
  dollar diplomacy II–359b, 475b
  Far Eastern policy II–488b
  Federal Children's Bureau IV–275b
  Foreign Service VI–389a
  international court III–456b–57a
  Latin American policy VI–163a
  literacy test III–342b
  Manchuria IV–235a
  match production IV–274b
  naval oil reserves V–13a
  Open Door policy V–159a
  Progressive movement V–427a–b
  Republican party split VI–384b–85a
  Roosevelt split VI–93a, 458a
  Sherman Antitrust Act VI–138b
  Sixteenth Amendment VI–297b
  tariff VI–464a–b, 467b
  "trust-busting" VII–122b
  Webb-Kenyon Act VII–265a
  Weeks Act VII–266b
  Winona speech VII–306b
TAFT COMMISSION VI–456b; V–281b, 283a
TAFT-HARTLEY ACT (1947) **VI–456b**; II–2b, 4a, 80b, 86b, 111a, 499a; III–407a, 419b; IV–74a, 467a; VII–178a
  efforts to amend I–102b, 103a
  National Labor Relations Board III–459a
  secondary boycotts VI–103b
  strikes VI–419b
TAFT-KATSURA MEMORANDUM (1905) **VI–457b**; II–488b; V–158b
Taft-Knox Treaties (1911) VII–112b
TAFT-ROOSEVELT SPLIT VI–458a; II–327b; VI–93a, 385a
Tagalogs (people) III–133a
Taggart, Thomas (pol.) I–343b
Taggart, William H. (dent.) II–331a
Tagliamento River I–102a; V–308a
Taglioni, Maria (dancer) II–287a
Tahgah-jute. *See* Logan, John
Tahiti (Society Islands) IV–364b
Tahoe, Lake VI–101b, 154a
Tahwaccaro (Indians) I–286a
Tailors II–81a, 81b; IV–61b
Tainter, Charles Sumner (inv.) V–289b
Tait, A. F. (art.) II–103a
Taiwan I–61b; II–28a
  exchange students II–471a
  immigration II–30a; III–341a,b
  military aid II–315b
  Southeast Asia Treaty Organization VI–350b
  tariff VI–470b
  U.S. Sixth Fleet V–22b
  wool VII–321b
Taiwi (Indian) VII–162b
Takagi, Takeo (nav. off.) II–225a; III–492b
Takahira, Kogoro (dipl.) VI–164a
Taku (China) I–322b, 356a
Talbot, John G. (nav. off.) VI–186a
Talbot, Silas (off.) II–190b
Talbot v. *Seeman* (1801) VII–224a
Tales (Baraka) IV–167b
Talese, Gay (au.) V–79a
Tales of a Wayside Inn (poem) IV–162a; VI–106a
Tales of Peter Parley About America V–264b
Tales of the Grotesque and Arabesque IV–162b
Taliaferro, Lawrence (off.) VI–322b; VII–196b
Taliesin (Spring Green, Wis.) I–165a
Taliesin West (Scottsdale, Ariz.) I–165a
Talishatchee (Ala.) II–256b
"Talking" movies II–424b
Talladega (Ala.) II–256b
Talladega College I–28b; II–113b; III–103b
Tallahassee (Fla.) I–238b; II–336a; III–39a; VI–348b–49a
Tallahatchie River VII–354b
Tallamook Lighthouse VI–146b
Tallapoosa River II–257a; III–278a, 305b
Tall Bull (Indian) VII–252b
Tallchief, Maria (dancer) II–288b
Talleyrand-Périgord, Charles Maurice de (states.) III–122b
  Louisiana IV–196a
  Spanish-American relations VI–359b
  XYZ Affair II–215a; III–96a; IV–347a; VII–347b
TALLMADGE AMENDMENT (1819) **VI–458b**; II–366a; IV–379a
Tallow trade. *See* Hide and Tallow Trade
TALL STORIES VI–458b; I–280b–81a; VI–49a, 299b–300a
Tally, Thomas L. IV–417b
Talmudical academies IV–11a
Talon, Jean (expl.) IV–109a; VI–219a
Tamanend (Indian) II–321a; VI–267b, 459a
Tama Reservation III–468a
Tamaroa (Indians) I–402a
Tamaulipas (Mex.) IV–348a
Tambourine II–291a
Tamiris, Helen (chor.) II–288a
Tammany (Indian). *See* Tamanend
TAMMANY HALL VI–459a; V–83a,b, 345a; VII–295a
  American Labor Party I–107a
  campaign of 1800 I–417a
  campaign of 1884 I–424a
  graft IV–137b
  high-minded men III–276b
  Locofoco party IV–175a
  Nast cartoons V–73a
  New York Evening Post V–71b
  New York mayoral election (1886) IV–101a
  party machine IV–214a
  sachems VI–183b
  Tweed Ring VII–131a
  Workingmen's Party VII–322a
TAMMANY SOCIETIES VI–460b; II–321a
  Bucktails I–374b
  Cleveland, Grover II–75a
  Martling Men IV–260a
  "wigwam" VII–295a
Tammany Tiger I–464b; IV–454b
Tampa (Fla.) III–39b
  airline service I–67b
  Capron Trail I–451b
  race riot VI–9a
  Rough Riders VI–165b
  Spanish exploration I–399b
Tampa (revenue cutter) V–20a
Tampa Bay VII–311a
  Narváez expedition IV–452a
  Seminole Wars II–278b
  Spanish exploration I–96b; II–184a, 336a
  Spanish posts IV–302b
Tampico (Mex.) IV–252a, 452a
  Mexican War IV–322a, 325a
  Veracruz incident VII–171a
Tampico affair. *See* Veracruz Incident

Tanaina (Indians) I–80b; III–360b
Tanaka, Shinichi (off.) IV–447a
Tanana (Indians) I–80b; III–252b, 360b
Tanana Valley I–77b–78a
Tanenhaus, Joseph (pol. sci.) V–347b, 348a
Taney, Robert G. (jur.) VI–445b
Taney, Roger B. (jur.)
arbitrary arrest I–195b–96a
commerce clause II–135b, 220a
corporate charters I–496a
Dred Scott Case II–370a–b; V–353b, 360b
Fifth Amendment II–370b
foreign corporations I–260b
Fugitive Slave Act I–2a
habeas corpus II–62a; III–237a; IV–314b
land grants IV–254a
martial law IV–206b
removal of deposits VI–85b
Tanganyika IV–236b
Tangerines II–43b
Tangiers (Mor.) I–266a
Tanglewood Tales I–335a
Tango (dance) II–290b
Tanguy, Yves (art.) II–105b
Tankers IV–311a; V–25a; VI–280a, 280b–81a,b
Tanks I–177a–b; II–314b; IV–430a, 431b
See also Armored vehicles
Tanner, Henry Schenk (cartog.) I–462b; II–355b; VII–74b
Tanning II–5a; III–413b; IV–9a
See also Leather Industry
Tanoan (lang.) III–301a,b, 367b, 368a; V–459b
Tanoan Pueblo (N.Mex.) I–7b
Tantalum III–14b, 14b
Tanzania I–22a; IV–236b
TAOS (N.Mex.) **VI–460b**
Arizona River I–174a
exploration II–228b
Fonda's expedition III–50b
Fort Bernard I–293a
Fowler expedition III–88a
Pueblo V–460a
Pueblo Indians III–367a,b
Taos Trail VI–461a
Utah fur trade VII–161a
western routes V–224b
Taos Pueblo (N.Mex.) VI–461a
TAOS TRAIL VI–461a; VI–215b
Taovaya (Indians) V–148a
Tape recorders V–290a; VII–90a
Tapir II–83b
Tappan (N.Y.) I–118b; VI–461a
Tappan, Arthur (mer., philan.) III–24b; VII–83a
Tappan, Henry P. (cler., educ.) II–470b
Tappan, Lewis (mer.) I–137a,b; III–24b; IV–307b; VII–83a
Tappan and Company IV–307b
Tappan brothers I–136a
TAPPAN PATENT VI–461a
TAR VI–461b; II–4b, 5a, 84b; V–14b, 267a,b, 327b
colonial production IV–243a
colonial trade II–453a
street paving V–230a
Tarabal (Indian) III–150b
Tarahumare (Indians) III–369a; IV–367a
peyote V–273a
Tarakan VII–337a
T A Ranch (Wyo.) VI–181b
TAR AND FEATHERS VI–461b; VI–122a, 253a
Loyalists IV–200b
smuggling VI–320b
Sons of Liberty VI–339a
Taranto (It.) VII–76b
TARASCON, BERTHOUD AND COMPANY VI–462a
Tarascon, John A. (bus.) VI–462a
Tarascon, Louis A. (bus.) VI–462a
TARAWA VI–462a; III–180a; IV–253a, 257b; VII–139a, 337a
Tarbell, Ida M. (au.) IV–424b; VI–157a
Tarentum (Pa.) IV–44a; VI–270b
"Tarheels" V–14b
Tar Heel State VI–395 (table)
TARIFF VI–462b; II–276a–b; VII–4a–b, 5a, 12a, 12b, 13a, 13b–14a, 87b, 88a,b, 89a, 124b
ad valorem and specific duties II–383b
agriculture I–42b, 44a
American System III–449a
big business I–389a
British trade III–493b
business development IV–243a,b
campaign of 1816 I–418a
campaign of 1844 I–420a
campaign of 1860 I–421b
campaign of 1872 I–422a,b
campaign of 1888 I–424a,b
campaign of 1892 I–424b
campaign of 1928 I–428a
Canadian–American reciprocity I–437a, 439a, 440a
Canadian fish I–277b
carpet manufacture I–460a
chemical industry II–5b
Civil War II–63b, 64b, 69a–b
Cleveland administration II–75a
cod fisheries II–93a
colonies VII–2b, 3a,b, 80b
commercial treaties VII–112a
Confederacy II–159b
Democratic party II–327a
Dingley Act IV–33a
East Indies trade II–388b
executive agreements II–472a
federal surplus II–333a; VI–449a
fishing bounties III–31b
Force Acts III–59b
Fort Hill letter III–78a
free trade III–112b
Friends of Domestic Industry III–124a
Gallatin's report on manufactures III–147a
Geneva conference III–161a
Gilded Age III–180b
Gorman–Wilson tariff V–354b
government regulation of business III–204a, 205a
Grenville Act III–228a
Hamilton's fiscal policies III–244b–45a, 245b–46a,b
Harrisburg Convention III–257a
Horizontal Tariff Bill III–301b
imposts III–349a
iron and steel manufacture III–473a
Jeffersonian Republicans VI–94b
Kasson Treaties IV–33a
Kennedy Round III–70a
laissez-faire doctrine IV–85b
land policies IV–91a,b
maritime regulation IV–254b
McKinley Tariff II–151a; III–20a, 263b; VI–277a
most-favored-nation principle IV–416b; VII–109a
nails IV–448b
narcotics IV–450a
Navigation Act of 1817 V–15b
Navigation Acts V–16b
Norfolk trade V–109b
"normalcy" V–110a
nullification I–404b; II–241a; V–125b–26a, 198a; VI–397a
opposition I–326a
Payne–Aldrich Bill VII–306b
Peking Tariff Conference V–242b
Philippines V–284a,b
"pop-gun" bills V–359a
presidential powers II–323a
prices V–403b
Progressive movement V–427a–b, 428b
protective I–113b, 113b, 245a
Puerto Rico II–323b; III–58a; V–461b
Reciprocal Trade Agreement Act V–45b
reciprocal trade agreements I–246a; VI–51b
Republican party VI–92b
retaliation in international law VI–104b
revenue VII–7a
Revenue Act of 1789 II–88b, 275b–76a
secessionist movement VI–250b
sectionalism VI–254a
silk VI–287a
silver purchases III–110b
Sixteenth Amendment VI–297b
South American trade VI–343b, 344a
Spanish goods I–10b
states' rights VI–404b
subsidies VI–425b–26a
sugar I–285b
sugarcane VI–436a
tea VII–15a, 16a
Vermont VII–172a
Ways and Means Committee VII–263b
Webster–Hayne debate VII–265b
Whig party VII–288a
wool VI–272b; VII–321b
World Economic Conference VII–324a
Wyoming VII–346a
Zollverein Treaty VII–370a
See also Duties
Tariff Act of 1890 III–113a
Tariff Act of 1909 III–113a
Tariff Act of 1930 VI–52a
Tariff Board VI–464a–b
Tariff Commission III–114a; VI–52a,b, 469a, 470a, 471b
Tariff Commission of 1882 VI–464a
Tariff Commission of 1916 VI–464b
"Tariff for revenue only" VI–462b–63a
Tariff of Abominations (1828) I–404b; VI–465b–66a
Tariff of 1789 VI–465a; VII–4b
Tariff of 1816 VI–465a–b; VII–12b
Tariff of 1921 VI–467b–68a
Tarleton, Banastre (off.) II–251a, 451b; III–30b; IV–8b; VI–130a
Battle of Cowpens VI–351b
Battle of Haw River III–265a
Battle of Waxhaw VII–261b–62a
Fishing Creek action III–31b
"Tarleton's quarter" VII–262a
Tarpley, Collin S. (pol.). *See* Tarpley Letter
TARPLEY LETTER (1849) **VII–1a**; IV–453b
Tarr farm (Pa.) V–318b
Tarrytown (N.Y.) IV–472a; VI–312b
Tartary V–95a

Tartuffe (privateer) V–423b
Task designations (U.S. Navy) V–24b
Task Force 16 IV–336a
Task Force 17 IV–336a
Task Force 38. *See* Task Force 58
TASK FORCE 58 VII–1a; V–285b
Task Force 77 VII–2a
Task Force 115 V–22a
Task Force 116 V–22a
Task Force 117 V–22a
Task forces
 World War II VII–343b
Task system (clothing ind.) II–82a
Tasmania VI–142a
Tassafaronga, Battle of (1942) VII–68a
Tate, Sharon (act.) VII–118b
Tatham, William (cartog.) I–462a
Tatholah (Indian) II–22a
Tattnall, Josiah (nav. off.) I–322b
Tatum, E. L. (biochem.) III–157b; IV–389a; V–100a
Taunton (Mass.) IV–47b, 175b, 266b
Taunton Britannia Company VI–291b
Taunton River II–341a
Taussig, Frank W. (econ., educ.) VI–464b
Taussig, Joseph K. (nav. off.) VII–328b
TAVERNS VII–2a
 Allegheny wagoners VII–216a
 curfew law II–274b
 Fraunces Tavern III–100a
 Indian Queen III–391b
 post roads V–375a
 Raleigh Tavern VI–44a
 stage lines VI–380a; VII–100a
 Tondee Tavern VII–71b
Tawakoni (Indians) V–148a
Tawi Tawi V–285b
Tax Adjustment Act (1945) VII–8b
Tax Adjustment Act (1966) VII–9b
Tax Appeals, U.S. Board of II–500b
TAXATION VII–2b
 Agricultural Adjustment Act III–299a; VI–138b
 Articles of Confederation I–197b–98a; II–165b, 167a
 Bank of the United States II–266b; III–245b; V–174a
 bootlegging I–339a
 campaign contributions I–414b
 capitalism I–449a,b
 capitation VI–377a
 chain stores I–489b
 Civil War II–63b, 66a, 69a
 colonial assemblies II–117a
 colonial policy VII–14a
 colonial suffrage VI–434a
 colonies II–118a, 309a–b, 494b
 commercial treaties VII–108b
 Confederacy II–164a; III–416a; VII–15a
 congressional powers II–171b, 178b, 195b, 199b, 275b, 313a, 453b, 476a
 contract clause II–213b
 corporations V–48b
 cost of government II–234a
 cost of living II–236b
 Crisis II–264b
 direct VI–377a
 endowed foundations III–83a–84a
 equal protection clause II–457b
 excess profits II–467a
 exports II–478a
 farmer's opposition I–41a
 federal aid II–502a, 502a
 federal deficit II–317a
 federal expenditures II–476a
 federal–state relations III–9a,b
 federal surplus VI–449b
 foreign investment II–301b
 Fries's Rebellion III–124a
 gasoline III–153a
 general welfare clause III–156b
 government regulation of business III–205a
 Great Britain II–191a
 Greenback party III–225a
 Guffey Coal Acts III–232a
 Hamilton's fiscal policies III–245a
 highways I–228b; VI–155b
 holding companies III–290a,b
 importation of slaves II–152a, 200a
 income II–206a, 502a; V–354b; VI–377a
 Income Tax Cases III–351a
 inheritance tax laws III–417b
 interstate trade barrier III–460b
 Ipswich protest III–469a
 irrigation III–477b
 Justice Department IV–22a
 justice of the peace IV–22b
 Kalamazoo Case IV–24b
 liquor IV–158b; V–45a
 local government II–502a; IV–171b, 172a–b
 Louisiana IV–194b
 Massachusetts IV–265b–66a
 matches IV–274b
 Minnesota IV–357b
 Molasses Act IV–387b
 mulct law IV–425b
 nails IV–448b
 narcotics control IV–450b
 Navigation Acts V–16b
 negative income tax VI–328b
 New Deal V–44a, 46a,b
 newspaper advertising III–229a
 New York State V–87b
 "normalcy" V–110a
 Ocala Platform V–132a
 oil depletion allowance V–272b
 original package doctrine V–172a,b
 payroll IV–71b
 per capita IV–65b
 philanthropy V–281a
 political subdivisions V–350a
 poll tax II–408a, 410a; V–355a
 prerevolutionary agitation IV–60b
 Progressive movement V–427a, 428b
 prohibitory taxes IV–211a
 property I–4b; II–502a; IV–103b
 public debt II–300a,b
 public revenue VI–105a; VII–108a
 publishers and broadcasters III–106a
 Puerto Rico III–58a; V–461b
 pump-priming V–464a
 Puritans VII–69a
 Readjuster movement VI–49a
 real estate VI–377a
 revolutionary war VI–121a
 road working days VI–156b
 sales II–502a; VI–200a
 salt VI–202a
 Sanborn contracts VI–207b
 school boards II–405a
 school taxes VI–226b, 228a
 Shays's Rebellion VI–271b
 single tax V–427a; VI–293a
 Sixteenth Amendment VI–297b
 Southern Commercial Conventions VI–352a
 Spanish-American War II–317a
 Stamp Act VI–381a–82a
 state government II–502a; VI–398b
 states' rights IV–105b
 state taxation of federal agencies IV–211b
 Supreme Court VI–447b
 Tax Court II–500b
 tobacco VII–67b
 Treasury Department I–12a
 Veazie Bank v. *Fenno* VII–168a
 voting V–434b
 voting rights II–207a
 Washington, D.C. VII–245b
 welfare programs II–234b
 West Jersey VII–278b
 whiskey II–353b; VII–290a–b
 Wisconsin VII–308b
 See also Tariff
TAXATION NO TYRANNY (pol. pamphlet) **VII–14a**
TAXATION WITHOUT REPRESENTATION VII–14a; II–191a, 307a, 325a; V–221a; VI–111a–b, 141a,b, 396a; VII–3b, 189b
 Dominion of New England V–50b
 Mutiny Act of 1765 IV–445b
 pamphleteering V–198b
 Stamp Act VI–381b–82a, 381b–82a
Tax clause III–349a
Tax Court of the United States I–12b–13a; II–500b; IV–16b
Taxicabs II–425b; III–1a
TAX IN KIND, CONFEDERATE VII–15a; VII–64a, 148b
Tax-paying qualifications III–91a
Tax Reform Act (1969) III–84a; VII–9b–10a
Tax shelters III–83b
Taylor, Allen (inv.) VII–61b
Taylor, Ann V–334a
Taylor, Buck VII–298b
Taylor, C. Gilbert (inv.) I–52b
Taylor, Daniel (off.) VI–411a–b
Taylor, David (nav. off.) I–51a
Taylor, Edward (poet) IV–161a
Taylor, Frederick W. (efficiency eng.) I–205b; III–15b, 405b–06a; IV–255a, 273a; VI–233b–34a,b
Taylor, George (legis.) II–308a
Taylor, Glen H. (pol.) I–429b; V–429a
Taylor, Graham (cler., educ.) VI–330b
Taylor, Isaac (surv.) II–322b
Taylor, James (mfr.) III–184b
Taylor, John, of Caroline (pol., agric.) VI–335a; VII–194a
Taylor, John L. (jur.) VI–250a
Taylor, John W. (law.) II–174 (table), 175 (table)
Taylor, Myron C. (law., bus.) VI–410b–11a
Taylor, Nathaniel G. (off.) III–378a
Taylor, Nathaniel W. (theol.) VI–81b
Taylor, Paul (dancer) II–290a
Taylor, Richard (off.) II–68b; III–298b; V–331a; VI–63a, 182a; VII–26b
Taylor, Robert L. (pol.) III–19a
Taylor, William S. (pol.) III–188a
Taylor, Zachary II–175 (table); V–152a, 395 (table), 398b
 —*Military Career:*
 Battle of Buena Vista

TAYLOR, ZACHARY (cont.)
I–375a
Battle of Credit Island II–255b
Battle of Lake Okeechobee VI–261a
Battle of Okeechobee V–147a
Battle of Palo Alto V–198b; VI–97a
Fort Brown I–371a
Fort Edwards II–406a
Mexican War IV–323b, 324a, 324b, 325a, 404b
—President:
campaign of 1848 I–420b
Compromise of 1850 II–150a
death I–421a; II–150a
Galphin claim III–148a
Hülsemann incident III–316a
Omnibus Bill V–155a
Republic IV–465b
Squier Treaty VI–378b
Taylor Grazing Act (1934) IV–95b, 96a
Taylor system. *See* Industrial Management
TBD Douglas Devastator (torpedo plane) I–55b
TBF bombers VII–343b
TBF Grumman Avenger (torpedo plane) I–55b
TC-3 (blimp) II–344a
Tchaikovsky, Pëtr Illich (comp.) II–287b
Tea I–201a,b
China trade II–28b; III–181a
clipper ships II–77a
Horizontal Tariff III–301b
pure food laws V–465b
TEA, DUTY ON VII–15a; I–347a–b; II–5a, 388a; III–244b; VI–110b, 343b; VII–3b, 17a, 80b, 81a, 112b
letters of "Junius" IV–20b
nonimportation agreements V–104b
protest I–208a; II–393a
tea parties VII–16a
Townshend Acts V–85b
Tea Act (1767) VII–15a
Tea Act (1773) VI–113b, 321a
Teach, Edward (Blackbeard) (pirate) I–374a
Teacher aids II–402b
Teacher education II–399b, 401a–b, 402b; IV–2b
Teachers VI–229a–b
middle class IV–334b
Minneapolis strike (1971) IV–75b
unions II–402b; IV–75b–76a
Teacher's College at Columbia University II–401a
Teacher's colleges II–401a
Teacher's institutes II–494a
TEACHERS' LOYALTY OATH VII–15b; IV–203a
Teacher's organizations II–399b
Teachers' rights IV–463a
Teacher training II–396b, 398a
Teaching II–394b–95a, 397a–b
academic freedom I–4b–5a
Carnegie Foundation I–456a–b
women VII–313a, 316a, 317a
Tead, Ordway III–407b
TEA GROWING IN THE SOUTH VII–16a
Teamsters Union IV–72a, 74b, 76b, 76b; V–400b
Teamsters v. *Vogt* (1957) V–309a
TEA PARTIES VII–16a; VI–113b
Boston I–208a, 346b, 347a–b
Edenton II–388a
New York City V–82b, 85b
Teapot Dome (Wyo.). *See* Teapot Dome Oil Scandal
TEAPOT DOME OIL SCANDAL VII–16b; II–231b; V–13b, 346b
TEA TRADE, PREREVOLUTIONARY VII–16b; III–52a
Boston Port Act I–346b
Charleston (S.C.) I–496b
duties VII–15a–b
East India Company II–388a
Peggy Stewart burning V–241b
smuggling VI–321a
Tebéssa (Alg.) IV–32b
Technetium IV–119a
Technical drawings
copyright II–224b
Technical instruction. *See* Engineering Education
Technicolor IV–418a
TECHNOCRACY MOVEMENT VII–17b; VI–269a; VII–79b
Technological unemployment VII–141a,b
Technology, Indian. *See* Indian Art and Technology
Tectonics III–165b, 167a,b
Tecumseh (Indian) II–256b; III–21b, 257b; IV–90a; VI–270a; VII–46a
Shawnee Prophet V–4a, 435a; VI–271a
War of 1812 IV–224b
See also Tecumseh, Crusade of
Tecumseh (monitor) II–286a; IV–383a
TECUMSEH, CRUSADE OF (c. 1806–13) **VII–17b**; V–141a; VII–233b–34a
Battle of Tippecanoe VII–63a
Fort Meigs IV–300b
Treaty of Fort Wayne VII–262b
Tecumseh, Fort (S. Dak.). *See* Pierre, Fort
Tedyuskung (Indian) II–389a
Teepee. *See* Tipi
Teeth. *See* Dentistry
Teeth, artificial II–331a
Teflon II–9a–b; V–328a
Tehachapi Mountains VII–271b
Tehachapi Pass V–225a
Tehama County (Calif.) I–340a
Tehauntepec (Mex.) III–145b
TEHERAN CONFERENCE (1943) **VII–18a**; I–403b; II–145b, 471b; VI–179a
Tehuantepec (Mex.) IV–218a, 324b; VII–58b
Tejas (Tex.) VI–210a
Telecommunications II–425b–26a
Bell Laboratories II–425b
licensing IV–148b
satellites II–142b
telephone I–287a
Telecommunications Policy, Office of I–480b; II–135b, 498a
Telecommunications Union, International II–143a
Telefon Hirmondo VI–14b
TELEGRAPH VII–18b; II–414a, 419a, 421b; IV–244a
American Telegraph and Cable Co. II–137a
army defense I–192a
Associated Press I–207a
balloons I–248a
Civil War I–481a; II–69a; VI–38a
electric battery I–276a
fire signal system III–25a
Fort Bridger I–363a
geographical longitudes I–211a
Henry, Joseph IV–317a
Interstate Commerce Commission III–458a
Iowa III–468b
Jackson, Charles T. I–119a
National Weather Service VII–264a
news transmission V–77a
ocean cables I–400b, 401a; VII–163a–b
off-track betting II–260a,b
Postal Telegraph II–137a; V–374b
price levels V–405a
public utilities V–456b
radio VI–14b
regulation III–1a,b
Signal Corps VI–286a
stock ticker VI–413b
taxation VII–7b, 8b
transfer of funds II–468a
typewriter VII–136a
United Press VII–152a
weather data II–75b
Western Union VII–276b
World War I I–481a
TELEGRAPHERS' STRIKE (1883) **VII–19b**
Telemetry II–425b, 426a; IV–333a
Telepathy V–212b, 213a
TELEPHONE VII–19b; II–413b, 417a,b, 419a; V–289b; VI–14b
communications satellites II–426a
electric circuit analysis II–38b
Federal Communications Commission I–13a
Interstate Commerce Commission III–458a
microwave technology IV–333a
miniaturization IV–352a
mutual societies II–220b
public utilities V–456b
radiotelephony VI–15a
regulation III–1a,b
relay technology II–153b
rural service I–39b; VI–175b
Signal Corps VI–286a
sound recording V–290a,b
taxation VII–7b, 8b, 9b, 13a
towboating VII–78a
transcontinental II–423b
urban structure VII–159b
vacuum tubes VII–163a,b
Western Union VII–276b
wiretapping II–427a–b
World War I I–481a
See also Bell Telephone Laboratories
TELEPHONE CASES VII–20b
Telephony II–424b
Telescope III–242a–b; V–131a,b
accessories I–212a
makers I–211a
Naval Observatory V–12b–13a
radar I–212b
radio I–212b
refracting I–211a
Schmidt I–212a
Teletype I–396a; II–153b; VII–264b
TELEVISION VII–21a; II–425b; III–409b; IV–271b; VI–16a,b; VII–19a
baseball I–271a,b
political campaigns I–430b
censorship I–480b–81a
communications satellites II–426a–b
Federal Communications Commission I–13a; III–1a,b
Federal Trade Commission I–480b
folklore III–49a
football III–57b
glass industry III–186a
imports VII–90a
libel IV–139b
licensing V–346b
McCarthy–Army hearings IV–210a–b
microwave transmission IV–333a
moon landing IV–406b,

407a
motion picture competition IV–418a,b
news services VII–152b
New York Times properties V–76b
New York World's Fair V–89a
political campaigns I–415b, 416b
presidential messages V–398b
public utilities V–456b
regulation IV–272a
rural service I–39b; VI–175b
sales II–332b
semiconductors VI–259b
slang VI–300a
soap advertising VI–323b
telephone VII–20b
tennis VII–30b
towboating VII–78a
trial proceedings III–105b
U.S. Information Agency II–499a
vacuum tube VII–164a
versus magazines IV–222b
weapon guidance IV–363b
See also Advertising
Television cathode–ray tube II–155b
Television Code I–20a, 480b–81a
Telfair, Edward (pol.) I–417a
Teller, Edward (phys.) III–324a; V–295b–96a, 300b, 302b, 303a
Teller, Henry M. (pol.) IV–154b; VII–22a
TELLER AMENDMENT (1898) **VII–22a**; II–268b–69a
Tellico (Tenn.) II–480a
Tellico, Treaty of (1798) III–383a
Tellico Treaty (1805) VI–357b–58a
Tell Me How Long the Train's Been Gone IV–167a
Telluride (Colo.) II–415a; VI–213b
Telluride (min.) III–191b
Telpherage systems II–414b
Telstar (satellite) VII–20b
Telstar (satellite) II–143a
Temin, Howard M. (biochem.) IV–391a
Temperance, American Society for the Promotion of VII–22b
Temperance Almanac I–91a
Temperance League. *See* National Temperance League
Temperance League of America I–134b
TEMPERANCE MOVEMENT VII–22a; IV–159a; VII–289b
Anti–Saloon League I–134a
Bible I–293b
Equal Rights party II–457b
high license III–276a
Kansas IV–26b
liquor laws IV–158a
Maine IV–226b
mechanics' institutes IV–281b
moral societies IV–409a
Nation, Carrie III–261b
Naval Home V–11b
New York State V–87a
phrenologists V–294a
physiology V–306a
Prohibition V–429b
Prohibition party V–430b
Quakers V–470b
secret societies VI–253a
Woman's Christian Temperance Union VII–312a
woman's rights movement VII–313b
Temperance Society, Washington VII–23a
Temperance Union, American VII–22b–23a
Temple (Salt Lake City) IV–117a; VI–203b
Temple, Henry John. *See* Palmerston, 3rd Viscount, Henry John Temple
Temple, Richard V–66a
Temple, Shirley (act.) I–488a; III–308b
Temple, Thomas (col. gov.) I–361a
Temple mounds IV–327a
Temple Street Parking Garage (New Haven, Conn.) I–166a
Temporary National Economic Committee III–434a; V–226b
Tenafly (N.J.) I–435a
Tenancy IV–102b, 104a
ground–rent leases IV–104b
land I–3b–4a
Tenant farmer I–40b–41a; IV–103–04a
blacks I–26a
manors IV–241b
New Deal I–30a
North Carolina V–116a
Oklahoma V–149a
poor whites V–359a
See also Sharecropper
Ten Cate and Vollenhoven (banking house) III–291a
Tender Land (opera) IV–439a
Tenedos (frigate) V–394a
Tenement House Act (1901) VII–24b
Tenement House Commission VII–24a,b
Tenement House Law (1867) VII–24a
TENEMENTS VII–23b; I–143a; VI–313b, 314b
clothing industry II–82a
public health VII–158a,b
TEN-FORTIES VII–24b
Ten–hour–day movement IV–61b, 62a, 173b
Tenino (Indians) III–363a
Ten lost tribes of Israel I–128a
Tenmarq wheat VII–286b
Ten Mile (Mont.) III–270a
Tennent, Gilbert (cler.) II–466a; III–214a; V–391b
Tennent, William (cler.) IV–179b; V–33a, 391b; VI–76b
TENNESSEE VII–24b; V–115b; VI–395 (table)
apportionment I–244b
Archaic culture II–385b
archives I–168b
backwoodsmen I–240a
Black Patch War I–316a
black suffrage VI–431b, 433b
campaign of 1836 I–419b
Carter's Valley settlement I–461b–62a
cattle drives I–473a
Cherokee II–15a, 51b; III–395a; IV–330a
Cherokee Wars IV–186a–b
Chickasaw II–22a–b
circuit riders II–39b
Civil War I–118b, 433a, 502a–b; II–21b, 62b, 163a, 271b, 272b, 295a–b, 295b, 363a; III–98a–b, 292a, 298a–b, 478b; IV–42a, 54a, 136b, 187a, 253b, 364b, 374b, 410a–b, 434b–35a, 453a; V–142a,b, 248a, 313b; VI–249b, 278a, 377a; VII–26b–27a, 127b, 128b–29a, 261b
Civil War neutrality IV–43a
coal mines II–85a, 86a
colleges and universities II–114b, 395b
constitution VI–391b
Constitutional Union party II–191b
cotton II–237b
Creek War II–256b; VII–239a
Cumberland Gap II–272a; V–224b
Cumberland Presbyterian Church II–272b
dams III–322a,b, 323b
desegregation I–31a
Dominicans II–362b
Ducktown mines II–163a
Emancipation Proclamation II–434b
exploration II–184a, 336b; IV–201a
fertilizer III–16b
feuds III–18a
folklore III–48b
Fort Loudoun IV–192a
Franklin (state) II–381a; III–87a
geological survey III–165a
Great Smoky Mountains III–222a
Great Smoky Mountains National Park V–218 (table)
Great Trading and War Path III–223a
Great Warrior Path III–387b
Henderson Land Company III–271b
Hermitage III–273b
Heroes of America VII–149a
historical society III–278b
Holston Treaty III–292a, 383a
horse racing III–304b
hydroelectric power II–423a
Indiana settlers III–369b–70a
Indian land titles IV–92b
Indian language II–282b
integration II–402a
iron mines II–163a
Jim Crow laws III–502b
King, Martin Luther, assassination I–31b
Knoxville Gazette V–70b
land speculation III–98b
land surveys V–452a
literature IV–163a
livestock industry I–37b
lyceum movement IV–207a
lynching legislation IV–208b
Manumission Society II–436a
martial law IV–259a
Melungeons IV–301a
Memphis IV–301b
military tract IV–344b
minimum–wage law IV–353b
Mississippi Territory IV–368a
Missouri settlers IV–377a
Muscle Shoals speculation IV–435a
Nashoba IV–452b
Nashville IV–452b
Natchez Trace IV–456a
Needham–Arthur expedition V–32a
"New West" V–81b
Night Riders V–96a
Nineteenth Amendment V–97a
Old Southwest VI–356a
Powell's Valley V–384b
race riots I–31b
railroads IV–453b; VI–25a, 33a, 35a
Reconstruction III–295a; VI–57a, 58b, 59a
Regulators I–74a
Republican party VI–337b
revolutionary war IV–48a; VI–124a
riflemen VI–269b
saltpeter II–5b; V–98a
Scioto Trail VI–239b
Scopes trial VI–239b
Scotch–Irish VI–240b
secession II–61b, 160b; VI–251b
settlement II–273a; IV–376a; VI–149b; VII–283a,b
Shawnee VI–270b
S. H. Kress and Company III–32b–33a
silver mining VI–292a
slavery VI–309a
Southwest Point VI–357b

TENNESSEE (cont.)
Southwest Territory VI–358a
statehood I–78b; VI–400a
stay and valuation acts VI–406a
suffrage III–91a
Tennessee River VII–27b
tobacco VII–66b, 67b
Tombigbee Valley VII–70b
tornadoes II–351a,b; VII–75b
train robberies VII–97b
Trans-Appalachia VII–97b
Transylvania Company VII–103a,b
trapping VII–104b
Treaty of Hopewell III–383a
Treaty of Old Town III–383b
Treaty of Tellico III–383a
Twelfth Amendment VII–132a
ungranted land V–443b
Union sentiment VI–354a; VII–148b
Washington District VII–250a
Watauga settlement II–477a; VII–253a
western lands VII–273b
western separatism VII–276a
westward movement V–179a; VII–284a
Wilderness Road I–89a; VII–296a
zinc VII–369a
TENNESSEE (ironclad) **VII–26a**; IV–383a
TENNESSEE, ARMY OF (Confederate) **VII–26b**; IV–365a; VI–26b; VII–127b, 150a
Battle of Ringgold Gap VI–141b
Knoxville IV–54a
TENNESSEE, ARMY OF THE (Union) **VII–26b**; I–184b; IV–370a
Shiloh VI–278b
Tennessee, University of VII–156a
TENNESSEE BOND CASES (1885) **VII–27a**
TENNESSEE CENTENNIAL EXPOSITION (1897) **VII–27a**
Tennessee Coal, Iron and Railroad Company V–208b
Tennessee Coal and Iron Company V–428a
Tennessee Cumberland Road II–273b
Tennessee Eastman Company V–328b
TENNESSEE RIVER VII–27a; II–247b; VI–149b
Acadians I–6a
Allegheny Mountains I–88b
Arthur expedition V–32a
Black Belt I–308b
cattle drives I–473a
Cherokee Wars II–15a
Chickasaw cession II–22a
Civil War II–253a; III–272b, 298a,b; IV–187a, 375a; VI–150b, 278a
dams III–321a, 322b, 323a,b; VII–26a
Fort Deposit II–333a
fur trade III–143b
Gaines' Trace III–146b
Holston exploration III–292b
hydroelectric power III–321b
Illinois Country III–330b
Iroquis cession VI–385b
Kentucky Dam IV–41b
Muscle Shoals II–423a; IV–435a; V–98a–b; VI–146b
railroads VI–37b
settlement II–274a
Southwest Point VI–357b
steamboating VI–406b, 407a
store boats VI–415b
Tennessee Valley Authority VII–28a–b
Treaty of Fort Stanwix III–382b
Treaty of Old Town III–383b
westward movement VI–148a
Tennessee Valley III–318b; VII–27b
Civil War VI–38a
Tennessee Valley Act (1933) V–44b
TENNESSEE VALLEY AUTHORITY VII–27b; I–216a, 391a; II–188a, 416b, 417a, 423a, 472b, 501a; III–201b, 203a, 321a,b, 459a; V–44b–45a, 455b; VII–26a, 124b, 260b–61a, 323a
civil service II–60a
dams III–322a,b, 323a,b
executive removal power VI–85a
fertilizer industry III–16b
forestry III–74a
mapmaking I–463b–64a
municipal power supply IV–428a
Muscle Shoals Dam V–98a,b
Nashville IV–453a
Tennessee Waltz (song) VI–395 (table)
TENNIS VII–28b; IV–220b; VII–323b
"TENNIS CABINET" VII–31a
Tennis Educational Foundation VII–30b
Tennyson, Alfred, Lord (poet) IV–223a
TENOR, OLD AND NEW VII–31a
"Ten percent plan" (Reconstruction) VI–55b, 58b; VII–39b
Ten Proprietors VII–219b
Tensaw, Lake Fort Mims IV–347b
Tenskwatawa (Indian). *See* Shawnee Prophet
Ten Sleep (Wyo.) III–181b
Tent III–381a
Tenth Airborne Division. *See* entries under Army, United States
Tenth Amendment I–299a; III–157a, 417b; V–352b; VI–97b, 404a
education II–395b
enumerated powers II–453b
implied powers III–349a
reserved powers III–9a; VI–98a
state police power V–339a
treatymaking power IV–381a
Tenth Army, U.S. V–147b
Tenth Cavalry IV–340a; VI–301a
Tenth Fleet V–24b
Tenth Infantry Division IV–411a
Tenth Mountain Division VI–298a
Tenth Muse Lately Sprung Up in America IV–160b
Tenure
civil service II–59b
federal judges IV–17a
state judges IV–18a
teachers I–5a; II–115b
Tenure, land. *See* Land Tenure
TENURE OF OFFICE ACT (1867) **VII–31b**; III–345b; VI–57a, 84b
Ten Years' War (Cuba, 1868–78) II–268a
Teotihuacán (Mex.) IV–327b
Tepee. *See* Tipi
Teran, Don Domingo de (col. gov.) VI–64b
Terborch, Gerard (art.) II–101b
Terman, F. E. (elec. eng.) VI–10b
Terman, Lewis M. (psych.) III–440a–b
Terminal Island Navy Yard V–29b
Terminal Railroad Association case (1912) VII–122b
Termination of reservation system. *See* Reservation System, Termination of
Ternay, Chevalier de, Charles Louis d'Arsac (off.) V–65b
Terny (Fr.) V–147a
Terracing (agric.) VI–334a, 335b
Terre aux Boeufs (La.) III–479a
Terrebonne Parish (La.) VII–57b
Terre Haute (Ind.) III–257b; VI–153b; VII–63a, 212a
Terre Haute (Ind.) *Express* (news.) III–206b
Terrier (missile) IV–363b
TERRITORIAL GOVERNMENTS VII–31b; V–162b–63a; VI–400b–01a; VII–33b–34a
Articles of Confederation II–166a–b
Canal Zone V–202a
Minnesota VI–413a
Northwest Territory V–122b
Oregon V–165b
organic law V–170a
Orleans Territory V–173a–b
Philippines V–283a,b
popular sovereignty V–360a
Southwest Territory VI–358a
Territorial governor VII–31b–32a
Territorial Sea and the Contiguous Zone, UN Convention on (1958) VII–33a
TERRITORIAL WATERS VII–32b; III–106b–07a
Declaration of Panama V–200a
Ecuador III–146b
prizes V–421b
Pueblo incident V–460a
rumrunners VI–170a
tidelands VII–57a
Territories
claim associations II–70a
Dakota II–284b
Emancipation Proclamation II–435a
enabling acts II–443b
federal revenue distribution IV–91b
fugitive slaves III–130a
slavery I–10b–11a, 138b, 139a; II–139a–b, 149b, 150a–b, 184b, 265a, 370a, 377b; III–109b, 111b
Utah II–334a
Territories, Office of VII–32b
Territories and Island Possessions, Division of VII–32b
TERRITORIES OF THE UNITED STATES VII–33b; II–474b–75b
Canal Zone V–201b–03a
congressional powers II–202b, 453b
courts IV–16b
government VII–32a–b
Guam III–230b
Insular Cases III–424b
insular possessions III–425a
Pacific Trust Territory VII–124b
Philippines V–282b–83b
Puerto Rico V–461a
Right of Way Law VI–140b
Samoa VI–205a
taxation VII–13b–14a
Virgin Islands VII–203b
See also Philippine Islands
Territory, annexation of. *See* Annexation of Territory
Territory Northwest of the River Ohio. *See* Northwest Territory

Territory South of the River
Ohio VII–25b
Terrorism III–231a
aerial hijacking
III–277b–78a
Terry, Alfred H. (off.)
II–496a; IV–168a; VI–46b
Terry, B. F. (off.) VII–34a–b
Terry, David S. (off., jur.)
I–203a; II–377a; V–30a
Terry, Eli (clockmaker)
II–78a, 79a–b; III–442b
TERRY'S TEXAS RANGERS VII–34a; VI–46b; VII–39b
Terry v. *Adams* (1953)
III–93a
Tertium Quids. *See* Quids
Tesla, Nikola (inv.) II–415a, 420a; III–409a
Tesson, Louis H. III–467b
Test ban. *See* Nuclear Test Ban Treaty
Testimony
congressional investigations
III–465a
Fifth Amendment I–299a
Testing Materials, American Society for III–408b
TEST LAWS VII–34b
ironclad oaths III–474a
Kansas oath IV–27a
Penn's Holy Experiment
III–293a
See also Loyalty Oaths
Test pilots IV–106a
Tesuque (N.Mex.) III–367b; V–459b
Tetanus IV–299a
Teterboro Airport V–368b
Tetley, Glen (chor.) II–289b
Tet offensive (1968) I–63a; II–316b; III–70b; VII–184a, 186a
Teton (Indians) II–283a; III–365a, 385a
Teton Range III–291a, 486a; V–310b
Teton Sioux (Indians)
II–380a; V–139a; VI–297a
Tetrahedral kite I–233a
Tetranucleotide II–357b
Teutonia (Pa.) II–147a
Tevis, Lloyd (capitalist)
I–116a
Tewa (lang.) III–301b, 367b; V–4a, 459b–60a
Tewksbury–Graham feud. *See* Graham–Tewksbury feud
Texaco II–156b; VII–40b
Texaco Oklahoma (tanker)
II–350a
TEXAN EMIGRATION AND LAND COMPANY VII–35b; VII–39a
TEXAN–SANTA FE EXPEDITIONS VII–36a; VII–38b
Texarkana (Tex.)
railroad VI–37a
TEXAS VII–36a; IV–115b, 200a; V–443b; VI–355a,b, 395 (table); VII–268a
Ab–Initio movement I–2a
acreage annexed V–445 (table)
Afro–American suffrage
III–93a
Alamo I–74a–b; VI–84a
annexation I–121b, 126a,b, 137b, 138b; II–313b, 475a; III–221a; IV–323a; VI–42b, 250b, 254a, 400a, 400b; VII–111b, 288b
Apache I–141b
architecture I–159b
Archive War I–169b
army posts IV–339b
Austin colony I–224a
Balcones Escarpment
I–246b
banking I–129b
Battle of Concepción
II–157a
bayous I–279a
Beale's colony
VI–143b–44a
birth and death registration
IV–149a
Black Cavalry I–309b
Black Infantry I–313b
blizzards I–320a–b
boll weevil II–238a
boundary VII–155a
boundary disputes
I–351a,b; II–139a, 150a–b
camels I–412b, 413a
campaign of 1844 I–420a
cattle I–1b, 38b, 472b–73b; II–31b–32a, 248b, 248b–49a, 251a,b; III–221b; IV–30b, 184a; V–139a, 148b; VI–364b; VII–294a
cattle fever I–1b; II–249a
cattle rustling I–473b
cattle trails I–2a, 358a
centennial III–81a
Champ d'Asile I–492a
chaparral I–494a
Chisholm Trail II–477b
Chrisholm Trail II–31b
citizenship V–6a
Civil War III–148b; IV–257a, 374b; V–198b; VI–63a, 144a, 150b
coal mines II–85a
coast survey II–88a
Colorado boundary
II–128a
Comanche II–133a–b
Compromise of 1850
II–150a–b
Confederate deserters
II–335b
cotton I–309a; II–237b, 238b; IV–104a
Delaware Indians II–321a
Democratic party
VII–210a
Denison Dam III–322b
Desert culture II–334b
Dodge City Trail II–358b
Dust Bowl II–382a
East Texas missions
II–389a
exploration I–269a; II–184b, 336b; III–108a, 119a, 220b
fair–trade laws II–482b
farmers' alliances
II–493b; V–365a
Fence War III–10a
Ferguson impeachment
III–11a
flour milling I–488a
Fort Belknap I–286a
Fort Brown I–371a
Fort Griffin III–228a
Fort Mason IV–263a
Fort Saint Louis VI–195a
Fort Sam Houston
VI–204b
Fort Worth III–80b
forty–niners III–82a
Franciscans III–94a
Fredonian Revolt
III–101a
French claims I–48b
French refugees III–121b
fruit growing II–43b; III–128b
Germaine girl captives
III–172a
Grand Prairie III–209a
Grange stores II–220b
Greer County dispute
III–200a, 228a; V–150a
Gulf of Mexico IV–326a
Gutiérrez–Magee expedition
III–236a
headright III–267a
horse III–302b
Horsehead Crossing
III–304a
horse racing III–304b
horse stealing III–306a
Hungarian settlement
V–42a
hurricanes II–351a,b; III–319b
impeachment III–344b
independence I–74b; IV–410a
Indian Country
III–379a,b
Indian culture III–367a
Indian land cession
IV–299b
Indian missions III–385b; IV–367b
Indian raids VII–252b
Indian reservations
II–133b
Indian Territory III–399b
Indian wars VII–239a, 239b
irrigation III–478b
joint–stock land banks
IV–6b
junior colleges II–400b
Kennedy assassination
IV–37b
Kiowa raids IV–50b
Ku Klux Klan IV–58b
La Salle's exploration
IV–110a, 372a
legislative resolution
VI–100a
livestock industry I–37b
Long expedition IV–184a
longhorns I–471b, 473a,b, 474a; IV–184b
Louisiana boundary
IV–192b, 197b
Louisiana boundry
IV–189a
Louisiana Purchase
VI–359a–b
lynching legislation
IV–208b
"manifest destiny"
IV IV–239a
maverick cattle IV–277b
Mexican border
IV–320b–21a,b
Mexican immigration
IV–322a
Mexican rule
IV–328a
Mexican War IV–324b; VI–60b
midcontinent oil region
IV–333b
Mier expedition
IV–337b
mineral patent law
IV–349b
minimum–wage law
IV–352b, 353b
missions I–48b, 159b; IV–302b; VI–207b
Mississippi emigration
IV–368b
mustangs IV–444b
Nacogdoches IV–448b
Narváez expedition
IV–452a
Natchitoches IV–456b, 457a
national parks and monuments V–217b, 219 (table)
naturalization of citizens
II–42b
Nolan expeditions V–101a
Nueces River V–125a
Okies V–149a
Oklahoma panhandle
V–205b
onions V–156a
open–range grazing
V–159b
Parker's Fort V–216b
petroleum I–336b; II–389a–b; V–270a, 271b; VI–356b, 357a; VII–336b
peyote V–272b
plantations VI–341b
popular sovereignty
V–155a
prairie V–387a
prairie dogs V–387b
presidios V–399b; VI–364a
privateering V–419b
railroads VI–26a–b, 32b, 33b, 35a, 36a,b, 37a
ranching I–472b; VI–44b–45a
Reconstruction I–2a; III–295a; VI–57b
Red River Indian War
VI–64a
Red River post VI–64b
referendum VI–66b
Reunion VI–105a
revolution I–116b, 116b; II–339b; III–22b, 198b, 304a; IV–274a, 457a; VI–209a, 213a–b; VII–37b–38a, 41a
rice I–486b; VI–136a
Rio Grande VI–143a, 150b
roundups VI–161a
sabbath–day houses
VI–182a
Saint–Denis' expedition
VI–189b
Salt War VI–204a
San Antonio VI–207a
San Francisco de los Tejas
VI–210a

TEXAS (cont.)
sanitariums VI–101a
Santa Fe trade VII–36a
secession II–61a; VI–251a
segregation VI–420b
settlement II–339b, 442b–43a; VII–35b–36b
Shawnee II–321a
sheep VII–321a
sheep wars VI–273a,b
Shreveport Rate Case VI–283b
silver mining VI–292a
single-tax plan VI–293b
slavery VI–307b, 309a
sorghum I–486b
Spanish posts IV–456b; VI–168b
Spanish settlements I–472b–73a
stagelines VI–379a
Staked Plain VI–380b
state fair VI–392b
state flag III–35a
suffrage III–92a
sugarcane VI–436a,b
survey system V–452a
Texians VII–42b
tidelands VII–57b–58a
tornadoes VII–76a
trading posts VII–77a, 96a, 238b
train robberies VII–97b
transcontinental railroad IV–28b
Treat Mission VII–108b
ungranted land V–443b
Van Zandt VII–167a
veterinary medicine VII–176b
vigilantes VII 187a,b
wagon trains VII–217b
westward movement VII–284a
wheat III–44a
white primary V–407b
windmills VII–304b
wire-cutting "wars" I–267a
World War I VII–325a
Zimmerman telegram VII–368b
See also El Paso
Texas (battleship) VI–216b
Texas (locomotive) I–118b
Texas, Our Texas (song) VI–395 (table)
Texas, University of II–109b; III–11a, 158a; IV–461a; VII–40b
Texas A&M University V–135a; VII–40b
Texas and New Orleans Railroad VI–37a
Texas and Pacific Railroad III–80b; IV–64b; VI–27a, 37a, 38b; VII–40a
Texas cattle fever. *See* Cattle Tick fever
TEXAS CENTENNIAL CENTRAL EXPOSITION (1936–37) **VII–41a**
Texas Company. *See* Texaco
TEXAS NAVY VII–41a; VII–38a
Texas Observer (news.) V–79a
Texas Panhandle I–15a
TEXAS PUBLIC LANDS VII–41b; VII–36a
Texas Public School Book Depository IV–37b
Texas Railroad Commission II–389b; VI–283b
TEXAS RANGERS VI–42a; I–355a; III–304a; V–339a; VII–39a
Colt six-shooter II–130b
Comanche II–133a
Fence War III–10a
Mexican War VI–60b
Salt War VI–204a
See also Terry's Texas Rangers
Texas Towers (radar platforms) I–58a–b
TEXAS* v. *WHITE (1869) **VII–42a**; VII–35b, 40a
Texcoco, Lake II–214b
TEXIAN VII–42b
Textbook of Physiology V–307a
Textbooks II–397a, 399b, 400a; IV–283b; VI–227b
TEXTILES VII–42b; V–212a; VII–83a, 83a
Augusta (Ga.) I–223a
chemical industry II–5a, 6a, 8b
child labor II–24b
city planning II–45b
Civil War II–163b
clothing industry II–81a
colonial industry III–413b
contract work V–309b
cotton II–237b
cotton gin I–34a
cotton manufacturing II–239a–b
Crompton loom II–266a
detergents VI–324a
Du Pont family III–80a
foreign trade VII–87a, 89b, 90a
French Canadian immigrants III–338b
Georgia III–169a
government regulation V–467b
health hazards IV–294b
hemp III–271a
household manufacture IV–246a
imports VII–84b
Industrial Revolution III–411a,b
Kentucky IV–41b
labor force IV–61a
Lawrence strike IV–120a
linen IV–157b
linsey-woolsey IV–158a
loom IV–187b
machinery II–415b; III–63a; IV–243b
machine tools IV–216a
Maine IV–226b–27a
Massachusetts IV–266b, 267b
mill air conditioning III–269b
Mound Builders IV–421b
New England II–255a
New Hampshire V–54b
New Jersey V–57b
New South V–67a
North Carolina II–163b; V–116b
nylon III–409b
panic of 1873 V–207b
Pawtucket V–230b–31a
Philadelphia V–247a, 277b, 278a
plant integration IV–272b
potash bleaching V–375b
Prairie du Chien V–388a
prices V–405a
Pueblo Indians III–367b
research III–408b
Rhode Island VI–133a,b
Salem VI–199b
Salt Lake City VI–203b
silk VI–286b
soap VI–323a,b
Society for Establishing Useful Manufactures VII–161a
South Carolina VI–348a
steam power VI–409b
synthetic fibers IV–245a
tariff VI–463a, 465b, 470b, 471a,b
Tennessee VII–26a
trade association VII–92a
unionization III–154a; IV–63b, 72b
Vermont VII–172b
Virginia VII–196a
wages IV–69b; VII–214b, 215a
Waltham (Mass.) I–345b
women workers VII–313a, 316b
wool VII–320b–21b
Textile workers
unionization IV–67b
Textile Workers Organizing Committee IV–73a
Textron II–169a
TF 58. *See* Task Force 58
Thacher, James (hist.) V–334a
Thacher, Thomas (physic.) VI–315a
Thackrah, C. Turner IV–293b
Thailand II–342b
aid II–315b; VII–229a
Korean War IV–55b, 56b
Southeast Asia Treaty Organization VI–350b
Vietnam War VII–182b
World War II III–46b
Thailand, Gulf of V–22a
Thala (Tun.) IV–32b
"Thaler" (dollar) II–94b
Thalidomide V–468a
Thalweg I–351b
THAMES, BATTLE OF THE (1813) **VII–45b**; I–436b; II–458b; V–141a; VII–18a, 234b
Thames Measurement (yachting) VII–349b
Thames River (Can.) II–338a
Thames River (Conn.) II–180a; VII–45b
Thames Valley (Conn.) IV–387a
Thamesville (Can.) VII–45b
"Thanatopsis" (poem) IV–161b
THANKSGIVING DAY VI–46a; II–496a–97a; IV–264b; V–68b, 425b
Tharp, Twyla (chor.) II–289b, 290a
Thatched House Society II–299a
Thatcher, Harvey D. (inv.) II–280a
Thatcher, Thomas (cler.) III–324b
Thatcher wheat VII–286b
Thaw, Harry K. IV–220b; VII–118a
Thayer, Charles VII–64a
Thayer, Eli (educ., pol.) II–439a; V–51a–b
Thayer, Sylvanus (off., educ.) I–184a; II–293a, 447a, 449b; IV–340b–41a
Thayer, Webster (jur.) VI–182b
Thayer School of Engineering II–293a
THEATER VII–46b
barnstorming I–268a
Boston Museum IV–436b
Federal Theatre Project V–46a; VII–323a
Madison Square Garden IV–220b
Manhattan IV–237b
minstrel shows IV–359b
moral codes IV–408a
New York City I–368b
playwrights IV–165b
Provincetown Players V–439b
showboats VI–283a
taxation VII–8b
vaudeville VII–167b
Theaters
discrimination II–457b
fires II–348a
New York City V–83b
Niblo's Garden V–93b
segregation III–502b; VI–256a
Theatorium (showboat) VI–283a
Theatre 47 (Dallas) VII–50b
Theatre Genesis (N.Y.C.) VII–51a
Theatre Guild VII–49b
Theatre Union VII–50a
"Theatrical Syndicate" VII–48b
Theistical Society of New York III–332a
Thélepte (Tun.) IV–32b
Theocracy I–307b
THEOCRACY IN NEW ENGLAND VII–51a; V–49b; VI–121a
freedom of the press III–104b
Massachusetts I–499b; IV–265a,b, 269a, 269b
New England Way V–51b
Plymouth colony IV–279a
Puritan II–35b
Theology
Arminianism I–176a
Calvinism I–176a
See also Religion; Religious Thought and Writings

Theology for the Social Gospel VI–78b, 82b
Theorem paintings III–47a,b
Theosophical Society V–172a; VII–52a
THEOSOPHY VII–51b; V–172a
"There'll Be a Hot Time in the Old Town Tonight" (song) VI–313a
Theresa of Avila, Saint I–455b
Thermodynamics II–11b
Thermonuclear warheads I–216a; IV–363a,b
Thetis (whaler) III–224a
Theüs, Jeremiah (paint.) V–186b
Thiamine III–44b
Thieu, Nguyen Van VII–185a
Thieves II–260a
Think tanks III–424b
Third Amendment I–297a
Third Army, French IV–404a
Third Army, U.S. *See* entries under Army, United States
Third Chickasaw Bluffs. *See* Prudhomme Bluffs
Third Communist International (1919) VI–327a
Third (III) Corps. *See* entries under Army, United States
Third Fleet IV–138a; V–24b; VII–1a,b, 337a, 343b
Third Infantry Division. *See* entries under Army, United States
Third Marine Amphibious Force IV–253b; VII–186a,b
Third Marine Division VII–186a,b
Third Marine Expeditionary Brigade VII–186a
THIRD PARTIES VII–52a
 American Labor Party I–107a
 Anti-Masonic Party I–132b
 Bull Moose party V–427a–29a
 campaign of 1924 IV–70a
 Citizens' Alliance II–42a
 Farmer-Labor party II–490b, 492b
 Farmers' Alliance II–493b
 Greenback party III–224b–25a
 labor parties IV–81a
 La Follette Progressive IV–84b
 Minnesota IV–357b
 Populists I–33a
 pressure groups V–400b
 Progressive party V–429a
 Prohibition party V–430b
 Quids VI–3a
 share-the-wealth movements VI–269b
 Union Labor party VII–146b
 Union party V–47b; VII–146a, 148a
 Union Rights party VII–148a
Third Plenary Council of Baltimore (1884) I–468b
Third Republic (Fr.) III–97a
Third Symphony (comp.) IV–439a
THIRD-TERM DOCTRINE VII–53a
 campaign of 1940 I–429a
 Twenty-second Amendment VII–132b
 Washington's Farewell Address VII–251b
Third World
 civil rights movement II–59a
 neutrality V–36a
 nonintervention III–463b
 Pan-Africanism V–199b–200a
 Students for a Democratic Society VI–421b
 U.S. foreign policy III–69a
 woman's rights VII–314b
Thirteenth Airborne Division V–213b
THIRTEENTH AMENDMENT VII–54a; I–28b, 94b, 134b, 139a; II–53b, 205a, 435a,b; III–86a, 437b; V–352b; VI–308b; VII–226b
 Black Codes I–310a
 black suffrage VI–431b
 Dred Scott Case II–370b
 Indian slaveholding III–401a
 judicial review IV–14a
 Misssissippi IV–369a
 Nevada V–39b
 peonage V–260b
 Radical Republicans VI–11a
 slave trade I–221b, 342a; VI–322a
 South Carolina VI–348a
 southern ratification VI–56b
 United States v. *Harris* VII–154b
Thirteenth (XIII) Corps IV–370a
Thirtieth Infantry Division VII–327a, 366b
Thirty-eighth parallel IV–55a
Thirty-second Infantry Division V–147a; VII–327a
Thirty-seventh Infantry Division VII–366b
Thirty Years War (1618–48) III–335a; VII–225a
Tho, Le Duc (dipl.) V–216a; VII–184b
Thom, Charles (bact.) I–241b
Thomas, Augustus (playwright) VII–49a
Thomas, Charles M. (nav. off.) I–276b
Thomas, Elmer (pol.) V–44a
Thomas, Fort (Ky.) V–66a
 See also Newport Barracks
Thomas, George H. (off.) I–502b; III–298a; IV–347a, 434b; V–142b, 377b
 Army of the Cumberland II–271b
 Battle of Missionary Ridge IV–365a
 Battle of Nashville IV–453a
 Tennessee campaign II–21b, 62b
Thomas, Isaiah (print.) II–108a; III–280b; V–69b
 Bible I–294b
 chapbooks I–494a
 children's books I–335a
Thomas, J. B. (pol.) IV–379a
Thomas, J. Parnell (pol.) III–308b
Thomas, Moses (auctioneer) I–332b
Thomas, Norman (Socialist, pol.) VI–321a, 326a
 V–47b
Thomas, Robert Bailey (pub.) I–91a; II–494a
Thomas, Seth (clockmaker) II–78a, 79a
Thomas, William (mfr.) VI–265a
Thomas, William H. (trader) III–395a
THOMAS AMENDMENT (1933) **VII–54b**; I–302a; III–194a; IV–395b; V–44a, 45a
Thomas Amendment of 1820. *See* Missouri Compromise
Thomas-Houston Company IV–153b
Thomas Jefferson Memorial Foundation IV–405a–b
Thomas-Morse Aircraft I–53a
Thomaston (Maine). *See* Saint Georges
Thomas Viaduct. *See* Latrobe's Folly
Thomas W. Lawson (schooner) VI–229b
Thomism V–288b
Thomist, The (period.) II–362b
Thompson, Benjamin, Count Rumford (phys.) I–97b; III–268b
Thompson, David (expl.) II–131b; VII–247b, 276a
Thompson, Dorothy (jour.) V–75a; VII–317b
Thompson, George (ref.) III–153a
Thompson, Jacob (pol.) I–435a; V–121b, 234b
Thompson, Jeremiah (mer.) I–308b
Thompson, John ("Snowshoe") (skier) VI–297b–98a
Thompson, John G. (offi.) IV–45b
Thompson, John Reuben (jour., poet) VI–353a
Thompson, Lewis Ryers (physic.) IV–287b
Thompson, Mary VI–205b
Thompson, M. Jeff (off.) III–101a
Thompson, Samuel (surv.) I–442a
Thompson, Smith (jur.) VI–445a
Thompson, Wiley (Indian agent) VI–260b
Thompson, William (off.) VII–55a
Thompson, William Hale ("Big Bill") (pol.) IV–214a
Thompson Act (1950) V–201b
Thomsen, Hans (dipl.) VII–333a–b
Thomson, Charles (pol.) II–305b, 384b; IV–8b; VI–246b
Thomson, David (col.) IV–396a; V–53b; VI–417b
Thomson, Elihu (elec. eng.) II–413b
Thomson, G. P. (phys.) I–287b
Thomson, James (math.) II–153a
Thomson, J. J. (phys.) I–218b; II–423b; V–297b, 299b; VII–21a
Thomson, John (rel. leader) V–391b
Thomson, Samuel (physic.) IV–288a
Thomson, Virgil (comp.) IV–439a
Thomson, William (Lord Kelvin) (math., phys.) III–166b
Thomson-Houston Company II–413b, 414a,b, 415a
Thomsonianism IV–284a
Thomson newspaper chain V–76b
Thonet, Michael III–136a
Thor (missile) I–62a; IV–363b
Thoreau, Henry (au.) I–111a, 344a; IV–162a, 267a; VII–361b
 civil disobedience II–50b
 Concord Group II–158a
 conservation II–187a
 Walden II–390b
Thorfinn Karlsefni (expl.) I–95b; VII–189b
Thorn, Jonathan (ship capt.) I–209a
Thornburgh, T. T. (off.) IV–300a
Thorndike, Edward L. (psych.) II–400a; V–442a
Thornhill v. *Alabama* (1940) V–308b
Thornton, Edward (dipl.) V–318a; VII–248b
Thornton, Matthew (physic.) II–305b, 307b
Thornton, William (arch.) I–162b, 451a; III–32b; V–226a
Thoroughfare Gap (Va.) I–382a
Thorp, John (machinist) VII–43a
Thorpe, Jack (music pub.) II–250b
Thorpe, Jim (James Francis) (athlete) I–455a

Thought, freedom of II–325b
Three–cent piece II–95b, 384b
Three–cornered hats II–371a
Three–cornered trade. *See* Triangular Trade
Three–fifths clause II–151b, 183a, 198a
Three–fifths compromise III–5a, 437b
See also Compromises of the U.S. Constitution; Constitution of the United States
308th Infantry Division IV–189b
307th Infantry Division IV–189b
339th Infantry Regiment I–158b–59a
332nd Infantry Regiment *See* entries under Army, United States
Three–mile limit III–106b
THREE NOTCH ROAD VII–54b
"308 Reports" VI–146b–47a
Three Places in New England (comp.) IV–439a
Three Rivers I–436a; II–385a; VI–201a
fur trade III–142a
Nicolet's explorations V–95a
THREE RIVERS, BATTLE OF (1776) **VII–55a**
"Three R's" IV–169a
Three Soldiers IV–164b
Thresher (submarine) II–350a
Thresher class (submarine) VI–423b
THRESHING MACHINE VII–55a; I–34b, 35b; II–133b; III–43a; VII–286b
THRIFT STAMPS VII–55b
Thrips III–421a
Throckmorton family III–18b
Throme, James (abolitionist) I–137a
"Thruway" authorities III–201b
Thucydides (hist.)
sea power VI–247b
"Thud Ridge" (Viet.) VI–302b
Thule air base (Green.) V–338a
Thunderbird (auto) I–232a
Thunderbolt (fighter plane) I–53a, 60a; VI–302a
Thunderchief (fighter plane) I–54a
Thunderjet (fighter plane) I–53b
"Thunder Road" (Viet.) VI–301a
Thunderstreak (fighter plane) I–53b
"Thunder trees" II–433a
Thurman, Allen G. (pol.) I–422b, 424a
Thurman, Wallace (au.) IV–166b
Thurmond, J. Strom (pol.) I–71b, 429b; III–22a; IV–195a
Thurot, François (buccaneer) I–374a
Thurston, Asa (miss.) IV–364b
Thurston, Robert H. (eng.) II–447b–48a
Thurstone, L. L. (statis.) III–440b
"Thus always to tyrants" (motto) VI–395 (table)
Thwaites, R. G. (hist.) III–272a–b, 501a; VII–253b
Thymine II–357b–58a; IV–389a, 390a
Thyrotron tubes II–154b
Tibet I–340a
Ticknor, George (educ.) II–108b, 398a; III–259b; IV–267a
Ticknor and Fields (pub.) I–334a
Ticks I–241b
Ticonderoga (carrier) I–54b; V–22a
Ticonderoga (N.Y.) II–266b; IV–85b
TICONDEROGA, CAPTURE OF (1775) **VII–56a**; I–345a, 435b; III–215b; IV–86b, 86b; VI–125a, 155b; VII–171b
Arnold, Benedict I–194b
Fort Chambly I–491b
Green Mountain Boys III–226b
TICONDEROGA, FORT (N.Y.) **VII–56b**; II–267a; VII–171a,b
French and Indian War III–115b; VI–162b
revolutionary war VII–164b
See also Carillon, Fort
TICONDEROGA, OPERATIONS AT (1758–59) **VII–56b**; I–358b; II–126b; III–116a,b; IV–86a; V–85b; VI–136b
TICONDEROGA, TAKING OF (1777) **VII–57a**; I–385a; III–311b; IV–86b; VI–123b
Tidal observations II–88a; III–454a
Tidal waves II–347b, 351b; III–149a
Tide detergent VI–324a
TIDELANDS VII–57a
TIDE MILLS VII–58a
Tide predictor II–153a
TIDEWATER VII–58a; II–485a; V–310a
agriculture VII–194a
climate observations IV–316b
settlement VI–192b
tobacco VII–66b
westward movement VII–283a
Tidewater Pipeline VI–383a
Tiegan, Henry (pol.) II–491a
Tientsin (China) I–356a; II–25b–26a; VII–334a
Tientsin, Treaties of I–386a; II–488a; VI–66a
See also Reed Treaty
Tierra Amarilla (N.Mex.) VI–7b
Tierra del Guego III–386a
Tiffany, Louis C. (paint.) III–186a
Tiffany and Company III–19a; VI–290a
Tiffin, Edward (pol., jur.) II–25b; V–141a
Tiger Tail (Indian) VI–261a
TIGRE ISLAND VII–58b
Tiguex (pueblo) II–228b
Tilden, Samuel J. (pol.) III–224b; V–87a–b
campaign of 1876 I–442b–23a; II–38b; VI–93a
Nast cartoons IV–454b
New York Public Library IV–145a
Tweed Ring VII–131b
Tilden, William T. II (athlete) VII–30a
Tiles I–377b
Tilghman, Lloyd (off.) III–272b
Till, Emmet I–31a
Tillamook (Indians) III–362a
Tillamook Lighthouse VI–146b
Tillich, Paul (theol.) IV–165a; VI–79b
Tillman, Benjamin R. (pol.) I–116b; VI–348a
See also Tillmanism
TILLMANISM VII–58b; I–319a
Tilsit, Treaty of (1807) II–291a
Timber and Stone Act (1878) IV–100a; V–166a, 444b, 450b
TIMBER CULTURE ACT (1873) **VII–59a**; II–336a; III–73a; IV–100a; V–444b; VI–67a; VII–114a
Timberlake, John B. (seaman) II–389b
TIMBERLANDS VII–59b; III–72b–76b; VI–48b
Forest Reserve Act IV–95a
Forest Service III–75a
government inspection III–422a
government sales III–444a
Great Lakes states IV–96a
Kentucky IV–41a
king's woods IV–49a
land speculation IV–97b, 99b
Louisiana IV–194b
Maine IV–227a
Natchez IV–455a
New South V–66b
Oregon land frauds V–166a
prairie V–387a
public land commission V–450b
public ownership V–445a
reforestation VI–67a
Washington State VII–247b
Weyerhaeuser Company IV–98a
See also Lumber Industry
Timber wolf VII–311b
Timby, Theodore R. (inv.) III–36b
Time (mag.) II–27b; IV–222b; VI–300a; VII–333b
Time–and–a–half pay VII–213b, 214a
Time–and–motion studies I–205b
Time deposits I–252a,b, 257a, 258a, 264a; II–1b–2a
Time locks II–79b
Time–On–Target I–200b
Timepieces, electronic VI–259a
Time signals II–424a
Times–Mirror Company v. *Superior Court* (1941) V–78b
Times Square (N.Y.C.) I–368b–69a
"TIMES THAT TRY MEN'S SOULS" VII–61a; II–264b
Time Table Conventions I–111b
Time Zones I–111b
Timmerman, Karl (off.) VI–84a
Timor (Indon.) IV–228b
Timpanogos Cave National Monument V–217b
Timucua (Indians) III–367a
Tin V–102a; VI–48b, 346a
TIN CAN VII–61b; I–445a; III–55a
"Tin goose" (plane) I–236a
TINIAN VII–62a; III–426a, 490a; IV–253a; V–21a, 285b; VII–139a
Tinicum (Pa.) V–80b
Tinicum Island V–246a
Tinker Air Field (Okla.) V–149a
Tinkham, A. W. (off.) VI–413a
Tinkle, Donald W. (zool.) VI–91b
Tinoco, Federico V–107b
TIN PAN ALLEY VII–62b; II–250a
TINTYPE VII–62b; V–291a
TINWARE PEDDLERS VII–62b; V–241b
Tiny Alice (play) VII–50b
Tioga (N.Dak.) V–117b
Tioga (Pa.) VI–438a
Tioga County (N.Y.) I–347b
Tipi I–166a; III–363b, 381a; VII–106b, 162b, 295a
Apache I–141b
Arapaho I–151b
Assiniboine I–206a
Dakota II–283a
Plains Indians IV–50b
Tipitapa, Peace of (1927) II–343a
TIPPECANOE, BATTLE OF (1811) **VII–63a**; III–369b; V–141a; VII–18a, 234a,

262b
Shawnee VI–270b
Shawnee Prophet V–435a; VI–271b
"TIPPECANOE AND TYLER TOO!" VII–63b; I–420a, 432b; VI–313a
Tippecanoe County (Ind.) V–435a
Tippecanoe Creek VII–63a
Tippecanoe River V–435a
Tippett, L. C. H. (statis.) VI–206b
Tipton, John (pol.) III–98b
Tires I–228b, 230a; IV–419b; VI–168a
Tiros (satellite) VII–264b
Tisne, Claude Charles du (expl.) III–119a, 303a; IV–376b, 380a
Tissot, Simon-André (physic.) III–325a; VI–266a,b
Titan (missile) I–64a; IV–363b, 432a; VI–159b
***TITANIC*, SINKING OF THE** (1912) **VII–64a**; II–424b; V–134b, 135a
Titanium III–15b
TITHES, SOUTHERN AGRICULTURAL VII–64a
TITHINGMEN VII–64b; V–338b
Titian (art.) II–103b
Title, abstract of IV–105b
Titles, foreign II–200b
Titles, land. *See* Land Titles
Titles of nobility. *See* Nobility, Titles of
Tituba (slave) VII–309b
Titus, Fort (Kans.) I–342a
Titusville (Pa.) II–369b, 464b; V–247a; VII–87a
oil exchange V–146b
oil pipeline V–319a
petroleum V–266b, 269a, 271a, 321a
Titusville Board of Trade V–146b
Titusville Pipe Company V–319a
Tiverton (R.I.) VI–438b
Tiwa (lang.) II–228b; III–367b; V–460a
Tizard, Henry (phys.) VI–10a
Tlingit (Indians) I–81a, 441b; III–238a, 361a–b, 362a; IV–59a
art and society IV–228b
scalping VI–224b
Sitka massacre I–75a
standard of living I–79a
TNT (nitrated toluene) II–8a
"To Anacreon in Heaven" (song) VI–387b
Toasters II–417b, 419a, 421b
Tobacco IV–409a
cytogenetics I–350a
fur trade III–140a,b
TOBACCO AND NARCOTICS, AMERICAN INDIAN VII–64b; III–367b, 369a, 381a; V–318a–b, 325b
cultivation I–36a, 47b, 48a
Eskimo trade II–461b
Hopi III–301a
Jimsonweed Cult III–503a
Southeast culture III–366a
TOBACCO AS MONEY VII–65b; II–140b; IV–101b, 392b; V–401b
beaver hats I–282a
Parson's Cause V–221b
taxation VII–3a
Two Penny Act VII–135a
Tobacco chewing I–367b
TOBACCO CONTRACT (1622) **VII–66a**; I–292b
Tobacco cooperatives. *See* Cooperatives, Tobacco
TOBACCO INDUSTRY VII–66b; VI–48a, 386a
Africa trade I–21a
Agricultural Adjustment Administration V–44a
antebellum South VI–341a
Baltimore I–249b, 250a
Black Patch War I–316a; IV–41b
coasting trade II–90b
colonial cultivation III–413a
colonial trade II–118b, 119a–b, 453b; VI–108a; VII–82b
Connecticut II–180b
cooperatives II–221b
Culpeper's Rebellion II–271a
excise taxes VI–105a
exports I–263a, 263a; VII–86a, 87a,b
farm tenancy I–41a
fertilizers II–8a
Florida III–39a
great fortunes III–80a–b
internal improvements III–447b
Jamestown III–489a
Kentucky IV–41b, 41b
log barns IV–179b
marketing associations II–221b
marketing quotas V–359a
Maryland IV–242a, 260b
Missouri IV–377a
monoply I–114a
Natchez IV–455a
Navigation Acts V–16a,b
New South V–67a
Night Riders V–96a
Norfolk V–109b, 110a
North Carolina V–116a–b
plantation system V–324b–25a
price-fixing V–401b
prices V–404a
price-support program II–222a
Puerto Rico V–461b
Richmond VI–136b, 137a
sharecropping VI–174b
Shenandoah Valley VI–275b
slavery IV–79a; VI–304b, 305a, 310a
smuggling VI–320b
soil depletion III–16b
South I–36b–37a, 38a
sweatshop VI–454a
tariff IV–308a; VI–466b, 467a; VII–370a
taxation VII–5a,b, 6a, 7a, 8b, 10b, 11b, 12b, 13a
tidewater II–485a; VII–58a
transport I–39b; VII–168a
triangular trade II–119a; VII–119b
Two Penny Act VII–135a
Virginia VII–192b, 193a, 194a
Wheeling VII–288a
Tobacco mosaic disease IV–389a
Tobacco plant (arch.) I–163a
Tobacco shops VII–319b
Tobacco trust III–443b; V–96a–b
Tobacco virus IV–378b
TOBACCO WAREHOUSES VII–67b; I–85a; VII–66a
Tobago V–214b
Tobasco (Mex.)
prizes V–424a
"To be, rather than to seem" (motto) VI–395 (table)
Tobey, Mark (paint.) II–107a; V–193a
Toboggan III–381a
Tocqueville, Alexis de (writ.) III–122b; V–353b
American West VII–267b
representative government VI–92a
science VI–231b–32a
stare decisis VI–386b
Tod, David (gov.) III–292a; VI–378b
"Today's Army Wants to Join You" (slogan) VI–61a
Today's Education (jour.) IV–463b
Todd, Andrew (bus.) VI–367a
Todd, Eli (physic.) IV–305b
Todd, Isaac (mer.) III–403b
Todd, Mary. *See* Lincoln, Mary Todd
Todd, Thomas (jur.) VI–445a
Todd, W. J. (cattleman) I–326a
TODD'S TAVERN, ACTION AT (1864) **VII–68a**
Todt Organization III–201a
Togau (Ger.) VII–341a
Togo, Heihachiro (nav. off.) V–11a
Togo, Republic of IV–236b
Togoland, British IV–236b
Tohopeka, Battle at. *See* Horseshoe Bend, Battle of
Toilet IV–167b
Tojo, Hideki (states.) V–239b; VI–198b
Tokyo (Jap.)
cherry trees gift III–491b
earthquake V–23a
war crimes trial VII–229b
World War II I–50a, 55b, 59b–60a, 66b; III–485a, 489b, 490a,b; V–21a; VII–341a
Tokyo Bay V–263a; VII–341a
"TOKYO EXPRESS" VII–68a; III–229b
Toledo (Ohio) II–317a, 459a; III–223b, 224b; V–141a,b, 142a; VII–68b
domestic trade VII–83b
Fort Industry III–414a
Hull's Trail III–316a
labor strike (1934) IV–71b
Miami and Erie Canal V–145b
National Greenback Labor party IV–63b
port authority V–368a
public land speculation I–107b
railroads VI–35b
Wabash and Erie Canal VII–212a
War of 1812 VI–42a
Toledo and Ohio Central Railroad VI–35b
Toledo Museum II–105a
Toledo, Peoria and Western Railroad VI–35a
Toledo Strip VII–157a
TOLEDO WAR (1835–36) **VI–68b**; IV–331a; V–141b, 144b
Toleration, religious. *See* Religious Liberty
Toleration Act (1689) V–470a
Toleration Act of 1819 V–54a
TOLERATION ACTS VII–68b
TOLL BRIDGES AND ROADS, PRIVATE VII–69a
Toll Gate Bill (1822) VI–450a
Tolliver, Floyd IV–259b
Tolls III–201b
National Road IV–470b
Panama Canal V–204b
Wilderness Road VII–296b
TOLLS EXEMPTION ACT (1912) **VII–69b**
Tolman, Richard (phys.) V–295a
Toloache. *See* Jimsonweed Cult
Tolowa (Indians) III–363a; VII–367b
Tolstoy, Leo (au.) I–117a
Toltec (Indians) III–356a; IV–327a
Toluene II–8a
TOMAHAWK VII–70a; III–365b
TOMAHAWK CLAIMS VII–70a; I–400a–b
Tomahita (Indians) V–32a
Tomato III–52b, 151a, 381a
cytogenetics I–350a
harvester I–35b
Indian cultivation I–36a
Tomato-canning clubs III–84b
Tombecbe, Fort (Ala.) II–167b; VII–70b
Tombigbee River II–167b; VII–70b
Black Belt I–308b
Chickasaw-French War

TOMBIGBEE RIVER (cont.)
I–197a; II–22b
Creek War IV–456a
Fort Confederation VI–366b; VII–270a
Fort Stoddert VI–414b
Gaines' Trace III–146b
land grants III–170a
Saint Stephens VI–197b
Tennessee River VII–27b
Three Notch Road VII–54b
TOMBIGBEE VALLEY VII–70b; I–402a
TOMBSTONE (Ariz.) **VII–70b**; I–172a, 336b; II–477b; VI–201b
Tome (N.Mex.) III–162b
Tomkins, Micah (Michael) VI–70b
Tompkins, Daniel D. (pol.) I–418a; III–276b; V–86b; VII–179 (table)
Tom Sawyer I–335b
TOMS BROOK, BATTLE AT (1864) **VII–71a**
Tom Show VII–48a
TOM THUMB (locomotive) **VII–71a**; IV–175a; VI–24b
Tonawanda (N.Y.) II–460a; V–139b
Ton-Dac. *See* Klondike River
Tondee, Lucy VII–71b
Tondee, Peter VII–71b
TONDEE TAVERN (Savannah) **VII–71b**
Toner, Joseph Meredith (physic.) IV–146b
Tongass National Forest (Alaska) I–80a
Tonkawa (Indians) I–286a; III–367a
Oklahoma lands V–148b, 149b
scouts VI–242a
Texas VII–36b
TONKIN GULF NAVAL EPISODE (1964) **VII–71b**; I–62b, 431a; VII–183a, 185b
TONKIN GULF RESOLUTION (1964) **VII–71b**; III–70b; VI–100a; VII–224b, 227b
TONNAGE ACT (1789) **VI–72a**
Tonnage duty, state II–200b
Tonopah (Nev.) III–191b; V–39b
TONQUIN (ship) **VII–72a**; I–209a
Tonti, Henry de (expl.) II–329a; III–119a, 143b
Arkansas post I–172b–73a,b; II–247b
Arkansas River I–174a
Fort Pimitoui V–315a
Fort Saint Louis III–329a; V–260b; VI–195a, 388a
Starved Rock II–257b
Tonti, Lorenzo (banker) VII–72a
Tontine Coffee House (N.Y.C.) VII–72a, 221b
TONTINE PLAN VII–72a; II–255a; III–427b, 432a–b, 433a
Tonto Apache (Indians) I–141b, 142b
Tonto National Monument V–217b
Tonyn, Fort (Fla.) III–42b
Tonyn, Patrick (gov.) III–42a
Toohoolhoolzote (Indian) II–74b
Tool dressers I–317a
Tools
Cleveland II–75a
colonial industry III–413b
fur trade III–140a
Hohokam culture III–289b
See also Machine Tools
Toombs, Robert (states.) II–139a, 160a, 241a; IV–326b; V–161a
"Toonerville Folks" (comic strip) V–72a
"TOO PROUD TO FIGHT" VII–72b
Tooth decay II–331b
Toovey, James (bookseller) II–109a
Topaz (Utah) III–491a
Topeka (Kans.) VII–72b
Atchison, Topeka and Santa Fe Railroad VI–32b
blizzard of 1888 I–320b
board of education I–372b
Kansas Free-State party IV–28a
Kansas State Historical Society IV–25b
proslavery legislature IV–118b
temperance movement IV–27a
tornado VII–76a
Topeka Commonwealth (news.) VII–187b
TOPEKA MOVEMENT AND CONSTITUTION VII–72b; IV–28a–b, 31a
Top hat II–371b, 372a
Topographical Engineers, Corps of II–440b, 449b; VI–146a
TOPOGRAPHIC MAPPING VII–73a; I–462a–64a; III–163b–64a; V–293a
Topsham (Maine) V–242a
Torbert, Alfred T. A. (off.) VII–117a, 358a
TORDESILLAS, TREATY OF (1494) **VII–75a**; II–323b; IV–221a
Torgau (Ger.) II–407b
Tories. *See* Loyalists
Torkillus, Reorus (cler.) V–80b
Tornado (bomber) I–50b
TORNADOES VII–75a; II–76b, 351a–52b
Galveston III–149a
military aid IV–341b
National Weather Service VII–264a
rainfall VI–41b
research IV–316a,b, 317b
Toronto (Can.)
Brulé exploration V–156b
hockey III–287b
rapid transit III–451b
Saint Lawrence River VI–192b
See also York, Capture and Destruction of
Toronto, Fort (Can.) V–156b–57a; VII–358b
Toroweap Point (Ariz.) III–208b
Torpedo boats VII–241a
See also Destroyers
Torpedoes III–270b, 291b; IV–430a
Torpedoes, Civil War. *See* Submarines and Torpedoes in the Civil War
Torpedo planes I–55a
TORPEDO WARFARE VII–76a; V–27a–b, 163b, 164a; VII–241a,b, 243a
Battle of the Philippine Sea V–286a
Civil War VI–424b–25a
research V–28a
World War II II–443a; VII–343a,b
Torquemada, Juan de VI–167a
TORRENS SYSTEM VI–76b; IV–105b, 105b
Torres, Manuel (dipl.) IV–115a
Torresolo, Griselio I–202b, 203a
Torrey, Charles T. (abolitionist) IV–143b; VII–138b
Torrey, Colonel (law.) I–262b
Torrey, John (bot.) I–349a; V–326b
Torrey brothers VII–77a
TORREYS' TRADING POST (Tex.) **VII–77a**; VII–96a
Torrijos, Omar (off.) V–203a
Tortuga Island I–373b; III–29a, 233a
Toscanelli, Paolo dal Posso IV–247a
Toscosa (Tex.) II–251b
Totalitarianism
academic freedom I–4b
Soviet Union I–179a
World War II II–315a
Total serialization (mus.) IV–439b
Total war IV–383a–b
Totem poles I–166b; III–238a, 361a,b, 374a
To the Finland Station IV–165b
"To the stars through difficulties" (motto) VI–393 (table)
Toulon (Fr.)
dry docks II–375a
TOULOUSE, FORT (Ala.) **VII–77a**
Tour, Charles de la III–120b
Tour, Claude de Saint-Étienne de la (fur trader) V–253b, 260a
Tourgée, Albion W. (au.) IV–163b
Tourism VI–471b
American Express Company I–102b
American Samoa VI–205b
Arizona I–172b
Arkansas I–173b
automobile I–99b, 228a
Bahama Islands I–243b
balance of payments VII–90b
balance of trade I–245b
Barbados I–266a
Beaufort (S.C.) I–281b
Bermuda I–292b
Colorado II–128b
Denver II–332a
El Paso II–433b
Florida III–40a, 42a
Great Lakes III–216b
Guam III–230b
Hawaii III–264b
Idaho III–328b
Massachusetts IV–268a–b
Montana IV–403b
Natchez IV–455a
Nevada V–40a
New Mexico V–60a
New Orleans V–62b; VII–187a
Oregon V–165b
Puerto Rico V–461b
Rhode Island VI–134a
Salem VI–199b
San Francisco VI–209b
Santa Fe VI–215a
South Dakota VI–350a
steamboats VI–407a
Tennessee VII–26a
Vermont VII–172b
Virginia VII–196a
Virginia City VII–199b
Virgin Islands VII–204a
Washington, D.C. VII–246a,b
Washington Monument VII–250b
West Virginia VII–282a
Williamsburg VII–302a–b
Wyoming VII–346a
Yellowstone Park VII–357b
Yosemite Park VII–361b, 362a
Tour of the Prairies IV–161b
Touro Synagogue (Newport) I–162a; V–65b
Tour Through the Western and Southern States in 1836 VI–163a
Tousey, Frank (pub.) II–341b
Toussaint L'Ouverture, Pierre Dominique (off.) V–342a
Toussand, Louis de (eng.) I–162b
Tovar, Pedro de (expl.) II–228b; III–208a
TOW (missile) IV–363b
Towa (lang.) III–367b; V–460a
Toward a Modern Diplomacy (report) III–72a
Toward a More Responsible Two-Party System: A Report V–353b

Toward a Stronger Foreign Service (report) III–72a
TOWBOATING VII–77a; IV–88b; VI–407a; VII–84a, 102a
Hudson River III–312b
Mississippi River IV–373a
Tow cloth III–271a
Towels IV–157b
Tower Buildings (N.Y.C.) VII–24b
Towers, John H. (nav. off.) VII–1b
Town. *See* Local Government; Town Government
Town, Ithiel (eng., arch.) I–163a–b, 363b
Town and Country (period.) I–17b
Town-and-temple complex I–157b, 158a
Town common II–45a
Towne, Benjamin (pub.) V–71a
Townes, Charles H. (phys.) IV–262b; V–100a, 296a
Towne Scientific School V–249a
"Town for the Motor Age." *See* Radburn (N.J.)
TOWN GOVERNMENT VII–78a; II–245a,b; IV–171a,b
elections II–411a
land distribution I–3b
New England V–50a
patronage V–228a
Town green II–45a
Town houses II–49a
Townley, Arthur Charles (farmer) V–106b
Town manager. *See* City Manager Plan
TOWN MEETINGS VII–78b; II–44a; VI–88b; VII–78a
Dorchester (Mass.) II–364b
meetinghouse IV–300a
New England V–50a–b
selectmen VI–257b
Towns
common lands II–141a
Towns, George W. (gov.) VII–148a
Town school II–285b, 394a; VI–226b
Town sealers. *See* Sealers, Town
Townsend, Francis E. (physic.). *See* Townsend Plan
Townsend, Henry (bus.) VI–412a
Townsend, Peter (ironmaster) III–313a
Townsend family III–134b, 138a
Townsendites. *See* Townsend Plan
TOWNSEND PLAN VII–79b; I–407b; V–46a, 401a; VI–269a
Townshend, Charles (states.) VI–110b; VII–14a, 80a
TOWNSHEND ACTS (1767) **VII–80a**; I–347a; II–123a, 309a, 494b; IV–445b; V–221a; VI–110b, 112a,b; VII–3b, 14a–b
committees of inspection III–421b
Maine IV–226a
New Jersey V–57a
New York City V–85b
nonimportation agreements V–104a
opposition IV–266a, 271a
smuggling VI–321a
Virginia Resolves VII–202b
writs of assistance VII–344b
Township school system VI–227a
TOWNSHIP SYSTEM VII–81a; IV–93b, 171a; V–452a–b
colonial land grants IV–91b
land sales IV–90b
Miami purchase IV–329b
New England IV–102b; V–50a–b
Northwest Territory V–122b
Ohio V–143b
Ordinance of 1785 V–162b
political subdivisions V–349b, 350a
roads VI–152b
school lands VI–228a
Seven Ranges survey VI–264a
surveyors VI–450b
taxation VII–11a
Virginia VII–195a
Townsley, James V–379a
Towson (Md.) IV–96b
TOWSON, FORT (Okla.) **VII–81b**; III–50b; VI–65a
Towson, Nathan (off.) VII–81b
Toynbee Hall (London) VI–330b
Toyota VII–90a
Toys
government regulation III–54a; V–467b
rubber VI–167b
Trace. *See* Buffalo Trails
Trachtenberg, Alan (au.) I–113a
Track and field
Olympic Games V–154a
Tracker (airplane) I–56b
Tractarianism II–455a
See also Oxford Movement
Traction engines I–35b
Traction machine II–429b
Tractor I–35b–36a, 39a, 227b, 443b; IV–419b; VII–55b
cotton farming II–238b
livestock industry IV–170a
"Old No. 1" I–35b
TRACTS VII–82a; VII–319a
political writings V–352b
temperance movement VII–22b
Vindication of the British Colonies VII–189b
See also Pamphleteering
Tracts and Other Papers, Relating Principally to the Origin, Settlement, and Progress of the Colonies in North America. *See* *Force's Tracts*
Tract societies I–335a
Tracy, Benjamin F. (law., offi.) VII–243a
Tracy, Lac. *See* Superior, Lake
Tracy, Marquis de, Alexandre de Prouville VI–443a
Trade, Boards of. *See* Chambers of Commerce
Trade, colonial. *See* Colonial Commerce
TRADE, DOMESTIC VII–82a; VII–87a–b
Alexandria Conference I–85a
Annapolis Convention II–192b
antitrust laws I–139b
bills of exchange II–468a, 468a
boards of trade I–491a
British credits III–63b
canal building II–321b, 322a
chambers of commerce I–491a
Chicago Board of Trade V–320b
Clayton Antitrust Act II–71b
coasting trade II–90b
congressional powers II–171b, 220a
fair-trade laws II–484a
farm products IV–219a
Federal Trade Commission II–500a, 500a–b
five-and-ten-cent stores III–33a
free trade III–112b
Friends of Domestic Industry III–124a
frontier merchant III–127b
fur trade III–139b
government regulation III–204a–05a
Great Lakes III–216b
Great Lakes steamships III–218a
Green Bay III–226a
hide and tallow trade III–274b
"Hot oil" Case III–307b
ice VI–69a
inland waterways VI–147a–b; VII–259b
internal improvements III–447b
Interstate Commerce Commission II–500a; III–457b
interstate commerce laws III–458b
interstate licensing regulations IV–148a
interstate trade barriers III–460b
labor-management disputes II–499a
liquor VII–265a
mackerel IV–217a–b
Mann Act IV–240a
Maritime Commission IV–254b
Massachusetts IV–266b
merchant marine IV–309a–b, 311a, 311b, 312b
Middlesex Canal IV–335b
Mississippi River IV–372b, 373a, 374a
narcotics regulation IV–450a,b
Nashville IV–453a
Natchez IV–455a
Natchez Trace IV–456b
National Recovery Administration II–481b
Navigation Act of 1817 V–15b
New York City V–82a, 87a
original package doctrine V–172a
paper V–212a,b
peddlers V–241b
Pennsylvania V–247a
Pittsburgh V–321b–22a
plantation system V–324b
Puerto Rico III–58a
Pure Food and Drug Act V–466a
railroad rate laws VI–21b
railroad rebates VI–49b
restraint of trade VI–101b
Saint Louis VI–194a–b
Santa Fe Trail VI–215a
Santee Canal VI–216b
Schenectady VI–225b
sectionalism VI–253b
state regulation II–220a
steamboat monopolies III–178a
trademarks VII–93a
trucking IV–420a
urban structure VII–159a
Washington State VII–247b
West I–278a
World War I IV–135b
See also Colonial Commerce; Indian Trade and Traders
TRADE, FOREIGN VII–85b; VII–82b, 84b
Africa I–21a
aluminum V–104a
antitrust laws I–139b
arbitration I–152a
Articles of Confederation II–165b, 166b, 167a
balance of trade I–244a, 244b
Baltimore IV–261a
Barbados I–266a
beef V–160a–b
bills of exchange II–468a
Bretton Woods Conference I–361b, 361b
China I–245a, 268b; II–26b–27a, 28b–29a, 77a, 275b; IV–34b
chromium III–13b
citrus industry III–39b–40a
Civil War I–245b; VI–405a; VII–146b
commercial treaties VII–108b, 112a–b
commission merchants and factors II–138a
congressional powers II–171b, 199b, 220a

TRADE, FOREIGN (cont.)
convoys II–217a
cotton I–245a,b; II–67b–68a
Cuba II–267b, 268b, 269a; VI–361a
Danish spoliation II–291a
Declaration of Independence II–307a
depression of 1920 II–334a
dollar diplomacy II–359b, 359b
East Indies II–388a–b
embargo of 1807 II–436a
enemy destination doctrine II–446a
enemy trading VII–93b
Erskine's Agreement II–460b
Essex Case II–464a
Export–Import Banks I–262b
Far East II–488a
farm products IV–219a
federal aid II–502a
fertilizers III–16b, 17b
flour III–43a
Fourteen Points III–86a
France I–245a; II–382b
free trade III–112b
French Decrees III–118b
furniture III–135b
Geneva tariff conference III–161a
Germany II–213a
ginseng III–180b
Great Britain I–121a, 122b–23b, 245a; III–4b, 63a,b
great fortunes III–78b–79a
Hamilton's fiscal policies III–244b–45a, 246b
hardware III–252a
Hawaii III–263a,b
"heroic age" IV–309b
Holland II–382b
"Hot oil" Case III–307b
ice VI–69a
imperialism III–347a
imposts III–349a
indigo III–405b
Industrial Revolution III–411a
international law III–456b
iron ore III–12b
isolationism III–479b
Jay's Treaty I–245a; III–493a–b
Korea IV–54b
Lake Michigan IV–332b
Lake Ontario V–157a
Latin America IV–115b
lead IV–123b
leather IV–128b
linen IV–157b
mackerel IV–217b
Macon's Bill No. 2 IV–219b
Manchuria IV–234b
manganese III–13a
Mann Act IV–240a
marine insurance III–427a–29a
Maritime Commission IV–254b
Massachusetts IV–266a–b
meat IV–280b, 281a
meat–packing IV–170a
merchant marine IV–309a
Mexico II–233a
most–favored–nation principle II–275a,b; IV–416b
motion pictures IV–417b–18a
Napoleonic Wars I–245a; II–460b
narcotics IV–449b–50b
naval competition V–10a
Navigation Acts V–15b
neutrality V–34a,b
Neutrality Acts of 1935–37 V–38a
neutral rights V–38b
New Deal V–45a,b
New England V–50a
New Orleans V–62a,b
New York City V–82a, 83a, 87a, 88a
Non–Intercourse Act II–437a; V–104b
Norfolk V–109b
Norris Farm Export Act V–111b
ocean shipping VI–280a
Open Door policy V–157b
Organization for Economic Cooperation and Development V–170a
original package doctrine V–172a
panic of 1785 V–206a
panic of 1837 V–206b
panic of 1893 V–207b
panic of 1929 V–209a,b
paper V–212b
Peking Tariff Conference V–242b
Perry's Japan expedition V–263a
petroleum V–270b
Philippines II–474b, 475a; V–284a,b
phosphate III–40a
pipe staves V–319a
piracy II–258a
plantation system V–324b–25a
Polly Case II–464a
potash V–376a
privateering IV–256a
Progressive movement V–428b
Prussia I–245a
Pure Food and Drug Act V–466a
reciprocal trade agreements III–69a; VI–51b
Reed Treaty VI–66a
revolutionary war VI–120b
rice VI–136a
rubber VI–167b, 168a
Rule of War of 1756 II–464a
Russia VI–177a,b, 178b
Saint Lawrence River VI–192b
Salem VI–199b
salmon VI–201b
salt VI–202a, 203a
San Francisco VI–209a,b
Savannah VI–220a,b
sea power VI–247b
Sound dues VI–340a
South America VI–343a
Spanish California II–212b
state regulation II–22a
Sweden I–245a
tar VI–461b
tariff VI–462b
tobacco VII–66b
Tonnage Act VII–72a
triangular trade VII–119a
tungsten III–15b
urban structure VII–159a,b
vanadium III–15a–b
War of 1812 VII–235a–b
War Trade Board VII–243b
Washington State VII–247b
Webb Export Act VII–264b
western separatism VII–276a
West Indies II–92b
whaling IV–449a
wheat III–44a; VII–286b
wool VII–321a–b
World War I II–314a; VII–327b
World War II II–217b
zinc V–103a; VII–369b
Trade, Free. *See* Free Trade
Trade Acts. *See* Navigation Acts
Trade Agreements. *See* Reciprocal Trade Agreements
Trade Agreements Act (1934). *See* Reciprocal Trade Agreements Act
Trade Agreements Extension Act (1945) VI–52b
Trade and Intercourse Act (1834). *See* Indian Trade and Intercourse Act
Trade and Plantation, Board of. *See* Board of Trade and Plantations
Trade assemblies IV–65a
TRADE ASSOCIATIONS VII–92a; VII–123a, 264b
Trade barriers. *See* Interstate Trade Barriers
Trade Commission, Federal. *See* Federal Trade Commission
Trade councils, central IV–62b
labor party IV–81b
Mechanics Union of Trade Association IV–61b
New York General Trades Union IV–61b–62a
TRADE DOLLAR VII–92b; II–264a; IV–395a
Trade Expansion Act (1962) III–114a; VI–52a, 53a, 469b–70a, 471b; VII–89a, 109a
Trade fairs, international II–419a
TRADEMARKS VII–93a; I–18a–b, 359b–60a; II–483a
commercial treaties VII–108b
Patent Office V–226b
silver work VI–289b–90a
Trademark Trial and Appeal Board V–226b
Trade Negotiations, Office of the Special Representative for II–498a
Traders Path (Pa.) I–88b
Tradescant, John (nat.) I–348b
Trades Union Congress IV–65a
Trade Union Council IV–81b
Trade Union Education League IV–70b
Trade unions II–142a; IV–10a
AFL I–103b
California II–29b
communism I–314b
Communist party II–144b–45a
TRADE WITH THE ENEMY ACTS VII–93b; VII–94a
New Deal V–43b–44a
War Trade Board VII–243b
World War I II–168b, 277a, 445b
TRADING COMPANIES VII–94b; IV–307b–08a; V–457a
British colonial policy II–122a–b
charter colonies I–499b
colonial charters II–118b
colonization I–500a; II–228b–29a, 231a
compact theory II–149a
corporations II–228b–29a
Great Migration III–220a
Massachusetts Bay II–35b; IV–269b
New England Company V–51a
New Sweden Company V–80b
Panton, Leslie and Company V–254a–b
Royal African Company I–22b
Virginia Company of London VII–199b
Virginia Company of Plymouth V–333b
TRADING POSTS, FRONTIER VII–95b; I–501b
architecture I–160a
Bellevue (Nebr.) V–30b–31a
Bent's Fort I–289b
Cabanne's I–399a
Cape Girardeau I–448a
Carson Valley V–39b
Carter's Valley I–461b–62a
Castine I–466a; III–120b
Chouteau's II–34a
Fort Benton I–289b; III–77b
Fort Bernard I–292b–93a
Fort Bridger I–363a
Fort Bute I–398a
Fort Lancaster IV–89a
Fort Leavenworth IV–129a
Fort Lisa IV–159b; V–30b
Fort Okanogan V–147a

Fort Orange II–383a
Fort Osage V–173b
Fort Peck V–241a
Fort Pierre V–310a
Fort Saint Marks VI–196b
Fort Union VII–145b
Fort Wayne VII–262a
Fort William IV–415a
Grand Portage III–209a
Indian factory system II–480a–b
Lake Superior VI–443a
Lassen's Post and Ranch IV–110a
Los Adaes IV–189a
Manchac IV–234b
Manuel's Fort IV–159b
merchants VII–273b
Minnesota IV–355b
Missouri IV–27a–b
Natchitoches IV–456b
Pembina V–244a
Saint Joseph VI–191b
Sault Sainte Marie VI–219b
Spokane House VI–375b
Torreys' VII–77a
Utah VII–161b
Venango VII–168b
Vincennes VII–188a
Walla Walla VII–221a
Warren's VII–238b
Washington State VII–247b
Westport VII–280b
Wichita VII–294a
Traffic pools V–358a
Trafford (Pa.) VI–49a
"T" rail VI–39b
TRAIL DRIVERS VII–96a; I–267b, 472b–73b, 473a
Trailer II–248a
Trail of Broken Treaties I–106b
TRAIL OF TEARS (1838) **VII–96b**; II–52b; III–389b, 394b–95a; V–148a; VII–190b
Trails VII–99b, 100a
California I–409b–10a
Camino del Diablo I–413a
Chisholm II–31b
Choctaw II–33a
Dodge City II–358b
Gila Trail III–179b
Great Basin III–215a–b
Great Trading and War Path III–223a
Great Trail III–223b
Hull's Trail III–316a
Nemacolin's Trail VII–244b
Pequot Trail V–261a
Platte River Trail V–330b
Santa Fe Trail VI–215a
Scioto Trail VI–239b
Smoky Hill Trail VI–320a
South Platte route VI–355a
Spanish Trail VI–368a
Taos Trail VI–461a
Trappers' Trail II–14b
Wilderness Road VII–296a
See also Buffalo Trails
Trails, Indian. *See* Indian Paths
Training and Doctrine Command I–187b
TRAINING DAY IN NEW ENGLAND VII–96b
Training of Teachers of Teachers II–402b
TRAIN ROBBERIES VII–97a; VI–252a
Train wrecking I–450a
Tramp printers. *See* Printers, Tramp
Tramways VI–24a, 39b
Tranquility Base (moon) IV–407a
Tranquilizers IV–306b–07a
Transactions of the American Dental Association II–330b
Transactions of the American Philosophical Society VI–235b
Transactions of the Medical Society of Pennsylvania IV–293b
TRANS-APPALACHIA VII–97b; IV–39b
Transatlantic cables. *See* Cables, Atlantic and Pacific
Transcendental Club VII–98a
TRANSCENDENTALISM VII–97b; III–112a; V–287a; VI–78a, 81b, 82a
Brook Farm I–369b; VI–325b
conservation II–187a
Fruitlands III–129b
Swedenborgianism V–58b
Unitarians II–170b
Transcontinental Air Transport I–68a
Transcontinental Treaty. *See* Adams–Onís Treaty
Transcription (biochem.) IV–390b, 391a
Transformer II–414b, 415b; III–156a
"Transient and Permanent in Christianity" (sermon) VI–81b–82a
Transistor I–287b; II–156b, 425b; III–410a; IV–352a; V–296a, 305a,b; VII–163a, 164a
computers II–426b
semiconductors VI–259a
solid-state physics V–303a
Transit authorities IV–428b
transition (mag.) IV–190a
Transit systems III–203a
Translation (biochem.) IV–390b, 391a
Transmission, auto IV–419b
TRANS-MISSISSIPPI-EXPOSITION (1898) **VII–98a**
Trans–Missouri region IV–423b
Trans–Missouri West V–177b
Transmitters, radio II–424a–b
Transoceanic Commercial Flight I–234a
"Transponder" principle II–143a
Transportation Act (1966) V–393a
Transport aircraft I–236a,b, 237a, 238a
TRANSPORTATION, DEPARTMENT OF VII–98a; I–391b, 399b; II–498a
Bureau of Public Roads II–135a
Coast Guard II–88b
consumer protection II–208b
Federal Highway Administration II–502b–03a
railroads VI–32a–b
railroad safety III–458a
Transportation, secretary of II–90b
Transportation Act (1940) III–458a–b
Transportation Act (1958) VI–30b, 32a
TRANSPORTATION ACT OF 1920 VII–99a; III–458a; VI–19b, 21a; VII–77a, 308b–09a
railroad pool V–358a
railroad rates VI–22a
railroads VI–29a,b
railway shopmen's strike VI–40b
TRANSPORTATION AND TRAVEL VII–99b
agriculture I–39b–40b, 42b
air transportation I–67b
Alaska I–77b–78a
Albuquerque I–83b
aluminum industry I–92b; V–104a
architecture I–163b
army logistics I–189b, 190a
automobile I–225a
Baltimore bell teams I–250b
barges I–40b
bicycles I–295a
buckboards I–374a
buggy I–461a
camels in the West I–412b–13a
canals I–40a, 442a
China Clipper II–28a
city planning II–45b
Civil War II–67a–b
colonial vehicles VII–168a
commerce clause II–135a
Concord coach II–158a
Conestoga wagon II–158b
Confederate army I–181a
covered wagon I–453a; II–248a
Dearborn wagon II–297b
Department of Commerce II–134b
domestic trade VII–83a–85a
electrical power II–413a, 414b–15a, 416a–b
electric railways VI–40a
Erie Canal II–460a; V–87a
Eskimo II–462a
Falls of the Ohio V–142b
federal aid II–502a
federal regulation II–229b–30a
federal–state relations III–9b
ferries III–11a
flour trade III–43a, 44b
foreign investments III–64a
frontier army I–192a,b
Fulton's Folly III–131b
fur trade III–403a–b
Gallatin's report III–147a
government ownership V–456a
government regulation I–390a, 449b
government traffic rates IV–94a,b
great fortunes III–79a
Great Lakes steamships III–218a
horse III–303a–b
housing III–310a
Hudson River III–312a–b
Illinois and Michigan Canal III–331a
immigration III–335a,b
Indiana III–370a,b
Industrial Revolution III–410b, 411a–b, 411b, 412a
industry IV–243b
inland waterways VII–259b
insurance III–427a–29b
internal improvements III–447b
Interstate Commerce Commission III–457b
interstate commerce laws III–458b
interurban II–416a
interurban electric lines III–461a
keelboats IV–35a
Lake Erie II–459a
Lake Michigan IV–332b
Lake Ontario V–157a
lumber industry IV–204a
Mackinaw boat IV–218a
merchant marine IV–309a
Michigan Territorial Road IV–332b
Mississippi River IV–372b, 373a, 374a
Missouri River IV–380a
motor trucks IV–419a
municipal ownership IV–427b, 428a–b
National Road IV–470a
National Waterways Commission V–1b
Newark V–41b
New England V–50a
New Jersey V–57b
New South V–67a
North Carolina V–115b, 116b
ocean passenger service IV–313a
Ohio V–141a,b
Ohio National Stage Company V–144b
Ohio River VI–147b

TRANSPORTATION AND TRAVEL (cont.)
Ohio state canals V–145b
Ohio Valley V–146a
oil V–269b
oil pipelines V–319b
passports V–225a
Pennsylvania V–247a
Pennsylvania canal system V–249b, 249b
Philippines V–283a
Phoenix V–289a
political campaigns I–415b
portages and water routes V–367a
port authorities V–368a–b
post roads V–374b
Potomac canals V–378a
prairie schooner V–389b
Progressive movement V–427a
public transit IV–77a
public utilities V–456b, 459a
Pullmans V–462a
rafting VI–18b
Railroad Administration VI–19a
railroad conventions VI–20b
railroad pools V–358a
railroad rate law VI–21b
railroad rate wars VI–22b
railroad rebates VI–49b
railroads VI–24a, 380b
Red River cart traffic VI–63b
Red River raft VI–65a
river and harbor improvements VI–145b
river navigation VI–148a
roads VI–152b
rural areas VI–175b
sailing packets V–183b
San Francisco VI–209b
Santee Canal VI–216a
Savannah VI–221a
Scientific American VI–231a–b
sectionalism VI–253b
segregation III–107a–b, 502b–03a; VI–255b–56a
Smoky Hill Trail VI–320a,b
snagboats VI–322a
snowshoes VI–323a
South Carolina Canal VI–349a
stagecoaches VI–380b
stagelines VI–379a–80b
state fairs VI–392b
state relations VI–402b
steamboating I–459a; VI–406b–08b
steam engine VI–408b–09a
street railways VI–418b
subsidies VI–425a
subways VI–429a
taverns VII–2a
taxation VII–5b, 7a, 8b, 13a
Texas VII–39a
toll bridges and roads VII–69a
towboating VII–77a
travois VII–106b
tunnels VII–127b
Union Pacific Railroad VII–147a
urban structure VII–159a,b
Vial's Road VII–178b
westward movement IV–99b–100a
whalebacks VII–285a
World War I II–243a; VII–326a
World War II VII–334b
Transportation industry
automation IV–75a
ferrous metals III–12a
Trans-Siberian railroad I–158b; VI–284a
Transuranium elements II–12b, 278b; V–300a,b
Trans World Airlines I–68b, 69a, 165b
diasters II–346b, 347a,b
hijacking III–277b
Transylvania
fourteenth colony III–87a
TRANSYLVANIA COMPANY VII–102b; I–337a; II–272a, 292a; III–271b; IV–92b; VII–203a, 253b
Boonesborough IV–40a; VI–356a
Cumberland Settlements II–273b
Fincastle County III–24b
Tennessee VII–25a
trails VI–153a
Treaty of Sycamore Shoals III–382b; VI–455a
Virginia lands IV–98b
Wilderness Road VII–296a
Transylvania Medical School (Ky.) IV–40b
Transylvania University (Ky.) I–324a, 410a; V–131a
TRAPPERS' RENDEZVOUS VII–103b; III–143a
Green River III–227a; IV–422a–b
holes of the mountains III–291a
Independence (Mo.) III–353b
Jackson Hole III–486a
Ogden's Hole V–140a
Pierre's Hole V–310b
Sault Sainte Marie VI–219b
Utah VII–161b
Trappers' Trail. *See* Cherokee Trail
TRAPPING VII–104b; III–140a, 402b
beaver VII–296b
mountain men IV–422a
rendezvous VII–103b
wolves VII–311b
Trapshooters Well (Kans.) II–408a
Trask, William (col.) III–128b
Travel. *See* Transportation and Travel
Travelers checks I–102b
Travelers Insurance Company III–431b, 435a
Traveling Hail (Indian) IV–356b
TRAVELING SALESMEN VII–105a; III–429a; VII–62b, 83a
See also Peddlers
"Travelling" (song) III–469a
Travel Service, U.S. II–135a
Travels Through North and South Carolina, Georgia, East and West Florida VI–90a
Travels Through the Interior Parts of North America. See Carver's *Travels*
Traverse, Lake VI–63b; VII–106a
TRAVERSE DES SIOUX, TREATY OF (1851) **VII–106a**; III–383b; VI–139a, 296a, 297a
Travers Racetrack (N.Y.) VI–218a
Travis, William Barret (off.)
Alamo I–74a, b; VII–37b
Anahuac attack I–116b
TRAVOIS VII–106b; III–363a
TREASON VII–106b
Burr, Aaron I–319b, 388b
capital punishment I–450a
Christiana Fugitive Affair II–34b
Civil War II–190a, 222b
colonial punishments V–464b, 465a
Constitution II–197a, 202a
conviction II–202b
Copperheads II–222b
Court of High Commission III–274b
Espionage Act of 1917 II–463a
impeachment II–202a
revolutionary war IV–201a
Vallandigham incident VII–164b
"Treason of the Senate" (article) IV–424b
TREASON TRIALS VII–107a
Brown, John VII–117b
Fries, John III–124a
Hull court-martial III–315b
Treasure Island III–189b
Treasure State VI–394 (table)
Treasury, secretary of the
comptroller of the currency II–152b
Customs Service II–276b
fur seal fisheries I–76a
lighthouses II–89a
TREASURY, UNITED STATES VII–107b; I–383a, 399a; II–498a; III–244b; VI–122b
Bank of the United States III–245b
Bureau of Standards IV–462a,b
Bureau of the Budget II–497b; V–136b
Civil War II–218b
Coast and Geodetic Survey II–87a
Coast Guard II–89b
comptroller II–152a
congressional appropriations II–200b
customs regulations II–276a
Deposit Act of 1836 II–333b
discretionary power I–12a
drug control IV–450b
enabling legislation II–178b
expenses of Congress II–172a,b
Export–Import Banks I–263a; II–500b
Federal Deposit Insurance Corporation II–501a
Federal Home Loan Banks System II–501a
federal mint IV–359b
Federal Reserve System III–6b, 7b
federal surplus VI–449a
fiscal policy V–137a
foreign service VI–389a
General Land Office I–463a; IV–95a
gold III–190a, 192a, 195b–96b; IV–53b; VI–371b
gold certificates III–190a
Gold Purchase Plan III–194b
greenbacks III–110a
hard money III–251b
Independent Treasury System III–354b
Intelligence Board III–439b
land sale surplus IV–91a
lend–lease legislation IV–134b
monetarist's formula IV–234b
Morgan–Belmont Agreement IV–410a
national bank notes IV–461b
open–market operations V–159b
police activities V–339a
Railroad Retirement Board II–499b
railroads VII–326a
Resumption Act VI–104a
sale of U.S. loans II–218b
Secret Service VI–252a
silver I–302a
silver purchases III–110b, 111a
specie circulars VI–369b
specie payments VI–370a,b
subtreasuries VI–427a
tariff legislation II–276a
taxes I–12a
World War I IV–143a; VII–94a, 331b
Treasury Act (1789) II–152a, 501b
Treasury bills IV–392a; VII–8b
Treasury Board IV–329b
Treasury bonds II–218b
Treasury Building (Washington, D.C.) I–163a

Treasury notes I–300a, 300a; III–111a
Civil War II–63b
Confederacy III–416a
Sherman Silver Purchase Act IV–395a; VI–277a
War of 1812 II–317a
World War I II–317a
Treat, James (dipl.). *See* Treat Mission
Treat, Robert (col. gov.) II–182b; V–41a
Treaties, citizenship II–42b
TREATIES, COMMERCIAL VII–108b; VII–111a,b, 112a–b
America VI–343a
Elgin–Marcy Reciprocity Treaty I–437a; II–431a
France III–96b
Hawaii III–263a
Jay's Treaty III–493a
Kasson Treaties IV–33a
McLane–Ocampo Treaty IV–218a
most–favored–nation principle IV–416b
Nicaragua V–94a
Plan of 1776 V–323b
Prussia I–245a
Spain III–492b
Sweden I–245a
Wheaton's Zollverein Treaty VII–370a
Treaties, compensated trade IV–416b
Treaties, Indian. *See* Indian Treaties
TREATIES, NEGOTIATION AND RATIFICATION OF VII–109b; VII–110a–b
constitutional provisions II–200b, 201b, 203a
diplomatic missions II–342b
executive and congressional powers II–472a
modus vivendi IV–385a
munitions definition IV–430a
Plan of 1776 V–323b
Root Arbitration Treaties V–232b; VI–163b
secret diplomacy II–342a
Senate ratification II–171b
two–thirds clause VI–359a
Treaties, Vienna Convention on the Law of (1968) III–457a
Treaties and Other International Agreements VI–405b
TREATIES WITH FOREIGN NATIONS VII–110a; III–455b, 456a, 457a; VI–405b
Adams–Onís I–10b, 351a; II–286a; III–68a; IV–320b
aerial hijacking III–277a–b
Barbary tribute VII–120a
Boundary Waters III–454b
Bryan–Chamorro I–373a–b
Clayton–Bulwer I–454a; II–72b, 285b; V–200b
Colombia canal I–454a
Convention of 1800 III–67b
Convention of 1818 II–216a; IV–6a
Cushing's IV–34b
Danish–American arbitration I–398b
Dominican Republic canal II–360b
Eisenhower Remón V–202b
executive agreements II–471b
extradition II–478b
Five–Power Naval III–33b
Four–Power III–85b
Franco–American Alliance II–215a, 218a; III–95a–b
Gadsden Purchase III–145a
Guadalupe Hidalgo III–68a, 230a; IV–321a, 324b
Hawaii III–263a
Hay–Bunau–Varilla III–265a; V–201a–b, 202a,b
Hay–Herrán III–265b; V–201a
Hay–Pauncefote III–266a; V–201a
Hay–Quesada III–479a
Hise III–278a
History and Digest of the International Arbitrations to Which the United States Has Been a Party IV–5b
Honduras canal I–454a
Honduras proposed loan III–297a
implied powers III–349a
International Court of Justice II–453a–b
Jay's Treaty III–67b, 493a
Kanagawa V–263a
Kellogg–Briand Pact IV–36a
mandates IV–236b
Migratory Bird Treaty IV–381a
nationalization of property IV–466a–b
Nicaragua V–94b
Nicaragua canal I–454a
Nine–Power Pact V–96b
Nuclear Test Ban III–70a; V–124b
nuclear weapons control III–161b
Olney–Pauncefote V–153a
outer space I–64a
Pact of Rio VI–143b
Peace of Paris V–214a
pelagic sealing VI–246a
Pinckney's I–459b; II–381a; III–67b; V–315a
Prussia V–440b
recognition policy VI–54b
Reed VI–66a
Root Arbitration VI–163a
Rush–Bagot Agreement III–68a
San Ildefonso VI–210b
seal of the United States VI–246b
sea otter hunting VI–247b
Sound dues VI–340a
Squier V–93b–94a; VI–378b
territorial waters VII–33a
Treaty of Ghent III–68a, 176b; VII–235b
Treaty of Paris (1898) V–215a
Treaty of Washington VII–248b
Versailles I–122b; IV–124a–25b; VII–172b, 330b–31a
Wanghia II–27a
war with Algiers II–303a
Washington Naval Conference VII–250b
Waterways Treaty VII–261a
Webster–Ashburton VII–265a
See also Definitive Treaty of Peace
Treatise Concerning Religious Affections VI–81a
Treatise of Military Discipline VI–126a
Treatise on Ecology and Paleoecology V–197b
Treatise on Invertebrate Paleontology V–197b
TREAT MISSION (1839) **VII–108b**; VII–41b
Treaty–making power III–417b
Articles of Confederation I–198b, 199a
Indian affairs III–383a
Missouri v. *Holland* IV–381a
proposed amendment I–362b–63a
states I–363a
Treaty on the Limitation of Strategic Armaments (1972) III–161b
Trecothic, Barlow VII–80b
TREDEGAR IRON WORKS VII–113b; II–163a
Tree, Maria (act.) III–297a
Tree planting III–76a; VII–60a
TREE PLANTING ON THE PLAINS VII–113b; III–74a, 76a; VI–42a; VII–59b
TREE–RING DATING VII–114a; VI–18a
Trees. *See* Forestry; Forest Service, United States; Timberlands
Trees, state VI–392a, 393–95 (table)
Trefaldighet, Fort. *See* Trinity, Fort
Trego County (Kans.) V–387b
Trego Motors IV–433a
Trelawney, Robert (col.). *See* Trelawney Plantation
TRELAWNEY PLANTATION VII–114b; IV–207b; VI–184a
Tremaine, Burton II–106b
Tremont (Mass.) VI–270a
Trenchard, Hugh (off.) I–66b, 328a
Trenchard, John (pol. writ.) VI–113a
TRENCHES IN AMERICAN WARFARE VII–115a; IV–253a
Trenholm, George A. (pol., fin.) VII–5b
Trent, William (trader) I–278a; III–219a, 370b, 403b; VII–166b
***TRENT* AFFAIR** (1861) **VII–115b**; I–121b, 438b; II–28a, 65b, 67b; III–350a
Trenton (N.J.)
New Sweden Colony V–80a–b
Phoenix V–289a
pottery III–183b, 184a,b
revolutionary war V–252b; VII–116a–b
steamboats III–32b
Trenton (warship) I–144a
TRENTON, BATTLE OF (1776) **VII–116a**; II–321a–b; III–173b; IV–413a; V–57b, 408a; VI–123b
TRENTON DECREE (1782) **VII–116b**
Trepassey (Newf.) V–30a
TRESPASS ACT (1783) **VII–116b**
Trevellick, Richard F. (labor leader) IV–62b
TREVETT* v. *WEEDEN (1786) **VII–117a**; IV–53b; VI–132b
TREVILIAN STATION, BATTLE AT (1864) **VII–117a**
Treviso (It.) I–102a
Trevithick, Richard (inv.) III–411b
Trial by jury I–94a, 297b, 299a; II–202a
Charter of Liberties I–500b
colonies II–308b
common–law suits II–204b
Declaration of Independence II–307a
Great Britain II–191a
See also Jury Trial
TRIALS, FAMOUS VII–117a
Haywood–Moyer–Pettibone Case III–266b
Hiss case III–278b
McLeod case IV–218a
McNamara case IV–218b
Mooney, Thomas J. IV–406a
Morgan trials IV–410b
Sacco–Vanzetti case VI–182b
Scopes trial VI–239b
Scottsboro case VI–241b
treason VII–107a
Webster–Fairbank trials VII–265a
Webster–Parkman murder case VII–266a
Zenger case III–104b;

TRIALS, FAMOUS (cont.)
VII–368a
Trials, perfunctory II–258a
TRIANGLE FIRE (1911)
VII–118b; II–82a, 348a, 372a; IV–68b
Triangle Shirtwaist Company. *See* Triangle Fire
Triangular pediment (arch.) I–161a
TRIANGULAR TRADE
VII–119a; II–119a; IV–309b; VI–170b, 310b; VII–86a, 277b–78a
middle passage IV–335a
molasses IV–388a
Sugar Islands VI–437b
Tribal courts, Indian. *See* Indian Tribal Courts
Triboelectric generators II–413a
Tribunals (federal) I–12b–13a
Tribunals, judicial. *See* Courts, legislative
Tribune Almanac and Political Register I–91a
Tribune Building (N.Y.C.) I–164a; VI–299a
TRIBUTE VII–120a; III–168a; VII–111b
TRICAP. *See* Triple capability unit
Trichinosis I–241b
Trickleculture III–151a
Trickster (myth.) III–386a–b
Tricorne VII–144a
Trident (submarine) IV–364a; V–11b, 26a
Trident missile system V–164a
Triennial Act (1641) II–181b
Trilling, Lionel (critic) IV–165b
Trilobites III–163b
Trimble, Robert (jur.) VI–445a
Trinchera Ranch (Colo.) VI–210b
Trinchera River VI–210b
Trincomalee (Cey.) VII–342b
Trinidad (Colo.) II–128b–29a; IV–278a
Trinitrotoluene V–383b
Trinity, Fort (Del.) V–42b
Trinity Bay (Newf.) I–401a
Trinity Church (Boston) I–164a; V–191a
Trinity Church (N.Y.C.) I–163a; II–132a; IV–100b
Trinity Dam III–323b
Trinity Island V–198a
Trinity River I–492a; II–389a; III–323b; VII–36b
Triode II–423b; VII–163a,b
TRIPARTITE AGREEMENT (1936) **VII–120b**
Triple Crown (horse racing) III–305a
Triple Entente II–314a
Tripoli III–234a
Barbary Wars III–464b; IV–44b; V–278b; VII–111b
extraterritoriality II–479a
tribute VII–120a,b
Tripoli, Bay of II–334a
Tripolitan War (1801–05) I–266a–b; II–89a, 313a
Constitution II–190b
Derna expedition II–334a
Philadelphia capture V–423b
U.S. Navy V–19a
Trist, Nicholas P. (dipl.). *See* Trist Mission
Tristan da Cunha III–302a
TriStar (transport plane) I–52b, 69a; II–347b
Tri-State Cooperative Association II–220b
Tri-State District IV–334a; VII–369a
Tri-State Regional Planning Commission III–460a
Tri-State tornado (1925) VII–75b
TRIST MISSION (1848)
VII–121a; II–342b, 471a; III–230a; IV–199b, 324a
Triton (submarine) VII–241b
Triumph of American Capitalism VI–157a
Triumph wheat VII–286b
Trois Rivières (Que.) VI–18b
Trolleys I–443b; III–461a; VI–212b
Boston VI–429a
municipal ownership IV–427b, 428a,b
Richmond VI–40a
urban structure VII–159b
Trollope, Frances I–367b, 368a
Tron, Charles A. VII–219b
Trona VII–346a
Troost, Gerard (min.) IV–348a
Tropical Forestry, Institute of III–76b
Tropical medicine IV–291b, 292b
Tropical Research Institute, Smithsonian VI–319b
Tropic of Cancer V–109b
Trop v. *Dulles* (1958) IV–15a
Trotsky, Leon (states.) II–144a
Trotskyites VI–326a, 455b
Trott, Benjamin (paint.) IV–352a
Trotter, William Monroe V–93a
Trouble in Tahiti (opera) IV–438b
Troup, George M. (gov.) VII–121a
TROUP AND CLARK PARTIES VII–121a
Trousers II–371b, 372b
Trout III–51a, 216b; IV–332b
Trowbridge, John T. (ed.) IV–223a
Troy (N.Y.) I–461a; II–399a; III–448a, 450a, 473a
Troy and Greenfield Railroad III–299a
Troy Trojans (basketball) I–273a
TRUAX* v. *CORRIGAN (1921) **VII–121a**
Truckee (Nev.) VII–97b
Truckee Lake II–364a
Truckee Meadows (Nev.) III–215a
Truckee Pass V–225a; VII–217b
Truckee River III–81b, 215a–b
Truck farming II–180b, 297b
Trucks
cattle rustling I–474a
cattle tending II–249b
Trucks, motor. *See* Motor Truck Transportation
Trudeau, Edward L. (physic.) VII–126b
Trudeau, Gary (cartoon.) V–72b
Trudeau, Pierre (states.) VII–91b, 259b
Trudeau, Zenon (col. gov.) III–144b; IV–377a
True American Society III–295b
True Whig Party (Liberia) IV–141b
Trujillo, Rafael (off., pol.) II–361b
Truk II–387a; IV–257b; VII–1b–2a, 125a, 337a
Truman, Harry S. (pres.) II–177 (table); III–353b; V–396 (table)
amnesty I–115b
Arab–American relations I–149b
armed forces desegregation VI–256b
arms control I–180a
atomic bomb VII–237a, 341a
atomic energy I–216a
attempted assassination I–202b, 203a
blacks I–30b
campaign of 1944 IV–73b
Central Intelligence Group I–484a
China policy II–28a
civil rights II–54a, 56b
coal miners II–86b
Committee on Civil Rights IV–208a,b
Committee on Government Contract Compliance II–456a
courts–martial VII–143b
elected president I–71b, 429b; II–480b
elected vice president I–429b
European Recovery Act VII–88b
executive orders II–473a
Fair Deal II–480b
Far Eastern policy II–489a–b
foreign aid I–179a,b; III–61a–b
foreign policy III–69b
full–employment law II–480b
Hawaii and Alaska statehood I–78a
health insurance IV–289b
hydrogen bomb III–324a
Indochina War VII–182b
inflation II–236b
integration of armed forces IV–340b
Israel III–481b
Korean War II–473a; IV–55b, 56a,b; V–124a
lend–lease IV–135a
loyalty program VII–310b
loyalty programs II–145b
MacArthur removal IV–56a; V–124a
Manchuria IV–235b
Marshall Plan II–315a
McCarran–Walter Act IV–209b
national health insurance IV–290a
National Science Foundation IV–470b
National Security Council VI–389b
Office of Civil Defense II–50a
Palestine I–124a
Pendergast machine V–244b
Philippines V–284b–85a
Point Four V–335a
Potsdam Conference II–97b; V–378b
presidential library III–284b
Progressive party V–429a
public debt III–7b
railroads seizure VI–30a
railroad strike of 1946 IV–74a
rearmament program IV–344a
Rio de Janeiro Conference VI–143a
seizure of steel mills II–179a, 473a
Soviet missile development IV–363b
special session of Congress II–479a
steel industry VI–411a
subversives VI–428b
succeeds to presidency I–429b
Taft–Hartley Act IV–74a; VI–456b
taxation VII–9a
term of office VII–132b
territorial waters VII–33a
transportation department VII–98a
vetoes VII–178a
vice–presidency VII–180 (table)
White House VII–291b, 292a
TRUMAN DOCTRINE
VII–121a; I–56a, 124a, 179a–b, 179a–b; II–98a; III–61a, 69b; V–113b–14a; VI–360b
Truman Library I–167b; III–353b
Trumball, Fort (Conn.) V–58b
Trumbull, Earl (eng.) I–363b
Trumbull, John (law., poet) III–259b; IV–161b
Trumbull, John (paint.) II–101a; V–187b, 188a,b

Trumbull, Jonathan, Jr. (states.) II–174 (table); IV–7b; VI–451b
Trumbull, Jonathan, Sr. (states.) VII–353a
Trumbull, Lyman (pol.) VI–11b, 56b; VII–54a
Trumbull County (Ohio) II–183b; VII–274b
Trumpeter swan VII–357b
Trunk hose (clothing) II–370b
Truscott, Lucian, Jr. (off.) I–141b
Truss bridges I–363b–64a, 377b, 378a
"TRUST-BUSTING" VII–121b; III–466a; IV–140b; VI–277a; VII–122b
Trust Company of America V–208b
Trustees of Dartmouth College v. Woodward. See Dartmouth College Case
TRUSTS VII–121b; II–229b
antitrust laws I–139b–40b
Beef Trust Cases III–343a
farmers II–493b
flour milling III–44a
investment companies III–467a
money trust V–462a–b
panic of 1907 V–208a
petroleum industry IV–399a
price–fixing V–402a
railroads VII–155a
regulation I–390b
Salt Trust IV–25a
Sherman Antitrust Act VI–276b–77a
smelting VI–317a
spermaceti trust VI–372b
Standard Oil III–80a; VI–383b
sugar trust VI–437b; VII–154a
tariff VI–463b
Trusts, charitable III–82a
Trusts, historical III–279b
TRUST TERRITORY OF THE PACIFIC VII–124b; III–425a, 425b–26a; VII–34a
American Samoa VI–205a
Marshall Islands IV–257b
Truteau, Jean B. (trader) II–285a; IV–380b; VI–367a
Truteau's Post (S.Dak.) IV–380b
Truth, Sojourner (ref.) V–280a; VII–316b
Truth in advertising I–19a; II–209a
Truth in labeling II–209a
Truth–in–Lending Act (1969) III–423b, 443b, 459a
Truth–in–Packaging Act (1966) III–459a
Truxtun, Thomas (nav. off.) I–13b; II–190a–b; V–15a, 19a, 423b; VII–240a
Tryon, William (col. gov.) I–162a; II–286a
Battle of Ridgefield VI–139a
Cherokee lands VII–125b
Danbury expedition IV–361a
Governors Island III–206b
New York–Quebec boundary VI–165b
Regulators I–73b; VI–72a
Sag Harbor VI–186a
Trespass Act VII–116b
Tryon County (N.Y.) V–172b
Tryon Mountain III–251a; VII–125b
TRYON'S LINE VII–125b; VI–165b
Tsimshian (Indians) I–79a, 441b; III–238a, 361a–b, 362a; IV–59a
Tsingtao (China) II–26b
Tsiolkovsky, K. E. (phys.) I–210a
Tsunami (seismic seawave) II–385b
Tsung Dao Lee (phys.) V–296a
Tsushima, Battle of (1905) V–11a
TUBAC (Ariz.) VII–125b; I–172a
TUBERCULOSIS VII–126a; I–241a,b; IV–295a,b, 298b; V–340b
cattle III–53a
deaths IV–150a,b
education of handicapped III–249a
garment workers IV–294a
Indian III–397a
opium II–373b
poor whites V–358b
sanitariums III–306b; VI–101a
social security VI–330a
Tubman, Harriet (ref.) VI–307a; VII–316b
Underground Railroad VII–138b
Tubman, William v. S. (states.) IV–142a
Tubutama mission V–314b
Tuck, Amos (law., pol.) II–293a
Tuckabatchee (Ga.) I–232a
Tucker, Benjamin E. (anarchist) I–116b, 117a
Tucker, Henry St. George (law., educ.) VII–197b
Tucker, Richard (col.) VI–184a
Tucker, William Ellis (potter) V–379b
Tuck School of Business Administration II–293a
Tucson (Ariz.) II–348b; III–179b
astronomical observatory I–212b
Camp Grant massacre I–433b
Indians I–172a
missions IV–367b
overland mail V–178a
presidio VII–125b
sanitariums VI–101a
San Xavier del Bac III–500b
Southern Overland Mail VI–353b
stagelines VI–379a
water supply II–130b
Tucumcari (gunboat) III–235a
Tudor, Antony (chor.) II–289b
Tuft, Otis (pressmaker) V–413a
Tufting II–239a
Tufts, James H. (philos.) V–386b
Tufts University IV–267b; V–24b
Tugboats II–90a; VII–260b
Tugua (Indians) IV–367b
Tugwell, Rexford G. (econ., prof.) I–359b; V–43b, 46a, 466b–67a
Tuition fees II–396b
Tulagi III–229b
Tulalip Reservation (Wash.) III–395b
Tulane Drama Review. See Drama Review
Tule Desert I–413a
Tule Lake (Calif.) III–491a
TULE LAKE, BATTLES OF (1873) VII–127a; IV–385a
Tuley, Murray F. (jur.) III–201a
Tulgas, Battle of (1918) I–159a
Tulip poplar VI–394 (table), 395 (table)
Tulip tree VI–393 (table)
Tull, Jethro (agric.) I–34a
TULLAHOMA CAMPAIGN (1863) VII–127b
Tulorosa Cave (N.Mex.) IV–385b
Tulsa (Okla.) VI–83b
Tumacacori National Monument V–217b
Tumbrels VII–168a
Tumpline III–381a
Tuna III–28b
Tunebooks IV–438a
Tungsten III–12a, 15b, 155b; VI–48b
lamp filaments II–417a; IV–89a
molybdenum production III–15a
South America VI–346a
Tungsten carbide III–15b, 156a
Tungsten steel III–15b
Tungsten wire IV–153b
Tunica (Indians) III–367a; IV–178b, 368a, 456a
Tunis
Barbary Wars VII–111b
consul II–334a
extraterritoriality II–479a
tribute I–266a; VII–120a,b
World War II IV–32b; V–113a; VII–338a
Tunisia
France III–97a
World War II I–60a, 308a; IV–32a–b; V–113a; VII–338a
Tunkhannock Creek Viaduct I–364b
TUNNELS VII–127b
health hazards IV–294b
Holland Tunnel III–312b
Hoosac Tunnel III–299a
insurance III–429a
Moffatt Tunnel VI–34a
Niagara Falls V–92a
Norfolk V–110a
Port Authority of New York and New Jersey V–368b
Saint Clair River VI–34a
subways VI–429a–b
Sutro tunnel VI–452b
Tunney, James Joseph (Gene) (pugilist) V–422b
Tuolumne River VII–362a
Tupelo (Miss.) I–7b; VI–26b
TUPELO, BATTLE AT (1864) VII–128b
Tupper, Benjamin (off.) V–143b
Turbans (dress) II–371b
TURBINE VII–129a; II–415b–16a; VI–410a; VII–257a–b
battleships II–369b
chromium III–13b
columbium III–14b
hydraulic II–422a
hydroelectric power III–321b
Niagara Falls power V–92a–b
steam locomotives IV–177a
steam power VI–410a
tungsten III–15b
Turbofan engine I–52b
Turbogenerators II–415b–16a
Turbogrinders III–44b
Turbojets I–68b
Turboprops I–68b
"TURF AND TWIG" VII–129b
Turgot, Anne Robert Jacques, Baron de l'Aulne (states., econ.) VI–118b
Turing, Alan (math.) II–154b, 427a
Turk atoll
World War II I–459a
Turkey I–149b; III–168a; V–22b
Baghdad Pact I–243a
British relations II–97b–98a
Cairo Conference I–403b
Declaration of Paris V–214a
extraterritoriality II–479a
fall of Constantinople II–386b
heroin II–262a
immigration to U.S. III–338b, 340b, 341a
Korean War IV–55b
Koszta, Martin IV–57b
mandated colonies IV–236a
North Atlantic Treaty Organization V–113b
Organization for Economic Cooperation and Development V–170b
Treaty of Versailles VII–173a
Truman Doctrine VII–121a
United Nations Declaration

TURKEY (cont.)
VII–151b
U.S. aid I–124a, 179a; II–98a, 315b; III–61a,b; VI–179b
U.S. arms shipments IV–363b
World War I I–176b; VII–327a, 330b
Turkeyfoot Rock (Ohio) III–316a
"Turkey in the Straw" (song) III–19a
TURKEYS, WILD VII–130a; III–51a, 52a, 150a, 381a
Turkey trot (dance) II–290b
Turkey wheat VII–286a,b
Turnbull, Andrew (col., physic.) III–38b; V–66a
Turnbull, Robert James (law.) II–264b
Turner, Asa (cler.) III–331b
Turner, Charles Yardley (paint.) V–191a
Turner, Frederick Jackson (hist.) III–125a–26a, 203a, 282b, 486a–b; V–81b; VI–342a; VII–269a
Turner, Henry McNeal (bp.) I–21a
Turner, James (engr.) II–466b
Turner, John, House (Salem) VI–199b
Turner, Jonathan Baldwin (educ.) IV–93b
Morrill Act IV–412a
Turner, Lorenzo (ling.) III–234a
Turner, Nat (slave) I–23b, 28a; II–403b; III–437a; V–4b; VI–304a
Turner, Richmond Kelly (nav. off.) III–180a, 229b, 485a
Saipan VI–198a
Turner, William (act.) I–268a
Turner, William (off.) IV–47b
Turner Joy (destroyer) VII–71b
Turner's, Nat, rebellion. *See* Nat Turner's Rebellion
Turner's Falls IV–347b
Turnpikes
agriculture I–40a
foreign investments I–245a; III–64a
Genesee Road III–157a
government ownership III–202b
internal improvements III–447b
Lancaster Pike IV–89b
Mohawk Valley IV–387a
See also Highways; Roads
Turnverein III–337a
Turpentine II–453a; IV–44a; V–14b
See also Naval Stores
Turquoise V–9b
Turtle (submarine) VI–422b
Turtle Creek I–358a
Turtle Mountain IV–118a
Turtles VI–90b, 91a
Tuscaloosa (Ala.) I–308b
Tuscaluza (Indian) IV–277a
Tuscarawas County (Ohio) II–359a; VII–369b
Tuscarawas River I–353b; III–187b, 227b
Fort Laurens IV–117a
Schoenbrunn missions VI–226a
Tuscarora (Indians) III–365b, 400b; VII–130b
education III–379b
French and Indian War III–115a
Iroquois League III–475a
Virginia trade VII–201b
TUSCARORA WAR (1711–13) **VII–130b**; I–458a
Tuscumbia (Ala.) III–298a
Tuskegee (Ala.) I–72a; VI–166a, 432b; VII–130b
TUSKEGEE INSTITUTE VII–130b; II–113b; VII–176b
Tuspan (Mex.) IV–322a
Tuspan River IV–322a
Tustenuggee, Halleck (Indian) VI–261a
Tutorial system III–260a
Tutuila Island III–425b; VI–205a
Tuve, Merle A. (phys.) V–300b
Tuxpan (Mex.) IV–252a
Tuzigoot National Monument V–217b
TVA. *See* Tennessee Valley Authority
Twachtman, John H. (paint.) V–192a
Twain, Mark (Samuel Clemens) (au.) IV–162b, 163b, 223a, 256a; V–68a, 336a; VI–146b
Gilded Age III–180b; VI–156b
Mississippi River IV–373a
on mustangs IV–445a
on stagecoach drivers V–178a
slang VI–300a
Tom Sawyer I–335b
Twana (Indians) III–362a
Tweed, William Marcy (pol.) V–347a; VII–295a
See also Tweed Ring
TWEED RING VII–131a; I–343a; II–232a; V–83b, 87a–b; VI–142a, 459b–60a
Nast cartoons III–257a; IV–454b; V–73a
party machine IV–214a
TWELFTH AMENDMENT VII–131b; I–94b, 417b; II–204b–05a, 409a, 412a; III–350b, 495a; VII–181a
Twelfth Army. *See* entries under Army, United States
Twelve-and-a-Quarter Million Acres Bill VI–327b
Twelve-hour day IV–69b
Twelve Men V–61a
Twelve-mile limit III–107a
Twelve-tone method (mus.) IV–439b
Twentieth Amendment I–95a; II–174a, 206b, 479a; III–350b; V–398b–99a
See also Lame-Duck Amendment
Twentieth Century (train) III–452a
Twentieth Century-Fox IV–418a; V–292b
Twentieth Century Fund V–77b
Twenty Associates VII–219b
Twenty-eighth Infantry Division. *See* entries under Army, United States
TWENTY-FIFTH AMENDMENT VII–133a; I–95a; II–207b–08a, 479a; V–397a–b, 398b; VI–93b
presidential disability II–172a
vice-presidency VII–181a
Twenty-fifth Infantry Division. *See* entries under Army, United States
TWENTY-FIRST AMENDMENT VII–132a; I–95a; II–206b–07a, 407a; IV–159a; V–45a, 430a; VII–23b, 265a
Twenty-first Army Group VII–339b
Twenty-first Infantry Division IV–205a
TWENTY-FOURTH AMENDMENT VII–133a; I–95a, 451a; II–207a–b, 408a, 410a; III–20b, 93a; V–355a, 434b; VI–97b, 98a, 435a; VII–208b, 209a–b
black suffrage VI–432b, 433a
poll tax IV–371b
Twenty-fourth Infantry Division. *See* entries under Army, United States
Twenty mule team I–340a
"Twenty Negro Law" II–162a
Twenty-ninth Infantry Division V–110b
Twenty-one Demands V–96b, 107b, 159a
TWENTY-ONE GUN SALUTE VII–132a
TWENTY-SECOND AMENDMENT VII–132b; I–95a; II–207a; VII–53b–54a
Twenty-seventh amendment I–95a
Twenty-seventh Infantry Division. *See* entries under Army, United States
Twenty-seventh Marine Regiment VII–186b
TWENTY-SIXTH AMENDMENT VII–133b; I–95a, 415a; II–55b, 208a, 325b, 408a–b; III–92a, 94a; V–108b; VI–97b, 98a, 435a; VII–208b
Twenty-sixth Infantry Division. *See* entries under Army, United States
Twenty-sixth Marine Regiment VII–186a
TWENTY-THIRD AMENDMENT VII–132b; I–95a; II–207a, 409a; III–92a; VII–208b, 245b
Twenty-third Infantry IV–445b
Twickenham (Ala.) III–318b
Twiggs, David E. (off.) I–488b; III–88b; VI–260a; VII–306a
Twiggs, John (off.) IV–44b
Twiller, Wouter van (col. gov.) III–309a–b
TWIN CITIES VII–133b; IV–357a,b
Indian population III–397b
North Carolina trade V–117b
railroads VI–32b, 33a,b
Sioux VI–295a
Twin Falls (Idaho) III–328b
Twining, Alexander C. VI–70a
Twining, Nathan F. (off.) V–332a
Twin Mustang (fighter plane) I–53b
Twin Oaks (commune) II–142b
"TWISTING THE BRITISH LION'S TAIL" VII–134b
Two bits (coin) II–94b
2, 4-D (growth regulant) III–421
Two Harbors (Minn.) VI–443b
285th Field Artillery Observation Battalion IV 230b
Two Kettle (Indian) II–283a
TWO-PARTY SYSTEM VII–134b; III–3b; V–343b
Democratic party II–326b
Jacksonian Democracy III–487a
legislature IV–133b
local government IV–134a
Maine IV–227a
party government V–222b–24a
party machine IV–213b
political patronage V–228b
presidential election II–409a
spoils system VI–375a
third parties VII–52b
TWO PENNY ACT (1755) **VII–135a**
Two Penny Act of 1769 V–221b
TWO-THIRDS RULE VII–135a; V–47b
Tydings, Millard E. (pol.) V–48b
TYDINGS-MCDUFFIE ACT (1934) **VII–135b**; V–284a
Tyger River II–451b
Tyler (Tex.) VI–36b
Tyler, Daniel (off.) I–309a, 381b
Tyler, Elizabeth IV–58b
Tyler, John (pres.) II–175 (table), 395b; V–395 (table); VII–300b

Border Slave State Convention I–341b
campaign of 1840 VII–63b
central bank III–354b
Dorr's Rebellion II–365b
Hawaii III–263a
Princeton explosion V–408b
San Francisco VI–209a–b
Texas annexation VII–38b
vice-presidency I–420a; VII–179 (table)
Virginia constitution VII–194b
Whig party VII–288b
Zollverein Treaty VII–370a
Tyler, Royall (jur., au.) VII–47a,b
Tyler Tap Railroad VI–36b
Typecasting V–412a–13a
Typefounding V–411b–12a,b
Typesetting V–77a–b, 412a–13a
TYPEWRITER VII–135b; I–395b–96a
electric II–153b
interchangeable manufacture IV–272b
Kentucky manufacture IV–41b
Typhoid fever II–280a, 454b; IV–150b, 285b, 291a,b, 292a, 297b; V–340a,b, 447b; VI–173b; VII–259b
Typhoons III–319a
Typhus IV–150b, 285b, 297b, 298a; VII–165a–b
Typhus Commission, United States of America IV–292a
Typographer I–395b; V–77b
Typographical Society of New York IV–60b
Typography V–411a–12a
Tyson, Edward (zool.) IV–231a

U

U-2 (reconnaissance plane) I–52b, 61b, 484b
U-2 incident (1960) III–70a; V–74a, 124b, 216a; VI–179b–80a
U-20 (submarine) IV–205a
U-134 (Ger. submarine) II–345a
Ua mau ke ea o ka aina i ka pono (motto) VI–393 (table)
UAW. *See* United Automobile Workers Union
U-boats V–21b; VII–325a
World War I I–158b
World War II I–54b–55a, 214a–b; IV–313b
See also Submarines
UCV. *See* United Confederate Veterans
Udall (Kans.) VII–76a
UDC. *See* United Daughters of the Confederacy
UDTS. *See* Underwater Demolition Teams
UFW. *See* United Farm Workers
UH-1BHuey (helicopter gunship) I–49b
UHF. *See* Ultra high frequency channels
Uhlenbeck, George (phys.) V–295b
Uhuru satellite I–212b
UINTAH, FORT (Utah) **VII–137a**; II–477b; VII–161b
Uintah Mountains II–477b
Uintah Valley II–477b
Uintoa County (Wyo.) I–363a
Ujházy, Ladislaus V–42a
Ukraine I–56b
Ukrainian Orthodox Church in America II–387a
Ukrainian Orthodox Church in America, Ecumenical Patriarchate II–387a
Ulam, Stanislaw M. (phys.) III–324a
Ulaswicz, Anthony T. VII–254a
Ulexite I–340a
Ulfsson, Gunnbjörn (expl.) II–461b
Ulibarri, Juan de (expl.) II–127b
Ulithi I–459a; VII–343b
World War II V–21a
Ulloa, Antonio de (col. gov.) IV–193a, 198b, 301b
Ulloa, Francisco de (expl.) II–129a
Ulrich, E. O. (paleon.) V–196a
Ulster County (N.Y.) II–462b; III–312a; VII–261b
Huguenots II–384a
Ultimate destination doctrine II–65b
ULTRA (Ger. intelligence) V–111a
Ultra high frequency channels III–1b
Ultrahigh frequency television stations VII–21b
Ultrasonics I–46b
Ultraviolet light I–303b
Ulysses I–479a
Umatilla River V–169a
Umiak I–446a
Umpqua River VI–318a
UMWA. *See* United Mine Workers of America
Unalaska Island I–85a
"Unanimous Declaration of the Thirteen United States of America" (1776) II–303b, 305b, 306a
Unassigned lands I–336a; V–148b, 149b
Uncas (Indian) IV–387a, 387a,b; V–261a
Uncle Remus: His Songs and Sayings I–335b; IV–162b
"UNCLE SAM" VII–137a; II–360a; VI–61a
Uncle Sam's Union Almanac I–91a
"Uncle Tomahawks" III–397a
***UNCLE TOM'S CABIN; OR, LIFE AMONG THE LOWLY* VII–137a**; I–137a; IV–162b; VI–307b; VII–48a, 138b
UNCOMPAHGRE (Colo.) **VII–137b**; VI–54a
Uncompahgre Peak V–268a
Uncompahgre River VII–137b
Uncompahgrite V–258a
"UNCONDITIONAL SURRENDER" (nickname) **VII–137b**
"Under God the People Rule" VI–395 (table)
Underground press V–79a
UNDERGROUND RAILROAD VII–138a; I–136b; VI–307a
Carlisle (Pa.) I–455a
fugitive slave acts III–130b
Ohio V–141b
Pearl case V–239a
Webster–Fairbank trials VII–265a
women VII–316b
Underground tests II–316a; V–125a
Underhill, John (off.) II–383a; III–309b; V–261a,b; VI–134a,b
UNDERWATER DEMOLITION TEAMS VII–139a
Underwear II–371b
Underwood, John C. (law., pol.) VII–195a
Underwood, J. T. (ind.) I–396b
Underwood, Oscar W. (pol.) III–38a; VI–467b
Underwood, William Lyman I I–444b
Underwood, William Lyman II I–445a
Underwood Constitution VII–195a
Underwood Tariff (1913) I–427a; VI–467b
Underwood typewriter VII–136b
Underwriting. *See* Insurance
Undistributed Profits Act (1933) VII–13a
"Uneeda" I–18a
UNEMPLOYMENT VII–139b; I–393 (table); IV–78a
automation I–225a
campaign of 1932 I–428b
child labor II–24a
Civilian Conservation Corps II–51a
counterfeiting II–244a
Coxey's Army II–252b; IV–67a
crime II–258b
Detroit II–337a
employment offices II–441b–42b
federal deficit II–317b
Federal Reserve System III–8a
Federal Theatre Project VII–50a
gold standard III–193b, 196b
grants-in-aid III–211b
Great Depression II–502a; III–322a; IV–70b, 71a–b
Indian III–396b
Indian relocation VI–83b
inflation II–236b
Insurance II–442a; VI–328a, 330a
Job Corps III–503b
Kelly's Industrial Army IV–36a
Michigan IV–332a
National Recovery Administration IV–469b
National Youth Administration VII–364b
New Deal V–44a,b, 45a,b, 46a
Nixon administration VI–471b, 472a
panic of 1837 V–206b
panic of 1857 V–207a
panic of 1873 V–207b
panic of 1893 V–208a
prices V–402a
recession of 1973–75 IV–75a; VII–85a, 91b
relief I–391a; II–476a; VI–73a,b
share-the-wealth movements VI–269a
slums VI–314b
Social Democracy VI–324b
social legislation VI–327a–b
social security VI–329a
social settlements VI–330a
taxation VII–7b, 9a–b, 10b, 11a, 13a
technological IV–65b; V–425b
veterans I–330a–b
West Virginia VII–282a
Works Progress Administration VII–322b
Unemployment compensation VI–73b, 74a
Unemployment insurance I–394a; IV–71a,b; V–464a; VII–140a, 215a
railroads VI–29b, 30b
UNICAMERAL LEGISLATURES VII–142a; II–183a; IV–133b
Articles of Confederation II–165b
city councils II–44a
Guam III–230b
Nebraska I–294b; V–31b
Pennsylvania II–118a
Vermont VII–171b
Virginia II–117a
Virgin Islands VII–204a
UNIFORM CODE OF MILITARY JUSTICE VII–142b; VII–154a

Uniform Commercial Code VI–399b
Uniform Consumer Credit Code III–423b
Uniform Crime Reports II–259a
Uniform Negotiable Instruments Law (1897) II–467b
UNIFORMS, ARMY VII–144a; II–81b, 371b, 371b
Uniform State Laws, National Conference of Commissioners on II–309b; III–423b; VI–399a–b, 402b
Uniform Time Act (1966) II–296b
Union (merchantman) I–290b
Union, Camp (Va.) V–335b
Union, Fort (Mont.) VII–357a
UNION, FORT (N.Mex.) **VII–145a**; III–187b; IV–217a; V–217b; VI–144a
UNION, FORT (N. Dak.) **VII–145b**; I–206a; II–34a, 284a, 285a; III–32a; IV–380b, 403a; VII–145b
"Union, Justice, and Confidence" VI–394 (table)
Union, preservation of the II–265a, 435a–b
"Union, The" (motto) VI–395 (table)
Union American Methodist Episcopal church IV–319a
Union and Loyal leagues. *See* Loyal Leagues
Union and Southern Rights party. *See* Union Rights Party
Union Army. *See* Army, Union
Union Bank (Miss.) VI–96a
Union Benevolent Association III–82b
UNION CANAL VII–145b; I–127b, 442b; VII–127b
Union Carbide IV–300b
Union City (N.J.) VI–144b
Union College (Schenectady, N.Y.) VI–226a
UNION COLONY (Colo.) **VII–146a**; III–477b
UNION DEMOCRATS VII–146a; VII–148a
Union Flotilla in the Western Waters IV–375a
Union Fur Company IV–415a
Union label IV–65b
UNION LABOR PARTY VII–146a; IV–81a; VII–146b
campaign of 1888 I–424b; III–225a
Union League II–63b, 66b, 222b
Union League of America. *See* Loyal Leagues
Union Mills Ford (Va.) I–381a
UNION NAVY VII–146b; V–19b
Arkansas destruction I–173b
Battle of Mobile Bay II–285b–86a
blacks I–28b; IV–339b
blockade II–62b–63a
blockade runners II–162b
British ships seized II–213a
Cairo VI–424b
Charleston (S.C.) I–497a
Christian Commission II–35a
Fort Donelson II–363a
Fulton III–131b
gunboats II–384a; III–234b
Hartford III–258b
Housatonic III–308a
ironclads III–474b
Kearsarge–Alabama encounter IV–35a
Lexington IV–136b
marines IV–252a
Mississippi River IV–371a, 374b–75a
Mississippi Squadron II–384a; IV–375a
Mobile Bay IV–382b, 382b
Monitor and *Marrimack* IV–396a–b
mortars IV–413b
New Ironsides II–294b; V–56a
New Orleans V–63b
Peninsular campaign V–245a
prizes V–421b, 424a
ships V–25a
sloops VI–313b
United States VII–153a
Wachusett affair VII–212b
warships VII–240b
Western Flotilla II–384a
West Indies blockade II–65a
Union of American Hebrew Congregations IV–9b
Union of Orthodox Jewish Congregations IV–11a
Union of Orthodox Rabbis IV–11a
Union Ordnance Corps IV–215a
Union Pacific Act (1862) I–453a
UNION PACIFIC RAILROAD VII–147a; I–485a–b; II–16b, 241b; III–79b, 221a, 328b; V–119a, 166a, 177a, 178b, 330b, 384a; VI–27a,b, 33b, 37a–b; VII–101a
buffalo I–375a
cattle shipments II–32a
Crédit Mobilier II–255b–56a
Fort Francis E. Warren VII–237b
Fort Wallace VII–221a
government loans III–450a
"Hell on Wheels" III–270b
hide and tallow trade III–274b
Kansas IV–26a
Kansas Pacific Railroad IV–30b
land grants IV–94a; VI–425a
Ogallala V–139a
Oregon Short Line V–168a
Saint Joseph VI–191b
Southern Branch VI–35a
Sun Valley VI–101b
Wyoming VII–345b, 346a
Union Pacific Railroad Company v. *Botsford* (1891) II–378b
Union Pacific Railway, Eastern Division. *See* Kansas Pacific Railroad
Union Pacific Railway Company IV–30b
Union Packet Line VI–407a
UNION PARTY VII–148a; V–395 (table); VI–92b
campaign of 1936 I–429a; V–47b
Democrats VII–146a
Loyal Leagues IV–201b
nullification V–198a
Union Pass V–225a
Union Prisons. *See* Prison Camps, Union
Union Railroad Station (Washington, D.C.) I–202b
UNION RIGHTS PARTY VII–148a
Unions IV–60b–77b, 471b
American Railway I–111b
Anthracite Strike I–127a
arbitration I–152a–53b
automobile I–230a
blacklisting I–314b–15a
Civil War II–69a
closed shop II–80a
clothing industry II–82b
collective bargaining II–110b–12a
Communists I–314b–15a
Department of Labor IV–78a,b
foreign contract labor II–214b
Gastonia riots III–154a
Industrial Brotherhood III–405b
industrial relations III–407a–08a
Industrial Workers of the World I–117a; III–412b
Landrum–Griffin Act IV–467a
lockout IV–174a
Locofoco party IV–175a
maritime IV–312a
National Labor Relations Act IV–466b
National Recovery Administration IV–469a
New York politics I–107a–b
occupational safety IV–293b
opposition IV–461b
political contributions V–448b
professional football III–57b
propaganda V–433a
public housing construction IV–429a
railroad brotherhoods VI–19b
scabs VI–223b
shop committees VI–282b
Socialist Labor party VI–325a
strikes VI–419a,b
Taft–Hartley Act IV–467a; VI–457b
United Mine Workers VII–151a
walking delegate VII–220b
Western Federation of Miners VII–272b
woman's rights movement VII–313b, 314b
women III–92a
"yellow–dog" contract VII–354b
See also American Federation of Labor–Congress of Industrial Organizations; Labor; Trade unio;sLabor
Union school VI–227a
Union Seminary V–392a
UNION SENTIMENT IN BORDER STATES VII–148b; VI–354a
Missouri V–402b
Parson Brownlow's Book V–221a
Tennessee VII–25b
UNION SENTIMENT IN THE SOUTH VII–148b; VI–354a
Jones County (Miss.) IV–8a
Kentucky IV–41a
North Carolina V–116a
Union shops
right–to–work laws IV–74b
Taft–Hartley Act IV–467a
Union Society (Savannah) I–293a
Union Stockyard and Transit Company VI–414a
Union Stock Yards (Chicago) II–17b, 18b; VI–414a,b
Union Theological Seminary II–133a
Uniontown (Pa.) I–358b, 364b; III–219a
radio VI–16b
Union Vale (N.Y.) I–284b
Unionville (Mont.) III–270a
Unitarians II–170a; III–112a; VI–78a, 81b, 82a
hymns III–326a
Quakers V–470a
Social Gospel VI–325a
transcendentalism VII–98a
Western Reserve VII–275a
See also Congregational Churches
Unitarian Universalist Association II–170a
Unitary school systems II–54b, 55a, 457a
United Aircraft and Transport I–236b, 237b
United Airlines I–68a,b, 69a; II–346b, 347a

UNITED AMERICANS, ORDER OF VII–149a
United Arab Republic IV–130a
United Automobile Workers I–103a, 230a; IV–72b
automation I–225a
break with AFL–CIO IV–76b
General Motors strike IV–74a
United Bible Societies I–100a, 294a
United Brethren, Church of the. *See* Evangelical United Brethren Church
United Brotherhood of Carpenters and Joiners I–103b
United Church V–123b
United Church of Christ II–170a; VI–79b
UNITED COLONIES OF NEW ENGLAND VII–149a; II–121b; IV–270a; VII–153a
fur trade III–141a
New Haven Colony V–55b
Treaty of Hartford III–258b
United Communist Party II–143b
United Company VI–190b
United Company of Spermaceti Candlers VI–372b
UNITED CONFEDERATE VETERANS VII–149b; VII–175a
United Copper Company V–208b
UNITED DAUGHTERS OF THE CONFEDERACY VII–150b; VI–348a
United Domestic Missionary Society of New York IV–365a
UNITED EMPIRE LOYALISTS VII–150b; V–156b
United Evangelical Lutheran Church V–123b
United Farm Workers Union I–42a,b, 357a; IV–76b–77a
United Foreign Missionary Society III–385b
United Garment Workers of America II–82b
United Hatters of North America II–286a–b
United Holy Church of America V–260a
United House of Prayer of Daddy Grace I–24a
United Jewish Appeal IV–10b; V–280a
United Kingdom
air defense I–58b
atomic bomb I–216a
atomic power reactor I–217b
exchange students II–471a
immigration to U.S. III–341b
iron and steel manufacture III–471 (tables)
North Atlantic Treaty Organization V–113b, 114b
Organization for Economic Cooperation and Development V–170b
United Nations Declaration VII–151b
U.S. immigration quotas IV–209b
Western Union Defense Organization V–114a
See also entries under England; Great Britain
United Labor Policy Committee IV–74b
United Lutheran Church VI–79b
United Methodist church IV–319a
UNITED MINE WORKERS OF AMERICA VII–150b; I–103b; II–86b, 87a; IV–65b–66a, 72a,b
Anthracite Strike IV–67a–67b
checkoff II–3b
coal strike of 1919 IV–69b
Colorado coal strikes II–129a
Guffey Coal Acts III–231b
health care IV–294b
Hitchman Coal Company v. *Mitchell* III–286a
internal conflicts IV–70b
leadership IV–76a
post–World War II IV–74a
United Mine Workers v. *Pennington* (1965) VI–103b
United Nations III–69b, 237b, 457a; IV–237b; V–234a; VII–113a
aerial hijacking III–277a
arms control I–180a
atomic energy I–216b
Bretton Woods Conference III–195b
China II–27b, 28a, 489a; III–70b
collective security V–36a, 39a; VI–142b
communication satellites II–143a
conciliation commissions IV–382a
Cuban missile crisis II–271a
Dumbarton Oaks Conference II–380b
freedom of the seas III–107a
General Assembly II–380b
Geneva Accords of 1954 III–160b
Geneva Conference (1954) IV–107a
human rights I–362b; III–317a
International Court of Justice III–452b; V–262a
International Labor Organization III–454b
international relief V–281a
Israel III–482a,b
Israeli–Arab relations I–150b
Korean War II–315b, 489a; IV–55a–57a, 253a; V–124a
League of Nations IV–125b
Manchuria IV–235b
Mexico IV–328b
mutual defense agreements V–114a
opposition II–294a
Organization of American States IV–112b
Palestine I–124a
Panama V–202b
postwar reconstruction II–301b
prison reform congresses V–416a
refugees V–342b
Security Council II–380b; IV–55b
Southeast Asia Treaty Organization VI–350b
Soviet Union VI–179a,b
Spain VI–360b
Suez crisis VI–430a
territorial waters VII–32b, 33a
Third World nations III–463b
treaty arbitration VII–112b
Trust Territory of the Pacific III–426a; VII–125a
U.S. intervention in Dominican Republic II–362a
veto power II–380b
war crimes VII–226a
Western Samoa VI–205a
Zionism III–481b
United Nations Building I–165b
United Nations Command IV–56b
United Nations Commission on Human Rights III–457a
UNITED NATIONS CONFERENCE (1945) **VII–151a**; IV–415b
United Nations Conference on the Law of the Sea (1958, 1960) III–107a
UNITED NATIONS DECLARATION (1942) **VII–151b**; I–215a; VII–151a, 351b
United Nations Economic and Social Council I–208b
United Nations International Law Commission III–457a
United Nations Monetary and Financial Conference (1944). *See* Bretton Woods Conference
United Nations Relief and Rehabilitation Agency III–60b–61a, 69b
United Nations Resolution on Permanent Sovereignty Over Natural Resources (1962) IV–466a
UNITED NATIVE AMERICANS, INC. VII–152a; V–210b
United Negro Improvement Association II–127b
United New Netherland Company II–383a
United Pentecostal Church V–260a
United Presbyterian Church in the United States of America (northern) V–392b
United Presbyterian Church of North America V–392a
United Press Association V–79b; VII–152a
UNITED PRESS INTERNATIONAL VII–152a; I–207a; V–74b, 79b
United Provinces of Buenos Aires. *See* Buenos Aires, United Provinces of
United Provinces of La Plata. *See* La Plata, United Provinces of
United Provinces of the New Granada and Venezuela I–93b
United Service Organizations VII–362b, 363a, 364a
United Shoe Machinery Company I–338b
United Society of Believers in Christ's Second Coming. *See* Shakers
UNITED STATES (frigate) **VII–153a**; III–21b; V–19a, 423b; VII–240a
United States (liner) VI–280a
United States (towboat) VII–77b
United States, Bank of the. *See* Bank of the United States
United States Catholic Conference I–469b
United States Catholic Miscellany (news.) I–467b
United States Code. *See* *Code, United States*
United States Employment Service. *See* Employment Service, United States
United States Escapee Program V–342b
United States Express Company I–102b
United States Flour Milling Company III–44a, 45a
United States Gazette (news.) IV–463b; V–69b
See also *Gazette of the United States*
United States–German Mixed Claims Commission IV–381b
United States Golf Association III–197b
United States Hotel (Saratoga Springs) VI–218a
United States Information Agency III–72a

United States–Italy Mixed Claims Commission IV–382a
United States Line II–438b; IV–312a
United States Magazine V–42b
United States Mail and Dixie in Difficulty (play) II–357a
United States Mail Steamship Company II–91a
United States–Mexican Commission IV–381b
United States Mining Company V–102a
UNITED STATES OF AMERICA (name) **VII–153a**
"Uncle Sam" VII–137a
"United States of North America" VII–153b
United States Open Championship (golf) III–197b
United States Pharmacopoeia V–273b
United States Pottery Company III–184a
United States Professional Golfers Association III–197b
United States Road II–273a
United States Rubber Company VI–167b
United States Steel case (1920) II–230a
United States Steel Corporation III–290b, 466a, 470b; IV–244b, 399a; VII–122b, 123a,b
antitrust suit V–428a
Great Lakes carriers III–218b
Mesabi Iron Range IV–315b
panic of 1907 V–208b
steel workers union IV–72b
strike of 1919 IV–69b
unionization VI–410b
United States Telegraph (news.) III–187b
United States Treaties and Other International Agreements VII–113b
United States v. *Addyston Pipe and Steel Company* (1898) *See* Addyston Pipe Company Case
United States v. *American Tobacco Company* (1911) VI–169a, 277a; VII–122b
United States v. *Arnold Schwinn and Company* (1967) VI–102b
United States v. *Belmont* (1937) VII–111a
United States v. *Brown Shoe Company* (1962) VI–103a
United States v. *Bulgaria* III–453b
United States v. *Burr* (1807) V–397a
United States v. *Butler* (1936) III–156b–57a; VII–7b
United States v. *California* (1947) VII–57b
UNITED STATES* v. *CLARK (1887) **VII–154a**
United States v. *Columbia Steel Company* (1948) VI–103a
UNITED STATES* v. *CRUIKSHANK (1876) **VII–154a**; III–60a; V–266a; VI–58a
United States v. *Curtiss–Wright Export Corporation* (1936) III–417b
United States v. *Darby Lumber Company* (1941) II–136b, 482a; III–247b; IV–80b; VII–214a
United States v. *Debs* (1894) II–299b; VI–276b–77a
UNITED STATES* v. *E. C. KNIGHT COMPANY (1895) **VII–154a**; I–11a; II–136a, 136b; III–351b; VII–122a
sugar trust VI–437b
United States v. *General Electric et al.* (1961) V–402a
United States v. *Guy W. Capps, Inc.* (1953) VII–111a
UNITED STATES* v. *HARRIS (1883) **VII–154a**; III–60a; IV–57b
United States v. *Hutcheson* (1941) VI–103b
United States v. *International Harvester Company* (1914) III–454b
United States v. *Kahriger* (1953) V–339b
United States v. *Kauten* (1943) II–185b
UNITED STATES* v. *LANZA (1922) **VII–154b**
UNITED STATES* v. *LEE (1882) **VII–154b**
United States v. *McGowan* (1938) III–395b
United States v. *National Lead* (1947) VI–102b
United States v. *Nixon* (1974) II–474a; III–465b; V–99a, 397b–98a
United States v. *Perkins* (1896) VII–6b
United States v. *Philadelphia National Bank* (1963) VI–103a
United States v. *Pink* (1942) VII–111a
UNITED STATES* v. *REESE (1876) **VII–155a**; III–60a, 438a; VI–58a
United States v. *Saint Louis Terminal Railway Association* (1912) VI–169a
United States v. *Schecter. See Schechter Poultry Corporation* v. *United States*
United States v. *Smith* (1806) VII–224a
United States v. *South–eastern Underwriters Association et al.* (1944) III–434a
United States v. *States of Louisiana, Texas, Mississippi, Alabama, and Florida* (1960) VII–57b
UNITED STATES* v. *TEXAS (1892) **VII–155a**
UNITED STATES* v. *TRANS-MISSOURI FREIGHT ASSOCIATION (1897) **VII–155a**; V–358a
United States v. *Trenton Potteries Company* (1927) V–402a; VI–102b
United States v. *United States District Court for the Eastern District of Michigan* (1972) II–427b
UNITED STATES* v. *WONG KIM ARK (1898) **VII–155b**; II–42a
United Steel Workers of America IV–76a
United Textile Workers Union IV–70b
United Transportation Union VI–20a
"UNITED WE STAND, DIVIDED WE FALL" VII–155b; VI–394 (table)
UNIT RULE VII–155b; III–169a
Unity (ship) VI–128a
Unity of the Brethren IV–409b
Unity Temple (Oak Park, Ill.) I–165a
UNIVAC (computer) II–156a, 426b
Universal Instructor in All Arts and Sciences: and Pennsylvania Gazette. See Pennsylvania Gazette
Universalists II–170b; III–112a, 326a; VII–275a
See also Congregational Churches
Universal military service II–313a; IV–343b
Universal military training I–108b
Universal Military Training and Service Act (1951) II–186b; IV–384b
Universal Negro Improvement Association I–21b, 30a; III–254a
Universal Oil Products Company of Chicago V–267a
Universal Peace Union V–235b; VII–236a,b
Universal Postal Union V–233a
Universal Suez Company VI–429b
Universal suffrage III–91a–92a, 107b
Universal Tontine Association III–427b, 432b
Universities. *See* Colleges and Universities
UNIVERSITIES, STATE VII–156a; II–114b, 115a, 395b, 397b, 399a, 401a
agricultural colleges IV–97a
antebellum South VI–343a
Florida III–40a
land grants II–399a; IV–93b, 96a
Louisiana IV–194b
New York II–132b, 401a; VI–158b
North Carolina V–115b, 116b
out–of–state students V–420b
Rutgers VI–181b
University, national. *See* National university
University Center (Philadelphia) VI–86b
University Hall (Harvard) III–260b
University of California Botanic Garden I–348b
University of Chicago Settlement VI–330b
University presses I–334b; IV–2b
University Settlement. *See* Neighborhood Guild
University Year for ACTION I–8b, 9a
Unknown Soldier I–207b; II–310a
UNKNOWN SOLDIER, TOMB OF THE VII–156b; I–175b; IV–301b
Unreasonable search and seizure. *See* Search and Seizure, Unreasonable
Un Souvenir de Solferino III–161b
Untermeyer, Samuel (law.) V–462a
Unzaga y Amezaga, Luis de (col. gov.) V–354b
Upchurch, John (rr. mech.) III–435a
Upcountry V–310a; VII–58b, 59a
Updike, John (au.) IV–165b
Upham, Thomas C. (philos., educ.) V–441b
Upholstering III–134b, 135a, 136a
UPI. *See* United Press International
Upjohn, Richard (arch.) I–163a
Upjohn Company V–274a
Upland (Pa.) III–219a; V–80b
See also Chester (Pa.)
UPPER AND LOWER LAKES VII–157a
Upper California. *See* Alta California
Upper Canada
Loyalists I–438a
rebellion I–458b
Upper Country. *See* Upper and Lower Lakes
Upper Creek (Indians) II–256b–57a
Upper Darby (Pa.) III–76b
Upper Falls Bridge V–93b
Upper Missouri Outfit I–105b; II–131b; IV–217a
UPPER PENINSULA OF MICHIGAN VII–157a; III–329b; IV–331a–b; V–144b; VII–68b

Upper Peru. *See* Bolivia
UPPER SANDUSKY (Ohio) **VII–157b**; VI–208b
Upper Sioux Agency (Minn.) III–267a; IV–356b
Upper Tract, Fort (W.Va.) VI–267a
Upperville (Va.) II–347b
Upper Volta II–437a–b
Upper Yosemite Falls VII–362a
"Up Salt River." *See* "Salt River"
Upshur, Abel P. (jur., states.) V–408b
Upshur County (Tex.) II–389a
Upton (N.Y.) II–133a; V–297a
Upton, Emory (off., hist.) II–367a
Upton, Francis H. VII–93a
Uptown Club (Montreal) III–286b
Uracil IV–389a
Uranium I–217b; II–423a; V–300a
  atomic bomb I–215b–16a; IV–237b, 238a,b
  Colorado IV–354b
  government purchase III–15a–b
  leasing of rights IV–90a
  mining hazards IV–294b
  molybdenum production III–15a
  New Mexico V–60a
  prospecting V–437b
  U.S. Geological Survey III–164a
  Wyoming VII–346a
Uranium Committee VII–334a
Uranium hexafluoride II–9a
Uranium–vanadium ores III–15a
Uravan (Colo.) IV–354b
Urban, Joseph (theat. designer) VII–49b
Urbana (Ohio) III–316a
Urban development II–41a–b, 47a–48b
Urban Development Corporation V–87b
Urban Growth and New Community Development Act (1970) II–48b
URBAN HEALTH VII–157b
  slums VI–313b
  See also Public Health
Urbanization
  Afro–Americans I–25b–26a, 29a
  Alabama I–72b
  effect on morality IV–408b
  land policy I–4b
  learned societies IV–126b
  local government IV–171a–b
  political bossism I–343a
Urban League, National. *See* National Urban League
Urban Planning Assistance Program II–47a
Urban property
  land tenure IV–102b
  speculation IV–100a–b
Urban renewal. *See* Renewal, Urban
URBAN STRUCTURE VII–159a
  Indians III–397b
  population changes V–363b–64b
  slums VI–313b
  suburban growth VI–427b
  Virginia VII–196b
  Washington, D.C. VII–245b
Urbino (It.) I–451b
Urethane V–328a
Urey, Harold (chem.) II–12b; V–99b, 299b
Urft Dam III–314a
Uribarri (expl.) I–174a
Uridine IV–390b
Urine I–303a
Urological Association, American IV–289a
Urrea, José (off.) VII–37b
URSULINE CONVENT BURNED (1834) **VII–160a**; I–467b; V–2b
URSULINES VII–160b
Ursus horribilis I–280b
Uruguay II–398a; VI–344b–45a; VII–151b
Uruguay River IV–363a
Urville, Jule Dumont d' V–198a
U.S. 12 (highway) IV–332b
U.S. 25 (highway) VII–296b
U.S. 30 (highway) III–59a; VII–165a
  See also Lincoln Highway
U.S. 40 (highway) II–273b; IV–470b; VI–320b
U.S. 112 (highway) IV–332b
U.S.A. IV–164b
USAAF. *See* Army Air Forces, United States
U.S. Aviation Underwriters, Inc. III–429b
U.S. Borax Company I–340b
U.S.–Canadian Communications Technology Satellite II–143b
U.S.–China Air Task Force II–26a
USEFUL MANUFACTURES, SOCIETY FOR ESTABLISHING VII–160b; V–57b
Use tax III–153a; VI–200a
U.S. Exploring Expedition (1838–42). *See* Wilkes Exploring Expedition
USGA. *See* United States Golf Association
Usher, John Palmer (law.) III–200b
Usher, N. L. I–268a
Ushijima, Mitsuru (off.) V–147b
U.S. Lawn Tennis Association VII–30a
U.S. Military Academy. *See* Military Academy, United States
U.S. National Herbarium V–327b
U.S. National Lawn Tennis Association VII–29a
U.S. Navy at War V–20b
USNLTA. *See* U.S. National Lawn Tennis Association
USO. *See* United Service Organizations
U.S. Olympic Committee V–153b
U.S. Petroleum Company V–321a
U.S. Rifle (Model 1873) VI–139b
U.S. Rifle (Model 1892) VI–140a
U.S. Rifle (Model 1903) VI–140a
U.S. Rifle M16 A1 VI–140a
Usury laws. *See* Interest laws
U.S. Veterinary Medical Association VII–176b
U.S. Voting Machine Company VII–210b
USWA. *See* United Steel Workers of America
UTAH VII–161a; II–334a; VI–395 (table)
  Anasazi culture I–117a
  Arbor Day I–154a
  army supply VI–176b
  Black Cavalry I–310a
  cliff dwellings IV–315b
  coal mines II–86a
  cobalt III–14a
  Colorado River Compact II–130a–b
  Compromise of 1850 II–139a, 150a–b; IV–28b; V–39b
  copper V–103b
  deserts II–477b
  dry farming II–375b
  flour milling I–488a
  Fort Robidou II–477b
  Fort Uintah II–477b; VII–137a
  freighting V–179a
  fur trapping I–201a
  gold III–192a
  Grand Canyon III–208a
  Great Basin III–214b
  Great Salt Lake III–222a
  Gunnison massacre III–235a
  hours of labor regulation IV–173b
  immigrants to I–363a
  Indians III–51b, 373b
  Indian wars VII–239b
  initiative III–418b
  irrigation III–477a
  Japanese–American relocation III–491a
  land grants for education IV–93b
  lead industry IV–123a
  lead–silver industry IV–122b
  minimum–wage law IV–353a
  mining III–65a
  Mormons I–363a, 397b; II–248a; III–213b, 221a; IV–249b, 339a; VI–87a; VII–100b, 107a, 284a
  Mountain Meadows massacre IV–421b
  Nataqua IV–454b
  national parks and monuments V–217b, 218–19 (table)
  Navaho V–8b
  Nez Perce War VII–239b
  Ogden's Hole III–291a; V–140a
  Paiute V–194a
  polygamy II–443b
  popular sovereignty V–155a
  potash III–17a–b
  private mints IV–360b
  Promontory Point V–430b
  referendum VI–66b
  Salt Lake City VI–203b
  seismic activity II–385a
  silver mining III–80a; VI–292b
  slavery II–150a–b; V–360a; VI–355b
  Smith explorations VI–318a
  Spanish Trail VII–217b, 256a
  Stansbury exploration VI–385a
  statehood II–443b
  state–making process VI–401a
  trails VII–100a
  U.S. Army I–184b
  Ute VII–162a
  Walker expedition VII–220a
  western routes V–224b, 224b, 225a
  woman's suffrage III–91b; VII–315a
  Wyoming VII–345b
Utah (Indians) I–281a; VII–137a
Utah, University of II–399a
Utah, We Love Thee (song) VI–395 (table)
Utah and Northern Railroad IV–403a
Utah Beach (Fr.) II–14a, 237a; V–110b, 111a,b
Utah Central Railroad VI–203b
Utah Indian War (1850–53) VII–239a
Utah Lake VII–272a
Utah War (1857–58). *See* Mormon Expedition
UTE (Indians) **VII–162a**; III–363a; VII–161a
  Arapaho I–151b
  Bannock I–264a–b
  Colorado II–128a
  Fort Massachusetts IV–268b
  Fort Union VII–145a
  Genizaro III–162b
  Gunnison massacre III–235a
  Meeker massacre IV–300a
  New Mexico V–59b
  removal from Colorado V–437b
  Sun Dance VI–441b
  Uncompahgre agency VII–137b
  wars VII–239b

Ute Creek IV–268b
Ute Pass Highway
V–311a
Utica (Ill.) I–477b; III–329a; IV–88a; VI–388a
Utica (N.Y.) III–32b, 157a; IV–445b; V–155b
Utilities. *See* Public Utilities
Uto-Aztecan (lang.) I–264a; II–133a; III–301a, 362b, 364a, 365a, 367a,b, 369a; IV–327a; V–194a, 314a, 459b; VII–162b
Utopian communities
II–142a–b
Utopianism IV–62a
Utopian socialism I–91a
UTRECHT, TREATY OF (1713) **VII–162b**; I–6a, 202a; II–92b, 126b, 267a; III–118a, 120b; V–214b; VI–3a, 359a
Acadia V–369b
Iroquois IV–386b
Louisiana boundary IV–198a
slave trade VI–310b
Uvalde (Tex.) VI–105a

V

V–1 (rocket) IV–363a; VII–340b, 340b
V–2 (rocket) I–212b; III–502a; IV–363a,b; V–14a–b
V–2 Bumper WAC (rocket) III–502a
VA. *See* Veterans Administration
Vacas de Cibola (buffalo) II–37a
Vaccination II–454b
public health V–447a
smallpox IV–275a; VI–315b–16a
Vaccines I–241b–42b
government control III–54a
government regulation V–467b
homeopathy III–293b
polio V–340b–41a
yellow fever VII–355b
Vacua Spencer Company II–421a
Vacuum cleaner II–417b, 421a
VACUUM TUBES **VII–163a**; II–156b, 423b; III–155b, 156a; V–305a; VI–259a
amplifiers IV–352a
computer memory II–155b
electric circuit analysis II–38b
radar VI–10a
radio VI–15a
sound amplification V–290a
telephone VII–20a,b
television VII–21a
V. A. Fogg (tanker) II–350a
Vagrancy II–258a, 259a; V–464b
Vahanian, Gabriel (theol.) VI–83a
Vail, Alfred (eng.) I–276a; VII–18b
Valachi, Joseph II–262b
VALCOUR ISLAND, BATTLE OF (1776) **VII–164a**; I–436a; III–234a; IV–86b; VII–171b
Valdese (N.C.) VII–219b
Valdez (Alaska) I–80a
Valencia (Ire.) I–401a
Valencia, Gabriel (off.) II–214b
Valencia County (N.Mex.) III–420b
Valentine, Curt (art dealer) II–105a
Valentine scrip IV–97b, 98a
Valenzuela (La.) III–479a
Valerianos, Apostolos. *See* Fuca, Juan de
Valhalla (yacht) VII–349a
Vallandigham, Clement L. (pol.)
Copperheads II–222b
New Departure policy V–49a
Northwest conspiracy V–121b
Sons of Liberty V–161b; VI–339a
See also Vallandigham Incident
VALLANDIGHAM INCIDENT (1863) **VII–164b**; I–196a, 304a; II–62a, 228a; III–156b
Vallejo (Calif.) V–29b
Vallejo, M. G. (off.) I–280b
Vallentine and Collins Line III–200a
Valley Campaign, Jackson's. *See* Jackson's Valley Campaign
Valley County (Mont.) V–241a
Valley Creek (Pa.) VII–165a
VALLEY FORGE (Pa.) **VII–164b**; VI–123b–24a, 126a
fortification VI–129a
Steuben's "Blue Book" I–183b
Washington's Lifeguard IV–152a
Valley Line VII–77b
Valley of Swans. *See* Zwaanendael Colony
Valley quail VI–393 (table)
Vallodolid (Sp.) I–399b
Valparaiso (Chile) II–463b; V–22b; VI–3b
Baltimore affair I–250b
Valuation acts. *See* Stay and Valuation Acts
Value-added tax VI–200b
Valverde (Tex.) II–363b; IV–8a
VALVERDE, BATTLE OF (1862) **VII–165b**; VI–144a
Vanadium III–12a, 15a–b; IV–354b; VI–48b
Van Alen, James H. VII–30b
Van Alen, William (arch.) I–164b; VI–299a
Van Allen radiation belts II–426a; III–454a
Van Alstyne, William (law.) II–473b–74a
Van Amburgh, Isaac A. (animal trainer) II–40b
Van Amringe, J. H. (educ.) I–109a
Van Arsdall, C. J., Jr. (nav. off.) V–11b
Van Buren (Ark.) V–389a
Van Buren, John D. (pol.) I–107b; IV–120a
Van Buren, Martin (pres.) II–175 (table); IV–51a; V–395 (table), 396b; VI–218a
Albany Regency I–82b
antislavery I–138b
Barnburners I–268a
campaign of 1812 I–418a
campaign of 1832 I–419a
campaign of 1836 I–419b
campaign of 1840 I–420a; V–207a
campaign of 1844 VI–138a
campaign of 1848 I–420b; III–111b
Caroline affair I–458b
Eaton affair II–389b
Hull court-martial III–315b
Independent Treasury System III–251b, 354b
Kendall v. *United States* IV–36b
Maysville veto IV–279b
navy yards VII–214a
New York constitutional convention V–86b
political parties V–223a
Tammany Hall VI–459b
ten-hour-day movement IV–62a
vice-presidency VII–179 (table)
Whig party VII–288a–b
Vance, Zebulon B. (pol.) II–163b, 165a; III–289b, 295a; VI–405a
Van Cortlandt, Stephanus (mer., col. off.) VI–170a
Van Cortlandt family (N.Y.) IV–92a
Vancouver (B.C.) I–401a; V–37b; VI–33a
VANCOUVER, FORT (Wash.) **VII–165b**; III–223b, 354b; V–97b
Hudson's Bay Company V–170a
Oregon Methodist Mission V–166b
Oregon Trail V–169a
Smith explorations VI–318a
Vancouver, George (expl.) I–84b; II–131b, 353a; V–164b, 167b, 327a; VII–166a
mapping of West Coast IV–248a
Northwest Coast III–238a
Puget Sound V–462a; VII–247b
Vancouver Island I–121a; IV–59a; V–165a, 167b
ferries III–11b
fur trade VII–166a
Haro Channel dispute III–256a
Indians II–30a
Nootka Indians IV–228b
Nootka Sound V–109a
Oregon Treaty VII–247b
Oregon Treaty of 1846 V–169b
Spanish exploration V–164b
VANCOUVER'S EXPLORATION (1791–92) **VII–166a**
Van Couwenhoven, Jacob (col.) V–266a
Van Curler, Arent VI–225b
Van Curler (Corlaer), Jacobus IV–185a
Vandalia (warship) I–144a; II–273b; III–329b; IV–32a
National Road IV–470b; VI–153b
VANDALIA COLONY **VII–166b**; III–209a; IV–92b
Vandalia Company III–209a; IV–371a; V–144a
Van Dam, Rip (col. gov.) VII–368a
Van de Graaff, Robert Jemison (phys.) II–12a, 278a; V–300b
Vandegrift, Alexander A. (off.) I–350a; III–229b
Vandenberg, Arthur H. (pol.) I–429a; III–480a; VII–151a
Van Denburgh, John (nat.) VI–91a
Van Depoele, Charles J. (inv.) II–414b, 415a; VI–40a
Vanderbilt, Cornelius (fin.) III–23a–b, 79a, 312b
Vanderbilt, Cornelius, Jr. V–74b
Vanderbilt, Harold S. (ind.) VII–348b
Vanderbilt, William H. (ind.) II–102b; V–443a; VII–222a
Vanderbilt, William K. (ind.) III–446b; IV–220b
Vanderbilt Cup road races I–226a, 231b
Vanderbilt mansions (N.Y.C.) V–191a
Vanderbilt University I–169a
Vanderburg, William (fur trader) VI–196a
Van der Donck, Adriaen (law., col.) V–266a; VII–70a
Vanderlyn, Pieter (paint.) V–186a

Van Devanter, Willis (jur.) V–47a; VII–269b
Van Deventer, Christopher (off.) VI–145a
Van Dorn, Earl (off.) II–22a, 225b; III–292b, 400a; VII–181b
Battle of Pea Ridge V–238b, 402b
Vandreuil–Cavagnal, Marquis de, Pierre François de Rigaud (col. gov.) IV–405b
Vane, Henry (col. gov.) I–133b
Van Eeghen (banking house) III–291a
Van Gogh, Vincent (paint.) II–104b
Vanguard (satellite) IV–458b, 459a,b
Van Horn, James (off.) VI–181b
VANHORNE'S LESSEE* v. *DORRANCE (1795) **VII–167a**
Vanity Fair (period.) I–464b
Van Lew, Elizabeth (spy) VI–373b
Van Ness, Cornelius P. (dipl.) VII–167a
VAN NESS CONVENTION (1834) **VII–167a**
Van Nostrand, David (pub.) I–334a
Van Ostade, Adriaen (paint.) II–101b
Van Rensselaer, Kiliaen (mer.) I–81b; III–313a; V–229a; VII–372b
Van Rensselaer, Stephen (off.) I–134a; V–90b; VI–3a; VII–234a
Van Rensselaer family IV–92a, 256b; V–86b
Van Ruysdael, Jacob (paint.) II–101b
Van Schaick, Goose (off.) VI–438a
Van Schaick, William (ship capt.) II–349b
Van Slyke, D. D. (biochem.) I–303b
Van Staphorst (banking house) III–291a
Van Sweringen, Mantis J. (bus.) V–209b; VI–35a
Van Sweringen, Oris P. (bus.) V–209b; VI–35a
Van Syckle, Samuel (bus.) V–269b, 318b–19a
Van Tuong Peninsula (Viet.) VII–186a
Van Twiller, Wouter (col. offi.) III–206b; IV–185a; V–61a
Vanuxem, Lardner (geol.) III–165a
Van Vechten, Carl (au.) IV–164b, 166a; V–96a
Van Vleck, John (phys.) V–304a
Van Wart, Isaac (sol.) I–118b
Van Winkle, Rip. *See* Rip van Winkle
Van Wyck, Robert A. (pol.) VI–460a
VAN ZANDT, FREE STATE OF VII–167a
Van Zandt, Isaac (dipl.) VII–167a
Vanzetti, Bartolomeo. *See* Sacco–Vanzetti Case VI–182b
Vaquero II–247a, 248b, 249a
Varagine, Jacobus de (au.) II–107b
Vardaman, James K. (pol.) IV–169a, 369a; VII–291a
Vardon, Harry (golfer) III–197b
Vare, Glenna. *See* Collett Vare, Glenna
Vare, William S. (pol.) VII–167b
VARE CASE VII–167b
Varennes, Pierre Gaultier de. *See* La Vérendrye, Sieur de
Vargas, Diego de (off.) IV–367b; V–59b, 461a; VI–461a
Variag (warship) VII–242a
Varian, Russell (phys.) IV–333a; VII–163b, 164a
Varian, Sigurd (phys.) IV–333a; VII–163b, 164a
Varieties of Religious Experience IV–448a
Variety shows. *See* Vaudeville
Variety stores I–490a; II–332b, 421b
See also Five–and–Ten–Cent Stores
Varley, Cromwell V–261b
Varlo, Charles V–333a
Varnum, Joseph B. (pol.) II–174 (table)
Varsity, Operation (1945) III–187b
Vas, Mrs. Petrus V–186a
Vasarely, Victor (art.) V–193b
Vaseline IV–44b
Vasquez, Benito (fur trader) VI–367a; VII–96a
Vasquez, Fort (Colo.) II–128a
Vasquez, Louis (trapper) I–363a
Vassar College I–272a; II–399a
Vassey, Richard (cler.) IV–318b
Vaterland. See Leviathan
Vatican
Confederate diplomacy II–65b
Vatican Council II (1962–65) I–468b, 470a
VAUDEVILLE VII–167b; VII–49b
dance II–290a
lyceums IV–207a
motion pictures IV–417a
showboats VI–283a
Vaudreuil–Cavagnal, Marquis de, Pierre François de Rigaud (col. gov.) III–116b, 117a; IV–268b
Vaughan, T. Wayland (geol., oceanog.) VI–242b
Vault (arch.) I–159b
Vaux (Fr.) I–70a, 286b; VII–326b
Vaux, Calvert (landscape arch.) IV–96b
Vaux–Andigny (Fr.) VI–338b
VBF (navy fighter–bomber) I–55a
VC. *See* Vietcong
Veatch, John A. (prospector) I–340a
VEAZIE BANK* v. *FENNO (1869) **VII–168a**
Veblen, Oswald (math.) II–155a; III–424a
Veblen, Thorstein (econ.) I–20a; III–424a
Vedanta Society V–171b
VE Day I–328b
Vedder, Elihu (paint.) V–190a, 191a, 192a
Vega (monoplane) I–51b
Vega (star) I–211a
Vegelahn v. *Gunther* (1896) II–110b
Vegetable gardens III–150b–51a
Vegetables III–52b, 53b, 54b; IV–255b
Vegetables, dried. *See* Dried Fruits and Vegetables
Vegetarianism I–125b; V–294a; VI–268a
VEHICLES, COLONIAL VII–168a; VII–99b
Veiller, Lawrence VII–24b
Veksler, Vladimir I. (phys.) IV–119b; V–301b
Velasco, Treaty of (1836) VII–38a–b
Velvet II–371a–b
Venable, James I–119a
Venables, Robert (off.) VII–270b
VENANGO (Pa.) **VII–168b**; II–381b; IV–130a,b
French post III–118a, 120a
garrison IV–250b
See also Franklin, Fort
Venango County (Pa.) IV–44a
Venegas, Miguel (cler.) III–27a
Venerable Society. *See* Society for the Propagation of the Gospel in Foreign Parts
VENEREAL DISEASE VII–168b; IV–306b
prostitution V–437b, 438a
sexual attitudes VI–266b–67a
World War I V–448a
Venezuela
Caracas Mixed Commissions I–452a
earthquake relief V–280b
Good Neighbor policy III–199a
iron ore III–12b; VI–281a–b
Miranda's intrigues IV–361b
oil industry IV–114a–b
rebels I–398b
United Nations Declaration VII–151b
U.S. trade VI–343b, 344a, 344b, 345a,b, 346a
VENEZUELA, BLOCKADE OF (1902) **VII–169b**; III–146b; IV–401a
VENEZUELA, PERRY'S MISSION TO (1819) **VII–170a**
VENEZUELA BOUNDARY CONTROVERSY VII–170a; I–122a, 439a; VII–134b
Monroe Doctrine IV–401a
Olney Corollary V–153a
Schomburgk line VI–226b
Vengeance (frigate). *See Constellation–Vengeance* Encounter
Venice (It.) III–106b
sea power VI–247b
Vening–Meinesz, F. A. (geol.) III–481a
Ventana Cave (Ariz.) II–334b; III–289a
Ventura County (Calif.) I–407a; II–348b
Venus
exploration III–502b
space missions I–210a
study I–212b
transit of I–110b; II–88a; V–130b
Veracruz (Mex.)
ABC Conference I–1b
Confederate expatriates I–455a
Cortes' expedition IV–326a
logwood trade IV–181b
Mexican War I–488b; IV–252a, 322a, 323b, 324a, 324b, 325a; V–19b
Santa Fe trade VI–215a
Spanish seizure IV–325b
VERACRUZ INCIDENT (1914) **VII–171a**; IV–328b; VI–104b
Verde River III–265b
Verdict of the People (paint.) V–190b
Verdigris River I–326a; II–34a; IV–199a
Verdun (Fr.) VI–197b
Vergennes (Vt.) IV–87a, 212a
Vergennes, Comte de, Charles Gravier (states.) II–208a, 318b; III–90a,b, 94b–95a,b, 306a
Franco–American alliance VI–119b
Natchez Indians IV–455b
Red Line Map VI–62b
Verhulst, Willem (col. gov.) V–60b
Verlé, Peter II–45b
Vermilion Iron Range III–473b; IV–357a
Vermillion River V–388b
VERMONT VII–171a; III–226b; IV–275b; V–49b; VI–395 (table)
birth and death registration IV–149a
black suffrage VI–431b

VERMONT (cont.)
boundary disputes I–351a; IV–92a
Champlain Canal III–312b
Civil War I–439a; VI–187a
coins I–483a
constitution VI–391b
dairy industry II–279b
Dummer's War II–380b
election of 1936 V–47b
fair-trade laws II–482b
farm prices V–404b
Fort Dummer II–380b
fourteenth colony III–87a
French and Indian War II–267a
Gore III–199b, 200a
grasshoppers III–212b
Haldimand negotiations III–240b
Hartford Convention III–259a
historical society III–278b
Hunters and Chasers of the Eastern Frontier III–318a
Jefferson–Burr election dispute III–495a
Lake Champlain IV–85b
legislature I–294b; IV–133b; VII–142a–b
maple sugar IV–246b
Masons I–132b
New Hampshire Grants V–53b, 54b, 88b
Onion River Land Company V–156a
osteopathy V–175a
pottery III–183b–84a
proposed British alliance IV–86b
railroads VI–25b, 32b
referendum VI–66b
revolutionary war III–311b
rivers VI–149a
secessionist movement VI–250a
Shays's Rebellion VI–272a
skiing VI–101a, 298a
slavery I–135b
statehood VI–400a
state university II–395b
suffrage III–91a,b
ungranted land V–443b
U.S. flag III–34b
voting behavior VII–210a
War of 1812 IV–212a
See also New England
Vermont (ship) VI–282a
Vermont, University of VII–156a
Vermont Gazette of Freeman's Depository (news.) V–70a
Vermont v. *New Hampshire* (1933) I–351a
Vernon (Tex.) II–358b
Vernon, Edward (nav. off.) III–498a
Verplanck, Gulian (law., legis.) VI–170a
Verplancks Point (N.Y.) IV–48a; VI–415b
Verplank, J. (off.) V–311a
Verrazano, Giovanni da (expl.) IV–247b; V–52b
Battery memorial I–275b
Cape Cod I–447a
Hudson River III–312a
Manhattan IV–237a
Narragansett Bay IV–451b
New York Bay I–96b; IV–452a
Rhode Island VI–131b
Verrazano, Hieronumus da (cartog.) IV–451b
Verrazano–Narrows Bridge I–364b; IV–452a
Verrill, Addison E. (zool.) IV–119b
Versailles (Fr.)
Peace of Paris V–214b
VERSAILLES, TREATY OF (1919) **VII–172b**; I–290b; III–457a; VII–330b–31a
congressional debate III–22a
Franco–American relations III–97a–b
freedom of the seas III–110a
Hitchcock Reservations III–285b
League of Nations IV–124a
Lodge Reservations IV–178a
mandates IV–236a
Reparation Commission VI–87b
reparations IV–117b
Russia VI–178b
Versailles Peace Conference
Pan-Africanism V–199b
Versailles Treaty (1783). *See* Definitive Treaty of Peace; Paris, Peace of
Vertical integration (bus.) I–389a
Vertue, George (critic) V–186a
Verville, Charles Gautier de VI–218b
Very high frequency channels III–1b
Vesey, Denmark (slave). *See* Vesey Rebellion
VESEY REBELLION (1822) **VII–174a**; I–23a, 28a, 497a; III–437a; VI–303b, 304a, 307a
Vesle River I–70b; V–147a
Vespucci, Amerigo (navig.) I–96a, 97a; IV–247a; V–130b
Vest II–371a,b
Vesta (yacht) VII–348b–49a
Vestal Gap V–224b
Vested interests. *See* "Interests"
Vestribygo (Green.) V–112b
Vestris, Mme. *See* Mathews, Lucia Elizabeth
Vetch, Samuel (off.) V–369b; VI–2b
Veterans
benefits I–13a, 108b, 331a–b; III–205a; VII–228 (table)
bonuses I–330b–32a
campaign of 1888 I–424a
congressional bloc I–322a
federal aid VI–327b
federal expenditures II–476a
GI Bill of Rights III–178b
land scrip IV–97a,b
Naval Home V–11b
revolutionary war I–12b
soldiers' homes VI–336a
World War I I–330a–b
VETERANS ADMINISTRATION VII–174b; I–13a; II–498b; V–257b–58b; VI–336b
hospital program IV–290b
loans I–376b–77a
national cemeteries I–478a
pensions II–277a
Veterans Bureau V–257a–b; VI–336b; VII–174b
Veterans of Foreign Wars VII–175a
Veterans of Future Wars VII–236b
VETERANS' ORGANIZATIONS VII–174b
American Legion I–108a
Grand Army of the Republic III–207b
National Tribune IV–471b
United Confederate Veterans VII–149b
United Daughters of the Confederacy VII–150b
Veteran's Readjustment Act (1952) I–331b–32a
Veteran's Readjustment Benefits Act (1966) I–332a
Veterinary College (Cornell Univ.) II–227b
Veterinary College of London VII–176a
Veterinary Corps, Army IV–290b
VETERINARY MEDICINE VII–175b
government regulation III–54a
livestock industry IV–170a
Tuskegee Institute VII–131a
University of Pennsylvania V–249a
Veto, royal, of colonial acts. *See* Royal Disallowance
VETO POWER OF THE PRESIDENT VII–177b; II–199b; III–3a, 484b; V–394a, 396a; VI–391a
legislative riders VI–138b
pocket veto V–334b
VF (navy fighter plane) I–55a
VFW. *See* Veterans of Foreign Wars
V.F.W. Magazine VII–175a
VHF. *See* Very high frequency channels
Vial, Pedro (expl.) VII–36a, 178b
VIAL'S ROAD VII–178b
Viburnum Trend (Mo.) IV–123a
Vice, Society for the Suppression of II–263b
VICE-PRESIDENCY VII–178b
District of Columbia electors VII–132b
election I–94b; II–171b, 194b–95a, 200b–01a, 204b, 409a–b
electoral votes II–412a
flag III–35b
impeachment II–202a; III–343b
nominating system V–101b
presidential disability V–397a,b
presidential succession I–95a; II–206b, 207b; III–351a; V–398b; VII–133a–b
qualifications II–205a
salary grab VI–198b
Secret Service VI–252b
Senate II–172b, 198b
Smithsonian Institution VI–319a
Twelfth Amendment VII–131b
two-thirds rule VII–135a
vacancies II–207b
Vick, Newitt (miss.) VII–181a
VICK ESTATE (Miss.) **VII–181a**
VICKSBURG (Miss.) **VII–181a**; II–319a
Afro-Americans I–25b, 29a
gambling III–149b
Southern Commercial Convention VI–352a
Spanish post VII–270a
Sultana disaster II–349a
Vick estate VII–181a
Waterways Experiment Station VI–147a
See also Walnut Hills
VICKSBURG IN THE CIVIL WAR VII–181b; II–22a, 62b, 63a, 295a; III–175b, 208b, 258b, 292a, 474b; IV–313b, 368b, 374a, 375a, 375a,b, 413b; V–19b–20a, 248a, 369a, 389a; VII–26b, 127b, 146b, 354a–b
Arkansas destruction I–173b
Battle at Big Black River I–295b
Battle of Champion's Hill I–492a
Battle of Jackson III–485b
Battle of Raymond VI–48b
capture I–502a–b; II–163a, 164b
Confederate surrender IV–85a
dummy battleships I–277a
Grant's siege I–279b
Grierson's Raid III–228a
Haines' Bluff III–238b
railroads VI–38a

Sherman's attack I–174a
Steele's Bayou expedition VI–410b
VICKSBURG RIOTS (1874) **VII–182a**
Victimless crimes II–259a; IV–19a
"Victor Charlie" VI–301a
Victoria (q.) I–438b; III–224a
Victoria (B.C.) I–76b; VI–214a; VII–166a
Victorian style furniture III–135b–36a
Victorio (Indian) I–142b, 310a, 313b; VII–239b
Victor of Japan V–290b
Victor Talking Machine Company V–290a
Victory, John F. IV–458a
Victory gardens II–50a; III–151a
VICTORY LOAN OF 1919 VII–182b; II–346a; IV–143a–b; VII–7a
Victory ships VI–279b–80a, 280b; VII–344a
Vidal, Gore (au.) IV–165a
Vieille, Paul (inv.) V–383b
Viele, Aernout (fur trader) V–143a
Vienna (Aus.) II–287a
International Exposition II–419a
medical education IV–284a
Strategic Arms Limitation Talks VI–417a
Vienna Convention on Consular Relations (1962) III–457a
Vienna Convention on Diplomatic Relations (1961) I–93a; III–457a
Vienna Convention on the Law of Treaties (1968) III–457a
Vienna Decree (1809) III–121b
Vienna Summit Conference (1961) VI–180a
Viereck, Peter (writ.) II–189b
Vierstraat Ridge (Belg.) VII–366b
Vietcong V–216a; VI–301a; VII–94a, 183a,b, 184a, 185a, 185b, 186a,b, 226a
Vietinghoff, Heinrich von (off.) III–201a
Vietminh
Geneva Accords of 1954 III–159b
Vietnam V–25a
fall of Dien Bien Phu III–70a
Vietnam, Democratic Republic of. *See* Vietnam, North
Vietnam, Laos, and Cambodia, Associated States of III–159b, 161a
Vietnam, North
embargo VII–94a
Geneva Accords of 1954 III–159b
International Court of Justice III–453a
U.S. Navy V–22a
Vietnam, Republic of. *See* Vietnam, South
Vietnam, South
Geneva Accords of 1954 III–160a–b
Southeast Asia Treaty Organization VI–350b
U.S. Navy V–21b–22a
Vietnam Era Veteran's Readjustment Act (1974) I–332a
Vietnamese Marine Corps IV–253a
Vietnam Veterans Against the War V–266a, 266a
VIETNAM WAR VII–182b; II–179a, 316a–b, 489a–b; III–3b, 70a–b, 348a, 463a,b; V–53a; VI–80a, 248b; VII–190b–91a, 192a
African–American relations I–22b
Afro-American troops IV–340b
air cavalry I–49a,b
aircraft IV–431b
aircraft carriers I–56a–57a, 56a,b
air force slang VI–302a–b
amnesty I–100b
Anglo–American relations I–124b
antiwar movement II–366a; IV–75a; V–237a–b; VI–14a; VII–118a, 237a, 246b, 366a
armored cavalry I–178b
army I–187a–b
army logistics I–190a
army slang VI–301a
atrocities I–219b; II–247a
aviation industry I 237b
balance of payments VII–90b
balance of trade I–246a
bombing I–328b; V–26b
booby traps I–332a
bunkers VII–115b
business cycles I–392 (table)
Cambodia I–411a, 411a–b
campaign of 1964 I–431a
campaign of 1968 I–431a–b; II–18b
campaign of 1972 I–432a
Canada I–439b–40a
censorship I–481b
chemical warfare II–9b
Coast Guard II–90a
cold war II–97b, 98b
collective security V–39a
conscientious objectors II–185b
conscription II–186b
Corps of Engineers II–450a
costs II–316b; VII–228 (table), 229a
declaration of war VII–224b, 227a,b
defoliation II–319a
demobilization II–324b
deserters I–115b; II–335b
"Doonesbury" comic strip V–72b
draft II–316b, 367b–68a; IV–384b; VII–208a
embargo VII–94a
federal deficit VI–449b; VII–222b
federal expenditures II–476a–b
financing II–317b
Franco–American relations III–97b
Geneva Conventions III–162a
guerrillas III–231b
gunboats III–235a
Hawks III–264b
helicopters I–188b; III–270b
Honolulu Conference III–297b
inflation I–391b; II–236b; III–415b
isolationism III–480a
labor's support IV–77a
Laos IV–107b
laws of war VII–226a
liberalism IV–141a
losses VII–232 (table), 233a
Manila Conference IV–239b
mines V–27b
missilery IV–363b
National Guard IV–341b
naval reserve V–29a
New Jersey V–26b
newspaper coverage V–74a–b
orphans V–281a
pacifism V–181a–b
paratroops V–213b
Paris peace talks V–216a
peace negotiations II–316b
Pentagon Papers III–105b; V–78b–79a, 258b; VII–254b
presidential war powers VII–237a,b
prisoner exchange II–469a
propaganda V–432b
public debt VI–294a
Quaker opposition V–470b
ranger companies VI–47a
recruitment VI–61a–b
refugees III–342b; V–342b
Reserve Officers' Training Corps VI–99a
rifles IV–430b; VI–140a
road construction VI–156a
snipers VI–270a
Southeast Asia Treaty Organization VI–350b
Soviet Union VI–180a
Strategic Arms Limitation Talks VI–417a
student protest VI–421a
Task Force 77 VII–2a
taxation VII–12a, 13b
Tonkin Gulf episode VII–71b
Tonkin Gulf Resolution VII–71b
underwater demolition teams VII–139a–b
Unknown Soldier VII–157a
U.S. foreign aid III–62a–b
U.S. Navy V–21b–22a
veterans I–108b, 332a
veterans' benefits V–257b, 258a
veterans' organizations VII–175a
warships VII–242a
withdrawal IV–344a
women VII–319a
wounded IV–290b
VIETNAM WAR, AIR FORCE IN VII–185a; I–62a–63a, 64a,b; VII–183b, 184b
bombing operations in North I–124b, 328b, 431a,b
bombing pauses IV–107b
mine planting IV–351b
reserves I–65a
VIETNAM WAR, MARINES IN VII–185a; IV–253a–b; VII–184a
VIEUX CARRÉ (New Orleans) **VII–187a**; V–62b
View From Apple Hill (paint.) V–190a
View From the Bridge (play) VII–50b
Vigil, Cornelio IV–110a
Vigilance Committee (Mass.) I–387a
VIGILANTES VII–187a; IV–68a; VI–253a
Anti-Horse Thief Association I–131b
cattle rustling I–474a
committees II–247a
cotton mill unionization IV–73a
Ku Klux Klan IV–58a,b
Loomis gang IV–187b
Montana IV–403a
Regulators VI–71b, 72a
Reno gang VII–97b
river gambling III–149b
San Francisco V–73b; VI–209b
Vigne, Jean III–315a
Vigneaud, Vincent du (chem.) I–303b–04a
Vigneulles-les-Hattonchatel (Fr.) VI–197b
Vigni, Saugrain de (writ.) III–122b
Vikings. *See* Norsemen in America; Vinland
Vilas, George H. VI–383a
Villa, Francisco (Pancho) (rev.) I–247a; IV–327b, 328a; VII–187b
Columbus raid IV–328b
Villa Americana (Braz.) I–360b
Village IV–102a
Village Hymns III–326a
Village of Euclid v. *Ambler Realty Company* (1926) II–47a; VII–370b
Villages, Indian. *See* Indian Villages
Village Voice (news.) V–79a

VILLA RAID AT COLUMBUS (1916) **VII–187b**; IV–327b, 328b
Villard, Henry (pub.) III–81a; V–71b
Villard, Oswald Garrison (ed., pub.) V–73b, 80a; VII–152b
Villasur, Don Pedro de (off.) VI–47b; VII–188a
VILLASUR EXPEDITION (1720) **VII–188a**; IV–379b
Villa Viscaya (Miami) IV–96b
VILLERE'S PLANTATION, BATTLE AT (1814) **VII–188a**
Villiers, George William Frederick, 4th Earl of Clarendon (states.) II–285a
VINCENNES (Ind.) **VII–188a**; II–356a; III–142b, 369b
Battle of Tippecanoe VII–63a,b
Fort Knox IV–53b
fur trade V–176a
Indiana Gazette V–70b
revolutionary war I–240a; II–71a–b; III–147b, 329a; IV–59b; VI–126b; VII–302b
Vincennes (ship) III–28b; VI–142a
VINCENNES, FRENCH DEFECTION AT (1797) **VII–189a**
Vincennes, Sieur de, François Marie Bissot (off.) I–197a; VII–188b
VINCENNES, TREATY OF (1803) **VII–189a**; III–383b
Vincent, Ambrose I–332b
Vincent, Jesse F. I–51a
Vincent, John (off.) VI–415a
Vincent, John H. (cler.) II–1a, 399b; VI–442b
Vinci, Leonardo da (paint., arch., sci.) III–481a
VINDICATION OF THE BRITISH COLONIES (tract) **VII–189b**
Vindicator (scout bomber) I–55a
Vinegar III–54b
Vines, Richard (col. gov.) III–200a; VI–184a; VII–114b
Vineyards III–477b
Vinita (Indian Terr.) I–214b
VINLAND VII–189b; IV–38a; V–112a
Vinland, Promontory of I–447a
Vinland Map V–112a; VII–190a
Vinland the Good I–95b
Vinson, Carl (pol.) VII–341b
Vinson, Fred M. (jur.) IV–14a; VI–446b
Vinson–Trammel Act (1934) VII–341b
Vinyl V–327b, 328a
Vinyl chloride VI–203a
Vinylite V–290b
VIOLENCE VII–190a; IV–151b
assassinations I–202a–03b
black suffrage VI–433a
Coeur d'Alene riots IV–66a
depression of 1873 IV–63a
feuds III–18a–b
Garrison mob III–153a
Gastonia riots III–154a
gun control IV–470a
Hamburg riot III–244a
Hatfield–McCoy feud III–262a
Haymarket Riot III–266a; IV–64b–65a
Herrin massacre III–274a
Homestead Strike III–297a; IV–66a
indemnities III–352a
Ku Klux Klan IV–58a,b, 59a
McNamara case IV–218b
miners strikes VII–272b
Molly Maguires IV–392a
Mooney case IV–406a
motion pictures IV–418b–19a
Mussel Slough incident IV–444a
organized crime II–261a
pacifism V–181a,b
Paxton Boys V–231a
Philadelphia riots V–279a
Pullman strike IV–67a; V–463b
race relations VI–7a–8a
race riots VI–8a
Railroad Conspiracy VI–20b
railroad strikes IV–64b; VI–38b
Red Shirts VI–65b
Regulators VI–71b, 72a
Rustler War VI–181b
Salt War VI–204a
schools II–402b
Stamp Act riot VI–382a
steel strikes IV–72b; VI–410b
Student Nonviolent Coordinating Committee VI–420b
syndicalism VI–455b
Tombstone VII–71a
Ursuline convent burned VII–160a
Vicksburg riots VII–182a
Wall Street explosion VII–222b
woman's rights movement VII–312b
See also Massacres
Violet (comic character) V–72b
Violet (flower) VI–395 (table)
Violin III–18b
Virchow, Rudolf (path.) V–273b
Vire River II–237a
Virgil (poet) II–455b
Virgin Birth of Christ VI–82b
VIRGINIA VII–192a; V–142a; VI–395 (table)
Acadians I–6a
Alexandria Conference I–85a; II–192b
American Colonization Society I–101a
Anglicanism VI–75a,b, 81a
Anglo–French rivalry III–115a
Annapolis Convention I–126a
antimiscegenation laws IV–362b
antislavery I–136a
apples III–128b
apprenticeship I–148a
archives I–168b
Articles of Confederation I–198a
assembly I–497a
Augusta Congress I–223a
backcountry I–239b–40a
Bacon's Rebellion I–240a; II–117a, 125a; III–436b
barbecue I–266b
beaver hats I–282a
Big Moccasin Gap I–297a
Bill of Rights I–298b
bills of credit I–300a
black suffrage VI 432a–
blast furnaces I–319a
Border Slave State Convention I–341b
border state I–341b
bossism I–343b
boundary disputes I–351b; II–274a; IV–263b
British debts I–366b; II–119a; VI–108b
Brown, John, trial VII–117b
buffalo I–375a
bushwhackers I–388b
cabin rights I–400b
capitol I–162b
Carolina settlers V–115a
Cartagena expedition I–461b
Cary's Rebellion I–465a
cattle I–37a, 471a; III–51b
Cherokee Wars II–14b; IV–186b
Chesapeake and Ohio Canal II–15b
Chickasaw Treaty II–23a
Chiswell's mines II–32b
Church of England II–36a
Civil War I–322b, 322b; II–231a, 373a; III–21a, 30b, 31a, 33a–b, 100a, 128a, 146a–b, 229a, 256a–b, 258a, 332b, 487a, 488a, 498b; IV–36a, 42a, 43b, 54a, 212b, 230b, 253b, 261b, 350a, 396b, 399b, 425a; V–59a, 113b, 245a–b, 248a,b, 264b, 369a–b; VI–47a, 137b–38a, 138a–b, 186b, 220a, 249b, 275a, 376a, 410a–b, 430b; VII–68a, 71a, 117a, 295b–96a, 301b, 304a–b, 358a
Antietam I–130a
Appomattox I–146b
Battle of Cross Keys II–266a
Battle of Fair Oaks II–482a
Belle Isle Prison I–287a
Blackburn's Ford I–309a
Boydton Plank Road I–357a
Brandy Station I–360a
Bristoe Campaign I–365a
Buckland Races I–374a
Bull Run I–381a–82a
Cedar Creek I–476b
Cedar Mountain I–476b
Chancellorsville I–493a
Dutch Gap Canal II–382b
Falling Waters skirmish II–484b
Sherman's march through Carolinas I–458b
supplies II–163a
Claiborne settlement II–70a
climate II–75b; IV–316b
coal mines II–85a, 86a
College of William and Mary II–395b, 396a; VII–300a
colonial assembly II–117a
colonial government I–204a
colonial governor II–120a
colonial lack of capital I–449a
colonial punishments V–465a
colonial suffrage VI–434a, 434a–b
colonial vehicles VII–168a,b
colonization I–16a; II–122b, 123b, 124b
committees of correspondence II–140a; VI–113b
commodities as money II–140b
constitution VI–390b, 391a,b
Constitutional Union party II–191b
courthouse towns II–45a
"crackers" II–253a
Crittenden Compromise II–265a
cruel and unusual punishment V–464a
Cumberland Gap II–272a
Cumberland Road II–273b
Cumberland settlements II–274a
Customs Service II–275b
dairy industry II–279b
Dale's Laws II–285a
Declaration of Independence II–308b
desegregation II–54b, 57b
Dismal Swamp II–353a
District of Columbia VII–132b
Donelson's line II–363a
Dunmore's War II–381a; V–335b
education II–470b; IV–116a
Emancipation Proclamation

II–434b
entail of estate II–452a
Fairfax proprietary II–481a
fall line II–485a
farm prices V–404b
Federalists III–4b
fencing laws III–10a
feuds III–18a
Fincastle County III–24b
First Families III–18b
fish III–26b
foreign trade VII–86a
Fort Henry V–31b–32a
Fortress Monroe IV–399b
free blacks IV–246b
Freemasons III–109a
French and Indian War III–219a–b
Friends of Domestic Industry III–124a
fugitive slave acts III–130a
furniture III–139b
fur trade III–141a,b
Gabriel's Insurrection III–145a, 437a
geological survey III–165a,b
Germanna III–173a
glebes III–186b
government I–290a
grandfather clause III–208b
Granville grant III–212b
Great Massacre III–219a
Great Trading and War Path III–223b
Greenbrier Company III–226a
Harpers Ferry raid III–256b, 437a
Heath Patent III–268a
Hening's Statutes III–271b
Heroes of America VII–149a
historical accounts III–280a,b
historical society III–278b
historic properties IV–472a
Holston Valley settlements III–292b
horse III–302b
horse racing III–304a–b
House of Burgesses II–117a
Huguenots III–121a, 315a
hundred III–317b
hurricanes II–352a; III–319b
Illinois III–329b
Illinois County III–331b
indentured servants I–21a, 26b
Indiana settlers III–369b
Indian factory III–380b
Indian land cessions III–251a, 382b; VI–385b
Indian lands IV–173a
Indian raids II–382a
Indians VII–65b
Indian trade VII–201b
Indian treaties IV–89b
Indian Treaty at Pittsburgh V–322a
inns VII–2a
Irish tract III–469b
iron II–163a; III–12a; V–409b; VI–376a
Iroquois Treaty III–476b
James River and Kanawha Canal III–448a, 488a–b
James River settlement II–123b
Jamestown III–488b
Jamestown Exposition III–489b
Jesuit missions III–498b, 499a
justice of the peace IV–22b
Kentucky IV–40a, 42b; VI–400a; VII–276a
Kentucky County IV–43a
land bounties IV–91a
land grants II–481a–b; IV–92a
land speculation IV–98b, 201a
land tenure IV–102b
lead industry IV–122a
legal tender IV–132a
liquor laws IV–158b
literacy test III–92b
lottery IV–190b
Loyalists IV–200a; VI–115b
mapping I–462a; IV–247b; VII–73b
Maryland boundary agreement III–459b
McDonald's Expedition IV–212a
migration from IV–338b
military bounties IV–92a
Military District VII–273a
military tracts IV–344b
militia IV–345b
mineral observations IV–348a
minimum-wage law IV–353b
Missouri settlers IV–377a; VI–194a
Monongahela River IV–398b
Mount Vernon IV–423a
national parks and monuments V–217b, 218 (table)
Nat Turner's Rebellion III–437a; V–4b
Natural Bridge V–5a
natural history V–325b–26a
Norfolk V–109b
Norsemen VII–190a
North American Land Company V–113a
North Carolina commerce V–115b–16a
Notes on the State of Virginia III–26b–27a
nullification V–125b
Ohio IV–181b; V–140a,b
Ohio Company of Virginia V–144a
Ohio Valley V–146a
Old Dominion V–151a
Old Southwest VI–356a
Parson's Cause V–221b
Pennsylvania boundary dispute I–223b–24a; III–250a; V–253a; VII–281b
petroleum V–269a
pioneers V–316b
pistole V–320b
plantations III–52a; V–324a, 324b, 325a
Plowden's New Albion V–332b
poll tax I–22b; V–355a; VII–133a
population enumerations VII–205b
port authority V–368a
postal service V–371a
potash V–375b
potatoes V–376b
Potomac River V–378a; VII–82b
pottery V–379a,b
Powell's Valley V–384b
Powhatan Confederacy V–385b
presidential electors I–416b
price-fixing V–401b, 402a
prices V–404a
primogeniture V–408a
provincial convention V–321b, 439b, 440a
public land states V–453a
public ownership V–455a
public schools II–396a
Quakers V–469b
quitrents VI–4a
railroads VI–25a, 25a, 33a, 35a, 36b, 38a
Raleigh Conference of Southern Governors VI–42b
Readjuster movement VI–49a
Reconstruction III–295a; VI–56a, 57b, 58b
religious liberty VII–69a
Republican party VI–337b
revolutionary war I–194a, 385a; II–15a, 251a; III–117b–18a, 215b, 232a, 236a, 308a, 400b; IV–8b, 48a; V–109b, 322b; VI–116b, 124b, 125a, 137a, 351b; VII–360a–61b
rice VI–135b
Richmond VI–136b
Richmond Junto VI–138a
Rip Raps contract VI–145a
roads VI–152b; VII–99b
royal colony VI–166a
royal disallowance I–145a
Ruffner pamphlet VI–168b
Saint Croix expedition VI–189a
saline wells VI–409b
Scioto Trail VI–239b
Scotch-Irish VI–240b
secession I–341b; II–61b; VI–251a–b
separation of powers V–385a
settlement V–333b–34a, 342a; VI–149b; VII–95a
sheep III–51b; VI–272b
Shenandoah Valley VI–275b
Sic semper tyrannis VI–285a
silver mining VI–292a
slave insurrections VI–303b
slavery I–21a, 26b, 27b, 28a, 36b; II–212b, 495a; IV–79a; VI–304b, 305a,b, 309a
smuggled goods V–320a
Somers' voyage VI–338a
Spanish colonization IV–302b
Spanish exploration III–38a
Spotswood's expedition IV–53a
state bill of rights I–300b
state debts VII–230b–31a
State of Franklin III–98b
steam navigation III–32a
suffrage III–91a
sumptuary laws VI–440a
Syms-Eaton School II–395a,b
taxation VII–3a
Tennessee settlement VII–25a
Thanksgiving Day VII–46a
theater VII–46b
tobacco IV–308a; VI–341a, 386a; VII–66b, 67a
tobacco as money VII–65b, 66a
tobacco warehouses VII–67b
toll roads III–450b
tornadoes VII–75b
trans-Appalachian territory IV–39b
transportation IV–428b
Transylvania III–87a
Transylvania Company III–271b; VII–103a–b
Tredegar Iron Works VII–113b
turnpike VII–69b
Tuscarora War VII–130b
Twin Oaks commune II–142b
Two Penny Act I–145a; VII–135a
Union sentiment VI–354a; VII–148b
U.S. Constitution II–192b, 193a,b, 196b, 198b, 203b, 478a; VII–111a
usury law III–443a
Vandalia Colony VII–166b
veterinary medicine VII–175b
Virginia and Kentucky Resolutions VII–198a
Voting Rights Act of 1965 VII–211a
War of 1812 VII–235b
Washington, D.C. VII–244b, 245b
Washington and Lee University VII–249a
Watauga settlement VII–253a
western lands II–166a; III–331a, 370b–71a, 496b–97a; IV–260b; V–162b, 205b, 443b; VI–356a; VII–202a, 273a,b, 274a

VIRGINIA (cont.)
West Virginia VI–400a–b; VII–203a–b, 281a–b
westward movement VII–260a, 283a,b
wheat VII–286a
Wilderness Road VII–296a
Williamsburg VII–301a–02b
winemaking VII–305a
witchcraft VII–310a
wolf bounties VII–311b
writs of assistance VII–345a
Yamasee War VII–352a
Yorktown VII–360a
zinc VII–369a
Virginia (col. ship) I–319b
Virginia (ironclad) II–163a; III–474b; V–29b; VI–44b
See also *Merrimack*
Virginia (ship of the line) VI–282a
VIRGINIA (steamboat) **VII–196b**; III–468a; IV–356a
VIRGINIA, ARMY OF VII–197a; III–267a
VIRGINIA, ARMY OF NORTHERN VII–197a; III–101a; VII–195a
VIRGINIA, UNIVERSITY OF VII–197b; II–396a; VII–156a
architecture I–163a; III–495a
history collection III–285a
Jefferson's influence II–398a
parapsychology V–213b
Virginia, Valley of II–381a; III–469b
VIRGINIA AND KENTUCKY RESOLUTIONS (1798, 1799) **VII–198a**; I–87a, 87a, 404b, 417a; III–9a; IV–40b; V–125b, 328b, 353a; VI–250a, 397a, 404b
Virginia Beach VII–196a
VIRGINIA CAPES, BATTLE OF (1781) **VII–198b**; VII–361a
Virginia–Carolina Chemical Company II–8b
Virginia Central Railroad I–325b; VII–117a
Virginia City (Mont.) IV–403a
gold I–84a, 357b; III–32a
stagelines VI–379b
VIRGINIA CITY (Nev.) **VII–199b**; V–68a
Bozeman Trail II–477b
Comstock Lode II–156b; III–191b; V–39b
silver mining I–329a, 336a
Sutro tunnel VI–452b
Virginia City–Corinne Road IV–403a
Virginia Commonwealth University VII–300b
VIRGINIA COMPANY OF LONDON VII–199b; I–16a, 319a, 499b, 500a; II–469b; III–62b, 132a–b; IV–37a, 116a; V–333b, 436b; VII–94b, 95a
charter I–204a, 292b; II–122b
Council for New England II–242a
dissolution II–138a
Heath Patent III–268a
ironworks III–472a
Jamestown III–488b, 489a; VI–341a; VII–192b, 193a
New Plymouth Colony V–65a
Old Dominion V–151a
patent II–122b
Pilgrims V–313a
plantation system V–324b
Plymouth colony IV–278b
Sandys–Southampton group II–117a
Somers' voyage VI–338a
tobacco contract VII–66a
winemaking VII–305a
Virginia Company of Plymouth. *See* Plymouth, Virginia Company of
VIRGINIA DECLARATION OF RIGHTS (1776) **VII–201a**; I–297b, 298b; II–247b; VII–193b–94a
VIRGINIA DYNASTY VII–201b; I–417b; VII–194a
VIRGINIA EXILES VII–201b
Virginia Garrison Regiment VII–302b
VIRGINIA INDIAN COMPANY VII–201b
VIRGINIA MILITARY RESERVE IN OHIO VII–202a; IV–91a, 344b, 345a; V–140b
Virginia Mountains II–157a
Virginia Museum of Fine Arts (Richmond) III–137b
Virginian Railroad IV–177a; VI–32a, 35a
VIRGINIAN RAILWAY COMPANY* v. *SYSTEM FEDERATION NO. 40 (1937) **VII–202a**
Virginian's Plan of Union II–121b
Virginia of Sagadahoc (ship) V–359b
Virginia Pass V–225a
VIRGINIA PATH VII–202b
Virginia Plan II–151b, 183a, 193b–94a
VIRGINIA RESOLUTIONS (1847) **VII–202b**
VIRGINIA RESOLVES VII–202b
Virginia Slims tennis circuit VII–30b–31a
Virginia State Army VI–126b
Virginia State Navy V–29b
Virginia Statute for Establishing Religious Freedom (1786) I–298b
VIRGINIA* v. *TRANSYLVANIA COMPANY (1778) **VII–203a**
VIRGINIA* v. *WEST VIRGINIA (1915) **VII–203a**
Virgin Islands Corporation VII–204a
Virgin Islands National Park V–220a
VIRGIN ISLANDS OF THE UNITED STATES VII–203b; I–126b, 454a; III–347a,b, 425a,b; VII–32b, 34a
acquisition II–475b; VII–112a
citizenship V–6a
logwood trade IV–181b
National Governors' Conference III–206b
national parks and monuments V–217b, 219 (table)
naturalization of citizens II–42b
***VIRGINIUS* AFFAIR** (1873) **VII–204a**; V–22b; VI–360a
Virgin River III–215a; V–384a; VI–368a; VII–256a
Virology I–240b–42b
"Virtue, Liberty, and Independence" (motto) VI–395 (table)
Virtue et armis (motto) VI–394 (table)
Virus IV–389a
DNA study II–358a
genetic material III–158a
Viscose rayon II–9a
Viscount Melville Sound V–122a
VISIBLE ADMIXTURE LAW (1859) **VII–204b**
"Visible saints" II–169b–70a
Vision of Life (paint.) V–190a
Vision quest II–283a; III–366a,b, 368a, 384b–85a, 392b; IV–50b, 236a
VISIT AND SEARCH VII–204b
impressment of seamen III–349b
neutral property V–34b
neutral rights V–38b
slave ships VI–353a
slave trade VI–311a
Visiting Guild for Crippled Children III–248b
VISTA. *See* Volunteers in Service to America
Visual Flight Rules II–346b
VITAL STATISTICS VII–205a
army medical department IV–291a
demography II–328a
life expectancy IV–149a
public health V–446b, 447a,b
research IV–285b
Vitamin A I–303a; IV–3b; V–128a
Vitamin B I–303a
Vitamin B–complex I–303b; V–128a
Vitamin B–6 V–128a
Vitamin B–12 V–128a
Vitamin D I–303a–b; IV–3b; V–128a,b
Vitamin E V–128a
Vitamins I–303a
See also Nutrition and Vitamins
Vitriol II–5a,b
Vittum, Harriet VI–330b
Vivekananda (swami) V–171b
Vivian, Grey and Company III–65a
Viviani, René (states.) I–246b
Viviparous Quadrupeds of North America IV–232b; V–413b
Vizcaíno, Sebastián (expl.) I–405a, 456a, 466b; VI–244b
San Diego VI–208a
Vizcaya (ship) VI–216b
VJ Day I–57a
Vladivostok (USSR) I–158b, 180b; II–316a; VI–283b–84a, 417a
Vlieland III–243a
Vocational education II–393b, 395b, 399a, 400b, 405b
Vocational Education, Federal Board for VI–318a
Vocational Education Act (1963) II–400b
Vocational rehabilitation II–502b
Vocational Rehabilitation, Office of III–267b
Vocational training I–5b
agriculture I–47a
Indians III–380b; VI–83b
mechanics' institutes IV–281b
reformatories VI–67b
Voice (Jewish news.) V–75b
VOICE OF AMERICA VII–207a; III–350b; V–432b
Voight, Henry (watchmaker) III–32a,b
Voit, Carl von (physiol.) I–302b, 303a
Volaperta, Giuseppi (art.) VII–262a
Volcano Islands III–485a
Volkswagon (auto) I–229b; VII–84b, 90a
Volleyball
Olympic Games V–154a
Volney, Comte de, Constantin F. de Chasseboeuf (scholar) III–122a
Volpe, John IV–268a
Volstead, Andrew J. (pol.). *See* Volstead Act
VOLSTEAD ACT (1919) **VII–207b**; I–339b; II–407a; IV–261a; V–429b
Volta, Alessandro (phys.) I–276a; II–413a; VII–18b
Volta Bureau III–248a
Voltaire (philos., au.) V–415a; VI–267b
Volta Laboratory V–289b
"Voluntariness" test (law) IV–361b–62a
Voluntary military companies. *See* Military Companies, Voluntary

Volunteer (merchantman) V–424a
Volunteer Air Reservists I–65a
Volunteer fire fighting III–25a
VOLUNTEERS VII–207b; II–316b; IV–346a
Civil War I–182a, 182a–b; II–161b, 186a, 302b, 313b; IV–383b; VII–264a
colonies II–450b
demobilization II–323b, 324a
draft II–366a
enlistment II–450b
Mexican War II–313b
military policy IV–343b
recruitment VI–60b
reenlistment VII–232b
Spanish–American War II–314a; VI–361b
Terry's Texas Rangers VII–34a
U.S. Army I–183a–85b, 187a, 188a
women VII–318a
World War I II–314a; IV–83b
Volunteers in Service to America I–8b; V–135b; VI–328b
Appalachia I–144b
Volunteers of Ireland VI–130a
Volunteer State VI–395 (table); VII–25b
Volvo (auto) I–229b
Vonore (Tenn.) VII–25a
Voodoo (fighter plane) I–54a
Voormezeele (Belg.) VII–366b
Voree (Wis.) VI–416b
VOS. *See* Scout observation aircraft
Vose, Robert C. (art dealer) II–102a
Vose Gallery II–102a
Voss, Gunter VII–371a
Vostok (satellite) IV–406b
Vostok Project I–210a
VOTER VII–208a
eighteen–year–olds VII–133b
franchise III–90b
manuals II–408b
nonvoting V–108b
political parties V–343a
presidential election II–409a–b
qualifications II–410a
Voters, registration of. *See* Registration of Voters
VOTING VII–209a; II–324b, 325b
Afro–Americans II–205b
age requirements I–95a; II–55b, 208a, 325b
civil rights movement II–58b
corruption V–346b
discrimination II–55b, 457b
election laws II–408a, 408a
Fifteenth Amendment I–94b; II–53b, 205b, 205b; III–20a
Force Acts III–59b
freedmen I–94b
government inspection III–422a
Indians I–385b
Jim Crow practices II–56b
League of Women Voters IV–125a
literacy tests IV–160a
Massachusetts IV–269a–b
Mississippi IV–368b
Nineteenth Amendment II–206a
party machine IV–213b
political emblems II–437b
polls II–410b–11a
poll tax V–355a; VII–133a
preferential V–390a
property qualifications V–434b
referendum VI–66a
registration VI–71a
repeating VI–88a
residency requirements VI–99b
statistics III–284a
Twenty–fourth Amendment II–207a–b
Twenty–sixth Amendment II–208a
women I–95a, 95a
See also Ballot; Franchise
VOTING, EDUCATIONAL TESTS FOR VII–209b; III–92b, 93a–b; IV–159b–160a; VII–211a
VOTING BEHAVIOR VII–209b; VII–208b–09a
nonvoting V–108b
opinion polls V–454a
party machine IV–213b
referendum VI–67a
registration VI–71b
third parties VII–53a
VOTING MACHINE VII–210b; I–249a; II–408b, 410b; IV–214b; VII–209a
VOTING RIGHTS ACT OF 1965 VII–211a; I–32a, 415a; II–55b, 56a, 59a, 325b, 408a, 472b; III–20a, 92a, 93a–b, 438a; VI–328b, 337b, 433a, 435a; VII–208b, 209b, 209b
backlash I–239b
congressional debate III–22a,b
literacy tests IV–160a
Voting Rights Act of 1970 I–415a; II–55b, 408a; VI–71a; VII–133b
Vought–Sikorsky Aircraft I–54a, 55a,b, 57a
Voyage a l'Quest des Monts Alléghanys, dans les États de l'Ohio, du Kentucky et du Tennessee, et Retour a Charleston par les Hautes Carolines III–122b
Voyage dans les États–Unis d'Amérique, fait en 1795, 1796 et 1797 III–122a
Voyage en Icarie III–327a
Voyage of Life (paint.) V–189a
Voyages (Champlain) IV–247b
Voyages dans l'Amérique Septentrionale dans les Années 1780, 1781 et 1782 III–122a
VOYAGEURS VII–211b; II–246a; III–142b, 403b
Grand Portage III–209a
Green Bay III–226a
half–breeds III–242b
Jesuit missions III–499b
Jolliet and Marquette expedition IV–7a
Missouri River IV–379b
North West Company V–121b
Pemmican V–244b
Prairie du Chien V–387b
Voyageurs National Park V–219 (table)
VP. *See* Patrol plane
Vrindaban commune II–142b
VSB. *See* Scout bomber
VSO. *See* Scout observation aircraft
VT (torpedo planes) I–55a
Vulcan (cannon) I–49b, 57b
Vulcan (Mich.) IV–303b
Vulcanite II–331a
Vulcanization VI–167a
Vulte Company I–237b
Vulture (ship) I–118a–b
Vyatka (riv.) I–158b–59a

W

W2XBS (television station) VII–21b
W3XK (television station) VII–21a
WAAC. *See* Women's Army Auxiliary Corps
Wabash (Indians) II–265b; III–144a
WABASH AND ERIE CANAL VII–212a; III–374b, 449a,b
Toledo VII–68b
Wabash Land Company III–331a; IV–98b
See also Illinois and Wabash Company
Wabash Railroad VI–32a, 35a
Wabash River II–265b, 477a; III–24b; V–145a
British boundary V–214b
canal III–374b
Cave–in–Rock I–476a
Charlotina I–499a
Fort Harrison III–257b
Fort Ouiatenon V–176a
Fort Recovery VI–60b
Fort Washington VII–247a
Fort Wayne VII–262a, 263a
French settlement V–146a
fur trade III–141b
Indian campaigns VII–212b
Indian land cessions VII–189b, 262b
"Pocket" V–334b
portage V–367b
Prophet's Town V–435a
revolutionary war IV–59b
salt VI–202a
Vincennes VII–188a–b
Wabash and Erie Canal VII–212a
Wabash, Saint Louis and Pacific Railroad Company v. *Illinois* (1886) II–135b; III–210a, 458a; V–457b; VI–21b, 28b
WABASH TOWNS, EXPEDITIONS AGAINST (1791) **VII–212b**
Wabash Valley III–227b
Wabeno IV–335b
WAC. *See* Women's Army Corps
Waccamaw River I–497a
WAC Corporal (rocket) III–502a
Wachita River. *See* Ouachita River
Wachovia (N.C.) I–293a; V–379a,b; VII–350a
***WACHUSETT* AFFAIR** (1864) **VII–212b**; III–40b
Wachusett Mountain IV–47b
Waco (Tex.) VII–37a
Balcones escarpment I–246b
Camp MacArthur I–434b–35a
Nolan expeditions V–101a
railroads VI–36b
tornado VII–76a
Torreys' trading post VII–77a, 96a
Waco Indians I–286a
Waddell, Hugh (off.) I–73b
Waddell, James (nav. off.) VI–274b
Waddell, William B. (bus.) VI–176b
Waddell family (Va.) III–469b
Waddie (cowboy) II–251b
Wade, Benjamin F. (pol.) II–139a, 140a
See also Wade–Davis Bill
Wade, J. F. (off.) I–142a
WADE–DAVIS BILL (1864) **VII–213a**; VI–11a, 55b–56a, 58b
Wade–ins I–31a; II–58a
Wadsworth (Nev.) III–215a
Wadsworth, James S. (law.) IV–99b
Wadsworth, Joseph (col.) II–182b
WADSWORTH AGREEMENT (1923) **VII–213a**
Wadsworth Athenaeum (Hartford, Conn.) II–289a; III–137b
Wadsworth charter II–183a

Wadsworth family IV–99a
WAF. *See* Women in the Air Force
Wage and Hour Division (Labor Dept.) II–482a
Wage–Hour Act. *See* Fair Labor Standards Act
Wages and Hours Bill (1938) II–481b–82a
WAGES AND HOURS OF LABOR, REGULATION OF VII–213a; III–3a, 204b; V–401b, 402a
Adamson Act IV–68b
colonial controls IV–60a–b, 79b
commerce clause II–137a
cost of living II–236a–b
eight-hour-day IV–63a
Fair Labor Standards Act II–481b; IV–78b, 80b; V–48a–b
Greenback party III–224b–25a
laissez-faire doctrine IV–85b
Lochner v. *New York* IV–173b
minimum-wage legislation IV–352b
National Industrial Recovery Act V–44b; VI–457a
National Recovery Administration II–481b; IV–469a,b
New Deal I–391a; IV–71b
Nixon administration I–431b
occupational medicine IV–293a
productivity studies V–425b
Progressive movement V–428b
Railroad Administration VI–19b
Railroad Labor Board VI–29b
Railroad Mediation Acts VI–21a
reduction of hours IV–80a
Schechter Poultry Corporation v. *United States* VI–225a
Seamen's Act of 1915 VI–246b
state laws IV–68b
sweatshop VI–454a
ten-hour day IV–61b, 62a
Walsh–Healy Act VII–223a
West Coast Hotel Company v. *Parrish* VII–269a
World War I VII–232b
World War II III–415a; V–255b–56a
WAGES AND SALARIES VII–214b; IV–61a,b
checkoff II–3a–b
Civil War IV–62b
collective bargaining II–110a–12b
colonial ministers V–221b
colonial period IV–79b
Congress VI–198b–99a
Consumer Price Index II–236b
industrial jobs IV–104a
inflation III–414a
Kansas VII–311a–b
labor force V–133a
merchant marine IV–312a
minimum wage IV–352b
New Deal IV–71a,b; V–46a,b
New Era V–52a
New York State V–87b
Nixon administration VI–472a
panic of 1873 V–207b
panic of 1929 V–209a, 209b
plantation overseer V–178b
political assessments V–341b
post–World War I IV–69b
post–World War II IV–74a
profit sharing V–426b
radicalism VI–13b
railroads VI–30a, 31b–32a, 38b
revolutionary war VI–120b
Social Gospel movement VI–325a
strikes VI–418b
sweatshop VI–453b
taxation VII–12a
wage boards I–12a
Works Progress Administration VI–73b
World War I VI–467b
World War II IV–73b
See also Minimum–Wage Legislation
Wagner, Robert, Sr. (pol.) VI–460a
Wagner, Robert F. (pol.) II–472b; IV–71b
Wagner Act. *See* National Labor Relations Act
WAGNER BATTERY, SIEGE OF (1863) **VII–215b**; IV–339b
Wagner–Connery Act (1935) IV–72a,b, 74a
See also National Labor Relations Act
Wagner–Crosser Railroad Retirement Act (1935) V–47a; VI–24a
Wagner–Ellender–Taft bill VI–86a
Wagner–Jauregg, J. (neurol.) IV–306b
Wagner–Peyser Act (1933) II–442a; IV–78b
WAGON BOX FIGHT (1867) **VII–215b**; IV–33b; VI–317b
WAGONERS OF THE ALLEGHENIES VII–216a
WAGON MANUFACTURE VII–216b; I–461a; III–413b
Conestoga VII–100a
prairie schooner V–389b
Wheeling VII–288a
Wagon master V–177a,b
Wagons IV–419a–b
freighting V–177a–b
westward movement I–452b
WAGON TRAIN CHARGE (1874) **VII–217a**
WAGON TRAINS VII–217a; I–452b–53a; VII–284b
Council Bluffs II–241b
Council Grove II–242b
Mountain Meadows massacre IV–421b
Oregon caravans V–166a, 169a
overland companies V–176b
overland freighting V–177a
Pawnee Rock V–230b
roads VI–156a
Santa Fe Trail VI–215a,b
Sioux wars VI–297a
water supply VI–377b
WAGON YARD VII–218b
Wahpekute (Indians) II–283a
Wahpeton (N. Dak.) VI–63b
Wahpeton Indians II–283a; III–383b
Waicuri–Pericue (Indians) III–363a
Waiilatpu (Wash.) I–476b; VII–293b
Waiilatpu Mission (Wash.) VII–221a
Wainwright, Jonathan M. (off.) I–274a; V–284a
Wainwright Building (Saint Louis) VI–299a
Waistcoat II–371a
Waite, Ezra (arch.) I–162a–b
Waite, Frederick C. (educ.) IV–283a
Waite, Merton B. (bact.) I–46a
Waite, Morrison R. (jur.) V–456b; VI–445b
WAKARUSA WAR (1855) **VII–218b**; I–342a; IV–28b; VI–270a
Wakashan (lang.) IV–228b
Wake (is.) II–475b; III–425a
WAKE, DEFENSE OF (1941) **VII–218b**; IV–253a; VII–336b
WAKEFIELD (Va.) **VII–219a**
Wakefield National Memorial Association VII–219a
Wakeman, Stephen H. I–333a
Waksman, Selman A. (microbiol.) V–100a
Walapai (Indians) III–262a, 369a
Walcott, Charles D. (paleon.) IV–106a; V–196a; VI–319a
Walcott, "Jersey Joe" (pugilist) V–423a
Wald, George (biol.) V–100a
Wald, Lillian D. (social worker) IV–275b; V–280a; VI–330b
Waldeck (Ger.) III–172b
Walden IV–162a
Walden, Elisha. *See* Walling, Elisha
WALDENSES VII–219b
Walden Two II–142b
Waldersee, Alfred von (off.) I–356a
Waldo, Peter (heretic) VII–219b
Waldo, Samuel (off., col.) VII–219b
Waldoboro (Maine). *See* Broad Bay
WALDO PATENT VII–219b
Waldorf Bar (N.Y.C.) VI–201b
Waldseemüller, Martin (geog.) I–96a, 97a; IV–247a,b
Wales
colonial trade II–453a
immigration to U.S. III–334b
tennis VII–29a
Wales, R. W. (nav. off.) V–238b
Walgreen Company VI–258b
Walke, Henry (nav. off.) I–459a
Walker, Dan (pol.) III–330a
Walker, David (abolitionist) I–28a
Walker, Edwin A. (off.) I–207a–b
Walker, Felix (pol.) I–383a
Walker, Francis Amasa (educ., econ.) I–482a; III–342a–b
Walker, Frank (offi.) II–446a
Walker, George C. (pol.) VI–12b
Walker, James J. (pol.) VI–460a
Walker, Joseph (av.) I–52b
Walker, Joseph R. (trapper) III–215a; VII–217b
See also Walker Expedition
Walker, Leroy Pope (law.) II–160a
Walker, Mickey (pugilist) V–423a
Walker, Robert H. (hist.) I–112a
Walker, Robert J. (pol.) IV–31a, 376a
Walker, Ronald H. (offi.) V–220b
Walker, Stanley (writ.) VII–41a
Walker, Thomas (physic., expl.) II–272a,b; IV–201a–b; V–384b; VII–238b
Kentucky IV–39b
Tennessee VII–25a
Walker, Thomas B. (lumberman) II–103b
Walker, W. H. (off.) IV–55b
Walker, William (adventurer) III–23a–b; IV–199b
Nicaragua V–94a
Walker, William H. (cameramaker) V–291b
Walker Act (1846) VI–466b
WALKER EXPEDITION (1833–34) **VII–220a**; I–330a; II–477b; VI–262b; VII–271b
Yosemite VII–361b
Walker Lake II–477b; III–215a; VII–220a

Walker River III–215a
Walker's Pass I–330a; II–477b; V–225a; VII–220a
Walker Tariff (1846) V–170a; VII–303b
WALKING DELEGATE VII–220b
WALKING PURCHASE VII–220b; III–123a, 382a; VI–270b–71a
Walking Treaty (1686) III–382b
WALK-IN-THE-WATER (steamboat) **VII–220b**; II–459a; IV–331a; VII–83b
Wall, David (pioneer) III–477a–b
Wallabout. *See* Brooklyn
Wallabout Bay III–498b; V–418b
Wallace (Kans.) VII–221a
Wallace, Davidson, and Johnson V–241b
WALLACE, FORT (Kans.) **VII–221a**
Wallace, George C. (pol.) I–72a
American Independent Party I–106b; VII–52b
attempted assassination I–203b, 432a
backlash I–239b
campaign of 1968 I–431b; IV–70a, 77a; VI–93b
Democratic party II–327b
Louisiana IV–195a
radical right II–189b
Wallace, Henry A. (pol.) II–134b; V–48a
campaign of 1944 I–429b
campaign of 1948 I–30b, 429b; II–146a, 480b; V–429a
New Deal V–43b, 44a–b
vice-presidency VII–180 (table)
Wallace, Henry C. (pol.) VI–378b
Wallace, Lew (off.) IV–398a; VI–275a, 278b
Wallace, Tom (jour.) IV–41a
Wallace, William ("Bigfoot") (frontiersman) VII–39a
Wallace, William H. L. (off.) VII–221a
Walla Walla (Wash.) III–477a; IV–426a
Walla Walla, Fort (Wash.) IV–403a; VII–221a
Oregon Trail V–169a
Walla Walla River VII–221a
WALLA WALLA SETTLEMENTS VII–221a; VII–248a
Whitman massacre VII–293b
Whitman mission I–476b; II–131b; V–167a
Walla Walla Valley
Indian treaties VI–412b
Yakima Wars VII–350b
Wall–Blackburn gang VI–379b
Wallboard IV–204b
Walleye (missile) IV–363b
Walling (Walden), Elisha (frontiersman) IV–185a
Walling, Henry Francis (cartog.) I–462b
Walling, William English (jour.) IV–460b
Wallingford (Conn.) II–147a; V–155b
Wallis, Frank E. (au.) II–99b
Wallkill Valley
Walloons VII–221b
WALLOONS VII–221b; III–121a, 312a
Fort Orange I–81b
New Amsterdam III–315a
New Netherland V–60b
New York Colony V–82a
Wallops Island (Va.) IV–458b
Wallowa Mountains V–165b
Wallowa Valley (Oreg.) V–89b
WALL STREET (N.Y.C.) **VII–221b**; III–189b; IV–237b
campaign of 1912 V–428b
gold exchange III–190a
regulation V–347a
WALL STREET EXPLOSION (1920) **VII–222b**
Wall Street Journal (news.) V–68a, 76b, 78a
Wallula (Wash.) VII–221b
Walnut Bayou II–94a
Walnut Canyon V–217b
Walnut Creek VII–238b, 368a
Walnut Grove (Pa.) IV–363a
Walnut Hills (Miss.) III–232b; IV–456a; V–100b
See also Vicksburg
Walnuts III–51a
Walnut Street jail (Phila.) V–415a
Walpi (Ariz.) III–300b
Walpole, Horace (au.) VI–112a
Walpole, Thomas III–208b
Walpole Company I–278b
Walpole Grant. *See* Grand Ohio Company; Vandalia Colony
Walpole Society II–100b
Walrus I–84a; III–208a; IV–233a; VI–182a
Walrussia (Alaska) I–75b
Walsenburg (Colo.) II–129a
Walsh, Frank P. (pol.) III–83b
Walsh, Thomas F. (miner) VI–213b
Walsh, Thomas J. (pol.) IV–403b; VII–16b
WALSH-HEALEY ACT (1936) **VII–223a**; IV–71b, 353b
Walter, Henry (rr. exec.) II–104a
Walter, Thomas Ustick (arch.) I–163a, 451a
Walter–Logan bill V–472a
Walter Reed Army Institute of Research IV–291b
Walters, William T. (bus.) II–102b, 103b
Walters Art Gallery (Md.) IV–261b
Waltham (Mass.) IV–266b
Boston Manufacturing Company IV–272b
federal records center III–284b
gardening III–151a
Lowell mill IV–61a–b
textiles I–345b; III–411b; VII–44b
Waltham Watch Company I–224b; II–78b
Walther, Carl F. W. (theol.) IV–206b
Waltomsac River I–289a
Walton, Ernest (phys.) II–278a; V–301a
Walton, G. (au.) IV–168b
Walton, George (law.) II–308a
Waltz II–290b
Walvis (ship) VII–372b
Walworth, Clarence (cler.) V–229b
Wampanoag (Indians) IV–47a–b, 264b
WAMPUM VII–223a; II–94b; III–365b; V–318b
Abnaki I–2b
as money IV–392b
fur trade III–140b
Iroquois III–475b
Wanamaker, John (mer.) I–17a, 18b; III–80b; VI–172b
Wanamaker's III–423a
Wanborough (Ill.) II–450b
Wanderbird (ship) I–448a–b
WANDERER (ship) **VII–223b**
Wanghia, Treaty of (1844) II–27a, 275a–b, 488a
Wankel engine I–229b
Wansey, Henry (trav.) I–68a, 367b
Wanting (China) IV–314a
Wanton, Joseph (col. gov.) VI–132b
Wapatomica (Indians) II–381b
Wapiti III–484b
WAPPINGER CONFEDERACY VII–223b
War
government regulation of business I–449b
logistics IV–180a
propaganda V–431b–32b
WAR, DECLARATION OF VII–223b; VII–226b–27b, 237a–b
congressional power II–171b, 195b, 200a, 313a
Japan V–240a
Ludlow Resolution IV–203a
Mexican War IV–323b
president II–171b
Spanish–American War VI–360b
War of 1812 VII–234a
World War I VII–325b
World War II VII–335a
WAR, LAWS OF VII–225a
confiscation of property III–343a–b
Declaration of Panama V–200a
Geneva Conventions III–161b
Hague peace conferences III–237a; V–233b
Kellogg–Briand Pact IV–36a
neutrality V–33b
neutral rights V–38b
regulation IV–342b
retaliation VI–104a
Rule of the War of 1756 VI–169a
submarines VI–424a
treason VII–106b
Treaty of Washington VII–249a
war crimes trials VII–229b
War, prisoners of II–468a
War, secretary of I–189b; II–139b, 166a
WAR AMENDMENTS VII–226b
War and National Defense Act (1917) II–463a–b
WAR AND ORDNANCE, BOARD OF VII–226b
WAR AND THE CONSTITUTION VII–226b
War atrocities. *See* Atrocities in War
War bonds I–257a,b; VII–8b
WAR BONNET CREEK, FIGHT ON (1876) **VII–227b**
Warburg, Felix (banker) III–79b
Warburg, James (fin.) V–45a
Warburg, Paul M. (banker) III–79b
War casualties
military medicine IV–290a
War Chronicle VII–332b
War claims
German–American debt agreement III–172a
Mexican War IV–325a
War Claims Acts (1948, 1962) II–169a
War Claims Commission IV–446b
War College, Army I–190b–91a
War College, National. *See* National War College
War Contracts Price Adjustment Board II–499b
War correspondents V–71a–b, 74a
WAR COSTS VII–228a; II–234a, 317a, 476a
American Revolution VI–120b
French and Indian War VI–110a
Korean War IV–56b
Philippine Insurrection V–282b
Spanish–American War VI–362b
taxation VII–7a
thrift stamps VII–56a

WAR COSTS (cont.)
Victory loan of 1919 VII–182b
Vietnam War VII–185a
World War II IV–134a; VI–449b; VII–8a,b
War crimes I–219a–b
WAR CRIMES TRIALS VII–229a; VII–226a
Homma, Masaharu I–274a
human rights III–317a
Malmédy massacre IV–230b
Nuremberg VI–424b
Ward (destroyer) V–239b
Ward, Artemas (off.) VII–251a,b
Ward, Holcombe VII–29b
Ward, John Quincy Adams (sculp.) VI–243b
Ward, Lester (off., soc.) V–196b
Ward, Lynd K. (art.) VII–319b
Ward, Montgomery (mer.) I–17b
Ward, Nathaniel (law.) IV–271a
Ward, Samuel (col. gov.) VI–132b
Ward, Samuel Ringgold (abolitionist) I–136b
War debts III–205a
balance of trade I–245a
Thomas Amendment VII–54b
World War I VII–331b
WAR DEMOCRATS VII–229b
Warden, Frew and Company VI–383a
WAR DEPARTMENT VII–229b; I–383b; II–498a; VI–122b; VII–226b
aircraft contracts VI–425b
air force I–59a
arbitrary arrest I–196a
army administration I–183b, 184a
army logistics I–189b
army supply I–184b; V–375a
blacks I–30a–b
Brownsville affair I–372a
Bureau of Indian Affairs III–371a,b
burial procedures I–478a
Chesapeake and Ohio Canal strike IV–61b
Civilian Conservation Corps II–51a
Civil War I–182a,b; II–63a, 67a, 68a–b, 451a
Colorado River exploration II–129b
discretionary power I–12a
Freedmen's Bureau III–103a
General Order No. 100 VII–225a
Indian affairs III–389a
Indian wars I–184a,b
loyalty testing IV–202b
mapmaking I–463a,b
Marcy's exploring expedition IV–249a
martial law IV–259a
military intelligence III–439a
military reserve II–367a
national parks and monuments V–217a
naval affairs V–17b
Office of Strategic Services V–138b
pensions I–12a
Purple Heart II–312b
railroad surveys VII–74b, 272a,b
Red River raft VI–65a
river and harbor improvements VI–146a
Signal Corps VI–285b
U.S. Military Academy IV–341a
veterans' pensions VII–174b
War Industries Board VII–232a
Weather Bureau I–45a
World War I I–101b, 186a
World War II VII–335b
Wright brothers I–233a
Warder, Bushnell and Glessner Company III–454b
WARD LEADER VII–230b
Wards, political V–344b–46a
Ward's Island IV–237a
Warehouse Act (1871) II–430b
WARE* v. *HYLTON (1797) **VII–230b**
Warfare, guerrilla III–231a–b
Warfare, psychological. *See* Psychological Warfare
Warfield, Benjamin B. (ed.) VI–82b
WAR FINANCE CORPORATION VII–231a; III–201b; V–111b; VII–328a
Warhawk (fighter plane) I–53a
WAR HAWKS VII–231a; III–350a; V–34b, 63a; VII–137a, 233b, 234a
campaign of 1812 I–418a
Canada I–438b
Kentucky IV–40b
War of 1812 I–436b
Warheads II–316a; V–163b
Warhol, Andy (art.) V–193a
WAR INDUSTRIES BOARD VII–231b; I–390b; V–44b; VII–326a, 327b, 328a
appliance industry II–418b
Council of National Defense II–243a
price controls V–401b
War Information, Office of II–499a; V–138a, 432b; VII–333b, 336a
WAR LABOR BOARD VII–232a; I–153a; IV–69a
shop committees VI–282b
steel strikes VI–410b
WAR LOSSES VII–232b; VII–190b
disease IV–291a
Korean War IV–56b; V–21b
Philippine Insurrection V–282b
Spanish–American War VI–362b
Vietnam War VII–182b, 185a, 187a
World War I V–20a; VII–327a–b
World War II V–20b
War materials. *See* Munitions
War Memorial Opera House (San Francisco) VI–209b
Warming, Eugen (bot.) II–391b
Warmouth, H. C. (gov.) IV–336a
Warms, William (nav. off.) II–349b
Warm Springs (Ga.) III–77b; V–340a
Warner, A. J. (pol.) VI–288a
Warner, Charles Dudley (au.) III–180b; IV–162b
Warner, Harry M. IV–417b
Warner, Olin L. (sculp.) VI–243b
Warner, Seth (off.)
Battle of Bennington I–289a–b
Battle of Hubbardton III–311b; VII–171b
Burgoyne's invasion I–385a
Crown Point II–267a
Green Mountain Boys III–226b
Warner, Thomas (inv.) III–442a
Warner, William (off., pol.)
Sioux Council VI–295b
Warner Brothers IV–418a; V–292b
Warner engine II–345a
Warnerke, Leon V–291b
Warner's Pass V–224b
Warner Theater (N.Y.C.) IV–418a
War of Austrian Succession (1740–48) III–115a; IV–46b
See also King George's War
WAR OF 1812 VII–233a; I–120b; II–313a–b; III–67b–68a
Afro-Americans IV–339b
Albatross I–83a
Algiers I–266b; II–303a
Argus–Pelican engagement I–170a
armed merchantmen IV–313a
armor plate I–179a
army uniforms VII–144a,b
artillery I–199b
Astoria I–209a
balance of trade I–245a
Battle at Maguaga IV–224b
Battle at Villere's Plantation VII–188a
Battle of Baltimore I–249b, 250b
Battle of Beaver Dams I–281b
Battle of Bladensburg I–317b
Battle of Chateaugay I–501b–02a
Battle of Lacolle Mill IV–82a
Battle of Lake Borgne I–342a; V–63a
Battle of Lake Erie II–458b, 459a; V–262b; VII–266b–67a
Battle of Lundy's Lane IV–204b
Battle of New Orleans I–342a–b; V–63a
Battle of Plattsburgh IV–87a; V–330b
Battle of Queenston Heights I–316b, 436b; VI–3a
Battle of Sandy Creek VI–209a
Battle of Stoney Creek VI–415a
Battle of the Thames VII–45b
Black Hawk I–311b
black powder V–383a
Black Rock bombardment I–316b
Blue Lights I–325b
bounties I–353a
British orders in council V–162a
Buffalo (N.Y.) I–375b
campaign of 1816 I–418a
Chesapeake–Leopard incident II–16a, 247a
Chesapeake–Shannon fight II–16a, 16a, 364a
conscription II–186a
Constellation–Vengeance encounter II–190b
Constitution–Cyane and *Levant* engagement II–191b
Constitution–Guerriere engagement II–191b
Constitution–Insurgente encounter II–190a
Constitution–Java engagement II–192a
costs VII–228 (table)
Craney Island Battle II–253b
Creek Indians II–52a
Dartmoor Prison II–292a
declaration of war VII–237a
demobilization II–323b
Demologos II–329a
desertion I–114b; II–335a
Detroit II–338a–b
enemy trading VII–93b
Enterprise–Boxer engagement II–452b
Essex II–463b
Essex Junto II–464a
exchange of prisoners II–468b
financing II–317a
floating batteries III–36a
foreign trade VII–87a
Fort Armstrong I–180b
Fort Bowyer I–356a
Fort Clark II–71a
Fort Dearborn II–297a
Fort Erie II–458a
Fort Fayette II–497a
Fort George II–458a; III–167b

Fort Madison IV–219b
Fort McHenry IV–213b
Fort Meigs IV–300b
Fort Miami IV–329a–b
Fort Osage V–173b
Fort Schlosser VI–226a
Fort Stephenson VI–208b, 412a
Fort Stoddert VI–414b
Fox–Wisconsin Waterway III–89b
Franco–American relations III–96b, 462a
free navigation of Mississippi IV–374a
free ships, free goods III–110a
French Creek action III–118a
French Mills III–120b
fur trade I–105a; III–144a; V–180b; VI–357b
General Armstrong III–155a
Great Lakes III–216b, 217a,b, 217b–18a
Green Bay III–226a
guerrillas III–231a
Gulf of Mexico IV–326b
gunboats III–234a–b
Hampden expedition III–247b
Hartford Convention VI–404b
Hornet–Peacock engagement III–301a
Hornet–Penquin engagement III–302a
hospitals I–191b
Hull court–martial III–315b
Hull's escape from Broke's squadron III–315b
Illinois III–329b
impressment III–350a; V–400a
Indiana III–369b
inflation III–414b
internal improvements VI–145b
isolationism III–480a
Kentucky support IV–40b
Lake Champlain IV–87a, 212a
land bounties IV–91a, 344b–45a
Lewes bombardment IV–135b
logistics I–189b
losses VII–232 (table)
Louisiana IV–193b
Loyalist veterans VI–130b
Mackinac IV–217b
Manitoulin Islands IV–240a
marine corps IV–251b
martial law IV–258b
Martin v. *Mott* IV–259b
Maryland IV–261a
Michigan IV–331a
militia IV–343b, 345b–46a
Mobile IV–382a, 383a; VI–359b
mobilization IV–383b
mutiny IV–445b
nationalism V–176b
Navy Department V–17b
New England I–347a; IV–266b; VI–253b, 397a
New Orleans I–490b
New York City IV–452a; V–83a
New York State V–86b
Niagara campaigns V–90b
Northwest garrisons IV–355b
ocean shipping III–428a
Ogdensburg V–139b
Ohio V–141a
Ohio Valley V–146a; VI–149b
opposition III–5a, 259a; V–235a
Oswego V–175b
Pass Christian V–224a
Peacock–Epervier engagement V–238b
Pensacola V–254b
pensions V–257a
Peoria V–260b
piracy V–320a
Pittsburgh V–322a
port cities II–41a
Prairie du Chien V–388a
President V–393b
privateers IV–256a; V–419a, 423b–24a
prize money V–423b–24a
profiteering V–426a
public debt II–299b; VI–294a
purchasing power IV–393a
Raisin River massacre VI–42a
rangers VI–46b
riflemen VI–269b
rockets VI–159a
Russia V–233a; VI–177b
Sackets Harbor VI–183b
Saint Lawrence River VI–192b
saltpeter II–5b
sea power VI–248a
sectionalism VI–342a
Shawnee VI–270b
Sioux treaties VI–295b–96a
sloops VI–313b
specie payments I–255a
"Star-Spangled Banner" VI–387b
Stonington bombardment VI–415a
submarines VI–422b
tariff VI–463a, 465a
taxation VII–5a, 12b
Tecumseh's crusade VII–18a
Tennessee VII–25b
textile industry III–411b
trade III–118b
treaties VII–111b
Treaty of Ghent III–176b
trenches VII–115a
"Uncle Sam" VII–137a
United States VII–153a
U.S. Army I–183b–84a
U.S. flag III–34b
U.S. Navy V–19a
U.S. neutral rights V–34b, 38b
U.S. shipping IV–309b
U.S. trade I–497a
veterans IV–97a
volunteers VII–208a
voyageurs VII–212a
war hawks VII–231a
warships VII–240a,b, 243b
Washington, D.C. I–249b, 250b, 451a; VII–249b
Washington Benevolent Society VII–249b
Washington Navy Yard V–29b
Wasp VII–252b
whiskey distillers II–353b
Wilkinson's Montreal expedition IV–406a
Wisconsin VII–307b
wool industry VI–272b
Yankee VII–352a
York VII–358b
See also Canada and the War of 1812
War of Jenkins' Ear. *See* Jenkins' Ear, War of
War of the League of Augsburg (1689) VII–291b
War of the Pacific (1879–83). *See* Nitrate War
War of the Roses IV–224a
War of the Spanish Succession (1701–14) VI–2a
War on Poverty I–309b; II–147b; V–135b, 382a; VI–328a,b, 331a
WAR OPPOSITION ORGANIZATIONS VII–236a; VII–365b, 366a
Civil War IV–5a
conscientious objectors II–185a
labor's attack IV–77a
peace movements V–235a
Quakers V–470b–71a
radicals VI–14a
Students for a Democratic Society VI–421a
Vietnam Veterans Against the War V–266a
Vietnam War VII–118a
War paint III–12a
War Powers Act (1941) V–74a; VII–335a, 336a
War Powers Act (1942) VII–336a
War Powers Act (1973) VII–224b, 227b, 237b
WAR POWERS OF THE PRESIDENT VII–237a; II–171b, 178b–79a, 472a–b; III–3b; V–394a–b; VII–226a–27b
congressional limitations II–179a
declaration of war VII–223b
Emancipation Proclamation II–434b
enemy–alien property VII–94a
enemy aliens II–445a
Ex parte Merryman IV–314b
Ex parte Milligan IV–346b
invasion II–202b
lend–lease IV–135a
Lincoln, Abraham V–421a–b
national defense II–313a
proclamations V–425a
railroads VI–38a
Roosevelt's seizure of coal mines IV–73b
World War I VII–327b
War Prizes. *See* Prize Cases, Civil War; Prize Courts; Prize Money
War Production Board VII–336a
War profits tax VII–7a
Warp yarn II–239a
Warrants
See also Arrest
Warrants, land. *See* Land warrants
War Relief Control Board V–281a
Warren (Pa.) V–367b
Warren (R.I.) I–372a; V–439b
Warren (ship) VI–128b
Warren, Abel (trader) VII–238b
Warren, Earl (jur.) III–349a; VI–447a,b
apportionment I–244b
Bill of Rights I–300a
Brown v. *Board of Education of Topeka* V–353b
California governor I–408a, 409a
citizenship II–54a
civil liberties IV–14a
due process clause V–184b
Erie rule II–460b
freedom of the press III–105a
Kennedy assassination I–202b; IV–38a; VII–238a
separate–but–equal doctrine II–57a
vice–presidential nomination I–429b
Warren, Fort (Mass.) V–414a; VII–115b
WARREN, FORT FRANCIS E. (Wyo.) **VII–237b**
Warren, Francis E. (pol.) VII–238a
Warren, George F. (econ.) III–192a; IV–234a; V–45a
Warren, Gouverneur IV–350a
Warren, Gouverneur K. (off.) I–357a, 365a; VI–276a, 376a
Warren, Henry E. (inv.) II–79b
Warren, John B. (nav. off.) VII–235a
Warren, John C. (surg.) I–119a
Warren, Joseph (physic., off.) I–382b, 383a; V–152a
Revere's ride VI–106a
Suffolk Resolves VI–430b
Warren, Josiah (anarchist) I–116b
Warren, Lyman (fur trader) II–13b
Warren, Mercy Otis (writ.) III–280b
Warren, Peter (nav. off.) IV–192a
Warren, Robert Penn (au.) IV–41a

Warren, Truman (fur trader) II–13b
Warren, William A. (sheriff) I–287a
Warren Association I–265a
Warren Bridge Company I–496a
WARREN COMMISSION VII–238a; I–202b; IV–38a
Warren County (Miss.) VII–182a
Warren County (Ohio) IV–421a; V–279b
Warren County (Va.) VII–196a
Warren Court I–408a
civil liberties IV–14b
Warren Plan. *See* Gold Purchase Plan
Warren Report (1964) VII–238a
Warrensburg (Mo.) I–317b
WARREN'S TRADING POSTS VII–238b
Warrenton Pike III–229a
War Resisters' International VII–236b
Warrington, Lewis (nav. off.) IV–416a; V–238b
"Warrior" (mule) IV–425b
Warrior (sloop) V–56a
Warrior River VII–70b
WARRIORS PATH, GREAT VII–238b; II–272a; VI–239b
War Risk Insurance, Bureau of II–277a; III–428b
WARS AND CAMPAIGNS, INDIAN VII–239a; II–313b; III–127a; VI–6a; VII–190b
Adobe Walls I–15a
Apache I–142a,b
army I–184a, 184b, 185a, 185a, 190b, 192a,b, 192a,b
army posts I–192b
army slang VI–300b–01a
artillery battalion I–199b
Astoria I–209a
atrocities I–219a
Bacon's Rebellion I–240a
Baker's Cabin massacre I–244a
Bannock I–264b
Battle of Ayubale I–238b
Battle of Bear River I–281a
Battle of Cabusto I–402a
Battle of Mississinewa IV–367b
Battle of Pierre's Hole V–310b
Battle of Tippecanoe V–435a
Big Bottom massacre I–296a
black cavalry I–310a
Black Hawk War I–242b, 311b; III–468a; VII–307b
Black Hills War I–313a; II–283b; IV–167b; VI–312b
black infantry I–314a
Boonesborough I–337a
bounties I–352b–53a
Brodhead's Allegheny campaign I–369a
Bryan's Station I–373b
Camp Grant massacre I–433a
Cayuse War I–476a; VII–293b–94a
Cherokee Wars II–14b; IV–186a–b
Chickasaw I–7b
Chickasaw–French War VII–25a, 70b
Conestoga Massacre V–231a
Crazy Snake Rebellion II–254a
Creek War I–232a, 387b; II–256b; III–278a, 305b, 366a; IV–456a
Cresap's War II–257b
Croghan's expedition II–265a
Dade Massacre II–257b
Dakota tribes II–283a
Deerfield Massacre II–312b
Delaware Prophet II–322b
De Soto expedition II–336b
Devil's Hole II–339b
Dodge–Leavenworth expedition II–358b, 358b
Dull Knife Campaign II–379b
Dummer's War V–111b
Dunmore's War I–499a; II–381a; V–335b
Dutch–Indian War II–382b
Falling Creek massacre III–472a
Federalist party III–4b
Forman's massacre III–77b
Fort C.F. Smith VI–317b
Fort Jefferson III–494a
Fort Laramie IV–108a
Fort Loudoun VII–25a
Fort Nisqually V–97b
Fort Randolph VI–45b
Fort Saint Clair VI–188a
Fort Washington VII–247a
French expeditions III–124b–25a
Grattan incident III–213a–b
Great Massacre III–219a
Great Plains III–221a
Great Swamp Fight VI–132a
guerrillas III–231a
gunboats VI–148a
Gunnison massacre III–235a
guns III–399b
Harney expedition III–256a
horse cavalry I–475a, 476a
Indian Bureau I–192a,b
Indian Key Massacre III–381b
Jesuit missions III–499b
Kentucky I–325a
King Philip's War I–380b; III–223a; IV–47a, 387a; V–53b, 439a; VI–132a
Leavenworth expedition IV–129b
Maine IV–226a
Mangas Coloradas wars IV–236b
Messiah War I–243a; IV–316a; VII–344a–b
Miami Trail IV–330a
Mille Lacs IV–346b
Modoc War IV–384b; VII–127a–b
Mountain Meadows massacre IV–421b
Navaho V–9a–b
New England I–465b, 466a
New Hampshire V–53b
New Netherland V–61a–b
Nez Perce I–281a, 296a; V–89b
North Carolina I–447b; V–115a
Ohio V–140b–41a
Oyster River Raid V–179b
Parker's Fort V–216b
Pawnee Rock V–230b
peace commissions III–378a
peace treaties III–404a
Pequot War V–261a
Piegan War V–310a
Pima Revolt V–314b
Plains Indians I–190b; III–363b, 364a–b
Platte Bridge fight V–330a
Pontiac's War I–323b, 353b, 353b, 359a; II–322b, 337b–38a, 392b; III–330a–b; IV–329a, 330b; V–231a, 356b, 399b
Powhatan Confederacy V–386a
Pueblo Revolt V–460b
Raleigh's first colony VI–43b
Red Cloud's War III–17b
Red River War VI–64a
Rogue River War V–165b
Saint Clair's defeat VI–188b
Saint Francis raid VI–190a
Sand Creek massacre VI–208a
Santa Fe Trail VI–215b
scalping VI–224a
scouts VI–241b–42a
Seminole Wars I–184a; III–88b, 462b; V–147a–b, 231b; VI–259b–61b; VII–311a
Sheridan's Washita operations VII–252b
Sioux I–283a,b, 358a; VI–296b
Sioux–Chippewa War IV–31b; VI–294b
Sioux Minnesota uprising IV–356b; V–81a; VI–295a, 296a; VII–319b
South Carolina VI–347a, 349b
South Platte route VI–355a
Spirit Lake massacre VI–374a
Squaw Campaign VI–378a
Sullivan–Clinton campaign IV–354b; VI–437b
Sully's Dakota expedition IV–45b
Sumner's Cheyenne expedition VI–439b
Tecumseh's crusade V–141a; VII–17b, 63a–b
Texas VII–36b, 38b, 42a
Tippecanoe VII–63a–b
Tuscarora War I–458a; VII–130b
Venango VII–168b
veterans I–331a; V–257b
Virginia III–489a
volunteers VII–208a
Wabash Towns VII–212b
Wagon Box fight VII–215b
Wagon Train charge VII–217a
War Bonnet Creek VII–227b
War of 1812 I–375b; II–35a, 71a, 255b, 297a, 338b
Washington Territory VI–412b
Wayne campaign II–458b, 484b; III–227b, 369b, 375b; VI–60b; VII–262b
Whitman massacre V–167a; VII–293b
Winnebago War VII–306a
Wounded Knee II–283b; VII–344a
Yakima Wars VII–350a
Yamasee War I–458a; VII–352a
York attack VII–358b
Zwaanendael Colony VII–372b
See also French and Indian War
War savings certificates VII–56a
Warsaw (Ill.) II–406a
Warsaw Pact (1955) III–69b; V–114a; VI–179b
War Settlements Act (1928) III–172a
War Shipping Administration VII–344a
WARSHIPS VII–240a; I–13b; IV–431b–32a; V–25a–26a
Alliance I–89a–b, 290b
Apia disaster I–144a
armament V–26a–27b
Battle of Santiago VI–216b
capital I–54a–b
Confederate navy V–17a; VI–44b
Continental navy VI–128a
Demologos II–329a
dreadnought II–369b
dry docks II–375a
Emergency Fleet Corporation III–438a
Exeter III–492b
Fast Carrier Task Force VII–1a–2a
figureheads III–21b
Five–Power Naval Treaty

III–33b
floating batteries III–36a
Florida III–40b
Fulton III–131b
Geneva Three–Power Naval Conference
III–160b–61a, 162a
Georgia III–169b
gunboats III–234a
Hartford III–258b
Houston III–492b
Intrepid III–464b
ironclads III–474b
ketch IV–44b
Lawrence IV–118b
Lexington IV–136b
London Naval Treaty (1930) IV–183a; VII–341b
London Naval Treaty (1936) IV–183b
lumber IV–204a
Michigan III–475a
monitors IV–397a
mortars IV–413b
Nautilus V–8a
naval competition V–10a
Naval War With France V–15a
navy yards V–29a
Neutrality Act (1935) IV–430a
New Ironsides V–56a
North Sea mine barrage V–119b
Oregon V–165b
Perth III–492b
President V–393b
Princeton V–408b
prize money V–423a
Shenandoah VI–274b
ships of the line VI–281b
Spanish–American War VI–361a,b
submarines VI–422b
Tennessee VII–26a
Texas navy VII–38a, 41a
torpedo warfare VII–76a
Union navy VII–147a
United States VII–153a
visit and search VII–205a
War of 1812 III–217b–18a
Washington Naval Conference VII–250b, 341b
Wasp VII–252b
"White Squadron" VII–293a
Willing VII–302b
World War I VII–328a–29a
World War II VI–279–80a; VII–334b, 339a, 343b
Yankee VII–352a
See also Aircraft Carriers; Battleships; Cruisers; Destroyers; Ironclad Warships Frigates; Submarines
"War time" II–296b
WAR TRADE BOARD VII–243b; VII–94a, 327b
Warville, Jean Pierre Brissot de (jour.) III–122a
Warwick (Pa.) VII–165a
Warwick (R.I.) II–117b; III–153b; VI–131b
See also Shawomet
Warwick (Va.) I–194a
Warwick, Earl of. *See* Rich, Robert, 2nd Earl of Warwick
WARWICK COMMISSION VII–244a; II–122b; IV–207b; VII–244a
Warwick Patent. *See* Connecticut, Old Patent of
Wasatch Mountains II–477b; III–214b; VI–203b
exploration VII–271b
irrigation III–477a
Mormon migration IV–411b
Old Spanish Trail VII–217b
Spanish Trail V–224b
Washakie (Indian) VII–244b
WASHAKIE, FORT (Wyo.) **VII–244a**
Washburn, Cadwallader C. (ind.) III–43b
Washburn, Captain (trapper) VII–105a
Washburn, Henry Bradford, Jr. (adm.) IV–437b
Washburn, Crosby and Company I–488a; III–44a
Washburne, Elihu B. (pol.) IV–6a
Washing machines II–417a,b, 420a, 420b
Washington (battleship) VII–242a
Washington (Ga.) II–294b
Washington (Jefferson's proposed state) III–497a
Washington (La.) I–461b
WASHINGTON (Pa.) **VII–244b**
Washington (ship of the line) VI–282a; VII–240b
Washington (steamboat) IV–374a; VI–148b, 408a
Washington, Augustine (planter) V–409b; VII–219a
Washington, Booker T. (educ.) I–309b; V–93a, 217b; VII–130b
Washington, Bushrod (jur.) I–101a; V–420b; VI–445a
WASHINGTON, D.C. VII–244b; I–208b
Afro–Americans I–25b
apartment houses I–143a
architecture I–162b–63a
arsenal IV–432b–33a
Baltimore and Ohio Railroad VI–25a
Bonus Army I–330a,b; V–257b
Border Slave State Convention I–341b
Bureau of Indian Affairs III–371b
Bureau of Standards IV–462b
burning I–250b
Camp Ordway I–435a
Catholic University of America I–468b
charitable institutions I–404a
chemistry education II–10b
civil rights movement II–56b, 58b; V–1b
Civil War I–381a,b, 382a; II–450a, 482b; III–78b, 487b; IV–261b, 398a; V–245a, 248a, 377a,b; VI–150a, 275a, 276a; VII–197a
commission rule II–319b
Constitution Hall II–294a
Corcoran Gallery II–103a
Coxey's Army II–252b; V–208a
DeGolyer Case II–319b
directory II–343b
Dominicans II–362b
Dulles Airport II–347b
Dumbarton Oaks IV–96b
Evangelical Alliance II–465b
fairs II–244b
fair–trade laws II–482b, 483b
federal mint IV–359b
Federal Reserve System III–5a
Folger Library II–109b
Forest Service III–76b
Gallaudet College III–248a; VI–327b
gambling III–149b
Genius of Universal Emancipation III–162b
Hirshhorn Museum and Sculpture Garden II–106a
homeopathy III–293b
inauguration of president III–350b
Indian protests I–106b
Indian treaty commission VI–317b
industrial armies IV–36a–b
inter–American conferences V–171a
International Monetary Fund III–457b
Interstate Commerce Commission III–458a
Japanese cherry trees III–491b
Kossuth's visit IV–57b
Lafayette's visit IV–84a
L'Enfant's plan II–45b, 46a, 338b
Library of Congress IV–146a
Lincoln Memorial VI–243b
Loyal Leagues IV–201b
National Academy of Sciences IV–457b
National Association of Manufacturers IV–461b
National Institute for the Promotion of Science IV–464b
National Labor Relations Board IV–467b
National Museum IV–468b
National Trust for Historic Preservation IV–471b
National Woman's Party VII–312b
natural history museum I–305a
Nautical Almanac Office V–12b
Naval Observatory V–12a, 13a
Naval Research Laboratory V–14a
navy yard V–27b, 29a,b
newspaper coverage V–71a
Office of Strategic Services V–138a
Old Capitol Prison I–466a–b
Organization of American States IV–112b
Pan–American Union IV–111b; V–205a
Potomac River V–378a
public transportation IV–428b
pure food and drug law V–465b
racial violence IV–46a
Railroad Administration VI–19b
railroads III–450a; IV–177a; VI–31b, 33a, 36a, 37a; VII–102b
"Resurrection City" IV–259b
riots I–31b–32a
School of Advanced International Studies IV–3b
Smithsonian Institution VI–318b
snowstorm I–320b
Soldiers' and Airmens' Home VI–336b
Students for a Democratic Society march VI–421a
subway III–451b; VI–429b
suffrage III–92a
telegraph VII–18b
temperance movement III–261b
territorial government II–319b
theater VII–50b
underground railroad V–239a
Union prison V–414a
urban renewal VI–86a,b
Vietnam War demonstrations V–237a,b
voting rights VII–132b
War of 1812 III–234b; VI–159a; VII–249b
Washington Monument VII–250a
Watergate VII–253b
water supply VII–259a
weather forecasts VII–264a
weather research laboratory II–76a
White House VII–291b
zinc industry VII–369a
WASHINGTON, FORT (N.Y.) **VII–246b**; IV–131b
WASHINGTON, FORT (Ohio) **VII–247a**; III–232b, 244a, 255a, 494a; IV–330a; VI–188b, 188b; VII–262b
Washington, George II–174 (table); III–26a, 47b, 51a, 315a; V–372b, 392b, 395 (table); VI–44a, 123a, 137a, 145b, 149b, 275b, 451a; VII–168b, 193b,

WASHINGTON, GEORGE (cont.)
194a, 221b, 250a, 262a
agricultural experiments I–46a
Alexandria Conference I–85b
Antifederalists I–131a
biographies III–281a
Burning Spring patent I–387a
canal proposals I–40a
cherry tree story I–494a
code of behavior IV–240b
communism II–144b
constitutional convention III–354a
estate I–175b
"Father of His Country" II–497a
Federalist party III–4a,b
Franco-American misunderstanding III–96a
Freemasons III–109a
gardening III–151a,b
Illuminati of New England III–332a
James River Company III–488a,b
landholdings II–353a
land speculation IV–98b
library I–333a; II–109a
lotteries IV–190b
Masons I–132a
Mazzei letter IV–279b
Miranda's intrigues IV–361b
Mount Vernon IV–96b, 423a; V–130a
mules IV–425b
Nemacolin's Trail VII–244b
New York residence I–368b
on dueling II–377a
on study abroad II–470b
Potomac Company V–378a
Rights of Man VI–141a
Saratoga Springs VI–217b
Society of the Cincinnati II–38a
statues VI–242b, 243a, 246a
U.S. Constitution II–193a, 196a, 203b
Virginia properties IV–92a–b
Virginia Resolves VII–203a
Wakefield VII–219a
Washington and Lee University VII–249a
Washington Elm VII–250a
wealth III–79a
western lands IV–371a; VII–252a
wheat growing VII–286a
—Military Career:
Battle of Harlem III–253b, 254b
Battle of Long Island IV–186a
Battle of Paoli V–211b
bonuses I–331a
Braddock's Road I–358b
commander in chief I–183a; III–100b
farewell to officers III–100a
French and Indian War I–88b, 282b; II–381b–82a; VI–267a
Battle of the Monongahela IV–398a
Braddock's expedition I–358a,b
Forbes expedition III–58b
Great Meadows III–219a
Le Boeuf mission III–115a,b; IV–130a; V–143a, 146a; VI–150a
LeBoeut mission IV–434b
Monongahela River IV–398b
Lifeguard IV–152a
Naval War With France V–15a
Pine Tree flag III–35a
revolutionary war II–231b; IV–266a; VI–123a–b, 124a,b, 125a,b, 351b
Arnold's march to Quebec I–193b
Arnold's treason I–194b
Battle of Cooch's Bridge II–218b
Battle of Edge Hill II–393a
Battle of Germantown III–173b
Battle of Long Island IV–185b
Battle of Monmouth IV–397b
Battle of Princeton V–408a
Battle of Trenton VII–116a
Battle of White Plains VII–293a
Boston I–344a, 344b–45a; VII–56b
Brandywine Creek I–360a
British prison ships V–418b
capture of André I–118b
Connolly's plot II–184a
Continental Army I–183a
Conway Cabal I–436a–b; II–218a
Corps of Engineers II–449b
Delaware crossing II–321a–b
eight months army VII–251b
espionage VI–372b–73a
foreign volunteers VI–126b
Fort Lee IV–131b; V–41a
Hale, Nathan III–241a–b
horse cavalry I–475b
Hudson River defense
insignia of rank I–189a
Jockey Hollow encampment IV–1a
manpower VI–117b
mapping I–463a
military code VII–142b
Morristown V–108a
Morristown encampment IV–413a; VI–377a
mutiny IV–445a; V–253a
navy VI–128a,b
Neshaminy Creek encampment V–33a
Newburgh Addresses V–42a
New York City V–82b
pine tree flag V–316a
Purple Heart II–312b
rangers VI–46b
Rochambeau's army III–117b
Stony Point VI–415b
Sullivan–Clinton campaign VI–437b
trenches VII–115a
Valley Forge VII–164b
western frontier VI–378a
West Point III–276a; VI–150a; VII–279b
Whitemarsh VII–292b
Wyoming massacre VII–346b
Yorktown VI–248a; VII–198b–99a, 361a
—President:
amnesty I–114b
Bank of the United States I–261a
British posts IV–329a
cabinet I–399b
Capitol building I–451a
China trade II–26b
circuit courts II–40a
civil service II–59b
Customs Service II–276a
Department of Agriculture I–45a
election I–416b–17a
executive agent II–342b, 471a
farewell address III–462a, 479b–80a; IV–399b; VII–251b
Federalist party II–325b
foreign policy III–67b
Franco-American relations III–96a–b
Gazette of the United States III–202a; V–69b
Genêt mission III–159b; IV–169b
government appointments I–145b
Hamilton's policies III–244b; IV–463b
Harpers Ferry armory IV–432b
implied powers III–348a–b
inauguration III–350b–51a
Indian factory system II–480a; VII–95b
Indian treaties VII–109b, 110b
Jacobin Clubs III–487b
Jay's Treaty I–120b, 126a; III–375b, 493b, 494a; IV–402b
military academy IV–340b
military policy IV–343a
national capital VII–244b
national university II–15b, 395b, 396a
neutrality III–238b; V–34b
Neutrality Proclamation III–455b, 462a; V–36b, 181a
newspaper attacks I–224a
Nootka Sound affair II–342b
Northwestern Indian Confederacy I–341a
Ohio Indian wars VI–188b
"permanent alliances" II–452b
Pinckney's Treaty I–126a; V–315b
political patronage VI–375a
postal service V–371b
Randolph resignation V–346a
regular army II–313a
Saint Clair's Indian campaign III–375a
selection of successor I–475a
Thanksgiving Day VII–46a
third-term doctrine VII–53b
title V–399a
trade restrictions V–104b
Trumbull, Jonathan IV–7b
Wayne's Indian campaign VII–262b
Whiskey Rebellion IV–258b; VII–290a
White House VII–291b
Zane's Trace VII–368a
Washington, George, Birthplace National Monument V–217b
Washington, Henry S. (chem.) V–268b
Washington, John (planter) VII–219a
Washington, John Augustine (off.) IV–423a
Washington, Lawrence (planter) IV–423a; V–409b
Washington, Lawrence Augustine I–387a
Washington, Martha Dandridge Custis IV–423a
Washington, My Home (song) VI–395 (table)
WASHINGTON, STATE OF VII–247a; V–180b; VI–395 (table)
Bannock War VII–239b
Bonneville Dam III–322a
boundary disputes I–351b
bridges I–365a
Cascade Tunnel VII–128b
Chief Joseph Dam III–322a
Columbia River II–132a; VI–150a
Donation Lands II–363a

Douglas fir III–74b
Farmer–Labor party of 1920 II–493a
forest fires III–74b
Fort Vancouver VII–165b
Grand Coulee Dam III–323a
Haro Channel dispute III–256a
horse III–303a
Hutterite communes II–142a
Ice Harbor Dam III–323a
Idaho III–328a; V–205b
Indians III–363a
Japanese–Americans II–445b
Jesuit missions III–500a
Makah IV–228b
Merwin Dam III–323b
minimum–wage law IV–80b, 353a; V–48a; VII–269a–b
national forests V–446a
national parks V–217a, 218–19 (table)
native plants V–327a
Nez Perce War V–89b
Nonpartisan League V–106b
Oregon III–328a; V–165a
public land states V–453a
Puget Sound V–462a
Quinault Reservation III–395b
recall VI–51a
referendum VI–66b
Rogue River War VII–239b
San Juan Island VI–214a
school lands VI–228–b
Seattle World's Fair VI–249a
single–tax plan VI–293b
Snake River VI–322b
Tulalip Reservation III–395b
United States v. *Lanza* VII–154b
U.S. boundary VII–248b
veterinary medicine VII–176b
Walla Walla settlements VII–221a
wheat I–486a; III–44a; VII–286a
woman's suffrage III–91b; VII–315a
Yakima Wars VII–350a
Washington, Treaty of (1826) III–401b
Washington, Treaty of (1837) VI–296a
Washington, Treaty of (1858) VI–296a
WASHINGTON, TREATY OF (1871) **VII–248b**; I–73b, 277b, 439a; III–30a, 31a, 243b, 456a; V–232b; VII–112b
British indemnities III–352a
Johnson–Clarendon Convention IV–4b
Washington, University of II–399a–b; V–135a
Washington Academy (Va.). *See* Washington and Lee University
WASHINGTON AND LEE UNIVERSITY VII–249a; III–488b
Washington Barracks, D.C. I–191a
WASHINGTON BENEVOLENT SOCIETY VII–249a
Washington Bottom (Ohio) VII–252a
Washington Bridge I–364a,b
WASHINGTON BURNED (1814) **VII–249b**; I–120b, 249b, 250b, 318a; III–176b–77a; VII–234b
congressional records IV–8b
Library of Congress IV–146a
patent files V–226a
White House VII–292a
Washington cent I–483a
Washington Conference on Limitation of Armaments (1921–22). *See* Washington Naval Conference
Washington County (Ala.) VI–197b
Washington County (Ga.) V–315b
Washington County (N.C.) III–87a; VII–250a
Washington County (Northwest Terr.) V–123a
Washington County (Pa.) III–188a
Washington County (R.I.) IV–49a
Washington County (Tenn.) VII–25a
Washington Crossing the Delaware (paint.) V–188b
WASHINGTON DISTRICT (N.C.) **VII–250a**; VII–253b
"Washington Ditch" II–353a
WASHINGTON ELM VII–250a
Washington Globe. *See Globe, Washington*
Washington Irving Island VII–190a
WASHINGTON MONUMENT VII–250a; I–163a; II–422b; VII–245a, 246b
Washington National Era (news.) VII–137b
Washington National Monument Society VII–250b
WASHINGTON NAVAL CONFERENCE (1921–22) **VII–250b**; II–314b, 370a, 488b; III–69a, 160b; IV–343b; V–10a, 233b; VII–242a, 341b
Anglo–American relations I–123a
carrier air power I–54b
Five–Power Treaty III–33b
Four–Power Treaty III–85b
Lansing–Ishii Agreement IV–107a
IV–183a
Nine–Power Pact V–96b
Open Door policy V–159a
parity V–216b
Peking commission II–479b
Soviet Union VI–178b
submarines VI–424a; VII–225b
Yap mandate VII–353b
Washington Navy Yard V–27b, 29b
Washington Park (Chicago) IV–337a
Washington Peace Conference. *See* Border Slave State Convention
Washington Post (news.) I–464b; V–73a; VII–317b
Nader's Raiders IV–448b
Pentagon Papers III–105b; V–78b
Watergate V–78a; VII–255b
Washington Post March (comp.) IV–441b
Washington Republican (news.) I–3a
WASHINGTON'S EIGHT MONTHS ARMY VII–251a; IV–360b–61a
WASHINGTON'S FAREWELL ADDRESS (1796) **VII–251b**; III–67b, 68a, 462a, 479b–80a; IV–399b
Washington's Mission to the French. *See* Le Boeuf, Fort, Washington's Mission to
Washington Square Players VII–49b
WASHINGTON'S WESTERN LANDS VII–252a; IV–92b, 98b, 371a; VII–249a
Washington Temperance Society VII–23a
Washington Territory V–165b; VI–20b, 412b
Washington Union (news.) III–187b
Washington University, Saint Louis V–349a
Washington. v. *Oregon* (1908) I–351b
WASHITA, SHERIDAN'S OPERATIONS ON (1868–69) **VII–252b**; VI–241b
Washita River II–91a, 359a, 381a; VI–443b; VII–252b
Washo (Indians) III–363a; V–39b
Washoe. *See* Comstock Lode
Washoe smelter (Mont.) VI–316b–17a
Washoe Valley II–157a
Wash sales (fin.) II–470a
Wasp (carrier) I–54b
Wasp (period.) II–266a
WASP (sloop) **VII–252b**; V–424a; VI–128a, 313b
WASPs. *See* Women Airforce Service Pilots
Wassaja (news.) V–76a
Wasser, Henry (educ.) I–113a
Wassily armchair III–136b
Waste Land IV–164a
Watauga, Fort (Tenn.) IV–186b; VII–296a
Watauga Association. *See* Watauga Settlement and Association
Watauga River II–15a; III–87a; VI–149b
Treaty of Sycamore Shoals VI–455a
Washington District VII–250a
See also Watauga Settlement and Association
WATAUGA SETTLEMENT AND ASSOCIATION VII–253a; II–274a, 477a; III–87a, 292b; VI–356a; VII–25a, 103a
backwoodsmen I–240a
Carter, John I–461b, 462a
State of Franklin III–98b
Watauga Valley III–400b
Watch and ward V–338b
Watch and Ward Society, New England I–478b, 479a
"WATCHFUL WAITING" VII–253b
Watchmaking industry. *See* Clock and Watch Industry; Clockmaking II–78a–b
Watchtower (period.) III–497b
Watchtower Bible and Tract Society III–497b
Watchung Mountains IV–413a
Waterbury (Conn.) II–78a, 79a; V–291a
Water cures I–219a; IV–288b
Waterford (N.Y.) II–460a
Waterford (Pa.) III–120a; V–246b
WATERGATE VII–253b; I–409a; II–231a, 259a; III–344b–45a; V–347a; VI–93b; VII–118b
AFL–CIO I–103a
campaign of 1972 I–432a
cartoons V–72b, 73a
executive privilege II–474a
newspaper coverage V–78a–b
Nixon resignation V–99a
subpoena of tapes V–397b–98a
WATER HOLES VII–256a; IV–98a; VI–377b
Waterhouse, Benjamin (physic.) IV–275a, 348b; VI–316a
Waterhouse, Daniel VI–316a
WATER LAW VII–256a; III–478a
Water lilies IV–378b
Waterloo (Ill.) I–286b
Waterman, Alan T. (adm.) IV–471a
Watermills VII–256b–57a
Water moccasin V–62b
WATERPOWER VII–256b
Ballinger–Pinchot controversy I–247b
Columbia River Treaty II–132a

WATERPOWER (cont.)
fall line II–485a
Falls of Saint Anthony VI–187a
flour milling III–42b, 43a, 44a, 45a
government ownership III–203a
Industrial Revolution III–411a,b
iron and steel manufacture III–472a–b
looms IV–187b
mill streams IV–347b
Niagara Falls V–91b
Point Four program V–335a
research III–99a
Rhode Island VI–131b, 133a
sawmills VI–222b
Society for Establishing Useful Manufactures VII–161a
textile industry II–237b; VII–45a
thresher VII–55b
tide mills VII–58a
turbines VII–129a–b
U.S. Geological Survey III–164a
Wisconsin VII–308a
wool industry VII–320b
See also Hydroelectric Power
Water Power Act of 1920 III–321a; V–446a
Water Quality Act (1965) VII–259b
Water Quality Improvement Act (1970) II–89b, 188b
Water rights
cow custom II–251a
farming IV–104a–b
Waters, Asa (mfr.) IV–432b
Waters, Henry Fitz Gilbert (geneal.) II–99a
Waters, Walter W. I–330b
WATER SUPPLY AND CONSERVATION VII–257b; VI–48b
agriculture I–42b, 45a
bacteriological tests I–241b
California I–407a–b, 408b
Canadian–American waterways I–440a–b
cattle V–160a
Corps of Engineers II–450a
Department of the Interior III–444a, 445a
detergent contamination VI–324a–b
ecology II–392a
electric energy II–417b
fire fighting III–25a
forests III–75b
government inspection III–422a
housing III–309b
irrigation III–477a
Kansas IV–26b
Kansas–Colorado water rights IV–27b
local government IV–172a
municipal ownership III–203a; IV–427b, 428a
New York City V–83a
Niagara Falls V–91b–92a
North Carolina V–116b
public health V–447a
public utilities V–456b
reclamation VI–53b, 425b
Rocky Mountains VI–160b
Rural Environmental Assistance Program VI–335b
sanitation VI–212a,b
Saratoga Springs VI–218a
Savannah VI–220b
South Carolina VI–348a
springs VI–377a
steam power VI–408b, 409a,b
timberlands VII–60a
tunnels VII–127b
urban health VII–158a,b
U.S. Geological Survey III–164a
Washington, D.C. VII–246a
Waterways Treaty VII–261a
Weeks Act VII–266b
windmills VII–304b, 304b
Watertown (Mass.) I–196b; VI–151a
Watertown (Wis.) II–398b
Waterville (Maine) IV–227a
Watervliet (N.Y.) I–196b; IV–432b–33a; VI–268a
WATERWAYS, INLAND VII–259b; VII–275b
admiralty law I–14b
barge traffic IV–312b
Civil War III–474a–b; V–17a
domestic trade VII–82b, 83a,b, 84a
Fox–Wisconsin III–89a
Great Lakes III–215b
Inland Waterways Corporation V–455a–b
Lakes–to–Gulf IV–87b
marine insurance III–429a–b
mill streams IV–347b
National Waterways Commission V–1b
Railroad Administration VI–19a
river and harbor improvements VI–145b
river navigation VI–148a
shipping IV–309a
steamboating VI–406b
towboating VII–77a
transportation VII–102a
War of 1812 V–19a; VII–235a
Waterways Commission, National. *See* National Waterways Commission
Waterways Experiment Station (Vicksburg) VI–147a
WATERWAYS TREATY (1909) **VII–261a**
Waterwheels VII–256b
Wathena (Kans.) IV–26a
Watie, Stand (Indian) V–49b
Watkins Point V–252a
Watkins v. *United States* (1957) II–210b; III–465b
WATLINGS ISLAND (B.W.I.) **VII–261a**; I–96a
Watrous (N.Mex.) VII–145a
Watson, Baxter (eng.) VI–422b
Watson, Elkanah (bus., agri.) II–244b; VI–392b
Watson, Fort (S.C.) III–286a,b
Watson, James D. (biochem.) I–304a; II–13a, 357b–58a; III–158a; IV–390a–b; V–100a
Watson, John (paint.) V–186a
Watson, John B. (psych.) V–442a
Watson, John Fanning (bus., antiq.) II–98b
Watson, Lloyd R. (beekeeper) I–284a
Watson, Morris (jour.) I–207a
Watson, Thomas A. (tech.) VII–20a
Watson, Thomas E. (pol.) III–169a; IV–335a; VI–172b
Watson, Thomas J. (bus.) I–397a
Watson, William (eng.) I–442a
Watson and the Shark (paint.) V–188b
Watsonville (Calif.) I–285a
Watson–Watt, Robert (eng.) VI–10a
Watt, James (eng., inv.) VI–408b, 410a
Watterson, Henry (jour.) IV–41a; V–73b
Watterston, George (librarian) IV–148a
Wattoquitchey Falls VI–190b
Watts (Los Angeles) I–31b, 408b; IV–457b; VI–8b–9a
Watts, Isaac (theol.) III–326a
Watts, John (mer.) V–242a; VI–109b
Watts Bar Dam III–323b
Watts Sherman House (Newport) I–164a
WAUHATCHIE, BATTLE OF (1863) **VII–261a**; VI–150b
Waurika (Okla.) II–32a
Waveguides I–287b; IV–333a
WAVES. *See* Women Accepted for Voluntary Emergency Service
"Waving the bloody shirt" I–422a
Wawasee, Lake II–391b
WAWAYANDA PATENT (1703) **VII–261b**
Wawona Tunnel Tree VII–362a
Wax III–44b
WAXHAW (S.C.) **VII–261b**
WAXHAW, BATTLE OF (1780) **VII–261b**
Waxhaw Creek VI–351b; VII–261b
WAX PORTRAITS VII–262a
Way, George (landowner) V–242a
Wayland, Francis (cler., educ.) I–372a
Waymouth, George (navig.) V–359b
Wayne, Anthony (off.) I–194a
Battle of Germantown III–173b
Battle of Paoli V–211b
Fort Massac IV–264a
Georgia campaign III–170a, 400b–01a
Loramie's store IV–188a
Stony Point III–276a; VI–415b
Yorktown VII–360b
See also Wayne Campaign; Wayne–Wilkinson Quarrel
WAYNE, FORT (Ind.) **VII–262a**; II–297a; III–369b; IV–59b; VII–263a
Central Canal III–374b
Fort Miami IV–329a
fur trade V–176a
Harmar's expedition III–255a; VII–247a
Indian factory II–480a
Lincoln Highway IV–156a
Miami Indians V–308a
portages V–367b
Saint Clair's defeat VI–188b
trading house III–142b
Vincennes Treaty VII–189b
Wasbash and Erie Canal VII–212a
WAYNE, FORT, TREATY OF (1809) **VII–262b**; III–404a
Wayne, James M. (jur.) VI–445b
WAYNE CAMPAIGN (1792–95) **VII–262b**; I–341a; II–338a; III–127a, 375b; V–123a
Battle of Fallen Timbers I–183b; II–484b; III–255a; IV–53b; VII–247a
Fort Defiance II–317a
Fort Fayette II–497b
Fort Greenville III–227b
Fort Pitt I–190b
Fort Recovery VI–60b
Hobson's Choice III–286b
Indiana III–369b
Lake Erie II–458b
Maumee Convention IV–276b
Michigan IV–330b
Ohio V–141a
Treaty of Greenville III–384b, 404a
Wayne–Wilkinson quarrel VII–263a
Wayne County (N.Y.) V–463b
Wayne County (Northwest Terr.) V–123a
Waynesboro (Va.) I–325b

Wayne State University
II–337b; III–285a
WAYNE–WILKINSON QUARREL VII–263a
Way of the Churches of Christ in New England . . .
V–52a
WAYS AND MEANS, COMMITTEE ON VII–263b; III–37b; VI–412a, 472b
Ways and Means for the Inhibitants of Delaware to Become Rich
III–427a–b
Way to Wealth. *See* Father Abraham's Speech
WCTU. *See* Woman's Christian Temperance Union
Wea (Indians) III–383a; VII–189b, 262b
Wealth
American Indians
IV–59a,b
balance of trade I–244b
See also Great Fortunes
Wealth of Nations III–246b
Wealth Tax Act (1935)
V–46b
Weapons V–163a–64a
fur trade III–140a
gliders III–187a
Green River knife
III–227a
harpoon II–462a
hydrogen bomb III–324a
Office of Scientific Research and Development
V–137a
prehistoric II–223a
recoilless rifle VI–140a
rifle VI–139a
Scientific American
VI–231a–b
See also Munitions
Weapons, nuclear V–296a
Weapons, tactical IV–363a
Weapon systems II–316a; VII–1a
"WE ARE COMING, FATHER ABRAHAM, THREE HUNDRED THOUSAND MORE" (song) **VII–263b**
Weather
almanacs I–90b
economy II–76b
experiments III–156a
See also Meteorology
Weather Bureau, United States. *See* Weather Service, National
Weatherford, Bill. *See* Red Eagle
WEATHER SERVICE, NATIONAL VII–264a;
I–45a; II–75b–76a, 88b, 135a; IV–291a
Allison Commission
I–90a,b
balloons I–248a
Coast Guard II–89b
mapmaking I–463b
polar exploration V–337b
Signal Corps VI–286a
"Weather Underground"
VI–421b
Weather vanes III–47a
Weaver, James B. (pol.)
I–424b–25a; III–225a, 468b; V–39b, 365b
Weavers (mus.) IV–441b
Weave shed II–239a
Weaving III–381a
Archaic culture II–386a
clothing industry II–81a
cotton industry II–239a
inventions II–237b
Navaho III–368b; V–9a,b
wool manufacture
VII–320b
See also Textiles
Webb, Beatrice (hist.)
II–110a
Webb, C. H. (archaeol.)
V–382b
Webb, Daniel (off.) VI–385a; VII–301a
Webb, Fort (N.Y.) VII–280a
Webb, James E. (offi.)
IV–459b
Webb, James Watson (jour., dipl.) VI–143b
Webb, John (arch.) I–161a
Webb, Sidney (hist.) II–110a
Webb, Walter Prescott (writ.)
VII–41a
WEBB EXPORT ACT (1918)
VII–264b; I–140a; VII–123a
Webb family III–79a
WEBB–KENYON ACT (1913)
VII–265a; IV–159a
Webb–Pomerene Export Trade Act (1918). *See* Webb Export Act
Weber, J. (phys.) IV–262b
Weber, Max (econ.) V–354a
Weber, Max (paint.) V–192b
Webern, Anton von (comp.)
IV–439b
Weber River IV–411b
Webster, Ambrose (watchmaker) II–78b
Webster, Arthur Gordon (phys.) V–295a
Webster, Daniel (states.)
IV–267a; V–161a; VI–218a
Bank of the United States
II–232a
Bunker Hill Monument
I–383a
campaign of 1836 I–419b
Compromise of 1850
II–150a
conservatism II–189a
Creole slave case II–257b
Dartmouth College Case
II–293b
Gibbons v. *Ogden*
III–178a; VI–407b
Hawaii III–263a
Hülsemann incident
III–316a
internal improvements
III–450b
land speculation IV–99b
lyceum movement
IV–207a
McCulloch v. *Maryland*
III–348b
McLeod Case VII–265a
Northeast boundary
V–118b
oratory IV–162b
state sovereignty VI–404a
tariff VI–465b
Webster–Hayne debate
VII–265b
Webster, Delia A.
VII–265a–b
Webster, John White (prof.)
VII–118a, 266a
Webster, Noah (educ.)
II–397a, 470b; IV–221b; V–199a
American Minerva V–69b
dictionaries II–340a
schoolbooks VI–227a
speller II–394a; VII–266a
Webster, Pelatiah (publicist)
V–199a
Webster, Robert (athlete)
V–154b
WEBSTER–ASHBURTON TREATY (1842)
VII–265a; I–121a, 438b; VII–111b
acreage ceded V–445 (table)
arbitration IV–5b
Aroostook War I–195a
Canadian–U.S. boundary
V–33b; VI–166a
Caroline affair I–458b
extradition VII–112b
Indian Stream Republic
III–402a
Maine–Canada boundary
IV–226b
Northeast boundary
V–118b
slave trade VI–311b, 322a
WEBSTER–FAIRBANK TRIALS (1844–45)
VII–265a
WEBSTER–HAYNE DEBATE (1830) **VII–265b**
WEBSTER–PARKMAN MURDER CASE
VII–266a; VII–118a
WEBSTER'S BLUE-BACKED SPELLER
VII–266a; VI–227a
Webster's International Dictionary II–340a
Webster's New International Dictionary II–340a
Webster's Spelling Book
IV–213a
Webster's Third International Dictionary II–340a
Weches (Tex.) VI–210a
"We dare defend our rights" (motto) VI–393 (table)
Weddell Sea V–338a
Wedderburn, Alexander (law.)
V–244a–b
Wedemeyer, Albert C. (off.)
II–26a; IV–235b
Wedge (tool) II–386a
Weed, Thurlow (jour., pol.)
I–132b; V–86b, 410a
Weeden, John (butcher)
VII–117a
Weed killers. *See* Insecticides and Herbicides
WEEHAWKEN (N.J.)
VII–266b; I–388a
"Weekend warrior" program
V–28b
Weekly Museum (news.)
V–71a
Weekly News-Letter. See Boston News-Letter
Weeks, John W. (pol.)
VII–266b
Weeks, Joseph D. (jour.)
II–235b
WEEKS ACT (1911)
VII–266b; III–73b, 75b
"Weeling." *See* Wheeling
Weems, Mason Locke (cler., au.) I–494a; III–281a
Wefald, Knud (pol.) II–491a
Weft yarn II–239a
"WE HAVE MET THE ENEMY, AND THEY ARE OURS" VII–266b;
II–459b
"We hold these truths to be self evident" II–306a–b
Weick, Fred E. (sci.)
IV–106b
Weidlein, Edward R. (chem.)
IV–300b
Weidman, Charles (dancer)
II–288a
Weightlifting
Olympic Games V–154b
Weights and measures
IV–462a,b
congressional powers
II–199b
consumer protection
II–208b
international regulation
VII–113a
interstate commerce
III–459a
town sealers VI–245a
Weights and Measures, Office of Construction of
IV–462b
Weights and Measures, Office of Standard II–87b
Weinberger, Caspar W. (offi.)
III–267b
Weiner, Lee II–20b, 21a
Weinglass, Leonard I. (law.)
II–21a
Weir, J. Alden (paint.)
V–192a
Weir, Robert (art.) II–101b
Weirton (W.Va.) II–349a
Weirton Steel Company
II–349a
Weisberger, Barbara (dancer)
II–289b
Weiser, Johann Conrad (Indian agent) II–388a; IV–89b; V–195a
Weishaupt, Adam (mystic, philos.) III–332a
Weisman, Frederick R. (art collector) II–106b
Weismann, August (biol.)
III–158b
Weiss, Carl A. I–203a; IV–184a
Weisskopf, Victor F. (phys.)
V–302b, 303a
Weissmuller, Johnny (athlete)
I–488a; V–154b
Weitzel, Godfrey (off.)
VII–292a
WEIZAC (computer)
II–156a

Welch, Joseph N. (law.) IV–210b
Welch, Robert H. W., Jr. (bus.) IV–1b
Welch, William H. (path.) IV–3a,b, 286b, 292a, 298a
WELCOME (ship) **VII–267a**
Weld, Isaac (trav.) I–367b, 368a
Weld, Theodore Dwight (abolitionist) I–28a, 136a, 137a; V–130a, 145b; VI–78b
Weldon (N.C.) VI–36b
Weldon Railroad V–265a
Welfare
aliens I–88a–b; II–457b
charity organization movement I–495b
county programs II–245b
farm tenancy I–40b
federal aid II–502a
federal–state relations III–9b
government costs II–234b
Health, Education, and Welfare Department III–267b
local government IV–171b
Michigan IV–332a
National Urban League V–1a
Nixon administration II–472b
state financing II–303a
Welfare and Pension Plans Disclosure Act (1958) IV–78b
Welfare clause. *See* General Welfare Clause
Welfare Island. *See* Roosevelt Island
Welfare state
campaign of 1964 I–431b
capital I–448b
Welland Canal I–440b; III–452a; V–157a; VI–192b, 193a
Weller, S. (prof.) V–197a
Weller, Thomas H. (biol.) V–100a, 340b
Welles, Gideon (pol.) II–435a; V–19b, 386a; VII–178b
Welles, Orson (act., prod.) VII–50a
Welles, Sumner (dipl.) II–269a, 361a–b; III–199a
Wellesley, Arthur. *See* Wellington, 1st Duke of
Wellesley College IV–267b
Wellfleet (Mass.) I–447a
Wellington (Kans.) I–336a
Wellington (Ohio) V–130b
Wellington, 1st Duke of, Arthur Wellesley (off., states.) III–43a, 177a; V–330b; VII–235b
Wellman, George (inv.) VII–43a
Wellman, Samuel T. (inv.) III–473a
Wells (Maine) III–200a; VI–2b
Wells, Butterfield and Company I–102a
Wells, David A. (econ.) VI–463b–64a
Wells, Henry (expressman) I–102a; VII–267a
Wells, Horace (dent.) I–119a; IV–285b
Wells, John I. (pressmaker) V–413a
Wells, R. W. II–390b
Wells, Samuel R. (phrenologist, pub.) V–294a
Wells, Wayne (athlete) V–154b
WELLS, FARGO AND COMPANY VII–267a; VI–379b; VII–101a
American Express I–102b
Holladay Stage Company III–291a; V–178a
Pioneer Stage Line V–318a
robberies VI–379b
Wells County (N.Dak.) V–388b
Welsback mantle IV–153a
Welsh
exploration I–96b
Minnesota IV–356b
Welty, Eudora (au.) IV–165a
Welwyn (Eng.) II–46b
"We must all hang together" II–306a
Wemyss, James (off.) III–30b
Wenatchee (Wash.) IV–177a
Wenatchee Valley VII–248a
Wenau Forest (Ger.) III–314a
Wendover (Utah) III–17b
Wentworth, Benning (col. gov.) III–226b; V–54b; VII–171b
Wentworth, John (col. gov.) II–292b; V–54a, 242a
Wentworth, Thomas. *See* Strafford, 1st Earl of
Wentworth and Flexner II–340b
Werden, John (col. offi.) V–436a
Wernwag, Lewis (eng.) I–363b
Wesberry v. *Sanders* (1964) I–147b; II–172a, 355b
Wesel (Ger.) III–187b
Wesley, John (cler.) II–39b; III–326a; IV–295b, 318a,b; V–259b; VI–77b
Savannah VI–220a
Sunday schools VI–442a
Wesleyan Methodist Church (Seneca Falls, N.Y.) VI–261b
Wesleyan Methodist Connection IV–318b
Wesleyans II–353a
Wesleyan University I–46b; III–58a
Wessagusset (Mass.) VII–279a
Wessells, Henry W. (off.) II–379b
WEST, AMERICAN VII–267b
camels in I–412b–13a
campaign of 1824 I–418b
caravans I–452a–b
fortifications III–78a
free blacks III–102a
French exploration III–118b
French travelers III–122b
frontier missions IV–365a,b
gambling III–149b
geological surveys III–165b–66a
geophysical explorations III–166b
Great American Desert III–213b
herd law versus free grass III–273a,b
horse stealing III–305b
hydroelectric power III–320b–21a
land speculation IV–99b–100a; V–88b
Lewis and Clark Expedition IV–136a
literary societies IV–160a
livestock industry I–37a,b
missions IV–366b
mountain men IV–422a
mountain passes V–224a
movers IV–423b
mustangs IV–444b
newspaper coverage V–71a
open–range grazing V–159b
outlaws II–258a
population growth V–363a
prairie fires V–388b
public land commissions V–450a
ranching VI–44b
reclamation VI–53b
Rocky Mountains VI–160a
rodeos VI–161a
Rustler War VI–181a
saddles VI–184b
sectionalism VI–253b, 254a
settlement IV–94b, 338a–39a
sheep wars VI–273a
Slade's Girls VI–299b
slang VI–299b–300a
Southwest VI–355a
springs VI–377b
timberlands VII–59b, 60b, 61a
Turner's frontier theory V–81b
U.S. Army exploration I–188a
Utah VII–161a
vigilantes VII–187a
water holes VII–256a
water law VII–256a
wheat I–38b
Wild West Show VII–298b
windmills VII–304b
West, Benjamin (paint.) V–185b, 186b–87a,b, 188a–b; VI–267b
West, Department of the II–434b
West, Edward (inv.) VII–280b
West, Jerry (athlete) V–154b
West, John C. (gov.) VI–348a
West, Nathanael (au.) IV–165a
West Africa
Axis bases II–314b
music IV–442b
slave trade I–26b–27a; IV–252a
trade I–21a
West Antarctica V–337b, 338a
Westar (satellite) II–143b
West Augusta (Pa.) V–322a
West Augusta, District of V–253a
West Branch (Iowa) I–167b; III–284b
Westchester County (N.Y.) V–130b, 186a
Dutch–Indian War II–383a
King's Ferry IV–48a
manors III–313a; IV–241b
Philipsborough V–286a
revolutionary war II–249b; V–33b
Westchester Light Horse Battalion II–249b
West Coast
Japanese–American relocation III–491a
mapping IV–247b, 248a
WEST COAST HOTEL COMPANY* v. *PARRISH (1937) **VII–269a**; I–12a; IV–80b, 353a; VII–214a
West Coast International Longshoremen's and Warehousemen's Union III–419b
West Company III–203b
Westcott, Edward N. (au.) IV–163a
West Country Puritans III–220a
Westerly (R.I.) V–261a
WESTERN, FORT (Maine) **VII–269b**
Western and Atlantic Railroad VI–33a
Western Archaic culture II–334b
WESTERN BOUNDARIES (1783–98) **VII–269b**
Western Clearings VI–372a
Western Company. *See* Compagnie de l'Occident
Western culture areas III–362a–63a
Western Department of Continental Army IV–216b
Western Desert (Africa) VII–338a
WESTERN DESIGN VII–270b; II–122b–23a
Western Dorsale mountains World War II IV–32b
Western Electric Company I–225a; III–406a; V–290a; VI–234a–b
WESTERN ENGINEER (steamboat) **VII–271a**; III–468a; IV–186b
Western Europe
cold war II–97b–98a
foreign investment

III–67a
North Atlantic Treaty Organization III–69b
WESTERN EXPLORATION VII–271a
Lederer's expeditions IV–131a
Lewis and Clark Expedition IV–136a
Missouri River IV–380a, 380b
mountain men IV–422a
mountain passes V–224a
Nebraska V–31a
Ohio River V–144b
Pike's southwestern expedition V–312a
Pike's upper Mississippi expedition V–312a
Powell's expeditions V–384a
Rocky Mountain Fur Company VI–160a
Rocky Mountains VI–160a–b
U.S. Army I–192a
WESTERN FEDERATION OF MINERS VII–272b; II–93b
Coeur d'Alene riots IV–66a
Haywood–Moyer–Pettibone Case III–266b
Industrial Workers of the World IV–67b
Western Flotilla II–384a
Western Hemisphere
Declaration of Panama V–36a
Good Neighbor policy III–198b
immigration III–333b, 334a, 337b, 341b, 342b
isolationism III–479b
Monroe Doctrine IV–399b
Organization of American States V–171a
Pan–American Union V–205a
World War II II–314b; IV–112a
See also Monroe Doctrine
Western hemlock VI–395 (table)
Western Inland Lock Navigation Company III–419b
Western Inland Lock Navigation Company Canal I–442a
WESTERN LANDS VII–273a; V–140b, 162a–63a; VI–356a–b
acreage ceded V–445 (table)
Articles of Confederation I–198a; II–166a
colonial land grants IV–91b
Georgia III–170b, 389a, 393b; VII–353b–54a
Jefferson's proposed states III–496b
Maryland IV–260b
military tracts IV–344b
Mississippi Company of Virginia IV–371a
North Carolina III–98b; V–115b
Ohio Company of Virginia V–144a
Old Northwest V–152a
panic of 1792 V–206a
panic of 1819 V–206a
public domain V–443b
sales II–166a
Seven Ranges survey VI–264a
speculation IV–99a–b
state claims II–166a
Tennessee VII–25b
Virginia III–331a, 370b–71a; VII–202a
Western Reserve VII–274a
Western meadowlark VI–393 (table), 394 (table), 395 (table)
WESTERN MERCHANTS AND THE INDIAN TRADE VII–273b
Western Missionary Society III–385b
Western Mountains VI–40a
Western Museum of Cincinnati IV–436b
Western Pacific Railroad VI–27b, 37b
Western posts, British I–120a, 366b, 438a–b; II–166b, 458b, 484b
Western Pueblo culture. *See* Mogollon
WESTERN RESERVE VII–274a; III–414a; V–140b; VII–273a
Connecticut claim II–183b
Firelands III–25b
Oberlin movement V–130a
Salt Springs Tract VI–204a
settlement IV–338b
Seven Ranges survey VI–264a
survey II–74b
WESTERN RESERVE, RELIGION IN VII–275a
Western Reserve Historical Society (Cleveland) III–137b, 278b; VII–274b
Western Reserve Synod VII–275a
Western Reserve University VII–274b
Western Samoa VI–205a
WESTERN SEA, SEARCH FOR THE VII–275a; IV–380a
WESTERN SEPARATISM VII–276a; IV–372b
Western Society of Engineers of Chicago II–448b
Western Union Building (N.Y.C.) VI–299a
Western Union Defense Organization V–114a
WESTERN UNION TELEGRAPH COMPANY VII–276b; I–401a; II–137a; V–374b; VI–413b; VII–18b, 19a
advertising I–19b
Alaska VII–367a
Gould fortune III–79a
Naval Observatory time V–12b
offtrack bookmakers II–260a,b
Promontory Point V–430b
telephone VII–20a,b
"yellow–dog" contracts VII–354b
Western World (news.) VI–366a
WEST FLORIDA, ANNEXATION OF VII–277a; I–274b, 275a; III–41b, 68a, 462b; IV–197b
Kemper raid IV–36b
Mississippi Territory IV–368a–b
Mobile Act IV–382b
Mobile seized IV–383a
Pearl River V–240b
revolution I–274b, 275a
See also Florida
WEST FLORIDA CONTROVERSY VII–277a; III–22b, 38b, 41b
Adams–Onís Treaty I–10b
Iberville boundary III–327a
Mobile Act IV–382b
Westham (Va.) I–194a
Westheimer, Irvin F. (bus.) I–296a
WEST INDIA TRADE VII–277b; II–119a; III–220a, 413a; V–355b; VI–108a,b, 111a, 343a–b, 386a–b; VII–82b, 86a–b, 87a V 355b–
alcoholic beverages II–261a
Anglo–American relations I–120a, 121a
apples III–128b
armed merchantmen IV–313a
Barbados I–265b
Civil War VII–146b
currency II–365b
Dutch West India Company II–383b
enemy trading VII–93b
flour III–42b, 43a, 45a
fruit III–52b
hats III–262a
ice VI–69a
Indian slaves III–401a
Jay's Treaty III–493a
mackerel IV–217a
meat IV–280a
meat–packing IV–170a
molasses IV–388a
Molasses Act II–116b; IV–388a; V–221a
Napoleonic Wars III–455b
Narragansett planters IV–451b
Naval War With France V–15a, 19a
Navigation Acts V–16a,b
New England IV–309b
Norfolk V–109b
onions V–156a
pipe staves V–319b
post–Revolution IV–266a
Queen Anne's War VI–2b
revolutionary war V–354a–b
rice II–453a; VI–136a
rum VI–170b, 321a
Salem fishing VI–199a
salt VI–202a
shipping VI–280b
slaves I–22b, 27a; IV–335a; VI–310b, 311a
soap trade VI–323b
South Carolina Interstate and West Indian Exposition VI–349b
Stamp Act VI–381b
Sugar Acts VI–435a
sugarcane VI–437a
Sugar Islands VI–437a
tafia VI–456b
triangular trade VII–119a
West Indies II–190a; IV–135b
Acadians I–6a
Afro–American literature IV–166a–b
antislavery III–332b
black nationalism V–200a
British army VI–126b, 127b
Champlain's voyage I–492b
cotton growing II–240a
Cromwell's western design VII–270b
French and Indian War III–117a
hurricanes III–319a
immigration to U.S. III–333a, 334b, 337b
indentured servants III–353a
Pan–Africanism V–199a
pirates II–484a; III–234b; IV–416a
presidios V–399b
Queen Anne's War VI–2b
quitrents VI–4a
revolutionary war VI–124a, 128b, 129b, 130a
rumrunners VI–170a
sugar I–444a; II–353b
Treaty of Paris V–214b
Wells, Fargo VII–267a
yellow fever VII–355a
See also Sugar Islands
West Indies, Danish. *See* Virgin Islands of the United States
Westinghouse, George (inv.) II–414a–b; IV–153b; V–247b; VI–28a
Westinghouse Bridge I–364b–65a
Westinghouse Company II–412b, 414b, 415a,b, 416a, 419b, 420a, 421b, 429b; VII–21b, 124a
commercial broadcasting II–424a
industrial research III–409a,b
lamp manufacture IV–153b
Niagara Falls power V–92b
radio VI–15a

Westinghouse Laboratories I–212a
WEST JERSEY VII–278a; V–56b–57a, 436b
assembly II–118a
plans of union II–121b
punishments V–464b
Quakers II–124b; V–469b
religious liberty VII–69a
WEST JERSEY CONCESSIONS (1677) **VII–278b**; II–157b
West Jersey Society VII–278b
Westminster (Mass.) I–490b
WESTMINSTER, TREATY OF (1674) **VII–279a**; IV–185b; V–82a
Westminster Assembly of Divines (1643–49) VI–262a; VII–279a
Westminster College (Fulton, Mo.) III–474b
WESTMINSTER CONFESSION OF FAITH (1647) **VII–279a**; I–410b; II–169b, 272b, 406a; VI–78a
Cambridge Platform I–412a
Presbyterianism V–391a,b, 392a
Westmoreland (Pa.) VII–347b
Westmoreland, William C. (off.) VII–183b, 184a
Westmoreland County (Pa.) I–223b; III–250a; V–253a,b
Miller's Run Gap V–224b
revolutionary war III–250b; VI–378a
Westmoreland County (Va.) VI–417b; VII–168b, 219a
Weston (Mo.) IV–129a
Weston (W.Va.) III–332b
Weston, Andrew (col.) VII–279a
Weston, Edward (inv.) V–41b
Weston, Thomas (mer.) V–313a,b; VII–279a
WESTON'S SETTLEMENT VII–279a
Westover (Va.) I–161b, 194a
Westover Manuscripts IV–161a
West Palm Beach (Fla.) III–320a
WEST POINT (N.Y.) **VII–279b**
Arnold's treason I–194b
bullion depository IV–360a
Hudson River chain III–312b
revolutionary war I–118a, 183b; III–275b, 276a; VI–129a, 150a, 217b, 377a; VII–165a
See also Military Academy, United States
West Point and Montgomery Railroad VI–166a
West Point Arms and Cannon Foundry IV–175b, 432b, 433a
Westport (Conn.) IV–361a; VI–139a
WESTPORT (Mo.) **VII–280a**; I–453a; II–242b; IV–27a,b
Civil War V–403a
Platte River Trail V–330b
WESTPORT, BATTLE OF (1864) **VII–280b**; V–403a
Westport Landing. *See* Westport (Mo.)
West Prussia
Treaty of Versailles VII–173a
West Rexburg Community (1841) II–147a
West Rock (Conn.) VI–70b
West Roxbury (Mass.) I–369b
West Shore Railroad VI–35b
West Side Story (musical) IV–438b; VII–50b
West Side Tennis Club (Forest Hills, N.Y.) VII–29b
WEST'S STEAMBOAT VII–280b
WESTSYLVANIA VII–281a
West Tennessee. *See* Tennessee
WEST VIRGINIA VII–281a; VI–251b, 354a, 395 (table), 400a; VII–195a
Adena culture I–11a
Augusta County I–223b
backcountry I–240a
black jury service VI–417b
black officeholders VI–432b
boundary dispute III–200a
Burning Springs Field II–464b
Charleston I–497b
civil disturbances IV–341b
Civil War I–457a–b; II–61b; III–272b, 332b, 498b; V–281a
coal II–75a, 85a, 86a; IV–70b
Eternal Center II–464b
exploration I–277b
feuds III–18a
Forman's massacre III–77b
Fort Henry III–272b
Fort Randolph VI–45b
Grave Creek Mound IV–420b
Greenbrier Company III–226a
Hatfield–McCoy feud III–262a
Indian land cession I–278a
ironclad oath VII–35a
Kanawha Salt Works IV–25a
Mason–Dixon Line IV–263a
military bounties IV–92a
Monongahela River IV–398b
National Road IV–470a
oil II–464b
panhandle V–205b
Peabody Fund V–231b
Potomac River V–378a
Pringle settlement II–477a
Radical Republicans VI–11a
railroad strike of 1877 IV–63b
rural free delivery VI–172b
sales taxes VI–200a
separation from Virginia I–341b
Shenandoah Valley VI–275b
state debts VII–203a–b
tornadoes VII–75b
ungranted land V–443b
unionization of coal miners III–286a
Virginia claims VII–273a
Vrindaban commune II–142b
Washington's western lands VII–252a
Wheeling VII–287b
West Virginia, My Home, Sweet Home (song) VI–395 (table)
West Virginia Hills (song) VI–395 (table)
West Virginia State Board of Education v. *Barnette* (1943) III–35a; IV–358b
West Virginia University VII–282a
Westwall. *See* Siegfried Line
WESTWARD MOVEMENT VII–282b; III–215a–b, 295b–97a; VII–267b, 268a
backcountry I–239b–40a
colonial land grants IV–92b
Confederation period II–166b
covered wagon II–248a
defense III–126b–27a
Donner party II–364a
Falls of the Ohio V–142b
fencing III–10b
flatboats III–35b
Forks of the Ohio V–143a
Fort Kearny IV–33b
Fort Laramie IV–108a
Fort Smith VI–317a
Fort Yuma VII–367a
Fox Indians III–88b
Gila Trail III–179b
"Go West, Young Man" III–206b
Great American Desert III–213b
Great Plains III–221a
group migration IV–338a
Hastings' Cutoff III–260b
Homestead Act IV–96a
Independence (Mo.) III–353b
Independence Rock III–354a
Indian Country III–379a–b
Indian removal III–404a
internal improvements III–447b
"Joe Bowers" IV–1a
jumping–off places IV–20b
Kansas IV–25b, 31a
Kansas–Nebraska Act IV–28b
Lancaster Pike IV–89b
land purchases IV–99b
land systems IV–102a
lead mining V–102b
long hunters IV–185a
"manifest destiny" IV–239a
manufacturing IV–243b
mapmaking I–462b, 463a
merchants III–127a; VII–274a
Miami purchase IV–329b
Michigan Territorial Road IV–332b
missionaries IV–365a,b, 366b
Mississippi Valley IV–376a
Missouri IV–377a, 377b
Mormons IV–411b
Mountain Meadows massacre IV–421b
mountain passes V–224a
Navigator handbook V–17a
New England opposition V–49b
Northwest Territory III–227b
Oatman Indian captives V–129b
Ohio Company of Associates V–143b
Ohio Valley V–146a
"Oh! Susanna" V–146b
Oregon caravans V–166a
Oregon Trail V–168b–69b
overland companies V–176b
oxen V–179a
Pawnee Rock V–230b
penole V–254a
pioneers V–316b
Pittsburgh V–321b
Platte River Trail V–330b
Powell's Valley V–384b
Prairie du Chien V–388a
prairie schooner V–389b
prospectors V–437a–b
Quakers V–470a; VI–347b
rafting VI–18b
railroads IV–30b, 94a,b
ranching VI–45a
Rocky Mountains VI–160b
Sage Plains VI–185b
Saint Joseph VI–191b
Santa Fe Trail VI–215b–16a
sectionalism VI–253b
slavery VI–305b
Smoky Hill Trail VI–320b
soil erosion VI–335a
Sooners VI–339b
Sublette's Cutoff VI–422a
telegraph VII–18b
Tennessee River VII–27b
trails VI–153a–54a
trans–Missouri region IV–423b
transportation VII–100a,b
trapping VII–104b
urban structure VII–159a

Utah VII–161a–b
wagon trains VII–217a
Washington (Pa.) VII–244b
water holes VII–256a
waterways VII–260a
Wilderness Road VII–296b
Willamette Valley VII–300a
Wyoming VII–345b
Wet bloc I–322a
Wetherill, Charles M. (chem.) II–10b
Wetherill, Samuel (chem.) II–5b; VII–369a
Wethersfield (Conn.) III–271b; VI–151a–b; VII–282b
New Haven settlers V–55b
onions V–156a
Pequot War V–261a
See also River Towns of Connecticut
Wetmore, Alexander (biol.) VI–319a
Wetumpka (Ala.) VII–77a
"We Wear the Mask" (poem) IV–166a
Weyerhaeuser, Frederick (bus.) III–80a
Weyerhaeuser Company IV–98a
Weyler y Nicolau, Valeriano (states.) II–268b; VI–360a
Weymouth (Mass.) IV–265a; VII–279a–b
Weymouth, George (expl.) I–96b; IV–37a, 396a; V–243b
Weyprecht, Karl (off.) III–454a
WHA. *See* World Hockey Association
WHALEBACKS VII–285a; III–218a
Whalebone III–413a
Whale fins II–453a
Whale oil IV–44a
WHALING VII–285a; IV–82a; V–158a; VI–245a; VII–87a
Aleut I–84a
arctic waters V–336b
Cape Cod I–447a
Civil War VI–274b
Coast Guard II–89b
colonial III–413a–b; VI–185b
Company of One Hundred Associates II–149b
Eskimo II–462a; III–358a
exports VII–86a
Fajardo Case II–484a
Grand Banks III–208a
Hawaii III–263a.b
Indian religion III–392b
Long Island IV–185b
Martha's Vineyard IV–258a
Nantucket IV–449a
Northwest Coast culture III–361a
preservation V–217b
Ringgold-Rodgers Exploring Expedition VI–142a
rockets VI–159a
Sag Harbor VI–186a
San Francisco VI–209a
spermaceti trust VI–372b
tallow VI–323a
War of 1812 II–463b
Whalley, Edward (off.) IV–48a; VI–70b
Wharton, Edith (au.) IV–164a
Wharton, Joseph IV–363a
Wharton, Richard (mer.) V–242a
Wharton, Samuel (mer.) I–278a; III–208b, 370b; VII–166b, 167a
Wharton family IV–98b, 200a
Wharton School of Business V–249a
What Is Church History? III–282a
"What Mr. Robinson Thinks" (poem) I–296b
WHEAT VII–286a; III–53a; VI–48a
Agricultural Adjustment Administration V–44a
as money IV–101b
Bonanza farming I–329a
California I–406a
cereals I–486a
Civil War II–66a
colonial crop I–37a
corn belt II–227a
Dodge City II–358b
domestic trade VII–83b
flour milling III–43a–45b
foreign trade VII–86a,b, 87b
Great Lakes shipping III–218a,b
Illinois III–329b
Indian agriculture I–48a
internal improvements III–447b
Kansas IV–26a
marketing quotas V–359a
McCormick reaper IV–211a
Minneapolis VII–134a
Minnesota IV–357a; VII–308a
Missouri IV–377a
Montana IV–403b
New York State V–87a
Nonpartisan League V–106b
Norfolk V–109b
North Dakota V–117a,b
Ohio V–141b
Oregon V–165b
panic of 1857 V–207a
prices V–404a
product enrichment V–128b
reaping IV–424a
Red River of the North VI–64b
Richmond VI–136b
Russian sale I–43b; VI–180a
Saint Lawrence Seaway I–440b
shipping IV–310b
soil VI–334b
South Dakota VI–350a
Southwest VI–355b
storage II–429b
tariff VI–344a
thresher VII–55b
towboating VII–77b
Virginia VII–194a
Washington State VII–248a
West I–38b
whiskey VII–289b
Wisconsin VII–308a
World War I VII–327b
Wheaties I–488a
Wheatley, John IV–166a
Wheatley, Phyllis (poet) IV–166a
Wheaton (Ill.) VI–17a
Wheaton, Frank (off.) VII–127a
Wheaton, Henry (dipl.) II–291b; VII–370a
Wheel
North American prehistory I–158a
Wheeler, Burton K. (pol.) I–428a; IV–84b, 403b
Wheeler, Cyrenus (inv.) IV–424a
Wheeler, Edward L. (au.) II–341b
Wheeler, Francis (nav. off.) IV–49b
Wheeler, George M. (topog., eng.) II–129b; VI–90b; VII–74b, 272b
Wheeler, Joe (off.) VI–278a
Wheeler, John A. (phys.) V–302a
Wheeler, Joseph (off.) VI–362a
Wheeler, Wayne B. (ref.) V–429b
Wheeler, William A. (pol.) I–422b, 423b; VII–179 (table), 287a
Wheeler and Melick VII–55b
Wheeler and Wilson Manufacturing Company VI–265a
WHEELER COMPROMISE (1876) **VII–287a**
Wheeler Dam III–323b
WHEELER-HOWARD ACT (1934) **VII–287a**; I–106b; II–296a; III–372a, 373a, 390a, 395b, 396a; V–48b–49a
Wheeler-Lea Act (1938) I–19a, 140a–b; V–467a
Wheeler Ranch (commune) II–142b
WHEELING (W.Va.) **VII–287b**; VII–194a–b, 281b
Allegheny wagoners VII–216a
bridges I–364b
Civil War VI–138b
Clark's Detroit expedition IV–173b
Cumberland Road II–273a,b; III–448b; VI–153b
Fort Henry III–76b, 272b
harness factory III–255b
iron and steel industry III–470b
National Road IV–470a
railroad II–15b
railroads VI–25b, 33a–b, 35a; VII–100b
steamboat construction VII–196b
Zane's Trace VII–368a
Wheeling and Lake Erie Railroad VI–35a
Wheeling Bridge VII–287b
WHEELING BRIDGE CASE (1849) **VII–288a**
Wheeling Creek VII–287b
Wheeling Island VII–287b
Wheelmaking VII–216b
Wheelock, Eleazar (miss., educ.) II–292b; V–279b
Wheelock, John (educ.) II–293a,b
Wheelwright, John (cler.) I–133b; V–53b, 185a
"When Work's All Done This Fall" (ballad) VI–382b
Where the Columbines Grow (song) VI–393 (table)
Whewell, W. (philos., math.) III–454a
Whey II–281a
WHIG PARTY VII–288a; II–327a; V–223b, 343b; VI–94b
Alabama I–71a, 308b
Anti-Masonic party VI–12b
antislavery IV–28a
backwoodsmen I–240a
campaign of 1836 I–419b
campaign of 1840 I–420a, 432b; VII–63b
campaign of 1844 I–420a; VI–42b
campaign of 1848 I–420b; V–329a
campaign of 1852 I–420b
campaign of 1860 I–421a
Connecticut II–180b
Conscience Whigs II–184b
Constitutional Union party II–191a
federal surplus VI–449a
Independent Treasury System III–251b, 354b
Indiana III–370a
Jacksonian Democracy III–487a
Kansas-Nebraska Act IV–29b
Louisiana IV–193b
Loyalists VI–116a
"manifest destiny" IV–239a
Missouri IV–377a
Mutiny Act of 1765 IV–445b
Nashville Convention IV–453a,b, 453b
National Intelligencer IV–465b
National Republican party IV–469b
New York City V–82a,b, 83a
New York State V–86b
nonimportation agreements V–104a
North Carolina IV–407b; V–115b, 116a
Pacific republic movement V–180b

WHIG PARTY (cont.)
panic of 1837 V–207a
Perry–Elliott controversy V–262b
presidents V–395 (table)
Reconstruction VI–93a
Republic IV–465b
revolutionary war VI–106a
Saint Louis Observer V–70b
scalawags VI–224a
scientific information III–165b
Scioto Gazette VI–239a
Silver Grays VI–288a
slavery issue II–327a
Topeka Constitution VII–72b
Union Rights party VII–148a
Vermont VII–172a
vice–presidents VII–179 (table)
Woolly Heads VII–321b
workingmen's parties IV–61b
Whig Workingmen's Party VII–322a
"While I breathe, I hope" (motto) VI–395 (table)
Whilte, William S. (jour.) V–75a
Whinnamice, Harry (pol.) IV–261a
Whinyates, Thomas (nav. off.) VII–253a
WHIP, PARTY VII–288b; II–172b
Whipped toppings II–282a
Whipping. *See* Flogging
Whipple, Abraham (nav. off.) III–154a; VI–128a, 129a
Whipple, Amiel W. (off.) VI–39a; VII–289a
Whipple, Fred (astron.) VI–17a
Whipple, George H. (path.) IV–3a; V–100a
Whipple, William (mer.) II–307b
WHIPPLE'S EXPEDITION (1853–56) **VII–289a**
Whipple truss (eng.) I–364a
Whipsaw strikes IV–174a
Whirlpool Rapids V–93b
Whirlwind (computer) II–156a
Whisk collars II–370b
WHISKEY VII–289a; V–184a
bourbon III–52a
Civil War II–163b
corn II–226a
distilling II–353b
duties III–244b
frontier merchant III–127a
fur trade III–140b
Indians I–289b
Kentucky IV–41b
moonshine IV–407b
price–fixing IV–399a
Prohibition V–429b
pure food and drug movement V–466a
rum trade VI–170b
saloons VI–201b
tariff VI–466b
taverns VII–2a
taxes VII–290a,b
temperance movement VII–22a
Whiskey jack. *See* Michabous, God of Michilimackinac
WHISKEY REBELLION (1794) **VII–289b**; I–41a; II–353b; III–436a–b; V–247a; VI–462a; VII–5a, 12b, 82b, 107a, 191a
amnesty I–114b
bounties I–353a
Fort Cumberland II–272a
martial law IV–258b
militia IV–345b
WHISKEY RING VII–290b; V–346a
WHISKEY TOWNS VII–290b
Whiskey trust VII–122a
WHISPERING CAMPAIGNS VII–291a
Whistler, Garland (off.) VI–135a
Whistler, James McNeil (paint.) V–191b, 192a, 413b
Whistler, John (off.) II–297a
Whistle–stop campaign I–429b
Whitcoat, Richard (cler.) IV–318b
Whitcomb, Chapman (au.) I–494a
Whitcomb, Richard T. (av. eng.) I–52a, 235a
White, Alfred T. (ref.) VII–24b
White, Andrew Dickson (educ.) I–106a; II–227b, 470b; III–282b; IV–163b
White, Byron R. (jur.) VI–447a
Hatch Act III–261b
White, Canvass (eng.) I–442b, 477b
White, Charles (art.) I–25a
White, David (paleobot., geol.) V–196b
White, E. B. (writ.) IV–166a
White, Edward D. (jur.) VI–102a–b, 446a, 446a; VII–155a
White, Edward H. (astronaut) II–347a
White, Elijah (physic., pioneer) I–453a
White, Harry D. (off.) VI–428b
White, Hugh L. (jur.) I–419b; VII–25b, 288b
White, James (landowner) VI–365b
White, Jim (cowboy) I–455b
White, John (art., col. gov.) III–26b; V–115a, 325b; VI–42b, 43a
White, John (cler.) II–364b; III–220a; V–51a
White, John (pol.) II–175 (table)
White, Josiah (eng.) I–127b, 364b, 442b
White, Leslie (anthrop.) I–129a
White, Maunsel (inv.) II–298b; III–15b; VI–234a
White, Robert (av.) I–52b
White, Stanford (arch.) I–164b; III–446b
Madison Square Garden IV–220b
murder VII–118a
World's Columbian Exposition VII–324b
White, Thomas W (ed.) VI–353a
White, William (cler.) I–23a; II–455a; VI–442b
White, William Alanson (psych.) IV–306a
White, William Allen (jour.) IV–26b; V–68a, 73b
White, Gallaher and White II–355b
White Army (Russ.) VI–284a
White birch VI–394 (table)
White Bird (Indian) II–74b
White Bird Canyon (Idaho) V–89b
White Boys IV–391b
White Bull (Indian) III–17b
WHITE CAPS VII–291a
White Captive (sculp.) VI–243a
WHITE CITIZENS COUNCILS VII–291a; II–57b; V–67b; VI–12b
"White City" (World's Columbian Exposition) I–164b
White–collar crime II–259a
"White–collar woes" IV–77b
White–collar workers I–103a; II–442a–b; IV–75a; V–132b
middle class IV–334b
profit sharing V–426b
White Earth River II–284b
White Eyes (Indian) V–322a
Whitefield, George (cler.) I–293a; III–214a–b; V–58b, 391b; VI–76b, 220a
"White fleet." *See* Battle Fleet Cruise Around the World
White gourd seed corn II–226a
Whitehall (Annapolis) I–161a
WHITEHALL, TREATY OF (1686) **VII–291a**
Whitehall Street (N.Y.C.) V–40a
Whitehead, Alfred North (math., philos.) V–288b; VI–79b
Whitehead, Robert (inv.) VII–76a, 243a
White–headed eagle II–384b
Whitehead torpedoes III–291b
"White hope" V–422b, 423a
White Horse (Yukon Terr.) IV–52a
White Horse (slave ship) VI–308b
WHITE HOUSE VII–291b; VII–246b
architecture I–162b
bathtub I–274b
burning I–120b, 318a; VII–249b
cabinet staff I–400a
First Lady III–26a
furniture collection III–137b
inauguration of president III–351a
Jefferson's fossils V–195a
National Governors' Conference III–206a
police force VI–252b
Telecommunications Policy Office I–480b
White House Conference (1908) II–187b
White House Conference on Children IV–275b
White House Conference on Conservation (1962) II–188a
White House Conference on Food, Nutrition and Health (1969) V–128b
White House Conference on Natural Beauty (1965) II–188b
White House Conference on the Care of Dependent Children (1909) V–381a
White House Conferences on Children and Youth II–400a
White House Conferences on Education II–400a
White House Office II–497b
WHITE HOUSE OF THE CONFEDERACY (Richmond) **VII–292a**; VI–137a
White Island III–479b
White–Jacket VI–301b
White lead II–5b
WHITE LEAGUE VII–292b; V–64a
WHITEMARSH (Pa.) **VII–292b**; II–393a; VII–165a
White Motor Company v. *United States* (1963) VI–102b
White Mountain Apache (Indians) I–141a; V–4a
White Mountains IV–423a; VI–100b, 417b
"White mule" (liquor) II–252a
White oak VI–393 (table), 393 (table), 394 (table)
White Oak (Md.) V–28a
White Oak Swamp (Va.) VI–220a; VII–292b–93a
WHITE OAK SWAMP, BATTLE AT (1862) **VII–292b**; III–100a
White Pass (Alaska) IV–52a
White Pass and Yukon Railroad IV–52a
White pine II–266b; III–74b; IV–204a; VI–393 (table), 394 (table), 394 (table)
White Pine Acts II–123a
WHITE PLAINS, BATTLE OF (1776) **VII–293a**; V–33b, 82b
White River III–256a, 374b; IV–300a; V–334b; VI–157a; VII–189b

White River Falls VI–190b
White Rock (Lake Huron) III–316a
White Russians I–158b
Whites, poor. *See* Poor Whites
White Sands Missile Range (N.Mex.) V–60a
White Sands National Monument V–217b
White Sea VI–245a; VII–329a
White's Fort (Tenn.) III–292a
White slavery
  Mann Act IV–240a
Whitesmithing I–317a; VI–291b
"WHITE SQUADRON" VII–293a
White Star line VII–64a
White Sticks (Indians) II–256b–57a
Whitestone Hill (N.Dak.) II–284a
White Sulphur Springs (W.Va.) IV–350a
White supremacy II–57b; III–59b, 169a; IV–58a, 369a
Whiteware V–379b
"WHITEWASH" VII–293b
"White-washed rebs" III–148b
Whitewater Canal I–442b; III–375a; VII–127b
Whitewater River III–374b
WHITE WOMAN OF THE GENESEE VII–293b
Whiting silver VI–290a
Whitin Machine Works VII–44a
Whitman (Wash.) VII–221a
Whitman, C. O. (biol.) IV–251a
Whitman, Malcolm (hist.) VII–29a, 29b
Whitman, Marcus (miss.) II–477b; III–477a; V–165a; VII–217b
  See also Whitman Massacre
Whitman, Walt (poet) IV–162b; V–294a
WHITMAN MASSACRE (1847) **VII–293b**; I–476b; IV–108a; V–167a; VII–221a
Whitman Mission. *See* Walla Walla Settlements; Whitman Massacre
Whitney, Asa (mer.) III–450b; VI–39a; VII–147a
Whitney, Eli (inv.)
  assembly line I–205b
  cotton gin I–27b, 34a, 38a; II–237b, 240a; V–325a; VI–305b; VII–43a
  interchangeable manufacture III–441a; IV–272a; V–163a
  musket manufacture IV–432b
Whitney, Eli, Jr. II–130b
Whitney, Henry H. (off.) III–150b
Whitney, J. H. (engr.) VII–319b
Whitney, John Hay (art collector) II–106b
Whitney, Milton (agric.) VI–334a
Whitney, Myra Clark. *See* Gaines Case
Whitney, William C. (fin.) II–75a, 104a
Whitney, William Dwight (philol.) II–340a
Whitney, Willis R. (chem.) II–417a; III–155b, 409a; IV–89a, 153b
Whitney family III–79a
Whitney Museum (N.Y.C.) II–106a, 107a; VI–244a
Whitside, S. M. (off.) IV–316a
Whittaker, Charles E. (jur.) VI–447a
Whittemore, Amos (inv.) VII–43a
Whittemore family II–103a
Whittier (Calif.) VI–210b
Whittier, John Greenleaf (poet) I–37b, 344a; III–124a; IV–162a, 267a,b
  hymns 326b
  Marais des Cygnes massacre IV–248b
Whittle engine I–234b
Whittlesey, Charles W. (off.) IV–189b
Whittling III–47a
Whitworth, Kathy (golfer) III–198b
Whole Booke of Psalmes. *See* Bay Psalm Book
Whooping cough IV–150b
Whorekill County (Del.) II–322b
Who's Afraid of Virginia Woolf? (play) VII–50b
Wichita (Indians) III–119b, 211a, 363b; V–230b; VII–239b, 294a
  Coronado's expedition II–228b
  Fort Sill VI–287b
  Kansas IV–25a
  Oklahoma V–148a, 149a,b
  trade II–34b
WICHITA (Kans.) **VII–294a**
  airplane manufacture I–236a
  cattle I–2a; II–32a, 251b; IV–26a; VI–45a
  temperance movement III–261b
Wichita, Camp (Okla.) VI–287a
Wichita County (Kans.) II–245b
Wichita Falls (Tex.) II–251b; VII–35b, 40b
Wichita Mountains III–119a; VI–64a, 287a; VII–252b
Wichita Mountains Wildlife Refuge (Okla.) IV–184b
Wichita State University II–347b
Wicker, Tom (jour.) V–75a
Wickersham, George W. (law.). *See* Wickersham Commission
Wickersham, James (jur., pol.) I–77b
WICKERSHAM COMMISSION VII–294b; II–263b, 407a; V–416a–b
Wickes, Lambert (nav. off.) V–18b; VI–128b
Wickford (R.I.) III–223a
Wickham, William C. (off.) VII–358a
Wickiup I–166a; III–363a; VII–294b
Wicox, Cadmus M. (off.) VI–274b
WIDE-AWAKES VII–294b
Widener, Joseph E. (capitalist) II–104a
Widener, Peter A. B. (bus.) III–80a
Wider Opportunities III–181b
Wied, Prince Maximilian zu (nat.) IV–236a; VI–90a
Wiegand, Karl H. von (jour.) V–74a
Wiegmann, Arend F. A. (nat.) III–16a; VI–90a
Wieland IV–161b
Wieman v. *Updegraff* (1952) VII–15b
Wiener, Norbert (math.) I–224b
Wiener v. *United States* (1958) IV–446b; VI–85a
Wigger, Lones (athlete) V–154b
Wiggin, Albert (fin.) III–466a
Wigglesworth, Edward (cler.) IV–149a, 150a; VII–207a
Wightman Cup VII–29b, 30a
Wigner, Eugene P. (phys.) V–100a, 301b–02a, 303a, 304a
Wigs II–233b, 371a; III–239b
Wigwag system VI–285b
WIGWAM (dwelling) **VII–294b**; I–2b, 160b, 166b
"WIGWAM" (Tammany Hall) **VII–295a**
Wilberforce, William (pol., humanitarian) VI–311a
Wilberforce University II–113b
Wilbur, Homer (lit. char.) I–296b
Wilbur, John (cler.) III–123b
Wilburite Friends III–123b; V–470b
Wilburton Field (Okla.) IV–334a
Wilck, Gerhard (off.) I–1a–b
Wilcox County (Ala.) VI–433a
Wildcat (animal) I–471a
Wildcat (fighter plane) I–55a
Wild Cat (Indian) VI–261a
Wildcat banking I–255b
WILDCAT MONEY VII–295a
WILDCAT OIL DRILLING VII–295a; II–389a; IV–334a; V–271b
Wildcat strike VI–418b
Wilder, Thornton (writ.) IV–164b, 189b; VII–50a
WILDERNESS, BATTLES OF THE (1864) **VII–295b**; II–62b; III–21a; VI–137b; VII–68a
  Atlanta campaign I–213b
  Bloody Angle I–322b
Wilderness Act (1964) II–188b; III–76a; IV–349b
Wilderness areas III–76b; IV–96a; VII–61a
  Gila Wilderness III–73b, 75b
Wilderness Preservation System, National II–188b
WILDERNESS ROAD VII–296a; I–89a; II–272a, 477a; III–387b; VI–153a, 239b; VII–25a
  Big Moccasin Gap I–297a
  Crab Orchard II–253a
  Cumberland River II–273a
  Kentucky settlers I–324b
  Powell's Valley V–384b
Wild game III–150a
Wild Hog (Indian) II–379b
WILDLIFE PRESERVATION VII–296b; IV–233a
  Alaska I–80b; V–217b
  Audubon Society I–222b
  bird sanctuaries I–305b
  Department of the Interior III–444a,b
  fish III–27b–28a
  Forest Service III–76a,b
  fur animals III–133b
  Girl Scouts III–181a
  Pacific tuna III–28b
  prairie dogs V–387b
  public lands IV–95b
  Rural Environmental Assistance Program VI–335b
  seals VI–245a,b
  sea otter VI–247a–b
  sea turtles VI–91a
  Texas longhorns IV–184b
  whales VII–285b–86a
  zoos VII–371b
  See also Forestry
Wildlife refuges III–444b; VII–297b
Wildlife Refuge System. *See* National Wildlife Refuge System
WILD RICE VII–298a; II–31b; III–140b, 366b
Wild River Indian reservation (Wyo.) VII–244a
Wild rivers
  Alaska I–80b
Wild West (series) II–341b
"Wild West, Rocky Mountain and Prairie Exhibition" VII–298b
WILD WEST SHOW VII–298b; I–369a; VI–161b; VII–97b
Wiley, Calvin H. (educ.) II–397a
Wiley, Harvey W. (chem.) IV–120a, 279b; V–465b–66a,b

Wiley, John, and Sons
I–334a
Wiley–Dondero Act (1954)
VI–193a
Wilkes, Charles (nav. off.)
II–65b
Trent affair VII–115b
See also Wilkes Exploring Expedition
Wilkes, John (pub.)
IV–143b; V–97b; VII–299b
Wilkes, Maurice (computer eng.) II–155b
Wilkes–Barre (Pa.) III–293a; VI–267b; VII–347a
canal V–250a,b
Hurricane Agnes IV–258b
settlement V–231a; VI–451b, 452a
Yankee–Pennamite Wars VII–353a
Wilkes County (Ga.) IV–44b
WILKES EXPLORING EXPEDITION (1838–42)
VII–299a; III–28b; V–22b, 23a, 134b, 195b; VI–90b; VII–272a, 285a
Antarctica V–336b
Depot of Charts and Instruments V–12a
oceanographic survey V–133b
Puget Sound V–462a
specimens IV–464b, 465a
WILKES FUND DISPUTE
VII–299b; VI–112b
Wilkes Land V–336b, 338a
Wilkie, Wendell L. (pol.)
VI–93b
Wilkins, George Hubert (expl., av.) V–337b
Wilkins, M. H. F. (biophys.)
II–358a; IV–390a
Wilkins, Roy (civil rights leader) IV–461a
Wilkins, William (law., pol.)
V–31a
Wilkinson, Benjamin (fur trader) VI–195b
WILKINSON, FORT (Ga.)
VII–299b
Wilkinson, James (off.)
V–59a; VII–299b
d'Arges Colony I–170a
Battle of Chrysler's Field II–35a
Battle of Lacolle Mill IV–82a
Bollman case I–327b
Burr conspiracy I–387b–88a; V–64a; VII–37a
Choctaw treaty I–9b; II–167b
Cox Insurrection II–252a
Fort Bellefontaine I–286b
Fort Charlotte I–499a
Fort Fayette II–497b
Fort Hamilton III–244a
Fort Saint Clair VI–188a
French Creek action III–118a
Indian treaties IV–456b
Louisiana purchase IV–197a
Mississippi exploration IV–131b
Mobile seized IV–382b, 383a
Montreal expedition III–120b–21a; IV–406a; VII–234b
neutral ground agreement V–33b
Oklahoma V–148a
Pike expeditions VII–271a–b
Saratoga surrender VI–217b
Spanish conspiracy VI–365b–66a
Wasbash Towns expedition VII–212b
Wayne's Indian campaign VII–263a–b
western separatism VII–276b
Wilkinson, Jemima II–147a
Wilkinson, Theodore S. (nav. off.) I–459a; V–119b
Will, Henry (metalworker)
VI–290b
Will, William (metalworker)
VI–290b
Willamette Heights (Oreg.)
IV–136a
Willamette River
hydroelectric power III–320b
Lookout Point Dam III–323a
McLoughlin land claim IV–218b
settlements VII–300a
Willamette Valley I–493a; III–223b; VI–153b
WILLAMETTE VALLEY SETTLEMENTS
VII–300a; II–131b; V–165a, 166b, 169a; VII–100b, 247b
Oregon Methodist mission V–166b–67a
Willapa Bay (Wash.)
VII–247b
Willard (Ohio) VII–274a
Willard, Aaron (clockmaker)
II–79a
Willard, Aaron, Jr. (clockmaker) II–78b
Willard, Alexander (clockmaker) II–79a
Willard, Archibald M. (paint.)
VI–374b
Willard, Benjamin (clockmaker) II–77b, 78b, 79a
Willard, Elizabeth Osgood Goodrich VI–266b
Willard, Frances Elizabeth C. (ref.) VII–312a,b
Willard, Jess (pugilist)
V–422b
Willard, Philander (clockmaker) II–79a
Willard, Samuel (theol.)
VI–81a
Willard, Simon (clockmaker)
II–78a, 79a
Willard, Simon (fur trader)
III–141a
Willard, Xerxes A. II–280a
Willert, W. H. (tech.)
V–328b
Willett, William II–296b
William I (Ger. emp.)
San Juan Island dispute VI–214a
William I (Neth. k.)
Netherlands award V–33a
Northeast boundary arbitration V–118a
William II (Ger. emp.)
VII–325a
Russo–Japanese War V–370b
Treaty of Versailles VII–173a
World War I IV–320a
World War I armistice I–176b
yacht racing VII–349a
William III (Br. k.) I–82b; II–123a; III–106b, 272a; IV–134a; V–52b, 84b; VII–300a, 301a
Province of Maine IV–226a
Queen Anne's War VI–2a
William, Fort (Can.)
III–209a; V–121a
William, Fort (Colo.) I–289b
William, Fort (Minn.)
VI–443a
William, Fort (N.Dak.)
IV–415a
William, Fort (Wyo.)
IV–108a
William A. Clark Library (Los Angeles) V–191b
WILLIAM AND MARY, COLLEGE OF
VII–300a; I–161b; II–395b, 396a; VII–193b, 301a
chemistry II–10a
curriculum II–397b
law school IV–120b
library II–107b–08a; IV–144a
Phi Beta Kappa V–276b
restoration VII–302a
theater VII–46b
WILLIAM AND MARY, FORT (N.H.)
VII–300b; V–54a
William and Mary style furniture III–134a, 138a
William Augustus, Fort (N.Y.)
V–139b
William Carter Fund
III–82a
William Henry, Fort (Maine)
V–243b
William Henry, Fort (N.Y.)
VI–136b; VII–301a
WILLIAM HENRY, FORT, MASSACRE AT (1757)
VII–301a; III–116a; IV–86a
William L. Clements Library (Univ. of Mich.)
IV–145b
William Mason Company
IV–175b
William Penn Charter School (Philadelphia) II–395a; VI–228b
William Pepper Laboratory of Clinical Medicine
IV–286a
Williams (Ariz.) III–208b
Williams, Aubrey (offi.)
VII–364b
Williams, Bert (act.)
III–253b
Williams, Bill (trapper)
II–477a; IV–422a; VI–241b
Williams, Daniel Day (theol.)
VI–79b
Williams, David (sol.)
I–118b
Williams, Ephraim (off.)
IV–87b, 268b
Williams, E. Virginia (dancer)
II–289b
Williams, F. C. (phys.)
II–155b, 156a
Williams, Francis (col. gov.)
VI–418a
Williams, Gaar (cartoon.)
V–72b
Williams, George (mer.)
VII–363a
Williams, George H. (pol.)
IV–6a; VII–248b
Williams, Hank (sing.)
IV–442a
Williams, Henry. *See Williams* v. *Mississippi*
Williams, Henry (art.)
VI–286b
Williams, Jesse (dairyman)
II–280b
Williams, John (law.)
VI–72a; VII–102b
Williams, John A. (au.)
I–25a
Williams, Jonathan (off.)
IV–340b
Williams, Joseph (off.)
IV–186b
Williams, N. H. (phys.)
IV–262b
Williams, Reelfoot (outlaw)
VI–379b
Williams, R. G. (ed.)
II–436a
Williams, Robert R. (chem.)
I–303b
Williams, Roger (cler.)
IV–270a; V–65b; VI–76a, 80b, 131b–32a; VII–82a
Baptist church I–264b
Indian mission III–385b
Pawtucket V–230b
Providence II–124a; V–439a
Rhode Island charters VI–134a
Rhode Island purchase I–149a
Salem VI–199a
Williams, Roger (sci.)
I–303b
Williams, Sam (math.)
II–154b
Williams, Tennessee (Thomas Lanier Williams) (playwright) IV–165b; VII–50b
Williams, Thomas (mer.)
V–241b–42a
Williams, William (bus.)
II–308a
Williams, William (paint.)
V–186b, 188a

Williams, William (off.) VI–374a
Williams, William A. (hist.) III–283a–b
Williams, William Carlos (poet) IV–165b
Williams, Wythe (jour.) V–74a
Williams and Company V–241b
Williams Bay (Wis.) V–131b
WILLIAMSBURG (Va.) **VII–301a**; I–161b; III–489a; IV–130b; VI–340b; VII–193b
Civil War II–482a–b; V–245a; VII–301b
climate observations IV–316b
Eastern State Hospital III–306b
French and Indian War III–219b
newspaper V–69a
revolutionary war III–308a; VI–137a
Spotswood's expedition IV–53a
theater VII–46b
WILLIAMSBURG, BATTLE OF (1862) **VII–301b**; V–245a
WILLIAMSBURG, COLONIAL VII–301b; III–137a, 430a–b; IV–437a; VII–196a
city plan II–45b
College of William and Mary VII–300b
gardens III–151b
Raleigh Tavern VI–44a
Williamsburg Bridge I–370b
Williamsburg section (Brooklyn) I–370a
Williams College IV–191a
Williams Gap V–224b
Williamson (W.Va.) III–262a
Williamson, Charles (off.) IV–135b; V–463b
Williamson, David (off.) III–188a; IV–351b; V–152b
Williamson, Hugh (states.) II–203b, 393a
Williamson, William P. (eng.) VI–44b
Williamson County (Ill.) III–274a; IV–70b
Williamson purchase. *See* Pulteney Purchase
Williams Pass V–224b
Williamsport (Md.) II–484b; V–248b; VII–304b
Williamsport (Pa.) V–250a
William's short route III–215a
Williamstown (Mass.) IV–268b
William Street (N.Y.C.) III–189b
WILLIAMS* v. *MISSISSIPPI (1898) **VII–302b**; IV–371b
William the Conqueror loyalty oaths IV–202a
William Young's Sons' Excelsior Pottery III–184a
"Willie and Joe" (comic strip) V–68a, 73a
WILLING (ship) **VII–302b**; III–147b
Willing, James III–147b; VII–302b–03a
WILLING EXPEDITION (1778–79) **VII–302b**; III–38b, 147b
Willink (banking house) III–291a
Willink, Van Staphorst, and Hubbard III–245a
Willis, Bailey (geol.) III–167a, 481a
Willis, Nathaniel (ed., jour.) IV–223a; VI–239a
Williston, S. W. (educ.) V–197a
Willkie, Wendell L. (pol.)
campaign of 1940 I–429a; IV–73a
Willoughby Run (Pa.) III–175b
Willow goldfinch VI–395 (table)
Willow ptarmigan VI–393 (table)
Will Rogers Field (Okla.) V–149a
Wills, Frank VII–255a
Wills, Helen (athlete) VII–30a
Wills Creek I–88b, 358b; II–271b; III–182a, 219b; IV–130a; V–144a; VI–150a
Wills Creek Post. *See* Cumberland, Fort
Willson, Augustus E. (pol.) V–96b
Willson, T. L. (chem.) II–7b, 422a,b
Will to Believe and Other Essays IV–163b
Willys (auto. mfg.) I–236a
Willys–Overland Company III–422b; IV–433a
Wilman, Henry Nelson (theol.) VI–83a
Wilmerding, Lucius I–333a
Wilmette (Ill.) V–172a
Wilmington (Del.) II–320b
Afro–American churches I–23a
bathtubs I–274b
Civil War V–19b
Du Pont II–5b; III–80a, 409a; V–383a
Fort Christina II–35a; V–42b
New Sweden Colony V–80a
paper and pulp industry V–212a
revolutionary war I–360a; III–173b; VI–123b
Underground Railroad VII–138b
yellow fever I–322a
Wilmington (N.C.) I–447b; V–116b
Civil War II–63a, 162b; VII–146b
race riot VII–303a
railroad VI–25b
revolutionary war III–232a; VI–351b; VII–360b
rice VI–135b
WILMINGTON RIOT (1898) **VII–303a**
Wilmot, David (law., pol.). *See* Wilmot Proviso
WILMOT PROVISO VII–303a; I–138b; III–111b; IV–379a–b; V–247a
Alabama Platform I–73b
Compromise of 1850 II–139a, 150a
Conscience Whigs II–184b
Democratic party I–145a, 268a
Dred Scott Case V–360b
sectionalism VI–254a
Virginia Resolutions VII–202b
Wilson, Alan Herries (phys.) V–304a; VI–259a
Wilson, Alexander (ornith.) I–304b; II–390a; V–190b, 413b
Wilson, Allen B. (inv.) VI–265a
Wilson, E. B. (zool.) III–157b, 158a
Wilson, E. D. (phys.) V–299b
Wilson, Edmund (critic) IV–165b
Wilson, Henry (pol.) I–422b; VII–179 (table)
Wilson, Jack (Indian) III–177b
Wilson, James (jur., pol.) I–297b; VI–445a
Articles of War VII–143a
Declaration of Independence II–308a
Parliament II–304a
prerevolutionary imperial idea III–346b
state sovereignty VI–403a
third–term doctrine VII–53b
U.S. Constitution II–193a, 194a,b, 194b, 196a,b, 203b
Wilson, James (off.) VI–377a; VII–358a
Wilson, James (offi.) V–466a–b
Wilson, James H. (off.) II–68b, 294b
Wilson, John (offi.) IV–95a
Wilson, Joseph (offi.) IV–95a
Wilson, Joseph M. (eng.) I–364a
Wilson, Lyle C. (jour.) VII–153a
Wilson, Malcolm (pol.) V–87b
Wilson, Mary Ellen VI–331b
Wilson, Mount III–241b–42b
Wilson, Samuel (meat packer) VII–137a
Wilson, "Tama Jim" (offi.) III–468b
Wilson, William B. (labor leader) IV–69a; V–247b; VII–167b
Wilson, William L. (pol.) VI–172b, 467a
Wilson, Woodrow II–176 (table); III–269b; V–100a, 161b, 385b, 396 (table), 396a; VII–198a, 236b
biography III–283a
monopolies V–58a
moral attitude IV–408b
political science V–347b
Princeton University V–409a
—President:
American Expeditionary Forces I–101b
amnesty I–115b
antitrust acts VI–277a
antitrust laws IV–69a
armed merchantmen IV–313b
Armistice Proclamation V–425a–b
campaign of 1912 I–426b–27a; III–91b; V–428b–29a; VI–93a, 458a; VII–40b
campaign of 1916 I–427a; VI–313a; VII–40b
China policy V–159a
Clayton Antitust Act II–71b
coal strike (1919) II–86b
Committee on Public Information II–139b
congressional committees II–173a
Congressional Government V–353b
conscientious objectors II–185b
conscription II–186a
Creel Committee VII–332b–33a
Cuba II–269a
daylight saving time II–296b; VI–139a
declaration of war VII–224b
diplomatic missions II–343a
disability V–397a
dollar diplomacy II–359b; VI–364a
Dominican Republic II–361a
Far Eastern policy II–488b
Flag Day III–34a
foreign policy III–69a
Fourteen Points I–215a; II–342a; III–85b; V–157b, 353b; VI–178a; VII–327a, 330b, 333a
gold embargo VI–371a
Haiti intervention III–239b–40a
House–Grey Memorandum III–309a
Inquiry III–420a
labor's support IV–68a, 68b
Latin American policy I–454b; VI–163a
League of Nations I–199a; II–472b; IV–124a; V–233b; VII–151a
Lind's mission to Mexico IV–157a
literacy test III–342b
"Little group of willful

WILSON, WOODROW (cont.)
men" IV–169a
Lusitania sinking IV–205b; VII–72b
martial law IV–259a
Mexican punitive expedition IV–328a
Monroe Doctrine IV–401b
Mooney case IV–406a
national banks III–6a
National Park Service V–219a
National Research Council IV–457a
navy VII–341b
New Freedom II–472b; V–53a; VII–122b–23a
Nineteenth Amendment V–97a
nonrecognition policy V–107b
"normalcy" V–110a
Panama Canal tolls V–204b; VII–70a
party government V–222a
"Peace without victory" V–238a, 353b
Philippines V–283b
preparedness movement V–390b–91a
Railroad Administration VI–19a, 29a
recognition policy III–456a; VI–55a
removal power IV–446a–b; VI–85a
Root mission to Russia VI–163b
secret diplomacy II–342a; VI–252a
Siberian expedition VI–283b
Soviet government VI–181a
tariff VI–464b, 467b, 469a
telephone VII–20a
third-term doctrine VII–53b
Transportation Act of 1920 VII–99a
Treaty of Versailles III–457a; IV–178b; VII–331a
U.S. flag III–34b
Veracruz incident VII–171a
Versailles Treaty III–110a
Volstead Act VII–207b
war debts VII–331b
War Department VII–230a
War Industries Board VII–231b
War Labor Board VII–232a
war powers II–179a
War Trade Board VII–243b
"watchful waiting" VII–253b
woman's suffrage VII–312b, 315a–b
woman suffrage III–92a
"world safe for democracy" II–326b; IV–383b
World War I I–122b, 158b–59a, 246b; VII–324b–26a, 327a,b, 328a, 368b
World War I armistice I–176b
World War I censorship I–481a
World War I mediation V–233a
Yap mandate VII–353b
Wilson, Woodrow, International Center for Scholars VI–319b
Wilson, Z. (off.) V–311a
Wilson Act (1890) IV–159a
Wilson Butte Cave (Idaho) I–155a
Wilson County (Kans.) I–326a
Wilson Creek (Mo.) II–379a
Wilson Dam III–323b–24a; VII–27b, 28a
Wilson–Gorman Tariff (1894) II–75a; VI–343b, 467a
Wilson Original Package Act (1890) V–172a–b
WILSON'S CREEK, BATTLE OF (1861) **VII–304a**; IV–137a, 377b; V–402b
Wilson v. *New* (1917) I–10a
Wilstach, W. P. (art collector) II–102a
Wilton (Maine) IV–227a
Wiltwyck (N.Y.) II–462b
Wimbledon (Eng.) VII–29a,b, 30a,b
Winant, John G. (pol.) III–455a
Winchell, James M. (comp.) III–326a
Winchester (Va.) I–476b
Civil War III–31a, 128a; IV–43b; V–59a; VI–276a; VII–304a–b
French and Indian War III–58b
Quaker exiles VII–201b
revolutionary war II–184a, 215a
WINCHESTER, BATTLE OF (1862) **VII–304a**; VI–373b
WINCHESTER, BATTLE OF (1864) **VII–304b**; VII–71a
Winchester, James (off.) VI–42a
Winchester Company IV–430b
Winchester rifle IV–430b
Wind and Current Chart of the North Atlantic IV–277a
Wind Cave National Park I–312b; V–218 (table)
Winder, John H. (off.) IV–139a
Winder, William H. (off.) I–318a, 476b–77a; VI–415a
Windham (Conn.) IV–387b; VI–451b; VII–347a
Windham County (Conn.) IV–207a
Windmill, Operation. Antarctic Developments Projects, U.S. Navy
Windmill Point (Md.) V–242b
WINDMILLS VII–304b; III–42b, 126a; V–160a; VII–58a, 257a
Window glass III–182b, 185b
Wind River I–452b; VII–103b, 217a
Wind River Mountains III–226b; V–225a
exploration VII–271b
Platte River Trail V–330b
South Pass VI–354b
Wind River Reservation (Wyo.) VII–346a
Wind River Shoshone (Indians) I–264a–b
Windships II–89a
Windsor (Can.) III–318a; VII–45b
Windsor (Conn.) II–179b, 181a, 182a, 309b; VI–151a–b; VII–282b
Pequot War V–261a
Plymouth Trading Post V–334b
See also River Towns of Connecticut
Windsor (Vt.) III–442a; VII–171b
Windsor chair I–490b; III–134b
Wind tunnels IV–106a
Windward (ship) V–240b
Windy City. *See* Chicago
WINE AND WINEMAKING VII–305a; III–52a, 54b, 129a; IV–76b
California I–406a; III–53b
colonial trade II–119a
duties III–228a, 244b
East India trade II–388a
fur trade III–140b
Indians III–398a,b; VII–65b
Navigation Acts V–16a
New England II–353b
pipe staves V–319b
Prohibition II–407a
smuggling VI–320b
Sugar Act VI–435b
taxation VII–7a, 8b
temperance movement VII–23a
triangular trade II–119a; VII–119b
World War I restrictions V–430a
Winecoff Hotel fire (1946) II–348b
Wine Islands VII–119b
"Wine of coca" II–374a
Wines, Enoch C. (ref., cler.) V–415b, 416a; VI–67b
Wingate, O. C. (off.) IV–314a
Wingfield, Edward Maria (col. offi.) III–488b
Wingfield, Walter Clopton VII–29a
Wings of the Dove IV–163b
Winkle, Rip Van. *See* Rip Van Winkle
Winland. *See* Vinland
WINNEBAGO (Indians) **VII–305b**; III–90a, 367a, 396b
Black Hawk War I–312a
Butte des Morts Council I–398a
citizenship III–377a
Fort Dearborn II–297a
Iowa III–468a
language II–282b; IV–235b
Maiden's Rock legend IV–224b
mounds IV–421a
nativistic movement V–4a
removal III–394b
revolutionary war VI–195a
Treaty at Prairie du Chien V–388b
wild rice VII–298b
Wisconsin VII–307b
Winnebago (Wis.) III–119a
WINNEBAGO, FORT (Wis.) **VII–306a**; III–90a
Winnebago, Lake I–398a; III–89a
Winnebago Act (1870) III–377a
Winnebago County (Ill.) III–84b
Winnebago Long Prairie Reservation (Minn.) VI–144b
Winnipeg (Can.) V–244a; VI–33a; VII–212a
Winnipeg, Lake III–242b; VII–275b
French post IV–118a
fur trade V–121a; VI–192b
Long's explorations IV–187a
Red River of the North VI–64a,b
Winnipeg River V–121a
Winnowing basket I–36a
Winnsboro (S.C.) II–251a
Winona (Indian) IV–224b
Winona (Minn.) VII–306b
WINONA SPEECH (1909) **VII–306b**
Winooski River III–226b; V–156a
Winslow (Maine) III–243b
Winslow, Edward (col.) IV–423b; V–184b, 334a–b
Winslow, Edward, Jr. (off.) I–206b
Winslow, Erving I–131b
Winslow, John (off.) IV–86a
Winslow, John A. (nav. off.) IV–35a; VII–147a
Winslow, Josiah (col. gov.) III–223a
Winsor, Justin (hist.) III–282a; IV–163a; V–334a
Winston, Joseph (off.) IV–48a
Winston Company II–340b
Winter, Ezra (paint.) V–191b
Winter, John (col.) IV–207b; VI–184a; VII–114b
Winter Games, Olympic. *See* Olympic Games
Winter Harbor (Maine) VI–184a
Winter Line III–235b
Winterset VI–183a
Winterthur (Del.) II–100b
Winterthur Museum (Del.) II–100b; III–137b; IV–437a

Winter wheat II–227a, 375b; VII–286a,b
Winthrop, Adam (landowner) V–242a
Winthrop, Fitz-John (col. gov.) IV–49b, 86a, 348a; V–84a, 84b
Winthrop, John (col. gov.) IV–265a; V–184b, 332b; VI–244a–b; VII–355a
Antinomian controversy I–133b
charity V–279b
criticism of artisans IV–60a
journal III–280a
literary narratives IV–161a
Massachusetts assembly II–117a
Massachusetts colony I–151b–52a, 344a, 411b, 498b
Salem VI–199a
Saugus furnace VI–218a
shipbuilding I–319b
theocracy VII–51b
Winthrop, John (phys., astron.) V–294a
Winthrop, John, Jr. (col. gov.) VI–151b
Atherton Company I–213a
Connecticut charter II–180a, 182b, 183a
Connecticut estate IV–103a
iron industry III–472a
library II–107a
manufacturing III–408a
mineral deposits IV–348a
New Haven Colony V–56a
saltpeter company II–5a
Saybrook VI–223a
training day VII–97a
Winthrop, Robert C. (law) II–175 (table)
"Winthrop Fleet" I–151b–52a
Winthrop v. *Lechmere* (1728) I–145a; III–464a
Winton Motor Carriage Company VI–257a
Wintun (Indians) III–363a; IV–381b
Winyah Bay (S.C.) VI–347a
Wire cutting "wars" I–267a
Wireless telegraphy. *See* Radio
Wire photos I–207b; VII–264b
Wire recording V–290a
Wiretapping. *See* Electronic Surveillance
Wirt, William (law.) III–281a; VI–455a
anti-Masonic movement I–132b
campaign of 1832 I–419a
Gibbons v. *Ogden* III–178a; VI–407b
Wirt County (W.Va.) II–464b
Wirth, Conrad L. (offi.) V–220a
Wirz, Henry (off.) I–118a
Wisakedjak. *See* Michabous, God of Michilimackinac
WISCONSIN VII–306b; VI–395 (table)
agricultural inspection III–422a
antibank movement I–129b
Black Hawk War VII–239a
blizzard I–320b
Border Slave State Convention I–341b
boundary disputes I–351a,b
Carver claim I–464b
Chequamegon Bay II–13b
Chippewa II–31b; III–360b, 394b
city planning II–46a–b
Civil War II–271b
conciliation process II–157b
dairy industry II–280b, 281a
direct primary V–102a
exploration II–380a; III–313a
factory safety and health standards IV–68b
ferries III–11b
forest fires II–348a
Fort Saint Antoine VI–187b
Fort Winnebago VII–306a
Fox Indians III–88b, 88b–89a
Fox-Wisconsin Waterway III–89a
fur trade III–209a; V–121a
German immigrants III–336b
ginseng III–181a
Granger laws III–209b
Green Bay III–225b
homeopathy III–293b
Indian Country III–379a
Indian factories II–480a
Indian hostilities I–311b–12a
Indian land cession II–21a; IV–107b
Indian migration I–398a–b
Indian reservation system VI–97a
Indians I–86a; IV–387a
Indian warfare III–399b
Iowa jurisidiction III–467b
iron III–216b
Jesuit missions III–499b
Lake Michigan IV–332b
lakes II–391a
land grant for education IV–412b
land speculation IV–99b
lead III–90a, 147a; IV–122a,b, 123a; V–102b
lotteries IV–191b
lumber industry IV–204a
Maiden's Rock IV–224b
Menominee Iron Range IV–303b
Mormons VI–87a
mounds III–365a; IV–420b
New England settlers V–50a
nickel III–14a
Nicolet's explorations V–95a
Nineteenth Amendment V–97a
Nonpartisan League V–106b
Northwest Territory III–329b
Old Copper culture II–386a
paper industry V–212a–b
Populist party V–365b
prairie V–387a
Prairie du Chien V–387b
Progressive party IV–84b; VII–308b
public employees IV–75b
public land sales V–452b
public land speculation I–107b
public land states V–453a
railroads VI–25b, 33b; VII–83b
recall VI–51a
retail sales VII–84b
Sauk Prairie VI–218b
school lands VI–228a
settlement IV–338b
Sioux-Chippewa War VI–294b
snowstorms II–351b
state fairs VI–392b
statehood I–351a; VI–413a
supreme court I–2a
taxation VII–11b
three-party system VII–135a
timberlands IV–99b; VII–60a
tobacco VII–66b–67a
tornadoes VII–75b
towns VII–81b
Treaty of Saint Louis III–383b
unemployment insurance IV–71a
unemployment legislation VI–328a
western lands VII–273a
westward movement VII–284a
wild rice VII–298a
Winnebago II–282b; VII–305b, 306a
Winnebago War VII–306b
workmen's compensation IV–80a
Wisconsin (battleship) VII–242a
Wisconsin, University of I–303a; IV–93b; VII–156b, 308a,b
Forest Products Laboratory III–75b
pharmacy V–275a,b
political science V–348b–49a
Wisconsin Agricultural Experiment Station I–303a,b
Wisconsin Dairyman's Association II–280b
Wisconsin Et Al. v. *Illinois and Chicago Sanitary District* . *See* Chicago Sanitary District Case
Wisconsin Evangelical Lutheran Synod IV–206b
Wisconsin Historical Society II–108b
WISCONSIN IDEA VII–308b; VII–308a
Wisconsin Phalanx II–147a
Wisconsin Progressives VII–53a
WISCONSIN RAILROAD COMMISSION* v. *CHICAGO, BURLINGTON AND QUINCY RAILROAD COMPANY (1922) **VII–308b**; II–136b
Wisconsin River III–89a; VII–305b, 306b
exploration III–119a, 329a; IV–372a; VII–73b
Fort Crawford II–253b
Fox-Wisconsin Waterway III–89a
fur trade III–144a
Sauk Prairie VI–218b
Wisconsin State Fair (1895) VI–392b
Wisconsin State Historical Society III–278b, 279b, 285a; VI–271b
Wisconsin Territory II–284b
Wisconsin v. *Illinois* (1933) II–20a
Wisconsin v. *Michigan* (1936) I–351b
Wisconsin Volunteer Infantry VI–135a
"Wisdom, Justice, Moderation" (motto) VI–393 (table)
"WISE, AND GOOD AND RICH" VII–309a; IV–267a; V–100b; VI–94a
Wise, Fort (Colo.) I–290a; IV–208b
Wise, Henry A. (gov.) VI–42b
Wise, Isaac Mayer (rabbi) IV–9b
Wise, John (aeron.) I–248a; II–343b
Wise, John (cler.) II–149a; III–469a; VI–223b
Wislizenus, Frederick (trav.) IV–1b
Wissler, Clark (anthrop.) I–129a
Wistar, Caspar (physic.) II–10b; VII–309b
Wistar, Casper (physic.) III–182b
Wistar, Richard (mfr.) III–182b
Wistar Association VII–309b
WISTAR PARTIES VII–309a
Wister, Owen (writ.) VII–346b
WITCHCRAFT VII–309b; II–258a, 376b
colonial punishment V–464b
Corey, Giles V–400a
folklore III–48b
"Holy Lord" hinges III–293b
Salem IV–265b; VI–199a

WITCHCRAFT (cont.)
sumptuary laws VI–440b
women VII–313a
Witch hazel III–381a
"WITCH–HUNT" VII–310a
Witheridge, John (mer.) V–243b
Witherspoon, John (states.) II–308a; V–409a
"With God All Things Are Possible" (motto) VI–395 (table)
WITHLACOOCHEE RIVER, BATTLES AT (1835,1836) **VII–311a**
"WITH MALICE TOWARD NONE, WITH CHARITY FOR ALL" VII–311a
Witnesses
Bill of Rights I–299a; II–204a,b
travel allowance IV–339a
Witt, Christopher (paint.) V–185b
Wittenberg, Henry (athlete) V–154b
Wittenmyer, Annie (ref.) VII–312a
Wiyot (Indians) I–86a; VII–367b
W.J. Barta (towboat) VII–77b
W. L. Clements Library (Univ. of Mich.) III–284b
WMs. *See* Women Marines
WNPC. *See* Women's National Political Caucus
"Wobblies." *See* Industrial Workers of the World
Woburn (Mass.) IV–360b; VI–167a
Wodziwob (Indian) III–177a–b; V–4a
Woerd, Charles Vander (watchmaker) II–78b
Wöhler, Friedrich (chem.) II–11b, 422a
Wolcott, Oliver (law.) II–305b, 308a
Wolcott, Oliver, Jr. (pol.) III–5a
Wolcott, Roger (col. gov.) VI–451b
Wolf, Fred D. (inv.) II–420b
Wolf, Henry (engr.) VII–319b
Wolfe, Bertram (Communist) II–144a
Wolfe, James (off.) I–3b; III–116b–17a
Quebec II–126a; IV–405b; VI–1a–b; VII–115a
Wolfe, Samuel M. (au.) III–271a
Wolfe, Thomas (au.) IV–164a, 189b
Wolfe, Tom (au.) IV–165a; V–79a
Wolfert's Roost (essay) VI–312b
***WOLFF PACKING COMPANY* v. *COURT OF INDUSTRIAL RELATIONS* (1923) VII–311a**
"Wolf packs" (U–boats) I–214b; II–217b; VII–343a
Wolf River II–22a
Wolfskill, William (trapper) VI–368a
Wolf v. *Colorado* (1949) VI–249a
Wollaston (Mass.) IV–265a
Wollaston, John (paint.) V–186b, 187a
Wolverine State VI–394 (table)
WOLVES VII–311b; III–150a; IV–233a; VII–357b
bounties I–352b
preservation V–217b
sign language VI–286b
Womack, Robert (cowboy) II–264a; V–437a
WOMAN'S CHRISTIAN TEMPERANCE UNION VII–312a; III–261b; V–429b; VII–313b
peace movements VII–236a
Woman's Education Association of Boston IV–250b
WOMAN'S PARTY, NATIONAL VII–312b; VII–315b
Woman's Peace Party VII–236b
WOMAN'S RIGHTS MOVEMENT VII–313a; I–100b; VII–316b–17a
antislavery I–137b
antiwar groups VII–236b
Bloomer dress I–323b
divorce II–356b
Edenton Tea Party II–393a
employment VII–141a
Equal Rights party II–457b
family structure II–486a–b
Farmer–Labor party II–491a
fashion II–372b
Kansas IV–26b
marriage IV–257a
Minor v. *Happersett* IV–359a
missionary work IV–365b
National Woman's Party VII–312b
New York State V–87a
Nineteenth Amendment V–97a
nurses V–127b
phrenologists V–294a
property rights V–434a
prostitution V–437b, 438a
Quakers V–470b
radicals VI–13a–b
Seneca Falls convention VI–261b
sexual attitudes VI–267a
social pacifism V–181b
suffrage III–91b–92a
Twenty–seventh Amendment I–95a
Woman's Christian Temperance Union VII–312a
work regulation VI–328a
See also Feminist movement
WOMAN'S SUFFRAGE VII–314b; II–325b; III–91b–92a; VI–431a; VII–208b, 312a, 317a
Alaska I–77b
colonial settlements VI–434b
Equal Rights party II–457b, 457b
Greenback party III–225a
League of Women Voters IV–126a
National Woman's Party VII–312b
Nineteenth Amendment I–95a, 297a, 297a; II–206a; V–97a
Progressive movement V–427a, 428a–b
Seneca Falls convention VI–262a
state government VI–398b
voter turnout V–108b
Washington State VII–248a
woman's rights movement VII–313b–14a
Wyoming VII–346a
Woman's Temperance Crusade VII–312a
Woman Suffrage Association, National American III–91b, 92a
Woman with Dog (sculp.) VI–244a
Womb chair III–137a
Women
advertising I–18b
agricultural workers II 495b–
basketball I–272a,b
campaign of 1920 I–427b
Charter of Liberties I–500b
commerce clause II–136a
cosmetics II–233b
dairy industry II–279b
education I–5b, 495a
etiquette IV–241a
farmers institutes II–494b
higher education II–23b, 115a,b, 227b, 399a
household electrification II–418a–b
Indian tribes I–288a
International Exposition of 1895 III–453b
labor legislation VII–213b
life expectancy IV–150a, 151a
Little League I–271b
Mann Act IV–240a
minimum wage VII–269a–b
patriotic societies II–294a
religious societies VI–77b
Russell Sage Foundation VI–177a
safety I–7b
unemployment VII–140b–41a
wages I–12a
Yale University VII–351a
See also Marriage
WOMEN, CITIZENSHIP OF MARRIED VII–315b; V–7a
Women Accepted for Voluntary Emergency Service VII–318a
Women Airforce Service Pilots VII–318b
Women in Community Service III–504a
WOMEN IN PUBLIC LIFE, BUSINESS, AND PROFESSIONS VII–316a; II–486a,b; III–92a; IV–257a
civil service II–61a
clothing industry II–81b
Council of National Defense II–243b
discrimination II–457b
Edenton Tea Party VII–16b
Equal Employment Opportunity Commission II–455b
Grasso, Ella II–180b
labor force V–133a
law IV–121b
medical education IV–3a
Pawtucket weavers' strike IV–61b
philanthropy V–280a
scientific societies VI–238b
teaching VI–229b
textile industry II–239b–40a
veterinary medicine VII–177b
World War II VII–88a
See also Woman's Rights Movement
Women in the Air Force VII–318b
WOMEN IN THE MILITARY SERVICES VII–318a
National Guard IV–346a–b
navy V–23b–24a
soldiers' homes VI–336b
uniforms VII–145a
World War I II–372a
Women in the Wilderness (Pa.) II–147a
Women Marines VII–318a
Womens Amateur Championship (golf) III–198a
Women's Armed Services Integration Act (1948) VII–318b
Women's Army Auxiliary Corps VII–318a
Women's Army Corps VII–145a, 318a
Women's Bureau IV–78a–b
Women's International League for Peace and Freedom VII–236b
"Women's Liberation" VII–317b
Women's Medical Specialist Corps IV–290b; VII–318b
Women's National Political Caucus VII–318a
Women's Peace Party V–236a
Women's Relief Corps III–207b

Women's studies II–402b
Women Strike for Peace V–237a
Women workers
equality of treatment IV–81a
industrial labor force IV–75a
legislation IV–68b
Massachusetts IV–293b
minimum wage IV–352b, 353a,b
protective legislation IV–80a,b
strikes IV–61b
textile factories IV–61a
World War I IV–69a
Wonder Book for Boys and Girls I–335a
Wonder-Working Providence of Sion's Saviour in New England III–280a
Wong Kim Ark VII–155b
Wood II–7a
building I–377a,b, 379a, 441b
canal construction IV–174b
distillation products II–8a
Wood, A. B. (min.) IV–124a
Wood, Abraham (off., expl.) I–277b; V–31b–32a, 145a; VII–201b
Wood, Fernando (pol.) II–222b; VI–459b
Wood, Grant (paint.) V–192b
Wood, John Ellis (off.) VI–336a
Wood, John S. (pol.) I–315a
Wood, Leonard (off., adm.) I–427b; II–268b; VI–165b; VII–31a
Cuba V–329b
Philippines V–283b
preparedness movement V–390b
War Department VII–230a
Wood, Robert E. (off.) III–480a
Wood, Samuel, and Sons I–494a
Wood, Samuel N. (off.) II–245b–46a
Wood, Walter A. (expl.) V–337b
Wood, William (au.) IV–231a
Woodbridge (N.J.) II–350b; III–183b, 184a
Woodbridge, William C. (educ.) II–397a
Wood Buffalo Park (Can.) VII–297a
Woodbury, Levi (jur.) II–464b; VI–445b
Woodbury, W. P. (off.) IV–33b
Wood carving VI–242b
Wood Creek VI–385a
Woodcuts IV–222a; V–413a
Wood End (Mass.) I–447a
WOOD ENGRAVING VII–319a
WOODEN INDIAN VII–319b
Woodford, William (off.) III–215b
Woodhouse, James (chem.) II–10b; III–408a; IV–348a
Woodhull, Victoria (ref.) VII–313b
Woodin, William H. (ind.) V–43b
WOOD LAKE, BATTLE OF (1862) **VII–319b**; VI–296b
Woodlands. *See* Forestry; Forest Service, United States; Timberlands
Woodlands (Tex.) II–48b
WOODLAND TRADITION VII–319b; I–11a,b
Fox III–88b
pipe V–318a,b
Winnebago VII–306a
See also Eastern Woodlands culture
Woodlawn Plantation (Mount Vernon, Va.) IV–472a
Wood lot IV–102a
Wood pulp
Alabama I–72a
paper I–16b
See also Paper and Pulp Manufacture
Wood River III–328a
Woodrow Wilson House (Washington, D.C.) IV–472a
Woodrow Wilson International Center for Scholars VI–319b
Woodrow Wilson School of Public and International Affairs V–409a
Woods, Andrew (fur trader) VI–196a
Woods, Robert (av. eng.) I–52a
Woods, Robert Archey (soc. worker) VI–330b
Woods, Rosemary VII–255b
Woods, William A. (jur.) V–463b
Woods, William B. (jur.) VI–446a
Woodsdale (Kans.) II–245b
Woods Hole (Mass.)
Fish Commission laboratories V–134b
Fish Commission laboratory III–28a–b
Marine Biological Laboratory IV–250b
Woods Hole Laboratory. *See* Marine Biological Laboratory, Woods Hole
Woods Hole Oceanographic Institution III–164b, 233b; IV–251a; V–135a
Woods Hole squid IV–250b
Woodsonville (Ky.) VII–34b
Woodstock (comic character) V–72b
Woodstock (Vt.) VI–101a
skiing VI–298a
Woodstock (Va.) VII–71a
"Woodstock Races" (1864) VII–71a
Wood v. *Brown* (1932) I–147b
Woodward (Okla.) VII–76a
Woodward, Augustus B. (jur.) II–45b, 338b; IV–331a
Woodward, Bob (jour.) V–78a; VII–255b
Woodward, C. Vann (hist.) IV–165a
Woodward, Joseph J. (med. off.) IV–291a
Woodward, Robert B. (chem.) V–100a
Woodward, Robert S. (math., phys.) I–457a; III–167a
Woodward, Samuel (physic.) IV–305b
Woodward, William H. (adm.) II–293b
Woodward Plan. *See* Detroit, Woodward Plan of
Woodworking I–490a
Indian III–374a
interchangeable manufacture III–442a–b
New Hampshire V–54b
prehistoric tools II–386a
Woodworth, C. M. (bot.) I–46a
Woodworth, Samuel (print., jour.) V–152a
Wooffendale, Robert (dent.) II–329b
Wool, John E. (off.) II–363b; VII–350a
Wool Act (1954) VII–321a
Woolco department stores III–33a
Woolen Act (1699) II–123a; VI–240a
Woolens II–119a, 371a
Woolens Bill (1827) III–257a
WOOL GROWING AND MANUFACTURE VII–320a; I–460b; VI–272b–73a; VII–42b–43a,b, 44a
as money II–140b
Boston I–344b
Civil War II–69a
clothing industry II–81a
colonial industry III–413b
colonial restrictions III–346b; IV–242b; VI–107b, 108a
household manufacture IV–246a
imports VII–87b
linsey-woolsey IV–158a
Maine IV–226b–27a
meat-packing by-products IV–281a
Navigation Acts V–16a,b
Ohio V–141b
prices V–404a
Rhode Island VI–133a,b
Santa Fe VI–215a
sheep ranching VI–45a–b
shipping IV–310b
soap VI–323a
South America VI–343b, 345a
tariff III–257a; VI–465b
tax II–164b
Tennessee VII–26a
textiles VII–83a
Vermont VII–172a,b
weaving IV–187b
WOOLLY HEADS VII–321b; II–184b
Woolman, Albert (sol.) III–207b
Woolman, John (Quaker) I–135a; III–123b; V–279b; VI–311a
pacifism V–181b
Woolsey, John M. (jur.) I–479a
Woolsey, Melancthon (off.) VI–209a
Woolsey, Theodore Dwight (educ.) V–347b
Woolsey, Theodore S. (jur.) II–100a
Woolwich (Eng.) II–375a
Woolworth, Frank W. (mer.) III–32b
Woolworth, F. W., Company VI–258b
Woolworth Building (N.Y.C.) I–164b; VI–299a
Woonsocket (R.I.) IV–347b
Wooster (Ohio) II–368b; III–223b
Wooster, David (off.) II–286a; VI–139a
Wootka Sound Convention (1790) VII–166a
Worcester (Mass.) I–9b; III–278b, 285a; IV–266b, 268b
Equal Rights Association III–91b
Massachusetts Spy V–69b
mental asylum IV–305b
minutemen IV–360b
railroad III–449b; VI–25a
tornado VII–76a
Worcester, Joseph (lexicog.) II–340a
Worcester, Samuel A. (miss.) VII–321b–22a
Worcester County (Mass.) IV–207a
Worcester Gazette (news.) V–69b
Worcester's Readers IV–213a
WORCESTER* v. *GEORGIA (1832) **VII–321b**
Worden, John (nav. off.) IV–396b
Work, Hubert (off.) VI–54a
Workable Program for Community Improvement II–47a
Work and Win (series) II–341b
Work council movement. *See* Shop Committee
Workers. *See* Labor; Labor, Department of
Workers' Alliance VII–323b
Workers' Party of America II–144a, 493a
Work force. *See* Occupations, Changes in
Workhouses III–306b; VI–327b
Workies VI–13b
Working Men's Advocate (period.) III–296a

Workingmen's Benevolent Association II–86b; IV–62b
WORKINGMEN'S PARTY VII–322a; II–29a; IV–61b, 61b
California I–406a,b; IV–33a
Chinese exclusion III–342a
labor reforms IV–80a
Workingmen's Party of California IV–64a
Workingmen's Protective Union II–220b
Working People's Nonpartisan Political League II–491a
Workmen's Circle. *See* Arbeter Ring
WORKMEN'S COMPENSATION VII–322a; I–7b; II–441a–b, 491a; III–204b, 426b, 431a–b, 435a–b; IV–294a–b; VI–328a, 331a
laissez-faire doctrine IV–85b
Progressive movement V–427a
Safety First movement VI–185a
state laws IV–68b, 80a
Washington State VII–248a
Works, John D. (pol.) IV–169a
WORKS PROGRESS ADMINISTRATION VII–322b; IV–71a; V–46a–b, 381b; VI–73b–74a; VII–140a
historical records III–281a
industrial research study III–409b
Mount Hood ski resort VI–101b
National Research Project V–425b
National Youth Administration VII–364a
school lunch program V–128b
zoos VII–371a
World Almanac I–91a
World Association of Girl Guides and Girl Scouts III–181a
World Bank I–254b, 361b; IV–113b; VI–468b
World Book (ency.) II–444b
World Championship of Tennis VII–30b
World Council of Churches II–353a, 387a
World Court. *See* International Court of Justice
World Cup (soccer) III–288a
WORLD ECONOMIC CONFERENCE (1933) **VII–324a**; VI–288b–89a
World Health Organization III–326a, 453a; VI–316a
World Hockey Association III–287b, 288a
World Peace Foundation VII–236b
World Publishing Company II–340b
World Safe for Democracy. *See* Democracy, World Safe for
WORLD'S COLUMBIAN EXPOSITION (1893) **VII–324a**; I–109a; II–18a; III–453b; IV–337b; VII–27a
apostolic delegation I–144a
architecture I–164b
Beaux Arts VI–243b
colonial architecture II–100a
Court of Honor II–46a
electric power and light II–415a, 419a
ferris wheel III–11b
Field Museum of Natural History III–19a
landscape architecture IV–96b
Midway Plaisance IV–337a
mural painting V–191a
wild west show VII–298b
World Series (baseball) I–271b
WORLD'S INDUSTRIAL AND COTTON CENTENNIAL EXPOSITION (1884) **VII–324b**
World's Parliament of Religions (1893) IV–448a; V–171b, 172a
World's Woman's Christian Temperance Union VII–312b
World Trade Center (N.Y.C.) V–368b; VI–299a
World War Foreign Debt Commission VII–331b
WORLD WAR I VII–324b; II–314a; V–124a, 233b; VI–378a
Afro-American troops IV–340a–b
air combat I–57b–58a, 59a–b
aircraft I–50a, 51a,b
aircraft armament I–57b
aircraft industry I–235b, 236a
Air Force I–64b, 233b
Aisne defensive I–70a
Aisne–Marne operation I–70a
aluminum industry I–92a
American Expeditionary Forces I–101b–02a; II–297a; IV–84a
American Relief Administration V–280b
amnesty I–115b
Anglo-American relations I–122b
applied physics V–295a–b
Arabic case I–151a
Archangel (Russia) I–158b
armed merchantmen IV–313b
armed merchantment IV–169a
armistice I–159a, 176b
armored vehicles I–177a
army I–186a, 188b–89a
army slang VI–301a
army uniforms VII–144b–45a
artillery I–200a
balloon warfare I–248a
battle deaths VII–190b
Battle of Belleau Wood I–286a–b
black enlistment I–29b
blockades I–321a–b
bombing I–66b, 328a
booby traps I–332a
"bully beef" II–436a
burial procedures I–478a
business cycles I–392 (table)
campaign of 1916 I–427a; III–269b
Camp Doniphan VI–287b
camps and cantonments I–434a–35a
Cantigny I–446a
censorship I–481a
Champagne–Marne operation I–491b
Château-Thierry I–502a
chemical industries II–8a; VII–281b
chief of naval operations V–13b
China incident II–28a
church support VI–79a,b
civil defense II–50a
commerce II–217b
confiscation of property II–168b
conscientious objectors II–185b
conscription and draft II–186a–b, 367a–b, 451a
contraband II–446b–47a; IV–182b
copper industry II–223b
Corps of Engineers II–450a
costs II–234a, 476a; VII–228 (table), 228b–29a
Council of National Defense II–243a
counterespionage VI–252a
Customs Intelligence Bureau II–277a
declaration of war VII–224b, 237a
demobilization II–324a; IV–341b
desertions II–335b
dirigibles II–343b
disease mortality IV–291a
dollar-a-year men II–359a
"doughboy" II–365b–66a
"embalmed beef" II–436a
Emergency Fleet Corporation V–455a; VI–281b
Employment Service II–442a
enemy aliens II–445b; III–350a–b
enemy trading VII–94a
Engineering Council II–449a
espionage VI–373b
Espionage Act II–463a–b
excess profits tax II–467a
exchange of prisoners II–468b
explosives V–383b
Federal Reserve System III–6b
financing II–317a; IV–143a
Ford's peace ship III–60a–b
foreign policy VI–439a
foreign trade VII–87b
Four-Minute Men II–139b; III–85a
Fourteen Points III–85b
freedom of speech III–104a
freedom of the press III–105a
freedom of the seas III–106b
free ships, free goods III–110a
Fuel Administration III–129b
general staff II–438a
German-language press V–75b
gold standard III–193b, 194a
horse cavalry I–476a
hospitals I–191b
House–Grey Memorandum III–309a
housing III–310a
immigration II–432b
Industrial Workers of the World III–412b
inflation III–415a; V–405b
influenza III–416b
Inquiry III–420a
intelligence tests III–440b
isolationism III–480a
Japan IV–106b
Jefferson Barracks III–494b
labor needs I–25b, 29a; IV–69a
Lafayette Escadrille IV–83b
land booms IV–6b
Latin American Commerce IV–111b
laws of war VII–225b
Liberty bonds III–85a–b
literature IV–164b
logistics I–190a
losses VII–232 (table), 233a
Lost Generation IV–189b
loyalty testing IV–202b
Lusitania sinking IV–205a
machine guns IV–215a
mapmaking I–463b
marines IV–252b
mental illness IV–304a, 306a–b
merchant marine IV–311a
merchant shipping II–217b, 314a–b
Meuse–Argonne offensive IV–189a, 319a
Michigan industry IV–331b
military decoration II–310b–11a
military photography V–293a
military policy IV–343b
military roads VI–156a
Mississippi River IV–373a
Montdidier–Noyon operation IV–404a
moral values IV–408b
motor trucks IV–419b

munitions IV–430b, 431a,b
Murmansk IV–435a
naturalization V–6b
neutrality III–69a, 456a; V–34a, 35a–b
neutral rights V–39a
newspaper coverage V–74a
nitrates V–98a–b
North Sea mine barrage IV–351a–b; V–27b, 119b
ocean shipping VI–280b
Officers' Reserve Corps V–138b
opposition IV–69b; V–236a–b
paratroops V–213b
peace groups VII–236b
"Peace without victory" V–238a
petroleum industry V–270b
pharmaceutical industry V–274a
Piave River operations V–307b
Pittman Act V–321b
political minorities IV–358b–59a
potash supply V–376a
preparedness V–390b
presidential authority II–179a
prices V–401b, 405b
profiteering V–426a
Progressive movement V–428b
Prohibition II–407a
propaganda V–432a; VII–82a, 332a–33a
prostitution V–438a
psychological warfare V–440b–41a
psychology V–442a–b
purchasing power of money IV–393a
radicals and radicalism VI–13b–14a
railroads VII–99a
rations II–436a
recruitment VI–61a
Red Cross VI–61b
Reparation Commission VI–87b
reparations III–352b; V–215a; VII–363b
Reserve Officers' Training Corps VI–98b
Root mission to Russia VI–163b
Russia VI–178a
Saint-Mihiel VI–197a
scientific research IV–457a
Sedition Act VI–255a
shipbuilding VI–279b
Siberian expedition VI–284a
Siegfried Line VI–285b
Socialist movement VI–326b
Somme offensive VI–338a–b
South American trade VI–343b–44a
submarines IV–311b, 431b; VI–423a, 424a–b
Sussex Case VI–452b
tariff VI–467b
taxation VII–7a, 12a, 12b–13a
temperance movement VII–23b
textile production V–67a
thrift stamps VII–55b
torpedo warfare V–27b; VII–76b
treason trials VII–107a–b
Treaty of Berlin I–290b
Treaty of Versailles VII–172b
trenches VII–115a
troop mobilization IV–384a
United States–German Mixed Claims Commission IV–381b
Unknown Soldiers II–310a; VII–156b
U.S. aid I–246b
U.S. entry I–122b, 286a; III–97a
U.S. Geological Survey III–164a
venereal disease V–448a; VII–169a
veterans I–108a,b, 330a–b, 331a
veterans' benefits V–257a–b, 258a
veterans' organizations VII–175a
Victory loan of 1919 VII–182b
Virgin Islands VII–203b
Wadsworth Agreement VII–213a
wages IV–69b
West Point graduates IV–341a
Williamsburg VII–301b
Wilson mediation V–233a
women II–372a; III–92a; VII–318a
Ypres–Lys operation VII–366b
Zimmerman telegram VII–368b
See also Versailles, Treaty of; War Industries Board
WORLD WAR I, ECONOMIC MOBILIZATION FOR VII–327b; I–153a; IV–384a; VII–123a, 326a
aircraft industry I–235b–36a; IV–433a–b
backyard gardening III–151a
grains V–430a
Hog Island Shipyard III–288a
Lever Act IV–135b
ordnance V–163b
public control of business I–390b
Railroad Administration VI–19a, 29a
War Finance Corporation VII–231a
War Industries Board VII–231b
War Labor Board VII–232a
War Trade Board VII–243b
zinc VII–369a
WORLD WAR I, NAVY IN VII–328a; II–314a; V–20a–b; VII–325b
admirals I–14a
aircraft carriers I–54a
convoys II–217b
Dreadnought II–370a
dry dock construction II–375b
Emergency Fleet Corporation II–438a–b
marine squadrons IV–252b
Navy Department V–18a
North Sea mine barrage V–119b
ordnance V–164a
warships VII–242b
WORLD WAR I PEACE CONFERENCE (1919) **VII–330b**; III–420a; VII–172b–74a
laws of war VII–225b
League of Nations IV–124a
Monroe Doctrine IV–401b
WORLD WAR I, U.S. RELIEF IN VII–329a; I–245b
Belgium I–285b–86a
war debts VII–331b
Young Men's Christian Association VII–363a
WORLD WAR I WAR DEBTS VII–331b; II–301a–b; III–66a, 69a; VII–326a
France III–97b
German reparations II–296a–b
Great Britain I–122b
Johnson Debt-Default Act IV–134b
Lausanne Agreement IV–117b
public debt II–300a
WORLD WAR II VII–333b; II–314b–15a, 489a; V–124a; VI–468a,b; VII–174a, 331a
Aachen I–1a
Afro-American troops IV–340b
air battle of Germany III–174a
aircraft I–50a, 53a–b, 234b
aircraft armament I–57b
aircraft carriers I–54b
Air Force I–59b–60b, 64a
air power I–66b–67b
air war against Japan III–489b
Alaska I–78a, 79b–80a
Aleutian Islands I–84b–85a, 439b
aluminum production I–92a
American First Committee I–97a
amnesty I–115b
amphibious warfare IV–252b; VII–139a
Anglo-American relations I–123a–b
antiwar demonstrations VII–365b
Antwerp I–140b–41a
Appam Case I–144b; V–422a
apprenticeship I–148b
Arizona economy I–172b
armed merchantmen IV–313b
armored vehicles I–178a,b
army I–186b–87a, 189a
army aviation I–188b
army logistics I–190a–b
army uniforms VII–145a
artillery I–200a–b
Atlantic I–214a–b
Atlantic Charter I–215a
Atlantic Intracoastal Waterway VI–149a
atomic bomb I–215b; IV–433b
atomic energy development I–215b, 217b
automobile industry I–230a,b
aviation industry I–235b, 237a,b
"baby boom" V–363a
Bahamas I–243b
balance of trade I–246a
balloon warfare I–248a
Bastogne I–273b
Bataan–Corregidor I–273b–74a; V–284a
battle deaths VII–190b
Battle of Bismark Sea I–307b–08a
Battle of Java Sea III–492b
Battle of Leyte Gulf IV–138a
Battle of Midway IV–337a
Battle of the Bulge I–273b, 379a–80a
biological and chemical warfare VI–105a
Bizerte V–113a
blockades I–321b
bombing I–328a–b; II–9b
booby traps I–332a
Bougainville I–350a–b
burial procedures I–478a
Burma and Ledo roads I–386b–87a
business cycles I–392 (table)
Cairo Conference I–403b
California I–407b–08a, 408b
campaign of 1940 I–429a
Canadian–American relations I–439b
Caroline Islands I–459a
Casablanca Conference I–465a
censorship I–481a–b; V–74a
Cherbourg II–13b
China–Burma–India Theater II–26a
Choiseul raid II–33a
church work VI–79b
civil defense II–50a
commercial airlines I–68a
communications II–424b–25a
Communist Party, USA

WORLD WAR II (cont.)
II–145a–b
confiscation of property II–168b–69a
conscientious objectors II–50b, 185b
conscription and draft II–186b, 367b, 451a
contraband II–213a, 213a
convoys II–217b
copper industry II–223b
cost of living II–236a
costs II–234a; VII–228 (table), 228b–29a
Cotentin Peninsula II–237a; V–110b
Customs Service II–277a
daylight saving time II–296b
D Day II–297a
Declaration of Panama V–200a
declaration of war VII–224b, 237a
defoliation II–319a
demobilization II–323b, 324a–b
desertion II–335b
dirigibles II–345a
dollar diplomacy II–359b
domestic support V–236b
drug testing V–467b
Dumbarton Oaks Conference II–380a
economic recovery V–170b
Elbe River II–407b
employment VII–141a,b, 323b–24a
employment services II–442a
enemy–alien property VII–94a
enemy aliens II–445b–46a
espionage VI–373b–74a
European Jews IV–11a
excess profits tax II–467a; III–205a
exchange of prisoners II–468b–69a
farmers' cooperatives II–221a
farm production VI–175b
fashions II–372b
federal debt VI–449b
Federal Reserve System III–7b
financing II–317b
Flying the Hump III–45b
Flying Tigers III–46b
foreign aid VII–332a
foreign investment II–301a
Foreign Service III–71b–72a
foreign trade VII–88a
foxholes VII–115b
Franco–American relations III–97b
freedom of the seas III–106b
Geneva Conventions III–162a
Gilbert Islands III–180a
gliders III–187a
Gothic Line III–200b
government controls of economy I–391a,b
government regulation of industries V–458b
gross national product II–300a–b
Guadalcanal III–229a
Guam III–230b, 425b
guerrillas III–231b
gunboats III–234b
Gustav Line III–235a; IV–404a
Hawaii III–264a
helicopters III–270a
Home Owners' Loan Association III–294b
Hoover Commissions III–299b
housing III–310a
Huertgen Forest III–314a–b
hydrogen bomb III–324a
Iceland III–327a–b
Indian migration to cities III–397b
industrial research III–409b–10a; IV–245a
inflation III–195a, 415a–b
isolationism III–480a
Italian campaign I–141a–b
Iwo Jima III–485a
Japanese–American relocation III–490b; IV–359a; VII–227b
Japanese–language press V–75b
Jedburgh Operation V–138b
Jefferson Barracks III–494b
Kasserine Pass IV–32a; V–113a
Korean occupation IV–55a
labor I–153a; IV–73a
Lae and Salamaua IV–83a
Latin America III–199b; IV–112a
Lawrence Radiation Laboratory IV–119a
laws of war VII–226b
lend–lease II–301b; III–60b; IV–134a; VII–237b
liberalism IV–140b
Liberia IV–141b
Lingayen Gulf IV–157b; V–284a
literature IV–164b
losses VII–232 (table), 233a
loyalty testing IV–203a
Luftwaffe I–328a
machine guns IV–215a; V–27a
Makin raid IV–229a
Malmédy massacre IV–230b
Manhattan Project IV–237b
mapmaking I–464a
marine insurance III–428b–29a
martial law IV–259a
merchant marine IV–312a
Merrill's Marauders IV–314a
Mexico IV–322b, 328b
Michigan IV–332a
Micronesia VII–125a,b
military justice VII–143a
military policy IV–343a, 343b
military roads VI–156a
mines IV–351b; V–27b
missile development IV–363a
mobilization IV–384a
Monroe Doctrine IV–402a
Monte Cassino IV–404a–b
Moscow Conference of Foreign Ministers IV–415b
municipal housing IV–428b
munitions IV–430b, 431b
"Murmansk run" IV–435a
Myitkyina IV–446b
national parks V–220a
natural gas V–5b
naturalization V–6b
naval competition V–10b
neutrality III–456a; V–34a, 35b–36a, 37a–38b
Neutrality Acts of 1935–37 V–38a
newspapers V–74a
New York World's Fair V–89a
Normandy invasion II–297a; V–110a
North African campaign I–55b; V–112b
nuclear fission V–300a–b
nuclear physics V–297a
occupation of Germany III–174b
oceanographic research V–135a; VI–242b
Office of Scientific Research and Development V–137a
Office of Strategic Services III–439a; V–137b
Ohio industry V–142a
Oise–Aisne operation V–146b
Okinawa V–147b
ordnance V–163b
Oregon V–166a
Pacific I–55b–56a
pacifists V–182a–b
paratroops V–213b
peace movement VII–236b
Pearl Harbor I–328a, 484a; V–239a
Peleliu V–242b
petroleum industry V–270b; VI–357a
pharmaceutical industry V–274a
Philippines V–284a–b
Pittsburgh steel V–322a
Ploesti oil fields V–332a
polar regions V–337b
pork barrel contracts V–366b
Potsdam Conference V–378b
presidential authority II–179a
price controls I–42a
price–fixing V–401b
prices V–406a
profiteering V–426a
propaganda V–432b; VII–333a–b
psychological warfare V–441a
public debt II–300a, 301b; VI–294a
purchasing power of money IV–393a
Rabaul VI–5a
racial discrimination VI–256a
radar II–425a; VI–9b–10b
railroads VI–30a
ranger battalions VI–46b–47a
Reconstruction Finance Corporation VI–60a
recruitment VI–61a
Red Cross VI–62a
refugees V–342a–b
Remagen VI–83b
reparations III–352b
repatriation of Soviet nationals IV–56b
Reserve Officers' Training Corps VI–98b–99a
Russia VI–178b–79a
Saint-Lô VI–193b
Saint Louis VI–194b
Saint-Vith VI–198a
Saipan VI–198a, 198a
Salerno VI–199b
savings bonds VI–222b
science VI–231b, 232a
sea power VI–248b
shipbuilding VI–279b, 280b–81a
ships IV–432a
Sicilian campaign VI–284b
silver VI–289a
ski regiments VI–298a–b
Smaller War Plants Corporation II–498b
solid–state physics V–304b
South American trade VI–344a
South Carolina VI–348a
Southeast Asia rubber VI–168a
southern industry V 67b–
Spain VI–360b
state debts II–303a
steel industry IV–72b
strategic decisions IV–180a
submarines IV–431b; VI–423a
Tarawa VI–462a
taxation VII–8a, 11b, 12a, 13a
Teheran Conference VII–18a
territorial waters VII–33a
Tinian VII–62a
Tokyo Express VII–68a
torpedo warfare VII–76b
treason VII–106b, 107a–b
trucks IV–420a
trusts VII–123b
Tunisia I–308a
Typhus Commission IV–292a
United Mine Workers VII–151a

United Nations Declaration VII–151b
United States–Italy Mixed Claims Commission IV–382a
Unknown Soldiers II–310a; VII–156b
U.S. Geological Survey III–164a
V-2 rocket VI–159a
venereal disease VII–169a
veterans I–108a,b, 330b, 331b
veterans' benefits V–257b, 258a
veterans' organizations VII–175a
victory gardens III–151a
visit and search VII–205a
wage controls V–255b–56a
Wake VII–218b
war crimes trials I–212b; VII–229a
war memorials I–275b
War Relief Control Board V–281a
West Point graduates IV–341a
Wisconsin VII–308a–b
women IV–73b; VII–314a, 318a–b
Yalta Conference VII–351b
yellow peril VII–357a
Young Men's Christian Association VII–363a
See also Pearl Harbor
WORLD WAR II, NAVY IN VII–341b; II–314b, 375b; V–20b–21b; VII–335a,b, 336a, 337a–38a, 338b–39a
admirals I–14a
barrage rocket IV–363a
Battle of Coral Sea II–225a
Battle of Eastern Solomons II–387a
Battle of Empress Augusta Bay II–443a
Battle of Java Sea III–492b
Battle of Komandorskiye Islands IV–54a
Battle of Leyte Gulf IV–138a
Battle of Lombok Strait IV–182a
Battle of Makassar Strait IV–228b–29a
Battle of Midway IV–336a
Battle of the Atlantic I–214a
Battle of the Philippine Sea V–285b
Bougainville I–350a
Caroline Islands I–459a
carrier battles I–55b–56a, 234b
Emergency Fleet Corporation II–438b
fleets V–24b
Japan III–489b
Lexington IV–136b
Lingayen Gulf IV–158a
Marshall Islands IV–257b
Navy Department V–18b
Normandy invasion V–110b
Okinawa V–147b
ordnance V–164a
psychological warfare V–441a
Rabaul VI–5a
reserve V–28b
Saipan VI–198a
Salerno VI–200a
sea power VI–248b
slang VI–301b–02a
Tarawa VI–462b
Task Force 58 VII–1a
Tokyo Express VII–68a
Wake VII–218b
warships VII–241b, 242b, 243a, 243a,b
WORLD WARS, PROPAGANDA IN THE VII–332a; V–432a–b; VII–325b
pamphleteering V–199a
U.S. neutrality V–35b
Voice of America VII–207a
Worm fence VI–19a
WORMLEY CONFERENCE (1876–77) **VII–344a**
Wormuth, Francis (pol. sci.) VII–227a
Worship, right of I–300b
Worshipful Company of Goldsmiths of the City of London VI–289b
Worsted industry VII–320b, 321a
Worth, William J. (off.) I–494b; III–267a; IV–329a, 391b; VI–261a
Worthington, Thomas (pol.) II–25b; IV–345a
"Worth thousands to the cause" V–239a
Wound chevrons II–312b
Wounded Knee (S.Dak.) I–107a; III–397a; V–210b
See also Wounded Knee, Battle of
WOUNDED KNEE, BATTLE OF (1890) **VII–344a**; I–219a; II–283b; III–177b; IV–316a; V–4b; VI–297a; VII–190b
Wovoka (Indian) III–177b; V–4b, 194b
WPA. *See* Works Progress Administration
Wrangel Island V–336b
Wrangell (Alaska) I–76a
Wray (Colo.) I–283a
Wren, Christopher (arch.) I–161a,b, 451a; II–45a
Wrenn, John H. II–109b
Wrestling
Olympic Games V–154a,b
Wright, Albert Hazen (nat.) V–91a
Wright, Anna (nat.) VI–91a
Wright, Benjamin (surv.) I–442a; II–459b
Wright, Carroll D. (statis.) V–425b
Wright, Chauncey (philos.) V–287b
Wright, Edward (cartog.) IV–247b
Wright, Elizur (actuary) III–432b
Wright, Fielding Lewis (pol.) I–71b, 429b
Wright, Frances (ref.) IV–452b; VII–322a
Wright, Frank Lloyd (arch.) I–164a, 165a; II–18a; III–136a
Wright, George (off.) VII–350b
Wright, Hendrick B. (pol.) II–222a
Wright, Henry (arch.) II–46b
Wright, Horatio G. (off.) V–142b; VI–186b, 376b
Wright, James (col. gov.) I–223b; III–168a,b; VI–220b
Wright, Marcus J. (off.) II–64a
Wright, Mickey (golfer) III–198b
Wright, Moses (surv.) III–291b
Wright, Nathan (cler.) I–24a
Wright, Orville (av.) I–50b–51a, 233a; II–346a
Wright, Patience Lovell (art.) VII–262a
Wright, Richard (au.) I–316a–b; IV–164b, 167a
Wright, R. M. (writ.) IV–240a
Wright, Silas (law., pol.) I–107b, 134a
Wright, Theodore S. (abolitionist) I–136b
Wright, Wilbur (av.) I–50b–51a, 233a
Wright Act (1887) III–477b
Wright Aeronautical Company I–236b
Wright–Bellanca engine I–51b
Wright Brothers I–59a, 232b, 235b
Wright–Martin Company I–235b
Wright–Patterson Air Force Base I–234b
Wrightstown (N.J.) I–434b
Wright Whirlwind motor IV–157a
Wrigley, William (ind.) I–466b
Wriston, Henry Merritt (educ.) I–372a–b
Wriston Report (1954) III–72a,b
"Writers in residence" IV–2b
Writing, Indian I–158a; IV–327a–b
Writings of George Washington III–281a
WRITS OF ASSISTANCE VII–344b; VI–249b; VII–14a–b, 117a
Wrought iron III–472a–b
W. T. Grant and Company III–33a
Wupatki National Monument V–217b
Wurf, Jerry (labor leader) IV–75b
Wurlitzer Company V–290b
Wurts brothers II–321b
Württemberg (Ger.) II–147a; III–255a, 335a; IV–338b
Wyandot (Indians) III–24b, 227b
Fort McIntosh treaties IV–216b
French and Indian War III–115a
Great Warriors Path VII–238b
Hull Treaty III–316a
land cession I–371b
Logstown Treaty IV–181b
Maumee Convention IV–276b
Oklahoma V–148b
removal III–394b
revolutionary war I–369a; III–400b; V–152b
Sandusky VI–208b
Treaty at Pittsburgh V–322a
Treaty of Fort Harmar III–255a
Treaty of Greenville III–383a
Upper Sandusky VII–157b
See also Huron
Wyandot County (Ohio) VII–157b
Wyandotte (Mich.) III–316a, 473a
WYANDOTTE CONSTITUTION (1859) **VII–345a**; IV–26a
Wyanoke Neck V–264b
Wyatt, Francis (col. gov.) V–376b
Wyatt family III–18b
Wyckoff Island V–240b
Wyeth (N.C.) I–19b
Wyeth, Nathaniel J. (trader, expl.) III–143b, 243b; V–168b, 310b
Wyeth, N. C. (illus., paint.) V–192b
Wyllys, Fort (N.Y.) VII–280a
Wyman, Seth (off.) IV–199a
Wynehamer v. *People* (1856) II–377b; V–339b
Wynne, James (statis.) VII–207a
WYOMING VII–345b; VI–395 (table)
Arapaho I–151b
Bannock I–264a
Black Hills I–312b–13a
cattle I–358a; II–249a; IV–280b
Cheyenne II–16b, 16b
Colorado River Compact II–130a
cow custom II–251a
Dakota Indians II–282b
Dakota Territory II–284b
exploration III–114a, 220b; IV–242a
Fort Bernard I–292b
Fort Bridger I–363a, 410a, 453a
Fort Connor I–357b
Fort Francis E. Warren

WYOMING (cont.)
VII–237b
Fort John IV–1b
Fort Laramie IV–108a
Fort Phil Kearny IV–33b
Fort Reno VI–87a
Fort Washakie VII–244a
Frémont exploration VII–271b
fur trapping I–452b
Green River III–226b
holes of the mountains III–291a
Independence Rock III–354a
Indian territory III–384a; IV–108b
Indian treaties IV–108b
Indian wars VII–239b
irrigation III–478a
Jackson Hole III–486a
Japanese–American relocation III–491a
Missouri River IV–380a
mountains I–296a–b
mustangs IV–445a
national parks and monuments V–217b, 218 (table)
Ninth Cavalry I–310a
open–range grazing V–160a
Oregon boundary V–165a
Oregon Territory III–328a
Overland Trail V–178b
Platte River Trail V–330b
Powell explorations V–384a
prairie dogs V–387b
public land I–247b
railroads VI–32b
ranches VI–45a
reclamation VI–53b
Rocky Mountains VI–160a,b
roundups VI–161a
Rustler War VI–181a
sheep wars VI–273b
Snake River VI–322b
South Pass I–485b; VI–354b
trappers' rendezvous VII–103b
Treaty of Fort Laramie III–383b
Union Pacific Railroad VII–147b
Union Pass V–225a
U.S. boundary IV–320b
woman's suffrage III–91b; VII–208b, 315a
Yellowstone National Park VII–357a
Wyoming (ship) VI–278b–79a, 395 (table)
Wyoming, Battle of. *See* Wyoming Massacre
Wyoming, University of III–285a
Wyoming County (N.Y.) VI–202b
WYOMING MASSACRE (1778) **VII–346b**; III–257b, 400b; V–231a; VI–267b, 452a; VII–347b
Wyoming Stock Growers' Association I–472a; II–16b
Wyoming Territory II–284b
Wyoming Valley (Pa.) I–398a; IV–92a, 98b; V–250b; VI–438a; VII–346b
WYOMING VALLEY, SETTLEMENT OF VII–346b
Connecticut claims II–183b
Forty Fort III–81b
Paxton Boys V–231a
Susquehanna Company VI–451b
Yankee–Pennamite Wars VII–353a
Wyon, Joseph Shephard (engr.) VI–246a
Wythe, George (states.) II–305b, 308b; IV–120b
Wythe County (Va.) II–32b
Wytheville (Va.) II–163a; III–381a
Wytschaete Ridge (Belg.) VII–366b

X

X–1 (rocket plane) I–52a, 235a; IV–106a, 458b
X–5 (turbojet plane) I–52a
X–15 (rocket plane) I–52a–b
XB–17 (bomber plane) I–59b
XC–35 (fighter plane) I–52a
Xenia (Ohio) II–25b; V–319b
Xerography I–275b, 397a
Ximinez, Juan II–389a
XIT Ranch VI–380b
XOP–1 (helicopter) I–56b
XP–59 (fighter plane) I–53b
X-rays III–155b, 156a; IV–391b; V–295b, 303b
X Y Company III–209a
XYZ AFFAIR (1798) **VII–347b**; II–215a; III–67b, 96a, 96b, 238b; IV–347a

Y

Y1B–9 (bomber aircraft) I–50a
Yablonski, Joseph A. (labor leader) IV–76a; VII–151a
Yachting IV–268b; VI–186a
YACHT RACING VII–348b
America I–95b
Newport V–65b
Olympic Games V–154a
Yadkin River VI–149b
YADKIN RIVER SETTLEMENTS VII–350a; III–182a
Yakima (Indians) III–500b; VII–239b, 350a–b
Yakima (Wash.) VI–173b
Yakima County (Wash.) VI–173b
YAKIMA INDIAN WARS (1855–58) **VII–350a**
Yakima River II–131b
Yakima Valley VII–248a
Yale, Elihu (mer.) VII–351a
Yale Art Gallery I–165b
YALE BAND VII–350b
Yale–Columbia Southern Observatory II–133a
Yale Daily News VII–351a
Yale Literary Magazine VII–351a
Yale Scientific School. *See* Sheffield Scientific School
YALE UNIVERSITY VII–350b; II–114b, 394b, 399b; IV–144a, 191a; VI–440b
Americana collections III–285a
American Journal of Sciences VI–235b
archives I–169a
art gallery III–138b; VI–243a
campus II–45a
classical curriculum II–398a
farmers institute II–494a
football III–56b, 58a
foreign students II–470b
Francis P. Garvan collection II–100b
Hartford Wits III–259b
Hawaiian missions IV–364b
hockey III–287b
Illinois Band III–331b
Jarvis art collection II–102a–b
law school IV–120b, 121a
library II–108a; IV–145a,b
moon hoax IV–406b
Nader's Raiders IV–448b
political science V–349a
psychology V–442b
rugby III–56b
science IV–348b; VI–232a
Sheffield Scientific School II–399a; VI–273b
Societé Anonyme art collection II–104b
technical instruction II–447a
YALTA CONFERENCE (1945) **VII–351b**; II–97b, 471b, 489a; VII–110a, 341a
Manchuria IV–235a–b
Soviet Union VI–179a
Yalu River I–57a, 61a, 219b
Korean War IV–56a, 57a
Yamamoto, Isoroku (nav. off.) IV–336a
Yamasee (Indians) VI–349a; VII–352a
Yamasee (lang.) III–41a
YAMASEE WAR (1715–16) **VII–352a**; I–458a; VI–349a
Yamashita, Tomoyuki (off.) IV–158a
Yamato (battleship) IV–336b; V–10b, 26b, 148b
Yamato class (battleship) VII–242a
Yancey, William L. (law., pol.) I–71b; II–65b, 162a; III–25a; V–161a
League of United Southerners IV–125b; VI–354a
states' rights II–160b
Wilmot Proviso I–73b
Yangtze River II–25b, 26a; III–234b; V–205b
YANKEE (brig) **VII–352a**
Yankee Doodle (paint.). *See* Spirit of '76
"YANKEE DOODLE" (song) **VI–352a**; I–335b
Yankee Harbor (S. Shetland Is.) V–198a
"Yankee ingenuity" VII–352b
YANKEE NOTIONS VII–352b; V–241b
YANKEE–PENNAMITE WARS VII–353a; II–183b; IV–92a; V–231a, 250b; VI–451b, 452a; VII–346b–47a
Yankee Sound (S. Shetland Is.) V–198a
"Yankee's Return From Camp" (ballad) VII–352b
"Yankie Doodles Intrenchments Near Boston 1776" (print) IV–7b
Yankton (Indians) II–283a; III–365a, 500a
Yankton (S.Dak.) II–285a; V–117a, 179a
Yanktonai (Indians) I–206a; II–283a; III–365a
VII–234b–35a
Yantic (steamer) III–224a
Yaphank (N.Y.) I–434b
YAP MANDATE VII–353b; IV–236b; VII–125a
Yaqui (Indians) III–369a; IV–367a
Yaquina Bay V–164b
Yard vessels V–25b
Yarmouth (Mass.) I–447a
Yarmouth (N.S., Can.) V–37b
Yarmouth (ship) V–18b
Yarrow, Henry C. (nat.) VI–90b
Yates, Robert (jur.) II–193a
Yates County (N.Y.) V–463b
Yates v. *United States* (1957) VI–317b; VII–118a
Yavapai (Indians) III–262a, 369a, 376b; V–129b
Yawl IV–44b
Yaws III–240a; VII–169a
Yazoo (Indians) III–499b
YAZOO–CHATTAHOOCHEE LINE VII–353b

YAZOO FRAUD VII–353b; III–170b; IV–99a; VI–356b; VII–273b, 273b
Blount conspiracy I–324a
Fletcher v. *Peck* III–36a
YAZOO PASS EXPEDITION (1863) **VII–354a**
Yazoo River II–22a,b; III–36a, 238b
Bourbon County I–354a
Civil War VI–410b, 424b; VII–181b, 354b
Florida boundary III–38b, 41b; VII–353b
Fort Adams I–9b
land fraud IV–99a
Natchez IV–456a
Vicksburg VII–181a
Ybarbo, Gil (rancher) VII–36b
Yeager, Charles (off.) I–52a, 235a
Yeardley, George (col. gov.) I–204a; II–117a
Yeast II–219a
Yeats, William Butler II–287b
Ye Bare and Ye Cubb (play) VII–46b
Yedo, Bay. *See* Tokyo Bay
Yellow Creek Massacre. *See* Cresap's War
Yellow Creek River II–257b
Yellow dent corn II–226a
"YELLOW-DOG" CONTRACT VII–354b; II–86a, 222a; IV–71a; VI–419b
YELLOW FEVER VII–355a; II–454b; III–81b; IV–295a,b, 298a
army research IV–291a,b
cities VII–158a
death IV–150a
environmental sanitation VI–211b, 212b
epidemics I–410a; V–446b
Jersey prison ship III–498b
Louisiana IV–194b
Memphis IV–302a
Mexican War IV–322a
New Orleans V–62b
New York City V–82b
Panama Canal V–201b
research I–46a, 188a, 241b
Rockefeller Foundation VI–158a
Savannah VI–220b
Spanish-American War VI–362b
statistics VII–205b, 206b
water supply VII–258a
Yellow Fever Commission I–241b
Yellow Hair (Indian). *See* Yellow Hand
Yellowhammer (bird) VI–393 (table)
Yellowhammer State VI–393 (table)
Yellow Hand (Hay-o-wei) (Indian) VII–228a
YELLOW JOURNALISM VII–356a; V–71b–72a; VI–84b, 360a, 361a
"Yellow Kid" (comic strip) V–71b, 72a; VII–356a
Yellowknives (Indians) I–441b; III–252b, 360b
Yellow Medicine (Minn.) III–267a; VI–296b
YELLOW PERIL VII–356a
Yellow pine VII–114b
Yellow Springs (Pa.) VII–165a
YELLOWSTONE (steamboat) **VII–357a**; I–470b; IV–380a
Yellowstone Lake VII–357b
YELLOWSTONE NATIONAL PARK V–357a; II–187b, 477a; III–444a; IV–96a; V–218 (table), 219b, 445b; VI–160b; VII–346a
Gardner's Hole III–291a
Jackson Hole III–486a
scenic roads VI–156a
Snake River VI–322b
wildlife preservation VII–297a,b, 298a
Yellowstone River II–284a, 496a; III–32a; VII–357b
Bent's Fort II–16b
Black Hills War IV–168a
Bozeman Pass V–225a
Bozeman Trail I–357b
Fort Union II–285a; VII–145b
fur trade III–143a; VI–160a
Hayden survey IV–233a
La Vérendrye exploration VI–192a–b
Leavenworth expedition IV–129b
Lewis and Clark expedition III–119b; IV–136b
Manuel's Fort IV–159b, 242a
Missouri Fur Company IV–403a
steamboating VII–357a
YELLOWSTONE RIVER EXPEDITIONS (1819–25) **VII–357b**; I–201a; IV–186b, 223b
YELLOW TAVERN, BATTLE AT (1864) **VII–358a**
Yellowware III–184a
Yemen
independence I–149b
trade with II–388a
U.S. relations I–150a
Yeo, James Lucas (nav. off.) VI–183b
Yeomanettes II–372a; VII–318a
Yeoman farmers I–33a; IV–102b
Yerba Buena (Calif.). *See* San Francisco
Yerby, Frank (au.) IV–167a
Yergan, Max I–22a
Yerger, Ex parte (1868) III–236b
Yerkes, Robert (psych.) III–440b
Yerkes Observatory (Wis.) I–211a; V–131b
Yeshiva (high school) IV–11a
Yeshiva College IV–11a
Yeshiva University V–83b
YF-12A (fighter plane) I–54a
YF-86 (fighter plane) I–53b–54a
Yiddish culture IV–10b
Yiddish-language press V–75b
Yiddish Theater (N.Y.C.) VII–49b
Y-Indian Guides VII–363b
Y-Indian Princesses VII–363b
YMCA *See* Young Men's Christian Association
YM-YWHAs. *See* Young Men's and Young Women's Hebrew Associations
Yogananda, Paramhansa V–171b
Yogurt II–282b
Yohogania County (Va.) I–223b
Yokohama (Jap.) V–23a, 263a; VI–278b
Yokut (Indians) III–362b, 363a
Yom Kippur War (1973) II–213a; III–482a; V–233a
Yonkers (N.Y.) III–197b
York (servant) IV–136b
"York" (locomotive) IV–175a–b
York (Maine) VII–358b
bridge I–363b
McIntyre Garrison IV–179a
settlement I–32a
YORK (Pa.) **VII–358a**
national capital V–247a
Pennsylvania Gazette V–68b, 251a
Whiskey Rebellion VII–290a
York, Alvin C. (sol.) IV–320a; VII–26a
YORK, ATTACK ON (1692) **VII–358b**; VI–323a
YORK, CAPTURE AND DESTRUCTION OF (1813) **VII–358b**; I–436b, 438b; III–167b
York, Duke of (James II) I–81b; IV–396a; VII–359a–60a
Delaware II–320a, 322b
Iroquois Treaty III–476b
Long Island grant IV–185b
Lower Counties-on-Delaware IV–199b
New Castle V–43a; VII–129b–30a
New York City V–82a
New York colony II–117b, 124a
royal land grants IV–91b
slave trade I–22b
York-Antwerp shipping convention I–14b–15a
York County (Mass.) III–200b
York County (Pa.) V–251b, 406b
York County (S.C.) IV–48b
York County (Va.) VII–360a
Yorke, Charles (states.) I–412b
Yorke, Philip, 1st Earl of Hardwicke (jur.) V–252a–b
York Factory (Can.) IV–118a
York (Pa.) *Gazette and Daily* (news.) V–73a, 74b–75a
York River I–363b; VI–149b; VII–358b, 360a
Civil War IV–397a; V–245a; VII–117a
revolutionary war VII–360b, 361a
settlements VII–192b
Williamsburg VII–301a
YORK'S, DUKE OF, PROPRIETARY VII–359a; V–436b; VII–274a, 347a
agents V–435b–36a
Charter of Liberties I–500b
Fishers Island III–31a
Monhegan Island IV–396a
Monmouth Purchase IV–398a
New Albion lands V–333a
New Haven Colony V–56a
New Jersey V–56b
New Netherland V–62a
New York City V–82a
New York Colony V–84b
Nicolls' commission V–95b
Pemaquid Point V–243b
Pennsylvania V–246a
Southampton VI–346b
Southold VI–354b
Yorkshire (N.Y.) II–379a
Yorkshire hog III–288b
Yorktown (carrier) I–54b, 56a; II–225a; V–20b
Battle of Midway IV–336a,b, 337a
YORKTOWN (Va.) **VII–360a**
Civil War V–245a; VII–301b
YORKTOWN CAMPAIGN (1781) **VII–360a**; II–465a; III–117b–18a; V–237b; VI–119b, 124b, 126a, 248a, 351b; VII–193b
Battle of Virginia Capes VII–198b
French troops V–66a; VI–116b, 117b
navy V–19a
Yorktown peninsula II–373a
Yoruba (people) VI–309b
YOSEMITE NATIONAL PARK VII–361b; II–477b; V–218 (table), 445b; VI–101b; VII–220a
Yosemite Valley I–330a; II–187b; VII–220a, 361b–62a
Yost, Casper S. (ed.) V–77b
You Bet (Calif.) I–281a
Youghiogheny River I–358b; II–15b; VI–149a, 150a
Youmans, Vincent (comp.) IV–442a

Young, Andrew (pol.) III–169a
Young, Arthur Henry ("Art") (cartoon.) V–73a
Young, Bennett H. (off.) VI–187a
Young, Brigham (Mormon) IV–117a; V–39b; VI–87a; VII–161b
Deseret II–334a
federal law IV–411a,b
Mormon Battalion IV–411a
Mormon migration IV–411b–12a
Mountain Meadows massacre IV–422a
Salt Lake City VI–203b
Salt Lake City plan II–45b
Young, Ewing (trapper) II–477b; III–143b; VI–461a
Young, H. H. (off.) VI–373b
Young, James (chem.) IV–44a; V–269b
Young, John (biol., physic.) V–306b
Young, John (gov.) I–134a
Young, John Russell (librarian) IV–148a
Young, J. Z. (biol.) IV–250b
Young, La Monte (mus.) IV–442b
Young, Lester (mus.) IV–440b
Young, Owen D. (law., bus.) I–254a; VI–88a; VII–363b
Young, W. J. (biochem.) V–127b
"YOUNG AMERICA" VI–362a; IV–324b
Younger, Thomas ("Cole") (outlaw) V–119b
Younger brothers (outlaws) III–231a; V–119b
Young Lords I–220a
YOUNG MEN'S AND YOUNG WOMEN'S HEBREW ASSOCIATIONS VII–362b; IV–11a
Young Men's Association for Mutual Improvement IV–409a
YOUNG MEN'S CHRISTIAN ASSOCIATION VII–363a; I–272b; IV–409a; VII–362b, 365a
settlement houses VI–330b
World War I relief VII–330b
Young Mill-Wright and Miller's Guide III–43a
YOUNG PLAN VII–363b; I–245b, 254a, 254a; II–296b; III–352b; IV–117b; VI–88a
Young's Sons' Excelsior Pottery III–184a
Youngstown (N.Y.) IV–60a; V–91a
Youngstown (Ohio) III–470b, 473b; V–141b; VII–274a
YOUNG WOMEN'S CHRISTIAN ASSOCIATION OF THE UNITED STATES OF AMERICA VII–363b; IV–409a; VII–313b, 330b
Young Women's Hebrew Associations. *See* Young Men's and Young Women's Hebrew Associations
YOUTH ADMINISTRATION, NATIONAL VII–364a; V–46a; VI–74a
YOUTH MOVEMENTS VII–365a
antiwar groups IV–75a; VII–236b–37a
consumer protection IV–448b
drug use IV–451a
Four-H clubs III–84b
mysticism IV–448a
National Indian Youth Council IV–464a
radicals VI–14a
Youth's Companion (mag.) IV–223a; V–331b
Youth's Friend and Scholar's Magazine IV–222b
YPRES–LYS OPERATION (1918) **VII–366b**; VI–338b
YUCATÁN (Mex.) **VI–366b**; I–48a
Isle of Pines III–479a
logwood trade IV–181b
marine research III–29a
Maya Indians III–355b, 386a
Monroe Doctrine IV–400b
pirates IV–416a
Polk Doctrine V–354a
Texas alliance VII–38a, 41b
Yucatán Channel IV–326b
Yucca House National Monument V–217b
Yucca plant IV–378b; VI–380b, 394 (table)
Yuchi (Indians) III–367a
Yuchian (lang.) II–282b
Yugoslavia
earthquake V–23a
immigration to U.S. III–338b, 339b, 340a–b, 341b
most-favored-nation status VI–470a
nationalization of U.S. property IV–466a
Organization for Economic Cooperation and Development V–170b
Paris Peace Conference V–215b
United Nations Declaration VII–151b
World War I relief VII–330a
Yukawa, Hideki (phys.) V–302b
YUKON (riv.) **VII–367a**; I–80b; IV–51b; VI–151a
Yukon, Fort (Can.) VII–367a
Yukon Indians V–437a
Yukon Territory I–441a,b; IV–51b–52a; VII–367a
Yuma (Ariz.) III–179b; V–129b; VI–154a; VII–367b
Yuma (Calif.) II–130a
Yuma (Indians) III–362a, 363a, 369a; IV–386a; VII–367a,b
YUMA, FORT (Calif.) **VII–367a**
Yuma Indian Reservation (Calif.) VII–367b
Yuman (lang.) III–262b
Yuma Valley II–130a
Yung Wing (student) II–470b
Yunnan province (China) III–46a
YUROK (Indians) **VII–367b**; I–86a; III–362a, 363a
YWCA. *See* Young Women's Christian Association of the United States of America

Z

Zacatecas (Mex.) II–23b
Zadeh, L. A. (phys.) II–39a
Zagoshkin, Lavrenti Alekseev VII–367a
Zaharias, Mildred ("Babe") Didrikson (athlete) III–198b
Zambia
Rhodes scholars VI–134b
Zane, Ebenezer (pioneer) VII–287b, 368a
ZANE'S TRACE AND GRANTS VII–368a; II–273b; IV–470b
Zanesville (Ohio) II–273b; III–449a; IV–444a, 470b; VII–368a
Zangara, Joseph (assassin) I–202b
Zanzibar IV–236b; VI–275a
slave trade VI–311b
Zapotec (Indians) IV–327a
Zapruder, Abraham VII–238b
ZARAH, FORT (Kans.) **VII–368a**
Zavala (steamer) VII–41b
Zavala, Manuel J. IV–322b–23a
Zeiger, H. J. (phys.) IV–262b
Zeisberger, David (miss.) VI–226a
Zeitung (news.) V–75b
Zelaya, José Santos (pol.) V–94a
Zen Buddhism V–171b
Zenger, John Peter (print.). *See* Zenger Trial
ZENGER TRIAL (1735) **VII–368a**; I–478b; II–266a; III–104b; IV–139b; V–69a, 82b, 85a; VII–117a
Zenith Radio Corporation VI–16b
Zenoni, John B. (fur trader) VI–196a
Zephyr (train) III–452a; VI–33a
Zeppelin, Ferdinand von (off., aeron.) I–232b
Zeppelins I–54a, 66b, 234a; II–344b
Zero (math.)
Maya IV–327b
Zero population growth II–486b
Zia (N.Mex.) I–8a; III–367b; V–460a
Zimmerman, Arthur (states.). *See* Zimmerman Telegram
ZIMMERMAN TELEGRAM (1917) **VII–368b**; VII–325a
ZINC INDUSTRY VII–368b; V–102a, 102b–03a; VI–48b
cobalt production III–14a
Coeur d'Alene IV–122b
copper ore II–224a
fuel IV–334a
Kansas IV–25a, 26a
Missouri IV–123a
Montana IV–403a
Oklahoma V–149a
Peru VI–346a
Saint Louis VI–194b
U.S. Geological Survey III–163a
Zinc oxide VII–369a,b
Zinn, Walter H. (phys.) I–217b
Zinzendorf, Count Nikolaus Ludwig von (rel. leader) V–311a; VI–76b
Hussites IV–409b
Zionism III–481b; IV–10a, 10b, 11a, 12a
Zionist Organization of America IV–10b
Zion National Park V–217a, 218 (table)
Zion Parnassus Academy VI–228b
Zirconium IV–350b
Zirkel, Ferdinand (geol.) V–268a
Zoar (Ohio) VII–369b
ZOAR SOCIETY VII–369b; II–147a; IV–338b
Zobel, O. J. (phys.) II–39a
Zollicoffer, Felix K. (off.) I–435a; IV–347a; VI–455a
ZOLLVEREIN TREATY, WHEATON'S (1844) **VII–370a**
Zoning
eminent domain II–400a
ZONING ORDINANCES VII–370a
city planning II–46b–47a, 49a
housing III–310b
national land system IV–102a–b
property owners' rights IV–101b
Zoological Institute of June, Titus and Angevine II–40b

Zoological Park, National (Washington, D.C.) VI–319b
ZOOLOGICAL PARKS VII–370b
North Carolina V–116b
San Diego VI–208b
Zoological Parks and Aquariums, American Association of VII–371a
Zoology
animal ecology II–391b
mammals IV–230b
Marine Biological Laboratory IV–250b–51a
National Museum collection IV–468b
reptiles VI–90a
Zoology of New York IV–232a
Zoonotic diseases IV–291b
Zorach, William (sculp.) VI–244a
Zoroastrianism VII–52a
ZOUAVES VII–371b; II–432b–33a; IV–342b
ZPG-1 (airship) II–345a–b
ZPG-2 (airship) II–345b
ZPG-2W (airship) II–345b
ZPG-3W (airship) II–345b
ZR-1 (airship) II–344a,b
ZR-2 (airship) II–344a
ZR-3 (airship) II–344b
ZRS-4 (airship) II–344b, 345a
ZRS-5 (airship) II–344b, 345a
Zuider Zee (Neth.) III–243a
Zuikaku (carrier) II–225a, 387b
Zukor, Adolph (prod.) IV–417b
ZUNI (Indians) **VII–372a**; III–208a, 301a, 367b, 368a, 396b; IV–386a; V–460a
Acoma I–7b
Apache I–141b
Cibola II–37a
Coronado's expedition II–228b
Navaho V–9a,b
Spanish contacts V–459b
Zuni (N.Mex.) I–409b–10a; II–461a
Zunian (lang.) III–367b
Zuni pueblo VI–162a
Zuni Reservation (N.Mex.) III–395b
Zuse, Konrad (math.) II–154b
ZWAANENDAEL COLONY VII–372b; II–322a
Zwicker, Ralph (off.) IV–210a,b
Zwicky, Fritz (phys.) V–295b
Zworykin, Vladimir K. (inv.) II–425b; VII–21b

DICTIONARY OF AMERICAN HISTORY